OFFICIAL BASEBALL REGISTER

1996 EDITION

Editors/Official Baseball Register

SEAN STEWART
KYLE VELTROP

Contributing Editor/Official Baseball Register

JOHN DUXBURY

PUBLISHING CO.

Efrem Zimbalist III, President and Chief Executive Officer, Times Mirror Magazines; **Nicholas H. Niles,** President and Chief Executive Officer; **Francis X. Farrell,** Senior Vice President, Publisher; **John D. Rawlings,** Senior Vice President, Editorial Director; **John Kastberg,** Vice President, General Manager; **Kathy Kinkeade,** Vice President, Production; **Mike Nahrstedt,** Managing Editor; **Mike Huguenin,** Assistant Managing Editor; **Joe Hoppel and Bill Marx,** Senior Editors; **Tom Dienhart and Dave Sloan,** Associate Editors; **Craig Carter,** Statistical Editor; **Sean Stewart and Kyle Veltrop,** Assistant Editors; **Fred Barnes,** Director of Graphics; **Angie Blackwell,** Art Director; **Albert Dickson,** Chief Photographer; **Paul Nisely,** Photo Editor; **Gary Brinker,** Director/Information Systems; **Bob Parajon,** Prepress Director; **Patrick Kolieboi,** Network Manager; **Terry Shea,** Database Analyst; **Marilyn Kasal,** Production Manager; **Mike Bruner,** Graphics Network Manager; **Michael Behrens,** Macintosh Production Artist.

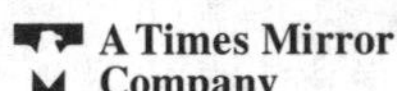

Major league statistics compiled by STATS, Inc., Skokie, Ill.

Minor league statistics compiled by Howe Sportsdata International Inc., Boston.

ISBN: 0-89204-545-0 (perfect-bound)
0-89204-548-5 (comb-bound)

10 9 8 7 6 5 4 3 2 1

CONTENTS

EXPLANATION OF FOOTNOTES AND ABBREVIATIONS

Note for statistical comparisons: Player strikes forced the cancellation of games in the 1972 season (10 days missed), the 1981 season (50 days missed), the 1994 season (52 days missed) and the 1995 season (18 games missed).

Positions are listed in descending order of games played; because of limited space, pinch-hitter and pinch-runner are listed in the regular-season section only if a player did not play a defensive position.

- * Led league. For fielding statistics, the player led the league at the position shown.
- • Tied for league lead. For fielding statistics, the player tied for the league lead at the position shown.
- † Led league, but number indicated is total figure for two or more positions. Actual league-leading figure for a position is mentioned in "Statistical Notes" section.
- ‡ Tied for league lead, but number indicated is total figure for two or more positions. Actual league-tying figure for a position is mentioned in "Statistical Notes" section.
- § Led or tied for league lead, but total figure is divided between two different teams. Actual league-leading or league-tying figure is mentioned in "Statistical Notes" section.
- ■ Indicates a player's movement from one major league organization to another major league organization or to an independent minor league organization.
- . . . Statistic unavailable, inapplicable, unofficial or mathematically impossible to calculate.
- — Manager statistic inapplicable.

LEAGUES: A.A., Am. Assoc.—American Association. **A.L.**—American. **App., Appal.**—Appalachian. **Ar., Ariz.**—Arizona. **Cal., Calif.**—California. **Car., Caro.**—Carolina. **CRL**—Cocoa Rookie. **DSL**—Dominican Summer. **East.**—Eastern. **Evan.**—Evangeline. **Fla. St., Florida St., FSL**—Florida State. **GCL**—Gulf Coast. **GSL**—Gulf States. **Int'l.**—International. **Jap. Pac, Jp. Pac.**—Japan Pacific. **Jp. Cen., Jp. Cn.**—Japan Central. **Mex.**—Mexican. **Mex. Cen.**—Mexican Center. **Mid., Midw.**—Midwest. **Miss.-O.V.**—Mississippi-Ohio Valley. **N.C. St.**—North Carolina State. **N.L.**—National. **North.**—Northern. **N'west**—Northwest. **NYP**—New York-Pennsylvania. **Pac. Coast, PCL**—Pacific Coast. **Pio.**—Pioneer. **S. Atl., SAL**—South Atlantic. **Soph.**—Sophomore. **Sou., South.**—Southern. **Taiw.**—Taiwan. **Tex.**—Texas. **W. Car., W. Caro.**—Western Carolinas.

TEAMS: Aguas.—Aguascalientes. **Alb./Colon.**—Albany/Colonie. **Ariz.**—Arizona. **Belling.**—Bellingham. **Birm.**—Birmingham. **Brevard Co.**—Brevard County. **Cant./Akr.**—Canton/Akron. **Ced. Rap.**—Cedar Rapids. **Cent. Ore.**—Central Oregon. **Central Vall.**—Central Valley. **Char., Charl.**—Charleston. **Chatt.**—Chattanooga. **Ciu. Juarez**—Ciudad Juarez. **Colo. Springs**—Colorado Springs. **Dall./Fort W.**—Dallas/Fort Worth. **Day. Beach.**—Daytona Beach. **Dom.**—Dominican. **Elizabeth.**—Elizabethton. **Estadio Quis.**—Estadio Quisqueya. **Eve.**—Everett. **Fort Lauder.**—Fort Lauderdale. **Fukuoka**—Fukuoka Daiei. **GC**—Gulf Coast. **GC Astros-Or.**—Gulf Coast Astros-Orange. **GC Royals-Bl.**—Gulf Coast Royals-Blue. **GC Whi. Sox**—Gulf Coast White Sox. **Grays Har.**—Grays Harbor. **Greens.**—Greensboro. **Greenw.**—Greenwood. **Guana.**—Guanajuato. **H.P.-Thomas.**—High Point-Thomasville. **Hunting.**—Huntington. **Jacksonv.**—Jacksonville. **Johns. City**—Johnson City. **Kane Co.**—Kane County. **Lake Charl.**—Lake Charles. **Matt.**—Mattoon. **M.C., Mex. City**—Mexico City. **Monc.**—Monclova. **Niag. F., Niag. Falls**—Niagara Falls. **Okla. City**—Oklahoma City. **Pan. City**—Panama City. **Phoe.**—Phoenix. **Pomp. Beach**—Pompano Beach. **Pres. Lions**—President Lions. **Prin. William**—Prince William. **Rancho Cuca.**—Rancho Cucamonga. **Salt.**—Saltillo. **San Bern.**—San Bernardino. **Schen.**—Schenectady. **Scran./W.B.**—Scranton/Wilkes-Barre. **S.C.**—South Carolina. **S.F. de Mac.**—San Francisco de Macoris. **San Luis Pot.**—San Luis Potosi. **S. Oregon**—Southern Oregon. **Spartan.**—Spartanburg. **St. Cath., St. Cathar.**—St. Catharines. **St. Peters.**—St. Petersburg. **States.**—Statesville. **Stock.**—Stockton. **T.-C.**—Tri-Cities. **Vanc.**—Vancouver. **Vent. Co.**—Ventura County. **Winst.-Salem**—Winston-Salem. **Wis. Rap.**—Wisconsin Rapids. **W.P. Beach**—West Palm Beach. **W.Va.**—West Virgina. **Yuc.**—Yucatan.

STATISTICS: A—assists. **AB**—at-bats. **Avg.**—average. **BB**—bases on balls. **CG**—complete games. **E**—errors. **ER**—earned runs. **ERA**—earned-run average. **G**—games. **GIDP**—grounded into double plays. **GS**—games started. **H**—hits. **HR**—home runs. **IP**—innings pitched. **L**—losses. **Pct.**—winning percentage. **PO**—putouts. **Pos.**—position. **R**—runs. **RBI**—runs batted in. **SB**—stolen bases. **ShO**—shutouts. **SO**—strikeouts. **Sv.**—saves. **W**—wins. **2B**—doubles. **3B**—triples.

ON THE COVER: Greg Maddux enjoyed another masterful season as his 19-2 record and 1.63 ERA earned him a fourth consecutive N.L. Cy Young Award. Maddux also helped the Atlanta Braves win the 1995 World Series. (Photo by Albert Dickson/The Sporting News).

Spine photo of Kirby Puckett by The Sporting News.

PLAYERS

ABBOTT, JIM — P — ANGELS

PERSONAL: Born September 19, 1967, in Flint, Mich. . . . 6-3/210. . . . Throws left, bats left. . . . Full name: James Anthony Abbott.
HIGH SCHOOL: Flint (Mich.) Central.
COLLEGE: Michigan.
TRANSACTIONS/CAREER NOTES: Selected by Toronto Blue Jays organization in 36th round of free-agent draft (June 3, 1985); did not sign. . . . Selected by California Angels organization in first round (eighth pick overall) of free-agent draft (June 1, 1988). . . . On disabled list (July 12-August 8, 1992). . . . Traded by Angels to New York Yankees for 1B J.T. Snow, P Jerry Nielsen and P Russ Springer (December 6, 1992). . . . On disabled list (June 10-25, 1993). . . . Granted free agency (December 23, 1994). . . . Signed by Chicago White Sox (April 8, 1995). . . . Traded by White Sox with P Tim Fortugno to Angels for P Andrew Lorraine, P Bill Simas, P John Snyder and OF McKay Christensen (July 27, 1995). . . . Granted free agency (October 31, 1995). . . . Re-signed by Angels (January 8, 1996).
HONORS: Named Golden Spikes Award winner by USA Baseball (1987). . . . Named lefthanded pitcher on The Sporting News college All-America team (1988). . . . Named lefthanded pitcher on The Sporting News A.L. All-Star team (1991).
STATISTICAL NOTES: Tied for A.L. lead with four balks in 1991. . . . Pitched 4-0 no-hit victory against Cleveland (September 4, 1993).
MISCELLANEOUS: Member of 1988 U.S. Olympic baseball team.

Year	Team (League)	W	L	Pct.	ERA	G	GS	CG	ShO	Sv.	IP	H	R	ER	BB	SO
1989	—California (A.L.)	12	12	.500	3.92	29	29	4	2	0	181 1/3	190	95	79	74	115
1990	—California (A.L.)	10	14	.417	4.51	33	33	4	1	0	211 2/3	*246	116	106	72	105
1991	—California (A.L.)	18	11	.621	2.89	34	34	5	1	0	243	222	85	78	73	158
1992	—California (A.L.)	7	15	.318	2.77	29	29	7	0	0	211	208	73	65	68	130
1993	—New York (A.L.)■	11	14	.440	4.37	32	32	4	1	0	214	221	115	104	73	95
1994	—New York (A.L.)	9	8	.529	4.55	24	24	2	0	0	160 1/3	167	88	81	64	90
1995	—Chicago (A.L.)■	6	4	.600	3.36	17	17	3	0	0	112 1/3	116	50	42	35	45
	—California (A.L.)■	5	4	.556	4.15	13	13	1	1	0	84 2/3	93	43	39	29	41
Major league totals (7 years)		78	82	.488	3.77	211	211	30	6	0	1418 1/3	1463	665	594	488	779

ABBOTT, KURT — SS — MARLINS

PERSONAL: Born June 2, 1969, in Zanesville, O. . . . 6-0/185. . . . Bats right, throws right. . . . Full name: Kurt Thomas Abbott.
HIGH SCHOOL: Dixie Hollins (St. Petersburg, Fla.).
JUNIOR COLLEGE: St. Petersburg (Fla.).
TRANSACTIONS/CAREER NOTES: Selected by Oakland Athletics organization in 15th round of free-agent draft (June 5, 1989). . . . On Modesto disabled list (May 26-June 6, 1991). . . . Traded by A's to Florida Marlins for OF Kerwin Moore (December 20, 1993). . . . On Florida disabled list (April 19-May 6, 1995); included rehabilitation assignment to Charlotte (April 30-May 6).
STATISTICAL NOTES: Led Arizona League shortstops with .922 fielding percentage in 1989. . . . Led Southern League shortstops with 87 double plays in 1992. . . . Career major league grand slams: 3.

				BATTING											FIELDING			
Year	Team (League)	Pos.	G	AB	R	H	2B	3B	HR	RBI	Avg.	BB	SO	SB	PO	A	E	Avg.
1989	—Arizona A's (Ariz.)	SS-2B-3B	36	155	27	42	5	3	0	25	.271	8	40	0	59	90	10	†.937
	—S. Oregon (N'west)	SS	5	10	2	1	0	0	0	1	.100	0	3	1	6	7	1	.929
1990	—Madison (Midwest)	SS-2B-3B	104	362	38	84	18	0	0	28	.232	47	74	21	180	268	40	.918
1991	—Modesto (Calif.)	SS	58	216	36	55	8	2	3	25	.255	29	55	6	78	130	9	.959
	—Huntsville (South.)	SS	53	182	18	46	6	1	0	11	.253	17	39	6	89	164	13	.951
1992	—Huntsville (South.)	SS	124	452	64	115	14	5	9	52	.254	31	75	16	196	342	29	*.949
	—Tacoma (PCL)	SS	11	39	2	6	1	0	0	1	.154	4	9	1	21	32	4	.930
1993	—Tacoma (PCL)	SS	133	480	75	153	36	11	12	79	.319	33	123	19	*210	367	30	.951
	—Oakland (A.L.)	OF-SS-2B	20	61	11	15	1	0	3	9	.246	3	20	2	36	13	2	.961
1994	—Florida (N.L.)■	SS	101	345	41	86	17	3	9	33	.249	16	98	3	162	260	15	.966
1995	—Charlotte (Int'l)	SS	5	18	3	5	0	0	1	3	.278	1	3	1	5	15	2	.909
	—Florida (N.L.)	SS	120	420	60	107	18	7	17	60	.255	36	110	4	149	290	19	.959
American League totals (1 year)			20	61	11	15	1	0	3	9	.246	3	20	2	36	13	2	.961
National League totals (2 years)			221	765	101	193	35	10	26	93	.252	52	208	7	311	550	34	.962
Major league totals (3 years)			241	826	112	208	36	10	29	102	.252	55	228	9	347	563	36	.962

ABBOTT, KYLE — P

PERSONAL: Born February 18, 1968, in Newburyport, Mass. . . . 6-4/215. . . . Throws left, bats left. . . . Full name: Lawrence Kyle Abbott. . . . Son of Larry Abbott, minor league pitcher (1964-70).
HIGH SCHOOL: Mission Viejo (Calif.).
COLLEGE: UC San Diego and Long Beach State.
TRANSACTIONS/CAREER NOTES: Selected by California Angels organization in first round (ninth pick overall) of free-agent draft (June 2, 1989). . . . Traded by Angels with OF Ruben Amaro to Philadelphia Phillies for OF Von Hayes (December 8, 1991). . . . Released by Phillies (November 24, 1993). . . . Signed by Kintetsu Buffaloes of Japan Pacific League (November 24, 1993). . . . Signed by Phillies (December 6, 1994). . . . On disabled list (July 24, 1995-remainder of season). . . . Granted free agency (October 16, 1995).
STATISTICAL NOTES: Led Pacific Coast League with 22 home runs allowed in 1991.

Year	Team (League)	W	L	Pct.	ERA	G	GS	CG	ShO	Sv.	IP	H	R	ER	BB	SO
1989	—Quad City (Midw.)	5	4	.556	2.57	13	12	0	0	0	73 2/3	55	26	21	30	95
1990	—Midland (Texas)	6	9	.400	4.14	24	24	2	0	0	128 1/3	124	75	59	73	91
	—Edmonton (PCL)	1	0	1.000	14.81	3	3	0	0	0	10 1/3	26	18	17	4	14
1991	—Edmonton (PCL)	•14	10	.583	3.99	27	27	4	2	0	*180 1/3	173	84	80	46	120
	—California (A.L.)	1	2	.333	4.58	5	3	0	0	0	19 2/3	22	11	10	13	12
1992	—Philadelphia (N.L.)■	1	14	.067	5.13	31	19	0	0	0	133 1/3	147	80	76	45	88
	—Scran./W.B. (Int'l)	4	1	.800	1.54	5	5	1	1	0	35	20	6	6	16	34
1993	—Scran./W.B. (Int'l)	12	10	.545	3.95	27	27	2	0	0	173	163	85	76	62	109
1994	—Kintetsu (Jp. Pac.)■	0	0	. . .	7.71	4	4	0	0	0	11 2/3	25	. . .	10	9	8
1995	—Philadelphia (N.L.)■	2	0	1.000	3.81	18	0	0	0	0	28 1/3	28	12	12	16	21
A.L. totals (1 year)		1	2	.333	4.58	5	3	0	0	0	19 2/3	22	11	10	13	12
N.L. totals (2 years)		3	14	.176	4.90	49	19	0	0	0	161 2/3	175	92	88	61	109
Major league totals (3 years)		4	16	.200	4.86	54	22	0	0	0	181 1/3	197	103	98	74	121

ABREU, BOB — OF — ASTROS

PERSONAL: Born March 11, 1974, in Aragua, Venezuela. . . . 6-0/160. . . . Bats left, throws right. . . . Full name: Bob Kelly Abreu. . . . Name pronounced a-BREW.
TRANSACTIONS/CAREER NOTES: Signed as non-drafted free agent by Houston Astros organization (August 21, 1990).
STATISTICAL NOTES: Led Gulf Coast League outfielders with 11 assists in 1991. . . . Led Texas League with .530 slugging percentage in 1994. . . . Led Pacific Coast League outfielders with 18 assists in 1995.

			BATTING											FIELDING			
Year Team (League)	**Pos.**	**G**	**AB**	**R**	**H**	**2B**	**3B**	**HR**	**RBI**	**Avg.**	**BB**	**SO**	**SB**	**PO**	**A**	**E**	**Avg.**
1991—GC Astros (GCL)	OF-SS	56	183	21	55	7	3	0	20	.301	17	27	10	70	†13	5	.943
1992—Asheville (S. Atl.)	OF	135	480	81	140	21	4	8	48	.292	63	79	15	167	15	11	.943
1993—Osceola (Fla. St.)	OF	129	474	62	134	21	17	5	55	.283	51	90	10	179	18	8	.961
1994—Jackson (Texas)	OF	118	400	61	121	25	9	16	73	.303	42	81	12	113	3	4	.967
1995—Tucson (PCL)	OF-2B	114	415	72	126	24	*17	10	75	.304	67	120	16	207	†18	7	.970

ACEVEDO, JUAN — P — METS

PERSONAL: Born May 5, 1970, in Juarez, Mexico. . . . 6-2/195. . . . Throws right, bats right. . . . Full name: Juan Carlos Acevedo. . . . Name pronounced ah-sah-VAY-doh.
HIGH SCHOOL: Dundee-Crown (Carpentersville, Ill.).
JUNIOR COLLEGE: Parkland College (Ill.).
TRANSACTIONS/CAREER NOTES: Selected by Colorado Rockies organization in 14th round of free-agent draft (June 1, 1992). . . . Traded by Rockies with P Arnold Gooch to New York Mets for P Bret Saberhagen and a player to be named later (July 31, 1995); Rockies acquired P David Swanson to complete deal (August 4, 1995).
HONORS: Named Eastern League Pitcher of the Year (1994).
STATISTICAL NOTES: Tied for Eastern League lead with four balks in 1994.

Year Team (League)	W	L	Pct.	ERA	G	GS	CG	ShO	Sv.	IP	H	R	ER	BB	SO
1992—Bend (Northwest)	0	0	...	13.50	1	0	0	0	0	2	4	3	3	1	3
—Visalia (California)	3	4	.429	5.43	12	12	1	0	0	64 2/3	75	46	39	33	37
1993—Central Valley (Cal.)	9	8	.529	4.40	27	20	1	0	0	118 2/3	119	68	58	58	107
1994—New Haven (East.)	*17	6	.739	*2.37	26	26	5	2	0	174 2/3	142	56	46	38	161
1995—Colorado (N.L.)	4	6	.400	6.44	17	11	0	0	0	65 2/3	82	53	47	20	40
—Colo. Springs (PCL)	1	1	.500	6.14	3	3	0	0	0	14 2/3	18	11	10	7	7
—Norfolk (Int'l)■	0	0	...	0.00	2	2	0	0	0	3	0	0	0	1	2
Major league totals (1 year)	4	6	.400	6.44	17	11	0	0	0	65 2/3	82	53	47	20	40

ACRE, MARK — P — ATHLETICS

PERSONAL: Born September 16, 1968, in Concord, Calif. . . . 6-8/240. . . . Throws right, bats right. . . . Full name: Mark Robert Acre.
HIGH SCHOOL: Corning (Calif.) Union.
COLLEGE: New Mexico State.
TRANSACTIONS/CAREER NOTES: Signed as non-drafted free agent by Oakland Athletics organization (August 5, 1991). . . . On Modesto disabled list (April 8-23, 1993). . . . On disabled list (August 10-September 1, 1995).

Year Team (League)	W	L	Pct.	ERA	G	GS	CG	ShO	Sv.	IP	H	R	ER	BB	SO
1991—Arizona A's (Ariz.)	2	0	1.000	2.70	6	0	0	0	0	10	10	3	3	6	6
1992—Reno (California)	4	4	.500	4.56	35	8	0	0	2	77	67	56	39	50	65
1993—Madison (Midwest)	0	0	...	0.29	28	0	0	0	20	31 1/3	9	1	1	13	41
—Huntsville (South.)	1	1	.500	2.42	19	0	0	0	10	22 1/3	22	10	6	3	21
1994—Tacoma (PCL)	1	1	.500	1.88	20	0	0	0	6	28 2/3	24	7	6	11	31
—Oakland (A.L.)	5	1	.833	3.41	34	0	0	0	0	34 1/3	24	13	13	23	21
1995—Oakland (A.L.)	1	2	.333	5.71	43	0	0	0	0	52	52	35	33	28	47
Major league totals (2 years)	6	3	.667	4.80	77	0	0	0	0	86 1/3	76	48	46	51	68

ADAMS, TERRY — P — CUBS

PERSONAL: Born March 6, 1973, in Mobile, Ala. . . . 6-3/205. . . . Throws right, bats right. . . . Full name: Terry Wayne Adams.
HIGH SCHOOL: Montgomery (Semmes, Ala.).
TRANSACTIONS/CAREER NOTES: Selected by Chicago Cubs organization in fourth round of free-agent draft (June 3, 1991). . . . On disabled list (June 21-September 21, 1993).

Year Team (League)	W	L	Pct.	ERA	G	GS	CG	ShO	Sv.	IP	H	R	ER	BB	SO
1991—Hunting. (Appal.)	0	*9	.000	5.77	14	13	0	0	0	57 2/3	67	*56	37	62	52
1992—Peoria (Midwest)	7	12	.368	4.41	25	25	3	1	0	157	144	95	77	86	96
1993—Daytona (Fla. St.)	3	5	.375	4.97	13	13	0	0	0	70 2/3	78	47	39	43	35
1994—Daytona (Fla. St.)	9	10	.474	4.38	39	7	0	0	7	84 1/3	87	47	41	46	64
1995—Orlando (Southern)	2	3	.400	1.43	37	0	0	0	19	37 2/3	23	9	6	16	26
—Iowa (Am. Assoc.)	0	0	...	0.00	7	0	0	0	5	6 1/3	3	0	0	2	10
—Chicago (N.L.)	1	1	.500	6.50	18	0	0	0	1	18	22	15	13	10	15
Major league totals (1 year)	1	1	.500	6.50	18	0	0	0	1	18	22	15	13	10	15

ADAMS, WILLIE — P — ATHLETICS

PERSONAL: Born October 8, 1972, in Gallup, N.M. . . . 6-7/215. . . . Throws right, bats right. . . . Full name: William Edward Adams.
HIGH SCHOOL: La Serna (Whittier, Calif.).
COLLEGE: Stanford.

A

TRANSACTIONS/CAREER NOTES: Selected by Detroit Tigers organization in 52nd round of free-agent draft (June 4, 1990); did not sign. . . . Selected by Oakland Athletics organization in supplemental round ("sandwich pick" between first and second round, 36th pick overall) of free-agent draft (June 3, 1993); pick received as part of compensation for Toronto Blue Jays signing Type A free-agent P Dave Stewart.

Year	Team (League)	W	L	Pct.	ERA	G	GS	CG	ShO	Sv.	IP	H	R	ER	BB	SO
1993—	Madison (Midwest)	0	2	.000	3.38	5	5	0	0	0	18 2/3	21	10	7	8	22
1994—	Modesto (Calif.)	7	1	.875	3.38	11	5	0	0	2	45 1/3	41	17	17	10	42
—	Huntsville (South.)	4	3	.571	4.30	10	10	0	0	0	60 2/3	58	32	29	23	33
1995—	Huntsville (South.)	6	5	.545	3.01	13	13	0	0	0	80 2/3	75	33	27	17	72
—	Edmonton (PCL)	2	5	.286	4.37	11	10	1	0	0	68	73	35	33	15	40

ADAMSON, JOEL — P — MARLINS

PERSONAL: Born July 2, 1971, in Lakewood, Calif. . . . 6-4/185. . . . Throws left, bats left. . . . Full name: Joel Lee Adamson.
HIGH SCHOOL: Artesia (Lakewood, Calif.).
COLLEGE: Cerritos College (Calif.).
TRANSACTIONS/CAREER NOTES: Selected by San Diego Padres organization in 31st round of free-agent draft (June 5, 1989); did not sign. . . . Selected by Philadelphia Phillies organization in seventh round of free-agent draft (June 4, 1990). . . . On Reading suspended list (June 1-8, 1992). . . . Traded by Phillies organization with P Matt Whisenant to Florida Marlins for P Danny Jackson (November 17, 1992). . . . On disabled list (August 6-25, 1994 and June 8-July 23, 1995).

Year	Team (League)	W	L	Pct.	ERA	G	GS	CG	ShO	Sv.	IP	H	R	ER	BB	SO
1990—	Princeton (Appal.)	2	5	.286	3.88	12	8	1	0	1	48 2/3	56	27	21	12	40
1991—	Spartanburg (SAL)	4	4	.500	2.56	14	14	1	1	0	81	72	29	23	22	84
—	Clearwater (Fla. St.)	2	1	.667	3.03	5	5	0	0	0	29 2/3	28	12	10	7	20
1992—	Clearwater (Fla. St.)	5	6	.455	3.41	15	15	1	1	0	89 2/3	90	35	34	19	52
—	Reading (Eastern)	3	6	.333	4.27	10	10	2	0	0	59	68	36	28	13	35
1993—	High Desert (Calif.)■	5	5	.500	4.58	22	20	•6	*3	0	129 2/3	160	83	66	30	72
—	Edmonton (PCL)	1	2	.333	6.92	5	5	0	0	0	26	39	21	20	13	7
1994—	Portland (Eastern)	5	6	.455	4.34	33	11	2	2	7	91 1/3	95	51	44	32	59
1995—	Charlotte (Int'l)	8	4	.667	3.29	19	18	2	0	0	115	113	51	42	20	80

AGUILERA, RICK — P — TWINS

PERSONAL: Born December 31, 1961, in San Gabriel, Calif. . . . 6-5/203. . . . Throws right, bats right. . . . Full name: Richard Warren Aguilera. . . . Name pronounced AG-yuh-LAIR-uh.
HIGH SCHOOL: Edgewood (West Covina, Calif.).
COLLEGE: Brigham Young.
TRANSACTIONS/CAREER NOTES: Selected by St. Louis Cardinals organization in 37th round of free-agent draft (June 3, 1980); did not sign. . . . Selected by New York Mets organization in third round of free-agent draft (June 6, 1983). . . . On New York disabled list (September 3-15, 1985). . . . On New York disabled list (May 23-August 24, 1987); included rehabilitation assignment to Tidewater (August 10-24). . . . On New York disabled list (April 19-June 19 and July 12-September 7, 1988); included rehabilitation assignments to St. Lucie (June 7-14) and Tidewater (June 15-19). . . . Traded by Mets with P David West and three players to be named later to Minnesota Twins for P Frank Viola (July 31, 1989); Portland, Twins organization, acquired P Kevin Tapani and P Tim Drummond (August 1, 1989), and Twins acquired P Jack Savage to complete deal (October 16, 1989). . . . Traded by Twins to Boston Red Sox for P Frank Rodriguez and a player to be named later (July 6, 1995); Twins acquired OF J.J. Johnson to complete deal (October 11, 1995). . . . Granted free agency (October 31, 1995). . . . Signed by Twins (December 11, 1995).
MISCELLANEOUS: Made an out in only appearance as pinch-hitter with New York (1989).

Year	Team (League)	W	L	Pct.	ERA	G	GS	CG	ShO	Sv.	IP	H	R	ER	BB	SO
1983—	Little Falls (NYP)	5	6	.455	3.72	16	15	4	•2	0	104	*109	55	43	26	84
1984—	Lynchburg (Caro.)	8	3	.727	2.34	13	13	6	•3	0	88 1/3	72	29	23	28	101
—	Jackson (Texas)	4	4	.500	4.57	11	11	2	1	0	67	68	37	34	19	71
1985—	Tidewater (Int'l)	6	4	.600	2.51	11	11	2	1	0	79	64	24	22	17	55
—	New York (N.L.)	10	7	.588	3.24	21	19	2	0	0	122 1/3	118	49	44	37	74
1986—	New York (N.L.)	10	7	.588	3.88	28	20	2	0	0	141 2/3	145	70	61	36	104
1987—	New York (N.L.)	11	3	.786	3.60	18	17	1	0	0	115	124	53	46	33	77
—	Tidewater (Int'l)	1	1	.500	0.69	3	3	0	0	0	13	8	2	1	1	10
1988—	New York (N.L.)	0	4	.000	6.93	11	3	0	0	0	24 2/3	29	20	19	10	16
—	St. Lucie (Fla. St.)	0	0	...	1.29	2	2	0	0	0	7	8	1	1	1	5
—	Tidewater (Int'l)	0	0	...	1.50	1	1	0	0	0	6	6	1	1	1	4
1989—	New York (N.L.)	6	6	.500	2.34	36	0	0	0	7	69 1/3	59	19	18	21	80
—	Minnesota (A.L.)■	3	5	.375	3.21	11	11	3	0	0	75 2/3	71	32	27	17	57
1990—	Minnesota (A.L.)	5	3	.625	2.76	56	0	0	0	32	65 1/3	55	27	20	19	61
1991—	Minnesota (A.L.)	4	5	.444	2.35	63	0	0	0	42	69	44	20	18	30	61
1992—	Minnesota (A.L.)	2	6	.250	2.84	64	0	0	0	41	66 2/3	60	28	21	17	52
1993—	Minnesota (A.L.)	4	3	.571	3.11	65	0	0	0	34	72 1/3	60	25	25	14	59
1994—	Minnesota (A.L.)	1	4	.200	3.63	44	0	0	0	23	44 2/3	57	23	18	10	46
1995—	Minnesota (A.L.)	1	1	.500	2.52	22	0	0	0	12	25	20	7	7	6	29
—	Boston (A.L.)■	2	2	.500	2.67	30	0	0	0	20	30 1/3	26	9	9	7	23
A.L. totals (7 years)		22	29	.431	2.91	355	11	3	0	204	449	393	171	145	120	388
N.L. totals (5 years)		37	27	.578	3.58	114	59	5	0	7	473	475	211	188	137	351
Major league totals (11 years)		59	56	.513	3.25	469	70	8	0	211	922	868	382	333	257	739

DIVISION SERIES RECORD

Year	Team (League)	W	L	Pct.	ERA	G	GS	CG	ShO	Sv.	IP	H	R	ER	BB	SO
1995—	Boston (A.L.)	0	0	...	13.50	1	0	0	0	0	2/3	3	1	1	0	1

CHAMPIONSHIP SERIES RECORD

Year	Team (League)	W	L	Pct.	ERA	G	GS	CG	ShO	Sv.	IP	H	R	ER	BB	SO
1986—	New York (N.L.)	0	0	...	0.00	2	0	0	0	0	5	2	1	0	2	2
1988—	New York (N.L.)	0	0	...	1.29	3	0	0	0	0	7	3	1	1	2	4
1991—	Minnesota (A.L.)	0	0	...	0.00	3	0	0	0	3	3 1/3	1	0	0	0	3
Champ. series totals (3 years)		0	0	...	0.59	8	0	0	0	3	15 1/3	6	2	1	4	9

WORLD SERIES RECORD

NOTES: Flied out in only appearance as pinch-hitter (1991). . . . Member of World Series championship teams (1986 and 1991).

Year	Team (League)	W	L	Pct.	ERA	G	GS	CG	ShO	Sv.	IP	H	R	ER	BB	SO
1986—	New York (N.L.)	1	0	1.000	12.00	2	0	0	0	0	3	8	4	4	1	4
1991—	Minnesota (A.L.)	1	1	.500	1.80	4	0	0	0	2	5	6	1	1	1	3
World Series totals (2 years)		2	1	.667	5.63	6	0	0	0	2	8	14	5	5	2	7

ALL-STAR GAME RECORD

Year	League	W	L	Pct.	ERA	GS	CG	ShO	Sv.	IP	H	R	ER	BB	SO
1991—	American	0	0	...	0.00	0	0	0	0	1 1/3	2	0	0	0	3
1992—	American	0	0	...	13.50	0	0	0	0	2/3	1	1	1	0	0
1993—	American	0	0	...	0.00	0	0	0	0	1	2	0	0	0	2
All-Star totals (3 years)		0	0	...	3.00	0	0	0	0	3	5	1	1	0	5

AHEARNE, PAT — P — TIGERS

PERSONAL: Born December 10, 1969, in San Francisco. . . . 6-3/195. . . . Throws right, bats right. . . . Full name: Patrick Howard Ahearne.

COLLEGE: Pepperdine.

TRANSACTIONS/CAREER NOTES: Selected by Detroit Tigers organization in seventh round of free-agent draft (June 1, 1992).

Year	Team (League)	W	L	Pct.	ERA	G	GS	CG	ShO	Sv.	IP	H	R	ER	BB	SO
1992—	Lakeland (Fla. St.)	0	0	...	1.93	1	1	0	0	0	4 2/3	4	2	1	0	4
1993—	Lakeland (Fla. St.)	6	15	.286	4.46	25	24	2	0	0	147 1/3	160	87	73	48	51
1994—	Trenton (Eastern)	7	5	.583	3.98	30	13	2	0	0	108 2/3	126	55	48	25	57
1995—	Toledo (Int'l)	7	9	.438	4.70	25	23	1	1	0	139 2/3	165	83	73	37	54
	—Detroit (A.L.)	0	2	.000	11.70	4	3	0	0	0	10	20	13	13	5	4
Major league totals (1 year)		0	2	.000	11.70	4	3	0	0	0	10	20	13	13	5	4

ALBERRO, JOSE — P — RANGERS

PERSONAL: Born June 29, 1969, in San Juan, Puerto Rico. . . . 6-2/190. . . . Throws right, bats right. . . . Full name: Jose E. Alberro.

HIGH SCHOOL: Escuela Superior (Arecibo, Puerto Rico).

TRANSACTIONS/CAREER NOTES: Signed as non-drafted free agent by Texas Rangers organization (June 11, 1991). . . . On Oklahoma City disabled list (June 18-August 9, 1993).

Year	Team (League)	W	L	Pct.	ERA	G	GS	CG	ShO	Sv.	IP	H	R	ER	BB	SO
1991—	GC Rangers (GCL)	2	0	1.000	1.48	19	0	0	0	6	30 1/3	17	6	5	9	40
	—Charlotte (Fla. St.)	0	1	.000	9.53	5	0	0	0	0	5 2/3	8	9	6	7	3
1992—	Gastonia (S. Atl.)	1	0	1.000	3.48	17	0	0	0	1	20 2/3	18	8	8	4	26
	—Charlotte (Fla. St.)	1	1	.500	1.20	28	0	0	0	15	45	37	10	6	9	29
1993—	Tulsa (Texas)	0	0	...	0.95	17	0	0	0	5	19	11	2	2	8	24
	—Okla. City (A.A.)	0	0	...	6.88	12	0	0	0	0	17	25	15	13	11	14
1994—	Okla. City (A.A.)	4	3	.571	4.52	52	0	0	0	11	69 2/3	79	40	35	36	50
1995—	Texas (A.L.)	0	0	...	7.40	12	0	0	0	0	20 2/3	26	18	17	12	10
	—Okla. City (A.A.)	4	2	.667	3.36	20	10	0	0	0	77 2/3	73	34	29	27	55
Major league totals (1 year)		0	0	...	7.40	12	0	0	0	0	20 2/3	26	18	17	12	10

ALCANTARA, ISRAEL — 3B — EXPOS

PERSONAL: Born May 6, 1973, in Santo Domingo, Dominican Republic. . . . 6-2/180. . . . Bats right, throws right.

TRANSACTIONS/CAREER NOTES: Signed as non-drafted free agent by Montreal Expos organization (July 2, 1990).

STATISTICAL NOTES: Led Gulf Coast League with four intentional bases on balls received in 1992. . . . Led Midwest League third basemen with 371 total chances in 1993.

			BATTING													FIELDING			
Year	Team (League)	Pos.	G	AB	R	H	2B	3B	HR	RBI	Avg.	BB	SO	SB	PO	A	E	Avg.
1991—	Dom. Expos (DSL)	...	68	239	42	68	9	2	•13	51	.285	32	41	8	...	...	...	...
1992—	GC Expos (GCL)	3B-2B-SS	59	*224	29	62	14	2	3	37	.277	17	35	6	55	137	14	.932
1993—	Burlington (Midw.)	3B	126	470	65	115	26	3	18	73	.245	20	125	6	*98	216	*57	.846
1994—	W.P. Beach (FSL)	3B	125	471	65	134	26	4	15	69	.285	26	130	9	97	199	*32	.902
1995—	Harrisburg (East.)	3B	71	237	25	50	12	2	10	29	.211	21	81	1	48	118	20	.892
	—W.P. Beach (FSL)	3B-OF	39	134	16	37	7	2	3	22	.276	9	35	3	34	58	9	.911

ALDRETE, MIKE — 1B/OF — ANGELS

PERSONAL: Born January 29, 1961, in Carmel, Calif. . . . 5-11/185. . . . Bats left, throws left. . . . Full name: Michael Peter Aldrete. . . . Brother of Rich Aldrete, minor league first baseman (1987-92). . . . Name pronounced owl-DRET-ee.

HIGH SCHOOL: Monterey (Calif.).

COLLEGE: Stanford (bachelor of arts degree in communication).

TRANSACTIONS/CAREER NOTES: Selected by San Francisco Giants organization in seventh round of free-agent draft (June 6, 1983). . . . Traded by Giants to Montreal Expos for OF Tracy Jones (December 8, 1988). . . . On Montreal disabled list (August 16-September 1, 1989); included rehabilitation assignment to Indianapolis (August 21-September 1). . . . Released by Expos (March 30, 1991). . . . Signed by San Diego Padres (April 5, 1991). . . . Released by Padres (May 10, 1991). . . . Signed by Colorado Springs, Cleveland Indians organization (May 17, 1991). . . . Released by Indians (March 31, 1992). . . . Signed by Colorado Springs (April 7, 1992). . . . Released by Charlotte, Indians organization (March 24, 1993). . . . Signed by Oakland Athletics organization (March 27, 1993). . . . On Tacoma disabled list (April 8-15, 1993). . . . Granted free agency (November 1, 1993). . . . Re-signed by A's (November 16, 1993). . . . Traded by A's to California Angles for OF Demond Smith (August 24, 1995). . . . Granted free agency (November 1, 1995). . . . Re-signed by Angels organization (December 6, 1995).

STATISTICAL NOTES: Led California League with 225 total bases in 1984. . . . Career major league grand slams: 1.

Year	Team (League)	Pos.	G	AB	R	H	2B	3B	HR	RBI	Avg.	BB	SO	SB	PO	A	E	Avg.
				BATTING											FIELDING			
1983—	Great Falls (Pio.)	1B-OF	38	132	30	55	11	2	4	31	.417	31	22	7	257	17	4	.986
—	Fresno (California)	1B	20	68	5	14	4	0	1	12	.206	11	17	2	189	9	2	.990
1984—	Fresno (California)	1B	136	457	89	155	28	3	12	72	.339	109	77	14	1180	74	8	*.994
1985—	Shreveport (Texas)	1B-OF	127	441	80	147	32	1	15	77	.333	94	57	16	854	41	9	.990
—	Phoenix (PCL)	OF	3	8	0	1	1	0	0	1	.125	0	3	0	3	0	0	1.000
1986—	Phoenix (PCL)	OF-1B	47	159	36	59	14	0	6	35	.371	36	24	0	131	8	1	.993
—	San Francisco (N.L.)	1B-OF	84	216	27	54	18	3	2	25	.250	33	34	1	317	36	1	.997
1987—	San Francisco (N.L.)	OF-1B	126	357	50	116	18	2	9	51	.325	43	50	6	328	18	3	.991
1988—	San Francisco (N.L.)	OF-1B	139	389	44	104	15	0	3	50	.267	56	65	6	272	8	4	.986
1989—	Montreal (N.L.)■	OF-1B	76	136	12	30	8	1	1	12	.221	19	30	1	109	9	1	.992
—	Indianapolis (A.A.)	1B-OF	10	31	4	4	1	0	0	2	.129	8	10	0	41	3	0	1.000
1990—	Montreal (N.L.)	OF-1B	96	161	22	39	7	1	1	18	.242	37	31	1	160	12	1	.994
1991—	San Diego (N.L.)■	OF	12	15	2	0	0	0	0	1	.000	3	4	0	7	1	0	1.000
—	Colo. Springs (PCL)■	OF-1B	23	76	4	22	5	0	0	8	.289	8	17	0	77	8	1	.988
—	Cleveland (A.L.)	1B-OF-DH	85	183	22	48	6	1	1	19	.262	36	37	1	334	23	2	.994
1992—	Colo. Springs (PCL)	1B-OF	128	463	69	149	42	2	8	84	.322	65	113	1	567	38	3	.995
1993—	Tacoma (PCL)■	OF-1B	37	122	20	39	11	2	7	21	.320	26	22	2	75	5	1	.988
—	Oakland (A.L.)	1B-OF-DH	95	255	40	68	13	1	10	33	.267	34	45	1	407	28	2	.995
1994—	Oakland (A.L.)	OF-1B-DH	76	178	23	43	5	0	4	18	.242	20	35	2	207	14	1	.995
1995—	Oakland (A.L.)	1B-OF	60	125	18	34	8	0	4	21	.272	19	23	0	191	10	3	.985
—	California (A.L.)■	DH-OF-1B	18	24	1	6	0	0	0	3	.250	0	8	0	8	0	0	1.000
American League totals (4 years)			334	765	104	199	32	2	19	94	.260	109	148	4	1147	75	8	.993
National League totals (6 years)			533	1274	157	343	66	7	16	157	.269	191	214	15	1193	84	10	.992
Major league totals (9 years)			867	2039	261	542	98	9	35	251	.266	300	362	19	2340	159	18	.993

CHAMPIONSHIP SERIES RECORD

Year	Team (League)	Pos.	G	AB	R	H	2B	3B	HR	RBI	Avg.	BB	SO	SB	PO	A	E	Avg.
				BATTING											FIELDING			
1987—	San Francisco (N.L.)	PH-OF	5	10	0	1	0	0	0	1	.100	0	2	0	5	0	0	1.000

ALEXANDER, MANNY — 2B — ORIOLES

PERSONAL: Born March 20, 1971, in San Pedro de Macoris, Dominican Republic. . . . 5-10/165. . . . Bats right, throws right. . . . Full name: Manuel DeJesus Alexander.

TRANSACTIONS/CAREER NOTES: Signed as non-drafted free agent by Baltimore Orioles organization (February 4, 1988). . . . On disabled list (April 26-July 23, 1990). . . . On Rochester disabled list (May 9-19 and June June 9-17, 1993). . . . On Baltimore disabled list (March 25-May 2, 1994).

STATISTICAL NOTES: Led Appalachian League shortstops with 349 total chances in 1989. . . . Led Carolina League shortstops with 651 total chances and 93 double plays in 1991.

Year	Team (League)	Pos.	G	AB	R	H	2B	3B	HR	RBI	Avg.	BB	SO	SB	PO	A	E	Avg.
				BATTING											FIELDING			
1988—				Dominican Summer League statistics unavailable.														
1989—	Bluefield (Appal.)	SS	65	*274	49	*85	13	2	2	34	.310	20	49	19	*140	177	*32	.908
1990—	Wausau (Midwest)	SS	44	152	16	27	3	1	0	11	.178	12	41	8	66	99	11	.938
1991—	Hagerstown (East.)	SS	3	9	3	3	1	0	0	2	.333	1	3	0	5	4	0	1.000
—	Frederick (Caro.)	SS	134	548	•81	*143	17	3	3	42	.261	44	68	47	*226	*393	32	*.951
1992—	Hagerstown (East.)	SS	127	499	69	129	23	8	2	41	.259	25	62	43	216	253	36	.929
—	Rochester (Int'l)	SS	6	24	3	7	1	0	0	3	.292	1	3	2	12	25	1	.974
—	Baltimore (A.L.)	SS	4	5	1	1	0	0	0	0	.200	0	3	0	3	3	0	1.000
1993—	Rochester (Int'l)	SS	120	471	55	115	23	8	6	51	.244	22	60	19	184	335	18	*.966
—	Baltimore (A.L.)	PR-DH	3	0	1	0	0	0	0	0	...	0	0	0	...	...	...	...
1994—	Rochester (Int'l)	SS-2B	111	426	63	106	23	6	6	39	.249	16	67	30	219	291	33	.939
1995—	Baltimore (A.L.)	2-S-3-DH	94	242	35	57	9	1	3	23	.236	20	30	11	139	170	10	.969
Major league totals (3 years)			101	247	37	58	9	1	3	23	.235	20	33	11	142	173	10	.969

ALFONSECA, ANTONIO — P — MARLINS

PERSONAL: Born April 16, 1972, in La Romano, Dominican Republic. . . . 6-4/180. . . . Throws right, bats right.

TRANSACTIONS/CAREER NOTES: Signed as non-drafted free agent by Montreal Expos organization (July 3, 1989). . . . Selected by Edmonton, Florida Marlins organization, from Harrisburg, Expos organization in Rule 5 minor league draft (December 13, 1993). . . . On disabled list (May 15-June 15, 1995).

Year	Team (League)	W	L	Pct.	ERA	G	GS	CG	ShO	Sv.	IP	H	R	ER	BB	SO
1990—	DSL Expos (DSL)	3	5	.375	3.60	13	13	1	0	0	60	60	29	24	32	19
1991—	GC Expos (GCL)	3	3	.500	3.88	11	10	0	0	0	51	46	33	22	25	38
1992—	GC Expos (GCL)	3	4	.429	3.68	12	10	1	1	0	66	55	31	27	35	62
1993—	Jamestown (NYP)	2	2	.500	6.15	15	4	0	0	1	33 2/3	31	26	23	22	29
1994—	Kane Co. (Mid.)■	6	5	.545	4.07	32	9	0	0	0	86 1/3	78	41	39	21	74
1995—	Portland (Eastern)	9	3	.750	3.64	19	17	1	0	0	96 1/3	81	43	39	42	75

ALFONZO, ED — SS — METS

PERSONAL: Born August 11, 1973, in St. Teresa, Venezuela. . . . 5-11/187. . . . Bats right, throws right. . . . Full name: Edgardo Antonio Alfonzo. . . . Brother of Roberto Alfonzo, second baseman, New York Mets organization (1993-94).

HIGH SCHOOL: Cecilio Acosto (Venezuela).

TRANSACTIONS/CAREER NOTES: Signed as non-drafted free agent by New York Mets organization (February 19, 1991). . . . On disabled list (August 11, 1995-remainder of season).

STATISTICAL NOTES: Led New York-Pennsylvania League shortstops with 389 total chances and 39 double plays in 1992.

			BATTING												FIELDING			
Year	Team (League)	Pos.	G	AB	R	H	2B	3B	HR	RBI	Avg.	BB	SO	SB	PO	A	E	Avg.
1991—	GC Mets (GCL)..........	2B-SS-3B	54	175	29	58	8	4	0	27	.331	34	12	6	99	108	9	.958
1992—	St. Lucie (Fla. St.)......	2B	4	5	0	0	0	0	0	0	.000	0	0	0	1	3	0	1.000
—	Pittsfield (NYP)..........	SS	74	*298	44	*106	13	5	1	44	*.356	18	31	7	*126	*237	*26	.933
1993—	St. Lucie (Fla. St.)......	SS	128	494	75	145	18	3	11	86	.294	57	51	26	183	425	29	.954
1994—	Binghamton (East.)....	SS-2B-1B	127	498	89	146	34	2	15	75	.293	64	55	14	206	408	27	.958
1995—	New York (N.L.)..........	3B-2B-SS	101	335	26	93	13	5	4	41	.278	12	37	1	81	171	7	.973
Major league totals (1 year)			101	335	26	93	13	5	4	41	.278	12	37	1	81	171	7	.973

ALICEA, LUIS — 2B — RED SOX

PERSONAL: Born July 29, 1965, in Santurce, Puerto Rico. . . . 5-9/176. . . . Bats both, throws right. . . . Full name: Luis Rene Alicea. . . . Name pronounced AH-la-SAY-uh.

HIGH SCHOOL: Liceo Castro (Rio Piedras, Puerto Rico).

COLLEGE: Florida State.

TRANSACTIONS/CAREER NOTES: Selected by St. Louis Cardinals organization in first round (23rd pick overall) of free-agent draft (June 2, 1986). . . . On St. Petersburg disabled list (April 6-June 4, 1990). . . . On Louisville disabled list (April 25-May 25, 1991). . . . On St. Louis disabled list (June 1-July 6, 1992); included rehabilitation assignment to Louisville (July 2-6). . . . Traded by Cardinals to Boston Red Sox for P Nate Minchey and OF Jeff McNeely (December 7, 1994).

HONORS: Named second baseman on The Sporting News college All-America team (1986).

STATISTICAL NOTES: Switch-hit home runs in one game (July 28, 1995). . . . Led A.L. second basemen with 699 total chances and 103 double plays in 1995. . . . Career major league grand slams: 1.

			BATTING												FIELDING			
Year	Team (League)	Pos.	G	AB	R	H	2B	3B	HR	RBI	Avg.	BB	SO	SB	PO	A	E	Avg.
1986—	Erie (NYP)..................	2B	47	163	40	46	6	1	3	18	.282	37	20	27	94	163	12	.955
—	Arkansas (Texas)........	2B-SS	25	68	8	16	3	0	0	3	.235	5	11	0	39	63	4	.962
1987—	Arkansas (Texas)........	2B	101	337	57	91	14	3	4	47	.270	49	28	13	184	251	11	*.975
—	Louisville (A.A.)..........	2B	29	105	18	32	10	2	2	20	.305	9	9	4	69	81	4	.974
1988—	Louisville (A.A.)..........	2B-SS-OF	49	191	21	53	11	6	1	21	.277	11	21	8	116	165	0	1.000
—	St. Louis (N.L.)..........	2B	93	297	20	63	10	4	1	24	.212	25	32	1	206	240	14	.970
1989—	Louisville (A.A.)..........	2B	124	412	53	102	20	3	8	48	.248	59	55	13	240	310	16	.972
1990—	St. Peters. (FSL).........	2B	29	95	14	22	1	4	0	12	.232	20	14	9	20	23	0	1.000
—	Arkansas (Texas)........	2B	14	49	11	14	3	1	0	4	.286	7	8	2	24	34	4	.935
—	Louisville (A.A.)..........	3B	25	92	10	32	6	3	0	10	.348	5	12	0	14	39	6	.898
1991—	Louisville (A.A.)..........	2B	31	112	26	44	6	3	4	16	.393	14	8	5	68	95	5	.970
—	St. Louis (N.L.)..........	2B-3B-SS	56	68	5	13	3	0	0	0	.191	8	19	0	19	23	0	1.000
1992—	Louisville (A.A.)..........	2B-SS	20	71	11	20	8	0	0	6	.282	16	6	0	44	52	4	.960
—	St. Louis (N.L.)..........	2B-SS	85	265	26	65	9	11	2	32	.245	27	40	2	136	233	7	.981
1993—	St. Louis (N.L.)..........	2B-OF-3B	115	362	50	101	19	3	3	46	.279	47	54	11	210	281	11	.978
1994—	St. Louis (N.L.)..........	2B-OF	88	205	32	57	12	5	5	29	.278	30	38	4	126	149	4	.986
1995—	Boston (A.L.)■..........	2B	132	419	64	113	20	3	6	44	.270	63	61	13	254	429	16	.977
American League totals (1 year)			132	419	64	113	20	3	6	44	.270	63	61	13	254	429	16	.977
National League totals (5 years)			437	1197	133	299	53	23	11	131	.250	137	183	18	697	926	36	.978
Major league totals (6 years)			569	1616	197	412	73	26	17	175	.255	200	244	31	951	1355	52	.978

DIVISION SERIES RECORD

			BATTING												FIELDING			
Year	Team (League)	Pos.	G	AB	R	H	2B	3B	HR	RBI	Avg.	BB	SO	SB	PO	A	E	Avg.
1995—	Boston (A.L.).............	2B	3	10	1	6	1	0	1	1	.600	2	2	1	6	11	1	.944

ALLANSON, ANDY — C

PERSONAL: Born December 22, 1961, in Richmond, Va. . . . 6-5/225. . . . Bats right, throws right. . . . Full name: Andrew Neal Allanson.

HIGH SCHOOL: Varina (Richmond, Va.).

COLLEGE: Richmond.

TRANSACTIONS/CAREER NOTES: Selected by Cleveland Indians organization in second round of free-agent draft (June 6, 1983). . . . On Cleveland disabled list (June 19-29, 1984 and July 16-August 5, 1988). . . . Released by Indians (March 27, 1990). . . . Signed by Oklahoma City, Texas Rangers organization (April 2, 1990). . . . Released by Oklahoma City (May 8, 1990). . . . Signed by Salinas, independent (July 23, 1990). . . . Released by Salinas (August 29, 1990). . . . Signed by Omaha, Kansas City Royals organization (January 18, 1991). . . . Traded by Royals to Detroit Tigers organization for C Jim Baxter (March 30, 1991). . . . Granted free agency (December 20, 1991). . . . Signed by Denver, Milwaukee Brewers organization (January 23, 1992). . . . On Milwaukee disabled list (May 18-June 30, 1992); included rehabilitation assignment to Denver (June 11-30). . . . Released by Brewers (October 15, 1992). . . . Signed by Phoenix, San Francisco Giants organization (January 14, 1993). . . . Granted free agency (October 15, 1993). . . . Re-signed by Giants organization (November 29, 1993). . . . Released by Phoenix (March 29, 1994). . . . Signed by San Bernardino, independent (April 5, 1994). . . . Contract sold by San Bernardino to Vancouver, California Angels organization (May 3, 1994). . . . On California disabled list (July 2, 1994-remainder of season). . . . Granted free agency (October 17, 1994). . . . Re-signed by Vancouver, Angels organization (March 17, 1995). . . . On California disabled list (June 9-30, 1995). . . . Released by Angels (October 13, 1995).

STATISTICAL NOTES: Led A.L. catchers with 762 total chances and 11 double plays in 1988. . . . Career major league grand slams: 1.

			BATTING												FIELDING			
Year	Team (League)	Pos.	G	AB	R	H	2B	3B	HR	RBI	Avg.	BB	SO	SB	PO	A	E	Avg.
1983—	Waterloo (Midw.)........	C	17	50	4	10	0	0	0	0	.200	7	10	1	99	8	3	.973
—	Batavia (NYP).............	C	51	145	27	38	3	0	0	6	.262	25	16	3	372	27	5	.988
1984—	Buffalo (Eastern)........	C	39	111	12	28	4	0	0	11	.252	15	18	0	154	15	3	.983
—	Waterloo (Midw.)........	C	46	144	14	39	5	0	0	10	.271	10	16	6	68	9	1	.987
1985—	Waterbury (East.).......	C	120	420	69	131	17	1	0	47	*.312	52	25	22	578	64	10	.985
1986—	Cleveland (A.L.)..........	C	101	293	30	66	7	3	1	29	.225	14	36	10	446	33	*20	.960

Year Team (League)	Pos.	G	AB	R	H	2B	3B	HR	RBI	Avg.	BB	SO	SB	PO	A	E	Avg.
		BATTING												FIELDING			
1987—Buffalo (A.A.)	C	76	276	21	75	8	0	4	39	.272	9	36	2	428	30	•12	.974
—Cleveland (A.L.)	C	50	154	17	41	6	0	3	16	.266	9	30	1	252	22	4	.986
1988—Cleveland (A.L.)	C	133	434	44	114	11	0	05	50	.263	25	63	5	*691	60	•11	.986
1989—Cleveland (A.L.)	C	111	323	30	75	9	1	3	17	.232	23	47	4	570	53	9	.986
1990—Okla. City (A.A.)■	C	13	40	3	4	0	0	0	4	.100	6	7	0	79	12	2	.978
—Salinas (Calif.)■	C	36	127	21	37	6	1	3	19	.291	19	22	6	223	28	2	.992
1991—Detroit (A.L.)■	C-1B-DH	60	151	10	35	10	0	1	16	.232	7	31	0	219	22	5	.980
1992—Milwaukee (A.L.)■	C	9	25	6	8	1	0	0	0	.320	1	2	3	30	3	2	.943
—Denver (A.A.)	C-1B-OF	72	266	42	79	16	3	4	31	.297	23	29	9	279	30	3	.990
1993—Phoenix (PCL)■	C-1-0-3	50	161	31	57	15	2	6	23	.354	10	18	7	243	26	8	.971
—San Francisco (N.L.)	C-1B	13	24	3	4	1	0	0	2	.167	1	2	0	38	0	0	1.000
1994—San Bern. (Calif.)■	1B-OF-C	20	61	13	14	2	1	1	9	.230	15	8	6	83	1	4	.955
—Vancouver (PCL)■	C-1B	40	138	18	36	11	0	3	22	.261	10	15	4	208	23	6	.975
1995—Lake Elsinore (Calif.)	C	22	82	22	26	9	0	4	22	.317	16	8	2	122	11	1	.993
—California (A.L.)	C	35	82	5	14	3	0	3	10	.171	7	12	0	164	15	1	.994
American League totals (7 years)		499	1462	142	353	47	4	16	138	.241	86	221	23	2372	208	52	.980
National League totals (1 year)		13	24	3	4	1	0	0	2	.167	1	2	0	38	0	0	1.000
Major league totals (8 years)		512	1486	145	357	48	4	16	140	.240	87	223	23	2410	208	52	.981

ALLENSWORTH, JERMAINE OF PIRATES

PERSONAL: Born January 11, 1972, in Anderson, Ind. . . . 6-0/178. . . . Bats right, throws right. . . . Full name: Jermaine LaMont Allensworth.
HIGH SCHOOL: Madison Heights (Anderson, Ind.).
COLLEGE: Purdue.
TRANSACTIONS/CAREER NOTES: Selected by Pittsburgh Pirates organization in supplemental round ("sandwich pick" between first and second round, 34th pick overall) of free-agent draft (June 3, 1993); pick received as part of compensation for Houston Astros signing Type A free-agent P Doug Drabek.

Year Team (League)	Pos.	G	AB	R	H	2B	3B	HR	RBI	Avg.	BB	SO	SB	PO	A	E	Avg.
		BATTING												FIELDING			
1993—Welland (NYP)	OF	67	263	44	81	16	4	1	32	.308	24	38	18	140	2	3	.979
1994—Carolina (South.)	OF	118	452	63	109	26	8	1	34	.241	39	79	16	245	5	6	.977
1995—Carolina (South.)	OF	56	219	37	59	14	2	1	14	.269	25	34	13	131	3	2	.985
—Calgary (PCL)	OF	51	190	46	60	13	4	3	11	.316	13	30	13	90	2	1	.989

ALOMAR, ROBERTO 2B ORIOLES

PERSONAL: Born February 5, 1968, in Ponce, Puerto Rico. . . . 6-0/185. . . . Bats both, throws right. . . . Full name: Roberto Velazquez Alomar. . . . Son of Sandy Alomar Sr., manager, Ft. Myers Cubs, Chicago Cubs organization, major league infielder with six teams (1964-78) and coach, San Diego Padres (1986-90); and brother of Sandy Alomar Jr., catcher, Cleveland Indians.
TRANSACTIONS/CAREER NOTES: Signed as non-drafted free agent by San Diego Padres organization (February 16, 1985). . . . Traded by Padres with OF Joe Carter to Toronto Blue Jays for 1B Fred McGriff and SS Tony Fernandez (December 5, 1990). . . . On suspended list (May 23-24, 1995). . . . Granted free agency (October 30, 1995). . . . Signed by Baltimore Orioles (December 21, 1995).
RECORDS: Holds A.L. career record for most consecutive errorless games by second baseman—104 (June 21, 1994 through July 3, 1995). . . . Holds A.L. single-season record for fewest double plays by second baseman (150 or more games)—66 (1992). . . . Shares A.L. single-season record for fewest errors by second baseman (150 or more games)—5 (1992).
HONORS: Won A.L. Gold Glove at second base (1991-95). . . . Named second baseman on THE SPORTING NEWS A.L. All-Star team (1992). . . . Named second baseman on THE SPORTING NEWS A.L. Silver Slugger team (1992).
STATISTICAL NOTES: Led South Atlantic League second basemen with 35 errors in 1985. . . . Led Texas League shortstops with 167 putouts and 34 errors in 1987. . . . Led N.L. with 17 sacrifice hits in 1989. . . . Led N.L. second basemen with 17 errors in 1990. . . . Switch-hit home runs in one game (May 10, 1991 and May 3, 1995). . . . Career major league grand slams: 1.

Year Team (League)	Pos.	G	AB	R	H	2B	3B	HR	RBI	Avg.	BB	SO	SB	PO	A	E	Avg.
		BATTING												FIELDING			
1985—Char., S.C. (S. Atl.)	2B-SS	*137	*546	89	160	14	3	0	54	.293	61	73	36	298	339	†36	.947
1986—Reno (California)	2B	90	356	53	123	16	4	4	49	*.346	32	38	14	198	265	18	.963
1987—Wichita (Texas)	SS-2B	130	536	88	171	41	4	12	68	.319	49	74	43	†188	309	†36	.932
1988—Las Vegas (PCL)	2B	9	37	5	10	1	0	2	14	.270	1	4	3	22	29	1	.981
—San Diego (N.L.)	2B	143	545	84	145	24	6	9	41	.266	47	83	24	319	459	16	.980
1989—San Diego (N.L.)	2B	158	623	82	184	27	1	7	56	.295	53	76	42	341	472	*28	.967
1990—San Diego (N.L.)	2B-SS	147	586	80	168	27	5	6	60	.287	48	72	24	316	404	†19	.974
1991—Toronto (A.L.)■	2B	161	637	88	188	41	11	9	69	.295	57	86	53	333	447	15	.981
1992—Toronto (A.L.)	2B-DH	152	571	105	177	27	8	8	76	.310	87	52	49	287	378	5	.993
1993—Toronto (A.L.)	2B	153	589	109	192	35	6	17	93	.326	80	67	55	254	439	14	.980
1994—Toronto (A.L.)	2B	107	392	78	120	25	4	8	38	.306	51	41	19	176	275	4	.991
1995—Toronto (A.L.)	2B	130	517	71	155	24	7	13	66	.300	47	45	30	*272	267	4	*.993
American League totals (5 years)		703	2706	451	832	152	36	55	342	.307	322	291	206	1322	1806	42	.987
National League totals (3 years)		448	1754	246	497	78	12	22	157	.283	148	231	90	976	1335	63	.973
Major league totals (8 years)		1151	4460	697	1329	230	48	77	499	.298	470	522	296	2298	3141	105	.981

CHAMPIONSHIP SERIES RECORD

NOTES: Named A.L. Championship Series Most Valuable Player (1992).

Year Team (League)	Pos.	G	AB	R	H	2B	3B	HR	RBI	Avg.	BB	SO	SB	PO	A	E	Avg.
		BATTING												FIELDING			
1991—Toronto (A.L.)	2B	5	19	3	9	0	0	0	4	.474	2	3	2	14	9	0	1.000
1992—Toronto (A.L.)	2B	6	26	4	11	1	0	2	4	.423	2	1	5	16	15	0	1.000
1993—Toronto (A.L.)	2B	6	24	3	7	1	0	0	4	.292	4	3	4	14	19	0	1.000
Championship series totals (3 years)		17	69	10	27	2	0	2	12	.391	8	7	11	44	43	0	1.000

WORLD SERIES RECORD

NOTES: Shares record for most at-bats in one inning—2 (October 20, 1993, eighth inning).... Member of World Series championship teams (1992 and 1993).

			BATTING											FIELDING			
Year Team (League)	Pos.	G	AB	R	H	2B	3B	HR	RBI	Avg.	BB	SO	SB	PO	A	E	Avg.
1992—Toronto (A.L.)	2B	6	24	3	5	1	0	0	0	.208	3	3	3	5	12	0	1.000
1993—Toronto (A.L.)	2B	6	25	5	12	2	1	0	6	.480	2	3	4	9	21	2	.938
World Series totals (2 years)		12	49	8	17	3	1	0	6	.347	5	6	7	14	33	2	.959

ALL-STAR GAME RECORD

NOTES: Shares single-game record for most stolen bases—2 (July 14, 1992).

		BATTING										FIELDING			
Year League	Pos.	AB	R	H	2B	3B	HR	RBI	Avg.	BB	SO	SB	PO	A	E	Avg.
1990—National	2B	1	0	0	0	0	0	0	.000	0	0	0	1	2	0	1.000
1991—American	2B	4	0	0	0	0	0	0	.000	0	0	0	2	5	0	1.000
1992—American	2B	3	1	1	0	0	0	0	.333	0	0	2	0	1	0	1.000
1993—American	2B	3	1	1	0	0	1	1	.333	0	0	0	0	0	0	...
1994—American	2B	3	1	1	0	0	0	0	.333	0	0	1	0	0	0	...
1995—American	PR-2B	1	0	0	0	0	0	0	.000	0	0	1	0	0	0	...
All-Star Game totals (6 years)		15	3	3	0	0	1	1	.200	0	0	4	3	8	0	1.000

ALOMAR, SANDY — C — INDIANS

PERSONAL: Born June 18, 1966, in Salinas, Puerto Rico.... 6-5/215.... Bats right, throws right.... Full name: Santos Velazquez Alomar Jr.... Son of Sandy Alomar Sr., manager, Ft. Myers Cubs, Chicago Cubs organization, major league infielder with six teams (1964-78) and coach, San Diego Padres (1986-90); and brother of Roberto Alomar, second baseman, Baltimore Orioles.

HIGH SCHOOL: Luis Munoz Rivera (Salinas, Puerto Rico).

TRANSACTIONS/CAREER NOTES: Signed as non-drafted free agent by San Diego Padres organization (October 21, 1983).... Traded by Padres with OF Chris James and 3B Carlos Baerga to Cleveland Indians for OF Joe Carter (December 6, 1989).... On Cleveland disabled list (May 15-June 17 and July 29, 1991-remainder of season); included rehabilitation assignments to Colorado Springs (June 8-17 and August 9-12).... On disabled list (May 2-18, 1992).... On suspended list (July 29-August 2, 1992).... On Cleveland disabled list (May 1-August 7, 1993); included rehabilitation assignment to Charlotte, S.C. (July 22-August 7).... On disabled list (April 24-May 11, 1994).... On Cleveland disabled list (April 19-June 29, 1995); included rehabilitation assignment to Canton/Akron (June 22-29).

HONORS: Named Minor League co-Player of the Year by The Sporting News (1988).... Named Pacific Coast League Player of the Year (1988-89).... Named Minor League Player of the Year by The Sporting News (1989).... Named A.L. Rookie Player of the Year by The Sporting News (1990).... Won A.L. Gold Glove at catcher (1990).... Named A.L. Rookie of the Year by Baseball Writers' Association of America (1990).

STATISTICAL NOTES: Led Northwest League catchers with .985 fielding percentage and 421 putouts in 1984.... Led Pacific Coast League catchers with 14 errors in 1988.... Led Pacific Coast League catchers with 573 putouts in 1988 and 702 in 1989.... Led Pacific Coast League catchers with 633 total chances in 1988 and 761 in 1989.... Career major league grand slams: 1.

MISCELLANEOUS: Batted as switch-hitter (1984-86).

			BATTING											FIELDING			
Year Team (League)	Pos.	G	AB	R	H	2B	3B	HR	RBI	Avg.	BB	SO	SB	PO	A	E	Avg.
1984—Spokane (N'west)	C-1B	59	219	13	47	5	0	0	21	.215	13	20	3	†465	51	8	†.985
1985—Char., S.C. (S. Atl.)	C-OF	100	352	38	73	7	0	3	43	.207	31	30	3	779	75	18	.979
1986—Beaumont (Texas)	C	100	346	36	83	15	1	4	27	.240	15	35	2	505	60	*18	.969
1987—Wichita (Texas)	C	103	375	50	115	19	1	8	65	.307	21	37	1	*606	50	*15	.978
1988—Las Vegas (PCL)	C-OF	93	337	59	100	9	5	16	71	.297	28	35	1	†574	46	†14	.978
—San Diego (N.L.)	PH	1	1	0	0	0	0	0	0	.000	0	1	0	...	...	...	...
1989—Las Vegas (PCL)	C-OF	131	*523	88	160	33	8	13	101	.306	42	58	3	†706	47	12	.984
—San Diego (N.L.)	C	7	19	1	4	1	0	1	6	.211	3	3	0	33	1	0	1.000
1990—Cleveland (A.L.)■	C	132	445	60	129	26	2	9	66	.290	25	46	4	686	46	*14	.981
1991—Cleveland (A.L.)	C-DH	51	184	10	40	9	0	0	7	.217	8	24	0	280	19	4	.987
—Colo. Springs (PCL)	C	12	35	5	14	2	0	1	10	.400	5	0	0	5	0	1	.833
1992—Cleveland (A.L.)	C-DH	89	299	22	75	16	0	2	26	.251	13	32	3	477	39	2	.996
1993—Cleveland (A.L.)	C	64	215	24	58	7	1	6	32	.270	11	28	3	342	25	6	.984
—Charlotte (Int'l)	C	12	44	8	16	5	0	1	8	.364	5	8	0	20	1	0	1.000
1994—Cleveland (A.L.)	C	80	292	44	84	15	1	14	43	.288	25	31	8	453	41	2	.996
1995—Cant./Akr. (East.)	C	6	15	3	6	1	0	0	1	.400	1	1	0	23	0	1	.958
—Cleveland (A.L.)	C	66	203	32	61	6	0	10	35	.300	7	26	3	364	22	2	.995
American League totals (6 years)		482	1638	192	447	79	4	41	209	.273	89	187	21	2602	192	30	.989
National League totals (2 years)		8	20	1	4	1	0	1	6	.200	3	4	0	33	1	0	1.000
Major league totals (8 years)		490	1658	193	451	80	4	42	215	.272	92	191	21	2635	193	30	.990

DIVISION SERIES RECORD

			BATTING											FIELDING			
Year Team (League)	Pos.	G	AB	R	H	2B	3B	HR	RBI	Avg.	BB	SO	SB	PO	A	E	Avg.
1995—Cleveland (A.L.)	C	3	11	1	2	1	0	0	1	.182	0	1	0	22	1	0	1.000

CHAMPIONSHIP SERIES RECORD

			BATTING											FIELDING			
Year Team (League)	Pos.	G	AB	R	H	2B	3B	HR	RBI	Avg.	BB	SO	SB	PO	A	E	Avg.
1995—Cleveland (A.L.)	C	5	15	0	4	1	1	0	1	.267	1	1	0	30	3	1	.971

WORLD SERIES RECORD

			BATTING											FIELDING			
Year Team (League)	Pos.	G	AB	R	H	2B	3B	HR	RBI	Avg.	BB	SO	SB	PO	A	E	Avg.
1995—Cleveland (A.L.)	C	5	15	0	3	2	0	0	1	.200	0	2	0	28	0	0	1.000

A

ALL-STAR GAME RECORD

Year League	Pos.	AB	R	H	2B	3B	HR	RBI	Avg.	BB	SO	SB	PO	A	E	Avg.
		BATTING											FIELDING			
1990—American	C	3	1	2	0	0	0	0	.667	0	0	0	3	0	0	1.000
1991—American	C	2	0	0	0	0	0	0	.000	0	0	0	2	0	0	1.000
1992—American	C	3	0	1	0	0	0	0	.333	0	0	0	3	0	0	1.000
All-Star Game totals (3 years)		8	1	3	0	0	0	0	.375	0	0	0	8	0	0	1.000

ALOU, MOISES — OF — EXPOS

PERSONAL: Born July 3, 1966, in Atlanta. . . . 6-3/195. . . . Bats right, throws right. . . . Full name: Moises Rojas Alou. . . . Son of Felipe Alou, manager, Montreal Expos and major league outfielder/first baseman with six teams (1958-74); nephew of Jesus Alou, major league outfielder with four teams (1963-75 and 1978-79); nephew of Matty Alou, major league outfielder with six teams (1960-74); and cousin of Mel Rojas, pitcher, Expos. . . . Name pronounced moy-SEZZ ah-LOO.

HIGH SCHOOL: C.E.E. (Santo Domingo, Dominican Republic).

COLLEGE: Canada College (Calif.).

TRANSACTIONS/CAREER NOTES: Selected by Pittsburgh Pirates organization in first round (second pick overall) of free-agent draft (January 14, 1986). . . . Traded by Pirates organization to Montreal Expos (August 16, 1990), completing deal in which Expos traded P Zane Smith to Pirates for P Scott Ruskin, SS Willie Greene and a player to be named later (August 8, 1990). . . . On Montreal disabled list (March 19, 1991-entire season; July 7-27, 1992; September 18, 1993-remainder of season; August 18-September 5, 1995 and September 11, 1995-remainder of season).

HONORS: Named outfielder on The Sporting News N.L. All-Star team (1994). . . . Named outfielder on The Sporting News N.L. Silver Slugger team (1994).

STATISTICAL NOTES: Led American Association outfielders with seven double plays in 1990. . . . Career major league grand slams: 1.

Year Team (League)	Pos.	G	AB	R	H	2B	3B	HR	RBI	Avg.	BB	SO	SB	PO	A	E	Avg.
			BATTING											FIELDING			
1986—Watertown (NYP)	OF	69	254	30	60	9	*8	6	35	.236	22	72	14	134	6	7	.952
1987—Macon (S. Atl.)	OF	4	8	1	1	0	0	0	0	.125	2	4	0	6	0	0	1.000
—Watertown (NYP)	OF	39	117	20	25	6	2	4	8	.214	16	36	6	43	1	2	.957
1988—Augusta (S. Atl.)	OF	105	358	58	112	23	5	7	62	.313	51	84	24	220	10	9	.962
1989—Salem (Carolina)	OF	86	321	50	97	29	2	14	53	.302	35	69	12	166	12	10	.947
—Harrisburg (East.)	OF	54	205	36	60	5	2	3	19	.293	17	38	8	89	1	2	.978
1990—Harrisburg (East.)	OF	36	132	19	39	12	2	3	22	.295	16	21	7	93	2	1	.990
—Buffalo (A.A.)	OF	75	271	38	74	4	6	5	31	.273	30	43	9	169	10	8	.957
—Pittsburgh (N.L.)	OF	2	5	0	1	0	0	0	0	.200	0	0	0	3	0	0	1.000
—Indianapolis (A.A.)■	OF	15	55	6	12	1	0	0	6	.218	3	7	4	27	2	0	1.000
—Montreal (N.L.)	OF	14	15	4	3	0	1	0	0	.200	0	3	0	6	1	0	1.000
1991—								Did not play.									
1992—Montreal (N.L.)	OF	115	341	53	96	28	2	9	56	.282	25	46	16	170	6	4	.978
1993—Montreal (N.L.)	OF	136	482	70	138	29	6	18	85	.286	38	53	17	254	11	4	.985
1994—Montreal (N.L.)	OF	107	422	81	143	31	5	22	78	.339	42	63	7	201	4	3	.986
1995—Montreal (N.L.)	OF	93	344	48	94	22	0	14	58	.273	29	56	4	147	5	3	.981
Major league totals (5 years)		467	1609	256	475	110	14	63	277	.295	134	221	44	781	27	14	.983

ALL-STAR GAME RECORD

Year League	Pos.	AB	R	H	2B	3B	HR	RBI	Avg.	BB	SO	SB	PO	A	E	Avg.
		BATTING											FIELDING			
1994—National	OF	1	0	1	1	0	0	1	1.000	0	0	0	0	0	0	...

ALSTON, GARVIN — P — ROCKIES

PERSONAL: Born December 8, 1971, in Mt. Vernon (N.Y.). . . . 6-1/185. . . . Throws right, bats right. . . . Full name: Garvin James Alston.

HIGH SCHOOL: Mount Vernon (N.Y.).

COLLEGE: Florida International.

TRANSACTIONS/CAREER NOTES: Selected by Colorado Rockies organization in 10th round of free-agent draft (June 1, 1992).

Year Team (League)	W	L	Pct.	ERA	G	GS	CG	ShO	Sv.	IP	H	R	ER	BB	SO
1992—Bend (Northwest)	5	4	.556	3.95	14	12	0	0	0	73	71	40	32	29	73
1993—Central Valley (Cal.)	5	9	.357	5.46	25	24	1	0	0	117	124	81	71	70	90
1994—Central Valley (Cal.)	5	9	.357	3.62	37	13	0	0	8	87	91	51	35	42	83
—New Haven (East.)	0	0	...	12.46	4	0	0	0	1	4 1/3	5	6	6	3	8
1995—New Haven (East.)	4	4	.500	2.84	47	0	0	0	6	66 2/3	47	24	21	26	73

ALVAREZ, TAVO — P — EXPOS

PERSONAL: Born November 25, 1971, in Obregon, Mexico. . . . 6-3/235. . . . Throws right, bats right. . . . Full name: Cesar Octavo Alvarez.

HIGH SCHOOL: Tucson (Ariz.).

TRANSACTIONS/CAREER NOTES: Selected by Montreal Expos organization in second round of free-agent draft (June 4, 1990); pick received as part of compensation for New York Yankees signing Type A free-agent P Pascual Perez. . . . On disabled list (August 30, 1991-remainder of season; June 17-24 and August 1-16, 1993). . . . On Ottawa disabled list (April 7, 1994-entire season).

Year Team (League)	W	L	Pct.	ERA	G	GS	CG	ShO	Sv.	IP	H	R	ER	BB	SO
1990—GC Expos (GCL)	5	2	.714	2.60	11	10	0	0	0	52	42	17	15	16	47
1991—Sumter (S. Atl.)	12	10	.545	3.24	25	25	3	1	0	152 2/3	151	68	55	58	158
1992—WP Beach (FSL)	13	4	.765	*1.49	19	19	•7	*4	0	139	124	30	23	24	83
—Harrisburg (East.)	4	1	.800	2.85	7	7	2	1	0	47 1/3	48	15	15	9	42
1993—Ottawa (Int'l)	7	10	.412	4.22	25	25	1	0	0	140 2/3	163	80	66	55	77
1994—							Did not play.								
1995—Harrisburg (East.)	2	1	.667	2.25	3	3	0	0	0	16	17	8	4	5	14
—Montreal (N.L.)	1	5	.167	6.75	8	8	0	0	0	37 1/3	46	30	28	14	17
Major league totals (1 year)	1	5	.167	6.75	8	8	0	0	0	37 1/3	46	30	28	14	17

ALVAREZ, WILSON — P — WHITE SOX

PERSONAL: Born March 24, 1970, in Maracaibo, Venezuela. . . . 6-1/235. . . . Throws left, bats left. . . . Full name: Wilson Eduardo Alvarez.
TRANSACTIONS/CAREER NOTES: Signed as non-drafted free agent by Texas Rangers organization (September 23, 1986). . . . Traded by Rangers with IF Scott Fletcher and OF Sammy Sosa to Chicago White Sox for OF Harold Baines and IF Fred Manrique (July 29, 1989).
STATISTICAL NOTES: Tied for Gulf Coast League lead with six home runs allowed in 1987. . . . Pitched 7-0 no-hit victory for Chicago against Baltimore (August 11, 1991).

Year	Team (League)	W	L	Pct.	ERA	G	GS	CG	ShO	Sv.	IP	H	R	ER	BB	SO
1987—	Gastonia (S. Atl.)	1	5	.167	6.47	8	6	0	0	0	32	39	24	23	23	19
—	GC Rangers (GCL)	2	5	.286	5.24	10	10	0	0	0	44 2/3	41	29	26	21	46
1988—	Gastonia (S. Atl.)	4	11	.267	2.98	23	23	1	0	0	127	113	63	42	49	134
—	Okla. City (A.A.)	1	1	.500	3.78	5	3	0	0	0	16 2/3	17	8	7	6	9
1989—	Charlotte (Fla. St.)	7	4	.636	2.11	13	13	3	2	0	81	68	29	19	21	51
—	Tulsa (Texas)	2	2	.500	2.06	7	7	1	1	0	48	40	14	11	16	29
—	Texas (A.L.)	0	1	.000	...	1	1	0	0	0	0	3	3	3	2	0
—	Birmingham (Sou.)■	2	1	.667	3.03	6	6	0	0	0	35 2/3	32	12	12	16	18
1990—	Birmingham (Sou.)	5	1	.833	4.27	7	7	1	0	0	46 1/3	44	24	22	25	36
—	Vancouver (PCL)	7	7	.500	6.00	17	15	1	0	0	75	91	54	50	51	35
1991—	Birmingham (Sou.)	10	6	.625	1.83	23	23	3	2	0	152 1/3	109	46	31	74	165
—	Chicago (A.L.)	3	2	.600	3.51	10	9	2	1	0	56 1/3	47	26	22	29	32
1992—	Chicago (A.L.)	5	3	.625	5.20	34	9	0	0	1	100 1/3	103	64	58	65	66
1993—	Chicago (A.L.)	15	8	.652	2.95	31	31	1	1	0	207 2/3	168	78	68	*122	155
—	Nashville (A.A.)	0	1	.000	2.84	1	1	0	0	0	6 1/3	7	7	2	2	8
1994—	Chicago (A.L.)	12	8	.600	3.45	24	24	2	1	0	161 2/3	147	72	62	62	108
1995—	Chicago (A.L.)	8	11	.421	4.32	29	29	3	0	0	175	171	96	84	93	118
Major league totals (6 years)		43	33	.566	3.81	129	103	8	3	1	701	639	339	297	373	479

CHAMPIONSHIP SERIES RECORD

Year	Team (League)	W	L	Pct.	ERA	G	GS	CG	ShO	Sv.	IP	H	R	ER	BB	SO
1993—	Chicago (A.L.)	1	0	1.000	1.00	1	1	1	0	0	9	7	1	1	2	6

ALL-STAR GAME RECORD

Year	League	W	L	Pct.	ERA	GS	CG	ShO	Sv.	IP	H	R	ER	BB	SO
1994—	American	0	0	...	0.00	0	0	0	0	1	0	0	0	0	0

AMARAL, RICH — OF — MARINERS

PERSONAL: Born April 1, 1962, in Visalia, Calif. . . . 6-0/175. . . . Bats right, throws right. . . . Full name: Richard Louis Amaral. . . . Name pronounced AM-ar-all.
HIGH SCHOOL: Estancia (Costa Mesa, Calif.).
JUNIOR COLLEGE: Orange Coast College (Calif.).
COLLEGE: UCLA.
TRANSACTIONS/CAREER NOTES: Selected by Chicago Cubs organization in second round of free-agent draft (June 6, 1983). . . . Selected by Chicago White Sox organization from Cubs organization in Rule 5 minor league draft (December 6, 1988). . . . Granted free agency (October 15, 1990). . . . Signed by Seattle Mariners organization (November 25, 1990). . . . On Seattle disabled list (May 29-July 17, 1991); included rehabilitation assignment to Calgary (July 11-17). . . . On disabled list (August 1-16, 1993).
HONORS: Named second baseman on The Sporting News college All-America team (1983).
STATISTICAL NOTES: Tied for New York-Pennsylvania League lead in double plays by second baseman with 39 in 1984. . . . Tied for Carolina League lead in errors by second baseman with 25 in 1985. . . . Led Pacific Coast League with .433 on-base percentage in 1991.

				BATTING											FIELDING			
Year	Team (League)	Pos.	G	AB	R	H	2B	3B	HR	RBI	Avg.	BB	SO	SB	PO	A	E	Avg.
1983—	Geneva (NYP)	2B-3B-SS	67	269	63	68	17	3	1	24	.253	45	47	22	135	205	14	.960
1984—	Quad Cities (Mid.)	2B-SS	34	119	21	25	1	0	0	7	.210	24	29	12	62	73	6	.957
1985—	Winst.-Salem (Car.)	2B-3B	124	428	62	116	15	5	3	36	.271	59	68	26	228	318	‡27	.953
1986—	Pittsfield (Eastern)	2B	114	355	43	89	12	0	0	24	.251	39	65	25	228	266	14	.972
1987—	Pittsfield (Eastern)	2B-1B	104	315	45	80	8	5	0	28	.254	43	50	28	242	274	18	.966
1988—	Pittsfield (Eastern)	2-3-1-S-O	122	422	66	117	15	4	4	47	.277	56	53	54	288	262	19	.967
1989—	Birm. (Southern)■	2B-SS-3B	122	432	*90	123	15	6	4	48	.285	88	66	57	198	256	23	.952
1990—	Vancouver (PCL)	S-3-2-O-1	130	462	87	139	*39	5	4	56	.301	88	68	20	154	260	15	.965
1991—	Calgary (PCL)■	SS-2B	86	347	79	120	26	2	3	36	*.346	53	37	30	148	284	15	.966
—	Seattle (A.L.)	2-3-S-DH-1	14	16	2	1	0	0	0	0	.063	1	5	0	13	16	2	.935
1992—	Calgary (PCL)	SS-2B-OF	106	403	79	128	21	8	0	21	.318	67	69	*53	192	329	22	.959
—	Seattle (A.L.)	S-3-O-1-2	35	100	9	24	3	0	1	7	.240	5	16	4	33	68	3	.971
1993—	Seattle (A.L.)	2-3-S-DH-1	110	373	53	108	24	1	1	44	.290	33	54	19	180	270	10	.978
1994—	Seattle (A.L.)	2-O-S-DH-1	77	228	37	60	10	2	4	18	.263	24	28	5	107	118	15	.938
—	Calgary (PCL)	2B-OF	13	56	13	18	7	0	0	12	.321	4	6	2	28	35	3	.955
1995—	Seattle (A.L.)	OF-DH	90	238	45	67	14	2	2	19	.282	21	33	21	121	6	1	.992
Major league totals (5 years)			326	955	146	260	51	5	8	88	.272	84	136	49	454	478	31	.968

CHAMPIONSHIP SERIES RECORD

				BATTING											FIELDING			
Year	Team (League)	Pos.	G	AB	R	H	2B	3B	HR	RBI	Avg.	BB	SO	SB	PO	A	E	Avg.
1995—	Seattle (A.L.)	PH	2	2	0	0	0	0	0	0	.000	0	1	0	0	0	0	...

AMARO, RUBEN — OF — BLUE JAYS

PERSONAL: Born February 12, 1965, in Philadelphia. . . . 5-10/175. . . . Bats both, throws right. . . . Full name: Ruben Amaro Jr. . . . Son of Ruben Amaro Sr., major league infielder with four teams (1958 and 1960-69).
HIGH SCHOOL: William Penn Charter (Philadelphia).

COLLEGE: Stanford (degree in human biology, 1987).
TRANSACTIONS/CAREER NOTES: Selected by California Angels organization in 11th round of free-agent draft (June 2, 1987). . . . Traded by Angels with P Kyle Abbott to Philadelphia Phillies for OF Von Hayes (December 8, 1991). . . . On Scranton/Wilkes-Barre disabled list (April 26-May 7, 1993). . . . Traded by Phillies to Cleveland Indians for P Heathcliff Slocumb (November 2, 1993). . . . On Cleveland disabled list (July 29-September 1, 1995); included rehabilitation assignment to Buffalo (August 13-28). . . . Released by Indians (November 9, 1995). . . . Signed by Toronto Blue Jays organization (January 24, 1996).
STATISTICAL NOTES: Led Northwest League in caught stealing with 11 in 1987. . . . Tied for Texas League lead in being hit by pitch with nine in 1990.

			BATTING												FIELDING			
Year	**Team (League)**	**Pos.**	**G**	**AB**	**R**	**H**	**2B**	**3B**	**HR**	**RBI**	**Avg.**	**BB**	**SO**	**SB**	**PO**	**A**	**E**	**Avg.**
1987—	Salem (Northwest).....	0-3-1-S-2	71	241	51	68	7	3	3	41	.282	49	28	27	243	53	17	.946
1988—	Palm Springs (Cal.)....	2-0-C-S	115	417	96	111	13	3	4	50	.266	105	61	42	258	188	18	.961
	—Midland (Texas)..........	2B	13	31	5	4	1	0	0	2	.129	4	5	4	14	30	1	.978
1989—	Quad City (Midw.)......	OF-2B	59	200	50	72	9	4	3	27	.360	45	25	20	94	34	4	.970
	—Midland (Texas)..........	OF	29	110	28	42	9	2	3	9	.382	10	19	7	34	2	2	.947
1990—	Midland (Texas)..........	OF	57	224	50	80	15	6	4	38	.357	29	23	8	97	8	0	1.000
	—Edmonton (PCL)........	OF-1B	82	318	53	92	15	4	3	32	.289	40	43	32	161	5	2	.988
1991—	Edmonton (PCL)........	OF-2B-1B	121	472	*95	154	*42	6	3	42	.326	63	48	36	167	23	5	.974
	—California (A.L.)..........	OF-2B-DH	10	23	0	5	1	0	0	2	.217	3	3	0	9	6	1	.938
1992—	Philadelphia (N.L.)■..	OF	126	374	43	82	15	6	7	34	.219	37	54	11	232	5	2	.992
	—Scran./W.B. (Int'l).......	OF	18	68	8	20	4	1	1	10	.294	9	6	2	35	1	0	1.000
1993—	Scran./W.B. (Int'l).......	OF-2B	101	412	76	120	30	5	9	37	.291	31	44	25	272	8	5	.982
	—Philadelphia (N.L.)......	OF	25	48	7	16	2	2	1	6	.333	6	5	0	25	1	1	.963
1994—	Charlotte (Int'l)■........	OF	43	181	39	58	12	4	3	17	.320	15	16	9	84	2	1	.989
	—Cleveland (A.L.)..........	OF-DH	26	23	5	5	1	0	2	5	.217	2	3	2	10	0	1	.909
1995—	Cleveland (A.L.)..........	OF-DH	28	60	5	12	3	0	1	7	.200	4	6	1	35	0	0	1.000
	—Buffalo (A.A.)..............	OF	54	213	42	65	15	3	6	22	.305	18	29	6	102	2	1	.990
American League totals (3 years)			64	106	10	22	5	0	3	14	.208	9	12	3	54	6	2	.968
National League totals (2 years)			151	422	50	98	17	8	8	40	.232	43	59	11	257	6	3	.989
Major league totals (5 years)			215	528	60	120	22	8	11	54	.227	52	71	14	311	12	5	.985

CHAMPIONSHIP SERIES RECORD

			BATTING												FIELDING			
Year	**Team (League)**	**Pos.**	**G**	**AB**	**R**	**H**	**2B**	**3B**	**HR**	**RBI**	**Avg.**	**BB**	**SO**	**SB**	**PO**	**A**	**E**	**Avg.**
1995—	Cleveland (A.L.)..........	PR-DH	3	1	1	0	0	0	0	0	.000	0	0	0	0	0	0	...

WORLD SERIES RECORD

			BATTING												FIELDING			
Year	**Team (League)**	**Pos.**	**G**	**AB**	**R**	**H**	**2B**	**3B**	**HR**	**RBI**	**Avg.**	**BB**	**SO**	**SB**	**PO**	**A**	**E**	**Avg.**
1995—	Cleveland (A.L.)..........	PH-OF	2	2	0	0	0	0	0	0	.000	0	1	0	0	0	0	...

ANDERSON, BRADY — OF — ORIOLES

PERSONAL: Born January 18, 1964, in Silver Spring, Md. . . . 6-1/195. . . . Bats left, throws left. . . . Full name: Brady Kevin Anderson.
HIGH SCHOOL: Carlsbad (Calif.).
COLLEGE: UC Irvine.
TRANSACTIONS/CAREER NOTES: Selected by Boston Red Sox organization in 10th round of free-agent draft (June 3, 1985). . . . Traded by Red Sox with P Curt Schilling to Baltimore Orioles for P Mike Boddicker (July 29, 1988). . . . On Baltimore disabled list (June 8-July 20, 1990); included rehabilitation assignments to Hagerstown (July 5-12) and Frederick (July 13-17). . . . On Baltimore disabled list (May 28-June 14, 1991 and June 23-July 8, 1993).
STATISTICAL NOTES: Led A.L. outfielders with six double plays in 1992. . . . Career major league grand slams: 1.

			BATTING												FIELDING			
Year	**Team (League)**	**Pos.**	**G**	**AB**	**R**	**H**	**2B**	**3B**	**HR**	**RBI**	**Avg.**	**BB**	**SO**	**SB**	**PO**	**A**	**E**	**Avg.**
1985—	Elmira (NYP)..............	OF	71	215	36	55	7	•6	5	21	.256	*67	32	13	119	5	3	.976
1986—	Winter Haven (FSL)....	OF	126	417	86	133	19	11	12	87	.319	*107	47	44	280	5	1	*.997
1987—	New Britain (East.).....	OF	52	170	30	50	4	3	6	35	.294	45	24	7	127	2	2	.985
	—Pawtucket (Int'l).........	OF	23	79	18	30	4	0	2	8	.380	16	8	2	48	1	0	1.000
1988—	Boston (A.L.).............	OF	41	148	14	34	5	3	0	12	.230	15	35	4	87	3	1	.989
	—Pawtucket (Int'l).........	OF	49	167	27	48	6	1	4	19	.287	26	33	8	115	4	2	.983
	—Baltimore (A.L.)■.......	OF	53	177	17	35	8	1	1	9	.198	8	40	6	156	1	3	.981
1989—	Baltimore (A.L.)..........	OF-DH	94	266	44	55	12	2	4	16	.207	43	45	16	191	3	3	.985
	—Rochester (Int'l).........	OF	21	70	14	14	1	2	1	8	.200	12	13	2	1	0	0	1.000
1990—	Baltimore (A.L.)..........	OF-DH	89	234	24	54	5	2	3	24	.231	31	46	15	149	3	2	.987
	—Hagerstown (East.).....	OF	9	34	8	13	0	2	1	5	.382	5	5	2	8	1	0	1.000
	—Frederick (Caro.)........	OF	2	7	2	3	1	0	0	3	.429	1	1	0	1	0	0	1.000
1991—	Baltimore (A.L.)..........	OF-DH	113	256	40	59	12	3	2	27	.230	38	44	12	150	3	3	.981
	—Rochester (Int'l).........	OF	7	26	5	10	3	0	0	2	.385	7	4	4	19	1	0	1.000
1992—	Baltimore (A.L.)..........	OF	159	623	100	169	28	10	21	80	.271	98	98	53	382	10	8	.980
1993—	Baltimore (A.L.)..........	OF-DH	142	560	87	147	36	8	13	66	.263	82	99	24	296	7	2	.993
1994—	Baltimore (A.L.)..........	OF	111	453	78	119	25	5	12	48	.263	57	75	31	247	4	1	.996
1995—	Baltimore (A.L.)..........	OF	143	554	108	145	33	10	16	64	.262	87	111	26	268	1	3	.989
Major league totals (8 years)			945	3271	512	817	164	44	72	346	.250	459	593	187	1926	35	26	.987

ALL-STAR GAME RECORD

			BATTING											FIELDING			
Year	**League**	**Pos.**	**AB**	**R**	**H**	**2B**	**3B**	**HR**	**RBI**	**Avg.**	**BB**	**SO**	**SB**	**PO**	**A**	**E**	**Avg.**
1992—	American....................	OF	3	0	0	0	0	0	0	.000	0	0	0	1	0	0	1.000

ANDERSON, BRIAN — P — ANGELS

PERSONAL: Born April 26, 1972, in Geneva, O. . . . 6-1/190. . . . Throws left, bats both. . . . Full name: Brian James Anderson.
HIGH SCHOOL: Geneva (O.).
COLLEGE: Wright State.
TRANSACTIONS/CAREER NOTES: Selected by California Angels organization in first round (third pick overall) of free-agent draft (June 3, 1993). . . . On California disabled list (May 7-June 7, 1994); included rehabilitation assignment to Lake Elsinore (May 27-June 7). . . . On California disabled list (May 6-June 20, 1995); included rehabilitation assignment to Lake Elsinore (June 4-20).
RECORDS: Shares major league record for most home runs allowed in one inning—4 (September 5, 1995, second inning).
HONORS: Named A.L. Rookie Pitcher of the Year by THE SPORTING NEWS (1994).
STATISTICAL NOTES: Tied for A.L. lead with five balks in 1994 and three in 1995.

Year	Team (League)	W	L	Pct.	ERA	G	GS	CG	ShO	Sv.	IP	H	R	ER	BB	SO
1993	—Midland (Texas)	0	1	.000	3.38	2	2	0	0	0	10 2/3	16	5	4	0	9
	—Vancouver (PCL)	0	1	.000	12.38	2	2	0	0	0	8	13	12	11	6	2
	—California (A.L.)	0	0	...	3.97	4	1	0	0	0	11 1/3	11	5	5	2	4
1994	—California (A.L.)	7	5	.583	5.22	18	18	0	0	0	101 2/3	120	63	59	27	47
	—Lake Elsinore (California)	0	1	.000	3.00	2	2	0	0	0	12	6	4	4	0	9
1995	—California (A.L.)	6	8	.429	5.87	18	17	1	0	0	99 2/3	110	66	65	30	45
	—Lake Elsinore (California)	1	1	.500	1.93	3	3	0	0	0	14	10	3	3	1	13
Major league totals (3 years)		13	13	.500	5.46	40	36	1	0	0	212 2/3	241	134	129	59	96

ANDERSON, GARRET — OF — ANGELS

PERSONAL: Born June 30, 1972, in Los Angeles. . . . 6-3/190. . . . Bats left, throws left. . . . Full name: Garret Joseph Anderson.
HIGH SCHOOL: John F. Kennedy (Granada Hills, Calif.) and Palos Verdes Estates (Calif.).
TRANSACTIONS/CAREER NOTES: Selected by California Angels organization in fourth round of free-agent draft (June 4, 1990).
HONORS: Named A.L. Rookie Player of the Year by THE SPORTING NEWS (1995).

			BATTING												FIELDING			
Year	Team (League)	Pos.	G	AB	R	H	2B	3B	HR	RBI	Avg.	BB	SO	SB	PO	A	E	Avg.
1990	—Ariz. Angels (Ariz.)	OF	32	127	5	27	2	0	0	14	.213	2	24	3	53	2	2	.965
	—Boise (Northwest)	OF	25	83	11	21	3	1	1	8	.253	4	18	0	38	0	2	.950
1991	—Quad City (Midw.)	OF	105	392	40	102	22	2	2	42	.260	20	89	5	158	7	10	.943
1992	—Palm Springs (Cal.)	OF	81	322	46	104	15	2	1	62	.323	21	61	1	137	4	6	.959
	—Midland (Texas)	OF	39	146	16	40	5	0	2	19	.274	9	30	2	62	6	1	.986
1993	—Vancouver (PCL)	OF-1B	124	467	57	137	34	4	4	71	.293	31	95	3	198	13	2	.991
1994	—Vancouver (PCL)	OF-1B	123	505	75	162	42	6	12	102	.321	28	93	3	196	10	2	.990
	—California (A.L.)	OF	5	13	0	5	0	0	0	1	.385	0	2	0	10	0	0	1.000
1995	—California (A.L.)	OF-DH	106	374	50	120	19	1	16	69	.321	19	65	6	213	7	5	.978
	—Vancouver (PCL)	OF	14	61	9	19	7	0	0	12	.311	5	14	0	22	0	1	.957
Major league totals (2 years)			111	387	50	125	19	1	16	70	.323	19	67	6	223	7	5	.979

ANDERSON, SCOTT — P

PERSONAL: Born May 1, 1962, in Corvallis, Ore. . . . 6-6/190. . . . Throws right, bats right. . . . Full name: Scott Richard Anderson.
HIGH SCHOOL: Newport (Bellevue, Wash.).
COLLEGE: Oregon State.
TRANSACTIONS/CAREER NOTES: Selected by Oakland Athletics organization in 16th round of free-agent draft (June 3, 1980); did not sign. . . . Selected by Texas Rangers organization in seventh round of free-agent draft (June 4, 1984). . . . Traded by Rangers organization to Indianapolis, Montreal Expos organization, for OF/1B Mike Berger (December 19, 1988). . . . Released by Expos (November 1, 1990). . . . Signed by Chunichi Dragons of Japan Central League (November 20, 1991). . . . Signed as free agent by Edmonton, Florida Marlins organization (January 26, 1993). . . . On disabled list (June 22-July 11, 1993). . . . Granted free agency (October 15, 1993). . . . Signed by New Orleans, Milwaukee Brewers organization (December 27, 1993). . . . On disabled list (April 25-June 7 and June 27-September 12, 1994). . . . Granted free agency (October 15, 1994). . . . Signed by Kansas City Royals organization (January 29, 1995). . . . On Omaha disabled list (April 28-June 1, 1995). . . . Granted free agency (October 16, 1995).

Year	Team (League)	W	L	Pct.	ERA	G	GS	CG	ShO	Sv.	IP	H	R	ER	BB	SO
1984	—Burlington (Midw.)	3	6	.333	2.50	14	13	2	0	0	86 1/3	79	33	24	28	81
1985	—Tulsa (Texas)	9	6	.600	3.67	28	•27	2	1	0	174 1/3	177	87	71	51	123
1986	—Tulsa (Texas)	0	0	...	1.45	10	0	0	0	5	18 2/3	11	4	3	8	13
	—Okla. City (A.A.)	5	7	.417	2.96	48	0	0	0	15	82	82	36	27	28	51
1987	—Texas (A.L.)	0	1	.000	9.53	8	0	0	0	0	11 1/3	17	12	12	8	6
	—Okla. City (A.A.)	5	3	.625	5.63	49	0	0	0	0	64	79	44	40	35	39
1988	—Okla. City (A.A.)	4	6	.400	4.55	38	10	0	0	0	97	101	51	49	49	44
1989	—Indianapolis (A.A.)■	7	8	.467	3.17	29	19	1	0	0	127 2/3	139	62	45	44	88
1990	—Indianapolis (A.A.)	12	10	.545	3.31	27	25	*6	2	0	182	166	74	67	61	116
	—Montreal (N.L.)	0	1	.000	3.00	4	3	0	0	0	18	12	6	6	5	16
1991	—Chunichi (Jp. Cn.)■	9	7	.563	4.09	23	17	6	4	0	132	131	62	60	45	80
1992	—Chunichi (Jp. Cn.)	9	14	.391	3.92	31	22	1	0	0	140	147	72	61	50	92
1993	—Edmonton (PCL)■	5	4	.556	3.53	44	1	0	0	4	66 1/3	74	30	26	15	52
1994	—New Orleans (A.A.)■	0	2	.000	7.03	8	3	0	0	0	24 1/3	34	20	19	6	17
1995	—Omaha (Am. Assoc.)■	5	3	.625	4.17	15	11	1	0	0	73 1/3	63	37	34	16	47
	—Kansas City (A.L.)	1	0	1.000	5.33	6	4	0	0	0	25 1/3	29	15	15	8	6
A.L. totals (2 years)		1	1	.500	6.63	14	4	0	0	0	36 2/3	46	27	27	16	12
N.L. totals (1 year)		0	1	.000	3.00	4	3	0	0	0	18	12	6	6	5	16
Major league totals (3 years)		1	2	.333	5.43	18	7	0	0	0	54 2/3	58	33	33	21	28

ANDREWS, SHANE — 3B — EXPOS

PERSONAL: Born August 28, 1971, in Dallas. . . . 6-1/215. . . . Bats right, throws right. . . . Full name: Darrell Shane Andrews.
HIGH SCHOOL: Carlsbad (N.M.) Senior.
TRANSACTIONS/CAREER NOTES: Selected by Montreal Expos organization in first round (11th pick overall) of free-agent draft (June 4, 1990). . . . On disabled list (August 3-11, 1993).
STATISTICAL NOTES: Led South Atlantic League third basemen with 98 putouts in 1992. . . . Led International League third basemen with 436 total chances in 1994. . . . Career major league grand slams: 1.

		BATTING												FIELDING			
Year Team (League)	**Pos.**	**G**	**AB**	**R**	**H**	**2B**	**3B**	**HR**	**RBI**	**Avg.**	**BB**	**SO**	**SB**	**PO**	**A**	**E**	**Avg.**
1990—GC Expos (GCL)	3B	56	190	31	46	7	1	3	24	.242	29	46	11	42	105	17	.896
1991—Sumter (S. Atl.)	3B	105	356	46	74	16	7	11	49	.208	65	132	5	71	205	29	.905
1992—Albany (S. Atl.)	3B-1B	136	453	76	104	18	1	*25	87	.230	*107	*174	8	†125	212	26	.928
1993—Harrisburg (East.)	3B-SS	124	442	77	115	29	2	18	70	.260	64	118	10	74	217	23	.927
1994—Ottawa (Int'l)	3B	137	460	79	117	25	2	16	85	.254	80	126	6	84	*320	*32	.927
1995—Montreal (N.L.)	3B-1B	84	220	27	47	10	1	8	31	.214	17	68	1	182	97	7	.976
Major league totals (1 year)		84	220	27	47	10	1	8	31	.214	17	68	1	182	97	7	.976

ANDUJAR, LUIS — P — WHITE SOX

PERSONAL: Born November 22, 1972, in Bani, Dominican Republic. . . . 6-2/175. . . . Throws right, bats right. . . . Full name: Luis Sanchez Andujar.
TRANSACTIONS/CAREER NOTES: Signed as non-drafted free agent by Chicago White Sox organization (February 25, 1991). . . . On disabled list (July 8-18, 1992). . . . On Birmingham disabled list (September 2, 1993-remainder of season). . . . On Birmingham disabled list (June 10-July 20 and August 9, 1994-remainder of season).
HONORS: Named Southern League Most Outstanding Pitcher (1995).
STATISTICAL NOTES: Pitched 1-0 no-hit victory for Birmingham against Memphis (August 8, 1995).

Year Team (League)	**W**	**L**	**Pct.**	**ERA**	**G**	**GS**	**CG**	**ShO**	**Sv.**	**IP**	**H**	**R**	**ER**	**BB**	**SO**
1991—GC White Sox (GCL)	4	4	.500	2.45	10	10	1	•1	0	62 1/3	60	27	17	10	52
1992—South Bend (Midw.)	6	5	.545	2.92	32	15	1	1	3	120 1/3	109	49	39	47	91
1993—Sarasota (Fla. St.)	6	6	.500	1.99	18	11	2	0	1	86	67	26	19	28	76
—Birmingham (Sou.)	5	0	1.000	1.82	6	6	0	0	0	39 2/3	31	9	8	18	48
1994—Birmingham (Sou.)	3	7	.300	5.05	15	15	0	0	0	76 2/3	90	50	43	25	64
—GC White Sox (GCL)	1	0	1.000	0.00	2	0	0	0	0	6	3	1	0	1	6
1995—Birmingham (Sou.)	14	8	.636	2.85	27	27	2	1	0	167 1/3	147	64	53	44	146
—Chicago (A.L.)	2	1	.667	3.26	5	5	0	0	0	30 1/3	26	12	11	14	9
Major league totals (1 year)	2	1	.667	3.26	5	5	0	0	0	30 1/3	26	12	11	14	9

ANTHONY, ERIC — OF — REDS

PERSONAL: Born November 8, 1967, in San Diego. . . . 6-2/195. . . . Bats left, throws left. . . . Full name: Eric Todd Anthony.
HIGH SCHOOL: Sharstown (Houston).
TRANSACTIONS/CAREER NOTES: Selected by Houston Astros organization in 34th round of free-agent draft (June 2, 1986). . . . On Houston disabled list (April 10-30, 1990); included rehabilitation assignment to Columbus (April 25-30). . . . Traded by Astros to Seattle Mariners for OF Mike Felder and P Mike Hampton (December 10, 1993). . . . On disabled list (June 25-July 10, 1994). . . . On suspended list (July 10-17, 1994). . . . Released by Mariners (December 21, 1994). . . . Signed by Cincinnati Reds (April 5, 1995). . . . On Cincinnati disabled list (April 17-June 7, July 15-August 14 and August 18-September 2, 1995); included rehabilitation assignments to Indianapolis (June 2-7 and August 11-14).
HONORS: Named Southern League Most Valuable Player (1989).
STATISTICAL NOTES: Led Gulf Coast League with 110 total bases in 1987. . . . Led South Atlantic League with .558 slugging percentage in 1988. . . . Led Southern League with .558 slugging percentage in 1989. . . . Career major league grand slams: 2.

		BATTING												FIELDING			
Year Team (League)	**Pos.**	**G**	**AB**	**R**	**H**	**2B**	**3B**	**HR**	**RBI**	**Avg.**	**BB**	**SO**	**SB**	**PO**	**A**	**E**	**Avg.**
1986—GC Astros (GCL)	OF	13	12	2	3	0	0	0	0	.250	5	5	1	2	1	0	1.000
1987—GC Astros (GCL)	OF	60	216	38	57	11	6	*10	*46	.264	26	58	2	100	•11	5	.957
1988—Asheville (S. Atl.)	OF	115	439	73	120	*36	1	*29	89	.273	40	101	10	152	8	14	.920
1989—Columbus (South.)	OF	107	403	67	121	16	2	*28	79	.300	35	127	14	178	17	8	.961
—Houston (N.L.)	OF	25	61	7	11	2	0	4	7	.180	9	16	0	34	1	0	1.000
—Tucson (PCL)	OF	12	46	10	10	3	0	3	11	.217	6	11	0	21	0	0	1.000
1990—Houston (N.L.)	OF	84	239	26	46	8	0	10	29	.192	29	78	5	124	5	4	.970
—Columbus (South.)	OF	4	12	2	2	0	0	1	3	.167	3	4	0	3	0	0	1.000
—Tucson (PCL)	OF	40	161	28	46	10	2	6	26	.286	17	40	8	84	7	4	.958
1991—Tucson (PCL)	OF-1B	79	318	57	107	22	2	9	63	.336	25	58	11	154	9	4	.976
—Houston (N.L.)	OF	39	118	11	18	6	0	1	7	.153	12	41	1	64	5	1	.986
1992—Houston (N.L.)	OF	137	440	45	105	15	1	19	80	.239	38	98	5	173	6	5	.973
1993—Houston (N.L.)	OF	145	486	70	121	19	4	15	66	.249	49	88	3	233	6	3	.988
1994—Seattle (A.L.)■	OF-DH	79	262	31	62	14	1	10	30	.237	23	66	6	126	4	2	.985
1995—Cincinnati (N.L.)■	OF-1B	47	134	19	36	6	0	5	23	.269	13	30	2	141	12	4	.975
—Indianapolis (A.A.)	1B-OF	7	24	7	7	0	0	4	8	.292	6	4	2	11	1	1	.923
American League totals (1 year)		79	262	31	62	14	1	10	30	.237	23	66	6	126	4	2	.985
National League totals (6 years)		477	1478	178	337	56	5	54	212	.228	150	351	16	769	35	17	.979
Major league totals (7 years)		556	1740	209	399	70	6	64	242	.229	173	417	22	895	39	19	.980

CHAMPIONSHIP SERIES RECORD

		BATTING												FIELDING			
Year Team (League)	**Pos.**	**G**	**AB**	**R**	**H**	**2B**	**3B**	**HR**	**RBI**	**Avg.**	**BB**	**SO**	**SB**	**PO**	**A**	**E**	**Avg.**
1995—Cincinnati (N.L.)	PH	2	1	0	0	0	0	0	0	.000	1	1	0	0	0	0	...

APPIER, KEVIN — P — ROYALS

PERSONAL: Born December 6, 1967, in Lancaster, Calif. . . . 6-2/195. . . . Throws right, bats right. . . . Full name: Robert Kevin Appier. . . . Name pronounced APE-e-er.
HIGH SCHOOL: Antelope Valley (Lancaster, Calif.).
JUNIOR COLLEGE: Antelope Valley (Calif.).
COLLEGE: Fresno State.
TRANSACTIONS/CAREER NOTES: Selected by Kansas City Royals organization in first round (ninth pick overall) of free-agent draft (June 2, 1987). . . . On disabled list (July 26-August 12, 1995).
HONORS: Named A.L. Rookie Pitcher of the Year by The Sporting News (1990).
STATISTICAL NOTES: Pitched 4-0 one-hit, complete-game victory for Kansas City against Detroit (July 7, 1990). . . . Pitched 1-0 one-hit, complete-game loss against Texas (July 27, 1993).

Year Team (League)	W	L	Pct.	ERA	G	GS	CG	ShO	Sv.	IP	H	R	ER	BB	SO
1987— Eugene (N'west)	5	2	.714	3.04	15	•15	0	0	0	77	81	43	26	29	72
1988— Baseball City (FSL)	10	9	.526	2.75	24	24	1	0	0	147 1/3	134	58	45	39	112
— Memphis (South.)	2	0	1.000	1.83	3	3	0	0	0	19 2/3	11	5	4	7	18
1989— Omaha (Am. Assoc.)	8	8	.500	3.95	22	22	3	2	0	139	141	70	61	42	109
— Kansas City (A.L.)	1	4	.200	9.14	6	5	0	0	0	21 2/3	34	22	22	12	10
1990— Omaha (Am. Assoc.)	2	0	1.000	1.50	3	3	0	0	0	18	15	3	3	3	17
— Kansas City (A.L.)	12	8	.600	2.76	32	24	3	3	0	185 2/3	179	67	57	54	127
1991— Kansas City (A.L.)	13	10	.565	3.42	34	31	6	3	0	207 2/3	205	97	79	61	158
1992— Kansas City (A.L.)	15	8	.652	2.46	30	30	3	0	0	208 1/3	167	59	57	68	150
1993— Kansas City (A.L.)	18	8	.692	*2.56	34	34	5	1	0	238 2/3	183	74	68	81	186
1994— Kansas City (A.L.)	7	6	.538	3.83	23	23	1	0	0	155	137	68	66	63	145
1995— Kansas City (A.L.)	15	10	.600	3.89	31	31	4	1	0	201 1/3	163	90	87	80	185
Major league totals (7 years)	81	54	.600	3.22	190	178	22	8	0	1218 1/3	1068	477	436	419	961

ALL-STAR GAME RECORD

Year League	W	L	Pct.	ERA	GS	CG	ShO	Sv.	IP	H	R	ER	BB	SO
1995— American	0	0	. . .	0.00	0	0	0	0	2	0	0	0	0	1

AQUINO, LUIS — P

PERSONAL: Born May 19, 1965, in Rio Piedras, Puerto Rico. . . . 6-1/190. . . . Throws right, bats right. . . . Full name: Luis Antonio Colon Aquino. . . . Name pronounced uh-KEE-no.
HIGH SCHOOL: Gabriela Mistra (Rio Piedras, Puerto Rico).
TRANSACTIONS/CAREER NOTES: Signed as non-drafted free agent by Toronto Blue Jays organization (June 15, 1981). . . . Traded by Blue Jays organization to Kansas City Royals organization for OF Juan Beniquez (July 14, 1987). . . . On disabled list (May 31-June 15, 1989 and July 21-September 24, 1990). . . . On Kansas City disabled list (April 11-July 19, 1992); included rehabilitation assignment to Omaha (July 8-19). . . . Contract sold by Royals to Florida Marlins (March 27, 1993). . . . On disabled list (July 4-August 3, 1993). . . . Granted free agency (December 20, 1993). . . . Re-signed by Marlins organization (January 17, 1994). . . . On Florida disabled list (May 31-July 8, 1994); included rehabilitation assignments to Portland (June 24-30) and Gulf Coast Marlins (June 30-July 8). . . . Granted free agency (October 17, 1994). . . . Signed by Montreal Expos (April 24, 1995). . . . Traded by Expos to San Francisco Giants for P Lou Pote (July 24, 1995). . . . On San Francisco disabled list (July 28-September 1, 1995); included rehabilitation assignment to San Jose (August 19-September 1). . . . Released by Giants (September 13, 1995). . . . Signed by Pawtucket, Boston Red Sox organization (October 9, 1995). . . . Released by Pawtucket (October 27, 1995).
STATISTICAL NOTES: Pitched 2-0 no-hit victory for Omaha against Columbus (June 20, 1988).

Year Team (League)	W	L	Pct.	ERA	G	GS	CG	ShO	Sv.	IP	H	R	ER	BB	SO
1982— GC Blue Jays (GCL)	4	7	.364	3.31	13	11	4	0	0	73 1/3	60	33	27	17	52
1983— Florence (S. Atl.)	7	9	.438	5.25	29	21	5	1	0	133 2/3	128	91	78	61	104
1984— Kinston (Carolina)	5	6	.455	2.70	*53	0	0	0	20	70	50	21	21	37	78
— Knoxville (South.)	0	0	. . .	9.00	3	0	0	0	0	4	3	4	4	3	7
1985— Knoxville (South.)	5	7	.417	2.60	50	0	0	0	*20	83	58	29	24	32	82
1986— Syracuse (Int'l)	3	7	.300	2.88	43	6	0	0	10	84 1/3	70	30	27	34	60
— Toronto (A.L.)	1	1	.500	6.35	7	0	0	0	0	11 1/3	14	8	8	3	5
1987— Syracuse (Int'l)	6	7	.462	4.78	26	11	0	0	0	84 2/3	75	46	45	51	68
— Omaha (Am. Assoc.)■	3	2	.600	2.31	14	4	1	0	1	50 2/3	42	15	13	16	29
1988— Omaha (Am. Assoc.)	8	3	.727	2.85	25	16	1	1	0	129 1/3	106	43	41	50	93
— Kansas City (A.L.)	1	0	1.000	2.79	7	5	1	1	0	29	33	15	9	17	11
1989— Kansas City (A.L.)	6	8	.429	3.50	34	16	2	1	0	141 1/3	148	62	55	35	68
1990— Kansas City (A.L.)	4	1	.800	3.16	20	3	1	0	0	68 1/3	59	25	24	27	28
1991— Kansas City (A.L.)	8	4	.667	3.44	38	18	1	1	3	157	152	67	60	47	80
1992— Kansas City (A.L.)	3	6	.333	4.52	15	13	0	0	0	67 2/3	81	35	34	20	11
— Omaha (Am. Assoc.)	0	0	. . .	2.61	2	2	0	0	0	10 1/3	13	3	3	4	3
1993— Florida (N.L.)■	6	8	.429	3.42	38	13	0	0	0	110 2/3	115	43	42	40	67
1994— Florida (N.L.)	2	1	.667	3.73	29	1	0	0	0	50 2/3	39	22	21	22	22
— Portland (Eastern)	0	1	.000	3.86	2	1	0	0	0	2 1/3	3	4	1	0	4
— GC Marlins (GCL)	0	0	. . .	1.42	3	3	0	0	0	6 1/3	3	1	1	1	9
1995— Montreal (N.L.)■	0	2	.000	3.86	29	0	0	0	2	37 1/3	47	24	16	11	22
— San Francisco (N.L.)■	0	1	.000	14.40	5	0	0	0	0	5	10	10	8	2	4
— San Jose (Calif.)	0	0	. . .	0.00	4	4	0	0	0	10 1/3	9	1	0	1	13
A.L. totals (6 years)	23	20	.535	3.60	121	55	5	3	3	474 2/3	487	212	190	149	203
N.L. totals (3 years)	8	12	.400	3.84	101	14	0	0	2	203 2/3	211	99	87	75	115
Major league totals (9 years)	31	32	.492	3.68	222	69	5	3	5	678 1/3	698	311	277	224	318

ARIAS, ALEX — SS/3B — MARLINS

PERSONAL: Born November 20, 1967, in New York. . . . 6-3/185. . . . Bats right, throws right. . . . Full name: Alejandro Arias. . . . Name pro-

nounced air-REE-ahs.
HIGH SCHOOL: George Washington (New York).
TRANSACTIONS/CAREER NOTES: Selected by Chicago Cubs organization in third round of free-agent draft (June 2, 1987). . . . Traded by Cubs with 3B Gary Scott to Florida Marlins for P Greg Hibbard (November 17, 1992).
STATISTICAL NOTES: Led Midwest League shortstops with 655 total chances and 83 double plays in 1989. . . . Led Southern League shortstops with 583 total chances and 81 double plays in 1991.

		BATTING												FIELDING			
Year Team (League)	**Pos.**	**G**	**AB**	**R**	**H**	**2B**	**3B**	**HR**	**RBI**	**Avg.**	**BB**	**SO**	**SB**	**PO**	**A**	**E**	**Avg.**
1987—Wytheville (Appal.)	SS-3B	61	233	41	69	7	0	0	24	.296	27	29	16	77	141	16	.932
1988—Char., W.Va. (SAL)	SS-3B-2B	127	472	57	122	12	1	0	33	.258	54	44	41	184	396	32	.948
1989—Peoria (Midwest)	SS	*136	506	74	140	10	*11	2	64	.277	49	67	31	*210	*408	37	.944
1990—Charlotte (South.)	SS	119	419	55	103	16	3	4	38	.246	42	53	12	171	284	*42	.915
1991—Charlotte (South.)	SS	134	488	69	134	26	0	4	47	.275	47	42	23	*203	*351	29	*.950
1992—Iowa (Am. Assoc.)	SS-2B	106	409	52	114	23	3	5	40	.279	44	27	14	183	290	14	.971
—Chicago (N.L.)	SS	32	99	14	29	6	0	0	7	.293	11	13	0	43	74	4	.967
1993—Florida (N.L.)■	2B-3B-SS	96	249	27	67	5	1	2	20	.269	27	18	1	94	144	6	.975
1994—Florida (N.L.)	SS-3B	59	113	4	27	5	0	0	15	.239	9	19	0	37	51	2	.978
1995—Florida (N.L.)	SS-3B-2B	94	216	22	58	9	2	3	26	.269	22	20	1	57	127	9	.953
Major league totals (4 years)		281	677	67	181	25	3	5	68	.267	69	70	2	231	396	21	.968

ARIAS, GEORGE — 3B — ANGELS

PERSONAL: Born March 12, 1972, in Tucson, Ariz. . . . 5-11/190. . . . Bats right, throws right. . . . Full name: George Albert Arias.
HIGH SCHOOL: Pueblo (Tucson, Ariz.).
COLLEGE: Arizona.
TRANSACTIONS/CAREER NOTES: Selected by California Angels organization in seventh round of free-agent draft (June 3, 1993).
STATISTICAL NOTES: Led California League third basemen with 467 total chances and 27 double plays in 1994.

		BATTING												FIELDING			
Year Team (League)	**Pos.**	**G**	**AB**	**R**	**H**	**2B**	**3B**	**HR**	**RBI**	**Avg.**	**BB**	**SO**	**SB**	**PO**	**A**	**E**	**Avg.**
1993—Ced. Rap. (Midw.)	3B-SS	74	253	31	55	13	3	9	41	.217	31	65	6	59	159	23	.905
1994—Lake Elsinore (Calif.)	3B	•134	514	89	144	28	3	23	80	.280	58	111	6	*122	*313	*32	.931
1995—Midland (Texas)	3B-SS	134	520	91	145	19	10	30	104	.279	63	119	3	128	300	29	.937

AROCHA, RENE — P — CARDINALS

PERSONAL: Born February 24, 1966, in Havana, Cuba. . . . 6-0/180. . . . Throws right, bats right.
HIGH SCHOOL: Regla (Cuba).
TRANSACTIONS/CAREER NOTES: Signed as non-drafted free agent by St. Louis Cardinals organization (November 21, 1991). . . . On disabled list (April 21-May 13, 1993 and July 31, 1995-remainder of season).
HONORS: Named American Association Most Valuable Pitcher (1992).
MISCELLANEOUS: Member of Cuban national baseball team (1986-91).

Year Team (League)	**W**	**L**	**Pct.**	**ERA**	**G**	**GS**	**CG**	**ShO**	**Sv.**	**IP**	**H**	**R**	**ER**	**BB**	**SO**
1992—Louisville (A.A.)	•12	7	.632	2.70	25	25	3	1	0	166 2/3	145	59	50	65	128
1993—St. Louis (N.L.)	11	8	.579	3.78	32	29	1	0	0	188	197	89	79	31	96
1994—St. Louis (N.L.)	4	4	.500	4.01	45	7	1	1	11	83	94	42	37	21	62
1995—St. Louis (N.L.)	3	5	.375	3.99	41	0	0	0	0	49 2/3	55	24	22	18	25
Major league totals (3 years)	18	17	.514	3.87	118	36	2	1	11	320 2/3	346	155	138	70	183

ARTEAGA, IVAN — P — ROCKIES

PERSONAL: Born July 20, 1972, in Puerto Cabello, Venezuela. . . . 6-2/227. . . . Throws right, bats left. . . . Full name: Ivan Jose Arteaga. . . . Name pronounced ar-tee-AH-guh.
TRANSACTIONS/CAREER NOTES: Signed as non-drafted free agent by Montreal Expos organization (May 11, 1989). . . . Not on disabled list but did not play (1992). . . . Traded by Expos with P Rodney Pedraza to Colorado Rockies for IF Freddie Benavides (January 7, 1994).
STATISTICAL NOTES: Tied for Eastern League lead with four balks in 1994.

Year Team (League)	**W**	**L**	**Pct.**	**ERA**	**G**	**GS**	**CG**	**ShO**	**Sv.**	**IP**	**H**	**R**	**ER**	**BB**	**SO**
1991—DSL Expos (DSL)	6	4	.600	1.91	14	13	3	1	0	85	58	24	18	45	60
1992—							Did not play.								
1993—Burlington (Midw.)	6	5	.545	2.83	20	20	2	0	0	127	114	57	40	47	111
—WP Beach (FSL)	0	3	.000	8.04	4	4	0	0	0	15 2/3	23	15	14	9	10
1994—New Haven (East.)■	8	9	.471	3.48	27	24	2	0	0	150	123	74	58	70	101
1995—New Haven (East.)	2	4	.333	5.56	14	11	0	0	0	34	36	26	21	21	18

RECORD AS POSITION PLAYER

		BATTING												FIELDING			
Year Team (League)	**Pos.**	**G**	**AB**	**R**	**H**	**2B**	**3B**	**HR**	**RBI**	**Avg.**	**BB**	**SO**	**SB**	**PO**	**A**	**E**	**Avg.**
1989—Dom. Expos (DSL)	IF	25	54	6	13	1	0	1	9	.241	13	16	0	...	...	...	...
1990—Dom. Expos (DSL)	IF	66	199	26	48	10	3	3	33	.241	52	50	2	...	...	...	...

ASHBY, ANDY — P — PADRES

PERSONAL: Born July 11, 1967, in Kansas City, Mo. . . . 6-5/190. . . . Throws right, bats right. . . . Full name: Andrew Jason Ashby.
HIGH SCHOOL: Park Hill (Kansas City, Mo.).
COLLEGE: Crowder College (Mo.).
TRANSACTIONS/CAREER NOTES: Signed as non-drafted free agent by Philadelphia Phillies organization (May 4, 1986). . . . On Spartanburg

disabled list (April 7-July 10, 1988 and April 6-26, 1989). . . . On Philadelphia disabled list (April 27-August 11, 1992); included rehabilitation assignments to Scranton/Wilkes-Barre (July 8-August 2 and August 6-10). . . . Selected by Colorado Rockies in first round (25th pick overall) of expansion draft (November 17, 1992). . . . Traded by Rockies to San Diego Padres (July 27, 1993), completing deal in which Padres traded P Bruce Hurst and P Greg W. Harris to Rockies for C Brad Ausmus, P Doug Bochtler and a player to be named later (July 26, 1993).
RECORDS: Shares major league record by striking out side on nine pitches (June 15, 1991, fourth inning).

Year Team (League)	W	L	Pct.	ERA	G	GS	CG	ShO	Sv.	IP	H	R	ER	BB	SO
1986—Bend (Northwest)	1	2	.333	4.95	16	6	0	0	2	60	56	40	33	34	45
1987—Spartanburg (SAL)	4	6	.400	5.60	13	13	1	0	0	64 1/3	73	45	40	38	52
—Utica (NYP)	3	7	.300	4.05	13	13	0	0	0	60	56	38	27	36	51
1988—Spartanburg (SAL)	1	1	.500	2.70	3	3	0	0	0	16 2/3	13	7	5	7	16
—Batavia (NYP)	3	1	.750	1.61	6	6	2	1	0	44 2/3	25	11	8	16	32
1989—Spartanburg (SAL)	5	9	.357	2.87	17	17	3	1	0	106 2/3	95	48	34	49	100
—Clearwater (Fla. St.)	1	4	.200	1.24	6	6	2	1	0	43 2/3	28	9	6	21	44
1990—Reading (Eastern)	10	7	.588	3.42	23	23	4	1	0	139 2/3	134	65	53	48	94
1991—Scran./W.B. (Int'l)	11	11	.500	3.46	26	26	•6	•3	0	161 1/3	144	78	62	60	113
—Philadelphia (N.L.)	1	5	.167	6.00	8	8	0	0	0	42	41	28	28	19	26
1992—Philadelphia (N.L.)	1	3	.250	7.54	10	8	0	0	0	37	42	31	31	21	24
—Scran./W.B. (Int'l)	0	3	.000	3.00	7	7	1	0	0	33	23	13	11	14	18
1993—Colorado (N.L.)■	0	4	.000	8.50	20	9	0	0	1	54	89	54	51	32	33
—Colo. Springs (PCL)	4	2	.667	4.10	7	6	1	0	0	41 2/3	45	25	19	12	35
—San Diego (N.L.)■	3	6	.333	5.48	12	12	0	0	0	69	79	46	42	24	44
1994—San Diego (N.L.)	6	11	.353	3.40	24	24	4	0	0	164 1/3	145	75	62	43	121
1995—San Diego (N.L.)	12	10	.545	2.94	31	•31	2	2	0	192 2/3	180	79	63	62	150
Major league totals (5 years)	23	39	.371	4.46	105	92	6	2	1	559	576	313	277	201	398

ASHLEY, BILLY — OF — DODGERS

PERSONAL: Born July 11, 1970, in Taylor, Mich. . . . 6-7/235. . . . Bats right, throws right. . . . Full name: Billy Manual Ashley.
HIGH SCHOOL: Belleville (Mich.).
TRANSACTIONS/CAREER NOTES: Selected by Los Angeles Dodgers organization in third round of free-agent draft (June 1, 1988). . . . On disabled list (April 10-May 1, May 19-31 and June 8-July 8, 1991). . . . On Albuquerque disabled list (May 1-16, 1994).
HONORS: Named Pacific Coast League Most Valuable Player (1994).
STATISTICAL NOTES: Led Texas League with .534 slugging percentage in 1992. . . . Led Pacific Coast League with .701 slugging percentage and tied for lead with seven intentional bases on balls received in 1994.

			BATTING											FIELDING			
Year Team (League)	Pos.	G	AB	R	H	2B	3B	HR	RBI	Avg.	BB	SO	SB	PO	A	E	Avg.
1988—GC Dodgers (GCL)	OF	9	26	3	4	0	0	0	0	.154	1	9	1	8	2	0	1.000
1989—GC Dodgers (GCL)	OF	48	160	23	38	6	2	1	19	.238	19	42	16	50	3	5	.914
1990—Bakersfield (Calif.)	OF	99	331	48	72	13	1	9	40	.218	25	135	17	122	3	10	.926
1991—Vero Beach (FSL)	OF	61	206	18	52	11	2	7	42	.252	7	69	9	39	1	0	1.000
1992—San Antonio (Tex.)	OF-1B	101	380	60	106	23	1	*24	66	.279	16	111	13	129	9	3	.979
—Albuquerque (PCL)	OF	25	95	11	20	7	0	2	10	.211	6	42	1	39	1	2	.952
—Los Angeles (N.L.)	OF	29	95	6	21	5	0	2	6	.221	5	34	0	34	2	6	.857
1993—Albuquerque (PCL)	OF	125	482	88	143	31	4	26	*100	.297	35	*143	6	211	7	*11	.952
—Los Angeles (N.L.)	OF	14	37	0	9	0	0	0	0	.243	2	11	0	11	3	0	1.000
1994—Los Angeles (N.L.)	OF	2	6	0	2	1	0	0	0	.333	0	2	0	3	0	0	1.000
—Albuquerque (PCL)	OF	107	388	93	134	19	4	*37	105	.345	53	116	6	119	2	12	.910
1995—Los Angeles (N.L.)	OF	81	215	17	51	5	0	8	27	.237	25	88	0	102	2	3	.972
Major league totals (4 years)		126	353	23	83	11	0	10	33	.235	32	135	0	150	7	9	.946

DIVISION SERIES RECORD

			BATTING											FIELDING			
Year Team (League)	Pos.	G	AB	R	H	2B	3B	HR	RBI	Avg.	BB	SO	SB	PO	A	E	Avg.
1995—Los Angeles (N.L.)	PH	1	0	0	0	0	0	0	0	...	1	0	0	...	...	...	...

ASSENMACHER, PAUL — P — INDIANS

PERSONAL: Born December 10, 1960, in Allen Park, Mich. . . . 6-3/210. . . . Throws left, bats left. . . . Full name: Paul Andre Assenmacher. . . . Name pronounced AHSS-en-mahk-ur.
HIGH SCHOOL: Aquinas (Southgate, Mich.).
COLLEGE: Aquinas, Mich. (degree in business administration).
TRANSACTIONS/CAREER NOTES: Signed as non-drafted free agent by Atlanta Braves organization (July 10, 1983). . . . On Atlanta disabled list (April 29-May 9, 1987 and August 10-25, 1988). . . . Traded by Braves organization to Chicago Cubs for two players to be named later (August 24, 1989); Braves acquired C Kelly Mann and P Pat Gomez to complete deal (September 1, 1989). . . . On disabled list (May 19-June 4, 1992). . . . Traded by Cubs to New York Yankees as part of a three-way deal in which Yankees sent P John Habyan to Kansas City Royals and Royals sent OF Tuffy Rhodes to Cubs (July 30, 1993). . . . Traded by Yankees to Chicago White Sox for P Brian Boehringer (March 21, 1994). . . . Granted free agency (October 24, 1994). . . . Signed by Cleveland Indians (April 10, 1995).
RECORDS: Shares major league record for most strikeouts in one inning—4 (August 22, 1989, fifth inning).

Year Team (League)	W	L	Pct.	ERA	G	GS	CG	ShO	Sv.	IP	H	R	ER	BB	SO
1983—GC Braves (GCL)	1	0	1.000	2.21	10	3	1	1	2	36 2/3	35	14	9	4	44
1984—Durham (Carolina)	6	11	.353	4.28	26	24	3	1	0	147 1/3	153	78	70	52	147
1985—Durham (Carolina)	3	2	.600	3.29	14	0	0	0	1	38 1/3	38	16	14	13	36
—Greenville (South.)	6	0	1.000	2.56	29	0	0	0	4	52 2/3	47	16	15	11	59
1986—Atlanta (N.L.)	7	3	.700	2.50	61	0	0	0	7	68 1/3	61	23	19	26	56
1987—Atlanta (N.L.)	1	1	.500	5.10	52	0	0	0	2	54 2/3	58	41	31	24	39
—Richmond (Int'l)	1	2	.333	3.65	4	4	0	0	0	24 2/3	30	11	10	8	21
1988—Atlanta (N.L.)	8	7	.533	3.06	64	0	0	0	5	79 1/3	72	28	27	32	71
1989—Atlanta (N.L.)	1	3	.250	3.59	49	0	0	0	0	57 2/3	55	26	23	16	64
—Chicago (N.L.)■	2	1	.667	5.21	14	0	0	0	0	19	19	11	11	12	15

Year	Team (League)	W	L	Pct.	ERA	G	GS	CG	ShO	Sv.	IP	H	R	ER	BB	SO
1990—	Chicago (N.L.)	7	2	.778	2.80	74	1	0	0	10	103	90	33	32	36	95
1991—	Chicago (N.L.)	7	8	.467	3.24	75	0	0	0	15	102 2/3	85	41	37	31	117
1992—	Chicago (N.L.)	4	4	.500	4.10	70	0	0	0	8	68	72	32	31	26	67
1993—	Chicago (N.L.)	2	1	.667	3.49	46	0	0	0	0	38 2/3	44	15	15	13	34
	—New York (A.L.)■	2	2	.500	3.12	26	0	0	0	0	17 1/3	10	6	6	9	11
1994—	Chicago (A.L.)■	1	2	.333	3.55	44	0	0	0	1	33	26	13	13	13	29
1995—	Cleveland (A.L.)■	6	2	.750	2.82	47	0	0	0	0	38 1/3	32	13	12	12	40
	A.L. totals (3 years)	9	6	.600	3.15	117	0	0	0	1	88 2/3	68	32	31	34	80
	N.L. totals (8 years)	39	30	.565	3.44	505	1	0	0	47	591 1/3	556	250	226	216	558
	Major league totals (10 years)	48	36	.571	3.40	622	1	0	0	48	680	624	282	257	250	638

DIVISION SERIES RECORD

Year	Team (League)	W	L	Pct.	ERA	G	GS	CG	ShO	Sv.	IP	H	R	ER	BB	SO
1995—	Cleveland (A.L.)	0	0	...	0.00	3	0	0	0	0	1 2/3	0	0	0	0	3

CHAMPIONSHIP SERIES RECORD

Year	Team (League)	W	L	Pct.	ERA	G	GS	CG	ShO	Sv.	IP	H	R	ER	BB	SO
1989—	Chicago (N.L.)	0	0	...	13.50	2	0	0	0	0	2/3	3	1	1	0	0
1995—	Cleveland (A.L.)	0	0	...	0.00	3	0	0	0	0	1 1/3	0	0	0	1	2
	Champ. series totals (2 years)	0	0	...	4.50	5	0	0	0	0	2	3	1	1	1	2

WORLD SERIES RECORD

Year	Team (League)	W	L	Pct.	ERA	G	GS	CG	ShO	Sv.	IP	H	R	ER	BB	SO
1995—	Cleveland (A.L.)	0	0	...	6.75	4	0	0	0	0	1 1/3	1	2	1	3	3

ASTACIO, PEDRO — P — DODGERS

PERSONAL: Born November 28, 1969, in Hato Mayor, Dominican Republic. . . . 6-2/195. . . . Throws right, bats right. . . . Full name: Pedro Julio Astacio. . . . Name pronounced ah-STA-see-oh.

HIGH SCHOOL: Pilar Rondon (Dominican Republic).

TRANSACTIONS/CAREER NOTES: Signed as non-drafted free agent by Los Angeles Dodgers organization (November 21, 1987). . . . On Albuquerque disabled list (April 26-May 21, 1992).

STATISTICAL NOTES: Led N.L. with nine balks in 1993.

Year	Team (League)	W	L	Pct.	ERA	G	GS	CG	ShO	Sv.	IP	H	R	ER	BB	SO
1989—	GC Dodgers (GCL)	7	3	.700	3.17	12	12	1	•1	0	76 2/3	77	30	27	12	52
1990—	Vero Beach (FSL)	1	5	.167	6.32	8	8	0	0	0	47	54	39	33	23	41
	—Yakima (N'west)	2	0	1.000	1.74	3	3	0	0	0	20 2/3	9	8	4	4	22
	—Bakersfield (Calif.)	5	2	.714	2.77	10	7	1	0	0	52	46	22	16	15	34
1991—	Vero Beach (FSL)	5	3	.625	1.67	9	9	3	1	0	59 1/3	44	19	11	8	45
	—San Antonio (Tex.)	4	11	.267	4.78	19	19	2	1	0	113	142	67	60	39	62
1992—	Albuquerque (PCL)	6	6	.500	5.47	24	15	1	0	0	98 2/3	115	68	60	44	66
	—Los Angeles (N.L.)	5	5	.500	1.98	11	11	4	4	0	82	80	23	18	20	43
1993—	Los Angeles (N.L.)	14	9	.609	3.57	31	31	3	2	0	186 1/3	165	80	74	68	122
1994—	Los Angeles (N.L.)	6	8	.429	4.29	23	23	3	1	0	149	142	77	71	47	108
1995—	Los Angeles (N.L.)	7	8	.467	4.24	48	11	1	1	0	104	103	53	49	29	80
	Major league totals (4 years)	32	30	.516	3.66	113	76	11	8	0	521 1/3	490	233	212	164	353

DIVISION SERIES RECORD

Year	Team (League)	W	L	Pct.	ERA	G	GS	CG	ShO	Sv.	IP	H	R	ER	BB	SO
1995—	Los Angeles (N.L.)	0	0	...	0.00	3	0	0	0	0	3 1/3	1	0	0	0	5

AUCOIN, DEREK — P — EXPOS

PERSONAL: Born March 27, 1970, in Lachine, Quebec. . . . 6-7/235. . . . Throws right, bats right. . . . Full name: Derek Alfred Aucoin.

HIGH SCHOOL: Ecole Secondaire (Terrebonne, Quebec).

COLLEGE: Douglas (New Westminster, B.C.).

TRANSACTIONS/CAREER NOTES: Signed as non-drafted free agent by Montreal Expos organization (July 17, 1989). . . . On temporarily inactive list (May 26-June 7, 1991). . . . On Ottawa disabled list (April 6-June 4, 1995).

Year	Team (League)	W	L	Pct.	ERA	G	GS	CG	ShO	Sv.	IP	H	R	ER	BB	SO
1989—	GC Expos (GCL)	2	1	.667	2.66	7	3	0	0	1	23 2/3	24	10	7	12	27
1990—	Jamestown (NYP)	1	3	.250	4.46	8	8	1	0	0	36 1/3	28	20	18	18	27
1991—	Sumter (S. Atl.)	3	6	.333	4.28	41	4	0	0	1	90 1/3	86	55	43	44	70
1992—	Rockford (Midw.)	3	2	.600	3.00	39	2	0	0	3	69	48	32	23	34	65
1993—	WP Beach (FSL)	4	4	.500	4.23	38	6	0	0	1	87 1/3	89	48	41	44	62
1994—	WP Beach (FSL)	0	0	...	0.00	7	0	0	0	2	7 1/3	3	0	0	2	10
	—Harrisburg (East.)	3	4	.429	3.26	31	0	0	0	4	47	36	19	17	29	48
1995—	Harrisburg (East.)	2	4	.333	4.96	29	0	0	0	1	52 2/3	52	34	29	28	48

AUDE, RICH — 1B — PIRATES

PERSONAL: Born July 13, 1971, in Van Nuys, Calif. . . . 6-5/215. . . . Bats right, throws right. . . . Full name: Richard Thomas Aude. . . . Name pronounced AW-day.

HIGH SCHOOL: Chatsworth (Calif.).

TRANSACTIONS/CAREER NOTES: Selected by Pittsburgh Pirates organization in second round of free-agent draft (June 5, 1989).

STATISTICAL NOTES: Led American Association first basemen with 1,239 total chances and 117 double plays in 1994.

				BATTING										FIELDING			
Year	Team (League)	Pos.	G	AB	R	H	2B	3B	HR	RBI	Avg.	BB	SO	SB	PO	A	E	Avg.
1989—	GC Pirates (GCL)	3B	24	88	13	19	3	0	0	7	.216	5	17	2	23	32	12	.821

Year	Team (League)	Pos.	G	AB	R	H	2B	3B	HR	RBI	Avg.	BB	SO	SB	PO	A	E	Avg.
							BATTING								FIELDING			
1990—	Augusta (S. Atl.)	1B-3B	128	475	48	111	23	1	6	61	.234	41	133	4	522	110	29	.956
1991—	Salem (Carolina)	1B-3B	103	366	45	97	12	2	3	43	.265	27	72	4	558	46	17	.973
1992—	Salem (Carolina)	1B-3B	122	447	63	128	26	4	9	60	.286	50	79	11	1120	58	10	.992
—	Carolina (South.)	1B-3B	6	20	4	4	1	0	2	3	.200	1	3	0	17	1	0	1.000
1993—	Carolina (South.)	1B	120	422	66	122	25	3	18	73	.289	50	79	8	790	49	13	.985
—	Buffalo (A.A.)	1B	21	64	17	24	9	0	4	16	.375	10	15	0	174	13	1	.995
—	Pittsburgh (N.L.)	1B-OF	13	26	1	3	1	0	0	4	.115	1	7	0	47	3	1	.980
1994—	Buffalo (A.A.)	1B	138	520	66	146	38	4	15	79	.281	41	83	9	*1156	75	8	.994
1995—	Pittsburgh (N.L.)	1B	42	109	10	27	8	0	2	19	.248	6	20	1	223	11	1	.996
—	Calgary (PCL)	1B	50	195	34	65	14	2	9	42	.333	12	30	3	447	31	6	.988
Major league totals (2 years)			55	135	11	30	9	0	2	23	.222	7	27	1	270	14	2	.993

AURILIA, RICH — SS — GIANTS

PERSONAL: Born September 2, 1971, in Brooklyn, N.Y. . . . 6-1/170. . . . Bats right, throws right. . . . Full name: Richard Aurilia.
HIGH SCHOOL: Xaverian (Brooklyn, N.Y.).
COLLEGE: St. John's.
TRANSACTIONS/CAREER NOTES: Selected by Texas Rangers organization in 24th round of free-agent draft (June 1, 1992). . . . On disabled list (April 9-16, 1993). . . . Traded by Rangers with IF/OF Desi Wilson to San Francisco Giants organization for P John Burkett (December 24, 1994).
STATISTICAL NOTES: Led Texas League shortstops with 635 total chances and tied for lead with 82 double plays in 1994.

Year	Team (League)	Pos.	G	AB	R	H	2B	3B	HR	RBI	Avg.	BB	SO	SB	PO	A	E	Avg.
							BATTING								FIELDING			
1992—	Butte (Pioneer)	SS	59	202	37	68	11	3	3	30	.337	42	18	13	78	154	14	*.943
1993—	Charlotte (Fla. St.)	SS	122	440	80	136	16	5	5	56	.309	75	57	15	200	445	24	.964
1994—	Tulsa (Texas)	SS	129	458	67	107	18	6	12	57	.234	53	74	10	*237	374	24	*.962
1995—	Shreveport (Texas)■	SS	64	226	29	74	17	1	4	42	.327	27	26	10	122	237	14	.962
—	Phoenix (PCL)	SS	71	258	42	72	12	0	5	34	.279	35	29	2	104	246	9	.975
—	San Francisco (N.L.)	SS	9	19	4	9	3	0	2	4	.474	1	2	1	8	16	0	1.000
Major league totals (1 year)			9	19	4	9	3	0	2	4	.474	1	2	1	8	16	0	1.000

AUSANIO, JOE — P — METS

PERSONAL: Born December 9, 1965, in Kingston, N.Y. . . . 6-1/205. . . . Throws right, bats right. . . . Full name: Joseph John Ausanio Jr. . . . Name pronounced oh-SONN-yo.
HIGH SCHOOL: Kingston (N.Y.).
COLLEGE: Jacksonville (Fla.).
TRANSACTIONS/CAREER NOTES: Selected by Atlanta Braves organization in 30th round of free-agent draft (June 4, 1984); did not sign. . . . Selected by Pittsburgh Pirates organization in 11th round of free-agent draft (June 1, 1988). . . . On Buffalo disabled list (June 24, 1991-remainder of season and August 28-September 15, 1992). . . . Claimed on waivers by Montreal Expos (November 12, 1992). . . . On Ottawa disabled list (April 8-July 20, 1993). . . . Selected by Columbus, New York Yankees organization, from Harrisburg, Expos organization, in Rule 5 minor league draft (December 13, 1993). . . . Granted free agency (October 16, 1995). . . . Signed by Norfolk, New York Mets organization (November 20, 1995).

Year	Team (League)	W	L	Pct.	ERA	G	GS	CG	ShO	Sv.	IP	H	R	ER	BB	SO
1988—	Watertown (NYP)	2	4	.333	1.32	28	0	0	0	*13	47 2/3	29	10	7	27	56
1989—	Salem (Carolina)	5	4	.556	2.12	54	0	0	0	*20	89	51	29	21	44	97
1990—	Harrisburg (East.)	3	2	.600	1.83	43	0	0	0	15	54	36	15	11	16	50
1991—	Carolina (South.)	0	0	. . .	0.00	3	0	0	0	2	3	0	0	0	0	2
—	Buffalo (A.A.)	2	2	.500	3.86	22	0	0	0	3	30 1/3	33	17	13	19	26
1992—	Buffalo (A.A.)	6	4	.600	2.90	53	0	0	0	15	83 2/3	64	35	27	40	66
1993—	GC Expos (GCL)■	0	0	. . .	0.00	5	0	0	0	0	5	3	1	0	1	6
—	Harrisburg (East.)	2	0	1.000	1.21	19	0	0	0	6	22 1/3	16	3	3	4	30
1994—	Columbus (Int'l)■	3	3	.500	2.39	44	0	0	0	13	60 1/3	45	21	16	16	69
—	New York (A.L.)	2	1	.667	5.17	13	0	0	0	0	15 2/3	16	9	9	6	15
1995—	New York (A.L.)	2	0	1.000	5.73	28	0	0	0	1	37 2/3	42	24	24	23	36
—	Columbus (Int'l)	1	0	1.000	7.50	11	0	0	0	3	12	12	10	10	5	20
Major league totals (2 years)		4	1	.800	5.57	41	0	0	0	1	53 1/3	58	33	33	29	51

AUSMUS, BRAD — C — PADRES

PERSONAL: Born April 14, 1969, in New Haven, Conn. . . . 5-11/190. . . . Bats right, throws right. . . . Full name: Bradley David Ausmus.
HIGH SCHOOL: Cheshire (Conn.).
COLLEGE: Dartmouth.
TRANSACTIONS/CAREER NOTES: Selected by New York Yankees organization in 47th round of free-agent draft (June 2, 1987); did not sign. . . . Selected by Colorado Rockies in third round (54th pick overall) of expansion draft (November 17, 1992). . . . Traded by Rockies with P Doug Bochtler and a player to be named later to San Diego Padres for P Bruce Hurst and P Greg W. Harris (July 26, 1993); Padres acquired P Andy Ashby to complete deal (July 27, 1993).
STATISTICAL NOTES: Led Gulf Coast League catchers with 434 total chances in 1988. . . . Led International League catchers with 666 putouts and 738 total chances in 1992. . . . Led N.L. catchers with 683 putouts and 749 total chances in 1994. . . . Led N.L. catchers with 14 double plays in 1995. . . . Tied for N.L. lead in assists by catcher with 63 in 1995.

Year	Team (League)	Pos.	G	AB	R	H	2B	3B	HR	RBI	Avg.	BB	SO	SB	PO	A	E	Avg.
							BATTING								FIELDING			
1988—	Oneonta (NYP)	C	2	4	0	1	0	0	0	0	.250	0	2	0	0	0	0	. . .
—	Sarasota (Fla. St.)	C	43	133	22	34	2	0	0	15	.256	11	25	5	*378	*47	9	.979
1989—	Oneonta (NYP)	C-3B	52	165	29	43	6	0	1	18	.261	22	28	6	401	43	7	.984

Year	Team (League)	Pos.	BATTING G	AB	R	H	2B	3B	HR	RBI	Avg.	BB	SO	SB	FIELDING PO	A	E	Avg.
1990—	Prin. William (Car.).....	C	107	364	46	86	12	2	0	27	.236	32	73	2	662	84	5	*.993
1991—	Prin. William (Car.).....	C	63	230	28	70	14	3	2	30	.304	24	37	17	419	54	5	.990
	—Alb./Colon. (East.)......	C	67	229	36	61	9	2	1	29	.266	27	36	14	470	56	4	.992
1992—	Alb./Colon. (East.)......	C	5	18	0	3	0	1	0	1	.167	2	3	2	30	2	1	.970
	—Columbus (Int'l).........	C-OF	111	364	48	88	14	3	2	35	.242	40	56	19	†666	63	9	.988
1993—	Colo. Springs (PCL)■	C-OF	76	241	31	65	10	4	2	33	.270	27	41	10	393	57	6	.987
	—San Diego (N.L.)■.....	C	49	160	18	41	8	1	5	12	.256	6	28	2	272	34	8	.975
1994—	San Diego (N.L.).........	C-1B	101	327	45	82	12	1	7	24	.251	30	63	5	†686	59	7	.991
1995—	San Diego (N.L.)........	C-1B	103	328	44	96	16	4	5	34	.293	31	56	16	656	‡63	6	.992
Major league totals (3 years)			253	815	107	219	36	6	17	70	.269	67	147	23	1614	156	21	.988

AVERY, STEVE — P — BRAVES

PERSONAL: Born April 14, 1970, in Trenton, Mich. . . . 6-4/205. . . . Throws left, bats left. . . . Full name: Steven Thomas Avery. . . . Son of Ken Avery, minor league pitcher (1962-63).
HIGH SCHOOL: John F. Kennedy (Taylor, Mich.).
TRANSACTIONS/CAREER NOTES: Selected by Atlanta Braves organization in first round (third pick overall) of free-agent draft (June 1, 1988).
HONORS: Named lefthanded pitcher on The Sporting News N.L. All-Star team (1993).
MISCELLANEOUS: Received base on balls in only appearance as pinch-hitter and appeared in one game as pinch-runner (1991).

Year	Team (League)	W	L	Pct.	ERA	G	GS	CG	ShO	Sv.	IP	H	R	ER	BB	SO
1988—	Pulaski (Appal.).................	7	1	.875	1.50	10	10	3	•2	0	66	38	16	11	19	80
1989—	Durham (Carolina).............	6	4	.600	1.45	13	13	3	1	0	86 2/3	59	22	14	20	90
	—Greenville (South.)...........	6	3	.667	2.77	13	13	1	0	0	84 1/3	68	32	26	34	75
1990—	Richmond (Int'l)................	5	5	.500	3.39	13	13	3	0	0	82 1/3	85	35	31	21	69
	—Atlanta (N.L.)...................	3	11	.214	5.64	21	20	1	1	0	99	121	79	62	45	75
1991—	Atlanta (N.L.)......................	18	8	.692	3.38	35	35	3	1	0	210 1/3	189	89	79	65	137
1992—	Atlanta (N.L.)......................	11	11	.500	3.20	35	•35	2	2	0	233 2/3	216	95	83	71	129
1993—	Atlanta (N.L.)......................	18	6	.750	2.94	35	35	3	1	0	223 1/3	216	81	73	43	125
1994—	Atlanta (N.L.)......................	8	3	.727	4.04	24	24	1	0	0	151 2/3	127	71	68	55	122
1995—	Atlanta (N.L.)......................	7	13	.350	4.67	29	29	3	1	0	173 1/3	165	92	90	52	141
Major league totals (6 years)......		65	52	.556	3.75	179	178	13	6	0	1091 1/3	1034	507	455	331	729

DIVISION SERIES RECORD

Year	Team (League)	W	L	Pct.	ERA	G	GS	CG	ShO	Sv.	IP	H	R	ER	BB	SO
1995—	Atlanta (N.L.)......................	0	0	...	13.50	1	0	0	0	0	2/3	1	1	1	0	1

CHAMPIONSHIP SERIES RECORD

NOTES: Named N.L. Championship Series Most Valuable Player (1991). . . . Holds career record for most consecutive scoreless innings—22 1/3 (1991-92). . . . Holds single-series record for most consecutive scoreless innings—16 1/3 (1991).

Year	Team (League)	W	L	Pct.	ERA	G	GS	CG	ShO	Sv.	IP	H	R	ER	BB	SO
1991—	Atlanta (N.L.)......................	2	0	1.000	0.00	2	2	0	0	0	16 1/3	9	0	0	4	17
1992—	Atlanta (N.L.)......................	1	1	.500	9.00	3	2	0	0	0	8	13	8	8	2	3
1993—	Atlanta (N.L.)......................	0	0	...	2.77	2	2	0	0	0	13	9	5	4	6	10
1995—	Atlanta (N.L.)......................	1	0	1.000	0.00	2	1	0	0	0	6	2	0	0	4	6
Champ. series totals (4 years)....		4	1	.800	2.49	9	7	0	0	0	43 1/3	33	13	12	16	36

WORLD SERIES RECORD

NOTES: Member of World Series championship team (1995).

Year	Team (League)	W	L	Pct.	ERA	G	GS	CG	ShO	Sv.	IP	H	R	ER	BB	SO
1991—	Atlanta (N.L.)......................	0	0	...	3.46	2	2	0	0	0	13	10	6	5	1	8
1992—	Atlanta (N.L.)......................	0	1	.000	3.75	2	2	0	0	0	12	11	5	5	3	11
1995—	Atlanta (N.L.)......................	1	0	1.000	1.50	1	1	0	0	0	6	3	1	1	5	3
World Series totals (3 years)		1	1	.500	3.19	5	5	0	0	0	31	24	12	11	9	22

ALL-STAR GAME RECORD

Year	League	W	L	Pct.	ERA	GS	CG	ShO	Sv.	IP	H	R	ER	BB	SO
1993—	National..............................	0	0	...	0.00	0	0	0	0	1	1	3	0	1	1

AYALA, BOBBY — P — MARINERS

PERSONAL: Born July 8, 1969, in Ventura, Calif. . . . 6-3/210. . . . Throws right, bats right. . . . Full name: Robert Joseph Ayala. . . . Name pronounced eye-YAH-luh.
HIGH SCHOOL: Rio Mesa (Oxnard, Calif.).
TRANSACTIONS/CAREER NOTES: Signed as non-drafted free agent by Cincinnati Reds organization (June 27, 1988). . . . Traded by Reds with C Dan Wilson to Seattle Mariners for P Erik Hanson and 2B Bret Boone (November 2, 1993).

Year	Team (League)	W	L	Pct.	ERA	G	GS	CG	ShO	Sv.	IP	H	R	ER	BB	SO
1988—	GC Reds (GCL)..................	0	4	.000	3.82	20	0	0	0	3	33	34	23	14	12	24
1989—	Greensboro (S. Atl.)...........	5	8	.385	4.10	22	19	1	0	0	105 1/3	97	73	48	50	70
1990—	Ced. Rap. (Midw.)..............	3	2	.600	3.38	18	7	3	1	1	53 1/3	40	24	20	18	59
	—Char., W.Va. (S. Atl.)..........	6	1	.857	2.43	21	4	2	1	2	74	48	23	20	21	73
1991—	Chattanooga (Sou.)...........	3	1	.750	4.67	39	8	1	0	4	90 2/3	79	52	47	58	92
1992—	Chattanooga (Sou.)...........	12	6	.667	3.54	27	27	3	3	0	162 2/3	152	75	64	58	154
	—Cincinnati (N.L.)...............	2	1	.667	4.34	5	5	0	0	0	29	33	15	14	13	23
1993—	Indianapolis (A.A.)............	0	2	.000	5.67	5	5	0	0	0	27	36	19	17	12	19
	—Cincinnati (N.L.)...............	7	10	.412	5.60	43	9	0	0	3	98	106	72	61	45	65
1994—	Seattle (A.L.)■..................	4	3	.571	2.86	46	0	0	0	18	56 2/3	42	25	18	26	76
1995—	Seattle (A.L.).....................	6	5	.545	4.44	63	0	0	0	19	71	73	42	35	30	77
A.L. totals (2 years)		10	8	.556	3.74	109	0	0	0	37	127 2/3	115	67	53	56	153
N.L. totals (2 years)		9	11	.450	5.31	48	14	0	0	3	127	139	87	75	58	88
Major league totals (4 years)......		19	19	.500	4.52	157	14	0	0	40	254 2/3	254	154	128	114	241

DIVISION SERIES RECORD

Year	Team (League)	W	L	Pct.	ERA	G	GS	CG	ShO	Sv.	IP	H	R	ER	BB	SO
1995—	Seattle (A.L.)	0	0	...	54.00	2	0	0	0	0	$\frac{2}{3}$	6	4	4	1	0

CHAMPIONSHIP SERIES RECORD

Year	Team (League)	W	L	Pct.	ERA	G	GS	CG	ShO	Sv.	IP	H	R	ER	BB	SO
1995—	Seattle (A.L.)	0	0	...	2.45	2	0	0	0	0	$3\frac{2}{3}$	3	1	1	3	3

AYBAR, MANUEL — P — CARDINALS

PERSONAL: Born October 5, 1974, in Bani, Dominican Republic. . . . 6-1/165. . . . Throws right, bats right. . . . Full name: Manuel A. Aybar.
TRANSACTIONS/CAREER NOTES: Signed as non-drafted free agent by St. Louis Cardinals organization (October 21, 1991).

Year	Team (League)	W	L	Pct.	ERA	G	GS	CG	ShO	Sv.	IP	H	R	ER	BB	SO
1992—	Estadio Quisqueya (DSL)	1	0	1.000	0.00	1	0	0	0	0	3	1	0	0	3	1
1993—	Estadio Quisqueya (DSL)	4	4	.500	3.15	13	11	1	0	0	$71\frac{1}{3}$	54	33	25	33	66
1994—	Ariz. Cardinals (Ariz.)	6	1	.857	2.12	13	13	1	0	0	$72\frac{1}{3}$	69	25	17	9	79
1995—	Savannah (S. Atl.)	3	8	.273	3.04	18	18	2	1	0	$112\frac{2}{3}$	82	46	38	36	99
—	St. Petersburg (FSL)	2	5	.286	3.35	9	9	0	0	0	$48\frac{1}{3}$	42	27	18	16	43

RECORD AS POSITION PLAYER

				BATTING											FIELDING			
Year	Team (League)	Pos.	G	AB	R	H	2B	3B	HR	RBI	Avg.	BB	SO	SB	PO	A	E	Avg.
1992—	Estadio Quis. (DSL)	IF	55	153	18	31	5	0	1	11	.203	10	27	2	53	131	19	.906

AYRAULT, JOE — C — BRAVES

PERSONAL: Born October 8, 1971, in Rochester, Mich. . . . 6-3/190. . . . Bats right, throws right. . . . Full name: Joseph Allen Ayrault. . . . Name pronounced AY-ralt.
HIGH SCHOOL: Sarasota (Fla.).
TRANSACTIONS/CAREER NOTES: Selected by Atlanta Braves organization in fifth round of free-agent draft (June 4, 1990). . . . On disabled list (August 9-22, 1992). . . . On temporarily inactive list (April 21-May 1, 1995).
STATISTICAL NOTES: Led Appalachian League catchers with 495 total chances and seven double plays and tied for lead with 12 passed balls in 1991.

				BATTING											FIELDING			
Year	Team (League)	Pos.	G	AB	R	H	2B	3B	HR	RBI	Avg.	BB	SO	SB	PO	A	E	Avg.
1990—	GC Braves (GCL)	C	30	87	8	24	2	2	0	12	.276	9	15	1	182	30	3	.986
1991—	Pulaski (Appal.)	C	55	202	22	52	12	0	3	27	.257	13	49	0	425	*64	6	.988
1992—	Macon (S. Atl.)	C	90	297	24	77	12	0	6	24	.259	24	68	1	584	101	19	.973
1993—	Durham (Carolina)	C	119	390	45	99	21	0	6	52	.254	23	103	1	*739	98	7	*.992
1994—	Greenville (South.)	C	107	350	38	80	24	0	6	40	.229	19	74	2	654	93	3	*.996
1995—	Greenville (South.)	C	89	302	27	74	20	0	7	42	.245	13	70	2	516	65	8	.986

BAERGA, CARLOS — 2B — INDIANS

PERSONAL: Born November 4, 1968, in San Juan, Puerto Rico. . . . 5-11/200. . . . Bats both, throws right. . . . Full name: Carlos Obed Ortiz Baerga. . . . Name pronounced by-AIR-guh.
HIGH SCHOOL: Barbara Ann Rooshart (Rio Piedra, Puerto Rico).
TRANSACTIONS/CAREER NOTES: Signed as non-drafted free agent by San Diego Padres organization (November 4, 1985). . . . Traded by Padres organization with C Sandy Alomar and OF Chris James to Cleveland Indians for OF Joe Carter (December 6, 1989).
RECORDS: Holds major league record for switch-hitting home runs in one inning (April 8, 1993, seventh inning). . . . Shares major league record for most home runs in one inning—2 (April 8, 1993, seventh inning).
HONORS: Named second baseman on The Sporting News A.L. All-Star team (1993 and 1995). . . . Named second baseman on The Sporting News A.L. Silver Slugger team (1993-94).
STATISTICAL NOTES: Led South Atlantic League second basemen with 29 errors in 1987. . . . Led Texas League shortstops with 61 double plays in 1988. . . . Led Pacific Coast League third basemen with 380 total chances in 1989. . . . Led A.L. second basemen with 138 double plays in 1992. . . . Led A.L. second basemen with 894 total chances in 1992 and 809 in 1993. . . . Collected six hits in one game (April 11, 1992). . . . Switch-hit home runs in one game (April 8, 1993). . . . Hit three home runs in one game (June 17, 1993). . . . Career major league grand slams: 1.

				BATTING											FIELDING			
Year	Team (League)	Pos.	G	AB	R	H	2B	3B	HR	RBI	Avg.	BB	SO	SB	PO	A	E	Avg.
1986—	Char., S.C. (S. Atl.)	2B-SS	111	378	57	102	14	4	7	41	.270	26	60	6	202	245	27	.943
1987—	Char., S.C. (S. Atl.)	2B-SS	134	515	83	157	23	•9	7	50	.305	38	107	26	253	341	†36	.943
1988—	Wichita (Texas)	SS-2B	122	444	67	121	28	1	12	65	.273	31	83	4	221	325	33	.943
1989—	Las Vegas (PCL)	3B	132	520	63	143	28	2	10	74	.275	30	98	6	*92	256	*32	.916
1990—	Cleveland (A.L.)■	3B-SS-2B	108	312	46	81	17	2	7	47	.260	16	57	0	79	164	17	.935
—	Colo. Springs (PCL)	3B	12	50	11	19	2	1	1	11	.380	5	4	1	18	31	4	.925
1991—	Cleveland (A.L.)	3B-2B-SS	158	593	80	171	28	2	11	69	.288	48	74	3	217	421	27	.959
1992—	Cleveland (A.L.)	2B-DH	161	657	92	205	32	1	20	105	.312	35	76	10	*400	*475	19	.979
1993—	Cleveland (A.L.)	2B-DH	154	624	105	200	28	6	21	114	.321	34	68	15	*347	*445	17	.979
1994—	Cleveland (A.L.)	2B-DH	103	442	81	139	32	2	19	80	.314	10	45	8	205	335	*15	.973
1995—	Cleveland (A.L.)	2B-DH	135	557	87	175	28	2	15	90	.314	35	31	11	231	*444	19	.973
Major league totals (6 years)			819	3185	491	971	165	15	93	505	.305	178	351	47	1479	2284	114	.971

DIVISION SERIES RECORD

				BATTING											FIELDING			
Year	Team (League)	Pos.	G	AB	R	H	2B	3B	HR	RBI	Avg.	BB	SO	SB	PO	A	E	Avg.
1995—	Cleveland (A.L.)	2B	3	14	2	4	1	0	0	1	.286	0	1	0	8	5	1	.929

CHAMPIONSHIP SERIES RECORD

Year	Team (League)	Pos.	G	AB	R	H	2B	3B	HR	RBI	Avg.	BB	SO	SB	PO	A	E	Avg.
				BATTING											FIELDING			
1995—	Cleveland (A.L.)	2B	6	25	3	10	0	0	1	4	.400	2	3	0	12	22		1.000

WORLD SERIES RECORD

Year	Team (League)	Pos.	G	AB	R	H	2B	3B	HR	RBI	Avg.	BB	SO	SB	PO	A	E	Avg.
				BATTING											FIELDING			
1995—	Cleveland (A.L.)	2B	6	26	1	5	2	0	0	4	.192	1	1	0	15	24	1	.975

ALL-STAR GAME RECORD

Year	League	Pos.	AB	R	H	2B	3B	HR	RBI	Avg.	BB	SO	SB	PO	A	E	Avg.
			BATTING											FIELDING			
1992—	American	2B	1	1	1	1	0	0	1	1.000	0	0	0	1	2	0	1.000
1993—	American	2B	2	1	0	0	0	0	0	.000	0	1	0	0	1	0	1.000
1995—	American	2B	3	1	3	1	0	0	0	1.000	0	0	0	1	2	0	1.000
All-Star Game totals (3 years)			6	3	4	2	0	0	1	.667	0	1	0	2	5	0	1.000

BAGWELL, JEFF — 1B — ASTROS

PERSONAL: Born May 27, 1968, in Boston. . . . 6-0/195. . . . Bats right, throws right. . . . Full name: Jeffrey Robert Bagwell.

HIGH SCHOOL: Xavier (Middletown, Conn.).

COLLEGE: Hartford.

TRANSACTIONS/CAREER NOTES: Selected by Boston Red Sox organization in fourth round of free-agent draft (June 5, 1989). . . . Traded by Red Sox to Houston Astros for P Larry Andersen (August 31, 1990). . . . On Houston disabled list (July 31-September 1, 1995); included rehabilitation assignment to Jackson (August 28-September 1).

RECORDS: Shares major league record for most home runs in one inning—2 (June 24, 1994, sixth inning).

HONORS: Named Eastern League Most Valuable Player (1990). . . . Named N.L. Rookie Player of the Year by The Sporting News (1991). . . . Named N.L. Rookie of the Year by Baseball Writers' Association of America (1991). . . . Named Major League Player of the Year by The Sporting News (1994). . . . Named first baseman on The Sporting News N.L. All-Star team (1994). . . . Won N.L. Gold Glove at first base (1994). . . . Named first baseman on The Sporting News N.L. Silver Slugger team (1994). . . . Named N.L. Most Valuable Player by Baseball Writers' Association of America (1994).

STATISTICAL NOTES: Led Eastern League with 220 total bases and 12 intentional bases on balls received in 1990. . . . Led N.L. in being hit by pitch with 13 in 1991. . . . Led N.L. with 13 sacrifice flies in 1992. . . . Hit three home runs in one game (June 24, 1994). . . . Led N.L. with .750 slugging percentage in 1994. . . . Led N.L. first basemen with 120 assists in 1994. . . . Tied for N.L. lead in errors by first basemen with nine and double plays by first basemen with 94 in 1994.

Year	Team (League)	Pos.	G	AB	R	H	2B	3B	HR	RBI	Avg.	BB	SO	SB	PO	A	E	Avg.
				BATTING											FIELDING			
1989—	GC Red Sox (GCL)	3B-2B	5	19	3	6	1	0	0	3	.316	3	0	0	2	12	2	.875
—	Winter Haven (FSL)	3B-2B-1B	64	210	27	65	13	2	2	19	.310	22	25	1	53	109	12	.931
1990—	New Britain (East.)	3B	136	481	63	*160	•34	7	4	61	.333	73	57	5	93	267	34	.914
1991—	Houston (N.L.)■	1B	156	554	79	163	26	4	15	82	.294	75	116	7	1270	106	12	.991
1992—	Houston (N.L.)	1B	•162	586	87	160	34	6	18	96	.273	84	97	10	1334	133	7	.995
1993—	Houston (N.L.)	1B	142	535	76	171	37	4	20	88	.320	62	73	13	1200	113	9	.993
1994—	Houston (N.L.)	1B-OF	110	400	*104	147	32	2	39	*116	.368	65	65	15	923	†121	‡9	.991
1995—	Houston (N.L.)	1B	114	448	88	130	29	0	21	87	.290	79	102	12	1004	*129	7	.994
—	Jackson (Texas)	1B	4	12	0	2	0	0	0	0	.167	3	2	0	24	6	0	1.000
Major league totals (5 years)			684	2523	434	771	158	16	113	469	.306	365	453	57	5731	602	44	.993

ALL-STAR GAME RECORD

Year	League	Pos.	AB	R	H	2B	3B	HR	RBI	Avg.	BB	SO	SB	PO	A	E	Avg.
			BATTING											FIELDING			
1994—	National	PH-1B	4	1	2	0	0	0	0	.500	0	1	0	3	2	0	1.000

BAILEY, CORY — P — CARDINALS

PERSONAL: Born January 24, 1971, in Herrin, Ill. . . . 6-1/208. . . . Throws right, bats right. . . . Full name: Phillip Cory Bailey.

HIGH SCHOOL: Marion (Ill.).

COLLEGE: Southeastern Illinois College.

TRANSACTIONS/CAREER NOTES: Selected by Boston Red Sox organization in 15th round of free-agent draft (June 3, 1991). . . . Traded by Red Sox with 3B Scott Cooper and a player to be named later to St. Louis Cardinals for P Rheal Cormier and OF Mark Whiten (April 8, 1995).

Year	Team (League)	W	L	Pct.	ERA	G	GS	CG	ShO	Sv.	IP	H	R	ER	BB	SO
1991—	GC Red Sox (GCL)	0	0	...	0.00	1	0	0	0	1	2	2	1	0	1	1
—	Elmira (NYP)	2	4	.333	1.85	28	0	0	0	*15	39	19	10	8	12	54
1992—	Lynchburg (Caro.)	5	7	.417	2.44	49	0	0	0	*23	66 1/3	43	20	18	30	87
1993—	Pawtucket (Int'l)	4	5	.444	2.88	52	0	0	0	20	65 2/3	48	21	21	31	59
—	Boston (A.L.)	0	1	.000	3.45	11	0	0	0	0	15 2/3	12	7	6	12	11
1994—	Pawtucket (Int'l)	4	3	.571	3.23	53	0	0	0	19	61 1/3	44	25	22	38	52
—	Boston (A.L.)	0	1	.000	12.46	5	0	0	0	0	4 1/3	10	6	6	3	4
1995—	Louisville (A.A.)■	5	3	.625	4.55	55	0	0	0	*25	59 1/3	51	30	30	30	49
—	St. Louis (N.L.)	0	0	...	7.36	3	0	0	0	0	3 2/3	2	3	3	2	5
A.L. totals (2 years)		0	2	.000	5.40	16	0	0	0	0	20	22	13	12	15	15
N.L. totals (1 year)		0	0	...	7.36	3	0	0	0	0	3 2/3	2	3	3	2	5
Major league totals (3 years)		0	2	.000	5.70	19	0	0	0	0	23 2/3	24	16	15	17	20

BAILEY, ROGER — P — ROCKIES

PERSONAL: Born October 3, 1970, in Chattahoochee, Fla. . . . 6-1/180. . . . Throws right, bats right. . . . Full name: Charles Roger Bailey.
HIGH SCHOOL: Chattahoochee (Fla.).
TRANSACTIONS/CAREER NOTES: Selected by Colorado Rockies organization in third round of free-agent draft (June 1, 1992).

Year	Team (League)	W	L	Pct.	ERA	G	GS	CG	ShO	Sv.	IP	H	R	ER	BB	SO
1992—	Bend (Northwest)	5	2	.714	2.20	11	11	1	0	0	65 1/3	48	19	16	30	81
1993—	Central Valley (Cal.)	4	7	.364	4.84	22	22	1	1	0	111 2/3	139	78	60	56	84
1994—	New Haven (East.)	9	9	.500	3.23	25	24	1	1	0	159	157	70	57	56	112
1995—	Colorado (N.L.)	7	6	.538	4.98	39	6	0	0	0	81 1/3	88	49	45	39	33
—	Colo. Springs (PCL)	0	0	...	2.70	3	3	0	0	0	16 2/3	15	9	5	8	7
Major league totals (1 year)		7	6	.538	4.98	39	6	0	0	0	81 1/3	88	49	45	39	33

BAINES, HAROLD — DH — WHITE SOX

PERSONAL: Born March 15, 1959, in St. Michaels, Md. . . . 6-2/195. . . . Bats left, throws left. . . . Full name: Harold Douglas Baines.
HIGH SCHOOL: St. Michaels (Easton, Md.).
TRANSACTIONS/CAREER NOTES: Selected by Chicago White Sox organization in first round (first pick overall) of free-agent draft (June 7, 1977). . . . On disabled list (April 7-May 8, 1987). . . . Traded by White Sox with IF Fred Manrique to Texas Rangers for SS Scott Fletcher, OF Sammy Sosa and P Wilson Alvarez (July 29, 1989). . . . Traded by Rangers to Oakland Athletics for two players to be named later (August 29, 1990); Rangers acquired P Joe Bitker and P Scott Chiamparino to complete deal (September 4, 1990). . . . Granted free agency (October 27, 1992); accepted arbitration. . . . Traded by A's to Baltimore Orioles for P Bobby Chouinard and P Allen Plaster (January 14, 1993). . . . On Baltimore disabled list (May 5-27, 1993); included rehabilitation assignment to Bowie (May 25-27). . . . Granted free agency (November 1, 1993). . . . Re-signed by Orioles (December 2, 1993). . . . Granted free agency (October 20, 1994). . . . Re-signed by Orioles (December 23, 1994). . . . Granted free agency (November 6, 1995). . . . Signed by White Sox (December 11, 1995).
RECORDS: Shares major league single-game record for most plate appearances—12 (May 8, finished May 9, 1984, 25 innings). . . . Shares A.L. record for longest errorless game by outfielder—25 innings (May 8, finished May 9, 1984). . . . Shares A.L. single-game record for most innings by outfielder—25 (May 8, finished May 9, 1984).
HONORS: Named outfielder on The Sporting News A.L. All-Star team (1985). . . . Named designated hitter on The Sporting News A.L. All-Star team (1988-89). . . . Named designated hitter on The Sporting News A.L. Silver Slugger team (1989).
STATISTICAL NOTES: Tied for American Association lead in double plays by outfielder with four in 1979. . . . Hit three home runs in one game (July 7, 1982; September 17, 1984 and May 7, 1991). . . . Led A.L. with 22 game-winning RBIs in 1983. . . . Led A.L. with .541 slugging percentage in 1984. . . . Career major league grand slams: 10.

				BATTING											FIELDING			
Year	Team (League)	Pos.	G	AB	R	H	2B	3B	HR	RBI	Avg.	BB	SO	SB	PO	A	E	Avg.
1977—	Appleton (Midw.)	OF	69	222	37	58	11	2	5	29	.261	36	62	2	94	10	7	.937
1978—	Knoxville (South.)	OF-1B	137	502	70	138	16	6	13	72	.275	43	91	3	291	22	13	.960
1979—	Iowa (Am. Assoc.)	OF	125	466	87	139	25	8	22	87	.298	33	80	5	222	•16	11	.956
1980—	Chicago (A.L.)	OF-DH	141	491	55	125	23	6	13	49	.255	19	65	2	229	6	9	.963
1981—	Chicago (A.L.)	OF-DH	82	280	42	80	11	7	10	41	.286	12	41	6	120	10	2	.985
1982—	Chicago (A.L.)	OF	161	608	89	165	29	8	25	105	.271	49	95	10	326	10	7	.980
1983—	Chicago (A.L.)	OF	156	596	76	167	33	2	20	99	.280	49	85	7	312	10	9	.973
1984—	Chicago (A.L.)	OF	147	569	72	173	28	10	29	94	.304	54	75	1	307	8	6	.981
1985—	Chicago (A.L.)	OF-DH	160	640	86	198	29	3	22	113	.309	42	89	1	318	8	2	.994
1986—	Chicago (A.L.)	OF-DH	145	570	72	169	29	2	21	88	.296	38	89	2	295	15	5	.984
1987—	Chicago (A.L.)	DH-OF	132	505	59	148	26	4	20	93	.293	46	82	0	13	0	0	1.000
1988—	Chicago (A.L.)	DH-OF	158	599	55	166	39	1	13	81	.277	67	109	0	14	1	2	.882
1989—	Chicago (A.L.)	DH-OF	70	333	55	107	20	1	13	56	.321	60	52	0	52	0	1	.981
—	Texas (A.L.)■	DH-OF	46	172	18	49	9	0	3	16	.285	13	27	0	2	0	1	.667
1990—	Texas (A.L.)	DH	103	321	41	93	10	1	13	44	.290	47	63	0	...	...	...	...
—	Oakland (A.L.)■	DH-OF	32	94	11	25	5	0	3	21	.266	20	17	0	5	0	1	.833
1991—	Oakland (A.L.)	DH-OF	141	488	76	144	25	1	20	90	.295	72	67	0	11	1	1	.923
1992—	Oakland (A.L.)	DH-OF	140	478	58	121	18	0	16	76	.253	59	61	1	27	0	1	.964
1993—	Baltimore (A.L.)■	DH	118	416	64	130	22	0	20	78	.313	57	52	0	...	...	...	...
—	Bowie (Eastern)	DH	2	6	0	0	0	0	0	0	.000	1	1	0	...	...	...	...
1994—	Baltimore (A.L.)	DH	94	326	44	96	12	1	16	54	.294	30	49	0	...	...	...	...
1995—	Baltimore (A.L.)	DH	127	385	60	115	19	1	24	63	.299	70	45	0	...	...	...	...
Major league totals (16 years)			2153	7871	1033	2271	387	48	301	1261	.289	804	1163	30	2031	69	47	.978

CHAMPIONSHIP SERIES RECORD

				BATTING											FIELDING			
Year	Team (League)	Pos.	G	AB	R	H	2B	3B	HR	RBI	Avg.	BB	SO	SB	PO	A	E	Avg.
1983—	Chicago (A.L.)	OF	4	16	0	2	0	0	0	0	.125	1	3	0	5	1	0	1.000
1990—	Oakland (A.L.)	DH	4	14	2	5	1	0	0	3	.357	2	1	1	...	...	...	...
1992—	Oakland (A.L.)	DH	6	25	6	11	2	0	1	4	.440	0	3	0	...	...	...	...
Championship series totals (3 years)			14	55	8	18	3	0	1	7	.327	3	7	1	5	1	0	1.000

WORLD SERIES RECORD

				BATTING											FIELDING			
Year	Team (League)	Pos.	G	AB	R	H	2B	3B	HR	RBI	Avg.	BB	SO	SB	PO	A	E	Avg.
1990—	Oakland (A.L.)	DH-PH	3	7	1	1	0	0	1	2	.143	1	2	0	...	...	...	...

ALL-STAR GAME RECORD

				BATTING									FIELDING			
Year	League	Pos.	AB	R	H	2B	3B	HR	RBI	Avg.	BB	SO	SB	PO	A	E	Avg.
1985—	American	PH	1	0	1	0	0	0	0	1.000	0	0	0	...	...	...	...
1986—	American	PH	1	0	0	0	0	0	0	.000	0	0	0	...	...	...	...
1987—	American	PH	1	0	0	0	0	0	0	.000	0	0	0	...	...	...	...
1989—	American	DH	3	1	1	0	0	0	1	.333	0	1	0	...	...	...	...
1991—	American	PH-DH	1	0	0	0	0	0	1	.000	0	0	0	...	...	...	...
All-Star Game totals (5 years)			7	1	2	0	0	0	2	.286	0	1	0	...	...	...	...

BAKER, SCOTT — P — ATHLETICS

PERSONAL: Born May 18, 1970, in San Jose, Calif. . . . 6-2/175. . . . Throws left, bats left.
HIGH SCHOOL: Basic (Henderson, Nev.).
COLLEGE: Taft (Calif.) College.
TRANSACTIONS/CAREER NOTES: Selected by St. Louis Cardinals organization in seventh round of free-agent draft (June 4, 1990). . . . Selected by Florida Marlins in third round (65th pick overall) of expansion draft (November 17, 1992). . . . Traded by Marlins to Oakland Athletics organization (November 20, 1992), completing deal in which A's traded SS Walt Weiss to Marlins for C Eric Helfand and a player to be named later (November 17, 1992). . . . On disabled list (August 10-17, 1993 and April 23-May 13, 1994). . . . On Edmonton temporarily inactive list (April 18-May 11, 1995).

Year Team (League)	W	L	Pct.	ERA	G	GS	CG	ShO	Sv.	IP	H	R	ER	BB	SO
1990—Johns. City (App.)	4	2	.667	2.28	*32	0	0	0	0	51 1/3	44	21	13	29	65
1991—Savannah (S. Atl.)	2	3	.400	2.89	8	8	0	0	0	46 2/3	42	27	15	25	41
—St. Petersburg (FSL)	3	9	.250	4.42	19	16	1	0	0	93 2/3	98	47	46	42	50
1992—St. Petersburg (FSL)	10	9	.526	1.96	24	24	0	0	0	151 2/3	123	48	33	54	125
1993—Huntsville (South.)■	10	4	.714	4.14	25	25	1	1	0	130 1/3	141	73	60	84	97
1994—Huntsville (South.)	10	4	.714	1.78	30	14	3	2	2	111	86	28	22	46	67
1995—Edmonton (PCL)	4	7	.364	5.28	22	20	1	0	0	107 1/3	123	69	63	46	56
—Oakland (A.L.)	0	0	...	9.82	1	0	0	0	0	3 2/3	5	4	4	5	3
Major league totals (1 year)	0	0	...	9.82	1	0	0	0	0	3 2/3	5	4	4	5	3

BALDWIN, JAMES — P — WHITE SOX

PERSONAL: Born July 15, 1971, in Southern Pines, N.C. . . . 6-3/210. . . . Throws right, bats right. . . . Full name: James Baldwin Jr.
HIGH SCHOOL: Pinecrest (Southern Pines, N.C.).
TRANSACTIONS/CAREER NOTES: Selected by Chicago White Sox organization in fourth round of free-agent draft (June 4, 1990). . . . On disabled list (August 3-19, 1994).
STATISTICAL NOTES: Led American Association with 27 home runs allowed in 1995. . . . Tied for American Association lead with three balks in 1995.

Year Team (League)	W	L	Pct.	ERA	G	GS	CG	ShO	Sv.	IP	H	R	ER	BB	SO
1990—GC White Sox (GCL)	1	6	.143	4.10	9	7	0	0	0	37 1/3	32	29	17	18	32
1991—GC White Sox (GCL)	3	1	.750	2.12	6	6	0	0	0	34	16	8	8	16	48
—Utica (NYP)	1	4	.200	5.30	7	7	1	0	0	37 1/3	40	26	22	27	23
1992—South Bend (Midw.)	9	5	.643	2.42	21	21	1	1	0	137 2/3	118	53	37	45	137
—Sarasota (Fla. St.)	1	2	.333	2.87	6	6	1	0	0	37 2/3	31	13	12	7	39
1993—Birmingham (Sou.)	8	5	.615	*2.25	17	17	•4	0	0	120	94	48	30	43	107
—Nashville (A.A.)	5	4	.556	2.61	10	10	1	0	0	69	43	21	20	36	61
1994—Nashville (A.A.)	12	6	.667	3.72	26	26	2	0	0	162	144	75	67	83	*156
1995—Chicago (A.L.)	0	1	.000	12.89	6	4	0	0	0	14 2/3	32	22	21	9	10
—Nashville (A.A.)	5	9	.357	5.85	18	18	0	0	0	95 1/3	120	76	62	44	89
Major league totals (1 year)	0	1	.000	12.89	6	4	0	0	0	14 2/3	32	22	21	9	10

BANKHEAD, SCOTT — P

PERSONAL: Born July 31, 1963, in Raleigh, N.C. . . . 5-10/185. . . . Throws right, bats right. . . . Full name: Michael Scott Bankhead.
HIGH SCHOOL: Reidsville (N.C.).
COLLEGE: North Carolina.
TRANSACTIONS/CAREER NOTES: Selected by Pittsburgh Pirates organization in 17th round of free-agent draft (June 8, 1981); did not sign. . . . Selected by Kansas City Royals organization in first round (16th pick overall) of free-agent draft (June 4, 1984). . . . Traded by Royals with P Steve Shields and OF Mike Kingery to Seattle Mariners for OF Danny Tartabull and P Rick Luecken (December 10, 1986). . . . On disabled list (June 24-July 13, 1987). . . . On Seattle disabled list (March 20-May 14, 1988); included rehabilitation assignments to San Bernardino (April 23-May 2) and Calgary (May 3-10). . . . On Seattle disabled list (April 16-May 18 and June 3, 1990-remainder of season); included rehabilitation assignment to Calgary (May 1-7). . . . On Seattle disabled list (May 11-31 and June 12-September 1, 1991); included rehabilitation assignments to San Bernardino (August 5-14), Bellingham (August 14-18) and Calgary (August 18-September 1). . . . Granted free agency (December 20, 1991). . . . Signed by Cincinnati Reds (January 22, 1992). . . . Granted free agency (October 28, 1992). . . . Signed by Boston Red Sox (December 8, 1992). . . . On Boston disabled list (May 11-June 12, and June 17-July 8, 1994); included rehabilitation assignments to Pawtucket (June 7-10 and July 5-8). . . . Traded by Red Sox to New York Yankees for a player to be named later and cash (August 31, 1994). . . . Granted free agency (October 17, 1994). . . . Re-signed by Yankees (November 1, 1994). . . . Released by Yankees (July 25, 1995). . . . Signed by Edmonton, Oakland Athletics organization (August 4, 1995). . . . Released by Edmonton (September 10, 1995).
MISCELLANEOUS: Member of 1984 U.S. Olympic baseball team.

Year Team (League)	W	L	Pct.	ERA	G	GS	CG	ShO	Sv.	IP	H	R	ER	BB	SO
1985—Memphis (South.)	8	6	.571	3.59	24	24	2	1	0	140 1/3	117	63	56	56	•128
1986—Omaha (Am. Assoc.)	2	2	.500	1.49	7	7	2	0	0	48 1/3	31	11	8	14	34
—Kansas City (A.L.)	8	9	.471	4.61	24	17	0	0	0	121	121	66	62	37	94
1987—Seattle (A.L.)■	9	8	.529	5.42	27	25	2	0	0	149 1/3	168	96	90	37	95
1988—San Bern. (Calif.)	0	0	...	1.64	2	2	0	0	0	11	6	3	2	4	6
—Calgary (PCL)	1	1	.500	7.36	2	2	0	0	0	11	15	9	9	5	5
—Seattle (A.L.)	7	9	.438	3.07	21	21	2	1	0	135	115	53	46	38	102
1989—Seattle (A.L.)	14	6	.700	3.34	33	33	3	2	0	210 1/3	187	84	78	63	140
1990—Seattle (A.L.)	0	2	.000	11.08	4	4	0	0	0	13	18	16	16	7	10
—Calgary (PCL)	0	1	.000	6.43	2	2	0	0	0	7	9	6	5	3	7
1991—Seattle (A.L.)	3	6	.333	4.90	17	9	0	0	0	60 2/3	73	35	33	21	28
—San Bern. (Calif.)	0	1	.000	5.06	2	2	0	0	0	5 1/3	4	4	3	2	4
—Bellingham (N'west)	1	0	1.000	0.00	1	0	0	0	0	4	1	0	0	1	8
—Calgary (PCL)	0	0	...	1.04	5	0	0	0	1	8 2/3	7	1	1	1	10
1992—Cincinnati (N.L.)■	10	4	.714	2.93	54	0	0	0	1	70 2/3	57	26	23	29	53
1993—Boston (A.L.)■	2	1	.667	3.50	40	0	0	0	0	64 1/3	59	28	25	29	47
1994—Boston (A.L.)	3	2	.600	4.54	27	0	0	0	0	37 2/3	34	21	19	12	25

Year	Team (League)	W	L	Pct.	ERA	G	GS	CG	ShO	Sv.	IP	H	R	ER	BB	SO
	—Pawtucket (Int'l)	0	1	.000	11.81	4	2	0	0	0	5 1/3	10	7	7	1	3
1995—	New York (A.L.)■	1	1	.500	6.00	20	1	0	0	0	39	44	26	26	16	20
	—Edmonton (PCL)■	1	3	.250	7.85	12	0	0	0	1	18 1/3	28	18	16	7	15
A.L. totals (9 years)		47	44	.516	4.28	213	110	7	3	0	830 1/3	819	425	395	260	561
N.L. totals (1 year)		10	4	.714	2.93	54	0	0	0	1	70 2/3	57	26	23	29	53
Major league totals (10 years)		57	48	.543	4.18	267	110	7	3	1	901	876	451	418	289	614

BANKS, BRIAN — OF — BREWERS

PERSONAL: Born September 28, 1970, in Mesa, Ariz. . . . 6-3/200. . . . Bats both, throws right. . . . Full name: Brian Glen Banks.
COLLEGE: Brigham Young.
TRANSACTIONS/CAREER NOTES: Selected by Milwaukee Brewers organization in second round of free-agent draft (June 3, 1993); pick received as part of compensation for Seattle Mariners signing Type A free-agent P Chris Bosio.
STATISTICAL NOTES: Tied for Midwest League lead in double plays by outfielder with four in 1994.

				BATTING											FIELDING			
Year	Team (League)	Pos.	G	AB	R	H	2B	3B	HR	RBI	Avg.	BB	SO	SB	PO	A	E	Avg.
1993—	Helena (Pioneer)	OF	12	48	8	19	1	1	2	8	.396	11	8	1	25	0	1	.962
	—Beloit (Midwest)	OF	38	147	21	36	5	1	4	19	.245	7	34	1	47	2	1	.980
1994—	Beloit (Midwest)	OF-1B-3B	65	237	41	71	13	1	9	47	.300	29	40	11	123	5	2	.985
	—Stockton (Calif.)	OF	67	246	29	58	9	1	4	28	.236	38	46	3	108	5	4	.966
1995—	El Paso (Texas)	OF-1B-3B	128	441	81	136	*39	10	12	78	.308	*81	113	9	245	11	10	.962

BANKS, WILLIE — P — PHILLIES

PERSONAL: Born February 27, 1969, in Jersey City, N.J. . . . 6-1/195. . . . Throws right, bats right. . . . Full name: Willie Anthony Banks.
HIGH SCHOOL: St. Anthony (Jersey City, N.J.).
TRANSACTIONS/CAREER NOTES: Selected by Minnesota Twins organization in first round (third pick overall) of free-agent draft (June 2, 1987). . . . Traded by Twins to Chicago Cubs for P Dave Stevens and C Matt Walbeck (November 24, 1993). . . . Traded by Cubs to Los Angeles Dodgers for P Dax Winslett (June 19, 1995). . . . Claimed on waivers by Florida Marlins (August 10, 1995). . . . Claimed on waivers by Philadelphia Phillies (October 4, 1995).
STATISTICAL NOTES: Led Appalachian League with 28 wild pitches and tied for lead with three balks in 1987. . . . Pitched 1-0 no-hit victory for Visalia against Palm Springs (May 24, 1989). . . . Led California League with 22 wild pitches in 1989. . . . Tied for Pacific Coast League lead with 14 wild pitches in 1991. . . . Tied for A.L. lead with five balks in 1993.
MISCELLANEOUS: Appeared in two games as pinch-runner and struck out in only appearance as pinch-hitter with Florida (1995).

Year	Team (League)	W	L	Pct.	ERA	G	GS	CG	ShO	Sv.	IP	H	R	ER	BB	SO
1987—	Elizabeth. (App.)	1	8	.111	6.99	13	13	0	0	0	65 2/3	73	*71	*51	*62	71
1988—	Kenosha (Midwest)	10	10	.500	3.72	24	24	0	0	0	125 2/3	109	73	52	*107	113
1989—	Visalia (California)	12	9	.571	2.59	27	27	7	•4	0	174	122	70	50	85	*173
	—Orlando (Southern)	1	0	1.000	5.14	1	1	0	0	0	7	10	4	4	0	9
1990—	Orlando (Southern)	7	9	.438	3.93	28	28	1	0	0	162 2/3	161	93	71	98	114
1991—	Portland (PCL)	9	8	.529	4.55	25	24	1	1	0	146 1/3	156	81	74	76	63
	—Minnesota (A.L.)	1	1	.500	5.71	5	3	0	0	0	17 1/3	21	15	11	12	16
1992—	Portland (PCL)	6	1	.857	1.92	11	11	2	1	0	75	62	20	16	34	41
	—Minnesota (A.L.)	4	4	.500	5.70	16	12	0	0	0	71	80	46	45	37	37
1993—	Minnesota (A.L.)	11	12	.478	4.04	31	30	0	0	0	171 1/3	186	91	77	78	138
1994—	Chicago (N.L.)■	8	12	.400	5.40	23	23	1	1	0	138 1/3	139	88	83	56	91
1995—	Chicago (N.L.)	0	1	.000	15.43	10	0	0	0	0	11 2/3	27	23	20	12	9
	—Los Angeles (N.L.)■	0	2	.000	4.03	6	6	0	0	0	29	36	21	13	16	23
	—Florida (N.L.)■	2	3	.400	4.32	9	9	0	0	0	50	43	27	24	30	30
A.L. totals (3 years)		16	17	.485	4.61	52	45	0	0	0	259 2/3	287	152	133	127	191
N.L. totals (2 years)		10	18	.357	5.50	48	38	1	1	0	229	245	159	140	114	153
Major league totals (5 years)		26	35	.426	5.03	100	83	1	1	0	488 2/3	532	311	273	241	344

BARBER, BRIAN — P — CARDINALS

PERSONAL: Born March 4, 1973, in Hamilton, O. . . . 6-1/175. . . . Throws right, bats right. . . . Full name: Brian Scott Barber.
HIGH SCHOOL: Dr. Phillips (Orlando, Fla.).
TRANSACTIONS/CAREER NOTES: Selected by St. Louis Cardinals organization in first round (22nd pick overall) of free-agent draft (June 3, 1991); pick received as part of compensation for New York Mets signing Type B free agent OF Vince Coleman. . . . On Louisville disabled list (April 21-May 14, 1994). . . . On Louisville suspended list (July 6-8, 1995).

Year	Team (League)	W	L	Pct.	ERA	G	GS	CG	ShO	Sv.	IP	H	R	ER	BB	SO
1991—	Johns. City (App.)	4	6	.400	5.40	14	13	0	0	0	73 1/3	62	48	44	38	84
1992—	Springfield (Midw.)	3	4	.429	3.73	8	8	0	0	0	50 2/3	39	21	21	24	56
	—St. Petersburg (FSL)	5	5	.500	3.26	19	19	1	0	0	113 1/3	99	51	41	46	102
1993—	Arkansas (Texas)	9	8	.529	4.02	24	24	1	0	0	143 1/3	154	70	64	56	126
	—Louisville (A.A.)	0	1	.000	4.76	1	1	0	0	0	5 2/3	4	3	3	4	5
1994—	Louisville (A.A.)	4	7	.364	5.38	19	18	0	0	1	85 1/3	79	58	51	46	95
	—Arkansas (Texas)	1	3	.250	3.25	6	6	0	0	0	36	31	15	13	16	54
1995—	Louisville (A.A.)	6	5	.545	4.70	20	19	0	0	0	107 1/3	105	67	56	40	94
	—St. Louis (N.L.)	2	1	.667	5.22	9	4	0	0	0	29 1/3	31	17	17	16	27
Major league totals (1 year)		2	1	.667	5.22	9	4	0	0	0	29 1/3	31	17	17	16	27

BARBERIE, BRET — 2B — CUBS

PERSONAL: Born August 16, 1967, in Long Beach, Calif. . . . 5-11/180. . . . Bats both, throws right. . . . Full name: Bret Edward Barberie.

. . . Son of Edward Barberie, minor league catcher/shortstop (1961-66). . . . Name pronounced BAR-ber-ee.
HIGH SCHOOL: Gahr (Cerritos, Calif.).
JUNIOR COLLEGE: Cerritos (Calif.).
COLLEGE: Southern California (received degree, 1988).
TRANSACTIONS/CAREER NOTES: Selected by St. Louis Cardinals organization in second round of free-agent draft (January 14, 1986); did not sign. . . . Selected by Oakland Athletics organization in secondary phase of free-agent draft (June 2, 1986); did not sign. . . . Selected by Kansas City Royals organization in 65th round of free-agent draft (June 2, 1987); did not sign. . . . Selected by Montreal Expos organization in seventh round of free-agent draft (June 1, 1988). . . . On Montreal disabled list (August 20-September 5, 1992). . . . Selected by Florida Marlins in first round (sixth pick overall) of expansion draft (November 17, 1992). . . . On Florida disabled list (April 17-May 28, 1993); included rehabilitation assignment to Edmonton (May 22-28). . . . On Florida disabled list (June 28-July 25, 1993); included rehabilitation assignment to Gulf Coast Marlins (July 23-25). . . . Traded by Marlins to Baltimore Orioles for P Jay Powell (December 6, 1994). . . . Granted free agency (December 21, 1995). . . . Signed by Chicago Cubs organization (January 24, 1996).
STATISTICAL NOTES: Switch-hit home runs in one game for Montreal (August 2, 1991). . . . Career major league grand slams: 1.
MISCELLANEOUS: Member of 1988 U.S. Olympic baseball team.

		BATTING												FIELDING			
Year Team (League)	**Pos.**	**G**	**AB**	**R**	**H**	**2B**	**3B**	**HR**	**RBI**	**Avg.**	**BB**	**SO**	**SB**	**PO**	**A**	**E**	**Avg.**
1989—W.P. Beach (FSL)	2B	124	457	63	122	16	4	4	34	.267	64	39	10	247	343	16	.974
1990—Jacksonv. (South.)	2B	133	431	71	112	18	3	7	56	.260	86	64	20	263	322	14	*.977
1991—Indianapolis (A.A.)	3-2-S-1	71	218	45	68	10	4	10	48	.312	59	47	10	83	162	13	.950
—Montreal (N.L.)	S-2-3-1	57	136	16	48	12	2	2	18	.353	20	22	0	53	90	5	.966
1992—Montreal (N.L.)	3B-2B-SS	111	285	26	66	11	0	1	24	.232	47	62	9	66	188	13	.951
—Indianapolis (A.A.)	2B-3B-SS	10	43	4	17	3	0	3	8	.395	1	9	0	25	20	3	.938
1993—Florida (N.L.)■	2B	99	375	45	104	16	2	5	33	.277	33	58	2	201	303	9	.982
—Edmonton (PCL)	2B	4	19	3	8	2	0	1	8	.421	0	2	0	8	12	1	.952
—GC Marlins (GCL)	2B	2	8	0	2	0	0	0	1	.250	1	1	0	3	4	0	1.000
1994—Florida (N.L.)	2B	107	372	40	112	20	2	5	31	.301	23	65	2	222	322	•14	.975
1995—Baltimore (A.L.)■	2B-DH-3B	90	237	32	57	14	0	2	25	.241	36	50	3	114	188	7	.977
American League totals (1 year)		90	237	32	57	14	0	2	25	.241	36	50	3	114	188	7	.977
National League totals (4 years)		374	1168	127	330	59	6	13	106	.283	123	207	13	542	903	41	.972
Major league totals (5 years)		464	1405	159	387	73	6	15	131	.275	159	257	16	656	1091	48	.973

BARCELO, MARC — P — TWINS

PERSONAL: Born January 10, 1972, in Van Nuys, Calif. . . . 6-3/215. . . . Throws right, bats right. . . . Full name: Marc Andrew Barcelo.
COLLEGE: Arizona State.
TRANSACTIONS/CAREER NOTES: Selected by Minnesota Twins organization in supplemental round ("sandwich pick" between first and second round, 33rd pick overall) of free-agent draft (June 3, 1993); pick received as part of compensation for Cincinnati Reds signing Type A free-agent P John Smiley.

Year Team (League)	**W**	**L**	**Pct.**	**ERA**	**G**	**GS**	**CG**	**ShO**	**Sv.**	**IP**	**H**	**R**	**ER**	**BB**	**SO**
1993—Fort Myers (Fla. St.)	1	1	.500	2.74	7	3	0	0	0	23	18	10	7	4	24
—Nashville (South.)	1	0	1.000	3.86	2	2	2	0	0	9 1/3	9	5	4	5	5
1994—Nashville (South.)	11	6	.647	2.65	29	•28	4	0	0	183 1/3	167	74	54	45	153
1995—Salt Lake (PCL)	8	13	.381	7.05	28	•28	2	0	0	143	*214	*131	*112	59	63

BARK, BRIAN — P — RED SOX

PERSONAL: Born August 26, 1968, in Baltimore. . . . 5-9/170. . . . Throws left, bats left. . . . Full name: Brian Stuart Bark. . . . Son of Jerry Bark, minor league pitcher (1965-68).
HIGH SCHOOL: Randallstown (Md.).
COLLEGE: North Carolina State.
TRANSACTIONS/CAREER NOTES: Selected by Baltimore Orioles organization in 28th round of free-agent draft (June 5, 1989); did not sign. . . . Selected by Atlanta Braves organization in 12th round of free-agent draft (June 4, 1990). . . . On Greenville disabled list (July 26-September 12, 1991). . . . Released by Richmond, Braves organization (June 1, 1995). . . . Signed by Pawtucket, Boston Red Sox organization (June 4, 1995).

Year Team (League)	**W**	**L**	**Pct.**	**ERA**	**G**	**GS**	**CG**	**ShO**	**Sv.**	**IP**	**H**	**R**	**ER**	**BB**	**SO**
1990—Pulaski (Appal.)	2	2	.500	2.66	5	5	0	0	0	23 2/3	17	19	7	13	33
1991—Durham (Carolina)	4	3	.571	2.51	13	13	0	0	0	82 1/3	66	23	23	24	76
—Greenville (South.)	2	1	.667	3.57	9	3	1	0	1	17 2/3	19	10	7	8	15
1992—Greenville (South.)	5	0	1.000	1.15	11	11	2	1	0	55	36	11	7	13	49
—Richmond (Int'l)	1	2	.333	6.00	22	4	0	0	2	42	63	32	28	15	50
1993—Richmond (Int'l)	12	9	.571	3.67	29	28	1	1	0	162	153	81	66	*72	110
1994—Richmond (Int'l)	4	9	.308	4.76	37	16	0	0	0	126 2/3	128	76	67	51	87
1995—Richmond (Int'l)	2	2	.500	3.54	13	5	0	0	0	40 2/3	42	16	16	17	22
—Pawtucket (Int'l)■	3	1	.750	2.27	30	0	0	0	7	31 2/3	21	8	8	14	21
—Boston (A.L.)	0	0	. . .	0.00	3	0	0	0	0	2 1/3	2	0	0	1	0
Major league totals (1 year)	0	0	. . .	0.00	3	0	0	0	0	2 1/3	2	0	0	1	0

BARRY, JEFF — OF — PADRES

PERSONAL: Born September 22, 1968, in Medford, Ore. . . . 6-0/200. . . . Bats both, throws right. . . . Full name: Jeffrey Finis Barry.
HIGH SCHOOL: Medford (Ore.).
COLLEGE: San Diego State.
TRANSACTIONS/CAREER NOTES: Selected by Montreal Expos organization in fourth round of free-agent draft (June 4, 1990). . . . On disabled list (September 5-20, 1991). . . . Traded by Expos organization to New York Mets organization for P Blaine Beatty (December 9, 1991). . . . On St. Lucie disabled list (April 16-September 18, 1992). . . . On disabled list (June 2-20, 1994). . . . On suspended list (August 14-15, 1994). . . . On Binghamton disabled list (August 26-September 5, 1995). . . . Traded by Mets to San Diego Padres for P Pedro A. Martinez (December 15, 1995).

STATISTICAL NOTES: Tied for Eastern League lead with nine sacrifice flies in 1995.

			BATTING											FIELDING			
Year Team (League)	Pos.	G	AB	R	H	2B	3B	HR	RBI	Avg.	BB	SO	SB	PO	A	E	Avg.
1990— Jamestown (NYP)	OF	70	263	40	76	18	1	5	38	.289	22	35	20	88	8	5	.950
1991— W.P. Beach (FSL)	OF	116	437	48	92	16	3	4	31	.211	34	68	20	200	14	7	.968
1992— St. Lucie (Fla. St.)■	DH	3	9	0	3	2	0	0	1	.333	0	0	0	...	...	...	...
— GC Mets (GCL)	DH	8	23	5	4	1	0	0	2	.174	6	2	2	...	...	...	...
1993— St. Lucie (Fla. St.)	OF	114	420	68	108	17	5	4	50	.257	49	37	17	167	12	1	.994
1994— Binghamton (East.)	OF	110	388	48	118	24	3	9	69	.304	35	62	10	144	6	5	.968
1995— Norfolk (Int'l)	1B	12	41	3	9	2	0	0	6	.220	3	6	0	117	9	2	.984
— Binghamton (East.)	OF-1B	80	290	49	78	17	6	11	53	.269	31	61	4	129	6	0	1.000
— New York (N.L.)	OF	15	15	2	2	1	0	0	0	.133	1	8	0	2	0	0	1.000
Major league totals (1 year)		15	15	2	2	1	0	0	0	.133	1	8	0	2	0	0	1.000

BARTEE, KIM — OF — ORIOLES

PERSONAL: Born July 21, 1972, in Omaha, Neb. . . . 6-0/175. . . . Bats both, throws right. . . . Full name: Kimera Anotchi Bartee.
HIGH SCHOOL: Central (Omaha, Neb.).
COLLEGE: Creighton.
TRANSACTIONS/CAREER NOTES: Selected by Baltimore Orioles organization in 14th round of free-agent draft (June 3, 1993). . . . On Bowie disabled list (June 8-August 8, 1995). . . . Traded by Orioles organization to Minnesota Twins organization (September 18, 1995), completing deal in which Orioles acquired P Scott Erickson from Twins for P Scott Klingenbeck and a player to be named later (July 7, 1995). . . . Selected by Orioles from Twins organization in Rule 5 major league draft (December 4, 1995).

			BATTING											FIELDING			
Year Team (League)	Pos.	G	AB	R	H	2B	3B	HR	RBI	Avg.	BB	SO	SB	PO	A	E	Avg.
1993— Bluefield (Appal.)	OF	66	264	59	65	15	2	4	37	.246	44	66	*27	124	5	4	.970
1994— Frederick (Caro.)	OF	130	514	97	150	22	4	10	57	.292	56	117	44	*304	7	6	.981
1995— GC Orioles (GCL)	OF	5	21	5	5	0	0	1	3	.238	3	2	1	15	0	0	1.000
— Bowie (Eastern)	OF	53	218	45	62	9	1	3	19	.284	23	45	22	155	4	6	.964
— Rochester (Int'l)	OF	15	52	5	8	2	1	0	3	.154	0	16	0	37	2	0	1.000

BARTON, SHAWN — P — GIANTS

PERSONAL: Born May 14, 1963, in Los Angeles. . . . 6-3/195. . . . Throws left, bats right. . . . Full name: Shawn Edward Barton.
HIGH SCHOOL: Saugus (Calif.).
JUNIOR COLLEGE: College of the Canyons (Calif.).
COLLEGE: Nevada.
TRANSACTIONS/CAREER NOTES: Selected by Philadelphia Phillies organization in 21st round of free-agent draft (June 4, 1984). . . . On disabled list (June 23-July 24, 1986). . . . Traded by Phillies organization with P Vladimir Perez to New York Mets organization for IF/OF Bill Almon (March 21, 1988). . . . Released by Mets organization (June 14, 1990). . . . Signed by Greenville, Atlanta Braves organization (June 19, 1990). . . . Released by Greenville (July 31, 1990). . . . Signed by Jacksonville, Seattle Mariners organization (February 20, 1991). . . . On Jacksonville disabled list (April 21-29, 1991). . . . On Calgary disabled list (June 21-July 17, 1992). . . . Granted free agency (October 15, 1993). . . . Signed by Phoenix, San Francisco Giants organization (January 30, 1994). . . . Released by Phoenix (April 4, 1994). . . . Re-signed by Phoenix (April 15, 1994).

Year Team (League)	W	L	Pct.	ERA	G	GS	CG	ShO	Sv.	IP	H	R	ER	BB	SO
1984— Bend (Northwest)	4	5	.444	2.16	13	8	1	0	0	58 1/3	46	28	14	24	47
1985— Peninsula (Caro.)	12	4	.750	2.30	22	22	7	*5	0	140 2/3	108	45	36	43	82
1986— Reading (Eastern)	8	7	.533	3.79	17	17	3	1	0	92 2/3	92	53	39	41	62
1987— Maine (Int'l)	1	1	.500	4.39	7	4	0	0	1	26 2/3	25	14	13	15	19
— Reading (Eastern)	6	5	.545	4.92	32	12	3	0	3	82 1/3	108	50	45	31	53
1988— Jackson (Texas)■	2	4	.333	3.27	22	8	0	0	1	71 2/3	74	33	26	26	58
— Tidewater (Int'l)	2	2	.500	3.06	19	2	0	0	0	32 1/3	34	13	11	11	27
1989— Tidewater (Int'l)	0	3	.000	4.28	38	0	0	0	5	33 2/3	41	22	16	9	27
1990— Tidewater (Int'l)	0	0	...	5.82	16	0	0	0	0	21 2/3	27	17	14	10	23
— Greenville (South.)■	0	1	.000	8.10	15	0	0	0	1	16 2/3	24	15	15	9	8
1991— Jacksonville (Sou.)■	3	3	.500	3.12	14	4	1	1	0	34 2/3	36	16	12	8	24
— Calgary (PCL)	2	0	1.000	2.61	17	0	0	0	1	31	25	11	9	8	22
1992— Calgary (PCL)	3	5	.375	4.25	30	0	0	0	4	53	57	31	25	24	31
— Seattle (A.L.)	0	1	.000	2.92	14	0	0	0	0	12 1/3	10	5	4	7	4
1993— Calgary (PCL)	3	1	.750	3.56	51	0	0	0	4	60 2/3	64	29	24	27	29
1994— Phoenix (PCL)■	1	2	.333	1.98	38	0	0	0	4	54 2/3	51	16	12	22	39
1995— Phoenix (PCL)	2	0	1.000	1.80	15	0	0	0	0	25	20	5	5	5	25
— San Francisco (N.L.)	4	1	.800	4.26	52	0	0	0	1	44 1/3	37	22	21	19	22
A.L. totals (1 year)	0	1	.000	2.92	14	0	0	0	0	12 1/3	10	5	4	7	4
N.L. totals (1 year)	4	1	.800	4.26	52	0	0	0	1	44 1/3	37	22	21	19	22
Major league totals (2 years)	4	2	.667	3.97	66	0	0	0	1	56 2/3	47	27	25	26	26

BASS, KEVIN — OF

PERSONAL: Born May 12, 1959, in Redwood City, Calif. . . . 6-0/190. . . . Bats both, throws right. . . . Full name: Kevin Charles Bass. . . . Brother of Richard Bass, minor league outfielder (1976-77); and cousin of James Lofton, wide receiver with five National Football League teams (1978-93).
HIGH SCHOOL: Menlo Park (Calif.).
TRANSACTIONS/CAREER NOTES: Selected by Milwaukee Brewers organization in second round of free-agent draft (June 7, 1977). . . . On disabled list (July 29-September 1, 1981). . . . Traded by Brewers organization with P Mike Madden and P Frank DiPino to Houston Astros (September 3, 1982), completing deal in which Houston traded P Don Sutton to Brewers for three players to be named later (August 30, 1982). . . . On disabled list (March 29-April 13, 1984). . . . On Houston disabled list (May 28-August 11, 1989); included rehabilitation assign-

ment to Tucson (August 4-22). . . . Granted free agency (November 13, 1989). . . . Signed by San Francisco Giants (November 16, 1989). . . . On San Francisco disabled list (May 27-September 3, 1990); included rehabilitation assignments to San Jose (August 20-26) and Phoenix (August 27-September 3). . . . On San Francisco disabled list (June 19-July 23, 1991); included rehabilitation assignments to San Jose (July 4-10) and Phoenix (July 10-23). . . . On San Francisco disabled list (March 29-April 19, 1992). . . . Traded by Giants to New York Mets for a player to be named later (August 8, 1992); Giants acquired OF Rob Katzaroff to complete deal (October 1, 1992). . . . Granted free agency (November 3, 1992). . . . Signed by Astros (January 5, 1993). . . . Granted free agency (November 1, 1993). . . . Re-signed by Astros (December 7, 1993). . . . Granted free agency (October 26, 1994). . . . Signed by Rochester, Baltimore Orioles organization (April 18, 1995). . . . Granted free agency (November 3, 1995).

STATISTICAL NOTES: Led Midwest League in being hit by pitch with 10 in 1978. . . . Led Eastern League outfielders with seven double plays in 1980. . . . Switch-hit home runs in one game four times (August 3 and September 2, 1987; August 20, 1989; and August 2, 1992, second game). . . . Career major league grand slams: 4.

		BATTING												FIELDING			
Year Team (League)	**Pos.**	**G**	**AB**	**R**	**H**	**2B**	**3B**	**HR**	**RBI**	**Avg.**	**BB**	**SO**	**SB**	**PO**	**A**	**E**	**Avg.**
1977—Newark (NYP)	OF	48	189	30	56	11	•7	1	33	.296	19	17	11	56	2	3	.951
1978—Burlington (Midw.)	OF	129	499	81	132	27	5	18	69	.265	40	63	36	*281	14	11	.964
1979—Holyoke (Eastern)	OF	135	490	69	129	15	4	8	54	.263	37	77	17	280	•16	*17	.946
1980—Holyoke (Eastern)	OF	136	490	79	147	*31	7	4	51	.300	41	59	35	305	14	*18	.947
1981—Vancouver (PCL)	OF	97	339	40	87	10	5	2	30	.257	43	36	29	175	14	7	.964
1982—Milwaukee (A.L.)	OF-DH	18	9	4	0	0	0	0	0	.000	1	1	0	7	0	0	1.000
—Vancouver (PCL)	OF	102	413	70	130	23	7	17	65	.315	44	44	23	199	15	10	.955
—Houston (N.L.)■	OF	12	24	2	1	0	0	0	1	.042	0	8	0	11	0	1	.917
1983—Houston (N.L.)	OF	88	195	25	46	7	3	2	18	.236	6	27	2	68	1	4	.945
1984—Houston (N.L.)	OF	121	331	33	86	17	5	2	29	.260	6	57	5	149	4	4	.975
1985—Houston (N.L.)	OF	150	539	72	145	27	5	16	68	.269	31	63	19	328	10	1	*.997
1986—Houston (N.L.)	OF	157	591	83	184	33	5	20	79	.311	38	72	22	303	12	5	.984
1987—Houston (N.L.)	OF	157	592	83	168	31	5	19	85	.284	53	77	21	287	11	4	.987
1988—Houston (N.L.)	OF	157	541	57	138	27	2	14	72	.255	42	65	31	267	7	6	.979
1989—Houston (N.L.)	OF	87	313	42	94	19	4	5	44	.300	29	44	11	186	6	3	.985
—Tucson (PCL)	OF	6	17	1	5	1	0	0	2	.294	1	2	0	8	0	0	1.000
1990—San Fran. (N.L.)■	OF	61	214	25	54	9	1	7	32	.252	14	26	2	88	2	3	.968
—San Jose (Calif.)	OF	6	22	2	8	1	0	0	4	.364	0	1	1	3	0	0	1.000
—Phoenix (PCL)	OF	8	33	2	8	2	0	0	4	.242	0	4	1	5	2	0	1.000
1991—San Francisco (N.L.)	OF	124	361	43	84	10	4	10	40	.233	36	56	7	159	9	4	.977
—San Jose (Calif.)	OF	5	19	1	2	2	0	0	1	.105	2	3	2	7	1	1	.889
—Phoenix (PCL)	OF	10	41	8	13	3	1	2	7	.317	2	4	1	20	0	0	1.000
1992—San Francisco (N.L.)	OF	89	265	25	71	11	3	7	30	.268	16	53	7	116	1	2	.983
—New York (N.L.)■	OF	46	137	15	37	12	2	2	9	.270	7	17	7	75	1	1	.987
1993—Houston (N.L.)■	OF	111	229	31	65	18	0	3	37	.284	26	31	7	83	3	1	.989
1994—Houston (N.L.)	OF	82	203	37	63	15	1	6	35	.310	28	24	2	82	3	2	.977
1995—Baltimore (A.L.)■	OF-DH	111	295	32	72	12	0	5	32	.244	24	47	8	123	3	2	.984
American League totals (2 years)		129	304	36	72	12	0	5	32	.237	25	48	8	130	3	2	.985
National League totals (13 years)		1442	4535	573	1236	236	40	113	579	.273	332	620	143	2202	70	41	.982
Major league totals (14 years)		1571	4839	609	1308	248	40	118	611	.270	357	668	151	2332	73	43	.982

CHAMPIONSHIP SERIES RECORD

NOTES: Shares single-game record for most times caught stealing—2 (October 15, 1986, 16 innings). . . . Shares N.L. single-series record for most times caught stealing—3 (1986).

		BATTING												FIELDING			
Year Team (League)	**Pos.**	**G**	**AB**	**R**	**H**	**2B**	**3B**	**HR**	**RBI**	**Avg.**	**BB**	**SO**	**SB**	**PO**	**A**	**E**	**Avg.**
1986—Houston (N.L.)	OF	6	24	0	7	2	0	0	0	.292	4	4	2	16	0	1	.941

ALL-STAR GAME RECORD

		BATTING											FIELDING			
Year League	**Pos.**	**AB**	**R**	**H**	**2B**	**3B**	**HR**	**RBI**	**Avg.**	**BB**	**SO**	**SB**	**PO**	**A**	**E**	**Avg.**
1986—National	PH	1	0	0	0	0	0	0	.000	0	0	0	...	...	...	...

BATES, JASON 2B/SS ROCKIES

PERSONAL: Born January 5, 1971, in Downey, Calif. . . . 5-11/181. . . . Bats both, throws right. . . . Full name: Jason Charles Bates.

HIGH SCHOOL: Ezperanza (Anaheim, Calif.).

COLLEGE: Arizona.

TRANSACTIONS/CAREER NOTES: Selected by Colorado Rockies organization in seventh round of free-agent draft (June 1, 1992).

STATISTICAL NOTES: Led Pacific Coast League shortstops with 87 double plays in 1994.

		BATTING												FIELDING			
Year Team (League)	**Pos.**	**G**	**AB**	**R**	**H**	**2B**	**3B**	**HR**	**RBI**	**Avg.**	**BB**	**SO**	**SB**	**PO**	**A**	**E**	**Avg.**
1992—Bend (Northwest)	SS	70	255	*57	73	10	3	6	31	.286	56	55	18	72	176	17	*.936
1993—Colo. Springs (PCL)	SS-2B	122	449	76	120	21	2	13	62	.267	45	99	9	174	319	29	.944
1994—Colo. Springs (PCL)	SS	125	458	68	131	19	5	10	76	.286	60	57	4	165	411	28	.954
1995—Colorado (N.L.)	2B-SS-3B	116	322	42	86	17	4	8	46	.267	42	70	3	170	255	5	.988
Major league totals (1 year)		116	322	42	86	17	4	8	46	.267	42	70	3	170	255	5	.988

DIVISION SERIES RECORD

		BATTING												FIELDING			
Year Team (League)	**Pos.**	**G**	**AB**	**R**	**H**	**2B**	**3B**	**HR**	**RBI**	**Avg.**	**BB**	**SO**	**SB**	**PO**	**A**	**E**	**Avg.**
1995—Colorado (N.L.)	3B-PH-2B	4	4	0	1	0	0	0	0	.250	0	0	0	1	3	0	1.000

BATISTA, MIGUEL P MARLINS

PERSONAL: Born February 19, 1971, in Santo Domingo, Dominican Republic. . . . 6-0/180. . . . Throws right, bats right. . . . Full name: Miguel

Jerez Decartes Batista.
HIGH SCHOOL: Nuevo Horizondes (Dominican Republic).
TRANSACTIONS/CAREER NOTES: Signed as non-drafted free agent by Montreal Expos organization (February 29, 1988).... Selected by Pittsburgh Pirates organization from Expos organization in Rule 5 major league draft (December 9, 1991).... Returned to Expos (April 23, 1992).... On disabled list (April 14-30 and May 7, 1994-remainder of season).... Released by Expos (November 18, 1994).... Signed by Florida Marlins organization (December 9, 1994).

Year	Team (League)	W	L	Pct.	ERA	G	GS	CG	ShO	Sv.	IP	H	R	ER	BB	SO
1988—		Dominican Summer League statistics unavailable.														
1989—	DSL Expos (DSL)	1	7	.125	4.24	13	11	0	0	0	68	56	46	32	50	60
1990—	GC Expos (GCL)	4	3	.571	2.06	9	6	0	0	0	39 1/3	33	16	9	17	21
	—Rockford (Midw.)	0	1	.000	8.76	3	2	0	0	0	12 1/3	16	13	12	5	7
1991—	Rockford (Midw.)	11	5	.688	4.04	23	23	2	1	0	133 2/3	126	74	60	57	90
1992—	Pittsburgh (N.L.)■	0	0	...	9.00	1	0	0	0	0	2	4	2	2	3	1
	—WP Beach (FSL)■	7	7	.500	3.79	24	24	1	0	0	135 1/3	130	69	57	54	92
1993—	Harrisburg (East.)	13	5	.722	4.34	26	26	0	0	0	141	139	79	68	86	91
1994—	Harrisburg (East.)	0	1	.000	2.38	3	3	0	0	0	11 1/3	8	3	3	9	5
1995—	Charlotte (Int'l)■	6	12	.333	4.80	34	18	0	0	0	116 1/3	118	79	62	60	58
Major league totals (1 year)		0	0	...	9.00	1	0	0	0	0	2	4	2	2	3	1

BATISTA, TONY — SS/2B — ATHLETICS

PERSONAL: Born December 9, 1973, in Puerto Plata, Dominican Republic.... 6-0/165.... Bats right, throws right.... Full name: Leocadio Francisco Batista.
TRANSACTIONS/CAREER NOTES: Signed as non-drafted free agent by Oakland Athletics organization (February 8, 1991).... On Tacoma disabled list (July 29, 1993-remainder of season).
STATISTICAL NOTES: Led California League shortstops with .950 fielding percentage in 1994.

				BATTING											FIELDING			
Year	Team (League)	Pos.	G	AB	R	H	2B	3B	HR	RBI	Avg.	BB	SO	SB	PO	A	E	Avg.
1992—	Arizona A's (Ariz.)	2B-SS-OF	45	167	32	41	6	2	0	22	.246	15	29	1	67	124	8	.960
1993—	Arizona A's (Ariz.)	3B-2B-SS	24	104	21	34	6	2	2	17	.327	6	14	6	34	54	3	.967
	—Tacoma (PCL)	OF	4	12	1	2	1	0	0	1	.167	1	4	0	6	9	0	1.000
1994—	Modesto (Calif.)	SS-2B	119	466	91	131	26	3	17	68	.281	54	108	7	182	372	30	†.949
1995—	Huntsville (South.)	SS-2B	120	419	55	107	23	1	16	61	.255	29	98	7	168	371	29	.949

BATISTE, KIM — 3B/SS — GIANTS

PERSONAL: Born March 15, 1968, in New Orleans.... 6-0/200.... Bats right, throws right.... Full name: Kimothy Emil Batiste.... Name pronounced buh-TEEST.
HIGH SCHOOL: St. Amant (La.).
TRANSACTIONS/CAREER NOTES: Selected by Philadelphia Phillies organization in third round of free-agent draft (June 2, 1987).... Released by Phillies organization (May 15, 1995).... Signed by Bowie, Baltimore Orioles organization (June 2, 1995).... Selected by San Francisco Giants from Orioles organization in Rule 5 major league draft (December 4, 1995).
STATISTICAL NOTES: Led Eastern League shortstops with 550 total chances in 1990.... Led International League third basemen with 75 putouts in 1995.... Career major league grand slams: 1.

				BATTING											FIELDING			
Year	Team (League)	Pos.	G	AB	R	H	2B	3B	HR	RBI	Avg.	BB	SO	SB	PO	A	E	Avg.
1987—	Utica (NYP)	SS-3B	46	150	15	26	8	1	2	10	.173	7	65	4	64	90	16	.906
1988—	Spartanburg (SAL)	SS	122	430	51	107	19	6	6	52	.249	14	100	16	202	363	60	.904
1989—	Clearwater (FSL)	SS-3B	114	385	36	90	12	4	3	33	.234	17	67	13	168	309	35	.932
1990—	Reading (Eastern)	SS	125	486	57	134	14	4	6	33	.276	13	73	28	*182	*333	*35	.936
1991—	Scran./W.B. (Int'l)	SS	122	462	54	135	25	6	1	41	.292	11	72	18	181	344	*37	.934
	—Philadelphia (N.L.)	SS	10	27	2	6	0	0	0	1	.222	1	8	0	10	22	1	.970
1992—	Philadelphia (N.L.)	SS	44	136	9	28	4	0	1	10	.206	4	18	0	69	85	13	.922
	—Scran./W.B. (Int'l)	SS	71	269	30	70	12	6	2	29	.260	7	42	6	105	160	16	.943
1993—	Philadelphia (N.L.)	3B-SS	79	156	14	44	7	1	5	29	.282	3	29	0	72	108	10	.947
1994—	Philadelphia (N.L.)	3B-SS	64	209	17	49	6	0	1	13	.234	1	32	1	52	116	12	.933
1995—	Scran./W.B. (Int'l)	3B	32	122	10	28	4	1	4	18	.230	2	14	1	24	56	4	.952
	—Bowie (Eastern)■	3B-SS	24	95	16	34	5	0	4	27	.358	6	14	2	15	42	8	.877
	—Rochester (Int'l)	3B-SS	66	260	31	73	13	1	3	29	.281	8	27	4	§54	107	11	.936
Major league totals (4 years)			197	528	42	127	17	1	7	53	.241	9	87	1	203	331	36	.937

CHAMPIONSHIP SERIES RECORD

				BATTING											FIELDING			
Year	Team (League)	Pos.	G	AB	R	H	2B	3B	HR	RBI	Avg.	BB	SO	SB	PO	A	E	Avg.
1993—	Philadelphia (N.L.)	3B	4	1	0	1	0	0	0	1	1.000	0	0	0	2	0	2	.500

WORLD SERIES RECORD

				BATTING											FIELDING			
Year	Team (League)	Pos.	G	AB	R	H	2B	3B	HR	RBI	Avg.	BB	SO	SB	PO	A	E	Avg.
1993—	Philadelphia (N.L.)	3B	2	0	0	0	0	0	0	0	...	0	0	0	0	1	0	1.000

BATTLE, ALLEN — OF — ATHLETICS

PERSONAL: Born November 29, 1968, in Grantham, N.C.... 6-0/170.... Bats right, throws right.... Full name: Allen Zelmo Battle.
HIGH SCHOOL: Southern Wayne (Dudley, N.C.).
COLLEGE: South Alabama.
TRANSACTIONS/CAREER NOTES: Selected by Chicago White Sox organization in 45th round of free-agent draft (June 4, 1990); did not sign.

. . . Selected by St. Louis Cardinals organization in 10th round of free-agent draft (June 3, 1991). . . . On disabled list (April 24-May 6, 1993). . . . Selected by White Sox from Cardinals organization in Rule 5 major league draft (December 13, 1993). . . . Returned to Cardinals organization (March 19, 1994). . . . Traded by Cardinals with P Bret Wagner, P Jay Witasick and P Carl Dale to Oakland Athletics for P Todd Stottlemyre (January 9, 1996).

							BATTING									FIELDING		
Year	Team (League)	Pos.	G	AB	R	H	2B	3B	HR	RBI	Avg.	BB	SO	SB	PO	A	E	Avg.
1991—	Johns. City (App.)	OF	17	62	26	24	6	1	0	7	.387	14	6	7	29	0	0	1.000
—	Savannah (S. Atl.)	OF	48	169	28	41	7	1	0	20	.243	27	34	12	83	2	1	.988
1992—	Springfield (Midw.)	OF	67	235	49	71	10	4	4	24	.302	41	34	22	136	3	4	.972
—	St. Peters. (FSL)	OF	60	222	34	71	9	2	1	15	.320	35	38	21	165	3	2	.988
1993—	Arkansas (Texas)	OF	108	390	71	107	24	*12	3	40	.274	45	75	20	241	5	5	.980
1994—	Louisville (A.A.)	OF	132	520	*104	•163	*44	7	6	69	.313	59	82	23	274	8	5	.983
1995—	St. Louis (N.L.)	OF	61	118	13	32	5	0	0	2	.271	15	26	3	61	0	1	.984
—	Louisville (A.A.)	OF	47	164	28	46	12	1	3	18	.280	28	32	7	106	1	2	.982
Major league totals (1 year)			61	118	13	32	5	0	0	2	.271	15	26	3	61	0	1	.984

BATTLE, HOWARD — 3B — PHILLIES

PERSONAL: Born March 25, 1972, in Biloxi, Miss. . . . 6-0/197. . . . Bats right, throws right. . . . Full name: Howard Dion Battle.
HIGH SCHOOL: Mercy Cross (Biloxi, Miss.).
TRANSACTIONS/CAREER NOTES: Selected by Toronto Blue Jays organization in fourth round of free-agent draft (June 4, 1990). . . . Traded by Blue Jays with P Ricardo Jordan to Philadelphia Phillies for P Paul Quantrill (December 6, 1995).
STATISTICAL NOTES: Led Southern League third basemen with 436 total chances in 1993.

							BATTING									FIELDING		
Year	Team (League)	Pos.	G	AB	R	H	2B	3B	HR	RBI	Avg.	BB	SO	SB	PO	A	E	Avg.
1990—	Medicine Hat (Pio.)	3B	61	233	25	62	17	1	5	32	.266	15	38	5	25	92	*34	.775
1991—	Myrtle Beach (SAL)	3B	138	520	82	145	33	4	20	87	.279	48	87	15	86	184	29	.903
1992—	Dunedin (Fla. St.)	3B	*136	520	76	132	27	3	17	85	.254	49	89	6	58	292	33	.914
1993—	Knoxville (South.)	3B	141	521	66	145	21	5	7	70	.278	45	94	12	88	*319	*29	.933
1994—	Syracuse (Int'l)	3B	139	517	72	143	26	8	14	75	.277	40	82	26	90	258	28	.926
1995—	Syracuse (Int'l)	3B-SS	118	443	43	111	17	4	8	48	.251	39	73	10	82	281	33	.917
—	Toronto (A.L.)	3B-DH	9	15	3	3	0	0	0	0	.200	4	8	1	1	6	0	1.000
Major league totals (1 year)			9	15	3	3	0	0	0	0	.200	4	8	1	1	6	0	1.000

BAUTISTA, DANNY — OF — TIGERS

PERSONAL: Born May 24, 1972, in Santo Domingo, Dominican Republic. . . . 5-11/170. . . . Bats right, throws right. . . . Full name: Daniel Bautista. . . . Stepson of Jesus de la Rosa, outfielder, Houston Astros (1974). . . . Name pronounced bough-TEES-tuh.
TRANSACTIONS/CAREER NOTES: Signed as non-drafted free agent by Detroit Tigers organization (June 24, 1989). . . . On disabled list (May 24-July 10, 1991). . . . On Toledo disabled list (June 8-July 31, 1994).
RECORDS: Shares major league single-game record (nine innings) for most strikeouts—5 (May 28, 1995).

							BATTING									FIELDING		
Year	Team (League)	Pos.	G	AB	R	H	2B	3B	HR	RBI	Avg.	BB	SO	SB	PO	A	E	Avg.
1989—						Dominican Summer League statistics unavailable.												
1990—	Bristol (Appal.)	OF	27	95	9	26	3	0	2	12	.274	8	21	2	43	2	0	1.000
1991—	Fayetteville (SAL)	OF	69	234	21	45	6	4	1	30	.192	21	65	7	137	6	4	.973
1992—	Fayetteville (SAL)	OF	121	453	59	122	22	0	5	52	.269	29	76	18	210	17	6	.974
1993—	London (Eastern)	OF	117	424	55	121	21	1	6	48	.285	32	69	28	256	13	3	.989
—	Detroit (A.L.)	OF-DH	17	61	6	19	3	0	1	9	.311	1	10	3	38	2	0	1.000
1994—	Detroit (A.L.)	OF-DH	31	99	12	23	4	1	4	15	.232	3	18	1	66	0	0	1.000
—	Toledo (Int'l)	OF	27	98	7	25	7	0	2	14	.255	6	23	2	54	1	1	.982
1995—	Detroit (A.L.)	OF	89	271	28	55	9	0	7	27	.203	12	68	4	164	3	2	.988
—	Toledo (Int'l)	OF	18	58	6	14	3	0	0	4	.241	1	10	1	32	1	2	.943
Major league totals (3 years)			137	431	46	97	16	1	12	51	.225	16	96	8	268	5	2	.993

BAUTISTA, JOSE — P — GIANTS

PERSONAL: Born July 25, 1964, in Bani, Dominican Republic. . . . 6-2/205. . . . Throws right, bats right. . . . Full name: Jose Joaquin Bautista. . . . Name pronounced bough-TEES-tuh.
HIGH SCHOOL: Bani (Dominican Republic) School.
TRANSACTIONS/CAREER NOTES: Signed as non-drafted free agent by New York Mets organization (April 25, 1981). . . . Selected by Baltimore Orioles from Mets organization in Rule 5 major league draft (December 7, 1987). . . . On Baltimore disabled list (May 20-June 11, 1989); included rehabilitation assignment to Rochester (May 29-June 11). . . . Loaned by Orioles to Miami, independent (April 24, 1991); returned to Orioles organization (June 1, 1991). . . . Loaned by Orioles organization to Oklahoma City (June 1-July 11, 1991). . . . Granted free agency (September 23, 1991). . . . Signed by Omaha, Kansas City Royals organization (December 20, 1991). . . . Granted free agency (October 15, 1992). . . . Signed by Chicago Cubs organization (December 17, 1992). . . . On suspended list (September 10-13, 1993). . . . On disabled list (August 6, 1994-remainder of season). . . . Granted free agency (December 23, 1994). . . . Signed by San Francisco Giants (April 6, 1995).
STATISTICAL NOTES: Pitched 6-0 no-hit victory against Prince William (May 26, 1985, first game).
MISCELLANEOUS: Appeared in two games as pinch-runner (1993).

Year	Team (League)	W	L	Pct.	ERA	G	GS	CG	ShO	Sv.	IP	H	R	ER	BB	SO
1981—	Kingsport (Appal.)	3	6	.333	4.64	13	11	3	2	0	66	84	54	34	17	34
1982—	Kingsport (Appal.)	0	4	.000	8.92	14	4	0	0	5	38 1/3	61	44	38	19	13
1983—	GC Mets (GCL)	4	3	.571	2.31	13	13	2	0	0	81 2/3	66	31	21	32	44
1984—	Columbia (S. Atl.)	13	4	.765	3.13	19	18	5	3	0	135	121	52	47	35	96
1985—	Lynchburg (Caro.)	15	8	.652	2.34	27	25	7	3	1	169	145	49	44	33	109
1986—	Jackson (Texas)	0	1	.000	8.31	7	4	0	0	0	21 2/3	36	22	20	8	13
—	Lynchburg (Caro.)	8	8	.500	3.94	18	18	5	1	0	118 2/3	120	58	52	24	62

Year	Team (League)	W	L	Pct.	ERA	G	GS	CG	ShO	Sv.	IP	H	R	ER	BB	SO
1987—	Jackson (Texas)	10	5	.667	3.24	28	25	2	0	0	169 1/3	174	76	61	43	95
1988—	Baltimore (A.L.)■	6	15	.286	4.30	33	25	3	0	0	171 2/3	171	86	82	45	76
1989—	Baltimore (A.L.)	3	4	.429	5.31	15	10	0	0	0	78	84	46	46	15	30
	—Rochester (Int'l)	4	4	.500	2.83	15	13	3	1	0	98 2/3	84	41	31	26	47
1990—	Baltimore (A.L.)	1	0	1.000	4.05	22	0	0	0	0	26 2/3	28	15	12	7	15
	—Rochester (Int'l)	7	8	.467	4.06	27	13	3	0	2	108 2/3	115	51	49	15	50
1991—	Baltimore (A.L.)	0	1	.000	16.88	5	0	0	0	0	5 1/3	13	10	10	5	3
	—Miami (Florida St.)■	8	2	*.800	2.71	11	11	4	•3	0	76 1/3	63	23	23	11	69
	—Okla. City (A.A.)■	0	3	.000	5.29	11	3	0	0	0	32 1/3	38	19	19	6	22
	—Rochester (Int'l)■	1	0	1.000	0.59	6	0	0	0	1	15 1/3	8	1	1	3	7
1992—	Omaha (Am. Assoc.)■	2	10	.167	4.90	40	7	1	0	2	108 1/3	125	66	59	28	60
	—Memphis (South.)	1	0	1.000	4.50	1	1	0	0	0	6	6	3	3	2	7
1993—	Chicago (N.L.)■	10	3	.769	2.82	58	7	1	0	2	111 2/3	105	38	35	27	63
1994—	Chicago (N.L.)	4	5	.444	3.89	58	0	0	0	1	69 1/3	75	30	30	17	45
1995—	San Francisco (N.L.)■	3	8	.273	6.44	52	6	0	0	0	100 2/3	120	77	72	26	45
	A.L. totals (4 years)	10	20	.333	4.79	75	35	3	0	0	281 2/3	296	157	150	72	124
	N.L. totals (3 years)	17	16	.515	4.38	168	13	1	0	3	281 2/3	300	145	137	70	153
	Major league totals (7 years)	27	36	.429	4.59	243	48	4	0	3	563 1/3	596	302	287	142	277

BAUTISTA, JUAN — SS — ORIOLES

PERSONAL: Born June 24, 1975, in San Pedro de Macoris, Dominican Republic. . . . 6-0/165. . . . Bats right, throws right. . . . Full name: Juan Aquino Bautista. . . . Name pronounced bough-TEES-tuh.

TRANSACTIONS/CAREER NOTES: Signed as non-drafted free agent by Baltimore Orioles organization (January 22, 1992). . . . On disabled list (April 7-July 14, 1994).

				BATTING											FIELDING			
Year	Team (League)	Pos.	G	AB	R	H	2B	3B	HR	RBI	Avg.	BB	SO	SB	PO	A	E	Avg.
1992—	Dom. Orioles (DSL)	IF	54	176	34	45	7	0	1	16	.256	28	20	4	79	167	35	.875
1993—	Albany (S. Atl.)	SS	98	295	24	70	17	2	0	28	.237	14	72	11	124	249	45	.892
1994—	GC Orioles (GCL)	SS	21	65	4	10	2	2	0	3	.154	2	19	3	18	25	4	.915
1995—	High Desert (Calif.)	SS	99	374	54	98	13	4	11	51	.262	18	74	22	154	253	40	.911
	—Bowie (Eastern)	SS	13	38	3	4	2	0	0	0	.105	3	5	1	21	28	5	.907

BEAMON, TREY — OF — PIRATES

PERSONAL: Born February 11, 1974, in Dallas. . . . 6-3/195. . . . Bats left, throws right. . . . Full name: Clifford Beamon.

HIGH SCHOOL: Warren Travis White (Dallas).

TRANSACTIONS/CAREER NOTES: Selected by Pittsburgh Pirates organization in second round of free-agent draft (June 1, 1992).

				BATTING											FIELDING			
Year	Team (League)	Pos.	G	AB	R	H	2B	3B	HR	RBI	Avg.	BB	SO	SB	PO	A	E	Avg.
1992—	GC Pirates (GCL)	OF	13	39	9	12	1	0	1	6	.308	4	0	0	25	0	2	.926
	—Welland (NYP)	OF	19	69	15	20	5	0	3	9	.290	8	9	4	38	1	0	1.000
1993—	Augusta (S. Atl.)	OF	104	373	64	101	18	6	0	45	.271	48	60	19	181	5	6	.969
1994—	Carolina (South.)	OF	112	434	69	140	18	9	5	47	*.323	33	53	24	170	11	10	.948
1995—	Calgary (PCL)	OF	118	452	74	151	29	5	5	62	.334	39	55	18	201	14	9	.960

BEAN, BILLY — OF

PERSONAL: Born May 11, 1964, in Santa Ana, Calif. . . . 6-0/195. . . . Bats left, throws left. . . . Full name: William Daro Bean.

HIGH SCHOOL: Santa Ana (Calif.).

COLLEGE: Loyola Marymount (degree in business administration).

TRANSACTIONS/CAREER NOTES: Selected by New York Yankees organization in 24th round of free-agent draft (June 3, 1985); did not sign. . . . Selected by Detroit Tigers organization in fourth round of free-agent draft (June 2, 1986). . . . Traded by Tigers organization to Los Angeles Dodgers organization for OF Steve Green and 1B/OF Domingo Michel (July 17, 1989). . . . Selected by Edmonton, Angels organization, from San Antonio, Dodgers organization, in Rule 5 minor league draft (December 9, 1991). . . . Released by Edmonton (January 21, 1992). . . . Signed by Kintetsu Buffaloes of Japan Pacific League (1992). . . . Released by Kintetsu (July 1992). . . . Signed by Edmonton, Angels organization (July 14, 1992). . . . Granted free agency (October 15, 1992). . . . Signed by Wichita, San Diego Padres organization (December 15, 1992). . . . Granted free agency (December 23, 1994). . . . Re-signed by Padres organization (February 26, 1995). . . . Granted free agency (October 16, 1995).

RECORDS: Shares modern record for most hits in first major league game (nine innings)—4 (April 25, 1987).

STATISTICAL NOTES: Career major league grand slams: 1.

				BATTING											FIELDING			
Year	Team (League)	Pos.	G	AB	R	H	2B	3B	HR	RBI	Avg.	BB	SO	SB	PO	A	E	Avg.
1986—	Glens Falls (East.)	OF	80	279	43	77	10	3	8	49	.276	36	27	3	189	4	3	.985
1987—	Toledo (Int'l)	OF	104	357	51	98	18	2	8	43	.275	38	52	14	228	1	7	.970
	—Detroit (A.L.)	OF	26	66	6	17	2	0	0	4	.258	5	11	1	54	1	0	1.000
1988—	Toledo (Int'l)	OF-1B	•138	484	59	124	19	1	6	40	.256	41	45	12	664	43	12	.983
	—Detroit (A.L.)	OF-1B-DH	10	11	2	2	0	1	0	0	.182	0	2	0	8	1	0	1.000
1989—	Detroit (A.L.)	OF-1B	9	11	0	0	0	0	0	0	.000	2	3	0	12	0	2	.857
	—Toledo (Int'l)	OF-1B	76	267	43	84	14	2	4	29	.315	27	35	7	231	14	4	.984
	—Albuquerque (PCL)■	OF	3	9	1	2	0	1	0	3	.222	2	0	0	7	0	0	1.000
	—Los Angeles (N.L.)	OF	51	71	7	14	4	0	0	3	.197	4	10	0	49	0	0	1.000
1990—	Albuquerque (PCL)	OF-1B-3B	129	427	85	126	26	5	7	67	.295	69	63	16	209	14	8	.965
1991—	Albuquerque (PCL)	OF	103	259	35	77	22	6	2	35	.297	23	32	7	112	5	1	.992
1992—	Kintetsu (Jp. Pac.)■	OF	7	24	2	5	2	0	0	2	.208	1	5	0	...	...	...	...
	—Edmonton (PCL)■	OF	39	138	17	34	8	2	1	24	.246	7	13	5	35	3	0	1.000

Year	Team (League)	Pos.	G	AB	R	H	2B	3B	HR	RBI	Avg.	BB	SO	SB	PO	A	E	Avg.
							BATTING								FIELDING			
1993—	Las Vegas (PCL)■	OF-1B	53	167	31	59	11	2	7	40	.353	32	14	3	149	20	1	.994
—	San Diego (N.L.)	OF-1B	88	177	19	46	9	0	5	32	.260	6	29	2	122	9	1	.992
1994—	San Diego (N.L.)	OF-1B	84	135	7	29	5	1	0	14	.215	7	25	0	96	5	0	1.000
1995—	Las Vegas (PCL)	OF-1B	119	445	67	129	34	2	15	77	.290	46	55	2	296	9	4	.987
—	San Diego (N.L.)	OF	4	7	1	0	0	0	0	0	.000	1	4	0	3	0	1	.750
American League totals (3 years)			45	88	8	19	2	1	0	4	.216	7	16	1	74	2	2	.974
National League totals (4 years)			227	390	34	89	18	1	5	49	.228	18	68	2	270	14	2	.993
Major league totals (6 years)			272	478	42	108	20	2	5	53	.226	25	84	3	344	16	4	.989

BECK, ROD — P — GIANTS

PERSONAL: Born August 3, 1968, in Burbank, Calif. . . . 6-1/236. . . . Throws right, bats right. . . . Full name: Rodney Roy Beck.

HIGH SCHOOL: Grant (Sherman Oaks, Calif.).

TRANSACTIONS/CAREER NOTES: Selected by Oakland Athletics organization in 13th round of free-agent draft (June 2, 1986). . . . Traded by A's organization to San Francisco Giants organization for P Charlie Corbell (March 23, 1988). . . . On disabled list (April 6-30, 1994).

Year	Team (League)	W	L	Pct.	ERA	G	GS	CG	ShO	Sv.	IP	H	R	ER	BB	SO
1986—	Medford (N'west)	1	3	.250	5.23	13	6	0	0	1	32 2/3	47	25	19	11	21
1987—	Medford (N'west)	5	8	.385	5.18	17	12	2	0	0	92	106	74	53	26	69
1988—	Clinton (Midwest)■	12	7	.632	3.00	28	23	5	1	0	177	177	68	59	27	123
1989—	San Jose (Calif.)	11	2	*.846	2.40	13	13	4	0	0	97 1/3	91	29	26	26	88
—	Shreveport (Texas)	7	3	.700	3.55	16	14	4	1	0	99	108	45	39	16	74
1990—	Shreveport (Texas)	10	3	.769	2.23	14	14	2	1	0	93	85	26	23	17	71
—	Phoenix (PCL)	4	7	.364	4.93	12	12	2	0	0	76 2/3	100	51	42	18	43
1991—	Phoenix (PCL)	4	3	.571	2.02	23	5	3	0	6	71 1/3	56	18	16	13	35
—	San Francisco (N.L.)	1	1	.500	3.78	31	0	0	0	1	52 1/3	53	22	22	13	38
1992—	San Francisco (N.L.)	3	3	.500	1.76	65	0	0	0	17	92	62	20	18	15	87
1993—	San Francisco (N.L.)	3	1	.750	2.16	76	0	0	0	48	79 1/3	57	20	19	13	86
1994—	San Francisco (N.L.)	2	4	.333	2.77	48	0	0	0	28	48 2/3	49	17	15	13	39
1995—	San Francisco (N.L.)	5	6	.455	4.45	60	0	0	0	33	58 2/3	60	31	29	21	42
Major league totals (5 years)		14	15	.483	2.80	280	0	0	0	127	331	281	110	103	75	292

ALL-STAR GAME RECORD

Year	League	W	L	Pct.	ERA	GS	CG	ShO	Sv.	IP	H	R	ER	BB	SO
1993—	National	0	0	...	9.00	0	0	0	0	1	2	1	1	0	1
1994—	National	0	0	...	0.00	0	0	0	0	1 2/3	1	0	0	0	1
All-Star totals (2 years)		0	0	...	3.38	0	0	0	0	2 2/3	3	1	1	0	2

BECKER, RICH — OF — TWINS

PERSONAL: Born February 1, 1972, in Aurora, Ill. . . . 5-10/199. . . . Bats left, throws left. . . . Full name: Richard Goodhard Becker.

HIGH SCHOOL: Aurora (Ill.) West.

TRANSACTIONS/CAREER NOTES: Selected by Minnesota Twins organization in third round of free-agent draft (June 4, 1990). . . . On Minnesota disabled list (September 13, 1993-remainder of season and April 29-May 17, 1994).

STATISTICAL NOTES: Led Appalachian League with .448 on-base percentage in 1990. . . . Led Midwest League with 215 total bases in 1991. . . . Led California League outfielders with 355 total chances in 1992. . . . Led A.L. outfielders with five double plays in 1995.

Year	Team (League)	Pos.	G	AB	R	H	2B	3B	HR	RBI	Avg.	BB	SO	SB	PO	A	E	Avg.
							BATTING								FIELDING			
1990—	Elizabeth. (Appal.)	OF	56	194	54	56	5	1	6	24	.289	*53	54	18	87	2	9	.908
1991—	Kenosha (Midwest)	OF	130	494	100	132	*38	3	13	53	.267	72	108	19	270	19	11	.963
1992—	Visalia (California)	OF	*136	506	*118	160	37	2	15	82	.316	*114	122	29	*332	17	6	.983
1993—	Nashville (South.)	OF	138	516	•93	148	25	7	15	66	.287	94	117	29	303	5	6	.981
—	Minnesota (A.L.)	OF	3	7	3	2	2	0	0	0	.286	5	4	1	7	0	1	.875
1994—	Minnesota (A.L.)	OF-DH	28	98	12	26	3	0	1	8	.265	13	25	6	87	2	1	.989
—	Salt Lake (PCL)	OF	71	282	64	89	21	3	2	38	.316	40	56	7	189	8	3	.985
1995—	Salt Lake (PCL)	OF	36	123	26	38	7	0	6	28	.309	26	24	6	108	5	1	.991
—	Minnesota (A.L.)	OF	106	392	45	93	15	1	2	33	.237	34	95	8	275	12	4	.986
Major league totals (3 years)			137	497	60	121	20	1	3	41	.243	52	124	15	369	14	6	.985

BECKETT, ROBBIE — P — PADRES

PERSONAL: Born July 16, 1972, in Austin, Tex. . . . 6-5/240. . . . Throws left, bats right. . . . Full name: Robert Joseph Beckett.

HIGH SCHOOL: McCallum (Austin, Tex.).

TRANSACTIONS/CAREER NOTES: Selected by San Diego Padres organization in first round (25th pick overall) of free-agent draft (June 4, 1990); pick received as part of compensation for Kansas City Royals signing Type A free-agent P Mark Davis.

STATISTICAL NOTES: Led California League with 25 wild pitches in 1993. . . . Led Southern League with 19 wild pitches in 1995. . . . Pitched 1-0 no-hit loss against Chattanooga (September 2, 1995, second game).

Year	Team (League)	W	L	Pct.	ERA	G	GS	CG	ShO	Sv.	IP	H	R	ER	BB	SO
1990—	Arizona Padres (Ariz.)	2	5	.286	4.38	10	10	0	0	0	49 1/3	40	28	24	*45	54
—	Riverside (Calif.)	2	1	.667	7.02	3	3	0	0	0	16 2/3	18	13	13	11	11
1991—	Char., S.C. (S. Atl.)	2	*14	.125	8.23	28	26	1	0	0	109 1/3	115	•111	*100	*117	96
1992—	Waterloo (Midw.)	4	10	.286	4.77	24	24	1	1	0	120 2/3	77	88	64	*140	147
1993—	Rancho Cuca. (Cal.)	2	4	.333	6.02	37	10	0	0	4	83 2/3	75	62	56	93	88
1994—	Las Vegas (PCL)	0	1	.000	11.79	23	0	0	0	0	23 2/3	27	36	31	39	30
1995—	Memphis (South.)	3	4	.429	4.80	36	8	2	1	0	86 1/3	65	57	46	73	98

BEDROSIAN, STEVE P

PERSONAL: Born December 6, 1957, in Methuen, Mass. . . . 6-3/205. . . . Throws right, bats right. . . . Full name: Stephen Wayne Bedrosian. . . . Name pronounced bed-ROHZ-ee-un.
HIGH SCHOOL: Methuen (Mass.).
JUNIOR COLLEGE: Northern Essex Community College (Mass.).
COLLEGE: New Haven (Conn.).
TRANSACTIONS/CAREER NOTES: Selected by Atlanta Braves organization in third round of free-agent draft (June 6, 1978). . . . On disabled list (June 24-September 18, 1979 and August 20-September 4, 1984). . . . Traded by Braves with OF Milt Thompson to Philadelphia Phillies for C Ozzie Virgil and P Pete Smith (December 10, 1985). . . . On Philadelphia disabled list (March 21-May 20, 1988); included rehabilitation assignment to Maine (May 9-19). . . . Traded by Phillies with a player to be named later to San Francisco Giants for P Dennis Cook, P Terry Mulholland and 3B Charlie Hayes (June 18, 1989); Giants organization acquired IF Rick Parker to complete deal (August 7, 1989). . . . Traded by Giants to Minnesota Twins for P Johnny Ard and a player to be named later (December 5, 1990); Giants acquired P Jimmy Williams to complete deal (December 18, 1990). . . . Granted free agency (November 7, 1991). . . . Signed by Braves organization (December 17, 1992). . . . Granted free agency (October 19, 1994). . . . Re-signed by Braves (October 28, 1994). . . . Announced retirement (August 11, 1995).
HONORS: Named N.L. Rookie Pitcher of the Year by The Sporting News (1982). . . . Named N.L. Fireman of the Year by The Sporting News (1987). . . . Named N.L. Cy Young Award winner by Baseball Writers' Association of America (1987).

Year	Team (League)	W	L	Pct.	ERA	G	GS	CG	ShO	Sv.	IP	H	R	ER	BB	SO
1978—	Kingsport (Appal.)	2	2	.500	3.08	6	6	1	0	0	38	38	18	13	25	29
—	Greenwood (W. Caro.)	5	1	.833	2.13	8	8	1	0	0	55	45	17	13	34	58
1979—	Savannah (South.)	5	5	.500	3.03	13	13	4	2	0	89	71	36	30	58	73
1980—	Savannah (South.)	14	10	.583	3.19	29	•29	9	2	0	*203	167	91	72	96	*161
1981—	Richmond (Int'l)	10	10	.500	2.69	26	25	8	1	0	184	143	76	55	99	144
—	Atlanta (N.L.)	1	2	.333	4.50	15	1	0	0	0	24	15	14	12	15	9
1982—	Atlanta (N.L.)	8	6	.571	2.42	64	3	0	0	11	137 2/3	102	39	37	57	123
1983—	Atlanta (N.L.)	9	10	.474	3.60	70	1	0	0	19	120	100	50	48	51	114
1984—	Atlanta (N.L.)	9	6	.600	2.37	40	4	0	0	11	83 2/3	65	23	22	33	81
1985—	Atlanta (N.L.)	7	15	.318	3.83	37	37	0	0	0	206 2/3	198	101	88	111	134
1986—	Philadelphia (N.L.)■	8	6	.571	3.39	68	0	0	0	29	90 1/3	79	39	34	34	82
1987—	Philadelphia (N.L.)	5	3	.625	2.83	65	0	0	0	40	89	79	31	28	28	74
1988—	Maine (Int'l)	0	0	...	0.00	5	0	0	0	0	6 2/3	6	0	0	2	5
—	Philadelphia (N.L.)	6	6	.500	3.75	57	0	0	0	28	74 1/3	75	34	31	27	61
1989—	Philadelphia (N.L.)	2	3	.400	3.21	28	0	0	0	6	33 2/3	21	13	12	17	24
—	San Francisco (N.L.)■	1	4	.200	2.65	40	0	0	0	17	51	35	18	15	22	34
1990—	San Francisco (N.L.)	9	9	.500	4.20	68	0	0	0	17	79 1/3	72	40	37	44	43
1991—	Minnesota (A.L.)■	5	3	.625	4.42	56	0	0	0	6	77 1/3	70	42	38	35	44
1992—							Out of organized baseball.									
1993—	Atlanta (N.L.)■	5	2	.714	1.63	49	0	0	0	0	49 2/3	34	11	9	14	33
1994—	Atlanta (N.L.)	0	2	.000	3.33	46	0	0	0	0	46	41	20	17	18	43
1995—	Atlanta (N.L.)	1	2	.333	6.11	29	0	0	0	0	28	40	21	19	12	22
A.L. totals (1 year)		5	3	.625	4.42	56	0	0	0	6	77 1/3	70	42	38	35	44
N.L. totals (13 years)		71	76	.483	3.31	676	46	0	0	178	1113 1/3	956	454	409	483	877
Major league totals (14 years)		76	79	.490	3.38	732	46	0	0	184	1190 2/3	1026	496	447	518	921

CHAMPIONSHIP SERIES RECORD

NOTES: Shares N.L. single-series record for most saves—3 (1989).

Year	Team (League)	W	L	Pct.	ERA	G	GS	CG	ShO	Sv.	IP	H	R	ER	BB	SO
1982—	Atlanta (N.L.)	0	0	...	18.00	2	0	0	0	0	1	3	2	2	1	2
1989—	San Francisco (N.L.)	0	0	...	2.70	4	0	0	0	3	3 1/3	4	1	1	2	2
1991—	Minnesota (A.L.)	0	0	...	0.00	2	0	0	0	0	1 1/3	3	2	0	2	2
1993—	Atlanta (N.L.)								Did not play.							
Champ. series totals (3 years)		0	0	...	4.76	8	0	0	0	3	5 2/3	10	5	3	5	6

WORLD SERIES RECORD

NOTES: Member of World Series championship team (1991).

Year	Team (League)	W	L	Pct.	ERA	G	GS	CG	ShO	Sv.	IP	H	R	ER	BB	SO
1989—	San Francisco (N.L.)	0	0	...	0.00	2	0	0	0	0	2 2/3	0	0	0	2	2
1991—	Minnesota (A.L.)	0	0	...	5.40	3	0	0	0	0	3 1/3	3	2	2	0	2
World Series totals (2 years)		0	0	...	3.00	5	0	0	0	0	6	3	2	2	2	4

ALL-STAR GAME RECORD

Year	League	W	L	Pct.	ERA	GS	CG	ShO	Sv.	IP	H	R	ER	BB	SO
1987—	National	0	0	...	0.00	0	0	0	0	1	0	0	0	2	0

BELCHER, TIM P

PERSONAL: Born October 19, 1961, in Sparta, O. . . . 6-3/220. . . . Throws right, bats right. . . . Full name: Timothy Wayne Belcher.
HIGH SCHOOL: Highland (Sparta, O.).
COLLEGE: Mt. Vernon (O.) Nazarene.
TRANSACTIONS/CAREER NOTES: Selected by Minnesota Twins organization in first round (first pick overall) of free-agent draft (June 6, 1983); did not sign. . . . Selected by New York Yankees organization in secondary phase of free-agent draft (January 17, 1984); did not sign. . . . Selected by Oakland Athletics organization in player compensation pool draft (February 8, 1984); A's received compensation for Baltimore Orioles signing Type A free-agent P Tom Underwood (February 7, 1984). . . . On disabled list (April 10-May 4 and May 5-July 23, 1986). . . . Traded by A's organization to Los Angeles Dodgers (September 3, 1987), completing deal in which Dodgers traded P Rick Honeycutt to A's for a player to be named later (August 29, 1987). . . . On disabled list (August 17, 1990-remainder of season). . . . Traded by Dodgers with P John Wetteland to Cincinnati Reds for OF Eric Davis and P Kip Gross (November 27, 1991). . . . Traded by Reds to Chicago White Sox for P Johnny Ruffin and P Jeff Pierce (July 31, 1993). . . . Granted free agency (October 26, 1993). . . . Signed by Detroit Tigers (February 7, 1994). . . . Granted free agency (October 20, 1994). . . . Signed by Reds organization (May 3, 1995). . . . Traded by Reds to Seattle Mariners organization for P Roger Salkeld (May 15, 1995). . . . Granted free agency (October 31, 1995).
HONORS: Named righthanded pitcher on The Sporting News college All-America team (1983). . . . Named N.L. Rookie Pitcher of the Year by

THE SPORTING NEWS (1988).

STATISTICAL NOTES: Pitched 6-0 one-hit, complete-game victory against Pittsburgh (July 21, 1990). . . . Pitched 4-0 one-hit, complete-game victory for Cincinnati against Atlanta (May 26, 1993).

Year	Team (League)	W	L	Pct.	ERA	G	GS	CG	ShO	Sv.	IP	H	R	ER	BB	SO
1984—	Madison (Midwest)	9	4	.692	3.57	16	16	3	1	0	98 1/3	80	45	39	48	111
—	Alb./Colon. (East.)	3	4	.429	3.33	10	10	2	0	0	54	37	30	20	41	40
1985—	Huntsville (South.)	11	10	.524	4.69	29	26	3	1	0	149 2/3	145	99	78	99	90
1986—	Huntsville (South.)	2	5	.286	6.57	9	9	0	0	0	37	50	28	27	22	25
1987—	Tacoma (PCL)	9	11	.450	4.42	29	28	2	1	0	163	143	89	80	*133	136
—	Los Angeles (N.L.)■	4	2	.667	2.38	6	5	0	0	0	34	30	11	9	7	23
1988—	Los Angeles (N.L.)	12	6	.667	2.91	36	27	4	1	4	179 2/3	143	65	58	51	152
1989—	Los Angeles (N.L.)	15	12	.556	2.82	39	30	•10	*8	1	230	182	81	72	80	200
1990—	Los Angeles (N.L.)	9	9	.500	4.00	24	24	5	2	0	153	136	76	68	48	102
1991—	Los Angeles (N.L.)	10	9	.526	2.62	33	33	2	1	0	209 1/3	189	76	61	75	156
1992—	Cincinnati (N.L.)■	15	14	.517	3.91	35	34	2	1	0	227 2/3	201	*104	*99	80	149
1993—	Cincinnati (N.L.)	9	6	.600	4.47	22	22	4	2	0	137	134	72	68	47	101
—	Chicago (A.L.)■	3	5	.375	4.40	12	11	1	1	0	71 2/3	64	36	35	27	34
1994—	Detroit (A.L.)■	7	*15	.318	5.89	25	•25	3	0	0	162	192	*124	106	78	76
1995—	Indianapolis (A.A.)■	0	0	...	1.80	2	2	0	0	0	10	6	2	2	1	8
—	Seattle (A.L.)■	10	12	.455	4.52	28	28	1	0	0	179 1/3	188	101	90	88	96
A.L. totals (3 years)		20	32	.385	5.03	65	64	5	1	0	413	444	261	231	193	206
N.L. totals (7 years)		74	58	.561	3.34	195	175	27	15	5	1170 2/3	1015	485	435	388	883
Major league totals (9 years)		94	90	.511	3.78	260	239	32	16	5	1583 2/3	1459	746	666	581	1089

DIVISION SERIES RECORD

Year	Team (League)	W	L	Pct.	ERA	G	GS	CG	ShO	Sv.	IP	H	R	ER	BB	SO
1995—	Seattle (A.L.)	0	1	.000	6.23	2	0	0	0	0	4 1/3	4	3	3	5	0

CHAMPIONSHIP SERIES RECORD

Year	Team (League)	W	L	Pct.	ERA	G	GS	CG	ShO	Sv.	IP	H	R	ER	BB	SO
1988—	Los Angeles (N.L.)	2	0	1.000	4.11	2	2	0	0	0	15 1/3	12	7	7	4	16
1993—	Chicago (A.L.)	1	0	1.000	2.45	1	0	0	0	0	3 2/3	3	1	1	3	1
1995—	Seattle (A.L.)	0	1	.000	6.35	1	1	0	0	0	5 2/3	9	4	4	2	1
Champ. series totals (3 years)		3	1	.750	4.38	4	3	0	0	0	24 2/3	24	12	12	9	18

WORLD SERIES RECORD

NOTES: Member of World Series championship team (1988).

Year	Team (League)	W	L	Pct.	ERA	G	GS	CG	ShO	Sv.	IP	H	R	ER	BB	SO
1988—	Los Angeles (N.L.)	1	0	1.000	6.23	2	2	0	0	0	8 2/3	10	7	6	6	10

BELINDA, STAN — P — RED SOX

PERSONAL: Born August 6, 1966, in Huntingdon, Pa. . . . 6-3/215. . . . Throws right, bats right. . . . Full name: Stanley Peter Belinda.

HIGH SCHOOL: State College (Pa.) Area.

JUNIOR COLLEGE: Allegany Community College (Md.).

TRANSACTIONS/CAREER NOTES: Selected by Pittsburgh Pirates organization in 10th round of free-agent draft (June 2, 1986). . . . On Gulf Coast Pirates disabled list (June 21-30, 1986). . . . Traded by Pirates to Kansas City Royals for P Jon Lieber and P Dan Miceli (July 31, 1993). . . . Granted free agency (December 23, 1994). . . . Signed by Boston Red Sox (April 9, 1995). . . . On Boston disabled list (April 21-May 6, 1995); included rehabilitation assignment to Sarasota (May 4-5).

Year	Team (League)	W	L	Pct.	ERA	G	GS	CG	ShO	Sv.	IP	H	R	ER	BB	SO
1986—	Watertown (NYP)	0	0	...	3.38	5	0	0	0	2	8	5	3	3	2	5
—	GC Pirates (GCL)	3	2	.600	2.66	17	0	0	0	7	20 1/3	23	12	6	2	17
1987—	Macon (S. Atl.)	6	4	.600	2.09	50	0	0	0	16	82	59	26	19	27	75
1988—	Salem (Carolina)	6	4	.600	2.76	53	0	0	0	14	71 2/3	54	33	22	32	63
1989—	Harrisburg (East.)	1	4	.200	2.33	32	0	0	0	13	38 2/3	32	13	10	25	33
—	Buffalo (A.A.)	2	2	.500	0.95	19	0	0	0	9	28 1/3	13	5	3	13	28
—	Pittsburgh (N.L.)	0	1	.000	6.10	8	0	0	0	0	10 1/3	13	8	7	2	10
1990—	Buffalo (A.A.)	3	1	.750	1.90	15	0	0	0	5	23 2/3	20	8	5	8	25
—	Pittsburgh (N.L.)	3	4	.429	3.55	55	0	0	0	8	58 1/3	48	23	23	29	55
1991—	Pittsburgh (N.L.)	7	5	.583	3.45	60	0	0	0	16	78 1/3	50	30	30	35	71
1992—	Pittsburgh (N.L.)	6	4	.600	3.15	59	0	0	0	18	71 1/3	58	26	25	29	57
1993—	Pittsburgh (N.L.)	3	1	.750	3.61	40	0	0	0	19	42 1/3	35	18	17	11	30
—	Kansas City (A.L.)■	1	1	.500	4.28	23	0	0	0	0	27 1/3	30	13	13	6	25
1994—	Kansas City (A.L.)	2	2	.500	5.14	37	0	0	0	1	49	47	36	28	24	37
1995—	Sarasota (Fla. St.)■	0	0	...	4.50	1	1	0	0	0	2	2	1	1	0	2
—	Boston (A.L.)	8	1	.889	3.10	63	0	0	0	10	69 2/3	51	25	24	28	57
A.L. totals (3 years)		11	4	.733	4.01	123	0	0	0	11	146	128	74	65	58	119
N.L. totals (5 years)		19	15	.559	3.52	222	0	0	0	61	260 2/3	204	105	102	106	223
Major league totals (7 years)		30	19	.612	3.70	345	0	0	0	72	406 2/3	332	179	167	164	342

DIVISION SERIES RECORD

Year	Team (League)	W	L	Pct.	ERA	G	GS	CG	ShO	Sv.	IP	H	R	ER	BB	SO
1995—	Boston (A.L.)	0	0	...	0.00	1	0	0	0	0	1/3	0	0	0	0	0

CHAMPIONSHIP SERIES RECORD

Year	Team (League)	W	L	Pct.	ERA	G	GS	CG	ShO	Sv.	IP	H	R	ER	BB	SO
1990—	Pittsburgh (N.L.)	0	0	...	2.45	3	0	0	0	0	3 2/3	3	1	1	0	4
1991—	Pittsburgh (N.L.)	1	0	1.000	0.00	3	0	0	0	0	5	0	0	0	3	4
1992—	Pittsburgh (N.L.)	0	0	...	0.00	2	0	0	0	0	1 2/3	2	0	0	1	2
Champ. series totals (3 years)		1	0	1.000	0.87	8	0	0	0	0	10 1/3	5	1	1	4	10

BELK, TIM — 1B — REDS

PERSONAL: Born April 6, 1970, in Cincinnati. . . . 6-3/200. . . . Bats right, throws right. . . . Full name: Timothy William Belk.
HIGH SCHOOL: Spring Woods (Houston).
JUNIOR COLLEGE: Alvin (Tex.) Community College.
COLLEGE: Texas and Lubbock (Tex.) Christian.
TRANSACTIONS/CAREER NOTES: Selected by Cincinnati Reds organization in 15th round of free-agent draft (June 1, 1992). . . . On Chattanooga disabled list (August 2-17, 1994). . . . On disabled list (June 16-July 26, 1995).
STATISTICAL NOTES: Led Pioneer League first basemen with 53 double plays in 1992. . . . Led Carolina League first basemen with 117 assists in 1993. . . . Led Southern League first basemen with 15 errors in 1994.

			BATTING											FIELDING			
Year Team (League)	Pos.	G	AB	R	H	2B	3B	HR	RBI	Avg.	BB	SO	SB	PO	A	E	Avg.
1992—Billings (Pioneer)	1B	73	273	60	78	13	0	12	56	.286	35	33	15	608	*40	12	.982
1993—Winst.-Salem (Car.)	1B-OF	134	509	89	•156	23	3	14	65	.306	48	76	9	1058	†118	18	.985
1994—Chatt. (South.)	1B-OF	118	411	64	127	35	3	10	86	.309	60	41	13	894	70	†15	.985
—Indianapolis (A.A.)	OF	6	18	1	2	1	0	0	0	.111	1	5	0	6	1	0	1.000
1995—Indianapolis (A.A.)	1B-OF	57	193	30	58	11	0	4	18	.301	16	30	2	440	21	5	.989

BELL, DAVID — 2B/3B — CARDINALS

PERSONAL: Born September 14, 1972, in Cincinnati. . . . 5-10/170. . . . Bats right, throws right. . . . Full name: David Michael Bell. . . . Son of Buddy Bell, manager, Detroit Tigers; brother of Mike Bell, third baseman, Texas Rangers organization; and grandson of Gus Bell, major league outfielder with four teams (1950-64).
HIGH SCHOOL: Moeller (Cincinnati).
TRANSACTIONS/CAREER NOTES: Selected by Cleveland Indians organization in seventh round of free-agent draft (June 4, 1990). . . . Traded by Indians with C Pepe McNeal and P Rick Heiserman to St. Louis Cardinals for P Ken Hill (July 27, 1995).
STATISTICAL NOTES: Led South Atlantic League in grounding into double plays with 22 in 1991. . . . Led South Atlantic League third basemen with 389 total chances in 1991. . . . Led Eastern League third basemen with 32 double plays in 1993. . . . Led International League third basemen with .950 fielding percentage in 1994.

			BATTING											FIELDING			
Year Team (League)	Pos.	G	AB	R	H	2B	3B	HR	RBI	Avg.	BB	SO	SB	PO	A	E	Avg.
1990—GC Indians (GCL)	3B	30	111	18	29	5	1	0	13	.261	10	8	1	29	50	7	.919
—Burlington (Appal.)	3B	12	42	4	7	1	1	0	2	.167	2	5	2	8	27	3	.921
1991—Columbus (S. Atl.)	3B	136	491	47	113	24	1	5	63	.230	37	50	3	90	*268	31	.920
1992—Kinston (Carolina)	3B	123	464	52	117	17	2	6	47	.252	54	66	2	83	264	20	.946
1993—Cant./Akr. (East.)	3B-2B-SS	129	483	69	141	20	2	9	60	.292	43	54	3	117	283	21	.950
1994—Charlotte (Int'l)	3B-SS-2B	134	481	66	141	17	4	18	88	.293	41	54	2	109	326	20	†.956
1995—Buffalo (A.A.)	3B-SS-2B	70	254	34	69	11	1	8	34	.272	22	37	0	46	172	11	.952
—Cleveland (A.L.)	3B	2	2	0	0	0	0	0	0	.000	0	0	0	0	2	0	1.000
—Louisville (A.A.)■	2B	18	76	9	21	3	1	1	9	.276	2	10	4	39	54	1	.989
—St. Louis (N.L.)	2B-3B	39	144	13	36	7	2	2	19	.250	4	25	1	77	108	7	.964
American League totals (1 year)		2	2	0	0	0	0	0	0	.000	0	0	0	0	2	0	1.000
National League totals (1 year)		39	144	13	36	7	2	2	19	.250	4	25	1	77	108	7	.964
Major league totals (1 year)		41	146	13	36	7	2	2	19	.247	4	25	1	77	110	7	.964

BELL, DEREK — OF — ASTROS

PERSONAL: Born December 11, 1968, in Tampa, Fla. . . . 6-2/215. . . . Bats right, throws right. . . . Full name: Derek Nathaniel Bell.
HIGH SCHOOL: King (Tampa, Fla.).
TRANSACTIONS/CAREER NOTES: Selected by Toronto Blue Jays organization in second round of free-agent draft (June 2, 1987). . . . On Knoxville disabled list (July 30, 1988-remainder of season; June 13-21 and July 2-12, 1990). . . . On Toronto disabled list (April 9-May 8, 1992); included rehabilitation assignment to Dunedin (April 27-May 4). . . . Traded by Blue Jays with OF Stoney Briggs to San Diego Padres for OF Darrin Jackson (March 30, 1993). . . . On suspended list (July 9-12, 1993 and July 9-17, 1994). . . . Traded by Padres with OF Phil Plantier, P Pedro Martinez, P Doug Brocail, IF Craig Shipley and SS Ricky Gutierrez to Houston Astros for 3B Ken Caminiti, OF Steve Finley, SS Andujar Cedeno, 1B Robert Petagine, P Brian Williams and a player to be named later (December 28, 1994).
HONORS: Named International League Most Valuable Player (1991).
STATISTICAL NOTES: Led International League with 243 total bases in 1991. . . . Led International League outfielders with seven double plays in 1991.

			BATTING											FIELDING			
Year Team (League)	Pos.	G	AB	R	H	2B	3B	HR	RBI	Avg.	BB	SO	SB	PO	A	E	Avg.
1987—St. Cathar. (NYP)	OF	74	273	46	72	11	3	10	42	.264	18	60	12	126	6	2	.985
1988—Knoxville (South.)	OF	14	52	5	13	3	1	0	4	.250	1	14	2	18	2	2	.909
1989—Knoxville (South.)	OF	136	513	72	124	22	6	16	75	.242	26	92	15	216	12	9	.962
1990—Syracuse (Int'l)	OF	109	402	57	105	13	5	7	56	.261	23	75	21	220	9	5	.979
1991—Syracuse (Int'l)	OF	119	457	*89	*158	22	•12	13	*93	*.346	57	69	27	278	*15	*16	.948
—Toronto (A.L.)	OF	18	28	5	4	0	0	0	1	.143	6	5	3	16	0	2	.889
1992—Toronto (A.L.)	OF-DH	61	161	23	39	6	3	2	15	.242	15	34	7	105	4	0	1.000
—Dunedin (Fla. St.)	OF	7	25	7	6	2	0	0	4	.240	4	4	3	13	0	2	.867
1993—San Diego (N.L.)■	OF-3B	150	542	73	142	19	1	21	72	.262	23	122	26	334	37	17	.956
1994—San Diego (N.L.)	OF	108	434	54	135	20	0	14	54	.311	29	88	24	247	3	10	.962
1995—Houston (N.L.)■	OF	112	452	63	151	21	2	8	86	.334	33	71	27	201	10	8	.963
American League totals (2 years)		79	189	28	43	6	3	2	16	.228	21	39	10	121	4	2	.984
National League totals (3 years)		370	1428	190	428	60	3	43	212	.300	85	281	77	782	50	35	.960
Major league totals (5 years)		449	1617	218	471	66	6	45	228	.291	106	320	87	903	54	37	.963

CHAMPIONSHIP SERIES RECORD

Year Team (League)	Pos.	G	AB	R	H	2B	3B	HR	RBI	Avg.	BB	SO	SB	PO	A	E	Avg.
			BATTING											FIELDING			
1992— Toronto (A.L.)	PR-OF	2	0	1	0	0	0	0	0	...	1	0	0	1	0	0	1.000

WORLD SERIES RECORD

NOTES: Member of World Series championship team (1992).

Year Team (League)	Pos.	G	AB	R	H	2B	3B	HR	RBI	Avg.	BB	SO	SB	PO	A	E	Avg.
			BATTING											FIELDING			
1992— Toronto (A.L.)	PH	2	1	1	0	0	0	0	0	.000	1	0	0	...	...	...	...

BELL, JAY — SS — PIRATES

PERSONAL: Born December 11, 1965, in Eglin AFB, Fla. . . . 6-0/182. . . . Bats right, throws right. . . . Full name: Jay Stuart Bell.
HIGH SCHOOL: Tate (Gonzalez, Fla.).
TRANSACTIONS/CAREER NOTES: Selected by Minnesota Twins organization in first round (eighth pick overall) of free-agent draft (June 4, 1984). . . . Traded by Twins with P Curt Wardle, OF Jim Weaver and a player to be named later to Cleveland Indians for P Bert Blyleven (August 1, 1985); Indians organization acquired P Rich Yett to complete deal (September 17, 1985). . . . Traded by Indians to Pittsburgh Pirates for SS Felix Fermin (March 25, 1989).
HONORS: Named shortstop on The Sporting News N.L. All-Star team (1993). . . . Won N.L. Gold Glove at shortstop (1993). . . . Named shortstop on The Sporting News N.L. Silver Slugger team (1993).
STATISTICAL NOTES: Led Appalachian League shortstops with 352 total chances and 43 double plays in 1984. . . . Led California League shortstops with 84 double plays in 1985. . . . Hit home run in first major league at-bat on first pitch (September 29, 1986). . . . Led Eastern League shortstops with 613 total chances in 1986. . . . Led American Association shortstops with 198 putouts, 322 assists, 30 errors and 550 total chances in 1987. . . . Led N.L. with 39 sacrifice hits in 1990 and 30 in 1991. . . . Led N.L. shortstops with 741 total chances in 1990, 754 in 1991, 816 in 1992, 794 in 1993 and 547 in 1994.. . . . Led N.L. shortstops with 94 double plays in 1992. . . . Career major league grand slams: 2.

Year Team (League)	Pos.	G	AB	R	H	2B	3B	HR	RBI	Avg.	BB	SO	SB	PO	A	E	Avg.
			BATTING											FIELDING			
1984— Elizabeth. (Appal.)	SS	66	245	43	54	12	1	6	30	.220	42	50	4	*109	*218	25	.929
1985— Visalia (California)	SS	106	376	56	106	16	6	9	59	.282	41	73	10	176	330	53	.905
— Waterbury (East.)■	SS	29	114	13	34	11	2	1	14	.298	9	16	3	41	79	6	.952
1986— Waterbury (East.)	SS	138	494	86	137	28	4	7	74	.277	87	65	10	197	*371	*45	.927
— Cleveland (A.L.)	2B-DH	5	14	3	5	2	0	1	4	.357	2	3	0	1	6	2	.778
1987— Buffalo (A.A.)	SS-2B	110	362	71	94	15	4	17	60	.260	70	84	6	†201	†325	†30	.946
— Cleveland (A.L.)	SS	38	125	14	27	9	1	2	13	.216	8	31	2	67	93	9	.947
1988— Cleveland (A.L.)	SS-DH	73	211	23	46	5	1	2	21	.218	21	53	4	103	170	10	.965
— Colo. Springs (PCL)	SS	49	181	35	50	12	2	7	24	.276	26	27	3	87	171	18	.935
1989— Pittsburgh (N.L.)■	SS	78	271	33	70	13	3	2	27	.258	19	47	5	109	197	10	.968
— Buffalo (A.A.)	SS-3B	86	298	49	85	15	3	10	54	.285	38	55	12	110	223	16	.954
1990— Pittsburgh (N.L.)	SS	159	583	93	148	28	7	7	52	.254	65	109	10	*260	459	22	.970
1991— Pittsburgh (N.L.)	SS	157	608	96	164	32	8	16	67	.270	52	99	10	239	*491	*24	.968
1992— Pittsburgh (N.L.)	SS	159	632	87	167	36	6	9	55	.264	55	103	7	*268	*526	22	.973
1993— Pittsburgh (N.L.)	SS	154	604	102	187	32	9	9	51	.310	77	122	16	*256	*527	11	*.986
1994— Pittsburgh (N.L.)	SS	110	424	68	117	35	4	9	45	.276	49	82	2	152	*380	15	.973
1995— Pittsburgh (N.L.)	SS-3B	138	530	79	139	28	4	13	55	.262	55	110	2	206	415	14	.978
American League totals (3 years)		116	350	40	78	16	2	5	38	.223	31	87	6	171	269	21	.954
National League totals (7 years)		955	3652	558	992	204	41	65	352	.272	372	672	52	1490	2995	118	.974
Major league totals (10 years)		1071	4002	598	1070	220	43	70	390	.267	403	759	58	1661	3264	139	.973

CHAMPIONSHIP SERIES RECORD

NOTES: Holds N.L. single-series record for most singles—9 (1991).

Year Team (League)	Pos.	G	AB	R	H	2B	3B	HR	RBI	Avg.	BB	SO	SB	PO	A	E	Avg.
			BATTING											FIELDING			
1990— Pittsburgh (N.L.)	SS	6	20	3	5	1	0	1	1	.250	4	3	0	4	22	1	.963
1991— Pittsburgh (N.L.)	SS	7	29	2	12	2	0	1	1	.414	0	10	0	13	19	1	.970
1992— Pittsburgh (N.L.)	SS	7	29	3	5	2	0	1	4	.172	3	4	0	6	8	1	.933
Championship series totals (3 years)		20	78	8	22	5	0	3	6	.282	7	17	0	23	49	3	.960

ALL-STAR GAME RECORD

Year League	Pos.	AB	R	H	2B	3B	HR	RBI	Avg.	BB	SO	SB	PO	A	E	Avg.
		BATTING											FIELDING			
1993— National	2B	1	0	0	0	0	0	0	.000	0	0	0	1	1	0	1.000

BELL, JUAN — 2B/SS — RED SOX

PERSONAL: Born March 29, 1968, in San Pedro de Macoris, Dominican Republic. . . . 5-11/175. . . . Bats both, throws right. . . . Full name: Juan Mathey Bell. . . . Brother of George Bell, designated hitter/outfielder, Toronto Blue Jays, Chicago Cubs and Chicago White Sox (1981-93); and brother of Rolando Bell, minor league infielder (1985-87).
HIGH SCHOOL: Gastone F. Deligne (San Pedro de Macoris, Dominican Republic).
TRANSACTIONS/CAREER NOTES: Signed as non-drafted free agent by Los Angeles Dodgers organization (September 1, 1984). . . . Traded by Dodgers organization with P Brian Holton and P Ken Howell to Baltimore Orioles for 1B Eddie Murray (December 4, 1988). . . . On Rochester disabled list (July 6-August 27, 1990). . . . Loaned by Rochester, Orioles organization, to Oklahoma City, Texas Rangers organization (June 2-August 11, 1992). . . . On Oklahoma City disabled list (June 8-July 24, 1992). . . . Traded by Orioles to Philadelphia Phillies for IF Steve Scarsone (August 11, 1992). . . . Claimed on waivers by Milwaukee Brewers (June 1, 1993). . . . Released by Brewers (March 29, 1994). . . . Signed by Montreal Expos organization (April 8, 1994). . . . Granted free agency (October 14, 1994). . . . Signed by Pawtucket, Boston Red Sox organization (November 7, 1994). . . . Granted free agency (October 6, 1995). . . . Re-signed by Red Sox organization (December 19, 1995).

STATISTICAL NOTES: Led Gulf Coast League shortstops with 293 total chances in 1986. . . . Led California League shortstops with 719 total chances in 1987.

MISCELLANEOUS: Batted righthanded only with Gulf Coast Dodgers (1986) and San Antonio (1988).

		BATTING												FIELDING			
Year Team (League)	**Pos.**	**G**	**AB**	**R**	**H**	**2B**	**3B**	**HR**	**RBI**	**Avg.**	**BB**	**SO**	**SB**	**PO**	**A**	**E**	**Avg.**
1985— GC Dodgers (GCL)	SS-2B	42	106	11	17	0	0	0	8	.160	12	20	2	56	73	20	.866
1986— GC Dodgers (GCL)	SS	59	217	38	52	6	2	0	26	.240	29	28	12	78	*193	22	.925
1987— Bakersfield (Calif.)......	SS	134	473	54	116	15	3	4	58	.245	73	91	21	235	*431	*53	.926
1988— San Antonio (Tex.)	SS	61	215	37	60	4	2	5	21	.279	16	37	11	106	182	20	.935
— Albuquerque (PCL).....	SS	73	257	42	77	9	3	8	45	.300	16	70	7	114	249	23	.940
1989— Rochester (Int'l)■......	SS	116	408	50	107	15	6	2	32	.262	39	92	17	190	297	36	.931
— Baltimore (A.L.)..........	DH-2B-SS	8	4	2	0	0	0	0	0	.000	0	1	1	2	6	0	1.000
1990— Rochester (Int'l)	SS	82	326	59	93	12	5	6	35	.285	36	59	16	131	240	22	.944
— Baltimore (A.L.)..........	SS	5	2	1	0	0	0	0	0	.000	0	1	0	1	1	0	1.000
1991— Baltimore (A.L.)..........	2-S-DH-O	100	209	26	36	9	2	1	15	.172	8	51	0	107	199	9	.971
1992— Rochester (Int'l)	SS-2B	39	138	21	27	6	3	2	14	.196	14	40	2	60	86	5	.967
— Okla. City (A.A.)■.......	SS	24	82	12	21	4	1	1	9	.256	4	19	2	35	62	5	.951
— Philadelphia (N.L.)■ ..	SS	46	147	12	30	3	1	1	8	.204	18	29	5	82	129	6	.972
1993— Philadelphia (N.L.)......	SS	24	65	5	13	6	1	0	7	.200	5	12	0	33	57	9	.909
— Milwaukee (A.L.)■.....	2-S-O-DH	91	286	42	67	6	2	5	29	.234	36	64	6	185	224	12	.971
1994— W.P. Beach (FSL)■.....	SS-2B	5	20	1	4	1	0	1	3	.200	3	2	0	21	20	1	.976
— Harrisburg (East.).......	SS-2B	11	45	7	13	4	2	0	6	.289	9	6	1	27	34	1	.984
— Ottawa (Int'l)	SS	7	24	5	6	1	0	0	1	.250	4	6	1	10	22	0	1.000
— Montreal (N.L.)...........	2B-3B-SS	38	97	12	27	4	0	2	10	.278	15	21	4	43	73	2	.983
1995— Pawtucket (Int'l)■......	SS-2B-3B	68	262	42	69	18	1	6	23	.263	21	46	4	108	144	14	.947
— Boston (A.L.)..............	SS-2B-3B	17	26	7	4	2	0	1	2	.154	2	10	0	15	24	3	.929
American League totals (5 years)		221	527	78	107	17	4	7	46	.203	46	127	7	310	454	24	.970
National League totals (3 years)		108	309	29	70	13	2	3	25	.227	38	62	9	158	259	17	.961
Major league totals (7 years)		329	836	107	177	30	6	10	71	.212	84	189	16	468	713	41	.966

BELLE, ALBERT — OF — INDIANS

PERSONAL: Born August 25, 1966, in Shreveport, La. . . . 6-2/210. . . . Bats right, throws right. . . . Full name: Albert Jojuan Belle. . . . Formerly known as Joey Belle.

HIGH SCHOOL: Huntington (Shreveport, La.).

COLLEGE: Louisiana State.

TRANSACTIONS/CAREER NOTES: Selected by Cleveland Indians organization in second round of free-agent draft (June 2, 1987). . . . On suspended list (July 12-18, 1991; August 4-8, 1992; June 4-7, 1993; and August 1-7, 1994).

RECORDS: Shares major league record for most home runs in two consecutive games—5 (September 18 [2] and 19 [3], 1995). . . . Shares A.L. single-season record for fewest errors by outfielder who led league in errors—9 (1991).

HONORS: Named outfielder on The Sporting News A.L. All-Star team (1993-95). . . . Named outfielder on The Sporting News A.L. Silver Slugger team (1993-95). . . . Named Major League Player of the Year by The Sporting News (1995).

STATISTICAL NOTES: Hit three home runs in one game (September 4, 1992 and September 19, 1995). . . . Led A.L. with 14 sacrifice flies in 1993. . . . Led A.L. outfielders with seven double plays in 1993. . . . Led A.L. with 294 total bases in 1994 and 377 in 1995. . . . Led A.L. with .690 slugging percentage in 1995. . . . Led A.L. in grounding into double plays with 24 in 1995. . . . Career major league grand slams: 5.

		BATTING												FIELDING			
Year Team (League)	**Pos.**	**G**	**AB**	**R**	**H**	**2B**	**3B**	**HR**	**RBI**	**Avg.**	**BB**	**SO**	**SB**	**PO**	**A**	**E**	**Avg.**
1987— Kinston (Carolina)	OF	10	37	5	12	2	0	3	9	.324	8	16	0	5	0	0	1.000
1988— Kinston (Carolina)	OF	41	153	21	46	16	0	8	39	.301	18	45	2	43	5	5	.906
— Waterloo (Midw.)	OF	9	28	2	7	1	0	1	2	.250	1	9	0	11	1	0	1.000
1989— Cant./Akr. (East.)	OF	89	312	48	88	20	0	20	69	.282	32	82	8	136	4	3	.979
— Cleveland (A.L.)..........	OF-DH	62	218	22	49	8	4	7	37	.225	12	55	2	92	3	2	.979
1990— Cleveland (A.L.)..........	DH-OF	9	23	1	4	0	0	1	3	.174	1	6	0	0	0	0	. . .
— Colo. Springs (PCL) ...	OF	24	96	16	33	3	1	5	19	.344	5	16	4	31	0	2	.939
— Cant./Akr. (East.)	DH	9	32	4	8	1	0	0	3	.250	3	7	0	. . .	. . .	. . .	. . .
1991— Cleveland (A.L.)..........	OF-DH	123	461	60	130	31	2	28	95	.282	25	99	3	170	8	•9	.952
— Colo. Springs (PCL) ...	OF	16	61	9	20	3	2	2	16	.328	2	8	1	19	1	1	.952
1992— Cleveland (A.L.)..........	DH-OF	153	585	81	152	23	1	34	112	.260	52	128	8	94	1	3	.969
1993— Cleveland (A.L.)..........	OF-DH	159	594	93	172	36	3	38	*129	.290	76	96	23	338	16	5	.986
1994— Cleveland (A.L.)..........	OF-DH	106	412	90	147	35	2	36	101	.357	58	71	9	205	8	6	.973
1995— Cleveland (A.L.)..........	OF-DH	143	546	•121	173	•52	1	*50	•126	.317	73	80	5	304	7	6	.981
Major league totals (7 years)		755	2839	468	827	185	13	194	603	.291	297	535	50	1203	43	31	.976

DIVISION SERIES RECORD

		BATTING												FIELDING			
Year Team (League)	**Pos.**	**G**	**AB**	**R**	**H**	**2B**	**3B**	**HR**	**RBI**	**Avg.**	**BB**	**SO**	**SB**	**PO**	**A**	**E**	**Avg.**
1995— Cleveland (A.L.)..........	OF	3	11	3	3	1	0	1	3	.273	4	3	0	7	0	1	.875

CHAMPIONSHIP SERIES RECORD

		BATTING												FIELDING			
Year Team (League)	**Pos.**	**G**	**AB**	**R**	**H**	**2B**	**3B**	**HR**	**RBI**	**Avg.**	**BB**	**SO**	**SB**	**PO**	**A**	**E**	**Avg.**
1995— Cleveland (A.L.)..........	OF	5	18	1	4	1	0	1	1	.222	3	5	0	4	0	2	.667

WORLD SERIES RECORD

		BATTING												FIELDING			
Year Team (League)	**Pos.**	**G**	**AB**	**R**	**H**	**2B**	**3B**	**HR**	**RBI**	**Avg.**	**BB**	**SO**	**SB**	**PO**	**A**	**E**	**Avg.**
1995— Cleveland (A.L.)..........	OF	6	17	4	4	0	0	2	4	.235	7	5	0	10	0	1	.909

ALL-STAR GAME RECORD

Year	League	Pos.	AB	R	H	2B	3B	HR	RBI	Avg.	BB	SO	SB	PO	A	E	Avg.
			BATTING											FIELDING			
1993—	American	PH-DH	1	2	1	0	0	0	1	1.000	1	0	0	...	...	...	...
1994—	American	OF	2	0	0	0	0	0	0	.000	0	0	0	1	0	0	1.000
1995—	American	OF	3	0	0	0	0	0	0	.000	0	1	0	1	0	0	1.000
All-Star Game totals (3 years)			6	2	1	0	0	0	1	.167	1	1	0	2	0	0	1.000

BELLIARD, RAFAEL — SS — BRAVES

PERSONAL: Born October 24, 1961, in Pueblo Nuevo, Mao, Dominican Republic. . . . 5-6/160. . . . Bats right, throws right. . . . Full name: Rafael Leonidas Matias Belliard. . . . Name pronounced BELL-ee-ard.

TRANSACTIONS/CAREER NOTES: Signed as non-drafted free agent by Pittsburgh Pirates organization (July 10, 1980). . . . On Buffalo disabled list (April 19-July 24, 1982). . . . On Pittsburgh disabled list (June 28-August 28, 1984; July 28-August 12, 1986; August 27, 1987-remainder of season; and May 19-June 3, 1988). . . . Granted free agency (November 5, 1990). . . . Signed by Atlanta Braves (December 18, 1990). . . . Granted free agency (October 25, 1994). . . . Re-signed by Braves (October 28, 1994).

STATISTICAL NOTES: Led Carolina League with 12 sacrifice hits and tied for lead in caught stealing with 15 in 1981. . . . Tied for Eastern League lead in double plays by shortstop with 69 in 1983. . . . Led N.L. shortstops with .977 fielding percentage in 1988.

Year	Team (League)	Pos.	G	AB	R	H	2B	3B	HR	RBI	Avg.	BB	SO	SB	PO	A	E	Avg.
				BATTING											FIELDING			
1980—	GC Pirates (GCL)	SS-2B-3B	12	42	6	9	1	0	0	2	.214	0	3	1	24	39	1	.984
—	Shelby (S. Atl.)	SS	8	24	1	3	0	0	0	2	.125	1	3	0	10	27	5	.881
1981—	Alexandria (Caro.)	SS	127	472	58	102	6	5	0	33	.216	26	92	42	•205	330	29	.949
1982—	Buffalo (Eastern)	SS	40	124	14	34	1	1	0	19	.274	8	16	6	56	87	5	.966
—	Pittsburgh (N.L.)	SS	9	2	3	1	0	0	0	0	.500	0	0	1	2	2	0	1.000
1983—	Lynn (Eastern)	SS-2B	127	431	63	113	13	2	2	37	.262	30	54	12	203	307	26	.951
—	Pittsburgh (N.L.)	SS	4	1	1	0	0	0	0	0	.000	0	1	0	1	3	0	1.000
1984—	Pittsburgh (N.L.)	SS-2B	20	22	3	5	0	0	0	0	.227	0	1	0	12	13	3	.893
1985—	Pittsburgh (N.L.)	SS	17	20	1	4	0	0	0	1	.200	0	5	0	13	23	2	.947
—	Hawaii (PCL)	SS-2B	100	341	35	84	12	4	1	18	.246	4	49	9	172	289	5	.989
1986—	Pittsburgh (N.L.)	SS-2B	117	309	33	72	5	2	0	31	.233	26	54	12	147	317	12	.975
1987—	Pittsburgh (N.L.)	SS-2B	81	203	26	42	4	3	1	15	.207	20	25	5	113	191	6	.981
—	Harrisburg (East.)	SS	37	145	24	49	5	2	0	9	.338	6	16	7	59	115	7	.961
1988—	Pittsburgh (N.L.)	SS-2B	122	286	28	61	0	4	0	11	.213	26	47	7	134	261	9	†.978
1989—	Pittsburgh (N.L.)	SS-2B-3B	67	154	10	33	4	0	0	8	.214	8	22	5	71	138	3	.986
1990—	Pittsburgh (N.L.)	2B-SS-3B	47	54	10	11	3	0	0	6	.204	5	13	1	37	36	2	.973
1991—	Atlanta (N.L.)■	SS	149	353	36	88	9	2	0	27	.249	22	63	3	168	361	18	.967
1992—	Atlanta (N.L.)	SS-2B	144	285	20	60	6	1	0	14	.211	14	43	0	152	291	14	.969
1993—	Atlanta (N.L.)	SS-2B	91	79	6	18	5	0	0	6	.228	4	13	0	53	99	1	.993
1994—	Atlanta (N.L.)	SS-2B	46	120	9	29	7	1	0	9	.242	2	29	0	45	86	1	.992
1995—	Atlanta (N.L.)	SS-2B	75	180	12	40	2	1	0	7	.222	6	28	2	74	181	1	.996
Major league totals (14 years)			989	2068	198	464	45	14	1	135	.224	133	344	36	1022	2002	72	.977

DIVISION SERIES RECORD

Year	Team (League)	Pos.	G	AB	R	H	2B	3B	HR	RBI	Avg.	BB	SO	SB	PO	A	E	Avg.
				BATTING											FIELDING			
1995—	Atlanta (N.L.)	SS	4	5	1	0	0	0	0	0	.000	0	1	0	2	5	0	1.000

CHAMPIONSHIP SERIES RECORD

Year	Team (League)	Pos.	G	AB	R	H	2B	3B	HR	RBI	Avg.	BB	SO	SB	PO	A	E	Avg.
				BATTING											FIELDING			
1990—	Pittsburgh (N.L.)								Did not play.									
1991—	Atlanta (N.L.)	SS	7	19	0	4	0	0	0	1	.211	3	3	0	9	15	1	.960
1992—	Atlanta (N.L.)	SS-2B-PR	4	2	1	0	0	0	0	0	.000	1	0	0	2	3	0	1.000
1993—	Atlanta (N.L.)	PH-2-PR-S	2	1	1	0	0	0	0	0	.000	0	1	0	0	0	0	...
1995—	Atlanta (N.L.)	SS	4	11	1	3	0	0	0	0	.273	0	3	0	6	7	1	.929
Championship series totals (4 years)			17	33	3	7	0	0	0	1	.212	4	7	0	17	25	2	.955

WORLD SERIES RECORD

NOTES: Member of World Series championship team (1995).

Year	Team (League)	Pos.	G	AB	R	H	2B	3B	HR	RBI	Avg.	BB	SO	SB	PO	A	E	Avg.
				BATTING											FIELDING			
1991—	Atlanta (N.L.)	SS	7	16	0	6	1	0	0	4	.375	1	2	0	8	21	0	1.000
1992—	Atlanta (N.L.)	SS-2B	4	4	0	0	0	0	0	0	.000	0	0	0	3	2	0	1.000
1995—	Atlanta (N.L.)	SS	6	16	0	0	0	0	0	1	.000	0	4	0	3	11	2	.875
World Series totals (3 years)			17	36	0	6	1	0	0	5	.167	1	6	0	14	34	2	.960

BELTRE, ESTEBAN — SS — RED SOX

PERSONAL: Born December 26, 1967, in Ingenio Quisfuella, Dominican Republic. . . . 5-10/172. . . . Bats right, throws right. . . . Full name: Esteban Valera Beltre. . . . Name pronounced BELL-tray.

HIGH SCHOOL: Eugenio Mariade Hostos (Dominican Republic).

TRANSACTIONS/CAREER NOTES: Signed as non-drafted free agent by Montreal Expos (May 9, 1984). . . . Loaned by Expos organization to Utica, independent (June 16-September 16, 1985). . . . Granted free agency (January 1, 1991). . . . Signed by Vancouver, Milwaukee Brewers organization (March 16, 1991). . . . Traded by Brewers organization to Chicago White Sox organization for OF John Cangelosi (May 23, 1991). . . . Traded by White Sox organization to Texas Rangers for P Scott Eyre (March 28, 1994). . . . Granted free agency (December 21, 1995). . . . Signed by Boston Red Sox (January 22, 1996).

STATISTICAL NOTES: Led American Association shortstops with 580 total chances in 1990 and 624 in 1993.

Year	Team (League)	Pos.	G	AB	R	H	2B	3B	HR	RBI	Avg.	BB	SO	SB	PO	A	E	Avg.
				BATTING											FIELDING			
1984—	Calgary (Pioneer)	SS	18	20	1	4	0	0	0	2	.200	2	8	1	13	13	10	.722
1985—	Utica (NYP)■	SS	72	241	19	48	6	2	0	22	.199	18	58	8	106	206	26	.923
1986—	W.P. Beach (FSL)■	SS	97	285	24	69	11	1	1	20	.242	16	59	4	116	273	23	.944
1987—	Jacksonv. (South.)	SS	142	491	55	104	15	4	4	34	.212	40	98	9	*198	*358	*35	.941
1988—	Jacksonv. (South.)	SS	35	113	5	17	2	0	0	6	.150	3	28	1	39	87	11	.920
	— W.P. Beach (FSL)	SS	69	226	23	63	5	6	0	15	.279	11	38	4	99	204	19	.941
1989—	Rockford (Midw.)	SS	104	375	42	80	15	3	2	33	.213	33	83	9	183	336	30	*.945
1990—	Indianapolis (A.A.)	SS	133	407	33	92	11	2	1	37	.226	32	77	8	215	*335	*30	.948
1991—	Denver (A.A.)■	SS	27	78	11	14	1	3	0	9	.179	9	16	3	52	64	13	.899
	— Vancouver (PCL)■	SS-2B	88	347	48	94	11	3	0	30	.271	23	61	8	129	243	26	.935
	— Chicago (A.L.)	SS	8	6	0	1	0	0	0	0	.167	1	1	1	1	5	0	1.000
1992—	Vancouver (PCL)	SS	40	161	17	43	5	2	0	16	.267	8	27	4	70	109	10	.947
	— Chicago (A.L.)	SS-DH	49	110	21	21	2	0	1	10	.191	3	18	1	53	92	12	.924
1993—	Nashville (A.A.)	SS	134	489	67	143	24	4	8	52	.292	33	102	18	190	*404	*30	.952
1994—	Texas (A.L.)■	SS-3B-2B	48	131	12	37	5	0	0	12	.282	16	25	2	59	132	9	.955
1995—	Texas (A.L.)	SS-2B-3B	54	92	7	20	8	0	0	7	.217	4	15	0	53	81	5	.964
Major league totals (4 years)			159	339	40	79	15	0	1	29	.233	24	59	4	166	310	26	.948

BENARD, MARVIN — OF — GIANTS

PERSONAL: Born January 20, 1970, in Bluefields, Nicaragua. . . . 5-9/180. . . . Bats left, throws left. . . . Full name: Marvin Larry Benard.
HIGH SCHOOL: Bell (Bell Gardens, Calif.).
JUNIOR COLLEGE: Los Angeles Harbor.
COLLEGE: Lewis-Clark State (Idaho).
TRANSACTIONS/CAREER NOTES: Selected by Philadelphia Phillies organization in 20th round of free-agent draft (June 4, 1990); did not sign. . . . Selected by San Francisco Giants organization in 50th round of free-agent draft (June 1, 1992). . . . On disabled list (April 17-28, 1993).
STATISTICAL NOTES: Tied for Texas League lead in grounding into double plays with 15 in 1994. . . . Led Texas League outfielders with five double plays in 1994.

Year	Team (League)	Pos.	G	AB	R	H	2B	3B	HR	RBI	Avg.	BB	SO	SB	PO	A	E	Avg.
				BATTING											FIELDING			
1992—	Everett (N'west)	OF	64	161	31	38	10	2	1	17	.236	24	39	17	90	8	3	.970
1993—	Clinton (Midwest)	OF	112	349	84	105	14	2	5	50	.301	56	66	42	179	10	5	.974
1994—	Shreveport (Texas)	OF	125	454	66	143	32	3	4	48	.315	31	58	24	259	17	*12	.958
1995—	Phoenix (PCL)	OF	111	378	70	115	14	6	6	32	.304	50	66	10	183	5	8	.959
	— San Francisco (N.L.)	OF	13	34	5	13	2	0	1	4	.382	1	7	1	19	0	0	1.000
Major league totals (1 year)			13	34	5	13	2	0	1	4	.382	1	7	1	19	0	0	1.000

BENES, ALAN — P — CARDINALS

PERSONAL: Born January 21, 1972, in Evansville, Ind. . . . 6-5/215. . . . Throws right, bats right. . . . Full name: Alan Paul Benes. . . . Brother of Andy Benes, pitcher, St. Louis Cardinals; and brother of Adam Benes, pitcher, St. Louis Cardinals organization. . . . Name pronounced BEN-ess.
HIGH SCHOOL: Lake Forest (Ill.).
COLLEGE: Creighton.
TRANSACTIONS/CAREER NOTES: Selected by San Diego Padres organization in 49th round of free-agent draft (June 4, 1990); did not sign. . . . Selected by St. Louis Cardinals organization in first round (16th pick overall) of free-agent draft (June 3, 1993). . . . On Louisville disabled list (May 3-August 9, 1995).

Year	Team (League)	W	L	Pct.	ERA	G	GS	CG	ShO	Sv.	IP	H	R	ER	BB	SO
1993—	Glens Falls (NYP)	0	4	.000	3.65	7	7	0	0	0	37	39	20	15	14	29
1994—	Savannah (S. Atl.)	2	0	1.000	1.48	4	4	0	0	0	24 1/3	21	5	4	7	24
	— St. Petersburg (FSL)	7	1	.875	1.61	11	11	0	0	0	78 1/3	55	18	14	15	69
	— Arkansas (Texas)	7	2	.778	2.98	13	13	1	0	0	87 2/3	58	38	29	26	75
	— Louisville (A.A.)	1	0	1.000	2.93	2	2	1	0	0	15 1/3	10	5	5	4	16
1995—	Louisville (A.A.)	4	2	.667	2.41	11	11	2	1	0	56	37	16	15	14	54
	— St. Louis (N.L.)	1	2	.333	8.44	3	3	0	0	0	16	24	15	15	4	20
Major league totals (1 year)		1	2	.333	8.44	3	3	0	0	0	16	24	15	15	4	20

BENES, ANDY — P — CARDINALS

PERSONAL: Born August 20, 1967, in Evansville, Ind. . . . 6-6/245. . . . Throws right, bats right. . . . Full name: Andrew Charles Benes. . . . Brother of Alan Benes, pitcher, St. Louis Cardinals; and brother of Adam Benes, pitcher, St. Louis Cardinals organization. . . . Name pronounced BEN-ess.
HIGH SCHOOL: Central (Evansville, Ind.).
COLLEGE: Evansville.
TRANSACTIONS/CAREER NOTES: Selected by San Diego Padres organization in first round (first pick overall) of free-agent draft (June 1, 1988). . . . On suspended list (September 28, 1993-remainder of season). . . . Traded by Padres with a player to be named later to Seattle Mariners for P Ron Villone and OF Marc Newfield (July 31, 1995); Mariners acquired P Greg Keagle to complete deal (September 16, 1995). . . . Granted free agency (October 31, 1995). . . . Signed by St. Louis Cardinals (December 23, 1995).
RECORDS: Holds major league single-season record for fewest hits allowed for leader in most hits allowed—230 (1992).
HONORS: Named N.L. Rookie Pitcher of the Year by The Sporting News (1989). . . . Named Texas League Pitcher of the Year (1989).
STATISTICAL NOTES: Tied for N.L. lead with five balks in 1990. . . . Pitched 7-0 one-hit, complete-game victory against New York (July 3, 1994).
MISCELLANEOUS: Member of 1988 U.S. Olympic baseball team.

Year	Team (League)	W	L	Pct.	ERA	G	GS	CG	ShO	Sv.	IP	H	R	ER	BB	SO
1989—	Wichita (Texas)	8	4	.667	2.16	16	16	5	*3	0	108 1/3	79	32	26	39	115
	—Las Vegas (PCL)	2	1	.667	8.10	5	5	0	0	0	26 2/3	41	29	24	12	29
	—San Diego (N.L.)	6	3	.667	3.51	10	10	0	0	0	66 2/3	51	28	26	31	66
1990—	San Diego (N.L.)	10	11	.476	3.60	32	31	2	0	0	192 1/3	177	87	77	69	140
1991—	San Diego (N.L.)	15	11	.577	3.03	33	33	4	1	0	223	194	76	75	59	167
1992—	San Diego (N.L.)	13	14	.481	3.35	34	34	2	2	0	231 1/3	*230	90	86	61	169
1993—	San Diego (N.L.)	15	15	.500	3.78	34	34	4	2	0	230 2/3	200	111	97	86	179
1994—	San Diego (N.L.)	6	*14	.300	3.86	25	25	2	2	0	172 1/3	155	82	74	51	*189
1995—	San Diego (N.L.)	4	7	.364	4.17	19	19	1	1	0	118 2/3	121	65	55	45	126
	—Seattle (A.L.)■	7	2	.778	5.86	12	12	0	0	0	63	72	42	41	33	45
A.L. totals (1 year)		7	2	.778	5.86	12	12	0	0	0	63	72	42	41	33	45
N.L. totals (7 years)		69	75	.479	3.57	187	186	15	8	0	1235	1128	539	490	402	1036
Major league totals (7 years)		76	77	.497	3.68	199	198	15	8	0	1298	1200	581	531	435	1081

DIVISION SERIES RECORD

Year	Team (League)	W	L	Pct.	ERA	G	GS	CG	ShO	Sv.	IP	H	R	ER	BB	SO
1995—	Seattle (A.L.)	0	0	...	5.40	2	2	0	0	0	11 2/3	10	7	7	9	8

CHAMPIONSHIP SERIES RECORD

Year	Team (League)	W	L	Pct.	ERA	G	GS	CG	ShO	Sv.	IP	H	R	ER	BB	SO
1995—	Seattle (A.L.)	0	1	.000	23.14	1	1	0	0	0	2 1/3	6	6	6	2	3

ALL-STAR GAME RECORD

Year	League	W	L	Pct.	ERA	GS	CG	ShO	Sv.	IP	H	R	ER	BB	SO
1993—	National	0	0	...	4.50	0	0	0	0	2	2	1	1	0	2

BENITEZ, ARMANDO — P — ORIOLES

PERSONAL: Born November 3, 1972, in Ramon Santana, Dominican Republic. . . . 6-4/180. . . . Throws right, bats right.
TRANSACTIONS/CAREER NOTES: Signed as non-drafted free agent by Baltimore Orioles organization (April 1, 1990).

Year	Team (League)	W	L	Pct.	ERA	G	GS	CG	ShO	Sv.	IP	H	R	ER	BB	SO
1990—		Dominican Summer League statistics unavailable.														
1991—	GC Orioles (GCL)	3	2	.600	2.72	14	3	0	0	0	36 1/3	35	16	11	11	33
1992—	Bluefield (Appal.)	1	2	.333	4.31	25	0	0	0	5	31 1/3	35	31	15	23	37
1993—	Albany (S. Atl.)	5	1	.833	1.52	40	0	0	0	14	53 1/3	31	10	9	19	83
	—Frederick (Caro.)	3	0	1.000	0.66	12	0	0	0	4	13 2/3	7	1	1	4	29
1994—	Bowie (Eastern)	8	4	.667	3.14	53	0	0	0	16	71 2/3	41	29	25	39	106
	—Baltimore (A.L.)	0	0	...	0.90	3	0	0	0	0	10	8	1	1	4	14
1995—	Baltimore (A.L.)	1	5	.167	5.66	44	0	0	0	2	47 2/3	37	33	30	37	56
	—Rochester (Int'l)	2	2	.500	1.25	17	0	0	0	8	21 2/3	10	4	3	7	37
Major league totals (2 years)		1	5	.167	4.84	47	0	0	0	2	57 2/3	45	34	31	41	70

BENITEZ, YAMIL — OF — EXPOS

PERSONAL: Born May 10, 1972, in San Juan, Puerto Rico. . . . 6-2/195. . . . Bats right, throws right. . . . Full name: Yamil Antonio Benitez.
TRANSACTIONS/CAREER NOTES: Signed as non-drafted free agent by Montreal Expos organization (October 26, 1989).

				BATTING											FIELDING			
Year	Team (League)	Pos.	G	AB	R	H	2B	3B	HR	RBI	Avg.	BB	SO	SB	PO	A	E	Avg.
1990—	GC Expos (GCL)	OF	22	83	6	19	1	0	1	5	.229	8	18	0	38	2	1	.976
1991—	GC Expos (GCL)	OF	54	197	20	47	9	5	5	38	.239	12	55	10	85	2	3	.967
1992—	Albany (S. Atl.)	OF	23	79	6	13	3	2	1	6	.165	5	49	0	30	0	1	.968
	—Jamestown (NYP)	OF	44	162	24	44	6	6	3	23	.272	14	52	19	61	2	1	.984
1993—	Burlington (Midw.)	OF	111	411	70	112	21	5	15	61	.273	29	99	18	167	4	10	.945
1994—	Harrisburg (East.)	OF	126	475	58	123	18	4	17	91	.259	36	134	18	252	11	9	.967
1995—	Ottawa (Int'l)	OF	127	474	66	123	24	6	18	69	.259	44	128	14	177	10	7	.964
	—Montreal (N.L.)	OF	14	39	8	15	2	1	2	7	.385	1	7	0	18	1	1	.950
Major league totals (1 year)			14	39	8	15	2	1	2	7	.385	1	7	0	18	1	1	.950

BENJAMIN, MIKE — 3B/SS — PHILLIES

PERSONAL: Born November 22, 1965, in Euclid, O. . . . 6-0/169. . . . Bats right, throws right. . . . Full name: Michael Paul Benjamin.
HIGH SCHOOL: Bellflower (Calif.).
JUNIOR COLLEGE: Cerritos (Calif.).
COLLEGE: Arizona State.
TRANSACTIONS/CAREER NOTES: Selected by Minnesota Twins organization in seventh round of free-agent draft (January 9, 1985); did not sign. . . . Selected by San Francisco Giants organization in third round of free-agent draft (June 2, 1987). . . . On San Francisco disabled list (March 31-June 5, 1992); included rehabilitation assignment to Phoenix (April 20-May 10). . . . On San Francisco disabled list (July 8-August 6, 1993); included rehabilitation assignment to San Jose (August 4-6). . . . Traded by Giants to Philadelphia Phillies for P Jeff Juden and OF/1B Tommy Eason (October 6, 1995).
RECORDS: Holds modern major league record for most hits in three consecutive games—14 (June 11 [4], 13 [4]and 14 [6], 1995).
STATISTICAL NOTES: Led Pacific Coast League shortstops with 626 total chances in 1990. . . . Collected six hits in one game (June 14, 1995).

				BATTING											FIELDING			
Year	Team (League)	Pos.	G	AB	R	H	2B	3B	HR	RBI	Avg.	BB	SO	SB	PO	A	E	Avg.
1987—	Fresno (California)	SS	64	212	25	51	6	4	6	24	.241	24	71	6	89	188	21	.930
1988—	Shreveport (Texas)	SS	89	309	48	73	19	5	6	37	.236	22	63	14	134	248	11	.972
	—Phoenix (PCL)	SS	37	106	13	18	4	1	0	6	.170	13	32	2	41	74	4	.966

Year	Team (League)	Pos.	G	AB	R	H	2B	3B	HR	RBI	Avg.	BB	SO	SB	PO	A	E	Avg.
			BATTING												FIELDING			
1989—	Phoenix (PCL)	SS-2B	113	363	44	94	17	6	3	36	.259	18	82	10	149	332	15	.970
—	San Francisco (N.L.)	SS	14	6	6	1	0	0	0	0	.167	0	1	0	4	4	0	1.000
1990—	Phoenix (PCL)	SS	118	419	61	105	21	7	5	39	.251	25	89	13	*216	*386	24	.962
—	San Francisco (N.L.)	SS	22	56	7	12	3	1	2	3	.214	3	10	1	29	53	1	.988
1991—	San Francisco (N.L.)	SS-3B	54	106	12	13	3	0	2	8	.123	7	26	3	64	123	3	.984
—	Phoenix (PCL)	SS	64	226	34	46	13	2	6	31	.204	20	67	3	109	252	9	.976
1992—	San Francisco (N.L.)	SS-3B	40	75	4	13	2	1	1	3	.173	4	15	1	34	71	1	.991
—	Phoenix (PCL)	SS-2B	31	108	15	33	10	2	0	17	.306	3	18	4	51	92	2	.986
1993—	San Francisco (N.L.)	SS-2B-3B	63	146	22	29	7	0	4	16	.199	9	23	0	74	133	5	.976
—	San Jose (Calif.)	SS-2B	2	8	1	0	0	0	0	0	.000	1	0	0	1	5	0	1.000
1994—	San Francisco (N.L.)	SS-2B-3B	38	62	9	16	5	1	1	9	.258	5	16	5	33	70	3	.972
1995—	San Francisco (N.L.)	3B-SS-2B	68	186	19	41	6	0	3	12	.220	8	51	11	51	121	4	.977
Major league totals (7 years)			299	637	79	125	26	3	13	51	.196	36	142	21	289	575	17	.981

BENNETT, ERIK — P

PERSONAL: Born September 13, 1968, in Yreka, Calif. . . . 6-2/205. . . . Throws right, bats right. . . . Full name: Erik Hans Bennett.
HIGH SCHOOL: Yreka (Calif.).
COLLEGE: Cal State Sacramento.
TRANSACTIONS/CAREER NOTES: Selected by Philadelphia Phillies organization in 17th round of free-agent draft (June 2, 1986); did not sign. . . . Selected by California Angels organization in fourth round of free-agent draft (June 5, 1989). . . . Claimed on waivers by Houston Astros (July 20, 1995). . . . Granted free agency (October 16, 1995).
STATISTICAL NOTES: Led Pacific Coast League with .900 winning percentage in 1995.

Year	Team (League)	W	L	Pct.	ERA	G	GS	CG	ShO	Sv.	IP	H	R	ER	BB	SO
1989—	Bend (Northwest)	6	8	.429	3.47	15	15	2	0	0	96	96	58	37	36	96
1990—	Quad City (Midw.)	7	7	.500	2.99	18	18	3	1	0	108 1/3	91	48	36	37	100
1991—	Palm Springs (Cal.)	2	3	.400	2.51	8	8	1	0	0	43	41	15	12	27	31
1992—	Quad City (Midw.)	3	3	.500	2.67	8	8	1	1	0	57 1/3	46	20	17	22	59
—	Palm Springs (Cal.)	4	2	.667	3.64	6	6	1	0	0	42	27	19	17	15	33
—	Midland (Texas)	1	3	.250	3.91	7	7	0	0	0	46	47	22	20	16	36
1993—	Midland (Texas)	5	4	.556	6.49	11	11	0	0	0	69 1/3	87	57	50	17	33
—	Vancouver (PCL)	6	6	.500	6.05	18	12	0	0	1	80 1/3	101	57	54	21	51
1994—	Vancouver (PCL)	1	4	.200	2.81	45	1	0	0	3	89 2/3	71	32	28	28	83
1995—	Vancouver (PCL)	6	0	1.000	4.26	28	0	0	0	2	50 2/3	44	24	24	18	39
—	California (A.L.)	0	0	...	0.00	1	0	0	0	0	1/3	0	0	0	0	0
—	Tucson (PCL)■	3	1	§.750	4.76	14	1	0	0	1	22 2/3	27	17	12	14	24
Major league totals (1 year)		0	0	...	0.00	1	0	0	0	0	1/3	0	0	0	0	0

BENNETT, GARY — C — PHILLIES

PERSONAL: Born April 17, 1972, in Waukegan, Ill. . . . 6-0/190. . . . Bats right, throws right. . . . Full name: Gary David Bennett Jr.
HIGH SCHOOL: East (Waukegan, Ill.).
TRANSACTIONS/CAREER NOTES: Selected by Philadelphia Phillies organization in 11th round of free-agent draft (June 4, 1990). . . . On Clearwater disabled list (September 5-15, 1993).
STATISTICAL NOTES: Led Eastern League with 22 passed balls in 1994. . . . Led Eastern League catchers with 13 double plays in 1995.

Year	Team (League)	Pos.	G	AB	R	H	2B	3B	HR	RBI	Avg.	BB	SO	SB	PO	A	E	Avg.
			BATTING												FIELDING			
1990—	Martinsville (App.)	C	16	52	3	14	2	1	0	10	.269	4	15	0	80	3	3	.965
1991—	Martinsville (App.)	C	41	136	15	32	7	0	1	16	.235	17	26	0	291	34	2	.994
1992—	Batavia (NYP)	C	47	146	22	30	2	0	0	12	.205	15	27	2	292	42	2	*.994
1993—	Spartanburg (SAL)	C	42	126	18	32	4	1	0	15	.254	12	22	0	199	35	2	.992
—	Clearwater (FSL)	C	17	55	5	18	0	0	1	6	.327	3	10	0	70	12	0	1.000
1994—	Clearwater (FSL)	C	19	55	6	13	3	0	0	10	.236	8	6	0	101	10	1	.991
—	Reading (Eastern)	C	63	208	13	48	9	0	3	22	.231	14	26	0	376	64	2	.995
1995—	Reading (Eastern)	C	86	271	27	64	11	0	4	40	.236	22	36	0	551	65	4	.994
—	Scran./W.B. (Int'l)	C	7	20	1	3	0	0	0	1	.150	2	2	0	38	4	0	1.000
—	Philadelphia (N.L.)	PH	1	1	0	0	0	0	0	0	.000	0	1	0	...	...	...	...
Major league totals (1 year)			1	1	0	0	0	0	0	0	.000	0	1	0	...	...	...	...

BENZINGER, TODD — 1B/OF

PERSONAL: Born February 11, 1963, in Dayton, Ky. . . . 6-1/195. . . . Bats both, throws right. . . . Full name: Todd Eric Benzinger. . . . Nephew of Don Gross, pitcher, Cincinnati Reds and Pittsburgh Pirates (1955-60). . . . Name pronounced BEN-zing-er.
HIGH SCHOOL: New Richmond (Richmond, O.).
TRANSACTIONS/CAREER NOTES: Selected by Boston Red Sox organization in fourth round of free-agent draft (June 8, 1981). . . . On disabled list (August 10, 1984-remainder of season; April 10-June 11, 1985; April 11-21 and June 26-July 17, 1986; and June 3-22, 1988). . . . Traded by Red Sox with P Jeff Sellers and a player to be named later to Cincinnati Reds for 1B Nick Esasky and P Rob Murphy (December 13, 1988); Reds acquired P Luis Vasquez to complete deal (January 12, 1989). . . . Traded by Reds to Kansas City Royals for 1B/OF Carmelo Martinez (July 11, 1991). . . . Traded by Royals to Los Angeles Dodgers for OF Chris Gwynn and 2B Domingo Mota (December 11, 1991). . . . Granted free agency (December 19, 1992). . . . Signed by San Francisco Giants (January 13, 1993). . . . Granted free agency (October 14, 1994). . . . Re-signed by Phoenix, Giants organization (April 8, 1995). . . . Released by Giants (May 15, 1995). . . . Signed by Columbus, New York Yankees organization (May 25, 1995). . . . Released by Columbus (June 9, 1995).
STATISTICAL NOTES: Switch-hit home runs in one game (August 30, 1993). . . . Career major league grand slams: 6.

Year Team (League)	Pos.	G	AB	R	H	2B	3B	HR	RBI	Avg.	BB	SO	SB	PO	A	E	Avg.
		BATTING												FIELDING			
1981—Elmira (NYP)	OF-1B	41	141	21	34	10	1	2	8	.241	20	32	4	131	9	2	.986
1982—Winst.-Salem (Car.)	OF-1B	121	443	54	97	19	1	5	46	.219	41	71	4	438	28	8	.983
1983—Winter Haven (FSL)	OF-1B-3B	125	480	56	134	34	5	7	68	.279	43	75	4	206	10	8	.964
1984—New Britain (East.)	OF-1B	110	391	49	101	25	5	10	60	.258	33	89	0	465	29	14	.972
1985—Pawtucket (Int'l)	OF	70	256	31	64	13	1	11	47	.250	12	49	0	106	3	3	.973
1986—Pawtucket (Int'l)	OF-1B	90	314	41	79	13	2	11	32	.252	23	76	7	156	4	2	.988
1987—Pawtucket (Int'l)	OF-1B	65	257	47	83	17	3	13	49	.323	16	41	7	256	16	2	.993
—Boston (A.L.)	OF-1B	73	223	36	62	11	1	8	43	.278	22	41	5	155	7	2	.988
1988—Boston (A.L.)	1B-OF-DH	120	405	47	103	28	1	13	70	.254	22	80	2	602	38	6	.991
1989—Cincinnati (N.L.)■	1B	161	*628	79	154	28	3	17	76	.245	44	120	3	1417	73	7	.995
1990—Cincinnati (N.L.)	1B-OF	118	376	35	95	14	2	5	46	.253	19	69	3	733	52	6	.992
1991—Cincinnati (N.L.)	1B-OF	51	123	7	23	3	2	1	11	.187	10	20	2	146	13	2	.988
—Kansas City (A.L.)■	1B-DH	78	293	29	86	15	3	2	40	.294	17	46	2	651	38	3	.996
1992—Los Angeles (N.L.)■	OF-1B	121	293	24	70	16	2	4	31	.239	15	54	2	263	18	1	.996
1993—San Fran. (N.L.)■	1B-OF-3B	86	177	25	51	7	2	6	26	.288	13	35	0	299	15	0	1.000
1994—San Francisco (N.L.)	1B	107	328	32	87	13	2	9	31	.265	17	84	2	780	54	5	.994
1995—San Francisco (N.L.)	1B	9	10	2	2	0	0	1	2	.200	2	3	0	15	0	0	1.000
—Columbus (Int'l)■	1B	12	50	4	14	3	0	1	4	.280	2	10	0	131	8	2	.986
American League totals (3 years)		271	921	112	251	54	5	23	153	.273	61	167	9	1408	83	11	.993
National League totals (7 years)		653	1935	204	482	81	13	43	223	.249	120	385	12	3653	225	21	.995
Major league totals (9 years)		924	2856	316	733	135	18	66	376	.257	181	552	21	5061	308	32	.994

CHAMPIONSHIP SERIES RECORD

Year Team (League)	Pos.	G	AB	R	H	2B	3B	HR	RBI	Avg.	BB	SO	SB	PO	A	E	Avg.
		BATTING												FIELDING			
1988—Boston (A.L.)	1B-PH	4	11	0	1	0	0	0	0	.091	1	3	0	21	1	0	1.000
1990—Cincinnati (N.L.)	PH-1B	5	9	0	3	0	0	0	0	.333	2	0	0	17	0	0	1.000
Championship series totals (2 years)		9	20	0	4	0	0	0	0	.200	3	3	0	38	1	0	1.000

WORLD SERIES RECORD

NOTES: Member of World Series championship team (1990).

Year Team (League)	Pos.	G	AB	R	H	2B	3B	HR	RBI	Avg.	BB	SO	SB	PO	A	E	Avg.
		BATTING												FIELDING			
1990—Cincinnati (N.L.)	1B-PH	4	11	1	2	0	0	0	0	.182	0	0	0	24	0	0	1.000

BERE, JASON — P — WHITE SOX

PERSONAL: Born May 26, 1971, in Cambridge, Mass. . . . 6-3/185. . . . Throws right, bats right. . . . Full name: Jason Phillip Bere. . . . Name pronounced burr-AY.

HIGH SCHOOL: Wilmington (Mass.).

JUNIOR COLLEGE: Middlesex Community College (Mass.).

TRANSACTIONS/CAREER NOTES: Selected by Chicago White Sox organization in 36th round of free-agent draft (June 4, 1990). . . . On Chicago disabled list (August 5-20, 1995); included rehabilitation assignment to South Bend (August 13-18).

Year Team (League)	W	L	Pct.	ERA	G	GS	CG	ShO	Sv.	IP	H	R	ER	BB	SO
1990—GC White Sox (GCL)	0	4	.000	2.37	16	2	0	0	1	38	26	19	10	19	41
1991—South Bend (Midw.)	9	12	.429	2.87	27	27	2	1	0	163	116	66	52	*100	158
1992—Sarasota (Fla. St.)	7	2	.778	2.41	18	18	1	1	0	116	84	35	31	34	106
—Birmingham (Sou.)	4	4	.500	3.00	8	8	4	2	0	54	44	22	18	20	45
—Vancouver (PCL)	0	0	...	0.00	1	0	0	0	0	1	2	0	0	0	2
1993—Nashville (A.A.)	5	1	.833	2.37	8	8	0	0	0	49 1/3	36	19	13	25	52
—Chicago (A.L.)	12	5	.706	3.47	24	24	1	0	0	142 2/3	109	60	55	81	129
1994—Chicago (A.L.)	12	2	*.857	3.81	24	24	0	0	0	141 2/3	119	65	60	80	127
1995—Chicago (A.L.)	8	•15	.348	7.19	27	27	1	0	0	137 2/3	151	120	110	106	110
—Nashville (A.A.)	1	0	1.000	3.38	1	1	0	0	0	5 1/3	6	2	2	2	7
Major league totals (3 years)	32	22	.593	4.80	75	75	2	0	0	422	379	245	225	267	366

CHAMPIONSHIP SERIES RECORD

Year Team (League)	W	L	Pct.	ERA	G	GS	CG	ShO	Sv.	IP	H	R	ER	BB	SO
1993—Chicago (A.L.)	0	0	...	11.57	1	1	0	0	0	2 1/3	5	3	3	2	3

ALL-STAR GAME RECORD

Year League	W	L	Pct.	ERA	GS	CG	ShO	Sv.	IP	H	R	ER	BB	SO
1994—American	0	1	.000	...	0	0	0	0	0	2	1	1	0	0

BERGMAN, SEAN — P — TIGERS

PERSONAL: Born April 11, 1970, in Joliet, Ill. . . . 6-4/205. . . . Throws right, bats right. . . . Full name: Sean Frederick Bergman.

HIGH SCHOOL: Joliet (Ill.) Catholic Academy.

COLLEGE: Southern Illinois.

TRANSACTIONS/CAREER NOTES: Selected by Detroit Tigers organization in fourth round of free-agent draft (June 3, 1991). . . . On Detroit disabled list (June 26-July 17, 1995); included rehabilitation assignment to Toledo (July 10-17).

Year Team (League)	W	L	Pct.	ERA	G	GS	CG	ShO	Sv.	IP	H	R	ER	BB	SO
1991—Niag. Falls (NYP)	5	7	.417	4.46	15	15	0	0	0	84 2/3	87	57	42	42	77
1992—Lakeland (Fla. St.)	5	2	.714	2.49	13	13	0	0	0	83	61	28	23	14	67
—London (Eastern)	4	7	.364	4.28	14	14	1	0	0	88 1/3	85	52	42	45	59
1993—Toledo (Int'l)	8	9	.471	4.38	19	19	3	0	0	117	124	62	57	53	91
—Detroit (A.L.)	1	4	.200	5.67	9	6	1	0	0	39 2/3	47	29	25	23	19

Year	Team (League)	W	L	Pct.	ERA	G	GS	CG	ShO	Sv.	IP	H	R	ER	BB	SO
1994—	Toledo (Int'l)	11	8	.579	3.72	25	25	2	0	0	154 2/3	147	77	64	53	145
	— Detroit (A.L.)	2	1	.667	5.60	3	3	0	0	0	17 2/3	22	11	11	7	12
1995—	Detroit (A.L.)	7	10	.412	5.12	28	28	1	1	0	135 1/3	169	95	77	67	86
	— Toledo (Int'l)	0	1	.000	6.00	1	1	0	0	0	3	4	2	2	0	4
Major league totals (3 years)		10	15	.400	5.28	40	37	2	1	0	192 2/3	238	135	113	97	117

BERROA, GERONIMO — OF/DH — ATHLETICS

PERSONAL: Born March 18, 1965, in Santo Domingo, Dominican Republic. . . . 6-0/195. . . . Bats right, throws right. . . . Full name: Geronimo Emiliano Berroa. . . . Name pronounced her-ON-i-mo bur-OH-uh.

TRANSACTIONS/CAREER NOTES: Signed as non-drafted free agent by Toronto Blue Jays organization (September 4, 1983). . . . Selected by Atlanta Braves from Blue Jays organization in Rule 5 major league draft (December 5, 1988). . . . Released by Braves (February 1, 1991). . . . Signed by Calgary, Seattle Mariners organization (February 27, 1991). . . . Contract sold by Mariners organization to Colorado Springs, Cleveland Indians organization (March 28, 1991). . . . Granted free agency (October 15, 1991). . . . Signed by Nashville, Cincinnati Reds organization (October 31, 1991). . . . Released by Reds (November 20, 1992). . . . Signed by Florida Marlins (December 9, 1992). . . . Granted free agency (October 15, 1993). . . . Signed by Oakland Athletics organization (January 20, 1994). . . . On disabled list (August 2, 1994-remainder of season).

STATISTICAL NOTES: Led Southern League with 297 total bases in 1987. . . . Led International League in being hit by pitch with 10 and tied for lead in sacrifice flies with eight in 1988. . . . Led International League in grounding into double plays with 17 in 1990. . . . Career major league grand slams: 1.

			BATTING												FIELDING			
Year	Team (League)	Pos.	G	AB	R	H	2B	3B	HR	RBI	Avg.	BB	SO	SB	PO	A	E	Avg.
1984—	GC Blue Jays (GCL)	OF-1B	62	235	31	59	16	1	3	34	.251	12	34	2	104	2	5	.955
1985—	Kinston (Carolina)	OF	19	43	4	8	0	0	1	4	.186	4	10	0	13	1	1	.933
	— Medicine Hat (Pio.)	OF	54	201	39	69	*22	2	6	45	.343	18	40	7	58	3	3	.953
	— Florence (S. Atl.)	OF	19	66	7	21	2	0	3	20	.318	6	13	0	24	0	2	.923
1986—	Ventura (Calif.)	OF	128	459	76	137	22	5	21	73	.298	38	92	12	194	9	14	.935
	— Knoxville (South.)	OF	1	4	0	0	0	0	0	0	.000	0	1	0	2	0	0	1.000
1987—	Knoxville (South.)	OF	134	523	87	150	33	3	36	108	.287	46	104	2	236	6	•15	.942
1988—	Syracuse (Int'l)	OF	131	470	55	122	•29	1	8	64	.260	38	88	7	243	12	5	.981
1989—	Atlanta (N.L.)■	OF	81	136	7	36	4	0	2	9	.265	7	32	0	67	1	2	.971
1990—	Richmond (Int'l)	OF	135	499	56	134	17	2	12	80	.269	34	89	4	200	10	7	.968
	— Atlanta (N.L.)	OF	7	4	0	0	0	0	0	0	.000	1	1	0	1	0	0	1.000
1991—	Colo. Springs (PCL)■	OF	125	478	81	154	31	7	18	91	.322	35	88	2	151	14	5	.971
1992—	Nashville (A.A.)■	OF	112	461	73	151	33	2	22	88	.328	32	69	8	194	16	5	.977
	— Cincinnati (N.L.)	OF	13	15	2	4	1	0	0	0	.267	2	1	0	2	1	0	1.000
1993—	Edmonton (PCL)■	OF-1B	90	327	64	107	33	4	16	68	.327	36	71	1	210	10	7	.969
	— Florida (N.L.)	OF	14	34	3	4	1	0	0	0	.118	2	7	0	9	1	2	.833
1994—	Oakland (A.L.)■	DH-OF-1B	96	340	55	104	18	2	13	65	.306	41	62	7	131	5	1	.993
1995—	Oakland (A.L.)	DH-OF	141	546	87	152	22	3	22	88	.278	63	98	7	129	5	4	.971
American League totals (2 years)			237	886	142	256	40	5	35	153	.289	104	160	14	260	10	5	.982
National League totals (4 years)			115	189	12	44	6	0	2	9	.233	12	41	0	79	3	4	.953
Major league totals (6 years)			352	1075	154	300	46	5	37	162	.279	116	201	14	339	13	9	.975

BERRY, SEAN — 3B — ASTROS

PERSONAL: Born March 22, 1966, in Santa Monica, Calif. . . . 5-11/200. . . . Bats right, throws right. . . . Full name: Sean Robert Berry.

HIGH SCHOOL: West Torrance (Torrance, Calif.).

COLLEGE: UCLA.

TRANSACTIONS/CAREER NOTES: Selected by Boston Red Sox organization in fourth round of free-agent draft (June 4, 1984); did not sign. . . . Selected by Kansas City Royals organization in secondary phase of free-agent draft (January 14, 1986). . . . On disabled list (April 16-May 3, 1987). . . . Traded by Royals with P Archie Corbin to Montreal Expos for P Bill Sampen and P Chris Haney (August 29, 1992). . . . Traded by Expos to Houston Astros for P Dave Veres and C Raul Chavez (December 20, 1995).

STATISTICAL NOTES: Led Northwest League third basemen with 11 double plays in 1986. . . . Career major league grand slams: 1.

			BATTING												FIELDING			
Year	Team (League)	Pos.	G	AB	R	H	2B	3B	HR	RBI	Avg.	BB	SO	SB	PO	A	E	Avg.
1986—	Eugene (N'west)	3B	65	238	53	76	20	2	5	44	.319	44	72	10	*63	96	21	.883
1987—	Fort Myers (FSL)	3B	66	205	26	52	7	2	2	30	.254	46	65	5	39	101	23	.859
1988—	Baseball City (FSL)	3B-SS-OF	94	304	34	71	6	4	4	30	.234	31	62	24	84	161	28	.897
1989—	Baseball City (FSL)	3-0-2-S	116	399	67	106	19	7	4	44	.266	44	68	37	100	199	24	.926
1990—	Memphis (South.)	3B	135	487	73	142	25	4	14	77	.292	44	89	18	79	238	27	.922
	— Kansas City (A.L.)	3B	8	23	2	5	1	1	0	4	.217	2	5	0	7	10	1	.944
1991—	Omaha (A.A.)	3B-SS-2B	103	368	62	97	21	9	11	54	.264	48	70	8	75	206	20	.934
	— Kansas City (A.L.)	3B	31	60	5	8	3	0	0	1	.133	5	23	0	13	52	2	.970
1992—	Omaha (A.A.)	3B	122	439	61	126	22	2	21	77	.287	39	87	6	86	239	21	*.939
	— Montreal (N.L.)■	3B	24	57	5	19	1	0	1	4	.333	1	11	2	10	19	4	.879
1993—	Montreal (N.L.)	3B	122	299	50	78	15	2	14	49	.261	41	70	12	66	153	15	.936
1994—	Montreal (N.L.)	3B	103	320	43	89	19	2	11	41	.278	32	50	14	66	147	14	.938
1995—	Montreal (N.L.)	3B-1B	103	314	38	100	22	1	14	55	.318	25	53	3	76	165	12	.953
American League totals (2 years)			39	83	7	13	4	1	0	5	.157	7	28	0	20	62	3	.965
National League totals (4 years)			352	990	136	286	57	5	40	149	.289	99	184	31	218	484	45	.940
Major league totals (6 years)			391	1073	143	299	61	6	40	154	.279	106	212	31	238	546	48	.942

BERRYHILL, DAMON — C — REDS

PERSONAL: Born December 3, 1963, in South Laguna, Calif. . . . 6-0/205. . . . Bats both, throws right. . . . Full name: Damon Scott Berryhill.

HIGH SCHOOL: Laguna Beach (Calif.).
COLLEGE: Orange Coast College (Calif.).
TRANSACTIONS/CAREER NOTES: Selected by Chicago White Sox organization in 13th round of free-agent draft (January 11, 1983); did not sign. . . . Selected by Chicago Cubs organization in first round (fourth pick overall) of free-agent draft (January 17, 1984). . . . On Chicago disabled list (June 30-July 15, 1988). . . . On Chicago disabled list (March 9-May 1, 1989); included rehabilitation assignment to Iowa (April 24-May 1). . . . On Chicago disabled list (August 19-September 29, 1989). . . . On Chicago disabled list (April 8-August 15, 1990); included rehabilitation assignments to Peoria (July 16-23) and Iowa (July 24-August 4). . . . Traded by Cubs with P Mike Bielecki to Atlanta Braves for P Turk Wendell and P Yorkis Perez (September 29, 1991). . . . Granted free agency (December 20, 1993). . . . Signed by Pawtucket, Boston Red Sox organization (February 1, 1994). . . . Granted free agency (October 31, 1994). . . . Signed by Indianapolis, Cincinnati Reds organization (November 4, 1994). . . . On disabled list (July 24-September 1, 1995).
STATISTICAL NOTES: Led Carolina League with 18 passed balls in 1985. . . . Led American Association catchers with .990 fielding percentage, 603 putouts, 66 assists, 676 total chances, 11 double plays and 15 passed balls in 1987. . . . Career major league grand slams: 1.
MISCELLANEOUS: Batted righthanded only (1984).

		BATTING												FIELDING			
Year Team (League)	Pos.	G	AB	R	H	2B	3B	HR	RBI	Avg.	BB	SO	SB	PO	A	E	Avg.
1984—Quad Cities (Mid.)	C-1B	62	217	30	60	14	0	0	31	.276	16	44	4	314	31	8	.977
1985—Winst.-Salem (Car.)	C-1B	117	386	31	90	25	1	9	50	.233	32	90	4	625	71	11	.984
1986—Pittsfield (Eastern)	C-OF	112	345	33	71	13	1	6	35	.206	37	54	2	449	61	12	.977
1987—Iowa (Am. Assoc.)	C-1B	121	429	54	123	22	1	18	67	.287	32	58	5	†607	†67	7	†.990
—Chicago (N.L.)	C	12	28	2	5	1	0	0	1	.179	3	5	0	37	3	4	.909
1988—Iowa (Am. Assoc.)	C	21	73	11	16	5	1	2	11	.219	7	21	0	117	15	0	1.000
—Chicago (N.L.)	C	95	309	19	80	19	1	7	38	.259	17	56	1	448	54	9	.982
1989—Iowa (Am. Assoc.)	C	7	30	4	6	1	0	2	4	.200	1	8	0	40	5	2	.957
—Chicago (N.L.)	C	91	334	37	86	13	0	5	41	.257	16	54	1	473	41	4	.992
1990—Peoria (Midwest)	C	7	26	10	10	2	0	3	8	.385	3	6	0	75	4	1	.988
—Iowa (Am. Assoc.)	C	22	79	8	17	1	0	3	6	.215	4	18	0	115	13	2	.985
—Chicago (N.L.)	C	17	53	6	10	4	0	1	9	.189	5	14	0	87	3	2	.978
1991—Chicago (N.L.)	C	62	159	13	30	7	0	5	14	.189	11	41	1	211	24	8	.967
—Iowa (Am. Assoc.)	C	26	97	20	32	4	1	8	24	.330	12	25	0	90	14	2	.981
—Atlanta (N.L.)■	C	1	1	0	0	0	0	0	0	.000	0	1	0	3	0	0	1.000
1992—Atlanta (N.L.)	C	101	307	21	70	16	1	10	43	.228	17	67	0	426	31	1	.998
1993—Atlanta (N.L.)	C	115	335	24	82	18	2	8	43	.245	21	64	0	570	52	6	.990
1994—Boston (A.L.)■	C-DH	82	255	30	67	17	2	6	34	.263	19	59	0	409	29	2	.995
1995—Cincinnati (N.L.)■	C-1B	34	82	6	15	3	0	2	11	.183	10	19	0	153	12	2	.988
American League totals (1 year)		82	255	30	67	17	2	6	34	.263	19	59	0	409	29	2	.995
National League totals (8 years)		528	1608	128	378	81	4	38	200	.235	100	321	3	2408	220	36	.986
Major league totals (9 years)		610	1863	158	445	98	6	44	234	.239	119	380	3	2817	249	38	.988

CHAMPIONSHIP SERIES RECORD

		BATTING												FIELDING			
Year Team (League)	Pos.	G	AB	R	H	2B	3B	HR	RBI	Avg.	BB	SO	SB	PO	A	E	Avg.
1992—Atlanta (N.L.)	C	7	24	1	4	1	0	0	1	.167	3	2	0	43	5	0	1.000
1993—Atlanta (N.L.)	C	6	19	2	4	0	0	1	3	.211	1	5	0	42	0	0	1.000
Championship series totals (2 years)		13	43	3	8	1	0	1	4	.186	4	7	0	85	5	0	1.000

WORLD SERIES RECORD

		BATTING												FIELDING			
Year Team (League)	Pos.	G	AB	R	H	2B	3B	HR	RBI	Avg.	BB	SO	SB	PO	A	E	Avg.
1992—Atlanta (N.L.)	C	6	22	1	2	0	0	1	3	.091	1	11	0	32	3	0	1.000

BERTOTTI, MIKE — P — WHITE SOX

PERSONAL: Born January 18, 1970, in Jersey City, N.J. . . . 6-1/185. . . . Throws left, bats left. . . . Full name: Michael David Bertotti.
COLLEGE: Iona.
TRANSACTIONS/CAREER NOTES: Selected by Chicago White Sox organization in 31st round of free-agent draft (June 3, 1991).

Year Team (League)	W	L	Pct.	ERA	G	GS	CG	ShO	Sv.	IP	H	R	ER	BB	SO
1991—Utica (NYP)	3	4	.429	5.79	14	5	0	0	0	37 1/3	38	33	24	36	33
1992—Utica (NYP)	2	2	.500	6.21	17	1	0	0	1	33 1/3	36	28	23	31	23
—South Bend (Midw.)	0	3	.000	3.72	11	0	0	0	1	19 1/3	12	8	8	22	17
1993—Hickory (S. Atl.)	3	3	.500	2.11	9	9	0	0	0	59 2/3	42	19	14	29	77
—South Bend (Midw.)	5	7	.417	3.49	17	16	2	2	0	111	93	51	43	44	108
1994—Prin. William (Caro.)	7	6	.538	3.53	16	15	2	1	0	104 2/3	90	48	41	43	103
—Birmingham (Sou.)	4	3	.571	2.90	10	10	1	1	0	68 1/3	55	25	22	21	44
1995—Birmingham (Sou.)	2	7	.222	5.00	12	12	1	0	0	63	60	38	35	36	53
—Nashville (A.A.)	2	3	.400	8.72	7	6	0	0	0	32	41	34	31	17	35
—Chicago (A.L.)	1	1	.500	12.56	4	4	0	0	0	14 1/3	23	20	20	11	15
Major league totals (1 year)	1	1	.500	12.56	4	4	0	0	0	14 1/3	23	20	20	11	15

BERUMEN, ANDRES — P — PADRES

PERSONAL: Born April 5, 1971, in Tijuana, Mexico. . . . 6-2/205. . . . Throws right, bats right. . . . Name pronounced buh-ROOM-un.
HIGH SCHOOL: Banning (Calif.).
TRANSACTIONS/CAREER NOTES: Selected by Kansas City Royals organization in 27th round of free-agent draft (June 5, 1989). . . . On Appleton disabled list (July 11-28, 1991). . . . Selected by Florida Marlins in second round (45th pick overall) of expansion draft (November 17, 1992). . . . Traded by Marlins with P Trevor Hoffman and P Jose Martinez to San Diego Padres for 3B Gary Sheffield and P Rich Rodriguez (June 24, 1993). . . . On Wichita disabled list (August 11, 1993-remainder of season). . . . On disabled list (May 4-13, 1994). . . . On San Diego disabled list (August 11, 1995-remainder of season); included rehabilitation assignment to Rancho Cucamonga (August 18-remainder of season).

Year	Team (League)	W	L	Pct.	ERA	G	GS	CG	ShO	Sv.	IP	H	R	ER	BB	SO
1989—	GC Royals (GCL)	2	4	.333	4.78	12	10	0	0	0	49	57	29	26	17	24
1990—	GC Royals (GCL)	0	2	.000	2.38	5	4	0	0	1	22 2/3	24	9	6	8	18
	— Baseball City (FSL)	3	5	.375	4.30	9	9	1	1	0	44	30	27	21	28	35
1991—	Appleton (Midw.)	2	6	.250	3.51	13	13	0	0	0	56 1/3	55	33	22	26	49
	— Baseball City (FSL)	0	5	.000	4.14	7	7	0	0	0	37	34	18	17	18	24
1992—	Appleton (Midw.)	5	2	.714	2.65	46	0	0	0	13	57 2/3	50	25	17	23	52
1993—	High Desert (Calif.)■	9	2	*.818	3.62	14	13	1	0	0	92	85	45	37	36	74
	— Wichita (Texas)■	3	1	.750	5.74	7	7	0	0	0	26 2/3	35	17	17	11	17
1994—	Las Vegas (PCL)	4	7	.364	6.54	43	6	0	0	1	75 2/3	93	70	55	57	49
1995—	San Diego (N.L.)	2	3	.400	5.68	37	0	0	0	1	44 1/3	37	29	28	36	42
	— Las Vegas (PCL)	0	0	...	5.40	3	0	0	0	0	3 1/3	4	2	2	2	3
	— Rancho Cuca. (Cal.)	0	0	...	2.45	4	0	0	0	1	7 1/3	6	2	2	1	11
Major league totals (1 year)		2	3	.400	5.68	37	0	0	0	1	44 1/3	37	29	28	36	42

BETTI, RICH — P — RED SOX

PERSONAL: Born September 16, 1973, in Natick, Mass. . . . 5-11/170. . . . Throws left, bats right. . . . Full name: Richard Paul Betti.
JUNIOR COLLEGE: Quinsigamond (Mass.).
TRANSACTIONS/CAREER NOTES: Selected by Atlanta Braves organization in 26th round of free-agent draft (June 3, 1993). . . . Released by Braves organization (March 27, 1994). . . . Signed by Boston Red Sox organization (July 11, 1995).

Year	Team (League)	W	L	Pct.	ERA	G	GS	CG	ShO	Sv.	IP	H	R	ER	BB	SO
1993—	GC Braves (GCL)	1	0	1.000	0.89	9	2	0	0	2	20 1/3	10	5	2	8	27
	— Danville (Appal.)	2	1	.667	2.10	11	5	0	0	0	34 1/3	20	13	8	19	28
1994—		Out of organized baseball.														
1995—	GC Red Sox (GCL)■	1	0	1.000	2.45	3	1	0	0	1	7 1/3	7	3	2	3	13
	— Utica (NYP)	2	1	.667	1.02	12	0	0	0	2	17 2/3	9	2	2	2	25
	— Michigan (Midwest)	0	0	...	0.00	1	0	0	0	0	2	0	0	0	1	1

BEVIL, BRIAN — P — ROYALS

PERSONAL: Born September 5, 1971, in Houston. . . . 6-3/190. . . . Throws right, bats right. . . . Full name: Brian Scott Bevil.
HIGH SCHOOL: MacArthur (Houston).
COLLEGE: Angelina (Tex.).
TRANSACTIONS/CAREER NOTES: Selected by Kansas City Royals organization in 30th round of free-agent draft (June 4, 1990). . . . On Memphis disabled list (July 24-1993-remainder of season). . . . On Wichita temporarily inactive list (April 24-May 9, 1995).

Year	Team (League)	W	L	Pct.	ERA	G	GS	CG	ShO	Sv.	IP	H	R	ER	BB	SO
1991—	GC Royals (GCL)	5	3	.625	1.93	13	12	2	0	0	65 1/3	56	20	14	19	70
1992—	Appleton (Midw.)	9	7	.563	3.40	26	26	4	•2	0	156	129	67	59	63	168
1993—	Wilmington (Caro.)	7	1	.875	2.30	12	12	2	0	0	74 1/3	46	21	19	23	61
	— Memphis (South.)	3	3	.500	4.36	6	6	0	0	0	33	36	17	16	14	26
1994—	Memphis (South.)	5	4	.556	3.51	17	17	0	0	0	100	75	42	39	40	78
1995—	Wichita (Texas)	5	7	.417	5.84	15	15	0	0	0	74	85	51	48	35	57
	— Omaha (Am. Assoc.)	1	3	.250	9.41	6	6	0	0	0	22	40	31	23	14	10

BICHETTE, DANTE — OF — ROCKIES

PERSONAL: Born November 18, 1963, in West Palm Beach, Fla. . . . 6-3/235. . . . Bats right, throws right. . . . Full name: Alphonse Dante Bichette. . . . Name pronounced bih-SHETT.
HIGH SCHOOL: Jupiter (Fla.).
JUNIOR COLLEGE: Palm Beach Community College (Fla.).
TRANSACTIONS/CAREER NOTES: Selected by California Angels organization in 17th round of free-agent draft (June 4, 1984). . . . Traded by Angels to Milwaukee Brewers for DH Dave Parker (March 14, 1991). . . . Traded by Brewers to Colorado Rockies for OF Kevin Reimer (November 17, 1992).
HONORS: Named outfielder on The Sporting News N.L. All-Star team (1995). . . . Named outfielder on The Sporting News N.L. Silver Slugger team (1995).
STATISTICAL NOTES: Led A.L. outfielders with seven double plays in 1991. . . . Led N.L. outfielders with four double plays in 1994. . . . Led N.L. with .620 slugging percentage in 1995. . . . Led N.L. with 359 total bases in 1995. . . . Career major league grand slams: 4.

			BATTING												FIELDING			
Year	Team (League)	Pos.	G	AB	R	H	2B	3B	HR	RBI	Avg.	BB	SO	SB	PO	A	E	Avg.
1984—	Salem (Northwest)	OF-1B-3B	64	250	27	58	9	2	4	30	.232	6	53	6	224	24	11	.958
1985—	Quad Cities (Mid.)	1B-OF-C	137	547	58	145	28	4	11	78	.265	25	89	25	300	21	15	.955
1986—	Palm Springs (Cal.)	OF-3B	68	290	39	79	15	0	10	73	.272	21	53	2	78	68	11	.930
	— Midland (Texas)	OF-3B	62	243	43	69	16	2	12	36	.284	18	50	3	131	30	11	.936
1987—	Edmonton (PCL)	OF-3B	92	360	54	108	20	3	13	50	.300	26	68	3	169	21	9	.955
1988—	Edmonton (PCL)	OF	132	509	64	136	29	•10	14	81	.267	25	78	7	218	*22	*15	.941
	— California (A.L.)	OF	21	46	1	12	2	0	0	8	.261	0	7	0	44	2	1	.979
1989—	California (A.L.)	OF-DH	48	138	13	29	7	0	3	15	.210	6	24	3	95	6	1	.990
	— Edmonton (PCL)	OF	61	226	39	55	11	2	11	40	.243	24	39	4	92	9	1	.990
1990—	California (A.L.)	OF	109	349	40	89	15	1	15	53	.255	16	79	5	183	12	7	.965
1991—	Milwaukee (A.L.)■	OF-3B	134	445	53	106	18	3	15	59	.238	22	107	14	270	14	7	.976
1992—	Milwaukee (A.L.)	OF-DH	112	387	37	111	27	2	5	41	.287	16	74	18	188	6	2	.990
1993—	Colorado (N.L.)■	OF	141	538	93	167	43	5	21	89	.310	28	99	14	308	14	9	.973
1994—	Colorado (N.L.)	OF	*116	*484	74	147	33	2	27	95	.304	19	70	21	211	10	2	.991
1995—	Colorado (N.L.)	OF	139	579	102	•197	38	2	*40	*128	.340	22	96	13	208	9	3	.986
American League totals (5 years)			424	1365	144	347	69	6	38	176	.254	60	291	40	780	40	18	.979
National League totals (3 years)			396	1601	269	511	114	9	88	312	.319	69	265	48	727	33	14	.982
Major league totals (8 years)			820	2966	413	858	183	15	126	488	.289	129	556	88	1507	73	32	.980

DIVISION SERIES RECORD

Year	Team (League)	Pos.	G	AB	R	H	2B	3B	HR	RBI	Avg.	BB	SO	SB	PO	A	E	Avg.
			BATTING												FIELDING			
1995	Colorado (N.L.)	OF	4	17	6	10	3	0	1	3	.588	1	3	0	9	0	0	1.000

ALL-STAR GAME RECORD

Year	League	Pos.	AB	R	H	2B	3B	HR	RBI	Avg.	BB	SO	SB	PO	A	E	Avg.
			BATTING											FIELDING			
1994	National	PH	1	0	1	0	0	0	0	1.000	0	0	0	...	...	...	...
1995	National	OF	1	0	0	0	0	0	0	.000	0	1	0	2	0	0	1.000
All-Star Game totals (2 years)			2	0	1	0	0	0	0	.500	0	1	0	2	0	0	1.000

BIELECKI, MIKE — P

PERSONAL: Born July 31, 1959, in Baltimore. . . . 6-3/195. . . . Throws right, bats right. . . . Full name: Michael Joseph Bielecki. . . . Name pronounced bill-LECK-ee.

HIGH SCHOOL: Dundalk (Baltimore).

JUNIOR COLLEGE: Valencia Community College (Fla.).

COLLEGE: Loyola College (Md.).

TRANSACTIONS/CAREER NOTES: Selected by Kansas City Royals organization in sixth round of free-agent draft (January 9, 1979); did not sign. . . . Selected by Pittsburgh Pirates organization in secondary phase of free-agent draft (June 5, 1979). . . . Traded by Pirates to Chicago Cubs for P Mike Curtis (March 31, 1988). . . . Traded by Cubs with C Damon Berryhill to Atlanta Braves for P Turk Wendell and P Yorkis Perez (September 29, 1991). . . . On disabled list (July 29, 1992-remainder of season). . . . Granted free agency (October 30, 1992). . . . Signed by Cleveland Indians (December 14, 1992). . . . Released by Indians (June 19, 1993). . . . Signed by Rochester, Baltimore Orioles organization (June 29, 1993). . . . Released by Rochester (August 15, 1993). . . . Signed by Braves organization (February 10, 1994). . . . Granted free agency (October 12, 1994). . . . Signed by Vancouver, California Angels organization (April 18, 1995). . . . On California disabled list (July 17, 1995-remainder of season); included rehabilitation assignments to Lake Elsinore (August 18-24) and Vancouver (August 24-September 1). . . . Granted free agency (November 1, 1995).

STATISTICAL NOTES: Tied for Eastern League lead with 24 home runs allowed in 1982.

Year	Team (League)	W	L	Pct.	ERA	G	GS	CG	ShO	Sv.	IP	H	R	ER	BB	SO
1979	GC Pirates (GCL)	1	4	.200	2.29	9	9	1	0	0	51	48	21	13	21	35
1980	Shelby (S. Atl.)	3	5	.375	4.55	29	6	1	0	3	99	106	60	50	58	78
1981	Greenwood (S. Atl.)	12	11	.522	3.42	28	•28	10	2	0	192	172	95	73	82	163
1982	Buffalo (Eastern)	7	12	.368	4.86	25	25	4	0	0	157 1/3	165	96	•85	75	135
1983	Lynn (Eastern)	•15	7	.682	3.19	25	25	7	1	0	163 2/3	126	73	58	69	*143
1984	Hawaii (Pac. Coast)	*19	3	.864	2.97	28	28	9	2	0	187 2/3	162	70	62	88	*162
—	Pittsburgh (N.L.)	0	0	...	0.00	4	0	0	0	0	4 1/3	4	0	0	0	1
1985	Pittsburgh (N.L.)	2	3	.400	4.53	12	7	0	0	0	45 2/3	45	26	23	31	22
—	Hawaii (Pac. Coast)	8	6	.571	3.83	20	20	2	0	0	129 1/3	117	58	55	56	111
1986	Pittsburgh (N.L.)	6	11	.353	4.66	31	27	0	0	0	148 2/3	149	87	77	83	83
1987	Vancouver (PCL)	12	10	.545	3.78	26	26	3	3	0	181	194	89	76	78	140
—	Pittsburgh (N.L.)	2	3	.400	4.73	8	8	2	0	0	45 2/3	43	25	24	12	25
1988	Chicago (N.L.)■	2	2	.500	3.35	19	5	0	0	0	48 1/3	55	22	18	16	33
—	Iowa (Am. Assoc.)	3	2	.600	2.63	23	3	1	1	5	54 2/3	34	19	16	20	50
1989	Chicago (N.L.)	18	7	.720	3.14	33	33	4	3	0	212 1/3	187	82	74	81	147
1990	Chicago (N.L.)	8	11	.421	4.93	36	29	0	0	1	168	188	101	92	70	103
1991	Chicago (N.L.)	13	11	.542	4.50	39	25	0	0	0	172	169	91	86	54	72
—	Atlanta (N.L.)■	0	0	...	0.00	2	0	0	0	0	1 2/3	2	0	0	2	3
1992	Atlanta (N.L.)	2	4	.333	2.57	19	14	1	1	0	80 2/3	77	27	23	27	62
1993	Cleveland (A.L.)■	4	5	.444	5.90	13	13	0	0	0	68 2/3	90	47	45	23	38
—	Rochester (Int'l)■	5	3	.625	5.03	9	9	0	0	0	48 1/3	56	33	27	16	31
1994	Atlanta (N.L.)■	2	0	1.000	4.00	19	1	0	0	0	27	28	12	12	12	18
1995	California (A.L.)■	4	6	.400	5.97	22	11	0	0	0	75 1/3	80	56	50	31	45
—	Lake Elsinore (California)	0	0	...	4.91	3	2	0	0	0	3 2/3	2	2	2	2	2
—	Vancouver (PCL)	1	0	1.000	0.00	3	1	0	0	0	5	2	3	0	2	4
A.L. totals (2 years)		8	11	.421	5.94	35	24	0	0	0	144	170	103	95	54	83
N.L. totals (10 years)		55	52	.514	4.05	222	149	7	4	1	954 1/3	947	473	429	388	569
Major league totals (12 years)		63	63	.500	4.29	257	173	7	4	1	1098 1/3	1117	576	524	442	652

CHAMPIONSHIP SERIES RECORD

Year	Team (League)	W	L	Pct.	ERA	G	GS	CG	ShO	Sv.	IP	H	R	ER	BB	SO
1989	Chicago (N.L.)	0	1	.000	3.65	2	2	0	0	0	12 1/3	7	5	5	6	11

BIGGIO, CRAIG — 2B — ASTROS

PERSONAL: Born December 14, 1965, in Smithtown, N.Y. . . . 5-11/180. . . . Bats right, throws right. . . . Full name: Craig Alan Biggio. . . . Name pronounced BEE-jee-oh.

HIGH SCHOOL: Kings Park (N.Y.).

COLLEGE: Seton Hall.

TRANSACTIONS/CAREER NOTES: Selected by Houston Astros organization in first round (22nd pick overall) of free-agent draft (June 2, 1987). . . . Granted free agency (October 31, 1995). . . . Re-signed by Astros (December 14, 1995).

HONORS: Named catcher on The Sporting News college All-America team (1987). . . . Named catcher on The Sporting News N.L. Silver Slugger team (1989). . . . Named second baseman on The Sporting News N.L. All-Star team (1994-95). . . . Won N.L. Gold Glove at second base (1994-95). . . . Named second baseman on The Sporting News N.L. Silver Slugger team (1994-95).

STATISTICAL NOTES: Led N.L. catchers with 889 putouts, 963 total chances and 13 passed balls in 1991. . . . Led N.L. in being hit by pitch with 22 in 1995. . . . Led N.L. second basemen with 728 total chances in 1995. . . . Career major league grand slams: 2.

Year	Team (League)	Pos.	G	AB	R	H	2B	3B	HR	RBI	Avg.	BB	SO	SB	PO	A	E	Avg.
				BATTING											FIELDING			
1987	Asheville (S. Atl.)	C-OF	64	216	59	81	17	2	9	49	.375	39	33	31	378	46	2	.995

Year Team (League)	Pos.	G	AB	R	H	2B	3B	HR	RBI	Avg.	BB	SO	SB	PO	A	E	Avg.
		BATTING												FIELDING			
1988—Tucson (PCL)	C-OF	77	281	60	90	21	4	3	41	.320	40	39	19	318	33	6	.983
—Houston (N.L.)	C	50	123	14	26	6	1	3	5	.211	7	29	6	292	28	3	.991
1989—Houston (N.L.)	C-OF	134	443	64	114	21	2	13	60	.257	49	64	21	742	56	9	.989
1990—Houston (N.L.)	C-OF	150	555	53	153	24	2	4	42	.276	53	79	25	657	60	13	.982
1991—Houston (N.L.)	C-2B-OF	149	546	79	161	23	4	4	46	.295	53	71	19	†894	73	11	.989
1992—Houston (N.L.)	2B	•162	613	96	170	32	3	6	39	.277	94	95	38	*344	413	12	.984
1993—Houston (N.L.)	2B	155	610	98	175	41	5	21	64	.287	77	93	15	306	*447	14	.982
1994—Houston (N.L.)	2B	114	437	88	139	*44	5	6	56	.318	62	58	*39	•225	*338	7	.988
1995—Houston (N.L.)	2B	141	553	*123	167	30	2	22	77	.302	80	85	33	299	*419	10	.986
Major league totals (8 years)		1055	3880	615	1105	221	24	79	389	.285	475	574	196	3759	1834	79	.986

ALL-STAR GAME RECORD

Year League	Pos.	AB	R	H	2B	3B	HR	RBI	Avg.	BB	SO	SB	PO	A	E	Avg.
		BATTING											FIELDING			
1991—National	C	1	0	0	0	0	0	0	.000	0	0	0	2	0	1	.667
1992—National	2B	2	0	0	0	0	0	0	.000	0	0	0	0	2	0	1.000
1994—National	2B	1	1	0	0	0	0	0	.000	0	0	0	2	1	0	1.000
1995—National	2B	2	1	1	0	0	1	1	.500	0	0	0	2	1	0	1.000
All-Star Game totals (4 years)		6	2	1	0	0	1	1	.167	0	0	0	6	4	1	.909

BIRKBECK, MIKE — P

PERSONAL: Born March 10, 1961, in Orrville, O. . . . 6-2/190. . . . Throws right, bats right. . . . Full name: Michael Lawrence Birkbeck.
HIGH SCHOOL: Orrville (O.).
COLLEGE: Akron.
TRANSACTIONS/CAREER NOTES: Selected by Chicago Cubs organization in 11th round of free-agent draft (June 7, 1982); did not sign. . . . Selected by Milwaukee Brewers organization in fourth round of free-agent draft (June 8, 1983). . . . On Milwaukee disabled list (June 2-September 5, 1987); included rehabilitation assignments to Beloit (June 19-23) and Denver (June 24-July 1). . . . On Milwaukee disabled list (May 31-August 29, 1989); included rehabilitation assignment to Denver (August 6-25). . . . Released by Brewers organization (October 16, 1990). . . . Signed by Cleveland Indians organization (April 8, 1991). . . . On Canton/Akron disabled list (April 10-May 8, 1991). . . . Released by Colorado Springs, Indians organization (September 25, 1991). . . . Signed by Tidewater, New York Mets organization (January 2, 1992). . . . On Tidewater disabled list (April 25-May 6 and July 11-26, 1992). . . . Granted free agency (October 16, 1992). . . . Signed by Richmond, Atlanta Braves organization (December 22, 1992). . . . Granted free agency (October 11, 1994). . . . Signed by Norfolk, Mets organization (December 19, 1994). . . . Released by Mets (June 13, 1995).

Year Team (League)	W	L	Pct.	ERA	G	GS	CG	ShO	Sv.	IP	H	R	ER	BB	SO
1983—Paintsville (Appal.)	3	1	.750	1.88	7	5	0	0	0	28 2/3	17	12	6	17	38
—Beloit (Midwest)	2	4	.333	3.43	7	7	0	0	0	42	35	22	16	17	38
1984—Beloit (Midwest)	14	3	.824	2.18	26	25	6	2	0	177 2/3	134	57	43	64	164
1985—El Paso (Texas)	9	9	.500	3.43	24	24	4	0	0	155	154	67	59	64	103
1986—Vancouver (PCL)	12	6	.667	4.62	23	23	2	0	0	134 1/3	160	82	69	39	81
—Milwaukee (A.L.)	1	1	.500	4.50	7	4	0	0	0	22	24	12	11	12	13
1987—Milwaukee (A.L.)	1	4	.200	6.20	10	10	1	0	0	45	63	33	31	19	25
—Beloit (Midwest)	0	0	...	2.08	1	1	0	0	0	4 1/3	4	4	1	1	7
—Denver (Am. Assoc.)	0	1	.000	9.64	1	1	0	0	0	4 2/3	9	11	5	3	1
1988—Milwaukee (A.L.)	10	8	.556	4.72	23	23	0	0	0	124	141	69	65	37	64
—Denver (Am. Assoc.)	4	1	.800	2.01	5	5	4	0	0	44 2/3	30	10	10	10	30
1989—Milwaukee (A.L.)	0	4	.000	5.44	9	9	1	0	0	44 2/3	57	32	27	22	31
—Denver (Am. Assoc.)	2	2	.500	3.04	5	5	0	0	0	23 2/3	26	9	8	10	9
1990—Denver (Am. Assoc.)	3	8	.273	5.33	21	20	0	0	0	96 1/3	102	73	57	36	69
1991—Cant./Akr. (East.)■	2	3	.400	3.89	21	2	0	0	5	39 1/3	39	17	17	18	40
—Colo. Springs (PCL)	0	0	...	0.00	3	1	0	0	0	7	4	0	0	3	3
1992—Tidewater (Int'l)■	4	10	.286	4.08	21	19	3	0	0	117	108	61	53	31	101
—New York (N.L.)	0	1	.000	9.00	1	1	0	0	0	7	12	7	7	1	2
1993—Richmond (Int'l)■	*13	8	.619	3.11	27	26	1	0	0	159 1/3	143	67	55	41	*136
1994—Richmond (Int'l)	13	6	.684	2.73	28	28	1	0	0	164 2/3	145	58	50	46	143
1995—Norfolk (Int'l)■	5	3	.625	2.36	9	9	0	0	0	53 1/3	52	20	14	13	39
—New York (N.L.)	0	1	.000	1.63	4	4	0	0	0	27 2/3	22	5	5	2	14
A.L. totals (4 years)	12	17	.414	5.12	49	46	2	0	0	235 2/3	285	146	134	90	133
N.L. totals (2 years)	0	2	.000	3.12	5	5	0	0	0	34 2/3	34	12	12	3	16
Major league totals (6 years)	12	19	.387	4.86	54	51	2	0	0	270 1/3	319	158	146	93	149

BLACK, BUD — P

PERSONAL: Born June 30, 1957, in San Mateo, Calif. . . . 6-2/188. . . . Throws left, bats left. . . . Full name: Harry Ralston Black.
HIGH SCHOOL: Mark Morris (Longview, Wash.).
JUNIOR COLLEGE: Lower Columbia College (Wash.).
COLLEGE: San Diego State (bachelor of arts degree in finance, 1979).
TRANSACTIONS/CAREER NOTES: Selected by San Francisco Giants organization in third round of free-agent draft (January 11, 1977); did not sign. . . . Selected by New York Mets organization in secondary phase of free-agent draft (June 7, 1977); did not sign. . . . Selected by Seattle Mariners organization in 17th round of free-agent draft (June 5, 1979). . . . Traded by Mariners to Kansas City Royals (March 2, 1982), completing deal in which Royals traded IF Manny Castillo to Mariners for a player to be named later (October 23, 1981). . . . On disabled list (June 8-July 4, 1987). . . . Traded by Royals to Cleveland Indians for 1B Pat Tabler (June 3, 1988). . . . On Cleveland disabled list (July 19-August 21, 1988); included rehabilitation assignment to Williamsport (August 16-21). . . . Granted free agency (November 4, 1988). . . . Re-signed by Indians (December 5, 1988). . . . Traded by Indians to Toronto Blue Jays for P Mauro Gozzo and two players to be named later (September 16, 1990); Indians acquired P Steve Cummings (September 21, 1990) and P Alex Sanchez (September 24, 1990) to complete deal. . . . Granted free agency (November 5, 1990). . . . Signed by San Francisco Giants (November 9, 1990). . . . On San Francisco disabled list (March 27-May 7, 1992); included rehabilitation assignment to Phoenix (April 23-May 7). . . . On San Francisco disabled list (April 9-29

and July 10-28, 1993). . . . On San Francisco disabled list (August 4, 1993-remainder of season); included rehabilitation assignment to San Jose (August 23-24). . . . On San Francisco disabled list (March 28-June 19, 1994); included rehabilitation assignments to Phoenix (May 30-June 14) and San Jose (June 14-19). . . . Granted free agency (October 14, 1994). . . . Signed by Indians organization (April 25, 1995). . . . Released by Indians (July 14, 1995).

RECORDS: Shares major league single-season record for fewest double plays by pitcher who led league in double plays—4 (1992). . . . Shares major league record for most hit batsmen in one inning—3 (July 8, 1988, fourth inning).

STATISTICAL NOTES: Led A.L. with seven balks in 1982. . . . Led N.L. with six balks in 1991 and tied for lead with seven in 1992. . . . Led N.L. with 23 home runs allowed in 1992.

MISCELLANEOUS: Made an out in only appearance as pinch-hitter (1991).

Year Team (League)	W	L	Pct.	ERA	G	GS	CG	ShO	Sv.	IP	H	R	ER	BB	SO
1979—Bellingham (N'west)	0	0	...	0.00	2	0	0	0	0	5	3	0	0	5	8
—San Jose (Calif.)	0	1	.000	3.00	17	2	0	0	1	27	17	11	9	16	24
1980—San Jose (Calif.)	5	3	.625	3.45	32	5	4	0	2	86	67	34	33	49	73
1981—Lynn (Eastern)	2	6	.250	3.00	22	11	2	1	2	87	78	38	29	23	86
—Spokane (PCL)	1	0	1.000	4.50	4	0	0	0	0	8	12	4	4	2	4
—Seattle (A.L.)	0	0	...	0.00	2	0	0	0	0	1	2	0	0	3	0
1982—Kansas City (A.L.)■	4	6	.400	4.58	22	14	0	0	0	88 1/3	92	48	45	34	40
—Omaha (Am. Assoc.)	3	1	.750	2.48	4	4	3	1	0	29	23	9	8	10	20
1983—Omaha (Am. Assoc.)	3	1	.750	3.34	5	5	3	0	0	35	31	13	13	13	32
—Kansas City (A.L.)	10	7	.588	3.79	24	24	3	0	0	161 1/3	159	75	68	43	58
1984—Kansas City (A.L.)	17	12	.586	3.12	35	35	8	1	0	257	226	99	89	64	140
1985—Kansas City (A.L.)	10	15	.400	4.33	33	33	5	2	0	205 2/3	216	111	99	59	122
1986—Kansas City (A.L.)	5	10	.333	3.20	56	4	0	0	9	121	100	49	43	43	68
1987—Kansas City (A.L.)	8	6	.571	3.60	29	18	0	0	1	122 1/3	126	63	49	35	61
1988—Kansas City (A.L.)	2	1	.667	4.91	17	0	0	0	0	22	23	12	12	11	19
—Cleveland (A.L.)■	2	3	.400	5.03	16	7	0	0	1	59	59	35	33	23	44
—Williamsport (East.)	1	0	1.000	0.00	1	1	0	0	0	5	0	0	0	0	5
1989—Cleveland (A.L.)	12	11	.522	3.36	33	32	6	3	0	222 1/3	213	95	83	52	88
1990—Cleveland (A.L.)	11	10	.524	3.53	29	29	5	2	0	191	171	79	75	58	103
—Toronto (A.L.)■	2	1	.667	4.02	3	2	0	0	0	15 2/3	10	7	7	3	3
1991—San Francisco (N.L.)■	12	*16	.429	3.99	34	34	3	3	0	214 1/3	201	104	95	71	104
1992—Phoenix (PCL)	2	0	1.000	0.86	3	3	1	1	0	21	21	3	2	5	7
—San Francisco (N.L.)	10	12	.455	3.97	28	28	2	1	0	177	178	88	78	59	82
1993—San Francisco (N.L.)	8	2	.800	3.56	16	16	0	0	0	93 2/3	89	44	37	33	45
—San Jose (Calif.)	0	0	...	9.00	1	1	0	0	0	1	2	1	1	0	2
1994—Phoenix (PCL)	1	0	1.000	1.17	3	3	0	0	0	15 1/3	14	4	2	7	8
—San Jose (Calif.)	1	0	1.000	0.00	1	1	0	0	0	7	6	0	0	2	5
—San Francisco (N.L.)	4	2	.667	4.47	10	10	0	0	0	54 1/3	50	31	27	16	28
1995—Cleveland (A.L.)■	4	2	.667	6.85	11	10	0	0	0	47 1/3	63	42	36	16	34
A.L. totals (11 years)	87	84	.509	3.80	310	208	27	8	11	1514	1460	715	639	444	780
N.L. totals (4 years)	34	32	.515	3.95	88	88	5	4	0	539 1/3	518	267	237	179	259
Major league totals (15 years)	121	116	.511	3.84	398	296	32	12	11	2053 1/3	1978	982	876	623	1039

CHAMPIONSHIP SERIES RECORD

Year Team (League)	W	L	Pct.	ERA	G	GS	CG	ShO	Sv.	IP	H	R	ER	BB	SO
1984—Kansas City (A.L.)	0	1	.000	7.20	1	1	0	0	0	5	7	4	4	1	3
1985—Kansas City (A.L.)	0	0	...	1.69	3	1	0	0	0	10 2/3	11	3	2	4	8
Champ. series totals (2 years)	0	1	.000	3.45	4	2	0	0	0	15 2/3	18	7	6	5	11

WORLD SERIES RECORD

NOTES: Member of World Series championship team (1985).

Year Team (League)	W	L	Pct.	ERA	G	GS	CG	ShO	Sv.	IP	H	R	ER	BB	SO
1985—Kansas City (A.L.)	0	1	.000	5.06	2	1	0	0	0	5 1/3	4	3	3	5	4

BLAIR, WILLIE — P — PADRES

PERSONAL: Born December 18, 1965, in Paintsville, Ky. . . . 6-1/185. . . . Throws right, bats right. . . . Full name: William Allen Blair.

HIGH SCHOOL: Johnson Central (Paintsville, Ky.).

COLLEGE: Morehead State.

TRANSACTIONS/CAREER NOTES: Selected by Toronto Blue Jays organization in 11th round of free-agent draft (June 2, 1986). . . . Traded by Blue Jays to Cleveland Indians for P Alex Sanchez (November 6, 1990). . . . Traded by Indians with C Eddie Taubensee to Houston Astros for OF Kenny Lofton and IF Dave Rohde (December 10, 1991). . . . Selected by Colorado Rockies in first round (21st pick overall) of expansion draft (November 17, 1992). . . . Granted free agency (December 20, 1994). . . . Signed by Las Vegas, San Diego Padres organization (April 10, 1995). . . . Granted free agency (December 21, 1995). . . . Re-signed by Padres (December 27, 1995).

STATISTICAL NOTES: Combined with starter Pat Hentgen and Enrique Burgos in 2-1 no-hit victory for Dunedin against Osceola (May 10, 1988).

Year Team (League)	W	L	Pct.	ERA	G	GS	CG	ShO	Sv.	IP	H	R	ER	BB	SO
1986—St. Cathar. (NYP)	5	0	1.000	1.68	21	0	0	0	*12	53 2/3	32	10	10	20	55
1987—Dunedin (Fla. St.)	2	9	.182	4.43	50	0	0	0	13	85 1/3	99	51	42	29	72
1988—Dunedin (Fla. St.)	2	0	1.000	2.70	4	0	0	0	0	6 2/3	5	2	2	4	5
—Knoxville (South.)	5	5	.500	3.62	34	9	0	0	3	102	94	49	41	35	76
1989—Syracuse (Int'l)	5	6	.455	3.97	19	17	3	1	0	106 2/3	94	55	47	38	76
1990—Toronto (A.L.)	3	5	.375	4.06	27	6	0	0	0	68 2/3	66	33	31	28	43
—Syracuse (Int'l)	0	2	.000	4.74	3	3	1	0	0	19	20	13	10	8	6
1991—Colo. Springs (PCL)■	9	6	.600	4.99	26	15	0	0	4	113 2/3	130	74	63	30	57
—Cleveland (A.L.)	2	3	.400	6.75	11	5	0	0	0	36	58	27	27	10	13
1992—Tucson (Pac. Coast)■	4	4	.500	2.39	21	2	1	0	2	52 2/3	50	20	14	12	35
—Houston (N.L.)	5	7	.417	4.00	29	8	0	0	0	78 2/3	74	47	35	25	48
1993—Colorado (N.L.)■	6	10	.375	4.75	46	18	1	0	0	146	184	90	77	42	84
1994—Colorado (N.L.)	0	5	.000	5.79	47	1	0	0	3	77 2/3	98	57	50	39	68
1995—San Diego (N.L.)■	7	5	.583	4.34	40	12	0	0	0	114	112	60	55	45	83
A.L. totals (2 years)	5	8	.385	4.99	38	11	0	0	0	104 2/3	124	60	58	38	56
N.L. totals (4 years)	18	27	.400	4.69	162	39	1	0	3	416 1/3	468	254	217	151	283
Major league totals (6 years)	23	35	.397	4.75	200	50	1	0	3	521	592	314	275	189	339

BLAUSER, JEFF — SS — BRAVES

PERSONAL: Born November 8, 1965, in Los Gatos, Calif. . . . 6-0/180. . . . Bats right, throws right. . . . Full name: Jeffrey Michael Blauser. . . . Name pronounced BLAU-zer.
HIGH SCHOOL: Placer (Sacramento, Calif.).
COLLEGE: Sacramento City College.
TRANSACTIONS/CAREER NOTES: Selected by St. Louis Cardinals organization in first round (eighth pick overall) of free-agent draft (January 17, 1984); did not sign. . . . Selected by Atlanta Braves organization in secondary phase of free-agent draft (June 4, 1984). . . . On disabled list (May 14-30, 1990 and May 2-20, 1994). . . . Granted free agency (October 15, 1994). . . . Re-signed by Braves (April 12, 1995).
STATISTICAL NOTES: Led Carolina League shortstops with 506 total chances in 1986. . . . Hit three home runs in one game (July 12, 1992). . . . Led N.L. in being hit by pitch with 16 in 1993. . . . Career major league grand slams: 1.

		BATTING												FIELDING			
Year Team (League)	Pos.	G	AB	R	H	2B	3B	HR	RBI	Avg.	BB	SO	SB	PO	A	E	Avg.
1984— Pulaski (Appal.)	SS	62	217	41	54	6	1	3	24	.249	38	47	14	61	162	24	.903
1985— Sumter (S. Atl.)	SS	125	422	74	99	19	0	5	49	.235	82	94	36	150	306	35	.929
1986— Durham (Carolina)	SS	123	447	94	128	27	3	13	52	.286	81	92	36	167	*314	25	*.951
1987— Richmond (Int'l)	SS-2B	33	113	11	20	1	0	1	12	.177	11	24	3	56	106	9	.947
— Atlanta (N.L.)	SS	51	165	11	40	6	3	2	15	.242	18	34	7	65	166	9	.963
— Greenville (South.)	SS	72	265	35	66	13	3	4	32	.249	34	49	5	101	225	8	.976
1988— Richmond (Int'l)	SS	69	271	40	77	19	1	5	23	.284	19	53	6	93	156	15	.943
— Atlanta (N.L.)	2B-SS	18	67	7	16	3	1	2	7	.239	2	11	0	35	59	4	.959
1989— Atlanta (N.L.)	3-2-S-O	142	456	63	123	24	2	12	46	.270	38	101	5	137	254	21	.949
1990— Atlanta (N.L.)	S-2-3-O	115	386	46	104	24	3	8	39	.269	35	70	3	169	288	16	.966
1991— Atlanta (N.L.)	SS-2B-3B	129	352	49	91	14	3	11	54	.259	54	59	5	136	219	17	.954
1992— Atlanta (N.L.)	SS-2B-3B	123	343	61	90	19	3	14	46	.262	46	82	5	119	225	14	.961
1993— Atlanta (N.L.)	SS	161	597	110	182	29	2	15	73	.305	85	109	16	189	426	19	.970
1994— Atlanta (N.L.)	SS	96	380	56	98	21	4	6	45	.258	38	64	1	126	290	13	.970
1995— Atlanta (N.L.)	SS	115	431	60	91	16	2	12	31	.211	57	107	8	151	337	15	.970
Major league totals (9 years)		950	3177	463	835	156	23	82	356	.263	373	637	50	1127	2264	128	.964

DIVISION SERIES RECORD

		BATTING												FIELDING			
Year Team (League)	Pos.	G	AB	R	H	2B	3B	HR	RBI	Avg.	BB	SO	SB	PO	A	E	Avg.
1995— Atlanta (N.L.)	SS	3	6	0	0	0	0	0	0	.000	1	3	0	5	11	1	.941

CHAMPIONSHIP SERIES RECORD

		BATTING												FIELDING			
Year Team (League)	Pos.	G	AB	R	H	2B	3B	HR	RBI	Avg.	BB	SO	SB	PO	A	E	Avg.
1991— Atlanta (N.L.)	SS-PH	2	2	0	0	0	0	0	0	.000	0	0	0	0	1	1	.500
1992— Atlanta (N.L.)	SS	7	24	3	5	0	1	1	4	.208	3	2	0	7	15	2	.917
1993— Atlanta (N.L.)	SS	6	25	5	7	1	0	2	4	.280	4	7	0	6	14	0	1.000
1995— Atlanta (N.L.)	SS	1	4	0	0	0	0	0	0	.000	1	2	0	4	6	0	1.000
Championship series totals (4 years)		16	55	8	12	1	1	3	8	.218	8	11	0	17	36	3	.946

WORLD SERIES RECORD

NOTES: Member of World Series championship team (1995).

		BATTING												FIELDING			
Year Team (League)	Pos.	G	AB	R	H	2B	3B	HR	RBI	Avg.	BB	SO	SB	PO	A	E	Avg.
1991— Atlanta (N.L.)	SS-PH	5	6	0	1	0	0	0	0	.167	1	1	0	3	3	0	1.000
1992— Atlanta (N.L.)	SS	6	24	2	6	0	0	0	0	.250	1	9	2	7	22	0	1.000
World Series totals (2 years)		11	30	2	7	0	0	0	0	.233	2	10	2	10	25	0	1.000

ALL-STAR GAME RECORD

		BATTING											FIELDING			
Year League	Pos.	AB	R	H	2B	3B	HR	RBI	Avg.	BB	SO	SB	PO	A	E	Avg.
1993— National	SS	1	0	0	0	0	0	0	.000	0	1	0	1	2	1	.750

BLAZIER, RON — P — PHILLIES

PERSONAL: Born July 30, 1971, in Altoona, Pa. . . . 6-5/205. . . . Throws right, bats right. . . . Full name: Ronald Patrick Blazier.
HIGH SCHOOL: Bellwood (Pa.)-Antis.
TRANSACTIONS/CAREER NOTES: Signed as non-drafted free agent by Philadelphia Phillies organization (July 14, 1989).

Year Team (League)	W	L	Pct.	ERA	G	GS	CG	ShO	Sv.	IP	H	R	ER	BB	SO
1990— Princeton (Appal.)	3	5	.375	4.46	14	13	1	0	0	78 2/3	77	46	39	29	45
1991— Batavia (NYP)	7	5	.583	4.60	24	8	0	0	2	72 1/3	81	40	37	17	77
1992— Spartanburg (SAL)	•14	7	.667	2.65	30	21	2	0	0	159 2/3	141	55	47	32	149
1993— Clearwater (Fla. St.)	9	8	.529	3.94	27	23	1	0	0	155 1/3	171	80	68	40	86
1994— Clearwater (Fla. St.)	•13	5	.722	3.38	29	*29	0	0	0	173 1/3	177	73	65	36	120
1995— Reading (Eastern)	4	5	.444	3.29	56	3	0	0	1	106 2/3	93	44	39	31	102

BLOMDAHL, BEN — P — TIGERS

PERSONAL: Born December 30, 1970, in Long Beach, Calif. . . . 6-2/185. . . . Throws right, bats right. . . . Full name: Benjamin Earl Blomdahl. . . . Name pronounced BLOOM-doll.
HIGH SCHOOL: Riverside (Calif.) Polytech.
JUNIOR COLLEGE: Riverside (Calif.) Community College.
TRANSACTIONS/CAREER NOTES: Selected by Detroit Tigers organization in 14th round of free-agent draft (June 4, 1990).
STATISTICAL NOTES: Pitched 1-0 perfect game for Fayetteville against Spartanburg (June 4, 1992, second game).

Year	Team (League)	W	L	Pct.	ERA	G	GS	CG	ShO	Sv.	IP	H	R	ER	BB	SO
1991—	Niag. Falls (NYP)	6	6	.500	4.46	16	13	0	0	0	78 2/3	72	43	39	50	30
1992—	Fayetteville (S. Atl.)	10	4	.714	2.70	17	17	2	2	0	103 1/3	94	46	31	26	65
—	Lakeland (Fla. St.)	5	3	.625	4.65	10	10	2	0	0	62	77	35	32	5	41
1993—	London (Eastern)	6	6	.500	3.71	17	17	3	0	0	119	108	58	49	42	72
—	Toledo (Int'l)	3	4	.429	4.88	11	10	0	0	0	62 2/3	67	34	34	19	27
1994—	Toledo (Int'l)	11	11	.500	4.46	28	28	0	0	0	165 1/3	*192	92	82	47	83
1995—	Detroit (A.L.)	0	0	...	7.77	14	0	0	0	1	24 1/3	36	21	21	13	15
—	Toledo (Int'l)	5	4	.556	3.54	41	0	0	0	3	56	55	24	22	13	39
Major league totals (1 year)		0	0	...	7.77	14	0	0	0	1	24 1/3	36	21	21	13	15

BLOWERS, MIKE — 3B — DODGERS

PERSONAL: Born April 24, 1965, in Wurzburg, West Germany. . . . 6-2/210. . . . Bats right, throws right. . . . Full name: Michael Roy Blowers.

HIGH SCHOOL: Bethel (Wash.).

JUNIOR COLLEGE: Tacoma (Wash.) Community College.

COLLEGE: Washington.

TRANSACTIONS/CAREER NOTES: Selected by Seattle Mariners organization in eighth round of free-agent draft (January 17, 1984); did not sign. . . . Selected by San Francisco Giants organization in secondary phase of free-agent draft (June 4, 1984); did not sign. . . . Selected by Baltimore Orioles organization in secondary phase of free-agent draft (January 9, 1985); did not sign. . . . Selected by Montreal Expos organization in 10th round of free-agent draft (June 2, 1986). . . . Traded by Expos to New York Yankees (August 31, 1989), completing deal in which Yankees traded P John Candelaria to Expos for a player to be named later (August 29, 1989). . . . Traded by Yankees to Mariners for a player to be named later and cash (May 17, 1991); Yankees acquired P Jim Blueberg to complete deal (June 22, 1991). . . . Traded by Mariners to Los Angeles Dodgers for 2B Miguel Cairo and 3B Willis Otanez (November 29, 1995).

RECORDS: Shares major league single-month record for most grand slams—3 (August 1995). . . . Shares A.L. single-game record for most errors by third baseman—4 (May 3, 1990).

STATISTICAL NOTES: Led Florida State League third basemen with .944 fielding percentage and 27 double plays in 1987. . . . Led Southern League third basemen with 125 putouts and 27 double plays in 1988. . . . Led American Association third basemen with .930 fielding percentage in 1989. . . . Career major league grand slams: 6.

				BATTING											FIELDING			
Year	Team (League)	Pos.	G	AB	R	H	2B	3B	HR	RBI	Avg.	BB	SO	SB	PO	A	E	Avg.
1986—	Jamestown (NYP)	SS-3B	32	95	13	24	9	2	1	6	.253	17	18	3	48	73	16	.883
—	GC Expos (GCL)	SS	31	115	14	25	3	1	2	17	.217	15	25	2	50	84	15	.899
1987—	W.P. Beach (FSL)	3B-SS-1B	136	491	68	124	30	3	16	71	.253	48	118	4	75	239	18	†.946
1988—	Jacksonv. (South.)	3B-SS-2B	137	460	58	115	20	6	15	60	.250	68	114	6	†125	241	34	.915
1989—	Indianapolis (A.A.)	3B-SS	131	461	49	123	29	6	14	56	.267	41	109	3	91	214	23	†.930
—	New York (A.L.)■	3B	13	38	2	10	0	0	0	3	.263	3	13	0	9	14	4	.852
1990—	New York (A.L.)	3B-DH	48	144	16	27	4	0	5	21	.188	12	50	1	26	63	10	.899
—	Columbus (Int'l)	3B-1B-2B	62	230	30	78	20	6	6	50	.339	29	40	3	64	89	8	.950
1991—	New York (A.L.)	3B	15	35	3	7	0	0	1	1	.200	4	3	0	4	16	3	.870
—	Calgary (PCL)■	3B-SS-1B	90	329	56	95	20	2	9	59	.289	40	74	3	56	163	19	.920
1992—	Calgary (PCL)	3B-1B-OF	83	300	56	95	28	2	9	67	.317	50	64	2	99	87	5	.974
—	Seattle (A.L.)	3B-1B	31	73	7	14	3	0	1	2	.192	6	20	0	28	44	1	.986
1993—	Seattle (A.L.)	3-DH-O-1-C	127	379	55	106	23	3	15	57	.280	44	98	1	70	225	15	.952
1994—	Seattle (A.L.)	3-1-DH-O	85	270	37	78	13	0	9	49	.289	25	60	2	142	109	9	.965
1995—	Seattle (A.L.)	3B-1B-OF	134	439	59	113	24	1	23	96	.257	53	128	2	116	174	16	.948
Major league totals (7 years)			453	1378	179	355	67	4	54	229	.258	147	372	6	395	645	58	.947

DIVISION SERIES RECORD

				BATTING											FIELDING			
Year	Team (League)	Pos.	G	AB	R	H	2B	3B	HR	RBI	Avg.	BB	SO	SB	PO	A	E	Avg.
1995—	Seattle (A.L.)	3B-1B	5	18	0	3	0	0	0	1	.167	3	7	0	2	6	0	1.000

CHAMPIONSHIP SERIES RECORD

NOTES: Hit home run in first at-bat (October 10, 1995).

				BATTING											FIELDING			
Year	Team (League)	Pos.	G	AB	R	H	2B	3B	HR	RBI	Avg.	BB	SO	SB	PO	A	E	Avg.
1995—	Seattle (A.L.)	3B	6	18	1	4	0	0	1	2	.222	0	4	0	5	9	0	1.000

BOCHTLER, DOUG — P — PADRES

PERSONAL: Born July 5, 1970, in West Palm Beach, Fla. . . . 6-3/200. . . . Throws right, bats right. . . . Full name: Douglas Eugene Bochtler. . . . Name pronounced BOCK-ler.

HIGH SCHOOL: John I. Leonard (Lake Worth, Fla.).

JUNIOR COLLEGE: Indian River Community College (Fla.).

TRANSACTIONS/CAREER NOTES: Selected by Montreal Expos organization in ninth round of free-agent draft (June 5, 1989). . . . On disabled list (June 18-September 6, 1992). . . . Selected by Colorado Rockies in second round (32nd pick overall) of expansion draft (November 17, 1992). . . . On Colorado Springs disabled list (April 18-26, 1993). . . . Traded by Rockies with C Brad Ausmus and a player to be named later to San Diego Padres for P Bruce Hurst and P Greg W. Harris (July 26, 1993); Padres acquired P Andy Ashby to complete deal (July 27, 1993). . . . On disabled list (June 16-24 and August 24, 1994-remainder of season).

Year	Team (League)	W	L	Pct.	ERA	G	GS	CG	ShO	Sv.	IP	H	R	ER	BB	SO
1989—	GC Expos (GCL)	2	2	.500	3.21	9	9	1	0	0	47 2/3	46	22	17	20	45
1990—	Rockford (Midw.)	9	12	.429	3.50	25	25	1	1	0	139	142	82	54	54	109
1991—	WP Beach (FSL)	•12	9	.571	2.92	26	24	7	2	0	160 1/3	148	63	52	55	109
1992—	Harrisburg (East.)	6	5	.545	2.32	13	13	2	1	0	77 2/3	50	25	20	36	89
1993—	Colo. Springs (PCL)■	1	4	.200	6.93	12	11	0	0	0	50 2/3	71	41	39	26	38
—	Central Valley (Cal.)	3	1	.750	3.40	8	8	0	0	0	47 2/3	40	23	18	28	43
—	Las Vegas (PCL)■	0	5	.000	5.22	7	7	1	0	0	39 2/3	52	26	23	11	30
1994—	Las Vegas (PCL)	3	7	.300	5.20	22	20	2	1	0	100 1/3	116	67	58	48	86

Year	Team (League)	W	L	Pct.	ERA	G	GS	CG	ShO	Sv.	IP	H	R	ER	BB	SO
1995—	Las Vegas (PCL)	2	3	.400	4.25	18	2	0	0	1	36	31	18	17	26	32
	—San Diego (N.L.)	4	4	.500	3.57	34	0	0	0	1	45 1/3	38	18	18	19	45
Major league totals (1 year)		4	4	.500	3.57	34	0	0	0	1	45 1/3	38	18	18	19	45

BOEHRINGER, BRIAN — P — YANKEES

PERSONAL: Born January 8, 1970, in St. Louis. . . . 6-2/190. . . . Throws right, bats both. . . . Full name: Brian Edward Boehringer. . . . Name pronounced BO-ring-er.

HIGH SCHOOL: Northwest (House Springs, Mo.).

JUNIOR COLLEGE: St. Louis Community College at Meramec.

COLLEGE: UNLV.

TRANSACTIONS/CAREER NOTES: Selected by Houston Astros organization in 10th round of free-agent draft (June 4, 1990); did not sign. . . . Selected by Chicago White Sox organization in fourth round of free-agent draft (June 3, 1991). . . . On Utica disabled list (June 29-August 25, 1991). . . . On disabled list (June 24-August 25, 1992). . . . Traded by White Sox organization to New York Yankees for P Paul Assenmacher (March 21, 1994).

STATISTICAL NOTES: Tied for Eastern League lead with four balks in 1994.

Year	Team (League)	W	L	Pct.	ERA	G	GS	CG	ShO	Sv.	IP	H	R	ER	BB	SO
1991—	GC White Sox (GCL)	1	1	.500	6.57	5	1	0	0	0	12 1/3	14	9	9	5	10
	—Utica (NYP)	1	1	.500	2.37	4	4	0	0	0	19	14	8	5	8	19
1992—	South Bend (Midw.)	6	7	.462	4.38	15	15	2	0	0	86 1/3	87	52	42	40	59
1993—	Sarasota (Fla. St.)	10	4	.714	2.80	18	17	3	0	0	119	103	47	37	51	92
	—Birmingham (Sou.)	2	1	.667	3.54	7	7	1	0	0	40 2/3	41	20	16	14	29
1994—	Alb./Colon. (East.)■	10	11	.476	3.62	27	27	5	1	0	171 2/3	165	85	69	57	145
1995—	New York (A.L.)	0	3	.000	13.75	7	3	0	0	0	17 2/3	24	27	27	22	10
	—Columbus (Int'l)	8	6	.571	2.77	17	17	3	0	0	104	101	39	32	31	58
Major league totals (1 year)		0	3	.000	13.75	7	3	0	0	0	17 2/3	24	27	27	22	10

BOEVER, JOE — P — TIGERS

PERSONAL: Born October 4, 1960, in St. Louis. . . . 6-1/200. . . . Throws right, bats right. . . . Full name: Joseph Martin Boever. . . . Name pronounced BAY-vur.

HIGH SCHOOL: Lindbergh (St. Louis).

JUNIOR COLLEGE: Crowder College (Mo.) and St. Louis Community College at Meramec.

COLLEGE: UNLV.

TRANSACTIONS/CAREER NOTES: Signed as non-drafted free agent by St. Louis Cardinals organization (June 25, 1982). . . . Traded by Cardinals to Atlanta Braves for P Randy O'Neal (July 25, 1987). . . . Traded by Braves to Philadelphia Phillies for P Marvin Freeman (July 23, 1990). . . . Granted free agency (December 20, 1991). . . . Signed by Houston Astros organization (January 27, 1992). . . . Granted free agency (December 19, 1992). . . . Signed by Oakland Athletics organization (January 21, 1993). . . . Released by A's (August 15, 1993). . . . Signed by Detroit Tigers (August 21, 1993). . . . Granted free agency (November 7, 1993). . . . Re-signed by Tigers (November 7, 1993). . . . Granted free agency (October 21, 1994). . . . Re-signed by Tigers (April 7, 1995).

Year	Team (League)	W	L	Pct.	ERA	G	GS	CG	ShO	Sv.	IP	H	R	ER	BB	SO
1982—	Erie (NYP)	2	3	.400	1.93	19	0	0	0	9	32 2/3	20	8	7	12	63
	—Springfield (Midw.)	0	0	. . .	2.25	3	0	0	0	0	4	3	1	1	2	7
1983—	St. Petersburg (FSL)	5	6	.455	3.02	53	0	0	0	*26	80 1/3	61	29	27	37	57
1984—	Arkansas (Texas)	0	1	.000	8.18	8	0	0	0	3	11	10	11	10	12	12
	—St. Petersburg (FSL)	6	4	.600	3.01	48	0	0	0	*14	77 2/3	52	31	26	45	81
1985—	Arkansas (Texas)	3	1	.750	1.19	27	0	0	0	9	37 2/3	21	5	5	23	45
	—Louisville (A.A.)	3	2	.600	2.04	21	0	0	0	1	35 1/3	28	11	8	22	37
	—St. Louis (N.L.)	0	0	. . .	4.41	13	0	0	0	0	16 1/3	17	8	8	4	20
1986—	St. Louis (N.L.)	0	1	.000	1.66	11	0	0	0	0	21 2/3	19	5	4	11	8
	—Louisville (A.A.)	4	5	.444	2.25	51	0	0	0	5	88	71	25	22	48	75
1987—	Louisville (A.A.)	3	2	.600	3.36	43	0	0	0	*21	59	52	22	22	27	79
	—Atlanta (N.L.)■	1	0	1.000	7.36	14	0	0	0	0	18 1/3	29	15	15	12	18
	—Richmond (Int'l)	1	0	1.000	1.00	6	0	0	0	1	9	8	1	1	4	8
1988—	Richmond (Int'l)	6	3	.667	2.14	48	0	0	0	*22	71 1/3	47	17	17	22	71
	—Atlanta (N.L.)	0	2	.000	1.77	16	0	0	0	1	20 1/3	12	4	4	1	7
1989—	Atlanta (N.L.)	4	11	.267	3.94	66	0	0	0	21	82 1/3	78	37	36	34	68
1990—	Atlanta (N.L.)	1	3	.250	4.68	33	0	0	0	8	42 1/3	40	23	22	35	35
	—Philadelphia (N.L.)■	2	3	.400	2.15	34	0	0	0	6	46	37	12	11	16	40
1991—	Philadelphia (N.L.)	3	5	.375	3.84	68	0	0	0	0	98 1/3	90	45	42	54	89
1992—	Houston (N.L.)■	3	6	.333	2.51	*81	0	0	0	2	111 1/3	103	38	31	45	67
1993—	Oakland (A.L.)■	4	2	.667	3.86	42	0	0	0	0	79 1/3	87	40	34	33	49
	—Detroit (A.L.)■	2	1	.667	2.74	19	0	0	0	3	23	14	10	7	11	14
1994—	Detroit (A.L.)	9	2	.818	3.98	46	0	0	0	3	81 1/3	80	40	36	37	49
1995—	Detroit (A.L.)	5	7	.417	6.39	60	0	0	0	3	98 2/3	128	74	70	44	71
A.L. totals (3 years)		20	12	.625	4.69	167	0	0	0	9	282 1/3	309	164	147	125	183
N.L. totals (8 years)		14	31	.311	3.41	336	0	0	0	38	457	425	187	173	212	352
Major league totals (11 years)		34	43	.442	3.90	503	0	0	0	47	739 1/3	734	351	320	337	535

BOGAR, TIM — IF — METS

PERSONAL: Born October 28, 1966, in Indianapolis. . . . 6-2/198. . . . Bats right, throws right. . . . Full name: Tim Paul Bogar.

HIGH SCHOOL: Buffalo Grove (Ill.).

COLLEGE: Eastern Illinois.

TRANSACTIONS/CAREER NOTES: Selected by New York Mets organization in eighth round of free-agent draft (June 2, 1987). . . . On disabled list (June 14, 1990-remainder of season). . . . On disabled list (August 16-September 1, 1993). . . . On New York disabled list (May 6-June 9, 1994); included rehabilitation assignment to Norfolk (June 4-9).

B

STATISTICAL NOTES: Order of frequency of positions played at Tidewater in 1991: SS-2B-3B-C-1B-OF-P.
MISCELLANEOUS: Played all nine positions in one game for Tidewater (September 4, 1991).

				BATTING											FIELDING			
Year	Team (League)	Pos.	G	AB	R	H	2B	3B	HR	RBI	Avg.	BB	SO	SB	PO	A	E	Avg.
1987—	Little Falls (NYP)	SS-2B	58	205	31	48	9	0	0	23	.234	18	39	2	79	194	24	.919
1988—	Columbia (S. Atl.)	2B-SS	45	142	19	40	4	2	3	21	.282	22	29	5	89	120	8	.963
—	St. Lucie (Fla. St.)	2B-SS-3B	76	236	34	65	7	1	2	30	.275	34	57	9	141	214	19	.949
1989—	Jackson (Texas)	SS	112	406	44	108	13	5	4	45	.266	41	57	8	185	351	29	.949
1990—	Tidewater (Int'l)	SS	33	117	10	19	2	0	0	4	.162	8	22	1	57	89	10	.936
1991—	Williamsport (East.)	3-2-1-S	63	243	33	61	12	2	2	25	.251	20	44	13	100	137	8	.967
—	Tidewater (Int'l)	S-2-3-C-1-0-P	65	218	23	56	11	0	1	23	.257	20	35	1	111	183	11	.964
1992—	Tidewater (Int'l)	2-S-3-P-1	129	481	54	134	32	1	5	38	.279	14	65	7	211	327	15	.973
1993—	New York (N.L.)	SS-3B-2B	78	205	19	50	13	0	3	25	.244	14	29	0	105	217	9	.973
1994—	New York (N.L.)	3-1-S-2-0	50	52	5	8	0	0	2	5	.154	4	11	1	77	38	1	.991
—	Norfolk (Int'l)	3B-2B	5	19	0	2	0	0	0	1	.105	1	4	0	5	11	0	1.000
1995—	New York (N.L.)	S-3-1-2-0	78	145	17	42	7	0	1	21	.290	9	25	1	82	100	6	.968
Major league totals (3 years)			206	402	41	100	20	0	6	51	.249	27	65	2	264	355	16	.975

RECORD AS PITCHER

Year	Team (League)	W	L	Pct.	ERA	G	GS	CG	ShO	Sv.	IP	H	R	ER	BB	SO
1991—	Tidewater (Int'l)	0	0	...	27.00	1	0	0	0	0	$^{1}/_{3}$	0	1	1	0	1
1992—	Tidewater (Int'l)	0	0	...	12.00	3	0	0	0	0	3	4	4	4	3	1

BOGGS, WADE 3B YANKEES

PERSONAL: Born June 15, 1958, in Omaha, Neb. . . . 6-2/197. . . . Bats left, throws right. . . . Full name: Wade Anthony Boggs.
HIGH SCHOOL: H.B. Plant (Tampa, Fla.).
JUNIOR COLLEGE: Hillsborough Community College (Fla.).
TRANSACTIONS/CAREER NOTES: Selected by Boston Red Sox organization in seventh round of free-agent draft (June 8, 1976). . . . On disabled list (April 20-May 2, 1979). . . . Granted free agency (October 26, 1992). . . . Signed by New York Yankees (December 15, 1992). . . . Granted free agency (November 11, 1995). . . . Re-signed by Yankees (December 5, 1995).
RECORDS: Holds major league records for most seasons and most consecutive seasons leading league in intentional bases on balls received—6 (1987-92). . . . Holds A.L. record for most consecutive seasons with 200 or more hits—7 (1983-89). . . . Holds A.L. rookie-season record for highest batting average (100 or more games)—.349 (1982). . . . Shares major league single-season record for most games with a hit—135 (1985). . . . Holds A.L. single-season record for most singles—187 (1985). . . . Shares A.L. single-season record for fewest double plays by third baseman (150 or more games)—17 (1988). . . . Shares major league single-season record for fewest chances accepted by third baseman (150 or more games)—349 (1990).
HONORS: Named third baseman on The Sporting News A.L. All-Star team (1983, 1985-88, 1991 and 1994). . . . Named third baseman on The Sporting News A.L. Silver Slugger team (1983, 1986-89, 1991 and 1993-94). . . . Won A.L. Gold Glove at third base (1994-95).
STATISTICAL NOTES: Led Eastern League third basemen with .953 fielding percentage in 1979. . . . Led International League with .3353 batting average in 1981. . . . Led A.L with .449 on-base percentage in 1983, .450 in 1985, .453 in 1986, .461 in 1987, .476 in 1988 and .430 in 1989. . . . Led A.L. third basemen with 30 double plays in 1984, 37 in 1987, 29 in 1989 and 29 in 1993. . . . Led A.L. third basemen with 486 total chances in 1985. . . . Led A.L. with 19 intentional bases on balls received in 1987, 1989, 1990 and 1992, with 25 in 1991 and tied for lead with 18 in 1988. . . . Led A.L. in grounding into double plays with 23 in 1988. . . . Led A.L. third basemen with .981 fielding percentage in 1995. . . . Career major league grand slams: 3.

				BATTING											FIELDING			
Year	Team (League)	Pos.	G	AB	R	H	2B	3B	HR	RBI	Avg.	BB	SO	SB	PO	A	E	Avg.
1976—	Elmira (NYP)	3B	57	179	29	47	6	0	0	15	.263	29	15	2	36	75	16	.874
1977—	Winst.-Salem (Car.)	3B-2B-SS	117	422	67	140	13	1	2	55	.332	65	22	8	145	223	27	.932
1978—	Bristol (Eastern)	3-S-2-0	109	354	63	110	14	2	1	32	.311	53	25	1	62	107	7	.960
1979—	Bristol (Eastern)	3B-SS-2B	113	406	56	132	17	2	0	41	.325	66	21	11	94	213	15	†.953
1980—	Pawtucket (Int'l)	3B-1B	129	418	51	128	21	0	1	45	.306	64	25	3	108	156	12	.957
1981—	Pawtucket (Int'l)	3B-1B	137	498	67	*167	*41	3	5	60	*.335	89	41	4	359	238	26	.958
1982—	Boston (A.L.)	1-3-DH-0	104	338	51	118	14	1	5	44	.349	35	21	1	489	168	8	.988
1983—	Boston (A.L.)	3B	153	582	100	210	44	7	5	74	*.361	92	36	3	118	368	*27	.947
1984—	Boston (A.L.)	3B-DH	158	625	109	203	31	4	6	55	.325	89	44	3	141	330	•20	.959
1985—	Boston (A.L.)	3B	161	653	107	*240	42	3	8	78	*.368	96	61	2	134	335	17	.965
1986—	Boston (A.L.)	3B	149	580	107	207	47	2	8	71	*.357	*105	44	0	*121	267	19	.953
1987—	Boston (A.L.)	3B-1B-DH	147	551	108	200	40	6	24	89	*.363	105	48	1	112	277	14	.965
1988—	Boston (A.L.)	3B-DH	155	584	*128	214	*45	6	5	58	*.366	*125	34	2	*122	250	11	.971
1989—	Boston (A.L.)	3B-DH	156	621	•113	205	*51	7	3	54	.330	107	51	2	*123	264	17	.958
1990—	Boston (A.L.)	3B-DH	155	619	89	187	44	5	6	63	.302	87	68	0	108	241	20	.946
1991—	Boston (A.L.)	3B	144	546	93	181	42	2	8	51	.332	89	32	1	89	276	12	.968
1992—	Boston (A.L.)	3B-DH	143	514	62	133	22	4	7	50	.259	74	31	1	70	229	15	.952
1993—	New York (A.L.)■	3B-DH	143	560	83	169	26	1	2	59	.302	74	49	0	75	*311	12	*.970
1994—	New York (A.L.)	3B-1B	97	366	61	125	19	1	11	55	.342	61	29	2	66	218	10	.966
1995—	New York (A.L.)	3B-1B	126	460	76	149	22	4	5	63	.324	74	50	1	114	198	5	†.984
Major league totals (14 years)			1991	7599	1287	2541	489	53	103	864	.334	1213	598	19	1882	3732	207	.964

DIVISION SERIES RECORD

				BATTING											FIELDING			
Year	Team (League)	Pos.	G	AB	R	H	2B	3B	HR	RBI	Avg.	BB	SO	SB	PO	A	E	Avg.
1995—	New York (A.L.)	3B	4	19	4	5	2	0	1	3	.263	3	5	0	4	8	0	1.000

CHAMPIONSHIP SERIES RECORD

NOTES: Shares single-series record for most sacrifice flies—2 (1988).

				BATTING											FIELDING			
Year	Team (League)	Pos.	G	AB	R	H	2B	3B	HR	RBI	Avg.	BB	SO	SB	PO	A	E	Avg.
1986—	Boston (A.L.)	3B	7	30	3	7	1	1	0	2	.233	4	1	0	7	13	2	.909
1988—	Boston (A.L.)	3B	4	13	2	5	0	0	0	3	.385	3	4	0	6	6	0	1.000
1990—	Boston (A.L.)	3B	4	16	1	7	1	0	1	1	.438	0	3	0	6	10	0	1.000
Championship series totals (3 years)			15	59	6	19	2	1	1	6	.322	7	8	0	19	29	2	.960

WORLD SERIES RECORD

Year	Team (League)	Pos.	G	AB	R	H	2B	3B	HR	RBI	Avg.	BB	SO	SB	PO	A	E	Avg.
			BATTING												FIELDING			
1986	Boston (A.L.)	3B	7	31	3	9	3	0	0	3	.290	4	2	0	4	15	0	1.000

ALL-STAR GAME RECORD

Year	League	Pos.	AB	R	H	2B	3B	HR	RBI	Avg.	BB	SO	SB	PO	A	E	Avg.
			BATTING											FIELDING			
1985	American	3B	0	0	0	0	0	0	0	...	1	0	0	0	0	0	...
1986	American	3B	3	0	1	0	0	0	0	.333	1	0	0	0	1	0	1.000
1987	American	3B	3	0	0	0	0	0	0	.000	0	0	0	0	3	0	1.000
1988	American	3B	3	0	1	0	0	0	0	.333	0	0	0	0	1	0	1.000
1989	American	3B	3	1	1	0	0	1	1	.333	0	0	0	1	1	0	1.000
1990	American	3B	2	0	2	0	0	0	0	1.000	1	0	0	0	4	0	1.000
1991	American	3B	2	1	1	0	0	0	0	.500	1	0	0	1	2	0	1.000
1992	American	3B	3	1	1	0	0	0	0	.333	0	1	0	1	0	0	1.000
1993	American	3B	1	0	0	0	0	0	0	.000	1	0	0	1	0	0	1.000
1994	American	3B	3	1	1	0	0	0	0	.333	0	2	0	0	2	0	1.000
1995	American	3B	2	0	1	0	0	0	0	.500	0	0	0	0	1	0	1.000
All-Star Game totals (11 years)			25	4	9	0	0	1	1	.360	5	3	0	4	15	0	1.000

BOHANON, BRIAN — P

PERSONAL: Born August 1, 1968, in Denton, Tex. . . . 6-2/220. . . . Throws left, bats left. . . . Full name: Brian Edward Bohanon.
HIGH SCHOOL: North Shore (Houston).
TRANSACTIONS/CAREER NOTES: Selected by Texas Rangers organization in first round (19th pick overall) of free-agent draft (June 2, 1987). . . . On disabled list (April 17, 1988-remainder of season). . . . On Charlotte disabled list (April 7-May 2, 1989). . . . On Texas disabled list (April 7-July 1, 1991); included rehabilitation assignments to Charlotte (June 1-10), Tulsa (June 10-23) and Oklahoma City (June 23-30). . . . On Texas disabled list (April 28-May 13, 1992). . . . On Texas disabled list (June 9-30, 1993); included rehabilitation assignment to Oklahoma City (June 21-30). . . . Granted free agency (December 23, 1994). . . . Signed by Toledo, Detroit Tigers organization (March 6, 1995). . . . Released by Tigers (October 13, 1995).

Year	Team (League)	W	L	Pct.	ERA	G	GS	CG	ShO	Sv.	IP	H	R	ER	BB	SO
1987	GC Rangers (GCL)	0	2	.000	4.71	5	4	0	0	0	21	15	13	11	5	21
1988	Charlotte (Fla. St.)	0	1	.000	5.40	2	2	0	0	0	6 2/3	6	4	4	5	9
1989	Charlotte (Fla. St.)	0	3	.000	1.81	11	7	0	0	1	54 2/3	40	16	11	20	33
	—Tulsa (Texas)	5	0	1.000	2.20	11	11	1	1	0	73 2/3	59	20	18	27	44
1990	Texas (A.L.)	0	3	.000	6.62	11	6	0	0	0	34	40	30	25	18	15
	—Okla. City (A.A.)	1	2	.333	3.66	14	4	0	0	1	32	35	16	13	8	22
1991	Charlotte (Fla. St.)	1	0	1.000	3.86	2	2	0	0	0	11 2/3	6	5	5	4	7
	—Tulsa (Texas)	0	1	.000	2.31	2	2	0	0	0	11 2/3	9	8	3	11	6
	—Okla. City (A.A.)	0	4	.000	2.91	7	7	0	0	0	46 1/3	49	19	15	15	37
	—Texas (A.L.)	4	3	.571	4.84	11	11	1	0	0	61 1/3	66	35	33	23	34
1992	Okla. City (A.A.)	4	2	.667	2.73	9	9	3	0	0	56	53	21	17	15	24
	—Texas (A.L.)	1	1	.500	6.31	18	7	0	0	0	45 2/3	57	38	32	25	29
	—Tulsa (Texas)	2	1	.667	1.27	6	6	1	0	0	28 1/3	25	7	4	9	25
1993	Texas (A.L.)	4	4	.500	4.76	36	8	0	0	0	92 2/3	107	54	49	46	45
	—Okla. City (A.A.)	0	1	.000	6.43	2	2	0	0	0	7	7	6	5	3	7
1994	Okla. City (A.A.)	5	10	.333	4.12	15	15	2	1	0	98 1/3	106	56	45	33	88
	—Texas (A.L.)	2	2	.500	7.23	11	5	0	0	0	37 1/3	51	31	30	8	26
1995	Detroit (A.L.)■	1	1	.500	5.54	52	10	0	0	1	105 2/3	121	68	65	41	63
Major league totals (6 years)		12	14	.462	5.59	139	47	1	0	1	376 2/3	442	256	234	161	212

BOLTON, RODNEY — P

PERSONAL: Born September 23, 1968, in Chattanooga, Tenn. . . . 6-2/190. . . . Throws right, bats right. . . . Full name: Rodney Earl Bolton.
HIGH SCHOOL: Ooltewah (Tenn.).
JUNIOR COLLEGE: Chattanooga State Community Technical College .
COLLEGE: Kentucky (bachelor's degree in marketing).
TRANSACTIONS/CAREER NOTES: Selected by Chicago White Sox in 13th round of free-agent draft (June 4, 1990). . . . On disabled list (September 15-October 9, 1992 and July 12, 1994-remainder of season). . . . Contract sold by White Sox to Fukuoka Daiei Hawks of Japan Pacific League (January 9, 1996).

Year	Team (League)	W	L	Pct.	ERA	G	GS	CG	ShO	Sv.	IP	H	R	ER	BB	SO
1990	Utica (NYP)	5	1	.833	0.41	6	6	1	1	0	44	27	4	2	11	45
	—South Bend (Midw.)	5	1	.833	1.94	7	7	3	1	0	51	34	14	11	12	50
1991	Sarasota (Fla. St.)	7	6	.538	1.91	15	15	5	2	0	103 2/3	81	29	22	23	77
	—Birmingham (Sou.)	8	4	.667	1.62	12	12	3	2	0	89	73	26	16	21	57
1992	Vancouver (PCL)	11	9	.550	2.93	27	27	3	2	0	*187 1/3	174	72	61	59	111
1993	Chicago (A.L.)	2	6	.250	7.44	9	8	0	0	0	42 1/3	55	40	35	16	17
	—Nashville (A.A.)	10	1	*.909	*2.88	18	16	1	0	1	115 2/3	108	40	37	37	75
1994	Nashville (A.A.)	7	5	.583	2.56	17	17	1	0	0	116	108	43	33	35	63
1995	Nashville (A.A.)	14	3	.824	*2.88	20	20	3	1	0	131 1/3	127	44	42	23	76
	—Chicago (A.L.)	0	2	.000	8.18	8	3	0	0	0	22	33	23	20	14	10
Major league totals (2 years)		2	8	.200	7.69	17	11	0	0	0	64 1/3	88	63	55	30	27

BONDS, BARRY — OF — GIANTS

PERSONAL: Born July 24, 1964, in Riverside, Calif. . . . 6-1/185. . . . Bats left, throws left. . . . Full name: Barry Lamar Bonds. . . . Son of Bobby Bonds, coach, San Francisco Giants; major league outfielder with eight teams (1968-81) and coach, Cleveland Indians (1984-87).
HIGH SCHOOL: Serra (San Mateo, Calif.).
COLLEGE: Arizona State.

TRANSACTIONS/CAREER NOTES: Selected by San Francisco Giants organization in second round of free-agent draft (June 7, 1982); did not sign. . . . Selected by Pittsburgh Pirates organization in first round (sixth pick overall) of free-agent draft (June 3, 1985). . . . On disabled list (June 15-July 4, 1992). . . . Granted free agency (October 26, 1992). . . . Signed by Giants (December 8, 1992).

RECORDS: Shares major league single-season record for fewest assists by outfielder who led league in assists—14 (1990). . . . Shares N.L. career records for most seasons leading league in intentional bases on balls received—4 (1992-95); and most consecutive seasons leading league in intentional bases on balls received—4 (1992-95).

HONORS: Named outfielder on The Sporting News college All-America team (1985). . . . Named Major League Player of the Year by The Sporting News (1990). . . . Named N.L. Player of the Year by The Sporting News (1990-91). . . . Named outfielder on The Sporting News N.L. All-Star team (1990-94). . . . Won N.L. Gold Glove as outfielder (1990-94). . . . Named outfielder on The Sporting News N.L. Silver Slugger team (1990-94). . . . Named N.L. Most Valuable Player by Baseball Writers' Association of America (1990 and 1992-93).

STATISTICAL NOTES: Led N.L. with .565 slugging percentage in 1990, .624 in 1992 and .677 in 1993. . . . Led N.L. with 32 intentional bases on balls received in 1992, 43 in 1993, 18 in 1994 and 22 in 1995. . . . Led N.L. with .456 on-base percentage in 1992, .458 in 1993 and .431 in 1995. . . . Led N.L. with 365 total bases in 1993. . . . Hit three home runs in one game (August 2, 1994). . . . Career major league grand slams: 4.

		BATTING												FIELDING			
Year Team (League)	**Pos.**	**G**	**AB**	**R**	**H**	**2B**	**3B**	**HR**	**RBI**	**Avg.**	**BB**	**SO**	**SB**	**PO**	**A**	**E**	**Avg.**
1985— Prin. William (Car.).....	OF	71	254	49	76	16	4	13	37	.299	37	52	15	202	4	5	.976
1986— Hawaii (PCL).............	OF	44	148	30	46	7	2	7	37	.311	33	31	16	109	4	2	.983
— Pittsburgh (N.L.)........	OF	113	413	72	92	26	3	16	48	.223	65	102	36	280	9	5	.983
1987— Pittsburgh (N.L.)........	OF	150	551	99	144	34	9	25	59	.261	54	88	32	330	15	5	.986
1988— Pittsburgh (N.L.)........	OF	144	538	97	152	30	5	24	58	.283	72	82	17	292	5	6	.980
1989— Pittsburgh (N.L.)........	OF	159	580	96	144	34	6	19	58	.248	93	93	32	365	14	6	.984
1990— Pittsburgh (N.L.)........	OF	151	519	104	156	32	3	33	114	.301	93	83	52	338	•14	6	.983
1991— Pittsburgh (N.L.)........	OF	153	510	95	149	28	5	25	116	.292	107	73	43	321	13	3	.991
1992— Pittsburgh (N.L.)........	OF	140	473	*109	147	36	5	34	103	.311	*127	69	39	310	4	3	.991
1993— San Fran. (N.L.)■.......	OF	159	539	129	181	38	4	*46	*123	.336	126	79	29	310	7	5	.984
1994— San Francisco (N.L.) ..	OF	112	391	89	122	18	1	37	81	.312	*74	43	29	198	10	3	.986
1995— San Francisco (N.L.) ..	OF	•144	506	109	149	30	7	33	104	.294	*120	83	31	279	12	6	.980
Major league totals (10 years)		1425	5020	999	1436	306	48	292	864	.286	931	795	340	3023	103	48	.985

CHAMPIONSHIP SERIES RECORD

NOTES: Shares record for most hits in one inning—2 (October 13, 1992, second inning).

		BATTING												FIELDING			
Year Team (League)	**Pos.**	**G**	**AB**	**R**	**H**	**2B**	**3B**	**HR**	**RBI**	**Avg.**	**BB**	**SO**	**SB**	**PO**	**A**	**E**	**Avg.**
1990— Pittsburgh (N.L.)........	OF	6	18	4	3	0	0	0	1	.167	6	5	2	13	0	0	1.000
1991— Pittsburgh (N.L.)........	OF	7	27	1	4	1	0	0	0	.148	2	4	3	14	1	1	.938
1992— Pittsburgh (N.L.)........	OF	7	23	5	6	1	0	1	2	.261	6	4	1	17	0	0	1.000
Championship series totals (3 years)		20	68	10	13	2	0	1	3	.191	14	13	6	44	1	1	.978

ALL-STAR GAME RECORD

		BATTING											FIELDING			
Year League	**Pos.**	**AB**	**R**	**H**	**2B**	**3B**	**HR**	**RBI**	**Avg.**	**BB**	**SO**	**SB**	**PO**	**A**	**E**	**Avg.**
1990— National.....................	OF	1	0	0	0	0	0	0	.000	1	0	0	2	0	0	1.000
1992— National.....................	OF	3	1	1	1	0	0	0	.333	0	0	0	2	0	0	1.000
1993— National.....................	OF	3	2	2	2	0	0	0	.667	0	0	0	1	0	0	1.000
1994— National.....................	OF	3	0	0	0	0	0	1	.000	0	2	0	1	0	0	1.000
1995— National.....................	OF	3	0	0	0	0	0	0	.000	0	1	0	0	0	0	...
All-Star Game totals (5 years)		13	3	3	3	0	0	1	.231	1	3	0	6	0	0	1.000

BONES, RICKY — P — BREWERS

PERSONAL: Born April 7, 1969, in Salinas, Puerto Rico. . . . 6-0/193. . . . Throws right, bats right. . . . Full name: Ricardo Bones. . . . Name pronounced BO-nuss.

TRANSACTIONS/CAREER NOTES: Signed as non-drafted free agent by San Diego Padres organization (May 13, 1986). . . . Traded by Padres with SS Jose Valentin and OF Matt Mieske to Milwaukee Brewers for 3B Gary Sheffield and P Geoff Kellogg (March 27, 1992).

STATISTICAL NOTES: Led Texas League with 22 home runs allowed in 1989.

MISCELLANEOUS: Appeared in one game as outfielder with no chances (1993).

Year Team (League)	**W**	**L**	**Pct.**	**ERA**	**G**	**GS**	**CG**	**ShO**	**Sv.**	**IP**	**H**	**R**	**ER**	**BB**	**SO**
1986— Spokane (N'west)..............	1	3	.250	5.59	18	9	0	0	0	58	63	44	36	29	46
1987— Char., S.C. (S. Atl.)............	12	5	.706	3.65	26	26	4	1	0	170 1/3	*183	81	69	45	130
1988— Riverside (Calif.)................	15	6	.714	3.64	25	25	5	2	0	175 1/3	162	80	71	64	129
1989— Wichita (Texas)...................	10	9	.526	5.74	24	24	2	0	0	136 1/3	162	103	87	47	88
1990— Wichita (Texas)...................	6	4	.600	3.48	21	21	2	1	0	137	138	66	53	45	96
— Las Vegas (PCL)...............	2	1	.667	3.47	5	5	0	0	0	36 1/3	45	17	14	10	25
1991— Las Vegas (PCL)................	8	6	.571	4.22	23	23	1	0	0	136 1/3	155	90	64	43	95
— San Diego (N.L.)...............	4	6	.400	4.83	11	11	0	0	0	54	57	33	29	18	31
1992— Milwaukee (A.L.)■............	9	10	.474	4.57	31	28	0	0	0	163 1/3	169	90	83	48	65
1993— Milwaukee (A.L.)...............	11	11	.500	4.86	32	31	3	0	0	203 2/3	222	122	110	63	63
1994— Milwaukee (A.L.)...............	10	9	.526	3.43	24	24	4	1	0	170 2/3	166	76	65	45	57
1995— Milwaukee (A.L.)...............	10	12	.455	4.63	32	31	3	0	0	200 1/3	218	108	103	83	77
A.L. totals (4 years)..................	40	42	.488	4.40	119	114	10	1	0	738	775	396	361	239	262
N.L. totals (1 year)....................	4	6	.400	4.83	11	11	0	0	0	54	57	33	29	18	31
Major league totals (5 years)......	44	48	.478	4.43	130	125	10	1	0	792	832	429	390	257	293

ALL-STAR GAME RECORD

Year League	**W**	**L**	**Pct.**	**ERA**	**GS**	**CG**	**ShO**	**Sv.**	**IP**	**H**	**R**	**ER**	**BB**	**SO**
1994— American..........................						Did not play.								

BONILLA, BOBBY — OF — ORIOLES

PERSONAL: Born February 23, 1963, in New York. . . . 6-3/240. . . . Bats both, throws right. . . . Full name: Roberto Martin Antonio Bonilla. . . . Name pronounced bo-NEE-yah.

HIGH SCHOOL: Lehman (Bronx, N.Y.).

COLLEGE: New York Technical College.

TRANSACTIONS/CAREER NOTES: Signed as non-drafted free agent by Pittsburgh Pirates organization (July 11, 1981). . . . On Pittsburgh disabled list (March 25-July 19, 1985). . . . Selected by Chicago White Sox from Pirates organization in Rule 5 major league draft (December 10, 1985). . . . Traded by White Sox to Pittsburgh Pirates for P Jose DeLeon (July 23, 1986). . . . Granted free agency (October 28, 1991). . . . Signed by New York Mets (December 2, 1991). . . . On suspended list (July 27-28, 1992). . . . On disabled list (August 3-19, 1992). . . . Traded by Mets with a player to be named later to Baltimore Orioles for OF Alex Ochoa and OF Damon Buford (July 28, 1995); Orioles acquired P Jimmy Williams to complete deal (August 17, 1995).

RECORDS: Shares major league single-inning record for most doubles—2 (July 21, 1995, eighth inning). . . . Holds N.L. career record for most games with switch-hit home runs—6.

HONORS: Named third baseman on The Sporting News N.L. All-Star team (1988). . . . Named third baseman on The Sporting News N.L. Silver Slugger team (1988). . . . Named outfielder on The Sporting News N.L. All-Star team (1990-91). . . . Named outfielder on The Sporting News N.L. Silver Slugger team (1990-91).

STATISTICAL NOTES: Led Eastern League outfielders with 15 errors in 1984. . . . Switch-hit home runs in one game six times (July 3, 1987; April 6, 1988; April 23 and June 10, 1993; May 4, 1994; and May 12, 1995). . . . Led N.L. third basemen with 489 total chances in 1988. . . . Led N.L. third basemen with 35 errors in 1989. . . . Led N.L. third basemen with 31 double plays in 1989. . . . Led N.L. with 15 sacrifice flies in 1990. . . . Career major league grand slams: 4.

		BATTING												FIELDING			
Year Team (League)	Pos.	G	AB	R	H	2B	3B	HR	RBI	Avg.	BB	SO	SB	PO	A	E	Avg.
1981—GC Pirates (GCL)	1B-C-3B	22	69	6	15	5	0	0	7	.217	7	17	2	124	23	5	.967
1982—GC Pirates (GCL)	1B	47	167	20	38	3	0	5	26	.228	11	20	2	318	36	*14	.962
1983—Alexandria (Caro.)	OF-1B	•136	504	88	129	19	7	11	59	.256	78	105	28	259	12	15	.948
1984—Nashua (Eastern)	OF-1B	136	484	74	128	19	5	11	71	.264	49	89	15	312	8	†15	.955
1985—Prin. William (Car.)	1B-3B	39	130	15	34	4	1	3	11	.262	16	29	1	180	9	2	.990
1986—Chicago (A.L.)■	OF-1B	75	234	27	63	10	2	2	26	.269	33	49	4	361	22	2	.995
—Pittsburgh (N.L.)■	OF-1B-3B	63	192	28	46	6	2	1	17	.240	29	39	4	90	16	3	.972
1987—Pittsburgh (N.L.)	3B-OF-1B	141	466	58	140	33	3	15	77	.300	39	64	3	142	139	16	.946
1988—Pittsburgh (N.L.)	3B	159	584	87	160	32	7	24	100	.274	85	82	3	121	*336	*32	.935
1989—Pittsburgh (N.L.)	3B-1B-OF	•163	616	96	173	37	10	24	86	.281	76	93	8	190	334	†35	.937
1990—Pittsburgh (N.L.)	OF-3B-1B	160	625	112	175	39	7	32	120	.280	45	103	4	315	35	15	.959
1991—Pittsburgh (N.L.)	OF-3B-1B	157	577	102	174	*44	6	18	100	.302	90	67	2	247	144	15	.963
1992—New York (N.L.)■	OF-1B	128	438	62	109	23	0	19	70	.249	66	73	4	277	9	4	.986
1993—New York (N.L.)	OF-3B-1B	139	502	81	133	21	3	34	87	.265	72	96	3	238	112	17	.954
1994—New York (N.L.)	3B	108	403	60	117	24	1	20	67	.290	55	101	1	78	215	*18	.942
1995—New York (N.L.)	3B-OF-1B	80	317	49	103	25	4	18	53	.325	31	48	0	164	80	14	.946
—Baltimore (A.L.)■	OF-3B	61	237	47	79	12	4	10	46	.333	23	31	0	80	48	5	.962
American League totals (2 years)		136	471	74	142	22	6	12	72	.301	56	80	4	441	70	7	.986
National League totals (10 years)		1298	4720	735	1330	284	43	205	777	.282	588	766	32	1862	1420	169	.951
Major league totals (10 years)		1434	5191	809	1472	306	49	217	849	.284	644	846	36	2303	1490	176	.956

CHAMPIONSHIP SERIES RECORD

		BATTING												FIELDING			
Year Team (League)	Pos.	G	AB	R	H	2B	3B	HR	RBI	Avg.	BB	SO	SB	PO	A	E	Avg.
1990—Pittsburgh (N.L.)	OF-3B	6	21	0	4	1	0	0	1	.190	3	1	0	4	5	1	.900
1991—Pittsburgh (N.L.)	OF	7	23	2	7	2	0	0	1	.304	6	2	0	12	1	0	1.000
Championship series totals (2 years)		13	44	2	11	3	0	0	2	.250	9	3	0	16	6	1	.957

ALL-STAR GAME RECORD

		BATTING											FIELDING			
Year League	Pos.	AB	R	H	2B	3B	HR	RBI	Avg.	BB	SO	SB	PO	A	E	Avg.
1988—National	3B	4	0	0	0	0	0	0	.000	0	0	0	0	2	0	1.000
1989—National	PH-DH	2	0	2	0	0	0	0	1.000	0	0	0	...	...	...	...
1990—National	1B	1	0	0	0	0	0	0	.000	0	0	0	1	0	0	1.000
1991—National	DH	4	0	2	0	0	0	1	.500	0	1	0	...	...	...	...
1993—National	OF	1	0	1	0	0	0	0	1.000	0	0	0	2	0	0	1.000
1995—National	3B	1	0	0	0	0	0	0	.000	0	1	0	0	0	0	...
All-Star Game totals (6 years)		13	0	5	0	0	0	1	.385	0	2	0	3	2	0	1.000

BOONE, BRET — 2B — REDS

PERSONAL: Born April 6, 1969, in El Cajon, Calif. . . . 5-10/180. . . . Bats right, throws right. . . . Full name: Bret Robert Boone. . . . Son of Bob Boone, manager, Kansas City Royals, and catcher, Philadelphia Phillies, California Angels and Royals (1972-90); brother of Aaron Boone, third baseman, Cincinnati Reds organization; grandson of Ray Boone, major league infielder with six teams (1948-60); and nephew of Rodney Boone, minor league catcher/outfielder (1972-75).

HIGH SCHOOL: El Dorado (Yorba Linda, Calif.).

COLLEGE: Southern California.

TRANSACTIONS/CAREER NOTES: Selected by Minnesota Twins organization in 28th round of free-agent draft (June 2, 1987); did not sign. . . . Selected by Seattle Mariners organization in fifth round of free-agent draft (June 4, 1990). . . . Traded by Mariners with P Erik Hanson to Cincinnati Reds for P Bobby Ayala and C Dan Wilson (November 2, 1993).

STATISTICAL NOTES: Tied for Southern League lead in grounding into double plays with 21 in 1991. . . . Led Southern League second basemen with 288 putouts in 1991. . . . Led Pacific Coast League second basemen with 90 double plays in 1992. . . . Led N.L. second basemen with 106 double plays in 1995.

		BATTING												FIELDING			
Year Team (League)	Pos.	G	AB	R	H	2B	3B	HR	RBI	Avg.	BB	SO	SB	PO	A	E	Avg.
1990—Peninsula (Caro.)	2B	74	255	42	68	13	2	8	38	.267	47	57	5	154	216	19	.951

Year Team (League)	Pos.	G	AB	R	H	2B	3B	HR	RBI	Avg.	BB	SO	SB	PO	A	E	Avg.
			BATTING											FIELDING			
1991—Jacksonv. (South.)	2B-3B	•139	475	64	121	18	1	19	75	.255	72	123	9	†300	369	21	.970
1992—Calgary (PCL)	2B-SS	118	439	73	138	26	5	13	73	.314	60	88	17	268	366	10	.984
—Seattle (A.L.)	2B-3B	33	129	15	25	4	0	4	15	.194	4	34	1	72	96	6	.966
1993—Calgary (PCL)	2B	71	274	48	91	18	3	8	56	.332	28	58	3	146	180	8	.976
—Seattle (A.L.)	2B-DH	76	271	31	68	12	2	12	38	.251	17	52	2	140	177	3	.991
1994—Cincinnati (N.L.)■	2B-3B	108	381	59	122	25	2	12	68	.320	24	74	3	191	269	12	.975
1995—Cincinnati (N.L.)	2B	138	513	63	137	34	2	15	68	.267	41	84	5	*311	362	4	*.994
American League totals (2 years)		109	400	46	93	16	2	16	53	.233	21	86	3	212	273	9	.982
National League totals (2 years)		246	894	122	259	59	4	27	136	.290	65	158	8	502	631	16	.986
Major league totals (4 years)		355	1294	168	352	75	6	43	189	.272	86	244	11	714	904	25	.985

DIVISION SERIES RECORD

Year Team (League)	Pos.	G	AB	R	H	2B	3B	HR	RBI	Avg.	BB	SO	SB	PO	A	E	Avg.
			BATTING											FIELDING			
1995—Cincinnati (N.L.)	2B	3	10	4	3	1	0	1	1	.300	1	3	1	7	5	0	1.000

CHAMPIONSHIP SERIES RECORD

Year Team (League)	Pos.	G	AB	R	H	2B	3B	HR	RBI	Avg.	BB	SO	SB	PO	A	E	Avg.
			BATTING											FIELDING			
1995—Cincinnati (N.L.)	2B	4	14	1	3	0	0	0	0	.214	1	2	0	9	13	0	1.000

BORBON, PEDRO — P — BRAVES

PERSONAL: Born November 15, 1967, in Mao, Dominican Republic. . . . 6-1/205. . . . Throws left, bats left. . . . Full name: Pedro Felix Borbon Jr. . . . Son of Pedro Borbon, major league pitcher with four teams (1969-80). . . . Name pronounced bor-BONE.

HIGH SCHOOL: DeWitt Clinton (Bronx, N.Y.).

JUNIOR COLLEGE: Ranger (Tex.) Junior College.

TRANSACTIONS/CAREER NOTES: Selected by Milwaukee Brewers organization in 35th round of free-agent draft (June 3, 1985); did not sign. . . . Selected by Los Angeles Dodgers organization in secondary phase of free-agent draft (January 14, 1986); did not sign. . . . Signed as non-drafted free agent by Chicago White Sox organization (June 4, 1988). . . . Released by White Sox organization (April 1, 1989). . . . Signed by Atlanta Braves organization (August 25, 1989).

STATISTICAL NOTES: Led Gulf Coast League with 14 balks in 1988.

Year Team (League)	W	L	Pct.	ERA	G	GS	CG	ShO	Sv.	IP	H	R	ER	BB	SO
1988—GC White Sox (GCL)	5	3	.625	2.41	16	11	1	1	1	$74\frac{2}{3}$	52	28	20	17	67
1989—							Did not play.								
1990—Burlington (Midw.)■	11	3	.786	1.47	14	14	6	2	0	$97\frac{2}{3}$	73	25	16	23	76
—Durham (Carolina)	4	5	.444	5.43	11	11	0	0	0	$61\frac{1}{3}$	73	40	37	16	37
1991—Durham (Carolina)	4	3	.571	2.27	37	6	1	0	5	91	85	40	23	35	79
—Greenville (South.)	0	1	.000	2.79	4	4	0	0	0	29	23	12	9	10	22
1992—Greenville (South.)	8	2	.800	3.06	39	10	0	0	3	94	73	36	32	42	79
—Atlanta (N.L.)	0	1	.000	6.75	2	0	0	0	0	$1\frac{1}{3}$	2	1	1	1	1
1993—Richmond (Int'l)	5	5	.500	4.23	52	0	0	0	1	$76\frac{2}{3}$	71	40	36	42	95
—Atlanta (N.L.)	0	0	. . .	21.60	3	0	0	0	0	$1\frac{2}{3}$	3	4	4	3	2
1994—Richmond (Int'l)	3	4	.429	2.79	59	0	0	0	4	$80\frac{2}{3}$	66	29	25	41	82
1995—Atlanta (N.L.)	2	2	.500	3.09	41	0	0	0	2	32	29	12	11	17	33
Major league totals (3 years)	2	3	.400	4.11	46	0	0	0	2	35	34	17	16	21	36

DIVISION SERIES RECORD

Year Team (League)	W	L	Pct.	ERA	G	GS	CG	ShO	Sv.	IP	H	R	ER	BB	SO
1995—Atlanta (N.L.)	0	0	. . .	0.00	1	0	0	0	0	1	1	0	0	0	3

WORLD SERIES RECORD

NOTES: Member of World Series championship team (1995).

Year Team (League)	W	L	Pct.	ERA	G	GS	CG	ShO	Sv.	IP	H	R	ER	BB	SO
1995—Atlanta (N.L.)	0	0	. . .	0.00	1	0	0	0	1	1	0	0	0	0	2

BORDERS, PAT — C — CARDINALS

PERSONAL: Born May 14, 1963, in Columbus, O. . . . 6-2/200. . . . Bats right, throws right. . . . Full name: Patrick Lance Borders. . . . Brother of Todd Borders, minor league catcher (1988).

HIGH SCHOOL: Lake Wales (Fla.).

TRANSACTIONS/CAREER NOTES: Selected by Toronto Blue Jays organization in sixth round of free-agent draft (June 7, 1982). . . . On Toronto disabled list (July 5-August 19, 1988); included rehabilitation assignment to Syracuse (July 30-August 19). . . . Granted free agency (October 21, 1994). . . . Signed by Kansas City Royals (April 10, 1995). . . . Traded by Royals to Houston Astros for a player to be named later (August 12, 1995); Royals acquired P Rick Huisman to complete deal (August 17, 1995). . . . On Houston suspended list (September 8-14, 1995). . . . Granted free agency (November 6, 1995). . . . Signed by St. Louis Cardinals organization (January 10, 1996).

STATISTICAL NOTES: Tied for Southern League lead with 16 passed balls in 1987. . . . Led A.L. catchers with 880 total chances in 1992 and 962 in 1993. . . . Led A.L. with nine passed balls in 1994. . . . Career major league grand slams: 1.

Year Team (League)	Pos.	G	AB	R	H	2B	3B	HR	RBI	Avg.	BB	SO	SB	PO	A	E	Avg.
			BATTING											FIELDING			
1982—Medicine Hat (Pio.)	3B	61	217	30	66	12	2	5	33	.304	24	52	1	23	96	*25	.826
1983—Florence (S. Atl.)	3B	131	457	62	125	31	4	5	54	.274	46	116	4	70	233	*41	.881
1984—Florence (S. Atl.)	1B-3B-OF	131	467	69	129	32	5	12	85	.276	56	109	3	650	77	25	.967
1985—Kinston (Carolina)	1B	127	460	43	120	16	1	10	60	.261	45	116	6	854	42	*20	.978
1986—Florence (S. Atl.)	C-OF	16	40	8	15	7	0	3	9	.375	2	9	0	22	1	0	1.000
—Knoxville (South.)	C-1B	12	34	3	12	1	0	2	5	.353	1	6	0	45	5	3	.943
—Kinston (Carolina)	C-1B-OF	49	174	24	57	10	0	6	26	.328	10	42	0	211	26	7	.971
1987—Dunedin (Fla. St.)	1B	3	11	0	4	0	0	0	1	.364	0	3	0	21	1	0	1.000

Year	Team (League)	Pos.	G	AB	R	H	2B	3B	HR	RBI	Avg.	BB	SO	SB	PO	A	E	Avg.
			BATTING												FIELDING			
	—Knoxville (South.)	C-3B	94	349	44	102	14	1	11	51	.292	20	56	2	432	49	12	.976
1988—	Toronto (A.L.)	C-DH-2-3	56	154	15	42	6	3	5	21	.273	3	24	0	205	19	7	.970
	—Syracuse (Int'l)	C	35	120	11	29	8	0	3	14	.242	16	22	0	202	17	2	.991
1989—	Toronto (A.L.)	C-DH	94	241	22	62	11	1	3	29	.257	11	45	2	261	27	6	.980
1990—	Toronto (A.L.)	C-DH	125	346	36	99	24	2	15	49	.286	18	57	0	515	46	4	.993
1991—	Toronto (A.L.)	C	105	291	22	71	17	0	5	36	.244	11	45	0	505	48	4	.993
1992—	Toronto (A.L.)	C	138	480	47	116	26	2	13	53	.242	33	75	1	784	*88	8	.991
1993—	Toronto (A.L.)	C	138	488	38	124	30	0	9	55	.254	20	66	2	869	*80	*13	.986
1994—	Toronto (A.L.)	C	85	295	24	73	13	1	3	26	.247	15	50	1	583	*60	8	.988
1995—	Kansas City (A.L.)■	C-DH	52	143	14	33	8	1	4	13	.231	7	22	0	182	18	0	1.000
	—Houston (N.L.)■	C	11	35	1	4	0	0	0	0	.114	2	7	0	70	5	1	.987
American League totals (8 years)			793	2438	218	620	135	10	57	282	.254	118	384	6	3904	386	50	.988
National League totals (1 year)			11	35	1	4	0	0	0	0	.114	2	7	0	70	5	1	.987
Major league totals (8 years)			804	2473	219	624	135	10	57	282	.252	120	391	6	3974	391	51	.988

CHAMPIONSHIP SERIES RECORD

Year	Team (League)	Pos.	G	AB	R	H	2B	3B	HR	RBI	Avg.	BB	SO	SB	PO	A	E	Avg.
			BATTING												FIELDING			
1989—	Toronto (A.L.)	PH-C	1	1	0	1	0	0	0	1	1.000	0	0	0	1	0	0	1.000
1991—	Toronto (A.L.)	C	5	19	0	5	1	0	0	2	.263	0	0	0	38	4	2	.955
1992—	Toronto (A.L.)	C	6	22	3	7	0	0	1	3	.318	1	1	0	38	3	1	.976
1993—	Toronto (A.L.)	C	6	24	1	6	1	0	0	3	.250	0	6	1	41	4	0	1.000
Championship series totals (4 years)			18	66	4	19	2	0	1	9	.288	1	7	1	118	11	3	.977

WORLD SERIES RECORD

NOTES: Named Most Valuable Player (1992). . . . Member of World Series championship teams (1992 and 1993).

Year	Team (League)	Pos.	G	AB	R	H	2B	3B	HR	RBI	Avg.	BB	SO	SB	PO	A	E	Avg.
			BATTING												FIELDING			
1992—	Toronto (A.L.)	C	6	20	2	9	3	0	1	3	.450	2	1	0	48	5	1	.981
1993—	Toronto (A.L.)	C	6	23	2	7	0	0	0	1	.304	2	1	0	50	2	1	.981
World Series totals (2 years)			12	43	4	16	3	0	1	4	.372	4	2	0	98	7	2	.981

BORDICK, MIKE SS ATHLETICS

PERSONAL: Born July 21, 1965, in Marquette, Mich. . . . 5-11/175. . . . Bats right, throws right. . . . Full name: Michael Todd Bordick.

HIGH SCHOOL: Hampden (Me.) Academy.

COLLEGE: Maine.

TRANSACTIONS/CAREER NOTES: Signed as non-drafted free agent by Oakland Athletics organization (July 10, 1986). . . . On Tacoma disabled list (April 14-May 13, 1991). . . . On Oakland disabled list (May 8-27, 1995); included rehabilitation assignment to Modesto (May 23-26).

STATISTICAL NOTES: Led Pacific Coast League shortstops with .972 fielding percentage and 82 double plays in 1990. . . . Led A.L. shortstops with 280 putouts and tied for lead with 108 double plays in 1993. . . . Career major league grand slams: 1.

Year	Team (League)	Pos.	G	AB	R	H	2B	3B	HR	RBI	Avg.	BB	SO	SB	PO	A	E	Avg.
			BATTING												FIELDING			
1986—	Medford (N'west)	SS	46	187	30	48	3	1	0	19	.257	40	21	6	68	143	18	.921
1987—	Modesto (Calif.)	SS	133	497	73	133	17	0	3	75	.268	87	92	8	216	305	17	*.968
1988—	Huntsville (South.)	2B-SS-3B	132	481	48	130	13	2	0	28	.270	87	50	7	260	406	24	.965
1989—	Tacoma (PCL)	2B-SS-3B	136	487	55	117	17	1	1	43	.240	58	51	4	261	431	33	.954
1990—	Oakland (A.L.)	3B-SS-2B	25	14	0	1	0	0	0	0	.071	1	4	0	9	8	0	1.000
	—Tacoma (PCL)	SS-2B	111	348	49	79	16	1	2	30	.227	46	40	3	210	366	16	†.973
1991—	Tacoma (PCL)	SS	26	81	15	22	4	1	2	14	.272	17	10	0	35	79	3	.974
	—Oakland (A.L.)	SS-2B-3B	90	235	21	56	5	1	0	21	.238	14	37	3	146	213	11	.970
1992—	Oakland (A.L.)	2B-SS	154	504	62	151	19	4	3	48	.300	40	59	12	311	449	16	.979
1993—	Oakland (A.L.)	SS-2B	159	546	60	136	21	2	3	48	.249	60	58	10	†285	420	13	.982
1994—	Oakland (A.L.)	SS-2B	114	391	38	99	18	4	2	37	.253	38	44	7	187	320	14	.973
1995—	Oakland (A.L.)	SS-DH	126	428	46	113	13	0	8	44	.264	35	48	11	*245	338	10	.983
	—Modesto (Calif.)	SS	1	2	0	0	0	0	0	0	.000	0	0	0	2	1	0	1.000
Major league totals (6 years)			668	2118	227	556	76	11	16	198	.263	188	250	43	1183	1748	64	.979

CHAMPIONSHIP SERIES RECORD

Year	Team (League)	Pos.	G	AB	R	H	2B	3B	HR	RBI	Avg.	BB	SO	SB	PO	A	E	Avg.
			BATTING												FIELDING			
1992—	Oakland (A.L.)	SS-2B	6	19	1	1	0	0	0	0	.053	1	2	1	15	14	0	1.000

WORLD SERIES RECORD

Year	Team (League)	Pos.	G	AB	R	H	2B	3B	HR	RBI	Avg.	BB	SO	SB	PO	A	E	Avg.
			BATTING												FIELDING			
1990—	Oakland (A.L.)	SS-PR	3	0	0	0	0	0	0	0	...	0	0	0	0	2	0	1.000

BORLAND, TOBY P PHILLIES

PERSONAL: Born May 29, 1969, in Quitman, La. . . . 6-6/193. . . . Throws right, bats right. . . . Full name: Toby Shawn Borland.

HIGH SCHOOL: Quitman (La.).

TRANSACTIONS/CAREER NOTES: Selected by Philadelphia Phillies organization in 27th round of free-agent draft (June 2, 1987). . . . On Philadelphia disabled list (June 14-July 8, 1995); included rehabilitation assignment to Scranton/Wilkes-Barre (June 22-July 8).

STATISTICAL NOTES: Tied for Eastern League lead with three balks in 1991. . . . Pitched one inning, combining with starter Craig Holman (two innings), Gregory Brown (two innings) and Ricky Bottalico (two innings) in seven-inning 2-0 no-hit victory for Reading against New

Britain (September 4, 1993, first game).

Year	Team (League)	W	L	Pct.	ERA	G	GS	CG	ShO	Sv.	IP	H	R	ER	BB	SO
1988—	Martinsville (App.)	2	3	.400	4.04	34	0	0	0	*12	49	42	26	22	29	43
1989—	Spartanburg (SAL)	4	5	.444	2.97	47	0	0	0	9	66 2/3	62	29	22	35	48
1990—	Clearwater (Fla. St.)	1	2	.333	2.26	44	0	0	0	5	59 2/3	44	21	15	35	44
	—Reading (Eastern)	4	1	.800	1.44	14	0	0	0	0	25	16	6	4	11	26
1991—	Reading (Eastern)	8	3	.727	2.70	*59	0	0	0	•24	76 2/3	68	31	23	56	72
1992—	Scran./W.B. (Int'l)	0	1	.000	7.24	27	0	0	0	1	27 1/3	25	23	22	26	25
	—Reading (Eastern)	2	4	.333	3.43	32	0	0	0	5	42	39	23	16	32	45
1993—	Reading (Eastern)	2	2	.500	2.52	44	0	0	0	13	53 2/3	38	17	15	20	74
	—Scran./W.B. (Int'l)	2	4	.333	5.76	26	0	0	0	1	29 2/3	31	20	19	20	26
1994—	Scran./W.B. (Int'l)	4	1	.800	1.68	27	1	0	0	4	53 2/3	36	12	10	21	61
	—Philadelphia (N.L.)	1	0	1.000	2.36	24	0	0	0	1	34 1/3	31	10	9	14	26
1995—	Philadelphia (N.L.)	1	3	.250	3.77	50	0	0	0	6	74	81	37	31	37	59
	—Scran./W.B. (Int'l)	0	0	...	0.00	8	0	0	0	1	11 1/3	5	0	0	6	15
	Major league totals (2 years)	2	3	.400	3.32	74	0	0	0	7	108 1/3	112	47	40	51	85

BOROWSKI, JOE — P — BRAVES

PERSONAL: Born May 4, 1971, in Bayonne, N.J. . . . 6-2/225. . . . Throws right, bats right. . . . Full name: Joseph Thomas Borowski.
HIGH SCHOOL: Marist (Bayonne, N.J.).
COLLEGE: Rutgers.
TRANSACTIONS/CAREER NOTES: Selected by Chicago White Sox organization in 32nd round of free-agent draft (June 5, 1989). . . . Traded by White Sox organization to Baltimore Orioles organization for IF Pete Rose (March 21, 1991). . . . Traded by Orioles with P Rachaad Stewart to Atlanta Braves for P Kent Mercker (December 17, 1995).

Year	Team (League)	W	L	Pct.	ERA	G	GS	CG	ShO	Sv.	IP	H	R	ER	BB	SO
1990—	GC White Sox (GCL)	2	•8	.200	5.58	12	11	0	0	0	61 1/3	74	*47	*38	25	67
1991—	Kane Co. (Mid.)■	7	2	.778	2.56	49	0	0	0	13	81	60	26	23	43	76
1992—	Frederick (Caro.)	5	6	.455	3.70	48	0	0	0	10	80 1/3	71	40	33	50	85
1993—	Frederick (Caro.)	1	1	.500	3.61	42	2	0	0	11	62 1/3	61	30	25	37	70
	—Bowie (Eastern)	3	0	1.000	0.00	9	0	0	0	0	17 2/3	11	0	0	11	17
1994—	Bowie (Eastern)	3	4	.429	1.91	49	0	0	0	14	66	52	14	14	28	73
1995—	Rochester (Int'l)	1	3	.250	4.04	28	0	0	0	6	35 2/3	32	16	16	18	32
	—Bowie (Eastern)	2	2	.500	3.92	16	0	0	0	7	20 2/3	16	9	9	7	32
	—Baltimore (A.L.)	0	0	...	1.23	6	0	0	0	0	7 1/3	5	1	1	4	3
	Major league totals (1 year)	0	0	...	1.23	6	0	0	0	0	7 1/3	5	1	1	4	3

BOSIO, CHRIS — P — MARINERS

PERSONAL: Born April 3, 1963, in Carmichael, Calif. . . . 6-3/235. . . . Throws right, bats right. . . . Full name: Christopher Louis Bosio. . . . Name pronounced BAHZ-ee-o.
HIGH SCHOOL: Cordova (Calif.).
COLLEGE: Sacramento (Calif.) City College.
TRANSACTIONS/CAREER NOTES: Selected by Pittsburgh Pirates organization in 29th round of free-agent draft (June 8, 1981); did not sign. . . . Selected by Milwaukee Brewers organization in secondary phase of free-agent draft (January 12, 1982). . . . On Milwaukee disabled list (June 29-July 15, 1990); included rehabilitation assignment to Beloit (July 9-15). . . . On Milwaukee disabled list (August 2, 1990-remainder of season). . . . On disabled list (July 1-16, 1991). . . . Granted free agency (October 26, 1992). . . . Signed by Seattle Mariners (December 3, 1992). . . . On disabled list (April 28-May 28 and June 7-25, 1993). . . . On suspended list (June 28-July 3, 1993). . . . On disabled list (July 10, 1994-remainder of season).
STATISTICAL NOTES: Pitched 7-0 no-hit victory against Boston (April 22, 1993).
MISCELLANEOUS: Appeared in one game as designated hitter but made no plate appearance (1993).

Year	Team (League)	W	L	Pct.	ERA	G	GS	CG	ShO	Sv.	IP	H	R	ER	BB	SO
1982—	Pikeville (Appal.)	3	2	.600	4.91	13	3	2	1	1	51 1/3	60	31	28	17	53
1983—	Beloit (Midwest)	3	10	.231	5.60	17	17	3	0	0	107 2/3	125	82	67	41	71
	—Paintsville (Appal.)	2	2	.500	2.84	7	7	2	2	0	44 1/3	30	18	14	18	43
1984—	Beloit (Midwest)	*17	6	.739	2.73	26	26	11	2	0	181	159	83	55	56	156
1985—	El Paso (Texas)	11	6	.647	3.82	28	25	6	1	2	181 1/3	186	108	77	49	*155
1986—	Vancouver (PCL)	7	3	.700	2.28	44	0	0	0	•16	67	47	18	17	13	60
	—Milwaukee (A.L.)	0	4	.000	7.01	10	4	0	0	0	34 2/3	41	27	27	13	29
1987—	Milwaukee (A.L.)	11	8	.579	5.24	46	19	2	1	2	170	187	102	99	50	150
1988—	Milwaukee (A.L.)	7	15	.318	3.36	38	22	9	1	6	182	190	80	68	38	84
	—Denver (Am. Assoc.)	1	0	1.000	3.86	2	2	1	0	0	14	13	6	6	4	12
1989—	Milwaukee (A.L.)	15	10	.600	2.95	33	33	8	2	0	234 2/3	225	90	77	48	173
1990—	Milwaukee (A.L.)	4	9	.308	4.00	20	20	4	1	0	132 2/3	131	67	59	38	76
	—Beloit (Midwest)	0	0	...	3.00	1	1	0	0	0	3	4	2	1	1	2
1991—	Milwaukee (A.L.)	14	10	.583	3.25	32	32	5	1	0	204 2/3	187	80	74	58	117
1992—	Milwaukee (A.L.)	16	6	.727	3.62	33	33	4	2	0	231 1/3	223	100	93	44	120
1993—	Seattle (A.L.)■	9	9	.500	3.45	29	24	3	1	1	164 1/3	138	75	63	59	119
1994—	Seattle (A.L.)	4	10	.286	4.32	19	19	4	0	0	125	137	72	60	40	67
1995—	Seattle (A.L.)	10	8	.556	4.92	31	31	0	0	0	170	211	98	93	69	85
	Major league totals (10 years)	90	89	.503	3.89	291	237	39	9	9	1649 1/3	1670	791	713	457	1020

DIVISION SERIES RECORD

Year	Team (League)	W	L	Pct.	ERA	G	GS	CG	ShO	Sv.	IP	H	R	ER	BB	SO
1995—	Seattle (A.L.)	0	0	...	10.57	2	2	0	0	0	7 2/3	10	9	9	4	2

CHAMPIONSHIP SERIES RECORD

Year	Team (League)	W	L	Pct.	ERA	G	GS	CG	ShO	Sv.	IP	H	R	ER	BB	SO
1995—	Seattle (A.L.)	0	1	.000	3.38	1	1	0	0	0	5 1/3	7	3	2	2	3

BOSKIE, SHAWN — P

PERSONAL: Born March 28, 1967, in Hawthorne, Nev. . . . 6-3/200. . . . Throws right, bats right. . . . Full name: Shawn Kealoha Boskie. . . . Name pronounced BAH-skee.
HIGH SCHOOL: Reno (Nev.).
JUNIOR COLLEGE: Modesto (Calif.) Junior College.
TRANSACTIONS/CAREER NOTES: Selected by Chicago Cubs organization in first round (10th pick overall) of free-agent draft (January 14, 1986). . . . On Chicago disabled list (August 5-September 26, 1990). . . . On Chicago disabled list (July 27-September 1, 1992); included rehabilitation assignment to Iowa (August 24-September 1). . . . On suspended list (August 31-September 3, 1993). . . . Granted free agency (December 20, 1993). . . . Re-signed by Cubs (December 22, 1993). . . . Traded by Cubs to Philadelphia Phillies for P Kevin Foster (April 12, 1994). . . . Traded by Phillies to Seattle Mariners for a player to be named later (July 21, 1994); Phillies acquired 1B Fred McNair to complete deal (September 7, 1994). . . . On Seattle disabled list (July 31, 1994-remainder of season). . . . Released by Mariners (November 18, 1994). . . . Signed by Vancouver, California Angels organization (March 6, 1995). . . . On California disabled list (July 6, 1995-remainder of season); included rehabilitation assignments to Lake Elsinore (August 10-24) and Vancouver (August 24-September 1). . . . Granted free agency (December 21, 1995).
STATISTICAL NOTES: Led Appalachian League with 15 wild pitches in 1986. . . . Led Carolina League with 17 hit batsmen in 1988. . . . Led Southern League with 19 hit batsmen in 1989.
MISCELLANEOUS: Appeared in one game as pinch-runner and made an out in only appearance as pinch-hitter with Chicago (1991). . . . Appeared in one game as pinch-runner with Philadelphia (1994).

Year	Team (League)	W	L	Pct.	ERA	G	GS	CG	ShO	Sv.	IP	H	R	ER	BB	SO
1986	—Wytheville (Appal.)	4	4	.500	5.33	14	12	1	0	0	54	42	41	32	57	40
1987	—Peoria (Midwest)	9	11	.450	4.35	26	25	1	0	0	149	149	91	72	56	100
1988	—Winst.-Salem (Car.)	12	7	.632	3.39	27	27	4	2	0	186	176	83	70	89	164
1989	—Charlotte (South.)	11	8	.579	4.38	28	28	5	0	0	181	*196	105	88	84	*164
1990	—Iowa (Am. Assoc.)	4	2	.667	3.18	8	8	1	0	0	51	46	22	18	21	51
	—Chicago (N.L.)	5	6	.455	3.69	15	15	1	0	0	97 2/3	99	42	40	31	49
1991	—Chicago (N.L.)	4	9	.308	5.23	28	20	0	0	0	129	150	78	75	52	62
	—Iowa (Am. Assoc.)	2	2	.500	3.57	7	6	2	0	0	45 1/3	43	19	18	11	29
1992	—Chicago (N.L.)	5	11	.313	5.01	23	18	0	0	0	91 2/3	96	55	51	36	39
	—Iowa (Am. Assoc.)	0	0	...	3.68	2	2	0	0	0	7 1/3	8	4	3	3	3
1993	—Chicago (N.L.)	5	3	.625	3.43	39	2	0	0	0	65 2/3	63	30	25	21	39
	—Iowa (Am. Assoc.)	6	1	.857	4.27	11	11	1	0	0	71 2/3	70	35	34	21	35
1994	—Chicago (N.L.)	0	0	...	0.00	2	0	0	0	0	3 2/3	3	0	0	0	2
	—Philadelphia (N.L.)■	4	6	.400	5.23	18	14	1	0	0	84 1/3	85	56	49	29	59
	—Seattle (A.L.)■	0	1	.000	6.75	2	1	0	0	0	2 2/3	4	2	2	1	0
1995	—California (A.L.)■	7	7	.500	5.64	20	20	1	0	0	111 2/3	127	73	70	25	51
	—Lake Elsinore (California)	0	0	...	4.09	3	3	0	0	0	11	15	7	5	4	8
	—Vancouver (PCL)	1	0	1.000	3.00	1	1	0	0	0	6	4	2	2	4	1
A.L. totals (2 years)		7	8	.467	5.67	22	21	1	0	0	114 1/3	131	75	72	26	51
N.L. totals (5 years)		23	35	.397	4.58	125	69	2	0	0	472	496	261	240	169	250
Major league totals (6 years)		30	43	.411	4.79	147	90	3	0	0	586 1/3	627	336	312	195	301

BOSTON, D.J. — 1B — BLUE JAYS

PERSONAL: Born September 6, 1971, in Cincinnati. . . . 6-7/230. . . . Bats left, throws left. . . . Full name: Donald Jeffrey Boston. . . . Brother of Daryl Boston, outfielder with four major league teams (1984-94).
HIGH SCHOOL: Woodward (Cincinnati).
JUNIOR COLLEGE: San Jacinto (Tex.).
TRANSACTIONS/CAREER NOTES: Selected by Toronto Blue Jays organization in 39th round of free-agent draft (June 4, 1990).
STATISTICAL NOTES: Led New York-Pennsylvania League first basemen with 701 total chances in 1992.

			BATTING												FIELDING			
Year	Team (League)	Pos.	G	AB	R	H	2B	3B	HR	RBI	Avg.	BB	SO	SB	PO	A	E	Avg.
1991	—Medicine Hat (Pio.)	1B	59	207	34	58	12	0	1	25	.280	33	33	4	514	37	•16	.972
1992	—St. Cathar. (NYP)	1B	72	256	25	60	7	1	5	36	.234	36	41	20	646	40	*15	.979
1993	—Hagerstown (SAL)	1B	127	464	77	146	35	4	13	93	.315	54	77	31	*1039	79	12	.989
1994	—Dunedin (Fla. St.)	1B-OF	119	433	59	125	20	1	7	52	.289	55	65	19	774	70	8	.991
1995	—Knoxville (South.)	1B	132	479	51	117	27	1	11	71	.244	47	100	12	1129	91	*17	.986

BOTTALICO, RICKY — P — PHILLIES

PERSONAL: Born August 26, 1969, in New Britain, Conn. . . . 6-1/208. . . . Throws right, bats left. . . . Full name: Richard Paul Bottalico. . . . Name pronounced ba-TAL-e-kah.
HIGH SCHOOL: South Catholic (Hartford, Conn.).
COLLEGE: Florida Southern and Central Connecticut State.
TRANSACTIONS/CAREER NOTES: Signed as non-drafted free agent by Philadelphia Phillies organization (July 21, 1991).
STATISTICAL NOTES: Pitched two innings, combining with starter Craig Holman (two innings), Gregory Brown (two innings) and Toby Borland (one inning) in seven-inning, 2-0 no-hit victory for Reading against New Britain (September 4, 1993, first game).

Year	Team (League)	W	L	Pct.	ERA	G	GS	CG	ShO	Sv.	IP	H	R	ER	BB	SO
1991	—Martinsville (App.)	3	2	.600	4.09	7	6	2	•1	0	33	32	20	15	13	38
	—Spartanburg (SAL)	2	0	1.000	0.00	2	2	0	0	0	15	4	0	0	2	11
1992	—Spartanburg (SAL)	5	10	.333	2.41	42	11	1	0	13	119 2/3	94	41	32	56	118
1993	—Clearwater (Fla. St.)	1	0	1.000	2.75	13	0	0	0	4	19 2/3	19	6	6	5	19
	—Reading (Eastern)	3	3	.500	2.25	49	0	0	0	20	72	63	22	18	26	65
1994	—Scran./W.B. (Int'l)	3	1	.750	8.87	19	0	0	0	3	22 1/3	32	27	22	22	22
	—Reading (Eastern)	2	2	.500	2.53	38	0	0	0	22	42 2/3	29	13	12	10	51
	—Philadelphia (N.L.)	0	0	...	0.00	3	0	0	0	0	3	3	0	0	1	3
1995	—Philadelphia (N.L.)	5	3	.625	2.46	62	0	0	0	1	87 2/3	50	25	24	42	87
Major league totals (2 years)		5	3	.625	2.38	65	0	0	0	1	90 2/3	53	25	24	43	90

BOURGEOIS, STEVE — P — GIANTS

PERSONAL: Born August 4, 1972, in Lutcher La. . . . 6-1/220. . . . Throws right, bats right. . . . Full name: Steven James Bourgeois.
HIGH SCHOOL: Riverside Academy (Reserve, La.).
JUNIOR COLLEGE: Delgado (La.) and Hinds (Miss.).
COLLEGE: Northeast Louisiana.
TRANSACTIONS/CAREER NOTES: Selected by San Fransisco Giants organization in 21st round of free-agent draft (June 3, 1993).
HONORS: Named Texas League Pitcher of the Year (1995).

Year	Team (League)	W	L	Pct.	ERA	G	GS	CG	ShO	Sv.	IP	H	R	ER	BB	SO
1993—	Everett (N'west)	5	3	.625	4.21	15	15	0	0	0	77	62	44	36	44	77
1994—	Clinton (Midwest)	8	5	.615	3.64	20	20	0	0	0	106 1/3	97	57	43	54	88
—	San Jose (Calif.)	4	0	1.000	5.40	7	7	0	0	0	36 2/3	40	22	22	22	27
1995—	Shreveport (Texas)	12	3	.800	2.85	22	22	2	•2	0	145 1/3	140	50	46	53	91
—	Phoenix (PCL)	1	1	.500	3.38	6	5	0	0	0	34 2/3	38	18	13	13	23

BOVEE, MIKE — P — ROYALS

PERSONAL: Born August 21, 1973, in San Diego. . . . 5-10/200. . . . Throws right, bats right. . . . Full name: Michael Craig Bovee.
HIGH SCHOOL: Mira Mesa (San Diego).
TRANSACTIONS/CAREER NOTES: Selected by Kansas City Royals organization in sixth round of free-agent draft (June 3, 1991). . . . On disabled list (June 26-July 14,1993). . . . On temporarily inactive list (April 24-May 12, 1995).

Year	Team (League)	W	L	Pct.	ERA	G	GS	CG	ShO	Sv.	IP	H	R	ER	BB	SO
1991—	GC Royals (GCL)	3	1	.750	2.04	11	11	0	0	0	61 2/3	52	19	14	12	*76
1992—	Appleton (Midw.)	9	10	.474	3.56	26	24	1	0	0	149 1/3	143	85	59	41	120
1993—	Rockford (Midw.)	5	9	.357	4.21	20	20	2	0	0	109	118	58	51	30	111
1994—	Wilmington (Caro.)	13	4	.765	*2.65	28	26	0	0	0	169 2/3	149	58	50	32	154
1995—	Wichita (Texas)	8	6	.571	4.18	20	20	1	0	0	114	118	60	53	43	72

BOWEN, RYAN — P — MARLINS

PERSONAL: Born February 10, 1968, in Hanford, Calif. . . . 6-0/185. . . . Throws right, bats right. . . . Full name: Ryan Eugene Bowen.
HIGH SCHOOL: Hanford (Calif.).
TRANSACTIONS/CAREER NOTES: Selected by Houston Astros organization in first round (13th pick overall) of free-agent draft (June 2, 1986). . . . Selected by Florida Marlins in third round (63rd pick overall) of expansion draft (November 17, 1992). . . . On Florida disabled list (May 10-August 7, 1994); included rehabilitation assignments to Brevard County (June 18-25) and Edmonton (June 25-July 5 and July 22-August 10). . . . On Florida disabled list (April 22-September 3, 1995); included rehabilitation assignments to Brevard County (August 14-30) and Charlotte (August 30-31).
MISCELLANEOUS: Appeared in three games as pinch-runner with Houston (1991). . . . Appeared in four games as pinch-runner with Houston (1992).

Year	Team (League)	W	L	Pct.	ERA	G	GS	CG	ShO	Sv.	IP	H	R	ER	BB	SO
1987—	Asheville (S. Atl.)	12	5	.706	4.04	26	26	6	2	0	160 1/3	143	86	72	78	126
1988—	Osceola (Florida St.)	1	0	1.000	3.95	4	4	0	0	0	13 2/3	12	8	6	10	12
1989—	Chatt. (South.)	8	6	.571	4.25	27	27	1	1	0	139 2/3	123	83	66	116	136
1990—	Chatt. (South.)	8	4	.667	3.74	18	18	2	2	0	113	103	59	47	49	109
—	Tucson (Pac. Coast)	1	3	.250	9.35	10	7	0	0	0	34 2/3	41	36	36	38	29
1991—	Tucson (Pac. Coast)	5	5	.500	4.38	18	18	2	2	0	98 2/3	114	56	48	56	78
—	Houston (N.L.)	6	4	.600	5.15	14	13	0	0	0	71 2/3	73	43	41	36	49
1992—	Houston (N.L.)	0	7	.000	10.96	11	9	0	0	0	33 2/3	48	43	41	30	22
—	Tucson (Pac. Coast)	7	6	.538	4.12	21	20	1	1	0	122 1/3	128	68	56	64	94
1993—	Florida (N.L.)■	8	12	.400	4.42	27	27	2	1	0	156 2/3	156	83	77	87	98
1994—	Florida (N.L.)	1	5	.167	4.94	8	8	1	0	0	47 1/3	50	28	26	19	32
—	Brevard Co. (FSL)	1	2	.333	2.16	4	1	0	0	0	16 2/3	7	6	4	9	15
—	Edmonton (PCL)	1	0	1.000	6.16	5	5	0	0	0	19	22	13	13	11	13
1995—	Brevard Co. (FSL)	0	2	.000	2.45	3	3	0	0	0	11	6	3	3	6	10
—	Charlotte (Int'l)	0	1	.000	9.64	1	1	0	0	0	4 2/3	5	5	5	4	3
—	Florida (N.L.)	2	0	1.000	3.78	4	3	0	0	0	16 2/3	23	11	7	12	15
Major league totals (5 years)		17	28	.378	5.30	64	60	3	1	0	326	350	208	192	184	216

BOZE, MARSHALL — P — BREWERS

PERSONAL: Born May 23, 1971, in San Manuel, Ariz. . . . 6-1/214. . . . Throws right, bats right. . . . Full name: Marshall Wayne Boze.
HIGH SCHOOL: Soldotna (Alaska).
COLLEGE: Southwestern College (Calif.).
TRANSACTIONS/CAREER NOTES: Selected by Milwaukee Brewers organization in 12th round of free-agent draft (June 4, 1990). . . . On temporarily inactive list (April 24-May 12, 1995).

Year	Team (League)	W	L	Pct.	ERA	G	GS	CG	ShO	Sv.	IP	H	R	ER	BB	SO
1990—	Ariz. Brewers (Ariz.)	1	0	1.000	7.84	15	0	0	0	3	20 2/3	27	22	18	13	17
1991—	Helena (Pioneer)	3	3	.500	7.07	16	8	0	0	0	56	59	49	44	47	64
—	Beloit (Midwest)	0	1	.000	5.68	3	1	0	0	0	6 1/3	8	4	4	7	4
1992—	Beloit (Midwest)	13	7	.650	2.83	26	22	4	1	0	146 1/3	117	59	46	82	126
1993—	Stockton (Calif.)	7	2	.778	2.65	14	14	0	0	0	88 1/3	82	36	26	41	54
—	El Paso (Texas)	10	3	.769	2.71	13	13	1	0	0	86 1/3	78	36	26	32	48
1994—	New Orleans (A.A.)	6	10	.375	4.73	29	•29	2	0	0	171 1/3	182	101	90	74	81
1995—	New Orleans (A.A.)	3	9	.250	4.27	23	19	1	0	1	111 2/3	134	65	53	45	47

BRADSHAW, TERRY — OF — CARDINALS

PERSONAL: Born February 3, 1969, in Franklin, Va. . . . 6-0/180. . . . Bats left, throws right. . . . Full name: Terry Leon Bradshaw.
HIGH SCHOOL: Windsor (Va.).
COLLEGE: Norfolk (Va.) State.
TRANSACTIONS/CAREER NOTES: Selected by New York Yankees organization in 17th round of free-agent draft (June 2, 1987); did not sign. . . . Selected by St. Louis Cardinals organization in ninth round of free-agent draft (June 4, 1990). . . . On Arkansas disabled list (April 10, 1992-entire season).
STATISTICAL NOTES: Led South Atlantic League outfielders with 309 total chances in 1991.

			BATTING											FIELDING			
Year Team (League)	Pos.	G	AB	R	H	2B	3B	HR	RBI	Avg.	BB	SO	SB	PO	A	E	Avg.
1990—Hamilton (NYP)	OF	68	235	37	55	5	1	3	13	.234	24	60	15	106	1	2	.982
1991—Savannah (S. Atl.)	OF	132	443	91	105	17	1	7	42	.237	99	118	*65	*297	4	8	.974
1992—								Did not play.									
1993—St. Peters. (FSL)	OF	125	461	84	134	25	6	5	51	.291	82	60	43	*293	10	1	*.997
1994—Arkansas (Texas)	OF	114	425	65	119	25	8	10	52	.280	50	69	13	212	7	1	*.995
—Louisville (A.A.)	OF	22	80	16	20	4	0	4	8	.250	6	10	5	39	0	1	.975
1995—Louisville (A.A.)	OF	111	389	65	110	24	•8	8	42	.283	53	60	20	248	1	•8	.969
—St. Louis (N.L.)	OF	19	44	6	10	1	1	0	2	.227	2	10	1	19	1	1	.952
Major league totals (1 year)		19	44	6	10	1	1	0	2	.227	2	10	1	19	1	1	.952

BRADY, DOUG — 2B/SS — WHITE SOX

PERSONAL: Born November 23, 1969, in Jacksonville, Ill. . . . 5-11/165. . . . Bats both, throws right. . . . Full name: Stephen Douglas Brady.
COLLEGE: Liberty (Va.).
TRANSACTIONS/CAREER NOTES: Selected by Chicago White Sox organization in 12th round of free-agent draft (June 3, 1991).
STATISTICAL NOTES: Led Southern League second basemen with 87 double plays in 1994. . . . Led American Association second basemen with .975 fielding percentage in 1995. . . . Led American Association second basemen with 238 putouts, 304 assists, 556 total chances and 88 double plays in 1995.

			BATTING											FIELDING			
Year Team (League)	Pos.	G	AB	R	H	2B	3B	HR	RBI	Avg.	BB	SO	SB	PO	A	E	Avg.
1991—Utica (NYP)	SS-2B	65	226	37	53	6	3	2	31	.235	31	31	21	75	105	23	.887
1992—South Bend (Mid.)	2B-SS	24	92	12	27	5	1	0	7	.293	17	13	16	24	44	3	.958
—GC Whi. Sox (GCL)	2B	3	8	1	1	0	0	0	2	.125	1	1	0	3	12	0	1.000
—Sarasota (Fla. St.)	SS-2B	56	184	21	50	6	0	2	27	.272	25	33	5	55	96	11	.932
1993—Sarasota (Fla. St.)	2B-SS	115	449	75	113	16	6	5	44	.252	55	54	26	208	370	24	.960
—Nashville (A.A.)	2B	2	3	0	0	0	0	0	0	.000	0	0	0	1	3	1	.800
1994—Birm. (Southern)	2B	127	516	59	128	18	8	4	47	.248	38	59	34	263	296	*21	.964
1995—Nashville (A.A.)	2B-SS	125	450	71	134	15	6	5	27	.298	31	76	32	†239	†307	15	†.973
—Chicago (A.L.)	2B-DH	12	21	4	4	1	0	0	3	.190	2	4	0	14	21	0	1.000
Major league totals (1 year)		12	21	4	4	1	0	0	3	.190	2	4	0	14	21	0	1.000

BRAGG, DARREN — OF — MARINERS

PERSONAL: Born September 7, 1969, in Waterbury, Conn. . . . 5-9/180. . . . Bats left, throws right. . . . Full name: Darren W. Bragg.
HIGH SCHOOL: Taft (Watertown, Conn.).
COLLEGE: Georgia Tech.
TRANSACTIONS/CAREER NOTES: Selected by Seattle Mariners organization in 22nd round of free-agent draft (June 30, 1991).
STATISTICAL NOTES: Led Carolina League in caught stealing with 19 in 1992. . . . Led Pacific Coast League outfielders with 344 total chances and five double plays in 1994.

			BATTING											FIELDING			
Year Team (League)	Pos.	G	AB	R	H	2B	3B	HR	RBI	Avg.	BB	SO	SB	PO	A	E	Avg.
1991—Peninsula (Caro.)	OF-2B	69	237	42	53	14	0	3	29	.224	66	72	21	167	9	4	.978
1992—Peninsula (Caro.)	OF	135	428	*83	117	29	5	9	58	.273	*105	76	44	262	11	4	.986
1993—Jacksonv. (South.)	OF-P	131	451	74	119	26	3	11	46	.264	81	82	19	306	14	10	.970
1994—Calgary (PCL)	OF	126	500	112	175	33	6	17	85	.350	68	72	28	317	20	7	.980
—Seattle (A.L.)	DH-OF	8	19	4	3	1	0	0	2	.158	2	5	0	1	0	0	1.000
1995—Seattle (A.L.)	OF-DH	52	145	20	34	5	1	3	12	.234	18	37	9	83	7	1	.989
—Tacoma (PCL)	OF	53	212	24	65	13	3	4	31	.307	23	39	10	115	7	4	.968
Major league totals (2 years)		60	164	24	37	6	1	3	14	.226	20	42	9	84	7	1	.989

RECORD AS PITCHER

Year Team (League)	W	L	Pct.	ERA	G	GS	CG	ShO	Sv.	IP	H	R	ER	BB	SO
1993—Jacksonville (Sou.)	0	0	...	9.00	1	0	0	0	0	1	3	1	1	0	0

BRANDENBURG, MARK — P — RANGERS

PERSONAL: Born July 14, 1970, in Houston. . . . 6-0/180. . . . Throws right, bats right. . . . Full name: Mark Clay Brandenburg.
HIGH SCHOOL: Humble (Tex.).
COLLEGE: Texas Tech.
TRANSACTIONS/CAREER NOTES: Selected by Texas Rangers organization in 26th round of free-agent draft (June 1, 1992). . . . On Oklahoma City suspended list (May 29-31, 1995).

Year Team (League)	W	L	Pct.	ERA	G	GS	CG	ShO	Sv.	IP	H	R	ER	BB	SO
1992—Butte (Pioneer)	7	1	.875	4.06	24	1	0	0	2	62	70	32	28	14	78
1993—Char., S.C. (S. Atl.)	6	3	.667	1.46	44	0	0	0	4	80	62	23	13	22	67

Year	Team (League)	W	L	Pct.	ERA	G	GS	CG	ShO	Sv.	IP	H	R	ER	BB	SO
1994	— Charlotte (Fla. St.)	0	2	.000	0.87	25	0	0	0	5	41 1/3	23	5	4	15	44
	— Tulsa (Texas)	5	4	.556	1.74	37	0	0	0	8	62	50	17	12	12	63
1995	— Okla. City (A.A.)	0	5	.000	2.02	35	0	0	0	2	58	52	16	13	15	51
	— Texas (A.L.)	0	1	.000	5.93	11	0	0	0	0	27 1/3	36	18	18	7	21
Major league totals (1 year)		0	1	.000	5.93	11	0	0	0	0	27 1/3	36	18	18	7	21

BRANSON, JEFF — 3B/SS — REDS

PERSONAL: Born January 26, 1967, in Waynesboro, Miss. . . . 6-0/180. . . . Bats left, throws right. . . . Full name: Jeffery Glenn Branson.
HIGH SCHOOL: Southern Choctaw (Silas, Ala.).
COLLEGE: Livingston (Ala.) University.
TRANSACTIONS/CAREER NOTES: Selected by Cincinnati Reds organization in second round of free-agent draft (June 1, 1988).
MISCELLANEOUS: Member of 1988 U.S. Olympic baseball team.

				BATTING											FIELDING			
Year	Team (League)	Pos.	G	AB	R	H	2B	3B	HR	RBI	Avg.	BB	SO	SB	PO	A	E	Avg.
1989	— Ced. Rap. (Midw.)	SS	127	469	70	132	28	1	10	68	.281	41	90	5	172	394	33	.945
1990	— Ced. Rap. (Midw.)	SS	62	239	37	60	13	4	6	24	.251	24	44	11	96	152	7	.973
	— Chatt. (South.)	2B-SS	63	233	19	49	9	1	2	29	.210	13	48	3	122	151	13	.955
1991	— Chatt. (South.)	SS-2B	88	304	35	80	13	3	2	28	.263	31	51	3	126	212	12	.966
	— Nashville (A.A.)	SS-2B-OF	43	145	10	35	4	1	0	11	.241	8	31	5	61	93	8	.951
1992	— Nashville (A.A.)	S-3-2-O	36	123	18	40	6	3	4	12	.325	9	19	0	59	76	5	.964
	— Cincinnati (N.L.)	2B-3B-SS	72	115	12	34	7	1	0	15	.296	5	16	0	46	63	7	.940
1993	— Cincinnati (N.L.)	S-2-3-1	125	381	40	92	15	1	3	22	.241	19	73	4	185	260	11	.976
1994	— Cincinnati (N.L.)	2-3-S-1	58	109	18	31	4	1	6	16	.284	5	16	0	39	52	1	.989
1995	— Cincinnati (N.L.)	3-S-2-1	122	331	43	86	18	2	12	45	.260	44	69	2	84	245	9	.973
Major league totals (4 years)			377	936	113	243	44	5	21	98	.260	73	174	6	354	620	28	.972

DIVISION SERIES RECORD

				BATTING											FIELDING			
Year	Team (League)	Pos.	G	AB	R	H	2B	3B	HR	RBI	Avg.	BB	SO	SB	PO	A	E	Avg.
1995	— Cincinnati (N.L.)	3B	3	7	0	2	1	0	0	2	.286	2	0	0	1	8	0	1.000

CHAMPIONSHIP SERIES RECORD

				BATTING											FIELDING			
Year	Team (League)	Pos.	G	AB	R	H	2B	3B	HR	RBI	Avg.	BB	SO	SB	PO	A	E	Avg.
1995	— Cincinnati (N.L.)	3B-PH	4	9	2	1	1	0	0	0	.111	0	2	1	1	3	0	1.000

BRANTLEY, JEFF — P — REDS

PERSONAL: Born September 5, 1963, in Florence, Ala. . . . 5-10/180. . . . Throws right, bats right. . . . Full name: Jeffrey Hoke Brantley.
HIGH SCHOOL: W.A. Berry (Florence, Ala.).
COLLEGE: Mississippi State.
TRANSACTIONS/CAREER NOTES: Selected by Montreal Expos organization in 13th round of free-agent draft (June 4, 1984); did not sign. . . . Selected by San Francisco Giants organization in sixth round of free-agent draft (June 3, 1985). . . . Granted free agency (December 20, 1993). . . . Signed by Cincinnati Reds (January 4, 1994). . . . Granted free agency (October 17, 1994). . . . Re-signed by Reds (October 28, 1994).
STATISTICAL NOTES: Tied for Pacific Coast League lead with 11 hit batsmen in 1987.
MISCELLANEOUS: Appeared in one game as pinch-runner with San Francisco (1989).

Year	Team (League)	W	L	Pct.	ERA	G	GS	CG	ShO	Sv.	IP	H	R	ER	BB	SO
1985	— Fresno (California)	8	2	.800	3.33	14	13	3	0	0	94 2/3	83	39	35	37	85
1986	— Shreveport (Texas)	8	10	.444	3.48	26	26	•8	3	0	165 2/3	139	78	64	68	125
1987	— Shreveport (Texas)	0	1	.000	3.09	2	2	0	0	0	11 2/3	12	7	4	4	7
	— Phoenix (PCL)	6	11	.353	4.65	29	28	2	0	0	170 1/3	187	110	88	82	111
1988	— Phoenix (PCL)	9	5	.643	4.33	27	19	1	0	0	122 2/3	130	65	59	39	83
	— San Francisco (N.L.)	0	1	.000	5.66	9	1	0	0	1	20 2/3	22	13	13	6	11
1989	— San Francisco (N.L.)	7	1	.875	4.07	59	1	0	0	0	97 1/3	101	50	44	37	69
	— Phoenix (PCL)	1	1	.500	1.26	7	0	0	0	3	14 1/3	6	2	2	6	20
1990	— San Francisco (N.L.)	5	3	.625	1.56	55	0	0	0	19	86 2/3	77	18	15	33	61
1991	— San Francisco (N.L.)	5	2	.714	2.45	67	0	0	0	15	95 1/3	78	27	26	52	81
1992	— San Francisco (N.L.)	7	7	.500	2.95	56	4	0	0	7	91 2/3	67	32	30	45	86
1993	— San Francisco (N.L.)	5	6	.455	4.28	53	12	0	0	0	113 2/3	112	60	54	46	76
1994	— Cincinnati (N.L.)■	6	6	.500	2.48	50	0	0	0	15	65 1/3	46	20	18	28	63
1995	— Cincinnati (N.L.)	3	2	.600	2.82	56	0	0	0	28	70 1/3	53	22	22	20	62
Major league totals (8 years)		38	28	.576	3.12	405	18	0	0	85	641	556	242	222	267	509

DIVISION SERIES RECORD

Year	Team (League)	W	L	Pct.	ERA	G	GS	CG	ShO	Sv.	IP	H	R	ER	BB	SO
1995	— Cincinnati (N.L.)	0	0	...	6.00	3	0	0	0	1	3	5	2	2	0	2

CHAMPIONSHIP SERIES RECORD

Year	Team (League)	W	L	Pct.	ERA	G	GS	CG	ShO	Sv.	IP	H	R	ER	BB	SO
1989	— San Francisco (N.L.)	0	0	...	0.00	3	0	0	0	0	5	1	0	0	2	3
1995	— Cincinnati (N.L.)	0	0	...	0.00	2	0	0	0	0	2 2/3	0	0	0	2	1
Champ. series totals (2 years)		0	0	...	0.00	5	0	0	0	0	7 2/3	1	0	0	4	4

WORLD SERIES RECORD

Year	Team (League)	W	L	Pct.	ERA	G	GS	CG	ShO	Sv.	IP	H	R	ER	BB	SO
1989	— San Francisco (N.L.)	0	0	...	4.15	3	0	0	0	0	4 1/3	5	2	2	3	1

ALL-STAR GAME RECORD

Year	League	W	L	Pct.	ERA	GS	CG	ShO	Sv.	IP	H	R	ER	BB	SO
1990—	National	0	1	.000	54.00	0	0	0	0	1/3	2	2	2	0	0

BREWER, BILLY — P — DODGERS

PERSONAL: Born April 15, 1968, in Fort Worth, Tex. . . . 6-1/175. . . . Throws left, bats left. . . . Full name: William Robert Brewer.
HIGH SCHOOL: Spring Hill (Longview, Tex.).
COLLEGE: Dallas Baptist.
TRANSACTIONS/CAREER NOTES: Selected by Cleveland Indians organization in 26th round of free-agent draft (June 5, 1989); did not sign. . . . Selected by Montreal Expos organization in 28th round of free-agent draft (June 4, 1990). . . . On disabled list (April 12-June 11, 1991). . . . Selected by Kansas City Royals from Expos organization in Rule 5 major league draft (December 7, 1992). . . . Traded by Royals to Los Angeles Dodgers for SS Jose Offerman (December 17, 1995).

Year	Team (League)	W	L	Pct.	ERA	G	GS	CG	ShO	Sv.	IP	H	R	ER	BB	SO
1990—	Jamestown (NYP)	2	2	.500	2.93	11	2	0	0	1	27 2/3	23	10	9	13	37
1991—	Rockford (Midw.)	3	3	.500	1.98	29	0	0	0	5	41	32	12	9	25	43
1992—	WP Beach (FSL)	2	2	.500	1.73	28	0	0	0	8	36 1/3	27	10	7	14	37
—	Harrisburg (East.)	2	0	1.000	5.01	20	0	0	0	0	23 1/3	25	15	13	18	18
1993—	Kansas City (A.L.)■	2	2	.500	3.46	46	0	0	0	0	39	31	16	15	20	28
1994—	Kansas City (A.L.)	4	1	.800	2.56	50	0	0	0	3	38 2/3	28	11	11	16	25
1995—	Kansas City (A.L.)	2	4	.333	5.56	48	0	0	0	0	45 1/3	54	28	28	20	31
—	Springfield (Midw.)	0	0	...	0.00	1	0	0	0	1	2	2	1	0	1	2
—	Omaha (Am. Assoc.)	0	0	...	0.00	6	0	0	0	0	7	1	0	0	7	5
Major league totals (3 years)		8	7	.533	3.95	144	0	0	0	3	123	113	55	54	56	84

BREWINGTON, JAMIE — P — GIANTS

PERSONAL: Born September 28, 1971, in Greenville, N.C. . . . 6-4/180. . . . Throws right, bats right. . . . Full name: Jamie Chancellor Brewington.
HIGH SCHOOL: J. H. Rose (Greenville, N.C.).
COLLEGE: Virginia Commonwealth.
TRANSACTIONS/CAREER NOTES: Selected by San Francisco Giants organization in 10th round of free-agent draft (June 1, 1992). . . . On San Jose temporarily inactive list (April 7-May 3, 1994).
MISCELLANEOUS: Appeared in one game as pinch-runner with San Francisco (1995).

Year	Team (League)	W	L	Pct.	ERA	G	GS	CG	ShO	Sv.	IP	H	R	ER	BB	SO
1992—	Everett (N'west)	5	2	.714	4.33	15	11	1	•1	0	68 2/3	65	40	33	47	63
1993—	Clinton (Midwest)	13	5	.722	4.78	25	25	1	0	0	133 2/3	126	78	71	61	111
1994—	San Jose (Calif.)	7	3	.700	3.20	13	13	0	0	0	76	61	38	27	25	65
—	Clinton (Midwest)	2	4	.333	4.92	10	10	0	0	0	53	46	29	29	24	62
1995—	Shreveport (Texas)	8	3	.727	3.06	16	16	1	1	0	88 1/3	72	39	30	55	74
—	San Francisco (N.L.)	6	4	.600	4.54	13	13	0	0	0	75 1/3	68	38	38	45	45
Major league totals (1 year)		6	4	.600	4.54	13	13	0	0	0	75 1/3	68	38	38	45	45

BRISCOE, JOHN — P — ATHLETICS

PERSONAL: Born September 22, 1967, in LaGrange, Ill. . . . 6-3/185. . . . Throws right, bats right. . . . Full name: John Eric Briscoe.
HIGH SCHOOL: Berkner (Tex.).
JUNIOR COLLEGE: Texarkana (Tex.) College.
COLLEGE: Texas Christian.
TRANSACTIONS/CAREER NOTES: Selected by Milwaukee Brewers organization in third round of free-agent draft (January 14, 1986); did not sign. . . . Selected by Toronto Blue Jays organization in secondary phase of free-agent draft (June 2, 1986); did not sign. . . . Selected by Oakland Athletics organization in third round of free-agent draft (June 1, 1988). . . . On Tacoma disabled list (June 22-July 31, 1992). . . . On Oakland disabled list (June 19-July 15, 1994); included rehabilitation assignment to Modesto (July 11-15). . . . On Oakland disabled list (April 22-July 25, 1995); included rehabilitation assignments to Modesto (July 4-13) and Edmonton (July 14-25).
MISCELLANEOUS: Appeared in one game as pinch-runner with Oakland (1994).

Year	Team (League)	W	L	Pct.	ERA	G	GS	CG	ShO	Sv.	IP	H	R	ER	BB	SO
1988—	Arizona A's (Ariz.)	1	1	.500	3.51	7	6	0	0	0	25 2/3	26	14	10	6	23
1989—	Madison (Midwest)	7	5	.583	4.21	21	20	1	0	0	117 2/3	121	66	55	57	69
1990—	Modesto (Calif.)	3	6	.333	4.59	29	12	1	0	4	86 1/3	72	50	44	52	66
—	Huntsville (South.)	0	0	...	13.50	3	0	0	0	0	4 2/3	9	7	7	7	7
1991—	Huntsville (South.)	2	0	1.000	0.00	2	0	0	0	0	4 1/3	1	2	0	2	6
—	Oakland (A.L.)	0	0	...	7.07	11	0	0	0	0	14	12	11	11	10	9
—	Tacoma (PCL)	3	5	.375	3.66	22	9	0	0	1	76 1/3	73	35	31	44	66
1992—	Oakland (A.L.)	0	1	.000	6.43	2	2	0	0	0	7	12	6	5	9	4
—	Tacoma (PCL)	2	5	.286	5.88	33	6	0	0	0	78	78	62	51	68	66
1993—	Huntsville (South.)	4	0	1.000	3.03	30	0	0	0	16	38 2/3	28	14	13	16	62
—	Oakland (A.L.)	1	0	1.000	8.03	17	0	0	0	0	24 2/3	26	25	22	26	24
—	Tacoma (PCL)	1	1	.500	2.92	9	0	0	0	6	12 1/3	13	5	4	9	16
1994—	Oakland (A.L.)	4	2	.667	4.01	37	0	0	0	1	49 1/3	31	24	22	39	45
—	Modesto (Calif.)	0	0	...	0.00	2	2	0	0	0	3	2	0	0	0	9
1995—	Modesto (Calif.)	0	0	...	1.59	4	4	0	0	0	5 2/3	5	1	1	2	5
—	Edmonton (PCL)	0	0	...	3.00	3	3	0	0	0	6	5	2	2	5	3
—	Oakland (A.L.)	0	1	.000	8.35	16	0	0	0	0	18 1/3	25	17	17	21	19
Major league totals (5 years)		5	4	.556	6.11	83	2	0	0	1	113 1/3	106	83	77	105	101

BRITO, BERNARDO OF

PERSONAL: Born December 4, 1963, in San Cristobal, Dominican Republic. . . . 6-1/190. . . . Bats right, throws right.
HIGH SCHOOL: Sabana Palenque (San Cristobal, Dominican Republic).
TRANSACTIONS/CAREER NOTES: Signed as non-drafted free agent by Cleveland Indians organization (October 8, 1980). . . . Released by Indians (March 25, 1988). . . . Signed by Minnesota Twins organization (March 31, 1988). . . . Granted free agency (December 19, 1992). . . . Re-signed by Twins organization (January 15, 1993). . . . Granted free agency (October 15, 1993). . . . Re-signed by Portland (October 24, 1993). . . . On disabled list (July 4-August 4, 1994). . . . Granted free agency (October 15, 1994). . . . Re-signed by Salt Lake, Twins organization (November 3, 1994). . . . Released by Twins (June 26, 1995).
STATISTICAL NOTES: Led New-York Pennsylvania League with 171 total bases in 1984. . . . Led Midwest League with 244 total bases in 1985.

			BATTING												FIELDING			
Year	Team (League)	Pos.	G	AB	R	H	2B	3B	HR	RBI	Avg.	BB	SO	SB	PO	A	E	Avg.
1981—	Batavia (NY-Penn)	OF	12	29	1	6	0	0	0	2	.207	2	9	0	2	0	0	1.000
1982—	Batavia (NY-Penn)	OF	41	123	10	29	2	0	4	15	.236	8	34	1	40	0	6	.870
1983—	Waterloo (Midw.)	OF	35	119	13	24	4	0	4	17	.202	10	40	3	41	2	3	.935
—	Batavia (NY-Penn)	OF	60	206	18	50	10	3	7	34	.243	15	65	5	54	7	8	.884
1984—	Batavia (NY-Penn)	OF	•76	*297	41	89	•19	3	*19	57	.300	14	67	3	100	8	8	.931
1985—	Waterloo (Midw.)	OF	135	498	66	128	27	1	*29	78	.257	24	133	1	160	15	9	.951
1986—	Waterbury (East.)	OF-SS	129	479	61	118	17	1	*18	75	.246	22	*127	0	67	1	1	.986
1987—	Williamsport (East.)	OF-1B	124	452	64	125	20	4	*24	79	.277	24	121	2	48	1	6	.891
1988—	Orlando (Southern)■	OF	135	508	55	122	20	4	24	76	.240	20	138	2	119	3	6	.953
1989—	Portland (PCL)	OF	111	355	51	90	12	7	22	74	.254	31	111	1	83	2	2	.977
1990—	Portland (PCL)	OF	113	376	48	106	26	3	*25	79	.282	27	102	1	40	0	2	.952
1991—	Portland (PCL)	OF	115	428	65	111	17	2	•27	83	.259	28	110	1	1	0	0	1.000
1992—	Portland (PCL)	OF	•140	*564	80	152	27	7	26	96	.270	32	*124	0	87	6	5	.949
—	Minnesota (A.L.)	OF-DH	8	14	1	2	1	0	0	2	.143	0	4	0	3	0	1	.750
1993—	Portland (PCL)	OF	85	319	64	108	18	3	20	72	.339	26	65	0	37	2	2	.951
—	Minnesota (A.L.)	OF-DH	27	54	8	13	2	0	4	9	.241	1	20	0	12	1	0	1.000
1994—	Salt Lake (PCL)	OF	108	437	85	135	24	2	29	122	.309	30	120	3	29	1	0	1.000
1995—	Salt Lake (PCL)	OF	51	186	31	57	10	1	15	49	.306	17	58	1	15	0	0	1.000
—	Minnesota (A.L.)	DH	5	5	1	1	0	0	1	1	.200	0	3	0	...	...	...	...
Major league totals (3 years)			40	73	10	16	3	0	5	12	.219	1	27	0	15	1	1	.941

BRITO, JORGE C ROCKIES

PERSONAL: Born June 22, 1966, in Moncion, Dominican Republic. . . . 6-1/190. . . . Bats right, throws right. . . . Full name: Jorge Manuel Brito.
HIGH SCHOOL: Academia La Trimitaria (Santo Domingo, Dominican Republic).
TRANSACTIONS/CAREER NOTES: Signed as non-drafted free agent by Oakland Athletics organization (May 6, 1986). . . . On Huntsville disabled list (August 3-September 11, 1992). . . . On disabled list (July 17-24 and July 30-August 11, 1993). . . . Granted free agency (October 15, 1993). . . . Signed by Colorado Rockies organization (December 3, 1993). . . . On New Haven disabled list (May 27-June 3, 1994). . . . On Colorado Springs temporarily inactive list (April 3-25, 1995).

			BATTING												FIELDING			
Year	Team (League)	Pos.	G	AB	R	H	2B	3B	HR	RBI	Avg.	BB	SO	SB	PO	A	E	Avg.
1986—	Medford (N'west)	C-1B	21	59	4	9	2	0	0	5	.153	4	17	0	121	11	4	.971
1987—	Medford (N'west)	C-1B-P	40	110	7	20	1	0	1	15	.182	12	54	0	224	31	5	.981
1988—	Modesto (Calif.)	C	96	300	38	65	15	0	5	27	.217	47	104	0	630	94	17	.977
1989—	Modesto (Calif.)	C	16	54	8	13	2	0	1	6	.241	5	14	0	97	16	1	.991
—	Huntsville (South.)	C	24	73	13	16	2	2	0	8	.219	20	23	1	164	25	3	.984
—	Tacoma (PCL)	C	5	15	2	3	1	0	0	0	.200	2	6	0	31	5	0	1.000
1990—	Huntsville (South.)	C	57	164	17	44	6	1	2	20	.268	30	49	0	307	36	0	1.000
1991—	Huntsville (South.)	C	65	203	26	41	11	0	1	23	.202	28	50	0	371	42	6	.986
—	Tacoma (PCL)	C	22	73	6	17	2	0	1	3	.233	4	20	0	113	13	2	.984
1992—	Tacoma (PCL)	C	18	35	4	5	2	0	0	1	.143	2	17	0	65	16	2	.976
—	Huntsville (South.)	C	33	72	10	15	2	0	2	6	.208	13	21	2	125	22	3	.980
1993—	Huntsville (South.)	C	18	36	6	10	3	0	4	11	.278	10	10	0	1	0	0	1.000
1994—	New Haven (East.)■	C-1B	63	100	18	46	11	1	5	25	.460	18	59	2	390	52	8	.982
—	Colo. Springs (PCL)	C	21	64	13	24	5	0	3	19	.375	7	14	0	122	13	1	.993
1995—	Colorado (N.L.)	C	18	51	5	11	3	0	0	7	.216	2	17	1	109	6	1	.991
—	Colo. Springs (PCL)	C	32	96	9	22	4	1	2	15	.229	2	20	0	163	14	3	.983
Major league totals (1 year)			18	51	5	11	3	0	0	7	.216	2	17	1	109	6	1	.991

RECORD AS PITCHER

Year	Team (League)	W	L	Pct.	ERA	G	GS	CG	ShO	Sv.	IP	H	R	ER	BB	SO
1987—	Medford (N'west)	0	0	...	0.00	1	0	0	0	0	1/3	0	0	0	0	0

BRITO, TILSON SS BLUE JAYS

PERSONAL: Born May 28, 1972, in Santo Domingo, Dominican Republic. . . . 6-0/170. . . . Bats right, throws right. . . . Full name: Tilson Manuel Brito.
TRANSACTIONS/CAREER NOTES: Signed as non-drafted free agent by Toronto Blue Jays organization (January 10, 1990). . . . On Syracuse disabled list (May 25-June 9, 1995).
STATISTICAL NOTES: Tied for Florida State League lead in errors by shortstop with 37 in 1993. . . . Led Southern League shortstops with 684 total chances and 85 double plays in 1994.

			BATTING												FIELDING			
Year	Team (League)	Pos.	G	AB	R	H	2B	3B	HR	RBI	Avg.	BB	SO	SB	PO	A	E	Avg.
1990—	Santo Dom. (DSL)	IF	39	130	31	33	8	2	0	14	.254	13	9	4	...	...	...	...
1991—	Santo Dom. (DSL)	IF	70	253	56	85	16	2	4	55	.336	44	19	11	...	...	...	...

Year	Team (League)	Pos.	G	BATTING AB	R	H	2B	3B	HR	RBI	Avg.	BB	SO	SB	FIELDING PO	A	E	Avg.
1992—	GC Blue Jays (GCL)	3B-2B-SS	54	189	36	58	10	4	3	36	.307	22	22	16	56	127	17	.915
—	Knoxville (South.)	SS	7	24	2	5	1	2	0	2	.208	0	9	0	6	19	5	.833
1993—	Dunedin (Fla. St.)	SS-3B-2B	126	465	80	125	21	3	6	44	.269	59	60	27	200	387	‡38	.939
1994—	Knoxville (South.)	SS	•139	476	61	127	17	7	5	57	.267	35	68	33	217	*424	43	.937
1995—	Syracuse (Int'l)	SS-2B	90	327	49	79	16	3	7	32	.242	29	69	17	123	240	18	.953

BROCAIL, DOUG — P — ASTROS

PERSONAL: Born May 16, 1967, in Clearfield, Pa. . . . 6-5/235. . . . Throws right, bats left. . . . Full name: Douglas Keith Brocail.
HIGH SCHOOL: Lamar (Colo.).
JUNIOR COLLEGE: Lamar (Colo.) Community College.
TRANSACTIONS/CAREER NOTES: Selected by San Diego Padres organization in first round (12th pick overall) of free-agent draft (January 14, 1986). . . . On Las Vegas disabled list (May 5-12, 1993). . . . On San Diego disabled list (April 2-June 28, 1994); included rehabilitation assignments to Wichita (May 26-June 3) and Las Vegas (June 3-23). . . . Traded by Padres with OF Phil Plantier, OF Derek Bell, P Pedro Martinez, IF Craig Shipley and SS Ricky Gutierrez to Houston Astros for 3B Ken Caminiti, OF Steve Finley, SS Andujar Cedeno, 1B Robert Petagine, P Brian Williams and a player to be named later (December 28, 1994).
MISCELLANEOUS: Appeared in six games as pinch-runner with San Diego (1993). . . . Appeared in two games as pinch-runner with San Diego (1994). . . . Appeared in one game as pinch-runner with Houston (1995).

Year	Team (League)	W	L	Pct.	ERA	G	GS	CG	ShO	Sv.	IP	H	R	ER	BB	SO
1986—	Spokane (N'west)	5	4	.556	3.81	16	•15	0	0	0	85	85	52	36	53	77
1987—	Char., S.C. (S. Atl.)	2	6	.250	4.09	19	18	0	0	0	92 1/3	94	51	42	28	68
1988—	Char., S.C. (S. Atl.)	8	6	.571	2.69	22	13	5	0	2	107	107	40	32	25	107
1989—	Wichita (Texas)	5	9	.357	5.21	23	22	1	1	0	134 2/3	158	88	78	50	95
1990—	Wichita (Texas)	2	2	.500	4.33	12	9	0	0	0	52	53	30	25	24	27
1991—	Wichita (Texas)	10	7	.588	3.87	34	16	3	•3	6	146 1/3	147	77	63	43	108
1992—	Las Vegas (PCL)	10	10	.500	3.97	29	25	4	0	0	172 1/3	187	82	76	63	103
—	San Diego (N.L.)	0	0	...	6.43	3	3	0	0	0	14	17	10	10	5	15
1993—	Las Vegas (PCL)	4	2	.667	3.68	10	8	0	0	1	51 1/3	51	26	21	14	32
—	San Diego (N.L.)	4	13	.235	4.56	24	24	0	0	0	128 1/3	143	75	65	42	70
1994—	Wichita (Texas)	0	0	...	0.00	2	0	0	0	0	4	3	1	0	1	2
—	Las Vegas (PCL)	0	0	...	7.11	7	3	0	0	0	12 2/3	21	12	10	2	8
—	San Diego (N.L.)	0	0	...	5.82	12	0	0	0	0	17	21	13	11	5	11
1995—	Houston (N.L.)■	6	4	.600	4.19	36	7	0	0	1	77 1/3	87	40	36	22	39
—	Tucson (Pac. Coast)	1	0	1.000	3.86	3	3	0	0	0	16 1/3	18	9	7	4	16
Major league totals (4 years)		10	17	.370	4.64	75	34	0	0	1	236 2/3	268	138	122	74	135

BROCK, CHRIS — P — BRAVES

PERSONAL: Born February 5, 1970, in Orlando, Fla. . . . 6-0/175. . . . Throws right, bats right. . . . Full name: Terrence Christopher Brock.
HIGH SCHOOL: Lyman (Longwood, Fla.).
COLLEGE: Florida State.
TRANSACTIONS/CAREER NOTES: Selected by Atlanta Braves organization in 12th round of free-agent draft (June 1, 1992). . . . On disabled list (July 26, 1995-remainder of season).

Year	Team (League)	W	L	Pct.	ERA	G	GS	CG	ShO	Sv.	IP	H	R	ER	BB	SO
1992—	Idaho Falls (Pio.)	6	4	.600	2.31	15	15	1	0	0	78	61	27	20	48	72
1993—	Macon (S. Atl.)	7	5	.583	2.70	14	14	1	0	0	80	61	37	24	33	92
—	Durham (Carolina)	5	2	.714	2.51	12	12	1	0	0	79	63	28	22	35	67
1994—	Greenville (South.)	7	6	.538	3.74	25	23	2	2	0	137 1/3	128	68	57	47	94
1995—	Richmond (Int'l)	2	8	.200	5.40	22	9	0	0	0	60	68	37	36	27	43

BROGNA, RICO — 1B — METS

PERSONAL: Born April 18, 1970, in Turner Falls, Mass. . . . 6-2/200. . . . Bats left, throws left. . . . Full name: Rico Joseph Brogna. . . . Name pronounced BRONE-yah.
HIGH SCHOOL: Watertown (Conn.).
TRANSACTIONS/CAREER NOTES: Selected by Detroit Tigers organization in first round (26th pick overall) of free-agent draft (June 1, 1988). . . . On Toledo disabled list (May 25-June 2, 1991). . . . Traded by Tigers to New York Mets for 1B Alan Zinter (March 31, 1994).
STATISTICAL NOTES: Led Eastern League first basemen with 1,261 total chances and 117 double plays in 1990. . . . Career major league grand slams: 1.

Year	Team (League)	Pos.	G	BATTING AB	R	H	2B	3B	HR	RBI	Avg.	BB	SO	SB	FIELDING PO	A	E	Avg.
1988—	Bristol (Appal.)	1B-OF	60	209	37	53	11	2	7	33	.254	25	42	3	319	26	6	.983
1989—	Lakeland (Fla. St.)	1B	128	459	47	108	20	7	5	51	.235	38	82	2	1098	83	13	.989
1990—	London (Eastern)	1B	137	488	70	128	21	3	*21	•77	.262	50	100	1	*1155	*93	13	.990
1991—	Toledo (Int'l)	1B	41	132	13	29	6	1	2	13	.220	4	26	2	311	37	5	.986
—	London (Eastern)	1B-OF	77	293	40	80	13	1	13	51	.273	25	59	0	368	46	6	.986
1992—	Toledo (Int'l)	1B	121	387	45	101	19	4	10	58	.261	31	85	1	896	76	9	.991
—	Detroit (A.L.)	1B-DH	9	26	3	5	1	0	1	3	.192	3	5	0	48	6	1	.982
1993—	Toledo (Int'l)	1B	129	483	55	132	30	3	11	59	.273	31	94	7	937	97	8	.992
1994—	Norfolk (Int'l)■	1B	67	258	33	63	14	5	12	37	.244	15	62	1	583	47	3	.995
—	New York (N.L.)	1B	39	131	16	46	11	2	7	20	.351	6	29	1	307	28	1	.997
1995—	New York (N.L.)	1B	134	495	72	143	27	2	22	76	.289	39	111	0	1111	93	3	*.998
American League totals (1 year)			9	26	3	5	1	0	1	3	.192	3	5	0	48	6	1	.982
National League totals (2 years)			173	626	88	189	38	4	29	96	.302	45	140	1	1418	121	4	.997
Major league totals (3 years)			182	652	91	194	39	4	30	99	.298	48	145	1	1466	127	5	.997

BRONKEY, JEFF — P

PERSONAL: Born September 18, 1965, in Kabul, Afghanistan. . . . 6-3/211. . . . Throws right, bats right. . . . Full name: Jacob Jeffery Bronkey.
HIGH SCHOOL: Klamath Union (Klamath Falls, Ore.).
COLLEGE: Oklahoma State.
TRANSACTIONS/CAREER NOTES: Selected by Philadelphia Phillies organization in eighth round of free-agent draft (June 6, 1983); did not sign. . . . Selected by Minnesota Twins organization in second round of free-agent draft (June 2, 1986). . . . Released by Twins organization (January 3, 1990). . . . Signed by Texas Rangers organization (May 25, 1990). . . . On Tulsa disabled list (May 21, 1991-remainder of season). . . . Traded by Rangers to Milwaukee Brewers for P David Pike (January 13, 1994). . . . On disabled list (May 25, 1994-remainder of season). . . . On Milwaukee disabled list (April 22-July 20 and August 14, 1995-remainder of season); included rehabilitation assignments to Beloit (June 15-16 and July 5-13) and New Orleans (July 13-21). . . . Released by Brewers (October 9, 1995).
STATISTICAL NOTES: Tied for Texas League lead with four balks in 1992.

Year	Team (League)	W	L	Pct.	ERA	G	GS	CG	ShO	Sv.	IP	H	R	ER	BB	SO
1986—	Kenosha (Midwest)	4	6	.400	3.83	14	6	1	0	0	49 1/3	41	24	21	30	25
1987—	Orlando (Southern)	1	6	.143	6.29	24	4	1	0	7	48 2/3	70	40	34	28	23
—	Visalia (California)	2	5	.286	3.82	27	0	0	0	5	35 1/3	26	21	15	32	31
1988—	Visalia (California)	4	6	.400	3.38	44	6	1	1	9	85 1/3	66	44	32	67	58
1989—	Orlando (Southern)	1	2	.333	5.40	16	13	0	0	0	61 2/3	74	53	37	35	47
1990—	Okla. City (A.A.)■	2	0	1.000	4.35	28	0	0	0	0	51 2/3	58	28	25	28	18
1991—	Okla. City (A.A.)	1	0	1.000	10.80	7	0	0	0	0	10	16	13	12	4	7
—	Tulsa (Texas)	0	0	...	9.39	4	0	0	0	0	7 2/3	11	9	8	5	5
1992—	Tulsa (Texas)	2	7	.222	2.55	45	0	0	0	13	70 2/3	51	27	20	25	58
—	Okla. City (A.A.)	0	1	.000	7.47	13	0	0	0	3	15 2/3	26	13	13	7	10
1993—	Okla. City (A.A.)	2	2	.500	2.65	29	0	0	0	14	37 1/3	29	11	11	7	19
—	Texas (A.L.)	1	1	.500	4.00	21	0	0	0	1	36	39	20	16	11	18
1994—	Milwaukee (A.L.)■	1	1	.500	4.35	16	0	0	0	1	20 2/3	20	10	10	12	13
1995—	Beloit (Midwest)	0	1	.000	3.68	3	3	0	0	0	7 1/3	5	5	3	3	8
—	New Orleans (A.A.)	0	1	.000	2.25	2	1	0	0	0	8	8	2	2	1	2
—	Milwaukee (A.L.)	0	0	...	3.65	8	0	0	0	0	12 1/3	15	6	5	6	5
Major league totals (3 years)		2	2	.500	4.04	45	0	0	0	2	69	74	36	31	29	36

BROSIUS, SCOTT — OF/3B — ATHLETICS

PERSONAL: Born August 15, 1966, in Hillsboro, Ore. . . . 6-1/185. . . . Bats right, throws right. . . . Full name: Scott David Brosius. . . . Name pronounced BRO-shus.
HIGH SCHOOL: Rex Putnam (Milwaukie, Ore.).
COLLEGE: Linfield College (Ore.).
TRANSACTIONS/CAREER NOTES: Selected by Oakland Athletics organization in 20th round of free-agent draft (June 2, 1987). . . . On Tacoma disabled list (April 17-May 29, 1991). . . . On Oakland disabled list (April 18-May 12, 1992); included rehabilitation assignment to Tacoma (May 6-12). . . . On Oakland disabled list (July 13-August 3, 1992); included rehabilitation assignment to Tacoma (July 27-August 3). . . . On Tacoma disabled list (July 28-August 5, 1993). . . . On disabled list (June 8-26, 1994).
STATISTICAL NOTES: Led Northwest League with seven sacrifice flies in 1987. . . . Led Southern League with 274 total bases in 1990. . . . Tied for Pacific Coast League lead in double plays by third baseman with 24 in 1992. . . . Career major league grand slams: 1.

			BATTING												FIELDING			
Year	Team (League)	Pos.	G	AB	R	H	2B	3B	HR	RBI	Avg.	BB	SO	SB	PO	A	E	Avg.
1987—	Medford (N'west)	3-S-2-1-P	65	255	34	73	18	1	3	49	.286	26	36	5	123	148	38	.877
1988—	Madison (Midwest)	S-3-O-1	132	504	82	153	28	2	9	58	.304	56	67	13	151	305	61	.882
1989—	Huntsville (South.)	2-O-3-S-1	128	461	68	125	22	2	7	60	.271	58	62	4	225	316	34	.941
1990—	Huntsville (South.)	SS-2B-3B	•142	547	94	*162	*39	2	23	88	.296	81	81	12	253	419	41	.942
—	Tacoma (PCL)	2B	3	7	2	1	0	1	0	0	.143	1	3	0	3	5	0	1.000
1991—	Tacoma (PCL)	3B-SS-2B	65	245	28	70	16	3	8	31	.286	18	29	4	49	168	14	.939
—	Oakland (A.L.)	2-O-3-DH	36	68	9	16	5	0	2	4	.235	3	11	3	31	16	0	1.000
1992—	Oakland (A.L.)	O-3-1-DH-S	38	87	13	19	2	0	4	13	.218	3	13	3	68	15	1	.988
—	Tacoma (PCL)	3B-OF	63	236	29	56	13	0	9	31	.237	23	44	8	50	167	10	.956
1993—	Oakland (A.L.)	O-1-3-S-DH	70	213	26	53	10	1	6	25	.249	14	37	6	173	29	2	.990
—	Tacoma (PCL)	3-O-2-1-S	56	209	38	62	13	2	8	41	.297	21	50	8	101	109	13	.942
1994—	Oakland (A.L.)	3B-OF-1B	96	324	31	77	14	1	14	49	.238	24	57	2	82	157	13	.948
1995—	Oakland (A.L.)	3-O-1-2-S-D	123	389	69	102	19	2	17	46	.262	41	67	4	208	121	15	.956
Major league totals (5 years)			363	1081	148	267	50	4	43	137	.247	85	185	18	562	338	31	.967

RECORD AS PITCHER

Year	Team (League)	W	L	Pct.	ERA	G	GS	CG	ShO	Sv.	IP	H	R	ER	BB	SO
1987—	Medford (N'west)	0	0	...	0.00	1	0	0	0	0	2	0	0	0	0	1

BROWN, BRANT — 1B — CUBS

PERSONAL: Born June 22, 1971, in Porterville, Calif. . . . 6-3/205. . . . Bats left, throws left. . . . Full name: Brant Michael Brown.
HIGH SCHOOL: Monache (Porterville, Calif.).
COLLEGE: Fresno State.
TRANSACTIONS/CAREER NOTES: Selected by Chicago Cubs organization in third round of free-agent draft (June 1, 1992). . . . On Daytona disabled list (April 10-25, 1993).

			BATTING												FIELDING			
Year	Team (League)	Pos.	G	AB	R	H	2B	3B	HR	RBI	Avg.	BB	SO	SB	PO	A	E	Avg.
1992—	Peoria (Midwest)	1B	70	248	28	68	14	0	3	27	.274	24	49	3	582	39	6	.990
1993—	Daytona (Fla. St.)	1B	75	266	26	91	8	7	3	33	.342	11	38	8	643	55	5	.993
—	Orlando (Southern)	1B	28	111	17	35	11	3	4	23	.315	6	19	2	237	27	3	.989
1994—	Orlando (Southern)	1B-OF	127	470	54	127	30	6	5	37	.270	37	86	11	1031	80	12	.989
1995—	Orlando (Southern)	1B-OF	121	446	67	121	27	4	6	53	.271	39	77	8	931	92	10	.990

BROWN, JARVIS — OF — ORIOLES

PERSONAL: Born March 26, 1967, in Waukegan, Ill. . . . 5-7/170. . . . Bats right, throws right. . . . Full name: Jarvis Ardel Brown.
HIGH SCHOOL: St. Joseph (Kenosha, Wis.).
COLLEGE: Triton College (Ill.).
TRANSACTIONS/CAREER NOTES: Selected by Minnesota Twins organization in first round (ninth pick overall) of free-agent draft (January 14, 1986). . . . On Portland disabled list (July 25-August 1, 1992). . . . Granted free agency (October 16, 1992). . . . Signed by San Diego Padres organization (November 20, 1992). . . . Claimed on waivers by Atlanta Braves (November 18, 1993). . . . Granted free agency (October 15, 1994). . . . Signed by New York Mets (December 7, 1994). . . . Released by Norfolk, Mets organization (May 29, 1995). . . . Signed by Indianapolis, Cincinnati Reds organization (June 12, 1995). . . . Traded by Reds organization to Baltimore Orioles organization for a player to be named later (June 14, 1995).
STATISTICAL NOTES: Led Midwest League outfielders with 334 total chances in 1988. . . . Led California League outfielders with seven double plays in 1989. . . . Tied for Southern League lead in double plays by outfielder with four in 1990.

				BATTING											FIELDING			
Year	Team (League)	Pos.	G	AB	R	H	2B	3B	HR	RBI	Avg.	BB	SO	SB	PO	A	E	Avg.
1986—	Elizabeth. (Appal.)	2B-OF-SS	49	180	28	41	4	0	3	23	.228	18	41	15	90	107	17	.921
1987—	Kenosha (Midwest)	2B-OF	43	117	22	37	4	1	3	16	.316	19	24	6	74	82	15	.912
—	Elizabeth. (Appal.)	OF	67	258	52	63	9	1	1	15	.244	48	50	30	106	6	*16	.875
1988—	Kenosha (Midwest)	OF	138	531	*108	*156	25	7	7	45	.294	71	89	72	311	15	8	.976
1989—	Visalia (California)	OF	141	545	*95	131	21	6	4	46	.240	73	112	49	291	16	6	.981
1990—	Orlando (Southern)	OF	135	527	*104	137	22	7	14	57	.260	80	79	33	316	12	10	.970
1991—	Portland (PCL)	OF	108	436	62	126	5	8	3	37	.289	36	66	27	243	11	4	.984
—	Minnesota (A.L.)	OF-DH	38	37	10	8	0	0	0	0	.216	2	8	7	21	0	1	.955
1992—	Minnesota (A.L.)	OF-DH	35	15	8	1	0	0	0	0	.067	2	4	2	20	0	1	.952
—	Portland (PCL)	OF	62	224	25	56	8	2	2	16	.250	20	37	17	135	4	4	.972
1993—	Las Vegas (PCL)■	OF	100	402	74	124	27	9	3	47	.308	41	55	22	217	*16	9	.963
—	San Diego (N.L.)	OF	47	133	21	31	9	2	0	8	.233	15	26	3	109	2	2	.982
1994—	Richmond (Int'l)■	OF	71	270	41	72	11	5	4	30	.267	36	35	8	172	6	6	.967
—	Atlanta (N.L.)	OF	17	15	3	2	1	0	1	1	.133	0	2	0	10	0	0	1.000
1995—	Norfolk (Int'l)■	OF	45	148	29	42	12	3	0	17	.284	18	29	6	71	1	3	.960
—	Bowie (Eastern)■	OF	58	219	50	61	12	1	6	23	.279	33	49	12	135	4	4	.972
—	Rochester (Int'l)	OF	17	70	12	22	4	2	0	4	.314	10	20	1	55	1	3	.949
—	Baltimore (A.L.)	OF	18	27	2	4	1	0	0	1	.148	7	9	1	16	0	0	1.000
American League totals (3 years)			91	79	20	13	1	0	0	1	.165	11	21	10	57	0	2	.966
National League totals (2 years)			64	148	24	33	10	2	1	9	.223	15	28	3	119	2	2	.984
Major league totals (5 years)			155	227	44	46	11	2	1	10	.203	26	49	13	176	2	4	.978

CHAMPIONSHIP SERIES RECORD

				BATTING											FIELDING			
Year	Team (League)	Pos.	G	AB	R	H	2B	3B	HR	RBI	Avg.	BB	SO	SB	PO	A	E	Avg.
1991—	Minnesota (A.L.)	PR-DH	1	0	1	0	0	0	0	0	...	0	0	0	...	...	...	...

WORLD SERIES RECORD

NOTES: Member of World Series championship team (1991).

				BATTING											FIELDING			
Year	Team (League)	Pos.	G	AB	R	H	2B	3B	HR	RBI	Avg.	BB	SO	SB	PO	A	E	Avg.
1991—	Minnesota (A.L.)	OF-PH-PR	3	2	0	0	0	0	0	0	.000	0	0	0	0	0	0	...

BROWN, KEVIN — P — MARLINS

PERSONAL: Born March 14, 1965, in McIntyre, Ga. . . . 6-4/195. . . . Throws right, bats right. . . . Full name: James Kevin Brown.
HIGH SCHOOL: Wilkinson County (Irwinton, Ga.).
COLLEGE: Georgia Tech.
TRANSACTIONS/CAREER NOTES: Selected by Texas Rangers organization in first round (fourth pick overall) of free-agent draft (June 2, 1986). . . . On disabled list (August 14-29, 1990 and March 27-April 11, 1993). . . . Granted free agency (October 15, 1994). . . . Signed by Baltimore Orioles (April 9, 1995). . . . On disabled list (June 23-July 17, 1995). . . . Granted free agency (November 3, 1995). . . . Signed by Florida Marlins (December 22, 1995).
HONORS: Named righthanded pitcher on The Sporting News college All-America team (1986).
STATISTICAL NOTES: Tied for A.L. lead with 13 hit batsmen in 1991.
MISCELLANEOUS: Made an out in only appearance as pinch-hitter (1990). . . . Appeared in one game as pinch-runner (1993).

Year	Team (League)	W	L	Pct.	ERA	G	GS	CG	ShO	Sv.	IP	H	R	ER	BB	SO
1986—	GC Rangers (GCL)	0	0	...	6.00	3	0	0	0	0	6	7	4	4	2	1
—	Tulsa (Texas)	0	0	...	4.50	3	2	0	0	0	10	9	7	5	5	10
—	Texas (A.L.)	1	0	1.000	3.60	1	1	0	0	0	5	6	2	2	0	4
1987—	Tulsa (Texas)	1	4	.200	7.29	8	8	0	0	0	42	53	36	34	18	26
—	Okla. City (A.A.)	0	5	.000	10.73	5	5	0	0	0	24 1/3	32	32	29	17	9
—	Charlotte (Fla. St.)	0	2	.000	2.72	6	6	1	0	0	36 1/3	33	14	11	17	21
1988—	Tulsa (Texas)	12	10	.545	3.51	26	26	5	0	0	174 1/3	174	94	68	61	118
—	Texas (A.L.)	1	1	.500	4.24	4	4	1	0	0	23 1/3	33	15	11	8	12
1989—	Texas (A.L.)	12	9	.571	3.35	28	28	7	0	0	191	167	81	71	70	104
1990—	Texas (A.L.)	12	10	.545	3.60	26	26	6	2	0	180	175	84	72	60	88
1991—	Texas (A.L.)	9	12	.429	4.40	33	33	0	0	0	210 2/3	233	116	103	90	96
1992—	Texas (A.L.)	•21	11	.656	3.32	35	35	11	1	0	*265 2/3	*262	117	98	76	173
1993—	Texas (A.L.)	15	12	.556	3.59	34	34	12	3	0	233	228	105	93	74	142
1994—	Texas (A.L.)	7	9	.438	4.82	26	•25	3	0	0	170	*218	109	91	50	123
1995—	Baltimore (A.L.)■	10	9	.526	3.60	26	26	3	1	0	172 1/3	155	73	69	48	117
Major league totals (9 years)		88	73	.547	3.78	213	212	43	7	0	1451	1477	702	610	476	859

ALL-STAR GAME RECORD

Year	League	W	L	Pct.	ERA	GS	CG	ShO	Sv.	IP	H	R	ER	BB	SO
1992—	American	1	0	1.000	0.00	1	0	0	0	1	0	0	0	0	1

BROWNE, BYRON — P — BREWERS

PERSONAL: Born August 8, 1970, in Camden, N.J. . . . 6-7/200. . . . Throws right, bats right. . . . Full name: Byron Ellis Browne Jr.
HIGH SCHOOL: St. Joseph (Mo.) Central.
COLLEGE: Grand Canyon (Ariz.).
TRANSACTIONS/CAREER NOTES: Selected by Milwaukee Brewers organization in 13th round of free-agent draft (June 3, 1991). . . . On Stockton disabled list (April 7-June 4, 1994). . . . On temporarily inactive list (April 24-May 8, 1995).
STATISTICAL NOTES: Led Midwest League with 24 wild pitches in 1992.

Year	Team (League)	W	L	Pct.	ERA	G	GS	CG	ShO	Sv.	IP	H	R	ER	BB	SO
1991—	Ariz. Brewers (Ar.)	1	6	.143	8.07	13	11	0	0	0	58	69	*65	*52	67	68
1992—	Beloit (Midwest)	9	8	.529	5.08	25	25	2	0	0	134 2/3	109	84	76	114	111
1993—	Stockton (Calif.)	10	5	.667	4.07	27	•27	0	0	0	143 2/3	117	73	65	117	110
1994—	Stockton (Calif.)	2	6	.250	2.76	11	11	1	0	0	62	46	30	19	30	67
	—El Paso (Texas)	2	1	.667	2.48	5	5	0	0	0	29	26	11	8	13	33
1995—	El Paso (Texas)	10	4	.714	3.43	25	20	2	1	0	126	106	55	48	78	110

BROWNE, JERRY — IF/OF

PERSONAL: Born February 3, 1966, in St. Croix, Virgin Islands. . . . 5-10/170. . . . Bats both, throws right. . . . Full name: Jerome Austin Browne.
HIGH SCHOOL: Central (Killshill, Va.).
TRANSACTIONS/CAREER NOTES: Signed as non-drafted free agent by Texas Rangers organization (March 3, 1983). . . . On disabled list (August 24-September 8, 1987). . . . Traded by Rangers with 1B Pete O'Brien and OF Oddibe McDowell to Cleveland Indians for 2B Julio Franco (December 6, 1988). . . . Released by Indians (March 31, 1992). . . . Signed by Tacoma, Oakland Athletics organization (April 11, 1992). . . . On Oakland disabled list (April 19-July 18, 1993); included rehabilitation assignment to Tacoma (July 6-11). . . . Granted free agency (October 26, 1993). . . . Signed by Florida Marlins organization (January 5, 1994). . . . Granted free agency (October 20, 1994). . . . Re-signed by Marlins (April 7, 1995). . . . On Florida disabled list (June 3-July 1 and August 19-September 3, 1995); included rehabilitation assignment to Brevard County (June 28-July 1). . . . Granted free agency (October 31, 1995).
STATISTICAL NOTES: Led Carolina League second basemen with 675 total chances in 1985. . . . Led Texas League second basemen with .984 fielding percentage in 1986. . . . Led A.L. with 16 sacrifice hits in 1992.

				BATTING											FIELDING			
Year	Team (League)	Pos.	G	AB	R	H	2B	3B	HR	RBI	Avg.	BB	SO	SB	PO	A	E	Avg.
1983—	GC Rangers (GCL)	2B	48	181	34	51	2	2	0	20	.282	31	16	8	92	123	14	.939
1984—	Burlington (Midw.)	SS-2B	127	420	70	99	10	1	0	18	.236	71	76	31	231	311	43	.926
1985—	Salem (Carolina)	2B	122	460	69	123	18	4	3	58	.267	82	62	24	*265	*390	20	.970
1986—	Tulsa (Texas)	2B-SS	128	491	82	149	15	7	2	57	.303	62	61	39	282	307	19	†.969
	—Texas (A.L.)	2B	12	24	6	10	2	0	0	3	.417	1	4	0	9	15	2	.923
1987—	Texas (A.L.)	2B-DH	132	454	63	123	16	6	1	38	.271	61	50	27	258	338	12	.980
1988—	Okla. City (A.A.)	2B	76	286	45	72	15	2	5	34	.252	37	29	14	190	231	10	.977
	—Texas (A.L.)	2B-DH	73	214	26	49	9	2	1	17	.229	25	33	7	112	139	11	.958
1989—	Cleveland (A.L.)■	2B-DH	153	598	83	179	31	4	5	45	.299	68	64	14	305	380	15	.979
1990—	Cleveland (A.L.)	2B	140	513	92	137	26	5	6	50	.267	72	46	12	286	382	10	.985
1991—	Cleveland (A.L.)	2-O-3-DH	107	290	28	66	5	2	1	29	.228	27	29	2	113	141	14	.948
1992—	Tacoma (PCL)■	2B	4	17	1	7	1	1	0	3	.412	3	1	0	9	16	0	1.000
	—Oakland (A.L.)	3-O-2-DH-S	111	324	43	93	12	2	3	40	.287	40	40	3	149	88	5	.979
1993—	Oakland (A.L.)	O-3-2-1	76	260	27	65	13	0	2	19	.250	22	17	4	149	28	6	.967
	—Tacoma (PCL)	3B-2B-OF	6	25	3	6	0	0	0	2	.240	0	4	1	7	12	2	.905
1994—	Florida (N.L.)■	3B-OF-2B	101	329	42	97	17	4	3	30	.295	52	23	3	118	128	15	.943
1995—	Florida (N.L.)	OF-2B-3B	77	184	21	47	4	0	1	17	.255	25	20	1	108	78	3	.984
	—Brevard Co. (FSL)	3B-OF	3	7	0	2	0	0	0	2	.286	1	1	0	3	1	1	.800
American League totals (8 years)			804	2677	368	722	114	21	19	241	.270	316	283	69	1381	1511	75	.975
National League totals (2 years)			178	513	63	144	21	4	4	47	.281	77	43	4	226	206	18	.960
Major league totals (10 years)			982	3190	431	866	135	25	23	288	.271	393	326	73	1607	1717	93	.973

CHAMPIONSHIP SERIES RECORD

NOTES: Shares single-game record for most singles—4 (October 12, 1992).

				BATTING											FIELDING			
Year	Team (League)	Pos.	G	AB	R	H	2B	3B	HR	RBI	Avg.	BB	SO	SB	PO	A	E	Avg.
1992—	Oakland (A.L.)	3B-OF-PH	4	10	3	4	0	0	0	2	.400	2	0	0	6	0	0	1.000

BROWNING, TOM — P — ROYALS

PERSONAL: Born April 28, 1960, in Casper, Wyo. . . . 6-1/190. . . . Throws left, bats left. . . . Full name: Thomas Leo Browning.
HIGH SCHOOL: Franklin Academy (Malone, N.Y.).
COLLEGE: Tennessee Wesleyan College and Le Moyne College (N.Y.).
TRANSACTIONS/CAREER NOTES: Selected by Cincinnati Reds organization in ninth round of free-agent draft (June 7, 1982). . . . Granted free agency (November 5, 1990). . . . Re-signed by Reds (November 21, 1990). . . . On disabled list (July 2, 1992-remainder of season; August 7, 1993-remainder of season; and May 10, 1994-remainder of season). . . . Granted free agency (October 11, 1994). . . . Signed by Omaha, Kansas City Royals organization (April 10, 1995). . . . On Kansas City disabled list (May 20, 1995-remainder of season); included rehabilitation assignment to Omaha (July 4-17). . . . Granted free agency (November 3, 1995). . . . Re-signed by Royals organization (December 7, 1995).
HONORS: Named N.L. Rookie Pitcher of the Year by THE SPORTING NEWS (1985).

STATISTICAL NOTES: Pitched seven-inning, 2-0 no-hit victory for Wichita against Iowa (July 31, 1984). . . . Tied for American Association lead with 24 home runs allowed in 1984. . . . Pitched 2-0 one-hit, complete-game victory against Chicago (June 4, 1986). . . . Pitched 12-0 one-hit, complete-game victory against San Diego (June 6, 1988). . . . Pitched 1-0 perfect game against Los Angeles (September 16, 1988). . . . Led N.L. with 36 home runs allowed in 1988, 31 in 1989 and 32 in 1991.

MISCELLANEOUS: Appeared in five games as pinch-runner (1988). . . . Appeared in two games as pinch-runner and struck out and made an out in two games as pinch-hitter (1989). . . . Appeared in three games as pinch-runner (1990).

Year	Team (League)	W	L	Pct.	ERA	G	GS	CG	ShO	Sv.	IP	H	R	ER	BB	SO
1982—	Billings (Pioneer)	4	•8	.333	3.89	14	14	3	0	0	88	96	53	38	41	*87
1983—	Tampa (Fla. St.)	8	1	.889	1.49	11	11	4	1	0	78 2/3	53	19	13	36	101
—	Waterbury (East.)	4	10	.286	3.53	18	18	3	1	0	117 1/3	100	62	46	63	101
1984—	Wichita (Am. Assoc.)	12	10	.545	3.95	30	28	8	1	0	189 1/3	169	88	83	73	*160
—	Cincinnati (N.L.)	1	0	1.000	1.54	3	3	0	0	0	23 1/3	27	4	4	5	14
1985—	Cincinnati (N.L.)	20	9	.690	3.55	38	38	6	4	0	261 1/3	242	111	103	73	155
1986—	Cincinnati (N.L.)	14	13	.519	3.81	39	•39	4	2	0	243 1/3	225	123	103	70	147
1987—	Cincinnati (N.L.)	10	13	.435	5.02	32	31	2	0	0	183	201	107	102	61	117
—	Nashville (A.A.)	2	3	.400	6.07	5	5	1	1	0	29 2/3	37	22	20	12	28
1988—	Cincinnati (N.L.)	18	5	.783	3.41	36	•36	5	2	0	250 2/3	205	98	95	64	124
1989—	Cincinnati (N.L.)	15	12	.556	3.39	37	*37	9	2	0	249 2/3	241	109	94	64	118
1990—	Cincinnati (N.L.)	15	9	.625	3.80	35	•35	2	1	0	227 2/3	235	98	96	52	99
1991—	Cincinnati (N.L.)	14	14	.500	4.18	36	36	1	0	0	230 1/3	241	*124	*107	56	115
1992—	Cincinnati (N.L.)	6	5	.545	5.07	16	16	0	0	0	87	108	49	49	28	33
1993—	Cincinnati (N.L.)	7	7	.500	4.74	21	20	0	0	0	114	159	61	60	20	53
1994—	Cincinnati (N.L.)	3	1	.750	4.20	7	7	2	1	0	40 2/3	34	20	19	13	22
1995—	Omaha (Am. Assoc.)■	2	1	.667	3.43	5	5	0	0	0	21	13	8	8	5	5
—	Kansas City (A.L.)	0	2	.000	8.10	2	2	0	0	0	10	13	9	9	5	3
—	Wichita (Texas)	1	0	1.000	7.50	1	1	0	0	0	6	10	5	5	1	5
A.L. totals (1 year)		0	2	.000	8.10	2	2	0	0	0	10	13	9	9	5	3
N.L. totals (11 years)		123	88	.583	3.92	300	298	31	12	0	1911	1918	904	832	506	997
Major league totals (12 years)		123	90	.577	3.94	302	300	31	12	0	1921	1931	913	841	511	1000

CHAMPIONSHIP SERIES RECORD

Year	Team (League)	W	L	Pct.	ERA	G	GS	CG	ShO	Sv.	IP	H	R	ER	BB	SO
1990—	Cincinnati (N.L.)	1	1	.500	3.27	2	2	0	0	0	11	9	4	4	6	5

WORLD SERIES RECORD

NOTES: Member of World Series championship team (1990).

Year	Team (League)	W	L	Pct.	ERA	G	GS	CG	ShO	Sv.	IP	H	R	ER	BB	SO
1990—	Cincinnati (N.L.)	1	0	1.000	4.50	1	1	0	0	0	6	6	3	3	2	2

ALL-STAR GAME RECORD

Year	League	W	L	Pct.	ERA	GS	CG	ShO	Sv.	IP	H	R	ER	BB	SO
1991—	National						Did not play.								

BRUMFIELD, JACOB — OF — PIRATES

PERSONAL: Born May 27, 1965, in Bogalusa, La. . . . 6-0/186. . . . Bats right, throws right. . . . Full name: Jacob Donnell Brumfield.

HIGH SCHOOL: Hammond (La.).

TRANSACTIONS/CAREER NOTES: Selected by Chicago Cubs organization in seventh round of free-agent draft (June 6, 1983). . . . On disabled list (June 21, 1984-remainder of season). . . . Released by Cubs organization (April 9, 1985). . . . Signed by Kansas City Royals organization (August 16, 1986). . . . Granted free agency (October 15, 1991). . . . Signed by Cincinnati Reds organization (November 12, 1991). . . . On Nashville disabled list (June 12-July 25, 1992). . . . Traded by Reds to Pittsburgh Pirates for OF Danny Clyburn (October 13, 1994). . . . On Pittsburgh disabled list (May 19-June 3, 1995); included rehabilitation assignment to Carolina (May 29-June 1).

STATISTICAL NOTES: Led Florida State League with .429 on-base percentage in 1990. . . . Led American Association in caught stealing with 16 in 1991.

			BATTING												FIELDING			
Year	Team (League)	Pos.	G	AB	R	H	2B	3B	HR	RBI	Avg.	BB	SO	SB	PO	A	E	Avg.
1983—	Pikeville (Appal.)	OF	42	113	17	29	0	1	3	15	.257	25	34	8	34	3	5	.881
1984—									Did not play.									
1985—									Did not play.									
1986—	Fort Myers (FSL)■	SS	12	41	3	13	3	1	1	5	.317	2	11	0	18	16	8	.810
1987—	Fort Myers (FSL)	OF-3B	114	379	56	93	14	*10	6	34	.245	45	78	43	235	53	19	.938
—	Memphis (South.)	OF	9	39	7	13	3	2	1	6	.333	3	8	2	35	0	2	.946
1988—	Memphis (South.)	OF	128	433	70	98	15	5	6	28	.226	52	104	47	239	2	6	.976
1989—	Memphis (South.)	OF	104	346	43	79	14	2	1	25	.228	53	74	28	217	2	8	.965
1990—	Baseball City (FSL)	OF	109	372	66	125	24	3	0	40	*.336	60	44	47	186	*17	8	.962
—	Omaha (A.A.)	OF	24	77	10	25	6	1	2	11	.325	7	14	10	45	3	0	1.000
1991—	Omaha (A.A.)	OF	111	397	62	106	14	7	3	43	.267	33	64	*36	227	10	2	.992
1992—	Cincinnati (N.L.)■	OF	24	30	6	4	0	0	0	2	.133	2	4	6	20	1	0	1.000
—	Nashville (A.A.)	OF	56	208	32	59	10	3	5	19	.284	26	35	22	137	4	6	.959
1993—	Indianapolis (A.A.)	OF	33	126	23	41	14	1	4	19	.325	6	14	11	74	4	4	.951
—	Cincinnati (N.L.)	OF-2B	103	272	40	73	17	3	6	23	.268	21	47	20	178	16	7	.965
1994—	Cincinnati (N.L.)	OF	68	122	36	38	10	2	4	11	.311	15	18	6	74	1	1	.987
1995—	Pittsburgh (N.L.)■	OF	116	402	64	109	23	2	4	26	.271	37	71	22	241	8	8	.969
—	Carolina (South.)	OF	3	12	2	5	0	0	2	2	.417	1	2	0	9	0	0	1.000
Major league totals (4 years)			311	826	146	224	50	7	14	62	.271	75	140	54	513	26	16	.971

BRUMLEY, MIKE — IF/OF — ASTROS

PERSONAL: Born April 9, 1963, in Oklahoma City. . . . 5-10/155. . . . Bats both, throws right. . . . Full name: Anthony Michael Brumley. . . . Son of Mike Brumley, catcher, Washington Senators (1964-66).

HIGH SCHOOL: Union (Broken Arrow, Okla.).
COLLEGE: Texas.
TRANSACTIONS/CAREER NOTES: Selected by Philadelphia Phillies organization in 16th round of free-agent draft (June 3, 1980); did not sign. . . . Selected by Boston Red Sox organization in second round of free-agent draft (June 6, 1983); pick received as compensation for Oakland Athletics signing Type A free-agent P Tom Burgmeier. . . . Traded by Red Sox organization with P Dennis Eckersley to Chicago Cubs for 1B/OF Bill Buckner (May 25, 1984). . . . Traded by Cubs with IF Keith Moreland to San Diego Padres for P Rich Gossage and P Ray Hayward (February 12, 1988). . . . Traded by Padres organization to Detroit Tigers for IF Luis Salazar (March 23, 1989). . . . Traded by Tigers organization to Baltimore Orioles for DH Larry Sheets (January 10, 1990). . . . Released by Orioles (April 3, 1990). . . . Signed by Seattle Mariners (April 6, 1990). . . . On Seattle disabled list (June 6-July 11, 1990); included rehabilitation assignment to Calgary (July 4-11). . . . Released by Mariners (September 27, 1990). . . . Signed by Pawtucket, Red Sox organization (January 23, 1991). . . . On Pawtucket disabled list (June 3-14 and 19-26, 1992). . . . Granted free agency (October 16, 1992). . . . Signed by Tucson, Houston Astros organization (February 22, 1993). . . . On Tucson disabled list (May 17-June 13, 1993). . . . Claimed on waivers by California Angels (October 4, 1993). . . . Released by Angels (March 29, 1994). . . . Signed by Tacoma, Oakland Athletics organization (April 5, 1994). . . . Released by Tacoma (May 27, 1994). . . . Signed by Edmonton, Florida Marlins organization (June 9, 1994). . . . Granted free agency (October 15, 1994). . . . Signed by Tucson, Astros organization (February 1, 1995). . . . On Tucson disabled list (April 25-May 2, 1995). . . . Granted free agency (October 17, 1995). . . . Re-signed by Astros organization (December 28, 1995).
STATISTICAL NOTES: Led American Association shortstops with 597 total chances in 1986.

			BATTING											FIELDING			
Year Team (League)	**Pos.**	**G**	**AB**	**R**	**H**	**2B**	**3B**	**HR**	**RBI**	**Avg.**	**BB**	**SO**	**SB**	**PO**	**A**	**E**	**Avg.**
1983—Winter Haven (FSL)	SS-OF	44	153	25	48	6	4	1	18	.314	16	31	4	51	92	20	.877
1984—New Britain (East.)	OF-SS	34	121	14	28	6	2	0	9	.231	18	33	3	71	6	6	.928
—Midland (Texas)■	OF	73	255	37	55	11	3	6	21	.216	48	49	5	128	4	5	.964
1985—Pittsfield (Eastern)	SS-OF	131	460	66	127	23	*14	3	58	.276	74	95	29	182	333	33	.940
1986—Iowa (Am. Assoc.)	SS	139	458	74	103	21	5	10	44	.225	63	102	35	177	*400	20	.966
1987—Iowa (Am. Assoc.)	SS-2B-OF	92	319	44	81	20	5	6	42	.254	35	61	27	147	240	24	.942
—Chicago (N.L.)	SS-2B	39	104	8	21	2	2	1	9	.202	10	30	7	43	93	5	.965
1988—Las Vegas (PCL)■	S-O-3-2	113	425	77	134	16	7	3	41	.315	56	84	41	139	322	28	.943
1989—Detroit (A.L.)■	S-2-3-DH-O	92	212	33	42	5	2	1	11	.198	14	45	8	80	160	12	.952
—Toledo (Int'l)	SS	8	26	4	6	2	2	0	1	.231	3	11	1	9	14	2	.920
1990—Seattle (A.L.)■	S-2-3-O	62	147	19	33	5	4	0	7	.224	10	22	2	63	123	5	.974
—Calgary (PCL)	SS	8	28	4	9	1	0	0	1	.321	1	3	3	13	23	2	.947
1991—Pawtucket (Int'l)■	SS-2B-OF	32	108	25	29	2	2	4	16	.269	24	21	8	49	77	7	.947
—Boston (A.L.)	S-3-2-O-DH	63	118	16	25	5	0	0	5	.212	10	22	2	46	116	7	.959
1992—Pawtucket (Int'l)	O-2-S-3	101	365	50	96	16	5	4	41	.263	37	76	14	133	83	13	.943
—Boston (A.L.)	PH-PR	2	1	0	0	0	0	0	0	.000	0	0	0	...	...	...	...
1993—Tucson (PCL)■	O-S-1-3	93	346	65	122	25	8	0	47	.353	44	71	24	161	76	14	.944
—Houston (N.L.)	OF-SS-3B	8	10	1	3	0	0	0	2	.300	1	3	0	1	1	0	1.000
1994—Tacoma (PCL)■	2-S-O-1-3	13	49	11	13	4	1	1	5	.265	7	9	3	18	36	2	.964
—Oakland (A.L.)	2-3-O-S	11	25	0	6	0	0	0	2	.240	1	8	0	10	9	2	.905
—Edmonton (PCL)■	2-S-O-P-3	72	263	43	76	20	3	11	36	.289	29	58	5	142	177	14	.958
1995—Tucson (PCL)■	O-S-3-2-1	94	330	56	86	20	10	4	33	.261	41	67	17	101	92	10	.951
—Houston (N.L.)	S-O-1-3	18	18	1	1	0	0	1	2	.056	0	6	1	3	2	1	.833
American League totals (5 years)		230	503	68	106	15	6	1	25	.211	35	97	12	199	408	26	.959
National League totals (3 years)		65	132	10	25	2	2	2	13	.189	11	39	8	47	96	6	.960
Major league totals (8 years)		295	635	78	131	17	8	3	38	.206	46	136	20	246	504	32	.959

RECORD AS PITCHER

Year Team (League)	**W**	**L**	**Pct.**	**ERA**	**G**	**GS**	**CG**	**ShO**	**Sv.**	**IP**	**H**	**R**	**ER**	**BB**	**SO**
1994—Edmonton (PCL)	0	0	...	0.00	2	0	0	0	0	$1^{2}/_{3}$	2	0	0	0	1

BRUSKE, JIM — P — DODGERS

PERSONAL: Born October 7, 1964, in East St. Louis, Ill. . . . 6-1/185. . . . Throws right, bats right. . . . Full name: James Scott Bruske.
HIGH SCHOOL: Palmdale (Calif.).
JUNIOR COLLEGE: Antelope Valley (Calif.).
COLLEGE: Loyola Marymount.
TRANSACTIONS/CAREER NOTES: Selected by San Diego Padres organization in seventh round of free-agent draft (January 9, 1985); did not sign. . . . Selected by Seattle Mariners organization in third round of secondary phase of free-agent draft (June 3, 1985); did not sign. . . . Selected by Cleveland Indians organization in first round (sixth player selected) of secondary phase of free-agent draft (June 2, 1986). . . . On Canton-Akron disabled list (May 8-25, 1991). . . . On Colorado Springs disabled list (May 7-June 9, 1992). . . . Released by Indians organization (June 9, 1992). . . . Signed by Houston Astros organization (June 22, 1992). . . . On disabled list (May 7-30 and June 9-October 12, 1994). . . . Granted free agency (October 15, 1994). . . . Signed by Los Angeles Dodgers organization (January 18, 1995). . . . On Albuquerque disabled list (May 3-11, 1995). . . . Granted free agency (October 16, 1995). . . . Re-signed by Dodgers organization (November 12, 1995).

Year Team (League)	**W**	**L**	**Pct.**	**ERA**	**G**	**GS**	**CG**	**ShO**	**Sv.**	**IP**	**H**	**R**	**ER**	**BB**	**SO**
1986—Batavia (NYP)	0	0	...	18.00	1	0	0	0	0	1	1	2	2	3	3
1989—Cant./Akr. (East.)	0	0	...	13.50	2	0	0	0	0	2	3	3	3	2	1
1990—Cant./Akr. (East.)	9	3	.750	3.28	32	13	3	2	0	118	118	53	43	42	62
1991—Cant./Akr. (East.)	5	2	.714	3.47	17	11	0	0	1	$80^{1}/_{3}$	73	36	31	27	35
—Colo. Springs (PCL)	4	0	1.000	2.45	7	1	0	0	2	$25^{2}/_{3}$	19	9	7	8	13
1992—Colo. Springs (PCL)	2	0	1.000	4.58	7	0	0	0	10	$17^{2}/_{3}$	24	11	9	6	8
—Jackson (Texas)■	4	3	.571	2.63	13	9	1	0	0	$61^{2}/_{3}$	54	23	18	14	48
1993—Jackson (Texas)	9	5	.643	2.31	15	15	1	0	0	$97^{1}/_{3}$	86	34	25	22	83
—Tucson (PCL)	4	2	.667	3.78	12	9	0	0	1	$66^{2}/_{3}$	77	36	28	18	42
1994—Tucson (PCL)	3	1	.750	4.15	7	7	0	0	0	39	47	22	18	8	25
1995—Los Angeles (N.L.)■	0	0	...	4.50	9	0	0	0	1	10	12	7	5	4	5
—Albuquerque (PCL)	7	5	.583	4.11	43	6	0	0	4	114	128	54	52	41	99
Major league totals (1 year)	0	0	...	4.50	9	0	0	0	1	10	12	7	5	4	5

RECORD AS POSITION PLAYER

Year	Team (League)	Pos.	G	AB	R	H	2B	3B	HR	RBI	Avg.	BB	SO	SB	PO	A	E	Avg.
				BATTING											FIELDING			
1986—	Batavia (NYP)	OF-P	56	181	23	44	2	2	3	14	.243	21	50	7	85	4	5	.947
1987—	Kinston (Carolina)	OF	123	439	62	102	16	3	7	61	.232	65	118	17	188	7	10	.951
1988—	Williamsport (East.)	OF	135	443	49	105	12	3	1	44	.237	45	*138	16	238	11	4	.984
1989—	Kinston (Carolina)	OF	63	217	29	63	12	1	5	36	.290	34	44	13	114	2	2	.983
—	Cant./Akr. (East.)	OF-P-SS	51	134	17	32	5	0	1	7	.239	19	28	3	75	4	0	1.000

BUECHELE, STEVE 3B

PERSONAL: Born September 26, 1961, in Lancaster, Calif. . . . 6-2/200. . . . Bats right, throws right. . . . Full name: Steven Bernard Buechele. . . . Name pronounced BOO-shell.
HIGH SCHOOL: Servite (Anaheim, Calif.).
COLLEGE: Stanford.
TRANSACTIONS/CAREER NOTES: Selected by Chicago White Sox organization in first round (ninth pick overall) of free-agent draft (June 5, 1979); did not sign. . . . Selected by Texas Rangers organization in fifth round of free-agent draft (June 7, 1982). . . . On Texas disabled list (April 22-May 25, 1990). . . . On Texas disabled list (June 18-July 20, 1990); included rehabilitation assignment to Oklahoma City (July 16-20). . . . On suspended list (August 24-27, 1990). . . . Traded by Rangers to Pittsburgh Pirates for P Kurt Miller and a player to be named later (August 30, 1991); Rangers acquired P Hector Fajardo to complete deal (September 6, 1991). . . . Granted free agency (October 28, 1991). . . . Re-signed by Pirates (December 12, 1991). . . . Traded by Pirates to Chicago Cubs for P Danny Jackson (July 11, 1992). . . . On disabled list (June 13-28, 1993). . . . On Chicago disabled list (June 12-July 6, 1995). . . . Released by Cubs (July 6, 1995). . . . Signed by Oklahoma City, Rangers organization (July 12, 1995). . . . Released by Rangers (July 31, 1995).
HONORS: Named American Association Most Valuable Player (1985).
STATISTICAL NOTES: Led A.L. third basemen with .991 fielding percentage in 1991. . . . Led N.L. third basemen with .975 fielding percentage in 1993. . . . Career major league grand slams: 1.

Year	Team (League)	Pos.	G	AB	R	H	2B	3B	HR	RBI	Avg.	BB	SO	SB	PO	A	E	Avg.
				BATTING											FIELDING			
1982—	Tulsa (Texas)	2B-3B	62	213	21	63	12	2	5	33	.296	18	42	2	111	174	8	.973
1983—	Tulsa (Texas)	2B-3B	117	437	62	121	12	4	14	62	.277	54	69	5	182	259	18	.961
—	Okla. City (A.A.)	2B-3B	9	34	6	9	5	0	1	4	.265	4	6	0	17	22	1	.975
1984—	Okla. City (A.A.)	2B-3B	131	447	48	118	25	3	7	59	.264	36	72	7	236	329	17	.971
1985—	Okla. City (A.A.)	3B-2B	89	350	56	104	20	7	9	64	.297	33	62	6	84	170	7	.973
—	Texas (A.L.)	3B-2B	69	219	22	48	6	3	6	21	.219	14	38	3	52	138	6	.969
1986—	Texas (A.L.)	3B-2B-OF	153	461	54	112	19	2	18	54	.243	35	98	5	174	292	12	.975
1987—	Texas (A.L.)	3B-2B-OF	136	363	45	86	20	0	13	50	.237	28	66	2	89	211	9	.971
1988—	Texas (A.L.)	3B-2B	155	503	68	126	21	4	16	58	.250	65	79	2	114	300	16	.963
1989—	Texas (A.L.)	3-2-S-DH	155	486	60	114	22	2	16	59	.235	36	107	1	128	288	12	.972
1990—	Texas (A.L.)	3B-2B	91	251	30	54	10	0	7	30	.215	27	63	1	72	160	8	.967
—	Okla. City (A.A.)	3B	6	21	1	3	0	0	1	1	.143	2	4	0	4	15	0	1.000
1991—	Texas (A.L.)	3B-2B-SS	121	416	58	111	17	2	18	66	.267	39	69	0	99	275	3	†.992
—	Pittsburgh (N.L.)■	3B	31	114	16	28	5	1	4	19	.246	10	28	0	22	64	4	.956
1992—	Pittsburgh (N.L.)	3B	80	285	27	71	14	1	8	43	.249	34	61	0	52	169	10	.957
—	Chicago (N.L.)■	3B-2B	65	239	25	66	9	3	1	21	.276	18	44	1	51	120	7	.961
1993—	Chicago (N.L.)	3B-1B	133	460	53	125	27	2	15	65	.272	48	87	1	97	232	8	†.976
1994—	Chicago (N.L.)	3B-1B-2B	104	339	33	82	11	1	14	52	.242	39	80	1	100	144	5	.980
1995—	Chicago (N.L.)	3B	32	106	10	20	2	0	1	9	.189	11	19	0	26	55	5	.942
—	Okla. City (A.A.)■	3B	3	13	1	4	0	0	1	3	.308	1	1	0	3	6	2	.818
—	Texas (A.L.)	3B	9	24	0	3	0	0	0	0	.125	4	3	0	7	10	0	1.000
American League totals (8 years)			889	2723	337	654	115	13	94	338	.240	248	523	14	735	1674	66	.973
National League totals (5 years)			445	1543	164	392	68	8	43	209	.254	160	319	3	348	784	39	.967
Major league totals (11 years)			1334	4266	501	1046	183	21	137	547	.245	408	842	17	1083	2458	105	.971

CHAMPIONSHIP SERIES RECORD

NOTES: Shares N.L. single-series record for most consecutive hits—5 (1991).

Year	Team (League)	Pos.	G	AB	R	H	2B	3B	HR	RBI	Avg.	BB	SO	SB	PO	A	E	Avg.
				BATTING											FIELDING			
1991—	Pittsburgh (N.L.)	3B	7	23	2	7	2	0	0	0	.304	4	6	0	8	14	0	1.000

BUFORD, DAMON OF METS

PERSONAL: Born June 12, 1970, in Baltimore. . . . 5-10/170. . . . Bats right, throws right. . . . Full name: Damon Jackson Buford. . . . Son of Don Buford, outfielder, Chicago White Sox and Baltimore Orioles (1963-72); and brother of Don Buford Jr., minor league infielder (1987-89).
HIGH SCHOOL: Birmingham (Calif.).
COLLEGE: Southern California.
TRANSACTIONS/CAREER NOTES: Selected by Baltimore Orioles organization in 10th round of free-agent draft (June 4, 1990). . . . Traded by Orioles with OF Alex Ochoa to New York Mets for 3B/OF Bobby Bonilla and a player to be named later (July 28, 1995); Orioles acquired P Jimmy Williams to complete deal (August 17, 1995).
STATISTICAL NOTES: Led Eastern League outfielders with 279 total chances in 1992. . . . Led International League outfielders with 347 total chances in 1994.

Year	Team (League)	Pos.	G	AB	R	H	2B	3B	HR	RBI	Avg.	BB	SO	SB	PO	A	E	Avg.
				BATTING											FIELDING			
1990—	Wausau (Midwest)	OF	41	160	31	48	7	2	1	14	.300	21	32	15	89	2	2	.978
1991—	Frederick (Caro.)	OF	133	505	71	138	25	6	8	54	.273	51	92	50	293	7	5	.984
1992—	Hagerstown (East.)	OF	101	373	53	89	17	3	1	30	.239	42	62	41	*264	13	2	.993
—	Rochester (Int'l)	OF	45	155	29	44	10	2	1	12	.284	14	23	23	100	1	3	.971
1993—	Rochester (Int'l)	OF	27	116	24	33	6	1	1	4	.284	7	16	10	73	3	3	.962

Year	Team (League)	Pos.	G	AB	R	H	2B	3B	HR	RBI	Avg.	BB	SO	SB	PO	A	E	Avg.
							BATTING								FIELDING			
	—Baltimore (A.L.)	OF-DH	53	79	18	18	5	0	2	9	.228	9	19	2	61	2	1	.984
1994	—Baltimore (A.L.)	DH-OF	4	2	2	1	0	0	0	0	.500	0	1	0	0	0	0	...
	—Rochester (Int'l)	OF	111	452	*89	122	21	4	16	66	.270	35	81	31	*339	4	4	.988
1995	—Baltimore (A.L.)	OF	24	32	6	2	0	0	0	2	.063	6	7	3	40	0	0	1.000
	—Rochester (Int'l)	OF	46	188	40	58	12	3	4	18	.309	17	26	17	115	2	2	.983
	—New York (N.L.)■	OF	44	136	24	32	5	0	4	12	.235	19	28	7	67	2	2	.972
American League totals (3 years)			81	113	26	21	5	0	2	11	.186	15	27	5	101	2	1	.990
National League totals (1 year)			44	136	24	32	5	0	4	12	.235	19	28	7	67	2	2	.972
Major league totals (3 years)			125	249	50	53	10	0	6	23	.213	34	55	12	168	4	3	.983

BUHNER, JAY — OF — MARINERS

PERSONAL: Born August 13, 1964, in Louisville, Ky. . . . 6-3/215. . . . Bats right, throws right. . . . Full name: Jay Campbell Buhner. . . . Name pronounced BYOO-ner.

HIGH SCHOOL: Clear Creek (League City, Tex.).

JUNIOR COLLEGE: McLennan Community College (Tex.).

TRANSACTIONS/CAREER NOTES: Selected by Atlanta Braves organization in ninth round of free-agent draft (June 6, 1983); did not sign. . . . Selected by Pittsburgh Pirates organization in secondary phase of free-agent draft (January 17, 1984). . . . Traded by Pirates organization with IF Dale Berra and P Alfonso Pulido to New York Yankees for OF Steve Kemp, IF Tim Foli and cash (December 20, 1984). . . . On disabled list (April 11-July 28, 1986). . . . Traded by Yankees with P Rich Balabon and a player to be named later to Seattle Mariners for DH Ken Phelps (July 21, 1988); Mariners acquired P Troy Evers to complete deal (October 12, 1988). . . . On Seattle disabled list (June 29-August 19, 1989); included rehabilitation assignment to Calgary (August 16-19). . . . On Seattle disabled list (March 31-June 1, 1990); included rehabilitation assignment to Calgary (May 18-June 1). . . . On Seattle disabled list (June 17-August 23, 1990). . . . Granted free agency (October 28, 1994). . . . Re-signed by Mariners (December 21, 1994). . . . On disabled list (June 6-22, 1995).

RECORDS: Shares major league records for most strikeouts in two consecutive nine-inning games—8 (August 23-24, 1990); and most strikeouts in three consecutive games—10 (August 23-25, 1990).

STATISTICAL NOTES: Tied for International League lead in double plays by outfielder with six in 1987. . . . Hit for the cycle (June 23, 1993). . . . Career major league grand slams: 6.

Year	Team (League)	Pos.	G	AB	R	H	2B	3B	HR	RBI	Avg.	BB	SO	SB	PO	A	E	Avg.
							BATTING								FIELDING			
1984	—Watertown (NYP)	OF	65	229	43	74	16	3	9	•58	.323	42	58	3	106	8	1	.991
1985	—Fort Lauder. (FSL)■	OF	117	409	65	121	18	10	11	76	.296	65	76	6	235	12	7	.972
1986	—Fort Lauder. (FSL)	OF	36	139	24	42	9	1	7	31	.302	15	30	1	84	7	3	.968
1987	—Columbus (Int'l)	OF	134	502	83	140	23	1	*31	85	.279	55	124	4	275	*20	6	.980
	—New York (A.L.)	OF	7	22	0	5	2	0	0	1	.227	1	6	0	11	1	0	1.000
1988	—Columbus (Int'l)	OF	38	129	26	33	5	0	8	18	.256	19	33	1	83	3	1	.989
	—New York (A.L.)	OF	25	69	8	13	0	0	3	13	.188	3	25	0	52	2	2	.964
	—Seattle (A.L.)■	OF	60	192	28	43	13	1	10	25	.224	25	68	1	134	7	1	.993
1989	—Calgary (PCL)	OF	56	196	43	61	12	1	11	45	.311	44	56	4	97	8	2	.981
	—Seattle (A.L.)	OF	58	204	27	56	15	1	9	33	.275	19	55	1	106	6	4	.966
1990	—Calgary (PCL)	OF	13	34	6	7	1	0	2	5	.206	7	11	0	14	1	0	1.000
	—Seattle (A.L.)	OF-DH	51	163	16	45	12	0	7	33	.276	17	50	2	55	1	2	.966
1991	—Seattle (A.L.)	OF	137	406	64	99	14	4	27	77	.244	53	117	0	244	15	5	.981
1992	—Seattle (A.L.)	OF	152	543	69	132	16	3	25	79	.243	71	146	0	314	14	2	.994
1993	—Seattle (A.L.)	OF-DH	158	563	91	153	28	3	27	98	.272	100	144	2	263	8	6	.978
1994	—Seattle (A.L.)	OF-DH	101	358	74	100	23	4	21	68	.279	66	63	0	178	11	2	.990
1995	—Seattle (A.L.)	OF-DH	126	470	86	123	23	0	40	121	.262	60	120	0	180	5	2	.989
Major league totals (9 years)			875	2990	463	769	146	16	169	548	.257	415	794	6	1537	70	26	.984

DIVISION SERIES RECORD

Year	Team (League)	Pos.	G	AB	R	H	2B	3B	HR	RBI	Avg.	BB	SO	SB	PO	A	E	Avg.
							BATTING								FIELDING			
1995	—Seattle (A.L.)	OF	5	24	2	11	1	0	1	3	.458	2	4	0	11	1	0	1.000

CHAMPIONSHIP SERIES RECORD

NOTES: Shares A.L. single-series record for most home runs—3 (1995). . . . Shares A.L. single-series record for most strike outs—8 (1995).

Year	Team (League)	Pos.	G	AB	R	H	2B	3B	HR	RBI	Avg.	BB	SO	SB	PO	A	E	Avg.
							BATTING								FIELDING			
1995	—Seattle (A.L.)	OF	6	23	5	7	2	0	3	5	.304	2	8	0	15	0	1	.938

BULLETT, SCOTT — OF — CUBS

PERSONAL: Born December 25, 1968, in Martinsburg, W.Va. . . . 6-2/220. . . . Bats left, throws left. . . . Full name: Scott Douglas Bullett.

HIGH SCHOOL: Martinsburg (W.Va.).

TRANSACTIONS/CAREER NOTES: Signed as non-drafted free agent by Pittsburgh Pirates organization (June 20, 1988). . . . Traded by Pirates to Chicago Cubs for P Travis Willis (March 29, 1994).

STATISTICAL NOTES: Led American Association in caught stealing with 17 in 1993. . . . Led American Association outfielders with 313 total chances in 1994.

Year	Team (League)	Pos.	G	AB	R	H	2B	3B	HR	RBI	Avg.	BB	SO	SB	PO	A	E	Avg.
							BATTING								FIELDING			
1988	—GC Pirates (GCL)	OF	21	61	6	11	1	0	0	8	.180	7	9	2	28	2	1	.968
1989	—GC Pirates (GCL)	OF-1B	46	165	24	42	7	3	1	16	.255	12	31	15	141	4	7	.954
1990	—Welland (NYP)	OF	74	255	46	77	11	4	3	33	.302	13	50	30	110	5	5	.958
1991	—Augusta (S. Atl.)	OF	95	384	61	109	22	6	1	36	.284	27	79	48	195	8	5	.976
	—Salem (Carolina)	OF	39	156	22	52	7	5	2	15	.333	8	29	15	87	3	4	.957
	—Pittsburgh (N.L.)	OF	11	4	2	0	0	0	0	0	.000	0	3	1	2	0	0	1.000
1992	—Carolina (South.)	OF	132	518	59	140	20	5	8	45	.270	28	98	29	260	7	6	.978

Year	Team (League)	Pos.	G	AB	R	H	2B	3B	HR	RBI	Avg.	BB	SO	SB	PO	A	E	Avg
				BATTING											FIELDING			
	—Buffalo (A.A.)	OF	3	10	1	4	0	2	0	0	.400	0	2	0	7	0	0	1.000
1993	—Buffalo (A.A.)	OF	110	408	62	117	13	6	1	30	.287	39	67	28	222	6	7	.970
	—Pittsburgh (N.L.)	OF	23	55	2	11	0	2	0	4	.200	3	15	3	35	1	0	1.000
1994	—Iowa (Am. Assoc.)■	OF	135	*530	75	•163	28	4	13	69	.308	19	110	27	*291	15	•7	.978
1995	—Chicago (N.L.)	OF	104	150	19	41	5	7	3	22	.273	12	30	8	59	1	2	.968
Major league totals (3 years)			138	209	23	52	5	9	3	26	.249	15	48	12	96	2	2	.980

BULLINGER, JIM — P — CUBS

PERSONAL: Born August 21, 1965, in New Orleans. . . . 6-2/190. . . . Throws right, bats right. . . . Full name: James Eric Bullinger. . . . Name pronounced BULL-in-jer.

HIGH SCHOOL: Archbishop Rummel (Metairie, La.).

COLLEGE: New Orleans.

TRANSACTIONS/CAREER NOTES: Selected by Chicago Cubs organization in ninth round of free-agent draft (June 2, 1986). . . . On Iowa disabled list (August 5-21, 1993). . . . On Chicago disabled list (May 21-June 22, 1995); included rehabilitation assignment to Orlando (June 13-18).

STATISTICAL NOTES: Led Carolina League shortstops with 92 double plays in 1987. . . . Hit home run in first major league at-bat (June 8, 1992, first game). . . . Pitched 3-1 one-hit, complete-game victory for Chicago against San Francisco (August 30, 1992).

MISCELLANEOUS: Struck out in only appearance as pinch-hitter with Chicago (1995).

Year	Team (League)	W	L	Pct.	ERA	G	GS	CG	ShO	Sv.	IP	H	R	ER	BB	SO
1989	—Charlotte (South.)	0	0	...	0.00	2	0	0	0	0	3	3	0	0	3	5
1990	—Winst.-Salem (Car.)	7	6	.538	3.70	14	13	3	0	0	90	81	43	37	46	85
	—Charlotte (South.)	3	4	.429	5.11	9	9	0	0	0	44	42	30	25	18	33
1991	—Iowa (Am. Assoc.)	3	4	.429	5.40	8	8	0	0	0	46 2/3	47	32	28	23	30
	—Charlotte (South.)	9	9	.500	3.53	20	20	•8	0	0	142 2/3	132	62	56	61	128
1992	—Iowa (Am. Assoc.)	1	2	.333	2.45	20	0	0	0	14	22	17	6	6	12	15
	—Chicago (N.L.)	2	8	.200	4.66	39	9	1	0	7	85	72	49	44	54	36
1993	—Iowa (Am. Assoc.)	4	6	.400	3.42	49	3	0	0	20	73 2/3	64	29	28	43	74
	—Chicago (N.L.)	1	0	1.000	4.32	15	0	0	0	1	16 2/3	18	9	8	9	10
1994	—Chicago (N.L.)	6	2	.750	3.60	33	10	1	0	2	100	87	43	40	34	72
1995	—Chicago (N.L.)	12	8	.600	4.14	24	24	1	1	0	150	152	80	69	65	93
	—Orlando (Southern)	0	0	...	0.00	1	1	0	0	0	4	3	0	0	1	2
Major league totals (4 years)		21	18	.538	4.12	111	43	3	1	10	351 2/3	329	181	161	162	211

RECORD AS POSITION PLAYER

Year	Team (League)	Pos.	G	AB	R	H	2B	3B	HR	RBI	Avg.	BB	SO	SB	PO	A	E	Avg.
				BATTING											FIELDING			
1986	—Geneva (NYP)	SS	*78	248	35	61	•16	1	3	33	.246	*48	50	7	104	207	26	.923
1987	—Winst.-Salem (Car.)	SS	129	437	58	112	12	3	9	48	.256	50	79	3	210	383	28	.955
1988	—Pittsfield (Eastern)	SS	88	242	21	41	6	1	3	33	.169	25	53	1	129	256	21	.948
	—Winst.-Salem (Car.)	SS	32	104	13	20	4	2	1	11	.192	13	26	4	49	80	11	.921
1989	—Charlotte (South.)	SS-3B	124	320	34	69	13	1	3	28	.216	39	56	3	188	281	26	.947

BUNCH, MELVIN — P — ROYALS

PERSONAL: Born November 4, 1971, in Texarkana, Tex. . . . 6-1/170. . . . Throws right, bats right. . . . Full name: Melvin Lynn Bunch Jr.

HIGH SCHOOL: Liberty Eylau (Texarkana, Tex.).

JUNIOR COLLEGE: Texarkana (Tex.) Community College.

TRANSACTIONS/CAREER NOTES: Selected by Kansas City Royals organization in 15th round of free-agent draft (June 1, 1992). . . . On disabled list (May 9-July 25, 1994).

Year	Team (League)	W	L	Pct.	ERA	G	GS	CG	ShO	Sv.	IP	H	R	ER	BB	SO
1992	—GC Royals (GCL)	2	1	.667	1.50	5	4	0	0	0	24	11	6	4	3	26
	—Eugene (N'west)	5	3	.625	2.78	10	10	0	0	0	64 2/3	62	23	20	13	69
1993	—Rockford (Midw.)	6	4	.600	2.12	19	11	1	0	4	85	79	24	20	18	71
	—Wilmington (Caro.)	5	3	.625	2.33	10	10	1	0	0	65 2/3	52	22	17	14	54
1994	—Wilmington (Caro.)	5	3	.625	3.39	15	12	0	0	0	61	52	30	23	15	62
1995	—Kansas City (A.L.)	1	3	.250	5.63	13	5	0	0	0	40	42	25	25	14	19
	—Omaha (Am. Assoc.)	1	7	.125	4.57	12	11	1	0	0	65	63	37	33	20	50
Major league totals (1 year)		1	3	.250	5.63	13	5	0	0	0	40	42	25	25	14	19

BURBA, DAVE — P — REDS

PERSONAL: Born July 7, 1966, in Dayton, O. . . . 6-4/240. . . . Throws right, bats right. . . . Full name: David Allen Burba. . . . Nephew of Ray Hathaway, pitcher, Brooklyn Dodgers (1945).

HIGH SCHOOL: Kenton Ridge (Springfield, O.).

COLLEGE: Ohio State.

TRANSACTIONS/CAREER NOTES: Selected by Seattle Mariners organization in second round of free-agent draft (June 2, 1987). . . . Traded by Mariners with P Bill Swift and P Mike Jackson to San Francisco Giants for OF Kevin Mitchell and P Mike Remlinger (December 11, 1991). . . . Traded by Giants with OF Darren Lewis and P Mark Portugal to Cincinnati Reds for OF Deion Sanders, P John Roper, P Ricky Pickett, P Scott Service and IF Dave McCarty (July 21, 1995).

Year	Team (League)	W	L	Pct.	ERA	G	GS	CG	ShO	Sv.	IP	H	R	ER	BB	SO
1987	—Bellingham (N'west)	3	1	.750	1.93	5	5	0	0	0	23 1/3	20	10	5	3	24
	—Salinas (Calif.)	1	6	.143	4.61	9	9	0	0	0	54 2/3	53	31	28	29	46
1988	—San Bern. (Calif.)	5	7	.417	2.68	20	20	0	0	0	114	106	41	34	54	102

Year	Team (League)	W	L	Pct.	ERA	G	GS	CG	ShO	Sv.	IP	H	R	ER	BB	SO
1989—	Williamsport (East.)	11	7	.611	3.16	25	25	5	1	0	156 2/3	138	69	55	55	89
1990—	Calgary (PCL)	10	6	.625	4.67	31	18	1	0	2	113 2/3	124	64	59	45	47
	—Seattle (A.L.)	0	0	...	4.50	6	0	0	0	0	8	8	6	4	2	4
1991—	Calgary (PCL)	6	4	.600	3.53	23	9	0	0	4	71 1/3	82	35	28	27	42
	—Seattle (A.L.)	2	2	.500	3.68	22	2	0	0	1	36 2/3	34	16	15	14	16
1992—	San Francisco (N.L.)■	2	7	.222	4.97	23	11	0	0	0	70 2/3	80	43	39	31	47
	—Phoenix (PCL)	5	5	.500	4.72	13	13	0	0	0	74 1/3	86	40	39	24	44
1993—	San Francisco (N.L.)	10	3	.769	4.25	54	5	0	0	0	95 1/3	95	49	45	37	88
1994—	San Francisco (N.L.)	3	6	.667	4.38	57	0	0	0	0	74	59	39	36	45	84
1995—	San Francisco (N.L.)	4	2	.667	4.98	37	0	0	0	0	43 1/3	38	26	24	25	46
	—Cincinnati (N.L.)■	6	2	.750	3.27	15	6	1	1	0	63 1/3	52	24	23	26	50
	A.L. totals (2 years)	2	2	.500	3.83	28	2	0	0	1	44 2/3	42	22	19	16	20
	N.L. totals (4 years)	25	20	.556	4.34	186	25	1	1	0	346 2/3	324	181	167	164	315
	Major league totals (6 years)	27	22	.551	4.28	214	27	1	1	1	391 1/3	366	203	186	180	335

DIVISION SERIES RECORD

Year	Team (League)	W	L	Pct.	ERA	G	GS	CG	ShO	Sv.	IP	H	R	ER	BB	SO
1995—	Cincinnati (N.L.)	1	0	1.000	0.00	1	0	0	0	0	1	2	0	0	1	0

CHAMPIONSHIP SERIES RECORD

Year	Team (League)	W	L	Pct.	ERA	G	GS	CG	ShO	Sv.	IP	H	R	ER	BB	SO
1995—	Cincinnati (N.L.)	0	0	...	0.00	2	0	0	0	0	3 2/3	3	0	0	4	0

BURGOS, ENRIQUE — P — GIANTS

PERSONAL: Born October 7, 1965, in Chorrera, Panama. . . . 6-4/230. . . . Throws left, bats left.

TRANSACTIONS/CAREER NOTES: Signed as non-drafted free agent by Toronto Blue Jays organization (January 31, 1983). . . . Loaned by Blue Jays organization to Miami, independent (May 17-July 3, 1989). . . . Granted free agency (October 22, 1989). . . . Played in Taiwan (1990-92). . . . Signed as free agent by Kansas City Royals organization (December 31, 1992). . . . Traded by Royals to San Francisco Giants for a player to be named (April 22, 1995); Royals acquired OF Brent Cookson to complete deal (June 25, 1995).

STATISTICAL NOTES: Combined with starter Pat Hentgen and Willie Blair in 2-1 no-hit victory for Dunedin against Osceola (May 10, 1988).

Year	Team (League)	W	L	Pct.	ERA	G	GS	CG	ShO	Sv.	IP	H	R	ER	BB	SO
1983—	GC Blue Jays (GCL)	0	•9	.000	4.78	13	8	1	0	0	49	52	37	26	32	19
1984—	Florence (S. Atl.)	0	0	...	18.00	2	0	0	0	0	1	2	2	2	1	1
	—GC Blue Jays (GCL)	4	5	.444	2.39	12	10	1	0	0	71 2/3	74	37	19	22	38
1985—	Florence (S. Atl.)	3	1	.750	6.61	26	0	0	0	1	47 2/3	55	39	35	44	32
	—Kinston (Carolina)	0	2	.000	11.88	7	1	0	0	0	8 1/3	12	11	11	10	5
1986—	Florence (S. Atl.)	3	8	.273	6.46	28	10	0	0	2	85	92	76	61	70	71
	—Vent. County (Calif.)	1	3	.250	3.94	9	9	0	0	0	45 2/3	46	27	20	31	37
1987—	Knoxville (South.)	2	3	.400	4.37	17	5	0	0	1	45 1/3	33	27	22	55	45
	—Myrtle Beach (SAL)	5	2	.714	2.11	23	0	0	0	7	38 1/3	22	15	9	24	46
1988—	Syracuse (Int'l)	0	0	...	7.71	2	0	0	0	0	2 1/3	4	2	2	2	2
	—Dunedin (Fla. St.)	1	5	.167	4.71	33	4	0	0	1	49 2/3	61	28	26	37	55
1989—	Dunedin (Fla. St.)	2	0	1.000	2.13	8	0	0	0	0	12 2/3	8	7	3	7	15
	—Miami (Florida St.)■	1	1	.500	3.92	15	1	0	0	0	20 2/3	20	14	9	13	18
	—Myrtle Beach (SAL)■	0	2	.000	2.70	16	1	0	0	1	16 2/3	16	11	5	20	15
1990—	Pres. Lions (Taiw.)■	9	8	.529	2.60	33	21	7	0	2	173	153	87	50	86	177
1991—	Pres. Lions (Taiw.)	7	9	.438	2.68	31	22	8	2	2	174 1/3	135	79	52	78	138
1992—	Pres. Lions (Taiw.)	7	9	.438	4.37	22	20	6	0	0	136	128	85	66	102	131
1993—	Omaha (Am. Assoc.)■	2	4	.333	3.16	48	0	0	0	9	62 2/3	36	26	22	37	91
	—Kansas City (A.L.)	0	1	.000	9.00	5	0	0	0	0	5	5	5	5	6	6
1994—	Omaha (Am. Assoc.)	1	4	.200	2.88	57	0	0	0	19	56 1/3	44	24	18	33	68
1995—	Phoenix (PCL)■	2	6	.250	6.14	41	2	0	0	2	58 2/3	63	44	40	40	77
	—San Francisco (N.L.)	0	0	...	8.64	5	0	0	0	0	8 1/3	14	8	8	6	12
	A.L. totals (1 year)	0	1	.000	9.00	5	0	0	0	0	5	5	5	5	6	6
	N.L. totals (1 year)	0	0	...	8.64	5	0	0	0	0	8 1/3	14	8	8	6	12
	Major league totals (2 years)	0	1	.000	8.78	10	0	0	0	0	13 1/3	19	13	13	12	18

BURKE, JOHN — P — ROCKIES

PERSONAL: Born February 9, 1970, in Durango, Colo. . . . 6-4/215. . . . Throws right, bats both. . . . Full name: John C. Burke.

HIGH SCHOOL: Cherry Creek (Englewood, Colo.).

COLLEGE: Florida.

TRANSACTIONS/CAREER NOTES: Selected by Houston Astros organization in first round (sixth pick overall) of free-agent draft (June 3, 1991); did not sign. . . . Selected by Colorado Rockies organization in first round (27th pick overall) of free-agent draft (June 1, 1992). . . . On Colorado Springs disabled list (April 7-June 22, 1994). . . . On disabled list (July 3-August 1 and August 20, 1995-remainder of season).

Year	Team (League)	W	L	Pct.	ERA	G	GS	CG	ShO	Sv.	IP	H	R	ER	BB	SO
1992—	Bend (Northwest)	2	0	1.000	2.41	10	10	0	0	0	41	38	13	11	18	32
1993—	Central Valley (Cal.)	7	8	.467	3.18	20	20	2	0	0	119	104	62	42	64	114
	—Colo. Springs (PCL)	3	2	.600	3.14	8	8	0	0	0	48 2/3	44	22	17	23	38
1994—	Colo. Springs (PCL)	0	0	...	19.64	8	0	0	0	0	11	16	25	24	22	6
	—Asheville (S. Atl.)	0	1	.000	1.06	4	4	0	0	0	17	5	3	2	5	16
1995—	Colo. Springs (PCL)	7	1	.875	4.55	19	17	0	0	1	87	79	46	44	48	65

BURKETT, JOHN P MARLINS

PERSONAL: Born November 28, 1964, in New Brighton, Pa. . . . 6-2/211. . . . Throws right, bats right. . . . Full name: John David Burkett. . . . Name pronounced bur-KETT.

HIGH SCHOOL: Beaver (Pa.).

TRANSACTIONS/CAREER NOTES: Selected by San Francisco Giants organization in sixth round of free-agent draft (June 6, 1983). . . . Traded by Giants to Texas Rangers for IF Rich Aurilia and OF Desi Wilson (December 22, 1994). . . . Granted free agency (April 7, 1995). . . . Signed by Florida Marlins (April 9, 1995).

STATISTICAL NOTES: Led N.L. with 10 hit batsmen in 1991.

MISCELLANEOUS: Had sacrifice hit in only appearance as pinch-hitter (1995).

Year	Team (League)	W	L	Pct.	ERA	G	GS	CG	ShO	Sv.	IP	H	R	ER	BB	SO
1983—	Great Falls (Pio.)	2	6	.250	6.26	13	9	0	0	0	50 1/3	73	44	35	30	38
1984—	Clinton (Midwest)	7	6	.538	4.33	20	20	2	0	0	126 2/3	128	81	61	38	83
1985—	Fresno (California)	7	4	.636	2.87	20	20	1	1	0	109 2/3	98	43	35	46	72
1986—	Fresno (California)	0	3	.000	5.47	4	4	0	0	0	24 2/3	34	19	15	8	14
—	Shreveport (Texas)	10	6	.625	2.66	22	21	4	2	0	128 2/3	99	46	38	42	73
1987—	Shreveport (Texas)	•14	8	.636	3.34	27	27	6	1	0	*177 2/3	181	75	66	53	126
—	San Francisco (N.L.)	0	0	...	4.50	3	0	0	0	0	6	7	4	3	3	5
1988—	Phoenix (PCL)	5	11	.313	5.21	21	21	0	0	0	114	141	79	66	49	74
—	Shreveport (Texas)	5	1	.833	2.13	7	7	2	1	0	50 2/3	33	15	12	18	34
1989—	Phoenix (PCL)	10	11	.476	5.05	28	•28	2	1	0	167 2/3	197	111	94	59	105
1990—	Phoenix (PCL)	2	1	.667	2.74	3	3	2	1	0	23	18	8	7	3	9
—	San Francisco (N.L.)	14	7	.667	3.79	33	32	2	0	1	204	201	92	86	61	118
1991—	San Francisco (N.L.)	12	11	.522	4.18	36	34	3	1	0	206 2/3	223	103	96	60	131
1992—	San Francisco (N.L.)	13	9	.591	3.84	32	32	3	1	0	189 2/3	194	96	81	45	107
1993—	San Francisco (N.L.)	•22	7	.759	3.65	34	34	2	1	0	231 2/3	224	100	94	40	145
1994—	San Francisco (N.L.)	6	8	.429	3.62	25	25	0	0	0	159 1/3	176	72	64	36	85
1995—	Florida (N.L.)■	14	14	.500	4.30	30	30	4	0	0	188 1/3	208	95	90	57	126
Major league totals (7 years)		81	56	.591	3.90	193	187	14	3	1	1185 2/3	1233	562	514	302	717

ALL-STAR GAME RECORD

Year	League	W	L	Pct.	ERA	GS	CG	ShO	Sv.	IP	H	R	ER	BB	SO
1993—	National	0	1	.000	40.50	0	0	0	0	2/3	4	3	3	0	1

B

BURKS, ELLIS OF ROCKIES

PERSONAL: Born September 11, 1964, in Vicksburg, Miss. . . . 6-2/198. . . . Bats right, throws right. . . . Full name: Ellis Rena Burks.

HIGH SCHOOL: Everman (Tex.).

JUNIOR COLLEGE: Ranger (Tex.) Junior College.

TRANSACTIONS/CAREER NOTES: Selected by Boston Red Sox organization in first round (20th pick overall) of free-agent draft (January 11, 1983). . . . On disabled list (March 26-April 12, 1988). . . . On Boston disabled list (June 15-August 1, 1989); included rehabilitation assignment to Pawtucket (July 26-August 1). . . . On disabled list (June 25, 1992-remainder of season). . . . Granted free agency (December 19, 1992). . . . Signed by Chicago White Sox (January 4, 1993). . . . Granted free agency (October 27, 1993). . . . Signed by Colorado Rockies (November 30, 1993). . . . On Colorado disabled list (May 18-July 31, 1994); included rehabilitation assignment to Colorado Springs (July 18-20). . . . On Colorado disabled list (April 17-May 5, 1995); included rehabilitation assignment to Colorado Springs (April 25-May 5).

RECORDS: Shares major league record for most home runs in one inning—2 (August 27, 1990, fourth inning).

HONORS: Named outfielder on The Sporting News A.L. All-Star team (1990). . . . Named outfielder on The Sporting News A.L. Silver Slugger team (1990). . . . Won A.L. Gold Glove as outfielder (1990).

STATISTICAL NOTES: Tied for Florida State League lead in double plays by outfielder with six in 1984. . . . Career major league grand slams: 8.

			BATTING												FIELDING			
Year	Team (League)	Pos.	G	AB	R	H	2B	3B	HR	RBI	Avg.	BB	SO	SB	PO	A	E	Avg.
1983—	Elmira (N.Y.-Penn)	OF	53	174	30	42	9	0	2	23	.241	17	43	9	89	5	2	.979
1984—	Winter Haven (FSL)	OF	112	375	52	96	15	4	6	43	.256	42	68	29	196	12	5	.977
1985—	New Britain (East.)	OF	133	476	66	121	25	7	10	61	.254	42	85	17	306	9	8	.975
1986—	New Britain (East.)	OF	124	462	70	126	20	3	14	55	.273	44	75	31	318	5	5	.985
1987—	Pawtucket (Int'l)	OF	11	40	11	9	3	1	3	6	.225	7	7	1	25	0	0	1.000
—	Boston (A.L.)	OF-DH	133	558	94	152	30	2	20	59	.272	41	98	27	320	15	4	.988
1988—	Boston (A.L.)	OF-DH	144	540	93	159	37	5	18	92	.294	62	89	25	370	9	9	.977
1989—	Boston (A.L.)	OF-DH	97	399	73	121	19	6	12	61	.303	36	52	21	245	7	6	.977
—	Pawtucket (Int'l)	OF	5	21	4	3	1	0	0	0	.143	2	3	0	16	0	0	1.000
1990—	Boston (A.L.)	OF-DH	152	588	89	174	33	8	21	89	.296	48	82	9	324	7	2	.994
1991—	Boston (A.L.)	OF-DH	130	474	56	119	33	3	14	56	.251	39	81	6	283	2	2	.993
1992—	Boston (A.L.)	OF-DH	66	235	35	60	8	3	8	30	.255	25	48	5	120	3	2	.984
1993—	Chicago (A.L.)■	OF	146	499	75	137	24	4	17	74	.275	60	97	6	313	6	6	.982
1994—	Colorado (N.L.)■	OF	42	149	33	48	8	3	13	24	.322	16	39	3	79	2	3	.964
—	Colo. Springs (PCL)	OF	2	8	4	4	1	0	1	2	.500	2	1	0	5	0	0	1.000
1995—	Colo. Springs (PCL)	OF	8	29	9	9	2	1	2	6	.310	4	8	0	16	0	0	1.000
—	Colorado (N.L.)	OF	103	278	41	74	10	6	14	49	.266	39	72	7	158	3	5	.970
American League totals (7 years)			868	3293	515	922	184	31	110	461	.280	311	547	99	1975	49	31	.985
National League totals (2 years)			145	427	74	122	18	9	27	73	.286	55	111	10	237	5	8	.968
Major league totals (9 years)			1013	3720	589	1044	202	40	137	534	.281	366	658	109	2212	54	39	.983

DIVISION SERIES RECORD

			BATTING												FIELDING			
Year	Team (League)	Pos.	G	AB	R	H	2B	3B	HR	RBI	Avg.	BB	SO	SB	PO	A	E	Avg.
1995—	Colorado (N.L.)	OF	2	6	1	2	1	0	0	2	.333	0	1	0	4	0	1	.800

CHAMPIONSHIP SERIES RECORD

Year	Team (League)	Pos.	G	AB	R	H	2B	3B	HR	RBI	Avg.	BB	SO	SB	PO	A	E	Avg.
			BATTING												FIELDING			
1988—	Boston (A.L.)	OF	4	17	2	4	1	0	0	1	.235	0	3	0	10	0	0	1.000
1990—	Boston (A.L.)	OF	4	15	1	4	2	0	0	0	.267	1	1	1	9	1	0	1.000
1993—	Chicago (A.L.)	OF	6	23	4	7	1	0	1	3	.304	3	5	0	15	0	0	1.000
Championship series totals (3 years)			14	55	7	15	4	0	1	4	.273	4	9	1	34	1	0	1.000

ALL-STAR GAME RECORD

NOTES: Named to A.L. All-Star team for 1990 game; replaced by Brook Jacoby due to injury.

Year	League	Pos.	AB	R	H	2B	3B	HR	RBI	Avg.	BB	SO	SB	PO	A	E	Avg.
			BATTING											FIELDING			
1990—	American							Selected, did not play—injured.									

B

BURNITZ, JEROMY — OF — INDIANS

PERSONAL: Born April 15, 1969, in Westminster, Calif. . . . 6-0/190. . . . Bats left, throws right. . . . Full name: Jeromy Neal Burnitz.

HIGH SCHOOL: Conroe (Tex.).

COLLEGE: Oklahoma State.

TRANSACTIONS/CAREER NOTES: Selected by Milwaukee Brewers organization in 24th round of free-agent draft (June 2, 1987); did not sign. . . . Selected by New York Mets organization in first round (17th pick overall) of free-agent draft (June 4, 1990). . . . On disabled list (August 23-September 18, 1992). . . . On Norfolk suspended list (August 11-13, 1994). . . . Traded by Mets with P Joe Roa to Cleveland Indians for P Paul Byrd, P Jerry DiPoto, P Dave Mlicki and a player to be named later (November 18, 1994); Mets acquired 2B Jesus Azuaje to complete deal (December 6, 1994).

STATISTICAL NOTES: Led New York-Pennsylvania League with .444 on-base percentage and tied for lead with six intentional bases on balls received in 1990. . . . Led American Association with .503 slugging percentage in 1995. . . . Led American Association with eight intentional bases on balls received in 1995. . . . Career major league grand slams: 1.

Year	Team (League)	Pos.	G	AB	R	H	2B	3B	HR	RBI	Avg.	BB	SO	SB	PO	A	E	Avg.
			BATTING												FIELDING			
1990—	Pittsfield (NYP)	OF	51	173	37	52	6	5	6	22	.301	45	39	12	79	2	0	1.000
—	St. Lucie (Fla. St.)	OF	11	32	6	5	1	0	0	3	.156	7	12	1	18	1	0	1.000
1991—	Williamsport (East.)	OF	135	457	80	103	16	•10	*31	•85	.225	*104	127	31	237	13	•11	.958
1992—	Tidewater (Int'l)	OF	121	445	56	108	21	3	8	40	.243	33	84	30	222	11	8	.967
1993—	Norfolk (Int'l)	OF	65	255	33	58	15	3	8	44	.227	25	53	10	133	9	1	.993
—	New York (N.L.)	OF	86	263	49	64	10	6	13	38	.243	38	66	3	165	6	4	.977
1994—	New York (N.L.)	OF	45	143	26	34	4	0	3	15	.238	23	45	1	63	1	2	.970
—	Norfolk (Int'l)	OF	85	314	58	75	15	5	14	49	.239	49	82	18	170	13	4	.979
1995—	Buffalo (A.A.)■	OF	128	443	72	126	26	7	19	*85	.284	50	83	13	241	12	5	.981
—	Cleveland (A.L.)	OF-DH	9	7	4	4	1	0	0	0	.571	0	0	0	10	0	0	1.000
American League totals (1 year)			9	7	4	4	1	0	0	0	.571	0	0	0	10	0	0	1.000
National League totals (2 years)			131	406	75	98	14	6	16	53	.241	61	111	4	228	7	6	.975
Major league totals (3 years)			140	413	79	102	15	6	16	53	.247	61	111	4	238	7	6	.976

BURROWS, TERRY — P — RANGERS

PERSONAL: Born November 28, 1968, in Lake Charles, La. . . . 6-1/185. . . . Throws left, bats left. . . . Full name: Terry Dale Burrows.

HIGH SCHOOL: Catholic-Point Coupee (New Roads, La.).

COLLEGE: McNeese State.

TRANSACTIONS/CAREER NOTES: Selected by Texas Rangers organization in seventh round of free-agent draft (June 4, 1990). . . . On disabled list (April 25-May 2, 1993). . . . On Oklahoma City disabled list (August 5-30, 1995).

STATISTICAL NOTES: Tied for American Association lead with five balks in 1993.

Year	Team (League)	W	L	Pct.	ERA	G	GS	CG	ShO	Sv.	IP	H	R	ER	BB	SO
1990—	Butte (Pioneer)	3	6	.333	4.02	14	11	1	0	0	62 2/3	56	35	28	35	64
1991—	Gastonia (S. Atl.)	12	8	.600	4.45	27	26	0	0	0	147 2/3	107	79	73	78	151
1992—	Charlotte (Fla. St.)	4	2	.667	2.03	14	14	0	0	0	80	71	22	18	25	66
—	Tulsa (Texas)	6	3	.667	2.13	14	13	1	0	0	76	66	22	18	35	59
—	Okla. City (A.A.)	1	0	1.000	1.13	1	1	0	0	0	8	3	1	1	5	0
1993—	Okla. City (A.A.)	7	*15	.318	6.39	27	25	1	0	0	138	171	*107	*98	76	74
1994—	Okla. City (A.A.)	3	5	.375	4.26	44	5	0	0	1	82 1/3	75	43	39	37	57
—	Texas (A.L.)	0	0	...	9.00	1	0	0	0	0	1	1	1	1	1	0
1995—	Texas (A.L.)	2	2	.500	6.45	28	3	0	0	1	44 2/3	60	37	32	19	22
—	Okla. City (A.A.)	0	1	.000	10.13	5	0	0	0	0	2 2/3	5	4	3	2	4
Major league totals (2 years)		2	2	.500	6.50	29	3	0	0	1	45 2/3	61	38	33	20	22

BURTON, DARREN — OF — ROYALS

PERSONAL: Born September 16, 1972, in Somerset, Ky. . . . 6-1/185. . . . Bats both, throws right. . . . Full name: Darren Scott Burton.

HIGH SCHOOL: Pulaski County (Somerset, Ky.).

TRANSACTIONS/CAREER NOTES: Selected by Kansas City Royals organization in fifth round of free-agent draft (June 4, 1990). . . . On disabled list (June 7-July 13, 1994). . . . Claimed on waivers by Cincinnati Reds (June 16, 1995). . . . Claimed on waivers by Chicago Cubs (June 22, 1995). . . . Claimed on waivers by Royals (November 27, 1995).

STATISTICAL NOTES: Led Midwest League outfielders with 313 total chances in 1991. . . . Led Florida State League outfielders with six double plays in 1992. . . . Tied for Carolina League lead with 13 sacrifice hits in 1993.

MISCELLANEOUS: Batted righthanded only (1990-91).

			BATTING											FIELDING			
Year	Team (League)	Pos.	G	AB	R	H	2B	3B	HR	RBI	Avg.	BB	SO	SB	PO	A	E	Avg.
1990—	GC Royals (GCL)	OF	15	58	10	12	0	1	0	2	.207	4	17	6	31	1	1	.970
1991—	Appleton (Midw.)	OF	*134	*531	78	143	32	6	2	51	.269	45	122	38	*288	16	9	.971
1992—	Baseball City (FSL)	OF	123	431	54	106	15	6	4	36	.246	49	93	16	282	16	5	.983
1993—	Wilmington (Caro.)	OF	134	549	82	152	23	5	10	45	.277	48	111	30	303	14	9	.972
1994—	Memphis (South.)	OF	97	373	55	95	12	3	3	37	.255	35	53	10	204	11	4	.982
1995—	Omaha (A.A.)	OF	2	5	0	0	0	0	0	0	.000	0	1	0	6	0	0	1.000
	—Wichita (Texas)	OF	41	163	13	39	9	1	1	20	.239	12	27	6	73	4	3	.963
	—Orlando (Southern)■	OF	62	222	40	68	16	2	4	21	.306	27	42	7	101	4	2	.981

BUSBY, MIKE — P — CARDINALS

PERSONAL: Born December 27, 1972, in Lomita, Calif. . . . 6-4/210. . . . Throws right, bats right. . . . Full name: Michael J. Busby.
HIGH SCHOOL: Banning (Wilmington, Calif.).
TRANSACTIONS/CAREER NOTES: Selected by St. Louis Cardinals organization in 14th round of free-agent draft (June 3, 1991).

Year	Team (League)	W	L	Pct.	ERA	G	GS	CG	ShO	Sv.	IP	H	R	ER	BB	SO
1991—	Ariz. Cardinals (Ariz.)	4	3	.571	3.51	11	11	0	0	0	59	67	35	23	29	71
1992—	Savannah (S. Atl.)	4	•13	.235	3.67	28	•28	1	0	0	149 2/3	145	96	61	67	84
1993—	Savannah (S. Atl.)	12	2	.857	2.44	23	21	1	1	0	143 2/3	116	49	39	31	125
1994—	St. Petersburg (FSL)	6	•13	.316	4.45	26	26	1	0	0	151 2/3	166	82	75	49	89
1995—	Arkansas (Texas)	7	6	.538	3.29	20	20	1	0	0	134	125	63	49	35	95
	—Louisville (A.A.)	2	2	.500	3.29	6	6	1	0	0	38 1/3	28	18	14	11	26

BUSCH, MIKE — 3B/1B — DODGERS

PERSONAL: Born July 7, 1968, in Davenport, Ia. . . . 6-5/220. . . . Bats right, throws right. . . . Full name: Michael Anthony Busch.
HIGH SCHOOL: North Scott (Eldridge, Ia.).
COLLEGE: Iowa State.
TRANSACTIONS/CAREER NOTES: Selected by Los Angeles Dodgers organization in fourth round of free-agent draft (June 4, 1990). . . . On disabled list (May 17-28 and June 6-September 10, 1991; and May 19-June 2, 1992).
STATISTICAL NOTES: Led Pioneer League with 134 total bases and .605 slugging percentage in 1990. . . . Led Pioneer League first basemen with 56 double plays in 1990. . . . Led Pacific Coast League third basemen with 312 total chances, 218 assists and 37 errors in 1993. . . . Led Pacific Coast League first basemen with 1,104 total chances, 1,008 putouts, 88 assists and 128 double plays in 1994.

			BATTING											FIELDING			
Year	Team (League)	Pos.	G	AB	R	H	2B	3B	HR	RBI	Avg.	BB	SO	SB	PO	A	E	Avg.
1990—	Great Falls (Pio.)	1B	61	220	48	72	19	2	*13	47	.327	38	49	3	481	*47	4	*.992
1991—	Bakersfield (Calif.)	1B	21	72	13	20	3	1	4	16	.278	12	21	0	161	17	7	.962
1992—	San Antonio (Tex.)	3B-OF-1B	115	416	58	99	14	2	18	51	.238	36	111	3	180	161	31	.917
1993—	Albuquerque (PCL)	3B-1B	122	431	87	122	32	4	22	70	.283	53	89	1	169	†231	†40	.909
1994—	Albuquerque (PCL)	1B-3B	126	460	73	121	23	3	27	83	.263	50	101	2	†1014	†94	8	.993
1995—	Albuquerque (PCL)	3B-1B-OF	121	443	68	119	32	1	18	62	.269	42	103	2	338	164	14	.973
	—Los Angeles (N.L.)	3B-1B	13	17	3	4	0	0	3	6	.235	0	7	0	10	6	1	.941
Major league totals (1 year)			13	17	3	4	0	0	3	6	.235	0	7	0	10	6	1	.941

BUSH, HOMER — 2B — PADRES

PERSONAL: Born November 12, 1972, in East St. Louis, Ill. . . . 5-10/175. . . . Bats right, throws right. . . . Full name: Homer Giles Bush.
HIGH SCHOOL: East St. Louis (Ill.).
COLLEGE: Southern Illinois-Edwardsville.
TRANSACTIONS/CAREER NOTES: Selected by San Diego Padres organization in seventh round of free-agent draft (June 3, 1991). . . . On Rancho Cucamonga disabled list (April 27-May 4 and May 9-26, 1994).

			BATTING											FIELDING			
Year	Team (League)	Pos.	G	AB	R	H	2B	3B	HR	RBI	Avg.	BB	SO	SB	PO	A	E	Avg.
1991—	Ariz. Padres (Ariz.)	3B	32	127	16	41	3	2	0	16	.323	4	33	11	25	60	10	.895
1992—	Char., S.C. (S. Atl.)	2B	108	367	37	86	10	5	0	18	.234	13	85	14	199	287	*34	.935
1993—	Waterloo (Midw.)	2B	130	472	63	*152	19	3	5	51	.322	19	87	39	215	289	38	.930
1994—	Rancho Cuca. (Cal.)	2B	39	161	37	54	10	3	0	16	.335	9	29	9	69	102	7	.961
	—Wichita (Texas)	2B	59	245	35	73	11	4	3	14	.298	10	39	20	101	135	8	.967
1995—	Memphis (South.)	2B	108	432	53	121	12	5	5	37	.280	15	83	34	235	268	16	.969

BUTCHER, MIKE — P — MARINERS

PERSONAL: Born May 10, 1965, in Davenport, Ia. . . . 6-1/200. . . . Throws right, bats right. . . . Full name: Michael Dana Butcher.
HIGH SCHOOL: United Township (East Moline, Ill.).
COLLEGE: Northeastern Oklahoma A&M.
TRANSACTIONS/CAREER NOTES: Selected by Cincinnati Reds organization in fourth round of free-agent draft (January 14, 1986); did not sign. . . . Selected by Kansas City Royals organization in secondary phase of free-agent draft (June 2, 1986). . . . Released by Royals organization (July 3, 1988). . . . Signed by California Angels organization (July 8, 1988). . . . On California disabled list (April 2-June 15, 1993); included rehabilitation assignment to Vancouver (May 17-June 15). . . . Granted free agency (October 16, 1995). . . . Signed by Seattle Mariners organization (December 14, 1995).

Year	Team (League)	W	L	Pct.	ERA	G	GS	CG	ShO	Sv.	IP	H	R	ER	BB	SO
1986—	Eugene (N'west)	5	4	.556	3.86	14	14	1	0	0	72 1/3	51	39	31	49	68
1987—	Appleton (Midw.)	10	4	.714	2.67	20	19	3	1	0	121 1/3	101	50	36	56	89

Year	Team (League)	W	L	Pct.	ERA	G	GS	CG	ShO	Sv.	IP	H	R	ER	BB	SO
	—Fort Myers (Fla. St.)	2	2	.500	5.46	5	5	1	0	0	31 1/3	33	20	19	8	17
1988	—Baseball City (FSL)	1	4	.200	3.86	6	6	0	0	0	32 2/3	32	19	14	10	20
	—Appleton (Midw.)	0	1	.000	3.00	4	4	0	0	0	18	17	7	6	5	7
	—Quad City (Midw.)■	0	0	...	4.50	3	0	0	0	0	6	6	3	3	4	7
	—Palm Springs (Cal.)	3	2	.600	5.70	7	7	0	0	0	42 2/3	57	33	27	19	37
1989	—Midland (Texas)	2	6	.250	6.55	15	15	0	0	0	68 2/3	92	54	50	41	49
1990	—Midland (Texas)	3	7	.300	6.21	35	8	0	0	0	87	109	68	60	55	84
1991	—Midland (Texas)	9	6	.600	5.22	41	6	0	0	3	88	93	54	51	46	70
1992	—Edmonton (PCL)	5	2	.714	3.07	26	0	0	0	4	29 1/3	24	12	10	18	32
	—California (A.L.)	2	2	.500	3.25	19	0	0	0	0	27 2/3	29	11	10	13	24
1993	—Vancouver (PCL)	2	3	.400	4.44	14	1	0	0	3	24 1/3	21	16	12	12	12
	—California (A.L.)	1	0	1.000	2.86	23	0	0	0	8	28 1/3	21	12	9	15	24
1994	—California (A.L.)	2	1	.667	6.67	33	0	0	0	1	29 2/3	31	24	22	23	19
	—Vancouver (PCL)	5	1	.833	3.77	19	0	0	0	5	28 2/3	29	14	12	11	30
1995	—California (A.L.)	6	1	.857	4.73	40	0	0	0	0	51 1/3	49	28	27	31	29
Major league totals (4 years)		11	4	.733	4.47	115	0	0	0	9	137	130	75	68	82	96

BUTLER, BRETT — OF — DODGERS

PERSONAL: Born June 15, 1957, in Los Angeles. . . . 5-10/161. . . . Bats left, throws left. . . . Full name: Brett Morgan Butler.

HIGH SCHOOL: Libertyville (Ill.).

TRANSACTIONS/CAREER NOTES: Selected by Atlanta Braves organization in 23rd round of free-agent draft (June 5, 1979). . . . Traded by Braves with IF Brook Jacoby to Cleveland Indians (October 21, 1983), completing deal in which Indians traded P Len Barker to Braves for three players to be named later (August 28, 1983); Indians acquired P Rick Behenna as partial completion of deal (September 2, 1983). . . . On disabled list (April 11-30, 1987). . . . Granted free agency (November 9, 1987). . . . Signed by San Francisco Giants (December 1, 1987). . . . Granted free agency (December 7, 1990). . . . Signed by Los Angeles Dodgers (December 14, 1990). . . . Granted free agency (October 21, 1994). . . . Granted free agency (April 3, 1995). . . . Signed by New York Mets (April 11, 1995). . . . Traded by Mets to Dodgers for OF Dwight Maness and OF Scott Hunter (August 18, 1995). . . . Granted free agency (November 7, 1995). . . . Re-signed by Dodgers (November 9, 1995).

RECORDS: Shares major league single-season records for fewest double plays by outfielder who led league in double plays—3 (1991); fewest double plays by outfielder (150 or more games)—0 (1990); highest fielding percentage by outfielder (150 or more games)—1.000 (1991 and 1993); and fewest errors by outfielder (150 games or more)—0 (1991 and 1993). . . . Holds N.L. record for most consecutive seasons leading league in singles—4 (1990-93). . . . Shares N.L. record for most years leading league in singles—4 (1990-93). . . . Shares modern N.L. single-game record for most bases on balls received—5 (April 12, 1990).

HONORS: Named International League Most Valuable Player (1981).

STATISTICAL NOTES: Tied for N.L. lead in double plays by outfielder with four in 1983 and three in 1991. . . . Led A.L. in caught stealing with 22 in 1984 and 20 in 1985. . . . Led N.L. in caught stealing with 28 in 1991. . . . Tied for N.L. lead in total chances by outfielder with 380 in 1991. . . . Led N.L. with 24 sacrifice hits in 1992. . . . Tied for N.L. lead with nine triples in 1995. . . . Career major league grand slams: 1.

				BATTING											FIELDING			
Year	Team (League)	Pos.	G	AB	R	H	2B	3B	HR	RBI	Avg.	BB	SO	SB	PO	A	E	Avg.
1979	—Greenw. (W. Car.)	OF	35	117	26	37	2	4	1	11	.316	24	27	20	45	2	0	1.000
	—GC Braves (GCL)	OF	30	111	36	41	7	5	3	20	.369	19	15	5	66	5	0	1.000
1980	—Anderson (S. Atl.)	OF	70	255	73	76	12	6	1	26	.298	67	29	44	190	5	1	.995
	—Durham (Carolina)	OF	66	224	47	82	15	6	2	39	.366	67	30	36	156	4	3	.982
1981	—Richmond (Int'l)	OF	125	466	*93	156	19	4	3	36	.335	*103	63	44	286	15	3	.990
	—Atlanta (N.L.)	OF	40	126	17	32	2	3	0	4	.254	19	17	9	76	2	1	.987
1982	—Atlanta (N.L.)	OF	89	240	35	52	2	0	0	7	.217	25	35	21	129	2	0	1.000
	—Richmond (Int'l)	OF	41	157	22	57	8	3	1	22	.363	22	19	12	101	2	1	.990
1983	—Atlanta (N.L.)	OF	151	549	84	154	21	*13	5	37	.281	54	56	39	284	13	4	.987
1984	—Cleveland (A.L.)■	OF	159	602	108	162	25	9	3	49	.269	86	62	52	448	13	4	.991
1985	—Cleveland (A.L.)	OF-DH	152	591	106	184	28	14	5	50	.311	63	42	47	437	19	1	*.998
1986	—Cleveland (A.L.)	OF	161	587	92	163	17	*14	4	51	.278	70	65	32	434	9	3	.993
1987	—Cleveland (A.L.)	OF	137	522	91	154	25	8	9	41	.295	91	55	33	393	4	4	.990
1988	—San Fran. (N.L.)■	OF	157	568	*109	163	27	9	6	43	.287	97	64	43	395	3	5	.988
1989	—San Francisco (N.L.)	OF	154	594	100	168	22	4	4	36	.283	59	69	31	407	11	6	.986
1990	—San Francisco (N.L.)	OF	160	622	108	•192	20	9	3	44	.309	90	62	51	420	4	6	.986
1991	—Los Angeles (N.L.)■	OF	*161	615	*112	182	13	5	2	38	.296	*108	79	38	*372	8	0	*1.000
1992	—Los Angeles (N.L.)	OF	157	553	86	171	14	11	3	39	.309	95	67	41	353	9	2	.995
1993	—Los Angeles (N.L.)	OF	156	607	80	181	21	10	1	42	.298	86	69	39	369	6	0	•1.000
1994	—Los Angeles (N.L.)	OF	111	417	79	131	13	•9	8	33	.314	68	52	27	260	8	2	.993
1995	—New York (N.L.)■	OF	90	367	54	114	13	7	1	25	.311	43	42	21	207	6	1	.995
	—Los Angeles (N.L.)■	OF	39	146	24	40	5	§2	0	13	.274	24	9	11	75	0	1	.987
American League totals (4 years)			609	2302	397	663	95	45	21	191	.288	310	224	164	1712	45	12	.993
National League totals (11 years)			1465	5404	888	1580	173	82	33	361	.292	768	621	371	3347	72	28	.992
Major league totals (15 years)			2074	7706	1285	2243	268	127	54	552	.291	1078	845	535	5059	117	40	.992

DIVISION SERIES RECORD

				BATTING											FIELDING			
Year	Team (League)	Pos.	G	AB	R	H	2B	3B	HR	RBI	Avg.	BB	SO	SB	PO	A	E	Avg.
1995	—Los Angeles (N.L.)	OF	3	15	1	4	0	0	0	1	.267	0	3	0	7	0	0	1.000

CHAMPIONSHIP SERIES RECORD

				BATTING											FIELDING			
Year	Team (League)	Pos.	G	AB	R	H	2B	3B	HR	RBI	Avg.	BB	SO	SB	PO	A	E	Avg.
1982	—Atlanta (N.L.)	OF-PH	2	1	0	0	0	0	0	0	.000	0	0	0	0	0	0	...
1989	—San Francisco (N.L.)	OF	5	19	6	4	0	0	0	0	.211	3	3	0	9	0	0	1.000
Championship series totals (2 years)			7	20	6	4	0	0	0	0	.200	3	3	0	9	0	0	1.000

WORLD SERIES RECORD

Year	Team (League)	Pos.	G	AB	R	H	2B	3B	HR	RBI	Avg.	BB	SO	SB	PO	A	E	Avg.
				BATTING											FIELDING			
1989—	San Francisco (N.L.)	OF	4	14	1	4	1	0	0	1	.286	2	1	2	9	0	0	1.000

ALL-STAR GAME RECORD

Year	League	Pos.	AB	R	H	2B	3B	HR	RBI	Avg.	BB	SO	SB	PO	A	E	Avg.
			BATTING											FIELDING			
1991—	National	PR-OF	1	0	0	0	0	0	0	.000	0	0	0	0	0	0	...

BYRD, PAUL — P — METS

PERSONAL: Born December 3, 1970, in Louisville, Ky. . . . 6-1/185. . . . Throws right, bats right. . . . Full name: Paul Gregory Byrd.
HIGH SCHOOL: St. Xavier (Louisville, Ky.).
COLLEGE: Louisiana State.
TRANSACTIONS/CAREER NOTES: Selected by Cincinnati Reds organization in 13th round of free-agent draft (June 1, 1988); did not sign. . . . Selected by Cleveland Indians organization in fourth round of free-agent draft (June 3, 1991). . . . On disabled list (August 12, 1992-remainder of season). . . . On disabled list (May 23-July 24, 1993). . . . Traded by Indians organization with P Dave Mlicki, P Jerry DiPoto and a player to be named to New York Mets organization for OF Jeromy Burnitz and P Joe Roa (November 18, 1994); Mets acquired 2B Jesus Azuaje to complete deal (December 6, 1994). . . . On Norfolk disabled list (June 1-19, 1995).
STATISTICAL NOTES: Led Carolina League with seven balks in 1991.

Year	Team (League)	W	L	Pct.	ERA	G	GS	CG	ShO	Sv.	IP	H	R	ER	BB	SO
1991—	Kinston (Carolina)	4	3	.571	3.16	14	11	0	0	0	62 2/3	40	27	22	36	62
1992—	Cant./Akr. (East.)	14	6	.700	3.01	24	24	4	0	0	152 1/3	122	68	51	75	118
1993—	Charlotte (Int'l)	7	4	.636	3.89	14	14	1	1	0	81	80	43	35	30	54
—	Cant./Akr. (East.)	0	0	...	3.60	2	1	0	0	0	10	7	4	4	3	8
1994—	Cant./Akr. (East.)	5	9	.357	3.81	21	20	4	1	0	139 1/3	135	70	59	52	106
—	Charlotte (Fla. St.)	2	2	.500	3.93	9	4	0	0	1	36 2/3	33	19	16	11	15
1995—	Norfolk (Int'l)■	3	5	.375	2.79	22	10	1	0	6	87	71	29	27	21	61
—	New York (N.L.)	2	0	1.000	2.05	17	0	0	0	0	22	18	6	5	7	26
Major league totals (1 year)		2	0	1.000	2.05	17	0	0	0	0	22	18	6	5	7	26

CACERES, EDGAR — IF — ROYALS

PERSONAL: Born June 6, 1964, in Lara, Venezuela. . . . 6-1/170. . . . Bats both, throws right. . . . Full name: Edgar F. Caceres.
HIGH SCHOOL: Obelisco (Lara, Venezuela).
TRANSACTIONS/CAREER NOTES: Signed as non-drafted free agent by Los Angeles Dodgers organization (November 4, 1983). . . . On disabled list (August 1, 1984-remainder of season). . . . Released by Dodgers organization (September 26, 1985). . . . Signed by Montreal Expos organization (December 16, 1985). . . . Traded by Expos organization (June 15, 1988); completing deal in which White Sox traded IF Tim Hulett to Expos for a player to be named later (April 13, 1988). . . . Granted free agency (October 15, 1990). . . . Signed by Milwaukee Brewers organization (January 30, 1992). . . . On disabled list (May 15-June 2, 1993). . . . Granted free agency (October 15, 1993). . . . Signed by Kansas City Royals organization (November 15, 1993). . . . On disabled list (May 25-June 30, 1994). . . . On Kansas City disabled list (July 16-31, 1995). . . . Granted free agency (October 16, 1995). . . . Re-signed by Royals organization (November 7, 1995).
STATISTICAL NOTES: Led Florida State League second basemen with .975 fielding percentage in 1986. . . . Led Florida State League third basemen with .943 fielding percentage in 1989.

Year	Team (League)	Pos.	G	AB	R	H	2B	3B	HR	RBI	Avg.	BB	SO	SB	PO	A	E	Avg.
				BATTING											FIELDING			
1984—	GC Dodgers (GCL)	2B	20	77	11	23	3	1	0	11	.299	10	6	5	54	62	5	.959
1985—	GC Dodgers (GCL)	3B-2B	53	176	37	53	6	0	0	22	.301	18	11	5	69	87	11	.934
1986—	W.P. Beach (FSL)■	2B-3B	111	382	52	106	9	5	0	37	.277	24	28	25	209	274	13	†.974
1987—	Jacksonv. (South.)	2B	18	62	7	8	0	1	0	3	.129	3	7	2	39	51	2	.978
—	W.P. Beach (FSL)	2B-3B-SS	105	390	55	105	14	1	2	37	.269	27	30	30	170	269	6	.987
1988—	Rockford (Midw.)	2B	36	117	25	31	2	0	0	8	.265	12	12	13	56	86	6	.959
—	Tampa (Fla. St.)■	2B-SS-3B	32	74	5	15	2	0	1	8	.203	10	8	3	42	56	0	1.000
1989—	Sarasota (Fla. St.)	3B-SS-2B	106	373	45	110	16	4	0	50	.295	24	38	8	83	176	16	†.942
1990—	Birm. (Southern)	SS-3B-2B	62	214	31	56	5	1	0	17	.262	15	26	7	74	170	10	.961
1991—									Did not play.									
1992—	El Paso (Texas)■	S-2-1-3	114	378	50	118	14	6	2	52	.312	23	41	9	219	256	12	.975
1993—	New Orleans (A.A.)	2-S-1-3-O	114	420	73	133	20	2	5	45	.317	35	39	7	282	259	8	.985
1994—	Omaha (A.A.)■	2-S-3-1-O	67	236	39	64	7	3	2	18	.271	16	23	5	132	184	3	.991
1995—	Kansas City (A.L.)	2-S-1-DH-3	55	117	13	28	6	2	1	17	.239	8	15	2	72	92	1	.994
—	Omaha (A.A.)	3-2-S-1-O-P	37	107	13	22	3	1	0	12	.206	8	10	3	61	69	3	.977
Major league totals (1 year)			55	117	13	28	6	2	1	17	.239	8	15	2	72	92	1	.994

RECORD AS PITCHER

Year	Team (League)	W	L	Pct.	ERA	G	GS	CG	ShO	Sv.	IP	H	R	ER	BB	SO
1995—	Omaha (Am. Assoc.)	0	0	...	9.00	1	0	0	0	0	2	4	2	2	1	1

CAIRO, MIGUEL — 2B — BLUE JAYS

PERSONAL: Born May 4, 1974, in Anaco, Venezuela. . . . 6-0/160. . . . Bats right, throws right. . . . Full name: Miguel Jesus Cairo.
TRANSACTIONS/CAREER NOTES: Signed as non-drafted free agent by Los Angeles Dodgers organization (November 4, 1983). . . . Traded by Dodgers with 3B Willis Ontanez to Seattle Mariners for 3B Mike Blowers (November 29, 1995). . . . Traded by Mariners with P Bill Risley to Toronto Blue Jays for P Edwin Hurtado and P Paul Menhart (December 18, 1995).
STATISTICAL NOTES: Led California League in caught stealing with 23 in 1994.

Year	Team (League)	Pos.	G	AB	R	H	2B	3B	HR	RBI	Avg.	BB	SO	SB	PO	A	E	Avg.
				BATTING											FIELDING			
1991—	Santo Dom. (DSL)	...	57	203	16	45	5	1	0	17	.222	0	17	8	...	...	...	...

Year	Team (League)	Pos.	G	AB	R	H	2B	3B	HR	RBI	Avg.	BB	SO	SB	PO	A	E	Avg.
			BATTING												FIELDING			
1992—	Vero Beach (FSL)	2B-3B	36	125	7	28	0	0	0	7	.224	11	12	5	69	76	10	.935
—	GC Dodgers (GCL)	SS-3B	21	76	10	23	5	2	0	9	.303	2	6	1	26	56	4	.953
1993—	Vero Beach (FSL)	2B-SS-3B	90	346	50	109	10	1	1	23	.315	28	22	23	172	244	18	.959
1994—	Bakersfield (Calif.)	2B-SS	133	533	76	155	23	4	2	48	.291	34	37	44	268	376	28	.958
1995—	San Antonio (Tex.)	2B-SS	107	435	53	121	20	1	1	41	.278	26	31	33	210	316	23	.958

CAMERON, MIKE — OF — WHITE SOX

PERSONAL: Born January 8, 1973, in LaGrange, Ga. . . . 6-2/190. . . . Bats right, throws right. . . . Full name: Michael Terrance Cameron.
HIGH SCHOOL: LaGrange (Ga.).
TRANSACTIONS/CAREER NOTES: Selected by Chicago White Sox organization in 18th round of free-agent draft (June 3, 1991).
STATISTICAL NOTES: Tied for Carolina League lead in double plays by outfielder with four in 1994.

Year	Team (League)	Pos.	G	AB	R	H	2B	3B	HR	RBI	Avg.	BB	SO	SB	PO	A	E	Avg.
			BATTING												FIELDING			
1991—	GC Whi. Sox (GCL)	OF	44	136	20	30	3	0	0	11	.221	17	29	13	55	3	3	.951
1992—	Utica (NYP)	OF	26	87	15	24	1	4	2	12	.276	11	26	3	60	3	0	1.000
—	South Bend (Mid.)	OF	35	114	19	26	8	1	1	9	.228	10	37	2	67	0	3	.957
1993—	South Bend (Mid.)	OF	122	411	52	98	14	5	0	30	.238	27	101	19	248	13	4	.985
1994—	Prin. William (Car.)	OF	131	468	86	116	15	*17	6	48	.248	60	101	22	275	10	6	.979
1995—	Birm. (Southern)	OF	107	350	64	87	20	5	11	60	.249	54	104	21	250	7	4	.985
—	Chicago (A.L.)	OF	28	38	4	7	2	0	1	2	.184	3	15	0	33	1	0	1.000
Major league totals (1 year)			28	38	4	7	2	0	1	2	.184	3	15	0	33	1	0	1.000

C

CAMINITI, KEN — 3B — PADRES

PERSONAL: Born April 21, 1963, in Hanford, Calif. . . . 6-0/200. . . . Bats both, throws right. . . . Full name: Kenneth Gene Caminiti. . . . Name pronounced CAM-uh-NET-ee.
HIGH SCHOOL: Leigh (San Jose, Calif.).
COLLEGE: San Jose State.
TRANSACTIONS/CAREER NOTES: Selected by Houston Astros organization in third round of free-agent draft (June 4, 1984). . . . On disabled list (April 19-May 11, 1992). . . . Traded by Astros with OF Steve Finley, SS Andujar Cedeno, 1B Robert Petagine, P Brian Williams and a player to be named later to San Diego Padres for OF Phil Plantier, OF Derek Bell, P Pedro Martinez, P Doug Brocail, IF Craig Shipley and SS Ricky Gutierrez (December 28, 1994).
RECORDS: Holds major league single-season record for most games with switch-hit home runs—3 (1995). . . . Holds major league record for most consecutive games with switch-hit home runs—2 (September 16-17, 1995).
HONORS: Named third baseman on The Sporting News college All-America team (1984). . . . Won N.L. Gold Glove at third base (1995).
STATISTICAL NOTES: Led Southern League third basemen with 34 double plays in 1986. . . . Led Pacific Coast League third basemen with 382 total chances and 25 double plays in 1988. . . . Switch-hit home runs in one game four times (July 3, 1994; September 16, September 17 and September 19, 1995). . . . Led N.L. third basemen with 424 total chances and 28 double plays in 1995. . . . Career major league grand slams: 2.

Year	Team (League)	Pos.	G	AB	R	H	2B	3B	HR	RBI	Avg.	BB	SO	SB	PO	A	E	Avg.
			BATTING												FIELDING			
1985—	Osceola (Fla. St.)	3B	126	468	83	133	26	9	4	73	.284	51	54	14	53	193	20	.925
1986—	Columbus (South.)	3B	137	513	82	154	29	3	12	81	.300	56	79	5	105	*299	33	.924
1987—	Columbus (South.)	3B	95	375	66	122	25	2	15	69	.325	25	58	11	55	205	21	.925
—	Houston (N.L.)	3B	63	203	10	50	7	1	3	23	.246	12	44	0	50	98	8	.949
1988—	Tucson (PCL)	3B	109	416	54	113	24	7	5	66	.272	29	54	13	*105	*250	27	.929
—	Houston (N.L.)	3B	30	83	5	15	2	0	1	7	.181	5	18	0	12	43	3	.948
1989—	Houston (N.L.)	3B	161	585	71	149	31	3	10	72	.255	51	93	4	126	335	22	.954
1990—	Houston (N.L.)	3B	153	541	52	131	20	2	4	51	.242	48	97	9	118	243	21	.945
1991—	Houston (N.L.)	3B	152	574	65	145	30	3	13	80	.253	46	85	4	129	293	23	.948
1992—	Houston (N.L.)	3B	135	506	68	149	31	2	13	62	.294	44	68	10	102	210	11	.966
1993—	Houston (N.L.)	3B	143	543	75	142	31	0	13	75	.262	49	88	8	123	264	24	.942
1994—	Houston (N.L.)	3B	111	406	63	115	28	2	18	75	.283	43	71	4	79	200	9	.969
1995—	San Diego (N.L.)■	3B	143	526	74	159	33	0	26	94	.302	69	94	12	102	*295	*27	.936
Major league totals (9 years)			1091	3967	483	1055	213	13	101	539	.266	367	658	51	841	1981	148	.950

ALL-STAR GAME RECORD

Year	League	Pos.	AB	R	H	2B	3B	HR	RBI	Avg.	BB	SO	SB	PO	A	E	Avg.
			BATTING											FIELDING			
1994—	National	3B	1	0	0	0	0	0	0	.000	0	0	0	0	0	0	...

CAMPBELL, KEVIN — P

PERSONAL: Born December 6, 1964, in Marianna, Ark. . . . 6-2/225. . . . Throws right, bats right. . . . Full name: Kevin Wade Campbell.
HIGH SCHOOL: Des Arc (Ark.).
COLLEGE: Arkansas.
TRANSACTIONS/CAREER NOTES: Selected by Philadelphia Phillies organization in 13th round of free-agent draft (June 6, 1983); did not sign. . . . Selected by Los Angeles Dodgers organization in fifth round of free-agent draft (June 2, 1986). . . . Traded by Dodgers organization to Oakland Athletics organization for P David Veres (January 15, 1991). . . . Granted free agency (December 19, 1992). . . . Re-signed by A's organization (January 21, 1993). . . . Granted free agency (October 15, 1993). . . . Signed by Portland, Minnesota Twins organization (December 6, 1993). . . . Released by Twins (May 16, 1995). . . . Signed by Tacoma, Seattle Mariners organization (May 28, 1995). . . . Granted free agency (October 16, 1995).

Year	Team (League)	W	L	Pct.	ERA	G	GS	CG	ShO	Sv.	IP	H	R	ER	BB	SO
1986—	Great Falls (Pio.)	5	6	.455	4.66	15	15	3	0	0	85	99	62	44	32	66

Year	Team (League)	W	L	Pct.	ERA	G	GS	CG	ShO	Sv.	IP	H	R	ER	BB	SO
1987—	Vero Beach (FSL)	7	14	.333	3.91	28	28	5	1	0	184	200	100	80	64	112
1988—	Vero Beach (FSL)	8	12	.400	2.75	26	26	5	1	0	163 2/3	166	67	50	49	115
1989—	San Antonio (Tex.)	1	5	.167	6.67	17	0	0	0	2	27	29	22	20	16	28
	—Bakersfield (Calif.)	5	3	.625	2.54	31	0	0	0	6	60 1/3	43	23	17	28	63
1990—	San Antonio (Tex.)	2	6	.250	2.33	49	0	0	0	8	81	67	29	21	25	84
1991—	Tacoma (PCL)■	9	2	*.818	1.80	35	0	0	0	2	75	53	18	15	35	56
	—Oakland (A.L.)	1	0	1.000	2.74	14	0	0	0	0	23	13	7	7	14	16
1992—	Tacoma (PCL)	2	2	.500	4.05	10	0	0	0	0	13 1/3	16	6	6	8	14
	—Oakland (A.L.)	2	3	.400	5.12	32	5	0	0	1	65	66	39	37	45	38
1993—	Tacoma (PCL)	3	5	.375	2.75	40	0	0	0	12	55 2/3	42	19	17	19	46
	—Oakland (A.L.)	0	0	...	7.31	11	0	0	0	0	16	20	13	13	11	9
1994—	Salt Lake (PCL)■	3	2	.600	3.60	29	0	0	0	7	40	39	17	16	14	35
	—Minnesota (A.L.)	1	0	1.000	2.92	14	0	0	0	0	24 2/3	20	8	8	5	15
1995—	Minnesota (A.L.)	0	0	...	4.66	6	0	0	0	0	9 2/3	8	5	5	5	5
	—Tacoma (PCL)■	3	2	.600	3.67	31	0	0	0	1	49	50	28	20	14	34
Major league totals (5 years)		4	3	.571	4.55	77	5	0	0	1	138 1/3	127	72	70	80	83

CANDIOTTI, TOM — P — DODGERS

PERSONAL: Born August 31, 1957, in Walnut Creek, Calif. . . . 6-2/215. . . . Throws right, bats right. . . . Full name: Thomas Caesar Candiotti. . . . Name pronounced KAN-dee-AH-tee.

HIGH SCHOOL: St. Mary's (Calif.).

COLLEGE: St. Mary's, Calif. (degree in business administration, 1979).

TRANSACTIONS/CAREER NOTES: Signed as non-drafted free agent by Victoria, independent (July 17, 1979). . . . Released by Victoria (January 4, 1980). . . . Signed by Ft. Myers, Kansas City Royals organization (January 5, 1980). . . . On Jacksonville disabled list (June 7-26, 1980). . . . Selected by Vancouver, Milwaukee Brewers organization, from Royals organization in Rule 5 minor league draft (December 9, 1980). . . . On disabled list (April 10-May 12, 1981 and April 13, 1982-remainder of season). . . . On Vancouver disabled list (May 30-June 15, 1984). . . . On Milwaukee disabled list (August 2-September 1, 1984); included rehabilitation assignment to Beloit (August 24-31). . . . Granted free agency (October 15, 1985). . . . Signed by Cleveland Indians (December 12, 1985). . . . On disabled list (August 4-19, 1988; July 2-17, 1989; and May 7-22, 1990). . . . Traded by Indians with OF Turner Ward to Toronto Blue Jays for P Denis Boucher, OF Glenallen Hill, OF Mark Whiten and a player to be named later (June 27, 1991); Indians acquired cash instead of player to complete deal (October 15, 1991). . . . Granted free agency (November 7, 1991). . . . Signed by Los Angeles Dodgers (December 3, 1991). . . . On disabled list (August 9-24, 1992). . . . Granted free agency (November 3, 1995). . . . Re-signed by Dodgers (December 15, 1995).

STATISTICAL NOTES: Pitched 2-0 one-hit, complete-game victory against New York (August 3, 1987).

Year	Team (League)	W	L	Pct.	ERA	G	GS	CG	ShO	Sv.	IP	H	R	ER	BB	SO
1979—	Victoria (N'west)	5	1	.833	2.44	12	9	3	0	1	70	63	23	19	16	66
1980—	Fort Myers (Fla. St.)■	3	2	.600	2.25	7	5	3	0	0	44	32	16	11	9	31
	—Jacksonville (Sou.)	7	8	.467	2.77	17	17	8	2	0	117	98	45	36	40	93
1981—	El Paso (Texas)■	7	6	.538	2.80	21	14	6	1	0	119	137	51	37	27	68
1982—		Did not play.														
1983—	El Paso (Texas)	1	0	1.000	2.92	7	0	0	0	2	24 2/3	23	10	8	7	18
	—Vancouver (PCL)	6	4	.600	2.81	15	14	5	2	0	99 1/3	87	35	31	16	61
	—Milwaukee (A.L.)	4	4	.500	3.23	10	8	2	1	0	55 2/3	62	21	20	16	21
1984—	Vancouver (PCL)	8	4	.667	2.89	15	15	4	0	0	96 2/3	96	36	31	22	53
	—Milwaukee (A.L.)	2	2	.500	5.29	8	6	0	0	0	32 1/3	38	21	19	10	23
	—Beloit (Midwest)	0	1	.000	2.70	2	2	0	0	0	10	12	5	3	5	12
1985—	El Paso (Texas)	1	0	1.000	2.76	4	4	2	1	0	29 1/3	29	11	9	7	16
	—Vancouver (PCL)	9	13	.409	3.94	24	24	0	0	0	150 2/3	178	83	66	36	97
1986—	Cleveland (A.L.)■	16	12	.571	3.57	36	34	*17	3	0	252 1/3	234	112	100	106	167
1987—	Cleveland (A.L.)	7	18	.280	4.78	32	32	7	2	0	201 2/3	193	132	107	93	111
1988—	Cleveland (A.L.)	14	8	.636	3.28	31	31	11	1	0	216 2/3	225	86	79	53	137
1989—	Cleveland (A.L.)	13	10	.565	3.10	31	31	4	0	0	206	188	80	71	55	124
1990—	Cleveland (A.L.)	15	11	.577	3.65	31	29	3	1	0	202	207	92	82	55	128
1991—	Cleveland (A.L.)	7	6	.538	2.24	15	15	3	0	0	108 1/3	88	35	27	28	86
	—Toronto (A.L.)■	6	7	.462	2.98	19	19	3	0	0	129 2/3	114	47	43	45	81
1992—	Los Angeles (N.L.)■	11	•15	.423	3.00	32	30	6	2	0	203 2/3	177	78	68	63	152
1993—	Los Angeles (N.L.)	8	10	.444	3.12	33	32	2	0	0	213 2/3	192	86	74	71	155
1994—	Los Angeles (N.L.)	7	7	.500	4.12	23	22	5	0	0	153	149	77	70	54	102
1995—	Los Angeles (N.L.)	7	14	.333	3.50	30	30	1	1	0	190 1/3	187	93	74	58	141
A.L. totals (8 years)		84	78	.519	3.51	213	205	50	8	0	1401 2/3	1349	626	548	461	878
N.L. totals (4 years)		33	46	.418	3.38	118	114	14	3	0	760 2/3	705	334	286	246	550
Major league totals (12 years)		117	124	.485	3.47	331	319	64	11	0	2165 1/3	2054	960	834	707	1428

CHAMPIONSHIP SERIES RECORD

Year	Team (League)	W	L	Pct.	ERA	G	GS	CG	ShO	Sv.	IP	H	R	ER	BB	SO
1991—	Toronto (A.L.)	0	1	.000	8.22	2	2	0	0	0	7 2/3	17	9	7	2	5

CANGELOSI, JOHN — OF — ASTROS

PERSONAL: Born March 10, 1963, in Brooklyn, N.Y. . . . 5-8/160. . . . Bats both, throws left. . . . Full name: John Anthony Cangelosi. . . . Name pronounced KAN-juh-LO-see.

HIGH SCHOOL: Miami Springs (Fla.) Senior.

JUNIOR COLLEGE: Miami-Dade North Community College.Miami

TRANSACTIONS/CAREER NOTES: Selected by Chicago White Sox organization in fourth round of free-agent draft (January 12, 1982). . . . Loaned by White Sox organization with IF Manny Salinas to Mexico City Reds of Mexican League (March 4-June 1, 1985) as part of deal in which IF Nelson Barrera was purchased by White Sox. . . . Traded by White Sox to Pittsburgh Pirates (March 30, 1987), completing deal in which Pirates traded P Jim Winn to White Sox for a player to be named later (March 27, 1987). . . . On Pittsburgh disabled list (June 6-27, 1988); included rehabilitation assignment to Buffalo (June 20-27). . . . Granted free agency (December 20, 1990). . . . Signed by Vancouver, White Sox organization (April 7, 1991). . . . Traded by White Sox organization to Milwaukee Brewers for SS Esteban Beltre (May 23, 1991).

. . . Granted free agency (October 15, 1991). . . . Signed by Texas Rangers organization (November 7, 1991). . . . Released by Rangers (July 19, 1992). . . . Signed by Toledo, Detroit Tigers organization (July 28, 1992). . . . Granted free agency (October 15, 1992). . . . Re-signed by Toledo (February 8, 1993). . . . On disabled list (April 8-May 4, 1993). . . . Granted free agency (October 15, 1993). . . . Signed by New York Mets organization (November 17, 1993). . . . On suspended list (June 15-18, 1994). . . . Released by Mets (July 8, 1994). . . . Signed by Tucson, Houston Astros organization (March 23, 1995). . . . Granted free agency (November 2, 1995). . . . Re-signed by Astros organization (December 7, 1995).

STATISTICAL NOTES: Led Midwest League in caught stealing with 35 in 1983. . . . Led International League in caught stealing with 18 in 1993.

			BATTING												FIELDING			
Year	**Team (League)**	**Pos.**	**G**	**AB**	**R**	**H**	**2B**	**3B**	**HR**	**RBI**	**Avg.**	**BB**	**SO**	**SB**	**PO**	**A**	**E**	**Avg.**
1982—	Niag. Falls (NYP)	OF	•76	277	60	80	15	4	5	38	.289	•56	51	45	118	5	4	.969
1983—	Appleton (Midw.)	OF	128	439	87	124	12	4	1	48	.282	99	81	*87	262	10	6	.978
1984—	Glens Falls (East.)	OF	138	464	91	133	17	1	1	38	.287	*101	66	65	310	11	11	.967
1985—	M.C. Reds (Mex.)	OF	61	201	46	71	9	4	1	30	.353	50	19	17	127	7	6	.957
	— Chicago (A.L.)	OF-DH	5	2	2	0	0	0	0	0	.000	0	1	0	1	0	0	1.000
	— Buffalo (A.A.)	OF	78	244	34	58	8	5	1	21	.238	46	32	14	148	9	2	.987
1986—	Chicago (A.L.)	OF-DH	137	438	65	103	16	3	2	32	.235	71	61	50	276	7	9	.969
1987—	Pittsburgh (N.L.)■	OF	104	182	44	50	8	3	4	18	.275	46	33	21	74	3	3	.963
1988—	Pittsburgh (N.L.)	OF-P	75	118	18	30	4	1	0	8	.254	17	16	9	52	0	2	.963
	— Buffalo (A.A.)	OF	37	145	23	48	6	0	0	10	.331	19	19	14	89	3	0	1.000
1989—	Pittsburgh (N.L.)	OF	112	160	18	35	4	2	0	9	.219	35	20	11	71	1	2	.973
1990—	Pittsburgh (N.L.)	OF	58	76	13	15	2	0	0	1	.197	11	12	7	24	0	0	1.000
	— Buffalo (A.A.)	OF	24	89	17	31	2	2	0	7	.348	12	8	5	49	0	1	.980
1991—	Vancouver (PCL)■	OF	30	102	15	25	1	0	0	10	.245	11	8	9	39	2	3	.932
	— Denver (A.A.)■	OF-1B-P	83	303	69	89	8	3	3	25	.294	59	29	26	118	10	3	.977
1992—	Texas (A.L.)■	OF-DH	73	85	12	16	2	0	1	6	.188	18	16	6	76	4	3	.964
	— Toledo (Int'l)■	OF	27	74	9	20	3	0	0	6	.270	7	13	11	48	1	0	1.000
1993—	Toledo (Int'l)	OF-P	113	439	73	128	23	4	6	42	.292	56	59	39	252	5	7	.973
1994—	New York (N.L.)■	OF	62	111	14	28	4	0	0	4	.252	19	20	5	64	5	0	1.000
1995—	Tucson (PCL)■	OF	30	106	18	39	4	1	0	9	.368	19	11	11	67	2	1	.986
	— Houston (N.L.)	OF-P	90	201	46	64	5	2	2	18	.318	48	42	21	92	4	5	.950
American League totals (3 years)			215	525	79	119	18	3	3	38	.227	89	78	56	353	11	12	.968
National League totals (6 years)			501	848	153	222	27	8	6	58	.262	176	143	74	377	13	12	.970
Major league totals (9 years)			716	1373	232	341	45	11	9	96	.248	265	221	130	730	24	24	.969

RECORD AS PITCHER

Year	**Team (League)**	**W**	**L**	**Pct.**	**ERA**	**G**	**GS**	**CG**	**ShO**	**Sv.**	**IP**	**H**	**R**	**ER**	**BB**	**SO**
1988—	Pittsburgh (N.L.)	0	0	...	0.00	1	0	0	0	0	2	1	0	0	0	0
1991—	Denver (Am. Assoc.)	0	0	...	2.45	2	0	0	0	0	3 2/3	3	1	1	2	1
1993—	Toledo (Int'l)	0	0	...	81.00	1	0	0	0	0	2/3	7	6	6	1	0
1995—	Houston (N.L.)	0	0	...	0.00	1	0	0	0	0	1	0	0	0	1	0
Major league totals (2 years)		0	0	...	0.00	2	0	0	0	0	3	1	0	0	1	0

CANIZARO, JAY — 2B/SS — GIANTS

PERSONAL: Born July 4, 1973, in Beaumont, Tex. . . . 5-9/170. . . . Bats right, throws right. . . . Full name: Jason Kyle Canizaro.

HIGH SCHOOL: West Orange-Stark (Orange, Tex.).

JUNIOR COLLEGE: Blinn (Tex.).

COLLEGE: Oklahoma State.

TRANSACTIONS/CAREER NOTES: Selected by San Francisco Giants organization in fourth round of free-agent draft (June 3, 1993).

STATISTICAL NOTES: Led Arizona League second basemen with 33 double plays in 1993. . . . Led Texas League second basemen with 19 errors in 1995.

			BATTING												FIELDING			
Year	**Team (League)**	**Pos.**	**G**	**AB**	**R**	**H**	**2B**	**3B**	**HR**	**RBI**	**Avg.**	**BB**	**SO**	**SB**	**PO**	**A**	**E**	**Avg.**
1993—	Ariz. Giants (Ariz.)	2B-SS	49	180	34	47	10	•6	3	*41	.261	22	40	12	102	106	10	.954
1994—	San Jose (Calif.)	2-S-3-O	126	464	77	117	16	2	15	69	.252	46	98	12	262	362	30	.954
1995—	Shreveport (Texas)	2B-SS	126	440	83	129	25	7	12	60	.293	58	98	16	254	333	‡23	.962

CANSECO, JOSE — OF/DH — RED SOX

PERSONAL: Born July 2, 1964, in Havana, Cuba. . . . 6-4/240. . . . Bats right, throws right. . . . Full name: Jose Canseco Jr. . . . Identical twin brother of Ozzie Canseco, outfielder, Oakland Athletics and St. Louis Cardinals (1990 and 1992-93). . . . Name pronounced can-SAY-co.

HIGH SCHOOL: Miami Coral Park Senior.

TRANSACTIONS/CAREER NOTES: Selected by Oakland Athletics organization in 15th round of free-agent draft (June 7, 1982). . . . On Huntsville disabled list (May 14-June 3, 1985). . . . On Oakland disabled list (March 23-July 13, 1989); included rehabilitation assignments to Huntsville (May 6 and June 28-July 13). . . . On disabled list (June 8-23, 1990 and July 1-16, 1992). . . . Traded by A's to Texas Rangers for OF Ruben Sierra, P Jeff Russell, P Bobby Witt and cash (August 31, 1992). . . . On disabled list (June 24, 1993-remainder of season). . . . Traded by Rangers to Boston Red Sox for OF Otis Nixon and 3B Luis Ortiz (December 9, 1994). . . . On Boston disabled list (May 15-June 20, 1995); included rehabilitation assignment to Pawtucket (June 18-20). . . . Granted free agency (October 30, 1995). . . . Re-signed by Red Sox (December 6, 1995).

RECORDS: Shares major league single-season record for most consecutive bases on balls received—7 (August 4-5, 1992). . . . Shares A.L. single-season record for fewest errors by outfielder who led league in errors—9 (1991).

HONORS: Named Minor League Player of the Year by The Sporting News (1985). . . . Named Southern League Most Valuable Player (1985). . . . Named A.L. Rookie Player of the Year by The Sporting News (1986). . . . Named A.L. Rookie of the Year by Baseball Writers' Association of America (1986). . . . Named A.L. Player of the Year by The Sporting News (1988). . . . Named outfielder on The Sporting News A.L. All-Star team (1988 and 1990-91). . . . Named outfielder on The Sporting News A.L. Silver Slugger team (1988 and 1990-91). . . . Named A.L. Most Valuable Player by Baseball Writers' Association of America (1988). . . . Named A.L. Comeback Player of the Year by The Sporting News (1994).

STATISTICAL NOTES: Led California League outfielders with eight double plays in 1984. . . . Hit three home runs in one game (July 3, 1988 and June 13, 1994). . . . Led A.L. with .569 slugging percentage in 1988. . . . Led A.L. in grounding into double plays with 20 in 1994. . . . Career major league grand slams: 4.

			BATTING											FIELDING			
Year Team (League)	**Pos.**	**G**	**AB**	**R**	**H**	**2B**	**3B**	**HR**	**RBI**	**Avg.**	**BB**	**SO**	**SB**	**PO**	**A**	**E**	**Avg.**
1982— Miami (Florida St.)	3B	6	9	0	1	0	0	0	0	.111	1	3	0	3	1	1	.800
— Idaho Falls (Pio.)	3B-OF	28	57	13	15	3	0	2	7	.263	9	13	3	6	17	3	.885
1983— Madison (Midwest)	OF	34	88	8	14	4	0	3	10	.159	10	36	2	23	2	1	.962
— Medford (N'west)	OF	59	197	34	53	15	2	11	40	.269	30	*78	6	46	5	5	.911
1984— Modesto (Calif.)	OF	116	410	61	113	21	2	15	73	.276	74	127	10	216	17	9	.963
1985— Huntsville (South.)	OF	58	211	47	67	10	2	25	80	.318	30	55	6	117	9	7	.947
— Tacoma (PCL)	OF	60	233	41	81	16	1	11	47	.348	40	66	5	81	7	2	.978
— Oakland (A.L.)	OF	29	96	16	29	3	0	5	13	.302	4	31	1	56	2	3	.951
1986— Oakland (A.L.)	OF-DH	157	600	85	144	29	1	33	117	.240	65	175	15	319	4	•14	.958
1987— Oakland (A.L.)	OF-DH	159	630	81	162	35	3	31	113	.257	50	157	15	263	12	7	.975
1988— Oakland (A.L.)	OF-DH	158	610	120	187	34	0	*42	*124	.307	78	128	40	304	11	7	.978
1989— Huntsville (South.)	OF	9	29	2	6	0	0	0	3	.207	5	11	1	9	0	0	1.000
— Oakland (A.L.)	OF-DH	65	227	40	61	9	1	17	57	.269	23	69	6	119	5	3	.976
1990— Oakland (A.L.)	OF-DH	131	481	83	132	14	2	37	101	.274	72	158	19	182	7	1	.995
1991— Oakland (A.L.)	OF-DH	154	572	115	152	32	1	•44	122	.266	78	152	26	245	5	•9	.965
1992— Oakland (A.L.)	OF-DH	97	366	66	90	11	0	22	72	.246	48	104	5	163	5	2	.988
— Texas (A.L.)■	OF-DH	22	73	8	17	4	0	4	15	.233	15	24	1	32	0	1	.970
1993— Texas (A.L.)	OF-DH-P	60	231	30	59	14	1	10	46	.255	16	62	6	94	4	3	.970
1994— Texas (A.L.)	DH	111	429	88	121	19	2	31	90	.282	69	114	15	...	...	...	...
1995— Boston (A.L.)■	DH-OF	102	396	64	121	25	1	24	81	.306	42	93	4	1	0	0	1.000
— Pawtucket (Int'l)	DH	2	6	1	1	0	0	0	1	.167	1	5	0	0	0	0	...
Major league totals (11 years)		1245	4711	796	1275	229	12	300	951	.271	560	1267	153	1778	55	50	.973

DIVISION SERIES RECORD

			BATTING											FIELDING			
Year Team (League)	**Pos.**	**G**	**AB**	**R**	**H**	**2B**	**3B**	**HR**	**RBI**	**Avg.**	**BB**	**SO**	**SB**	**PO**	**A**	**E**	**Avg.**
1995— Boston (A.L.)	DH-OF	3	13	0	0	0	0	0	0	.000	2	2	0	4	0	0	1.000

CHAMPIONSHIP SERIES RECORD

NOTES: Shares A.L. single-series record for most home runs—3 (1988).

			BATTING											FIELDING			
Year Team (League)	**Pos.**	**G**	**AB**	**R**	**H**	**2B**	**3B**	**HR**	**RBI**	**Avg.**	**BB**	**SO**	**SB**	**PO**	**A**	**E**	**Avg.**
1988— Oakland (A.L.)	OF	4	16	4	5	1	0	3	4	.313	1	2	1	6	0	0	1.000
1989— Oakland (A.L.)	OF-PH	5	17	1	5	0	0	1	3	.294	3	7	0	6	1	1	.875
1990— Oakland (A.L.)	OF	4	11	3	2	0	0	0	1	.182	5	5	2	14	0	0	1.000
Championship series totals (3 years)		13	44	8	12	1	0	4	8	.273	9	14	3	26	1	1	.964

WORLD SERIES RECORD

NOTES: Hit home run in first at-bat (October 15, 1988). . . . Shares single-game record for most grand slams—1 (October 15, 1988). . . . Shares record for most runs batted in in one inning—4 (October 15, 1988, second inning). . . . Member of World Series championship team (1989).

			BATTING											FIELDING			
Year Team (League)	**Pos.**	**G**	**AB**	**R**	**H**	**2B**	**3B**	**HR**	**RBI**	**Avg.**	**BB**	**SO**	**SB**	**PO**	**A**	**E**	**Avg.**
1988— Oakland (A.L.)	OF	5	19	1	1	0	0	1	5	.053	2	4	1	8	0	0	1.000
1989— Oakland (A.L.)	OF	4	14	5	5	0	0	1	3	.357	4	3	1	6	0	0	1.000
1990— Oakland (A.L.)	OF-PH-DH	4	12	1	1	0	0	1	2	.083	2	3	0	4	0	0	1.000
World Series totals (3 years)		13	45	7	7	0	0	3	10	.156	8	10	2	18	0	0	1.000

ALL-STAR GAME RECORD

			BATTING									FIELDING			
Year League	**Pos.**	**AB**	**R**	**H**	**2B**	**3B**	**HR**	**RBI**	**Avg.**	**BB**	**SO**	**SB**	**PO**	**A**	**E**	**Avg.**
1986— American							Did not play.									
1988— American	OF	4	0	0	0	0	0	0	.000	0	1	0	3	0	0	1.000
1989— American							Selected, did not play—injured.									
1990— American	OF	4	0	0	0	0	0	0	.000	1	1	1	1	0	0	1.000
1992— American							Selected, did not play—injured.									
All-Star Game totals (2 years)		8	0	0	0	0	0	0	.000	1	2	1	4	0	0	1.000

RECORD AS PITCHER

Year Team (League)	**W**	**L**	**Pct.**	**ERA**	**G**	**GS**	**CG**	**ShO**	**Sv.**	**IP**	**H**	**R**	**ER**	**BB**	**SO**
1993— Texas (A.L.)	0	0	...	27.00	1	0	0	0	0	1	2	3	3	3	0

CARABALLO, RAMON 2B RED SOX

PERSONAL: Born May 23, 1969, in Rio San Juan, Dominican Republic. . . . 5-7/150. . . . Bats both, throws right. . . . Name pronounced CAR-uh-BY-oh.

HIGH SCHOOL: Liceo Antorcha del Futero (Dominican Republic).

TRANSACTIONS/CAREER NOTES: Signed as non-drafted free agent by Atlanta Braves organization (April 10, 1988). . . . On Richmond disabled list (May 6-13, 1994). . . . Traded by Braves organization to St. Louis Cardinals organization for a player to be named later (November 28, 1994); Braves acquired 1B Aldo Pecorilli to complete deal (December 9, 1994). . . . On Louisville suspended list (May 19-21, 1995). . . . On Louisville disabled list (August 26, 1995-remainder of season). . . . Granted free agency (October 16, 1995). . . . Signed by Pawtucket, Boston Red Sox organization (November 20, 1995).

STATISTICAL NOTES: Led Carolina League in caught stealing with 23 in 1991. . . . Led International League in caught stealing with 16 in 1992.

			BATTING											FIELDING			
Year Team (League)	**Pos.**	**G**	**AB**	**R**	**H**	**2B**	**3B**	**HR**	**RBI**	**Avg.**	**BB**	**SO**	**SB**	**PO**	**A**	**E**	**Avg.**
1989— GC Braves (GCL)	SS-OF-2B	20	77	9	19	3	1	1	10	.247	10	14	5	39	47	6	.935

Year Team (League)	Pos.	G	AB	R	H	2B	3B	HR	RBI	Avg.	BB	SO	SB	PO	A	E	Avg.
		BATTING												FIELDING			
—Sumter (S. Atl.)	SS	45	171	22	45	10	5	1	32	.263	16	38	9	57	151	18	.920
1990—Burlington (Midw.)	SS	102	390	83	113	18	*14	7	55	.290	49	68	41	139	280	35	.923
1991—Durham (Carolina)	2B	120	444	73	111	13	8	6	52	.250	38	91	*53	217	341	*28	.952
1992—Greenville (South.)	2B	24	93	15	29	4	4	1	8	.312	14	13	10	32	74	6	.946
—Richmond (Int'l)	2B	101	405	42	114	20	3	2	40	.281	22	60	19	217	284	14	*.973
1993—Richmond (Int'l)	2B-OF	126	470	73	128	25	9	3	41	.272	30	81	20	211	345	23	.960
—Atlanta (N.L.)	2B	6	0	0	0	0	0	0	0	...	0	0	0	4	3	0	1.000
1994—Richmond (Int'l)	2B-SS-OF	22	75	5	10	1	0	0	0	.133	7	12	4	23	40	3	.955
—Greenville (South.)	SS-2B	72	243	32	58	4	6	9	30	.239	12	46	4	72	181	15	.944
1995—Louisville (A.A.)■	2B-SS	69	245	38	78	10	1	8	25	.318	19	42	14	134	201	7	.980
—St. Louis (N.L.)	2B	34	99	10	20	4	1	2	3	.202	6	33	3	56	73	6	.956
Major league totals (2 years)		40	99	10	20	4	1	2	3	.202	6	33	3	60	76	6	.958

CARMONA, RAFAEL — P — MARINERS

PERSONAL: Born October 2, 1972, in Rio Piedras, Puerto Rico. . . . 6-2/185. . . . Throws right, bats left.
HIGH SCHOOL: Juano Colon (Comerio, Puerto Rico).
TRANSACTIONS/CAREER NOTES: Selected by Seattle Mariners organization in 13th round of free-agent draft (June 3, 1993).

Year Team (League)	W	L	Pct.	ERA	G	GS	CG	ShO	Sv.	IP	H	R	ER	BB	SO
1993—Bellingham (N'west)	2	3	.400	3.79	23	0	0	0	2	35 2/3	33	19	15	14	30
1994—Riverside (Calif.)	8	2	.800	2.81	50	0	0	0	21	67 1/3	48	22	21	19	63
1995—Port City (Southern)	0	1	.000	1.80	15	0	0	0	4	15	11	5	3	3	17
—Seattle (A.L.)	2	4	.333	5.66	15	3	0	0	1	47 2/3	55	31	30	34	28
—Tacoma (PCL)	4	3	.571	5.06	8	8	1	1	0	48	52	29	27	19	37
Major league totals (1 year)	2	4	.333	5.66	15	3	0	0	1	47 2/3	55	31	30	34	28

CARR, CHUCK — OF — BREWERS

PERSONAL: Born August 10, 1968, in San Bernardino, Calif. . . . 5-10/165. . . . Bats both, throws right. . . . Full name: Charles Lee Glenn Carr Jr.
HIGH SCHOOL: Fontana (Calif.).
TRANSACTIONS/CAREER NOTES: Selected by Cincinnati Reds organization in ninth round of free-agent draft (June 2, 1986). . . . Released by Reds organization (March 1987). . . . Signed by Bellingham, Seattle Mariners organization (June 15, 1987). . . . Traded by Mariners organization to New York Mets organization for P Reggie Dobie (November 18, 1988). . . . On Tidewater disabled list (April 10-17 and July 15-August 9, 1991). . . . On New York disabled list (August 29-September 13, 1991). . . . Traded by Mets to St. Louis Cardinals for P Clyde Keller (December 13, 1991). . . . On Louisville disabled list (July 31-August 7, 1992). . . . Selected by Florida Marlins in first round (14th pick overall) of expansion draft (November 17, 1992). . . . On Florida disabled list (July 1-18, 1993); included rehabilitation assignment to Gulf Coast Marlins (July 11-14). . . . On Florida disabled list (May 15-June 11, 1995); included rehabilitation assignments to Charlotte (May 26-30 and June 5-11). . . . Traded by Marlins to Milwaukee Brewers for P Juan Gonzalez (December 4, 1995).
STATISTICAL NOTES: Led N.L. in caught stealing with 22 in 1993. . . . Career major league grand slams: 1.

Year Team (League)	Pos.	G	AB	R	H	2B	3B	HR	RBI	Avg.	BB	SO	SB	PO	A	E	Avg.
		BATTING												FIELDING			
1986—GC Reds (GCL)	2B	44	123	13	21	5	0	0	10	.171	10	27	9	75	100	11	.941
1987—Belling. (N'west)■	S-O-2-3	44	165	31	40	1	1	1	11	.242	12	38	20	50	58	14	.885
1988—Wausau (Midwest)	OF-SS	82	304	58	91	14	2	6	30	.299	14	49	41	170	17	12	.940
—Vermont (Eastern)	OF	41	159	26	39	4	2	1	13	.245	8	33	21	105	6	6	.949
1989—Jackson (Texas)■	OF	116	444	45	107	13	1	0	22	.241	27	66	47	280	11	8	.973
1990—Jackson (Texas)	OF	93	361	60	93	19	9	3	24	.258	43	77	48	226	12	8	.967
—Tidewater (Int'l)	OF	20	81	13	21	5	1	0	8	.259	4	12	6	40	3	0	1.000
—New York (N.L.)	OF	4	2	0	0	0	0	0	0	.000	0	2	1	0	0	0	...
1991—Tidewater (Int'l)	OF	64	246	34	48	6	1	1	11	.195	18	37	27	141	8	6	.961
—New York (N.L.)	OF	12	11	1	2	0	0	0	1	.182	0	2	1	9	0	0	1.000
1992—Arkansas (Texas)■	OF	28	111	17	29	5	1	1	6	.261	8	23	8	70	3	1	.986
—Louisville (A.A.)	OF	96	377	68	116	11	9	3	28	.308	31	60	*53	244	9	5	.981
—St. Louis (N.L.)	OF	22	64	8	14	3	0	0	3	.219	9	6	10	39	1	0	1.000
1993—Florida (N.L.)■	OF	142	551	75	147	19	2	4	41	.267	49	74	*58	393	7	6	.985
—GC Marlins (GCL)	OF	3	12	4	5	1	0	1	3	.417	0	2	3	9	0	1	.900
1994—Florida (N.L.)	OF	106	433	61	114	19	2	2	30	.263	22	71	32	297	4	6	.980
1995—Florida (N.L.)	OF	105	308	54	70	20	0	2	20	.227	46	49	25	217	8	3	.987
—Charlotte (Int'l)	OF	7	23	5	5	0	1	1	2	.217	2	1	2	9	0	0	1.000
Major league totals (6 years)		391	1369	199	347	61	4	8	95	.253	126	204	127	955	20	15	.985

CARRARA, GIOVANNI — P — BLUE JAYS

PERSONAL: Born March 4, 1968, in Edo Anzuategni, Venezuela. . . . 6-2/230. . . . Throws right, bats right.
TRANSACTIONS/CAREER NOTES: Signed as non-drafted free agent by Toronto Blue Jays organization (January 23, 1990).

Year Team (League)	W	L	Pct.	ERA	G	GS	CG	ShO	Sv.	IP	H	R	ER	BB	SO
1990—Santo Dom. (DSL)	8	2	.800	2.62	15	14	4	0	0	86	88	31	25	28	55
1991—St. Cathar. (NYP)	5	2	.714	1.71	15	13	2	•2	0	89 2/3	66	26	17	21	83
1992—Dunedin (Fla. St.)	0	1	.000	4.63	5	4	0	0	0	23 1/3	22	13	12	11	16
—Myrtle Beach (SAL)	11	7	.611	3.14	22	16	1	1	0	100 1/3	86	40	35	36	100
1993—Dunedin (Fla. St.)	6	11	.353	3.45	27	24	1	0	0	140 2/3	136	69	54	59	108
1994—Knoxville (South.)	13	7	.650	3.89	26	26	1	0	0	164 1/3	158	85	71	59	96
1995—Syracuse (Int'l)	7	7	.500	3.96	21	21	0	0	0	131 2/3	116	72	58	56	81
—Toronto (A.L.)	2	4	.333	7.21	12	7	1	0	0	48 2/3	64	46	39	25	27
Major league totals (1 year)	2	4	.333	7.21	12	7	1	0	0	48 2/3	64	46	39	25	27

CARRASCO, HECTOR — P — REDS

PERSONAL: Born October 22, 1969, in San Pedro de Macoris, Dominican Republic. . . . 6-2/180. . . . Throws right, bats right. . . . Full name: Hector Pacheco Pipo Carrasco.

HIGH SCHOOL: Liceo Mattias Mella (San Pedro de Macoris, Dominican Republic).

TRANSACTIONS/CAREER NOTES: Signed as non-drafted free agent by New York Mets organization (March 20, 1988). . . . Released by Mets organization (January 6, 1992). . . . Signed by Houston Astros organization (January 21, 1992). . . . Traded by Astros organization with P Brian Griffiths to Florida Marlins organization for P Tom Edens (November 17, 1992). . . . Traded by Marlins to Cincinnati Reds (September 10, 1993), completing deal in which Reds traded P Chris Hammond to Marlins for 3B Gary Scott and a player to be named later (March 27, 1993). . . . On disabled list (May 12-June 1, 1994).

Year Team (League)	W	L	Pct.	ERA	G	GS	CG	ShO	Sv.	IP	H	R	ER	BB	SO
1988— GC Mets (GCL)	0	2	.000	4.17	14	2	0	0	0	36 2/3	37	29	17	13	21
1989— Kingsport (Appal.)	1	6	.143	5.74	12	10	0	0	0	53 1/3	69	49	34	34	55
1990— Kingsport (Appal.)	0	0	. . .	4.05	3	1	0	0	0	6 2/3	8	3	3	1	5
1991— Pittsfield (NYP)	0	1	.000	5.40	12	1	0	0	1	23 1/3	25	17	14	21	20
1992— Asheville (S. Atl.)■	5	5	.500	2.99	49	0	0	0	8	78 1/3	66	30	26	47	67
1993— Kane Co. (Mid.)■	6	12	.333	4.11	28	*28	0	0	0	149	153	90	68	76	127
1994— Cincinnati (N.L.)■	5	6	.455	2.24	45	0	0	0	6	56 1/3	42	17	14	30	41
1995— Cincinnati (N.L.)	2	7	.222	4.12	64	0	0	0	5	87 1/3	86	45	40	46	64
Major league totals (2 years)	7	13	.350	3.38	109	0	0	0	11	143 2/3	128	62	54	76	105

CHAMPIONSHIP SERIES RECORD

Year Team (League)	W	L	Pct.	ERA	G	GS	CG	ShO	Sv.	IP	H	R	ER	BB	SO
1995— Cincinnati (N.L.)	0	0	. . .	0.00	1	0	0	0	0	1 1/3	1	0	0	0	3

CARREON, MARK — OF — GIANTS

PERSONAL: Born July 9, 1963, in Chicago. . . . 6-0/195. . . . Bats right, throws left. . . . Full name: Mark Steven Carreon. . . . Son of Camilo Carreon, catcher, Chicago White Sox, Cleveland Indians and Baltimore Orioles (1959-66). . . . Name pronounced CARE-ee-on.

HIGH SCHOOL: Salpointe (Tucson, Ariz.).

TRANSACTIONS/CAREER NOTES: Selected by New York Mets organization in eighth round of free-agent draft (June 8, 1981). . . . On New York disabled list (March 28-April 24, 1989); included rehabilitation assignment to Tidewater (April 5-24). . . . On disabled list (August 21, 1990-remainder of season). . . . Traded by Mets with P Tony Castillo to Detroit Tigers for P Paul Gibson and P Randy Marshall (January 22, 1992). . . . On Detroit disabled list (June 10-28, 1992). . . . Granted free agency (December 19, 1992). . . . Signed by San Francisco Giants organization (January 13, 1993). . . . On disabled list (July 10-26, 1994).

STATISTICAL NOTES: Led Carolina League with 11 sacrifice flies in 1983.

		BATTING												FIELDING			
Year Team (League)	Pos.	G	AB	R	H	2B	3B	HR	RBI	Avg.	BB	SO	SB	PO	A	E	Avg.
1981— Kingsport (Appal.)	OF-C	64	232	30	67	8	0	1	36	.289	24	13	12	101	7	4	.964
1982— Shelby (S. Atl.)	OF	133	486	*120	160	29	6	2	79	.329	78	37	33	183	8	5	.974
1983— Lynchburg (Caro.)	OF	128	491	94	164	13	8	1	67	.334	76	39	36	173	8	14	.928
1984— Jackson (Texas)	OF	119	435	64	122	14	3	1	43	.280	38	24	12	146	1	4	.974
1985— Tidewater (Int'l)	OF	7	15	1	2	1	0	1	2	.133	2	5	0	2	0	0	1.000
— Jackson (Texas)	OF	123	447	96	140	23	5	6	51	.313	87	32	23	201	8	1	.995
1986— Tidewater (Int'l)	OF	115	426	62	123	23	2	10	64	.289	50	42	11	192	6	6	.971
1987— Tidewater (Int'l)	OF	133	525	83	164	*41	5	10	89	.312	34	46	31	237	8	5	.980
— New York (N.L.)	OF	9	12	0	3	0	0	0	1	.250	1	1	0	4	0	1	.800
1988— Tidewater (Int'l)	OF	102	365	48	96	13	3	14	55	.263	40	53	11	111	6	2	.983
— New York (N.L.)	OF	7	9	5	5	2	0	1	1	.556	2	1	0	1	0	0	1.000
1989— Tidewater (Int'l)	OF-1B	32	122	22	34	4	0	1	21	.279	13	20	8	26	0	0	1.000
— New York (N.L.)	OF	68	133	20	41	6	0	6	16	.308	12	17	2	57	0	1	.983
1990— New York (N.L.)	OF	82	188	30	47	12	0	10	26	.250	15	29	1	87	1	0	1.000
1991— New York (N.L.)	OF	106	254	18	66	6	0	4	21	.260	12	26	2	96	4	3	.971
1992— Detroit (A.L.)■	OF-DH	101	336	34	78	11	1	10	41	.232	22	57	3	178	5	4	.979
1993— San Fran. (N.L.)■	OF-1B	78	150	22	49	9	1	7	33	.327	13	16	1	54	4	3	.951
1994— San Francisco (N.L.)	OF	51	100	8	27	4	0	3	20	.270	7	20	0	44	0	1	.978
1995— San Francisco (N.L.)	1B-OF	117	396	53	119	24	0	17	65	.301	23	37	0	732	45	7	.991
American League totals (1 year)		101	336	34	78	11	1	10	41	.232	22	57	3	178	5	4	.979
National League totals (8 years)		518	1242	156	357	63	1	48	183	.287	85	147	6	1075	54	16	.986
Major league totals (9 years)		619	1578	190	435	74	2	58	224	.276	107	204	9	1253	59	20	.985

CARTER, ANDY — P — GIANTS

PERSONAL: Born November 9, 1968, in Philadelphia. . . . 6-5/220. . . . Throws left, bats left. . . . Full name: Andrew Godfrey Carter.

HIGH SCHOOL: Springfield (Pa.).

COLLEGE: Delaware.

TRANSACTIONS/CAREER NOTES: Selected by Philadelphia Phillies organization in 37th round of free-agent draft (June 2, 1987). . . . On Scranton/Wilkes-Barre disabled list (June 26-August 8, 1995). . . . Granted free agency (October 16, 1995). . . . Signed by Phoenix, San Francisco Giants organization (November 15, 1995).

STATISTICAL NOTES: Pitched 4-0 no-hit victory against Augusta (August 18, 1988).

Year Team (League)	W	L	Pct.	ERA	G	GS	CG	ShO	Sv.	IP	H	R	ER	BB	SO
1987— Utica (NYP)	0	1	.000	5.65	12	1	0	0	0	28 2/3	27	25	18	19	19
1988— Spartanburg (SAL)	11	6	.647	2.30	25	25	4	1	0	156 2/3	110	55	40	75	99
1989— Clearwater (Fla. St.)	1	5	.167	4.85	12	12	2	1	0	68 2/3	73	46	37	32	31
— Spartanburg (SAL)	6	5	.545	3.28	15	15	1	1	0	90 2/3	73	38	33	51	72
1990— Clearwater (Fla. St.)	4	*14	.222	4.88	26	26	2	0	0	131	121	82	71	69	90
1991— Reading (Eastern)	11	5	.688	4.84	20	20	1	0	0	102 1/3	86	57	55	57	64
1992— Reading (Eastern)	0	4	.000	9.24	7	6	0	0	0	25 1/3	37	28	26	15	17

Year	Team (League)	W	L	Pct.	ERA	G	GS	CG	ShO	Sv.	IP	H	R	ER	BB	SO
	—Clearwater (Fla. St.)	3	4	.429	1.86	16	13	1	1	0	87	60	30	18	13	68
1993	—Reading (Eastern)	1	1	.500	2.82	4	4	0	0	0	22 1/3	15	8	7	12	16
	—Scran./W.B. (Int'l)	7	7	.500	4.54	30	13	0	0	1	109	104	59	55	35	68
1994	—Scran./W.B. (Int'l)	1	0	1.000	2.61	25	0	0	0	2	31	22	10	9	13	27
	—Philadelphia (N.L.)	0	2	.000	4.46	20	0	0	0	0	34 1/3	34	18	17	12	18
1995	—Scran./W.B. (Int'l)	1	2	.333	4.35	14	1	0	0	0	20 2/3	17	10	10	13	18
	—Philadelphia (N.L.)	0	0	...	6.14	4	0	0	0	0	7 1/3	4	5	5	2	6
Major league totals (2 years)		0	2	.000	4.75	24	0	0	0	0	41 2/3	38	23	22	14	24

CARTER, JOE — OF — BLUE JAYS

PERSONAL: Born March 7, 1960, in Oklahoma City. . . . 6-3/225. . . . Bats right, throws right. . . . Full name: Joseph Chris Carter. . . . Brother of Fred Carter, minor league outfielder (1985-88).

HIGH SCHOOL: Millwood (Oklahoma City).

COLLEGE: Wichita State.

TRANSACTIONS/CAREER NOTES: Selected by Chicago Cubs organization in first round (second pick overall) of free-agent draft (June 8, 1981). . . . On disabled list (April 9-19, 1982). . . . Traded by Cubs organization with OF Mel Hall, P Don Schulze and P Darryl Banks to Cleveland Indians for C Ron Hassey, P Rick Sutcliffe and P George Frazier (June 13, 1984). . . . On Cleveland disabled list (July 2-17, 1984). . . . Traded by Indians to San Diego Padres for C Sandy Alomar, OF Chris James and 3B Carlos Baerga (December 6, 1989). . . . Traded by Padres with 2B Roberto Alomar to Toronto Blue Jays for 1B Fred McGriff and SS Tony Fernandez (December 5, 1990). . . . Granted free agency (October 30, 1992). . . . Re-signed by Blue Jays (December 7, 1992).

RECORDS: Shares major league records for most home runs in two consecutive games—5 (July 18 [2] and 19 [3], 1989). . . . Shares major league single-season record for most games with three or more home runs—2 (1989). . . . Shares major league record for most home runs in one inning—2 (October 3, 1993, second inning). . . . Holds A.L. career record for most games with three or more home runs—5.

HONORS: Named outfielder on The Sporting News college All-America team (1980-81). . . . Named College Player of the Year by The Sporting News (1981). . . . Named outfielder on The Sporting News A.L. All-Star team (1991-92). . . . Named outfielder on The Sporting News A.L. Silver Slugger team (1991-92).

STATISTICAL NOTES: Led American Association with 265 total bases in 1983. . . . Hit three home runs in one game five times (August 29, 1986; May 28, 1987; June 24 and July 19, 1989; and August 23, 1993). . . . Led A.L. first basemen with 12 errors in 1987. . . . Led A.L. in being hit by pitch with 10 in 1991. . . . Led A.L. with 13 sacrifice flies in 1992 and 1994. . . . Career major league grand slams: 7.

			BATTING												FIELDING			
Year	Team (League)	Pos.	G	AB	R	H	2B	3B	HR	RBI	Avg.	BB	SO	SB	PO	A	E	Avg.
1981	—Midland (Texas)	OF	67	249	42	67	15	3	5	35	.269	8	30	12	100	10	4	.965
1982	—Midland (Texas)	OF	110	427	84	136	22	8	25	98	.319	26	51	15	182	6	5	.974
1983	—Iowa (Am. Assoc.)	OF	124	*522	82	160	27	6	22	83	.307	17	•103	40	204	9	12	.947
	—Chicago (N.L.)	OF	23	51	6	9	1	1	0	1	.176	0	21	1	26	0	0	1.000
1984	—Iowa (Am. Assoc.)	OF	61	248	45	77	12	7	14	67	.310	20	31	11	142	6	2	.987
	—Cleveland (A.L.)■	OF-1B	66	244	32	67	6	1	13	41	.275	11	48	2	169	11	6	.968
1985	—Cleveland (A.L.)	O-1-DH-2-3	143	489	64	128	27	0	15	59	.262	25	74	24	311	17	6	.982
1986	—Cleveland (A.L.)	OF-1B	162	663	108	200	36	9	29	*121	.302	32	95	29	800	55	10	.988
1987	—Cleveland (A.L.)	1B-OF-DH	149	588	83	155	27	2	32	106	.264	27	105	31	782	46	†17	.980
1988	—Cleveland (A.L.)	OF	157	621	85	168	36	6	27	98	.271	27	98	27	444	8	7	.985
1989	—Cleveland (A.L.)	OF-1B-DH	•162	•651	84	158	32	4	35	105	.243	39	112	13	443	20	9	.981
1990	—San Diego (N.L.)■	OF-1B	*162	*634	79	147	27	1	24	115	.232	48	93	22	492	16	11	.979
1991	—Toronto (A.L.)■	OF-DH	•162	638	89	174	42	3	33	108	.273	49	112	20	283	13	8	.974
1992	—Toronto (A.L.)	OF-DH-1B	158	622	97	164	30	7	34	119	.264	36	109	12	284	13	9	.971
1993	—Toronto (A.L.)	OF-DH	155	603	92	153	33	5	33	121	.254	47	113	8	289	7	8	.974
1994	—Toronto (A.L.)	OF-DH	111	435	70	118	25	2	27	103	.271	33	64	11	205	4	2	.991
1995	—Toronto (A.L.)	OF-1B-DH	139	558	70	141	23	0	25	76	.253	37	87	12	316	12	7	.979
American League totals (11 years)			1564	6112	874	1626	317	39	303	1057	.266	363	1017	189	4326	206	89	.981
National League totals (2 years)			185	685	85	156	28	2	24	116	.228	48	114	23	518	16	11	.980
Major league totals (13 years)			1749	6797	959	1782	345	41	327	1173	.262	411	1131	212	4844	222	100	.981

CHAMPIONSHIP SERIES RECORD

NOTES: Shares A.L. single-game record for most at-bats—6 (October 11, 1992, 11 innings).

			BATTING												FIELDING			
Year	Team (League)	Pos.	G	AB	R	H	2B	3B	HR	RBI	Avg.	BB	SO	SB	PO	A	E	Avg.
1991	—Toronto (A.L.)	OF-DH	5	19	3	5	2	0	1	4	.263	1	5	0	4	1	0	1.000
1992	—Toronto (A.L.)	OF-1B	6	26	2	5	0	0	1	3	.192	2	4	2	16	1	1	.944
1993	—Toronto (A.L.)	OF	6	27	2	7	0	0	0	2	.259	1	5	0	12	1	0	1.000
Championship series totals (3 years)			17	72	7	17	2	0	2	9	.236	4	14	2	32	3	1	.972

WORLD SERIES RECORD

NOTES: Holds career record for most sacrifice flies—4. . . . Holds single-series record for most sacrifice flies—3 (1993). . . . Member of World Series championship teams (1992 and 1993).

			BATTING												FIELDING			
Year	Team (League)	Pos.	G	AB	R	H	2B	3B	HR	RBI	Avg.	BB	SO	SB	PO	A	E	Avg.
1992	—Toronto (A.L.)	OF-1B	6	22	2	6	2	0	2	3	.273	3	2	0	27	1	0	1.000
1993	—Toronto (A.L.)	OF	6	25	6	7	1	0	2	8	.280	0	4	0	13	0	2	.867
World Series totals (2 years)			12	47	8	13	3	0	4	11	.277	3	6	0	40	1	2	.953

ALL-STAR GAME RECORD

			BATTING											FIELDING			
Year	League	Pos.	AB	R	H	2B	3B	HR	RBI	Avg.	BB	SO	SB	PO	A	E	Avg.
1991	—American	OF	1	1	1	0	0	0	0	1.000	1	0	0	1	0	0	1.000
1992	—American	OF	3	1	2	0	0	0	1	.667	0	0	0	1	0	0	1.000
1993	—American	OF	3	0	1	0	0	0	0	.333	0	1	0	1	0	0	1.000
1994	—American	OF	3	1	0	0	0	0	0	.000	0	0	0	1	0	0	1.000
All-Star Game totals (4 years)			10	3	4	0	0	0	1	.400	1	1	0	4	0	0	1.000

CARTER, JOHN — P — METS

PERSONAL: Born February 16, 1972, in Chicago. . . . 6-1/195. . . . Throws right, bats right. . . . Full name: John Christopher Carter.
HIGH SCHOOL: Neal F. Simeon (Chicago).
COLLEGE: Kishwaukee College (Ill.).
TRANSACTIONS/CAREER NOTES: Selected by Pittsburgh Pirates organization in 37th round of free-agent draft (June 4, 1990). . . . Traded by Pirates organization with OF Tony Mitchell to Cleveland Indians organization for OF Alex Cole (July 4, 1992). . . . On disabled list (April 20-27 and August 15, 1994-remainder of season). . . . On disabled list (May 22, 1995-remainder of season). . . . Claimed on waivers by Kansas City Royals (November 16, 1995). . . . Traded by Royals to New York Mets (November 16, 1995), completing deal in which Royals acquired P John Jacome and P Allen McDill for P Derek Wallace and a player to be named later (July 21, 1995).

Year	Team (League)	W	L	Pct.	ERA	G	GS	CG	ShO	Sv.	IP	H	R	ER	BB	SO
1991—	GC Pirates (GCL)	5	4	.556	3.29	10	9	0	0	0	41	42	20	15	13	28
1992—	Welland (NYP)	0	3	.000	3.45		3	0	0	0	15 2/3	12	11	6	7	15
	—Augusta (S. Atl.)	0	0	. . .	0.00	1	1	0	0	0	5	3	0	0	1	4
	—Watertown (NYP)■	4	4	.500	4.14	13	11	3	0	0	63	55	36	29	32	39
1993—	Columbus (S. Atl.)	*17	7	.708	2.79	29	•29	1	0	0	180 1/3	147	72	56	48	134
1994—	Cant./Akr. (East.)	9	6	.600	4.33	22	22	3	1	0	131	134	68	63	53	73
1995—	Cant./Akr. (East.)	1	2	.333	3.95	5	5	0	0	0	27 1/3	27	13	12	13	14

CASANOVA, RAUL — C — PADRES

PERSONAL: Born August 23, 1972, in Humacao, Puerto Rico. . . . 5-11/200. . . . Bats both, throws right.
HIGH SCHOOL: Ponce (Puerto Rico).
TRANSACTIONS/CAREER NOTES: Selected by New York Mets organization in eighth round of free-agent draft (June 4, 1990). . . . Traded by Mets organization to San Diego Padres organization (December 7, 1992), completing deal in which Padres traded SS Tony Fernandez to Mets for P Wally Whitehurst, OF D.J. Dozier and a player to be named later (October 26, 1992).

				BATTING											FIELDING			
Year	Team (League)	Pos.	G	AB	R	H	2B	3B	HR	RBI	Avg.	BB	SO	SB	PO	A	E	Avg.
1990—	GC Mets (GCL)	C	23	65	4	5	0	0	0	1	.077	4	16	0	141	20	8	.953
1991—	GC Mets (GCL)	C	32	111	19	27	4	2	0	9	.243	12	22	3	211	24	5	.979
	—Kingsport (Appal.)	C	5	18	0	1	0	0	0	0	.056	1	10	0	35	4	1	.975
1992—	Columbia (S. Atl.)	C	5	18	2	3	0	0	0	1	.167	1	4	0	29	1	0	1.000
	—Kingsport (Appal.)	C	42	137	25	37	9	1	4	27	.270	26	25	3	286	34	6	.982
1993—	Waterloo (Midw.)■	C-3B	76	227	32	58	12	0	6	30	.256	21	46	0	361	50	10	.976
1994—	Rancho Cuca. (Cal.)	C	123	471	83	*160	27	2	23	120	*.340	43	97	1	593	55	14	.979
1995—	Memphis (South.)	C	89	306	42	83	18	0	12	44	.271	25	51	4	531	55	*12	.980

CASIAN, LARRY — P — CUBS

PERSONAL: Born October 28, 1965, in Lynwood, Calif. . . . 6-0/175. . . . Throws left, bats right. . . . Full name: Lawrence Paul Casian. . . . Name pronounced CASS-ee-un.
HIGH SCHOOL: Lakewood (Calif.).
COLLEGE: Cal State Fullerton.
TRANSACTIONS/CAREER NOTES: Selected by Minnesota Twins organization in sixth round of free-agent draft (June 2, 1987). . . . On Minnesota disabled list (April 14-May 28, 1993); included rehabilitation assignment to Portland (May 14-27). . . . Claimed on waivers by Cleveland Indians (July 14, 1994). . . . Released by Indians (November 4, 1994). . . . Signed by Iowa, Cubs organization (December 12, 1994). . . . On Chicago disabled list (June 14-August 1, 1995); included rehabilitation assignment to Iowa (July 13-August 1).
STATISTICAL NOTES: Pitched two innings, combining with starter David West (six innings) and Greg Johnson (one inning) in 5-0 no-hit victory for Portland against Vancouver (June 7, 1992).

Year	Team (League)	W	L	Pct.	ERA	G	GS	CG	ShO	Sv.	IP	H	R	ER	BB	SO
1987—	Visalia (California)	10	3	.769	2.51	18	15	2	1	2	97	89	35	27	49	96
1988—	Orlando (Southern)	9	9	.500	2.95	27	26	4	1	0	174	165	72	57	62	104
	—Portland (PCL)	0	1	.000	0.00	1	0	0	0	0	2 2/3	5	3	0	0	2
1989—	Portland (PCL)	7	12	.368	4.52	28	27	0	0	0	169 1/3	201	97	85	63	65
1990—	Portland (PCL)	9	9	.500	4.48	37	23	1	0	0	156 2/3	171	90	78	59	89
	—Minnesota (A.L.)	2	1	.667	3.22	5	3	0	0	0	22 1/3	26	9	8	4	11
1991—	Minnesota (A.L.)	0	0	. . .	7.36	15	0	0	0	0	18 1/3	28	16	15	7	6
	—Portland (PCL)	3	2	.600	3.46	34	6	0	0	1	52	51	25	20	16	24
1992—	Portland (PCL)	4	0	1.000	2.32	58	0	0	0	11	62	54	16	16	13	43
	—Minnesota (A.L.)	1	0	1.000	2.70	6	0	0	0	0	6 2/3	7	2	2	1	2
1993—	Minnesota (A.L.)	5	3	.625	3.02	54	0	0	0	1	56 2/3	59	23	19	14	31
	—Portland (PCL)	1	0	1.000	0.00	7	0	0	0	2	7 2/3	9	0	0	2	2
1994—	Minnesota (A.L.)	1	3	.250	7.08	33	0	0	0	1	40 2/3	57	34	32	12	18
	—Cleveland (A.L.)■	0	2	.000	8.64	7	0	0	0	0	8 1/3	16	9	8	4	2
1995—	Iowa (Am. Assoc.)■	0	0	. . .	2.13	13	0	0	0	1	12 2/3	9	3	3	2	9
	—Chicago (N.L.)	1	0	1.000	1.93	42	0	0	0	0	23 1/3	23	6	5	15	11
A.L. totals (5 years)		9	9	.500	4.94	120	3	0	0	2	153	193	93	84	42	70
N.L. totals (1 year)		1	0	1.000	1.93	42	0	0	0	0	23 1/3	23	6	5	15	11
Major league totals (6 years)		10	9	.526	4.54	162	3	0	0	2	176 1/3	216	99	89	57	81

CASTELLANO, PEDRO — 3B/1B — ROCKIES

PERSONAL: Born March 11, 1970, in Lara, Venezuela. . . . 6-1/180. . . . Bats right, throws right. . . . Full name: Pedro Orlando Castellano. . . . Name pronounced KASS-ta-YAH-no.
HIGH SCHOOL: Jose Dominguez (Lara, Venezuela).
TRANSACTIONS/CAREER NOTES: Signed as non-drafted free agent by Chicago Cubs organization (April 14, 1988). . . . Selected by Colorado

Rockies in third round (64th pick overall) of expansion draft (November 17, 1992). . . . On disabled list (May 7-26 and August 7, 1994-remainder of the season). . . . Granted free agency (October 16, 1995). . . . Re-signed by Rockies organization (October 25, 1995).
HONORS: Named Carolina League Most Valuable Player (1991).

			BATTING												FIELDING			
Year	**Team (League)**	**Pos.**	**G**	**AB**	**R**	**H**	**2B**	**3B**	**HR**	**RBI**	**Avg.**	**BB**	**SO**	**SB**	**PO**	**A**	**E**	**Avg.**
1989—	Wytheville (Appal.)	SS-3B-1B	66	244	•55	76	17	4	9	42	.311	46	44	5	91	138	19	.923
1990—	Peoria (Midwest)	3B-SS	117	417	61	115	27	4	2	44	.276	63	73	7	93	213	17	.947
—	Winst.-Salem (Car.)	3B	19	66	6	13	0	0	1	8	.197	10	11	1	14	37	2	.962
1991—	Charlotte (South.)	3B	7	19	2	8	0	0	0	2	.421	1	6	0	2	11	0	1.000
—	Winst.-Salem (Car.)	3B-SS	129	459	59	139	25	3	10	*87	.303	72	97	11	132	318	26	.945
1992—	Iowa (Am. Assoc.)	3B-SS-1B	74	238	25	59	14	4	2	20	.248	32	42	2	43	133	10	.946
—	Charlotte (South.)	3B-SS	45	147	16	33	3	0	1	15	.224	19	21	0	36	104	10	.933
1993—	Colo. Springs (PCL)■	3B-1B	90	304	61	95	21	2	12	60	.313	36	63	3	312	145	13	.972
—	Colorado (N.L.)	3-1-S-2	34	71	12	13	2	0	3	7	.183	8	16	1	55	33	4	.957
1994—	Colo. Springs (PCL)	3B-1B	33	120	23	42	11	2	4	24	.350	13	17	1	85	54	0	1.000
1995—	Colorado (N.L.)	3B	4	5	0	0	0	0	0	0	.000	2	3	0	1	0	0	1.000
—	Colo. Springs (PCL)	3B-1B	99	334	40	89	23	2	9	47	.266	24	56	2	222	119	5	.986
Major league totals (2 years)			38	76	12	13	2	0	3	7	.171	10	19	1	56	33	4	.957

CASTILLA, VINNY 3B ROCKIES

PERSONAL: Born July 4, 1967, in Oaxaca, Mexico. . . . 6-1/200. . . . Bats right, throws right. . . . Full name: Vinicio Soria Castilla.
HIGH SCHOOL: Instituto Carlos Gracida (Oaxaca, Mexico).
TRANSACTIONS/CAREER NOTES: Signed as non-drafted free agent by Saltillo of Mexican League. . . . Contract sold by Saltillo to Atlanta Braves organization (March 19, 1990). . . . Selected by Colorado Rockies in second round (40th pick overall) of expansion draft (November 17, 1992). . . . On disabled list (May 20-June 4, 1993).
HONORS: Named third baseman on THE SPORTING NEWS N.L. All-Star team (1995). . . . Named third baseman on THE SPORTING NEWS N.L. Silver Slugger team (1995).
STATISTICAL NOTES: Led International League shortstops with 550 total chances and 72 double plays in 1992.

			BATTING												FIELDING			
Year	**Team (League)**	**Pos.**	**G**	**AB**	**R**	**H**	**2B**	**3B**	**HR**	**RBI**	**Avg.**	**BB**	**SO**	**SB**	**PO**	**A**	**E**	**Avg.**
1987—	Saltillo (Mexican)	3B	13	27	0	5	2	0	0	1	.185	0	5	0	10	31	1	.976
1988—	Salt.-Monc. (Mex.)■	SS	50	124	22	30	2	2	5	18	.242	8	29	1	53	105	13	.924
1989—	Saltillo (Mexican)■	SS-3B	128	462	70	142	25	13	10	58	.307	33	70	11	224	427	34	.950
1990—	Sumter (S. Atl.)■	SS	93	339	47	91	15	2	9	53	.268	28	54	2	139	320	23	.952
—	Greenville (South.)	SS	46	170	20	40	5	1	4	16	.235	13	23	4	71	167	7	.971
1991—	Greenville (South.)	SS	66	259	34	70	17	3	7	44	.270	9	35	0	86	221	11	.965
—	Richmond (Int'l)	SS	67	240	25	54	7	4	7	36	.225	14	32	1	93	208	12	.962
—	Atlanta (N.L.)	SS	12	5	1	1	0	0	0	0	.200	0	2	0	6	6	0	1.000
1992—	Richmond (Int'l)	SS	127	449	49	113	29	1	7	44	.252	21	68	1	162	357	*31	.944
—	Atlanta (N.L.)	SS-3B	9	16	1	4	1	0	0	1	.250	1	4	0	2	12	1	.933
1993—	Colorado (N.L.)■	SS	105	337	36	86	9	7	9	30	.255	13	45	2	141	282	11	.975
1994—	Colorado (N.L.)	S-2-3-1	52	130	16	43	11	1	3	18	.331	7	23	2	67	78	2	.986
—	Colo. Springs (PCL)	3B-2B-SS	22	78	13	19	6	1	1	11	.244	7	11	0	20	60	3	.964
1995—	Colorado (N.L.)	3B-SS	139	527	82	163	34	2	32	90	.309	30	87	2	86	264	15	.959
Major league totals (5 years)			317	1015	136	297	55	10	44	139	.293	51	161	6	302	642	29	.970

DIVISION SERIES RECORD

			BATTING												FIELDING			
Year	**Team (League)**	**Pos.**	**G**	**AB**	**R**	**H**	**2B**	**3B**	**HR**	**RBI**	**Avg.**	**BB**	**SO**	**SB**	**PO**	**A**	**E**	**Avg.**
1995—	Colorado (N.L.)	3B	4	15	3	7	1	0	3	6	.467	0	1	0	3	13	1	.941

ALL-STAR GAME RECORD

			BATTING											FIELDING			
Year	**League**	**Pos.**	**AB**	**R**	**H**	**2B**	**3B**	**HR**	**RBI**	**Avg.**	**BB**	**SO**	**SB**	**PO**	**A**	**E**	**Avg.**
1995—	National	3B	2	0	0	0	0	0	0	.000	0	1	0	0	0	0	. . .

CASTILLO, ALBERTO C METS

PERSONAL: Born February 10, 1970, in San Juan de la Maguana, Dominican Republic. . . . 6-0/184. . . . Bats right, throws right. . . . Full name: Alberto Terrero Castillo.
HIGH SCHOOL: Mercedes Maria Mateo (Dominican Republic).
TRANSACTIONS/CAREER NOTES: Signed as non-drafted free agent by New York Mets organization (April 15, 1987). . . . On disabled list (July 3, 1992-remainder of season and June 1-July 13, 1994). . . . On suspended list (August 27-29, 1994).

			BATTING												FIELDING			
Year	**Team (League)**	**Pos.**	**G**	**AB**	**R**	**H**	**2B**	**3B**	**HR**	**RBI**	**Avg.**	**BB**	**SO**	**SB**	**PO**	**A**	**E**	**Avg.**
1987—	Kingsport (Appal.)	C	7	9	1	1	0	0	0	0	.111	5	3	1	21	4	0	1.000
1988—	GC Mets (GCL)	C	22	68	7	18	4	0	0	10	.265	4	4	2	126	13	1	.993
—	Kingsport (Appal.)	C	24	75	7	22	3	0	1	14	.293	15	14	0	161	18	5	.973
1989—	Kingsport (Appal.)	C-1B	27	74	15	19	4	0	3	12	.257	11	14	2	140	19	1	.994
—	Pittsfield (NYP)	C	34	123	13	29	8	0	1	13	.236	7	26	2	186	26	2	.991
—	St. Lucie (Fla. St.)	. . .	1	0	0	0	0	0	0	0	. . .	0	0	0	0	0	0	. . .
1990—	Columbia (S. Atl.)	C	30	103	8	24	4	3	1	14	.233	10	21	1	187	22	5	.977
—	Pittsfield (NYP)	C-OF-1B	58	187	19	41	8	1	4	24	.219	26	35	3	378	61	9	.980
1991—	Columbia (S. Atl.)	C	90	267	35	74	20	3	3	47	.277	43	44	6	*734	86	15	.982
1992—	St. Lucie (Fla. St.)	C	60	162	11	33	6	0	3	17	.204	16	37	0	317	40	12	.967
1993—	St. Lucie (Fla. St.)	C	105	333	37	86	21	0	5	42	.258	28	46	0	*604	80	12	.983
1994—	Binghamton (East.)	C-1B	90	315	33	78	14	0	7	42	.248	41	46	1	643	54	6	.991
1995—	Norfolk (Int'l)	C	69	217	23	58	13	1	4	31	.267	26	32	2	469	44	7	.987
—	New York (N.L.)	C	13	29	2	3	0	0	0	0	.103	3	9	1	66	9	2	.974
Major league totals (1 year)			13	29	2	3	0	0	0	0	.103	3	9	1	66	9	2	.974

CASTILLO, FRANK — P — CUBS

PERSONAL: Born April 1, 1969, in El Paso, Tex. . . . 6-1/200. . . . Throws right, bats right. . . . Full name: Frank Anthony Castillo.
HIGH SCHOOL: Eastwood (El Paso, Tex.).
TRANSACTIONS/CAREER NOTES: Selected by Chicago Cubs organization in sixth round of free-agent draft (June 2, 1987). . . . On disabled list (April 1-July 23, 1988). . . . On Iowa disabled list (April 12-June 6, 1991). . . . On Chicago disabled list (August 11-27, 1991). . . . On suspended list (September 20-24, 1993). . . . On Chicago disabled list (March 20-May 12, 1994); included rehabilitation assignments to Daytona (April 24), Orlando (April 25-May 2) and Iowa (May 2-10). . . . On Iowa disabled list (June 21-July 1, 1994).
HONORS: Named Appalachian League Player of the Year (1987).
STATISTICAL NOTES: Pitched 4-0 no-hit victory against Huntsville (July 13, 1990, first game). . . . Pitched 7-0 one-hit, complete-game victory against St. Louis (September 25, 1995).

Year	Team (League)	W	L	Pct.	ERA	G	GS	CG	ShO	Sv.	IP	H	R	ER	BB	SO
1987—	Wytheville (Appal.)	*10	1	*.909	2.29	12	12	•5	0	0	90 1/3	86	31	23	21	83
—	Geneva (NYP)	1	0	1.000	0.00	1	1	0	0	0	6	3	1	0	1	6
1988—	Peoria (Midwest)	6	1	.857	0.71	9	8	2	2	0	51	25	5	4	10	58
1989—	Winst.-Salem (Car.)	9	6	.600	2.51	18	18	8	1	0	129 1/3	118	42	36	24	114
—	Charlotte (South.)	3	4	.429	3.84	10	10	4	0	0	68	73	35	29	12	43
1990—	Charlotte (South.)	6	6	.500	3.88	18	18	4	1	0	111 1/3	113	54	48	27	112
1991—	Iowa (Am. Assoc.)	3	1	.750	2.52	4	4	1	1	0	25	20	7	7	7	20
—	Chicago (N.L.)	6	7	.462	4.35	18	18	4	0	0	111 2/3	107	56	54	33	73
1992—	Chicago (N.L.)	10	11	.476	3.46	33	33	0	0	0	205 1/3	179	91	79	63	135
1993—	Chicago (N.L.)	5	8	.385	4.84	29	25	2	0	0	141 1/3	162	83	76	39	84
1994—	Daytona (Fla. St.)	0	1	.000	4.50	1	1	0	0	0	4	7	3	2	0	1
—	Orlando (Southern)	1	0	1.000	1.29	1	1	0	0	0	7	4	2	1	1	2
—	Iowa (Am. Assoc.)	4	2	.667	3.27	11	11	0	0	0	66	57	30	24	10	64
—	Chicago (N.L.)	2	1	.667	4.30	4	4	1	0	0	23	25	13	11	5	19
1995—	Chicago (N.L.)	11	10	.524	3.21	29	29	2	2	0	188	179	75	67	52	135
Major league totals (5 years)		34	37	.479	3.86	113	109	9	2	0	669 1/3	652	318	287	192	446

CASTILLO, TONY — P — BLUE JAYS

PERSONAL: Born March 1, 1963, in Lara, Venezuela. . . . 5-10/190. . . . Throws left, bats left. . . . Full name: Antonio Jose Castillo.
TRANSACTIONS/CAREER NOTES: Signed as non-drafted free agent by Toronto Blue Jays organization (February 16, 1983). . . . On disabled list (April 10, 1986-entire season). . . . Traded by Blue Jays organization with a player to be named later to Atlanta Braves for P Jim Acker (August 24, 1989); Braves organization acquired C Francisco Cabrera to complete deal (August 24, 1989). . . . Traded by Braves with a player to be named later to New York Mets for P Alejandro Pena (August 28, 1991); Mets acquired P Joe Roa to complete deal (August 29, 1991). . . . Traded by Mets with OF Mark Carreon to Detroit Tigers for P Paul Gibson and P Randy Marshall (January 22, 1992). . . . On disabled list (June 8-August 29, 1992). . . . Granted free agency (October 15, 1992). . . . Signed by Syracuse, Blue Jays organization (January 11, 1993).

Year	Team (League)	W	L	Pct.	ERA	G	GS	CG	ShO	Sv.	IP	H	R	ER	BB	SO
1983—	GC Blue Jays (GCL)	0	0	. . .	3.00	1	0	0	0	1	3	3	1	1	0	4
1984—	Florence (S. Atl.)	11	8	.579	3.41	25	24	4	1	0	137 1/3	123	71	52	50	96
1985—	Kinston (Carolina)	11	7	.611	1.90	36	12	0	0	3	127 2/3	111	44	27	48	136
1986—								Did not play.								
1987—	Dunedin (Fla. St.)	6	2	.750	3.36	39	0	0	0	6	69 2/3	62	30	26	19	62
1988—	Dunedin (Fla. St.)	4	3	.571	1.48	30	0	0	0	12	42 2/3	31	9	7	10	46
—	Knoxville (South.)	1	0	1.000	0.00	5	0	0	0	2	8	2	0	0	1	11
—	Toronto (A.L.)	1	0	1.000	3.00	14	0	0	0	0	15	10	5	5	2	14
1989—	Toronto (A.L.)	1	1	.500	6.11	17	0	0	0	1	17 2/3	23	14	12	10	10
—	Syracuse (Int'l)	1	3	.250	2.81	27	0	0	0	5	41 2/3	33	15	13	15	37
—	Atlanta (N.L.)■	0	1	.000	4.82	12	0	0	0	0	9 1/3	8	5	5	4	5
1990—	Atlanta (N.L.)	5	1	.833	4.23	52	3	0	0	1	76 2/3	93	41	36	20	64
—	Richmond (Int'l)	3	1	.750	2.52	5	4	1	1	0	25	14	7	7	6	27
1991—	Richmond (Int'l)	5	6	.455	2.90	23	17	0	0	0	118	89	47	38	32	78
—	Atlanta (N.L.)	1	1	.500	7.27	7	0	0	0	0	8 2/3	13	9	7	5	8
—	New York (N.L.)■	1	0	1.000	1.90	10	3	0	0	0	23 2/3	27	7	5	6	10
1992—	Toledo (Int'l)■	2	3	.400	3.63	12	9	0	0	2	44 2/3	48	23	18	14	24
1993—	Syracuse (Int'l)■	0	0	. . .	0.00	1	1	0	0	0	6	4	2	0	0	2
—	Toronto (A.L.)	3	2	.600	3.38	51	0	0	0	0	50 2/3	44	19	19	22	28
1994—	Toronto (A.L.)	5	2	.714	2.51	41	0	0	0	1	68	66	22	19	28	43
1995—	Toronto (A.L.)	1	5	.167	3.22	55	0	0	0	13	72 2/3	64	27	26	24	38
A.L. totals (5 years)		11	10	.524	3.25	178	0	0	0	15	224	207	87	81	86	133
N.L. totals (3 years)		7	3	.700	4.03	81	6	0	0	1	118 1/3	141	62	53	35	87
Major league totals (7 years)		18	13	.581	3.52	259	6	0	0	16	342 1/3	348	149	134	121	220

CHAMPIONSHIP SERIES RECORD

Year	Team (League)	W	L	Pct.	ERA	G	GS	CG	ShO	Sv.	IP	H	R	ER	BB	SO
1993—	Toronto (A.L.)	0	0	. . .	0.00	2	0	0	0	0	2	0	0	0	1	1

WORLD SERIES RECORD

NOTES: Member of World Series championship team (1993).

Year	Team (League)	W	L	Pct.	ERA	G	GS	CG	ShO	Sv.	IP	H	R	ER	BB	SO
1993—	Toronto (A.L.)	1	0	1.000	8.10	2	0	0	0	0	3 1/3	6	3	3	3	1

CASTRO, JUAN — SS — DODGERS

PERSONAL: Born June 20, 1972, in Los Mochis, Mexico. . . . 5-10/163. . . . Bats right, throws right.
HIGH SCHOOL: CBTIS 43 (Los Mochis, Mexico).
TRANSACTIONS/CAREER NOTES: Signed as non-drafted free agent by Los Angeles Dodgers organization (June 13, 1991).
STATISTICAL NOTES: Tied for Texas League lead in double plays by shortstop with 82 in 1994.

			BATTING												FIELDING			
Year	Team (League)	Pos.	G	AB	R	H	2B	3B	HR	RBI	Avg.	BB	SO	SB	PO	A	E	Avg.
1991—	Great Falls (Pio.)	SS-2B	60	217	36	60	4	2	1	27	.276	33	31	7	90	155	21	.921
1992—	Bakersfield (Calif.)	SS	113	446	56	116	15	4	4	42	.260	37	64	14	180	309	38	.928
1993—	San Antonio (Tex.)	SS-2B	118	424	55	117	23	8	7	41	.276	30	40	12	169	314	28	.945
1994—	San Antonio (Tex.)	SS	123	445	55	128	25	4	4	44	.288	31	66	4	187	377	29	.951
1995—	Albuquerque (PCL)	SS-2B	104	341	51	91	18	4	3	43	.267	20	42	4	152	344	14	.973
—	Los Angeles (N.L.)	3B-SS	11	4	0	1	0	0	0	0	.250	1	1	0	3	7	0	1.000
Major league totals (1 year)			11	4	0	1	0	0	0	0	.250	1	1	0	3	7	0	1.000

CEDENO, ANDUJAR — SS — PADRES

PERSONAL: Born August 21, 1969, in La Romana, Dominican Republic. . . . 6-1/170. . . . Bats right, throws right.

TRANSACTIONS/CAREER NOTES: Signed as non-drafted free agent by Houston Astros organization (October 1, 1986). . . . Traded by Astros with 3B Ken Caminiti, OF Steve Finley, 1B Robert Petagine, P Brian Williams and a player to be named later to San Diego Padres for OF Phil Plantier, OF Derek Bell, P Pedro Martinez, P Doug Brocail, IF Craig Shipley and SS Ricky Gutierrez (December 28, 1994).

RECORDS: Shares major league record for most strikeouts in three consecutive games—10 (July 5 [2], 6 [5]and 7 [3], 1994).

STATISTICAL NOTES: Led Southern League shortstops with 572 total chances in 1990. . . . Led Southern League with 12 sacrifice hits in 1990. . . . Hit for the cycle (August 25, 1992). . . . Led N.L. shortstops with 71 double plays in 1994.

			BATTING												FIELDING			
Year	Team (League)	Pos.	G	AB	R	H	2B	3B	HR	RBI	Avg.	BB	SO	SB	PO	A	E	Avg.
1988—	GC Rangers (GCL)	SS	46	165	25	47	5	2	1	20	.285	11	34	10	58	145	25	.890
1989—	Asheville (S. Atl.)	SS-3B	126	487	76	*146	23	6	14	93	.300	29	124	23	182	346	62	.895
1990—	Columbus (South.)	SS	132	495	57	119	21	*11	19	64	.240	33	135	6	167	354	*51	.911
—	Houston (N.L.)	SS	7	8	0	0	0	0	0	0	.000	0	5	0	3	2	1	.833
1991—	Tucson (PCL)	SS	93	347	49	105	19	6	7	55	.303	19	68	5	131	262	31	.927
—	Houston (N.L.)	SS	67	251	27	61	13	2	9	36	.243	9	74	4	88	151	18	.930
1992—	Houston (N.L.)	SS	71	220	15	38	13	2	2	13	.173	14	71	2	82	175	11	.959
—	Tucson (PCL)	SS	74	280	27	82	18	4	6	56	.293	18	49	6	112	211	22	.936
1993—	Houston (N.L.)	SS-3B	149	505	69	143	24	4	11	56	.283	48	97	9	155	376	25	.955
1994—	Houston (N.L.)	SS	98	342	38	90	26	0	9	49	.263	29	79	1	130	282	*23	.947
1995—	San Diego (N.L.)■	SS-3B	120	390	42	82	16	2	6	31	.210	28	92	5	139	305	17	.963
Major league totals (6 years)			512	1716	191	414	92	10	37	185	.241	128	418	21	597	1291	95	.952

CEDENO, DOMINGO — SS/2B — BLUE JAYS

PERSONAL: Born November 4, 1968, in La Romana, Dominican Republic. . . . 6-1/170. . . . Bats both, throws right.

TRANSACTIONS/CAREER NOTES: Signed as non-drafted free agent by Toronto Blue Jays organization (August 4, 1987). . . . On disabled list (April 22-May 28, 1991).

STATISTICAL NOTES: Led Florida State League shortstops with 633 total chances and 74 double plays in 1990. . . . Led Southern League with 12 sacrifice hits in 1991.

			BATTING												FIELDING			
Year	Team (League)	Pos.	G	AB	R	H	2B	3B	HR	RBI	Avg.	BB	SO	SB	PO	A	E	Avg.
1988—						Dominican Summer League statistics unavailable.												
1989—	Myrtle Beach (SAL)	SS	9	35	4	7	0	0	0	2	.200	3	12	1	12	20	7	.821
—	Dunedin (Fla. St.)	SS	9	28	3	6	0	1	0	1	.214	3	10	0	9	21	1	.968
—	Medicine Hat (Pio.)	SS	53	194	28	45	6	4	1	20	.232	23	65	6	100	141	•25	.906
1990—	Dunedin (Fla. St.)	SS	124	493	64	109	12	10	7	61	.221	48	127	10	*215	*382	36	.943
1991—	Knoxville (South.)	SS	100	336	39	75	7	6	1	26	.223	29	81	11	140	272	24	.945
1992—	Knoxville (South.)	2B-SS	106	337	31	76	7	7	2	21	.226	18	88	8	189	254	28	.941
—	Syracuse (Int'l)	2B-SS	18	57	4	11	4	0	0	5	.193	3	14	0	36	43	0	1.000
1993—	Syracuse (Int'l)	SS-2B	103	382	58	104	16	10	2	28	.272	33	67	15	150	242	21	.949
—	Toronto (A.L.)	SS-2B	15	46	5	8	0	0	0	7	.174	1	10	1	10	39	1	.980
1994—	Toronto (A.L.)	2-S-3-O	47	97	14	19	2	3	0	10	.196	10	31	1	40	64	8	.929
—	Syracuse (Int'l)	2B-OF-SS	22	80	11	23	5	1	1	9	.288	8	13	3	42	33	2	.974
1995—	Toronto (A.L.)	SS-2B-3B	51	161	18	38	6	1	4	14	.236	10	35	0	85	132	3	.986
Major league totals (3 years)			113	304	37	65	8	4	4	31	.214	21	76	2	135	235	12	.969

CEDENO, ROGER — OF — DODGERS

PERSONAL: Born August 16, 1974, in Valencia, Venezuela. . . . 6-1/165. . . . Bats both, throws right. . . . Full name: Roger Leandro Cedeno.

TRANSACTIONS/CAREER NOTES: Signed as non-drafted free agent by Los Angeles Dodgers organization (March 28, 1991). . . . On disabled list (June 27-July 14, 1994).

STATISTICAL NOTES: Tied for Pioneer League lead with three intentional bases on balls received in 1992. . . . Led Texas League in caught stealing with 20 in 1993. . . . Led Pacific Coast League in caught stealing with 18 in 1995.

			BATTING												FIELDING			
Year	Team (League)	Pos.	G	AB	R	H	2B	3B	HR	RBI	Avg.	BB	SO	SB	PO	A	E	Avg.
1991—	Santo Dom. (DSL)	OF	58	209	25	50	1	1	0	7	.239	0	0	26	...	...	...	...
1992—	Great Falls (Pio.)	OF	69	256	60	81	6	5	2	27	.316	51	53	*40	113	6	8	.937
1993—	San Antonio (Tex.)	OF	122	465	70	134	12	8	4	30	.288	45	90	28	213	6	9	.961
—	Albuquerque (PCL)	OF	6	18	1	4	1	1	0	4	.222	3	3	0	12	0	1	.923
1994—	Albuquerque (PCL)	OF	104	383	84	123	18	5	4	49	.321	51	57	30	194	7	8	.962
1995—	Albuquerque (PCL)	OF	99	367	67	112	19	9	2	44	.305	53	56	23	189	3	3	.985
—	Los Angeles (N.L.)	OF	40	42	4	10	2	0	0	3	.238	3	10	1	43	0	1	.977
Major league totals (1 year)			40	42	4	10	2	0	0	3	.238	3	10	1	43	0	1	.977

CHAMBERLAIN, WES — OF — ROYALS

PERSONAL: Born April 13, 1966, in Chicago. . . . 6-2/225. . . . Bats right, throws right. . . . Full name: Wesley Polk Chamberlain.
HIGH SCHOOL: Neal F. Simeon (Chicago).
COLLEGE: Jackson State.
TRANSACTIONS/CAREER NOTES: Selected by Pittsburgh Pirates organization in fifth round of free-agent draft (June 4, 1984); did not sign. . . . Selected by Pirates organization in fourth round of free-agent draft (June 2, 1987). . . . Traded by Pirates organization with OF Julio Peguero and a player to be named later to Philadelphia Phillies for OF/1B Carmelo Martinez (August 30, 1990); Phillies acquired OF Tony Longmire to complete deal (September 28, 1990). . . . On Philadelphia disabled list (August 19, 1992-remainder of season). . . . On disabled list (June 16-July 4, 1993). . . . On Philadelphia disabled list (March 25-April 19, 1994); included rehabilitation assignment to Clearwater (April 12-19). . . . Traded by Phillies with P Mike Sullivan to Boston Red Sox for P Paul Quantrill and OF Billy Hatcher (May 31, 1994). . . . Signed by Boston Red Sox (April 7, 1995). . . . Traded by Red Sox organization to Kansas City Royals organization for OF Chris James (August 14, 1995).
HONORS: Named Eastern League Most Valuable Player (1989).
STATISTICAL NOTES: Tied for New York-Pennsylvania League lead in double plays by outfielder with three in 1987. . . . Led Eastern League with 239 total bases in 1989. . . . Career major league grand slams: 2.

			BATTING												FIELDING			
Year	Team (League)	Pos.	G	AB	R	H	2B	3B	HR	RBI	Avg.	BB	SO	SB	PO	A	E	Avg.
1987—	Watertown (NYP)	OF	66	258	50	67	13	4	5	35	.260	25	48	22	121	9	7	.949
1988—	Augusta (S. Atl.)	OF	27	107	22	36	7	2	1	17	.336	11	11	1	49	4	1	.981
—	Salem (Carolina)	OF	92	365	66	100	15	1	11	50	.274	38	59	14	161	11	9	.950
1989—	Harrisburg (East.)	OF	129	471	65	*144	26	3	21	*87	.306	32	82	11	205	*14	*15	.936
1990—	Buffalo (A.A.)	OF	123	416	43	104	24	2	6	52	.250	34	58	14	203	16	9	.961
—	Philadelphia (N.L.)■	OF	18	46	9	13	3	0	2	4	.283	1	9	4	23	0	1	.958
1991—	Philadelphia (N.L.)	OF	101	383	51	92	16	3	13	50	.240	31	73	9	199	4	3	.985
—	Scran./W.B. (Int'l)	OF	39	144	12	37	7	2	2	20	.257	8	13	7	63	2	3	.956
1992—	Philadelphia (N.L.)	OF	76	275	26	71	18	0	9	41	.258	10	55	4	132	3	4	.971
—	Scran./W.B. (Int'l)	OF	34	127	16	42	6	2	4	26	.331	11	13	6	51	4	0	1.000
1993—	Philadelphia (N.L.)	OF	96	284	34	80	20	2	12	45	.282	17	51	2	131	10	1	.993
1994—	Clearwater (FSL)	OF	6	25	5	9	1	0	3	6	.360	1	1	0	5	0	0	1.000
—	Philadelphia (N.L.)	OF	24	69	7	19	5	0	2	6	.275	3	12	0	27	3	0	1.000
—	Boston (A.L.)■	OF-DH	51	164	13	42	9	1	4	20	.256	12	38	0	69	5	0	1.000
1995—	Boston (A.L.)	OF-DH	19	42	4	5	1	0	1	1	.119	3	11	1	20	1	1	.955
—	Pawtucket (Int'l)	OF-1B	48	183	28	64	17	1	12	40	.350	3	45	5	67	3	4	.946
—	Omaha (A.A.)■	OF	16	64	2	14	3	0	1	6	.219	2	15	0	24	2	0	1.000
American League totals (2 years)			70	206	17	47	10	1	5	21	.228	15	49	1	89	6	1	.990
National League totals (5 years)			315	1057	127	275	62	5	38	146	.260	62	200	19	512	20	9	.983
Major league totals (6 years)			385	1263	144	322	72	6	43	167	.255	77	249	20	601	26	10	.984

CHAMPIONSHIP SERIES RECORD

			BATTING												FIELDING			
Year	Team (League)	Pos.	G	AB	R	H	2B	3B	HR	RBI	Avg.	BB	SO	SB	PO	A	E	Avg.
1993—	Philadelphia (N.L.)	OF-PH	4	11	1	4	3	0	0	1	.364	1	3	0	2	2	0	1.000

WORLD SERIES RECORD

			BATTING												FIELDING			
Year	Team (League)	Pos.	G	AB	R	H	2B	3B	HR	RBI	Avg.	BB	SO	SB	PO	A	E	Avg.
1993—	Philadelphia (N.L.)	PH	2	2	0	0	0	0	0	0	.000	0	1	0	...	...	...	...

CHARLTON, NORM — P — MARINERS

PERSONAL: Born January 6, 1963, in Fort Polk, La. . . . 6-3/205. . . . Throws left, bats both. . . . Full name: Norman Wood Charlton III.
HIGH SCHOOL: James Madison (San Antonio).
COLLEGE: Rice (degrees in political science, religion and physical education, 1986).
TRANSACTIONS/CAREER NOTES: Selected by Montreal Expos organization in supplemental round ("sandwich pick" between first and second round, 28th pick overall) of free-agent draft (June 4, 1984); pick received as compensation for San Francisco Giants signing Type B free-agent 2B Manny Trillo. . . . Traded by Expos organization with a player to be named later to Cincinnati Reds for IF Wayne Krenchicki (March 31, 1986); Reds acquired 2B Tim Barker to complete deal (April 2, 1986). . . . On Cincinnati disabled list (April 6-June 26, 1987); included rehabilitation assignment to Nashville (June 9-26). . . . On disabled list (May 26-June 11 and June 17-July 19, 1991). . . . On suspended list (September 29 and October 4-6, 1991). . . . Traded by Reds to Seattle Mariners for OF Kevin Mitchell (November 17, 1992). . . . On suspended list (July 9-16, 1993). . . . On disabled list (July 21-August 5 and August 8, 1993-remainder of season). . . . Granted free agency (November 18, 1993). . . . Signed by Philadelphia Phillies organization (February 3, 1994). . . . On disabled list (March 31, 1994-entire season). . . . Granted free agency (October 28, 1994). . . . Re-signed by Phillies organization (December 22, 1994). . . . Released by Phillies (July 10, 1995). . . . Signed by Seattle Mariners (July 14, 1995).
STATISTICAL NOTES: Led American Association with 13 wild pitches in 1988.
MISCELLANEOUS: Appeared in one game as pinch-runner (1990). . . . Appeared in two games as pinch-runner (1991).

Year	Team (League)	W	L	Pct.	ERA	G	GS	CG	ShO	Sv.	IP	H	R	ER	BB	SO
1984—	WP Beach (FSL)	1	4	.200	4.58	8	8	0	0	0	39 1/3	51	27	20	22	27
1985—	WP Beach (FSL)	7	10	.412	4.57	24	23	5	2	0	128	135	79	65	79	71
1986—	Vermont (Eastern)■	10	6	.625	2.83	22	22	6	1	0	136 2/3	109	55	43	74	96
1987—	Nashville (A.A.)	2	8	.200	4.30	18	17	3	1	0	98 1/3	97	57	47	44	74
1988—	Nashville (A.A.)	11	10	.524	3.02	27	27	8	1	0	182	149	69	61	56	*161
—	Cincinnati (N.L.)	4	5	.444	3.96	10	10	0	0	0	61 1/3	60	27	27	20	39
1989—	Cincinnati (N.L.)	8	3	.727	2.93	69	0	0	0	0	95 1/3	67	38	31	40	98
1990—	Cincinnati (N.L.)	12	9	.571	2.74	56	16	1	1	2	154 1/3	131	53	47	70	117
1991—	Cincinnati (N.L.)	3	5	.375	2.91	39	11	0	0	1	108 1/3	92	37	35	34	77
1992—	Cincinnati (N.L.)	4	2	.667	2.99	64	0	0	0	26	81 1/3	79	39	27	26	90
1993—	Seattle (A.L.)■	1	3	.250	2.34	34	0	0	0	18	34 2/3	22	12	9	17	48
1994—	Philadelphia■	Did not play.														

Year	Team (League)	W	L	Pct.	ERA	G	GS	CG	ShO	Sv.	IP	H	R	ER	BB	SO
1995—	Philadelphia (N.L.)	2	5	.286	7.36	25	0	0	0	0	22	23	19	18	15	12
—	Seattle (A.L.)■	2	1	.667	1.51	30	0	0	0	14	47 2/3	23	12	8	16	58
A.L. totals (2 years)		3	4	.429	1.86	64	0	0	0	32	82 1/3	45	24	17	33	106
N.L. totals (6 years)		33	29	.532	3.19	263	37	1	1	29	522 2/3	452	213	185	205	433
Major league totals (7 years)		36	33	.522	3.00	327	37	1	1	61	605	497	237	202	238	539

DIVISION SERIES RECORD

Year	Team (League)	W	L	Pct.	ERA	G	GS	CG	ShO	Sv.	IP	H	R	ER	BB	SO
1995—	Seattle (A.L.)	1	0	1.000	2.45	4	0	0	0	1	7 1/3	4	2	2	3	9

CHAMPIONSHIP SERIES RECORD

Year	Team (League)	W	L	Pct.	ERA	G	GS	CG	ShO	Sv.	IP	H	R	ER	BB	SO
1990—	Cincinnati (N.L.)	1	1	.500	1.80	4	0	0	0	0	5	4	2	1	3	3
1995—	Seattle (A.L.)	1	0	1.000	0.00	3	0	0	0	1	6	1	0	0	1	5
Champ. series totals (2 years)		2	1	.667	0.82	7	0	0	0	1	11	5	2	1	4	8

WORLD SERIES RECORD

NOTES: Member of World Series championship team (1990).

Year	Team (League)	W	L	Pct.	ERA	G	GS	CG	ShO	Sv.	IP	H	R	ER	BB	SO
1990—	Cincinnati (N.L.)	0	0	...	0.00	1	0	0	0	0	1	1	0	0	0	0

ALL-STAR GAME RECORD

Year	League	W	L	Pct.	ERA	GS	CG	ShO	Sv.	IP	H	R	ER	BB	SO
1992—	National	0	0	...	0.00	0	0	0	0	1	0	0	0	0	1

CHRISTIANSEN, JASON P PIRATES

PERSONAL: Born September 21, 1969, in Omaha, Neb. . . . 6-5/234. . . . Throws left, bats right. . . . Full name: Jason Samuel Christiansen.
HIGH SCHOOL: Elkhorn (Neb.).
JUNIOR COLLEGE: Iowa Western.
COLLEGE: Cameron (Okla.).
TRANSACTIONS/CAREER NOTES: Signed as non-drafted free agent by Pittsburgh Pirates organization (July 5, 1991).

Year	Team (League)	W	L	Pct.	ERA	G	GS	CG	ShO	Sv.	IP	H	R	ER	BB	SO
1991—	GC Pirates (GCL)	1	0	1.000	0.00	6	0	0	0	1	8	4	0	0	1	8
—	Welland (NYP)	0	1	.000	2.53	8	1	0	0	0	21 1/3	15	9	6	12	17
1992—	Augusta (S. Atl.)	1	0	1.000	1.80	10	0	0	0	2	20	12	4	4	8	21
—	Salem (Carolina)	3	1	.750	3.24	38	0	0	0	2	50	47	20	18	22	59
1993—	Salem (Carolina)	1	1	.500	3.15	57	0	0	0	4	71 1/3	48	30	25	24	70
—	Carolina (South.)	0	0	...	0.00	2	0	0	0	0	2 2/3	3	0	0	1	2
1994—	Carolina (South.)	2	1	.667	2.09	28	0	0	0	2	38 2/3	30	10	9	14	43
—	Buffalo (A.A.)	3	1	.750	2.41	33	0	0	0	0	33 2/3	19	9	9	16	39
1995—	Pittsburgh (N.L.)	1	3	.250	4.15	63	0	0	0	0	56 1/3	49	28	26	34	53
Major league totals (1 year)		1	3	.250	4.15	63	0	0	0	0	56 1/3	49	28	26	34	53

CHRISTOPHER, MIKE P TIGERS

PERSONAL: Born November 3, 1963, in Petersburg, Va. . . . 6-5/205. . . . Throws right, bats right. . . . Full name: Michael Wayne Christopher.
HIGH SCHOOL: Dinwiddie (Va.) County.
COLLEGE: East Carolina.
TRANSACTIONS/CAREER NOTES: Selected by New York Yankees organization in seventh round of free-agent draft (June 3, 1985). . . . On Albany/Colonie disabled list (May 2-20, 1989). . . . Selected by Los Angeles Dodgers organization from Yankees organization in Rule 5 minor league draft (December 5, 1989). . . . Traded by Dodgers with P Dennis Cook to Cleveland Indians for P Rudy Seanez (December 10, 1991). . . . Released by Indians (November 29, 1993). . . . Signed by Toledo, Detroit Tigers organization (January 21, 1994). . . . Granted free agency (October 15, 1994). . . . Re-signed by Tigers organization (December 26, 1994).

Year	Team (League)	W	L	Pct.	ERA	G	GS	CG	ShO	Sv.	IP	H	R	ER	BB	SO
1985—	Oneonta (NYP)	8	1	.889	1.46	15	9	2	2	0	80 1/3	58	21	13	22	84
1986—	Fort Lauder. (FSL)	7	3	.700	2.63	15	14	3	1	0	102 2/3	92	37	30	36	56
—	Alb./Colon. (East.)	3	5	.375	5.04	11	11	2	0	0	60 2/3	75	48	34	12	34
1987—	Fort Lauder. (FSL)	13	8	.619	2.44	24	24	9	4	0	169 1/3	183	63	46	28	81
1988—	Alb./Colon. (East.)	13	7	.650	3.83	24	24	5	1	0	152 2/3	166	75	65	44	67
1989—	Alb./Colon. (East.)	6	1	.857	2.52	8	8	3	0	0	53 2/3	48	17	15	7	33
—	Columbus (Int'l)	5	6	.455	4.81	13	11	1	0	0	73	95	45	39	21	42
1990—	Albuquerque (PCL)■	6	1	.857	1.97	54	0	0	0	8	68 2/3	62	20	15	23	47
1991—	Albuquerque (PCL)	7	2	.778	2.44	63	0	0	0	16	77 1/3	73	25	21	30	67
—	Los Angeles (N.L.)	0	0	...	0.00	3	0	0	0	0	4	2	0	0	3	2
1992—	Colo. Springs (PCL)■	4	4	.500	2.91	49	0	0	0	26	58 2/3	59	21	19	13	39
—	Cleveland (A.L.)	0	0	...	3.00	10	0	0	0	0	18	17	8	6	10	13
1993—	Cleveland (A.L.)	0	0	...	3.86	9	0	0	0	0	11 2/3	14	6	5	2	8
—	Charlotte (Int'l)	3	6	.333	3.22	50	0	0	0	22	50 1/3	51	21	18	6	36
1994—	Toledo (Int'l)■	3	6	.333	3.52	63	0	0	0	11	71 2/3	76	33	28	18	60
1995—	Toledo (Int'l)	2	4	.333	2.23	36	0	0	0	21	36 1/3	38	14	9	8	32
—	Detroit (A.L.)	4	0	1.000	3.82	36	0	0	0	1	61 1/3	71	28	26	14	34
A.L. totals (3 years)		4	0	1.000	3.66	55	0	0	0	1	91	102	42	37	26	55
N.L. totals (1 year)		0	0	...	0.00	3	0	0	0	0	4	2	0	0	3	2
Major league totals (4 years)		4	0	1.000	3.51	58	0	0	0	1	95	104	42	37	29	57

CIANFROCCO, ARCHI — 1B — PADRES

PERSONAL: Born October 6, 1966, in Rome, N.Y. . . . 6-5/215. . . . Bats right, throws right. . . . Full name: Angelo Dominic Cianfrocco. . . . Name pronounced AR-kee SEE-un-FROCK-oh.
HIGH SCHOOL: Rome (N.Y.) Free Academy.
JUNIOR COLLEGE: Onondaga Community College (N.Y.).
COLLEGE: Purdue.
TRANSACTIONS/CAREER NOTES: Selected by Pittsburgh Pirates organization in 11th round of free-agent draft (January 14, 1986); did not sign. . . . Selected by Pirates organization in secondary phase of free-agent draft (June 2, 1986); did not sign. . . . Selected by Montreal Expos organization in fifth round of free-agent draft (June 2, 1987). . . . On disabled list (June 27, 1990-remainder of season). . . . On Ottawa disabled list (June 3-10, 1993). . . . Traded by Expos to San Diego Padres for P Tim Scott (June 23, 1993). . . . Released by Padres (November 28, 1994). . . . Re-signed by Padres organization (December 1, 1994).
STATISTICAL NOTES: Led Southern League third basemen with 37 errors in 1989. . . . Led Eastern League in being hit by pitch with nine in 1991. . . . Led Eastern League first basemen with 95 assists and 110 double plays in 1991. . . . Career major league grand slams: 1.

			BATTING												FIELDING			
Year	Team (League)	Pos.	G	AB	R	H	2B	3B	HR	RBI	Avg.	BB	SO	SB	PO	A	E	Avg.
1987—	Jamestown (NYP)	2B-SS-1B	70	251	28	62	8	4	2	27	.247	9	59	2	125	179	22	.933
1988—	Rockford (Midw.)	3B	126	455	54	115	34	0	15	65	.253	26	99	6	94	240	29	*.920
1989—	Jacksonv. (South.)	3B-2B-1B	132	429	46	105	22	7	7	50	.245	37	126	3	99	221	†38	.894
1990—	Jacksonv. (South.)	1B-3B-OF	62	196	18	43	10	0	5	29	.219	12	45	0	244	54	7	.977
1991—	Harrisburg (East.)	1B-OF	124	456	71	144	21	•10	9	77	.316	38	112	11	1023	†95	11	.990
1992—	Montreal (N.L.)	1B-3B-OF	86	232	25	56	5	2	6	30	.241	11	66	3	387	66	8	.983
—	Indianapolis (A.A.)	1B-3B-SS	15	59	12	18	3	0	4	16	.305	5	15	1	62	14	5	.938
1993—	Montreal (N.L.)	1B	12	17	3	4	1	0	1	1	.235	0	5	0	45	2	0	1.000
—	Ottawa (Int'l)	OF-1B-3B	50	188	21	56	14	2	4	27	.298	7	33	4	188	26	3	.986
—	San Diego (N.L.)■	3B-1B	84	279	27	68	10	2	11	47	.244	17	64	2	198	95	10	.967
1994—	San Diego (N.L.)	3B-1B-SS	59	146	9	32	8	0	4	13	.219	3	39	2	58	67	7	.947
—	Las Vegas (PCL)	OF-3B	32	112	11	34	11	1	1	21	.304	12	23	0	43	6	2	.961
1995—	Las Vegas (PCL)	1-3-O-C	89	322	51	100	20	2	10	58	.311	16	61	5	412	100	17	.968
—	San Diego (N.L.)	1-S-O-2-3	51	118	22	31	7	0	5	31	.263	11	28	0	111	50	3	.982
Major league totals (4 years)			292	792	86	191	31	4	27	122	.241	42	202	7	799	280	28	.975

CIRILLO, JEFF — 3B — BREWERS

PERSONAL: Born September 23, 1969, in Pasadena, Calif. . . . 6-2/188. . . . Bats right, throws right. . . . Full name: Jeffrey Howard Cirillo.
HIGH SCHOOL: Providence (Burbank, Calif.).
COLLEGE: Southern California.
TRANSACTIONS/CAREER NOTES: Selected by Chicago Cubs organization in 37th round of free-agent draft (June 2, 1987); did not sign. . . . Selected by Milwaukee Brewers organization in 11th round of free-agent draft (June 3, 1991). . . . On New Orleans disabled list (July 22-August 6, 1993).
STATISTICAL NOTES: Led Pioneer League in grounding into double plays with 11 in 1991. . . . Led Pioneer League third basemen with 60 putouts, 104 assists and 179 total chances in 1991. . . . Tied for Midwest League lead with six intentional bases on balls received in 1992.

			BATTING												FIELDING			
Year	Team (League)	Pos.	G	AB	R	H	2B	3B	HR	RBI	Avg.	BB	SO	SB	PO	A	E	Avg.
1991—	Helena (Pioneer)	3B-OF	•70	286	60	100	16	2	10	51	.350	31	28	3	†71	†104	15	.921
1992—	Stockton (Calif.)	3B	7	27	2	6	1	0	0	5	.222	2	0	0	7	10	0	1.000
—	Beloit (Midwest)	3B-2B	126	444	65	135	27	3	9	71	.304	84	85	21	115	309	26	.942
1993—	El Paso (Texas)	2B-3B	67	249	53	85	16	2	9	41	.341	26	37	2	83	142	9	.962
—	New Orleans (A.A.)	3B-2B-SS	58	215	31	63	13	2	3	32	.293	29	33	2	46	145	5	.974
1994—	New Orleans (A.A.)	3B-2B-SS	61	236	45	73	18	2	10	46	.309	28	39	4	67	139	8	.963
—	Milwaukee (A.L.)	3B-2B	39	126	17	30	9	0	3	12	.238	11	16	0	23	60	3	.965
1995—	Milwaukee (A.L.)	3-2-1-S	125	328	57	91	19	4	9	39	.277	47	42	7	113	230	15	.958
Major league totals (2 years)			164	454	74	121	28	4	12	51	.267	58	58	7	136	290	18	.959

CLARK, DAVE — OF — PIRATES

PERSONAL: Born September 3, 1962, in Tupelo, Miss. . . . 6-2/213. . . . Bats left, throws right. . . . Full name: David Earl Clark. . . . Brother of Louis Clark, wide receiver, Seattle Seahawks (1987-92).
HIGH SCHOOL: Shannon (Miss.).
COLLEGE: Jackson State.
TRANSACTIONS/CAREER NOTES: Selected by Cleveland Indians organization in first round (11th pick overall) of free-agent draft (June 6, 1983). . . . Traded by Indians to Chicago Cubs for OF Mitch Webster (November 20, 1989). . . . Released by Cubs (April 1, 1991). . . . Signed by Omaha, Kansas City Royals organization (April 29, 1991). . . . Released by Royals (December 20, 1991). . . . Signed by Pittsburgh Pirates organization (January 29, 1992). . . . On Buffalo disabled list (May 11-18, 1992). . . . On disabled list (July 26-September 11, 1995).
HONORS: Named outfielder on The Sporting News college All-America team (1983).

			BATTING												FIELDING			
Year	Team (League)	Pos.	G	AB	R	H	2B	3B	HR	RBI	Avg.	BB	SO	SB	PO	A	E	Avg.
1983—	Waterloo (Midw.)	OF	58	159	20	44	8	1	4	20	.277	19	32	2	37	4	1	.976
1984—	Waterloo (Midw.)	OF	110	363	74	112	16	3	15	63	.309	57	68	20	128	10	4	.972
—	Buffalo (Eastern)	OF	17	56	12	10	1	0	3	10	.179	9	13	1	23	2	1	.962
1985—	Waterbury (East.)	OF	132	463	75	140	24	7	12	64	.302	86	79	27	204	11	11	.951
1986—	Maine (Int'l)	OF	106	355	56	99	17	2	19	58	.279	52	70	6	150	4	6	.963
—	Cleveland (A.L.)	OF-DH	18	58	10	16	1	0	3	9	.276	7	11	1	26	0	0	1.000
1987—	Buffalo (A.A.)	OF	108	420	83	143	22	3	30	80	.340	52	62	14	181	*22	6	.971
—	Cleveland (A.L.)	OF-DH	29	87	11	18	5	0	3	12	.207	2	24	1	24	1	0	1.000
1988—	Cleveland (A.L.)	DH-OF	63	156	11	41	4	1	3	18	.263	17	28	0	36	0	2	.947
—	Colo. Springs (PCL)	OF	47	165	27	49	10	2	4	31	.297	27	37	4	85	6	3	.968

										BATTING						FIELDING			
Year	Team (League)	Pos.	G	AB	R	H	2B	3B	HR	RBI	Avg.	BB	SO	SB	PO	A	E	Avg.
1989—	Cleveland (A.L.)	DH-OF	102	253	21	60	12	0	8	29	.237	30	63	0	27	0	1	.964
1990—	Chicago (N.L.)■	OF	84	171	22	47	4	2	5	20	.275	8	40	7	60	2	0	1.000
1991—	Omaha (A.A.)■	OF-1B	104	359	45	108	24	3	13	64	.301	30	53	6	264	11	4	.986
—	Kansas City (A.L.)	OF-DH	11	10	1	2	0	0	0	1	.200	1	1	0	0	0	0	...
1992—	Buffalo (A.A.)■	OF-1B	78	253	43	77	17	6	11	55	.304	34	51	6	171	6	6	.967
—	Pittsburgh (N.L.)	OF	23	33	3	7	0	0	2	7	.212	6	8	0	10	0	0	1.000
1993—	Pittsburgh (N.L.)	OF	110	277	43	75	11	2	11	46	.271	38	58	1	132	3	6	.957
1994—	Pittsburgh (N.L.)	OF	86	223	37	66	11	1	10	46	.296	22	48	2	107	5	3	.974
1995—	Pittsburgh (N.L.)	OF	77	196	30	55	6	0	4	24	.281	24	38	3	98	1	4	.961
American League totals (5 years)			223	564	54	137	22	1	17	69	.243	57	127	2	113	1	3	.974
National League totals (5 years)			380	900	135	250	32	5	32	143	.278	98	192	13	407	11	13	.970
Major league totals (10 years)			603	1464	189	387	54	6	49	212	.264	155	319	15	520	12	16	.971

CLARK, JERALD — OF/1B

PERSONAL: Born August 10, 1963, in Crockett, Tex. . . . 6-4/205. . . . Bats right, throws right. . . . Full name: Jerald Dwayne Clark. . . . Brother of Phil Clark, outfielder/first baseman, Detroit Tigers and San Diego Padres (1992-95); and brother of Isaiah Clark, minor league infielder (1984-90).

HIGH SCHOOL: Crockett (Tex.).

COLLEGE: Lamar.

TRANSACTIONS/CAREER NOTES: Selected by Los Angeles Dodgers organization in 23rd round of free-agent draft (June 4, 1984); did not sign. . . . Selected by San Diego Padres organization in 12th round of free-agent draft (June 3, 1985). . . . On disabled list (May 1-20, 1991). . . . Selected by Colorado Rockies in first round (seventh pick overall) of expansion draft (November 17, 1992). . . . Granted free agency (December 20, 1993). . . . Signed by Yakult Swallows of Japan Central League (January 25, 1994). . . . Signed as free agent by Fort Myers, Minnesota Twins organization (March 7, 1995). . . . On disabled list (June 17-July 17 and July 18, 1995-remainder of season). . . . Granted free agency (October 5, 1995).

HONORS: Named Northwest League Most Valuable Player (1985).

STATISTICAL NOTES: Career major league grand slams: 1.

										BATTING						FIELDING			
Year	Team (League)	Pos.	G	AB	R	H	2B	3B	HR	RBI	Avg.	BB	SO	SB	PO	A	E	Avg.
1985—	Spokane (N'west)	OF	73	283	45	92	•24	3	2	50	.325	34	38	9	145	7	6	.962
1986—	Reno (California)	OF	95	389	76	118	34	3	7	58	.303	29	46	5	135	6	5	.966
—	Beaumont (Texas)	OF	16	56	9	18	4	1	0	6	.321	5	9	1	39	1	2	.952
1987—	Wichita (Texas)	OF	132	531	86	165	36	8	18	95	.311	40	82	6	262	10	3	.989
1988—	Las Vegas (PCL)	OF-3B-1B	107	408	65	123	27	7	9	67	.301	17	66	6	194	11	7	.967
—	San Diego (N.L.)	OF	6	15	0	3	1	0	0	3	.200	0	4	0	10	1	0	1.000
1989—	Las Vegas (PCL)	OF-1B	107	419	84	131	27	4	22	83	.313	38	81	5	213	8	8	.965
—	San Diego (N.L.)	OF	17	41	5	8	2	0	1	7	.195	3	9	0	16	2	1	.947
1990—	San Diego (N.L.)	1B-OF	53	101	12	27	4	1	5	11	.267	5	24	0	102	6	1	.991
—	Las Vegas (PCL)	1B-OF	40	161	30	49	7	4	12	32	.304	5	35	2	236	10	2	.992
1991—	San Diego (N.L.)	OF-1B	118	369	26	84	16	0	10	47	.228	31	90	2	245	10	2	.992
1992—	San Diego (N.L.)	OF-1B	146	496	45	120	22	6	12	58	.242	22	97	3	344	10	3	.992
1993—	Colorado (N.L.)■	OF-1B	140	478	65	135	26	6	13	67	.282	20	60	9	476	23	12	.977
1994—	Yakult (Jap. Cen.)■	...	99	376	61	110	15	1	20	53	.293	23	66	3	...	...	...	...
1995—	Minnesota (A.L.)■	OF-1B-DH	36	109	17	37	8	3	3	15	.339	2	11	3	80	4	0	1.000
American League totals (1 year)			36	109	17	37	8	3	3	15	.339	2	11	3	80	4	0	1.000
National League totals (6 years)			480	1500	153	377	71	13	41	193	.251	81	284	14	1193	52	19	.985
Major league totals (7 years)			516	1609	170	414	79	16	44	208	.257	83	295	17	1273	56	19	.986

CLARK, MARK — P — INDIANS

PERSONAL: Born May 12, 1968, in Bath, Ill. . . . 6-5/225. . . . Throws right, bats right. . . . Full name: Mark William Clark.

HIGH SCHOOL: Balyki (Bath, Ill.).

JUNIOR COLLEGE: Lincoln Land Community College (Ill.).

TRANSACTIONS/CAREER NOTES: Selected by St. Louis Cardinals organization in ninth round of free-agent draft (June 1, 1988). . . . On Arkansas disabled list (April 12-May 8, 1991). . . . Traded by Cardinals with SS Juan Andujar to Cleveland Indians for OF Mark Whiten (March 31, 1993). . . . On Cleveland disabled list (July 17-September 9, 1993 and July 21, 1994-remainder of season).

Year	Team (League)	W	L	Pct.	ERA	G	GS	CG	ShO	Sv.	IP	H	R	ER	BB	SO
1988—	Hamilton (NYP)	6	7	.462	3.05	15	15	2	0	0	94 1/3	88	39	32	32	60
1989—	Savannah (S. Atl.)	•14	9	.609	2.44	27	27	4	2	0	173 2/3	143	61	47	52	132
1990—	St. Petersburg (FSL)	3	2	.600	3.05	10	10	1	1	0	62	63	33	21	14	58
—	Arkansas (Texas)	5	11	.313	3.82	19	19	*5	0	0	115 1/3	111	56	49	37	87
1991—	Arkansas (Texas)	5	5	.500	4.00	15	15	4	1	0	92 1/3	99	50	41	30	76
—	Louisville (A.A.)	3	2	.600	2.98	7	6	1	1	0	45 1/3	43	17	15	15	29
—	St. Louis (N.L.)	1	1	.500	4.03	7	2	0	0	0	22 1/3	17	10	10	11	13
1992—	Louisville (A.A.)	4	4	.500	2.80	9	9	4	*3	0	61	56	20	19	15	38
—	St. Louis (N.L.)	3	10	.231	4.45	20	20	1	1	0	113 1/3	117	59	56	36	44
1993—	Cleveland (A.L.)■	7	5	.583	4.28	26	15	1	0	0	109 1/3	119	55	52	25	57
—	Charlotte (Int'l)	1	0	1.000	2.08	2	2	0	0	0	13	9	5	3	2	12
1994—	Cleveland (A.L.)	11	3	.786	3.82	20	20	4	1	0	127 1/3	133	61	54	40	60
1995—	Cleveland (A.L.)	9	7	.563	5.27	22	21	2	0	0	124 2/3	143	77	73	42	68
—	Buffalo (A.A.)	4	0	1.000	3.57	5	5	0	0	0	35 1/3	39	14	14	10	17
A.L. totals (3 years)		27	15	.643	4.46	68	56	7	1	0	361 1/3	395	193	179	107	185
N.L. totals (2 years)		4	11	.267	4.38	27	22	1	1	0	135 2/3	134	69	66	47	57
Major league totals (5 years)		31	26	.544	4.44	95	78	8	2	0	497	529	262	245	154	242

CLARK, PHIL — OF/1B

PERSONAL: Born May 6, 1968, in Crockett, Tex. . . . 6-0/205. . . . Bats right, throws right. . . . Full name: Phillip Benjamin Clark. . . . Brother of Jerald Clark, outfielder/first baseman, San Diego Padres, Colorado Rockies and Minnesota Twins (1988-93 and 1995); and brother of Isaiah Clark, minor league infielder (1984-90).

HIGH SCHOOL: Crockett (Tex.).

TRANSACTIONS/CAREER NOTES: Selected by Detroit Tigers organization in first round (18th pick overall) of free-agent draft (June 2, 1986). . . . Claimed on waivers by San Diego Padres (April 2, 1993). . . . Released by Padres (November 13, 1995).

STATISTICAL NOTES: Led Appalachian League catchers with 11 errors in 1986. . . . Led South Atlantic League catchers with 23 passed balls and tied for lead in errors by catcher with 21 in 1987. . . . Tied for Eastern League lead in double plays by catcher with eight in 1989.

			BATTING											FIELDING			
Year	**Team (League)**	**Pos.**	**G**	**AB**	**R**	**H**	**2B**	**3B**	**HR**	**RBI**	**Avg.**	**BB**	**SO**	**SB**	**PO**	**A**	**E**	**Avg.**
1986—	Bristol (Appal.)	C-OF	66	247	40	*82	4	2	4	36	*.332	19	42	12	354	25	†11	.972
1987—	Fayetteville (SAL)	C-OF-3B	135	*542	83	160	26	•9	8	79	.295	25	43	25	480	82	‡28	.953
1988—	Lakeland (Fla. St.)	C-OF	109	403	60	120	17	4	9	66	.298	15	43	16	413	35	8	.982
1989—	London (Eastern)	C-OF-3B	104	373	43	108	15	4	8	42	.290	31	49	2	505	56	7	.988
1990—	Toledo (Int'l)	C-OF	75	207	15	47	14	1	2	22	.227	14	35	1	156	13	2	.988
1991—	Toledo (Int'l)	OF-C	110	362	47	92	14	4	4	45	.254	21	49	6	196	12	13	.941
1992—	Toledo (Int'l)	OF-C	79	271	29	76	20	0	10	39	.280	16	35	4	145	13	7	.958
—	Detroit (A.L.)	OF-DH	23	54	3	22	4	0	1	5	.407	6	9	1	27	0	2	.931
1993—	San Diego (N.L.)■	0-1-C-3	102	240	33	75	17	0	9	33	.313	8	31	2	243	35	8	.972
1994—	San Diego (N.L.)	1-0-C-3	61	149	14	32	6	0	5	20	.215	5	17	1	148	14	4	.976
1995—	San Diego (N.L.)	OF-1B	75	97	12	21	3	0	2	7	.216	8	18	0	32	0	0	1.000
American League totals (1 year)			23	54	3	22	4	0	1	5	.407	6	9	1	27	0	2	.931
National League totals (3 years)			238	486	59	128	26	0	16	60	.263	21	66	3	423	49	12	.975
Major league totals (4 years)			261	540	62	150	30	0	17	65	.278	27	75	4	450	49	14	.973

CLARK, TERRY — P

PERSONAL: Born October 10, 1960, in Los Angeles. . . . 6-2/196. . . . Throws right, bats right. . . . Full name: Terry Lee Clark.

COLLEGE: Mount San Antonio College (Calif.).

TRANSACTIONS/CAREER NOTES: Selected by St. Louis Cardinals organization in 22nd round of free-agent draft (June 5, 1979). . . . On disabled list (May 27-August 22, 1984). . . . Granted free agency (October 15, 1985). . . . Signed by Midland, California Angels organization (February 25, 1986). . . . On California disabled list (March 19-May 3, 1989); included rehabilitation assignments to Palm Springs (April 12-20) and Edmonton (April 21-May 1). . . . Released by Angels (October 6, 1989). . . . Signed by Tucson, Houston Astros organization (January 26, 1990). . . . Granted free agency (October 15, 1991). . . . Signed by Colorado Springs, Cleveland Indians organization (January 6, 1992). . . . Released by Colorado Springs (July 23, 1992). . . . Signed by Rancho Cucamonga, San Diego Padres organization (July 1, 1993). . . . Granted free agency (October 15, 1993). . . . Signed by Atlanta Braves organization (November 24, 1993). . . . Granted free agency (May 16, 1995). . . . Signed by Rochester, Baltimore Orioles organization (June 1, 1995). . . . Granted free agency (December 21, 1995).

Year	**Team (League)**	**W**	**L**	**Pct.**	**ERA**	**G**	**GS**	**CG**	**ShO**	**Sv.**	**IP**	**H**	**R**	**ER**	**BB**	**SO**
1979—	Johns. City (App.)	4	2	.667	1.97	•23	0	0	0	*8	32	31	10	7	11	22
1980—	Gastonia (S. Atl.)	4	7	.364	3.17	49	0	0	0	0	88	82	34	31	22	50
1981—	Gastonia (S. Atl.)	4	5	.444	2.16	*53	0	0	0	0	75	56	23	18	25	66
1982—	St. Petersburg (FSL)	10	7	.588	2.55	*58	0	0	0	0	88 1/3	81	25	34	61	
1983—	Arkansas (Texas)	6	6	.500	3.21	52	0	0	0	15	81 1/3	68	31	29	19	63
1984—	Louisville (A.A.)	1	3	.250	4.72	18	1	0	0	1	34 1/3	41	19	18	12	24
1985—	Arkansas (Texas)	6	5	.545	4.93	42	7	0	0	2	96 2/3	102	64	53	38	67
1986—	Midland (Texas)■	9	4	.692	3.29	57	2	0	0	4	90 1/3	98	49	33	28	66
1987—	Edmonton (PCL)	8	9	.471	3.84	33	20	5	1	4	154 2/3	140	79	66	56	88
1988—	Edmonton (PCL)	7	6	.538	4.51	16	16	3	0	0	113 2/3	128	62	57	33	59
—	California (A.L.)	6	6	.500	5.07	15	15	2	1	0	94	120	54	53	31	39
1989—	Edmonton (PCL)	11	5	.688	3.58	21	20	4	0	0	138 1/3	130	62	55	33	90
—	California (A.L.)	0	2	.000	4.91	4	2	0	0	0	11	13	8	6	3	7
1990—	Tucson (Pac. Coast)■	11	4	.733	3.54	29	22	3	1	1	155	172	73	61	41	80
—	Houston (N.L.)	0	0	. . .	13.50	1	1	0	0	0	4	9	7	6	3	2
1991—	Tucson (Pac. Coast)	•14	7	.667	4.66	26	26	2	0	0	164	•200	104	85	37	97
1992—	Colo. Springs (PCL)■	4	4	.500	3.77	9	9	2	0	0	59 2/3	62	30	25	13	33
1993—	Rancho Cuca. (Cal.)■	0	2	.000	4.66	8	0	0	0	0	9 2/3	7	5	5	4	7
—	Wichita (Texas)	3	0	1.000	2.43	19	0	0	0	0	29 2/3	27	10	8	7	30
1994—	Richmond (Int'l)■	5	4	.556	3.02	61	0	0	0	26	83 2/3	72	33	28	27	74
1995—	Atlanta (N.L.)	0	0	. . .	4.91	3	0	0	0	0	3 2/3	3	2	2	5	2
—	Rochester (Int'l)■	1	2	.333	2.70	9	0	0	0	5	10	5	3	3	2	10
—	Baltimore (A.L.)	2	5	.286	3.46	38	0	0	0	1	39	40	15	15	15	18
A.L. totals (3 years)		8	13	.381	4.63	57	17	2	1	1	144	173	77	74	49	64
N.L. totals (2 years)		0	0	. . .	9.39	4	1	0	0	0	7 2/3	129	8	8	4	
Major league totals (4 years)		8	13	.381	4.87	61	18	2	1	1	151 2/3	185	86	82	57	68

CLARK, TONY — 1B/OF — TIGERS

PERSONAL: Born June 15, 1972, in Newton, Kan. . . . 6-8/250. . . . Bats both, throws right. . . . Full name: Anthony Christopher Clark.

HIGH SCHOOL: Valhalla (El Cajon, Calif.) and Christian (El Cajon, Calif.).

COLLEGE: Arizona and San Diego State.

TRANSACTIONS/CAREER NOTES: Selected by Detroit Tigers organization in first round (second pick overall) of free-agent draft (June 4, 1990). . . . On Niagara Falls temporarily inactive list (June 17, 1991-remainder of season and August 17, 1992-remainder of season). . . . On disabled list (August 24, 1993-remainder of season).

					BATTING										FIELDING		
Year	Team (League)	Pos.	G	AB	R	H	2B	3B	HR	RBI	Avg.	BB	SO	SB	PO	A	E	Avg.
1990—	Bristol (Appal.)	OF	25	73	2	12	2	0	1	8	.164	6	28	0	23	3	0	1.000
1991—									Did not play.									
1992—	Niag. Falls (NYP)	OF	27	85	12	26	9	0	5	17	.306	9	34	1	18	1	0	1.000
1993—	Lakeland (Fla. St.)	OF	36	117	14	31	4	1	1	22	.265	18	32	0	34	0	2	.944
1994—	Trenton (Eastern)	1B	107	394	50	110	25	0	21	86	.279	40	113	0	505	48	•13	.977
	—Toledo (Int'l)	1B	25	92	10	24	4	0	2	13	.261	12	25	2	144	12	0	1.000
1995—	Toledo (Int'l)	1B	110	405	50	98	17	2	14	63	.242	52	*129	0	615	51	*13	.981
	—Detroit (A.L.)	1B	27	101	10	24	5	1	3	11	.238	8	30	0	253	18	4	.985
Major league totals (1 year)			27	101	10	24	5	1	3	11	.238	8	30	0	253	18	4	.985

CLARK, WILL 1B RANGERS

PERSONAL: Born March 13, 1964, in New Orleans. . . . 6-1/196. . . . Bats left, throws left. . . . Full name: William Nuschler Clark Jr.
HIGH SCHOOL: Jesuit (New Orleans).
COLLEGE: Mississippi State.
TRANSACTIONS/CAREER NOTES: Selected by Kansas City Royals organization in fourth round of free-agent draft (June 7, 1982); did not sign. . . . Selected by San Francisco Giants organization in first round (second pick overall) of free-agent draft (June 3, 1985). . . . On San Francisco disabled list (June 4-July 24, 1986); included rehabilitation assignment to Phoenix (July 7-24). . . . On disabled list (August 26-September 10, 1993). . . . Granted free agency (October 25, 1993). . . . Signed by Texas Rangers (November 22, 1993).
HONORS: Named designated hitter on The Sporting News college All-America team (1984). . . . Named Golden Spikes Award winner by USA Baseball (1985). . . . Named first baseman on The Sporting News college All-America team (1985). . . . Named first baseman on The Sporting News N.L. All-Star team (1988-89 and 1991). . . . Named first baseman on The Sporting News N.L. Silver Slugger team (1989 and 1991). . . . Won N.L. Gold Glove at first base (1991).
STATISTICAL NOTES: Led N.L. first basemen with 130 double plays in 1987, 126 in 1988, 118 in 1990, 115 in 1991 and 130 in 1992. . . . Led N.L. with 27 intentional bases on balls received in 1988. . . . Led N.L. first basemen with 1,608 total chances in 1988, 1,566 in 1989 and 1,587 in 1990. . . . Led N.L. with .536 slugging percentage and tied for lead with 303 total bases in 1991. . . . Led A.L. first basemen with 1,051 total chances in 1994. . . . Career major league grand slams: 3.
MISCELLANEOUS: Member of 1984 U.S. Olympic baseball team. . . . Hit home run in first minor league at-bat (June 21, 1985) and first major league at-bat (April 8, 1986); both were on the first swing.

					BATTING										FIELDING		
Year	Team (League)	Pos.	G	AB	R	H	2B	3B	HR	RBI	Avg.	BB	SO	SB	PO	A	E	Avg.
1985—	Fresno (California)	1B-OF	65	217	41	67	14	0	10	48	.309	62	46	11	523	51	6	.990
1986—	San Francisco (N.L.)	1B	111	408	66	117	27	2	11	41	.287	34	76	4	942	72	11	.989
	—Phoenix (PCL)	DH	6	20	3	5	0	0	0	1	.250	4	2	1	. . .	. . .	. . .	. . .
1987—	San Francisco (N.L.)	1B	150	529	89	163	29	5	35	91	.308	49	98	5	1253	103	13	.991
1988—	San Francisco (N.L.)	1B	*162	575	102	162	31	6	29	*109	.282	*100	129	9	*1492	104	12	.993
1989—	San Francisco (N.L.)	1B	159	588	•104	196	38	9	23	111	.333	74	103	8	*1445	111	10	.994
1990—	San Francisco (N.L.)	1B	154	600	91	177	25	5	19	95	.295	62	97	8	*1456	119	12	.992
1991—	San Francisco (N.L.)	1B	148	565	84	170	32	7	29	116	.301	51	91	4	1273	110	4	*.997
1992—	San Francisco (N.L.)	1B	144	513	69	154	40	1	16	73	.300	73	82	12	1275	105	10	.993
1993—	San Francisco (N.L.)	1B	132	491	82	139	27	2	14	73	.283	63	68	2	1078	88	14	.988
1994—	Texas (A.L.)■	1B-DH	110	389	73	128	24	2	13	80	.329	71	59	5	*968	73	•10	.990
1995—	Texas (A.L.)	1B-DH	123	454	85	137	27	3	16	92	.302	68	50	0	1076	88	7	.994
American League totals (2 years)			233	843	158	265	51	5	29	172	.314	139	109	5	2044	161	17	.992
National League totals (8 years)			1160	4269	687	1278	249	37	176	709	.299	506	744	52	10214	812	86	.992
Major league totals (10 years)			1393	5112	845	1543	300	42	205	881	.302	645	853	57	12258	973	103	.992

CHAMPIONSHIP SERIES RECORD

NOTES: Named N.L. Championship Series Most Valuable Player (1989). . . . Holds single-series records for most hits—13; and most total bases—24 (1989). . . . Holds single-game record for most runs batted in—6 (October 4, 1989). . . . Shares single-series records for most runs—8; and most long hits—6 (1989). . . . Shares single-game records for most runs—4; and most grand slams—1 (October 4, 1989). . . . Shares record for most runs batted in in one inning—4 (October 4, 1989, fourth inning). . . . Shares N.L. single-series record for most consecutive hits—5 (1989). . . . Shares N.L. single-game record for most hits—4 (October 4, 1989).

					BATTING										FIELDING		
Year	Team (League)	Pos.	G	AB	R	H	2B	3B	HR	RBI	Avg.	BB	SO	SB	PO	A	E	Avg.
1987—	San Francisco (N.L.)	1B	7	25	3	9	2	0	1	3	.360	3	6	1	63	7	1	.986
1989—	San Francisco (N.L.)	1B	5	20	8	13	3	1	2	8	.650	2	2	0	43	6	0	1.000
Championship series totals (2 years)			12	45	11	22	5	1	3	11	.489	5	8	1	106	13	1	.992

WORLD SERIES RECORD

					BATTING										FIELDING		
Year	Team (League)	Pos.	G	AB	R	H	2B	3B	HR	RBI	Avg.	BB	SO	SB	PO	A	E	Avg.
1989—	San Francisco (N.L.)	1B	4	16	2	4	1	0	0	0	.250	1	3	0	40	2	0	1.000

ALL-STAR GAME RECORD

					BATTING									FIELDING		
Year	League	Pos.	AB	R	H	2B	3B	HR	RBI	Avg.	BB	SO	SB	PO	A	E	Avg.
1988—	National	1B	2	0	0	0	0	0	0	.000	0	0	0	4	1	0	1.000
1989—	National	1B	2	0	0	0	0	0	0	.000	0	1	0	5	0	0	1.000
1990—	National	1B	3	0	1	0	0	0	0	.333	0	0	0	6	0	0	1.000
1991—	National	1B	2	0	1	0	0	0	0	.500	1	0	0	2	0	0	1.000
1992—	National	PH-1B	2	1	1	0	0	1	3	.500	0	1	0	1	0	0	1.000
1994—	American	1B	2	0	2	0	0	0	0	1.000	0	0	1	7	0	0	1.000
All-Star Game totals (6 years)			13	1	5	0	0	1	3	.385	1	2	1	25	1	0	1.000

CLAUDIO, PATRICIO — OF — PIRATES

PERSONAL: Born April 12, 1972, in Santiago, Dominican Republic. . . . 6-0/160. . . . Bats both, throws right. . . . Full name: Patricio Ortiz Claudio.

TRANSACTIONS/CAREER NOTES: Signed as non-drafted free agent by Cleveland Indians (December 20, 1990). . . . Loaned by Indians to Bakersfield, independent (April 5-May 13, 1995). . . . Selected by Pittsburgh Pirates from Indians organization in Rule 5 major league draft (December 4, 1995).

STATISTICAL NOTES: Led Carolina League in caught stealing with 20 in 1994.

			BATTING												FIELDING			
Year	**Team (League)**	**Pos.**	**G**	**AB**	**R**	**H**	**2B**	**3B**	**HR**	**RBI**	**Avg.**	**BB**	**SO**	**SB**	**PO**	**A**	**E**	**Avg.**
1991—	Dom. Indians (DSL) ...	OF	56	185	52	63	10	2	3	21	.341	22	32	16	...	...	...	...
1992—	Burlington (Appal.).....	OF-3B	48	165	31	43	4	0	2	12	.261	20	43	20	61	1	3	.954
1993—	Columbus (S. Atl.)......	OF	98	312	48	80	8	6	0	26	.256	23	67	40	182	7	3	.984
1994—	Kinston (Carolina)	OF	121	454	56	111	16	2	1	24	.244	42	117	34	250	6	5	.981
1995—	Bakersfield (Calif.)■...	OF	32	128	19	36	9	3	1	9	.281	13	26	5	67	5	3	.960
—	Kinston (Carolina)■ ...	OF	89	298	37	79	7	4	5	27	.265	26	73	27	233	5	3	.988

CLAYTON, ROYCE — SS — CARDINALS

PERSONAL: Born January 2, 1970, in Burbank, Calif. . . . 6-0/183. . . . Bats right, throws right. . . . Full name: Royce Spencer Clayton.

HIGH SCHOOL: St. Bernard (Inglewood, Calif.).

TRANSACTIONS/CAREER NOTES: Selected by San Francisco Giants organization in first round (15th pick overall) of free-agent draft (June 1, 1988); pick received as compensation for Cincinnati Reds signing Type B free-agent OF Eddie Milner. . . . Traded by Giants with a player to be named later to St. Louis Cardinals for P Allen Watson, P Rich DeLucia and P Doug Creek (December 14, 1995); Cardinals acquired 2B Chris Wimmer to complete deal (January 16, 1996).

STATISTICAL NOTES: Led Texas League shortstops with 80 double plays in 1991. . . . Led N.L. shortstops with 103 double plays in 1993. . . . Led N.L. shortstops with 654 total chances in 1995.

			BATTING												FIELDING			
Year	**Team (League)**	**Pos.**	**G**	**AB**	**R**	**H**	**2B**	**3B**	**HR**	**RBI**	**Avg.**	**BB**	**SO**	**SB**	**PO**	**A**	**E**	**Avg.**
1988—	Everett (N'west)..........	SS	60	212	35	55	4	0	3	29	.259	27	54	10	75	166	35	.873
1989—	Clinton (Midwest).......	SS	104	385	39	91	13	3	0	24	.236	39	101	28	182	332	31	.943
—	San Jose (Calif.).........	SS	28	92	5	11	2	0	0	4	.120	13	27	10	53	71	8	.939
1990—	San Jose (Calif.).........	SS	123	460	80	123	15	10	7	71	.267	68	98	33	*202	358	37	.938
1991—	Shreveport (Texas).....	SS	126	485	84	136	22	8	5	68	.280	61	104	36	174	379	29	.950
—	San Francisco (N.L.) ..	SS	9	26	0	3	1	0	0	2	.115	1	6	0	16	6	3	.880
1992—	San Francisco (N.L.) ..	SS-3B	98	321	31	72	7	4	4	24	.224	26	63	8	142	257	11	.973
—	Phoenix (PCL)...........	SS	48	192	30	46	6	2	3	18	.240	17	25	15	81	150	7	.971
1993—	San Francisco (N.L.) ..	SS	153	549	54	155	21	5	6	70	.282	38	91	11	251	449	27	.963
1994—	San Francisco (N.L.) ..	SS	108	385	38	91	14	6	3	30	.236	30	74	23	177	330	14	.973
1995—	San Francisco (N.L.) ..	SS	138	509	56	124	29	3	5	58	.244	38	109	24	*223	•411	20	.969
Major league totals (5 years)			506	1790	179	445	72	18	18	184	.249	133	343	66	809	1453	75	.968

CLEMENS, ROGER — P — RED SOX

PERSONAL: Born August 4, 1962, in Dayton, O. . . . 6-4/230. . . . Throws right, bats right. . . . Full name: William Roger Clemens.

HIGH SCHOOL: Spring Woods (Houston).

JUNIOR COLLEGE: San Jacinto North (Tex.).

COLLEGE: Texas.

TRANSACTIONS/CAREER NOTES: Selected by New York Mets organization in 12th round of free-agent draft (June 8, 1981); did not sign. . . . Selected by Boston Red Sox organization in first round (19th pick overall) of free-agent draft (June 6, 1983). . . . On disabled list (July 8-August 3 and August 21, 1985-remainder of season). . . . On suspended list (April 26-May 3, 1991). . . . On Boston disabled list (June 19-July 16, 1993); included rehabilitation assignment to Pawtucket (July 11-16). . . . On Boston disabled list (April 16-June 2, 1995); included rehabilitation assignments to Sarasota (May 25-28) and Pawtucket (May 28-June 2).

RECORDS: Holds major league single-game record for most strikeouts (nine-inning game)—20 (April 29, 1986). . . . Shares major league record for most putouts by pitcher in one inning—3 (June 27, 1992, sixth inning). . . . Shares A.L. record for most consecutive seasons with 200 or more strikeouts—7 (1986-92). . . . Shares A.L. single-game record for most consecutive strikeouts—8 (April 29, 1986).

HONORS: Named Major League Player of the Year by The Sporting News (1986). . . . Named A.L. Pitcher of the Year by The Sporting News (1986 and 1991). . . . Named righthanded pitcher on The Sporting News A.L. All-Star team (1986-87 and 1991). . . . Named A.L. Most Valuable Player by Baseball Writers' Association of America (1986). . . . Named A.L. Cy Young Award winner by Baseball Writers' Association of America (1986-87 and 1991).

STATISTICAL NOTES: Struck out 15 batters in one game (August 21, 1984 and July 9, 1988). . . . Struck out 20 batters in one game (April 29, 1986). . . . Struck out 16 batters in one game (May 9 and July 15, 1988). . . . Pitched 6-0 one-hit, complete-game victory against Cleveland (September 10, 1988). . . . Led A.L. with 14 hit batsmen in 1995.

Year	**Team (League)**	**W**	**L**	**Pct.**	**ERA**	**G**	**GS**	**CG**	**ShO**	**Sv.**	**IP**	**H**	**R**	**ER**	**BB**	**SO**
1983—	Winter Haven (FSL)............	3	1	.750	1.24	4	4	3	1	0	29	22	4	4	0	36
—	New Britain (East.)............	4	1	.800	1.38	7	7	1	1	0	52	31	8	8	12	59
1984—	Pawtucket (Int'l)..................	2	3	.400	1.93	7	6	3	1	0	46 2/3	39	12	10	14	50
—	Boston (A.L.).......................	9	4	.692	4.32	21	20	5	1	0	133 1/3	146	67	64	29	126
1985—	Boston (A.L.).......................	7	5	.583	3.29	15	15	3	1	0	98 1/3	83	38	36	37	74
1986—	Boston (A.L.).......................	*24	4	*.857	*2.48	33	33	10	1	0	254	179	77	70	67	238
1987—	Boston (A.L.).......................	•20	9	.690	2.97	36	36	*18	*7	0	281 2/3	248	100	93	83	256
1988—	Boston (A.L.).......................	18	12	.600	2.93	35	35	•14	*8	0	264	217	93	86	62	*291
1989—	Boston (A.L.).......................	17	11	.607	3.13	35	35	8	3	0	253 1/3	215	101	88	93	230
1990—	Boston (A.L.).......................	21	6	.778	*1.93	31	31	7	•4	0	228 1/3	193	59	49	54	209
1991—	Boston (A.L.).......................	18	10	.643	*2.62	35	•35	13	*4	0	*271 1/3	219	93	79	65	*241
1992—	Boston (A.L.).......................	18	11	.621	*2.41	32	32	11	*5	0	246 2/3	203	80	66	62	208
1993—	Boston (A.L.).......................	11	14	.440	4.46	29	29	2	1	0	191 2/3	175	99	95	67	160
—	Pawtucket (Int'l)..................	0	0	...	0.00	1	1	0	0	0	3 2/3	1	0	0	4	8

Year	Team (League)	W	L	Pct.	ERA	G	GS	CG	ShO	Sv.	IP	H	R	ER	BB	SO
1994—	Boston (A.L.)	9	7	.563	2.85	24	24	3	1	0	170 2/3	124	62	54	71	168
1995—	Sarasota (Fla. St.)	0	0	...	0.00	1	1	0	0	0	4	0	0	0	2	7
—	Pawtucket (Int'l)	0	0	...	0.00	1	1	0	0	0	5	1	0	0	3	5
—	Boston (A.L.)	10	5	.667	4.18	23	23	0	0	0	140	141	70	65	60	132
Major league totals (12 years)		182	98	.650	3.00	349	348	94	36	0	2533 1/3	2143	939	845	750	2333

DIVISION SERIES RECORD

Year	Team (League)	W	L	Pct.	ERA	G	GS	CG	ShO	Sv.	IP	H	R	ER	BB	SO
1995—	Boston (A.L.)	0	0	...	3.86	1	1	0	0	0	7	5	3	3	1	5

CHAMPIONSHIP SERIES RECORD

NOTES: Holds single-series record for most hits allowed—22 (1986). . . . Shares single-series record for most earned runs allowed—11 (1986). . . . Shares single-game records for most earned runs allowed—7 (October 7, 1986); and most consecutive strikeouts—4 (October 6, 1988). . . . Holds A.L. single-series record for most innings pitched—22 2/3 (1986). . . . Shares A.L. single-game record for most runs allowed—8 (October 7, 1986).

Year	Team (League)	W	L	Pct.	ERA	G	GS	CG	ShO	Sv.	IP	H	R	ER	BB	SO
1986—	Boston (A.L.)	1	1	.500	4.37	3	3	0	0	0	22 2/3	22	12	11	7	17
1988—	Boston (A.L.)	0	0	...	3.86	1	1	0	0	0	7	6	3	3	0	8
1990—	Boston (A.L.)	0	1	.000	3.52	2	2	0	0	0	7 2/3	7	3	3	5	4
Champ. series totals (3 years)		1	2	.333	4.10	6	6	0	0	0	37 1/3	35	18	17	12	29

WORLD SERIES RECORD

Year	Team (League)	W	L	Pct.	ERA	G	GS	CG	ShO	Sv.	IP	H	R	ER	BB	SO
1986—	Boston (A.L.)	0	0	...	3.18	2	2	0	0	0	11 1/3	9	5	4	6	11

ALL-STAR GAME RECORD

NOTES: Named Most Valuable Player (1986).

Year	League	W	L	Pct.	ERA	GS	CG	ShO	Sv.	IP	H	R	ER	BB	SO
1986—	American	1	0	1.000	0.00	1	0	0	0	3	0	0	0	0	2
1988—	American	0	0	...	0.00	0	0	0	0	1	0	0	0	0	1
1990—	American						Did not play.								
1991—	American	0	0	...	9.00	0	0	0	0	1	1	1	1	0	0
1992—	American	0	0	...	0.00	0	0	0	0	1	2	0	0	0	0
All-Star totals (4 years)		1	0	1.000	1.50	1	0	0	0	6	3	1	1	0	3

CLONTZ, BRAD — P — BRAVES

PERSONAL: Born April 25, 1971, in Stuart, Va. . . . 6-1/180. . . . Throws right, bats right. . . . Full name: John Bradley Clontz.
HIGH SCHOOL: Patrick County (Stuart, Va.).
COLLEGE: Virginia Tech.
TRANSACTIONS/CAREER NOTES: Selected by Atlanta Braves organization in 10th round of free-agent draft (June 1, 1992).
HONORS: Named Southern League Outstanding Pitcher (1994).

Year	Team (League)	W	L	Pct.	ERA	G	GS	CG	ShO	Sv.	IP	H	R	ER	BB	SO
1992—	Pulaski (Appal.)	0	0	...	1.59	4	0	0	0	1	5 2/3	3	1	1	2	7
—	Macon (S. Atl.)	2	1	.667	3.91	17	0	0	0	2	23	19	14	10	10	18
1993—	Durham (Carolina)	1	7	.125	2.75	51	0	0	0	10	75 1/3	69	32	23	26	79
1994—	Greenville (South.)	1	2	.333	1.20	39	0	0	0	*27	45	32	13	6	10	49
—	Richmond (Int'l)	0	0	...	2.10	24	0	0	0	11	25 2/3	19	6	6	9	21
1995—	Atlanta (N.L.)	8	1	.889	3.65	59	0	0	0	4	69	71	29	28	22	55
Major league totals (1 year)		8	1	.889	3.65	59	0	0	0	4	69	71	29	28	22	55

DIVISION SERIES RECORD

Year	Team (League)	W	L	Pct.	ERA	G	GS	CG	ShO	Sv.	IP	H	R	ER	BB	SO
1995—	Atlanta (N.L.)	0	0	...	0.00	1	0	0	0	0	1 1/3	0	0	0	0	2

CHAMPIONSHIP SERIES RECORD

Year	Team (League)	W	L	Pct.	ERA	G	GS	CG	ShO	Sv.	IP	H	R	ER	BB	SO
1995—	Atlanta (N.L.)	0	0	...	0.00	1	0	0	0	0	1/3	1	0	0	0	0

WORLD SERIES RECORD

NOTES: Member of World Series championship team (1995).

Year	Team (League)	W	L	Pct.	ERA	G	GS	CG	ShO	Sv.	IP	H	R	ER	BB	SO
1995—	Atlanta (N.L.)	0	0	...	2.70	2	0	0	0	0	3 1/3	2	1	1	0	2

COLBRUNN, GREG — 1B — MARLINS

PERSONAL: Born July 26, 1969, in Fontana, Calif. . . . 6-0/200. . . . Bats right, throws right. . . . Full name: Gregory Joseph Colbrunn.
HIGH SCHOOL: Fontana (Calif.).
TRANSACTIONS/CAREER NOTES: Selected by Montreal Expos organization in sixth round of free-agent draft (June 2, 1987). . . . On disabled list (April 10, 1991-entire season). . . . On Indianapolis disabled list (April 9-May 5, 1992). . . . On Montreal disabled list (August 2-18, 1992); included rehabilitation assignment to Indianapolis (August 13-18). . . . On Montreal disabled list (April 5-21, 1993); included rehabilitation assignment to West Palm Beach (April 9-20). . . . On Montreal disabled list (July 12, 1993-remainder of season); included rehabilitation assignment to Ottawa (July 27-August 2). . . . Claimed on waivers by Florida Marlins (October 7, 1993). . . . On Florida disabled list (April 9-May 27, and July 15-30, 1994); included rehabilitation assignments to Brevard County (May 12-18 and July 28-30) and Edmonton (May 18-27).
STATISTICAL NOTES: Career major league grand slams: 1.

			BATTING											FIELDING			
Year	Team (League)	Pos.	G	AB	R	H	2B	3B	HR	RBI	Avg.	BB	SO	SB	PO	A	E	Avg.
1988—	Rockford (Midw.)	C	115	417	55	111	18	2	7	46	.266	22	60	5	595	81	15	.978
1989—	W.P. Beach (FSL)	C	59	228	20	54	8	0	0	25	.237	6	29	3	376	49	5	.988

Year	Team (League)	Pos.	G	AB	R	H	2B	3B	HR	RBI	Avg.	BB	SO	SB	PO	A	E	Avg.
				BATTING											FIELDING			
	—Jacksonv. (South.)	C	55	178	21	49	11	1	3	18	.275	13	33	0	304	34	4	.988
1990—	Jacksonv. (South.)	C	125	458	57	138	29	1	13	76	.301	38	78	1	698	58	15	.981
1991—									Did not play.									
1992—	Indianapolis (A.A.)	1B	57	216	32	66	19	1	11	48	.306	7	41	1	441	27	4	.992
	—Montreal (N.L.)	1B	52	168	12	45	8	0	2	18	.268	6	34	3	363	29	3	.992
1993—	W.P. Beach (FSL)	1B	8	31	6	12	2	1	1	5	.387	4	1	0	74	5	1	.988
	—Montreal (N.L.)	1B	70	153	15	39	9	0	4	23	.255	6	33	4	372	27	2	.995
	—Ottawa (Int'l)	1B	6	22	4	6	1	0	0	8	.273	1	2	1	50	1	0	1.000
1994—	Florida (N.L.)■	1B	47	155	17	47	10	0	6	31	.303	9	27	1	304	26	4	.988
	—Brevard Co. (FSL)	1B	7	11	3	6	2	0	1	2	.545	1	0	0	16	1	1	.944
	—Edmonton (PCL)	1B	7	17	2	4	0	0	1	2	.235	0	1	0	28	1	1	.967
1995—	Florida (N.L.)	1B	138	528	70	146	22	1	23	89	.277	22	69	11	1066	90	5	.996
Major league totals (4 years)			307	1004	114	277	49	1	35	161	.276	43	163	19	2105	172	14	.994

COLE, ALEX — OF — RED SOX

C

PERSONAL: Born August 17, 1965, in Fayetteville, N.C. . . . 6-0/170. . . . Bats left, throws left. . . . Full name: Alexander Cole Jr.
HIGH SCHOOL: George Wythe (Richmond, Va.).
JUNIOR COLLEGE: Manatee Junior College (Fla.).
TRANSACTIONS/CAREER NOTES: Selected by Pittsburgh Pirates organization in 11th round of free-agent draft (January 17, 1984); did not sign. . . . Selected by St. Louis Cardinals organization in second round of free-agent draft (January 9, 1985). . . . Traded by Cardinals organization with P Steve Peters to San Diego Padres for P Omar Olivares (February 27, 1990). . . . Traded by Padres organization to Cleveland Indians for C Tom Lampkin (July 11, 1990). . . . On Cleveland disabled list (May 4-26, 1991); included rehabilitation assignment to Colorado Springs (May 17-26). . . . Traded by Indians to Pirates for OF Tony Mitchell and P John Carter (July 4, 1992). . . . Selected by Colorado Rockies in first round (17th pick overall) of expansion draft (November 17, 1992). . . . Granted free agency (October 21, 1993). . . . Signed by Minnesota Twins organization (February 16, 1994). . . . On disabled list (May 31-September 19, 1995). . . . Granted free agency (October 10, 1995). . . . Signed by Boston Red Sox (January 22, 1996).
STATISTICAL NOTES: Led Appalachian League outfielders with 142 total chances in 1985. . . . Led Appalachian League in caught stealing with eight in 1985. . . . Led Florida State League in caught stealing with 22 in 1986. . . . Led Texas League in caught stealing with 29 in 1987. . . . Tied for Texas League lead in double plays by outfielder with five in 1987. . . . Led American Association outfielders with 342 total chances in 1989. . . . Tied for Pacific Coast League lead in caught stealing with 18 in 1990.

Year	Team (League)	Pos.	G	AB	R	H	2B	3B	HR	RBI	Avg.	BB	SO	SB	PO	A	E	Avg.
				BATTING											FIELDING			
1985—	Johns. City (App.)	OF	66	232	*60	61	5	1	1	13	.263	30	27	*46	*127	*12	3	.979
1986—	St. Peters. (FSL)	OF	74	286	76	98	9	1	0	26	.343	54	37	56	201	4	8	.962
	—Louisville (A.A.)	OF	63	200	25	50	2	4	1	16	.250	17	30	24	135	6	9	.940
1987—	Arkansas (Texas)	OF	125	477	68	122	12	4	2	27	.256	44	55	*68	289	14	10	.968
1988—	Louisville (A.A.)	OF	120	392	44	91	7	8	0	24	.232	42	59	40	276	13	1	.997
1989—	St. Peters. (FSL)	OF	8	32	2	6	0	0	0	1	.188	3	7	4	13	0	0	1.000
	—Louisville (A.A.)	OF	127	455	75	128	5	5	2	29	.281	71	76	*47	*320	14	8	.977
1990—	Las Vegas (PCL)■	OF	90	341	58	99	7	4	0	28	.290	47	62	32	152	6	6	.963
	—Col. Springs (PCL)■	OF	14	49	13	21	2	0	0	3	.429	8	7	6	29	0	3	.906
	—Cleveland (A.L.)	OF	63	227	43	68	5	4	0	13	.300	28	38	40	145	3	6	.961
1991—	Cleveland (A.L.)	OF-DH	122	387	58	114	17	3	0	21	.295	58	47	27	256	6	8	.970
	—Colo. Springs (PCL)	OF	8	32	6	6	0	1	0	3	.188	4	3	1	18	2	2	.909
1992—	Cleveland (A.L.)	OF-DH	41	97	11	20	1	0	0	5	.206	10	21	9	33	1	1	.971
	—Pittsburgh (N.L.)■	OF	64	205	33	57	3	7	0	10	.278	18	46	7	85	5	1	.989
1993—	Colorado (N.L.)■	OF	126	348	50	89	9	4	0	24	.256	43	58	30	219	5	4	.982
1994—	Minnesota (A.L.)■	OF-DH	105	345	68	102	15	5	4	23	.296	44	60	29	245	4	8	.969
1995—	Minnesota (A.L.)	OF-DH	28	79	10	27	3	2	1	14	.342	8	15	1	44	1	3	.938
American League totals (5 years)			359	1135	190	331	41	14	5	76	.292	148	181	106	723	15	26	.966
National League totals (2 years)			190	553	83	146	12	11	0	34	.264	61	104	37	304	10	5	.984
Major league totals (6 years)			549	1688	273	477	53	25	5	110	.283	209	285	143	1027	25	31	.971

CHAMPIONSHIP SERIES RECORD

Year	Team (League)	Pos.	G	AB	R	H	2B	3B	HR	RBI	Avg.	BB	SO	SB	PO	A	E	Avg.
				BATTING											FIELDING			
1992—	Pittsburgh (N.L.)	OF-PH	4	10	2	2	0	0	0	1	.200	3	2	0	7	1	0	1.000

COLEMAN, VINCE — OF

PERSONAL: Born September 22, 1961, in Jacksonville, Fla. . . . 6-1/185. . . . Bats both, throws right. . . . Full name: Vincent Maurice Coleman. . . . Cousin of Greg Coleman, punter, Cleveland Browns and Minnesota Vikings (1977-88).
HIGH SCHOOL: Raines (Jacksonville, Fla.).
COLLEGE: Florida A&M (degree in physical education).
TRANSACTIONS/CAREER NOTES: Selected by Philadelphia Phillies organization in 20th round of free-agent draft (June 8, 1981); did not sign. . . . Selected by St. Louis Cardinals organization in 10th round of free-agent draft (June 7, 1982). . . . Granted free agency (November 5, 1990). . . . Signed by New York Mets (December 5, 1990). . . . On disabled list (June 15-July 25 and August 14-September 27, 1991). . . . On New York disabled list (April 10-May 1, 1992). . . . On New York disabled list (May 2-28, 1992); included rehabilitation assignment to St. Lucie (May 23-28). . . . On New York disabled list (June 27-July 27, 1992). . . . Traded by Mets with cash to Kansas City Royals for OF Kevin McReynolds (January 5, 1994). . . . Granted free agency (October 20, 1994). . . . Re-signed by Omaha, Royals organization (April 26, 1995). . . . Traded by Royals to Seattle Mariners for a player to be named later (August 15, 1995); Royals acquired P Jim Converse to complete deal (August 18, 1995). . . . Granted free agency (October 31, 1995).
RECORDS: Holds major league rookie-season records for most stolen bases—110; and most times caught stealing—25 (1985). . . . Holds major league career record for most consecutive stolen bases without being caught stealing—50 (September 18, 1988 through July 26, 1989). . . . Shares major league single-game record for most sacrifice flies—3 (May 1, 1986). . . . Shares N.L. record for most consecutive seasons leading league in stolen bases—6 (1985-90). . . . Shares A.L. single-season record for fewest times caught stealing (50 or more

stolen bases)—8 (1994).

HONORS: Named South Atlantic League Most Valuable Player (1983).... Named N.L. Rookie Player of the Year by The Sporting News (1985).... Named N.L. Rookie of the Year by Baseball Writers' Association of America (1985).

STATISTICAL NOTES: Led South Atlantic League in caught stealing with 31 in 1983.... Led American Association in caught stealing with 36 in 1984.... Led American Association outfielders with 381 total chances in 1984.... Led N.L. in caught stealing with 25 in 1985, 22 in 1987 and tied for lead with 27 in 1988.... Career major league grand slams: 1.

			BATTING												FIELDING			
Year	Team (League)	Pos.	G	AB	R	H	2B	3B	HR	RBI	Avg.	BB	SO	SB	PO	A	E	Avg.
1982—	Johns. City (App.)	OF	58	212	40	53	2	1	0	16	.250	29	49	•43	123	7	8	.942
1983—	Macon (S. Atl.)	OF	113	446	99	156	8	7	0	53	*.350	56	85	*145	225	18	8	.968
1984—	Louisville (A.A.)	OF	152	*608	*97	156	21	7	4	48	.257	55	112	*101	357	14	•10	.974
1985—	Louisville (A.A.)	OF	5	21	1	3	0	0	0	0	.143	0	2	0	8	0	0	1.000
—	St. Louis (N.L.)	OF	151	636	107	170	20	10	1	40	.267	50	115	*110	305	16	7	.979
1986—	St. Louis (N.L.)	OF	154	600	94	139	13	8	0	29	.232	60	98	*107	300	12	•9	.972
1987—	St. Louis (N.L.)	OF	151	623	121	180	14	10	3	43	.289	70	126	*109	274	16	9	.970
1988—	St. Louis (N.L.)	OF	153	616	77	160	20	10	3	38	.260	49	111	*81	290	14	9	.971
1989—	St. Louis (N.L.)	OF	145	563	94	143	21	9	2	28	.254	50	90	*65	247	5	•10	.962
1990—	St. Louis (N.L.)	OF	124	497	73	145	18	9	6	39	.292	35	88	*77	244	12	5	.981
1991—	New York (N.L.)■	OF	72	278	45	71	7	5	1	17	.255	39	47	37	132	5	3	.979
1992—	New York (N.L.)	OF	71	229	37	63	11	1	2	21	.275	27	41	24	112	2	1	.991
—	St. Lucie (Fla. St.)	OF	6	22	4	8	0	0	0	2	.364	2	6	3	9	0	0	1.000
1993—	New York (N.L.)	OF	92	373	64	104	14	8	2	25	.279	21	58	38	162	5	3	.982
1994—	Kansas City (A.L.)■	OF-DH	104	438	61	105	14	12	2	33	.240	29	72	50	164	11	7	.962
1995—	Omaha (A.A.)	OF	9	38	7	15	2	0	1	5	.395	2	6	3	19	0	1	.950
—	Kansas City (A.L.)	OF-DH	75	293	39	84	13	4	4	20	.287	27	48	26	107	7	3	.974
—	Seattle (A.L.)■	OF	40	162	27	47	10	2	1	9	.290	10	32	16	83	2	1	.988
American League totals (2 years)			219	893	127	236	37	18	7	62	.264	66	152	92	354	20	11	.971
National League totals (9 years)			1113	4415	712	1175	138	70	20	280	.266	401	774	648	2066	87	56	.975
Major league totals (11 years)			1332	5308	839	1411	175	88	27	342	.266	467	926	740	2420	107	67	.974

DIVISION SERIES RECORD

			BATTING												FIELDING			
Year	Team (League)	Pos.	G	AB	R	H	2B	3B	HR	RBI	Avg.	BB	SO	SB	PO	A	E	Avg.
1995—	Seattle (A.L.)	OF	5	23	6	5	0	1	1	1	.217	2	4	1	14	0	0	1.000

CHAMPIONSHIP SERIES RECORD

NOTES: Shares N.L. career record for most times caught stealing—4.

			BATTING												FIELDING			
Year	Team (League)	Pos.	G	AB	R	H	2B	3B	HR	RBI	Avg.	BB	SO	SB	PO	A	E	Avg.
1985—	St. Louis (N.L.)	OF	3	14	2	4	0	0	0	1	.286	0	2	1	8	0	0	1.000
1987—	St. Louis (N.L.)	OF	7	26	3	7	1	0	0	4	.269	4	6	1	9	1	0	1.000
1995—	Seattle (A.L.)	OF-PH	6	200	0	2	0	0	0	0	.010	2	6	4	12	0	0	1.000
Championship series totals (3 years)			16	240	5	13	1	0	0	5	.054	6	14	6	29	1	0	1.000

WORLD SERIES RECORD

			BATTING												FIELDING			
Year	Team (League)	Pos.	G	AB	R	H	2B	3B	HR	RBI	Avg.	BB	SO	SB	PO	A	E	Avg.
1985—	St. Louis (N.L.)								Did not play.									
1987—	St. Louis (N.L.)	OF	7	28	5	4	2	0	0	2	.143	2	10	6	10	2	0	1.000
World Series totals (1 year)			7	28	5	4	2	0	0	2	.143	2	10	6	10	2	0	1.000

ALL-STAR GAME RECORD

			BATTING										FIELDING			
Year	League	Pos.	AB	R	H	2B	3B	HR	RBI	Avg.	BB	SO	SB	PO	A	E	Avg.
1988—	National	OF	2	1	1	0	0	0	0	.500	0	0	1	3	0	0	1.000
1989—	National	PR-OF	0	0	0	0	0	0	0	...	0	0	0	0	0	0	...
All-Star Game totals (2 years)			2	1	1	0	0	0	0	.500	0	0	1	3	0	0	1.000

COLES, DARNELL OF/3B

PERSONAL: Born June 2, 1962, in San Bernardino, Calif.... 6-1/185.... Bats right, throws right.

HIGH SCHOOL: Eisenhower (Rialto, Calif.).

COLLEGE: Orange Coast College (Calif.).

TRANSACTIONS/CAREER NOTES: Selected by Seattle Mariners organization in first round (sixth pick overall) of free-agent draft (June 3, 1980).... On Seattle disabled list (March 29-April 24, 1984); included rehabilitation assignment to Salt Lake (April 12-24).... On Calgary disabled list (August 8-September 9, 1985).... Traded by Mariners to Detroit Tigers for P Rich Monteleone (December 12, 1985).... On disabled list (June 16-July 1, 1986).... On Detroit disabled list (May 25-June 27, 1987); included rehabilitation assignment to Toledo (June 16-27).... Traded by Tigers organization with a player to be named later to Pittsburgh Pirates for 3B Jim Morrison (August 7, 1987); Pirates organization acquired P Morris Madden to complete deal (August 12, 1987).... Traded by Pirates to Mariners for OF Glenn Wilson (July 22, 1988).... Traded by Mariners to Tigers for OF Tracy Jones (June 18, 1990).... Granted free agency (November 5, 1990).... Signed by Phoenix, San Francisco Giants organization (March 30, 1991).... Granted free agency (October 16, 1991).... Signed by Cincinnati Reds organization (November 12, 1991).... On Cincinnati disabled list (August 26, 1992-remainder of season).... Granted free agency (October 28, 1992).... Signed by Toronto Blue Jays (November 27, 1992).... Granted free agency (October 14, 1994).... Signed by Louisville, St. Louis Cardinals organization (March 9, 1995).... Released by Cardinals (August 25, 1995).

STATISTICAL NOTES: Led Midwest League shortstops with 66 double plays in 1981.... Hit three home runs in one game (September 30, 1987, second game; and July 5, 1994).... Career major league grand slams: 3.

			BATTING												FIELDING			
Year	Team (League)	Pos.	G	AB	R	H	2B	3B	HR	RBI	Avg.	BB	SO	SB	PO	A	E	Avg.
1980—	Belling. (N'west)	SS	35	117	23	25	3	1	2	12	.214	22	24	1	37	80	*28	.807
1981—	Wausau (Midwest)	SS	111	354	53	97	20	3	9	48	.274	42	67	9	154	335	52	.904

Year	Team (League)	Pos.	G	BATTING AB	R	H	2B	3B	HR	RBI	Avg.	BB	SO	SB	FIELDING PO	A	E	Avg.
1982—	Bakersfield (Calif.)	SS	136	482	91	146	24	4	11	55	.303	68	61	27	200	419	*73	.895
1983—	Chatt. (South.)	SS	72	261	49	75	10	4	5	24	.287	41	39	12	131	232	30	.924
—	Salt Lake (PCL)	SS	61	234	43	74	12	5	10	41	.316	20	19	11	100	178	25	.917
—	Seattle (A.L.)	3B	27	92	9	26	7	0	1	6	.283	7	12	0	17	47	4	.941
1984—	Salt Lake (PCL)	3B	69	242	57	77	22	3	14	68	.318	48	41	7	45	164	16	.929
—	Seattle (A.L.)	3B-OF-DH	48	143	15	23	3	1	0	6	.161	17	26	2	31	63	8	.922
1985—	Calgary (PCL)	3B-SS-OF	31	97	16	31	8	0	4	24	.320	17	15	2	16	49	5	.929
—	Seattle (A.L.)	S-3-O-DH	27	59	8	14	4	0	1	5	.237	9	17	0	25	44	6	.920
1986—	Detroit (A.L.)■	3-DH-O-S	142	521	67	142	30	2	20	86	.273	45	84	6	111	242	23	.939
1987—	Detroit (A.L.)	3-1-O-DH-S	53	149	14	27	5	1	4	15	.181	15	23	0	84	67	17	.899
—	Toledo (Int'l)	3B-OF-SS	10	37	7	12	5	0	1	8	.324	4	2	0	7	8	1	.938
—	Pittsburgh (N.L.)■	OF-3B-1B	40	119	20	27	8	0	6	24	.227	19	20	1	39	20	3	.952
1988—	Pittsburgh (N.L.)	OF-1B-3B	68	211	20	49	13	1	5	36	.232	20	41	1	100	0	2	.980
—	Seattle (A.L.)■	OF-DH-1B	55	195	32	57	10	1	10	34	.292	17	26	3	66	3	1	.986
1989—	Seattle (A.L.)	O-3-1-DH	146	535	54	135	21	3	10	59	.252	27	61	5	317	76	12	.970
1990—	Seattle (A.L.)	OF-3B-DH	37	107	9	23	5	1	2	16	.215	4	17	0	34	0	6	.850
—	Detroit (A.L.)■	DH-O-3-1	52	108	13	22	2	0	1	4	.204	12	21	0	35	22	3	.950
1991—	Phoenix (PCL)■	3B-OF-1B	83	328	43	95	23	2	6	65	.290	27	43	0	102	118	17	.928
—	San Francisco (N.L.)	OF-1B	11	14	1	3	0	0	0	0	.214	0	2	0	4	0	0	1.000
1992—	Nashville (A.A.)■	3B-1B	22	81	19	24	5	0	6	16	.296	8	13	1	69	35	5	.954
—	Cincinnati (N.L.)	3B-1B-OF	55	141	16	44	11	2	3	18	.312	3	15	1	161	42	0	1.000
1993—	Toronto (A.L.)■	O-3-DH-1	64	194	26	49	9	1	4	26	.253	16	29	1	77	20	7	.933
1994—	Toronto (A.L.)	O-1-3-DH	48	143	15	30	6	1	4	15	.210	10	25	0	103	9	4	.966
1995—	St. Louis (N.L.)■	3B-1B-OF	63	138	13	31	7	0	3	16	.225	16	20	0	136	33	3	.983
American League totals (10 years)			699	2246	262	548	102	11	57	272	.244	179	341	17	900	593	91	.943
National League totals (5 years)			237	623	70	154	39	3	17	94	.247	58	98	3	440	95	8	.985
Major league totals (13 years)			936	2869	332	702	141	14	74	366	.245	237	439	20	1340	688	99	.953

CHAMPIONSHIP SERIES RECORD

Year	Team (League)	Pos.	G	BATTING AB	R	H	2B	3B	HR	RBI	Avg.	BB	SO	SB	FIELDING PO	A	E	Avg.
1993—	Toronto (A.L.)								Did not play.									

WORLD SERIES RECORD

NOTES: Member of World Series championship team (1993).

Year	Team (League)	Pos.	G	BATTING AB	R	H	2B	3B	HR	RBI	Avg.	BB	SO	SB	FIELDING PO	A	E	Avg.
1993—	Toronto (A.L.)								Did not play.									

CONE, DAVID — P — YANKEES

PERSONAL: Born January 2, 1963, in Kansas City, Mo. . . . 6-1/190. . . . Throws right, bats left. . . . Full name: David Brian Cone.

HIGH SCHOOL: Rockhurst (Kansas City, Mo.).

TRANSACTIONS/CAREER NOTES: Selected by Kansas City Royals organization in third round of free-agent draft (June 8, 1981). . . . On disabled list (April 8, 1983-entire season). . . . Traded by Royals with C Chris Jelic to New York Mets for C Ed Hearn, P Rick Anderson and P Mauro Gozzo (March 27, 1987). . . . On New York disabled list (May 28-August 14, 1987); included rehabilitation assignment to Tidewater (July 30-August 14). . . . Traded by Mets to Toronto Blue Jays for IF Jeff Kent and a player to be named later (August 27, 1992); Mets acquired OF Ryan Thompson to complete deal (September 1, 1992). . . . Granted free agency (October 30, 1992). . . . Signed by Royals (December 8, 1992). . . . Traded by Royals to Blue Jays for P David Sinnes, IF Chris Stynes and IF Tony Medrano (April 6, 1995). . . . Traded by Blue Jays to New York Yankees for P Marty Janzen, P Jason Jarvis and P Mike Gordon (July 28, 1995). . . . Granted free agency (November 3, 1995). . . . Re-signed by Yankees (December 21, 1995).

RECORDS: Shares major league record for striking out side on nine pitches (August 30, 1991, seventh inning). . . . Shares N.L. single-game record for most strikeouts—19 (October 6, 1991).

HONORS: Named righthanded pitcher on The Sporting News A.L. All-Star team (1994). . . . Named A.L. Cy Young Award winner by Baseball Writers' Association of America (1994).

STATISTICAL NOTES: Led Southern League with 27 wild pitches in 1984. . . . Pitched 6-0 one-hit, complete-game victory against San Diego (August 29, 1988). . . . Tied for N.L. lead with 10 balks in 1988. . . . Pitched 1-0 one-hit, complete-game victory against St. Louis (September 20, 1991). . . . Struck out 19 batters in one game (October 6, 1991). . . . Pitched 4-0 one-hit, complete-game victory against California (May 22, 1994). . . . Led A.L. with 229.1 innings pitched in 1995.

MISCELLANEOUS: Singled in only appearance as pinch-hitter (1990).

Year	Team (League)	W	L	Pct.	ERA	G	GS	CG	ShO	Sv.	IP	H	R	ER	BB	SO
1981—	GC Royals-Bl. (GCL)	6	4	.600	2.55	14	12	0	0	0	67	52	24	19	33	45
1982—	Char., S.C. (S. Atl.)	9	2	.818	2.06	16	16	1	1	0	104 2/3	84	38	24	47	87
—	Fort Myers (Fla. St.)	7	1	.875	2.12	10	9	6	1	0	72 2/3	56	21	17	25	57
1983—								Did not play.								
1984—	Memphis (South.)	8	12	.400	4.28	29	29	9	1	0	178 2/3	162	103	85	114	110
1985—	Omaha (Am. Assoc.)	9	15	.375	4.65	28	27	5	1	0	158 2/3	157	90	82	*93	115
1986—	Omaha (Am. Assoc.)	8	4	.667	2.79	39	2	2	0	14	71	60	23	22	25	63
—	Kansas City (A.L.)	0	0	. . .	5.56	11	0	0	0	0	22 2/3	29	14	14	13	21
1987—	New York (N.L.)■	5	6	.455	3.71	21	13	1	0	1	99 2/3	87	46	41	44	68
—	Tidewater (Int'l)	0	1	.000	5.73	3	3	0	0	0	11	10	8	7	6	7
1988—	New York (N.L.)	20	3	*.870	2.22	35	28	8	4	0	231 2/3	178	67	57	80	213
1989—	New York (N.L.)	14	8	.636	3.52	34	33	7	2	0	219 2/3	183	92	86	74	190
1990—	New York (N.L.)	14	10	.583	3.23	31	30	6	2	0	211 2/3	177	84	76	65	*233
1991—	New York (N.L.)	14	14	.500	3.29	34	34	5	2	0	232 2/3	204	95	85	73	*241
1992—	New York (N.L.)	13	7	.650	2.88	27	27	7	•5	0	196 2/3	162	75	63	*82	214
—	Toronto (A.L.)■	4	3	.571	2.55	8	7	0	0	0	53	39	16	15	29	47
1993—	Kansas City (A.L.)■	11	14	.440	3.33	34	34	6	1	0	254	205	102	94	114	191
1994—	Kansas City (A.L.)	16	5	.762	2.94	23	23	4	3	0	171 2/3	130	60	56	54	132

Year Team (League)	W	L	Pct.	ERA	G	GS	CG	ShO	Sv.	IP	H	R	ER	BB	SO
1995— Toronto (A.L.)■	9	6	.600	3.38	17	17	5	2	0	130 2/3	113	53	49	41	102
— New York (A.L.)■	9	2	.818	3.82	13	13	1	0	0	§99	82	42	42	47	89
A.L. totals (5 years)	49	30	.620	3.33	106	94	16	6	0	730 2/3	598	287	270	298	582
N.L. totals (6 years)	80	48	.625	3.08	182	165	34	15	1	1191 2/3	991	459	408	418	1159
Major league totals (10 years)	129	78	.623	3.17	288	259	50	21	1	1922	1589	746	678	716	1741

DIVISION SERIES RECORD

Year Team (League)	W	L	Pct.	ERA	G	GS	CG	ShO	Sv.	IP	H	R	ER	BB	SO
1995— New York (A.L.)	1	0	1.000	4.60	2	2	0	0	0	15 2/3	15	8	8	9	14

CHAMPIONSHIP SERIES RECORD

Year Team (League)	W	L	Pct.	ERA	G	GS	CG	ShO	Sv.	IP	H	R	ER	BB	SO
1988— New York (N.L.)	1	1	.500	4.50	3	2	1	0	0	12	10	6	6	5	9
1992— Toronto (A.L.)	1	1	.500	3.00	2	2	0	0	0	12	11	7	4	5	9
Champ. series totals (2 years)	2	2	.500	3.75	5	4	1	0	0	24	21	13	10	10	18

WORLD SERIES RECORD

NOTES: Member of World Series championship team (1992).

Year Team (League)	W	L	Pct.	ERA	G	GS	CG	ShO	Sv.	IP	H	R	ER	BB	SO
1992— Toronto (A.L.)	0	0	...	3.48	2	2	0	0	0	10 1/3	9	5	4	8	8

ALL-STAR GAME RECORD

Year League	W	L	Pct.	ERA	GS	CG	ShO	Sv.	IP	H	R	ER	BB	SO
1988— National	0	0	...	0.00	0	0	0	0	1	0	0	0	0	1
1992— National	0	0	...	0.00	0	0	0	0	1	0	0	0	0	1
1994— American	0	0	...	13.50	0	0	0	0	2	4	3	3	0	3
All-Star totals (3 years)	0	0	...	6.75	0	0	0	0	4	4	3	3	0	5

CONINE, JEFF — OF — MARLINS

PERSONAL: Born June 27, 1966, in Tacoma, Wash. . . . 6-1/220. . . . Bats right, throws right. . . . Full name: Jeffrey Guy Conine.

HIGH SCHOOL: Eisenhower (Yakima, Wash.).

COLLEGE: UCLA.

TRANSACTIONS/CAREER NOTES: Selected by Kansas City Royals organization in 58th round of free-agent draft (June 2, 1987). . . . On disabled list (June 28, 1991-remainder of season). . . . Selected by Florida Marlins in first round (22nd pick overall) of expansion draft (November 17, 1992).

RECORDS: Shares major league rookie-season record for most games—162 (1993).

HONORS: Named Southern League Most Valuable Player (1990).

STATISTICAL NOTES: Led Southern League first basemen with 1,164 putouts, 95 assists, 22 errors, 1,281 total chances and 108 double plays in 1990. . . . Led N.L. with 12 sacrifice flies in 1995. . . . Career major league grand slams: 2.

		BATTING												FIELDING			
Year Team (League)	Pos.	G	AB	R	H	2B	3B	HR	RBI	Avg.	BB	SO	SB	PO	A	E	Avg.
1988— Baseball City (FSL)	1B-3B	118	415	63	113	23	9	10	59	.272	46	77	26	661	51	22	.970
1989— Baseball City (FSL)	1B	113	425	68	116	12	7	14	60	.273	40	91	32	830	65	18	.980
1990— Memphis (South.)	1B-3B	137	487	89	156	37	8	15	95	.320	94	88	21	†1164	†95	†22	.983
— Kansas City (A.L.)	1B	9	20	3	5	2	0	0	2	.250	2	5	0	39	4	1	.977
1991— Omaha (A.A.)	1B-OF	51	171	23	44	9	1	3	15	.257	26	39	0	392	41	7	.984
1992— Omaha (A.A.)	1B-OF	110	397	69	120	24	5	20	72	.302	54	67	4	845	60	6	.993
— Kansas City (A.L.)	OF-1B	28	91	10	23	5	2	0	9	.253	8	23	0	75	3	0	1.000
1993— Florida (N.L.)■	OF-1B	*162	595	75	174	24	3	12	79	.292	52	135	2	403	25	2	.995
1994— Florida (N.L.)	OF-1B	115	451	60	144	27	6	18	82	.319	40	92	1	408	24	6	.986
1995— Florida (N.L.)	OF-1B	133	483	72	146	26	2	25	105	.302	66	94	2	292	18	6	.981
American League totals (2 years)		37	111	13	28	7	2	0	11	.252	10	28	0	114	7	1	.992
National League totals (3 years)		410	1529	207	464	77	11	55	266	.303	158	321	5	1103	67	14	.988
Major league totals (5 years)		447	1640	220	492	84	13	55	277	.300	168	349	5	1217	74	15	.989

ALL-STAR GAME RECORD

NOTES: Named Most Valuable Player (1995). . . . Hit home run in first at-bat (July 11, 1995).

		BATTING											FIELDING			
Year League	Pos.	AB	R	H	2B	3B	HR	RBI	Avg.	BB	SO	SB	PO	A	E	Avg.
1994— National							Did not play.									
1995— National	PH	1	1	1	0	0	1	1	1.000	0	0	0	...	...	...	...
All-Star Game totals (1 year)		1	1	1	0	0	1	1	1.000	0	0	0	...	...	...	...

CONVERSE, JIM — P — ROYALS

PERSONAL: Born August 17, 1971, in San Francisco. . . . 5-9/185. . . . Throws right, bats right. . . . Full name: James Daniel Converse.

HIGH SCHOOL: Orangevale (Calif.)-Casa Roble.

TRANSACTIONS/CAREER NOTES: Selected by Seattle Mariners organization in 16th round of free-agent draft (June 4, 1990). . . . Traded by Mariners to Kansas City Royals (August 18, 1995), completing deal in which Mariners acquired OF Vince Coleman for a player to be named later (August 15, 1995).

HONORS: Named Southern League co-Pitcher of the Year (1992).

STATISTICAL NOTES: Led Northwest League with 10 balks in 1990. . . . Tied for Pacific Coast League lead in balks with four in 1995.

Year Team (League)	W	L	Pct.	ERA	G	GS	CG	ShO	Sv.	IP	H	R	ER	BB	SO
1990— Bellingham (N'west)	2	4	.333	3.92	12	12	0	0	0	66 2/3	50	31	29	32	75
1991— Peninsula (Caro.)	6	15	.286	4.97	26	26	1	0	0	137 2/3	143	90	76	97	137
1992— Jacksonville (Sou.)	12	7	.632	2.66	27	26	2	0	0	159	134	61	47	*82	*157
1993— Calgary (PCL)	7	8	.467	5.40	23	22	•4	0	0	121 2/3	144	86	73	64	78
— Seattle (A.L.)	1	3	.250	5.31	4	4	0	0	0	20 1/3	23	12	12	14	10

Year	Team (League)	W	L	Pct.	ERA	G	GS	CG	ShO	Sv.	IP	H	R	ER	BB	SO
1994—	Calgary (PCL)	5	3	.625	5.11	14	14	0	0	0	74	105	48	42	21	53
—	Seattle (A.L.)	0	5	.000	8.69	13	8	0	0	0	48 2/3	73	49	47	40	39
1995—	Seattle (A.L.)	0	3	.000	7.36	6	1	0	0	1	11	16	9	9	8	9
—	Tacoma (PCL)	4	7	.364	5.99	17	12	0	0	0	73 2/3	96	57	49	36	43
—	Omaha (Am. Assoc.)■	1	0	1.000	0.00	4	0	0	0	0	5	1	0	0	1	9
—	Kansas City (A.L.)	1	0	1.000	5.84	9	0	0	0	0	12 1/3	12	8	8	8	5
Major league totals (3 years)		2	11	.154	7.41	32	13	0	0	1	92 1/3	124	78	76	70	63

COOK, DENNIS — P — RANGERS

PERSONAL: Born October 4, 1962, in Lamarque, Tex. . . . 6-3/190. . . . Throws left, bats left. . . . Full name: Dennis Bryan Cook.
HIGH SCHOOL: Dickinson (Tex.).
JUNIOR COLLEGE: Angelina College (Tex.).
COLLEGE: Texas.
TRANSACTIONS/CAREER NOTES: Selected by San Diego Padres organization in sixth round of free-agent draft (January 11, 1983); did not sign. . . . Selected by San Francisco Giants organization in 18th round of free-agent draft (June 3, 1985). . . . Traded by Giants with P Terry Mulholland and 3B Charlie Hayes to Philadelphia Phillies for P Steve Bedrosian and a player to be named later (June, 18, 1989); Giants organization acquired IF Rick Parker to complete deal (August 7, 1989). . . . Traded by Phillies to Los Angeles Dodgers for C Darrin Fletcher (September 13, 1990). . . . Traded by Dodgers with P Mike Christopher to Cleveland Indians for P Rudy Seanez (December 10, 1991). . . . Granted free agency (October 15, 1993). . . . Signed by Chicago White Sox organization (January 5, 1994). . . . Claimed on waivers by Indians (October 17, 1994). . . . Traded by Indians to Texas Rangers for SS Guillermo Mercedes (June 22, 1995).
HONORS: Named Texas League Pitcher of the Year (1987).
STATISTICAL NOTES: Led A.L. with five balks in 1992.
MISCELLANEOUS: Appeared in one game as pinch-runner with Philadelphia (1989). . . . Appeared in one game as pinch-runner and singled once and scored once in five games as pinch-hitter with Philadelphia (1990).

Year	Team (League)	W	L	Pct.	ERA	G	GS	CG	ShO	Sv.	IP	H	R	ER	BB	SO
1985—	Clinton (Midwest)	5	4	.556	3.36	13	13	1	0	0	83	73	35	31	27	40
1986—	Fresno (California)	12	7	.632	3.97	27	25	2	1	1	170	141	92	75	100	*173
1987—	Shreveport (Texas)	9	2	.818	2.13	16	16	1	1	0	105 2/3	94	32	25	20	98
—	Phoenix (PCL)	2	5	.286	5.23	12	11	1	0	0	62	72	45	36	26	24
1988—	Phoenix (PCL)	11	9	.550	3.88	26	25	5	1	0	141 1/3	138	73	61	51	110
—	San Francisco (N.L.)	2	1	.667	2.86	4	4	1	1	0	22	9	8	7	11	13
1989—	Phoenix (PCL)	7	4	.636	3.12	12	12	3	1	0	78	73	29	27	19	85
—	San Francisco (N.L.)	1	0	1.000	1.80	2	2	1	0	0	15	13	3	3	5	9
—	Philadelphia (N.L.)■	6	8	.429	3.99	21	16	1	1	0	106	97	56	47	33	58
1990—	Philadelphia (N.L.)	8	3	.727	3.56	42	13	2	1	1	141 2/3	132	61	56	54	58
—	Los Angeles (N.L.)■	1	1	.500	7.53	5	3	0	0	0	14 1/3	23	13	12	2	6
1991—	Albuquerque (PCL)	7	3	.700	3.63	14	14	1	0	0	91 2/3	73	46	37	32	84
—	Los Angeles (N.L.)	1	0	1.000	0.51	20	1	0	0	0	17 2/3	12	3	1	7	8
—	San Antonio (Tex.)	1	3	.250	2.49	7	7	1	0	0	50 2/3	43	20	14	10	45
1992—	Cleveland (A.L.)■	5	7	.417	3.82	32	25	1	0	0	158	156	79	67	50	96
1993—	Cleveland (A.L.)	5	5	.500	5.67	25	6	0	0	0	54	62	36	34	16	34
—	Charlotte (Int'l)	3	2	.600	5.06	12	6	0	0	0	42 2/3	46	26	24	6	40
1994—	Chicago (A.L.)■	3	1	.750	3.55	38	0	0	0	0	33	29	17	13	14	26
1995—	Cleveland (A.L.)■	0	0	. . .	6.39	11	0	0	0	0	12 2/3	16	9	9	10	13
—	Texas (A.L.)■	0	2	.000	4.00	35	1	0	0	2	45	47	23	20	16	40
A.L. totals (4 years)		13	15	.464	4.25	141	32	1	0	2	302 2/3	310	164	143	106	209
N.L. totals (4 years)		19	13	.594	3.58	94	39	5	3	1	316 2/3	286	144	126	112	152
Major league totals (8 years)		32	28	.533	3.91	235	71	6	3	3	619 1/3	596	308	269	218	361

COOKE, STEVE — P — PIRATES

PERSONAL: Born January 14, 1970, in Kauai, Hawaii. . . . 6-6/236. . . . Throws left, bats right. . . . Full name: Stephen Montague Cooke.
HIGH SCHOOL: Tigard (Ore.).
COLLEGE: Southern Idaho.
TRANSACTIONS/CAREER NOTES: Selected by Philadelphia Phillies organization in 53rd round of free-agent draft (June 1, 1988); did not sign. . . . Selected by Pittsburgh Pirates organization in 35th round of free-agent draft (June 5, 1989). . . . On Buffalo disabled list (May 18-28, 1992). . . . On Pittsburgh disabled list (April 16, 1995-entire season); included rehabilitation assignments to Augusta (July 18) and Carolina (July 24-26).

Year	Team (League)	W	L	Pct.	ERA	G	GS	CG	ShO	Sv.	IP	H	R	ER	BB	SO
1990—	Welland (NYP)	2	3	.400	2.35	11	11	0	0	0	46	36	21	12	17	43
1991—	Augusta (S. Atl.)	5	4	.556	2.82	11	11	1	0	0	60 2/3	50	28	19	35	52
—	Salem (Carolina)	1	0	1.000	4.85	2	2	0	0	0	13	14	8	7	2	5
—	Carolina (South.)	0	0	. . .	2.84	3	9	1	1	0	12 2/3	9	4	4	7	18
1992—	Carolina (South.)	2	2	.500	3.00	6	6	0	0	0	36	31	13	12	12	38
—	Buffalo (A.A.)	6	3	.667	3.75	13	13	0	0	0	74 1/3	71	35	31	36	52
—	Pittsburgh (N.L.)	2	0	1.000	3.52	11	0	0	0	1	23	22	9	9	4	10
1993—	Pittsburgh (N.L.)	10	10	.500	3.89	32	32	3	1	0	210 2/3	207	101	91	59	132
1994—	Pittsburgh (N.L.)	4	11	.267	5.02	25	23	2	0	0	134 1/3	157	79	75	46	74
1995—	Augusta (S. Atl.)	1	0	1.000	0.00	1	1	0	0	0	5	2	0	0	1	6
—	Carolina (South.)	0	0	. . .	7.20	1	1	0	0	0	5	5	4	4	5	4
Major league totals (3 years)		16	21	.432	4.28	68	55	5	1	1	368	386	189	175	109	216

COOKSON, BRENT — OF — RED SOX

PERSONAL: Born September 7, 1969, in Van Nuys, Calif. . . . 6-0/195. . . . Bats right, throws right. . . . Full name: Brent Adam Cookson.

HIGH SCHOOL: Santa Paula (Calif.).
COLLEGE: Long Beach State.
TRANSACTIONS/CAREER NOTES: Selected by Oakland Athletics organization in 15th round of free-agent draft (June 3, 1991). . . . Signed as free agent by San Francisco Giants organization (February 1, 1992). . . . On suspended list (June 6-July 29 and August 26-September 7, 1993). . . . On Phoenix disabled list (July 2-14 and July 25-September 6, 1994). . . . Traded by Giants organization to Kansas City Royals organization (June 25, 1995), completing deal in which Giants acquired P Enrique Burgos for a player to be named later (April 22, 1995). . . . Claimed on waivers by Boston Red Sox (October 6, 1995).

			BATTING												FIELDING			
Year	Team (League)	Pos.	G	AB	R	H	2B	3B	HR	RBI	Avg.	BB	SO	SB	PO	A	E	Avg.
1991	—Arizona A's (Ariz.)	OF	1	1	0	0	0	0	0	0	.000	0	1	0	0	0	0	...
	—S. Oregon (N'west)	OF	6	9	0	0	0	0	0	0	.000	0	7	0	6	0	1	.857
1992	—Clinton (Midwest)■	OF	46	145	30	31	5	1	8	20	.214	22	48	9	65	5	2	.972
	—San Jose (Calif.)	OF	68	255	44	74	8	4	12	49	.290	25	69	9	96	3	5	.952
1993	—San Jose (Calif.)	OF	67	234	43	60	10	1	17	50	.256	43	73	14	90	4	3	.969
1994	—Shreveport (Texas)	OF	62	207	32	67	21	3	11	41	.324	18	57	4	84	4	3	.967
	—Phoenix (PCL)	OF	14	43	7	12	0	1	1	6	.279	5	14	0	20	1	0	1.000
1995	—Phoenix (PCL)	OF	68	210	38	63	9	3	15	46	.300	25	36	3	86	2	3	.967
	—Omaha (A.A.)■	OF	40	137	28	55	13	0	4	20	.401	17	24	0	56	3	0	1.000
	—Kansas City (A.L.)	OF-DH	22	35	2	5	1	0	0	5	.143	2	7	1	14	0	0	1.000
Major league totals (1 year)			22	35	2	5	1	0	0	5	.143	2	7	1	14	0	0	1.000

COOMER, RON — 3B — TWINS

PERSONAL: Born November 18, 1966, in Crest Hill, Ill. . . . 5-11/195. . . . Bats right, throws right. . . . Full name: Ronald Bryan Coomer.
HIGH SCHOOL: Lockport (Ill.) Township.
COLLEGE: Taft (Calif.) College.
TRANSACTIONS/CAREER NOTES: Selected by Oakland Athletics organization in 14th round of free-agent draft (June 2, 1987). . . . Released by A's organization (August 1, 1990). . . . Signed by Chicago White Sox organization (March 18, 1991). . . . On disabled list (June 5-19, 1992). . . . On Birmingham disabled list (June 12-21, 1993). . . . Traded by White Sox organization to Los Angeles Dodgers organization for P Isidro Martinez (December 27, 1993). . . . Traded by Dodgers with P Greg Hansell, P Jose Parra and a player to be named later to Minnesota Twins for P Kevin Tapani and P Mark Guthrie (July 31, 1995); Twins acquired OF Chris Latham to complete deal (October 30, 1995).
STATISTICAL NOTES: Led Southern League with eight sacrifice flies and tied for lead in grounding into double plays with 21 in 1991. . . . Led Southern League third basemen with 94 putouts, 396 total chances, 24 double plays and tied for lead with 26 errors in 1991. . . . Led Pacific Coast League with 293 total bases in 1994. . . . Led Pacific Coast League third basemen with .952 fielding percentage, 399 total chances and 299 assists in 1994.

			BATTING												FIELDING			
Year	Team (League)	Pos.	G	AB	R	H	2B	3B	HR	RBI	Avg.	BB	SO	SB	PO	A	E	Avg.
1987	—Medford (N'west)	3B-1B	45	168	23	58	10	2	1	26	.345	19	22	1	54	78	11	.923
1988	—Modesto (Calif.)	3B-1B	131	495	67	138	23	2	17	85	.279	60	88	2	78	105	16	.920
1989	—Madison (Midwest)	3B-1B	61	216	28	69	15	0	4	28	.319	30	34	0	67	64	6	.956
1990	—Huntsville (South.)	2B-1B-3B	66	194	22	43	7	0	3	27	.222	21	40	3	200	100	11	.965
1991	—Birm. (Southern)■	3B-1B	137	505	*81	129	27	5	13	76	.255	59	78	0	†113	278	†26	.938
1992	—Vancouver (PCL)	3B	86	262	29	62	10	0	9	40	.237	16	36	3	49	115	13	.927
1993	—Birm. (Southern)	3B-1B	69	262	44	85	18	0	13	50	.324	15	43	1	43	106	11	.931
	—Nashville (A.A.)	3B	59	211	34	66	19	0	13	51	.313	10	29	1	30	107	16	.895
1994	—Albuquerque (PCL)■	3B-2B	127	535	89	181	34	6	22	*123	.338	26	62	4	81	†299	19	†.952
1995	—Albuquerque (PCL)	3B-1B	85	323	54	104	23	2	16	76	.322	18	28	5	335	93	9	.979
	—Minnesota (A.L.)■	1-3-DH-O	37	101	15	26	3	1	5	19	.257	9	11	0	138	32	2	.988
Major league totals (1 year)			37	101	15	26	3	1	5	19	.257	9	11	0	138	32	2	.988

COOPER, SCOTT — 3B

PERSONAL: Born October 13, 1967, in St. Louis. . . . 6-3/205. . . . Bats left, throws right. . . . Full name: Scott Kendrick Cooper.
HIGH SCHOOL: Pattonville (Maryland Heights, Mo.).
TRANSACTIONS/CAREER NOTES: Selected by Boston Red Sox organization in third round of free-agent draft (June 2, 1986). . . . On disabled list (August 4, 1994-remainder of season). . . . Traded by Red Sox with P Cory Bailey and a player to be named later to St. Louis Cardinals for P Rheal Cormier and OF Mark Whiten (April 8, 1995). . . . Granted free agency (December 21, 1995).
STATISTICAL NOTES: Led Carolina League with 234 total bases in 1988. . . . Led International League third basemen with 94 putouts and tied for lead with 240 assists in 1990. . . . Led International League with 11 intentional bases on balls received in 1991. . . . Led International League third basemen with 106 putouts, 232 assists, 26 errors and 364 total chances in 1991. . . . Hit for the cycle (April 12, 1994). . . . Career major league grand slams: 1.

			BATTING												FIELDING			
Year	Team (League)	Pos.	G	AB	R	H	2B	3B	HR	RBI	Avg.	BB	SO	SB	PO	A	E	Avg.
1986	—Elmira (N.Y.-Penn)	3B	51	191	23	55	9	0	9	43	.288	19	32	1	22	62	9	.903
1987	—Greensboro (S. Atl.)	3B-1B-P	119	370	52	93	21	2	15	63	.251	58	69	1	150	153	21	.935
1988	—Lynchburg (Caro.)	3B-1B-OF	130	497	90	•148	*45	7	9	73	.298	58	74	0	116	198	27	.921
1989	—New Britain (East.)	3B	124	421	50	104	24	2	7	39	.247	55	84	1	91	212	22	.932
1990	—Pawtucket (Int'l)	3B-SS	124	433	56	115	17	1	12	44	.266	39	75	2	†96	†244	22	.939
	—Boston (A.L.)	PH-PR	2	1	0	0	0	0	0	0	.000	0	1	0	...	...	...	...
1991	—Pawtucket (Int'l)	3B-SS	137	483	55	134	21	2	15	72	.277	50	58	3	†115	†241	†26	.932
	—Boston (A.L.)	3B	14	35	6	16	4	2	0	7	.457	2	2	0	6	22	2	.933
1992	—Boston (A.L.)	1-3-DH-S-2	123	337	34	93	21	0	5	33	.276	37	33	1	472	136	9	.985
1993	—Boston (A.L.)	3B-1B-SS	156	526	67	147	29	3	9	63	.279	58	81	5	112	244	24	.937
1994	—Boston (A.L.)	3B	104	369	49	104	16	4	13	53	.282	30	65	0	51	219	16	.944
1995	—St. Louis (N.L.)■	3B	118	374	29	86	18	2	3	40	.230	49	85	0	65	243	18	.945
American League totals (5 years)			399	1268	156	360	70	9	27	156	.284	127	182	6	641	621	51	.961
National League totals (1 year)			118	374	29	86	18	2	3	40	.230	49	85	0	65	243	18	.945
Major league totals (6 years)			517	1642	185	446	88	11	30	196	.272	176	267	6	706	864	69	.958

ALL-STAR GAME RECORD

Year	League	Pos.	AB	R	H	2B	3B	HR	RBI	Avg.	BB	SO	SB	PO	A	E	Avg.
			BATTING											FIELDING			
1993—	American	3B	2	0	0	0	0	0	0	.000	0	1	0	1	0	0	1.000
1994—	American	3B	2	1	1	1	0	0	1	.500	0	0	0	0	2	0	1.000
All-Star Game totals (2 years)			4	1	1	1	0	0	1	.250	0	1	0	1	2	0	1.000

RECORD AS PITCHER

Year	Team (League)	W	L	Pct.	ERA	G	GS	CG	ShO	Sv.	IP	H	R	ER	BB	SO
1987—	Greensboro (S. Atl.)	0	0	...	0.00	2	0	0	0	0	2	2	1	0	2	3

CORA, JOEY — 2B — MARINERS

PERSONAL: Born May 14, 1965, in Caguas, Puerto Rico. . . . 5-8/162. . . . Bats both, throws right. . . . Full name: Jose Manuel Cora.
COLLEGE: Vanderbilt.
TRANSACTIONS/CAREER NOTES: Selected by San Diego Padres organization in first round (23rd pick overall) of free-agent draft (June 3, 1985); pick received as compensation for New York Yankees signing free-agent P Ed Whitson. . . . On disabled list (June 22-August 15, 1986). . . . Traded by Padres with IF Kevin Garner and OF Warren Newson to Chicago White Sox for P Adam Peterson and P Steve Rosenberg (March 31, 1991). . . . On Chicago disabled list (June 22-July 11, 1991); included rehabilitation assignment to South Bend (July 9-11). . . . On Chicago disabled list (June 30-July 15, 1994); included rehabilitation assignment to South Bend (July 11-15). . . . Granted free agency (December 23, 1994). . . . Signed by Seattle Mariners (April 6, 1995).
STATISTICAL NOTES: Led Pacific Coast League second basemen with 24 errors in 1988 and 1989. . . . Led A.L. with 19 sacrifice hits in 1993. . . . Led A.L. second basemen with 19 errors in 1993 and 22 in 1995.

Year	Team (League)	Pos.	G	AB	R	H	2B	3B	HR	RBI	Avg.	BB	SO	SB	PO	A	E	Avg.
				BATTING											FIELDING			
1985—	Spokane (N'west)	2B	43	170	48	55	11	2	3	26	.324	27	24	13	92	123	9	.960
1986—	Beaumont (Texas)	2B-SS	81	315	54	96	5	5	3	41	.305	47	29	24	217	267	19	.962
1987—	San Diego (N.L.)	2B-SS	77	241	23	57	7	2	0	13	.237	28	26	15	123	200	10	.970
—	Las Vegas (PCL)	2B-SS	81	293	50	81	9	1	1	24	.276	62	39	12	186	249	9	.980
1988—	Las Vegas (PCL)	2B-3B-OF	127	460	73	136	15	3	3	55	.296	44	19	31	285	346	†26	.960
1989—	Las Vegas (PCL)	2B-SS	119	507	79	157	25	4	0	37	.310	42	31	*40	245	349	†27	.957
—	San Diego (N.L.)	SS-3B-2B	12	19	5	6	1	0	0	1	.316	1	0	1	11	15	2	.929
1990—	San Diego (N.L.)	SS-2B-C	51	100	12	27	3	0	0	2	.270	6	9	8	59	49	11	.908
—	Las Vegas (PCL)	SS-2B	51	211	41	74	13	9	0	24	.351	29	16	15	125	148	14	.951
1991—	Chicago (A.L.)■	2B-SS-DH	100	228	37	55	2	3	0	18	.241	20	21	11	107	192	10	.968
—	South Bend (Mid.)	2B	1	5	1	1	0	0	0	0	.200	0	1	1	2	4	0	1.000
1992—	Chicago (A.L.)	2-DH-S-3	68	122	27	30	7	1	0	9	.246	22	13	10	60	84	3	.980
1993—	Chicago (A.L.)	2B-3B	153	579	95	155	15	13	2	51	.268	67	63	20	296	413	†19	.974
1994—	Chicago (A.L.)	2B-DH	90	312	55	86	13	4	2	30	.276	38	32	8	162	195	8	.978
—	South Bend (Mid.)	2B	3	11	3	5	1	0	0	1	.455	2	1	1	4	8	1	.923
1995—	Seattle (A.L.)■	2B-SS	120	427	64	127	19	2	3	39	.297	37	31	18	205	262	†23	.953
American League totals (5 years)			531	1668	278	453	56	23	7	147	.272	184	160	67	830	1146	63	.969
National League totals (3 years)			140	360	40	90	11	2	0	16	.250	35	35	24	193	264	23	.952
Major league totals (8 years)			671	2028	318	543	67	25	7	163	.268	219	195	91	1023	1410	86	.966

DIVISION SERIES RECORD

Year	Team (League)	Pos.	G	AB	R	H	2B	3B	HR	RBI	Avg.	BB	SO	SB	PO	A	E	Avg.
				BATTING											FIELDING			
1995—	Seattle (A.L.)	2B	5	19	7	6	1	0	1	1	.316	3	0	1	10	12	1	.957

CHAMPIONSHIP SERIES RECORD

Year	Team (League)	Pos.	G	AB	R	H	2B	3B	HR	RBI	Avg.	BB	SO	SB	PO	A	E	Avg.
				BATTING											FIELDING			
1993—	Chicago (A.L.)	2B	6	22	1	3	0	0	0	1	.136	3	6	0	18	20	3	.927
1995—	Seattle (A.L.)	2B	6	23	3	4	1	0	0	0	.174	1	0	2	15	12	1	.964
Championship series totals (2 years)			12	45	4	7	1	0	0	1	.156	4	6	2	33	32	4	.942

CORDERO, WIL — SS — RED SOX

PERSONAL: Born October 3, 1971, in Mayaguez, Puerto Rico. . . . 6-2/195. . . . Bats right, throws right. . . . Full name: Wilfredo Nieva Cordero. . . . Name pronounced cor-DARE-oh.
HIGH SCHOOL: Centro de Servicios Educacion de Mayaguez (Puerto Rico).
TRANSACTIONS/CAREER NOTES: Signed as non-drafted free agent by Montreal Expos organization (May 24, 1988). . . . On Indianapolis disabled list (August 1, 1991-remainder of season; and May 12-June 11 and July 7-20, 1992). . . . Traded by Expos with P Bryan Eversgerd to Boston Red Sox for P Rheal Cormier, 1B Ryan McGuire and P Shayne Bennett (January 10, 1996).
HONORS: Named shortstop on The Sporting News N.L. Silver Slugger team (1994).
STATISTICAL NOTES: Career major league grand slams: 1.

Year	Team (League)	Pos.	G	AB	R	H	2B	3B	HR	RBI	Avg.	BB	SO	SB	PO	A	E	Avg.
				BATTING											FIELDING			
1988—	Jamestown (NYP)	SS	52	190	18	49	3	0	2	22	.258	15	44	3	82	159	31	.886
1989—	W.P. Beach (FSL)	SS	78	289	37	80	12	2	6	29	.277	33	58	2	121	224	29	.922
—	Jacksonv. (South.)	SS	39	121	9	26	6	1	3	17	.215	12	33	1	62	93	7	.957
1990—	Jacksonv. (South.)	SS	131	444	63	104	18	4	7	40	.234	56	122	9	179	349	41	.928
1991—	Indianapolis (A.A.)	SS	98	360	48	94	16	4	11	52	.261	26	89	9	157	287	27	.943
1992—	Indianapolis (A.A.)	SS	52	204	32	64	11	1	6	27	.314	24	54	6	75	146	12	.948
—	Montreal (N.L.)	SS-2B	45	126	17	38	4	1	2	8	.302	9	31	0	51	92	8	.947
1993—	Montreal (N.L.)	SS-3B	138	475	56	118	32	2	10	58	.248	34	60	12	163	373	36	.937
1994—	Montreal (N.L.)	SS	110	415	65	122	30	3	15	63	.294	41	62	16	124	316	22	.952
1995—	Montreal (N.L.)	SS-OF	131	514	64	147	35	2	10	49	.286	36	88	9	168	281	22	.953
Major league totals (4 years)			424	1530	202	425	101	8	37	178	.278	120	241	37	506	1062	88	.947

ALL-STAR GAME RECORD

Year	League	Pos.	BATTING AB	R	H	2B	3B	HR	RBI	Avg.	BB	SO	SB	FIELDING PO	A	E	Avg.
1994—	National	SS	2	0	0	0	0	0	0	.000	0	0	0	1	1	0	1.000

CORDOVA, MARTY — OF — TWINS

PERSONAL: Born July 10, 1969, in Las Vegas. . . . 6-0/193. . . . Bats right, throws right. . . . Full name: Martin Keevin Cordova.
HIGH SCHOOL: Bishop Gorman (Las Vegas).
JUNIOR COLLEGE: Orange Coast College (Calif.).
COLLEGE: UNLV.
TRANSACTIONS/CAREER NOTES: Selected by San Diego Padres organization in eighth round of free-agent draft (June 2, 1987); did not sign. . . . Selected by Minnesota Twins organization in 10th round of free-agent draft (June 5, 1989). . . . On disabled list (April 12-May 20, 1991 and April 7-May 11, 1994).
HONORS: Named California League Most Valuable Player (1992). . . . Named A.L. Rookie of the Year by Baseball Writers' Association of America (1995).
STATISTICAL NOTES: Led California League with 302 total bases and .589 slugging percentage and tied for lead in grounding into double plays with 20 in 1992.

Year	Team (League)	Pos.	G	BATTING AB	R	H	2B	3B	HR	RBI	Avg.	BB	SO	SB	FIELDING PO	A	E	Avg.
1989—	Elizabeth. (Appal.)	OF-3B	38	148	32	42	2	3	8	29	.284	14	29	2	6	9	4	.789
1990—	Kenosha (Midwest)	OF	81	269	35	58	7	5	7	25	.216	28	73	6	87	5	5	.948
1991—	Visalia (California)	OF	71	189	31	40	6	1	7	19	.212	17	46	2	58	2	5	.923
1992—	Visalia (California)	OF	134	513	103	175	31	6	*28	*131	.341	76	99	13	173	10	3	.984
1993—	Nashville (South.)	OF	138	508	83	127	30	5	19	77	.250	64	*153	10	209	7	2	*.991
1994—	Salt Lake (PCL)	OF	103	385	69	138	25	4	19	66	.358	39	63	17	187	13	8	.962
1995—	Minnesota (A.L.)	OF	137	512	81	142	27	4	24	84	.277	52	111	20	345	12	5	.986
Major league totals (1 year)			137	512	81	142	27	4	24	84	.277	52	111	20	345	12	5	.986

CORMIER, RHEAL — P — EXPOS

PERSONAL: Born April 23, 1967, in Moncton, New Brunswick, Canada. . . . 5-10/187. . . . Throws left, bats left. . . . Full name: Rheal Paul Cormier. . . . Name pronounced ree-AL COR-mee-AY.
JUNIOR COLLEGE: Community College of Rhode Island.
TRANSACTIONS/CAREER NOTES: Selected by St. Louis Cardinals organization in sixth round of free-agent draft (June 6, 1988). . . . On Louisville disabled list (April 10-29, 1991). . . . On disabled list (August 12-September 7, 1993). . . . On St. Louis disabled list (April 28-May 13 and May 21-August 3, 1994); included rehabilitation assignments to Arkansas (July 7-18) and Louisville (July 18-30). . . . Traded by Cardinals with OF Mark Whiten to Boston Red Sox for 3B Scott Cooper, P Cory Bailey and a player to be named later (April 8, 1995). . . . Traded by Red Sox with 1B Ryan McGuire and P Shayne Bennett to Montreal Expos for SS Wil Cordero and P Bryan Eversgerd (January 10, 1996).
MISCELLANEOUS: Member of 1988 Canadian Olympic baseball team.

Year	Team (League)	W	L	Pct.	ERA	G	GS	CG	ShO	Sv.	IP	H	R	ER	BB	SO
1989—	St. Petersburg (FSL)	12	7	.632	2.23	26	26	4	1	0	169 2/3	141	63	42	33	122
1990—	Arkansas (Texas)	5	•12	.294	5.04	22	21	3	1	0	121 1/3	133	81	68	30	102
—	Louisville (A.A.)	1	1	.500	2.25	4	4	0	0	0	24	18	8	6	3	9
1991—	Louisville (A.A.)	7	9	.438	4.23	21	21	3	*3	0	127 2/3	140	64	60	31	74
—	St. Louis (N.L.)	4	5	.444	4.12	11	10	2	0	0	67 2/3	74	35	31	8	38
1992—	Louisville (A.A.)	0	1	.000	6.75	1	1	0	0	0	4	8	4	3	0	1
—	St. Louis (N.L.)	10	10	.500	3.68	31	30	3	0	0	186	194	83	76	33	117
1993—	St. Louis (N.L.)	7	6	.538	4.33	38	21	1	0	0	145 1/3	163	80	70	27	75
1994—	St. Louis (N.L.)	3	2	.600	5.45	7	7	0	0	0	39 2/3	40	24	24	7	26
—	Arkansas (Texas)	1	0	1.000	1.93	2	2	0	0	0	9 1/3	9	2	2	0	11
—	Louisville (A.A.)	1	2	.333	4.50	3	3	1	0	0	22	21	11	11	8	13
1995—	Boston (A.L.)■	7	5	.583	4.07	48	12	0	0	0	115	131	60	52	31	69
A.L. totals (1 year)		7	5	.583	4.07	48	12	0	0	0	115	131	60	52	31	69
N.L. totals (4 years)		24	23	.511	4.12	87	68	6	0	0	438 2/3	471	222	201	75	256
Major league totals (5 years)		31	28	.525	4.11	135	80	6	0	0	553 2/3	602	282	253	106	325

DIVISION SERIES RECORD

Year	Team (League)	W	L	Pct.	ERA	G	GS	CG	ShO	Sv.	IP	H	R	ER	BB	SO
1995—	Boston (A.L.)	0	0	...	13.50	2	0	0	0	0	2/3	2	1	1	1	2

CORNELIUS, REID — P — METS

PERSONAL: Born June 2, 1970, in Thomasville, Ala. . . . 6-0/200. . . . Throws right, bats right. . . . Full name: Jonathan Reid Cornelius.
HIGH SCHOOL: Thomasville (Alabaster, Ala.).
TRANSACTIONS/CAREER NOTES: Selected by Montreal Expos organization in 11th round of free-agent draft (June 1, 1988). . . . On West Palm Beach disabled list (May 27-August 2, 1990 and May 20-June 3, 1991). . . . On Harrisburg disabled list (August 6, 1991-remainder of season and April 27-September 6, 1992). . . . On disabled list (July 12-28, 1994). . . . Traded by Expos to New York Mets for 1B/OF David Segui (June 8, 1995).

Year	Team (League)	W	L	Pct.	ERA	G	GS	CG	ShO	Sv.	IP	H	R	ER	BB	SO
1989—	Rockford (Midw.)	5	6	.455	4.27	17	17	0	0	0	84 1/3	71	58	40	63	66
1990—	WP Beach (FSL)	2	3	.400	3.38	11	11	0	0	0	56	54	25	21	25	47
1991—	WP Beach (FSL)	8	3	.727	2.39	17	17	0	0	0	109 1/3	79	31	29	43	81
—	Harrisburg (East.)	2	1	.667	2.89	3	3	1	1	0	18 2/3	15	6	6	7	12
1992—	Harrisburg (East.)	1	0	1.000	3.13	4	4	0	0	0	23	11	8	8	8	17
1993—	Harrisburg (East.)	10	7	.588	4.17	27	27	1	0	0	157 2/3	146	95	73	82	119
1994—	Ottawa (Int'l)	9	8	.529	4.38	25	24	1	0	0	148	149	89	72	75	87
1995—	Montreal (N.L.)	0	0	...	8.00	8	0	0	0	0	9	11	8	8	5	4

Year	Team (League)	W	L	Pct.	ERA	G	GS	CG	ShO	Sv.	IP	H	R	ER	BB	SO
	—Ottawa (Int'l)	1	1	.500	6.75	4	3	0	0	0	10 2/3	16	12	8	5	7
	—Norfolk (Int'l)■	7	0	1.000	0.90	10	10	1	0	0	70 1/3	57	10	7	19	43
	—New York (N.L.)	3	7	.300	5.15	10	10	0	0	0	57 2/3	64	36	33	25	35
Major league totals (1 year)		3	7	.300	5.54	18	10	0	0	0	66 2/3	75	44	41	30	39

CORNETT, BRAD — P — BLUE JAYS

PERSONAL: Born February 4, 1969, in LaMesa, Tex. . . . 6-3/190. . . . Throws right, bats right. . . . Full name: Brad Bryan Cornett.

HIGH SCHOOL: Odessa Periman (Tex.).

COLLEGE: Lubbock (Tex.) Christian.

TRANSACTIONS/CAREER NOTES: Signed as non-drafted free agent by Toronto Blue Jays organization (June 15, 1992). . . . On Toronto disabled list (May 13-June 12, 1995). . . . On Syracuse disabled list (July 21-September 3, 1995).

Year	Team (League)	W	L	Pct.	ERA	G	GS	CG	ShO	Sv.	IP	H	R	ER	BB	SO
1992	—St. Cathar. (NYP)	4	1	.800	3.60	25	0	0	0	1	60	54	30	24	10	64
1993	—Hagerstown (S. Atl.)	10	8	.556	2.40	31	21	3	1	3	172 1/3	164	77	46	31	161
1994	—Knoxville (South.)	2	3	.400	2.41	7	7	1	0	0	37 1/3	34	18	10	6	26
	—Syracuse (Int'l)	1	2	.333	1.42	3	3	0	0	0	19	18	8	3	9	12
	—Toronto (A.L.)	1	3	.250	6.68	9	4	0	0	0	31	40	25	23	11	22
1995	—Toronto (A.L.)	0	0	...	9.00	5	0	0	0	0	5	9	6	5	3	4
	—Syracuse (Int'l)	0	1	.000	4.91	3	3	0	0	0	11	13	6	6	4	3
Major league totals (2 years)		1	3	.250	7.00	14	4	0	0	0	36	49	31	28	14	26

C

CORREA, RAMSER — P — DODGERS

PERSONAL: Born November 13, 1970, in Carolina, Puerto Rico. . . . 6-5/200. . . . Throws right, bats right. . . . Full name: Ramser Andino Correa. . . . Brother of Edwin Correa, pitcher, Chicago White Sox and Texas Rangers (1985-87); and pitching coach, Great Falls Dodgers of Pioneer League.

HIGH SCHOOL: Academia Adventista Metropolitana (Carolina, Puerto Rico).

TRANSACTIONS/CAREER NOTES: Signed as a non-drafted free agent by Milwaukee Brewers organization (May 28, 1987). . . . On disabled list (June 20-June 30, 1988; May 11, 1990-remainder of season; April 12-June 16, 1991; and June 12-July 13, 1992). . . . On El Paso disabled list (April 9-May 17, 1993). . . . Granted free agency (October 15, 1993). . . . Signed by Cleveland Indians organization (December 14, 1993). . . . On Canton/Akron temporarily inactive list (April 26-May 6, 1994). . . . Granted free agency (October 15, 1994). . . . Signed by Los Angeles Dodgers organization (November 24, 1994).

Year	Team (League)	W	L	Pct.	ERA	G	GS	CG	ShO	Sv.	IP	H	R	ER	BB	SO
1987	—Helena (Pioneer)	0	1	.000	16.50	3	2	0	0	0	6	10	12	11	8	0
1988	—Helena (Pioneer)	2	2	.500	3.95	13	7	0	0	0	43 2/3	38	22	19	24	34
1989	—Helena (Pioneer)	0	0	...	0.00	2	1	0	0	0	3	3	0	0	2	2
1990	—Beloit (Midwest)	3	0	1.000	2.19	4	4	0	0	0	24 2/3	24	8	6	9	30
1991	—Stockton (Calif.)	2	1	.667	2.94	10	8	0	0	0	33 2/3	31	14	11	20	21
1992	—Stockton (Calif.)	3	2	.600	3.58	35	4	0	0	0	70 1/3	71	31	28	38	55
1993	—Stockton (Calif.)	4	3	.571	4.52	21	10	0	0	3	67 2/3	78	38	34	30	32
	—El Paso (Texas)	1	0	1.000	5.06	5	1	0	0	0	10 2/3	15	15	6	7	5
1994	—Cant./Akr. (East.)■	2	4	.333	4.28	19	8	0	0	0	67 1/3	72	41	32	51	41
	—Kinston (Carolina)	2	1	.667	4.42	4	4	0	0	0	18 1/3	14	11	9	19	17
1995	—San Antonio (Texas.)■	1	4	.200	4.53	42	0	0	0	17	49 2/3	54	29	25	21	34
	—Albuquerque (PCL)	0	0	...	0.00	2	0	0	0	0	4	5	0	0	1	3

CORREIA, ROD — SS/2B — ANGELS

PERSONAL: Born September 13, 1967, in Providence, R.I. . . . 5-11/185. . . . Bats right, throws right. . . . Full name: Ronald Douglas Correia. . . . Name pronounced KOR-ee-ah.

HIGH SCHOOL: Dighton-Rehoboth (Mass.) Regional

COLLEGE: Southeastern Massachusetts.

TRANSACTIONS/CAREER NOTES: Selected by Oakland Athletics organization in 15th round of free-agent draft (June 1, 1988). . . . On Tacoma disabled list (May 7-14, 1991). . . . Traded by A's organization to California Angels organization for OF Dan Grunhard (January 17, 1992).

STATISTICAL NOTES: Led Texas League shortstops with 621 total chances in 1992.

			BATTING												FIELDING			
Year	Team (League)	Pos.	G	AB	R	H	2B	3B	HR	RBI	Avg.	BB	SO	SB	PO	A	E	Avg.
1988	—S. Oregon (N'west)	2B-SS	56	207	23	52	7	3	1	19	.251	18	42	6	97	137	15	.940
1989	—Modesto (Calif.)	2-S-0-3	107	339	31	71	9	3	0	26	.209	34	64	7	183	197	20	.950
1990	—Modesto (Calif.)	2-3-0-S	87	246	27	60	6	3	0	16	.244	22	41	4	125	167	18	.942
1991	—Modesto (Calif.)	3B-2B	5	19	8	5	0	0	0	3	.263	2	1	1	7	6	1	.929
	—Tacoma (PCL)	3B-2B	17	56	9	14	0	0	1	7	.250	4	6	0	23	41	3	.955
	—Huntsville (South.)	2-S-0-3	87	290	25	64	10	1	1	22	.221	31	50	2	142	162	17	.947
1992	—Midland (Texas)■	SS	123	482	73	140	23	1	6	56	.290	28	72	20	*204	*385	32	.948
1993	—Vancouver (PCL)	SS-2B	60	207	43	56	10	4	4	28	.271	15	25	11	105	159	14	.950
	—California (A.L.)	S-2-DH-3	64	128	12	34	5	0	0	9	.266	6	20	2	87	121	3	.986
1994	—Vancouver (PCL)	SS-2B	106	376	54	103	12	3	6	49	.274	25	54	8	155	334	23	.955
	—California (A.L.)	2B-SS	6	17	4	4	1	0	0	0	.235	0	0	0	12	9	0	1.000
1995	—Vancouver (PCL)	SS-2B-3B	73	264	42	80	6	5	1	39	.303	26	33	8	125	222	16	.956
	—California (A.L.)	S-2-3-DH	14	21	3	5	1	1	0	3	.238	0	5	0	6	20	5	.839
Major league totals (3 years)			84	166	19	43	7	1	0	12	.259	6	25	2	105	150	8	.970

CORSI, JIM — P — ATHLETICS

PERSONAL: Born September 9, 1961, in Newton, Mass. . . . 6-1/220. . . . Throws right, bats right. . . . Full name: James Bernard Corsi.
HIGH SCHOOL: Newton (Mass.) North.
COLLEGE: St. Leo (Fla.) College (bachelor of arts degree in management).
TRANSACTIONS/CAREER NOTES: Selected by New York Yankees organization in 25th round of free-agent draft (June 7, 1982). . . . On Fort Lauderdale disabled list (April 8-May 11, 1983). . . . Released by Yankees organization (April 3, 1984). . . . Signed by Greensboro, Boston Red Sox organization (April 1, 1985). . . . Released by Red Sox organization (January 31, 1986). . . . Re-signed by Red Sox organization (April 5, 1986). . . . Released by Red Sox organization (April 2, 1987). . . . Signed by Modesto, Oakland Athletics organization (April 12, 1987). . . . On Oakland disabled list (March 29, 1990-entire season); included rehabilitation assignment to Tacoma (June 29-July 25). . . . Granted free agency (December 20, 1990). . . . Signed by Tucson, Houston Astros organization (March 19, 1991). . . . Released by Astros (November 18, 1991). . . . Signed by Tacoma, A's organization (March 16, 1992). . . . Selected by Florida Marlins in second round (49th pick overall) of expansion draft (November 17, 1992). . . . On Florida disabled list (March 27-April 30, 1993); included rehabilitation assignment to High Desert (April 20-30). . . . On Florida disabled list (July 6, 1993-remainder of season). . . . Granted free agency (October 15, 1993). . . . Re-signed by Marlins organization (January 24, 1994). . . . On Brevard County disabled list (April 11-July 5, 1994). . . . Granted free agency (October 15, 1994). . . . Signed by Edmonton, A's organization (January 20, 1995). . . . On Oakland disabled list (June 22-August 8, 1995).

Year	Team (League)	W	L	Pct.	ERA	G	GS	CG	ShO	Sv.	IP	H	R	ER	BB	SO
1982	Oneonta (NYP)	0	0	...	10.80	1	0	0	0	0	3 1/3	5	4	4	2	6
	Paintsville (Appal.)	0	2	.000	2.90	8	4	0	0	0	31	32	11	10	13	20
1983	Greensboro (S. Atl.)	2	2	.500	4.09	12	7	1	0	1	50 2/3	59	37	23	33	37
	Oneonta (NYP)	3	6	.333	4.25	11	10	2	0	0	59 1/3	76	38	28	21	47
1984		Out of organized baseball.														
1985	Greensboro (S. Atl.)■	5	8	.385	4.23	41	2	1	0	9	78 2/3	94	49	37	23	84
1986	New Britain (East.)	2	3	.400	2.28	29	0	0	0	3	51 1/3	52	13	13	20	38
1987	Modesto (Calif.)■	3	1	.750	3.60	19	0	0	0	6	30	23	16	12	10	45
	Huntsville (South.)	8	1	.889	2.81	28	0	0	0	4	48	30	17	15	15	33
1988	Tacoma (PCL)	2	5	.286	2.75	50	0	0	0	16	59	60	25	18	23	48
	Oakland (A.L.)	0	1	.000	3.80	11	1	0	0	0	21 1/3	20	10	9	6	10
1989	Tacoma (PCL)	2	3	.400	4.13	23	0	0	0	8	28 1/3	40	17	13	9	23
	Oakland (A.L.)	1	2	.333	1.88	22	0	0	0	0	38 1/3	26	8	8	10	21
1990	Tacoma (PCL)	0	0	...	1.50	5	0	0	0	0	6	9	2	1	1	3
1991	Tucson (PCL)■	0	0	...	0.00	2	0	0	0	0	3	2	0	0	0	4
	Houston (N.L.)	0	5	.000	3.71	47	0	0	0	0	77 2/3	76	37	32	23	53
1992	Tacoma (PCL)■	0	0	...	1.23	26	0	0	0	12	29 1/3	22	8	4	10	21
	Oakland (A.L.)	4	2	.667	1.43	32	0	0	0	0	44	44	12	7	18	19
1993	High Desert (Calif.)■	0	1	.000	3.00	3	3	0	0	0	9	11	3	3	2	6
	Florida (N.L.)	0	2	.000	6.64	15	0	0	0	0	20 1/3	28	15	15	10	7
1994	Brevard Co. (FSL)	0	1	.000	1.64	6	0	0	0	0	11	8	3	2	0	11
	Edmonton (PCL)	0	1	.000	4.50	15	0	0	0	0	22	29	15	11	10	15
1995	Edmonton (PCL)■	0	0	...	0.00	3	0	0	0	3	3	0	0	0	1	3
	Oakland (A.L.)	2	4	.333	2.20	38	0	0	0	2	45	31	14	11	26	26
A.L. totals (4 years)		7	9	.438	2.12	103	1	0	0	2	148 2/3	121	44	35	60	76
N.L. totals (2 years)		0	7	.000	4.32	62	0	0	0	0	98	104	52	47	33	60
Major league totals (6 years)		7	16	.304	2.99	165	1	0	0	2	246 2/3	225	96	82	93	136

CHAMPIONSHIP SERIES RECORD

Year	Team (League)	W	L	Pct.	ERA	G	GS	CG	ShO	Sv.	IP	H	R	ER	BB	SO
1992	Oakland (A.L.)	0	0	...	0.00	3	0	0	0	0	2	2	0	0	3	0

COUNSELL, CRAIG — SS/2B — ROCKIES

PERSONAL: Born August 21, 1970, in South Bend, Ind. . . . 6-0/170. . . . Bats left, throws right. . . . Full name: Craig John Counsell. . . . Son of John Counsell, outfielder, Minnesota Twins organization (1964-68).
HIGH SCHOOL: Whitefish Bay (Milwaukee).
COLLEGE: Notre Dame.
TRANSACTIONS/CAREER NOTES: Selected by Colorado Rockies organization in 11th round of free-agent draft (June 1, 1992). . . . On disabled list (April 7-May 13, July 30-August 6 and August 7-27, 1994).
STATISTICAL NOTES: Led California League shortstops with 621 total chances in 1993. . . . Led Pacific Coast League shortstops with 598 total chances and 86 double plays in 1995.

			BATTING												FIELDING			
Year	Team (League)	Pos.	G	AB	R	H	2B	3B	HR	RBI	Avg.	BB	SO	SB	PO	A	E	Avg.
1992	Bend (Northwest)	2B-SS	18	61	11	15	6	1	0	8	.246	9	10	1	23	36	2	.967
1993	Central Valley (Cal.)	SS	131	471	79	132	26	3	5	59	.280	95	68	14	*233	353	35	.944
1994	New Haven (East.)	SS-2B	83	300	47	84	20	1	5	37	.280	37	32	4	122	242	27	.931
1995	Colo. Springs (PCL)	SS	118	399	60	112	22	6	5	53	.281	34	47	10	182	386	30	.950
	Colorado (N.L.)	SS	3	1	0	0	0	0	0	0	.000	1	0	0	1	1	0	1.000
Major league totals (1 year)			3	1	0	0	0	0	0	0	.000	1	0	0	1	1	0	1.000

COURTRIGHT, JOHN — P — TWINS

PERSONAL: Born May 30, 1970, in Marion, O. . . . 6-2/185. . . . Throws left, bats left. . . . Full name: John Charles Courtright.
HIGH SCHOOL: Harding (Marion, O.).
COLLEGE: Duke.
TRANSACTIONS/CAREER NOTES: Selected by Cincinnati Reds organization in eighth round of free-agent draft (June 3, 1991). . . . Traded by Reds to Minnesota Twins for 1B Dave McCarthy (June 8, 1995).

Year	Team (League)	W	L	Pct.	ERA	G	GS	CG	ShO	Sv.	IP	H	R	ER	BB	SO
1991—	Billings (Pioneer)	1	0	1.000	0.00	1	1	0	0	0	6	2	0	0	1	4
1992—	Char., W.Va. (S. Atl.)	10	5	.667	2.50	27	26	1	1	0	173	147	64	48	55	147
1993—	Chattanooga (Sou.)	5	11	.313	3.50	27	27	1	0	0	175	179	81	68	70	96
1994—	Chattanooga (Sou.)	1	2	.333	5.40	4	4	0	0	0	21 2/3	19	16	13	14	12
	—Indianapolis (A.A.)	9	10	.474	3.55	24	23	2	2	0	142	144	61	56	46	73
1995—	Indianapolis (A.A.)	2	1	.667	4.28	13	2	0	0	0	33 2/3	29	18	16	15	13
	—Cincinnati (N.L.)	0	0	...	9.00	1	0	0	0	0	1	2	1	1	0	0
	—Salt Lake (PCL)■	3	7	.300	6.80	18	17	1	0	0	84 2/3	108	70	64	36	42
Major league totals (1 year)		0	0	...	9.00	1	0	0	0	0	1	2	1	1	0	0

COX, DANNY — P — BLUE JAYS

PERSONAL: Born September 21, 1959, in Northampton, England. . . . 6-4/250. . . . Throws right, bats right. . . . Full name: Danny Bradford Cox.

HIGH SCHOOL: Warner Robins (Ga.).

JUNIOR COLLEGE: Chattahoochee Valley (Ala.).

COLLEGE: Troy (Ala.) State.

TRANSACTIONS/CAREER NOTES: Selected by St. Louis Cardinals organization in 13th round of free-agent draft (June 8, 1981). . . . On Arkansas disabled list (April 8-21, 1983). . . . On St. Louis disabled list (March 30-April 24, 1986); included rehabilitation assignment to Louisville (April 17-24). . . . On disabled list (July 10-August 8, 1987). . . . On St. Louis disabled list (April 30-June 27, 1988); included rehabilitation assignment to Louisville (June 16-27). . . . On St. Louis disabled list (August 7, 1988-remainder of season). . . . On disabled list (March 27, 1989-entire season). . . . Granted free agency (November 13, 1989). . . . Re-signed by Cardinals (November 30, 1989). . . . On St. Louis disabled list (March 31, 1990-entire season); included rehabilitation assignments to Louisville (May 17-31 and June 13-18), Springfield (June 6-7) and Arkansas (June 8-12). . . . Granted free agency (October 19, 1990). . . . Signed by Scranton/Wilkes-Barre, Philadelphia Phillies organization (December 17, 1990). . . . On Philadelphia disabled list (May 19-June 17, 1991); included rehabilitation assignment to Scranton/Wilkes-Barre (June 14-15). . . . Granted free agency (October 31, 1991). . . . Re-signed by Phillies organization (December 9, 1991). . . . Released by Phillies (June 7, 1992). . . . Signed by Buffalo, Pittsburgh Pirates organization (June 19, 1992). . . . On Buffalo disabled list (July 11-24, 1992). . . . Granted free agency (November 3, 1992). . . . Signed by Toronto Blue Jays organization (December 8, 1992). . . . Granted free agency (October 29, 1993). . . . Re-signed by Blue Jays organization (November 8, 1993). . . . On Toronto disabled list (March 25-July 9, 1994); included rehabilitation assignment to Dunedin (June 27-July 8). . . . Granted free agency (October 20, 1994). . . . Re-signed by Blue Jays organization (December 14, 1994). . . . On Toronto disabled list (July 23-August 31, 1995); included rehabilitation assignment to Syracuse (August 16-18). . . . Granted free agency (November 1, 1995). . . . Re-signed by Blue Jays organization (December 6, 1995).

HONORS: Named Appalachian League Player of the Year (1981).

STATISTICAL NOTES: Pitched 11-0 no-hit victory against Bristol (August 9, 1981). . . . Tied for N.L. lead with seven hit batsmen in 1984. . . . Pitched seven innings, combining with Bob Gaddy (two innings) in no-hit victory for Clearwater against Baseball City (April 21, 1991).

Year	Team (League)	W	L	Pct.	ERA	G	GS	CG	ShO	Sv.	IP	H	R	ER	BB	SO
1981—	Johns. City (App.)	9	4	.692	*2.06	13	13	*10	*4	0	*109	80	27	25	36	*87
1982—	Springfield (Midw.)	5	3	.625	2.56	15	13	2	0	0	84 1/3	82	46	24	29	68
1983—	St. Petersburg (FSL)	2	2	.500	2.53	5	5	2	0	0	32	26	10	9	14	22
	—Arkansas (Texas)	8	3	.727	2.29	11	11	7	1	0	86 1/3	60	31	22	24	73
	—Louisville (A.A.)	0	0	...	2.45	2	2	0	0	0	11	10	3	3	0	8
	—St. Louis (N.L.)	3	6	.333	3.25	12	12	0	0	0	83	92	38	30	23	36
1984—	St. Louis (N.L.)	9	11	.450	4.03	29	27	1	1	0	156 1/3	171	81	70	54	70
	—Louisville (A.A.)	4	1	.800	2.13	6	6	4	0	0	42 1/3	34	16	10	7	34
1985—	St. Louis (N.L.)	18	9	.667	2.88	35	35	10	4	0	241	226	91	77	64	131
1986—	St. Louis (N.L.)	12	13	.480	2.90	32	32	8	0	0	220	189	85	71	60	108
1987—	St. Louis (N.L.)	11	9	.550	3.88	31	31	2	0	0	199 1/3	224	99	86	71	101
1988—	St. Louis (N.L.)	3	8	.273	3.98	13	13	0	0	0	86	89	40	38	25	47
	—Louisville (A.A.)	0	0	...	3.09	3	3	0	0	0	11 2/3	11	7	4	6	7
1989—								Did not play.								
1990—	Louisville (A.A.)	0	3	.000	15.55	4	3	0	0	0	11	22	20	19	10	6
	—Springfield (Midw.)	0	0	...	0.00	1	1	0	0	0	5	1	0	0	0	3
	—Arkansas (Texas)	1	0	1.000	1.29	1	1	0	0	0	7	3	1	1	1	3
1991—	Clearwater (Fla. St.)■	3	0	1.000	0.00	3	3	0	0	0	18	4	0	0	4	15
	—Philadelphia (N.L.)	4	6	.400	4.57	23	17	0	0	0	102 1/3	98	57	52	39	46
	—Scran./W.B. (Int'l)	1	0	1.000	3.00	1	1	0	0	0	6	5	2	2	2	3
1992—	Philadelphia (N.L.)	2	2	.500	5.40	9	7	0	0	0	38 1/3	46	28	23	19	30
	—Buffalo (A.A.)■	1	1	.500	1.70	8	8	0	0	0	42 1/3	28	11	8	18	30
	—Pittsburgh (N.L.)	3	1	.750	3.33	16	0	0	0	3	24 1/3	20	9	9	8	18
1993—	Toronto (A.L.)■	7	6	.538	3.12	44	0	0	0	2	83 2/3	73	31	29	29	84
1994—	Dunedin (Fla. St.)	0	0	...	0.00	4	4	0	0	0	8	1	0	0	4	8
	—Toronto (A.L.)	1	1	.500	1.45	10	0	0	0	3	18 2/3	7	3	3	7	14
1995—	Toronto (A.L.)	1	3	.250	7.40	24	0	0	0	0	45	57	40	37	33	38
	—Syracuse (Int'l)	0	0	...	0.00	4	0	0	0	0	7	2	0	0	5	9
A.L. totals (3 years)		9	10	.474	4.21	78	0	0	0	5	147 1/3	137	74	69	69	136
N.L. totals (8 years)		65	65	.500	3.57	200	174	21	5	3	1150 2/3	1155	528	456	363	587
Major league totals (11 years)		74	75	.497	3.64	278	174	21	5	8	1298	1292	602	525	432	723

CHAMPIONSHIP SERIES RECORD

NOTES: Shares single-series record for most complete games pitched—2 (1987). . . . Shares N.L. career record for most complete games pitched—2.

Year	Team (League)	W	L	Pct.	ERA	G	GS	CG	ShO	Sv.	IP	H	R	ER	BB	SO
1985—	St. Louis (N.L.)	1	0	1.000	3.00	1	1	0	0	0	6	4	2	2	5	4
1987—	St. Louis (N.L.)	1	1	.500	2.12	2	2	2	1	0	17	17	4	4	3	11
1992—	Pittsburgh (N.L.)	0	0	...	0.00	2	0	0	0	0	1 1/3	1	0	0	1	1
1993—	Toronto (A.L.)	0	0	...	0.00	2	0	0	0	0	5	3	0	0	2	5
Champ. series totals (4 years)		2	1	.667	1.84	7	3	2	1	0	29 1/3	25	6	6	11	21

C

WORLD SERIES RECORD

NOTES: Shares single-game record for most earned runs allowed—7 (October 18, 1987). . . . Shares record for most earned runs allowed in one inning—6 (October 18, 1987, fourth inning). . . . Member of World Series championship team (1993).

Year	Team (League)	W	L	Pct.	ERA	G	GS	CG	ShO	Sv.	IP	H	R	ER	BB	SO
1985	St. Louis (N.L.)	0	0	...	1.29	2	2	0	0	0	14	14	2	2	4	13
1987	St. Louis (N.L.)	1	2	.333	7.71	3	2	0	0	0	11 2/3	13	10	10	8	9
1993	Toronto (A.L.)	0	0	...	8.10	3	0	0	0	0	3 1/3	6	3	3	5	6
World Series totals (3 years)		1	2	.333	4.66	8	4	0	0	0	29	33	15	15	17	28

COX, STEVE — 1B — ATHLETICS

PERSONAL: Born October 31, 1974, in Delano, Calif. . . . 6-4/200. . . . Bats left, throws left. . . . Full name: Charles Steven Cox.

HIGH SCHOOL: Monache (Porterville, Calif.).

TRANSACTIONS/CAREER NOTES: Selected by Oakland Athletics organization in fifth round of free-agent draft (June 1, 1992). . . . On disabled list (July 23, 1993-remainder of season).

STATISTICAL NOTES: Led California League with 10 sacrifice flies in 1995.

				BATTING											FIELDING			
Year	Team (League)	Pos.	G	AB	R	H	2B	3B	HR	RBI	Avg.	BB	SO	SB	PO	A	E	Avg.
1992	Scottsdale (Ariz.)	1B	52	184	30	43	4	1	1	35	.234	27	51	2	407	28	11	.975
1993	S. Oregon (N'west)	1B	15	57	10	18	4	1	2	16	.316	5	15	0	104	11	2	.983
1994	West. Mich. (Mid.)	1B-OF	99	311	37	75	19	2	6	32	.241	41	95	2	727	49	10	.987
1995	Modesto (Calif.)	1B	132	483	95	144	29	3	*30	*110	.298	84	88	5	991	77	17	.984

CRABTREE, TIM — P — BLUE JAYS

PERSONAL: Born October 13, 1969, in Jackson, Mich. . . . 6-4/205. . . . Throws right, bats right. . . . Full name: Timothy Lyle Crabtree.

HIGH SCHOOL: Grass Lake (Mich.).

COLLEGE: Michigan State.

TRANSACTIONS/CAREER NOTES: Selected by Toronto Blue Jays organization in second round of free-agent draft (June 1, 1992).

Year	Team (League)	W	L	Pct.	ERA	G	GS	CG	ShO	Sv.	IP	H	R	ER	BB	SO
1992	St. Cathar. (NYP)	6	3	.667	1.57	12	12	2	0	0	69	45	19	12	22	47
	—Knoxville (South.)	0	2	.000	0.95	3	3	1	0	0	19	14	8	2	4	13
1993	Knoxville (South.)	9	14	.391	4.08	27	27	2	2	0	158 2/3	178	93	72	59	67
1994	Syracuse (Int'l)	2	6	.250	4.17	51	9	0	0	2	108	125	58	50	49	58
1995	Syracuse (Int'l)	0	2	.000	5.40	26	0	0	0	5	31 2/3	38	25	19	12	22
	—Toronto (A.L.)	0	2	.000	3.09	31	0	0	0	0	32	30	16	11	13	21
Major league totals (1 year)		0	2	.000	3.09	31	0	0	0	0	32	30	16	11	13	21

CRAWFORD, CARLOS — P — PHILLIES

PERSONAL: Born October 4, 1971, in Charlotte, N.C. . . . 6-1/190. . . . Throws right, bats right. . . . Full name: Carlos Lamonte Crawford.

HIGH SCHOOL: South Mecklenburg (Charlotte, N.C.).

COLLEGE: Montreat (N.C.)-Anderson College.

TRANSACTIONS/CAREER NOTES: Selected by Cleveland Indians organization in 51st round of free-agent draft (June 4, 1990). . . . On Buffalo disabled list (April 22-May 15, 1995). . . . Claimed on waivers by Philadelphia Phillies (November 16, 1995).

Year	Team (League)	W	L	Pct.	ERA	G	GS	CG	ShO	Sv.	IP	H	R	ER	BB	SO
1990	GC Indians (GCL)	2	3	.400	4.36	10	9	0	0	0	53 2/3	68	43	26	25	39
1991	Burlington (Appal.)	6	3	.667	2.46	13	13	2	•1	0	80 1/3	62	28	22	14	80
1992	Columbus (S. Atl.)	10	11	.476	2.92	28	•28	•6	•3	0	•188 1/3	167	78	61	85	127
1993	Kinston (Carolina)	7	9	.438	3.65	28	28	4	1	0	165	158	87	67	46	124
1994	Cant./Akr. (East.)	12	6	.667	3.45	26	25	3	0	0	175	164	83	67	59	99
1995	Buffalo (A.A.)	0	1	.000	5.64	13	3	0	0	1	30 1/3	36	22	19	12	15
	—Cant./Akr. (East.)	2	2	.500	2.61	8	8	2	0	0	51 2/3	47	19	15	15	36

CRAWFORD, JOE — P — RED SOX

PERSONAL: Born May 2, 1970, in Gainesville, Fla. . . . 6-3/225. . . . Throws left, bats left. . . . Full name: Joseph Randal Crawford.

HIGH SCHOOL: Hillsboro (O.).

COLLEGE: Kent.

TRANSACTIONS/CAREER NOTES: Selected by New York Mets organization in 17th round of free-agent draft (June 3, 1991). . . . On disabled list (April 28-May 30, 1992). . . . Selected by Boston Red Sox from Mets organization in Rule 5 major league draft (December 4, 1995).

Year	Team (League)	W	L	Pct.	ERA	G	GS	CG	ShO	Sv.	IP	H	R	ER	BB	SO
1991	Kingsport (Appal.)	0	0	...	1.11	19	0	0	0	11	32 1/3	16	5	4	8	43
	—Columbia (S. Atl.)	0	0	...	0.00	3	0	0	0	0	3	0	0	0	0	6
1992	St. Lucie (Fla. St.)	3	3	.500	2.06	25	1	0	0	3	43 2/3	29	18	10	15	32
1993	St. Lucie (Fla. St.)	3	3	.500	3.65	34	0	0	0	5	37	38	15	15	14	24
1994	St. Lucie (Fla. St.)	1	1	.500	1.48	33	0	0	0	5	42 2/3	22	8	7	9	31
	—Binghamton (East.)	1	0	1.000	5.52	13	0	0	0	0	14 2/3	20	10	9	8	9
1995	Binghamton (East.)	7	2	.778	2.23	42	1	0	0	0	60 2/3	48	17	15	17	43
	—Norfolk (Int'l)	1	1	.500	1.93	8	0	0	0	1	18 2/3	9	5	4	4	13

CREEK, DOUG — P — GIANTS

PERSONAL: Born March 1, 1969, in Winchester, Va. . . . 5-10/205. . . . Throws left, bats left. . . . Full name: Paul Douglas Creek.
HIGH SCHOOL: Martinsburg (W.Va.).
COLLEGE: Georgia Tech.
TRANSACTIONS/CAREER NOTES: Selected by California Angels organization in fifth round of free-agent draft (June 4, 1990); did not sign. . . . Selected by St. Louis Cardinals organization in seventh round of free-agent draft (June 3, 1991). . . . On Arkansas disabled list (April 10-May 21, 1992; July 25-August 1, 1993; and June 25-July 10, 1994). . . . Traded by Cardinals with P Allen Watson and P Rich DeLucia to San Francisco Giants for SS Royce Clayton and a player to be named later (December 14, 1995); Cardinals acquired 2B Chris Wimmer to complete deal (January 16, 1996).

Year Team (League)	W	L	Pct.	ERA	G	GS	CG	ShO	Sv.	IP	H	R	ER	BB	SO
1991— Hamilton (NYP)	3	2	.600	5.12	9	5	0	0	1	38 2/3	39	22	22	18	45
— Savannah (S. Atl.)	2	1	.667	4.45	5	5	0	0	0	28 1/3	24	14	14	17	32
1992— Springfield (Midw.)	4	1	.800	2.58	6	6	0	0	0	38 1/3	32	11	11	13	43
— St. Petersburg (FSL)	5	4	.556	2.82	13	13	0	0	0	73 1/3	57	31	23	37	63
1993— Louisville (A.A.)	0	0	...	3.21	2	2	0	0	0	14	10	5	5	9	9
— Arkansas (Texas)	11	10	.524	4.02	25	25	1	1	0	147 2/3	142	75	66	48	128
1994— Louisville (A.A.)	1	4	.200	8.54	7	7	0	0	0	26 1/3	37	26	25	23	16
— Arkansas (Texas)	3	10	.231	4.40	17	17	1	0	0	92	96	54	45	36	65
1995— Louisville (A.A.)	3	2	.600	3.23	26	0	0	0	0	30 2/3	20	12	11	21	29
— Arkansas (Texas)	4	2	.667	2.88	26	0	0	0	1	34 1/3	24	12	11	16	50
— St. Louis (N.L.)	0	0	...	0.00	6	0	0	0	0	6 2/3	2	0	0	3	10
Major league totals (1 year)	0	0	...	0.00	6	0	0	0	0	6 2/3	2	0	0	3	10

CREEK, RYAN — P — ASTROS

PERSONAL: Born September 24, 1972, in Winchester, Va. . . . 6-1/180. . . . Throws right, bats right. . . . Full name: Ryan Matthew Creek.
JUNIOR COLLEGE: Louisburg (N.C.) College.
TRANSACTIONS/CAREER NOTES: Selected by Houston Astros organization in 34th round of free-agent draft (June 1, 1992). . . . On disabled list (June 5-July 10, 1994).

Year Team (League)	W	L	Pct.	ERA	G	GS	CG	ShO	Sv.	IP	H	R	ER	BB	SO
1993— GC Astros (GCL)	•7	3	.700	2.34	12	11	2	1	1	69 1/3	53	22	18	30	62
1994— Quad City (Midw.)	3	5	.375	4.99	21	15	0	0	0	74	86	62	41	41	66
1995— Jackson (Texas)	9	7	.563	3.63	26	24	1	1	0	143 2/3	137	74	58	64	120

CRESPO, FELIPE — 2B — BLUE JAYS

PERSONAL: Born March 5, 1973, in Rio Piedras, Puerto Rico. . . . 5-11/210. . . . Bats both, throws right. . . . Full name: Felipe Javier Clauso Crespo.
HIGH SCHOOL: Notre Dame (Caguas, Puerto Rico).
TRANSACTIONS/CAREER NOTES: Selected by Toronto Blue Jays organization in third round of free-agent draft (June 4, 1990). . . . On disabled list (May 26-July 2, 1995).
STATISTICAL NOTES: Led Southern League third basemen with 127 putouts and 42 errors in 1994.

			BATTING											FIELDING			
Year Team (League)	Pos.	G	AB	R	H	2B	3B	HR	RBI	Avg.	BB	SO	SB	PO	A	E	Avg.
1991— Medicine Hat (Pio.)	2B	49	184	40	57	11	4	4	31	.310	25	31	6	*97	133	*23	.909
1992— Myrtle Beach (SAL)	2B-3B	81	263	43	74	14	3	1	29	.281	58	38	7	161	149	22	.934
1993— Dunedin (Fla. St.)	2B	96	345	51	103	16	8	6	39	.299	47	40	18	198	269	25	.949
1994— Knoxville (South.)	3B-2B	129	502	74	135	30	4	8	49	.269	57	95	20	†127	270	†42	.904
1995— Syracuse (Int'l)	2B	88	347	56	102	20	5	13	41	.294	41	56	12	160	220	*25	.938

CROGHAN, ANDY — P — YANKEES

PERSONAL: Born October 26, 1969, in Fullerton, Calif. . . . 6-5/220. . . . Throws right, bats right. . . . Full name: Andrew Joseph Croghan.
COLLEGE: Long Beach State.
TRANSACTIONS/CAREER NOTES: Selected by New York Yankees organization in 16th round of free-agent draft (June 3, 1991). . . . On disabled list (May 15-27 and July 2, 1995-remainder of season).

Year Team (League)	W	L	Pct.	ERA	G	GS	CG	ShO	Sv.	IP	H	R	ER	BB	SO
1991— Oneonta (NYP)	5	4	.556	5.63	14	14	0	0	0	78 1/3	92	59	*49	28	54
1992— Greensboro (S. Atl.)	10	8	.556	4.49	33	19	1	0	0	122 1/3	128	78	61	57	98
1993— Prin. William (Caro.)	5	11	.313	4.80	39	14	1	0	11	105	117	66	56	27	80
1994— Alb./Colon. (East.)	0	1	.000	1.72	36	0	0	0	16	36 2/3	33	7	7	14	38
— Columbus (Int'l)	2	2	.500	4.13	21	0	0	0	8	24	25	11	11	13	28
1995— Columbus (Int'l)	1	1	.500	3.60	20	0	0	0	4	25	21	10	10	22	22

CROMER, TRIPP — SS — CARDINALS

PERSONAL: Born November 21, 1967, in Lake City, S.C. . . . 6-2/165. . . . Bats right, throws right. . . . Full name: Roy Bunyan Cromer III. . . . Son of Roy Cromer, scout, St. Louis Cardinals and minor league pitcher/second baseman (1960-63); brother of Brandon Cromer, shortstop, Toronto Blue Jays organization; brother of D.T. Cromer, outfielder/first baseman, Oakland Athletics organization; and brother of Burke Cromer, pitcher, Atlanta Braves organization (1992-93).
HIGH SCHOOL: Lake City (S.C.).
COLLEGE: South Carolina.
TRANSACTIONS/CAREER NOTES: Selected by St. Louis Cardinals organization in third round of free-agent draft (June 5, 1989). . . . On Arkansas disabled list (May 14-26, 1992). . . . On Louisville disabled list (April 30-May 28 and July 5-August 3, 1993).

				BATTING										FIELDING			
Year Team (League)	Pos.	G	AB	R	H	2B	3B	HR	RBI	Avg.	BB	SO	SB	PO	A	E	Avg.
1989—Hamilton (NYP)	SS	35	137	18	36	6	3	0	6	.263	17	30	4	66	85	11	.932
1990—St. Peters. (FSL)	SS	121	408	53	88	12	5	5	38	.216	46	78	7	202	334	32	.944
1991—St. Peters. (FSL)	SS	43	137	11	28	3	1	0	10	.204	9	17	0	79	134	3	.986
—Arkansas (Texas)	SS	73	227	28	52	12	1	1	18	.229	15	37	0	117	198	10	.969
1992—Arkansas (Texas)	SS	110	339	30	81	16	6	7	29	.239	22	82	4	135	315	18	*.962
—Louisville (A.A.)	SS	6	25	5	5	1	1	1	7	.200	1	6	0	13	20	0	1.000
1993—Louisville (A.A.)	SS	85	309	39	85	8	4	11	33	.275	15	60	1	123	253	12	.969
—St. Louis (N.L.)	SS	10	23	1	2	0	0	0	0	.087	1	6	0	13	18	3	.912
1994—Louisville (A.A.)	SS	124	419	53	115	23	9	9	50	.274	33	85	5	165	370	12	*.978
—St. Louis (N.L.)	SS	2	0	1	0	0	0	0	0	...	0	0	0	0	0	1	.000
1995—St. Louis (N.L.)	SS-2B	105	345	36	78	19	0	5	18	.226	14	66	0	126	292	17	.961
Major league totals (3 years)		117	368	38	80	19	0	5	18	.217	15	72	0	139	310	21	.955

CROW, DEAN — P — MARINERS

PERSONAL: Born August 21, 1972, in Garland, Tex. . . . 6-4/215. . . . Throws right, bats left. . . . Full name: Paul Dean Crow Jr.
HIGH SCHOOL: Stratford (Texas).
JUNIOR COLLEGE: San Jacinto (Tex.).
COLLEGE: Miami of Ohio, then Baylor.
TRANSACTIONS/CAREER NOTES: Selected by Seattle Mariners organization in 10th round of free-agent draft (June 3, 1993). . . . On disabled list (June 15-26 and July 18, 1994-remainder of season).

Year Team (League)	W	L	Pct.	ERA	G	GS	CG	ShO	Sv.	IP	H	R	ER	BB	SO
1993—Bellingham (N'west)	5	3	.625	1.89	25	0	0	0	4	47 2/3	31	14	10	21	38
1994—Appleton (Midw.)	2	4	.333	7.04	16	0	0	0	2	15 2/3	25	15	12	7	11
1995—Riverside (Calif.)	3	4	.429	2.63	51	0	0	0	22	61 2/3	54	21	18	13	46

CRUZ, FAUSTO — SS/3B — ATHLETICS

PERSONAL: Born May 1, 1972, in Monte Cristi, Dominican Republic. . . . 5-10/165. . . . Bats right, throws right. . . . Full name: Fausto Santiago Cruz.
TRANSACTIONS/CAREER NOTES: Signed as non-drafted free agent by Oakland Athletics organization (January 15, 1990).
STATISTICAL NOTES: Led Arizona League in grounding into double plays with 10 in 1991. . . . Tied for Arizona League lead with seven sacrifice flies in 1991. . . . Led Arizona League shortstops with 254 total chances and 27 double plays in 1991.

				BATTING										FIELDING			
Year Team (League)	Pos.	G	AB	R	H	2B	3B	HR	RBI	Avg.	BB	SO	SB	PO	A	E	Avg.
1990—					Dominican Summer League statistics unavailable.												
1991—Arizona A's (Ariz.)	SS	52	180	38	50	2	1	2	36	.278	32	23	3	*92	147	15	*.941
—Modesto (Calif.)	SS-2B	18	58	9	12	1	0	0	0	.207	8	13	1	22	44	7	.904
1992—Reno (California)	SS	127	489	86	156	22	11	9	90	.319	70	66	8	*278	382	*54	.924
1993—Modesto (Calif.)	SS	43	165	21	39	3	0	1	20	.236	25	34	6	90	117	12	.945
—Huntsville (South.)	SS-3B	63	251	45	84	15	2	3	31	.335	20	42	2	100	143	12	.953
—Tacoma (PCL)	3-S-2-O	21	74	13	18	2	1	0	6	.243	5	16	3	34	43	3	.963
1994—Tacoma (PCL)	SS-3B	65	218	27	70	19	0	1	17	.321	17	32	2	97	175	18	.938
—Oakland (A.L.)	SS-3B-2B	17	28	2	3	0	0	0	0	.107	4	6	0	17	23	2	.952
1995—Edmonton (PCL)	SS	114	448	72	126	23	2	11	67	.281	34	67	7	*196	355	24	.958
—Oakland (A.L.)	SS	8	23	0	5	0	0	0	5	.217	3	5	1	9	24	1	.971
Major league totals (2 years)		25	51	2	8	0	0	0	5	.157	7	11	1	26	47	3	.961

CUMBERLAND, CHRIS — P — YANKEES

PERSONAL: Born January 15, 1973, in Clearwater, Fla. . . . 6-1/190. . . . Throws left, bats right. . . . Full name: Christopher Mark Cumberland.
JUNIOR COLLEGE: Pasco Hernando (Fla.).
TRANSACTIONS/CAREER NOTES: Selected by New York Yankees organization in 48th round of free-agent draft (June 1, 1992). . . . On Greensboro disabled list (April 6-August 12, 1995).

Year Team (League)	W	L	Pct.	ERA	G	GS	CG	ShO	Sv.	IP	H	R	ER	BB	SO
1993—Oneonta (NYP)	4	4	.500	3.34	15	15	0	0	0	89	*109	43	33	28	62
1994—Greensboro (S. Atl.)	14	5	.737	2.94	22	22	1	1	0	137 2/3	123	55	45	41	95
1995—GC Yankees (GCL)	0	1	.000	1.29	4	4	0	0	0	7	3	1	1	1	7
—Tampa (Fla. St.)	1	2	.333	1.82	5	5	0	0	0	24 2/3	28	10	5	5	10

CUMMINGS, JOHN — P — DODGERS

PERSONAL: Born May 10, 1969, in Torrance, Calif. . . . 6-3/200. . . . Throws left, bats left. . . . Full name: John Russell Cummings.
HIGH SCHOOL: Canyon (Anaheim, Calif.).
COLLEGE: Southern California.
TRANSACTIONS/CAREER NOTES: Selected by New York Yankees organization in 32nd round of free-agent draft (June 1, 1988); did not sign. . . . Selected by Seattle Mariners organization in eighth round of free-agent draft (June 4, 1990). . . . On Calgary disabled list (August 1-8, 1993). . . . On Seattle disabled list (May 11-28, 1994); included rehabilitation assignment to Appleton (May 23-26). . . . Claimed on waivers by Los Angeles Dodgers (May 25, 1995).
HONORS: Named Carolina League Pitcher of the Year (1992).

Year Team (League)	W	L	Pct.	ERA	G	GS	CG	ShO	Sv.	IP	H	R	ER	BB	SO
1990—Bellingham (N'west)	1	1	.500	2.12	6	6	0	0	0	34	25	11	8	9	39
—San Bern. (Calif.)	2	4	.333	4.20	7	7	1	0	0	40 2/3	47	27	19	20	30
1991—San Bern. (Calif.)	4	10	.286	4.06	29	20	0	0	1	124	129	79	56	61	120

Year	Team (League)	W	L	Pct.	ERA	G	GS	CG	ShO	Sv.	IP	H	R	ER	BB	SO
1992—	Peninsula (Caro.)	*16	6	.727	2.57	27	27	4	1	0	168 1/3	149	71	48	63	*144
1993—	Seattle (A.L.)	0	6	.000	6.02	10	8	1	0	0	46 1/3	59	34	31	16	19
	—Jacksonville (Sou.)	2	2	.500	3.15	7	7	1	0	0	45 2/3	50	24	16	9	35
	—Calgary (PCL)	3	4	.429	4.13	11	10	0	0	0	65 1/3	69	40	30	21	42
1994—	Seattle (A.L.)	2	4	.333	5.63	17	8	0	0	0	64	66	43	40	37	33
	—Appleton (Midw.)	0	0	...	3.00	1	1	0	0	0	3	2	1	1	0	6
	—Calgary (PCL)	1	0	1.000	1.50	1	1	0	0	0	6	3	1	1	2	4
	—Riverside (Calif.)	0	1	.000	6.75	1	1	0	0	0	2 2/3	5	2	2	1	2
1995—	Seattle (A.L.)	0	0	...	11.81	4	0	0	0	0	5 1/3	8	8	7	7	4
	—Tacoma (PCL)	0	1	.000	7.71	1	1	0	0	0	2 1/3	6	4	2	3	3
	—San Antonio (Tex.)■	0	2	.000	3.95	6	5	0	0	0	27 1/3	28	13	12	7	13
	—Los Angeles (N.L.)	3	1	.750	3.00	35	0	0	0	0	39	38	16	13	10	21
A.L. totals (3 years)		2	10	.167	6.07	31	16	1	0	0	115 2/3	133	85	78	60	56
N.L. totals (1 year)		3	1	.750	3.00	35	0	0	0	0	39	38	16	13	10	21
Major league totals (3 years)		5	11	.313	5.30	66	16	1	0	0	154 2/3	171	101	91	70	77

DIVISION SERIES RECORD

Year	Team (League)	W	L	Pct.	ERA	G	GS	CG	ShO	Sv.	IP	H	R	ER	BB	SO
1995—	Los Angeles (N.L.)	0	0	...	20.25	2	0	0	0	0	1 1/3	3	3	3	2	3

CUMMINGS, MIDRE — OF — PIRATES

PERSONAL: Born October 14, 1971, in St. Croix, Virgin Islands. . . . 6-0/203. . . . Bats left, throws right. . . . Full name: Midre Almeric Cummings.

HIGH SCHOOL: Miami Edison Senior.

TRANSACTIONS/CAREER NOTES: Selected by Minnesota Twins organization in supplemental round ("sandwich pick" between first and second round, 29th pick overall) of free-agent draft (June 4, 1990); pick received as part of compensation for Boston Red Sox signing Type A free-agent P Jeff Reardon. . . . Traded by Twins organization with P Denny Neagle to Pittsburgh Pirates organization for P John Smiley (March 17, 1992). . . . On Buffalo disabled list (April 21-June 6, 1994). . . . On Calgary disabled list (June 17-July 1, 1995).

MISCELLANEOUS: Batted as switch-hitter (1990-92).

			BATTING												FIELDING			
Year	Team (League)	Pos.	G	AB	R	H	2B	3B	HR	RBI	Avg.	BB	SO	SB	PO	A	E	Avg.
1990—	GC Twins (GCL)	OF	47	177	28	56	3	4	5	28	.316	13	32	14	73	2	6	.926
1991—	Kenosha (Midwest)	OF	106	382	59	123	20	4	4	54	*.322	22	66	28	166	6	•13	.930
1992—	Salem (Carolina)■	OF	113	420	55	128	20	5	14	75	.305	35	67	23	151	10	6	.964
1993—	Carolina (South.)	OF	63	237	33	70	17	2	6	26	.295	14	23	5	99	7	4	.964
	—Buffalo (A.A.)	OF	60	232	36	64	12	1	9	21	.276	22	45	5	90	1	2	.978
	—Pittsburgh (N.L.)	OF	13	36	5	4	1	0	0	3	.111	4	9	0	21	0	0	1.000
1994—	Buffalo (A.A.)	OF	49	183	23	57	12	4	2	22	.311	13	26	5	117	2	0	1.000
	—Pittsburgh (N.L.)	OF	24	86	11	21	4	0	1	12	.244	4	18	0	49	1	2	.962
1995—	Pittsburgh (N.L.)	OF	59	152	13	37	7	1	2	15	.243	13	30	1	79	2	1	.988
	—Calgary (PCL)	OF	45	159	19	44	9	1	1	16	.277	6	27	1	96	4	6	.943
Major league totals (3 years)			96	274	29	62	12	1	3	30	.226	21	57	1	149	3	3	.981

CURTIS, CHAD — OF — TIGERS

PERSONAL: Born November 6, 1968, in Marion, Ind. . . . 5-10/175. . . . Bats right, throws right. . . . Full name: Chad David Curtis.

HIGH SCHOOL: Benson (Ariz.) Union.

JUNIOR COLLEGE: Yavapi College (Ariz.) and Cochise (Ariz.) Community College.

COLLEGE: Grand Canyon (Ariz.).

TRANSACTIONS/CAREER NOTES: Selected by California Angels organization in 45th round of free-agent draft (June 5, 1989). . . . On disabled list (June 5-20, 1991). . . . On suspended list (June 8-12, 1993). . . . Traded by Angels to Detroit Tigers for OF/3B Tony Phillips (April 12, 1995).

RECORDS: Shares A.L. single-season record for fewest errors by outfielder who led league in errors—9 (1993).

STATISTICAL NOTES: Led Midwest League with 223 total bases in 1990. . . . Tied for A.L. lead in caught stealing with 24 in 1993. . . . Led A.L. outfielders with 448 total chances and tied for lead with nine errors in 1993. . . . Led A.L. outfielders with 345 total chances in 1994.

			BATTING												FIELDING			
Year	Team (League)	Pos.	G	AB	R	H	2B	3B	HR	RBI	Avg.	BB	SO	SB	PO	A	E	Avg.
1989—	Ariz. Angels (Ariz.)	2B-OF	32	122	30	37	4	4	3	20	.303	14	20	17	62	58	6	.952
	—Quad City (Midw.)	OF	23	78	7	19	3	0	2	11	.244	6	17	7	34	1	1	.972
1990—	Quad City (Midw.)	2B-OF	135	*492	87	*151	28	1	14	65	.307	57	76	64	216	221	26	.944
1991—	Edmonton (PCL)	3B-2B-OF	115	431	81	136	28	7	9	61	.316	51	56	46	124	220	25	.932
1992—	California (A.L.)	OF-DH	139	441	59	114	16	2	10	46	.259	51	71	43	250	*16	6	.978
1993—	California (A.L.)	OF-2B	152	583	94	166	25	3	6	59	.285	70	89	48	426	13	‡9	.980
1994—	California (A.L.)	OF	114	453	67	116	23	4	11	50	.256	37	69	25	*332	9	4	.988
1995—	Detroit (A.L.)■	OF	144	586	96	157	29	3	21	67	.268	70	93	27	362	5	3	.992
Major league totals (4 years)			549	2063	316	553	93	12	48	222	.268	228	322	143	1370	43	22	.985

CURTIS, CHRIS — P — RANGERS

PERSONAL: Born May 8, 1971, in Hearne, Tex. . . . 6-2/185. . . . Throws right, bats right. . . . Full name: Christopher Eugene Curtis.

HIGH SCHOOL: Duncansville (Tex.).

JUNIOR COLLEGE: Blinn (Tex.).

COLLEGE: Dallas Baptist.

TRANSACTIONS/CAREER NOTES: Selected by Texas Rangers organization in fourth round of free-agent draft (June 3, 1991). . . . On suspended list (May 23-25, 1995).

STATISTICAL NOTES: Led Texas League with seven balks in 1994.

Year Team (League)	W	L	Pct.	ERA	G	GS	CG	ShO	Sv.	IP	H	R	ER	BB	SO
1991—GC Rangers (GCL)	4	0	1.000	2.06	7	7	7	0	0	35	27	9	8	9	23
—Butte (Pioneer)	0	2	.000	9.95	6	3	0	0	0	12 2/3	27	23	14	4	7
1992—Gastonia (S. Atl.)	8	11	.421	2.63	24	24	1	1	0	147	117	60	43	54	107
1993—Charlotte (Fla. St.)	8	8	.500	3.99	27	26	1	0	0	151	159	76	67	51	55
1994—Tulsa (Texas)	3	*13	.188	5.36	25	23	3	1	0	142 2/3	173	102	85	57	62
1995—Okla. City (A.A.)	3	5	.375	5.00	51	0	0	0	5	77 1/3	81	53	43	39	40

CUYLER, MILT — OF — RED SOX

PERSONAL: Born October 7, 1968, in Macon, Ga. . . . 5-10/185. . . . Bats both, throws right. . . . Full name: Milton Cuyler Jr. . . . Name pronounced KY-ler.

HIGH SCHOOL: Southwest Macon (Macon, Ga.).

TRANSACTIONS/CAREER NOTES: Selected by Detroit Tigers organization in second round of free-agent draft (June 2, 1986). . . . On disabled list (July 26, 1992-remainder of season and August 9, 1993-remainder of season). . . . On Detroit disabled list (May 26-July 25, 1994); included rehabilitation assignment to Toledo (July 8-25). . . . On Toledo disabled list (July 1-16, 1995). . . . Released by Tigers (November 30, 1995). . . . Signed by Boston Red Sox organization (December 21, 1995).

STATISTICAL NOTES: Led South Atlantic League with 17 sacrifice hits in 1987. . . . Led Florida State League in caught stealing with 25 in 1988. . . . Led Eastern League outfielders with 293 total chances in 1989. . . . Led International League in caught stealing with 14 in 1990. . . . Career major league grand slams: 2.

		BATTING												FIELDING			
Year Team (League)	Pos.	G	AB	R	H	2B	3B	HR	RBI	Avg.	BB	SO	SB	PO	A	E	Avg.
1986—Bristol (Appal.)	OF	45	174	24	40	3	5	1	11	.230	15	35	12	97	0	4	.960
1987—Fayetteville (SAL)	OF	94	366	65	107	8	4	2	34	.292	34	78	27	237	13	7	.973
1988—Lakeland (Fla. St.)	OF	132	483	*100	143	11	3	2	32	.296	71	83	50	257	8	4	.985
1989—Toledo (Int'l)	OF	24	83	4	14	3	2	0	6	.169	8	27	4	48	3	2	.962
—London (Eastern)	OF	98	366	69	96	8	7	7	34	.262	47	74	32	*272	13	8	.973
1990—Toledo (Int'l)	OF	124	461	77	119	11	8	2	42	.258	60	77	*52	290	4	7	.977
—Detroit (A.L.)	OF	19	51	8	13	3	1	0	8	.255	5	10	1	38	2	1	.976
1991—Detroit (A.L.)	OF	154	475	77	122	15	7	3	33	.257	52	92	41	411	7	6	.986
1992—Detroit (A.L.)	OF	89	291	39	70	11	1	3	28	.241	10	62	8	232	4	4	.983
1993—Detroit (A.L.)	OF	82	249	46	53	11	7	0	19	.213	19	53	13	211	2	7	.968
1994—Detroit (A.L.)	OF	48	116	20	28	3	1	1	11	.241	13	21	5	78	1	2	.975
—Toledo (Int'l)	OF	15	64	8	22	4	1	0	2	.344	3	11	4	33	0	3	.917
1995—Detroit (A.L.)	OF-DH	41	88	15	18	1	4	0	5	.205	8	16	2	50	2	4	.929
—Toledo (Int'l)	OF	54	203	33	62	10	4	6	28	.305	20	40	6	95	1	4	.960
Major league totals (6 years)		433	1270	205	304	44	21	7	104	.239	107	254	70	1020	18	24	.977

DAAL, OMAR — P — EXPOS

PERSONAL: Born March 1, 1972, in Maracaibo, Venezuela. . . . 6-3/185. . . . Throws left, bats left. . . . Full name: Omar Jose Cordaro Daal.

HIGH SCHOOL: Valencia (Venezuela) Superior.

TRANSACTIONS/CAREER NOTES: Signed as non-drafted free agent by Los Angeles Dodgers organization (August 24, 1990). . . . Traded by Dodgers to Montreal Expos for P Rick Clelland (December 14, 1995).

Year Team (League)	W	L	Pct.	ERA	G	GS	CG	ShO	Sv.	IP	H	R	ER	BB	SO
1990—Santo Dom. (DSL)	3	6	.333	1.18	17	13	6	0	2	91 2/3	61	29	12	29	91
1991—Santo Dom. (DSL)	7	2	.778	1.16	13	13	0	0	0	93	30	17	12	32	81
1992—Albuquerque (PCL)	0	2	.000	7.84	12	0	0	0	0	10 1/3	14	9	9	11	9
—San Antonio (Tex.)	2	6	.250	5.02	35	5	0	0	5	57 1/3	60	39	32	33	52
1993—Albuquerque (PCL)	1	1	.500	3.38	6	0	0	0	2	5 1/3	5	2	2	3	2
—Los Angeles (N.L.)	2	3	.400	5.09	47	0	0	0	0	35 1/3	36	20	20	21	19
1994—Albuquerque (PCL)	4	2	.667	5.19	11	5	0	0	1	34 2/3	38	20	20	16	28
—Los Angeles (N.L.)	0	0	...	3.29	24	0	0	0	0	13 2/3	12	5	5	5	9
1995—Albuquerque (PCL)	2	3	.400	4.05	17	9	0	0	1	53 1/3	56	28	24	26	46
—Los Angeles (N.L.)	4	0	1.000	7.20	28	0	0	0	0	20	29	16	16	15	11
Major league totals (3 years)	6	3	.667	5.35	99	0	0	0	0	69	77	41	41	41	39

DALESANDRO, MARK — 3B/C — ANGELS

PERSONAL: Born May 14, 1968, in Chicago. . . . 6-0/185. . . . Bats right, throws right. . . . Full name: Mark Anthony Dalesandro. . . . Name pronounced DEE-uh-SAN-droh.

HIGH SCHOOL: St. Ignatius College Prep School (Chicago).

COLLEGE: Illinois.

TRANSACTIONS/CAREER NOTES: Selected by California Angels organization in 18th round of free-agent draft (June 4, 1990).

STATISTICAL NOTES: Tied for California League lead in grounding into double plays with 20 in 1992.

		BATTING												FIELDING			
Year Team (League)	Pos.	G	AB	R	H	2B	3B	HR	RBI	Avg.	BB	SO	SB	PO	A	E	Avg.
1990—Boise (Northwest)	OF-3B-1B	55	224	35	75	10	2	6	44	.335	18	42	6	37	23	6	.909
1991—Quad City (Midw.)	3B-1B	125	487	63	133	17	8	5	69	.273	34	58	1	198	186	25	.939
1992—Palm Springs (Cal.)	1B-3B	126	492	72	146	30	3	7	92	.297	33	50	6	594	114	15	.979
1993—Palm Springs (Cal.)	C-1B	46	176	22	43	5	3	1	25	.244	15	20	3	271	42	7	.978
—Midland (Texas)	3B-C-1B	57	235	33	69	9	0	2	36	.294	8	30	1	137	60	12	.943
—Vancouver (PCL)	3B	26	107	16	32	8	1	2	15	.299	6	13	1	19	59	7	.918
1994—Vancouver (PCL)	3-C-1-O	51	199	29	63	9	1	1	31	.317	7	19	1	153	71	11	.953
—California (A.L.)	C-3B-OF	19	25	5	5	1	0	1	2	.200	2	4	0	19	5	1	.960
1995—California (A.L.)	C-DH-OF	11	10	1	1	1	0	0	0	.100	0	2	0	11	0	0	1.000
—Vancouver (PCL)	O-3-C-1	34	123	16	41	13	1	1	18	.333	6	12	2	56	8	2	.970
Major league totals (2 years)		30	35	6	6	2	0	1	2	.171	2	6	0	30	5	1	.972

DAMON, JOHNNY — OF — ROYALS

PERSONAL: Born November 5, 1973, in Fort Riley, Kan. . . . 6-0/175. . . . Bats left, throws left. . . . Full name: Johnny David Damon.
HIGH SCHOOL: Dr. Phillips (Orlando, Fla.).
TRANSACTIONS/CAREER NOTES: Selected by Kansas City Royals organization in supplemental round ("sandwich pick" between first and second round, 35th pick overall) of free-agent draft (June 1, 1992); pick received as part of compensation for San Diego Padres signing Type A free-agent IF Kurt Stillwell.
HONORS: Named Texas League Player of the Year (1995).
STATISTICAL NOTES: Led Gulf Coast League with 109 total bases in 1992. . . . Led Midwest League outfielders with five double plays in 1993. . . . Led Texas League with .434 on-base percentage in 1995. . . . Led Texas League with .534 slugging percentage in 1995. . . . Led Texas League with 13 intentional bases on balls received in 1995.

			BATTING												FIELDING			
Year	Team (League)	Pos.	G	AB	R	H	2B	3B	HR	RBI	Avg.	BB	SO	SB	PO	A	E	Avg.
1992—	GC Royals (GCL)	OF	50	192	*58	67	12	*9	4	24	*.349	31	21	33	77	7	1	.988
—	Baseball City (FSL)	OF	1	1	0	0	0	0	0	0	.000	0	0	0	0	0	0	...
1993—	Rockford (Midw.)	OF	127	511	82	148	25	*13	5	50	.290	52	83	59	240	14	6	.977
1994—	Wilmington (Caro.)	OF	119	472	96	149	25	13	6	75	.316	62	55	44	‡273	9	3	.989
1995—	Wichita (Texas)	OF	111	423	83	145	15	9	16	54	.343	67	35	26	296	11	5	.984
—	Kansas City (A.L.)	OF	47	188	32	53	11	5	3	23	.282	12	22	7	110	0	1	.991
Major league totals (1 year)			47	188	32	53	11	5	3	23	.282	12	22	7	110	0	1	.991

DANIELS, LEE — P — BRAVES

PERSONAL: Born March 31, 1971, in Rochelle, Ga. . . . 6-4/190. . . . Throws right, bats right. . . . Full name: Lee Andrew Daniels.
HIGH SCHOOL: Wilcox County (Rochelle, Ga.).
JUNIOE COLLEGE: Hawamba Junior College (Miss.).
TRANSACTIONS/CAREER NOTES: Selected by Toronto Blue Jays organization in 68th round of free-agent draft (June 5, 1989). . . . Claimed on waivers by Atlanta Braves organization (April 17, 1995).
STATISTICAL NOTES: Led Pioneer League outfielders with 127 total chances and tied for lead in putouts by outfielder with 117 in 1991.

Year	Team (League)	W	L	Pct.	ERA	G	GS	CG	ShO	Sv.	IP	H	R	ER	BB	SO
1991—	Medicine Hat (Pio.)	0	0	...	0.00	1	0	0	0	0	1 1/3	1	0	0	0	2
1992—	St. Cathar. (NYP)	3	6	.333	4.34	17	4	0	0	0	58	61	34	28	20	37
1993—	Dunedin (Fla. St.)	0	1	.000	6.23	2	1	0	0	0	4 1/3	6	4	3	2	5
—	Hagerstown (S. Atl.)	2	4	.333	3.43	33	0	0	0	12	39 1/3	31	20	15	26	38
1994—	Dunedin (Fla. St.)	3	6	.333	3.75	49	0	0	0	15	60	55	30	25	26	48
1995—	Durham (Carolina)■	1	4	.200	4.24	21	0	0	0	4	23 1/3	26	13	11	14	24

RECORD AS POSITION PLAYER

			BATTING												FIELDING			
Year	Team (League)	Pos.	G	AB	R	H	2B	3B	HR	RBI	Avg.	BB	SO	SB	PO	A	E	Avg.
1990—	Medicine Hat (Pio.)	OF	31	95	3	16	3	0	0	9	.168	7	39	4	37	2	6	.867
1991—	Medicine Hat (Pio.)	OF	61	219	43	54	4	1	2	22	.247	34	65	18	‡117	5	5	.961

DARENSBOURG, VIC — P — MARLINS

PERSONAL: Born November 13, 1970, in Los Angeles. . . . 5-10/165. . . . Throws left, bats left. . . . Full name: Victor Anthony Darensbourg.
HIGH SCHOOL: Westchester (Los Angeles).
COLLEGE: Lewis & Clark (Ore.).
TRANSACTIONS/CAREER NOTES: Signed as non-drafted free agent by Florida Marlins organization (June 11, 1992). . . . On Florida disabled list (September 15, 1995-remainder of season).

Year	Team (League)	W	L	Pct.	ERA	G	GS	CG	ShO	Sv.	IP	H	R	ER	BB	SO
1992—	GC Marlins (GCL)	2	1	.667	0.64	8	4	0	0	2	42	28	5	3	11	37
1993—	Kane Co. (Mid.)	9	1	.900	2.14	46	0	0	0	16	71 1/3	58	17	17	28	89
—	High Desert (Calif.)	0	0	...	0.00	1	0	0	0	0	1	0	0	0	0	1
1994—	Portland (Eastern)	10	7	.588	3.81	35	21	1	1	4	149	146	76	63	60	103
1995—		Did not play.														

DARLING, RON — P

PERSONAL: Born August 19, 1960, in Honolulu. . . . 6-3/195. . . . Throws right, bats right. . . . Full name: Ronald Maurice Darling Jr. . . . Brother of Eddie Darling, minor league first baseman (1981-82).
HIGH SCHOOL: St. John's (Worcester, Mass.).
COLLEGE: Yale.
TRANSACTIONS/CAREER NOTES: Selected by Texas Rangers organization in first round (ninth pick overall) of free-agent draft (June 8, 1981). . . . Traded by Rangers organization with P Walt Terrell to New York Mets organization for OF Lee Mazzilli (April 1, 1982). . . . On disabled list (September 12, 1987-remainder of season). . . . Traded by Mets with P Mike Thomas to Montreal Expos for P Tim Burke (July 15, 1991). . . . Traded by Expos to Oakland Athletics for P Matt Grott and P Russell Cormier (July 31, 1991). . . . Granted free agency (October 31, 1991). . . . Re-signed by A's (January 17, 1992). . . . Granted free agency (October 28, 1992). . . . Re-signed by A's (December 17, 1992). . . . Released by A's (August 21, 1995).
RECORDS: Shares N.L. single-season record for fewest assists by pitcher who led league in assists—47 (both in 1985 and 1986).
HONORS: Won N.L. Gold Glove at pitcher (1989).
STATISTICAL NOTES: Led N.L. pitchers with six errors in 1991.
MISCELLANEOUS: Appeared in two games as pinch-runner (1989). . . . Appeared in one game as pinch-runner (1990). . . . Appeared in one game as pinch-runner (1992). . . . Appeared in one game as pinch-runner (1993). . . . Appeared in one game as pinch-runner and made an out in one game as pinch-hitter (1994). . . . Appeared in one game as pinch-runner (1995).

D

Year	Team (League)	W	L	Pct.	ERA	G	GS	CG	ShO	Sv.	IP	H	R	ER	BB	SO
1981—	Tulsa (Texas)	4	2	.667	4.44	13	13	2	2	0	71	72	43	35	33	53
1982—	Tidewater (Int'l)■	7	9	.438	3.73	26	26	6	2	0	152	143	76	63	95	114
1983—	Tidewater (Int'l)	10	9	.526	4.02	27	27	5	1	0	159	137	83	71	102	107
	—New York (N.L.)	1	3	.250	2.80	5	5	1	0	0	35 1/3	31	11	11	17	23
1984—	New York (N.L.)	12	9	.571	3.81	33	33	2	2	0	205 2/3	179	97	87	104	136
1985—	New York (N.L.)	16	6	.727	2.90	36	35	4	2	0	248	214	93	80	*114	167
1986—	New York (N.L.)	15	6	.714	2.81	34	34	4	2	0	237	203	84	74	81	184
1987—	New York (N.L.)	12	8	.600	4.29	32	32	2	0	0	207 2/3	183	111	99	96	167
1988—	New York (N.L.)	17	9	.654	3.25	34	34	7	4	0	240 2/3	218	97	87	60	161
1989—	New York (N.L.)	14	14	.500	3.52	33	33	4	0	0	217 1/3	214	100	85	70	153
1990—	New York (N.L.)	7	9	.438	4.50	33	18	1	0	0	126	135	73	63	44	99
1991—	New York (N.L.)	5	6	.455	3.87	17	17	0	0	0	102 1/3	96	50	44	28	58
	—Montreal (N.L.)■	0	2	.000	7.41	3	3	0	0	0	17	25	16	14	5	11
	—Oakland (A.L.)■	3	7	.300	4.08	12	12	0	0	0	75	64	34	34	38	60
1992—	Oakland (A.L.)	15	10	.600	3.66	33	33	4	3	0	206 1/3	198	98	84	72	99
1993—	Oakland (A.L.)	5	9	.357	5.16	31	29	3	0	0	178	198	107	102	72	95
1994—	Oakland (A.L.)	10	11	.476	4.50	25	•25	4	0	0	160	162	89	80	59	108
1995—	Oakland (A.L.)	4	7	.364	6.23	21	21	1	0	0	104	124	79	72	46	69
A.L. totals (5 years)		37	44	.457	4.63	122	120	12	3	0	723 1/3	746	407	372	287	431
N.L. totals (9 years)		99	72	.579	3.54	260	244	25	10	0	1637	1498	732	644	619	1159
Major league totals (13 years)		136	116	.540	3.87	382	364	37	13	0	2360 1/3	2244	1139	1016	906	1590

CHAMPIONSHIP SERIES RECORD

NOTES: Appeared in one game as pinch-runner (1988).

Year	Team (League)	W	L	Pct.	ERA	G	GS	CG	ShO	Sv.	IP	H	R	ER	BB	SO
1986—	New York (N.L.)	0	0	...	7.20	1	1	0	0	0	5	6	4	4	2	5
1988—	New York (N.L.)	0	1	.000	7.71	2	2	0	0	0	7	11	9	6	4	7
1992—	Oakland (A.L.)	0	1	.000	3.00	1	1	0	0	0	6	4	3	2	2	3
Champ. series totals (3 years)		0	2	.000	6.00	4	4	0	0	0	18	21	16	12	8	15

WORLD SERIES RECORD

NOTES: Shares single-game record for most wild pitches—2 (October 18, 1986). . . . Member of World Series championship team (1986).

Year	Team (League)	W	L	Pct.	ERA	G	GS	CG	ShO	Sv.	IP	H	R	ER	BB	SO
1986—	New York (N.L.)	1	1	.500	1.53	3	3	0	0	0	17 2/3	13	4	3	10	12

ALL-STAR GAME RECORD

Year	League	W	L	Pct.	ERA	GS	CG	ShO	Sv.	IP	H	R	ER	BB	SO
1985—	National						Did not play.								

DARWIN, DANNY P

PERSONAL: Born October 25, 1955, in Bonham, Tex. . . . 6-3/195. . . . Throws right, bats right. . . . Full name: Daniel Wayne Darwin. . . . Brother of Jeff Darwin, pitcher, Chicago White Sox organization.

HIGH SCHOOL: Bonham (Tex.).

COLLEGE: Grayson County (Tex.) College.

TRANSACTIONS/CAREER NOTES: Signed as non-drafted free agent by Texas Rangers organization (May 10, 1976). . . . On disabled list (April 25-May 4 and May 22-June 11, 1977; June 5-26, 1980; March 25-April 10 and August 9-September 1, 1983). . . . Traded by Rangers with a player to be named later to Milwaukee Brewers as part of a six-player, four-team deal in which Kansas City Royals acquired C Jim Sundberg from Brewers, Rangers acquired C Don Slaught from Royals, New York Mets organization acquired P Frank Wills from Royals and Brewers organization acquired P Tim Leary from Mets (January 18, 1985); Brewers organization acquired C Bill Hance from Rangers to complete deal (January 30, 1985). . . . Granted free agency (November 12, 1985). . . . Re-signed by Brewers (December 22, 1985). . . . Traded by Brewers organization to Houston Astros for P Don August and a player to be named later (August 15, 1986); Brewers organization acquired P Mark Knudson to complete deal (August 21, 1986). . . . Granted free agency (November 9, 1987). . . . Re-signed by Astros (January 8, 1988). . . . Granted free agency (December 7, 1990). . . . Signed by Boston Red Sox (December 19, 1990). . . . On disabled list (April 23-May 22 and July 5, 1991-remainder of season; and June 16, 1994-remainder of season). . . . Granted free agency (October 21, 1994). . . . Signed by Toronto Blue Jays (April 10, 1995). . . . Released by Blue Jays (July 18, 1995). . . . Signed by Oklahoma City, Rangers organization (July 31, 1995). . . . Granted free agency (November 11, 1995).

STATISTICAL NOTES: Tied for Western Carolinas League lead with five balks in 1976. . . . Tied for Texas League lead with eight hit batsmen in 1977. . . . Pitched 5-0 one-hit, complete-game victory against Boston (April 29, 1981). . . . Pitched 4-1 one-hit, complete-game victory against Minnesota (August 19, 1985). . . . Tied for A.L. lead with 34 home runs allowed in 1985. . . Pitched 5-0 one-hit, complete-game victory against Chicago (August 18, 1993).

MISCELLANEOUS: Appeared in four games as pinch-runner (1990).

Year	Team (League)	W	L	Pct.	ERA	G	GS	CG	ShO	Sv.	IP	H	R	ER	BB	SO
1976—	Asheville (W. Caro.)	6	3	.667	3.62	16	16	6	1	0	102	96	54	41	48	76
1977—	Tulsa (Texas)	13	4	.765	2.51	23	23	6	•4	0	154	130	53	43	72	129
1978—	Tucson (Pac. Coast)	8	9	.471	6.26	23	23	4	0	0	125	147	100	87	83	126
	—Texas (A.L.)	1	0	1.000	4.00	3	1	0	0	0	9	11	4	4	1	8
1979—	Tucson (Pac. Coast)	6	6	.500	3.60	13	13	4	1	0	95	89	43	38	42	65
	—Texas (A.L.)	4	4	.500	4.04	20	6	1	0	0	78	50	36	35	30	58
1980—	Texas (A.L.)	13	4	.765	2.62	53	2	0	0	8	110	98	37	32	50	104
1981—	Texas (A.L.)	9	9	.500	3.64	22	22	6	2	0	146	115	67	59	57	98
1982—	Texas (A.L.)	10	8	.556	3.44	56	1	0	0	7	89	95	38	34	37	61
1983—	Texas (A.L.)	8	13	.381	3.49	28	26	9	2	0	183	175	86	71	62	92
1984—	Texas (A.L.)	8	12	.400	3.94	35	32	5	2	0	223 2/3	249	110	98	54	123
1985—	Milwaukee (A.L.)■	8	18	.308	3.80	39	29	11	1	2	217 2/3	212	112	92	65	125
1986—	Milwaukee (A.L.)	6	8	.429	3.52	27	14	5	1	0	130 1/3	120	62	51	35	80
	—Houston (N.L.)■	5	2	.714	2.32	12	8	1	0	0	54 1/3	50	19	14	9	40
1987—	Houston (N.L.)	9	10	.474	3.59	33	30	3	1	0	195 2/3	184	87	78	69	134
1988—	Houston (N.L.)	8	13	.381	3.84	44	20	3	0	3	192	189	86	82	48	129
1989—	Houston (N.L.)	11	4	.733	2.36	68	0	0	0	7	122	92	34	32	33	104
1990—	Houston (N.L.)	11	4	.733	*2.21	48	17	3	0	2	162 2/3	136	42	40	31	109

Year	Team (League)	W	L	Pct.	ERA	G	GS	CG	ShO	Sv.	IP	H	R	ER	BB	SO
1991—	Boston (A.L.)■	3	6	.333	5.16	12	12	0	0	0	68	71	39	39	15	42
1992—	Boston (A.L.)	9	9	.500	3.96	51	15	2	0	3	161 1/3	159	76	71	53	124
1993—	Boston (A.L.)	15	11	.577	3.26	34	34	2	1	0	229 1/3	196	93	83	49	130
1994—	Boston (A.L.)	7	5	.583	6.30	13	13	0	0	0	75 2/3	101	54	53	24	54
1995—	Toronto (A.L.)■	1	8	.111	7.62	13	11	1	0	0	65	91	60	55	24	36
—	Okla. City (A.A.)■	0	0	...	0.00	1	1	0	0	0	3	1	0	0	0	4
—	Texas (A.L.)	2	2	.500	7.15	7	4	0	0	0	34	40	27	27	7	22
A.L. totals (14 years)		104	117	.471	3.98	413	222	42	9	20	1820	1783	901	804	563	1157
N.L. totals (5 years)		44	33	.571	3.05	205	75	10	1	12	726 2/3	651	268	246	190	516
Major league totals (18 years)		148	150	.497	3.71	618	297	52	10	32	2546 2/3	2434	1169	1050	753	1673

DARWIN, JEFF — P — WHITE SOX

PERSONAL: Born July 6, 1969, in Sherman, Tex. . . . 6-3/180. . . . Throws right, bats right. . . . Full name: Jeffrey Scott Darwin. . . . Brother of Danny Darwin, major league pitcher with six teams (1978-95).

HIGH SCHOOL: Bonham (Tex.).

JUNIOR COLLEGE: Alvin (Tex.) Community College.

TRANSACTIONS/CAREER NOTES: Selected by Seattle Mariners organization in 46th round of free-agent draft (June 2, 1987); did not sign. . . . Selected by Mariners organization in 13th round of free-agent draft (June 1, 1988). . . . On disabled list (June 3-August 2, 1991). . . . Traded by Mariners with OF Henry Cotto to Florida Marlins for 3B Dave Magadan (June 27, 1993). . . . Traded by Marlins with cash to Mariners for 3B Dave Magadan (November 9, 1993). . . . Traded by Mariners organization to Chicago White Sox organization (October 9, 1995), completing deal in which Mariners acquired OF Warren Newson from White Sox for a player to be named later (July 18, 1995).

STATISTICAL NOTES: Led Carolina League with nine balks in 1990.

Year	Team (League)	W	L	Pct.	ERA	G	GS	CG	ShO	Sv.	IP	H	R	ER	BB	SO
1989—	Bellingham (N'west)	1	7	.125	4.92	12	12	0	0	0	64	73	42	35	24	47
1990—	Peninsula (Caro.)	8	•14	.364	4.01	25	25	1	0	0	150 1/3	153	86	67	57	89
1991—	San Bern. (Calif.)	3	9	.250	6.20	16	14	0	0	0	74	80	53	51	31	58
1992—	Peninsula (Caro.)	5	11	.313	3.35	32	20	4	•2	3	139 2/3	132	58	52	40	122
1993—	Jacksonville (Sou.)	3	5	.375	2.97	27	0	0	0	7	36 1/3	29	17	12	17	39
—	Edmonton (PCL)■	2	2	.500	8.51	25	0	0	0	2	30 2/3	50	34	29	10	22
1994—	Calgary (PCL)■	1	2	.333	3.44	42	0	0	0	11	70 2/3	60	32	27	28	54
—	Seattle (A.L.)	0	0	...	13.50	2	0	0	0	0	4	7	6	6	3	1
1995—	Tacoma (PCL)	7	2	.778	2.70	46	0	0	0	12	63 1/3	51	21	19	21	51
Major league totals (1 year)		0	0	...	13.50	2	0	0	0	0	4	7	6	6	3	1

D

DAULTON, DARREN — C — PHILLIES

PERSONAL: Born January 3, 1962, in Arkansas City, Kan. . . . 6-2/207. . . . Bats left, throws right. . . . Full name: Darren Arthur Daulton.

HIGH SCHOOL: Arkansas City (Kan.).

JUNIOR COLLEGE: Crowley County (Kan.) Community College.

TRANSACTIONS/CAREER NOTES: Selected by Philadelphia Phillies organization in 25th round of free-agent draft (June 3, 1980). . . . On disabled list (July 20-August 28, 1984). . . . On Philadelphia disabled list (May 17-August 9, 1985); included rehabilitation assignment to Portland (July 20-August 7). . . . On Philadelphia disabled list (June 22, 1986-remainder of season; April 1-16, 1987; August 28, 1988-remainder of season; and May 6-21, 1991). . . . On Philadelphia disabled list (May 28-June 18 and September 7, 1991-remainder of season); included rehabilitation assignments to Scranton/Wilkes-Barre (June 15-17) and Reading (June 17-18). . . . On disabled list (June 29, 1994-remainder of season and August 26, 1995-remainder of season).

HONORS: Named catcher on THE SPORTING NEWS N.L. All-Star team (1992). . . . Named catcher on THE SPORTING NEWS N.L. Silver Slugger team (1992).

STATISTICAL NOTES: Tied for Eastern League lead with 10 sacrifice flies in 1983. . . . Tied for N.L. lead in double plays by catcher with 10 in 1990. . . . Led N.L. catchers with 1,057 total chances and 19 double plays in 1993. . . . Career major league grand slams: 5.

				BATTING											FIELDING			
Year	Team (League)	Pos.	G	AB	R	H	2B	3B	HR	RBI	Avg.	BB	SO	SB	PO	A	E	Avg.
1980—	Helena (Pioneer)	C	37	100	13	20	2	1	1	10	.200	23	29	5	224	17	4	.984
1981—	Spartanburg (SAL)	C-OF-3B	98	270	44	62	11	1	3	29	.230	56	35	14	378	34	4	.990
1982—	Peninsula (Caro.)	C-1B	110	324	65	78	21	2	11	44	.241	89	51	17	654	63	9	.988
1983—	Reading (Eastern)	C-1B-OF	113	362	77	95	16	4	19	83	.262	106	87	28	557	57	14	.978
—	Philadelphia (N.L.)	C	2	3	1	1	0	0	0	0	.333	1	1	0	8	0	0	1.000
1984—	Portland (PCL)	C	80	252	45	75	19	4	7	38	.298	57	49	3	322	26	6	.983
1985—	Portland (PCL)	C	23	64	13	19	5	3	2	10	.297	16	13	6	110	9	0	1.000
—	Philadelphia (N.L.)	C	36	103	14	21	3	1	4	11	.204	16	37	3	160	15	1	.994
1986—	Philadelphia (N.L.)	C	49	138	18	31	4	0	8	21	.225	38	41	2	244	21	4	.985
1987—	Clearwater (FSL)	C-1B	9	22	1	5	3	0	1	5	.227	4	3	0	27	5	3	.914
—	Maine (Int'l)	C-1B	20	70	9	15	1	1	3	10	.214	16	15	5	138	12	0	1.000
—	Philadelphia (N.L.)	C-1B	53	129	10	25	6	0	3	13	.194	16	37	0	210	13	2	.991
1988—	Philadelphia (N.L.)	C-1B	58	144	13	30	6	0	1	12	.208	17	26	2	205	15	6	.973
1989—	Philadelphia (N.L.)	C	131	368	29	74	12	2	8	44	.201	52	58	2	627	56	11	.984
1990—	Philadelphia (N.L.)	C	143	459	62	123	30	1	12	57	.268	72	72	7	683	*70	8	.989
1991—	Philadelphia (N.L.)	C	89	285	36	56	12	0	12	42	.196	41	66	5	493	33	8	.985
—	Scran./W.B. (Int'l)	C	2	9	1	2	0	0	1	1	.222	0	0	0	14	1	0	1.000
—	Reading (Eastern)	C	1	4	0	1	0	0	0	0	.250	1	0	0	6	2	0	1.000
1992—	Philadelphia (N.L.)	C	145	485	80	131	32	5	27	*109	.270	88	103	11	760	69	11	.987
1993—	Philadelphia (N.L.)	C	147	510	90	131	35	4	24	105	.257	117	111	5	*981	67	9	.991
1994—	Philadelphia (N.L.)	C	69	257	43	77	17	1	15	56	.300	33	43	4	435	42	3	.994
1995—	Philadelphia (N.L.)	C	98	342	44	85	19	3	9	55	.249	55	52	3	631	45	4	.994
Major league totals (12 years)			1020	3223	440	785	176	17	123	525	.244	546	647	44	5437	446	67	.989

CHAMPIONSHIP SERIES RECORD

NOTES: Shares single-game record for most bases on balls received—4 (October 10, 1993).

Year	Team (League)	Pos.	G	AB	R	H	2B	3B	HR	RBI	Avg.	BB	SO	SB	PO	A	E	Avg.
								BATTING							FIELDING			
1993—	Philadelphia (N.L.)......	C	6	19	2	5	1	0	1	3	.263	6	3	0	54	3	0	1.000

WORLD SERIES RECORD

Year	Team (League)	Pos.	G	AB	R	H	2B	3B	HR	RBI	Avg.	BB	SO	SB	PO	A	E	Avg.
								BATTING							FIELDING			
1993—	Philadelphia (N.L.)......	C	6	23	4	5	2	0	1	4	.217	4	5	0	31	4	0	1.000

ALL-STAR GAME RECORD

Year	League	Pos.	AB	R	H	2B	3B	HR	RBI	Avg.	BB	SO	SB	PO	A	E	Avg.
							BATTING							FIELDING			
1992—	National......................	C	3	1	0	0	0	0	0	.000	0	0	0	5	0	0	1.000
1993—	National......................	C	3	0	0	0	0	0	0	.000	0	1	0	4	0	0	1.000
1995—	National......................	C	0	0	0	0	0	0	0	...	0	0	0	3	0	0	1.000
All-Star Game totals (3 years)			6	1	0	0	0	0	0	.000	0	1	0	12	0	0	1.000

DAVIS, CHILI — DH — ANGELS

PERSONAL: Born January 17, 1960, in Kingston, Jamaica. . . . 6-3/217. . . . Bats both, throws right. . . . Full name: Charles Theodore Davis.
HIGH SCHOOL: Dorsey (Los Angeles).
TRANSACTIONS/CAREER NOTES: Selected by San Francisco Giants organization in 11th round of free-agent draft (June 7, 1977). . . . On Phoenix disabled list (August 19-28, 1981). . . . Granted free agency (November 9, 1987). . . . Signed by California Angels (December 1, 1987). . . . On disabled list (July 17-August 9, 1990). . . . Granted free agency (December 7, 1990). . . . Signed by Minnesota Twins (January 29, 1991). . . . Granted free agency (November 3, 1992). . . . Signed by Angels (December 11, 1992). . . . On disabled list (June 20-July 18, 1995).
RECORDS: Shares A.L. single-season record for most games with switch-hit home runs—2 (1994).
STATISTICAL NOTES: Switch-hit home runs in one game eight times (June 5, 1983; June 27 and September 15, 1987; July 30, 1988; July 1, 1989; October 2, 1992; and May 11 and July 30, 1994). . . . Tied for A.L. lead with 10 sacrifice flies in 1988. . . . Career major league grand slams: 6.
MISCELLANEOUS: Original nickname was Chili Bowl, which was prompted by a friend who saw Davis after he received a haircut in the sixth grade. The nickname was later shortened to Chili.

D

Year	Team (League)	Pos.	G	AB	R	H	2B	3B	HR	RBI	Avg.	BB	SO	SB	PO	A	E	Avg.
								BATTING							FIELDING			
1978—	Ced. Rap. (Midw.)	C-OF	124	424	63	119	18	5	16	73	.281	36	103	15	365	45	25	.943
1979—	Fresno (California)......	OF-C	134	490	91	132	24	5	21	95	.269	80	91	30	339	43	20	.950
1980—	Shreveport (Texas).....	OF-C	129	442	50	130	30	4	12	67	.294	52	94	19	184	20	12	.944
1981—	San Francisco (N.L.) ..	OF	8	15	1	2	0	0	0	0	.133	1	2	2	7	0	0	1.000
—	Phoenix (PCL)...........	OF	88	334	76	117	16	6	19	75	.350	46	54	40	175	7	6	.968
1982—	San Francisco (N.L.) ..	OF	154	641	86	167	27	6	19	76	.261	45	115	24	404	•16	12	.972
1983—	San Francisco (N.L.) ..	OF	137	486	54	113	21	2	11	59	.233	55	108	10	357	7	9	.976
—	Phoenix (PCL)...........	OF	10	44	12	13	2	0	2	9	.295	4	6	5	15	0	2	.882
1984—	San Francisco (N.L.) ..	OF	137	499	87	157	21	6	21	81	.315	42	74	12	292	9	9	.971
1985—	San Francisco (N.L.) ..	OF	136	481	53	130	25	2	13	56	.270	62	74	15	279	10	6	.980
1986—	San Francisco (N.L.) ..	OF	153	526	71	146	28	3	13	70	.278	84	96	16	303	9	•9	.972
1987—	San Francisco (N.L.) ..	OF	149	500	80	125	22	1	24	76	.250	72	109	16	265	6	7	.975
1988—	California (A.L.)■......	OF-DH	158	600	81	161	29	3	21	93	.268	56	118	9	299	10	*19	.942
1989—	California (A.L.).........	OF-DH	154	560	81	152	24	1	22	90	.271	61	109	3	270	5	6	.979
1990—	California (A.L.).........	DH-OF	113	412	58	109	17	1	12	58	.265	61	89	1	77	5	3	.965
1991—	Minnesota (A.L.)■.....	DH-OF	153	534	84	148	34	1	29	93	.277	95	117	5	2	0	0	1.000
1992—	Minnesota (A.L.)	DH-OF-1B	138	444	63	128	27	2	12	66	.288	73	76	4	6	0	0	1.000
1993—	California (A.L.)■.......	DH-P	153	573	74	139	32	0	27	112	.243	71	135	4	0	0	0	...
1994—	California (A.L.).........	DH-OF	108	392	72	122	18	1	26	84	.311	69	84	3	5	0	0	1.000
1995—	California (A.L.).........	DH	119	424	81	135	23	0	20	86	.318	89	79	3	...	...	...	...
American League totals (8 years)			1096	3939	594	1094	204	9	169	682	.278	575	807	32	659	20	28	.960
National League totals (7 years)			874	3148	432	840	144	20	101	418	.267	361	578	95	1907	57	52	.974
Major league totals (15 years)			1970	7087	1026	1934	348	29	270	1100	.273	936	1385	127	2566	77	80	.971

CHAMPIONSHIP SERIES RECORD

NOTES: Shares A.L. single-series record for most strikeouts—8 (1991).

Year	Team (League)	Pos.	G	AB	R	H	2B	3B	HR	RBI	Avg.	BB	SO	SB	PO	A	E	Avg.
								BATTING							FIELDING			
1987—	San Francisco (N.L.) ..	OF	6	20	2	3	1	0	0	0	.150	1	4	0	11	1	1	.923
1991—	Minnesota (A.L.)	DH	5	17	3	5	2	0	0	2	.294	5	8	1	...	...	...	...
Championship series totals (2 years)			11	37	5	8	3	0	0	2	.216	6	12	1	11	1	1	.923

WORLD SERIES RECORD

NOTES: Member of World Series championship team (1991).

Year	Team (League)	Pos.	G	AB	R	H	2B	3B	HR	RBI	Avg.	BB	SO	SB	PO	A	E	Avg.
								BATTING							FIELDING			
1991—	Minnesota (A.L.)	DH-PH-OF	6	18	4	4	0	0	2	4	.222	2	3	0	1	0	0	1.000

ALL-STAR GAME RECORD

Year	League	Pos.	AB	R	H	2B	3B	HR	RBI	Avg.	BB	SO	SB	PO	A	E	Avg.
							BATTING							FIELDING			
1984—	National......................	PH	1	0	0	0	0	0	0	.000	0	0	0	...	...	...	...
1986—	National......................	OF	1	0	0	0	0	0	0	.000	0	1	0	0	0	0	...
1994—	American....................	PH	1	0	0	0	0	0	0	.000	0	0	0	...	...	...	...
All-Star Game totals (3 years)			3	0	0	0	0	0	0	.000	0	1	0	0	0	0	...

RECORD AS PITCHER

Year	Team (League)	W	L	Pct.	ERA	G	GS	CG	ShO	Sv.	IP	H	R	ER	BB	SO
1993—	California (A.L.)	0	0	...	0.00	1	0	0	0	0	2	0	0	0	0	0

DAVIS, JEFF — P — RANGERS

PERSONAL: Born August 20, 1972, in Fall River, Mass. . . . 6-0/170. . . . Throws right, bats right. . . . Full name: Jeff Marc Davis.
HIGH SCHOOL: Durfee (Fall River, Mass.).
JUNIOR COLLEGE: Massasoit (Mass.).
TRANSACTIONS/CAREER NOTES: Selected by Texas Rangers organization in 28th round of free-agent draft (June 3, 1993).

Year	Team (League)	W	L	Pct.	ERA	G	GS	CG	ShO	Sv.	IP	H	R	ER	BB	SO
1993—	Erie (N.Y.-Penn)	0	5	.000	3.65	27	0	0	0	13	37	32	18	15	10	41
1994—	Char., S.C. (S. Atl.)	2	3	.400	3.99	45	0	0	0	19	49 2/3	53	25	22	11	72
1995—	Charlotte (Fla. St.)	12	7	.632	2.89	26	26	0	0	0	165 1/3	159	74	53	37	105
	—Tulsa (Texas)	1	0	1.000	0.00	1	1	0	0	0	7	2	0	0	1	4

DAVIS, RUSS — 3B — MARINERS

PERSONAL: Born September 13, 1969, in Birmingham, Ala. . . . 6-0/195. . . . Bats right, throws right. . . . Full name: Russell Stuart Davis.
JUNIOR COLLEGE: Shelton State Junior College (Ala.).
TRANSACTIONS/CAREER NOTES: Selected by New York Yankees organization in 29th round of free-agent draft (June 1, 1988). . . . On disabled list (July 13-August 1, 1993). . . . On Columbus disabled list (April 7-15 and August 26, 1994-remainder of season). . . . Traded by Yankees with P Sterling Hitchcock to Seattle Mariners for 1B Tino Martinez, P Jeff Nelson and P Jim Mecir (December 7, 1995).
HONORS: Named Eastern League Most Valuable Player (1992).
STATISTICAL NOTES: Tied for New York-Pennsylvania League lead in double plays by third baseman with 11 in 1989. . . . Led Carolina League third basemen with 336 total chances and 18 double plays in 1990. . . . Tied for Eastern League lead in fielding percentage by third basemen with .917, putouts with 83, assists with 205, errors with 26 and total chances with 314 in 1991. . . . Led Eastern League with 237 total bases and .483 slugging percentage in 1992. . . . Led International League third basemen with 25 errors in 1993.

			BATTING												FIELDING			
Year	Team (League)	Pos.	G	AB	R	H	2B	3B	HR	RBI	Avg.	BB	SO	SB	PO	A	E	Avg.
1988—	GC Yankees (GCL)	2B-3B	58	213	33	49	11	3	2	30	.230	16	39	6	64	105	15	.918
1989—	Fort Lauder. (FSL)	3B-2B	48	147	8	27	5	1	2	22	.184	11	38	3	32	72	17	.860
	—Oneonta (NYP)	3B	65	236	33	68	7	5	7	42	.288	19	44	3	27	87	17	.870
1990—	Prin. William (Car.)	3B	137	510	55	127	*37	3	16	71	.249	37	136	3	*68	*244	24	.929
1991—	Alb./Colon. (East.)	3B-2B	135	473	57	103	23	3	8	58	.218	50	102	3	‡83	‡206	‡26	‡.917
1992—	Alb./Colon. (East.)	3B	132	491	77	140	23	4	22	71	.285	49	93	3	78	185	23	.920
1993—	Columbus (Int'l)	3B-SS	113	424	63	108	24	1	26	83	.255	40	118	1	85	245	†26	.927
1994—	Columbus (Int'l)	3B-1B	117	416	76	115	30	2	25	69	.276	62	93	3	86	250	23	.936
	—New York (A.L.)	3B	4	14	0	2	0	0	0	1	.143	0	4	0	2	6	0	1.000
1995—	Columbus (Int'l)	3B-1B	20	76	12	19	4	1	2	15	.250	17	23	0	17	31	7	.873
Major league totals (1 year)			4	14	0	2	0	0	0	1	.143	0	4	0	2	6	0	1.000

DIVISION SERIES RECORD

			BATTING												FIELDING			
Year	Team (League)	Pos.	G	AB	R	H	2B	3B	HR	RBI	Avg.	BB	SO	SB	PO	A	E	Avg.
1995—	New York (A.L.)	3B	2	5	0	1	0	0	0	0	.200	0	2	0	0	1	0	1.000

DAVIS, TIM — P — MARINERS

PERSONAL: Born July 14, 1970, in Marianna, Fla. . . . 5-11/165. . . . Throws left, bats left. . . . Full name: Timothy Howard Davis.
HIGH SCHOOL: Liberty County (Bristol, Fla.).
JUNIOR COLLEGE: Gulf Coast Community College (Fla.).
COLLEGE: Florida State.
TRANSACTIONS/CAREER NOTES: Selected by Minnesota Twins organization in 34th round of free-agent draft (June 3, 1991); did not sign. . . . Selected by Seattle Mariners organization in sixth round of free-agent draft (June 1, 1992). . . . On Tacoma disabled list (June 7-September 8, 1995). . . . On Seattle disabled list (September 8, 1995-remainder of season).

Year	Team (League)	W	L	Pct.	ERA	G	GS	CG	ShO	Sv.	IP	H	R	ER	BB	SO
1993—	Appleton (Midw.)	10	2	.833	1.85	16	10	3	2	2	77 2/3	54	20	16	33	89
	—Riverside (Calif.)	3	0	1.000	1.76	18	0	0	0	7	30 2/3	14	6	6	9	56
1994—	Seattle (A.L.)	2	2	.500	4.01	42	1	0	0	2	49 1/3	57	25	22	25	28
	—Calgary (PCL)	3	1	.750	1.82	6	6	1	0	0	39 2/3	35	13	8	8	43
1995—	Seattle (A.L.)	2	1	.667	6.38	5	5	0	0	0	24	30	21	17	18	19
	—Tacoma (PCL)	0	1	.000	5.40	2	2	0	0	0	13 1/3	15	8	8	4	13
Major league totals (2 years)		4	3	.571	4.79	47	6	0	0	2	73 1/3	87	46	39	43	47

DAVISON, SCOTT — P — MARINERS

PERSONAL: Born October 16, 1970, in Inglewood, Calif. . . . 6-0/190. . . . Throws right, bats right. . . . Full name: Scott Ray Davison.
HIGH SCHOOL: Redondo Union (Redondo Beach, Calif.).
TRANSACTIONS/CAREER NOTES: Selected by Montreal Expos organization in fifth round of free-agent draft (June 1, 1988). . . . Released by Harrisburg, Expos organization (February 5, 1992). . . . Signed by Bellingham, Seattle Mariners organization (May 17, 1994).

Year	Team (League)	W	L	Pct.	ERA	G	GS	CG	ShO	Sv.	IP	H	R	ER	BB	SO
1992—							Out of organized baseball.									
1993—							Out of organized baseball.									
1994—	Bellingham (N'west)	0	1	.000	1.80	13	0	0	0	7	15	11	5	3	6	21
	—Appleton (Midw.)	0	1	.000	3.68	4	0	0	0	0	7 1/3	7	4	3	2	7

Year	Team (League)	W	L	Pct.	ERA	G	GS	CG	ShO	Sv.	IP	H	R	ER	BB	SO
	—Calgary (PCL)	0	1	.000	6.14	11	0	0	0	0	14 2/3	20	10	10	6	17
1995	—Tacoma (PCL)	1	1	.500	5.32	8	3	0	0	0	22	21	14	13	4	12
	—Port City (Southern)	2	0	1.000	0.89	34	0	0	0	10	40 2/3	22	4	4	16	50
	—Seattle (A.L.)	0	0	...	6.23	3	0	0	0	0	4 1/3	7	3	3	1	3
Major league totals (1 year)		0	0	...	6.23	3	0	0	0	0	4 1/3	7	3	3	1	3

RECORD AS POSITION PLAYER

				BATTING										FIELDING			
Year	Team (League)	Pos.	G	AB	R	H	2B	3B	HR	RBI	Avg.	BB	SO	SB	PO	A	E	Avg.
1988	—GC Expos (GCL)	2B-SS	30	98	11	19	3	0	0	8	.194	9	21	8	22	53	5	.938
1989	—Jamestown (NYP)	SS-2B	59	230	29	55	10	3	0	18	.239	21	57	19	77	168	24	.911
1990	—Rockford (Midw.)	SS-3B	127	441	52	95	13	7	1	48	.215	60	115	22	182	403	28	.954
1991	—W.P. Beach (FSL)	SS-2B-OF	82	250	19	42	6	4	1	24	.168	31	66	11	125	194	17	.949

DAWSON, ANDRE OF MARLINS

PERSONAL: Born July 10, 1954, in Miami. . . . 6-3/197. . . . Bats right, throws right. . . . Full name: Andre Nolan Dawson.

HIGH SCHOOL: Southwest Miami.

COLLEGE: Florida A&M.

TRANSACTIONS/CAREER NOTES: Selected by Montreal Expos organization in 11th round of free-agent draft (June 4, 1975). . . . On disabled list (June 5-30, 1986). . . . Granted free agency (November 12, 1986). . . . Signed by Chicago Cubs (March 9, 1987). . . . On disabled list (May 7-June 12, 1989). . . . On suspended list (September 17, 1991). . . . Granted free agency (November 4, 1992). . . . Signed by Boston Red Sox (December 9, 1992). . . . On disabled list (May 6-25, 1993; May 25-June 10 and July 20-August 4, 1994). . . . Granted free agency (October 21, 1994). . . . Signed by Florida Marlins (April 10, 1995). . . . On Florida disabled list (July 3-August 1, 1995); included rehabilitation assignment to Brevard County (July 19-24). . . . Granted free agency (November 7, 1995). . . . Re-signed by Marlins organization (January 5, 1996).

RECORDS: Holds major league single-game record for most intentional bases on balls received—5 (May 22, 1990, 16 innings). . . . Shares major league records for most total bases—8; and most home runs—2, in one inning (July 30, 1978, third inning, and September 24, 1985, fifth inning); and most runs batted in in one inning—6 (September 24, 1985, fifth inning). . . . Shares major league single-season record for fewest double plays by outfielder (150 or more games)—0 (1987).

HONORS: Named N.L. Rookie Player of the Year by The Sporting News (1977). . . . Named N.L. Rookie of the Year by Baseball Writers' Association of America (1977). . . . Named outfielder on The Sporting News N.L. Silver Slugger team (1980-81, 1983 and 1987). . . . Won N.L. Gold Glove as outfielder (1980-85 and 1987-88). . . . Named N.L. Player of the Year by The Sporting News (1981 and 1987). . . . Named outfielder on The Sporting News N.L. All-Star team (1981, 1983 and 1987). . . . Named N.L. Most Valuable Player by Baseball Writers' Association of America (1987).

STATISTICAL NOTES: Led Pioneer League with 166 total bases, in being hit by pitch with six and tied for lead with five sacrifice flies in 1975. . . . Led N.L. in being hit by pitch with 12 in 1978, seven in 1981 and tied for lead with six in 1980 and nine in 1983. . . . Led N.L. outfielders with 344 total chances in 1981, 435 in 1982 and 450 in 1983. . . . Hit for the cycle (April 29, 1987). . . . Led N.L. with 341 total bases in 1983 and 353 in 1987. . . . Led N.L. with 18 sacrifice flies in 1983. . . . Hit three home runs in one game (September 24, 1985 and August 1, 1987). . . . Tied for N.L. lead with 16 game-winning RBIs in 1987. . . . Tied for N.L. lead with 21 intentional bases on balls received in 1990. . . . Career major league grand slams: 7.

				BATTING										FIELDING			
Year	Team (League)	Pos.	G	AB	R	H	2B	3B	HR	RBI	Avg.	BB	SO	SB	PO	A	E	Avg.
1975	—Lethbridge (Pio.)	OF	•72	*300	52	*99	14	7	*13	50	.330	23	59	11	*142	7	*10	.937
1976	—Quebec City (East.)	OF	40	143	27	51	6	0	8	27	.357	12	21	9	89	3	6	.939
	—Denver (A.A.)	OF	74	240	51	84	19	4	20	46	.350	23	50	10	97	2	2	.980
	—Montreal (N.L.)	OF	24	85	9	20	4	1	0	7	.235	5	13	1	61	1	2	.969
1977	—Montreal (N.L.)	OF	139	525	64	148	26	9	19	65	.282	34	93	21	352	9	4	.989
1978	—Montreal (N.L.)	OF	157	609	84	154	24	8	25	72	.253	30	128	28	411	17	5	.988
1979	—Montreal (N.L.)	OF	155	639	90	176	24	12	25	92	.275	27	115	35	394	7	5	.988
1980	—Montreal (N.L.)	OF	151	577	96	178	41	7	17	87	.308	44	69	34	410	14	6	.986
1981	—Montreal (N.L.)	OF	103	394	71	119	21	3	24	64	.302	35	50	26	*327	10	7	.980
1982	—Montreal (N.L.)	OF	148	608	107	183	37	7	23	83	.301	34	96	39	*419	8	8	.982
1983	—Montreal (N.L.)	OF	159	633	104	•189	36	10	32	113	.299	38	81	25	*435	6	9	.980
1984	—Montreal (N.L.)	OF	138	533	73	132	23	6	17	86	.248	41	80	13	297	11	8	.975
1985	—Montreal (N.L.)	OF	139	529	65	135	27	2	23	91	.255	29	92	13	248	9	7	.973
1986	—Montreal (N.L.)	OF	130	496	65	141	32	2	20	78	.284	37	79	18	200	11	3	.986
1987	—Chicago (N.L.)■	OF	153	621	90	178	24	2	*49	*137	.287	32	103	11	271	12	4	.986
1988	—Chicago (N.L.)	OF	157	591	78	179	31	8	24	79	.303	37	73	12	267	7	3	.989
1989	—Chicago (N.L.)	OF	118	416	62	105	18	6	21	77	.252	35	62	8	227	4	3	.987
1990	—Chicago (N.L.)	OF	147	529	72	164	28	5	27	100	.310	42	65	16	250	10	5	.981
1991	—Chicago (N.L.)	OF	149	563	69	153	21	4	31	104	.272	22	80	4	243	7	3	.988
1992	—Chicago (N.L.)	OF	143	542	60	150	27	2	22	90	.277	30	70	6	223	11	2	.992
1993	—Boston (A.L.)■	DH-OF	121	461	44	126	29	1	13	67	.273	17	49	2	42	0	0	1.000
1994	—Boston (A.L.)	DH	75	292	34	70	18	0	16	48	.240	9	53	2	...	...	...	...
1995	—Florida (N.L.)■	OF	79	226	30	58	10	3	8	37	.257	9	45	0	76	3	8	.908
	—Brevard Co. (FSL)	DH	3	10	0	1	0	0	0	0	.100	0	2	0	...	...	...	...
American League totals (2 years)			196	753	78	196	47	1	29	115	.260	26	102	4	42	0	0	1.000
National League totals (18 years)			2389	9116	1289	2562	454	97	407	1462	.281	561	1394	310	5111	157	92	.983
Major league totals (20 years)			2585	9869	1367	2758	501	98	436	1577	.279	587	1496	314	5153	157	92	.983

DIVISION SERIES RECORD

				BATTING										FIELDING			
Year	Team (League)	Pos.	G	AB	R	H	2B	3B	HR	RBI	Avg.	BB	SO	SB	PO	A	E	Avg.
1981	—Montreal (N.L.)	OF	5	20	1	6	0	1	0	0	.300	1	6	2	12	1	1	.929

CHAMPIONSHIP SERIES RECORD

				BATTING										FIELDING			
Year	Team (League)	Pos.	G	AB	R	H	2B	3B	HR	RBI	Avg.	BB	SO	SB	PO	A	E	Avg.
1981	—Montreal (N.L.)	OF	5	20	2	3	0	0	0	0	.150	0	4	0	12	0	0	1.000

Year	League	Pos.		AB	R	H	2B	3B	HR	RBI	Avg.	BB	SO	SB	PO	A	E	Avg.
			BATTING												FIELDING			
1989—	Chicago (N.L.)	OF	5	19	0	2	1	0	0	3	.105	2	6	0	4	0	0	1.000
Championship series totals (2 years)			10	39	2	5	1	0	0	3	.128	2	10	0	16	0	0	1.000

ALL-STAR GAME RECORD

Year	League	Pos.	AB	R	H	2B	3B	HR	RBI	Avg.	BB	SO	SB	PO	A	E	Avg.
			BATTING											FIELDING			
1981—	National	OF	4	0	1	0	0	0	0	.250	0	1	1	4	0	0	1.000
1982—	National	OF	4	0	1	0	0	0	0	.250	0	0	0	4	0	0	1.000
1983—	National	OF	3	0	0	0	0	0	0	.000	0	1	0	3	0	0	1.000
1987—	National	OF	3	0	1	1	0	0	0	.333	0	1	0	3	0	0	1.000
1988—	National	OF	2	0	1	0	0	0	0	.500	0	0	0	0	0	0	...
1989—	National	OF	1	0	0	0	0	0	0	.000	0	0	0	1	0	0	1.000
1990—	National	OF	2	0	0	0	0	0	0	.000	0	1	0	1	0	0	1.000
1991—	National	OF	2	1	1	0	0	1	1	.500	0	0	0	0	0	0	...
All-Star Game totals (8 years)			21	1	5	1	0	1	1	.238	0	4	1	16	0	0	1.000

DECKER, STEVE — C

PERSONAL: Born October 25, 1965, in Rock Island, Ill. . . . 6-3/220. . . . Bats right, throws right. . . . Full name: Steven Michael Decker.
HIGH SCHOOL: Rock Island (Ill.).
COLLEGE: Lewis-Clark State College (Idaho).
TRANSACTIONS/CAREER NOTES: Selected by San Francisco Giants organization in 21st round of free-agent draft (June 1, 1988). . . . Selected by Florida Marlins in second round (35th pick overall) of expansion draft (November 17, 1992). . . . On disabled list (May 18, 1993-remainder of season). . . . On disabled list (April 8-May 14, 1994). . . . Granted free agency (October 16, 1995).
STATISTICAL NOTES: Led Pacific Coast League catchers with 626 putouts and 694 total chances in 1992.

Year	Team (League)	Pos.	G	AB	R	H	2B	3B	HR	RBI	Avg.	BB	SO	SB	PO	A	E	Avg.
				BATTING											FIELDING			
1988—	Everett (N'west)	C	13	42	11	22	2	0	2	13	.524	7	5	0	37	3	2	.952
—	San Jose (Calif.)	C	47	175	31	56	9	0	4	34	.320	21	21	0	199	26	5	.978
1989—	San Jose (Calif.)	C-1B	64	225	27	65	12	0	3	46	.289	44	36	8	417	51	7	.985
—	Shreveport (Texas)	C-1B	44	142	19	46	8	0	1	18	.324	11	24	0	229	22	5	.980
1990—	Shreveport (Texas)	C	116	403	52	118	22	1	15	80	.293	40	64	3	650	71	10	.986
—	San Francisco (N.L.)	C	15	54	5	16	2	0	3	8	.296	1	10	0	75	11	1	.989
1991—	San Francisco (N.L.)	C	79	233	11	48	7	1	5	24	.206	16	44	0	385	41	7	.984
—	Phoenix (PCL)	C	31	111	20	28	5	1	6	14	.252	13	29	0	156	16	1	.994
1992—	Phoenix (PCL)	C-1B	125	450	50	127	22	2	8	74	.282	47	64	2	†650	65	5	.993
—	San Francisco (N.L.)	C	15	43	3	7	1	0	0	1	.163	6	7	0	94	4	0	1.000
1993—	Florida (N.L.)■	C	8	15	0	0	0	0	0	1	.000	3	3	0	28	2	1	.968
1994—	Edmonton (PCL)	C-1B	73	259	38	101	23	0	11	48	.390	27	24	0	295	34	8	.976
1995—	Florida (N.L.)	C-1B	51	133	12	30	2	1	3	13	.226	19	22	1	299	24	5	.985
Major league totals (5 years)			168	478	31	101	12	2	11	47	.211	45	86	1	881	82	14	.986

DEDRICK, JIM — P — ORIOLES

PERSONAL: Born April 4, 1968, in Los Angeles. . . . 6-0/185. . . . Throws right, bats both. . . . Full name: James Michael Dedrick.
HIGH SCHOOL: Huntington Beach (Calif.).
JUNIOR COLLEGE: Orange Coast Community College (Calif.).
COLLEGE: Southern California College.
TRANSACTIONS/CAREER NOTES: Selected by Baltimore Orioles organization in 33rd round of free-agent draft (June 4, 1990). . . . On disabled list (May 21-June 12 and July 12-August 1, 1991).

Year	Team (League)	W	L	Pct.	ERA	G	GS	CG	ShO	Sv.	IP	H	R	ER	BB	SO
1990—	Wausau (Midwest)	0	1	.000	2.70	3	1	0	0	0	10	6	4	3	4	8
1991—	Kane Co. (Mid.)	4	5	.444	2.95	16	15	0	0	0	88 1/3	84	38	29	38	71
1992—	Frederick (Caro.)	8	4	.667	3.06	38	5	1	0	3	108 2/3	94	41	37	42	86
1993—	Bowie (Eastern)	8	3	.727	2.54	38	6	1	1	3	106 1/3	84	36	30	32	78
—	Rochester (Int'l)	1	0	1.000	2.57	1	1	1	0	0	7	6	2	2	0	3
1994—	Rochester (Int'l)	3	6	.333	3.82	44	1	0	0	1	99	98	56	42	35	70
1995—	Rochester (Int'l)	4	0	1.000	1.77	24	2	0	0	1	45 2/3	45	9	9	14	31
—	Bowie (Eastern)	4	2	.667	2.98	10	10	0	0	0	60 1/3	59	24	20	25	48
—	Baltimore (A.L.)	0	0	...	2.35	6	0	0	0	0	7 2/3	8	2	2	6	3
Major league totals (1 year)		0	0	...	2.35	6	0	0	0	0	7 2/3	8	2	2	6	3

DeJEAN, MIKE — P — ROCKIES

PERSONAL: Born September 28, 1970, in Baton Rouge, La. . . . 6-2/205. . . . Throws right, bats right. . . . Full name: Michel DeJean.
HIGH SCHOOL: Walker (La.).
COLLEGE: Livingston (La.).
TRANSACTIONS/CAREER NOTES: Selected by New York Yankees organization in 24th round of free-agent draft (June 1, 1992). . . . On disabled list (June 4-July 21 and July 26, 1993-remainder of season). . . . Traded by Yankees with a player to be named later to Colorado Rockies for C Joe Girardi (November 20, 1995); Rockies acquired P Steve Shoemaker to complete deal (December 6, 1995).

Year	Team (League)	W	L	Pct.	ERA	G	GS	CG	ShO	Sv.	IP	H	R	ER	BB	SO
1992—	Oneonta (NYP)	0	0	...	0.44	20	0	0	0	16	20 2/3	12	3	1	3	20
1993—	Greensboro (S. Atl.)	2	3	.400	5.00	20	0	0	0	9	18	22	12	10	8	16
1994—	Tampa (Fla. St.)	0	2	.000	2.38	34	0	0	0	16	34	39	15	9	13	22
—	Albany (East.)	0	2	.000	4.38	16	0	0	0	4	24 2/3	22	14	12	15	13
1995—	Norwich (Eastern)	5	5	.500	2.99	59	0	0	0	20	78 1/3	58	29	26	34	57

DE LA ROSA, MAXIMO — P — INDIANS

PERSONAL: Born July 12, 1971, in Villa Mella, Dominican Republic. . . . 5-11/170. . . . Throws right, bats right.
HIGH SCHOOL: Ramon Mella (Villa Mella, Dominican Republic).
TRANSACTIONS/CAREER NOTES: Signed as non-drafted free agent by Cleveland Indians organization (February 24, 1990).

Year	Team (League)	W	L	Pct.	ERA	G	GS	CG	ShO	Sv.	IP	H	R	ER	BB	SO
1993—	Burlington (Appal.)	7	2	.778	3.77	14	•14	2	1	0	76 1/3	53	38	32	37	69
1994—	Kinston (Carolina)	0	11	.000	5.04	13	13	0	0	0	69 2/3	82	56	39	38	53
	—Columbus (S. Atl.)	4	2	.667	3.35	14	14	0	0	0	75 1/3	49	33	28	38	71
1995—	Kinston (Carolina)	5	2	.714	2.19	43	0	0	0	8	61 2/3	46	23	15	37	61
	—Cant./Akr. (East.)	0	0	...	54.00	1	0	0	0	0	1/3	1	2	2	1	0

RECORD AS POSITION PLAYER

				BATTING											FIELDING			
Year	Team (League)	Pos.	G	AB	R	H	2B	3B	HR	RBI	Avg.	BB	SO	SB	PO	A	E	Avg.
1990—	Dom. Indians (DSL)	OF	61	225	51	63	14	1	1	31	.280	36	24	15	...	...	...	...
1991—	Dom. Indians (DSL)	OF	60	219	43	67	8	2	4	36	.306	28	23	15	...	...	...	...
1992—	Burlington (Appal.)	OF	62	222	27	54	5	1	1	30	.243	24	52	4	100	3	4	.963

DeLEON, JOSE — P

PERSONAL: Born December 20, 1960, in Rancho Viejo, LaVega, Dominican Republic. . . . 6-3/226. . . . Throws right, bats right. . . . Full name: Jose Chestaro DeLeon. . . . Name pronounced DAY-lee-own.
HIGH SCHOOL: Perth Amboy (N.J.).
TRANSACTIONS/CAREER NOTES: Selected by Pittsburgh Pirates organization in third round of free-agent draft (June 5, 1979); pick received as compensation for Montreal Expos signing free-agent C Duffy Dyer. . . . On disabled list (July 5-29, 1982). . . . Traded by Pirates organization to Chicago White Sox for OF Bobby Bonilla (July 23, 1986). . . . Traded by White Sox to St. Louis Cardinals for P Rick Horton, OF Lance Johnson and cash (February 9, 1988). . . . Released by Cardinals (August 31, 1992). . . . Signed by Philadelphia Phillies (September 9, 1992). . . . Traded by Phillies to Chicago White Sox for P Bobby Thigpen (August 10, 1993). . . . Granted free agency (November 1, 1993). . . . Re-signed by White Sox organization (December 7, 1993). . . . Granted free agency (October 25, 1994). . . . Signed by Chicago White Sox (April 7, 1995). . . . Traded by White Sox to Montreal Expos for P Jeff Shaw (October 28, 1995). . . . Granted free agency (October 16, 1995).
STATISTICAL NOTES: Led Gulf Coast League with seven home runs allowed and tied for lead with nine wild pitches in 1979. . . . Tied for South Atlantic League lead with 19 home runs allowed in 1980. . . . Pitched 2-0 one-hit, complete-game loss against Cincinnati (August 24, 1984).
MISCELLANEOUS: Appeared in one game as outfielder with one putout (1988).

Year	Team (League)	W	L	Pct.	ERA	G	GS	CG	ShO	Sv.	IP	H	R	ER	BB	SO
1979—	GC Pirates (GCL)	2	4	.333	6.41	11	9	2	0	1	59	76	47	42	38	33
1980—	Shelby (S. Atl.)	10	15	.400	4.82	26	26	7	0	0	168	160	108	*90	69	118
1981—	Buffalo (Eastern)	12	6	.667	3.11	25	25	2	0	0	159	136	72	55	94	158
1982—	Portland (PCL)	10	7	.588	5.97	24	23	3	0	0	119	138	81	79	65	94
1983—	Hawaii (PCL)	11	6	.647	*3.04	20	20	6	1	0	127 1/3	90	50	43	68	128
	—Pittsburgh (N.L.)	7	3	.700	2.83	15	15	3	2	0	108	75	36	34	47	118
1984—	Pittsburgh (N.L.)	7	13	.350	3.74	30	28	5	1	0	192 1/3	147	86	80	92	153
1985—	Pittsburgh (N.L.)	2	*19	.095	4.70	31	25	1	0	3	162 2/3	138	93	85	89	149
	—Hawaii (PCL)	4	0	1.000	0.88	5	5	4	2	0	41	15	4	4	10	45
1986—	Hawaii (PCL)	5	8	.385	2.46	15	14	7	1	0	106	87	32	29	44	83
	—Pittsburgh (N.L.)	1	3	.250	8.27	9	1	0	0	1	16 1/3	17	16	15	17	11
	—Chicago (A.L.)■	4	5	.444	2.96	13	13	1	0	0	79	49	30	26	42	68
1987—	Chicago (A.L.)	11	12	.478	4.02	33	31	2	0	0	206	177	106	92	97	153
1988—	St. Louis (N.L.)■	13	10	.565	3.67	34	34	3	1	0	225 1/3	198	95	92	86	208
1989—	St. Louis (N.L.)	16	12	.571	3.05	36	36	5	3	0	244 2/3	173	96	83	80	*201
1990—	St. Louis (N.L.)	7	*19	.269	4.43	32	32	0	0	0	182 2/3	168	96	90	86	164
1991—	St. Louis (N.L.)	5	9	.357	2.71	28	28	1	0	0	162 2/3	144	57	49	61	118
1992—	St. Louis (N.L.)	2	7	.222	4.57	29	15	0	0	0	102 1/3	95	56	52	43	72
	—Philadelphia (N.L.)■	0	1	.000	3.00	3	3	0	0	0	15	16	7	5	5	7
1993—	Philadelphia (N.L.)	3	0	1.000	3.26	24	3	0	0	0	47	39	25	17	27	34
	—Chicago (A.L.)■	0	0	...	1.74	11	0	0	0	0	10 1/3	5	2	2	3	6
1994—	Chicago (A.L.)	3	2	.600	3.36	42	0	0	0	2	67	48	28	25	31	67
1995—	Chicago (A.L.)	5	3	.625	5.19	38	0	0	0	0	67 2/3	60	41	39	28	53
	—Montreal (N.L.)■	0	1	.000	7.56	7	0	0	0	0	8 1/3	7	7	7	7	12
A.L. totals (5 years)		23	22	.511	3.85	137	44	3	0	2	430	339	207	184	201	347
N.L. totals (11 years)		63	97	.394	3.74	278	220	18	7	4	1467 1/3	1217	670	609	640	1247
Major league totals (13 years)		86	119	.420	3.76	415	264	21	7	6	1897 1/3	1556	877	793	841	1594

CHAMPIONSHIP SERIES RECORD

Year	Team (League)	W	L	Pct.	ERA	G	GS	CG	ShO	Sv.	IP	H	R	ER	BB	SO
1993—	Chicago (A.L.)	0	0	...	1.93	2	0	0	0	0	4 2/3	7	1	1	1	6

DELGADO, CARLOS — 1B/OF — BLUE JAYS

PERSONAL: Born June 25, 1972, in Aguadilla, Puerto Rico. . . . 6-3/225. . . . Bats left, throws right. . . . Full name: Carlos Juan Delgado.
HIGH SCHOOL: Jose de Diego (Aguadilla, Puerto Rico).
TRANSACTIONS/CAREER NOTES: Signed as non-drafted free agent by Toronto Blue Jays organization (October 9, 1988).
HONORS: Named Florida State League Most Valuable Player (1992). . . . Named Southern League Most Valuable Player (1993).
STATISTICAL NOTES: Led New York-Pennsylvania League catchers with 540 total chances and six double plays in 1990. . . . Led South Atlantic League with 29 passed balls in 1991. . . . Led Florida State League with 281 total bases, .579 slugging percentage, .402 on-base percentage and 11 intentional bases on balls received in 1992. . . . Led Florida State League catchers with 784 total chances in 1992. . . . Led Southern League with .524 slugging percentage, .430 on-base percentage and 18 intentional bases on balls received in 1993. . . . Led Southern League catchers with 800 total chances in 1993. . . . Led International League with .610 slugging percentage in 1995. . . . Led International League with seven intentional bases on balls received in 1995.

Year	Team (League)	Pos.	G	AB	R	H	2B	3B	HR	RBI	Avg.	BB	SO	SB	PO	A	E	Avg.
			BATTING												FIELDING			
1989—	St. Cathar. (NYP)	C	31	89	9	16	5	0	0	11	.180	23	39	0	63	13	2	.974
1990—	St. Cathar. (NYP)	C	67	228	30	64	13	0	6	39	.281	35	65	2	*471	*62	7	.987
1991—	Myrtle Beach (SAL)	C	132	441	72	126	18	2	18	70	.286	75	97	9	679	*100	19	.976
	—Syracuse (Int'l)	C	1	3	0	0	0	0	0	0	.000	0	2	0	5	0	0	1.000
1992—	Dunedin (Fla. St.)	C	133	485	83	*157	•30	2	*30	*100	.324	59	91	2	*684	89	11	.986
1993—	Knoxville (South.)	C	140	468	91	142	28	0	*25	*102	.303	*102	98	10	*683	*103	*14	.983
	—Toronto (A.L.)	DH-C	2	1	0	0	0	0	0	0	.000	1	0	0	2	0	0	1.000
1994—	Toronto (A.L.)	OF-C	43	130	17	28	2	0	9	24	.215	25	46	1	56	2	2	.967
	—Syracuse (Int'l)	C-1B	85	307	52	98	11	0	19	58	.319	42	58	1	235	25	7	.974
1995—	Toronto (A.L.)	OF-DH-1B	37	91	7	15	3	0	3	11	.165	6	26	0	54	2	0	1.000
	—Syracuse (Int'l)	1B-OF	91	333	59	106	23	4	22	74	.318	45	78	0	724	49	4	.995
Major league totals (3 years)			82	222	24	43	5	0	12	35	.194	32	72	1	112	4	2	.983

DeLUCIA, RICH — P — GIANTS

PERSONAL: Born October 7, 1964, in Reading, Pa. . . . 6-0/185. . . . Throws right, bats right. . . . Full name: Richard Anthony DeLucia. . . . Name pronounced duh-LOO-sha.

HIGH SCHOOL: Wyomissing (Pa.) Area.

COLLEGE: Tennessee.

TRANSACTIONS/CAREER NOTES: Selected by Toronto Blue Jays organization in 15th round of free-agent draft (June 3, 1985); did not sign. . . . Selected by Seattle Mariners organization in sixth round of free-agent draft (June 2, 1986). . . . On disabled list (April 10, 1987-remainder of season). . . . On disabled list (May 31-July 2 and July 7, 1989-remainder of season). . . . On Seattle disabled list (August 5-September 1, 1992); included rehabilitation assignment to Calgary (August 26-31). . . . On Seattle disabled list (June 28-July 22, 1993); included rehabilitation assignment to Calgary (July 16-22). . . . Released by Mariners (March 29, 1994). . . . Signed by Cincinnati Reds organization (April 2, 1994). . . . Granted free agency (October 15, 1994). . . . Signed by Rochester, Baltimore Orioles organization (November 17, 1994). . . . Selected by St. Louis Cardinals from Orioles organization in Rule 5 major league draft (December 5, 1994). . . . Traded by Cardinals with P Allen Watson and P Doug Creek to San Francisco Giants for SS Royce Clayton and a player to be named later (December 14, 1995); Cardinals acquired 2B Chris Wimmer to complete deal (January 16, 1996).

STATISTICAL NOTES: Pitched seven-inning, 1-0 no-hit victory against Everett (July 17, 1986). . . . Led A.L. with 31 home runs allowed in 1991.

Year	Team (League)	W	L	Pct.	ERA	G	GS	CG	ShO	Sv.	IP	H	R	ER	BB	SO
1986—	Bellingham (N'west)	8	2	.800	*1.70	13	11	1	•1	0	74	44	20	14	24	69
1987—	Salinas (Calif.)	0	0	. . .	9.00	1	0	0	0	0	1	2	1	1	0	1
1988—	San Bern. (Calif.)	7	8	.467	3.10	22	22	0	0	0	127 2/3	110	57	44	59	118
1989—	Williamsport (East.)	3	4	.429	3.79	10	10	0	0	0	54 2/3	59	28	23	13	41
1990—	San Bern. (Calif.)	4	1	.800	2.05	5	5	1	0	0	30 2/3	19	9	7	3	35
	—Williamsport (East.)	6	6	.500	2.11	18	18	2	1	0	115	92	30	27	30	76
	—Calgary (PCL)	2	2	.500	3.62	5	5	1	0	0	32 1/3	30	17	13	12	23
	—Seattle (A.L.)	1	2	.333	2.00	5	5	1	0	0	36	30	9	8	9	20
1991—	Seattle (A.L.)	12	13	.480	5.09	32	31	0	0	0	182	176	107	103	78	98
1992—	Seattle (A.L.)	3	6	.333	5.49	30	11	0	0	1	83 2/3	100	55	51	35	66
	—Calgary (PCL)	4	2	.667	2.45	8	5	2	1	1	40 1/3	32	11	11	14	38
1993—	Seattle (A.L.)	3	6	.333	4.64	30	1	0	0	0	42 2/3	46	24	22	23	48
	—Calgary (PCL)	1	5	.167	5.73	8	7	0	0	1	44	45	30	28	20	38
1994—	Indianapolis (A.A.)■	5	1	.833	2.30	36	0	0	0	19	43	22	12	11	24	52
	—Cincinnati (N.L.)	0	0	. . .	4.22	8	0	0	0	0	10 2/3	9	6	5	5	15
1995—	St. Louis (N.L.)■	8	7	.533	3.39	56	1	0	0	0	82 1/3	63	38	31	36	76
A.L. totals (4 years)		19	27	.413	4.81	97	48	1	0	1	344 1/3	352	195	184	145	232
N.L. totals (2 years)		8	7	.533	3.48	64	1	0	0	0	93	72	44	36	41	91
Major league totals (6 years)		27	34	.443	4.53	161	49	1	0	1	437 1/3	424	239	220	186	323

DESHAIES, JIM — P

PERSONAL: Born June 23, 1960, in Massena, N.Y. . . . 6-5/222. . . . Throws left, bats left. . . . Full name: James Joseph Deshaies. . . . Name pronounced duh-SHAYS.

HIGH SCHOOL: Massena (N.Y.) Central.

COLLEGE: Le Moyne College, N.Y. (bachelor of arts degree, 1982).

TRANSACTIONS/CAREER NOTES: Selected by Montreal Expos organization in 13th round of free-agent draft (June 6, 1978); did not sign. . . . Selected by New York Yankees organization in 21st round of free-agent draft (June 7, 1982). . . . On Columbus disabled list (April 10-25 and August 4-14, 1985). . . . Traded by Yankees organization with two players to be named later to Houston Astros for P Joe Niekro (September 15, 1985); Astros organization acquired IF Neder Horta (September 24, 1985) and P Dody Rather (January 11, 1986) to complete deal. . . . On disabled list (April 21-May 7, 1986 and July 26-August 16, 1987). . . . Granted free agency (October 28, 1991). . . . Signed by Oakland Athletics organization (January 27, 1992). . . . Released by A's organization (March 23, 1992). . . . Signed by San Diego Padres organization (April 28, 1992). . . . Granted free agency (October 27, 1992). . . . Signed by Minnesota Twins (December 9, 1992). . . . Traded by Twins to San Francisco Giants for P Aaron Fultz, SS Andres Duncan and a player to be named later (August 28, 1993); Twins acquired P Greg Brummett to complete deal (September 1, 1993). . . . Granted free agency (October 25, 1993). . . . Signed by Twins (January 13, 1994). . . . Granted free agency (October 24, 1994). . . . Signed by Scranton/Wilkes-Barre, Philadelphia Phillies organization (February 26, 1995). . . . Released by Phillies (July 31, 1995).

RECORDS: Holds modern major league record for most consecutive strikeouts at start of game—8 (September 23, 1986).

STATISTICAL NOTES: Pitched seven-inning, 5-1 no-hit victory for Nashville against Columbus (May 4, 1984). . . . Led International League with four balks in 1985. . . . Led N.L. with seven balks in 1986. . . . Led A.L. with 30 home runs allowed in 1994.

MISCELLANEOUS: Struck out in only appearance as pinch-hitter (1989).

Year	Team (League)	W	L	Pct.	ERA	G	GS	CG	ShO	Sv.	IP	H	R	ER	BB	SO
1982—	Oneonta (NYP)	6	5	.545	3.32	15	14	6	1	0	108 1/3	93	50	40	40	*137
1983—	Fort Lauder. (FSL)	11	3	.786	2.52	20	19	5	2	0	117 2/3	105	44	33	58	128
1984—	Nashville (South.)	3	2	.600	2.80	7	7	1	0	0	45	33	20	14	29	42
	—Columbus (Int'l)	10	5	.667	*2.39	18	18	9	•4	0	135 2/3	99	45	36	62	117
	—New York (A.L.)	0	1	.000	11.57	2	2	0	0	0	7	14	9	9	7	5

Year	Team (League)	W	L	Pct.	ERA	G	GS	CG	ShO	Sv.	IP	H	R	ER	BB	SO
1985—	Columbus (Int'l)	8	6	.571	4.31	21	21	3	0	0	131 2/3	124	67	63	59	106
—	Houston (N.L.)■	0	0	...	0.00	2	0	0	0	0	3	1	0	0	0	2
1986—	Houston (N.L.)	12	5	.706	3.25	26	26	1	1	0	144	124	58	52	59	128
1987—	Houston (N.L.)	11	6	.647	4.62	26	25	1	0	0	152	149	81	78	57	104
1988—	Houston (N.L.)	11	14	.440	3.00	31	31	3	2	0	207	164	77	69	72	127
1989—	Houston (N.L.)	15	10	.600	2.91	34	34	6	3	0	225 2/3	180	80	73	79	153
1990—	Houston (N.L.)	7	12	.368	3.78	34	34	2	0	0	209 1/3	186	93	88	84	119
1991—	Houston (N.L.)	5	12	.294	4.98	28	28	1	0	0	161	156	90	89	72	98
1992—	Las Vegas (PCL)■	6	3	.667	4.03	18	8	0	0	1	58	60	28	26	17	46
—	San Diego (N.L.)	4	7	.364	3.28	15	15	0	0	0	96	92	40	35	33	46
1993—	Minnesota (A.L.)■	11	13	.458	4.41	27	27	1	0	0	167 1/3	159	85	82	51	80
—	San Francisco (N.L.)■	2	2	.500	4.24	5	4	0	0	0	17	24	9	8	6	5
1994—	Minnesota (A.L.)■	6	12	.333	7.39	25	•25	0	0	0	130 1/3	170	109	*107	54	78
1995—	Scran./W.B. (Int'l)■	7	8	.467	3.45	19	19	2	1	0	117 1/3	105	51	45	26	79
—	Philadelphia (N.L.)	0	1	.000	20.25	2	2	0	0	0	5 1/3	15	12	12	1	6
A.L. totals (3 years)		17	26	.395	5.85	54	54	1	0	0	304 2/3	343	203	198	112	163
N.L. totals (10 years)		67	69	.493	3.72	203	199	14	6	0	1220 1/3	1091	540	504	463	788
Major league totals (12 years)		84	95	.469	4.14	257	253	15	6	0	1525	1434	743	702	575	951

CHAMPIONSHIP SERIES RECORD

Year	Team (League)	W	L	Pct.	ERA	G	GS	CG	ShO	Sv.	IP	H	R	ER	BB	SO
1986—	Houston (N.L.)	Did not play.														

DeSHIELDS, DELINO — 2B — DODGERS

PERSONAL: Born January 15, 1969, in Seaford, Del. . . . 6-1/175. . . . Bats left, throws right. . . . Full name: Delino Lamont DeShields. . . . Name pronounced duh-LINE-oh.

HIGH SCHOOL: Seaford (Del.).

COLLEGE: Villanova.

TRANSACTIONS/CAREER NOTES: Selected by Montreal Expos organization in first round (12th pick overall) of free-agent draft (June 2, 1987). . . . On disabled list (June 16-July 12, 1990 and August 12-September 11, 1993). . . . Traded by Expos to Los Angeles Dodgers for P Pedro J. Martinez (November 19, 1993). . . . On disabled list (May 26-June 20, 1994).

RECORDS: Shares modern N.L. record for most hits in first major league game—4 (April 9, 1990).

STATISTICAL NOTES: Led Gulf Coast League shortstops with 22 errors in 1987. . . . Career major league grand slams: 1.

			BATTING												FIELDING			
Year	Team (League)	Pos.	G	AB	R	H	2B	3B	HR	RBI	Avg.	BB	SO	SB	PO	A	E	Avg.
1987—	GC Expos (GCL)	SS-3B	31	111	17	24	5	2	1	4	.216	21	30	16	47	90	†22	.862
—	Jamestown (NYP)	SS	34	96	16	21	1	2	1	5	.219	24	28	14	25	57	21	.796
1988—	Rockford (Midw.)	SS	129	460	97	116	26	6	12	46	.252	95	110	59	173	344	42	.925
1989—	Jacksonv. (South.)	SS	93	307	55	83	10	6	3	35	.270	76	80	37	127	218	34	.910
—	Indianapolis (A.A.)	SS	47	181	29	47	8	4	2	14	.260	16	53	16	73	101	13	.930
1990—	Montreal (N.L.)	2B	129	499	69	144	28	6	4	45	.289	66	96	42	236	371	12	.981
1991—	Montreal (N.L.)	2B	151	563	83	134	15	4	10	51	.238	95	*151	56	285	405	*27	.962
1992—	Montreal (N.L.)	2B	135	530	82	155	19	8	7	56	.292	54	108	46	251	360	15	.976
1993—	Montreal (N.L.)	2B	123	481	75	142	17	7	2	29	.295	72	64	43	243	381	11	.983
1994—	Los Angeles (N.L.)■	2B-SS	89	320	51	80	11	3	2	33	.250	54	53	27	156	282	7	.984
1995—	Los Angeles (N.L.)	2B	127	425	66	109	18	3	8	37	.256	63	83	39	204	330	•11	.980
Major league totals (6 years)			754	2818	426	764	108	31	33	251	.271	404	555	253	1375	2129	83	.977

DIVISION SERIES RECORD

			BATTING												FIELDING			
Year	Team (League)	Pos.	G	AB	R	H	2B	3B	HR	RBI	Avg.	BB	SO	SB	PO	A	E	Avg.
1995—	Los Angeles (N.L.)	2B	3	12	1	3	0	0	0	0	.250	1	3	0	8	7	0	1.000

DeSILVA, JOHN — P

PERSONAL: Born September 30, 1967, in Fort Bragg, Calif. . . . 6-0/190. . . . Throws right, bats right. . . . Full name: John Reed DeSilva.

HIGH SCHOOL: Fort Bragg (Calif.).

COLLEGE: Brigham Young.

TRANSACTIONS/CAREER NOTES: Selected by Chicago White Sox organization in 30th round of free-agent draft (June 1, 1988); did not sign. . . . Selected by Detroit Tigers organization in eighth round of free-agent draft (June 5, 1989). . . . On Toledo disabled list (June 15-July 2, 1991; and April 4-21 and April 30-June 26, 1992). . . . Traded by Tigers to Los Angeles Dodgers (September 7, 1993), completing deal in which Dodgers traded OF Eric Davis to Tigers for a player to be named later (August 31, 1993). . . . On Albuquerque temporarily inactive list (June 16-24, 1994). . . . Traded by Dodgers organization to Baltimore Orioles organization for P John O'Donoghue (December 19, 1994). . . . Granted free agency (October 11, 1995).

Year	Team (League)	W	L	Pct.	ERA	G	GS	CG	ShO	Sv.	IP	H	R	ER	BB	SO
1989—	Niag. Falls (NYP)	3	0	1.000	1.88	4	4	0	0	0	24	15	5	5	8	24
—	Fayetteville (S. Atl.)	2	2	.500	2.68	9	9	1	0	0	53 2/3	40	23	16	21	54
1990—	Lakeland (Fla. St.)	8	1	.889	1.48	14	14	0	0	0	91	54	18	15	25	113
—	London (Eastern)	5	6	.455	3.84	14	14	1	1	0	89	87	47	38	27	76
1991—	London (Eastern)	5	4	.556	2.81	11	11	2	1	0	73 2/3	51	24	23	24	80
—	Toledo (Int'l)	5	4	.556	4.60	11	11	1	0	0	58 2/3	62	33	30	21	56
1992—	Toledo (Int'l)	0	3	.000	8.53	7	2	0	0	0	19	26	18	18	8	21
—	London (Eastern)	2	4	.333	4.13	9	9	1	1	0	52 1/3	51	24	24	13	53
1993—	Toledo (Int'l)	7	10	.412	3.69	25	24	1	0	0	161	145	73	66	60	136
—	Detroit (A.L.)	0	0	...	9.00	1	0	0	0	0	1	2	1	1	0	0
—	Los Angeles (N.L.)■	0	0	...	6.75	3	0	0	0	0	5 1/3	6	4	4	1	6
1994—	Albuquerque (PCL)	3	5	.375	7.83	25	6	0	0	1	66 2/3	90	62	58	27	39

Year	Team (League)	W	L	Pct.	ERA	G	GS	CG	ShO	Sv.	IP	H	R	ER	BB	SO
	—San Antonio (Tex.)	1	3	.250	5.09	25	2	0	0	2	46	46	29	26	18	46
1995—	Rochester (Int'l)■	11	9	.550	4.18	26	25	2	0	0	150 2/3	156	78	70	51	82
	—Baltimore (A.L.)	1	0	1.000	7.27	2	2	0	0	0	8 2/3	8	7	7	7	1
A.L. totals (2 years)		1	0	1.000	7.45	3	2	0	0	0	9 2/3	10	8	8	7	1
N.L. totals (1 year)		0	0	...	6.75	3	0	0	0	0	5 1/3	6	4	4	1	6
Major league totals (2 years)		1	0	1.000	7.20	6	2	0	0	0	15	16	12	12	8	7

DETTMER, JOHN — P — ORIOLES

PERSONAL: Born March 4, 1970, in Cahokia, Ill. . . . 6-0/185. . . . Throws right, bats right. . . . Full name: John Franklin Dettmer.
HIGH SCHOOL: Lafayette (Ballwin, Mo.).
COLLEGE: Missouri.
TRANSACTIONS/CAREER NOTES: Selected by San Diego Padres organization in 41st round of free-agent draft (June 3, 1991); did not sign. . . . Selected by Texas Rangers organization in 11th round of free-agent draft (June 1, 1992). . . . Traded by Rangers to Baltimore Orioles organization for OF Jack Voigt (May 16, 1995). . . . On Rochester suspended list (June 10-12, 1995).

Year	Team (League)	W	L	Pct.	ERA	G	GS	CG	ShO	Sv.	IP	H	R	ER	BB	SO
1992—	Gastonia (S. Atl.)	10	1	*.909	2.02	15	15	3	1	0	98	74	25	22	17	102
1993—	Charlotte (Fla. St.)	*16	3	*.842	2.15	27	27	5	2	0	163	132	44	39	33	128
1994—	Tulsa (Texas)	6	1	.857	2.41	10	10	2	0	0	74 2/3	57	23	20	12	65
	—Okla. City (A.A.)	3	2	.600	5.63	8	8	1	1	0	46 1/3	59	33	29	11	26
	—Texas (A.L.)	0	6	.000	4.33	11	9	0	0	0	54	63	42	26	20	27
1995—	Texas (A.L.)	0	0	...	27.00	1	0	0	0	0	1/3	2	1	1	0	0
	—Okla. City (A.A.)	0	0	...	2.08	5	0	0	0	0	8 2/3	10	3	2	4	10
	—Rochester (Int'l)■	4	7	.364	4.68	21	11	1	1	1	82 2/3	98	52	43	16	46
Major league totals (2 years)		0	6	.000	4.47	12	9	0	0	0	54 1/3	65	43	27	20	27

DEVAREZ, CESAR — C — ORIOLES

PERSONAL: Born September 22, 1969, in San Francisco de Macoris, Dominican Republic. . . . 5-10/175. . . . Bats right, throws right. . . . Full name: Cesar Salvatore Devarez.
TRANSACTIONS/CAREER NOTES: Signed as non-drafted free agent by Baltimore Orioles organization (February 6, 1988). . . . On disabled list (July 16-August 29, 1991 and August 10, 1994-remainder of season).
STATISTICAL NOTES: Led Eastern League catchers with 11 double plays and 19 passed balls in 1992.

				BATTING											FIELDING			
Year	Team (League)	Pos.	G	AB	R	H	2B	3B	HR	RBI	Avg.	BB	SO	SB	PO	A	E	Avg.
1989—	Bluefield (Appal.)	C	12	42	3	9	4	0	0	7	.214	1	5	0	59	12	3	.959
1990—	Wausau (Midwest)	C-3B	56	171	7	34	4	1	3	19	.199	7	28	2	320	31	8	.978
1991—	Frederick (Caro.)	C-OF	74	235	25	59	13	2	3	29	.251	14	28	2	443	70	5	.990
1992—	Hagerstown (East.)	C	110	319	20	72	8	1	2	32	.226	17	49	2	655	82	8	.989
1993—	Frederick (Caro.)	C	38	124	15	36	8	0	2	16	.290	12	18	1	238	38	1	.996
	—Bowie (Eastern)	C	57	174	14	39	7	1	0	17	.224	5	21	5	316	36	5	.986
1994—	Bowie (Eastern)	C	73	249	43	78	13	4	6	48	.313	8	25	7	508	61	9	.984
1995—	Rochester (Int'l)	C	67	240	32	60	12	1	1	21	.250	7	25	2	331	40	2	.995
	—Baltimore (A.L.)	C	6	4	0	0	0	0	0	0	.000	0	0	0	14	0	0	1.000
Major league totals (1 year)			6	4	0	0	0	0	0	0	.000	0	0	0	14	0	0	1.000

DEVEREAUX, MIKE — OF — ORIOLES

PERSONAL: Born April 10, 1963, in Casper, Wyo. . . . 6-0/195. . . . Bats right, throws right. . . . Full name: Michael Devereaux. . . . Name pronounced DEH-ver-oh.
HIGH SCHOOL: Kelly Walsh (Casper, Wyo.).
JUNIOR COLLEGE: Mesa (Ariz.) Community College.
COLLEGE: Arizona State (bachelor of arts degree in finance).
TRANSACTIONS/CAREER NOTES: Selected by Cleveland Indians organization in 26th round of free-agent draft (June 4, 1984); did not sign. . . . Selected by Los Angeles Dodgers organization in fifth round of free-agent draft (June 3, 1985). . . . Traded by Dodgers to Baltimore Orioles for P Mike Morgan (March 12, 1989). . . . On Baltimore disabled list (May 17-June 15, 1990); included rehabilitation assignments to Frederick (June 9-10) and Hagerstown (June 11-15). . . . On Baltimore disabled list (May 3-27, 1993); included rehabilitation assignment to Bowie (May 25-27). . . . On disabled list (June 16-July 1, 1994). . . . Granted free agency (Decemberer 23, 1994). . . . Signed by Chicago White Sox (April 8, 1995). . . . Traded by White Sox to Atlanta Braves for OF Andre King (August 25, 1995). . . . Granted free agency (November 3, 1995). . . . Signed by Orioles (January 11, 1996).
HONORS: Named outfielder on The Sporting News A.L. All-Star team (1992).
STATISTICAL NOTES: Led Pioneer League with 152 total bases in 1985. . . . Led Texas League with 11 sacrifice flies in 1987. . . . Led Texas League outfielders with 349 total chances in 1987. . . . Career major league grand slams: 3.

				BATTING											FIELDING			
Year	Team (League)	Pos.	G	AB	R	H	2B	3B	HR	RBI	Avg.	BB	SO	SB	PO	A	E	Avg.
1985—	Great Falls (Pio.)	OF	•70	*289	*73	*103	17	10	4	*67	.356	32	29	*40	100	4	5	.954
1986—	San Antonio (Tex.)	OF	115	431	69	130	22	2	10	53	.302	58	47	31	292	13	4	.987
1987—	San Antonio (Tex.)	OF	*135	*562	90	169	28	9	26	91	.301	48	65	33	*339	7	3	*.991
	—Albuquerque (PCL)	OF	3	11	2	3	1	0	1	1	.273	0	2	1	4	1	0	1.000
	—Los Angeles (N.L.)	OF	19	54	7	12	3	0	0	4	.222	3	10	3	21	1	0	1.000
1988—	Albuquerque (PCL)	OF	109	423	88	144	26	4	13	76	.340	44	46	33	211	5	7	.969
	—Los Angeles (N.L.)	OF	30	43	4	5	1	0	0	2	.116	2	10	0	29	0	0	1.000
1989—	Baltimore (A.L.)■	OF-DH	122	391	55	104	14	3	8	46	.266	36	60	22	288	1	5	.983
1990—	Baltimore (A.L.)	OF-DH	108	367	48	88	18	1	12	49	.240	28	48	13	281	4	5	.983
	—Frederick (Caro.)	OF	2	8	3	4	0	0	1	3	.500	1	2	1	4	2	0	1.000
	—Hagerstown (East.)	OF	4	20	4	5	3	0	0	3	.250	0	1	0	13	0	1	.929
1991—	Baltimore (A.L.)	OF	149	608	82	158	27	10	19	59	.260	47	115	16	399	10	3	.993

			BATTING												FIELDING			
Year	**Team (League)**	**Pos.**	**G**	**AB**	**R**	**H**	**2B**	**3B**	**HR**	**RBI**	**Avg.**	**BB**	**SO**	**SB**	**PO**	**A**	**E**	**Avg.**
1992—	Baltimore (A.L.)	OF	156	653	76	180	29	11	24	107	.276	44	94	10	431	5	5	.989
1993—	Baltimore (A.L.)	OF	131	527	72	132	31	3	14	75	.250	43	99	3	311	8	4	.988
—	Bowie (Eastern)	OF	2	7	1	2	1	0	0	2	.286	0	2	0	5	0	0	1.000
1994—	Baltimore (A.L.)	OF-DH	85	301	35	61	8	2	9	33	.203	22	72	1	203	3	1	.995
1995—	Chicago (A.L.)■	OF	92	333	48	102	21	1	10	55	.306	25	51	6	187	4	3	.985
—	Atlanta (N.L.)■	OF	29	55	7	14	3	0	1	8	.255	2	11	2	41	0	0	1.000
American League totals (6 years)			843	3180	416	825	148	31	96	424	.259	245	539	71	2100	35	26	.988
National League totals (3 years)			78	152	18	31	7	0	1	14	.204	7	31	5	91	1	0	1.000
Major league totals (9 years)			921	3332	434	856	155	31	97	438	.257	252	570	76	2191	36	26	.988

DIVISION SERIES RECORD

			BATTING												FIELDING			
Year	**Team (League)**	**Pos.**	**G**	**AB**	**R**	**H**	**2B**	**3B**	**HR**	**RBI**	**Avg.**	**BB**	**SO**	**SB**	**PO**	**A**	**E**	**Avg.**
1995—	Atlanta (N.L.)	OF	4	5	1	1	0	0	0	0	.200	0	0	0	2	0	0	1.000

CHAMPIONSHIP SERIES RECORD

NOTES: Named N.L. Championship Series Most Valuable Player (1995).

			BATTING												FIELDING			
Year	**Team (League)**	**Pos.**	**G**	**AB**	**R**	**H**	**2B**	**3B**	**HR**	**RBI**	**Avg.**	**BB**	**SO**	**SB**	**PO**	**A**	**E**	**Avg.**
1995—	Atlanta (N.L.)	OF	4	13	2	4	1	0	1	5	.308	1	2	0	2	0	0	1.000

WORLD SERIES RECORD

NOTES: Member of World Series championship team (1995).

			BATTING												FIELDING			
Year	**Team (League)**	**Pos.**	**G**	**AB**	**R**	**H**	**2B**	**3B**	**HR**	**RBI**	**Avg.**	**BB**	**SO**	**SB**	**PO**	**A**	**E**	**Avg.**
1995—	Atlanta (N.L.)	OF-PH-DH	5	4	0	1	0	0	0	1	.250	2	1	0	0	0	1	.000

DEWEY, MARK — P — GIANTS

PERSONAL: Born January 3, 1965, in Grand Rapids, Mich. . . . 6-0/216. . . . Throws right, bats right. . . . Full name: Mark Alan Dewey.
HIGH SCHOOL: Jenison (Mich.).
COLLEGE: Grand Valley State (Mich.).
TRANSACTIONS/CAREER NOTES: Selected by San Francisco Giants organization in 23rd round of free-agent draft (June 2, 1987). . . . Claimed on waivers by New York Mets (May 9, 1991). . . . On Norfolk disqualified list (April 8-May 10, 1993). . . . Claimed on waivers by Pittsburgh Pirates (May 11, 1993). . . . On disabled list (May 9-24, 1994). . . . Granted free agency (October 14, 1994). . . . Signed by Phoenix, Giants organization (November 14, 1994). . . . On disabled list (June 16-September 13, 1995).

Year	**Team (League)**	**W**	**L**	**Pct.**	**ERA**	**G**	**GS**	**CG**	**ShO**	**Sv.**	**IP**	**H**	**R**	**ER**	**BB**	**SO**
1987—	Everett (N'west)	7	3	.700	3.30	19	10	1	0	1	84 2/3	88	39	31	26	67
1988—	Clinton (Midwest)	10	4	.714	*1.43	37	7	1	0	7	119 1/3	95	36	19	14	76
1989—	San Jose (Calif.)	1	6	.143	3.15	59	0	0	0	*30	68 2/3	62	35	24	23	60
1990—	Shreveport (Texas)	1	5	.167	1.88	33	0	0	0	13	38 1/3	37	11	8	10	23
—	Phoenix (PCL)	2	3	.400	2.67	19	0	0	0	8	30 1/3	26	14	9	10	27
—	San Francisco (N.L.)	1	1	.500	2.78	14	0	0	0	0	22 2/3	22	7	7	5	11
1991—	Phoenix (PCL)	1	2	.333	3.97	10	0	0	0	4	11 1/3	16	7	5	7	4
—	Tidewater (Int'l)■	•12	3	•.800	3.34	48	0	0	0	9	64 2/3	61	30	24	36	38
1992—	Tidewater (Int'l)	5	7	.417	4.31	43	0	0	0	9	54 1/3	61	29	26	18	55
—	New York (N.L.)	1	0	1.000	4.32	20	0	0	0	0	33 1/3	37	16	16	10	24
1993—	Buffalo (A.A.)■	2	0	1.000	1.23	22	0	0	0	6	29 1/3	21	9	4	5	17
—	Pittsburgh (N.L.)	1	2	.333	2.36	21	0	0	0	7	26 2/3	14	8	7	10	14
1994—	Pittsburgh (N.L.)	2	1	.667	3.68	45	0	0	0	1	51 1/3	61	22	21	19	30
1995—	San Francisco (N.L.)■	1	0	1.000	3.13	27	0	0	0	0	31 2/3	30	12	11	17	32
Major league totals (5 years)		6	4	.600	3.37	127	0	0	0	8	165 2/3	164	65	62	61	111

DIAZ, ALEX — OF — MARINERS

PERSONAL: Born October 5, 1968, in Brooklyn, N.Y. . . . 5-11/180. . . . Bats both, throws right. . . . Full name: Alexis Diaz. . . . Son of Mario Caballero Diaz, minor league infielder (1959-64).
HIGH SCHOOL: Manuel Mendez Licihea (Puerto Rico).
TRANSACTIONS/CAREER NOTES: Signed as non-drafted free agent by New York Mets organization (August 24, 1986). . . . Traded by Mets with OF Darren Reed to Montreal Expos for OF Terrel Hansen and P David Sommer (April 2, 1991). . . . On suspended list (August 30, 1991-remainder of season). . . . Traded by Expos organization to Milwaukee Brewers organization for IF George Canale (October 15, 1991). . . . On Milwaukee disabled list (May 3-August 30, 1993); included rehabilitation assignment to New Orleans (August 13-30). . . . Granted free agency (December 20, 1993). . . . Re-signed by Brewers (December 21, 1993). . . . On disabled list (July 31, 1994-remainder of season). . . . Claimed on waivers by Seattle Mariners (October 14, 1994).

			BATTING												FIELDING			
Year	**Team (League)**	**Pos.**	**G**	**AB**	**R**	**H**	**2B**	**3B**	**HR**	**RBI**	**Avg.**	**BB**	**SO**	**SB**	**PO**	**A**	**E**	**Avg.**
1987—	Kingsport (Appal.)	SS	54	212	29	56	9	1	0	13	.264	16	31	*34	67	126	18	.915
—	Little Falls (NYP)	SS	12	47	7	16	4	1	0	8	.340	2	3	2	13	22	4	.897
1988—	Columbia (S. Atl.)	SS	123	481	82	126	14	*11	0	37	.262	21	49	28	175	299	*72	.868
—	St. Lucie (Fla. St.)	SS	3	6	2	0	0	0	0	1	.000	0	4	0	3	3	3	.667
1989—	St. Lucie (Fla. St.)	SS-OF	102	416	54	106	11	10	1	33	.255	20	38	43	151	244	28	.934
—	Jackson (Texas)	2B	23	95	11	26	5	1	2	9	.274	3	11	3	25	65	3	.968
1990—	Tidewater (Int'l)	OF-2B-SS	124	437	55	112	15	2	1	36	.256	30	39	23	196	101	11	.964
1991—	Indianapolis (A.A.)■	O-S-3-2	108	370	48	90	14	4	1	21	.243	27	46	17	207	45	8	.969
1992—	Denver (A.A.)■	OF-2B-SS	106	455	67	122	17	4	1	41	.268	24	36	42	240	43	7	.976
—	Milwaukee (A.L.)	OF-DH	22	9	5	1	0	0	0	1	.111	0	0	3	10	0	0	1.000
1993—	Milwaukee (A.L.)	OF-DH	32	69	9	22	2	0	0	1	.319	0	12	5	46	1	1	.979

Year	Team (League)	Pos.	G	AB	R	H	2B	3B	HR	RBI	Avg.	BB	SO	SB	PO	A	E	Avg.
				BATTING											FIELDING			
	—New Orleans (A.A.).....	OF	16	55	8	16	2	0	0	5	.291	3	6	7	38	1	0	1.000
1994—	Milwaukee (A.L.)........	OF-2B-DH	79	187	17	47	5	7	1	17	.251	10	19	5	138	11	2	.987
1995—	Seattle (A.L.)■..........	OF	103	270	44	67	14	0	3	27	.248	13	27	18	145	4	2	.987
	—Tacoma (PCL)...........	OF	10	40	3	10	1	0	0	4	.250	2	5	1	15	1	0	1.000
Major league totals (4 years)			236	535	75	137	21	7	4	46	.256	23	58	31	339	16	5	.986

DIVISION SERIES RECORD

Year	Team (League)	Pos.	G	AB	R	H	2B	3B	HR	RBI	Avg.	BB	SO	SB	PO	A	E	Avg.
				BATTING											FIELDING			
1995—	Seattle (A.L.).............	OF-PH	2	3	0	1	0	0	0	0	.333	1	1	0	1	1	0	1.000

CHAMPIONSHIP SERIES RECORD

Year	Team (League)	Pos.	G	AB	R	H	2B	3B	HR	RBI	Avg.	BB	SO	SB	PO	A	E	Avg.
				BATTING											FIELDING			
1995—	Seattle (A.L.).............	PH-OF	4	7	0	3	1	0	0	0	.429	1	1	0	1	0	0	1.000

DIAZ, EINAR C INDIANS

PERSONAL: Born December 28, 1972, in Chiniqui, Panama. . . . 5-10/165. . . . Bats right, throws right. . . . Full name: Einar Antonio Diaz.
TRANSACTIONS/CAREER NOTES: Signed as non-drafted free agent by Cleveland Indians organization (October 5, 1990).
STATISTICAL NOTES: Led Appalachian League third basemen with 125 assists and .959 fielding percentage in 1992. . . . Led Appalachian League catchers with 54 assists and nine errors in 1993. . . . Led South Atlantic League in grounding into double plays with 18 in 1994. . . . Led South Atlantic League catchers with 966 total chances, 845 putouts, 112 assists and tied for lead with eight double plays in 1994. . . . Led Carolina League catchers with 107 assists and .992 fielding percentage in 1995.

Year	Team (League)	Pos.	G	AB	R	H	2B	3B	HR	RBI	Avg.	BB	SO	SB	PO	A	E	Avg.
				BATTING											FIELDING			
1991—	Dom. Indians (DSL)...	...	62	239	35	67	6	3	1	29	.280	14	5	10	...	...	...	...
1992—	Burlington (Appal.).....	3B-SS	52	178	19	37	3	0	1	14	.208	20	9	2	27	†137	7	†.959
1993—	Burlington (Appal.).....	C-3B	60	231	40	69	15	3	5	33	.299	8	7	7	315	†55	†10	.974
	—Columbus (S. Atl.)......	C	1	5	0	0	0	0	0	0	.000	0	1	0	3	1	0	1.000
1994—	Columbus (S. Atl.)......	C-3B	120	491	67	137	23	2	16	71	.279	17	34	4	†848	†134	9	.991
1995—	Kinston (Carolina)......	C-3B	104	373	46	98	21	0	6	43	.263	12	29	3	676	†111	7	†.991

DIAZ, MARIO IF INDIANS

PERSONAL: Born January 10, 1962, in Humacao, Puerto Rico. . . . 5-10/160. . . . Bats right, throws right. . . . Full name: Mario Rafael Torres Diaz.
HIGH SCHOOL: Teodor Aguilar Mora (Humacao, Puerto Rico).
TRANSACTIONS/CAREER NOTES: Signed as non-drafted free agent by Seattle Mariners organization (December 21, 1978). . . . On Seattle disabled list (May 6-23, 1988); included rehabilitation assignment to Calgary (May 16-23). . . . On Seattle disabled list (March 31-May 4, 1990). . . . Traded by Mariners organization to Tidewater, New York Mets organization, for P Brian Givens (June 19, 1990). . . . Granted free agency (October 15, 1990). . . . Signed by Texas Rangers (December 14, 1990). . . . On disabled list (June 24-July 11, 1991). . . . Granted free agency (October 15, 1991). . . . Signed by Denver, Milwaukee Brewers organization (December 16, 1991). . . . Released by Denver (April 1, 1992). . . . Signed by Calgary, Mariners organization (April 4, 1992). . . . On Calgary disabled list (April 20-May 4, 1992). . . . Released by Calgary (May 29, 1992). . . . Signed by Oklahoma City, Rangers organization (June 19, 1992). . . . Granted free agency (October 15, 1992). . . . Re-signed by Oklahoma City (January 13, 1993). . . . Granted free agency (October 15, 1993). . . . Signed by Florida Marlins organization (December 15, 1993). . . . Released by Edmonton, Marlins organization (March 30, 1994). . . . Signed by Pawtucket, Boston Red Sox organization (April 9, 1994). . . . Released by Pawtucket (May 25, 1994). . . . Signed by Marlins (May 30, 1994). . . . Granted free agency (February 17, 1995). . . . Re-signed by Charlotte, Marlins organization (April 5, 1995). . . . Granted free agency (October 16, 1995). . . . Signed by Cleveland Indians organization (January 4, 1996).
STATISTICAL NOTES: Led Southern League with 14 sacrifice hits in 1985.

Year	Team (League)	Pos.	G	AB	R	H	2B	3B	HR	RBI	Avg.	BB	SO	SB	PO	A	E	Avg.
				BATTING											FIELDING			
1979—	Belling. (N'west).........	SS-3B-2B	32	96	12	19	2	0	1	5	.198	5	17	0	28	69	8	.924
1980—	Wausau (Midwest).....	SS-2B	110	349	28	63	5	0	3	21	.181	19	37	5	172	328	41	.924
1981—	Lynn (Eastern)...........	SS	106	314	16	63	8	1	1	22	.201	16	42	1	163	318	18	*.964
1982—	Lynn (Eastern)...........	SS-1B	53	162	19	35	7	1	1	13	.216	19	24	2	384	172	18	.969
	—Salt Lake (PCL)..........	SS	5	19	2	7	1	0	0	2	.368	0	2	0	4	15	1	.950
	—Wausau (Midwest).....	SS	56	187	15	49	8	1	1	23	.262	7	23	3	78	148	16	.934
1983—	Bakersfield (Calif.)......	SS-2B	51	171	23	41	5	1	0	10	.240	10	26	3	92	146	22	.915
	—Chatt. (South.)...........	SS	33	111	18	30	6	5	2	13	.270	5	15	0	48	80	10	.928
1984—	Chatt. (South.)...........	SS-2B	108	322	23	67	7	1	1	19	.208	21	18	6	179	313	26	.950
1985—	Chatt. (South.)...........	SS	115	400	38	101	6	7	0	38	.253	21	20	3	186	314	31	.942
1986—	Calgary (PCL)............	SS	109	379	40	107	17	6	1	41	.282	13	29	1	194	302	16	.969
1987—	Calgary (PCL)............	SS	108	376	52	106	17	3	4	52	.282	20	28	1	195	280	21	.958
	—Seattle (A.L.)............	SS	11	23	4	7	0	1	0	3	.304	0	4	0	10	25	1	.972
1988—	Calgary (PCL)............	SS	46	164	16	54	18	0	1	30	.329	9	10	1	65	138	12	.944
	—Seattle (A.L.)............	S-2-1-3	28	72	6	22	5	0	0	9	.306	3	5	0	31	47	1	.987
1989—	Seattle (A.L.).............	SS-2B-3B	52	74	9	10	0	0	1	7	.135	7	7	0	35	54	5	.947
	—Calgary (PCL)............	2B-SS-1B	37	127	22	43	8	1	2	9	.339	8	7	1	64	73	9	.938
1990—	Calgary (PCL)............	3B-SS-2B	32	105	10	35	5	1	1	19	.333	1	8	0	35	61	2	.980
	—Tidewater (Int'l)■.......	SS-3B	29	104	15	33	8	0	1	9	.317	6	6	1	38	92	6	.956
	—New York (N.L.).........	SS-2B	16	22	0	3	1	0	0	1	.136	0	3	0	5	18	1	.958
1991—	Texas (A.L.)■............	S-2-3-DH	96	182	24	48	7	0	1	22	.264	15	18	0	93	143	7	.971
1992—	Calgary (PCL)■..........	SS-OF	18	52	8	14	4	0	0	11	.269	0	6	1	23	26	4	.925
	—Okla. City (A.A.)■......	SS-3B-2B	43	167	24	56	11	0	3	20	.335	2	12	1	81	109	5	.974
	—Texas (A.L.)...............	SS-2B-3B	19	31	2	7	1	0	0	1	.226	1	2	0	16	26	1	.977
1993—	Okla. City (A.A.)..........	3B-2B-SS	48	177	24	58	12	2	3	20	.328	7	15	3	53	105	3	.981

Year Team (League)	Pos.	G	AB	R	H	2B	3B	HR	RBI	Avg.	BB	SO	SB	PO	A	E	Avg.
		BATTING												FIELDING			
—Texas (A.L.)	SS-3B-1B	71	205	24	56	10	1	2	24	.273	8	13	1	90	153	3	.988
1994—Pawtucket (Int'l)■	3B-SS-2B	30	120	14	40	6	1	3	19	.333	4	7	0	18	44	1	.984
—Florida (N.L.)■	3B-2B-SS	32	77	10	25	4	2	0	11	.325	6	6	0	20	39	1	.983
1995—Florida (N.L.)	2B-SS-3B	49	87	5	20	3	0	1	6	.230	1	12	0	22	30	2	.963
American League totals (6 years)		277	587	69	150	23	2	4	66	.256	34	49	1	275	448	18	.976
National League totals (3 years)		97	186	15	48	8	2	1	18	.258	7	21	0	47	87	4	.971
Major league totals (9 years)		374	773	84	198	31	4	5	84	.256	41	70	1	322	535	22	.975

DIBBLE, ROB — P — CUBS

PERSONAL: Born January 24, 1964, in Bridgeport, Conn. . . . 6-4/230. . . . Throws right, bats left. . . . Full name: Robert Keith Dibble.

HIGH SCHOOL: Southington (Conn.).

COLLEGE: Florida Southern.

TRANSACTIONS/CAREER NOTES: Selected by St. Louis Cardinals organization in 11th round of free-agent draft (June 7, 1982); did not sign. . . . Selected by Cincinnati Reds organization in secondary phase of free-agent draft (June 6, 1983). . . . On suspended list (May 31-June 2 and July 25-28, 1989). . . . On disabled list (July 10-25, 1989). . . . On suspended list (July 19-23 and July 31-August 3, 1991). . . . On disabled list (March 28-April 16, 1992). . . . On suspended list (July 9-12, 1992). . . . On disabled list (April 22-May 28 and September 22, 1993-remainder of season). . . . On Cincinnati disabled list (March 30, 1994-entire season); included rehabilitation assignments to Indianapolis (March 30-April 5 and July 26-August 10). . . . Granted free agency (October 11, 1994). . . . Signed by Nashville, Chicago White Sox organization (February 28, 1995). . . . Released by White Sox (July 17, 1995). . . . Signed by New Orleans, Milwaukee Brewers organization (July 31, 1995). . . . On Milwaukee suspended list (August 6-9, 1995). . . . Granted free agency (October 30, 1995). . . . Signed by Chicago Cubs organization (December 13, 1995).

RECORDS: Shares major league record by striking out side on nine pitches (June 4, 1989, eighth inning). . . . Shares N.L. single-game record for most consecutive strikeouts by relief pitcher—6 (April 23, 1991).

Year Team (League)	W	L	Pct.	ERA	G	GS	CG	ShO	Sv.	IP	H	R	ER	BB	SO
1983—Billings (Pioneer)	0	1	.000	7.82	5	2	0	0	0	12 2/3	18	13	11	11	7
—Eugene (N'west)	3	2	.600	5.73	7	7	1	0	0	37 2/3	38	28	24	18	17
1984—Tampa (Fla. St.)	5	2	.714	2.92	15	11	2	0	0	64 2/3	59	31	21	29	39
1985—Ced. Rap. (Midw.)	5	5	.500	3.84	45	1	0	0	12	65 2/3	67	37	28	28	73
1986—Vermont (Eastern)	3	2	.600	3.09	31	1	1	0	10	55 1/3	53	29	19	28	37
—Denver (Am. Assoc.)	1	0	1.000	5.40	5	0	0	0	0	6 2/3	9	4	4	2	3
1987—Nashville (A.A.)	2	4	.333	4.72	44	0	0	0	4	61	72	34	32	27	51
1988—Nashville (A.A.)	2	1	.667	2.31	31	0	0	0	13	35	21	9	9	14	41
—Cincinnati (N.L.)	1	1	.500	1.82	37	0	0	0	0	59 1/3	43	12	12	21	59
1989—Cincinnati (N.L.)	10	5	.667	2.09	74	0	0	0	2	99	62	23	23	39	141
1990—Cincinnati (N.L.)	8	3	.727	1.74	68	0	0	0	11	98	62	22	19	34	136
1991—Cincinnati (N.L.)	3	5	.375	3.17	67	0	0	0	31	82 1/3	67	32	29	25	124
1992—Cincinnati (N.L.)	3	5	.375	3.07	63	0	0	0	25	70 1/3	48	26	24	31	110
1993—Cincinnati (N.L.)	1	4	.200	6.48	45	0	0	0	19	41 2/3	34	33	30	42	49
1994—Indianapolis (A.A.)	0	2	.000	22.85	6	5	0	0	0	4 1/3	5	11	11	10	5
1995—Birmingham (Sou.)■	0	1	.000	7.36	8	0	0	0	1	7 1/3	4	6	6	5	15
—Chicago (A.L.)	0	1	.000	6.28	16	0	0	0	1	14 1/3	7	10	10	27	16
—New Orleans (A.A.)■	0	1	.000	0.00	4	0	0	0	0	4	1	2	0	2	6
—Milwaukee (A.L.)	1	1	.500	8.25	15	0	0	0	0	12	9	11	11	19	10
A.L. totals (1 year)	1	2	.333	7.18	31	0	0	0	1	26 1/3	16	21	21	46	26
N.L. totals (6 years)	26	23	.531	2.74	354	0	0	0	88	450 2/3	316	148	137	192	619
Major league totals (7 years)	27	25	.519	2.98	385	0	0	0	89	477	332	169	158	238	645

CHAMPIONSHIP SERIES RECORD

NOTES: Named N.L. Championship Series co-Most Valuable Player (1990).

Year Team (League)	W	L	Pct.	ERA	G	GS	CG	ShO	Sv.	IP	H	R	ER	BB	SO
1990—Cincinnati (N.L.)	0	0	...	0.00	4	0	0	0	1	5	0	0	0	1	10

WORLD SERIES RECORD

NOTES: Member of World Series championship team (1990).

Year Team (League)	W	L	Pct.	ERA	G	GS	CG	ShO	Sv.	IP	H	R	ER	BB	SO
1990—Cincinnati (N.L.)	1	0	1.000	0.00	3	0	0	0	0	4 2/3	3	0	0	1	4

ALL-STAR GAME RECORD

Year League	W	L	Pct.	ERA	GS	CG	ShO	Sv.	IP	H	R	ER	BB	SO
1990—National	0	0	...	0.00	0	0	0	0	1	1	0	0	1	0
1991—National	0	0	...	0.00	0	0	0	0	1	0	0	0	1	1
All-Star totals (2 years)	0	0	...	0.00	0	0	0	0	2	1	0	0	2	1

DiPOTO, JERRY — P — METS

PERSONAL: Born May 24, 1968, in Jersey City, N.J. . . . 6-2/200. . . . Throws right, bats right. . . . Full name: Gerard Peter DiPoto III.

HIGH SCHOOL: Toms River (N.J.).

COLLEGE: Virginia Commonwealth.

TRANSACTIONS/CAREER NOTES: Selected by Cleveland Indians organization in third round of free-agent draft (June 5, 1989). . . . On Cleveland disabled list (March 25-June 12, 1994); included rehabilitation assignment to Charlotte (May 10-June 8). . . . Traded by Indians with P Paul Byrd, P Dave Mlicki and a player to be named later to New York Mets for OF Jeromy Burnitz and P Joe Roa (November 18, 1994); Mets acquired 2B Jesus Azuaje to complete deal (December 6, 1994).

STATISTICAL NOTES: Led Eastern League with 15 wild pitches and tied for lead with three balks in 1991.

Year Team (League)	W	L	Pct.	ERA	G	GS	CG	ShO	Sv.	IP	H	R	ER	BB	SO
1989—Watertown (NYP)	6	5	.545	3.61	14	14	1	0	0	87 1/3	75	42	35	39	98
1990—Kinston (Carolina)	11	4	.733	3.78	24	24	1	0	0	145 1/3	129	75	61	77	143
—Cant./Akr. (East.)	1	0	1.000	2.57	3	2	0	0	0	14	11	5	4	4	12

Year	Team (League)	W	L	Pct.	ERA	G	GS	CG	ShO	Sv.	IP	H	R	ER	BB	SO
1991—	Cant./Akr. (East.)	6	11	.353	3.81	28	26	2	0	0	156	143	83	66	74	97
1992—	Colo. Springs (PCL)	9	9	.500	4.94	50	9	0	0	2	122	148	78	67	66	62
1993—	Charlotte (Int'l)	6	3	.667	1.93	34	0	0	0	12	46 2/3	34	10	10	13	44
	—Cleveland (A.L.)	4	4	.500	2.40	46	0	0	0	11	56 1/3	57	21	15	30	41
1994—	Charlotte (Int'l)	3	2	.600	3.15	25	2	0	0	9	34 1/3	37	13	12	12	26
	—Cleveland (A.L.)	0	0	...	8.04	7	0	0	0	0	15 2/3	26	14	14	10	9
1995—	New York (N.L.)■	4	6	.400	3.78	58	0	0	0	2	78 2/3	77	41	33	29	49
A.L. totals (2 years)		4	4	.500	3.63	53	0	0	0	11	72	83	35	29	40	50
N.L. totals (1 year)		4	6	.400	3.78	58	0	0	0	2	78 2/3	77	41	33	29	49
Major league totals (3 years)		8	10	.444	3.70	111	0	0	0	13	150 2/3	160	76	62	69	99

DiSARCINA, GARY — SS — ANGELS

PERSONAL: Born November 19, 1967, in Malden, Mass. . . . 6-1/178. . . . Bats right, throws right. . . . Full name: Gary Thomas DiSarcina. . . . Brother of Glenn DiSarcina, shortstop, Chicago White Sox organization. . . . Name pronounced DEE-sar-SEE-na.
HIGH SCHOOL: Billerica (Mass.) Memorial.
COLLEGE: Massachusetts.
TRANSACTIONS/CAREER NOTES: Selected by California Angels organization in sixth round of free-agent draft (June 1, 1988). . . . On disabled list (August 27, 1993-remainder of season and August 4-September 17, 1995).
STATISTICAL NOTES: Led Pacific Coast League shortstops with .968 fielding percentage and 419 assists in 1991. . . . Led A.L. shortstops with 761 total chances in 1992.

			BATTING												FIELDING			
Year	Team (League)	Pos.	G	AB	R	H	2B	3B	HR	RBI	Avg.	BB	SO	SB	PO	A	E	Avg.
1988—	Bend (Northwest)	SS	71	295	40	90	11	•5	2	39	.305	27	34	7	104	*237	27	.927
1989—	Midland (Texas)	SS	126	441	65	126	18	7	4	54	.286	24	54	11	206	*411	30	*.954
	—California (A.L.)	SS	2	0	0	0	0	0	0	0	...	0	0	0	0	0	0	...
1990—	Edmonton (PCL)	SS	97	330	46	70	12	2	4	37	.212	25	46	5	165	289	24	.950
	—California (A.L.)	SS-2B	18	57	8	8	1	1	0	0	.140	3	10	1	17	57	4	.949
1991—	Edmonton (PCL)	SS-2B	119	390	61	121	21	4	4	58	.310	29	32	16	191	†425	20	†.969
	—California (A.L.)	SS-2B-3B	18	57	5	12	2	0	0	3	.211	3	4	0	29	45	4	.949
1992—	California (A.L.)	SS	157	518	48	128	19	0	3	42	.247	20	50	9	250	*486	•25	.967
1993—	California (A.L.)	SS	126	416	44	99	20	1	3	45	.238	15	38	5	193	362	14	.975
1994—	California (A.L.)	SS	112	389	53	101	14	2	3	33	.260	18	28	3	159	*358	9	.983
1995—	California (A.L.)	SS	99	362	61	111	28	6	5	41	.307	20	25	7	146	275	6	.986
Major league totals (7 years)			532	1799	219	459	84	10	14	164	.255	79	155	25	794	1583	62	.975

ALL-STAR GAME RECORD

			BATTING											FIELDING			
Year	League	Pos.	AB	R	H	2B	3B	HR	RBI	Avg.	BB	SO	SB	PO	A	E	Avg.
1995—	American	PR-SS	1	0	0	0	0	0	0	.000	0	0	0	0	0	0	...

DISHMAN, GLENN — P — PADRES

PERSONAL: Born November 5, 1970, in Baltimore. . . . 6-1/195. . . . Throws left, bats right. . . . Full name: Glenelg Edward Dishman.
HIGH SCHOOL: Moreau (Hayward, Calif.).
COLLEGE: Texas Christian.
TRANSACTIONS/CAREER NOTES: Signed as non-drafted free agent by San Diego Padres organization (June 10, 1993).
STATISTICAL NOTES: Pitched 1-0 no-hit victory for Spokane against Yakima (July 17, 1993).

Year	Team (League)	W	L	Pct.	ERA	G	GS	CG	ShO	Sv.	IP	H	R	ER	BB	SO
1993—	Spokane (N'west)	6	3	.667	2.20	12	12	2	•2	0	77 2/3	59	25	19	13	79
	—Rancho Cuca. (Cal.)	0	1	.000	7.15	2	2	0	0	0	11 1/3	14	9	9	5	6
1994—	Wichita (Texas)	11	8	.579	2.82	27	•27	1	0	0	169 1/3	156	73	53	42	*165
	—Las Vegas (PCL)	1	1	.500	3.46	2	2	0	0	0	13	15	7	5	1	12
1995—	Las Vegas (PCL)	6	3	.667	2.55	14	14	3	1	0	106	91	37	30	20	64
	—San Diego (N.L.)	4	8	.333	5.01	19	16	0	0	0	97	104	60	54	34	43
Major league totals (1 year)		4	8	.333	5.01	19	16	0	0	0	97	104	60	54	34	43

DOHERTY, JOHN — P — TIGERS

PERSONAL: Born June 11, 1967, in Bronx, N.Y. . . . 6-4/210. . . . Throws right, bats right. . . . Full name: John Harold Doherty.
HIGH SCHOOL: Eastchester (N.Y.).
COLLEGE: Concordia College, N.Y. (received degree).
TRANSACTIONS/CAREER NOTES: Selected by Detroit Tigers organization in 19th round of free-agent draft (June 5, 1989). . . . On disabled list (June 9-28, 1992). . . . On suspended list (September 25-30, 1992). . . . On disabled list (May 20-June 4, 1993 and July 10, 1994-remainder of season).
STATISTICAL NOTES: Tied for Eastern League lead with three balks in 1991.

Year	Team (League)	W	L	Pct.	ERA	G	GS	CG	ShO	Sv.	IP	H	R	ER	BB	SO
1989—	Niag. Falls (NYP)	1	1	.500	0.95	26	1	0	0	14	47 1/3	30	7	5	6	45
1990—	Fayetteville (S. Atl.)	1	0	1.000	5.79	7	0	0	0	1	9 1/3	17	12	6	1	6
	—Lakeland (Fla. St.)	5	1	.833	1.10	30	0	0	0	10	41	33	7	5	5	23
1991—	London (Eastern)	3	3	.500	2.22	53	0	0	0	15	65	62	29	16	21	42
1992—	Detroit (A.L.)	7	4	.636	3.88	47	11	0	0	3	116	131	61	50	25	37
1993—	Detroit (A.L.)	14	11	.560	4.44	32	31	3	2	0	184 2/3	205	104	91	48	63
1994—	Detroit (A.L.)	6	7	.462	6.48	18	17	2	0	0	101 1/3	139	75	73	26	28
1995—	Detroit (A.L.)	5	9	.357	5.10	48	2	0	0	6	113	130	66	64	37	46
Major league totals (4 years)		32	31	.508	4.86	145	61	5	2	9	515	605	306	278	136	174

DONNELS, CHRIS — IF

PERSONAL: Born April 21, 1966, in Los Angeles. . . . 6-0/185. . . . Bats left, throws right. . . . Full name: Chris Barton Donnels. . . . Name pronounced DON-uls.
HIGH SCHOOL: South Torrance (Calif.).
COLLEGE: Loyola Marymount.
TRANSACTIONS/CAREER NOTES: Selected by New York Mets organization in first round (24th pick overall) of free-agent draft (June 2, 1987). . . . On Tidewater disabled list (June 20-28, 1991). . . . Selected by Florida Marlins in third round (67th pick overall) of expansion draft (November 17, 1992). . . . Claimed on waivers by Houston Astros (December 18, 1992). . . . On Houston disabled list (April 23-May 12, 1995); included rehabilitation assignment to Jackson (May 8-12). . . . Traded by Astros to Boston Red Sox for player to be named (June 10, 1995). . . . Released by Red Sox (October 26, 1995).
HONORS: Named Florida State League Most Valuable Player (1989).
STATISTICAL NOTES: Led Florida State League with .510 slugging percentage and 15 intentional bases on balls received in 1989. . . . Led Florida State League third basemen with 93 putouts, 202 assists and 320 total chances in 1989. . . . Led Texas League third basemen with 79 putouts, 242 assists, 31 errors, 352 total chances and 24 double plays in 1990.

		BATTING												FIELDING			
Year Team (League)	Pos.	G	AB	R	H	2B	3B	HR	RBI	Avg.	BB	SO	SB	PO	A	E	Avg.
1987— Kingsport (Appal.)	3B	26	86	18	26	4	0	3	16	.302	17	17	4	16	44	6	.909
— Columbia (S. Atl.)	3B	41	136	20	35	7	0	2	17	.257	24	27	3	32	86	10	.922
1988— St. Lucie (Fla. St.)	3B	65	198	25	43	14	2	3	22	.217	32	53	4	40	116	15	.912
— Columbia (S. Atl.)	3B	42	133	19	32	6	0	2	13	.241	30	25	5	29	84	7	.942
1989— St. Lucie (Fla. St.)	3B-1B	117	386	70	121	23	1	17	*78	.313	83	65	18	†242	†209	28	.942
1990— Jackson (Texas)	3B-1B-2B	130	419	66	114	24	0	12	63	.272	*111	81	11	†95	†244	†32	.914
1991— Tidewater (Int'l)	3B-2B	84	287	45	87	19	2	8	56	.303	62	56	1	88	189	14	.952
— New York (N.L.)	1B-3B	37	89	7	20	2	0	0	5	.225	14	19	1	131	34	2	.988
1992— Tidewater (Int'l)	3B-1B-2B	81	279	35	84	15	3	5	32	.301	58	45	12	160	156	16	.952
— New York (N.L.)	3B-2B	45	121	8	21	4	0	0	6	.174	17	25	1	34	77	5	.957
1993— Houston (N.L.)■	3B-1B-2B	88	179	18	46	14	2	2	24	.257	19	33	2	169	54	8	.965
1994— Houston (N.L.)	3B-1B-2B	54	86	12	23	5	0	3	5	.267	13	18	1	42	28	0	1.000
1995— Jackson (Texas)	3B	4	12	1	2	1	0	0	1	.167	4	4	0	6	7	1	.929
— Houston (N.L.)	3B-2B	19	30	4	9	0	0	0	2	.300	3	6	0	3	7	2	.833
— Boston (A.L.)■	3B-1B-2B	40	91	13	23	2	2	2	11	.253	9	18	0	54	41	4	.960
— Pawtucket (Int'l)	3B	4	15	1	6	0	0	1	4	.400	1	3	0	2	3	1	.833
American League totals (1 year)		40	91	13	23	2	2	2	11	.253	9	18	0	54	41	4	.960
National League totals (5 years)		243	505	49	119	25	2	5	42	.236	66	101	5	379	200	17	.971
Major league totals (5 years)		283	596	62	142	27	4	7	53	.238	75	119	5	433	241	21	.970

DOSTER, DAVE — 2B — PHILLIES

PERSONAL: Born October 8, 1970, in Fort Wayne, Ind. . . . 5-10/185. . . . Bats right, throws right. . . . Full name: David Eric Doster.
HIGH SCHOOL: New Haven (Ind.).
COLLEGE: Indiana State.
TRANSACTIONS/CAREER NOTES: Selected by Philadelphia Phillies organization in 27th round of free-agent draft (June 3, 1993).
STATISTICAL NOTES: Led Florida State League second basemen with 743 total chances and 115 double plays in 1994. . . . Led Eastern League with 254 total bases in 1995. . . . Led Eastern League second basemen with 420 assists, 693 total chances and 91 double plays in 1995.

		BATTING												FIELDING			
Year Team (League)	Pos.	G	AB	R	H	2B	3B	HR	RBI	Avg.	BB	SO	SB	PO	A	E	Avg.
1993— Spartanburg (SAL)	2B	60	223	34	61	15	0	3	20	.274	25	36	1	111	205	13	.960
— Clearwater (FSL)	2B-3B	9	28	4	10	3	1	0	2	.357	2	2	2	16	29	5	.900
1994— Clearwater (FSL)	2B	131	480	76	135	*42	4	13	74	.281	54	71	12	*278	*445	20	.973
1995— Reading (Eastern)	2B-OF	139	*551	84	146	39	3	21	79	.265	51	61	11	261	†420	12	.983

DOUGHERTY, JIM — P — ASTROS

PERSONAL: Born March 8, 1968, in Brentwood, N.Y. . . . 6-0/210. . . . Throws right, bats right. . . . Full name: James E. Dougherty.
HIGH SCHOOL: Ross (Brentwood, N.Y.).
COLLEGE: North Carolina.
TRANSACTIONS/CAREER NOTES: Selected by Houston Astros organization in 26th round of free-agent draft (June 4, 1990). . . . On disabled list (August 22, 1994-remainder of season).

Year Team (League)	W	L	Pct.	ERA	G	GS	CG	ShO	Sv.	IP	H	R	ER	BB	SO
1991— Asheville (S. Atl.)	3	1	.750	1.52	62	0	0	0	28	83	63	17	14	25	78
1992— Osceola (Florida St.)	5	2	.714	1.56	57	0	0	0	31	81	66	21	14	22	77
1993— Jackson (Texas)	2	2	.500	1.87	52	0	0	0	*36	53	39	15	11	21	55
1994— Tucson (Pac. Coast)	5	4	.556	4.12	55	0	0	0	*21	59	70	32	27	30	49
1995— Houston (N.L.)	8	4	.667	4.92	56	0	0	0	0	67 2/3	76	37	37	25	49
— Tucson (Pac. Coast)	1	0	1.000	3.27	8	0	0	0	1	11	11	4	4	5	12
Major league totals (1 year)	8	4	.667	4.92	56	0	0	0	0	67 2/3	76	37	37	25	49

DRABEK, DOUG — P — ASTROS

PERSONAL: Born July 25, 1962, in Victoria, Tex. . . . 6-1/185. . . . Throws right, bats right. . . . Full name: Douglas Dean Drabek. . . . Name pronounced DRAY-bek.
HIGH SCHOOL: St. Joseph (Victoria, Tex.).
COLLEGE: Houston.
TRANSACTIONS/CAREER NOTES: Selected by Cleveland Indians organization in fourth round of free-agent draft (June 3, 1980); did not sign.

. . . Selected by Chicago White Sox organization in 11th round of free-agent draft (June 6, 1983). . . . Traded by White Sox with P Kevin Hickey to New York Yankees organization (August 13, 1984), completing deal in which Yankees traded IF Roy Smalley to White Sox for two players to be named later (July 18, 1984). . . . Traded by Yankees with P Brian Fisher and P Logan Easley to Pittsburgh Pirates for P Rick Rhoden, P Cecilio Guante and P Pat Clements (November 26, 1986). . . . On disabled list (April 26-May 18, 1987). . . . Granted free agency (October 26, 1992). . . . Signed by Houston Astros (December 1, 1992). . . . On suspended list (September 12-17, 1995).

RECORDS: Shares major league single-season record for fewest double plays by pitcher who led league in double plays—4 (1992).

HONORS: Named N.L. Pitcher of the Year by The Sporting News (1990). . . . Named righthanded pitcher on The Sporting News N.L. All-Star team (1990). . . . Named N.L. Cy Young Award winner by Baseball Writers' Association of America (1990).

STATISTICAL NOTES: Pitched 11-0 one-hit, complete-game victory against Philadelphia (August 3, 1990). . . . Pitched 8-0 one-hit, complete-game victory against St. Louis (May 27, 1991).

MISCELLANEOUS: Appeared in five games as pinch-runner (1989). . . . Appeared in one game as pinch-runner (1991). . . . Made an out in only appearance as pinch-hitter (1992). . . . Appeared in one game as pinch-runner (1994). . . . Appeared in two games as pinch-runner (1995).

Year Team (League)	W	L	Pct.	ERA	G	GS	CG	ShO	Sv.	IP	H	R	ER	BB	SO
1983— Niag. Falls (NYP)	6	7	.462	3.65	16	13	3	0	0	103 2/3	99	52	42	48	103
1984— Appleton (Midw.)	1	0	1.000	1.80	1	1	0	0	0	5	3	1	1	3	6
— Glens Falls (East.)	12	5	.706	2.24	19	17	7	3	0	124 2/3	90	34	31	44	75
— Nashville (South.)■	1	2	.333	2.32	4	4	2	0	0	31	30	11	8	10	22
1985— Alb./Colon. (East.)	13	7	.650	2.99	26	26	9	2	0	*192 2/3	153	71	64	55	*153
1986— Columbus (Int'l)	1	4	.200	7.29	8	8	0	0	0	42	50	36	34	25	23
— New York (A.L.)	7	8	.467	4.10	27	21	0	0	0	131 2/3	126	64	60	50	76
1987— Pittsburgh (N.L.)■	11	12	.478	3.88	29	28	1	1	0	176 1/3	165	86	76	46	120
1988— Pittsburgh (N.L.)	15	7	.682	3.08	33	32	3	1	0	219 1/3	194	83	75	50	127
1989— Pittsburgh (N.L.)	14	12	.538	2.80	35	34	8	5	0	244 1/3	215	83	76	69	123
1990— Pittsburgh (N.L.)	*22	6	.786	2.76	33	33	9	3	0	231 1/3	190	78	71	56	131
1991— Pittsburgh (N.L.)	15	14	.517	3.07	35	35	5	2	0	234 2/3	245	92	80	62	142
1992— Pittsburgh (N.L.)	15	11	.577	2.77	34	34	10	4	0	256 2/3	218	84	79	54	177
1993— Houston (N.L.)■	9	*18	.333	3.79	34	34	7	2	0	237 2/3	242	108	100	60	157
1994— Houston (N.L.)	12	6	.667	2.84	23	23	6	2	0	164 2/3	132	58	52	45	121
1995— Houston (N.L.)	10	9	.526	4.77	31	•31	2	1	0	185	205	104	98	54	143
A.L. totals (1 year)	7	8	.467	4.10	27	21	0	0	0	131 2/3	126	64	60	50	76
N.L. totals (9 years)	123	95	.564	3.26	287	284	51	21	0	1950	1806	776	707	496	1241
Major league totals (10 years)	130	103	.558	3.32	314	305	51	21	0	2081 2/3	1932	840	767	546	1317

CHAMPIONSHIP SERIES RECORD

NOTES: Holds single-series record for most games lost—3 (1992). . . . Shares N.L. career record for most complete games pitched—2.

Year Team (League)	W	L	Pct.	ERA	G	GS	CG	ShO	Sv.	IP	H	R	ER	BB	SO
1990— Pittsburgh (N.L.)	1	1	.500	1.65	2	2	1	0	0	16 1/3	12	4	3	3	13
1991— Pittsburgh (N.L.)	1	1	.500	0.60	2	2	1	0	0	15	10	1	1	5	10
1992— Pittsburgh (N.L.)	0	3	.000	3.71	3	3	0	0	0	17	18	11	7	6	10
Champ. series totals (3 years)	2	5	.286	2.05	7	7	2	0	0	48 1/3	40	16	11	14	33

ALL-STAR GAME RECORD

Year League	W	L	Pct.	ERA	GS	CG	ShO	Sv.	IP	H	R	ER	BB	SO
1994— National	0	0	. . .	13.50	0	0	0	0	2/3	4	3	1	0	1

DREIFORT, DARREN P DODGERS

PERSONAL: Born May 18, 1972, in Wichita, Kan. . . . 6-2/205. . . . Throws right, bats right. . . . Full name: Darren John Dreifort. . . . Name pronounced DRY-fert.

HIGH SCHOOL: Wichita (Kan.) Heights.

COLLEGE: Wichita State.

TRANSACTIONS/CAREER NOTES: Selected by New York Mets organization in 11th round of free-agent draft (June 4, 1990); did not sign. . . . Selected by Los Angeles Dodgers organization in first round (second pick overall) of free-agent draft (June 3, 1993). . . . On San Antonio disabled list (July 7-28, 1994). . . . On Albuquerque disabled list (August 27, 1994-remainder of season). . . . On disabled list (April 23, 1995-entire season).

HONORS: Named righthanded pitcher on The Sporting News college All-America team (1992-93). . . . Named Golden Spikes Award winner by USA Baseball (1993).

MISCELLANEOUS: Member of 1992 U.S. Olympic baseball team. . . . Singled with an RBI in one game as pinch-hitter with Los Angeles (1994).

Year Team (League)	W	L	Pct.	ERA	G	GS	CG	ShO	Sv.	IP	H	R	ER	BB	SO
1993—							Did not play.								
1994— Los Angeles (N.L.)	0	5	.000	6.21	27	0	0	0	6	29	45	21	20	15	22
— San Antonio (Tex.)	3	1	.750	2.80	8	8	0	0	0	35 1/3	36	14	11	13	32
— Albuquerque (PCL)	1	0	1.000	5.68	1	1	0	0	0	6 1/3	8	4	4	3	3
1995—							Did not play—injured.								
Major league totals (1 year)	0	5	.000	6.21	27	0	0	0	6	29	45	21	20	15	22

DUNBAR, MATT P YANKEES

PERSONAL: Born October 15, 1968, in Tallahassee, Fla. . . . 6-0/175. . . . Throws left, bats left. . . . Full name: Matthew Marshall Dunbar.

HIGH SCHOOL: Dunedin (Fla.).

COLLEGE: Florida State.

TRANSACTIONS/CAREER NOTES: Selected by New York Yankees organization in 25th round of free-agent draft (June 4, 1990). . . . Selected by Florida Marlins from Yankees organization in Rule 5 major league draft (December 5, 1994). . . . Returned to Yankees organization (May 25, 1995).

Year Team (League)	W	L	Pct.	ERA	G	GS	CG	ShO	Sv.	IP	H	R	ER	BB	SO
1990— GC Yankees (GCL)	0	0	. . .	3.00	3	0	0	0	1	6	4	2	2	3	7
— Oneonta (NYP)	1	4	.200	4.15	19	2	0	0	0	30 1/3	32	23	14	24	24

Year	Team (League)	W	L	Pct.	ERA	G	GS	CG	ShO	Sv.	IP	H	R	ER	BB	SO
1991—	Greensboro (S. Atl.)	2	2	.500	2.22	24	2	1	0	1	44 2/3	36	14	11	15	40
1992—	Prin. William (Caro.)	5	4	.556	2.87	44	0	0	0	2	81 2/3	68	37	26	33	68
1993—	Prin. William (Caro.)	6	2	.750	1.73	49	0	0	0	4	73	50	21	14	30	66
	—Albany (Eastern)	1	0	1.000	2.66	15	0	0	0	0	23 2/3	23	8	7	6	18
1994—	Columbus (Int'l)	0	1	.000	1.73	19	0	0	0	2	26	20	5	5	10	21
	—Albany (Eastern)	2	1	.667	2.04	34	0	0	0	4	39 2/3	30	10	9	14	41
1995—	Florida (N.L.)■	0	1	.000	11.57	8	0	0	0	0	7	12	9	9	11	5
	—Columbus (Int'l)■	2	3	.400	4.06	36	0	0	0	0	44 1/3	50	22	20	19	33
Major league totals (1 year)		0	1	.000	11.57	8	0	0	0	0	7	12	9	9	11	5

DUNCAN, MARIANO — 2B/SS — YANKEES

PERSONAL: Born March 13, 1963, in San Pedro de Macoris, Dominican Republic. . . . 6-0/185. . . . Bats right, throws right.

TRANSACTIONS/CAREER NOTES: Signed as non-drafted free agent by Los Angeles Dodgers organization (January 17, 1982). . . . On Los Angeles disabled list (August 19-September 17, 1986; June 19-July 4 and August 16, 1987-remainder of season; May 28-June 12 and July 1-16, 1989). . . . Traded by Dodgers with P Tim Leary to Cincinnati Reds for OF Kal Daniels and IF Lenny Harris (July 18, 1989). . . . On disabled list (May 14-30, 1990 and August 8-23, 1991). . . . Granted free agency (October 30, 1991). . . . Signed by Philadelphia Phillies (December 10, 1991). . . . On disabled list (July 3-18, 1993 and July 24-August 8, 1994). . . . On suspended list (September 20-24, 1993). . . . Granted free agency (October 18, 1994). . . . Re-signed by Phillies organization (April 14, 1995). . . . Claimed on waivers by Reds (August 8, 1995). . . . Granted free agency (October 31, 1995). . . . Signed by New York Yankees (December 11, 1995).

STATISTICAL NOTES: Led Texas League second basemen with 84 double plays in 1984. . . . Led N.L. shortstops with 21 errors in 1987. . . . Career major league grand slams: 3.

MISCELLANEOUS: Batted as switch-hitter (1982-88).

			BATTING												FIELDING			
Year	Team (League)	Pos.	G	AB	R	H	2B	3B	HR	RBI	Avg.	BB	SO	SB	PO	A	E	Avg.
1982—	Lethbridge (Pio.)	SS-2B	30	55	9	13	3	1	1	8	.236	8	21	1	23	35	15	.795
1983—	Vero Beach (FSL)	OF-SS-2B	109	384	73	102	10	*15	0	42	.266	44	87	*56	169	157	37	.898
1984—	San Antonio (Tex.)	2B-OF-SS	125	502	80	127	14	•11	2	44	.253	41	110	41	283	335	22	.966
1985—	Los Angeles (N.L.)	SS-2B	142	562	74	137	24	6	6	39	.244	38	113	38	224	430	30	.956
1986—	Los Angeles (N.L.)	SS	109	407	47	93	7	0	8	30	.229	30	78	48	172	317	25	.951
1987—	Los Angeles (N.L.)	SS-2B-OF	76	261	31	56	8	1	6	18	.215	17	62	11	101	213	†21	.937
	—Albuquerque (PCL)	SS	6	22	6	6	0	0	0	0	.273	2	5	3	8	15	2	.920
1988—	Albuquerque (PCL)	SS-2B	56	227	48	65	4	8	0	25	.286	10	40	33	104	153	18	.935
1989—	Los Angeles (N.L.)	SS-2B	49	84	9	21	5	1	0	8	.250	0	15	3	28	44	5	.935
	—Cincinnati (N.L.)■	SS-OF-2B	45	174	23	43	10	1	3	13	.247	8	36	6	73	111	9	.953
1990—	Cincinnati (N.L.)	2B-SS-OF	125	435	67	133	22	*11	10	55	.306	24	67	13	265	303	18	.969
1991—	Cincinnati (N.L.)	2B-SS-OF	100	333	46	86	7	4	12	40	.258	12	57	5	169	212	9	.977
1992—	Philadelphia (N.L.)■	0-2-S-3	142	574	71	153	40	3	8	50	.267	17	108	23	256	210	16	.967
1993—	Philadelphia (N.L.)	2B-SS	124	496	68	140	26	4	11	73	.282	12	88	6	180	304	21	.958
1994—	Philadelphia (N.L.)	2-3-S-1	88	347	49	93	22	1	8	48	.268	17	72	10	147	188	12	.965
1995—	Philadelphia (N.L.)	2-S-1-3	52	196	20	56	12	1	3	23	.286	0	43	1	156	119	10	.965
	—Cincinnati (N.L.)■	2-1-S-O	29	69	16	20	2	1	3	13	.290	5	19	0	59	26	1	.988
Major league totals (10 years)			1081	3938	521	1031	185	34	78	410	.262	180	758	164	1830	2477	177	.961

DIVISION SERIES RECORD

			BATTING												FIELDING			
Year	Team (League)	Pos.	G	AB	R	H	2B	3B	HR	RBI	Avg.	BB	SO	SB	PO	A	E	Avg.
1995—	Cincinnati (N.L.)	PH-2B	2	3	1	2	0	0	0	1	.667	0	0	1	0	1	0	1.000

CHAMPIONSHIP SERIES RECORD

NOTES: Holds single-game record for most triples—2 (October 9, 1993). . . . Shares single-series record for most triples—2 (1993). . . . Shares N.L. career record for most triples—3.

			BATTING												FIELDING			
Year	Team (League)	Pos.	G	AB	R	H	2B	3B	HR	RBI	Avg.	BB	SO	SB	PO	A	E	Avg.
1985—	Los Angeles (N.L.)	SS	5	18	2	4	2	1	0	1	.222	1	3	1	7	16	1	.958
1990—	Cincinnati (N.L.)	2B	6	20	1	6	0	0	1	4	.300	0	8	0	6	11	1	.944
1993—	Philadelphia (N.L.)	2B	3	15	3	4	0	2	0	0	.267	0	5	0	5	6	1	.917
1995—	Cincinnati (N.L.)	PH-1B	3	3	0	0	0	0	0	0	.000	1	1	0	9	0	0	1.000
Championship series totals (4 years)			17	56	6	14	2	3	1	5	.250	2	17	1	27	33	3	.952

WORLD SERIES RECORD

NOTES: Member of World Series championship team (1990).

			BATTING												FIELDING			
Year	Team (League)	Pos.	G	AB	R	H	2B	3B	HR	RBI	Avg.	BB	SO	SB	PO	A	E	Avg.
1990—	Cincinnati (N.L.)	2B	4	14	1	2	0	0	0	1	.143	2	2	1	9	9	0	1.000
1993—	Philadelphia (N.L.)	2B-DH	6	29	5	10	0	1	0	2	.345	1	7	3	11	17	1	.966
World Series totals (2 years)			10	43	6	12	0	1	0	3	.279	3	9	4	20	26	1	.979

ALL-STAR GAME RECORD

		BATTING											FIELDING			
Year	League	Pos.	AB	R	H	2B	3B	HR	RBI	Avg.	BB	SO	SB	PO	A	E	Avg.
1994—	National	2B	1	0	0	0	0	0	0	.000	0	0	0	0	2	0	1.000

DUNN, STEVE — 1B — INDIANS

PERSONAL: Born April 18, 1970, in Champaign, Ill. . . . 6-4/225. . . . Bats left, throws left. . . . Full name: Steven Robert Dunn.

HIGH SCHOOL: Robinson Secondary (Fairfax, Va.).

TRANSACTIONS/CAREER NOTES: Selected by Minnesota Twins organization in fourth round of free-agent draft (June 1, 1988). . . . On disabled list (April 20-June 2, 1993). . . . Released by Twins (November 20, 1995). . . . Signed by Cleveland Indians organization (January 4, 1996).

STATISTICAL NOTES: Led Midwest League with eight intentional bases on balls received in 1990. . . . Led California League first basemen with 1,244 total chances and 117 double plays in 1992.

		BATTING												FIELDING			
Year Team (League)	**Pos.**	**G**	**AB**	**R**	**H**	**2B**	**3B**	**HR**	**RBI**	**Avg.**	**BB**	**SO**	**SB**	**PO**	**A**	**E**	**Avg.**
1988—Elizabeth. (Appal.)	1B	26	95	9	27	4	0	2	14	.284	8	22	0	187	14	5	.976
1989—Kenosha (Midwest)	1B	63	219	17	48	8	0	0	23	.219	18	55	2	470	54	7	.987
—Elizabeth. (Appal.)	1B	57	210	34	64	12	3	6	42	.305	22	41	0	480	36	3	*.994
1990—Kenosha (Midwest)	1B	130	478	48	142	29	1	10	72	.297	49	105	13	1125	97	10	.992
1991—Visalia (California)	1B	125	458	64	105	16	1	13	59	.229	58	103	9	1122	*131	11	*.991
1992—Visalia (California)	1B	125	492	93	150	36	3	26	113	.305	41	103	8	*1125	106	13	.990
1993—Nashville (South.)	1B	97	366	48	96	20	2	14	60	.262	35	88	1	700	73	10	.987
1994—Salt Lake (PCL)	1B	90	330	61	102	21	2	15	73	.309	24	75	0	535	63	12	.980
—Minnesota (A.L.)	1B	14	35	2	8	5	0	0	4	.229	1	12	0	91	8	1	.990
1995—Salt Lake (PCL)	1B	109	402	57	127	31	1	12	83	.316	30	63	3	916	59	9	.991
—Minnesota (A.L.)	1B	5	6	0	0	0	0	0	0	.000	1	3	0	5	0	0	1.000
Major league totals (2 years)		19	41	2	8	5	0	0	4	.195	2	15	0	96	8	1	.990

DUNN, TODD OF BREWERS

PERSONAL: Born July 29, 1970, in Tulsa, Okla. . . . 6-5/220. . . . Bats right, throws right. . . . Full name: Todd Kent Dunn.
COLLEGE: North Florida.
TRANSACTIONS/CAREER NOTES: Selected by Milwaukee Brewers organization in supplemental round ("sandwich pick" between first and second round, 35th pick overall) of free-agent draft (June 3, 1993); pick received as compensation for Seattle Mariners signing Type A free-agent P Chris Bosio. . . . On disabled list (July 9-September 1, 1995).

		BATTING												FIELDING			
Year Team (League)	**Pos.**	**G**	**AB**	**R**	**H**	**2B**	**3B**	**HR**	**RBI**	**Avg.**	**BB**	**SO**	**SB**	**PO**	**A**	**E**	**Avg.**
1993—Helena (Pioneer)	OF-1B	43	150	33	46	11	2	10	42	.307	22	52	5	91	1	4	.958
1994—Beloit (Midwest)	OF	129	429	72	94	13	2	23	63	.219	50	131	18	236	14	9	.965
1995—Stockton (Calif.)	OF	67	249	44	73	20	2	7	40	.293	19	67	14	116	6	4	.968

DUNSTON, SHAWON SS GIANTS

PERSONAL: Born March 21, 1963, in Brooklyn, N.Y. . . . 6-1/180. . . . Bats right, throws right. . . . Full name: Shawon Donnell Dunston.
HIGH SCHOOL: Thomas Jefferson (Brooklyn, N.Y.).
TRANSACTIONS/CAREER NOTES: Selected by Chicago Cubs organization in first round (first pick overall) of free-agent draft (June 7, 1982). . . . On disabled list (May 31-June 10, 1983). . . . On Chicago disabled list (June 16-August 21, 1987); included rehabilitation assignment to Iowa (August 14-21). . . . On disabled list (May 5, 1992-remainder of season and March 27-September 1, 1993). . . . On suspended list (September 8-12, 1995). . . . Granted free agency (October 31, 1995). . . . Signed by San Francisco Giants (January 8, 1996).
RECORDS: Shares modern major league single-game record for most triples—3 (July 28, 1990).
HONORS: Named shortstop on The Sporting News N.L. All-Star team (1989).
STATISTICAL NOTES: Led N.L. shortstops with 817 total chances and tied for lead in double plays with 96 in 1986. . . . Career major league grand slams: 2.

		BATTING												FIELDING			
Year Team (League)	**Pos.**	**G**	**AB**	**R**	**H**	**2B**	**3B**	**HR**	**RBI**	**Avg.**	**BB**	**SO**	**SB**	**PO**	**A**	**E**	**Avg.**
1982—GC Cubs (GCL)	SS-3B	53	190	27	61	11	0	2	28	.321	11	22	32	61	129	24	.888
1983—Quad Cities (Mid.)	SS	117	455	65	141	17	8	4	62	.310	7	51	58	172	326	47	.914
1984—Midland (Texas)	SS	73	298	44	98	13	3	3	34	.329	11	38	11	164	203	32	.920
—Iowa (Am. Assoc.)	SS	61	210	25	49	11	1	7	27	.233	4	40	9	90	165	26	.907
1985—Chicago (N.L.)	SS	74	250	40	65	12	4	4	18	.260	19	42	11	144	248	17	.958
—Iowa (Am. Assoc.)	SS	73	272	24	73	9	6	2	28	.268	5	48	17	138	176	12	.963
1986—Chicago (N.L.)	SS	150	581	66	145	36	3	17	68	.250	21	114	13	*320	*465	*32	.961
1987—Chicago (N.L.)	SS	95	346	40	85	18	3	5	22	.246	10	68	12	160	271	14	.969
—Iowa (Am. Assoc.)	SS	5	19	1	8	1	0	0	2	.421	0	3	1	6	12	1	.947
1988—Chicago (N.L.)	SS	155	575	69	143	23	6	9	56	.249	16	108	30	*257	455	20	.973
1989—Chicago (N.L.)	SS	138	471	52	131	20	6	9	60	.278	30	86	19	213	379	17	.972
1990—Chicago (N.L.)	SS	146	545	73	143	22	8	17	66	.262	15	87	25	255	392	20	.970
1991—Chicago (N.L.)	SS	142	492	59	128	22	7	12	50	.260	23	64	21	*261	383	21	.968
1992—Chicago (N.L.)	SS	18	73	8	23	3	1	0	2	.315	3	13	2	28	42	1	.986
1993—Chicago (N.L.)	SS	7	10	3	4	2	0	0	2	.400	0	1	0	5	0	0	1.000
1994—Chicago (N.L.)	SS	88	331	38	92	19	0	11	35	.278	16	48	3	121	218	12	.966
1995—Chicago (N.L.)	SS	127	477	58	141	30	6	14	69	.296	10	75	10	187	336	17	.969
Major league totals (11 years)		1140	4151	506	1100	207	44	98	448	.265	163	706	146	1951	3189	171	.968

CHAMPIONSHIP SERIES RECORD

		BATTING												FIELDING			
Year Team (League)	**Pos.**	**G**	**AB**	**R**	**H**	**2B**	**3B**	**HR**	**RBI**	**Avg.**	**BB**	**SO**	**SB**	**PO**	**A**	**E**	**Avg.**
1989—Chicago (N.L.)	SS	5	19	2	6	0	0	0	0	.316	1	1	1	10	14	1	.960

ALL-STAR GAME RECORD

		BATTING											FIELDING			
Year League	**Pos.**	**AB**	**R**	**H**	**2B**	**3B**	**HR**	**RBI**	**Avg.**	**BB**	**SO**	**SB**	**PO**	**A**	**E**	**Avg.**
1988—National							Did not play.									
1990—National	SS	2	0	0	0	0	0	0	.000	0	0	0	0	0	0	. . .
All-Star Game totals (1 year)		2	0	0	0	0	0	0	.000	0	0	0	0	0	0	. . .

DURAN, ROBERTO — P — DODGERS

PERSONAL: Born March 6, 1973, in Moca, Dominican Republic. . . . 6-0/167. . . . Throws left, bats left.
HIGH SCHOOL: Liceo Domingo Fantino (Moca, Dominican Republic).
TRANSACTIONS/CAREER NOTES: Signed as non-drafted free agent by Los Angeles Dodgers organization (February 10, 1990). . . . On disabled list (May 8, 1991-remainder of season).

Year	Team (League)	W	L	Pct.	ERA	G	GS	CG	ShO	Sv.	IP	H	R	ER	BB	SO
1990—	Santo Dom. (DSL)	0	2	.000	13.27	9	8	0	0	0	19 2/3	18	31	29	36	23
1991—	Santo Dom. (DSL)	1	1	.500	3.18	3	3	0	0	0	11 1/3	8	8	4	8	22
1992—	Vero Beach (FSL)	0	0	...	9.00	2	1	0	0	0	5	6	5	5	4	5
	—GC Dodgers (GCL)	4	3	.571	2.79	9	8	0	0	0	38 2/3	22	17	12	31	57
1993—	Vero Beach (FSL)	1	1	.500	3.72	8	0	0	0	0	9 2/3	10	4	4	8	9
	—Yakima (N'west)	2	2	.500	6.98	20	3	0	0	0	40	37	34	31	42	50
1994—	Bakersfield (Calif.)	6	5	.545	4.82	42	4	0	0	10	65 1/3	61	43	35	48	86
1995—	Vero Beach (FSL)	7	4	.636	3.38	23	22	0	0	0	101 1/3	82	42	38	70	114

DURANT, MIKE — C — TWINS

PERSONAL: Born September 14, 1969, in Columbus, O. . . . 6-2/200. . . . Bats right, throws right. . . . Full name: Michael Joseph Durant.
HIGH SCHOOL: Watterson (Columbus, O.).
COLLEGE: Ohio State.
TRANSACTIONS/CAREER NOTES: Selected by Houston Astros organization in 19th round of free-agent draft (June 1, 1988); did not sign. . . . Selected by Minnesota Twins organization in second round of free-agent draft (June 3, 1991).
STATISTICAL NOTES: Led Southern League catchers with .992 fielding percentage in 1993.

			BATTING											FIELDING			
Year	Team (League)	Pos.	G	AB	R	H	2B	3B	HR	RBI	Avg.	BB	SO	SB	PO	A	E	Avg.
1991—	Kenosha (Midwest)	C-3B-OF	66	217	27	44	10	0	2	20	.203	25	35	20	335	50	12	.970
1992—	Visalia (California)	C	119	418	61	119	18	2	6	57	.285	55	35	19	672	79	14	.982
1993—	Nashville (South.)	C-OF	123	437	58	106	23	1	8	57	.243	44	68	17	591	61	5	†992
1994—	Salt Lake (PCL)	C	103	343	67	102	24	4	4	51	.297	35	47	9	569	44	*11	.982
1995—	Salt Lake (PCL)	C-OF-1B	85	295	40	74	15	3	2	23	.251	20	31	11	370	30	5	.988

DURHAM, RAY — 2B — WHITE SOX

PERSONAL: Born November 30, 1971, in Charlotte, N.C. . . . 5-8/170. . . . Bats both, throws right.
HIGH SCHOOL: Harding (Charlotte, N.C.).
TRANSACTIONS/CAREER NOTES: Selected by Chicago White Sox organization in fifth round of free-agent draft (June 4, 1990). . . . On Utica suspended list (April 1-May 22, 1992). . . . On Sarasota disabled list (June 16-July 9, 1992).
STATISTICAL NOTES: Led Southern League in caught stealing with 25 in 1993. . . . Led Southern League second basemen with 541 total chances in 1993. . . . Led American Association with 261 total bases in 1994. . . . Led American Association second basemen with 701 total chances and 92 double plays in 1994. . . . Career major league grand slams: 1.

			BATTING											FIELDING			
Year	Team (League)	Pos.	G	AB	R	H	2B	3B	HR	RBI	Avg.	BB	SO	SB	PO	A	E	Avg.
1990—	GC Whi. Sox (GCL)	2B-SS	35	116	18	32	3	3	0	13	.276	15	36	23	61	85	15	.907
1991—	Utica (N.Y.-Penn)	2B	39	142	29	36	2	7	0	17	.254	25	44	12	54	101	12	.928
	—GC Whi. Sox (GCL)	2B	6	23	3	7	1	0	0	4	.304	3	5	5	18	15	0	1.000
1992—	Sarasota (Fla. St.)	2B	57	202	37	55	6	3	0	7	.272	32	36	28	66	107	10	.945
	—GC Whi. Sox (GCL)	2B	5	13	3	7	2	0	0	2	.538	3	1	1	4	3	0	1.000
1993—	Birm. (Southern)	2B	137	528	83	143	22	*10	3	37	.271	42	100	39	227	284	*30	.945
1994—	Nashville (A.A.)	2B	133	527	89	156	33	•12	16	66	.296	46	91	34	*254	*429	*19	*.973
1995—	Chicago (A.L.)	2B-DH	125	471	68	121	27	6	7	51	.257	31	83	18	245	298	15	.973
Major league totals (1 year)			125	471	68	121	27	6	7	51	.257	31	83	18	245	298	15	.973

DYE, JERMAINE — OF — BRAVES

PERSONAL: Born January 28, 1974, in Oakland, Calif. . . . 6-0/195. . . . Bats right, throws right. . . . Full name: Jermaine Terrell Dye.
JUNIOR COLLEGE: Cosumnes River (Calif.).
TRANSACTIONS/CAREER NOTES: Selected by Atlanta Braves organization in 17th round of free-agent draft (June 3, 1993). . . . On disabled list (July 13-August 9, 1995).
STATISTICAL NOTES: Led South Atlantic League outfielders with six double plays in 1994.

			BATTING											FIELDING			
Year	Team (League)	Pos.	G	AB	R	H	2B	3B	HR	RBI	Avg.	BB	SO	SB	PO	A	E	Avg.
1993—	GC Braves (GCL)	OF-3B	31	124	17	43	14	0	0	27	.347	5	13	5	46	9	3	.948
	—Danville (Appal.)	OF	25	94	6	26	6	1	2	12	.277	8	10	19	51	1	2	.963
1994—	Macon (S. Atl.)	OF	135	506	73	151	*41	1	15	98	.298	33	82	19	263	*22	9	.969
1995—	Greenville (South.)	OF	104	403	50	115	26	4	15	71	.285	27	74	4	234	*22	5	.981

DYER, MIKE — P — PIRATES

PERSONAL: Born September 8, 1966, in Upland, Calif. . . . 6-3/200. . . . Throws right, bats right. . . . Full name: Michael Lawrence Dyer.
HIGH SCHOOL: Charter Oak (Covina, Calif.).
COLLEGE: Citrus College (Calif.).

TRANSACTIONS/CAREER NOTES: Selected by Minnesota Twins organization in fourth round of free-agent draft (January 14, 1986). . . . On Portland disabled list (April 15, 1990-remainder of season; April 11, 1991-entire season and April 9-25, 1992). . . . Granted free agency (October 15, 1992). . . . Signed by Iowa, Chicago Cubs organization (February 18, 1993). . . . Released by Iowa (May 25, 1993). . . . Signed by Canton/Akron, Cleveland Indians organization (June 8, 1993). . . . Granted free agency (October 15, 1993). . . . Signed by Pittsburgh Pirates organization (January 5, 1994).

Year Team (League)	W	L	Pct.	ERA	G	GS	CG	ShO	Sv.	IP	H	R	ER	BB	SO
1986— Elizabeth. (App.)	5	7	.417	3.48	14	•14	3	1	0	72 1/3	70	50	28	42	62
1987— Kenosha (Midwest)	16	5	.762	3.07	27	27	2	0	0	167	124	72	57	84	163
1988— Orlando (Southern)	11	13	.458	3.99	27	27	3	0	0	162 1/3	155	84	72	86	125
1989— Portland (PCL)	3	6	.333	4.43	15	15	2	0	0	89 1/3	80	56	44	51	63
— Minnesota (A.L.)	4	7	.364	4.82	16	12	1	0	0	71	74	43	38	37	37
1990— Portland (PCL)	0	1	.000	34.71	2	2	0	0	0	2 1/3	6	10	9	9	0
1991—							Did not play.								
1992— Portland (PCL)	7	6	.538	5.06	27	16	0	0	1	105	119	62	59	56	85
1993— Iowa (Am. Assoc.)■	1	0	1.000	4.81	14	0	0	0	0	24 1/3	18	14	13	20	18
— Cant./Akr. (East.)■	7	4	.636	5.55	17	17	0	0	0	94	90	64	58	55	75
1994— Buffalo (A.A.)■	3	3	.500	2.34	29	0	0	0	12	34 2/3	33	11	9	16	26
— Pittsburgh (N.L.)	1	1	.500	5.87	14	0	0	0	4	15 1/3	15	12	10	12	13
1995— Pittsburgh (N.L.)	4	5	.444	4.34	55	0	0	0	0	74 2/3	81	40	36	30	53
A.L. totals (1 year)	4	7	.364	4.82	16	12	1	0	0	71	74	43	38	37	37
N.L. totals (2 years)	5	6	.455	4.60	69	0	0	0	4	90	96	52	46	42	66
Major league totals (3 years)	9	13	.409	4.70	85	12	1	0	4	161	170	95	84	79	103

DYKSTRA, LENNY — OF — PHILLIES

PERSONAL: Born February 10, 1963, in Santa Ana, Calif. . . . 5-10/188. . . . Bats left, throws left. . . . Full name: Leonard Kyle Dykstra. . . . Grandson of Pete Leswick, National Hockey League player (1936-37 and 1944-45); and nephew of Tony Leswick, NHL player (1945-46 through 1955-56 and 1957-58). . . . Name pronounced DIKE-struh.

HIGH SCHOOL: Garden Grove (Calif.).

TRANSACTIONS/CAREER NOTES: Selected by New York Mets organization in 12th round of free-agent draft (June 8, 1981). . . . Traded by Mets with P Roger McDowell and a player to be named later to Philadelphia Phillies for OF Juan Samuel (June 18, 1989); Phillies organization acquired P Tom Edens to complete deal (July 27, 1989). . . . On disabled list (May 6-July 15 and August 27, 1991-remainder of season; April 8-24, June 29-July 16 and August 16, 1992-remainder of season). . . . On Philadelphia disabled list (June 18-July 23, 1994); included rehabilitation assignment to Scranton/Wilkes-Barre (July 19-23). . . . On disabled list (June 4-June 24 and July 28, 1995-remainder of season).

RECORDS: Holds N.L. single-season record for fewest assists by outfielder (150 or more games)—2 (1993).

HONORS: Named Carolina League Player of the Year (1983). . . . Named outfielder on The Sporting News N.L. All-Star team (1993). . . . Named outfielder on The Sporting News N.L. Silver Slugger team (1993).

STATISTICAL NOTES: Led Carolina League in caught stealing with 23 in 1983. . . . Led N.L. outfielders with 452 total chances in 1990 and 481 in 1993. . . . Led N.L. with .418 on-base percentage in 1990. . . . Career major league grand slams: 1.

		BATTING											FIELDING			
Year Team (League)	Pos.	G	AB	R	H	2B	3B	HR	RBI	Avg.	BB	SO	SB	PO	A	E	Avg.
1981— Shelby (S. Atl.)	OF-SS	48	157	34	41	7	2	0	18	.261	37	31	15	86	3	4	.957
1982— Shelby (S. Atl.)	OF	120	413	95	120	13	7	3	38	.291	95	40	77	239	11	14	.947
1983— Lynchburg (Caro.)	OF	•136	*525	*132	*188	24	*14	8	81	*.358	*107	35	*105	268	9	7	.975
1984— Jackson (Texas)	OF	131	501	*100	138	25	7	6	52	.275	73	45	53	256	5	2	*.992
1985— Tidewater (Int'l)	OF	58	229	44	71	8	6	1	25	.310	31	20	26	184	4	5	.974
— New York (N.L.)	OF	83	236	40	60	9	3	1	19	.254	30	24	15	165	6	1	.994
1986— New York (N.L.)	OF	147	431	77	127	27	7	8	45	.295	58	55	31	283	8	3	.990
1987— New York (N.L.)	OF	132	431	86	123	37	3	10	43	.285	40	67	27	239	4	3	.988
1988— New York (N.L.)	OF	126	429	57	116	19	3	8	33	.270	30	43	30	270	3	1	.996
1989— New York (N.L.)	OF	56	159	27	43	12	1	3	13	.270	23	15	13	124	1	2	.984
— Philadelphia (N.L.)■	OF	90	352	39	78	20	3	4	19	.222	37	38	17	208	9	2	.991
1990— Philadelphia (N.L.)	OF	149	590	106	•192	35	3	9	60	.325	89	48	33	*439	7	6	.987
1991— Philadelphia (N.L.)	OF	63	246	48	73	13	5	3	12	.297	37	20	24	167	3	4	.977
1992— Philadelphia (N.L.)	OF	85	345	53	104	18	0	6	39	.301	40	32	30	253	6	3	.989
1993— Philadelphia (N.L.)	OF	161	*637	*143	*194	44	6	19	66	.305	*129	64	37	*469	2	10	.979
1994— Philadelphia (N.L.)	OF	84	315	68	86	26	5	5	24	.273	68	44	15	235	4	4	.984
— Scran./W.B. (Int'l)	OF	3	7	1	2	1	1	0	1	.286	1	1	0	2	0	0	1.000
1995— Philadelphia (N.L.)	OF	62	254	37	67	15	1	2	18	.264	33	28	10	153	2	2	.987
Major league totals (11 years)		1238	4425	781	1263	275	40	78	391	.285	614	478	282	3005	55	41	.987

CHAMPIONSHIP SERIES RECORD

NOTES: Shares single-series record for most times hit by pitch—2 (1988).

		BATTING											FIELDING			
Year Team (League)	Pos.	G	AB	R	H	2B	3B	HR	RBI	Avg.	BB	SO	SB	PO	A	E	Avg.
1986— New York (N.L.)	OF-PH	6	23	3	7	1	1	1	3	.304	2	4	1	10	0	0	1.000
1988— New York (N.L.)	OF-PH	7	14	6	6	3	0	1	3	.429	4	0	0	9	0	0	1.000
1993— Philadelphia (N.L.)	OF	6	25	5	7	1	0	2	2	.280	5	8	0	13	0	0	1.000
Championship series totals (3 years)		19	62	14	20	5	1	4	8	.323	11	12	1	32	0	0	1.000

WORLD SERIES RECORD

NOTES: Member of World Series championship team (1986).

		BATTING											FIELDING			
Year Team (League)	Pos.	G	AB	R	H	2B	3B	HR	RBI	Avg.	BB	SO	SB	PO	A	E	Avg.
1986— New York (N.L.)	OF-PH	7	27	4	8	0	0	2	3	.296	2	7	0	14	0	0	1.000
1993— Philadelphia (N.L.)	OF	6	23	9	8	1	0	4	8	.348	7	4	4	18	1	0	1.000
World Series totals (2 years)		13	50	13	16	1	0	6	11	.320	9	11	4	32	1	0	1.000

ALL-STAR GAME RECORD

Year League	Pos.	BATTING AB	R	H	2B	3B	HR	RBI	Avg.	BB	SO	SB	FIELDING PO	A	E	Avg.
1990—National	OF	4	0	1	0	0	0	0	.250	0	0	0	3	0	0	1.000
1994—National		Selected, did not play—injured.														
1995—National	OF	2	0	0	0	0	0	0	.000	1	0	0	1	0	0	1.000
All-Star Game totals (2 years)		6	0	1	0	0	0	0	.167	1	0	0	4	0	0	1.000

EASLEY, DAMION — 2B — ANGELS

PERSONAL: Born November 11, 1969, in New York. . . . 5-11/185. . . . Bats right, throws right. . . . Full name: Jacinto Damion Easley.

HIGH SCHOOL: Lakewood (Calif.).

COLLEGE: Long Beach (Calif.) City College.

TRANSACTIONS/CAREER NOTES: Selected by California Angels organization in 30th round of free-agent draft (June 1, 1988). . . . On disabled list (June 19-July 4 and July 28, 1993-remainder of season; and May 30-June 17, 1994).

Year Team (League)	Pos.	G	BATTING AB	R	H	2B	3B	HR	RBI	Avg.	BB	SO	SB	FIELDING PO	A	E	Avg.
1989—Bend (Northwest)	2B	36	131	34	39	5	1	4	21	.298	25	21	9	49	89	22	.863
1990—Quad City (Midw.)	SS	103	365	59	100	19	3	10	56	.274	41	60	25	136	206	41	.893
1991—Midland (Texas)	SS	127	452	73	115	24	5	6	57	.254	58	67	23	186	388	*47	.924
1992—Edmonton (PCL)	SS-3B	108	429	61	124	18	3	3	44	.289	31	44	26	152	342	30	.943
—California (A.L.)	3B-SS	47	151	14	39	5	0	1	12	.258	8	26	9	30	102	5	.964
1993—California (A.L.)	2B-3B-DH	73	230	33	72	13	2	2	22	.313	28	35	6	111	157	6	.978
1994—California (A.L.)	3B-2B	88	316	41	68	16	1	6	30	.215	29	48	4	122	179	7	.977
1995—California (A.L.)	2B-SS	114	357	35	77	14	2	4	35	.216	32	47	5	186	276	10	.979
Major league totals (4 years)		322	1054	123	256	48	5	13	99	.243	97	156	24	449	714	28	.976

ECKERSLEY, DENNIS — P — ATHLETICS

PERSONAL: Born October 3, 1954, in Oakland, Calif. . . . 6-2/195. . . . Throws right, bats right. . . . Full name: Dennis Lee Eckersley.

HIGH SCHOOL: Washington (Fremont, Calif.).

TRANSACTIONS/CAREER NOTES: Selected by Cleveland Indians organization in third round of free-agent draft (June 6, 1972). . . . Traded by Indians with C Fred Kendall to Boston Red Sox for P Rick Wise, P Mike Paxton, 3B Ted Cox and C Bo Diaz (March 30, 1978). . . . Traded by Red Sox with OF Mike Brumley to Chicago Cubs for 1B/OF Bill Buckner (May 25, 1984). . . . Granted free agency (November 8, 1984). . . . Re-signed by Cubs (November 28, 1984). . . . On disabled list (August 11-September 7, 1985). . . . Traded by Cubs with IF Dan Rohn to Oakland Athletics for OF Dave Wilder, IF Brian Guinn and P Mark Leonette (April 3, 1987). . . . On disabled list (May 29-July 13, 1989). . . . Granted free agency (October 25, 1994). . . . Re-signed by A's (April 3, 1995).

RECORDS: Holds A.L. career records for most saves—323; and most consecutive errorless games by pitcher—470 (May 1, 1987 through May 4, 1995).

HONORS: Named A.L. Rookie Pitcher of the Year by THE SPORTING NEWS (1975). . . . Named A.L. Fireman of the Year by THE SPORTING NEWS (1988 and 1992). . . . Named A.L. co-Fireman of the Year by THE SPORTING NEWS (1991). . . . Named A.L. Most Valuable Player by Baseball Writers' Association of America (1992). . . . Named A.L. Cy Young Award winner by Baseball Writers' Association of America (1992).

STATISTICAL NOTES: Led Texas League with 10 hit batsmen in 1974. . . . Pitched 1-0 no-hit victory against California (May 30, 1977). . . . Pitched 2-0 one-hit, complete-game victory against Milwaukee (August 12, 1977, first game). . . . Led A.L. with 30 home runs allowed in 1978. . . . Pitched 3-1 one-hit, complete-game victory against Toronto (September 26, 1980).

Year Team (League)	W	L	Pct.	ERA	G	GS	CG	ShO	Sv.	IP	H	R	ER	BB	SO
1972—Reno (California)	5	5	.500	4.80	12	12	3	1	0	75	87	46	40	33	56
1973—Reno (California)	12	8	.600	3.65	31	*31	11	•5	0	202	182	97	82	91	218
1974—San Antonio (Tex.)	•14	3	*.824	3.40	23	23	10	2	0	167	141	66	63	60	*163
1975—Cleveland (A.L.)	13	7	.650	2.60	34	24	6	2	2	187	147	61	54	90	152
1976—Cleveland (A.L.)	13	12	.520	3.44	36	30	9	3	1	199	155	82	76	78	200
1977—Cleveland (A.L.)	14	13	.519	3.53	33	33	12	3	0	247	214	100	97	54	191
1978—Boston (A.L.)■	20	8	.714	2.99	35	35	16	3	0	268	258	99	89	71	162
1979—Boston (A.L.)	17	10	.630	2.99	33	33	17	2	0	247	234	89	82	59	150
1980—Boston (A.L.)	12	14	.462	4.27	30	30	8	0	0	198	188	101	94	44	121
1981—Boston (A.L.)	9	8	.529	4.27	23	23	8	2	0	154	160	82	73	35	79
1982—Boston (A.L.)	13	13	.500	3.73	33	33	11	3	0	224 1/3	228	101	93	43	127
1983—Boston (A.L.)	9	13	.409	5.61	28	28	2	0	0	176 1/3	223	119	110	39	77
1984—Boston (A.L.)	4	4	.500	5.01	9	9	2	0	0	64 2/3	71	38	36	13	33
—Chicago (N.L.)■	10	8	.556	3.03	24	24	2	0	0	160 1/3	152	59	54	36	81
1985—Chicago (N.L.)	11	7	.611	3.08	25	25	6	2	0	169 1/3	145	61	58	19	117
1986—Chicago (N.L.)	6	11	.353	4.57	33	32	1	0	0	201	226	109	102	43	137
1987—Oakland (A.L.)■	6	8	.429	3.03	54	2	0	0	16	115 2/3	99	41	39	17	113
1988—Oakland (A.L.)	4	2	.667	2.35	60	0	0	0	45	72 2/3	52	20	19	11	70
1989—Oakland (A.L.)	4	0	1.000	1.56	51	0	0	0	33	57 2/3	32	10	10	3	55
1990—Oakland (A.L.)	4	2	.667	0.61	63	0	0	0	48	73 1/3	41	9	5	4	73
1991—Oakland (A.L.)	5	4	.556	2.96	67	0	0	0	43	76	60	26	25	9	87
1992—Oakland (A.L.)	7	1	.875	1.91	69	0	0	0	*51	80	62	17	17	11	93
1993—Oakland (A.L.)	2	4	.333	4.16	64	0	0	0	36	67	67	32	31	13	80
1994—Oakland (A.L.)	5	4	.556	4.26	45	0	0	0	19	44 1/3	49	26	21	13	47
1995—Oakland (A.L.)	4	6	.400	4.83	52	0	0	0	29	50 1/3	53	29	27	11	40
A.L. totals (19 years)	165	133	.554	3.45	819	280	91	18	323	2602 1/3	2393	1082	998	618	1950
N.L. totals (3 years)	27	26	.509	3.63	82	81	9	2	0	530 2/3	523	229	214	98	335
Major league totals (21 years)	192	159	.547	3.48	901	361	100	20	323	3133	2916	1311	1212	716	2285

CHAMPIONSHIP SERIES RECORD

NOTES: Named A.L. Championship Series Most Valuable Player (1988). . . . Holds career record for most saves—10. . . . Holds single-series record for most saves—4 (1988). . . . Shares career record for most games pitched—15. . . . Shares A.L. career records for most games pitched—14; and most games as relief pitcher—14.

Year	Team (League)	W	L	Pct.	ERA	G	GS	CG	ShO	Sv.	IP	H	R	ER	BB	SO
1984—	Chicago (N.L.)	0	1	.000	8.44	1	1	0	0	0	5 1/3	9	5	5	0	0
1988—	Oakland (A.L.)	0	0	...	0.00	4	0	0	0	4	6	1	0	0	2	5
1989—	Oakland (A.L.)	0	0	...	1.59	4	0	0	0	3	5 2/3	4	1	1	0	2
1990—	Oakland (A.L.)	0	0	...	0.00	3	0	0	0	2	3 1/3	2	0	0	0	3
1992—	Oakland (A.L.)	0	0	...	6.00	3	0	0	0	1	3	8	2	2	0	2
Champ. series totals (5 years)		0	1	.000	3.09	15	1	0	0	10	23 1/3	24	8	8	2	12

WORLD SERIES RECORD

NOTES: Member of World Series championship team (1989).

Year	Team (League)	W	L	Pct.	ERA	G	GS	CG	ShO	Sv.	IP	H	R	ER	BB	SO
1988—	Oakland (A.L.)	0	1	.000	10.80	2	0	0	0	0	1 2/3	2	2	2	1	2
1989—	Oakland (A.L.)	0	0	...	0.00	2	0	0	0	1	1 2/3	0	0	0	0	0
1990—	Oakland (A.L.)	0	1	.000	6.75	2	0	0	0	0	1 1/3	3	1	1	0	1
World Series totals (3 years)		0	2	.000	5.79	6	0	0	0	1	4 2/3	5	3	3	1	3

ALL-STAR GAME RECORD

Year	League	W	L	Pct.	ERA	GS	CG	ShO	Sv.	IP	H	R	ER	BB	SO
1977—	American	0	0	...	0.00	0	0	0	0	2	0	0	0	0	1
1982—	American	0	1	.000	9.00	1	0	0	0	3	2	3	3	2	1
1988—	American	0	0	...	0.00	0	0	0	1	1	0	0	0	0	1
1990—	American	0	0	...	0.00	0	0	0	1	1	1	0	0	0	1
1991—	American	0	0	...	0.00	0	0	0	1	1	0	0	0	0	1
1992—	American	0	0	...	0.00	0	0	0	0	2/3	3	2	0	0	2
All-Star totals (6 years)		0	1	.000	3.12	1	0	0	3	8 2/3	6	5	3	2	7

EDDY, CHRIS — P — ROYALS

PERSONAL: Born November 27, 1969, in Dallas. . . . 6-3/200. . . . Throws left, bats left. . . . Full name: Christopher Mark Eddy.
HIGH SCHOOL: Duncanville (Tex.).
COLLEGE: Texas Christian.
TRANSACTIONS/CAREER NOTES: Selected by Kansas City Royals organization in third round of free-agent draft (June 1, 1992). . . . Selected by Oakland Athletics from Royals organization in Rule 5 major league draft (December 5, 1994). . . . Returned to Royals organization (May 15, 1995). . . . On Omaha disabled list (June 30-July 15 and July 24-August 5, 1995).

Year	Team (League)	W	L	Pct.	ERA	G	GS	CG	ShO	Sv.	IP	H	R	ER	BB	SO
1992—	Eugene (N'west)	4	2	.667	1.59	23	0	0	0	5	45 1/3	25	13	8	23	63
1993—	Wilmington (Caro.)	2	2	.500	2.83	55	0	0	0	14	54	39	23	17	37	67
1994—	Memphis (South.)	9	2	*.818	3.91	43	0	0	0	1	78 1/3	74	37	34	32	86
1995—	Oakland (A.L.)■	0	0	...	7.36	6	0	0	0	0	3 2/3	7	3	3	2	2
—	Omaha (Am. Assoc.)■	1	1	.500	7.27	14	0	0	0	0	17 1/3	20	15	14	12	12
—	Wichita (Texas)	1	0	1.000	4.00	9	0	0	0	1	9	8	4	4	3	10
Major league totals (1 year)		0	0	...	7.36	6	0	0	0	0	3 2/3	7	3	3	2	2

EDENFIELD, KEN — P — ANGELS

PERSONAL: Born March 18, 1967, in Jesup, Ga. . . . 6-1/165. . . . Throws right, bats right. . . . Full name: Kenneth Edward Edenfield.
HIGH SCHOOL: Morristown (Tenn.) Hamblen East.
COLLEGE: Western Kentucky.
TRANSACTIONS/CAREER NOTES: Selected by California Angels organization in 21st round of free-agent draft (June 4, 1990).

Year	Team (League)	W	L	Pct.	ERA	G	GS	CG	ShO	Sv.	IP	H	R	ER	BB	SO
1990—	Boise (Northwest)	8	4	.667	1.65	31	0	0	0	9	54 2/3	38	15	10	17	57
1991—	Quad City (Midw.)	8	5	.615	2.59	47	0	0	0	15	87	69	30	25	30	106
1992—	Palm Springs (Cal.)	0	0	...	0.49	13	0	0	0	7	18 1/3	12	1	1	7	20
—	Midland (Texas)	1	5	.167	5.98	31	0	0	0	2	49 2/3	60	35	33	24	43
1993—	Midland (Texas)	5	8	.385	4.61	48	3	1	0	4	93 2/3	93	56	48	35	84
—	Vancouver (PCL)	0	0	...	0.00	2	0	0	0	0	3 2/3	1	0	0	1	5
1994—	Vancouver (PCL)	9	4	.692	3.39	51	0	0	0	4	87 2/3	69	38	33	36	84
1995—	Vancouver (PCL)	7	2	.778	3.45	33	0	0	0	0	66	56	24	23	25	44
—	California (A.L.)	0	0	...	4.26	7	0	0	0	0	12 2/3	15	7	6	5	6
Major league totals (1 year)		0	0	...	4.26	7	0	0	0	0	12 2/3	15	7	6	5	6

EDENS, TOM — P

PERSONAL: Born June 9, 1961, in Ontario, Ore. . . . 6-2/188. . . . Throws right, bats left. . . . Full name: Thomas Patrick Edens.
HIGH SCHOOL: Fruitland (Idaho).
COLLEGE: Lewis-Clark State College, Idaho (degree in business).
TRANSACTIONS/CAREER NOTES: Selected by Cincinnati Reds organization in 12th round of free-agent draft (June 5, 1979); did not sign. . . . Selected by Kansas City Royals organization in 14th round of free-agent draft (June 6, 1983). . . . Traded by Royals organization to New York Mets organization for IF Tucker Ashford (April 1, 1984). . . . On Columbia disabled list (April 9-19 and May 21-June 18, 1984). . . . On disabled list (June 25-August 12, 1985). . . . Traded by Mets organization to Philadelphia Phillies organization (July 27, 1989), completing deal in which Phillies traded 2B Juan Samuel to Mets for OF Lenny Dykstra, P Roger McDowell and a player to be named later (June 18, 1989). . . . Granted free agency (October 15, 1989). . . . Signed by Denver, Milwaukee Brewers organization (December 6, 1989). . . . Granted free agency (December 20, 1990). . . . Signed by Minnesota Twins (January 14, 1991). . . . Selected by Florida Marlins in second round (43rd pick overall) of expansion draft (November 17, 1992). . . . Traded by Marlins to Houston Astros for P Brian Griffiths and P Hector Carrasco (November 17, 1992). . . . On Houston disabled list (March 29-May 6, 1993); included rehabilitation assignments to Osceola (April 19-24) and Tucson (April 24-May 3). . . . Traded by Astros to Phillies for OF Milt Thompson (July 31, 1994). . . . Released by Phillies (November 18, 1994). . . . Signed by Iowa, Chicago Cubs organization (April 8, 1995). . . . On Iowa disabled list (July 21-August 28, 1995). . . . Released by Cubs (September 6, 1995).

STATISTICAL NOTES: Pitched seven-inning, 6-1 no-hit victory against Helena (August 22, 1983, second game).

Year	Team (League)	W	L	Pct.	ERA	G	GS	CG	ShO	Sv.	IP	H	R	ER	BB	SO
1983—	Butte (Pioneer)	2	3	.400	4.32	13	12	1	0	0	58 1/3	65	47	28	33	44
1984—	Columbia (S. Atl.)■	7	4	.636	3.12	16	15	4	1	0	95 1/3	65	44	33	58	60
—	Lynchburg (Caro.)	1	1	.500	2.51	3	2	0	0	0	14 1/3	11	6	4	8	15
1985—	Lynchburg (Caro.)	6	4	.600	3.84	16	16	0	0	0	82	86	40	35	34	48
1986—	Jackson (Texas)	9	4	.692	2.55	16	16	4	0	0	106	76	36	30	41	72
—	Tidewater (Int'l)	5	3	.625	4.55	11	11	2	1	0	61 1/3	71	33	31	28	31
1987—	Tidewater (Int'l)	9	7	.563	3.59	25	22	0	0	1	138	140	69	55	55	61
—	New York (N.L.)	0	0	...	6.75	2	2	0	0	0	8	15	6	6	4	4
1988—	Tidewater (Int'l)	7	6	.538	3.46	24	21	3	0	0	135 1/3	128	67	52	53	89
1989—	Tidewater (Int'l)	1	5	.167	5.26	18	8	0	0	1	65	76	43	38	28	31
—	Scran./W.B. (Int'l)■	1	1	.500	3.21	7	6	0	0	0	42	45	16	15	11	16
1990—	Denver (Am. Assoc.)■	1	1	.500	5.40	19	0	0	0	4	36 2/3	32	23	22	22	26
—	Milwaukee (A.L.)	4	5	.444	4.45	35	6	0	0	2	89	89	52	44	33	40
1991—	Portland (PCL)■	10	7	.588	3.01	25	24	3	1	0	161 1/3	145	67	54	62	100
—	Minnesota (A.L.)	2	2	.500	4.09	8	6	0	0	0	33	34	15	15	10	19
1992—	Minnesota (A.L.)	6	3	.667	2.83	52	0	0	0	3	76 1/3	65	26	24	36	57
1993—	Osceola (Florida St.)■	1	0	1.000	0.00	3	1	0	0	0	4	5	0	0	1	4
—	Tucson (Pac. Coast)	1	0	1.000	6.14	5	0	0	0	0	7 1/3	9	5	5	3	6
—	Houston (N.L.)	1	1	.500	3.12	38	0	0	0	0	49	47	17	17	19	21
1994—	Houston (N.L.)	4	1	.800	4.50	39	0	0	0	1	50	55	25	25	17	38
—	Philadelphia (N.L.)■	1	0	1.000	2.25	3	0	0	0	0	4	4	1	1	1	1
1995—	Chicago (N.L.)■	1	0	1.000	6.00	5	0	0	0	0	3	6	3	2	3	2
—	Iowa (Am. Assoc.)	2	0	1.000	3.46	20	3	0	0	1	41 2/3	36	17	16	17	28
A.L. totals (3 years)		12	10	.545	3.77	95	12	0	0	5	198 1/3	188	93	83	79	116
N.L. totals (4 years)		7	2	.778	4.03	87	2	0	0	1	114	127	52	51	44	66
Major league totals (7 years)		19	12	.613	3.86	182	14	0	0	6	312 1/3	315	145	134	123	182

EDMONDS, JIM — OF — ANGELS

PERSONAL: Born June 27, 1970, in Fullerton, Calif. . . . 6-1/190. . . . Bats left, throws left. . . . Full name: James Patrick Edmonds. . . . Name pronounced ED-muns.

HIGH SCHOOL: Diamond Bar (Calif.).

TRANSACTIONS/CAREER NOTES: Selected by California Angels organization in seventh round of free-agent draft (June 1, 1988). . . . On disabled list (June 19-September 2, 1989; April 10-May 7 and May 23, 1991-remainder of season). . . . On Vancouver disabled list (June 29-July 19, 1993).

HONORS: Named outfielder on The Sporting News A.L. All-Star team (1995).

			BATTING												FIELDING			
Year	Team (League)	Pos.	G	AB	R	H	2B	3B	HR	RBI	Avg.	BB	SO	SB	PO	A	E	Avg.
1988—	Bend (Northwest)	OF	35	122	23	27	4	0	0	13	.221	20	44	4	59	1	1	.984
1989—	Quad City (Midw.)	OF	31	92	11	24	4	0	1	4	.261	7	34	1	47	2	3	.942
1990—	Palm Springs (Cal.)	OF	91	314	36	92	18	6	3	56	.293	27	75	5	199	9	10	.954
1991—	Palm Springs (Cal.)	OF-1B-P	60	187	28	55	15	1	2	27	.294	40	57	2	97	6	0	1.000
1992—	Midland (Texas)	OF	70	246	42	77	15	2	8	32	.313	41	83	3	139	6	5	.967
—	Edmonton (PCL)	OF	50	194	37	58	15	2	6	36	.299	14	55	3	79	5	1	.988
1993—	Vancouver (PCL)	OF	95	356	59	112	28	4	9	74	.315	41	81	6	167	4	3	.983
—	California (A.L.)	OF	18	61	5	15	4	1	0	4	.246	2	16	0	47	4	1	.981
1994—	California (A.L.)	OF-1B	94	289	35	79	13	1	5	37	.273	30	72	4	301	20	3	.991
1995—	California (A.L.)	OF	141	558	120	162	30	4	33	107	.290	51	130	1	401	8	1	.998
Major league totals (3 years)			253	908	160	256	47	6	38	148	.282	83	218	5	749	32	5	.994

ALL-STAR GAME RECORD

			BATTING											FIELDING			
Year	League	Pos.	AB	R	H	2B	3B	HR	RBI	Avg.	BB	SO	SB	PO	A	E	Avg.
1995—	American	PH-OF	1	0	0	0	0	0	0	.000	0	1	0	0	0	0	...

RECORD AS PITCHER

Year	Team (League)	W	L	Pct.	ERA	G	GS	CG	ShO	Sv.	IP	H	R	ER	BB	SO
1991—	Palm Springs (Cal.)	0	0	...	0.00	1	0	0	0	0	2	1	0	0	3	2

EDMONDSON, BRIAN — P — METS

PERSONAL: Born January 29, 1973, in Fontana, Calif. . . . 6-2/185. . . . Throws right, bats right. . . . Full name: Brian Christopher Edmondson.

HIGH SCHOOL: Norte Vista (Riverside, Calif.).

TRANSACTIONS/CAREER NOTES: Selected by Detroit Tigers organization in third round of free-agent draft (June 3, 1991); pick received as part of compensation for Milwaukee Brewers signing Type B free agent P Edwin Nunez. . . . Claimed on waivers by New York Mets (April 24, 1995).

STATISTICAL NOTES: Tied for Appalachian League lead with seven home runs allowed in 1991.

Year	Team (League)	W	L	Pct.	ERA	G	GS	CG	ShO	Sv.	IP	H	R	ER	BB	SO
1991—	Bristol (Appal.)	4	4	.500	4.57	12	12	1	0	0	69	72	38	35	23	42
1992—	Fayetteville (S. Atl.)	10	6	.625	3.36	28	27	3	1	0	155 1/3	145	69	58	67	125
1993—	Lakeland (Fla. St.)	8	5	.615	2.99	19	19	1	0	0	114 1/3	115	44	38	43	64
—	London (Eastern)	0	4	.000	6.26	5	5	1	0	0	23	30	23	16	13	17
1994—	Trenton (Eastern)	11	9	.550	4.56	26	26	2	0	0	162	171	89	82	61	90
1995—	Binghamton (East.)■	7	11	.389	4.76	23	22	2	1	0	134 1/3	150	82	71	59	69

EDSELL, GEOFF — P — ANGELS

PERSONAL: Born December 12, 1971, in Butler, Pa. . . . 6-3/190. . . . Throws right, bats right. . . . Full name: Geoffrey Scott Edsell.
HIGH SCHOOL: Montoursville (Pa.).
COLLEGE: Old Dominion.
TRANSACTIONS/CAREER NOTES: Selected by California Angels organization in sixth round of free-agent draft (June 3, 1993).

Year	Team (League)	W	L	Pct.	ERA	G	GS	CG	ShO	Sv.	IP	H	R	ER	BB	SO
1993—	Boise (Northwest)	4	3	.571	6.89	13	13	1	0	0	64	64	52	49	40	63
1994—	Ced. Rap. (Midw.)	11	5	.688	3.02	17	17	4	1	0	125 1/3	109	54	42	65	84
	— Lake Elsinore (California)	2	2	.500	4.05	9	7	0	0	0	40	38	21	18	24	26
1995—	Lake Elsinore (California)	8	12	.400	3.67	23	22	1	1	0	139 2/3	127	81	57	67	134
	— Midland (Texas)	2	3	.400	5.91	5	5	1	0	0	32	39	26	21	16	19

EENHOORN, ROBERT — SS — YANKEES

PERSONAL: Born February 9, 1968, in Rotterdam, The Netherlands. . . . 6-3/185. . . . Bats right, throws right. . . . Full name: Robert F. Eenhoorn.
COLLEGE: Davidson.
TRANSACTIONS/CAREER NOTES: Selected by New York Yankees organization in second round of free-agent draft (June 4, 1990); pick received as compensation for Pittsburgh Pirates signing Type B free-agent P Walt Terrell. . . . On Prince William disabled list (May 30-June 28 and July 1-September 2, 1991). . . . On disabled list (July 28, 1993-remainder of season).
MISCELLANEOUS: Member of The Netherlands' 1988 Olympic baseball team.

			BATTING												FIELDING			
Year	Team (League)	Pos.	G	AB	R	H	2B	3B	HR	RBI	Avg.	BB	SO	SB	PO	A	E	Avg.
1990—	Oneonta (NYP)	SS	57	220	30	59	9	3	2	18	.268	18	29	11	83	135	9	*.960
1991—	GC Yankees (GCL)	SS	13	40	6	14	4	1	1	7	.350	3	8	1	12	29	4	.911
	— Prin. William (Car.)	SS	29	108	15	26	6	1	1	12	.241	13	21	0	45	69	6	.950
1992—	Fort Lauder. (FSL)	SS	57	203	23	62	5	2	4	33	.305	19	25	6	60	138	16	.925
	— Alb./Colon. (East.)	SS	60	196	24	46	11	2	1	23	.235	10	17	2	88	153	13	.949
1993—	Alb./Colon. (East.)	SS	82	314	48	88	24	3	6	46	.280	21	39	3	143	221	31	.922
1994—	Columbus (Int'l)	SS-2B	99	343	38	82	10	2	5	39	.239	14	43	2	135	325	17	.964
	— New York (A.L.)	SS	3	4	1	2	1	0	0	0	.500	0	0	0	0	1	0	1.000
1995—	Columbus (Int'l)	2B-3B-SS	92	318	36	80	11	3	5	32	.252	20	54	2	168	231	8	.980
	— New York (A.L.)	2B-SS	5	14	1	2	1	0	0	2	.143	1	3	0	11	8	1	.950
Major league totals (2 years)			8	18	2	4	2	0	0	2	.222	1	3	0	11	9	1	.952

EILAND, DAVE — P — CARDINALS

PERSONAL: Born July 5, 1966, in Dade City, Fla. . . . 6-3/212. . . . Throws right, bats right. . . . Full name: David William Eiland. . . . Name pronounced EYE-land.
HIGH SCHOOL: Zephyrhills (Fla.).
COLLEGE: South Florida and Florida.
TRANSACTIONS/CAREER NOTES: Selected by New York Yankees organization in seventh round of free-agent draft (June 2, 1987). . . . On disabled list (May 28-July 12, 1991); included rehabilitation assignment to Columbus (June 16-July 12). . . . Released by Yankees (January 19, 1992). . . . Signed by San Diego Padres organization (January 27, 1992). . . . On San Diego disabled list (May 4-June 26, 1992); included rehabilitation assignment to Las Vegas (May 27-June 25). . . . On San Diego disabled list (July 5-August 26, 1992); included rehabilitation assignment to Las Vegas (July 28-August 26). . . . Granted free agency (December 7, 1992). . . . Signed by Wichita, Padres organization (February 28, 1993). . . . Granted free agency (May 27, 1993). . . . Signed by Charlotte, Cleveland Indians organization (May 29, 1993). . . . Traded by Indians organization to Texas Rangers organization for P Gerald Alexander and P Allan Anderson (August 4, 1993). . . . Granted free agency (October 15, 1993). . . . Signed by Columbus, Yankees organization (March 12, 1994). . . . Granted free agency (October 3, 1995). . . . Signed by St. Louis Cardinals organization (December 6, 1995).
HONORS: Named International League Most Valuable Pitcher (1990).
STATISTICAL NOTES: Hit home run in first major league at-bat (April 10, 1992).

Year	Team (League)	W	L	Pct.	ERA	G	GS	CG	ShO	Sv.	IP	H	R	ER	BB	SO
1987—	Oneonta (NYP)	4	0	1.000	1.84	5	5	0	0	0	29 1/3	20	6	6	3	16
	— Fort Lauder. (FSL)	5	3	.625	1.88	8	8	4	1	0	62 1/3	57	17	13	8	28
1988—	Alb./Colon. (East.)	9	5	.643	2.56	18	18	•7	2	0	119 1/3	95	39	34	22	66
	— Columbus (Int'l)	1	1	.500	2.59	4	4	0	0	0	24 1/3	25	8	7	6	13
	— New York (A.L.)	0	0	. . .	6.39	3	3	0	0	0	12 2/3	15	9	9	4	7
1989—	Columbus (Int'l)	9	4	.692	3.76	18	18	2	0	0	103	107	47	43	21	45
	— New York (A.L.)	1	3	.250	5.77	6	6	0	0	0	34 1/3	44	25	22	13	11
1990—	Columbus (Int'l)	*16	5	.762	2.87	27	26	*11	•3	0	175 1/3	155	63	56	32	96
	— New York (A.L.)	2	1	.667	3.56	5	5	0	0	0	30 1/3	31	14	12	5	16
1991—	New York (A.L.)	2	5	.286	5.33	18	13	0	0	0	72 2/3	87	51	43	23	18
	— Columbus (Int'l)	6	1	.857	2.40	9	9	2	0	0	60	54	22	16	7	18
1992—	San Diego (N.L.)■	0	2	.000	5.67	7	7	0	0	0	27	33	21	17	5	10
	— Las Vegas (PCL)	4	5	.444	5.23	14	14	0	0	0	63 2/3	78	43	37	11	31
1993—	San Diego (N.L.)	0	3	.000	5.21	10	9	0	0	0	48 1/3	58	33	28	17	14
	— Charlotte (Int'l)■	1	3	.250	5.30	8	8	0	0	0	35 2/3	42	22	21	12	13
	— Okla. City (A.A.)■	3	1	.750	4.29	7	7	1	0	0	35 2/3	39	18	17	9	15
1994—	Columbus (Int'l)■	9	6	.600	3.58	26	26	0	0	0	140 2/3	141	72	56	33	84
1995—	Columbus (Int'l)	8	7	.533	3.14	19	18	1	1	0	109	109	44	38	22	62
	— New York (A.L.)	1	1	.500	6.30	4	1	0	0	0	10	16	10	7	3	6
A.L. totals (5 years)		6	10	.375	5.23	36	28	0	0	0	160	193	109	93	48	58
N.L. totals (2 years)		0	5	.000	5.38	17	16	0	0	0	75 1/3	91	54	45	22	24
Major league totals (7 years)		6	15	.286	5.28	53	44	0	0	0	235 1/3	284	163	138	70	82

EISCHEN, JOEY P DODGERS

PERSONAL: Born May 25, 1970, in West Covina, Calif. . . . 6-1/190. . . . Throws left, bats left. . . . Full name: Joseph Raymond Eischen. . . . Name pronounced EYE-shen.

HIGH SCHOOL: West Covina (Calif.).

COLLEGE: Pasadena (Calif.) City College.

TRANSACTIONS/CAREER NOTES: Selected by Chicago White Sox organization in fifth round of free-agent draft (June 1, 1988); did not sign. . . . Selected by Texas Rangers organization in fourth round of free-agent draft (June 5, 1989). . . . Traded by Rangers organization with P Jonathan Hurst and a player to be named later to Montreal Expos organization for P Oil Can Boyd (July 21, 1991); Expos organization acquired P Travis Buckley to complete deal (September 1, 1991). . . . Traded by Expos with OF Roberto Kelly to Los Angeles Dodgers for OF Henry Rodriguez and IF Jeff Treadway (May 23, 1995).

HONORS: Named Eastern League Pitcher of the Year (1993).

STATISTICAL NOTES: Led Pioneer League with 11 balks in 1989. . . . Led Florida State League with 86 runs allowed in 1991. . . . Pitched 5-0 no-hit victory against Vero Beach (June 16, 1992, first game).

Year	Team (League)	W	L	Pct.	ERA	G	GS	CG	ShO	Sv.	IP	H	R	ER	BB	SO
1989—	Butte (Pioneer)	3	7	.300	5.30	12	12	0	0	0	52 2/3	50	45	31	38	57
1990—	Gastonia (S. Atl.)	3	7	.300	2.70	17	14	0	0	0	73 1/3	51	36	22	40	69
1991—	Charlotte (Fla. St.)	4	10	.286	3.41	18	18	1	0	0	108 1/3	99	59	41	55	80
	—WP Beach (FSL)■	4	2	.667	5.17	8	8	1	0	0	38 1/3	35	§27	22	24	26
1992—	WP Beach (FSL)	9	8	.529	3.08	27	26	3	2	0	169 2/3	128	68	58	*83	167
1993—	Harrisburg (East.)	*14	4	*.778	3.62	20	20	0	0	0	119 1/3	122	62	48	60	110
	—Ottawa (Int'l)	2	2	.500	3.54	6	6	0	0	0	40 2/3	34	18	16	15	29
1994—	Ottawa (Int'l)	2	6	.250	4.94	48	2	0	0	2	62	54	38	34	40	57
	—Montreal (N.L.)	0	0	...	54.00	1	0	0	0	0	2/3	4	4	4	0	1
1995—	Ottawa (Int'l)	2	1	.667	1.72	11	0	0	0	0	15 2/3	9	4	3	8	13
	—Los Angeles (N.L.)■	0	0	...	3.10	17	0	0	0	0	20 1/3	19	9	7	11	15
	—Albuquerque (PCL)	3	0	1.000	0.00	13	0	0	0	2	16 1/3	8	0	0	3	14
Major league totals (2 years)		0	0	...	4.71	18	0	0	0	0	21	23	13	11	11	16

EISENREICH, JIM OF PHILLIES

PERSONAL: Born April 18, 1959, in St. Cloud, Minn. . . . 5-11/195. . . . Bats left, throws left. . . . Full name: James Michael Eisenreich. . . . Name pronounced EYES-en-rike.

HIGH SCHOOL: Technical (St. Cloud, Minn.).

COLLEGE: St. Cloud (Minn.) State.

TRANSACTIONS/CAREER NOTES: Selected by Minnesota Twins organization in 16th round of free-agent draft (June 3, 1980). . . . On disabled list (May 6-28 and June 18-September 1, 1982). . . . On disabled list (April 7, 1983); then transferred to voluntarily retired list (May 27, 1983-remainder of season). . . . On disabled list (April 26-May 18, 1984). . . . On voluntarily retired list (June 4, 1984-September 29, 1986). . . . Claimed on waivers by Kansas City Royals (October 2, 1986). . . . On Kansas City disabled list (August 25-September 9, 1987 and July 22-August 6, 1989). . . . Granted free agency (October 30, 1991). . . . Re-signed by Royals (January 31, 1992). . . . On disabled list (August 12-September 7, 1992). . . . Granted free agency (October 30, 1992). . . . Signed by Philadelphia Phillies (January 20, 1993). . . . Granted free agency (October 29, 1993). . . . Re-signed by Phillies (November 24, 1993). . . . Granted free agency (November 1, 1995). . . . Re-signed by Phillies (December 7, 1995).

HONORS: Named Appalachian League co-Player of the Year (1980).

STATISTICAL NOTES: Career major league grand slams: 3.

				BATTING											FIELDING			
Year	Team (League)	Pos.	G	AB	R	H	2B	3B	HR	RBI	Avg.	BB	SO	SB	PO	A	E	Avg.
1980—	Elizabeth. (Appal.)	OF	67	258	47	77	12	•4	3	41	.298	35	32	12	151	7	3	.981
	—Wis. Rap. (Midw.)	DH	5	16	4	7	0	0	0	5	.438	1	0	1	...	...	...	...
1981—	Wis. Rap. (Midw.)	OF	*134	489	101	•152	*27	0	23	99	.311	84	70	9	*295	17	9	.972
1982—	Minnesota (A.L.)	OF	34	99	10	30	6	0	2	9	.303	11	13	0	72	0	2	.973
1983—	Minnesota (A.L.)	OF	2	7	1	2	1	0	0	0	.286	1	1	0	6	1	0	1.000
1984—	Minnesota (A.L.)	OF-DH	12	32	1	7	1	0	0	3	.219	2	4	2	5	0	0	1.000
1985—								Out of organized baseball.										
1986—								Out of organized baseball.										
1987—	Memphis (South.)■	DH	70	275	60	105	36	•10	11	57	.382	47	44	13	...	...	...	...
	—Kansas City (A.L.)	DH	44	105	10	25	8	2	4	21	.238	7	13	1	...	...	...	...
1988—	Kansas City (A.L.)	OF-DH	82	202	26	44	8	1	1	19	.218	6	31	9	109	0	4	.965
	—Omaha (A.A.)	OF	36	142	28	41	8	3	4	14	.289	9	20	9	73	1	1	.987
1989—	Kansas City (A.L.)	OF-DH	134	475	64	139	33	7	9	59	.293	37	44	27	273	4	3	.989
1990—	Kansas City (A.L.)	OF-DH	142	496	61	139	29	7	5	51	.280	42	51	12	261	6	1	*.996
1991—	Kansas City (A.L.)	OF-1B-DH	135	375	47	113	22	3	2	47	.301	20	35	5	243	12	5	.981
1992—	Kansas City (A.L.)	OF-DH	113	353	31	95	13	3	2	28	.269	24	36	11	180	1	1	.995
1993—	Philadelphia (N.L.)■	OF-1B	153	362	51	115	17	4	7	54	.318	26	36	5	223	6	1	.996
1994—	Philadelphia (N.L.)	OF	104	290	42	87	15	4	4	43	.300	33	31	6	179	4	2	.989
1995—	Philadelphia (N.L.)	OF	129	377	46	119	22	2	10	55	.316	38	44	10	205	2	0	*1.000
American League totals (9 years)			698	2144	251	594	121	23	25	237	.277	150	228	67	1149	24	16	.987
National League totals (3 years)			386	1029	139	321	54	10	21	152	.312	97	111	21	607	12	3	.995
Major league totals (12 years)			1084	3173	390	915	175	33	46	389	.288	247	339	88	1756	36	19	.990

CHAMPIONSHIP SERIES RECORD

				BATTING											FIELDING			
Year	Team (League)	Pos.	G	AB	R	H	2B	3B	HR	RBI	Avg.	BB	SO	SB	PO	A	E	Avg.
1993—	Philadelphia (N.L.)	OF-PH	6	15	0	2	1	0	0	1	.133	0	2	0	6	0	0	1.000

WORLD SERIES RECORD

				BATTING											FIELDING			
Year	Team (League)	Pos.	G	AB	R	H	2B	3B	HR	RBI	Avg.	BB	SO	SB	PO	A	E	Avg.
1993—	Philadelphia (N.L.)	OF	6	26	3	6	0	0	1	7	.231	2	4	0	18	0	0	1.000

ELDRED, CAL — P — BREWERS

PERSONAL: Born November 24, 1967, in Cedar Rapids, Ia. . . . 6-4/235. . . . Throws right, bats right. . . . Full name: Calvin John Eldred.
HIGH SCHOOL: Urbana (Ia.) Community.
COLLEGE: Iowa.
TRANSACTIONS/CAREER NOTES: Selected by Milwaukee Brewers organization in first round (17th pick overall) of free-agent draft (June 5, 1989). . . . On disabled list (May 15, 1995-remainder of season).
HONORS: Named A.L. Rookie Pitcher of the Year by The Sporting News (1992).
STATISTICAL NOTES: Led American Association with 12 hit batsmen in 1991.

Year	Team (League)	W	L	Pct.	ERA	G	GS	CG	ShO	Sv.	IP	H	R	ER	BB	SO
1989—	Beloit (Midwest)	2	1	.667	2.30	5	5	0	0	0	31 1/3	23	10	8	11	32
1990—	Stockton (Calif.)	4	2	.667	1.62	7	7	3	1	0	50	31	12	9	19	75
	— El Paso (Texas)	5	4	.556	4.49	19	19	0	0	0	110 1/3	126	61	55	47	93
1991—	Denver (Am. Assoc.)	13	9	.591	3.75	29	*29	3	1	0	*185	161	82	77	84	*168
	— Milwaukee (A.L.)	2	0	1.000	4.50	3	3	0	0	0	16	20	9	8	6	10
1992—	Denver (Am. Assoc.)	10	6	.625	3.00	19	19	4	1	0	141	122	49	47	42	99
	— Milwaukee (A.L.)	11	2	.846	1.79	14	14	2	1	0	100 1/3	76	21	20	23	62
1993—	Milwaukee (A.L.)	16	16	.500	4.01	36	•36	8	1	0	*258	232	120	115	91	180
1994—	Milwaukee (A.L.)	11	11	.500	4.68	25	•25	6	0	0	179	158	96	93	84	98
1995—	Milwaukee (A.L.)	1	1	.500	3.42	4	4	0	0	0	23 2/3	24	10	9	10	18
Major league totals (5 years)		41	30	.577	3.82	82	82	16	2	0	577	510	256	245	214	368

ELLIOTT, DONNIE — P

PERSONAL: Born September 20, 1968, in Pasadena, Tex. . . . 6-5/225. . . . Throws right, bats right. . . . Full name: Donald Glenn Elliott.
HIGH SCHOOL: Deer Park (Tex.).
COLLEGE: San Jacinto (Tex.).
TRANSACTIONS/CAREER NOTES: Selected by Philadelphia Phillies organization in seventh round of free-agent draft (June 2, 1987). . . . Selected by Seattle Mariners from Phillies organization in Rule 5 major league draft (December 9, 1991). . . . Returned to Phillies (April 1, 1992). . . . Traded by Phillies to Atlanta Braves for P Ben Rivera (May 28, 1992). . . . Traded by Braves with OF Mel Nieves and OF Vince Moore to San Diego Padres for 1B Fred McGriff (July 18, 1993). . . . On San Diego disabled list (July 10, 1994-remainder of season). . . . On San Diego disabled list (April 24-September 18, 1995); included rehabilitation assignments to Las Vegas (May 5-9, May 18-June 6 and August 19-September 3). . . . Released by Padres (October 12, 1995).
STATISTICAL NOTES: Tied for Appalachian League lead with nine balks in 1988.

Year	Team (League)	W	L	Pct.	ERA	G	GS	CG	ShO	Sv.	IP	H	R	ER	BB	SO
1988—	Martinsville (App.)	4	2	.667	3.66	15	10	0	0	1	59	47	37	24	31	77
1989—	Batavia (N.Y.-Penn)	4	1	.800	1.42	8	8	0	0	0	57	45	21	9	14	48
	— Spartanburg (SAL)	2	3	.400	2.47	7	7	1	1	0	43 2/3	46	19	12	14	36
1990—	Spartanburg (SAL)	4	8	.333	3.50	20	20	0	0	0	105 1/3	101	52	41	46	109
1991—	Spartanburg (SAL)	3	4	.429	4.24	10	10	0	0	0	51	42	37	24	36	81
	— Clearwater (Fla. St.)	8	5	.615	2.78	18	18	1	1	0	107	78	34	33	51	103
1992—	Clearwater (Fla. St.)	1	1	.500	3.00	3	3	0	0	0	18	12	6	6	8	12
	— Reading (Eastern)	3	3	.500	2.52	6	6	0	0	0	35 2/3	37	10	10	11	23
	— Greenville (South.)■	7	2	.778	2.08	19	17	0	0	0	103 2/3	76	28	24	35	100
1993—	Richmond (Int'l)	8	5	.615	4.72	18	18	1	0	0	103	108	65	54	39	99
	— Las Vegas (PCL)■	2	5	.286	6.37	8	7	0	0	0	41	48	32	29	24	44
1994—	Las Vegas (PCL)	2	0	1.000	5.40	6	0	0	0	0	13 1/3	13	11	8	11	12
	— San Diego (N.L.)	0	1	.000	3.27	30	1	0	0	0	33	31	12	12	21	24
1995—	Las Vegas (PCL)	1	0	1.000	4.50	7	0	0	0	1	8	8	4	4	4	2
	— San Diego (N.L.)	0	0	. . .	0.00	1	0	0	0	0	2	2	0	0	1	3
Major league totals (2 years)		0	1	.000	3.09	31	1	0	0	0	35	33	12	12	22	27

ELLIS, ROBERT — P — WHITE SOX

PERSONAL: Born December 15, 1970, in Baton Rouge, La. . . . 6-5/220. . . . Throws right, bats right. . . . Full name: Robert Randolph Ellis.
HIGH SCHOOL: Belaire (Baton Rouge, La.).
JUNIOR COLLEGE: Panola Junior College (Tex.).
COLLEGE: Northwestern State (La.).
TRANSACTIONS/CAREER NOTES: Selected by Chicago White Sox organization in third round of free-agent draft (June 4, 1990). . . . On South Bend disabled list (May 20-July 1, 1992). . . . On disabled list (July 25, 1994-remainder of season and May 17, 1995-remainder of season).

Year	Team (League)	W	L	Pct.	ERA	G	GS	CG	ShO	Sv.	IP	H	R	ER	BB	SO
1991—	Utica (N.Y.-Penn)	3	•9	.250	4.62	15	15	1	1	0	87 2/3	86	*66	45	61	66
1992—	South Bend (Midw.)	6	5	.545	2.34	18	18	1	1	0	123	90	46	32	35	97
	— GC White Sox (GCL)	1	0	1.000	10.80	1	1	0	0	0	5	10	6	6	1	4
1993—	Sarasota (Fla. St.)	7	8	.467	2.51	15	15	*8	2	0	104	81	37	29	31	79
	— Birmingham (Sou.)	6	3	.667	3.10	12	12	2	1	0	81 1/3	68	33	28	21	77
1994—	Nashville (A.A.)	4	10	.286	6.09	19	19	1	0	0	105	126	77	71	55	76
1995—	Nashville (A.A.)	1	1	.500	2.18	4	4	0	0	0	20 2/3	16	7	5	10	9

ELSTER, KEVIN — SS — RANGERS

PERSONAL: Born August 3, 1964, in San Pedro, Calif. . . . 6-2/200. . . . Bats right, throws right. . . . Full name: Kevin Daniel Elster.
HIGH SCHOOL: Marina (Huntington Beach, Calif.).
COLLEGE: Golden West College (Calif.).
TRANSACTIONS/CAREER NOTES: Selected by New York Mets organization in second round of free-agent draft (January 17, 1984). . . . On Jackson disabled list (August 11, 1985-remainder of season). . . . On disabled list (August 4, 1990-remainder of season; May 6-21, 1991;

and April 13, 1992-remainder of season). . . . Granted free agency (December 19, 1992). . . . Signed by Los Angeles Dodgers organization (January 12, 1993). . . . On Albuquerque disabled list (April 8-May 2, 1993). . . . Released by Dodgers (May 17, 1993). . . . Signed by Florida Marlins organization (May 22, 1993). . . . Released by Edmonton, Marlins organization (June 4, 1993). . . . Signed by San Diego Padres organization (December 17, 1993). . . . Released by Las Vegas, Padres organization (March 21, 1994). . . . Signed by Columbus, New York Yankees organization (May 1, 1994). . . . On Columbus temporarily inactive list (May 1-June 1, 1994). . . . On New York disabled list (July 7, 1994-remainder of season); included rehabilitation assignment to Albany (August 1-20). . . . Released by Yankees (June 8, 1995). . . . Signed by Omaha, Kansas City Royals organization (June 29, 1995). . . . Released by Omaha (July 3, 1995). . . . Signed by Scranton/Wilkes-Barre, Philadelphia Phillies organization (July 7, 1995). . . . Granted free agency (October 5, 1995). . . . Signed by Texas Rangers (January 16, 1996).
RECORDS: Holds major league single-season record for fewest putouts by shortstop who led league in putouts—235 (1989). . . . Holds N.L. career record for most consecutive errorless games by shortstop—88 (July 20, 1988 through May 8, 1989).
STATISTICAL NOTES: Led New York-Pennsylvania League shortstops with 358 total chances and 45 double plays in 1984. . . . Led Texas League shortstops with 589 total chances and 83 double plays in 1986.

			BATTING											FIELDING			
Year Team (League)	**Pos.**	**G**	**AB**	**R**	**H**	**2B**	**3B**	**HR**	**RBI**	**Avg.**	**BB**	**SO**	**SB**	**PO**	**A**	**E**	**Avg.**
1984—Little Falls (NYP)	SS	71	257	35	66	7	3	3	35	.257	35	41	13	*128	214	16	*.955
1985—Lynchburg (Caro.)	SS	59	224	41	66	9	0	7	26	.295	33	21	8	82	195	16	.945
—Jackson (Texas)	SS	59	214	30	55	13	0	2	22	.257	19	29	2	107	220	10	.970
1986—Jackson (Texas)	SS	127	435	69	117	19	3	2	52	.269	61	46	6	*196	*365	28	*.952
—New York (N.L.)	SS	19	30	3	5	1	0	0	0	.167	3	8	0	16	35	2	.962
1987—Tidewater (Int'l)	SS	134	*549	83	*170	33	7	8	74	.310	35	62	7	219	419	21	.968
—New York (N.L.)	SS	5	10	1	4	2	0	0	1	.400	0	1	0	4	6	1	.909
1988—New York (N.L.)	SS	149	406	41	87	11	1	9	37	.214	35	47	2	196	345	13	.977
1989—New York (N.L.)	SS	151	458	52	106	25	2	10	55	.231	34	77	4	*235	374	15	.976
1990—New York (N.L.)	SS	92	314	36	65	20	1	9	45	.207	30	54	2	159	251	17	.960
1991—New York (N.L.)	SS	115	348	33	84	16	2	6	36	.241	40	53	2	149	299	14	.970
1992—New York (N.L.)	SS	6	18	0	4	0	0	0	0	.222	0	2	0	8	10	0	1.000
1993—San Antonio (Tex.)■	SS	10	39	5	11	2	1	0	7	.282	4	4	0	14	31	4	.918
1994—Tampa (Fla. St.)■	2B-3B	3	11	2	2	1	0	0	2	.182	2	2	0	4	7	1	.917
—Alb./Colon. (East.)	SS-3B-2B	41	135	19	33	7	0	2	21	.244	21	16	2	64	112	7	.962
1995—New York (A.L.)	SS-2B	10	17	1	2	1	0	0	0	.118	1	5	0	10	14	0	1.000
—Omaha (A.A.)■	SS	11	42	5	10	4	0	0	6	.238	5	8	0	22	30	0	1.000
—Scran./W.B. (Int'l)■	SS	5	17	2	5	3	0	0	2	.294	2	3	0	6	12	1	.947
—Philadelphia (N.L.)	SS-1B-3B	26	53	10	11	4	1	1	9	.208	7	14	0	37	38	1	.987
American League totals (1 year)		10	17	1	2	1	0	0	0	.118	1	5	0	10	14	0	1.000
National League totals (8 years)		563	1637	176	366	79	7	35	183	.224	149	256	10	804	1358	63	.972
Major league totals (8 years)		573	1654	177	368	80	7	35	183	.222	150	261	10	814	1372	63	.972

CHAMPIONSHIP SERIES RECORD

			BATTING											FIELDING			
Year Team (League)	**Pos.**	**G**	**AB**	**R**	**H**	**2B**	**3B**	**HR**	**RBI**	**Avg.**	**BB**	**SO**	**SB**	**PO**	**A**	**E**	**Avg.**
1986—New York (N.L.)	SS-PR	4	3	0	0	0	0	0	0	.000	0	1	0	2	3	0	1.000
1988—New York (N.L.)	SS-PR	5	8	1	2	1	0	0	1	.250	3	0	0	7	7	2	.875
Championship series totals (2 years)		9	11	1	2	1	0	0	1	.182	3	1	0	9	10	2	.905

WORLD SERIES RECORD

NOTES: Member of World Series championship team (1986).

			BATTING											FIELDING			
Year Team (League)	**Pos.**	**G**	**AB**	**R**	**H**	**2B**	**3B**	**HR**	**RBI**	**Avg.**	**BB**	**SO**	**SB**	**PO**	**A**	**E**	**Avg.**
1986—New York (N.L.)	SS	1	1	0	0	0	0	0	0	.000	0	0	0	3	3	1	.857

EMBREE, ALAN — P — INDIANS

PERSONAL: Born January 23, 1970, in Vancouver, Wash. . . . 6-2/190. . . . Throws left, bats left. . . . Full name: Alan Duane Embree.
HIGH SCHOOL: Prairie (Vancouver, Wash.).
TRANSACTIONS/CAREER NOTES: Selected by Cleveland Indians organization in fifth round of free-agent draft (June 5, 1989). . . . On Cleveland disabled list (April 1-June 2 and June 2, 1993-remainder of season); included rehabilitation assignment to Canton/Akron (June 2-15).

Year Team (League)	W	L	Pct.	ERA	G	GS	CG	ShO	Sv.	IP	H	R	ER	BB	SO
1990—Burlington (Appal.)	4	4	.500	2.64	15	•15	0	0	0	81 2/3	87	36	24	30	58
1991—Columbus (S. Atl.)	10	8	.556	3.59	27	26	3	1	0	155 1/3	126	80	62	77	137
1992—Kinston (Carolina)	10	5	.667	3.30	15	15	1	0	0	101	89	48	37	32	115
—Cant./Akr. (East.)	7	2	.778	2.28	12	12	0	0	0	79	61	24	20	28	56
—Cleveland (A.L.)	0	2	.000	7.00	4	4	0	0	0	18	19	14	14	8	12
1993—Cant./Akr. (East.)	0	0	...	3.38	1	1	0	0	0	5 1/3	3	2	2	3	4
1994—Cant./Akr. (East.)	9	•16	.360	5.50	30	27	2	1	0	157	183	106	96	64	81
1995—Buffalo (A.A.)	3	4	.429	0.89	30	0	0	0	5	40 2/3	31	10	4	19	56
—Cleveland (A.L.)	3	2	.600	5.11	23	0	0	0	1	24 2/3	23	16	14	16	23
Major league totals (2 years)	3	4	.429	5.91	27	4	0	0	1	42 2/3	42	30	28	24	35

CHAMPIONSHIP SERIES RECORD

Year Team (League)	W	L	Pct.	ERA	G	GS	CG	ShO	Sv.	IP	H	R	ER	BB	SO
1995—Cleveland (A.L.)	0	0	...	0.00	1	0	0	0	0	1/3	0	0	0	0	1

WORLD SERIES RECORD

Year Team (League)	W	L	Pct.	ERA	G	GS	CG	ShO	Sv.	IP	H	R	ER	BB	SO
1995—Cleveland (A.L.)	0	0	...	2.70	4	0	0	0	0	3 1/3	2	1	1	2	2

ENCARNACION, ANGELO — C — PIRATES

PERSONAL: Born April 18, 1973, in Santo Domingo, Dominican Republic. . . . 5-8/177. . . . Bats right, throws right. . . . Full name: Angelo

Benjamin Encarnacion.
HIGH SCHOOL: Francisco Espaillat College (Dominican Republic).
TRANSACTIONS/CAREER NOTES: Signed as non-drafted free agent by Pittsburgh Pirates organization (June 1, 1990).... On Salem disabled list (June 28-July 16, 1993).... On disabled list (July 27, 1994-remainder of season).
STATISTICAL NOTES: Led South Atlantic League catchers with 15 double plays in 1992.

							BATTING							FIELDING			
Year	**Team (League)**	**Pos.**	**G**	**AB**	**R**	**H**	**2B**	**3B**	**HR**	**RBI**	**Avg.**	**BB**	**SO**	**SB**	**PO**	**A**	**E**	**Avg.**
1990—	Dom. Pirates (DSL)	...	30	96	18	32	2	0	0	19	.333	6	5	8	...	...	...	...
1991—	Welland (NYP)	C	50	181	21	46	3	2	0	15	.254	5	27	4	366	74	*18	.961
1992—	Augusta (S. Atl.)	C	94	314	39	80	14	3	1	29	.255	25	37	2	676	*121	*22	.973
1993—	Salem (Carolina)	C	70	238	20	61	12	1	3	24	.256	13	27	1	450	82	*21	.962
—	Buffalo (A.A.)	C-OF	3	9	1	3	0	0	0	2	.333	0	0	0	14	1	0	1.000
1994—	Carolina (South.)	C	67	227	26	66	17	0	3	32	.291	11	28	2	400	71	*15	.969
1995—	Calgary (PCL)	C	21	80	8	20	3	0	1	6	.250	1	12	1	113	14	2	.984
—	Pittsburgh (N.L.)	C	58	159	18	36	7	2	2	10	.226	13	28	1	278	43	7	.979
Major league totals (1 year)			58	159	18	36	7	2	2	10	.226	13	28	1	278	43	7	.979

ERICKS, JOHN — P — PIRATES

PERSONAL: Born September 16, 1967, in Oak Lawn, Ill.... 6-7/251.... Throws right, bats right.... Full name: John Edward Ericks III.
HIGH SCHOOL: Chicago Christian (Palos Heights, Ill.).
COLLEGE: Illinois.
TRANSACTIONS/CAREER NOTES: Selected by St. Louis Cardinals organization in first round (22nd pick overall) of free-agent draft (June 1, 1988); pick received as part of compensation for New York Yankees signing Type A free-agent 1B Jack Clark.... On Arkansas disabled list (May 19, 1990-remainder of season).... On disabled list (May 11-23 and July 7-September 8, 1992).... Released by Cardinals (September 8, 1992).... Signed by Carolina, Pittsburgh Pirates organization (February 12, 1993).... On disabled list (April 8, 1993-entire season).... On Carolina disabled list (August 8-19, 1994).

Year	**Team (League)**	**W**	**L**	**Pct.**	**ERA**	**G**	**GS**	**CG**	**ShO**	**Sv.**	**IP**	**H**	**R**	**ER**	**BB**	**SO**
1988—	Johns. City (App.)	3	2	.600	3.73	9	9	1	0	0	41	27	20	17	27	41
1989—	Savannah (S. Atl.)	11	10	.524	2.04	28	28	1	0	0	167 1/3	90	59	38	101	*211
1990—	St. Petersburg (FSL)	2	1	.667	1.57	4	4	0	0	0	23	16	5	4	6	25
—	Arkansas (Texas)	1	2	.333	9.39	4	4	1	1	0	15 1/3	17	19	16	19	19
1991—	Arkansas (Texas)	5	14	.263	4.77	25	25	1	0	0	139 2/3	138	94	74	84	103
1992—	Arkansas (Texas)	2	6	.250	4.08	13	13	1	0	0	75	69	36	34	29	71
1993—								Did not play.								
1994—	Salem (Carolina)■	4	2	.667	3.10	17	5	0	0	1	52 1/3	42	22	18	20	71
—	Carolina (South.)	2	4	.333	2.68	11	11	0	0	0	57	42	22	17	19	64
1995—	Calgary (PCL)	2	1	.667	2.48	5	5	0	0	0	29	20	8	8	13	25
—	Pittsburgh (N.L.)	3	9	.250	4.58	19	18	1	0	0	106	108	59	54	50	80
Major league totals (1 year)		3	9	.250	4.58	19	18	1	0	0	106	108	59	54	50	80

ERICKSON, SCOTT — P — ORIOLES

PERSONAL: Born February 2, 1968, in Long Beach, Calif.... 6-4/222.... Throws right, bats right.... Full name: Scott Gavin Erickson.
HIGH SCHOOL: Homestead (Cupertino, Calif.).
JUNIOR COLLEGE: San Jose City College.
COLLEGE: Arizona.
TRANSACTIONS/CAREER NOTES: Selected by New York Mets organization in 36th round of free-agent draft (June 2, 1986); did not sign.... Selected by Houston Astros organization in 34th round of free-agent draft (June 2, 1987); did not sign.... Selected by Toronto Blue Jays organization in 44th round of free-agent draft (June 1, 1988); did not sign.... Selected by Minnesota Twins organization in fourth round of free-agent draft (June 5, 1989).... On disabled list (June 30-July 15, 1991; April 3-18, 1993 and May 15-31, 1994).... Traded by Twins to Baltimore Orioles for P Scott Klingenbeck and a player to be named later (July 7, 1995); Twins acquired OF Kim Bartee to complete deal (September 18, 1995).
STATISTICAL NOTES: Pitched 5-0 one-hit, complete-game victory against Boston (July 24, 1992, first game).... Pitched 6-0 no-hit victory against Milwaukee (April 27, 1994).... Tied for A.L. lead with nine hit batsmen in 1994.

Year	**Team (League)**	**W**	**L**	**Pct.**	**ERA**	**G**	**GS**	**CG**	**ShO**	**Sv.**	**IP**	**H**	**R**	**ER**	**BB**	**SO**
1989—	Visalia (California)	3	4	.429	2.97	12	12	2	0	0	78 2/3	79	29	26	22	59
1990—	Orlando (Southern)	8	3	.727	3.03	15	15	3	1	0	101	75	38	34	24	69
—	Minnesota (A.L.)	8	4	.667	2.87	19	17	1	0	0	113	108	49	36	51	53
1991—	Minnesota (A.L.)	•20	8	.714	3.18	32	32	5	3	0	204	189	80	72	71	108
1992—	Minnesota (A.L.)	13	12	.520	3.40	32	32	5	3	0	212	197	86	80	83	101
1993—	Minnesota (A.L.)	8	*19	.296	5.19	34	34	1	0	0	218 2/3	*266	*138	126	71	116
1994—	Minnesota (A.L.)	8	11	.421	5.44	23	23	2	1	0	144	173	95	87	59	104
1995—	Minnesota (A.L.)	4	6	.400	5.95	15	15	0	0	0	87 2/3	102	61	58	32	45
—	Baltimore (A.L.)■	9	4	.692	3.89	17	16	7	2	0	108 2/3	111	47	47	35	61
Major league totals (6 years)		70	64	.522	4.19	172	169	21	9	0	1088	1146	556	506	402	588

CHAMPIONSHIP SERIES RECORD

Year	**Team (League)**	**W**	**L**	**Pct.**	**ERA**	**G**	**GS**	**CG**	**ShO**	**Sv.**	**IP**	**H**	**R**	**ER**	**BB**	**SO**
1991—	Minnesota (A.L.)	0	0	...	4.50	1	1	0	0	0	4	3	2	2	5	2

WORLD SERIES RECORD

NOTES: Member of World Series championship team (1991).

Year	**Team (League)**	**W**	**L**	**Pct.**	**ERA**	**G**	**GS**	**CG**	**ShO**	**Sv.**	**IP**	**H**	**R**	**ER**	**BB**	**SO**
1991—	Minnesota (A.L.)	0	0	...	5.06	2	2	0	0	0	10 2/3	10	7	6	4	5

ESHELMAN, VAUGHN — P — RED SOX

PERSONAL: Born May 22, 1969, in Philadelphia. . . . 6-3/215. . . . Throws left, bats left. . . . Full name: Vaughn Michael Eshelman.
HIGH SCHOOL: Westfield (Houston).
JUNIOR COLLEGE: Blinn College (Tex.).
COLLEGE: Houston.
TRANSACTIONS/CAREER NOTES: Selected by Baltimore Orioles organization in fourth round of free-agent draft (June 3, 1991). . . . On disabled list (April 9, 1992-entire season). . . . Selected by Boston Red Sox from Orioles organization in Rule 5 major league draft (December 5, 1994). . . . On Boston disabled list (May 25-June 13, July 6-24 and August 25-September 9, 1995); included rehabilitation assignment to Trenton (July 14-24).

Year Team (League)	W	L	Pct.	ERA	G	GS	CG	ShO	Sv.	IP	H	R	ER	BB	SO
1991—Bluefield (Appal.)	1	0	1.000	0.64	3	3	0	0	0	14	10	1	1	9	15
—Kane Co. (Mid.)	5	3	.625	2.32	11	11	2	1	0	77 2/3	57	23	20	35	90
1992—							Did not play.								
1993—Frederick (Caro.)	7	10	.412	3.89	24	24	2	1	0	143 1/3	128	70	62	59	122
1994—Bowie (Eastern)	11	9	.550	4.00	27	25	2	2	0	166 1/3	175	81	74	60	133
1995—Boston (A.L.)■	6	3	.667	4.85	23	14	0	0	0	81 2/3	86	47	44	36	41
—Trenton (Eastern)	0	1	.000	0.00	2	2	0	0	0	7	3	1	0	0	7
Major league totals (1 year)	6	3	.667	4.85	23	14	0	0	0	81 2/3	86	47	44	36	41

ESPINOZA, ALVARO — 3B/SS — INDIANS

PERSONAL: Born February 19, 1962, in Valencia, Carabobo, Venezuela. . . . 6-0/190. . . . Bats right, throws right. . . . Full name: Alvaro Alberto Ramirez Espinoza. . . . Name pronounced ESS-pin-OH-zuh.
HIGH SCHOOL: Valencia (Carabobo, Venezuela).
TRANSACTIONS/CAREER NOTES: Signed as non-drafted free agent by Houston Astros organization (October 30, 1978). . . . Released by Astros organization (September 30, 1980). . . . Signed by Wisconsin Rapids, Minnesota Twins organization (March 18, 1982). . . . On Toledo disabled list (June 7-25, 1984 and June 6-July 2, 1985). . . . Granted free agency (October 15, 1987). . . . Signed by Columbus, New York Yankees organization (November 17, 1987). . . . Released by Yankees (March 17, 1992). . . . Signed by Colorado Springs, Cleveland Indians organization (April 3, 1992). . . . Granted free agency (November 2, 1995). . . . Re-signed by Indians organization (December 7, 1995).
RECORDS: Shares major league single-season record for fewest runs batted in (150 or more games)—20 (1990).
STATISTICAL NOTES: Led Gulf Coast League shortstops with 114 putouts, 217 assists, 25 errors, 356 total chances and 33 double plays in 1980. . . . Led California League shortstops with 660 total chances in 1983. . . . Tied for International League lead with 16 sacrifice hits in 1984. . . . Led International League shortstops with 159 putouts in 1986. . . . Led Pacific Coast League shortstops with 631 total chances and 112 double plays in 1992.

			BATTING											FIELDING			
Year Team (League)	Pos.	G	AB	R	H	2B	3B	HR	RBI	Avg.	BB	SO	SB	PO	A	E	Avg.
1979—GC Astros (GCL)	SS-2B-3B	11	32	3	7	0	0	0	5	.219	4	6	0	18	27	1	.978
1980—GC Astros-Or. (GCL)	SS-3B	59	200	24	43	5	0	0	14	.215	15	18	6	†114	†219	†25	.930
1981—							Out of organized baseball.										
1982—Wis. Rap. (Midw.)■	SS-3B-1B	112	379	41	101	9	0	5	29	.266	16	66	9	237	241	33	.935
1983—Visalia (California)	SS	130	486	57	155	20	1	4	57	.319	14	50	6	*256	364	40	.939
1984—Toledo (Int'l)	SS	104	344	22	80	12	5	0	30	.233	3	49	3	157	293	19	.959
—Minnesota (A.L.)	SS	1	0	0	0	0	0	0	0	...	0	0	0	0	0	0	...
1985—Toledo (Int'l)	SS	82	266	24	61	11	0	1	33	.229	14	30	1	132	245	16	.959
—Minnesota (A.L.)	SS	32	57	5	15	2	0	0	9	.263	1	9	0	25	69	5	.949
1986—Toledo (Int'l)	SS-2B	73	253	18	71	8	1	2	27	.281	6	30	1	†170	205	12	.969
—Minnesota (A.L.)	2B-SS	37	42	4	9	1	0	0	1	.214	1	10	0	23	52	4	.949
1987—Portland (PCL)	SS-3B-1B	91	291	28	80	3	2	4	28	.275	12	37	2	158	236	20	.952
1988—Columbus (Int'l)■	SS-2B-3B	119	435	42	107	10	5	2	30	.246	7	53	4	221	404	19	.970
—New York (A.L.)	2B-SS	3	3	0	0	0	0	0	0	.000	0	0	0	5	2	0	1.000
1989—New York (A.L.)	SS	146	503	51	142	23	1	0	41	.282	14	60	3	237	471	22	.970
1990—New York (A.L.)	SS	150	438	31	98	12	2	2	20	.224	16	54	1	268	447	17	.977
1991—New York (A.L.)	SS-3B-P	148	480	51	123	23	2	5	33	.256	16	57	4	225	441	21	.969
1992—Colo. Springs (PCL)■	SS	122	483	64	145	36	6	9	79	.300	21	55	2	191	*414	26	.959
1993—Cleveland (A.L.)	3B-SS-2B	129	263	34	73	15	0	4	27	.278	8	36	2	66	157	12	.949
1994—Cleveland (A.L.)	3-S-2-1	90	231	27	55	13	0	1	19	.238	6	33	1	93	210	10	.968
1995—Cleveland (A.L.)	2-3-S-1-DH	66	143	15	36	4	0	2	17	.252	2	16	0	50	101	5	.968
Major league totals (10 years)		802	2160	218	551	93	5	14	167	.255	64	275	11	992	1950	96	.968

DIVISION SERIES RECORD

			BATTING											FIELDING			
Year Team (League)	Pos.	G	AB	R	H	2B	3B	HR	RBI	Avg.	BB	SO	SB	PO	A	E	Avg.
1995—Cleveland (A.L.)	3B	1	1	0	0	0	0	0	0	.000	0	0	0	0	0	0	...

CHAMPIONSHIP SERIES RECORD

			BATTING											FIELDING			
Year Team (League)	Pos.	G	AB	R	H	2B	3B	HR	RBI	Avg.	BB	SO	SB	PO	A	E	Avg.
1995—Cleveland (A.L.)	3B	4	8	1	1	0	0	0	0	.125	0	3	0	0	3	1	.750

WORLD SERIES RECORD

			BATTING											FIELDING			
Year Team (League)	Pos.	G	AB	R	H	2B	3B	HR	RBI	Avg.	BB	SO	SB	PO	A	E	Avg.
1995—Cleveland (A.L.)	PR-3B	2	2	1	1	0	0	0	0	.500	0	0	0	1	1	0	1.000

RECORD AS PITCHER

Year Team (League)	W	L	Pct.	ERA	G	GS	CG	ShO	Sv.	IP	H	R	ER	BB	SO
1991—New York (A.L.)	0	0	...	0.00	1	0	0	0	0	2/3	0	0	0	0	0

ESTES, SHAWN — P — GIANTS

PERSONAL: Born February 18, 1973, in San Bernardino, Calif. . . . 6-2/185. . . . Throws left, bats both. . . . Full name: Aaron Shawn Estes.
HIGH SCHOOL: Douglas (Minden, Nev.).
TRANSACTIONS/CAREER NOTES: Selected by Seattle Mariners organization in first round (11th pick overall) of free-agent draft (June 3, 1991). . . . On disabled list (August 19, 1993-remainder of season). . . . On Appleton disabled list (April 8-July 19 and July 25-August 15, 1994). . . . Traded by Mariners with IF Wilson Delgado to San Francisco Giants for P Salomon Torres (May 21, 1995).

Year	Team (League)	W	L	Pct.	ERA	G	GS	CG	ShO	Sv.	IP	H	R	ER	BB	SO
1991—	Bellingham (N'west)	1	3	.250	6.88	9	9	0	0	0	34	27	33	26	55	35
1992—	Bellingham (N'west)	3	3	.500	4.32	15	15	0	0	0	77	84	55	37	45	77
1993—	Appleton (Midw.)	5	9	.357	7.24	19	18	0	0	0	83 1/3	108	85	67	52	65
1994—	Appleton (Midw.)	0	2	.000	4.58	5	4	0	0	0	19 2/3	19	13	10	17	28
	—Ariz. Mariners (Ar.)	0	3	.000	3.15	5	5	0	0	0	20	16	9	7	6	31
1995—	Wis. Rap. (Midw.)	0	0	...	0.90	2	2	0	0	0	10	5	1	1	5	11
	—Burlington (Midw.)■	0	0	...	4.11	4	4	0	0	0	15 1/3	13	8	7	12	22
	—San Jose (Calif.)	5	2	.714	2.17	9	8	0	0	0	49 2/3	32	13	12	17	61
	—Shreveport (Texas)	2	0	1.000	2.01	4	4	0	0	0	22 1/3	14	5	5	10	18
	—San Francisco (N.L.)	0	3	.000	6.75	3	3	0	0	0	17 1/3	16	14	13	5	14
Major league totals (1 year)		0	3	.000	6.75	3	3	0	0	0	17 1/3	16	14	13	5	14

EUSEBIO, TONY — C — ASTROS

PERSONAL: Born April 27, 1967, in San Jose de Los Llamos, Dominican Republic. . . . 6-2/180. . . . Bats right, throws right. . . . Full name: Raul Antonio Eusebio. . . . Name pronounced you-SAY-bee-o.
HIGH SCHOOL: San Rafael (Dominican Republic).
TRANSACTIONS/CAREER NOTES: Signed as non-drafted free agent by Houston Astros organization (May 30, 1985). . . . On disabled list (August 5, 1990-remainder of season; April 16-23, 1992 and August 24, 1993-remainder of season).
STATISTICAL NOTES: Tied for Southern League lead in double plays by catcher with eight in 1989. . . . Led Texas League catchers with .9963 fielding percentage and 12 double plays in 1992. . . . Career major league grand slams: 2.

			BATTING												FIELDING			
Year	Team (League)	Pos.	G	AB	R	H	2B	3B	HR	RBI	Avg.	BB	SO	SB	PO	A	E	Avg.
1985—	GC Astros (GCL)	C	1	1	0	0	0	0	0	0	.000	0	0	0	4	0	0	1.000
1985—						Dominican Summer League statistics unavailable.												
1986—						Dominican Summer League statistics unavailable.												
1987—	GC Astros (GCL)	C-1B	42	125	26	26	1	2	1	15	.208	18	19	8	204	24	4	.983
1988—	Osceola (Fla. St.)	C-OF	118	392	45	96	6	3	0	40	.245	40	69	19	611	66	8	.988
1989—	Columbus (South.)	C	65	203	20	38	6	1	0	18	.187	38	47	7	355	46	7	.983
	—Osceola (Fla. St.)	C	52	175	22	50	6	3	0	30	.286	19	27	5	290	40	5	.985
1990—	Columbus (South.)	C	92	318	36	90	18	0	4	37	.283	21	80	6	558	69	4	*.994
1991—	Jackson (Texas)	C	66	222	27	58	8	3	2	31	.261	25	54	3	424	48	7	.985
	—Tucson (PCL)	C	5	20	5	8	1	0	0	2	.400	3	3	1	40	1	0	1.000
	—Houston (N.L.)	C	10	19	4	2	1	0	0	0	.105	6	8	0	49	4	1	.981
1992—	Jackson (Texas)	C	94	339	33	104	9	3	5	44	.307	25	58	1	493	51	2	*.996
1993—	Tucson (PCL)	C	78	281	39	91	20	1	1	43	.324	22	40	1	450	46	3	.994
1994—	Houston (N.L.)	C	55	159	18	47	9	1	5	30	.296	8	33	0	263	24	2	.993
1995—	Houston (N.L.)	C	113	368	46	110	21	1	6	58	.299	31	59	0	645	49	5	.993
Major league totals (3 years)			178	546	68	159	31	2	11	88	.291	45	100	0	957	77	8	.992

EVANS, BART — P — ROYALS

PERSONAL: Born December 30, 1970, in Springfield, Mo. . . . 6-1/190. . . . Throws right, bats right. . . . Full name: Bart Steven Evans.
HIGH SCHOOL: Mansfield (Mo.).
COLLEGE: Southwest Missouri State.
TRANSACTIONS/CAREER NOTES: Selected by Kansas City Royals organization in ninth round of free-agent draft (June 1, 1992). . . . On disabled list (June 17, 1993-remainder of season). . . . On Wichita temporarily inactive list (April 24-May 10, 1995).
HONORS: Named Southern League Pitcher of the Year (1994).

Year	Team (League)	W	L	Pct.	ERA	G	GS	CG	ShO	Sv.	IP	H	R	ER	BB	SO
1992—	Eugene (N'west)	1	1	.500	6.23	13	1	0	0	0	26	17	20	18	31	39
1993—	Rockford (Midw.)	10	4	.714	4.36	27	16	0	0	0	99	95	52	48	60	120
1994—	Wilmington (Caro.)	10	3	.769	2.98	26	26	0	0	0	145	107	53	48	61	145
1995—	Wichita (Texas)	0	4	.000	10.48	7	7	0	0	0	22 1/3	22	28	26	45	13
	—Wilmington (Caro.)	4	1	.800	2.89	16	6	0	0	2	46 2/3	30	21	15	44	47

EVANS, TOM — 3B — BLUE JAYS

PERSONAL: Born July 9, 1974, in Kirkland, Wash. . . . 6-1/208. . . . Bats right, throws right. . . . Full name: Thomas John Evans.
HIGH SCHOOL: Juanita (Kirkland, Wash.).
TRANSACTIONS/CAREER NOTES: Selected by Toronto Blue Jays organization in fourth round of free-agent draft (June 1, 1992). . . . On disabled list (April 7-May 17, 1994).
STATISTICAL NOTES: Led Florida State League third basemen with 435 total chances in 1995.

			BATTING												FIELDING			
Year	Team (League)	Pos.	G	AB	R	H	2B	3B	HR	RBI	Avg.	BB	SO	SB	PO	A	E	Avg.
1992—	Medicine Hat (Pio.)	3B	52	166	17	36	3	0	1	21	.217	33	29	4	53	115	20	.894
1993—	Hagerstown (SAL)	3B-1B-SS	119	389	47	100	25	1	7	54	.257	53	92	9	92	181	27	.910
1994—	Hagerstown (SAL)	3B	95	322	52	88	16	2	13	48	.273	51	80	2	60	196	36	.877
1995—	Dunedin (Fla. St.)	3B	130	444	63	124	29	3	9	66	.279	51	80	7	*92	*309	34	.922

EVERETT, CARL — OF — METS

PERSONAL: Born June 3, 1971, in Tampa, Fla. . . . 6-0/190. . . . Bats both, throws right. . . . Full name: Carl Edward Everett.
HIGH SCHOOL: Hillsborough (Tampa, Fla.).
TRANSACTIONS/CAREER NOTES: Selected by New York Yankees organization in first round (10th pick overall) of free-agent draft (June 4, 1990). . . . On Fort Lauderdale disabled list (July 7-August 15, 1992). . . . Selected by Florida Marlins in second round (27th pick overall) of expansion draft (November 17, 1992). . . . On High Desert disabled list (April 8-13, 1993). . . . On Florida disabled list (July 23-August 10, 1994). . . . On Edmonton suspended list (August 29, 1994-remainder of season). . . . Traded by Marlins to New York Mets for 2B Quilvio Veras (November 29, 1994).
STATISTICAL NOTES: Led South Atlantic League in being hit by pitch with 23 in 1991. . . . Career major league grand slams: 1.

		BATTING												FIELDING			
Year Team (League)	Pos.	G	AB	R	H	2B	3B	HR	RBI	Avg.	BB	SO	SB	PO	A	E	Avg.
1990—GC Yankees (GCL)	OF	48	185	28	48	8	5	1	14	.259	15	38	15	64	5	5	.932
1991—Greensboro (S. Atl.)	OF	123	468	96	127	18	0	4	40	.271	57	122	28	250	14	7	.974
1992—Fort Lauder. (FSL)	OF	46	183	30	42	8	2	2	9	.230	12	40	11	111	5	3	.975
—Prin. William (Car.)	OF	6	22	7	7	0	0	4	9	.318	5	7	1	12	1	0	1.000
1993—High Desert (Calif.)■	OF	59	253	48	73	12	6	10	52	.289	22	73	24	124	6	2	.985
—Florida (N.L.)	OF	11	19	0	2	0	0	0	0	.105	1	9	1	6	0	1	.857
—Edmonton (PCL)	OF	35	136	28	42	13	4	6	16	.309	19	45	12	69	12	2	.976
1994—Edmonton (PCL)	OF	78	321	63	108	17	2	11	47	.336	19	65	16	167	11	2	.989
—Florida (N.L.)	OF	16	51	7	11	1	0	2	6	.216	3	15	4	28	2	0	1.000
1995—New York (N.L.)■	OF	79	289	48	75	13	1	12	54	.260	39	67	2	148	9	3	.981
—Norfolk (Int'l)	OF-SS	67	260	52	78	16	4	6	35	.300	20	47	12	133	7	0	1.000
Major league totals (2 years)		106	359	55	88	14	1	14	60	.245	43	91	7	182	11	4	.980

EVERSGERD, BRYAN — P — RED SOX

PERSONAL: Born February 11, 1969, in Centralia, Ill. . . . 6-1/190. . . . Throws left, bats right. . . . Full name: Bryan David Eversgerd.
HIGH SCHOOL: Carlyle (Ill.).
TRANSACTIONS/CAREER NOTES: Signed as non-drafted free agent by St. Louis Cardinals organization (June 14, 1989). . . . Traded by Cardinals with P Kirk Bullinger and OF Darond Stovall to Montreal Expos for P Ken Hill (April 5, 1995). . . . Traded by Expos with SS Wil Cordero to Boston Red Sox for P Rheal Cormier, 1B Ryan McGuire and P Shayne Bennett (January 10, 1996).

Year Team (League)	W	L	Pct.	ERA	G	GS	CG	ShO	Sv.	IP	H	R	ER	BB	SO
1989—Johnson City (Appal.)	2	3	.400	3.64	16	1	0	0	0	29 2/3	30	16	12	12	19
1990—Springfield (Midw.)	6	8	.429	4.14	20	15	2	0	0	104 1/3	123	60	48	26	55
1991—Savannah (S. Atl.)	1	5	.167	3.47	72	0	0	0	1	93 1/3	71	43	36	34	97
1992—St. Petersburg (FSL)	3	2	.600	2.68	57	1	0	0	0	74	65	25	22	25	57
—Arkansas (Texas)	0	1	.000	6.75	6	0	0	0	0	5 1/3	7	4	4	2	4
1993—Arkansas (Texas)	4	4	.500	2.18	*62	0	0	0	0	66	60	24	16	19	68
1994—Louisville (A.A.)	1	1	.500	4.50	9	0	0	0	0	12	11	7	6	8	8
—St. Louis (N.L.)	2	3	.400	4.52	40	0	0	0	0	67 1/3	75	36	34	20	47
1995—Montreal (N.L.)■	0	0	...	5.14	25	0	0	0	0	21	22	13	12	9	8
—Ottawa (Int'l)	6	2	.750	2.38	38	0	0	0	2	53	49	21	14	26	45
Major league totals (2 years)	2	3	.400	4.67	65	1	0	0	0	88 2/3	97	49	46	29	55

FABREGAS, JORGE — C — ANGELS

PERSONAL: Born March 13, 1970, in Miami. . . . 6-3/205. . . . Bats left, throws right.
HIGH SCHOOL: Christopher Columbus (Miami).
COLLEGE: Miami (Fla.).
TRANSACTIONS/CAREER NOTES: Selected by Cleveland Indians organization in 11th round of free-agent draft (June 1, 1988); did not sign. . . . Selected by California Angels organization in supplemental round "sandwich pick" between first and second round, 34th pick overall) of free agent draft (June 3, 1991); pick received as part of compensation for Minnesota Twins signing Type A free agent OF/DH Chili Davis. . . . On disabled list (April 12-May 4 and July 28-September 5, 1992).
STATISTICAL NOTES: Led Texas League with 17 passed balls in 1993.

		BATTING												FIELDING			
Year Team (League)	Pos.	G	AB	R	H	2B	3B	HR	RBI	Avg.	BB	SO	SB	PO	A	E	Avg.
1992—Palm Springs (Cal.)	C	70	258	35	73	13	0	0	40	.283	30	27	0	436	63	*17	.967
1993—Midland (Texas)	C	113	409	63	118	26	3	6	56	.289	31	60	1	620	99	•11	.985
—Vancouver (PCL)	C	4	13	1	3	1	0	0	1	.231	1	3	0	30	3	0	1.000
1994—Vancouver (PCL)	C	66	211	17	47	6	1	1	24	.223	12	25	1	365	41	4	.990
—California (A.L.)	C	43	127	12	36	3	0	0	16	.283	7	18	2	217	16	3	.987
1995—California (A.L.)	C	73	227	24	56	10	0	1	22	.247	17	28	0	391	36	6	.986
—Vancouver (PCL)	C	21	73	9	18	3	0	4	10	.247	9	12	0	112	12	4	.969
Major league totals (2 years)		116	354	36	92	13	0	1	38	.260	24	46	2	608	52	9	.987

FAJARDO, HECTOR — P

PERSONAL: Born November 6, 1970, in Michoacan, Mexico. . . . 6-4/200. . . . Throws right, bats right. . . . Full name: Hector Navarrete Fajardo.
TRANSACTIONS/CAREER NOTES: Contract sold by Mexico City to Pittsburgh Pirates organization (April 2, 1989). . . . Traded by Pirates to Texas Rangers (September 6, 1991), completing deal in which Rangers traded 3B Steve Buechele to Pirates for P Kurt Miller and a player to be named later (August 30, 1991). . . . On Texas disabled list (March 28-July 27, 1992); included rehabilitation assignments to Gulf Coast Rangers (July 16-21) and Charlotte (July 21-27). . . . On Texas disabled list (March 27-August 31, 1993); included rehabilitation assignments

to Gulf Coast Rangers (July 28-August 12) and Charlotte (August 18-31). . . . On Texas restricted list (April 20-May 30, 1995). . . . Traded by Rangers organization to Montreal Expos organization (August 5, 1995), completing deal in which Rangers acquired OF Lou Frazier for a player to be named later (July 30, 1995). . . . Released by Expos (October 11, 1995).

Year	Team (League)	W	L	Pct.	ERA	G	GS	CG	ShO	Sv.	IP	H	R	ER	BB	SO
1989—	Mex. City Reds (Mex.)	0	0	...	6.30	3	0	0	0	0	10	8	7	7	7	6
—	GC Pirates (GCL)■	0	5	.000	5.97	10	6	0	0	0	34 2/3	38	24	23	20	19
1990—	GC Pirates (GCL)	1	1	.500	3.86	5	4	0	0	0	21	23	10	9	8	17
—	Augusta (S. Atl.)	2	2	.500	3.86	7	7	0	0	0	39 2/3	41	18	17	15	28
1991—	Augusta (S. Atl.)	4	3	.571	2.69	11	11	1	1	0	60 1/3	44	26	18	24	79
—	Salem (Carolina)	0	1	.000	2.35	1	1	1	0	0	7 2/3	4	3	2	1	7
—	Carolina (South.)	3	4	.429	4.13	10	10	1	0	0	61	55	32	28	24	53
—	Pittsburgh (N.L.)	0	0	...	9.95	2	2	0	0	0	6 1/3	10	7	7	7	8
—	Buffalo (A.A.)	1	0	1.000	0.96	8	0	0	0	1	9 1/3	6	1	1	3	12
—	Texas (A.L.)■	0	2	.000	5.68	4	3	0	0	0	19	25	13	12	4	15
1992—	GC Rangers (GCL)	0	1	.000	5.68	1	1	0	0	0	6 1/3	5	4	4	2	9
—	Charlotte (Fla. St.)	2	2	.500	2.78	4	4	0	0	0	22 2/3	22	9	7	8	12
—	Tulsa (Texas)	2	1	.667	2.16	5	4	0	0	0	25	19	6	6	7	26
—	Okla. City (A.A.)	1	0	1.000	0.00	1	1	0	0	0	7	8	0	0	2	6
1993—	GC Rangers (GCL)	3	1	.750	1.80	6	6	0	0	0	30	21	8	6	5	27
—	Charlotte (Fla. St.)	0	0	...	1.80	2	1	0	0	0	5	5	1	1	1	3
—	Texas (A.L.)	0	0	...	0.00	1	0	0	0	0	2/3	0	0	0	0	1
1994—	Okla. City (A.A.)	5	1	.833	2.45	8	8	1	1	0	51 1/3	44	16	14	12	43
—	Texas (A.L.)	5	7	.417	6.91	18	12	0	0	0	83 1/3	95	67	64	26	45
1995—	Texas (A.L.)	0	0	...	7.80	5	0	0	0	0	15	19	13	13	5	9
—	Ottawa (Int'l)■	0	0	...	4.11	11	0	0	0	0	15 1/3	18	7	7	6	9
A.L. totals (4 years)		5	9	.357	6.79	28	15	0	0	0	118	139	93	89	35	70
N.L. totals (1 year)		0	0	...	9.95	2	2	0	0	0	6 1/3	10	7	7	7	8
Major league totals (4 years)		5	9	.357	6.95	30	17	0	0	0	124 1/3	149	100	96	42	78

FALTEISEK, STEVE — P — EXPOS

PERSONAL: Born January 28, 1972, in Mineola, N.Y. . . . 6-2/200. . . . Throws right, bats right. . . . Full name: Steven James Falteisek.
HIGH SCHOOL: Memorial (Floral Park, N.Y.).
COLLEGE: South Alabama.
TRANSACTIONS/CAREER NOTES: Selected by Montreal Expos organization in 10th round of free-agent draft (June 1, 1992).

Year	Team (League)	W	L	Pct.	ERA	G	GS	CG	ShO	Sv.	IP	H	R	ER	BB	SO
1992—	Jamestown (NYP)	3	*8	.273	3.56	15	•15	2	0	0	*96	84	47	38	31	82
1993—	Burlington (Midw.)	3	5	.375	5.90	14	14	0	0	0	76 1/3	86	59	50	35	63
1994—	WP Beach (FSL)	9	4	.692	2.54	27	24	0	0	0	159 2/3	144	72	45	49	91
1995—	Harrisburg (East.)	9	6	.600	2.95	25	25	•5	0	0	168	152	74	55	64	112
—	Ottawa (Int'l)	2	0	1.000	1.17	3	3	1	1	0	23	17	4	3	5	18

FANEYTE, RIKKERT — OF — RANGERS

PERSONAL: Born May 31, 1969, in Amsterdam, The Netherlands. . . . 6-1/170. . . . Bats right, throws right. . . . Name pronounced fuh-NY-tuh.
JUNIOR COLLEGE: Miami-Dade Community College-Kendall.
TRANSACTIONS/CAREER NOTES: Selected by San Francisco Giants organization in 16th round of free-agent draft (June 4, 1990). . . . On temporarily inactive list (April 12-May 8, 1991). . . . On disabled list (May 13-June 22, 1992). . . . Traded by Giants to Texas Rangers for a player to be named later (December 1, 1995).

				BATTING											FIELDING			
Year	Team (League)	Pos.	G	AB	R	H	2B	3B	HR	RBI	Avg.	BB	SO	SB	PO	A	E	Avg.
1991—	Clinton (Midwest)	OF	107	384	73	98	14	7	6	52	.255	61	106	18	211	9	3	*.987
1992—	San Jose (Calif.)	OF	94	342	69	90	13	2	9	43	.263	73	65	17	172	13	3	.984
1993—	Phoenix (PCL)	OF	115	426	71	133	23	2	11	71	.312	40	72	15	223	11	3	.987
—	San Francisco (N.L.)	OF	7	15	2	2	0	0	0	0	.133	2	4	0	10	0	0	1.000
1994—	Phoenix (PCL)	OF	94	365	62	122	17	6	6	57	.334	30	63	15	218	10	3	.987
—	San Francisco (N.L.)	OF	19	26	1	3	3	0	0	4	.115	3	11	0	9	0	1	.900
1995—	Phoenix (PCL)	OF	38	135	22	37	8	1	1	17	.274	15	22	2	83	2	5	.944
—	San Francisco (N.L.)	OF	46	86	7	17	4	1	0	4	.198	11	27	1	49	3	1	.981
Major league totals (3 years)			72	127	10	22	7	1	0	8	.173	16	42	1	68	3	2	.973

FARMER, MIKE — P — ROCKIES

PERSONAL: Born July 3, 1968, in Gary, Ind. . . . 6-1/193. . . . Throws left, bats both. . . . Full name: Michael Anthony Farmer.
HIGH SCHOOL: Roosevelt (Gary, Ind.).
COLLEGE: Jackson State.
TRANSACTIONS/CAREER NOTES: Signed as free agent by Philadelphia Phillies organization (August 9, 1989). . . . On disabled list (July 27-August 25, 1993). . . . Selected by Colorado Springs, Colorado Rockies organization, from Reading, Phillies organization, in Rule 5 minor league draft (December 13, 1993). . . . On New Haven disabled list (June 27, 1994-remainder of season).
STATISTICAL NOTES: Tied for Appalachian League lead in double plays by outfielder with two in 1990.
MISCELLANEOUS: Batted righthanded only (1991). . . . Assigned by Rockies to New Haven of the Eastern League (April 3, 1995).

Year	Team (League)	W	L	Pct.	ERA	G	GS	CG	ShO	Sv.	IP	H	R	ER	BB	SO
1992—	Clearwater (Fla. St.)	3	3	.500	1.87	11	9	1	1	0	53	33	16	11	13	41
1993—	Reading (Eastern)	5	10	.333	5.03	22	18	0	0	0	102	125	62	57	34	64
1994—	Central Valley (Cal.)■	1	4	.200	4.71	14	3	0	0	1	28 2/3	28	17	15	11	28
—	New Haven (East.)	0	0	...	1.29	10	0	0	0	2	14	7	2	2	5	13
1995—	New Haven (East.)	10	5	.667	4.89	40	12	0	0	0	110 1/3	117	63	60	35	77

RECORD AS POSITION PLAYER

Year	Team (League)	Pos.	G	AB	R	H	2B	3B	HR	RBI	Avg.	BB	SO	SB	PO	A	E	Avg.
				BATTING											FIELDING			
1990—	Martinsville (App.)	OF	55	194	33	52	11	5	10	34	.268	13	56	11	85	8	4	.959
1991—	Spartanburg (SAL)	OF	132	483	65	115	16	5	12	77	.238	32	130	33	228	11	6	.976
1992—	Clearwater (FSL)	OF	94	303	37	73	10	2	2	32	.241	15	61	12	163	7	7	.960

FARRELL, JOHN — P — MARINERS

PERSONAL: Born August 4, 1962, in Neptune, N.J. . . . 6-4/210. . . . Throws right, bats right. . . . Full name: John Edward Farrell.

HIGH SCHOOL: Shore Regional (West Long Branch, N.J.).

COLLEGE: Oklahoma State.

TRANSACTIONS/CAREER NOTES: Selected by Oakland Athletics organization in ninth round of free-agent draft (June 3, 1980); did not sign. . . . Selected by Cleveland Indians organization in 16th round of free-agent draft (June 6, 1983); did not sign. . . . Selected by Indians organization in second round of free-agent draft (June 4, 1984). . . . On disabled list (August 28-September 20, 1988 and March 19-April 16, 1989). . . . On Cleveland disabled list (June 25-September 21, 1990); included rehabilitation assignment to Canton/Akron (July 16-30). . . . On disabled list (April 5, 1991-entire season). . . . Granted free agency (November 22, 1991). . . . Signed by Edmonton, California Angels organization (February 12, 1992). . . . On California disabled list (April 5, 1992-entire season). . . . Granted free agency (June 7, 1994). . . . Signed by Charlotte, Cleveland Indians organization (June 22, 1994). . . . Granted free agency (October 15, 1994). . . . Re-signed by Charlotte (November 1, 1994). . . . Granted free agency (November 1, 1995). . . . Signed by Seattle Mariners organization (January 19, 1996).

STATISTICAL NOTES: Tied for Eastern League lead with 10 hit batsmen in 1986. . . . Led American Association with 26 home runs allowed in 1987. . . . Led American Association with 16 hit batsmen in 1995.

Year	Team (League)	W	L	Pct.	ERA	G	GS	CG	ShO	Sv.	IP	H	R	ER	BB	SO
1984—	Waterloo (Midw.)	0	5	.000	6.44	9	9	2	0	0	43 1/3	59	34	31	33	29
—	Maine (Int'l)	2	1	.667	3.76	5	5	0	0	0	26 1/3	20	11	11	20	12
1985—	Waterbury (East.)	7	13	.350	5.19	25	25	5	1	0	149	161	*106	86	76	75
1986—	Waterbury (East.)	9	10	.474	3.06	26	26	9	•3	0	173 1/3	158	82	59	54	104
1987—	Buffalo (A.A.)	6	12	.333	5.83	25	24	2	0	0	156	155	109	101	64	91
—	Cleveland (A.L.)	5	1	.833	3.39	10	9	1	0	0	69	68	29	26	22	28
1988—	Cleveland (A.L.)	14	10	.583	4.24	31	30	4	0	0	210 1/3	216	106	99	67	92
1989—	Cleveland (A.L.)	9	14	.391	3.63	31	31	7	2	0	208	196	97	84	71	132
1990—	Cleveland (A.L.)	4	5	.444	4.28	17	17	1	0	0	96 2/3	108	49	46	33	44
—	Cant./Akr. (East.)	1	1	.500	7.20	2	2	0	0	0	10	13	8	8	2	5
1991—								Did not play.								
1992—								Did not play.								
1993—	California (A.L.)■	3	12	.200	7.35	21	17	0	0	0	90 2/3	110	74	74	44	45
—	Vancouver (PCL)	4	5	.444	3.99	12	12	2	0	0	85 2/3	83	44	38	28	71
1994—	Vancouver (PCL)	4	4	.500	3.25	8	8	•4	1	0	61	60	24	22	16	35
—	California (A.L.)	1	2	.333	9.00	3	3	0	0	0	13	16	14	13	8	10
—	Charlotte (Int'l)■	4	7	.364	5.61	15	14	1	1	0	78 2/3	72	51	49	21	55
1995—	Buffalo (A.A.)	11	9	.550	4.54	29	*28	2	0	0	*184 1/3	*198	*97	*93	61	92
—	Cleveland (A.L.)	0	0	...	3.86	1	0	0	0	0	4 2/3	7	4	2	0	4
Major league totals (7 years)		36	44	.450	4.47	114	107	13	2	0	692 1/3	721	373	344	245	355

FASANO, SAL — C — ROYALS

PERSONAL: Born August 10, 1971, in Chicago. . . . 6-2/220. . . . Bats right, throws right.

HIGH SCHOOL: Hoffman Estates (Ill.).

COLLEGE: Evansville.

TRANSACTIONS/CAREER NOTES: Selected by Kansas City Royals organization in 37th round of free-agent draft (June 3, 1993).

STATISTICAL NOTES: Led Northwest League catchers with seven double plays in 1993.

Year	Team (League)	Pos.	G	AB	R	H	2B	3B	HR	RBI	Avg.	BB	SO	SB	PO	A	E	Avg.
				BATTING											FIELDING			
1993—	Eugene (N'west)	C	49	176	25	47	11	1	10	36	.267	19	49	4	276	38	1	.997
1994—	Rockford (Midw.)	C-1B	97	345	61	97	16	1	25	81	.281	33	66	8	527	86	12	.981
—	Wilmington (Caro.)	C-1B	23	90	15	29	7	0	7	32	.322	13	24	0	80	9	4	.957
1995—	Wilmington (Caro.)	C-1B	23	88	12	20	2	1	2	7	.227	5	16	0	132	12	0	1.000
—	Wichita (Texas)	C-1B	87	317	60	92	19	2	20	66	.290	27	61	3	589	64	14	.979

FASSERO, JEFF — P — EXPOS

PERSONAL: Born January 5, 1963, in Springfield, Ill. . . . 6-1/195. . . . Throws left, bats left. . . . Full name: Jeffrey Joseph Fassero. . . . Name pronounced fuh-SAIR-oh.

HIGH SCHOOL: Griffin (Springfield, Ill.).

JUNIOR COLLEGE: Lincoln Land Community College (Ill.).

COLLEGE: Mississippi.

TRANSACTIONS/CAREER NOTES: Selected by St. Louis Cardinals organization in 22nd round of free-agent draft (June 4, 1984). . . . Selected by Chicago White Sox organization from Cardinals organization in Rule 5 minor league draft (December 5, 1989). . . . Released by White Sox organization (April 3, 1990). . . . Signed by Cleveland Indians organization (April 9, 1990). . . . Granted free agency (October 15, 1990). . . . Signed by Indianapolis, Montreal Expos organization (January 3, 1991). . . . On disabled list (July 24-August 11, 1994).

STATISTICAL NOTES: Pitched 5-0 no-hit victory for Arkansas against Jackson (June 12, 1989).

Year	Team (League)	W	L	Pct.	ERA	G	GS	CG	ShO	Sv.	IP	H	R	ER	BB	SO
1984—	Johns. City (App.)	4	7	.364	4.59	13	11	2	0	1	66 2/3	65	42	34	39	59
1985—	Springfield (Midw.)	4	8	.333	4.01	29	15	1	0	1	119	125	78	53	45	65
1986—	St. Petersburg (FSL)	13	7	.650	2.45	26	•26	6	1	0	*176	156	63	48	56	112
1987—	Arkansas (Texas)	10	7	.588	4.10	28	27	2	1	0	151 1/3	168	90	69	67	118
1988—	Arkansas (Texas)	5	5	.500	3.58	70	1	0	0	17	78	97	48	31	41	72

Year	Team (League)	W	L	Pct.	ERA	G	GS	CG	ShO	Sv.	IP	H	R	ER	BB	SO
1989—	Louisville (A.A.)	3	10	.231	5.22	22	19	0	0	0	112	136	79	65	47	73
—	Arkansas (Texas)	4	1	.800	1.64	6	6	2	1	0	44	32	11	8	12	38
1990—	Cant./Akr. (East.)■	5	4	.556	2.80	*61	0	0	0	6	64 1/3	66	24	20	24	61
1991—	Indianapolis (A.A.)■	3	0	1.000	1.47	18	0	0	0	4	18 1/3	11	3	3	7	12
—	Montreal (N.L.)	2	5	.286	2.44	51	0	0	0	8	55 1/3	39	17	15	17	42
1992—	Montreal (N.L.)	8	7	.533	2.84	70	0	0	0	1	85 2/3	81	35	27	34	63
1993—	Montreal (N.L.)	12	5	.706	2.29	56	15	1	0	1	149 2/3	119	50	38	54	140
1994—	Montreal (N.L.)	8	6	.571	2.99	21	21	1	0	0	138 2/3	119	54	46	40	119
1995—	Montreal (N.L.)	13	14	.481	4.33	30	30	1	0	0	189	207	102	91	74	164
Major league totals (5 years)		43	37	.538	3.16	228	66	3	0	10	618 1/3	565	258	217	219	528

FELDER, KEN — OF — BREWERS

PERSONAL: Born February 9, 1971, in Harrisburg, Pa. . . . 6-3/220. . . . Bats right, throws right. . . . Full name: Kenneth Wesley Felder.
HIGH SCHOOL: Niceville (Fla.).
COLLEGE: Florida State.
TRANSACTIONS/CAREER NOTES: Selected by San Diego Padres organization in second round of free-agent draft (June 5, 1989); did not sign. . . . Selected by Milwaukee Brewers organization in first round (12th pick overall) of free-agent draft (June 1, 1992). . . . On disabled list (May 13-July 3 and July 26-September 3, 1993).

				BATTING											FIELDING			
Year	**Team (League)**	**Pos.**	**G**	**AB**	**R**	**H**	**2B**	**3B**	**HR**	**RBI**	**Avg.**	**BB**	**SO**	**SB**	**PO**	**A**	**E**	**Avg.**
1992—	Helena (Pioneer)	OF	74	276	58	60	8	1	15	48	.217	35	102	11	94	5	7	.934
1993—	Beloit (Midwest)	OF	32	99	12	18	4	2	3	8	.182	10	40	1	38	1	4	.907
1994—	Stockton (Calif.)	OF	121	435	56	119	21	2	10	60	.274	32	112	4	206	10	10	.956
1995—	El Paso (Texas)	OF	114	367	51	100	24	4	12	55	.272	48	94	2	156	14	6	.966

FERMIN, FELIX — SS — MARINERS

PERSONAL: Born October 9, 1963, in Mao, Valverde, Dominican Republic. . . . 5-11/185. . . . Bats right, throws right. . . . Full name: Felix Jose Fermin. . . . Name pronounced fair-MEEN.
COLLEGE: U.C.E. College (San Pedro de Macoris, Dominican Republic).
TRANSACTIONS/CAREER NOTES: Signed as non-drafted free agent by Pittsburgh Pirates organization (June 11, 1983). . . . On Pittsburgh disabled list (July 19-August 24, 1987); included rehabilitation assignment to Harrisburg (August 12-24). . . . Traded by Pirates to Cleveland Indians for SS Jay Bell (March 25, 1989). . . . On Cleveland disabled list (April 23-May 12, 1991); included rehabilitation assignment to Colorado Springs (May 5-12). . . . Traded by Indians with 1B Reggie Jefferson and cash to Seattle Mariners for SS Omar Vizquel (December 20, 1993). . . . Granted free agency (October 24, 1994). . . . Re-signed by Mariners (November 29, 1994). . . . On Seattle disabled list (May 6-27, 1995); included rehabilitation assignment to Tacoma (May 26-27).
RECORDS: Shares major league single-game record for most sacrifice hits—4 (August 22, 1989, 10 innings). . . . Holds A.L. single-season records for fewest long hits (150 or more games)—10 (1989); and fewest errors by shortstop who led league in errors—23 (1993).
STATISTICAL NOTES: Tied for New York-Pennsylvania League lead in double plays by shortstop with 38 in 1983. . . . Led Eastern League shortstops with .964 fielding percentage, 251 putouts and 661 total chances in 1985. . . . Led Eastern League shortstops with .968 fielding percentage in 1987. . . . Led A.L. with 32 sacrifice hits in 1989. . . . Led A.L. shortstops with 26 errors in 1989.

				BATTING											FIELDING			
Year	**Team (League)**	**Pos.**	**G**	**AB**	**R**	**H**	**2B**	**3B**	**HR**	**RBI**	**Avg.**	**BB**	**SO**	**SB**	**PO**	**A**	**E**	**Avg.**
1983—	Watertown (NYP)	SS	67	234	27	46	6	1	0	14	.197	16	30	5	94	223	30	.914
—	GC Pirates (GCL)	SS	1	4	1	1	0	0	0	1	.250	0	0	0	1	4	0	1.000
1984—	Prin. William (Car.)	SS	119	382	34	94	13	1	0	41	.246	29	32	32	181	376	23	*.960
1985—	Nashua (Eastern)	SS-2B	137	443	32	100	10	2	0	27	.226	37	30	29	†251	387	24	†.964
1986—	Hawaii (PCL)	SS-2B	39	125	13	32	5	0	0	9	.256	7	13	1	60	99	7	.958
—	Prin. William (Car.)	SS	84	322	58	90	10	1	0	26	.280	25	19	40	158	205	19	.950
1987—	Harrisburg (East.)	SS-2B	100	399	62	107	9	5	0	35	.268	27	22	22	177	288	15	†.969
—	Pittsburgh (N.L.)	SS	23	68	6	17	0	0	0	4	.250	4	9	0	36	62	2	.980
1988—	Buffalo (A.A.)	SS	87	352	38	92	11	1	0	31	.261	17	18	8	131	268	10	.976
—	Pittsburgh (N.L.)	SS	43	87	9	24	0	2	0	2	.276	8	10	3	51	76	6	.955
1989—	Cleveland (A.L.)■	SS-2B	156	484	50	115	9	1	0	21	.238	41	27	6	253	517	†26	.967
1990—	Cleveland (A.L.)	SS-2B	148	414	47	106	13	2	1	40	.256	26	22	3	214	423	16	.975
1991—	Cleveland (A.L.)	SS	129	424	30	111	13	2	0	31	.262	26	27	5	214	372	12	.980
—	Colo. Springs (PCL)	SS	2	8	1	2	0	0	0	1	.250	0	0	0	2	5	0	1.000
1992—	Cleveland (A.L.)	S-3-2-1	79	215	27	58	7	2	0	13	.270	18	10	0	79	168	8	.969
1993—	Cleveland (A.L.)	SS	140	480	48	126	16	2	2	45	.263	24	14	4	211	346	*23	.960
1994—	Seattle (A.L.)■	SS-2B	101	379	52	120	21	0	1	35	.317	11	22	4	169	250	10	.977
1995—	Seattle (A.L.)	SS-2B	73	200	21	39	6	0	0	15	.195	6	6	2	107	168	6	.979
—	Tacoma (PCL)	SS	1	3	0	1	0	0	0	0	.333	0	0	0	0	0	0	...
American League totals (7 years)			826	2596	275	675	85	9	4	200	.260	152	128	24	1247	2244	101	.972
National League totals (2 years)			66	155	15	41	0	2	0	6	.265	12	19	3	87	138	8	.966
Major league totals (9 years)			892	2751	290	716	85	11	4	206	.260	164	147	27	1334	2382	109	.972

DIVISION SERIES RECORD

				BATTING											FIELDING			
Year	**Team (League)**	**Pos.**	**G**	**AB**	**R**	**H**	**2B**	**3B**	**HR**	**RBI**	**Avg.**	**BB**	**SO**	**SB**	**PO**	**A**	**E**	**Avg.**
1995—	Seattle (A.L.)	2B-SS	3	1	0	0	0	0	0	0	.000	0	1	0	3	3	0	1.000

CHAMPIONSHIP SERIES RECORD

				BATTING											FIELDING			
Year	**Team (League)**	**Pos.**	**G**	**AB**	**R**	**H**	**2B**	**3B**	**HR**	**RBI**	**Avg.**	**BB**	**SO**	**SB**	**PO**	**A**	**E**	**Avg.**
1995—	Seattle (A.L.)	2B-SS	2	2	0	0	0	0	0	0	.000	0	0	0	0	0	0	...

FERMIN, RAMON — P — ATHLETICS

PERSONAL: Born November 25, 1972, in San Francisco de Macoris, Dominican Republic. . . . 6-3/180. . . . Throws right, bats right. . . . Full name: Ramon Antonio Ventura Fermin.

TRANSACTIONS/CAREER NOTES: Signed as non-drafted free agent by Oakland Athletics organization (December 1, 1989).

Year	Team (League)	W	L	Pct.	ERA	G	GS	CG	ShO	Sv.	IP	H	R	ER	BB	SO
1991	—Arizona A's (Ariz.)	3	0	1.000	2.13	7	3	1	0	0	25 1/3	20	6	6	4	11
	—Modesto (Calif.)	1	0	1.000	4.38	3	2	0	0	0	12 1/3	16	7	6	3	5
1992	—Madison (Midwest)	5	5	.500	2.43	14	14	1	0	0	77 2/3	66	33	21	35	37
	—Modesto (Calif.)	2	3	.400	5.70	14	5	0	0	1	42 2/3	50	31	27	19	18
1993	—Modesto (Calif.)	4	6	.400	6.15	31	5	0	0	1	67 1/3	78	56	46	37	47
1994	—Modesto (Calif.)	9	6	.600	3.59	29	18	0	0	5	133	129	71	53	42	120
1995	—Huntsville (South.)	6	7	.462	3.86	32	13	0	0	7	100 1/3	105	53	43	45	58
	—Oakland (A.L.)	0	0	...	13.50	1	0	0	0	0	1 1/3	4	2	2	1	0
Major league totals (1 year)		0	0	...	13.50	1	0	0	0	0	1 1/3	4	2	2	1	0

FERNANDEZ, ALEX — P — WHITE SOX

PERSONAL: Born August 13, 1969, in Miami Beach, Fla. . . . 6-1/215. . . . Throws right, bats right. . . . Full name: Alexander Fernandez.

HIGH SCHOOL: Pace (Miami).

JUNIOR COLLEGE: Miami-Dade (South) Community College.

COLLEGE: Miami (Fla.).

TRANSACTIONS/CAREER NOTES: Selected by Milwaukee Brewers organization in first round (24th pick overall) of free-agent draft (June 1, 1988); did not sign. . . . Selected by Chicago White Sox organization in first round (fourth pick overall) of free-agent draft (June 4, 1990).

HONORS: Named Golden Spikes Award winner by USA Baseball (1990).

STATISTICAL NOTES: Pitched 7-0 one-hit, complete-game victory for Chicago against Milwaukee (May 4, 1992).

Year	Team (League)	W	L	Pct.	ERA	G	GS	CG	ShO	Sv.	IP	H	R	ER	BB	SO
1990	—GC White Sox (GCL)	1	0	1.000	3.60	2	2	0	0	0	10	11	4	4	1	16
	—Sarasota (Fla. St.)	1	1	.500	1.84	2	2	0	0	0	14 2/3	8	4	3	3	23
	—Birmingham (Sou.)	3	0	1.000	1.08	4	4	0	0	0	25	20	7	3	6	27
	—Chicago (A.L.)	5	5	.500	3.80	13	13	3	0	0	87 2/3	89	40	37	34	61
1991	—Chicago (A.L.)	9	13	.409	4.51	34	32	2	0	0	191 2/3	186	100	96	88	145
1992	—Chicago (A.L.)	8	11	.421	4.27	29	29	4	2	0	187 2/3	199	100	89	50	95
	—Vancouver (PCL)	2	1	.667	0.94	4	3	2	1	0	28 2/3	15	8	3	6	27
1993	—Chicago (A.L.)	18	9	.667	3.13	34	34	3	1	0	247 1/3	221	95	86	67	169
1994	—Chicago (A.L.)	11	7	.611	3.86	24	24	4	3	0	170 1/3	163	83	73	50	122
1995	—Chicago (A.L.)	12	8	.600	3.80	30	30	5	2	0	203 2/3	200	98	86	65	159
Major league totals (6 years)		63	53	.543	3.86	164	162	21	8	0	1088 1/3	1058	516	467	354	751

CHAMPIONSHIP SERIES RECORD

Year	Team (League)	W	L	Pct.	ERA	G	GS	CG	ShO	Sv.	IP	H	R	ER	BB	SO
1993	—Chicago (A.L.)	0	2	.000	1.80	2	2	0	0	0	15	15	6	3	6	10

FERNANDEZ, SID — P — PHILLIES

PERSONAL: Born October 12, 1962, in Honolulu. . . . 6-1/230. . . . Throws left, bats left. . . . Full name: Charles Sidney Fernandez.

HIGH SCHOOL: Kaiser (Honolulu).

TRANSACTIONS/CAREER NOTES: Selected by Los Angeles Dodgers organization in third round of free-agent draft (June 8, 1981). . . . Traded by Dodgers with IF Ross Jones to New York Mets for P Carlos Diaz and a player to be named later (December 8, 1983); Dodgers acquired IF Bob Bailor to complete deal (December 12, 1983). . . . On disabled list (August 4-22, 1987). . . . On New York disabled list (March 12-July 18, 1991); included rehabilitation assignment to St. Lucie (June 22-27), Tidewater (June 27-July 7 and July 14-16) and Williamsport (July 7-14). . . . On New York disabled list (May 1-July 29, 1993); included rehabilitation assignment to St. Lucie (July 11-17) and Binghamton (July 17-29). . . . Granted free agency (October 25, 1993). . . . Signed by Baltimore Orioles (November 22, 1993). . . . On Baltimore disabled list (March 25-April 17 and June 19-July 4, 1994); included rehabilitation assignments to Albany (April 7-12) and Rochester (April 12-17). . . . On Baltimore disabled list (June 5-28, 1995); included rehabilitation assignment to Bowie (June 14-28). . . . Released by Orioles (July 10, 1995). . . . Signed by Philadelphia Phillies (July 13, 1995). . . . Granted free agency (November 3, 1995). . . . Re-signed by Phillies (November 27, 1995).

HONORS: Named Texas League Pitcher of the Year (1983).

STATISTICAL NOTES: Pitched 5-0 no-hit victory for Vero Beach against Winter Haven (April 24, 1982). . . . Pitched 1-0 no-hit victory for Vero Beach against Fort Lauderdale (June 8, 1982). . . . Struck out 16 batters in one game (July 14, 1989).

Year	Team (League)	W	L	Pct.	ERA	G	GS	CG	ShO	Sv.	IP	H	R	ER	BB	SO
1981	—Lethbridge (Pio.)	5	1	.833	*1.54	11	11	2	1	0	76	43	21	13	31	*128
1982	—Vero Beach (FSL)	8	1	.889	1.91	12	12	5	4	0	84 2/3	38	19	18	38	*137
	—Albuquerque (PCL)	6	5	.545	5.42	13	13	5	0	0	88	76	54	53	52	86
1983	—San Antonio (Tex.)	•13	4	.765	*2.82	24	24	4	1	0	153	111	61	48	96	*209
	—Los Angeles (N.L.)	0	1	.000	6.00	2	1	0	0	0	6	7	4	4	7	9
1984	—Tidewater (Int'l)■	6	5	.545	2.56	17	17	3	0	0	105 2/3	69	39	30	63	123
	—New York (N.L.)	6	6	.500	3.50	15	15	0	0	0	90	74	40	35	34	62
1985	—Tidewater (Int'l)	4	1	.800	2.04	5	5	1	0	0	35 1/3	17	8	8	21	42
	—New York (N.L.)	9	9	.500	2.80	26	26	3	0	0	170 1/3	108	56	53	80	180
1986	—New York (N.L.)	16	6	.727	3.52	32	31	2	1	1	204 1/3	161	82	80	91	200
1987	—New York (N.L.)	12	8	.600	3.81	28	27	3	1	0	156	130	75	66	67	134
1988	—New York (N.L.)	12	10	.545	3.03	31	31	1	1	0	187	127	69	63	70	189
1989	—New York (N.L.)	14	5	.737	2.83	35	32	6	2	0	219 1/3	157	73	69	75	198
1990	—New York (N.L.)	9	14	.391	3.46	30	30	2	1	0	179 1/3	130	79	69	67	181
1991	—St. Lucie (Fla. St.)	0	0	...	0.00	1	1	0	0	0	3	1	0	0	1	4
	—Tidewater (Int'l)	1	0	1.000	1.15	3	3	0	0	0	15 2/3	9	2	2	6	22
	—Williamsport (East.)	0	0	...	0.00	1	1	0	0	0	6	3	0	0	1	5

Year	Team (League)	W	L	Pct.	ERA	G	GS	CG	ShO	Sv.	IP	H	R	ER	BB	SO
	—New York (N.L.)	1	3	.250	2.86	8	8	0	0	0	44	36	18	14	9	31
1992	—New York (N.L.)	14	11	.560	2.73	32	32	5	2	0	214 2/3	162	67	65	67	193
1993	—New York (N.L.)	5	6	.455	2.93	18	18	1	1	0	119 2/3	82	42	39	36	81
	—St. Lucie (Fla. St.)	0	0	...	4.50	1	1	0	0	0	4	3	2	2	1	7
	—Binghamton (East.)	0	1	.000	1.80	2	2	0	0	0	10	6	2	2	3	11
1994	—Albany (S. Atl.)■	0	0	...	0.00	1	1	0	0	0	3	0	0	0	2	4
	—Rochester (Int'l)	0	0	...	4.50	1	1	0	0	0	4	3	2	2	1	4
	—Baltimore (A.L.)	6	6	.500	5.15	19	19	2	0	0	115 1/3	109	66	66	46	95
1995	—Baltimore (A.L.)	0	4	.000	7.39	8	7	0	0	0	28	36	26	23	17	31
	—Bowie (Eastern)	1	0	1.000	0.75	2	2	1	1	0	12	4	2	1	3	10
	—Philadelphia (N.L.)■	6	1	.857	3.34	11	11	0	0	0	64 2/3	48	25	24	21	79
A.L. totals (2 years)		6	10	.375	5.59	27	26	2	0	0	143 1/3	145	92	89	63	126
N.L. totals (12 years)		104	80	.565	3.16	268	262	23	9	1	1655 1/3	1222	630	581	624	1537
Major league totals (13 years)		110	90	.550	3.35	295	288	25	9	1	1798 2/3	1367	722	670	687	1663

CHAMPIONSHIP SERIES RECORD

Year	Team (League)	W	L	Pct.	ERA	G	GS	CG	ShO	Sv.	IP	H	R	ER	BB	SO
1986	—New York (N.L.)	0	1	.000	4.50	1	1	0	0	0	6	3	3	3	1	5
1988	—New York (N.L.)	0	1	.000	13.50	1	1	0	0	0	4	7	6	6	1	5
Champ. series totals (2 years)		0	2	.000	8.10	2	2	0	0	0	10	10	9	9	2	10

WORLD SERIES RECORD

NOTES: Member of World Series championship team (1986).

Year	Team (League)	W	L	Pct.	ERA	G	GS	CG	ShO	Sv.	IP	H	R	ER	BB	SO
1986	—New York (N.L.)	0	0	...	1.35	3	0	0	0	0	6 2/3	6	1	1	1	10

ALL-STAR GAME RECORD

Year	League	W	L	Pct.	ERA	GS	CG	ShO	Sv.	IP	H	R	ER	BB	SO
1986	—National	0	0	...	0.00	0	0	0	0	1	0	0	0	2	3
1987	—National	0	0	...	0.00	0	0	0	1	1	0	0	0	1	1
All-Star totals (2 years)		0	0	...	0.00	0	0	0	1	2	0	0	0	3	4

FERNANDEZ, TONY SS YANKEES

PERSONAL: Born June 30, 1962, in San Pedro de Macoris, Dominican Republic. . . . 6-2/175. . . . Bats both, throws right. . . . Full name: Octavio Antonio Castro Fernandez.

HIGH SCHOOL: Gasto Fernando (San Pedro de Macoris, Dominican Republic).

TRANSACTIONS/CAREER NOTES: Signed as non-drafted free agent by Toronto Blue Jays organization (April 24, 1979). . . . On Syracuse disabled list (August 10-27, 1981). . . . On disabled list (April 8-May 2, 1989). . . . Traded by Blue Jays with 1B Fred McGriff to San Diego Padres for OF Joe Carter and 2B Roberto Alomar (December 5, 1990). . . . Traded by Padres to New York Mets for P Wally Whitehurst, OF D.J. Dozier and a player to be named later (October 26, 1992); Padres acquired C Raul Casanova from Mets to complete deal (December 7, 1992). . . . Traded by Mets to Blue Jays for OF Darrin Jackson (June 11, 1993). . . . Granted free agency (November 3, 1993). . . . Signed by Cincinnati Reds organization (March 8, 1994). . . . Granted free agency (October 13, 1994). . . . Signed by New York Yankees (December 15, 1994). . . . On disabled list (May 21-June 8, 1995).

RECORDS: Shares major league career record for highest fielding percentage by shortstop (1,000 or more games)—.980. . . . Shares major league record for most times caught stealing in one inning—2 (June 26, 1992, fifth inning). . . . Holds A.L. career record for highest fielding percentage by shortstop (1,000 or more games)—.982. . . . Holds A.L. single-season record for most games by shortstop—163 (1986). . . . Shares A.L. single-season record for most games by switch-hitter—163 (1986).

HONORS: Named shortstop on The Sporting News A.L. All-Star team (1986). . . . Won A.L. Gold Glove at shortstop (1986-89).

STATISTICAL NOTES: Led International League shortstops with 87 double plays in 1983. . . . Led A.L. shortstops with 791 total chances in 1985 and 786 in 1990. . . . Led N.L. third basemen with .991 fielding percentage in 1994. . . . Hit for the cycle (September 3, 1995, 10 innings). . . . Career major league grand slams: 2.

			BATTING											FIELDING			
Year	Team (League)	Pos.	G	AB	R	H	2B	3B	HR	RBI	Avg.	BB	SO	SB	PO	A	E	Avg.
1980	—Kinston (Carolina)	SS	62	187	28	52	6	2	0	12	.278	28	17	7	93	205	28	.914
1981	—Kinston (Carolina)	SS	75	280	57	89	10	6	1	13	.318	49	20	15	121	227	19	.948
	—Syracuse (Int'l)	SS	31	115	13	32	6	2	1	9	.278	7	15	9	69	80	3	.980
1982	—Syracuse (Int'l)	SS	134	523	78	158	21	6	4	56	.302	42	31	22	*246	364	23	*.964
1983	—Syracuse (Int'l)	SS	117	437	65	131	18	6	5	38	.300	57	27	35	*211	361	26	.957
	—Toronto (A.L.)	SS-DH	15	34	5	9	1	1	0	2	.265	2	2	0	16	17	0	1.000
1984	—Syracuse (Int'l)	SS	26	94	12	24	1	0	0	6	.255	13	9	1	46	72	5	.959
	—Toronto (A.L.)	SS-3B-DH	88	233	29	63	5	3	3	19	.270	17	15	5	119	195	9	.972
1985	—Toronto (A.L.)	SS	161	564	71	163	31	10	2	51	.289	43	41	13	283	*478	30	.962
1986	—Toronto (A.L.)	SS	*163	*687	91	213	33	9	10	65	.310	27	52	25	*294	445	13	*.983
1987	—Toronto (A.L.)	SS	146	578	90	186	29	8	5	67	.322	51	48	32	*270	396	14	.979
1988	—Toronto (A.L.)	SS	154	648	76	186	41	4	5	70	.287	45	65	15	247	470	14	.981
1989	—Toronto (A.L.)	SS	140	573	64	147	25	9	11	64	.257	29	51	22	260	475	6	*.992
1990	—Toronto (A.L.)	SS	161	635	84	175	27	*17	4	66	.276	71	70	26	*297	*480	9	.989
1991	—San Diego (N.L.)■	SS	145	558	81	152	27	5	4	38	.272	55	74	23	247	440	20	.972
1992	—San Diego (N.L.)	SS	155	622	84	171	32	4	4	37	.275	56	62	20	240	405	11	.983
1993	—New York (N.L.)■	SS	48	173	20	39	5	2	1	14	.225	25	19	6	83	150	6	.975
	—Toronto (A.L.)■	SS	94	353	45	108	18	9	4	50	.306	31	26	15	196	260	7	.985
1994	—Cincinnati (N.L.)■	3B-SS-2B	104	366	50	102	18	6	8	50	.279	44	40	12	67	195	4	†.985
1995	—New York (A.L.)■	SS-2B	108	384	57	94	20	2	5	45	.245	42	40	6	148	283	10	.977
American League totals (10 years)			1230	4689	612	1344	230	72	49	499	.287	358	410	159	2130	3499	112	.980
National League totals (4 years)			452	1719	235	464	82	17	17	139	.270	180	195	61	637	1190	41	.978
Major league totals (13 years)			1682	6408	847	1808	312	89	66	638	.282	538	605	220	2767	4689	153	.980

DIVISION SERIES RECORD

			BATTING											FIELDING			
Year Team (League)	Pos.	G	AB	R	H	2B	3B	HR	RBI	Avg.	BB	SO	SB	PO	A	E	Avg.
1995— New York (A.L.)	SS	5	21	0	5	2	0	0	0	.238	2	2	0	9	15	0	1.000

CHAMPIONSHIP SERIES RECORD

			BATTING											FIELDING			
Year Team (League)	Pos.	G	AB	R	H	2B	3B	HR	RBI	Avg.	BB	SO	SB	PO	A	E	Avg.
1985— Toronto (A.L.)	SS	7	24	2	8	2	0	0	2	.333	1	2	0	11	15	2	.929
1989— Toronto (A.L.)	SS	5	20	6	7	3	0	0	1	.350	1	2	5	9	15	0	1.000
1993— Toronto (A.L.)	SS	6	22	1	7	0	0	0	1	.318	2	4	0	12	8	0	1.000
Championship series totals (3 years)		18	66	9	22	5	0	0	4	.333	4	8	5	32	38	2	.972

WORLD SERIES RECORD

NOTES: Member of World Series championship team (1993).

			BATTING											FIELDING			
Year Team (League)	Pos.	G	AB	R	H	2B	3B	HR	RBI	Avg.	BB	SO	SB	PO	A	E	Avg.
1993— Toronto (A.L.)	SS	6	21	2	7	1	0	0	9	.333	3	3	0	11	8	0	1.000

ALL-STAR GAME RECORD

		BATTING											FIELDING			
Year League	Pos.	AB	R	H	2B	3B	HR	RBI	Avg.	BB	SO	SB	PO	A	E	Avg.
1986— American	SS	0	0	0	0	0	0	0	...	0	0	0	0	0	0	...
1987— American	SS	2	0	0	0	0	0	0	.000	0	0	0	1	3	0	1.000
1989— American	PR-SS	1	0	0	0	0	0	0	.000	0	0	0	2	2	0	1.000
1992— National	SS	2	1	1	0	0	0	0	.500	0	0	0	3	0	0	1.000
All-Star Game totals (4 years)		5	1	1	0	0	0	0	.200	0	0	0	6	5	0	1.000

FETTERS, MIKE P BREWERS

PERSONAL: Born December 19, 1964, in Van Nuys, Calif. . . . 6-4/224. . . . Throws right, bats right. . . . Full name: Michael Lee Fetters.
HIGH SCHOOL: Iolani (Hawaii).
COLLEGE: Pepperdine.
TRANSACTIONS/CAREER NOTES: Selected by Los Angeles Dodgers organization in 22nd round of free-agent draft (June 6, 1983); did not sign. . . . Selected by California Angels organization in supplemental round ("sandwich pick" between first and second round, 27th pick overall) of free-agent draft (June 2, 1986); pick received as compensation for Baltimore Orioles signing Type A free-agent OF/IF Juan Beniquez. . . . Traded by Angels with P Glenn Carter to Milwaukee Brewers for P Chuck Crim (December 10, 1991). . . . On disabled list (May 3-19, 1992 and May 25-June 9, 1995).

Year Team (League)	W	L	Pct.	ERA	G	GS	CG	ShO	Sv.	IP	H	R	ER	BB	SO
1986— Salem (Northwest)	4	2	.667	3.38	12	12	1	0	0	72	60	39	27	51	72
1987— Palm Springs (Cal.)	9	7	.563	3.57	19	19	2	0	0	116	106	62	46	73	105
1988— Midland (Texas)	8	8	.500	5.92	20	20	2	0	0	114	116	78	75	67	101
— Edmonton (PCL)	2	0	1.000	1.93	2	2	1	0	0	14	8	3	3	10	11
1989— Edmonton (PCL)	12	8	.600	3.80	26	26	•6	2	0	168	160	80	71	72	*144
— California (A.L.)	0	0	...	8.10	1	0	0	0	0	3 1/3	5	4	3	1	4
1990— Edmonton (PCL)	1	1	.500	0.99	5	5	1	1	0	27 1/3	22	9	3	13	26
— California (A.L.)	1	1	.500	4.12	26	2	0	0	1	67 2/3	77	33	31	20	35
1991— Edmonton (PCL)	2	7	.222	4.87	11	11	1	0	0	61	65	39	33	26	43
— California (A.L.)	2	5	.286	4.84	19	4	0	0	0	44 2/3	53	29	24	28	24
1992— Milwaukee (A.L.)■	5	1	.833	1.87	50	0	0	0	2	62 2/3	38	15	13	24	43
1993— Milwaukee (A.L.)	3	3	.500	3.34	45	0	0	0	0	59 1/3	59	29	22	22	23
1994— Milwaukee (A.L.)	1	4	.200	2.54	42	0	0	0	17	46	41	16	13	27	31
1995— Milwaukee (A.L.)	0	3	.000	3.38	40	0	0	0	22	34 2/3	40	16	13	20	33
Major league totals (7 years)	12	17	.414	3.36	223	6	0	0	42	318 1/3	313	142	119	142	193

FIELDER, CECIL 1B/DH TIGERS

PERSONAL: Born September 21, 1963, in Los Angeles. . . . 6-3/250. . . . Bats right, throws right. . . . Full name: Cecil Grant Fielder.
HIGH SCHOOL: Nogales (La Puente, Calif.).
COLLEGE: UNLV.
TRANSACTIONS/CAREER NOTES: Selected by Baltimore Orioles organization in 31st round of free-agent draft (June 8, 1981); did not sign. . . . Selected by Kansas City Royals organization in secondary phase of free-agent draft (June 7, 1982). . . . Traded by Royals organization to Toronto Blue Jays organization for OF Leon Roberts (February 4, 1983). . . . Contract sold by Blue Jays to Hanshin Tigers of Japan Central League (December 22, 1988). . . . Signed as free agent by Detroit Tigers (January 15, 1990).
RECORDS: Shares major league records for most consecutive years leading league in runs batted in—3 (1990-92); and most years without a stolen base (150 games or more per year)—4. . . . Shares major league single-season record for most games with three home runs—2 (1990).
HONORS: Named A.L. Player of the Year by THE SPORTING NEWS (1990). . . . Named first baseman on THE SPORTING NEWS A.L. All-Star team (1990-91). . . . Named first baseman on THE SPORTING NEWS A.L. Silver Slugger team (1990-91).
STATISTICAL NOTES: Led Pioneer League with 176 total bases and in being hit by pitch with eight in 1982. . . . Led A.L. with 339 total bases and .592 slugging percentage in 1990. . . . Led A.L. first basemen with 137 double plays in 1990. . . . Hit three home runs in one game (May 6 and June 6, 1990). . . . Career major league grand slams: 8.

			BATTING											FIELDING			
Year Team (League)	Pos.	G	AB	R	H	2B	3B	HR	RBI	Avg.	BB	SO	SB	PO	A	E	Avg.
1982— Butte (Pioneer)	1B	69	273	73	88	*28	0	*20	68	.322	37	62	3	247	18	4	.985
1983— Florence (S. Atl.)■	1B	140	500	81	156	28	2	16	94	.312	58	90	2	957	64	16	.985
1984— Kinston (Carolina)	1B	61	222	42	63	12	1	19	49	.284	28	44	2	533	24	9	.984
— Knoxville (South.)	1B	64	236	33	60	12	2	9	44	.254	22	48	0	173	10	4	.979
1985— Knoxville (South.)	1B	96	361	52	106	26	2	18	81	.294	45	83	0	444	26	6	.987

Year	Team (League)	Pos.	G	AB	R	H	2B	3B	HR	RBI	Avg.	BB	SO	SB	PO	A	E	Avg.
			BATTING												FIELDING			
	—Toronto (A.L.)	1B	30	74	6	23	4	0	4	16	.311	6	16	0	171	17	4	.979
1986—	Toronto (A.L.)	DH-1-3-O	34	83	7	13	2	0	4	13	.157	6	27	0	37	4	1	.976
	—Syracuse (Int'l)	OF-1B	88	325	47	91	13	3	18	68	.280	32	91	0	•117	5	1	.992
1987—	Toronto (A.L.)	DH-1B-3B	82	175	30	47	7	1	14	32	.269	20	48	0	98	6	0	1.000
1988—	Toronto (A.L.)	DH-1-3-2	74	174	24	40	6	1	9	23	.230	14	53	0	101	12	1	.991
1989—	Hanshin (Jp. Cn.)■	...	106	384	60	116	11	0	38	81	.302	67	107	0	...	...	...	...
1990—	Detroit (A.L.)■	1B-DH	159	573	104	159	25	1	*51	*132	.277	90	*182	0	1190	111	14	.989
1991—	Detroit (A.L.)	1B-DH	•162	624	102	163	25	0	•44	*133	.261	78	151	0	1055	83	8	.993
1992—	Detroit (A.L.)	1B-DH	155	594	80	145	22	0	35	*124	.244	73	151	0	957	92	10	.991
1993—	Detroit (A.L.)	1B-DH	154	573	80	153	23	0	30	117	.267	90	125	0	971	78	10	.991
1994—	Detroit (A.L.)	1B-DH	109	425	67	110	16	2	28	90	.259	50	110	0	887	*108	7	.993
1995—	Detroit (A.L.)	1B-DH	136	494	70	120	18	1	31	82	.243	75	116	0	631	73	5	.993
Major league totals (10 years)			1095	3789	570	973	148	6	250	762	.257	502	979	0	6098	584	60	.991

CHAMPIONSHIP SERIES RECORD

Year	Team (League)	Pos.	G	AB	R	H	2B	3B	HR	RBI	Avg.	BB	SO	SB	PO	A	E	Avg.
			BATTING												FIELDING			
1985—	Toronto (A.L.)	PH	3	3	0	1	1	0	0	0	.333	0	0	0	...	...	...	...

ALL-STAR GAME RECORD

Year	League	Pos.	AB	R	H	2B	3B	HR	RBI	Avg.	BB	SO	SB	PO	A	E	Avg.
			BATTING											FIELDING			
1990—	American	PH-1B	1	0	0	0	0	0	0	.000	0	0	0	3	1	0	1.000
1991—	American	1B	3	0	0	0	0	0	0	.000	0	1	0	6	2	0	1.000
1993—	American	1B	1	0	0	0	0	0	0	.000	0	0	0	4	0	0	1.000
All-Star Game totals (3 years)			5	0	0	0	0	0	0	.000	0	1	0	13	3	0	1.000

FIGGA, MIKE — C — YANKEES

PERSONAL: Born July 31, 1970, in Tampa, Fla. . . . 6-0/200. . . . Bats right, throws right. . . . Full name: Michael Anthony Figga.
JUNIOR COLLEGE: Central Florida Community College.
TRANSACTIONS/CAREER NOTES: Selected by New York Yankees organization in 44th round of free-agent draft (June 5, 1989).
STATISTICAL NOTES: Led Gulf Coast League catchers with 296 total chances in 1990.

Year	Team (League)	Pos.	G	AB	R	H	2B	3B	HR	RBI	Avg.	BB	SO	SB	PO	A	E	Avg.
			BATTING												FIELDING			
1990—	GC Yankees (GCL)	C	40	123	19	35	1	1	2	18	.285	17	33	4	*270	19	7	.976
1991—	Prin. William (Car.)	C	55	174	15	34	6	0	3	17	.195	19	51	2	278	33	5	.984
1992—	Fort Lauder. (FSL)	C	80	249	12	44	13	0	1	15	.177	13	78	3	568	71	12	.982
	—Prin. William (Car.)	C	3	10	0	2	1	0	0	0	.200	2	3	1	27	1	0	1.000
1993—	San Bern. (Calif.)	C	83	308	48	82	17	1	25	71	.266	17	84	2	491	70	12	.979
	—Alb./Colon. (East.)	C	6	22	3	5	0	0	0	2	.227	2	9	1	31	2	1	.971
1994—	Tampa (Fla. St.)	C	111	420	48	116	17	5	15	75	.276	22	94	3	703	79	10	.987
	—Alb./Colon. (East.)	C	1	2	1	1	1	0	0	0	.500	0	1	0	5	0	0	1.000
1995—	Norwich (Eastern)	C	109	399	59	108	22	4	13	61	.271	43	90	1	640	92	11	.985
	—Columbus (Int'l)	C	8	25	2	7	1	0	1	3	.280	3	5	0	29	4	0	1.000

FINLEY, CHUCK — P — ANGELS

PERSONAL: Born November 26, 1962, in Monroe, La. . . . 6-6/214. . . . Throws left, bats left. . . . Full name: Charles Edward Finley.
HIGH SCHOOL: West Monroe (La.).
COLLEGE: Northeast Louisiana.
TRANSACTIONS/CAREER NOTES: Selected by California Angels organization in 15th round of free-agent draft (June 4, 1984); did not sign. . . . Selected by Angels organization in secondary phase of free-agent draft (January 9, 1985). . . . On disabled list (August 22-September 15, 1989 and April 6-22, 1992). . . . Granted free agency (November 7, 1995). . . . Re-signed by Angels (January 4, 1996).
HONORS: Named lefthanded pitcher on The Sporting News A.L. All-Star team (1989-90).
STATISTICAL NOTES: Pitched 5-0 one-hit, complete-game victory against Boston (May 26, 1989). . . . Struck out 15 batters in one game (June 24, 1989 and May 23, 1995).

Year	Team (League)	W	L	Pct.	ERA	G	GS	CG	ShO	Sv.	IP	H	R	ER	BB	SO
1985—	Salem (Northwest)	3	1	.750	4.66	18	0	0	0	5	29	34	21	15	10	32
1986—	Quad Cities (Midw.)	1	0	1.000	0.00	10	0	0	0	6	12	4	0	0	3	16
	—California (A.L.)	3	1	.750	3.30	25	0	0	0	0	46 1/3	40	17	17	23	37
1987—	California (A.L.)	2	7	.222	4.67	35	3	0	0	0	90 2/3	102	54	47	43	63
1988—	California (A.L.)	9	15	.375	4.17	31	31	2	0	0	194 1/3	191	95	90	82	111
1989—	California (A.L.)	16	9	.640	2.57	29	29	9	1	0	199 2/3	171	64	57	82	156
1990—	California (A.L.)	18	9	.667	2.40	32	32	7	2	0	236	210	77	63	81	177
1991—	California (A.L.)	18	9	.667	3.80	34	34	4	2	0	227 1/3	205	102	96	101	171
1992—	California (A.L.)	7	12	.368	3.96	31	31	4	1	0	204 1/3	212	99	90	98	124
1993—	California (A.L.)	16	14	.533	3.15	35	35	*13	2	0	251 1/3	243	108	88	82	187
1994—	California (A.L.)	10	10	.500	4.32	25	•25	7	2	0	*183 1/3	178	95	88	71	148
1995—	California (A.L.)	15	12	.556	4.21	32	32	2	1	0	203	192	106	95	93	195
Major league totals (10 years)		114	98	.538	3.58	309	252	48	11	0	1836 1/3	1744	817	731	756	1369

CHAMPIONSHIP SERIES RECORD

Year	Team (League)	W	L	Pct.	ERA	G	GS	CG	ShO	Sv.	IP	H	R	ER	BB	SO
1986—	California (A.L.)	0	0	...	0.00	3	0	0	0	0	2	1	0	0	0	1

F

ALL-STAR GAME RECORD

Year League	W	L	Pct.	ERA	GS	CG	ShO	Sv.	IP	H	R	ER	BB	SO
1989— American						Did not play.								
1990— American	0	0	...	0.00	0	0	0	0	1	0	0	0	1	1
1995— American						Did not play.								
All-Star totals (1 years)	0	0	...	0.00	0	0	0	0	1	0	0	0	1	1

FINLEY, STEVE OF PADRES

PERSONAL: Born March 12, 1965, in Union City, Tenn. . . . 6-2/180. . . . Bats left, throws left. . . . Full name: Steven Allen Finley.

HIGH SCHOOL: Paducah (Ky.) Tilghman.

COLLEGE: Southern Illinois (degree in physiology).

TRANSACTIONS/CAREER NOTES: Selected by Atlanta Braves organization in 11th round of free-agent draft (June 2, 1986); did not sign. . . . Selected by Baltimore Orioles organization in 13th round of free-agent draft (June 2, 1987). . . . On Baltimore disabled list (April 4-22, 1989). . . . On Baltimore disabled list (July 29-September 1, 1989); included rehabilitation assignment to Hagerstown (August 21-23). . . . Traded by Orioles with P Pete Harnisch and P Curt Schilling to Houston Astros for 1B Glenn Davis (January 10, 1991). . . . On disabled list (April 25-May 14, 1993). . . . On Houston disabled list (June 13-July 3, 1994); included rehabilitation assignment to Jackson (June 28-July 3). . . . Traded by Astros with 3B Ken Caminiti, SS Andujar Cedeno, 1B Robert Petagine, P Brian Williams and a player to be named later to San Diego Padres for OF Phil Plantier, OF Derek Bell, P Pedro Martinez, P Doug Brocail, IF Craig Shipley and SS Ricky Gutierrez (December 28, 1994).

HONORS: Won N.L. Gold Glove as outfielder (1995).

STATISTICAL NOTES: Led International League outfielders with 315 total chances in 1988. . . . Career major league grand slams: 2.

			BATTING											FIELDING			
Year Team (League)	Pos.	G	AB	R	H	2B	3B	HR	RBI	Avg.	BB	SO	SB	PO	A	E	Avg.
1987— Newark (NYP)	OF	54	222	40	65	13	2	3	33	.293	22	24	26	122	7	4	.970
— Hagerstown (Car.)	OF	15	65	9	22	3	2	1	5	.338	1	6	7	32	3	0	1.000
1988— Hagerstown (Car.)	OF	8	28	2	6	2	0	0	3	.214	4	3	4	17	0	0	1.000
— Charlotte (South.)	OF	10	40	7	12	4	2	1	6	.300	4	3	2	14	0	0	1.000
— Rochester (Int'l)	OF	120	456	61	*143	19	7	5	54	*.314	28	55	20	*289	14	*12	.962
1989— Baltimore (A.L.)	OF-DH	81	217	35	54	5	2	2	25	.249	15	30	17	144	1	2	.986
— Rochester (Int'l)	OF	7	25	2	4	0	0	0	2	.160	1	5	3	17	2	0	1.000
— Hagerstown (East.)	OF	11	48	11	20	3	1	0	7	.417	4	3	4	35	2	3	.925
1990— Baltimore (A.L.)	OF-DH	142	464	46	119	16	4	3	37	.256	32	53	22	298	4	7	.977
1991— Houston (N.L.)■	OF	159	596	84	170	28	10	8	54	.285	42	65	34	323	13	5	.985
1992— Houston (N.L.)	OF	•162	607	84	177	29	13	5	55	.292	58	63	44	417	8	3	.993
1993— Houston (N.L.)	OF	142	545	69	145	15	*13	8	44	.266	28	65	19	329	12	4	.988
1994— Houston (N.L.)	OF	94	373	64	103	16	5	11	33	.276	28	52	13	214	9	4	.982
— Jackson (Texas)	OF	5	13	3	4	0	0	0	0	.308	4	0	1	6	0	0	1.000
1995— San Diego (N.L.)■	OF	139	562	104	167	23	8	10	44	.297	59	62	36	291	8	7	.977
American League totals (2 years)		223	681	81	173	21	6	5	62	.254	47	83	39	442	5	9	.980
National League totals (5 years)		696	2683	405	762	111	49	42	230	.284	215	307	146	1574	50	23	.986
Major league totals (7 years)		919	3364	486	935	132	55	47	292	.278	262	390	185	2016	55	32	.985

FLAHERTY, JOHN C TIGERS

PERSONAL: Born October 21, 1967, in New York. . . . 6-1/202. . . . Bats right, throws right. . . . Full name: John Timothy Flaherty.

HIGH SCHOOL: St. Joseph's Regional (Montvale, N.J.).

COLLEGE: George Washington.

TRANSACTIONS/CAREER NOTES: Selected by Boston Red Sox organization in 25th round of free-agent draft (June 1, 1988). . . . Traded by Red Sox to Detroit Tigers for C Rich Rowland (April 1, 1994).

STATISTICAL NOTES: Tied for Florida State League lead with 19 passed balls in 1989.

			BATTING											FIELDING			
Year Team (League)	Pos.	G	AB	R	H	2B	3B	HR	RBI	Avg.	BB	SO	SB	PO	A	E	Avg.
1988— Elmira (N.Y.-Penn)	C	46	162	17	38	3	0	3	16	.235	12	23	2	235	39	7	.975
1989— Winter Haven (FSL)	C-1B	95	334	31	87	14	2	4	28	.260	20	44	1	369	60	9	.979
1990— Pawtucket (Int'l)	C-3B	99	317	35	72	18	0	4	32	.227	24	43	1	509	59	10	.983
— Lynchburg (Caro.)	C	1	4	0	0	0	0	0	1	.000	0	1	0	3	2	0	1.000
1991— New Britain (East.)	C	67	225	27	65	9	0	3	18	.289	31	22	0	337	46	9	.977
— Pawtucket (Int'l)	C	45	156	18	29	7	0	3	13	.186	15	14	0	270	18	•9	.970
1992— Boston (A.L.)	C	35	66	3	13	2	0	0	2	.197	3	7	0	102	7	2	.982
— Pawtucket (Int'l)	C	31	104	11	26	3	0	0	7	.250	5	8	0	158	17	4	.978
1993— Pawtucket (Int'l)	C	105	365	29	99	22	0	6	35	.271	26	41	0	626	78	10	.986
— Boston (A.L.)	C	13	25	3	3	2	0	0	2	.120	2	6	0	35	9	0	1.000
1994— Toledo (Int'l)■	C	44	151	20	39	10	2	7	17	.258	6	21	3	286	24	2	.994
— Detroit (A.L.)	C-DH	34	40	2	6	1	0	0	4	.150	1	11	0	78	9	0	1.000
1995— Detroit (A.L.)	C	112	354	39	86	22	1	11	40	.243	18	47	0	569	33	*11	.982
Major league totals (4 years)		194	485	47	108	27	1	11	48	.223	24	71	0	784	58	13	.985

FLEMING, DAVE P

PERSONAL: Born November 7, 1969, in Queens, N.Y. . . . 6-3/205. . . . Throws left, bats left. . . . Full name: David Anthony Fleming.

HIGH SCHOOL: Mahopac (N.Y.).

COLLEGE: Georgia.

TRANSACTIONS/CAREER NOTES: Selected by Seattle Mariners organization in third round of free-agent draft (June 4, 1990). . . . On Seattle disabled list (March 26-May 23, 1993); included rehabilitation assignment to Jacksonville (May 3-21). . . . Traded by Mariners organization

to Kansas City Royals organization for P Bob Milacki (July 7, 1995). . . . Granted free agency (December 21, 1995).
HONORS: Named lefthanded pitcher on THE SPORTING NEWS A.L. All-Star team (1992).

Year	Team (League)	W	L	Pct.	ERA	G	GS	CG	ShO	Sv.	IP	H	R	ER	BB	SO
1990—	San Bern. (Calif.)	7	3	.700	2.60	12	12	4	0	0	79 2/3	64	29	23	30	77
1991—	Jacksonville (Sou.)	10	6	.625	2.64	21	20	6	1	0	140	129	50	41	25	109
—	Seattle (A.L.)	1	0	1.000	6.62	9	3	0	0	0	17 2/3	19	13	13	3	11
—	Calgary (PCL)	2	0	1.000	1.13	3	2	1	0	0	16	11	2	2	3	16
1992—	Seattle (A.L.)	17	10	.630	3.39	33	33	7	4	0	228 1/3	225	95	86	60	112
1993—	Jacksonville (Sou.)	0	2	.000	4.41	4	4	0	0	0	16 1/3	16	9	8	7	10
—	Seattle (A.L.)	12	5	.706	4.36	26	26	1	1	0	167 1/3	189	84	81	67	75
1994—	Seattle (A.L.)	7	11	.389	6.46	23	23	0	0	0	117	152	93	84	65	65
1995—	Seattle (A.L.)	1	5	.167	7.50	16	7	1	0	0	48	57	44	40	34	26
—	Omaha (Am. Assoc.)■	1	0	1.000	3.38	3	3	0	0	0	16	17	6	6	7	8
—	Kansas City (A.L.)	0	1	.000	3.66	9	5	0	0	0	32	27	17	13	19	14
—	GC Royals (GCL)	0	0	...	0.00	1	1	0	0	0	3	2	1	0	0	1
Major league totals (5 years)		38	32	.543	4.67	116	97	9	5	0	610 1/3	669	346	317	248	303

FLETCHER, DARRIN — C — EXPOS

PERSONAL: Born October 3, 1966, in Elmhurst, Ill. . . . 6-1/200. . . . Bats left, throws right. . . . Full name: Darrin Glen Fletcher. . . . Son of Tom Fletcher, pitcher, Detroit Tigers (1962).
HIGH SCHOOL: Oakwood (Ill.).
COLLEGE: Illinois.
TRANSACTIONS/CAREER NOTES: Selected by Los Angeles Dodgers organization in sixth round of free-agent draft (June 2, 1987). . . . Traded by Dodgers to Philadelphia Phillies for P Dennis Cook (September 13, 1990). . . . Traded by Phillies with cash to Montreal Expos for P Barry Jones (December 9, 1991). . . . On Montreal disabled list (May 12-June 15, 1992); included rehabilitation assignment to Indianapolis (May 31-June 14).
STATISTICAL NOTES: Tied for Texas League lead in double plays by catcher with nine in 1988. . . . Led Pacific Coast League catchers with 787 total chances in 1990. . . . Led N.L. with 12 sacrifice flies in 1994.

				BATTING											FIELDING			
Year	Team (League)	Pos.	G	AB	R	H	2B	3B	HR	RBI	Avg.	BB	SO	SB	PO	A	E	Avg.
1987—	Vero Beach (FSL)	C	43	124	13	33	7	0	0	15	.266	22	12	0	212	35	3	.988
1988—	San Antonio (Tex.)	C	89	279	19	58	8	0	1	20	.208	17	42	2	529	64	5	*.992
1989—	Albuquerque (PCL)	C	100	315	34	86	16	1	5	44	.273	30	38	1	632	63	9	.987
—	Los Angeles (N.L.)	C	5	8	1	4	0	0	1	2	.500	1	0	0	16	1	0	1.000
1990—	Albuquerque (PCL)	C	105	350	58	102	23	1	13	65	.291	40	37	1	*715	64	8	.990
—	Los Angeles (N.L.)	C	2	1	0	0	0	0	0	0	.000	0	1	0	0	0	0	...
—	Philadelphia (N.L.)■	C	9	22	3	3	1	0	0	1	.136	1	5	0	30	3	0	1.000
1991—	Scran./W.B. (Int'l)	C-1B	90	306	39	87	13	1	8	50	.284	23	29	1	491	44	5	.991
—	Philadelphia (N.L.)	C	46	136	5	31	8	0	1	12	.228	5	15	0	242	22	2	.992
1992—	Montreal (N.L.)■	C	83	222	13	54	10	2	2	26	.243	14	28	0	360	33	2	.995
—	Indianapolis (A.A.)	C	13	51	2	13	2	0	1	9	.255	2	10	0	65	7	1	.986
1993—	Montreal (N.L.)	C	133	396	33	101	20	1	9	60	.255	34	40	0	620	41	8	.988
1994—	Montreal (N.L.)	C	94	285	28	74	18	1	10	57	.260	25	23	0	479	20	2	.996
1995—	Montreal (N.L.)	C	110	350	42	100	21	1	11	45	.286	32	23	0	613	44	4	.994
Major league totals (7 years)			482	1420	125	367	78	5	34	203	.258	112	135	0	2360	164	18	.993

ALL-STAR GAME RECORD

				BATTING									FIELDING			
Year	League	Pos.	AB	R	H	2B	3B	HR	RBI	Avg.	BB	SO	SB	PO	A	E	Avg.
1994—	National	C	0	0	0	0	0	0	0	...	0	0	0	3	0	0	1.000

FLETCHER, PAUL — P — ATHLETICS

PERSONAL: Born January 14, 1967, in Gallipolis, O. . . . 6-1/193. . . . Throws right, bats right. . . . Full name: Edward Paul Fletcher.
HIGH SCHOOL: Ravenswood (W.Va.).
COLLEGE: South Carolina-Aiken and West Virginia State College.
TRANSACTIONS/CAREER NOTES: Selected by Philadelphia Phillies organization in 40th round of free-agent draft (June 1, 1988). . . . On Reading disabled list (May 5-23, 1992). . . . Granted free agency (October 16, 1995). . . . Signed by Oakland Athletics organization (November 6, 1995).
STATISTICAL NOTES: Led New York-Pennsylvania League with 13 home runs allowed in 1989. . . . Led International League with 21 wild pitches in 1993.

Year	Team (League)	W	L	Pct.	ERA	G	GS	CG	ShO	Sv.	IP	H	R	ER	BB	SO
1988—	Martinsville (App.)	1	3	.250	4.67	15	14	1	0	1	69 1/3	81	44	36	33	61
1989—	Batavia (NYP)	7	5	.583	3.28	14	14	3	0	0	82 1/3	77	41	30	28	58
1990—	Spartanburg (SAL)	2	4	.333	3.28	9	9	1	0	0	49 1/3	46	24	18	18	53
—	Clearwater (Fla. St.)	5	8	.385	3.38	20	18	2	0	1	117 1/3	104	56	44	49	104
1991—	Clearwater (Fla. St.)	0	1	.000	1.23	14	4	0	0	1	29 1/3	22	6	4	8	27
—	Reading (Eastern)	7	9	.438	3.51	21	19	3	1	0	120 2/3	111	56	47	56	90
1992—	Reading (Eastern)	9	4	.692	2.83	22	20	2	1	0	127	103	45	40	47	103
—	Scran./W.B. (Int'l)	3	0	1.000	2.78	4	4	0	0	0	22 2/3	17	8	7	2	26
1993—	Scran./W.B. (Int'l)	4	12	.250	5.66	34	19	2	1	0	140	146	99	*88	60	116
—	Philadelphia (N.L.)	0	0	...	0.00	1	0	0	0	0	1/3	0	0	0	0	0
1994—	Scran./W.B. (Int'l)	4	9	.308	4.68	42	13	3	1	3	138 1/3	144	78	72	54	92
1995—	Scran./W.B. (Int'l)	4	1	.800	3.10	52	0	0	0	2	61	45	33	21	28	48
—	Philadelphia (N.L.)	1	0	1.000	5.40	10	0	0	0	0	13 1/3	15	8	8	9	10
Major league totals (2 years)		1	0	1.000	5.27	11	0	0	0	0	13 2/3	15	8	8	9	10

FLETCHER, SCOTT 2B

PERSONAL: Born July 30, 1958, in Fort Walton Beach, Fla. . . . 5-11/173. . . . Bats right, throws right. . . . Full name: Scott Brian Fletcher. . . . Son of Richard Fletcher, minor league pitcher (1952-59).
HIGH SCHOOL: Wadsworth (O.).
JUNIOR COLLEGE: Valencia Community College (Fla.).
COLLEGE: Toledo and Georgia Southern.
TRANSACTIONS/CAREER NOTES: Selected by Los Angeles Dodgers organization in 33rd round of free-agent draft (June 8, 1976); did not sign. . . . Selected by Oakland Athletics organization in secondary phase of free-agent draft (January 10, 1978); did not sign. . . . Selected by Houston Astros organization in secondary phase of free-agent draft (June 6, 1978); did not sign. . . . Selected by Chicago Cubs organization in secondary phase of free-agent draft (June 5, 1979). . . . Traded by Cubs with P Dick Tidrow, P Randy Martz and IF Pat Tabler to Chicago White Sox for P Steve Trout and P Warren Brusstar (January 25, 1983). . . . Traded by White Sox with P Ed Correa and a player to be named later to Texas Rangers for IF Wayne Tolleson and P Dave Schmidt (November 25, 1985); Rangers acquired IF Jose Mota to complete deal (December 12, 1985). . . . Granted free agency (November 4, 1988). . . . Re-signed by Rangers (November 30, 1988). . . . On Texas disabled list (July 5-20, 1989). . . . Traded by Rangers with OF Sammy Sosa and P Wilson Alvarez to Chicago White Sox for OF Harold Baines and IF Fred Manrique (July 29, 1989). . . . Granted free agency (November 4, 1991). . . . Signed by Milwaukee Brewers organization (February 23, 1992). . . . Granted free agency (October 30, 1992). . . . Signed by Boston Red Sox (December 1, 1992). . . . On disabled list (June 10-25, 1993). . . . On Boston disabled list (May 22-June 20, 1994); included rehabilitation assignment to Pawtucket (June 18-20). . . . Granted free agency (October 14, 1994). . . . Signed by Toledo, Detroit Tigers organization (April 24, 1995). . . . On disabled list (June 10-July 1, 1995) . . . . Granted free agency (October 31, 1995).
STATISTICAL NOTES: Led Texas League second basemen with 354 putouts, 390 assists, 29 errors, 773 total chances and 112 double plays in 1980. . . . Led American Association in being hit by pitch with nine and grounding into double plays with 20 in 1981. . . . Led American Association shortstops with 607 total chances in 1982. . . . Led A.L. second basemen with 115 double plays in 1990.

			BATTING												FIELDING			
Year	**Team (League)**	**Pos.**	**G**	**AB**	**R**	**H**	**2B**	**3B**	**HR**	**RBI**	**Avg.**	**BB**	**SO**	**SB**	**PO**	**A**	**E**	**Avg.**
1979	Geneva (NYP)	SS	67	261	59	81	12	3	4	43	.310	56	29	10	99	195	18	*.942
1980	Midland (Texas)	2B-SS	130	501	*111	164	16	*11	6	65	.327	82	65	20	†354	†390	†29	.962
1981	Iowa (Am. Assoc.)	SS	119	458	66	117	26	4	4	33	.255	51	72	24	*222	337	28	.952
	Chicago (N.L.)	2B-SS-3B	19	46	6	10	4	0	0	1	.217	2	4	0	34	44	3	.963
1982	Iowa (Am. Assoc.)	SS	129	502	90	157	26	3	4	60	.313	46	62	20	224	•357	26	.957
	Chicago (N.L.)	SS	11	24	4	4	0	0	0	1	.167	4	5	1	11	23	0	1.000
1983	Chicago (A.L.)■	S-2-3-DH	114	262	42	62	16	5	3	31	.237	29	22	5	126	308	16	.964
1984	Chicago (A.L.)	SS-2B-3B	149	456	46	114	13	3	3	35	.250	46	46	10	234	439	19	.973
1985	Chicago (A.L.)	3-S-2-DH	119	301	38	77	8	1	2	31	.256	35	47	5	123	208	8	.976
1986	Texas (A.L.)■	S-3-2-DH	147	530	82	159	34	5	3	50	.300	47	59	12	216	388	16	.974
1987	Texas (A.L.)	SS	156	588	82	169	28	4	5	63	.287	61	66	13	249	413	23	.966
1988	Texas (A.L.)	SS	140	515	59	142	19	4	0	47	.276	62	34	8	215	414	11	.983
1989	Texas (A.L.)	SS	83	314	47	75	14	1	0	22	.239	38	41	1	124	190	13	.960
	Chicago (A.L.)■	2B-SS-DH	59	232	30	63	11	1	1	21	.272	26	19	1	117	172	2	.993
1990	Chicago (A.L.)	2B	151	509	54	123	18	3	4	56	.242	45	63	1	305	436	9	.988
1991	Chicago (A.L.)	2B-3B	90	248	14	51	10	1	1	28	.206	17	26	0	178	192	3	.992
1992	Milwaukee (A.L.)■	2B-SS-3B	123	386	53	106	18	3	3	51	.275	30	33	17	236	382	9	.986
1993	Boston (A.L.)■	2-S-DH-3	121	480	81	137	31	5	5	45	.285	37	35	16	217	371	11	.982
1994	Boston (A.L.)	2B-DH	63	185	31	42	9	1	3	11	.227	16	14	8	118	163	1	.996
	Pawtucket (Int'l)	2B	2	9	0	2	0	0	0	0	.222	0	1	0	1	7	1	.889
1995	Detroit (A.L.)■	2B-SS-1B	67	182	19	42	10	1	1	17	.231	19	27	1	111	162	0	1.000
American League totals (13 years)			1582	5188	678	1362	239	38	34	508	.263	508	532	98	2569	4238	141	.980
National League totals (2 years)			30	70	10	14	4	0	0	2	.200	6	9	1	45	67	3	.974
Major league totals (15 years)			1612	5258	688	1376	243	38	34	510	.262	514	541	99	2614	4305	144	.980

CHAMPIONSHIP SERIES RECORD

			BATTING												FIELDING			
Year	**Team (League)**	**Pos.**	**G**	**AB**	**R**	**H**	**2B**	**3B**	**HR**	**RBI**	**Avg.**	**BB**	**SO**	**SB**	**PO**	**A**	**E**	**Avg.**
1983	Chicago (A.L.)	SS	3	7	0	0	0	0	0	0	.000	1	0	0	3	8	0	1.000

FLORA, KEVIN OF METS

PERSONAL: Born June 10, 1969, in Fontana, Calif. . . . 6-0/185. . . . Bats right, throws right. . . . Full name: Kevin Scot Flora.
HIGH SCHOOL: Bonita (Calif.).
TRANSACTIONS/CAREER NOTES: Selected by California Angels organization in second round of free-agent draft (June 2, 1987). . . . On disabled list (June 21, 1988-remainder of season and June 14-September 8, 1992). . . . On temporarily inactive list (April 24-July 16 and September 3, 1993-remainder of season). . . . On Vancouver temporarily inactive list (June 11-July 13, 1994). . . . On Lake Elsinore disabled list (August 3-14, 1994). . . . On Vancouver disabled list (July 3-11, 1995). . . . Traded by Angels organization with a player to be named later to Philadelphia Phillies organization for OF Dave Gallagher (August 9, 1995); Phillies acquired P Russ Springer from Angels to complete deal (August 15, 1995). . . . Granted free agency (October 16, 1995). . . . Signed by Angels organization (January 16, 1996). . . . Traded by Angels to New York Mets for SS Aaron Ledesma (January 18, 1996).
STATISTICAL NOTES: Led Midwest League shortstops with 46 errors in 1989.

			BATTING												FIELDING			
Year	**Team (League)**	**Pos.**	**G**	**AB**	**R**	**H**	**2B**	**3B**	**HR**	**RBI**	**Avg.**	**BB**	**SO**	**SB**	**PO**	**A**	**E**	**Avg.**
1987	Salem (Northwest)	SS	35	88	17	24	5	1	0	12	.273	21	14	8	35	81	22	.841
1988	Quad City (Midw.)	SS	48	152	19	33	3	4	0	15	.217	18	33	5	64	121	23	.889
1989	Quad City (Midw.)	SS-2B	120	372	46	81	8	4	1	21	.218	57	107	30	156	281	†46	.905
1990	Midland (Texas)	SS-2B	71	232	35	53	17	5	5	32	.228	23	53	11	98	213	26	.923
1991	Midland (Texas)	2B	124	484	97	138	14	*15	12	67	.285	37	92	40	272	*348	24	.963
	California (A.L.)	2B	3	8	1	1	0	0	0	0	.125	1	5	1	8	3	2	.846
1992	Edmonton (PCL)	2B	52	170	35	55	8	4	3	19	.324	29	25	9	111	118	11	.954
1993	Vancouver (PCL)	2B-OF	30	94	17	31	2	0	1	12	.330	10	20	6	21	22	2	.956
1994	Vancouver (PCL)	2B	6	12	5	2	1	0	0	1	.167	4	4	1	5	7	1	.923
	Lake Elsinore (Calif.)	2B	19	72	13	13	3	2	0	6	.181	12	17	7	9	4	4	.765
1995	California (A.L.)	DH	2	1	1	0	0	0	0	0	.000	0	1	0	...	...	...	...

Year	Team (League)	Pos.	BATTING												FIELDING			
			G	AB	R	H	2B	3B	HR	RBI	Avg.	BB	SO	SB	PO	A	E	Avg.
	—Vancouver (PCL)	OF	38	124	22	37	7	0	3	14	.298	16	33	7	65	4	1	.986
	—Philadelphia (N.L.)■	OF	24	75	12	16	3	0	2	7	.213	4	22	1	33	1	0	1.000
American League totals (2 years)			5	9	2	1	0	0	0	0	.111	1	6	1	8	3	2	.846
National League totals (1 year)			24	75	12	16	3	0	2	7	.213	4	22	1	33	1	0	1.000
Major league totals (2 years)			29	84	14	17	3	0	2	7	.202	5	28	2	41	4	2	.957

FLORENCE, DON — P

PERSONAL: Born March 16, 1967, in Manchester, N.H. . . . 6-0/195. . . . Throws left, bats right. . . . Full name: Donald Emery Florence.
HIGH SCHOOL: Memorial (Manchester, N.H.).
JUNIOR COLLEGE: Crowder College (Mo.).
TRANSACTIONS/CAREER NOTES: Signed as non-drafted free agent by Boston Red Sox organization (October 7, 1987). . . . Granted free agency (October 17, 1994). . . . Signed by New York Mets organization (November 16, 1994). . . . Granted free agency (October 16, 1995).

Year	Team (League)	W	L	Pct.	ERA	G	GS	CG	ShO	Sv.	IP	H	R	ER	BB	SO
1988	—Winter Haven (FSL)	6	8	.429	3.95	27	16	4	0	0	120 2/3	136	68	53	50	56
1989	—Winter Haven (FSL)	2	7	.222	2.88	51	2	0	0	15	93 2/3	81	46	30	34	71
1990	—New Britain (East.)	6	4	.600	3.50	34	4	0	0	1	79 2/3	85	37	31	26	39
1991	—New Britain (East.)	3	8	.273	5.44	55	2	0	0	2	84 1/3	84	58	51	43	73
1992	—New Britain (East.)	3	1	.750	2.41	58	0	0	0	6	74 2/3	65	23	20	27	51
1993	—Pawtucket (Int'l)	7	8	.467	3.36	57	0	0	0	2	59	56	24	22	18	46
1994	—Pawtucket (Int'l)	1	4	.200	3.66	61	0	0	0	7	59	66	24	24	24	43
1995	—Norfolk (Int'l)■	0	1	.000	0.96	41	0	0	0	4	47	37	6	5	17	29
	—New York (N.L.)	3	0	1.000	1.50	14	0	0	0	0	12	17	3	2	6	5
Major league totals (1 year)		3	0	1.000	1.50	14	0	0	0	0	12	17	3	2	6	5

FLORIE, BRYCE — P — PADRES

PERSONAL: Born May 21, 1970, in Charleston, S.C. . . . 5-11/190. . . . Throws right, bats right. . . . Full name: Bryce Bettencourt Florie.
HIGH SCHOOL: Hanahan (Charleston, S.C.).
COLLEGE: Trident Technical College (S.C.).
TRANSACTIONS/CAREER NOTES: Selected by San Diego Padres organization in fifth round of free-agent draft (June 1, 1988).
STATISTICAL NOTES: Led Texas League with 25 wild pitches in 1993.

Year	Team (League)	W	L	Pct.	ERA	G	GS	CG	ShO	Sv.	IP	H	R	ER	BB	SO
1988	—Arizona Padres (Ar.)	4	5	.444	7.98	11	6	0	0	0	38 1/3	52	44	34	22	29
1989	—Spokane (N'west)	4	5	.444	7.08	14	14	0	0	0	61	79	•66	48	40	50
	—Char., S.C. (S. Atl.)	1	7	.125	6.95	12	12	0	0	0	44	54	47	34	42	22
1990	—Waterloo (Midw.)	4	5	.444	4.39	14	14	1	0	0	65 2/3	60	37	32	37	38
1991	—Waterloo (Midw.)	7	6	.538	3.92	23	23	2	0	0	133	119	66	58	79	90
1992	—High Desert (Calif.)	9	7	.563	4.12	26	24	0	0	0	137 2/3	99	79	63	*114	106
	—Char., S.C. (S. Atl.)	0	1	.000	1.80	1	1	0	0	0	5	5	3	1	0	5
1993	—Wichita (Texas)	11	8	.579	3.96	27	•27	0	0	0	154 2/3	128	80	68	*100	133
1994	—Las Vegas (PCL)	2	5	.286	5.15	50	0	0	0	1	71 2/3	76	47	41	47	67
	—San Diego (N.L.)	0	0	...	0.96	9	0	0	0	0	9 1/3	8	1	1	3	8
1995	—San Diego (N.L.)	2	2	.500	3.01	47	0	0	0	1	68 2/3	49	30	23	38	68
Major league totals (2 years)		2	2	.500	2.77	56	0	0	0	1	78	57	31	24	41	76

FLOYD, CLIFF — 1B — EXPOS

F

PERSONAL: Born December 5, 1972, in Chicago. . . . 6-4/235. . . . Bats left, throws right. . . . Full name: Cornelius Clifford Floyd.
HIGH SCHOOL: Thornwood (South Holland, Ill.).
TRANSACTIONS/CAREER NOTES: Selected by Montreal Expos organization in first round (14th pick overall) of free-agent draft (June 3, 1991). . . . On disabled list (May 16-September 11, 1995).
HONORS: Named Minor League Player of the Year by The Sporting News (1993). . . . Named Eastern League Most Valuable Player (1993).
STATISTICAL NOTES: Led South Atlantic League with 261 total bases and nine intentional bases on balls received in 1992. . . . Led Eastern League with .600 slugging percentage and 12 intentional bases on balls received in 1993.

Year	Team (League)	Pos.	BATTING												FIELDING			
			G	AB	R	H	2B	3B	HR	RBI	Avg.	BB	SO	SB	PO	A	E	Avg.
1991	—GC Expos (GCL)	1B	56	214	35	56	9	3	6	30	.262	19	37	13	451	27	*15	.970
1992	—Albany (S. Atl.)	OF-1B	134	516	83	157	24	*16	16	*97	.304	45	75	32	423	29	17	.964
	—W.P. Beach (FSL)	OF	1	4	0	0	0	0	0	1	.000	0	1	0	2	0	0	1.000
1993	—Harrisburg (East.)	1B-OF	101	380	82	125	17	4	•26	*101	.329	54	71	31	564	27	19	.969
	—Ottawa (Int'l)	1B	32	125	12	30	2	2	2	18	.240	16	34	2	272	23	5	.983
	—Montreal (N.L.)	1B	10	31	3	7	0	0	1	2	.226	0	9	0	79	4	0	1.000
1994	—Montreal (N.L.)	1B-OF	100	334	43	94	19	4	4	41	.281	24	63	10	565	42	6	.990
1995	—Montreal (N.L.)	1B-OF	29	69	6	9	1	0	1	8	.130	7	22	3	146	12	3	.981
Major league totals (3 years)			139	434	52	110	20	4	6	51	.253	31	94	13	790	58	9	.989

FOLEY, TOM — IF

PERSONAL: Born September 9, 1959, in Columbus, Ga. . . . 6-1/185. . . . Bats left, throws right. . . . Full name: Thomas Michael Foley.
HIGH SCHOOL: Palmetto (Miami).
JUNIOR COLLEGE: Miami-Dade (South) Community College.
TRANSACTIONS/CAREER NOTES: Selected by Cincinnati Reds organization in seventh round of free-agent draft (June 7, 1977). . . . Traded

by Reds with C Alan Knicely, a player to be named later and cash to Philadelphia Phillies for C Bo Diaz and P Greg Simpson (August 8, 1985); Phillies acquired P Freddie Toliver to complete deal (August 27, 1985).... On Philadelphia disabled list (March 23-April 29, 1986); included rehabilitation assignment to Reading (April 25-29).... Traded by Phillies with P Larry Sorensen to Montreal Expos for P Dan Schatzeder and IF Skeeter Barnes (July 24, 1986).... On disabled list (May 17-June 2, 1987 and July 26-August 12, 1989).... Released by Expos (October 6, 1992).... Signed by Pittsburgh Pirates (December 14, 1992).... On disabled list (July 19-August 4, 1993 and May 29-June 16, 1994).... Granted free agency (October 17, 1994).... Signed by Ottawa, Expos organization (April 24, 1995).... On Montreal disabled list (June 15-July 3, 1995).... Released by Expos (July 26, 1995).

STATISTICAL NOTES: Led Pioneer League in caught stealing with 10 in 1977.... Led Western Carolinas League shortstops with 98 double plays in 1978.... Led Florida State League shortstops with 71 double plays in 1979.

			BATTING											FIELDING			
Year	Team (League)	Pos.	G	AB	R	H	2B	3B	HR	RBI	Avg.	BB	SO	SB	PO	A	E	Avg.
1977	Billings (Pioneer)	3B-SS	59	209	37	53	7	1	2	21	.254	37	43	7	53	109	24	.871
1978	Shelby (W. Caro.)	SS	124	424	55	98	19	1	2	41	.231	50	43	8	*217	•352	30	*.950
1979	Tampa (Fla. St.)	SS	125	414	38	95	12	6	0	37	.229	37	39	5	223	*394	35	.946
1980	Waterbury (East.)	2B	131	477	49	119	16	4	4	41	.249	47	50	3	*222	329	31	.947
1981	Indianapolis (A.A.)	SS	103	347	47	81	12	2	6	27	.233	27	27	6	175	267	27	.942
1982	Indianapolis (A.A.)	SS	129	427	65	115	20	9	8	63	.269	42	48	1	*227	343	27	.955
1983	Cincinnati (N.L.)	SS-2B	68	98	7	20	4	1	0	9	.204	13	17	1	54	76	2	.985
1984	Cincinnati (N.L.)	SS-2B-3B	106	277	26	70	8	3	5	27	.253	24	36	3	119	228	11	.969
1985	Cincinnati (N.L.)	2B-SS-3B	43	92	7	18	5	1	0	6	.196	6	16	1	52	74	3	.977
	—Philadelphia (N.L.)■	SS	46	158	17	42	8	0	3	17	.266	13	18	1	75	128	4	.981
1986	Reading (Eastern)	SS-2B	3	11	2	2	2	0	0	0	.182	1	0	0	2	11	0	1.000
	—Philadelphia (N.L.)	SS-2B-3B	39	61	8	18	2	1	0	5	.295	10	11	2	36	43	2	.975
	—Montreal (N.L.)■	SS-2B-3B	64	202	18	52	13	2	1	18	.257	20	26	8	81	147	4	.983
1987	Montreal (N.L.)	SS-2B-3B	106	280	35	82	18	3	5	28	.293	11	40	6	134	190	9	.973
1988	Montreal (N.L.)	2B-SS-3B	127	377	33	100	21	3	5	43	.265	30	49	2	204	324	15	.972
1989	Montreal (N.L.)	2-3-S-P	122	375	34	86	19	2	7	39	.229	45	53	2	203	317	8	.985
1990	Montreal (N.L.)	S-2-3-1	73	164	11	35	2	1	0	12	.213	12	22	0	80	123	5	.976
1991	Montreal (N.L.)	SS-3B-2B	86	168	12	35	11	1	0	15	.208	14	30	2	52	84	5	.965
1992	Montreal (N.L.)	S-2-1-3-O	72	115	7	20	3	1	0	5	.174	8	21	3	74	97	5	.972
1993	Pittsburgh (N.L.)■	2-1-3-S	86	194	18	49	11	1	3	22	.253	11	26	0	116	105	5	.978
1994	Pittsburgh (N.L.)	2-3-S-1	59	123	13	29	7	0	3	15	.236	13	18	0	51	94	3	.980
1995	Ottawa (Int'l)■	2B-SS-3B	23	62	13	19	5	0	0	7	.306	8	7	1	45	62	1	.991
	—Montreal (N.L.)	1B-2B	11	24	2	5	2	0	0	2	.208	2	4	1	23	7	0	1.000
Major league totals (13 years)			1108	2708	248	661	134	20	32	263	.244	232	387	32	1354	2037	81	.977

RECORD AS PITCHER

Year	Team (League)	W	L	Pct.	ERA	G	GS	CG	ShO	Sv.	IP	H	R	ER	BB	SO
1989	Montreal (N.L.)	0	0	...	27.00	1	0	0	0	0	1/3	1	1	1	0	0

FONVILLE, CHAD — SS/2B — DODGERS

PERSONAL: Born March 5, 1971, in Jacksonville, N.C.... 5-6/155.... Bats both, throws right.... Full name: Chad Everette Fonville.

HIGH SCHOOL: White Oak (Jacksonville, N.C.).

COLLEGE: Louisburg (N.C.).

TRANSACTIONS/CAREER NOTES: Selected by San Francisco Giants organization in 11th round of free-agent draft (June 1, 1992).... Selected by Montreal Expos from Giants organization in Rule 5 major league draft (December 5, 1994).... Claimed on waivers by Los Angeles Dodgers (May 31, 1995).... On disabled list (April 8-June 10, 1994).

STATISTICAL NOTES: Led Northwest League second basemen with 131 putouts and tied for lead with 17 errors in 1992.

			BATTING											FIELDING			
Year	Team (League)	Pos.	G	AB	R	H	2B	3B	HR	RBI	Avg.	BB	SO	SB	PO	A	E	Avg.
1992	Everett (N'west)	2B-SS	63	260	56	71	9	1	1	33	.273	31	39	36	†134	141	‡18	.939
1993	Clinton (Midwest)	SS-3B-2B	120	447	80	137	16	10	1	44	.306	40	48	52	167	319	36	.931
1994	San Jose (Calif.)	SS-2B-OF	68	283	58	87	9	6	0	26	.307	34	34	22	119	203	22	.936
1995	Montreal (N.L.)■	2B	14	12	2	4	0	0	0	0	.333	0	3	0	0	0	0	...
	—Los Angeles (N.L.)■	SS-2B-OF	88	308	41	85	6	1	0	16	.276	23	39	20	125	195	11	.967
Major league totals (1 year)			102	320	43	89	6	1	0	16	.278	23	42	20	125	195	11	.967

DIVISION SERIES RECORD

			BATTING											FIELDING			
Year	Team (League)	Pos.	G	AB	R	H	2B	3B	HR	RBI	Avg.	BB	SO	SB	PO	A	E	Avg.
1995	Los Angeles (N.L.)	SS	3	12	1	6	0	0	0	0	.500	0	1	0	1	7	1	.889

FORDYCE, BROOK — C — REDS

PERSONAL: Born May 7, 1970, in New London, Conn.... 6-1/185.... Bats right, throws right.... Full name: Brook Alexander Fordyce.... Name pronounced FOR-dice.

HIGH SCHOOL: St. Bernard's (Uncasville, Conn.).

TRANSACTIONS/CAREER NOTES: Selected by New York Mets organization in third round of free-agent draft (June 5, 1989). ... On disabled list (June 19-July 2 and July 18-August 30, 1994).... On suspended list (August 30-September 1, 1994).... Claimed on waivers by Cleveland Indians (May 15, 1995).... Granted free agency (October 16, 1995).... Signed by Cincinnati Reds organization (December 7, 1995).

STATISTICAL NOTES: Led Appalachian League catchers with .991 fielding percentage in 1989.... Led South Atlantic League in slugging percentage with .478 and tied for lead in grounding into double plays with 18 in 1990.... Led South Atlantic League with 30 passed balls in 1990.... Led Eastern League catchers with 795 total chances in 1992.... Led International League catchers with 810 total chances and tied for lead in double plays by catcher with 11 in 1993.

			BATTING											FIELDING			
Year	Team (League)	Pos.	G	AB	R	H	2B	3B	HR	RBI	Avg.	BB	SO	SB	PO	A	E	Avg.
1989	Kingsport (Appal.)	C-OF-3B	69	226	45	74	15	0	9	38	.327	30	26	10	311	28	4	†.988

F

		BATTING												FIELDING			
Year Team (League)	Pos.	G	AB	R	H	2B	3B	HR	RBI	Avg.	BB	SO	SB	PO	A	E	Avg.
1990—Columbia (S. Atl.)	C	104	372	45	117	29	1	10	54	.315	39	42	4	574	63	15	.977
1991—St. Lucie (Fla. St.)	C	115	406	42	97	19	3	7	55	.239	37	50	4	630	87	13	.982
1992—Binghamton (East.)	C	118	425	59	118	30	0	11	61	.278	37	78	1	*713	*79	3	*.996
1993—Norfolk (Int'l)	C	116	409	33	106	21	2	2	41	.259	26	62	2	*735	67	8	.990
1994—Norfolk (Int'l)	C	66	229	26	60	13	3	3	32	.262	19	26	1	330	33	7	.981
1995—New York (N.L.)	...	4	2	1	1	1	0	0	0	.500	1	0	0	0	0	0	...
—Buffalo (A.A.)■	C-OF	58	176	18	44	13	0	0	9	.250	14	20	1	306	18	3	.991
Major league totals (1 year)		4	2	1	1	1	0	0	0	.500	1	0	0	0	0	0	...

FORTUGNO, TIM — P

PERSONAL: Born April 11, 1962, in Clinton, Mass. . . . 6-0/195. . . . Throws left, bats left. . . . Full name: Timothy Shawn Fortugno. . . . Name pronounced for-TOON-yo.

HIGH SCHOOL: Uxbridge (Mass.).

COLLEGE: Golden West College (Calif.).

TRANSACTIONS/CAREER NOTES: Selected by Oakland Athletics organization in first round (ninth pick overall) of free-agent draft (January 17, 1984); did not sign. . . . Selected by Cleveland Indians organization in secondary phase of free-agent draft (June 4, 1984); did not sign. . . . Signed as free agent by Seattle Mariners organization (June 6, 1986). . . . Traded by Mariners with OF Phil Bradley to Philadelphia Phillies organization for OF Glenn Wilson, OF Dave Brundage and P Mike Jackson (December 9, 1987). . . . Released by Phillies (March 30, 1989). . . . Signed as free agent by Reno, independent (April 3, 1989). . . . Contract sold by Reno to Milwaukee Brewers organization (May 5, 1989). . . . Selected by California Angels from Brewers organization in Rule 5 major league draft (December 9, 1991). . . . Released by Angels (March 16, 1993). . . . Signed by Montreal Expos organization (March 23, 1993). . . . Released by Ottawa, Expos organization (July 19, 1993). . . . Signed Calgary, Mariners organization (December 19, 1993). . . . Released by Calgary (March 30, 1994). . . . Signed by Chattanooga, Cincinnati Reds organization (April 6, 1994). . . . Claimed on waivers by Chicago White Sox (January 6, 1995). . . . Traded by White Sox with P Jim Abbott to Angels for P Andrew Lorraine, P Bill Simas, P John Snyder and OF McKay Christensen (July 27, 1995). . . . Granted free agency (October 16, 1995).

STATISTICAL NOTES: Pitched seven-inning 6-0 no-hit victory against Modesto (August 12, 1987). . . . Tied for A.L. lead with three balks in 1995.

Year Team (League)	W	L	Pct.	ERA	G	GS	CG	ShO	Sv.	IP	H	R	ER	BB	SO
1986—Bellingham (N'west)	0	0	...	1.13	6	0	0	0	1	8	2	2	1	12	11
—Wausau (Midwest)	1	1	.500	2.61	19	0	0	0	3	31	18	17	9	26	38
1987—Salinas (Calif.)	8	2	.800	2.80	46	4	1	1	6	93 1/3	43	36	29	84	141
1988—Reading (Eastern)■	1	4	.200	4.44	29	4	0	0	0	50 2/3	42	29	25	36	48
—Clearwater (Fla. St.)	1	3	.250	2.42	9	3	0	0	0	26	17	10	7	15	28
1989—Reno-Stock. (Cal.)■	4	4	.500	1.97	18	7	1	0	1	68 2/3	37	26	15	40	90
—El Paso (Texas)■	0	3	.000	7.96	10	4	0	0	0	26	29	24	23	21	22
1990—Beloit (Midwest)	8	4	.667	1.56	31	0	0	0	7	63 1/3	38	16	11	38	106
—El Paso (Texas)	2	3	.400	3.14	12	2	0	0	2	28 2/3	23	12	10	22	24
1991—El Paso (Texas)	5	1	.833	1.99	20	3	0	0	1	54 1/3	40	15	12	25	73
—Denver (Am. Assoc.)	0	1	.000	3.57	26	0	0	0	2	35 1/3	30	15	14	20	39
1992—Edmonton (PCL)■	6	4	.600	3.56	26	7	0	0	1	73 1/3	69	36	29	33	82
—California (A.L.)	1	1	.500	5.18	14	5	1	1	1	41 2/3	37	24	24	19	31
1993—Ottawa (Int'l)■	2	1	.667	3.60	28	4	0	0	1	40	28	17	16	31	42
1994—Chattanooga (Sou.)■	0	1	.000	2.70	22	0	0	0	8	26 2/3	19	15	8	16	36
—Cincinnati (N.L.)	1	0	1.000	4.20	25	0	0	0	0	30	32	14	14	14	29
1995—Chicago (A.L.)■	1	3	.250	5.59	37	0	0	0	0	38 2/3	30	24	24	19	24
—Vancouver (PCL)■	1	1	.500	1.54	10	0	0	0	1	11 2/3	8	2	2	4	7
A.L. totals (2 years)	2	4	.333	5.38	51	5	1	1	1	80 1/3	67	48	48	38	55
N.L. totals (1 year)	1	0	1.000	4.20	25	0	0	0	0	30	32	14	14	14	29
Major league totals (3 years)	3	4	.429	5.06	76	5	1	1	1	110 1/3	99	62	62	52	84

FOSSAS, TONY — P — CARDINALS

PERSONAL: Born September 23, 1957, in Havana, Cuba. . . . 6-0/200. . . . Throws left, bats left. . . . Full name: Emilio Anthony Fossas.

HIGH SCHOOL: St. Mary's (Brookline, Mass.).

COLLEGE: South Florida.

TRANSACTIONS/CAREER NOTES: Selected by Minnesota Twins organization in ninth round of free-agent draft (June 6, 1978); did not sign. . . . Selected by Texas Rangers organization in 12th round of free-agent draft (June 5, 1979). . . . Released by Rangers organization (February 18, 1982). . . . Signed by Midland, Chicago Cubs organization (March 11, 1982). . . . Loaned by Cubs organization to Tabasco of Mexican League (March 15-April 7, 1982). . . . Released by Cubs organization (April 7, 1982). . . . Signed by Burlington, Rangers organization (May 3, 1982). . . . Granted free agency (October 15, 1985). . . . Signed by Edmonton, California Angels organization (December 13, 1985). . . . On disabled list (June 2, 1986-remainder of season). . . . Granted free agency (October 15, 1987). . . . Signed by Oklahoma City, Rangers organization (December 1, 1987). . . . Granted free agency (October 15, 1988). . . . Signed by Denver, Milwaukee Brewers organization (January 21, 1989). . . . Released by Brewers organization (December 6, 1990). . . . Signed by Boston Red Sox organization (January 23, 1991). . . . Released by Red Sox (December 11, 1992). . . . Re-signed by Red Sox organization (January 18, 1993). . . . Granted free agency (December 20, 1993). . . . Re-signed by Red Sox organization (January 20, 1994). . . . Granted free agency (December 23, 1994). . . . Signed by New Jersey, St. Louis Cardinals organization (April 11, 1995).

Year Team (League)	W	L	Pct.	ERA	G	GS	CG	ShO	Sv.	IP	H	R	ER	BB	SO
1979—GC Rangers (GCL)	6	3	.667	3.00	10	9	1	0	0	60	54	28	20	26	49
—Tulsa (Texas)	1	1	.500	6.55	2	2	0	0	0	11	14	10	8	4	3
1980—Asheville (S. Atl.)	8	2	.800	3.15	30	•27	8	2	2	*197	*187	84	69	69	140
1981—Tulsa (Texas)	5	6	.455	4.16	38	12	1	1	2	106	113	65	49	44	57
1982—Tabasco (Mexican)■	0	3	.000	5.56	3	3	0	0	0	11 1/3	15	14	7	10	6
—Burlington (Midw.)■	8	9	.471	3.08	25	18	10	1	0	146 1/3	121	63	50	33	115
1983—Tulsa (Texas)	8	7	.533	4.20	24	16	6	1	0	133	123	77	62	46	103
—Okla. City (A.A.)	1	2	.333	7.90	10	5	0	0	0	35 1/3	55	33	31	12	23
1984—Tulsa (Texas)	0	1	.000	4.50	4	0	0	0	2	10	12	5	5	3	7

Year	Team (League)	W	L	Pct.	ERA	G	GS	CG	ShO	Sv.	IP	H	R	ER	BB	SO
	—Okla. City (A.A.)	5	9	.357	4.31	29	15	3	0	0	121	143	65	58	34	74
1985	—Okla. City (A.A.)	7	6	.538	4.75	30	13	2	0	2	110	121	65	58	36	49
1986	—Edmonton (PCL)■	3	3	.500	4.57	7	7	2	1	0	43 1/3	53	23	22	12	15
1987	—Edmonton (PCL)	6	8	.429	4.99	40	15	1	0	0	117 1/3	152	76	65	29	54
1988	—Okla. City (A.A.)■	3	0	1.000	2.84	52	0	0	0	4	66 2/3	64	21	21	16	42
	—Texas (A.L.)	0	0	...	4.76	5	0	0	0	0	5 2/3	11	3	3	2	0
1989	—Denver (Am. Assoc.)■	5	1	.833	2.04	24	1	0	0	0	35 1/3	27	9	8	11	35
	—Milwaukee (A.L.)	2	2	.500	3.54	51	0	0	0	1	61	57	27	24	22	42
1990	—Milwaukee (A.L.)	2	3	.400	6.44	32	0	0	0	0	29 1/3	44	23	21	10	24
	—Denver (Am. Assoc.)	5	2	.714	1.51	25	0	0	0	4	35 2/3	29	8	6	10	45
1991	—Boston (A.L.)■	3	2	.600	3.47	64	0	0	0	1	57	49	27	22	28	29
1992	—Boston (A.L.)	1	2	.333	2.43	60	0	0	0	2	29 2/3	31	9	8	14	19
1993	—Boston (A.L.)	1	1	.500	5.18	71	0	0	0	0	40	38	28	23	15	39
1994	—Boston (A.L.)	2	0	1.000	4.76	44	0	0	0	1	34	35	18	18	15	31
	—Pawtucket (Int'l)	2	0	1.000	0.00	11	0	0	0	0	9 2/3	4	1	0	3	8
1995	—St. Louis (N.L.)■	3	0	1.000	1.47	58	0	0	0	0	36 2/3	28	6	6	10	40
A.L. totals (7 years)		11	10	.524	4.17	327	0	0	0	5	256 2/3	265	135	119	106	184
N.L. totals (1 year)		3	0	1.000	1.47	58	0	0	0	0	36 2/3	28	6	6	10	40
Major league totals (8 years)		14	10	.583	3.84	385	0	0	0	5	293 1/3	293	141	125	116	224

FOSTER, KEVIN — P — CUBS

PERSONAL: Born January 13, 1969, in Evanston, Ill. . . . 6-1/170. . . . Throws right, bats right. . . . Full name: Kevin Christopher Foster.
HIGH SCHOOL: Evanston (Ill.) Township.
COLLEGE: Kishwaukee College (Ill.).
TRANSACTIONS/CAREER NOTES: Selected by Montreal Expos organization in 29th round of free-agent draft (June 2, 1987). . . . On Albany (Ga.) suspended list (April 9-May 6, 1992). . . . Traded by Expos organization with P Dave Wainhouse to Seattle Mariners for IF Frank Bolick and a player to be named later (November 20, 1992); Expos organization acquired C Miah Bradbury to complete deal (December 8, 1992). . . . Traded by Mariners to Philadelphia Phillies for P Bob Ayrault (June 12, 1993). . . . Traded by Phillies to Chicago Cubs for P Shawn Boskie (April 12, 1994).
STATISTICAL NOTES: Led N.L. with 32 home runs allowed in 1995.
MISCELLANEOUS: Appeared in three games as pinch-runner (1995).

Year	Team (League)	W	L	Pct.	ERA	G	GS	CG	ShO	Sv.	IP	H	R	ER	BB	SO
1990	—GC Expos (GCL)	2	0	1.000	5.06	4	0	0	0	0	10 2/3	9	6	6	6	11
	—Gate City (Pioneer)	1	7	.125	4.58	10	10	0	0	0	55	43	42	28	34	52
1991	—Sumter (S. Atl.)	10	4	.714	2.74	34	11	1	1	1	102	62	36	31	68	111
1992	—WP Beach (FSL)	7	2	.778	1.95	16	11	0	0	0	69 1/3	45	19	15	31	66
1993	—Jacksonville (Sou.)■	4	4	.500	3.97	12	12	1	1	0	65 2/3	53	32	29	29	72
	—Scran./W.B. (Int'l)■	1	1	.500	3.93	17	9	1	0	0	71	63	32	31	29	59
	—Philadelphia (N.L.)	0	1	.000	14.85	2	1	0	0	0	6 2/3	13	11	11	7	6
1994	—Reading (Eastern)	0	1	.000	6.00	1	1	0	0	0	6	7	4	4	1	3
	—Orlando (Southern)■	1	0	1.000	0.95	3	3	1	1	0	19	8	2	2	2	21
	—Iowa (Am. Assoc.)	3	1	.750	4.28	6	6	1	0	0	33 2/3	28	17	16	14	35
	—Chicago (N.L.)	3	4	.429	2.89	13	13	0	0	0	81	70	31	26	35	75
1995	—Chicago (N.L.)	12	11	.522	4.51	30	28	0	0	0	167 2/3	149	90	84	65	146
Major league totals (3 years)		15	16	.484	4.27	45	42	0	0	0	255 1/3	232	132	121	107	227

RECORD AS POSITION PLAYER

			BATTING											FIELDING			
Year	Team (League)	Pos.	G	AB	R	H	2B	3B	HR	RBI	Avg.	BB	SO	SB	PO	A	E	Avg.
1988	—GC Expos (GCL)	3B-2B-SS	49	164	21	42	10	1	2	21	.256	21	33	16	38	92	18	.878
1989	—Rockford (Midw.)	3B-2B	44	117	9	19	3	2	1	15	.162	18	44	1	29	70	12	.892
1990	—W.P. Beach (FSL)	3B	3	6	0	1	0	1	0	2	.167	1	1	0	2	1	0	1.000

FOX, ANDY — 3B — YANKEES

PERSONAL: Born January 12, 1971, in Sacramento, Calif. . . . 6-4/205. . . . Bats left, throws right. . . . Full name: Andrew Junipero Fox.
HIGH SCHOOL: Christian Brothers (Sacramento, Calif.).
TRANSACTIONS/CAREER NOTES: Selected by New York Yankees organization in second round of free-agent draft (June 5, 1989). . . . On disabled list (June 11-21, 1991; April 9-22, 1992 and June 10-August 1, 1993).
STATISTICAL NOTES: Led Carolina League third basemen with 96 putouts in 1992. . . . Led Eastern League third basemen with 30 errors in 1994. . . . Led International League third basemen with 22 double plays in 1995.

				BATTING										FIELDING			
Year	Team (League)	Pos.	G	AB	R	H	2B	3B	HR	RBI	Avg.	BB	SO	SB	PO	A	E	Avg.
1989	—GC Yankees (GCL)	3B	40	141	26	35	9	2	3	25	.248	31	29	6	37	78	10	.920
1990	—Greensboro (S. Atl.)	3B	134	455	68	99	19	4	9	55	.218	92	132	26	93	238	*45	.880
1991	—Prin. William (Car.)	3B	126	417	60	96	22	2	10	46	.230	81	104	15	85	247	*29	.920
1992	—Prin. William (Car.)	3B-SS	125	473	75	113	18	3	7	42	.239	54	81	28	†97	304	27	.937
1993	—Alb./Colon. (East.)	3B	65	236	44	65	16	1	3	24	.275	32	54	12	59	150	19	.917
1994	—Alb./Colon. (East.)	3B-SS-2B	121	472	75	105	20	3	11	43	.222	62	102	22	110	261	†34	.916
1995	—Norwich (Eastern)	SS	44	175	23	36	3	5	5	17	.206	19	36	8	77	127	9	.958
	—Columbus (Int'l)	3-S-O-2	82	302	61	105	16	6	9	37	.348	43	41	22	84	211	9	.970

FOX, CHAD — P — BRAVES

PERSONAL: Born September 3, 1970, in Conroe, Tex. . . . 6-3/183. . . . Throws right, bats right. . . . Full name: Chad Douglas Fox.
HIGH SCHOOL: Westfield (Houston).

COLLEGE: Tarleton State (Tex.).

TRANSACTIONS/CAREER NOTES: Selected by Cincinnati Reds organization in 23rd round of free-agent draft (June 1, 1992). . . . Traded by Reds organization with a player to be named later to Atlanta Braves for OF Mike Kelly (January 9, 1996).

STATISTICAL NOTES: Led Carolina League with 20 wild pitches in 1994.

Year	Team (League)	W	L	Pct.	ERA	G	GS	CG	ShO	Sv.	IP	H	R	ER	BB	SO
1992—	Princeton (Appal.)	4	2	.667	4.74	15	8	0	0	0	49 1/3	55	43	26	34	37
1993—	Char., W.Va. (S. Atl.)	9	12	.429	5.37	27	26	0	0	0	135 2/3	138	100	81	97	81
1994—	Winst.-Salem (Car.)	12	5	.706	3.86	25	25	1	0	0	156 1/3	121	77	67	*94	137
1995—	Chattanooga (Sou.)	4	5	.444	5.06	20	17	0	0	0	80	76	49	45	52	56

FOX, ERIC — OF

PERSONAL: Born August 15, 1963, in LeMoore, Calif. . . . 5-10/180. . . . Bats both, throws left. . . . Full name: Eric Hollis Fox.

HIGH SCHOOL: Capistrano Valley (San Juan Capistrano, Calif.).

COLLEGE: Fresno State (degree in physical education).

TRANSACTIONS/CAREER NOTES: Selected by Toronto Blue Jays organization in 22nd round of free-agent draft (June 4, 1984); did not sign. . . . Selected by Philadelphia Phillies organization in 13th round of free-agent draft (June 3, 1985); did not sign. . . . Selected by Seattle Mariners organization in secondary phase of free-agent draft (January 14, 1986). . . . Released by Mariners organization (March 29, 1989). . . . Signed by Huntsville, Oakland Athletics organization (March 29, 1989). . . . On disabled list (June 21, 1990-remainder of season). . . . Granted free agency (December 19, 1992). . . . Re-signed by A's organization (February 2, 1993). . . . Granted free agency (October 15, 1993). . . . Re-signed by A's organization (December 1, 1993). . . . Granted free agency (October 15, 1994). . . . Signed by Oklahoma City, Texas Rangers organization (November 25, 1994). . . . Granted free agency (October 16, 1995).

STATISTICAL NOTES: Led California League in caught stealing with 27 in 1986. . . . Led California League outfielders with 337 total chances and seven double plays in 1986. . . . Tied for Southern League lead in double plays by outfielder with five in 1987. . . . Led Southern League outfielders with 321 total chances in 1989. . . . Career major league grand slams: 1.

			BATTING												FIELDING			
Year	Team (League)	Pos.	G	AB	R	H	2B	3B	HR	RBI	Avg.	BB	SO	SB	PO	A	E	Avg.
1986—	Salinas (Calif.)	OF	133	526	80	137	17	3	5	42	.260	69	78	41	*314	18	5	.985
1987—	Chatt. (South.)	OF	134	523	76	139	28	•10	8	54	.266	40	93	22	378	11	8	.980
1988—	Vermont (Eastern)	OF	129	478	55	120	20	6	3	39	.251	39	69	33	308	8	4	.988
1989—	Huntsville (South.)■	OF	139	498	84	125	10	5	15	51	.251	72	85	49	*306	10	5	.984
1990—	Tacoma (PCL)	OF	62	221	37	61	9	2	4	34	.276	20	34	8	130	3	5	.964
1991—	Tacoma (PCL)	OF	127	522	85	141	24	8	4	52	.270	57	82	17	306	14	6	.982
1992—	Tacoma (PCL)	OF	37	121	16	24	3	1	1	7	.198	16	25	5	78	4	0	1.000
—	Huntsville (South.)	OF	59	240	42	65	16	2	5	14	.271	27	43	16	125	4	0	1.000
—	Oakland (A.L.)	OF-DH	51	143	24	34	5	2	3	13	.238	13	29	3	92	3	1	.990
1993—	Oakland (A.L.)	OF-DH	29	56	5	8	1	0	1	5	.143	2	7	0	47	0	0	1.000
—	Tacoma (PCL)	OF	92	317	49	99	14	5	11	52	.312	41	48	18	198	6	4	.981
1994—	Tacoma (PCL)	OF	52	191	30	60	15	2	3	19	.314	20	28	7	97	4	0	1.000
—	Oakland (A.L.)	OF	26	44	7	9	2	0	1	1	.205	3	8	2	32	1	0	1.000
1995—	Texas (A.L.)■	OF-DH	10	15	2	0	0	0	0	0	.000	3	4	0	13	0	0	1.000
—	Okla. City (A.A.)	OF	92	349	52	97	22	5	6	50	.278	30	68	5	157	4	3	.982
Major league totals (4 years)			116	258	38	51	8	2	5	19	.198	21	48	5	184	4	1	.995

CHAMPIONSHIP SERIES RECORD

			BATTING												FIELDING			
Year	Team (League)	Pos.	G	AB	R	H	2B	3B	HR	RBI	Avg.	BB	SO	SB	PO	A	E	Avg.
1992—	Oakland (A.L.)	PR-DH-OF	4	1	0	0	0	0	0	0	.000	1	0	2	1	0	0	1.000

FRANCO, JOHN — P — METS

PERSONAL: Born September 17, 1960, in Brooklyn, N.Y. . . . 5-10/185. . . . Throws left, bats left. . . . Full name: John Anthony Franco.

HIGH SCHOOL: Lafayette (Brooklyn, N.Y.).

COLLEGE: St. John's.

TRANSACTIONS/CAREER NOTES: Selected by Los Angeles Dodgers organization in fifth round of free-agent draft (June 8, 1981). . . . Traded by Dodgers organization with P Brett Wise to Cincinnati Reds organization for IF Rafael Landestoy (May 9, 1983). . . . Traded by Reds with OF Don Brown to New York Mets for P Randy Myers and P Kip Gross (December 6, 1989). . . . On disabled list (June 30-August 1 and August 26, 1992-remainder of season; April 17-May 7 and August 3-26, 1993). . . . Granted free agency (October 18, 1994). . . . Re-signed by Mets (April 5, 1995).

HONORS: Named N.L. Fireman of the Year by The Sporting News (1988, 1990 and 1994).

Year	Team (League)	W	L	Pct.	ERA	G	GS	CG	ShO	Sv.	IP	H	R	ER	BB	SO
1981—	Vero Beach (FSL)	7	4	.636	3.53	13	11	3	0	0	79	78	41	31	41	60
1982—	Albuquerque (PCL)	1	2	.333	7.24	5	5	0	0	0	27 1/3	41	22	22	15	24
—	San Antonio (Tex.)	10	5	.667	4.96	17	17	3	0	0	105 1/3	137	70	58	46	76
1983—	Albuquerque (PCL)	0	0	...	5.40	11	0	0	0	0	15	10	11	9	11	8
—	Indianapolis (A.A.)■	6	10	.375	4.85	23	18	2	0	2	115	148	69	62	42	54
1984—	Wichita (Am. Assoc.)	1	0	1.000	5.79	6	0	0	0	0	9 1/3	8	6	6	4	11
—	Cincinnati (N.L.)	6	2	.750	2.61	54	0	0	0	4	79 1/3	74	28	23	36	55
1985—	Cincinnati (N.L.)	12	3	.800	2.18	67	0	0	0	12	99	83	27	24	40	61
1986—	Cincinnati (N.L.)	6	6	.500	2.94	74	0	0	0	29	101	90	40	33	44	84
1987—	Cincinnati (N.L.)	8	5	.615	2.52	68	0	0	0	32	82	76	26	23	27	61
1988—	Cincinnati (N.L.)	6	6	.500	1.57	70	0	0	0	*39	86	60	18	15	27	46
1989—	Cincinnati (N.L.)	4	8	.333	3.12	60	0	0	0	32	80 2/3	77	35	28	36	60
1990—	New York (N.L.)■	5	3	.625	2.53	55	0	0	0	*33	67 2/3	66	22	19	21	56
1991—	New York (N.L.)	5	9	.357	2.93	52	0	0	0	30	55 1/3	61	27	18	18	45
1992—	New York (N.L.)	6	2	.750	1.64	31	0	0	0	15	33	24	6	6	11	20
1993—	New York (N.L.)	4	3	.571	5.20	35	0	0	0	10	36 1/3	46	24	21	19	29
1994—	New York (N.L.)	1	4	.200	2.70	47	0	0	0	*30	50	47	20	15	19	42
1995—	New York (N.L.)	5	3	.625	2.44	48	0	0	0	29	51 2/3	48	17	14	17	41
Major league totals (12 years)		68	54	.557	2.62	661	0	0	0	295	822	752	290	239	315	600

ALL-STAR GAME RECORD

Year	League	W	L	Pct.	ERA	GS	CG	ShO	Sv.	IP	H	R	ER	BB	SO
1986—	National						Did not play.								
1987—	National	0	0	...	0.00	0	0	0	0	2/3	0	0	0	0	0
1989—	National						Did not play.								
1990—	National	0	0	...	0.00	0	0	0	0	1	0	0	0	0	0
1991—	National						Did not play.								
All-Star totals (2 years)		0	0	...	0.00	0	0	0	0	1 2/3	0	0	0	0	0

FRANCO, JULIO — 1B/DH — INDIANS

PERSONAL: Born August 23, 1961, in San Pedro de Macoris, Dominican Republic. . . . 6-1/190. . . . Bats right, throws right. . . . Full name: Julio Cesar Franco.

HIGH SCHOOL: Divine Providence (San Pedro de Macoris, Dominican Republic).

TRANSACTIONS/CAREER NOTES: Signed as non-drafted free agent by Philadelphia Phillies organization (June 23, 1978). . . . Traded by Phillies with 2B Manny Trillo, OF George Vukovich, P Jay Baller and C Jerry Willard to Cleveland Indians for OF Von Hayes (December 9, 1982). . . . On disabled list (July 13-August 8, 1987). . . . Traded by Indians to Texas Rangers for 1B Pete O'Brien, OF Oddibe McDowell and 2B Jerry Browne (December 6, 1988). . . . On disabled list (March 28-April 19, May 4-June 1 and July 9, 1992-remainder of season). . . . Granted free agency (October 27, 1993). . . . Signed by Chicago White Sox (December 15, 1993). . . . Granted free agency (October 21, 1994). . . . Signed by Chiba Lotte Marines of Japan Pacific League (December 28, 1994). . . . Signed as free agent by Indians (December 7, 1995).

HONORS: Named Carolina League Most Valuable Player (1980). . . . Named second baseman on The Sporting News A.L. Silver Slugger team (1988-1991). . . . Named second baseman on The Sporting News A.L. All-Star team (1989-1991). . . . Named designated hitter on The Sporting News A.L. Silver Slugger team (1994).

STATISTICAL NOTES: Led Northwest League with 153 total bases in 1979. . . . Led Northwest League shortstops with 45 double plays in 1979. . . . Led Carolina League shortstops with 73 double plays in 1980. . . . Led American Association shortstops with 42 errors in 1982. . . . Led A.L. shortstops with 35 errors in 1985. . . . Led A.L. in grounding into double plays with 28 in 1986 and 27 in 1989. . . . Career major league grand slams: 5.

			BATTING												FIELDING			
Year	Team (League)	Pos.	G	AB	R	H	2B	3B	HR	RBI	Avg.	BB	SO	SB	PO	A	E	Avg.
1978—	Butte (Pioneer)	SS	47	141	34	43	5	2	3	28	.305	17	30	4	37	52	25	.781
1979—	Cent. Ore. (N'west)	SS	•71	299	57	*98	15	5	•10	45	.328	24	59	22	103	*256	31	.921
1980—	Peninsula (Caro.)	SS	•140	*555	105	178	25	6	11	*99	.321	33	66	44	179	*412	42	.934
1981—	Reading (Eastern)	SS	*139	*532	70	160	17	3	8	74	.301	52	60	27	246	437	30	.958
1982—	Okla. City (A.A.)	SS-3B	120	463	80	139	19	5	21	66	.300	39	56	33	211	350	†42	.930
—	Philadelphia (N.L.)	SS-3B	16	29	3	8	1	0	0	3	.276	2	4	0	8	25	0	1.000
1983—	Cleveland (A.L.)■	SS	149	560	68	153	24	8	8	80	.273	27	50	32	247	438	28	.961
1984—	Cleveland (A.L.)	SS-DH	160	*658	82	188	22	5	3	79	.286	43	68	19	280	481	*36	.955
1985—	Cleveland (A.L.)	SS-2B-DH	160	636	97	183	33	4	6	90	.288	54	74	13	252	437	†36	.950
1986—	Cleveland (A.L.)	SS-2B-DH	149	599	80	183	30	5	10	74	.306	32	66	10	248	413	19	.972
1987—	Cleveland (A.L.)	SS-2B-DH	128	495	86	158	24	3	8	52	.319	57	56	32	175	313	18	.964
1988—	Cleveland (A.L.)	2B-DH	152	613	88	186	23	6	10	54	.303	56	72	25	310	434	14	.982
1989—	Texas (A.L.)■	2B-DH	150	548	80	173	31	5	13	92	.316	66	69	21	256	386	13	.980
1990—	Texas (A.L.)	2B-DH	157	582	96	172	27	1	11	69	.296	82	83	31	310	444	•19	.975
1991—	Texas (A.L.)	2B	146	589	108	201	27	3	15	78	*.341	65	78	36	294	372	14	.979
1992—	Texas (A.L.)	DH-2B-OF	35	107	19	25	7	0	2	8	.234	15	17	1	21	17	3	.927
1993—	Texas (A.L.)	DH	144	532	85	154	31	3	14	84	.289	62	95	9	...	...	...	...
1994—	Chicago (A.L.)■	DH-1B	112	433	72	138	19	2	20	98	.319	62	75	8	88	7	3	.969
1995—	Chiba Lot. (Jp. Pc.)■	1B	127	474	60	145	25	3	10	58	.306	...	...	11	...	...	...	...
American League totals (12 years)			1642	6352	961	1914	298	45	120	858	.301	621	803	237	2481	3742	203	.968
National League totals (1 year)			16	29	3	8	1	0	0	3	.276	2	4	0	8	25	0	1.000
Major league totals (13 years)			1658	6381	964	1922	299	45	120	861	.301	623	807	237	2489	3767	203	.969

ALL-STAR GAME RECORD

NOTES: Named Most Valuable Player (1990).

			BATTING										FIELDING			
Year	League	Pos.	AB	R	H	2B	3B	HR	RBI	Avg.	BB	SO	SB	PO	A	E	Avg.
1989—	American	2B	3	0	1	0	0	0	0	.333	0	0	0	1	1	0	1.000
1990—	American	PH-2B	3	0	1	1	0	0	2	.333	0	0	0	1	0	0	1.000
1991—	American							Did not play.									
All-Star Game totals (2 years)			6	0	2	1	0	0	2	.333	0	0	0	2	1	0	1.000

FRANCO, MATT — 1B — CUBS

PERSONAL: Born August 19, 1969, in Santa Monica, Calif. . . . 6-2/210. . . . Bats left, throws right. . . . Full name: Matthew Neil Franco.

HIGH SCHOOL: Westlake (Calif.) Village.

TRANSACTIONS/CAREER NOTES: Selected by Chicago Cubs organization in seventh round of free-agent draft (June 2, 1987). . . . On disabled list (May 6-13, 1994).

STATISTICAL NOTES: Led Midwest League in grounding into double plays with 19 in 1990.

			BATTING												FIELDING			
Year	Team (League)	Pos.	G	AB	R	H	2B	3B	HR	RBI	Avg.	BB	SO	SB	PO	A	E	Avg.
1987—	Wytheville (Appal.)	3B-1B-2B	62	202	25	50	10	1	1	21	.248	26	41	4	95	88	23	.888
1988—	Wytheville (Appal.)	3B-1B	20	79	14	31	9	1	0	16	.392	7	5	0	31	24	6	.902
—	Geneva (NYP)	3B-1B	44	164	19	42	2	0	3	21	.256	19	13	2	190	43	14	.943
1989—	Char., W.Va. (SAL)	3-1-O-S	109	377	42	102	16	1	5	48	.271	57	40	2	113	189	22	.932
—	Peoria (Midwest)	3B	16	58	4	13	4	0	0	9	.224	5	5	0	11	32	6	.878
1990—	Peoria (Midwest)	1B-3B	123	443	52	125	*33	2	6	65	.282	43	39	4	810	75	18	.980
1991—	Winst.-Salem (Car.)	1B-3B-SS	104	307	47	66	12	1	4	41	.215	46	42	4	711	53	11	.986
1992—	Charlotte (South.)	3B-1B-OF	108	343	35	97	18	3	2	31	.283	26	46	3	248	69	13	.961

Year	Team (League)	Pos.	BATTING G	AB	R	H	2B	3B	HR	RBI	Avg.	BB	SO	SB	FIELDING PO	A	E	Avg.
1993—	Orlando (Southern)	1B-3B	68	237	31	75	20	1	7	37	.316	29	30	3	444	40	4	.992
—	Iowa (Am. Assoc.)	1-0-2-P	62	199	24	58	17	4	5	29	.291	16	30	4	450	39	2	.996
1994—	Iowa (Am. Assoc.)	1B-3B-OF	128	437	63	121	32	4	11	71	.277	52	66	3	976	81	7	.993
1995—	Iowa (Am. Assoc.)	3-1-P-C	121	455	51	128	28	5	6	58	.281	37	44	1	283	179	19	.960
—	Chicago (N.L.)	2B-1B-3B	16	17	3	5	1	0	0	1	.294	0	4	0	2	2	0	1.000
Major league totals (1 year)			16	17	3	5	1	0	0	1	.294	0	4	0	2	2	0	1.000

RECORD AS PITCHER

Year	Team (League)	W	L	Pct.	ERA	G	GS	CG	ShO	Sv.	IP	H	R	ER	BB	SO
1993—	Iowa (Am. Assoc.)	0	0	...	36.00	1	0	0	0	0	1	5	4	4	1	1
1995—	Iowa (Am. Assoc.)	0	0	...	0.00	1	0	0	0	0	1	1	0	0	1	1

FRANKLIN, MICAH — OF — TIGERS

PERSONAL: Born April 25, 1972, in San Francisco. . . . 6-0/200. . . . Bats both, throws right. . . . Full name: Micah Ishanti Franklin.
HIGH SCHOOL: Lincoln (San Francisco).
TRANSACTIONS/CAREER NOTES: Selected by New York Mets organization in third round of free-agent draft (June 4, 1990). . . . On Pittsfield suspended list (July 20-24, 1991). . . . Released by Pittsfield, Mets organization (March 11, 1992). . . . Signed by Cincinnati Reds organization (March 27, 1992). . . . Traded by Reds organization to Pittsburgh Pirates organization (October 13, 1994), completing deal in which Pirates traded 1B Brian R. Hunter to Reds for a player to be named later (July 27, 1994). . . . Claimed on waivers by Detroit Tigers (November 20, 1995).
STATISTICAL NOTES: Led Pioneer League with 17 caught stealing and tied for lead with three intentional bases on balls received in 1992.

Year	Team (League)	Pos.	BATTING G	AB	R	H	2B	3B	HR	RBI	Avg.	BB	SO	SB	FIELDING PO	A	E	Avg.
1990—	Kingsport (Appal.)	2B	39	158	29	41	10	3	7	25	.259	8	44	5	72	98	13	.929
1991—	Pittsfield (NYP)	2B	26	94	17	27	4	2	0	14	.287	21	20	12	48	81	14	.902
—	Erie (NYP)	OF-2B	39	153	28	37	4	0	2	8	.242	25	35	4	45	9	6	.900
1992—	Billings (Pioneer)■	OF	*75	251	58	84	13	2	11	60	.335	53	65	18	42	3	2	.957
1993—	Char., W.Va. (SAL)	OF	102	343	56	90	14	4	17	68	.262	47	109	6	134	5	7	.952
—	Winst.-Salem (Car.)	OF	20	69	10	16	1	1	3	6	.232	10	19	0	36	1	1	.974
1994—	Chatt. (South.)	OF	79	279	46	77	17	0	10	40	.276	33	79	2	112	3	6	.950
—	Winst.-Salem (Car.)■	OF	42	150	44	45	7	0	21	44	.300	27	48	7	65	3	4	.944
1995—	Calgary (PCL)■	OF	110	358	64	105	28	0	21	71	.293	47	95	3	162	3	6	.965

FRASCATORE, JOHN — P — CARDINALS

PERSONAL: Born February 4, 1970, in Queens, N.Y. . . . 6-1/200. . . . Throws right, bats right. . . . Full name: John Vincent Frascatore. . . . Name pronounced FRASS-kuh-TOR-ee.
HIGH SCHOOL: Oceanside (N.Y.).
COLLEGE: C.W. Post (N.Y.).
TRANSACTIONS/CAREER NOTES: Selected by St. Louis Cardinals organization in 24th round of free-agent draft (June 3, 1991).

Year	Team (League)	W	L	Pct.	ERA	G	GS	CG	ShO	Sv.	IP	H	R	ER	BB	SO
1991—	Hamilton (NYP)	2	7	.222	9.20	30	1	0	0	1	30 1/3	44	38	31	22	18
1992—	Savannah (S. Atl.)	5	7	.417	3.84	50	0	0	0	23	58 2/3	49	32	25	29	56
1993—	Springfield (Midw.)	7	12	.368	3.78	27	26	2	1	0	157 1/3	157	84	66	33	126
1994—	Arkansas (Texas)	7	3	.700	3.10	12	12	4	1	0	78 1/3	76	37	27	15	63
—	Louisville (A.A.)	8	3	.727	3.39	13	12	2	1	0	85	82	34	32	33	58
—	St. Louis (N.L.)	0	1	.000	16.20	1	1	0	0	0	3 1/3	7	6	6	2	2
1995—	Louisville (A.A.)	2	8	.200	3.95	28	10	1	0	5	82	89	54	36	34	55
—	St. Louis (N.L.)	1	1	.500	4.41	14	4	0	0	0	32 2/3	39	19	16	16	21
Major league totals (2 years)		1	2	.333	5.50	15	5	0	0	0	36	46	25	22	18	23

FRASER, WILLIE — P

PERSONAL: Born May 26, 1964, in New York. . . . 6-1/206. . . . Throws right, bats right. . . . Full name: William Patrick Fraser.
HIGH SCHOOL: Newburgh (N.Y.).
COLLEGE: Concordia College (N.Y.).
TRANSACTIONS/CAREER NOTES: Selected by California Angels organization in first round (15th pick overall) of free-agent draft (June 3, 1985). . . . Traded by Angels organization with OF Devon White and a player to be named later to Toronto Blue Jays for OF Junior Felix, IF Luis Sojo and a player to be named later (December 2, 1990); Blue Jays acquired P Marcus Moore and Angels acquired C Ken Rivers to complete deal (December 4, 1990). . . . Claimed on waivers by St. Louis Cardinals (June 26, 1991). . . . Granted free agency (December 20, 1991). . . . Signed by Angels organization (January 14, 1992). . . . Released by Midland, Angels organization (November 20, 1992). . . . Signed by Toledo, Detroit Tigers organization (February 13, 1993). . . . Released by Toledo (September 6, 1993). . . . Signed by Edmonton, Florida Marlins organization (January 3, 1994). . . . On Edmonton disabled list (April 8-15, 1994). . . . Granted free agency (October 15, 1994). . . . Signed by Ottawa, Montreal Expos organization (January 17, 1995). . . . Granted free agency (October 16, 1995).
STATISTICAL NOTES: Pitched 2-1 one-hit, complete-game victory against Seattle (August 10, 1988). . . . Led A.L. with 33 home runs allowed in 1988.

Year	Team (League)	W	L	Pct.	ERA	G	GS	CG	ShO	Sv.	IP	H	R	ER	BB	SO
1985—	Quad Cities (Midw.)	2	6	.250	5.40	13	13	1	0	0	81 2/3	95	53	49	32	72
1986—	Palm Springs (Cal.)	9	2	.818	3.55	19	19	2	0	0	124 1/3	115	60	49	29	99
—	Edmonton (PCL)	4	1	.800	3.15	6	6	2	2	0	40	25	15	14	8	24
—	California (A.L.)	0	0	...	8.31	1	1	0	0	0	4 1/3	6	4	4	1	2
1987—	California (A.L.)	10	10	.500	3.92	36	23	5	1	1	176 2/3	160	85	77	63	106
1988—	California (A.L.)	12	13	.480	5.41	34	32	2	0	0	194 2/3	203	129	117	80	86
1989—	California (A.L.)	4	7	.364	3.24	44	0	0	0	2	91 2/3	80	33	33	23	46
1990—	California (A.L.)	5	4	.556	3.08	45	0	0	0	2	76	69	29	26	24	32

Year	Team (League)	W	L	Pct.	ERA	G	GS	CG	ShO	Sv.	IP	H	R	ER	BB	SO
	—Edmonton (PCL)	1	0	1.000	3.14	3	3	0	0	0	14 1/3	11	8	5	6	12
1991	—Syracuse (Int'l)■	0	1	.000	3.68	7	0	0	0	1	14 2/3	12	7	6	6	12
	—Toronto (A.L.)	0	2	.000	6.15	13	1	0	0	0	26 1/3	33	20	18	11	12
	—St. Louis (N.L.)■	3	3	.500	4.93	35	0	0	0	0	49 1/3	44	28	27	21	25
1992	—Edmonton (PCL)■	7	6	.538	4.90	44	7	0	0	6	90	110	59	49	24	49
1993	—Toledo (Int'l)■	10	7	.588	4.69	53	1	0	0	8	71	79	44	37	24	63
1994	—Edmonton (PCL)■	1	5	.167	5.00	41	0	0	0	3	54	65	36	30	14	53
	—Florida (N.L.)	2	0	1.000	5.84	9	0	0	0	0	12 1/3	20	9	8	6	7
1995	—Ottawa (Int'l)■	7	6	.538	3.19	19	19	1	1	0	107 1/3	94	44	38	18	84
	—Montreal (N.L.)	2	1	.667	5.61	22	0	0	0	2	25 2/3	25	17	16	9	12
A.L. totals (6 years)		31	36	.463	4.34	173	57	7	1	5	569 2/3	551	300	275	202	284
N.L. totals (3 years)		7	4	.636	5.26	66	0	0	0	2	87 1/3	89	54	51	36	44
Major league totals (8 years)		38	40	.487	4.47	239	57	7	1	7	657	640	354	326	238	328

FRAZIER, LOU — OF — RANGERS

PERSONAL: Born January 26, 1965, in St. Louis. . . . 6-2/175. . . . Bats both, throws right. . . . Full name: Arthur Louis Frazier.
HIGH SCHOOL: Jennings (Mo.).
JUNIOR COLLEGE: Scottsdale (Ariz.) Community College.
TRANSACTIONS/CAREER NOTES: Selected by Detroit Tigers organization in 10th round of free-agent draft (June 3, 1985); did not sign. . . . Selected by Cleveland Indians organization in secondary phase of free-agent draft (January 14, 1986); did not sign. . . . Selected by Houston Astros organization in secondary phase of free-agent draft (June 2, 1986). . . . Traded by Astros organization to Detroit Tigers organization for IF Doug Strange (March 30, 1990). . . . Granted free agency (October 15, 1992). . . . Signed by Montreal Expos organization (December 8, 1992). . . . Traded by Expos to Texas Rangers for a player to be named later (July 30, 1995); Expos acquired P Hector Fajardo to complete deal (August 5, 1995).
STATISTICAL NOTES: Led Eastern League in caught stealing with 23 in 1992.

			BATTING											FIELDING			
Year	Team (League)	Pos.	G	AB	R	H	2B	3B	HR	RBI	Avg.	BB	SO	SB	PO	A	E	Avg.
1986	—GC Astros (GCL)	SS	51	178	39	51	7	2	1	23	.287	32	25	17	81	131	31	.872
1987	—Asheville (S. Atl.)	SS	108	399	83	103	9	2	1	33	.258	68	89	75	172	297	48	.907
1988	—Osceola (Fla. St.)	2-S-O-1	130	468	79	110	11	3	0	34	.235	90	104	*87	220	282	28	.947
1989	—Columbus (South.)	2B-OF	135	460	65	106	10	1	4	31	.230	76	101	43	228	254	15	.970
1990	—London (Eastern)■	O-2-S-3	81	242	29	53	4	1	0	15	.219	27	52	20	123	68	15	.927
1991	—London (Eastern)	OF-2B	122	439	69	105	9	4	3	40	.239	77	87	42	210	36	12	.953
1992	—London (Eastern)	OF-2B	129	477	85	120	16	3	0	34	.252	*95	107	*58	255	12	10	.964
1993	—Montreal (N.L.)■	OF-1B-2B	112	189	27	54	7	1	1	16	.286	16	24	17	98	9	2	.982
1994	—Montreal (N.L.)	OF-2B-1B	76	140	25	38	3	1	0	14	.271	18	23	20	61	4	1	.985
1995	—Montreal (N.L.)	OF-2B	35	63	6	12	2	0	0	3	.190	8	12	4	36	1	1	.974
	—Ottawa (Int'l)	OF	31	110	11	24	3	0	1	10	.218	13	20	10	73	3	2	.974
	—Texas (A.L.)■	OF-DH	49	99	19	21	2	0	0	8	.212	7	20	9	69	2	2	.973
American League totals (1 year)			49	99	19	21	2	0	0	8	.212	7	20	9	69	2	2	.973
National League totals (3 years)			223	392	58	104	12	2	1	33	.265	42	59	41	195	14	4	.981
Major league totals (3 years)			272	491	77	125	14	2	1	41	.255	49	79	50	264	16	6	.979

FREEMAN, MARVIN — P — ROCKIES

PERSONAL: Born April 10, 1963, in Chicago. . . . 6-7/222. . . . Throws right, bats right.
HIGH SCHOOL: Chicago Vocational.
COLLEGE: Jackson State.
TRANSACTIONS/CAREER NOTES: Selected by Montreal Expos organization in ninth round of free-agent draft (June 8, 1981); did not sign. . . . Selected by Philadelphia Phillies organization in second round of free-agent draft (June 4, 1984). . . . On Philadelphia disabled list (April 25, 1989-remainder of season); included rehabilitation assignment to Scranton/Wilkes-Barre (August 24-September 1). . . . Traded by Phillies organization to Richmond, Atlanta Braves organization, for P Joe Boever (July 23, 1990). . . . On disabled list (August 18, 1991-remainder of season and May 26-June 10, 1992). . . . On Atlanta disabled list (June 4-August 7, 1993); included rehabilitation assignment to Richmond (July 31-August 7). . . . Released by Braves (October 25, 1993). . . . Signed by Colorado Rockies (October 29, 1993). . . . On disabled list (August 13-September 1, 1995).
STATISTICAL NOTES: Pitched 6-0 no-hit victory for Maine against Richmond (July 28, 1988, second game).

Year	Team (League)	W	L	Pct.	ERA	G	GS	CG	ShO	Sv.	IP	H	R	ER	BB	SO
1984	—Bend (Northwest)	8	5	.615	2.61	15	•15	2	1	0	89 2/3	64	41	26	52	79
1985	—Clearwater (Fla. St.)	6	5	.545	3.06	14	13	3	3	0	88 1/3	72	32	30	36	55
	—Reading (Eastern)	1	7	.125	5.37	11	11	2	0	0	65 1/3	51	41	39	52	35
1986	—Reading (Eastern)	13	6	.684	4.03	27	•27	4	2	0	163	130	89	73	*111	113
	—Philadelphia (N.L.)	2	0	1.000	2.25	3	3	0	0	0	16	6	4	4	10	8
1987	—Maine (Int'l)	0	7	.000	6.26	10	10	2	0	0	46	56	38	32	30	29
	—Reading (Eastern)	3	3	.500	5.07	9	9	0	0	0	49 2/3	45	30	28	32	40
1988	—Maine (Int'l)	5	5	.500	4.62	18	14	2	1	0	74	62	43	38	46	37
	—Philadelphia (N.L.)	2	3	.400	6.10	11	11	0	0	0	51 2/3	55	36	35	43	37
1989	—Scran./W.B. (Int'l)	1	1	.500	4.50	5	5	0	0	0	14	11	8	7	5	8
	—Philadelphia (N.L.)	0	0	. . .	6.00	1	1	0	0	0	3	2	2	2	5	0
1990	—Scran./W.B. (Int'l)	2	4	.333	5.09	7	7	0	0	0	35 1/3	39	23	20	19	33
	—Philadelphia (N.L.)	0	2	.000	5.57	16	3	0	0	1	32 1/3	34	21	20	14	26
	—Richmond (Int'l)■	2	3	.400	4.62	7	7	1	1	0	39	33	20	20	22	23
	—Atlanta (N.L.)	1	0	1.000	1.72	9	0	0	0	0	15 2/3	7	3	3	3	12
1991	—Atlanta (N.L.)	1	0	1.000	3.00	34	0	0	0	1	48	37	19	16	13	34
1992	—Atlanta (N.L.)	7	5	.583	3.22	58	0	0	0	3	64 1/3	61	26	23	29	41
1993	—Atlanta (N.L.)	2	0	1.000	6.08	21	0	0	0	0	23 2/3	24	16	16	10	25
	—Richmond (Int'l)	0	0	. . .	2.25	2	2	0	0	0	4	4	1	1	1	5
1994	—Colorado (N.L.)■	10	2	*.833	2.80	19	18	0	0	0	112 2/3	113	39	35	23	67

Year	Team (League)	W	L	Pct.	ERA	G	GS	CG	ShO	Sv.	IP	H	R	ER	BB	SO
1995—	Colorado (N.L.)	3	7	.300	5.89	22	18	0	0	0	94 2/3	122	64	62	41	61
Major league totals (9 years)		28	19	.596	4.21	194	54	0	0	5	462	461	230	216	191	311

CHAMPIONSHIP SERIES RECORD

Year	Team (League)	W	L	Pct.	ERA	G	GS	CG	ShO	Sv.	IP	H	R	ER	BB	SO
1992—	Atlanta (N.L.)	0	0	...	14.73	3	0	0	0	0	3 2/3	8	6	6	2	1

WORLD SERIES RECORD

Year	Team (League)	W	L	Pct.	ERA	G	GS	CG	ShO	Sv.	IP	H	R	ER	BB	SO
1992—	Atlanta (N.L.)							Did not play.								

FREY, STEVE P

PERSONAL: Born July 29, 1963, in Southampton, Pa. . . . 5-9/170. . . . Throws left, bats right. . . . Full name: Steven Francis Frey. . . . Name pronounced FRY.

HIGH SCHOOL: William Tennent (Warminster, Pa.).

JUNIOR COLLEGE: Bucks County (Pa.) Community College.

TRANSACTIONS/CAREER NOTES: Selected by New York Yankees organization in 15th round of free-agent draft (June 6, 1983). . . . Traded by Yankees organization with OF Darren Reed and C Phil Lombardi to New York Mets for SS Rafael Santana and P Victor Garcia (December 11, 1987). . . . Traded by Mets organization to Indianapolis, Montreal Expos organization, for C Mark Bailey and 3B Tom O'Malley (March 28, 1989). . . . On Montreal disabled list (May 25-June 15, 1990); included rehabilitation assignment to Indianapolis (June 11-15). . . . Contract sold by Expos organization to California Angels organization (March 29, 1992). . . . On disabled list (August 19-September 4, 1992). . . . Granted free agency (December 20, 1993). . . . Signed by San Francisco Giants (January 5, 1994). . . . Traded by Giants to Seattle Mariners for future considerations (May 21, 1995). . . . On Seattle disabled list (June 12-July 2, 1995). . . . Released by Mariners (July 29, 1995). . . . Signed by Philadelphia Phillies (August 16, 1995). . . . Granted free agency (October 13, 1995).

Year	Team (League)	W	L	Pct.	ERA	G	GS	CG	ShO	Sv.	IP	H	R	ER	BB	SO
1983—	Oneonta (NYP)	4	6	.400	2.74	28	0	0	0	9	72 1/3	47	27	22	35	86
1984—	Fort Lauder. (FSL)	4	2	.667	2.09	47	0	0	0	4	64 2/3	46	26	15	34	66
1985—	Fort Lauder. (FSL)	1	1	.500	1.21	19	0	0	0	7	22 1/3	11	4	3	12	15
—	Alb./Colon. (East.)	4	7	.364	3.82	40	0	0	0	3	61 1/3	53	30	26	25	54
1986—	Alb./Colon. (East.)	3	4	.429	2.10	40	0	0	0	4	73	50	25	17	18	62
—	Columbus (Int'l)	0	2	.000	8.05	11	0	0	0	0	19	29	17	17	10	11
1987—	Alb./Colon. (East.)	0	2	.000	1.93	14	0	0	0	1	28	20	6	6	7	19
—	Columbus (Int'l)	2	1	.667	3.04	23	0	0	0	6	47 1/3	45	19	16	10	35
1988—	Tidewater (Int'l)■	6	3	.667	3.13	58	1	0	0	6	54 2/3	38	23	19	25	58
1989—	Indianapolis (A.A.)■	2	1	.667	1.78	21	0	0	0	3	25 1/3	18	7	5	6	23
—	Montreal (N.L.)	3	2	.600	5.48	20	0	0	0	0	21 1/3	29	15	13	11	15
1990—	Montreal (N.L.)	8	2	.800	2.10	51	0	0	0	9	55 2/3	44	15	13	29	29
—	Indianapolis (A.A.)	0	0	...	0.00	2	0	0	0	1	3	0	0	0	1	3
1991—	Montreal (N.L.)	0	1	.000	4.99	31	0	0	0	1	39 2/3	43	31	22	23	21
—	Indianapolis (A.A.)	3	1	.750	1.51	30	0	0	0	3	35 2/3	25	6	6	15	45
1992—	California (A.L.)■	4	2	.667	3.57	51	0	0	0	4	45 1/3	39	18	18	22	24
1993—	California (A.L.)	2	3	.400	2.98	55	0	0	0	13	48 1/3	41	20	16	26	22
1994—	San Francisco (N.L.)■	1	0	1.000	4.94	44	0	0	0	0	31	37	17	17	15	20
1995—	San Francisco (N.L.)	0	1	.000	4.26	9	0	0	0	0	6 1/3	7	6	3	2	5
—	Seattle (A.L.)■	0	3	.000	4.76	13	0	0	0	0	11 1/3	16	7	6	6	7
—	Scran./W.B. (Int'l)■	0	0	...	1.80	4	0	0	0	0	5	3	1	1	2	3
—	Philadelphia (N.L.)	0	0	...	0.84	9	0	0	0	1	10 2/3	3	1	1	2	2
A.L. totals (3 years)		6	8	.429	3.43	119	0	0	0	17	105	96	45	40	54	53
N.L. totals (5 years)		12	6	.667	3.77	164	0	0	0	11	164 2/3	163	85	69	82	92
Major league totals (7 years)		18	14	.563	3.64	283	0	0	0	28	269 2/3	259	130	109	136	145

FRYE, JEFF 2B

PERSONAL: Born August 31, 1966, in Oakland, Calif. . . . 5-9/165. . . . Bats right, throws right. . . . Full name: Jeffrey Dustin Frye.

HIGH SCHOOL: Panama (Okla.).

COLLEGE: Southeastern Oklahoma.

TRANSACTIONS/CAREER NOTES: Selected by Texas Rangers organization in 30th round of free-agent draft (June 1, 1988). . . . On Texas disabled list (March 27, 1993-entire season; June 9-24, 1994; and June 3-18 and June 21-July 6, 1995). . . . Granted free agency (December 21, 1995).

STATISTICAL NOTES: Led Pioneer League second basemen with 44 double plays in 1988. . . . Tied for American Association lead in being hit by pitch with 11 in 1992.

			BATTING												FIELDING			
Year	Team (League)	Pos.	G	AB	R	H	2B	3B	HR	RBI	Avg.	BB	SO	SB	PO	A	E	Avg.
1988—	Butte (Pioneer)	2B	54	185	47	53	7	1	0	14	.286	35	25	16	96	149	7	.972
1989—	Gastonia (S. Atl.)	2B	125	464	85	145	26	3	1	40	*.313	72	53	33	242	340	14	*.977
1990—	Charlotte (Fla. St.)	2B	131	503	77	137	16	7	0	50	.272	80	66	29	252	350	13	*.979
1991—	Tulsa (Texas)	2B	131	503	92	152	32	11	4	41	.302	71	60	15	262	322	*26	.957
1992—	Okla. City (A.A.)	2B	87	337	64	101	26	2	2	28	.300	51	39	11	212	248	7	.985
—	Texas (A.L.)	2B	67	199	24	51	9	1	1	12	.256	16	27	1	120	196	7	.978
1993—									Did not play.									
1994—	Okla. City (A.A.)	2B	17	68	7	19	3	0	1	5	.279	6	7	2	28	44	1	.986
—	Texas (A.L.)	2B-DH-3B	57	205	37	67	20	3	0	18	.327	29	23	6	90	136	4	.983
1995—	Texas (A.L.)	2B	90	313	38	87	15	2	4	29	.278	24	45	3	173	248	11	.975
Major league totals (3 years)			214	717	99	205	44	6	5	59	.286	69	95	10	383	580	22	.978

F

FRYMAN, TRAVIS — 3B — TIGERS

PERSONAL: Born March 25, 1969, in Lexington, Ky. . . . 6-1/194. . . . Bats right, throws right. . . . Full name: David Travis Fryman.
HIGH SCHOOL: Tates Creek (Lexington, Ky.).
TRANSACTIONS/CAREER NOTES: Selected by Detroit Tigers organization in supplemental round ("sandwich pick" between first and second round, 30th pick overall) of free-agent draft (June 2, 1987); pick received as compensation for Philadelphia Phillies signing Type A free-agent C Lance Parrish.
HONORS: Named shortstop on THE SPORTING NEWS A.L. All-Star team (1992). . . . Named shortstop on THE SPORTING NEWS A.L. Silver Slugger team (1992). . . . Named third baseman on THE SPORTING NEWS A.L. All-Star team (1993).
STATISTICAL NOTES: Led Appalachian League shortstops with 313 total chances in 1987. . . . Hit for the cycle (July 28, 1993). . . . Tied for A.L. lead with 13 sacrifice flies in 1994. . . . Led A.L. third basemen with 313 total chances in 1994 and 337 in 1995. . . . Led A.L. third basemen with 38 double plays in 1995. . . . Career major league grand slams: 3.

			BATTING											FIELDING			
Year Team (League)	Pos.	G	AB	R	H	2B	3B	HR	RBI	Avg.	BB	SO	SB	PO	A	E	Avg.
1987—Bristol (Appal.)	SS	67	248	25	58	9	0	2	20	.234	22	39	6	*103	187	•23	.927
1988—Fayetteville (SAL)	SS-2B	123	411	44	96	17	4	0	47	.234	24	83	16	174	390	32	.946
1989—London (Eastern)	SS	118	426	52	113	*30	1	9	56	.265	19	78	5	192	346	*27	.952
1990—Toledo (Int'l)	SS	87	327	38	84	22	2	10	53	.257	17	59	4	128	277	26	.940
—Detroit (A.L.)	3B-SS-DH	66	232	32	69	11	1	9	27	.297	17	51	3	47	145	14	.932
1991—Detroit (A.L.)	3B-SS	149	557	65	144	36	3	21	91	.259	40	149	12	153	354	23	.957
1992—Detroit (A.L.)	SS-3B	161	*659	87	175	31	4	20	96	.266	45	144	8	220	489	22	.970
1993—Detroit (A.L.)	SS-3B-DH	151	607	98	182	37	5	22	97	.300	77	128	9	169	382	23	.960
1994—Detroit (A.L.)	3B	114	*464	66	122	34	5	18	85	.263	45	*128	2	78	*221	14	.955
1995—Detroit (A.L.)	3B	144	567	79	156	21	5	15	81	.275	63	100	4	107	*337	14	.969
Major league totals (6 years)		785	3086	427	848	170	23	105	477	.275	287	700	38	774	1928	110	.961

ALL-STAR GAME RECORD

		BATTING											FIELDING			
Year League	Pos.	AB	R	H	2B	3B	HR	RBI	Avg.	BB	SO	SB	PO	A	E	Avg.
1992—American	SS	1	1	1	0	0	0	1	1.000	1	0	0	0	3	0	1.000
1993—American	SS	1	0	0	0	0	0	0	.000	0	0	0	1	1	0	1.000
1994—American	PH	1	0	0	0	0	0	0	.000	0	0	0	...	...	...	...
All-Star Game totals (3 years)		3	1	1	0	0	0	1	.333	1	0	0	1	4	0	1.000

GAETTI, GARY — 3B — CARDINALS

PERSONAL: Born August 19, 1958, in Centralia, Ill. . . . 6-0/200. . . . Bats right, throws right. . . . Full name: Gary Joseph Gaetti. . . . Name pronounced guy-ETT-ee.
HIGH SCHOOL: Centralia (Ill.).
JUNIOR COLLEGE: Lake Land College (Ill.).
COLLEGE: Northwest Missouri State.
TRANSACTIONS/CAREER NOTES: Selected by St. Louis Cardinals organization in fourth round of free-agent draft (January 10, 1978); did not sign. . . . Selected by Chicago White Sox organization in secondary phase of free-agent draft (June 6, 1978); did not sign. . . . Selected by Minnesota Twins organization in secondary phase of free-agent draft (June 5, 1979). . . . Granted free agency (November 9, 1987). . . . Re-signed by Twins (January 7, 1988). . . . On disabled list (August 21-September 5, 1988 and August 26-September 13, 1989). . . . Granted free agency (December 7, 1990). . . . Signed by California Angels (January 23, 1991). . . . Released by Angels (June 3, 1993). . . . Signed by Kansas City Royals (June 19, 1993). . . . Granted free agency (October 25, 1993). . . . Re-signed by Royals organization (December 16, 1993). . . . On disabled list (July 5-20, 1994). . . . Granted free agency (October 28, 1994). . . . Re-signed by Omaha, Royals organization (December 20, 1994). . . . Granted free agency (November 3, 1995). . . . Signed by Cardinals (December 18, 1995).
RECORDS: Shares major league rookie-season record for most sacrifice flies—13 (1982).
HONORS: Won A.L. Gold Glove at third base (1986-89). . . . Named third baseman on THE SPORTING NEWS A.L. Silver Slugger team (1995).
STATISTICAL NOTES: Tied for Appalachian League lead in errors by third baseman with 18 in 1979. . . . Led Midwest League third basemen with 492 total chances and 35 double plays in 1980. . . . Led Southern League third basemen with 122 putouts, 281 assists, 32 errors and 435 total chances in 1981. . . . Hit home run in first major league at-bat (September 20, 1981). . . .Led A.L. with 13 sacrifice flies in 1982. . . . Led A.L. third basemen with 131 putouts in 1983, 142 in 1984 and 146 in 1985. . . . Led A.L. third basemen with 46 double plays in 1983, 36 in both 1986 and 1990 and 39 in 1991. . . . Led A.L. third basemen with 496 total chances in 1984, 473 in 1986, 438 in 1990 and 481 in 1991. . . . Led A.L. third basemen with 334 assists in both 1984 and 1986 and 318 in 1990. . . . Tied for A.L. lead in errors by third baseman with 20 in 1984. . . . Led A.L. in grounding into double plays with 25 in 1987. . . . Led A.L. third basemen with .982 fielding percentage in 1994. . . . Career major league grand slams: 8.

			BATTING											FIELDING			
Year Team (League)	Pos.	G	AB	R	H	2B	3B	HR	RBI	Avg.	BB	SO	SB	PO	A	E	Avg.
1979—Elizabeth. (Appal.)	3B-SS	66	230	50	59	15	2	14	42	.257	43	40	6	70	134	‡21	.907
1980—Wis. Rap. (Midw.)	3B	138	503	77	134	27	3	*22	82	.266	67	120	24	*94	*363	•35	.929
1981—Orlando (Southern)	3B-1B	137	495	92	137	19	2	30	93	.277	58	105	15	†143	†283	†32	.930
—Minnesota (A.L.)	3B-DH	9	26	4	5	0	0	2	3	.192	0	6	0	5	17	0	1.000
1982—Minnesota (A.L.)	3B-SS-DH	145	508	59	117	25	4	25	84	.230	37	107	0	106	291	17	.959
1983—Minnesota (A.L.)	3B-SS-DH	157	584	81	143	30	3	21	78	.245	54	121	7	†131	361	17	.967
1984—Minnesota (A.L.)	3B-OF-SS	•162	588	55	154	29	4	5	65	.262	44	81	11	†163	†335	‡21	.960
1985—Minnesota (A.L.)	3-O-1-DH	160	560	71	138	31	0	20	63	.246	37	89	13	†162	316	18	.964
1986—Minnesota (A.L.)	3-S-O-2	157	596	91	171	34	1	34	108	.287	52	108	14	120	†335	21	.956
1987—Minnesota (A.L.)	3B-DH	154	584	95	150	36	2	31	109	.257	37	92	10	•134	261	11	.973
1988—Minnesota (A.L.)	3B-DH-SS	133	468	66	141	29	2	28	88	.301	36	85	7	105	191	7	.977
1989—Minnesota (A.L.)	3B-DH-1B	130	498	63	125	11	4	19	75	.251	25	87	6	115	253	10	.974
1990—Minnesota (A.L.)	3B-SS	154	577	61	132	27	5	16	85	.229	36	101	6	125	†319	18	.961
1991—California (A.L.)■	3B	152	586	58	144	22	1	18	66	.246	33	104	5	111	*353	17	.965
1992—California (A.L.)	3B-1B-DH	130	456	41	103	13	2	12	48	.226	21	79	3	423	196	22	.966
1993—California (A.L.)	3B-1B-DH	20	50	3	9	2	0	0	4	.180	5	12	1	38	7	1	.978
—Kansas City (A.L.)■	3B-1B-DH	82	281	37	72	18	1	14	46	.256	16	75	0	147	146	6	.980
1994—Kansas City (A.L.)	3B-1B	90	327	53	94	15	3	12	57	.287	19	63	0	99	166	4	†.985

Year	Team (League)	Pos.	G	AB	R	H	2B	3B	HR	RBI	Avg.	BB	SO	SB	PO	A	E	Avg.
			BATTING												FIELDING			
1995—	Kansas City (A.L.)	3B-1B-DH	137	514	76	134	27	0	35	96	.261	47	91	3	182	228	16	.962
Major league totals (15 years)			1972	7203	914	1832	349	32	292	1075	.254	499	1301	86	2166	3775	206	.966

CHAMPIONSHIP SERIES RECORD

NOTES: Named A.L. Championship Series Most Valuable Player (1987). . . . Hit home run in first at-bat (October 7, 1987).

Year	Team (League)	Pos.	G	AB	R	H	2B	3B	HR	RBI	Avg.	BB	SO	SB	PO	A	E	Avg.
			BATTING												FIELDING			
1987—	Minnesota (A.L.)	3B	5	20	5	6	1	0	2	5	.300	1	3	0	8	7	0	1.000

WORLD SERIES RECORD

NOTES: Shares records for most at-bats—2; and most hits—2, in one inning (October 17, 1987, fourth inning). . . . Member of World Series championship team (1987).

Year	Team (League)	Pos.	G	AB	R	H	2B	3B	HR	RBI	Avg.	BB	SO	SB	PO	A	E	Avg.
			BATTING												FIELDING			
1987—	Minnesota (A.L.)	3B	7	27	4	7	2	1	1	4	.259	2	5	2	6	15	0	1.000

ALL-STAR GAME RECORD

Year	League	Pos.	AB	R	H	2B	3B	HR	RBI	Avg.	BB	SO	SB	PO	A	E	Avg.
			BATTING											FIELDING			
1988—	American....................	PH	1	0	0	0	0	0	0	.000	0	0	0	...	...	...	...
1989—	American....................	3B	1	0	0	0	0	0	0	.000	0	1	0	1	0	0	1.000
All-Star Game totals (2 years)			2	0	0	0	0	0	0	.000	0	1	0	1	0	0	1.000

GAGNE, GREG — SS — DODGERS

PERSONAL: Born November 12, 1961, in Fall River, Mass. . . . 5-11/180. . . . Bats right, throws right. . . . Full name: Gregory Carpenter Gagne. . . . Name pronounced GAG-nee.

HIGH SCHOOL: Somerset (Mass.).

TRANSACTIONS/CAREER NOTES: Selected by New York Yankees organization in fifth round of free-agent draft (June 5, 1979). . . . On disabled list (September 4-22, 1980). . . . Traded by Yankees organization with P Ron Davis, P Paul Boris and cash to Minnesota Twins for SS Roy Smalley (April 10, 1982). . . . On Toledo disabled list (June 13-July 18, 1984). . . . On disabled list (August 10-September 1, 1985). . . . Granted free agency (October 27, 1992). . . . Signed by Kansas City Royals (December 8, 1992). . . . On disabled list (June 22-July 13, 1995). . . . Granted free agency (November 7, 1995). . . . Signed by Los Angeles Dodgers (November 30, 1995).

RECORDS: Shares major league single-game record for most inside-the-park home runs—2 (October 4, 1986).

STATISTICAL NOTES: Led International League shortstops with 599 total chances in 1983. . . . Led A.L. shortstops with 26 errors in 1986. . . . Led A.L. in caught stealing with 17 in 1994. . . . Career major league grand slams: 2.

Year	Team (League)	Pos.	G	AB	R	H	2B	3B	HR	RBI	Avg.	BB	SO	SB	PO	A	E	Avg.
			BATTING												FIELDING			
1979—	Paintsville (Appal.)	SS	41	106	10	19	2	3	0	7	.179	13	25	2	28	62	14	.865
1980—	Greensboro (S. Atl.) ...	SS-3B-2B	98	337	39	91	20	5	3	32	.270	22	46	8	133	233	35	.913
1981—	Greensboro (S. Atl.) ...	2B-SS-3B	104	364	71	108	21	3	9	48	.297	49	72	14	172	280	25	.948
1982—	Fort Lauder. (FSL)	SS	1	3	0	1	0	0	0	0	.333	1	1	0	3	5	0	1.000
—	Orlando (Southern)■.	SS-2B	136	504	73	117	23	5	11	57	.232	57	100	8	185	403	39	.938
1983—	Toledo (Int'l)..............	SS	119	392	61	100	22	4	17	66	.255	36	70	6	201	*364	*34	.943
—	Minnesota (A.L.)	SS	10	27	2	3	1	0	0	3	.111	0	6	0	10	14	2	.923
1984—	Toledo (Int'l)..............	3B-SS-2B	70	236	31	66	7	2	9	27	.280	34	52	2	58	168	20	.919
—	Minnesota (A.L.)	PR-PH	2	1	0	0	0	0	0	0	.000	0	0	0	...	...	...	...
1985—	Minnesota (A.L.)	SS-DH	114	293	37	66	15	3	2	23	.225	20	57	10	149	269	14	.968
1986—	Minnesota (A.L.)	SS-2B	156	472	63	118	22	6	12	54	.250	30	108	12	228	381	†26	.959
1987—	Minnesota (A.L.)	S-O-2-DH	137	437	68	116	28	7	10	40	.265	25	84	6	196	391	18	.970
1988—	Minnesota (A.L.)	S-O-2-3	149	461	70	109	20	6	14	48	.236	27	110	15	202	373	18	.970
1989—	Minnesota (A.L.)	SS-OF	149	460	69	125	29	7	9	48	.272	17	80	11	218	389	18	.971
1990—	Minnesota (A.L.)	SS-OF	138	388	38	91	22	3	7	38	.235	24	76	8	184	377	14	.976
1991—	Minnesota (A.L.)	SS-3B-DH	139	408	52	108	23	3	8	42	.265	26	72	11	181	377	9	.984
1992—	Minnesota (A.L.)	SS	146	439	53	108	23	0	7	39	.246	19	83	6	208	438	18	.973
1993—	Kansas City (A.L.)■ ...	SS	159	540	66	151	32	3	10	57	.280	33	93	10	266	451	10	*.986
1994—	Kansas City (A.L.)	SS	107	375	39	97	23	3	7	51	.259	27	79	10	*189	323	12	.977
1995—	Kansas City (A.L.)	SS-DH	120	430	58	110	25	4	6	49	.256	38	60	3	174	389	•18	.969
Major league totals (13 years)			1526	4731	615	1202	263	45	92	492	.254	286	908	102	2205	4172	177	.973

CHAMPIONSHIP SERIES RECORD

Year	Team (League)	Pos.	G	AB	R	H	2B	3B	HR	RBI	Avg.	BB	SO	SB	PO	A	E	Avg.
			BATTING												FIELDING			
1987—	Minnesota (A.L.)	SS	5	18	5	5	3	0	2	3	.278	3	4	0	9	13	2	.917
1991—	Minnesota (A.L.)	SS	5	17	1	4	0	0	0	1	.235	1	5	0	9	9	2	.900
Championship series totals (2 years)			10	35	6	9	3	0	2	4	.257	4	9	0	18	22	4	.909

WORLD SERIES RECORD

NOTES: Shares record for most at-bats in one inning—2 (October 18, 1987, fourth inning). . . . Member of World Series championship teams (1987 and 1991).

Year	Team (League)	Pos.	G	AB	R	H	2B	3B	HR	RBI	Avg.	BB	SO	SB	PO	A	E	Avg.
			BATTING												FIELDING			
1987—	Minnesota (A.L.)	SS	7	30	5	6	1	0	1	3	.200	1	6	0	6	20	2	.929
1991—	Minnesota (A.L.)	SS	7	24	1	4	1	0	1	3	.167	0	7	0	13	24	0	1.000
World Series totals (2 years)			14	54	6	10	2	0	2	6	.185	1	13	0	19	44	2	.969

GALARRAGA, ANDRES — 1B — ROCKIES

PERSONAL: Born June 18, 1961, in Caracas, Venezuela. . . . 6-3/235. . . . Bats right, throws right. . . . Full name: Andres Jose Galarraga. . . . Name pronounced GAHL-ah-RAH-guh.

HIGH SCHOOL: Enrique Felmi (Caracas, Venezuela).

TRANSACTIONS/CAREER NOTES: Signed as non-drafted free agent by Montreal Expos organization (January 19, 1979). . . . On disabled list (July 10-August 19 and August 20-September 4, 1986; and May 26-July 4, 1991). . . . Traded by Expos to St. Louis Cardinals for P Ken Hill (November 25, 1991). . . . On St. Louis disabled list (April 8-May 22, 1992); included rehabilitation assignment to Louisville (May 13-22). . . . Granted free agency (October 27, 1992). . . . Signed by Colorado Rockies (November 16, 1992). . . . On disabled list (May 10-27 and July 25-August 21, 1993). . . . Granted free agency (October 25, 1993). . . . Re-signed by Rockies (December 6, 1993). . . . On disabled list (July 29, 1994-remainder of season).

HONORS: Named Southern League Most Valuable Player (1984). . . . Named first baseman on The Sporting News N.L. Silver Slugger team (1988). . . . Won N.L. Gold Glove at first base (1989-90). . . . Named N.L. Comeback Player of the Year by The Sporting News (1993).

STATISTICAL NOTES: Led Southern League with 271 total bases, .508 slugging percentage and 10 intentional bases on balls received and tied for lead in being hit by pitch with nine in 1984. . . . Led Southern League first basemen with 1,428 total chances and 130 double plays in 1984. . . . Led N.L. in being hit by pitch with 10 in 1987 and tied for lead with 13 in 1989. . . . Led N.L. with 329 total bases in 1988. . . . Hit three home runs in one game (June 25, 1995). . . . Collected six hits in one game (July 3, 1995). . . . Led N.L. first basemen with 1,432 total chances and 129 double plays in 1995. . . . Career major league grand slams: 7.

			BATTING												FIELDING			
Year	Team (League)	Pos.	G	AB	R	H	2B	3B	HR	RBI	Avg.	BB	SO	SB	PO	A	E	Avg.
1979	W.P. Beach (FSL)	1B	7	23	3	3	0	0	0	1	.130	2	11	0	2	1	0	1.000
	Calgary (Pioneer)	1B-3B-C	42	112	14	24	3	1	4	16	.214	9	42	1	187	21	5	.977
1980	Calgary (Pioneer)	1-3-C-O	59	190	27	50	11	4	4	22	.263	7	55	3	287	52	21	.942
1981	Jamestown (NYP)	C-1-0-3	47	154	24	40	5	4	6	26	.260	15	44	0	154	15	0	1.000
1982	W.P. Beach (FSL)	1B-OF	105	338	39	95	20	2	14	51	.281	34	77	2	462	36	9	.982
1983	W.P. Beach (FSL)	1B-OF-3B	104	401	55	116	18	3	10	66	.289	33	68	7	861	77	13	.986
1984	Jacksonv. (South.)	1B	143	533	81	154	28	4	27	87	.289	59	122	2	*1302	*110	16	.989
1985	Indianapolis (A.A.)	1B-OF	121	439	*75	118	15	8	25	87	.269	45	103	3	930	63	14	.986
	Montreal (N.L.)	1B	24	75	9	14	1	0	2	4	.187	3	18	1	173	22	1	.995
1986	Montreal (N.L.)	1B	105	321	39	87	13	0	10	42	.271	30	79	6	805	40	4	.995
1987	Montreal (N.L.)	1B	147	551	72	168	40	3	13	90	.305	41	127	7	*1300	103	10	.993
1988	Montreal (N.L.)	1B	157	609	99	*184	*42	8	29	92	.302	39	*153	13	1464	103	15	.991
1989	Montreal (N.L.)	1B	152	572	76	147	30	1	23	85	.257	48	*158	12	1335	91	11	.992
1990	Montreal (N.L.)	1B	155	579	65	148	29	0	20	87	.256	40	*169	10	1300	94	10	.993
1991	Montreal (N.L.)	1B	107	375	34	82	13	2	9	33	.219	23	86	5	887	80	9	.991
1992	St. Louis (N.L.)■	1B	95	325	38	79	14	2	10	39	.243	11	69	5	777	62	8	.991
	Louisville (A.A.)	1B	11	34	3	6	0	1	2	3	.176	0	8	1	61	7	2	.971
1993	Colorado (N.L.)■	1B	120	470	71	174	35	4	22	98	*.370	24	73	2	1018	103	11	.990
1994	Colorado (N.L.)	1B	103	417	77	133	21	0	31	85	.319	19	93	8	953	65	8	.992
1995	Colorado (N.L.)	1B	143	554	89	155	29	3	31	106	.280	32	*146	12	*1299	120	*13	.991
Major league totals (11 years)			1308	4848	669	1371	267	23	200	761	.283	310	1171	81	11311	883	100	.992

DIVISION SERIES RECORD

			BATTING												FIELDING			
Year	Team (League)	Pos.	G	AB	R	H	2B	3B	HR	RBI	Avg.	BB	SO	SB	PO	A	E	Avg.
1995	Colorado (N.L.)	1B	4	18	1	5	1	0	0	2	.278	0	6	0	41	2	0	1.000

ALL-STAR GAME RECORD

			BATTING											FIELDING			
Year	League	Pos.	AB	R	H	2B	3B	HR	RBI	Avg.	BB	SO	SB	PO	A	E	Avg.
1988	National	1B	2	0	0	0	0	0	0	.000	0	1	0	6	0	0	1.000
1993	National	1B	1	0	0	0	0	0	0	.000	0	0	0	0	0	0	...
All-Star Game totals (2 years)			3	0	0	0	0	0	0	.000	0	1	0	6	0	0	1.000

GALLAGHER, DAVE — OF

PERSONAL: Born September 20, 1960, in Trenton, N.J. . . . 6-0/185. . . . Bats right, throws right. . . . Full name: David Thomas Gallagher.

HIGH SCHOOL: Steinert (Trenton, N.J.).

JUNIOR COLLEGE: Mercer County (N.J.) Community College.

TRANSACTIONS/CAREER NOTES: Selected by Oakland Athletics organization in first round (third pick overall) of free-agent draft (January 8, 1980); did not sign. . . . Selected by Cleveland Indians organization in secondary phase of free-agent draft (June 3, 1980). . . . On disabled list (May 2-June 6, 1983). . . . Traded by Indians organization to Seattle Mariners organization for P Mark Huismann (May 12, 1987). . . . Released by Mariners organization (September 30, 1987). . . . Signed by Vancouver, Chicago White Sox organization (December 7, 1987). . . . On Chicago disabled list (April 29-May 28, 1990). . . . Claimed on waivers by Baltimore Orioles (August 1, 1990). . . . Traded by Orioles to California Angels for P David Martinez and P Mike Hook (December 4, 1990). . . . Traded by Angels to New York Mets for OF Hubie Brooks (December 10, 1991). . . . On New York disabled list (April 25-June 8, 1992); included rehabilitation assignment to Tidewater (June 5-8). . . . Granted free agency (December 19, 1992). . . . Re-signed by Mets (January 21, 1993). . . . Traded by Mets to Atlanta Braves for P Pete Smith (November 24, 1993). . . . Granted free agency (October 17, 1994). . . . Signed by Scranton/Wilkes-Barre, Philadelphia Phillies organization (April 10, 1995). . . . Traded by Phillies to California Angels for 2B Kevin Flora and a player to be named later (August 9, 1995); Phillies acquired P Russ Springer to complete deal (August 15, 1995). . . . On California disabled list (August 22-September 11, 1995). . . . Granted free agency (November 6, 1995).

STATISTICAL NOTES: Led Midwest League with 21 sacrifice hits in 1982. . . . Tied for Eastern League lead in double plays by outfielder with four in 1983. . . . Led International League outfielders with 369 total chances in 1985. . . . Led International League with 12 sacrifice hits in 1986. . . . Career major league grand slams: 1.

			BATTING												FIELDING			
Year	Team (League)	Pos.	G	AB	R	H	2B	3B	HR	RBI	Avg.	BB	SO	SB	PO	A	E	Avg.
1980	Batavia (NYP)	OF	69	241	33	66	6	3	5	36	.274	29	16	11	114	4	2	.983
1981	Waterloo (Midw.)	OF-3B	127	435	55	102	22	1	3	34	.234	38	67	12	224	22	7	.972
1982	Chatt. (South.)	OF	15	54	10	12	2	1	0	4	.222	5	8	2	32	1	0	1.000

Year	Team (League)	Pos.	G	AB	R	H	2B	3B	HR	RBI	Avg.	BB	SO	SB	PO	A	E	Avg.
				BATTING											FIELDING			
	—Waterloo (Midw.)	OF	110	409	61	118	25	7	6	47	.289	41	57	19	232	15	4	*.984
1983—	Buffalo (Eastern)	OF-3B	107	376	64	127	21	3	2	47	*.338	83	21	12	223	13	5	.979
1984—	Maine (Int'l)	OF	116	380	49	94	19	5	6	49	.247	49	42	4	208	7	3	.986
1985—	Maine (Int'l)	OF	132	488	71	118	22	3	9	55	.242	65	38	16	*357	9	3	*.992
1986—	Maine (Int'l)	OF	132	497	59	145	23	5	8	44	.292	41	41	19	341	*14	1	*.997
1987—	Cleveland (A.L.)	OF	15	36	2	4	1	1	0	1	.111	2	5	2	34	1	1	.972
	—Buffalo (A.A.)	OF	12	46	10	12	4	0	0	6	.261	11	3	1	34	1	0	1.000
	—Calgary (PCL)■	OF	75	268	45	82	27	2	3	46	.306	37	36	12	143	5	4	.974
1988—	Vancouver (PCL)■	OF	34	131	23	44	8	1	4	27	.336	12	21	5	79	2	0	1.000
	—Chicago (A.L.)	OF-DH	101	347	59	105	15	3	5	31	.303	29	40	5	228	5	0	1.000
1989—	Chicago (A.L.)	OF-DH	161	601	74	160	22	2	1	46	.266	46	79	5	390	8	3	.993
1990—	Chicago (A.L.)	OF-DH	45	75	5	21	3	1	0	5	.280	3	9	0	50	1	1	.981
	—Baltimore (A.L.)■	OF-DH	23	51	7	11	1	0	0	2	.216	4	3	1	46	2	1	.980
1991—	California (A.L.)■	OF-DH	90	270	32	79	17	0	1	30	.293	24	43	2	180	8	0	1.000
1992—	New York (N.L.)■	OF	98	175	20	42	11	1	1	21	.240	19	16	4	105	4	2	.982
	—Tidewater (Int'l)	OF	3	12	1	3	0	0	0	0	.250	3	2	0	13	1	0	1.000
1993—	New York (N.L.)	OF-1B	99	201	34	55	12	2	6	28	.274	20	18	1	139	7	0	1.000
1994—	Atlanta (N.L.)■	OF-1B	89	152	27	34	5	0	2	14	.224	22	17	0	94	4	1	.990
1995—	Philadelphia (N.L.)■	OF	62	157	12	50	12	0	1	12	.318	16	20	0	89	1	0	1.000
	—California (A.L.)■	OF-DH	11	16	1	3	1	0	0	0	.188	2	1	0	9	1	0	1.000
American League totals (6 years)			446	1396	180	383	60	7	7	115	.274	110	180	15	937	26	6	.994
National League totals (4 years)			348	685	93	181	40	3	10	75	.264	77	71	5	427	16	3	.993
Major league totals (9 years)			794	2081	273	564	100	10	17	190	.271	187	251	20	1364	42	9	.994

GALLAHER, KEVIN — P — ASTROS

PERSONAL: Born August 1, 1968, in Fairfax, Va. . . . 6-3/190. . . . Throws right, bats right. . . . Full name: Kevin John Gallaher.

HIGH SCHOOL: Bishop Denis J. O'Connell (Arlington, Va.).

COLLEGE: St. Bonaventure.

TRANSACTIONS/CAREER NOTES: Signed as non-drafted free agent by Houston Astros organization (May 8, 1991). . . . On Kissimmee disabled list (April 21-June 14, 1995).

STATISTICAL NOTES: Pitched six innings, combining with Jimmy Daspit (one inning) in seven-inning 3-0 no-hit victory for Jackson against Tulsa (April 10, 1994).

Year	Team (League)	W	L	Pct.	ERA	G	GS	CG	ShO	Sv.	IP	H	R	ER	BB	SO
1991—	Auburn (NYP)	2	5	.286	6.94	16	8	0	0	0	48	59	48	37	37	25
1992—	Osceola (Florida St.)	0	1	.000	2.84	1	1	0	0	0	6 1/3	2	2	2	3	5
	—Burlington (Midw.)	6	10	.375	3.85	20	20	1	0	0	117	108	70	50	80	89
1993—	Osceola (Florida St.)	7	7	.500	3.80	21	21	1	1	0	135	132	68	57	57	93
	—Jackson (Texas)	0	2	.000	2.63	4	4	0	0	0	24	14	7	7	10	30
1994—	Jackson (Texas)	6	6	.500	3.91	18	18	0	0	0	106	88	57	46	67	112
	—Tucson (Pac. Coast)	3	4	.429	5.37	9	9	2	0	0	53 2/3	55	35	32	25	58
1995—	Kissimmee (Florida State)	1	1	.500	5.71	7	7	0	0	0	17 1/3	8	11	11	24	21
	—Tucson (Pac. Coast)	1	1	.500	6.43	3	3	0	0	0	14	19	11	10	9	11
	—Jackson (Texas)	2	2	.500	3.40	6	6	1	0	0	42 1/3	31	18	16	23	28

GALLEGO, MIKE — 2B/SS — CARDINALS

PERSONAL: Born October 31, 1960, in Whittier, Calif. . . . 5-8/175. . . . Bats right, throws right. . . . Full name: Michael Anthony Gallego. . . . Name pronounced guy-YAY-go.

HIGH SCHOOL: St. Paul (Sante Fe Springs, Calif.).

COLLEGE: UCLA.

TRANSACTIONS/CAREER NOTES: Selected by Oakland Athletics organization in second round of free-agent draft (June 8, 1981); pick received as compensation for Chicago White Sox signing free-agent C/1B Jim Essian. . . . On Tacoma temporarily inactive list (April 10-May 20, 1983). . . . On Oakland disabled list (June 13-July 29, 1987). . . . Granted free agency (October 28, 1991). . . . Signed by New York Yankees (January 9, 1992). . . . On New York disabled list (March 28-May 17, 1992); included rehabilitation assignment to Fort Lauderdale (May 14-17). . . . On New York disabled list (July 8-September 18, 1992; June 11-26, 1993 and June 29-July 19, 1994). . . . Granted free agency (October 24, 1994). . . . Signed by A's (April 12, 1995). . . . On Oakland disabled list (May 18-August 10, 1995); included rehabilitation assignment to Edmonton (August 3-10). . . . Granted free agency (November 1, 1995). . . . Signed by St. Louis Cardinals (January 9, 1996).

STATISTICAL NOTES: Led Pacific Coast League in being hit by pitch with eight in 1986. . . . Tied for A.L. lead with 17 sacrifice hits in 1990. . . . Career major league grand slams: 1.

Year	Team (League)	Pos.	G	AB	R	H	2B	3B	HR	RBI	Avg.	BB	SO	SB	PO	A	E	Avg.
				BATTING											FIELDING			
1981—	Modesto (Calif.)	2B	60	202	38	55	9	3	0	23	.272	31	31	9	127	161	13	.957
1982—	West Haven (East.)	2B-SS	54	139	17	25	1	0	0	5	.180	13	25	3	85	111	4	.980
	—Tacoma (PCL)	2B-3B-SS	44	136	12	30	3	1	0	11	.221	7	12	4	73	111	8	.958
1983—	Tacoma (PCL)	2B	2	2	0	0	0	0	0	0	.000	0	1	0	0	1	0	1.000
	—Alb./Colon. (East.)	2B-SS-3B	90	274	31	61	6	0	0	18	.223	43	25	3	184	260	4	.991
1984—	Tacoma (PCL)	2B-SS-3B	101	288	29	70	8	1	0	18	.243	27	39	7	167	231	13	.968
1985—	Oakland (A.L.)	2B-SS-3B	76	77	13	16	5	1	1	9	.208	12	14	1	57	94	1	.993
	—Modesto (Calif.)	2B-SS-3B	6	25	1	5	1	0	0	2	.200	2	8	1	12	11	1	.958
1986—	Tacoma (PCL)	SS-3B-2B	132	443	58	122	16	5	4	46	.275	39	58	3	197	417	23	.964
	—Oakland (A.L.)	2B-3B-SS	20	37	2	10	2	0	0	4	.270	1	6	0	24	51	1	.987
1987—	Tacoma (PCL)	2B	10	41	6	11	0	2	0	6	.268	10	7	1	15	25	1	.976
	—Oakland (A.L.)	2B-3B-SS	72	124	18	31	6	0	2	14	.250	12	21	0	75	122	8	.961
1988—	Oakland (A.L.)	2B-SS-3B	129	277	38	58	8	0	2	20	.209	34	53	2	155	254	8	.981
1989—	Oakland (A.L.)	S-2-3-DH	133	357	45	90	14	2	3	30	.252	35	43	7	211	363	19	.968
1990—	Oakland (A.L.)	2-S-3-O-DH	140	389	36	80	13	2	3	34	.206	35	50	5	207	379	13	.978

Year	Team (League)	Pos.	G	AB	R	H	2B	3B	HR	RBI	Avg.	BB	SO	SB	PO	A	E	Avg.
				BATTING											FIELDING			
1991—	Oakland (A.L.)	2B-SS	159	482	67	119	15	4	12	49	.247	67	84	6	283	446	12	.984
1992—	Fort Lauder. (FSL)■	SS	3	10	0	2	1	0	0	2	.200	1	4	1	3	5	0	1.000
—	New York (A.L.)	2B-SS	53	173	24	44	7	1	3	14	.254	20	22	0	112	153	6	.978
1993—	New York (A.L.)	S-2-3-DH	119	403	63	114	20	1	10	54	.283	50	65	3	169	368	13	.976
1994—	New York (A.L.)	SS-2B	89	306	39	73	17	1	6	41	.239	38	46	0	143	311	11	.976
1995—	Oakland (A.L.)	2B-SS-3B	43	120	11	28	0	0	0	8	.233	9	24	0	46	90	5	.965
—	Edmonton (PCL)	2B-3B-SS	6	18	1	5	1	0	0	1	.278	0	4	0	3	8	0	1.000
Major league totals (11 years)			1033	2745	356	663	107	12	42	277	.242	313	428	24	1482	2631	97	.977

CHAMPIONSHIP SERIES RECORD

NOTES: Shares A.L. single-series record for most sacrifice hits—2 (1989).

Year	Team (League)	Pos.	G	AB	R	H	2B	3B	HR	RBI	Avg.	BB	SO	SB	PO	A	E	Avg.
				BATTING											FIELDING			
1988—	Oakland (A.L.)	2B	4	12	1	1	0	0	0	0	.083	0	3	0	7	6	0	1.000
1989—	Oakland (A.L.)	SS-2B	4	11	3	3	1	0	0	1	.273	0	2	0	6	14	0	1.000
1990—	Oakland (A.L.)	SS-2B	4	10	1	4	1	0	0	2	.400	1	1	0	8	9	0	1.000
Championship series totals (3 years)			12	33	5	8	2	0	0	3	.242	1	6	0	21	29	0	1.000

WORLD SERIES RECORD

NOTES: Member of World Series championship team (1989).

Year	Team (League)	Pos.	G	AB	R	H	2B	3B	HR	RBI	Avg.	BB	SO	SB	PO	A	E	Avg.
				BATTING											FIELDING			
1988—	Oakland (A.L.)	PR-2B	1	0	0	0	0	0	0	0	...	0	0	0	0	0	0	...
1989—	Oakland (A.L.)	2B-PH-3B	2	1	0	0	0	0	0	0	.000	0	0	0	0	0	0	...
1990—	Oakland (A.L.)	SS	4	11	0	1	0	0	0	1	.091	1	3	1	7	10	1	.944
World Series totals (3 years)			7	12	0	1	0	0	0	1	.083	1	3	1	7	10	1	.944

GANDARILLAS, GUS — P — TWINS

PERSONAL: Born July 19, 1971, in Coral Gables, Fla. . . . 6-0/183. . . . Throws right, bats right. . . . Full name: Gustavo Gandarillas. . . . Name pronounced gan-dar-REE-yas..

HIGH SCHOOL: Hialeah (Fla.)-Miami Lakes.

JUNIOR COLLEGE: Miami-Dade (South) Community College.

COLLEGE: Miami (Fla.).

TRANSACTIONS/CAREER NOTES: Selected by Minnesota Twins organization in third round of free-agent draft (June 1, 1992).

STATISTICAL NOTES: Led Appalachian League pitchers with 29 games finished in 1992.

Year	Team (League)	W	L	Pct.	ERA	G	GS	CG	ShO	Sv.	IP	H	R	ER	BB	SO
1992—	Elizabeth. (App.)	1	2	.333	3.00	*29	0	0	0	•13	36	24	14	12	10	34
1993—	Fort Wayne (Midw.)	5	5	.500	3.26	52	0	0	0	25	66 1/3	66	37	24	22	59
1994—	Fort Myers (Fla. St.)	4	1	.800	0.77	37	0	0	0	20	46 2/3	37	7	4	13	39
—	Nashville (South.)	2	2	.500	3.16	28	0	0	0	8	37	34	13	13	10	29
1995—	Salt Lake (PCL)	2	3	.400	6.44	22	0	0	0	2	29 1/3	34	23	21	19	17
—	New Britain (East.)	2	4	.333	6.12	25	0	0	0	7	32 1/3	38	26	22	16	25

GANT, RON — OF — CARDINALS

PERSONAL: Born March 2, 1965, in Victoria, Tex. . . . 6-0/200. . . . Bats right, throws right. . . . Full name: Ronald Edwin Gant.

HIGH SCHOOL: Victoria (Tex.).

TRANSACTIONS/CAREER NOTES: Selected by Atlanta Braves organization in fourth round of free-agent draft (June 6, 1983). . . . On suspended list (July 31, 1991). . . . Released by Braves (March 15, 1994). . . . Signed by Cincinnati Reds (June 21, 1994). . . . On Cincinnati disabled list (June 21, 1994-remainder of season). . . . On suspended list (September 11-15, 1995). . . . Granted free agency (October 30, 1995). . . . Signed by St. Louis Cardinals (December 23, 1995).

HONORS: Named outfielder on THE SPORTING NEWS N.L. All-Star team (1991). . . . Named outfielder on THE SPORTING NEWS N.L. Silver Slugger team (1991). . . . Named N.L. Comeback Player of the Year by THE SPORTING NEWS (1995).

STATISTICAL NOTES: Led South Atlantic League second basemen with 75 double plays in 1984. . . . Led Carolina League with 271 total bases in 1986. . . . Led Southern League second basemen with 783 total chances and 108 double plays in 1987. . . . Led N.L. second basemen with 26 errors in 1988. . . . Career major league grand slams: 2.

Year	Team (League)	Pos.	G	AB	R	H	2B	3B	HR	RBI	Avg.	BB	SO	SB	PO	A	E	Avg.
				BATTING											FIELDING			
1983—	GC Braves (GCL)	SS	56	193	32	45	2	2	1	14	.233	41	34	4	68	134	22	.902
1984—	Anderson (S. Atl.)	2B	105	359	44	85	14	6	3	38	.237	29	65	13	248	263	31	.943
1985—	Sumter (S. Atl.)	2B-SS-OF	102	305	46	78	14	4	7	37	.256	33	59	19	160	200	10	.973
1986—	Durham (Carolina)	2B	137	512	108	142	31	10	*26	102	.277	78	85	35	240	384	26	.960
1987—	Greenville (South.)	2B	140	527	78	130	27	3	14	82	.247	59	91	24	*328	*434	21	*.973
—	Atlanta (N.L.)	2B	21	83	9	22	4	0	2	9	.265	1	11	4	45	59	3	.972
1988—	Richmond (Int'l)	2B	12	45	3	14	2	2	0	4	.311	2	10	1	22	23	5	.900
—	Atlanta (N.L.)	2B-3B	146	563	85	146	28	8	19	60	.259	46	118	19	316	417	†31	.959
1989—	Atlanta (N.L.)	3B-OF	75	260	26	46	8	3	9	25	.177	20	63	9	70	103	17	.911
—	Sumter (S. Atl.)	OF	12	39	13	15	4	1	1	5	.385	11	3	4	19	1	2	.909
—	Richmond (Int'l)	OF-3B	63	225	42	59	13	2	11	27	.262	29	42	6	111	14	5	.962
1990—	Atlanta (N.L.)	OF	152	575	107	174	34	3	32	84	.303	50	86	33	357	7	8	.978
1991—	Atlanta (N.L.)	OF	154	561	101	141	35	3	32	105	.251	71	104	34	338	7	6	.983
1992—	Atlanta (N.L.)	OF	153	544	74	141	22	6	17	80	.259	45	101	32	277	5	4	.986
1993—	Atlanta (N.L.)	OF	157	606	113	166	27	4	36	117	.274	67	117	26	271	5	*11	.962
1994—									Did not play.									
1995—	Cincinnati (N.L.)■	OF	119	410	79	113	19	4	29	88	.276	74	108	23	191	7	3	.985
Major league totals (8 years)			977	3602	594	949	177	31	176	568	.263	374	708	180	1865	610	83	.968

DIVISION SERIES RECORD

Year	Team (League)	Pos.	G	AB	R	H	2B	3B	HR	RBI	Avg.	BB	SO	SB	PO	A	E	Avg.
				BATTING											FIELDING			
1995—	Cincinnati (N.L.)	OF	3	13	3	3	0	0	1	2	.231	0	3	0	8	1	0	1.000

CHAMPIONSHIP SERIES RECORD

NOTES: Shares single-game record for most grand slams—1 (October 7, 1992). . . . Shares records for most runs batted in in one inning—4 (October 7, 1992, fifth inning); and most stolen bases in one inning—2 (October 10, 1991, third inning). . . . Holds N.L. single-series record for most stolen bases—7 (1991). . . . Shares N.L. single-game record for most stolen bases—3 (October 10, 1991).

Year	Team (League)	Pos.	G	AB	R	H	2B	3B	HR	RBI	Avg.	BB	SO	SB	PO	A	E	Avg.
				BATTING											FIELDING			
1991—	Atlanta (N.L.)	OF	7	27	4	7	1	0	1	3	.259	2	4	7	15	2	0	1.000
1992—	Atlanta (N.L.)	OF	7	22	5	4	0	0	2	6	.182	4	4	1	16	0	0	1.000
1993—	Atlanta (N.L.)	OF	6	27	4	5	3	0	0	3	.185	2	9	0	10	1	1	.917
1995—	Cincinnati (N.L.)	OF	4	16	1	3	0	0	0	1	.188	0	3	0	9	0	0	1.000
Championship series totals (4 years)			24	92	14	19	4	0	3	13	.207	8	20	8	50	3	1	.981

WORLD SERIES RECORD

Year	Team (League)	Pos.	G	AB	R	H	2B	3B	HR	RBI	Avg.	BB	SO	SB	PO	A	E	Avg.
				BATTING											FIELDING			
1991—	Atlanta (N.L.)	OF	7	30	3	8	0	1	0	4	.267	2	3	1	19	0	0	1.000
1992—	Atlanta (N.L.)	OF-PR-PH	4	8	2	1	1	0	0	0	.125	1	2	2	3	1	0	1.000
World Series totals (2 years)			11	38	5	9	1	1	0	4	.237	3	5	3	22	1	0	1.000

ALL-STAR GAME RECORD

Year	League	Pos.	AB	R	H	2B	3B	HR	RBI	Avg.	BB	SO	SB	PO	A	E	Avg.
			BATTING											FIELDING			
1992—	National	PH-OF	2	0	0	0	0	0	0	.000	0	0	0	1	0	0	1.000
1995—	National	DH	2	0	0	0	0	0	0	.000	0	1	0	...	...	...	...
All-Star Game totals (2 years)			4	0	0	0	0	0	0	.000	0	1	0	1	0	0	1.000

GARCES, RICHARD P

PERSONAL: Born May 18, 1971, in Maracay, Venezuela. . . . 6-0/215. . . . Throws right, bats right. . . . Full name: Richard Aron Garces Jr. . . . Name pronounced gar-SESS.

HIGH SCHOOL: Jose Felix Rivas (Maracay, Venezuela).

COLLEGE: Venezuela Universidad.

TRANSACTIONS/CAREER NOTES: Signed as non-drafted free agent by Minnesota Twins organization (December 29, 1987). . . . On Portland suspended list (May 17-September 16, 1991). . . . On Portland disabled list (July 28, 1991-remainder of season). . . . Granted free agency (October 15, 1994). . . . Signed by Iowa, Chicago Cubs organization (January 30, 1995). . . . Claimed on waivers by Florida Marlins (August 9, 1995). . . . Granted free agency (October 16, 1995).

Year	Team (League)	W	L	Pct.	ERA	G	GS	CG	ShO	Sv.	IP	H	R	ER	BB	SO
1988—	Elizabeth. (App.)	5	4	.556	2.29	17	3	1	0	5	59	51	22	15	27	69
1989—	Kenosha (Midwest)	9	10	.474	3.41	24	24	4	1	0	142 2/3	117	70	54	62	84
1990—	Visalia (California)	2	2	.500	1.81	47	0	0	0	*28	54 2/3	33	14	11	16	75
—	Orlando (Southern)	2	1	.667	2.08	15	0	0	0	8	17 1/3	17	4	4	14	22
—	Minnesota (A.L.)	0	0	...	1.59	5	0	0	0	2	5 2/3	4	2	1	4	1
1991—	Portland (PCL)	0	1	.000	4.85	10	0	0	0	3	13	10	7	7	8	13
—	Orlando (Southern)	2	1	.667	3.31	10	0	0	0	0	16 1/3	12	6	6	14	17
1992—	Orlando (Southern)	3	3	.500	4.54	58	0	0	0	13	73 1/3	76	46	37	39	72
1993—	Portland (PCL)	1	3	.250	8.33	35	7	0	0	0	54	70	55	50	64	48
—	Minnesota (A.L.)	0	0	...	0.00	3	0	0	0	0	4	4	2	0	2	3
1994—	Nashville (South.)	4	5	.444	3.72	40	1	0	0	3	77 1/3	70	40	32	31	76
1995—	Iowa (Am. Assoc.)■	0	2	.000	2.86	23	0	0	0	7	28 1/3	25	10	9	8	36
—	Chicago (N.L.)	0	0	...	3.27	7	0	0	0	0	11	11	6	4	3	6
—	Florida (N.L.)■	0	2	.000	5.40	11	0	0	0	0	13 1/3	14	9	8	8	16
A.L. totals (2 years)		0	0	...	0.93	8	0	0	0	2	9 2/3	8	4	1	6	4
N.L. totals (1 year)		0	2	.000	4.44	18	0	0	0	0	24 1/3	25	15	12	11	22
Major league totals (3 years)		0	2	.000	3.44	26	0	0	0	2	34	33	19	13	17	26

GARCIA, CARLOS 2B PIRATES

PERSONAL: Born October 15, 1967, in Tachira, Venezuela. . . . 6-1/205. . . . Bats right, throws right. . . . Full name: Carlos Jesus Garcia.

HIGH SCHOOL: Bolivar (Venezuela).

TRANSACTIONS/CAREER NOTES: Signed as non-drafted free agent by Pittsburgh Pirates organization (January 9, 1987). . . . On disabled list (July 28-August 14, 1995).

STATISTICAL NOTES: Led N.L. second basemen with 80 double plays in 1994.

Year	Team (League)	Pos.	G	AB	R	H	2B	3B	HR	RBI	Avg.	BB	SO	SB	PO	A	E	Avg.
				BATTING											FIELDING			
1987—	Macon (S. Atl.)	SS	110	373	44	95	14	3	3	38	.255	23	80	20	161	262	42	.910
1988—	Augusta (S. Atl.)	SS	73	269	32	78	13	2	1	45	.290	22	46	11	138	207	29	.922
—	Salem (Carolina)	SS	62	236	21	65	9	3	1	28	.275	10	32	8	131	151	24	.922
1989—	Salem (Carolina)	SS	81	304	45	86	12	4	7	49	.283	18	51	19	137	262	32	.926
—	Harrisburg (East.)	SS	54	188	28	53	5	5	3	25	.282	8	36	6	84	131	7	.968
1990—	Harrisburg (East.)	SS	65	242	36	67	11	2	5	25	.277	16	36	12	101	209	14	.957
—	Buffalo (A.A.)	SS	63	197	23	52	10	0	5	18	.264	16	41	7	106	170	19	.936
—	Pittsburgh (N.L.)	SS	4	4	1	2	0	0	0	0	.500	0	2	0	0	4	0	1.000
1991—	Buffalo (A.A.)	SS	127	463	62	123	21	6	7	60	.266	33	78	30	*212	332	*31	.946
—	Pittsburgh (N.L.)	SS-3B-2B	12	24	2	6	0	2	0	1	.250	1	8	0	11	18	1	.967

Year	Team (League)	Pos.	G	AB	R	H	2B	3B	HR	RBI	Avg.	BB	SO	SB	PO	A	E	Avg.
				BATTING											FIELDING			
1992—	Buffalo (A.A.)	SS-2B	113	426	73	129	28	9	13	70	.303	24	64	21	192	314	28	.948
—	Pittsburgh (N.L.)	2B-SS	22	39	4	8	1	0	0	4	.205	0	9	0	25	35	2	.968
1993—	Pittsburgh (N.L.)	2B-SS	141	546	77	147	25	5	12	47	.269	31	67	18	299	347	11	.983
1994—	Pittsburgh (N.L.)	2B	98	412	49	114	15	2	6	28	.277	16	67	18	•225	315	12	.978
1995—	Pittsburgh (N.L.)	2B-SS	104	367	41	108	24	2	6	50	.294	25	55	8	234	298	15	.973
Major league totals (6 years)			381	1392	174	385	65	11	24	130	.277	73	208	44	794	1017	41	.978

CHAMPIONSHIP SERIES RECORD

Year	Team (League)	Pos.	G	AB	R	H	2B	3B	HR	RBI	Avg.	BB	SO	SB	PO	A	E	Avg.
				BATTING											FIELDING			
1992—	Pittsburgh (N.L.)	2B	1	1	0	0	0	0	0	0	.000	0	0	0	0	0	0	...

ALL-STAR GAME RECORD

Year	League	Pos.	AB	R	H	2B	3B	HR	RBI	Avg.	BB	SO	SB	PO	A	E	Avg.
			BATTING											FIELDING			
1994—	National	2B	2	0	1	0	0	0	0	.500	0	0	0	0	1	0	1.000

GARCIA, FREDDY — 3B — PIRATES

PERSONAL: Born August 1, 1972, in La Romana, Dominican Republic. . . . 6-2/205. . . . Bats right, throws right. . . . Full name: Freddy Adrian Garcia.

TRANSACTIONS/CAREER NOTES: Signed as non-drafted free agent by Toronto Blue Jays organization (May 16, 1991). . . . Selected by Pittsburgh Pirates from Blue Jays organization in Rule 5 major league draft (December 5, 1994).

STATISTICAL NOTES: Led Pioneer League third basemen with 267 total chances and tied for lead in double plays with 18 in 1993. . . . Led New York-Pennsylvania League third basemen with 257 total chances and 18 double plays in 1994.

Year	Team (League)	Pos.	G	AB	R	H	2B	3B	HR	RBI	Avg.	BB	SO	SB	PO	A	E	Avg.
				BATTING											FIELDING			
1991—	Villa Mella (DSL)	IF	53	154	28	39	4	1	1	19	.253	39	36	8	...	—	...	...
1992—	Blue Jays East (DSL)	IF	70	249	56	73	13	2	12	62	.293	61	52	5	146	32	5	.973
1993—	Medicine Hat (Pio.)	3B	72	264	47	63	8	2	11	42	.239	31	71	4	*63	*175	•29	.891
1994—	St. Cathar. (NYP)	3B	73	260	46	74	10	2	*13	40	.285	33	57	1	63	*169	25	.903
1995—	Pittsburgh (N.L.)■	OF-3B	42	57	5	8	1	1	0	1	.140	8	17	0	19	15	1	.971
Major league totals (1 year)			42	57	5	8	1	1	0	1	.140	8	17	0	19	15	1	.971

GARCIA, KARIM — OF — DODGERS

PERSONAL: Born October 29, 1975, in Ciudad Obregon, Mexico. . . . 6-0/172. . . . Bats left, throws left. . . . Full name: Gustavo Garcia.

HIGH SCHOOL: Preparatoria Abierta (Ciudad Obregon, Mexico).

TRANSACTIONS/CAREER NOTES: Signed as non-drafted free agent by Los Angeles Dodgers organization (July 16, 1992).

HONORS: Named Minor League Player of the Year by The Sporting News (1995).

Year	Team (League)	Pos.	G	AB	R	H	2B	3B	HR	RBI	Avg.	BB	SO	SB	PO	A	E	Avg.
				BATTING											FIELDING			
1993—	Bakersfield (Calif.)	OF	123	460	61	111	20	9	19	54	.241	37	109	5	193	12	*13	.940
1994—	Vero Beach (FSL)	OF	121	452	72	120	28	10	*21	84	.265	37	112	8	229	12	5	.980
1995—	Albuquerque (PCL)	OF	124	474	88	151	26	10	20	•91	.319	38	102	12	185	7	*14	.932
—	Los Angeles (N.L.)	OF	13	20	1	4	0	0	0	0	.200	0	4	0	5	2	0	1.000
Major league totals (1 year)			13	20	1	4	0	0	0	0	.200	0	4	0	5	2	0	1.000

GARDINER, MIKE — P

PERSONAL: Born October 19, 1965, in Sarnia, Ont. . . . 6-0/200. . . . Throws right, bats both. . . . Full name: Michael James Gardiner.

HIGH SCHOOL: Sarnia (Ont.) Collegiate.

COLLEGE: Indiana State (degree in business, 1987).

TRANSACTIONS/CAREER NOTES: Selected by Seattle Mariners organization in 18th round of free-agent draft (June 2, 1987). . . . On disabled list (May 9-June 10, 1988). . . . Traded by Mariners to Boston Red Sox for P Rob Murphy (April 1, 1991). . . . On Boston disabled list (June 27-July 15, 1991). . . . Traded by Red Sox with P Terry Powers to Montreal Expos for OF Ivan Calderon (December 8, 1992). . . . Released by Expos (August 22, 1993). . . . Signed by Toledo, Detroit Tigers organization (August 28, 1993). . . . Granted free agency (December 23, 1994). . . . Re-signed by Tigers organization (April 14, 1995). . . . On Detroit disabled list (May 8-June 22 and July 3-September 1, 1995); included rehabilitation assignments to Toledo (June 8-22 and August 7-September 1). . . . Released by Tigers (September 1, 1995).

HONORS: Named Eastern League Pitcher of the Year (1990).

MISCELLANEOUS: Member of 1984 Canadian Olympic baseball team.

Year	Team (League)	W	L	Pct.	ERA	G	GS	CG	ShO	Sv.	IP	H	R	ER	BB	SO
1987—	Bellingham (N'west)	2	0	1.000	0.00	2	1	0	0	0	10	6	0	0	1	11
—	Wausau (Midwest)	3	5	.375	5.22	13	13	2	0	0	81	91	54	47	33	80
1988—	Wausau (Midwest)	2	1	.667	3.16	11	6	0	0	1	31 1/3	31	16	11	13	24
1989—	Wausau (Midwest)	4	0	1.000	0.59	15	1	0	0	7	30 1/3	21	5	2	11	48
—	Williamsport (East.)	4	6	.400	2.84	30	3	1	0	2	63 1/3	54	25	20	32	60
1990—	Williamsport (East.)	12	8	.600	*1.90	26	26	5	1	0	*179 2/3	136	47	38	29	*149
—	Seattle (A.L.)	0	2	.000	10.66	5	3	0	0	0	12 2/3	22	17	15	5	6
1991—	Pawtucket (Int'l)■	7	1	.875	2.34	8	8	2	1	0	57 2/3	39	16	15	11	42
—	Boston (A.L.)	9	10	.474	4.85	22	22	0	0	0	130	140	79	70	47	91
1992—	Boston (A.L.)	4	10	.286	4.75	28	18	0	0	0	130 2/3	126	78	69	58	79
—	Pawtucket (Int'l)	1	3	.250	3.31	5	5	2	0	0	32 2/3	32	14	12	9	37
1993—	Montreal (N.L.)■	2	3	.400	5.21	24	2	0	0	0	38	40	28	22	19	21

Year	Team (League)	W	L	Pct.	ERA	G	GS	CG	ShO	Sv.	IP	H	R	ER	BB	SO
	— Ottawa (Int'l)	1	1	.500	2.16	5	5	0	0	0	25	17	8	6	9	25
	— Toledo (Int'l)■	0	1	.000	5.40	4	0	0	0	1	5	6	3	3	2	10
	— Detroit (A.L.)	0	0	...	3.97	10	0	0	0	0	11 1/3	12	5	5	7	4
1994	— Detroit (A.L.)	2	2	.500	4.14	38	1	0	0	5	58 2/3	53	35	27	23	31
1995	— Detroit (A.L.)	0	0	...	14.59	9	0	0	0	0	12 1/3	27	20	20	2	7
	— Toledo (Int'l)	0	1	.000	4.41	11	1	0	0	0	16 1/3	19	8	8	13	10
A.L. totals (6 years)		15	24	.385	5.21	112	44	0	0	5	355 2/3	380	234	206	142	218
N.L. totals (1 year)		2	3	.400	5.21	24	2	0	0	0	38	40	28	22	19	21
Major league totals (6 years)		17	27	.386	5.21	136	46	0	0	5	393 2/3	420	262	228	161	239

GARDNER, MARK — P — MARLINS

PERSONAL: Born March 1, 1962, in Los Angeles. . . . 6-1/205. . . . Throws right, bats right. . . . Full name: Mark Allan Gardner.
HIGH SCHOOL: Clovis (Calif.).
JUNIOR COLLEGE: Fresno (Calif.) City College.
COLLEGE: Fresno State.
TRANSACTIONS/CAREER NOTES: Selected by California Angels organization in sixth round of free-agent draft (January 11, 1983); did not sign. . . . Selected by Cleveland Indians organization in 17th round of free-agent draft (June 4, 1984); did not sign. . . . Selected by Montreal Expos organization in eighth round of free-agent draft (June 3, 1985). . . . On disabled list (September 20, 1990-remainder of season). . . . On Montreal disabled list (April 2-May 14, 1991); included rehabilitation assignment to Indianapolis (April 11-May 8). . . . Traded by Expos with P Doug Piatt to Kansas City Royals for C Tim Spehr and P Jeff Shaw (December 9, 1992). . . . On Kansas City disabled list (July 7-August 27, 1993); included rehabilitation assignment to Omaha (July 28-August 26). . . . Released by Royals (December 8, 1993). . . . Signed by Edmonton, Florida Marlins organization (January 6, 1994). . . . On Florida disabled list (June 8-26, 1994); included rehabilitation assignment to Brevard County (June 18-22). . . . Granted free agency (February 17, 1995). . . . Re-signed by Marlins (April 7, 1995). . . . Granted free agency (October 16, 1995). . . . Re-signed by Marlins organization (December 8, 1995).
RECORDS: Shares major league record for most hit batsmen in one inning—3 (August 15, 1992, first inning).
HONORS: Named American Association Pitcher of the Year (1989).
STATISTICAL NOTES: Led N.L. with nine hit batsmen in 1990. . . . Pitched nine hitless innings against Los Angeles Dodgers, but gave up two hits in 10th inning and lost, 1-0, when reliever Jeff Fassero gave up game-winning hit in 10th (July 26, 1991).

Year	Team (League)	W	L	Pct.	ERA	G	GS	CG	ShO	Sv.	IP	H	R	ER	BB	SO
1985	— Jamestown (NYP)	0	0	...	2.77	3	3	0	0	0	13	9	4	4	4	16
	— WP Beach (FSL)	5	4	.556	2.37	10	9	4	0	0	60 2/3	54	24	16	18	44
1986	— Jacksonville (Sou.)	10	11	.476	3.84	29	28	3	1	0	168 2/3	144	88	72	90	140
1987	— Indianapolis (A.A.)	3	3	.500	5.67	9	9	0	0	0	46	48	32	29	28	41
	— Jacksonville (Sou.)	4	6	.400	4.19	17	17	1	0	0	101	101	50	47	42	78
1988	— Jacksonville (Sou.)	6	3	.667	1.60	15	15	4	2	0	112 1/3	72	24	20	36	130
	— Indianapolis (A.A.)	4	2	.667	2.77	13	13	3	1	0	84 1/3	65	30	26	32	71
1989	— Indianapolis (A.A.)	12	4	*.750	2.37	24	23	4	2	0	163 1/3	122	51	43	59	*175
	— Montreal (N.L.)	0	3	.000	5.13	7	4	0	0	0	26 1/3	26	16	15	11	21
1990	— Montreal (N.L.)	7	9	.438	3.42	27	26	3	3	0	152 2/3	129	62	58	61	135
1991	— Indianapolis (A.A.)	2	0	1.000	3.48	6	6	0	0	0	31	26	13	12	16	38
	— Montreal (N.L.)	9	11	.450	3.85	27	27	0	0	0	168 1/3	139	78	72	75	107
1992	— Montreal (N.L.)	12	10	.545	4.36	33	30	0	0	0	179 2/3	179	91	87	60	132
1993	— Kansas City (A.L.)■	4	6	.400	6.19	17	16	0	0	0	91 2/3	92	65	63	36	54
	— Omaha (Am. Assoc.)	4	2	.667	2.79	8	8	1	0	0	48 1/3	34	17	15	19	41
1994	— Florida (N.L.)■	4	4	.500	4.87	20	14	0	0	0	92 1/3	97	53	50	30	57
	— Edmonton (PCL)	1	0	1.000	0.00	1	1	0	0	0	6	4	0	0	1	11
	— Brevard Co. (FSL)	1	0	1.000	0.00	1	1	0	0	0	5	1	0	0	1	3
1995	— Florida (N.L.)	5	5	.500	4.49	39	11	1	1	1	102 1/3	109	60	51	43	87
A.L. totals (1 year)		4	6	.400	6.19	17	16	0	0	0	91 2/3	92	65	63	36	54
N.L. totals (6 years)		37	42	.468	4.15	153	112	4	4	1	721 2/3	679	360	333	280	539
Major league totals (7 years)		41	48	.461	4.38	170	128	4	4	1	813 1/3	771	425	396	316	593

GATES, BRENT — 2B — ATHLETICS

PERSONAL: Born March 14, 1970, in Grand Rapids, Mich. . . . 6-1/180. . . . Bats both, throws right. . . . Full name: Brent Robert Gates.
HIGH SCHOOL: Grandville (Mich.).
COLLEGE: Minnesota.
TRANSACTIONS/CAREER NOTES: Selected by Oakland Athletics organization in first round (26th pick overall) of free-agent draft (June 3, 1991). . . . On disabled list (April 10-May 5 and July 17, 1994-remainder of season).
STATISTICAL NOTES: Led California League second basemen with 735 total chances and 105 double plays in 1992.

				BATTING											FIELDING			
Year	Team (League)	Pos.	G	AB	R	H	2B	3B	HR	RBI	Avg.	BB	SO	SB	PO	A	E	Avg.
1991	— S. Oregon (N'west)	SS-2B-3B	58	219	41	63	11	0	3	26	.288	30	33	8	77	177	15	.944
	— Madison (Midwest)	SS-3B	4	12	4	4	2	0	0	1	.333	3	2	1	6	10	0	1.000
1992	— Modesto (Calif.)	2B	133	505	94	162	39	2	10	88	.321	85	60	9	*293	*420	•22	.970
1993	— Huntsville (South.)	2B	12	45	7	15	4	0	1	11	.333	7	9	0	32	28	0	1.000
	— Tacoma (PCL)	2B	12	44	7	15	7	0	1	4	.341	4	6	2	27	36	1	.984
	— Oakland (A.L.)	2B	139	535	64	155	29	2	7	69	.290	56	75	7	281	431	14	.981
1994	— Oakland (A.L.)	2B-1B	64	233	29	66	11	1	2	24	.283	21	32	3	113	159	8	.971
1995	— Oakland (A.L.)	2B-DH-1B	136	524	60	133	24	4	5	56	.254	46	84	3	241	428	12	.982
Major league totals (3 years)			339	1292	153	354	64	7	14	149	.274	123	191	13	635	1018	34	.980

GENTILE, SCOTT — P — EXPOS

PERSONAL: Born December 21, 1970, in New Britain, Conn. . . . 5-10/205. . . . Throws right, bats right. . . . Full name: Scott Patrick Gentile.

. . . Name pronounced JEN-teel.
HIGH SCHOOL: Berlin (Conn.).
COLLEGE: Western Connecticut State.
TRANSACTIONS/CAREER NOTES: Selected by Montreal Expos organization in fourth round of free-agent draft (June 1, 1992). . . . On disabled list (August 22, 1993-remainder of season and July 15-August 13, 1995).

Year Team (League)	W	L	Pct.	ERA	G	GS	CG	ShO	Sv.	IP	H	R	ER	BB	SO
1992— Jamestown (NYP)	4	4	.500	3.88	13	13	0	0	0	62 2/3	59	32	27	34	44
1993— WP Beach (FSL)	8	9	.471	4.03	25	25	0	0	0	138 1/3	132	72	62	54	108
1994— Harrisburg (East.)	0	1	.000	17.42	6	2	0	0	0	10 1/3	16	21	20	25	14
— WP Beach (FSL)	5	2	.714	1.93	53	1	0	0	26	65 1/3	44	16	14	19	90
1995— Harrisburg (East.)	2	2	.500	3.44	37	0	0	0	11	49 2/3	36	19	19	15	48

GIAMBI, JASON 3B ATHLETICS

PERSONAL: Born January 8, 1971, in West Covina, Calif. . . . 6-2/200. . . . Bats left, throws right. . . . Full name: Jason Gilbert Giambi. . . . Name pronounced GEE-om-bee.
HIGH SCHOOL: South Hills (Covina, Calif.).
COLLEGE: Long Beach State.
TRANSACTIONS/CAREER NOTES: Selected by Milwaukee Brewers organization in 43rd round of free-agent draft (June 5, 1989); did not sign. . . . Selected by Oakland Athletics organization in second round of free-agent draft (June 1, 1992). . . . On disabled list (July 28-August 28, 1993). . . . On Huntsville disabled list (April 7-14, 1994).
MISCELLANEOUS: Member of 1992 U.S. Olympic baseball team.

		BATTING												FIELDING			
Year Team (League)	Pos.	G	AB	R	H	2B	3B	HR	RBI	Avg.	BB	SO	SB	PO	A	E	Avg.
1992— S. Oregon (N'west)	3B	13	41	9	13	3	0	3	13	.317	9	6	1	5	20	1	.962
1993— Modesto (Calif.)	3B	89	313	72	91	16	2	12	60	.291	73	47	2	49	145	19	.911
1994— Huntsville (South.)	3B-1B	56	193	31	43	9	0	6	30	.223	27	31	0	111	77	11	.945
— Tacoma (PCL)	3B-SS	52	176	28	56	20	0	4	38	.318	25	32	1	39	110	8	.949
1995— Edmonton (PCL)	3B-1B	55	190	34	65	26	1	3	41	.342	34	26	0	38	98	9	.938
— Oakland (A.L.)	3B-1B-DH	54	176	27	45	7	0	6	25	.256	28	31	2	194	55	4	.984
Major league totals (1 year)		54	176	27	45	7	0	6	25	.256	28	31	2	194	55	4	.984

GIANNELLI, RAY OF/1B

PERSONAL: Born February 5, 1966, in Brooklyn, N.Y. . . . 6-0/195. . . . Bats left, throws right. . . . Full name: Raymond John Giannelli.
HIGH SCHOOL: Copiague (N.Y.).
COLLEGE: New York Institute of Technology.
TRANSACTIONS/CAREER NOTES: Selected by Baltimore Orioles organization in 22nd round of free-agent draft (June 2, 1987); did not sign. . . . Selected by Toronto Blue Jays organization in 38th round of free-agent draft (June 1, 1988). . . . On disabled list (June 19-July 20, 1992). . . . Granted free agency (October 15, 1994). . . . Signed by St. Louis Cardinals organization (November 18, 1994). . . . On Louisville suspended list (May 25-27, 1995). . . . Granted free agency (October 16, 1995).

		BATTING												FIELDING			
Year Team (League)	Pos.	G	AB	R	H	2B	3B	HR	RBI	Avg.	BB	SO	SB	PO	A	E	Avg.
1988— Medicine Hat (Pio.)	3B-C	47	123	17	30	8	3	4	28	.244	19	22	0	29	30	6	.908
1989— Myrtle Beach (SAL)	3B	127	458	76	138	17	1	18	84	.301	78	53	2	65	161	22	.911
1990— Dunedin (Fla. St.)	1B-3B	118	416	64	120	18	1	*18	57	.288	66	56	5	711	120	13	.985
1991— Knoxville (South.)	3B	112	362	53	100	14	3	7	37	.276	64	66	8	70	161	21	.917
— Toronto (A.L.)	3B	9	24	2	4	1	0	0	0	.167	5	9	1	0	12	1	.923
1992— Syracuse (Int'l)	OF-2B	84	249	23	57	9	2	5	22	.229	48	44	2	127	18	5	.967
1993— Syracuse (Int'l)	2B-3B-1B	127	411	51	104	18	4	11	42	.253	38	79	1	132	211	10	.972
1994— Syracuse (Int'l)	1-2-C-3	114	327	43	94	19	1	10	51	.287	48	77	0	617	56	16	.977
1995— Louisville (A.A.)■	0-1-3-2	119	390	56	115	19	1	16	70	.295	44	85	3	239	26	5	.981
— St. Louis (N.L.)	1B-OF	9	11	0	1	0	0	0	0	.091	3	4	0	10	0	0	1.000
American League totals (1 year)		9	24	2	4	1	0	0	0	.167	5	9	1	0	12	1	.923
National League totals (1 year)		9	11	0	1	0	0	0	0	.091	3	4	0	10	0	0	1.000
Major league totals (2 years)		18	35	2	5	1	0	0	0	.143	8	13	1	10	12	1	.957

GIBRALTER, STEVE OF REDS

PERSONAL: Born October 9, 1972, in Dallas. . . . 6-0/190. . . . Bats right, throws right. . . . Full name: Stephan Benson Gibralter. . . . Brother of David Gibralter, third baseman, Boston Red Sox organization.
HIGH SCHOOL: Duncanville (Tex.).
TRANSACTIONS/CAREER NOTES: Selected by Cincinnati Reds organization in sixth round of free-agent draft (June 4, 1990). . . . On Indianapolis disabled list (July 16, 1995-remainder of season).
HONORS: Named Midwest League Most Valuable Player (1992).
STATISTICAL NOTES: Led Gulf Coast League outfielders with 115 total chances in 1990. . . . Tied for South Atlantic League lead in double plays by outfielder with three in 1991. . . . Led Midwest League with 257 total bases in 1992. . . . Led Southern League with 334 total bases in 1993.

		BATTING												FIELDING			
Year Team (League)	Pos.	G	AB	R	H	2B	3B	HR	RBI	Avg.	BB	SO	SB	PO	A	E	Avg.
1990— GC Reds (GCL)	OF	52	174	26	45	11	3	4	27	.259	23	30	9	100	•9	6	.948
1991— Char., W.Va. (SAL)	OF	*140	*544	72	145	*36	7	6	71	.267	31	117	11	234	15	10	.961
1992— Ced. Rap. (Midw.)	OF	•137	529	*92	*162	32	3	*19	*99	.306	51	99	12	*311	7	7	.978
1993— Chatt. (South.)	OF	132	477	65	113	25	3	11	47	.237	20	108	7	*319	7	8	.976
1994— Chatt. (South.)	OF	133	460	71	124	28	3	14	63	.270	47	114	10	304	7	5	.984
1995— Indianapolis (A.A.)	OF	79	263	49	83	19	3	18	63	.316	25	70	0	207	2	5	.977
— Cincinnati (N.L.)	OF	4	3	0	1	0	0	0	0	.333	0	0	0	1	0	0	1.000
Major league totals (1 year)		4	3	0	1	0	0	0	0	.333	0	0	0	1	0	0	1.000

GIBSON, KIRK — DH/OF

PERSONAL: Born May 28, 1957, in Pontiac, Mich. . . . 6-3/225. . . . Bats left, throws left. . . . Full name: Kirk Harold Gibson.
HIGH SCHOOL: Kettering (Detroit).
COLLEGE: Michigan State.
TRANSACTIONS/CAREER NOTES: Selected by Detroit Tigers organization in first round (12th pick overall) of free-agent draft (June 6, 1978). . . . On restricted list (August 15, 1978-March 1, 1979). . . . On disabled list (April 13-May 21, 1979; June 18-October 6, 1980; and July 11, 1982-remainder of season). . . . Granted free agency (November 12, 1985). . . . Re-signed by Tigers (January 8, 1986). . . . On disabled list (April 23-June 2, 1986). . . . On Detroit disabled list (March 30-May 5, 1987); included rehabilitation assignment to Toledo (April 28-May 5). . . . Granted free agency (January 22, 1988). . . . Signed by Los Angeles Dodgers (January 29, 1988). . . . On disabled list (April 26-May 23 and July 23, 1989-remainder of season). . . . On Los Angeles disabled list (March 31-June 2, 1990); included rehabilitation assignment to Albuquerque (May 24-June 2). . . . Granted free agency (November 5, 1990). . . . Signed by Kansas City Royals (December 1, 1990). . . . Traded by Royals to Pittsburgh Pirates for P Neal Heaton (March 10, 1992). . . . Released by Pirates (May 5, 1992). . . . Signed by Tigers (February 10, 1993). . . . Granted free agency (November 5, 1993). . . . Re-signed by Tigers (February 4, 1994). . . . Granted free agency (October 28, 1994). . . . Re-signed by Tigers (April 7, 1995). . . . Announced retirement (August 11, 1995).
HONORS: Named outfielder on The Sporting News college All-America team (1978). . . . Named outfielder on The Sporting News N.L. Silver Slugger team (1988). . . . Named N.L. Most Valuable Player by Baseball Writers' Association of America (1988).
STATISTICAL NOTES: Career major league grand slams: 4.
MISCELLANEOUS: Named as wide receiver on The Sporting News college football All-America team (1978). . . . Selected by St. Louis Cardinals in seventh round (173rd pick overall) of 1979 NFL draft.

							BATTING									FIELDING		
Year	Team (League)	Pos.	G	AB	R	H	2B	3B	HR	RBI	Avg.	BB	SO	SB	PO	A	E	Avg.
1978	Lakeland (Fla. St.)	OF	54	175	27	42	5	4	8	40	.240	22	54	13	115	2	6	.951
1979	Evansville (A.A.)	OF	89	327	50	80	13	5	9	42	.245	34	110	20	100	5	9	.921
	— Detroit (A.L.)	OF	12	38	3	9	3	0	1	4	.237	1	3	3	15	0	0	1.000
1980	Detroit (A.L.)	OF-DH	51	175	23	46	2	1	9	16	.263	10	45	4	122	1	1	.992
1981	Detroit (A.L.)	OF-DH	83	290	41	95	11	3	9	40	.328	18	64	17	142	1	4	.973
1982	Detroit (A.L.)	OF-DH	69	266	34	74	16	2	8	35	.278	25	41	9	167	4	1	.994
1983	Detroit (A.L.)	DH-OF	128	401	60	91	12	9	15	51	.227	53	96	14	116	2	3	.975
1984	Detroit (A.L.)	OF-DH	149	531	92	150	23	10	27	91	.282	63	103	29	245	4	•12	.954
1985	Detroit (A.L.)	OF-DH	154	581	96	167	37	5	29	97	.287	71	137	30	286	1	•11	.963
1986	Detroit (A.L.)	OF-DH	119	441	84	118	11	2	28	86	.268	68	107	34	190	2	2	.990
1987	Toledo (Int'l)	DH	6	17	2	4	0	0	0	3	.235	2	3	2	...	...	...	...
	— Detroit (A.L.)	OF-DH	128	487	95	135	25	3	24	79	.277	71	117	26	253	6	7	.974
1988	Los Angeles (N.L.)■	OF	150	542	106	157	28	1	25	76	.290	73	120	31	311	6	*12	.964
1989	Los Angeles (N.L.)	OF	71	253	35	54	8	2	9	28	.213	35	55	12	146	3	3	.980
1990	Albuquerque (PCL)	OF	5	14	6	6	2	0	1	4	.429	4	3	1	2	0	1	.667
	— Los Angeles (N.L.)	OF	89	315	59	82	20	0	8	38	.260	39	65	26	191	4	1	.995
1991	Kansas City (A.L.)■	OF-DH	132	462	81	109	17	6	16	55	.236	69	103	18	162	3	4	.976
1992	Pittsburgh (N.L.)■	OF	16	56	6	11	0	0	2	5	.196	3	12	3	25	1	0	1.000
1993	Detroit (A.L.)■	DH-OF	116	403	62	105	18	6	13	62	.261	44	87	15	76	0	1	.987
1994	Detroit (A.L.)	DH-OF	98	330	71	91	17	2	23	72	.276	42	69	4	76	3	1	.988
1995	Detroit (A.L.)	DH-OF	70	227	37	59	12	2	9	35	.260	33	61	9	0	0	0	...
American League totals (13 years)			1309	4632	779	1249	204	51	211	723	.270	568	1033	212	1850	27	47	.976
National League totals (4 years)			326	1166	206	304	56	3	44	147	.261	150	252	72	673	14	16	.977
Major league totals (17 years)			1635	5798	985	1553	260	54	255	870	.268	718	1285	284	2523	41	63	.976

CHAMPIONSHIP SERIES RECORD

NOTES: Named A.L. Championship Series Most Valuable Player (1984). . . . Shares single-series record for most game-winning RBIs—2 (1988). . . . Shares A.L. single-series record for most strikeouts—8 (1987).

							BATTING									FIELDING		
Year	Team (League)	Pos.	G	AB	R	H	2B	3B	HR	RBI	Avg.	BB	SO	SB	PO	A	E	Avg.
1984	Detroit (A.L.)	OF	3	12	2	5	1	0	1	2	.417	2	1	1	7	0	0	1.000
1987	Detroit (A.L.)	OF	5	21	4	6	1	0	1	4	.286	3	8	3	10	1	0	1.000
1988	Los Angeles (N.L.)	OF	7	26	2	4	0	0	2	6	.154	3	6	2	17	1	1	.947
Championship series totals (3 years)			15	59	8	15	2	0	4	12	.254	8	15	6	34	2	1	.973

WORLD SERIES RECORD

NOTES: Member of World Series championship teams (1984 and 1988).

							BATTING									FIELDING		
Year	Team (League)	Pos.	G	AB	R	H	2B	3B	HR	RBI	Avg.	BB	SO	SB	PO	A	E	Avg.
1984	Detroit (A.L.)	OF	5	18	4	6	0	0	2	7	.333	4	4	3	5	1	2	.750
1988	Los Angeles (N.L.)	PH	1	1	1	1	0	0	1	2	1.000	0	0	0	...	...	...	...
World Series totals (2 years)			6	19	5	7	0	0	3	9	.368	4	4	3	5	1	2	.750

GIL, BENJI — SS — RANGERS

PERSONAL: Born October 6, 1972, in Tijuana, Mexico. . . . 6-2/182. . . . Bats right, throws right. . . . Full name: Romar Benjamin Gil.
HIGH SCHOOL: Castle Park (Chula Vista, Calif.).
TRANSACTIONS/CAREER NOTES: Selected by Texas Rangers organization in first round (19th pick overall) of free-agent draft (June 3, 1991).
STATISTICAL NOTES: Led American Association shortstops with 660 total chances and 85 double plays in 1994. . . . Career major league grand slams: 1.

							BATTING									FIELDING		
Year	Team (League)	Pos.	G	AB	R	H	2B	3B	HR	RBI	Avg.	BB	SO	SB	PO	A	E	Avg.
1991	Butte (Pioneer)	SS	32	129	25	37	4	3	2	15	.287	14	36	9	61	88	14	.914
1992	Gastonia (S. Atl.)	SS	132	482	75	132	21	1	9	55	.274	50	106	26	226	384	45	.931
1993	Texas (A.L.)	SS	22	57	3	7	0	0	0	2	.123	5	22	1	27	76	5	.954
	— Tulsa (Texas)	SS	101	342	45	94	9	1	17	59	.275	35	89	20	159	285	19	.959
1994	Okla. City (A.A.)	SS	*139	487	62	121	20	6	10	55	.248	33	120	14	*222	*401	*37	.944
1995	Texas (A.L.)	SS	130	415	36	91	20	3	9	46	.219	26	147	2	226	409	17	.974
Major league totals (2 years)			152	472	39	98	20	3	9	48	.208	31	169	3	253	485	22	.971

GILES, BRIAN — OF — INDIANS

PERSONAL: Born January 21, 1971, in El Cajon, Calif. . . . 5-11/195. . . . Bats left, throws left. . . . Full name: Brian S. Giles.
HIGH SCHOOL: Granite Hills (El Cajon, Calif.).
TRANSACTIONS/CAREER NOTES: Selected by Cleveland Indians organization in 17th round of free-agent draft (June 5, 1989). . . . On Canton/Akron disabled list (May 15-July 7, 1992).
STATISTICAL NOTES: Led International League with 10 intentional bases on balls received in 1994. . . . Led International League outfielders with five double plays in 1994.

			BATTING											FIELDING			
Year Team (League)	Pos.	G	AB	R	H	2B	3B	HR	RBI	Avg.	BB	SO	SB	PO	A	E	Avg.
1989—Burlington (Appal.)	OF	36	129	18	40	7	0	0	20	.310	11	19	6	52	3	1	.982
1990—Watertown (NYP)	OF	70	246	44	71	15	2	1	23	.289	48	23	11	108	8	1	.991
1991—Kinston (Carolina)	OF	125	394	71	122	14	0	4	47	.310	68	70	19	187	10	5	.975
1992—Cant./Akr. (East.)	OF	23	74	6	16	4	0	0	3	.216	10	10	3	45	0	0	1.000
—Kinston (Carolina)	OF	42	140	28	37	5	1	3	18	.264	30	21	3	74	3	1	.987
1993—Cant./Akr. (East.)	OF	123	425	64	139	17	6	6	64	.327	57	43	18	186	3	5	.974
1994—Charlotte (Int'l)	OF	128	434	74	136	18	3	16	58	.313	55	61	8	242	12	4	.984
1995—Buffalo (A.A.)	OF	123	413	67	128	18	•8	15	67	.310	54	40	7	248	4	5	.981
—Cleveland (A.L.)	OF-DH	6	9	6	5	0	0	1	3	.556	0	1	0	2	1	0	1.000
Major league totals (1 year)		6	9	6	5	0	0	1	3	.556	0	1	0	2	1	0	1.000

GILKEY, BERNARD — OF — METS

PERSONAL: Born September 24, 1966, in St. Louis. . . . 6-0/190. . . . Bats right, throws right. . . . Full name: Otis Bernard Gilkey.
HIGH SCHOOL: University City (Mo.).
TRANSACTIONS/CAREER NOTES: Signed as non-drafted free agent by St. Louis Cardinals organization (August 22, 1984). . . . On disabled list (April 10-25, 1986 and May 29, 1987-remainder of season). . . . On St. Louis disabled list (June 14-July 11, 1991 and April 29-May 14, 1993). . . . On suspended list (July 8-9, 1994). . . . Granted free agency (April 7, 1995). . . . Re-signed by Cardinals (April 8, 1995). . . . On St. Louis disabled list (June 28-July 17, 1995); included rehabilitation assignment to Louisville (July 15-17). . . . Traded by Cardinals to New York Mets for P Eric Ludwick, P Erik Hiljus and OF Yudith Ozorio (January 22, 1996).
STATISTICAL NOTES: Led New York-Pennsylvania League outfielders with 185 total chances in 1985. . . . Led Texas League in caught stealing with 22 in 1989. . . . Led American Association in caught stealing with 33 in 1990. . . . Led N.L. outfielders with 19 assists in 1993. . . . Tied for N.L. lead in double plays by outfielder with four in 1995.

			BATTING											FIELDING			
Year Team (League)	Pos.	G	AB	R	H	2B	3B	HR	RBI	Avg.	BB	SO	SB	PO	A	E	Avg.
1985—Erie (NYP)	OF	•77	*294	57	60	9	1	7	27	.204	55	57	34	*164	*13	*8	.957
1986—Savannah (S. Atl.)	OF	105	374	64	88	15	4	6	36	.235	84	57	32	220	7	5	.978
1987—Springfield (Midw.)	OF	46	162	30	37	5	0	0	9	.228	39	28	18	79	5	4	.955
1988—Springfield (Midw.)	OF	125	491	84	120	18	7	6	36	.244	65	54	54	165	10	6	.967
1989—Arkansas (Texas)	OF	131	500	*104	139	25	3	6	57	.278	70	54	*53	236	*22	9	.966
1990—Louisville (A.A.)	OF	132	499	83	147	26	8	3	46	.295	*75	49	45	236	18	•11	.958
—St. Louis (N.L.)	OF	18	64	11	19	5	2	1	3	.297	8	5	6	47	2	2	.961
1991—St. Louis (N.L.)	OF	81	268	28	58	7	2	5	20	.216	39	33	14	164	6	1	.994
—Louisville (A.A.)	OF	11	41	5	6	2	0	0	2	.146	6	10	1	33	1	0	1.000
1992—St. Louis (N.L.)	OF	131	384	56	116	19	4	7	43	.302	39	52	18	217	9	5	.978
1993—St. Louis (N.L.)	OF-1B	137	557	99	170	40	5	16	70	.305	56	66	15	251	†20	8	.971
1994—St. Louis (N.L.)	OF	105	380	52	96	22	1	6	45	.253	39	65	15	168	9	3	.983
1995—St. Louis (N.L.)	OF	121	480	73	143	33	4	17	69	.298	42	70	12	206	10	3	.986
—Louisville (A.A.)	OF	2	6	3	2	1	0	1	1	.333	1	0	0	2	0	0	1.000
Major league totals (6 years)		593	2133	319	602	126	18	52	250	.282	223	291	80	1053	56	22	.981

GIOVANOLA, ED — SS — BRAVES

PERSONAL: Born March 4, 1969, in Los Gatos, Calif. . . . 5-10/170. . . . Bats left, throws right. . . . Full name: Edward Thomas Giovanola.
HIGH SCHOOL: Bellarmine College Prepatory (San Jose, Calif.).
COLLEGE: Santa Clara.
TRANSACTIONS/CAREER NOTES: Selected by Atlanta Braves organization in seventh round of free-agent draft (June 4, 1990). . . . On disabled list (May 29-June 5 and June 23-July 23, 1992). . . . On Richmond disabled list (June 28-July 21, 1995).
STATISTICAL NOTES: Led International League with .417 on-base percentage in 1995.

			BATTING											FIELDING			
Year Team (League)	Pos.	G	AB	R	H	2B	3B	HR	RBI	Avg.	BB	SO	SB	PO	A	E	Avg.
1990—Idaho Falls (Pio.)	2B	25	98	25	38	6	0	0	13	.388	17	9	6	32	72	2	.981
—Sumter (S. Atl.)	2B	35	119	20	29	4	0	0	8	.244	34	17	8	61	125	3	.984
1991—Durham (Carolina)	3-S-2-O	101	299	50	76	9	0	6	27	.254	57	39	18	112	182	15	.951
1992—Greenville (South.)	3B	75	270	39	72	5	0	5	30	.267	29	40	4	35	168	18	.919
1993—Greenville (South.)	3B-2B	120	384	70	108	21	5	5	43	.281	84	49	6	94	281	14	.964
1994—Greenville (South.)	3B	25	84	13	20	6	1	4	16	.238	10	12	2	20	41	2	.968
—Richmond (Int'l)	3-S-2-O	98	344	48	97	16	2	6	30	.282	31	49	7	94	211	16	.950
1995—Richmond (Int'l)	SS-3B	99	321	45	103	18	2	4	36	.321	55	37	8	125	286	15	.965
—Atlanta (N.L.)	2B-3B-SS	13	14	2	1	0	0	0	0	.071	3	5	0	9	7	0	1.000
Major league totals (1 year)		13	14	2	1	0	0	0	0	.071	3	5	0	9	7	0	1.000

GIRARDI, JOE — C — YANKEES

PERSONAL: Born October 14, 1964, in Peoria, Ill. . . . 5-11/195. . . . Bats right, throws right. . . . Full name: Joseph Elliott Girardi. . . . Name pronounced jeh-RAR-dee.
HIGH SCHOOL: Spalding Institute (Peoria, Ill.).

COLLEGE: Northwestern (degree in industrial engineering, 1986).
TRANSACTIONS/CAREER NOTES: Selected by Chicago Cubs organization in fifth round of free-agent draft (June 2, 1986).... On disabled list (August 27, 1986-remainder of season and August 7, 1988-remainder of season).... On Chicago disabled list (April 17-August 6, 1991); included rehabilitation assignment to Iowa (July 23-August 6).... Selected by Colorado Rockies in first round (19th pick overall) of expansion draft (November 17, 1992).... On Colorado disabled list (June 5-August 11, 1993); included rehabilitation assignment to Colorado Springs (August 1-11).... On disabled list (July 11-26, 1994).... Traded by Rockies to New York Yankees for P Mike DeJean and a player to be named later (November 20, 1995); Rockies acquired P Steve Shoemaker to complete deal (December 6, 1995).
STATISTICAL NOTES: Led Carolina League catchers with 661 total chances and tied for lead with 17 passed balls in 1987.... Led Eastern League catchers with .992 fielding percentage, 448 putouts, 76 assists and 528 total chances and tied for lead with five double plays in 1988. ... Tied for N.L. lead with 16 passed balls in 1990.

			BATTING											FIELDING			
Year	**Team (League)**	**Pos.**	**G**	**AB**	**R**	**H**	**2B**	**3B**	**HR**	**RBI**	**Avg.**	**BB**	**SO**	**SB**	**PO**	**A**	**E**	**Avg.**
1986—	Peoria (Midwest)	C	68	230	36	71	13	1	3	28	.309	17	36	6	405	34	5	.989
1987—	Winst.-Salem (Car.)	C	99	364	51	102	9	8	8	46	.280	33	64	9	*569	*74	18	.973
1988—	Pittsfield (Eastern)	C-OF	104	357	44	97	14	1	7	41	.272	29	51	7	†460	†76	6	†.989
1989—	Chicago (N.L.)	C	59	157	15	39	10	0	1	14	.248	11	26	2	332	28	7	.981
—	Iowa (Am. Assoc.)	C	32	110	12	27	4	2	2	11	.245	5	19	3	172	21	1	.995
1990—	Chicago (N.L.)	C	133	419	36	113	24	2	1	38	.270	17	50	8	653	61	11	.985
1991—	Chicago (N.L.)	C	21	47	3	9	2	0	0	6	.191	6	6	0	95	11	3	.972
—	Iowa (Am. Assoc.)	C	12	36	3	8	1	0	0	4	.222	4	8	2	62	5	3	.957
1992—	Chicago (N.L.)	C	91	270	19	73	3	1	1	12	.270	19	38	0	369	51	4	.991
1993—	Colorado (N.L.)■	C	86	310	35	90	14	5	3	31	.290	24	41	6	478	46	6	.989
—	Colo. Springs (PCL)	C	8	31	6	15	1	1	1	6	.484	0	3	1	40	3	1	.977
1994—	Colorado (N.L.)	C	93	330	47	91	9	4	4	34	.276	21	48	3	549	56	5	.992
1995—	Colorado (N.L.)	C	125	462	63	121	17	2	8	55	.262	29	76	3	730	60	10	.988
Major league totals (7 years)			608	1995	218	536	79	14	18	190	.269	127	285	22	3206	313	46	.987

DIVISION SERIES RECORD

			BATTING											FIELDING			
Year	**Team (League)**	**Pos.**	**G**	**AB**	**R**	**H**	**2B**	**3B**	**HR**	**RBI**	**Avg.**	**BB**	**SO**	**SB**	**PO**	**A**	**E**	**Avg.**
1995—	Colorado (N.L.)	C	4	16	0	2	0	0	0	0	.125	0	2	0	25	3	1	.966

CHAMPIONSHIP SERIES RECORD

			BATTING											FIELDING			
Year	**Team (League)**	**Pos.**	**G**	**AB**	**R**	**H**	**2B**	**3B**	**HR**	**RBI**	**Avg.**	**BB**	**SO**	**SB**	**PO**	**A**	**E**	**Avg.**
1989—	Chicago (N.L.)	C	4	10	1	1	0	0	0	0	.100	1	2	0	20	0	0	1.000

GIVENS, BRIAN — P — BREWERS

PERSONAL: Born November 6, 1965, in Lompoc, Calif.... 6-6/220.... Throws left, bats right.... Full name: Brian Alan Givens.
HIGH SCHOOL: Overland (Aurora, Colo.).
JUNIOR COLLEGE: Trinidad State (Colo.).
TRANSACTIONS/CAREER NOTES: Selected by New York Mets organization in 10th round of free-agent draft (January 17, 1984).... On Lynchburg disabled list (May 21-June 13, 1987).... On Jackson disabled list (April 7-May 13 and May 19-June 12, 1989).... Traded by Mets organization to Seattle Mariners organization for SS Mario Diaz (June 19, 1990).... On Calgary disabled list (July 1, 1990-remainder of season; April 11-May 26 and June 11-September 16, 1991 and April 9-June 2, 1992).... Released by Mariners organization (June 2, 1992).... Signed by Kansas City Royals organization (August 6, 1992).... On disabled list (September 1-18, 1992).... On Memphis disabled list (May 1-July 25, 1993).... Granted free agency (October 15, 1993).... Signed by Chicago White Sox organization (December 8, 1993).... On disabled list (June 22-July 5, 1994).... Granted free agency (October 15, 1994).... Signed by Milwaukee Brewers organization (October 31, 1994).
STATISTICAL NOTES: Led Appalachian League with 20 wild pitches in 1984.... Led Carolina League with 29 wild pitches in 1987.

Year	**Team (League)**	**W**	**L**	**Pct.**	**ERA**	**G**	**GS**	**CG**	**ShO**	**Sv.**	**IP**	**H**	**R**	**ER**	**BB**	**SO**
1984—	Kingsport (Appal.)	4	1	.800	6.50	14	10	0	0	0	44 1/3	41	36	32	52	51
1985—	Little Falls (NYP)	3	4	.429	2.93	11	11	3	1	0	73 2/3	54	28	24	43	81
—	Columbia (S. Atl.)	1	2	.333	2.95	3	3	1	0	0	21 1/3	15	7	7	13	25
1986—	Columbia (S. Atl.)	8	7	.533	3.77	27	27	2	1	0	172	147	89	72	100	*189
1987—	Lynchburg (Caro.)	6	8	.429	4.65	21	20	3	0	0	112 1/3	112	79	58	69	96
—	Tidewater (Int'l)	0	1	.000	24.55	1	1	0	0	0	3 2/3	9	10	10	6	3
1988—	Jackson (Texas)	6	*14	.300	3.78	26	26	4	3	0	164 1/3	140	78	69	68	*156
1989—	St. Lucie (Fla. St.)	0	1	.000	0.00	1	1	0	0	0	5	7	6	0	1	8
—	Jackson (Texas)	3	5	.375	3.39	13	13	2	0	0	85	76	39	32	55	68
1990—	Tidewater (Int'l)	4	6	.400	4.12	15	15	0	0	0	83	99	45	38	39	53
—	Calgary (PCL)■	0	1	.000	12.71	2	2	0	0	0	5 2/3	7	8	8	8	4
1991—	San Bern. (Calif.)	1	0	1.000	1.80	1	1	0	0	0	5	4	2	1	1	4
—	Calgary (PCL)	1	0	1.000	4.91	3	3	0	0	0	14 2/3	16	8	8	6	8
1992—	Memphis (South.)■	0	0	...	3.24	7	0	0	0	0	8 1/3	5	5	3	7	9
1993—	GC Royals (GCL)	0	1	.000	3.38	4	4	0	0	0	8	7	3	3	1	11
—	Memphis (South.)	1	3	.250	4.58	14	4	0	0	2	35 1/3	37	22	18	11	29
1994—	Birmingham (Sou.)■	4	7	.364	3.68	36	13	1	1	1	110	103	57	45	52	111
1995—	New Orleans (A.A.)■	7	4	.636	2.55	16	11	2	1	0	77 2/3	67	28	22	33	75
—	Milwaukee (A.L.)	5	7	.417	4.95	19	19	0	0	0	107 1/3	116	71	59	54	73
Major league totals (1 year)		5	7	.417	4.95	19	19	0	0	0	107 1/3	116	71	59	54	73

GLANVILLE, DOUG — OF — CUBS

PERSONAL: Born August 25, 1970, in Hackensack, N.J.... 6-2/170.... Bats right, throws right.... Full name: Douglas Metunwa Glanville.
HIGH SCHOOL: Teaneck (N.J.).
COLLEGE: Pennsylvania.
TRANSACTIONS/CAREER NOTES: Selected by Chicago Cubs organization in first round (12th pick overall) of free-agent draft (June 3, 1991).

G

STATISTICAL NOTES: Led Carolina League outfielders with 312 total chances in 1992. . . . Led Southern League in caught stealing with 20 in 1994. . . . Led Southern League outfielders with 339 total chances in 1994.

			BATTING											FIELDING			
Year Team (League)	Pos.	G	AB	R	H	2B	3B	HR	RBI	Avg.	BB	SO	SB	PO	A	E	Avg.
1991—Geneva (NYP)	OF	36	152	29	46	8	0	2	12	.303	11	25	17	77	4	0	1.000
1992—Winst.-Salem (Car.)	OF	120	485	72	125	18	4	4	36	.258	40	78	32	*293	12	7	.978
1993—Daytona (Fla. St.)	OF	61	239	47	70	10	1	2	21	.293	28	24	18	123	11	7	.950
—Orlando (Southern)	OF	73	296	42	78	14	4	9	40	.264	12	41	15	168	8	5	.972
1994—Orlando (Southern)	OF	130	483	53	127	22	2	5	52	.263	24	49	26	*322	14	3	.991
1995—Iowa (Am. Assoc.)	OF	112	419	48	113	16	2	4	37	.270	16	64	13	209	9	4	.982

GLAVINE, TOM — P — BRAVES

PERSONAL: Born March 25, 1966, in Concord, Mass. . . . 6-1/185. . . . Throws left, bats left. . . . Full name: Thomas Michael Glavine. . . . Name pronounced GLAV-in.

HIGH SCHOOL: Billerica (Mass.).

TRANSACTIONS/CAREER NOTES: Selected by Atlanta Braves organization in second round of free-agent draft (June 4, 1984).

HONORS: Named N.L. Pitcher of the Year by The Sporting News (1991). . . . Named lefthanded pitcher on The Sporting News N.L. All-Star team (1991-92). . . . Named pitcher on The Sporting News N.L. Silver Slugger team (1991 and 1995). . . . Named N.L. Cy Young Award winner by Baseball Writers' Association of America (1991).

STATISTICAL NOTES: Led Gulf Coast League with 12 wild pitches in 1984.

MISCELLANEOUS: Selected by Los Angeles Kings in fourth round (69th pick overall) of NHL entry draft (June 9, 1984). . . . Appeared in eight games as pinch-runner (1988). . . . Appeared in one game as pinch-runner (1989). . . . Appeared in one game as pinch-runner (1990). . . . Received a base on balls and scored once in one game as pinch-hitter and appeared in one game as pinch-runner (1991). . . . Singled and struck out in two games as pinch-hitter (1992). . . . Struck out in only appearance as pinch-hitter (1994).

Year Team (League)	W	L	Pct.	ERA	G	GS	CG	ShO	Sv.	IP	H	R	ER	BB	SO
1984—GC Braves (GCL)	2	3	.400	3.34	8	7	0	0	0	32 1/3	29	17	12	13	34
1985—Sumter (S. Atl.)	9	6	.600	*2.35	26	26	2	1	0	168 2/3	114	58	44	73	174
1986—Greenville (South.)	11	6	.647	3.41	22	22	2	1	0	145 1/3	129	62	55	70	114
—Richmond (Int'l)	1	5	.167	5.63	7	7	1	1	0	40	40	29	25	27	12
1987—Richmond (Int'l)	6	12	.333	3.35	22	22	4	1	0	150 1/3	142	70	56	56	91
—Atlanta (N.L.)	2	4	.333	5.54	9	9	0	0	0	50 1/3	55	34	31	33	20
1988—Atlanta (N.L.)	7	*17	.292	4.56	34	34	1	0	0	195 1/3	201	111	99	63	84
1989—Atlanta (N.L.)	14	8	.636	3.68	29	29	6	4	0	186	172	88	76	40	90
1990—Atlanta (N.L.)	10	12	.455	4.28	33	33	1	0	0	214 1/3	232	111	102	78	129
1991—Atlanta (N.L.)	•20	11	.645	2.55	34	34	•9	1	0	246 2/3	201	83	70	69	192
1992—Atlanta (N.L.)	•20	8	.714	2.76	33	33	7	•5	0	225	197	81	69	70	129
1993—Atlanta (N.L.)	•22	6	.786	3.20	36	•36	4	2	0	239 1/3	236	91	85	90	120
1994—Atlanta (N.L.)	13	9	.591	3.97	25	25	2	0	0	165 1/3	173	76	73	70	140
1995—Atlanta (N.L.)	16	7	.696	3.08	29	29	3	1	0	198 2/3	182	76	68	66	127
Major league totals (9 years)	124	82	.602	3.52	262	262	33	13	0	1721	1649	751	673	579	1031

DIVISION SERIES RECORD

Year Team (League)	W	L	Pct.	ERA	G	GS	CG	ShO	Sv.	IP	H	R	ER	BB	SO
1995—Atlanta (N.L.)	0	0	. . .	2.57	1	1	0	0	0	7	5	3	2	1	3

CHAMPIONSHIP SERIES RECORD

NOTES: Holds records for most runs allowed in one inning—8 (October 13, 1992, second inning); and most earned runs allowed in one inning—7 (October 13, 1992, second inning). . . . Shares single-game record for most earned runs allowed—7 (October 13, 1992). . . . Shares record for most hits allowed in one inning—6 (October 13, 1992, second inning). . . . Shares N.L. career record for most hit batsmen—2. . . . Shares N.L. single-series record for most hit batsmen—2 (1992).

Year Team (League)	W	L	Pct.	ERA	G	GS	CG	ShO	Sv.	IP	H	R	ER	BB	SO
1991—Atlanta (N.L.)	0	2	.000	3.21	2	2	0	0	0	14	12	5	5	6	11
1992—Atlanta (N.L.)	0	2	.000	12.27	2	2	0	0	0	7 1/3	13	11	10	3	2
1993—Atlanta (N.L.)	1	0	1.000	2.57	1	1	0	0	0	7	6	2	2	0	5
1995—Atlanta (N.L.)	0	0	. . .	1.29	1	1	0	0	0	7	7	1	1	2	5
Champ. series totals (4 years)	1	4	.200	4.58	6	6	0	0	0	35 1/3	38	19	18	11	23

WORLD SERIES RECORD

NOTES: Shares records for most bases on balls allowed in one inning—4 (October 24, 1991, sixth inning); and most consecutive bases on balls allowed in one inning—3 (October 24, 1991, sixth inning). . . . Named Most Valuable Player (1995). . . . Member of World Series championship team (1995).

Year Team (League)	W	L	Pct.	ERA	G	GS	CG	ShO	Sv.	IP	H	R	ER	BB	SO
1991—Atlanta (N.L.)	1	1	.500	2.70	2	2	1	0	0	13 1/3	8	6	4	7	8
1992—Atlanta (N.L.)	1	1	.500	1.59	2	2	2	0	0	17	10	3	3	4	8
1995—Atlanta (N.L.)	2	0	1.000	1.29	2	2	0	0	0	14	4	2	2	6	11
World Series totals (3 years)	4	2	.667	1.83	6	6	3	0	0	44 1/3	22	11	9	17	27

ALL-STAR GAME RECORD

NOTES: Holds single-game record for most hits allowed—9 (July 14, 1992). . . . Holds record for most hits allowed in one inning—7 (July 14, 1992, first inning).

Year League	W	L	Pct.	ERA	GS	CG	ShO	Sv.	IP	H	R	ER	BB	SO
1991—National	0	0	. . .	0.00	1	0	0	0	2	1	0	0	1	3
1992—National	0	1	.000	27.00	1	0	0	0	1 2/3	9	5	5	0	2
1993—National						Did not play.								
All-Star totals (2 years)	0	1	.000	12.27	2	0	0	0	3 2/3	10	5	5	1	5

GOFF, JERRY — C — ASTROS

PERSONAL: Born April 12, 1964, in San Rafael, Calif. . . . 6-3/207. . . . Bats left, throws right. . . . Full name: Jerry Leroy Goff.

HIGH SCHOOL: San Rafael (Calif.).
JUNIOR COLLEGE: Marin Community College (Calif.).
COLLEGE: California.
TRANSACTIONS/CAREER NOTES: Selected by Oakland Athletics organization in seventh round of free-agent draft (January 11, 1983); did not sign. . . . Selected by New York Yankees organization in 12th round of free-agent draft (January 17, 1984); did not sign. . . . Selected by Seattle Mariners organization in third round of free-agent draft (June 2, 1986). . . . Traded by Mariners organization to Montreal Expos for P Pat Pacillo (February 27, 1990). . . . On disabled list (June 14-July 11 and July 21-September 6, 1991). . . . Granted free agency (October 16, 1992). . . . Signed by Buffalo, Pittsburgh Pirates organization (January 20, 1993). . . . Granted free agency (October 14, 1994). . . . Signed by Tucson, Houston Astros organization (February 8, 1995). . . . Granted free agency (October 11, 1995). . . . Re-signed by Astros organization (December 28, 1995).
STATISTICAL NOTES: Led Northwest League catchers with seven double plays in 1986. . . . Led Midwest League with 32 passed balls in 1987. . . . Led Eastern League catchers with 17 errors in 1988. . . . Led Pacific Coast League with 14 passed balls in 1989. . . . Led American Association catchers with 499 putouts in 1993. . . . Led American Association catchers with eight double plays and 15 passed balls in 1994. . . . Led Pacific Coast League with 12 passed balls in 1995.

			BATTING											FIELDING			
Year Team (League)	Pos.	G	AB	R	H	2B	3B	HR	RBI	Avg.	BB	SO	SB	PO	A	E	Avg.
1986— Belling. (N'west)	C	54	168	26	32	7	2	7	25	.190	42	54	4	286	35	12	.964
1987— Wausau (Midwest)	C-1B-3B	109	336	51	78	17	2	13	47	.232	65	87	4	589	90	16	.977
1988— San Bern. (Calif.)	C	65	215	38	62	11	0	13	43	.288	52	59	2	383	64	6	.987
— Vermont (Eastern)	C-OF	63	195	27	41	7	1	7	23	.210	23	58	2	283	40	†17	.950
1989— Williamsport (East.)	C-OF	33	119	9	22	5	0	3	8	.185	14	42	1	180	21	6	.971
— Calgary (PCL)	C-1-3-O	76	253	40	59	16	0	11	50	.233	23	62	1	346	63	12	.971
1990— Indianapolis (A.A.)■	C-3-1-2	39	143	23	41	10	2	5	26	.287	24	33	3	162	24	6	.969
— Montreal (N.L.)	C-1B-3B	52	119	14	27	1	0	3	7	.227	21	36	0	216	17	9	.963
1991— Indianapolis (A.A.)	C-3B-1B	57	191	32	48	10	2	9	37	.251	22	51	2	204	44	13	.950
1992— Indianapolis (A.A.)	3B-C-1B	94	314	37	75	17	1	14	39	.239	32	97	0	136	145	24	.921
— Montreal (N.L.)	PH	3	3	0	0	0	0	0	0	.000	0	3	0	...	...	...	...
1993— Buffalo (A.A.)■	C-3B	104	362	52	91	27	3	14	69	.251	55	82	1	†500	53	7	.988
— Pittsburgh (N.L.)	C	14	37	5	11	2	0	2	6	.297	8	9	0	54	7	1	.984
1994— Pittsburgh (N.L.)	C	8	25	0	2	0	0	0	1	.080	0	11	0	34	4	2	.950
— Buffalo (A.A.)	C	79	277	28	70	19	1	4	32	.253	32	64	0	361	35	3	.992
1995— Tucson (PCL)■	C-1B-3B	68	207	23	46	11	1	6	34	.222	29	56	0	351	39	5	.987
— Houston (N.L.)	C	12	26	2	4	2	0	1	3	.154	4	13	0	80	6	0	1.000
Major league totals (5 years)		89	210	21	44	5	0	6	17	.210	33	72	0	384	34	12	.972

GOHR, GREG — P — TIGERS

PERSONAL: Born October 29, 1967, in Santa Clara, Calif. . . . 6-3/205. . . . Throws right, bats right. . . . Full name: Gregory James Gohr.
HIGH SCHOOL: Bellarmine Prep (San Jose, Calif.).
COLLEGE: Santa Clara.
TRANSACTIONS/CAREER NOTES: Selected by Detroit Tigers organization in first round (21st pick overall) of free-agent draft (June 5, 1989). . . . On disabled list (July 27-August 18 and August 25-September 8, 1992). . . . On Detroit disabled list (July 20-August 10, 1994). . . . On Detroit disabled list (April 19-September 1, 1995); including rehabilitation assignments to Toledo (May 10-26 and August 21-September 1).
STATISTICAL NOTES: Led International League with 14 wild pitches in 1991.

Year Team (League)	W	L	Pct.	ERA	G	GS	CG	ShO	Sv.	IP	H	R	ER	BB	SO
1989— Fayetteville (S. Atl.)	0	2	.000	7.15	4	4	0	0	0	11 1/3	11	9	9	6	10
1990— Lakeland (Fla. St.)	13	5	.722	2.62	25	25	0	0	0	137 2/3	125	52	40	50	90
1991— London (Eastern)	0	0	...	0.00	2	2	0	0	0	11	9	0	0	2	10
— Toledo (Int'l)	10	8	.556	4.61	26	26	2	1	0	148 1/3	125	86	76	66	96
1992— Toledo (Int'l)	8	10	.444	3.99	22	20	2	0	0	130 2/3	124	65	58	46	94
1993— Detroit (A.L.)	0	0	...	5.96	16	0	0	0	0	22 2/3	26	15	15	14	23
— Toledo (Int'l)	3	10	.231	5.80	18	17	2	0	0	107	127	74	69	38	77
1994— Toledo (Int'l)	6	4	.600	3.56	12	12	0	0	0	73 1/3	75	34	29	18	56
— Detroit (A.L.)	2	2	.500	4.50	8	6	0	0	0	34	36	19	17	21	21
1995— Toledo (Int'l)	0	2	.000	2.87	6	4	0	0	0	15 2/3	16	9	5	8	15
— Detroit (A.L.)	1	0	1.000	0.87	10	0	0	0	0	10 1/3	9	1	1	3	12
Major league totals (3 years)	3	2	.600	4.43	34	6	0	0	0	67	71	35	33	38	56

GOMES, WAYNE — P — PHILLIES

PERSONAL: Born January 15, 1973, in Langley AFB, Va. . . . 6-2/205. . . . Throws right, bats right. . . . Full name: Wayne M. Gomes.
HIGH SCHOOL: Phoebus (Hampton, Va.).
COLLEGE: Old Dominion.
TRANSACTIONS/CAREER NOTES: Selected by Philadelphia Phillies organization in first round (fourth pick overall) of free-agent draft (June 3, 1993). . . . On disabled list (May 12-June 23, 1995).
STATISTICAL NOTES: Led Florida State League with 27 wild pitches in 1994. . . . Tied for Eastern League lead with six balks in 1995.

Year Team (League)	W	L	Pct.	ERA	G	GS	CG	ShO	Sv.	IP	H	R	ER	BB	SO
1993— Batavia (NYP)	1	0	1.000	1.23	5	0	0	0	0	7 1/3	1	1	1	8	11
— Clearwater (Fla. St.)	0	0	...	1.17	9	0	0	0	4	7 2/3	4	1	1	9	13
1994— Clearwater (Fla. St.)	6	8	.429	4.74	23	21	1	1	0	104 1/3	85	63	55	82	102
1995— Reading (Eastern)	7	4	.636	3.96	22	22	1	1	0	104 2/3	89	54	46	70	102

GOMEZ, CHRIS — SS — TIGERS

PERSONAL: Born June 16, 1971, in Los Angeles. . . . 6-1/183. . . . Bats right, throws right. . . . Full name: Christopher Cory Gomez.
HIGH SCHOOL: Lakewood (Calif.).
COLLEGE: Long Beach State.

TRANSACTIONS/CAREER NOTES: Selected by California Angels organization in 37th round of free-agent draft (June 5, 1989); did not sign. . . . Selected by Detroit Tigers organization in third round of free-agent draft (June 1, 1992).

			BATTING												FIELDING			
Year	Team (League)	Pos.	G	AB	R	H	2B	3B	HR	RBI	Avg.	BB	SO	SB	PO	A	E	Avg.
1992	London (Eastern)	SS	64	220	20	59	13	2	1	19	.268	20	34	1	100	174	14	.951
1993	Toledo (Int'l)	SS	87	277	29	68	12	2	0	20	.245	23	37	6	133	261	16	.961
	—Detroit (A.L.)	SS-2B-DH	46	128	11	32	7	1	0	11	.250	9	17	2	69	118	5	.974
1994	Detroit (A.L.)	SS-2B	84	296	32	76	19	0	8	53	.257	33	64	5	140	210	8	.978
1995	Detroit (A.L.)	SS-2B-DH	123	431	49	96	20	2	11	50	.223	41	96	4	210	361	15	.974
Major league totals (3 years)			253	855	92	204	46	3	19	114	.239	83	177	11	419	689	28	.975

GOMEZ, LEO — 3B — CUBS

PERSONAL: Born March 2, 1967, in Canovanas, Puerto Rico. . . . 6-0/208. . . . Bats right, throws right. . . . Full name: Leonardo Gomez.
HIGH SCHOOL: Luis Hernaes Nevones (Canovanas, Puerto Rico).
TRANSACTIONS/CAREER NOTES: Signed as non-drafted free agent by Baltimore Orioles organization (December 13, 1985). . . . On disabled list (July 3-31, 1986 and May 3, 1988-remainder of season). . . . On Baltimore disabled list (July 8-September 1, 1993); included rehabilitation assignment to Rochester (August 26-September 1). . . . On disabled list (July 31, 1995-remainder of season). . . . Granted free agency (December 21, 1995). . . . Signed by Chicago Cubs organization (January 24, 1996).
STATISTICAL NOTES: Led Eastern League third basemen with 256 assists in 1989. . . . Led International League third basemen with 26 double plays in 1990. . . . Career major league grand slams: 1.

			BATTING												FIELDING			
Year	Team (League)	Pos.	G	AB	R	H	2B	3B	HR	RBI	Avg.	BB	SO	SB	PO	A	E	Avg.
1986	Bluefield (Appal.)	3B-2B-SS	27	88	23	31	7	1	7	28	.352	25	27	1	15	38	7	.883
1987	Hagerstown (Car.)	3B-SS	131	466	94	152	*38	2	19	110	*.326	95	85	6	75	233	33	.903
1988	Charlotte (South.)	3B-1B	24	89	6	26	5	0	1	10	.292	10	17	1	19	50	8	.896
1989	Hagerstown (East.)	3B-SS	134	448	71	126	23	3	18	78	.281	*89	102	2	79	†257	25	.931
1990	Rochester (Int'l)	3B-1B	131	430	*97	119	26	4	26	*97	.277	89	89	2	92	204	20	.937
	—Baltimore (A.L.)	3B	12	39	3	9	0	0	0	1	.231	8	7	0	11	20	4	.886
1991	Baltimore (A.L.)	3B-DH-1B	118	391	40	91	17	2	16	45	.233	40	82	1	78	184	7	.974
	—Rochester (Int'l)	3B-1B	28	101	13	26	6	0	6	19	.257	16	18	0	24	46	4	.946
1992	Baltimore (A.L.)	3B	137	468	62	124	24	0	17	64	.265	63	78	2	106	246	18	.951
1993	Baltimore (A.L.)	3B-DH	71	244	30	48	7	0	10	25	.197	32	60	0	48	145	10	.951
	—Rochester (Int'l)	3B	4	15	3	3	1	0	0	1	.200	3	4	0	1	5	0	1.000
1994	Baltimore (A.L.)	3B-DH-1B	84	285	46	78	20	0	15	56	.274	41	55	0	56	141	5	.975
1995	Baltimore (A.L.)	3B-DH-1B	53	127	16	30	5	0	4	12	.236	18	23	0	28	68	2	.980
Major league totals (6 years)			475	1554	197	380	73	2	62	203	.245	202	305	3	327	804	46	.961

GOMEZ, PAT — P

PERSONAL: Born March 17, 1968, in Roseville, Calif. . . . 5-11/185. . . . Throws left, bats left. . . . Full name: Patrick Alexander Gomez.
HIGH SCHOOL: San Juan (Citrus Heights, Calif.).
TRANSACTIONS/CAREER NOTES: Selected by Chicago Cubs organization in fourth round of free-agent draft (June 2, 1986). . . . Traded by Cubs organization with C Kelly Mann to Atlanta Braves (September 1, 1989), completing deal in which Braves traded P Paul Assenmacher to Cubs for two players to be named later (August 24, 1989). . . . Traded by Braves organization to Texas Rangers organization for 3B Jose Oliva (December 9, 1992). . . . Traded by Rangers organization to San Diego Padres for P Terry Bross (December 16, 1992). . . . On San Diego disabled list (June 26, 1993-remainder of season); included rehabilitation assignment to Las Vegas but did not play (July 18-23). . . . Granted free agency (October 5, 1993). . . . Signed by San Francisco Giants organization (February 27, 1994). . . . On San Francisco disabled list (May 13-August 22, 1995); included rehabilitation assignments to Phoenix (June 26-30) and San Jose (August 13-22). . . . Released by Giants (October 18, 1995).
MISCELLANEOUS: Struck out in one game as pinch-hitter (1993).

Year	Team (League)	W	L	Pct.	ERA	G	GS	CG	ShO	Sv.	IP	H	R	ER	BB	SO
1986	Wytheville (Appal.)	3	6	.333	5.17	11	11	0	0	0	54	57	51	31	46	55
1987	Peoria (Midwest)	3	6	.333	4.31	20	17	1	0	0	94	88	55	45	71	95
1988	Char., W.Va. (S. Atl.)	2	7	.222	5.38	36	9	0	0	5	78 2/3	75	53	47	52	97
1989	Winst.-Salem (Car.)	11	6	.647	2.75	23	21	3	1	0	137 2/3	115	59	42	60	127
	—Charlotte (South.)■	1	0	1.000	2.51	2	2	0	0	0	14 1/3	14	5	4	3	11
1990	Richmond (Int'l)	1	1	.500	8.80	4	4	0	0	0	15 1/3	19	16	15	10	8
	—Greenville (South.)	6	8	.429	4.49	23	21	0	0	0	124 1/3	126	75	62	71	94
1991	Greenville (South.)	5	2	.714	1.81	13	13	0	0	0	79 2/3	58	20	16	31	71
	—Richmond (Int'l)	2	9	.182	4.39	16	14	0	0	0	82	99	55	40	41	41
1992	Richmond (Int'l)	3	5	.375	5.45	23	11	0	0	0	71	79	47	43	42	48
	—Greenville (South.)	7	0	1.000	1.13	8	8	1	1	0	47 2/3	25	8	6	19	38
1993	San Diego (N.L.)■	1	2	.333	5.12	27	1	0	0	0	31 2/3	35	19	18	19	26
1994	Phoenix (PCL)■	1	0	1.000	4.76	11	0	0	0	1	11 1/3	14	6	6	4	10
	—San Francisco (N.L.)	0	1	.000	3.78	26	0	0	0	0	33 1/3	23	14	14	20	14
1995	San Francisco (N.L.)	0	0	...	5.14	18	0	0	0	0	14	16	8	8	12	15
	—Phoenix (PCL)	0	0	...	27.00	2	0	0	0	0	1 1/3	5	5	4	3	1
	—San Jose (Calif.)	0	0	...	1.42	3	2	0	0	0	6 1/3	5	2	1	5	5
Major league totals (3 years)		1	3	.250	4.56	71	1	0	0	0	79	74	41	40	51	55

GONZALES, RENE — IF — RANGERS

PERSONAL: Born September 3, 1961, in Austin, Tex. . . . 6-3/201. . . . Bats right, throws right. . . . Full name: Rene Adrian Gonzales.
HIGH SCHOOL: Rosemead (Calif.).
JUNIOR COLLEGE: Glendale (Calif.) College.
COLLEGE: Cal State Los Angeles.

TRANSACTIONS/CAREER NOTES: Selected by Montreal Expos organization in fifth round of free-agent draft (June 7, 1982).... Traded by Expos to Baltimore Orioles (December 16, 1986), completing deals in which Orioles traded P Dennis Martinez (June 16, 1986) and C John Stefero (December 8, 1986) to Expos for a player to be named later.... Traded by Orioles to Toronto Blue Jays for P Rob Blumberg (January 15, 1991).... Granted free agency (November 18, 1991).... Signed by California Angels organization (January 10, 1992).... On disabled list (August 12, 1992-remainder of season).... Granted free agency (October 26, 1992).... Re-signed by Angels (December 18, 1992).... Granted free agency (October 29, 1993).... Signed by Orioles organization (February 3, 1994).... Released by Rochester, Orioles organization (April 6, 1994).... Signed by Charlotte, Cleveland Indians organization (April 6, 1994).... Granted free agency (October 25, 1994).... Signed by Midland, Angels organization (April 16, 1995).... On Vancouver disabled list (April 25-May 2, 1995).... Granted free agency (October 30, 1995).... Signed by Texas Rangers organization (January 9, 1996).

STATISTICAL NOTES: Led Southern League shortstops with 102 double plays in 1983.... Led American Association shortstops with 79 double plays in 1985.

		BATTING												FIELDING			
Year Team (League)	**Pos.**	**G**	**AB**	**R**	**H**	**2B**	**3B**	**HR**	**RBI**	**Avg.**	**BB**	**SO**	**SB**	**PO**	**A**	**E**	**Avg.**
1982—Memphis (South.)	SS	56	183	10	39	3	1	1	11	.213	9	44	2	77	183	14	.949
1983—Memphis (South.)	SS	144	476	67	128	12	2	2	44	.269	40	53	5	*258	449	20	*.972
1984—Indianapolis (A.A.)	SS-3B-2B	114	359	41	84	12	2	2	32	.234	20	33	10	161	349	13	.975
—Montreal (N.L.)	SS	29	30	5	7	1	0	0	2	.233	2	5	0	17	28	2	.957
1985—Indianapolis (A.A.)	SS	130	340	21	77	11	1	0	25	.226	22	49	3	203	*345	23	.960
1986—Indianapolis (A.A.)	3B-SS-2B	116	395	57	108	14	2	3	43	.273	41	47	8	208	297	23	.956
—Montreal (N.L.)	SS-3B	11	26	1	3	0	0	0	0	.115	2	7	0	7	19	0	1.000
1987—Baltimore (A.L.)■	3B-2B-SS	37	60	14	16	2	1	1	7	.267	3	11	1	22	43	2	.970
—Rochester (Int'l)	3-S-2-1-O	42	170	20	51	9	3	0	24	.300	13	17	4	72	108	3	.984
1988—Baltimore (A.L.)	3-2-S-1-O	92	237	13	51	6	0	2	15	.215	13	32	2	66	185	8	.969
1989—Baltimore (A.L.)	2B-3B-SS	71	166	16	36	4	0	1	11	.217	12	30	5	103	146	7	.973
1990—Baltimore (A.L.)	2-3-S-O	67	103	13	22	3	1	1	12	.214	12	14	1	68	114	2	.989
1991—Toronto (A.L.)■	S-3-2-1	71	118	16	23	3	0	1	6	.195	12	22	0	61	118	7	.962
1992—California (A.L.)■	3-2-1-S	104	329	47	91	17	1	7	38	.277	41	46	7	191	229	9	.979
1993—California (A.L.)	3-1-S-2-P	118	335	34	84	17	0	2	31	.251	49	45	5	234	170	12	.971
1994—Charlotte (Int'l)■	S-3-1-O	42	133	26	30	4	0	2	17	.226	38	21	1	79	106	3	.984
—Cleveland (A.L.)	3-1-S-2	22	23	6	8	1	1	1	5	.348	5	3	2	17	21	1	.974
1995—Midland (Texas)	2B	5	17	1	3	0	0	0	2	.176	4	1	0	11	16	1	.964
—Vancouver (PCL)■	S-3-2-1	50	165	27	45	12	0	4	18	.273	24	25	0	53	120	10	.945
—California (A.L.)	3B-2B-SS	30	18	1	6	1	0	1	3	.333	0	4	0	6	12	0	1.000
American League totals (9 years)		612	1389	160	337	54	4	17	128	.243	147	207	23	768	1038	48	.974
National League totals (2 years)		40	56	6	10	1	0	0	2	.179	4	12	0	24	47	2	.973
Major league totals (11 years)		652	1445	166	347	55	4	17	130	.240	151	219	23	792	1085	50	.974

CHAMPIONSHIP SERIES RECORD

		BATTING												FIELDING			
Year Team (League)	**Pos.**	**G**	**AB**	**R**	**H**	**2B**	**3B**	**HR**	**RBI**	**Avg.**	**BB**	**SO**	**SB**	**PO**	**A**	**E**	**Avg.**
1991—Toronto (A.L.)	PR-1B-SS	2	0	0	0	0	0	0	0	...	0	0	0	2	0	0	1.000

RECORD AS PITCHER

Year Team (League)	**W**	**L**	**Pct.**	**ERA**	**G**	**GS**	**CG**	**ShO**	**Sv.**	**IP**	**H**	**R**	**ER**	**BB**	**SO**
1993—California (A.L.)	0	0	...	0.00	1	0	0	0	0	1	0	0	0	0	0

GONZALEZ, ALEX SS BLUE JAYS

PERSONAL: Born April 8, 1973, in Miami.... 6-0/185.... Bats right, throws right.... Full name: Alexander Scott Gonzalez.

HIGH SCHOOL: Miami Killian.

TRANSACTIONS/CAREER NOTES: Selected by Toronto Blue Jays organization in 14th round of free-agent draft (June 3, 1991).... On Toronto disabled list (April 29-May 27, 1994); included rehabilitation assignment to Syracuse (May 14-27).

STATISTICAL NOTES: Led Gulf Coast League shortstops with 247 total chances in 1991.... Led Southern League with 253 total bases in 1993.... Led Southern League shortstops with 682 total chances and 92 double plays in 1993.... Led International League shortstops with 542 total chances in 1994.

		BATTING												FIELDING			
Year Team (League)	**Pos.**	**G**	**AB**	**R**	**H**	**2B**	**3B**	**HR**	**RBI**	**Avg.**	**BB**	**SO**	**SB**	**PO**	**A**	**E**	**Avg.**
1991—GC Blue Jays (GCL)	SS	53	191	29	40	5	4	0	10	.209	12	41	7	66	*160	21	.915
1992—Myrtle Beach (SAL)	SS	134	535	83	145	22	9	10	62	.271	38	119	26	*248	*406	48	.932
1993—Knoxville (S. Atl.)	SS	*142	561	*93	162	29	7	16	69	.289	39	110	38	*224	*428	30	*.956
1994—Toronto (A.L.)	SS	15	53	7	8	3	1	0	1	.151	4	17	3	18	49	6	.918
—Syracuse (Int'l)	SS	110	437	69	124	22	4	12	57	.284	53	92	23	*163	*348	*31	.943
1995—Toronto (A.L.)	SS-3B-DH	111	367	51	89	19	4	10	42	.243	44	114	4	164	227	19	.954
Major league totals (2 years)		126	420	58	97	22	5	10	43	.231	48	131	7	182	276	25	.948

GONZALEZ, JUAN OF RANGERS

PERSONAL: Born October 16, 1969, in Vega Baja, Puerto Rico.... 6-3/215.... Bats right, throws right.... Full name: Juan Alberto Vazquez Gonzalez.

HIGH SCHOOL: Vega Baja (Puerto Rico).

TRANSACTIONS/CAREER NOTES: Signed as non-drafted free agent by Texas Rangers organization (May 30, 1986).... On disabled list (April 27-June 17, 1988; March 30-April 26, 1991; and April 16-June 1 and July 27-August 16, 1995).

HONORS: Named American Association Most Valuable Player (1990).... Named outfielder on The Sporting News A.L. Silver Slugger team (1992-93).... Named outfielder on The Sporting News A.L. All-Star team (1993).

STATISTICAL NOTES: Led Texas League with 254 total bases in 1989.... Led American Association with 252 total bases in 1990.... Hit three home runs in one game (June 7, 1992 and August 28, 1993).... Led A.L. with .632 slugging percentage in 1993.... Career major league grand slams: 4.

Year Team (League)	Pos.	BATTING G	AB	R	H	2B	3B	HR	RBI	Avg.	BB	SO	SB	FIELDING PO	A	E	Avg.
1986—GC Rangers (GCL)	OF	60	*233	24	56	4	1	0	36	.240	21	57	7	89	6	•6	.941
1987—Gastonia (S. Atl.)	OF	127	509	69	135	21	2	14	74	.265	30	92	9	234	10	12	.953
1988—Charlotte (Fla. St.)	OF	77	277	25	71	14	3	8	43	.256	25	64	5	139	5	4	.973
1989—Tulsa (Texas)	OF	133	502	73	147	30	7	21	85	.293	31	98	1	292	15	9	.972
—Texas (A.L.)	OF	24	60	6	9	3	0	1	7	.150	6	17	0	53	0	2	.964
1990—Okla. City (A.A.)	OF	128	496	78	128	29	4	*29	*101	.258	32	109	2	220	7	8	.966
—Texas (A.L.)	OF-DH	25	90	11	26	7	1	4	12	.289	2	18	0	33	0	0	1.000
1991—Texas (A.L.)	OF-DH	142	545	78	144	34	1	27	102	.264	42	118	4	310	6	6	.981
1992—Texas (A.L.)	OF-DH	155	584	77	152	24	2	*43	109	.260	35	143	0	379	9	10	.975
1993—Texas (A.L.)	OF-DH	140	536	105	166	33	1	*46	118	.310	37	99	4	265	5	4	.985
1994—Texas (A.L.)	OF	107	422	57	116	18	4	19	85	.275	30	66	6	223	9	2	.991
1995—Texas (A.L.)	DH-OF	90	352	57	104	20	2	27	82	.295	17	66	0	6	1	0	1.000
Major league totals (7 years)		683	2589	391	717	139	11	167	515	.277	169	527	14	1269	30	24	.982

ALL-STAR GAME RECORD

Year League	Pos.	BATTING AB	R	H	2B	3B	HR	RBI	Avg.	BB	SO	SB	FIELDING PO	A	E	Avg.
1993—American	OF	1	0	0	0	0	0	0	.000	1	1	0	1	0	0	1.000

GONZALEZ, LUIS — OF — CUBS

PERSONAL: Born September 3, 1967, in Tampa, Fla. . . . 6-2/185. . . . Bats left, throws right. . . . Full name: Luis Emilio Gonzalez.
HIGH SCHOOL: Jefferson (Tampa, Fla.).
COLLEGE: South Alabama.
TRANSACTIONS/CAREER NOTES: Selected by Houston Astros organization in fourth round of free-agent draft (June 1, 1988). . . . On disabled list (May 26-July 5, 1989 and August 29-September 13, 1991). . . . On Houston disabled list (July 21-August 5, 1992). . . . Traded by Astros with C Scott Servais to Chicago Cubs for C Rick Wikins (June 28, 1995).
STATISTICAL NOTES: Tied for Southern League lead with 12 sacrifice flies and nine intentional bases on balls received in 1990. . . . Led N.L. with 10 sacrifice flies in 1993.

Year Team (League)	Pos.	BATTING G	AB	R	H	2B	3B	HR	RBI	Avg.	BB	SO	SB	FIELDING PO	A	E	Avg.
1988—Asheville (S. Atl.)	3B	31	115	13	29	7	1	2	14	.252	12	17	2	19	62	6	.931
—Auburn (NYP)	3B-SS-1B	39	157	32	49	10	3	5	27	.312	12	19	2	37	83	13	.902
1989—Osceola (Fla. St.)	DH	86	287	46	82	16	7	6	38	.286	37	49	2	...	...	...	...
1990—Columbus (South.)	1B-3B	138	495	86	131	30	6	•24	89	.265	54	100	27	1039	88	23	.980
—Houston (N.L.)	3B-1B	12	21	1	4	2	0	0	0	.190	2	5	0	22	10	0	1.000
1991—Houston (N.L.)	OF	137	473	51	120	28	9	13	69	.254	40	101	10	294	6	5	.984
1992—Houston (N.L.)	OF	122	387	40	94	19	3	10	55	.243	24	52	7	261	5	2	.993
—Tucson (PCL)	OF	13	44	11	19	4	2	1	9	.432	5	7	4	26	0	1	.963
1993—Houston (N.L.)	OF	154	540	82	162	34	3	15	72	.300	47	83	20	347	10	8	.978
1994—Houston (N.L.)	OF	112	392	57	107	29	4	8	67	.273	49	57	15	228	5	2	.991
1995—Houston (N.L.)	OF	56	209	35	54	10	4	6	35	.258	18	30	1	94	2	2	.980
—Chicago (N.L.)■	OF	77	262	34	76	19	4	7	34	.290	39	33	5	172	5	4	.978
Major league totals (6 years)		670	2284	300	617	141	27	59	332	.270	219	361	58	1418	43	23	.985

GOODWIN, CURTIS — OF — REDS

PERSONAL: Born September 30, 1972, in Oakland, Calif. . . . 5-11/180. . . . Bats left, throws left. . . . Full name: Curtis LaMar Goodwin.
HIGH SCHOOL: San Leandro (Calif.).
TRANSACTIONS/CAREER NOTES: Selected by Baltimore Orioles organization in 12th round of free-agent draft (June 3, 1991). . . . On Baltimore disabled list (August 20-September 4, 1995). . . . Traded by Orioles with OF Trovin Valdez to Cincinnati Reds for P David Wells (December 26, 1995).
STATISTICAL NOTES: Led Midwest League outfielders with 327 total chances and seven double plays in 1992. . . . Led Eastern League with 13 sacrifice hits in 1994. . . . Led Eastern League outfielders with 323 total chances in 1994.

Year Team (League)	Pos.	BATTING G	AB	R	H	2B	3B	HR	RBI	Avg.	BB	SO	SB	FIELDING PO	A	E	Avg.
1991—GC Orioles (GCL)	OF	48	151	32	39	5	0	0	9	.258	38	25	26	77	5	1	.988
1992—Kane Co. (Midw.)	OF	134	*542	85	153	7	5	1	42	.282	38	106	52	301	15	11	.966
1993—Frederick (Caro.)	OF	•138	*555	*98	•156	15	*10	2	42	.281	52	90	*61	271	9	7	.976
1994—Bowie (Eastern)	OF	*142	*597	*105	*171	18	8	2	37	.286	40	78	*59	*301	12	10	.969
1995—Rochester (Int'l)	OF	36	140	24	37	3	3	0	7	.264	12	15	17	81	1	3	.965
—Baltimore (A.L.)	OF-DH	87	289	40	76	11	3	1	24	.263	15	53	22	202	1	2	.990
Major league totals (1 year)		87	289	40	76	11	3	1	24	.263	15	53	22	202	1	2	.990

GOODWIN, TOM — OF — ROYALS

PERSONAL: Born July 27, 1968, in Fresno, Calif. . . . 6-1/175. . . . Bats left, throws right. . . . Full name: Thomas Jones Goodwin.
HIGH SCHOOL: Central (Fresno, Calif.).
COLLEGE: Fresno State.
TRANSACTIONS/CAREER NOTES: Selected by Pittsburgh Pirates organization in sixth round of free-agent draft (June 2, 1986); did not sign. . . . Selected by Los Angeles Dodgers organization in first round (22nd pick overall) of free-agent draft (June 5, 1989). . . . Claimed on waivers by Kansas City Royals (January 6, 1994).
HONORS: Named outfielder on The Sporting News college All-America team (1989).
STATISTICAL NOTES: Tied for Pacific Coast League lead in caught stealing with 23 in 1991. . . . Led American Association in caught stealing with 20 in 1994. . . . Led A.L. with 14 sacrifice hits in 1995.

MISCELLANEOUS: Member of 1988 U.S. Olympic baseball team.

			BATTING												FIELDING			
Year	Team (League)	Pos.	G	AB	R	H	2B	3B	HR	RBI	Avg.	BB	SO	SB	PO	A	E	Avg.
1989—	Great Falls (Pio.)	OF	63	240	*55	74	12	3	2	33	.308	28	30	*60	67	3	1	.986
1990—	San Antonio (Tex.)	OF	102	428	76	119	15	4	0	28	.278	38	72	*60	264	7	3	*.989
—	Bakersfield (Calif.)	OF	32	134	24	39	6	2	0	13	.291	11	22	22	55	2	0	1.000
1991—	Albuquerque (PCL)	OF	132	509	84	139	19	4	1	45	.273	59	83	48	284	6	3	.990
—	Los Angeles (N.L.)	OF	16	7	3	1	0	0	0	0	.143	0	0	1	8	0	0	1.000
1992—	Albuquerque (PCL)	OF	82	319	48	96	10	4	2	28	.301	37	47	27	184	5	1	.995
—	Los Angeles (N.L.)	OF	57	73	15	17	1	1	0	3	.233	6	10	7	43	0	0	1.000
1993—	Los Angeles (N.L.)	OF	30	17	6	5	1	0	0	1	.294	1	4	1	8	0	0	1.000
—	Albuquerque (PCL)	OF	85	289	48	75	5	5	1	28	.260	30	51	21	145	1	2	.986
1994—	Kansas City (A.L.)■	DH-OF	2	2	0	0	0	0	0	0	.000	0	1	0	1	0	0	1.000
—	Omaha (A.A.)	OF	113	429	67	132	17	7	2	34	.308	23	60	*50	276	3	2	.993
1995—	Kansas City (A.L.)	OF-DH	133	480	72	138	16	3	4	28	.288	38	72	50	292	6	3	.990
American League totals (2 years)			135	482	72	138	16	3	4	28	.286	38	73	50	293	6	3	.990
National League totals (3 years)			103	97	24	23	2	1	0	4	.237	7	14	9	59	0	0	1.000
Major league totals (5 years)			238	579	96	161	18	4	4	32	.278	45	87	59	352	6	3	.992

GORDON, MIKE — P — BLUE JAYS

PERSONAL: Born November 30, 1972, in Quincy, Fla. . . . 6-3/210. . . . Throws right, bats left. . . . Full name: Michael C. Gordon.
HIGH SCHOOL: James A. Shanks (Quincy, Fla.).
TRANSACTIONS/CAREER NOTES: Selected by New York Yankees organization in 11th round of free-agent draft (June 1, 1992). . . . Traded by Yankees organization with P Jason Jarvis and P Marty Janzen to Toronto Blue Jays organization for P David Cone (July 28, 1995).

Year	Team (League)	W	L	Pct.	ERA	G	GS	CG	ShO	Sv.	IP	H	R	ER	BB	SO
1992—	GC Yankees (GCL)	3	4	.429	3.04	11	10	0	0	0	53 1/3	33	21	18	33	55
1993—	GC Yankees (GCL)	4	2	.667	1.67	11	9	0	0	0	64 2/3	43	23	12	27	61
—	Oneonta (NYP)	0	3	.000	6.91	3	3	1	0	0	14 1/3	13	12	11	11	15
1994—	Greensboro (S. Atl.)	2	10	.167	6.46	23	22	0	0	0	107 1/3	128	88	77	54	116
1995—	Tampa (Fla. St.)	4	6	.400	3.04	21	21	1	0	0	124 1/3	111	54	42	49	96
—	Dunedin (Fla. St.)■	1	2	.333	5.89	7	6	0	0	0	36 2/3	44	32	24	24	36

GORDON, TOM — P — RED SOX

PERSONAL: Born November 18, 1967, in Sebring, Fla. . . . 5-9/180. . . . Throws right, bats right. . . . Full name: Thomas Gordon. . . . Brother of Tony Gordon, minor league pitcher (1988-94).
HIGH SCHOOL: Avon Park (Fla.).
TRANSACTIONS/CAREER NOTES: Selected by Kansas City Royals organization in sixth round of free-agent draft (June 2, 1986). . . . On disabled list (August 12-September 1, 1992 and May 8-24, 1995). . . . Granted free agency (October 30, 1995). . . . Signed by Boston Red Sox (December 21, 1995).
HONORS: Named A.L. Rookie Pitcher of the Year by The Sporting News (1989).
STATISTICAL NOTES: Tied for Northwest League lead with four balks in 1987.
MISCELLANEOUS: Appeared in one game as pinch-runner (1991). . . . Appeared in one game as pinch-runner (1995).

Year	Team (League)	W	L	Pct.	ERA	G	GS	CG	ShO	Sv.	IP	H	R	ER	BB	SO
1986—	GC Royals (GCL)	3	1	.750	1.02	9	7	2	1	0	44	31	12	5	23	47
—	Omaha (Am. Assoc.)	0	0	...	47.25	1	0	0	0	0	1 1/3	6	7	7	2	3
1987—	Eugene (N'west)	•9	0	•1.000	2.86	15	13	0	0	1	72 1/3	48	33	23	47	91
—	Fort Myers (Fla. St.)	1	0	1.000	2.63	3	3	0	0	0	13 2/3	5	4	4	17	11
1988—	Appleton (Midw.)	7	5	.583	2.06	17	17	5	1	0	118	69	30	27	43	*172
—	Memphis (South.)	6	0	1.000	0.38	6	6	2	2	0	47 1/3	16	3	2	17	62
—	Omaha (Am. Assoc.)	3	0	1.000	1.33	3	3	0	0	0	20 1/3	11	3	3	15	29
—	Kansas City (A.L.)	0	2	.000	5.17	5	2	0	0	0	15 2/3	16	9	9	7	18
1989—	Kansas City (A.L.)	17	9	.654	3.64	49	16	1	1	1	163	122	67	66	86	153
1990—	Kansas City (A.L.)	12	11	.522	3.73	32	32	6	1	0	195 1/3	192	99	81	99	175
1991—	Kansas City (A.L.)	9	14	.391	3.87	45	14	1	0	1	158	129	76	68	87	167
1992—	Kansas City (A.L.)	6	10	.375	4.59	40	11	0	0	0	117 2/3	116	67	60	55	98
1993—	Kansas City (A.L.)	12	6	.667	3.58	48	14	2	0	1	155 2/3	125	65	62	77	143
1994—	Kansas City (A.L.)	11	7	.611	4.35	24	24	0	0	0	155 1/3	136	79	75	87	126
1995—	Kansas City (A.L.)	12	12	.500	4.43	31	31	2	0	0	189	204	110	93	89	119
Major league totals (8 years)		79	71	.527	4.02	274	144	12	2	3	1149 2/3	1040	572	514	587	999

GORECKI, RICK — P — DODGERS

PERSONAL: Born August 27, 1973, in Evergreen Park, Ill. . . . 6-3/167. . . . Throws right, bats right. . . . Full name: Richard Gorecki.
HIGH SCHOOL: Oak Forest (Ill.).
TRANSACTIONS/CAREER NOTES: Selected by Los Angeles Dodgers organization in 10th round of free-agent draft (June 3, 1991). . . . On disabled list (May 27-June 3 and June 20-July 17, 1994). . . . On Los Angeles disabled list (April 23, 1995-entire season); included rehabilitation assignments to Vero Beach (June 26-29 and July 9-August 3).

Year	Team (League)	W	L	Pct.	ERA	G	GS	CG	ShO	Sv.	IP	H	R	ER	BB	SO
1991—	Great Falls (Pio.)	0	3	.000	4.41	13	10	0	0	0	51	44	34	25	27	56
1992—	Bakersfield (Calif.)	11	7	.611	4.05	25	24	0	0	0	129	122	68	58	90	115
1993—	San Antonio (Tex.)	6	9	.400	3.35	26	26	0	0	0	156	136	76	58	62	118
1994—	Albuquerque (PCL)	8	6	.571	5.07	22	21	0	0	0	103	119	65	58	60	73
1995—	Vero Beach (FSL)	1	2	.333	0.67	6	5	0	0	0	27	19	6	2	9	24

GOTT, JIM — P

PERSONAL: Born August 3, 1959, in Hollywood, Calif. . . . 6-4/229. . . . Throws right, bats right. . . . Full name: James William Gott.
HIGH SCHOOL: San Marino (Calif.).
COLLEGE: Brigham Young.
TRANSACTIONS/CAREER NOTES: Selected by St. Louis Cardinals organization in fourth round of free-agent draft (June 7, 1977). . . . On Arkansas disabled list (August 16-September 1, 1979). . . . Selected by Toronto Blue Jays from Cardinals organization in Rule 5 major league draft (December 7, 1981). . . . Traded by Blue Jays with P Jack McKnight and IF Augie Schmidt to San Francisco Giants for P Gary Lavelle (January 26, 1985). . . . On San Francisco disabled list (May 9, 1986-remainder of season); included rehabilitation assignment to Phoenix (June 9-24). . . . Released by Giants organization (December 19, 1986). . . . Re-signed by Giants (April 7, 1987). . . . Claimed on waivers by Pittsburgh Pirates (August 3, 1987). . . . On disabled list (April 7, 1989-remainder of season). . . . Granted free agency (November 13, 1989). . . . Signed by Los Angeles Dodgers (December 7, 1989). . . . On Los Angeles disabled list (April 7-May 25, 1990); included rehabilitation assignment to Bakersfield (May 4-25). . . . On Los Angeles disabled list (June 7-July 12, 1994); included rehabilitation assignment to Bakersfield (July 8-12). . . . Granted free agency (October 7, 1994). . . . Signed by Pirates (April 7, 1995). . . . On disabled list (May 29-June 15, June 27-July 12 and August 4, 1995-remainder of season). . . . Released by Pirates (October 6, 1995).
STATISTICAL NOTES: Led Western Carolinas League with 21 wild pitches in 1979.

Year Team (League)	W	L	Pct.	ERA	G	GS	CG	ShO	Sv.	IP	H	R	ER	BB	SO
1977— Calgary (Pioneer)	3	4	.429	9.55	14	•14	0	0	0	65	71	*82	*69	*83	60
1978— Gastonia (W. Caro.)	9	6	.600	3.97	22	22	4	0	0	145	100	67	64	•113	130
— St. Petersburg (FSL)	1	3	.250	1.29	5	5	2	0	0	28	23	9	4	12	15
1979— St. Petersburg (FSL)	0	3	.000	6.50	4	4	0	0	0	18	18	13	13	13	9
— Gastonia (W. Caro.)	5	5	.500	5.61	19	11	1	0	0	77	63	57	48	88	102
— Arkansas (Texas)	0	1	.000	5.40	2	1	0	0	0	5	3	6	3	13	7
1980— St. Petersburg (FSL)	5	11	.313	4.60	25	21	4	1	0	137	138	96	70	113	103
1981— Arkansas (Texas)	5	9	.357	3.44	28	19	4	0	0	131	133	68	50	65	93
1982— Toronto (A.L.)■	5	10	.333	4.43	30	23	1	1	0	136	134	76	67	66	82
1983— Toronto (A.L.)	9	14	.391	4.74	34	30	6	1	0	176 2/3	195	103	93	68	121
1984— Toronto (A.L.)	7	6	.538	4.02	35	12	1	1	2	109 2/3	93	54	49	49	73
1985— San Francisco (N.L.)■	7	10	.412	3.88	26	26	2	0	0	148 1/3	144	73	64	51	78
1986— San Francisco (N.L.)	0	0	...	7.62	9	2	0	0	1	13	16	12	11	13	9
— Phoenix (PCL)	0	0	...	6.75	2	2	0	0	0	2 2/3	2	2	2	3	2
1987— San Francisco (N.L.)	1	0	1.000	4.50	30	3	0	0	0	56	53	32	28	32	63
— Pittsburgh (N.L.)■	0	2	.000	1.45	25	0	0	0	13	31	28	11	5	8	27
1988— Pittsburgh (N.L.)	6	6	.500	3.49	67	0	0	0	34	77 1/3	68	30	30	22	76
1989— Pittsburgh (N.L.)	0	0	...	0.00	1	0	0	0	0	2/3	1	0	0	1	1
1990— Bakersfield (Calif.)■	0	0	...	2.77	7	3	0	0	0	13	13	5	4	4	16
— Los Angeles (N.L.)	3	5	.375	2.90	50	0	0	0	3	62	59	27	20	34	44
1991— Los Angeles (N.L.)	4	3	.571	2.96	55	0	0	0	2	76	63	28	25	32	73
1992— Los Angeles (N.L.)	3	3	.500	2.45	68	0	0	0	6	88	72	27	24	41	75
1993— Los Angeles (N.L.)	4	8	.333	2.32	62	0	0	0	25	77 2/3	71	23	20	17	67
1994— Los Angeles (N.L.)	5	3	.625	5.94	37	0	0	0	2	36 1/3	46	24	24	20	29
— Bakersfield (Calif.)	0	0	...	1.80	3	2	0	0	1	5	5	1	1	0	4
1995— Pittsburgh (N.L.)■	2	4	.333	6.03	25	0	0	0	3	31 1/3	38	26	21	12	19
A.L. totals (3 years)	21	30	.412	4.45	99	65	8	3	2	422 1/3	422	233	209	183	276
N.L. totals (11 years)	35	44	.443	3.51	455	31	2	0	89	697 2/3	659	313	272	283	561
Major league totals (14 years)	56	74	.431	3.87	554	96	10	3	91	1120	1081	546	481	466	837

GRACE, MARK — 1B — CUBS

PERSONAL: Born June 28, 1964, in Winston-Salem, N.C. . . . 6-2/190. . . . Bats left, throws left. . . . Full name: Mark Eugene Grace.
HIGH SCHOOL: Tustin (Calif.).
COLLEGE: San Diego State.
TRANSACTIONS/CAREER NOTES: Selected by Minnesota Twins organization in 15th round of free-agent draft (January 17, 1984); did not sign. . . . Selected by Chicago Cubs organization in 24th round of free-agent draft (June 3, 1985). . . . On disabled list (June 5-23, 1989). . . . Granted free agency (October 15, 1994). . . . Re-signed by Cubs (April 7, 1995). . . . Granted free agency (November 3, 1995). . . . Re-signed by Cubs (December 19, 1995).
RECORDS: Shares major league record for most assists by first baseman in one inning—3 (May 23, 1990, fourth inning). . . . Holds N.L. single-season record for most assists by first baseman—180 (1990).
HONORS: Named Eastern League Most Valuable Player (1987). . . . Named N.L. Rookie Player of the Year by THE SPORTING NEWS (1988). . . . Won N.L. Gold Glove at first base (1992-93 and 1995).
STATISTICAL NOTES: Led Midwest League first basemen with 103 double plays in 1986. . . . Led Eastern League with .545 slugging percentage in 1987. . . . Led N.L. first basemen with 1,695 total chances in 1991, 1,725 in 1992 and 1,573 in 1993. . . . Tied for N.L. lead in grounding into double plays with 25 in 1993. . . . Led N.L. first basemen with 134 double plays in 1993. . . . Hit for the cycle (May 9, 1993).

			BATTING											FIELDING			
Year Team (League)	Pos.	G	AB	R	H	2B	3B	HR	RBI	Avg.	BB	SO	SB	PO	A	E	Avg.
1986— Peoria (Midwest)	1B-OF	126	465	81	159	30	4	15	95	*.342	60	28	6	1050	69	13	.989
1987— Pittsfield (Eastern)	1B	123	453	81	151	29	8	17	*101	.333	48	24	5	1054	*96	6	*.995
1988— Iowa (Am. Assoc.)	1B	21	67	11	17	4	0	0	14	.254	13	4	1	189	20	1	.995
— Chicago (N.L.)	1B	134	486	65	144	23	4	7	57	.296	60	43	3	1182	87	•17	.987
1989— Chicago (N.L.)	1B	142	510	74	160	28	3	13	79	.314	80	42	14	1230	126	6	.996
1990— Chicago (N.L.)	1B	157	589	72	182	32	1	9	82	.309	59	54	15	1324	*180	12	.992
1991— Chicago (N.L.)	1B	160	*619	87	169	28	5	8	58	.273	70	53	3	*1520	*167	8	.995
1992— Chicago (N.L.)	1B	158	603	72	185	37	5	9	79	.307	72	36	6	*1580	*141	4	.998
1993— Chicago (N.L.)	1B	155	594	86	193	39	4	14	98	.325	71	32	8	*1456	112	5	.997
1994— Chicago (N.L.)	1B	106	403	55	120	23	3	6	44	.298	48	41	0	925	78	7	.993
1995— Chicago (N.L.)	1B	143	552	97	180	*51	3	16	92	.326	65	46	6	1211	114	7	.995
Major league totals (8 years)		1155	4356	608	1333	261	28	82	589	.306	525	347	55	10428	1005	66	.994

CHAMPIONSHIP SERIES RECORD

NOTES: Hit home run in first at-bat (October 4, 1989).

			BATTING												FIELDING			
Year	**Team (League)**	**Pos.**	**G**	**AB**	**R**	**H**	**2B**	**3B**	**HR**	**RBI**	**Avg.**	**BB**	**SO**	**SB**	**PO**	**A**	**E**	**Avg.**
1989—	Chicago (N.L.)	1B	5	17	3	11	3	1	1	8	.647	4	1	1	44	3	0	1.000

ALL-STAR GAME RECORD

			BATTING										FIELDING			
Year	**League**	**Pos.**	**AB**	**R**	**H**	**2B**	**3B**	**HR**	**RBI**	**Avg.**	**BB**	**SO**	**SB**	**PO**	**A**	**E**	**Avg.**
1993—	National	DH	3	0	0	0	0	0	0	.000	0	0	0	...	...	...	...
1995—	National	1B	0	0	0	0	0	0	0	...	0	0	0	1	0	0	1.000
All-Star Game totals (2 years)			3	0	0	0	0	0	0	.000	0	0	0	1	0	0	1.000

GRACE, MIKE — P — PHILLIES

PERSONAL: Born June 20, 1970, in Joliet, Ill. . . . 6-4/220. . . . Throws right, bats right. . . . Full name: Michael James Grace.
HIGH SCHOOL: Joliet (Ill.) Catholic.
COLLEGE: Bradley.
TRANSACTIONS/CAREER NOTES: Selected by Philadelphia Phillies organization in 10th round of free-agent draft (June 3, 1991). . . . On disabled list (April 9-June 8, July 8-20 and July 27, 1992-remainder of season; April 8, 1993-entire season; and April 7-June 14, 1994).

Year	Team (League)	W	L	Pct.	ERA	G	GS	CG	ShO	Sv.	IP	H	R	ER	BB	SO
1991—	Batavia (NYP)	1	2	.333	1.39	6	6	0	0	0	32 1/3	20	9	5	14	36
	—Spartanburg (SAL)	3	1	.750	1.89	6	6	0	0	0	33 1/3	24	7	7	9	23
1992—	Spartanburg (SAL)	0	1	.000	4.94	6	6	0	0	0	27 1/3	25	16	15	8	21
1993—								Did not play.								
1994—	Spartanburg (SAL)	5	5	.500	4.82	15	15	0	0	0	80 1/3	84	50	43	20	45
1995—	Reading (Eastern)	13	6	.684	3.54	24	24	2	0	0	147 1/3	137	65	58	35	118
	—Scran./W.B. (Int'l)	2	0	1.000	1.59	2	2	1	0	0	17	17	3	3	2	13
	—Philadelphia (N.L.)	1	1	.500	3.18	2	2	0	0	0	11 1/3	10	4	4	4	7
Major league totals (1 year)		1	1	.500	3.18	2	2	0	0	0	11 1/3	10	4	4	4	7

GRAFFANINO, TONY — 2B — BRAVES

PERSONAL: Born June 6, 1972, in Amityville, N.Y. . . . 6-1/175. . . . Bats right, throws right. . . . Full name: Anthony Joseph Graffanino. . . . Name pronounced GRAF-uh-NEE-noh.
HIGH SCHOOL: East Islip (Islip Terrace, N.Y.).
TRANSACTIONS/CAREER NOTES: Selected by Atlanta Braves organization in 10th round of free-agent draft (June 4, 1990). . . . On disabled list (July 3, 1995-remainder of season).
STATISTICAL NOTES: Led Pioneer League shortstops with 41 double plays in 1991. . . . Led Carolina League second basemen with .968 fielding percentage in 1993.

				BATTING											FIELDING			
Year	**Team (League)**	**Pos.**	**G**	**AB**	**R**	**H**	**2B**	**3B**	**HR**	**RBI**	**Avg.**	**BB**	**SO**	**SB**	**PO**	**A**	**E**	**Avg.**
1990—	Pulaski (Appal.)	SS	42	131	23	27	5	1	0	11	.206	26	17	6	60	105	24	.873
1991—	Idaho Falls (Pio.)	SS	66	274	53	95	16	4	4	56	.347	27	37	19	112	187	*29	.912
1992—	Macon (S. Atl.)	2B	112	400	50	96	15	5	10	31	.240	50	84	9	178	239	17	.961
1993—	Durham (Carolina)	2B-SS	123	459	78	126	30	5	15	69	.275	45	78	24	186	263	15	†.968
1994—	Greenville (South.)	2B	124	440	66	132	28	3	7	52	.300	50	53	29	254	326	14	.976
1995—	Richmond (Int'l)	2B	50	179	20	34	6	0	4	17	.190	15	49	2	102	127	4	.983

GRAHE, JOE — P

PERSONAL: Born August 14, 1967, in West Palm Beach, Fla. . . . 6-0/200. . . . Throws right, bats right. . . . Full name: Joseph Milton Grahe. . . . Name pronounced GRAY.
HIGH SCHOOL: Palm Beach Gardens (West Palm Beach, Fla.).
JUNIOR COLLEGE: Palm Beach Junior College (Fla.).
COLLEGE: Miami (Fla.).
TRANSACTIONS/CAREER NOTES: Selected by Milwaukee Brewers organization in 28th round of free-agent draft (June 2, 1986); did not sign. . . . Selected by Oakland Athletics organization in fifth round of free-agent draft (June 1, 1988); did not sign. . . . Selected by California Angels organization in second round of free-agent draft (June 5, 1989). . . . On California disabled list (June 5-July 15, 1993); included rehabilitation assignment to Vancouver (July 2-15). . . . Granted free agency (November 26, 1994). . . . Signed by Colorado Rockies organization (December 15, 1994). . . . On Colorado Springs disabled list (April 6-May 11, 1995). . . . On Colorado disabled list (July 18-September 1, 1995). . . . Released by Rockies (October 10, 1995).

Year	Team (League)	W	L	Pct.	ERA	G	GS	CG	ShO	Sv.	IP	H	R	ER	BB	SO
1990—	Midland (Texas)	7	5	.583	5.29	18	18	1	0	0	119	145	75	70	34	58
	—Edmonton (PCL)	3	0	1.000	1.35	5	5	2	0	0	40	35	10	6	11	21
	—California (A.L.)	3	4	.429	4.98	8	8	0	0	0	43 1/3	51	30	24	23	25
1991—	Edmonton (PCL)	9	3	.750	4.01	14	14	3	1	0	94 1/3	121	55	42	30	55
	—California (A.L.)	3	7	.300	4.81	18	10	1	0	0	73	84	43	39	33	40
1992—	California (A.L.)	5	6	.455	3.52	46	7	0	0	21	94 2/3	85	37	37	39	39
	—Edmonton (PCL)	1	0	1.000	3.20	3	3	0	0	0	19 2/3	18	7	7	5	12
1993—	California (A.L.)	4	1	.800	2.86	45	0	0	0	11	56 2/3	54	22	18	25	31
	—Vancouver (PCL)	1	1	.500	4.50	4	2	0	0	0	6	4	3	3	2	5
1994—	California (A.L.)	2	5	.286	6.65	40	0	0	0	13	43 1/3	68	33	32	18	26
1995—	Colorado (N.L.)■	4	3	.571	5.08	17	9	0	0	0	56 2/3	69	42	32	27	27
	—Colo. Springs (PCL)	1	1	.500	3.27	2	2	1	0	0	11	7	4	4	3	4
A.L. totals (5 years)		17	23	.425	4.34	157	25	1	0	45	311	342	165	150	138	161
N.L. totals (1 year)		4	3	.571	5.08	17	9	0	0	0	56 2/3	69	42	32	27	27
Major league totals (6 years)		21	26	.447	4.46	174	34	1	0	45	367 2/3	411	207	182	165	188

GRANGER, JEFF — P — ROYALS

PERSONAL: Born December 16, 1971, in San Pedro, Calif. . . . 6-4/200. . . . Throws left, bats right. . . . Full name: Jeffrey Adam Granger.
HIGH SCHOOL: Orangefield (Tex.).
COLLEGE: Texas A&M.
TRANSACTIONS/CAREER NOTES: Selected by Minnesota Twins organization in 14th round of free-agent draft (June 4, 1990); did not sign. . . . Selected by Kansas City Royals organization in first round (fifth pick overall) of free-agent draft (June 3, 1993). . . . On disabled list (June 20-July 3, 1996).
HONORS: Named lefthanded pitcher on THE SPORTING NEWS college All-America team (1993).
STATISTICAL NOTES: Tied for Southern League lead with 14 wild pitches in 1994.

Year	Team (League)	W	L	Pct.	ERA	G	GS	CG	ShO	Sv.	IP	H	R	ER	BB	SO
1993—	Eugene (N'west)	3	3	.500	3.00	8	7	0	0	0	36	28	17	12	10	56
—	Kansas City (A.L.)	0	0	. . .	27.00	1	0	0	0	0	1	3	3	3	2	1
1994—	Memphis (South.)	7	7	.500	3.87	25	25	0	0	0	139 2/3	155	72	60	61	112
—	Kansas City (A.L.)	0	1	.000	6.75	2	2	0	0	0	9 1/3	13	8	7	6	3
1995—	Wichita (Texas)	4	7	.364	5.93	18	18	0	0	0	95 2/3	122	76	63	40	81
Major league totals (2 years)		0	1	.000	8.71	3	2	0	0	0	10 1/3	16	11	10	8	4

GREBECK, CRAIG — IF — MARLINS

PERSONAL: Born December 29, 1964, in Johnstown, Pa. . . . 5-7/148. . . . Bats right, throws right. . . . Full name: Craig Allen Grebeck. . . . Name pronounced GRAY-bek.
HIGH SCHOOL: Lakewood (Calif.).
COLLEGE: Cal State Dominguez Hills.
TRANSACTIONS/CAREER NOTES: Signed as non-drafted free agent by Chicago White Sox organization (August 13, 1986). . . . On disabled list (August 9, 1992-remainder of season). . . . On Chicago disabled list (May 21-June 30, 1994); included rehabilitation assignment to Nashville (June 23-30). . . . Granted free agency (December 21, 1995). . . . Signed by Florida Marlins organization (December 22, 1995).
STATISTICAL NOTES: Led Southern League in grounding into double plays with 15 in 1989. . . . Career major league grand slams: 1.

							BATTING								FIELDING			
Year	Team (League)	Pos.	G	AB	R	H	2B	3B	HR	RBI	Avg.	BB	SO	SB	PO	A	E	Avg.
1987—	Peninsula (Caro.)	SS-3B	104	378	63	106	22	3	15	67	.280	37	62	3	137	278	16	.963
1988—	Birm. (Southern)	2B	133	450	57	126	21	1	9	53	.280	65	72	5	238	368	19	.970
1989—	Birm. (Southern)	SS-3B-2B	•143	•533	85	*153	25	4	5	80	.287	63	77	14	234	364	28	.955
1990—	Chicago (A.L.)	3B-SS-2B	59	119	7	20	3	1	1	9	.168	8	24	0	36	98	3	.978
—	Vancouver (PCL)	SS-3B-2B	12	41	8	8	0	0	1	3	.195	6	7	1	28	26	1	.982
1991—	Chicago (A.L.)	3B-2B-SS	107	224	37	63	16	3	6	31	.281	38	40	1	104	183	10	.966
1992—	Chicago (A.L.)	SS-3B-OF	88	287	24	77	21	2	3	35	.268	30	34	0	112	283	8	.980
1993—	Chicago (A.L.)	SS-2B-3B	72	190	25	43	5	0	1	12	.226	26	26	1	91	185	5	.982
1994—	Chicago (A.L.)	2B-SS-3B	35	97	17	30	5	0	0	5	.309	12	5	0	44	65	2	.982
—	Nashville (A.A.)	SS	5	15	3	6	2	0	0	4	.400	1	2	0	5	12	1	.944
1995—	Chicago (A.L.)	SS-3B-2B	53	154	19	40	12	0	1	18	.260	21	23	0	76	127	7	.967
Major league totals (6 years)			414	1071	129	273	62	6	12	110	.255	135	152	2	463	941	35	.976

CHAMPIONSHIP SERIES RECORD

							BATTING								FIELDING			
Year	Team (League)	Pos.	G	AB	R	H	2B	3B	HR	RBI	Avg.	BB	SO	SB	PO	A	E	Avg.
1993—	Chicago (A.L.)	PH-3B	1	1	0	1	0	0	0	0	1.000	0	0	0	0	0	0	. . .

GREEN, SHAWN — OF — BLUE JAYS

PERSONAL: Born November 10, 1972, in Des Plaines, Ill. . . . 6-4/190. . . . Bats left, throws left. . . . Full name: Shawn David Green.
HIGH SCHOOL: Tustin (Calif.).
TRANSACTIONS/CAREER NOTES: Selected by Toronto Blue Jays organization in first round (16th pick overall) of free-agent draft (June 3, 1991); pick received as compensation for San Francisco Giants signing Type A free-agent P Bud Black. . . . On disabled list (June 30-July 23, 1992). . . . On Knoxville disabled list (June 11-July 24, 1993).
STATISTICAL NOTES: Tied for Florida State League lead with eight sacrifice flies in 1992.

							BATTING								FIELDING			
Year	Team (League)	Pos.	G	AB	R	H	2B	3B	HR	RBI	Avg.	BB	SO	SB	PO	A	E	Avg.
1992—	Dunedin (Fla. St.)	OF	114	417	44	114	21	3	1	49	.273	28	66	22	182	3	5	.974
1993—	Knoxville (South.)	OF	99	360	40	102	14	2	4	34	.283	26	72	4	172	3	8	.956
—	Toronto (A.L.)	OF-DH	3	6	0	0	0	0	0	0	.000	0	1	0	1	0	0	1.000
1994—	Syracuse (Int'l)	OF	109	433	82	149	27	3	13	61	*.344	40	54	19	220	5	1	*.996
—	Toronto (A.L.)	OF	14	33	1	3	1	0	0	1	.091	1	8	1	12	2	0	1.000
1995—	Toronto (A.L.)	OF	121	379	52	109	31	4	15	54	.288	20	68	1	207	9	6	.973
Major league totals (3 years)			138	418	53	112	32	4	15	55	.268	21	77	2	220	11	6	.975

GREEN, TYLER — P — PHILLIES

PERSONAL: Born February 18, 1970, in Springfield, O. . . . 6-5/211. . . . Throws right, bats right. . . . Full name: Tyler Scott Green.
HIGH SCHOOL: Thomas Jefferson (Denver).
COLLEGE: Wichita State.
TRANSACTIONS/CAREER NOTES: Selected by Cincinnati Reds organization in third round of free-agent draft (June 1, 1988); did not sign. . . . Selected by Philadelphia Phillies organization in first round (10th pick overall) of free-agent draft (June 3, 1991). . . . On Clearwater disabled list (August 7, 1991-remainder of season). . . . On Scranton/Wilkes-Barre disabled list (July 10, 1992-remainder of season and May 3-22, 1993).

STATISTICAL NOTES: Pitched 3-1 no-hit victory for Scranton/Wilkes-Barre against Ottawa (July 4, 1993, first game). . . . Led International League with 12 hit batsmen in 1994.
MISCELLANEOUS: Appeared in one game as pinch-runner (1995).

Year	Team (League)	W	L	Pct.	ERA	G	GS	CG	ShO	Sv.	IP	H	R	ER	BB	SO
1991—	Batavia (NYP)	1	0	1.000	1.20	3	3	0	0	0	15	7	2	2	6	19
—	Clearwater (Fla. St.)	2	0	1.000	1.38	2	2	0	0	0	13	3	2	2	8	20
1992—	Reading (Eastern)	6	3	.667	1.88	12	12	0	0	0	62 1/3	46	16	13	20	67
—	Scran./W.B. (Int'l)	0	1	.000	6.10	2	2	0	0	0	10 1/3	7	7	7	12	15
1993—	Philadelphia (N.L.)	0	0	...	7.36	3	2	0	0	0	7 1/3	16	9	6	5	7
—	Scran./W.B. (Int'l)	6	10	.375	3.95	28	14	4	0	0	118 1/3	102	62	52	43	87
1994—	Scran./W.B. (Int'l)	7	*16	.304	5.56	27	26	4	0	0	162	179	*110	*100	*77	95
1995—	Philadelphia (N.L.)	8	9	.471	5.31	26	25	4	2	0	140 2/3	157	86	83	66	85
Major league totals (2 years)		8	9	.471	5.41	29	27	4	2	0	148	173	95	89	71	92

ALL-STAR GAME RECORD

Year	League	W	L	Pct.	ERA	GS	CG	ShO	Sv.	IP	H	R	ER	BB	SO
1995—	National	0	0	...	0.00	0	0	0	0	1	2	0	0	0	1

GREENE, CHARLIE — C — METS

PERSONAL: Born January 23, 1971, in Miami. . . . 6-1/177. . . . Bats right, throws right. . . . Full name: Charles P. Greene.
HIGH SCHOOL: Miami Killian.
JUNIOR COLLEGE: Miami-Dade (South) Community College.
TRANSACTIONS/CAREER NOTES: Selected by San Diego Padres organization in 19th round of free-agent draft (June 3, 1991). . . . Selected by Norfolk, New York Mets organization, from Padres organization in Rule 5 minor league draft (December 13, 1993).
STATISTICAL NOTES: Tied for Midwest League lead in double plays by catcher with 11 in 1993.

				BATTING											FIELDING			
Year	Team (League)	Pos.	G	AB	R	H	2B	3B	HR	RBI	Avg.	BB	SO	SB	PO	A	E	Avg.
1991—	Ariz. Padres (Ariz.)	C-1B-3B	49	183	27	52	15	1	5	38	.284	16	26	6	334	30	3	.992
1992—	Char., S.C. (S. Atl.)	C-3B	98	298	22	55	9	1	1	24	.185	11	60	1	561	119	14	.980
1993—	Waterloo (Midw.)	C-1-3-S	84	213	19	38	8	0	2	20	.178	13	33	0	460	96	16	.972
1994—	St. Lucie (Fla. St.)■	C	69	224	23	57	4	0	0	21	.254	9	31	0	380	65	13	.972
—	Binghamton (East.)	C	30	106	13	18	4	0	0	2	.170	6	18	0	190	30	3	.987
1995—	Binghamton (East.)	C	100	346	26	82	13	0	2	34	.237	15	47	2	670	54	4	*.995
—	Norfolk (Int'l)	C	27	88	6	17	3	0	0	4	.193	3	28	0	157	25	0	1.000

GREENE, RICK — P — TIGERS

PERSONAL: Born January 2, 1971, in Fort Knox, Ky. . . . 6-5/200. . . . Throws right, bats right. . . . Full name: Richard Douglas Greene.
HIGH SCHOOL: Coral Gables (Fla.).
COLLEGE: Louisiana State.
TRANSACTIONS/CAREER NOTES: Selected by Detroit Tigers organization in first round (16th pick overall) of free-agent draft (June 1, 1992). . . . On disabled list (May 23-July 17, 1995).
MISCELLANEOUS: Member of 1992 U.S. Olympic baseball team.

Year	Team (League)	W	L	Pct.	ERA	G	GS	CG	ShO	Sv.	IP	H	R	ER	BB	SO
1992—							Did not play—injured.									
1993—	Lakeland (Fla. St.)	2	3	.400	6.20	26	0	0	0	2	40 2/3	57	28	28	16	32
—	London (Eastern)	2	2	.500	6.52	23	0	0	0	0	29	31	22	21	20	19
1994—	Trenton (Eastern)	1	1	.500	7.91	20	0	0	0	3	19 1/3	17	17	17	21	5
—	Lakeland (Fla. St.)	0	4	.000	4.32	19	2	0	0	4	33 1/3	50	23	16	10	28
1995—	Jacksonville (Sou.)	6	2	.750	3.49	32	0	0	0	0	38 2/3	45	19	15	15	29

GREENE, TODD — C — ANGELS

PERSONAL: Born May 8, 1971, in Augusta, Ga. . . . 5-9/195. . . . Bats right, throws right. . . . Full name: Todd Anthony Greene.
HIGH SCHOOL: Evans (Ga.).
COLLEGE: Georgia Southern.
TRANSACTIONS/CAREER NOTES: Selected by California Angels organization in 12th round of free-agent draft (June 3, 1993).
HONORS: Named California League Most Valuable Player (1994). . . . Named California League Rookie of the Year (1994).
STATISTICAL NOTES: Led California League with 306 total bases, 12 intentional bases on balls received and .584 slugging percentage in 1994. . . . Led California League catchers with 15 errors, 13 double plays and 44 passed balls in 1994.

				BATTING											FIELDING			
Year	Team (League)	Pos.	G	AB	R	H	2B	3B	HR	RBI	Avg.	BB	SO	SB	PO	A	E	Avg.
1993—	Boise (Northwest)	OF	•76	*305	55	82	15	3	*15	*71	.269	34	44	4	136	4	3	.979
1994—	Lake Elsinore (Calif.)	C-OF-1B	133	524	98	158	*39	2	*35	*124	.302	64	96	10	624	90	†15	.979
1995—	Midland (Texas)	C-1B	82	318	59	104	19	1	26	57	.327	17	55	3	314	44	3	.992
—	Lake Elsinore (Calif.)	C	43	168	28	42	3	1	14	35	.250	11	36	1	175	17	1	.995

GREENE, TOMMY — P — PHILLIES

PERSONAL: Born April 6, 1967, in Lumberton, N.C. . . . 6-5/225. . . . Throws right, bats right. . . . Full name: Ira Thomas Greene.
HIGH SCHOOL: Whiteville (N.C.).
TRANSACTIONS/CAREER NOTES: Selected by Atlanta Braves organization in first round (14th pick overall) of free-agent draft (June 3, 1985). . . . Traded by Braves to Scranton/Wilkes-Barre, Philadelphia Phillies organization (August 9, 1990), as partial completion of deal in which Braves traded OF Dale Murphy and a player to be named later to Phillies for P Jeff Parrett and two players to be named later (August 3, 1990);

Braves acquired OF Jim Vatcher (August 9, 1990) and SS Victor Rosario (September 4, 1990) to complete deal. . . . On Philadelphia disabled list (May 13-September 1, 1992); included rehabilitation assignments to Scranton/Wilkes-Barre (May 29-June 4, August 12-20 and August 21-September 1) and Reading (August 20-21). . . . On disabled list (July 28-August 12, 1993). . . . On Philadelphia disabled list (April 8-26, 1994); included rehabilitation assignment to Clearwater (April 21-26). . . . On Philadelphia disabled list (May 23, 1994-remainder of season); included rehabilitation assignments to Scranton/Wilkes-Barre (July 27) and Reading (July 28-August 11). . . . On Philadelphia disabled list (April 19-June 29, July 4-August 5 and August 28-September 12, 1995); included rehabilitation assignments to Clearwater (June 13-28) and Scranton/Wilkes-Barre (July 14-August 3 and September 1-11).

STATISTICAL NOTES: Pitched 2-0 no-hit victory against Montreal (May 23, 1991). . . . Led N.L. with 15 wild pitches in 1993.

MISCELLANEOUS: Made two outs in two games as pinch-hitter (1991). . . . Appeared in one game as pinch-runner (1993).

Year	Team (League)	W	L	Pct.	ERA	G	GS	CG	ShO	Sv.	IP	H	R	ER	BB	SO
1985	Pulaski (Appal.)	2	5	.286	7.64	12	12	1	1	0	50 2/3	49	45	43	27	32
1986	Sumter (S. Atl.)	11	7	.611	4.69	28	*28	5	•3	0	174 2/3	162	95	91	82	169
1987	Greenville (South.)	11	8	.579	3.29	23	23	4	2	0	142 1/3	103	60	52	66	101
1988	Richmond (Int'l)	7	17	.292	4.77	29	29	4	•3	0	177 1/3	169	98	94	70	130
1989	Richmond (Int'l)	9	12	.429	3.61	26	26	2	1	0	152	136	74	61	50	125
	—Atlanta (N.L.)	1	2	.333	4.10	4	4	1	1	0	26 1/3	22	12	12	6	17
1990	Atlanta (N.L.)	1	0	1.000	8.03	5	2	0	0	0	12 1/3	14	11	11	9	4
	—Richmond (Int'l)	5	8	.385	3.72	19	18	2	0	0	109	88	49	45	65	65
	—Scran./W.B. (Int'l)■	0	0	...	0.00	1	1	0	0	0	7	5	0	0	2	4
	—Philadelphia (N.L.)	2	3	.400	4.15	10	7	0	0	0	39	36	20	18	17	17
1991	Philadelphia (N.L.)	13	7	.650	3.38	36	27	3	2	0	207 2/3	177	85	78	66	154
1992	Philadelphia (N.L.)	3	3	.500	5.32	13	12	0	0	0	64 1/3	75	39	38	34	39
	—Reading (Eastern)	0	0	...	9.00	1	1	0	0	0	2	3	2	2	2	2
	—Scran./W.B. (Int'l)	2	1	.667	2.49	5	5	1	1	0	21 2/3	15	7	6	4	21
1993	Philadelphia (N.L.)	16	4	.800	3.42	31	30	7	2	0	200	175	84	76	62	167
1994	Philadelphia (N.L.)	2	0	1.000	4.54	7	7	0	0	0	35 2/3	37	20	18	22	28
	—Clearwater (Fla. St.)	0	0	...	0.00	1	1	0	0	0	5	2	0	0	1	4
	—Scran./W.B. (Int'l)	0	0	...	0.00	1	1	0	0	0	4	3	1	0	1	6
	—Reading (Eastern)	1	0	1.000	4.35	2	2	0	0	0	10 1/3	12	5	5	3	12
1995	Clearwater (Fla. St.)	0	3	.000	3.15	3	3	0	0	0	20	12	7	7	7	20
	—Philadelphia (N.L.)	0	5	.000	8.29	11	6	0	0	0	33 2/3	45	32	31	20	24
	—Scran./W.B. (Int'l)	3	0	1.000	2.22	4	4	0	0	0	28 1/3	18	8	7	6	19
Major league totals (7 years)		38	24	.613	4.10	117	95	11	5	0	619	581	303	282	236	450

CHAMPIONSHIP SERIES RECORD

NOTES: Shares single-game record for most earned runs allowed—7 (October 7, 1993).

Year	Team (League)	W	L	Pct.	ERA	G	GS	CG	ShO	Sv.	IP	H	R	ER	BB	SO
1993	Philadelphia (N.L.)	1	1	.500	9.64	2	2	0	0	0	9 1/3	12	10	10	7	7

WORLD SERIES RECORD

Year	Team (League)	W	L	Pct.	ERA	G	GS	CG	ShO	Sv.	IP	H	R	ER	BB	SO
1993	Philadelphia (N.L.)	0	0	...	27.00	1	1	0	0	0	2 1/3	7	7	7	4	1

GREENE, WILLIE — 3B — REDS

PERSONAL: Born September 23, 1971, in Milledgeville, Ga. . . . 5-11/185. . . . Bats left, throws right. . . . Full name: Willie Louis Greene.

HIGH SCHOOL: Jones County (Gray, Ga.).

TRANSACTIONS/CAREER NOTES: Selected by Pittsburgh Pirates organization in first round (18th pick overall) of free-agent draft (June 5, 1989). . . . Traded by Pirates organization with P Scott Ruskin and a player to be named later to Montreal Expos organization for P Zane Smith (August 8, 1990); Expos acquired OF Moises Alou to complete deal (August 16, 1990). . . . Traded by Expos organization with OF Dave Martinez and P Scott Ruskin to Cincinnati Reds organization for P John Wetteland and P Bill Risley (December 11, 1991). . . . On Cincinnati disabled list (August 21, 1993-remainder of season). . . . On Indianapolis disabled list (June 7-19, 1995).

STATISTICAL NOTES: Led Florida State League third basemen with 31 errors in 1991. . . . Led Southern League third basemen with 24 double plays in 1992. . . . Led American Association third basemen with 23 errors in 1993.

			BATTING												FIELDING			
Year	Team (League)	Pos.	G	AB	R	H	2B	3B	HR	RBI	Avg.	BB	SO	SB	PO	A	E	Avg.
1989	Princeton (Appal.)	SS	39	136	22	44	6	4	2	24	.324	9	29	4	33	69	19	.843
	—GC Pirates (GCL)	SS	23	86	17	24	3	3	5	11	.279	9	6	4	25	49	3	.961
1990	Augusta (S. Atl.)	SS-2B	86	291	59	75	12	4	11	47	.258	61	58	7	117	209	34	.906
	—Salem (Carolina)	SS	17	60	9	11	1	1	3	9	.183	7	18	0	22	43	2	.970
	—Rockford (Midw.)■	SS	11	35	4	14	3	0	0	2	.400	6	7	2	14	37	4	.927
1991	W.P. Beach (FSL)	3B-SS	99	322	46	70	9	3	12	43	.217	50	93	10	72	184	†32	.889
1992	Ced. Rap. (Midw.)■	3B	34	120	26	34	8	2	12	40	.283	18	27	3	13	60	8	.901
	—Chatt. (South.)	3B	96	349	47	97	19	2	15	66	.278	46	90	9	*77	174	14	*.947
	—Cincinnati (N.L.)	3B	29	93	10	25	5	2	2	13	.269	10	23	0	15	40	3	.948
1993	Indianapolis (A.A.)	3B-SS	98	341	62	91	19	0	22	58	.267	51	83	2	77	171	†23	.915
	—Cincinnati (N.L.)	SS-3B	15	50	7	8	1	1	2	5	.160	2	19	0	19	37	1	.982
1994	Cincinnati (N.L.)	3B-OF	16	37	5	8	2	0	0	3	.216	6	14	0	2	21	1	.958
	—Indianapolis (A.A.)	3B-SS	114	435	77	124	24	1	23	80	.285	56	88	8	93	249	17	.953
1995	Cincinnati (N.L.)	3B	8	19	1	2	0	0	0	0	.105	3	7	0	1	13	0	1.000
	—Indianapolis (A.A.)	3B-SS-OF	91	325	57	79	12	2	19	45	.243	38	67	3	60	160	12	.948
Major league totals (4 years)			68	199	23	43	8	3	4	21	.216	21	63	0	37	111	5	.967

GREENWELL, MIKE — OF — RED SOX

PERSONAL: Born July 18, 1963, in Louisville, Ky. . . . 6-0/200. . . . Bats left, throws right. . . . Full name: Michael Lewis Greenwell.

HIGH SCHOOL: North Fort Myers (Fla.).

TRANSACTIONS/CAREER NOTES: Selected by Boston Red Sox organization in third round of free-agent draft (June 7, 1982). . . . On disabled list (April 21-May 2 and May 13-July 25, 1983; July 30-August 14, 1989; May 2-17 and June 22, 1992-remainder of season; May 18-June 2, 1993; and August 4, 1994-remainder of season). . . . On Boston disabled list (June 30-July 21, 1995); included rehabilitation assignment

to Pawtucket (July 20-21).
RECORDS: Holds A.L. single-season record for most game-winning runs batted in—23 (1988).
HONORS: Named outfielder on THE SPORTING NEWS A.L. All-Star team (1988). . . . Named outfielder on THE SPORTING NEWS A.L. Silver Slugger team (1988).
STATISTICAL NOTES: Led Carolina League in being hit by pitch with 15 in 1984. . . . Hit for the cycle (September 14, 1988). . . . Led A.L. with 23 game-winning RBIs and tied for lead with 18 intentional bases on balls received in 1988. . . . Career major league grand slams: 2.

			BATTING											FIELDING			
Year Team (League)	**Pos.**	**G**	**AB**	**R**	**H**	**2B**	**3B**	**HR**	**RBI**	**Avg.**	**BB**	**SO**	**SB**	**PO**	**A**	**E**	**Avg.**
1982—Elmira (N.Y.-Penn)	3B-2B	72	268	57	72	10	1	6	36	.269	37	37	5	96	151	31	.888
1983—Winst.-Salem (Car.)	OF	48	158	23	44	8	0	3	21	.278	19	23	4	28	1	1	.967
1984—Winst.-Salem (Car.)	3B-OF	130	454	70	139	23	6	16	84	.306	56	40	9	126	132	30	.896
1985—Pawtucket (Int'l)	OF	117	418	47	107	21	1	13	52	.256	38	45	3	178	8	7	.964
—Boston (A.L.)	OF	17	31	7	10	1	0	4	8	.323	3	4	1	14	0	0	1.000
1986—Pawtucket (Int'l)	OF-3B	89	320	62	96	21	1	18	59	.300	43	20	6	130	20	8	.949
—Boston (A.L.)	OF-DH	31	35	4	11	2	0	0	4	.314	5	7	0	18	1	0	1.000
1987—Boston (A.L.)	OF-DH-C	125	412	71	135	31	6	19	89	.328	35	40	5	165	8	6	.966
1988—Boston (A.L.)	OF-DH	158	590	86	192	39	8	22	119	.325	87	38	16	302	6	6	.981
1989—Boston (A.L.)	OF-DH	145	578	87	178	36	0	14	95	.308	56	44	13	220	11	8	.967
1990—Boston (A.L.)	OF	159	610	71	181	30	6	14	73	.297	65	43	8	287	13	7	.977
1991—Boston (A.L.)	OF-DH	147	544	76	163	26	6	9	83	.300	43	35	15	263	9	3	.989
1992—Boston (A.L.)	OF-DH	49	180	16	42	2	0	2	18	.233	18	19	2	85	1	0	1.000
1993—Boston (A.L.)	OF-DH	146	540	77	170	38	6	13	72	.315	54	46	5	261	6	2	.993
1994—Boston (A.L.)	OF-DH	95	327	60	88	25	1	11	45	.269	38	26	2	141	10	1	.993
1995—Boston (A.L.)	OF-DH	120	481	67	143	25	4	15	76	.297	38	35	9	201	11	6	.972
—Pawtucket (Int'l)	DH	1	4	0	2	2	0	0	0	.500	1	0	1	...	...	...	...
Major league totals (11 years)		1192	4328	622	1313	255	37	123	682	.303	442	337	76	1957	76	39	.981

DIVISION SERIES RECORD

			BATTING											FIELDING			
Year Team (League)	**Pos.**	**G**	**AB**	**R**	**H**	**2B**	**3B**	**HR**	**RBI**	**Avg.**	**BB**	**SO**	**SB**	**PO**	**A**	**E**	**Avg.**
1995—Boston (A.L.)	OF	3	15	0	3	0	0	0	0	.200	0	1	0	8	0	0	1.000

CHAMPIONSHIP SERIES RECORD

			BATTING											FIELDING			
Year Team (League)	**Pos.**	**G**	**AB**	**R**	**H**	**2B**	**3B**	**HR**	**RBI**	**Avg.**	**BB**	**SO**	**SB**	**PO**	**A**	**E**	**Avg.**
1986—Boston (A.L.)	PH	2	2	0	1	0	0	0	0	.500	0	0	0	...	...	...	...
1988—Boston (A.L.)	OF	4	14	2	3	1	0	1	3	.214	3	0	0	4	0	0	1.000
1990—Boston (A.L.)	OF	4	14	1	0	0	0	0	0	.000	2	2	0	3	0	1	.750
Championship series totals (3 years)		10	30	3	4	1	0	1	3	.133	5	2	0	7	0	1	.875

WORLD SERIES RECORD

			BATTING											FIELDING			
Year Team (League)	**Pos.**	**G**	**AB**	**R**	**H**	**2B**	**3B**	**HR**	**RBI**	**Avg.**	**BB**	**SO**	**SB**	**PO**	**A**	**E**	**Avg.**
1986—Boston (A.L.)	PH	4	3	0	0	0	0	0	0	.000	1	2	0	...	...	...	...

ALL-STAR GAME RECORD

		BATTING											FIELDING			
Year League	**Pos.**	**AB**	**R**	**H**	**2B**	**3B**	**HR**	**RBI**	**Avg.**	**BB**	**SO**	**SB**	**PO**	**A**	**E**	**Avg.**
1988—American	OF	1	0	0	0	0	0	0	.000	0	0	0	1	0	0	1.000
1989—American	OF	0	0	0	0	0	0	0	...	0	0	0	1	0	0	1.000
All-Star Game totals (2 years)		1	0	0	0	0	0	0	.000	0	0	0	2	0	0	1.000

GREER, KENNY P

PERSONAL: Born May 12, 1967, in Boston. . . . 6-2/215. . . . Throws right, bats right. . . . Full name: Kenneth William Greer.
HIGH SCHOOL: Portsmouth (N.H.).
COLLEGE: Massachusetts.
TRANSACTIONS/CAREER NOTES: Selected by New York Yankees organization in 10th round of free-agent draft (June 1, 1988). . . . On Columbus disabled list (June 19-July 15, 1993). . . . Traded by Yankees to New York Mets for P Frank Tanana (September 17, 1993). . . . On Norfolk disabled list (April 15-June 30, 1994). . . . On Norfolk suspended list (July 21-23, 1994). . . . Granted free agency (October 15, 1994). . . . Signed by Phoenix, San Francisco Giants organization (November 29, 1994). . . . Granted free agency (October 15, 1995).

Year Team (League)	**W**	**L**	**Pct.**	**ERA**	**G**	**GS**	**CG**	**ShO**	**Sv.**	**IP**	**H**	**R**	**ER**	**BB**	**SO**
1988—Oneonta (N.Y.-Penn)	5	5	.500	2.40	15	15	4	0	0	112 1/3	109	46	30	18	60
1989—Prin. William (Caro.)	7	3	.700	4.19	29	13	3	1	2	111 2/3	101	56	52	22	44
1990—Fort Lauder. (FSL)	4	9	.308	5.44	38	5	0	0	1	89 1/3	115	64	54	33	55
—Prin. William (Caro.)	1	0	1.000	2.35	1	1	0	0	0	7 2/3	7	2	2	2	7
1991—Fort Lauder. (FSL)	4	3	.571	4.24	31	1	0	0	0	57 1/3	49	31	27	22	46
1992—Prin. William (Caro.)	1	2	.333	3.67	13	0	0	0	1	27	25	11	11	9	30
—Alb./Colon. (East.)	4	1	.800	1.83	40	1	0	0	4	68 2/3	48	19	14	30	53
—Columbus (Int'l)	0	0	...	9.00	1	0	0	0	0	1	3	2	1	1	1
1993—Columbus (Int'l)	9	4	.692	4.42	46	0	0	0	6	79 1/3	78	41	39	36	50
—New York (N.L.)■	1	0	1.000	0.00	1	0	0	0	0	1	0	0	0	0	2
1994—Norfolk (Int'l)■	1	1	.500	3.77	25	0	0	0	1	31	35	14	13	11	8
—GC Mets (GCL)	0	0	...	3.00	4	2	0	0	0	6	7	2	2	0	3
1995—Phoenix (PCL)■	5	2	.714	3.98	38	0	0	0	1	63 1/3	65	29	28	19	41
—San Francisco (N.L.)	0	2	.000	5.25	8	0	0	0	0	12	15	12	7	5	7
Major league totals (2 years)	1	2	.333	4.85	9	0	0	0	0	13	15	12	7	5	9

GREER, RUSTY — 1B — RANGERS

PERSONAL: Born January 21, 1969, in Fort Rucker, Ala. . . . 6-0/190. . . . Bats left, throws left. . . . Full name: Thurman Clyde Greer III.
HIGH SCHOOL: Albertville (Ala.).
COLLEGE: Montevallo (Ala.).
TRANSACTIONS/CAREER NOTES: Selected by Texas Rangers organization in 10th round of free-agent draft (June 4, 1990). . . . On disabled list (July 31-August 22, 1992).
STATISTICAL NOTES: Led Florida State League with .395 on-base percentage in 1991. . . . Career major league grand slams: 1.

			BATTING												FIELDING			
Year	Team (League)	Pos.	G	AB	R	H	2B	3B	HR	RBI	Avg.	BB	SO	SB	PO	A	E	Avg.
1990	Butte (Pioneer)	OF	62	226	48	78	12	6	10	50	.345	41	23	9	84	5	*8	.918
1991	Charlotte (Fla. St.)	OF-1B	111	388	52	114	25	1	5	48	.294	66	48	12	213	15	7	.970
—	Tulsa (Texas)	OF	20	64	12	19	3	2	3	12	.297	17	6	2	34	0	0	1.000
1992	Tulsa (Texas)	1B-OF	106	359	47	96	22	4	5	37	.267	60	63	2	814	50	11	.987
1993	Tulsa (Texas)	1B	129	474	76	138	25	6	15	59	.291	53	79	10	1055	93	8	.993
—	Okla. City (A.A.)	OF	8	27	6	6	2	0	1	4	.222	6	7	0	16	0	0	1.000
1994	Okla. City (A.A.)	OF-1B	31	111	18	35	12	1	3	13	.315	18	24	1	52	3	3	.948
—	Texas (A.L.)	OF-1B	80	277	36	87	16	1	10	46	.314	46	46	0	216	4	6	.973
1995	Texas (A.L.)	OF-1B	131	417	58	113	21	2	13	61	.271	55	66	3	240	9	6	.976
Major league totals (2 years)			211	694	94	200	37	3	23	107	.288	101	112	3	456	13	12	.975

GREGG, TOMMY — 1B/OF — MARLINS

PERSONAL: Born July 29, 1963, in Boone, N.C. . . . 6-1/190. . . . Bats left, throws left. . . . Full name: William Thomas Gregg Jr.
HIGH SCHOOL: R.J. Reynolds (Winston-Salem, N.C.).
COLLEGE: Wake Forest.
TRANSACTIONS/CAREER NOTES: Selected by Cleveland Indians organization in ninth round of free-agent draft (June 8, 1981); did not sign. . . . Selected by Indians organization in 32nd round of free-agent draft (June 4, 1984); did not sign. . . . Selected by Pittsburgh Pirates organization in seventh round of free-agent draft (June 3, 1985). . . . Traded by Pirates to Atlanta Braves (September 1, 1988), completing deal in which Braves traded IF Ken Oberkfell and cash to Pirates for a player to be named later (August 28, 1988). . . . On disabled list (April 20-June 2, 1989). . . . On Atlanta disabled list (April 28-June 9, 1991); included rehabilitation assignment to Richmond (June 5-9). . . . On Atlanta disabled list (March 24-July 21, 1992); included rehabilitation assignments to Richmond (May 30-June 7, July 8-13 and July 16-20). . . . Claimed on waivers by Cincinnati Reds (December 1, 1992). . . . Released by Indianapolis, Reds organization (March 26, 1993). . . . Re-signed by Indianapolis (March 27, 1993). . . . On Indianapolis disabled list (May 15-22 and June 7-17, 1993). . . . Granted free agency (August 30, 1993). . . . Signed by Buffalo, Pittsburgh Pirates organization (April 30, 1995). . . . Loaned by Buffalo to Mexico City Red Devils of Mexican League (April 30, 1995). . . . Granted free agency (October 15, 1994). . . . Signed by Charlotte, Florida Marlins organization (January 11, 1995). . . . On Florida disabled list (August 11-September 1, 1995); included rehabilitation assignment to Charlotte (August 26-September 1). . . . Granted free agency (October 16, 1995). . . . Re-signed by Marlins organization (November 2, 1995).
STATISTICAL NOTES: Led Eastern League with 14 intentional bases on balls received in 1987. . . . Career major league grand slams: 1.

			BATTING												FIELDING			
Year	Team (League)	Pos.	G	AB	R	H	2B	3B	HR	RBI	Avg.	BB	SO	SB	PO	A	E	Avg.
1985	Macon (S. Atl.)	OF	72	259	43	81	14	2	1	18	.313	49	38	16	117	4	1	.992
1986	Nashua (Eastern)	OF-1B	126	421	55	113	13	4	1	29	.268	66	48	11	216	7	4	.982
1987	Harrisburg (East.)	OF	133	461	99	171	22	9	10	82	*.371	84	47	35	242	12	7	.973
—	Pittsburgh (N.L.)	OF	10	8	3	2	1	0	0	0	.250	0	2	0	1	0	0	1.000
1988	Buffalo (A.A.)	OF	72	252	34	74	12	0	6	27	.294	25	26	7	134	3	2	.986
—	Pittsburgh (N.L.)	OF	14	15	4	3	1	0	1	3	.200	1	4	0	4	0	0	1.000
—	Atlanta (N.L.)■	OF	11	29	1	10	3	0	0	4	.345	2	2	0	22	1	0	1.000
1989	Atlanta (N.L.)	OF-1B	102	276	24	67	8	0	6	23	.243	18	45	3	321	17	2	.994
1990	Atlanta (N.L.)	1B-OF	124	239	18	63	13	1	5	32	.264	24	39	4	356	34	6	.985
1991	Atlanta (N.L.)	OF-1B	72	107	13	20	8	1	1	4	.187	12	24	2	121	9	0	1.000
—	Richmond (Int'l)	OF	3	13	3	6	0	0	1	4	.462	1	2	1	5	0	0	1.000
1992	Richmond (Int'l)	OF	39	125	17	36	9	2	0	12	.288	19	27	3	53	0	2	.964
—	Atlanta (N.L.)	OF	18	19	1	5	0	0	1	1	.263	1	7	1	15	0	0	1.000
1993	Indianapolis (A.A.)■	1B-OF	71	198	34	63	12	5	7	30	.318	26	28	3	330	29	7	.981
—	Cincinnati (N.L.)	OF	10	12	1	2	0	0	0	1	.167	0	0	0	2	0	0	1.000
1994	MC Red Dev. (Mex.)■	1B	85	287	69	101	19	3	7	64	.352	56	28	12	703	46	8	.989
1995	Charlotte (Int'l)■	1B-OF	34	124	30	48	10	1	9	32	.387	21	13	7	140	13	1	.994
—	Florida (N.L.)	OF-1B	72	156	20	37	5	0	6	20	.237	16	33	3	80	1	1	.988
Major league totals (8 years)			433	861	85	209	39	2	20	88	.243	74	156	13	922	62	9	.991

CHAMPIONSHIP SERIES RECORD

			BATTING												FIELDING			
Year	Team (League)	Pos.	G	AB	R	H	2B	3B	HR	RBI	Avg.	BB	SO	SB	PO	A	E	Avg.
1991	Atlanta (N.L.)	PH	4	4	0	1	0	0	0	0	.250	0	2	0	...	...	...	...

WORLD SERIES RECORD

			BATTING												FIELDING			
Year	Team (League)	Pos.	G	AB	R	H	2B	3B	HR	RBI	Avg.	BB	SO	SB	PO	A	E	Avg.
1991	Atlanta (N.L.)	PH	4	3	0	0	0	0	0	0	.000	0	2	0	...	...	...	...

GRIFFEY JR., KEN — OF — MARINERS

PERSONAL: Born November 21, 1969, in Donora, Pa. . . . 6-3/205. . . . Bats left, throws left. . . . Full name: George Kenneth Griffey Jr. . . . Son of Ken Griffey Sr., hitting coach, Colorado Rockies, and major league outfielder with four teams (1973-91); and brother of Craig Griffey, outfielder, Seattle Mariners organization.
HIGH SCHOOL: Moeller (Cincinnati).
TRANSACTIONS/CAREER NOTES: Selected by Seattle Mariners organization in first round (first pick overall) of free-agent draft (June 2,

1987). . . . On San Bernardino disabled list (June 9-August 15, 1988). . . . On disabled list (July 24-August 20, 1989 and June 9-25, 1992). . . . On Seattle disabled list (May 27-August 15, 1995); included rehabilitation assignment to Tacoma (August 13-15).

RECORDS: Shares major league record for most consecutive games with one or more home runs—8 (July 20 through July 28, 1993).

HONORS: Won A.L. Gold Glove as outfielder (1990-95). . . . Named outfielder on THE SPORTING NEWS A.L. All-Star team (1991 and 1993-94). . . . Named outfielder on THE SPORTING NEWS A.L. Silver Slugger team (1991 and 1993-94).

STATISTICAL NOTES: Led A.L. outfielders with six double plays in 1989. . . . Led A.L. with 359 total bases in 1993. . . . Career major league grand slams: 8.

		BATTING												FIELDING			
Year Team (League)	Pos.	G	AB	R	H	2B	3B	HR	RBI	Avg.	BB	SO	SB	PO	A	E	Avg.
1987—Belling. (N'west)	OF	54	182	43	57	9	1	14	40	.313	44	42	13	117	4	1	*.992
1988—San Bern. (Calif.)	OF	58	219	50	74	13	3	11	42	.338	34	39	32	145	3	2	.987
—Vermont (Eastern)	OF	17	61	10	17	5	1	2	10	.279	5	12	4	40	2	1	.977
1989—Seattle (A.L.)	OF-DH	127	455	61	120	23	0	16	61	.264	44	83	16	302	12	•10	.969
1990—Seattle (A.L.)	OF	155	597	91	179	28	7	22	80	.300	63	81	16	330	8	7	.980
1991—Seattle (A.L.)	OF-DH	154	548	76	179	42	1	22	100	.327	71	82	18	360	15	4	.989
1992—Seattle (A.L.)	OF-DH	142	565	83	174	39	4	27	103	.308	44	67	10	359	8	1	.997
1993—Seattle (A.L.)	OF-DH-1B	156	582	113	180	38	3	45	109	.309	96	91	17	317	8	3	.991
1994—Seattle (A.L.)	OF-DH	111	433	94	140	24	4	*40	90	.323	56	73	11	225	12	4	.983
1995—Seattle (A.L.)	OF-DH	72	260	52	67	7	0	17	42	.258	52	53	4	190	5	2	.990
—Tacoma (PCL)	DH	1	3	0	0	0	0	0	0	.000	0	1	0	...	...	...	...
Major league totals (7 years)		917	3440	570	1039	201	19	189	585	.302	426	530	92	2083	68	31	.986

DIVISION SERIES RECORD

NOTES: Shares postseason single-series record for most home runs-5 (1995).

		BATTING												FIELDING			
Year Team (League)	Pos.	G	AB	R	H	2B	3B	HR	RBI	Avg.	BB	SO	SB	PO	A	E	Avg.
1995—Seattle (A.L.)	OF	5	23	9	9	0	0	5	7	.391	2	4	1	15	1		1.000

CHAMPIONSHIP SERIES RECORD

		BATTING												FIELDING			
Year Team (League)	Pos.	G	AB	R	H	2B	3B	HR	RBI	Avg.	BB	SO	SB	PO	A	E	Avg.
1995—Seattle (A.L.)	OF	6	21	2	7	2	0	1	2	.333	4	4	2	13	0	1	.929

ALL-STAR GAME RECORD

NOTES: Holds career record for highest batting average (five or more games)—.571. . . . Named Most Valuable Player (1992).

		BATTING											FIELDING			
Year League	Pos.	AB	R	H	2B	3B	HR	RBI	Avg.	BB	SO	SB	PO	A	E	Avg.
1990—American	OF	2	0	0	0	0	0	0	.000	1	0	0	2	0	0	1.000
1991—American	OF	3	0	2	0	0	0	0	.667	0	0	0	2	0	0	1.000
1992—American	OF	3	2	3	1	0	1	2	1.000	0	0	0	1	0	0	1.000
1993—American	OF	3	1	1	0	0	0	1	.333	0	1	0	2	0	0	1.000
1994—American	OF	3	0	2	1	0	0	1	.667	0	0	0	2	0	0	1.000
1995—American		Selected, did not play—injured.														
All-Star Game totals (5 years)		14	3	8	2	0	1	4	.571	1	1	0	9	0	0	1.000

GRIMSLEY, JASON P

PERSONAL: Born August 7, 1967, in Cleveland, Tex. . . . 6-3/180. . . . Throws right, bats right. . . . Full name: Jason Alan Grimsley.

HIGH SCHOOL: Tarkington (Cleveland, Tex.).

TRANSACTIONS/CAREER NOTES: Selected by Philadelphia Phillies organization in 10th round of free-agent draft (June 3, 1985). . . . On Clearwater disabled list (April 8-May 10, 1988). . . . On Philadelphia disabled list (June 6-August 22, 1991); included rehabilitation assignments to Scranton/Wilkes-Barre (June 15-30 and August 7-21). . . . Traded by Phillies to Houston Astros for P Curt Schilling (April 2, 1992). . . . On disabled list (May 14-June 14, 1992). . . . Released by Astros (March 30, 1993). . . . Signed by Cleveland Indians organization (April 7, 1993). . . . On Charlotte disabled list (April 15-26, 1993). . . . Granted free agency (October 16, 1995).

STATISTICAL NOTES: Led New York-Pennsylvania League with 11 hit batsmen and 18 wild pitches in 1986. . . . Pitched 3-0 no-hit victory for Reading against Harrisburg (May 3, 1989, first game). . . . Led International League with 18 wild pitches in 1990.

MISCELLANEOUS: Appeared in one game as pinch-runner with Philadelphia (1990).

Year Team (League)	W	L	Pct.	ERA	G	GS	CG	ShO	Sv.	IP	H	R	ER	BB	SO
1985—Bend (Northwest)	0	1	.000	13.50	6	1	0	0	0	11 1/3	12	21	17	25	10
1986—Utica (NYP)	1	•10	.091	6.40	14	14	3	0	0	64 2/3	63	61	46	*77	46
1987—Spartanburg (SAL)	7	4	.636	3.16	23	9	3	0	0	88 1/3	59	48	31	54	98
1988—Clearwater (Fla. St.)	4	7	.364	3.73	16	15	2	0	0	101 1/3	80	48	42	37	90
—Reading (Eastern)	1	3	.250	7.17	5	4	0	0	0	21 1/3	20	19	17	13	14
1989—Reading (Eastern)	11	8	.579	2.98	26	26	8	2	0	172	121	65	57	*109	134
—Philadelphia (N.L.)	1	3	.250	5.89	4	4	0	0	0	18 1/3	19	13	12	19	7
1990—Scran./W.B. (Int'l)	8	5	.615	3.93	22	22	0	0	0	128 1/3	111	68	56	78	99
—Philadelphia (N.L.)	3	2	.600	3.30	11	11	0	0	0	57 1/3	47	21	21	43	41
1991—Philadelphia (N.L.)	1	7	.125	4.87	12	12	0	0	0	61	54	34	33	41	42
—Scran./W.B. (Int'l)	2	3	.400	4.35	9	9	0	0	0	51 2/3	48	28	25	37	43
1992—Tucson (Pac. Coast)■	8	7	.533	5.05	26	20	0	0	0	124 2/3	152	79	70	55	90
1993—Charlotte (Int'l)■	6	6	.500	3.39	28	19	3	1	0	135 1/3	138	64	51	49	102
—Cleveland (A.L.)	3	4	.429	5.31	10	6	0	0	0	42 1/3	52	26	25	20	27
1994—Charlotte (Int'l)	7	0	1.000	3.42	10	10	2	0	0	71	58	36	27	17	60
—Cleveland (A.L.)	5	2	.714	4.57	14	13	1	0	0	82 2/3	91	47	42	34	59
1995—Cleveland (A.L.)	0	0	...	6.09	15	2	0	0	1	34	37	24	23	32	25
—Buffalo (A.A.)	5	3	.625	2.91	10	10	2	0	0	68	61	26	22	19	40
A.L. totals (3 years)	8	6	.571	5.09	39	21	1	0	1	159	180	97	90	86	111
N.L. totals (3 years)	5	12	.294	4.35	27	27	0	0	0	136 2/3	120	68	66	103	90
Major league totals (6 years)	13	18	.419	4.75	66	48	1	0	1	295 2/3	300	165	156	189	201

G

GRISSOM, MARQUIS — OF — BRAVES

PERSONAL: Born April 17, 1967, in Atlanta. . . . 5-11/190. . . . Bats right, throws right. . . . Full name: Marquis Dean Grissom. . . . Name pronounced mar-KEESE.

HIGH SCHOOL: Lakeshore (College Park, Ga.).

COLLEGE: Florida A&M.

TRANSACTIONS/CAREER NOTES: Selected by Montreal Expos organization in third round of free-agent draft (June 1, 1988). . . . On Montreal disabled list (May 29-June 30, 1990); included rehabilitation assignment to Indianapolis (June 25-30). . . . Traded by Expos to Atlanta Braves for OF Roberto Kelly, OF Tony Tarasco and P Esteban Yan (April 6, 1995).

HONORS: Won N.L. Gold Glove as outfielder (1993-95).

STATISTICAL NOTES: Led New York-Pennsylvania League with 146 total bases in 1988. . . . Led N.L. outfielders with 333 total chances in 1994. . . . Career major league grand slams: 1.

		BATTING												FIELDING			
Year Team (League)	**Pos.**	**G**	**AB**	**R**	**H**	**2B**	**3B**	**HR**	**RBI**	**Avg.**	**BB**	**SO**	**SB**	**PO**	**A**	**E**	**Avg.**
1988—Jamestown (NYP)	OF	74	*291	*69	94	14	7	8	39	.323	35	39	23	123	•11	3	.978
1989—Jacksonv. (South.)	OF	78	278	43	83	15	4	3	31	.299	24	31	24	141	7	3	.980
—Indianapolis (A.A.)	OF	49	187	28	52	10	4	2	21	.278	14	23	16	106	5	0	1.000
—Montreal (N.L.)	OF	26	74	16	19	2	0	1	2	.257	12	21	1	32	1	2	.943
1990—Montreal (N.L.)	OF	98	288	42	74	14	2	3	29	.257	27	40	22	165	5	2	.988
—Indianapolis (A.A.)	OF	5	22	3	4	0	0	2	3	.182	0	5	1	16	0	0	1.000
1991—Montreal (N.L.)	OF	148	558	73	149	23	9	6	39	.267	34	89	*76	350	•15	6	.984
1992—Montreal (N.L.)	OF	159	*653	99	180	39	6	14	66	.276	42	81	*78	401	7	7	.983
1993—Montreal (N.L.)	OF	157	630	104	188	27	2	19	95	.298	52	76	53	416	8	7	.984
1994—Montreal (N.L.)	OF	110	475	96	137	25	4	11	45	.288	41	66	36	*321	7	5	.985
1995—Atlanta (N.L.)■	OF	139	551	80	142	23	3	12	42	.258	47	61	29	309	9	2	.994
Major league totals (7 years)		837	3229	510	889	153	26	66	318	.275	255	434	295	1994	52	31	.985

DIVISION SERIES RECORD

		BATTING												FIELDING			
Year Team (League)	**Pos.**	**G**	**AB**	**R**	**H**	**2B**	**3B**	**HR**	**RBI**	**Avg.**	**BB**	**SO**	**SB**	**PO**	**A**	**E**	**Avg.**
1995—Atlanta (N.L.)	OF	4	21	5	11	2	0	3	4	.524	0	3	2	9	0	0	1.000

CHAMPIONSHIP SERIES RECORD

		BATTING												FIELDING			
Year Team (League)	**Pos.**	**G**	**AB**	**R**	**H**	**2B**	**3B**	**HR**	**RBI**	**Avg.**	**BB**	**SO**	**SB**	**PO**	**A**	**E**	**Avg.**
1995—Atlanta (N.L.)	OF	4	19	2	5	0	1	0	0	.263	1	4	0	8	0	1	.889

WORLD SERIES RECORD

NOTES: Member of World Series championship team (1995).

		BATTING												FIELDING			
Year Team (League)	**Pos.**	**G**	**AB**	**R**	**H**	**2B**	**3B**	**HR**	**RBI**	**Avg.**	**BB**	**SO**	**SB**	**PO**	**A**	**E**	**Avg.**
1995—Atlanta (N.L.)	OF	6	25	3	9	1	0	0	1	.360	1	3	3	13	0	0	1.000

ALL-STAR GAME RECORD

		BATTING											FIELDING			
Year League	**Pos.**	**AB**	**R**	**H**	**2B**	**3B**	**HR**	**RBI**	**Avg.**	**BB**	**SO**	**SB**	**PO**	**A**	**E**	**Avg.**
1993—National	OF	3	0	0	0	0	0	0	.000	0	1	0	1	0	0	1.000
1994—National	OF	1	1	1	0	0	1	1	1.000	1	0	0	2	1	0	1.000
All-Star Game totals (2 years)		4	1	1	0	0	1	1	.250	1	1	0	3	1	0	1.000

GROOM, BUDDY — P — ATHLETICS

PERSONAL: Born July 10, 1965, in Dallas. . . . 6-2/200. . . . Throws left, bats left. . . . Full name: Wedsel Gary Groom.

HIGH SCHOOL: Red Oak (Tex.).

COLLEGE: University of Mary Hardin-Baylor (Tex.).

TRANSACTIONS/CAREER NOTES: Selected by Chicago White Sox organization in 12th round of free-agent draft (June 2, 1987). . . . Selected by Detroit Tigers organization from White Sox organization in Rule 5 minor league draft (December 3, 1990). . . . Traded by Tigers to Florida Marlins for a player to be named later (August 7, 1995); Tigers acquired P Mike Myers to complete deal (August 9, 1995). . . . Granted free agency (October 16, 1995). . . . Signed by Oakland Athletics organization (November 27, 1995).

Year Team (League)	**W**	**L**	**Pct.**	**ERA**	**G**	**GS**	**CG**	**ShO**	**Sv.**	**IP**	**H**	**R**	**ER**	**BB**	**SO**
1987—GC White Sox (GCL)	1	0	1.000	0.75	4	1	0	0	1	12	12	1	1	2	8
—Day. Beach (FSL)	7	2	.778	3.59	11	10	2	0	0	67 2/3	60	30	27	33	29
1988—Tampa (Fla. St.)	13	10	.565	2.54	27	27	8	0	0	*195	181	69	55	51	118
1989—Birmingham (Sou.)	13	8	.619	4.52	26	26	3	1	0	167 1/3	172	101	84	78	94
1990—Birmingham (Sou.)	6	8	.429	5.07	20	20	0	0	0	115 1/3	135	81	65	48	66
1991—Toledo (Int'l)■	2	5	.286	4.32	24	6	0	0	1	75	75	39	36	25	49
—London (Eastern)	7	1	.875	3.48	11	7	0	0	0	51 2/3	51	20	20	12	39
1992—Toledo (Int'l)	7	7	.500	2.80	16	16	1	0	0	109 1/3	102	41	34	23	71
—Detroit (A.L.)	0	5	.000	5.82	12	7	0	0	1	38 2/3	48	28	25	22	15
1993—Toledo (Int'l)	9	3	.750	2.74	16	15	0	0	0	102	98	34	31	30	78
—Detroit (A.L.)	0	2	.000	6.14	19	3	0	0	0	36 2/3	48	25	25	13	15
1994—Toledo (Int'l)	0	0	. . .	2.25	5	0	0	0	0	4	2	1	1	0	6
—Detroit (A.L.)	0	1	.000	3.94	40	0	0	0	1	32	31	14	14	13	27
1995—Detroit (A.L.)	1	3	.250	7.52	23	4	0	0	1	40 2/3	55	35	34	26	23
—Toledo (Int'l)	2	3	.400	1.91	6	5	1	0	0	33	31	14	7	4	24
—Florida (N.L.)■	1	2	.333	7.20	14	0	0	0	0	15	26	12	12	6	12
A.L. totals (4 years)	1	11	.083	5.96	94	14	0	0	3	148	182	102	98	74	80
N.L. totals (1 year)	1	2	.333	7.20	14	0	0	0	0	15	26	12	12	6	12
Major league totals (4 years)	2	13	.133	6.07	108	14	0	0	3	163	208	114	110	80	92

GROSS, KEVIN — P — RANGERS

PERSONAL: Born June 8, 1961, in Downey, Calif. . . . 6-5/227. . . . Throws right, bats right. . . . Full name: Kevin Frank Gross.
HIGH SCHOOL: Fillmore (Calif.).
JUNIOR COLLEGE: Oxnard (Calif.) College.
COLLEGE: California Lutheran College.
TRANSACTIONS/CAREER NOTES: Selected by Baltimore Orioles organization in 32nd round of free-agent draft (June 5, 1979); did not sign. . . . Selected by Philadelphia Phillies organization in secondary phase of free-agent draft (January 13, 1981). . . . Traded by Phillies to Montreal Expos for P Floyd Youmans and P Jeff Parrett (December 6, 1988). . . . On disabled list (June 28-July 20, 1990). . . . Granted free agency (November 5, 1990). . . . Signed by Los Angeles Dodgers (December 3, 1990). . . . Granted free agency (October 20, 1994). . . . Signed by Texas Rangers (December 13, 1994).
STATISTICAL NOTES: Led N.L. with 28 home runs allowed in 1986. . . . Led N.L. with 11 hit batsmen in 1988 and tied for lead with eight in 1986 and 10 in 1987. . . . Pitched 2-0 no-hit victory against San Francisco (August 17, 1992).
MISCELLANEOUS: Made an out in only appearance as pinch-hitter (1990). . . . Singled and scored and struck out in two games as pinch-hitter (1991).

Year	Team (League)	W	L	Pct.	ERA	G	GS	CG	ShO	Sv.	IP	H	R	ER	BB	SO
1981—	Spartanburg (SAL)	13	12	.520	3.56	28	•28	8	2	0	192	173	94	76	62	123
1982—	Reading (Eastern)	10	15	.400	4.23	26	24	8	2	0	151	138	81	71	89	136
1983—	Portland (PCL)	3	5	.375	6.75	15	15	0	0	0	80	82	60	60	45	61
—	Philadelphia (N.L.)	4	6	.400	3.56	17	17	1	1	0	96	100	46	38	35	66
1984—	Philadelphia (N.L.)	8	5	.615	4.12	44	14	1	0	1	129	140	66	59	44	84
1985—	Philadelphia (N.L.)	15	13	.536	3.41	38	31	6	2	0	205 2/3	194	86	78	81	151
1986—	Philadelphia (N.L.)	12	12	.500	4.02	37	36	7	2	0	241 2/3	240	115	108	94	154
1987—	Philadelphia (N.L.)	9	16	.360	4.35	34	33	3	1	0	200 2/3	205	107	97	87	110
1988—	Philadelphia (N.L.)	12	14	.462	3.69	33	33	5	1	0	231 2/3	209	101	95	*89	162
1989—	Montreal (N.L.)■	11	12	.478	4.38	31	31	4	3	0	201 1/3	188	105	*98	88	158
1990—	Montreal (N.L.)	9	12	.429	4.57	31	26	2	1	0	163 1/3	171	86	83	65	111
1991—	Los Angeles (N.L.)■	10	11	.476	3.58	46	10	0	0	3	115 2/3	123	55	46	50	95
1992—	Los Angeles (N.L.)	8	13	.381	3.17	34	30	4	3	0	204 2/3	182	82	72	77	158
1993—	Los Angeles (N.L.)	13	13	.500	4.14	33	32	3	0	0	202 1/3	224	110	93	74	150
1994—	Los Angeles (N.L.)	9	7	.563	3.60	25	23	1	0	1	157 1/3	162	64	63	43	124
1995—	Texas (A.L.)■	9	•15	.375	5.54	31	30	4	0	0	183 2/3	200	124	113	89	106
A.L. totals (1 year)		9	15	.375	5.54	31	30	4	0	0	183 2/3	200	124	113	89	106
N.L. totals (12 years)		120	134	.472	3.89	403	316	37	14	5	2149 1/3	2138	1023	930	827	1523
Major league totals (13 years)		129	149	.464	4.02	434	346	41	14	5	2333	2338	1147	1043	916	1629

WORLD SERIES RECORD

Year	Team (League)	W	L	Pct.	ERA	G	GS	CG	ShO	Sv.	IP	H	R	ER	BB	SO
1983—	Philadelphia (N.L.)							Did not play.								

ALL-STAR GAME RECORD

Year	League	W	L	Pct.	ERA	GS	CG	ShO	Sv.	IP	H	R	ER	BB	SO
1988—	National	0	0	. . .	0.00	0	0	0	0	1	0	0	0	0	1

GROTEWOLD, JEFF — C/1B

PERSONAL: Born December 8, 1965, in Madera, Calif. . . . 6-0/215. . . . Bats left, throws right. . . . Full name: Jeffrey Scott Grotewold.
HIGH SCHOOL: Rim of the World (Lake Arrowhead, Calif.).
COLLEGE: San Diego.
TRANSACTIONS/CAREER NOTES: Signed as free agent by Philadelphia Phillies organization (December 17, 1986). . . . On Scranton/Wilkes-Barre disabled list (June 23-July 16, 1991). . . . Traded by Phillies to Minnesota Twins for OF Mica Lewis (March 25, 1993). . . . On disabled list (May 15-July 9, 1993). . . . Granted free agency (October 15, 1993). . . . Signed by Toledo, Detroit Tigers organization (January 12, 1994). . . . Released by Toledo (March 31, 1994). . . . Played with San Bernardino, independent (1994). . . . Granted free agency (October 15, 1994). . . . Signed by Kansas City Royals organization (February 15, 1995). . . . Granted free agency (October 16, 1995).
STATISTICAL NOTES: Tied for South Atlantic League lead with 10 intentional bases on balls received in 1987. . . . Tied for Florida State League lead with nine intentional bases on balls received in 1988. . . . Led Eastern League with .464 slugging percentage in 1990. . . . Led American Association with .434 on-base percentage in 1995. . . . Led American Association first basemen with 15 errors in 1995.

				BATTING											FIELDING			
Year	Team (League)	Pos.	G	AB	R	H	2B	3B	HR	RBI	Avg.	BB	SO	SB	PO	A	E	Avg.
1987—	Spartanburg (SAL)	C-1B	113	381	56	96	22	2	15	70	.252	47	114	4	547	61	20	.968
1988—	Clearwater (FSL)	1B	125	442	35	97	23	2	6	39	.219	42	103	2	797	68	17	.981
1989—	Clearwater (FSL)	1B-C	91	301	32	84	17	2	6	55	.279	32	43	8	309	33	2	.994
—	Reading (Eastern)	1B	25	80	9	16	2	0	0	11	.200	8	14	0	83	8	1	.989
1990—	Reading (Eastern)	1B-C-OF	127	412	56	111	33	1	15	72	.269	62	83	2	579	54	10	.984
1991—	Scran./W.B. (Int'l)	1B-C	87	276	33	71	13	5	5	38	.257	25	61	0	444	38	6	.988
1992—	Scran./W.B. (Int'l)	1B	17	51	8	15	1	1	1	8	.294	7	10	0	64	2	1	.985
—	Philadelphia (N.L.)	OF-C-1B	72	65	7	13	2	0	3	5	.200	9	16	0	6	0	0	1.000
1993—	Portland (PCL)■	C-1B-3B	52	151	27	38	6	3	6	30	.252	27	41	2	157	12	11	.939
1994—	San Bern. (Calif.)■	1B-OF-C	32	117	19	36	10	0	6	25	.308	15	29	0	189	16	4	.981
1995—	Omaha (A.A.)■	1B-3B	105	350	70	103	19	0	17	60	.294	*82	88	0	750	52	†15	.982
—	Kansas City (A.L.)	DH-1B	15	36	4	10	1	0	1	6	.278	9	7	0	3	0	1	.750
American League totals (1 year)			15	36	4	10	1	0	1	6	.278	9	7	0	3	0	1	.750
National League totals (1 year)			72	65	7	13	2	0	3	5	.200	9	16	0	6	0	0	1.000
Major league totals (2 years)			87	101	11	23	3	0	4	11	.228	18	23	0	9	0	1	.900

GROTT, MATT — P

PERSONAL: Born December 5, 1967, in La Porte, Ind. . . . 6-1/210. . . . Throws left, bats left. . . . Full name: Matthew Allen Grott.

G

HIGH SCHOOL: Apollo (Glendale, Ariz.).
COLLEGE: Phoenix College.
TRANSACTIONS/CAREER NOTES: Signed as non-drafted free agent by Oakland Athletics organization (July 28, 1989).... Traded by A's organization with P Russell Cormier to Montreal Expos organization for P Ron Darling (July 31, 1991).... Selected by Cincinnati Reds organization from Harrisburg, Expos organization in Rule 5 minor league draft (December 9, 1991).... On disabled list (April 7-19, June 9-17 and June 20-August 17, 1994).... Granted free agency (October 3, 1995).

Year Team (League)	W	L	Pct.	ERA	G	GS	CG	ShO	Sv.	IP	H	R	ER	BB	SO
1989—Arizona A's (Ariz.)	3	1	.750	2.31	9	5	0	0	0	35	29	10	9	9	44
1990—Madison (Midwest)	2	0	1.000	0.36	22	0	0	0	12	25	15	5	1	14	36
—Modesto (Calif.)	2	0	1.000	2.04	12	0	0	0	4	17 2/3	10	7	4	14	28
—Huntsville (South.)	0	0	...	2.87	10	0	0	0	1	15 2/3	8	5	5	10	12
1991—Huntsville (South.)	2	9	.182	5.15	42	0	0	0	3	57 2/3	65	40	33	37	65
—Harrisburg (East.)■	2	1	.667	4.70	10	1	0	0	1	15 1/3	14	8	8	8	16
1992—Chattanooga (Sou.)■	1	2	.333	2.68	32	0	0	0	6	40 1/3	39	16	12	25	44
1993—Indianapolis (A.A.)	7	5	.583	3.59	33	9	0	0	1	100 1/3	88	45	40	40	73
1994—Indianapolis (A.A.)	10	3	.769	*2.55	26	16	2	1	1	116 1/3	106	44	33	32	64
1995—Indianapolis (A.A.)	7	3	.700	4.24	25	18	2	1	2	114 2/3	99	61	54	24	74
—Cincinnati (N.L.)	0	0	...	21.60	2	0	0	0	0	1 2/3	6	4	4	0	2
Major league totals (1 year)	0	0	...	21.60	2	0	0	0	0	1 2/3	6	4	4	0	2

GRUDZIELANEK, MARK — SS/3B — EXPOS

PERSONAL: Born June 30, 1970, in Milwaukee.... 6-1/185.... Bats right, throws right.... Full name: Mark James Grudzielanek.... Name pronounced gruzz-ELL-uh-neck.
HIGH SCHOOL: J.M. Hanks (El Paso, Tex.).
JUNIOR COLLEGE: Trinidad (Colo.) State Junior College.
TRANSACTIONS/CAREER NOTES: Selected by Montreal Expos organization in 11th round of free-agent draft (June 3, 1991).... On disabled list (July 13-August 9, 1993 and May 12-19, 1994).
HONORS: Named Eastern League Most Valuable Player (1994).
STATISTICAL NOTES: Led Eastern League shortstops with .959 fielding percentage in 1994.

		BATTING												FIELDING		
Year Team (League)	Pos.	G	AB	R	H	2B	3B	HR	RBI	Avg.	BB	SO	SB	PO	A	E	Avg.
1991—Jamestown (NYP)	SS	72	275	44	72	9	3	2	32	.262	18	43	14	112	206	23	.933
1992—Rockford (Midw.)	SS	128	496	64	122	12	5	5	54	.246	22	59	25	173	290	41	.919
1993—W.P. Beach (FSL)	2-S-O-3	86	300	41	80	11	6	1	34	.267	14	42	17	105	135	13	.949
1994—Harrisburg (East.)	SS-3B	122	488	92	157	•37	3	11	66	.322	43	66	32	178	344	23	†.958
1995—Montreal (N.L.)	SS-3B-2B	78	269	27	66	12	2	1	20	.245	14	47	8	94	198	10	.967
—Ottawa (Int'l)	SS	49	181	26	54	9	1	1	22	.298	10	17	12	58	156	14	.939
Major league totals (1 year)		78	269	27	66	12	2	1	20	.245	14	47	8	94	198	10	.967

GRZANICH, MIKE — P — ASTROS

PERSONAL: Born August 24, 1972, in Canton, Ill.... 6-1/180.... Throws right, bats right.... Full name: Michael Edward Grzanich.
JUNIOR COLLEGE: Parkland College (Ill.).
TRANSACTIONS/CAREER NOTES: Selected by Houston Astros organization in 19th round of free-agent draft (June 1, 1992).
STATISTICAL NOTES: Led New York-Pennsylvania League with 11 home runs allowed in 1993.

Year Team (League)	W	L	Pct.	ERA	G	GS	CG	ShO	Sv.	IP	H	R	ER	BB	SO
1992—GC Astros (GCL)	2	5	.286	4.54	17	17	0	0	3	33 2/3	38	21	17	14	29
1993—Auburn (NYP)	5	•8	.385	4.82	16	14	•4	•1	0	93 1/3	106	*63	50	27	71
1994—Quad City (Midw.)	11	7	.611	3.09	23	22	3	0	0	142 2/3	145	55	49	43	101
1995—Jackson (Texas)	5	3	.625	2.74	50	0	0	0	8	65 2/3	55	22	20	38	44

GUARDADO, EDDIE — P — TWINS

PERSONAL: Born October 2, 1970, in Stockton, Calif.... 6-0/193.... Throws left, bats right.... Full name: Edward Adrian Guardado.... Name pronounced gwar-DAH-doh.
HIGH SCHOOL: Franklin (Stockton, Calif.).
COLLEGE: San Joaquin Delta College (Calif.).
TRANSACTIONS/CAREER NOTES: Selected by Minnesota Twins organization in 21st round of free-agent draft (June 4, 1990).
STATISTICAL NOTES: Pitched 5-0 no-hit victory against Pulaski (August 26, 1991).

Year Team (League)	W	L	Pct.	ERA	G	GS	CG	ShO	Sv.	IP	H	R	ER	BB	SO
1991—Elizabeth. (App.)	8	4	.667	1.86	14	13	3	•1	0	92	67	30	19	31	*106
1992—Kenosha (Midwest)	5	10	.333	4.37	18	18	2	1	0	101	106	57	49	30	103
—Visalia (California)	7	0	1.000	1.64	7	7	1	1	0	49 1/3	47	13	9	10	39
1993—Nashville (South.)	4	0	1.000	1.24	10	10	2	2	0	65 1/3	53	10	9	10	57
—Minnesota (A.L.)	3	8	.273	6.18	19	16	0	0	0	94 2/3	123	68	65	36	46
1994—Salt Lake (PCL)	12	7	.632	4.83	24	24	2	0	0	151	171	90	81	51	87
—Minnesota (A.L.)	0	2	.000	8.47	4	4	0	0	0	17	26	16	16	4	8
1995—Minnesota (A.L.)	4	9	.308	5.12	51	5	0	0	2	91 1/3	99	54	52	45	71
Major league totals (3 years)	7	19	.269	5.90	74	25	0	0	2	203	248	138	133	85	125

GUBICZA, MARK — P — ROYALS

PERSONAL: Born August 14, 1962, in Philadelphia.... 6-5/230.... Throws right, bats right.... Full name: Mark Steven Gubicza.... Son of Anthony Gubicza, minor league pitcher (1950-51).... Name pronounced GOO-ba-zah.

HIGH SCHOOL: William Penn Charter (Philadelphia).
TRANSACTIONS/CAREER NOTES: Selected by Kansas City Royals organization in second round of free-agent draft (June 8, 1981); pick received as compensation for St. Louis Cardinals signing free-agent C Darrell Porter. . . . On disabled list (June 29, 1982-remainder of season; June 6-21, 1986; and July 1, 1990-remainder of season). . . . On Kansas City disabled list (March 30-May 14, 1991); included rehabilitation assignment to Omaha (April 20-May 13). . . . On Kansas City disabled list (July 11, 1992-remainder of season). . . . Granted free agency (October 30, 1992). . . . Re-signed by Royals (November 25, 1992). . . . Granted free agency (November 3, 1993). . . . Re-signed by Royals (December 7, 1993). . . . Granted free agency (October 18, 1994). . . . Re-signed by Royals (December 12, 1994). . . . Granted free agency (October 31, 1995). . . . Re-signed by Royals (December 7, 1995).
STATISTICAL NOTES: Pitched 7-0 one-hit, complete-game victory against Oakland (June 15, 1995).

Year	Team (League)	W	L	Pct.	ERA	G	GS	CG	ShO	Sv.	IP	H	R	ER	BB	SO
1981—	GC Royals-Gold (GCL)	•8	1	.889	2.25	11	11	0	0	0	56	39	18	14	23	40
1982—	Fort Myers (Fla. St.)	2	5	.286	4.13	11	11	0	0	0	48	49	33	22	25	36
1983—	Jacksonville (Sou.)	14	12	.538	3.08	28	28	5	0	0	196	146	81	67	93	*146
1984—	Kansas City (A.L.)	10	14	.417	4.05	29	29	4	2	0	189	172	90	85	75	111
1985—	Kansas City (A.L.)	14	10	.583	4.06	29	28	0	0	0	177 1/3	160	88	80	77	99
1986—	Kansas City (A.L.)	12	6	.667	3.64	35	24	3	2	0	180 2/3	155	77	73	84	118
1987—	Kansas City (A.L.)	13	18	.419	3.98	35	35	10	2	0	241 2/3	231	114	107	120	166
1988—	Kansas City (A.L.)	20	8	.714	2.70	35	35	8	4	0	269 2/3	237	94	81	83	183
1989—	Kansas City (A.L.)	15	11	.577	3.04	36	•36	8	2	0	255	252	100	86	63	173
1990—	Kansas City (A.L.)	4	7	.364	4.50	16	16	2	0	0	94	101	48	47	38	71
1991—	Omaha (Am. Assoc.)	2	1	.667	3.31	3	3	0	0	0	16 1/3	20	7	6	4	12
—	Kansas City (A.L.)	9	12	.429	5.68	26	26	0	0	0	133	168	90	84	42	89
1992—	Kansas City (A.L.)	7	6	.538	3.72	18	18	2	1	0	111 1/3	110	47	46	36	81
1993—	Kansas City (A.L.)	5	8	.385	4.66	49	6	0	0	2	104 1/3	128	61	54	43	80
1994—	Kansas City (A.L.)	7	9	.438	4.50	22	22	0	0	0	130	158	74	65	26	59
1995—	Kansas City (A.L.)	12	14	.462	3.75	33	*33	3	2	0	213 1/3	222	97	89	62	81
Major league totals (12 years)		128	123	.510	3.85	363	308	40	15	2	2099 1/3	2094	980	897	749	1311

CHAMPIONSHIP SERIES RECORD

Year	Team (League)	W	L	Pct.	ERA	G	GS	CG	ShO	Sv.	IP	H	R	ER	BB	SO
1985—	Kansas City (A.L.)	1	0	1.000	3.24	2	1	0	0	0	8 1/3	4	3	3	4	4

WORLD SERIES RECORD

NOTES: Member of World Series championship team (1985).

Year	Team (League)	W	L	Pct.	ERA	G	GS	CG	ShO	Sv.	IP	H	R	ER	BB	SO
1985—	Kansas City (A.L.)							Did not play.								

ALL-STAR GAME RECORD

Year	League	W	L	Pct.	ERA	GS	CG	ShO	Sv.	IP	H	R	ER	BB	SO
1988—	American	0	0	...	4.50	0	0	0	0	2	3	1	1	0	2
1989—	American	0	0	...	0.00	0	0	0	0	1	0	0	0	0	1
All-Star totals (2 years)		0	0	...	3.00	0	0	0	0	3	3	1	1	0	3

GUERRERO, WILTON — SS — DODGERS

PERSONAL: Born October 24, 1974, in Don Gregorio, Dominican Republic. . . . 5-11/145. . . . Bats right, throws right.
HIGH SCHOOL: Escuela Primaria (Don Gregorio, Dominican Republic).
TRANSACTIONS/CAREER NOTES: Signed as non-drafted free agent by Los Angeles Dodgers organization (October 8, 1991).
STATISTICAL NOTES: Led Florida State League in caught stealing with 20 in 1994. . . . Led Texas League in caught stealing with 22 in 1995.

			BATTING												FIELDING			
Year	Team (League)	Pos.	G	AB	R	H	2B	3B	HR	RBI	Avg.	BB	SO	SB	PO	A	E	Avg.
1992—	Dom. Dodgers (DSL)	SS	61	225	52	87	7	4	0	38	.387	34	21	15	104	215	21	.938
1993—	Great Falls (Pio.)	SS	66	256	44	76	5	1	0	21	.297	24	33	20	76	184	21	.925
—	Dom. Dodgers (DSL)	SS	8	31	6	11	0	1	0	4	.355	4	3	2	15	18	1	.971
1994—	Vero Beach (FSL)	SS	110	402	55	118	11	4	1	32	.294	29	71	23	111	292	17	.960
1995—	San Antonio (Tex.)	SS	95	382	53	133	13	6	0	26	*.348	26	63	21	121	263	19	.953
—	Albuquerque (PCL)	SS-OF	14	49	10	16	1	1	0	2	.327	1	7	2	13	39	9	.852

GUETTERMAN, LEE — P — MARINERS

PERSONAL: Born November 22, 1958, in Chattanooga, Tenn. . . . 6-8/230. . . . Throws left, bats left. . . . Full name: Arthur Lee Guetterman.
HIGH SCHOOL: Oceanside (Calif.).
COLLEGE: Liberty, Va. (bachelor of science degree in physical education, 1981).
TRANSACTIONS/CAREER NOTES: Selected by Seattle Mariners organization in fourth round of free-agent draft (June 8, 1981); pick received as compensation for California Angels signing free-agent OF Juan Beniquez. . . . On Chattanooga disabled list (August 1-15, 1984). . . . On disabled list (April 11-May 31, 1985). . . . Traded by Mariners with P Clay Parker, P Wade Taylor and P Niels Jensen to New York Yankees for P Steve Trout, OF Steve Norkaitis and OF Henry Cotto (December 22, 1987). . . . On disabled list (July 19-August 3, 1990). . . . Traded by Yankees to New York Mets for P Tim Burke (June 9, 1992). . . . Granted free agency (October 30, 1992). . . . Signed by Los Angeles Dodgers organization (January 13, 1993). . . . Released by Dodgers organization (March 30, 1993). . . . Signed by Louisville, St. Louis Cardinals organization (May 1, 1993). . . . Granted free agency (October 25, 1993). . . . Signed by Vancouver, California Angels organization (February 28, 1994). . . . Released by Angels organization (March 29, 1994). . . . Signed by San Diego Padres organization (May 12, 1994). . . . Released by Las Vegas, Padres organization (June 24, 1994). . . . Signed by Calgary, Seattle Mariners organization (August 8, 1994). . . . Granted free agency (October 15, 1994). . . . Re-signed by Mariners organization (December 23, 1994). . . . Granted free agency (November 8, 1995). . . . Re-signed by Mariners organization (December 7, 1995).

Year	Team (League)	W	L	Pct.	ERA	G	GS	CG	ShO	Sv.	IP	H	R	ER	BB	SO
1981—	Bellingham (N'west)	6	4	.600	2.68	13	13	3	0	0	84	85	36	25	42	55
1982—	Bakersfield (Calif.)	7	11	.389	4.44	26	26	4	1	0	154	172	100	76	69	82
1983—	Bakersfield (Calif.)	12	6	.667	3.22	25	25	6	1	0	156 1/3	164	72	56	45	93
1984—	Chattanooga (Sou.)	11	7	.611	3.38	24	24	4	2	0	157	174	68	59	38	47
—	Seattle (A.L.)	0	0	...	4.15	3	0	0	0	0	4 1/3	9	2	2	2	2

Year	Team (League)	W	L	Pct.	ERA	G	GS	CG	ShO	Sv.	IP	H	R	ER	BB	SO
1985—	Calgary (PCL)	5	8	.385	5.79	20	18	2	0	0	110 1/3	138	86	71	44	48
1986—	Seattle (A.L.)	0	4	.000	7.34	41	4	1	0	0	76	108	67	62	30	38
—	Calgary (PCL)	1	0	1.000	5.59	4	4	0	0	0	19 1/3	24	12	12	7	8
1987—	Calgary (PCL)	5	1	.833	2.86	16	2	1	0	1	44	41	14	14	17	29
—	Seattle (A.L.)	11	4	*.733	3.81	25	17	2	1	0	113 1/3	117	60	48	35	42
1988—	New York (A.L.)■	1	2	.333	4.65	20	2	0	0	0	40 2/3	49	21	21	14	15
—	Columbus (Int'l)	9	6	.600	2.76	18	18	6	0	0	120 2/3	109	46	37	26	49
1989—	New York (A.L.)	5	5	.500	2.45	70	0	0	0	13	103	98	31	28	26	51
1990—	New York (A.L.)	11	7	.611	3.39	64	0	0	0	2	93	80	37	35	26	48
1991—	New York (A.L.)	3	4	.429	3.68	64	0	0	0	6	88	91	42	36	25	35
1992—	New York (A.L.)	1	1	.500	9.53	15	0	0	0	0	22 2/3	35	24	24	13	5
—	New York (N.L.)■	3	4	.429	5.82	43	0	0	0	2	43 1/3	57	28	28	14	15
1993—	Louisville (A.A.)■	2	1	.667	2.94	25	0	0	0	2	33 2/3	35	11	11	12	20
—	St. Louis (N.L.)	3	3	.500	2.93	40	0	0	0	1	46	41	18	15	16	19
1994—	Las Vegas (PCL)■	1	1	.500	2.11	15	1	0	0	0	21 1/3	21	6	5	4	18
—	Calgary (PCL)■	4	0	1.000	2.75	12	0	0	0	2	19 2/3	19	9	6	3	17
1995—	Tacoma (PCL)	1	2	.333	2.95	33	1	0	0	4	36 2/3	33	12	12	9	21
—	Seattle (A.L.)	0	0	....	6.88	23	0	0	0	1	17	21	13	13	11	11
A.L. totals (9 years)		32	27	.542	4.34	325	23	3	1	22	608	297	284	269	182	247
N.L. totals (2 years)		6	7	.462	4.33	83	0	0	0	3	89 1/3	98	46	43	30	34
Major league totals (11 years)		38	34	.528	4.34	408	23	3	1	25	647 1/3	706	343	312	212	281

GUEVARA, GIOMAR — SS/2B — MARINERS

PERSONAL: Born October 23, 1972, in Miranda, Venezuela. . . . 5-8/150. . . . Bats both, throws right. . . . Full name: Giomar Antonio Guevara.
TRANSACTIONS/CAREER NOTES: Signed as non-drafted free agent by Seattle Mariners organization (November 13, 1990).

				BATTING											FIELDING			
Year	Team (League)	Pos.	G	AB	R	H	2B	3B	HR	RBI	Avg.	BB	SO	SB	PO	A	E	Avg.
1991—				Dominican Summer League statistics unavailable.														
1992—	Santo Dom. (DSL)	IF	45	163	30	51	13	4	1	24	.313	19	30	14	37	103	10	.933
1993—	Belling. (N'west)	SS	62	211	31	48	8	3	1	23	.227	34	46	4	83	172	16	.941
1994—	Appleton (Midw.)	SS-2B	110	385	57	116	23	3	8	46	.301	42	77	9	171	270	23	.950
—	Jacksonv. (South.)	SS	7	20	2	4	2	0	1	3	.200	2	9	0	12	25	3	.925
1995—	Riverside (Calif.)	SS	83	292	53	71	12	3	2	34	.243	30	71	7	123	231	27	.929

GUILLEN, OZZIE — SS — WHITE SOX

PERSONAL: Born January 20, 1964, in Oculare del Tuy, Miranda, Venezuela. . . . 5-11/164. . . . Bats left, throws right. . . . Full name: Oswaldo Jose Barrios Guillen. . . . Name pronounced GHEE-un.
TRANSACTIONS/CAREER NOTES: Signed as non-drafted free agent by San Diego Padres organization (December 17, 1980). . . . Traded by Padres organization with P Tim Lollar, P Bill Long and 3B Luis Salazar to Chicago White Sox for P LaMarr Hoyt, P Kevin Kristan and P Todd Simmons (December 6, 1984). . . . On disabled list (April 22, 1992-remainder of season).
RECORDS: Shares major league single-season record for fewest bases on balls received (150 or more games)—11 (1991). . . . Holds A.L. single-season record for fewest putouts by shortstop (150 or more games)—220 (1985).
HONORS: Named A.L. Rookie Player of the Year by The Sporting News (1985). . . . Named A.L. Rookie of the Year by Baseball Writers' Association of America (1985). . . . Won A.L. Gold Glove at shortstop (1990).
STATISTICAL NOTES: Tied for California League lead with 14 sacrifice hits in 1982. . . . Led Pacific Coast League shortstops with 362 assists and 549 total chances in 1984. . . . Led A.L. shortstops with 760 total chances in 1987 and 863 in 1988. . . . Led A.L. shortstops with 105 double plays in 1987. . . . Career major league grand slams: 1.
MISCELLANEOUS: Batted as switch-hitter (1981-84).

				BATTING											FIELDING			
Year	Team (League)	Pos.	G	AB	R	H	2B	3B	HR	RBI	Avg.	BB	SO	SB	PO	A	E	Avg.
1981—	GC Padres (GCL)	SS-2B	55	189	26	49	4	1	0	16	.259	13	24	8	105	135	15	.941
1982—	Reno (California)	SS	130	528	*103	*183	33	1	2	54	.347	16	53	25	*240	399	41	.940
1983—	Beaumont (Texas)	SS	114	427	62	126	20	4	2	48	.295	15	29	7	185	327	*38	.931
1984—	Las Vegas (PCL)	SS-2B	122	463	81	137	26	6	5	53	.296	13	40	9	172	†364	17	.969
1985—	Chicago (A.L.)■	SS	150	491	71	134	21	9	1	33	.273	12	36	7	220	382	12	*.980
1986—	Chicago (A.L.)	SS-DH	159	547	58	137	19	4	2	47	.250	12	52	8	261	459	22	.970
1987—	Chicago (A.L.)	SS	149	560	64	156	22	7	2	51	.279	22	52	25	266	475	19	.975
1988—	Chicago (A.L.)	SS	156	566	58	148	16	7	0	39	.261	25	40	25	273	*570	20	.977
1989—	Chicago (A.L.)	SS	155	597	63	151	20	8	1	54	.253	15	48	36	272	512	22	.973
1990—	Chicago (A.L.)	SS	160	516	61	144	21	4	1	58	.279	26	37	13	252	474	17	.977
1991—	Chicago (A.L.)	SS	154	524	52	143	20	3	3	49	.273	11	38	21	249	439	21	.970
1992—	Chicago (A.L.)	SS	12	40	5	8	4	0	0	7	.200	1	5	1	20	39	0	1.000
1993—	Chicago (A.L.)	SS	134	457	44	128	23	4	4	50	.280	10	41	5	189	361	16	.972
1994—	Chicago (A.L.)	SS	100	365	46	105	9	5	1	39	.288	14	35	5	139	237	16	.959
1995—	Chicago (A.L.)	SS-DH	122	415	50	103	20	3	1	41	.248	13	25	6	167	319	12	.976
Major league totals (11 years)			1451	5078	572	1357	195	54	16	468	.267	161	409	152	2308	4267	177	.974

CHAMPIONSHIP SERIES RECORD

				BATTING											FIELDING			
Year	Team (League)	Pos.	G	AB	R	H	2B	3B	HR	RBI	Avg.	BB	SO	SB	PO	A	E	Avg.
1993—	Chicago (A.L.)	SS	6	22	4	6	1	0	0	2	.273	0	2	1	12	14	0	1.000

ALL-STAR GAME RECORD

NOTES: Named to A.L. All-Star team; replaced by Kurt Stillwell due to injury (1988).

Year League	Pos.	AB	R	H	2B	3B	HR	RBI	Avg.	BB	SO	SB	PO	A	E	Avg.
			BATTING										FIELDING			
1988— American			Selected, did not play—injured.													
1990— American	SS	2	0	0	0	0	0	0	.000	0	0	0	0	2	0	1.000
1991— American	SS	0	0	0	0	0	0	0	...	0	0	0	1	0	0	1.000
All-Star Game totals (2 years)		2	0	0	0	0	0	0	.000	0	0	0	1	2	0	1.000

GULAN, MIKE — 3B — CARDINALS

PERSONAL: Born December 18, 1970, in Steubenville, O. . . . 6-1/192. . . . Bats right, throws right. . . . Full name: Michael W. Gulan. . . . Name pronounced GOO-len.
HIGH SCHOOL: Catholic Central (Steubenville, O.).
COLLEGE: Kent.
TRANSACTIONS/CAREER NOTES: Selected by St. Louis Cardinals organization in second round of free-agent draft (June 1, 1992). . . . On disabled list (April 27-May 12, 1994).

Year Team (League)	Pos.	G	AB	R	H	2B	3B	HR	RBI	Avg.	BB	SO	SB	PO	A	E	Avg.
				BATTING										FIELDING			
1992— Hamilton (NYP)	3B-1B	62	242	33	66	8	4	7	36	.273	23	53	12	51	113	11	.937
1993— Springfield (Midw.)	3B	132	455	81	118	28	4	23	76	.259	34	135	8	78	*255	28	.922
1994— St. Peters. (FSL)	3B	120	466	39	113	30	2	8	56	.242	26	108	2	86	218	26	.921
1995— Arkansas (Texas)	3B	64	242	47	76	16	3	12	48	.314	11	52	4	33	150	14	.929
— Louisville (A.A.)	3B	58	195	21	46	10	4	5	27	.236	10	53	2	38	90	7	.948

GUNDERSON, ERIC — P — RED SOX

PERSONAL: Born March 29, 1966, in Portland, Ore. . . . 6-0/195. . . . Throws left, bats right. . . . Full name: Eric Andrew Gunderson.
HIGH SCHOOL: Aloha (Portland, Ore.).
COLLEGE: Portland (Ore.) State.
TRANSACTIONS/CAREER NOTES: Selected by San Francisco Giants organization in second round of free-agent draft (June 2, 1987). . . . Released by Giants (March 31, 1992). . . . Signed by Jacksonville, Seattle Mariners organization (April 10, 1992). . . . On Jacksonville disabled list (April 10-17, 1992). . . . On Seattle suspended list (September 30-October 4, 1992). . . . Released by Mariners (April 29, 1993). . . . Signed by Binghamton, New York Mets organization (June 10, 1993). . . . Granted free agency (October 15, 1993). . . . Signed by San Diego Padres organization (December 24, 1993). . . . Released by Las Vegas (April 2, 1994). . . . Signed by St. Lucie, Mets organization (May 5, 1994). . . . Claimed on waivers by Mariners (August 4, 1995). . . . Claimed on waivers by Boston Red Sox (August 10, 1995).
STATISTICAL NOTES: Led California League with 17 hit batsmen in 1988.

Year Team (League)	W	L	Pct.	ERA	G	GS	CG	ShO	Sv.	IP	H	R	ER	BB	SO
1987— Everett (N'west)	8	4	.667	2.46	15	•15	*5	•3	0	98 2/3	80	34	27	34	*99
1988— San Jose (Calif.)	12	5	.706	2.65	20	20	5	•4	0	149 1/3	131	56	44	52	151
— Shreveport (Texas)	1	2	.333	5.15	7	6	0	0	0	36 2/3	45	25	21	13	28
1989— Shreveport (Texas)	8	2	*.800	2.72	11	11	2	1	0	72 2/3	68	24	22	23	61
— Phoenix (PCL)	2	4	.333	5.04	14	14	2	1	0	85 2/3	93	51	48	36	56
1990— San Francisco (N.L.)	1	2	.333	5.49	7	4	0	0	0	19 2/3	24	14	12	11	14
— Phoenix (PCL)	5	7	.417	8.23	16	16	0	0	0	82	137	87	75	46	41
— Shreveport (Texas)	2	2	.500	3.25	8	8	1	1	0	52 2/3	51	24	19	17	44
1991— San Francisco (N.L.)	0	0	...	5.40	2	0	0	0	1	3 1/3	6	4	2	1	2
— Phoenix (PCL)	7	6	.538	6.14	40	14	0	0	3	107	153	85	73	44	53
1992— Jacksonville (Sou.)■	2	0	1.000	2.31	15	0	0	0	2	23 1/3	18	10	6	7	23
— Calgary (PCL)	0	2	.000	6.02	27	1	0	0	5	52 1/3	57	37	35	31	50
— Seattle (A.L.)	2	1	.667	8.68	9	0	0	0	0	9 1/3	12	12	9	5	2
1993— Calgary (PCL)	0	1	.000	18.90	5	0	0	0	0	6 2/3	14	15	14	8	3
— Binghamton (East.)■	2	1	.667	5.24	20	1	0	0	1	22 1/3	20	14	13	14	26
— Norfolk (Int'l)	3	2	.600	3.71	6	5	1	0	0	34	41	16	14	9	26
1994— St. Lucie (Fla. St.)	1	0	1.000	0.00	3	0	0	0	1	4 2/3	4	0	0	0	6
— Norfolk (Int'l)	3	1	.750	3.68	19	2	1	1	1	36 2/3	25	16	15	17	31
— New York (N.L.)	0	0	...	0.00	14	0	0	0	0	9	5	0	0	4	4
1995— New York (N.L.)	1	1	.500	3.70	30	0	0	0	0	24 1/3	25	10	10	8	19
— Boston (A.L.)■	2	1	.667	5.11	19	0	0	0	0	12 1/3	13	7	7	9	9
A.L. totals (2 years)	4	2	.667	6.65	28	0	0	0	0	21 2/3	25	19	16	14	11
N.L. totals (4 years)	2	3	.400	3.83	53	4	0	0	1	56 1/3	60	28	24	24	39
Major league totals (5 years)	6	5	.545	4.62	81	4	0	0	1	78	85	47	40	38	50

GUTHRIE, MARK — P — DODGERS

PERSONAL: Born September 22, 1965, in Buffalo, N.Y. . . . 6-4/207. . . . Throws left, bats right. . . . Full name: Mark Andrew Guthrie.
HIGH SCHOOL: Venice (Fla.).
COLLEGE: Louisiana State.
TRANSACTIONS/CAREER NOTES: Selected by St. Louis Cardinals organization in fourth round of free-agent draft (June 2, 1986); did not sign. . . . Selected by Minnesota Twins organization in seventh round of free-agent draft (June 2, 1987). . . . On disabled list (May 29, 1993-remainder of season). . . . Traded by Twins with P Kevin Tapani to Los Angeles Dodgers for 1B/3B Ron Coomer, P Greg Hansell, P Jose Parra and a player to be named later (July 31, 1995); Twins acquired OF Chris Latham to complete deal (October 30, 1995).
MISCELLANEOUS: Appeared in one game as pinch-runner (1991).

Year Team (League)	W	L	Pct.	ERA	G	GS	CG	ShO	Sv.	IP	H	R	ER	BB	SO
1987— Visalia (California)	2	1	.667	4.50	4	1	0	0	0	12	10	7	6	5	9
1988— Visalia (California)	12	9	.571	3.31	25	25	4	1	0	171 1/3	169	81	63	86	182
1989— Orlando (Southern)	8	3	.727	1.97	14	14	0	0	0	96	75	32	21	38	103
— Portland (PCL)	3	4	.429	3.65	7	7	1	0	0	44 1/3	45	21	18	16	35
— Minnesota (A.L.)	2	4	.333	4.55	13	8	0	0	0	57 1/3	66	32	29	21	38

G

Year	Team (League)	W	L	Pct.	ERA	G	GS	CG	ShO	Sv.	IP	H	R	ER	BB	SO
1990	—Minnesota (A.L.)	7	9	.438	3.79	24	21	3	1	0	144 2/3	154	65	61	39	101
	—Portland (PCL)	1	3	.250	2.98	9	8	1	0	0	42 1/3	47	19	14	12	39
1991	—Minnesota (A.L.)	7	5	.583	4.32	41	12	0	0	2	98	116	52	47	41	72
1992	—Minnesota (A.L.)	2	3	.400	2.88	54	0	0	0	5	75	59	27	24	23	76
1993	—Minnesota (A.L.)	2	1	.667	4.71	22	0	0	0	0	21	20	11	11	16	15
1994	—Minnesota (A.L.)	4	2	.667	6.14	50	2	0	0	1	51 1/3	65	43	35	18	38
1995	—Minnesota (A.L.)	5	3	.625	4.46	36	0	0	0	0	42 1/3	47	22	21	16	48
	—Los Angeles (N.L.)■	0	2	.000	3.66	24	0	0	0	0	19 2/3	19	11	8	9	19
A.L. totals (7 years)		29	27	.518	4.19	240	43	3	1	8	489 2/3	527	252	228	174	388
N.L. totals (1 year)		0	2	.000	3.66	24	0	0	0	0	19 2/3	19	11	8	9	19
Major league totals (7 years)		29	29	.500	4.17	264	43	3	1	8	509 1/3	546	263	236	183	407

DIVISION SERIES RECORD

Year	Team (League)	W	L	Pct.	ERA	G	GS	CG	ShO	Sv.	IP	H	R	ER	BB	SO
1995	—Los Angeles (N.L.)	0	0	...	6.75	3	0	0	0	0	1 1/3	2	1	1	1	1

CHAMPIONSHIP SERIES RECORD

Year	Team (League)	W	L	Pct.	ERA	G	GS	CG	ShO	Sv.	IP	H	R	ER	BB	SO
1991	—Minnesota (A.L.)	1	0	1.000	0.00	2	0	0	0	0	2 2/3	0	0	0	0	0

WORLD SERIES RECORD

NOTES: Member of World Series championship team (1991).

Year	Team (League)	W	L	Pct.	ERA	G	GS	CG	ShO	Sv.	IP	H	R	ER	BB	SO
1991	—Minnesota (A.L.)	0	1	.000	2.25	4	0	0	0	0	4	3	1	1	4	3

GUTIERREZ, RICKY — SS — ASTROS

PERSONAL: Born May 23, 1970, in Miami. . . . 6-1/175. . . . Bats right, throws right. . . . Full name: Ricardo Gutierrez.
HIGH SCHOOL: American (Hialeah, Fla.).
TRANSACTIONS/CAREER NOTES: Selected by Baltimore Orioles organization in supplemental round ("sandwich pick" between first and second round, 28th pick overall) of free-agent draft (June 1, 1988); pick received as compensation for Orioles failing to sign 1987 No. 1 pick P Brad DuVall. . . . Traded by Orioles to San Diego Padres (September 4, 1992), completing deal in which Padres traded P Craig Lefferts to Orioles for P Erik Schullstrom and a player to be named later (August 31, 1992). . . . Traded by Padres with OF Phil Plantier, OF Derek Bell, P Pedro Martinez, P Doug Brocail and IF Craig Shipley to Houston Astros for 3B Ken Caminiti, OF Steve Finley, SS Andujar Cedeno, 1B Robert Petagine, P Brian Williams and a player to be named later (December 28, 1994).
STATISTICAL NOTES: Led Appalachian League shortstops with 309 total chances in 1988.

				BATTING											FIELDING			
Year	Team (League)	Pos.	G	AB	R	H	2B	3B	HR	RBI	Avg.	BB	SO	SB	PO	A	E	Avg.
1988	—Bluefield (Appal.)	SS	62	208	35	51	8	2	2	19	.245	44	40	5	*100	175	34	.890
1989	—Frederick (Caro.)	SS	127	456	48	106	16	2	3	41	.232	39	89	15	190	372	34	*.943
1990	—Frederick (Caro.)	SS	112	425	54	117	16	4	1	46	.275	38	59	12	192	286	26	.948
	—Hagerstown (East.)	SS	20	64	4	15	0	1	0	6	.234	3	8	2	31	36	4	.944
1991	—Hagerstown (East.)	SS	84	292	47	69	6	4	0	30	.236	57	52	11	158	196	22	.941
	—Rochester (Int'l)	SS-3B	49	157	23	48	5	3	0	15	.306	24	27	4	61	129	8	.960
1992	—Rochester (Int'l)	2B-SS	125	431	54	109	9	3	0	41	.253	53	77	14	251	283	15	.973
	—Las Vegas (PCL)■	SS	3	6	0	1	0	0	0	1	.167	1	3	0	1	8	0	1.000
1993	—Las Vegas (PCL)	2B-SS	5	24	4	10	4	0	0	4	.417	0	4	4	11	14	2	.926
	—San Diego (N.L.)	S-2-0-3	133	438	76	110	10	5	5	26	.251	50	97	4	194	305	14	.973
1994	—San Diego (N.L.)	SS-2B	90	275	27	66	11	2	1	28	.240	32	54	2	93	202	22	.931
1995	—Houston (N.L.)■	SS-3B	52	156	22	43	6	0	0	12	.276	10	33	5	64	108	8	.956
	—Tucson (PCL)	SS	64	236	46	71	12	4	1	26	.301	28	28	9	91	167	6	.977
Major league totals (3 years)			275	869	125	219	27	7	6	66	.252	92	184	11	351	615	44	.956

GUZMAN, JOSE — P — CUBS

PERSONAL: Born April 9, 1963, in Santa Isabel, Puerto Rico. . . . 6-3/200. . . . Throws right, bats right. . . . Full name: Jose Alberto Mirabel Guzman.
HIGH SCHOOL: John F. Kennedy (Santa Isabel, Puerto Rico).
TRANSACTIONS/CAREER NOTES: Signed as non-drafted free agent by Texas Rangers organization (February 10, 1981). . . . On disabled list (March 26-September 1, 1989). . . . On Texas disabled list (March 31-August 9, 1990); included rehabilitation assignments to Charlotte (June 6-19), Oklahoma City (July 17-19 and July 29-30) and Tulsa (July 20-25). . . . Released by Rangers (April 2, 1991). . . . Re-signed by Rangers organization (April 8, 1991). . . . Granted free agency (October 26, 1992). . . . Signed by Chicago Cubs (December 1, 1992). . . . On Chicago disabled list (April 12-May 17 and May 31, 1994-remainder of season); included rehabilitation assignments to Orlando (May 9-13) and Peoria (May 13-17). . . . On Chicago disabled list (April 24, 1995-entire season); included rehabilitation assignment to Fort Myers (June 28-July 4).
HONORS: Named A.L. Comeback Player of the Year by The Sporting News (1991).
STATISTICAL NOTES: Pitched 1-0 one-hit, complete-game victory against Atlanta (April 6, 1993).

Year	Team (League)	W	L	Pct.	ERA	G	GS	CG	ShO	Sv.	IP	H	R	ER	BB	SO
1981	—GC Rangers (GCL)	3	3	.500	5.31	14	4	0	0	0	39	44	30	23	14	13
1982	—GC Rangers (GCL)	5	4	.556	2.18	12	9	1	0	0	66	51	21	16	13	42
1983	—Burlington (Midw.)	12	8	.600	2.97	25	24	2	1	0	154 2/3	135	68	51	52	146
1984	—Tulsa (Texas)	7	9	.438	4.17	25	25	7	1	0	140 1/3	137	75	65	55	82
1985	—Okla. City (A.A.)	10	5	.667	3.13	25	23	4	1	1	149 2/3	131	60	52	40	76
	—Texas (A.L.)	3	2	.600	2.76	5	5	0	0	0	32 2/3	27	13	10	14	24
1986	—Texas (A.L.)	9	15	.375	4.54	29	29	2	0	0	172 1/3	199	101	87	60	87
1987	—Texas (A.L.)	14	14	.500	4.67	37	30	6	0	0	208 1/3	196	115	108	82	143
1988	—Texas (A.L.)	11	13	.458	3.70	30	30	6	2	0	206 2/3	180	99	85	82	157
1989	—							Did not play.								
1990	—Charlotte (Fla. St.)	0	1	.000	2.16	2	2	0	0	0	8 1/3	10	3	2	4	7
	—Okla. City (A.A.)	0	3	.000	5.65	7	7	0	0	0	28 2/3	35	20	18	9	26

Year	Team (League)	W	L	Pct.	ERA	G	GS	CG	ShO	Sv.	IP	H	R	ER	BB	SO
	—Tulsa (Texas)	0	0	...	6.00	1	1	0	0	0	3	3	2	2	0	2
1991	—Okla. City (A.A.)	1	1	.500	3.92	3	3	0	0	0	20 2/3	18	9	9	4	18
	—Texas (A.L.)	13	7	.650	3.08	25	25	5	1	0	169 2/3	152	67	58	84	125
1992	—Texas (A.L.)	16	11	.593	3.66	33	33	5	0	0	224	229	103	91	73	179
1993	—Chicago (N.L.)■	12	10	.545	4.34	30	30	2	1	0	191	188	98	92	74	163
1994	—Chicago (N.L.)	2	2	.500	9.15	4	4	0	0	0	19 2/3	22	20	20	13	11
	—Orlando (Southern)	0	0	...	1.80	1	1	0	0	0	5	3	1	1	3	4
1995	—GC Cubs (GCL)	0	0	...	1.50	2	2	0	0	0	6	5	1	1	0	3
A.L. totals (6 years)		66	62	.516	3.90	159	152	24	3	0	1013 2/3	983	498	439	395	715
N.L. totals (2 years)		14	12	.538	4.78	34	34	2	1	0	210 2/3	210	118	112	87	174
Major league totals (8 years)		80	74	.519	4.05	193	186	26	4	0	1224 1/3	1193	616	551	482	889

GUZMAN, JUAN — P — BLUE JAYS

PERSONAL: Born October 28, 1966, in Santo Domingo, Dominican Republic. . . . 5-11/195. . . . Throws right, bats right. . . . Full name: Juan Andres Correa Guzman.

HIGH SCHOOL: Liceo Las Americas (Dominican Republic).

TRANSACTIONS/CAREER NOTES: Signed as non-drafted free agent by Los Angeles Dodgers organization (March 16, 1985). . . . Traded by Dodgers to Toronto Blue Jays organization for IF Mike Sharperson (September 22, 1987). . . . On Toronto disabled list (August 4-29, 1992); included rehabilitation assignment to Syracuse (August 24-25). . . . On Toronto disabled list (May 16-June 5 and August 10-29, 1995); included rehabilitation assignment to Syracuse (August 25-26).

RECORDS: Holds A.L. single-season record for most wild pitches—26 (1993).

HONORS: Named A.L. Rookie Pitcher of the Year by The Sporting News (1991).

STATISTICAL NOTES: Led Gulf Coast League with 15 wild pitches in 1985. . . . Led Florida State League with 16 wild pitches in 1986. . . . Led Southern League with 21 wild pitches in 1990. . . . Led A.L. with 26 wild pitches in 1993 and tied for lead with 13 wild pitches in 1994.

Year	Team (League)	W	L	Pct.	ERA	G	GS	CG	ShO	Sv.	IP	H	R	ER	BB	SO
1985	—GC Dodgers (GCL)	5	1	.833	3.86	21	3	0	0	4	42	39	26	18	25	43
1986	—Vero Beach (FSL)	10	9	.526	3.49	20	24	3	0	0	131 1/3	114	69	51	90	96
1987	—Bakersfield (Calif.)	5	6	.455	4.75	22	21	0	0	0	110	106	71	58	84	113
1988	—Knoxville (South.)■	4	5	.444	2.36	46	2	0	0	6	84	52	29	22	61	90
1989	—Syracuse (Int'l)	1	1	.500	3.98	14	0	0	0	0	20 1/3	13	9	9	30	28
	—Knoxville (South.)	1	4	.200	6.23	22	8	0	0	0	47 2/3	34	36	33	60	50
1990	—Knoxville (South.)	11	9	.550	4.24	37	21	2	0	1	157	145	84	74	80	138
1991	—Syracuse (Int'l)	4	5	.444	4.03	12	11	0	0	0	67	46	39	30	42	67
	—Toronto (A.L.)	10	3	.769	2.99	23	23	1	0	0	138 2/3	98	53	46	66	123
1992	—Toronto (A.L.)	16	5	.762	2.64	28	28	1	0	0	180 2/3	135	56	53	72	165
	—Syracuse (Int'l)	0	0	...	6.00	1	1	0	0	0	3	6	2	2	1	3
1993	—Toronto (A.L.)	14	3	*.824	3.99	33	33	2	1	0	221	211	107	98	110	194
1994	—Toronto (A.L.)	12	11	.522	5.68	25	•25	2	0	0	147 1/3	165	102	93	76	124
1995	—Toronto (A.L.)	4	14	.222	6.32	24	24	3	0	0	135 1/3	151	101	95	73	94
	—Syracuse (Int'l)	0	0	...	0.00	1	1	0	0	0	5	1	0	0	3	5
Major league totals (5 years)		56	36	.609	4.21	133	133	9	1	0	823	760	419	385	397	700

CHAMPIONSHIP SERIES RECORD

Year	Team (League)	W	L	Pct.	ERA	G	GS	CG	ShO	Sv.	IP	H	R	ER	BB	SO
1991	—Toronto (A.L.)	1	0	1.000	3.18	1	1	0	0	0	5 2/3	4	2	2	4	2
1992	—Toronto (A.L.)	2	0	1.000	2.08	2	2	0	0	0	13	12	3	3	5	11
1993	—Toronto (A.L.)	2	0	1.000	2.08	2	2	0	0	0	13	8	4	3	9	9
Champ. series totals (3 years)		5	0	1.000	2.27	5	5	0	0	0	31 2/3	24	9	8	18	22

WORLD SERIES RECORD

NOTES: Member of World Series championship teams (1992 and 1993).

Year	Team (League)	W	L	Pct.	ERA	G	GS	CG	ShO	Sv.	IP	H	R	ER	BB	SO
1992	—Toronto (A.L.)	0	0	...	1.13	1	1	0	0	0	8	8	2	1	1	7
1993	—Toronto (A.L.)	0	1	.000	3.75	2	2	0	0	0	12	10	6	5	8	12
World Series totals (2 years)		0	1	.000	2.70	3	3	0	0	0	20	18	8	6	9	19

ALL-STAR GAME RECORD

Year	League	W	L	Pct.	ERA	GS	CG	ShO	Sv.	IP	H	R	ER	BB	SO
1992	—American	0	0	...	0.00	0	0	0	0	1	2	0	0	1	2

GWYNN, CHRIS — OF — PADRES

PERSONAL: Born October 13, 1964, in Los Angeles. . . . 6-0/220. . . . Bats left, throws left. . . . Full name: Christopher Karlton Gwynn. . . . Brother of Tony Gwynn, outfielder, San Diego Padres.

HIGH SCHOOL: Long Beach (Calif.) Polytechnic.

COLLEGE: San Diego State.

TRANSACTIONS/CAREER NOTES: Selected by California Angels organization in fifth round of free-agent draft (June 7, 1982); did not sign. . . . Selected by Los Angeles Dodgers organization in first round (10th pick overall) of free-agent draft (June 3, 1985). . . . On Los Angeles disabled list (June 12-July 6, 1989). . . . On Los Angeles disabled list (July 16, 1989-remainder of season); included rehabilitation assignment to Albuquerque (August 3-11). . . . Traded by Dodgers with 2B Domingo Mota to Kansas City Royals for 1B/OF Todd Benzinger (December 11, 1991). . . . On disabled list (May 29-July 16 and July 27, 1992-remainder of season). . . . Released by Royals (March 29, 1994). . . . Signed by Dodgers (April 10, 1994). . . . Granted free agency (October 21, 1994). . . . Re-signed by Albuquerque, Dodgers organization (April 10, 1995). . . . On disabled list (August 8-29, 1995). . . . Granted free agency (October 12, 1995). . . . Signed by San Diego Padres organization (January 13, 1996).

HONORS: Named outfielder on The Sporting News college All-America team (1985).

STATISTICAL NOTES: Career major league grand slams: 1.

MISCELLANEOUS: Member of 1984 U.S. Olympic baseball team.

Year	Team (League)	Pos.	G	AB	R	H	2B	3B	HR	RBI	Avg.	BB	SO	SB	PO	A	E	Avg.
				BATTING											FIELDING			
1985—	Vero Beach (FSL)	OF	52	179	19	46	8	6	0	17	.257	16	34	2	43	2	0	1.000
1986—	San Antonio (Tex.)	OF	111	401	46	115	22	1	6	67	.287	16	44	2	186	11	2	.990
1987—	Albuquerque (PCL)	OF	110	362	54	101	12	3	5	41	.279	36	38	5	141	5	1	.993
—	Los Angeles (N.L.)	OF	17	32	2	7	1	0	0	2	.219	1	7	0	12	0	0	1.000
1988—	Albuquerque (PCL)	OF	112	411	57	123	22	•10	5	61	.299	39	39	1	134	3	4	.972
—	Los Angeles (N.L.)	OF	12	11	1	2	0	0	0	0	.182	1	2	0	0	0	0	...
1989—	Albuquerque (PCL)	OF	26	89	14	29	9	1	0	12	.326	7	7	3	27	0	0	1.000
—	Los Angeles (N.L.)	OF	32	68	8	16	4	1	0	7	.235	2	9	1	26	1	0	1.000
1990—	Los Angeles (N.L.)	OF	101	141	19	40	2	1	5	22	.284	7	28	0	39	1	0	1.000
1991—	Los Angeles (N.L.)	OF	94	139	18	35	5	1	5	22	.252	10	23	1	37	2	0	1.000
1992—	Kansas City (A.L.)■	OF-DH	34	84	10	24	3	2	1	7	.286	3	10	0	33	0	0	1.000
1993—	Kansas City (A.L.)	OF-DH-1B	103	287	36	86	14	4	1	25	.300	24	34	0	161	7	1	.994
1994—	Los Angeles (N.L.)■	OF	58	71	9	19	0	0	3	13	.268	7	7	0	14	0	0	1.000
1995—	Los Angeles (N.L.)	OF-1B	67	84	8	18	3	2	1	10	.214	6	23	0	26	1	0	1.000
American League totals (2 years)			137	371	46	110	17	6	2	32	.296	27	44	0	194	7	1	.995
National League totals (7 years)			381	546	65	137	15	5	14	76	.251	34	99	2	154	5	0	1.000
Major league totals (9 years)			518	917	111	247	32	11	16	108	.269	61	143	2	348	12	1	.997

DIVISION SERIES RECORD

Year	Team (League)	Pos.	G	AB	R	H	2B	3B	HR	RBI	Avg.	BB	SO	SB	PO	A	E	Avg.
				BATTING											FIELDING			
1995—	Los Angeles (N.L.)	PH	1	1	0	0	0	0	0	0	.000	0	1	0	...	...	...	...

GWYNN, TONY — OF — PADRES

PERSONAL: Born May 9, 1960, in Los Angeles. . . . 5-11/215. . . . Bats left, throws left. . . . Full name: Anthony Keith Gwynn. . . . Brother of Chris Gwynn, outfielder, San Diego Padres organization.

HIGH SCHOOL: Long Beach (Calif.) Polytechnic.

COLLEGE: San Diego State.

TRANSACTIONS/CAREER NOTES: Selected by San Diego Padres organization in third round of free-agent draft (June 8, 1981). . . . On San Diego disabled list (August 26-September 10, 1982). . . . On San Diego disabled list (March 26-June 21, 1983); included rehabilitation to Las Vegas (May 31-June 20). . . . On disabled list (May 8-29, 1988).

RECORDS: Holds N.L. career record for most years leading league in singles—6 (1984, 1986-87, 1989, 1994 and 1995). . . . Holds N.L. single-season record for lowest batting average by leader—.313 (1988). . . . Shares N.L. single-season record for most times collecting five or more hits in one game—4 (1993).

HONORS: Named Northwest League Most Valuable Player (1981). . . . Named outfielder on The Sporting News N.L. All-Star team (1984, 1986-87, 1989 and 1994). . . . Named outfielder on The Sporting News N.L. Silver Slugger team (1984, 1986-87, 1989 and 1994-95). . . . Won N.L. Gold Glove as outfielder (1986-87 and 1989-91).

STATISTICAL NOTES: Led N.L. with .410 on-base percentage in 1984. . . . Led N.L. outfielders with 360 total chances in 1986. . . . Collected six hits in one game (August 4, 1993, 12 innings). . . . Led N.L. in grounding into double plays with 20 in 1994. . . . Career major league grand slams: 1.

MISCELLANEOUS: Selected by San Diego Clippers in 10th round (210th pick overall) of 1981 NBA draft (June 9, 1981).

Year	Team (League)	Pos.	G	AB	R	H	2B	3B	HR	RBI	Avg.	BB	SO	SB	PO	A	E	Avg.
				BATTING											FIELDING			
1981—	Walla Walla (N'west)	OF	42	178	46	59	12	1	12	37	*.331	23	21	17	76	2	3	.963
—	Amarillo (Texas)	OF	23	91	22	42	8	2	4	19	.462	5	7	5	41	1	0	1.000
1982—	Hawaii (PCL)	OF	93	366	65	120	23	2	5	46	.328	18	18	14	208	11	4	.982
—	San Diego (N.L.)	OF	54	190	33	55	12	2	1	17	.289	14	16	8	110	1	1	.991
1983—	Las Vegas (PCL)	OF	17	73	15	25	6	0	0	7	.342	6	5	3	23	2	3	.893
—	San Diego (N.L.)	OF	86	304	34	94	12	2	1	37	.309	23	21	7	163	9	1	.994
1984—	San Diego (N.L.)	OF	158	606	88	*213	21	10	5	71	*.351	59	23	33	345	11	4	.989
1985—	San Diego (N.L.)	OF	154	622	90	197	29	5	6	46	.317	45	33	14	337	14	4	.989
1986—	San Diego (N.L.)	OF	160	*642	•107	*211	33	7	14	59	.329	52	35	37	*337	19	4	.989
1987—	San Diego (N.L.)	OF	157	589	119	*218	36	13	7	54	*.370	82	35	56	298	13	6	.981
1988—	San Diego (N.L.)	OF	133	521	64	163	22	5	7	70	*.313	51	40	26	264	8	5	.982
1989—	San Diego (N.L.)	OF	158	604	82	*203	27	7	4	62	*.336	56	30	40	353	13	6	.984
1990—	San Diego (N.L.)	OF	141	573	79	177	29	10	4	72	.309	44	23	17	327	11	5	.985
1991—	San Diego (N.L.)	OF	134	530	69	168	27	11	4	62	.317	34	19	8	291	8	3	.990
1992—	San Diego (N.L.)	OF	128	520	77	165	27	3	6	41	.317	46	16	3	270	9	5	.982
1993—	San Diego (N.L.)	OF	122	489	70	175	41	3	7	59	.358	36	19	14	244	8	5	.981
1994—	San Diego (N.L.)	OF	110	419	79	*165	35	1	12	64	*.394	48	19	5	191	6	3	.985
1995—	San Diego (N.L.)	OF	135	535	82	•197	33	1	9	90	*.368	35	15	17	245	8	2	.992
Major league totals (14 years)			1830	7144	1073	2401	384	80	87	804	.336	625	344	285	3775	138	54	.986

CHAMPIONSHIP SERIES RECORD

Year	Team (League)	Pos.	G	AB	R	H	2B	3B	HR	RBI	Avg.	BB	SO	SB	PO	A	E	Avg.
				BATTING											FIELDING			
1984—	San Diego (N.L.)	OF	5	19	6	7	3	0	0	3	.368	1	2	0	9	0	0	1.000

WORLD SERIES RECORD

Year	Team (League)	Pos.	G	AB	R	H	2B	3B	HR	RBI	Avg.	BB	SO	SB	PO	A	E	Avg.
				BATTING											FIELDING			
1984—	San Diego (N.L.)	OF	5	19	1	5	0	0	0	0	.263	3	2	1	12	1	1	.929

ALL-STAR GAME RECORD

NOTES: Shares single-game record for most at-bats in nine-inning game—5 (July 12, 1994).

Year	League	Pos.	AB	R	H	2B	3B	HR	RBI	Avg.	BB	SO	SB	PO	A	E	Avg.
			BATTING											FIELDING			
1984—	National	OF	3	0	1	0	0	0	0	.333	0	0	0	0	0	0	...

G

1985— National	OF	1	0	0	0	0	0	0	.000	0	0	0	1	0	0	1.000
1986— National	OF	3	0	0	0	0	0	0	.000	0	0	0	1	0	0	1.000
1987— National	PH	1	0	0	0	0	0	0	.000	0	0	0	...	...	...	...
1989— National	OF	2	1	1	0	0	0	0	.500	1	1	1	2	0	0	1.000
1990— National	PH	0	0	0	0	0	0	0	...	1	0	0	...	...	...	...
1991— National	OF	4	1	2	0	0	0	0	.500	0	0	0	6	0	0	1.000
1992— National	OF	2	0	0	0	0	0	0	.000	1	0	0	0	2	0	1.000
1993— National	OF	1	0	0	0	0	0	0	.000	0	0	0	0	0	0	...
1994— National	OF	5	2	2	1	0	0	2	.400	0	0	0	2	0	0	1.000
1995— National	OF	2	0	0	0	0	0	0	.000	0	0	0	1	0	0	1.000
All-Star Game totals (11 years)		24	4	6	1	0	0	2	.250	3	1	1	13	2	0	1.000

HABYAN, JOHN — P — ROCKIES

PERSONAL: Born January 29, 1964, in Bayshore, N.Y. . . . 6-2/195. . . . Throws right, bats right. . . . Full name: John Gabriel Habyan. . . . Name pronounced HAY-bee-un.

HIGH SCHOOL: St. John The Baptist (Brentwood, N.Y.).

TRANSACTIONS/CAREER NOTES: Selected by Baltimore Orioles organization in third round of free-agent draft (June 7, 1982). . . . On Baltimore disabled list (March 30-June 9, 1989). . . . Traded by Orioles to New York Yankees organization for OF Stanley Jefferson (July 20, 1989). . . . Traded by Yankees to Kansas City Royals as part of a three-way deal in which Royals sent OF Tuffy Rhodes to Cubs and Cubs sent P Paul Assenmacher to Yankees (July 30, 1993). . . . Granted free agency (December 20, 1993). . . . Signed by St. Louis Cardinals organization (January 5, 1994). . . . On disabled list (June 29-July 21, 1994). . . . Traded by Cardinals to California Angels for 1B Mark Sweeney and a player to be named later (July 8, 1995). . . . Granted free agency (October 30, 1995). . . . Signed by Colorado Rockies organization (January 12, 1996).

STATISTICAL NOTES: Pitched 6-0 no-hit victory for Charlotte against Columbus (May 13, 1985).

Year Team (League)	W	L	Pct.	ERA	G	GS	CG	ShO	Sv.	IP	H	R	ER	BB	SO
1982— Bluefield (Appal.)	•9	2	.818	3.54	12	12	2	1	0	81 1/3	68	35	32	24	55
— Hagerstown (Caro.)	0	0	...	67.50	1	1	0	0	0	2/3	5	5	5	2	1
1983— Hagerstown (Caro.)	2	3	.400	5.81	11	11	1	0	0	48	54	41	31	29	42
— Newark (NYP)	5	3	.625	3.39	11	11	1	1	0	71 2/3	68	34	27	29	64
1984— Hagerstown (Caro.)	9	4	.692	3.54	13	13	4	0	0	81 1/3	64	41	32	33	81
— Charlotte (South.)	4	7	.364	4.44	13	13	1	0	0	77	84	46	38	34	55
1985— Charlotte (South.)	13	5	.722	3.27	28	28	8	2	0	189 2/3	157	73	69	90	123
— Baltimore (A.L.)	1	0	1.000	0.00	2	0	0	0	0	2 2/3	3	1	0	0	2
1986— Rochester (Int'l)	12	7	.632	4.29	26	25	5	1	0	157 1/3	168	82	75	69	93
— Baltimore (A.L.)	1	3	.250	4.44	6	5	0	0	0	26 1/3	24	17	13	18	14
1987— Rochester (Int'l)	3	2	.600	3.86	7	7	2	1	0	49	47	23	21	20	39
— Baltimore (A.L.)	6	7	.462	4.80	27	13	0	0	1	116 1/3	110	67	62	40	64
1988— Rochester (Int'l)	9	9	.500	4.46	23	23	8	1	0	147 1/3	161	78	73	46	91
— Baltimore (A.L.)	1	0	1.000	4.30	7	0	0	0	0	14 2/3	22	10	7	4	4
1989— Rochester (Int'l)	1	2	.333	2.17	7	5	0	0	0	37 1/3	38	15	9	5	22
— Columbus (Int'l)■	2	3	.400	5.44	8	8	2	0	0	46 1/3	65	29	28	9	30
1990— Columbus (Int'l)	7	7	.500	3.21	36	11	1	0	6	112	99	52	40	30	77
— New York (A.L.)	0	0	...	2.08	6	0	0	0	0	8 2/3	10	2	2	2	4
1991— New York (A.L.)	4	2	.667	2.30	66	0	0	0	2	90	73	28	23	20	70
1992— New York (A.L.)	5	6	.455	3.84	56	0	0	0	7	72 2/3	84	32	31	21	44
1993— New York (A.L.)	2	1	.667	4.04	36	0	0	0	1	42 1/3	45	20	19	16	29
— Kansas City (A.L.)■	0	0	...	4.50	12	0	0	0	0	14	14	7	7	4	10
1994— St. Louis (N.L.)■	1	0	1.000	3.23	52	0	0	0	1	47 1/3	50	17	17	20	46
1995— St. Louis (N.L.)	3	2	.600	2.88	31	0	0	0	0	40 2/3	32	18	13	15	35
— California (A.L.)■	1	2	.333	4.13	28	0	0	0	0	32 2/3	36	16	15	12	25
A.L. totals (9 years)	21	21	.500	3.83	246	18	0	0	11	420 1/3	421	200	179	137	266
N.L. totals (2 years)	4	2	.667	3.07	83	0	0	0	1	88	82	35	30	35	81
Major league totals (10 years)	25	23	.521	3.70	329	18	0	0	12	508 1/3	503	235	209	172	347

HAJEK, DAVE — 2B — ASTROS

PERSONAL: Born October 14, 1967, in Roseville, Calif. . . . 5-10/165. . . . Bats right, throws right. . . . Full name: David Vincent Hajek.

COLLEGE: California Poly-Pomona.

TRANSACTIONS/CAREER NOTES: Signed as a non-drafted free agent by Houston Astros organization (August 9, 1989).

STATISTICAL NOTES: Led South Atlantic League with 10 sacrifice flies and 24 times caught stealing in 1990. . . . Led Pacific Coast League second basemen with 298 putouts, 434 assists, 748 total chances, 123 double plays and .979 fielding percentage in 1994. . . . Led Pacific Coast League second basemen with 269 putouts, 398 assists, 679 total chances and 100 double plays in 1995.

		BATTING												FIELDING			
Year Team (League)	Pos.	G	AB	R	H	2B	3B	HR	RBI	Avg.	BB	SO	SB	PO	A	E	Avg.
1990— Asheville (S. Atl.)	2B-SS-3B	135	498	86	156	28	0	6	60	.313	61	50	43	222	373	33	.947
1991— Osceola (Fla. St.)	0-2-S-3	63	232	35	61	9	4	0	20	.263	23	30	8	71	47	3	.975
— Jackson (Texas)	3B-2B-SS	37	94	10	18	6	0	0	9	.191	7	12	2	29	65	6	.940
1992— Osceola (Fla. St.)	2B-SS-P	5	18	3	2	1	0	0	1	.111	1	1	1	11	19	1	.968
— Jackson (Texas)	2-3-O-S-P	103	326	36	88	12	3	1	18	.270	31	25	8	140	226	10	.973
1993— Jackson (Texas)	3-2-O-S-P	110	332	50	97	20	2	5	27	.292	17	14	6	144	221	9	.976
1994— Tucson (PCL)	2-3-S-P	129	484	71	157	29	5	7	70	.324	29	23	12	†299	†435	16	†.979
1995— Tucson (PCL)	2B-OF	131	502	99	164	37	4	4	79	.327	39	27	12	†271	†398	12	.982
— Houston (N.L.)	PH	5	2	0	0	0	0	0	0	.000	1	1	1	...	...	...	...
Major league totals (1 year)		5	2	0	0	0	0	0	0	.000	1	1	1	...	...	...	...

RECORD AS PITCHER

Year Team (League)	W	L	Pct.	ERA	G	GS	CG	ShO	Sv.	IP	H	R	ER	BB	SO
1992— Osceola (Florida St.)	1	0	1.000	0.00	1	0	0	0	0	2	1	0	0	1	0

G H

Year	Team (League)	W	L	Pct.	ERA	G	GS	CG	ShO	Sv.	IP	H	R	ER	BB	SO
	—Jackson (Texas)	0	0	...	3.00	2	0	0	0	0	3	3	1	1	0	3
1993—	Jackson (Texas)	0	0	...	27.00	2	0	0	0	0	2	4	6	6	1	2
1994—	Tucson (Pac. Coast)	0	0	...	0.00	1	0	0	0	0	4 1/3	1	0	0	1	0

HALE, CHIP — 2B/3B — TWINS

PERSONAL: Born December 2, 1964, in Santa Clara, Calif. . . . 5-11/191. . . . Bats left, throws right. . . . Full name: Walter William Hale III.
HIGH SCHOOL: Campolindo (Moraga, Calif.).
COLLEGE: Arizona (received degree).
TRANSACTIONS/CAREER NOTES: Selected by Minnesota Twins organization in 17th round of free-agent draft (June 2, 1987).
STATISTICAL NOTES: Led Pacific Coast League second basemen with 332 assists in 1989. . . . Led Pacific Coast League second basemen with .982 fielding percentage, 311 putouts, 679 total chances and 101 double plays in 1990. . . . Led Pacific Coast League second basemen with 552 total chances and 85 double plays in 1991. . . . Led Pacific Coast League second basemen with .986 fielding percentage and 273 putouts in 1992.

				BATTING											FIELDING			
Year	Team (League)	Pos.	G	AB	R	H	2B	3B	HR	RBI	Avg.	BB	SO	SB	PO	A	E	Avg.
1987—	Kenosha (Midwest)	2B	87	339	65	117	12	7	7	65	*.345	33	26	3	164	233	10	.975
1988—	Orlando (Southern)	2B	133	482	62	126	20	1	11	65	.261	64	31	8	254	322	*23	.962
1989—	Portland (PCL)	2B-3B	108	411	49	112	16	9	2	34	.273	35	55	3	217	†333	10	.982
	—Minnesota (A.L.)	2B-3B-DH	28	67	6	14	3	0	0	4	.209	1	6	0	15	40	1	.982
1990—	Portland (PCL)	2B-SS-3B	130	479	71	134	24	2	3	40	.280	68	57	6	†312	362	13	†.981
	—Minnesota (A.L.)	2B	1	2	0	0	0	0	0	2	.000	0	1	0	2	6	0	1.000
1991—	Portland (PCL)	2B	110	352	45	85	16	3	1	37	.241	47	22	3	*236	306	10	*.982
1992—	Portland (PCL)	2B-OF-P	132	474	77	135	25	8	1	53	.285	73	45	3	†278	361	9	†.986
1993—	Portland (PCL)	2B-3B-SS	55	211	37	59	15	3	1	24	.280	21	13	2	79	134	11	.951
	—Minnesota (A.L.)	2-DH-3-S-1	69	186	25	62	6	1	3	27	.333	18	17	2	39	63	4	.962
1994—	Minnesota (A.L.)	3-DH-1-2-0	67	118	13	31	9	0	1	11	.263	16	14	0	45	51	3	.970
1995—	Minnesota (A.L.)	DH-2-3-1	69	103	10	27	4	0	2	18	.262	11	20	0	16	6	0	1.000
	—Salt Lake (PCL)	3B-2B-1B	16	49	5	14	4	0	0	2	.286	7	5	0	33	26	0	1.000
Major league totals (5 years)			234	476	54	134	22	1	6	62	.282	46	58	2	117	166	8	.973

RECORD AS PITCHER

Year	Team (League)	W	L	Pct.	ERA	G	GS	CG	ShO	Sv.	IP	H	R	ER	BB	SO
1992—	Portland (PCL)	0	0	...	18.00	1	0	0	0	0	1	5	4	2	0	0

HALL, DARREN — P — DODGERS

PERSONAL: Born July 14, 1964, in Marysville, O. . . . 6-3/205. . . . Throws right, bats right. . . . Full name: Michael Darren Hall.
HIGH SCHOOL: Nimitz (Irving, Tex.).
COLLEGE: Dallas Baptist.
TRANSACTIONS/CAREER NOTES: Selected by Toronto Blue Jays organization in 28th round of free-agent draft (June 2, 1986). . . . On disabled list (June 26, 1990-remainder of season; June 19-July 4 and July 24, 1995-remainder of season). . . . Granted free agency (October 16, 1995). . . . Signed by Los Angeles Dodgers (November 1, 1995).
STATISTICAL NOTES: Tied for Pioneer League lead with 12 wild pitches in 1986.

Year	Team (League)	W	L	Pct.	ERA	G	GS	CG	ShO	Sv.	IP	H	R	ER	BB	SO
1986—	Medicine Hat (Pio.)	5	7	.417	3.83	17	•16	1	1	0	89 1/3	91	64	38	47	60
1987—	Myrtle Beach (SAL)	5	5	.500	3.51	41	0	0	0	6	66 2/3	57	31	26	28	68
1988—	Dunedin (Fla. St.)	1	1	.500	1.93	4	0	0	0	1	9 1/3	6	2	2	5	15
	—Knoxville (South.)	3	2	.600	2.23	37	0	0	0	17	40 1/3	28	11	10	17	33
1989—	Dunedin (Fla. St.)	1	4	.200	3.53	16	14	0	0	0	51	46	25	20	21	42
	—Knoxville (South.)	0	2	.000	3.66	13	0	0	0	1	19 2/3	21	12	8	10	10
1990—	Knoxville (South.)	3	5	.375	4.86	28	0	0	0	1	33 1/3	29	23	18	33	28
1991—	Knoxville (South.)	5	3	.625	2.60	42	0	0	0	2	69 1/3	56	23	20	27	78
1992—	Syracuse (Int'l)	4	6	.400	4.30	55	0	0	0	5	69	62	36	33	35	49
1993—	Syracuse (Int'l)	6	7	.462	5.33	60	0	0	0	13	79 1/3	75	51	47	31	68
1994—	Syracuse (Int'l)	1	0	1.000	1.59	6	0	0	0	3	5 2/3	5	2	1	2	7
	—Toronto (A.L.)	2	3	.400	3.41	30	0	0	0	17	31 2/3	26	12	12	14	28
1995—	Toronto (A.L.)	0	2	.000	4.41	17	0	0	0	3	16 1/3	21	9	8	9	11
Major league totals (2 years)		2	5	.286	3.75	47	0	0	0	20	48	47	21	20	23	39

HALL, JOE — OF — ORIOLES

PERSONAL: Born March 6, 1966, in Paducah, Ky. . . . 6-0/180. . . . Bats right, throws right. . . . Full name: Joseph Geroy Hall.
HIGH SCHOOL: Saint Mary (Paducah, Ky.).
COLLEGE: Southern Illinois.
TRANSACTIONS/CAREER NOTES: Selected by St. Louis Cardinals organization in 10th round of free-agent draft (June 1, 1988). . . . Traded by Cardinals organization to Chicago White Sox organization for OF Willie Magallanes (April 3, 1991). . . . On disabled list (July 30-August 15, 1992 and July 30-August 12, 1993). . . . On Chicago disabled list (May 14-July 21, 1994); included rehabilitation assignments to South Bend (June 9-19 and June 22-29). . . . Released by White Sox (April 22, 1995). . . . Signed by Toledo, Detroit Tigers organization (May 8, 1995). . . . Granted free agency (October 16, 1995). . . . Signed by Rochester, Baltimore Orioles organizaiton (November 13, 1995).
STATISTICAL NOTES: Led Florida State League in caught stealing with 28 in 1989. . . . Led Pacific Coast League third basemen with .938 fielding percentage in 1991.

				BATTING											FIELDING			
Year	Team (League)	Pos.	G	AB	R	H	2B	3B	HR	RBI	Avg.	BB	SO	SB	PO	A	E	Avg.
1988—	Hamilton (NYP)	0-1-C-3	70	274	46	78	9	1	2	37	.285	30	37	30	291	21	4	.987
	—Springfield (Midw.)	3B-OF	1	1	0	0	0	0	0	0	.000	0	1	0	0	0	0	...

Year Team (League)	Pos.	BATTING												FIELDING			
Year Team (League)	Pos.	G	AB	R	H	2B	3B	HR	RBI	Avg.	BB	SO	SB	PO	A	E	Avg.
1989—St. Peters. (FSL)	3B-OF-2B	134	504	72	147	9	3	0	54	.292	60	57	45	190	147	25	.931
1990—Arkansas (Texas)	0-3-1-C	115	399	44	108	13	4	4	44	.271	35	41	21	179	40	15	.936
1991—Vancouver (PCL)■	3-0-1-C	118	427	41	106	16	1	4	39	.248	23	45	11	114	205	19	‡.944
1992—Vancouver (PCL)	3-0-C-1	112	367	46	104	19	7	6	56	.283	60	44	11	160	101	16	.942
1993—Nashville (A.A.)	0-3-C-P	116	424	66	123	33	5	10	58	.290	52	56	10	189	66	7	.973
1994—Chicago (A.L.)	OF-DH	17	28	6	11	3	0	1	5	.393	2	4	0	11	0	1	.917
—Birm. (Southern)	OF-C-3B	19	67	9	14	6	0	0	6	.209	15	11	0	31	7	0	1.000
—Nashville (A.A.)	0-C-1-3	22	72	14	21	7	0	4	21	.292	16	10	0	57	8	0	1.000
1995—Toledo (Int'l)■	OF-3B-2B	91	319	52	102	19	2	11	47	.320	36	50	4	148	26	4	.978
—Detroit (A.L.)	OF-DH	7	15	2	2	0	0	0	0	.133	2	3	0	11	1	0	1.000
Major league totals (2 years)		24	43	8	13	3	0	1	5	.302	4	7	0	22	1	1	.958

RECORD AS PITCHER

Year Team (League)	W	L	Pct.	ERA	G	GS	CG	ShO	Sv.	IP	H	R	ER	BB	SO
1993—Nashville (A.A.)	0	0	...	0.00	1	0	0	0	0	1	1	0	0	0	1

HAMELIN, BOB — 1B/DH — ROYALS

PERSONAL: Born November 29, 1967, in Elizabeth, N.J. . . . 6-0/235. . . . Bats left, throws left. . . . Full name: Robert James Hamelin III.
HIGH SCHOOL: Irvine (Calif.).
JUNIOR COLLEGE: Rancho Santiago College (Calif.).
COLLEGE: UCLA.
TRANSACTIONS/CAREER NOTES: Selected by Kansas City Royals organization in second round of free-agent draft (June 1, 1988). . . . On disabled list (June 25-July 2 and August 3, 1989-remainder of season; August 8, 1990-remainder of season; and May 27, 1991-remainder of season). . . . On Omaha disabled list (April 9-June 10, 1992).
RECORDS: Shares major league single-game record (nine innings) for most strikeouts—5 (May 24, 1995).
HONORS: Named A.L. Rookie Player of the Year by The Sporting News (1994). . . . Named A.L. Rookie of the Year by Baseball Writers' Association of America (1994).
STATISTICAL NOTES: Led Northwest League first basemen with 682 total chances in 1988. . . . Led American Association first basemen with 1,205 total chances and 116 double plays in 1993.

Year Team (League)	Pos.	BATTING												FIELDING			
Year Team (League)	Pos.	G	AB	R	H	2B	3B	HR	RBI	Avg.	BB	SO	SB	PO	A	E	Avg.
1988—Eugene (N'west)	1B	70	235	42	70	19	1	*17	61	.298	56	67	9	*642	25	*15	.978
1989—Memphis (South.)	1B	68	211	45	62	12	5	16	47	.294	52	52	3	487	27	8	.985
1990—Omaha (A.A.)	1B	90	271	31	63	11	2	8	30	.232	62	78	2	396	32	4	.991
1991—Omaha (A.A.)	1B	37	127	13	24	3	1	4	19	.189	16	32	0	55	4	0	1.000
1992—Baseball City (FSL)	1B	11	44	7	12	0	1	1	6	.273	2	11	0	18	1	3	.864
—Memphis (South.)	1B	35	120	23	40	8	0	6	22	.333	26	17	0	173	9	2	.989
—Omaha (A.A.)	1B	27	95	9	19	3	1	5	15	.200	14	15	0	230	13	3	.988
1993—Omaha (A.A.)	1B	•137	479	77	124	19	3	29	84	.259	*82	94	8	*1104	*90	•11	.991
—Kansas City (A.L.)	1B	16	49	2	11	3	0	2	5	.224	6	15	0	129	9	2	.986
1994—Kansas City (A.L.)	DH-1B	101	312	64	88	25	1	24	65	.282	56	62	4	234	18	2	.992
1995—Kansas City (A.L.)	DH-1B	72	208	20	35	7	1	7	25	.168	26	56	0	66	9	0	1.000
—Omaha (A.A.)	1B	36	119	25	35	12	0	10	32	.294	31	34	2	157	19	6	.967
Major league totals (3 years)		189	569	86	134	35	2	33	95	.236	88	133	4	429	36	4	.991

HAMILTON, DARRYL — OF — RANGERS

PERSONAL: Born December 3, 1964, in Baton Rouge, La. . . . 6-1/180. . . . Bats left, throws right. . . . Full name: Darryl Quinn Hamilton.
HIGH SCHOOL: University (Baton Rouge, La.).
COLLEGE: Nicholls State (La.).
TRANSACTIONS/CAREER NOTES: Selected by Milwaukee Brewers organization in 11th round of free-agent draft (June 2, 1986). . . . On disabled list (May 22-June 15, 1991; May 6-24, 1992; May 2-17, 1993; May 11-26 and June 10, 1994-remainder of season). . . . Granted free agency (November 1, 1995). . . . Signed by Texas Rangers (December 14, 1995).
STATISTICAL NOTES: Led California League with nine intentional bases on balls received in 1987. . . . Career major league grand slams: 2.

Year Team (League)	Pos.	BATTING												FIELDING			
Year Team (League)	Pos.	G	AB	R	H	2B	3B	HR	RBI	Avg.	BB	SO	SB	PO	A	E	Avg.
1986—Helena (Pioneer)	OF	65	248	*72	•97	12	•6	0	35	*.391	51	18	34	132	9	0	*1.000
1987—Stockton (Calif.)	OF	125	494	102	162	17	6	8	61	.328	74	59	42	221	8	1	*.996
1988—Denver (A.A.)	OF	72	277	55	90	11	4	0	32	.325	39	28	28	160	2	2	.988
—Milwaukee (A.L.)	OF-DH	44	103	14	19	4	0	1	11	.184	12	9	7	75	1	0	1.000
1989—Denver (A.A.)	OF	129	497	72	142	24	4	2	40	.286	42	58	20	263	11	0	*1.000
1990—Milwaukee (A.L.)	OF-DH	89	156	27	46	5	0	1	18	.295	9	12	10	120	1	1	.992
1991—Milwaukee (A.L.)	OF	122	405	64	126	15	6	1	57	.311	33	38	16	234	3	1	.996
1992—Milwaukee (A.L.)	OF	128	470	67	140	19	7	5	62	.298	45	42	41	279	10	0	*1.000
1993—Milwaukee (A.L.)	OF-DH	135	520	74	161	21	1	9	48	.310	45	62	21	340	10	3	.992
1994—Milwaukee (A.L.)	OF-DH	36	141	23	37	10	1	1	13	.262	15	17	3	60	2	0	1.000
1995—Milwaukee (A.L.)	OF-DH	112	398	54	108	20	6	5	44	.271	47	35	11	262	4	3	.989
Major league totals (7 years)		666	2193	323	637	94	21	23	253	.290	206	215	109	1370	31	8	.994

HAMILTON, JOEY — P — PADRES

PERSONAL: Born September 9, 1970, in Statesboro, Ga. . . . 6-4/230. . . . Throws right, bats right. . . . Full name: Johns Joseph Hamilton.
HIGH SCHOOL: Statesboro (Ga.).
COLLEGE: Georgia Southern.

TRANSACTIONS/CAREER NOTES: Selected by Baltimore Orioles organization in 28th round of free-agent draft (June 1, 1988); did not sign. . . . Selected by San Diego Padres organization in first round (eighth pick overall) of free-agent draft (June 3, 1991). . . . On Rancho Cucamonga disabled list (April 5-20, 1993).

HONORS: Named right-handed pitcher on THE SPORTING NEWS college All-America second team (1990).

Year	Team (League)	W	L	Pct.	ERA	G	GS	CG	ShO	Sv.	IP	H	R	ER	BB	SO
1992—	Char., S.C. (S. Atl.)	2	2	.500	3.38	7	7	0	0	0	34 2/3	37	24	13	4	35
—	High Desert (Calif.)	4	3	.571	2.74	9	8	0	0	0	49 1/3	46	20	15	18	43
—	Wichita (Texas)	3	0	1.000	2.86	6	6	0	0	0	34 2/3	33	12	11	11	26
1993—	Rancho Cuca. (Cal.)	1	0	1.000	4.09	2	2	0	0	0	11	11	5	5	2	6
—	Wichita (Texas)	4	9	.308	3.97	15	15	0	0	0	90 2/3	101	55	40	36	20
—	Las Vegas (PCL)	3	2	.600	4.40	8	8	0	0	0	47	49	25	23	22	33
1994—	Las Vegas (PCL)	3	5	.375	2.73	9	9	1	1	0	59 1/3	69	25	18	22	32
—	San Diego (N.L.)	9	6	.600	2.98	16	16	1	1	0	108 2/3	98	40	36	29	61
1995—	San Diego (N.L.)	6	9	.400	3.08	31	30	2	2	0	204 1/3	189	89	70	56	123
Major league totals (2 years)		15	15	.500	3.05	47	46	3	3	0	313	287	129	106	85	184

HAMMAKER, ATLEE P

PERSONAL: Born January 24, 1958, in Carmel, Calif. . . . 6-2/204. . . . Throws left, bats both. . . . Full name: Charlton Atlee Hammaker. . . . Name pronounced HAM-ek-er.

HIGH SCHOOL: Mt. Vernon (Alexandria, Va.).

COLLEGE: East Tennessee State.

TRANSACTIONS/CAREER NOTES: Selected by Kansas City Royals organization in first round (21st pick overall) of free-agent draft (June 5, 1979). . . . On disabled list (July 6-October 26, 1979 and August 3-22, 1980). . . . Traded by Royals with P Craig Chamberlain, P Renie Martin and a player to be named later to San Francisco Giants for P Vida Blue and P Bob Tufts (March 30, 1982); Giants organization acquired 2B Brad Wellman to complete deal (April 19, 1982). . . . On disabled list (July 26-August 21, 1983). . . . On San Francisco disabled list (April 2-June 26 and August 4-September 1, 1984); included rehabilitation assignment to Phoenix (June 16-25). . . . On disabled list (April 7, 1986-entire season). . . . Released by Giants (December 9, 1986). . . . Re-signed by Giants (February 4, 1987). . . . On San Francisco disabled list (April 2-30, 1987); included rehabilitation assignment to Phoenix (April 10-30). . . . Granted free agency (November 9, 1987). . . . Re-signed by Giants (January 8, 1988). . . . On San Francisco disabled list (June 19-July 17 and August 3-September 21, 1989; and June 18-July 11, 1990). . . . Released by Giants (August 12, 1990). . . . Signed by San Diego Padres (August 24, 1990). . . . On San Diego disabled list (March 31-June 9, 1991); included rehabilitation assignments to High Desert (May 12-23) and Las Vegas (May 23-June 9). . . . On San Diego disabled list (June 14-September 3, 1991); included rehabilitation assignment to Wichita (August 13-September 3). . . . Granted free agency (October 31, 1991). . . . Signed by Chicago White Sox organization (February 12, 1992). . . . Released by White Sox organization (March 18, 1992). . . . Re-signed by Prince William, White Sox organization (April 12, 1994). . . . Released by White Sox (August 18, 1995).

Year	Team (League)	W	L	Pct.	ERA	G	GS	CG	ShO	Sv.	IP	H	R	ER	BB	SO
1979—	GC Royals (GCL)	1	0	1.000	1.80	1	1	0	0	0	5	3	1	1	1	6
—	Fort Myers (Fla. St.)	0	1	.000	1.80	1	1	0	0	0	5	9	5	1	0	5
1980—	Jacksonville (Sou.)	8	9	.471	3.35	20	20	6	1	0	137	131	64	51	37	88
1981—	Omaha (Am. Assoc.)	11	5	.688	3.64	21	21	8	1	0	146	147	70	59	40	63
—	Kansas City (A.L.)	1	3	.250	5.54	10	6	0	0	0	39	44	24	24	12	11
1982—	Phoenix (PCL)■	0	1	.000	6.35	1	1	0	0	0	5 2/3	13	5	4	2	6
—	San Francisco (N.L.)	12	8	.600	4.11	29	27	4	1	0	175	189	86	80	28	102
1983—	San Francisco (N.L.)	10	9	.526	*2.25	23	23	8	3	0	172 1/3	147	57	43	32	127
1984—	Phoenix (PCL)	0	1	.000	4.50	2	2	0	0	0	8	14	7	4	2	5
—	San Francisco (N.L.)	2	0	1.000	2.18	6	6	0	0	0	33	32	10	8	9	24
1985—	San Francisco (N.L.)	5	12	.294	3.74	29	29	1	1	0	170 2/3	161	81	71	47	100
1986—								Did not play.								
1987—	Phoenix (PCL)	1	2	.333	4.15	3	3	0	0	0	17 1/3	19	9	8	6	8
—	Shreveport (Texas)	0	1	.000	1.29	1	1	0	0	0	7	6	2	1	0	3
—	San Francisco (N.L.)	10	10	.500	3.58	31	27	2	0	0	168 1/3	159	73	67	57	107
1988—	San Francisco (N.L.)	9	9	.500	3.73	43	17	3	1	5	144 2/3	136	68	60	41	65
1989—	San Francisco (N.L.)	6	6	.500	3.76	28	9	0	0	0	76 2/3	78	34	32	23	30
1990—	San Francisco (N.L.)	4	5	.444	4.28	25	6	0	0	0	67 1/3	69	33	32	21	28
—	San Diego (N.L.)■	0	4	.000	4.66	9	1	0	0	0	19 1/3	16	11	10	6	16
1991—	High Desert (Calif.)	0	0	...	2.25	2	2	0	0	0	8	9	3	2	3	3
—	Las Vegas (PCL)	0	0	...	6.46	3	3	0	0	0	15 1/3	21	11	11	3	9
—	San Diego (N.L.)	0	1	.000	5.79	1	1	0	0	0	4 2/3	8	7	3	3	1
—	Wichita (Texas)	0	1	.000	3.52	5	0	0	0	0	7 2/3	10	3	3	0	9
1992—								Out of organized baseball.								
1993—								Out of organized baseball.								
1994—	Birmingham (Sou.)■	1	0	1.000	2.00	13	0	0	0	0	18	13	11	4	10	17
—	Nashville (A.A.)	2	1	.667	2.79	21	0	0	0	3	29	24	9	9	11	29
—	Chicago (A.L.)	0	0	...	0.00	2	0	0	0	0	1 1/3	1	0	0	0	1
1995—	Chicago (A.L.)	0	0	...	12.79	13	0	0	0	0	6 1/3	11	9	9	8	3
—	Nashville (A.A.)	1	2	.333	1.27	15	0	0	0	1	28 1/3	27	4	4	7	20
A.L. totals (3 years)		1	3	.250	6.36	25	6	0	0	0	46 2/3	56	33	33	20	15
N.L. totals (9 years)		58	64	.475	3.54	224	146	18	6	5	1032	995	460	406	267	600
Major league totals (12 years)		59	67	.468	3.66	249	152	18	6	5	1078 2/3	1051	493	439	287	615

CHAMPIONSHIP SERIES RECORD

Year	Team (League)	W	L	Pct.	ERA	G	GS	CG	ShO	Sv.	IP	H	R	ER	BB	SO
1987—	San Francisco (N.L.)	0	1	.000	7.88	2	2	0	0	0	8	12	7	7	0	7
1989—	San Francisco (N.L.)	0	0	...	0.00	1	0	0	0	0	1	1	0	0	0	0
Champ. series totals (2 years)		0	1	.000	7.00	3	2	0	0	0	9	13	7	7	0	7

WORLD SERIES RECORD

Year	Team (League)	W	L	Pct.	ERA	G	GS	CG	ShO	Sv.	IP	H	R	ER	BB	SO
1989—	San Francisco (N.L.)	0	0	...	15.43	2	0	0	0	0	2 1/3	8	4	4	0	2

ALL-STAR GAME RECORD

NOTES: Holds single-game records for most runs—7; and most earned runs allowed—7 (July 6, 1983, third inning). . . . Shares record for most home runs allowed in one inning—2 (July 6, 1983, third inning).

Year	League	W	L	Pct.	ERA	GS	CG	ShO	Sv.	IP	H	R	ER	BB	SO
1983—	National	0	0	...	94.50	0	0	0	0	2/3	6	7	7	1	0

HAMMOND, CHRIS — P — MARLINS

PERSONAL: Born January 21, 1966, in Atlanta. . . . 6-1/195. . . . Throws left, bats left. . . . Full name: Christopher Andrew Hammond. . . . Brother of Steve Hammond, outfielder, Kansas City Royals (1982).
HIGH SCHOOL: Vestavia Hills (Birmingham, Ala.).
JUNIOR COLLEGE: Gulf Coast Community College (Fla.).
COLLEGE: Alabama-Birmingham.
TRANSACTIONS/CAREER NOTES: Selected by Cincinnati Reds organization in sixth round of free-agent draft (January 14, 1986). . . . On disabled list (July 27-September 1, 1991). . . . Traded by Reds to Florida Marlins for 3B Gary Scott and a player to be named later (March 27, 1993); Reds acquired P Hector Carrasco to complete deal (September 10, 1993). . . . On Florida disabled list (June 11-August 3, 1994); included rehabilitation assignments to Portland (June 24-25) and Brevard County (July 25-30). . . . On Florida disabled list (April 16-May 13 and August 3-19, 1995); included rehabilitation assignments to Brevard County (May 4-9) and Charlotte (May 9-13).
HONORS: Named American Association Pitcher of the Year (1990).
STATISTICAL NOTES: Career major league grand slams: 1.
MISCELLANEOUS: Appeared in two games as pinch-runner (1992). . . . Struck out in one game as pinch-hitter (1993).

Year	Team (League)	W	L	Pct.	ERA	G	GS	CG	ShO	Sv.	IP	H	R	ER	BB	SO
1986—	GC Reds (GCL)	3	2	.600	2.81	7	7	1	0	0	41 2/3	27	21	13	17	53
—	Tampa (Fla. St.)	0	2	.000	3.32	5	5	0	0	0	21 2/3	25	8	8	13	5
1987—	Tampa (Fla. St.)	11	11	.500	3.55	25	24	6	0	0	170	174	81	67	60	126
1988—	Chattanooga (Sou.)	*16	5	.762	*1.72	26	26	4	2	0	182 2/3	127	48	35	77	127
1989—	Nashville (A.A.)	11	7	.611	3.38	24	24	3	1	0	157 1/3	144	69	59	96	142
1990—	Nashville (A.A.)	*15	1	*.938	*2.17	24	24	5	*3	0	149	118	43	36	63	*149
—	Cincinnati (N.L.)	0	2	.000	6.35	3	3	0	0	0	11 1/3	13	9	8	12	4
1991—	Cincinnati (N.L.)	7	7	.500	4.06	20	18	0	0	0	99 2/3	92	51	45	48	50
1992—	Cincinnati (N.L.)	7	10	.412	4.21	28	26	0	0	0	147 1/3	149	75	69	55	79
1993—	Florida (N.L.)■	11	12	.478	4.66	32	32	1	0	0	191	207	106	99	66	108
1994—	Florida (N.L.)	4	4	.500	3.07	13	13	1	1	0	73 1/3	79	30	25	23	40
—	Portland (Eastern)	0	0	...	0.00	1	1	0	0	0	2	0	0	0	0	2
—	Brevard Co. (FSL)	0	0	...	1.23	2	2	0	0	0	7 1/3	4	3	1	3	5
1995—	Brevard Co. (FSL)	0	0	...	0.00	1	1	0	0	0	4	3	1	0	0	4
—	Charlotte (Int'l)	0	0	...	0.00	1	1	0	0	0	4	3	1	0	2	3
—	Florida (N.L.)	9	6	.600	3.80	25	24	3	2	0	161	157	73	68	47	126
Major league totals (6 years)		38	41	.481	4.13	121	116	5	3	0	683 2/3	697	344	314	251	407

HAMMONDS, JEFFREY — OF — ORIOLES

PERSONAL: Born March 5, 1971, in Plainfield, N.J. . . . 6-0/195. . . . Bats right, throws right. . . . Full name: Jeffrey Bryan Hammonds. . . . Brother of Reggie Hammonds, outfielder, Pittsburgh Pirates organization (1984-86).
HIGH SCHOOL: Scotch Plains (N.J.)-Fanwood.
COLLEGE: Stanford.
TRANSACTIONS/CAREER NOTES: Selected by Toronto Blue Jays organization in ninth round of free-agent draft (June 5, 1989); did not sign. . . . Selected by Baltimore Orioles organization in first round (fourth pick overall) of free-agent draft (June 1, 1992). . . . On Hagerstown temporarily inactive list (August 6-September 14, 1992). . . . On Rochester disabled list (May 17-28, 1993). . . . On Baltimore disabled list (August 8-September 1, 1993); included rehabilitation assignment to Bowie (August 28-September 1). . . . On Baltimore disabled list (September 28, 1993-remainder of season; May 4-June 16, 1994; and July 18-September 3, 1995).
HONORS: Named outfielder on The Sporting News college All-America team (1990 and 1992).
MISCELLANEOUS: Member of 1992 U.S. Olympic baseball team.

			BATTING												FIELDING			
Year	Team (League)	Pos.	G	AB	R	H	2B	3B	HR	RBI	Avg.	BB	SO	SB	PO	A	E	Avg.
1992—									Did not play.									
1993—	Bowie (Eastern)	OF	24	92	13	26	3	0	3	10	.283	9	18	4	48	2	0	1.000
—	Rochester (Int'l)	OF	36	151	25	47	9	1	5	23	.311	5	27	6	72	1	0	1.000
—	Baltimore (A.L.)	OF-DH	33	105	10	32	8	0	3	19	.305	2	16	4	47	2	2	.961
1994—	Baltimore (A.L.)	OF	68	250	45	74	18	2	8	31	.296	17	39	5	147	5	6	.962
1995—	Baltimore (A.L.)	OF-DH	57	178	18	43	9	1	4	23	.242	9	30	4	88	1	1	.989
—	Bowie (Eastern)	OF	9	31	7	12	3	1	1	11	.387	10	7	3	12	0	1	.923
Major league totals (3 years)			158	533	73	149	35	3	15	73	.280	28	85	13	282	8	9	.970

HAMPTON, MIKE — P — ASTROS

PERSONAL: Born September 9, 1972, in Brooksville, Fla. . . . 5-10/180. . . . Throws left, bats right. . . . Full name: Michael William Hampton.
HIGH SCHOOL: Crystal River (Fla.).
TRANSACTIONS/CAREER NOTES: Selected by Seattle Mariners organization in sixth round of free-agent draft (June 4, 1990). . . . Traded by Mariners with OF Mike Felder to Houston Astros for OF Eric Anthony (December 10, 1993). . . . On disabled list (May 15-June 13, 1995).
STATISTICAL NOTES: Led Arizona League with 10 wild pitches in 1990. . . . Pitched 6-0 no-hit victory for San Bernardino against Visalia (May 31, 1991).

Year	Team (League)	W	L	Pct.	ERA	G	GS	CG	ShO	Sv.	IP	H	R	ER	BB	SO
1990—	Ariz. Mariners (Ariz.)	•7	2	.778	2.66	14	•13	0	0	0	64 1/3	52	32	19	40	59
1991—	San Bern. (Calif.)	1	7	.125	5.25	18	15	1	1	0	73 2/3	71	58	43	47	57
—	Bellingham (N'west)	5	2	.714	1.58	9	9	0	0	0	57	32	15	10	26	65
1992—	San Bern. (Calif.)	13	8	.619	3.12	25	25	6	•2	0	170	163	75	59	66	132
—	Jacksonville (Sou.)	0	1	.000	4.35	2	2	1	0	0	10 1/3	13	5	5	1	6

Year	Team (League)	W	L	Pct.	ERA	G	GS	CG	ShO	Sv.	IP	H	R	ER	BB	SO
1993—	Seattle (A.L.)	1	3	.250	9.53	13	3	0	0	1	17	28	20	18	17	8
	—Jacksonville (Sou.)	6	4	.600	3.71	15	14	1	0	0	87 1/3	71	43	36	33	84
1994—	Houston (N.L.)■	2	1	.667	3.70	44	0	0	0	0	41 1/3	46	19	17	16	24
1995—	Houston (N.L.)	9	8	.529	3.35	24	24	0	0	0	150 2/3	141	73	56	49	115
A.L. totals (1 year)		1	3	.250	9.53	13	3	0	0	1	17	28	20	18	17	8
N.L. totals (2 years)		11	9	.550	3.42	68	24	0	0	0	192	187	92	73	65	139
Major league totals (3 years)		12	12	.500	3.92	81	27	0	0	1	209	215	112	91	82	147

HANCOCK, LEE — P — PIRATES

PERSONAL: Born June 27, 1967, in Van Nuys, Calif. . . . 6-4/220. . . . Throws left, bats left. . . . Full name: Leland David Hancock.
HIGH SCHOOL: Saratoga (Calif.).
COLLEGE: Cal Poly-San Luis Obispo.
TRANSACTIONS/CAREER NOTES: Selected by Seattle Mariners organization in fourth round of free-agent draft (June 1, 1988). . . . Traded by Mariners to Pittsburgh Pirates organization for P Scott Medvin (May 18, 1990). . . . On Buffalo disabled list (May 13-20, 1992). . . . On Carolina disabled list (June 28-July 27 and August 7-14, 1992).

Year	Team (League)	W	L	Pct.	ERA	G	GS	CG	ShO	Sv.	IP	H	R	ER	BB	SO
1988—	Bellingham (N'west)	6	5	.545	2.60	16	•16	2	0	0	100 1/3	83	37	29	31	102
1989—	San Bern. (Calif.)	12	7	.632	2.60	26	26	5	0	0	173	131	69	50	82	119
1990—	Williamsport (East.)	3	2	.600	2.68	7	7	0	0	0	47	39	20	14	20	27
	—Harrisburg (East.)■	6	7	.462	3.44	20	19	3	1	0	117 2/3	106	51	45	57	65
	—Buffalo (A.A.)	0	0	...	...	1	0	0	0	0	0	0	0	0	1	0
1991—	Carolina (South.)	4	7	.364	3.77	37	11	0	0	4	98	93	48	41	42	66
1992—	Carolina (South.)	1	1	.500	2.23	23	1	0	0	0	40 1/3	32	13	10	12	40
	—Buffalo (A.A.)	0	2	.000	2.00	10	0	0	0	0	9	9	2	2	3	5
1993—	Carolina (South.)	7	3	.700	2.53	25	11	0	0	0	99 2/3	87	42	28	32	85
	—Buffalo (A.A.)	2	6	.250	4.91	11	11	0	0	0	66	73	38	36	14	30
1994—	Buffalo (A.A.)	4	5	.444	3.43	37	7	0	0	1	86 2/3	103	35	33	22	39
1995—	Calgary (PCL)	6	10	.375	5.07	34	17	1	0	0	113 2/3	146	78	64	27	49
	—Pittsburgh (N.L.)	0	0	...	1.93	11	0	0	0	0	14	10	3	3	2	6
Major league totals (1 year)		0	0	...	1.93	11	0	0	0	0	14	10	3	3	2	6

HANCOCK, RYAN — P — ANGELS

PERSONAL: Born November 11, 1971, in Santa Clara, Calif. . . . 6-2/215. . . . Throws right, bats right. . . . Full name: Ryan Lee Hancock.
HIGH SCHOOL: Monta Vista (Cupertino, Calif.).
COLLEGE: Brigham Young.
TRANSACTIONS/CAREER NOTES: Selected by California Angels organization in second round of free-agent draft (June 3, 1993).

Year	Team (League)	W	L	Pct.	ERA	G	GS	CG	ShO	Sv.	IP	H	R	ER	BB	SO
1993—	Boise (Northwest)	1	0	1.000	3.31	3	3	0	0	0	16 1/3	14	9	6	8	18
1994—	Lake Elsinore (California)	9	6	.600	3.79	18	18	3	1	0	116 1/3	113	62	49	36	95
	—Midland (Texas)	3	4	.429	5.81	8	8	0	0	0	48	63	34	31	11	35
1995—	Midland (Texas)	12	9	.571	4.56	28	*28	*5	1	0	*175 2/3	*222	*107	*89	45	79

HANEY, CHRIS — P — ROYALS

PERSONAL: Born November 16, 1968, in Baltimore. . . . 6-3/195. . . . Throws left, bats left. . . . Full name: Christopher Deane Haney. . . . Son of Larry Haney, major league catcher with five teams (1966-70 and 1972-78) and coach, Milwaukee Brewers (1978-91).
HIGH SCHOOL: Orange County (Va.).
COLLEGE: UNC Charlotte.
TRANSACTIONS/CAREER NOTES: Selected by Milwaukee Brewers organization in 25th round of free-agent draft (June 2, 1987); did not sign. . . . Selected by Montreal Expos organization in second round of free-agent draft (June 4, 1990). . . . On Indianapolis disabled list (June 17-25, 1992). . . . Traded by Expos with P Bill Sampen to Kansas City Royals for 3B Sean Berry and P Archie Corbin (August 29, 1992). . . . On disabled list (July 13, 1995-remainder of season).
MISCELLANEOUS: Appeared in one game as pinch-runner with Montreal (1992).

Year	Team (League)	W	L	Pct.	ERA	G	GS	CG	ShO	Sv.	IP	H	R	ER	BB	SO
1990—	Jamestown (NYP)	3	0	1.000	0.96	6	5	0	0	1	28	17	3	3	10	26
	—Rockford (Midw.)	2	4	.333	2.21	8	8	3	0	0	53	40	15	13	6	45
	—Jacksonville (Sou.)	1	0	1.000	0.00	1	1	0	0	0	6	6	0	0	3	6
1991—	Harrisburg (East.)	5	3	.625	2.16	12	12	3	0	0	83 1/3	65	21	20	31	68
	—Montreal (N.L.)	3	7	.300	4.04	16	16	0	0	0	84 2/3	94	49	38	43	51
	—Indianapolis (A.A.)	1	1	.500	4.35	2	2	0	0	0	10 1/3	14	10	5	6	8
1992—	Montreal (N.L.)	2	3	.400	5.45	9	6	1	1	0	38	40	25	23	10	27
	—Indianapolis (A.A.)	5	2	.714	5.14	15	15	0	0	0	84	88	50	48	42	61
	—Kansas City (A.L.)■	2	3	.400	3.86	7	7	1	1	0	42	35	18	18	16	27
1993—	Omaha (Am. Assoc.)	6	1	.857	2.27	8	7	2	0	0	47 2/3	43	13	12	14	32
	—Kansas City (A.L.)	9	9	.500	6.02	23	23	1	1	0	124	141	87	83	53	65
1994—	Kansas City (A.L.)	2	2	.500	7.31	6	6	0	0	0	28 1/3	36	25	23	11	18
	—Omaha (Am. Assoc.)	8	7	.533	5.25	18	18	1	0	0	104 2/3	125	77	61	37	78
1995—	Kansas City (A.L.)	3	4	.429	3.65	16	13	1	0	0	81 1/3	78	35	33	33	31
A.L. totals (4 years)		16	18	.471	5.13	52	49	3	2	0	275 2/3	290	165	157	113	141
N.L. totals (2 years)		5	10	.333	4.48	25	22	1	1	0	122 2/3	134	74	61	53	78
Major league totals (5 years)		21	28	.429	4.93	77	71	4	3	0	398 1/3	424	239	218	166	219

HANEY, TODD — 2B — CUBS

PERSONAL: Born July 30, 1965, in Galveston, Tex. . . . 5-9/165. . . . Bats right, throws right. . . . Full name: Todd Michael Haney.
HIGH SCHOOL: Richfield (Waco, Tex.).
JUNIOR COLLEGE: Panola Junior College (Tex.).
COLLEGE: Texas.
TRANSACTIONS/CAREER NOTES: Selected by Seattle Mariners organization in 38th round of free-agent draft (June 2, 1987). . . . Traded by Mariners organization to Detroit Tigers organization for P Dave Richards (January 21, 1991). . . . Released by Tigers organization (April 4, 1991). . . . Signed by Montreal Expos organization (April 7, 1991). . . . On Indianapolis disabled list (April 12-July 16, 1992). . . . Granted free agency (October 15, 1993). . . . Signed by Chicago Cubs organization (December 14, 1993). . . . Granted free agency (October 15, 1994). . . . Re-signed by Cubs organization (January 9, 1995).
STATISTICAL NOTES: Led Midwest League second basemen with 29 double plays in 1988. . . . Led American Association second basemen with .974 fielding percentage, 381 assists and 74 double plays in 1991.

			BATTING											FIELDING			
Year	Team (League)	Pos.	G	AB	R	H	2B	3B	HR	RBI	Avg.	BB	SO	SB	PO	A	E	Avg.
1987—	Belling. (N'west)	2B	66	252	57	64	11	2	5	27	.254	44	33	18	148	170	16	.952
1988—	Wausau (Midwest)	2B-SS	132	452	66	127	23	2	7	52	.281	56	54	35	282	318	30	.952
1989—	San Bern. (Calif.)	2B	25	107	10	27	5	0	0	7	.252	7	14	2	47	14	3	.953
—	Williamsport (East.)	2B	115	401	59	108	20	4	2	31	.269	49	43	13	213	313	*18	.967
1990—	Williamsport (East.)	2B	1	2	0	1	1	0	0	0	.500	1	0	0	1	1	0	1.000
—	Calgary (PCL)	2B	108	419	81	142	15	6	1	36	.339	37	38	16	206	292	15	.971
1991—	Indianapolis (A.A.)■	2B-SS	132	510	68	159	32	3	2	39	.312	47	49	12	232	†385	16	†.975
1992—	Indianapolis (A.A.)	2B	57	200	30	53	14	0	6	33	.265	37	34	1	113	161	7	.975
—	Montreal (N.L.)	2B	7	10	0	3	1	0	0	1	.300	0	0	0	2	6	0	1.000
1993—	Ottawa (Int'l)	2B-SS	136	506	69	147	30	4	3	46	.291	36	56	11	245	401	15	.977
1994—	Iowa (Am. Assoc.)■	2B-OF	83	305	48	89	22	1	3	35	.292	28	29	9	159	199	8	.978
—	Chicago (N.L.)	2B-3B	17	37	6	6	0	0	1	2	.162	3	3	2	20	28	1	.980
1995—	Iowa (Am. Assoc.)	2-S-3-O	90	326	38	102	20	2	4	30	.313	28	21	2	123	182	10	.968
—	Chicago (N.L.)	2B-3B	25	73	11	30	8	0	2	6	.411	7	11	0	34	61	2	.979
Major league totals (3 years)			49	120	17	39	9	0	3	9	.325	10	14	2	56	95	3	.981

HANSELL, GREG — P — TWINS

PERSONAL: Born March 12, 1971, in Bellflower, Calif. . . . 6-5/215. . . . Throws right, bats right. . . . Full name: Gregory Michael Hansell.
HIGH SCHOOL: John F. Kennedy (La Palma, Calif.).
TRANSACTIONS/CAREER NOTES: Selected by Boston Red Sox organization in 10th round of free-agent draft (June 5, 1989). . . . Traded by Red Sox organization with OF Ed Perozo and a player to be named later to New York Mets organization for 1B Mike Marshall (July 27, 1990); Mets acquired C Paul Williams to complete deal (November 19, 1990). . . . Traded by Mets organization with P Bob Ojeda to Los Angeles Dodgers organization for OF Hubie Brooks (December 15, 1990). . . . On disabled list (June 19-July 8, 1993). . . . Traded by Dodgers with 3B/1B Ron Coomer, P Jose Parra and a player to be named later to Minnesota Twins for P Kevin Tapani and P Mark Guthrie (July 31, 1995); Twins acquired OF Chris Latham to complete deal (October 30, 1995).
STATISTICAL NOTES: Tied for Florida State League lead with 14 losses and 27 games started in 1990.

Year	Team (League)	W	L	Pct.	ERA	G	GS	CG	ShO	Sv.	IP	H	R	ER	BB	SO
1989—	GC Red Sox (GCL)	3	2	.600	2.53	10	8	0	0	2	57	51	23	16	23	44
1990—	Winter Haven (FSL)	7	10	.412	3.59	21	21	2	1	0	115 1/3	95	63	46	64	79
—	St. Lucie (Fla. St.)■	2	§4	.333	2.84	6	§6	0	0	0	38	34	22	12	15	16
1991—	Bakersfield (Calif.)■	14	5	.737	2.87	25	25	0	0	0	150 2/3	142	56	48	42	132
1992—	San Antonio (Tex.)	6	4	.600	2.83	14	14	0	0	0	92 1/3	80	40	29	33	64
—	Albuquerque (PCL)	1	5	.167	5.24	13	13	0	0	0	68 2/3	84	46	40	35	38
1993—	Albuquerque (PCL)	5	10	.333	6.93	26	20	0	0	0	101 1/3	131	86	78	60	60
1994—	Albuquerque (PCL)	10	2	*.833	2.99	47	6	0	0	8	123 1/3	109	44	41	31	101
1995—	Los Angeles (N.L.)	0	1	.000	7.45	20	0	0	0	0	19 1/3	29	17	16	6	13
—	Albuquerque (PCL)	1	1	.500	8.44	8	1	0	0	1	16	25	15	15	6	15
—	Salt Lake (PCL)■	3	1	.750	5.01	7	5	0	0	0	32 1/3	39	20	18	4	17
Major league totals (1 year)		0	1	.000	7.45	20	0	0	0	0	19 1/3	29	17	16	6	13

HANSEN, DAVE — 3B — DODGERS

PERSONAL: Born November 24, 1968, in Long Beach, Calif. . . . 6-0/195. . . . Bats left, throws right. . . . Full name: David Andrew Hansen.
HIGH SCHOOL: Rowland (Long Beach, Calif.).
TRANSACTIONS/CAREER NOTES: Selected by Los Angeles Dodgers organization in second round of free-agent draft (June 2, 1986). . . . On disabled list (May 9-28, 1994).
STATISTICAL NOTES: Led California League third basemen with 45 errors in 1987. . . . Led Florida State League with 210 total bases and tied for lead with nine sacrifice flies in 1988. . . . Led Florida State League third basemen with 383 total chances and 24 double plays in 1988. . . . Led Pacific Coast League third basemen with .926 fielding percentage, 254 assists, 349 total chances and 25 double plays in 1990. . . . Career major league grand slams: 1.

			BATTING											FIELDING			
Year	Team (League)	Pos.	G	AB	R	H	2B	3B	HR	RBI	Avg.	BB	SO	SB	PO	A	E	Avg.
1986—	Great Falls (Pio.)	O-3-C-2	61	204	39	61	7	3	1	36	.299	27	28	9	54	10	7	.901
1987—	Bakersfield (Calif.)	3B-OF	132	432	68	113	22	1	3	38	.262	65	61	4	79	198	†45	.860
1988—	Vero Beach (FSL)	3B	135	512	68	*149	•28	6	7	*81	.291	56	46	2	*102	*263	18	*.953
1989—	San Antonio (Tex.)	3B	121	464	72	138	21	4	6	52	.297	50	44	3	*92	208	16	*.949
—	Albuquerque (PCL)	3B	6	30	6	8	1	0	2	10	.267	2	3	0	3	8	3	.786
1990—	Albuquerque (PCL)	3B-OF-SS	135	487	90	154	20	3	11	92	.316	*90	54	9	71	†255	26	†.926
—	Los Angeles (N.L.)	3B	5	7	0	1	0	0	0	1	.143	0	0	0	0	1	1	.500
1991—	Albuquerque (PCL)	3B-SS	68	254	42	77	11	1	5	40	.303	49	33	4	43	125	6	.966
—	Los Angeles (N.L.)	3B-SS	53	56	3	15	4	0	1	5	.268	2	12	1	5	19	0	1.000

H

Year	Team (League)	Pos.	G	AB	R	H	2B	3B	HR	RBI	Avg.	BB	SO	SB	PO	A	E	Avg.
			BATTING												FIELDING			
1992—	Los Angeles (N.L.)	3B	132	341	30	73	11	0	6	22	.214	34	49	0	61	183	8	*.968
1993—	Los Angeles (N.L.)	3B	84	105	13	38	3	0	4	30	.362	21	13	0	11	27	3	.927
1994—	Los Angeles (N.L.)	3B	40	44	3	15	3	0	0	5	.341	5	5	0	0	6	1	.857
1995—	Los Angeles (N.L.)	3B	100	181	19	52	10	0	1	14	.287	28	28	0	27	70	7	.933
Major league totals (6 years)			414	734	68	194	31	0	12	77	.264	90	107	1	104	306	20	.953

DIVISION SERIES RECORD

Year	Team (League)	Pos.	G	AB	R	H	2B	3B	HR	RBI	Avg.	BB	SO	SB	PO	A	E	Avg.
			BATTING												FIELDING			
1995—	Los Angeles (N.L.)	PH	3	3	0	2	0	0	0	0	.667	0	0	0	...	...	...	...

HANSON, ERIK — P — BLUE JAYS

PERSONAL: Born May 18, 1965, in Kinnelon, N.J. . . . 6-6/215. . . . Throws right, bats right. . . . Full name: Erik Brian Hanson.

HIGH SCHOOL: Peddie Prep (Highstown, N.J.).

COLLEGE: Wake Forest.

TRANSACTIONS/CAREER NOTES: Selected by Montreal Expos organization in seventh round of free-agent draft (June 6, 1983); did not sign. . . . Selected by Seattle Mariners organization in second round of free-agent draft (June 2, 1986). . . . On inactive list (June 12-August 18, 1986). . . . On Seattle disabled list (May 25-August 4, 1989); included rehabilitation assignments to Calgary (June 14-22 and July 24-August 4). . . . On Seattle disabled list (May 12-28 and May 29-June 22, 1991); included rehabilitation assignment to Calgary (June 16-20). . . . On disabled list (August 23-September 12, 1992). . . . Traded by Mariners with 2B Bret Boone to Cincinnati Reds for P Bobby Ayala and C Dan Wilson (November 2, 1993). . . . On disabled list (August 9, 1994-remainder of season). . . . Granted free agency (October 31, 1994). . . . Signed by Boston Red Sox (April 11, 1995). . . . Granted free agency (November 1, 1995). . . . Signed by Toronto Blue Jays (December 22, 1995).

STATISTICAL NOTES: Pitched 5-0 no-hit victory for Calgary against Las Vegas (August 21, 1988, second game).

MISCELLANEOUS: Scored once in two games as pinch-runner; after pinch-running in one game, became designated hitter but made no plate appearance (1993).

Year	Team (League)	W	L	Pct.	ERA	G	GS	CG	ShO	Sv.	IP	H	R	ER	BB	SO
1986—	Chattanooga (Sou.)	0	0	...	3.86	3	2	0	0	0	9 1/3	10	4	4	4	11
1987—	Chattanooga (Sou.)	8	10	.444	2.60	21	21	1	0	0	131 1/3	102	56	38	43	131
—	Calgary (PCL)	1	3	.250	3.61	8	7	0	0	0	47 1/3	38	23	19	21	43
1988—	Calgary (PCL)	12	7	.632	4.23	27	26	2	1	0	161 2/3	167	92	76	57	*154
—	Seattle (A.L.)	2	3	.400	3.24	6	6	0	0	0	41 2/3	35	17	15	12	36
1989—	Seattle (A.L.)	9	5	.643	3.18	17	17	1	0	0	113 1/3	103	44	40	32	75
—	Calgary (PCL)	4	2	.667	6.87	8	8	1	0	0	38	51	30	29	11	37
1990—	Seattle (A.L.)	18	9	.667	3.24	33	33	5	1	0	236	205	88	85	68	211
1991—	Seattle (A.L.)	8	8	.500	3.81	27	27	2	1	0	174 2/3	182	82	74	56	143
—	Calgary (PCL)	0	0	...	1.50	1	1	0	0	0	6	1	1	1	2	5
1992—	Seattle (A.L.)	8	*17	.320	4.82	31	30	6	1	0	186 2/3	209	110	100	57	112
1993—	Seattle (A.L.)	11	12	.478	3.47	31	30	7	0	0	215	215	91	83	60	163
1994—	Cincinnati (N.L.)■	5	5	.500	4.11	22	21	0	0	0	122 2/3	137	60	56	23	101
1995—	Boston (A.L.)■	15	5	.750	4.24	29	29	1	1	0	186 2/3	187	94	88	59	139
A.L. totals (7 years)		71	59	.546	3.78	174	172	22	4	0	1154	1136	526	485	344	879
N.L. totals (1 year)		5	5	.500	4.11	22	21	0	0	0	122 2/3	137	60	56	23	101
Major league totals (8 years)		76	64	.543	3.81	196	193	22	4	0	1276 2/3	1273	586	541	367	980

DIVISION SERIES RECORD

Year	Team (League)	W	L	Pct.	ERA	G	GS	CG	ShO	Sv.	IP	H	R	ER	BB	SO
1995—	Boston (A.L.)	0	1	.000	4.50	1	1	1	0	0	8	4	4	4	4	5

ALL-STAR GAME RECORD

Year	League	W	L	Pct.	ERA	GS	CG	ShO	Sv.	IP	H	R	ER	BB	SO
1995—	American						Did not play.								

HARE, SHAWN — OF

PERSONAL: Born March 26, 1967, in St. Louis. . . . 6-1/200. . . . Bats left, throws left. . . . Full name: Shawn Robert Hare.

HIGH SCHOOL: Rochester Adams (Mich.).

COLLEGE: Central Michigan.

TRANSACTIONS/CAREER NOTES: Signed as non-drafted free agent by Detroit Tigers organization (August 28, 1988). . . . On Toledo disabled list (April 26-May 11, 1991). . . . On Detroit disabled list (August 3, 1992-remainder of season). . . . Claimed on waivers by New York Mets (May 12, 1994). . . . Granted free agency (October 15, 1994). . . . Signed by Oklahoma City, Texas Rangers organization (January 24, 1995). . . . Granted free agency (October 16, 1995).

STATISTICAL NOTES: Led International League with nine intentional bases on balls received in 1990.

Year	Team (League)	Pos.	G	AB	R	H	2B	3B	HR	RBI	Avg.	BB	SO	SB	PO	A	E	Avg.
			BATTING												FIELDING			
1989—	Lakeland (Fla. St.)	OF-1B	93	290	32	94	16	4	2	36	.324	41	32	11	142	4	2	.986
1990—	Toledo (Int'l)	OF-1B	127	429	53	109	25	4	9	55	.254	49	77	9	198	6	7	.967
1991—	Toledo (Int'l)	OF-1B	80	252	44	78	18	2	9	42	.310	30	53	1	231	19	5	.980
—	London (Eastern)	OF	31	125	20	34	12	0	4	28	.272	12	23	2	55	5	3	.952
—	Detroit (A.L.)	OF-DH	9	19	0	1	1	0	0	0	.053	2	1	0	9	1	0	1.000
1992—	Toledo (Int'l)	OF-1B	57	203	31	67	12	2	5	34	.330	31	28	6	173	7	3	.984
—	Detroit (A.L.)	OF-1B	15	26	0	3	1	0	0	5	.115	2	4	0	33	2	0	1.000
1993—	Toledo (Int'l)	OF-1B-P	130	470	81	124	29	3	20	76	.264	34	90	8	190	5	5	.975
1994—	Toledo (Int'l)	OF-1B	29	99	19	30	6	0	5	9	.303	17	28	5	55	2	2	.966
—	Norfolk (Int'l)■	OF-1B	64	209	26	58	15	1	6	28	.278	33	42	4	138	8	3	.980
—	New York (N.L.)	OF	22	40	7	9	1	1	0	2	.225	4	11	0	23	0	0	1.000
1995—	Texas (A.L.)■	OF-DH-1B	18	24	2	6	1	0	0	2	.250	4	6	0	10	1	0	1.000

Year	Team (League)	Pos.	G	AB	R	H	2B	3B	HR	RBI	Avg.	BB	SO	SB	PO	A	E	Avg.
				BATTING											FIELDING			
	—Okla. City (A.A.)	OF	68	238	27	63	13	3	4	30	.265	23	47	3	110	4	4	.966
American League totals (3 years)			42	69	2	10	3	0	0	7	.145	8	11	0	52	4	0	1.000
National League totals (1 year)			22	40	7	9	1	1	0	2	.225	4	11	0	23	0	0	1.000
Major league totals (4 years)			64	109	9	19	4	1	0	9	.174	12	22	0	75	4	0	1.000

RECORD AS PITCHER

Year	Team (League)	W	L	Pct.	ERA	G	GS	CG	ShO	Sv.	IP	H	R	ER	BB	SO
1993—	Toledo (Int'l)	0	0	...	0.00	1	0	0	0	0	1	2	0	0	0	1

HARIKKALA, TIM — P — MARINERS

PERSONAL: Born July 15, 1971, in West Palm Beach, Fla. ... 6-2/185. ... Throws right, bats right. ... Full name: Timothy Allan Harikkala. ... Name pronounced ha-RICK-a-la.
HIGH SCHOOL: Lake Worth Christian (Lantana, Fla.).
COLLEGE: Florida Atlantic.
TRANSACTIONS/CAREER NOTES: Selected by Seattle Mariners organization in 34th round of free-agent draft (June 1, 1992).

Year	Team (League)	W	L	Pct.	ERA	G	GS	CG	ShO	Sv.	IP	H	R	ER	BB	SO
1992—	Bellingham (N'west)	2	0	1.000	2.70	15	2	0	0	1	33 1/3	37	15	10	16	18
1993—	Bellingham (N'west)	1	0	1.000	1.13	4	0	0	0	0	8	3	1	1	2	12
	—Appleton (Midw.)	3	3	.500	6.52	15	4	0	0	0	38 2/3	50	30	28	12	33
1994—	Appleton (Midw.)	8	3	.727	1.92	13	13	3	0	0	93 2/3	69	31	20	24	63
	—Riverside (Calif.)	4	0	1.000	0.62	4	4	0	0	0	29	16	6	2	10	30
	—Jacksonville (Sou.)	4	1	.800	3.98	9	9	0	0	0	54 1/3	70	30	24	19	22
1995—	Seattle (A.L.)	0	0	...	16.20	1	0	0	0	0	3 1/3	7	6	6	1	1
	—Tacoma (PCL)	5	12	.294	4.24	25	24	4	1	0	146 1/3	151	78	69	55	73
Major league totals (1 year)		0	0	...	16.20	1	0	0	0	0	3 1/3	7	6	6	1	1

HARKEY, MIKE — P

PERSONAL: Born October 25, 1966, in San Diego. ... 6-5/235. ... Throws right, bats right. ... Full name: Michael Anthony Harkey.
HIGH SCHOOL: Ganesha (Pomona, Calif.).
COLLEGE: Cal State Fullerton.
TRANSACTIONS/CAREER NOTES: Selected by San Diego Padres organization in 18th round of free-agent draft (June 4, 1984); did not sign. ... Selected by Chicago Cubs organization in first round (fourth pick overall) of free-agent draft (June 2, 1987). ... On disabled list (April 5-28 and July 4, 1989-remainder of season; May 29-June 13, 1990; and April 27, 1991-remainder of season). ... On Chicago disabled list (March 28-July 20, 1992); included rehabilitation assignments to Peoria (June 9-13 and June 19-20), Iowa (June 20-July 9) and Charlotte (July 15-16). ... On Chicago disabled list (March 27-April 14, 1993); included rehabilitation assignment to Orlando (April 9-10). ... On Chicago disabled list (June 13-July 5, 1993). ... Granted free agency (December 20, 1993). ... Signed by Colorado Rockies (January 4, 1994). ... Granted free agency (October 18, 1994). ... Signed by Edmonton, Oakland Athletics organization (March 8, 1995). ... Claimed on waivers by California Angels (July 19, 1995). ... Granted free agency (December 21, 1995).
RECORDS: Shares major league record for most putouts by pitcher in one inning—3 (May 23, 1990, fourth inning).
HONORS: Named N.L. Rookie Pitcher of the Year by The Sporting News (1990).

Year	Team (League)	W	L	Pct.	ERA	G	GS	CG	ShO	Sv.	IP	H	R	ER	BB	SO
1987—	Peoria (Midwest)	2	3	.400	3.55	12	12	3	0	0	76	81	45	30	28	48
	—Pittsfield (Eastern)	0	0	...	0.00	1	0	0	0	0	2	1	0	0	0	2
1988—	Pittsfield (Eastern)	9	2	*.818	1.37	13	13	3	1	0	85 2/3	66	29	13	35	73
	—Iowa (Am. Assoc.)	7	2	.778	3.55	12	12	3	1	0	78 2/3	55	36	31	33	62
	—Chicago (N.L.)	0	3	.000	2.60	5	5	0	0	0	34 2/3	33	14	10	15	18
1989—	Iowa (Am. Assoc.)	2	7	.222	4.43	12	12	0	0	0	63	67	37	31	35	37
1990—	Chicago (N.L.)	12	6	.667	3.26	27	27	2	1	0	173 2/3	153	71	63	59	94
1991—	Chicago (N.L.)	0	2	.000	5.30	4	4	0	0	0	18 2/3	21	11	11	6	15
1992—	Peoria (Midwest)	1	0	1.000	3.00	2	2	0	0	0	12	15	6	4	3	17
	—Iowa (Am. Assoc.)	0	1	.000	5.56	4	4	0	0	0	22 2/3	21	15	14	13	16
	—Charlotte (South.)	0	1	.000	5.63	1	1	0	0	0	8	9	5	5	0	5
	—Chicago (N.L.)	4	0	1.000	1.89	7	7	0	0	0	38	34	13	8	15	21
1993—	Orlando (Southern)	0	0	...	1.69	1	1	0	0	0	5 1/3	4	1	1	2	5
	—Chicago (N.L.)	10	10	.500	5.26	28	28	1	0	0	157 1/3	187	100	92	43	67
1994—	Colorado (N.L.)■	1	6	.143	5.79	24	13	0	0	0	91 2/3	125	61	59	35	39
	—Colo. Springs (PCL)	1	1	.500	12.60	2	2	0	0	0	10	19	14	14	3	4
1995—	Oakland (A.L.)■	4	6	.400	6.27	14	12	0	0	0	66	75	46	46	31	28
	—California (A.L.)■	4	3	.571	4.55	12	8	1	0	0	61 1/3	80	32	31	16	28
A.L. totals (1 year)		8	9	.471	5.44	26	20	1	0	0	127 1/3	155	78	77	47	56
N.L. totals (6 years)		27	27	.500	4.25	95	84	3	1	0	514	553	270	243	173	254
Major league totals (7 years)		35	36	.493	4.49	121	104	4	1	0	641 1/3	708	348	320	220	310

HARKRIDER, TIMOTHY — SS — ANGELS

PERSONAL: Born September 5, 1971, in Carthage, Tex. ... 6-0/180. ... Bats both, throws right. ... Full name: Timothy T. Harkrider.
HIGH SCHOOL: Carthage (Tex.).
COLLEGE: Texas.
TRANSACTIONS/CAREER NOTES: Selected by California Angels organization in eighth round of free-agent draft (June 3, 1993).
STATISTICAL NOTES: Led Texas League shortstops with 95 double plays in 1995.

Year	Team (League)	Pos.	G	AB	R	H	2B	3B	HR	RBI	Avg.	BB	SO	SB	PO	A	E	Avg.
				BATTING											FIELDING			
1993—	Boise (Northwest)	SS	3	10	4	4	2	0	0	1	.400	5	0	0	6	4	1	.909

Year	Team (League)	Pos.	G	AB	R	H	2B	3B	HR	RBI	Avg.	BB	SO	SB	PO	A	E	Avg.
				BATTING											FIELDING			
	—Ced. Rap. (Midw.)	SS-3B	54	190	29	48	11	0	0	14	.253	22	28	7	64	124	13	.935
1994	—Midland (Texas)	SS-OF	112	409	69	111	20	1	1	49	.271	64	51	13	150	297	24	.949
1995	—Midland (Texas)	SS	124	460	66	134	22	4	2	39	.291	48	36	3	177	*402	32	.948

HARNISCH, PETE P METS

PERSONAL: Born September 23, 1966, in Commack, N.Y. . . . 6-0/207. . . . Throws right, bats right. . . . Full name: Peter Thomas Harnisch.
HIGH SCHOOL: Commack (N.Y.).
COLLEGE: Fordham.
TRANSACTIONS/CAREER NOTES: Selected by Baltimore Orioles organization in supplemental round ("sandwich pick" between first and second round, 27th pick overall) of free-agent draft (June 2, 1987); pick received as compensation for Cleveland Indians signing Type A free-agent C Rick Dempsey. . . . Traded by Orioles with P Curt Schilling and OF Steve Finley to Houston Astros for 1B Glenn Davis (January 10, 1991). . . . On suspended list (July 7-9, 1992). . . . On Houston disabled list (May 23-June 30, 1994); included rehabilitation assignment to Tucson (June 25-26). . . . Traded by Astros to New York Mets for two players to be named later (November 28, 1994); Astros acquired P Andy Beckerman (December 6, 1994) and P Juan Castillo (April 12, 1995) to complete deal. . . . Granted free agency (December 23, 1994). . . . Signed by Mets (April 7, 1995). . . . On disabled list (August 2, 1995-remainder of season).
RECORDS: Shares major league record for striking out side on nine pitches (September 6, 1991, seventh inning).
STATISTICAL NOTES: Pitched 4-0 one-hit, complete-game victory against Chicago (July 10, 1993.) . . . Pitched 3-0 one-hit, complete-game victory against San Diego (September 17, 1993).
MISCELLANEOUS: Appeared in one game as pinch-runner with Houston (1994).

Year	Team (League)	W	L	Pct.	ERA	G	GS	CG	ShO	Sv.	IP	H	R	ER	BB	SO
1987	—Bluefield (Appal.)	3	1	.750	2.56	9	9	0	0	0	52 2/3	38	19	15	26	64
	—Hagerstown (Caro.)	1	2	.333	2.25	4	4	0	0	0	20	17	7	5	14	18
1988	—Charlotte (South.)	7	6	.538	2.58	20	20	4	2	0	132 1/3	113	55	38	52	141
	—Rochester (Int'l)	4	1	.800	2.16	7	7	3	2	0	58 1/3	44	16	14	14	43
	—Baltimore (A.L.)	0	2	.000	5.54	2	2	0	0	0	13	13	8	8	9	10
1989	—Baltimore (A.L.)	5	9	.357	4.62	18	17	2	0	0	103 1/3	97	55	53	64	70
	—Rochester (Int'l)	5	5	.500	2.58	12	12	3	1	0	87 1/3	60	27	25	35	59
1990	—Baltimore (A.L.)	11	11	.500	4.34	31	31	3	0	0	188 2/3	189	96	91	86	122
1991	—Houston (N.L.)■	12	9	.571	2.70	33	33	4	2	0	216 2/3	169	71	65	83	172
1992	—Houston (N.L.)	9	10	.474	3.70	34	34	0	0	0	206 2/3	182	92	85	64	164
1993	—Houston (N.L.)	16	9	.640	2.98	33	33	5	*4	0	217 2/3	171	84	72	79	185
1994	—Houston (N.L.)	8	5	.615	5.40	17	17	1	0	0	95	100	59	57	39	62
	—Tucson (Pac. Coast)	0	0	...	0.00	1	1	0	0	0	5	2	0	0	1	1
1995	—New York (N.L.)■	2	8	.200	3.68	18	18	0	0	0	110	111	55	45	24	82
A.L. totals (3 years)		16	22	.421	4.49	51	50	5	0	0	305	299	159	152	159	202
N.L. totals (5 years)		47	41	.534	3.45	135	135	10	6	0	846	733	361	324	289	665
Major league totals (8 years)		63	63	.500	3.72	186	185	15	6	0	1151	1032	520	476	448	867

ALL-STAR GAME RECORD

Year	League	W	L	Pct.	ERA	GS	CG	ShO	Sv.	IP	H	R	ER	BB	SO
1991	—National	0	0	...	0.00	0	0	0	0	1	2	0	0	0	1

HARPER, BRIAN C

PERSONAL: Born October 16, 1959, in Los Angeles. . . . 6-2/206. . . . Bats right, throws right. . . . Full name: Brian David Harper.
HIGH SCHOOL: San Pedro (Calif.).
TRANSACTIONS/CAREER NOTES: Selected by California Angels organization in fourth round of free-agent draft (June 7, 1977). . . . On disabled list (July 1-17, 1980). . . . Traded by Angels to Pittsburgh Pirates for SS Tim Foli (December 11, 1981). . . . On disabled list (April 12-May 10 and May 16-June 4, 1984). . . . Traded by Pirates with P John Tudor to St. Louis Cardinals for OF/1B George Hendrick and C Steve Barnard (December 12, 1984). . . . Released by Cardinals (April 1, 1986). . . . Signed by Detroit Tigers (April 25, 1986). . . . Released by Tigers (March 23, 1987). . . . Signed by San Jose, independent (May 3, 1987). . . . Contract sold by San Jose to Oakland Athletics organization (May 12, 1987). . . . Released by A's organization (October 12, 1987). . . . Signed by Portland, Minnesota Twins organization (January 4, 1988). . . . Granted free agency (November 4, 1991). . . . Re-signed by Twins (December 19, 1991). . . . Granted free agency (November 2, 1993). . . . Signed by Milwaukee Brewers organization (February 13, 1994). . . . On disabled list (March 30-April 14 and June 26, 1994-remainder of season). . . . Granted free agency (October 20, 1994). . . . Signed by Edmonton, A's organization (April 20, 1995). . . . Announced retirement (May 4, 1995).
STATISTICAL NOTES: Led Texas League with 19 passed balls in 1979. . . . Led Pacific Coast League with 339 total bases in 1981. . . . Led Pacific Coast League catchers with 19 errors in 1981. . . . Tied for American Association lead in errors by catcher with 13 in 1986. . . . Led Pacific Coast League with 12 sacrifice flies in 1987. . . . Led A.L. catchers with 11 errors in 1989. . . . Led A.L. with 12 passed balls in 1992 and 18 in 1993. . . . Career major league grand slams: 2.

Year	Team (League)	Pos.	G	AB	R	H	2B	3B	HR	RBI	Avg.	BB	SO	SB	PO	A	E	Avg.
				BATTING											FIELDING			
1977	—Idaho Falls (Pio.)	C	52	186	28	60	9	3	1	33	.323	13	31	4	352	36	13	.968
1978	—Quad Cities (Mid.)	C	129	508	80	149	31	2	24	*101	.293	37	66	1	430	46	16	.967
1979	—El Paso (Texas)	C	132	531	85	167	*37	3	14	90	.315	50	47	10	443	66	*29	.946
	—California (A.L.)	DH	1	2	0	0	0	0	0	0	.000	0	1	0	...	...	...	...
1980	—El Paso (Texas)	C	105	400	61	114	23	3	12	66	.285	38	46	3	214	30	7	.972
1981	—Salt Lake (PCL)	C-OF-1B	134	549	99	*192	45	9	28	122	.350	39	33	0	421	30	†24	.949
	—California (A.L.)	OF-DH	4	11	1	3	0	0	0	1	.273	0	0	1	5	0	1	.833
1982	—Pittsburgh (N.L.)■	OF	20	29	4	8	1	0	2	4	.276	1	4	0	10	0	0	1.000
	—Portland (PCL)	OF-3B-C	101	395	71	112	29	8	17	73	.284	25	29	3	164	36	8	.962
1983	—Pittsburgh (N.L.)	OF-1B	61	131	16	29	4	1	7	20	.221	2	15	0	40	0	0	1.000
1984	—Pittsburgh (N.L.)	OF-C	46	112	4	29	4	0	2	11	.259	5	11	0	57	3	1	.984
1985	—St. Louis (N.L.)■	O-3-C-1	43	52	5	13	4	0	0	8	.250	2	3	0	15	5	0	1.000
1986	—Nashville (A.A.)■	C-OF-1B	95	317	41	83	11	1	11	45	.262	26	27	3	377	55	‡15	.966
	—Detroit (A.L.)	O-DH-1-C	19	36	2	5	1	0	0	3	.139	3	3	0	25	2	1	.964

Year	Team (League)	Pos.	G	AB	R	H	2B	3B	HR	RBI	Avg.	BB	SO	SB	PO	A	E	Avg.
			BATTING												FIELDING			
1987—	San Jose (Calif.)■	3B-OF-C	8	29	5	9	0	0	3	8	.310	2	0	0	21	12	5	.868
—	Tacoma (PCL)■	OF-C-P	94	323	41	100	17	0	9	62	.310	28	23	1	163	10	5	.972
—	Oakland (A.L.)	DH-OF	11	17	1	4	1	0	0	3	.235	0	4	0	0	0	0	...
1988—	Portland (PCL)■	C-3-O-P	46	170	34	60	10	1	13	42	.353	14	7	2	181	25	5	.976
—	Minnesota (A.L.)	C-DH-3B	60	166	15	49	11	1	3	20	.295	10	12	0	208	15	2	.991
1989—	Minnesota (A.L.)	C-DH-O-1-3	126	385	43	125	24	0	8	57	.325	13	16	2	462	36	†11	.978
1990—	Minnesota (A.L.)	C-DH-3-1	134	479	61	141	42	3	6	54	.294	19	27	3	686	58	11	.985
1991—	Minnesota (A.L.)	C-DH-1B	123	441	54	137	28	1	10	69	.311	14	22	1	643	33	8	.988
1992—	Minnesota (A.L.)	C-DH	140	502	58	154	25	0	9	73	.307	26	22	0	744	58	13	.984
1993—	Minnesota (A.L.)	C-DH	147	530	52	161	26	1	12	73	.304	29	29	1	736	64	10	.988
1994—	Milwaukee (A.L.)■	DH-C-OF	64	251	23	73	15	0	4	32	.291	9	18	0	143	14	3	.981
1995—	Oakland (A.L.)■	C	2	7	0	0	0	0	0	0	.000	0	1	0	6	0	0	1.000
American League totals (12 years)			831	2827	310	852	173	6	52	385	.301	123	155	8	3658	280	60	.985
National League totals (4 years)			170	324	29	79	13	1	11	43	.244	10	33	0	122	8	1	.992
Major league totals (16 years)			1001	3151	339	931	186	7	63	428	.295	133	188	8	3780	288	61	.985

CHAMPIONSHIP SERIES RECORD

Year	Team (League)	Pos.	G	AB	R	H	2B	3B	HR	RBI	Avg.	BB	SO	SB	PO	A	E	Avg.
			BATTING												FIELDING			
1985—	St. Louis (N.L.)	PH	1	1	0	0	0	0	0	0	.000	0	0	0	...	...	...	...
1991—	Minnesota (A.L.)	C	5	18	1	5	2	0	0	1	.278	0	2	0	23	1	1	.960
Championship series totals (2 years)			6	19	1	5	2	0	0	1	.263	0	2	0	23	1	1	.960

WORLD SERIES RECORD

NOTES: Member of World Series championship team (1991).

Year	Team (League)	Pos.	G	AB	R	H	2B	3B	HR	RBI	Avg.	BB	SO	SB	PO	A	E	Avg.
			BATTING												FIELDING			
1985—	St. Louis (N.L.)	PH	4	4	0	1	0	0	0	1	.250	0	1	0	...	...	...	...
1991—	Minnesota (A.L.)	C-PH	7	21	2	8	2	0	0	1	.381	2	2	0	33	5	2	.950
World Series totals (2 years)			11	25	2	9	2	0	0	2	.360	2	3	0	33	5	2	.950

RECORD AS PITCHER

Year	Team (League)	W	L	Pct.	ERA	G	GS	CG	ShO	Sv.	IP	H	R	ER	BB	SO
1987—	Tacoma (PCL)	0	0	...	3.00	1	0	0	0	0	3	3	1	1	0	1
1988—	Portland (PCL)	0	0	...	9.00	1	0	0	0	0	1	2	1	1	2	0

HARRIGER, DENNY — P — PADRES

PERSONAL: Born July 21, 1969, in Kittanning, Pa. . . . 5-11/185. . . . Throws right, bats right. . . . Full name: Dennis Scott Harriger.
HIGH SCHOOL: Ford City (Pa.).
TRANSACTIONS/CAREER NOTES: Selected by New York Mets organization in 18th round of free-agent draft (June 2, 1987). . . . On St. Lucie disabled list (April 11-May 30, 1991). . . . Granted free agency (October 15, 1993). . . . Signed by San Diego Padres organization (November 9, 1993).

Year	Team (League)	W	L	Pct.	ERA	G	GS	CG	ShO	Sv.	IP	H	R	ER	BB	SO
1987—	Kingsport (Appal.)	2	5	.286	4.33	12	7	0	0	0	43 2/3	43	31	21	22	24
1988—	Kingsport (Appal.)	7	2	.778	2.14	13	13	2	1	0	92 1/3	83	35	22	24	59
1989—	Pittsfield (NYP)	2	0	1.000	1.71	3	3	1	1	0	21	20	4	4	0	17
—	St. Lucie (Fla. St.)	5	3	.625	3.19	11	11	0	0	0	67 2/3	72	33	24	17	17
1990—	St. Lucie (Fla. St.)	5	3	.625	3.52	27	7	1	0	2	71 2/3	73	36	28	20	47
1991—	Columbia (S. Atl.)	2	0	1.000	0.00	2	2	1	1	0	11	5	0	0	2	13
—	St. Lucie (Fla. St.)	6	1	.857	2.27	14	11	2	1	0	71 1/3	67	20	18	12	37
1992—	Binghamton (East.)	2	2	.500	3.80	11	0	0	0	0	21 1/3	22	11	9	7	8
—	St. Lucie (Fla. St.)	7	3	.700	2.24	27	10	0	0	3	88 1/3	89	30	22	14	65
1993—	Binghamton (East.)	13	10	.565	2.95	35	24	•4	*3	1	170 2/3	174	69	56	40	89
1994—	Las Vegas (PCL)■	6	11	.353	5.95	30	25	3	0	0	157 1/3	216	*122	104	44	87
1995—	Las Vegas (PCL)	9	9	.500	4.07	29	•28	*7	*2	0	177	187	94	80	60	97

HARRIS, GENE — P — REDS

PERSONAL: Born December 5, 1964, in Sebring, Fla. . . . 5-11/195. . . . Throws right, bats right. . . . Full name: Tyrone Eugene Harris.
HIGH SCHOOL: Okeechobee (Fla.).
COLLEGE: Tulane.
TRANSACTIONS/CAREER NOTES: Selected by Montreal Expos organization in fifth round of free-agent draft (June 2, 1986). . . . Traded by Expos organization with P Randy Johnson and P Brian Holman to Seattle Mariners for P Mark Langston and a player to be named later (May 25, 1989); Indianapolis, Expos organization, acquired P Mike Campbell to complete deal (July 31, 1989). . . . On Seattle disabled list (July 29, 1989-remainder of season). . . . On Seattle disqualified list (April 25-June 26, 1991 and May 3-29, 1992). . . . Traded by Mariners to San Diego Padres for OF Will Taylor (May 11, 1992). . . . On Las Vegas suspended list (July 2-16, 1992). . . . Traded by Padres to Detroit Tigers for 3B Scott Livingstone and SS Jorge Velandia (May 11, 1994). . . . On Detroit disabled list (May 29-July 23, 1994); included rehabilitation assignment to Toledo (July 6-23). . . . Granted free agency (December 23, 1994). . . . Signed by Philadelphia Phillies (April 6, 1995). . . . Traded by Phillies to Baltimore Orioles for OF Andy Van Slyke (June 18, 1995). . . . On Baltimore disabled list (June 25, 1995-remainder of season). . . . Granted free agency (October 18, 1995). . . . Signed by Cincinnati Reds (January 12, 1996).
MISCELLANEOUS: Appeared in one game as pinch-runner (Seattle 1989 and San Diego 1992).

Year	Team (League)	W	L	Pct.	ERA	G	GS	CG	ShO	Sv.	IP	H	R	ER	BB	SO
1986—	Jamestown (NYP)	0	2	.000	2.21	4	4	0	0	0	20 1/3	15	8	5	11	16
—	Burlington (Midw.)	4	2	.667	1.35	7	6	4	3	0	53 1/3	37	12	8	15	32
—	WP Beach (FSL)	0	0	...	4.09	2	2	0	0	0	11	14	7	5	7	5
1987—	WP Beach (FSL)	9	7	.563	4.37	26	26	7	1	0	179	178	101	87	77	121
1988—	Jacksonville (Sou.)	9	5	.643	2.63	18	18	*7	0	0	126 2/3	95	43	37	45	103

Year	Team (League)	W	L	Pct.	ERA	G	GS	CG	ShO	Sv.	IP	H	R	ER	BB	SO
1989	—Montreal (N.L.)	1	1	.500	4.95	11	0	0	0	0	20	16	11	11	10	11
	—Indianapolis (A.A.)	2	0	1.000	0.00	6	0	0	0	2	11	4	0	0	10	9
	—Calgary (PCL)■	0	0	...	0.00	5	0	0	0	2	6	4	0	0	1	4
	—Seattle (A.L.)	1	4	.200	6.48	10	6	0	0	1	33 1/3	47	27	24	15	14
1990	—Calgary (PCL)	3	0	1.000	2.35	6	0	0	0	2	7 2/3	7	2	2	4	9
	—Seattle (A.L.)	1	2	.333	4.74	25	0	0	0	0	38	31	25	20	30	43
1991	—Seattle (A.L.)	0	0	...	4.05	8	0	0	0	1	13 1/3	15	8	6	10	6
	—Calgary (PCL)	4	0	1.000	3.34	25	0	0	0	4	35	37	16	13	11	23
1992	—Seattle (A.L.)	0	0	...	7.00	8	0	0	0	0	9	8	7	7	6	6
	—San Diego (N.L.)■	0	2	.000	2.95	14	1	0	0	0	21 1/3	15	8	7	9	19
	—Las Vegas (PCL)	0	2	.000	3.67	18	0	0	0	4	34 1/3	36	15	14	16	35
1993	—San Diego (N.L.)	6	6	.500	3.03	59	0	0	0	23	59 1/3	57	27	20	37	39
1994	—San Diego (N.L.)	1	1	.500	8.03	13	0	0	0	0	12 1/3	21	11	11	8	9
	—Detroit (A.L.)■	0	0	...	7.15	11	0	0	0	1	11 1/3	13	10	9	4	10
	—Toledo (Int'l)	0	1	.000	5.19	7	1	0	0	1	8 2/3	11	6	5	1	6
1995	—Philadelphia (N.L.)■	2	2	.500	4.26	21	0	0	0	0	19	19	9	9	8	9
	—Baltimore (A.L.)■	0	0	...	4.50	3	0	0	0	0	4	4	2	2	1	4
A.L. totals (6 years)		2	6	.250	5.61	65	6	0	0	3	109	118	79	68	66	83
N.L. totals (5 years)		10	12	.455	3.95	118	1	0	0	23	132	128	66	58	72	87
Major league totals (7 years)		12	18	.400	4.71	183	7	0	0	26	241	246	145	126	138	170

HARRIS, GREG A. P

PERSONAL: Born November 2, 1955, in Lynwood, Calif. . . . 6-0/175. . . . Throws right, bats both. . . . Full name: Greg Allen Harris.

HIGH SCHOOL: Los Alamitos (Calif.).

COLLEGE: Long Beach (Calif.) City College.

TRANSACTIONS/CAREER NOTES: Selected by California Angels organization in 10th round of free-agent draft (June 5, 1974); did not sign. . . . Selected by New York Mets organization in secondary phase of free-agent draft (January 9, 1975); did not sign. . . . Selected by Mets organization in seventh round of free-agent draft (January 7, 1976); did not sign. . . . Signed as non-drafted free agent by Mets organization (September 17, 1976). . . . Traded by Mets with C Alex Trevino and P Jim Kern to Cincinnati Reds for OF George Foster (February 10, 1982). . . . Claimed on waivers by Montreal Expos (September 27, 1983). . . . Traded by Expos to San Diego Padres for IF Al Newman (July 20, 1984). . . . Contract sold by Padres to Texas Rangers (February 13, 1985). . . . Released by Rangers (December 21, 1987). . . . Signed by Cleveland Indians (January 19, 1988). . . . Released by Indians (March 24, 1988). . . . Signed by Maine, Philadelphia Phillies organization (April 1, 1988). . . . Granted free agency (November 4, 1988). . . . Re-signed by Phillies (December 7, 1988). . . . Claimed on waivers by Boston Red Sox (August 7, 1989). . . . Granted free agency (November 13, 1989). . . . Re-signed by Red Sox (February 15, 1990). . . . Released by Red Sox (June 27, 1994). . . . Signed by New York Yankees (July 3, 1994). . . . Released by Yankees (July 13, 1994). . . . Signed by Ottawa, Expos organization (March 29, 1995). . . . Granted free agency (October 17, 1995).

MISCELLANEOUS: Pitched both left- and right-handed in one inning against Cincinnati (September 28, 1995, ninth inning).

Year	Team (League)	W	L	Pct.	ERA	G	GS	CG	ShO	Sv.	IP	H	R	ER	BB	SO
1977	—Jackson (Texas)	3	6	.333	5.42	30	8	0	0	0	83	96	63	50	36	56
1978	—Lynchburg (Caro.)	8	9	.471	2.16	21	21	10	2	0	154	114	52	37	74	102
	—Jackson (Texas)	2	3	.400	3.00	6	5	1	1	0	33	24	13	11	10	18
1979	—Jackson (Texas)	9	11	.450	*2.26	25	25	11	2	0	163	125	58	41	81	89
1980	—Tidewater (Int'l)	2	9	.182	2.70	39	11	1	0	2	110	99	45	33	40	92
1981	—Tidewater (Int'l)	4	0	1.000	2.06	7	7	2	0	0	48	37	14	11	16	26
	—New York (N.L.)	3	5	.375	4.43	16	14	0	0	1	69	65	36	34	28	54
1982	—Indianapolis (A.A.)■	4	1	.800	3.00	8	8	3	1	0	48	27	18	16	24	44
	—Cincinnati (N.L.)	2	6	.250	4.83	34	10	1	0	1	91 1/3	96	56	49	37	67
1983	—Indianapolis (A.A.)	9	12	.429	4.14	28	0	0	0	0	152 1/3	155	83	70	66	*146
	—Cincinnati (N.L.)	0	0	...	27.00	1	21	5	0	0	1	2	3	3	3	1
1984	—Montreal (N.L.)■	0	1	.000	2.04	15	0	0	0	2	17 2/3	10	4	4	7	15
	—Indianapolis (A.A.)	4	4	.500	4.43	14	6	0	0	1	44 2/3	44	27	22	29	45
	—San Diego (N.L.)■	2	1	.667	2.70	19	1	0	0	1	36 2/3	28	14	11	18	30
1985	—Texas (A.L.)■	5	4	.556	2.47	58	0	0	0	11	113	74	35	31	43	111
1986	—Texas (A.L.)	10	8	.556	2.83	73	0	0	0	20	111 1/3	103	40	35	42	95
1987	—Texas (A.L.)	5	10	.333	4.86	42	19	0	0	0	140 2/3	157	92	76	56	106
1988	—Maine (Int'l)■	0	1	.000	1.93	3	0	0	0	1	4 2/3	5	3	1	1	5
	—Philadelphia (N.L.)	4	6	.400	2.36	66	1	0	0	1	107	80	34	28	52	71
1989	—Philadelphia (N.L.)	2	2	.500	3.58	44	0	0	0	1	75 1/3	64	34	30	43	51
	—Boston (A.L.)■	2	2	.500	2.57	15	0	0	0	0	28	21	12	8	15	25
1990	—Boston (A.L.)	13	9	.591	4.00	34	30	1	0	0	184 1/3	186	90	82	77	117
1991	—Boston (A.L.)	11	12	.478	3.85	53	21	1	0	2	173	157	79	74	69	127
1992	—Boston (A.L.)	4	9	.308	2.51	70	2	1	0	4	107 2/3	82	38	30	60	73
1993	—Boston (A.L.)	6	7	.462	3.77	*80	0	0	0	8	112 1/3	95	55	47	60	103
1994	—Boston (A.L.)	3	4	.429	8.28	35	0	0	0	2	45 2/3	60	44	42	23	44
	—New York (A.L.)■	0	1	.000	5.40	3	0	0	0	0	5	4	5	3	3	4
1995	—Ottawa (Int'l)■	3	0	1.000	1.06	11	0	0	0	1	17	7	3	2	3	17
	—Montreal (N.L.)	2	3	.400	2.61	45	0	0	0	0	48 1/3	45	18	14	16	47
A.L. totals (9 years)		59	66	.472	3.77	463	72	3	0	47	1021	939	490	428	448	805
N.L. totals (7 years)		15	24	.385	3.49	240	47	6	0	7	446 1/3	390	199	173	204	336
Major league totals (15 years)		74	90	.451	3.69	703	119	9	0	54	1467 1/3	1329	689	601	652	1141

CHAMPIONSHIP SERIES RECORD

NOTES: Shares single-game record for most earned runs allowed—7 (October 2, 1984). . . . Shares record for most hits allowed in one inning—6 (October 2, 1984, fifth inning).

Year	Team (League)	W	L	Pct.	ERA	G	GS	CG	ShO	Sv.	IP	H	R	ER	BB	SO
1984	—San Diego (N.L.)	0	0	...	31.50	1	0	0	0	0	2	9	8	7	3	2
1990	—Boston (A.L.)	0	1	.000	27.00	1	0	0	0	0	1/3	3	1	1	0	0
Champ. series totals (2 years)		0	1	.000	30.86	2	0	0	0	0	2 1/3	12	9	8	3	2

WORLD SERIES RECORD

Year	Team (League)	W	L	Pct.	ERA	G	GS	CG	ShO	Sv.	IP	H	R	ER	BB	SO
1984—	San Diego (N.L.)	0	0	...	0.00	1	0	0	0	0	5 1/3	3	0	0	3	5

HARRIS, GREG W. P

PERSONAL: Born December 1, 1963, in Greensboro, N.C. . . . 6-2/195. . . . Throws right, bats right. . . . Full name: Gregory Wade Harris.
HIGH SCHOOL: Jordan Matthews (Siler City, N.C.).
COLLEGE: Elon College (N.C.).
TRANSACTIONS/CAREER NOTES: Selected by San Diego Padres organization in 10th round of free-agent draft (June 3, 1985). . . . On San Diego disabled list (April 23-July 4, 1991); included rehabilitation assignment to Las Vegas (June 12-30). . . . On San Diego disabled list (June 1-21 and June 22-August 22, 1992); included rehabilitation assignments to High Desert (August 7-12) and Las Vegas (August 12-22). . . . Traded by Padres with P Bruce Hurst to Colorado Rockies for C Brad Ausmus, P Doug Bochtler and a player to be named later (July 26, 1993); Padres acquired P Andy Ashby to complete deal (July 27, 1993). . . . Released by Rockies (November 30, 1994). . . . Signed by Salt Lake, Minnesota Twins organization (April 11, 1995). . . . On Salt Lake disabled list (April 27-May 21, 1995). . . . Released by Twins (August 4, 1995).
STATISTICAL NOTES: Pitched 7-0 no-hit victory against Midland (August 26, 1987). . . . Led Texas League with 32 home runs allowed and six balks in 1987. . . . Led N.L. with 32 home runs allowed in 1993.

Year	Team (League)	W	L	Pct.	ERA	G	GS	CG	ShO	Sv.	IP	H	R	ER	BB	SO
1985—	Spokane (N'west)	5	4	.556	3.40	13	13	1	0	0	87 1/3	80	36	33	36	90
1986—	Char., S.C. (S. Atl.)	13	7	.650	2.63	27	27	8	2	0	*191 1/3	176	69	56	54	176
1987—	Wichita (Texas)	12	11	.522	4.28	27	27	*7	•2	0	174 1/3	205	103	83	49	170
1988—	Las Vegas (PCL)	9	5	.643	4.11	26	25	5	2	0	159 2/3	160	84	73	65	147
—	San Diego (N.L.)	2	0	1.000	1.50	3	1	1	0	0	18	13	3	3	3	15
1989—	San Diego (N.L.)	8	9	.471	2.60	56	8	0	0	6	135	106	43	39	52	106
1990—	San Diego (N.L.)	8	8	.500	2.30	73	0	0	0	9	117 1/3	92	35	30	49	97
1991—	San Diego (N.L.)	9	5	.643	2.23	20	20	3	2	0	133	116	42	33	27	95
—	Las Vegas (PCL)	1	2	.333	7.40	4	4	0	0	0	20 2/3	24	20	17	8	16
1992—	San Diego (N.L.)	4	8	.333	4.12	20	20	1	0	0	118	113	62	54	35	66
—	High Desert (Calif.)	0	0	...	0.00	1	1	0	0	0	5 1/3	2	0	0	1	5
—	Las Vegas (PCL)	2	0	1.000	0.56	2	2	0	0	0	16	8	1	1	1	15
1993—	San Diego (N.L.)	10	9	.526	3.67	22	22	4	0	0	152	151	65	62	39	83
—	Colorado (N.L.)■	1	8	.111	6.50	13	13	0	0	0	73 1/3	88	62	53	30	40
1994—	Colorado (N.L.)	3	12	.200	6.65	29	19	1	0	1	130	154	*99	*96	52	82
1995—	Minnesota (A.L.)■	0	5	.000	8.82	7	6	0	0	0	32 2/3	50	35	32	16	21
—	Fort Myers (Fla. St.)	1	1	.500	0.95	3	3	1	0	0	19	12	3	2	4	11
A.L. totals (1 year)		0	5	.000	8.82	7	6	0	0	0	32 2/3	50	35	32	16	21
N.L. totals (7 years)		45	59	.433	3.80	236	103	10	2	16	876 2/3	833	411	370	287	584
Major league totals (8 years)		45	64	.413	3.98	243	109	10	2	16	909 1/3	883	446	402	303	605

HARRIS, LENNY 3B/1B REDS

PERSONAL: Born October 28, 1964, in Miami. . . . 5-10/210. . . . Bats left, throws right. . . . Full name: Leonard Anthony Harris.
HIGH SCHOOL: Jackson (Miami).
JUNIOR COLLEGE: Miami-Dade (North) Community College.
TRANSACTIONS/CAREER NOTES: Selected by Cincinnati Reds organization in fifth round of free-agent draft (June 6, 1983). . . . Loaned by Reds organization to Glens Falls, Detroit Tigers organization (May 6-28, 1988). . . . Traded by Reds with OF Kal Daniels to Los Angeles Dodgers for P Tim Leary and SS Mariano Duncan (July 18, 1989). . . . Granted free agency (October 8, 1993). . . . Signed by Reds (December 1, 1993).
STATISTICAL NOTES: Led Florida State League third basemen with 34 double plays in 1985. . . . Led Eastern League third basemen with 116 putouts, 28 errors and 360 total chances in 1986. . . . Led American Association in caught stealing with 22 in 1988. . . . Led American Association second basemen with 23 errors in 1988. . . . Career major league grand slams: 1.

			BATTING												FIELDING			
Year	Team (League)	Pos.	G	AB	R	H	2B	3B	HR	RBI	Avg.	BB	SO	SB	PO	A	E	Avg.
1983—	Billings (Pioneer)	3B	56	224	37	63	8	1	1	26	.281	13	35	7	34	95	22	.854
1984—	Ced. Rap. (Midw.)	3B	132	468	52	115	15	3	6	53	.246	42	59	31	111	204	*34	.903
1985—	Tampa (Fla. St.)	3B	132	499	66	129	11	8	3	51	.259	37	57	15	89	*277	*35	.913
1986—	Vermont (Eastern)	3B-SS	119	450	68	114	17	2	10	52	.253	29	38	36	†119	220	†28	.924
1987—	Nashville (A.A.)	SS-3B	120	403	45	100	12	3	2	31	.248	27	43	30	124	210	34	.908
1988—	Nashville (A.A.)	2B-SS-3B	107	422	46	117	20	2	0	35	.277	22	36	*45	203	247	†25	.947
—	Glens Falls (East.)■	2B	17	65	9	22	5	1	1	7	.338	9	6	6	40	49	5	.947
—	Cincinnati (N.L.)■	3B-2B	16	43	7	16	1	0	0	8	.372	5	4	4	14	33	1	.979
1989—	Cincinnati (N.L.)	2B-SS-3B	61	188	17	42	4	0	2	11	.223	9	20	10	92	134	13	.946
—	Nashville (A.A.)	2B	8	34	6	9	2	0	3	6	.265	0	5	0	23	20	0	1.000
—	Los Angeles (N.L.)■	0-2-3-S	54	147	19	37	6	1	1	15	.252	11	13	4	55	34	2	.978
1990—	Los Angeles (N.L.)	3-2-0-S	137	431	61	131	16	4	2	29	.304	29	31	15	140	205	11	.969
1991—	Los Angeles (N.L.)	3-2-S-0	145	429	59	123	16	1	3	38	.287	37	32	12	125	250	20	.949
1992—	Los Angeles (N.L.)	2-3-0-S	135	347	28	94	11	0	0	30	.271	24	24	19	199	248	27	.943
1993—	Los Angeles (N.L.)	2-3-S-0	107	160	20	38	6	1	2	11	.238	15	15	3	61	99	3	.982
1994—	Cincinnati (N.L.)■	3-1-0-2	66	100	13	31	3	1	0	14	.310	5	13	7	27	29	6	.903
1995—	Cincinnati (N.L.)	3-1-0-2	101	197	32	41	8	3	2	16	.208	14	20	10	147	68	4	.982
Major league totals (8 years)			822	2042	256	553	71	11	12	172	.271	149	172	84	860	1100	87	.957

CHAMPIONSHIP SERIES RECORD

			BATTING												FIELDING			
Year	Team (League)	Pos.	G	AB	R	H	2B	3B	HR	RBI	Avg.	BB	SO	SB	PO	A	E	Avg.
1995—	Cincinnati (N.L.)	PH	3	2	0	2	0	0	0	1	1.000	0	0	1	...	...	...	...

HARRIS, PEP — P — INDIANS

PERSONAL: Born September 23, 1972, in Lancaster, S.C. . . . 6-2/185. . . . Throws right, bats right. . . . Full name: Hernando Petrocelli Harris.
HIGH SCHOOL: Lancaster (S.C.).
TRANSACTIONS/CAREER NOTES: Selected by Cleveland Indians organization in seventh round of free-agent draft (June 3, 1991). . . . On disabled list (June 4-15, 1992 and April 9-May 1, 1993).

Year	Team (League)	W	L	Pct.	ERA	G	GS	CG	ShO	Sv.	IP	H	R	ER	BB	SO
1991	—Burlington (Appal.)	4	3	.571	3.29	13	13	0	0	0	65 2/3	67	30	24	31	47
1992	—Columbus (S. Atl.)	7	4	.636	3.67	18	17	0	0	0	90 2/3	88	51	37	51	57
1993	—Columbus (S. Atl.)	7	8	.467	4.24	26	17	0	0	0	119	113	67	56	44	82
1994	—Cant./Akr. (East.)	2	0	1.000	2.21	24	0	0	0	12	20 1/3	9	5	5	13	15
	—Kinston (Carolina)	4	1	.800	1.93	27	0	0	0	8	32 2/3	21	14	7	16	37
1995	—Cant./Akr. (East.)	6	3	.667	2.39	32	7	0	0	10	83	78	34	22	23	40
	—Buffalo (A.A.)	2	1	.667	2.48	14	0	0	0	0	32 2/3	32	11	9	15	18

HARTGRAVES, DEAN — P — ASTROS

PERSONAL: Born August 12, 1966, in Bakersfield, Calif. . . . 6-0/185. . . . Throws left, bats right. . . . Full name: Dean Charles Hartgraves.
JUNIOR COLLEGE: College of the Siskiyous (Calif.).
COLLEGE: Fresno State.
TRANSACTIONS/CAREER NOTES: Selected by New York Mets organization in 12th round of free-agent draft (January 14, 1986); did not sign. . . . Selected by Houston Astros organization in 20th round of free-agent draft (June 2, 1987). . . . On disabled list (April 8-20 and July 12-September 20, 1993).
STATISTICAL NOTES: Pitched 3-0 no-hit victory against Myrtle Beach (August 12, 1988, second game).

Year	Team (League)	W	L	Pct.	ERA	G	GS	CG	ShO	Sv.	IP	H	R	ER	BB	SO
1987	—Auburn (NYP)	0	5	.000	3.98	23	0	0	0	2	31 2/3	31	24	14	27	42
1988	—Asheville (S. Atl.)	5	9	.357	4.49	34	13	2	1	0	118 1/3	131	70	59	47	83
1989	—Asheville (S. Atl.)	5	8	.385	4.11	19	19	4	0	0	120 1/3	140	66	55	49	87
	—Osceola (Florida St.)	3	3	.500	2.95	7	6	1	1	0	39 2/3	36	20	13	12	21
1990	—Chatt. (South.)	8	8	.500	4.70	33	14	0	0	0	99 2/3	108	66	52	48	64
1991	—Jackson (Texas)	6	5	.545	2.68	19	9	3	0	0	74	60	25	22	25	44
	—Tucson (Pac. Coast)	3	0	1.000	3.09	16	3	1	1	0	43 2/3	47	17	15	20	18
1992	—Jackson (Texas)	9	6	.600	2.76	22	22	3	2	0	146 2/3	127	54	45	40	92
	—Tucson (Pac. Coast)	0	1	.000	24.75	5	1	0	0	0	8	26	24	22	9	6
1993	—Tucson (Pac. Coast)	1	6	.143	6.37	23	10	2	0	0	77 2/3	90	65	55	40	42
1994	—Tucson (Pac. Coast)	7	2	.778	5.07	47	4	0	0	3	97 2/3	106	64	55	36	54
1995	—Tucson (Pac. Coast)	3	2	.600	2.11	14	0	0	0	5	21 1/3	21	6	5	5	15
	—Houston (N.L.)	2	0	1.000	3.22	40	0	0	0	0	36 1/3	30	14	13	16	24
Major league totals (1 year)		2	0	1.000	3.22	40	0	0	0	0	36 1/3	30	14	13	16	24

HARTLEY, MIKE — P

PERSONAL: Born August 31, 1961, in Hawthorne, Calif. . . . 6-1/195. . . . Throws right, bats right. . . . Full name: Michael Edward Hartley.
HIGH SCHOOL: El Cajon Valley (Calif.).
COLLEGE: Grossmont College (Calif.).
TRANSACTIONS/CAREER NOTES: Signed as non-drafted free agent by St. Louis Cardinals organization (November 27, 1981). . . . Selected by Los Angeles Dodgers organization from Cardinals organization in Rule 5 minor league draft (December 9, 1986). . . . Traded by Dodgers with OF Braulio Castillo to Philadelphia Phillies for P Roger McDowell (July 31, 1991). . . . On Philadelphia disabled list (March 31-May 13, 1992); included rehabilitation assignment to Scranton/Wilkes-Barre (April 12-25). . . . Traded by Phillies to Minnesota Twins for P David West (December 5, 1992). . . . Granted free agency (October 12, 1993). . . . Signed by Midland, California Angels organization (November 22, 1993). . . . Contract sold by Angels organization to Chiba Lotte Marines of Japan Pacific League (November 1993). . . . Selected by Calgary, Seattle Mariners organization, from Midland, Angels organization, in Rule 5 minor league draft (December 13, 1993); Angels organization compensated Mariners with cash for already having sold contract to Chiba Lotte. . . . Signed as free agent by Pawtucket, Boston Red Sox organization (April 17, 1995). . . . Released by Pawtucket (August 3, 1995). . . . Signed by Rochester, Baltimore Orioles organization (August 9, 1995). . . . Granted free agency (October 14, 1995).

Year	Team (League)	W	L	Pct.	ERA	G	GS	CG	ShO	Sv.	IP	H	R	ER	BB	SO
1982	—Johns. City (App.)	3	1	.750	2.79	8	5	0	0	0	29	32	12	9	8	13
1983	—St. Petersburg (FSL)	1	3	.250	3.34	9	4	1	0	0	29 2/3	25	14	11	24	18
	—Macon (S. Atl.)	2	3	.400	10.24	7	7	1	0	0	29	36	36	33	30	12
	—Erie (NYP)	1	3	.250	6.75	7	7	0	0	0	32	36	27	24	31	25
1984	—St. Petersburg (FSL)	8	14	.364	4.20	31	31	4	1	0	139 1/3	142	81	65	84	88
1985	—Springfield (Midw.)	2	7	.222	5.12	33	33	0	0	0	114 1/3	119	77	65	62	100
1986	—Springfield (Midw.)	0	0	...	9.60	8	0	0	0	1	15	22	17	16	14	10
	—Savannah (S. Atl.)	5	7	.417	2.89	39	0	0	0	8	56	38	31	18	37	55
1987	—Bakersfield (Calif.)■	5	4	.556	2.57	33	0	0	0	15	56	44	19	16	24	72
	—San Antonio (Tex.)	3	4	.429	1.32	25	0	0	0	3	41	21	8	6	18	37
	—Albuquerque (PCL)	0	1	.000	6.75	2	0	0	0	0	2 2/3	5	3	2	3	3
1988	—San Antonio (Tex.)	5	1	.833	0.80	30	0	0	0	9	45	25	5	4	18	57
	—Albuquerque (PCL)	2	2	.500	4.35	18	0	0	0	3	20 2/3	22	11	10	12	16
1989	—Albuquerque (PCL)	7	4	.636	2.79	58	0	0	0	18	77 1/3	53	31	24	34	76
	—Los Angeles (N.L.)	0	1	.000	1.50	5	0	0	0	0	6	2	1	1	0	4
1990	—Los Angeles (N.L.)	6	3	.667	2.95	32	6	1	1	1	79 1/3	58	32	26	30	76
	—Albuquerque (PCL)	0	0	...	0.00	3	0	0	0	2	3	3	0	0	2	3
1991	—Los Angeles (N.L.)	2	0	1.000	4.42	40	0	0	0	1	57	53	29	28	37	44
	—Philadelphia (N.L.)■	2	1	.667	3.76	18	0	0	0	1	26 1/3	21	11	11	10	19
1992	—Scran./W.B. (Int'l)	1	2	.333	4.09	3	3	0	0	0	11	9	6	5	7	10
	—Philadelphia (N.L.)	7	6	.538	3.44	46	0	0	0	0	55	54	23	21	23	53
1993	—Minnesota (A.L.)■	1	2	.333	4.00	53	0	0	0	1	81	86	38	36	36	57

Year Team (League)	W	L	Pct.	ERA	G	GS	CG	ShO	Sv.	IP	H	R	ER	BB	SO
1994—Chiba Lotte (Jap. Pac.)■	1	6	.143	6.69	14	...	0	0	1	40 1/3	8	7	7	2	2
1995—Boston (A.L.)■	0	0	...	9.00	5	0	0	0	0	7	8	7	7	2	2
—Pawtucket (Int'l)	1	1	.500	4.05	26	1	0	0	1	46 2/3	47	21	21	12	39
—Rochester (Int'l)■	0	1	.000	0.82	8	0	0	0	0	11	4	1	1	2	12
—Baltimore (A.L.)	1	0	1.000	1.29	3	0	0	0	0	7	5	1	1	1	4
A.L. totals (2 years)	2	2	.500	4.17	61	0	0	0	1	95	99	46	44	39	63
N.L. totals (4 years)	17	11	.607	3.50	141	6	1	1	3	223 2/3	188	96	87	100	196
Major league totals (6 years)	19	13	.594	3.70	202	6	1	1	4	318 2/3	287	142	131	139	259

HARVEY, BRYAN — P — ANGELS

PERSONAL: Born June 2, 1963, in Chattanooga, Tenn. . . . 6-2/212. . . . Throws right, bats right. . . . Full name: Bryan Stanley Harvey.
HIGH SCHOOL: Bandys (Catawba, N.C.).
COLLEGE: UNC Charlotte.
TRANSACTIONS/CAREER NOTES: Signed as non-drafted free agent by California Angels organization (August 20, 1984). . . . On disabled list (April 12-22, 1985; June 7-22 and July 1, 1992-remainder of season). . . . Selected by Florida Marlins in first round (20th pick overall) of expansion draft (November 17, 1992). . . . On Florida disabled list (April 26-May 25, May 26-June 22 and June 30, 1994-remainder of season); included rehabilitation assignments to Brevard County (May 9-10, May 25 and June 9-22). . . . On disabled list (April 29, 1995-remainder of season). . . . Granted free agency (October 30, 1995). . . . Signed by Angels (December 20, 1995).
HONORS: Named A.L. Rookie Pitcher of the Year by The Sporting News (1988). . . . Named A.L. co-Fireman of the Year by The Sporting News (1991).

Year Team (League)	W	L	Pct.	ERA	G	GS	CG	ShO	Sv.	IP	H	R	ER	BB	SO
1985—Quad City (Midw.)	5	6	.455	3.53	30	7	0	0	4	81 2/3	66	37	32	37	111
1986—Palm Springs (Cal.)	3	4	.429	2.68	43	0	0	0	15	57	38	24	17	38	68
1987—Midland (Texas)	2	2	.500	2.04	43	0	0	0	20	53	40	14	12	28	78
—California (A.L.)	0	0	...	0.00	3	0	0	0	0	5	6	0	0	2	3
1988—Edmonton (PCL)	0	0	...	3.18	5	0	0	0	2	5 2/3	7	2	2	4	10
—California (A.L.)	7	5	.583	2.13	50	0	0	0	17	76	59	22	18	20	67
1989—California (A.L.)	3	3	.500	3.44	51	0	0	0	25	55	36	21	21	41	78
1990—California (A.L.)	4	4	.500	3.22	54	0	0	0	25	64 1/3	45	24	23	35	82
1991—California (A.L.)	2	4	.333	1.60	67	0	0	0	*46	78 2/3	51	20	14	17	101
1992—California (A.L.)	0	4	.000	2.83	25	0	0	0	13	28 2/3	22	12	9	11	34
1993—Florida (N.L.)■	1	5	.167	1.70	59	0	0	0	45	69	45	14	13	13	73
1994—Florida (N.L.)	0	0	...	5.23	12	0	0	0	6	10 1/3	12	6	6	4	10
—Brevard Co. (FSL)	0	0	...	1.50	7	1	0	0	0	6	2	1	1	2	6
1995—Florida (N.L.)	0	0	...	...	1	0	0	0	0	0	2	3	3	1	0
A.L. totals (6 years)	16	20	.444	2.49	250	0	0	0	126	307 2/3	219	99	85	126	365
N.L. totals (3 years)	1	5	.167	2.50	72	0	0	0	51	79 1/3	59	23	22	18	83
Major league totals (9 years)	17	25	.405	2.49	322	0	0	0	177	387	278	122	107	144	448

ALL-STAR GAME RECORD

Year League	W	L	Pct.	ERA	GS	CG	ShO	Sv.	IP	H	R	ER	BB	SO
1991—American						Did not play.								
1993—National	0	0	...	0.00	0	0	0	0	1	1	0	0	0	2
All-Star totals (1 year)	0	0	...	0.00	0	0	0	0	1	1	0	0	0	2

HASELMAN, BILL — C — RED SOX

PERSONAL: Born May 25, 1966, in Long Branch, N.J. . . . 6-3/220. . . . Bats right, throws right. . . . Full name: William Joseph Haselman.
HIGH SCHOOL: Saratoga (Calif.).
COLLEGE: UCLA.
TRANSACTIONS/CAREER NOTES: Selected by Texas Rangers organization in first round (23rd pick overall) of free-agent draft (June 2, 1987); pick received as compensation for New York Yankees signing Type A free-agent OF Gary Ward. . . . On disabled list (March 28-May 4, 1992). . . . Claimed on waivers by Seattle Mariners (May 29, 1992). . . . On suspended list (July 22-25, 1993). . . . Granted free agency (October 15, 1994). . . . Signed by Boston Red Sox (November 7, 1994).
STATISTICAL NOTES: Led Texas League with 12 passed balls in 1989. . . . Led Texas League catchers with 676 putouts, 90 assists, 20 errors, 786 total chances and 20 passed balls in 1990. . . . Led American Association catchers with 673 putouts and 751 total chances in 1991. . . . Career major league grand slams: 1.

		BATTING												FIELDING			
Year Team (League)	Pos.	G	AB	R	H	2B	3B	HR	RBI	Avg.	BB	SO	SB	PO	A	E	Avg.
1987—Gastonia (S. Atl.)	C	61	235	35	72	13	1	8	33	.306	19	46	1	26	2	2	.933
1988—Charlotte (Fla. St.)	C	122	453	56	111	17	2	10	54	.245	45	99	8	249	30	6	.979
1989—Tulsa (Texas)	C	107	352	38	95	17	2	7	36	.270	40	88	5	508	63	9	.984
1990—Tulsa (Texas)	C-1-O-3	120	430	68	137	39	2	18	80	.319	43	96	3	†722	†93	†20	.976
—Texas (A.L.)	DH-C	7	13	0	2	0	0	0	3	.154	1	5	0	8	0	0	1.000
1991—Okla. City (A.A.)	C-O-1-3	126	442	57	113	22	2	9	60	.256	61	89	10	†706	71	11	.986
1992—Okla. City (A.A.)	OF-C	17	58	8	14	5	0	1	9	.241	13	12	1	45	7	3	.945
—Calgary (PCL)■	C-OF	88	302	49	77	14	2	19	53	.255	41	89	3	227	23	6	.977
—Seattle (A.L.)	C-OF	8	19	1	5	0	0	0	0	.263	0	7	0	19	2	0	1.000
1993—Seattle (A.L.)	C-DH-OF	58	137	21	35	8	0	5	16	.255	12	19	2	236	17	2	.992
1994—Seattle (A.L.)	C-DH-OF	38	83	11	16	7	1	1	8	.193	3	11	1	157	6	3	.982
—Calgary (PCL)	C-1B	44	163	44	54	10	0	15	46	.331	30	33	1	219	16	5	.979
1995—Boston (A.L.)■	C-DH-1-3	64	152	22	37	6	1	5	23	.243	17	30	0	259	16	3	.989
Major league totals (5 years)		175	404	55	95	21	2	11	50	.235	33	72	3	679	41	8	.989

DIVISION SERIES RECORD

		BATTING												FIELDING			
Year Team (League)	Pos.	G	AB	R	H	2B	3B	HR	RBI	Avg.	BB	SO	SB	PO	A	E	Avg.
1995—Boston (A.L.)	C	1	2	0	0	0	0	0	0	.000	0	0	0	6	0	0	1.000

H

HATCHER, BILLY OF ROYALS

PERSONAL: Born October 4, 1960, in Williams, Ariz. . . . 5-10/190. . . . Bats right, throws right. . . . Full name: William Augustus Hatcher.

HIGH SCHOOL: Williams (Ariz.).

JUNIOR COLLEGE: Yavapai College (Ariz.).

TRANSACTIONS/CAREER NOTES: Selected by Chicago Cubs organization in sixth round of free-agent draft (January 13, 1981). . . . On Chicago disabled list (August 19-September 3, 1985). . . . Traded by Cubs with a player to be named later to Houston Astros for OF Jerry Mumphrey (December 16, 1985); Astros organization acquired P Steve Engel to complete deal (July 24, 1986). . . . On disabled list (June 28-July 13, 1986 and July 7-22, 1987). . . . Traded by Astros to Pittsburgh Pirates for OF Glenn Wilson (August 18, 1989). . . . Traded by Pirates to Cincinnati Reds for P Mike Roesler and IF Jeff Richardson (April 3, 1990). . . . On disabled list (May 5-22, 1992). . . . Traded by Reds to Boston Red Sox for P Tom Bolton (July 9, 1992). . . . Granted free agency (November 2, 1992). . . . Re-signed by Red Sox (November 27, 1992). . . . Traded by Red Sox with P Paul Quantrill to Philadelphia Phillies for OF Wes Chamberlain and P Mike Sullivan (May 31, 1994). . . . Granted free agency (October 15, 1994). . . . Signed by Texas Rangers (April 25, 1995). . . . Released by Rangers (May 16, 1995). . . . Signed by Omaha, Kansas City Royals organization (June 8, 1995).

RECORDS: Shares major league single-game record for most doubles—4 (August 21, 1990).

STATISTICAL NOTES: Led New York-Pennsylvania League in being hit by pitch with eight in 1981. . . . Led American Association in being hit by pitch with nine in 1984. . . . Tied for N.L. lead in double plays by outfielder with six in 1987. . . . Career major league grand slams: 2.

			BATTING											FIELDING			
Year	Team (League)	Pos.	G	AB	R	H	2B	3B	HR	RBI	Avg.	BB	SO	SB	PO	A	E	Avg.
1981	Geneva (NYP)	OF	•75	289	57	81	15	3	4	40	.280	36	41	13	138	7	11	.929
1982	Salinas (Calif.)	OF	138	549	92	171	18	8	8	59	.311	40	47	84	235	10	12	.953
1983	Midland (Texas)	OF	135	545	*132	163	33	11	10	80	.299	65	61	56	286	17	•13	.959
1984	Iowa (Am. Assoc.)	OF	150	595	96	164	27	18	9	59	.276	51	54	56	303	15	7	.978
	—Chicago (N.L.)	OF	8	9	1	1	0	0	0	0	.111	1	0	2	2	1	0	1.000
1985	Iowa (Am. Assoc.)	OF	67	279	39	78	14	5	5	19	.280	24	40	17	157	4	4	.976
	—Chicago (N.L.)	OF	53	163	24	40	12	1	2	10	.245	8	12	2	77	2	1	.988
1986	Houston (N.L.)■	OF	127	419	55	108	15	4	6	36	.258	22	52	38	226	7	4	.983
1987	Houston (N.L.)	OF	141	564	96	167	28	3	11	63	.296	42	70	53	276	16	4	.986
1988	Houston (N.L.)	OF	145	530	79	142	25	4	7	52	.268	37	56	32	280	7	5	.983
1989	Houston (N.L.)	OF	108	395	49	90	15	3	3	44	.228	30	53	22	223	1	2	.991
	—Pittsburgh (N.L.)■	OF	27	86	10	21	4	0	1	7	.244	0	9	2	27	0	0	1.000
1990	Cincinnati (N.L.)■	OF	139	504	68	139	28	5	5	25	.276	33	42	30	308	10	1	*.997
1991	Cincinnati (N.L.)	OF	138	442	45	116	25	3	4	41	.262	26	55	11	248	4	5	.981
1992	Cincinnati (N.L.)	OF	43	94	10	27	3	0	2	10	.287	5	11	0	29	0	1	.967
	—Boston (A.L.)■	OF	75	315	37	75	16	2	1	23	.238	17	41	4	145	5	5	.968
1993	Boston (A.L.)	OF-2B	136	508	71	146	24	3	9	57	.287	28	46	14	284	6	2	.993
1994	Boston (A.L.)	OF-DH	44	164	24	40	9	1	1	18	.244	11	14	4	87	3	3	.968
	—Philadelphia (N.L.)■	OF	43	134	15	33	5	1	2	13	.246	6	14	4	68	4	0	1.000
1995	Texas (A.L.)■	OF-DH	6	12	2	1	1	0	0	0	.083	1	1	0	9	1	0	1.000
	—Omaha (A.A.)■	OF	26	105	14	29	5	1	1	12	.276	9	6	4	52	0	1	.981
American League totals (4 years)			261	999	134	262	50	6	11	98	.262	57	102	22	525	15	10	.982
National League totals (10 years)			972	3340	452	884	160	24	43	301	.265	210	374	196	1764	52	23	.987
Major league totals (12 years)			1233	4339	586	1146	210	30	54	399	.264	267	476	218	2289	67	33	.986

CHAMPIONSHIP SERIES RECORD

NOTES: Shares single-game record for most at-bats—7 (October 15, 1986, 16 innings).

			BATTING											FIELDING			
Year	Team (League)	Pos.	G	AB	R	H	2B	3B	HR	RBI	Avg.	BB	SO	SB	PO	A	E	Avg.
1986	Houston (N.L.)	OF	6	25	4	7	0	0	1	2	.280	3	2	3	11	0	1	.917
1990	Cincinnati (N.L.)	OF	4	15	2	5	1	0	1	2	.333	0	2	0	5	1	0	1.000
Championship series totals (2 years)			10	40	6	12	1	0	2	4	.300	3	4	3	16	1	1	.944

WORLD SERIES RECORD

NOTES: Holds single-series records for highest batting average—.750 (1990); and most consecutive hits—7 (October 16 [3] and 17 [4], 1990). . . . Shares record for most at-bats in one inning—2 (October 19, 1990, third inning). . . . Member of World Series championship team (1990).

			BATTING											FIELDING			
Year	Team (League)	Pos.	G	AB	R	H	2B	3B	HR	RBI	Avg.	BB	SO	SB	PO	A	E	Avg.
1990	Cincinnati (N.L.)	OF	4	12	6	9	4	1	0	2	.750	2	0	0	11	0	0	1.000

HATTEBERG, SCOTT C RED SOX

PERSONAL: Born December 14, 1969, in Salem, Ore. . . . 6-1/192. . . . Bats left, throws right. . . . Full name: Scott Allen Hatteberg. . . . Name pronounced HAT-ee-berg.

HIGH SCHOOL: Eisenhower (Yakima, Wash.).

COLLEGE: Washington State.

TRANSACTIONS/CAREER NOTES: Selected by Philadelphia Phillies organization in 12th round of free-agent draft (June 1, 1988); did not sign. . . . Selected by Boston Red Sox organization in supplemental round ("sandwich pick" between first and second round, 43rd pick overall) of free-agent draft (June 3, 1991); pick received as part of compensation for Kansas City signing Type A free-agent P Mike Boddicker. . . . On disabled list (July 27-August 3, 1992).

			BATTING											FIELDING			
Year	Team (League)	Pos.	G	AB	R	H	2B	3B	HR	RBI	Avg.	BB	SO	SB	PO	A	E	Avg.
1991	Winter Haven (FSL)	C	56	191	21	53	7	3	1	25	.277	22	22	1	261	35	5	.983
	—Lynchburg (Caro.)	C	8	25	4	5	1	0	0	2	.200	7	6	0	35	2	0	1.000
1992	New Britain (East.)	C	103	297	28	69	13	2	1	30	.232	41	49	1	473	44	11	.979
1993	New Britain (East.)	C	68	227	35	63	10	2	7	28	.278	42	38	1	410	45	10	.978
	—Pawtucket (Int'l)	C	18	53	6	10	0	0	1	2	.189	6	12	0	131	4	5	.964
1994	New Britain (East.)	C	20	68	6	18	4	1	1	9	.265	7	9	0	125	14	1	.993
	—Pawtucket (Int'l)	C	78	238	26	56	14	0	7	19	.235	32	49	2	467	36	7	.986

H

Year	Team (League)	Pos.	G	AB	R	H	2B	3B	HR	RBI	Avg.	BB	SO	SB	PO	A	E	Avg.
			BATTING												FIELDING			
1995—	Pawtucket (Int'l)	C	85	251	36	68	15	1	7	27	.271	40	39	2	446	45	•8	.984
—	Boston (A.L.)	C	2	2	1	1	0	0	0	0	.500	0	0	0	4	0	0	1.000
Major league totals (1 year)			2	2	1	1	0	0	0	0	.500	0	0	0	4	0	0	1.000

HAWKINS, LaTROY P TWINS

PERSONAL: Born December 21, 1972, in Gary, Ind. . . . 6-5/193. . . . Throws right, bats right.

HIGH SCHOOL: West Side (Gary, Ind.).

TRANSACTIONS/CAREER NOTES: Selected by Minnesota Twins organization in seventh round of free-agent draft (June 3, 1991).

Year	Team (League)	W	L	Pct.	ERA	G	GS	CG	ShO	Sv.	IP	H	R	ER	BB	SO
1991—	GC Twins (GCL)	4	3	.571	4.75	11	11	0	0	0	55	62	34	29	26	47
1992—	GC Twins (GCL)	3	2	.600	3.22	6	6	1	0	0	36 1/3	36	19	13	10	35
—	Elizabeth. (App.)	0	1	.000	3.38	5	5	1	0	0	26 2/3	21	12	10	11	36
1993—	Fort Wayne (Midw.)	•15	5	.750	*2.06	26	23	4	•3	0	157 1/3	110	53	36	41	*179
1994—	Fort Myers (Fla. St.)	4	0	1.000	2.33	6	6	1	1	0	38 2/3	32	10	10	6	36
—	Nashville (South.)	9	2	*.818	2.33	11	11	1	0	0	73 1/3	50	23	19	28	53
—	Salt Lake (PCL)	5	4	.556	4.08	12	12	1	0	0	81 2/3	92	42	37	33	37
1995—	Minnesota (A.L.)	2	3	.400	8.67	6	6	1	0	0	27	39	29	26	12	9
—	Salt Lake (PCL)	9	7	.563	3.55	22	22	4	1	0	144 1/3	150	63	57	40	74
Major league totals (1 year)		2	3	.400	8.67	6	6	1	0	0	27	39	29	26	12	9

HAYES, CHARLIE 3B PIRATES

PERSONAL: Born May 29, 1965, in Hattiesburg, Miss. . . . 6-0/215. . . . Bats right, throws right. . . . Full name: Charles Dewayne Hayes.

HIGH SCHOOL: Forrest County Agricultural (Brooklyn, Miss.).

TRANSACTIONS/CAREER NOTES: Selected by San Francisco Giants organization in fourth round of free-agent draft (June 6, 1983). . . . On disabled list (July 20, 1983-remainder of season). . . . Traded by Giants with P Dennis Cook and P Terry Mulholland to Philadelphia Phillies for P Steve Bedrosian and a player to be named later (June 18, 1989); Giants organization acquired IF Rick Parker to complete deal (August 7, 1989). . . . Traded by Phillies to New York Yankees (February 19, 1992), completing deal in which Yankees traded P Darrin Chapin to Phillies for a player to be named later (January 8, 1992). . . . Selected by Colorado Rockies in first round (third pick overall) of expansion draft (November 17, 1992). . . . On suspended list (August 10-13, 1993). . . . Granted free agency (December 23, 1994). . . . Signed by Phillies (April 6, 1995). . . . Granted free agency (November 2, 1995). . . . Signed by Pittsburgh Pirates (December 28, 1995).

STATISTICAL NOTES: Led Texas League third basemen with 27 double plays in 1986. . . . Led Texas League third basemen with 334 total chances in 1987. . . . Led Pacific Coast League in grounding into double plays with 19 in 1988. . . . Led N.L. third basemen with 324 assists and tied for lead with 465 total chances in 1990. . . . Tied for A.L. lead in double plays by third baseman with 29 in 1992. . . . Tied for N.L. lead in grounding into double plays with 25 in 1993. . . . Led N.L. in grounding into double plays with 23 in 1995. . . . Career major league grand slams: 2.

Year	Team (League)	Pos.	G	AB	R	H	2B	3B	HR	RBI	Avg.	BB	SO	SB	PO	A	E	Avg.
			BATTING												FIELDING			
1983—	Great Falls (Pio.)	3B-OF	34	111	9	29	4	2	0	9	.261	7	26	1	13	32	9	.833
1984—	Clinton (Midwest)	3B	116	392	41	96	17	2	2	51	.245	34	110	4	68	216	28	.910
1985—	Fresno (California)	3B	131	467	73	132	17	2	4	68	.283	56	95	7	*100	233	18	*.949
1986—	Shreveport (Texas)	3B	121	434	52	107	23	2	5	45	.247	28	83	1	89	*259	25	.933
1987—	Shreveport (Texas)	3B	128	487	66	148	33	3	14	75	.304	26	76	5	*100	*212	22	*.934
1988—	Phoenix (PCL)	OF-3B	131	492	71	151	26	4	7	71	.307	34	91	4	206	100	23	.930
—	San Francisco (N.L.)	OF-3B	7	11	0	1	0	0	0	0	.091	0	3	0	5	0	0	1.000
1989—	Phoenix (PCL)	3-0-1-S-2	61	229	25	65	15	1	7	27	.284	15	48	5	76	76	8	.950
—	San Francisco (N.L.)	3B	3	5	0	1	0	0	0	0	.200	0	1	0	2	1	0	1.000
—	Scran./W.B. (Int'l)■	3B	7	27	4	11	3	1	1	3	.407	0	3	0	8	8	0	1.000
—	Philadelphia (N.L.)	3B	84	299	26	77	15	1	8	43	.258	11	49	3	49	173	22	.910
1990—	Philadelphia (N.L.)	3B-1B-2B	152	561	56	145	20	0	10	57	.258	28	91	4	151	†329	20	.960
1991—	Philadelphia (N.L.)	3B-SS	142	460	34	106	23	1	12	53	.230	16	75	3	88	240	15	.956
1992—	New York (A.L.)■	3B-1B	142	509	52	131	19	2	18	66	.257	28	100	3	125	249	13	.966
1993—	Colorado (N.L.)■	3B-SS	157	573	89	175	*45	2	25	98	.305	43	82	11	123	292	20	.954
1994—	Colorado (N.L.)	3B	113	423	46	122	23	4	10	50	.288	36	71	3	72	216	17	.944
1995—	Philadelphia (N.L.)■	3B	141	529	58	146	30	3	11	85	.276	50	88	5	•104	264	14	.963
American League totals (1 year)			142	509	52	131	19	2	18	66	.257	28	100	3	125	249	13	.966
National League totals (7 years)			799	2861	309	773	156	11	76	386	.270	184	460	29	594	1515	108	.951
Major league totals (8 years)			941	3370	361	904	175	13	94	452	.268	212	560	32	719	1764	121	.954

HAYNES, JIMMY P ORIOLES

PERSONAL: Born September 5, 1972, in La Grange, Ga. . . . 6-4/185. . . . Throws right, bats right. . . . Full name: Jimmy Wayne Haynes.

HIGH SCHOOL: Troup (La Grange, Ga.).

TRANSACTIONS/CAREER NOTES: Selected by Baltimore Orioles organization in seventh round of free-agent draft (June 3, 1991).

Year	Team (League)	W	L	Pct.	ERA	G	GS	CG	ShO	Sv.	IP	H	R	ER	BB	SO
1991—	GC Orioles (GCL)	3	2	.600	1.60	14	8	1	0	2	62	44	27	11	21	67
1992—	Kane Co. (Mid.)	7	11	.389	2.56	24	24	4	0	0	144	131	66	41	45	141
1993—	Frederick (Caro.)	12	8	.600	3.03	27	27	2	1	0	172 1/3	139	73	58	61	174
1994—	Bowie (Eastern)	13	8	.619	2.90	25	25	5	1	0	173 2/3	154	67	56	46	*177
—	Rochester (Int'l)	1	0	1.000	6.75	3	3	0	0	0	13 1/3	20	12	10	6	14
1995—	Rochester (Int'l)	•12	8	.600	3.29	26	25	3	1	0	167	162	77	61	49	*140
—	Baltimore (A.L.)	2	1	.667	2.25	4	3	0	0	0	24	11	6	6	12	22
Major league totals (1 year)		2	1	.667	2.25	4	3	0	0	0	24	11	6	6	12	22

HELFAND, ERIC — C — INDIANS

PERSONAL: Born March 25, 1969, in Erie, Pa. . . . 6-0/195. . . . Bats left, throws right. . . . Full name: Eric James Helfand. . . . Name pronounced HELL-fand.

HIGH SCHOOL: Patrick Henry (San Diego).

COLLEGE: Nebraska, then Arizona State.

TRANSACTIONS/CAREER NOTES: Selected by Seattle Mariners organization in eighth round of free-agent draft (June 2, 1987); did not sign. . . . Selected by Oakland Athletics in second round of free-agent draft (June 4, 1990); pick received as part of compensation for Kansas City Royals signing Type A free-agent P Storm Davis. . . . On Modesto disabled list (June 9-July 30, 1991). . . . Selected by Florida Marlins in first round (18th pick overall) of expansion draft (November 17, 1992). . . . Traded by Marlins with a player to be named later to A's for SS Walt Weiss (November 17, 1992); A's acquired P Scott Baker to complete deal (November 20, 1992). . . . On Tacoma disabled list (June 27-July 14, 1994). . . . Granted free agency (November 22, 1995). . . . Signed by Cleveland Indians organization (December 19, 1995).

STATISTICAL NOTES: Tied for Northwest League lead with 13 passed balls in 1990. . . . Led Southern League catchers with 12 double plays in 1993.

		BATTING												FIELDING			
Year Team (League)	Pos.	G	AB	R	H	2B	3B	HR	RBI	Avg.	BB	SO	SB	PO	A	E	Avg.
1990—S. Oregon (N'west)	C	57	207	29	59	12	0	2	39	.285	20	49	4	383	33	5	.988
1991—Modesto (Calif.)	C	67	242	35	62	15	1	7	38	.256	37	56	0	314	48	8	.978
1992—Modesto (Calif.)	C	72	249	40	72	15	0	10	44	.289	47	46	0	422	47	13	.973
—Huntsville (South.)	C	37	114	13	26	7	0	2	9	.228	5	32	0	180	21	2	.990
1993—Huntsville (South.)	C-OF	100	302	38	69	15	2	10	48	.228	43	78	1	603	63	10	.985
—Oakland (A.L.)	C	8	13	1	3	0	0	0	1	.231	0	1	0	25	5	0	1.000
1994—Tacoma (PCL)	C	57	178	22	36	10	0	2	25	.202	23	37	0	255	27	5	.983
—Oakland (A.L.)	C	7	6	1	1	0	0	0	1	.167	0	1	0	12	2	0	1.000
1995—Edmonton (PCL)	C	19	56	5	12	4	2	1	12	.214	9	10	0	79	11	3	.968
—Oakland (A.L.)	C	38	86	9	14	2	1	0	7	.163	11	25	0	167	13	1	.994
Major league totals (3 years)		53	105	11	18	2	1	0	9	.171	11	27	0	204	20	1	.996

HELLING, RICK — P — RANGERS

PERSONAL: Born December 15, 1970, in Devils Lake, N.D. . . . 6-3/215. . . . Throws right, bats right. . . . Full name: Ricky Allen Helling.

HIGH SCHOOL: Shanley (Fargo, N.D.) and Lakota (N.D.).

JUNIOR COLLEGE: Kiswaukee College (Ill.).

COLLEGE: North Dakota, then Stanford.

TRANSACTIONS/CAREER NOTES: Selected by New York Mets organization in 50th round of free-agent draft (June 4, 1990); did not sign. . . . Selected by Texas Rangers organization in first round (22nd pick overall) of free-agent draft (June 1, 1992).

MISCELLANEOUS: Member of 1992 U.S. Olympic baseball team.

Year Team (League)	W	L	Pct.	ERA	G	GS	CG	ShO	Sv.	IP	H	R	ER	BB	SO
1992—Charlotte (Fla. St.)	1	1	.500	2.29	3	3	0	0	0	19 2/3	13	5	5	4	20
1993—Tulsa (Texas)	12	8	.600	3.60	26	26	2	•2	0	177 1/3	150	76	71	46	*188
—Okla. City (A.A.)	1	1	.500	1.64	2	2	1	0	0	11	5	3	2	3	17
1994—Texas (A.L.)	3	2	.600	5.88	9	9	1	1	0	52	62	34	34	18	25
—Okla. City (A.A.)	4	12	.250	5.78	20	20	2	0	0	132 1/3	153	93	85	43	85
1995—Texas (A.L.)	0	2	.000	6.57	3	3	0	0	0	12 1/3	17	11	9	8	5
—Okla. City (A.A.)	4	8	.333	5.33	20	20	3	0	0	109 2/3	132	73	65	41	80
Major league totals (2 years)	3	4	.429	6.02	12	12	1	1	0	64 1/3	79	45	43	26	30

HEMOND, SCOTT — C

PERSONAL: Born November 18, 1965, in Taunton, Mass. . . . 6-0/215. . . . Bats right, throws right. . . . Full name: Scott Matthew Hemond. . . . Name pronounced HEE-mund.

HIGH SCHOOL: Dunedin (Fla.).

COLLEGE: South Florida.

TRANSACTIONS/CAREER NOTES: Selected by Kansas City Royals organization in fifth round of free-agent draft (June 6, 1983); did not sign. . . . Selected by Oakland Athletics organization in first round (12th pick overall) of free-agent draft (June 2, 1986). . . . On Tacoma disabled list (May 18-July 6, 1990). . . . On Oakland disabled list (May 10-August 6, 1992); included rehabilitation assignments to Huntsville (June 5-15) and Tacoma (July 17-August 6). . . . Claimed on waivers by Chicago White Sox (August 6, 1992). . . . Claimed on waivers by A's (March 29, 1993). . . . Granted free agency (December 23, 1994). . . . Signed by St. Louis Cardinals (April 7, 1995). . . . Granted free agency (December 21, 1995).

HONORS: Named catcher on The Sporting News college All-America team (1986).

STATISTICAL NOTES: Led Southern League third basemen with 299 assists and 427 total chances in 1988.

		BATTING												FIELDING			
Year Team (League)	Pos.	G	AB	R	H	2B	3B	HR	RBI	Avg.	BB	SO	SB	PO	A	E	Avg.
1986—Madison (Midwest)	C	22	85	9	26	2	0	2	13	.306	5	19	2	121	11	2	.985
1987—Madison (Midwest)	C-OF	90	343	60	99	21	4	8	52	.289	40	79	27	408	53	16	.966
—Huntsville (South.)	C-3B	33	110	10	20	3	1	1	8	.182	4	30	5	161	32	6	.970
1988—Huntsville (South.)	3B-C	133	482	51	106	22	4	9	53	.220	48	114	29	93	†302	38	.912
1989—Huntsville (South.)	3B-C	132	490	89	130	26	6	5	62	.265	62	77	45	272	198	31	.938
—Oakland (A.L.)	DH-PR	4	0	2	0	0	0	0	0	...	0	0	0	...	...	...	...
1990—Tacoma (PCL)	2-C-3-S	72	218	32	53	11	0	8	35	.243	24	52	11	138	177	12	.963
—Oakland (A.L.)	3B-2B	7	13	0	2	0	0	0	1	.154	0	5	0	2	5	0	1.000
1991—Tacoma (PCL)	2-C-3-S	92	327	50	89	19	5	3	31	.272	39	69	11	280	177	12	.974
—Oakland (A.L.)	C-2-DH-3-S	23	23	4	5	0	0	0	0	.217	1	7	1	27	14	1	.976
1992—Oakland (A.L.)	C-S-O-3-DH	17	27	7	6	1	0	0	1	.222	3	7	1	32	5	1	.974
—Huntsville (South.)	C-2B	9	27	3	9	0	0	0	2	.333	4	8	2	22	5	0	1.000
—Tacoma (PCL)	2B-C	8	33	6	8	3	0	0	3	.242	5	6	1	35	16	2	.962
—Chicago (A.L.)■	DH-O-3-C	8	13	1	3	1	0	0	1	.231	1	6	0	2	1	0	1.000

Year	Team (League)	Pos.	G	AB	R	H	2B	3B	HR	RBI	Avg.	BB	SO	SB	PO	A	E	Avg.
				BATTING											FIELDING			
1993—	Oakland (A.L.)■	C-O-DH-2-1	91	215	31	55	16	0	6	26	.256	32	55	14	404	39	4	.991
1994—	Oakland (A.L.)	C-2-3-1-DH-0	91	198	23	44	11	0	3	20	.222	16	51	7	245	93	6	.983
1995—	St. Louis (N.L.)■	C-2B	57	118	11	17	1	0	3	9	.144	12	31	0	189	22	3	.986
—	Louisville (A.A.)	C	1	3	1	0	0	0	0	0	.000	0	0	0	6	0	0	1.000
American League totals (6 years)			241	489	68	115	29	0	9	49	.235	53	131	23	712	157	12	.986
National League totals (1 year)			57	118	11	17	1	0	3	9	.144	12	31	0	189	22	3	.986
Major league totals (7 years)			298	607	79	132	30	0	12	58	.217	65	162	23	901	179	15	.986

HENDERSON, RICKEY — OF — PADRES

PERSONAL: Born December 25, 1958, in Chicago. . . . 5-10/190. . . . Bats right, throws left. . . . Full name: Rickey Henley Henderson.

HIGH SCHOOL: Technical (Oakland, Calif.).

TRANSACTIONS/CAREER NOTES: Selected by Oakland Athletics organization in fourth round of free-agent draft (June 8, 1976). . . . Traded by A's with P Bert Bradley and cash to New York Yankees for OF Stan Javier, P Jay Howell, P Jose Rijo, P Eric Plunk and P Tim Birtsas (December 5, 1984). . . . On New York disabled list (March 30-April 22, 1985); included rehabilitation assignment to Fort Lauderdale (April 19-22). . . . On disabled list (June 5-29 and July 26-September 1, 1987). . . . Traded by Yankees to A's for P Greg Cadaret, P Eric Plunk and OF Luis Polonia (June 21, 1989). . . . Granted free agency (November 13, 1989). . . . Re-signed by A's (November 28, 1989). . . . On disabled list (April 12-27, 1991; May 28-June 17 and June 30-July 16, 1992). . . . Traded by A's to Toronto Blue Jays for P Steve Karsay and a player to be named later (July 31, 1993); A's acquired OF Jose Herrera to complete deal (August 6, 1993). . . . Granted free agency (October 29, 1993). . . . Signed by A's (December 17, 1993). . . . On disabled list (May 11-27, 1994). . . . Granted free agency (October 30, 1995). . . . Signed by San Diego Padres (December 29, 1995).

RECORDS: Holds major league career records for most stolen bases—1,149; and most home runs as leadoff batter—67. . . . Holds major league single-season records for most stolen bases—130 (1982); and most times caught stealing—42 (1982). . . . Holds major league record for most years leading league in stolen bases—11. . . . Holds A.L. career record for most times caught stealing—265. . . . Holds A.L. single-season record for most home runs as leadoff batter—9 (1986). . . . Holds A.L. records for most years with 50 or more stolen bases—11; and most consecutive years with 50 or more stolen bases—7 (1980-86). . . . Shares A.L. single-season record for fewest times caught stealing (50 or more stolen bases)—8 (1993). . . . Shares A.L. record for most stolen bases in two consecutive games—7 (July 3 [4], 15 innings, and 4 [3], 1983).

HONORS: Named outfielder on The Sporting News A.L. All-Star team (1981, 1985 and 1990). . . . Named outfielder on The Sporting News A.L. Silver Slugger team (1981, 1985 and 1990). . . . Won A.L. Gold Glove as outfielder (1981). . . . Won The Sporting News Silver Shoe Award (1982). . . . Won The Sporting News Golden Shoe Award (1983). . . . Named A.L. Most Valuable Player by Baseball Writers' Association of America (1990).

STATISTICAL NOTES: Led California League in caught stealing with 22 in 1977. . . . Led Eastern League in caught stealing with 28 in 1978. . . . Led Eastern League outfielders with four double plays in 1978. . . . Led A.L. in caught stealing with 26 in 1980, 22 in 1981, 42 in 1982, 19 in 1983 and tied for lead with 18 in 1986. . . . Led A.L. outfielders with 341 total chances in 1981. . . . Tied for A.L. lead in double plays by outfielder with five in 1988. . . . Led A.L. with 77 stolen bases and 126 bases on balls in 1989. . . . Tied for A.L. lead with 113 runs scored in 1989. . . . Led A.L. with .439 on-base percentage in 1990. . . . Career major league grand slams: 1.

Year	Team (League)	Pos.	G	AB	R	H	2B	3B	HR	RBI	Avg.	BB	SO	SB	PO	A	E	Avg.
				BATTING											FIELDING			
1976—	Boise (Northwest)	OF	46	140	34	47	13	2	3	23	.336	33	32	29	99	3	*12	.895
1977—	Modesto (Calif.)	OF	134	481	120	166	18	4	11	69	.345	104	67	*95	278	15	*20	.936
1978—	Jersey City (East.)	OF	133	455	81	141	14	4	0	34	.310	83	67	*81	305	•15	7	.979
1979—	Ogden (Pac. Coast)	OF	71	259	66	80	11	8	3	26	.309	53	41	44	149	6	6	.963
—	Oakland (A.L.)	OF	89	351	49	96	13	3	1	26	.274	34	39	33	215	5	6	.973
1980—	Oakland (A.L.)	OF-DH	158	591	111	179	22	4	9	53	.303	117	54	*100	407	15	7	.984
1981—	Oakland (A.L.)	OF	108	423	*89	*135	18	7	6	35	.319	64	68	*56	*327	7	7	.979
1982—	Oakland (A.L.)	OF-DH	149	536	119	143	24	4	10	51	.267	*116	94	*130	379	2	9	.977
1983—	Oakland (A.L.)	OF-DH	145	513	105	150	25	7	9	48	.292	*103	80	*108	349	9	3	.992
1984—	Oakland (A.L.)	OF	142	502	113	147	27	4	16	58	.293	86	81	*66	341	7	11	.969
1985—	Fort Lauder. (FSL)■	OF	3	6	5	1	0	1	0	3	.167	5	2	1	6	0	0	1.000
—	New York (A.L.)	OF-DH	143	547	*146	172	28	5	24	72	.314	99	65	*80	439	7	9	.980
1986—	New York (A.L.)	OF-DH	153	608	*130	160	31	5	28	74	.263	89	81	*87	426	4	6	.986
1987—	New York (A.L.)	OF-DH	95	358	78	104	17	3	17	37	.291	80	52	41	189	3	4	.980
1988—	New York (A.L.)	OF-DH	140	554	118	169	30	2	6	50	.305	82	54	*93	320	7	12	.965
1989—	New York (A.L.)	OF	65	235	41	58	13	1	3	22	.247	56	29	25	144	3	1	.993
—	Oakland (A.L.)■	OF-DH	85	306	§72	90	13	2	9	35	.294	§70	39	§52	191	3	3	.985
1990—	Oakland (A.L.)	OF-DH	136	489	*119	159	33	3	28	61	.325	97	60	*65	289	5	5	.983
1991—	Oakland (A.L.)	OF-DH	134	470	105	126	17	1	18	57	.268	98	73	*58	249	10	8	.970
1992—	Oakland (A.L.)	OF-DH	117	396	77	112	18	3	15	46	.283	95	56	48	231	9	4	.984
1993—	Oakland (A.L.)	OF-DH	90	318	77	104	19	1	17	47	.327	85	46	31	182	5	5	.974
—	Toronto (A.L.)■	OF	44	163	37	35	3	1	4	12	.215	35	19	22	76	1	2	.975
1994—	Oakland (A.L.)■	OF-DH	87	296	66	77	13	0	6	20	.260	72	45	22	166	4	4	.977
1995—	Oakland (A.L.)	OF-DH	112	407	67	122	31	1	9	54	.300	72	66	32	162	5	2	.988
Major league totals (17 years)			2192	8063	1719	2338	395	57	235	858	.290	1550	1101	1149	5082	111	108	.980

DIVISION SERIES RECORD

Year	Team (League)	Pos.	G	AB	R	H	2B	3B	HR	RBI	Avg.	BB	SO	SB	PO	A	E	Avg.
				BATTING											FIELDING			
1981—	Oakland (A.L.)	OF	3	11	3	2	0	0	0	0	.182	2	0	2	8	0	0	1.000

CHAMPIONSHIP SERIES RECORD

NOTES: Named A.L. Championship Series Most Valuable Player (1989). . . . Holds career record for most stolen bases—16. . . . Holds single-series record for most stolen bases—8 (1989). . . . Holds single-game record for most stolen bases—4 (October 4, 1989). . . . Shares records for most at-bats in one inning—2; most hits in one inning—2; most singles in one inning—2 (October 6, 1990, ninth inning); and most stolen bases in one inning—2 (October 4, 1989, fourth and seventh innings). . . . Shares single-series record for most runs—8 (1989). . . . Shares A.L. career record for most bases on balls received—17. . . . Shares A.L. single-game record for most at-bats—6 (October 5, 1993).

Year	Team (League)	Pos.	G	AB	R	H	2B	3B	HR	RBI	Avg.	BB	SO	SB	PO	A	E	Avg.
			BATTING												FIELDING			
1981—	Oakland (A.L.)	OF	3	11	0	4	2	1	0	1	.364	1	2	2	6	0	1	.857
1989—	Oakland (A.L.)	OF	5	15	8	6	1	1	2	5	.400	7	0	8	13	0	1	.929
1990—	Oakland (A.L.)	OF	4	17	1	5	0	0	0	3	.294	1	2	2	10	0	0	1.000
1992—	Oakland (A.L.)	OF	6	23	5	6	0	0	0	1	.261	4	4	2	15	0	3	.833
1993—	Toronto (A.L.)	OF	6	25	4	3	2	0	0	0	.120	4	5	2	9	0	1	.900
Championship series totals (5 years)			24	91	18	24	5	2	2	10	.264	17	13	16	53	0	6	.898

WORLD SERIES RECORD

NOTES: Shares single-game record for most at-bats—6 (October 28, 1989). . . . Member of World Series championship teams (1989 and 1993).

Year	Team (League)	Pos.	G	AB	R	H	2B	3B	HR	RBI	Avg.	BB	SO	SB	PO	A	E	Avg.
			BATTING												FIELDING			
1989—	Oakland (A.L.)	OF	4	19	4	9	1	2	1	3	.474	2	2	3	9	0	0	1.000
1990—	Oakland (A.L.)	OF	4	15	2	5	2	0	1	1	.333	3	4	3	12	1	0	1.000
1993—	Toronto (A.L.)	OF	6	22	6	5	2	0	0	2	.227	5	2	1	8	0	0	1.000
World Series totals (3 years)			14	56	12	19	5	2	2	6	.339	10	8	7	29	1	0	1.000

ALL-STAR GAME RECORD

NOTES: Shares single-game record for most singles—3 (July 13, 1982).

Year	League	Pos.	AB	R	H	2B	3B	HR	RBI	Avg.	BB	SO	SB	PO	A	E	Avg.
			BATTING											FIELDING			
1980—	American	OF	1	0	0	0	0	0	0	.000	0	1	0	0	0	0	...
1982—	American	OF	4	1	3	0	0	0	0	.750	0	0	1	3	0	1	.750
1983—	American	OF	1	0	0	0	0	0	1	.000	0	0	0	0	0	0	...
1984—	American	OF	2	0	0	0	0	0	0	.000	0	0	0	0	0	0	...
1985—	American	OF	3	1	1	0	0	0	0	.333	0	1	1	1	0	0	1.000
1986—	American	OF	3	0	0	0	0	0	0	.000	0	1	0	2	0	0	1.000
1987—	American	OF	3	0	1	0	0	0	0	.333	0	0	0	0	0	0	...
1988—	American	OF	2	0	1	0	0	0	0	.500	1	0	0	1	0	0	1.000
1990—	American	OF	3	0	0	0	0	0	0	.000	0	1	0	2	0	0	1.000
1991—	American	OF	2	1	1	0	0	0	0	.500	0	0	0	0	0	0	...
All-Star Game totals (10 years)			24	3	7	0	0	0	1	.292	1	4	2	9	0	1	.900

HENDERSON, ROD — P — EXPOS

PERSONAL: Born March 11, 1971, in Greensburg, Ky. . . . 6-4/193. . . . Throws right, bats right. . . . Full name: Rodney Wood Henderson.
HIGH SCHOOL: Glasgow (Ky.).
COLLEGE: Kentucky.
TRANSACTIONS/CAREER NOTES: Selected by Montreal Expos organization in second round of free-agent draft (June 1, 1992). . . . On disabled list (June 19, 1992-remainder of season). . . . On Montreal disabled list (July 18, 1995-remainder of season).

Year	Team (League)	W	L	Pct.	ERA	G	GS	CG	ShO	Sv.	IP	H	R	ER	BB	SO
1992—	Jamestown (NYP)	0	0	...	6.00	1	1	0	0	0	3	2	3	2	5	2
1993—	WP Beach (FSL)	12	7	.632	2.90	22	22	1	1	0	143	110	50	46	44	127
—	Harrisburg (East.)	5	0	1.000	1.82	5	5	0	0	0	29 2/3	20	10	6	15	25
1994—	Harrisburg (East.)	2	0	1.000	1.50	2	2	0	0	0	12	5	2	2	4	16
—	Montreal (N.L.)	0	1	.000	9.45	3	2	0	0	0	6 2/3	9	9	7	7	3
—	Ottawa (Int'l)	6	9	.400	4.62	23	21	0	0	1	122 2/3	123	67	63	67	100
1995—	Harrisburg (East.)	3	6	.333	4.31	12	12	0	0	0	56 1/3	51	28	27	18	53
Major league totals (1 year)		0	1	.000	9.45	3	2	0	0	0	6 2/3	9	9	7	7	3

HENKE, TOM — P

PERSONAL: Born December 21, 1957, in Kansas City, Mo. . . . 6-5/225. . . . Throws right, bats right. . . . Full name: Thomas Anthony Henke. . . . Name pronounced HEN-kee.
HIGH SCHOOL: Blair Oaks (Jefferson City, Mo.).
COLLEGE: East Central College (Mo.).
TRANSACTIONS/CAREER NOTES: Selected by Seattle Mariners organization in 20th round of free-agent draft (June 5, 1979); did not sign. . . . Selected by Chicago Cubs organization in secondary phase of free-agent draft (January 8, 1980); did not sign. . . . Selected by Texas Rangers organization in secondary phase of free-agent draft (June 3, 1980). . . . Selected by Toronto Blue Jays organization in player compensation pool draft (January 24, 1985); pick received as compensation for Rangers signing Type A free-agent DH Cliff Johnson (December 5, 1984). . . . On Toronto disabled list (April 12-May 17, 1991); included rehabilitation assignment to Dunedin but did not pitch (May 13-17). . . . Granted free agency (October 27, 1992). . . . Signed by Rangers (December 15, 1992). . . . On disabled list (May 17-June 17, 1994). . . . Granted free agency (October 28, 1994). . . . Signed by St. Louis Cardinals (December 12, 1994). . . . Granted free agency (November 1, 1995).
HONORS: Named International League Pitcher of the Year (1985).

Year	Team (League)	W	L	Pct.	ERA	G	GS	CG	ShO	Sv.	IP	H	R	ER	BB	SO
1980—	GC Rangers (GCL)	3	3	.500	0.95	8	4	1	1	0	38	33	11	4	12	34
—	Asheville (S. Atl.)	0	2	.000	7.83	5	5	0	0	0	23	25	21	20	20	19
1981—	Asheville (S. Atl.)	8	6	.571	2.93	28	8	0	0	3	92	77	36	30	35	67
—	Tulsa (Texas)	4	3	.571	3.94	15	0	0	0	1	32	31	16	14	14	37
1982—	Tulsa (Texas)	3	6	.333	2.67	*52	1	0	0	14	87 2/3	69	35	26	40	100
—	Texas (A.L.)	1	0	1.000	1.15	8	0	0	0	0	15 2/3	14	2	2	8	9
1983—	Okla. City (A.A.)	9	6	.600	3.01	47	0	0	0	2	77 2/3	71	33	26	33	90
—	Texas (A.L.)	1	0	1.000	3.38	8	0	0	0	1	16	16	6	6	4	17
1984—	Texas (A.L.)	1	1	.500	6.35	25	0	0	0	2	28 1/3	36	21	20	20	25
—	Okla. City (A.A.)	6	2	.750	2.64	39	0	0	0	7	64 2/3	59	21	19	25	65
1985—	Syracuse (Int'l)■	2	1	.667	0.88	39	0	0	0	•18	51 1/3	13	5	5	18	60

Year Team (League)	W	L	Pct.	ERA	G	GS	CG	ShO	Sv.	IP	H	R	ER	BB	SO
—Toronto (A.L.)	3	3	.500	2.03	28	0	0	0	13	40	29	12	9	8	42
1986—Toronto (A.L.)	9	5	.643	3.35	63	0	0	0	27	91 1/3	63	39	34	32	118
1987—Toronto (A.L.)	0	6	.000	2.49	72	0	0	0	*34	94	62	27	26	25	128
1988—Toronto (A.L.)	4	4	.500	2.91	52	0	0	0	25	68	60	23	22	24	66
1989—Toronto (A.L.)	8	3	.727	1.92	64	0	0	0	20	89	66	20	19	25	116
1990—Toronto (A.L.)	2	4	.333	2.17	61	0	0	0	32	74 2/3	58	18	18	19	75
1991—Toronto (A.L.)	0	2	.000	2.32	49	0	0	0	32	50 1/3	33	13	13	11	53
1992—Toronto (A.L.)	3	2	.600	2.26	57	0	0	0	34	55 2/3	40	19	14	22	46
1993—Texas (A.L.)■	5	5	.500	2.91	66	0	0	0	40	74 1/3	55	25	24	27	79
1994—Texas (A.L.)	3	6	.333	3.79	37	0	0	0	15	38	33	16	16	12	39
1995—St. Louis (N.L.)■	1	1	.500	1.82	52	0	0	0	36	54 1/3	42	11	11	18	48
A.L. totals (13 years)	40	41	.494	2.73	590	0	0	0	275	735 1/3	565	241	223	237	813
N.L. totals (1 year)	1	1	.500	1.82	52	0	0	0	36	54 1/3	42	11	11	18	48
Major league totals (14 years)	41	42	.494	2.67	642	0	0	0	311	789 2/3	607	252	234	255	861

CHAMPIONSHIP SERIES RECORD

Year Team (League)	W	L	Pct.	ERA	G	GS	CG	ShO	Sv.	IP	H	R	ER	BB	SO
1985—Toronto (A.L.)	2	0	1.000	4.26	3	0	0	0	0	6 1/3	5	3	3	4	4
1989—Toronto (A.L.)	0	0	...	0.00	3	0	0	0	0	2 2/3	0	0	0	0	3
1991—Toronto (A.L.)	0	0	...	0.00	2	0	0	0	0	2 2/3	0	0	0	1	5
1992—Toronto (A.L.)	0	0	...	0.00	4	0	0	0	3	4 2/3	4	0	0	2	2
Champ. series totals (4 years)	2	0	1.000	1.65	12	0	0	0	3	16 1/3	9	3	3	7	14

WORLD SERIES RECORD

NOTES: Member of World Series championship team (1992).

Year Team (League)	W	L	Pct.	ERA	G	GS	CG	ShO	Sv.	IP	H	R	ER	BB	SO
1992—Toronto (A.L.)	0	0	...	2.70	3	0	0	0	2	3 1/3	2	1	1	2	1

ALL-STAR GAME RECORD

Year League	W	L	Pct.	ERA	GS	CG	ShO	Sv.	IP	H	R	ER	BB	SO
1987—American	0	0	...	0.00	0	0	0	0	2 2/3	2	0	0	0	1
1995—National	0	0	...	0.00	0	0	0	0	2/3	0	0	0	0	1
All-Star totals (2 years)	0	0	...	0.00	0	0	0	0	3 1/3	2	0	0	0	2

HENNEMAN, MIKE P RANGERS

PERSONAL: Born December 11, 1961, in St. Charles, Mo. . . . 6-4/205. . . . Throws right, bats right. . . . Full name: Michael Alan Henneman. . . . Name pronounced HENN-uh-min.

HIGH SCHOOL: St. Pius X (Festus, Mo.).

COLLEGE: Oklahoma State.

TRANSACTIONS/CAREER NOTES: Selected by Toronto Blue Jays organization in 27th round of free-agent draft (June 7, 1982); did not sign. . . . Selected by Philadelphia Phillies organization in secondary phase of free-agent draft (June 6, 1983); did not sign. . . . Selected by Detroit Tigers organization in fourth round of free-agent draft (June 4, 1984). . . . On disabled list (May 22-June 6, 1988; April 24-May 15, 1989; and July 19-August 8, 1994). . . . Traded by Tigers to Houston Astros for a player to be named later (August 10, 1995); Tigers acquired 3B/OF Phil Nevin to complete deal (August 15, 1995). . . . Granted free agency (November 1, 1995). . . . Signed by Texas Rangers (December 22, 1995).

HONORS: Named A.L. Rookie Pitcher of the Year by The Sporting News (1987).

MISCELLANEOUS: Struck out in only appearance as pinch-hitter with Detroit (1987).

Year Team (League)	W	L	Pct.	ERA	G	GS	CG	ShO	Sv.	IP	H	R	ER	BB	SO
1984—Birmingham (Sou.)	4	2	.667	2.43	29	1	0	0	6	59 1/3	48	22	16	33	39
1985—Birmingham (Sou.)	3	5	.375	5.76	46	0	0	0	9	70 1/3	88	50	45	28	40
1986—Nashville (A.A.)	2	5	.286	2.95	31	0	0	0	1	58	57	27	19	23	39
1987—Toledo (Int'l)	1	1	.500	1.47	11	0	0	0	4	18 1/3	5	3	3	3	19
—Detroit (A.L.)	11	3	.786	2.98	55	0	0	0	7	96 2/3	86	36	32	30	75
1988—Detroit (A.L.)	9	6	.600	1.87	65	0	0	0	22	91 1/3	72	23	19	24	58
1989—Detroit (A.L.)	11	4	.733	3.70	60	0	0	0	8	90	84	46	37	51	69
1990—Detroit (A.L.)	8	6	.571	3.05	69	0	0	0	22	94 1/3	90	36	32	33	50
1991—Detroit (A.L.)	10	2	.833	2.88	60	0	0	0	21	84 1/3	81	29	27	34	61
1992—Detroit (A.L.)	2	6	.250	3.96	60	0	0	0	24	77 1/3	75	36	34	20	58
1993—Detroit (A.L.)	5	3	.625	2.64	63	0	0	0	24	71 2/3	69	28	21	32	58
1994—Detroit (A.L.)	1	3	.250	5.19	30	0	0	0	8	34 2/3	43	27	20	17	27
1995—Detroit (A.L.)	0	1	.000	1.53	29	0	0	0	18	29 1/3	24	5	5	9	24
—Houston (N.L.)■	0	1	.000	3.00	21	0	0	0	8	21	21	7	7	4	19
A.L. totals (9 years)	57	34	.626	3.05	491	0	0	0	154	669 2/3	624	266	227	250	480
N.L. totals (1 year)	0	1	.000	3.00	21	0	0	0	8	21	21	7	7	4	19
Major league totals (9 years)	57	35	.620	3.05	512	0	0	0	162	690 2/3	645	273	234	254	499

CHAMPIONSHIP SERIES RECORD

Year Team (League)	W	L	Pct.	ERA	G	GS	CG	ShO	Sv.	IP	H	R	ER	BB	SO
1987—Detroit (A.L.)	1	0	1.000	10.80	3	0	0	0	0	5	6	6	6	6	3

ALL-STAR GAME RECORD

Year League	W	L	Pct.	ERA	GS	CG	ShO	Sv.	IP	H	R	ER	BB	SO
1989—American						Did not play.								

HENRIQUEZ, OSCAR P ASTROS

PERSONAL: Born January 28, 1974, in LaGuaria, Venezuela. . . . 6-6/220. . . . Throws right, bats right. . . . Full name: Oscar Eduardo Henriquez.

TRANSACTIONS/CAREER NOTES: Signed as non-drafted free agent by Houston Astros organization (May 28, 1991). . . . On disabled list

(June 15, 1994-remainder of season).

Year	Team (League)	W	L	Pct.	ERA	G	GS	CG	ShO	Sv.	IP	H	R	ER	BB	SO
1992—		Dominican League statistics unavailable.														
1993—	Asheville (S. Atl.)	9	10	.474	4.44	27	26	2	1	0	150	154	95	74	70	117
1994—		Did not play.														
1995—	Kissimmee (Florida State)	3	4	.429	5.04	20	0	0	0	1	44 2/3	40	29	25	30	36

HENRY, BUTCH — P — RED SOX

PERSONAL: Born October 7, 1968, in El Paso, Tex. . . . 6-1/205. . . . Throws left, bats left. . . . Full name: Floyd Bluford Henry III.

HIGH SCHOOL: Eastwood (El Paso, Tex.).

TRANSACTIONS/CAREER NOTES: Selected by Cincinnati Reds organization in 15th round of free-agent draft (June 2, 1987). . . . On disabled list (April 28, 1989-remainder of season). . . . Traded by Reds with C Terry McGriff and P Keith Kaiser to Houston Astros (September 7, 1990), completing deal in which Astros traded 2B Bill Doran to Reds for three players to be named later (August 30, 1990). . . . Selected by Colorado Rockies in second round (36th pick overall) of expansion draft (November 17, 1992). . . . Traded by Rockies to Montreal Expos for P Kent Bottenfield (July 16, 1993). . . . On disabled list (August 16, 1995-remainder of season). . . . Claimed on waivers by Boston Red Sox (October 13, 1995).

Year	Team (League)	W	L	Pct.	ERA	G	GS	CG	ShO	Sv.	IP	H	R	ER	BB	SO
1987—	Billings (Pioneer)	4	0	1.000	4.63	9	5	0	0	1	35	37	21	18	12	38
1988—	Ced. Rap. (Midw.)	16	2	*.889	2.26	27	27	1	1	0	187	144	59	47	56	163
1989—	Chattanooga (Sou.)	1	3	.250	3.42	7	7	0	0	0	26 1/3	22	12	10	12	19
1990—	Chattanooga (Sou.)	8	8	.500	4.21	24	22	2	0	0	143 1/3	151	74	67	58	95
1991—	Tucson (Pac. Coast)■	10	11	.476	4.80	27	27	2	0	0	153 2/3	192	92	82	42	97
1992—	Houston (N.L.)	6	9	.400	4.02	28	28	2	1	0	165 2/3	185	81	74	41	96
1993—	Colorado (N.L.)■	2	8	.200	6.59	20	15	1	0	0	84 2/3	117	66	62	24	39
—	Montreal (N.L.)■	1	1	.500	3.93	10	1	0	0	0	18 1/3	18	10	8	4	8
—	Ottawa (Int'l)	3	1	.750	3.73	5	5	1	0	0	31 1/3	34	15	13	1	25
1994—	Ottawa (Int'l)	2	0	1.000	0.00	2	2	1	1	0	14	11	0	0	2	11
—	Montreal (N.L.)	8	3	.727	2.43	24	15	0	0	1	107 1/3	97	30	29	20	70
1995—	Montreal (N.L.)	7	9	.438	2.84	21	21	1	1	0	126 2/3	133	47	40	28	60
Major league totals (4 years)		24	30	.444	3.81	103	80	4	2	1	502 2/3	550	234	213	117	273

HENRY, DOUG — P — METS

PERSONAL: Born December 10, 1963, in Sacramento, Calif. . . . 6-4/205. . . . Throws right, bats right. . . . Full name: Richard Douglas Henry.

HIGH SCHOOL: Tennyson (Hayward, Calif.).

COLLEGE: Arizona State.

TRANSACTIONS/CAREER NOTES: Selected by New York Mets organization in 16th round of free-agent draft (June 7, 1982); did not sign. . . . Selected by Milwaukee Brewers organization in eighth round of free-agent draft (June 3, 1985). . . . On El Paso disabled list (April 5-June 5 and June 18-August 9, 1989). . . . On Milwaukee disabled list (March 25-April 26, 1994); included rehabilitation assignments to El Paso (April 8-22) and New Orleans (April 22-26). . . . Traded by Brewers to New York Mets for two players to be named later (November 30, 1994); Brewers acquired C Javier Gonzales (December 6, 1994) and IF Fernando Vina (December 22, 1994) to complete deal.

STATISTICAL NOTES: Combined with Michael Ignasiak in 6-3 no-hit victory for Stockton against San Jose (April 15, 1990, first game).

Year	Team (League)	W	L	Pct.	ERA	G	GS	CG	ShO	Sv.	IP	H	R	ER	BB	SO
1986—	Beloit (Midwest)	7	8	.467	4.65	27	24	4	1	1	143 1/3	153	95	74	56	115
1987—	Beloit (Midwest)	8	9	.471	4.88	31	15	1	0	2	132 2/3	145	83	72	51	106
1988—	Stockton (Calif.)	7	1	.875	1.78	23	1	1	0	7	70 2/3	46	19	14	31	71
—	El Paso (Texas)	4	0	1.000	3.15	14	3	3	1	0	45 2/3	33	16	16	19	50
1989—	Stockton (Calif.)	0	1	.000	0.00	4	3	0	0	0	11	9	4	0	3	9
—	El Paso (Texas)	0	0	...	13.50	1	1	0	0	0	2	3	3	3	3	2
1990—	Stockton (Calif.)	1	0	1.000	1.13	4	0	0	0	1	8	4	1	1	3	13
—	El Paso (Texas)	1	0	1.000	2.93	15	0	0	0	9	30 2/3	31	13	10	11	25
—	Denver (Am. Assoc.)	2	3	.400	4.44	27	0	0	0	8	50 2/3	46	26	25	27	54
1991—	Denver (Am. Assoc.)	3	2	.600	2.18	32	0	0	0	14	57 2/3	47	16	14	20	47
—	Milwaukee (A.L.)	2	1	.667	1.00	32	0	0	0	15	36	16	4	4	14	28
1992—	Milwaukee (A.L.)	1	4	.200	4.02	68	0	0	0	29	65	64	34	29	24	52
1993—	Milwaukee (A.L.)	4	4	.500	5.56	54	0	0	0	17	55	67	37	34	25	38
1994—	El Paso (Texas)	1	0	1.000	5.40	6	0	0	0	3	8 1/3	7	5	5	2	10
—	New Orleans (A.A.)	1	0	1.000	1.84	10	0	0	0	3	14 2/3	5	3	3	10	10
—	Milwaukee (A.L.)	2	3	.400	4.60	25	0	0	0	0	31 1/3	32	17	16	23	20
1995—	New York (N.L.)■	3	6	.333	2.96	51	0	0	0	4	67	48	23	22	25	62
A.L. totals (4 years)		9	12	.429	3.99	179	0	0	0	61	187 1/3	179	92	83	86	138
N.L. totals (1 year)		3	6	.333	2.96	51	0	0	0	4	67	48	23	22	25	62
Major league totals (5 years)		12	18	.400	3.72	230	0	0	0	65	254 1/3	227	115	105	111	200

HENRY, DWAYNE — P

PERSONAL: Born February 16, 1962, in Elkton, Md. . . . 6-3/230. . . . Throws right, bats right. . . . Full name: Dwayne Allen Henry.

HIGH SCHOOL: Middletown (Del.).

TRANSACTIONS/CAREER NOTES: Selected by Texas Rangers organization in second round of free-agent draft (June 3, 1980). . . . On disabled list (May 4, 1982-remainder of season). . . . On Tulsa disabled list (April 8-July 9, 1983). . . . On Texas disabled list (May 31-July 8, 1986); included rehabilitation assignment to Oklahoma City (June 18-July 8). . . . Traded by Rangers to Atlanta Braves for P David Miller and cash (March 30, 1989). . . . Released by Braves organization (November 13, 1990). . . . Signed by Tucson, Houston Astros organization (March 29, 1991). . . . Claimed on waivers by Cincinnati Reds (November 26, 1991). . . . Contract sold by Reds to Seattle Mariners (April 13, 1993). . . . On disabled list (July 3-August 2, 1993). . . . Released by Mariners (October 4, 1993). . . . Signed by Chunichi Dragons of Japan Central League (December 6, 1993). . . . Signed as free agent by Toledo, Detroit Tigers organization (March 19, 1995). . . . Released by Tigers (October 12, 1995).

Year	Team (League)	W	L	Pct.	ERA	G	GS	CG	ShO	Sv.	IP	H	R	ER	BB	SO
1980—	GC Rangers (GCL)	5	1	.833	2.67	11	11	1	1	0	54	36	23	16	28	47
1981—	Asheville (S. Atl.)	8	7	.533	4.43	25	25	1	0	0	134	120	81	66	58	86
1982—	Burlington (Midw.)	2	0	1.000	0.00	4	4	0	0	0	18 2/3	6	0	0	6	25
1983—	Tulsa (Texas)	0	0	...	5.79	9	2	0	0	1	14	16	14	9	19	14
—	GC Rangers (GCL)	0	0	...	4.00	3	2	0	0	0	9	10	6	4	1	11
1984—	Tulsa (Texas)	5	8	.385	3.39	33	12	1	1	8	85	65	42	32	60	79
—	Texas (A.L.)	0	1	.000	8.31	3	0	0	0	0	4 1/3	5	4	4	7	2
1985—	Tulsa (Texas)	7	6	.538	2.66	34	11	0	0	9	81 1/3	51	32	24	44	97
—	Texas (A.L.)	2	2	.500	2.57	16	0	0	0	3	21	16	7	6	7	20
1986—	Texas (A.L.)	1	0	1.000	4.66	19	0	0	0	0	19 1/3	14	11	10	2	17
—	Okla. City (A.A.)	2	1	.667	5.89	28	1	0	0	3	44 1/3	51	30	29	27	41
1987—	Okla. City (A.A.)	4	4	.500	4.96	30	8	0	0	3	69	66	39	38	50	55
—	Texas (A.L.)	0	0	...	9.00	5	0	0	0	0	10	12	10	10	9	7
1988—	Okla. City (A.A.)	5	5	.500	5.59	46	3	0	0	7	75 2/3	57	51	47	54	98
—	Texas (A.L.)	0	1	.000	8.71	11	0	0	0	1	10 1/3	15	10	10	9	10
1989—	Richmond (Int'l)■	11	5	.688	2.44	41	6	0	0	1	84 2/3	43	28	23	61	101
—	Atlanta (N.L.)	0	2	.000	4.26	12	0	0	0	1	12 2/3	12	6	6	5	16
1990—	Atlanta (N.L.)	2	2	.500	5.63	34	0	0	0	0	38 1/3	41	26	24	25	34
—	Richmond (Int'l)	1	1	.500	2.33	13	0	0	0	2	27	12	7	7	16	36
1991—	Houston (N.L.)■	3	2	.600	3.19	52	0	0	0	2	67 2/3	51	25	24	39	51
1992—	Cincinnati (N.L.)■	3	3	.500	3.33	60	0	0	0	0	83 2/3	59	31	31	44	72
1993—	Cincinnati (N.L.)	0	1	.000	3.86	3	0	0	0	0	4 2/3	6	8	2	4	2
—	Seattle (A.L.)■	2	1	.667	6.67	31	1	0	0	2	54	56	40	40	35	35
1994—	Chunichi (Jap. Cen.)■	3	7	.300	3.48	31	0	0	0	0	67 1/3	49	...	26	47	70
1995—	Toledo (Int'l)■	1	1	.500	3.35	41	0	0	0	11	48 1/3	43	21	18	24	52
—	Detroit (A.L.)	1	0	1.000	6.23	10	0	0	0	5	8 2/3	11	6	6	10	9
A.L. totals (7 years)		6	5	.545	6.06	95	1	0	0	11	127 2/3	129	88	86	79	100
N.L. totals (5 years)		8	10	.444	3.78	161	0	0	0	3	207	169	96	87	117	175
Major league totals (11 years)		14	15	.483	4.65	256	1	0	0	14	334 2/3	298	184	173	196	275

HENTGEN, PAT — P — BLUE JAYS

PERSONAL: Born November 13, 1968, in Detroit. . . . 6-2/200. . . . Throws right, bats right. . . . Full name: Patrick George Hentgen. . . . Name pronounced HENT-ghen.

HIGH SCHOOL: Fraser (Mich.).

TRANSACTIONS/CAREER NOTES: Selected by Toronto Blue Jays organization in fifth round of free-agent draft (June 2, 1986). . . . On Toronto disabled list (August 13-September 29, 1992); included rehabilitation assignment to Syracuse (September 1-8).

STATISTICAL NOTES: Combined with relievers Willie Blair and Enrique Burgos in 2-1 no-hit victory against Osceola (May 10, 1988).

Year	Team (League)	W	L	Pct.	ERA	G	GS	CG	ShO	Sv.	IP	H	R	ER	BB	SO
1986—	St. Cathar. (NYP)	0	4	.000	4.50	13	11	0	0	1	40	38	27	20	30	30
1987—	Myrtle Beach (SAL)	11	5	.688	2.35	32	*31	2	2	0	*188	145	62	49	60	131
1988—	Dunedin (Fla. St.)	3	12	.200	3.45	31	*30	0	0	0	151 1/3	139	80	58	65	125
1989—	Dunedin (Fla. St.)	9	8	.529	2.68	29	28	0	0	0	151 1/3	123	53	45	71	148
1990—	Knoxville (South.)	9	5	.643	3.05	28	26	0	0	0	153 1/3	121	57	52	68	142
1991—	Syracuse (Int'l)	8	9	.471	4.47	31	•28	1	0	0	171	146	91	85	*90	*155
—	Toronto (A.L.)	0	0	...	2.45	3	1	0	0	0	7 1/3	5	2	2	3	3
1992—	Toronto (A.L.)	5	2	.714	5.36	28	2	0	0	0	50 1/3	49	30	30	32	39
—	Syracuse (Int'l)	1	2	.333	2.66	4	4	0	0	0	20 1/3	15	6	6	8	17
1993—	Toronto (A.L.)	19	9	.679	3.87	34	32	3	0	0	216 1/3	215	103	93	74	122
1994—	Toronto (A.L.)	13	8	.619	3.40	24	24	6	3	0	174 2/3	158	74	66	59	147
1995—	Toronto (A.L.)	10	14	.417	5.11	30	30	2	0	0	200 2/3	*236	*129	*114	90	135
Major league totals (5 years)		47	33	.588	4.23	119	89	11	3	0	649 1/3	663	338	305	258	446

CHAMPIONSHIP SERIES RECORD

Year	Team (League)	W	L	Pct.	ERA	G	GS	CG	ShO	Sv.	IP	H	R	ER	BB	SO
1993—	Toronto (A.L.)	0	1	.000	18.00	1	1	0	0	0	3	9	6	6	2	3

WORLD SERIES RECORD

NOTES: Member of World Series championship team (1993).

Year	Team (League)	W	L	Pct.	ERA	G	GS	CG	ShO	Sv.	IP	H	R	ER	BB	SO
1993—	Toronto (A.L.)	1	0	1.000	1.50	1	1	0	0	0	6	5	1	1	3	6

ALL-STAR GAME RECORD

Year	League	W	L	Pct.	ERA	GS	CG	ShO	Sv.	IP	H	R	ER	BB	SO
1993—	American						Did not play.								
1994—	American	0	0	...	0.00	0	0	0	0	1	1	0	0	0	0
All-Star totals (1 years)		0	0	...	0.00	0	0	0	0	1	1	0	0	0	0

HEREDIA, GIL — P — RANGERS

PERSONAL: Born October 26, 1965, in Nogales, Ariz. . . . 6-1/205. . . . Throws right, bats right. . . . Full name: Gilbert Heredia. . . . Name pronounced err-AY-dee-uh.

HIGH SCHOOL: Nogales (Ariz.).

JUNIOR COLLEGE: Pima Community College (Ariz.).

COLLEGE: Arizona.

TRANSACTIONS/CAREER NOTES: Selected by Pittsburgh Pirates organization in first round (16th pick overall) of free-agent draft (January 17, 1984); did not sign. . . . Selected by Baltimore Orioles organization in sixth round of free-agent draft (January 9, 1985); did not sign. . . . Selected by San Francisco Giants organization in ninth round of free-agent draft (June 2, 1987). . . . Loaned by Giants organization to San Luis Potosi of Mexican League (1989). . . . Claimed on waivers by Montreal Expos (August 18, 1992). . . . Granted free agency (December

21, 1995). . . . Signed by Texas Rangers organization (January 5, 1996).

Year	Team (League)	W	L	Pct.	ERA	G	GS	CG	ShO	Sv.	IP	H	R	ER	BB	SO
1987—	Everett (N'west)	2	0	1.000	3.60	3	3	1	0	0	20	24	8	8	1	14
—	Fresno (California)	5	3	.625	2.90	11	11	5	2	0	80 2/3	62	28	26	23	60
1988—	San Jose (Calif.)	13	12	.520	3.49	27	27	9	0	0	*206 1/3	•216	107	80	46	121
1989—	Shreveport (Texas)	1	0	1.000	2.55	7	2	1	0	0	24 2/3	28	10	7	4	8
—	San Luis Pot. (Mex.)■	14	9	.609	2.99	24	24	15	3	0	180 2/3	183	73	60	35	125
1990—	Phoenix (PCL)■	9	7	.563	4.10	29	19	0	0	1	147	159	81	67	37	75
1991—	Phoenix (PCL)	9	11	.450	*2.82	33	15	•5	1	1	140 1/3	155	60	44	28	75
—	San Francisco (N.L.)	0	2	.000	3.82	7	4	0	0	0	33	27	14	14	7	13
1992—	Phoenix (PCL)	5	5	.500	2.01	22	7	1	1	1	80 2/3	83	30	18	13	37
—	San Francisco (N.L.)	2	3	.400	5.40	13	4	0	0	0	30	32	20	18	16	15
—	Indianapolis (A.A.)■	2	0	1.000	1.02	3	3	0	0	0	17 2/3	18	2	2	3	10
—	Montreal (N.L.)	0	0	...	1.84	7	1	0	0	0	14 2/3	12	3	3	4	7
1993—	Ottawa (Int'l)	8	4	.667	2.98	16	16	1	0	0	102 2/3	97	46	34	26	66
—	Montreal (N.L.)	4	2	.667	3.92	20	9	1	0	2	57 1/3	66	28	25	14	40
1994—	Montreal (N.L.)	6	3	.667	3.46	39	3	0	0	0	75 1/3	85	34	29	13	62
1995—	Montreal (N.L.)	5	6	.455	4.31	40	18	0	0	1	119	137	60	57	21	74
Major league totals (5 years)		17	16	.515	3.99	126	39	1	0	3	329 1/3	359	159	146	75	211

HEREDIA, WILSON — P — MARLINS

PERSONAL: Born March 30, 1972, in La Romana, Dominican Republic. . . . 6-0/175. . . . Throws right, bats right.
TRANSACTIONS/CAREER NOTES: Signed as non-drafted free agent by Texas Rangers organization (February 28, 1990). . . . On disabled list (June 3-August 17, 1994). . . . Traded by Rangers to Florida Marlins (August 11, 1995), completing deal in which Rangers acquired P Bobby Witt for two players to be named later (August 8, 1995); Marlins acquired OF Scott Podsednik to complete deal (October 2, 1995).

Year	Team (League)	W	L	Pct.	ERA	G	GS	CG	ShO	Sv.	IP	H	R	ER	BB	SO
1990—	San Pedro (DSL)	5	7	.417	4.86	15	15	8	1	0	111	119	69	60	48	58
1991—	GC Rangers (GCL)	2	4	.333	2.14	17	0	0	0	4	33 2/3	25	18	8	20	22
1992—	Gastonia (S. Atl.)	1	2	.333	5.12	39	1	0	0	5	63 1/3	71	45	36	30	64
1993—	Charlotte (Fla. St.)	1	5	.167	3.76	34	0	0	0	15	38 1/3	30	17	16	20	26
1994—	Tulsa (Texas)	3	2	.600	3.77	18	1	0	0	0	43	35	23	18	8	53
1995—	Texas (A.L.)	0	1	.000	3.75	6	0	0	0	0	12	9	5	5	15	6
—	Okla. City (A.A.)	1	4	.200	6.82	8	7	0	0	0	31 2/3	40	26	24	25	21
—	Tulsa (Texas)	4	2	.667	3.18	8	7	1	1	1	45 1/3	42	19	16	21	34
—	Portland (Eastern)■	4	0	1.000	2.00	4	4	0	0	0	27	22	7	6	14	19
Major league totals (1 year)		0	1	.000	3.75	6	0	0	0	0	12	9	5	5	15	6

HERMANSON, DUSTIN — P — PADRES

PERSONAL: Born December 21, 1972, in Springfield, O. . . . 6-2/195. . . . Throws right, bats right. . . . Full name: Dustin Michael Hermanson.
HIGH SCHOOL: Kenton Ridge (Springfield, O.).
COLLEGE: Kent.
TRANSACTIONS/CAREER NOTES: Selected by Pittsburgh Pirates organization in 39th round of free-agent draft (June 3, 1991); did not sign. . . . Selected by San Diego Padres organization in first round (third pick overall) of free-agent draft (June 2, 1994).

Year	Team (League)	W	L	Pct.	ERA	G	GS	CG	ShO	Sv.	IP	H	R	ER	BB	SO
1994—	Wichita (Texas)	1	0	1.000	0.43	16	0	0	0	8	21	13	1	1	6	30
—	Las Vegas (PCL)	0	0	...	6.14	7	0	0	0	3	7 1/3	6	5	5	5	6
1995—	Las Vegas (PCL)	0	1	.000	3.50	31	0	0	0	11	36	35	23	14	29	42
—	San Diego (N.L.)	3	1	.750	6.82	26	0	0	0	0	31 2/3	35	26	24	22	19
Major league totals (1 year)		3	1	.750	6.82	26	0	0	0	0	31 2/3	35	26	24	22	19

HERNANDEZ, CARLOS — C — DODGERS

PERSONAL: Born May 24, 1967, in San Felix, Bolivar, Venezuela. . . . 5-11/215. . . . Bats right, throws right. . . . Full name: Carlos Alberto Hernandez.
HIGH SCHOOL: Escuela Tecnica Industrial (San Felix, Bolivar, Venezuela).
TRANSACTIONS/CAREER NOTES: Signed as non-drafted free agent by Los Angeles Dodgers organization (October 10, 1984). . . . On Albuquerque disabled list (May 27-June 20, 1990). . . . On disabled list (April 4-22, 1994).
STATISTICAL NOTES: Tied for Gulf Coast League lead in double plays by catcher with three in 1986. . . . Led Texas League catchers with 737 total chances in 1989. . . . Led Pacific Coast League catchers with 684 total chances in 1991.

				BATTING											FIELDING			
Year	Team (League)	Pos.	G	AB	R	H	2B	3B	HR	RBI	Avg.	BB	SO	SB	PO	A	E	Avg.
1985—	GC Dodgers (GCL)	3B-1B	22	49	3	12	1	0	0	0	.245	3	8	0	48	16	2	.970
1986—	GC Dodgers (GCL)	C-3B	57	205	19	64	7	0	1	31	.312	5	18	1	217	36	10	.962
1987—	Bakersfield (Calif.)	C	48	162	22	37	6	1	3	22	.228	14	23	8	181	26	8	.963
1988—	Bakersfield (Calif.)	C	92	333	37	103	15	2	5	52	.309	16	39	3	480	88	14	.976
—	Albuquerque (PCL)	C	3	8	0	1	0	0	0	1	.125	0	0	0	11	0	1	.917
1989—	San Antonio (Tex.)	C	99	370	37	111	16	3	8	41	.300	12	46	2	*629	*90	*18	.976
—	Albuquerque (PCL)	C	4	14	1	3	0	0	0	1	.214	2	1	0	23	3	3	.897
1990—	Albuquerque (PCL)	C	52	143	11	45	8	1	0	16	.315	8	25	2	207	31	8	.967
—	Los Angeles (N.L.)	C	10	20	2	4	1	0	0	1	.200	0	2	0	37	2	0	1.000
1991—	Albuquerque (PCL)	C	95	345	60	119	24	2	8	44	.345	24	36	5	*592	*77	*15	.978
—	Los Angeles (N.L.)	C-3B	15	14	1	3	1	0	0	1	.214	0	5	1	24	4	1	.966
1992—	Los Angeles (N.L.)	C	69	173	11	45	4	0	3	17	.260	11	21	0	295	37	7	.979
1993—	Los Angeles (N.L.)	C	50	99	6	25	5	0	2	7	.253	2	11	0	181	15	7	.966
1994—	Los Angeles (N.L.)	C	32	64	6	14	2	0	2	6	.219	1	14	0	104	13	0	1.000
1995—	Los Angeles (N.L.)	C	45	94	3	14	1	0	2	8	.149	7	25	0	210	25	4	.983
Major league totals (6 years)			221	464	29	105	14	0	9	40	.226	21	78	1	851	96	19	.980

H

HERNANDEZ, JEREMY — P — RED SOX

PERSONAL: Born July 6, 1966, in Burbank, Calif. . . . 6-7/210. . . . Throws right, bats right. . . . Full name: Jeremy Stuart Hernandez.
HIGH SCHOOL: Francis Poly (Sun Valley, Calif.).
COLLEGE: Cal State Northridge.
TRANSACTIONS/CAREER NOTES: Selected by St. Louis Cardinals organization in second round of free-agent draft (June 2, 1987). . . . Traded by Cardinals organization to Charleston, S.C., San Diego Padres organization, for OF Randell Byers (April 24, 1989). . . . Traded by Padres to Cleveland Indians for OF Tracy Sanders and P Fernando Hernandez (June 1, 1993). . . . Traded by Indians to Florida Marlins for P Matt Turner (April 3, 1994). . . . On disabled list (June 2, 1994-remainder of season). . . . On Florida disabled list (April 16-June 4 and June 19-September 1, 1995); included rehabilitation assignments to Brevard County (May 15-30) and Charlotte (May 30-June 4 and June 19-August 2). . . . Signed as free agent by Boston Red Sox (January 22, 1996).
STATISTICAL NOTES: Led Texas League with 18 home runs allowed in 1990.

Year Team (League)	W	L	Pct.	ERA	G	GS	CG	ShO	Sv.	IP	H	R	ER	BB	SO
1987— Erie (NYP)	5	4	.556	2.81	16	16	1	0	0	99 1/3	87	36	31	41	62
1988— Springfield (Midw.)	12	6	.667	3.54	24	24	3	1	0	147 1/3	133	73	58	34	97
1989— St. Petersburg (FSL)	0	2	.000	7.71	3	3	0	0	0	14	17	14	12	5	5
— Char., S.C. (S. Atl.)■	3	5	.375	3.53	10	10	2	1	0	58 2/3	65	37	23	16	39
— Riverside (Calif.)	5	2	.714	1.75	9	9	4	1	0	67	55	17	13	11	65
— Wichita (Texas)	2	1	.667	8.53	4	3	0	0	0	19	30	18	18	8	9
1990— Wichita (Texas)	7	6	.538	4.53	26	26	1	0	0	155	163	92	78	50	101
1991— Las Vegas (PCL)	4	8	.333	4.74	56	0	0	0	13	68 1/3	76	36	36	25	67
— San Diego (N.L.)	0	0	...	0.00	9	0	0	0	2	14 1/3	8	1	0	5	9
1992— San Diego (N.L.)	1	4	.200	4.17	26	0	0	0	1	36 2/3	39	17	17	11	25
— Las Vegas (PCL)	2	4	.333	2.91	42	0	0	0	11	55 2/3	53	19	18	20	38
1993— San Diego (N.L.)	0	2	.000	4.72	21	0	0	0	0	34 1/3	41	19	18	7	26
— Cleveland (A.L.)■	6	5	.545	3.14	49	0	0	0	8	77 1/3	75	33	27	27	44
1994— Florida (N.L.)■	3	3	.500	2.70	21	0	0	0	9	23 1/3	16	9	7	14	13
1995— Brevard Co. (FSL)	0	0	...	2.35	4	2	0	0	0	7 2/3	5	2	2	2	5
— Charlotte (Int'l)	0	2	.000	5.58	15	3	0	0	0	30 2/3	37	20	19	15	24
— Florida (N.L.)	0	0	...	11.57	7	0	0	0	0	7	12	9	9	3	5
A.L. totals (1 year)	6	5	.545	3.14	49	0	0	0	8	77 1/3	75	33	27	27	44
N.L. totals (5 years)	4	9	.308	3.97	84	0	0	0	12	115 2/3	116	55	51	40	78
Major league totals (5 years)	10	14	.417	3.64	133	0	0	0	20	193	191	88	78	67	122

HERNANDEZ, JOSE — SS — CUBS

PERSONAL: Born July 14, 1969, in Vega Alta, Puerto Rico. . . . 6-1/180. . . . Bats right, throws right. . . . Full name: Jose Antonio Hernandez.
HIGH SCHOOL: Maestro Ladi (Vega Alta, Puerto Rico).
COLLEGE: American University (Puerto Rico).
TRANSACTIONS/CAREER NOTES: Signed as non-drafted free agent by Texas Rangers organization (January 13, 1987). . . . Claimed on waivers by Cleveland Indians (April 3, 1992). . . . Traded by Indians to Chicago Cubs for P Heathcliff Slocumb (June 1, 1993).
STATISTICAL NOTES: Led Gulf Coast League third basemen with .950 fielding percentage, 47 putouts and 11 double plays in 1988. . . . Led Florida State League shortstops with .959 fielding percentage in 1990. . . . Career major league grand slams: 1.

		BATTING												FIELDING			
Year Team (League)	Pos.	G	AB	R	H	2B	3B	HR	RBI	Avg.	BB	SO	SB	PO	A	E	Avg.
1987— GC Rangers (GCL)	SS	24	52	5	9	1	1	0	2	.173	9	25	2	30	38	5	.932
1988— GC Rangers (GCL)	3-2-S-1-O	55	162	19	26	7	1	1	13	.160	12	36	4	†68	115	8	†.958
1989— Gastonia (S. Atl.)	3-S-2-O	91	215	35	47	7	6	1	16	.219	33	67	9	101	169	17	.941
1990— Charlotte (Fla. St.)	SS-OF	121	388	43	99	14	7	1	44	.255	50	122	11	192	372	25	†.958
1991— Tulsa (Texas)	SS	91	301	36	72	17	4	1	20	.239	26	75	4	151	300	15	*.968
— Okla. City (A.A.)	SS	14	46	6	14	1	1	1	3	.304	4	10	0	32	43	3	.962
— Texas (A.L.)	SS-3B	45	98	8	18	2	1	0	4	.184	3	31	0	49	111	4	.976
1992— Cant./Akr. (East.)■	SS	130	404	56	103	16	4	3	46	.255	37	108	7	*226	320	*40	.932
— Cleveland (A.L.)	SS	3	4	0	0	0	0	0	0	.000	0	2	0	3	3	1	.857
1993— Cant./Akr. (East.)	SS-3B	45	150	19	30	6	0	2	17	.200	10	39	9	75	135	7	.968
— Orlando (Southern)■	SS	71	263	42	80	8	3	8	33	.304	20	60	8	136	205	14	.961
— Iowa (Am. Assoc.)	SS	6	24	3	6	1	0	0	3	.250	0	2	0	14	26	1	.976
1994— Chicago (N.L.)	3-S-2-O	56	132	18	32	2	3	1	9	.242	8	29	2	46	86	4	.971
1995— Chicago (N.L.)	SS-2B-3B	93	245	37	60	11	4	13	40	.245	13	69	1	113	189	9	.971
American League totals (2 years)		48	102	8	18	2	1	0	4	.176	3	33	0	52	114	5	.971
National League totals (2 years)		149	377	55	92	13	7	14	49	.244	21	98	3	159	275	13	.971
Major league totals (4 years)		197	479	63	110	15	8	14	53	.230	24	131	3	211	389	18	.971

HERNANDEZ, ROBERTO — P — WHITE SOX

PERSONAL: Born November 11, 1964, in Santurce, Puerto Rico. . . . 6-4/235. . . . Throws right, bats right. . . . Full name: Roberto Manuel Hernandez.
HIGH SCHOOL: New Hampton (N.H.) Prep.
COLLEGE: South Carolina-Aiken.
TRANSACTIONS/CAREER NOTES: Selected by California Angels organization in first round (16th pick overall) of free-agent draft (June 2, 1986); pick received as compensation for Baltimore Orioles signing Type A free-agent OF/IF Juan Beniquez. . . . On disabled list (May 6-21 and June 4-August 14, 1987). . . . Traded by Angels with OF Mark Doran to Chicago White Sox organization for OF Mark Davis (August 2, 1989). . . . On Vancouver disabled list (May 17-August 10, 1991).

Year Team (League)	W	L	Pct.	ERA	G	GS	CG	ShO	Sv.	IP	H	R	ER	BB	SO
1986— Salem (Northwest)	2	2	.500	4.58	10	10	0	0	0	55	57	37	28	42	38
1987— Quad City (Midw.)	2	3	.400	6.86	7	6	0	0	1	21	24	21	16	12	21
1988— Quad City (Midw.)	9	10	.474	3.17	24	24	6	1	0	164 2/3	157	70	58	48	114
— Midland (Texas)	0	2	.000	6.57	3	3	0	0	0	12 1/3	16	13	9	8	7

Year	Team (League)	W	L	Pct.	ERA	G	GS	CG	ShO	Sv.	IP	H	R	ER	BB	SO
1989—	Midland (Texas)	2	7	.222	6.89	12	12	0	0	0	64	94	57	49	30	42
—	Palm Springs (Cal.)	1	4	.200	4.64	7	7	0	0	0	42 2/3	49	27	22	16	33
—	South Bend (Midw.)■	1	1	.500	3.33	4	4	0	0	0	24 1/3	19	9	9	7	17
1990—	Birmingham (Sou.)	8	5	.615	3.67	17	17	1	0	0	108	103	57	44	43	62
—	Vancouver (PCL)	3	5	.375	2.84	11	11	3	1	0	79 1/3	73	33	25	26	49
1991—	Birmingham (Sou.)	2	1	.667	1.99	4	4	0	0	0	22 2/3	11	5	5	6	25
—	Vancouver (PCL)	4	1	.800	3.22	7	7	0	0	0	44 2/3	41	17	16	23	40
—	GC White Sox (GCL)	0	0	...	0.00	1	1	0	0	0	6	2	0	0	0	7
—	Chicago (A.L.)	1	0	1.000	7.80	9	3	0	0	0	15	18	15	13	7	6
1992—	Chicago (A.L.)	7	3	.700	1.65	43	0	0	0	12	71	45	15	13	20	68
—	Vancouver (PCL)	3	3	.500	2.61	9	0	0	0	2	20 2/3	13	9	6	11	23
1993—	Chicago (A.L.)	3	4	.429	2.29	70	0	0	0	38	78 2/3	66	21	20	20	71
1994—	Chicago (A.L.)	4	4	.500	4.91	45	0	0	0	14	47 2/3	44	29	26	19	50
1995—	Chicago (A.L.)	3	7	.300	3.92	60	0	0	0	32	59 2/3	63	30	26	28	84
Major league totals (5 years)		18	18	.500	3.24	227	3	0	0	96	272	236	110	98	94	279

CHAMPIONSHIP SERIES RECORD

Year	Team (League)	W	L	Pct.	ERA	G	GS	CG	ShO	Sv.	IP	H	R	ER	BB	SO
1993—	Chicago (A.L.)	0	0	...	0.00	4	0	0	0	1	4	4	0	0	0	1

HERNANDEZ, XAVIER — P — REDS

PERSONAL: Born August 16, 1965, in Port Arthur, Tex. . . . 6-2/195. . . . Throws right, bats left. . . . Full name: Francis Xavier Hernandez.
HIGH SCHOOL: Thomas Jefferson (Port Arthur, Tex.).
COLLEGE: Southwestern Louisiana.
TRANSACTIONS/CAREER NOTES: Selected by Toronto Blue Jays organization in fourth round of free-agent draft (June 2, 1986). . . . On disabled list (June 7-27, 1987). . . . Selected by Houston Astros from Blue Jays organization in Rule 5 major league draft (December 4, 1989). . . . On Houston disabled list (June 3-26, 1991); included rehabilitation assignment to Tucson (June 14-26). . . . Traded by Astros to New York Yankees for P Domingo Jean and IF Andy Stankiewicz (November 27, 1993). . . . On disabled list (July 27-August 11, 1994). . . . Granted free agency (November 28, 1994). . . . Signed by Cincinnati Reds (December 1, 1994). . . . On suspended list (September 16-21, 1995).
MISCELLANEOUS: Appeared in two games as pinch-runner (1990).

Year	Team (League)	W	L	Pct.	ERA	G	GS	CG	ShO	Sv.	IP	H	R	ER	BB	SO
1986—	St. Cathar. (NYP)	5	5	.500	2.67	13	10	1	1	0	70 2/3	55	27	21	16	69
1987—	St. Cathar. (NYP)	3	3	.500	5.07	13	11	0	0	0	55	57	39	31	16	49
1988—	Myrtle Beach (SAL)	13	6	.684	2.55	23	22	2	2	0	148	116	52	42	28	111
—	Knoxville (South.)	2	4	.333	2.90	11	11	2	0	0	68 1/3	73	32	22	15	33
1989—	Knoxville (South.)	1	1	.500	4.13	4	4	1	0	0	24	25	11	11	11	17
—	Syracuse (Int'l)	5	6	.455	3.53	15	15	2	1	0	99 1/3	95	42	39	22	47
—	Toronto (A.L.)	1	0	1.000	4.76	7	0	0	0	0	22 2/3	25	15	12	8	7
1990—	Houston (N.L.)■	2	1	.667	4.62	34	1	0	0	0	62 1/3	60	34	32	24	24
1991—	Houston (N.L.)	2	7	.222	4.71	32	6	0	0	3	63	66	34	33	32	55
—	Tucson (Pac. Coast)	2	1	.667	2.75	16	3	0	0	4	36	35	16	11	9	34
1992—	Houston (N.L.)	9	1	.900	2.11	77	0	0	0	7	111	81	31	26	42	96
1993—	Houston (N.L.)	4	5	.444	2.61	72	0	0	0	9	96 2/3	75	37	28	28	101
1994—	New York (A.L.)■	4	4	.500	5.85	31	0	0	0	6	40	48	27	26	21	37
1995—	Cincinnati (N.L.)■	7	2	.778	4.60	59	0	0	0	3	90	95	47	46	31	84
A.L. totals (2 years)		5	4	.556	5.46	38	0	0	0	6	62 2/3	73	42	38	29	44
N.L. totals (5 years)		24	16	.600	3.51	274	7	0	0	22	423	377	183	165	157	360
Major league totals (7 years)		29	20	.592	3.76	312	7	0	0	28	485 2/3	450	225	203	186	404

CHAMPIONSHIP SERIES RECORD

Year	Team (League)	W	L	Pct.	ERA	G	GS	CG	ShO	Sv.	IP	H	R	ER	BB	SO
1995—	Cincinnati (N.L.)	0	0	...	27.00	1	0	0	0	0	2/3	3	2	2	0	0

HERRERA, JOSE — OF — ATHLETICS

PERSONAL: Born August 30, 1972, in Santo Domingo, Dominican Republic. . . . 6-0/165. . . . Bats left, throws left. . . . Full name: Jose Ramon Catalino Herrera.
TRANSACTIONS/CAREER NOTES: Signed as non-drafted free agent by Toronto Blue Jays organization (January 10, 1990). . . . Traded by Blue Jays organization to Oakland Athletics organization (August 6, 1993), completing deal in which A's traded OF Rickey Henderson to Blue Jays for P Steve Karsay and a player to be named later (July 31, 1993).

			BATTING												FIELDING			
Year	Team (League)	Pos.	G	AB	R	H	2B	3B	HR	RBI	Avg.	BB	SO	SB	PO	A	E	Avg.
1990—	Santo Dom. (DSL)	OF	50	164	18	42	7	0	2	18	.256	14	16	2	...	...	...	...
1991—	Medicine Hat (Pio.)	OF	40	143	21	35	5	1	1	11	.245	6	38	6	50	5	3	.948
—	St. Cathar. (NYP)	OF	3	9	3	3	1	0	0	2	.333	1	2	0	8	1	0	1.000
1992—	Medicine Hat (Pio.)	OF	72	265	45	72	9	2	0	21	.272	32	62	32	132	3	*10	.931
1993—	Hagerstown (SAL)	OF	95	388	60	123	22	5	5	42	.317	26	63	36	150	6	9	.945
—	Madison (Midwest)■	OF	4	14	1	3	0	0	0	0	.214	0	6	1	6	1	0	1.000
1994—	Modesto (Calif.)■	OF	103	370	59	106	20	3	11	56	.286	38	76	21	138	9	3	.980
1995—	Huntsville (South.)	OF	92	358	37	101	11	4	6	45	.282	27	58	9	176	6	8	.958
—	Oakland (A.L.)	OF-DH	33	70	9	17	1	2	0	2	.243	6	11	1	41	2	2	.956
Major league totals (1 year)			33	70	9	17	1	2	0	2	.243	6	11	1	41	2	2	.956

HERSHISER, OREL — P — INDIANS

PERSONAL: Born September 16, 1958, in Buffalo, N.Y. . . . 6-3/195. . . . Throws right, bats right. . . . Full name: Orel Leonard Hershiser IV. . . . Brother of Gordie Hershiser, minor league pitcher (1987-88). . . . Name pronounced her-SHY-zer.

HIGH SCHOOL: Cherry Hill (N.J.) East.

COLLEGE: Bowling Green State.

TRANSACTIONS/CAREER NOTES: Selected by Los Angeles Dodgers organization in 17th round of free-agent draft (June 5, 1979). . . . On disabled list (April 27, 1990-remainder of season). . . . On Los Angeles disabled list (March 31-May 29, 1991); included rehabilitation assignments to Bakersfield (May 8-13 and May 18-24), Albuquerque (May 13-18) and San Antonio (May 24-29). . . . Granted free agency (November 1, 1991). . . . Re-signed by Dodgers (December 3, 1991). . . . Granted free agency (October 17, 1994). . . . Signed by Cleveland Indians (April 8, 1995). . . . On disabled list (June 22-July 7, 1995).

RECORDS: Holds major league single-season record for most consecutive scoreless innings—59 (August 30, sixth inning through September 28, 10th inning, 1988). . . . Shares N.L. single-season record for fewest games lost by pitcher who led league in games lost—15 (1989 and 1992). . . . Shares N.L. single-month record for most shutouts—5 (September 1988).

HONORS: Named Major League Player of the Year by The Sporting News (1988). . . . Named N.L. Pitcher of the Year by The Sporting News (1988). . . . Named righthanded pitcher on The Sporting News N.L. All-Star team (1988). . . . Won N.L. Gold Glove at pitcher (1988). . . . Named N.L. Cy Young Award winner by Baseball Writers' Association of America (1988). . . . Named pitcher on The Sporting News N.L. Silver Slugger team (1993).

STATISTICAL NOTES: Pitched 2-0 one-hit, complete-game victory against San Diego (April 26, 1985). . . . Pitched 6-0 one-hit, complete-game victory against Pittsburgh (July 23, 1985). . . . Tied for N.L. lead with 19 sacrifice hits in 1988.

MISCELLANEOUS: Had sacrifice hit in only appearance as pinch-hitter (1988). . . . Singled once in two games as pinch-hitter (1992). . . . Started one game at third base but replaced before first plate appearance and never played in field (1993).

Year Team (League)	W	L	Pct.	ERA	G	GS	CG	ShO	Sv.	IP	H	R	ER	BB	SO
1979— Clinton (Midwest)	4	0	1.000	2.09	15	4	1	0	2	43	33	15	10	17	33
1980— San Antonio (Tex.)	5	9	.357	3.55	49	3	1	0	14	109	120	59	43	59	75
1981— San Antonio (Tex.)	7	6	.538	4.68	42	4	3	0	*15	102	94	54	53	50	95
1982— Albuquerque (PCL)	9	6	.600	3.71	47	7	2	0	4	123 2/3	121	73	51	63	93
1983— Albuquerque (PCL)	10	8	.556	4.09	49	10	6	0	16	134 1/3	132	73	61	57	95
— Los Angeles (N.L.)	0	0	. . .	3.38	8	0	0	0	1	8	7	6	3	6	5
1984— Los Angeles (N.L.)	11	8	.579	2.66	45	20	8	•4	2	189 2/3	160	65	56	50	150
1985— Los Angeles (N.L.)	19	3	*.864	2.03	36	34	9	5	0	239 2/3	179	72	54	68	157
1986— Los Angeles (N.L.)	14	14	.500	3.85	35	35	8	1	0	231 1/3	213	112	99	86	153
1987— Los Angeles (N.L.)	16	16	.500	3.06	37	35	10	1	1	*264 2/3	247	105	90	74	190
1988— Los Angeles (N.L.)	•23	8	.742	2.26	35	34	•15	*8	1	*267	208	73	67	73	178
1989— Los Angeles (N.L.)	15	•15	.500	2.31	35	33	8	4	0	*256 2/3	226	75	66	77	178
1990— Los Angeles (N.L.)	1	1	.500	4.26	4	4	0	0	0	25 1/3	26	12	12	4	16
1991— Bakersfield (Calif.)	2	0	1.000	0.82	2	2	0	0	0	11	5	2	1	1	6
— Albuquerque (PCL)	0	0	. . .	0.00	1	1	0	0	0	5	5	0	0	0	5
— San Antonio (Tex.)	0	1	.000	2.57	1	1	0	0	0	7	11	3	2	1	5
— Los Angeles (N.L.)	7	2	.778	3.46	21	21	0	0	0	112	112	43	43	32	73
1992— Los Angeles (N.L.)	10	•15	.400	3.67	33	33	1	0	0	210 2/3	209	101	86	69	130
1993— Los Angeles (N.L.)	12	14	.462	3.59	33	33	5	1	0	215 2/3	201	106	86	72	141
1994— Los Angeles (N.L.)	6	6	.500	3.79	21	21	1	0	0	135 1/3	146	67	57	42	72
1995— Cleveland (A.L.)■	16	6	.727	3.87	26	26	1	1	0	167 1/3	151	76	72	51	111
A.L. totals (1 year)	16	6	.727	3.87	26	26	1	1	0	167 1/3	151	76	72	51	111
N.L. totals (12 years)	134	102	.568	3.00	343	303	65	24	5	2156	1934	837	719	653	1443
Major league totals (13 years)	150	108	.581	3.06	369	329	66	25	5	2323 1/3	2085	913	791	704	1554

DIVISION SERIES RECORD

Year Team (League)	W	L	Pct.	ERA	G	GS	CG	ShO	Sv.	IP	H	R	ER	BB	SO
1995— Cleveland (A.L.)	1	0	1.000	0.00	1	1	0	0	0	7 1/3	3	0	0	2	7

CHAMPIONSHIP SERIES RECORD

NOTES: Named N.L. Championship Series Most Valuable Player (1988). . . . Holds single-series record for most innings pitched—24 2/3 (1988). . . . Holds N.L. single-game record for most hit batsmen—2 (October 12, 1988). . . . Shares N.L. career records for most complete games—2; and most hit batsmen—2. . . . Shares N.L. single-series record for most hit batsmen—2 (1988). . . . Named A.L. Championship Series Most Valuable Player (1995).

Year Team (League)	W	L	Pct.	ERA	G	GS	CG	ShO	Sv.	IP	H	R	ER	BB	SO
1983— Los Angeles (N.L.)							Did not play.								
1985— Los Angeles (N.L.)	1	0	1.000	3.52	2	2	1	0	0	15 1/3	17	6	6	6	5
1988— Los Angeles (N.L.)	1	0	1.000	1.09	4	3	1	1	1	24 2/3	18	5	3	7	15
1995— Cleveland (A.L.)	2	0	1.000	1.29	2	2	0	0	0	14	9	3	2	3	15
Champ. series totals (3 years)	4	0	1.000	1.83	8	7	2	1	1	54	44	14	11	16	35

WORLD SERIES RECORD

NOTES: Named Most Valuable Player (1988). . . . Member of World Series championship team (1988).

Year Team (League)	W	L	Pct.	ERA	G	GS	CG	ShO	Sv.	IP	H	R	ER	BB	SO
1988— Los Angeles (N.L.)	2	0	1.000	1.00	2	2	2	1	0	18	7	2	2	6	17
1995— Cleveland (A.L.)	1	1	.500	2.57	2	2	0	0	0	14	8	5	4	4	13
World Series totals (2 years)	3	1	.750	1.69	4	4	2	1	0	32	15	7	6	10	30

ALL-STAR GAME RECORD

Year League	W	L	Pct.	ERA	GS	CG	ShO	Sv.	IP	H	R	ER	BB	SO
1987— National	0	0	. . .	0.00	0	0	0	0	2	1	0	0	1	0
1988— National	0	0	. . .	0.00	0	0	0	0	1	0	0	0	0	0
1989— National						Did not play.								
All-Star totals (2 years)	0	0	. . .	0.00	0	0	0	0	3	1	0	0	1	0

HIATT, PHIL 3B TIGERS

H

PERSONAL: Born May 1, 1969, in Pensacola, Fla. . . . 6-3/200. . . . Bats right, throws right. . . . Full name: Philip Farrell Hiatt.

HIGH SCHOOL: Catholic (Pensacola, Fla.).

COLLEGE: Louisiana Tech.

TRANSACTIONS/CAREER NOTES: Selected by Kansas City Royals organization in eighth round of free-agent draft (June 4, 1990). . . . On Omaha disabled list (April 15-May 2, 1994). . . . On disabled list (May 5-20, 1995). . . . Traded by Royals to Detroit Tigers (September 14,

1995), completing deal in which Royals acquired 1B/OF Juan Samuel for a player to be named later (September 8, 1995).
STATISTICAL NOTES: Led Northwest League third basemen with 145 assists, 200 total chances and 18 double plays in 1990.

							BATTING								FIELDING		
Year Team (League)	**Pos.**	**G**	**AB**	**R**	**H**	**2B**	**3B**	**HR**	**RBI**	**Avg.**	**BB**	**SO**	**SB**	**PO**	**A**	**E**	**Avg.**
1990— Eugene (N'west)	3B-SS	73	289	33	85	18	5	2	44	.294	17	70	15	41	†151	16	.923
1991— Baseball City (FSL)	3B	81	315	41	94	21	6	5	33	.298	22	70	28	65	146	12	.946
— Memphis (South.)	3B	56	206	29	47	7	1	6	33	.228	9	63	6	36	112	13	.919
1992— Memphis (South.)	3B-OF-1B	129	487	71	119	20	5	27	83	.244	25	157	5	139	150	20	.935
— Omaha (A.A.)	3B	5	14	3	3	0	0	2	4	.214	2	3	1	2	13	1	.938
1993— Kansas City (A.L.)	3B-DH	81	238	30	52	12	1	7	36	.218	16	82	6	45	114	16	.909
— Omaha (A.A.)	3B	12	51	8	12	2	0	3	10	.235	4	20	0	11	24	2	.946
1994— Omaha (A.A.)	OF	6	22	2	4	1	0	1	2	.182	0	4	1	7	1	0	1.000
— Memphis (South.)	OF	108	400	57	120	26	4	17	66	.300	40	116	12	218	*18	6	.975
1995— Kansas City (A.L.)	OF-DH	52	113	11	23	6	0	4	12	.204	9	37	1	63	4	3	.957
— Omaha (A.A.)	OF	20	76	7	12	5	0	2	8	.158	2	25	0	37	1	1	.974
Major league totals (2 years)		133	351	41	75	18	1	11	48	.214	25	119	7	108	118	19	.922

HIBBARD, GREG — P — MARINERS

PERSONAL: Born September 13, 1964, in New Orleans. . . . 6-0/190. . . . Throws left, bats left. . . . Full name: James Gregory Hibbard.
HIGH SCHOOL: Harrison Central (Gulfport, Miss.).
JUNIOR COLLEGE: Mississippi Gulf Coast Junior College.
COLLEGE: Alabama.
TRANSACTIONS/CAREER NOTES: Selected by Houston Astros organization in eighth round of free-agent draft (January 17, 1984); did not sign. . . . Selected by Kansas City Royals organization in 16th round of free-agent draft (June 2, 1986). . . . Traded by Royals with P Melido Perez, P John Davis and P Chuck Mount to Chicago White Sox for P Floyd Bannister and 3B Dave Cochrane (December 10, 1987). . . . Selected by Florida Marlins in first round (12th pick overall) of expansion draft (November 17, 1992). . . . Traded by Marlins to Chicago Cubs for 3B Gary Scott and SS Alex Arias (November 17, 1992). . . . On disabled list (June 12-July 2, 1993). . . . Granted free agency (December 20, 1993). . . . Signed by Seattle Mariners (January 14, 1994). . . . On disabled list (June 24, 1994-remainder of season and April 21, 1995-entire season).
MISCELLANEOUS: Appeared in one game as pinch-runner (1993).

Year Team (League)	**W**	**L**	**Pct.**	**ERA**	**G**	**GS**	**CG**	**ShO**	**Sv.**	**IP**	**H**	**R**	**ER**	**BB**	**SO**
1986— Eugene (N'west)	5	2	.714	3.46	26	1	0	0	5	39	30	23	15	19	44
1987— Appleton (Midw.)	7	2	.778	1.11	9	9	2	1	0	64 2/3	53	17	8	18	61
— Fort Myers (Fla. St.)	2	1	.667	1.88	3	3	3	1	0	24	20	5	5	3	20
— Memphis (South.)	7	6	.538	3.23	16	16	3	1	0	106	102	48	38	21	56
1988— Vancouver (PCL)■	11	11	.500	4.12	25	24	4	1	0	144 1/3	155	74	66	44	65
1989— Vancouver (PCL)	2	3	.400	2.64	9	9	2	1	0	58	47	24	17	11	45
— Chicago (A.L.)	6	7	.462	3.21	23	23	2	0	0	137 1/3	142	58	49	41	55
1990— Chicago (A.L.)	14	9	.609	3.16	33	33	3	1	0	211	202	80	74	55	92
1991— Chicago (A.L.)	11	11	.500	4.31	32	29	5	0	0	194	196	107	93	57	71
— Vancouver (PCL)	0	0	...	3.38	1	1	0	0	0	5 1/3	4	3	2	3	3
1992— Chicago (A.L.)	10	7	.588	4.40	31	28	0	0	1	176	187	92	86	57	69
1993— Chicago (N.L.)■	15	11	.577	3.96	31	31	1	0	0	191	209	96	84	47	82
1994— Seattle (A.L.)■	1	5	.167	6.69	15	14	0	0	0	80 2/3	115	78	60	31	39
1995—							Did not play.								
A.L. totals (5 years)	42	39	.519	4.08	134	127	10	1	1	799	842	415	362	241	326
N.L. totals (1 year)	15	11	.577	3.96	31	31	1	0	0	191	209	96	84	47	82
Major league totals (6 years)	57	50	.533	4.05	165	158	11	1	1	990	1051	511	446	288	408

HICKERSON, BRYAN — P — REDS

PERSONAL: Born October 13, 1963, in Bemidji, Minn. . . . 6-2/190. . . . Throws left, bats left. . . . Full name: Bryan David Hickerson.
HIGH SCHOOL: Bemidji (Minn.).
COLLEGE: Minnesota (degree in sports and exercise science, 1987).
TRANSACTIONS/CAREER NOTES: Selected by St. Louis Cardinals organization in ninth round of free-agent draft (June 3, 1985); did not sign. . . . Selected by Minnesota Twins organization in seventh round of free-agent draft (June 2, 1986). . . . Loaned by Twins to San Francisco Giants organization (April 1-June 14, 1987). . . . Traded by Twins organization to Giants organization (June 15, 1987), completing trade in which Twins traded P Jose Dominguez and P Ray Velasquez to Giants for P David Blakely and OF Dan Gladden (March 31, 1987). . . . On disabled list (July 14-August 17, 1987 and April 8, 1988-entire season). . . . Claimed on waivers by Chicago Cubs (November 22, 1994). . . . Traded by Cubs to Colorado Rockies for future considerations (July 31, 1995). . . . Released by Rockies (October 10, 1995). . . . Signed by Cincinnati Reds organization (January 2, 1996).
MISCELLANEOUS: Had two-run triple in only appearance as pinch-hitter for Colorado (1995).

Year Team (League)	**W**	**L**	**Pct.**	**ERA**	**G**	**GS**	**CG**	**ShO**	**Sv.**	**IP**	**H**	**R**	**ER**	**BB**	**SO**
1986— Visalia (California)	4	3	.571	4.23	11	11	3	0	0	72 1/3	72	37	34	25	69
1987— Clinton (Midwest)■	11	0	*1.000	1.24	17	10	2	1	1	94	60	17	13	37	103
— Shreveport (Texas)■	1	2	.333	3.94	4	3	0	0	0	16	20	7	7	4	23
1988—							Did not play.								
1989— San Jose (Calif.)	11	6	.647	2.55	21	21	1	1	0	134	111	52	38	57	110
1990— Shreveport (Texas)	3	6	.333	4.23	27	6	0	0	1	66	71	37	31	26	63
— Phoenix (PCL)	0	4	.000	5.50	12	4	0	0	0	34 1/3	48	25	21	16	26
1991— Shreveport (Texas)	3	4	.429	3.00	23	0	0	0	2	39	36	15	13	14	41
— Phoenix (PCL)	1	1	.500	3.80	12	0	0	0	2	21 1/3	29	10	9	5	21
— San Francisco (N.L.)	2	2	.500	3.60	17	6	0	0	0	50	53	20	20	17	43
1992— San Francisco (N.L.)	5	3	.625	3.09	61	1	0	0	0	87 1/3	74	31	30	21	68
1993— San Francisco (N.L.)	7	5	.583	4.26	47	15	0	0	0	120 1/3	137	58	57	39	69
1994— San Francisco (N.L.)	4	8	.333	5.40	28	14	0	0	1	98 1/3	118	60	59	38	59
1995— Chicago (N.L.)■	2	3	.400	6.82	38	0	0	0	1	31 2/3	36	28	24	15	28
— Colorado (N.L.)■	1	0	1.000	11.88	18	0	0	0	0	16 2/3	33	24	22	13	12
Major league totals (5 years)	21	21	.500	4.72	209	36	0	0	2	404 1/3	451	221	212	143	279

HIDALGO, RICHARD — OF — ASTROS

PERSONAL: Born July 2, 1975, in Caracas, Venezuela. . . . 6-3/190. . . . Bats right, throws right. . . . Full name: Richard Jose Hidalgo.
TRANSACTIONS/CAREER NOTES: Signed as non-drafted free agent by Houston Astros organization (July 2, 1991).

			BATTING												FIELDING			
Year	**Team (League)**	**Pos.**	**G**	**AB**	**R**	**H**	**2B**	**3B**	**HR**	**RBI**	**Avg.**	**BB**	**SO**	**SB**	**PO**	**A**	**E**	**Avg.**
1992	GC Astros (GCL)	OF	51	184	20	57	7	3	1	27	.310	13	27	14	67	6	0	1.000
1993	Asheville (S. Atl.)	OF	111	403	49	109	23	3	10	55	.270	30	76	21	197	*30	6	.974
1994	Quad City (Midw.)	OF	124	476	68	139	*47	6	12	76	.292	23	80	12	202	*23	11	.953
1995	Jackson (Texas)	OF	133	489	59	130	28	6	14	59	.266	32	76	8	238	14	5	.981

HIGGINSON, BOBBY — OF — TIGERS

PERSONAL: Born August 18, 1970, in Philadelphia. . . . 5-11/180. . . . Bats left, throws right. . . . Full name: Robert Leigh Higginson.
COLLEGE: Temple.
TRANSACTIONS/CAREER NOTES: Selected by Detroit Tigers organization in 12th round of free-agent draft (June 1, 1992).

			BATTING												FIELDING			
Year	**Team (League)**	**Pos.**	**G**	**AB**	**R**	**H**	**2B**	**3B**	**HR**	**RBI**	**Avg.**	**BB**	**SO**	**SB**	**PO**	**A**	**E**	**Avg.**
1992	Niag. Falls (NYP)	OF	70	232	35	68	17	4	2	37	.293	33	47	12	109	5	2	.983
1993	Lakeland (Fla. St.)	OF	61	223	42	67	11	7	3	25	.300	40	31	8	88	7	2	.979
	London (Eastern)	OF	63	224	25	69	15	4	4	35	.308	19	37	3	100	11	2	.982
1994	Toledo (Int'l)	OF	137	476	81	131	28	3	23	67	.275	46	99	16	282	10	8	.973
1995	Detroit (A.L.)	OF-DH	131	410	61	92	17	5	14	43	.224	62	107	6	247	*13	4	.985
Major league totals (1 year)			131	410	61	92	17	5	14	43	.224	62	107	6	247	13	4	.985

HIGHTOWER, VEE — OF — CUBS

PERSONAL: Born April 25, 1972, in Pittsburgh. . . . 6-5/215. . . . Bats both, throws right. . . . Full name: Vegrin Joseph Hightower.
HIGH SCHOOL: Mt. Lebanon (Pa.).
COLLEGE: Vanderbilt.
TRANSACTIONS/CAREER NOTES: Selected by Chicago Cubs organization in third round of free-agent draft (June 3, 1993). . . . On disabled list (July 23, 1993-remainder of season; April 8-May 19 and August 6, 1994-remainder of season).

			BATTING												FIELDING			
Year	**Team (League)**	**Pos.**	**G**	**AB**	**R**	**H**	**2B**	**3B**	**HR**	**RBI**	**Avg.**	**BB**	**SO**	**SB**	**PO**	**A**	**E**	**Avg.**
1993	Peoria (Midwest)	OF	2	10	0	2	0	0	0	0	.200	0	1	1	0	0	0	...
1994	Peoria (Midwest)	OF	46	147	28	35	6	4	1	10	.238	28	30	6	32	0	0	1.000
1995	Rockford (Midw.)	OF	64	238	51	63	11	1	7	36	.265	39	52	23	29	1	1	.968

HILL, GLENALLEN — OF — GIANTS

PERSONAL: Born March 22, 1965, in Santa Cruz, Calif. . . . 6-2/220. . . . Bats right, throws right.
HIGH SCHOOL: Santa Cruz (Calif.).
TRANSACTIONS/CAREER NOTES: Selected by Toronto Blue Jays organization in ninth round of free-agent draft (June 6, 1983). . . . On disabled list (July 6-21, 1990). . . . Traded by Blue Jays with P Denis Boucher, OF Mark Whiten and a player to be named later to Cleveland Indians for P Tom Candiotti and OF Turner Ward (June 27, 1991); Indians acquired cash instead of player to complete deal (October 15, 1991). . . . On Cleveland disabled list (September 8, 1991-remainder of season). . . . On Cleveland disabled list (April 23-May 22, 1992); included rehabilitation assignment to Canton/Akron (May 18-22). . . . Traded by Indians to Chicago Cubs for OF Candy Maldonado (August 19, 1993). . . . Granted free agency (October 27, 1993). . . . Re-signed by Cubs (November 24, 1993). . . . Granted free agency (April 7, 1995). . . . Signed by San Francisco Giants (April 9, 1995).
STATISTICAL NOTES: Led Southern League with 287 total bases and tied for lead with 13 sacrifice flies in 1986. . . . Led International League with 279 total bases and .578 slugging percentage in 1989. . . . Career major league grand slams: 2.

			BATTING												FIELDING			
Year	**Team (League)**	**Pos.**	**G**	**AB**	**R**	**H**	**2B**	**3B**	**HR**	**RBI**	**Avg.**	**BB**	**SO**	**SB**	**PO**	**A**	**E**	**Avg.**
1983	Medicine Hat (Pio.)	OF	46	133	34	63	3	4	6	27	.474	17	49	4	63	3	6	.917
1984	Florence (S. Atl.)	OF	129	440	75	105	19	5	16	64	.239	63	*150	30	281	9	16	.948
1985	Kinston (Carolina)	OF	131	466	57	98	13	0	20	56	.210	57	*211	42	234	12	13	.950
1986	Knoxville (South.)	OF	141	*570	87	159	23	6	*31	96	.279	39	*153	18	230	9	*21	.919
1987	Syracuse (Int'l)	OF	*137	536	65	126	25	6	16	77	.235	25	*152	22	176	10	10	.949
1988	Syracuse (Int'l)	OF	51	172	21	40	7	0	4	19	.233	15	59	7	101	2	1	.990
	Knoxville (South.)	OF	79	269	37	71	13	2	12	38	.264	28	75	10	130	6	5	.965
1989	Syracuse (Int'l)	OF	125	483	*86	*155	31	*15	*21	72	.321	34	107	21	242	3	*7	.972
	Toronto (A.L.)	OF-DH	19	52	4	15	0	0	1	7	.288	3	12	2	27	0	1	.964
1990	Toronto (A.L.)	OF-DH	84	260	47	60	11	3	12	32	.231	18	62	8	115	4	2	.983
1991	Toronto (A.L.)	DH-OF	35	99	14	25	5	2	3	11	.253	7	24	2	29	0	1	.967
	Cleveland (A.L.)■	OF-DH	37	122	15	32	3	0	5	14	.262	16	30	4	89	0	2	.978
1992	Cleveland (A.L.)	OF-DH	102	369	38	89	16	1	18	49	.241	20	73	9	126	5	6	.956
	Cant./Akr. (East.)	OF	3	9	1	1	1	0	0	1	.111	3	4	0	4	0	1	.800
1993	Cleveland (A.L.)	OF-DH	66	174	19	39	7	2	5	25	.224	11	50	7	62	1	4	.940
	Chicago (N.L.)■	OF	31	87	14	30	7	0	10	22	.345	6	21	1	42	2	2	.957
1994	Chicago (N.L.)	OF	89	269	48	80	12	1	10	38	.297	29	57	19	149	0	2	.987
1995	San Fran. (N.L.)■	OF	132	497	71	131	29	4	24	86	.264	39	98	25	226	10	10	.959
American League totals (5 years)			343	1076	137	260	42	8	44	138	.242	75	251	32	448	10	16	.966
National League totals (3 years)			252	853	133	241	48	5	44	146	.283	74	176	45	417	12	14	.968
Major league totals (7 years)			595	1929	270	501	90	13	88	284	.260	149	427	77	865	22	30	.967

HILL, KEN — P — RANGERS

PERSONAL: Born December 14, 1965, in Lynn, Mass. . . . 6-2/205. . . . Throws right, bats right. . . . Full name: Kenneth Wade Hill.
HIGH SCHOOL: Classical (Lynn, Mass.).
COLLEGE: North Adams (Mass.) State.
TRANSACTIONS/CAREER NOTES: Signed as non-drafted free agent by Detroit Tigers organization (February 14, 1985). . . . Traded by Tigers with a player to be named later to St. Louis Cardinals for C Mike Heath (August 10, 1986); Cardinals acquired 1B Mike Laga to complete deal (September 2, 1986). . . . On St. Louis disabled list (March 26-May 9, 1988). . . . On St. Louis disabled list (August 11-September 1, 1991); included rehabilitation assignment to Louisville (August 29-30). . . . Traded by Cardinals to Montreal Expos for 1B Andres Galarraga (November 25, 1991). . . . On Montreal disabled list (June 26-July 17, 1993); included rehabilitation assignment to Ottawa (July 12-15). . . . Traded by Expos to Cardinals for P Brian Eversgerd, P Kirk Bullinger and OF Darond Stovall (April 5, 1995). . . . Traded by Cardinals to Cleveland Indians for 3B/2B David Bell, P Rick Heiserman and C Pepe McNeal (July 27, 1995). . . . Granted free agency (November 1, 1995). . . . Signed by Texas Rangers (December 22, 1995).
RECORDS: Shares N.L. single-season record for fewest games lost by pitcher who led league in games lost—15 (1989).
STATISTICAL NOTES: Pitched 6-0 one-hit, complete-game victory against New York (June 8, 1992). . . . Led N.L. with 16 sacrifice hits in 1994.
MISCELLANEOUS: Made an out in one game as pinch-hitter with Montreal (1993). . . . Had sacrifice hit in one game as pinch-hitter (1994).

Year	Team (League)	W	L	Pct.	ERA	G	GS	CG	ShO	Sv.	IP	H	R	ER	BB	SO
1985	Gastonia (S. Atl.)	3	6	.333	4.96	15	12	0	0	0	69	60	51	38	57	48
1986	Gastonia (S. Atl.)	9	5	.643	2.79	22	16	1	0	0	122 2/3	95	51	38	80	86
—	Glens Falls (East.)	0	1	.000	5.14	1	1	0	0	0	7	4	4	4	6	4
—	Arkansas (Texas)■	1	2	.333	4.50	3	3	1	0	0	18	18	10	9	7	9
1987	Arkansas (Texas)	3	5	.375	5.20	18	8	0	0	2	53 2/3	60	33	31	30	48
—	St. Petersburg (FSL)	1	3	.250	4.17	18	4	0	0	2	41	38	19	19	17	32
1988	St. Louis (N.L.)	0	1	.000	5.14	4	1	0	0	0	14	16	9	8	6	6
—	Arkansas (Texas)	9	9	.500	4.92	22	22	3	1	0	115 1/3	129	76	63	50	107
1989	Louisville (A.A.)	0	2	.000	3.50	3	3	0	0	0	18	13	8	7	10	18
—	St. Louis (N.L.)	7	•15	.318	3.80	33	33	2	1	0	196 2/3	186	92	83	*99	112
1990	St. Louis (N.L.)	5	6	.455	5.49	17	14	1	0	0	78 2/3	79	49	48	33	58
—	Louisville (A.A.)	6	1	.857	1.79	12	12	2	1	0	85 1/3	47	20	17	27	104
1991	St. Louis (N.L.)	11	10	.524	3.57	30	30	0	0	0	181 1/3	147	76	72	67	121
—	Louisville (A.A.)	0	0	...	0.00	1	1	0	0	0	1	0	0	0	0	2
1992	Montreal (N.L.)■	16	9	.640	2.68	33	33	3	3	0	218	187	76	65	75	150
1993	Montreal (N.L.)	9	7	.563	3.23	28	28	2	0	0	183 2/3	163	84	66	74	90
—	Ottawa (Int'l)	0	0	...	0.00	1	1	0	0	0	4	1	0	0	1	0
1994	Montreal (N.L.)	•16	5	.762	3.32	23	23	2	1	0	154 2/3	145	61	57	44	85
1995	St. Louis (N.L.)■	6	7	.462	5.06	18	18	0	0	0	110 1/3	125	71	62	45	50
—	Cleveland (A.L.)■	4	1	.800	3.98	12	11	1	0	0	74 2/3	77	36	33	32	48
A.L. totals (1 year)		4	1	.800	3.98	12	11	1	0	0	74 2/3	77	36	33	32	48
N.L. totals (8 years)		70	60	.538	3.65	186	180	10	5	0	1137 1/3	1048	518	461	443	672
Major league totals (8 years)		74	61	.548	3.67	198	191	11	5	0	1212	1125	554	494	475	720

DIVISION SERIES RECORD

Year	Team (League)	W	L	Pct.	ERA	G	GS	CG	ShO	Sv.	IP	H	R	ER	BB	SO
1995	Cleveland (A.L.)	1	0	1.000	0.00	1	0	0	0	0	1 1/3	1	0	0	0	2

CHAMPIONSHIP SERIES RECORD

Year	Team (League)	W	L	Pct.	ERA	G	GS	CG	ShO	Sv.	IP	H	R	ER	BB	SO
1995	Cleveland (A.L.)	1	0	1.000	0.00	1	1	0	0	0	7	5	0	0	3	6

WORLD SERIES RECORD

Year	Team (League)	W	L	Pct.	ERA	G	GS	CG	ShO	Sv.	IP	H	R	ER	BB	SO
1995	Cleveland (A.L.)	0	1	.000	4.26	2	1	0	0	0	6 1/3	7	3	3	4	1

ALL-STAR GAME RECORD

Year	League	W	L	Pct.	ERA	GS	CG	ShO	Sv.	IP	H	R	ER	BB	SO
1994	National	0	0	...	0.00	0	0	0	0	2	0	0	0	1	0

HITCHCOCK, STERLING — P — MARINERS

PERSONAL: Born April 29, 1971, in Fayetteville, N.C. . . . 6-1/192. . . . Throws left, bats left. . . . Full name: Sterling Alex Hitchcock.
HIGH SCHOOL: Armwood (Seffner, Fla.).
TRANSACTIONS/CAREER NOTES: Selected by New York Yankees organization in ninth round of free-agent draft (June 5, 1989). . . . On disabled list (June 26-August 14, 1991). . . . On Columbus disabled list (May 23-July 21, 1993). . . . Traded by Yankees with 3B Russ Davis to Seattle Mariners for 1B Tino Martinez, P Jeff Nelson and P Jim Mecir (December 7, 1995).
STATISTICAL NOTES: Pitched 1-0 no-hit victory against Sumter (July 16, 1990).

Year	Team (League)	W	L	Pct.	ERA	G	GS	CG	ShO	Sv.	IP	H	R	ER	BB	SO
1989	GC Yankees (GCL)	*9	1	.900	1.64	13	•13	0	0	0	76 2/3	48	16	14	27	*98
1990	Greensboro (S. Atl.)	12	12	.500	2.91	27	27	6	*5	0	173 1/3	122	68	56	60	*171
1991	Prin. William (Caro.)	7	7	.500	2.64	19	19	2	0	0	119 1/3	111	49	35	26	101
1992	Alb./Colon. (East.)	6	9	.400	2.58	24	24	2	0	0	146 2/3	116	51	42	42	*155
—	New York (A.L.)	0	2	.000	8.31	3	3	0	0	0	13	23	12	12	6	6
1993	Columbus (Int'l)	3	5	.375	4.81	16	16	0	0	0	76 2/3	80	43	41	28	85
—	New York (A.L.)	1	2	.333	4.65	6	6	0	0	0	31	32	18	16	14	26
1994	New York (A.L.)	4	1	.800	4.20	23	5	1	0	2	49 1/3	48	24	23	29	37
—	Columbus (Int'l)	3	4	.429	4.32	10	9	1	0	0	50	53	30	24	18	47
—	Alb./Colon. (East.)	1	0	1.000	1.80	1	1	0	0	0	5	4	1	1	0	7
1995	New York (A.L.)	11	10	.524	4.70	27	27	4	1	0	168 1/3	155	91	88	68	121
Major league totals (4 years)		16	15	.516	4.78	59	41	5	1	2	261 2/3	258	145	139	117	190

H

DIVISION SERIES RECORD

Year	Team (League)	W	L	Pct.	ERA	G	GS	CG	ShO	Sv.	IP	H	R	ER	BB	SO
1995—	New York (A.L.)	0	0	...	5.40	2	0	0	0	0	1 2/3	2	2	1	2	1

HOCKING, DENNY — SS — TWINS

PERSONAL: Born April 2, 1970, in Torrance, Calif. . . . 5-10/174. . . . Bats both, throws right. . . . Full name: Dennis Lee Hocking.
HIGH SCHOOL: West Torrance (Calif.).
COLLEGE: El Camino College (Calif.).
TRANSACTIONS/CAREER NOTES: Selected by Minnesota Twins organization in 52nd round of free-agent draft (June 5, 1989). . . . On Nashville disabled list (April 8-29, 1993).
STATISTICAL NOTES: Led California League shortstops with 721 total chances in 1992. . . . Led Pacific Coast League shortstops with .966 fielding percentage and 390 assists in 1995.

			BATTING												FIELDING			
Year	Team (League)	Pos.	G	AB	R	H	2B	3B	HR	RBI	Avg.	BB	SO	SB	PO	A	E	Avg.
1990—	Elizabeth. (Appal.)	SS-2B-3B	54	201	45	59	6	2	6	30	.294	40	26	14	77	179	20	.928
1991—	Kenosha (Midwest)	SS	125	432	72	110	17	8	2	36	.255	77	69	22	193	308	42	.923
1992—	Visalia (California)	SS	135	*550	117	*182	34	9	7	81	.331	72	77	38	214	*469	38	.947
1993—	Nashville (South.)	SS-2B	107	409	54	109	9	4	8	50	.267	34	66	15	144	300	30	.937
—	Minnesota (A.L.)	SS-2B	15	36	7	5	1	0	0	0	.139	6	8	1	19	23	1	.977
1994—	Salt Lake (PCL)	SS	112	394	61	110	14	6	5	57	.279	28	57	13	143	342	26	.949
—	Minnesota (A.L.)	SS	11	31	3	10	3	0	0	2	.323	0	4	2	11	27	0	1.000
1995—	Salt Lake (PCL)	SS-2B	117	397	51	112	24	2	8	75	.282	25	41	12	173	†393	20	†.966
—	Minnesota (A.L.)	SS	9	25	4	5	0	2	0	3	.200	2	2	1	13	20	1	.971
Major league totals (3 years)			35	92	14	20	4	2	0	5	.217	8	14	4	43	70	2	.983

HOFFMAN, TREVOR — P — PADRES

PERSONAL: Born October 13, 1967, in Bellflower, Calif. . . . 6-0/205. . . . Throws right, bats right. . . . Full name: Trevor William Hoffman. . . . Brother of Glenn Hoffman, minor league field coordinator, Los Angeles Dodgers, and major league infielder with Boston Red Sox, Dodgers and California Angels (1980-89).
HIGH SCHOOL: Savanna (Anaheim, Calif.).
JUNIOR COLLEGE: Cypress (Calif.) College.
COLLEGE: Arizona.
TRANSACTIONS/CAREER NOTES: Selected by Cincinnati Reds organization in 11th round of free-agent draft (June 5, 1989). . . . Selected by Florida Marlins in first round (eighth pick overall) of expansion draft (November 17, 1992). . . . Traded by Marlins with P Jose Martinez and P Andres Berumen to San Diego Padres for 3B Gary Sheffield and P Rich Rodriguez (June 24, 1993).

Year	Team (League)	W	L	Pct.	ERA	G	GS	CG	ShO	Sv.	IP	H	R	ER	BB	SO
1991—	Ced. Rap. (Midw.)	1	1	.500	1.87	27	0	0	0	12	33 2/3	22	8	7	13	52
—	Chattanooga (Sou.)	1	0	1.000	1.93	14	0	0	0	8	14	10	4	3	7	23
1992—	Chattanooga (Sou.)	3	0	1.000	1.52	6	6	0	0	0	29 2/3	22	6	5	11	31
—	Nashville (A.A.)	4	6	.400	4.27	42	5	0	0	6	65 1/3	57	32	31	32	63
1993—	Florida (N.L.)■	2	2	.500	3.28	28	0	0	0	2	35 2/3	24	13	13	19	26
—	San Diego (N.L.)■	2	4	.333	4.31	39	0	0	0	3	54 1/3	56	30	26	20	53
1994—	San Diego (N.L.)	4	4	.500	2.57	47	0	0	0	20	56	39	16	16	20	68
1995—	San Diego (N.L.)	7	4	.636	3.88	55	0	0	0	31	53 1/3	48	25	23	14	52
Major league totals (3 years)		15	14	.517	3.52	169	0	0	0	56	199 1/3	167	84	78	73	199

RECORD AS POSITION PLAYER

			BATTING												FIELDING			
Year	Team (League)	Pos.	G	AB	R	H	2B	3B	HR	RBI	Avg.	BB	SO	SB	PO	A	E	Avg.
1989—	Billings (Pioneer)	SS	61	201	22	50	5	0	1	20	.249	19	40	1	*116	140	•25	.911
1990—	Char., W.Va. (SAL)	SS-3B	103	278	41	59	10	1	2	23	.212	38	53	3	114	209	30	.915

HOILES, CHRIS — C — ORIOLES

PERSONAL: Born March 20, 1965, in Bowling Green, O. . . . 6-0/213. . . . Bats right, throws right. . . . Full name: Christopher Allen Hoiles.
HIGH SCHOOL: Elmwood (Wayne, O.).
COLLEGE: Eastern Michigan.
TRANSACTIONS/CAREER NOTES: Selected by Detroit Tigers organization in 19th round of free-agent draft (June 2, 1986). . . . Traded by Tigers organization with P Cesar Mejia and P Robinson Garces to Baltimore Orioles (September 9, 1988), completing deal in which Orioles traded OF Fred Lynn to Tigers for three players to be named later (August 31, 1988). . . . On Rochester disabled list (June 18-July 7, 1989). . . . On Baltimore disabled list (June 22-August 18, 1992); included rehabilitation assignment to Hagerstown (August 11-18). . . . On disabled list (August 3-24, 1993 and July 16-31, 1995).
STATISTICAL NOTES: Led Appalachian League first basemen with .996 fielding percentage, 515 putouts and 551 total chances in 1986. . . . Led Appalachian League with 143 total bases in 1986. . . . Led Eastern League with .500 slugging percentage in 1988. . . . Tied for Eastern League lead in double plays by catcher with five in 1988. . . . Led A.L. catchers with .998 fielding percentage in 1991. . . . Led A.L. catchers with 658 total chances in 1994. . . . Career major league grand slams: 3.

			BATTING												FIELDING			
Year	Team (League)	Pos.	G	AB	R	H	2B	3B	HR	RBI	Avg.	BB	SO	SB	PO	A	E	Avg.
1986—	Bristol (Appal.)	1B-C	•68	253	42	81	*19	2	13	*57	.320	30	20	10	†563	38	4	†.993
1987—	Glens Falls (East.)	C-1B-3B	108	380	47	105	12	0	13	53	.276	35	37	1	406	88	11	.978
1988—	Glens Falls (East.)	C-1B	103	360	67	102	21	3	•17	73	.283	50	56	4	438	57	7	.986
—	Toledo (Int'l)	C	22	69	4	11	1	0	2	6	.159	2	12	1	71	2	1	.986
1989—	Rochester (Int'l)■	C-1B	96	322	41	79	19	1	10	51	.245	31	58	1	431	33	7	.985
—	Baltimore (A.L.)	C-DH	6	9	0	1	1	0	0	1	.111	1	3	0	11	0	0	1.000
1990—	Rochester (Int'l)	C-1B	74	247	52	86	20	1	18	56	.348	44	48	4	268	13	5	.983

Year	Team (League)	Pos.	G	AB	R	H	2B	3B	HR	RBI	Avg.	BB	SO	SB	PO	A	E	Avg.
				BATTING											FIELDING			
	—Baltimore (A.L.)	C-DH-1B	23	63	7	12	3	0	1	6	.190	5	12	0	62	6	0	1.000
1991	—Baltimore (A.L.)	C-1B	107	341	36	83	15	0	11	31	.243	29	61	0	443	44	1	†.998
1992	—Baltimore (A.L.)	C-DH	96	310	49	85	10	1	20	40	.274	55	60	0	500	31	3	.994
	—Hagerstown (East.)	C	7	24	7	11	1	0	1	5	.458	2	5	0	16	5	0	1.000
1993	—Baltimore (A.L.)	C-DH	126	419	80	130	28	0	29	82	.310	69	94	1	696	64	5	.993
1994	—Baltimore (A.L.)	C	99	332	45	82	10	0	19	53	.247	63	73	2	*615	36	7	.989
1995	—Baltimore (A.L.)	C-DH	114	352	53	88	15	1	19	58	.250	67	80	1	659	33	3	*.996
Major league totals (7 years)			571	1826	270	481	82	2	99	271	.263	289	383	4	2986	214	19	.994

HOLBERT, AARON — SS — CARDINALS

PERSONAL: Born January 9, 1973, in Torrance, Calif. . . . 6-0/160. . . . Bats right, throws right. . . . Full name: Aaron Keith Holbert. . . . Brother of Ray Holbert, shortstop, Houston Astros.

HIGH SCHOOL: David Starr Jordan (Long Beach, Calif.).

TRANSACTIONS/CAREER NOTES: Selected by St. Louis Cardinals organization in first round (18th pick overall) of free-agent draft (June 4, 1990); pick received as part of compensation for Boston Red Sox signing Type A free-agent C Tony Pena. . . . On disabled list (June 5-July 17, 1991). . . . On Arkansas disabled list (May 10-July 30, 1994). . . . On disabled list (May 15-22 and July 28-August 4, 1995). . . . On suspended list (May 23-25, 1995).

STATISTICAL NOTES: Led Florida State League in caught stealing with 22 in 1993.

Year	Team (League)	Pos.	G	AB	R	H	2B	3B	HR	RBI	Avg.	BB	SO	SB	PO	A	E	Avg.
				BATTING											FIELDING			
1990	—Johns. City (App.)	SS	54	174	27	30	4	1	1	18	.172	24	31	4	87	136	*30	.881
1991	—Springfield (Midw.)	SS	59	215	22	48	5	1	1	24	.223	15	28	5	112	181	15	.951
1992	—Savannah (S. Atl.)	SS	119	438	53	117	17	4	1	34	.267	40	57	62	190	314	47	.915
1993	—St. Peters. (FSL)	SS-2B	121	457	60	121	18	3	2	31	.265	28	61	45	220	351	32	.947
1994	—Arkansas (Texas)	SS	59	233	41	69	10	6	2	19	.296	14	25	9	94	192	17	.944
	—Ariz. Cardinals (Ar.)	SS	5	12	3	2	0	0	0	0	.167	2	2	2	2	17	1	.950
1995	—Louisville (A.A.)	SS	112	401	57	103	16	4	9	40	.257	20	60	14	153	302	*31	.936

HOLBERT, RAY — SS — ASTROS

PERSONAL: Born September 25, 1970, in Torrance, Calif. . . . 6-0/175. . . . Bats right, throws right. . . . Full name: Ray Arthur Holbert III. . . . Brother of Aaron Holbert, shortstop, St. Louis Cardinals organization.

HIGH SCHOOL: David Starr Jordan (Long Beach, Calif.).

TRANSACTIONS/CAREER NOTES: Selected by San Diego Padres organization in third round of free-agent draft (June 1, 1988). . . . On disabled list (July 7-28, 1992). . . . On San Diego disabled list (July 30, 1995-remainder of season). . . . Traded by Padres to Houston Astros for P Pedro A. Martinez (October 10, 1995).

STATISTICAL NOTES: Led Arizona League shortstops with .927 fielding percentage and 132 assists in 1988. . . . Led Midwest League shortstops with 642 total chances and 75 double plays in 1990. . . . Led Texas League with nine sacrifice flies in 1993. . . . Led Pacific Coast League with 10 sacrifice hits in 1994. . . . Led Pacific Coast League shortstops with 34 errors in 1994. . . . Career major league grand slams: 1.

Year	Team (League)	Pos.	G	AB	R	H	2B	3B	HR	RBI	Avg.	BB	SO	SB	PO	A	E	Avg.
				BATTING											FIELDING			
1988	—Ariz. Padres (Ariz.)	SS-3B	49	170	38	44	1	0	3	19	.259	38	32	20	59	†137	15	†.929
1989	—Waterloo (Midw.)	SS-3B	117	354	37	55	7	1	0	20	.155	41	99	13	205	303	32	.941
1990	—Waterloo (Midw.)	SS	133	411	51	84	10	1	3	39	.204	51	117	16	*233	*378	31	.952
1991	—High Desert (Calif.)	SS	122	386	76	102	14	2	4	51	.264	56	83	19	196	331	*37	.934
1992	—Wichita (Texas)	SS	95	304	46	86	7	3	2	23	.283	42	68	26	150	217	17	.956
1993	—Wichita (Texas)	SS	112	388	56	101	13	5	5	48	.260	54	87	30	155	267	30	.934
1994	—Las Vegas (PCL)	SS-OF	118	426	68	128	21	5	8	52	.300	50	99	27	157	333	†34	.935
	—San Diego (N.L.)	SS	5	5	1	1	0	0	0	0	.200	0	4	0	0	0	0	. . .
1995	—San Diego (N.L.)	SS-2B-OF	63	73	11	13	2	1	2	5	.178	8	20	4	27	58	5	.944
	—Las Vegas (PCL)	2B	9	26	3	3	1	0	0	3	.115	5	10	1	9	26	1	.972
Major league totals (2 years)			68	78	12	14	2	1	2	5	.179	8	24	4	27	58	5	.944

HOLDRIDGE, DAVID — P — ANGELS

PERSONAL: Born February 5, 1969, in Wayne, Mich. . . . 6-3/185. . . . Throws right, bats right. . . . Full name: David Allen Holdridge.

HIGH SCHOOL: Ocean View (Huntington Beach, Calif.).

TRANSACTIONS/CAREER NOTES: Selected by California Angels organization in supplemental round ("sandwich pick" between first and second round, 31st pick overall) of free-agent draft (June 2, 1987); pick received as compensation for Oakland Athletics signing Type A free-agent DH/OF Reggie Jackson. . . . Traded by Angels organization to Philadelphia Phillies organization for C Lance Parrish (October 3, 1988). . . . On Reading disabled list (May 27-June 25, 1991). . . . Selected by Angels from Phillies organization in Rule 5 major league draft (December 9, 1991).

STATISTICAL NOTES: Tied for Florida State League lead with 11 home runs allowed in 1989. . . . Tied for Eastern League lead with 13 home runs allowed in 1990. . . . Led California League with 21 wild pitches in 1992.

Year	Team (League)	W	L	Pct.	ERA	G	GS	CG	ShO	Sv.	IP	H	R	ER	BB	SO
1988	—Quad City (Midw.)	6	12	.333	3.87	28	28	0	0	0	153 2/3	151	92	66	66	110
1989	—Clearwater (Fla. St.)■	7	10	.412	5.71	24	24	3	0	0	132 1/3	147	*100	*84	77	77
1990	—Reading (Eastern)	8	12	.400	4.58	24	24	1	0	0	127 2/3	114	74	65	*79	78
1991	—Reading (Eastern)	0	2	.000	5.47	7	7	0	0	0	26 1/3	26	24	16	34	19
	—Clearwater (Fla. St.)	0	0	. . .	7.56	15	0	0	0	1	25	34	23	21	21	23
1992	—Palm Springs (Cal.)■	12	12	.500	4.25	28	27	3	•2	0	159	169	99	75	87	135
1993	—Midland (Texas)	8	10	.444	6.08	27	•27	1	1	0	151	*202	*117	*102	55	123
1994	—Midland (Texas)	7	4	.636	3.93	38	2	0	0	2	66 1/3	66	33	29	23	59
	—Vancouver (PCL)	0	0	. . .	5.14	4	0	0	0	0	7	12	7	4	4	4

Year	Team (League)	W	L	Pct.	ERA	G	GS	CG	ShO	Sv.	IP	H	R	ER	BB	SO
1995—	Vancouver (PCL)	0	2	.000	4.61	11	0	0	0	1	13 2/3	18	10	7	7	13
—	Lake Elsinore (California)	3	0	1.000	0.98	12	0	0	0	0	18 1/3	13	3	2	5	24
—	Midland (Texas)	1	0	1.000	1.78	14	0	0	0	1	25 1/3	20	8	5	8	23

HOLIFIELD, RICK — OF — PHILLIES

PERSONAL: Born March 25, 1970, in Bronx, N.Y. . . . 6-2/180. . . . Bats left, throws left. . . . Full name: Marshall Rickey Holifield. . . . Name pronounced HOLE-lee-field.

HIGH SCHOOL: Ganesha (Pomona, Calif.).

TRANSACTIONS/CAREER NOTES: Selected by Toronto Blue Jays organization in 21st round of free-agent draft (June 1, 1988). . . . Claimed on waivers by Philadelphia Phillies (June 24, 1994).

STATISTICAL NOTES: Led Florida State League in being hit by pitch with 16 and tied for lead with 214 total bases and .526 slugging percentage in 1993.

							BATTING								FIELDING		
Year	Team (League)	Pos.	G	AB	R	H	2B	3B	HR	RBI	Avg.	BB	SO	SB	PO	A	E	Avg.
1988—	Medicine Hat (Pio.)	OF	31	96	16	26	4	1	1	6	.271	9	27	6	36	5	*14	.745
1989—	St. Cathar. (NYP)	OF	60	209	22	46	7	1	4	21	.220	15	74	4	115	4	2	.983
1990—	Myrtle Beach (SAL)	OF	99	279	37	56	9	2	3	18	.201	28	88	13	171	2	10	.945
1991—	Myrtle Beach (SAL)	OF	114	324	37	71	15	5	1	25	.219	34	94	16	152	8	5	.970
1992—	Myrtle Beach (SAL)	OF	93	281	32	56	15	2	8	27	.199	23	81	6	157	4	11	.936
1993—	Dunedin (Fla. St.)	OF	127	407	84	112	18	12	*20	68	.275	56	*129	30	255	9	•12	.957
1994—	Knoxville (South.)	OF	71	238	31	59	10	9	4	31	.248	24	64	23	96	7	7	.936
—	Scran./W.B. (Int'l)■	OF	18	55	5	7	1	0	0	0	.127	3	19	0	41	0	0	1.000
—	Reading (Eastern)	OF	42	155	29	44	8	3	7	19	.284	18	34	21	89	3	0	1.000
1995—	Scran./W.B. (Int'l)	OF	76	223	32	46	6	3	3	24	.206	24	52	21	131	4	5	.964
—	Reading (Eastern)	OF	30	93	18	23	3	1	1	5	.247	22	18	5	84	3	1	.989

HOLLANDSWORTH, TODD — OF — DODGERS

PERSONAL: Born April 20, 1973, in Dayton, O. . . . 6-2/193. . . . Bats left, throws left. . . . Full name: Todd Mathew Hollandsworth.

HIGH SCHOOL: Newport (Bellevue, Wash.).

TRANSACTIONS/CAREER NOTES: Selected by Los Angeles Dodgers organization in third round of free-agent draft (June 3, 1991); pick received as part of compensation for Kansas City Royals signing Type B free agent OF/DH Kirk Gibson. . . . On Los Angeles disabled list (May 3-July 7 and August 9-September 12, 1995); included rehabilitation assignments to San Bernardino (June 6-7) and Albuquerque (June 27-July 7).

							BATTING								FIELDING		
Year	Team (League)	Pos.	G	AB	R	H	2B	3B	HR	RBI	Avg.	BB	SO	SB	PO	A	E	Avg.
1991—	Yakima (N'west)	OF	56	203	34	48	5	1	8	33	.236	27	57	11	106	1	7	.939
1992—	Bakersfield (Calif.)	OF	119	430	70	111	23	5	13	58	.258	50	113	27	230	8	6	.975
1993—	San Antonio (Tex.)	OF	126	474	57	119	24	9	17	63	.251	29	101	24	246	13	12	.956
1994—	Albuquerque (PCL)	OF	132	505	80	144	31	5	19	91	.285	46	96	15	237	5	13	.949
1995—	Los Angeles (N.L.)	OF	41	103	16	24	2	0	5	13	.233	10	29	2	60	1	4	.938
—	San Bern. (Calif.)	OF	1	2	0	1	0	0	0	0	.500	0	1	0	0	0	0	...
—	Albuquerque (PCL)	OF	10	38	9	9	2	0	2	4	.237	6	8	1	19	3	0	1.000
Major league totals (1 year)			41	103	16	24	2	0	5	13	.233	10	29	2	60	1	4	.938

DIVISION SERIES RECORD

							BATTING								FIELDING		
Year	Team (League)	Pos.	G	AB	R	H	2B	3B	HR	RBI	Avg.	BB	SO	SB	PO	A	E	Avg.
1995—	Los Angeles (N.L.)	OF-PH	2	2	0	0	0	0	0	0	.000	0	0	0	0	0	0	...

HOLLINS, DAMON — OF — BRAVES

PERSONAL: Born June 12, 1974, in Fairfield, Calif. . . . 5-11/180. . . . Bats right, throws left. . . . Full name: Damon Jamall Hollins.

TRANSACTIONS/CAREER NOTES: Selected by Atlanta Braves organization in fourth round of free-agent draft (June 1, 1992).

STATISTICAL NOTES: Led Southern League outfielders with 356 total chances in 1995.

							BATTING								FIELDING		
Year	Team (League)	Pos.	G	AB	R	H	2B	3B	HR	RBI	Avg.	BB	SO	SB	PO	A	E	Avg.
1992—	GC Braves (GCL)	OF	49	179	35	41	12	1	1	15	.229	30	22	15	83	6	1	.989
1993—	Danville (Appal.)	OF	62	240	37	77	15	2	7	51	.321	19	30	10	95	*11	6	.946
1994—	Durham (Carolina)	OF	131	485	76	131	28	0	23	88	.270	45	115	12	279	11	*13	.957
1995—	Greenville (South.)	OF	129	466	64	115	26	2	18	77	.247	44	120	6	*330	18	8	.978

HOLLINS, DAVE — 3B/1B — TWINS

PERSONAL: Born May 25, 1966, in Buffalo, N.Y. . . . 6-1/210. . . . Bats both, throws right. . . . Full name: David Michael Hollins.

HIGH SCHOOL: Orchard Park (N.Y.).

COLLEGE: South Carolina.

TRANSACTIONS/CAREER NOTES: Selected by San Diego Padres organization in sixth round of free-agent draft (June 2, 1987). . . . Selected by Philadelphia Phillies from Padres organization in Rule 5 major league draft (December 4, 1989). . . . On Philadelphia disabled list (August 16-September 6, 1991); included rehabilitation assignment to Scranton/Wilkes-Barre (September 2-5). . . . On suspended list (September 29-October 3, 1992). . . . On disabled list (June 11-28, 1993). . . . On Philadelphia disabled list (May 23-July 23 and July 25, 1994-remainder of season); included rehabilitation assignment to Scranton/Wilkes-Barre (July 16-23). . . . On Philadelphia disabled list (June 12-27, 1995). . . . Traded by Phillies to Boston Red Sox for OF Mark Whiten (July 24, 1995). . . . On Boston disabled list (August 9, 1995-remainder of season). . . . Granted free agency (December 21, 1995). . . . Signed by Minnesota Twins (December 23, 1995).

H

STATISTICAL NOTES: Led Northwest League with seven intentional bases on balls received in 1987. . . . Led Northwest League third basemen with 241 total chances in 1987. . . . Led Texas League with 10 sacrifice flies in 1989. . . . Led N.L. in being hit by pitch with 19 in 1992. . . . Career major league grand slams: 2.

		BATTING												FIELDING			
Year Team (League)	**Pos.**	**G**	**AB**	**R**	**H**	**2B**	**3B**	**HR**	**RBI**	**Avg.**	**BB**	**SO**	**SB**	**PO**	**A**	**E**	**Avg.**
1987—Spokane (N'west)	3B	75	278	52	86	14	4	2	44	.309	53	36	20	*59	*167	15	*.938
1988—Riverside (Calif.)	3B-1B-SS	139	516	90	157	32	1	9	92	.304	82	67	13	102	248	29	.923
1989—Wichita (Texas)	3B	131	459	69	126	29	4	9	79	.275	63	88	8	77	209	25	.920
1990—Philadelphia (N.L.)■	3B-1B	72	114	14	21	0	0	5	15	.184	10	28	0	27	37	4	.941
1991—Philadelphia (N.L.)	3B-1B	56	151	18	45	10	2	6	21	.298	17	26	1	67	62	8	.942
—Scran./W.B. (Int'l)	3B-1B	72	229	37	61	11	6	8	35	.266	43	43	4	67	105	10	.945
1992—Philadelphia (N.L.)	3B-1B	156	586	104	158	28	4	27	93	.270	76	110	9	120	253	18	.954
1993—Philadelphia (N.L.)	3B	143	543	104	148	30	4	18	93	.273	85	109	2	73	215	27	.914
1994—Philadelphia (N.L.)	3B-OF	44	162	28	36	7	1	4	26	.222	23	32	1	39	48	11	.888
—Scran./W.B. (Int'l)	OF	6	19	6	4	0	0	1	3	.211	5	4	0	12	1	2	.867
1995—Philadelphia (N.L.)	1B	65	205	46	47	12	2	7	25	.229	53	38	1	532	30	7	.988
—Boston (A.L.)■	DH-OF	5	13	2	2	0	0	0	1	.154	4	7	0	3	0	0	1.000
American League totals (1 year)		5	13	2	2	0	0	0	1	.154	4	7	0	3	0	0	1.000
National League totals (6 years)		536	1761	314	455	87	13	67	273	.258	264	343	14	858	645	75	.952
Major league totals (6 years)		541	1774	316	457	87	13	67	274	.258	268	350	14	861	645	75	.953

CHAMPIONSHIP SERIES RECORD

		BATTING												FIELDING			
Year Team (League)	**Pos.**	**G**	**AB**	**R**	**H**	**2B**	**3B**	**HR**	**RBI**	**Avg.**	**BB**	**SO**	**SB**	**PO**	**A**	**E**	**Avg.**
1993—Philadelphia (N.L.)	3B	6	20	2	4	1	0	2	4	.200	5	4	1	5	4	0	1.000

WORLD SERIES RECORD

		BATTING												FIELDING			
Year Team (League)	**Pos.**	**G**	**AB**	**R**	**H**	**2B**	**3B**	**HR**	**RBI**	**Avg.**	**BB**	**SO**	**SB**	**PO**	**A**	**E**	**Avg.**
1993—Philadelphia (N.L.)	3B	6	23	5	6	1	0	0	2	.261	6	5	0	9	9	0	1.000

ALL-STAR GAME RECORD

		BATTING											FIELDING			
Year League	**Pos.**	**AB**	**R**	**H**	**2B**	**3B**	**HR**	**RBI**	**Avg.**	**BB**	**SO**	**SB**	**PO**	**A**	**E**	**Avg.**
1993—National	3B	1	0	1	1	0	0	0	1.000	0	0	0	1	0	0	1.000

HOLLINS, STACY — P — ATHLETICS

PERSONAL: Born July 31, 1972, in Conroe, Tex. . . . 6-3/180. . . . Throws right, bats right. . . . Full name: Stacy Evan Hollins.
HIGH SCHOOL: Willis (Tex.).
JUNIOR COLLEGE: San Jacinto Junior College (Tex.).
TRANSACTIONS/CAREER NOTES: Selected by Oakland Athletics organization in 43rd round of free-agent draft (June 1, 1992). . . . On Huntsville temporarily inactive list (April 18-May 6, 1995).
STATISTICAL NOTES: Led Midwest League with 12 home runs allowed in 1993. . . . Pitched 3-0 no-hit victory against Springfield (July 7, 1993).

Year Team (League)	W	L	Pct.	ERA	G	GS	CG	ShO	Sv.	IP	H	R	ER	BB	SO
1992—Arizona A's (Ariz.)	6	3	.667	3.39	15	14	3	2	0	*93	*89	47	35	19	*93
1993—Madison (Midwest)	10	11	.476	5.14	26	26	2	1	0	150 2/3	145	100	*86	52	105
1994—Modesto (Calif.)	13	6	.684	3.39	29	22	0	0	0	143 1/3	133	57	54	55	131
1995—Huntsville (South.)	3	8	.273	5.33	15	15	0	0	0	82 2/3	80	52	49	42	62
—Edmonton (PCL)	0	7	.000	10.31	7	7	0	0	0	29 2/3	47	43	34	21	25

HOLMES, DARREN — P — ROCKIES

PERSONAL: Born April 25, 1966, in Asheville, N.C. . . . 6-0/202. . . . Throws right, bats right. . . . Full name: Darren Lee Holmes.
HIGH SCHOOL: T.C. Roberson (Asheville, N.C.).
TRANSACTIONS/CAREER NOTES: Selected by Los Angeles Dodgers organization in 16th round of free-agent draft (June 4, 1984). . . . On disabled list (June 5, 1986-remainder of season). . . . Loaned by Dodgers organization to San Luis Potosi (1988). . . . Traded by Dodgers to Milwaukee Brewers for C Bert Heffernan (December 20, 1990). . . . On Milwaukee disabled list (July 3-18, 1991); included rehabilitation assignment to Beloit (July 13-18). . . . Selected by Colorado Rockies in first round (fifth pick overall) of expansion draft (November 17, 1992). . . . On Colorado disabled list (May 30-June 24, and July 21-August 11, 1994); included rehabilitation assignments to Asheville (June 14-19) and Colorado Springs (June 20).

Year Team (League)	W	L	Pct.	ERA	G	GS	CG	ShO	Sv.	IP	H	R	ER	BB	SO
1984—Great Falls (Pio.)	2	5	.286	6.65	18	6	1	0	0	44 2/3	53	41	33	30	29
1985—Vero Beach (FSL)	4	3	.571	3.11	33	0	0	0	2	63 2/3	57	31	22	35	46
1986—Vero Beach (FSL)	3	6	.333	2.92	11	10	0	0	0	64 2/3	55	30	21	39	59
1987—Vero Beach (FSL)	6	4	.600	4.52	19	19	1	0	0	99 2/3	111	60	50	53	46
1988—San Luis Pot. (Mex.)■	9	9	.500	4.64	23	23	7	1	0	139 2/3	151	88	72	92	110
—Albuquerque (PCL)■	0	1	.000	5.06	2	1	0	0	0	5 1/3	6	3	3	1	1
1989—San Antonio (Tex.)	5	8	.385	3.83	17	16	3	2	1	110 1/3	102	59	47	44	81
—Albuquerque (PCL)	1	4	.200	7.45	9	8	0	0	0	38 2/3	50	32	32	18	31
1990—Albuquerque (PCL)	12	2	*.857	3.11	56	0	0	0	13	92 2/3	78	34	32	39	99
—Los Angeles (N.L.)	0	1	.000	5.19	14	0	0	0	0	17 1/3	15	10	10	11	19
1991—Denver (Am. Assoc.)■	0	0	...	9.00	1	0	0	0	0	1	1	1	1	2	2
—Milwaukee (A.L.)	1	4	.200	4.72	40	0	0	0	3	76 1/3	90	43	40	27	59
—Beloit (Midwest)	0	0	...	0.00	2	0	0	0	2	2	0	0	0	0	3
1992—Denver (Am. Assoc.)	0	0	...	1.38	12	0	0	0	7	13	7	2	2	1	12
—Milwaukee (A.L.)	4	4	.500	2.55	41	0	0	0	6	42 1/3	35	12	12	11	31
1993—Colorado (N.L.)■	3	3	.500	4.05	62	0	0	0	25	66 2/3	56	31	30	20	60

Year	Team (League)	W	L	Pct.	ERA	G	GS	CG	ShO	Sv.	IP	H	R	ER	BB	SO
	—Colo. Springs (PCL)	1	0	1.000	0.00	3	2	0	0	0	8 2/3	1	1	0	1	9
1994	—Colorado (N.L.)	0	3	.000	6.35	29	0	0	0	3	28 1/3	35	25	20	24	33
	—Colo. Springs (PCL)	0	1	.000	8.22	4	2	0	0	0	7 2/3	11	7	7	3	12
	—Asheville (S. Atl.)	0	0	...	0.00	2	1	0	0	0	3	1	0	0	0	7
1995	—Colorado (N.L.)	6	1	.857	3.24	68	0	0	0	14	66 2/3	59	26	24	28	61
A.L. totals (2 years)		5	8	.385	3.94	81	0	0	0	9	118 2/3	125	55	52	38	90
N.L. totals (4 years)		9	8	.529	4.22	173	0	0	0	42	179	165	92	84	83	173
Major league totals (6 years)		14	16	.467	4.11	254	0	0	0	51	297 2/3	290	147	136	121	263

DIVISION SERIES RECORD

Year	Team (League)	W	L	Pct.	ERA	G	GS	CG	ShO	Sv.	IP	H	R	ER	BB	SO
1995	—Colorado (N.L.)	1	0	1.000	0.00	3	0	0	0	0	1 2/3	6	2	0	9	2

HOLT, CHRIS — P — ASTROS

PERSONAL: Born September 18, 1971, in Dallas. . . . 6-4/205. . . . Throws right, bats right. . . . Full name: Christopher Michael Holt.
COLLEGE: Navarro College (Tex.).
TRANSACTIONS/CAREER NOTES: Selected by Houston Astros organization in third round of free-agent draft (June 1, 1992).

Year	Team (League)	W	L	Pct.	ERA	G	GS	CG	ShO	Sv.	IP	H	R	ER	BB	SO
1992	—Auburn (NYP)	2	5	.286	4.45	14	14	0	0	0	83	75	48	41	24	81
1993	—Quad City (Midw.)	11	10	.524	2.27	26	26	*10	•3	0	*186 1/3	162	70	47	54	176
1994	—Jackson (Texas)	10	9	.526	3.45	26	25	5	•2	0	167	169	78	64	22	111
1995	—Jackson (Texas)	2	2	.500	1.67	5	5	1	1	0	32 1/3	27	8	6	5	24
	—Tucson (Pac. Coast)	5	8	.385	4.10	20	19	0	0	0	118 2/3	155	65	54	32	69

HOLZEMER, MARK — P — ANGELS

PERSONAL: Born August 20, 1969, in Littleton, Colo. . . . 6-0/165. . . . Throws left, bats left. . . . Full name: Mark Harold Holzemer. . . . Name pronounced HOLE-zeh-mer.
HIGH SCHOOL: J.K. Mullen (Denver).
JUNIOR COLLEGE: Seminole (Okla.) Junior College.
TRANSACTIONS/CAREER NOTES: Selected by California Angels organization in fourth round of free-agent draft (June 2, 1987). . . . On Midland disabled list (July 2-September 18, 1990; April 12-May 25 and June 7-26, 1991).
STATISTICAL NOTES: Led Pacific Coast League with 15 wild pitches in 1994.

Year	Team (League)	W	L	Pct.	ERA	G	GS	CG	ShO	Sv.	IP	H	R	ER	BB	SO
1988	—Bend (Northwest)	4	6	.400	5.24	13	13	1	1	0	68 2/3	59	51	40	47	72
1989	—Quad City (Midw.)	12	7	.632	3.36	25	25	3	1	0	139 1/3	122	68	52	64	131
1990	—Midland (Texas)	1	7	.125	5.26	15	15	1	0	0	77	92	55	45	41	54
1991	—Midland (Texas)	0	0	...	1.42	2	2	0	0	0	6 1/3	3	2	1	5	7
	—Palm Springs (Cal.)	0	4	.000	2.86	6	6	0	0	0	22	15	14	7	16	19
1992	—Palm Springs (Cal.)	3	2	.600	3.00	5	5	2	0	0	30	23	10	10	13	32
	—Midland (Texas)	2	5	.286	3.83	7	7	2	0	0	44 2/3	45	22	19	13	36
	—Edmonton (PCL)	5	7	.417	6.67	17	16	4	0	0	89	114	69	66	55	49
1993	—Vancouver (PCL)	9	6	.600	4.82	24	23	2	0	0	145 2/3	158	94	78	70	80
	—California (A.L.)	0	3	.000	8.87	5	4	0	0	0	23 1/3	34	24	23	13	10
1994	—Vancouver (PCL)	5	10	.333	6.60	29	17	0	0	0	117 1/3	144	93	86	58	77
1995	—Vancouver (PCL)	3	2	.600	2.47	28	4	0	0	2	54 2/3	45	18	15	24	35
	—California (A.L.)	0	1	.000	5.40	12	0	0	0	0	8 1/3	11	6	5	7	5
Major league totals (2 years)		0	4	.000	7.96	17	4	0	0	0	31 2/3	45	30	28	20	15

HONEYCUTT, RICK — P — CARDINALS

PERSONAL: Born June 29, 1954, in Chattanooga, Tenn. . . . 6-1/191. . . . Throws left, bats left. . . . Full name: Frederick Wayne Honeycutt.
HIGH SCHOOL: Lakeview (Fort Oglethorpe, Ga.).
COLLEGE: Tennessee (degree in health education).
TRANSACTIONS/CAREER NOTES: Selected by Baltimore Orioles organization in 14th round of free-agent draft (June 6, 1972); did not sign. . . . Selected by Pittsburgh Pirates organization in 17th round of free-agent draft (June 8, 1976). . . . Traded by Pirates organization to Seattle Mariners (August 22, 1977), completing deal in which Mariners traded P Dave Pagan to Pirates for a player to be named later (July 27, 1977). . . . On disabled list (May 20-June 26, 1978). . . . Traded by Mariners with C Larry Cox, OF Willie Horton, OF Leon Roberts and SS Mario Mendoza to Texas Rangers for P Brian Allard, P Ken Clay, P Steve Finch, P Jerry Don Gleaton, SS Rick Auerbach and OF Richie Zisk (December 12, 1980). . . . Traded by Rangers to Los Angeles Dodgers for P Dave Stewart and a player to be named later (August 19, 1983); Rangers acquired P Ricky Wright to complete deal (September 16, 1983). . . . Traded by Dodgers to Oakland Athletics for a player to be named later (August 29, 1987); Dodgers acquired P Tim Belcher to complete deal (September 3, 1987). . . . Granted free agency (November 4, 1988). . . . Re-signed by A's (December 21, 1988). . . . On Oakland disabled list (April 1-June 16, 1991); included rehabilitation assignments to Modesto (June 6-14) and Madison (June 14-16). . . . Granted free agency (October 30, 1992). . . . Re-signed by A's (December 7, 1992). . . . On disabled list (June 15-July 24, 1993). . . . Granted free agency (November 1, 1993). . . . Signed by Rangers (November 24, 1993). . . . On disabled list (June 22-July 15, 1994). . . . Granted free agency (October 25, 1994). . . . Signed by Edmonton, A's organization (April 8-9, 1995). . . . Contract sold by A's to New York Yankees (September 25, 1995). . . . Contract sold by Yankees to St. Louis Cardinals (December 21, 1995).
STATISTICAL NOTES: Pitched 1-0 one-hit, complete-game victory against San Diego (April 27, 1984).
MISCELLANEOUS: Played two games as first baseman and one game as shortstop (1976). . . . Appeared as shortstop with no chances with Shreveport (1977). . . . Made an out in both appearances as pinch-hitter and appeared in one game as pinch-runner (1990).

Year	Team (League)	W	L	Pct.	ERA	G	GS	CG	ShO	Sv.	IP	H	R	ER	BB	SO
1976	—Niag. Falls (NYP)	5	3	.625	2.60	13	12	•7	0	0	*97	91	36	28	20	*98
1977	—Shreveport (Texas)	10	6	.625	*2.47	21	21	6	0	0	135	144	53	37	42	82
	—Seattle (A.L.)■	0	1	.000	4.34	10	3	0	0	0	29	26	16	14	11	17
1978	—Seattle (A.L.)	5	11	.313	4.90	26	24	4	1	0	134	150	81	73	49	50

Year	Team (League)	W	L	Pct.	ERA	G	GS	CG	ShO	Sv.	IP	H	R	ER	BB	SO
1979—	Seattle (A.L.)	11	12	.478	4.04	33	28	8	0	0	194	201	103	87	67	83
1980—	Seattle (A.L.)	10	17	.370	3.95	30	30	9	2	0	203	221	99	89	60	79
1981—	Texas (A.L.)■	11	6	.647	3.30	20	20	8	2	0	128	120	49	47	17	40
1982—	Texas (A.L.)	5	17	.227	5.27	30	26	4	1	0	164	201	103	96	54	64
1983—	Texas (A.L.)	14	8	.636	*2.42	25	25	5	2	0	174 2/3	168	59	47	37	56
—	Los Angeles (N.L.)■	2	3	.400	5.77	9	7	1	0	0	39	46	26	25	13	18
1984—	Los Angeles (N.L.)	10	9	.526	2.84	29	28	6	2	0	183 2/3	180	72	58	51	75
1985—	Los Angeles (N.L.)	8	12	.400	3.42	31	25	1	0	1	142	141	71	54	49	67
1986—	Los Angeles (N.L.)	11	9	.550	3.32	32	28	0	0	0	171	164	71	63	45	100
1987—	Los Angeles (N.L.)	2	12	.143	4.59	27	20	1	1	0	115 2/3	133	74	59	45	92
—	Oakland (A.L.)■	1	4	.200	5.32	7	4	0	0	0	23 2/3	25	17	14	9	10
1988—	Oakland (A.L.)	3	2	.600	3.50	55	0	0	0	7	79 2/3	74	36	31	25	47
1989—	Oakland (A.L.)	2	2	.500	2.35	64	0	0	0	12	76 2/3	56	26	20	26	52
1990—	Oakland (A.L.)	2	2	.500	2.70	63	0	0	0	7	63 1/3	46	23	19	22	38
1991—	Oakland (A.L.)	2	4	.333	3.58	43	0	0	0	0	37 2/3	37	16	15	20	26
—	Modesto (Calif.)	0	0	...	0.00	3	3	0	0	0	5	4	1	0	1	5
—	Madison (Midwest)	0	1	.000	18.00	1	1	0	0	0	1	4	2	2	0	2
1992—	Oakland (A.L.)	1	4	.200	3.69	54	0	0	0	3	39	41	19	16	10	32
1993—	Oakland (A.L.)	1	4	.200	2.81	52	0	0	0	1	41 2/3	30	18	13	20	21
1994—	Texas (A.L.)■	1	2	.333	7.20	42	0	0	0	1	25	37	21	20	9	18
1995—	Oakland (A.L.)	5	1	.833	2.42	49	0	0	0	2	44 2/3	37	13	12	9	21
—	New York (A.L.)■	0	0	...	27.00	3	0	0	0	0	1	2	3	3	1	0
A.L. totals (16 years)		74	97	.433	3.80	606	160	38	8	33	1459	1472	702	616	446	654
N.L. totals (5 years)		33	45	.423	3.58	128	108	9	3	1	651 1/3	664	314	259	203	352
Major league totals (19 years)		107	142	.430	3.73	734	268	47	11	34	2110 1/3	2136	1016	875	649	1006

CHAMPIONSHIP SERIES RECORD

NOTES: Shares career record for most games as relief pitcher—15.

Year	Team (League)	W	L	Pct.	ERA	G	GS	CG	ShO	Sv.	IP	H	R	ER	BB	SO
1983—	Los Angeles (N.L.)	0	0	...	21.60	2	0	0	0	0	1 2/3	4	4	4	0	2
1985—	Los Angeles (N.L.)	0	0	...	13.50	2	0	0	0	0	1 1/3	4	2	2	2	1
1988—	Oakland (A.L.)	1	0	1.000	0.00	3	0	0	0	0	2	0	0	0	2	0
1989—	Oakland (A.L.)	0	0	...	32.40	3	0	0	0	0	1 2/3	6	6	6	5	1
1990—	Oakland (A.L.)	0	0	...	0.00	3	0	0	0	1	1 2/3	0	0	0	0	0
1992—	Oakland (A.L.)	0	0	...	0.00	2	0	0	0	0	2	0	0	0	0	1
Champ. series totals (6 years)		1	0	1.000	10.45	15	0	0	0	1	10 1/3	14	12	12	9	5

WORLD SERIES RECORD

NOTES: Member of World Series championship team (1989).

Year	Team (League)	W	L	Pct.	ERA	G	GS	CG	ShO	Sv.	IP	H	R	ER	BB	SO
1988—	Oakland (A.L.)	1	0	1.000	0.00	3	0	0	0	0	3 1/3	0	0	0	0	5
1989—	Oakland (A.L.)	0	0	...	6.75	3	0	0	0	0	2 2/3	4	2	2	0	2
1990—	Oakland (A.L.)	0	0	...	0.00	1	0	0	0	0	1 2/3	2	0	0	1	0
World Series totals (3 years)		1	0	1.000	2.35	7	0	0	0	0	7 2/3	6	2	2	1	7

ALL-STAR GAME RECORD

Year	League	W	L	Pct.	ERA	GS	CG	ShO	Sv.	IP	H	R	ER	BB	SO
1980—	American						Did not play.								
1983—	American	0	0	...	9.00	0	0	0	0	2	5	2	2	0	0
All-Star totals (1 year)		0	0	...	9.00	0	0	0	0	2	5	2	2	0	0

HOOK, CHRIS — P — GIANTS

PERSONAL: Born August 4, 1968, in San Diego. . . . 6-5/230. . . . Throws right, bats right. . . . Full name: Christopher Wayne Hook.
HIGH SCHOOL: Lloyd Memorial (Erlanger, Ky.).
COLLEGE: Northern Kentucky.
TRANSACTIONS/CAREER NOTES: Signed as non-drafted free agent by Cincinnati Reds organization (June 14, 1989). . . . Traded by Reds organization with P Scott Robinson to San Francisco Giants organization for OF Adam Hyzdu (March 31, 1994). . . . On disabled list (June 20- August 2, 1994).

Year	Team (League)	W	L	Pct.	ERA	G	GS	CG	ShO	Sv.	IP	H	R	ER	BB	SO
1989—	GC Reds (GCL)	4	1	.800	3.18	14	9	0	0	0	51	43	19	18	17	39
1990—	Char., W.Va. (S. Atl.)	6	5	.545	4.07	30	16	0	0	0	119 1/3	117	65	54	62	87
1991—	Char., W.Va. (S. Atl.)	8	2	.800	2.41	45	0	0	0	2	71	52	26	19	40	79
1992—	Ced. Rap. (Midw.)	14	8	.636	2.72	26	25	1	0	0	159	138	59	48	53	144
1993—	Chattanooga (Sou.)	12	8	.600	3.62	28	•28	1	0	0	166 2/3	163	85	67	66	122
1994—	Phoenix (PCL)■	7	2	.778	4.60	27	11	0	0	2	90	109	48	46	29	57
1995—	Phoenix (PCL)	0	0	...	1.50	4	0	0	0	0	6	2	1	1	3	5
—	San Francisco (N.L.)	5	1	.833	5.50	45	0	0	0	0	52 1/3	55	33	32	29	40
Major league totals (1 year)		5	1	.833	5.50	45	0	0	0	0	52 1/3	55	33	32	29	40

HOPE, JOHN — P — PIRATES

PERSONAL: Born December 21, 1970, in Fort Lauderdale, Fla. . . . 6-3/206. . . . Throws right, bats right. . . . Full name: John Alan Hope.
HIGH SCHOOL: Stranahan (Fort Lauderdale, Fla.).
TRANSACTIONS/CAREER NOTES: Selected by Pittsburgh Pirates organization in supplemental round ("sandwich pick" between second and third round) of free-agent draft (June 5, 1989); pick received as compensation for New York Yankees signing Type C free-agent P Dave LaPoint. . . . On Buffalo disabled list (August 8-September 8, 1994). . . . On Calgary disabled list (June 2-27 and August 1-September 8, 1995).

Year	Team (League)	W	L	Pct.	ERA	G	GS	CG	ShO	Sv.	IP	H	R	ER	BB	SO
1989—	GC Pirates (GCL)	0	1	.000	4.80	4	3	0	0	0	15	15	12	8	6	14
1990—								Did not play.								
1991—	Welland (NYP)	2	0	1.000	0.53	3	3	0	0	0	17	12	1	1	3	15
	—Augusta (S. Atl.)	4	2	.667	3.50	7	7	0	0	0	46 1/3	29	20	18	19	37
	—Salem (Carolina)	2	2	.500	6.18	6	5	0	0	0	27 2/3	38	20	19	4	18
1992—	Salem (Carolina)	11	8	.579	3.47	27	27	4	0	0	176 1/3	169	75	68	46	106
1993—	Carolina (South.)	9	4	.692	4.37	21	20	0	0	0	111 1/3	123	69	54	29	66
	—Buffalo (A.A.)	2	1	.667	6.33	4	4	0	0	0	21 1/3	30	16	15	2	6
	—Pittsburgh (N.L.)	0	2	.000	4.03	7	7	0	0	0	38	47	19	17	8	8
1994—	Buffalo (A.A.)	4	9	.308	3.87	18	17	0	0	0	100	98	56	43	23	54
	—Pittsburgh (N.L.)	0	0	...	5.79	9	0	0	0	0	14	18	12	9	4	6
1995—	Calgary (PCL)	7	1	.875	2.79	13	13	3	1	0	80 2/3	76	29	25	11	41
	—Pittsburgh (N.L.)	0	0	...	30.86	3	0	0	0	0	2 1/3	8	8	8	4	2
Major league totals (3 years)		0	2	.000	5.63	19	7	0	0	0	54 1/3	73	39	34	16	16

HORN, SAM — DH/1B

PERSONAL: Born November 2, 1963, in Dallas. . . . 6-5/235. . . . Bats left, throws left. . . . Full name: Samuel Lee Horn.

HIGH SCHOOL: Morse (San Diego).

TRANSACTIONS/CAREER NOTES: Selected by Boston Red Sox organization in first round (16th pick overall) of free-agent draft (June 7, 1982); pick received as compensation for Texas Rangers signing Type A free-agent P Frank Tanana. . . . On disabled list (April 28-June 23, 1983). . . . On Boston disabled list (June 8-July 28, 1989); included rehabilitation assignment to Pawtucket (July 13-28). . . . Released by Red Sox organization (December 20, 1989). . . . Signed by Rochester, Baltimore Orioles organization (February 20, 1990). . . . On Baltimore disabled list (May 8-29, 1990); included rehabilitation assignment to Rochester (May 21-29). . . . Granted free agency (December 19, 1992). . . . Signed by Canton/Akron, Cleveland Indians organization (March 4, 1993). . . . Released by Indians (December 13, 1993). . . . Signed by New York Yankees organization (December 22, 1993). . . . Released by Columbus, Yankees organization (June 23, 1994). . . . Signed by Calgary, Pittsburgh Pirates organization (January 26, 1995). . . . Released by Calgary (June 24, 1995). . . . Signed by Oklahoma City, Texas Rangers organization (July 20, 1995). . . . Granted free agency (October 16, 1995).

RECORDS: Shares major league single-game record for most strikeouts—6 (July 17, 1991, 15 innings). . . . Shares A.L. record for most home runs in first two major league games—2 (July 25-26, 1987).

STATISTICAL NOTES: Led Carolina League with .538 slugging percentage in 1984. . . . Led International League with .649 slugging percentage in 1987 and .600 in 1993. . . . Tied for International League lead with 10 intentional bases on balls received in 1988. . . . Career major league grand slams: 3.

				BATTING											FIELDING			
Year	Team (League)	Pos.	G	AB	R	H	2B	3B	HR	RBI	Avg.	BB	SO	SB	PO	A	E	Avg.
1982—	Elmira (NYP)	1B	61	213	47	64	13	1	11	48	.300	40	59	2	368	29	11	.973
1983—	Winst.-Salem (Car.)	1B	68	217	33	52	9	0	9	29	.240	50	78	0	363	24	10	.975
1984—	Winst.-Salem (Car.)	1B	127	403	67	126	22	3	21	89	.313	76	107	5	978	*70	*29	.973
1985—	New Britain (East.)	1B	134	457	64	129	*32	0	11	82	.282	64	107	4	751	63	*23	.973
1986—	New Britain (East.)	1B	100	345	41	85	13	0	8	46	.246	49	80	1	356	28	9	.977
	—Pawtucket (Int'l)	1B	20	77	8	15	2	0	3	14	.195	5	23	0	61	4	0	1.000
1987—	Pawtucket (Int'l)	1B	94	333	57	107	19	0	30	84	.321	33	88	0	28	2	2	.938
	—Boston (A.L.)	DH	46	158	31	44	7	0	14	34	.278	17	55	0	...	...	...	...
1988—	Boston (A.L.)	DH	24	61	4	9	0	0	2	8	.148	11	20	0	...	...	...	...
	—Pawtucket (Int'l)	1B	83	279	33	65	10	0	10	31	.233	44	82	0	6	1	1	.875
1989—	Boston (A.L.)	DH-1B	33	54	1	8	2	0	0	4	.148	8	16	0	5	0	0	1.000
	—Pawtucket (Int'l)	DH	51	164	15	38	9	1	8	27	.232	20	46	0	...	...	...	...
1990—	Baltimore (A.L.)■	DH-1B	79	246	30	61	13	0	14	45	.248	32	62	0	58	6	2	.970
	—Rochester (Int'l)	1B	17	58	16	24	3	0	9	26	.414	9	13	0	27	1	2	.933
	—Hagerstown (East.)	DH	7	23	2	6	2	0	1	3	.261	6	5	0	...	...	...	...
1991—	Baltimore (A.L.)	DH	121	317	45	74	16	0	23	61	.233	41	99	0	...	...	...	...
1992—	Baltimore (A.L.)	DH	63	162	13	38	10	1	5	19	.235	21	60	0	...	...	...	...
1993—	Charlotte (Int'l)■	1B	122	402	62	108	17	1	*38	96	.269	60	131	1	58	0	1	.983
	—Cleveland (A.L.)	DH	12	33	8	15	1	0	4	8	.455	1	5	0	...	...	...	...
1994—	Columbus (Int'l)■	1B	59	197	22	48	9	1	8	26	.244	22	58	1	120	9	5	.963
1995—	Calgary (PCL)■	1B	36	99	21	33	8	2	8	22	.333	14	21	0	157	5	4	.976
	—Okla. City (A.A.)■	1B	46	156	26	48	9	0	12	42	.308	25	49	0	11	0	0	1.000
	—Texas (A.L.)	DH	11	9	0	1	0	0	0	0	.111	1	6	0	...	...	...	...
Major league totals (8 years)			389	1040	132	250	49	1	62	179	.240	132	323	0	63	6	2	.972

HORSMAN, VINCE — P

PERSONAL: Born March 9, 1967, in Halifax, Nova Scotia. . . . 6-2/180. . . . Throws left, bats right. . . . Full name: Vincent Stanley Joseph Horsman.

HIGH SCHOOL: Prince Andrew (Dartmouth, Nova Scotia).

TRANSACTIONS/CAREER NOTES: Signed as non-drafted free agent by Toronto Blue Jays organization (September 26, 1984). . . . On Knoxville disabled list (April 11-24, 1991). . . . Claimed on waivers by Oakland Athletics (March 20, 1992). . . . Released by A's (December 5, 1994). . . . Signed by Salt Lake, Minnesota Twins organization (April 6, 1995). . . . Released by Salt Lake (August 8, 1995).

STATISTICAL NOTES: Led South Atlantic League with 20 home runs allowed in 1987.

Year	Team (League)	W	L	Pct.	ERA	G	GS	CG	ShO	Sv.	IP	H	R	ER	BB	SO
1985—	Medicine Hat (Pio.)	0	3	.000	6.25	18	1	0	0	1	40 1/3	56	31	28	23	30
1986—	Florence (S. Atl.)	4	3	.571	4.07	29	9	1	1	1	90 2/3	93	56	41	49	64
1987—	Myrtle Beach (SAL)	7	7	.500	3.32	30	28	0	0	0	149	144	74	55	37	109
1988—	Dunedin (Fla. St.)	3	1	.750	1.36	14	2	0	0	1	39 2/3	28	7	6	12	34
	—Knoxville (South.)	3	2	.600	4.63	20	6	1	0	0	58 1/3	57	34	30	28	40
1989—	Dunedin (Fla. St.)	5	6	.455	2.51	35	1	0	0	8	79	72	24	22	27	60
	—Knoxville (South.)	0	0	...	1.80	4	0	0	0	1	5	3	1	1	2	3
1990—	Dunedin (Fla. St.)	4	7	.364	3.24	28	0	0	0	1	50	53	21	18	15	41

H

Year	Team (League)	W	L	Pct.	ERA	G	GS	CG	ShO	Sv.	IP	H	R	ER	BB	SO
	—Knoxville (South.)	2	1	.667	4.63	8	0	0	0	0	11 2/3	11	7	6	5	10
1991	—Knoxville (South.)	4	1	.800	2.34	42	2	0	0	3	80 2/3	79	23	21	19	80
	—Toronto (A.L.)	0	0	...	0.00	4	0	0	0	0	4	2	0	0	3	2
1992	—Oakland (A.L.)■	2	1	.667	2.49	58	0	0	0	1	43 1/3	39	13	12	21	18
1993	—Tacoma (PCL)	1	2	.333	4.28	26	0	0	0	3	33 2/3	37	25	16	9	23
	—Oakland (A.L.)	2	0	1.000	5.40	40	0	0	0	0	25	25	15	15	15	17
1994	—Tacoma (PCL)	1	0	1.000	2.57	7	0	0	0	0	7	5	2	2	1	6
	—Oakland (A.L.)	0	1	.000	4.91	33	0	0	0	0	29 1/3	29	17	16	11	20
1995	—Minnesota (A.L.)■	0	0	...	7.00	6	0	0	0	0	9	12	8	7	4	4
	—Salt Lake (PCL)	1	0	1.000	10.38	16	0	0	0	0	13	23	15	15	4	10
Major league totals (5 years)		4	2	.667	4.07	141	0	0	0	1	110 2/3	107	53	50	54	61

HOSEY, DWAYNE — OF — RED SOX

PERSONAL: Born March 11, 1967, in Sharon, Pa. . . . 5-10/175. . . . Bats both, throws right. . . . Full name: Dwayne Samuel Hosey.
COLLEGE: Pasadena (Calif.) City College.
TRANSACTIONS/CAREER NOTES: Selected by Chicago White Sox organization in 13th round of free-agent draft (June 2, 1987). . . . Released by White Sox organization (January 13, 1989). . . . Signed by Oakland Athletics organization (February 23, 1989). . . . Selected by Milwaukee Brewers from A's organization in Rule 5 major league draft (December 9, 1991). . . . Drafted by San Diego Padres organization from Brewers organization (December 9, 1991). . . . Granted free agency (October 15, 1993). . . . Signed by Omaha, Kansas City Royals organization (January 8, 1994). . . . On Omaha disabled list (May 25-June 16, 1995). . . . Claimed on waivers by Boston Red Sox (August 31, 1995).
HONORS: Named American Association Most Valuable Player (1994).
STATISTICAL NOTES: Led American Association with .628 slugging percentage and tied for lead with 10 intentional bases on balls received in 1994. . . . Led American Association outfielders with five double plays in 1994.

				BATTING										FIELDING			
Year	Team (League)	Pos.	G	AB	R	H	2B	3B	HR	RBI	Avg.	BB	SO	SB	PO	A	E	Avg.
1987	—GC Whi. Sox (GCL)	OF	41	129	26	36	2	1	1	10	.279	18	22	19	65	3	0	1.000
1988	—South Bend (Mid.)	OF	95	311	53	71	11	0	2	24	.228	28	55	36	147	10	9	.946
	—Utica (NYP)	OF	3	7	0	1	0	0	0	0	.143	2	1	1	6	0	1	.857
1989	—Madison (Midwest)■	OF	123	470	72	115	16	6	11	51	.245	44	82	33	207	8	14	.939
1990	—Modesto (Calif.)	OF	113	453	77	133	21	5	16	61	.294	50	70	30	210	13	9	.961
1991	—Huntsville (South.)	OF	28	102	16	25	6	0	1	7	.245	9	15	5	49	2	2	.962
	—Stockton (Calif.)■	OF	85	356	55	97	12	7	15	62	.272	31	55	22	112	8	8	.938
1992	—Wichita (Texas)■	OF	125	427	56	108	23	5	9	68	.253	40	70	16	195	9	8	.962
1993	—Wichita (Texas)	OF	86	326	52	95	19	2	18	61	.291	25	44	13	85	0	7	.924
	—Las Vegas (PCL)	OF	32	110	21	29	4	4	3	12	.264	11	17	7	43	1	2	.957
1994	—Omaha (A.A.)■	OF	112	406	95	135	23	8	27	80	.333	61	85	27	162	13	6	.967
1995	—Omaha (A.A.)	OF	75	271	59	80	21	4	12	50	.295	29	45	15	125	10	4	.971
	—Boston (A.L.)■	OF-DH	24	68	20	23	8	1	3	7	.338	8	16	6	46	1	0	1.000
Major league totals (1 year)			24	68	20	23	8	1	3	7	.338	8	16	6	46	1	0	1.000

DIVISION SERIES RECORD

				BATTING										FIELDING			
Year	Team (League)	Pos.	G	AB	R	H	2B	3B	HR	RBI	Avg.	BB	SO	SB	PO	A	E	Avg.
1995	—Boston (A.L.)	OF	3	12	1	0	0	0	0	0	.000	2	3	1	7	0	0	1.000

HOUSTON, TYLER — C — BRAVES

PERSONAL: Born January 17, 1971, in Las Vegas. . . . 6-2/210. . . . Bats left, throws right. . . . Full name: Tyler Sam Houston.
HIGH SCHOOL: Valley (Las Vegas).
TRANSACTIONS/CAREER NOTES: Selected by Atlanta Braves organization in first round (second pick overall) of free-agent draft (June 5, 1989). . . . On Greenville disabled list (June 25-July 5, 1993).
STATISTICAL NOTES: Led Pioneer League with 14 passed balls in 1989.

				BATTING										FIELDING			
Year	Team (League)	Pos.	G	AB	R	H	2B	3B	HR	RBI	Avg.	BB	SO	SB	PO	A	E	Avg.
1989	—Idaho Falls (Pio.)	C	50	176	30	43	11	0	4	24	.244	25	41	4	148	15	5	.970
1990	—Sumter (S. Atl.)	C	117	442	58	93	14	3	13	56	.210	49	101	6	498	55	*18	.968
1991	—Macon (S. Atl.)	C	107	351	41	81	16	3	8	47	.231	39	70	10	591	75	10	.985
1992	—Durham (Carolina)	C-3B-1B	117	402	39	91	17	1	7	38	.226	20	89	5	493	65	15	.974
1993	—Greenville (South.)	C-OF	84	262	27	73	14	1	5	33	.279	13	50	5	410	34	9	.980
	—Richmond (Int'l)	C	13	36	4	5	1	1	1	3	.139	1	8	0	69	2	3	.959
1994	—Richmond (Int'l)	1B-C-OF	97	312	33	76	15	2	4	33	.244	16	44	3	619	54	7	.990
1995	—Richmond (Int'l)	1-C-O-3	103	349	41	89	10	3	12	42	.255	18	62	3	579	69	11	.983

HOWARD, CHRIS — P — RANGERS

PERSONAL: Born November 18, 1965, in Lynn, Mass. . . . 6-0/185. . . . Throws left, bats right.
HIGH SCHOOL: St. Mary's (Lynn, Mass.).
JUNIOR COLLEGE: Miami-Dade (South) Community College.
TRANSACTIONS/CAREER NOTES: Selected by Milwaukee Brewers organization in eighth round of free-agent draft (January 9, 1985); did not sign. . . . Signed as non-drafted free agent by New York Yankees organization (June 16, 1986). . . . Released by Yankees organization (May 1, 1990). . . . Signed by Cleveland Indians organization (May 10, 1990). . . . Released by Indians organization (June 6, 1990). . . . Signed by Chicago White Sox organization (January 27, 1991). . . . On Vancouver disabled list (May 30-July 4 and July 9-August 18, 1992). . . . Granted free agency (December 20, 1993). . . . Signed by Boston Red Sox organization (January 20, 1994). . . . Traded by Red Sox to Texas Rangers for OF Jack Voigt (August 31, 1995).
STATISTICAL NOTES: Pitched in relief, combining with Jose Ventura and John Hudek in 4-1 no-hit victory against Charlotte (April 18, 1991).

Year	Team (League)	W	L	Pct.	ERA	G	GS	CG	ShO	Sv.	IP	H	R	ER	BB	SO
1987—	Prin. William (Caro.)	0	0	...	10.29	4	0	0	0	0	7	9	8	8	8	1
1988—	Prin. William (Caro.)	2	2	.500	2.34	31	0	0	0	3	50	44	18	13	23	48
—	Alb./Colon. (East.)	0	0	...	13.50	2	0	0	0	0	1 1/3	3	2	2	1	1
1989—	Fort Lauder. (FSL)	2	0	1.000	1.78	13	0	0	0	0	25 1/3	19	6	5	13	25
—	Alb./Colon. (East.)	0	1	.000	3.44	24	0	0	0	2	34	29	14	13	17	33
1990—	Alb./Colon. (East.)	0	0	...	14.40	2	0	0	0	0	5	9	8	8	7	2
—	Kinston (Carolina)■	1	1	.500	2.45	8	0	0	0	0	14 2/3	21	5	4	6	16
1991—	Birmingham (Sou.)■	6	1	.857	2.04	38	0	0	0	9	53	43	14	12	16	52
1992—	Vancouver (PCL)	3	1	.750	2.92	20	0	0	0	0	24 2/3	18	9	8	22	23
—	GC White Sox (GCL)	0	0	...	4.50	1	0	0	0	0	2	3	1	1	0	3
1993—	Nashville (A.A.)	4	3	.571	3.38	43	0	0	0	3	66 2/3	55	32	25	16	53
—	Chicago (A.L.)	1	0	1.000	0.00	3	0	0	0	0	2 1/3	2	0	0	3	1
1994—	Pawtucket (Int'l)■	3	0	1.000	2.22	13	0	0	0	0	24 1/3	14	6	6	10	21
—	Boston (A.L.)	1	0	1.000	3.63	37	0	0	0	1	39 2/3	35	17	16	12	22
1995—	Sarasota (Fla. St.)	0	2	.000	5.23	6	5	0	0	0	10 1/3	10	6	6	4	7
—	Pawtucket (Int'l)	3	1	.750	3.92	17	0	0	0	0	20 2/3	25	11	9	4	19
—	Texas (A.L.)■	0	0	...	0.00	4	0	0	0	0	4	3	0	0	1	2
Major league totals (3 years)		2	0	1.000	3.13	44	0	0	0	1	46	40	17	16	16	25

RECORD AS POSITION PLAYER

				BATTING											FIELDING			
Year	Team (League)	Pos.	G	AB	R	H	2B	3B	HR	RBI	Avg.	BB	SO	SB	PO	A	E	Avg.
1986—	Oneonta (NYP)	OF	9	23	2	2	0	0	0	4	.087	5	4	1	4	1	1	.833
—	GC Yankees (GCL)	OF-1B	43	131	15	39	5	1	0	16	.298	13	25	2	101	4	3	.972
1987—	Prin. William (Car.)	OF	86	258	35	62	11	1	5	27	.240	10	43	2	135	15	7	.955
1988—	Prin. William (Car.)	1B-OF	40	11	2	1	0	0	0	0	.091	0	2	0	10	9	0	1.000

HOWARD, DAVID — 2B/SS — ROYALS

PERSONAL: Born February 26, 1967, in Sarasota, Fla. . . . 6-0/175. . . . Bats both, throws right. . . . Full name: David Wayne Howard. . . . Son of Bruce Howard, pitcher, Chicago White Sox, Baltimore Orioles and Washington Senators (1963-68).

HIGH SCHOOL: Riverview (Sarasota, Fla.).

JUNIOR COLLEGE: Manatee Junior College (Fla.).

TRANSACTIONS/CAREER NOTES: Selected by Kansas City Royals organization in 32nd round of free-agent draft (June 2, 1986). . . . On disabled list (May 12-31 and July 23-August 9, 1989). . . . On Kansas City disabled list (April 22-July 6, 1992); included rehabilitation assignments to Baseball City (June 16-20) and Omaha (June 20-July 5). . . . On Kansas City disabled list (April 19-May 17, 1993); included rehabilitation assignment to Omaha (May 10-17). . . . On Kansas City disabled list (June 7-August 10, 1993); included rehabilitation assignment to Omaha (July 15-23 and July 31-August 10). . . . On disabled list (May 27-June 17, 1995).

				BATTING											FIELDING			
Year	Team (League)	Pos.	G	AB	R	H	2B	3B	HR	RBI	Avg.	BB	SO	SB	PO	A	E	Avg.
1987—	Fort Myers (FSL)	SS	89	289	26	56	9	4	1	19	.194	30	68	11	123	273	28	.934
1988—	Appleton (Midw.)	SS	110	368	48	82	9	4	1	22	.223	25	80	10	151	275	43	.908
1989—	Baseball City (FSL)	S-O-3-2	83	267	36	63	7	3	3	30	.236	23	44	12	141	225	18	.953
1990—	Memphis (South.)	SS-2B	116	384	41	96	10	4	5	44	.250	39	73	15	194	321	32	.941
1991—	Omaha (A.A.)	SS-2B	14	41	2	5	0	0	0	2	.122	7	11	1	30	43	3	.961
—	Kansas City (A.L.)	S-2-3-O-DH	94	236	20	51	7	0	1	17	.216	16	45	3	129	248	12	.969
1992—	Kansas City (A.L.)	SS-OF	74	219	19	49	6	2	1	18	.224	15	43	3	124	204	8	.976
—	Baseball City (FSL)	SS	3	9	3	4	1	0	0	0	.444	2	0	0	3	7	1	.909
—	Omaha (A.A.)	SS	19	68	5	8	1	0	0	5	.118	3	8	1	25	52	8	.906
1993—	Kansas City (A.L.)	2-S-3-O	15	24	5	8	0	1	0	2	.333	2	5	1	17	28	3	.938
—	Omaha (A.A.)	SS	47	157	15	40	8	2	0	18	.255	7	20	3	76	137	8	.964
1994—	Kansas City (A.L.)	3-S-2-DH-P-O	46	83	9	19	4	0	1	13	.229	11	23	3	27	79	1	.991
1995—	Kansas City (A.L.)	2-S-O-DH-1	95	255	23	62	13	4	0	19	.243	24	41	6	167	195	29	.926
Major league totals (5 years)			324	817	76	189	30	7	3	69	.231	68	157	16	464	754	53	.958

RECORD AS PITCHER

Year	Team (League)	W	L	Pct.	ERA	G	GS	CG	ShO	Sv.	IP	H	R	ER	BB	SO
1994—	Kansas City (A.L.)	0	0	...	4.50	1	0	0	0	0	2	2	1	1	5	0

HOWARD, THOMAS — OF — REDS

PERSONAL: Born December 11, 1964, in Middletown, O. . . . 6-2/205. . . . Bats both, throws right. . . . Full name: Thomas Sylvester Howard.

HIGH SCHOOL: Valley View (Germantown, O.).

COLLEGE: Ball State.

TRANSACTIONS/CAREER NOTES: Selected by San Diego Padres organization in first round (11th pick overall) of free-agent draft (June 2, 1986). . . . On disabled list (June 5-July 17, 1989). . . . Traded by Padres to Cleveland Indians for SS Jason Hardtke and a player to be named later (April 14, 1992); Padres acquired C Christopher Maffett to complete deal (July 10, 1992). . . . Traded by Indians to Cincinnati Reds (August 20, 1993), completing deal in which Reds traded 1B Randy Milligan to Indians for a player to be named later (August 17, 1993).

HONORS: Named outfielder on The Sporting News college All-America team (1986).

				BATTING											FIELDING			
Year	Team (League)	Pos.	G	AB	R	H	2B	3B	HR	RBI	Avg.	BB	SO	SB	PO	A	E	Avg.
1986—	Spokane (N'west)	OF	13	55	16	23	3	3	2	17	.418	3	9	2	24	3	0	1.000
—	Reno (California)	OF	61	223	35	57	7	3	10	39	.256	34	49	10	104	5	6	.948
1987—	Wichita (Texas)	OF	113	401	72	133	27	4	14	60	.332	36	72	26	226	6	6	.975
1988—	Wichita (Texas)	OF	29	103	15	31	9	2	0	16	.301	13	14	6	51	2	2	.964
—	Las Vegas (PCL)	OF	44	167	29	42	9	1	0	15	.251	12	31	3	74	3	2	.975
1989—	Las Vegas (PCL)	OF	80	303	45	91	18	3	3	31	.300	30	56	22	178	7	2	.989
1990—	Las Vegas (PCL)	OF	89	341	58	112	26	8	5	51	.328	44	63	27	159	6	2	.988

Year	Team (League)	Pos.	G	AB	R	H	2B	3B	HR	RBI	Avg.	BB	SO	SB	PO	A	E	Avg.
				BATTING											FIELDING			
	— San Diego (N.L.)	OF	20	44	4	12	2	0	0	0	.273	0	11	0	19	0	1	.950
1991	— San Diego (N.L.)	OF	106	281	30	70	12	3	4	22	.249	24	57	10	182	4	1	.995
	— Las Vegas (PCL)	OF	25	94	22	29	3	1	2	16	.309	10	16	11	54	2	2	.966
1992	— San Diego (N.L.)	PH	5	3	1	1	0	0	0	0	.333	0	0	0	...	...	...	...
	— Cleveland (A.L.)■	OF-DH	117	358	36	99	15	2	2	32	.277	17	60	15	185	5	2	.990
1993	— Cleveland (A.L.)	OF-DH	74	178	26	42	7	0	3	23	.236	12	42	5	81	3	2	.977
	— Cincinnati (N.L.)■	OF	38	141	22	39	8	3	4	13	.277	12	21	5	73	4	1	.987
1994	— Cincinnati (N.L.)	OF	83	178	24	47	11	0	5	24	.264	10	30	4	80	2	3	.965
1995	— Cincinnati (N.L.)	OF	113	281	42	85	15	2	3	26	.302	20	37	17	127	2	2	.985
American League totals (2 years)			191	536	62	141	22	2	5	55	.263	29	102	20	266	8	4	.986
National League totals (6 years)			365	928	123	254	48	8	16	85	.274	66	156	36	481	12	8	.984
Major league totals (6 years)			556	1464	185	395	70	10	21	140	.270	95	258	56	747	20	12	.985

DIVISION SERIES RECORD

Year	Team (League)	Pos.	G	AB	R	H	2B	3B	HR	RBI	Avg.	BB	SO	SB	PO	A	E	Avg.
				BATTING											FIELDING			
1995	— Cincinnati (N.L.)	OF	3	10	0	1	1	0	0	0	.100	0	2	0	5	0	0	1.000

CHAMPIONSHIP SERIES RECORD

Year	Team (League)	Pos.	G	AB	R	H	2B	3B	HR	RBI	Avg.	BB	SO	SB	PO	A	E	Avg.
				BATTING											FIELDING			
1995	— Cincinnati (N.L.)	PH-OF	4	8	0	2	1	0	0	1	.250	2	0	0	2	0	0	1.000

HOWE, STEVE P

PERSONAL: Born March 10, 1958, in Pontiac, Mich. . . . 6-2/198. . . . Throws left, bats left. . . . Full name: Steven Roy Howe.

HIGH SCHOOL: Clarkston (Mich.).

COLLEGE: Michigan.

TRANSACTIONS/CAREER NOTES: Selected by Los Angeles Dodgers organization in first round (16th pick overall) of free-agent draft (June 5, 1979); pick received as compensation for Pittsburgh Pirates signing free-agent OF/2B Lee Lacy. . . . On disabled list (May 28-June 29, 1983). . . . On suspended list (July 16-17 and September 23, 1983-remainder of season; and December 15, 1983-entire 1984 season). . . . On restricted list (July 1-3, 1985). . . . Released by Dodgers (July 3, 1985). . . . Signed by Minnesota Twins (August 12, 1985). . . . Released by Twins (September 17, 1985). . . . Signed by San Jose, independent (March 20, 1986). . . . On suspended list (May 15-June 24 and July 15, 1986-remainder of season). . . . Released by San Jose (December 31, 1986). . . . Signed by Tabasco of Mexican League (1987). . . . Signed by Texas Rangers organization (July 12, 1987). . . . Released by Rangers (January 19, 1988). . . . Signed by Salinas, independent (April 7, 1990). . . . Released by Salinas (October 24, 1990). . . . Signed by New York Yankees organization (February 21, 1991). . . . On New York disabled list (August 11-September 2, 1991). . . . On disqualified list (June 8-November 12, 1992). . . . Granted free agency (November 8, 1992). . . . Re-signed by Yankees (December 8, 1992). . . . On New York disabled list (May 7-June 5, 1993); included rehabilitation assignment to Columbus (May 31-June 5). . . . On New York disabled list (May 2-20, 1994); included rehabilitation assignment to Albany (May 18-20). . . . Granted free agency (November 3, 1995).

HONORS: Named lefthanded pitcher on The Sporting News college All-America team (1979). . . . Named N.L. Rookie of the Year by Baseball Writers' Association of America (1980).

Year	Team (League)	W	L	Pct.	ERA	G	GS	CG	ShO	Sv.	IP	H	R	ER	BB	SO
1979	— San Antonio (Tex.)	6	2	.750	3.13	13	13	5	1	0	95	78	36	33	22	57
1980	— Los Angeles (N.L.)	7	9	.438	2.65	59	0	0	0	17	85	83	33	25	22	39
1981	— Los Angeles (N.L.)	5	3	.625	2.50	41	0	0	0	8	54	51	17	15	18	32
1982	— Los Angeles (N.L.)	7	5	.583	2.08	66	0	0	0	13	99 1/3	87	27	23	17	49
1983	— Los Angeles (N.L.)	4	7	.364	1.44	46	0	0	0	18	68 2/3	55	15	11	12	52
1984	—							Did not play.								
1985	— Los Angeles (N.L.)	1	1	.500	4.91	19	0	0	0	3	22	30	17	12	5	11
	— Minnesota (A.L.)■	2	3	.400	6.16	13	0	0	0	0	19	28	16	13	7	10
1986	— San Jose (Calif.)■	3	2	.600	1.47	14	8	0	0	2	49	40	14	8	5	37
1987	— Tabasco (Mexican)■	1	0	1.000	0.00	10	0	0	0	4	12 1/3	7	0	0	7	5
	— Okla. City (A.A.)■	2	2	.500	3.48	7	3	0	0	0	20 2/3	26	8	8	5	14
	— Texas (A.L.)	3	3	.500	4.31	24	0	0	0	1	31 1/3	33	15	15	8	19
1988	—							Out of organized baseball.								
1989	—							Out of organized baseball.								
1990	— Salinas (Calif.)■	0	1	.000	2.12	10	6	0	0	0	17	19	8	4	5	14
1991	— Columbus (Int'l)■	2	1	.667	0.00	12	0	0	0	5	18	11	1	0	8	13
	— New York (A.L.)	3	1	.750	1.68	37	0	0	0	3	48 1/3	39	12	9	7	34
1992	— New York (A.L.)	3	0	1.000	2.45	20	0	0	0	6	22	9	7	6	3	12
1993	— New York (A.L.)	3	5	.375	4.97	51	0	0	0	4	50 2/3	58	31	28	10	19
	— Columbus (Int'l)	0	1	.000	10.13	2	2	0	0	0	2 2/3	6	3	3	1	1
1994	— New York (A.L.)	3	0	1.000	1.80	40	0	0	0	15	40	28	8	8	7	18
	— Alb./Colon. (East.)	0	0	...	0.00	1	1	0	0	0	1 1/3	2	2	0	0	2
1995	— New York (A.L.)	6	3	.667	4.96	56	0	0	0	2	49	66	29	27	17	28
A.L. totals (7 years)		23	15	.605	3.66	241	0	0	0	31	260 1/3	261	118	106	59	140
N.L. totals (5 years)		24	25	.490	2.35	231	0	0	0	59	329	306	109	86	74	183
Major league totals (11 years)		47	40	.540	2.93	472	0	0	0	90	589 1/3	567	227	192	133	323

DIVISION SERIES RECORD

Year	Team (League)	W	L	Pct.	ERA	G	GS	CG	ShO	Sv.	IP	H	R	ER	BB	SO
1981	— Los Angeles (N.L.)	0	0	...	0.00	2	0	0	0	0	2	1	0	0	0	2
1995	— New York (A.L.)	0	0	...	18.00	2	0	0	0	0	1	4	2	2	0	0
Div. series totals (2 years)		0	0	...	6.00	4	0	0	0	0	3	5	2	2	0	2

CHAMPIONSHIP SERIES RECORD

Year	Team (League)	W	L	Pct.	ERA	G	GS	CG	ShO	Sv.	IP	H	R	ER	BB	SO
1981	— Los Angeles (N.L.)	0	0	...	0.00	2	0	0	0	0	2	1	0	0	0	2

WORLD SERIES RECORD

NOTES: Member of World Series championship team (1981).

Year	Team (League)	W	L	Pct.	ERA	G	GS	CG	ShO	Sv.	IP	H	R	ER	BB	SO
1981—	Los Angeles (N.L.)	1	0	1.000	3.86	3	0	0	0	1	7	7	3	3	1	4

ALL-STAR GAME RECORD

Year	League	W	L	Pct.	ERA	GS	CG	ShO	Sv.	IP	H	R	ER	BB	SO
1982—	National	0	0	...	0.00	0	0	0	0	1/3	0	0	0	0	0

HUBBARD, MIKE — C — CUBS

PERSONAL: Born February 16, 1971, in Lynchburg, Va. . . . 6-1/195. . . . Bats right, throws right. . . . Full name: Michael Wayne Hubbard.
HIGH SCHOOL: Amherst (Va.) County.
COLLEGE: James Madison.
TRANSACTIONS/CAREER NOTES: Selected by Chicago Cubs organization in eighth round of free-agent draft (June 1, 1992).

			BATTING												FIELDING			
Year	Team (League)	Pos.	G	AB	R	H	2B	3B	HR	RBI	Avg.	BB	SO	SB	PO	A	E	Avg.
1992—	Geneva (NYP)	C	50	183	25	44	4	4	3	25	.240	7	29	6	325	27	5	.986
1993—	Daytona (Fla. St.)	C-2B	68	245	25	72	10	3	1	20	.294	18	41	10	354	66	9	.979
1994—	Orlando (Southern)	C-3B-1B	104	357	52	102	13	3	11	39	.286	29	58	7	498	78	12	.980
1995—	Iowa (Am. Assoc.)	C-3B	75	254	28	66	6	3	5	23	.260	26	60	6	447	34	9	.982
—	Chicago (N.L.)	C	15	23	2	4	0	0	0	1	.174	2	2	0	33	0	1	.971
Major league totals (1 year)			15	23	2	4	0	0	0	1	.174	2	2	0	33	0	1	.971

HUBBARD, TRENIDAD — OF — ROCKIES

PERSONAL: Born May 11, 1966, in Chicago. . . . 5-8/183. . . . Bats right, throws right. . . . Full name: Trenidad Aviel Hubbard. . . . Cousin of Joe Cribbs, running back, Buffalo Bills (1980-83 and 1985).
HIGH SCHOOL: South Shore (Chicago).
COLLEGE: Southern (La.).
TRANSACTIONS/CAREER NOTES: Selected by Houston Astros organization in 12th round of free-agent draft (June 2, 1986). . . . Granted free agency (October 15, 1992). . . . Signed by Colorado Rockies organization (October 30, 1992). . . . On disabled list (June 15-24, 1993). . . . Granted free agency (October 15, 1993). . . . Re-signed by Rockies organization (December 3, 1993). . . . Granted free agency (October 15, 1994). . . . Re-signed by Colorado Springs, Rockies organization (November 14, 1994).
STATISTICAL NOTES: Led Texas League second basemen with 296 putouts, 653 total chances and 81 double plays in 1991. . . . Tied for Pacific Coast League lead in caught stealing with 18 in 1993. . . . Led Pacific Coast League with .416 on-base percentage in 1995.
MISCELLANEOUS: Batted lefthanded on occasion though not a switch-hitter (1986-91).

			BATTING												FIELDING			
Year	Team (League)	Pos.	G	AB	R	H	2B	3B	HR	RBI	Avg.	BB	SO	SB	PO	A	E	Avg.
1986—	Auburn (NYP)	2B-OF	70	242	42	75	12	1	1	32	.310	28	42	35	131	110	18	.931
1987—	Asheville (S. Atl.)	2-O-C-3-P	101	284	39	67	8	1	1	35	.236	28	42	28	124	108	14	.943
1988—	Osceola (Fla. St.)	2-C-O-3-1	130	446	68	116	15	11	3	65	.260	61	72	44	261	150	12	.972
1989—	Columbus (South.)	2-C-O-3	104	348	55	92	7	8	3	37	.264	43	53	28	321	122	15	.967
—	Tucson (PCL)	OF-3B-C	21	50	3	11	2	0	0	2	.220	1	10	3	20	9	1	.967
1990—	Columbus (South.)	2-O-C-3	95	335	39	84	14	4	4	35	.251	32	51	17	216	116	11	.968
—	Tucson (PCL)	2B-3B-C	12	27	5	6	2	2	0	2	.222	3	6	1	20	22	3	.933
1991—	Jackson (Texas)	2-O-1-P	126	455	78	135	21	3	2	41	.297	65	81	39	†299	338	21	.968
—	Tucson (PCL)	2B	2	4	0	0	0	0	0	0	.000	0	0	0	1	2	0	1.000
1992—	Tucson (PCL)	2B-3B	115	420	69	130	16	4	2	33	.310	45	68	34	238	353	18	.970
1993—	Colo. Springs (PCL)■	O-2-3-S	117	439	83	138	24	8	7	56	.314	47	57	33	208	29	6	.975
1994—	Colo. Springs (PCL)	OF	79	320	78	116	22	5	8	38	.363	44	40	28	183	5	7	.964
—	Colorado (N.L.)	OF	18	25	3	7	1	1	1	3	.280	3	4	0	4	0	0	1.000
1995—	Colo. Springs (PCL)	OF	123	480	*102	163	29	7	12	66	.340	61	59	*37	285	11	6	.980
—	Colorado (N.L.)	OF	24	58	13	18	4	0	3	9	.310	8	6	2	16	1	0	1.000
Major league totals (2 years)			42	83	16	25	5	1	4	12	.301	11	10	2	20	1	0	1.000

DIVISION SERIES RECORD

			BATTING												FIELDING			
Year	Team (League)	Pos.	G	AB	R	H	2B	3B	HR	RBI	Avg.	BB	SO	SB	PO	A	E	Avg.
1995—	Colorado (N.L.)	PH	3	2	0	0	0	0	0	0	.000	0	0	0	...	...	...	...

RECORD AS PITCHER

Year	Team (League)	W	L	Pct.	ERA	G	GS	CG	ShO	Sv.	IP	H	R	ER	BB	SO
1987—	Asheville (S. Atl.)	0	0	...	0.00	1	0	0	0	0	1	1	0	0	1	0
1991—	Jackson (Texas)	0	0	...	0.00	1	0	0	0	0	1	0	0	0	2	0

HUCKABY, KENNETH — C — DODGERS

PERSONAL: Born January 27, 1971, in San Leandro, Calif. . . . 6-1/205. . . . Bats right, throws right. . . . Full name: Kenneth Paul Huckaby.
HIGH SCHOOL: Manteca (Calif.).
JUNIOR COLLEGE: San Joaquin Delta (Calif.).
TRANSACTIONS/CAREER NOTES: Selected by Los Angeles Dodgers organization in second round of free-agent draft (June 3, 1991). . . . On disabled list (May 26-June 5 and July 2-21, 1992). . . . On San Antonio disabled list (May 4-13, 1994).
STATISTICAL NOTES: Led Florida State League catchers with 14 double plays in 1993. . . . Led Pacific Coast League catchers with 592 total chances in 1995.

Year	Team (League)	Pos.	G	AB	R	H	2B	3B	HR	RBI	Avg.	BB	SO	SB	PO	A	E	Avg.
			BATTING												FIELDING			
1991—	Great Falls (Pio.)	C	57	213	39	55	16	0	3	37	.258	17	38	3	456	48	*12	.977
1992—	Vero Beach (FSL)	C	73	261	14	63	9	00	0	21	.241	7	42	1	442	56	9	.982
1993—	San Antonio (Tex.)	C	28	82	4	18	1	0	0	5	.220	2	7	0	149	29	4	.978
	—Vero Beach (FSL)	C	79	281	22	75	14	1	4	41	.267	11	35	2	481	*99	12	.980
1994—	San Antonio (Tex.)	C	11	41	3	11	1	0	1	9	.268	1	1	1	73	8	6	.931
	—Bakersfield (Calif.)	C	77	270	29	81	18	1	2	30	.300	10	37	2	591	93	10	.986
1995—	Albuquerque (PCL)	C-1B	89	278	30	90	16	2	1	40	.324	12	26	3	518	61	16	.973

HUDEK, JOHN — P — ASTROS

PERSONAL: Born August 8, 1966, in Tampa, Fla. . . . 6-1/200. . . . Throws right, bats both. . . . Full name: John Raymond Hudek. . . . Name pronounced HOO-dek.

HIGH SCHOOL: H.B. Plant (Tampa, Fla.).

COLLEGE: Florida Southern.

TRANSACTIONS/CAREER NOTES: Selected by Texas Rangers organization in 30th round of free-agent draft (June 3, 1985); did not sign. . . . Selected by Chicago White Sox organization in 10th round of free-agent draft (June 1, 1988). . . . Selected by Detroit Tigers from White Sox organization in Rule 5 major league draft (December 7, 1992). . . . On Toledo disabled list (April 8-28 and June 17-July 1, 1993). . . . Claimed on waivers by Houston Astros (July 29, 1993). . . . On disabled list (June 26, 1995-remainder of season).

STATISTICAL NOTES: Combined with starter Jose Ventura and Chris Howard in 4-1 no-hit victory against Charlotte (April 18, 1991).

Year	Team (League)	W	L	Pct.	ERA	G	GS	CG	ShO	Sv.	IP	H	R	ER	BB	SO
1988—	South Bend (Midw.)	7	2	.778	1.98	26	0	0	0	8	54 2/3	45	19	12	21	35
1989—	Sarasota (Fla. St.)	1	3	.250	1.67	27	0	0	0	15	43	22	10	8	13	39
	—Birmingham (Sou.)	1	1	.500	4.24	18	0	0	0	11	17	14	8	8	9	10
1990—	Birmingham (Sou.)	6	6	.500	4.58	42	10	0	0	4	92 1/3	84	59	47	52	67
1991—	Birmingham (Sou.)	5	10	.333	3.84	51	0	0	0	13	65 2/3	58	39	28	28	49
1992—	Birmingham (Sou.)	0	1	.000	2.31	5	0	0	0	1	11 2/3	9	4	3	11	9
	—Vancouver (PCL)	8	1	.889	3.16	39	3	1	1	2	85 1/3	69	36	30	45	61
1993—	Toledo (Int'l)■	1	3	.250	5.82	16	5	0	0	0	38 2/3	44	26	25	22	32
	—Tucson (Pac. Coast)■	3	1	.750	3.79	13	1	0	0	0	19	17	11	8	11	18
1994—	Tucson (Pac. Coast)	0	0	...	4.91	6	0	0	0	2	7 1/3	3	4	4	3	14
	—Houston (N.L.)	0	2	.000	2.97	42	0	0	0	16	39 1/3	24	14	13	18	39
1995—	Houston (N.L.)	2	2	.500	5.40	19	0	0	0	7	20	19	12	12	5	29
Major league totals (2 years)		2	4	.333	3.79	61	0	0	0	23	59 1/3	43	26	25	23	68

ALL-STAR GAME RECORD

Year	League	W	L	Pct.	ERA	GS	CG	ShO	Sv.	IP	H	R	ER	BB	SO
1994—	National	0	0	...	27.00	0	0	0	0	2/3	1	2	2	1	1

HUDLER, REX — 2B/OF — ANGELS

PERSONAL: Born September 2, 1960, in Tempe, Ariz. . . . 6-0/195. . . . Bats right, throws right. . . . Full name: Rex Allen Hudler.

HIGH SCHOOL: Bullard (Fresno, Calif.).

TRANSACTIONS/CAREER NOTES: Selected by New York Yankees organization in first round (18th pick overall) of free-agent draft (June 6, 1978); pick received as compensation for Chicago White Sox signing free-agent DH/OF Ron Blomberg. . . . On Fort Lauderdale disabled list (May 18-31, 1979; May 10-June 15, 1980; and May 11-June 11, 1981). . . . Traded by Yankees with P Rich Bordi to Baltimore Orioles for OF Gary Roenicke and a player to be named later (December 12, 1985); Yankees acquired OF Leo Hernandez to complete deal (December 16, 1985). . . . On Baltimore disabled list (March 23-June 16, 1987); included rehabilitation assignment to Rochester (May 28-June 16). . . . Granted free agency (October 15, 1987). . . . Signed by Indianapolis, Montreal Expos organization (December 18, 1987). . . . Traded by Expos to St. Louis Cardinals for P John Costello (April 23, 1990). . . . On disabled list (May 7-June 29, 1992). . . . Released by Cardinals (December 7, 1992). . . . Signed by Yakult Swallows of Japan Central League (1993). . . . Signed as free agent by San Francisco Giants organization (December 20, 1993). . . . Released by Phoenix, Giants organization (March 22, 1994). . . . Signed by California Angels (March 28, 1994). . . . On disabled list (May 28-June 14, 1994). . . . Granted free agency (October 18, 1994). . . . Re-signed by Angels (December 6, 1994).

STATISTICAL NOTES: Led International League second basemen with 95 double plays in 1984.

Year	Team (League)	Pos.	G	AB	R	H	2B	3B	HR	RBI	Avg.	BB	SO	SB	PO	A	E	Avg.
			BATTING												FIELDING			
1978—	Oneonta (NYP)	SS	58	221	33	62	5	5	0	24	.281	21	29	16	123	21	22	.867
1979—	Fort Lauder. (FSL)	S-3-2-0	116	414	37	104	14	1	1	25	.251	15	73	23	164	314	45	.914
1980—	Fort Lauder. (FSL)	3-2-0-1	37	125	14	26	4	0	0	6	.208	2	25	2	55	71	5	.962
	—Greensboro (S. Atl.)	2B	20	75	7	17	3	1	2	9	.227	4	14	1	51	52	5	.954
1981—	Fort Lauder. (FSL)	2-S-3-0	79	259	35	77	11	1	2	26	.297	13	31	6	104	238	19	.947
1982—	Nashville (South.)	2B-SS-OF	89	299	27	71	14	1	0	24	.237	9	51	9	136	219	20	.947
	—Fort Lauder. (FSL)	2B	9	32	2	8	1	0	1	6	.250	4	5	0	23	25	2	.960
1983—	Fort Lauder. (FSL)	2B-SS	91	345	55	93	15	2	2	50	.270	26	44	30	195	245	15	.967
	—Columbus (Int'l)	2B-3B-SS	40	118	17	36	5	0	1	11	.305	6	25	1	55	95	4	.974
1984—	Columbus (Int'l)	2B	114	394	49	115	26	1	1	35	.292	16	61	11	266	348	16	.975
	—New York (A.L.)	2B	9	7	2	1	1	0	0	0	.143	1	5	0	4	7	0	1.000
1985—	Columbus (Int'l)	2-S-0-3-1	106	380	62	95	13	4	3	18	.250	17	51	29	192	234	17	.962
	—New York (A.L.)	2B-1B-SS	20	51	4	8	0	1	0	1	.157	1	9	0	42	51	2	.979
1986—	Rochester (Int'l)■	2-3-0-S	77	219	29	57	12	3	2	13	.260	16	32	12	135	191	15	.956
	—Baltimore (A.L.)	2B-3B	14	1	1	0	0	0	0	0	.000	0	0	1	2	3	1	.833
1987—	Rochester (Int'l)	OF-2B-SS	31	106	22	27	5	1	5	10	.255	2	15	9	51	15	2	.971
1988—	Indianapolis (A.A.)■	0-2-S-3	67	234	36	71	11	3	7	25	.303	10	35	14	102	96	4	.980
	—Montreal (N.L.)	2B-SS-OF	77	216	38	59	14	2	4	14	.273	10	34	29	116	168	10	.966
1989—	Montreal (N.L.)	2B-OF-SS	92	155	21	38	7	0	6	13	.245	6	23	15	59	59	7	.944
1990—	Montreal (N.L.)	PH	4	3	1	1	0	0	0	0	.333	0	1	0	0	0	0	...
	—St. Louis (N.L.)■	0-2-1-3-S	89	217	30	61	11	2	7	22	.281	12	31	18	158	42	5	.976
1991—	St. Louis (N.L.)	OF-1B-2B	101	207	21	47	10	2	1	15	.227	10	29	12	130	6	2	.986
1992—	St. Louis (N.L.)	2B-OF-1B	61	98	17	24	4	0	3	5	.245	2	23	2	44	39	3	.965

			BATTING												FIELDING			
Year	**Team (League)**	**Pos.**	**G**	**AB**	**R**	**H**	**2B**	**3B**	**HR**	**RBI**	**Avg.**	**BB**	**SO**	**SB**	**PO**	**A**	**E**	**Avg.**
1993—	Yakult (Jp. Cen.)■	...	120	410	48	123	26	3	14	64	.300	32	77	1	...	...	...	...
1994—	California (A.L.)■	2-O-DH-3-1	56	124	17	37	8	0	8	20	.298	6	28	2	71	61	5	.964
1995—	California (A.L.)	2-O-DH-1	84	223	30	59	16	0	6	27	.265	10	48	13	122	115	4	.983
American League totals (5 years)			183	406	54	105	25	1	14	48	.259	18	90	16	241	237	12	.976
National League totals (5 years)			424	896	128	230	46	6	21	69	.257	40	141	76	507	314	27	.968
Major league totals (10 years)			607	1302	182	335	71	7	35	117	.257	58	231	92	748	551	39	.971

HUDSON, JOE — P — RED SOX

PERSONAL: Born September 29, 1970, in Philadelphia. . . . 6-1/180. . . . Throws right, bats right. . . . Full name: Joseph Paul Hudson.
HIGH SCHOOL: Holy Cross (Delran, N.J.).
COLLEGE: West Virginia.
TRANSACTIONS/CAREER NOTES: Selected by Boston Red Sox organization in 27th round of free-agent draft (June 1, 1992).

Year	**Team (League)**	**W**	**L**	**Pct.**	**ERA**	**G**	**GS**	**CG**	**ShO**	**Sv.**	**IP**	**H**	**R**	**ER**	**BB**	**SO**
1992—	Elmira (NYP)	3	3	.500	4.38	19	7	0	0	0	72	76	46	35	33	38
1993—	Lynchburg (Caro.)	8	6	.571	4.06	49	1	0	0	0	84 1/3	97	49	38	38	62
1994—	Sarasota (Fla. St.)	3	1	.750	2.23	30	0	0	0	7	48 1/3	42	20	12	27	33
—	New Britain (East.)	5	3	.625	3.92	23	0	0	0	0	39	49	18	17	18	24
1995—	Trenton (Eastern)	0	1	.000	1.71	22	0	0	0	8	31 2/3	20	8	6	17	24
—	Boston (A.L.)	0	1	.000	4.11	39	0	0	0	1	46	53	21	21	23	29
Major league totals (1 year)		0	1	.000	4.11	39	0	0	0	1	46	53	21	21	23	29

DIVISION SERIES RECORD

Year	**Team (League)**	**W**	**L**	**Pct.**	**ERA**	**G**	**GS**	**CG**	**ShO**	**Sv.**	**IP**	**H**	**R**	**ER**	**BB**	**SO**
1995—	Boston (A.L.)	0	0	...	0.00	1	0	0	0	0	1	2	0	0	1	0

HUFF, MIKE — OF — BLUE JAYS

PERSONAL: Born August 11, 1963, in Honolulu. . . . 6-1/190. . . . Bats right, throws right. . . . Full name: Michael Kale Huff.
HIGH SCHOOL: New Trier (Winnetka, Ill.).
COLLEGE: Northwestern (degree in industrial engineering, 1985).
TRANSACTIONS/CAREER NOTES: Selected by Los Angeles Dodgers organization in 16th round of free-agent draft (June 3, 1985). . . . On disabled list (May 11, 1987-remainder of season). . . . Selected by Cleveland Indians from Dodgers organization in Rule 5 major league draft (December 3, 1990). . . . Claimed on waivers by Chicago White Sox (July 12, 1991). . . . On disabled list (August 25-September 9, 1991). . . . On Chicago disabled list (June 17-September 1, 1992); included rehabilitation assignment to Vancouver (July 31) and South Bend (August 21-September 1). . . . Traded by White Sox to Toronto Blue Jays for 1B Domingo Martinez (March 29, 1994). . . . On Toronto disabled list (July 16-31, 1994); included rehabilitation assignment to Syracuse (July 29-31). . . . On disabled list (May 12-31 and July 3-18, 1995). . . . Granted free agency (October 19, 1995). . . . Re-signed by Blue Jays (December 20, 1995).
STATISTICAL NOTES: Tied for Texas League lead in double plays by outfielder with four in 1988. . . . Led American Association with .411 on-base percentage in 1993. . . . Tied for American Association lead in double plays by outfielder with five in 1993.

			BATTING												FIELDING			
Year	**Team (League)**	**Pos.**	**G**	**AB**	**R**	**H**	**2B**	**3B**	**HR**	**RBI**	**Avg.**	**BB**	**SO**	**SB**	**PO**	**A**	**E**	**Avg.**
1985—	Great Falls (Pio.)	OF	•70	247	70	78	6	6	0	35	.316	56	44	28	120	5	5	.962
1986—	Vero Beach (FSL)	OF	113	362	73	106	6	8	2	32	.293	67	67	28	257	10	1	.996
1987—	San Antonio (Tex.)	OF	31	135	23	42	5	1	3	18	.311	9	21	2	52	2	2	.964
1988—	San Antonio (Tex.)	OF	102	395	68	120	18	10	2	40	.304	37	55	33	222	12	2	.992
—	Albuquerque (PCL)	OF	2	4	0	1	1	0	0	0	.250	0	0	0	2	0	0	1.000
1989—	Albuquerque (PCL)	OF-2B	115	471	75	150	29	7	10	78	.318	38	75	32	209	13	2	.991
—	Los Angeles (N.L.)	OF	12	25	4	5	1	0	1	2	.200	3	6	0	18	0	0	1.000
1990—	Albuquerque (PCL)	OF-2B	*138	474	99	154	28	11	7	84	.325	82	68	27	285	29	5	.984
1991—	Cleveland (A.L.)■	OF-2B	51	146	28	35	6	1	2	10	.240	25	30	11	97	6	1	.990
—	Chicago (A.L.)■	OF-2B-DH	51	97	14	26	4	1	1	15	.268	12	18	3	71	1	1	.986
1992—	Chicago (A.L.)	OF-DH	60	115	13	24	5	0	0	8	.209	10	24	1	68	2	0	1.000
—	Vancouver (PCL)	OF	1	4	1	1	0	0	0	0	.250	1	0	0	4	0	0	1.000
—	South Bend (Mid.)	OF-3B-1B	12	40	7	15	2	1	1	5	.375	11	7	2	15	2	1	.944
1993—	Nashville (A.A.)	OF-2B	92	344	65	101	12	6	8	32	.294	64	43	18	207	11	3	.986
—	Chicago (A.L.)	OF	43	44	4	8	2	0	1	6	.182	9	15	1	40	0	0	1.000
1994—	Toronto (A.L.)■	OF	80	207	31	63	15	3	3	25	.304	27	27	2	126	4	1	.992
—	Syracuse (Int'l)	OF	2	8	2	0	0	0	0	0	.000	1	2	1	2	0	0	1.000
1995—	Toronto (A.L.)	OF	61	138	14	32	9	1	1	9	.232	22	21	1	95	3	2	.980
American League totals (5 years)			346	747	104	188	41	6	8	73	.252	105	135	19	497	16	5	.990
National League totals (1 year)			12	25	4	5	1	0	1	2	.200	3	6	0	18	0	0	1.000
Major league totals (6 years)			358	772	108	193	42	6	9	75	.250	108	141	19	515	16	5	.991

HUGHES, BOBBY — C — BREWERS

PERSONAL: Born March 10, 1971, in Burbank, Calif. . . . 6-4/237. . . . Bats right, throws right. . . . Full name: Robert E. Hughes.
HIGH SCHOOL: Notre Dame (Sherman Oaks, Calif.).
JUNIOR COLLEGE: College of the Canyons (Calif.).
COLLEGE: Loyola Marymount, then Southern California.
TRANSACTIONS/CAREER NOTES: Selected by Detroit Tigers organization in 47th round of free-agent draft (June 3, 1991); did not sign. . . . Selected by Milwaukee Brewers organization in second round of free-agent draft (June 1, 1992).
STATISTICAL NOTES: Led Midwest League catchers with 17 errors in 1993.

Year	Team (League)	Pos.	G	BATTING AB	R	H	2B	3B	HR	RBI	Avg.	BB	SO	SB	FIELDING PO	A	E	Avg.
1992—	Helena (Pioneer)	OF-C	11	40	5	7	1	1	0	6	.175	4	14	0	64	9	1	.986
1993—	Beloit (Midwest)	C-1B	98	321	42	89	11	3	17	56	.277	23	76	1	573	67	†18	.973
1994—	Stockton (Calif.)	C-1B-3B	95	322	54	81	24	3	11	53	.252	33	83	2	517	63	8	.986
	—El Paso (Texas)	C	12	36	3	10	4	1	0	12	.278	5	7	0	52	8	1	.984
1995—	Stockton (Calif.)	C-1B	52	179	22	42	9	2	8	31	.235	17	41	2	252	50	4	.987
	—El Paso (Texas)	C	51	173	11	46	12	0	7	27	.266	12	30	0	299	29	8	.976

HUISMAN, RICK — P — ROYALS

PERSONAL: Born May 17, 1969, in Oak Park, Ill. . . . 6-3/210. . . . Throws right, bats right. . . . Full name: Richard Allen Huisman. . . . Name pronounced HIGHS-man.

HIGH SCHOOL: Timothy Christian (Elmhurst, Ill.).

COLLEGE: Lewis (Ill.).

TRANSACTIONS/CAREER NOTES: Selected by San Francisco Giants organization in third round of free-agent draft (June 4, 1990). . . . On Phoenix disabled list (April 8-May 18, 1993). . . . Claimed on waivers by Houston Astros (August 27, 1993). . . . Traded by Astros to Kansas City Royals (August 17, 1995), completing deal in which Astros acquired C Pat Borders for a player to be named later (August 12, 1995).

HONORS: Named California League Pitcher of the Year (1991).

Year	Team (League)	W	L	Pct.	ERA	G	GS	CG	ShO	Sv.	IP	H	R	ER	BB	SO
1990—	Everett (N'west)	0	0	. . .	4.50	1	0	0	0	0	2	3	1	1	2	2
	—Clinton (Midwest)	6	5	.545	2.05	14	13	0	0	0	79	56	19	18	33	103
1991—	San Jose (Calif.)	*16	4	.800	*1.83	26	26	7	*4	0	*182 1/3	126	45	37	73	*216
1992—	Shreveport (Texas)	7	4	.636	2.35	17	16	1	1	0	103 1/3	79	33	27	31	100
	—Phoenix (PCL)	3	2	.600	2.41	9	8	0	0	0	56	45	16	15	24	44
1993—	San Jose (Calif.)	2	1	.667	2.31	4	4	1	0	0	23 1/3	19	6	6	12	15
	—Phoenix (PCL)	3	4	.429	5.97	14	14	0	0	0	72 1/3	78	54	48	45	59
	—Tucson (Pac. Coast)■	1	0	1.000	7.36	2	0	0	0	0	3 2/3	6	5	3	1	4
1994—	Jackson (Texas)	3	0	1.000	1.61	49	0	0	0	31	50 1/3	32	10	9	24	63
1995—	Tucson (Pac. Coast)	6	1	.857	4.45	42	0	0	0	6	54 2/3	58	33	27	28	47
	—Omaha (Am. Assoc.)■	0	0	. . .	1.80	5	0	0	0	1	5	3	1	1	1	13
	—Kansas City (A.L.)	0	0	. . .	7.45	7	0	0	0	0	9 2/3	14	8	8	1	12
Major league totals (1 year)		0	0	. . .	7.45	7	0	0	0	0	9 2/3	14	8	8	1	12

HULETT, TIM — 3B

PERSONAL: Born January 12, 1960, in Springfield, Ill. . . . 6-0/199. . . . Bats right, throws right. . . . Full name: Timothy Craig Hulett. . . . Name pronounced HYOO-lit.

HIGH SCHOOL: Lanphier (Springfield, Ill.).

JUNIOR COLLEGE: Miami-Dade (North) Community College.

COLLEGE: South Florida.

TRANSACTIONS/CAREER NOTES: Selected by Texas Rangers organization in 39th round of free-agent draft (June 6, 1978); did not sign. . . . Selected by Chicago White Sox organization in secondary phase of free-agent draft (January 8, 1980). . . . Traded by White Sox organization to Montreal Expos for a player to be named later (April 13, 1988); White Sox acquired 2B Edgar Caceres to complete deal (June 15, 1988). . . . Granted free agency (October 15, 1988). . . . Signed by Rochester, Baltimore Orioles organization (November 21, 1988). . . . On Baltimore disabled list (April 4-June 12, 1990); included rehabilitation assignment to Rochester (May 29-June 21). . . . On disabled list (July 21-August 6, 1992). . . . Granted free agency (November 7, 1993). . . . Re-signed by Orioles (December 2, 1993). . . . Granted free agency (October 21, 1994). . . . Signed by Louisville, St. Louis Cardinals organization (April 1, 1995). . . . On St. Louis disabled list (April 23-May 8, 1995); included rehabilitation assignment to Louisville (May 5-8). . . . Released by Cardinals (May 16, 1995). . . . Signed by Oklahoma City, Texas Rangers organization (June 1, 1995). . . . Announced retirement (July 22, 1995).

STATISTICAL NOTES: Led Eastern League second basemen with 332 putouts, 415 assists, 763 total chances and 112 double plays in 1981. . . . Led Eastern League second basemen with .975 fielding percentage, 343 putouts, 386 assists, 748 total chances and 95 double plays in 1982. . . . Led American Association second basemen with 730 total chances in 1983. . . . Led American Association with nine sacrifice flies in 1983 and 1988. . . . Tied for A.L. lead in errors by third baseman with 23 in 1985. . . . Led International League third basemen with 23 double plays in 1989.

Year	Team (League)	Pos.	G	BATTING AB	R	H	2B	3B	HR	RBI	Avg.	BB	SO	SB	FIELDING PO	A	E	Avg.
1980—	Glens Falls (East.)	SS	6	23	2	4	0	0	0	0	.174	3	5	0	14	13	2	.931
	—Iowa (Am. Assoc.)	3B	3	8	1	2	0	0	0	0	.250	0	0	1	0	6	3	.667
	—Appleton (Midw.)	2B-3B-SS	79	278	49	72	11	1	13	47	.259	34	56	5	162	258	17	.961
1981—	Glens Falls (East.)	2B-3B	134	437	59	99	27	1	10	55	.227	64	86	0	†333	†422	16	.979
1982—	Glens Falls (East.)	2B-SS	•140	*536	*113	145	28	5	22	87	.271	95	135	1	†352	†398	21	†.973
1983—	Denver (A.A.)	2B	133	477	77	130	19	4	21	88	.273	61	64	5	*286	*424	*20	.973
	—Chicago (A.L.)	2B	6	5	0	1	0	0	0	0	.200	0	0	1	8	6	2	.875
1984—	Chicago (A.L.)	3B-2B	8	7	1	0	0	0	0	0	.000	1	4	1	4	15	0	1.000
	—Denver (A.A.)	2B-3B-SS	139	475	72	125	32	6	16	80	.263	67	88	3	269	371	28	.958
1985—	Chicago (A.L.)	3B-2B-OF	141	395	52	106	19	4	5	37	.268	30	81	6	117	256	‡24	.940
1986—	Chicago (A.L.)	3B-2B	150	520	53	120	16	5	17	44	.231	21	91	4	179	331	15	.971
1987—	Chicago (A.L.)	3B-2B	68	240	20	52	10	0	7	28	.217	10	41	0	55	142	9	.956
	—Hawaii (PCL)	3B-2B	42	157	13	37	5	2	1	24	.236	9	28	4	47	81	11	.921
1988—	Indianapolis (A.A.)■	3B-2B	126	427	36	100	29	2	7	59	.234	34	106	2	118	211	25	.929
1989—	Rochester (Int'l)■	3-S-2-P	122	461	61	129	32	12	3	50	.280	38	81	2	149	289	20	.956
	—Baltimore (A.L.)	2B-3B	33	97	12	27	5	0	3	18	.278	10	17	0	70	71	4	.972
1990—	Rochester (Int'l)	2B-SS-3B	14	43	10	16	2	1	2	4	.372	11	7	0	22	35	1	.983
	—Baltimore (A.L.)	3B-2B-DH	53	153	16	39	7	1	3	16	.255	15	41	1	44	101	4	.973
1991—	Baltimore (A.L.)	3-2-DH-S	79	206	29	42	9	0	7	18	.204	13	49	0	47	96	4	.973
1992—	Baltimore (A.L.)	3-DH-2-S	57	142	11	41	7	2	2	21	.289	10	31	0	25	92	7	.944
1993—	Baltimore (A.L.)	3-S-2-DH	85	260	40	78	15	0	2	23	.300	23	56	1	58	176	8	.967
1994—	Baltimore (A.L.)	2B-3B-SS	36	92	11	21	2	1	2	15	.228	12	24	0	60	93	3	.981

H

Year	Team (League)	Pos.	G	AB	R	H	2B	3B	HR	RBI	Avg.	BB	SO	SB	PO	A	E	Avg.
			BATTING												FIELDING			
1995—	Louisville (A.A.)■	2B	3	10	1	3	1	0	0	3	.300	2	0	0	6	5	0	1.000
—	St. Louis (N.L.)	2B-SS	4	11	0	2	0	0	0	0	.182	0	3	0	6	13	2	.905
—	Okla. City (A.A.)■	SS-2B-3B	39	141	14	30	6	1	1	7	.213	7	33	0	54	88	10	.934
American League totals (11 years)			716	2117	245	527	90	13	48	220	.249	145	435	14	667	1379	80	.962
National League totals (1 year)			4	11	0	2	0	0	0	0	.182	0	3	0	6	13	2	.905
Major league totals (12 years)			720	2128	245	529	90	13	48	220	.249	145	438	14	673	1392	82	.962

RECORD AS PITCHER

Year	Team (League)	W	L	Pct.	ERA	G	GS	CG	ShO	Sv.	IP	H	R	ER	BB	SO
1989—	Rochester (Int'l)	0	0	...	0.00	1	0	0	0	0	2/3	0	0	0	0	0

HULSE, DAVID — OF — BREWERS

PERSONAL: Born February 25, 1968, in San Angelo, Tex. . . . 5-11/170. . . . Bats left, throws left. . . . Full name: David Lindsey Hulse. . . . Name pronounced HULTZ.

HIGH SCHOOL: San Angelo (Tex.) Central.

COLLEGE: Schreiner College (Tex.).

TRANSACTIONS/CAREER NOTES: Selected by Texas Rangers organization in 13th round of free-agent draft (June 4, 1990). . . . On disabled list (July 26-August 15, 1991). . . . On disabled list (July 25-August 12, 1993). . . . Traded by Rangers to Milwaukee Brewers for P Scott Taylor (April 14, 1995).

Year	Team (League)	Pos.	G	AB	R	H	2B	3B	HR	RBI	Avg.	BB	SO	SB	PO	A	E	Avg.
			BATTING												FIELDING			
1990—	Butte (Pioneer)	OF	64	257	54	*92	12	2	2	36	*.358	25	30	24	102	5	6	.947
1991—	Charlotte (Fla. St.)	OF	88	310	41	86	4	5	0	17	.277	36	74	44	129	6	3	.978
1992—	Tulsa (Texas)	OF	88	354	40	101	14	3	3	20	.285	20	86	17	84	2	4	.956
—	Okla. City (A.A.)	OF	8	30	7	7	1	1	0	3	.233	1	4	2	13	0	1	.929
—	Texas (A.L.)	OF-DH	32	92	14	28	4	0	0	2	.304	3	18	3	61	0	1	.984
1993—	Texas (A.L.)	OF-DH	114	407	71	118	9	10	1	29	.290	26	57	29	244	3	3	.988
1994—	Texas (A.L.)	OF-DH	77	310	58	79	8	4	1	19	.255	21	53	18	179	0	4	.978
—	Okla. City (A.A.)	OF	25	99	10	28	5	2	0	6	.283	6	21	6	78	1	2	.975
1995—	Milwaukee (A.L.)■	OF	119	339	46	85	11	6	3	47	.251	18	60	15	180	2	3	.984
Major league totals (4 years)			342	1148	189	310	32	20	5	97	.270	68	188	65	664	5	11	.984

HUNDLEY, TODD — C — METS

PERSONAL: Born May 27, 1969, in Martinsville, Va. . . . 5-11/185. . . . Bats both, throws right. . . . Full name: Todd Randolph Hundley. . . . Son of Randy Hundley, major league catcher with four teams (1964-77).

HIGH SCHOOL: William Fremd (Palatine, Ill.).

COLLEGE: William Rainey Harper College (Ill.).

TRANSACTIONS/CAREER NOTES: Selected by New York Mets organization in second round of free-agent draft (June 2, 1987); pick received as compensation for Baltimore Orioles signing Type B free-agent 3B/1B Ray Knight. . . . On Tidewater disabled list (June 29-July 6, 1991). . . . On disabled list (July 23, 1995-remainder of season).

STATISTICAL NOTES: Led South Atlantic League in intentional bases on balls received with 10 and in grounding into double plays with 20 in 1989. . . . Led South Atlantic League catchers with 826 putouts and 930 total chances in 1989. . . . Tied for International League lead in errors by catcher with nine and double plays with 12 in 1991. . . . Switch-hit home runs in one game (June 18, 1994). . . . Career major league grand slams: 3.

Year	Team (League)	Pos.	G	AB	R	H	2B	3B	HR	RBI	Avg.	BB	SO	SB	PO	A	E	Avg.
			BATTING												FIELDING			
1987—	Little Falls (NYP)	C	34	103	12	15	4	0	1	10	.146	12	27	0	181	25	7	.967
1988—	Little Falls (NYP)	C	52	176	23	33	8	0	2	18	.188	16	31	1	345	54	8	.980
—	St. Lucie (Fla. St.)	C	1	1	0	0	0	0	0	0	.000	2	1	0	4	0	1	.800
1989—	Columbia (S. Atl.)	C-OF	125	439	67	118	23	4	11	66	.269	54	67	6	†829	91	13	.986
1990—	Jackson (Texas)	C-3B	81	279	27	74	12	2	1	35	.265	34	44	5	474	63	9	.984
—	New York (N.L.)	C	36	67	8	14	6	0	0	2	.209	6	18	0	162	8	2	.988
1991—	Tidewater (Int'l)	C-1B	125	454	62	124	24	4	14	66	.273	51	95	1	585	63	‡9	.986
—	New York (N.L.)	C	21	60	5	8	0	1	1	7	.133	6	14	0	85	11	0	1.000
1992—	New York (N.L.)	C	123	358	32	75	17	0	7	32	.209	19	76	3	700	48	3	.996
1993—	New York (N.L.)	C	130	417	40	95	17	2	11	53	.228	23	62	1	592	63	8	.988
1994—	New York (N.L.)	C	91	291	45	69	10	1	16	42	.237	25	73	2	448	28	5	.990
1995—	New York (N.L.)	C	90	275	39	77	11	0	15	51	.280	42	64	1	488	29	7	.987
Major league totals (6 years)			491	1468	169	338	61	4	50	187	.230	121	307	7	2475	187	25	.991

HUNTER, BRIAN L. — OF — ASTROS

PERSONAL: Born March 5, 1971, in Portland, Ore. . . . 6-4/180. . . . Bats right, throws right. . . . Full name: Brian Lee Hunter.

HIGH SCHOOL: Fort Vancouver (Vancouver, Wash.).

TRANSACTIONS/CAREER NOTES: Selected by Houston Astros organization in second round of free-agent draft (June 5, 1989); pick received as part of compensation for Texas Rangers signing Type A free-agent P Nolan Ryan. . . . On Houston disabled list (July 5-23, 1995); included rehabilitation assignment to Jackson (July 21-23).

Year	Team (League)	Pos.	G	AB	R	H	2B	3B	HR	RBI	Avg.	BB	SO	SB	PO	A	E	Avg.
			BATTING												FIELDING			
1989—	GC Astros (GCL)	OF	51	206	15	35	2	0	0	13	.170	7	42	12	95	4	2	.980
1990—	Asheville (S. Atl.)	OF	127	444	84	111	14	6	0	16	.250	60	72	45	219	13	11	.955
1991—	Osceola (Fla. St.)	OF	118	392	51	94	15	3	1	30	.240	45	75	32	250	7	9	.966
1992—	Osceola (Fla. St.)	OF	131	489	62	146	18	9	1	62	.299	31	76	39	295	10	9	.971

								BATTING							FIELDING			
Year	Team (League)	Pos.	G	AB	R	H	2B	3B	HR	RBI	Avg.	BB	SO	SB	PO	A	E	Avg.
1993—	Jackson (Texas)	OF	133	523	84	154	22	5	10	52	.294	34	85	*35	276	9	*14	.953
1994—	Tucson (PCL)	OF	128	513	*113	*191	28	9	10	51	*.372	52	52	*49	244	14	5	.981
	— Houston (N.L.)	OF	6	24	2	6	1	0	0	0	.250	1	6	2	14	1	1	.938
1995—	Tucson (PCL)	OF	38	155	28	51	5	1	1	16	.329	17	13	11	91	1	0	1.000
	— Houston (N.L.)	OF	78	321	52	97	14	5	2	28	.302	21	52	24	182	8	9	.955
	— Jackson (Texas)	OF	2	6	1	3	0	0	0	0	.500	1	0	0	5	0	0	1.000
Major league totals (2 years)			84	345	54	103	15	5	2	28	.299	22	58	26	196	9	10	.953

HUNTER, BRIAN R. — 1B — REDS

PERSONAL: Born March 4, 1968, in El Toro, Calif. . . . 6-0/195. . . . Bats right, throws left. . . . Full name: Brian Ronald Hunter.

HIGH SCHOOL: Paramount (Calif.).

COLLEGE: Cerritos College (Calif.).

TRANSACTIONS/CAREER NOTES: Selected by Atlanta Braves organization in eighth round of free-agent draft (June 2, 1987). . . . On Atlanta disabled list (April 18-May 18, 1993). . . . Traded by Braves to Pittsburgh Pirates for a player to be named later (November 17, 1993); Braves acquired SS Jose Delgado to complete deal (June 6, 1994). . . . Traded by Pirates to Cincinnati Reds for a player to be named later (July 27, 1994); Pirates acquired OF Micah Franklin to complete deal (October 13, 1994). . . . On Cincinnati disabled list (June 19-July 24 and August 14-September 1, 1995); included rehabilitation assignment to Indianapolis (August 22-31).

STATISTICAL NOTES: Led Appalachian League first basemen with 43 double plays in 1987. . . . Led Midwest League first basemen with 21 errors in 1988. . . . Tied for Southern League lead with nine sacrifice flies in 1989. . . . Career major league grand slams: 2.

								BATTING							FIELDING			
Year	Team (League)	Pos.	G	AB	R	H	2B	3B	HR	RBI	Avg.	BB	SO	SB	PO	A	E	Avg.
1987—	Pulaski (Appal.)	1B-OF	65	251	38	58	10	2	8	30	.231	18	47	3	498	29	11	.980
1988—	Burlington (Midw.)	1B-OF	117	417	58	108	17	0	•22	71	.259	45	90	7	987	69	†22	.980
	— Durham (Carolina)	OF-1B	13	49	13	17	3	0	3	9	.347	7	8	2	52	6	0	1.000
1989—	Greenville (South.)	OF-1B	124	451	57	114	19	2	19	82	.253	33	62	5	248	15	4	.985
1990—	Richmond (Int'l)	OF-1B	43	137	13	27	4	0	5	16	.197	18	37	2	126	5	3	.978
	— Greenville (South.)	OF-1B	88	320	45	77	13	1	14	55	.241	43	62	6	189	19	8	.963
1991—	Richmond (Int'l)	OF	48	181	28	47	7	0	10	30	.260	11	24	3	121	4	4	.969
	— Atlanta (N.L.)	1B-OF	97	271	32	68	16	1	12	50	.251	17	48	0	624	46	8	.988
1992—	Atlanta (N.L.)	1B-OF	102	238	34	57	13	2	14	41	.239	21	50	1	542	50	4	.993
1993—	Atlanta (N.L.)	1B-OF	37	80	4	11	3	1	0	8	.138	2	15	0	168	13	1	.995
	— Richmond (Int'l)	1B-OF	30	99	16	24	7	0	6	26	.242	10	21	4	174	15	0	1.000
1994—	Pittsburgh (N.L.)■	1B-OF	76	233	28	53	15	1	11	47	.227	15	55	0	496	37	5	.991
	— Cincinnati (N.L.)■	OF-1B	9	23	6	7	1	0	4	10	.304	2	1	0	20	1	0	1.000
1995—	Cincinnati (N.L.)	1B-OF	40	79	9	17	6	0	1	9	.215	11	21	2	171	13	3	.984
	— Indianapolis (A.A.)	OF-1B	9	36	7	13	5	0	4	11	.361	6	11	0	42	2	1	.978
Major league totals (5 years)			361	924	113	213	54	5	42	165	.231	68	190	3	2021	160	21	.990

CHAMPIONSHIP SERIES RECORD

								BATTING							FIELDING			
Year	Team (League)	Pos.	G	AB	R	H	2B	3B	HR	RBI	Avg.	BB	SO	SB	PO	A	E	Avg.
1991—	Atlanta (N.L.)	1B	5	18	2	6	2	0	1	4	.333	0	2	0	30	4	0	1.000
1992—	Atlanta (N.L.)	1B-PH	3	5	1	1	0	0	0	0	.200	0	1	0	7	0	0	1.000
Championship series totals (2 years)			8	23	3	7	2	0	1	4	.304	0	3	0	37	4	0	1.000

WORLD SERIES RECORD

								BATTING							FIELDING			
Year	Team (League)	Pos.	G	AB	R	H	2B	3B	HR	RBI	Avg.	BB	SO	SB	PO	A	E	Avg.
1991—	Atlanta (N.L.)	OF-1B-PH	7	21	2	4	1	0	1	3	.190	0	2	0	6	1	0	1.000
1992—	Atlanta (N.L.)	1B-PH-PR	4	5	0	1	0	0	0	2	.200	0	1	0	14	1	0	1.000
World Series totals (2 years)			11	26	2	5	1	0	1	5	.192	0	3	0	20	2	0	1.000

HURST, BILL — P — MARLINS

PERSONAL: Born April 28, 1970, in Miami Beach, Fla. . . . 6-7/215. . . . Throws right, bats right. . . . Full name: William H. Hurst.

HIGH SCHOOL: Miami Palmetto.

JUNIOR COLLEGE: Central Florida Community College.

TRANSACTIONS/CAREER NOTES: Selected by St. Louis Cardinals organization in 20th round of free-agent draft (June 5, 1989). . . . On Savannah disabled list (August 10, 1990-remainder of season). . . . On disabled list (April 29, 1991-remainder of season and April 10, 1992-entire season). . . . Released by Cardinals organization (December 10, 1992). . . . Signed by Florida Marlins organization (March 12, 1995).

Year	Team (League)	W	L	Pct.	ERA	G	GS	CG	ShO	Sv.	IP	H	R	ER	BB	SO
1990—	Johns. City (App.)	0	0	. . .	1.64	2	2	0	0	0	11	5	2	2	6	12
	— Savannah (S. Atl.)	2	1	.667	3.38	7	7	0	0	0	32	22	17	12	27	14
1991—	Johns. City (App.)	0	0	. . .	10.80	2	0	0	0	0	1 2/3	0	2	2	2	2
1992—								Did not play.								
1993—								Did not play.								
1994—								Did not play.								
1995—	Brevard County (FSL)■	1	4	.200	3.02	39	4	0	0	12	50 2/3	33	20	17	41	35

HURST, JIMMY — OF — WHITE SOX

PERSONAL: Born March 1, 1972, in Druid City, Ala. . . . 6-6/225. . . . Bats right, throws right.

HIGH SCHOOL: Central High of Tuscaloosa (Ala.).

JUNIOR COLLEGE: Three Rivers Community College (Mo.).

TRANSACTIONS/CAREER NOTES: Selected by Chicago White Sox organization in 12th round of free-agent draft (June 4, 1990).
STATISTICAL NOTES: Tied for Midwest League lead in errors by outfielder with 12 in 1993.

			BATTING											FIELDING			
Year	Team (League)	Pos.	G	AB	R	H	2B	3B	HR	RBI	Avg.	BB	SO	SB	PO	A	E	Avg.
1991—	GC Whi. Sox (GCL)	OF	36	121	14	31	4	0	0	12	.256	13	32	6	37	4	1	.976
1992—	Utica (NYP)	OF	68	220	31	50	8	5	6	35	.227	27	78	11	81	6	6	.935
1993—	South Bend (Mid.)	OF-1B	123	464	79	113	26	0	20	79	.244	37	141	15	98	8	‡12	.898
1994—	Prin. William (Car.)	OF	127	455	90	126	31	6	25	91	.277	72	128	15	145	6	5	.968
1995—	Birm. (Southern)	OF	91	301	47	57	11	0	12	34	.189	33	95	12	131	3	10	.931

HURTADO, EDWIN — P — MARINERS

PERSONAL: Born February 1, 1970, in Barquisimeto, Venezuela. . . . 6-3/215. . . . Throws right, bats right. . . . Full name: Edwin Amilgar Hurtado.
TRANSACTIONS/CAREER NOTES: Signed as non-drafted free agent by Toronto Blue Jays organization (December 10, 1990). . . . Traded by Blue Jays with P Paul Menhart to Seattle Mariners for P Bill Risley and 2B Miguel Cairo (December 18, 1995).

Year	Team (League)	W	L	Pct.	ERA	G	GS	CG	ShO	Sv.	IP	H	R	ER	BB	SO
1991—	Santo Dom. (DSL)	7	1	.875	1.61	13	13	2	1	0	84	59	21	15	48	92
1992—	Santo Dom. (DSL)	11	0	*1.000	1.36	16	15	2	1	0	92 1/3	65	17	14	37	110
1993—	St. Cathar. (NYP)	10	2	.833	2.50	15	15	3	•1	0	101	69	34	28	34	87
1994—	Hagerstown (S. Atl.)	11	2	.846	2.95	33	16	1	0	2	134 1/3	118	53	44	46	121
1995—	Knoxville (South.)	2	4	.333	4.45	11	11	0	0	0	54 2/3	54	34	27	25	38
—	Toronto (A.L.)	5	2	.714	5.45	14	10	1	0	0	77 2/3	81	50	47	40	33
Major league totals (1 year)		5	2	.714	5.45	14	10	1	0	0	77 2/3	81	50	47	40	33

HUSKEY, BUTCH — 3B — METS

PERSONAL: Born November 10, 1971, in Anadarko, Okla. . . . 6-3/244. . . . Bats right, throws right. . . . Full name: Robert Leon Huskey.
HIGH SCHOOL: Eisenhower (Lawton, Okla.).
TRANSACTIONS/CAREER NOTES: Selected by New York Mets in seventh round of free-agent draft (June 5, 1989).
HONORS: Named International League Most Valuable Player (1995).
STATISTICAL NOTES: Led Gulf Coast League third basemen with 50 putouts and 23 errors in 1989. . . . Led Appalachian League third basemen with 217 total chances and tied for lead with 11 double plays in 1990. . . . Led South Atlantic League with 256 total bases in 1991. . . . Led South Atlantic League third basemen with 21 double plays in 1991. . . . Led Florida State League third basemen with 456 total chances and 28 double plays in 1992. . . . Led Eastern League third basemen with 101 putouts, 297 assists, 34 errors and 432 total chances in 1993. . . . Led International League third basemen with 31 double plays in 1994.

			BATTING											FIELDING			
Year	Team (League)	Pos.	G	AB	R	H	2B	3B	HR	RBI	Avg.	BB	SO	SB	PO	A	E	Avg.
1989—	GC Mets (GCL)	3B-1B	54	190	27	50	14	2	6	34	.263	14	36	4	†73	106	†23	.886
1990—	Kingsport (Appal.)	3B	*72	*279	39	75	13	0	14	53	.269	24	74	7	45	*150	•22	.899
1991—	Columbia (S. Atl.)	3B	134	492	88	141	27	5	*26	*99	.287	54	89	22	*102	218	31	.912
1992—	St. Lucie (Fla. St.)	3B	134	493	65	125	17	1	18	75	.254	33	74	7	*108	*310	*38	.917
1993—	Binghamton (East.)	3B-SS	*139	*526	72	132	23	1	25	98	.251	48	102	11	†101	†297	†34	.921
—	New York (N.L.)	3B	13	41	2	6	1	0	0	3	.146	1	13	0	9	27	3	.923
1994—	Norfolk (Int'l)	3B	127	474	59	108	23	3	10	57	.228	37	88	16	*95	297	25	.940
1995—	Norfolk (Int'l)	3B-OF-1B	109	394	66	112	18	1	*28	87	.284	39	88	8	248	132	13	.967
—	New York (N.L.)	3B-OF	28	90	8	17	1	0	3	11	.189	10	16	1	16	60	6	.927
Major league totals (2 years)			41	131	10	23	2	0	3	14	.176	11	29	1	25	87	9	.926

HUSON, JEFF — IF — ORIOLES

PERSONAL: Born August 15, 1964, in Scottsdale, Ariz. . . . 6-3/180. . . . Bats left, throws right. . . . Full name: Jeffrey Kent Huson. . . . Name pronounced HYOO-son.
HIGH SCHOOL: Mingus Union (Cottonwood, Ariz.).
JUNIOR COLLEGE: Glendale (Ariz.) Community College.
COLLEGE: Wyoming.
TRANSACTIONS/CAREER NOTES: Signed as non-drafted free agent by Montreal Expos organization (August 18, 1985). . . . Traded by Expos to Oklahoma City, Texas Rangers organization, for P Drew Hall (April 2, 1990). . . . On Texas disabled list (August 8-31, 1991); included rehabilitation assignment to Oklahoma City (August 29-31). . . . On Texas disabled list (March 27-May 27, 1993); included rehabilitation assignment to Oklahoma City (May 24-27). . . . On Texas disabled list (June 5-July 15, 1993); included rehabilitation assignment to Oklahoma City (July 10-15). . . . On Texas disabled list (July 24-August 23, 1993); included rehabilitation assignment to Oklahoma City (July 31-August 19). . . . On Texas disabled list (March 25-June 6, 1994); included rehabilitation assignment to Oklahoma City (May 17-June 5). . . . Released by Rangers (November 30, 1994). . . . Signed by Rochester, Baltimore Orioles organization (December 31, 1994).

			BATTING											FIELDING			
Year	Team (League)	Pos.	G	AB	R	H	2B	3B	HR	RBI	Avg.	BB	SO	SB	PO	A	E	Avg.
1986—	Burlington (Midw.)	SS-3B-2B	133	457	85	132	19	1	16	72	.289	76	68	32	183	324	37	.932
—	Jacksonv. (South.)	3B	1	4	0	0	0	0	0	0	.000	0	0	0	0	1	0	1.000
1987—	W.P. Beach (FSL)	SS-OF-2B	131	455	54	130	15	4	1	53	.286	50	30	33	234	347	34	.945
1988—	Jacksonv. (South.)	S-2-0-3	128	471	72	117	18	1	0	34	.248	59	45	*56	217	285	26	.951
—	Montreal (N.L.)	S-2-3-0	20	42	7	13	2	0	0	3	.310	4	3	2	18	41	4	.937
1989—	Indianapolis (A.A.)	SS-OF-2B	102	378	70	115	17	4	3	35	.304	50	26	30	172	214	17	.958
—	Montreal (N.L.)	SS-2B-3B	32	74	1	12	5	0	0	2	.162	6	6	3	40	65	8	.929
1990—	Texas (A.L.)■	SS-3B-2B	145	396	57	95	12	2	0	28	.240	46	54	12	183	304	19	.962
1991—	Texas (A.L.)	SS-2B-3B	119	268	36	57	8	3	2	26	.213	39	32	8	143	269	15	.965
—	Okla. City (A.A.)	SS	2	6	0	3	1	0	0	2	.500	0	1	0	5	3	0	1.000
1992—	Texas (A.L.)	S-2-0-DH	123	318	49	83	14	3	4	24	.261	41	43	18	178	250	9	.979
1993—	Okla. City (A.A.)	3-S-2-0	24	76	11	22	5	0	1	10	.289	13	10	1	39	52	3	.968

Year	Team (League)	Pos.	G	AB	R	H	2B	3B	HR	RBI	Avg.	BB	SO	SB	PO	A	E	Avg.
				BATTING											FIELDING			
	—Texas (A.L.)	S-2-DH-3	23	45	3	6	1	1	0	2	.133	0	10	0	25	42	6	.918
1994	—Okla. City (A.A.)	2-3-0-S	83	302	47	91	20	2	1	27	.301	30	32	18	140	165	7	.978
1995	—Rochester (Int'l)■	SS-2B	60	223	28	56	9	0	3	21	.251	26	29	16	110	203	7	.978
	—Baltimore (A.L.)	3-2-DH-S	66	161	24	40	4	2	1	19	.248	15	20	5	59	89	1	.993
American League totals (5 years)			476	1188	169	281	39	11	7	99	.237	141	159	43	588	954	50	.969
National League totals (2 years)			52	116	8	25	7	0	0	5	.216	10	9	5	58	106	12	.932
Major league totals (7 years)			528	1304	177	306	46	11	7	104	.235	151	168	48	646	1060	62	.965

HUTTON, MARK — P — YANKEES

PERSONAL: Born February 6, 1970, in South Adelaide, Australia. . . . 6-6/240. . . . Throws right, bats right. . . . Full name: Mark Steven Hutton.
TRANSACTIONS/CAREER NOTES: Signed as non-drafted free agent by New York Yankees organization (December 15, 1988). . . . On Columbus disabled list (April 23-May 15, 1993). . . . On Columbus temporarily inactive list (April 11-16, 1994). . . . On Columbus disabled list (June 2-11, July 5-August 12, August 18-27 and August 28-September 4, 1994) . . . On disabled list (June 8-26 and July 11, 1995-remainder of season).

Year	Team (League)	W	L	Pct.	ERA	G	GS	CG	ShO	Sv.	IP	H	R	ER	BB	SO
1989	—Oneonta (NYP)	6	2	.750	4.07	12	12	0	0	0	66 1/3	70	39	30	24	62
1990	—Greensboro (S. Atl.)	1	10	.091	6.31	21	19	0	0	0	81 1/3	77	78	57	62	72
1991	—Fort Lauder. (FSL)	5	8	.385	2.45	24	24	3	0	0	147	98	54	40	65	117
	—Columbus (Int'l)	1	0	1.000	1.50	1	1	0	0	0	6	3	2	1	5	5
1992	—Alb./Colon. (East.)	13	7	.650	3.59	25	25	1	0	0	165 1/3	146	75	66	66	128
	—Columbus (Int'l)	0	1	.000	5.40	1	0	0	0	0	5	7	4	3	2	4
1993	—Columbus (Int'l)	10	4	.714	3.18	21	21	0	0	0	133	98	52	47	53	112
	—New York (A.L.)	1	1	.500	5.73	7	4	0	0	0	22	24	17	14	17	12
1994	—Columbus (Int'l)	2	5	.286	3.63	22	5	0	0	3	34 2/3	31	16	14	12	27
	—New York (A.L.)	0	0	...	4.91	2	0	0	0	0	3 2/3	4	3	2	0	1
1995	—Columbus (Int'l)	2	6	.250	8.43	11	11	0	0	0	52 1/3	64	51	49	24	23
Major league totals (2 years)		1	1	.500	5.61	9	4	0	0	0	25 2/3	28	20	16	17	13

HYERS, TIM — 1B — TIGERS

PERSONAL: Born October 3, 1971, in Atlanta. . . . 6-1/195. . . . Bats left, throws left. . . . Full name: Timothy James Hyers.
HIGH SCHOOL: Newton County (Covington, Ga.).
TRANSACTIONS/CAREER NOTES: Selected by Toronto Blue Jays organization in supplemental round ("sandwich pick" between second and third round) of free-agent draft (June 4, 1990); pick received as compensation for Detroit Tigers signing Type C free-agent OF Lloyd Moseby. . . . Selected by San Diego Padres from Blue Jays organization in Rule 5 major league draft (December 13, 1993). . . . On San Diego disabled list (June 22-August 10, 1994); included rehabilitation assignment to Las Vegas (July 26-August 10). . . . Traded by Padres to Detroit Tigers for a player to be named later (November 14, 1995).
STATISTICAL NOTES: Led Pioneer League first basemen with 565 total chances in 1990. . . . Led Florida State League first basemen with 1,260 total chances in 1992. . . . Led Southern League first basemen with 1,330 total chances and 105 double plays in 1993.

Year	Team (League)	Pos.	G	AB	R	H	2B	3B	HR	RBI	Avg.	BB	SO	SB	PO	A	E	Avg.
				BATTING											FIELDING			
1990	—Medicine Hat (Pio.)	1B	61	224	29	49	7	2	2	19	.219	29	22	4	*516	38	*11	.981
1991	—Myrtle Beach (SAL)	1B	132	398	31	81	8	0	3	37	.204	27	52	6	915	84	14	.986
1992	—Dunedin (Fla. St.)	1B	124	464	54	114	24	3	8	59	.246	41	54	2	*1149	102	9	.993
1993	—Knoxville (South.)	1B	140	487	72	149	26	3	3	61	.306	53	51	12	*1209	*116	5	*.996
1994	—San Diego (N.L.)■	1B-OF	52	118	13	30	3	0	0	7	.254	9	15	3	258	23	4	.986
	—Las Vegas (PCL)	OF-1B	14	47	4	12	1	0	1	5	.255	4	4	0	27	2	0	1.000
1995	—San Diego (N.L.)	1B	6	5	0	0	0	0	0	0	.000	0	1	0	1	1	0	1.000
	—Las Vegas (PCL)	1B-OF	82	259	46	75	12	1	1	23	.290	24	33	0	490	25	3	.994
Major league totals (2 years)			58	123	13	30	3	0	0	7	.244	9	16	3	259	24	4	.986

IBANEZ, RAUL — C — MARINERS

PERSONAL: Born June 2, 1972, in New York, N.Y. . . . 6-2/200. . . . Bats left, throws right. . . . Full name: Raul Javier Ibanez.
HIGH SCHOOL: Sunset (Miami, Fla.).
JUNIOR COLLEGE: Miami-Dade (South) Community College.
TRANSACTIONS/CAREER NOTES: Selected by Seattle Mariners organization in 36th round of free-agent draft (June 1, 1992). . . . On disabled list (June 4-July 16, 1994).
STATISTICAL NOTES: Led California League with .612 slugging percentage in 1995. . . . Led California League with 25 passed balls in 1995.

Year	Team (League)	Pos.	G	AB	R	H	2B	3B	HR	RBI	Avg.	BB	SO	SB	PO	A	E	Avg.
				BATTING											FIELDING			
1992	—Ariz. Mariners (Ariz.)	1B-C-OF	33	120	25	37	8	2	1	16	.308	9	18	1	51	3	4	.931
1993	—Appleton (Midw.)	1B-C-OF	52	157	26	43	9	0	5	21	.274	24	31	0	98	2	2	.980
	—Belling. (N'west)	C	43	134	16	38	5	2	0	15	.284	21	23	0	137	15	1	.993
1994	—Appleton (Midw.)	C-1B-OF	91	327	55	102	30	3	7	59	.312	32	37	10	304	28	10	.971
1995	—Riverside (Calif.)	C-1B	95	361	59	120	23	9	20	108	.332	41	49	4	465	54	12	.977

IGNASIAK, MICHAEL — P

PERSONAL: Born March 12, 1966, in Anchorville, Mich. . . . 5-11/190. . . . Throws right, bats both. . . . Full name: Michael James Ignasiak. . . . Name pronounced ig-NAH-shik.
HIGH SCHOOL: St. Mary's (Orchard Lake, Mich.).
COLLEGE: Michigan.

TRANSACTIONS/CAREER NOTES: Selected by St. Louis Cardinals organization in fourth round of free-agent draft (June 2, 1987); did not sign. . . . Selected by Milwaukee Brewers organization in eighth round of free-agent draft (June 1, 1988). . . . On Milwaukee disabled list (August 31-September 28, 1991 and August 3, 1994-remainder of season). . . . On New Orleans disabled list (April 7-22, 1994). . . . On Milwaukee disabled list (May 15-June 19, 1995); included rehabilitation assignments to Beloit (June 13-14) and New Orleans (June 14-19). . . . Granted free agency (October 11, 1995).

STATISTICAL NOTES: Combined with reliever Doug Henry in 6-3 no-hit victory for Stockton against San Jose (April 15, 1990, first game).

Year	Team (League)	W	L	Pct.	ERA	G	GS	CG	ShO	Sv.	IP	H	R	ER	BB	SO
1988—	Beloit (Midwest)	2	4	.333	2.72	9	9	1	0	0	56 1/3	52	21	17	12	66
—	Helena (Pioneer)	2	0	1.000	3.09	7	0	0	0	1	11 2/3	10	5	4	7	18
1989—	Stockton (Calif.)	11	6	.647	2.72	28	•28	4	•4	0	179	140	67	54	97	142
1990—	Stockton (Calif.)	3	1	.750	3.94	6	6	1	1	0	32	18	14	14	17	23
—	El Paso (Texas)	6	3	.667	4.35	15	15	1	0	0	82 2/3	96	45	40	34	39
1991—	Denver (Am. Assoc.)	9	5	.643	4.25	24	22	1	0	1	137 2/3	119	68	65	57	103
—	Milwaukee (A.L.)	2	1	.667	5.68	4	1	0	0	0	12 2/3	7	8	8	8	10
1992—	Denver (Am. Assoc.)	7	4	.636	2.93	*62	0	0	0	10	92	83	37	30	33	64
1993—	New Orleans (A.A.)	6	0	1.000	1.09	35	0	0	0	9	57 2/3	26	10	7	20	61
—	Milwaukee (A.L.)	1	1	.500	3.65	27	0	0	0	0	37	32	17	15	21	28
1994—	New Orleans (A.A.)	0	1	.000	5.14	8	2	0	0	0	21	25	13	12	4	16
—	Milwaukee (A.L.)	3	1	.750	4.53	23	5	0	0	0	47 2/3	51	25	24	13	24
1995—	Milwaukee (A.L.)	4	1	.800	5.90	25	0	0	0	0	39 2/3	51	27	26	23	26
—	Beloit (Midwest)	0	0	...	0.00	1	1	0	0	0	3	0	0	0	2	4
—	New Orleans (A.A.)	1	1	.500	2.50	4	2	0	0	0	18	9	5	5	8	19
Major league totals (4 years)		10	4	.714	4.80	79	6	0	0	0	137	141	77	73	65	88

INGRAM, GAREY — 2B — DODGERS

PERSONAL: Born July 25, 1970, in Columbus, Ga. . . . 5-11/185. . . . Bats right, throws right. . . . Full name: Garey Lamar Ingram.

HIGH SCHOOL: Columbus (Ga.).

COLLEGE: Middle Georgia College.

TRANSACTIONS/CAREER NOTES: Selected by Los Angeles Dodgers organization in 43rd round of free-agent draft (June 1, 1988); did not sign. . . . Selected by Dodgers organization in 44th round of free-agent draft (June 5, 1989). . . . On Bakersfield disabled list (June 28-July 6, 1991). . . . On San Antonio disabled list (April 14-June 16, 1992; April 26-May 3, May 14-June 10 and July 29-August 8, 1993).

STATISTICAL NOTES: Tied for California League lead in being hit by pitch with 14 in 1991. . . . Led Texas League in being hit by pitch with 12 in 1992. . . . Tied for Texas League lead in errors by second baseman with 27 in 1993.

MISCELLANEOUS: Hit home run in first major league at-bat (May 19, 1994).

				BATTING											FIELDING			
Year	Team (League)	Pos.	G	AB	R	H	2B	3B	HR	RBI	Avg.	BB	SO	SB	PO	A	E	Avg.
1990—	Great Falls (Pio.)	DH	56	198	43	68	12	*8	2	21	.343	22	37	10	...	...	...	...
1991—	Bakersfield (Calif.)	OF	118	445	75	132	16	4	9	61	.297	52	70	30	174	5	9	.952
—	San Antonio (Tex.)	OF	1	1	0	0	0	0	0	0	.000	0	1	0	2	0	0	1.000
1992—	San Antonio (Tex.)	OF	65	198	34	57	9	5	2	17	.288	28	43	11	112	4	4	.967
1993—	San Antonio (Tex.)	2B-OF	84	305	43	82	14	5	6	33	.269	31	50	19	101	184	‡27	.913
1994—	San Antonio (Tex.)	2B-OF-SS	99	345	68	89	24	3	8	28	.258	43	61	19	152	205	8	.978
—	Los Angeles (N.L.)	2B	26	78	10	22	1	0	3	8	.282	7	22	0	44	68	2	.982
—	Albuquerque (PCL)	OF	2	8	2	2	0	0	0	0	.250	0	1	1	0	0	0	...
1995—	Los Angeles (N.L.)	3B-2B-OF	44	55	5	11	2	0	0	3	.200	9	8	3	17	26	8	.843
—	Albuquerque (PCL)	2B-OF	63	232	28	57	11	4	1	30	.246	21	40	10	115	144	6	.977
Major league totals (2 years)			70	133	15	33	3	0	3	11	.248	16	30	3	61	94	10	.939

INGRAM, RICCARDO — OF — PADRES

PERSONAL: Born September 10, 1966, in Douglas, Ga. . . . 6-0/198. . . . Bats right, throws right. . . . Full name: Riccardo Benay Ingram.

HIGH SCHOOL: Coffee (Douglas, Ga.).

COLLEGE: Georgia Tech.

TRANSACTIONS/CAREER NOTES: Selected by Detroit Tigers organization in fourth round of free-agent draft (June 2, 1987). . . . Granted free agency (October 15, 1994). . . . Signed by Salt Lake, Minnesota Twins organization (January 26, 1995). . . . Granted free agency (October 16, 1995). . . . Signed by San Diego Padres organization (November 16, 1995).

STATISTICAL NOTES: Led Pacific Coast League in grounding into double plays with 22 in 1995.

				BATTING											FIELDING			
Year	Team (League)	Pos.	G	AB	R	H	2B	3B	HR	RBI	Avg.	BB	SO	SB	PO	A	E	Avg.
1988—	Lakeland (Fla. St.)	OF	37	117	10	24	3	1	0	10	.205	10	30	2	33	2	0	1.000
—	Fayetteville (SAL)	OF	17	50	7	9	2	1	0	3	.180	2	15	0	14	5	0	1.000
1989—	Lakeland (Fla. St.)	OF	109	365	40	88	13	3	6	30	.241	29	56	5	119	5	4	.969
1990—	London (Eastern)	OF	92	271	27	69	10	2	0	26	.255	27	49	3	108	8	4	.967
1991—	London (Eastern)	OF	118	421	58	114	14	1	18	64	.271	40	77	6	181	6	5	.974
1992—	Toledo (Int'l)	OF	121	410	45	103	15	6	8	41	.251	31	52	8	155	5	5	.970
1993—	Toledo (Int'l)	OF-3B	123	415	41	112	20	4	13	62	.270	32	66	9	167	2	2	.988
1994—	Toledo (Int'l)	OF-P	90	314	39	90	16	4	9	56	.287	24	45	11	128	2	3	.977
—	Detroit (A.L.)	OF-DH	12	23	3	5	0	0	0	2	.217	1	2	0	13	1	0	1.000
1995—	Salt Lake (PCL)■	OF-1B	122	477	80	*166	*43	2	12	85	*.348	41	60	4	198	10	2	.990
—	Minnesota (A.L.)	DH	4	8	0	1	0	0	0	1	.125	2	1	0	...	...	...	...
Major league totals (2 years)			16	31	3	6	0	0	0	3	.194	3	3	0	13	1	0	1.000

RECORD AS PITCHER

Year	Team (League)	W	L	Pct.	ERA	G	GS	CG	ShO	Sv.	IP	H	R	ER	BB	SO
1994—	Toledo (Int'l)	0	0	...	0.00	1	0	0	0	0	1	0	0	0	0	1

ISRINGHAUSEN, JASON — P — METS

PERSONAL: Born September 7, 1972, in Brighton, Ill. . . . 6-3/195. . . . Throws right, bats right. . . . Full name: Jason Derek Isringhausen.
HIGH SCHOOL: Piasa (Ill.) Southwest.
JUNIOR COLLEGE: Lewis & Clark (Ill.).
TRANSACTIONS/CAREER NOTES: Selected by New York Mets organization in 44th round of free-agent draft (June 3, 1991).
HONORS: Named International League Most Valuable Pitcher (1995).

Year	Team (League)	W	L	Pct.	ERA	G	GS	CG	ShO	Sv.	IP	H	R	ER	BB	SO
1992—	GC Mets (GCL)	2	4	.333	4.34	6	6	0	0	0	29	26	19	14	17	25
—	Kingsport (Appal.)	4	1	.800	3.25	7	6	1	1	0	36	32	22	13	12	24
1993—	Pittsfield (NYP)	7	4	.636	3.29	15	15	2	0	0	90 1/3	68	45	33	28	*104
1994—	St. Lucie (Fla. St.)	6	4	.600	2.23	14	14	•6	•3	0	101	76	31	25	27	59
—	Binghamton (East.)	5	4	.556	3.02	14	14	2	0	0	92 1/3	78	35	31	23	69
1995—	Binghamton (East.)	2	1	.667	2.85	6	6	1	0	0	41	26	15	13	12	59
—	Norfolk (Int'l)	9	1	*.900	1.55	12	12	3	*3	0	87	64	17	15	24	75
—	New York (N.L.)	9	2	.818	2.81	14	14	1	0	0	93	88	29	29	31	55
Major league totals (1 year)		9	2	.818	2.81	14	14	1	0	0	93	88	29	29	31	55

JACKSON, DAMIAN — SS — INDIANS

PERSONAL: Born August 16, 1973, in Los Angeles. . . . 5-10/160. . . . Bats right, throws right. . . . Full name: Damian Jacques Jackson.
HIGH SCHOOL: Ygnacio (Concord, Calif.).
JUNIOR COLLEGE: Laney (Calif.).
TRANSACTIONS/CAREER NOTES: Selected by Cleveland Indians organization in 44th round of free-agent draft (June 3, 1991).
STATISTICAL NOTES: Led Appalachian League shortstops with 342 total chances and 45 double plays in 1992. . . . Led Eastern League shortstops with 241 putouts, 446 assists, 54 errors, 741 total chances and 85 double plays in 1994. . . . Led Eastern League in caught stealing with 22 in 1995. . . . Tied for Eastern League lead in double plays by shortstop with 80 in 1995.

				BATTING										FIELDING			
Year	Team (League)	Pos.	G	AB	R	H	2B	3B	HR	RBI	Avg.	BB	SO	SB	PO	A	E	Avg.
1992—	Burlington (Appal.)	SS	62	226	32	56	12	1	0	23	.248	32	31	29	*102	*217	23	.933
1993—	Columbus (S. Atl.)	SS	108	350	70	94	19	3	6	45	.269	41	61	26	191	324	52	.908
1994—	Cant./Akr. (East.)	SS-OF	138	531	85	143	29	5	5	60	.269	60	121	37	†241	†446	†54	.927
1995—	Cant./Akr. (East.)	SS	131	484	67	120	20	2	3	34	.248	65	103	40	*220	337	*36	.939

JACKSON, DANNY — P — CARDINALS

PERSONAL: Born January 5, 1962, in San Antonio. . . . 6-0/220. . . . Throws left, bats right. . . . Full name: Danny Lynn Jackson.
HIGH SCHOOL: Central (Aurora, Colo.).
JUNIOR COLLEGE: Trinidad State Junior College (Colo.).
COLLEGE: Oklahoma.
TRANSACTIONS/CAREER NOTES: Selected by Oakland Athletics organization in 24th round of free-agent draft (June 3, 1980); did not sign. . . . Selected by Kansas City Royals organization in secondary phase of free-agent draft (January 17, 1982). . . . On Jacksonville disabled list (September 8, 1982-remainder of season). . . . On disabled list (April 4-21, 1986). . . . Traded by Royals with SS Angel Salazar to Cincinnati Reds for P Ted Power and SS Kurt Stillwell (November 6, 1987). . . . On disabled list (June 18-July 6 and July 25-September 1, 1989). . . . On Cincinnati disabled list (April 30-May 17, 1990); included rehabilitation assignment to Nashville (May 13-17). . . . On Cincinnati disabled list (July 18-August 8, 1990); included rehabilitation assignment to Charleston, W.Va. (August 5-8). . . . On Cincinnati disabled list (August 14-30, 1990); included rehabilitation assignment to Nashville (August 30). . . . Granted free agency (November 5, 1990). . . . Signed by Chicago Cubs (November 21, 1990). . . . On Chicago disabled list (April 20-June 9, 1991). . . . On Chicago disabled list (June 20-August 3, 1991); included rehabilitation assignment to Iowa (July 29-30). . . . Traded by Cubs to Pittsburgh Pirates for 3B Steve Buechele (July 11, 1992). . . . Selected by Florida Marlins in third round (53rd pick overall) of expansion draft (November 17, 1992). . . . Traded by Marlins to Philadelphia Phillies for P Joel Adamson and P Matt Whisenant (November 17, 1992). . . . Granted free agency (October 17, 1994). . . . Signed by St. Louis Cardinals (December 12, 1994). . . . On St. Louis disabled list (June 8-26 and August 12, 1995-remainder of season); included rehabilitation assignment to Louisville (June 20-26).
HONORS: Named lefthanded pitcher on The Sporting News N.L. All-Star team (1988 and 1994).
MISCELLANEOUS: Appeared in one game as pinch-runner (1989). . . . Appeared in one game as pinch-runner (1994).

Year	Team (League)	W	L	Pct.	ERA	G	GS	CG	ShO	Sv.	IP	H	R	ER	BB	SO
1982—	Char., S.C. (S. Atl.)	10	1	.909	2.62	13	13	3	0	0	96 1/3	80	37	28	39	62
—	Jacksonville (Sou.)	7	2	.778	2.39	14	14	3	1	0	98	78	30	26	42	74
1983—	Omaha (Am. Assoc.)	7	8	.467	3.97	23	22	5	•2	0	136	126	74	60	73	93
—	Kansas City (A.L.)	1	1	.500	5.21	4	3	0	0	0	19	26	12	11	6	9
1984—	Kansas City (A.L.)	2	6	.250	4.26	15	11	1	0	0	76	84	41	36	35	40
—	Omaha (Am. Assoc.)	5	8	.385	3.67	16	16	•10	•3	0	110 1/3	91	50	45	45	82
1985—	Kansas City (A.L.)	14	12	.538	3.42	32	32	4	3	0	208	209	94	79	76	114
1986—	Kansas City (A.L.)	11	12	.478	3.20	32	27	4	1	1	185 2/3	177	83	66	79	115
1987—	Kansas City (A.L.)	9	18	.333	4.02	36	34	11	2	0	224	219	115	100	109	152
1988—	Cincinnati (N.L.)■	•23	8	.742	2.73	35	35	•15	6	0	260 2/3	206	86	79	71	161
1989—	Cincinnati (N.L.)	6	11	.353	5.60	20	20	1	0	0	115 2/3	122	78	72	57	70
1990—	Cincinnati (N.L.)	6	6	.500	3.61	22	21	0	0	0	117 1/3	119	54	47	40	76
—	Nashville (A.A.)	1	0	1.000	0.00	2	2	0	0	0	11	9	0	0	4	3
—	Char., W.Va. (S. Atl.)	0	0	...	6.00	1	1	0	0	0	3	2	2	2	1	2
1991—	Chicago (N.L.)■	1	5	.167	6.75	17	14	0	0	0	70 2/3	89	59	53	48	31
—	Iowa (Am. Assoc.)	0	0	...	1.80	1	1	0	0	0	5	2	1	1	2	4
1992—	Chicago (N.L.)	4	9	.308	4.22	19	19	0	0	0	113	117	59	53	48	51
—	Pittsburgh (N.L.)■	4	4	.500	3.36	15	15	0	0	0	88 1/3	94	40	33	29	46
1993—	Philadelphia (N.L.)■	12	11	.522	3.77	32	32	2	1	0	210 1/3	214	105	88	80	120
1994—	Philadelphia (N.L.)	14	6	.700	3.26	25	25	4	1	0	179 1/3	183	71	65	46	129
1995—	St. Louis (N.L.)■	2	12	.143	5.90	19	19	2	1	0	100 2/3	120	82	66	48	52
—	Louisville (A.A.)	1	0	1.000	1.29	1	1	1	0	0	7	8	1	1	2	2
A.L. totals (5 years)		37	49	.430	3.69	119	107	20	6	1	712 2/3	715	345	292	305	430
N.L. totals (8 years)		72	72	.500	3.98	204	200	24	9	0	1256	1264	634	556	467	736
Major league totals (13 years)		109	121	.474	3.88	323	307	44	15	1	1968 2/3	1979	979	848	772	1166

J

CHAMPIONSHIP SERIES RECORD

Year	Team (League)	W	L	Pct.	ERA	G	GS	CG	ShO	Sv.	IP	H	R	ER	BB	SO
1985—	Kansas City (A.L.)	1	0	1.000	0.00	2	1	1	1	0	10	10	0	0	1	7
1990—	Cincinnati (N.L.)	1	0	1.000	2.38	2	2	0	0	0	11 1/3	8	3	3	7	8
1992—	Pittsburgh (N.L.)	0	1	.000	21.60	1	1	0	0	0	1 2/3	4	4	4	2	0
1993—	Philadelphia (N.L.)	1	0	1.000	1.17	1	1	0	0	0	7 2/3	9	1	1	2	6
Champ. series totals (4 years)		3	1	.750	2.35	6	5	1	1	0	30 2/3	31	8	8	12	21

WORLD SERIES RECORD

NOTES: Member of World Series championship teams (1985 and 1990).

Year	Team (League)	W	L	Pct.	ERA	G	GS	CG	ShO	Sv.	IP	H	R	ER	BB	SO
1985—	Kansas City (A.L.)	1	1	.500	1.69	2	2	1	0	0	16	9	3	3	5	12
1990—	Cincinnati (N.L.)	0	0	...	10.13	1	1	0	0	0	2 2/3	6	4	3	2	0
1993—	Philadelphia (N.L.)	0	1	.000	7.20	1	1	0	0	0	5	6	4	4	1	1
World Series totals (3 years)		1	2	.333	3.80	4	4	1	0	0	23 2/3	21	11	10	8	13

ALL-STAR GAME RECORD

Year	League	W	L	Pct.	ERA	GS	CG	ShO	Sv.	IP	H	R	ER	BB	SO
1988—	National						Did not play.								
1994—	National	0	0	...	...	0	0	0	0	0	3	1	1	0	0
All-Star totals (1 year)		0	0	...		0	0	0	0	3	1	1	0	0	

JACKSON, MIKE — P

PERSONAL: Born December 22, 1964, in Houston. . . . 6-2/223. . . . Throws right, bats right. . . . Full name: Michael Ray Jackson.

HIGH SCHOOL: Forest Brook (Houston).

JUNIOR COLLEGE: Hill Junior College (Tex.).

TRANSACTIONS/CAREER NOTES: Selected by Philadelphia Phillies organization in 29th round of free-agent draft (June 6, 1983); did not sign. . . . Selected by Phillies organization in secondary phase of free-agent draft (January 17, 1984). . . . On Philadelphia disabled list (August 6-21, 1987). . . . Traded by Phillies organization with OF Glenn Wilson and OF Dave Brundage to Seattle Mariners for OF Phil Bradley and P Tim Fortugno (December 9, 1987). . . . Traded by Mariners with P Bill Swift and P Dave Burba to San Francisco Giants for OF Kevin Mitchell and P Mike Remlinger (December 11, 1991). . . . On disabled list (July 24-August 9, 1993; June 17-July 2 and July 7, 1994-remainder of season). . . . Granted free agency (October 17, 1994). . . . Signed by Cincinnati Reds (April 8, 1995). . . . On Cincinnati disabled list (April 20-June 5, 1995); included rehabilitation assignments to Chattanooga (May 21-30) and Indianapolis (May 30-June 5). . . . Granted free agency (November 3, 1995).

STATISTICAL NOTES: Led Carolina League with seven balks in 1985. . . . Tied for N.L. lead with eight balks in 1987.

Year	Team (League)	W	L	Pct.	ERA	G	GS	CG	ShO	Sv.	IP	H	R	ER	BB	SO
1984—	Spartanburg (SAL)	7	2	.778	2.68	14	0	0	0	0	80 2/3	53	35	24	50	77
1985—	Peninsula (Caro.)	7	9	.438	4.60	31	18	0	0	1	125 1/3	127	71	64	53	96
1986—	Reading (Eastern)	2	3	.400	1.66	30	0	0	0	6	43 1/3	25	9	8	22	42
—	Portland (PCL)	3	1	.750	3.18	17	0	0	0	3	22 2/3	18	8	8	13	23
—	Philadelphia (N.L.)	0	0	...	3.38	9	0	0	0	0	13 1/3	12	5	5	4	3
1987—	Philadelphia (N.L.)	3	10	.231	4.20	55	7	0	0	1	109 1/3	88	55	51	56	93
—	Maine (Int'l)	1	0	1.000	0.82	2	2	0	0	0	11	9	2	1	5	13
1988—	Seattle (A.L.)■	6	5	.545	2.63	62	0	0	0	4	99 1/3	74	37	29	43	76
1989—	Seattle (A.L.)	4	6	.400	3.17	65	0	0	0	7	99 1/3	81	43	35	54	94
1990—	Seattle (A.L.)	5	7	.417	4.54	63	0	0	0	3	77 1/3	64	42	39	44	69
1991—	Seattle (A.L.)	7	7	.500	3.25	72	0	0	0	14	88 2/3	64	35	32	34	74
1992—	San Francisco (N.L.)■	6	6	.500	3.73	67	0	0	0	2	82	76	35	34	33	80
1993—	San Francisco (N.L.)	6	6	.500	3.03	*81	0	0	0	1	77 1/3	58	28	26	24	70
1994—	San Francisco (N.L.)	3	2	.600	1.49	36	0	0	0	4	42 1/3	23	8	7	11	51
1995—	Chattanooga (Sou.)■	0	0	...	0.00	3	2	0	0	0	3	2	0	0	0	2
—	Indianapolis (A.A.)	0	0	...	0.00	2	1	0	0	0	2	0	0	0	0	1
—	Cincinnati (N.L.)	6	1	.857	2.39	40	0	0	0	2	49	38	13	13	19	41
A.L. totals (4 years)		22	25	.468	3.33	262	0	0	0	28	364 2/3	283	157	135	175	313
N.L. totals (6 years)		24	25	.490	3.28	288	7	0	0	10	373 1/3	295	144	136	147	338
Major league totals (10 years)		46	50	.479	3.30	550	7	0	0	38	738	578	301	271	322	651

DIVISION SERIES RECORD

Year	Team (League)	W	L	Pct.	ERA	G	GS	CG	ShO	Sv.	IP	H	R	ER	BB	SO
1995—	Cincinnati (N.L.)	0	0	...	0.00	3	0	0	0	0	3 2/3	4	0	0	0	1

CHAMPIONSHIP SERIES RECORD

Year	Team (League)	W	L	Pct.	ERA	G	GS	CG	ShO	Sv.	IP	H	R	ER	BB	SO
1995—	Cincinnati (N.L.)	0	1	.000	23.14	3	0	0	0	0	2 1/3	5	6	6	4	1

JACOBS, RYAN — P — BRAVES

PERSONAL: Born February 3, 1974, in Richmond, Va. . . . 6-2/175. . . . Throws left, bats right. . . . Full name: Ryan Christopher Jacobs.

TRANSACTIONS/CAREER NOTES: Selected by Atlanta Braves organization in 33rd round of free-agent draft (June 1, 1992).

Year	Team (League)	W	L	Pct.	ERA	G	GS	CG	ShO	Sv.	IP	H	R	ER	BB	SO
1992—	GC Braves (GCL)	1	3	.250	2.57	12	2	0	0	1	35	30	18	10	8	40
1993—	Danville (Appal.)	4	3	.571	4.01	10	10	0	0	0	42 2/3	35	24	19	25	32
1994—	Macon (S. Atl.)	8	7	.533	2.88	27	18	1	1	1	121 2/3	105	54	39	62	81
1995—	Durham (Carolina)	11	6	.647	3.51	29	25	1	0	0	148 2/3	145	72	58	57	99

JACOBSEN, JOE — P — TWINS

PERSONAL: Born December 26, 1971, in Fresno, Calif. . . . 6-3/225. . . . Throws right, bats right. . . . Full name: Joseph Jacobsen.

HIGH SCHOOL: Clovis (Calif.) West.
JUNIOR COLLEGE: Fresno City College.
TRANSACTIONS/CAREER NOTES: Signed as non-drafted free agent by Los Angeles Dodgers organization (May 30, 1992). . . . Selected by Minnesota Twins from Dodgers organization in Rule 5 major league draft (December 4, 1995).

Year	Team (League)	W	L	Pct.	ERA	G	GS	CG	ShO	Sv.	IP	H	R	ER	BB	SO
1992—	GC Dodgers (GCL)	1	1	.500	1.73	6	3	0	0	0	26	17	7	5	6	25
	— Great Falls (Pio.)	2	2	.500	5.29	6	6	1	0	0	32 1/3	37	22	19	9	24
1993—	Bakersfield (Calif.)	1	0	1.000	4.58	6	0	0	0	2	19 2/3	22	16	10	8	23
	— Yakima (N'west)	1	0	1.000	2.39	25	0	0	0	3	37 2/3	27	16	10	28	55
1994—	San Antonio (Tex.)	2	1	.667	2.52	18	0	0	0	1	25	21	9	7	12	15
	— Bakersfield (Calif.)	1	0	1.000	1.23	3	0	0	0	0	7 1/3	2	1	1	1	5
	— Vero Beach (FSL)	0	5	.000	2.72	37	0	0	0	15	43	40	15	13	23	44
1995—	Vero Beach (FSL)	1	3	.250	3.67	47	0	0	0	*32	49	42	22	20	23	54
	— San Bern. (Calif.)	0	0	. . .	0.00	4	0	0	0	2	3 2/3	4	2	0	2	5

JACOME, JASON — P — ROYALS

PERSONAL: Born November 24, 1970, in Tulsa, Okla. . . . 6-0/180. . . . Throws left, bats left. . . . Full name: Jason James Jacome.
HIGH SCHOOL: Rincon (Tucson, Ariz.).
JUNIOR COLLEGE: Pima Community College (Ariz.).
TRANSACTIONS/CAREER NOTES: Selected by New York Mets organization in 12th round of free-agent draft (June 3, 1991). . . . On Norfolk disabled list (June 5-16 and June 17-July 21, 1995). . . . Traded by Mets with P Allen McDill to Kansas City Royals for P Derek Wallace and a player to be named later (July 21, 1995); Mets acquired P John Carter to complete deal (November 16, 1995).

Year	Team (League)	W	L	Pct.	ERA	G	GS	CG	ShO	Sv.	IP	H	R	ER	BB	SO
1991—	Kingsport (Appal.)	5	4	.556	1.63	12	7	3	•1	2	55 1/3	35	18	10	13	48
1992—	Columbia (S. Atl.)	4	1	.800	1.03	8	8	1	0	0	52 2/3	40	7	6	15	49
	— St. Lucie (Fla. St.)	6	7	.462	2.83	17	17	5	1	0	114 1/3	98	45	36	30	66
1993—	St. Lucie (Fla. St.)	6	3	.667	3.08	14	14	2	2	0	99 1/3	106	37	34	23	66
	— Binghamton (East.)	8	4	.667	3.21	14	14	0	0	0	87	85	36	31	38	56
1994—	Norfolk (Int'l)	8	6	.571	2.84	19	19	4	1	0	126 2/3	138	57	40	42	80
	— New York (N.L.)	4	3	.571	2.67	8	8	1	1	0	54	54	17	16	17	30
1995—	New York (N.L.)	0	4	.000	10.29	5	5	0	0	0	21	33	24	24	15	11
	— Norfolk (Int'l)	2	4	.333	3.92	8	8	0	0	0	43 2/3	40	21	19	13	31
	— Kansas City (A.L.)■	4	6	.400	5.36	15	14	1	0	0	84	101	52	50	21	39
A.L. totals (1 year)		4	6	.400	5.36	15	14	1	0	0	84	101	52	50	21	39
N.L. totals (2 years)		4	7	.364	4.80	13	13	1	1	0	75	87	41	40	32	41
Major league totals (2 years)		8	13	.381	5.09	28	27	2	1	0	159	188	93	90	53	80

JAHA, JOHN — 1B — BREWERS

PERSONAL: Born May 27, 1966, in Portland, Ore. . . . 6-1/222. . . . Bats right, throws right. . . . Full name: John Emile Jaha. . . . Name pronounced JAH-ha.
HIGH SCHOOL: David Douglas (Portland, Ore.).
TRANSACTIONS/CAREER NOTES: Selected by Milwaukee Brewers organization in 14th round of free-agent draft (June 4, 1984). . . . On disabled list (April 6-August 1, 1990 and May 21-June 6, 1995). . . . On Milwaukee disabled list (June 24-July 27, 1995); included rehabilitation assignments to Beloit (July 16-20) and New Orleans (July 20-27).
HONORS: Named Texas League Most Valuable Player (1991).
STATISTICAL NOTES: Led Northwest League with 144 total bases and tied for lead with four intentional bases on balls received in 1986. . . . Led Texas League with 301 total bases, .619 slugging percentage and .438 on-base percentage in 1991. . . . Led Texas League first basemen with 81 assists in 1991. . . . Career major league grand slams: 3.

				BATTING											FIELDING			
Year	Team (League)	Pos.	G	AB	R	H	2B	3B	HR	RBI	Avg.	BB	SO	SB	PO	A	E	Avg.
1985—	Helena (Pioneer)	3B	24	68	13	18	3	0	2	14	.265	14	23	4	9	32	1	.976
1986—	Tri-Cities (N'west)	1B-3B	•73	258	65	82	13	2	*15	67	.318	*70	75	9	352	101	18	.962
1987—	Beloit (Midwest)	3B-1B-SS	122	376	68	101	22	0	7	47	.269	102	86	10	493	113	18	.971
1988—	Stockton (Calif.)	1B	99	302	58	77	14	6	8	54	.255	69	85	10	793	60	5	*.994
1989—	Stockton (Calif.)	1B-3B	140	479	83	140	26	5	25	91	.292	*112	115	8	1081	62	8	.993
1990—	Stockton (Calif.)	DH	26	84	12	22	5	0	4	19	.262	18	25	0	. . .	. . .	. . .	. . .
1991—	El Paso (Texas)	1B-3B	130	486	*121	167	38	3	*30	*134	.344	78	101	12	883	†87	10	.990
1992—	Denver (A.A.)	1B	79	274	61	88	18	2	18	69	.321	50	60	6	654	50	7	.990
	— Milwaukee (A.L.)	1B-DH-OF	47	133	17	30	3	1	2	10	.226	12	30	10	286	22	0	1.000
1993—	Milwaukee (A.L.)	1B-3B-2B	153	515	78	136	21	0	19	70	.264	51	109	13	1187	128	10	.992
1994—	Milwaukee (A.L.)	1B-DH	84	291	45	70	14	0	12	39	.241	32	75	3	660	47	8	.989
	— New Orleans (A.A.)	1B	18	62	8	25	7	1	2	16	.403	12	8	2	122	14	1	.993
1995—	Milwaukee (A.L.)	1B-DH	88	316	59	99	20	2	20	65	.313	36	66	2	649	60	2	.997
	— Beloit (Midwest)	DH	1	4	1	0	0	0	0	0	.000	0	1	0	0	0	0	. . .
	— New Orleans (A.A.)	1B	3	10	2	4	1	0	1	3	.400	2	1	0	9	2	0	1.000
Major league totals (4 years)			372	1255	199	335	58	3	53	184	.267	131	280	28	2782	257	20	.993

JAMES, CHRIS — OF

PERSONAL: Born October 4, 1962, in Rusk, Tex. . . . 6-1/202. . . . Bats right, throws right. . . . Full name: Donald Christopher James. . . . Brother of Craig James, ESPN college football analyst, and running back with Washington Federals of United States Football League and New England Patriots (1983-88).
HIGH SCHOOL: Stratford (Houston).
COLLEGE: Blinn College (Tex.).
TRANSACTIONS/CAREER NOTES: Signed as non-drafted free agent by Philadelphia Phillies organization (October 30, 1981). . . . On

Philadelphia disabled list (May 6-July 21, 1986); included rehabilitation assignment to Portland (July 3-21). . . . Traded by Phillies to San Diego Padres for IF Randy Ready and OF John Kruk (June 2, 1989). . . . Traded by Padres with C Sandy Alomar and 3B Carlos Baerga to Cleveland Indians for OF Joe Carter (December 6, 1989). . . . On disabled list (September 11, 1991-remainder of season). . . . Granted free agency (December 20, 1991). . . . Signed by San Francisco Giants (January 15, 1992). . . . On disabled list (August 15-September 1, 1992). . . . Granted free agency (October 29, 1992). . . . Signed by Houston Astros organization (January 8, 1993). . . . Traded by Astros to Texas Rangers for P Dave Gandolph (September 17, 1993). . . . On disabled list (May 26-June 19 and July 16-August 3, 1994). . . . Granted free agency (October 21, 1994). . . . Signed by Kansas City Royals (April 8, 1995). . . . On Kansas City disabled list (April 16-June 30, 1995); included rehabilitation assignment to Omaha (May 12-15). . . . Traded by Royals to Boston Red Sox for OF Wes Chamberlain (August 14, 1995). . . . On Boston disabled list (August 30-September 14, 1995). . . . Granted free agency (October 14, 1995).

STATISTICAL NOTES: Led South Atlantic League with 257 total bases and tied for lead in being hit by pitch with 12 in 1983. . . . Led Eastern League third basemen with 39 errors in 1984. . . . Led Pacific Coast League outfielders with 351 total chances in 1985. . . . Tied for Pacific Coast League lead in being hit by pitch with seven in 1985. . . . Career major league grand slams: 3.

				BATTING										FIELDING			
Year Team (League)	Pos.	G	AB	R	H	2B	3B	HR	RBI	Avg.	BB	SO	SB	PO	A	E	Avg.
1982— Bend (Northwest)	3B-OF	63	227	47	72	*19	3	12	50	.317	20	56	10	93	54	10	.936
1983— Spartanburg (SAL)	OF-3B	129	499	94	148	23	4	26	*121	.297	41	93	11	150	88	16	.937
1984— Reading (Eastern)	3B-OF	128	457	66	117	19	*12	8	57	.256	40	74	19	104	209	†39	.889
1985— Portland (PCL)	OF	135	507	78	160	35	8	11	73	.316	33	72	23	*328	16	7	.980
1986— Portland (PCL)	OF-3B	69	266	30	64	6	2	12	41	.241	17	45	3	83	44	8	.941
— Philadelphia (N.L.)	OF	16	46	5	13	3	0	1	5	.283	1	13	0	19	0	0	1.000
1987— Philadelphia (N.L.)	OF	115	358	48	105	20	6	17	54	.293	27	67	3	198	5	2	.990
— Maine (Int'l)	OF-3B	13	40	5	9	2	1	0	3	.225	3	9	0	22	4	0	1.000
1988— Philadelphia (N.L.)	OF-3B	150	566	57	137	24	1	19	66	.242	31	73	7	282	51	9	.974
1989— Philadelphia (N.L.)	OF-3B	45	179	14	37	4	0	2	19	.207	4	23	3	66	16	4	.953
— San Diego (N.L.)■	OF-3B	87	303	41	80	13	2	11	46	.264	22	45	2	149	11	4	.976
1990— Cleveland (A.L.)■	DH-OF	140	528	62	158	32	4	12	70	.299	31	71	4	25	1	0	1.000
1991— Cleveland (A.L.)	DH-OF-1B	115	437	31	104	16	2	5	41	.238	18	61	3	173	10	0	1.000
1992— San Fran. (N.L.)■	OF	111	248	25	60	10	4	5	32	.242	14	45	2	112	2	3	.974
1993— Houston (N.L.)■	OF	65	129	19	33	10	1	6	19	.256	15	34	2	65	4	3	.958
— Texas (A.L.)■	OF	8	31	5	11	1	0	3	7	.355	3	6	0	14	0	0	1.000
1994— Texas (A.L.)	OF	52	133	28	34	8	4	7	19	.256	20	38	0	63	2	0	1.000
1995— Omaha (A.A.)■	DH	3	12	3	2	1	0	1	3	.167	1	2	0	...	...	...	...
— Kansas City (A.L.)	DH-OF	26	58	6	18	3	0	2	7	.310	6	10	1	9	0	0	1.000
— Boston (A.L.)■	OF-DH	16	24	2	4	1	0	0	1	.167	1	4	0	14	0	0	1.000
American League totals (5 years)		357	1211	134	329	61	10	29	145	.272	79	190	8	298	13	0	1.000
National League totals (6 years)		589	1829	209	465	84	14	61	241	.254	114	300	19	891	89	25	.975
Major league totals (10 years)		946	3040	343	794	145	24	90	386	.261	193	490	27	1189	102	25	.981

JAMES, DION OF

PERSONAL: Born November 9, 1962, in Philadelphia. . . . 6-1/185. . . . Bats left, throws left.

HIGH SCHOOL: McClatchy (Sacramento, Calif.).

TRANSACTIONS/CAREER NOTES: Selected by Milwaukee Brewers organization in first round (25th pick overall) of free-agent draft (June 3, 1980). . . . On disabled list (July 1-August 1, 1982). . . . On Milwaukee disabled list (March 31-April 28, 1985); included rehabilitation assignment to Vancouver (April 12-28). . . . On Milwaukee disabled list (May 20-September 1, 1985). . . . Traded by Brewers organization to Atlanta Braves for OF Brad Komminsk (January 20, 1987). . . . Traded by Braves to Cleveland Indians for OF Oddibe McDowell (July 2, 1989). . . . Released by Indians (October 30, 1990). . . . Signed by New York Yankees (April 3, 1992). . . . Granted free agency (October 27, 1993). . . . Signed by Chunichi Dragons of Japan Central League (December 6, 1993). . . . Signed as free agent by New York Yankees (April 24, 1995). . . . Granted free agency (November 3, 1995).

STATISTICAL NOTES: Led California League outfielders with .988 fielding percentage in 1981.

				BATTING										FIELDING			
Year Team (League)	Pos.	G	AB	R	H	2B	3B	HR	RBI	Avg.	BB	SO	SB	PO	A	E	Avg.
1980— Butte (Pioneer)	OF-1B	59	224	57	71	14	1	0	27	.317	42	11	15	80	4	7	.923
— Burlington (Midw.)	OF	3	10	0	1	0	0	0	1	.100	4	1	0	8	1	0	1.000
1981— Stockton (Calif.)	OF-1B	124	451	70	137	17	3	2	49	.304	62	43	45	250	10	3	†.989
1982— El Paso (Texas)	OF	106	422	103	136	25	3	9	72	.322	61	46	16	237	9	7	.972
1983— Vancouver (PCL)	OF	129	467	84	157	29	5	8	68	.336	63	33	22	289	6	2	.993
— Milwaukee (A.L.)	OF-DH	11	20	1	2	0	0	0	1	.100	2	2	1	12	1	0	1.000
1984— Milwaukee (A.L.)	OF	128	387	52	114	19	5	1	30	.295	32	41	10	252	7	3	.989
1985— Vancouver (PCL)	OF	10	37	2	4	2	0	0	5	.108	4	6	0	17	0	0	1.000
— Milwaukee (A.L.)	OF-DH	18	49	5	11	1	0	0	3	.224	6	6	0	20	0	0	1.000
1986— Vancouver (PCL)	OF-1B	130	485	85	137	25	6	6	55	.282	61	66	30	348	7	5	.986
1987— Atlanta (N.L.)■	OF	134	494	80	154	37	6	10	61	.312	110	112	21	262	4	1	*.996
1988— Atlanta (N.L.)	OF	132	386	46	99	17	5	3	30	.256	58	59	9	222	5	3	.987
1989— Atlanta (N.L.)	OF-1B	63	170	15	44	7	0	1	11	.259	25	23	1	126	7	0	1.000
— Cleveland (A.L.)■	OF-DH-1B	71	245	26	75	11	0	4	29	.306	24	26	1	85	1	3	.966
1990— Cleveland (A.L.)	1B-OF-DH	87	248	28	68	15	2	1	22	.274	27	23	5	282	17	4	.987
1991—		Out of organized baseball.															
1992— New York (A.L.)■	OF-DH	67	145	24	38	8	0	3	17	.262	22	15	1	62	1	0	1.000
1993— New York (A.L.)	OF-DH-1B	115	343	62	114	21	2	7	36	.332	31	31	0	141	4	5	.967
1994— Chunichi (Jp. Cn.)■	OF	100	373	38	98	11	0	8	40	.263	25	46	4	...	...	...	...
1995— New York (A.L.)■	OF-DH-1B	85	209	22	60	6	1	2	26	.287	20	16	4	61	4	1	.985
American League totals (8 years)		582	1646	220	482	81	10	18	164	.293	164	160	22	915	35	16	.983
National League totals (3 years)		329	1050	141	297	61	11	14	102	.283	193	194	31	610	16	4	.994
Major league totals (10 years)		911	2696	361	779	142	21	32	266	.289	357	354	53	1525	51	20	.987

DIVISION SERIES RECORD

				BATTING										FIELDING			
Year Team (League)	Pos.	G	AB	R	H	2B	3B	HR	RBI	Avg.	BB	SO	SB	PO	A	E	Avg.
1995— New York (A.L.)	OF	4	12	0	1	0	0	0	0	.083	1	1	0	6	0	0	1.000

JAMES, MIKE — P — ANGELS

PERSONAL: Born August 15, 1967, in Fort Walton Beach, Fla. . . . 6-4/216. . . . Throws right, bats right. . . . Full name: Michael Elmo James.
HIGH SCHOOL: Fort Walton Beach (Fla.).
JUNIOR COLLEGE: Lurleen B. Wallace State Junior College (Ala.).
TRANSACTIONS/CAREER NOTES: Selected by Los Angeles Dodgers organization in 43rd round of free-agent draft (June 2, 1987). . . . On Albuquerque disabled list (July 12-August 26, 1992). . . . On Vero Beach disabled list (July 2-9, 1993). . . . Traded by Dodgers to California Angels for OF Reggie Williams (October 26, 1993). . . . On California disabled list (May 11-June 1, 1995); included rehabilitation assignment to Lake Elsinore (May 25-June 1).

Year	Team (League)	W	L	Pct.	ERA	G	GS	CG	ShO	Sv.	IP	H	R	ER	BB	SO
1988—	Great Falls (Pio.)	7	1	*.875	3.76	14	12	0	0	0	67	61	36	28	41	59
1989—	Bakersfield (Calif.)	11	8	.579	3.78	27	27	1	1	0	159 2/3	144	82	67	78	127
1990—	San Antonio (Tex.)	11	4	.733	3.32	26	26	3	0	0	157	144	73	58	78	97
1991—	Albuquerque (PCL)	1	3	.250	6.60	13	8	0	0	0	45	51	36	33	30	39
—	San Antonio (Tex.)	9	5	.643	4.53	15	15	2	1	0	89 1/3	88	54	45	51	74
1992—	Albuquerque (PCL)	2	1	.667	5.59	18	6	0	0	1	46 2/3	55	35	29	22	33
—	San Antonio (Tex.)	2	1	.667	2.67	8	8	0	0	0	54	39	16	16	20	52
1993—	Albuquerque (PCL)	1	0	1.000	7.47	16	0	0	0	2	31 1/3	38	28	26	19	32
—	Vero Beach (FSL)	2	3	.400	4.92	30	1	0	0	5	60 1/3	54	37	33	33	60
1994—	Vancouver (PCL)■	5	3	.625	5.22	37	10	0	0	8	91 1/3	101	56	53	34	66
1995—	California (A.L.)	3	0	1.000	3.88	46	0	0	0	1	55 2/3	49	27	24	26	36
—	Lake Elsinore (California)	0	0	...	9.53	5	1	0	0	0	5 2/3	9	6	6	3	8
Major league totals (1 year)		3	0	1.000	3.88	46	0	0	0	1	55 2/3	49	27	24	26	36

JANICKI, PETE — P — ANGELS

PERSONAL: Born January 26, 1971, in Parma, O. . . . 6-4/190. . . . Throws right, bats right. . . . Full name: Peter Anthony Janicki.
HIGH SCHOOL: El Dorado (Placentia, Calif.).
COLLEGE: UCLA.
TRANSACTIONS/CAREER NOTES: Selected by Boston Red Sox organization in ninth round of free-agent draft (June 5, 1989); did not sign. . . . Selected by California Angels organization in first round (eighth pick overall) of free-agent draft (June 1, 1992). . . . On Palm Springs disabled list (April 12-22, 1993). . . . On California disabled list (April 22, 1993-remainder of season). . . . On Lake Elsinore disabled list (August 3-September 2, 1994).
STATISTICAL NOTES: Led Texas League with 15 wild pitches in 1994.

Year	Team (League)	W	L	Pct.	ERA	G	GS	CG	ShO	Sv.	IP	H	R	ER	BB	SO
1993—	Palm Springs (Cal.)	0	0	...	10.80	1	1	0	0	0	1 2/3	3	2	2	2	2
1994—	Midland (Texas)	2	6	.250	6.94	14	14	1	0	0	70	86	68	54	33	54
—	Lake Elsinore (California)	1	2	.333	6.75	3	3	0	0	0	12	17	12	9	4	12
1995—	Lake Elsinore (California)	9	4	.692	3.06	20	20	0	0	0	123 1/3	130	66	42	28	106
—	Vancouver (PCL)	1	4	.200	7.03	9	9	0	0	0	48 2/3	64	38	38	23	34

JANZEN, MARTY — P — BLUE JAYS

PERSONAL: Born May 31, 1973, in Homestead, Fla. . . . 6-3/197. . . . Throws right, bats right. . . . Full name: Martin Thomas Janzen.
TRANSACTIONS/CAREER NOTES: Signed as non-drafted free agent by New York Yankees organization (August 8, 1991). . . . On disabled list (June 17, 1993-remainder of season). . . . Traded by Yankees organization with P Jason Jarvis and P Mike Gordon to Toronto Blue Jays organization for P David Cone (July 28, 1995).

Year	Team (League)	W	L	Pct.	ERA	G	GS	CG	ShO	Sv.	IP	H	R	ER	BB	SO
1992—	GC Yankees (GCL)	7	2	.778	2.36	12	•11	0	0	0	68 2/3	55	21	18	15	73
—	Greensboro (S. Atl.)	0	0	...	3.60	2	0	0	0	1	5	5	2	2	1	5
1993—	GC Yankees (GCL)	0	1	.000	1.21	5	5	0	0	0	22 1/3	20	5	3	3	19
1994—	Greensboro (S. Atl.)	3	7	.300	3.89	17	17	0	0	0	104	98	57	45	25	92
1995—	Tampa (Fla. St.)	10	3	.769	2.61	18	18	1	0	0	113 2/3	102	38	33	30	104
—	Norwich (Eastern)	1	2	.333	4.95	3	3	0	0	0	20	17	11	11	7	16
—	Knoxville (South.)■	5	1	.833	2.63	7	7	2	1	0	48	35	14	14	14	44

JARVIS, KEVIN — P — REDS

PERSONAL: Born August 1, 1969, in Lexington, Ky. . . . 6-2/200. . . . Throws right, bats left. . . . Full name: Kevin Thomas Jarvis.
HIGH SCHOOL: Tates Creek (Lexington, Ky.).
COLLEGE: Wake Forest.
TRANSACTIONS/CAREER NOTES: Selected by Cincinnati Reds organization in 21st round of free-agent draft (June 3, 1991).

Year	Team (League)	W	L	Pct.	ERA	G	GS	CG	ShO	Sv.	IP	H	R	ER	BB	SO
1991—	Princeton (Appal.)	5	6	.455	2.42	13	13	4	•1	0	85 2/3	73	34	23	29	79
1992—	Ced. Rap. (Midw.)	0	0	...	0.00	1	0	0	0	0	1	1	0	0	0	0
—	Char., W.Va. (S. Atl.)	6	8	.429	3.11	28	18	2	1	0	133	123	59	46	37	131
1993—	Winst.-Salem (Car.)	8	7	.533	3.41	21	20	2	1	0	145	133	68	55	48	101
—	Chattanooga (Sou.)	3	1	.750	1.69	7	3	2	0	0	37 1/3	26	7	7	11	18
1994—	Cincinnati (N.L.)	1	1	.500	7.13	6	3	0	0	0	17 2/3	22	14	14	5	10
—	Indianapolis (A.A.)	10	2	•.833	3.54	21	20	2	0	0	132 1/3	136	55	52	34	90
1995—	Indianapolis (A.A.)	4	2	.667	4.45	10	10	2	1	0	60 2/3	62	33	30	18	37
—	Cincinnati (N.L.)	3	4	.429	5.70	19	11	1	1	0	79	91	56	50	32	33
Major league totals (2 years)		4	5	.444	5.96	25	14	1	1	0	96 2/3	113	70	64	37	43

JAVIER, STAN — OF — GIANTS

PERSONAL: Born January 9, 1964, in San Francisco de Macoris, Dominican Republic. . . . 6-0/185. . . . Bats both, throws right. . . . Full name: Stanley Julian Javier. . . . Son of Julian Javier, infielder, St. Louis Cardinals and Cincinnati Reds (1960-72). . . . Name pronounced HA-vee-AIR.

HIGH SCHOOL: La Altagracia (San Francisco de Macoris, Dominican Republic).

TRANSACTIONS/CAREER NOTES: Signed as non-drafted free agent by St. Louis Cardinals organization (March 26, 1981). . . . Traded by Cardinals organization with SS Bobby Meacham to New York Yankees organization for OF Bob Helsom, P Marty Mason and P Steve Fincher (December 14, 1982). . . . Traded by Yankees organization with P Jay Howell, P Jose Rijo, P Eric Plunk and P Tim Birtsas to Oakland A's for OF Rickey Henderson, P Bert Bradley and cash (December 5, 1984). . . . On Oakland disabled list (August 3-September 1, 1987); included rehabilitation assignment to Tacoma (August 20-September 1). . . . On disabled list (August 18-September 2, 1988 and July 7-24, 1989). . . . Traded by A's to Los Angeles Dodgers for 2B Willie Randolph (May 13, 1990). . . . Traded by Dodgers to Philadelphia Phillies for P Steve Searcy and a player to be named later (July 2, 1992); Dodgers acquired IF Julio Peguero to complete deal (July 28, 1992). . . . Granted free agency (October 27, 1992). . . . Signed by California Angels organization (January 15, 1993). . . . Granted free agency (October 29, 1993). . . . Signed by A's (December 7, 1993). . . . Granted free agency (November 2, 1995). . . . Signed by San Francisco Giants (December 8, 1995).

STATISTICAL NOTES: Led A.L. outfielders with 1.000 fielding percentage in 1995.

			BATTING												FIELDING			
Year	**Team (League)**	**Pos.**	**G**	**AB**	**R**	**H**	**2B**	**3B**	**HR**	**RBI**	**Avg.**	**BB**	**SO**	**SB**	**PO**	**A**	**E**	**Avg.**
1981—	Johns. City (App.)	OF	53	144	30	36	5	4	3	19	.250	40	33	2	53	2	3	.948
1982—	Johns. City (App.)	OF	57	185	45	51	3	•4	8	36	.276	42	55	11	94	8	4	.962
1983—	Greensboro (S. Atl.)■	OF	129	489	109	152	*34	6	12	77	.311	75	95	33	250	10	15	.945
1984—	New York (A.L.)	OF	7	7	1	1	0	0	0	0	.143	0	1	0	3	0	0	1.000
—	Nashville (South.)	OF	76	262	40	76	17	4	7	38	.290	39	57	17	202	4	7	.967
—	Columbus (Int'l)	OF	32	99	12	22	3	1	0	7	.222	12	26	1	77	4	2	.976
1985—	Huntsville (South.)■	OF	140	486	105	138	22	8	9	64	.284	*112	92	61	363	8	7	.981
1986—	Tacoma (PCL)	OF-1B	69	248	50	81	16	2	4	51	.327	47	46	18	172	9	6	.968
—	Oakland (A.L.)	OF-DH	59	114	13	23	8	0	0	8	.202	16	27	8	118	1	0	1.000
1987—	Oakland (A.L.)	OF-1B-DH	81	151	22	28	3	1	2	9	.185	19	33	3	149	5	3	.981
—	Tacoma (PCL)	OF-1B	15	51	6	11	2	0	0	2	.216	4	12	3	26	0	2	.929
1988—	Oakland (A.L.)	OF-1B-DH	125	397	49	102	13	3	2	35	.257	32	63	20	274	7	5	.983
1989—	Oakland (A.L.)	OF-2B-1B	112	310	42	77	12	3	1	28	.248	31	45	12	221	8	2	.991
1990—	Oakland (A.L.)	OF-DH	19	33	4	8	0	2	0	3	.242	3	6	0	19	0	0	1.000
—	Los Angeles (N.L.)■	OF	104	276	56	84	9	4	3	24	.304	37	44	15	204	2	0	1.000
1991—	Los Angeles (N.L.)	OF-1B	121	176	21	36	5	3	1	11	.205	16	36	7	90	4	3	.969
1992—	Los Angeles (N.L.)	OF	56	58	6	11	3	0	1	5	.190	6	11	1	17	0	0	1.000
—	Philadelphia (N.L.)■	OF	74	276	36	72	14	1	0	24	.261	31	43	17	212	7	3	.986
1993—	California (A.L.)■	O-1-2-DH	92	237	33	69	10	4	3	28	.291	27	33	12	167	4	4	.977
1994—	Oakland (A.L.)■	OF-1B-3B	109	419	75	114	23	0	10	44	.272	49	76	24	274	4	4	.986
1995—	Oakland (A.L.)	OF-3B	130	442	81	123	20	2	8	56	.278	49	63	36	332	3	0	†1.000
American League totals (9 years)			734	2110	320	545	89	15	26	211	.258	226	347	115	1557	32	18	.989
National League totals (3 years)			355	786	119	203	31	8	5	64	.258	90	134	40	523	13	6	.989
Major league totals (11 years)			1089	2896	439	748	120	23	31	275	.258	316	481	155	2080	45	24	.989

CHAMPIONSHIP SERIES RECORD

			BATTING												FIELDING			
Year	**Team (League)**	**Pos.**	**G**	**AB**	**R**	**H**	**2B**	**3B**	**HR**	**RBI**	**Avg.**	**BB**	**SO**	**SB**	**PO**	**A**	**E**	**Avg.**
1988—	Oakland (A.L.)	OF-PR	2	4	0	2	0	0	0	1	.500	1	0	0	5	0	0	1.000
1989—	Oakland (A.L.)	OF	1	2	0	0	0	0	0	0	.000	0	1	0	1	0	0	1.000
Championship series totals (2 years)			3	6	0	2	0	0	0	1	.333	1	1	0	6	0	0	1.000

WORLD SERIES RECORD

NOTES: Member of World Series championship team (1989).

			BATTING												FIELDING			
Year	**Team (League)**	**Pos.**	**G**	**AB**	**R**	**H**	**2B**	**3B**	**HR**	**RBI**	**Avg.**	**BB**	**SO**	**SB**	**PO**	**A**	**E**	**Avg.**
1988—	Oakland (A.L.)	PR-OF	3	4	0	2	0	0	0	2	.500	0	1	0	1	0	0	1.000
1989—	Oakland (A.L.)	OF	1	0	0	0	0	0	0	0	...	0	0	0	0	0	0	...
World Series totals (2 years)			4	4	0	2	0	0	0	2	.500	0	1	0	1	0	0	1.000

JEFFERIES, GREGG — 1B — PHILLIES

PERSONAL: Born August 1, 1967, in Burlingame, Calif. . . . 5-10/184. . . . Bats both, throws right. . . . Full name: Gregory Scott Jefferies.

HIGH SCHOOL: Serra (San Mateo, Calif.).

TRANSACTIONS/CAREER NOTES: Selected by New York Mets organization in first round (20th pick overall) of free-agent draft (June 3, 1985). . . . On disabled list (April 27-May 13, 1991). . . . Traded by Mets with OF Kevin McReynolds and 2B Keith Miller to Kansas City Royals for P Bret Saberhagen and IF Bill Pecota (December 11, 1991). . . . Traded by Royals with OF Ed Gerald to St. Louis Cardinals for OF Felix Jose and IF/OF Craig Wilson (February 12, 1993). . . . Granted free agency (October 18, 1994). . . . Signed by Philadelphia Phillies (December 14, 1994). . . . On disabled list (June 17-July 2, 1995).

HONORS: Named Appalachian League Player of the Year (1985). . . . Named Carolina League Most Valuable Player (1986). . . . Named Texas League Most Valuable Player (1987).

STATISTICAL NOTES: Led Carolina League with .549 slugging percentage in 1986. . . . Led Texas League with 18 intentional bases on balls received in 1987. . . . Tied for International League lead with 10 intentional bases on balls received in 1988. . . . Led International League third basemen with 240 assists in 1988. . . . Led A.L. third basemen with 26 errors in 1992. . . . Tied for N.L. lead with 94 double plays by first basemen in 1994. . . . Hit for the cycle (August 25, 1995). . . . Career major league grand slams: 1.

			BATTING												FIELDING			
Year	**Team (League)**	**Pos.**	**G**	**AB**	**R**	**H**	**2B**	**3B**	**HR**	**RBI**	**Avg.**	**BB**	**SO**	**SB**	**PO**	**A**	**E**	**Avg.**
1985—	Kingsport (Appal.)	SS-2B	47	166	27	57	18	2	3	29	.343	14	16	21	78	130	21	.908
—	Columbia (S. Atl.)	2B-SS	20	64	7	18	2	2	1	12	.281	4	4	7	28	26	2	.964
1986—	Columbia (S. Atl.)	SS	25	112	29	38	6	1	5	24	.339	9	10	13	36	83	7	.944
—	Lynchburg (Caro.)	SS	95	390	66	138	25	9	11	80	*.354	33	29	43	138	273	20	.954

Year Team (League)	Pos.	G	AB	R	H	2B	3B	HR	RBI	Avg.	BB	SO	SB	PO	A	E	Avg.
		BATTING												FIELDING			
— Jackson (Texas)	SS-3B	5	19	1	8	1	1	0	7	.421	2	2	1	7	9	1	.941
1987— Jackson (Texas)	SS-3B	134	510	81	187	*48	5	20	101	.367	49	43	26	167	388	35	.941
— New York (N.L.)	PH	6	6	0	3	1	0	0	2	.500	0	0	0	...	...	...	...
1988— Tidewater (Int'l)	3-S-2-O	132	504	62	142	28	4	7	61	.282	32	35	32	110	†330	27	.942
— New York (N.L.)	3B-2B	29	109	19	35	8	2	6	17	.321	8	10	5	33	46	2	.975
1989— New York (N.L.)	2B-3B	141	508	72	131	28	2	12	56	.258	39	46	21	242	280	14	.974
1990— New York (N.L.)	2B-3B	153	604	96	171	*40	3	15	68	.283	46	40	11	242	341	16	.973
1991— New York (N.L.)	2B-3B	136	486	59	132	19	2	9	62	.272	47	38	26	170	271	17	.963
1992— Kansas City (A.L.)■	3B-DH-2B	152	604	66	172	36	3	10	75	.285	43	29	19	96	304	†26	.939
1993— St. Louis (N.L.)■	1B-2B	142	544	89	186	24	3	16	83	.342	62	32	46	1281	77	9	.993
1994— St. Louis (N.L.)	1B	103	397	52	129	27	1	12	55	.325	45	26	12	889	53	7	.993
1995— Philadelphia (N.L.)■	1B-OF	114	480	69	147	31	2	11	56	.306	35	26	9	579	36	3	.995
American League totals (1 year)		152	604	66	172	36	3	10	75	.285	43	29	19	96	304	26	.939
National League totals (8 years)		824	3134	456	934	178	15	81	399	.298	282	218	130	3436	1104	68	.985
Major league totals (9 years)		976	3738	522	1106	214	18	91	474	.296	325	247	149	3532	1408	94	.981

CHAMPIONSHIP SERIES RECORD

Year Team (League)	Pos.	G	AB	R	H	2B	3B	HR	RBI	Avg.	BB	SO	SB	PO	A	E	Avg.
		BATTING												FIELDING			
1988— New York (N.L.)	3B	7	27	2	9	2	0	0	1	.333	4	0	0	5	8	1	.929

ALL-STAR GAME RECORD

Year League	Pos.	AB	R	H	2B	3B	HR	RBI	Avg.	BB	SO	SB	PO	A	E	Avg.
		BATTING											FIELDING			
1993— National	PH-DH	1	0	0	0	0	0	0	.000	0	1	0	...	...	...	...
1994— National	1B	1	2	1	1	0	0	0	1.000	0	0	0	6	0	0	1.000
All-Star Game totals (2 years)		2	2	1	1	0	0	0	.500	0	1	0	6	0	0	1.000

JEFFERSON, REGGIE — 1B — RED SOX

PERSONAL: Born September 25, 1968, in Tallahassee, Fla. . . . 6-4/215. . . . Bats left, throws left. . . . Full name: Reginald Jirod Jefferson.

HIGH SCHOOL: Lincoln (Tallahassee, Fla.).

TRANSACTIONS/CAREER NOTES: Selected by Cincinnati Reds organization in third round of free-agent draft (June 2, 1986). . . . On disabled list (May 25, 1990-remainder of season). . . . Traded by Reds to Cleveland Indians for 1B Tim Costo (June 14, 1991). . . . On Cleveland disabled list (June 24-July 1, 1991); included rehabilitation assignment to Canton/Akron (June 25-July 1). . . . On Cleveland disabled list (March 28-July 4, 1992); included rehabilitation assignment to Colorado Springs (June 15-July 4). . . . On Colorado Springs suspended list (September 6-9, 1992). . . . Traded by Indians with SS Felix Fermin and cash to Seattle Mariners for SS Omar Vizquel (December 20, 1993). . . . On disabled list (May 21-June 10, 1994). . . . Granted free agency (March 11, 1995). . . . Signed by Boston Red Sox (April 9, 1995). . . . On disabled list (July 10-September 19, 1995).

STATISTICAL NOTES: Led Gulf Coast League first basemen with 624 total chances in 1986. . . . Career major league grand slams: 2.

MISCELLANEOUS: Batted as switch-hitter (1986 and 1989-May 1994).

Year Team (League)	Pos.	G	AB	R	H	2B	3B	HR	RBI	Avg.	BB	SO	SB	PO	A	E	Avg.
		BATTING												FIELDING			
1986— GC Reds (GCL)	1B	59	208	28	54	4	•5	3	33	.260	24	40	10	*581	*36	7	.989
1987— Billings (Pioneer)	1B	8	22	10	8	1	0	1	9	.364	4	2	1	21	1	0	1.000
— Ced. Rap. (Midw.)	1B	15	54	9	12	5	0	3	11	.222	1	12	1	120	11	1	.992
1988— Ced. Rap. (Midw.)	1B	135	517	76	149	26	2	18	*90	.288	40	89	2	1084	91	13	.989
1989— Chatt. (South.)	1B	135	487	66	140	19	3	17	80	.287	43	73	2	1004	79	16	.985
1990— Nashville (A.A.)	1B	37	126	24	34	11	2	5	23	.270	14	30	1	314	20	4	.988
1991— Nashville (A.A.)	1B	28	103	15	33	3	1	3	20	.320	10	22	3	196	13	2	.991
— Cincinnati (N.L.)	1B	5	7	1	1	0	0	1	1	.143	1	2	0	14	1	0	1.000
— Cleveland (A.L.)■	1B	26	101	10	20	3	0	2	12	.198	3	22	0	252	24	2	.993
— Cant./Akr. (East.)	1B	6	25	2	7	1	0	0	4	.280	1	5	0	46	3	0	1.000
— Colo. Springs (PCL)	1B	39	136	29	42	11	0	3	21	.309	16	28	0	289	25	3	.991
1992— Colo. Springs (PCL)	1B	57	218	49	68	11	4	11	44	.312	29	50	1	363	34	5	.988
— Cleveland (A.L.)	1B-DH	24	89	8	30	6	2	1	6	.337	1	17	0	129	12	1	.993
1993— Cleveland (A.L.)	DH-1B	113	366	35	91	11	2	10	34	.249	28	78	1	112	10	3	.976
1994— Seattle (A.L.)■	DH-1B-OF	63	162	24	53	11	0	8	32	.327	17	32	0	95	10	2	.981
1995— Boston (A.L.)■	DH-1B-OF	46	121	21	35	8	0	5	26	.289	9	24	0	28	4	0	1.000
American League totals (5 years)		272	839	98	229	39	4	26	110	.273	58	173	1	616	60	8	.988
National League totals (1 year)		5	7	1	1	0	0	1	1	.143	1	2	0	14	1	0	1.000
Major league totals (5 years)		277	846	99	230	39	4	27	111	.272	59	175	1	630	61	8	.989

DIVISION SERIES RECORD

Year Team (League)	Pos.	G	AB	R	H	2B	3B	HR	RBI	Avg.	BB	SO	SB	PO	A	E	Avg.
		BATTING												FIELDING			
1995— Boston (A.L.)	DH	1	4	1	1	0	0	0	0	.250	0	1	0	...	...	...	...

JENNINGS, ROBIN — OF — CUBS

PERSONAL: Born April 11, 1972, in Singapore. . . . 6-2/205. . . . Bats left, throws left. . . . Full name: Robin Christopher Jennings.

HIGH SCHOOL: Annandale (Va.).

JUNIOR COLLEGE: Manatee (Fla.).

TRANSACTIONS/CAREER NOTES: Selected by Baltimore Orioles organization in 30th round of free-agent draft (June 4, 1990); did not sign. . . . Selected by Chicago Cubs organization in 33rd round of free-agent draft (June 3, 1991).

STATISTICAL NOTES: Tied for New York-Pennsylvania League lead in double plays by outfielder with two in 1992. . . . Led Midwest League outfielders with 20 assists in 1993.

Year	Team (League)	Pos.	G	BATTING AB	R	H	2B	3B	HR	RBI	Avg.	BB	SO	SB	FIELDING PO	A	E	Avg.
1992—	Geneva (NYP)	OF	72	275	39	82	12	2	7	47	.298	20	43	10	96	*9	4	.963
1993—	Peoria (Midwest)	OF-1B	132	474	64	146	29	5	3	65	.308	46	73	11	219	†31	7	.973
1994—	Daytona (Fla. St.)	OF	128	476	54	133	24	5	8	60	.279	45	54	2	165	8	8	.956
1995—	Orlando (Southern)	OF	132	490	71	145	27	7	17	79	.296	44	61	7	242	15	10	.963

JENSEN, MARCUS — C — GIANTS

PERSONAL: Born December 14, 1972, in Oakland, Calif. . . . 6-4/195. . . . Bats both, throws right. . . . Full name: Marcus C. Jensen.
HIGH SCHOOL: Skyline (Oakland, Calif.).
TRANSACTIONS/CAREER NOTES: Selected by San Francisco Giants organization in supplemental round ("sandwich pick" between first and second round, 33rd pick overall) of free-agent draft (June 4, 1990); pick received as part of compensation for San Diego Padres signing Type A free-agent P Craig Lefferts. . . . On disabled list (June 1-14, 1993).
STATISTICAL NOTES: Tied for Arizona League lead with three intentional bases on balls received in 1991. . . . Led California League catchers with 722 total chances in 1994. . . . Led Texas League catchers with 546 total chances in 1995.

Year	Team (League)	Pos.	G	BATTING AB	R	H	2B	3B	HR	RBI	Avg.	BB	SO	SB	FIELDING PO	A	E	Avg.
1990—	Everett (N'west)	C	51	171	21	29	3	0	2	12	.170	24	60	0	191	27	3	.986
1991—	Ariz. Giants (Ariz.)	C-1B	48	155	28	44	8	3	2	30	.284	34	22	4	226	29	7	.973
1992—	Clinton (Midwest)	C-1B	86	264	35	62	14	0	4	33	.235	54	87	4	493	68	10	.982
1993—	Clinton (Midwest)	C	104	324	53	85	24	2	11	56	.262	66	98	1	641	73	7	.990
1994—	San Jose (Calif.)	C	118	418	56	101	18	0	7	47	.242	61	100	1	*627	86	9	.988
1995—	Shreveport (Texas)	C	95	321	55	91	22	8	4	45	.283	41	68	0	*471	70	5	.991

JETER, DEREK — SS — YANKEES

PERSONAL: Born June 26, 1974, in Pequannock, N.J. . . . 6-3/185. . . . Bats right, throws right.
HIGH SCHOOL: Central (Kalamazoo, Mich.).
COLLEGE: Michigan.
TRANSACTIONS/CAREER NOTES: Selected by New York Yankees organization in first round (sixth pick overall) of free-agent draft (June 1, 1992).
HONORS: Named Minor League Player of the Year by THE SPORTING NEWS (1994).

Year	Team (League)	Pos.	G	BATTING AB	R	H	2B	3B	HR	RBI	Avg.	BB	SO	SB	FIELDING PO	A	E	Avg.
1992—	GC Yankees (GCL)	SS	47	173	19	35	10	0	3	25	.202	19	36	2	67	132	12	.943
—	Greensboro (S. Atl.)	SS	11	37	4	9	0	0	1	4	.243	7	16	0	14	25	9	.813
1993—	Greensboro (S. Atl.)	SS	128	515	85	152	14	11	5	71	.295	56	95	18	158	292	56	.889
1994—	Tampa (Fla. St.)	SS	69	292	61	96	13	8	0	39	.329	23	30	28	93	204	12	.961
—	Alb./Colon. (East.)	SS	34	122	17	46	7	2	2	13	.377	15	16	12	42	105	6	.961
—	Columbus (Int'l)	SS	35	126	25	44	7	1	3	16	.349	20	15	10	54	93	7	.955
1995—	Columbus (Int'l)	SS	123	486	*96	154	27	9	2	45	.317	61	56	20	189	394	*29	.953
—	New York (A.L.)	SS	15	48	5	12	4	1	0	7	.250	3	11	0	17	34	2	.962
Major league totals (1 year)			15	48	5	12	4	1	0	7	.250	3	11	0	17	34	2	.962

JOHNS, DOUG — P — ATHLETICS

PERSONAL: Born December 19, 1967, in South Bend, Ind. . . . 6-2/185. . . . Throws left, bats right. . . . Full name: Douglas Alan Johns.
HIGH SCHOOL: Nova (Fort Lauderdale, Fla.).
COLLEGE: Virginia.
TRANSACTIONS/CAREER NOTES: Selected by Oakland Athletics organization in 16th round of free-agent draft (June 4, 1990).
STATISTICAL NOTES: Pitched 3-0 no-hit victory against Burlington (July 17, 1991).

Year	Team (League)	W	L	Pct.	ERA	G	GS	CG	ShO	Sv.	IP	H	R	ER	BB	SO
1990—	Arizona A's (Ariz.)	3	1	.750	1.84	8	7	1	0	0	44	36	17	9	9	38
—	S. Oregon (N'west)	0	2	.000	5.73	6	2	0	0	1	11	13	9	7	11	9
1991—	Madison (Midwest)	12	6	.667	3.23	38	14	1	1	2	128 1/3	108	59	46	54	104
1992—	Reno (California)	13	10	.565	3.26	27	26	4	1	0	*179 1/3	194	98	65	64	101
—	Huntsville (South.)	0	0	. . .	3.94	3	1	0	0	0	16	21	11	7	5	4
1993—	Huntsville (South.)	7	5	.583	2.97	40	6	0	0	1	91	82	41	30	31	56
1994—	Huntsville (South.)	3	0	1.000	1.20	9	0	0	0	0	15	16	2	2	12	9
—	Tacoma (PCL)	9	8	.529	2.89	22	19	2	1	0	134	114	55	43	48	65
1995—	Edmonton (PCL)	9	5	.643	3.41	23	21	0	0	0	132	148	55	50	43	70
—	Oakland (A.L.)	5	3	.625	4.61	11	9	1	1	0	54 2/3	44	32	28	26	25
Major league totals (1 year)		5	3	.625	4.61	11	9	1	1	0	54 2/3	44	32	28	26	25

JOHNS, KEITH — SS — CARDINALS

PERSONAL: Born July 19, 1971, in Jacksonville, Fla. . . . 6-1/175. . . . Bats right, throws right. . . . Full name: Robert Keith Johns.
HIGH SCHOOL: Sandalwood (Jacksonville, Fla.).
COLLEGE: Mississippi.
TRANSACTIONS/CAREER NOTES: Selected by St. Louis Cardinals organization in sixth round of free-agent draft (June 1, 1992). . . . On disabled list (April 13-27, 1994).
STATISTICAL NOTES: Led Florida State League shortstops with 588 total chances in 1994.

Year	Team (League)	Pos.	G	AB	R	H	2B	3B	HR	RBI	Avg.	BB	SO	SB	PO	A	E	Avg.
				BATTING											FIELDING			
1992—	Hamilton (NYP)	SS	70	275	36	78	11	1	1	28	.284	27	42	15	106	183	22	.929
1993—	Springfield (Midw.)	SS	132	467	74	121	24	1	2	40	.259	70	68	40	151	*415	34	.943
1994—	St. Peters. (FSL)	SS	122	464	52	106	20	0	3	47	.228	37	49	18	*186	372	30	.949
1995—	Arkansas (Texas)	SS	111	396	69	111	13	2	2	28	.280	55	53	14	159	354	26	.952
	—Louisville (A.A.)	2B-3B-SS	5	10	0	0	0	0	0	0	.000	0	2	0	7	9	0	1.000

JOHNSON, BRIAN C PADRES

PERSONAL: Born January 8, 1968, in Oakland, Calif. . . . 6-2/200. . . . Bats right, throws right. . . . Full name: Brian David Johnson.
HIGH SCHOOL: Skyline (Oakland, Calif.).
COLLEGE: Stanford.
TRANSACTIONS/CAREER NOTES: Selected by Montreal Expos organization in 36th round of free-agent draft (June 2, 1986); did not sign. . . . Selected by New York Yankees organization in 16th round of free-agent draft (June 5, 1989). . . . Selected by Las Vegas, San Diego Padres organization from Albany/Colonie, Yankees organization, in Rule 5 minor league draft (December 9, 1991). . . . On disabled list (April 22-May 16, 1992).
STATISTICAL NOTES: Led South Atlantic League catchers with 752 putouts and 844 total chances in 1990. . . . Led Florida State League catchers with 654 putouts in 1991. . . . Career major league grand slams: 2.

Year	Team (League)	Pos.	G	AB	R	H	2B	3B	HR	RBI	Avg.	BB	SO	SB	PO	A	E	Avg.
				BATTING											FIELDING			
1989—	GC Yankees (GCL)	C	17	61	7	22	1	1	0	8	.361	4	5	0	84	14	1	.990
1990—	Greensboro (S. Atl.)	C-3B-1B	137	496	58	118	15	0	7	51	.238	57	65	4	†773	91	13	.985
1991—	Alb./Colon. (East.)	C-1B	2	8	0	0	0	0	0	0	.000	0	2	0	10	2	0	1.000
	—Fort Lauder. (FSL)	C-1B-3B	113	394	35	94	19	0	1	44	.239	34	67	4	†738	65	13	.984
1992—	Wichita (Texas)■	C-3B	75	245	30	71	20	0	3	26	.290	22	32	3	472	40	3	.994
1993—	Las Vegas (PCL)	C-3B-OF	115	416	58	141	35	6	10	71	.339	41	53	0	513	67	9	.985
1994—	San Diego (N.L.)	C-1B	36	93	7	23	4	1	3	16	.247	5	21	0	185	15	0	1.000
	—Las Vegas (PCL)	C	15	51	6	11	1	0	2	9	.216	8	6	0	61	5	0	1.000
1995—	San Diego (N.L.)	C-1B	68	207	20	52	9	0	3	29	.251	11	39	0	403	32	4	.991
Major league totals (2 years)			104	300	27	75	13	1	6	45	.250	16	60	0	588	47	4	.994

JOHNSON, CHARLES C MARLINS

PERSONAL: Born July 20, 1971, in Fort Pierce, Fla. . . . 6-2/215. . . . Bats right, throws right. . . . Full name: Charles Edward Johnson Jr.
HIGH SCHOOL: Westwood (Fort Pierce, Fla.).
COLLEGE: Miami (Fla.).
TRANSACTIONS/CAREER NOTES: Selected by Montreal Expos organization in first round (10th pick overall) of free-agent draft (June 5, 1989); did not sign. . . . Selected by Florida Marlins organization in first round (28th pick overall) of free-agent draft (June 1, 1992). . . . On Florida disabled list (August 9-September 1, 1995); included rehabilitation assignment to Portland (August 30-September 1).
HONORS: Named catcher on The Sporting News college All-America team (1992). . . . Won N.L. Gold Glove at catcher (1995).
STATISTICAL NOTES: Led Midwest League with 230 total bases in 1993. . . . Led Midwest League catchers with 1,004 total chances in 1993.
MISCELLANEOUS: Member of 1992 U.S. Olympic baseball team.

Year	Team (League)	Pos.	G	AB	R	H	2B	3B	HR	RBI	Avg.	BB	SO	SB	PO	A	E	Avg.
				BATTING											FIELDING			
1993—	Kane Co. (Midw.)	C	135	488	74	134	29	5	19	*94	.275	62	111	9	*852	*140	12	.988
1994—	Portland (Eastern)	C	132	443	64	117	29	1	*28	80	.264	*74	97	4	713	*84	7	.991
	—Florida (N.L.)	C	4	11	5	5	1	0	1	4	.455	1	4	0	18	2	0	1.000
1995—	Florida (N.L.)	C	97	315	40	79	15	1	11	39	.251	46	71	0	641	•63	6	.992
	—Portland (Eastern)	C	2	7	0	0	0	0	0	0	.000	1	3	0	21	2	1	.958
Major league totals (2 years)			101	326	45	84	16	1	12	43	.258	47	75	0	659	65	6	.992

JOHNSON, EARL OF PADRES

PERSONAL: Born October 3, 1971, in Detroit. . . . 5-10/165. . . . Bats both, throws right. . . . Full name: Earl R. Johnson.
HIGH SCHOOL: Osborn (Detroit).
JUNIOR COLLEGE: Henry Ford Community College (Mich.).
TRANSACTIONS/CAREER NOTES: Signed as non-drafted free agent by San Diego Padres organization (August 24, 1991). . . . On Rancho Cucamonga disabled list (July 20-August 2, 1995).
STATISTICAL NOTES: Tied for Midwest League lead in double plays by outfielder with four in 1994.

Year	Team (League)	Pos.	G	AB	R	H	2B	3B	HR	RBI	Avg.	BB	SO	SB	PO	A	E	Avg.
				BATTING											FIELDING			
1992—	Ariz. Padres (Ariz.)	OF	35	101	20	17	1	0	0	1	.168	10	28	19	60	5	0	1.000
1993—	Spokane (N'west)	OF	63	199	33	49	3	1	0	14	.246	16	49	19	139	8	5	.967
1994—	Springfield (Midw.)	OF	136	533	80	149	11	3	1	43	.280	37	94	*80	277	15	10	.967
1995—	R. Cucamonga (Cal.)	OF	81	341	51	100	11	3	0	25	.293	25	51	34	225	16	7	.972
	—Memphis (South.)	OF	2	10	0	2	0	0	0	25	.200	1	0	0	4	0	1	.800

JOHNSON, HOWARD OF/3B

PERSONAL: Born November 29, 1960, in Clearwater, Fla. . . . 5-10/195. . . . Bats both, throws right. . . . Full name: Howard Michael Johnson.
HIGH SCHOOL: Clearwater (Fla.).
JUNIOR COLLEGE: St. Petersburg (Fla.) Junior College.
TRANSACTIONS/CAREER NOTES: Selected by Detroit Tigers organization in secondary phase of free-agent draft (January 9, 1979). . . . On Evansville disabled list (June 2-August 8, 1983). . . . Traded by Tigers to New York Mets for P Walt Terrell (December 7, 1984). . . . On dis-

abled list (June 2-23, 1986; August 2, 1992-remainder of season and June 11-July 2, 1993). . . . On suspended list (July 8-10, 1993). . . . On disabled list (July 23, 1993-remainder of season). . . . Granted free agency (October 26, 1993). . . . Signed by Colorado Rockies (November 19, 1993). . . . Granted free agency (October 21, 1994). . . . Signed by Iowa, Chicago Cubs organization (April 14, 1995). . . . Granted free agency (November 3, 1995).

RECORDS: Holds N.L. career record for most home runs by switch-hitter—209. . . . Holds N.L. single-season record for most home runs by switch-hitter—38 (1991). . . . Shares N.L. record for most home runs by switch-hitter in two consecutive seasons—61 (1990-91).

HONORS: Named third baseman on The Sporting News N.L. All-Star team (1989). . . . Named third baseman on The Sporting News N.L. Silver Slugger team (1989 and 1991).

STATISTICAL NOTES: Led Florida State League with 16 sacrifice hits in 1980. . . . Led Florida State League third basemen with 21 double plays in 1980. . . . Led American Association third basemen with 19 double plays in 1982. . . . Tied for N.L. lead with 16 game-winning RBIs in 1987. . . . Switch-hit home runs in one game (August 31, 1991). . . . Led N.L. with 15 sacrifice flies in 1991. . . . Career major league grand slams: 6.

			BATTING											FIELDING			
Year	Team (League)	Pos.	G	AB	R	H	2B	3B	HR	RBI	Avg.	BB	SO	SB	PO	A	E	Avg.
1979—	Lakeland (Fla. St.)	3B-SS-OF	132	456	49	107	9	6	3	49	.235	69	85	18	130	240	36	.911
1980—	Lakeland (Fla. St.)	3B	130	474	83	135	*28	1	10	69	.285	73	75	31	*110	*264	13	*.966
1981—	Birm. (Southern)	3B	138	488	84	130	28	7	22	83	.266	75	93	19	103	218	26	.925
1982—	Evansville (A.A.)	3B-OF	98	366	70	116	16	4	23	67	.317	46	62	35	69	139	23	.900
—	Detroit (A.L.)	3B-DH-OF	54	155	23	49	5	0	4	14	.316	16	30	7	36	40	7	.916
1983—	Detroit (A.L.)	3B-DH	27	66	11	14	0	0	3	5	.212	7	10	0	10	30	7	.851
—	Evansville (A.A.)	3B	3	9	1	2	1	0	0	0	.222	4	2	0	1	11	2	.857
1984—	Detroit (A.L.)	3-S-DH-1-O	116	355	43	88	14	1	12	50	.248	40	67	10	63	150	14	.938
1985—	New York (N.L.)■	3B-SS-OF	126	389	38	94	18	4	11	46	.242	34	78	6	78	190	18	.937
1986—	New York (N.L.)	3B-SS-OF	88	220	30	54	14	0	10	39	.245	31	64	8	52	136	20	.904
1987—	New York (N.L.)	3B-SS-OF	157	554	93	147	22	1	36	99	.265	83	113	32	118	305	26	.942
1988—	New York (N.L.)	3B-SS	148	495	85	114	21	1	24	68	.230	86	104	23	110	274	18	.955
1989—	New York (N.L.)	3B-SS	153	571	•104	164	41	3	36	101	.287	77	126	41	97	217	24	.929
1990—	New York (N.L.)	3B-SS	154	590	89	144	37	3	23	90	.244	69	100	34	150	335	28	.945
1991—	New York (N.L.)	3B-OF-SS	156	564	108	146	34	4	*38	*117	.259	78	120	30	161	264	31	.932
1992—	New York (N.L.)	OF	100	350	48	78	19	0	7	43	.223	55	79	22	206	3	4	.981
1993—	New York (N.L.)	3B	72	235	32	56	8	2	7	26	.238	43	43	6	52	135	11	.944
1994—	Colorado (N.L.)■	OF-1B	93	227	30	48	10	2	10	40	.211	39	73	11	98	3	2	.981
1995—	Chicago (N.L.)■	3-O-2-1-S	87	169	26	33	4	1	7	22	.195	34	46	1	45	65	7	.940
American League totals (3 years)			197	576	77	151	19	1	19	69	.262	63	107	17	109	220	28	.922
National League totals (11 years)			1334	4364	683	1078	228	21	209	691	.247	629	946	214	1167	1927	189	.942
Major league totals (14 years)			1531	4940	760	1229	247	22	228	760	.249	692	1053	231	1276	2147	217	.940

CHAMPIONSHIP SERIES RECORD

			BATTING											FIELDING			
Year	Team (League)	Pos.	G	AB	R	H	2B	3B	HR	RBI	Avg.	BB	SO	SB	PO	A	E	Avg.
1984—	Detroit (A.L.)								Did not play.									
1986—	New York (N.L.)	PH	2	2	0	0	0	0	0	0	.000	0	0	0	...	...	...	...
1988—	New York (N.L.)	SS-PH-3B	6	18	3	1	0	0	0	0	.056	1	6	1	6	9	1	.938
Championship series totals (2 years)			8	20	3	1	0	0	0	0	.050	1	6	1	6	9	1	.938

WORLD SERIES RECORD

NOTES: Member of World Series championship teams (1984 and 1986).

			BATTING											FIELDING			
Year	Team (League)	Pos.	G	AB	R	H	2B	3B	HR	RBI	Avg.	BB	SO	SB	PO	A	E	Avg.
1984—	Detroit (A.L.)	PH	1	1	0	0	0	0	0	0	.000	0	0	0	...	...	...	...
1986—	New York (N.L.)	3B-PH-SS	2	5	0	0	0	0	0	0	.000	0	2	0	1	0	0	1.000
World Series totals (2 years)			3	6	0	0	0	0	0	0	.000	0	2	0	1	0	0	1.000

ALL-STAR GAME RECORD

			BATTING										FIELDING			
Year	League	Pos.	AB	R	H	2B	3B	HR	RBI	Avg.	BB	SO	SB	PO	A	E	Avg.
1989—	National	3B	3	0	1	0	0	0	1	.333	0	0	1	0	0	0	...
1991—	National	3B	2	0	0	0	0	0	0	.000	0	1	0	0	0	0	...
All-Star Game totals (2 years)			5	0	1	0	0	0	1	.200	0	1	1	0	0	0	...

JOHNSON, J.J. OF TWINS

PERSONAL: Born August 31, 1973, in Sharon, Conn. . . . 6-0/195. . . . Bats right, throws right. . . . Full name: Jermaine Jay Johnson.

HIGH SCHOOL: Stissing Mount (Pine Plains, N.Y.).

TRANSACTIONS/CAREER NOTES: Selected by Boston Red Sox organization in supplemental round ("sandwich pick" between first and second round, 37th pick overall) of free-agent draft (June 3, 1991); pick received as part of compensation for San Diego Padres signing Type A free-agent P Larry Andersen. . . . Traded by Red Sox organization to Minnesota Twins organization (October 11, 1995), completing deal in which Twins traded P Rick Aguilera to Red Sox for P Frank Rodriguez and a player to be named later (July 6, 1995).

			BATTING											FIELDING			
Year	Team (League)	Pos.	G	AB	R	H	2B	3B	HR	RBI	Avg.	BB	SO	SB	PO	A	E	Avg.
1991—	GC Red Sox (GCL)	OF	31	110	14	19	1	0	0	9	.173	10	16	3	40	3	2	.956
1992—	Elmira (NYP)	OF	30	114	8	26	3	1	1	12	.228	4	32	8	44	1	3	.938
1993—	Utica (N.Y.-Penn)	OF	43	170	33	49	17	4	2	27	.288	9	34	5	87	3	4	.957
—	Lynchburg (Caro.)	OF	25	94	10	24	3	0	4	17	.255	7	20	1	38	2	2	.952
1994—	Lynchburg (Caro.)	OF	131	515	66	120	28	4	14	51	.233	36	132	4	209	9	7	.969
1995—	Sarasota (Fla. St.)	OF	107	391	49	108	162	16	4	43	.276	26	74	7	159	8	8	.954
—	Trenton (Eastern)	OF	2	6	1	3	0	0	0	1	.500	0	0	0	1	0	0	1.000

JOHNSON, LANCE OF METS

PERSONAL: Born July 6, 1963, in Lincoln Heights, O. . . . 5-11/160. . . . Bats left, throws left. . . . Full name: Kenneth Lance Johnson.
HIGH SCHOOL: Princeton (Cincinnati).
JUNIOR COLLEGE: Triton College (Ill.).
COLLEGE: South Alabama.
TRANSACTIONS/CAREER NOTES: Selected by Pittsburgh Pirates organization in 30th round of free-agent draft (June 8, 1981); did not sign. . . . Selected by Seattle Mariners organization in 31st round of free-agent draft (June 7, 1982); did not sign. . . . Selected by St. Louis Cardinals organization in sixth round of free-agent draft (June 4, 1984). . . . Traded by Cardinals with P Rick Horton and cash to Chicago White Sox for P Jose DeLeon (February 9, 1988). . . . Granted free agency (November 8, 1995). . . . Signed by New York Mets (December 14, 1995).
RECORDS: Holds major league record for most consecutive years leading league in triples—4 (1991-94). . . . Shares A.L. single-season record for fewest errors by outfielder who led league in errors—9 (1993). . . . Shares A.L. single-game record for most triples—3 (September 23, 1995).
HONORS: Named American Association Most Valuable Player (1987).
STATISTICAL NOTES: Led New York-Pennsylvania League outfielders with 201 total chances in 1984. . . . Led Texas League in caught stealing with 15 in 1986. . . . Led American Association outfielders with 333 total chances in 1987. . . . Led Pacific Coast League outfielders with five double plays in 1988. . . . Led Pacific Coast League outfielders with 273 total chances in 1989. . . . Led Pacific Coast League in caught stealing with 18 in 1989. . . . Led A.L. in caught stealing with 22 in 1990. . . . Collected six hits in one game (September 23, 1995). . . . Career major league grand slams: 1

		BATTING												FIELDING			
Year Team (League)	Pos.	G	AB	R	H	2B	3B	HR	RBI	Avg.	BB	SO	SB	PO	A	E	Avg.
1984—Erie (N.Y.-Penn)	OF	71	283	*63	*96	7	5	1	28	.339	45	20	29	*188	5	8	.960
1985—St. Peters. (FSL)	OF	129	497	68	134	17	10	2	55	.270	58	39	33	338	16	5	.986
1986—Arkansas (Texas)	OF	127	445	82	128	24	6	2	33	.288	59	57	*49	262	11	7	.975
1987—Louisville (A.A.)	OF	116	477	89	159	21	11	5	50	.333	49	45	42	*319	6	•8	.976
—St. Louis (N.L.)	OF	33	59	4	13	2	1	0	7	.220	4	6	6	27	0	2	.931
1988—Chicago (A.L.)■	OF-DH	33	124	11	23	4	1	0	6	.185	6	11	6	63	1	2	.970
—Vancouver (PCL)	OF	100	411	71	126	12	6	2	36	.307	42	52	49	262	9	5	.982
1989—Vancouver (PCL)	OF	106	408	69	124	11	7	0	28	.304	46	36	33	*261	7	5	.982
—Chicago (A.L.)	OF-DH	50	180	28	54	8	2	0	16	.300	17	24	16	113	0	2	.983
1990—Chicago (A.L.)	OF-DH	151	541	76	154	18	9	1	51	.285	33	45	36	353	5	10	.973
1991—Chicago (A.L.)	OF	159	588	72	161	14	•13	0	49	.274	26	58	26	425	11	2	.995
1992—Chicago (A.L.)	OF	157	567	67	158	15	*12	3	47	.279	34	33	41	433	11	6	.987
1993—Chicago (A.L.)	OF	147	540	75	168	18	*14	0	47	.311	36	33	35	*427	7	•9	.980
1994—Chicago (A.L.)	OF-DH	106	412	56	114	11	*14	3	54	.277	26	23	26	317	1	0	*1.000
1995—Chicago (A.L.)	OF-DH	142	*607	98	*186	18	12	10	57	.306	32	31	40	338	8	3	.991
American League totals (8 years)		945	3559	483	1018	106	77	17	327	.286	210	258	226	2469	44	34	.987
National League totals (1 year)		33	59	4	13	2	1	0	7	.220	4	6	6	27	0	2	.931
Major league totals (9 years)		978	3618	487	1031	108	78	17	334	.285	214	264	232	2496	44	36	.986

CHAMPIONSHIP SERIES RECORD

		BATTING												FIELDING			
Year Team (League)	Pos.	G	AB	R	H	2B	3B	HR	RBI	Avg.	BB	SO	SB	PO	A	E	Avg.
1987—St. Louis (N.L.)	PR	1	0	1	0	0	0	0	0	...	0	0	1	...	...	...	...
1993—Chicago (A.L.)	OF	6	23	2	5	1	1	1	6	.217	2	1	1	15	0	0	1.000
Championship series totals (2 years)		7	23	3	5	1	1	1	6	.217	2	1	2	15	0	0	1.000

WORLD SERIES RECORD

		BATTING												FIELDING			
Year Team (League)	Pos.	G	AB	R	H	2B	3B	HR	RBI	Avg.	BB	SO	SB	PO	A	E	Avg.
1987—St. Louis (N.L.)	PR	1	0	0	0	0	0	0	0	...	0	0	1	...	...	...	...

JOHNSON, MARK 1B PIRATES

PERSONAL: Born October 17, 1967, in Worcester, Mass. . . . 6-4/230. . . . Bats left, throws left. . . . Full name: Mark Patrick Johnson.
HIGH SCHOOL: Holy Name (Worcester, Mass.).
COLLEGE: Dartmouth.
TRANSACTIONS/CAREER NOTES: Selected by Pittsburgh Pirates organization in 42nd round of free-agent draft (June 5, 1989); did not sign. . . . Selected by Pirates organization in 20th round of free-agent draft (June 4, 1990). . . . On Calgary disabled list (August 26-September 8, 1995).
HONORS: Named Southern League Most Valuable Player (1994).
STATISTICAL NOTES: Led Southern League with 11 intentional bases on balls received in 1994.

		BATTING												FIELDING			
Year Team (League)	Pos.	G	AB	R	H	2B	3B	HR	RBI	Avg.	BB	SO	SB	PO	A	E	Avg.
1990—Welland (NYP)	1B	5	8	2	4	1	0	0	2	.500	2	0	0	2	1	0	1.000
—Augusta (S. Atl.)	1B	43	144	12	36	7	0	0	19	.250	24	18	4	240	18	5	.981
1991—Augusta (S. Atl.)	1B	49	139	23	36	7	4	2	25	.259	29	1	15	319	33	9	.975
—Salem (Carolina)	1B-OF-3B	37	103	12	26	2	0	2	13	.252	18	25	0	32	28	3	.952
1992—Carolina (South.)	1B	122	383	40	89	16	1	7	45	.232	55	94	16	610	41	8	.988
1993—Carolina (South.)	1B-OF	125	399	48	93	18	4	14	52	.233	66	93	6	500	40	4	.993
1994—Carolina (South.)	1B-OF	111	388	69	107	20	2	*23	85	.276	67	89	6	570	52	6	.990
1995—Pittsburgh (N.L.)	1B	79	221	32	46	6	1	13	28	.208	37	66	5	527	36	8	.986
—Calgary (PCL)	1B	9	23	7	7	4	0	2	8	.304	6	4	1	65	5	2	.972
Major league totals (1 year)		79	221	32	46	6	1	13	28	.208	37	66	5	527	36	8	.986

JOHNSON, RANDY — P — MARINERS

PERSONAL: Born September 10, 1963, in Walnut Creek, Calif. . . . 6-10/230. . . . Throws left, bats right. . . . Full name: Randall David Johnson.
HIGH SCHOOL: Livermore (Calif.).
COLLEGE: Southern California.
TRANSACTIONS/CAREER NOTES: Selected by Atlanta Braves organization in third round of free-agent draft (June 7, 1982); did not sign. . . . Selected by Montreal Expos organization in second round of free-agent draft (June 3, 1985). . . . Traded by Expos organization with P Brian Holman and P Gene Harris to Seattle Mariners for P Mark Langston and a player to be named later (May 25, 1989); Indianapolis, Expos organization, acquired P Mike Campbell to complete deal (July 31, 1989). . . . On disabled list (June 11-27, 1992).
HONORS: Named A.L. Pitcher of the Year by The Sporting News (1995). . . . Named lefthanded pitcher on The Sporting News A.L. All-Star team (1995). . . . Named A.L. Cy Young Award winner by Baseball Writers' Association of America (1995).
STATISTICAL NOTES: Led American Association with 20 balks in 1988. . . . Pitched 2-0 no-hit victory against Detroit (June 2, 1990). . . . Pitched 4-0 one-hit, complete-game victory against Oakland (August 14, 1991). . . . Struck out 15 batters in one game (September 16, 1992; June 14 and September 16, 1993; June 4 and August 11, 1994; June 24 and September 23, 1995). . . . Struck out 18 batters in one game (September 27, 1992). . . . Led A.L. with 18 hit batsmen in 1992 and 16 in 1993. . . . Pitched 7-0 one-hit, complete-game victory against Oakland (May 16, 1993). . . . Struck out 16 batters in one game (July 15, 1995).
MISCELLANEOUS: Appeared in one game as outfielder with no chances (1993).

Year	Team (League)	W	L	Pct.	ERA	G	GS	CG	ShO	Sv.	IP	H	R	ER	BB	SO
1985—	Jamestown (NYP)	0	3	.000	5.93	8	8	0	0	0	27 1/3	29	22	18	24	21
1986—	WP Beach (FSL)	8	7	.533	3.16	26	•26	2	1	0	119 2/3	89	49	42	*94	133
1987—	Jacksonville (Sou.)	11	8	.579	3.73	25	24	0	0	0	140	100	63	58	128	*163
1988—	Indianapolis (A.A.)	8	7	.533	3.26	20	19	0	0	0	113 1/3	85	52	41	72	111
—	Montreal (N.L.)	3	0	1.000	2.42	4	4	1	0	0	26	23	8	7	7	25
1989—	Montreal (N.L.)	0	4	.000	6.67	7	6	0	0	0	29 2/3	29	25	22	26	26
—	Indianapolis (A.A.)	1	1	.500	2.00	3	3	0	0	0	18	13	5	4	9	17
—	Seattle (A.L.)■	7	9	.438	4.40	22	22	2	0	0	131	118	75	64	70	104
1990—	Seattle (A.L.)	14	11	.560	3.65	33	33	5	2	0	219 2/3	174	103	89	*120	194
1991—	Seattle (A.L.)	13	10	.565	3.98	33	33	2	1	0	201 1/3	151	96	89	*152	228
1992—	Seattle (A.L.)	12	14	.462	3.77	31	31	6	2	0	210 1/3	154	104	88	*144	*241
1993—	Seattle (A.L.)	19	8	.704	3.24	35	34	10	3	1	255 1/3	185	97	92	99	*308
1994—	Seattle (A.L.)	13	6	.684	3.19	23	23	*9	*4	0	172	132	65	61	72	*204
1995—	Seattle (A.L.)	18	2	*.900	*2.48	30	30	6	3	0	214 1/3	159	65	59	65	*294
A.L. totals (7 years)		96	60	.615	3.47	207	206	40	15	1	1404	1073	605	542	722	1573
N.L. totals (2 years)		3	4	.429	4.69	11	10	1	0	0	55 2/3	52	33	29	33	51
Major league totals (8 years)		99	64	.607	3.52	218	216	41	15	1	1459 2/3	1125	638	571	755	1624

DIVISION SERIES RECORD

Year	Team (League)	W	L	Pct.	ERA	G	GS	CG	ShO	Sv.	IP	H	R	ER	BB	SO
1995—	Seattle (A.L.)	2	0	1.000	2.70	2	1	0	0	0	10	5	3	3	6	16

CHAMPIONSHIP SERIES RECORD

Year	Team (League)	W	L	Pct.	ERA	G	GS	CG	ShO	Sv.	IP	H	R	ER	BB	SO
1995—	Seattle (A.L.)	0	1	.000	2.35	2	2	0	0	0	15 1/3	12	6	4	2	13

ALL-STAR GAME RECORD

Year	League	W	L	Pct.	ERA	GS	CG	ShO	Sv.	IP	H	R	ER	BB	SO
1990—	American						Did not play.								
1993—	American	0	0	. . .	0.00	0	0	0	0	2	0	0	0	0	1
1994—	American	0	0	. . .	9.00	0	0	0	0	1	2	1	1	0	0
1995—	American	0	0	. . .	0.00	1	0	0	0	2	0	0	0	1	3
All-Star totals (3 years)		0	0	. . .	1.80	1	0	0	0	5	2	1	1	1	4

JOHNSTON, JOEL — P

PERSONAL: Born March 8, 1967, in West Chester, Pa. . . . 6-4/234. . . . Throws right, bats right. . . . Full name: Joel Raymond Johnston.
HIGH SCHOOL: Newtown (West Chester, Pa.).
COLLEGE: Penn State.
TRANSACTIONS/CAREER NOTES: Selected by Kansas City Royals organization in third round of free-agent draft (June 1, 1988). . . . Traded by Royals with P Dennis Moeller to Pittsburgh Pirates for 2B Jose Lind (November 19, 1992). . . . On Buffalo disabled list (April 24-May 25, 1993). . . . Released by Buffalo (May 25, 1994). . . . Signed by Syracuse, Toronto Blue Jays organization (June 1, 1994). . . . On Syracuse disabled list (July 19, 1994-remainder of season). . . . Granted free agency (October 15, 1994). . . . Signed by Pawtucket, Boston Red Sox organization (December 16, 1994). . . . Released by Pawtucket (July 22, 1995). . . . Signed by Colorado Springs, Colorado Rockies organization (July 26, 1995). . . . On Colorado Springs suspended list (August 25-27, 1995). . . . Released by Colorado Springs (September 12, 1995).

Year	Team (League)	W	L	Pct.	ERA	G	GS	CG	ShO	Sv.	IP	H	R	ER	BB	SO
1988—	Eugene (N'west)	4	7	.364	5.20	14	14	0	0	0	64	64	49	37	34	64
1989—	Baseball City (FSL)	9	4	.692	4.92	26	26	0	0	0	131 2/3	135	84	72	63	76
1990—	Memphis (South.)	0	0	. . .	6.75	4	3	0	0	0	6 2/3	5	9	5	16	6
—	Baseball City (FSL)	2	4	.333	4.88	31	7	1	0	7	55 1/3	36	37	30	49	60
—	Omaha (Am. Assoc.)	0	0	. . .	0.00	2	0	0	0	0	3	1	0	0	1	3
1991—	Omaha (Am. Assoc.)	4	7	.364	5.21	47	0	0	0	8	74 1/3	60	43	43	42	63
—	Kansas City (A.L.)	1	0	1.000	0.40	13	0	0	0	0	22 1/3	9	1	1	9	21
1992—	Kansas City (A.L.)	0	0	. . .	13.50	5	0	0	0	0	2 2/3	3	4	4	2	0
—	Omaha (Am. Assoc.)	5	2	.714	6.39	42	0	0	0	2	74 2/3	80	54	53	45	48
1993—	Buffalo (A.A.)■	1	3	.250	7.76	26	0	0	0	1	31 1/3	30	28	27	25	26
—	Pittsburgh (N.L.)	2	4	.333	3.38	33	0	0	0	2	53 1/3	38	20	20	19	31
1994—	Pittsburgh (N.L.)	0	0	. . .	29.70	4	0	0	0	0	3 1/3	14	12	11	4	5
—	Buffalo (A.A.)	0	0	. . .	5.14	13	0	0	0	2	14	8	8	8	14	11
—	Syracuse (Int'l)■	0	2	.000	6.75	11	2	0	0	0	20	20	18	15	18	17
1995—	Pawtucket (Int'l)■	1	2	.333	6.75	30	0	0	0	6	41 1/3	54	31	31	19	39
—	Boston (A.L.)	0	1	.000	11.25	4	0	0	0	0	4	2	5	5	3	4

Year	Team (League)	W	L	Pct.	ERA	G	GS	CG	ShO	Sv.	IP	H	R	ER	BB	SO
	— Colo. Springs (PCL)■	2	2	.500	5.96	18	0	0	0	0	22 2/3	26	16	15	12	14
A.L. totals (3 years)		1	1	.500	3.10	22	0	0	0	0	29	14	10	10	14	25
N.L. totals (2 years)		2	4	.333	4.92	37	0	0	0	2	56 2/3	52	32	31	23	36
Major league totals (5 years)		3	5	.375	4.31	59	0	0	0	2	85 2/3	66	42	41	37	61

JOHNSTONE, JOHN — P — ASTROS

PERSONAL: Born November 25, 1968, in Liverpool, N.Y. . . . 6-3/195. . . . Throws right, bats right. . . . Full name: John William Johnstone.
HIGH SCHOOL: Bishop Ludden (Syracuse, N.Y.).
JUNIOR COLLEGE: Onondaga Community College (N.Y.).
TRANSACTIONS/CAREER NOTES: Selected by New York Mets organization in 20th round of free-agent draft (June 2, 1987). . . . On disabled list (June 24-July 7, 1992). . . . Selected by Florida Marlins in second round (31st pick overall) of expansion draft (November 17, 1992). . . . On disabled list (May 8, 1995-remainder of season). . . . Granted free agency (December 21, 1995). . . . Signed by Houston Astros organization (December 28, 1995).

Year	Team (League)	W	L	Pct.	ERA	G	GS	CG	ShO	Sv.	IP	H	R	ER	BB	SO
1987	— Kingsport (Appal.)	1	1	.500	7.45	17	1	0	0	0	29	42	28	24	20	21
1988	— GC Mets (GCL)	3	4	.429	2.68	12	12	3	0	0	74	65	29	22	25	57
1989	— Pittsfield (NYP)	*11	2	.846	2.77	15	15	2	1	0	104	101	47	32	28	60
1990	— St. Lucie (Fla. St.)	*15	6	.714	2.24	25	25	*9	3	0	172 2/3	145	53	43	60	120
1991	— Williamsport (East.)	7	9	.438	3.97	27	•27	2	0	0	165 1/3	159	94	73	79	100
1992	— Binghamton (East.)	7	7	.500	3.74	24	24	2	0	0	149 1/3	132	66	62	36	121
1993	— Edmonton (PCL)■	4	*15	.211	5.18	30	21	1	0	4	144 1/3	167	95	83	59	126
	— Florida (N.L.)	0	2	.000	5.91	7	0	0	0	0	10 2/3	16	8	7	7	5
1994	— Edmonton (PCL)	5	3	.625	4.46	29	0	0	0	4	42 1/3	46	23	21	9	43
	— Florida (N.L.)	1	2	.333	5.91	17	0	0	0	0	21 1/3	23	20	14	16	23
1995	— Florida (N.L.)	0	0	...	3.86	4	0	0	0	0	4 2/3	7	2	2	2	3
Major league totals (3 years)		1	4	.200	5.65	28	0	0	0	0	36 2/3	46	30	23	25	31

JONES, BOBBY J. — P — METS

PERSONAL: Born February 10, 1970, in Fresno, Calif. . . . 6-4/225. . . . Throws right, bats right. . . . Full name: Robert Joseph Jones.
HIGH SCHOOL: Fresno (Calif.).
COLLEGE: Fresno State.
TRANSACTIONS/CAREER NOTES: Selected by New York Mets organization in supplemental round ("sandwich pick" between first and second round, 36th pick overall) of free-agent draft (June 3, 1991); pick received as part of compensation for Los Angeles Dodgers signing Type A free-agent OF Darryl Strawberry.
HONORS: Named Eastern League Pitcher of the Year (1992).
STATISTICAL NOTES: Led International League with 11 hit batsmen in 1993. . . . Led N.L. with 18 sacrifice hits in 1995.

Year	Team (League)	W	L	Pct.	ERA	G	GS	CG	ShO	Sv.	IP	H	R	ER	BB	SO
1991	— Columbia (S. Atl.)	3	1	.750	1.85	5	5	5	0	0	24 1/3	20	5	5	3	35
1992	— Binghamton (East.)	12	4	.750	*1.88	24	24	4	*4	0	158	118	40	33	43	143
1993	— Norfolk (Int'l)	12	10	.545	3.63	24	24	6	*3	0	166	149	72	67	32	126
	— New York (N.L.)	2	4	.333	3.65	9	9	0	0	0	61 2/3	61	35	25	22	35
1994	— New York (N.L.)	12	7	.632	3.15	24	24	1	1	0	160	157	75	56	56	80
1995	— New York (N.L.)	10	10	.500	4.19	30	30	3	1	0	195 2/3	209	107	91	53	127
Major league totals (3 years)		24	21	.533	3.71	63	63	4	2	0	417 1/3	427	217	172	131	242

JONES, BOBBY M. — P — ROCKIES

PERSONAL: Born April 11, 1972, in Orange, N.J. . . . 6-0/175. . . . Throws left, bats right. . . . Full name: Robert M. Jones.
JUNIOR COLLEGE: Chipola (Fla.).
TRANSACTIONS/CAREER NOTES: Selected by Milwaukee Brewers organization in 44th round of free-agent draft (June 3, 1991). . . . Selected by Colorado Rockies organization from Brewers organization in Rule 5 minor league draft (December 5, 1994).

Year	Team (League)	W	L	Pct.	ERA	G	GS	CG	ShO	Sv.	IP	H	R	ER	BB	SO
1992	— Helena (Pioneer)	5	4	.556	4.36	14	13	1	0	0	76 1/3	93	51	37	23	53
1993	— Beloit (Midwest)	10	10	.500	4.11	25	25	4	0	0	144 2/3	159	82	66	65	115
1994	— Stockton (Calif.)	6	12	.333	4.21	26	26	2	0	0	147 2/3	131	90	69	64	147
1995	— New Haven (Eastern)■	5	2	.714	2.58	27	8	0	0	3	73 1/3	61	27	21	36	70
	— Colo. Springs (PCL)	1	2	.333	7.30	11	8	0	0	0	40 2/3	50	38	33	33	48

JONES, CHIPPER — 3B — BRAVES

PERSONAL: Born April 24, 1972, in De Land, Fla. . . . 6-3/195. . . . Bats both, throws right. . . . Full name: Larry Wayne Jones.
HIGH SCHOOL: The Bolles School (Jacksonville, Fla.).
TRANSACTIONS/CAREER NOTES: Selected by Atlanta Braves organization in first round (first pick overall) of free-agent draft (June 4, 1990). . . . On Atlanta disabled list (March 20, 1994-entire season).
HONORS: Named N.L. Rookie Player of the Year by The Sporting News (1995).
STATISTICAL NOTES: Led South Atlantic League with 10 sacrifice flies in 1991. . . . Led South Atlantic League shortstops with 692 total chances and 71 double plays in 1991. . . . Led International League with 268 total bases in 1993. . . . Led International League shortstops with 619 total chances in 1993.

			BATTING												FIELDING			
Year	Team (League)	Pos.	G	AB	R	H	2B	3B	HR	RBI	Avg.	BB	SO	SB	PO	A	E	Avg.
1990	— GC Braves (GCL)	SS	44	140	20	32	1	1	1	18	.229	14	25	5	64	140	18	.919
1991	— Macon (S. Atl.)	SS	136	473	*104	154	24	11	15	98	.326	69	70	40	*217	*419	56	.919

Year	Team (League)	Pos.	G	AB	R	H	2B	3B	HR	RBI	Avg.	BB	SO	SB	PO	A	E	Avg.
			BATTING												FIELDING			
1992—	Durham (Carolina)......	SS	70	264	43	73	22	1	4	31	.277	31	34	10	106	200	14	.956
—	Greenville (South.).....	SS	67	266	43	92	17	11	9	42	.346	11	32	14	92	218	18	.945
1993—	Richmond (Int'l).........	SS	139	536	*97	*174	31	*12	13	89	.325	57	70	23	195	381	*43	.931
—	Atlanta (N.L.).............	SS	8	3	2	2	1	0	0	0	.667	1	1	0	1	1	0	1.000
1994—	Atlanta (N.L.).............								Did not play.									
1995—	Atlanta (N.L.).............	3B-OF	140	524	87	139	22	3	23	86	.265	73	99	8	103	255	25	.935
Major league totals (2 years)			148	527	89	141	23	3	23	86	.268	74	100	8	104	256	25	.935

DIVISION SERIES RECORD

Year	Team (League)	Pos.	G	AB	R	H	2B	3B	HR	RBI	Avg.	BB	SO	SB	PO	A	E	Avg.
			BATTING												FIELDING			
1995—	Atlanta (N.L.).............	3B	4	18	4	7	2	0	2	4	.389	2	2	0	3	4	0	1.000

CHAMPIONSHIP SERIES RECORD

Year	Team (League)	Pos.	G	AB	R	H	2B	3B	HR	RBI	Avg.	BB	SO	SB	PO	A	E	Avg.
			BATTING												FIELDING			
1995—	Atlanta (N.L.).............	3B	4	16	3	7	0	0	1	3	.438	3	1	1	4	13	0	1.000

WORLD SERIES RECORD

NOTES: Member of World Series championship team (1995).

Year	Team (League)	Pos.	G	AB	R	H	2B	3B	HR	RBI	Avg.	BB	SO	SB	PO	A	E	Avg.
			BATTING												FIELDING			
1995—	Atlanta (N.L.).............	3B	6	21	3	6	3	0	0	1	.286	4	3	0	6	12	1	.947

JONES, CHRIS — OF — METS

PERSONAL: Born December 16, 1965, in Utica, N.Y. . . . 6-2/205. . . . Bats right, throws right. . . . Full name: Christopher Carlos Jones.
HIGH SCHOOL: Liverpool (N.Y.).
TRANSACTIONS/CAREER NOTES: Selected by Cincinnati Reds organization in third round of free-agent draft (June 4, 1984). . . . Released by Reds (December 13, 1991). . . . Signed by Houston Astros organization (December 19, 1991). . . . Granted free agency (October 16, 1992). . . . Signed by Colorado Rockies (October 26, 1992). . . . Granted free agency (December 20, 1993). . . . Re-signed by Rockies organization (December 22, 1993). . . . Granted free agency (October 15, 1994). . . . Signed by New York Mets (December 7, 1994).

Year	Team (League)	Pos.	G	AB	R	H	2B	3B	HR	RBI	Avg.	BB	SO	SB	PO	A	E	Avg.
			BATTING												FIELDING			
1984—	Billings (Pioneer)........	3B	21	73	8	11	2	0	2	13	.151	2	24	4	6	27	5	.868
1985—	Billings (Pioneer)........	OF	63	240	43	62	12	5	4	33	.258	19	72	13	112	4	*13	.899
1986—	Ced. Rap. (Midw.)......	OF	128	473	65	117	13	9	20	78	.247	20	126	23	218	15	11	.955
1987—	Vermont (Eastern)......	OF	113	383	50	88	11	4	10	39	.230	23	99	13	207	12	8	.965
1988—	Chatt. (South.)............	OF	116	410	50	111	20	7	4	61	.271	29	102	11	185	15	8	.962
1989—	Chatt. (South.)............	OF	103	378	47	95	18	2	10	54	.251	23	68	10	197	8	7	.967
—	Nashville (A.A.)..........	OF	21	49	8	8	1	0	2	5	.163	0	16	2	25	0	1	.962
1990—	Nashville (A.A.)..........	OF	134	436	53	114	23	3	10	52	.261	23	86	12	209	17	8	.966
1991—	Nashville (A.A.)..........	OF	73	267	29	65	5	4	9	33	.243	19	65	10	110	5	6	.950
—	Cincinnati (N.L.).........	OF	52	89	14	26	1	2	2	6	.292	2	31	2	27	1	0	1.000
1992—	Houston (N.L.)■........	OF	54	63	7	12	2	1	1	4	.190	7	21	3	27	0	2	.931
—	Tucson (PCL).............	OF	45	170	25	55	9	8	3	28	.324	18	34	7	86	7	2	.979
1993—	Colo. Springs (PCL)■	OF	46	168	41	47	5	5	12	40	.280	19	47	8	107	5	3	.974
—	Colorado (N.L.)..........	OF	86	209	29	57	11	4	6	31	.273	10	48	9	114	2	2	.983
1994—	Colo. Springs (PCL)...	OF	98	386	77	124	22	4	20	75	.321	35	72	12	191	11	*15	.931
—	Colorado (N.L.)..........	OF	21	40	6	12	2	1	0	2	.300	2	14	0	16	0	1	.941
1995—	New York (N.L.)■......	OF-1B	79	182	33	51	6	2	8	31	.280	13	45	2	122	6	2	.985
—	Norfolk (Int'l)............	OF	33	114	20	38	12	1	3	19	.333	11	20	5	62	4	1	.985
Major league totals (5 years)			292	583	89	158	22	10	17	74	.271	34	159	16	306	9	7	.978

JONES, DAX — OF — GIANTS

PERSONAL: Born August 4, 1970, in Pittsburgh. . . . 6-0/180. . . . Bats right, throws right. . . . Full name: Dax Xenos Jones.
HIGH SCHOOL: Waukegan (Ill.) West.
COLLEGE: Creighton.
TRANSACTIONS/CAREER NOTES: Selected by Toronto Blue Jays organization in 49th round of free-agent draft (June 1, 1988); did not sign. . . . Selected by San Francisco Giants organization in eighth round of free-agent draft (June 3, 1991). . . . On Clinton disabled list (May 22-June 13, 1992). . . . On disabled list (July 7-28, 1994).
STATISTICAL NOTES: Tied for Northwest League lead in double plays by outfielder with two in 1991.

Year	Team (League)	Pos.	G	AB	R	H	2B	3B	HR	RBI	Avg.	BB	SO	SB	PO	A	E	Avg.
			BATTING												FIELDING			
1991—	Everett (N'west)..........	OF	53	180	42	55	5	•6	5	29	.306	27	26	15	77	•10	6	.935
1992—	Clinton (Midwest).......	OF	79	295	45	88	12	4	1	42	.298	21	32	18	159	13	8	.956
—	Shreveport (Texas).....	OF	19	66	10	20	0	2	1	7	.303	4	6	2	24	3	3	.900
1993—	Shreveport (Texas).....	OF	118	436	59	124	19	5	4	36	.284	26	53	13	236	13	7	.973
1994—	Phoenix (PCL)............	OF	111	399	55	111	25	5	4	52	.278	21	42	16	283	*21	7	.977
1995—	Phoenix (PCL)............	OF	112	404	47	108	21	3	2	45	.267	31	52	11	284	9	6	.980

JONES, DOUG — P — CUBS

PERSONAL: Born June 24, 1957, in Covina, Calif. . . . 6-2/195. . . . Throws right, bats right. . . . Full name: Douglas Reid Jones.
HIGH SCHOOL: Lebanon (Ind.).
JUNIOR COLLEGE: Central Arizona College.

COLLEGE: Butler.

TRANSACTIONS/CAREER NOTES: Selected by Milwaukee Brewers organization in third round of free-agent draft (January 10, 1978).... On disabled list (June 20-July 12, 1978).... On Vancouver disabled list (April 11-September 1, 1983 and April 25-May 30, 1984).... Granted free agency (October 15, 1984).... Signed by Waterbury, Cleveland Indians organization (April 3, 1985).... Granted free agency (December 20, 1991).... Signed by Houston Astros organization (January 24, 1992).... Traded by Astros with P Jeff Juden to Philadelphia Phillies for P Mitch Williams (December 2, 1993).... Granted free agency (October 15, 1994).... Signed by Baltimore Orioles (April 8, 1995).... Granted free agency (November 3, 1995).... Signed by Chicago Cubs (December 28, 1995).

HONORS: Named N.L. co-Fireman of the Year by The Sporting News (1992).

Year	Team (League)	W	L	Pct.	ERA	G	GS	CG	ShO	Sv.	IP	H	R	ER	BB	SO
1978—	Newark (NYP)	2	4	.333	5.21	15	3	1	0	2	38	49	30	22	15	27
1979—	Burlington (Midw.)	10	10	.500	*1.75	28	20	*16	•3	0	*190	144	63	37	73	115
1980—	Stockton (Calif.)	6	2	.750	2.84	11	11	5	1	0	76	63	32	24	31	54
—	Vancouver (PCL)	3	2	.600	3.23	8	8	1	1	0	53	52	19	19	15	28
—	Holyoke (Eastern)	5	3	.625	2.90	8	8	4	2	0	62	57	23	20	26	39
1981—	El Paso (Texas)	5	7	.417	5.80	15	15	3	1	0	90	121	67	58	28	62
—	Vancouver (PCL)	5	3	.625	3.04	11	10	2	0	0	80	79	29	27	22	38
1982—	Milwaukee (A.L.)	0	0	...	10.13	4	0	0	0	0	2 2/3	5	3	3	1	1
—	Vancouver (PCL)	5	8	.385	2.97	23	9	4	0	2	106	109	48	35	31	60
1983—	Vancouver (PCL)	0	1	.000	10.29	3	1	0	0	0	7	10	8	8	5	4
1984—	Vancouver (PCL)	1	0	1.000	10.13	3	0	0	0	0	8	9	9	9	3	2
—	El Paso (Texas)	6	8	.429	4.28	16	16	7	0	0	109 1/3	120	61	52	35	62
1985—	Waterbury (East.)■	9	4	.692	3.65	39	1	0	0	7	116	123	59	47	36	113
1986—	Maine (Int'l)	5	6	.455	*2.09	43	3	0	0	9	116 1/3	105	35	27	27	98
—	Cleveland (A.L.)	1	0	1.000	2.50	11	0	0	0	1	18	18	5	5	6	12
1987—	Cleveland (A.L.)	6	5	.545	3.15	49	0	0	0	8	91 1/3	101	45	32	24	87
—	Buffalo (A.A.)	5	2	.714	2.04	23	0	0	0	7	61 2/3	49	18	14	12	61
1988—	Cleveland (A.L.)	3	4	.429	2.27	51	0	0	0	37	83 1/3	69	26	21	16	72
1989—	Cleveland (A.L.)	7	10	.412	2.34	59	0	0	0	32	80 2/3	76	25	21	13	65
1990—	Cleveland (A.L.)	5	5	.500	2.56	66	0	0	0	43	84 1/3	66	26	24	22	55
1991—	Cleveland (A.L.)	4	8	.333	5.54	36	4	0	0	7	63 1/3	87	42	39	17	48
—	Colo. Springs (PCL)	2	2	.500	3.28	17	2	1	1	7	35 2/3	30	14	13	5	29
1992—	Houston (N.L.)■	11	8	.579	1.85	80	0	0	0	36	111 2/3	96	29	23	17	93
1993—	Houston (N.L.)	4	10	.286	4.54	71	0	0	0	26	85 1/3	102	46	43	21	66
1994—	Philadelphia (N.L.)■	2	4	.333	2.17	47	0	0	0	27	54	55	14	13	6	38
1995—	Baltimore (A.L.)■	0	4	.000	5.01	52	0	0	0	22	46 2/3	55	30	26	16	42
A.L. totals (8 years)		26	36	.419	3.27	328	4	0	0	150	470 1/3	477	202	171	115	382
N.L. totals (3 years)		17	22	.436	2.83	198	0	0	0	89	251	253	89	79	44	197
Major league totals (11 years)		43	58	.426	3.12	526	4	0	0	239	721 1/3	730	291	250	159	579

ALL-STAR GAME RECORD

Year	League	W	L	Pct.	ERA	GS	CG	ShO	Sv.	IP	H	R	ER	BB	SO
1988—	American	0	0	...	0.00	0	0	0	0	2/3	0	0	0	0	1
1989—	American	0	0	...	0.00	0	0	0	1	1 1/3	1	0	0	0	0
1990—	American						Did not play.								
1992—	National	0	0	...	27.00	0	0	0	0	1	4	3	3	0	2
1994—	National	1	0	1.000	0.00	0	0	0	0	1	2	0	0	0	2
All-Star totals (4 years)		1	0	1.000	6.75	0	0	0	1	4	7	3	3	0	5

JONES, TERRY — OF — ROCKIES

PERSONAL: Born February 15, 1971, in Birmingham, Ala.... 5-10/165.... Bats both, throws right.

COLLEGE: North Alabama.

TRANSACTIONS/CAREER NOTES: Selected by Colorado Rockies organization in 40th round of free-agent draft (June 3, 1993).

STATISTICAL NOTES: Led California League outfielders with 342 total chances and tied for lead with four double plays in 1994.

				BATTING											FIELDING			
Year	Team (League)	Pos.	G	AB	R	H	2B	3B	HR	RBI	Avg.	BB	SO	SB	PO	A	E	Avg.
1993—	Bend (Northwest)	OF	33	138	21	40	5	4	0	18	.290	12	19	16	57	7	1	.985
—	Central Vall. (Cal.)	OF	21	73	16	21	1	0	0	7	.288	10	15	5	36	2	1	.974
1994—	Central Vall. (Cal.)	OF	129	*536	94	157	20	1	2	34	.293	42	85	44	*312	*16	14	.959
1995—	New Haven (Eastern)	OF	124	472	78	127	12	1	1	26	.269	39	104	*51	264	18	*10	.966

JONES, TODD — P — ASTROS

PERSONAL: Born April 24, 1968, in Marietta, Ga.... 6-3/200.... Throws right, bats left.... Full name: Todd Barton Jones.

HIGH SCHOOL: Osborne (Ga.).

COLLEGE: Jacksonville (Ala.) State.

TRANSACTIONS/CAREER NOTES: Selected by New York Mets organization in 41st round of free-agent draft (June 2, 1986); did not sign.... Selected by Houston Astros organization in supplemental round ("sandwich pick" between first and second round, 27th pick overall) of free-agent draft (June 5, 1989); pick received as part of compensation for Texas Rangers signing Type A free-agent P Nolan Ryan.... On suspended list (September 14-16, 1993).

Year	Team (League)	W	L	Pct.	ERA	G	GS	CG	ShO	Sv.	IP	H	R	ER	BB	SO
1989—	Auburn (NYP)	2	3	.400	5.44	11	9	1	0	0	49 2/3	47	39	30	42	71
1990—	Osceola (Florida St.)	12	10	.545	3.51	27	•27	1	0	0	151 1/3	124	81	59	*109	106
1991—	Osceola (Florida St.)	4	4	.500	4.35	14	14	0	0	0	72 1/3	69	38	35	35	51
—	Jackson (Texas)	4	3	.571	4.88	10	10	0	0	0	55 1/3	51	37	30	39	37
1992—	Jackson (Texas)	3	7	.300	3.14	*61	0	0	0	25	66	52	28	23	44	60
—	Tucson (Pac. Coast)	0	1	.000	4.50	3	0	0	0	0	4	1	2	2	10	4
1993—	Tucson (Pac. Coast)	4	2	.667	4.44	41	0	0	0	12	48 2/3	49	26	24	31	45
—	Houston (N.L.)	1	2	.333	3.13	27	0	0	0	2	37 1/3	28	14	13	15	25

Year	Team (League)	W	L	Pct.	ERA	G	GS	CG	ShO	Sv.	IP	H	R	ER	BB	SO
1994—	Houston (N.L.)	5	2	.714	2.72	48	0	0	0	5	72⅔	52	23	22	26	63
1995—	Houston (N.L.)	6	5	.545	3.07	68	0	0	0	15	99⅔	89	38	34	52	96
Major league totals (3 years)		12	9	.571	2.96	143	0	0	0	22	209⅔	169	75	69	93	184

JORDAN, BRIAN — OF — CARDINALS

PERSONAL: Born March 29, 1967, in Baltimore. . . . 6-1/205. . . . Bats right, throws right. . . . Full name: Brian O'Neal Jordan.
HIGH SCHOOL: Milford (Baltimore).
COLLEGE: Richmond.
TRANSACTIONS/CAREER NOTES: Selected by Cleveland Indians organization in 20th round of free-agent draft (June 3, 1985); did not sign. . . . Selected by St. Louis Cardinals organization in supplemental round ("sandwich pick" between first and second round, 30th pick overall) of free-agent draft (June 1, 1988); pick received as part of compensation for New York Yankees signing Type A free-agent 1B/OF Jack Clark. . . . On disabled list (May 1-8 and June 3-10, 1991). . . . On temporarily inactive list (July 3, 1991-remainder of season). . . . On St. Louis disabled list (May 23-June 22, 1992); included rehabilitation assignment to Louisville (June 10-22). . . . On Louisville disabled list (June 7-14, 1993). . . . On disabled list (July 10, 1994-remainder of season).
STATISTICAL NOTES: Career major league grand slams: 1.

			BATTING												FIELDING			
Year	Team (League)	Pos.	G	AB	R	H	2B	3B	HR	RBI	Avg.	BB	SO	SB	PO	A	E	Avg.
1988—	Hamilton (NYP)	OF	19	71	12	22	3	1	4	12	.310	6	15	3	32	1	1	.971
1989—	St. Peters. (FSL)	OF	11	43	7	15	4	1	2	11	.349	0	8	0	22	2	0	1.000
1990—	Arkansas (Texas)	OF	16	50	4	8	1	0	0	0	.160	0	11	0	28	0	2	.933
—	St. Peters. (FSL)	OF	9	30	3	5	0	1	0	1	.167	2	11	0	23	0	0	1.000
1991—	Louisville (A.A.)	OF	61	212	35	56	11	4	4	24	.264	17	41	10	144	3	2	.987
1992—	Louisville (A.A.)	OF	43	155	23	45	3	1	4	16	.290	8	21	13	89	3	1	.989
—	St. Louis (N.L.)	OF	55	193	17	40	9	4	5	22	.207	10	48	7	101	4	1	.991
1993—	St. Louis (N.L.)	OF	67	223	33	69	10	6	10	44	.309	12	35	6	140	4	4	.973
—	Louisville (A.A.)	OF	38	144	24	54	13	2	5	35	.375	16	17	9	75	2	0	1.000
1994—	St. Louis (N.L.)	OF-1B	53	178	14	46	8	2	5	15	.258	16	40	4	105	6	1	.991
1995—	St. Louis (N.L.)	OF	131	490	83	145	20	4	22	81	.296	22	79	24	267	4	1	.996
Major league totals (4 years)			306	1084	147	300	47	16	42	162	.277	60	202	41	613	18	7	.989

RECORD AS FOOTBALL PLAYER

TRANSACTIONS/CAREER NOTES: Selected by Buffalo Bills in seventh round (173rd pick overall) of 1989 NFL draft. . . . Signed by Bills (July 17, 1989). . . . Claimed on waivers by Atlanta Falcons (September 5, 1989). . . . On injured reserve with ankle injury (September 9-October 22, 1989). . . . On developmental squad (October 23-December 2, 1989). . . . Granted free agency (February 1, 1992).
PRO STATISTICS: 1989—Recovered two fumbles. 1990—Recovered one fumble. 1991—Credited with two safeties and recovered one fumble.
MISCELLANEOUS: Played safety.

			INTERCEPTIONS				SACKS	PUNT RETURNS				KICKOFF RETURNS				TOTAL		
Year	Team	G	No.	Yds.	Avg.	TD	No.	No.	Yds.	Avg.	TD	No.	Yds.	Avg.	TD	TD	Pts.	Fum.
1989—	Atlanta NFL	4	0	0	...	0	0.0	4	34	8.5	0	3	27	9.0	0	0	0	1
1990—	Atlanta NFL	16	3	14	4.7	0	0.0	2	19	9.5	0	0	0	...	0	0	0	0
1991—	Atlanta NFL	16	2	3	1.5	0	4.0	14	116	8.3	0	5	100	20.0	0	0	4	0
Pro totals (3 years)		36	5	17	3.4	0	4.0	20	169	8.5	0	8	127	15.9	0	0	4	1

JORDAN, KEVIN — 2B — PHILLIES

PERSONAL: Born October 9, 1969, in San Francisco. . . . 6-1/193. . . . Bats right, throws right. . . . Full name: Kevin Wayne Jordan.
HIGH SCHOOL: Lowell (San Francisco).
JUNIOR COLLEGE: Canada College (Calif.).
COLLEGE: Nebraska.
TRANSACTIONS/CAREER NOTES: Selected by Los Angeles Dodgers organization in 10th round of free-agent draft (June 5, 1989); did not sign. . . . Selected by New York Yankees organization in 20th round of free-agent draft (June 4, 1990). . . . Traded by Yankees with P Bobby Munoz and P Ryan Karp to Philadelphia Phillies for P Terry Mulholland and a player to be named later (February 9, 1994). . . . On disabled list (May 1-June 20, 1994).
STATISTICAL NOTES: Led Eastern League with 234 total bases in 1993. . . . Led Eastern League second basemen with 93 double plays in 1993.

			BATTING												FIELDING			
Year	Team (League)	Pos.	G	AB	R	H	2B	3B	HR	RBI	Avg.	BB	SO	SB	PO	A	E	Avg.
1990—	Oneonta (NYP)	2B	73	276	47	92	13	•7	4	54	.333	23	31	19	131	158	8	.973
1991—	Fort Lauder. (FSL)	2B-1B	121	448	61	122	25	5	4	53	.272	37	66	14	182	306	16	.968
1992—	Prin. William (Car.)	2B-3B	112	438	67	136	29	8	8	63	.311	27	54	6	192	288	20	.960
1993—	Alb./Colon. (East.)	2B	135	513	87	145	*33	4	16	87	.283	41	53	8	261	359	21	.967
1994—	Scran./W.B. (Int'l)■	2B-3B	81	314	44	91	22	1	12	57	.290	29	28	0	160	237	16	.961
1995—	Scran./W.B. (Int'l)	2B	106	410	61	127	29	4	5	60	.310	28	36	3	217	279	12	.976
—	Philadelphia (N.L.)	2B-3B	24	54	6	10	1	0	2	6	.185	2	9	0	29	35	1	.985
Major league totals (1 year)			24	54	6	10	1	0	2	6	.185	2	9	0	29	35	1	.985

JORDAN, RICARDO — P — PHILLIES

PERSONAL: Born June 27, 1970, in Delray Beach, Fla. . . . 6-0/180. . . . Throws left, bats left.
HIGH SCHOOL: Atlantic (Delray Beach, Fla.).
JUNIOR COLLEGE: Miami-Dade (South) Community College.
TRANSACTIONS/CAREER NOTES: Selected by Toronto Blue Jays organization in 37th round of free-agent draft (June 4, 1990). . . . Traded by Blue Jays with 3B Howard Battle to Philadelphia Phillies for P Paul Quantrill (December 6, 1995).

Year	Team (League)	W	L	Pct.	ERA	G	GS	CG	ShO	Sv.	IP	H	R	ER	BB	SO
1990—	Dunedin (Fla. St.)	0	2	.000	2.38	13	2	0	0	0	22 2/3	15	9	6	19	16
1991—	Myrtle Beach (SAL)	9	8	.529	2.74	29	23	3	1	1	144 2/3	101	58	44	79	152
1992—	Dunedin (Fla. St.)	0	5	.000	3.83	45	0	0	0	15	47	44	26	20	28	49
1993—	Knoxville (South.)	1	4	.200	2.45	25	0	0	0	2	36 2/3	33	17	10	18	35
—	Dunedin (Fla. St.)	2	0	1.000	4.38	15	0	0	0	1	24 2/3	20	13	12	15	24
1994—	Knoxville (South.)	4	3	.571	2.66	53	0	0	0	17	64 1/3	54	25	19	23	70
1995—	Syracuse (Int'l)	0	0	...	6.57	13	0	0	0	0	12 1/3	15	9	9	7	17
—	Toronto (A.L.)	1	0	1.000	6.60	15	0	0	0	1	15	18	11	11	13	10
Major league totals (1 year)		1	0	1.000	6.60	15	0	0	0	1	15	18	11	11	13	10

JORDAN, RICKY 1B ANGELS

PERSONAL: Born May 26, 1965, in Richmond, Calif. . . . 6-3/205. . . . Bats right, throws right. . . . Full name: Paul Scott Jordan.
HIGH SCHOOL: Grant (Sacramento, Calif.).
TRANSACTIONS/CAREER NOTES: Selected by Philadelphia Phillies organization in first round (22nd pick overall) of free-agent draft (June 6, 1983). . . . On Philadelphia disabled list (June 13-July 4, 1990); included rehabilitation assignment to Scranton/Wilkes-Barre (June 29-July 4). . . . On Philadelphia disabled list (March 28-May 11, 1992); included rehabilitation assignment to Scranton/Wilkes-Barre (May 6-11). . . . Granted free agency (October 17, 1994). . . . Signed by Vancouver, California Angels organizaton (April 26, 1995). . . . On Vancouver disabled list (April 27-June 12 and July 21, 1995-remainder of season).
STATISTICAL NOTES: Led Eastern League first basemen with 17 errors and 100 double plays in 1986. . . . Tied for Eastern League lead with nine sacrifice flies in 1987. . . . Led Eastern League first basemen with 1,255 total chances and 110 double plays in 1987. . . . Hit home run in first major league at-bat (July 17, 1988). . . . Career major league grand slams: 2.

			BATTING												FIELDING			
Year	Team (League)	Pos.	G	AB	R	H	2B	3B	HR	RBI	Avg.	BB	SO	SB	PO	A	E	Avg.
1983—	Helena (Pioneer)	1B	60	247	32	73	7	1	5	33	.296	12	35	3	486	35	7	.987
1984—	Spartanburg (SAL)	1B	128	490	72	143	23	4	10	76	.292	32	63	8	1129	69	14	.988
1985—	Clearwater (FSL)	1B	*139	528	60	146	22	8	7	62	.277	25	59	26	1252	86	*20	.985
1986—	Reading (Eastern)	1B-OF	133	478	44	131	19	3	2	60	.274	21	44	17	1052	87	†17	.985
1987—	Reading (Eastern)	1B	132	475	78	151	28	3	16	95	.318	28	22	15	*1193	54	8	.994
1988—	Maine (Int'l)	1B	87	338	42	104	23	1	7	36	.308	6	30	10	809	41	4	.995
—	Philadelphia (N.L.)	1B	69	273	41	84	15	1	11	43	.308	7	39	1	579	35	5	.992
1989—	Philadelphia (N.L.)	1B	144	523	63	149	22	3	12	75	.285	23	62	4	1271	61	9	.993
1990—	Philadelphia (N.L.)	1B	92	324	32	78	21	0	5	44	.241	13	39	2	743	37	4	.995
—	Scran./W.B. (Int'l)	1B	27	104	8	29	1	0	2	11	.279	5	18	0	225	8	1	.996
1991—	Philadelphia (N.L.)	1B	101	301	38	82	21	3	9	49	.272	14	49	0	626	37	9	.987
1992—	Scran./W.B. (Int'l)	1B	4	19	1	5	0	0	0	2	.263	1	2	0	47	3	0	1.000
—	Philadelphia (N.L.)	1B-OF	94	276	33	84	19	0	4	34	.304	5	44	3	427	27	2	.996
1993—	Philadelphia (N.L.)	1B	90	159	21	46	4	1	5	18	.289	8	32	0	201	4	2	.990
1994—	Philadelphia (N.L.)	1B	72	220	29	62	14	2	8	37	.282	6	32	0	430	15	3	.993
1995—	Vancouver (PCL)■	1B	19	63	5	14	2	0	2	9	.222	3	7	0	4	0	0	1.000
Major league totals (7 years)			662	2076	257	585	116	10	54	300	.282	76	297	10	4277	216	34	.992

CHAMPIONSHIP SERIES RECORD

			BATTING												FIELDING			
Year	Team (League)	Pos.	G	AB	R	H	2B	3B	HR	RBI	Avg.	BB	SO	SB	PO	A	E	Avg.
1993—	Philadelphia (N.L.)	PH	2	1	0	0	0	0	0	0	.000	1	0	0	...	...	...	...

WORLD SERIES RECORD

			BATTING												FIELDING			
Year	Team (League)	Pos.	G	AB	R	H	2B	3B	HR	RBI	Avg.	BB	SO	SB	PO	A	E	Avg.
1993—	Philadelphia (N.L.)	DH-PH	3	10	0	2	0	0	0	0	.200	0	2	0	...	...	...	...

JOSE, FELIX OF

PERSONAL: Born May 8, 1965, in Santo Domingo, Dominican Republic. . . . 6-1/220. . . . Bats both, throws right. . . . Full name: Domingo Felix Jose.
HIGH SCHOOL: Eldo Foreda Reyez de Munoz (Santo Domingo, Dominican Republic).
TRANSACTIONS/CAREER NOTES: Signed as non-drafted free agent by Oakland Athletics organization (January 3, 1984). . . . Traded by A's with 3B Stan Royer and P Daryl Green to St. Louis Cardinals for OF Willie McGee (August 29, 1990). . . . On St. Louis disabled list (March 28-April 29, 1992); included rehabilitation assignments to Louisville (April 17-22) and St. Petersburg (April 22-29). . . . Traded by Cardinals with IF/OF Craig Wilson to Kansas City Royals for 3B Gregg Jefferies and OF Ed Gerald (February 12, 1993). . . . On Kansas City disabled list (March 25-April 15, 1994); included rehabilitation assignment to Memphis (April 7-13). . . . Granted free agency (December 12, 1994). . . . Re-signed by Royals organization (April 19, 1995). . . . Released by Royals (May 14, 1995). . . . Signed by Iowa, Chicago Cubs organization (May 24, 1995). . . . Released by Iowa (June 1, 1995).
STATISTICAL NOTES: Career major league grand slams: 2.

			BATTING												FIELDING			
Year	Team (League)	Pos.	G	AB	R	H	2B	3B	HR	RBI	Avg.	BB	SO	SB	PO	A	E	Avg.
1984—	Idaho Falls (Pio.)	OF	45	152	16	33	6	0	1	18	.217	18	37	5	48	6	1	.982
1985—	Madison (Midwest)	OF	117	409	46	89	13	3	3	33	.218	32	82	6	187	9	12	.942
1986—	Modesto (Calif.)	OF	127	516	77	147	22	8	14	77	.285	36	89	14	215	12	14	.942
1987—	Huntsville (South.)	OF	91	296	29	67	11	1	5	42	.226	28	61	9	131	7	8	.945
1988—	Tacoma (PCL)	OF	134	508	72	161	29	5	12	83	.317	53	75	16	253	11	8	.971
—	Oakland (A.L.)	OF	8	6	2	2	1	0	0	1	.333	0	1	1	8	0	0	1.000
1989—	Tacoma (PCL)	OF	104	387	59	111	26	0	14	63	.287	41	82	11	186	7	*10	.951
—	Oakland (A.L.)	OF	20	57	3	11	2	0	0	5	.193	4	13	0	35	2	1	.974
1990—	Oakland (A.L.)	OF-DH	101	341	42	90	12	0	8	39	.264	16	65	8	212	5	5	.977
—	St. Louis (N.L.)■	OF	25	85	12	23	4	1	3	13	.271	8	16	4	42	0	0	1.000
1991—	St. Louis (N.L.)	OF	154	568	69	173	40	6	8	77	.305	50	113	20	268	•15	3	.990

Year	League	Pos.		AB	R	H	2B	3B	HR	RBI	Avg.	BB	SO	SB	PO	A	E	Avg.
				BATTING											FIELDING			
1992—	Louisville (A.A.)	OF	2	7	0	1	0	0	0	0	.143	1	0	0	2	0	0	1.000
—	St. Peters. (FSL)	OF	6	18	2	8	1	1	0	2	.444	1	2	1	6	0	0	1.000
—	St. Louis (N.L.)	OF	131	509	62	150	22	3	14	75	.295	40	100	28	273	11	6	.979
1993—	Kansas City (A.L.)■	OF-DH	149	499	64	126	24	3	6	43	.253	36	95	31	237	6	7	.972
1994—	Memphis (South.)	OF	6	21	3	7	2	0	0	6	.333	5	6	1	9	0	0	1.000
—	Kansas City (A.L.)	OF	99	366	56	111	28	1	11	55	.303	35	75	10	192	7	4	.980
1995—	Kansas City (A.L.)	OF	9	30	2	4	1	0	0	1	.133	2	9	0	15	2	0	1.000
—	Iowa (Am. Assoc.)■	OF	10	37	2	5	3	0	0	1	.135	1	6	0	12	0	0	1.000
American League totals (6 years)			386	1299	169	344	68	4	25	144	.265	93	258	50	699	22	17	.977
National League totals (3 years)			310	1162	143	346	66	10	25	165	.298	98	229	52	583	26	9	.985
Major league totals (8 years)			696	2461	312	690	134	14	50	309	.280	191	487	102	1282	48	26	.981

ALL-STAR GAME RECORD

Year	League	Pos.	AB	R	H	2B	3B	HR	RBI	Avg.	BB	SO	SB	PO	A	E	Avg.
			BATTING											FIELDING			
1991—	National	OF	2	0	1	0	0	0	0	.500	0	0	0	1	0	0	1.000

JOYNER, WALLY — 1B — PADRES

PERSONAL: Born June 16, 1962, in Atlanta. . . . 6-2/200. . . . Bats left, throws left. . . . Full name: Wallace Keith Joyner.

HIGH SCHOOL: Redan (Stone Mountain, Ga.).

COLLEGE: Brigham Young.

TRANSACTIONS/CAREER NOTES: Selected by California Angels organization in third round of free-agent draft (June 6, 1983); pick received as compensation for New York Yankees signing free-agent DH Don Baylor. . . . On disabled list (July 12, 1990-remainder of season). . . . Granted free agency (October 28, 1991). . . . Signed by Kansas City Royals (December 9, 1991). . . . On disabled list (June 26-July 14, 1994). . . . Traded by Royals with P Aaron Dorlarque to San Diego Padres for 2B/OF Bip Roberts and P Bryan Wolff (December 21, 1995).

RECORDS: Shares major league record for most home runs in month of October—4 (1987).

STATISTICAL NOTES: Tied for Eastern League lead with eight intentional bases on balls received in 1984. . . . Led Pacific Coast League first basemen with 1,229 total chances and 121 double plays in 1985. . . . Led A.L. with 12 sacrifice flies in 1986. . . . Hit three home runs in one game (October 3, 1987). . . . Led A.L. first basemen with 1,520 total chances in 1988 and 1,441 in 1991. . . . Led A.L. first basemen with 148 double plays in 1988 and 138 in 1992. . . . Career major league grand slams: 5.

Year	Team (League)	Pos.	G	AB	R	H	2B	3B	HR	RBI	Avg.	BB	SO	SB	PO	A	E	Avg.
				BATTING											FIELDING			
1983—	Peoria (Midwest)	1B	54	192	25	63	16	2	3	33	.328	19	25	1	480	45	6	.989
1984—	Waterbury (East.)	1B-OF	134	467	81	148	24	7	12	72	.317	67	60	0	906	86	9	.991
1985—	Edmonton (PCL)	1B	126	477	68	135	29	5	12	73	.283	60	64	2	*1107	*107	•15	.988
1986—	California (A.L.)	1B	154	593	82	172	27	3	22	100	.290	57	58	5	1222	139	15	.989
1987—	California (A.L.)	1B	149	564	100	161	33	1	34	117	.285	72	64	8	1276	92	10	.993
1988—	California (A.L.)	1B	158	597	81	176	31	2	13	85	.295	55	51	8	*1369	*143	8	.995
1989—	California (A.L.)	1B	159	593	78	167	30	2	16	79	.282	46	58	3	*1487	99	4	*.997
1990—	California (A.L.)	1B	83	310	35	83	15	0	8	41	.268	41	34	2	727	62	4	.995
1991—	California (A.L.)	1B	143	551	79	166	34	3	21	96	.301	52	66	2	*1335	98	8	.994
1992—	Kansas City (A.L.)■	1B-DH	149	572	66	154	36	2	9	66	.269	55	50	11	1236	137	10	.993
1993—	Kansas City (A.L.)	1B	141	497	83	145	36	3	15	65	.292	66	67	5	1116	145	7	.994
1994—	Kansas City (A.L.)	1B-DH	97	363	52	113	20	3	8	57	.311	47	43	3	777	64	8	.991
1995—	Kansas City (A.L.)	1B-DH	131	465	69	144	28	0	12	83	.310	69	65	3	1111	118	3	*.998
Major league totals (10 years)			1364	5105	725	1481	290	19	158	789	.290	560	556	50	11656	1097	77	.994

CHAMPIONSHIP SERIES RECORD

Year	Team (League)	Pos.	G	AB	R	H	2B	3B	HR	RBI	Avg.	BB	SO	SB	PO	A	E	Avg.
				BATTING											FIELDING			
1986—	California (A.L.)	1B	3	11	3	5	2	0	1	2	.455	2	0	0	24	1	0	1.000

ALL-STAR GAME RECORD

Year	League	Pos.	AB	R	H	2B	3B	HR	RBI	Avg.	BB	SO	SB	PO	A	E	Avg.
			BATTING											FIELDING			
1986—	American	1B	1	0	0	0	0	0	0	.000	0	0	0	3	1	0	1.000

JUDEN, JEFF — P — GIANTS

PERSONAL: Born January 19, 1971, in Salem, Mass. . . . 6-8/265. . . . Throws right, bats right. . . . Full name: Jeffrey Daniel Juden. . . . Cousin of Daniel Juden, right winger, Tampa Bay Lightning organization. . . . Name pronounced JOO-den.

HIGH SCHOOL: Salem (Mass.).

TRANSACTIONS/CAREER NOTES: Selected by Houston Astros organization in first round (12th pick overall) of free-agent draft (June 5, 1989). . . . On disabled list (June 14-21, 1992). . . . Traded by Astros with P Doug Jones to Philadelphia Phillies for P Mitch Williams (December 2, 1993). . . . On Scranton/Wilkes-Barre disabled list (June 22-July 24 and July 25, 1994-remainder of season). . . . Traded by Phillies with OF/1B Tommy Eason to San Francisco Giants for IF Mike Benjamin (October 6, 1995).

STATISTICAL NOTES: Led Pacific Coast League with seven balks in 1992. . . . Career major league grand slams: 1.

Year	Team (League)	W	L	Pct.	ERA	G	GS	CG	ShO	Sv.	IP	H	R	ER	BB	SO
1989—	Sarasota (Fla. St.)	1	4	.200	3.40	9	8	0	0	0	39 2/3	33	21	15	17	49
1990—	Osceola (Florida St.)	10	1	*.909	2.27	15	15	2	1	0	91	72	37	23	42	85
—	Chatt. (South.)	1	3	.250	5.37	11	11	0	0	0	52	55	36	31	42	40
1991—	Jackson (Texas)	6	3	.667	3.10	16	16	0	0	0	95 2/3	84	43	33	44	75
—	Tucson (Pac. Coast)	3	2	.600	3.18	10	10	0	0	0	56 2/3	56	28	20	25	51
—	Houston (N.L.)	0	2	.000	6.00	4	3	0	0	0	18	19	14	12	7	11
1992—	Tucson (Pac. Coast)	9	10	.474	4.04	26	26	0	0	0	147	149	84	66	71	120
1993—	Tucson (Pac. Coast)	11	6	.647	4.63	27	27	0	0	0	169	174	102	87	*76	156

Year	Team (League)	W	L	Pct.	ERA	G	GS	CG	ShO	Sv.	IP	H	R	ER	BB	SO
	—Houston (N.L.)	0	1	.000	5.40	2	0	0	0	0	5	4	3	3	4	7
1994	—Philadelphia (N.L.)■	1	4	.200	6.18	6	5	0	0	0	27 2/3	29	25	19	12	22
	—Scran./W.B. (Int'l)	2	2	.500	8.53	6	6	0	0	0	25 1/3	30	28	24	19	28
1995	—Scran./W.B. (Int'l)	6	4	.600	4.10	14	13	0	0	0	83 1/3	73	43	38	33	65
	—Philadelphia (N.L.)	2	4	.333	4.02	13	10	1	0	0	62 2/3	53	31	28	31	47
Major league totals (4 years)		3	11	.214	4.92	25	18	1	0	0	113 1/3	105	73	62	54	87

JUELSGAARD, JAROD — P — MARLINS

PERSONAL: Born June 27, 1968, in Harlan, Ia. . . . 6-3/195. . . . Throws right, bats right. . . . Full name: Jarod Del Juelsgaard.
HIGH SCHOOL: Elk Horn (Ia.)-Kimballton.
JUNIOR COLLEGE: Waldorf (Ia.).
COLLEGE: Iowa State.
TRANSACTIONS/CAREER NOTES: Selected by San Francisco Giants organization in 27th round of free-agent draft (June 3, 1991). . . . Traded by Giants organization with IF Andres Santana to Florida Marlins organization for P Brian Griffiths (April 3, 1993).

Year	Team (League)	W	L	Pct.	ERA	G	GS	CG	ShO	Sv.	IP	H	R	ER	BB	SO
1991	—Everett (N'west)	3	5	.375	4.33	20	6	0	0	3	62 1/3	61	36	30	27	46
1992	—Clinton (Midwest)	6	9	.400	5.28	35	9	1	0	2	76 2/3	86	58	45	52	60
1993	—Kane Co. (Mid.)■	3	0	1.000	3.81	11	2	1	0	0	26	21	11	11	7	18
	—High Desert (Calif.)	6	5	.545	5.56	17	16	0	0	0	79 1/3	81	57	49	58	58
1994	—Portland (Eastern)	4	9	.308	6.60	36	12	0	0	0	92 2/3	115	74	68	55	55
1995	—Portland (Eastern)	3	1	.750	3.89	48	0	0	0	2	71 2/3	65	35	31	44	44

JUSTICE, DAVID — OF — BRAVES

PERSONAL: Born April 14, 1966, in Cincinnati. . . . 6-3/200. . . . Bats left, throws left. . . . Full name: David Christopher Justice.
HIGH SCHOOL: Covington (Ky.) Latin.
COLLEGE: Thomas More College (Ky.).
TRANSACTIONS/CAREER NOTES: Selected by Atlanta Braves organization in fourth round of free-agent draft (June 3, 1985). . . . On Atlanta disabled list (June 27-August 20, 1991); included rehabilitation assignment to Macon (August 16-20). . . . On disabled list (April 12-27, 1992 and June 2-17, 1995).
RECORDS: Holds major league single-season record for fewest errors by outfielder who led league in errors—8 (1992).
HONORS: Named N.L. Rookie Player of the Year by The Sporting News (1990). . . . Named N.L. Rookie of the Year by Baseball Writers' Association of America (1990). . . . Named outfielder on The Sporting News N.L. All-Star team (1993). . . . Named outfielder on The Sporting News N.L. Silver Slugger team (1993).
STATISTICAL NOTES: Tied for Appalachian League lead with five sacrifice flies in 1985. . . . Career major league grand slams: 1.

							BATTING								FIELDING			
Year	Team (League)	Pos.	G	AB	R	H	2B	3B	HR	RBI	Avg.	BB	SO	SB	PO	A	E	Avg.
1985	—Pulaski (Appal.)	OF	66	204	39	50	8	0	•10	46	.245	40	30	0	86	2	4	.957
1986	—Sumter (S. Atl.)	OF	61	220	48	66	16	0	10	61	.300	48	28	10	124	7	4	.970
	—Durham (Carolina)	OF-1B	67	229	47	64	9	1	12	44	.279	46	24	2	163	5	1	.994
1987	—Greenville (South.)	OF	93	348	38	79	12	4	6	40	.227	53	48	3	199	4	8	.962
1988	—Richmond (Int'l)	OF	70	227	27	46	9	1	8	28	.203	39	55	4	136	5	4	.972
	—Greenville (South.)	OF	58	198	34	55	13	1	9	37	.278	37	41	6	100	3	5	.954
1989	—Richmond (Int'l)	OF-1B	115	391	47	102	24	3	12	58	.261	59	66	12	220	15	6	.975
	—Atlanta (N.L.)	OF	16	51	7	12	3	0	1	3	.235	3	9	2	24	0	0	1.000
1990	—Richmond (Int'l)	OF-1B	12	45	7	16	5	1	2	7	.356	7	6	0	23	4	2	.931
	—Atlanta (N.L.)	1B-OF	127	439	76	124	23	2	28	78	.282	64	92	11	604	42	14	.979
1991	—Atlanta (N.L.)	OF	109	396	67	109	25	1	21	87	.275	65	81	8	204	9	7	.968
	—Macon (S. Atl.)	OF	3	10	2	2	0	0	2	5	.200	2	1	0	1	0	0	1.000
1992	—Atlanta (N.L.)	OF	144	484	78	124	19	5	21	72	.256	79	85	2	313	8	*8	.976
1993	—Atlanta (N.L.)	OF	157	585	90	158	15	4	40	120	.270	78	90	3	323	9	5	.985
1994	—Atlanta (N.L.)	OF	104	352	61	110	16	2	19	59	.313	69	45	2	192	6	*11	.947
1995	—Atlanta (N.L.)	OF	120	411	73	104	17	2	24	78	.253	73	68	4	233	8	4	.984
Major league totals (7 years)			777	2718	452	741	118	16	154	497	.273	431	470	32	1893	82	49	.976

DIVISION SERIES RECORD

							BATTING								FIELDING			
Year	Team (League)	Pos.	G	AB	R	H	2B	3B	HR	RBI	Avg.	BB	SO	SB	PO	A	E	Avg.
1995	—Atlanta (N.L.)	OF	4	13	2	3	0	0	0	0	.231	5	2	0	6	0	1	.857

CHAMPIONSHIP SERIES RECORD

							BATTING								FIELDING			
Year	Team (League)	Pos.	G	AB	R	H	2B	3B	HR	RBI	Avg.	BB	SO	SB	PO	A	E	Avg.
1991	—Atlanta (N.L.)	OF	7	25	4	5	1	0	1	2	.200	3	7	0	17	0	1	.944
1992	—Atlanta (N.L.)	OF	7	25	5	7	1	0	2	6	.280	6	2	0	19	3	0	1.000
1993	—Atlanta (N.L.)	OF	6	21	2	3	1	0	0	4	.143	3	3	0	14	0	1	.933
1995	—Atlanta (N.L.)	OF	3	11	1	3	0	0	0	1	.273	2	1	0	0	0	0	...
Championship series totals (4 years)			23	82	12	18	3	0	3	13	.220	14	13	0	50	3	2	.964

WORLD SERIES RECORD

NOTES: Member of World Series championship team (1995).

							BATTING								FIELDING			
Year	Team (League)	Pos.	G	AB	R	H	2B	3B	HR	RBI	Avg.	BB	SO	SB	PO	A	E	Avg.
1991	—Atlanta (N.L.)	OF	7	27	5	7	0	0	2	6	.259	5	5	2	21	1	1	.957
1992	—Atlanta (N.L.)	OF	6	19	4	3	0	0	1	3	.158	6	5	1	15	0	1	.938
1995	—Atlanta (N.L.)	OF	6	20	3	5	1	0	1	5	.250	5	1	0	16	0	0	1.000
World Series totals (3 years)			19	66	12	15	1	0	4	14	.227	16	11	3	52	1	2	.964

J K

ALL-STAR GAME RECORD

Year	League	Pos.	AB	R	H	2B	3B	HR	RBI	Avg.	BB	SO	SB	PO	A	E	Avg.
			BATTING											FIELDING			
1993—	National	OF	3	0	1	0	0	0	0	.333	0	0	0	1	0	1	.500
1994—	National	OF	2	0	0	0	0	0	0	.000	0	0	0	1	0	0	1.000
All-Star Game totals (2 years)			5	0	1	0	0	0	0	.200	0	0	0	2	0	1	.667

KAMIENIECKI, SCOTT — P — YANKEES

PERSONAL: Born April 19, 1964, in Mt. Clemens, Mich. . . . 6-0/195. . . . Throws right, bats right. . . . Full name: Scott Andrew Kamieniecki. . . . Name pronounced KAM-ah-NIK-ee.

HIGH SCHOOL: Redford St. Mary's (Detroit).

COLLEGE: Michigan (degree in physical education).

TRANSACTIONS/CAREER NOTES: Selected by Detroit Tigers organization in second round of free-agent draft (June 7, 1982); did not sign. . . . Selected by Milwaukee Brewers organization in 23rd round of free-agent draft (June 3, 1985); did not sign. . . . Selected by New York Yankees organization in 14th round of free-agent draft (June 2, 1986). . . . On New York disabled list (August 3, 1991-remainder of season). . . . On New York disabled list (April 2-29, 1992); included rehabilitation assignments to Fort Lauderdale (April 9-17) and Columbus (April 17-29). . . . On New York disabled list (May 6-July 15, 1995); included rehabilitation assignments to Tampa (July 5-10) and Columbus (July 10-12).

Year	Team (League)	W	L	Pct.	ERA	G	GS	CG	ShO	Sv.	IP	H	R	ER	BB	SO
1987—	Alb./Colon. (East.)	1	3	.250	5.35	10	7	0	0	0	37	41	25	22	33	19
—	Prin. William (Caro.)	9	5	.643	4.17	19	19	1	0	0	112 1/3	91	61	52	78	84
1988—	Prin. William (Caro.)	6	7	.462	4.40	15	15	•7	2	0	100 1/3	115	62	49	50	72
—	Fort Lauder. (FSL)	3	6	.333	3.62	12	11	1	1	0	77	71	36	31	40	51
1989—	Alb./Colon. (East.)	10	9	.526	3.70	24	23	6	3	1	151	142	67	62	57	*140
1990—	Alb./Colon. (East.)	10	9	.526	3.20	22	21	3	1	0	132	113	55	47	61	99
1991—	Columbus (Int'l)	6	3	.667	2.36	11	11	3	1	0	76 1/3	61	25	20	20	58
—	New York (A.L.)	4	4	.500	3.90	9	9	0	0	0	55 1/3	54	24	24	22	34
1992—	Fort Lauder. (FSL)	1	0	1.000	1.29	1	1	1	0	0	7	8	1	1	0	3
—	Columbus (Int'l)	1	0	1.000	0.69	2	2	0	0	0	13	6	1	1	4	12
—	New York (A.L.)	6	14	.300	4.36	28	28	4	0	0	188	193	100	91	74	88
1993—	New York (A.L.)	10	7	.588	4.08	30	20	2	0	1	154 1/3	163	73	70	59	72
—	Columbus (Int'l)	1	0	1.000	1.50	1	1	0	0	0	6	5	1	1	0	4
1994—	New York (A.L.)	8	6	.571	3.76	22	16	1	0	0	117 1/3	115	53	49	59	71
1995—	New York (A.L.)	7	6	.538	4.01	17	16	1	0	0	89 2/3	83	43	40	49	43
—	Tampa (Fla. St.)	1	0	1.000	1.80	1	1	0	0	0	5	6	2	1	1	2
—	Columbus (Int'l)	1	0	1.000	0.00	1	1	0	0	0	6 2/3	2	0	0	1	10
Major league totals (5 years)		35	37	.486	4.08	106	89	8	0	1	604 2/3	608	293	274	263	308

DIVISION SERIES RECORD

Year	Team (League)	W	L	Pct.	ERA	G	GS	CG	ShO	Sv.	IP	H	R	ER	BB	SO
1995—	New York (A.L.)	0	0	...	7.20	1	1	0	0	0	5	9	5	4	4	4

KARCHNER, MATT — P — WHITE SOX

PERSONAL: Born June 28, 1967, in Berwick, Pa. . . . 6-4/210. . . . Throws right, bats right. . . . Full name: Matthew Dean Karchner.

HIGH SCHOOL: Berwick (Pa.).

COLLEGE: Bloomsburg (Pa.).

TRANSACTIONS/CAREER NOTES: Selected by Kansas City Royals organization in eighth round of free-agent draft (June 5, 1989). . . . On disabled list (August 1-8, 1991). . . . Selected by Montreal Expos from Royals organization in Rule 5 major league draft (December 9, 1991). . . . Returned to Royals (April 4, 1992). . . . On disabled list (September 2-18, 1992 and May 10, 1993-remainder of season). . . . Selected by Nashville, Chicago White Sox organization, from Memphis, Royals organization, in Rule 5 minor league draft (December 13, 1993).

Year	Team (League)	W	L	Pct.	ERA	G	GS	CG	ShO	Sv.	IP	H	R	ER	BB	SO
1989—	Eugene (N'west)	1	1	.500	3.90	8	5	0	0	0	30	30	19	13	8	25
1990—	Appleton (Midw.)	2	7	.222	4.82	27	11	1	0	0	71	70	42	38	31	58
1991—	Baseball City (FSL)	6	3	.667	1.97	38	0	0	0	5	73	49	28	16	25	65
1992—	Memphis (South.)	8	8	.500	4.47	33	18	2	0	1	141	161	83	70	35	88
1993—	Memphis (South.)	3	2	.600	4.20	6	5	0	0	0	30	34	16	14	4	14
1994—	Birmingham (Sou.)■	5	2	.714	1.26	39	0	0	0	6	43	36	10	6	14	29
—	Nashville (A.A.)	4	2	.667	1.37	17	0	0	0	2	26 1/3	18	5	4	7	19
1995—	Nashville (A.A.)	3	3	.500	1.45	28	0	0	0	9	37 1/3	39	7	6	10	29
—	Chicago (A.L.)	4	2	.667	1.69	31	0	0	0	0	32	33	8	6	12	24
Major league totals (1 year)		4	2	.667	1.69	31	0	0	0	0	32	33	8	6	12	24

KARKOVICE, RON — C — WHITE SOX

PERSONAL: Born August 8, 1963, in Union, N.J. . . . 6-1/219. . . . Bats right, throws right. . . . Full name: Ronald Joseph Karkovice. . . . Name pronounced CAR-ko-VICE.

HIGH SCHOOL: Boone (Orlando, Fla.).

TRANSACTIONS/CAREER NOTES: Selected by Chicago White Sox organization in first round (14th pick overall) of free-agent draft (June 7, 1982). . . . On disabled list (May 20-July 3, 1991; June 20-July 6, 1993 and July 18, 1994-remainder of season).

STATISTICAL NOTES: Led Gulf Coast League catchers with 394 total chances and tied for lead with five double plays in 1982. . . . Led Midwest League catchers with .996 fielding percentage in 1983. . . . Led Eastern League catchers with 13 double plays in 1985. . . . Career major league grand slams: 5.

Year	Team (League)	Pos.	G	AB	R	H	2B	3B	HR	RBI	Avg.	BB	SO	SB	PO	A	E	Avg.
				BATTING											FIELDING			
1982—	GC Whi. Sox (GCL)	C	60	214	34	56	6	0	7	32	.262	29	*73	5	*331	*51	12	.970

Year	Team (League)	Pos.	G	AB	R	H	2B	3B	HR	RBI	Avg.	BB	SO	SB	PO	A	E	Avg.
							BATTING								FIELDING			
1983—	Appleton (Midw.)	C-OF	97	326	54	78	17	3	13	48	.239	31	90	10	682	91	4	†.995
1984—	Glens Falls (East.)	C	88	260	37	56	9	1	13	39	.215	25	102	3	442	*68	11	.979
—	Denver (A.A.)	C	31	86	7	19	1	0	2	10	.221	8	25	1	149	28	3	.983
1985—	Glens Falls (East.)	C	99	324	37	70	9	3	11	37	.216	49	104	6	573	*103	*14	.980
1986—	Birm. (Southern)	C	97	319	63	90	13	1	20	53	.282	61	109	2	463	72	10	.982
—	Chicago (A.L.)	C	37	97	13	24	7	0	4	13	.247	9	37	1	227	19	1	.996
1987—	Chicago (A.L.)	C-DH	39	85	7	6	0	0	2	7	.071	7	40	3	147	20	3	.982
—	Hawaii (PCL)	C-OF	34	104	15	19	3	0	4	11	.183	8	37	3	108	13	3	.976
1988—	Vancouver (PCL)	C	39	116	12	29	10	0	2	13	.250	8	26	2	202	16	3	.986
—	Chicago (A.L.)	C	46	115	10	20	4	0	3	9	.174	7	30	4	190	24	1	.995
1989—	Chicago (A.L.)	C-DH	71	182	21	48	9	2	3	24	.264	10	56	0	299	47	5	.986
1990—	Chicago (A.L.)	C-DH	68	183	30	45	10	0	6	20	.246	16	52	2	296	31	2	.994
1991—	Chicago (A.L.)	C-OF	75	167	25	41	13	0	5	22	.246	15	42	0	309	28	4	.988
1992—	Chicago (A.L.)	C-OF	123	342	39	81	12	1	13	50	.237	30	89	10	536	53	6	.990
1993—	Chicago (A.L.)	C	128	403	60	92	17	1	20	54	.228	29	126	2	769	63	5	.994
1994—	Chicago (A.L.)	C	77	207	33	44	9	1	11	29	.213	36	68	0	417	19	3	.993
1995—	Chicago (A.L.)	C	113	323	44	70	14	1	13	51	.217	39	84	2	629	42	6	.991
Major league totals (10 years)			777	2104	282	471	95	6	80	279	.224	198	624	24	3819	346	36	.991

CHAMPIONSHIP SERIES RECORD

Year	Team (League)	Pos.	G	AB	R	H	2B	3B	HR	RBI	Avg.	BB	SO	SB	PO	A	E	Avg.
							BATTING								FIELDING			
1993—	Chicago (A.L.)	C-PR	6	15	0	0	0	0	0	0	.000	1	7	0	30	2	0	1.000

KARL, SCOTT — P — BREWERS

PERSONAL: Born August 9, 1971, in Fontana, Calif. . . . 6-2/195. . . . Throws left, bats left. . . . Full name: Randall Scott Karl.
HIGH SCHOOL: Carlsbad (Calif.).
COLLEGE: Hawaii.
TRANSACTIONS/CAREER NOTES: Selected by Milwaukee Brewers organization in sixth round of free-agent draft (June 1, 1992). . . . On New Orleans disabled list (April 27-May 31, 1994).
STATISTICAL NOTES: Tied for Texas League lead with seven balks in 1993.

Year	Team (League)	W	L	Pct.	ERA	G	GS	CG	ShO	Sv.	IP	H	R	ER	BB	SO
1992—	Helena (Pioneer)	7	0	•1.000	*1.46	9	9	1	1	0	61 2/3	54	13	10	16	57
1993—	El Paso (Texas)	13	8	.619	2.45	27	•27	•4	•2	0	*180	172	67	49	35	95
1994—	New Orleans (A.A.)	5	5	.500	3.84	15	13	2	0	0	89	92	38	38	33	54
—	El Paso (Texas)	5	1	.833	2.96	8	8	3	0	0	54 2/3	44	21	18	15	51
1995—	New Orleans (A.A.)	3	4	.429	3.30	8	6	1	1	0	46 1/3	47	18	17	12	29
—	Milwaukee (A.L.)	6	7	.462	4.14	25	18	1	0	0	124	141	65	57	50	59
Major league totals (1 year)		6	7	.462	4.14	25	18	1	0	0	124	141	65	57	50	59

KARP, RYAN — P — PHILLIES

PERSONAL: Born April 5, 1970, in Los Angeles. . . . 6-4/214. . . . Throws left, bats left. . . . Full name: Ryan Jason Karp.
HIGH SCHOOL: Beverly Hills (Calif.).
JUNIOR COLLEGE: Los Angeles Harbor.
COLLEGE: Miami (Fla.), then Florida International.
TRANSACTIONS/CAREER NOTES: Selected by Houston Astros organization in 73rd round of free-agent draft (June 5, 1989); did not sign. . . . Selected by New York Yankees organization in ninth round of free-agent draft (June 1, 1992). . . . Traded by Yankees organization with P Bobby Munoz and 2B Kevin Jordan to Philadelphia Phillies organization for P Terry Mulholland and a player to be named later (February 9, 1994); Yankees acquired P Jeff Patterson to complete deal (November 8, 1994). . . . On disabled list (May 13-June 25, 1994). . . . On Scranton/Wilkes-Barre disabled list (April 17-May 12, 1995).
HONORS: Named South Atlantic League Most Outstanding Pitcher (1993).

Year	Team (League)	W	L	Pct.	ERA	G	GS	CG	ShO	Sv.	IP	H	R	ER	BB	SO
1992—	Oneonta (NYP)	6	4	.600	4.09	14	13	1	1	0	70 1/3	66	38	32	30	58
1993—	Greensboro (S. Atl.)	13	1	*.929	1.81	17	17	0	0	0	109 1/3	73	26	22	40	132
—	Prin. William (Caro.)	3	2	.600	2.20	8	8	1	1	0	49	35	17	12	12	34
—	Albany (Eastern)	0	0	. . .	4.15	3	3	0	0	0	13	13	7	6	9	10
1994—	Reading (Eastern)■	4	11	.267	4.45	21	21	0	0	0	121 1/3	123	67	60	54	96
1995—	Reading (Eastern)	1	2	.333	3.06	7	7	0	0	0	47	44	18	16	15	37
—	Philadelphia (N.L.)	0	0	. . .	4.50	1	0	0	0	0	2	1	1	1	3	2
—	Scran./W.B. (Int'l)	7	1	.875	4.20	13	13	0	0	0	81 1/3	81	43	38	31	73
Major league totals (1 year)		0	0	. . .	4.50	1	0	0	0	0	2	1	1	1	3	2

KARROS, ERIC — 1B — DODGERS

PERSONAL: Born November 4, 1967, in Hackensack, N.J. . . . 6-4/222. . . . Bats right, throws right. . . . Full name: Eric Peter Karros. . . . Name pronounced CARE-ose.
HIGH SCHOOL: Patrick Henry (San Diego).
COLLEGE: UCLA.
TRANSACTIONS/CAREER NOTES: Selected by Los Angeles Dodgers organization in sixth round of free-agent draft (June 1, 1988).
HONORS: Named N.L. Rookie Player of the Year by The Sporting News (1992). . . . Named N.L. Rookie of the Year by Baseball Writers' Association of America (1992). . . . Named first baseman on The Sporting News N.L. All-Star team (1995). . . . Named first baseman on The Sporting News N.L. Silver Slugger team (1995).
STATISTICAL NOTES: Tied for Pioneer League lead in errors by first baseman with 14 in 1988. . . . Led California League first basemen with

1,232 putouts, 110 assists and 1,358 total chances in 1989. . . . Led Texas League with 282 total bases in 1990. . . . Led Texas League first basemen with 1,337 total chances and 129 double plays in 1990. . . . Led Pacific Coast League with 269 total bases in 1991. . . . Tied for Pacific Coast League lead with eight intentional bases on balls received in 1991. . . . Led Pacific Coast League first basemen with 1,095 putouts, 109 assists and 1,215 total chances in 1991.

			BATTING												FIELDING			
Year	Team (League)	Pos.	G	AB	R	H	2B	3B	HR	RBI	Avg.	BB	SO	SB	PO	A	E	Avg.
1988—	Great Falls (Pio.)	1B-3B	66	268	68	98	12	1	12	55	.366	32	35	8	516	31	‡19	.966
1989—	Bakersfield (Calif.)	1B-3B	*142	545	86	*165	*40	1	15	86	.303	63	99	18	†1238	†113	19	.986
1990—	San Antonio (Tex.)	1B	•131	509	91	*179	*45	2	18	78	*.352	57	79	8	*1223	*106	8	*.994
1991—	Albuquerque (PCL)	1B-3B	132	488	88	154	33	8	22	101	.316	58	80	3	†1095	†109	11	.991
—	Los Angeles (N.L.)	1B	14	14	0	1	1	0	0	1	.071	1	6	0	33	2	0	1.000
1992—	Los Angeles (N.L.)	1B	149	545	63	140	30	1	20	88	.257	37	103	2	1211	126	9	.993
1993—	Los Angeles (N.L.)	1B	158	619	74	153	27	2	23	80	.247	34	82	0	1335	*147	12	.992
1994—	Los Angeles (N.L.)	1B	111	406	51	108	21	1	14	46	.266	29	53	2	896	118	•9	.991
1995—	Los Angeles (N.L.)	1B	143	551	83	164	29	3	32	105	.298	61	115	4	1234	109	7	.995
Major league totals (5 years)			575	2135	271	566	108	7	89	320	.265	162	359	8	4709	502	37	.993

DIVISION SERIES RECORD

			BATTING												FIELDING			
Year	Team (League)	Pos.	G	AB	R	H	2B	3B	HR	RBI	Avg.	BB	SO	SB	PO	A	E	Avg.
1995—	Los Angeles (N.L.)	1B	3	12	3	6	1	0	2	4	.500	1	0	0	14	0	0	1.000

KARSAY, STEVE — P — ATHLETICS

PERSONAL: Born March 24, 1972, in College Point, N.Y. . . . 6-3/205. . . . Throws right, bats right. . . . Full name: Stefan Andrew Karsay. . . . Name pronounced CAR-say.

HIGH SCHOOL: Christ the King (Queens, N.Y.).

TRANSACTIONS/CAREER NOTES: Selected by Toronto Blue Jays organization in first round (22nd pick overall) of free-agent draft (June 4, 1990). . . . On Knoxville disabled list (July 3-16, 1993). . . . Traded by Blue Jays with a player to be named later to Oakland Athletics for OF Rickey Henderson (July 31, 1993); A's acquired OF Jose Herrera to complete deal (August 6, 1993). . . . On disabled list (April 26, 1994-remainder of season and April 24, 1995-entire season).

Year	Team (League)	W	L	Pct.	ERA	G	GS	CG	ShO	Sv.	IP	H	R	ER	BB	SO
1990—	St. Cathar. (NYP)	1	1	.500	0.79	5	5	0	0	0	22 2/3	11	4	2	12	25
1991—	Myrtle Beach (SAL)	4	9	.308	3.58	20	20	1	0	0	110 2/3	96	58	44	48	100
1992—	Dunedin (Fla. St.)	6	3	.667	2.73	16	16	3	2	0	85 2/3	56	32	26	29	87
1993—	Knoxville (South.)	8	4	.667	3.38	19	18	1	0	0	104	98	42	39	32	100
—	Huntsville (South.)■	0	0	...	5.14	2	2	0	0	0	14	13	8	8	3	22
—	Oakland (A.L.)	3	3	.500	4.04	8	8	0	0	0	49	49	23	22	16	33
1994—	Oakland (A.L.)	1	1	.500	2.57	4	4	1	0	0	28	26	8	8	8	15
1995—		Did not play.														
Major league totals (2 years)		4	4	.500	3.51	12	12	1	0	0	77	75	31	30	24	48

KAUFMAN, BRAD — P — PADRES

PERSONAL: Born April 26, 1972, in Marshalltown, Ia. . . . 6-2/210. . . . Throws right, bats right. . . . Full name: Bradley Joseph Kaufman.

HIGH SCHOOL: North Tama County (Traer, Ia.).

COLLEGE: Iowa State.

TRANSACTIONS/CAREER NOTES: Selected by San Diego Padres organization in 16th round of free-agent draft (June 3, 1993).

Year	Team (League)	W	L	Pct.	ERA	G	GS	CG	ShO	Sv.	IP	H	R	ER	BB	SO
1993—	Spokane (N'west)	5	4	.556	6.88	25	8	1	0	4	53 2/3	56	56	41	41	48
1994—	Springfield (Midw.)	10	9	.526	3.34	31	20	3	0	0	145 1/3	124	62	54	63	122
1995—	Memphis (South.)	11	10	.524	5.76	27	27	0	0	0	148 1/3	142	*112	•95	*90	119

KEAGLE, GREG — P — TIGERS

PERSONAL: Born June 20, 1971, in Corning, N.Y. . . . 6-1/185. . . . Throws right, bats right. . . . Full name: Gregory Charles Keagle.

HIGH SCHOOL: Horseheads (N.Y.) Central.

TRANSACTIONS/CAREER NOTES: Selected by San Diego Padres organization in sixth round of free-agent draft (June 3, 1993). . . . Traded by Padres organization to Seattle Mariners organization (September 16, 1995), completing deal in which Padres traded P Andy Benes and a player to be named later to Mariners for P Ron Villone and OF Marc Newfield (July 31, 1995). . . . Selected by Detroit Tigers from Mariners organization in Rule 5 major league draft (December 4, 1995).

Year	Team (League)	W	L	Pct.	ERA	G	GS	CG	ShO	Sv.	IP	H	R	ER	BB	SO
1993—	Spokane (N'west)	3	3	.500	3.25	15	15	1	0	0	83	80	37	30	40	77
1994—	Rancho Cuca. (Cal.)	11	1	.917	2.05	14	14	1	1	0	92	62	23	21	41	91
—	Wichita (Texas)	3	9	.250	6.27	13	13	0	0	0	70 1/3	84	53	49	32	57
1995—	Memphis (South.)	4	9	.308	5.11	15	15	1	0	0	81	82	52	46	41	82
—	Rancho Cuca. (Cal.)	0	0	...	4.50	2	2	0	0	0	14	14	9	7	2	11
—	Las Vegas (PCL)	7	6	.538	4.28	14	13	0	0	0	75 2/3	76	47	36	42	49

KELLY, MIKE — OF — REDS

PERSONAL: Born June 2, 1970, in Los Angeles. . . . 6-4/195. . . . Bats right, throws right. . . . Full name: Michael Raymond Kelly.

HIGH SCHOOL: Los Alamitos (Calif.).

COLLEGE: Arizona State.

TRANSACTIONS/CAREER NOTES: Selected by New York Mets organization in 24th round of free-agent draft (June 1, 1988); did not sign. . . . Selected by Atlanta Braves organization in first round (second pick overall) of free-agent draft (June 3, 1991). . . . Traded by Braves to

Cincinnati Reds for P Chad Fox and a player to be named later (January 9, 1996).
HONORS: Named College Player of the Year by The Sporting News (1990).... Named outfielder on The Sporting News college All-America team (1990).... Named Golden Spikes Award winner by USA Baseball (1991).

Year	Team (League)	Pos.	G	BATTING AB	R	H	2B	3B	HR	RBI	Avg.	BB	SO	SB	FIELDING PO	A	E	Avg.
1991	—Durham (Carolina)	OF	35	124	29	31	6	1	6	17	.250	19	47	6	4	0	0	1.000
1992	—Greenville (South.)	OF	133	471	83	108	18	4	25	71	.229	65	*162	22	244	7	3	.988
1993	—Richmond (Int'l)	OF	123	424	63	103	13	1	19	58	.243	36	109	11	270	6	2	*.993
1994	—Atlanta (N.L.)	OF	30	77	14	21	10	1	2	9	.273	2	17	0	25	0	1	.962
	—Richmond (Int'l)	OF	81	313	46	82	14	4	15	45	.262	32	96	9	181	5	1	.995
1995	—Richmond (Int'l)	OF	15	45	5	13	1	0	2	8	.289	5	17	0	24	0	0	1.000
	—Atlanta (N.L.)	OF	97	137	26	26	6	1	3	17	.190	11	49	7	63	0	4	.940
Major league totals (2 years)			127	214	40	47	16	2	5	26	.220	13	66	7	88	0	5	.946

KELLY, PAT — 2B — YANKEES

PERSONAL: Born October 14, 1967, in Philadelphia.... 6-0/182.... Bats right, throws right.... Full name: Patrick Franklin Kelly.
HIGH SCHOOL: Catashuqua (Pa.).
COLLEGE: West Chester (Pa.).
TRANSACTIONS/CAREER NOTES: Selected by New York Yankees organization in ninth round of free-agent draft (June 1, 1988).... On New York disabled list (April 21-May 7, 1992); included rehabilitation assignment to Albany/Colonie (May 5-7).... On New York disabled list (June 22-July 7, 1994); included rehabilitation assignment to Albany/Colonie (July 6-7).... On New York disabled list (May 27-July 7, 1995); included rehabilitation assignments to Gulf Coast Yankees (July 3-4) and Tampa (July 4-7).
STATISTICAL NOTES: Led Carolina League second basemen with 76 double plays and tied for lead with 641 total chances in 1989.... Led Eastern League second basemen with 667 total chances and 97 double plays in 1990.... Led A.L. with 14 sacrifice hits in 1994.

Year	Team (League)	Pos.	G	BATTING AB	R	H	2B	3B	HR	RBI	Avg.	BB	SO	SB	FIELDING PO	A	E	Avg.
1988	—Oneonta (NYP)	2B-SS	71	280	49	92	11	6	2	34	.329	15	45	25	124	207	16	.954
1989	—Prin. William (Car.)	2B	124	436	61	116	21	*7	3	45	.266	32	79	31	244	*372	25	.961
1990	—Alb./Colon. (East.)	2B	126	418	67	113	19	6	8	44	.270	37	79	31	*266	*381	*20	.970
1991	—Columbus (Int'l)	2B	31	116	27	39	9	2	3	19	.336	9	16	8	53	97	4	.974
	—New York (A.L.)	3B-2B	96	298	35	72	12	4	3	23	.242	15	52	12	78	204	18	.940
1992	—New York (A.L.)	2B-DH	106	318	38	72	22	2	7	27	.226	25	72	8	203	296	11	.978
	—Alb./Colon. (East.)	2B	2	6	1	0	0	0	0	0	.000	2	4	0	4	8	0	1.000
1993	—New York (A.L.)	2B	127	406	49	111	24	1	7	51	.273	24	68	14	245	369	14	.978
1994	—New York (A.L.)	2B	93	286	35	80	21	2	3	41	.280	19	51	6	180	258	10	.978
	—Alb./Colon. (East.)	2B	1	4	1	1	0	0	0	0	.250	0	1	1	2	2	0	1.000
1995	—New York (A.L.)	2B-DH	89	270	32	64	12	1	4	29	.237	23	65	8	161	255	7	.983
	—GC Yankees (GCL)	2B	1	2	2	0	0	0	0	1	.000	1	0	0	3	3	0	1.000
	—Tampa (Fla. St.)	2B	3	17	0	4	1	0	0	2	.235	0	1	0	8	14	0	1.000
Major league totals (5 years)			511	1578	189	399	91	10	24	171	.253	106	308	48	867	1382	60	.974

DIVISION SERIES RECORD

Year	Team (League)	Pos.	G	BATTING AB	R	H	2B	3B	HR	RBI	Avg.	BB	SO	SB	FIELDING PO	A	E	Avg.
1995	—New York (A.L.)	2B-PR	5	3	3	0	0	0	0	1	.000	1	3	0	2	4	0	1.000

KELLY, ROBERTO — OF

PERSONAL: Born October 1, 1964, in Panama City, Panama.... 6-2/202.... Bats right, throws right.... Full name: Roberto Conrado Kelly.
HIGH SCHOOL: Panama City (Panama).
COLLEGE: Jose Dolores Moscote College (Panama).
TRANSACTIONS/CAREER NOTES: Signed as non-drafted free agent by New York Yankees organization (February 21, 1982).... On disabled list (July 10-August 23, 1986).... On New York disabled list (June 29-September 1, 1988; May 26-June 12, 1989; and July 6-August 13, 1991).... Traded by Yankees to Cincinnati Reds for OF Paul O'Neill and 1B Joe DeBerry (November 3, 1992).... On disabled list (July 14, 1993-remainder of season).... Traded by Reds with P Roger Etheridge to Atlanta Braves for OF Deion Sanders (May 29, 1994).... Traded by Braves with OF Tony Tarasco and P Esteban Yan to Montreal Expos for OF Marquis Grissom (April 6, 1995).... Traded by Expos with P Joey Eischen to Los Angeles Dodgers for OF Henry Rodriguez and IF Jeff Treadway (May 23, 1995).... Granted free agency (November 6, 1995).
RECORDS: Holds major league single-season record for most times reaching base on catcher's interference—8 (1992).... Shares major league single-season record for fewest double plays by outfielder (150 or more games)—0 (1990).
STATISTICAL NOTES: Led International League outfielders with 345 total chances in 1987.... Led A.L. outfielders with 430 total chances in 1990.... Career major league grand slams: 1.
MISCELLANEOUS: Batted as switch-hitter (1985).

Year	Team (League)	Pos.	G	BATTING AB	R	H	2B	3B	HR	RBI	Avg.	BB	SO	SB	FIELDING PO	A	E	Avg.
1982	—GC Yankees (GCL)	SS-OF	31	86	13	17	1	1	1	18	.198	10	18	3	47	79	19	.869
1983	—Oneonta (NYP)	OF-3B	48	167	17	36	1	2	2	17	.216	12	20	12	70	3	5	.936
	—Greensboro (S. Atl.)	OF-SS	20	49	6	13	0	0	0	3	.265	3	5	3	30	2	0	1.000
1984	—Greensboro (S. Atl.)	OF-1B	111	361	68	86	13	2	1	26	.238	57	49	42	228	5	4	.983
1985	—Fort Lauder. (FSL)	OF	114	417	86	103	4	*13	3	38	.247	58	70	49	187	1	1	.995
1986	—Alb./Colon. (East.)	OF	86	299	42	87	11	4	2	43	.291	29	63	10	206	8	7	.968
1987	—Columbus (Int'l)	OF	118	471	77	131	19	8	13	62	.278	33	116	*51	*331	4	10	.971
	—New York (A.L.)	OF-DH	23	52	12	14	3	0	1	7	.269	5	15	9	42	0	2	.955
1988	—New York (A.L.)	OF-DH	38	77	9	19	4	1	1	7	.247	3	15	5	70	1	1	.986
	—Columbus (Int'l)	OF	30	120	25	40	8	1	3	16	.333	6	29	11	51	1	0	1.000
1989	—New York (A.L.)	OF	137	441	65	133	18	3	9	48	.302	41	89	35	353	9	6	.984
1990	—New York (A.L.)	OF	*162	641	85	183	32	4	15	61	.285	33	148	42	420	5	5	.988

Year Team (League)	Pos.	G	AB	R	H	2B	3B	HR	RBI	Avg.	BB	SO	SB	PO	A	E	Avg.
			BATTING											FIELDING			
1991—New York (A.L.)	OF	126	486	68	130	22	2	20	69	.267	45	77	32	268	8	4	.986
1992—New York (A.L.)	OF	152	580	81	158	31	2	10	66	.272	41	96	28	389	8	7	.983
1993—Cincinnati (N.L.)■	OF	78	320	44	102	17	3	9	35	.319	17	43	21	198	3	1	.995
1994—Cincinnati (N.L.)	OF	47	179	29	54	8	0	3	21	.302	11	35	9	118	2	1	.992
—Atlanta (N.L.)■	OF	63	255	44	73	15	3	6	24	.286	24	36	10	128	3	2	.985
1995—Montreal (N.L.)■	OF	24	95	11	26	4	0	1	9	.274	7	14	4	42	1	0	1.000
—Los Angeles (N.L.)■	OF	112	409	47	114	19	2	6	48	.279	15	65	15	183	2	6	.969
American League totals (6 years)		638	2277	320	637	110	12	56	258	.280	168	440	151	1542	31	25	.984
National League totals (3 years)		324	1258	175	369	63	8	25	137	.293	74	193	59	669	11	10	.986
Major league totals (9 years)		962	3535	495	1006	173	20	81	395	.285	242	633	210	2211	42	35	.985

DIVISION SERIES RECORD

Year Team (League)	Pos.	G	AB	R	H	2B	3B	HR	RBI	Avg.	BB	SO	SB	PO	A	E	Avg.
			BATTING											FIELDING			
1995—Los Angeles (N.L.)	OF	3	11	0	4	0	0	0	0	.364	1	0	0	8	0	1	.889

ALL-STAR GAME RECORD

Year League	Pos.	AB	R	H	2B	3B	HR	RBI	Avg.	BB	SO	SB	PO	A	E	Avg.
		BATTING											FIELDING			
1992—American	OF	2	0	1	1	0	0	2	.500	0	1	0	1	0	0	1.000
1993—National	OF	1	0	0	0	0	0	0	.000	0	1	0	0	1	0	1.000
All-Star Game totals (2 years)		3	0	1	1	0	0	2	.333	0	2	0	1	1	0	1.000

KENDALL, JASON — C — PIRATES

PERSONAL: Born June 26, 1974, in San Diego. . . . 6-0/181. . . . Bats right, throws right. . . . Full name: Jason Daniel Kendall. . . . Son of Fred Kendall, catcher/first baseman with San Diego Padres, Cleveland Indians and Boston Red Sox (1969-80).
HIGH SCHOOL: Torrance (Calif.).
TRANSACTIONS/CAREER NOTES: Selected by Pittsburgh Pirates organization in first round (23rd pick overall) of free-agent draft (June 1, 1992).
HONORS: Named Southern League Most Valuable Player (1995).
STATISTICAL NOTES: Led Gulf Coast League with 13 passed balls in 1992. . . . Led Southern League with .414 on-base percentage in 1995. . . . Led Southern League catchers with 754 total chances in 1995.

Year Team (League)	Pos.	G	AB	R	H	2B	3B	HR	RBI	Avg.	BB	SO	SB	PO	A	E	Avg.
			BATTING											FIELDING			
1992—GC Pirates (GCL)	C	33	111	7	29	2	0	0	10	.261	8	9	2	182	36	5	.978
1993—Augusta (S. Atl.)	C	102	366	43	101	17	4	1	40	.276	22	30	8	472	65	20	.964
1994—Salem (Carolina)	C	101	371	68	118	19	2	7	66	.318	47	21	14	409	33	9	.980
—Carolina (South.)	C	13	47	6	11	2	0	0	6	.234	2	3	0	54	9	2	.969
1995—Carolina (South.)	C	117	429	87	140	26	1	8	71	.326	56	22	10	*692	54	8	.989

KENT, JEFF — 2B — METS

PERSONAL: Born March 7, 1968, in Bellflower, Calif. . . . 6-1/185. . . . Bats right, throws right. . . . Full name: Jeffrey Franklin Kent.
HIGH SCHOOL: Edison (Huntington Beach, Calif.).
COLLEGE: California.
TRANSACTIONS/CAREER NOTES: Selected by Toronto Blue Jays organization in 20th round of free-agent draft (June 5, 1989). . . . Traded by Blue Jays with a player to be named later to New York Mets for P David Cone (August 27, 1992); Mets acquired OF Ryan Thompson to complete deal (September 1, 1992). . . . On disabled list (July 6-21, 1995).
STATISTICAL NOTES: Led Florida State League second basemen with 680 total chances and 83 double plays in 1990. . . . Led Southern League second basemen with 673 total chances and 96 double plays in 1991. . . . Led N.L. second basemen with 18 errors in 1993. . . . Career major league grand slams: 2.

Year Team (League)	Pos.	G	AB	R	H	2B	3B	HR	RBI	Avg.	BB	SO	SB	PO	A	E	Avg.
			BATTING											FIELDING			
1989—St. Cathar. (NYP)	SS-3B	73	268	34	60	14	1	*13	37	.224	33	81	5	103	178	29	.906
1990—Dunedin (Fla. St.)	2B	132	447	72	124	32	2	16	60	.277	53	98	17	*261	*404	15	.978
1991—Knoxville (South.)	2B	•139	445	68	114	*34	1	2	61	.256	80	104	25	249	*395	*29	.957
1992—Toronto (A.L.)	3B-2B-1B	65	192	36	46	13	1	8	35	.240	20	47	2	62	112	11	.941
—New York (N.L.)■	2B-SS-3B	37	113	16	27	8	1	3	15	.239	7	29	0	62	93	3	.981
1993—New York (N.L.)	2B-3B-SS	140	496	65	134	24	0	21	80	.270	30	88	4	261	341	†22	.965
1994—New York (N.L.)	2B	107	415	53	121	24	5	14	68	.292	23	84	1	222	337	•14	.976
1995—New York (N.L.)	2B	125	472	65	131	22	3	20	65	.278	29	89	3	245	354	10	.984
American League totals (1 year)		65	192	36	46	13	1	8	35	.240	20	47	2	62	112	11	.941
National League totals (4 years)		409	1496	199	413	78	9	58	228	.276	89	290	8	790	1125	49	.975
Major league totals (4 years)		474	1688	235	459	91	10	66	263	.272	109	337	10	852	1237	60	.972

KEY, JIMMY — P — YANKEES

PERSONAL: Born April 22, 1961, in Huntsville, Ala. . . . 6-1/185. . . . Throws left, bats right. . . . Full name: James Edward Key.
HIGH SCHOOL: Butler (Huntsville, Ala.).
COLLEGE: Clemson.
TRANSACTIONS/CAREER NOTES: Selected by Chicago White Sox organization in 10th round of free-agent draft (June 5, 1979); did not sign. . . . Selected by Toronto Blue Jays organization in third round of free-agent draft (June 7, 1982). . . . On Toronto disabled list (April 15-June 29, 1988); included rehabilitation assignment to Dunedin (June 10-27). . . . On disabled list (August 4-19, 1989). . . . On Toronto disabled list (May 23-June 22, 1990); included rehabilitation assignment to Dunedin (June 7-18). . . . Granted free agency (October 27, 1992). . . .

Signed by New York Yankees (December 10, 1992). . . . On disabled list (May 17, 1995-remainder of season).

HONORS: Named A.L. Pitcher of the Year by The Sporting News (1987 and 1994). . . . Named lefthanded pitcher on The Sporting News A.L. All-Star team (1987 and 1993-94).

STATISTICAL NOTES: Pitched 5-0 one-hit, complete-game victory against Chicago (May 22, 1986). . . . Pitched 5-0 one-hit, complete-game victory against California (April 27, 1993).

MISCELLANEOUS: Appeared in one game as pinch-runner (1985).

Year Team (League)	W	L	Pct.	ERA	G	GS	CG	ShO	Sv.	IP	H	R	ER	BB	SO
1982— Medicine Hat (Pio.)	2	1	.667	2.30	5	5	1	0	0	31 1/3	27	12	8	10	25
— Florence (S. Atl.)	5	2	.714	3.72	9	9	0	0	0	58	59	33	24	18	49
1983— Knoxville (South.)	6	5	.545	2.85	14	14	2	0	0	101	86	35	32	40	57
— Syracuse (Int'l)	4	8	.333	4.13	16	15	2	0	0	89 1/3	87	58	41	33	71
1984— Toronto (A.L.)	4	5	.444	4.65	63	0	0	0	10	62	70	37	32	32	44
1985— Toronto (A.L.)	14	6	.700	3.00	35	32	3	0	0	212 2/3	188	77	71	50	85
1986— Toronto (A.L.)	14	11	.560	3.57	36	35	4	2	0	232	222	98	92	74	141
1987— Toronto (A.L.)	17	8	.680	*2.76	36	36	8	1	0	261	210	93	80	66	161
1988— Toronto (A.L.)	12	5	.706	3.29	21	21	2	2	0	131 1/3	127	55	48	30	65
— Dunedin (Fla. St.)	2	0	1.000	0.00	4	4	0	0	0	21 1/3	15	2	0	1	11
1989— Toronto (A.L.)	13	14	.481	3.88	33	33	5	1	0	216	226	99	93	27	118
1990— Toronto (A.L.)	13	7	.650	4.25	27	27	0	0	0	154 2/3	169	79	73	22	88
— Dunedin (Fla. St.)	2	0	1.000	2.50	3	3	0	0	0	18	21	7	5	3	14
1991— Toronto (A.L.)	16	12	.571	3.05	33	33	2	2	0	209 1/3	207	84	71	44	125
1992— Toronto (A.L.)	13	13	.500	3.53	33	33	4	2	0	216 2/3	205	88	85	59	117
1993— New York (A.L.)■	18	6	.750	3.00	34	34	4	2	0	236 2/3	219	84	79	43	173
1994— New York (A.L.)	*17	4	.810	3.27	25	•25	1	0	0	168	177	68	61	52	97
1995— New York (A.L.)	1	2	.333	5.64	5	5	0	0	0	30 1/3	40	20	19	6	14
Major league totals (12 years)	152	93	.620	3.40	381	314	33	12	10	2130 2/3	2060	882	804	505	1228

CHAMPIONSHIP SERIES RECORD

Year Team (League)	W	L	Pct.	ERA	G	GS	CG	ShO	Sv.	IP	H	R	ER	BB	SO
1985— Toronto (A.L.)	0	1	.000	5.19	2	2	0	0	0	8 2/3	15	5	5	2	5
1989— Toronto (A.L.)	1	0	1.000	4.50	1	1	0	0	0	6	7	3	3	2	2
1991— Toronto (A.L.)	0	0	...	3.00	1	1	0	0	0	6	5	2	2	1	1
1992— Toronto (A.L.)	0	0	...	0.00	1	0	0	0	0	3	2	0	0	2	1
Champ. series totals (4 years)	1	1	.500	3.80	5	4	0	0	0	23 2/3	29	10	10	7	9

WORLD SERIES RECORD

NOTES: Member of World Series championship team (1992).

Year Team (League)	W	L	Pct.	ERA	G	GS	CG	ShO	Sv.	IP	H	R	ER	BB	SO
1992— Toronto (A.L.)	2	0	1.000	1.00	2	1	0	0	0	9	6	2	1	0	6

ALL-STAR GAME RECORD

Year League	W	L	Pct.	ERA	GS	CG	ShO	Sv.	IP	H	R	ER	BB	SO
1985— American	0	0	...	0.00	0	0	0	0	1/3	0	0	0	0	0
1991— American	1	0	1.000	0.00	0	0	0	0	1	1	0	0	0	1
1993— American	0	0	...	9.00	0	0	0	0	1	2	1	1	0	1
1994— American	0	0	...	4.50	1	0	0	0	2	1	1	1	0	1
All-Star totals (4 years)	1	0	1.000	4.15	1	0	0	0	4 1/3	4	2	2	0	3

KEYSER, BRIAN — P — WHITE SOX

PERSONAL: Born October 31, 1966, in Castro Valley, Calif. . . . 6-1/180. . . . Throws right, bats right.

HIGH SCHOOL: Chico (Calif.).

COLLEGE: Stanford.

TRANSACTIONS/CAREER NOTES: Selected by Chicago White Sox organization in 19th round of free-agent draft (June 5, 1989).

Year Team (League)	W	L	Pct.	ERA	G	GS	CG	ShO	Sv.	IP	H	R	ER	BB	SO
1989— Utica (NYP)	4	4	.500	2.98	14	13	2	0	0	93 2/3	79	37	31	22	70
1990— Sarasota (Fla. St.)	6	7	.462	3.66	38	10	2	1	2	115 2/3	107	54	47	40	83
1991— Sarasota (Fla. St.)	6	7	.462	2.30	27	14	2	1	2	129	110	40	33	45	94
— Birmingham (Sou.)	0	1	.000	5.00	3	3	0	0	0	18	19	10	10	9	9
1992— Birmingham (Sou.)	9	10	.474	3.73	28	27	7	3	0	183 1/3	173	86	76	60	99
1993— Birmingham (Sou.)	0	2	.000	5.73	2	2	1	0	0	11	15	9	7	5	8
— Nashville (A.A.)	9	5	.643	4.66	30	16	2	0	1	121 2/3	142	70	63	27	44
1994— Birmingham (Sou.)	0	0	...	1.50	1	1	0	0	0	6	4	1	1	1	5
— Nashville (A.A.)	9	5	.643	2.79	37	10	2	1	2	135 2/3	123	49	42	36	76
1995— Nashville (A.A.)	2	4	.333	2.36	10	10	2	1	0	72 1/3	49	23	19	9	40
— Chicago (A.L.)	5	6	.455	4.97	23	10	0	0	0	92 1/3	114	53	51	27	48
Major league totals (1 year)	5	6	.455	4.97	23	10	0	0	0	92 1/3	114	53	51	27	48

KIEFER, MARK — P — BREWERS

PERSONAL: Born November 13, 1968, in Orange, Calif. . . . 6-4/184. . . . Throws right, bats right. . . . Full name: Mark Andrew Kiefer.

HIGH SCHOOL: Garden Grove (Calif.).

COLLEGE: Cal State Fullerton.

TRANSACTIONS/CAREER NOTES: Selected by Milwaukee Brewers organization in 21st round of free-agent draft (June 2, 1987). . . . On New Orleans disabled list (April 8-May 25, 1993). . . . On El Paso disabled list (June 2-17, 1993).

STATISTICAL NOTES: Led American Association with 25 home runs allowed in 1992.

Year Team (League)	W	L	Pct.	ERA	G	GS	CG	ShO	Sv.	IP	H	R	ER	BB	SO
1988— Helena (Pioneer)	4	4	.500	2.65	15	9	2	0	0	68	76	30	20	17	51
1989— Beloit (Midwest)	9	6	.600	2.32	30	15	7	2	1	131 2/3	106	44	34	32	100
1990— Ariz. Brewers (Ar.)	0	0	...	3.38	1	1	0	0	0	2 2/3	3	1	1	1	2

Year	Team (League)	W	L	Pct.	ERA	G	GS	CG	ShO	Sv.	IP	H	R	ER	BB	SO
	—Stockton (Calif.)	5	2	.714	3.30	11	10	0	0	0	60	65	23	22	17	37
1991—	El Paso (Texas)	7	1	.875	3.33	12	12	0	0	0	75 2/3	62	33	28	43	72
	—Denver (Am. Assoc.)	9	5	.643	4.62	17	17	3	2	0	101 1/3	104	55	52	41	68
1992—	Denver (Am. Assoc.)	7	*13	.350	4.59	27	26	1	0	0	162 2/3	168	95	83	65	*145
1993—	El Paso (Texas)	3	4	.429	4.01	11	11	0	0	0	51 2/3	48	29	23	19	44
	—New Orleans (A.A.)	3	2	.600	5.08	5	5	0	0	0	28 1/3	28	20	16	17	23
	—Milwaukee (A.L.)	0	0	...	0.00	6	0	0	0	1	9 1/3	3	0	0	5	7
1994—	Milwaukee (A.L.)	1	0	1.000	8.44	7	0	0	0	0	10 2/3	15	12	10	8	8
	—New Orleans (A.A.)	9	7	.563	3.90	21	21	0	0	0	124 2/3	111	61	54	48	116
1995—	Milwaukee (A.L.)	4	1	.800	3.44	24	0	0	0	0	49 2/3	37	20	19	27	41
	—New Orleans (A.A.)	8	2	.800	2.82	12	12	1	0	0	70 1/3	60	22	22	19	52
Major league totals (3 years)		5	1	.833	3.75	37	0	0	0	1	69 2/3	55	32	29	40	56

K

KIESCHNICK, BROOKS — OF — CUBS

PERSONAL: Born June 6, 1972, in Robstown, Tex. . . . 6-4/225. . . . Bats left, throws right. . . . Full name: Michael Brooks Kieschnick. . . . Name pronounced KEY-shnik.
HIGH SCHOOL: Carroll (Corpus Christi, Tex.).
COLLEGE: Texas.
TRANSACTIONS/CAREER NOTES: Selected by Chicago Cubs organization in first round (10th pick overall) of free-agent draft (June 3, 1993).
STATISTICAL NOTES: Led American Association with 250 total bases in 1995.

				BATTING											FIELDING			
Year	Team (League)	Pos.	G	AB	R	H	2B	3B	HR	RBI	Avg.	BB	SO	SB	PO	A	E	Avg.
1993—	GC Cubs (GCL)	OF	3	9	0	2	1	0	0	0	.222	0	1	0	3	1	0	1.000
	—Daytona (Fla. St.)	OF	6	22	1	4	2	0	0	2	.182	1	4	0	9	1	0	1.000
	—Orlando (Southern)	OF	25	91	12	31	8	0	2	10	.341	7	19	1	22	1	3	.885
1994—	Orlando (Southern)	OF-1B-3B	126	468	57	132	25	3	14	55	.282	33	78	3	259	14	6	.978
1995—	Iowa (Am. Assoc.)	OF-1B	138	505	61	*149	30	1	*23	73	.295	58	91	2	179	15	2	.990

KILE, DARRYL — P — ASTROS

PERSONAL: Born December 2, 1968, in Garden Grove, Calif. . . . 6-5/185. . . . Throws right, bats right. . . . Full name: Darryl Andrew Kile.
COLLEGE: Chaffey College (Calif.).
TRANSACTIONS/CAREER NOTES: Selected by Houston Astros organization in 30th round of free-agent draft (June 2, 1987). . . . On Tucson disabled list (June 25-July 5, 1992).
STATISTICAL NOTES: Led N.L. with 15 hit batsmen in 1993. . . . Pitched 7-1 no-hit victory against New York (September 8, 1993). . . . Tied for N.L. lead with 10 wild pitches in 1994.

Year	Team (League)	W	L	Pct.	ERA	G	GS	CG	ShO	Sv.	IP	H	R	ER	BB	SO
1988—	GC Astros (GCL)	5	3	.625	3.17	12	12	0	0	0	59 2/3	48	34	21	33	54
1989—	Chatt. (South.)	11	6	.647	2.58	20	20	6	•2	0	125 2/3	74	47	36	68	108
	—Tucson (Pac. Coast)	2	1	.667	5.96	6	6	1	1	0	25 2/3	33	20	17	13	18
1990—	Tucson (Pac. Coast)	5	10	.333	6.64	26	23	1	0	0	123 1/3	147	97	91	68	77
1991—	Houston (N.L.)	7	11	.389	3.69	37	22	0	0	0	153 2/3	144	81	63	84	100
1992—	Houston (N.L.)	5	10	.333	3.95	22	22	2	0	0	125 1/3	124	61	55	63	90
	—Tucson (Pac. Coast)	4	1	.800	3.99	9	9	0	0	0	56 1/3	50	31	25	32	43
1993—	Houston (N.L.)	15	8	.652	3.51	32	26	4	2	0	171 2/3	152	73	67	69	141
1994—	Houston (N.L.)	9	6	.600	4.57	24	24	0	0	0	147 2/3	153	84	75	*82	105
1995—	Houston (N.L.)	4	12	.250	4.96	25	21	0	0	0	127	114	81	70	73	113
	—Tucson (Pac. Coast)	2	1	.667	8.51	4	4	0	0	0	24 1/3	29	23	23	12	15
Major league totals (5 years)		40	47	.460	4.09	140	115	6	2	0	725 1/3	687	380	330	371	549

ALL-STAR GAME RECORD

Year	League	W	L	Pct.	ERA	GS	CG	ShO	Sv.	IP	H	R	ER	BB	SO
1993—	National						Did not play.								

KING, ANDRE — OF — REDS

PERSONAL: Born November 26, 1973, in Kingston, Jamaica . . . 6-1/180. . . . Bats right, throws right. . . . Full name: Andre Omar King.
HIGH SCHOOL: Stranahan (Fort Lauderdale, Fla.).
TRANSACTIONS/CAREER NOTES: Selected by Atlanta Braves organization in second round of free-agent draft (June 3, 1993). . . . Traded by Braves to Chicago White Sox organization for OF Mike Devereaux (August 26, 1995). . . . Selected by St. Louis Cardinals from White Sox organization in Rule 5 major league draft (December 4, 1995). . . . Traded by Cardinals to Cincinnati Reds as part of a three-team deal in which Reds sent SS Luis Ordaz to Cardinals and P Mike Remlinger to Kansas City Royals. Royals then sent OF Miguel Mejia to Cardinals to complete deal (December 4, 1995).
STATISTICAL NOTES: Led Carolina League outfielders with 279 putouts and 1.000 fielding percentage in 1995.

				BATTING											FIELDING			
Year	Team (League)	Pos.	G	AB	R	H	2B	3B	HR	RBI	Avg.	BB	SO	SB	PO	A	E	Avg.
1993—	Danville (Appal.)	OF	60	223	41	69	10	6	0	18	.309	36	40	15	133	1	6	.957
1994—	Macon (S. Atl.)	OF	129	496	80	122	22	6	4	38	.246	34	139	31	269	5	9	.968
1995—	Durham (Carolina)	OF	111	421	59	106	22	3	9	33	.252	39	126	15	261	9	0	1.000
	—Prin. William (Car.)■	OF	9	32	4	5	1	1	0	3	.156	6	9	1	§18	0	0	§1.000

KING, BRETT — SS — GIANTS

PERSONAL: Born July 20, 1972, in Orlando, Fla. . . . 6-1/190. . . . Bats right, throws right. . . . Full name: Brett Alan King.

HIGH SCHOOL: Apopka (Fla.).
COLLEGE: South Florida.
TRANSACTIONS/CAREER NOTES: Selected by San Francisco Giants organization in supplemental round ("sandwich pick" between second and third round) of free-agent draft (June 3, 1993); pick received as part of compensation for Houston Astros signing Type C free-agent OF Chris James.
STATISTICAL NOTES: Led Northwest League shortstops with 340 total chances in 1993.

			BATTING											FIELDING			
Year	Team (League)	Pos.	G	AB	R	H	2B	3B	HR	RBI	Avg.	BB	SO	SB	PO	A	E	Avg.
1993—	Everett (N'west)	SS	69	243	43	55	10	0	2	24	.226	40	63	26	120	*193	*27	.921
1994—	San Jose (Calif.)	SS	48	188	24	47	8	2	1	11	.250	19	62	6	73	160	27	.896
	—Clinton (Midwest)	SS	68	261	45	57	13	2	5	30	.218	23	86	12	112	217	25	.929
1995—	San Jose (Calif.)	SS	107	394	61	108	29	4	3	41	.274	41	86	28	165	269	23	.950

KING, JEFF — 3B/1B — PIRATES

PERSONAL: Born December 26, 1964, in Marion, Ind. . . . 6-1/184. . . . Bats right, throws right. . . . Full name: Jeffrey Wayne King. . . . Son of Jack King, minor league catcher (1954-55).
HIGH SCHOOL: Rampart (Colorado Springs, Colo.).
COLLEGE: Arkansas.
TRANSACTIONS/CAREER NOTES: Selected by Chicago Cubs organization in 23rd round of free-agent draft (June 6, 1983); did not sign. . . . Selected by Pittsburgh Pirates organization in first round (first pick overall) of free-agent draft (June 2, 1986). . . . On Pittsburgh disabled list (May 5-31, 1991); included rehabilitation assignment to Buffalo (May 25-31). . . . On Pittsburgh disabled list (June 13-October 7, 1991); included rehabilitation assignment to Buffalo (August 28-September 6). . . . On disabled list (May 25-June 9, 1994 and June 16-July 1, 1995).
RECORDS: Shares major league single-inning record for most home runs—2 (August 8, 1995, second inning).
HONORS: Named College Player of the Year by The Sporting News (1986). . . . Named third baseman on The Sporting News college All-America team (1986).
STATISTICAL NOTES: Led Carolina League with .565 slugging percentage in 1987. . . . Led N.L. third basemen with 353 assists and 475 total chances in 1993. . . . Led N.L. third basemen with 27 double plays in 1994. . . . Career major league grand slams: 3.

			BATTING											FIELDING			
Year	Team (League)	Pos.	G	AB	R	H	2B	3B	HR	RBI	Avg.	BB	SO	SB	PO	A	E	Avg.
1986—	Prin. William (Car.)	3B	37	132	18	31	4	1	6	20	.235	19	34	1	25	50	8	.904
1987—	Salem (Carolina)	1B-3B	90	310	68	86	9	1	26	71	.277	61	88	6	572	106	13	.981
	—Harrisburg (East.)	1B	26	100	12	24	7	0	2	25	.240	4	27	0	107	10	1	.992
1988—	Harrisburg (East.)	3B	117	411	49	105	21	1	14	66	.255	46	87	5	97	208	24	.927
1989—	Buffalo (A.A.)	1B-3B	51	169	26	43	5	2	6	29	.254	57	60	11	213	61	8	.972
	—Pittsburgh (N.L.)	1-3-2-S	75	215	31	42	13	3	5	19	.195	20	34	4	403	59	4	.991
1990—	Pittsburgh (N.L.)	3B-1B	127	371	46	91	17	1	14	53	.245	21	50	3	61	215	18	.939
1991—	Pittsburgh (N.L.)	3B	33	109	16	26	1	1	4	18	.239	14	15	3	15	62	2	.975
	—Buffalo (A.A.)	3B	9	18	3	4	1	1	0	2	.222	6	3	1	2	8	1	.909
1992—	Pittsburgh (N.L.)	3-2-1-S-O	130	480	56	111	21	2	14	65	.231	27	56	4	368	234	12	.980
	—Buffalo (A.A.)	3B-1B-2B	7	29	6	10	2	0	2	5	.345	2	2	1	21	12	0	1.000
1993—	Pittsburgh (N.L.)	3B-SS-2B	158	611	82	180	35	3	9	98	.295	59	54	8	108	†362	18	.963
1994—	Pittsburgh (N.L.)	3B-2B	94	339	36	89	23	0	5	42	.263	30	38	3	61	198	13	.952
1995—	Pittsburgh (N.L.)	3-1-2-S	122	445	61	118	27	2	18	87	.265	55	63	7	352	206	17	.970
Major league totals (7 years)			739	2570	328	657	137	12	69	382	.256	226	310	32	1368	1336	84	.970

CHAMPIONSHIP SERIES RECORD

NOTES: Shares single-series record for most doubles—4 (1992).

			BATTING											FIELDING			
Year	Team (League)	Pos.	G	AB	R	H	2B	3B	HR	RBI	Avg.	BB	SO	SB	PO	A	E	Avg.
1990—	Pittsburgh (N.L.)	3B-PH	5	10	0	1	0	0	0	0	.100	1	5	0	1	4	0	1.000
1992—	Pittsburgh (N.L.)	3B	7	29	4	7	4	0	0	2	.241	0	1	0	11	19	1	.968
Championship series totals (2 years)			12	39	4	8	4	0	0	2	.205	1	6	0	12	23	1	.972

KING, KEVIN — P — MARINERS

PERSONAL: Born February 11, 1969, in Atwater, Calif. . . . 6-4/200. . . . Throws left, bats left. . . . Full name: Kevin Ray King.
HIGH SCHOOL: Braggs (Okla.).
COLLEGE: Oklahoma.
TRANSACTIONS/CAREER NOTES: Selected by Toronto Blue Jays organization in ninth round of free-agent draft (June 2, 1987); did not sign. . . . Selected by Seattle Mariners organization in seventh round of free-agent draft (June 4, 1990). . . . On disabled list (May 29-July 20, 1991).

Year	Team (League)	W	L	Pct.	ERA	G	GS	CG	ShO	Sv.	IP	H	R	ER	BB	SO
1990—	Bellingham (N'west)	3	2	.600	4.78	6	6	0	0	0	32	37	18	17	10	27
	—Peninsula (Caro.)	4	2	.667	4.46	7	7	0	0	0	36 1/3	42	23	18	13	20
1991—	Peninsula (Caro.)	6	7	.462	4.37	17	17	2	1	0	92 2/3	99	55	45	38	59
1992—	San Bern. (Calif.)	7	*16	.304	5.32	27	27	0	0	0	165 2/3	*226	*118	*98	55	101
1993—	Riverside (Calif.)	3	2	.600	1.57	25	0	0	0	5	46	37	10	8	20	28
	—Jacksonville (Sou.)	2	0	1.000	3.14	16	0	0	0	1	28 2/3	25	10	10	7	13
	—Seattle (A.L.)	0	1	.000	6.17	13	0	0	0	0	11 2/3	9	8	8	4	8
1994—	Seattle (A.L.)	0	2	.000	7.04	19	0	0	0	0	15 1/3	21	13	12	17	6
	—Calgary (PCL)	1	2	.333	5.65	25	0	0	0	1	36 2/3	46	27	23	18	29
1995—	Seattle (A.L.)	0	0	...	12.27	2	0	0	0	0	3 2/3	7	5	5	1	3
	—Tacoma (PCL)	0	0	...	7.56	16	0	0	0	0	16 2/3	33	14	14	7	10
	—Port City (Southern)	1	2	.333	3.77	20	0	0	0	0	31	35	15	13	11	19
Major league totals (3 years)		0	3	.000	7.34	34	0	0	0	0	30 2/3	37	26	25	22	17

KINGERY, MIKE OF PIRATES

PERSONAL: Born March 29, 1961, in St. James, Minn. . . . 6-0/185. . . . Bats left, throws left. . . . Full name: Michael Scott Kingery.
HIGH SCHOOL: Atwater (Minn.).
JUNIOR COLLEGE: Willmar (Minn.) Community College.
COLLEGE: St. Cloud State (Minn.).
TRANSACTIONS/CAREER NOTES: Signed as non-drafted free agent by Kansas City Royals organization (August 27, 1979). . . . On disabled list (July 29-August 15, 1981). . . . Traded by Royals with P Scott Bankhead and P Steve Shields to Seattle Mariners for OF Danny Tartabull and P Rick Luecken (December 10, 1986). . . . Granted free agency (April 6, 1990). . . . Signed by Phoenix, San Francisco Giants organization (April 14, 1990). . . . Released by Giants (October 6, 1991). . . . Signed by Oakland Athletics organization (December 27, 1991). . . . Granted free agency (October 16, 1992). . . . Signed by Royals organization (January 23, 1993). . . . Granted free agency (October 15, 1993). . . . Signed by Colorado Rockies organization (December 3, 1993). . . . Granted free agency (November 1, 1995). . . . Signed by Pittsburgh Pirates (December 14, 1995).
STATISTICAL NOTES: Tied for South Atlantic League lead in double plays by outfielder with five in 1982. . . . Led Florida State League with 11 intentional bases on balls received in 1983. . . . Tied for American Association lead in double plays by outfielder with five in 1993. . . . Career major league grand slams: 1.

			BATTING												FIELDING			
Year	Team (League)	Pos.	G	AB	R	H	2B	3B	HR	RBI	Avg.	BB	SO	SB	PO	A	E	Avg.
1980	—GC Royals (GCL)	OF	44	143	12	32	3	3	0	13	.224	21	23	4	78	5	2	.976
1981	—Char., S.C. (S. Atl.)	OF	69	213	33	57	3	4	3	25	.268	26	45	12	80	7	4	.956
1982	—Char., S.C. (S. Atl.)	OF	140	513	65	163	19	4	8	75	.318	62	77	25	250	21	7	.975
1983	—Fort Myers (FSL)	OF	123	436	68	116	9	7	2	51	.266	56	70	31	200	16	5	.977
1984	—Memphis (South.)	OF	139	455	65	135	19	3	4	58	.297	93	61	18	291	18	6	.981
1985	—Omaha (A.A.)	OF	132	444	51	113	25	6	2	49	.255	61	58	16	247	17	5	.981
1986	—Omaha (A.A.)	OF	79	298	47	99	14	8	3	47	.332	39	30	22	171	10	1	.995
	—Kansas City (A.L.)	OF	62	209	25	54	8	5	3	14	.258	12	30	7	102	6	3	.973
1987	—Seattle (A.L.)■	OF-DH	120	354	38	99	25	4	9	52	.280	27	43	7	226	15	2	.992
1988	—Seattle (A.L.)	OF-1B	57	123	21	25	6	0	1	9	.203	19	23	3	102	6	2	.982
	—Calgary (PCL)	OF-1B	47	170	29	54	12	2	1	14	.318	33	23	6	144	4	3	.980
1989	—Calgary (PCL)	OF-1B	107	396	72	115	22	9	4	47	.290	47	52	7	289	10	1	.997
	—Seattle (A.L.)	OF	31	76	14	17	3	0	2	6	.224	7	14	1	70	0	0	1.000
1990	—Phoenix (PCL)■	OF	35	100	12	24	9	2	1	16	.240	18	15	2	61	4	1	.985
	—San Francisco (N.L.)	OF	105	207	24	61	7	1	0	24	.295	12	19	6	126	7	3	.978
1991	—San Francisco (N.L.)	OF-1B	91	110	13	20	2	2	0	8	.182	15	21	1	60	2	1	.984
	—Phoenix (PCL)	OF	13	44	8	15	3	0	1	13	.341	6	6	0	32	0	0	1.000
1992	—Oakland (A.L.)■	OF	12	28	3	3	0	0	0	1	.107	1	3	0	14	0	0	1.000
	—Tacoma (PCL)	OF-1B	99	363	44	111	18	4	1	37	.306	33	27	8	218	13	3	.987
1993	—Omaha (A.A.)■	OF	116	399	61	105	19	5	10	41	.263	36	24	9	212	15	1	*.996
1994	—Colorado (N.L.)■	OF-1B	105	301	56	105	27	8	4	41	.349	30	26	5	187	5	4	.980
1995	—Colorado (N.L.)	OF-1B	119	350	66	94	18	4	8	37	.269	45	40	13	205	5	5	.977
American League totals (5 years)			282	790	101	198	42	9	15	82	.251	66	113	18	514	27	7	.987
National League totals (4 years)			420	968	159	280	54	15	12	110	.289	102	106	25	578	19	13	.979
Major league totals (9 years)			702	1758	260	478	96	24	27	192	.272	168	219	43	1092	46	20	.983

DIVISION SERIES RECORD

			BATTING												FIELDING			
Year	Team (League)	Pos.	G	AB	R	H	2B	3B	HR	RBI	Avg.	BB	SO	SB	PO	A	E	Avg.
1995	—Colorado (N.L.)	OF	4	10	1	2	0	0	0	0	.200	0	1	0	5	0	0	1.000

KIRBY, WAYNE OF INDIANS

PERSONAL: Born January 22, 1964, in Williamsburg, Va. . . . 5-10/190. . . . Bats left, throws right. . . . Full name: Wayne Edward Kirby. . . . Brother of Terry Kirby, running back, Miami Dolphins.
HIGH SCHOOL: Tabb (Va.).
COLLEGE: Newport News (Va.) Apprentice School.
TRANSACTIONS/CAREER NOTES: Selected by Los Angeles Dodgers organization in 13th round of free-agent draft (January 11, 1983). . . . Granted free agency (October 15, 1990). . . . Signed by Cleveland Indians organization (December 3, 1990). . . . Granted free agency (October 15, 1991). . . . Re-signed by Colorado Springs, Indians organization (December 12, 1991).
STATISTICAL NOTES: Led Pacific Coast League in caught stealing with 20 in 1992.

			BATTING												FIELDING			
Year	Team (League)	Pos.	G	AB	R	H	2B	3B	HR	RBI	Avg.	BB	SO	SB	PO	A	E	Avg.
1983	—GC Dodgers (GCL)	OF	60	216	43	63	7	1	0	13	.292	34	19	23	89	9	1	.990
1984	—Vero Beach (FSL)	OF	76	224	39	61	6	3	0	21	.272	21	30	11	101	3	5	.954
	—Great Falls (Pio.)	OF	20	84	19	26	2	2	1	11	.310	12	9	19	35	3	2	.950
	—Bakersfield (Calif.)	OF	23	84	14	23	3	0	0	10	.274	4	5	8	10	1	3	.786
1985	—Vero Beach (FSL)	OF	122	437	70	123	9	3	0	28	.281	41	41	31	231	10	4	.984
1986	—Vero Beach (FSL)	OF-2B	114	387	60	101	9	4	2	31	.261	37	30	28	264	18	4	.986
1987	—Bakersfield (Calif.)	OF	105	416	77	112	14	3	0	34	.269	49	42	56	213	13	12	.950
	—San Antonio (Tex.)	OF	24	80	7	19	1	2	1	9	.238	4	7	6	47	1	3	.941
1988	—Bakersfield (Calif.)	OF	12	47	12	13	0	1	0	4	.277	11	4	9	20	2	2	.917
	—San Antonio (Tex.)	OF	100	334	50	80	9	2	0	21	.240	21	43	26	181	4	2	.989
1989	—San Antonio (Tex.)	OF	44	140	14	30	3	1	0	7	.214	18	17	11	77	3	4	.952
	—Albuquerque (PCL)	OF	78	310	62	106	18	8	0	30	.342	26	27	29	149	8	2	.987
1990	—Albuquerque (PCL)	OF	119	342	56	95	14	5	0	30	.278	28	36	29	185	11	9	.956
1991	—Colo. Springs (PCL)■	OF-2B	118	385	66	113	14	4	1	39	.294	34	36	29	227	14	6	.976
	—Cleveland (A.L.)	OF	21	43	4	9	2	0	0	5	.209	2	6	1	40	1	0	1.000
1992	—Colo. Springs (PCL)	OF	123	470	•101	*162	18	*16	11	74	.345	36	28	51	274	14	7	.976
	—Cleveland (A.L.)	DH-OF	21	18	9	3	1	0	1	1	.167	3	2	0	3	0	0	1.000
1993	—Charlotte (Int'l)	OF	17	76	10	22	6	2	3	7	.289	3	10	4	38	1	0	1.000

Year	Team (League)	Pos.	G	AB	R	H	2B	3B	HR	RBI	Avg.	BB	SO	SB	PO	A	E	Avg.
			BATTING												FIELDING			
	—Cleveland (A.L.)	OF-DH	131	458	71	123	19	5	6	60	.269	37	58	17	273	*19	5	.983
1994	—Cleveland (A.L.)	OF-DH	78	191	33	56	6	0	5	23	.293	13	30	11	92	2	4	.959
1995	—Cleveland (A.L.)	OF-DH	101	188	29	39	10	2	1	14	.207	13	32	10	94	2	1	.990
Major league totals (5 years)			352	898	146	230	38	7	13	103	.256	68	128	39	502	24	10	.981

DIVISION SERIES RECORD

Year	Team (League)	Pos.	G	AB	R	H	2B	3B	HR	RBI	Avg.	BB	SO	SB	PO	A	E	Avg.
			BATTING												FIELDING			
1995	—Cleveland (A.L.)	PR-OF	3	1	0	1	0	0	0	0	1.000	0	0	0	...	...	...	...

CHAMPIONSHIP SERIES RECORD

Year	Team (League)	Pos.	G	AB	R	H	2B	3B	HR	RBI	Avg.	BB	SO	SB	PO	A	E	Avg.
			BATTING												FIELDING			
1995	—Cleveland (A.L.)	OF-PR	5	5	2	1	0	0	0	0	.200	0	0	1	3	0	0	1.000

WORLD SERIES RECORD

Year	Team (League)	Pos.	G	AB	R	H	2B	3B	HR	RBI	Avg.	BB	SO	SB	PO	A	E	Avg.
			BATTING												FIELDING			
1995	—Cleveland (A.L.)	PH-PR-OF	3	1	0	0	0	0	0	0	.000	0	1	0	1	0	0	1.000

KIRKREIT, DARON — P — INDIANS

PERSONAL: Born August 7, 1972, in Anaheim, Calif. . . . 6-6/225. . . . Throws right, bats right.
COLLEGE: California-Riverside.
TRANSACTIONS/CAREER NOTES: Selected by Cleveland Indians organization in first round (11th pick overall) of free-agent draft (June 3, 1993). . . . On Kinston disabled list (July 10, 1995-remainder of season).
MISCELLANEOUS: Member of 1992 U.S. Olympic baseball team.

Year	Team (League)	W	L	Pct.	ERA	G	GS	CG	ShO	Sv.	IP	H	R	ER	BB	SO
1993	—Watertown (NYP)	4	1	.800	2.23	7	7	1	0	0	36 1/3	33	14	9	11	44
1994	—Kinston (Carolina)	8	7	.533	2.68	20	19	4	0	0	127 2/3	92	48	38	40	116
	—Cant./Akr. (East.)	3	5	.375	6.22	9	9	0	0	0	46 1/3	53	35	32	25	54
1995	—Kinston (Carolina)	0	1	.000	5.93	3	3	0	0	0	13 2/3	14	9	9	6	14
	—Cant./Akr. (East.)	2	9	.182	5.69	14	14	1	0	0	80 2/3	74	54	51	46	67

KLESKO, RYAN — OF — BRAVES

PERSONAL: Born June 12, 1971, in Westminster, Calif. . . . 6-3/220. . . . Bats left, throws left. . . . Full name: Ryan Anthony Klesko.
HIGH SCHOOL: Westminster (Calif.).
TRANSACTIONS/CAREER NOTES: Selected by Atlanta Braves organization in fifth round of free-agent draft (June 5, 1989). . . . On Atlanta disabled list (May 3-18, 1995); included rehabilitation assignment to Greenville (May 13-17).
HONORS: Named Southern League Most Valuable Player (1991).
STATISTICAL NOTES: Career major league grand slams: 1.

Year	Team (League)	Pos.	G	AB	R	H	2B	3B	HR	RBI	Avg.	BB	SO	SB	PO	A	E	Avg.
			BATTING												FIELDING			
1989	—GC Braves (GCL)	DH	17	57	14	23	5	4	1	16	.404	6	6	4	...	...	...	...
	—Sumter (S. Atl.)	1B	25	90	17	26	6	0	1	12	.289	11	14	1	173	11	4	.979
1990	—Sumter (S. Atl.)	1B	63	231	41	85	15	1	10	38	.368	31	30	13	575	43	14	.978
	—Durham (Carolina)	1B	77	292	40	80	16	1	7	47	.274	32	53	10	490	34	13	.976
1991	—Greenville (South.)	1B	126	419	64	122	22	3	14	67	.291	75	60	14	1043	57	*17	.985
1992	—Richmond (Int'l)	1B	123	418	63	105	22	2	17	59	.251	41	72	3	947	51	*11	.989
	—Atlanta (N.L.)	1B	13	14	0	0	0	0	0	1	.000	0	5	0	25	0	0	1.000
1993	—Richmond (Int'l)	1B-OF	98	343	59	94	14	2	22	74	.274	47	69	4	587	45	12	.981
	—Atlanta (N.L.)	1B-OF	22	17	3	6	1	0	2	5	.353	3	4	0	8	0	0	1.000
1994	—Atlanta (N.L.)	OF-1B	92	245	42	68	13	3	17	47	.278	26	48	1	89	3	7	.929
1995	—Atlanta (N.L.)	OF-1B	107	329	48	102	25	2	23	70	.310	47	72	5	131	4	8	.944
	—Greenville (South.)	OF	4	13	1	3	0	0	1	4	.231	2	1	0	2	0	0	1.000
Major league totals (4 years)			234	605	93	176	39	5	42	123	.291	76	129	6	253	7	15	.945

DIVISION SERIES RECORD

Year	Team (League)	Pos.	G	AB	R	H	2B	3B	HR	RBI	Avg.	BB	SO	SB	PO	A	E	Avg.
			BATTING												FIELDING			
1995	—Atlanta (N.L.)	OF	4	15	5	7	1	0	0	1	.467	0	3	0	3	0	0	1.000

CHAMPIONSHIP SERIES RECORD

Year	Team (League)	Pos.	G	AB	R	H	2B	3B	HR	RBI	Avg.	BB	SO	SB	PO	A	E	Avg.
			BATTING												FIELDING			
1995	—Atlanta (N.L.)	OF-PH	4	7	0	0	0	0	0	0	.000	3	4	0	1	0	0	1.000

WORLD SERIES RECORD

NOTES: Member of World Series championship team (1995).

Year	Team (League)	Pos.	G	AB	R	H	2B	3B	HR	RBI	Avg.	BB	SO	SB	PO	A	E	Avg.
			BATTING												FIELDING			
1995	—Atlanta (N.L.)	OF-DH	6	16	4	5	0	0	3	4	.313	3	4	0	1	0	0	1.000

KLINE, STEVE — P — INDIANS

PERSONAL: Born August 22, 1972, in Sunbury, Pa. . . . 6-2/200. . . . Throws left, bats both. . . . Full name: Steven James Kline.

COLLEGE: West Virginia.
TRANSACTIONS/CAREER NOTES: Selected by Cleveland Indians organization in eighth round of free-agent draft (June 3, 1993).... On disabled list (May 23-August 5, 1995).

Year	Team (League)	W	L	Pct.	ERA	G	GS	CG	ShO	Sv.	IP	H	R	ER	BB	SO
1993—	Burlington (Appal.)	1	1	.500	4.91	2	1	0	0	0	7 1/3	11	4	4	2	4
—	Watertown (NYP)	5	4	.556	3.19	13	13	2	1	0	79	77	36	28	12	45
1994—	Columbus (S. Atl.)	*18	5	.783	3.01	28	•28	2	1	0	*185 2/3	175	67	62	36	*174
1995—	Cant./Akr. (East.)	2	3	.400	2.42	14	14	0	0	0	89 1/3	86	34	24	30	45

KLINGENBECK, SCOTT — P — TWINS

PERSONAL: Born February 3, 1971, in Cincinnati.... 6-2/205.... Throws right, bats right.... Full name: Scott Edward Klingenbeck.
HIGH SCHOOL: Oak Hills (Cincinnati).
COLLEGE: Ohio State.
TRANSACTIONS/CAREER NOTES: Selected by Detroit Tigers organization in 57th round of free-agent draft (June 5, 1989); did not sign.... Selected by Baltimore Orioles organization in fifth round of free-agent draft (June 1, 1992).... On Bowie disabled list (July 11-30, 1994).... Traded by Orioles with a player to be named later to Minnesota Twins for P Scott Erickson (July 7, 1995); Twins acquired OF Kim Bartee to complete deal (September 18, 1995).

Year	Team (League)	W	L	Pct.	ERA	G	GS	CG	ShO	Sv.	IP	H	R	ER	BB	SO
1992—	Kane Co. (Mid.)	3	4	.429	2.63	11	11	0	0	0	68 1/3	50	31	20	28	64
1993—	Frederick (Caro.)	13	4	*.765	2.98	23	23	0	0	0	139	151	62	46	35	146
1994—	Bowie (Eastern)	7	5	.583	3.63	25	25	3	0	0	143 2/3	151	76	58	37	120
—	Baltimore (A.L.)	1	0	1.000	3.86	1	1	0	0	0	7	6	4	3	4	5
1995—	Rochester (Int'l)	3	1	.750	2.72	8	7	0	0	0	43	46	14	13	10	29
—	Baltimore (A.L.)	2	2	.500	4.88	6	5	0	0	0	31 1/3	32	17	17	18	15
—	Minnesota (A.L.)■	0	2	.000	8.57	18	4	0	0	0	48 1/3	69	48	46	24	27
Major league totals (2 years)		3	4	.429	6.85	25	10	0	0	0	86 2/3	107	69	66	46	47

KMAK, JOE — C

PERSONAL: Born May 3, 1963, in Napa, Calif.... 6-0/185.... Bats right, throws right.... Full name: Joseph Robert Kmak.... Name pronounced KAY-mak.
HIGH SCHOOL: Serra (San Mateo, Calif.).
COLLEGE: UC Santa Barbara.
TRANSACTIONS/CAREER NOTES: Selected by San Francisco Giants organization in 10th round of free-agent draft (June 3, 1985).... Signed as free agent by Milwaukee Brewers organization (January 20, 1990).... On disabled list (June 7-July 26, 1992).... Claimed on waivers by New York Mets (November 18, 1993).... Granted free agency (October 15, 1994).... Signed by Iowa, Chicago Cubs organization (December 24, 1994).... On Chicago disabled list (August 28, 1995-remainder of season).... Granted free agency (October 16, 1995).
STATISTICAL NOTES: Led American Association catchers with 10 double plays in 1991.

			BATTING												FIELDING			
Year	Team (League)	Pos.	G	AB	R	H	2B	3B	HR	RBI	Avg.	BB	SO	SB	PO	A	E	Avg.
1985—	Everett (N'west)	C	40	129	21	40	10	1	1	14	.310	20	23	0	175	21	3	.985
1986—	Fresno (California)	C	60	163	23	44	5	0	1	9	.270	15	38	3	203	26	3	.987
1987—	Fresno (California)	C	48	154	18	34	8	0	0	12	.221	15	32	1	323	35	4	.989
—	Shreveport (Texas)	C	15	41	5	8	0	1	0	3	.195	3	4	0	87	11	2	.980
1988—	Shreveport (Texas)	C	71	178	16	40	5	2	1	14	.225	11	19	0	325	35	6	.984
1989—	Reno (California)	C	78	248	39	68	10	5	4	34	.274	40	41	8	459	60	5	.990
1990—	El Paso (Texas)■	C	35	109	8	31	3	2	2	11	.284	7	22	0	194	28	2	.991
—	Denver (A.A.)	C	28	95	12	22	3	0	1	10	.232	4	16	2	160	20	6	.968
1991—	Denver (A.A.)	C	100	295	34	70	17	2	1	33	.237	28	45	7	579	*77	5	*.992
1992—	Denver (A.A.)	C	67	225	27	70	11	4	3	31	.311	19	39	6	351	54	3	.993
1993—	Milwaukee (A.L.)	C	51	110	9	24	5	0	0	7	.218	14	13	6	172	23	0	1.000
—	New Orleans (A.A.)	C	24	76	9	23	3	2	1	13	.303	8	14	1	106	18	2	.984
1994—	Norfolk (Int'l)■	C	86	264	28	66	5	0	5	31	.250	31	51	2	392	55	10	.978
1995—	Iowa (Am. Assoc.)■	C	34	98	6	17	3	0	2	7	.173	6	24	0	209	26	2	.992
—	Chicago (N.L.)	C-3B	19	53	7	13	3	0	1	6	.245	6	12	0	93	9	0	1.000
American League totals (1 year)			51	110	9	24	5	0	0	7	.218	14	13	6	172	23	0	1.000
National League totals (1 year)			19	53	7	13	3	0	1	6	.245	6	12	0	93	9	0	1.000
Major league totals (2 years)			70	163	16	37	8	0	1	13	.227	20	25	6	265	32	0	1.000

KNOBLAUCH, CHUCK — 2B — TWINS

PERSONAL: Born July 7, 1968, in Houston.... 5-9/181.... Bats right, throws right.... Full name: Edward Charles Knoblauch.... Son of Ray Knoblauch, minor league pitcher (1947-56); and nephew of Ed Knoblauch, minor league outfielder (1938-42 and 1947-55).... Name pronounced NOB-lock.
HIGH SCHOOL: Bellaire (Houston).
COLLEGE: Texas A&M.
TRANSACTIONS/CAREER NOTES: Selected by Philadelphia Phillies organization in 18th round of free-agent draft (June 2, 1986); did not sign.... Selected by Minnesota Twins organization in first round (25th pick overall) of free-agent draft (June 5, 1989).
HONORS: Named A.L. Rookie Player of the Year by THE SPORTING NEWS (1991).... Named A.L. Rookie of the Year by Baseball Writers' Association of America (1991).... Named second baseman on THE SPORTING NEWS A.L. All-Star team (1994).... Named second baseman on THE SPORTING NEWS A.L. Silver Slugger team (1995).

			BATTING												FIELDING			
Year	Team (League)	Pos.	G	AB	R	H	2B	3B	HR	RBI	Avg.	BB	SO	SB	PO	A	E	Avg.
1989—	Kenosha (Midwest)	SS	51	196	29	56	13	1	2	19	.286	32	23	9	60	124	21	.898
—	Visalia (California)	SS	18	77	20	28	10	0	0	21	.364	6	11	4	23	52	10	.882

Year	Team (League)	Pos.	G	AB	R	H	2B	3B	HR	RBI	Avg.	BB	SO	SB	PO	A	E	Avg.
				BATTING											FIELDING			
1990—	Orlando (Southern)	2B	118	432	74	125	23	6	2	53	.289	63	31	23	275	300	20	.966
1991—	Minnesota (A.L.)	2B	151	565	78	159	24	6	1	50	.281	59	40	25	249	460	18	.975
1992—	Minnesota (A.L.)	2B-DH-SS	155	600	104	178	19	6	2	56	.297	88	60	34	306	415	6	.992
1993—	Minnesota (A.L.)	2B-SS-OF	153	602	82	167	27	4	2	41	.277	65	44	29	302	431	9	.988
1994—	Minnesota (A.L.)	2B-SS	109	445	85	139	*45	3	5	51	.312	41	56	35	191	285	3	.994
1995—	Minnesota (A.L.)	2B-SS	136	538	107	179	34	8	11	63	.333	78	95	46	254	400	10	.985
Major league totals (5 years)			704	2750	456	822	149	27	21	261	.299	331	295	169	1302	1991	46	.986

CHAMPIONSHIP SERIES RECORD

Year	Team (League)	Pos.	G	AB	R	H	2B	3B	HR	RBI	Avg.	BB	SO	SB	PO	A	E	Avg.
				BATTING											FIELDING			
1991—	Minnesota (A.L.)	2B	5	20	5	7	2	0	0	3	.350	3	3	2	8	14	0	1.000

WORLD SERIES RECORD

NOTES: Member of World Series championship team (1991).

Year	Team (League)	Pos.	G	AB	R	H	2B	3B	HR	RBI	Avg.	BB	SO	SB	PO	A	E	Avg.
				BATTING											FIELDING			
1991—	Minnesota (A.L.)	2B	7	26	3	8	1	0	0	2	.308	4	2	4	15	14	1	.967

ALL-STAR GAME RECORD

Year	League	Pos.	AB	R	H	2B	3B	HR	RBI	Avg.	BB	SO	SB	PO	A	E	Avg.
			BATTING											FIELDING			
1992—	American	PH-2B	1	0	0	0	0	0	0	.000	1	0	0	0	0	0	...
1994—	American	2B	3	1	0	0	0	0	0	.000	0	2	0	1	2	0	1.000
All-Star Game totals (2 years)			4	1	0	0	0	0	0	.000	1	2	0	1	2	0	1.000

KNORR, RANDY — C — BLUE JAYS

PERSONAL: Born November 12, 1968, in San Gabriel, Calif. . . . 6-2/220. . . . Bats right, throws right. . . . Full name: Randy Duane Knorr. . . . Name pronounced NOR.

HIGH SCHOOL: Baldwin Park (Calif.).

TRANSACTIONS/CAREER NOTES: Selected by Toronto Blue Jays organization in 10th round of free-agent draft (June 2, 1986). . . . On disabled list (June 24-July 4, 1986 and May 10, 1989-remainder of season). . . . On Syracuse disabled list (May 11-23, 1992). . . . On Toronto disabled list (August 20-September 30, 1992). . . . On Toronto disabled list (July 1-August 11, 1995); included rehabilitation assignment to Syracuse (July 21-August 9).

STATISTICAL NOTES: Led South Atlantic League catchers with 960 total chances and 25 passed balls in 1988.

Year	Team (League)	Pos.	G	AB	R	H	2B	3B	HR	RBI	Avg.	BB	SO	SB	PO	A	E	Avg.
				BATTING											FIELDING			
1986—	Medicine Hat (Pio.)	1B	55	215	21	58	13	0	4	52	.270	17	53	0	451	29	10	.980
1987—	Myrtle Beach (SAL)	C-1B-2B	46	129	17	34	4	0	6	21	.264	6	46	0	95	7	1	.990
—	Medicine Hat (Pio.)	C	26	106	21	31	7	0	10	24	.292	5	26	0	70	5	4	.949
1988—	Myrtle Beach (SAL)	C	117	364	43	85	13	0	9	42	.234	41	91	0	*870	75	15	.984
1989—	Dunedin (Fla. St.)	C	33	122	13	32	6	0	6	23	.262	6	21	0	186	20	2	.990
1990—	Knoxville (South.)	C	116	392	51	108	12	1	13	64	.276	31	83	0	599	72	15	.978
1991—	Knoxville (South.)	C-1B	24	74	7	13	4	0	0	4	.176	10	18	2	136	16	2	.987
—	Syracuse (Int'l)	C	91	342	29	89	20	0	5	44	.260	23	58	1	477	49	7	.987
—	Toronto (A.L.)	C	3	1	0	0	0	0	0	0	.000	1	1	0	6	1	0	1.000
1992—	Syracuse (Int'l)	C	61	228	27	62	13	1	11	27	.272	17	38	1	220	22	3	.988
—	Toronto (A.L.)	C	8	19	1	5	0	0	1	2	.263	1	5	0	33	3	0	1.000
1993—	Toronto (A.L.)	C	39	101	11	25	3	2	4	20	.248	9	29	0	168	20	0	1.000
1994—	Toronto (A.L.)	C	40	124	20	30	2	0	7	19	.242	10	35	0	247	21	2	.993
1995—	Toronto (A.L.)	C	45	132	18	28	8	0	3	16	.212	11	28	0	243	22	8	.971
—	Syracuse (Int'l)	C	18	67	6	18	5	1	1	6	.269	5	14	0	129	14	3	.979
Major league totals (5 years)			135	377	50	88	13	2	15	57	.233	32	98	0	697	67	10	.987

CHAMPIONSHIP SERIES RECORD

Year	Team (League)	Pos.	G	AB	R	H	2B	3B	HR	RBI	Avg.	BB	SO	SB	PO	A	E	Avg.
				BATTING											FIELDING			
1992—	Toronto (A.L.)								Did not play.									
1993—	Toronto (A.L.)								Did not play.									

WORLD SERIES RECORD

NOTES: Member of World Series championship teams (1992 and 1993).

Year	Team (League)	Pos.	G	AB	R	H	2B	3B	HR	RBI	Avg.	BB	SO	SB	PO	A	E	Avg.
				BATTING											FIELDING			
1992—	Toronto (A.L.)								Did not play.									
1993—	Toronto (A.L.)	C	1	0	0	0	0	0	0	0	...	0	0	0	3	0	0	1.000
World Series totals (1 year)			1	0	0	0	0	0	0	0	...	0	0	0	3	0	0	1.000

KONUSZEWSKI, DENNIS — P — PIRATES

PERSONAL: Born February 4, 1971, in Bridgeport, Mich. . . . 6-3/210. . . . Throws right, bats right. . . . Full name: Dennis John Konuszewski. . . . Name pronounced kon-ah-SHES-key.

HIGH SCHOOL: Bridgeport (Mich.).

COLLEGE: Michigan.

TRANSACTIONS/CAREER NOTES: Selected by Pittsburgh Pirates organization in seventh round of free-agent draft (June 1, 1992).

Year	Team (League)	W	L	Pct.	ERA	G	GS	CG	ShO	Sv.	IP	H	R	ER	BB	SO
1992—	Welland (NYP)	0	0	...	1.29	2	2	0	0	0	7	6	1	1	4	4
—	Augusta (S. Atl.)	3	3	.500	2.31	17	8	0	0	1	62 1/3	50	19	16	19	45
1993—	Salem (Carolina)	4	10	.286	4.62	39	13	0	0	1	103 1/3	121	66	53	43	81
1994—	Carolina (South.)	6	5	.545	3.59	51	0	0	0	1	77 2/3	81	39	31	31	53
1995—	Carolina (South.)	7	7	.500	3.65	48	0	0	0	2	61 2/3	63	33	25	26	48
—	Pittsburgh (N.L.)	0	0	...	54.00	1	0	0	0	0	1/3	3	2	2	1	0
Major league totals (1 year)		0	0	...	54.00	1	0	0	0	0	1/3	3	2	2	1	0

KOWITZ, BRIAN — OF

PERSONAL: Born August 7, 1969, in Baltimore. . . . 5-10/182. . . . Bats left, throws left. . . . Full name: Brian Mark Kowitz.
HIGH SCHOOL: Boys Latin (Baltimore).
COLLEGE: Clemson.
TRANSACTIONS/CAREER NOTES: Selected by Atlanta Braves organization in ninth round of free-agent draft (June 4, 1990). . . . Selected by Minnesota Twins from Braves organization in Rule 5 major league draft (December 5, 1994). . . . Returned to Braves organization (April 24, 1995). . . . Granted free agency (November 27, 1995).

			BATTING												FIELDING			
Year	Team (League)	Pos.	G	AB	R	H	2B	3B	HR	RBI	Avg.	BB	SO	SB	PO	A	E	Avg.
1990—	Pulaski (Appal.)	OF	43	182	40	59	13	1	8	19	.324	16	16	13	66	2	6	.919
—	Greenville (South.)	OF	20	68	4	9	0	0	0	4	.132	8	10	1	40	1	0	1.000
1991—	Durham (Carolina)	OF	86	323	41	82	13	5	3	21	.254	23	56	18	169	1	0	1.000
—	Greenville (South.)	OF	35	112	15	26	5	0	3	17	.232	10	7	1	56	2	0	1.000
1992—	Durham (Carolina)	OF	105	382	53	115	14	7	7	64	.301	44	53	22	205	6	2	*.991
—	Greenville (South.)	OF	21	56	9	16	4	0	0	6	.286	6	10	1	29	3	1	.970
1993—	Greenville (South.)	OF	122	450	63	125	20	5	5	48	.278	60	56	13	257	6	3	.989
—	Richmond (Int'l)	OF	12	45	10	12	1	3	0	8	.267	5	8	1	20	1	1	.955
1994—	Richmond (Int'l)	OF	124	466	68	140	29	7	8	57	.300	43	53	22	222	10	2	.991
1995—	Richmond (Int'l)	OF	100	353	53	99	14	5	2	34	.280	41	43	11	217	2	7	.969
—	Atlanta (N.L.)	OF	10	24	3	4	1	0	0	3	.167	2	5	0	6	0	0	1.000
Major league totals (1 year)			10	24	3	4	1	0	0	3	.167	2	5	0	6	0	0	1.000

KREUTER, CHAD — C — WHITE SOX

PERSONAL: Born August 26, 1964, in Greenbrae, Calif. . . . 6-2/200. . . . Bats both, throws right. . . . Full name: Chad Michael Kreuter. . . . Name pronounced CREW-ter.
HIGH SCHOOL: Redwood (Calif.).
COLLEGE: Pepperdine.
TRANSACTIONS/CAREER NOTES: Selected by Texas Rangers organization in fifth round of free-agent draft (June 3, 1985). . . . Granted free agency (October 15, 1991). . . . Signed by Toledo, Detroit Tigers organization (January 2, 1992). . . . Granted free agency (December 23, 1994). . . . Signed by Seattle Mariners (April 8, 1995). . . . On Seattle disabled list (June 19-July 6, 1995). . . . On Tacoma disabled list (August 4-25, 1995). . . . Granted free agency (October 16, 1995). . . . Signed by Chicago White Sox organization (December 11, 1995).
RECORDS: Shares major league single-game record for most sacrifice flies—3 (July 30, 1994). . . . Shares major league record for most hits in one inning in first major league game—2 (September 14, 1988, fifth inning).
STATISTICAL NOTES: Led Carolina League catchers with 21 errors and 17 double plays and tied for lead with 113 assists in 1986. . . . Tied for Texas League lead in double plays by catcher with nine in 1988. . . . Led A.L. with 21 passed balls in 1989. . . . Switch-hit home runs in one game (September 7, 1993). . . . Career major league grand slams: 1.
MISCELLANEOUS: Batted righthanded only (1985 and 1990).

			BATTING												FIELDING			
Year	Team (League)	Pos.	G	AB	R	H	2B	3B	HR	RBI	Avg.	BB	SO	SB	PO	A	E	Avg.
1985—	Burlington (Midw.)	C	69	199	25	53	9	0	4	26	.266	38	48	3	349	34	8	.980
1986—	Salem (Carolina)	C-OF-3B	125	387	55	85	21	2	6	49	.220	67	82	5	613	‡115	†21	.972
1987—	Charlotte (Fla. St.)	C-OF-3B	85	281	36	61	18	1	9	40	.217	31	32	1	380	54	8	.982
1988—	Tulsa (Texas)	C	108	358	46	95	24	6	3	51	.265	55	66	2	603	71	•13	.981
—	Texas (A.L.)	C	16	51	3	14	2	1	1	5	.275	7	13	0	93	8	1	.990
1989—	Texas (A.L.)	C	87	158	16	24	3	0	5	9	.152	27	40	0	453	26	4	.992
—	Okla. City (A.A.)	C	26	87	10	22	3	0	0	6	.253	13	11	1	146	14	2	.988
1990—	Texas (A.L.)	C	22	22	2	1	1	0	0	2	.045	8	9	0	39	4	1	.977
—	Okla. City (A.A.)	C	92	291	41	65	17	1	7	35	.223	52	80	0	559	64	10	.984
1991—	Texas (A.L.)	C	3	4	0	0	0	0	0	0	.000	0	1	0	5	0	0	1.000
—	Okla. City (A.A.)	C	24	70	14	19	6	0	1	12	.271	18	16	2	146	23	7	.960
—	Tulsa (Texas)	C	42	128	23	30	5	1	2	10	.234	29	23	1	269	27	4	.987
1992—	Detroit (A.L.)■	C-DH	67	190	22	48	9	0	2	16	.253	20	38	0	271	22	5	.983
1993—	Detroit (A.L.)	C-DH-1B	119	374	59	107	23	3	15	51	.286	49	92	2	522	70	7	.988
1994—	Detroit (A.L.)	C-1B-OF	65	170	17	38	8	0	1	19	.224	28	36	0	280	22	4	.987
1995—	Seattle (A.L.)■	C	26	75	12	17	5	0	1	8	.227	5	22	0	151	12	4	.976
—	Tacoma (PCL)	C	15	48	6	14	5	0	1	11	.292	8	11	0	70	10	1	.988
Major league totals (8 years)			405	1044	131	249	51	4	25	110	.239	144	251	2	1814	164	26	.987

KRIVDA, RICK — P — ORIOLES

PERSONAL: Born January 19, 1970, in McKeesport, Pa. . . . 6-1/180. . . . Throws left, bats right. . . . Full name: Rick Michael Krivda.
HIGH SCHOOL: McKeesport (Pa.) Area.
COLLEGE: California (Pa.).
TRANSACTIONS/CAREER NOTES: Selected by Baltimore Orioles organization in 23rd round of free-agent draft (June 3, 1991).

Year	Team (League)	W	L	Pct.	ERA	G	GS	CG	ShO	Sv.	IP	H	R	ER	BB	SO
1991—	Bluefield (Appal.)	7	1	.875	1.88	15	8	0	0	1	67	48	20	14	24	79

Year	Team (League)	W	L	Pct.	ERA	G	GS	CG	ShO	Sv.	IP	H	R	ER	BB	SO
1992—	Kane Co. (Mid.)	12	5	.706	3.03	18	18	2	0	0	121 2/3	108	53	41	41	124
—	Frederick (Caro.)	5	1	.833	2.98	9	9	1	1	0	57 1/3	51	23	19	15	64
1993—	Bowie (Eastern)	7	5	.583	3.08	22	22	0	0	0	125 2/3	114	46	43	50	108
—	Rochester (Int'l)	3	0	1.000	1.89	5	5	0	0	0	33 1/3	20	7	7	16	23
1994—	Rochester (Int'l)	9	10	.474	3.53	28	26	3	2	0	163	149	75	64	73	122
1995—	Rochester (Int'l)	6	5	.545	3.19	16	16	1	0	0	101 2/3	96	44	36	32	74
—	Baltimore (A.L.)	2	7	.222	4.54	13	13	1	0	0	75 1/3	76	40	38	25	53
Major league totals (1 year)		2	7	.222	4.54	13	13	1	0	0	75 1/3	76	40	38	25	53

KROON, MARC — P — PADRES

PERSONAL: Born April 2, 1973, in Bronx, N.Y. . . . 6-2/195. . . . Throws right, bats right. . . . Full name: Marc Jason Kroon.
HIGH SCHOOL: South Mountain (Phoenix).
TRANSACTIONS/CAREER NOTES: Selected by New York Mets organization in supplemental round ("sandwich pick" between second and third round) of free-agent draft (June 3, 1991); pick received as part of compensation for Toronto Blue Jays signing Type C free agent 1B/DH Pat Tabler. . . . Traded by Mets organization to San Diego Padres organization (December 13, 1993), completing the deal in which Mets traded OF Randy Curtis and a player to named later to Padres for P Frank Seminara, OF Tracy Jones and SS Pablo Martinez (December 10, 1993).

Year	Team (League)	W	L	Pct.	ERA	G	GS	CG	ShO	Sv.	IP	H	R	ER	BB	SO
1991—	GC Mets (GCL)	2	3	.400	4.53	12	10	1	0	0	47 2/3	39	33	24	22	39
1992—	Kingsport (Appal.)	3	5	.375	4.10	12	12	0	0	0	68	52	41	31	57	60
1993—	Capital City (S. Atl.)	2	11	.154	3.47	29	19	0	0	2	124 1/3	123	65	48	70	122
1994—	Rancho Cuca. (Cal.)■	11	6	.647	4.83	26	26	0	0	0	143 1/3	143	86	77	81	153
1995—	Memphis (South.)	7	5	.583	3.51	22	19	0	0	2	115 1/3	90	49	45	61	123
—	San Diego (N.L.)	0	1	.000	10.80	2	0	0	0	0	1 2/3	1	2	2	2	2
Major league totals (1 year)		0	1	.000	10.80	2	0	0	0	0	1 2/3	1	2	2	2	2

KRUEGER, BILL — P

PERSONAL: Born April 24, 1958, in Waukegan, Ill. . . . 6-5/205. . . . Throws left, bats left. . . . Full name: William Culp Krueger. . . . Name pronounced CREW-ger.
HIGH SCHOOL: McMinnville (Ore.).
COLLEGE: Portland (degree in business administration, 1979).
TRANSACTIONS/CAREER NOTES: Signed as non-drafted free agent by Oakland Athletics organization (July 12, 1980). . . . On disabled list (August 5, 1983-remainder of season). . . . On Oakland disabled list (May 6-August 8, 1986); included rehabilitation assignments to Madison (July 4-8) and Tacoma (July 10-18 and July 21-27). . . . Traded by A's organization to Los Angeles Dodgers organization for P Tim Meeks (June 23, 1987). . . . Released by Dodgers (November 12, 1987). . . . Re-signed by Dodgers organization (January 1, 1988). . . . Traded by Dodgers to Pittsburgh Pirates for P Jim Neidlinger (October 3, 1988). . . . Released by Pirates (March 28, 1989). . . . Signed by Denver, Milwaukee Brewers organization (April 7, 1989). . . . On Milwaukee disabled list (August 10-31, 1990); included rehabilitation assignment to Beloit (August 29-31). . . . Granted free agency (November 5, 1990). . . . Signed by Seattle Mariners (December 19, 1990). . . . Granted free agency (October 30, 1991). . . . Signed by Minnesota Twins organization (January 29, 1992). . . . Traded by Twins to Montreal Expos for OF Darren Reed (August 31, 1992). . . . Granted free agency (October 30, 1992). . . . Signed by Detroit Tigers (December 11, 1992). . . . On Detroit disabled list (July 4-August 22, 1993); included rehabilitation assignment to Toledo (August 9-22). . . . Released by Tigers (June 4, 1994). . . . Signed by Las Vegas, San Diego Padres organization (June 14, 1994). . . . Granted free agency (October 26, 1994). . . . Re-signed by Las Vegas (April 10, 1995). . . . Released by Padres (May 16, 1995). . . . Signed by Tacoma, Mariners organization (June 12, 1995). . . . Granted free agency (October 6, 1995).
STATISTICAL NOTES: Pitched seven-inning 2-0 no-hit victory for Albuquerque against Phoenix (August 14, 1988, second game).

Year	Team (League)	W	L	Pct.	ERA	G	GS	CG	ShO	Sv.	IP	H	R	ER	BB	SO
1980—	Medford (N'west)	0	4	.000	5.11	9	7	1	0	1	44	54	38	25	29	48
1981—	Modesto (Calif.)	3	5	.375	3.67	16	13	5	1	0	98	87	49	40	52	76
—	West Haven (East.)	3	6	.333	3.57	11	11	1	0	0	68	74	36	27	31	36
1982—	West Haven (East.)	15	9	.625	2.83	28	•27	7	•3	0	181	160	69	57	81	163
1983—	Oakland (A.L.)	7	6	.538	3.61	17	16	2	0	0	109 2/3	104	54	44	53	58
1984—	Tacoma (PCL)	2	2	.500	3.69	5	5	2	0	0	31 2/3	29	17	13	21	20
—	Oakland (A.L.)	10	10	.500	4.75	26	24	1	0	0	142	156	95	75	85	61
1985—	Oakland (A.L.)	9	10	.474	4.52	32	23	2	0	0	151 1/3	165	95	76	69	56
—	Tacoma (PCL)	0	1	.000	9.31	2	2	0	0	0	9 2/3	12	10	10	6	10
1986—	Oakland (A.L.)	1	2	.333	6.03	11	3	0	0	1	34 1/3	40	25	23	13	10
—	Madison (Midwest)	0	0	. . .	0.00	1	0	0	0	0	2	1	0	0	1	1
—	Tacoma (PCL)	3	3	.500	4.64	8	8	2	1	0	52 1/3	53	32	27	27	41
1987—	Oakland (A.L.)	0	3	.000	9.53	9	0	0	0	0	5 2/3	9	7	6	8	2
—	Tacoma (PCL)	3	3	.500	3.47	10	10	1	1	0	62 1/3	64	26	24	27	37
—	Los Angeles (N.L.)■	0	0	. . .	0.00	2	0	0	0	0	2 1/3	3	2	0	1	2
1988—	Albuquerque (PCL)	*15	5	.750	*3.01	27	26	7	*4	0	173 1/3	167	74	58	69	114
—	Los Angeles (N.L.)	0	0	. . .	11.57	1	1	0	0	0	2 1/3	4	3	3	2	1
1989—	Denver (Am. Assoc.)■	1	1	.500	2.03	2	2	0	0	0	13 1/3	10	4	3	6	9
—	Milwaukee (A.L.)	3	2	.600	3.84	34	5	0	0	3	93 2/3	96	43	40	33	72
1990—	Milwaukee (A.L.)	6	8	.429	3.98	30	17	0	0	0	129	137	70	57	54	64
—	Beloit (Midwest)	1	0	1.000	1.50	1	1	0	0	0	6	4	1	1	0	4
1991—	Seattle (A.L.)■	11	8	.579	3.60	35	25	1	0	0	175	194	82	70	60	91
1992—	Minnesota (A.L.)■	10	6	.625	4.30	27	27	2	2	0	161 1/3	166	82	77	46	86
—	Montreal (N.L.)■	0	2	.000	6.75	9	2	0	0	0	17 1/3	23	13	13	7	13
1993—	Detroit (A.L.)■	6	4	.600	3.40	32	7	0	0	0	82	90	43	31	30	60
—	Toledo (Int'l)	1	0	1.000	1.59	3	3	0	0	0	11 1/3	11	2	2	3	8
1994—	Detroit (A.L.)	0	2	.000	9.61	16	2	0	0	0	19 2/3	26	24	21	17	17
—	Las Vegas (PCL)■	1	0	1.000	2.70	3	3	0	0	0	16 2/3	19	7	5	2	19
—	San Diego (N.L.)	3	2	.600	4.83	8	7	1	0	0	41	42	24	22	7	30
1995—	San Diego (N.L.)	0	0	. . .	7.04	6	0	0	0	0	7 2/3	13	6	6	4	6
—	Tacoma (PCL)■	5	3	.625	4.26	10	8	0	0	0	50 2/3	52	30	24	9	39
—	Seattle (A.L.)	2	1	.667	5.85	6	5	0	0	0	20	37	17	13	4	10
A.L. totals (12 years)		65	62	.512	4.27	275	154	8	2	4	1123 2/3	1220	637	533	472	587
N.L. totals (5 years)		3	4	.429	5.60	26	10	1	0	0	70 2/3	85	48	44	21	52
Major league totals (13 years)		68	66	.507	4.35	301	164	9	2	4	1194 1/3	1305	685	577	493	639

KRUK, JOHN — 1B

PERSONAL: Born February 9, 1961, in Charleston, W.Va. . . . 5-10/220. . . . Bats left, throws left. . . . Full name: John Martin Kruk.
HIGH SCHOOL: Keyser (W.Va.).
JUNIOR COLLEGE: Allegany Community College (Md.).
TRANSACTIONS/CAREER NOTES: Selected by Pittsburgh Pirates organization in third round of free-agent draft (January 13, 1981); did not sign. . . . Selected by San Diego Padres organization in secondary phase of free-agent draft (June 8, 1981). . . . On San Diego disabled list (May 5-21, 1989). . . . Traded by Padres with IF Randy Ready to Philadelphia Phillies for OF Chris James (June 2, 1989). . . . On Philadelphia disabled list (July 3-July 28, 1989). . . . On Philadelphia disabled list (March 25-April 11, 1994); included rehabilitation assignment to Reading (April 8-11). . . . On Philadelphia disabled list (May 12-June 1, 1994); included rehabilitation assignment to Scranton/Wilkes-Barre (May 28-June 1). . . . Granted free agency (October 15, 1994). . . . Signed by Nashville, Chicago White Sox organization (May 18, 1995). . . . On Chicago disabled list (June 3-June 19, 1995).
STATISTICAL NOTES: Led Texas League with 13 sacrifice flies in 1983. . . . Led Pacific Coast League outfielders with four double plays in 1984. . . . Career major league grand slams: 4.

			BATTING												FIELDING			
Year	Team (League)	Pos.	G	AB	R	H	2B	3B	HR	RBI	Avg.	BB	SO	SB	PO	A	E	Avg.
1981—	Walla Walla (N'west)	OF-1B	63	157	31	38	10	0	1	13	.242	56	45	7	108	5	2	.983
1982—	Reno (California)	OF-1B	125	441	82	137	30	8	11	92	.311	72	55	17	253	11	7	.974
1983—	Beaumont (Texas)	OF-1B-P	133	498	94	170	41	9	10	88	.341	69	54	13	304	22	8	.976
1984—	Las Vegas (PCL)	OF	115	340	56	111	25	6	11	57	.326	45	37	2	183	7	2	.990
1985—	Las Vegas (PCL)	OF-1B	123	422	61	148	29	4	7	59	*.351	67	48	2	356	18	7	.982
1986—	San Diego (N.L.)	OF-1B	122	278	33	86	16	2	4	38	.309	48	58	2	139	6	3	.980
—	Las Vegas (PCL)	OF-1B	6	28	6	13	3	1	0	9	.464	4	5	0	22	1	0	1.000
1987—	San Diego (N.L.)	1B-OF	138	447	72	140	14	2	20	91	.313	73	93	18	911	78	5	.995
1988—	San Diego (N.L.)	1B-OF	120	378	54	91	17	1	9	44	.241	80	68	5	634	37	3	.996
1989—	San Diego (N.L.)	OF	31	76	7	14	0	0	3	6	.184	17	14	0	48	3	2	.962
—	Philadelphia (N.L.)■	OF-1B	81	281	46	93	13	6	5	38	.331	27	39	3	164	6	2	.988
1990—	Philadelphia (N.L.)	OF-1B	142	443	52	129	25	8	7	67	.291	69	70	10	543	45	4	.993
1991—	Philadelphia (N.L.)	1B-OF	152	538	84	158	27	6	21	92	.294	67	100	7	848	53	3	.997
1992—	Philadelphia (N.L.)	1B-OF	144	507	86	164	30	4	10	70	.323	92	88	3	1037	58	8	.993
1993—	Philadelphia (N.L.)	1B	150	535	100	169	33	5	14	85	.316	111	87	6	1149	69	8	.993
1994—	Reading (Eastern)	1B	3	9	1	3	0	1	0	0	.333	2	1	0	20	1	0	1.000
—	Philadelphia (N.L.)	1B	75	255	35	77	17	0	5	38	.302	42	51	4	539	46	3	.995
—	Scran./W.B. (Int'l)	1B	4	16	2	2	0	0	1	3	.125	0	3	0	32	1	1	.971
1995—	Chicago (A.L.)■	DH-1B	45	159	13	49	7	0	2	23	.308	26	33	0	10	0	1	.909
American League totals (1 year)			45	159	13	49	7	0	2	23	.308	26	33	0	10	0	1	.909
National League totals (9 years)			1155	3738	569	1121	192	34	98	569	.300	626	668	58	6012	401	41	.994
Major league totals (10 years)			1200	3897	582	1170	199	34	100	592	.300	652	701	58	6022	401	42	.994

CHAMPIONSHIP SERIES RECORD

			BATTING												FIELDING			
Year	Team (League)	Pos.	G	AB	R	H	2B	3B	HR	RBI	Avg.	BB	SO	SB	PO	A	E	Avg.
1993—	Philadelphia (N.L.)	1B	6	24	4	6	2	1	1	5	.250	4	5	0	43	2	0	1.000

WORLD SERIES RECORD

			BATTING												FIELDING			
Year	Team (League)	Pos.	G	AB	R	H	2B	3B	HR	RBI	Avg.	BB	SO	SB	PO	A	E	Avg.
1993—	Philadelphia (N.L.)	1B	6	23	4	8	1	0	0	4	.348	7	7	0	42	3	0	1.000

ALL-STAR GAME RECORD

			BATTING											FIELDING			
Year	League	Pos.	AB	R	H	2B	3B	HR	RBI	Avg.	BB	SO	SB	PO	A	E	Avg.
1991—	National							Did not play.									
1992—	National	OF	2	1	2	0	0	0	0	1.000	0	0	0	0	1	1	.500
1993—	National	1B	3	0	0	0	0	0	0	.000	0	2	0	7	0	0	1.000
All-Star Game totals (2 years)			5	1	2	0	0	0	0	.400	0	2	0	7	1	1	.889

RECORD AS PITCHER

Year	Team (League)	W	L	Pct.	ERA	G	GS	CG	ShO	Sv.	IP	H	R	ER	BB	SO
1983—	Beaumont (Texas)	0	0	...	0.00	3	0	0	0	0	5	5	0	0	2	3

LACY, KERRY — P — RANGERS

PERSONAL: Born August 7, 1972, in Chattanooga, Tenn. . . . 6-2/195. . . . Throws right, bats right. . . . Full name: Kerry Ardeen Lacy.
HIGH SCHOOL: North Sand Mountain (Higdon, Ala.).
COLLEGE: Chattanooga (Tenn.) State.
TRANSACTIONS/CAREER NOTES: Selected by Texas Rangers organization in 15th round of free-agent draft (June 3, 1991).

Year	Team (League)	W	L	Pct.	ERA	G	GS	CG	ShO	Sv.	IP	H	R	ER	BB	SO
1991—	Butte (Pioneer)	2	1	.667	5.59	24	2	0	0	1	48 1/3	47	34	30	36	45
1992—	Gastonia (S. Atl.)	3	7	.300	3.88	49	1	0	0	17	55 2/3	55	35	24	42	57
1993—	Char., S.C. (S. Atl.)	0	6	.000	3.15	58	0	0	0	36	60	49	25	21	32	54
—	Charlotte (Fla. St.)	0	0	...	1.93	4	0	0	0	2	4 2/3	2	2	1	3	3
1994—	Tulsa (Texas)	2	6	.250	3.68	41	0	0	0	12	63 2/3	49	30	26	37	46
1995—	Tulsa (Texas)	2	7	.222	4.28	28	7	0	0	9	82	94	47	39	39	49
—	Okla. City (A.A.)	0	0	...	0.00	1	0	0	0	1	2 1/3	0	0	0	0	1

LADELL, CLEVELAND — OF — REDS

PERSONAL: Born September 19, 1970, in Paris, Tex. . . . 5-11/170. . . . Bats right, throws right. . . . Full name: Cleveland Marquis Ladell.
HIGH SCHOOL: Paris (Tex.).
COLLEGE: Northwood (Texas).
TRANSACTIONS/CAREER NOTES: Selected by Cincinnati Reds organization in 14th round of free-agent draft (June 1, 1992).
STATISTICAL NOTES: Led Appalachian League outfielders with 159 total chances in 1992. . . . Led Carolina league with 240 total bases in 1993. . . . Led Carolina League outfielders with 310 putouts and 334 total chances in 1993.

					BATTING									FIELDING			
Year Team (League)	Pos.	G	AB	R	H	2B	3B	HR	RBI	Avg.	BB	SO	SB	PO	A	E	Avg.
1992—Princeton (Appal.)	OF	64	241	37	64	6	4	4	32	.266	13	45	24	*147	8	4	.975
—Char., W.Va. (SAL)	OF	8	30	3	6	0	0	0	0	.200	3	14	3	27	1	0	1.000
1993—Winst.-Salem (Car.)	OF-C	132	531	90	151	15	7	20	66	.284	16	95	24	†310	12	12	.964
1994—Winst.-Salem (Car.)	OF	75	283	46	71	11	3	12	40	.251	26	63	17	198	4	5	.976
—Chatt. (South.)	OF	33	99	9	16	4	1	1	9	.162	4	26	4	50	1	0	1.000
1995—Chatt. (South.)	OF	135	517	76	151	28	7	5	43	.292	39	88	28	312	6	5	.985

LAKER, TIM — C — EXPOS

PERSONAL: Born November 27, 1969, in Encino, Calif. . . . 6-3/200. . . . Bats right, throws right. . . . Full name: Timothy John Laker.
HIGH SCHOOL: Simi Valley (Calif.).
COLLEGE: Oxnard (Calif.) College.
TRANSACTIONS/CAREER NOTES: Selected by Kansas City Royals organization in 49th round of free-agent draft (June 2, 1987); did not sign. . . . Selected by Montreal Expos organization in sixth round of free-agent draft (June 1, 1988). . . . On Ottawa disabled list (April 30-May 14, 1993).
STATISTICAL NOTES: Led New York-Pennsylvania League with 16 passed balls in 1989. . . . Led Midwest League catchers with 125 assists, 18 errors and 944 total chances in 1990. . . . Tied for International League lead in errors by catcher with 11 in 1993. . . . Led International League with 20 passed balls in 1994.

					BATTING									FIELDING			
Year Team (League)	Pos.	G	AB	R	H	2B	3B	HR	RBI	Avg.	BB	SO	SB	PO	A	E	Avg.
1988—Jamestown (NYP)	C-OF	47	152	14	34	9	0	0	17	.224	8	30	2	236	22	2	.992
1989—Rockford (Midw.)	C	14	48	4	11	1	1	0	4	.229	3	6	1	91	6	4	.960
—Jamestown (NYP)	C	58	216	25	48	9	1	2	24	.222	16	40	8	437	61	8	.984
1990—Rockford (Midw.)	C-OF	120	425	46	94	18	3	7	57	.221	32	83	7	802	†125	†18	.981
—W.P. Beach (FSL)	C	2	3	0	0	0	0	0	0	.000	0	1	0	2	0	0	1.000
1991—Harrisburg (East.)	C	11	35	4	10	1	0	1	5	.286	2	5	0	67	4	3	.959
—W.P. Beach (FSL)	C	100	333	35	77	15	2	5	33	.231	22	51	10	560	87	*14	.979
1992—Harrisburg (East.)	C	117	409	55	99	19	3	15	68	.242	39	89	3	630	62	*14	.980
—Montreal (N.L.)	C	28	46	8	10	3	0	0	4	.217	2	14	1	102	8	1	.991
1993—Montreal (N.L.)	C	43	86	3	17	2	1	0	7	.198	2	16	2	136	18	2	.987
—Ottawa (Int'l)	C-1B	56	204	26	47	10	0	4	23	.230	21	41	3	341	37	‡11	.972
1994—Ottawa (Int'l)	C	118	424	68	131	32	2	12	71	.309	47	96	11	643	*89	•11	.985
1995—Montreal (N.L.)	C	64	141	17	33	8	1	3	20	.234	14	38	0	265	27	7	.977
Major league totals (3 years)		135	273	28	60	13	2	3	31	.220	18	68	3	503	53	10	.982

LAMPKIN, TOM — C — GIANTS

PERSONAL: Born March 4, 1964, in Cincinnati. . . . 5-11/185. . . . Bats left, throws right. . . . Full name: Thomas Michael Lampkin.
HIGH SCHOOL: Blanchet (Seattle).
COLLEGE: Portland.
TRANSACTIONS/CAREER NOTES: Selected by Cleveland Indians organization in 11th round of free-agent draft (June 2, 1986). . . . On disabled list (July 6, 1989-remainder of season). . . . Traded by Indians organization to San Diego Padres for OF Alex Cole (July 11, 1990). . . . Traded by Padres to Milwaukee Brewers for cash (March 25, 1993). . . . Granted free agency (December 20, 1993). . . . Signed by San Francisco Giants organization (January 5, 1994).
STATISTICAL NOTES: Led Pacific Coast League catchers with 11 double plays in 1992. . . . Led Pacific Coast League catchers with 595 putouts in 1994.

					BATTING									FIELDING			
Year Team (League)	Pos.	G	AB	R	H	2B	3B	HR	RBI	Avg.	BB	SO	SB	PO	A	E	Avg.
1986—Batavia (NYP)	C	63	190	24	49	5	1	1	20	.258	31	14	4	323	36	8	.978
1987—Waterloo (Midw.)	C	118	398	49	106	19	2	7	55	.266	34	41	5	689	*100	15	.981
1988—Williamsport (East.)	C	80	263	38	71	10	0	3	23	.270	25	20	1	431	60	9	.982
—Colo. Springs (PCL)	C	34	107	14	30	5	0	0	7	.280	9	2	0	171	28	5	.975
—Cleveland (A.L.)	C	4	4	0	0	0	0	0	0	.000	1	0	0	3	0	0	1.000
1989—Colo. Springs (PCL)	C	63	209	26	67	10	3	4	32	.321	10	18	4	305	21	8	.976
1990—Colo. Springs (PCL)	C-2B	69	199	32	44	7	5	1	18	.221	19	19	7	312	36	12	.967
—San Diego (N.L.)■	C	26	63	4	14	0	1	1	4	.222	4	9	0	91	10	3	.971
—Las Vegas (PCL)	C	1	2	0	1	0	0	0	0	.500	0	1	0	3	0	0	1.000
1991—San Diego (N.L.)	C	38	58	4	11	3	1	0	3	.190	3	9	0	49	5	0	1.000
—Las Vegas (PCL)	C-1B-OF	45	164	25	52	11	1	2	29	.317	10	19	2	211	26	6	.975
1992—Las Vegas (PCL)	C	108	340	45	104	17	4	3	48	.306	53	27	15	506	*64	12	.979
—San Diego (N.L.)	C-OF	9	17	3	4	0	0	0	0	.235	6	1	2	30	3	0	1.000
1993—New Orleans (A.A.)■	C-OF	25	80	18	26	5	0	2	10	.325	18	4	5	152	12	3	.982
—Milwaukee (A.L.)	C-OF-DH	73	162	22	32	8	0	4	25	.198	20	26	7	242	24	6	.978
1994—Phoenix (PCL)■	C-OF	118	453	76	136	32	8	8	70	.300	42	49	8	†595	59	10	.985
1995—San Francisco (N.L.)	C-OF	65	76	8	21	2	0	1	9	.276	9	8	2	62	5	0	1.000
American League totals (2 years)		77	166	22	32	8	0	4	25	.193	21	26	7	245	24	6	.978
National League totals (4 years)		138	214	19	50	5	2	2	16	.234	22	27	4	232	23	3	.988
Major league totals (6 years)		215	380	41	82	13	2	6	41	.216	43	53	11	477	47	9	.983

LANE, AARON — P — ORIOLES

PERSONAL: Born June 2, 1971, in Springfield, Ill. . . . 6-1/180. . . . Throws left, bats left. . . . Full name: Joseph Aaron Lane.
HIGH SCHOOL: Taylorville (Ill.).
JUNIOR COLLEGE: Lincoln Land (Ill.).
COLLEGE: New Orleans.
TRANSACTIONS/CAREER NOTES: Selected by Baltimore Orioles organization in 18th round of free-agent draft (June 3, 1991); did not sign. . . . Selected by Orioles organization in 24th round of free-agent draft (June 1, 1992).

Year Team (League)	W	L	Pct.	ERA	G	GS	CG	ShO	Sv.	IP	H	R	ER	BB	SO
1992— Bluefield (Appal.)	5	1	.833	3.00	14	7	0	0	0	45	36	24	15	24	39
1993— Albany (S. Atl.)	2	10	.167	4.97	29	11	0	0	0	76	92	62	42	42	48
1994— Albany (S. Atl.)	3	2	.600	2.30	35	0	0	0	11	54 2/3	42	20	14	24	56
— Frederick (Caro.)	1	1	.500	3.68	5	0	0	0	2	7 1/3	10	3	3	3	6
1995— Bowie (Eastern)	5	3	.625	4.17	40	0	0	0	2	45 1/3	45	23	21	21	31
— Rochester (Int'l)	0	0	...	6.30	9	0	0	0	0	10	11	11	7	5	9

LANGSTON, MARK — P — ANGELS

PERSONAL: Born August 20, 1960, in San Diego. . . . 6-2/184. . . . Throws left, bats right. . . . Full name: Mark Edward Langston.
HIGH SCHOOL: Buchser (Santa Clara, Calif.).
COLLEGE: San Jose State.
TRANSACTIONS/CAREER NOTES: Selected by Chicago Cubs organization in 15th round of free-agent draft (June 6, 1978); did not sign. . . . Selected by Seattle Mariners organization in third round of free-agent draft (June 8, 1981); pick received as compensation for Texas Rangers signing free-agent IF Bill Stein. . . . On disabled list (June 7-July 22, 1985). . . . Traded by Mariners with a player to be named later to Montreal Expos for P Randy Johnson, P Brian Holman and P Gene Harris (May 25, 1989); Indianapolis, Expos organization, acquired P Mike Campbell to complete deal (July 31, 1989). . . . Granted free agency (November 13, 1989). . . . Signed by California Angels (December 1, 1989). . . . On disabled list (April 10-May 11, 1994).
RECORDS: Holds major league single-season record for fewest assists by pitcher who led league in assists—42 (1990).
HONORS: Named A.L. Rookie Pitcher of the Year by THE SPORTING NEWS (1984). . . . Won A.L. Gold Glove at pitcher (1987-88 and 1991-95).
STATISTICAL NOTES: Pitched seven innings, combining with Mike Witt (two innings) in 1-0 no-hit victory against Seattle (April 11, 1990). . . . Struck out 15 batters in one game (June 25, 1986). . . . Struck out 16 batters in one game (May 10, 1988). . . . Pitched 3-0 one-hit, complete-game victory against Texas (September 24, 1988).
MISCELLANEOUS: Scored in only appearance as pinch-runner and struck out twice in two appearances as designated hitter (1992).

Year Team (League)	W	L	Pct.	ERA	G	GS	CG	ShO	Sv.	IP	H	R	ER	BB	SO
1981— Bellingham (N'west)	7	3	.700	3.39	13	13	5	1	0	85	81	37	32	46	97
1982— Bakersfield (Calif.)	12	7	.632	2.54	26	26	7	3	0	177 1/3	143	71	50	102	161
1983— Chattanooga (Sou.)	14	9	.609	3.59	28	28	10	0	0	198	187	104	79	102	142
1984— Seattle (A.L.)	17	10	.630	3.40	35	33	5	2	0	225	188	99	85	*118	*204
1985— Seattle (A.L.)	7	14	.333	5.47	24	24	2	0	0	126 2/3	122	85	77	91	72
1986— Seattle (A.L.)	12	14	.462	4.85	37	36	9	0	0	239 1/3	234	*142	*129	123	*245
1987— Seattle (A.L.)	19	13	.594	3.84	35	35	14	3	0	272	242	132	116	114	*262
1988— Seattle (A.L.)	15	11	.577	3.34	35	35	9	3	0	261 1/3	222	108	97	110	235
1989— Seattle (A.L.)	4	5	.444	3.56	10	10	2	1	0	73 1/3	60	30	29	19	60
— Montreal (N.L.)■	12	9	.571	2.39	24	24	6	4	0	176 2/3	138	57	47	93	175
1990— California (A.L.)■	10	17	.370	4.40	33	33	5	1	0	223	215	120	109	104	195
1991— California (A.L.)	19	8	.704	3.00	34	34	7	0	0	246 1/3	190	89	82	96	183
1992— California (A.L.)	13	14	.481	3.66	32	32	9	2	0	229	206	103	93	74	174
1993— California (A.L.)	16	11	.593	3.20	35	35	7	0	0	256 1/3	220	100	91	85	196
1994— California (A.L.)	7	8	.467	4.68	18	18	2	1	0	119 1/3	121	67	62	54	109
1995— California (A.L.)	15	7	.682	4.63	31	31	2	1	0	200 1/3	212	109	103	64	142
A.L. totals (12 years)	154	132	.538	3.91	359	356	73	14	0	2472	2232	1184	1073	1052	2077
N.L. totals (1 year)	12	9	.571	2.39	24	24	6	4	0	176 2/3	138	57	47	93	175
Major league totals (12 years)	166	141	.541	3.81	383	380	79	18	0	2648 2/3	2370	1241	1120	1145	2252

ALL-STAR GAME RECORD

Year League	W	L	Pct.	ERA	GS	CG	ShO	Sv.	IP	H	R	ER	BB	SO
1987— American	0	0	...	0.00	0	0	0	0	2	0	0	0	0	3
1991— American						Did not play.								
1992— American	0	0	...	9.00	0	0	0	0	1	2	1	1	0	1
1993— American	0	0	...	9.00	1	0	0	0	2	3	2	2	1	2
All-Star totals (3 years)	0	0	...	5.40	1	0	0	0	5	5	3	3	1	6

LANKFORD, RAY — OF — CARDINALS

PERSONAL: Born June 5, 1967, in Modesto, Calif. . . . 5-11/198. . . . Bats left, throws left. . . . Full name: Raymond Lewis Lankford.
HIGH SCHOOL: Grace Davis (Modesto, Calif.).
JUNIOR COLLEGE: Modesto (Calif.) Junior College.
TRANSACTIONS/CAREER NOTES: Selected by Chicago Cubs organization in third round of free-agent draft (January 14, 1986); did not sign. . . . Selected by St. Louis Cardinals organization in third round of free-agent draft (June 2, 1987). . . . On disabled list (June 24-July 9, 1993).
RECORDS: Shares major league single-season record for fewest double plays by outfielder (150 or more games)—0 (1992).
HONORS: Named Texas League Most Valuable Player (1989).
STATISTICAL NOTES: Led Appalachian League outfielders with 155 total chances in 1987. . . . Led Appalachian League in caught stealing with 11 in 1987. . . . Led Midwest League with 242 total bases in 1988. . . . Led Texas League outfielders with 387 total chances in 1989. . . . Led American Association outfielders with 352 total chances in 1990. . . . Tied for American Association lead with nine intentional bases on balls received in 1990. . . . Hit for the cycle (September 15, 1991). . . . Led N.L. in caught stealing with 24 in 1992. . . . Career major league grand slams: 1.

Year	Team (League)	Pos.	G	AB	R	H	2B	3B	HR	RBI	Avg.	BB	SO	SB	PO	A	E	Avg.
			BATTING												FIELDING			
1987—	Johns. City (App.)	OF	66	253	45	78	17	4	3	32	.308	19	43	14	*143	7	5	.968
1988—	Springfield (Midw.)	OF	135	532	90	151	26	*16	11	66	.284	60	92	33	284	5	7	.976
1989—	Arkansas (Texas)	OF	*134	498	98	*158	28	*12	11	98	.317	65	57	38	*367	9	11	.972
1990—	Louisville (A.A.)	OF	132	473	61	123	25	8	10	72	.260	72	81	30	*333	8	•11	.969
—	St. Louis (N.L.)	OF	39	126	12	36	10	1	3	12	.286	13	27	8	92	1	1	.989
1991—	St. Louis (N.L.)	OF	151	566	83	142	23	*15	9	69	.251	41	114	44	367	7	6	.984
1992—	St. Louis (N.L.)	OF	153	598	87	175	40	6	20	86	.293	72	*147	42	*438	5	2	.996
1993—	St. Louis (N.L.)	OF	127	407	64	97	17	3	7	45	.238	81	111	14	312	6	7	.978
1994—	St. Louis (N.L.)	OF	109	416	89	111	25	5	19	57	.267	58	113	11	260	5	6	.978
1995—	St. Louis (N.L.)	OF	132	483	81	134	35	2	25	82	.277	63	110	24	300	7	3	.990
Major league totals (6 years)			711	2596	416	695	150	32	83	351	.268	328	622	143	1769	31	25	.986

LANSING, MIKE — 2B — EXPOS

PERSONAL: Born April 3, 1968, in Rawlins, Wyo. . . . 6-0/185. . . . Bats right, throws right. . . . Full name: Michael Thomas Lansing.
HIGH SCHOOL: Natrona County (Casper, Wyo.).
COLLEGE: Wichita State.
TRANSACTIONS/CAREER NOTES: Selected by Baltimore Orioles organization in ninth round of free-agent draft (June 5, 1989); did not sign. . . . Selected by Miami, independent, in sixth round of free-agent draft (June 4, 1990). . . . On disabled list (April 29-May 9, 1991). . . . Contract sold by Miami to Montreal Expos organization (September 18, 1991). . . . On disabled list (May 31-June 15, 1995).
STATISTICAL NOTES: Led Eastern League shortstops with 76 double plays in 1992. . . . Career major league grand slams: 1.

Year	Team (League)	Pos.	G	AB	R	H	2B	3B	HR	RBI	Avg.	BB	SO	SB	PO	A	E	Avg.
			BATTING												FIELDING			
1990—	Miami (Florida St.)	SS	61	207	20	50	5	2	2	11	.242	29	35	15	104	166	10	.964
1991—	Miami (Florida St.)	SS-2B	104	384	54	110	20	7	6	55	.286	40	75	29	148	273	27	.940
1992—	Harrisburg (East.)■	SS	128	483	66	135	20	6	6	54	.280	52	64	46	189	*373	20	*.966
1993—	Montreal (N.L.)	3B-SS-2B	141	491	64	141	29	1	3	45	.287	46	56	23	136	336	24	.952
1994—	Montreal (N.L.)	2B-3B-SS	106	394	44	105	21	2	5	35	.266	30	37	12	164	283	10	.978
1995—	Montreal (N.L.)	2B-SS	127	467	47	119	30	2	10	62	.255	28	65	27	306	373	6	.991
Major league totals (3 years)			374	1352	155	365	80	5	18	142	.270	104	158	62	606	992	40	.976

LARKIN, ANDY — P — MARLINS

PERSONAL: Born June 27, 1974, in Chelan, Wash. . . . 6-4/175. . . . Throws right, bats right.
HIGH SCHOOL: South Medford (Medford, Ore).
TRANSACTIONS/CAREER NOTES: Selected by Florida Marlins organization in 25th round of free-agent draft (June 1, 1992). . . . On disabled list (June 14-August 23, 1995).
STATISTICAL NOTES: Pitched 6-0 no-hit victory against Welland (July 25, 1993). . . . Led New York-Pennsylvania League with 12 hit batsmen in 1993. . . . Led Midwest League with 19 hit batsmen in 1994.

Year	Team (League)	W	L	Pct.	ERA	G	GS	CG	ShO	Sv.	IP	H	R	ER	BB	SO
1992—	GC Marlins (GCL)	1	2	.333	5.23	14	4	0	0	2	41 1/3	41	26	24	19	20
1993—	Elmira (NYP)	5	7	.417	2.97	14	14	•4	•1	0	88	74	43	29	23	89
1994—	Kane Co. (Mid.)	9	7	.563	2.83	21	21	3	1	0	140	125	53	44	27	125
1995—	Portland (Eastern)	1	2	.333	3.38	9	9	0	0	0	40	29	16	15	11	23

LARKIN, BARRY — SS — REDS

PERSONAL: Born April 28, 1964, in Cincinnati. . . . 6-0/195. . . . Bats right, throws right. . . . Full name: Barry Louis Larkin.
HIGH SCHOOL: Moeller (Cincinnati).
COLLEGE: Michigan.
TRANSACTIONS/CAREER NOTES: Selected by Cincinnati Reds organization in second round of free-agent draft (June 7, 1982); did not sign. . . . Selected by Reds organization in first round (fourth pick overall) of free-agent draft (June 3, 1985). . . . On disabled list (April 13-May 2, 1987). . . . On Cincinnati disabled list (July 11-September 1, 1989); included rehabilitation assignment to Nashville (August 27-September 1). . . . On disabled list (May 18-June 4, 1991; April 19-May 8, 1992; and August 5, 1993-remainder of season).
RECORDS: Shares major league record for most home runs in two consecutive games—5 (June 27 [2] and 28 [3], 1991).
HONORS: Named shortstop on The Sporting News college All-America team (1985). . . . Named American Association Most Valuable Player (1986). . . . Named shortstop on The Sporting News N.L. All-Star team (1988-92 and 1994-95). . . . Named shortstop on The Sporting News N.L. Silver Slugger team (1988-92 and 1995). . . . Won N.L. Gold Glove at shortstop (1994-95). . . . Named N.L. Most Valuable Player by Baseball Writers' Association of America (1995).
STATISTICAL NOTES: Led American Association with .525 slugging percentage in 1986. . . . Tied for N.L. lead in double plays by shortstop with 86 in 1990. . . . Hit three home runs in one game (June 28, 1991).
MISCELLANEOUS: Member of 1984 U.S. Olympic baseball team.

Year	Team (League)	Pos.	G	AB	R	H	2B	3B	HR	RBI	Avg.	BB	SO	SB	PO	A	E	Avg.
			BATTING												FIELDING			
1985—	Vermont (Eastern)	SS	72	255	42	68	13	2	1	31	.267	23	21	12	110	166	17	.942
1986—	Denver (A.A.)	SS-2B	103	413	67	136	31	10	10	51	.329	31	43	19	172	287	18	.962
—	Cincinnati (N.L.)	SS-2B	41	159	27	45	4	3	3	19	.283	9	21	8	51	125	4	.978
1987—	Cincinnati (N.L.)	SS	125	439	64	107	16	2	12	43	.244	36	52	21	168	358	19	.965
1988—	Cincinnati (N.L.)	SS	151	588	91	174	32	5	12	56	.296	41	24	40	231	470	•29	.960
1989—	Cincinnati (N.L.)	SS	97	325	47	111	14	4	4	36	.342	20	23	10	142	267	10	.976
—	Nashville (A.A.)	SS	2	5	2	5	1	0	0	0	1.000	0	0	0	1	3	0	1.000
1990—	Cincinnati (N.L.)	SS	158	614	85	185	25	6	7	67	.301	49	49	30	254	*469	17	.977
1991—	Cincinnati (N.L.)	SS	123	464	88	140	27	4	20	69	.302	55	64	24	226	372	15	.976
1992—	Cincinnati (N.L.)	SS	140	533	76	162	32	6	12	78	.304	63	58	15	233	408	11	.983

			BATTING												FIELDING			
Year	Team (League)	Pos.	G	AB	R	H	2B	3B	HR	RBI	Avg.	BB	SO	SB	PO	A	E	Avg.
1993—	Cincinnati (N.L.)	SS	100	384	57	121	20	3	8	51	.315	51	33	14	159	281	16	.965
1994—	Cincinnati (N.L.)	SS	110	427	78	119	23	5	9	52	.279	64	58	26	*178	312	10	.980
1995—	Cincinnati (N.L.)	SS	131	496	98	158	29	6	15	66	.319	61	49	51	192	341	11	.980
Major league totals (10 years)			1176	4429	711	1322	222	44	102	537	.298	449	431	239	1834	3403	142	.974

DIVISION SERIES RECORD

			BATTING												FIELDING			
Year	Team (League)	Pos.	G	AB	R	H	2B	3B	HR	RBI	Avg.	BB	SO	SB	PO	A	E	Avg.
1995—	Cincinnati (N.L.)	SS	3	13	2	5	0	0	0	1	.385	1	2	4	3	8	0	1.000

CHAMPIONSHIP SERIES RECORD

			BATTING												FIELDING			
Year	Team (League)	Pos.	G	AB	R	H	2B	3B	HR	RBI	Avg.	BB	SO	SB	PO	A	E	Avg.
1990—	Cincinnati (N.L.)	SS	6	23	5	6	2	0	0	1	.261	3	1	3	21	15	1	.973
1995—	Cincinnati (N.L.)	SS	4	18	1	7	2	1	0	0	.389	1	1	1	10	15	1	.962
Championship series totals (2 years)			10	41	6	13	4	1	0	1	.317	4	2	4	31	30	2	.968

WORLD SERIES RECORD

NOTES: Shares record for most at-bats in one inning—2 (October 19, 1990, third inning). . . . Member of World Series championship team (1990).

			BATTING												FIELDING			
Year	Team (League)	Pos.	G	AB	R	H	2B	3B	HR	RBI	Avg.	BB	SO	SB	PO	A	E	Avg.
1990—	Cincinnati (N.L.)	SS	4	17	3	6	1	1	0	1	.353	2	0	0	1	14	0	1.000

ALL-STAR GAME RECORD

			BATTING											FIELDING			
Year	League	Pos.	AB	R	H	2B	3B	HR	RBI	Avg.	BB	SO	SB	PO	A	E	Avg.
1988—	National	SS	2	0	0	0	0	0	0	.000	0	1	0	0	1	0	1.000
1989—	National		Did not play.														
1990—	National	PR-SS	0	0	0	0	0	0	0	...	0	0	1	1	2	0	1.000
1991—	National	SS	1	0	0	0	0	0	0	.000	0	0	0	0	2	0	1.000
1993—	National	SS	2	0	0	0	0	0	1	.000	0	1	0	2	1	0	1.000
1994—	National		Selected, did not play—injured.														
1995—	National	SS	3	0	0	0	0	0	0	.000	0	0	0	2	3	0	1.000
All-Star Game totals (5 years)			8	0	0	0	0	0	1	.000	0	2	1	5	9	0	1.000

LATHAM, CHRIS — OF — TWINS

PERSONAL: Born May 26, 1973, in Coeur d'Alene, Idaho. . . . 6-0/195. . . . Bats both, throws right.
HIGH SCHOOL: Basic Technical (Las Vegas).
TRANSACTIONS/CAREER NOTES: Selected by Los Angeles Dodgers organization in 11th round of free-agent draft (June 3, 1991). . . . Traded by Dodgers organization to Minnesota Twins (October 30, 1995), completing deal in which Twins traded P Mark Guthrie and P Kevin Tapani to Dodgers for 1B/3B Ron Coomer, P Greg Hansell, P Jose Parra and a player to be named later (July 31, 1995).
STATISTICAL NOTES: Led Northwest League with 148 total bases and 20 caught stealing in 1994. . . . Tied for Northwest League lead with seven intentional bases on balls received in 1994. . . . Led Northwest League outfielders with 154 total chances in 1994.

			BATTING												FIELDING			
Year	Team (League)	Pos.	G	AB	R	H	2B	3B	HR	RBI	Avg.	BB	SO	SB	PO	A	E	Avg.
1991—	GC Dodgers (GCL)	2B	43	109	17	26	2	1	0	11	.239	16	45	14	47	63	10	.917
1992—	Great Falls (Pio.)	2B	17	37	8	12	2	0	0	3	.324	8	8	1	17	24	6	.872
—	GC Dodgers (GCL)	2B-SS-3B	14	48	4	11	2	0	0	2	.229	5	17	2	26	14	1	.976
1993—	Yakima (N'west)	OF	54	192	46	50	2	*6	4	17	.260	39	53	25	83	5	6	.936
—	Bakersfield (Calif.)	OF	6	27	1	5	1	0	0	3	.185	4	5	2	12	0	1	.923
1994—	Bakersfield (Calif.)	OF	52	191	29	41	5	2	2	15	.215	28	49	28	88	4	7	.929
—	Yakima (N'west)	OF	71	288	*69	*98	19	*8	5	32	*.340	55	66	33	*144	6	4	.974
1995—	Vero Beach (FSL)	OF	71	259	53	74	13	4	6	39	.286	56	54	42	125	5	7	.949
—	San Antonio (Tex.)	OF	58	214	38	64	14	5	9	37	.299	33	59	11	135	2	4	.972
—	Albuquerque (PCL)	OF	5	18	2	3	0	1	0	3	.167	1	4	1	7	0	0	1.000

LaVALLIERE, MIKE — C

PERSONAL: Born August 18, 1960, in Charlotte, N.C. . . . 5-9/205. . . . Bats left, throws right. . . . Full name: Michael Eugene LaValliere. . . . Son of Guy LaValliere, minor league catcher (1952 and 1955-61). . . . Name pronounced luh-VAL-yur.
HIGH SCHOOL: Trinity (Manchester, N.H.).
COLLEGE: University of Massachusetts Lowell.
TRANSACTIONS/CAREER NOTES: Signed as non-drafted free agent by Philadelphia Phillies organization (July 12, 1981). . . . Traded by Phillies to St. Louis Cardinals for a player to be named later (December 3, 1984); returned to Phillies due to injured status (December 13, 1984). . . . Granted free agency (December 23, 1984). . . . Signed by Louisville, Cardinals organization (January 23, 1985). . . . On Louisville disabled list (July 18-29, 1985). . . . Traded by Cardinals with OF Andy Van Slyke and P Mike Dunne to Pittsburgh Pirates for C Tony Pena (April 1, 1987). . . . On Pittsburgh disabled list (April 17-July 4, 1989); included rehabilitation assignment to Buffalo (June 26-July 4). . . . Granted free agency (October 31, 1991). . . . Re-signed by Pirates (January 3, 1992). . . . Released by Pirates (April 11, 1993). . . . Signed by Chicago White Sox organization (April 23, 1993). . . . On Chicago disabled list (June 27-July 12 and August 4-23, 1995); included rehabilitation assignment to South Bend (July 8-9). . . . Granted free agency (October 13, 1995).
HONORS: Won N.L. Gold Glove at catcher (1987). . . . Named catcher on The Sporting News N.L. All-Star team (1988).
STATISTICAL NOTES: Career major league grand slams: 1.

			BATTING												FIELDING			
Year	Team (League)	Pos.	G	AB	R	H	2B	3B	HR	RBI	Avg.	BB	SO	SB	PO	A	E	Avg.
1981—	Spartanburg (SAL)	3B-OF	39	123	15	33	9	0	2	23	.268	31	16	3	16	32	5	.906

Year	Team (League)	Pos.	G	AB	R	H	2B	3B	HR	RBI	Avg.	BB	SO	SB	PO	A	E	Avg.
			BATTING												FIELDING			
1982—	Peninsula (Caro.)	C-3B	66	178	20	49	4	2	2	23	.275	26	20	3	306	35	6	.983
1983—	Reading (Eastern)	C-3B-P	81	218	24	64	16	2	4	43	.294	32	26	1	243	59	4	.987
1984—	Reading (Eastern)	C-3-2-P	55	147	19	37	6	0	6	22	.252	36	15	0	113	45	2	.988
—	Portland (PCL)	C	37	122	20	38	6	3	5	21	.311	15	11	0	186	16	1	.995
—	Philadelphia (N.L.)	C	6	7	0	0	0	0	0	0	.000	2	2	0	20	2	0	1.000
1985—	St. Louis (N.L.)■	C	12	34	2	5	1	0	0	6	.147	7	3	0	48	5	0	1.000
—	Louisville (A.A.)	C	83	231	19	47	12	1	4	26	.203	48	20	0	420	53	5	.990
1986—	St. Louis (N.L.)	C	110	303	18	71	10	2	3	30	.234	36	37	0	468	47	6	.988
1987—	Pittsburgh (N.L.)■	C	121	340	33	102	19	0	1	36	.300	43	32	0	584	70	5	.992
1988—	Pittsburgh (N.L.)	C	120	352	24	92	18	0	2	47	.261	50	34	3	565	55	8	.987
1989—	Pittsburgh (N.L.)	C	68	190	15	60	10	0	2	23	.316	29	24	0	306	24	3	.991
—	Buffalo (A.A.)	C	7	18	0	2	0	0	0	1	.111	3	4	0	15	1	0	1.000
1990—	Pittsburgh (N.L.)	C	96	279	27	72	15	0	3	31	.258	44	20	0	478	36	5	.990
1991—	Pittsburgh (N.L.)	C	108	336	25	97	11	2	3	41	.289	33	27	2	565	46	1	*.998
1992—	Pittsburgh (N.L.)	C-3B	95	293	22	75	13	1	2	29	.256	44	21	0	421	63	3	.994
1993—	Pittsburgh (N.L.)	C	1	5	0	1	0	0	0	0	.200	0	0	0	12	0	0	1.000
—	Sarasota (Fla. St.)■	C	32	108	6	33	2	0	0	14	.306	19	5	2	141	14	2	.987
—	Chicago (A.L.)	C	37	97	6	25	2	0	0	8	.258	4	14	0	164	28	0	1.000
1994—	Chicago (A.L.)	C	59	139	6	39	4	0	1	24	.281	20	15	0	305	21	3	.991
1995—	Chicago (A.L.)	C	46	98	7	24	6	0	1	19	.245	9	15	0	202	20	1	.996
—	South Bend (Mid.)	C	2	5	1	3	1	0	0	1	.600	1	0	0	3	0	0	1.000
American League totals (3 years)			142	334	19	88	12	0	2	51	.263	33	44	0	671	69	4	.995
National League totals (10 years)			737	2139	166	575	97	5	16	243	.269	288	200	5	3467	348	31	.992
Major league totals (12 years)			879	2473	185	663	109	5	18	294	.268	321	244	5	4138	417	35	.992

CHAMPIONSHIP SERIES RECORD

Year	Team (League)	Pos.	G	AB	R	H	2B	3B	HR	RBI	Avg.	BB	SO	SB	PO	A	E	Avg.
			BATTING												FIELDING			
1990—	Pittsburgh (N.L.)	C	3	6	1	0	0	0	0	0	.000	3	1	0	17	2	0	1.000
1991—	Pittsburgh (N.L.)	C-PH	3	6	0	2	0	0	0	1	.333	2	0	0	14	3	0	1.000
1992—	Pittsburgh (N.L.)	C	3	10	1	2	0	0	0	0	.200	0	3	0	14	0	0	1.000
1993—	Chicago (A.L.)	C	2	3	0	1	0	0	0	0	.333	1	0	0	8	0	0	1.000
Championship series totals (4 years)			11	25	2	5	0	0	0	1	.200	6	4	0	53	5	0	1.000

RECORD AS PITCHER

Year	Team (League)	W	L	Pct.	ERA	G	GS	CG	ShO	Sv.	IP	H	R	ER	BB	SO
1983—	Reading (Eastern)	0	0	...	5.40	4	0	0	0	0	3 1/3	3	3	2	2	2
1984—	Reading (Eastern)	0	0	...	18.00	1	0	0	0	0	1	3	2	2	1	1

LAWTON, MATT — OF — TWINS

PERSONAL: Born November 3, 1971, in Gulfport, Miss. . . . 5-10/196. . . . Bats left, throws right. . . . Full name: Matthew Lawton III.
HIGH SCHOOL: Harrison Central (Gulfport, Miss.).
JUNIOR COLLEGE: Gulf Coast Community College (Fla.).
TRANSACTIONS/CAREER NOTES: Selected by Minnesota Twins organization in 12th round of free-agent draft (June 3, 1991).
STATISTICAL NOTES: Led Florida State League with .407 on-base percentage in 1994.

Year	Team (League)	Pos.	G	AB	R	H	2B	3B	HR	RBI	Avg.	BB	SO	SB	PO	A	E	Avg.
			BATTING												FIELDING			
1992—	GC Twins (GCL)	2B	53	173	39	45	8	3	2	26	.260	27	27	20	129	142	12	.958
1993—	Fort Wayne (Mid.)	OF	111	340	50	97	21	3	9	38	.285	65	42	23	65	6	3	.959
1994—	Fort Myers (FSL)	OF	122	446	79	134	30	1	7	51	.300	80	64	42	188	13	6	.971
1995—	New Britain (East.)	OF	114	412	75	111	19	5	13	54	.269	56	70	26	221	12	2	*.991
—	Minnesota (A.L.)	OF-DH	21	60	11	19	4	1	1	12	.317	7	11	1	34	1	1	.972
Major league totals (1 year)			21	60	11	19	4	1	1	12	.317	7	11	1	34	1	1	.972

LEDESMA, AARON — SS — ANGELS

PERSONAL: Born June 3, 1971, in Union City, Calif. . . . 6-2/200. . . . Bats right, throws right. . . . Full name: Aaron David Ledesma.
HIGH SCHOOL: James Logan (Union City, Calif.).
COLLEGE: Chabot College (Calif.).
TRANSACTIONS/CAREER NOTES: Selected by New York Mets organization in second round of free-agent draft (June 4, 1990). . . . On disabled list (April 13-May 24, 1991 and July 19, 1993-remainder of season). . . . On suspended list (July 29-31, 1994). . . . Traded by Mets to California Angels for OF Kevin Flora (January 18, 1996).
STATISTICAL NOTES: Led Florida State League shortstops with 641 total chances and 79 double plays in 1992. . . . Led International League shortstops with 68 double plays in 1994.

Year	Team (League)	Pos.	G	AB	R	H	2B	3B	HR	RBI	Avg.	BB	SO	SB	PO	A	E	Avg.
			BATTING												FIELDING			
1990—	Kingsport (Appal.)	SS	66	243	50	81	11	1	5	38	.333	30	28	27	78	*170	24	.912
1991—	Columbia (S. Atl.)	SS	33	115	19	39	8	0	1	14	.339	8	16	3	44	64	10	.915
1992—	St. Lucie (Fla. St.)	SS	134	456	51	120	17	2	2	50	.263	46	66	20	185	*411	45	.930
1993—	Binghamton (East.)	SS	66	206	23	55	12	0	5	22	.267	14	43	2	36	65	10	.910
1994—	Norfolk (Int'l)	SS	119	431	49	118	20	1	3	57	.274	28	41	18	157	347	26	*.951
1995—	Norfolk (Int'l)	3B-1B-SS	56	201	26	60	12	1	0	28	.299	10	22	6	73	94	10	.944
—	New York (N.L.)	3B-1B-SS	21	33	4	8	0	0	0	3	.242	6	7	0	5	12	2	.895
Major league totals (1 year)			21	33	4	8	0	0	0	3	.242	6	7	0	5	12	2	.895

LEE, MANNY SS

PERSONAL: Born June 17, 1965, in San Pedro de Macoris, Dominican Republic. . . . 5-9/166. . . . Bats both, throws right. . . . Full name: Manuel Lora Lee.

TRANSACTIONS/CAREER NOTES: Signed as non-drafted free agent by New York Mets organization (May 10, 1982). . . . On disabled list (April 9-22, 1984). . . . Traded by Mets organization with OF Gerald Young to Houston Astros (August 31, 1984) as partial completion of deal in which Mets acquired IF Ray Knight from Astros for three players to be named later (August 28, 1984); Astros acquired P Mitch Cook to complete deal (September 10, 1984). . . . Selected by Toronto Blue Jays from Astros organization in Rule 5 major league draft (December 3, 1984). . . . On disabled list (March 28-April 12 and May 12-June 1, 1988; and April 30-June 6, 1989). . . . Granted free agency (November 4, 1992). . . . Signed by Texas Rangers (December 19, 1992). . . . On disabled list (March 27-April 16 and May 15-July 24, 1993; and June 4-19, 1994). . . . Granted free agency (October 28, 1994). . . . Signed by New Jersey, St. Louis Cardinals organization (April 18, 1995). . . . On St. Louis disabled list (April 27-June 16, 1995); included rehabilitation assignment to Louisville (May 16-25 and May 26-June 2). . . . Released by Cardinals (June 22, 1995).

STATISTICAL NOTES: Led A.L. second basemen with .993 fielding percentage in 1990.

							BATTING							FIELDING			
Year	Team (League)	Pos.	G	AB	R	H	2B	3B	HR	RBI	Avg.	BB	SO	SB	PO	A	E	Avg.
1982—	Kingsport (Appal.)	2B-SS	16	54	2	12	1	0	0	3	.222	3	12	0	34	34	6	.919
1983—	GC Mets (GCL)	2B-SS	32	97	8	24	2	1	0	12	.247	13	14	2	44	79	8	.939
—	Little Falls (NYP)	2B	17	45	10	13	0	0	0	5	.289	9	11	2	34	40	3	.961
1984—	Columbia (S. Atl.)	SS-2B	102	346	84	114	12	5	2	33	*.329	60	42	24	126	277	34	.922
1985—	Toronto (A.L.)■	2-S-DH-3	64	40	9	8	0	0	0	0	.200	2	9	1	34	56	3	.968
1986—	Syracuse (Int'l)	SS-2B	76	236	34	58	6	1	1	19	.246	21	39	7	132	237	18	.953
—	Knoxville (South.)	SS-2B	41	158	21	43	1	2	0	11	.272	20	29	8	70	117	8	.959
—	Toronto (A.L.)	2B-SS-3B	35	78	8	16	0	1	1	7	.205	4	10	0	36	76	2	.982
1987—	Toronto (A.L.)	2B-SS-DH	56	121	14	31	2	3	1	11	.256	6	13	2	77	110	5	.974
—	Syracuse (Int'l)	SS	74	251	25	71	9	5	3	26	.283	18	50	2	120	177	23	.928
1988—	Toronto (A.L.)	2-S-3-DH	116	381	38	111	16	3	2	38	.291	26	64	3	250	308	12	.979
1989—	Toronto (A.L.)	2-S-3-DH-O	99	300	27	78	9	2	3	34	.260	20	60	4	152	201	11	.970
1990—	Toronto (A.L.)	2B-SS	117	391	45	95	12	4	6	41	.243	26	90	3	265	301	4	†.993
1991—	Toronto (A.L.)	SS	138	445	41	104	18	3	0	29	.234	24	107	7	194	360	19	.967
1992—	Toronto (A.L.)	SS	128	396	49	104	10	1	3	39	.263	50	73	6	187	331	7	.987
1993—	Texas (A.L.)■	SS-DH	73	205	31	45	3	1	1	12	.220	22	39	2	96	205	10	.968
1994—	Texas (A.L.)	SS-2B	95	335	41	93	18	2	2	38	.278	21	66	3	151	282	13	.971
1995—	St. Louis (N.L.)■	2B	1	1	1	1	0	0	0	0	1.000	0	0	0	2	2	1	.800
—	Louisville (A.A.)	SS	6	22	2	6	0	0	0	0	.273	0	2	1	4	3	0	1.000
—	St. Peters. (FSL)	SS-2B	6	17	2	6	1	0	0	3	.353	2	3	0	2	10	2	.857
American League totals (10 years)			921	2692	303	685	88	20	19	249	.254	201	531	31	1442	2230	86	.977
National League totals (1 year)			1	1	1	1	0	0	0	0	1.000	0	0	0	2	2	1	.800
Major league totals (11 years)			922	2693	304	686	88	20	19	249	.255	201	531	31	1444	2232	87	.977

CHAMPIONSHIP SERIES RECORD

							BATTING							FIELDING			
Year	Team (League)	Pos.	G	AB	R	H	2B	3B	HR	RBI	Avg.	BB	SO	SB	PO	A	E	Avg.
1985—	Toronto (A.L.)	PR-2B	1	0	0	0	0	0	0	0	...	0	0	0	0	0	0	...
1989—	Toronto (A.L.)	2B	2	8	2	2	0	0	0	0	.250	0	1	0	4	1	0	1.000
1991—	Toronto (A.L.)	SS	5	16	3	2	0	0	0	0	.125	1	5	0	8	16	1	.960
1992—	Toronto (A.L.)	SS	6	18	2	5	1	1	0	3	.278	1	2	0	12	15	3	.900
Championship series totals (4 years)			14	42	7	9	1	1	0	3	.214	2	8	0	24	32	4	.933

WORLD SERIES RECORD

NOTES: Member of World Series championship team (1992).

							BATTING							FIELDING			
Year	Team (League)	Pos.	G	AB	R	H	2B	3B	HR	RBI	Avg.	BB	SO	SB	PO	A	E	Avg.
1992—	Toronto (A.L.)	SS	6	19	1	2	0	0	0	0	.105	1	2	0	14	10	1	.960

LEE, MARK P ORIOLES

PERSONAL: Born July 20, 1964, in Williston, N.D. . . . 6-3/200. . . . Throws left, bats left. . . . Full name: Mark Owen Lee.

HIGH SCHOOL: Natrona County (Casper, Wyo.).

JUNIOR COLLEGE: Trinidad (Colo.) State Junior College.

COLLEGE: Florida International.

TRANSACTIONS/CAREER NOTES: Selected by Detroit Tigers organization in 15th round of free-agent draft (June 3, 1985). . . . Traded by Tigers organization with C Rey Palacios to Kansas City Royals for P Ted Power (August 31, 1988). . . . Released by Royals organization (March 31, 1990). . . . Signed by Stockton, Milwaukee Brewers organization (May 23, 1990). . . . Granted free agency (October 10, 1992). . . . Signed by Texas Rangers organization (December 8, 1992). . . . Granted free agency (October 15, 1993). . . . Signed by Iowa, Chicago Cubs organization (January 12, 1994). . . . Granted free agency (October 15, 1994). . . . Signed by Rochester, Baltimore Orioles organization (November 18, 1994).

Year	Team (League)	W	L	Pct.	ERA	G	GS	CG	ShO	Sv.	IP	H	R	ER	BB	SO
1985—	Bristol (Appal.)	3	0	1.000	1.09	15	1	0	0	5	33	18	5	4	12	40
1986—	Lakeland (Fla. St.)	2	5	.286	5.17	41	0	0	0	10	62 2/3	73	44	36	21	39
1987—	Glens Falls (East.)	0	0	...	8.64	7	0	0	0	0	8 1/3	13	9	8	1	3
—	Lakeland (Fla. St.)	3	2	.600	2.55	30	0	0	0	4	53	48	17	15	18	42
1988—	Lakeland (Fla. St.)	1	0	1.000	1.42	10	0	0	0	1	19	16	7	3	4	15
—	Glens Falls (East.)	3	0	1.000	2.42	14	0	0	0	1	26	27	10	7	4	25
—	Toledo (Int'l)	0	1	.000	2.79	22	0	0	0	0	19 1/3	18	7	6	7	13
—	Kansas City (A.L.)■	0	0	...	3.60	4	0	0	0	0	5	6	2	2	1	0
1989—	Memphis (South.)	5	11	.313	5.21	25	24	0	0	0	122 2/3	149	84	71	44	79
1990—	Stockton (Calif.)■	1	0	1.000	2.35	5	0	0	0	1	7 2/3	5	2	2	3	7
—	Denver (Am. Assoc.)	3	1	.750	2.25	20	0	0	0	4	28	25	7	7	6	35
—	Milwaukee (A.L.)	1	0	1.000	2.11	11	0	0	0	0	21 1/3	20	5	5	4	14

Year	Team (League)	W	L	Pct.	ERA	G	GS	CG	ShO	Sv.	IP	H	R	ER	BB	SO
1991—	Milwaukee (A.L.)	2	5	.286	3.86	62	0	0	0	1	67 2/3	72	33	29	31	43
1992—	Denver (Am. Assoc.)	2	4	.333	4.19	48	0	0	0	1	68 2/3	78	45	32	26	57
1993—	Okla. City (A.A.)■	5	3	.625	4.34	52	1	0	0	4	101 2/3	112	61	49	43	65
1994—	Iowa (Am. Assoc.)■	1	3	.250	3.38	54	0	0	0	10	61 1/3	69	27	23	21	42
1995—	Rochester (Int'l)■	4	2	.667	1.57	25	0	0	0	3	28 2/3	18	6	5	5	35
—	Baltimore (A.L.)	2	0	1.000	4.86	39	0	0	0	1	33 1/3	31	18	18	18	27
Major league totals (4 years)		5	5	.500	3.82	116	0	0	0	2	127 1/3	129	58	54	54	84

LEFTWICH, PHIL — P — ANGELS

PERSONAL: Born May 19, 1969, in Lynchburg, Va. . . . 6-5/205. . . . Throws right, bats right. . . . Full name: Phillip Dale Leftwich.
HIGH SCHOOL: Brookville (Lynchburg, Va.).
COLLEGE: Radford (Va.).
TRANSACTIONS/CAREER NOTES: Selected by California Angels organization in second round of free-agent draft (June 4, 1990). . . . On California disabled list (June 7-28, 1994); included rehabilitation assignment to Lake Elsinore (June 23-25). . . . On California disabled list (April 18-August 27, 1995); included rehabilitation assignments to Mesa (July 12-August 2) and Vancouver (August 2-25).

Year	Team (League)	W	L	Pct.	ERA	G	GS	CG	ShO	Sv.	IP	H	R	ER	BB	SO
1990—	Boise (Northwest)	8	2	.800	1.86	15	15	0	0	0	92	88	36	19	22	81
1991—	Quad City (Midw.)	11	9	.550	3.28	26	26	5	1	0	173	158	70	63	59	163
—	Midland (Texas)	1	0	1.000	3.00	1	1	0	0	0	6	5	2	2	5	3
1992—	Midland (Texas)	6	9	.400	5.88	21	21	0	0	0	121	156	90	79	37	85
1993—	Vancouver (PCL)	7	7	.500	4.64	20	20	3	1	0	126	138	74	65	45	102
—	California (A.L.)	4	6	.400	3.79	12	12	1	0	0	80 2/3	81	35	34	27	31
1994—	California (A.L.)	5	10	.333	5.68	20	20	1	0	0	114	127	75	72	42	67
—	Lake Elsinore (California)	1	0	1.000	0.00	1	1	0	0	0	6	3	0	0	1	4
1995—	Arizona Angels (Ar.)	1	1	.500	0.45	4	4	0	0	0	20	13	4	1	2	32
—	Vancouver (PCL)	2	0	1.000	3.19	6	5	1	0	0	36 2/3	28	13	13	9	25
Major league totals (2 years)		9	16	.360	4.90	32	32	2	0	0	194 2/3	208	110	106	69	98

LEIPER, DAVE — P — PHILLIES

PERSONAL: Born June 18, 1962, in Whittier, Calif. . . . 6-1/175. . . . Throws left, bats left. . . . Full name: David Paul Leiper.
HIGH SCHOOL: Lowell (Calif.).
COLLEGE: Fullerton College.
TRANSACTIONS/CAREER NOTES: Selected by Texas Rangers organization in second round of free-agent draft (January 13, 1981); did not sign. . . . Selected by San Francisco Giants organization in secondary phase of free-agent draft (June 8, 1981); did not sign. . . . Selected by Oakland Athletics organization in secondary phase of free-agent draft (January 12, 1982). . . . On disabled list (April 11-May 13, 1985). . . . Traded by A's organization to San Diego Padres organization (August 31, 1987); partial completion of trade in which Padres traded P Storm Davis to Athletics organization for two players to be named later (August 20, 1987); Padres aquired 1B Rob Nelson to complete deal (September 8, 1987). . . . On disabled list (March 27-April 18 and May 3-23, 1988). . . . On disabled list (June 14-July 15, 1989); included rehabilitation assignment to Las Vegas (June 27-July 15). . . . Released by Padres organization (December 19, 1989). . . . Signed by A's organization (January 16, 1990). . . . On Oakland disabled list (April 13-August 20, 1990). . . . Granted free agency (October 15, 1990). . . . Signed by Edmonton, California Angels organization (April 6, 1991). . . . On disabled list (May 26-July 15, 1991). . . . Released by Edmonton, Angels organization (July 15, 1991). . . . Signed by Milwaukee Brewers organization (December 9, 1991). . . . Released by Denver, Brewers organization (March 29, 1992). . . . Signed by Buffalo, Pittsburgh Pirates organization (July 2, 1993). . . . On Buffalo disabled list (July 2-August 5, 1993). . . . Granted free agency (October 15, 1993). . . . Signed by A's organization (November 17, 1993). . . . Traded by A's organization to Montreal Expos organization for OF Kevin Northrup (July 25, 1995). . . . Granted free agency (December 21, 1995). . . . Signed by Philadelphia Phillies organization (January 9, 1996).

Year	Team (League)	W	L	Pct.	ERA	G	GS	CG	ShO	Sv.	IP	H	R	ER	BB	SO
1982—	Idaho Falls (Pio.)	9	3	.750	4.11	14	13	4	1	0	85 1/3	94	49	39	27	77
1983—	Madison (Midwest)	5	4	.556	3.74	16	15	0	0	0	79 1/3	89	43	33	37	60
1984—	Modesto (Calif.)	5	0	1.000	0.25	19	0	0	0	7	35 1/3	12	2	1	14	30
—	Tacoma (PCL)	2	3	.400	3.03	28	0	0	0	11	32 2/3	33	11	11	14	13
—	Oakland (A.L.)	1	0	1.000	9.00	8	0	0	0	0	7	12	7	7	5	3
1985—	Modesto (Calif.)	1	0	1.000	7.80	21	0	0	0	1	30	53	31	26	19	24
1986—	Tacoma (PCL)	2	1	.667	4.85	20	0	0	0	2	26	30	17	14	9	13
—	Oakland (A.L.)	2	2	.500	4.83	33	0	0	0	1	31 2/3	28	17	17	18	15
1987—	Tacoma (PCL)	0	0	...	0.00	5	0	0	0	1	9	3	0	0	1	6
—	Oakland (A.L.)	2	1	.667	3.78	45	0	0	0	1	52 1/3	49	28	22	18	33
—	San Diego (N.L.)■	1	0	1.000	4.50	12	0	0	0	1	16	16	8	8	5	10
1988—	San Diego (N.L.)	3	0	1.000	2.17	35	0	0	0	1	54	45	19	13	14	33
1989—	San Diego (N.L.)	0	1	.000	5.02	22	0	0	0	0	28 2/3	40	19	16	20	7
—	Las Vegas (PCL)	2	2	.500	5.85	11	0	0	0	3	20	23	15	13	10	12
1990—	Tacoma (PCL)■	0	1	.000	5.82	6	0	0	0	2	17	19	12	11	9	8
—	Modesto (Calif.)	1	0	1.000	0.00	3	1	0	0	0	9	2	0	0	1	6
1991—	Edmonton (PCL)■	1	0	1.000	7.64	13	0	0	0	1	17 2/3	30	15	15	5	8
1992—								Did not play.								
1993—	GC Pirates (GCL)■	0	0	...	1.69	7	4	0	0	0	21 1/3	17	4	4	0	24
—	Carolina (South.)	2	1	.667	1.48	8	4	2	1	0	30 1/3	26	6	5	5	16
1994—	Tacoma (PCL)■	1	1	.500	2.05	17	0	0	0	4	26 1/3	25	8	6	8	24
—	Oakland (A.L.)	0	0	...	1.93	26	0	0	0	1	18 2/3	13	4	4	6	14
1995—	Oakland (A.L.)	1	1	.500	3.57	24	0	0	0	0	22 2/3	23	10	9	13	10
—	Edmonton (PCL)	1	0	1.000	13.50	2	0	0	0	0	1 1/3	4	2	2	2	1
—	Ottawa (Int'l)■	0	0	...	0.00	2	0	0	0	0	3	1	0	0	1	2
—	Montreal (N.L.)	0	2	.000	2.86	26	0	0	0	2	22	16	8	7	6	12
A.L. totals (5 years)		6	4	.600	4.01	136	0	0	0	3	132 1/3	125	66	59	60	75
N.L. totals (4 years)		4	3	.571	3.28	95	0	0	0	4	120 2/3	117	54	44	45	62
Major league totals (7 years)		10	7	.588	3.66	231	0	0	0	7	253	242	120	103	105	137

LEITER, AL — P — MARLINS

PERSONAL: Born October 23, 1965, in Toms River, N.J. . . . 6-3/215. . . . Throws left, bats left. . . . Full name: Alois Terry Leiter. . . . Brother of Mark Leiter, pitcher, San Francisco Giants; and brother of Kurt Leiter, minor league pitcher (1982-84 and 1986). . . . Name pronounced LIE-ter.

HIGH SCHOOL: Central Regional (Bayville, N.J.).

TRANSACTIONS/CAREER NOTES: Selected by New York Yankees organization in second round of free-agent draft (June 4, 1984). . . . On New York disabled list (June 22-July 26, 1988); included rehabilitation assignment to Columbus (July 17-25). . . . Traded by Yankees to Toronto Blue Jays for OF Jesse Barfield (April 30, 1989). . . . On Toronto disabled list (May 11, 1989-remainder of season); included rehabilitation assignment to Dunedin (August 12-29). . . . On Syracuse disabled list (May 20-June 13, 1990). . . . On Toronto disabled list (April 27, 1991-remainder of season); included rehabilitation assignments to Dunedin (May 20-28 and July 19-August 7). . . . On disabled list (April 24-May 9, 1993 and June 9-24, 1994). . . . Granted free agency (November 6, 1995). . . . Signed by Florida Marlins (December 14, 1995).

STATISTICAL NOTES: Tied for A.L. lead with five balks in 1994. . . . Led A.L. with 14 wild pitches in 1995.

Year	Team (League)	W	L	Pct.	ERA	G	GS	CG	ShO	Sv.	IP	H	R	ER	BB	SO
1984—	Oneonta (N.Y.-Penn)	3	2	.600	3.63	10	10	0	0	0	57	52	32	23	26	48
1985—	Oneonta (N.Y.-Penn)	3	2	.600	2.37	6	6	2	0	0	38	27	14	10	25	34
—	Fort Lauder. (FSL)	1	6	.143	6.48	17	17	1	0	0	82	87	70	59	57	44
1986—	Fort Lauder. (FSL)	4	8	.333	4.05	22	21	1	1	0	117 2/3	96	64	53	90	101
1987—	Columbus (Int'l)	1	4	.200	6.17	5	5	0	0	0	23 1/3	21	18	16	15	23
—	Alb./Colon. (East.)	3	3	.500	3.35	15	14	2	0	0	78	64	34	29	37	71
—	New York (A.L.)	2	2	.500	6.35	4	4	0	0	0	22 2/3	24	16	16	15	28
1988—	New York (A.L.)	4	4	.500	3.92	14	14	0	0	0	57 1/3	49	27	25	33	60
—	Columbus (Int'l)	0	2	.000	3.46	4	4	0	0	0	13	5	7	5	14	12
1989—	New York (A.L.)	1	2	.333	6.08	4	4	0	0	0	26 2/3	23	20	18	21	22
—	Toronto (A.L.)■	0	0	...	4.05	1	1	0	0	0	6 2/3	9	3	3	2	4
—	Dunedin (Fla. St.)	0	2	.000	5.63	3	3	0	0	0	8	11	5	5	5	4
1990—	Dunedin (Fla. St.)	0	0	...	2.63	6	6	0	0	0	24	18	8	7	12	14
—	Syracuse (Int'l)	3	8	.273	4.62	15	14	1	1	0	78	59	43	40	68	69
—	Toronto (A.L.)	0	0	...	0.00	4	0	0	0	0	6 1/3	1	0	0	2	5
1991—	Toronto (A.L.)	0	0	...	27.00	3	0	0	0	0	1 2/3	3	5	5	5	1
—	Dunedin (Fla. St.)	0	0	...	1.86	4	3	0	0	0	9 2/3	5	2	2	7	5
1992—	Syracuse (Int'l)	8	9	.471	3.86	27	27	2	0	0	163 1/3	159	82	70	64	108
—	Toronto (A.L.)	0	0	...	9.00	1	0	0	0	0	1	1	1	1	2	0
1993—	Toronto (A.L.)	9	6	.600	4.11	34	12	1	1	2	105	93	52	48	56	66
1994—	Toronto (A.L.)	6	7	.462	5.08	20	20	1	0	0	111 2/3	125	68	63	65	100
1995—	Toronto (A.L.)	11	11	.500	3.64	28	28	2	1	0	183	162	80	74	*108	153
Major league totals (9 years)		33	32	.508	4.36	113	83	4	2	2	522	490	272	253	309	439

CHAMPIONSHIP SERIES RECORD

Year	Team (League)	W	L	Pct.	ERA	G	GS	CG	ShO	Sv.	IP	H	R	ER	BB	SO
1993—	Toronto (A.L.)	0	0	...	3.38	2	0	0	0	0	2 2/3	4	1	1	2	2

WORLD SERIES RECORD

NOTES: Member of World Series championship team (1993).

Year	Team (League)	W	L	Pct.	ERA	G	GS	CG	ShO	Sv.	IP	H	R	ER	BB	SO
1993—	Toronto (A.L.)	1	0	1.000	7.71	3	0	0	0	0	7	12	6	6	2	5

LEITER, MARK — P — GIANTS

PERSONAL: Born April 13, 1963, in Joliet, Ill. . . . 6-3/210. . . . Throws right, bats right. . . . Full name: Mark Edward Leiter. . . . Brother of Al Leiter, pitcher, Florida Marlins; and brother of Kurt Leiter, minor league pitcher (1982-84 and 1986). . . . Name pronounced LIE-ter.

HIGH SCHOOL: Central Regional (Bayville, N.J.).

JUNIOR COLLEGE: Connors State College (Okla.).

COLLEGE: Ramapo College of New Jersey.

TRANSACTIONS/CAREER NOTES: Selected by Baltimore Orioles organization in fourth round of free-agent draft (January 11, 1983). . . . On disabled list (April 10, 1986-entire season; April 10, 1987-entire season; and April 10-June 13, 1988). . . . Released by Orioles organization (June 13, 1988). . . . Signed by Fort Lauderdale, New York Yankees organization (September 29, 1988). . . . Traded by Yankees to Detroit Tigers for IF Torey Lovullo (March 19, 1991). . . . On Detroit disabled list (June 6-23, 1991; July 24-August 24, 1992; and August 4-September 1, 1993). . . . Released by Tigers (March 15, 1994). . . . Signed by California Angels (March 21, 1994). . . . Granted free agency (December 23, 1994). . . . Signed by Phoenix, San Francisco Giants organization (April 10, 1995).

STATISTICAL NOTES: Tied for A.L. lead with nine hit batsmen in 1994. . . . Led N.L. with 17 hit batsmen in 1995.

Year	Team (League)	W	L	Pct.	ERA	G	GS	CG	ShO	Sv.	IP	H	R	ER	BB	SO
1983—	Bluefield (Appal.)	2	1	.667	2.70	6	6	2	0	0	36 2/3	33	17	11	13	35
—	Hagerstown (Caro.)	1	5	.167	7.25	8	8	0	0	0	36	42	31	29	28	18
1984—	Hagerstown (Caro.)	8	•13	.381	5.62	27	24	5	1	0	139 1/3	132	96	87	*108	105
1985—	Hagerstown (Caro.)	2	8	.200	3.46	34	6	1	0	8	83 1/3	77	44	32	29	82
—	Charlotte (South.)	0	1	.000	1.42	5	0	0	0	1	6 1/3	3	1	1	2	8
1986—								Did not play.								
1987—								Did not play.								
1988—								Did not play.								
1989—	Fort Lauder. (FSL)■	2	2	.500	1.53	6	4	1	0	1	35 1/3	27	9	6	5	22
—	Columbus (Int'l)	9	6	.600	5.00	22	12	0	0	0	90	102	50	50	34	70
1990—	Columbus (Int'l)	9	4	.692	3.60	30	14	2	1	1	122 2/3	114	56	49	27	115
—	New York (A.L.)	1	1	.500	6.84	8	3	0	0	0	26 1/3	33	20	20	9	21
1991—	Toledo (Int'l)■	1	0	1.000	0.00	5	0	0	0	1	6 2/3	6	0	0	3	7
—	Detroit (A.L.)	9	7	.563	4.21	38	15	1	0	1	134 2/3	125	66	63	50	103
1992—	Detroit (A.L.)	8	5	.615	4.18	35	14	1	0	0	112	116	57	52	43	75
1993—	Detroit (A.L.)	6	6	.500	4.73	27	13	1	0	0	106 2/3	111	61	56	44	70
1994—	California (A.L.)■	4	7	.364	4.72	40	7	0	0	2	95 1/3	99	56	50	35	71
1995—	San Francisco (N.L.)■	10	12	.455	3.82	30	29	7	1	0	195 2/3	185	91	83	55	129
A.L. totals (5 years)		28	26	.519	4.57	148	52	3	0	3	475	484	260	241	181	340
N.L. totals (1 year)		10	12	.455	3.82	30	29	7	1	0	195 2/3	185	91	83	55	129
Major league totals (6 years)		38	38	.500	4.35	178	81	10	1	3	670 2/3	669	351	324	236	469

L

LEIUS, SCOTT 3B/SS

PERSONAL: Born September 24, 1965, in Yonkers, N.Y. . . . 6-3/208. . . . Bats right, throws right. . . . Full name: Scott Thomas Leius. . . . Name pronounced LAY-us.

HIGH SCHOOL: Mamaroneck (N.Y.).

COLLEGE: Concordia College (N.Y.).

TRANSACTIONS/CAREER NOTES: Selected by Minnesota Twins organization in 13th round of free-agent draft (June 2, 1986). . . . On disabled list (August 3, 1989-remainder of season and April 22, 1993-remainder of season). . . . Granted free agency (October 10, 1995).

STATISTICAL NOTES: Led Appalachian League shortstops with 174 assists and 33 double plays in 1986. . . . Led Midwest League shortstops with 74 double plays in 1987.

				BATTING											FIELDING			
Year	Team (League)	Pos.	G	AB	R	H	2B	3B	HR	RBI	Avg.	BB	SO	SB	PO	A	E	Avg.
1986—	Elizabeth. (Appal.)	SS-3B	61	237	37	66	14	1	4	23	.278	26	45	5	67	†176	18	.931
1987—	Kenosha (Midwest)	SS	126	414	65	99	16	4	8	51	.239	50	88	6	183	331	31	.943
1988—	Visalia (California)	SS	93	308	44	73	14	4	3	46	.237	42	50	3	154	234	15	.963
1989—	Orlando (Southern)	SS	99	346	49	105	22	2	4	45	*.303	38	74	3	148	257	22	.948
1990—	Portland (PCL)	SS-2B	103	352	34	81	13	5	2	23	.230	35	66	5	155	323	18	.964
—	Minnesota (A.L.)	SS-3B	14	25	4	6	1	0	1	4	.240	2	2	0	20	25	0	1.000
1991—	Minnesota (A.L.)	3B-SS-OF	109	199	35	57	7	2	5	20	.286	30	35	5	56	129	7	.964
1992—	Minnesota (A.L.)	3B-SS	129	409	50	102	18	2	2	35	.249	34	61	6	63	261	15	.956
1993—	Minnesota (A.L.)	SS	10	18	4	3	0	0	0	2	.167	2	4	0	10	26	2	.947
1994—	Minnesota (A.L.)	3B-SS	97	350	57	86	16	1	14	49	.246	37	58	2	63	185	8	.969
1995—	Minnesota (A.L.)	3B-SS-DH	117	372	51	92	16	5	4	45	.247	49	54	2	60	187	14	.946
Major league totals (6 years)			476	1373	201	346	58	10	26	155	.252	154	214	15	272	813	46	.959

CHAMPIONSHIP SERIES RECORD

				BATTING											FIELDING			
Year	Team (League)	Pos.	G	AB	R	H	2B	3B	HR	RBI	Avg.	BB	SO	SB	PO	A	E	Avg.
1991—	Minnesota (A.L.)	3B-PH	3	4	0	0	0	0	0	0	.000	1	1	0	1	4	0	1.000

WORLD SERIES RECORD

NOTES: Member of World Series championship team (1991).

				BATTING											FIELDING			
Year	Team (League)	Pos.	G	AB	R	H	2B	3B	HR	RBI	Avg.	BB	SO	SB	PO	A	E	Avg.
1991—	Minnesota (A.L.)	3B-PH-SS	7	14	2	5	0	0	1	2	.357	1	2	0	5	8	1	.929

LEMKE, MARK 2B BRAVES

PERSONAL: Born August 13, 1965, in Utica, N.Y. . . . 5-9/167. . . . Bats both, throws right. . . . Full name: Mark Alan Lemke. . . . Name pronounced LEM-kee.

HIGH SCHOOL: Notre Dame (Utica, N.Y.).

TRANSACTIONS/CAREER NOTES: Selected by Atlanta Braves organization in 27th round of free-agent draft (June 6, 1983). . . . On Atlanta disabled list (May 29-July 17, 1990); included rehabilitation assignment to Gulf Coast Braves (July 9-17). . . . On disabled list (June 25-July 18, 1995).

STATISTICAL NOTES: Led Gulf Coast League second basemen with .977 fielding percentage, 175 putouts, 207 assists, 391 total chances and 39 double plays in 1984. . . . Led Carolina League second basemen with .982 fielding percentage, 355 assists and 83 double plays in 1987. . . . Led Southern League with 239 total bases in 1988. . . . Led Southern League second basemen with 739 total chances and 105 double plays in 1988. . . . Led International League second basemen with 731 total chances and 105 double plays in 1989. . . . Led N.L. second basemen with 785 total chances and 100 double plays in 1993.

				BATTING											FIELDING			
Year	Team (League)	Pos.	G	AB	R	H	2B	3B	HR	RBI	Avg.	BB	SO	SB	PO	A	E	Avg.
1983—	GC Braves (GCL)	2B	53	209	37	55	6	0	0	19	.263	30	19	10	81	101	11	.943
1984—	Anderson (S. Atl.)	2B-3B	42	121	18	18	2	0	0	5	.149	14	14	3	67	83	4	.974
—	GC Braves (GCL)	2B-SS	•63	*243	41	67	11	0	3	32	.276	29	14	2	†175	†209	9	†.977
1985—	Sumter (S. Atl.)	2B	90	231	25	50	6	0	0	20	.216	34	22	2	119	174	11	.964
1986—	Sumter (S. Atl.)	3B-2B	126	448	99	122	24	2	18	66	.272	87	31	11	134	274	16	.962
1987—	Durham (Carolina)	2B-3B	127	489	75	143	28	3	20	68	.292	54	45	10	248	†355	11	†.982
—	Greenville (South.)	3B	6	26	0	6	0	0	0	4	.231	0	4	0	4	12	1	.941
1988—	Greenville (South.)	2B	•143	*567	81	*153	30	4	16	80	.270	52	92	18	*281	*440	18	.976
—	Atlanta (N.L.)	2B	16	58	8	13	4	0	0	2	.224	4	5	0	47	51	3	.970
1989—	Richmond (Int'l)	2B	*146	*518	69	143	22	7	5	61	.276	66	45	4	*299	*417	*15	.979
—	Atlanta (N.L.)	2B	14	55	4	10	2	1	2	10	.182	5	7	0	25	40	0	1.000
1990—	Atlanta (N.L.)	3B-2B-SS	102	239	22	54	13	0	0	21	.226	21	22	0	90	193	4	.986
—	GC Braves (GCL)	2B-3B	4	11	2	4	0	0	1	5	.364	1	3	0	5	11	1	.941
1991—	Atlanta (N.L.)	2B-3B	136	269	36	63	11	2	2	23	.234	29	27	1	162	215	10	.974
1992—	Atlanta (N.L.)	2B-3B	155	427	38	97	7	4	6	26	.227	50	39	0	236	335	9	.984
1993—	Atlanta (N.L.)	2B	151	493	52	124	19	2	7	49	.252	65	50	1	*329	442	14	.982
1994—	Atlanta (N.L.)	2B	104	350	40	103	15	0	3	31	.294	38	37	0	209	300	3	*.994
1995—	Atlanta (N.L.)	2B	116	399	42	101	16	5	5	38	.253	44	40	2	205	305	5	.990
Major league totals (8 years)			794	2290	242	565	87	14	25	200	.247	256	227	4	1303	1881	48	.985

DIVISION SERIES RECORD

				BATTING											FIELDING			
Year	Team (League)	Pos.	G	AB	R	H	2B	3B	HR	RBI	Avg.	BB	SO	SB	PO	A	E	Avg.
1995—	Atlanta (N.L.)	2B	4	19	3	4	1	0	0	1	.211	1	3	0	8	16	0	1.000

CHAMPIONSHIP SERIES RECORD

NOTES: Holds N.L. career record for most games with one club—24.

Year	Team (League)	Pos.	G	AB	R	H	2B	3B	HR	RBI	Avg.	BB	SO	SB	PO	A	E	Avg.
				BATTING											FIELDING			
1991—	Atlanta (N.L.)	2B	7	20	1	4	1	0	0	1	.200	4	0	0	12	10	1	.957
1992—	Atlanta (N.L.)	2B-3B	7	21	2	7	1	0	0	2	.333	5	3	0	11	17	0	1.000
1993—	Atlanta (N.L.)	2B	6	24	2	5	2	0	0	4	.208	1	6	0	6	19	2	.926
1995—	Atlanta (N.L.)	2B	4	18	2	3	0	0	0	1	.167	1	0	0	13	16	0	1.000
Championship series totals (4 years)			24	83	7	19	4	0	0	8	.229	11	9	0	42	62	3	.972

WORLD SERIES RECORD

NOTES: Shares single-game record for most triples—2 (October 24, 1991). . . . Member of World Series championship team (1995).

Year	Team (League)	Pos.	G	AB	R	H	2B	3B	HR	RBI	Avg.	BB	SO	SB	PO	A	E	Avg.
				BATTING											FIELDING			
1991—	Atlanta (N.L.)	2B	6	24	4	10	1	3	0	4	.417	2	4	0	14	19	1	.971
1992—	Atlanta (N.L.)	2B	6	19	0	4	0	0	0	2	.211	1	3	0	18	12	0	1.000
1995—	Atlanta (N.L.)	2B	6	22	1	6	0	0	0	0	.273	3	2	0	10	24	1	.971
World Series totals (3 years)			18	65	5	20	1	3	0	6	.308	6	9	0	42	55	2	.980

LEONARD, MARK — OF — GIANTS

PERSONAL: Born August 14, 1964, in Mountain View, Calif. . . . 6-0/212. . . . Bats left, throws right. . . . Full name: Mark David Leonard.
HIGH SCHOOL: Fremont (Calif.).
COLLEGE: UC Santa Barbara.
TRANSACTIONS/CAREER NOTES: Selected by San Francisco Giants organization in 29th round of free-agent draft (June 2, 1986). . . . Loaned by Giants organization to Tri-Cities, independent (June 23-September 1, 1986). . . . On Phoenix disabled list (August 6, 1989-remainder of season). . . . On San Francisco disabled list (August 8-September 5, 1990); included rehabilitation assignment to Phoenix (August 27-September 5). . . . On San Francisco disabled list (April 19-June 15, 1992); included rehabilitation assignment to Phoenix (May 26-June 14). . . . Traded by Giants to Baltimore Orioles for IF Steve Scarsone (March 20, 1993). . . . Released by Orioles (December 12, 1993). . . . Signed by Phoenix, Giants organization (January 28, 1994). . . . On Phoenix temporarily inactive list (April 13-May 1, 1995).
STATISTICAL NOTES: Led California League with 283 total bases, 11 sacrifice flies and 13 intentional bases on balls received in 1988.

Year	Team (League)	Pos.	G	AB	R	H	2B	3B	HR	RBI	Avg.	BB	SO	SB	PO	A	E	Avg.
				BATTING											FIELDING			
1986—	Eve.-T.-C. (N'west)■	OF-1B-C	38	128	21	33	6	0	4	17	.258	27	21	4	63	2	4	.942
1987—	Clinton (Midwest)■	1B	128	413	57	132	31	2	15	80	.320	71	61	5	610	47	9	.986
1988—	San Jose (Calif.)■	OF-1B	*142	510	102	176	*50	6	15	*118	.345	*118	82	11	178	120	9	.971
1989—	Shreveport (Texas)	OF	63	219	29	68	15	3	10	52	.311	33	40	1	90	5	0	1.000
—	Phoenix (PCL)	OF	27	78	7	21	4	0	0	6	.269	9	15	1	29	1	3	.909
1990—	Phoenix (PCL)	OF	109	390	76	130	22	2	19	82	.333	76	81	6	120	3	1	.992
—	San Francisco (N.L.)	OF	11	17	3	3	1	0	1	2	.176	3	8	0	10	0	0	1.000
1991—	San Francisco (N.L.)	OF	64	129	14	31	7	1	2	14	.240	12	25	0	41	0	0	1.000
—	Phoenix (PCL)	OF	41	146	27	37	7	0	8	25	.253	21	29	1	45	3	3	.941
1992—	San Francisco (N.L.)	OF	55	128	13	30	7	0	4	16	.234	16	31	0	61	2	1	.984
—	Phoenix (PCL)	OF	39	139	17	47	4	1	5	25	.338	21	29	1	62	2	1	.985
1993—	Rochester (Int'l)■	OF	97	330	57	91	23	1	17	58	.276	60	81	0	127	2	2	.985
—	Baltimore (A.L.)	OF-DH	10	15	1	1	1	0	0	3	.067	3	7	0	5	0	1	.833
1994—	Phoenix (PCL)■	OF	89	314	51	93	19	2	11	49	.296	50	53	2	104	6	3	.973
—	San Francisco (N.L.)	OF	14	11	2	4	1	1	0	2	.364	3	2	0	1	0	0	1.000
1995—	Phoenix (PCL)	OF-1B	112	392	73	116	25	3	14	79	.296	*81	63	3	243	10	5	.981
—	San Francisco (N.L.)	OF	14	21	4	4	1	0	1	4	.190	5	2	0	9	0	0	1.000
American League totals (1 year)			10	15	1	1	1	0	0	3	.067	3	7	0	5	0	1	.833
National League totals (5 years)			158	306	36	72	17	2	8	38	.235	39	68	0	122	2	1	.992
Major league totals (6 years)			168	321	37	73	18	2	8	41	.227	42	75	0	127	2	2	.985

LESHER, BRIAN — OF/1B — ATHLETICS

PERSONAL: Born March 5, 1971, in Belgium. . . . 6-5/205. . . . Bats right, throws left. . . . Full name: Brian Herbert Lesher.
COLLEGE: Delaware.
TRANSACTIONS/CAREER NOTES: Selected by Oakland Athletics organization in 25th round of free-agent draft (June 1, 1992).

Year	Team (League)	Pos.	G	AB	R	H	2B	3B	HR	RBI	Avg.	BB	SO	SB	PO	A	E	Avg.
				BATTING											FIELDING			
1992—	S. Oregon (N'west)	OF-1B	46	136	21	26	7	1	3	18	.191	12	35	3	63	3	4	.943
1993—	Madison (Midwest)	OF	119	394	63	108	13	5	5	47	.274	46	102	20	193	9	5	.976
1994—	Modesto (Calif.)	OF-1B	117	393	76	114	21	0	14	68	.290	81	84	11	332	20	11	.970
1995—	Huntsville (South.)	OF-1B	127	471	78	123	23	2	19	71	.261	64	110	7	198	7	6	.972

LESKANIC, CURTIS — P — ROCKIES

PERSONAL: Born April 2, 1968, in Homestead, Pa. . . . 6-0/180. . . . Throws right, bats right. . . . Full name: Curtis John Leskanic.
HIGH SCHOOL: Steel Valley (Munhall, Pa.).
COLLEGE: Louisiana State.
TRANSACTIONS/CAREER NOTES: Selected by Cleveland Indians organization in eighth round of free-agent draft (June 5, 1989). . . . On disabled list (April 23-June 25, 1990). . . . Traded by Indians organization with P Oscar Munoz to Minnesota Twins organization for 1B Paul Sorrento (March 28, 1992). . . . Selected by Colorado Rockies in third round (66th pick overall) of expansion draft (November 17, 1992). . . . Loaned by Rockies organization to Wichita, Padres organization (April 7-May 20, 1993).

Year	Team (League)	W	L	Pct.	ERA	G	GS	CG	ShO	Sv.	IP	H	R	ER	BB	SO
1990—	Kinston (Carolina)	6	5	.545	3.68	14	14	2	0	0	73 1/3	61	34	30	30	71

Year	Team (League)	W	L	Pct.	ERA	G	GS	CG	ShO	Sv.	IP	H	R	ER	BB	SO
1991—	Kinston (Carolina)	•15	8	.652	2.79	28	28	0	0	0	174 1/3	143	63	54	91	*163
1992—	Orlando (Southern)■	9	11	.450	4.30	26	23	3	0	0	152 2/3	158	84	73	64	126
—	Portland (PCL)	1	2	.333	9.98	5	3	0	0	0	15 1/3	16	17	17	8	14
1993—	Wichita (Texas)■	3	2	.600	3.45	7	7	0	0	0	44 1/3	37	20	17	17	42
—	Colo. Springs (PCL)■	4	3	.571	4.47	9	7	1	1	0	44 1/3	39	24	22	26	38
—	Colorado (N.L.)	1	5	.167	5.37	18	8	0	0	0	57	59	40	34	27	30
1994—	Colo. Springs (PCL)	5	7	.417	3.31	21	21	2	0	0	130 1/3	129	60	48	54	98
—	Colorado (N.L.)	1	1	.500	5.64	8	3	0	0	0	22 1/3	27	14	14	10	17
1995—	Colorado (N.L.)	6	3	.667	3.40	*76	0	0	0	10	98	83	38	37	33	107
Major league totals (3 years)		8	9	.471	4.31	102	11	0	0	10	177 1/3	169	92	85	70	154

DIVISION SERIES RECORD

Year	Team (League)	W	L	Pct.	ERA	G	GS	CG	ShO	Sv.	IP	H	R	ER	BB	SO
1995—	Colorado (N.L.)	0	1	.000	6.00	3	0	0	0	0	3	3	2	2	0	4

LEVIS, JESSE — C — INDIANS

PERSONAL: Born April 14, 1968, in Philadelphia. . . . 5-9/180. . . . Bats left, throws right.
HIGH SCHOOL: Northeast (Philadelphia).
COLLEGE: North Carolina.
TRANSACTIONS/CAREER NOTES: Selected by Philadelphia Phillies organization in 36th round of free-agent draft (June 2, 1986); did not sign. . . . Selected by Cleveland Indians organization in fourth round of free-agent draft (June 5, 1989).
STATISTICAL NOTES: Led Eastern League catchers with 733 total chances in 1991.

L

			BATTING												FIELDING			
Year	Team (League)	Pos.	G	AB	R	H	2B	3B	HR	RBI	Avg.	BB	SO	SB	PO	A	E	Avg.
1989—	Burlington (Appal.)	C	27	93	11	32	4	0	4	16	.344	10	7	1	189	27	2	.991
—	Kinston (Carolina)	C	27	87	11	26	6	0	2	11	.299	12	15	1	95	17	2	.982
—	Colo. Springs (PCL)	PH	1	1	0	0	0	0	0	0	.000	0	0	0	...	...	...	...
1990—	Kinston (Carolina)	C	107	382	63	113	18	3	7	64	.296	64	42	4	517	63	5	.991
1991—	Cant./Akr. (East.)	C	115	382	31	101	17	3	6	45	.264	40	36	2	*644	*77	12	.984
1992—	Colo. Springs (PCL)	C	87	253	39	92	20	1	6	44	.364	37	25	1	375	47	4	.991
—	Cleveland (A.L.)	C-DH	28	43	2	12	4	0	1	3	.279	0	5	0	59	5	1	.985
1993—	Charlotte (Int'l)	C	47	129	10	32	6	1	2	20	.248	15	12	0	266	22	4	.986
—	Cleveland (A.L.)	C	31	63	7	11	2	0	0	4	.175	2	10	0	109	7	1	.991
1994—	Charlotte (Int'l)	C	111	375	55	107	20	0	10	59	.285	55	39	2	452	34	4	.992
—	Cleveland (A.L.)	PH	1	1	0	1	0	0	0	0	1.000	0	0	0	...	...	...	...
1995—	Buffalo (A.A.)	C	66	196	26	61	16	0	4	20	.311	32	11	0	338	20	2	.994
—	Cleveland (A.L.)	C	12	18	1	6	2	0	0	3	.333	1	0	0	33	5	0	1.000
Major league totals (4 years)			72	125	10	30	8	0	1	10	.240	3	15	0	201	17	2	.991

LEWIS, DARREN — OF — WHITE SOX

PERSONAL: Born August 28, 1967, in Berkeley, Calif. . . . 6-0/189. . . . Bats right, throws right. . . . Full name: Darren Joel Lewis.
HIGH SCHOOL: Moreau (Hayward, Calif.).
JUNIOR COLLEGE: Chabot College (Calif.).
COLLEGE: California.
TRANSACTIONS/CAREER NOTES: Selected by Los Angeles Dodgers organization in sixth round of free-agent draft (January 14, 1986); did not sign. . . . Selected by Toronto Blue Jays organization in 45th round of free-agent draft (June 2, 1987); did not sign. . . . Selected by Oakland Athletics organization in 18th round of free-agent draft (June 1, 1988). . . . Traded by A's with a player to be named later to San Francisco Giants for IF Ernest Riles (December 4, 1990); Giants acquired P Pedro Pena to complete deal (December 17, 1990). . . . On disabled list (August 20-September 4, 1993). . . . Traded by Giants with P Mark Portugal and P Dave Burba to Cincinnati Reds for OF Deion Sanders, P John Roper, P Ricky Pickett, P Scott Service and IF Dave McCarty (July 21, 1995). . . . Released by Reds (December 1, 1995). . . . Signed by Chicago White Sox (December 14, 1995).
RECORDS: Holds major league records for most consecutive errorless games by outfielder—392 (August 21, 1990 through June 29, 1994); and most consecutive chances accepted without an error by outfielder—938 (August 21, 1990 through June 29, 1994). . . . Holds N.L. records for most consecutive errorless games by outfielder—369 (July 13, 1991 through June 29, 1994); and most consecutive chances accepted without an error by outfielder—905 (July 13, 1991 through June 29, 1994).
HONORS: Won N.L. Gold Glove as outfielder (1994).
STATISTICAL NOTES: Led California League outfielders with 324 total chances in 1989.

			BATTING												FIELDING			
Year	Team (League)	Pos.	G	AB	R	H	2B	3B	HR	RBI	Avg.	BB	SO	SB	PO	A	E	Avg.
1988—	Arizona A's (Ariz.)	OF	5	15	8	5	3	0	0	4	.333	6	5	4	15	1	0	1.000
—	Madison (Midwest)	OF-2B	60	199	38	49	4	1	0	11	.246	46	37	31	195	3	4	.980
1989—	Modesto (Calif.)	OF	129	503	74	150	23	5	4	39	.298	59	84	27	*311	8	5	.985
—	Huntsville (South.)	OF	9	31	7	10	1	1	1	7	.323	2	6	0	16	0	0	1.000
1990—	Huntsville (South.)	OF	71	284	52	84	11	3	3	23	.296	36	28	21	186	6	0	1.000
—	Tacoma (PCL)	OF	60	247	32	72	5	2	2	26	.291	16	35	16	132	9	2	.986
—	Oakland (A.L.)	OF-DH	25	35	4	8	0	0	0	1	.229	7	4	2	33	0	0	1.000
1991—	Phoenix (PCL)■	OF	81	315	63	107	12	10	2	52	.340	41	36	32	243	5	2	.992
—	San Francisco (N.L.)	OF	72	222	41	55	5	3	1	15	.248	36	30	13	159	2	0	1.000
1992—	San Francisco (N.L.)	OF	100	320	38	74	8	1	1	18	.231	29	46	28	225	3	0	1.000
—	Phoenix (PCL)	OF	42	158	22	36	5	2	0	6	.228	11	15	9	93	2	0	1.000
1993—	San Francisco (N.L.)	OF	136	522	84	132	17	7	2	48	.253	30	40	46	344	4	0	•1.000
1994—	San Francisco (N.L.)	OF	114	451	70	116	15	•9	4	29	.257	53	50	30	279	5	2	.993
1995—	San Francisco (N.L.)	OF	74	309	47	78	10	3	1	16	.252	17	37	21	200	2	1	.995
—	Cincinnati (N.L.)■	OF	58	163	19	40	3	0	0	8	.245	17	20	11	121	3	1	.992
American League totals (1 year)			25	35	4	8	0	0	0	1	.229	7	4	2	33	0	0	1.000
National League totals (5 years)			554	1987	299	495	58	23	9	134	.249	182	223	149	1328	19	4	.997
Major league totals (6 years)			579	2022	303	503	58	23	9	135	.249	189	227	151	1361	19	4	.997

DIVISION SERIES RECORD

Year	Team (League)	Pos.	G	BATTING AB	R	H	2B	3B	HR	RBI	Avg.	BB	SO	SB	FIELDING PO	A	E	Avg.
1995—	Cincinnati (N.L.)	OF-PH	3	3	0	0	0	0	0	0	.000	0	1	0	3	0	0	1.000

CHAMPIONSHIP SERIES RECORD

Year	Team (League)	Pos.	G	BATTING AB	R	H	2B	3B	HR	RBI	Avg.	BB	SO	SB	FIELDING PO	A	E	Avg.
1995—	Cincinnati (N.L.)	OF-PR	2	1	0	0	0	0	0	0	.000	0	0	0	2	0	0	1.000

LEWIS, JAMES — P — INDIANS

PERSONAL: Born January 31, 1970, in Jacksonville, Fla. . . . 6-4/190. . . . Throws right, bats right. . . . Full name: James Howard Lewis Jr.
HIGH SCHOOL: Terry Parker (Jacksonville, Fla.).
JUNIOR COLLEGE: Florida Community College.
COLLEGE: Florida State.
TRANSACTIONS/CAREER NOTES: Selected by St. Louis Cardinals organization in fifth round of free-agent draft (June 4, 1990); did not sign. . . . Selected by Houston Astros organization in second round of free-agent draft (June 3, 1991); pick received as part of compensation for Milwaukee Brewers signing Type A free agent 1B Franklin Stubbs. . . . On disabled list (June 17-August 13, 1993). . . . Selected by Cleveland Indians from Astros organization in Rule 5 major league draft (December 5, 1994). . . . On disabled list (August 1-14, 1995).

Year	Team (League)	W	L	Pct.	ERA	G	GS	CG	ShO	Sv.	IP	H	R	ER	BB	SO
1991—	Auburn (NYP)	3	2	.600	3.76	7	7	0	0	0	38 1/3	30	20	16	14	26
1992—	Osceola (Florida St.)	5	1	.833	1.12	13	13	1	0	0	80 1/3	54	18	10	32	65
	—Jackson (Texas)	3	5	.375	4.11	12	12	2	1	0	70	64	33	32	30	43
	—Tucson (Pac. Coast)	0	0	...	0.00	1	1	0	0	0	1	0	0	0	2	0
1993—	Osceola (Florida St.)	0	0	...	2.35	4	4	0	0	0	7 2/3	8	4	2	2	3
1994—	Osceola (Florida St.)	1	8	.111	3.14	16	16	0	0	0	63	64	37	22	16	33
	—Jackson (Texas)	2	1	.667	2.44	8	8	0	0	0	48	41	13	13	10	39
1995—	Buffalo (A.A.)■	6	4	.600	3.64	18	16	1	0	1	94	101	42	38	25	50

LEWIS, MARK — 3B/SS — TIGERS

PERSONAL: Born November 30, 1969, in Hamilton, O. . . . 6-1/190. . . . Bats right, throws right. . . . Full name: Mark David Lewis.
HIGH SCHOOL: Hamilton (O.).
TRANSACTIONS/CAREER NOTES: Selected by Cleveland Indians organization in first round (second pick overall) of free-agent draft (June 1, 1988). . . . On Kinston disabled list (May 29-June 20, 1989). . . . Traded by Indians to Cincinnati Reds for IF Tim Costo (December 14, 1994). . . . Traded by Reds to Detroit Tigers (November 16, 1995), completing deal in which Reds acquired P David Wells for P C.J. Nitkowski, P David Tuttle and a player to be named later (July 31, 1995).
STATISTICAL NOTES: Tied for A.L. lead in errors by shortstop with 25 in 1992. . . . Tied for International League lead in grounding into double plays with 19 in 1993. . . . Led International League shortstops with 81 double plays in 1993.

Year	Team (League)	Pos.	G	BATTING AB	R	H	2B	3B	HR	RBI	Avg.	BB	SO	SB	FIELDING PO	A	E	Avg.
1988—	Burlington (Appal.)	SS	61	227	39	60	13	1	7	43	.264	25	44	14	70	*177	23	.915
1989—	Kinston (Carolina)	SS	93	349	50	94	16	3	1	32	.269	34	50	17	130	244	32	.921
	—Cant./Akr. (East.)	SS	7	25	4	5	1	0	0	1	.200	1	3	0	15	28	2	.956
1990—	Cant./Akr. (East.)	SS	102	390	55	106	19	3	10	60	.272	23	49	8	152	286	31	.934
	—Colo. Springs (PCL)	SS	34	124	16	38	8	1	1	21	.306	9	13	2	52	84	11	.925
1991—	Colo. Springs (PCL)	SS-2B-3B	46	179	29	50	10	3	2	31	.279	18	23	3	65	135	10	.952
	—Cleveland (A.L.)	2B-SS	84	314	29	83	15	1	0	30	.264	15	45	2	129	231	9	.976
1992—	Cleveland (A.L.)	SS-3B	122	413	44	109	21	0	5	30	.264	25	69	4	184	336	‡26	.952
1993—	Charlotte (Int'l)	SS	126	507	93	144	30	4	17	67	.284	34	76	9	168	*403	23	.961
	—Cleveland (A.L.)	SS	14	52	6	13	2	0	1	5	.250	0	7	3	22	31	2	.964
1994—	Cleveland (A.L.)	SS-3B-2B	20	73	6	15	5	0	1	8	.205	2	13	1	17	40	6	.905
	—Charlotte (Int'l)	SS-2B-3B	86	328	56	85	16	1	8	34	.259	35	48	2	117	199	12	.963
1995—	Cincinnati (N.L.)■	3B-2B-SS	81	171	25	58	13	1	3	30	.339	21	33	0	19	107	4	.969
American League totals (4 years)			240	852	85	220	43	1	7	73	.258	42	134	10	352	638	43	.958
National League totals (1 year)			81	171	25	58	13	1	3	30	.339	21	33	0	19	107	4	.969
Major league totals (5 years)			321	1023	110	278	56	2	10	103	.272	63	167	10	371	745	47	.960

DIVISION SERIES RECORD

Year	Team (League)	Pos.	G	BATTING AB	R	H	2B	3B	HR	RBI	Avg.	BB	SO	SB	FIELDING PO	A	E	Avg.
1995—	Cincinnati (N.L.)	3B-PH	2	2	2	1	0	0	1	5	.500	1	0	0	0	0	1	.000

CHAMPIONSHIP SERIES RECORD

Year	Team (League)	Pos.	G	BATTING AB	R	H	2B	3B	HR	RBI	Avg.	BB	SO	SB	FIELDING PO	A	E	Avg.
1995—	Cincinnati (N.L.)	3B	2	4	0	1	0	0	0	0	.250	1	1	0	2	3	0	1.000

LEWIS, RICHIE — P

PERSONAL: Born January 25, 1966, in Muncie, Ind. . . . 5-10/175. . . . Throws right, bats right. . . . Full name: Richie Todd Lewis.
HIGH SCHOOL: South Side (Muncie, Ind.).
COLLEGE: Florida State (received degree, 1987).
TRANSACTIONS/CAREER NOTES: Selected by Montreal Expos organization in second round of free-agent draft (June 2, 1987). . . . On disabled list (June 2-August 12 and August 22, 1988-remainder of season; and July 28, 1989-remainder of season). . . . On Jacksonville disabled list (June 1-8 and June 11, 1990-remainder of season). . . . Traded by Expos to Baltimore Orioles for P Chris Myers (August 24, 1991). . . . Selected by Florida Marlins in second round (51st pick overall) of expansion draft (November 17, 1992). . . . On Charlotte disabled list

(April 6-25, 1995). . . . Granted free agency (October 16, 1995).
HONORS: Named righthanded pitcher on The Sporting News college All-America team (1987).
STATISTICAL NOTES: Tied for N.L. lead with 10 wild pitches in 1994.

Year	Team (League)	W	L	Pct.	ERA	G	GS	CG	ShO	Sv.	IP	H	R	ER	BB	SO
1987—	Indianapolis (A.A.)	0	0	...	9.82	2	0	0	0	0	3 2/3	6	4	4	2	3
1988—	Jacksonville (Sou.)	5	3	.625	3.38	12	12	1	0	0	61 1/3	37	32	23	56	60
1989—	Jacksonville (Sou.)	5	4	.556	2.58	17	17	0	0	0	94 1/3	80	37	27	55	105
1990—	WP Beach (FSL)	0	1	.000	4.80	10	0	0	0	2	15	12	12	8	11	14
	—Jacksonville (Sou.)	0	0	...	1.26	11	0	0	0	5	14 1/3	7	2	2	5	14
1991—	Harrisburg (East.)	6	5	.545	3.74	34	6	0	0	5	74 2/3	67	33	31	40	82
	—Indianapolis (A.A.)	1	0	1.000	3.58	5	4	0	0	0	27 2/3	35	12	11	20	22
	—Rochester (Int'l)■	1	0	1.000	2.81	2	2	0	0	0	16	13	5	5	7	18
1992—	Rochester (Int'l)	10	9	.526	3.28	24	23	6	1	0	159 1/3	136	63	58	61	154
	—Baltimore (A.L.)	1	1	.500	10.80	2	2	0	0	0	6 2/3	13	8	8	7	4
1993—	Florida (N.L.)■	6	3	.667	3.26	57	0	0	0	0	77 1/3	68	37	28	43	65
1994—	Florida (N.L.)	1	4	.200	5.67	45	0	0	0	0	54	62	44	34	38	45
1995—	Charlotte (Int'l)	5	2	.714	3.20	17	8	1	0	0	59	50	22	21	20	45
	—Florida (N.L.)	0	1	.000	3.75	21	1	0	0	0	36	30	15	15	15	32
A.L. totals (1 year)		1	1	.500	10.80	2	2	0	0	0	6 2/3	13	8	8	7	4
N.L. totals (3 years)		7	8	.467	4.14	123	1	0	0	0	167 1/3	160	96	77	96	142
Major league totals (4 years)		8	9	.471	4.40	125	3	0	0	0	174	173	104	85	103	146

LEYRITZ, JIM — C/DH/1B — YANKEES

PERSONAL: Born December 27, 1963, in Lakewood, O. . . . 6-0/195. . . . Bats right, throws right. . . . Full name: James Joseph Leyritz. . . . Name pronounced LAY-rits.
JUNIOR COLLEGE: Middle Georgia College.
COLLEGE: Kentucky.
TRANSACTIONS/CAREER NOTES: Signed as non-drafted free agent by New York Yankees organization (August 24, 1985).
STATISTICAL NOTES: Led Florida State League with 25 passed balls in 1987. . . . Tied for Eastern League lead in being hit by pitch with nine in 1989. . . . Career major league grand slams: 2.

			BATTING												FIELDING			
Year	Team (League)	Pos.	G	AB	R	H	2B	3B	HR	RBI	Avg.	BB	SO	SB	PO	A	E	Avg.
1986—	Oneonta (NYP)	C	23	91	12	33	3	1	4	15	.363	5	10	1	170	21	2	.990
	—Fort Lauder. (FSL)	C	12	34	3	10	1	1	0	1	.294	4	5	0	32	8	1	.976
1987—	Fort Lauder. (FSL)	C	102	374	48	115	22	0	6	51	.307	38	54	2	458	*76	13	.976
1988—	Alb./Colon. (East.)	C-3B-1B	112	382	40	92	18	3	5	50	.241	43	62	3	418	73	6	.988
1989—	Alb./Colon. (East.)	C-OF-3B	114	375	53	118	18	2	10	66	*.315	65	51	2	421	41	3	.994
1990—	Columbus (Int'l)	3-2-1-0-C	59	204	36	59	11	1	8	32	.289	37	33	4	75	96	13	.929
	—New York (A.L.)	3B-OF-C	92	303	28	78	13	1	5	25	.257	27	51	2	117	107	13	.945
1991—	New York (A.L.)	3-C-1-DH	32	77	8	14	3	0	0	4	.182	13	15	0	38	21	3	.952
	—Columbus (Int'l)	C-3-S-2	79	270	50	72	24	1	11	48	.267	38	50	1	209	48	5	.981
1992—	New York (A.L.)	DH-C-O-3-1-2	63	144	17	37	6	0	7	26	.257	14	22	0	96	15	1	.991
1993—	New York (A.L.)	1-O-DH-C	95	259	43	80	14	0	14	53	.309	37	59	0	333	15	2	.994
1994—	New York (A.L.)	C-DH-1B	75	249	47	66	12	0	17	58	.265	35	61	0	282	15	0	1.000
1995—	New York (A.L.)	C-1B-DH	77	264	37	71	12	0	7	37	.269	37	73	1	417	24	3	.993
Major league totals (6 years)			434	1296	180	346	60	1	50	203	.267	163	281	3	1283	197	22	.985

DIVISION SERIES RECORD

			BATTING												FIELDING			
Year	Team (League)	Pos.	G	AB	R	H	2B	3B	HR	RBI	Avg.	BB	SO	SB	PO	A	E	Avg.
1995—	New York (A.L.)	C-PH	2	7	1	1	0	0	1	2	.143	0	1	0	13	0	0	1.000

LIEBER, JON — P — PIRATES

PERSONAL: Born April 2, 1970, in Council Bluffs, Ia. . . . 6-3/220. . . . Throws right, bats left. . . . Full name: Jonathan Ray Lieber. . . . Name pronounced LEE-ber.
HIGH SCHOOL: Abraham Lincoln (Council Bluffs, Ia.).
JUNIOR COLLEGE: Iowa Western Community College-Council Bluffs.
COLLEGE: South Alabama.
TRANSACTIONS/CAREER NOTES: Selected by Chicago Cubs organization in ninth round of free-agent draft (June 3, 1991); did not sign. . . . Selected by Kansas City Royals organization in second round of free-agent draft (June 1, 1992); pick received as part of compensation for New York Yankees signing Type A free agent OF Danny Tartabull. . . . Traded by Royals organization with P Dan Miceli to Pittsburgh Pirates organization for P Stan Belinda (July 31, 1993).

Year	Team (League)	W	L	Pct.	ERA	G	GS	CG	ShO	Sv.	IP	H	R	ER	BB	SO
1992—	Eugene (N'west)	3	0	1.000	1.16	5	5	0	0	0	31	26	6	4	2	23
	—Baseball City (FSL)	3	3	.500	4.65	7	6	0	0	0	31	45	20	16	8	19
1993—	Wilmington (Caro.)	9	3	.750	2.67	17	16	2	0	0	114 2/3	125	47	34	9	89
	—Memphis (South.)	2	1	.667	6.86	4	4	0	0	0	21	32	16	16	6	17
	—Carolina (South.)■	4	2	.667	3.97	6	6	0	0	0	34	39	15	15	10	28
1994—	Carolina (South.)	2	0	1.000	1.29	3	3	1	1	0	21	13	4	3	2	21
	—Buffalo (A.A.)	1	1	.500	1.69	3	3	0	0	0	21 1/3	16	4	4	1	21
	—Pittsburgh (N.L.)	6	7	.462	3.73	17	17	1	0	0	108 2/3	116	62	45	25	71
1995—	Pittsburgh (N.L.)	4	7	.364	6.32	21	12	0	0	0	72 2/3	103	56	51	14	45
	—Calgary (PCL)	1	5	.167	7.01	14	14	0	0	0	77	122	69	60	19	34
Major league totals (2 years)		10	14	.417	4.76	38	29	1	0	0	181 1/3	219	118	96	39	116

LIEBERTHAL, MIKE — C — PHILLIES

PERSONAL: Born January 18, 1972, in Glendale, Calif. . . . 6-0/178. . . . Bats right, throws right. . . . Full name: Michael Scott Lieberthal. . . . Name pronounced LEE-ber-thal.
HIGH SCHOOL: Westlake (Westlake Village, Calif.).
TRANSACTIONS/CAREER NOTES: Selected by Philadelphia Phillies organization in first round (third pick overall) of free-agent draft (June 4, 1990). . . . On Scranton/Wilkes-Barre disabled list (August 31, 1992-remainder of season).

		BATTING												FIELDING			
Year Team (League)	Pos.	G	AB	R	H	2B	3B	HR	RBI	Avg.	BB	SO	SB	PO	A	E	Avg.
1990— Martinsville (App.)	C	49	184	26	42	9	0	4	22	.228	11	40	2	421	*52	5	*.990
1991— Spartanburg (SAL)	C	72	243	34	74	17	0	0	31	.305	23	25	1	565	68	10	.984
— Clearwater (FSL)	C	16	52	7	15	2	0	0	7	.288	3	12	0	128	9	1	.993
1992— Reading (Eastern)	C	86	309	30	88	16	1	2	37	.285	19	26	4	524	48	7	.988
— Scran./W.B. (Int'l)	C	16	45	4	9	1	0	0	4	.200	2	5	0	86	6	1	.989
1993— Scran./W.B. (Int'l)	C	112	382	35	100	17	0	7	40	.262	24	32	2	659	75	•11	.985
1994— Scran./W.B. (Int'l)	C	84	296	23	69	16	0	1	32	.233	21	29	1	472	50	9	.983
— Philadelphia (N.L.)	C	24	79	6	21	3	1	1	5	.266	3	5	0	122	4	4	.969
1995— Philadelphia (N.L.)	C	16	47	1	12	2	0	0	4	.255	5	5	0	95	10	1	.991
— Scran./W.B. (Int'l)	C-3B	85	278	44	78	20	2	6	42	.281	44	26	1	503	46	5	.991
Major league totals (2 years)		40	126	7	33	5	1	1	9	.262	8	10	0	217	14	5	.979

LILLIQUIST, DEREK — P

PERSONAL: Born February 20, 1966, in Winter Park, Fla. . . . 5-10/195. . . . Throws left, bats left. . . . Full name: Derek Jansen Lilliquist.
HIGH SCHOOL: Sarasota (Fla.).
COLLEGE: Georgia.
TRANSACTIONS/CAREER NOTES: Selected by Boston Red Sox organization in 15th round of free-agent draft (June 4, 1984); did not sign. . . . Selected by Atlanta Braves in first round (sixth pick overall) of free-agent draft (June 2, 1987). . . . Traded by Braves to San Diego Padres for P Mark Grant (July 12, 1990). . . . Claimed on waivers by Cleveland Indians (November 20, 1991). . . . Claimed on waivers by Braves (November 9, 1994). . . . Granted free agency (December 23, 1994). . . . Signed by Pawtucket, Boston Red Sox organization (April 22, 1995). . . . Released by Red Sox (July 16, 1995). . . . Signed by Albuquerque, Los Angeles Dodgers organization (August 1, 1995). . . . Granted free agency (October 16, 1995).
HONORS: Named lefthanded pitcher on The Sporting News college All-America team (1987).
MISCELLANEOUS: Singled once and scored once in four games as pinch-hitter (1989). . . . Made an out in only appearance as pinch-hitter with Atlanta (1990). . . . Made an out in only appearance as pinch-hitter with San Diego (1990).

Year Team (League)	W	L	Pct.	ERA	G	GS	CG	ShO	Sv.	IP	H	R	ER	BB	SO
1987— GC Braves (GCL)	0	0	...	0.00	2	2	0	0	0	13	3	0	0	2	16
— Durham (Carolina)	2	1	.667	2.88	3	3	2	0	0	25	13	9	8	6	29
1988— Richmond (Int'l)	10	12	.455	3.38	28	28	2	0	0	170 2/3	179	70	64	36	80
1989— Atlanta (N.L.)	8	10	.444	3.97	32	30	0	0	0	165 2/3	202	87	73	34	79
1990— Atlanta (N.L.)	2	8	.200	6.28	12	11	0	0	0	61 2/3	75	45	43	19	34
— Richmond (Int'l)	4	0	1.000	2.57	5	5	1	0	0	35	31	11	10	11	24
— San Diego (N.L.)■	3	3	.500	4.33	16	7	1	1	0	60 1/3	61	29	29	23	29
1991— Las Vegas (PCL)	4	6	.400	5.38	33	14	0	0	2	105 1/3	142	79	63	33	89
— San Diego (N.L.)	0	2	.000	8.79	6	2	0	0	0	14 1/3	25	14	14	4	7
1992— Cleveland (A.L.)■	5	3	.625	1.75	71	0	0	0	6	61 2/3	39	13	12	18	47
1993— Cleveland (A.L.)	4	4	.500	2.25	56	2	0	0	10	64	64	20	16	19	40
1994— Cleveland (A.L.)	1	3	.250	4.91	36	0	0	0	1	29 1/3	34	17	16	8	15
1995— Boston (A.L.)■	2	1	.667	6.26	28	0	0	0	0	23	27	17	16	9	9
— Albuquerque (PCL)■	0	0	...	2.70	13	0	0	0	5	13 1/3	18	4	4	3	9
A.L. totals (4 years)	12	11	.522	3.03	191	2	0	0	17	178	164	67	60	54	111
N.L. totals (3 years)	13	23	.361	4.74	66	50	1	1	0	302	363	175	159	80	149
Major league totals (7 years)	25	34	.424	4.11	257	52	1	1	17	480	527	242	219	134	260

LIMA, JOSE — P — TIGERS

PERSONAL: Born September 30, 1972, in Santiago, Dominican Republic. . . . 6-2/170. . . . Throws right, bats right. . . . Full name: Jose D. Lima.
TRANSACTIONS/CAREER NOTES: Signed as non-drafted free agent by Detroit Tigers organization (July 5, 1989).
STATISTICAL NOTES: Led Florida State League with 14 home runs allowed in 1992. . . . Led Eastern League with 13 balks in 1993. . . . Pitched 3-0 no-hit victory for Toledo against Pawtucket (August 17, 1994).

Year Team (League)	W	L	Pct.	ERA	G	GS	CG	ShO	Sv.	IP	H	R	ER	BB	SO
1990— Bristol (Appal.)	3	8	.273	5.02	14	12	1	0	1	75 1/3	89	49	42	22	64
1991— Lakeland (Fla. St.)	0	1	.000	10.38	4	1	0	0	0	8 2/3	16	10	10	2	5
— Fayetteville (S. Atl.)	1	3	.250	4.97	18	7	0	0	0	58	53	38	32	25	60
1992— Lakeland (Fla. St.)	5	11	.313	3.16	25	25	5	2	0	151	132	57	53	21	137
1993— London (Eastern)	8	•13	.381	4.07	27	27	2	0	0	177	160	96	80	59	138
1994— Toledo (Int'l)	7	9	.438	3.60	23	22	3	2	0	142 1/3	124	70	57	48	117
— Detroit (A.L.)	0	1	.000	13.50	3	1	0	0	0	6 2/3	11	10	10	3	7
1995— Lakeland (Fla. St.)	3	1	.750	2.57	4	4	0	0	0	21	23	11	6	0	20
— Toledo (Int'l)	5	3	.625	3.01	11	11	1	0	0	74 2/3	69	26	25	14	40
— Detroit (A.L.)	3	9	.250	6.11	15	15	0	0	0	73 2/3	85	52	50	18	37
Major league totals (2 years)	3	10	.231	6.72	18	16	0	0	0	80 1/3	96	62	60	21	44

LIND, JOSE — 2B

PERSONAL: Born May 1, 1964, in Toabaja, Puerto Rico. . . . 5-11/180. . . . Bats right, throws right. . . . Full name: Jose Salgado Lind. . . . Brother of Orlando Lind, minor league pitcher (1983-93). . . . Name pronounced LEEND.

HIGH SCHOOL: Jose Alegria (Dorado, Puerto Rico).

TRANSACTIONS/CAREER NOTES: Signed as non-drafted free agent by Pittsburgh Pirates organization (December 3, 1982). . . . Traded by Pirates to Kansas City Royals for P Joel Johnston and P Dennis Moeller (November 19, 1992). . . . On Kansas City disqualified list (June 2-July 13, 1995). . . . Released by Royals (July 13, 1995). . . . Signed by Vancouver, California Angels organization (July 25, 1995). . . . Released by Angels (August 31, 1995).

HONORS: Won N.L. Gold Glove at second base (1992).

STATISTICAL NOTES: Led Eastern League second basemen with 705 total chances and 84 double plays in 1986. . . . Led Pacific Coast League second basemen with 764 total chances and 84 double plays in 1987. . . . Led N.L. second basemen with 786 total chances in 1990 and 796 in 1991.

			BATTING											FIELDING			
Year Team (League)	Pos.	G	AB	R	H	2B	3B	HR	RBI	Avg.	BB	SO	SB	PO	A	E	Avg.
1983—GC Pirates (GCL)	2B-SS	45	163	26	49	3	4	0	18	.301	13	18	12	102	125	9	.962
1984—Macon (S. Atl.)	2B-SS	121	396	39	82	5	2	0	30	.207	29	48	17	271	306	32	.947
1985—Prin. William (Car.)	2-S-3-0	105	377	42	104	9	4	0	28	.276	32	42	11	164	221	14	.965
1986—Nashua (Eastern)	2B	134	•520	58	137	18	5	1	33	.263	43	28	29	*314	*378	13	*.982
1987—Vancouver (PCL)	2B	128	*533	75	143	16	3	3	30	.268	35	52	21	*311	*432	21	.973
—Pittsburgh (N.L.)	2B	35	143	21	46	8	4	0	11	.322	8	12	2	53	139	1	.995
1988—Pittsburgh (N.L.)	2B	154	611	82	160	24	4	2	49	.262	42	75	15	333	473	11	.987
1989—Pittsburgh (N.L.)	2B	153	578	52	134	21	3	2	48	.232	39	64	15	309	438	18	.976
1990—Pittsburgh (N.L.)	2B	152	514	46	134	28	5	1	48	.261	35	52	8	*330	449	7	.991
1991—Pittsburgh (N.L.)	2B	150	502	53	133	16	6	3	54	.265	30	56	7	*349	438	9	.989
1992—Pittsburgh (N.L.)	2B	135	468	38	110	14	1	0	39	.235	26	29	3	311	428	6	*.992
1993—Kansas City (A.L.)■	2B	136	431	33	107	13	2	0	37	.248	13	36	3	269	362	4	*.994
1994—Kansas City (A.L.)	2B-DH	85	290	34	78	16	2	1	31	.269	16	34	9	149	252	5	.988
1995—Kansas City (A.L.)	2B	29	97	4	26	3	0	0	6	.268	3	8	0	56	75	1	.992
—Vancouver (PCL)■	2B	10	36	2	8	2	0	0	5	.222	1	4	1	23	21	0	1.000
—California (A.L.)	2B	15	43	5	7	2	0	0	1	.163	3	4	0	24	40	0	1.000
American League totals (3 years)		265	861	76	218	34	4	1	75	.253	35	82	12	498	729	10	.992
National League totals (6 years)		779	2816	292	717	111	23	8	249	.255	180	288	50	1685	2365	52	.987
Major league totals (9 years)		1044	3677	368	935	145	27	9	324	.254	215	370	62	2183	3094	62	.988

CHAMPIONSHIP SERIES RECORD

			BATTING											FIELDING			
Year Team (League)	Pos.	G	AB	R	H	2B	3B	HR	RBI	Avg.	BB	SO	SB	PO	A	E	Avg.
1990—Pittsburgh (N.L.)	2B	6	21	1	5	1	1	1	2	.238	1	4	0	19	19	0	1.000
1991—Pittsburgh (N.L.)	2B	7	25	0	4	0	0	0	3	.160	0	6	0	12	24	1	.973
1992—Pittsburgh (N.L.)	2B	7	27	5	6	2	1	1	5	.222	1	4	0	16	23	2	.951
Championship series totals (3 years)		20	73	6	15	3	2	2	10	.205	2	14	0	47	66	3	.974

LINTON, DOUG — P — ROYALS

PERSONAL: Born September 2, 1965, in Santa Ana, Calif. . . . 6-1/190. . . . Throws right, bats right. . . . Full name: Douglas Warren Linton.

HIGH SCHOOL: Canyon (Anaheim, Calif.).

COLLEGE: UC Irvine.

TRANSACTIONS/CAREER NOTES: Selected by Toronto Blue Jays organization in 43rd round of free-agent draft (June 2, 1986). . . . On disabled list (April 30-May 24 and July 29-September 2, 1987). . . . On Knoxville disabled list (April 7-July 21, 1988). . . . On disabled list (April 7-July 21, 1989). . . . Claimed on waivers by California Angels (June 17, 1993). . . . Released by Angels (September 14, 1993). . . . Signed by New York Mets organization (December 17, 1993). . . . On Norfolk suspended list (July 21-29, 1994). . . . Granted free agency (October 15, 1994). . . . Signed by Kansas City Royals organization (April 25, 1995). . . . Granted free agency (October 11, 1995). . . . Re-signed by Royals organization (October 22, 1995).

STATISTICAL NOTES: Led International League with 21 home runs allowed and tied for lead with 10 hit batsmen in 1991.

Year Team (League)	W	L	Pct.	ERA	G	GS	CG	ShO	Sv.	IP	H	R	ER	BB	SO
1987—Myrtle Beach (SAL)	14	2	.875	*1.55	20	19	2	0	1	122	94	34	21	25	155
—Knoxville (South.)	0	0	...	9.00	1	1	0	0	0	3	5	3	3	1	1
1988—Dunedin (Fla. St.)	2	1	.667	1.63	12	0	0	0	2	27 2/3	19	5	5	9	28
1989—Dunedin (Fla. St.)	1	2	.333	2.96	9	1	0	0	2	27 1/3	27	12	9	9	35
—Knoxville (South.)	5	4	.556	2.60	14	13	3	•2	0	90	68	28	26	23	93
1990—Syracuse (Int'l)	10	10	.500	3.40	26	26	8	•3	0	*177 1/3	174	77	67	67	113
1991—Syracuse (Int'l)	10	12	.455	5.01	30	26	3	1	0	161 2/3	181	108	90	56	93
1992—Syracuse (Int'l)	12	10	.545	3.74	25	25	7	1	0	170 2/3	176	83	71	70	126
—Toronto (A.L.)	1	3	.250	8.63	8	3	0	0	0	24	31	23	23	17	16
1993—Syracuse (Int'l)	2	6	.250	5.32	13	7	0	0	2	47 1/3	48	29	28	14	42
—Toronto (A.L.)	0	1	.000	6.55	4	1	0	0	0	11	11	8	8	9	4
—California (A.L.)■	2	0	1.000	7.71	19	0	0	0	0	25 2/3	35	22	22	14	19
1994—Norfolk (Int'l)■	2	1	.667	2.00	3	3	0	0	0	18	11	6	4	1	15
—New York (N.L.)	6	2	.750	4.47	32	3	0	0	0	50 1/3	74	27	25	20	29
1995—Kansas City (A.L.)■	0	1	.000	7.25	7	2	0	0	0	22 1/3	22	21	18	10	13
—Omaha (Am. Assoc.)	7	7	.500	4.40	18	18	2	1	0	108 1/3	129	60	53	24	85
A.L. totals (3 years)	3	5	.375	7.70	38	6	0	0	0	83	99	74	71	50	52
N.L. totals (1 year)	6	2	.750	4.47	32	3	0	0	0	50 1/3	74	27	25	20	29
Major league totals (4 years)	9	7	.563	6.48	70	9	0	0	0	133 1/3	173	101	96	70	81

LIRA, FELIPE — P — TIGERS

PERSONAL: Born April 26, 1972, in Miranda, Venezuela. . . . 6-0/170. . . . Throws right, bats right. . . . Full name: Antonio Felipe Lira.

TRANSACTIONS/CAREER NOTES: Signed as non-drafted free agent by Detroit Tigers organization (February 20, 1990). . . . On Lakeland disabled list (April 10-June 10, 1991).

STATISTICAL NOTES: Pitched seven-inning, 4-0 no-hit victory against Columbus (May 4, 1994). . . . Led International League with 16 wild pitches in 1994.

Year	Team (League)	W	L	Pct.	ERA	G	GS	CG	ShO	Sv.	IP	H	R	ER	BB	SO
1990—	Bristol (Appal.)	5	5	.500	2.41	13	10	2	1	1	78 1/3	70	26	21	16	71
—	Lakeland (Fla. St.)	0	0	. . .	5.40	1	0	0	0	0	1 2/3	3	1	1	3	4
1991—	Fayetteville (S. Atl.)	5	5	.500	4.66	15	13	0	0	1	73 1/3	79	43	38	19	56
1992—	Lakeland (Fla. St.)	11	5	.688	2.39	32	8	2	1	1	109	95	36	29	16	84
1993—	London (Eastern)	10	4	.714	3.38	22	22	2	0	0	152	157	63	57	39	122
—	Toledo (Int'l)	1	2	.333	4.60	5	5	0	0	0	31 1/3	32	18	16	11	23
1994—	Toledo (Int'l)	7	12	.368	4.70	26	26	1	1	0	151 1/3	171	91	79	45	110
1995—	Detroit (A.L.)	9	13	.409	4.31	37	22	0	0	1	146 1/3	151	74	70	56	89
Major league totals (1 year)		9	13	.409	4.31	37	22	0	0	1	146 1/3	151	74	70	56	89

LIRIANO, NELSON — 2B — PIRATES

L

PERSONAL: Born June 3, 1964, in Puerto Plata, Dominican Republic. . . . 5-10/181. . . . Bats both, throws right. . . . Full name: Nelson Arturo Liriano. . . . Name pronounced LEER-ee-ON-oh.

HIGH SCHOOL: Jose Debeaw (Puerto Plata, Dominican Republic).

TRANSACTIONS/CAREER NOTES: Signed as non-drafted free agent by Toronto Blue Jays organization (November 1, 1982). . . . Traded by Blue Jays with OF Pedro Munoz to Minnesota Twins for P John Candelaria (July 27, 1990). . . . Released by Twins (April 2, 1991). . . . Signed by Omaha, Kansas City Royals organization (May 1, 1991). . . . Granted free agency (October 15, 1991). . . . Signed by Colorado Springs, Cleveland Indians organization (January 31, 1992). . . . Granted free agency (October 15, 1992). . . . Signed by Colorado Rockies (October 26, 1992). . . . On Colorado Springs disabled list (April 7-30, 1993). . . . Claimed on waivers by Pittsburgh Pirates (October 14, 1994).

STATISTICAL NOTES: Led Carolina League second basemen with 79 double plays in 1985. . . . Led International League second basemen with 611 total chances and 96 double plays in 1987. . . . Career major league grand slams: 1.

				BATTING											FIELDING			
Year	Team (League)	Pos.	G	AB	R	H	2B	3B	HR	RBI	Avg.	BB	SO	SB	PO	A	E	Avg.
1983—	Florence (S. Atl.)	2B	129	478	87	124	24	5	6	57	.259	70	81	27	214	323	34	.940
1984—	Kinston (Carolina)	2B	132	*512	68	126	22	4	5	50	.246	46	86	10	260	*357	*21	.967
1985—	Kinston (Carolina)	2B	134	451	68	130	23	1	6	36	.288	39	55	25	*261	328	•25	.959
1986—	Knoxville (South.)	2B-3B-SS	135	557	88	159	25	*15	7	59	.285	48	63	35	239	324	22	.962
1987—	Syracuse (Int'l)	2B	130	531	72	133	19	•10	10	55	.250	44	76	36	*246	*346	*19	.969
—	Toronto (A.L.)	2B	37	158	29	38	6	2	2	10	.241	16	22	13	83	107	1	.995
1988—	Toronto (A.L.)	2B-DH-3B	99	276	36	73	6	2	3	23	.264	11	40	12	121	177	12	.961
—	Syracuse (Int'l)	2B	8	31	2	6	1	1	0	1	.194	2	4	2	14	23	0	1.000
1989—	Toronto (A.L.)	2B-DH	132	418	51	110	26	3	5	53	.263	43	51	16	267	330	12	.980
1990—	Toronto (A.L.)	2B	50	170	16	36	7	2	1	15	.212	16	20	3	93	132	4	.983
—	Minnesota (A.L.)■	2B-DH-SS	53	185	30	47	5	7	0	13	.254	22	24	5	83	128	7	.968
1991—	Omaha (A.A.)■	2B-SS	86	292	50	80	16	9	2	36	.274	31	39	6	149	218	9	.976
—	Kansas City (A.L.)	2B	10	22	5	9	0	0	0	1	.409	0	2	0	11	23	0	1.000
1992—	Colo. Springs (PCL)■	2B-3B-SS	106	361	73	110	19	9	5	52	.305	48	50	20	144	230	9	.977
1993—	Central Vall. (Cal.)■	3B-SS-2B	6	22	3	8	0	2	0	4	.364	6	0	0	4	10	0	1.000
—	Colo. Springs (PCL)	2B-SS-3B	79	293	48	105	23	6	6	46	.358	32	34	9	143	232	15	.962
—	Colorado (N.L.)	SS-2B-3B	48	151	28	46	6	3	2	15	.305	18	22	6	65	103	6	.966
1994—	Colorado (N.L.)	2B-SS-3B	87	255	39	65	17	5	3	31	.255	42	44	0	145	225	10	.974
1995—	Pittsburgh (N.L.)■	2B-3B-SS	107	259	29	74	12	1	5	38	.286	24	34	2	130	137	5	.982
American League totals (5 years)			381	1229	167	313	50	16	11	115	.255	108	159	49	658	897	36	.977
National League totals (3 years)			242	665	96	185	35	9	10	84	.278	84	100	8	340	465	21	.975
Major league totals (8 years)			623	1894	263	498	85	25	21	199	.263	192	259	57	998	1362	57	.976

CHAMPIONSHIP SERIES RECORD

				BATTING											FIELDING			
Year	Team (League)	Pos.	G	AB	R	H	2B	3B	HR	RBI	Avg.	BB	SO	SB	PO	A	E	Avg.
1989—	Toronto (A.L.)	2B	3	7	1	3	0	0	0	1	.429	2	0	3	4	3	1	.875

LISTACH, PAT — 2B/SS — BREWERS

PERSONAL: Born September 12, 1967, in Natchitoches, La. . . . 5-9/180. . . . Bats both, throws right. . . . Full name: Patrick Alan Listach. . . . Name pronounced LISS-tatch.

HIGH SCHOOL: Natchitoches (La.) Central.

JUNIOR COLLEGE: McLennan Community College (Tex.).

COLLEGE: Arizona State.

TRANSACTIONS/CAREER NOTES: Selected by Seattle Mariners organization in 23rd round of free-agent draft (June 2, 1987); did not sign. . . . Selected by Milwaukee Brewers organization in fifth round of free-agent draft (June 1, 1988). . . . On Milwaukee disabled list (June 2-July 18, 1993); included rehabilitation assignment to Beloit (July 14-18, 1993). . . . On Milwaukee disabled list (April 24, 1994-remainder of season); included rehabilitation assignment to New Orleans (August 5-7).

HONORS: Named A.L. Rookie Player of the Year by The Sporting News (1992). . . . Named A.L. Rookie of the Year by Baseball Writers' Association of America (1992).

STATISTICAL NOTES: Led California League second basemen with 276 putouts in 1990.

MISCELLANEOUS: Batted righthanded only (1988-89 and 1991).

Year	Team (League)	Pos.	G	AB	R	H	2B	3B	HR	RBI	Avg.	BB	SO	SB	PO	A	E	Avg.
				BATTING											FIELDING			
1988—	Beloit (Midwest)	SS	53	200	40	48	5	1	1	18	.240	18	20	20	66	117	24	.884
1989—	Stockton (Calif.)	2B-SS	132	480	73	110	11	4	2	34	.229	58	106	37	250	351	29	.954
1990—	Stockton (Calif.)	2B-SS-OF	•139	503	*116	137	21	6	2	39	.272	*105	122	78	≠319	356	25	.964
1991—	El Paso (Texas)	SS-2B	49	186	40	47	5	2	0	13	.253	25	56	14	86	131	22	.908
	— Denver (A.A.)	2B-SS-OF	89	286	51	72	10	4	1	31	.252	45	66	23	182	237	9	.979
1992—	Milwaukee (A.L.)	SS-OF-2B	149	579	93	168	19	6	1	47	.290	55	124	54	238	449	24	.966
1993—	Milwaukee (A.L.)	SS-OF	98	356	50	87	15	1	3	30	.244	37	70	18	135	267	10	.976
	— Beloit (Midwest)	SS	4	12	2	3	0	0	0	1	.250	1	2	2	3	7	0	1.000
1994—	Milwaukee (A.L.)	SS	16	54	8	16	3	0	0	2	.296	3	8	2	18	51	3	.958
	— New Orleans (A.A.)	OF	2	5	1	2	0	0	0	0	.400	0	0	0	0	0	0	...
1995—	Milwaukee (A.L.)	2-S-O-3	101	334	35	73	8	2	0	25	.219	25	61	13	169	273	6	.987
Major league totals (4 years)			364	1323	186	344	45	9	4	104	.260	120	263	87	560	1040	43	.974

LIVINGSTONE, SCOTT — 3B — PADRES

PERSONAL: Born July 15, 1965, in Dallas. . . . 6-0/190. . . . Bats left, throws right. . . . Full name: Scott Louis Livingstone.
HIGH SCHOOL: Lake Highlands (Dallas).
COLLEGE: Texas A&M.
TRANSACTIONS/CAREER NOTES: Selected by Toronto Blue Jays organization in sixth round of free-agent draft (June 4, 1984); did not sign. . . . Selected by New York Yankees organization in 26th round of free-agent draft (June 2, 1986); did not sign. . . . Selected by Oakland Athletics organization in third round of free-agent draft (June 2, 1987); did not sign. . . . Selected by Detroit Tigers organization in second round of free-agent draft (June 1, 1988). . . . On disabled list (July 14-23 and July 28-August 7, 1990). . . . Traded by Tigers with SS Jorge Velandia to San Diego Padres for P Gene Harris (May 11, 1994).
HONORS: Named designated hitter on The Sporting News college All-America team (1987-88).
STATISTICAL NOTES: Tied for Eastern League lead in total chances by third baseman with 360 in 1989.

Year	Team (League)	Pos.	G	AB	R	H	2B	3B	HR	RBI	Avg.	BB	SO	SB	PO	A	E	Avg.
				BATTING											FIELDING			
1988—	Lakeland (Fla. St.)	3B	53	180	28	51	8	1	2	25	.283	11	25	1	30	115	8	.948
1989—	London (Eastern)	3B-SS	124	452	46	98	18	1	14	71	.217	52	67	1	100	265	25	.936
1990—	Toledo (Int'l)	3B	103	345	44	94	19	0	6	36	.272	21	40	1	66	181	13	.950
1991—	Toledo (Int'l)	3B-1B	92	331	48	100	13	3	3	62	.302	40	52	2	65	137	16	.927
	— Detroit (A.L.)	3B	44	127	19	37	5	0	2	11	.291	10	25	2	32	67	2	.980
1992—	Detroit (A.L.)	3B	117	354	43	100	21	0	4	46	.282	21	36	1	67	189	10	.962
1993—	Detroit (A.L.)	3B-DH	98	304	39	89	10	2	2	39	.293	19	32	1	33	94	6	.955
1994—	Detroit (A.L.)	DH-1B-3B	15	23	0	5	1	0	0	1	.217	1	4	0	6	3	0	1.000
	— San Diego (N.L.)■	3B	57	180	11	49	12	1	2	10	.272	6	22	2	20	78	6	.942
1995—	San Diego (N.L.)	1B-3B-2B	99	196	26	66	15	0	5	32	.337	15	22	2	300	33	3	.991
American League totals (4 years)			274	808	101	231	37	2	8	97	.286	51	97	4	138	353	18	.965
National League totals (2 years)			156	376	37	115	27	1	7	42	.306	21	44	4	320	111	9	.980
Major league totals (5 years)			430	1184	138	346	64	3	15	139	.292	72	141	8	458	464	27	.972

LLOYD, GRAEME — P — BREWERS

PERSONAL: Born April 9, 1967, in Victoria, Australia. . . . 6-7/234. . . . Throws left, bats left. . . . Full name: Graeme John Lloyd. . . . Name pronounced GRAM.
HIGH SCHOOL: Geelong Technical School (Victoria, Australia).
TRANSACTIONS/CAREER NOTES: Signed as non-drafted free agent by Toronto Blue Jays organization (January 26, 1988). . . . On Myrtle Beach disabled list (June 29-September 1, 1989). . . . Selected by Philadelphia Phillies from Blue Jays organization in Rule 5 major league draft (December 7, 1992). . . . Traded by Phillies to Milwaukee Brewers for P John Trisler (December 8, 1992). . . . On disabled list (August 20-September 4, 1993 and July 25-September 10, 1995). . . . On suspended list (September 5-9, 1993).

Year	Team (League)	W	L	Pct.	ERA	G	GS	CG	ShO	Sv.	IP	H	R	ER	BB	SO
1988—	Myrtle Beach (SAL)	3	2	.600	3.62	41	0	0	0	2	59 2/3	71	33	24	30	43
1989—	Dunedin (Fla. St.)	0	0	...	10.13	2	0	0	0	0	2 2/3	6	3	3	1	0
	— Myrtle Beach (SAL)	0	0	...	5.40	1	1	0	0	0	5	5	4	3	0	3
1990—	Myrtle Beach (SAL)	5	2	.714	2.72	19	6	0	0	6	49 2/3	51	20	15	16	42
1991—	Dunedin (Fla. St.)	2	5	.286	2.24	50	0	0	0	24	60 1/3	54	17	15	25	39
	— Knoxville (South.)	0	0	...	0.00	2	0	0	0	0	1 2/3	1	0	0	1	2
1992—	Knoxville (South.)	4	8	.333	1.96	49	7	1	0	14	92	79	30	20	25	65
1993—	Milwaukee (A.L.)■	3	4	.429	2.83	55	0	0	0	0	63 2/3	64	24	20	13	31
1994—	Milwaukee (A.L.)	2	3	.400	5.17	43	0	0	0	3	47	49	28	27	15	31
1995—	Milwaukee (A.L.)	0	5	.000	4.50	33	0	0	0	4	32	28	16	16	8	13
Major league totals (3 years)		5	12	.294	3.97	131	0	0	0	7	142 2/3	141	68	63	36	75

LOAIZA, ESTEBAN — P — PIRATES

PERSONAL: Born December 31, 1971, in Tijuana, Mexico. . . . 6-4/190. . . . Throws right, bats right. . . . Full name: Esteban Antonio Loaiza. . . . Name pronounced low-WAY-zah.
HIGH SCHOOL: Mar Vista (Imperial Beach, Calif.).
TRANSACTIONS/CAREER NOTES: Signed as non-drafted free agent by Pittsburgh Pirates organization (March 21, 1991). . . . On disabled list (April 7-28 and July 7-14, 1994).
MISCELLANEOUS: Made an out in only appearance as pinch-hitter (1995).

Year	Team (League)	W	L	Pct.	ERA	G	GS	CG	ShO	Sv.	IP	H	R	ER	BB	SO
1991—	GC Pirates (GCL)	5	1	.833	2.26	11	11	1	•1	0	51 2/3	48	17	13	14	41
1992—	Augusta (S. Atl.)	10	8	.556	3.89	26	25	3	0	0	143 1/3	134	72	62	60	123
1993—	Salem (Carolina)	6	7	.462	3.39	17	17	3	0	0	109	113	53	41	30	61

Year Team (League)	W	L	Pct.	ERA	G	GS	CG	ShO	Sv.	IP	H	R	ER	BB	SO
—Carolina (South.)	2	1	.667	3.77	7	7	1	0	0	43	39	18	18	12	40
—M.C. Red Devils (Mex.)	1	1	.500	5.18	4	3	0	0	0	24 1/3	32	18	14	4	15
1994—Carolina (South.)	10	5	.667	3.79	24	24	3	0	0	154 1/3	169	69	65	30	115
1995—Pittsburgh (N.L.)	8	9	.471	5.16	32	•31	1	0	0	172 2/3	205	*115	*99	55	85
Major league totals (1 year)	8	9	.471	5.16	32	31	1	0	0	172 2/3	205	115	99	55	85

LOCKHART, KEITH — 2B/3B — ROYALS

PERSONAL: Born November 10, 1964, in Whittier, Calif. . . . 5-10/170. . . . Bats left, throws right. . . . Full name: Keith Virgil Lockhart.
HIGH SCHOOL: Northview (Covina, Calif.).
JUNIOR COLLEGE: Mount San Antonio.
COLLEGE: Oral Roberts.
TRANSACTIONS/CAREER NOTES: Selected by Cincinnati Reds organization in 11th round of free-agent draft (June 2, 1986). . . . Contract sold by Reds organization to Tacoma, Oakland Athletics organization (February 4, 1992). . . . Granted free agency (October 15, 1992). . . . Signed by St. Louis Cardinals organization (December 12, 1992). . . . Granted free agency (October 15, 1993). . . . Signed by San Diego Padres organization (January 7, 1994). . . . Granted free agency (October 15, 1994). . . . Signed by Omaha, Kansas City Royals organization (November 14, 1994).
STATISTICAL NOTES: Led Midwest League third basemen with 33 double plays in 1987. . . . Led Southern League with 11 sacrifice flies in 1988. . . . Led American Association second basemen with 631 total chances in 1989. . . . Order of frequency of positions played in 1994 for Las Vegas: OF-SS-2B-3B-P-C.

			BATTING											FIELDING			
Year Team (League)	Pos.	G	AB	R	H	2B	3B	HR	RBI	Avg.	BB	SO	SB	PO	A	E	Avg.
1986—Billings (Pioneer)	2B-3B	53	202	51	70	11	3	7	31	.347	35	22	4	81	150	17	.931
—Ced. Rap. (Midw.)	2B-3B	13	42	4	8	2	0	0	1	.190	6	6	1	17	15	0	1.000
1987—Ced. Rap. (Midw.)	3B-2B	*140	511	101	160	37	5	23	84	.313	86	70	20	85	292	28	.931
1988—Chatt. (South.)	3B-2B	139	515	74	137	27	3	12	67	.266	61	59	7	102	323	36	.922
1989—Nashville (A.A.)	2B	131	479	77	128	21	6	14	58	.267	61	41	4	*279	*335	17	.973
1990—Nashville (A.A.)	2B-3B-OF	126	431	48	112	25	4	9	63	.260	51	74	8	173	248	9	.979
1991—Nashville (A.A.)	3B-2B-OF	116	411	53	107	25	3	8	36	.260	24	64	3	153	241	13	.968
1992—Tacoma (PCL)■	2B-3B-SS	107	363	44	101	25	3	5	37	.278	29	21	5	199	239	11	.976
1993—Louisville (A.A.)■	3-2-0-1	132	467	66	140	24	3	13	68	.300	60	43	3	157	239	12	.971
1994—San Diego (N.L.)■	3-2-S-0	27	43	4	9	0	0	2	6	.209	4	10	1	10	21	1	.969
—Las Vegas (PCL)	0-I-P-C	89	331	61	106	15	5	7	43	.320	26	37	3	143	113	10	.962
1995—Omaha (A.A.)■	3B	44	148	24	56	7	1	5	19	.378	16	10	1	31	72	8	.928
—Kansas City (A.L.)	2B-3B-DH	94	274	41	88	19	3	6	33	.321	14	21	8	111	178	8	.973
American League totals (1 year)		94	274	41	88	19	3	6	33	.321	14	21	8	111	178	8	.973
National League totals (1 year)		27	43	4	9	0	0	2	6	.209	4	10	1	10	21	1	.969
Major league totals (2 years)		121	317	45	97	19	3	8	39	.306	18	31	9	121	199	9	.973

RECORD AS PITCHER

Year Team (League)	W	L	Pct.	ERA	G	GS	CG	ShO	Sv.	IP	H	R	ER	BB	SO
1994—Las Vegas (PCL)	0	0	...	0.00	1	1	0	0	0	1	0	0	0	0	0

LOFTON, KENNY — OF — INDIANS

PERSONAL: Born May 31, 1967, in East Chicago, Ind. . . . 6-0/180. . . . Bats left, throws left. . . . Full name: Kenneth Lofton.
HIGH SCHOOL: Washington (East Chicago, Ind.).
COLLEGE: Arizona.
TRANSACTIONS/CAREER NOTES: Selected by Houston Astros organization in 17th round of free-agent draft (June 1, 1988). . . . Traded by Astros with IF Dave Rohde to Cleveland Indians for P Willie Blair and C Eddie Taubensee (December 10, 1991). . . . On disabled list (July 17-August 1, 1995).
RECORDS: Holds A.L. rookie-season record for most stolen bases—66 (1992). . . . Shares A.L. single-season record for fewest errors by outfielder who led league in errors—9 (1993).
HONORS: Won A.L. Gold Glove as outfielder (1993-95).
STATISTICAL NOTES: Tied for Pacific Coast League lead in caught stealing with 23 in 1991. . . . Led Pacific Coast League outfielders with 344 total chances in 1991. . . . Career major league grand slams: 1.

			BATTING											FIELDING			
Year Team (League)	Pos.	G	AB	R	H	2B	3B	HR	RBI	Avg.	BB	SO	SB	PO	A	E	Avg.
1988—Auburn (NYP)	OF	48	187	23	40	6	1	1	14	.214	19	51	26	94	5	4	.961
1989—Auburn (NYP)	OF	34	110	21	29	3	1	0	8	.264	14	30	26	37	4	8	.837
—Asheville (S. Atl.)	OF	22	82	14	27	2	0	1	9	.329	12	10	14	38	1	2	.951
1990—Osceola (Fla. St.)	OF	124	481	98	*159	15	5	2	35	.331	61	77	62	246	13	7	.974
1991—Tucson (PCL)	OF	130	*545	93	*168	19	*17	2	50	.308	52	95	40	*308	*27	9	.974
—Houston (N.L.)	OF	20	74	9	15	1	0	0	0	.203	5	19	2	41	1	1	.977
1992—Cleveland (A.L.)■	OF	148	576	96	164	15	8	5	42	.285	68	54	*66	420	14	8	.982
1993—Cleveland (A.L.)	OF	148	569	116	185	28	8	1	42	.325	81	83	*70	402	11	•9	.979
1994—Cleveland (A.L.)	OF	112	459	105	*160	32	9	12	57	.349	52	56	*60	276	•13	2	.993
1995—Cleveland (A.L.)	OF-DH	118	481	93	149	22	*13	7	53	.310	40	49	*54	248	•11	8	.970
American League totals (4 years)		526	2085	410	658	97	38	25	194	.316	241	242	250	1346	49	27	.981
National League totals (1 year)		20	74	9	15	1	0	0	0	.203	5	19	2	41	1	1	.977
Major league totals (5 years)		546	2159	419	673	98	38	25	194	.312	246	261	252	1387	50	28	.981

DIVISION SERIES RECORD

			BATTING											FIELDING			
Year Team (League)	Pos.	G	AB	R	H	2B	3B	HR	RBI	Avg.	BB	SO	SB	PO	A	E	Avg.
1995—Cleveland (A.L.)	OF	3	13	1	2	0	0	0	0	.154	1	3	0	9	0	2	.818

CHAMPIONSHIP SERIES RECORD

Year	Team (League)	Pos.	G	AB	R	H	2B	3B	HR	RBI	Avg.	BB	SO	SB	PO	A	E	Avg.
				BATTING											FIELDING			
1995—	Cleveland (A.L.)	OF	6	24	4	11	0	2	0	3	.458	4	6	5	15	0	0	1.000

WORLD SERIES RECORD

NOTES: Shares single-inning record for most stolen bases—2 (October 21, 1995).

Year	Team (League)	Pos.	G	AB	R	H	2B	3B	HR	RBI	Avg.	BB	SO	SB	PO	A	E	Avg.
				BATTING											FIELDING			
1995—	Cleveland (A.L.)	OF	6	25	6	5	1	0	0	0	.200	3	1	6	12	0	0	1.000

ALL-STAR GAME RECORD

Year	League	Pos.	AB	R	H	2B	3B	HR	RBI	Avg.	BB	SO	SB	PO	A	E	Avg.
			BATTING											FIELDING			
1994—	American	OF	2	0	1	0	0	0	2	.500	0	1	1	1	0	0	1.000
1995—	American	OF	3	0	0	0	0	0	0	.000	0	1	0	0	0	0	...
All-Star Game totals (2 years)			5	0	1	0	0	0	2	.200	0	2	1	1	0	0	1.000

LOISELLE, RICH — P — ASTROS

PERSONAL: Born January 12, 1972, in Neenah, Wis. . . . 6-5/225. . . . Throws right, bats right. . . . Full name: Richard Frank Loiselle.
HIGH SCHOOL: Lawton (Okla.).
COLLEGE: Odessa (Tex.) College.
TRANSACTIONS/CAREER NOTES: Selected by San Diego Padres organization in 38th round of free-agent draft (June 3, 1991). . . . Traded by Padres organization with P Jeff Tabaka to Houston Astros organization for OF Phil Plantier (July 19, 1995). . . . On Tucson disabled list (August 2, 1995-remainder of season).

Year	Team (League)	W	L	Pct.	ERA	G	GS	CG	ShO	Sv.	IP	H	R	ER	BB	SO
1991—	Arizona Padres (Ariz.)	2	3	.400	3.52	12	12	0	0	0	61 1/3	72	40	24	26	47
1992—	Charleston (A. A.)	4	8	.333	3.71	19	19	2	2	0	97	93	51	40	42	64
1993—	Waterloo (Midw.)	1	5	.167	3.94	14	10	1	1	0	59 1/3	55	28	26	29	47
	—Rancho Cuca. (Cal.)	5	8	.385	5.77	14	14	1	0	0	82 2/3	109	64	53	34	53
1994—	Rancho Cuca. (Cal.)	9	10	.474	3.96	27	27	0	0	0	156 2/3	160	83	69	76	120
1995—	Memphis (South.)	6	3	.667	3.55	13	13	1	0	0	78 2/3	82	46	31	33	48
	—Las Vegas (PCL)	2	2	.500	7.24	8	7	1	1	0	27 1/3	36	27	22	9	16
	—Tucson (Pac. Coast)■	0	0	...	2.61	2	1	0	0	0	10 1/3	8	4	3	4	4

LOMON, KEVIN — P — BRAVES

PERSONAL: Born November 20, 1971, in Fort Smith, Ark. . . . 6-1/195. . . . Throws right, bats right. . . . Full name: Kevin Dale Lomon.
COLLEGE: Westark (Ark.).
TRANSACTIONS/CAREER NOTES: Selected by Atlanta Braves organization in 14th round of free-agent draft (June 3, 1991). . . . Selected by New York Mets from Braves organization in Rule 5 major league draft (December 5, 1994). . . . Returned to Braves organization (May 30, 1995).

Year	Team (League)	W	L	Pct.	ERA	G	GS	CG	ShO	Sv.	IP	H	R	ER	BB	SO
1991—	Pulaski (Appal.)	6	0	1.000	0.61	10	5	1	•1	1	44	17	9	3	13	70
	—Macon (S. Atl.)	1	0	1.000	1.80	1	0	0	0	0	5	2	1	1	1	2
1992—	Durham (Carolina)	8	9	.471	4.93	27	27	0	0	0	135	147	83	74	63	113
1993—	Durham (Carolina)	4	2	.667	3.71	14	14	1	0	0	85	80	36	35	30	68
	—Greenville (South.)	3	4	.429	3.86	13	13	1	1	0	79 1/3	76	41	34	31	68
1994—	Richmond (Int'l)	10	8	.556	3.86	28	26	0	0	0	147	159	69	63	53	97
1995—	New York (N.L.)■	0	1	.000	6.75	6	0	0	0	0	9 1/3	17	8	7	5	6
	—Richmond (Int'l)■	1	2	.333	3.00	32	3	0	0	1	60	62	23	20	32	52
Major league totals (1 year)		0	1	.000	6.75	6	0	0	0	0	9 1/3	17	8	7	5	6

LONG, JOEY — P — PADRES

PERSONAL: Born July 15, 1970, in Sidney, O. . . . 6-2/220. . . . Throws left, bats right.
HIGH SCHOOL: Graham (St. Paris, O.).
COLLEGE: Kent.
TRANSACTIONS/CAREER NOTES: Selected by San Diego Padres organization in fifth round of free-agent draft (June 3, 1991). . . . On Chandler disabled list (June 24, 1992-remainder of season).

Year	Team (League)	W	L	Pct.	ERA	G	GS	CG	ShO	Sv.	IP	H	R	ER	BB	SO
1991—	Spokane (N'west)	1	*9	.100	6.99	13	11	0	0	0	56 2/3	78	57	44	39	40
1992—								Did not play.								
1993—	Waterloo (Midw.)	4	3	.571	4.86	33	7	0	0	0	96 1/3	96	56	52	36	90
1994—	Rancho Cuca. (Cal.)	2	4	.333	4.67	46	0	0	0	3	52	69	36	27	22	52
1995—	Las Vegas (PCL)	1	3	.250	4.60	25	0	0	0	0	31 1/3	38	22	16	16	13
	—Memphis (South.)	0	2	.000	3.32	25	0	0	0	0	21 2/3	28	15	8	10	18

LONGMIRE, TONY — OF — PHILLIES

PERSONAL: Born August 12, 1968, in Vallejo, Calif. . . . 6-1/218. . . . Bats left, throws right. . . . Full name: Anthony Eugene Longmire.
HIGH SCHOOL: Hogan (Vallejo, Calif.).
TRANSACTIONS/CAREER NOTES: Selected by Pittsburgh Pirates organization in eighth round of free-agent draft (June 2, 1986). . . . On Salem disabled list (August 27, 1988-remainder of season). . . . On disabled list (April 10-May 24 and June 25, 1990-remainder of season). . . . Traded by Pirates organization to Philadelphia Phillies (September 28, 1990), completing deal in which Phillies traded OF/1B Carmelo

Martinez to Pirates for OF Wes Chamberlain, OF Julio Peguero and a player to be named later (August 30, 1990). . . . On Philadelphia disabled list (March 28, 1992-entire season).
MISCELLANEOUS: Batted as switch-hitter (1986-87, Harrisburg 1988 and 1990).

		BATTING												FIELDING			
Year Team (League)	**Pos.**	**G**	**AB**	**R**	**H**	**2B**	**3B**	**HR**	**RBI**	**Avg.**	**BB**	**SO**	**SB**	**PO**	**A**	**E**	**Avg.**
1986— GC Pirates (GCL)	OF	15	40	6	11	2	1	0	6	.275	2	2	1	19	0	2	.905
1987— Macon (S. Atl.)	OF	127	445	63	117	15	4	5	62	.263	41	73	18	167	5	8	.956
1988— Salem (Carolina)	OF	64	218	46	60	12	2	11	40	.275	36	44	4	91	3	3	.969
— Harrisburg (East.)	OF	32	94	7	14	2	2	0	4	.149	9	12	0	46	2	2	.960
1989— GC Pirates (GCL)	OF	2	5	0	0	0	0	0	0	.000	1	1	0	0	0	0	...
— Salem (Carolina)	OF	14	62	8	20	3	1	1	6	.323	1	13	0	14	3	0	1.000
— Harrisburg (East.)	OF	37	127	15	37	7	0	3	22	.291	12	21	1	62	1	2	.969
1990— Harrisburg (East.)	OF	24	91	9	27	6	0	1	13	.297	7	11	5	46	4	2	.962
1991— Reading (Eastern)■	OF	85	323	43	93	22	1	9	56	.288	32	45	10	134	3	4	.972
— Scran./W.B. (Int'l)	OF	36	111	11	29	3	2	0	9	.261	8	20	4	54	1	4	.932
1992—								Did not play.									
1993— Scran./W.B. (Int'l)	OF	120	447	63	136	*36	4	6	67	.304	41	71	12	195	5	5	.976
— Philadelphia (N.L.)	OF	11	13	1	3	0	0	0	1	.231	0	1	0	4	0	0	1.000
1994— Philadelphia (N.L.)	OF	69	139	10	33	11	0	0	17	.237	10	27	2	45	3	3	.941
1995— Philadelphia (N.L.)	OF	59	104	21	37	7	0	3	19	.356	11	19	1	33	2	0	1.000
Major league totals (3 years)		139	256	32	73	18	0	3	37	.285	21	47	3	82	5	3	.967

CHAMPIONSHIP SERIES RECORD

		BATTING												FIELDING			
Year Team (League)	**Pos.**	**G**	**AB**	**R**	**H**	**2B**	**3B**	**HR**	**RBI**	**Avg.**	**BB**	**SO**	**SB**	**PO**	**A**	**E**	**Avg.**
1993— Philadelphia (N.L.)	PH	1	1	0	0	0	0	0	0	.000	0	1	0	...	...	...	...

WORLD SERIES RECORD

		BATTING												FIELDING			
Year Team (League)	**Pos.**	**G**	**AB**	**R**	**H**	**2B**	**3B**	**HR**	**RBI**	**Avg.**	**BB**	**SO**	**SB**	**PO**	**A**	**E**	**Avg.**
1993— Philadelphia (N.L.)								Did not play.									

LOONEY, BRIAN — P — RED SOX

PERSONAL: Born September 26, 1969, in New Haven, Conn. . . . 5-10/185. . . . Throws left, bats left. . . . Full name: Brian James Looney.
HIGH SCHOOL: The Gunnery School (Washington, Conn.).
COLLEGE: Boston College.
TRANSACTIONS/CAREER NOTES: Selected by San Diego Padres organization in 43rd round of free-agent draft (June 1, 1988); did not sign. . . . Selected by Montreal Expos organization in 10th round of free-agent draft (June 3, 1991). . . . Traded by Expos to Boston Red Sox for a player to be named later (November 9, 1994). . . . On Boston disabled list (August 22-September 14, 1995).

Year Team (League)	W	L	Pct.	ERA	G	GS	CG	ShO	Sv.	IP	H	R	ER	BB	SO
1991— Jamestown (NYP)	7	1	.875	*1.16	11	11	2	1	0	62 1/3	42	12	8	28	64
1992— Rockford (Midw.)	3	1	.750	3.16	17	0	0	0	0	31 1/3	28	13	11	23	34
— Albany (S. Atl.)	3	2	.600	2.14	11	11	1	1	0	67 1/3	51	22	16	30	56
1993— WP Beach (FSL)	4	6	.400	3.14	18	16	0	0	0	106	108	48	37	29	109
— Harrisburg (East.)	3	2	.600	2.38	8	8	1	1	0	56 2/3	36	15	15	17	76
— Montreal (N.L.)	0	0	...	3.00	3	1	0	0	0	6	8	2	2	2	7
1994— Ottawa (Int'l)	7	7	.500	4.33	27	16	0	0	0	124 2/3	134	71	60	67	90
— Montreal (N.L.)	0	0	...	22.50	1	0	0	0	0	2	4	5	5	0	2
1995— Pawtucket (Int'l)■	4	7	.364	3.49	18	18	1	0	0	100 2/3	106	44	39	33	78
— Boston (A.L.)	0	1	.000	17.36	3	1	0	0	0	4 2/3	12	9	9	4	2
A.L. totals (1 year)	0	1	.000	17.36	3	1	0	0	0	4 2/3	12	9	9	4	2
N.L. totals (2 years)	0	0	...	7.88	4	1	0	0	0	8	12	7	7	2	9
Major league totals (3 years)	0	1	.000	11.37	7	2	0	0	0	12 2/3	24	16	16	6	11

LOPEZ, ALBIE — P — INDIANS

PERSONAL: Born August 18, 1971, in Mesa, Ariz. . . . 6-2/205. . . . Throws right, bats right. . . . Full name: Albert Anthony Lopez.
HIGH SCHOOL: Westwood (Mesa, Ariz.).
JUNIOR COLLEGE: Mesa (Ariz.) Community College.
TRANSACTIONS/CAREER NOTES: Selected by San Francisco Giants organization in 46th round of free-agent draft (June 5, 1989); did not sign. . . . Selected by Seattle Mariners organization in 19th round of free-agent draft (June 4, 1990); did not sign. . . . Selected by Cleveland Indians organization in 20th round of free-agent draft (June 3, 1991).

Year Team (League)	W	L	Pct.	ERA	G	GS	CG	ShO	Sv.	IP	H	R	ER	BB	SO
1991— Burlington (Appal.)	4	5	.444	3.44	13	13	0	0	0	73 1/3	61	33	28	23	81
1992— Columbus (S. Atl.)	7	2	.778	2.88	16	16	1	0	0	97	80	41	31	33	117
— Kinston (Carolina)	5	2	.714	3.52	10	10	1	1	0	64	56	28	25	26	44
1993— Cant./Akr. (East.)	9	4	.692	3.11	16	16	2	0	0	110	79	44	38	47	80
— Cleveland (A.L.)	3	1	.750	5.98	9	9	0	0	0	49 2/3	49	34	33	32	25
— Charlotte (Int'l)	1	0	1.000	2.25	3	2	0	0	0	12	8	3	3	2	7
1994— Charlotte (Int'l)	13	3	.813	3.94	22	22	3	0	0	144	136	68	63	42	105
— Cleveland (A.L.)	1	2	.333	4.24	4	4	1	1	0	17	20	11	8	6	18
1995— Buffalo (A.A.)	5	10	.333	4.44	18	18	1	1	0	101 1/3	101	57	50	51	82
— Cleveland (A.L.)	0	0	...	3.13	6	2	0	0	0	23	17	8	8	7	22
Major league totals (3 years)	4	3	.571	4.92	19	15	1	1	0	89 2/3	86	53	49	45	65

LOPEZ, JAVIER — C — BRAVES

PERSONAL: Born November 5, 1970, in Ponce, Puerto Rico. . . . 6-3/185. . . . Bats right, throws right. . . . Full name: Javier Torres Lopez.
HIGH SCHOOL: Academia Cristo Rey (Urb la Ramble Ponce, Puerto Rico).
TRANSACTIONS/CAREER NOTES: Signed as non-drafted free agent by Atlanta Braves organization (November 6, 1987). . . . On Greenville disabled list (July 18-August 2, 1992).
HONORS: Named Southern League Most Valuable Player (1992).
STATISTICAL NOTES: Led Midwest League catchers with 11 double plays and 31 passed balls in 1990. . . . Led Carolina League catchers with 701 total chances and 14 double plays in 1991. . . . Led Southern League catchers with 763 total chances and 19 passed balls in 1992. . . . Led International League catchers with 15 passed balls in 1993. . . . Tied for N.L. lead with 10 passed balls in 1994.

			BATTING												FIELDING			
Year	Team (League)	Pos.	G	AB	R	H	2B	3B	HR	RBI	Avg.	BB	SO	SB	PO	A	E	Avg.
1988—	GC Braves (GCL)	C	31	94	8	18	4	0	1	9	.191	3	19	1	131	30	7	.958
1989—	Pulaski (Appal.)	C	51	153	27	40	8	1	3	27	.261	5	35	3	264	26	5	.983
1990—	Burlington (Midw.)	C	116	422	48	112	17	3	11	55	.265	14	84	0	724	79	11	.986
1991—	Durham (Carolina)	C	113	384	43	94	14	2	11	51	.245	25	88	10	*610	85	6	.991
1992—	Greenville (South.)	C	115	442	63	142	28	3	16	60	.321	24	47	7	*680	75	8	.990
	—Atlanta (N.L.)	C	9	16	3	6	2	0	0	2	.375	0	1	0	28	2	0	1.000
1993—	Richmond (Int'l)	C	100	380	56	116	23	2	17	74	.305	12	53	1	718	70	10	.987
	—Atlanta (N.L.)	C	8	16	1	6	1	1	1	2	.375	0	2	0	37	2	1	.975
1994—	Atlanta (N.L.)	C	80	277	27	68	9	0	13	35	.245	17	61	0	559	35	3	.995
1995—	Atlanta (N.L.)	C	100	333	37	105	11	4	14	51	.315	14	57	0	625	50	8	.988
Major league totals (4 years)			197	642	68	185	23	5	28	90	.288	31	121	0	1249	89	12	.991

DIVISION SERIES RECORD

			BATTING												FIELDING			
Year	Team (League)	Pos.	G	AB	R	H	2B	3B	HR	RBI	Avg.	BB	SO	SB	PO	A	E	Avg.
1995—	Atlanta (N.L.)	C	3	9	0	4	0	0	0	3	.444	0	3	0	22	3	0	1.000

CHAMPIONSHIP SERIES RECORD

			BATTING												FIELDING			
Year	Team (League)	Pos.	G	AB	R	H	2B	3B	HR	RBI	Avg.	BB	SO	SB	PO	A	E	Avg.
1992—	Atlanta (N.L.)	C	1	1	0	0	0	0	0	0	.000	0	0	0	2	0	0	1.000
1995—	Atlanta (N.L.)	C	3	14	2	5	1	0	1	3	.357	0	1	0	28	2	0	1.000
Championship series totals (2 years)			4	15	2	5	1	0	1	3	.333	0	1	0	30	2	0	1.000

WORLD SERIES RECORD

NOTES: Member of World Series championship team (1995).

			BATTING												FIELDING			
Year	Team (League)	Pos.	G	AB	R	H	2B	3B	HR	RBI	Avg.	BB	SO	SB	PO	A	E	Avg.
1992—	Atlanta (N.L.)								Did not play.									
1995—	Atlanta (N.L.)	C-PH	6	17	1	3	2	0	1	3	.176	1	1	0	32	4	0	1.000
World Series totals (1 year)			6	17	1	3	2	0	1	3	.176	1	1	0	32	4	0	1.000

LOPEZ, LUIS — 2B/SS — PADRES

PERSONAL: Born September 4, 1970, in Cidra, Puerto Rico. . . . 5-11/175. . . . Bats both, throws right. . . . Full name: Luis Santos Lopez.
HIGH SCHOOL: San Jose (Caguas, Puerto Rico).
TRANSACTIONS/CAREER NOTES: Signed as non-drafted free agent by San Diego Padres organization (September 9, 1987). . . . On Las Vegas disabled list (July 3-14, 1994). . . . Granted free agency (October 15, 1994). . . . Re-signed by Padres (April 20, 1995). . . . On disabled list (April 24, 1995-entire season).
STATISTICAL NOTES: Led South Atlantic League shortstops with 703 total chances and 78 double plays in 1989. . . . Led Pacific Coast League shortstops with 30 errors in 1992. . . . Tied for Pacific Coast League lead with 13 sacrifice hits in 1993. . . . Career major league grand slams: 1.

			BATTING												FIELDING			
Year	Team (League)	Pos.	G	AB	R	H	2B	3B	HR	RBI	Avg.	BB	SO	SB	PO	A	E	Avg.
1988—	Spokane (N'west)	SS	70	312	50	95	13	1	0	35	.304	18	59	14	*118	217	*47	.877
1989—	Char., S.C. (S. Atl.)	SS	127	460	50	102	15	1	1	29	.222	17	85	12	*256	*373	*74	.895
1990—	Riverside (Calif.)	SS	14	46	5	17	3	1	1	4	.370	3	3	4	18	38	6	.903
1991—	Wichita (Texas)	2B-SS	125	452	43	121	17	1	1	41	.268	18	70	6	274	339	26	.959
1992—	Las Vegas (PCL)	SS-OF	120	395	44	92	8	8	1	31	.233	19	65	6	200	358	†30	.949
1993—	Las Vegas (PCL)	SS-2B	131	491	52	150	36	6	6	58	.305	27	62	8	230	380	29	.955
	—San Diego (N.L.)	2B	17	43	1	5	1	0	0	1	.116	0	8	0	23	34	1	.983
1994—	Las Vegas (PCL)	2B	12	49	2	10	2	2	0	6	.204	1	5	0	28	43	2	.973
	—San Diego (N.L.)	SS-2B-3B	77	235	29	65	16	1	2	20	.277	15	39	3	101	174	14	.952
1995—									Did not play—injured.									
Major league totals (2 years)			94	278	30	70	17	1	2	21	.252	15	47	3	124	208	15	.957

LOPEZ, MENDY — 3B/SS — ROYALS

PERSONAL: Born October 15, 1974, in Santo Domingo, Dominican Republic. . . . 6-2/165. . . . Bats right, throws right.
HIGH SCHOOL: Liceo Los Trinitanos (Santo Domingo, Dominican Republic).
TRANSACTIONS/CAREER NOTES: Signed as non-drafted free agent by Kansas City Royals organization (February 26, 1992).
STATISTICAL NOTES: Led Gulf Coast League shortstops with 80 putouts, 154 assists, 241 total chances, 39 double plays and .971 fielding percentage in 1994.

Year	Team (League)	Pos.	G	AB	R	H	2B	3B	HR	RBI	Avg.	BB	SO	SB	PO	A	E	Avg.
			BATTING												FIELDING			
1992—	Dom. Royals (DSL)	SS	49	145	22	40	1	0	1	23	.276	22	15	7	81	155	26	.901
1993—	Dom. Royals (DSL)	IF	28	98	15	27	5	2	0	20	.276	11	5	2	52	75	15	.894
1994—	GC Royals (GCL)	SS-3B-2B	59	*235	56	85	*19	3	5	*50	.362	22	27	10	†84	†195	12	†.959
1995—	Wilmington (Caro.)	3B-SS	130	428	42	116	29	3	2	36	.271	28	73	18	84	335	25	.944

LORETTA, MARK — SS — BREWERS

PERSONAL: Born August 14, 1971, in Santa Monica, Calif. . . . 6-0/175. . . . Bats right, throws right. . . . Full name: Mark David Loretta.
HIGH SCHOOL: St. Francis (La Canada, Calif.).
COLLEGE: Northwestern.
TRANSACTIONS/CAREER NOTES: Selected by Milwaukee Brewers organization in seventh round of free-agent draft (June 3, 1993).
STATISTICAL NOTES: Led American Association shortstops with 200 putouts and 591 total chances in 1995.

Year	Team (League)	Pos.	G	AB	R	H	2B	3B	HR	RBI	Avg.	BB	SO	SB	PO	A	E	Avg.
			BATTING												FIELDING			
1993—	Helena (Pioneer)	SS	6	28	5	9	1	0	1	8	.321	1	4	0	11	18	0	1.000
—	Stockton (Calif.)	SS-3B	53	201	36	73	4	1	4	31	.363	22	17	8	75	173	15	.943
1994—	El Paso (Texas)	SS-P	77	302	50	95	13	6	0	38	.315	27	33	8	125	271	11	.973
—	New Orleans (A.A.)	SS-2B	43	138	16	29	7	0	1	14	.210	12	13	2	68	121	11	.945
1995—	New Orleans (A.A.)	SS-3B-2B	127	479	48	137	22	5	7	79	.286	34	47	8	†204	376	25	.959
—	Milwaukee (A.L.)	SS-2B-DH	19	50	13	13	3	0	1	3	.260	4	7	1	18	42	1	.984
Major league totals (1 year)			19	50	13	13	3	0	1	3	.260	4	7	1	18	42	1	.984

RECORD AS PITCHER

Year	Team (League)	W	L	Pct.	ERA	G	GS	CG	ShO	Sv.	IP	H	R	ER	BB	SO
1994—	El Paso (Texas)	0	0	...	...	1	0	0	0	0	0	0	1	1	1	0

LORRAINE, ANDREW — P — ATHLETICS

PERSONAL: Born August 11, 1972, in Los Angeles. . . . 6-3/195. . . . Throws left, bats left. . . . Full name: Andrew Jason Lorraine.
HIGH SCHOOL: William S. Hart (Newhall, Calif.).
COLLEGE: Stanford.
TRANSACTIONS/CAREER NOTES: Selected by New York Mets organization in 38th round of free-agent draft (June 4, 1990); did not sign. . . . Selected by California Angels organization in fourth round of free-agent draft (June 3, 1993). . . . Traded by Angels with OF McKay Christensen, P Bill Simas and P John Snyder to Chicago White Sox for P Jim Abbott and P Tim Fortugno (July 27, 1995). . . . Traded by White Sox with OF Charles Poe to Oakland Athletics for OF/DH Danny Tartabull (January 22, 1996).

Year	Team (League)	W	L	Pct.	ERA	G	GS	CG	ShO	Sv.	IP	H	R	ER	BB	SO
1993—	Boise (Northwest)	4	1	.800	1.29	6	6	3	1	0	42	33	6	6	6	39
1994—	Vancouver (PCL)	12	4	.750	3.42	22	22	•4	•2	0	142	156	63	54	34	90
—	California (A.L.)	0	2	.000	10.61	4	3	0	0	0	18 2/3	30	23	22	11	10
1995—	Vancouver (PCL)	6	6	.500	3.96	18	18	4	1	0	97 2/3	105	49	43	30	51
—	Nashville (A.A.)■	4	1	.800	6.00	7	7	0	0	0	39	51	29	26	12	26
—	Chicago (A.L.)	0	0	...	3.38	5	0	0	0	0	8	3	3	3	2	5
Major league totals (2 years)		0	2	.000	8.44	9	3	0	0	0	26 2/3	33	26	25	13	15

LOWE, DEREK — P — MARINERS

PERSONAL: Born June 1, 1973, in Dearborn, Mich. . . . 6-6/170. . . . Throws right, bats right. . . . Full name: Derek Christopher Lowe.
HIGH SCHOOL: Edsel Ford (Dearborn, Mich.).
TRANSACTIONS/CAREER NOTES: Selected by Seattle Mariners organization in eighth round of free-agent draft (June 3, 1991). . . . On Port City disabled list (April 18-July 8, 1995).
STATISTICAL NOTES: Led Southern League with seven balks in 1994.

Year	Team (League)	W	L	Pct.	ERA	G	GS	CG	ShO	Sv.	IP	H	R	ER	BB	SO
1991—	Ariz. Mariners (Ariz.)	5	3	.625	2.41	12	12	0	0	0	71	58	26	19	21	60
1992—	Bellingham (N'west)	7	3	.700	2.42	14	13	2	•1	0	85 2/3	69	34	23	22	66
1993—	Riverside (Calif.)	12	9	.571	5.26	27	26	3	2	0	154	189	104	90	60	80
1994—	Jacksonville (Sou.)	7	10	.412	4.94	26	26	2	0	0	151 1/3	177	92	83	50	75
1995—	Port City (Southern)	1	6	.143	6.08	10	10	1	0	0	53 1/3	70	41	36	22	30
—	Ariz. Mariners (Ariz.)	1	0	1.000	0.93	2	2	0	0	0	9 2/3	5	1	1	2	11

LOWERY, TERRELL — OF — RANGERS

PERSONAL: Born October 25, 1970, in Oakland, Calif. . . . 6-3/180. . . . Bats right, throws right. . . . Full name: Quenton Terrell Lowery. . . . Brother of Josh Lowery, minor league shortstop (1989-90).
HIGH SCHOOL: Oakland (Calif.) Technical.
COLLEGE: Loyola Marymount.
TRANSACTIONS/CAREER NOTES: Selected by Texas Rangers organization in second round of free-agent draft (June 3, 1991). . . . On Butte disabled list (June 17-27, 1992). . . . On restricted list (June 27, 1992-February 5, 1993). . . . On Oklahoma City disabled list (April 6-August 24, 1995).
STATISTICAL NOTES: Led Texas League outfielders with 303 total chances in 1994.

Year	Team (League)	Pos.	G	AB	R	H	2B	3B	HR	RBI	Avg.	BB	SO	SB	PO	A	E	Avg.
			BATTING												FIELDING			
1991—	Butte (Pioneer)	OF	54	214	38	64	10	7	3	33	.299	29	44	23	92	7	6	.943
1992—			Did not play.															
1993—	Charlotte (Fla. St.)	OF	65	257	46	77	7	9	3	36	.300	46	47	14	156	5	4	.976
—	Tulsa (Texas)	OF	66	258	29	62	5	1	3	14	.240	28	50	10	152	6	2	.988

			BATTING												FIELDING		
Year	Team (League)	Pos.	G	AB	R	H	2B	3B	HR	RBI	Avg.	BB	SO	SB	PO	A	E	Avg.
1994—	Tulsa (Texas)	OF	129	496	89	142	34	8	8	54	.286	59	113	33	*280	16	7	.977
1995—	GC Rangers (GCL)	OF	10	34	10	9	3	1	3	7	.265	6	7	1	7	0	0	1.000
—	Charlotte (Fla. St.)	OF	11	35	4	9	2	2	0	4	.257	6	6	1	18	0	0	1.000

LUDWICK, ERIC — P — CARDINALS

PERSONAL: Born December 14, 1971, in Whiteman AFB, Mo. . . . 6-5/210. . . . Throws right, bats right. . . . Full name: Eric D. Ludwick.
HIGH SCHOOL: El Dorado (Las Vegas).
COLLEGE: California, then UNLV.
TRANSACTIONS/CAREER NOTES: Selected by New York Mets organization in second round of free-agent draft (June 3, 1993). . . . Traded by Mets with P Erik Hiljus and OF Yudith Ozorio to St. Louis Cardinals for OF Bernard Gilkey (January 22, 1996).

Year	Team (League)	W	L	Pct.	ERA	G	GS	CG	ShO	Sv.	IP	H	R	ER	BB	SO
1993—	Pittsfield (NYP)	4	4	.500	3.18	10	10	1	0	0	51	51	27	18	18	40
1994—	St. Lucie (Fla. St.)	7	13	.350	4.55	27	27	3	0	0	150 1/3	162	*102	76	77	77
1995—	Binghamton (East.)	12	5	.706	2.95	23	22	3	2	0	143 1/3	108	52	47	68	131
—	Norfolk (Int'l)	1	1	.500	5.85	4	3	0	0	0	20	22	15	13	7	9

LUKE, MATT — OF — YANKEES

PERSONAL: Born February 26, 1971, in Long Beach, Calif. . . . 6-5/220. . . . Bats left, throws left. . . . Full name: Matthew Clifford Luke.
HIGH SCHOOL: El Dorado (Calif.).
COLLEGE: California.
TRANSACTIONS/CAREER NOTES: Selected by New York Yankees organization in eighth round of free-agent draft (June 1, 1992). . . . On Tampa disabled list (April 22-May 9, 1994).
STATISTICAL NOTES: Led South Atlantic League with 267 total bases in 1993.

			BATTING												FIELDING		
Year	Team (League)	Pos.	G	AB	R	H	2B	3B	HR	RBI	Avg.	BB	SO	SB	PO	A	E	Avg.
1992—	Oneonta (NYP)	OF-1B	69	271	30	67	11	*7	2	34	.247	19	32	4	230	16	7	.972
1993—	Greensboro (S. Atl.)	OF	135	*549	83	•157	37	5	21	91	.286	47	79	11	218	11	3	*.987
1994—	Tampa (Fla. St.)	OF	57	222	52	68	11	2	16	42	.306	28	27	4	100	12	5	.957
—	Alb./Colon. (East.)	OF-1B	63	236	34	67	11	2	8	40	.284	28	50	6	158	8	3	.982
1995—	Norwich (Eastern)	OF	93	365	48	95	17	5	8	53	.260	20	68	5	178	12	4	.979
—	Columbus (Int'l)	OF	23	77	11	23	4	1	3	12	.299	2	12	1	36	1	2	.949

LYDY, SCOTT — OF — ATHLETICS

PERSONAL: Born October 26, 1968, in Mesa, Ariz. . . . 6-5/195. . . . Bats right, throws right. . . . Full name: Donald Scott Lydy. . . . Name pronounced LY-dee.
HIGH SCHOOL: Mountain View (Mesa, Ariz.).
JUNIOR COLLEGE: South Mountain Community College (Ariz.).
TRANSACTIONS/CAREER NOTES: Selected by Oakland Athletics organization in second round of free-agent draft (June 5, 1989).

			BATTING												FIELDING		
Year	Team (League)	Pos.	G	AB	R	H	2B	3B	HR	RBI	Avg.	BB	SO	SB	PO	A	E	Avg.
1989—	S. Oregon (N'west)	OF	67	230	37	48	11	2	3	28	.209	31	72	8	109	3	6	.949
1990—	Arizona A's (Ariz.)	1B	18	50	8	17	6	0	2	11	.340	10	14	0	6	1	0	1.000
—	Madison (Midwest)	OF	54	174	33	33	6	2	4	19	.190	25	62	7	85	3	4	.957
1991—	Madison (Midwest)	OF	127	464	64	120	26	2	12	69	.259	66	109	24	222	14	8	.967
1992—	Reno (California)	OF	33	124	29	49	13	2	2	27	.395	26	30	9	41	6	4	.922
—	Huntsville (South.)	OF	109	387	64	118	20	3	9	65	.305	67	95	16	137	4	7	.953
1993—	Tacoma (PCL)	OF	95	341	70	100	22	6	9	41	.293	50	87	12	182	9	6	.970
—	Oakland (A.L.)	OF-DH	41	102	11	23	5	0	2	7	.225	8	39	2	67	2	3	.958
1994—	Tacoma (PCL)	OF-1B	135	508	98	160	37	3	17	73	.315	58	108	22	294	4	6	.980
1995—	Edmonton (PCL)	OF	104	400	78	116	29	7	16	65	.290	33	66	15	202	12	7	.968
Major league totals (1 year)			41	102	11	23	5	0	2	7	.225	8	39	2	67	2	3	.958

LYONS, BARRY — C/1B — RANGERS

PERSONAL: Born June 3, 1960, in Biloxi, Miss. . . . 6-1/200. . . . Bats right, throws right. . . . Full name: Barry Stephen Lyons.
HIGH SCHOOL: Biloxi (Miss.).
COLLEGE: Delta State (Miss.).
TRANSACTIONS/CAREER NOTES: Selected by Detroit Tigers organization in 25th round of free-agent draft (June 8, 1981); did not sign. . . . Selected by New York Mets organization in 15th round of free-agent draft (June 7, 1982). . . . On Tidewater disabled list (August 4, 1986-remainder of season). . . . On New York disabled list (June 27-July 25, 1989); included rehabilitation assignment to Tidewater (July 19-25). . . . On New York disabled list (May 16-July 9, 1990); included rehabilitation assignment to Tidewater (June 19-July 9). . . . Released by Mets (September 4, 1990). . . . Signed by Los Angeles Dodgers (September 21, 1990). . . . Granted free agency (June 12, 1991). . . . Signed by Edmonton, California Angels organization (June 19, 1991). . . . Released by Angels (October 24, 1991). . . . Signed by Houston Astros organization (January 15, 1992). . . . On Tucson disabled list (May 26-June 23, 1992). . . . Granted free agency (October 15, 1992). . . . Signed by St. Louis Cardinals organization (January 4, 1993). . . . On disabled list (June 22-July 2, 1993). . . . Released by Louisville, Cardinals organization (September 1, 1993). . . . Signed by Indianapolis, Cincinnati Reds organization (February 11, 1994). . . . Granted free agency (October 15, 1994). . . . Signed by Chicago White Sox (April 25, 1995). . . . Released by White Sox (November 30, 1995). . . . Signed by Texas Rangers organization (January 16, 1996).
HONORS: Named Carolina League Player of the Year (1984).
STATISTICAL NOTES: Led Carolina League catchers with .989 fielding percentage and 72 assists in 1984. . . . Led Texas League in grounding into double plays with 19 in 1985. . . . Led Texas League catchers with 19 errors in 1985. . . . Led American Association catchers with 641 total chances, 583 putouts and 14 errors in 1994.

Year	Team (League)	Pos.	G	AB	R	H	2B	3B	HR	RBI	Avg.	BB	SO	SB	PO	A	E	Avg.
			BATTING												FIELDING			
1982	Shelby (S. Atl.)	C-1B	45	164	23	46	12	0	4	46	.280	24	10	0	226	21	8	.969
1983	Lynchburg (Caro.)	C	2	7	0	1	0	0	0	2	.143	0	0	0	21	4	0	1.000
	—Columbia (S. Atl.)	C-1B-OF	92	316	55	94	9	2	5	45	.297	42	32	3	387	33	17	.961
1984	Lynchburg (Caro.)	C-1B-OF	115	412	59	130	17	3	12	87	.316	45	40	1	894	†86	13	†.987
1985	Jackson (Texas)	C-1B	126	486	69	149	34	6	11	108	.307	25	67	3	834	65	†23	.975
1986	New York (N.L.)	C	6	9	1	0	0	0	0	2	.000	1	2	0	16	0	1	.941
	—Tidewater (Int'l)	1B-C	61	234	28	69	16	0	4	46	.295	18	32	0	423	25	6	.987
1987	New York (N.L.)	C	53	130	15	33	4	1	4	24	.254	8	24	0	223	17	4	.984
1988	New York (N.L.)	C-1B	50	91	5	21	7	1	0	11	.231	3	12	0	130	9	3	.979
1989	New York (N.L.)	C	79	235	15	58	13	0	3	27	.247	11	28	0	463	29	10	.980
	—Tidewater (Int'l)	C-1B	5	20	1	2	0	1	0	2	.100	0	4	0	43	5	1	.980
1990	New York (N.L.)	C	24	80	8	19	0	0	2	7	.238	2	9	0	180	12	4	.980
	—Tidewater (Int'l)	C-1B	57	164	8	28	5	0	0	17	.171	16	25	0	291	23	5	.984
	—Los Angeles (N.L.)■	C	3	5	1	1	0	0	1	2	.200	0	1	0	3	0	0	1.000
1991	Los Angeles (N.L.)	C	9	9	0	0	0	0	0	0	.000	0	2	0	12	1	0	1.000
	—Edmonton (PCL)■	C-1B	47	165	15	51	13	0	2	23	.309	10	11	0	247	26	8	.972
	—California (A.L.)	1B	2	5	0	1	0	0	0	0	.200	0	0	0	10	1	0	1.000
1992	Tucson (PCL)■	C-1B	71	277	32	83	24	0	4	45	.300	9	35	1	549	50	4	.993
1993	Louisville (A.A.)■	1B-C	107	401	36	108	19	0	18	65	.269	15	64	0	641	53	8	.989
1994	Indianapolis (A.A.)■	C-1B	114	431	63	133	25	1	14	66	.309	28	59	0	†651	54	†14	.981
1995	Chicago (A.L.)■	C-DH-1B	27	64	8	17	2	0	5	16	.266	4	14	0	97	14	2	.982
	—Nashville (A.A.)	C-1B	71	265	37	68	16	1	8	38	.257	20	56	0	300	22	1	.997
American League totals (2 years)			29	69	8	18	2	0	5	16	.261	4	14	0	107	15	2	.984
National League totals (6 years)			224	559	45	132	24	2	10	73	.236	25	78	0	1027	68	22	.980
Major league totals (7 years)			253	628	53	150	26	2	15	89	.239	29	92	0	1134	83	24	.981

MAAS, KEVIN — DH/1B — YANKEES

PERSONAL: Born January 20, 1965, in Castro Valley, Calif. . . . 6-3/204. . . . Bats left, throws left. . . . Full name: Kevin Christian Maas. . . . Brother of Jason Maas, minor league outfielder/infielder (1985-91).

HIGH SCHOOL: Bishop O'Dowd (Oakland, Calif.).

COLLEGE: California.

TRANSACTIONS/CAREER NOTES: Selected by New York Yankees organization in 22nd round of free-agent draft (June 2, 1986). . . . On disabled list (April 19-30 and July 27, 1989-remainder of season). . . . Released by Yankees (March 29, 1994). . . . Signed by Wichita, San Diego Padres organization (April 13, 1994). . . . Released by Las Vegas, Padres organization (May 23, 1994). . . . Signed by Indianapolis, Cincinnati Reds organization (May 27, 1994). . . . Released by Reds (December 1, 1994). . . . Signed by Salt Lake, Minnesota Twins organization (December 22, 1994). . . . On Minnesota disabled list (May 4-20, 1995). . . . Granted free agency (June 30, 1995). . . . Signed by Columbus, Yankees organization (July 1, 1995). . . . On Columbus disabled list (July 1-9, 1995).

Year	Team (League)	Pos.	G	AB	R	H	2B	3B	HR	RBI	Avg.	BB	SO	SB	PO	A	E	Avg.
			BATTING												FIELDING			
1986	Oneonta (NYP)	1B	28	101	14	36	10	0	0	18	.356	7	9	5	222	19	1	.996
1987	Fort Lauder. (FSL)	1B	116	439	77	122	28	4	11	73	.278	53	108	14	667	51	10	.986
1988	Prin. William (Car.)	1B	29	108	24	32	7	0	12	35	.296	17	28	3	288	25	5	.984
	—Alb./Colon. (East.)	1B	109	372	66	98	14	3	16	55	.263	64	103	5	902	73	12	.988
1989	Columbus (Int'l)	OF	83	291	42	93	23	2	6	45	.320	40	73	2	78	3	3	.964
1990	Columbus (Int'l)	1B	57	194	37	55	15	2	13	41	.284	34	45	2	219	19	4	.983
	—New York (A.L.)	1B-DH	79	254	42	64	9	0	21	41	.252	43	76	1	486	35	9	.983
1991	New York (A.L.)	DH-1B	148	500	69	110	14	1	23	63	.220	83	128	5	317	23	6	.983
1992	New York (A.L.)	DH-1B	98	286	35	71	12	0	11	35	.248	25	63	3	142	4	2	.986
1993	New York (A.L.)	DH-1B	59	151	20	31	4	0	9	25	.205	24	32	1	115	5	2	.984
	—Columbus (Int'l)	1B	28	104	14	29	6	0	4	18	.279	19	22	0	270	20	7	.976
1994	Wichita (Texas)■	1B-OF	4	15	4	8	3	0	3	8	.533	3	0	0	26	0	0	1.000
	—Las Vegas (PCL)	1B-OF	29	90	15	22	6	2	4	12	.244	9	25	1	161	8	2	.988
	—Indianapolis (A.A.)■	OF-1B	78	283	55	82	18	2	19	45	.290	29	49	2	184	15	4	.980
1995	Minnesota (A.L.)■	DH-1B	22	57	5	11	4	0	1	5	.193	7	11	0	43	1	3	.936
	—GC Yankees (GCL)■	OF	2	9	1	4	0	0	1	3	.444	0	0	0	3	0	0	1.000
	—Columbus (Int'l)	OF-1B	44	161	28	45	7	2	9	33	.280	23	40	0	115	8	0	1.000
Major league totals (5 years)			406	1248	171	287	43	1	65	169	.230	182	310	10	1103	68	22	.982

MABRY, JOHN — 1B/OF — CARDINALS

PERSONAL: Born October 17, 1970, in Wilmington, Del. . . . 6-4/195. . . . Bats left, throws right. . . . Full name: John Steven Mabry.

HIGH SCHOOL: Bohemia Manor (Chesapeake City, Md.).

COLLEGE: West Chester (Pa.).

TRANSACTIONS/CAREER NOTES: Selected by St. Louis Cardinals organization in sixth round of free-agent draft (June 3, 1991). . . . On disabled list (April 22-30 and May 6-18, 1992).

STATISTICAL NOTES: Led Texas League in grounding into double plays with 17 in 1993. . . . Led Texas League outfielders with six double plays in 1993.

Year	Team (League)	Pos.	G	AB	R	H	2B	3B	HR	RBI	Avg.	BB	SO	SB	PO	A	E	Avg.
			BATTING												FIELDING			
1991	Hamilton (NYP)	OF	49	187	25	58	11	0	1	31	.310	17	18	9	73	*10	5	.943
	—Savannah (S. Atl.)	OF	22	86	10	20	6	1	0	8	.233	7	12	1	36	1	1	.974
1992	Springfield (Midw.)	OF	115	438	63	115	13	6	11	57	.263	24	39	2	171	14	6	.969
1993	Arkansas (Texas)	OF	*136	528	68	153	32	2	16	72	.290	27	68	7	262	15	3	*.989
	—Louisville (A.A.)	OF	4	7	0	1	0	0	0	1	.143	0	1	0	3	0	0	1.000
1994	Louisville (A.A.)	OF	122	477	76	125	30	1	15	68	.262	32	67	2	237	4	2	.992
	—St. Louis (N.L.)	OF	6	23	2	7	3	0	0	3	.304	2	4	0	16	0	0	1.000

Year	Team (League)	Pos.	G	AB	R	H	2B	3B	HR	RBI	Avg.	BB	SO	SB	PO	A	E	Avg.
				BATTING											FIELDING			
1995—	St. Louis (N.L.)	1B-OF	129	388	35	119	21	1	5	41	.307	24	45	0	652	58	4	.994
—	Louisville (A.A.)	OF	4	12	0	1	0	0	0	0	.083	0	0	0	8	0	1	.889
Major league totals (2 years)			135	411	37	126	24	1	5	44	.307	26	49	0	668	58	4	.995

MacDONALD, BOB — P

PERSONAL: Born April 27, 1965, in East Orange, N.J. . . . 6-2/204. . . . Throws left, bats left. . . . Full name: Robert Joseph MacDonald.
HIGH SCHOOL: Point Pleasant Beach (N.J.).
COLLEGE: Rutgers.
TRANSACTIONS/CAREER NOTES: Selected by Toronto Blue Jays organization in 19th round of free-agent draft (June 2, 1987). . . . Contract sold by Blue Jays to Detroit Tigers (March 30, 1993). . . . Granted free agency (December 20, 1993). . . . Signed by Houston Astros organization (February 11, 1994). . . . Released by Tucson, Astros organization (April 1, 1994). . . . Signed by Calgary, Seattle Mariners organization (April 8, 1994). . . . Released by Calgary (June 13, 1994). . . . Signed by Birmingham, Chicago White Sox organization (July 1, 1994). . . . Granted free agency (October 15, 1994). . . . Signed by New York Yankees organization (February 15, 1995). . . . Granted free agency (October 16, 1995).

Year	Team (League)	W	L	Pct.	ERA	G	GS	CG	ShO	Sv.	IP	H	R	ER	BB	SO
1987—	St. Cathar. (NYP)	0	0	...	4.50	1	1	0	0	0	4	8	4	2	0	4
—	Medicine Hat (Pio.)	3	1	.750	2.92	13	0	0	0	2	24 2/3	22	13	8	12	26
—	Myrtle Beach (SAL)	2	1	.667	5.66	10	0	0	0	0	20 2/3	24	18	13	7	12
1988—	Myrtle Beach (SAL)	3	4	.429	1.69	52	0	0	0	15	53 1/3	42	13	10	18	43
1989—	Knoxville (South.)	3	5	.375	3.29	43	0	0	0	9	63	52	27	23	23	58
—	Syracuse (Int'l)	1	0	1.000	5.63	12	0	0	0	0	16	16	10	10	6	12
1990—	Syracuse (Int'l)	0	2	.000	5.40	9	0	0	0	2	8 1/3	4	5	5	9	6
—	Knoxville (South.)	1	2	.333	1.89	36	0	0	0	15	57	37	17	12	29	54
—	Toronto (A.L.)	0	0	...	0.00	4	0	0	0	0	2 1/3	0	0	0	2	0
1991—	Syracuse (Int'l)	1	0	1.000	4.50	7	0	0	0	1	6	5	3	3	5	8
—	Toronto (A.L.)	3	3	.500	2.85	45	0	0	0	0	53 2/3	51	19	17	25	24
1992—	Toronto (A.L.)	1	0	1.000	4.37	27	0	0	0	0	47 1/3	50	24	23	16	26
—	Syracuse (Int'l)	2	3	.400	4.63	17	0	0	0	2	23 1/3	25	13	12	12	14
1993—	Detroit (A.L.)■	3	3	.500	5.35	68	0	0	0	3	65 2/3	67	42	39	33	39
1994—	Calgary (PCL)■	2	2	.500	7.55	25	0	0	0	1	31	39	28	26	14	26
—	Birmingham (Sou.)■	4	4	.500	1.78	23	3	0	0	2	55 2/3	40	16	11	6	38
—	Nashville (A.A.)	0	0	...	0.00	2	0	0	0	0	1 2/3	1	0	0	0	0
1995—	Columbus (Int'l)■	2	1	.667	2.33	13	0	0	0	0	19 1/3	22	7	5	5	13
—	New York (A.L.)	1	1	.500	4.86	33	0	0	0	0	46 1/3	50	25	25	22	41
Major league totals (5 years)		8	7	.533	4.35	177	0	0	0	3	215 1/3	218	110	104	98	130

CHAMPIONSHIP SERIES RECORD

Year	Team (League)	W	L	Pct.	ERA	G	GS	CG	ShO	Sv.	IP	H	R	ER	BB	SO
1991—	Toronto (A.L.)	0	0	...	9.00	1	0	0	0	0	1	1	1	1	1	0

MACFARLANE, MIKE — C — ROYALS

PERSONAL: Born April 12, 1964, in Stockton, Calif. . . . 6-1/210. . . . Bats right, throws right. . . . Full name: Michael Andrew Macfarlane.
HIGH SCHOOL: Lincoln (Stockton, Calif.).
COLLEGE: Santa Clara.
TRANSACTIONS/CAREER NOTES: Selected by Kansas City Royals organization in fourth round of free-agent draft (June 3, 1985). . . . On disabled list (April 9-July 9, 1986 and July 16-September 14, 1991). . . . Granted free agency (October 17, 1994). . . . Signed by Boston Red Sox (April 8, 1995). . . . Granted free agency (November 6, 1995). . . . Signed by Royals (December 16, 1995).
STATISTICAL NOTES: Tied for A.L. lead in being hit by pitch with 15 in 1992. . . . Led A.L. in being hit by pitch with 18 in 1994. . . . Led A.L. catchers with nine double plays in 1994. . . . Led A.L. with 26 passed balls in 1995. . . . Career major league grand slams: 4.

Year	Team (League)	Pos.	G	AB	R	H	2B	3B	HR	RBI	Avg.	BB	SO	SB	PO	A	E	Avg.
				BATTING											FIELDING			
1985—	Memphis (South.)	C	65	223	29	60	15	4	8	39	.269	11	30	0	295	24	9	.973
1986—	Memphis (South.)	OF	40	141	26	34	7	2	12	29	.241	10	26	0	0	0	0	...
1987—	Omaha (A.A.)	C	87	302	53	79	25	1	13	50	.262	22	50	0	408	37	6	.987
—	Kansas City (A.L.)	C	8	19	0	4	1	0	0	3	.211	2	2	0	29	2	0	1.000
1988—	Kansas City (A.L.)	C	70	211	25	56	15	0	4	26	.265	21	37	0	309	18	2	.994
—	Omaha (A.A.)	C	21	76	8	18	7	2	2	8	.237	4	15	0	85	5	1	.989
1989—	Kansas City (A.L.)	C-DH	69	157	13	35	6	0	2	19	.223	7	27	0	249	17	1	.996
1990—	Kansas City (A.L.)	C-DH	124	400	37	102	24	4	6	58	.255	25	69	1	660	23	6	.991
1991—	Kansas City (A.L.)	C-DH	84	267	34	74	18	2	13	41	.277	17	52	1	391	28	3	.993
1992—	Kansas City (A.L.)	C-DH	129	402	51	94	28	3	17	48	.234	30	89	1	527	43	4	.993
1993—	Kansas City (A.L.)	C	117	388	55	106	27	0	20	67	.273	40	83	2	647	68	11	.985
1994—	Kansas City (A.L.)	C-DH	92	314	53	80	17	3	14	47	.255	35	71	1	498	39	4	.993
1995—	Boston (A.L.)■	C-DH	115	364	45	82	18	1	15	51	.225	38	78	2	618	49	5	.993
Major league totals (9 years)			808	2522	313	633	154	13	91	360	.251	215	508	8	3928	287	36	.992

DIVISION SERIES RECORD

Year	Team (League)	Pos.	G	AB	R	H	2B	3B	HR	RBI	Avg.	BB	SO	SB	PO	A	E	Avg.
				BATTING											FIELDING			
1995—	Boston (A.L.)	C	3	9	0	3	0	0	0	1	.333	0	3	0	18	0	2	.900

MADDUX, GREG — P — BRAVES

PERSONAL: Born April 14, 1966, in San Angelo, Tex. . . . 6-0/175. . . . Throws right, bats right. . . . Full name: Gregory Alan Maddux. . . .

M

Brother of Mike Maddux, pitcher, Boston Red Sox.

HIGH SCHOOL: Valley (Las Vegas).

TRANSACTIONS/CAREER NOTES: Selected by Chicago Cubs organization in second round of free-agent draft (June 4, 1984).... Granted free agency (October 26, 1992).... Signed by Atlanta Braves (December 9, 1992).

RECORDS: Holds major league single-season record for fewest complete games by pitcher who led league in complete games—8 (1993). ... Shares major league career record for most years leading league in putouts by pitcher—5.... Shares major league single-game record for most putouts by pitcher—7 (April 29, 1990).... Shares modern N.L. single-season record for most putouts by pitcher—39 (each in 1990-91 and 1993).

HONORS: Won N.L. Gold Glove at pitcher (1990-95).... Named righthanded pitcher on The Sporting News N.L. All-Star team (1992-95). ... Named N.L. Cy Young Award winner by Baseball Writers' Association of America (1992-95).... Named N.L. Pitcher of the Year by The Sporting News (1993-95).

STATISTICAL NOTES: Led Appalachian League with eight hit batsmen in 1984.... Led American Association with 12 hit batsmen in 1986. ... Led N.L. with 14 hit batsmen in 1992.... Pitched 3-1 one-hit, complete-game victory against Houston (May 28, 1995).

MISCELLANEOUS: Appeared in three games as pinch-runner (1988).... Singled and scored and struck out in two appearances as pinch-hitter (1991).

Year Team (League)	W	L	Pct.	ERA	G	GS	CG	ShO	Sv.	IP	H	R	ER	BB	SO
1984— Pikeville (Appal.)	6	2	.750	2.63	14	12	2	•2	0	85 2/3	63	35	25	41	62
1985— Peoria (Midwest)	13	9	.591	3.19	27	27	6	0	0	186	176	86	66	52	125
1986— Pittsfield (Eastern)	4	3	.571	2.73	8	8	4	2	0	62 2/3	49	22	19	15	35
— Iowa (Am. Assoc.)	10	1	*.909	3.02	18	18	5	•2	0	128 1/3	127	49	43	30	65
— Chicago (N.L.)	2	4	.333	5.52	6	5	1	0	0	31	44	20	19	11	20
1987— Chicago (N.L.)	6	14	.300	5.61	30	27	1	1	0	155 2/3	181	111	97	74	101
— Iowa (Am. Assoc.)	3	0	1.000	0.98	4	4	2	•2	0	27 2/3	17	3	3	12	22
1988— Chicago (N.L.)	18	8	.692	3.18	34	34	9	3	0	249	230	97	88	81	140
1989— Chicago (N.L.)	19	12	.613	2.95	35	35	7	1	0	238 1/3	222	90	78	82	135
1990— Chicago (N.L.)	15	15	.500	3.46	35	•35	8	2	0	237	*242	*116	91	71	144
1991— Chicago (N.L.)	15	11	.577	3.35	37	*37	7	2	0	*263	232	113	98	66	198
1992— Chicago (N.L.)	•20	11	.645	2.18	35	•35	9	4	0	*268	201	68	65	70	199
1993— Atlanta (N.L.)■	20	10	.667	*2.36	36	•36	*8	1	0	*267	228	85	70	52	197
1994— Atlanta (N.L.)	•16	6	.727	*1.56	25	25	*10	•3	0	*202	150	44	35	31	156
1995— Atlanta (N.L.)	*19	2	*.905	*1.63	28	28	*10	•3	0	•209 2/3	147	39	38	23	181
Major league totals (10 years)	150	93	.617	2.88	301	297	70	20	0	2120 2/3	1877	783	679	561	1471

DIVISION SERIES RECORD

Year Team (League)	W	L	Pct.	ERA	G	GS	CG	ShO	Sv.	IP	H	R	ER	BB	SO
1995— Atlanta (N.L.)	1	0	1.000	4.50	2	2	0	0	0	14	19	7	7	2	7

CHAMPIONSHIP SERIES RECORD

NOTES: Shares single-series record for most earned runs allowed—11 (1989).... Holds N.L. single-series record for most runs allowed—12 (1989).... Scored once in one game as pinch-runner (1989).

Year Team (League)	W	L	Pct.	ERA	G	GS	CG	ShO	Sv.	IP	H	R	ER	BB	SO
1989— Chicago (N.L.)	0	1	.000	13.50	2	2	0	0	0	7 1/3	13	12	11	4	5
1993— Atlanta (N.L.)	1	1	.500	4.97	2	2	0	0	0	12 2/3	11	8	7	7	11
1995— Atlanta (N.L.)	1	0	1.000	1.13	1	1	0	0	0	8	7	1	1	2	4
Champ. series totals (3 years)	2	2	.500	6.11	5	5	0	0	0	28	31	21	19	13	20

WORLD SERIES RECORD

NOTES: Member of World Series championship team (1995).

Year Team (League)	W	L	Pct.	ERA	G	GS	CG	ShO	Sv.	IP	H	R	ER	BB	SO
1995— Atlanta (N.L.)	1	1	.500	2.25	2	2	1	0	0	16	9	6	4	3	8

ALL-STAR GAME RECORD

Year League	W	L	Pct.	ERA	GS	CG	ShO	Sv.	IP	H	R	ER	BB	SO
1988— National						Did not play.								
1992— National	0	0	...	6.75	0	0	0	0	1 1/3	1	1	1	0	0
1994— National	0	0	...	3.00	1	0	0	0	3	3	1	1	0	2
1995— National						Selected, did not play—injured.								
All-Star totals (2 years)	0	0	...	4.15	1	0	0	0	4 1/3	4	2	2	0	2

MADDUX, MIKE — P — RED SOX

PERSONAL: Born August 27, 1961, in Dayton, O.... 6-2/185.... Throws right, bats left.... Full name: Michael Ausley Maddux.... Brother of Greg Maddux, pitcher, Atlanta Braves.

HIGH SCHOOL: Rancho (Las Vegas).

COLLEGE: Texas-El Paso.

TRANSACTIONS/CAREER NOTES: Selected by Cincinnati Reds organization in 36th round of free-agent draft (June 5, 1979); did not sign. ... Selected by Philadelphia Phillies organization in fifth round of free-agent draft (June 7, 1982).... On Philadelphia disabled list (April 21-June 1, 1988); included rehabilitation assignment to Maine (May 13-22).... Released by Phillies organization (November 20, 1989).... Signed by Los Angeles Dodgers (December 21, 1989).... Granted free agency (October 15, 1990).... Signed by San Diego Padres (March 30, 1991).... On disabled list (April 5-26, 1992).... Traded by Padres to New York Mets for P Roger Mason and P Mike Freitas (December 17, 1992).... On disabled list (April 27-May 13, 1994).... Granted free agency (October 18, 1994).... Signed by Calgary, Pittsburgh Pirates organization (April 10, 1995).... Released by Pirates (May 16, 1995).... Signed by Boston Red Sox (May 30, 1995).... Granted free agency (November 6, 1995).... Re-signed by Red Sox (December 15, 1995).

MISCELLANEOUS: Appeared in one game as pinch-runner with Philadelphia (1988).

Year Team (League)	W	L	Pct.	ERA	G	GS	CG	ShO	Sv.	IP	H	R	ER	BB	SO
1982— Bend (Northwest)	3	6	.333	3.99	11	10	3	0	0	65 1/3	68	35	29	26	59
1983— Spartanburg (SAL)	4	6	.400	5.44	13	13	3	0	0	84 1/3	98	62	51	47	85
— Peninsula (Caro.)	8	4	.667	3.62	14	14	6	0	0	99 1/3	92	46	40	35	78
— Reading (Eastern)	0	0	...	6.00	1	1	0	0	0	3	4	2	2	1	2
1984— Reading (Eastern)	3	•12	.200	5.04	20	19	4	0	0	116	143	82	65	49	77
— Portland (PCL)	2	4	.333	5.84	8	8	1	0	0	44 2/3	58	32	29	17	22

Year	Team (League)	W	L	Pct.	ERA	G	GS	CG	ShO	Sv.	IP	H	R	ER	BB	SO
1985—	Portland (PCL)	9	12	.429	5.31	27	26	6	1	0	166	195	106	98	51	96
1986—	Portland (PCL)	5	2	.714	2.36	12	12	3	0	0	84	70	26	22	22	65
—	Philadelphia (N.L.)	3	7	.300	5.42	16	16	0	0	0	78	88	56	47	34	44
1987—	Maine (Int'l)	6	6	.500	4.35	18	16	3	1	0	103 1/3	116	58	50	26	71
—	Philadelphia (N.L.)	2	0	1.000	2.65	7	2	0	0	0	17	17	5	5	5	15
1988—	Philadelphia (N.L.)	4	3	.571	3.76	25	11	0	0	0	88 2/3	91	41	37	34	59
—	Maine (Int'l)	0	2	.000	4.18	5	3	1	0	0	23 2/3	25	18	11	10	18
1989—	Philadelphia (N.L.)	1	3	.250	5.15	16	4	2	1	1	43 2/3	52	29	25	14	26
—	Scran./W.B. (Int'l)	7	7	.500	3.66	19	17	3	1	0	123	119	55	50	26	100
1990—	Albuquerque (PCL)■	8	5	.615	4.25	20	19	2	0	0	108	122	59	51	32	85
—	Los Angeles (N.L.)	0	1	.000	6.53	11	2	0	0	0	20 2/3	24	15	15	4	11
1991—	San Diego (N.L.)■	7	2	.778	2.46	64	1	0	0	5	98 2/3	78	30	27	27	57
1992—	San Diego (N.L.)	2	2	.500	2.37	50	1	0	0	5	79 2/3	71	25	21	24	60
1993—	New York (N.L.)■	3	8	.273	3.60	58	0	0	0	5	75	67	34	30	27	57
1994—	New York (N.L.)	2	1	.667	5.11	27	0	0	0	2	44	45	25	25	13	32
1995—	Pittsburgh (N.L.)■	1	0	1.000	9.00	8	0	0	0	0	9	14	9	9	3	4
—	Boston (A.L.)■	4	1	.800	3.61	36	4	0	0	1	89 2/3	86	40	36	15	65
A.L. totals (1 year)		4	1	.800	3.61	36	4	0	0	1	89 2/3	86	40	36	15	65
N.L. totals (10 years)		25	27	.481	3.91	282	37	2	1	18	554 1/3	547	269	241	185	365
Major league totals (10 years)		29	28	.509	3.87	318	41	2	1	19	644	633	309	277	200	430

DIVISION SERIES RECORD

Year	Team (League)	W	L	Pct.	ERA	G	GS	CG	ShO	Sv.	IP	H	R	ER	BB	SO
1995—	Boston (A.L.)	0	0	...	0.00	2	0	0	0	0	3	2	0	0	1	1

MADURO, CALVIN — P — ORIOLES

PERSONAL: Born September 5, 1974, in Santa Cruz, Aruba. . . . 6-0/175. . . . Throws right, bats right. . . . Full name: Calvin Gregory Maduro.
HIGH SCHOOL: Tourist Economy School (Santa Cruz, Aruba).
TRANSACTIONS/CAREER NOTES: Signed as non-drafted free agent by Baltimore Orioles organization (September 9, 1991).

Year	Team (League)	W	L	Pct.	ERA	G	GS	CG	ShO	Sv.	IP	H	R	ER	BB	SO
1992—	GC Orioles (GCL)	1	4	.200	2.27	13	•12	1	1	0	71 1/3	56	29	18	26	66
1993—	Bluefield (Appal.)	•9	4	.692	3.96	14	•14	*3	0	0	*91	90	46	40	17	*83
1994—	Frederick (Caro.)	9	8	.529	4.25	27	26	0	0	0	152 1/3	132	86	72	59	137
1995—	Frederick (Caro.)	8	5	.615	2.94	20	20	2	2	0	122 1/3	109	43	40	34	120
—	Bowie (Eastern)	0	6	.000	5.09	7	7	0	0	0	35 1/3	39	28	20	27	26

MAGADAN, DAVE — 3B/1B — CUBS

PERSONAL: Born September 30, 1962, in Tampa, Fla. . . . 6-3/205. . . . Bats left, throws right. . . . Full name: David Joseph Magadan. . . . Cousin of Lou Piniella, manager, Seattle Mariners, and major league outfielder/designated hitter with four teams (1964 and 1968-84). . . . Name pronounced MAG-uh-dun.
HIGH SCHOOL: Jesuit (Tampa, Fla.).
COLLEGE: Alabama.
TRANSACTIONS/CAREER NOTES: Selected by Boston Red Sox organization in 12th round of free-agent draft (June 3, 1980); did not sign. . . . Selected by New York Mets organization in second round of free-agent draft (June 6, 1983). . . . On disabled list (August 7-September 10, 1984; March 29-April 17, 1987; May 5-20, 1988; and August 9, 1992-remainder of season). . . . Granted free agency (October 27, 1992). . . . Signed by Florida Marlins organization (December 8, 1992). . . . Traded by Marlins to Seattle Mariners for OF Henry Cotto and P Jeff Darwin (June 27, 1993). . . . Traded by Mariners to Marlins for P Jeff Darwin and cash (November 9, 1993). . . . On disabled list (March 29-April 13 and July 21, 1994-remainder of season). . . . Granted free agency (October 19, 1994). . . . Signed by Houston Astros (April 15, 1995). . . . Granted free agency (October 30, 1995). . . . Signed by Chicago Cubs (December 26, 1995).
HONORS: Named Golden Spikes Award winner by USA Baseball (1983). . . . Named designated hitter on The Sporting News college All-America team (1983).
STATISTICAL NOTES: Led Carolina League with 10 intentional bases on balls received in 1984. . . . Led Texas League third basemen with 87 putouts, 275 assists, 393 total chances and 31 errors in 1985. . . . Led International League third basemen with .934 fielding percentage, 283 assists and 31 double plays in 1986. . . . Led N.L. first basemen with .998 fielding percentage in 1990.

				BATTING										FIELDING			
Year	Team (League)	Pos.	G	AB	R	H	2B	3B	HR	RBI	Avg.	BB	SO	SB	PO	A	E	Avg.
1983—	Columbia (S. Atl.)	1B	64	220	41	74	13	1	3	32	.336	51	29	2	520	37	7	.988
1984—	Lynchburg (Caro.)	1B	112	371	78	130	22	4	0	62	*.350	104	43	2	896	64	16	.984
1985—	Jackson (Texas)	3B-1B	134	466	84	144	22	0	0	76	.309	*106	57	0	†106	†276	†31	.925
1986—	Tidewater (Int'l)	3B-1B	133	473	68	147	33	6	1	64	.311	84	45	2	78	†284	25	†.935
—	New York (N.L.)	1B	10	18	3	8	0	0	0	3	.444	3	1	0	48	5	0	1.000
1987—	New York (N.L.)	3B-1B	85	192	21	61	13	1	3	24	.318	22	22	0	88	92	4	.978
1988—	New York (N.L.)	1B-3B	112	314	39	87	15	0	1	35	.277	60	39	0	459	99	10	.982
1989—	New York (N.L.)	1B-3B	127	374	47	107	22	3	4	41	.286	49	37	1	587	89	7	.990
1990—	New York (N.L.)	1B-3B	144	451	74	148	28	6	6	72	.328	74	55	2	837	99	3	†.997
1991—	New York (N.L.)	1B	124	418	58	108	23	0	4	51	.258	83	50	1	1035	90	5	.996
1992—	New York (N.L.)	3B-1B	99	321	33	91	9	1	3	28	.283	56	44	1	54	136	11	.945
1993—	Florida (N.L.)■	3B-1B	66	227	22	65	12	0	4	29	.286	44	30	0	55	122	7	.962
—	Seattle (A.L.)■	1B-3B-DH	71	228	27	59	11	0	1	21	.259	36	33	2	325	72	5	.988
1994—	Florida (N.L.)■	3B-1B	74	211	30	58	7	0	1	17	.275	39	25	0	127	78	4	.981
1995—	Houston (N.L.)■	3B-1B	127	348	44	109	24	0	2	51	.313	71	56	2	121	163	18	.940
American League totals (1 year)			71	228	27	59	11	0	1	21	.259	36	33	2	325	72	5	.988
National League totals (10 years)			968	2874	371	842	153	11	28	351	.293	501	359	7	3411	973	69	.985
Major league totals (10 years)			1039	3102	398	901	164	11	29	372	.290	537	392	9	3736	1045	74	.985

CHAMPIONSHIP SERIES RECORD

Year	Team (League)	Pos.	G	AB	R	H	2B	3B	HR	RBI	Avg.	BB	SO	SB	PO	A	E	Avg.
				BATTING											FIELDING			
1988—	New York (N.L.)	PH	3	3	0	0	0	0	0	0	.000	0	2	0	...	...	...	...

MAGNANTE, MIKE — P — ROYALS

PERSONAL: Born June 17, 1965, in Glendale, Calif. . . . 6-1/195. . . . Throws left, bats left. . . . Full name: Michael Anthony Magnante. . . . Name pronounced mag-NAN-tee.

HIGH SCHOOL: John Burroughs (Burbank, Calif.).

COLLEGE: UCLA (bachelor of science in applied mathematics).

TRANSACTIONS/CAREER NOTES: Selected by Kansas City Royals organization in 11th round of free-agent draft (June 1, 1988). . . . On disabled list (June 17, 1990-remainder of season; July 2-20, 1992; and July 16-31, 1994).

Year	Team (League)	W	L	Pct.	ERA	G	GS	CG	ShO	Sv.	IP	H	R	ER	BB	SO
1988—	Eugene (N'west)	1	1	.500	0.56	3	3	0	0	0	16	10	6	1	2	26
—	Appleton (Midw.)	3	2	.600	3.21	9	8	0	0	0	47 2/3	48	20	17	15	40
—	Baseball City (FSL)	1	1	.500	4.13	4	4	1	0	0	24	19	12	11	8	19
1989—	Memphis (South.)	8	9	.471	3.66	26	26	4	1	0	157 1/3	137	70	64	53	118
1990—	Omaha (Am. Assoc.)	2	5	.286	4.11	13	13	2	0	0	76 2/3	72	39	35	25	56
1991—	Omaha (Am. Assoc.)	6	1	.857	3.02	10	10	2	0	0	65 2/3	53	23	22	23	50
—	Kansas City (A.L.)	0	1	.000	2.45	38	0	0	0	0	55	55	19	15	23	42
1992—	Kansas City (A.L.)	4	9	.308	4.94	44	12	0	0	0	89 1/3	115	53	49	35	31
1993—	Omaha (Am. Assoc.)	2	6	.250	3.67	33	13	0	0	2	105 1/3	97	46	43	29	74
—	Kansas City (A.L.)	1	2	.333	4.08	7	6	0	0	0	35 1/3	37	16	16	11	16
1994—	Kansas City (A.L.)	2	3	.400	4.60	36	1	0	0	0	47	55	27	24	16	21
1995—	Omaha (Am. Assoc.)	5	1	.833	2.84	15	8	0	0	0	57	55	23	18	13	38
—	Kansas City (A.L.)	1	1	.500	4.23	28	0	0	0	0	44 2/3	45	23	21	16	28
Major league totals (5 years)		8	16	.333	4.15	153	19	0	0	0	271 1/3	307	138	125	101	138

MAHAY, RON — OF — RED SOX

PERSONAL: Born June 28, 1971, in Crestwood, Ill. . . . 6-2/190. . . . Bats left, throws left. . . . Full name: Ronald Matthew Mahay.

HIGH SCHOOL: Alan B. Shepard (Palos Heights, Ill.).

JUNIOR COLLEGE: South Suburban (Ill.).

TRANSACTIONS/CAREER NOTES: Selected by Boston Red Sox organization in 18th round of free-agent draft (June 3, 1991). . . . On disabled list (May 5-September 28, 1992). . . . On Lynchburg disabled list (August 6-September 9, 1993). . . . On disabled list (August 23-September 1, 1994). . . . On Pawtucket temporarily inactive list (April 19-25, 1995).

Year	Team (League)	Pos.	G	AB	R	H	2B	3B	HR	RBI	Avg.	BB	SO	SB	PO	A	E	Avg.
				BATTING											FIELDING			
1991—	GC Red Sox (GCL)	OF	54	187	30	51	6	5	1	29	.273	33	40	2	97	2	3	.971
1992—	Winter Haven (FSL)	OF	19	63	6	16	2	1	0	4	.254	2	19	0	33	2	1	.972
1993—	Lynchburg (Caro.)	OF-C	73	254	28	54	8	1	5	23	.213	11	63	2	174	7	5	.973
—	New Britain (East.)	OF	8	25	2	3	0	0	1	2	.120	1	6	1	15	1	2	.889
1994—	Sarasota (Fla. St.)	OF	105	367	43	102	18	0	4	46	.278	39	67	3	189	16	4	.981
1995—	Pawtucket (Int'l)	OF	11	44	5	14	4	0	0	3	.318	4	9	1	30	2	0	1.000
—	Trenton (Eastern)	OF	93	310	37	73	12	3	5	28	.235	44	90	5	187	9	6	.970
—	Boston (A.L.)	OF	5	20	3	4	2	0	1	3	.200	1	6	0	9	0	0	1.000
Major league totals (1 year)			5	20	3	4	2	0	1	3	.200	1	6	0	9	0	0	1.000

MAHOMES, PAT — P — TWINS

PERSONAL: Born August 9, 1970, in Bryan, Tex. . . . 6-4/212. . . . Throws right, bats right. . . . Full name: Patrick Lavon Mahomes. . . . Name pronounced muh-HOMES.

HIGH SCHOOL: Lindale (Tex.).

TRANSACTIONS/CAREER NOTES: Selected by Minnesota Twins organization in sixth round of free-agent draft (June 1, 1988). . . . On disabled list (July 6-23, 1994).

MISCELLANEOUS: Appeared in one game as pinch-runner (1994).

Year	Team (League)	W	L	Pct.	ERA	G	GS	CG	ShO	Sv.	IP	H	R	ER	BB	SO
1988—	Elizabeth. (App.)	6	3	.667	3.69	13	13	3	0	0	78	66	45	32	51	93
1989—	Kenosha (Midwest)	13	7	.650	3.28	25	25	3	1	0	156 1/3	120	66	57	•100	167
1990—	Visalia (California)	11	11	.500	3.30	28	*28	5	1	0	•185 1/3	136	77	68	*118	178
1991—	Orlando (Southern)	8	5	.615	*1.78	18	17	2	0	0	116	77	30	23	57	136
—	Portland (PCL)	3	5	.375	3.44	9	9	2	0	0	55	50	26	21	36	41
1992—	Minnesota (A.L.)	3	4	.429	5.04	14	13	0	0	0	69 2/3	73	41	39	37	44
—	Portland (PCL)	9	5	.643	3.41	17	16	3	*3	1	111	97	43	42	43	87
1993—	Minnesota (A.L.)	1	5	.167	7.71	12	5	0	0	0	37 1/3	47	34	32	16	23
—	Portland (PCL)	11	4	•.733	*3.03	17	16	3	1	0	115 2/3	89	47	39	54	94
1994—	Minnesota (A.L.)	9	5	.643	4.73	21	21	0	0	0	120	121	68	63	62	53
1995—	Minnesota (A.L.)	4	10	.286	6.37	47	7	0	0	3	94 2/3	100	74	67	47	67
Major league totals (4 years)		17	24	.415	5.62	94	46	0	0	3	321 2/3	341	217	201	162	187

MALAVE, JOSE — OF — RED SOX

PERSONAL: Born May 31, 1971, in Cumana, Venezuela. . . . 6-2/212. . . . Bats right, throws right. . . . Full name: Jose Francisco Malave. . . . Brother of Omar Malave, manager, Hagerstown, Toronto Blue Jays organization, and minor league infielder (1981-89). . . . Name pronounced muh-LAH-vee.

HIGH SCHOOL: Modesto Silva (Cumana, Venezuela).
TRANSACTIONS/CAREER NOTES: Signed as non-drafted free agent by Boston Red Sox organization (August 15, 1989). . . . On disabled list (May 29-June 26 and August 3, 1993-remainder of season; and April 25-May 16, 1995).
STATISTICAL NOTES: Led Eastern League with .563 slugging percentage and 262 total bases in 1994.

			BATTING												FIELDING			
Year	**Team (League)**	**Pos.**	**G**	**AB**	**R**	**H**	**2B**	**3B**	**HR**	**RBI**	**Avg.**	**BB**	**SO**	**SB**	**PO**	**A**	**E**	**Avg.**
1990—	Elmira (NYP)	OF	13	29	4	4	1	0	0	3	.138	2	12	1	4	0	1	.800
1991—	GC Red Sox (GCL)	1B-OF	37	146	24	47	4	2	2	28	.322	10	23	6	277	8	7	.976
1992—	Winter Haven (FSL)	OF	8	25	1	4	0	0	0	0	.160	0	11	0	8	0	1	.889
	— Elmira (NYP)	OF-1B	65	268	44	87	9	1	12	46	.325	14	48	8	306	22	5	.985
1993—	Lynchburg (Caro.)	OF	82	312	42	94	27	1	8	54	.301	36	54	2	129	10	10	.933
1994—	New Britain (East.)	OF	122	465	87	139	•37	7	24	*92	.299	52	81	4	166	5	*11	.940
1995—	Pawtucket (Int'l)	OF	91	318	55	86	12	1	23	57	.270	30	67	0	113	2	4	.966

MALDONADO, CANDY — OF

PERSONAL: Born September 5, 1960, in Humacao, Puerto Rico. . . . 6-0/205. . . . Bats right, throws right. . . . Full name: Candido Guadarrama Maldonado.
HIGH SCHOOL: Trina Padilla de Sanz (Humacao, Puerto Rico).
TRANSACTIONS/CAREER NOTES: Signed as non-drafted free agent by Los Angeles Dodgers organization (June 6, 1978). . . . On disabled list (August 16-September 16, 1980). . . . Traded by Dodgers to San Francisco Giants for C Alex Trevino (December 11, 1985). . . . On disabled list (June 28-August 7, 1987). . . . Granted free agency (November 13, 1989). . . . Signed by Cleveland Indians (November 28, 1989). . . . Granted free agency (November 5, 1990). . . . Signed by Milwaukee Brewers (April 2, 1991). . . . On disabled list (April 11-June 25, 1991). . . . Traded by Brewers to Toronto Blue Jays for P Rob Wishnevski and a player to be named later (August 9, 1991); Brewers acquired IF William Suero to complete deal (August 14, 1991). . . . Granted free agency (October 30, 1992). . . . Signed by Chicago Cubs (December 11, 1992). . . . Traded by Cubs to Indians for OF Glenallen Hill (August 19, 1993). . . . Granted free agency (October 15, 1994). . . . Signed by Syracuse, Blue Jays organization (April 12, 1995). . . . Traded by Blue Jays to Texas Rangers for a player to be named later (August 31, 1995). . . . Granted free agency (November 2, 1995).
RECORDS: Shares major league single-game record for most sacrifice flies—3 (August 29, 1987).
HONORS: Named California League co-Most Valuable Player (1980).
STATISTICAL NOTES: Tied for Pioneer League lead with six sacrifice flies in 1978. . . . Led California League with 247 total bases in 1980. . . . Hit for the cycle (May 4, 1987). . . . Career major league grand slams: 3.

			BATTING												FIELDING			
Year	**Team (League)**	**Pos.**	**G**	**AB**	**R**	**H**	**2B**	**3B**	**HR**	**RBI**	**Avg.**	**BB**	**SO**	**SB**	**PO**	**A**	**E**	**Avg.**
1978—	Lethbridge (Pio.)	OF	57	210	45	61	15	5	12	48	.290	22	48	2	112	6	8	.937
1979—	Clinton (Midwest)	OF	50	158	25	37	13	1	2	26	.234	17	29	5	81	5	2	.977
	— Lethbridge (Pio.)	OF	59	234	42	70	*20	3	5	33	.299	18	56	4	81	5	4	.956
1980—	Lodi (California)	OF	121	456	75	139	27	3	25	*102	.305	41	63	12	211	13	11	.953
1981—	Albuquerque (PCL)	OF	126	460	96	154	40	9	21	104	.335	50	104	13	221	21	8	.968
	— Los Angeles (N.L.)	OF	11	12	0	1	0	0	0	0	.083	0	5	0	8	0	0	1.000
1982—	Albuquerque (PCL)	OF	138	541	91	163	28	6	24	96	.301	48	89	4	303	15	10	.970
	— Los Angeles (N.L.)	OF	6	4	0	0	0	0	0	0	.000	1	2	0	5	0	0	1.000
1983—	Los Angeles (N.L.)	OF	42	62	5	12	1	1	1	6	.194	5	14	0	26	0	0	1.000
	— Albuquerque (PCL)	OF-3B	38	144	23	46	6	1	4	20	.319	14	23	3	66	11	4	.951
1984—	Los Angeles (N.L.)	OF-3B	116	254	25	68	14	0	5	28	.268	19	29	0	124	5	8	.942
1985—	Los Angeles (N.L.)	OF	121	213	20	48	7	1	5	19	.225	19	40	1	121	6	2	.984
1986—	San Fran. (N.L.)■	OF-3B	133	405	49	102	31	3	18	85	.252	20	77	4	161	11	3	.983
1987—	San Francisco (N.L.)	OF	118	442	69	129	28	4	20	85	.292	34	78	8	176	7	5	.973
1988—	San Francisco (N.L.)	OF	142	499	53	127	23	1	12	68	.255	37	89	6	251	5	10	.962
1989—	San Francisco (N.L.)	OF	129	345	39	75	23	0	9	41	.217	37	69	4	181	6	5	.974
1990—	Cleveland (A.L.)■	OF-DH	155	590	76	161	32	2	22	95	.273	49	134	3	293	9	2	.993
1991—	Milwaukee (A.L.)■	OF	34	111	11	23	6	0	5	20	.207	13	23	1	41	0	1	.976
	— Toronto (A.L.)■	OF-DH	52	177	26	49	9	0	7	28	.277	23	53	3	98	2	1	.990
1992—	Toronto (A.L.)	OF-DH	137	489	64	133	25	4	20	66	.272	59	112	2	260	12	6	.978
1993—	Chicago (N.L.)■	OF	70	140	8	26	5	0	3	15	.186	13	40	0	50	3	5	.914
	— Cleveland (A.L.)■	OF-DH	28	81	11	20	2	0	5	20	.247	11	18	0	39	1	1	.976
1994—	Cleveland (A.L.)	DH-OF	42	92	14	18	5	1	5	12	.196	19	31	1	6	0	0	1.000
1995—	Toronto (A.L.)■	OF-DH	61	160	22	43	13	0	7	25	.269	25	45	1	78	2	1	.988
	— Texas (A.L.)■	OF	13	30	6	7	3	0	2	5	.233	7	5	0	20	1	0	1.000
American League totals (6 years)			522	1730	230	454	95	7	73	271	.262	206	421	11	835	27	12	.986
National League totals (10 years)			888	2376	268	588	132	10	73	347	.247	185	443	23	1103	43	38	.968
Major league totals (15 years)			1410	4106	498	1042	227	17	146	618	.254	391	864	34	1938	70	50	.976

CHAMPIONSHIP SERIES RECORD

			BATTING												FIELDING			
Year	**Team (League)**	**Pos.**	**G**	**AB**	**R**	**H**	**2B**	**3B**	**HR**	**RBI**	**Avg.**	**BB**	**SO**	**SB**	**PO**	**A**	**E**	**Avg.**
1983—	Los Angeles (N.L.)	PH	2	2	0	0	0	0	0	0	.000	0	1	0	...	...	...	...
1985—	Los Angeles (N.L.)	OF-PH	4	7	0	1	0	0	0	1	.143	0	3	0	4	0	1	.800
1987—	San Francisco (N.L.)	OF	5	19	2	4	1	0	0	2	.211	0	3	0	7	0	0	1.000
1989—	San Francisco (N.L.)	OF-PH	3	3	1	0	0	0	0	1	.000	2	0	0	2	0	0	1.000
1991—	Toronto (A.L.)	OF	5	20	1	2	1	0	0	1	.100	1	6	0	4	0	0	1.000
1992—	Toronto (A.L.)	OF	6	22	3	6	0	0	2	6	.273	3	4	0	9	1	0	1.000
Championship series totals (6 years)			25	73	7	13	2	0	2	11	.178	6	17	0	26	1	1	.964

WORLD SERIES RECORD

NOTES: Member of World Series championship team (1992).

			BATTING												FIELDING			
Year	**Team (League)**	**Pos.**	**G**	**AB**	**R**	**H**	**2B**	**3B**	**HR**	**RBI**	**Avg.**	**BB**	**SO**	**SB**	**PO**	**A**	**E**	**Avg.**
1989—	San Francisco (N.L.)	OF-PH	4	11	1	1	0	1	0	0	.091	0	4	0	5	0	0	1.000
1992—	Toronto (A.L.)	OF-PH	6	19	1	3	0	0	1	2	.158	2	5	0	8	2	0	1.000
World Series totals (2 years)			10	30	2	4	0	1	1	2	.133	2	9	0	13	2	0	1.000

MANTEI, MATT — P — MARLINS

PERSONAL: Born July 7, 1973, in Tampa, Fla. . . . 6-1/181. . . . Throws right, bats right. . . . Full name: Matthew Bruce Mantei. . . . Name pronounced MAN-tay.

HIGH SCHOOL: River Valley (Three Oaks, Mich.).

TRANSACTIONS/CAREER NOTES: Selected by Seattle Mariners organization in 25th round of free-agent draft (June 3, 1991). . . . Selected by Florida Marlins from Mariners organization in Rule 5 major league draft (December 5, 1994). . . . On Florida disabled list (April 20-June 18 and July 29-September 1, 1995); included rehabilitation assignments to Portland and Charlotte (May 13-June 18).

Year Team (League)	W	L	Pct.	ERA	G	GS	CG	ShO	Sv.	IP	H	R	ER	BB	SO
1991— Ariz. Mariners (Ariz.)	1	4	.200	6.69	17	5	0	0	0	40 1/3	54	40	30	28	29
1992— Ariz. Mariners (Ariz.)	1	1	.500	5.63	3	3	0	0	0	16	18	10	10	5	19
1993— Bellingham (N'west)	1	1	.500	5.96	26	0	0	0	*12	25 2/3	26	19	17	15	34
1994— Appleton (Midw.)	5	1	.833	2.06	48	0	0	0	26	48	42	14	11	21	70
1995— Portland (Eastern)■	1	0	1.000	2.38	8	0	0	0	1	11 1/3	10	3	3	5	15
— Charlotte (Int'l)	0	1	.000	2.57	6	0	0	0	0	7	1	3	2	5	10
— Florida (N.L.)	0	1	.000	4.73	12	0	0	0	0	13 1/3	12	8	7	13	15
Major league totals (1 year)	0	1	.000	4.73	12	0	0	0	0	13 1/3	12	8	7	13	15

MANTO, JEFF — 3B — ORIOLES

PERSONAL: Born August 23, 1964, in Bristol, Pa. . . . 6-3/210. . . . Bats right, throws right. . . . Full name: Jeffrey Paul Manto.

HIGH SCHOOL: Bristol (Pa.).

COLLEGE: Temple.

TRANSACTIONS/CAREER NOTES: Selected by New York Yankees organization in 35th round of free-agent draft (June 7, 1982); did not sign. . . . Selected by California Angels organization in 14th round of free-agent draft (June 3, 1985). . . . On disabled list (July 16, 1986-remainder of season). . . . Traded by Angels organization with P Colin Charland to Cleveland Indians for P Scott Bailes (January 9, 1990). . . . Released by Indians (November 27, 1991). . . . Signed by Richmond, Atlanta Braves organization (January 23, 1992). . . . On disabled list (May 4-14, 1992). . . . Granted free agency (October 15, 1992). . . . Signed by Philadelphia Phillies organization (December 16, 1992). . . . Granted free agency (October 15, 1993). . . . Signed by New York Mets organization (December 16, 1993). . . . Traded by Mets organization to Baltimore Orioles organization for future considerations (May 19, 1994). . . . On Baltimore disabled list (June 26-July 13, 1995); included rehabilitation assignments to Bowie (July 9-10) and Frederick (July 10-13).

RECORDS: Shares major league record for most consecutive home runs in three games—4 (June 8 [1], 9[2]and 10 [1], 1995).

HONORS: Named Texas League Most Valuable Player (1988). . . . Named International League Most Valuable Player (1994).

STATISTICAL NOTES: Led California League third basemen with 245 assists and 365 total chances in 1987. . . . Tied for Texas League lead in errors by third baseman with 32 in 1988. . . . Led Texas League in grounding into double plays with 17 in 1988. . . . Led Pacific Coast League with .446 on-base percentage in 1990. . . . Led Pacific Coast League third basemen with .943 fielding percentage, 265 assists and 22 double plays in 1989. . . . Led International League with 12 sacrifice flies in 1992. . . . Led International League with .404 on-base percentage, 260 total bases, 31 home runs, 100 RBIs and tied for lead in being hit by pitch with 11 in 1994.

			BATTING											FIELDING			
Year Team (League)	Pos.	G	AB	R	H	2B	3B	HR	RBI	Avg.	BB	SO	SB	PO	A	E	Avg.
1985— Quad Cities (Mid.)	OF-3B	74	233	34	46	5	2	11	34	.197	40	74	3	87	8	3	.969
1986— Quad Cities (Mid.)	3B	73	239	31	59	13	0	8	49	.247	37	70	2	48	114	28	.853
1987— Palm Springs (Cal.)	3B-1B	112	375	61	96	21	4	7	63	.256	102	85	8	93	†246	37	.902
1988— Midland (Texas)	3B-2B-1B	120	408	88	123	23	3	24	101	.301	62	76	7	82	208	‡32	.901
1989— Edmonton (PCL)	3B-1B	127	408	89	113	25	3	23	67	.277	91	81	4	140	†266	21	†.951
1990— Colo. Springs (PCL)■	3B-1B	96	316	73	94	27	1	18	82	.297	78	65	10	340	131	10	.979
— Cleveland (A.L.)	1B-3B	30	76	12	17	5	1	2	14	.224	21	18	0	185	24	2	.991
1991— Cleveland (A.L.)	3-1-C-O	47	128	15	27	7	0	2	13	.211	14	22	2	109	63	8	.956
— Colo. Springs (PCL)	3-1-C-S-O	43	153	36	49	16	0	6	36	.320	33	24	1	169	53	11	.953
1992— Richmond (Int'l)■	3B-2B-1B	127	450	65	131	24	1	13	68	.291	57	63	1	89	245	23	.936
1993— Scran./W.B. (Int'l)■	3B-1B-C	106	388	62	112	30	1	17	88	.289	55	58	4	401	134	8	.985
— Philadelphia (N.L.)	3B-SS	8	18	0	1	0	0	0	0	.056	0	3	0	2	8	0	1.000
1994— Norfolk (Int'l)■	3B-1B-2B	37	115	20	30	6	0	4	17	.261	27	28	1	73	46	4	.967
— Rochester (Int'l)■	3B-1B	94	329	61	102	25	2	§27	§83	.310	43	47	2	277	102	15	.962
1995— Baltimore (A.L.)	3B-DH-1B	89	254	31	65	9	0	17	38	.256	24	69	0	68	103	6	.966
— Bowie (Eastern)	DH	1	4	1	1	0	0	0	0	.250	0	2	0	0	0	0	...
— Frederick (Caro.)	3B	2	8	1	3	0	0	1	3	.375	0	1	0	0	2	0	1.000
American League totals (3 years)		166	458	58	109	21	1	21	65	.238	59	109	2	362	190	16	.972
National League totals (1 year)		8	18	0	1	0	0	0	0	.056	0	3	0	2	8	0	1.000
Major league totals (4 years)		174	476	58	110	21	1	21	65	.231	59	112	2	364	198	16	.972

MANWARING, KIRT — C — GIANTS

PERSONAL: Born July 15, 1965, in Elmira, N.Y. . . . 5-11/203. . . . Bats right, throws right. . . . Full name: Kirt Dean Manwaring.

HIGH SCHOOL: Horseheads (N.Y.).

COLLEGE: Coastal Carolina (S.C.).

TRANSACTIONS/CAREER NOTES: Selected by Boston Red Sox organization in 12th round of free-agent draft (June 6, 1983); did not sign. . . . Selected by San Francisco Giants organization in second round of free-agent draft (June 2, 1986). . . . On disabled list (August 31-September 15, 1989 and June 24-July 18, 1990). . . . On San Francisco disabled list (May 30-July 11, 1991); included rehabilitation assignments to Phoenix (July 1-8) and San Jose (July 8-11). . . . On San Francisco disabled list (July 22-August 6, 1992).

HONORS: Won N.L. Gold Glove at catcher (1993).

STATISTICAL NOTES: Led Texas League catchers with 688 total chances and eight double plays in 1987. . . . Led N.L. catchers with 12 double plays in 1992 and 10 in 1994.

			BATTING											FIELDING			
Year Team (League)	Pos.	G	AB	R	H	2B	3B	HR	RBI	Avg.	BB	SO	SB	PO	A	E	Avg.
1986— Clinton (Midwest)	C	49	147	18	36	7	1	2	16	.245	14	26	1	243	31	5	.982
1987— Shreveport (Texas)	C	98	307	27	82	13	2	2	22	.267	19	33	1	603	*81	4	.994

Year	Team (League)	Pos.	G	AB	R	H	2B	3B	HR	RBI	Avg.	BB	SO	SB	PO	A	E	Avg.
				BATTING											FIELDING			
	—San Francisco (N.L.) ..	C	6	7	0	1	0	0	0	0	.143	0	1	0	9	1	1	.909
1988—	Phoenix (PCL)...........	C	81	273	29	77	12	2	2	35	.282	14	32	3	411	51	6	.987
	—San Francisco (N.L.) ..	C	40	116	12	29	7	0	1	15	.250	2	21	0	162	24	4	.979
1989—	San Francisco (N.L.) ..	C	85	200	14	42	4	2	0	18	.210	11	28	2	289	32	6	.982
1990—	Phoenix (PCL)...........	C	74	247	20	58	10	2	3	14	.235	24	34	0	352	45	4	*.990
	—San Francisco (N.L.) ..	C	8	13	0	2	0	1	0	1	.154	0	3	0	22	3	0	1.000
1991—	San Francisco (N.L.) ..	C	67	178	16	40	9	0	0	19	.225	9	22	1	315	28	4	.988
	—Phoenix (PCL)...........	C	24	81	8	18	0	0	4	14	.222	8	15	0	100	15	3	.975
	—San Jose (Calif.).........	C	1	3	1	0	0	0	0	0	.000	1	1	0	16	0	0	1.000
1992—	San Francisco (N.L.) ..	C	109	349	24	85	10	5	4	26	.244	29	42	2	564	68	4	.994
1993—	San Francisco (N.L.) ..	C	130	432	48	119	15	1	5	49	.275	41	76	1	739	70	2	*.998
1994—	San Francisco (N.L.) ..	C	97	316	30	79	17	1	1	29	.250	25	50	1	541	52	4	.993
1995—	San Francisco (N.L.) ..	C	118	379	21	95	15	2	4	36	.251	27	72	1	607	55	7	.990
Major league totals (9 years)			660	1990	165	492	77	12	15	193	.247	144	315	8	3248	333	32	.991

CHAMPIONSHIP SERIES RECORD

Year	Team (League)	Pos.	G	AB	R	H	2B	3B	HR	RBI	Avg.	BB	SO	SB	PO	A	E	Avg.
				BATTING											FIELDING			
1989—	San Francisco (N.L.) ..	C-PH	3	2	0	0	0	0	0	0	.000	0	0	0	5	0	0	1.000

WORLD SERIES RECORD

Year	Team (League)	Pos.	G	AB	R	H	2B	3B	HR	RBI	Avg.	BB	SO	SB	PO	A	E	Avg.
				BATTING											FIELDING			
1989—	San Francisco (N.L.) ..	C	1	1	1	1	1	0	0	0	1.000	0	0	0	0	0	0	...

MANZANILLO, JOSIAS P

PERSONAL: Born October 16, 1967, in San Pedro de Macoris, Dominican Republic. . . . 6-0/190. . . . Throws right, bats right. . . . Brother of Ravelo Manzanillo, pitcher, Chicago White Sox and Pittsburgh Pirates (1988 and 1994-95). . . . Name pronounced hose-EYE-ess MAN-zan-EE-oh.

TRANSACTIONS/CAREER NOTES: Signed as non-drafted free agent by Boston Red Sox organization (January 10, 1983). . . . On disabled list (June 8, 1987-remainder of season and April 8, 1988-entire season). . . . Granted free agency (March 24, 1992). . . . Signed by Omaha, Kansas City Royals organization (April 3, 1992). . . . Granted free agency (October 15, 1992). . . . Signed by Milwaukee Brewers (November 20, 1992). . . . Traded by Brewers to New York Mets for OF Wayne Housie (June 12, 1993). . . . On New York disabled list (July 27, 1994-remainder of season). . . . Claimed on waivers by New York Yankees (June 5, 1995). . . . On New York Yankees disabled list (July 6, 1995-remainder of season). . . . Granted free agency (October 16, 1995).

Year	Team (League)	W	L	Pct.	ERA	G	GS	CG	ShO	Sv.	IP	H	R	ER	BB	SO
1983—	Elmira (NYP)	1	5	.167	7.98	12	4	0	0	0	38 1/3	52	44	34	20	19
1984—	Elmira (NYP)	2	3	.400	5.26	14	0	0	0	1	25 2/3	27	24	15	26	15
1985—	Greensboro (S. Atl.)	1	1	.500	9.75	7	0	0	0	0	12	12	13	13	18	10
	—Elmira (N.Y.-Penn)............	2	4	.333	3.86	19	4	0	0	1	39 2/3	36	19	17	36	43
1986—	Winter Haven (FSL)............	13	5	.722	2.27	23	21	3	2	0	142 2/3	110	51	36	81	102
1987—	New Britain (East.)	2	0	1.000	4.50	2	2	0	0	0	10	8	5	5	8	12
1988—	....							Did not play.								
1989—	New Britain (East.)	9	10	.474	3.66	26	•26	3	1	0	147 2/3	129	78	60	85	93
1990—	New Britain (East.)	4	4	.500	3.41	12	12	2	1	0	74	66	34	28	37	51
	—Pawtucket (Int'l)................	4	7	.364	5.55	15	15	5	0	0	82 2/3	75	57	51	45	77
1991—	Pawtucket (Int'l)................	5	5	.500	5.61	20	16	0	0	0	102 2/3	109	69	64	53	65
	—New Britain (East.)	2	2	.500	2.90	7	7	0	0	0	49 2/3	37	25	16	28	35
	—Boston (A.L.)......................	0	0	...	18.00	1	0	0	0	0	1	2	2	2	3	1
1992—	Omaha (Am. Assoc.)■.......	7	10	.412	4.36	26	21	0	0	0	136 1/3	138	76	66	71	114
	—Memphis (South.).............	0	2	.000	7.36	2	0	0	0	0	7 1/3	6	6	6	6	8
1993—	Milwaukee (A.L.)■.............	1	1	.500	9.53	10	1	0	0	1	17	22	20	18	10	10
	—New Orleans (A.A.)............	0	1	.000	9.00	1	0	0	0	0	1	1	1	1	0	3
	—Norfolk (Int'l)■	1	5	.167	3.11	14	12	2	1	0	84	82	40	29	25	79
	—New York (N.L.).................	0	0	...	3.00	6	0	0	0	0	12	8	7	4	9	11
1994—	Norfolk (Int'l)	0	1	.000	4.38	8	0	0	0	3	12 1/3	12	6	6	6	10
	—New York (N.L.).................	3	2	.600	2.66	37	0	0	0	2	47 1/3	34	15	14	13	48
1995—	New York (N.L.).................	1	2	.333	7.88	12	0	0	0	0	16	18	15	14	6	14
	—New York (A.L.)■..............	0	0	...	2.08	11	0	0	0	0	17 1/3	19	4	4	9	11
A.L. totals (3 years)		1	1	.500	6.11	22	1	0	0	1	35 1/3	43	26	24	22	22
N.L. totals (3 years)		4	4	.500	3.82	55	0	0	0	2	75 1/3	60	37	32	28	73
Major league totals (4 years)		5	5	.500	4.55	77	1	0	0	3	110 2/3	103	63	56	50	95

MANZANILLO, RAVELO P

PERSONAL: Born October 17, 1963, in San Pedro de Macoris, Dominican Republic. . . . 5-10/190. . . . Throws left, bats left. . . . Brother of Josias Manzanillo, pitcher with four major league teams (1991 and 1993-95). . . . Name pronounced MAN-zan-EE-oh..

TRANSACTIONS/CAREER NOTES: Signed as non-drafted free agent by Pittsburgh Pirates organization (August 21, 1980). . . . On disabled list (July 30, 1984-remainder of season). . . . Released by Pirates organization (May 1, 1986). . . . Signed by Baltimore Orioles organization (January 3, 1987). . . . Released by Orioles organization (April 5, 1987). . . . Signed by Tampa, Chicago White Sox organization (February 2, 1988). . . . Granted free agency (October 15, 1990). . . . Signed by Toronto Blue Jays organization (December 4, 1990). . . . On disabled list (May 20-July 11 and August 10-30, 1991). . . . Granted free agency (October 15, 1991). . . . Signed by Pirates organization (January 5, 1994). . . . On Calgary disabled list (June 14-July 20 and August 1, 1995-remainder of season). . . . Granted free agency (October 15, 1995).

STATISTICAL NOTES: Led N.L. with five balks in 1994.

Year	Team (League)	W	L	Pct.	ERA	G	GS	CG	ShO	Sv.	IP	H	R	ER	BB	SO
1981—	GC Pirates (GCL)...............	3	1	.750	1.13	9	7	0	0	0	48	35	11	6	10	34
1982—	Greenwood (S. Atl.)...........	9	9	.500	4.97	27	25	7	2	1	157 2/3	156	•108	87	109	93

Year	Team (League)	W	L	Pct.	ERA	G	GS	CG	ShO	Sv.	IP	H	R	ER	BB	SO
1983—	Alexandria (Caro.)	7	7	.500	4.44	22	20	1	0	0	105 1/3	107	68	52	79	66
1984—	Nashua (Eastern)	4	4	.500	4.24	14	13	2	1	0	74 1/3	56	40	35	62	50
1985—	Nashua (Eastern)	6	10	.375	4.67	33	17	2	0	5	123 1/3	99	70	64	96	62
1986—	Veracruz (Mex.)	1	3	.250	5.57	5	5	1	0	0	21	19	16	13	20	16
1987—	■							Did not play.								
1988—	Tampa (Fla. St.)■	10	6	.625	3.04	24	20	2	2	0	130 1/3	93	53	44	49	140
	—Chicago (A.L.)	0	1	.000	5.79	2	2	0	0	0	9 1/3	7	6	6	12	10
1989—	Birmingham (Sou.)	8	7	.533	3.90	22	22	2	0	0	129 1/3	105	66	56	72	89
1990—	Vancouver (PCL)	7	3	.700	3.61	38	6	0	0	4	92 1/3	74	41	37	60	64
1991—	Syracuse (Int'l)■	3	0	1.000	3.42	12	0	0	0	1	23 2/3	26	10	9	14	20
1992—								Played in Taiwan.								
1993—								Did not play.								
1994—	Pittsburgh (N.L.)■	4	2	.667	4.14	46	0	0	0	1	50	45	30	23	42	39
1995—	Pittsburgh (N.L.)	0	0	...	4.91	5	0	0	0	0	3 2/3	3	3	2	2	1
	—Calgary (PCL)	0	2	.000	12.75	8	1	0	0	0	12	23	18	17	10	2
A.L. totals (1 year)		0	1	.000	5.79	2	2	0	0	0	9 1/3	7	6	6	12	10
N.L. totals (2 years)		4	2	.667	4.19	51	0	0	0	1	53 2/3	48	33	25	44	40
Major league totals (3 years)		4	3	.571	4.43	53	2	0	0	1	63	55	39	31	56	50

MARQUEZ, ISIDRO — P

PERSONAL: Born May 15, 1965, in Navojoa, Sonora, Mexico. . . . 6-3/190. . . . Throws right, bats right. . . . Full name: Isidro Espinoza Marquez.
HIGH SCHOOL: Cobach (Sonora, Mexico).
TRANSACTIONS/CAREER NOTES: Signed as free agent by Tampico of Mexican League (March 8, 1985). . . . Contract sold by San Luis of Mexican League to Los Angeles Dodgers organization (May 13, 1988). . . . Loaned by Dodgers organization to Mexico City Tigers of Mexican League (July 4, 1993-remainder of season). . . .Traded by Dodgers organization to Chicago White Sox organization for 3B Ron Coomer (December 28, 1993). . . . Granted free agency (October 16, 1995).

Year	Team (League)	W	L	Pct.	ERA	G	GS	CG	ShO	Sv.	IP	H	R	ER	BB	SO
1985—	Tampico (Mexican)	0	0	...	3.90	12	0	0	0	0	27 2/3	28	13	12	14	17
1986—	San Luis Pot. (Mex.)	3	2	.600	5.87	25	15	2	1	0	92	96	71	60	69	74
1987—	San Luis Pot. (Mex.)	0	0	...	4.15	1	1	0	0	0	4 1/3	5	3	2	5	1
1988—	San Luis Pot. (Mex.)	6	3	.667	2.25	10	10	4	1	0	72	54	22	18	27	56
	—Bakersfield (Calif.)■	8	4	.667	3.09	20	20	1	1	0	125 1/3	114	54	43	77	106
1989—	San Antonio (Tex.)	1	4	.200	4.33	39	0	0	0	4	62 1/3	61	33	30	34	52
	—Bakersfield (Calif.)	6	0	1.000	0.75	17	0	0	0	8	36	21	5	3	11	44
1990—	San Antonio (Tex.)	3	1	.750	4.86	13	0	0	0	0	16 2/3	20	10	9	8	15
1991—	San Antonio (Tex.)	4	1	.800	2.09	34	0	0	0	3	47 1/3	42	16	11	19	36
	—Albuquerque (PCL)	0	0	...	0.00	1	0	0	0	3	1	1	0	0	1	1
1992—	M.C. Tigers (Mex.)	5	5	.500	3.49	52	0	0	0	25	87 2/3	75	39	34	40	57
1993—	San Antonio (Tex.)	1	4	.200	2.84	30	0	0	0	12	31 2/3	34	13	10	8	25
	—Albuquerque (PCL)	1	0	1.000	1.50	9	0	0	0	2	12	7	2	2	3	10
	—M.C. Tigers (Mex.)■	3	1	.750	1.90	14	0	0	0	5	23 2/3	21	5	5	11	12
1994—	Nashville (A.A.)■	3	3	.500	2.83	39	0	0	0	11	63 2/3	48	32	20	27	63
1995—	Nashville (A.A.)	7	4	.636	4.75	46	0	0	0	4	72	80	41	38	27	57
	—Chicago (A.L.)	0	1	.000	6.75	7	0	0	0	0	6 2/3	9	5	5	2	8
Major league totals (1 year)		0	1	.000	6.75	7	0	0	0	0	6 2/3	9	5	5	2	8

MARRERO, ELIESER — C — CARDINALS

PERSONAL: Born November 17, 1973, in Havana, Cuba. . . . 6-1/180. . . . Bats right, throws right.
HIGH SCHOOL: Coral Gables (Fla.).
TRANSACTIONS/CAREER NOTES: Selected by St. Louis Cardinals organization in third round of free-agent draft (June 3, 1993).

				BATTING											FIELDING			
Year	Team (League)	Pos.	G	AB	R	H	2B	3B	HR	RBI	Avg.	BB	SO	SB	PO	A	E	Avg.
1993—	Johns. City (App.)	C	18	61	10	22	8	0	2	14	.361	12	9	2	154	18	1	.994
1994—	Savannah (S. Atl.)	C	116	421	71	110	16	3	21	79	.261	39	92	5	821	92	•15	.984
1995—	St. Peters. (FSL)	C	107	383	43	81	16	1	10	55	.211	23	55	9	574	52	10	.984

MARSH, TOM — OF — PHILLIES

PERSONAL: Born December 27, 1965, in Toledo, O. . . . 6-2/196. . . . Bats right, throws right. . . . Full name: Thomas Owen Marsh.
HIGH SCHOOL: Calvin M. Woodward (Toledo, O.).
COLLEGE: Toledo.
TRANSACTIONS/CAREER NOTES: Selected by Toronto Blue Jays organization in 70th round of free-agent draft (June 2, 1987); did not sign. . . . Selected by Philadelphia Phillies organization in 16th round of free-agent draft (June 1, 1988). . . . On Reading disabled list (June 22-September 7, 1990 and May 8-June 14, 1991). . . . On Philadelphia disabled list (June 27-July 28, 1992). . . . On disabled list (May 15-July 20, 1993). . . . On Philadelphia disabled list (August 16-September 1, 1995); included rehabilitation assignment to Scranton/Wilkes-Barre (August 28-September 1).
STATISTICAL NOTES: Led International League outfielders with five double plays in 1993. . . . Career major league grand slams: 1.

				BATTING											FIELDING			
Year	Team (League)	Pos.	G	AB	R	H	2B	3B	HR	RBI	Avg.	BB	SO	SB	PO	A	E	Avg.
1988—	Batavia (NYP)	OF	62	216	35	55	14	1	8	27	.255	18	54	6	99	9	4	.964
1989—	Spartanburg (SAL)	OF	79	288	42	73	18	1	10	42	.253	29	66	8	128	10	8	.945
	—Clearwater (FSL)	OF	43	141	12	24	2	1	1	10	.170	7	30	5	97	1	1	.990
1990—	Spartanburg (SAL)	C	24	75	14	21	2	1	4	15	.280	8	21	5	46	6	0	1.000
	—Reading (Eastern)	OF	41	132	13	34	6	1	1	10	.258	8	27	5	93	3	3	.970
1991—	Reading (Eastern)	OF	67	236	27	62	12	5	7	35	.263	11	47	8	142	3	2	.986
1992—	Scran./W.B. (Int'l)	OF	45	158	26	38	7	2	8	25	.241	10	30	5	35	1	1	.973

Year	Team (League)	Pos.	G	AB	R	H	2B	3B	HR	RBI	Avg.	BB	SO	SB	PO	A	E	Avg.
			BATTING												FIELDING			
	—Philadelphia (N.L.)	OF	42	125	7	25	3	2	2	16	.200	2	23	0	66	0	2	.971
1993—	Scran./W.B. (Int'l)	OF	78	315	45	90	16	8	12	57	.286	14	47	10	145	10	7	.957
1994—	Philadelphia (N.L.)	OF	8	18	3	5	1	1	0	3	.278	1	1	0	8	0	1	.889
	—Scran./W.B. (Int'l)	OF	114	448	52	120	31	5	9	59	.268	13	58	5	252	•14	7	.974
1995—	Scran./W.B. (Int'l)	OF	78	296	46	91	22	5	10	47	.307	13	39	9	156	4	1	.994
	—Philadelphia (N.L.)	OF	43	109	13	32	3	1	3	15	.294	4	25	0	44	2	3	.939
Major league totals (3 years)			93	252	23	62	7	4	5	34	.246	7	49	0	118	2	6	.952

MARTIN, AL — OF — PIRATES

PERSONAL: Born November 24, 1967, in West Covina, Calif. . . . 6-2/210. . . . Bats left, throws left. . . . Full name: Albert Lee Martin. . . . Formerly known as Albert Scales-Martin.

HIGH SCHOOL: Rowland Heights (Calif.).

COLLEGE: Southern California.

TRANSACTIONS/CAREER NOTES: Selected by Atlanta Braves organization in eighth round of free-agent draft (June 3, 1985). . . . Granted free agency (October 15, 1991). . . . Signed by Pittsburgh Pirates organization (November 11, 1991). . . . On suspended list (September 17-20, 1993). . . . On disabled list (July 11, 1994-remainder of season).

STATISTICAL NOTES: Led Gulf Coast League first basemen with 15 errors in 1985. . . . Led American Association with .557 slugging percentage in 1992. . . . Led American Association outfielders with six double plays in 1992.

Year	Team (League)	Pos.	G	AB	R	H	2B	3B	HR	RBI	Avg.	BB	SO	SB	PO	A	E	Avg.
			BATTING												FIELDING			
1985—	GC Braves (GCL)	1B-OF	40	138	16	32	3	0	0	9	.232	19	36	1	246	13	†15	.945
1986—	Sumter (S. Atl.)	1B	44	156	23	38	5	0	1	24	.244	23	36	6	299	12	8	.975
	—Idaho Falls (Pio.)	OF-1B	63	242	39	80	17	•6	4	44	.331	20	53	11	272	15	8	.973
1987—	Sumter (S. Atl.)	OF-1B	117	375	59	95	18	5	12	64	.253	44	69	27	137	7	9	.941
1988—	Burlington (Midw.)	OF	123	480	69	134	21	3	7	42	.279	30	88	40	224	4	8	.966
1989—	Durham (Carolina)	OF	128	457	*84	124	26	3	9	48	.271	34	107	27	169	7	7	.962
1990—	Greenville (South.)	OF	133	455	64	110	17	4	11	50	.242	43	102	20	200	8	7	.967
1991—	Greenville (South.)	OF-1B	86	301	38	73	13	3	7	38	.243	32	84	19	134	7	6	.959
	—Richmond (Int'l)	OF	44	151	20	42	11	1	5	18	.278	7	33	11	73	4	2	.975
1992—	Buffalo (A.A.)■	OF	125	420	85	128	16	*15	20	59	.305	35	93	20	222	10	8	.967
	—Pittsburgh (N.L.)	OF	12	12	1	2	0	1	0	2	.167	0	5	0	6	0	0	1.000
1993—	Pittsburgh (N.L.)	OF	143	480	85	135	26	8	18	64	.281	42	122	16	268	6	7	.975
1994—	Pittsburgh (N.L.)	OF	82	276	48	79	12	4	9	33	.286	34	56	15	129	8	3	.979
1995—	Pittsburgh (N.L.)	OF	124	439	70	124	25	3	13	41	.282	44	92	20	206	8	5	.977
Major league totals (4 years)			361	1207	204	340	63	16	40	140	.282	120	275	51	609	22	15	.977

M

MARTIN, NORBERTO — 2B — WHITE SOX

PERSONAL: Born December 10, 1966, in Santo Domingo, Dominican Republic. . . . 5-10/164. . . . Bats right, throws right. . . . Full name: Norberto Edonal Martin. . . . Name pronounced mar-TEEN.

TRANSACTIONS/CAREER NOTES: Signed as non-drafted free agent by Chicago White Sox organization (March 27, 1984). . . . On Peninsula disabled list (April 10-May 5, 1986). . . . On Appleton disabled list (May 14, 1986-remainder of season). . . . On disabled list (April 7, 1989-entire season and May 5-June 9, 1991).

STATISTICAL NOTES: Led Gulf Coast League shortstops with 37 errors in 1984. . . . Led Pacific Coast League second basemen with 681 total chances in 1992. . . . Led American Association second basemen with 291 putouts, 438 assists, 18 errors and 747 total chances in 1993. . . . Career major league grand slams: 1.

Year	Team (League)	Pos.	G	AB	R	H	2B	3B	HR	RBI	Avg.	BB	SO	SB	PO	A	E	Avg.
			BATTING												FIELDING			
1984—	GC Whi. Sox (GCL)	SS-OF	56	205	36	56	8	2	1	30	.273	21	31	18	66	149	†37	.853
1985—	Appleton (Midw.)	SS	30	196	15	19	2	0	0	5	.097	9	23	2	39	86	12	.912
	—Niag. Falls (NYP)	SS	60	217	22	55	9	0	1	13	.253	7	41	6	85	173	35	.881
1986—	Appleton (Midw.)	SS	9	33	4	10	2	0	0	2	.303	2	5	1	13	16	6	.829
	—GC Whi. Sox (GCL)	PR	1	0	0	0	0	0	0	0	...	0	0	0	...	...	...	...
1987—	Char., W.Va. (SAL)	SS-OF-2B	68	250	44	78	14	1	5	35	.312	17	40	14	84	152	25	.904
	—Peninsula (Caro.)	2B	41	162	21	42	6	1	1	18	.259	18	19	11	94	108	15	.931
1988—	Tampa (Fla. St.)	2B	101	360	44	93	10	4	2	33	.258	17	49	24	196	268	20	.959
1989—									Did not play.									
1990—	Vancouver (PCL)	2B	130	508	77	135	20	4	3	45	.266	27	63	10	283	324	17	.973
1991—	Vancouver (PCL)	2B-SS	93	338	39	94	9	0	0	20	.278	21	38	11	196	265	16	.966
1992—	Vancouver (PCL)	2B	135	497	72	143	12	7	0	29	.288	29	44	29	266	*395	•20	.971
1993—	Nashville (A.A.)	2B-SS	•137	*580	87	*179	21	6	9	74	.309	26	59	31	†292	†442	†18	.976
	—Chicago (A.L.)	2B-DH	8	14	3	5	0	0	0	2	.357	1	1	0	13	9	1	.957
1994—	Nashville (A.A.)	S-3-2-O	43	172	26	44	8	0	2	12	.256	10	14	4	47	72	10	.922
	—Chicago (A.L.)	2-S-3-O-DH	45	131	19	36	7	1	1	16	.275	9	16	4	58	77	2	.985
1995—	Chicago (A.L.)	2-O-DH-3-S	72	160	17	43	7	4	2	17	.269	3	25	5	52	67	7	.944
Major league totals (3 years)			125	305	39	84	14	5	3	35	.275	13	42	9	123	153	10	.965

MARTINEZ, CARLOS — 3B/1B — RANGERS

PERSONAL: Born August 11, 1965, in La Guaira, Venezuela. . . . 6-5/215. . . . Bats right, throws right. . . . Full name: Carlos Alberto Martinez.

TRANSACTIONS/CAREER NOTES: Signed as non-drafted free agent by New York Yankees organization (November 17, 1983). . . . On Fort Lauderdale disabled list (April 11-May 1, 1986). . . . Traded by Yankees organization with C Ron Hassey and a player to be named later to Chicago White Sox for C Joel Skinner, IF Wayne Tolleson and OF/DH Ron Kittle (July 30, 1986); White Sox organization acquired C Bill Lindsey to complete deal (December 24, 1986). . . . On Chicago disabled list (June 22-July 13, 1989); included rehabilitation assignment to South

Bend (July 8-12). . . . Granted free agency (February 23, 1991). . . . Signed by Cleveland Indians (March 2, 1991). . . . On suspended list (October 5-6, 1991). . . . On Cleveland disabled list (March 28-May 29, 1992); included rehabilitation assignment to Colorado Springs (May 20-29). . . . Released by Indians organization (April 1994). . . . Signed by Vancouver, California Angels organization (December 28, 1994). . . . Released by Angels (July 21, 1995). . . . Re-signed by Angels organization (July 28, 1995). . . . Released by Angels organization (August 22, 1995). . . . Signed by Texas Rangers organization (November 30, 1995).

STATISTICAL NOTES: Career major league grand slams: 1.

			BATTING											FIELDING			
Year Team (League)	**Pos.**	**G**	**AB**	**R**	**H**	**2B**	**3B**	**HR**	**RBI**	**Avg.**	**BB**	**SO**	**SB**	**PO**	**A**	**E**	**Avg.**
1984— GC Yankees (GCL)	SS	31	91	9	14	1	1	0	4	.154	6	15	3	53	103	14	.918
1985— Fort Lauder. (FSL)	SS	93	311	39	77	15	7	6	44	.248	14	65	8	123	254	25	.938
1986— Fort Lauder. (FSL)	SS	5	16	1	1	0	0	0	0	.063	0	6	0	7	18	0	1.000
— Alb./Colon. (East.)	SS-3B	69	253	34	70	18	2	8	39	.277	6	46	2	120	161	32	.898
— Buffalo (A.A.)■	SS-3B	17	54	6	16	1	0	2	6	.296	2	12	0	24	20	5	.898
1987— Birm. (Southern)	3B	9	30	2	7	1	0	0	0	.233	1	6	2	5	17	2	.917
— Hawaii (PCL)	OF-3B-SS	83	304	32	75	15	1	3	36	.247	14	50	3	109	91	18	.917
1988— Birm. (Southern)	OF-3B-SS	133	498	67	138	22	3	14	73	.277	36	82	25	196	139	20	.944
— Chicago (A.L.)	3B-DH	17	55	5	9	1	0	0	0	.164	0	12	1	7	33	4	.909
1989— Vancouver (PCL)	1B	18	64	12	25	3	1	2	9	.391	5	14	2	178	10	1	.995
— Chicago (A.L.)	3-1-O-DH	109	350	44	105	22	0	5	32	.300	21	57	4	283	134	20	.954
— South Bend (Mid.)	3B	3	11	2	6	3	0	0	3	.545	1	1	2	0	9	3	.750
1990— Chicago (A.L.)	1B-DH-OF	92	272	18	61	6	5	4	24	.224	10	40	0	632	38	8	.988
1991— Cant./Akr. (East.)■	OF-1B	80	295	48	97	22	2	11	73	.329	22	47	11	37	1	2	.950
— Cleveland (A.L.)	DH-1B	72	257	22	73	14	0	5	30	.284	10	43	3	229	12	8	.968
1992— Colo. Springs (PCL)	1B	9	32	7	10	1	0	0	5	.313	1	5	0	57	4	4	.938
— Cleveland (A.L.)	1B-3B-DH	69	228	23	60	9	1	5	35	.263	7	21	1	276	57	4	.988
1993— Cleveland (A.L.)	3B-1B-DH	80	262	26	64	10	0	5	31	.244	20	29	1	162	51	9	.959
— Charlotte (Int'l)	1B-3B	20	79	17	29	7	1	3	12	.367	4	15	2	85	23	2	.982
1994—							Out of organized baseball.										
1995— Vancouver (PCL)■	3B	25	97	17	24	3	0	1	6	.247	7	17	1	17	48	2	.970
— California (A.L.)	3B-1B-DH	26	61	7	11	1	0	1	9	.180	6	7	0	25	25	1	.980
Major league totals (7 years)		465	1485	145	383	63	6	25	161	.258	74	209	10	1614	350	54	.973

MARTINEZ, DAVE OF WHITE SOX

PERSONAL: Born September 26, 1964, in New York. . . . 5-10/175. . . . Bats left, throws left. . . . Full name: David Martinez.

HIGH SCHOOL: Lake Howell (Casselberry, Fla.).

JUNIOR COLLEGE: Valencia Community College (Fla.).

TRANSACTIONS/CAREER NOTES: Selected by Texas Rangers organization in 40th round of free-agent draft (June 7, 1982); did not sign. . . . Selected by Chicago Cubs organization in secondary phase of free-agent draft (January 11, 1983). . . . On disabled list (April 27, 1984-remainder of season). . . . Traded by Cubs to Montreal Expos for OF Mitch Webster (July 14, 1988). . . . On disqualified list (October 4-5, 1991). . . . Traded by Expos with P Scott Ruskin and SS Willie Greene to Cincinnati Reds for P John Wetteland and P Bill Risley (December 11, 1991). . . . Granted free agency (October 27, 1992). . . . Signed by San Francisco Giants (December 9, 1992). . . . On San Francisco disabled list (April 30-June 4, 1993); included rehabilitation assignment to Phoenix (June 1-4). . . . Granted free agency (October 14, 1994). . . . Signed by Chicago White Sox (April 5, 1995). . . . Granted free agency (November 3, 1995). . . . Re-signed by White Sox (November 14, 1995).

STATISTICAL NOTES: Career major league grand slams: 2.

			BATTING											FIELDING			
Year Team (League)	**Pos.**	**G**	**AB**	**R**	**H**	**2B**	**3B**	**HR**	**RBI**	**Avg.**	**BB**	**SO**	**SB**	**PO**	**A**	**E**	**Avg.**
1983— Quad Cities (Mid.)	OF	44	119	17	29	6	2	0	10	.244	26	30	10	47	8	1	.982
— Geneva (NYP)	OF	64	241	35	63	15	2	5	33	.261	40	52	16	132	6	8	.945
1984— Quad Cities (Mid.)	OF	12	41	6	9	2	2	0	5	.220	9	13	3	13	2	1	.938
1985— Winst.-Salem (Car.)	OF	115	386	52	132	14	4	5	54	*.342	62	35	38	206	11	7	.969
1986— Iowa (Am. Assoc.)	OF	83	318	52	92	11	5	5	32	.289	36	34	42	214	7	2	.991
— Chicago (N.L.)	OF	53	108	13	15	1	1	1	7	.139	6	22	4	77	2	1	.988
1987— Chicago (N.L.)	OF	142	459	70	134	18	8	8	36	.292	57	96	16	283	10	6	.980
1988— Chicago (N.L.)	OF	75	256	27	65	10	1	4	34	.254	21	46	7	162	2	5	.970
— Montreal (N.L.)■	OF	63	191	24	49	3	5	2	12	.257	17	48	16	119	2	1	.992
1989— Montreal (N.L.)	OF	126	361	41	99	16	7	3	27	.274	27	57	23	199	7	7	.967
1990— Montreal (N.L.)	OF-P	118	391	60	109	13	5	11	39	.279	24	48	13	257	6	3	.989
1991— Montreal (N.L.)	OF	124	396	47	117	18	5	7	42	.295	20	54	16	213	10	4	.982
1992— Cincinnati (N.L.)■	OF-1B	135	393	47	100	20	5	3	31	.254	42	54	12	382	18	6	.985
1993— San Fran. (N.L.)■	OF	91	241	28	58	12	1	5	27	.241	27	39	6	131	6	1	.993
— Phoenix (PCL)	OF	3	15	4	7	0	0	0	2	.467	1	1	1	5	1	0	1.000
1994— San Francisco (N.L.)	OF-1B	97	235	23	58	9	3	4	27	.247	21	22	3	256	18	3	.989
1995— Chicago (A.L.)■	O-1-DH-P	119	303	49	93	16	4	5	37	.307	32	41	8	392	25	3	.993
American League totals (1 year)		119	303	49	93	16	4	5	37	.307	32	41	8	392	25	3	.993
National League totals (9 years)		1024	3031	380	804	120	41	48	282	.265	262	486	116	2079	81	37	.983
Major league totals (10 years)		1143	3334	429	897	136	45	53	319	.269	294	527	124	2471	106	40	.985

RECORD AS PITCHER

Year Team (League)	**W**	**L**	**Pct.**	**ERA**	**G**	**GS**	**CG**	**ShO**	**Sv.**	**IP**	**H**	**R**	**ER**	**BB**	**SO**
1990— Montreal (N.L.)	0	0	. . .	54.00	1	0	0	0	0	1/3	2	2	2	2	0
1995— Chicago (A.L.)	0	0	. . .	0.00	1	0	0	0	0	1	0	0	0	2	0
A.L. totals (1 year)	0	0	. . .	0.00	1	0	0	0	0	1	0	0	0	2	0
N.L. totals (1 year)	0	0	. . .	54.00	1	0	0	0	0	1/3	2	2	2	2	0
Major league totals (2 years)	0	0	. . .	13.50	2	0	0	0	0	1 1/3	2	2	2	4	0

MARTINEZ, DENNIS — P — INDIANS

PERSONAL: Born May 14, 1955, in Granada, Nicaragua. . . . 6-1/180. . . . Throws right, bats right. . . . Full name: Jose Dennis Martinez.

TRANSACTIONS/CAREER NOTES: Signed as non-drafted free agent by Baltimore Orioles organization (December 10, 1973). . . . On Baltimore disabled list (March 28-April 20, 1980). . . . On Baltimore disabled list (June 3-July 10, 1980); included rehabilitation assignment to Miami (July 1-10). . . . On Baltimore disabled list (April 28-June 16, 1986); included rehabilitation assignment to Rochester (May 21-June 10). . . . Traded by Orioles to Montreal Expos for a player to be named later (June 16, 1986); Orioles acquired IF Rene Gonzales to complete deal (December 16, 1986). . . . Granted free agency (November 12, 1986). . . . Signed by Miami, independent (April 14, 1987). . . . Released by Miami (May 6, 1987). . . . Signed by Expos organization (May 6, 1987). . . . Granted free agency (November 9, 1987). . . . Re-signed by Expos (December 18, 1987). . . . Granted free agency (October 25, 1993). . . . Signed by Cleveland Indians (December 2, 1993).

RECORDS: Shares major league single-season record for fewest complete games by pitcher who led league in complete games—9 (1991).

HONORS: Named International League Pitcher of the Year (1976).

STATISTICAL NOTES: Pitched 4-0 one-hit, complete-game victory against California (June 5, 1985). . . . Tied for N.L. lead with 10 balks in 1988. . . . Pitched 2-0 perfect game against Los Angeles (July 28, 1991).

MISCELLANEOUS: Had sacrifice hit in one game as pinch-hitter (1991). . . . Had sacrifice fly in one game as pinch-hitter (1993).

Year	Team (League)	W	L	Pct.	ERA	G	GS	CG	ShO	Sv.	IP	H	R	ER	BB	SO
1974—	Miami (Florida St.)	15	6	.714	2.06	25	25	10	4	0	179	124	48	41	53	162
1975—	Miami (Florida St.)	12	4	.750	2.61	20	20	9	3	0	145	125	54	42	35	114
	—Asheville (South.)	4	1	.800	2.60	6	6	4	1	0	45	45	16	13	12	18
	—Rochester (Int'l)	0	0	...	5.40	2	0	0	0	0	5	7	4	3	2	4
1976—	Rochester (Int'l)	*14	8	.636	*2.50	25	23	*16	1	0	180	148	64	50	50	*140
	—Baltimore (A.L.)	1	2	.333	2.57	4	2	1	0	0	28	23	8	8	8	18
1977—	Baltimore (A.L.)	14	7	.667	4.10	42	13	5	0	4	167	157	86	76	64	107
1978—	Baltimore (A.L.)	16	11	.593	3.52	40	38	15	2	0	276	257	121	108	93	142
1979—	Baltimore (A.L.)	15	16	.484	3.67	40	*39	*18	3	0	*292	279	129	119	78	132
1980—	Baltimore (A.L.)	6	4	.600	3.96	25	12	2	0	1	100	103	44	44	44	42
	—Miami (Florida St.)	0	0	...	0.00	2	2	0	0	0	12	3	1	0	5	7
1981—	Baltimore (A.L.)	•14	5	.737	3.32	25	24	9	2	0	179	173	84	66	62	88
1982—	Baltimore (A.L.)	16	12	.571	4.21	40	39	10	2	0	252	262	123	118	87	111
1983—	Baltimore (A.L.)	7	16	.304	5.53	32	25	4	0	0	153	209	108	94	45	71
1984—	Baltimore (A.L.)	6	9	.400	5.02	34	20	2	0	0	141 2/3	145	81	79	37	77
1985—	Baltimore (A.L.)	13	11	.542	5.15	33	31	3	1	0	180	203	110	103	63	68
1986—	Baltimore (A.L.)	0	0	...	6.75	4	0	0	0	0	6 2/3	11	5	5	2	2
	—Rochester (Int'l)	2	1	.667	6.05	4	4	0	0	0	19 1/3	18	14	13	9	14
	—Montreal (N.L.)■	3	6	.333	4.59	19	15	1	1	0	98	103	52	50	28	63
1987—	Miami (Florida St.)■	1	1	.500	6.16	3	3	0	0	0	19	21	14	13	3	11
	—Indianapolis (A.A.)■	3	2	.600	4.46	7	7	1	1	0	38 1/3	32	20	19	13	30
	—Montreal (N.L.)	11	4	*.733	3.30	22	22	2	1	0	144 2/3	133	59	53	40	84
1988—	Montreal (N.L.)	15	13	.536	2.72	34	34	9	2	0	235 1/3	215	94	71	55	120
1989—	Montreal (N.L.)	16	7	.696	3.18	34	33	5	2	0	232	227	88	82	49	142
1990—	Montreal (N.L.)	10	11	.476	2.95	32	32	7	2	0	226	191	80	74	49	156
1991—	Montreal (N.L.)	14	11	.560	*2.39	31	31	•9	*5	0	222	187	70	59	62	123
1992—	Montreal (N.L.)	16	11	.593	2.47	32	32	6	0	0	226 1/3	172	75	62	60	147
1993—	Montreal (N.L.)	15	9	.625	3.85	35	34	2	0	1	224 2/3	211	110	96	64	138
1994—	Cleveland (A.L.)■	11	6	.647	3.52	24	24	7	3	0	176 2/3	166	75	69	44	92
1995—	Cleveland (A.L.)	12	5	.706	3.08	28	28	3	2	0	187	174	71	64	46	99
A.L. totals (13 years)		131	104	.557	4.01	371	295	79	15	5	2139	2162	1045	953	673	1049
N.L. totals (8 years)		100	72	.581	3.06	239	233	41	13	1	1609	1439	628	547	407	973
Major league totals (20 years)		231	176	.568	3.60	610	528	120	28	6	3748	3601	1673	1500	1080	2022

DIVISION SERIES RECORD

Year	Team (League)	W	L	Pct.	ERA	G	GS	CG	ShO	Sv.	IP	H	R	ER	BB	SO
1995—	Cleveland (A.L.)	0	0	...	3.00	1	1	0	0	0	6	5	2	2	0	2

CHAMPIONSHIP SERIES RECORD

Year	Team (League)	W	L	Pct.	ERA	G	GS	CG	ShO	Sv.	IP	H	R	ER	BB	SO
1979—	Baltimore (A.L.)	0	0	...	3.24	1	1	0	0	0	8 1/3	8	3	3	0	4
1983—	Baltimore (A.L.)							Did not play.								
1995—	Cleveland (A.L.)	1	1	.500	2.03	2	2	0	0	0	13 1/3	10	3	3	3	7
Champ. series totals (2 years)		1	1	.500	2.49	3	3	0	0	0	21 2/3	18	6	6	3	11

WORLD SERIES RECORD

NOTES: Member of World Series championship team (1983).

Year	Team (League)	W	L	Pct.	ERA	G	GS	CG	ShO	Sv.	IP	H	R	ER	BB	SO
1979—	Baltimore (A.L.)	0	0	...	18.00	2	1	0	0	0	2	6	4	4	0	0
1983—	Baltimore (A.L.)							Did not play.								
1995—	Cleveland (A.L.)	0	1	.000	3.48	2	2	0	0	0	10 1/3	12	4	4	8	5
World Series totals (2 years)		0	1	.000	5.84	4	3	0	0	0	12 1/3	18	8	8	8	5

ALL-STAR GAME RECORD

Year	League	W	L	Pct.	ERA	GS	CG	ShO	Sv.	IP	H	R	ER	BB	SO
1990—	National	0	0	...	0.00	0	0	0	0	1	0	0	0	0	1
1991—	National	0	1	.000	13.50	0	0	0	0	2	4	3	3	0	0
1992—	National	0	0	...	0.00	0	0	0	0	1	0	0	0	1	1
1995—	American	0	0	...	4.50	0	0	0	0	2	1	1	1	0	0
All-Star totals (4 years)		0	1	.000	6.00	0	0	0	0	6	5	4	4	1	2

MARTINEZ, EDGAR — DH/3B — MARINERS

PERSONAL: Born January 2, 1963, in New York. . . . 5-11/200. . . . Bats right, throws right. . . . Cousin of Carmelo Martinez, major league first baseman/outfielder with six teams (1983-91).

HIGH SCHOOL: Dorado (Puerto Rico).
COLLEGE: American College (Puerto Rico.).
TRANSACTIONS/CAREER NOTES: Signed as non-drafted free agent by Seattle Mariners organization (December 19, 1982). . . . On Seattle disabled list (April 4-May 17, 1993). . . . On Seattle disabled list (June 15-July 21, 1993); included rehabilitation assignment to Jacksonville (July 17-21). . . . On Seattle disabled list (August 17, 1993-remainder of season). . . . On disabled list (April 16-May 6, 1994).
RECORDS: Shares A.L. single-game record for most errors by third baseman—4 (May 6, 1990).
HONORS: Named third baseman on THE SPORTING NEWS A.L. All-Star team (1992). . . . Named third baseman on THE SPORTING NEWS A.L. Silver Slugger team (1992). . . . Named designated hitter on THE SPORTING NEWS A.L. All-Star team (1995). . . . Named designated hitter on THE SPORTING NEWS A.L. Silver Slugger team (1995).
STATISTICAL NOTES: Led Southern League third basemen with 360 total chances and 34 double plays in 1985. . . . Led Southern League with 12 sacrifice flies in 1985. . . . Led Southern League third basemen with .960 fielding percentage in 1986. . . . Led Pacific Coast League third basemen with 389 total chances and 31 double plays in 1987. . . . Led A.L. with .479 on-base percentage in 1995. . . . Career major league grand slams: 2.

			BATTING											FIELDING			
Year	Team (League)	Pos.	G	AB	R	H	2B	3B	HR	RBI	Avg.	BB	SO	SB	PO	A	E	Avg.
1983—	Belling. (N'west)	3B	32	104	14	18	1	1	0	5	.173	18	24	1	22	58	6	.930
1984—	Wausau (Midwest)	3B	126	433	72	131	32	2	15	66	.303	84	57	11	85	246	25	.930
1985—	Chatt. (South.)	3B	111	357	43	92	15	5	3	47	.258	71	30	1	*94	*247	19	*.947
—	Calgary (PCL)	3B-2B	20	68	8	24	7	1	0	14	.353	12	7	1	15	44	4	.937
1986—	Chatt. (South.)	3B-2B	132	451	71	119	29	5	6	74	.264	89	35	2	94	263	15	†.960
1987—	Calgary (PCL)	3B	129	438	75	144	31	1	10	66	.329	82	47	3	*91	*278	20	.949
—	Seattle (A.L.)	3B-DH	13	43	6	16	5	2	0	5	.372	2	5	0	13	19	0	1.000
1988—	Calgary (PCL)	3B-2B	95	331	63	120	19	4	8	64	*.363	66	40	9	48	185	20	.921
—	Seattle (A.L.)	3B	14	32	0	9	4	0	0	5	.281	4	7	0	5	8	1	.929
1989—	Seattle (A.L.)	3B	65	171	20	41	5	0	2	20	.240	17	26	2	40	72	6	.949
—	Calgary (PCL)	3B-2B	32	113	30	39	11	0	3	23	.345	22	13	2	22	56	12	.867
1990—	Seattle (A.L.)	3B-DH	144	487	71	147	27	2	11	49	.302	74	62	1	89	259	*27	.928
1991—	Seattle (A.L.)	3B-DH	150	544	98	167	35	1	14	52	.307	84	72	0	84	299	15	.962
1992—	Seattle (A.L.)	3B-DH-1B	135	528	100	181	•46	3	18	73	*.343	54	61	14	88	211	17	.946
1993—	Seattle (A.L.)	DH-3B	42	135	20	32	7	0	4	13	.237	28	19	0	5	11	2	.889
—	Jacksonv. (South.)	DH	4	14	2	5	0	0	1	3	.357	2	0	0	...	...	...	...
1994—	Seattle (A.L.)	3B-DH	89	326	47	93	23	1	13	51	.285	53	42	6	44	128	9	.950
1995—	Seattle (A.L.)	DH-3B-1B	•145	511	•121	182	•52	0	29	113	*.356	116	87	4	30	4	2	.944
Major league totals (9 years)			797	2777	483	868	204	9	91	381	.313	432	381	27	398	1011	79	.947

DIVISION SERIES RECORD

RECORDS: Holds postseason single-game record for most RBIs-7 (October 7, 1995).

			BATTING											FIELDING			
Year	Team (League)	Pos.	G	AB	R	H	2B	3B	HR	RBI	Avg.	BB	SO	SB	PO	A	E	Avg.
1995—	Seattle (A.L.)	DH	5	21	6	12	3	0	2	10	.571	6	2	0	...	...	...	...

CHAMPIONSHIP SERIES RECORD

			BATTING											FIELDING			
Year	Team (League)	Pos.	G	AB	R	H	2B	3B	HR	RBI	Avg.	BB	SO	SB	PO	A	E	Avg.
1995—	Seattle (A.L.)	DH	6	23	0	2	0	0	0	0	.087	2	5	1	...	...	...	...

ALL-STAR GAME RECORD

			BATTING										FIELDING			
Year	League	Pos.	AB	R	H	2B	3B	HR	RBI	Avg.	BB	SO	SB	PO	A	E	Avg.
1992—	American	PH	1	0	0	0	0	0	0	.000	0	0	0	...	...	...	...
1995—	American	DH	3	0	0	0	0	0	0	.000	0	1	0	...	...	...	...
All-Star Game totals (2 years)			4	0	0	0	0	0	0	.000	0	1	0	...	...	...	...

MARTINEZ, GABBY SS BREWERS

PERSONAL: Born January 7, 1974, in San Juan, Puerto Rico. . . . 6-2/170. . . . Bats both, throws right. . . . Full name: Gabriel Martinez.
HIGH SCHOOL: Luchetti (Santurce, Puerto Rico).
TRANSACTIONS/CAREER NOTES: Selected by Milwaukee Brewers organization in supplemental round ("sandwich pick" between first and second round, 38th pick overall) of free-agent draft (June 1, 1992).

			BATTING											FIELDING			
Year	Team (League)	Pos.	G	AB	R	H	2B	3B	HR	RBI	Avg.	BB	SO	SB	PO	A	E	Avg.
1992—	Ariz. Brewers (Ariz.)	SS	48	165	29	43	7	2	0	24	.261	12	19	7	58	129	21	.899
1993—	Beloit (Midwest)	SS	94	285	40	69	14	5	0	24	.242	14	52	22	109	242	23	.939
1994—	Stockton (Calif.)	SS-OF	112	364	37	90	18	3	0	32	.247	17	66	19	151	236	32	.924
1995—	Stockton (Calif.)	SS	64	213	25	55	13	3	1	20	.258	10	25	13	96	158	21	.924
—	El Paso (Texas)	SS	44	133	13	37	3	2	0	11	.278	2	22	5	65	103	9	.949

MARTINEZ, JESUS P DODGERS

PERSONAL: Born March 13, 1974, in Santo Domingo, Dominican Republic. . . . 6-2/145. . . . Throws left, bats left. . . . Brother of Ramon Martinez, pitcher, Los Angeles Dodgers; and brother of Pedro J. Martinez, pitcher, Montreal Expos.
HIGH SCHOOL: Liceo Las Americas (Santo Domingo, Dominican Republic).
TRANSACTIONS/CAREER NOTES: Signed as non-drafted free agent by Los Angeles Dodgers organization (August 22, 1990).
STATISTICAL NOTES: Tied for Texas League lead with four balks in 1995.

Year	Team (League)	W	L	Pct.	ERA	G	GS	CG	ShO	Sv.	IP	H	R	ER	BB	SO
1991—	Santo Dom. (DSL)	3	2	.600	3.57	14	14	0	0	0	70 2/3	58	34	28	45	83
1992—	GC Dodgers (GCL)	1	4	.200	3.29	7	7	1	0	0	41	38	19	15	11	39
—	Great Falls (Pio.)	0	3	.000	13.25	6	6	0	0	0	18 1/3	36	30	27	21	23

Year	Team (League)	W	L	Pct.	ERA	G	GS	CG	ShO	Sv.	IP	H	R	ER	BB	SO
1993—	Bakersfield (Calif.)	4	*13	.235	4.14	30	21	0	0	0	145 2/3	144	95	67	75	108
1994—	Vero Beach (FSL)	7	9	.438	6.26	18	18	1	1	0	87 2/3	91	65	61	43	69
	— San Antonio (Tex.)	0	1	.000	4.50	1	1	0	0	0	4	3	2	2	2	3
1995—	San Antonio (Tex.)	6	9	.400	3.54	24	24	1	0	0	139 2/3	129	64	55	71	83
	— Albuquerque (PCL)	1	1	.500	4.50	2	0	0	0	0	4	4	2	2	4	5

MARTINEZ, PEDRO A. — P — METS

PERSONAL: Born November 29, 1968, in Santo Domingo, Dominican Republic. . . . 6-2/185. . . . Throws left, bats right. . . . Full name: Pedro Aquino Martinez. . . . Formerly known as Pedro Aquino.

HIGH SCHOOL: Ramon Matia Melle (Santo Domingo, Dominican Republic).

TRANSACTIONS/CAREER NOTES: Signed as non-drafted free agent by San Diego Padres organization (September 30, 1986). . . . Traded by Padres with OF Phil Plantier, OF Derek Bell, P Doug Brocail, IF Craig Shipley and SS Ricky Gutierrez to Houston Astros for 3B Ken Caminiti, OF Steve Finley, SS Andujar Cedeno, 1B Robert Petagine, P Brian Williams and a player to be named later (December 28, 1994). . . . Traded by Astros to Padres for SS Ray Holbert (October 10, 1995). . . . Traded by Padres to New York Mets for OF Jeff Barry (December 15, 1995).

Year	Team (League)	W	L	Pct.	ERA	G	GS	CG	ShO	Sv.	IP	H	R	ER	BB	SO
1987—	Spokane (N'west)	4	1	.800	3.83	18	5	1	0	0	51 2/3	57	31	22	36	42
1988—	Spokane (N'west)	8	3	.727	4.24	15	15	1	0	0	99 2/3	108	55	47	32	89
1989—	Char., S.C. (S. Atl.)	•14	8	.636	*1.97	27	27	5	2	0	*187	147	53	41	64	158
1990—	Wichita (Texas)	6	10	.375	4.80	24	23	2	0	0	129 1/3	139	83	69	70	88
1991—	Wichita (Texas)	11	10	.524	5.23	26	26	3	2	0	156 2/3	169	99	*91	57	95
1992—	Wichita (Texas)	11	7	.611	2.99	26	26	1	0	0	168 1/3	153	66	56	52	142
1993—	Las Vegas (PCL)	3	5	.375	4.72	15	14	1	0	0	87 2/3	94	49	46	40	65
	— San Diego (N.L.)	3	1	.750	2.43	32	0	0	0	0	37	23	11	10	13	32
1994—	San Diego (N.L.)	3	2	.600	2.90	48	1	0	0	3	68 1/3	52	31	22	49	52
1995—	Houston (N.L.)■	0	0	...	7.40	25	0	0	0	0	20 2/3	29	18	17	16	17
	— Tucson (Pac. Coast)	1	1	.500	6.62	20	3	0	0	2	34	44	28	25	13	21
	Major league totals (3 years)	6	3	.667	3.50	105	1	0	0	3	126	104	60	49	78	101

MARTINEZ, PEDRO J. — P — EXPOS

PERSONAL: Born July 25, 1971, in Manoguayabo, Dominican Republic. . . . 5-11/170. . . . Throws right, bats right. . . . Full name: Pedro Jaime Martinez. . . . Brother of Ramon J. Martinez, pitcher, Los Angeles Dodgers; and brother of Jesus Martinez, pitcher, Dodgers organization.

COLLEGE: Ohio Dominican College (Dominican Republic).

TRANSACTIONS/CAREER NOTES: Signed as non-drafted free agent by Los Angeles Dodgers organization (June 18, 1988). . . . On Albuquerque disabled list (June 20-July 2 and July 13-August 25, 1992). . . . Traded by Dodgers to Montreal Expos for 2B Delino DeShields (November 19, 1993).

HONORS: Named Minor League Player of the Year by The Sporting News (1991).

STATISTICAL NOTES: Led N.L. with 11 hit batsmen in 1994. . . . Pitched nine perfect innings against San Diego before being relieved after yielding leadoff double in 10th inning (June 3, 1995).

MISCELLANEOUS: Started one game at third base for Los Angeles, but replaced before first plate appearance and never played in field (1993).

Year	Team (League)	W	L	Pct.	ERA	G	GS	CG	ShO	Sv.	IP	H	R	ER	BB	SO
1988—	Santo Dom. (DSL)	5	1	.833	3.10	8	7	1	0	0	49 1/3	45	25	17	16	28
1989—	Santo Dom. (DSL)	7	2	.778	2.73	13	7	2	3	1	85 2/3	59	30	26	25	63
1990—	Great Falls (Pio.)	8	3	.727	3.62	14	•14	0	0	0	77	74	39	31	40	82
1991—	Bakersfield (Calif.)	8	0	1.000	2.05	10	10	0	0	0	61 1/3	41	17	14	19	83
	— San Antonio (Tex.)	7	5	.583	1.76	12	12	4	•3	0	76 2/3	57	21	15	31	74
	— Albuquerque (PCL)	3	3	.500	3.66	6	6	0	0	0	39 1/3	28	17	16	16	35
1992—	Albuquerque (PCL)	7	6	.538	3.81	20	20	3	1	0	125 1/3	104	57	53	57	124
	— Los Angeles (N.L.)	0	1	.000	2.25	2	1	0	0	0	8	6	2	2	1	8
1993—	Albuquerque (PCL)	0	0	...	3.00	1	1	0	0	0	3	1	1	1	1	4
	— Los Angeles (N.L.)	10	5	.667	2.61	65	2	0	0	2	107	76	34	31	57	119
1994—	Montreal (N.L.)■	11	5	.688	3.42	24	23	1	1	1	144 2/3	115	58	55	45	142
1995—	Montreal (N.L.)	14	10	.583	3.51	30	30	2	2	0	194 2/3	158	79	76	66	174
	Major league totals (4 years)	35	21	.625	3.25	121	56	3	3	3	454 1/3	355	173	164	169	443

MARTINEZ, RAMON J. — P — DODGERS

PERSONAL: Born March 22, 1968, in Santo Domingo, Dominican Republic. . . . 6-4/186. . . . Throws right, bats both. . . . Full name: Ramon Jaime Martinez. . . . Brother of Pedro J. Martinez, pitcher, Montreal Expos; and brother of Jesus Martinez, pitcher, Los Angeles Dodgers organization.

HIGH SCHOOL: Liceo Secunderia Las Americas (Dominican Republic).

TRANSACTIONS/CAREER NOTES: Signed as non-drafted free agent by Los Angeles Dodgers organization (September 1, 1984). . . . On suspended list (July 8-12, 1993). . . . Granted free agency (November 1, 1995). . . . Re-signed by Dodgers (November 16, 1995).

STATISTICAL NOTES: Struck out 18 batters in one game (June 4, 1990). . . . Pitched 7-0 no-hit victory against Florida (July 14, 1995).

MISCELLANEOUS: Member of 1984 Dominican Republic Olympic baseball team. . . . Appeared in one game as pinch-runner (1989). . . . Appeared in one game as pinch-runner (1992).

Year	Team (League)	W	L	Pct.	ERA	G	GS	CG	ShO	Sv.	IP	H	R	ER	BB	SO
1985—	GC Dodgers (GCL)	4	1	.800	2.59	23	6	0	0	1	59	57	30	17	23	42
1986—	Bakersfield (Calif.)	4	8	.333	4.75	20	20	2	1	0	106	119	73	56	63	78
1987—	Vero Beach (FSL)	16	5	.762	2.17	25	25	6	1	0	170 1/3	128	45	41	78	148
1988—	San Antonio (Tex.)	8	4	.667	2.46	14	14	2	1	0	95	79	29	26	34	89
	— Albuquerque (PCL)	5	2	.714	2.76	10	10	1	1	0	58 2/3	43	24	18	32	49
	— Los Angeles (N.L.)	1	3	.250	3.79	9	6	0	0	0	35 2/3	27	17	15	22	23
1989—	Albuquerque (PCL)	10	2	.833	2.79	18	18	2	1	0	113	92	40	35	50	127

Year	Team (League)	W	L	Pct.	ERA	G	GS	CG	ShO	Sv.	IP	H	R	ER	BB	SO
	—Los Angeles (N.L.)	6	4	.600	3.19	15	15	2	2	0	98 2/3	79	39	35	41	89
1990—	Los Angeles (N.L.)	20	6	.769	2.92	33	33	*12	3	0	234 1/3	191	89	76	67	223
1991—	Los Angeles (N.L.)	17	13	.567	3.27	33	33	6	4	0	220 1/3	190	89	80	69	150
1992—	Los Angeles (N.L.)	8	11	.421	4.00	25	25	1	1	0	150 2/3	141	82	67	69	101
1993—	Los Angeles (N.L.)	10	12	.455	3.44	32	32	4	3	0	211 2/3	202	88	81	*104	127
1994—	Los Angeles (N.L.)	12	7	.632	3.97	24	24	4	•3	0	170	160	83	75	56	119
1995—	Los Angeles (N.L.)	17	7	.708	3.66	30	30	4	2	0	206 1/3	176	95	84	*81	138
Major league totals (8 years)		91	63	.591	3.48	201	198	33	18	0	1327 2/3	1166	582	513	509	970

DIVISION SERIES RECORD

Year	Team (League)	W	L	Pct.	ERA	G	GS	CG	ShO	Sv.	IP	H	R	ER	BB	SO
1995—	Los Angeles (N.L.)	0	1	.000	14.54	1	1	0	0	0	4 1/3	10	7	7	2	3

MARTINEZ, SANDY — C — BLUE JAYS

PERSONAL: Born October 3, 1972, in Villa Mella, Dominican Republic. . . . 6-2/200. . . . Bats left, throws right. . . . Full name: Angel Sandy Martinez.

TRANSACTIONS/CAREER NOTES: Signed as non-drafted free agent by Toronto Blue Jays organization (January 10, 1990). . . . On disabled list (May 15-June 8, 1993).

STATISTICAL NOTES: Led Pioneer League with 24 passed balls in 1992. . . . Led Florida State League catchers with 14 errors in 1994.

				BATTING											FIELDING			
Year	Team (League)	Pos.	G	AB	R	H	2B	3B	HR	RBI	Avg.	BB	SO	SB	PO	A	E	Avg.
1990—	Santo Dom. (DSL)	C	44	145	21	35	2	0	0	10	.241	18	15	1	...	...	...	...
1991—	Dunedin (Fla. St.)	C	12	38	3	7	1	0	0	3	.184	7	7	0	82	9	2	.978
	—Medicine Hat (Pio.)	C	34	98	8	17	1	0	2	16	.173	12	29	0	141	19	3	.982
1992—	Dunedin (Fla. St.)	C	4	15	4	3	1	0	2	4	.200	0	3	0	11	2	1	.929
	—Medicine Hat (Pio.)	C-1B-SS	57	206	27	52	15	0	4	39	.252	14	62	0	275	58	5	.985
1993—	Hagerstown (SAL)	C	94	338	41	89	16	1	9	46	.263	19	71	1	493	68	14	.976
1994—	Dunedin (Fla. St.)	C-1B	122	450	50	117	14	6	7	52	.260	22	79	1	615	79	†14	.980
1995—	Knoxville (South.)	C	41	144	14	33	8	1	2	22	.229	6	34	0	219	30	5	.980
	—Toronto (A.L.)	C	62	191	12	46	12	0	2	25	.241	7	45	0	329	28	5	.986
Major league totals (1 year)			62	191	12	46	12	0	2	25	.241	7	45	0	329	28	5	.986

MARTINEZ, TINO — 1B — YANKEES

PERSONAL: Born December 7, 1967, in Tampa, Fla. . . . 6-2/210. . . . Bats left, throws right. . . . Full name: Constantino Martinez.

HIGH SCHOOL: Jefferson (Tampa, Fla.).

COLLEGE: Tampa (Fla.).

TRANSACTIONS/CAREER NOTES: Selected by Boston Red Sox organization in third round of free-agent draft (June 3, 1985); did not sign. . . . Selected by Seattle Mariners organization in first round (14th pick overall) of free-agent draft (June 1, 1988). . . . On disabled list (August 10, 1993-remainder of season). . . . Traded by Mariners with P Jeff Nelson and P Jim Mecir to New York Yankees for P Sterling Hitchcock and 3B Russ Davis (December 7, 1995).

HONORS: Named first baseman on The Sporting News college All-America team (1988). . . . Named Pacific Coast League Most Valuable Player (1991).

STATISTICAL NOTES: Led Eastern League with 13 intentional bases on balls received in 1989. . . . Led Eastern League first basemen with 1,348 total chances and 106 double plays in 1989. . . . Tied for Pacific Coast League lead with 11 intentional bases on balls received in 1990. . . . Led Pacific Coast League first basemen with .991 fielding percentage, 1,051 putouts, 98 assists, 1,159 total chances and 117 double plays in 1990. . . . Led Pacific Coast League first basemen with .992 fielding percentage and 122 double plays in 1991. . . . Career major league grand slams: 3.

MISCELLANEOUS: Member of 1988 U.S. Olympic baseball team.

				BATTING											FIELDING			
Year	Team (League)	Pos.	G	AB	R	H	2B	3B	HR	RBI	Avg.	BB	SO	SB	PO	A	E	Avg.
1989—	Williamsport (East.)	1B	*137	*509	51	131	29	2	13	64	.257	59	54	7	*1260	*81	7	*.995
1990—	Calgary (PCL)	1B-3B	128	453	83	145	28	1	17	93	.320	74	37	8	†1051	†98	10	†.991
	—Seattle (A.L.)	1B	24	68	4	15	4	0	0	5	.221	9	9	0	155	12	0	1.000
1991—	Calgary (PCL)	1B-3B	122	442	94	144	34	5	18	86	.326	82	44	3	1078	106	9	†.992
	—Seattle (A.L.)	1B-DH	36	112	11	23	2	0	4	9	.205	11	24	0	249	22	2	.993
1992—	Seattle (A.L.)	1B-DH	136	460	53	118	19	2	16	66	.257	42	77	2	678	58	4	.995
1993—	Seattle (A.L.)	1B-DH	109	408	48	108	25	1	17	60	.265	45	56	0	932	60	3	.997
1994—	Seattle (A.L.)	1B-DH	97	329	42	86	21	0	20	61	.261	29	52	1	705	45	2	.997
1995—	Seattle (A.L.)	1B-DH	141	519	92	152	35	3	31	111	.293	62	91	0	1048	101	8	.993
Major league totals (6 years)			543	1896	250	502	106	6	88	312	.265	198	309	3	3767	298	19	.995

DIVISION SERIES RECORD

				BATTING											FIELDING			
Year	Team (League)	Pos.	G	AB	R	H	2B	3B	HR	RBI	Avg.	BB	SO	SB	PO	A	E	Avg.
1995—	Seattle (A.L.)	1B	5	22	4	9	1	0	1	5	.409	3	4	0	39	5	0	1.000

CHAMPIONSHIP SERIES RECORD

				BATTING											FIELDING			
Year	Team (League)	Pos.	G	AB	R	H	2B	3B	HR	RBI	Avg.	BB	SO	SB	PO	A	E	Avg.
1995—	Seattle (A.L.)	1B	6	22	1	3	0	0	0	0	.136	3	7	0	45	5	1	.980

ALL-STAR GAME RECORD

			BATTING										FIELDING			
Year	League	Pos.	AB	R	H	2B	3B	HR	RBI	Avg.	BB	SO	SB	PO	A	E	Avg.
1995—	American	PH	1	0	1	0	0	0	0	1.000	0	0	0	...	...	...	...

MARZANO, JOHN — C — MARINERS

PERSONAL: Born February 14, 1963, in Philadelphia. . . . 5-11/195. . . . Bats right, throws right. . . . Full name: John Robert Marzano.
HIGH SCHOOL: Central (Philadelphia).
COLLEGE: Temple.
TRANSACTIONS/CAREER NOTES: Selected by Minnesota Twins organization in third round of free-agent draft (June 8, 1981); pick received as compensation for California Angels signing free-agent P Geoff Zahn. . . . Selected by Boston Red Sox organization in first round (14th pick overall) of free-agent draft (June 4, 1984). . . . On disabled list (June 13-28, 1986). . . . On Boston disabled list (April 6-July 26, 1992); included rehabilitation assignment to Pawtucket (July 7-26). . . . Released by Red Sox (March 24, 1993). . . . Signed by Charlotte, Cleveland Indians organization (May 5, 1993). . . . On disabled list (May 12-23, 1993). . . . Released by Charlotte (May 23, 1993). . . . Signed by Philadelphia Phillies organization (December 14, 1993). . . . Granted free agency (October 15, 1994). . . . Signed by Oklahoma City, Texas Rangers organization (April 2, 1995). . . . On Oklahoma City suspended list (June 8-10, 1995). . . . Granted free agency (October 16, 1995). . . . Signed by Seattle Mariners organization (December 14, 1995).
HONORS: Named catcher on The Sporting News college All-America team (1984).
STATISTICAL NOTES: Led Eastern League in being hit by pitch with 12 in 1986. . . . Led American Association catchers with 620 total chances and 12 double plays in 1995.
MISCELLANEOUS: Member of 1984 U.S. Olympic baseball team.

			BATTING												FIELDING			
Year	Team (League)	Pos.	G	AB	R	H	2B	3B	HR	RBI	Avg.	BB	SO	SB	PO	A	E	Avg.
1985	New Britain (East.)	C	103	350	36	86	14	6	4	51	.246	19	43	4	530	70	12	.980
1986	New Britain (East.)	C-3B	118	445	55	126	28	2	10	62	.283	24	66	2	509	76	14	.977
1987	Pawtucket (Int'l)	C	70	255	46	72	22	0	10	35	.282	21	50	2	326	36	8	.978
	—Boston (A.L.)	C	52	168	20	41	11	0	5	24	.244	7	41	0	337	24	5	.986
1988	Boston (A.L.)	C	10	29	3	4	1	0	0	1	.138	1	3	0	77	4	0	1.000
	—Pawtucket (Int'l)	C	33	111	7	22	2	1	0	5	.198	8	17	1	151	24	8	.956
	—New Britain (East.)	C	35	112	11	23	6	1	0	5	.205	10	13	1	117	11	3	.977
1989	Pawtucket (Int'l)	C	106	322	27	68	11	0	8	36	.211	15	53	1	574	62	10	.985
	—Boston (A.L.)	C	7	18	5	8	3	0	1	3	.444	0	2	0	29	4	0	1.000
1990	Boston (A.L.)	C	32	83	8	20	4	0	0	6	.241	5	10	0	153	14	0	1.000
	—Pawtucket (Int'l)	C-3B	26	75	16	24	4	1	2	8	.320	11	9	6	100	12	0	1.000
1991	Boston (A.L.)	C	49	114	10	30	8	0	0	9	.263	1	16	0	174	20	3	.985
1992	Pawtucket (Int'l)	C	18	62	5	18	1	0	2	12	.290	3	11	0	53	4	2	.966
	—Boston (A.L.)	C-DH	19	50	4	4	2	1	0	1	.080	2	12	0	81	9	3	.968
1993	Charlotte (Int'l)■	C	3	9	0	1	0	0	0	0	.111	1	1	0	12	1	1	.929
1994	Scran./W.B. (Int'l)■	C-OF	88	280	25	59	19	2	1	19	.211	24	32	2	311	31	7	.980
1995	Okla. City (A.A.)■	C	120	427	55	132	*41	3	9	56	.309	33	54	3	*551	*64	5	.992
	—Texas (A.L.)	C	2	6	1	2	0	0	0	0	.333	0	0	0	7	1	0	1.000
Major league totals (7 years)			171	468	51	109	29	1	6	44	.233	16	84	0	858	76	11	.988

MASTELLER, DAN — 1B/OF — TWINS

PERSONAL: Born March 17, 1968, in Toledo, O. . . . 6-0/190. . . . Bats left, throws left. . . . Full name: Dan Patrick Masteller.
HIGH SCHOOL: Charles F. Brush (Lyndhurst, O.).
COLLEGE: Michigan State.
TRANSACTIONS/CAREER NOTES: Selected by Minnesota Twins organization in 11th round of free-agent draft (June 5, 1989). . . . On Nashville disabled list (April 5-May 29, 1993).
STATISTICAL NOTES: Led California League first basemen with 1,234 total chances and 100 double plays in 1990.

			BATTING												FIELDING			
Year	Team (League)	Pos.	G	AB	R	H	2B	3B	HR	RBI	Avg.	BB	SO	SB	PO	A	E	Avg.
1989	Elizabeth. (Appal.)	OF	9	38	8	13	0	0	2	9	.342	6	2	2	10	1	0	1.000
	—Visalia (California)	OF-1B	53	181	24	46	5	1	3	16	.254	18	36	0	58	4	3	.954
1990	Visalia (California)	1B	135	473	71	133	20	5	4	73	.281	81	76	2	*1119	*95	20	.984
1991	Orlando (Southern)	1B-OF	124	370	44	91	14	5	5	35	.246	43	43	6	550	27	8	.986
1992	Orlando (Southern)	OF-1B	116	365	42	96	24	4	8	42	.263	23	36	2	360	28	6	.985
1993	Nashville (South.)	1B-OF	36	121	19	33	3	0	3	16	.273	11	19	2	155	4	2	.988
	—Portland (PCL)	1B-OF	61	211	35	68	13	4	7	47	.322	24	25	3	341	29	5	.987
1994	Salt Lake (PCL)	OF-1B-P	96	338	53	102	26	3	8	58	.302	21	27	4	299	19	3	.991
1995	Salt Lake (PCL)	OF-1B	48	152	25	46	10	7	4	18	.303	15	17	4	137	14	1	.993
	—Minnesota (A.L.)	1B-OF-DH	71	198	21	47	12	0	3	21	.237	18	19	1	365	21	2	.995
Major league totals (1 year)			71	198	21	47	12	0	3	21	.237	18	19	1	365	21	2	.995

RECORD AS PITCHER

Year	Team (League)	W	L	Pct.	ERA	G	GS	CG	ShO	Sv.	IP	H	R	ER	BB	SO
1994	Salt Lake (PCL)	0	0	...	0.00	1	0	0	0	0	1	0	0	0	0	0

MATHENY, MIKE — C — BREWERS

PERSONAL: Born September 22, 1970, in Columbus, O. . . . 6-3/205. . . . Bats right, throws right. . . . Full name: Michael Scott Matheny.
HIGH SCHOOL: Reynoldsburg (O.).
COLLEGE: Michigan.
TRANSACTIONS/CAREER NOTES: Selected by Toronto Blue Jays organization in 31st round of free-agent draft (June 1, 1988); did not sign. . . . Selected by Milwaukee Brewers organization in eighth round of free-agent draft (June 3, 1991).
STATISTICAL NOTES: Led California League catchers with 20 double plays in 1992. . . . Led Texas League catchers with 18 double plays in 1993.

			BATTING												FIELDING			
Year	Team (League)	Pos.	G	AB	R	H	2B	3B	HR	RBI	Avg.	BB	SO	SB	PO	A	E	Avg.
1991	Helena (Pioneer)	C	64	253	35	72	14	0	2	34	.285	19	52	2	456	68	5	*.991
1992	Stockton (Calif.)	C	106	333	42	73	13	2	6	46	.219	35	81	2	582	114	8	*.989

Year	Team (League)	Pos.	G	AB	R	H	2B	3B	HR	RBI	Avg.	BB	SO	SB	PO	A	E	Avg.
				BATTING											FIELDING			
1993—	El Paso (Texas)	C	107	339	39	86	21	2	2	28	.254	17	73	1	524	*100	9	.986
1994—	Milwaukee (A.L.)	C	28	53	3	12	3	0	1	2	.226	3	13	0	81	8	1	.989
—	New Orleans (A.A.)	C-1B	57	177	20	39	10	1	4	21	.220	16	39	1	345	43	5	.987
1995—	New Orleans (A.A.)	C	6	17	3	6	2	0	3	4	.353	0	5	0	30	4	0	1.000
—	Milwaukee (A.L.)	C	80	166	13	41	9	1	0	21	.247	12	28	2	261	18	4	.986
Major league totals (2 years)			108	219	16	53	12	1	1	23	.242	15	41	2	342	26	5	.987

MATHEWS, TERRY — P — MARLINS

PERSONAL: Born October 5, 1964, in Alexandria, La. . . . 6-2/225. . . . Throws right, bats left. . . . Full name: Terry Alan Mathews.
HIGH SCHOOL: Menard (Alexandria, La.).
COLLEGE: Northeast Louisiana.
TRANSACTIONS/CAREER NOTES: Selected by Texas Rangers organization in fifth round of free-agent draft (June 2, 1987). . . . On Texas disabled list (July 29-September 12, 1992). . . . Released by Rangers organization (April 4, 1993). . . . Signed by Houston Astros organization (April 4, 1993). . . . Granted free agency (October 15, 1993). . . . Signed by Edmonton, Florida Marlins organization (November 9, 1993). . . . On Florida disabled list (August 19-September 3, 1995); included rehabilitation assignment to Charlotte (August 29-September 1).
MISCELLANEOUS: Grounded into double play in only appearance as pinch-hitter with Florida (1995).

Year	Team (League)	W	L	Pct.	ERA	G	GS	CG	ShO	Sv.	IP	H	R	ER	BB	SO
1987—	Gastonia (S. Atl.)	3	3	.500	5.59	34	1	0	0	0	48 1/3	53	35	30	32	46
1988—	Charlotte (Fla. St.)	13	6	.684	2.80	27	26	2	1	0	163 2/3	141	68	51	49	94
1989—	Tulsa (Texas)	2	5	.286	6.15	10	10	1	0	0	45 1/3	53	40	31	24	32
—	Charlotte (Fla. St.)	4	2	.667	3.64	10	10	0	0	0	59 1/3	55	28	24	17	30
1990—	Tulsa (Texas)	5	7	.417	4.27	14	14	4	2	0	86 1/3	88	50	41	36	48
—	Okla. City (A.A.)	2	7	.222	3.69	12	11	1	1	0	70 2/3	81	39	29	15	36
1991—	Okla. City (A.A.)	5	6	.455	3.49	18	13	1	0	1	95 1/3	98	39	37	34	63
—	Texas (A.L.)	4	0	1.000	3.61	34	2	0	0	1	57 1/3	54	24	23	18	51
1992—	Texas (A.L.)	2	4	.333	5.95	40	0	0	0	0	42 1/3	48	29	28	31	26
—	Okla. City (A.A.)	1	1	.500	4.32	9	2	0	0	1	16 2/3	17	8	8	7	13
1993—	Jackson (Texas)■	6	5	.545	3.67	17	17	0	0	0	103	116	55	42	29	74
—	Tucson (Pac. Coast)	5	0	1.000	3.55	16	4	0	0	2	33	40	14	13	11	34
1994—	Edmonton (PCL)■	4	4	.500	4.29	13	12	3	0	0	84	88	43	40	22	46
—	Florida (N.L.)	2	1	.667	3.35	24	2	0	0	0	43	45	16	16	9	21
1995—	Florida (N.L.)	4	4	.500	3.38	57	0	0	0	3	82 2/3	70	32	31	27	72
—	Charlotte (Int'l)	0	0	. . .	4.91	2	0	0	0	0	3 2/3	5	2	2	0	5
A.L. totals (2 years)		6	4	.600	4.61	74	2	0	0	1	99 2/3	102	53	51	49	77
N.L. totals (2 years)		6	5	.545	3.37	81	2	0	0	3	125 2/3	115	48	47	36	93
Major league totals (4 years)		12	9	.571	3.91	155	4	0	0	4	225 1/3	217	101	98	85	170

MATHEWS, T.J. — P — CARDINALS

PERSONAL: Born January 19, 1970, in Belleville, Ill. . . . 6-2/200. . . . Throws right, bats right. . . . Full name: Timothy Jay Mathews. . . . Son of Nelson Mathews, outfielder, Chicago Cubs and Kansas City Athletics (1960-65).
HIGH SCHOOL: Columbia (Ill.).
COLLEGE: UNLV.
TRANSACTIONS/CAREER NOTES: Selected by St. Louis Cardinals organization in 36th round of free-agent draft (June 1, 1992). . . . On Louisville disabled list (May 30-June 6, 1995).
STATISTICAL NOTES: Pitched 4-0 no-hit victory against Burlington (August 13, 1993).

Year	Team (League)	W	L	Pct.	ERA	G	GS	CG	ShO	Sv.	IP	H	R	ER	BB	SO
1992—	Hamilton (NYP)	10	1	*.909	2.18	14	14	1	0	0	86 2/3	70	25	21	30	89
1993—	Springfield (Midw.)	12	9	.571	2.71	25	25	5	2	0	159 1/3	121	59	48	29	144
1994—	St. Petersburg (FSL)	5	5	.500	2.44	11	11	1	0	0	66 1/3	52	22	18	23	62
—	Arkansas (Texas)	5	5	.500	3.15	16	16	1	0	0	97	83	37	34	24	93
1995—	Louisville (A.A.)	9	4	.692	2.70	32	7	0	0	1	66 2/3	60	35	20	27	50
—	St. Louis (N.L.)	1	1	.500	1.52	23	0	0	0	2	29 2/3	21	7	5	11	28
Major league totals (1 year)		1	1	.500	1.52	23	0	0	0	2	29 2/3	21	7	5	11	28

MATTINGLY, DON — 1B

PERSONAL: Born April 20, 1961, in Evansville, Ind. . . . 6-0/200. . . . Bats left, throws left. . . . Full name: Donald Arthur Mattingly.
HIGH SCHOOL: Evansville (Ind.) Memorial.
TRANSACTIONS/CAREER NOTES: Selected by New York Yankees organization in 19th round of free-agent draft (June 5, 1979). . . . On disabled list (June 9-24, 1987; May 27-June 14, 1988; July 26-September 11, 1990; May 14-June 10, 1993; and June 28-July 13, 1994). . . . Granted free agency (November 11, 1995).
RECORDS: Holds major league records for most home runs in seven consecutive games—9 (July 8-17, 1987); and eight consecutive games—10 (July 8-18, 1987). . . . Holds major league single-season records for most grand slams—6 (1987); and most at-bats without a stolen base—677 (1986). . . . Shares major league single-game records for most sacrifice flies—3 (May 3, 1986); and most putouts and chances accepted by first baseman in nine-inning game—22 (July 20, 1987). . . . Shares major league records for most doubles in one inning—2 (April 11, 1987, seventh inning); and most consecutive games with one or more home runs—8 (July 8 through July 18, 1987). . . . Shares major league career record for highest fielding percentage for first baseman—.996. . . . Holds A.L. single-season record for most at-bats by lefthander—677 (1986).
HONORS: Named South Atlantic League Most Valuable Player (1980). . . . Named A.L. Player of the Year by The Sporting News (1984-86). . . . Named first baseman on The Sporting News A.L. All-Star team (1984-87). . . . Named Major League Player of the Year by The Sporting News (1985). . . . Won A.L. Gold Glove at first base (1985-89 and 1991-94). . . . Named first baseman on The Sporting News A.L. Silver Slugger team (1985-87). . . . Named A.L. Most Valuable Player by Baseball Writers' Association of America (1985).
STATISTICAL NOTES: Led South Atlantic League with 12 sacrifice flies in 1980. . . . Led A.L. first basemen with .996 fielding percentage in

both 1984 and 1986. . . . Led A.L. with 370 total bases in 1985 and 388 in 1986. . . . Led A.L. with 21 game-winning RBIs in 1985 and tied for lead with 15 in 1986. . . . Led A.L. with 15 sacrifice flies in 1985. . . . Tied for A.L. lead in double plays by first baseman with 154 in 1985. . . . Led A.L. with .573 slugging percentage in 1986. . . . Led A.L. first basemen with 1,377 putouts and 1,483 total chances in 1986. . . . Led A.L. first basemen with 135 double plays in 1991. . . . Career major league grand slams: 6.

		BATTING												FIELDING			
Year Team (League)	Pos.	G	AB	R	H	2B	3B	HR	RBI	Avg.	BB	SO	SB	PO	A	E	Avg.
1979— Oneonta (NYP)	OF-1B	53	166	20	58	10	2	3	31	.349	30	6	2	29	2	2	.939
1980— Greensboro (S. Atl.)	OF-1B	133	494	92	*177	32	5	9	105	*.358	59	33	8	205	16	8	.965
1981— Nashville (South.)	OF-1B	141	547	74	173	*35	4	7	98	.316	64	55	4	846	69	12	.987
1982— Columbus (Int'l)	OF-1B	130	476	67	150	24	2	10	75	.315	50	24	1	271	17	5	.983
— New York (A.L.)	OF-1B	7	12	0	2	0	0	0	1	.167	0	1	0	15	1	0	1.000
1983— New York (A.L.)	OF-1B-2B	91	279	34	79	15	4	4	32	.283	21	31	0	350	15	3	.992
— Columbus (Int'l)	1B-OF	43	159	35	54	11	3	8	37	.340	29	14	2	325	29	1	.997
1984— New York (A.L.)	1B-OF	153	603	91	*207	*44	2	23	110	*.343	41	33	1	1143	126	6	†.995
1985— New York (A.L.)	1B	159	652	107	211	*48	3	35	*145	.324	56	41	2	1318	87	7	*.995
1986— New York (A.L.)	1B-3B-DH	162	677	117	*238	*53	2	31	113	.352	53	35	0	†1378	111	7	†.995
1987— New York (A.L.)	1B-DH	141	569	93	186	38	2	30	115	.327	51	38	1	1239	91	5	*.996
1988— New York (A.L.)	1B-OF-DH	144	599	94	186	37	0	18	88	.311	41	29	1	1250	99	9	.993
1989— New York (A.L.)	1B-DH-OF	158	631	79	191	37	2	23	113	.303	51	30	3	1276	87	7	.995
1990— New York (A.L.)	1B-DH-OF	102	394	40	101	16	0	5	42	.256	28	20	1	800	78	3	.997
1991— New York (A.L.)	1B-DH	152	587	64	169	35	0	9	68	.288	46	42	2	1119	77	5	.996
1992— New York (A.L.)	1B-DH	157	640	89	184	40	0	14	86	.288	39	43	3	1209	116	4	*.997
1993— New York (A.L.)	1B-DH	134	530	78	154	27	2	17	86	.291	61	42	0	1258	84	3	*.998
1994— New York (A.L.)	1B	97	372	62	113	20	1	6	51	.304	60	24	0	919	68	2	*.998
1995— New York (A.L.)	1B-DH	128	458	59	132	32	2	7	49	.288	40	35	0	997	80	7	.994
Major league totals (14 years)		1785	7003	1007	2153	442	20	222	1099	.307	588	444	14	14271	1120	68	.996

DIVISION SERIES RECORD

		BATTING												FIELDING			
Year Team (League)	Pos.	G	AB	R	H	2B	3B	HR	RBI	Avg.	BB	SO	SB	PO	A	E	Avg.
1995— New York (A.L.)	1B	5	24	3	10	4	0	1	6	.417	1	5	0	36	4	1	.976

ALL-STAR GAME RECORD

		BATTING											FIELDING			
Year League	Pos.	AB	R	H	2B	3B	HR	RBI	Avg.	BB	SO	SB	PO	A	E	Avg.
1984— American	PH	1	0	0	0	0	0	0	.000	0	0	0	. . .	. . .	. . .	. . .
1985— American	1B	1	0	0	0	0	0	0	.000	0	0	0	4	0	0	1.000
1986— American	PH-1B	3	0	0	0	0	0	0	.000	0	2	0	7	0	0	1.000
1987— American	1B	0	0	0	0	0	0	0	. . .	2	0	0	10	0	0	1.000
1988— American	1B	2	0	0	0	0	0	0	.000	0	0	0	2	1	1	.750
1989— American	1B	1	0	1	1	0	0	0	1.000	0	0	0	4	0	0	1.000
All-Star Game totals (6 years)		8	0	1	1	0	0	0	.125	2	2	0	27	1	1	.966

MAUSER, TIM P

PERSONAL: Born October 4, 1966, in Fort Worth, Tex. . . . 6-0/200. . . . Throws right, bats right. . . . Full name: Timothy Edward Mauser.
HIGH SCHOOL: Arlington Heights (Tex.).
COLLEGE: Texas Christian.
TRANSACTIONS/CAREER NOTES: Selected by Philadelphia Phillies organization in third round of free-agent draft (June 1, 1988). . . . Traded by Phillies to San Diego Padres for P Roger Mason (July 3, 1993). . . . On disabled list (May 4-20, 1994). . . . Granted free agency (October 16, 1995).
STATISTICAL NOTES: Pitched 9-0 no-hit victory for Reading against New Britain (August 30, 1989, second game).

Year Team (League)	W	L	Pct.	ERA	G	GS	CG	ShO	Sv.	IP	H	R	ER	BB	SO
1988— Spartanburg (SAL)	2	1	.667	1.96	4	3	0	0	0	23	15	6	5	5	18
— Reading (Eastern)	2	3	.400	3.49	5	5	0	0	0	28 1/3	27	14	11	6	17
1989— Clearwater (Fla. St.)	6	7	.462	2.69	16	16	5	0	0	107	105	40	32	40	73
— Reading (Eastern)	7	4	.636	3.63	11	11	4	2	0	72	62	36	29	33	54
1990— Reading (Eastern)	3	4	.429	3.30	8	8	1	0	0	46 1/3	35	20	17	15	40
— Scran./W.B. (Int'l)	5	7	.417	3.66	16	16	4	1	0	98 1/3	75	48	40	34	54
1991— Scran./W.B. (Int'l)	6	11	.353	3.72	26	18	1	0	1	128 1/3	119	66	53	55	75
— Philadelphia (N.L.)	0	0	. . .	7.59	3	0	0	0	0	10 2/3	18	10	9	3	6
1992— Scran./W.B. (Int'l)	8	6	.571	2.97	45	5	0	0	4	100	87	37	33	45	75
1993— Scran./W.B. (Int'l)	2	0	1.000	0.87	19	0	0	0	10	20 2/3	10	2	2	5	25
— Philadelphia (N.L.)	0	0	. . .	4.96	8	0	0	0	0	16 1/3	15	9	9	7	14
— San Diego (N.L.)■	0	1	.000	3.58	28	0	0	0	0	37 2/3	36	19	15	17	32
1994— San Diego (N.L.)	2	4	.333	3.49	35	0	0	0	2	49	50	21	19	19	32
1995— San Diego (N.L.)	0	1	.000	9.53	5	0	0	0	0	5 2/3	4	6	6	9	9
— Las Vegas (PCL)	3	4	.429	4.80	35	0	0	0	0	50 2/3	63	39	27	20	32
Major league totals (4 years)	2	6	.250	4.37	79	0	0	0	2	119 1/3	123	65	58	55	93

MAXCY, BRIAN P TIGERS

PERSONAL: Born May 4, 1971, in Amory, Miss. . . . 6-1/170. . . . Throws right, bats right. . . . Full name: David Brian Maxcy.
COLLEGE: Mississippi.
TRANSACTIONS/CAREER NOTES: Selected by Detroit Tigers organization in 29th round of free-agent draft (June 1, 1992). . . . On Toledo disabled list (August 6-September 13, 1994 and April 6-23, 1995).

Year Team (League)	W	L	Pct.	ERA	G	GS	CG	ShO	Sv.	IP	H	R	ER	BB	SO
1992— Bristol (Appal.)	4	2	.667	3.47	14	7	2	•2	3	49 1/3	41	24	19	17	43
1993— Fayetteville (S. Atl.)	12	4	.750	2.93	39	12	1	1	9	113 2/3	111	51	37	42	101
1994— Trenton (Eastern)	0	0	. . .	0.00	5	0	0	0	1	10 2/3	6	1	0	4	5

Year	Team (League)	W	L	Pct.	ERA	G	GS	CG	ShO	Sv.	IP	H	R	ER	BB	SO
	—Toledo (Int'l)	2	3	.400	1.62	24	1	0	0	3	44 1/3	31	12	8	18	43
1995—	Toledo (Int'l)	1	3	.250	5.26	20	0	0	0	2	25 2/3	32	20	15	11	11
	—Detroit (A.L.)	4	5	.444	6.88	41	0	0	0	0	52 1/3	61	48	40	31	20
Major league totals (1 year)		4	5	.444	6.88	41	0	0	0	0	52 1/3	61	48	40	31	20

MAXWELL, JASON — SS — CUBS

PERSONAL: Born March 21, 1972, in Lewisburg, Tenn. . . . 6-1/175. . . . Bats right, throws right. . . . Full name: Jason Ramond Maxwell.
HIGH SCHOOL: Marshall County (Lewisburg, Tenn.).
COLLEGE: Middle Tennessee.
TRANSACTIONS/CAREER NOTES: Selected by Chicago Cubs organization in 74th round of free-agent draft (June 3, 1993).

			BATTING											FIELDING			
Year	Team (League)	Pos.	G	AB	R	H	2B	3B	HR	RBI	Avg.	BB	SO	SB	PO	A	E	Avg.
1993—	Hunting. (Appal.)	SS	61	179	50	52	7	2	7	38	.291	35	39	6	60	140	9	.957
1994—	Daytona (Fla. St.)	SS	116	368	71	85	18	2	10	31	.231	55	96	7	167	333	*38	.929
1995—	Daytona (Fla. St.)	SS	117	388	66	102	13	3	10	58	.263	63	68	12	181	325	16	*.969

MAY, DARRELL — P — BRAVES

PERSONAL: Born June 13, 1972, in San Bernardino, Calif. . . . 6-2/170. . . . Throws left, bats left. . . . Full name: Darrell Kevin May.
HIGH SCHOOL: Rogue River (Ore.).
COLLEGE: Sacramento (Calif.) City College.
TRANSACTIONS/CAREER NOTES: Selected by Atlanta Braves organization in 46th round of free-agent draft (June 1, 1992).

Year	Team (League)	W	L	Pct.	ERA	G	GS	CG	ShO	Sv.	IP	H	R	ER	BB	SO
1992—	GC Braves (GCL)	4	3	.571	1.36	12	7	0	0	1	53	34	13	8	13	61
1993—	Macon (S. Atl.)	10	4	.714	2.24	17	17	0	0	0	104 1/3	81	29	26	22	111
	—Durham (Carolina)	5	2	.714	2.09	9	9	0	0	0	51 2/3	44	18	12	16	47
1994—	Greenville (South.)	5	3	.625	3.11	11	11	1	0	0	63 2/3	61	25	22	17	42
	—Durham (Carolina)	8	2	*.800	3.01	12	12	1	0	0	74 2/3	74	29	25	17	73
1995—	Greenville (South.)	2	8	.200	3.55	15	15	0	0	0	91 1/3	81	44	36	20	79
	—Richmond (Int'l)	4	2	.667	3.71	9	9	0	0	0	51	53	21	21	16	42
	—Atlanta (N.L.)	0	0	...	11.25	2	0	0	0	0	4	10	5	5	0	1
Major league totals (1 year)		0	0	...	11.25	2	0	0	0	0	4	10	5	5	0	1

MAY, DERRICK — OF — ASTROS

PERSONAL: Born July 14, 1968, in Rochester, N.Y. . . . 6-4/225. . . . Bats left, throws right. . . . Full name: Derrick Brant May. . . . Son of Dave May, major league outfielder with five teams (1967-78).
HIGH SCHOOL: Newark (Del.).
TRANSACTIONS/CAREER NOTES: Selected by Chicago Cubs organization in first round (ninth pick overall) of free-agent draft (June 2, 1986). . . . On Iowa disabled list (April 14-May 27 and June 6-24, 1991). . . . Granted free agency (April 7, 1995). . . . Signed by New Orleans, Milwaukee Brewers organization (April 12, 1995). . . . Traded by Brewers to Houston Astros for a player to be named later (June 21, 1995).
STATISTICAL NOTES: Tied for Carolina League lead in double plays by outfielder with four in 1988. . . . Career major league grand slams: 2.

			BATTING											FIELDING			
Year	Team (League)	Pos.	G	AB	R	H	2B	3B	HR	RBI	Avg.	BB	SO	SB	PO	A	E	Avg.
1986—	Wytheville (Appal.)	OF	54	178	25	57	6	1	0	23	.320	16	15	17	47	3	5	.909
1987—	Peoria (Midwest)	OF	128	439	60	131	19	8	9	52	.298	42	106	5	181	13	8	.960
1988—	Winst.-Salem (Car.)	OF	130	485	76	•148	29	*9	8	65	.305	37	82	13	209	13	10	.957
1989—	Charlotte (South.)	OF	136	491	72	145	26	5	9	70	.295	34	77	19	239	8	•13	.950
1990—	Iowa (Am. Assoc.)	OF-1B	119	459	55	136	27	1	8	69	.296	23	50	5	159	10	8	.955
	—Chicago (N.L.)	OF	17	61	8	15	3	0	1	11	.246	2	7	1	34	1	1	.972
1991—	Iowa (Am. Assoc.)	OF	82	310	47	92	18	4	3	49	.297	19	38	7	130	2	5	.964
	—Chicago (N.L.)	OF	15	22	4	5	2	0	1	3	.227	2	1	0	11	1	0	1.000
1992—	Iowa (Am. Assoc.)	OF	8	30	6	11	4	1	2	8	.367	3	3	0	11	1	0	1.000
	—Chicago (N.L.)	OF	124	351	33	96	11	0	8	45	.274	14	40	5	153	3	5	.969
1993—	Chicago (N.L.)	OF	128	465	62	137	25	2	10	77	.295	31	41	10	220	8	7	.970
1994—	Chicago (N.L.)	OF	100	345	43	98	19	2	8	51	.284	30	34	3	155	4	1	.994
1995—	Milwaukee (A.L.)■	OF	32	113	15	28	3	1	1	9	.248	5	18	0	65	1	2	.971
	—Houston (N.L.)■	OF-1B	78	206	29	62	15	1	8	41	.301	19	24	5	74	0	2	.974
American League totals (1 year)			32	113	15	28	3	1	1	9	.248	5	18	0	65	1	2	.971
National League totals (6 years)			462	1450	179	413	75	5	36	228	.285	98	147	24	647	17	16	.976
Major league totals (6 years)			494	1563	194	441	78	6	37	237	.282	103	165	24	712	18	18	.976

MAYNE, BRENT — C — METS

PERSONAL: Born April 19, 1968, in Loma Linda, Calif. . . . 6-1/190. . . . Bats left, throws right. . . . Full name: Brent Danem Mayne.
HIGH SCHOOL: Costa Mesa (Calif.).
JUNIOR COLLEGE: Orange Coast College (Calif.).
COLLEGE: Cal State Fullerton.
TRANSACTIONS/CAREER NOTES: Selected by Kansas City Royals organization in first round (13th pick overall) of free-agent draft (June 5, 1989). . . . On disabled list (July 24, 1989-remainder of season). . . . Traded by Royals to New York Mets for OF Al Shirley (December 19, 1995).
STATISTICAL NOTES: Led A.L. catchers with 11 double plays in 1995. . . . Career major league grand slams: 1.

Year	Team (League)	Pos.	G	AB	R	H	2B	3B	HR	RBI	Avg.	BB	SO	SB	PO	A	E	Avg.
							BATTING								FIELDING			
1989—	Baseball City (FSL)	C	7	24	5	13	3	1	0	8	.542	0	3	0	31	2	0	1.000
1990—	Memphis (South.)	C	115	412	48	110	16	3	2	61	.267	52	51	5	591	61	11	.983
—	Kansas City (A.L.)	C	5	13	2	3	0	0	0	1	.231	3	3	0	29	3	1	.970
1991—	Kansas City (A.L.)	C-DH	85	231	22	58	8	0	3	31	.251	23	42	2	425	38	6	.987
1992—	Kansas City (A.L.)	C-3B-DH	82	213	16	48	10	0	0	18	.225	11	26	0	281	33	3	.991
1993—	Kansas City (A.L.)	C-DH	71	205	22	52	9	1	2	22	.254	18	31	3	356	27	2	.995
1994—	Kansas City (A.L.)	C-DH	46	144	19	37	5	1	2	20	.257	14	27	1	246	14	1	.996
1995—	Kansas City (A.L.)	C	110	307	23	77	18	1	1	27	.251	25	41	0	540	40	3	.995
Major league totals (6 years)			399	1113	104	275	50	3	8	119	.247	94	170	6	1877	155	16	.992

McANDREW, JAMIE — P — BREWERS

PERSONAL: Born September 2, 1967, in Williamsport, Pa. . . . 6-2/190. . . . Throws right, bats right. . . . Full name: James Brian McAndrew. . . . Son of Jim McAndrew, pitcher, New York Mets and San Diego Padres (1968-74).

HIGH SCHOOL: Ponderosa (Fla.).

COLLEGE: Florida.

TRANSACTIONS/CAREER NOTES: Selected by Seattle Mariners organization in 23rd round of free-agent draft (June 2, 1986); did not sign. . . . Selected by Los Angeles Dodgers organization in supplemental round ("sandwich pick" between first and second round, 28th pick overall) of free-agent draft (June 5, 1989); pick received as part of compensation for New York Yankees signing Type A free-agent 2B Steve Sax. . . . On San Antonio disabled list (May 2-July 6, 1992). . . . Selected by Florida Marlins in third round (57th pick overall) of expansion draft (November 17, 1992). . . . Traded by Marlins to Milwaukee Brewers for P Tom McGraw (April 2, 1993). . . . On New Orleans disabled list (April 7, 1994-entire season). . . . On Milwaukee disabled list (August 29-September 28, 1995).

Year	Team (League)	W	L	Pct.	ERA	G	GS	CG	ShO	Sv.	IP	H	R	ER	BB	SO
1989—	Great Falls (Pio.)	*11	0	*1.000	1.65	13	13	1	0	0	76 1/3	49	16	14	27	72
1990—	San Antonio (Tex.)	7	3	.700	1.93	12	12	0	0	0	79 1/3	68	28	17	32	50
—	Bakersfield (Calif.)	10	3	.769	2.27	14	14	1	1	0	95	88	31	24	29	82
1991—	Albuquerque (PCL)	12	10	.545	5.04	28	26	0	0	1	155 1/3	167	105	87	76	91
1992—	Albuquerque (PCL)	1	3	.250	5.83	5	5	0	0	0	29 1/3	41	20	19	14	9
—	San Antonio (Tex.)	3	4	.429	3.58	11	8	0	0	0	50 1/3	50	26	20	19	35
1993—	New Orleans (A.A.)■	11	6	.647	3.94	27	25	5	1	0	166 2/3	172	78	73	45	97
1994—							Did not play.									
1995—	New Orleans (A.A.)	7	5	.583	3.97	17	17	3	1	0	104 1/3	102	48	46	44	62
—	Milwaukee (A.L.)	2	3	.400	4.71	10	4	0	0	0	36 1/3	37	21	19	12	19
Major league totals (1 year)		2	3	.400	4.71	10	4	0	0	0	36 1/3	37	21	19	12	19

McCARTY, DAVID — OF/1B — GIANTS

PERSONAL: Born November 23, 1969, in Houston. . . . 6-5/207. . . . Bats right, throws left. . . . Full name: David Andrew McCarty.

HIGH SCHOOL: Sharpstown (Houston).

COLLEGE: Stanford.

TRANSACTIONS/CAREER NOTES: Selected by Minnesota Twins organization in first round (third pick overall) of free-agent draft (June 3, 1991). . . . Traded by Twins to Cincinnati Reds for P John Courtright (June 8, 1995). . . . Traded by Reds with OF Deion Sanders, P Ricky Pickett, P Scott Service and P John Roper to San Francisco Giants for OF Darren Lewis, P Mark Portugal and P Dave Burba (July 21, 1995).

Year	Team (League)	Pos.	G	AB	R	H	2B	3B	HR	RBI	Avg.	BB	SO	SB	PO	A	E	Avg.
							BATTING								FIELDING			
1991—	Visalia (California)	OF	15	50	16	19	3	0	3	8	.380	13	7	3	23	1	0	1.000
—	Orlando (Southern)	OF	28	88	18	23	4	0	3	11	.261	10	20	0	38	4	1	.977
1992—	Orlando (Southern)	OF-1B	129	456	75	124	16	2	18	79	.272	55	89	6	357	32	9	.977
—	Portland (PCL)	OF-1B	7	26	7	13	2	0	1	8	.500	5	3	1	40	3	1	.977
1993—	Portland (PCL)	OF-1B	40	143	42	55	11	0	8	31	.385	27	25	5	185	21	2	.990
—	Minnesota (A.L.)	OF-1B-DH	98	350	36	75	15	2	2	21	.214	19	80	2	412	38	8	.983
1994—	Minnesota (A.L.)	1B-OF	44	131	21	34	8	2	1	12	.260	7	32	2	243	28	5	.982
—	Salt Lake (PCL)	OF-1B	55	186	32	47	9	3	3	19	.253	35	34	1	191	16	5	.976
1995—	Minnesota (A.L.)	1B-OF	25	55	10	12	3	1	0	4	.218	4	18	0	130	10	1	.993
—	Indianapolis (A.A.)■	1B	37	140	31	47	10	1	8	32	.336	15	30	0	335	14	2	.994
—	Phoenix (PCL)■	1B-OF	37	151	31	53	19	2	4	19	.351	17	27	1	330	32	2	.995
—	San Francisco (N.L.)	OF-1B	12	20	1	5	1	0	0	2	.250	2	4	1	19	0	1	.950
American League totals (3 years)			167	536	67	121	26	5	3	37	.226	30	130	4	785	76	14	.984
National League totals (1 year)			12	20	1	5	1	0	0	2	.250	2	4	1	19	0	1	.950
Major league totals (3 years)			179	556	68	126	27	5	3	39	.227	32	134	5	804	76	15	.983

McCASKILL, KIRK — P — WHITE SOX

PERSONAL: Born April 9, 1961, in Kapuskasing, Ont. . . . 6-1/205. . . . Throws right, bats right. . . . Full name: Kirk Edward McCaskill. . . . Son of Ted McCaskill, National Hockey League and World Hockey Association player (1967-68, 1972-73 and 1973-74).

HIGH SCHOOL: Trinity Pawling (Pawling, N.Y.).

COLLEGE: Vermont.

TRANSACTIONS/CAREER NOTES: Selected by California Angels organization in fourth round of free-agent draft (June 7, 1982). . . . On suspended list (August 30, 1983); transferred to disqualified list (September 26, 1983-April 25, 1984). . . . On California disabled list (April 24-July 11, 1987); included rehabilitation assignments to Palm Springs (June 24-July 2) and Edmonton (July 3-8). . . . On disabled list (August 9, 1988-remainder of season). . . . Granted free agency (October 30, 1991). . . . Signed by Chicago White Sox (December 28, 1991). . . . On Chicago disabled list (June 15-10, 1993); included rehabilitation assignment to South Bend (June 25-30). . . . Granted free agency (October 25, 1994). . . . Signed by Chicago White Sox (April 7, 1995).

STATISTICAL NOTES: Pitched 7-1 one-hit, complete-game victory against Texas (June 25, 1986). . . . Pitched 9-0 one-hit, complete-game victory against Toronto (April 28, 1989).

Year	Team (League)	W	L	Pct.	ERA	G	GS	CG	ShO	Sv.	IP	H	R	ER	BB	SO
1982—	Salem (Northwest)	5	5	.500	4.29	11	11	1	0	0	71 1/3	63	43	34	51	87
1983—	Redwood (Calif.)	6	5	.545	2.33	16	15	4	0	0	108 1/3	78	39	28	60	100
—	Nashua (Eastern)	4	8	.333	4.45	13	13	3	0	0	87	90	47	43	43	63
1984—	Edmonton (PCL)	7	11	.389	5.73	24	22	2	0	0	143	162	104	91	74	75
1985—	Edmonton (PCL)	1	1	.500	2.04	3	3	0	0	0	17 2/3	17	7	4	6	18
—	California (A.L.)	12	12	.500	4.70	30	29	6	1	0	189 2/3	189	105	99	64	102
1986—	California (A.L.)	17	10	.630	3.36	34	33	10	2	0	246 1/3	207	98	92	92	202
1987—	California (A.L.)	4	6	.400	5.67	14	13	1	1	0	74 2/3	84	52	47	34	56
—	Palm Springs (Cal.)	2	0	1.000	0.00	2	2	0	0	0	10	4	1	0	3	7
—	Edmonton (PCL)	1	0	1.000	3.00	1	1	0	0	0	6	3	2	2	4	4
1988—	California (A.L.)	8	6	.571	4.31	23	23	4	2	0	146 1/3	155	78	70	61	98
1989—	California (A.L.)	15	10	.600	2.93	32	32	6	4	0	212	202	73	69	59	107
1990—	California (A.L.)	12	11	.522	3.25	29	29	2	1	0	174 1/3	161	77	63	72	78
1991—	California (A.L.)	10	*19	.345	4.26	30	30	1	0	0	177 2/3	193	93	84	66	71
1992—	Chicago (A.L.)■	12	13	.480	4.18	34	34	0	0	0	209	193	116	97	95	109
1993—	Chicago (A.L.)	4	8	.333	5.23	30	14	0	0	2	113 2/3	144	71	66	36	65
—	South Bend (Midw.)	1	0	1.000	1.50	1	1	0	0	0	6	3	2	1	3	5
1994—	Chicago (A.L.)	1	4	.200	3.42	40	0	0	0	3	52 2/3	51	22	20	22	37
1995—	Chicago (A.L.)	6	4	.600	4.89	55	1	0	0	2	81	97	50	44	33	50
Major league totals (11 years)		101	103	.495	4.03	351	238	30	11	7	1677 1/3	1676	835	751	634	975

CHAMPIONSHIP SERIES RECORD

NOTES: Holds single-series record for most runs allowed—13 (1986). . . . Shares record for most hits allowed in one inning—6 (October 14, 1986, third inning).

Year	Team (League)	W	L	Pct.	ERA	G	GS	CG	ShO	Sv.	IP	H	R	ER	BB	SO
1986—	California (A.L.)	0	2	.000	7.71	2	2	0	0	0	9 1/3	16	13	8	5	7
1993—	Chicago (A.L.)	0	0	...	0.00	3	0	0	0	0	3 2/3	3	0	0	1	3
Champ. series totals (2 years)		0	2	.000	5.54	5	2	0	0	0	13	19	13	8	6	10

RECORD AS HOCKEY PLAYER

PERSONAL: Played center/right wing. . . . Shot right.

CAREER NOTES: Selected by Winnipeg Jets in fourth round (64th pick overall) of National Hockey League entry draft (June 1981).

		REGULAR SEASON					PLAYOFFS				
Season Team	League	Gms.	G	A	Pts.	PIM	Gms.	G	A	Pts.	PIM
83-84—Sherbrooke Jets	AHL	78	10	12	22	21	—	—	—	—	—

M

McCLAIN, SCOTT — 3B — ORIOLES

PERSONAL: Born May 19, 1972, in Simi Valley, Calif. . . . 6-4/210. . . . Bats right, throws right. . . . Full name: Scott Michael McClain.

HIGH SCHOOL: Atascadero (Calif.).

TRANSACTIONS/CAREER NOTES: Selected by Baltimore Orioles organization in 22nd round of free-agent draft (June 4, 1990).

STATISTICAL NOTES: Led Carolina League third basemen with 113 putouts in 1993. . . . Led Eastern League third basemen with 111 putouts in 1994.

				BATTING											FIELDING			
Year	Team (League)	Pos.	G	AB	R	H	2B	3B	HR	RBI	Avg.	BB	SO	SB	PO	A	E	Avg.
1990—	Bluefield (Appal.)	3B-OF-P	40	107	20	21	2	0	4	15	.196	22	35	2	27	46	8	.901
1991—	Kane Co. (Midw.)	3B	25	81	9	18	0	0	0	4	.222	17	25	1	12	53	4	.942
—	Bluefield (Appal.)	3B-2B-SS	41	148	16	39	5	0	0	24	.264	15	39	5	33	79	15	.882
1992—	Kane Co. (Midw.)	3B-SS	96	316	43	84	12	2	3	30	.266	48	62	7	97	192	26	.917
1993—	Frederick (Caro.)	3B-SS-1B	133	427	65	111	22	2	9	54	.260	70	88	10	†114	239	24	.936
1994—	Bowie (Eastern)	3B-SS	133	427	71	103	29	1	11	58	.241	72	89	6	†111	224	22	.938
1995—	Bowie (Eastern)	3B	70	259	41	72	14	1	13	61	.278	25	44	2	57	165	16	.933
—	Rochester (Int'l)	3B	61	199	32	50	9	1	8	22	.251	23	34	0	41	130	11	.940

RECORD AS PITCHER

Year	Team (League)	W	L	Pct.	ERA	G	GS	CG	ShO	Sv.	IP	H	R	ER	BB	SO
1990—	Bluefield (Appal.)	0	0	...	9.00	1	0	0	0	0	1	1	1	1	0	0

McCRACKEN, QUINTON — OF — ROCKIES

PERSONAL: Born March 16, 1970, in Wilmington, N.C. . . . 5-7/173. . . . Bats both, throws right. . . . Full name: Quinton Antoine McCracken.

HIGH SCHOOL: South Brunswick (Southport, N.C.).

COLLEGE: Duke.

TRANSACTIONS/CAREER NOTES: Selected by Colorado Rockies organization in 25th round of free-agent draft (June 1, 1992).

STATISTICAL NOTES: Led California League with 12 sacrifice hits in 1993. . . . Led Eastern League in caught stealing with 19 in 1994.

				BATTING											FIELDING			
Year	Team (League)	Pos.	G	AB	R	H	2B	3B	HR	RBI	Avg.	BB	SO	SB	PO	A	E	Avg.
1992—	Bend (Northwest)	2B-OF	67	232	37	65	13	2	0	27	.280	25	39	18	98	129	17	.930
1993—	Central Vall. (Cal.)	OF-2B	127	483	94	141	17	7	2	58	.292	78	90	60	153	75	13	.946
1994—	New Haven (East.)	OF	136	544	94	151	27	4	5	39	.278	48	72	36	273	6	8	.972
1995—	New Haven (East.)	OF	55	221	33	79	11	4	1	26	.357	21	32	26	92	10	3	.971
—	Colo. Springs (PCL)	OF	61	244	55	88	14	6	3	28	.361	23	30	17	104	5	1	.991
—	Colorado (N.L.)	OF	3	1	0	0	0	0	0	0	.000	0	1	0	0	0	0	...
Major league totals (1 year)			3	1	0	0	0	0	0	0	.000	0	1	0	0	0	0	...

McCURRY, JEFF — P — TIGERS

PERSONAL: Born January 21, 1970, in Tokyo, Japan. . . . 6-7/210. . . . Throws right, bats right. . . . Full name: Jeffrey Dee McCurry.
HIGH SCHOOL: St. Thomas (Houston).
COLLEGE: San Jacinto (North) College (Tex.).
TRANSACTIONS/CAREER NOTES: Selected by Pittsburgh Pirates organization in 20th round of free-agent draft (June 5, 1989); did not sign. . . . Selected by Pirates organization in 14th round of free-agent draft (June 4, 1990). . . . On Welland disabled list (June 19-July 12, 1991). . . . Claimed on waivers by Detroit Tigers (November 20, 1995).

Year	Team (League)	W	L	Pct.	ERA	G	GS	CG	ShO	Sv.	IP	H	R	ER	BB	SO
1991—	GC Pirates (GCL)	1	0	1.000	2.57	6	1	0	0	0	14	19	10	4	4	8
—	Welland (NYP)	2	1	.667	0.57	9	0	0	0	0	15 2/3	11	4	1	10	18
1992—	Augusta (S. Atl.)	2	1	.667	3.30	19	0	0	0	7	30	36	14	11	15	34
—	Salem (Carolina)	6	2	.750	2.87	30	0	0	0	3	62 2/3	49	22	20	24	52
1993—	Salem (Carolina)	1	4	.200	3.89	41	0	0	0	22	44	41	21	19	15	32
—	Carolina (South.)	2	1	.667	2.79	23	0	0	0	0	29	24	11	9	14	14
1994—	Carolina (South.)	6	5	.545	3.21	48	2	0	0	11	81 1/3	74	35	29	30	60
1995—	Calgary (PCL)	0	0	...	1.80	3	0	0	0	0	5	3	1	1	2	2
—	Pittsburgh (N.L.)	1	4	.200	5.02	55	0	0	0	1	61	82	38	34	30	27
Major league totals (1 year)		1	4	.200	5.02	55	0	0	0	1	61	82	38	34	30	27

McDAVID, RAY — OF — EXPOS

PERSONAL: Born July 20, 1971, in San Diego. . . . 6-2/200. . . . Bats left, throws right. . . . Full name: Ray Darnell McDavid.
HIGH SCHOOL: Clairemont (San Diego).
COLLEGE: Arizona Western College.
TRANSACTIONS/CAREER NOTES: Selected by San Diego Padres organization in ninth round of free-agent draft (June 5, 1989). . . . On Las Vegas disabled list (May 24-August 9, 1995). . . . Claimed on waivers by Montreal Expos (December 21, 1995).

				BATTING											FIELDING			
Year	Team (League)	Pos.	G	AB	R	H	2B	3B	HR	RBI	Avg.	BB	SO	SB	PO	A	E	Avg.
1990—	Ariz. Padres (Ariz.)	OF	13	41	4	6	0	2	0	1	.146	6	5	3	30	2	1	.970
1991—	Char., S.C. (S. Atl.)	OF	127	425	93	105	16	9	10	45	.247	*106	119	60	269	9	6	.979
1992—	High Desert (Calif.)	OF	123	428	94	118	22	5	24	94	.276	94	126	43	206	4	4	.981
1993—	Wichita (Texas)	OF	126	441	65	119	18	5	11	55	.270	70	104	33	259	8	10	.964
1994—	Las Vegas (PCL)	OF	128	476	85	129	24	6	13	62	.271	67	110	24	293	9	13	.959
—	San Diego (N.L.)	OF	9	28	2	7	1	0	0	2	.250	1	8	1	11	0	0	1.000
1995—	Las Vegas (PCL)	OF	52	166	28	45	8	1	5	27	.271	30	35	7	134	0	0	1.000
—	Ariz. Padres (Ariz.)	OF	9	28	13	13	2	1	1	6	.464	8	7	3	1	0	0	1.000
—	San Diego (N.L.)	OF	11	17	2	3	0	0	0	0	.176	2	6	1	5	0	0	1.000
Major league totals (2 years)			20	45	4	10	1	0	0	2	.222	3	14	2	16	0	0	1.000

McDONALD, BEN — P — BREWERS

PERSONAL: Born November 24, 1967, in Baton Rouge, La. . . . 6-7/214. . . . Throws right, bats right. . . . Full name: Larry Benard McDonald.
HIGH SCHOOL: Denham Springs (La.).
COLLEGE: Louisiana State.
TRANSACTIONS/CAREER NOTES: Selected by Atlanta Braves organization in 27th round of free-agent draft (June 2, 1986); did not sign. . . . Selected by Baltimore Orioles organization in first round (first pick overall) of free-agent draft (June 5, 1989). . . . On Baltimore disabled list (April 6-May 22, 1990); included rehabilitation assignments to Hagerstown (April 24-29 and May 14) and Rochester (April 30-May 13 and May 15-21). . . . On Baltimore disabled list (March 29-April 19, 1991). . . . On Baltimore disabled list (May 23-July 1, 1991); included rehabilitation assignment to Rochester (June 19-July 1). . . . On Baltimore disabled list (June 17-July 14 and July 20-September 11, 1995); included rehabilitation assignment to Rochester (August 31-September 11). . . . Granted free agency (December 21, 1995). . . . Signed by Milwaukee Brewers (January 20, 1996).
HONORS: Named Golden Spikes Award winner by USA Baseball (1989). . . . Named College Player of the Year by The Sporting News (1989). . . . Named righthanded pitcher on The Sporting News college All-America team (1989).
STATISTICAL NOTES: Pitched 7-0 one-hit, complete-game victory against Kansas City (July 20, 1993). . . . Pitched 4-0 one-hit, complete-game victory against Milwaukee (August 5, 1994).
MISCELLANEOUS: Member of 1988 U.S. Olympic baseball team.

Year	Team (League)	W	L	Pct.	ERA	G	GS	CG	ShO	Sv.	IP	H	R	ER	BB	SO
1989—	Frederick (Caro.)	0	0	...	2.00	2	2	0	0	0	9	10	2	2	0	9
—	Baltimore (A.L.)	1	0	1.000	8.59	6	0	0	0	0	7 1/3	8	7	7	4	3
1990—	Hagerstown (East.)	0	1	.000	6.55	3	3	0	0	0	11	11	8	8	3	15
—	Rochester (Int'l)	3	3	.500	2.86	7	7	0	0	0	44	33	18	14	21	37
—	Baltimore (A.L.)	8	5	.615	2.43	21	15	3	2	0	118 2/3	88	36	32	35	65
1991—	Baltimore (A.L.)	6	8	.429	4.84	21	21	1	0	0	126 1/3	126	71	68	43	85
—	Rochester (Int'l)	0	1	.000	7.71	2	2	0	0	0	7	10	7	6	5	7
1992—	Baltimore (A.L.)	13	13	.500	4.24	35	35	4	2	0	227	213	113	107	74	158
1993—	Baltimore (A.L.)	13	14	.481	3.39	34	34	7	1	0	220 1/3	185	92	83	86	171
1994—	Baltimore (A.L.)	14	7	.667	4.06	24	24	5	1	0	157 1/3	151	75	71	54	94
1995—	Baltimore (A.L.)	3	6	.333	4.16	14	13	1	0	0	80	67	40	37	38	62
—	Rochester (Int'l)	0	0	...	2.45	1	1	0	0	0	3 2/3	1	2	1	4	1
Major league totals (7 years)		58	53	.523	3.89	155	142	21	6	0	937	838	434	405	334	638

McDONALD, JASON — SS/OF — ATHLETICS

PERSONAL: Born March 20, 1972, in Modesto, Calif. . . . 5-8/175. . . . Bats both, throws right. . . . Full name: Jason Adam McDonald.
HIGH SCHOOL: Elk Grove (Calif.) Unified School.
COLLEGE: Houston.

TRANSACTIONS/CAREER NOTES: Selected by Oakland Athletics organization in fourth round of free-agent draft (June 3, 1993).
STATISTICAL NOTES: Led California League shortstops with 43 errors in 1995.

			BATTING											FIELDING			
Year	Team (League)	Pos.	G	AB	R	H	2B	3B	HR	RBI	Avg.	BB	SO	SB	PO	A	E	Avg.
1993—	S. Oregon (N'west)	2B	35	112	26	33	5	2	0	8	.295	31	17	22	70	77	7	.955
1994—	West. Mich. (Mid.)	2B-OF-SS	116	404	67	96	11	*9	2	31	.238	81	87	52	253	167	21	.952
1995—	Modesto (Calif.)	SS-OF-2B	133	493	109	129	25	7	6	50	.262	*110	84	*70	247	246	†50	.908

McDOWELL, JACK — P — INDIANS

PERSONAL: Born January 16, 1966, in Van Nuys, Calif. . . . 6-5/188. . . . Throws right, bats right. . . . Full name: Jack Burns McDowell.
HIGH SCHOOL: Notre Dame (Van Nuys, Calif.).
COLLEGE: Stanford.
TRANSACTIONS/CAREER NOTES: Selected by Boston Red Sox organization in 20th round of free-agent draft (June 4, 1984); did not sign. . . . Selected by Chicago White Sox organization in first round (fifth pick overall) of free-agent draft (June 2, 1987). . . . On suspended list (August 20-24, 1991). . . . Traded by White Sox to New York Yankees for P Keith Heberling and a player to be named later (December 14, 1994); White Sox acquired OF Lyle Mouton to complete deal (April 22, 1995). . . . Granted free agency (October 31, 1995). . . . Signed by Cleveland Indians (December 14, 1995).
HONORS: Named righthanded pitcher on The Sporting News A.L. All-Star team (1992-93). . . . Named A.L. Pitcher of the Year by The Sporting News (1993). . . . Named A.L. Cy Young Award winner by Baseball Writers' Association of America (1993).
STATISTICAL NOTES: Pitched 15-1 one-hit, complete-game victory against Milwaukee (July 14, 1991).

Year	Team (League)	W	L	Pct.	ERA	G	GS	CG	ShO	Sv.	IP	H	R	ER	BB	SO
1987—	GC White Sox (GCL)	0	1	.000	2.57	2	1	0	0	0	7	4	3	2	1	12
—	Birmingham (Sou.)	1	2	.333	7.84	4	4	1	1	0	20 2/3	19	20	18	8	17
—	Chicago (A.L.)	3	0	1.000	1.93	4	4	0	0	0	28	16	6	6	6	15
1988—	Chicago (A.L.)	5	10	.333	3.97	26	26	1	0	0	158 2/3	147	85	70	68	84
1989—	Vancouver (PCL)	5	6	.455	6.13	16	16	1	0	0	86 2/3	97	60	59	50	65
—	GC White Sox (GCL)	2	0	1.000	0.75	4	4	0	0	0	24	19	2	2	4	25
1990—	Chicago (A.L.)	14	9	.609	3.82	33	33	4	0	0	205	189	93	87	77	165
1991—	Chicago (A.L.)	17	10	.630	3.41	35	•35	*15	3	0	253 2/3	212	97	96	82	191
1992—	Chicago (A.L.)	20	10	.667	3.18	34	34	*13	1	0	260 2/3	247	95	92	75	178
1993—	Chicago (A.L.)	*22	10	.688	3.37	34	34	10	*4	0	256 2/3	261	104	96	69	158
1994—	Chicago (A.L.)	10	9	.526	3.73	25	•25	6	2	0	181	186	82	75	42	127
1995—	New York (A.L.)■	15	10	.600	3.93	30	30	*8	2	0	217 2/3	211	106	95	78	157
	Major league totals (8 years)	106	68	.609	3.56	221	221	57	12	0	1561 1/3	1469	668	617	497	1075

DIVISION SERIES RECORD

Year	Team (League)	W	L	Pct.	ERA	G	GS	CG	ShO	Sv.	IP	H	R	ER	BB	SO
1995—	New York (A.L.)	0	2	.000	9.00	2	1	0	0	0	7	8	7	7	4	6

CHAMPIONSHIP SERIES RECORD

NOTES: Holds single-game record for most hits allowed—13 (October 5, 1993). . . . Shares single-game record for most earned runs allowed—7 (October 5, 1993).

Year	Team (League)	W	L	Pct.	ERA	G	GS	CG	ShO	Sv.	IP	H	R	ER	BB	SO
1993—	Chicago (A.L.)	0	2	.000	10.00	2	2	0	0	0	9	18	10	10	5	5

ALL-STAR GAME RECORD

Year	League	W	L	Pct.	ERA	GS	CG	ShO	Sv.	IP	H	R	ER	BB	SO
1991—	American	0	0	. . .	0.00	0	0	0	0	2	1	0	0	2	0
1992—	American	0	0	. . .	0.00	0	0	0	0	1	0	0	0	0	0
1993—	American	1	0	1.000	0.00	0	0	0	0	1	0	0	0	0	0
	All-Star totals (3 years)	1	0	1.000	0.00	0	0	0	0	4	1	0	0	2	0

McDOWELL, ROGER — P — ORIOLES

PERSONAL: Born December 21, 1960, in Cincinnati. . . . 6-1/197. . . . Throws right, bats right. . . . Full name: Roger Alan McDowell.
HIGH SCHOOL: Colerain (Cincinnati).
COLLEGE: Bowling Green State.
TRANSACTIONS/CAREER NOTES: Selected by New York Mets organization in third round of free-agent draft (June 7, 1982). . . . On disabled list (April 10-August 14, 1984 and March 29-May 14, 1987). . . . Traded by Mets with OF Lenny Dykstra and a player to be named later to Philadelphia Phillies for OF Juan Samuel (June 18, 1989); Phillies organization acquired P Tom Edens to complete deal (July 27, 1989). . . . On disabled list (July 1-18, 1991). . . . Traded by Phillies to Los Angeles Dodgers for P Mike Hartley and OF Braulio Castillo (July 31, 1991). . . . Granted free agency (October 28, 1992). . . . Re-signed by Dodgers (December 5, 1992). . . . Granted free agency (October 11, 1994). . . . Signed by Texas Rangers (April 11, 1995). . . . Granted free agency (November 3, 1995). . . . Signed by Baltimore Orioles (December 18, 1995).
MISCELLANEOUS: Appeared in one game as outfielder with no chances (1986). . . . Appeared in one game as pinch-runner (1988). . . . Appeared in two games as outfielder with no chances with Los Angeles (1991).

Year	Team (League)	W	L	Pct.	ERA	G	GS	CG	ShO	Sv.	IP	H	R	ER	BB	SO
1982—	Shelby (S. Atl.)	6	4	.600	3.28	12	11	4	0	0	71 1/3	61	34	26	30	40
—	Lynchburg (Caro.)	2	0	1.000	2.15	4	4	2	1	0	29 1/3	26	12	7	11	23
1983—	Jackson (Texas)	11	12	.478	4.86	27	26	9	1	0	172 1/3	203	111	93	71	115
1984—	Jackson (Texas)	0	0	. . .	3.68	3	2	0	0	0	7 1/3	9	3	3	1	8
1985—	New York (N.L.)	6	5	.545	2.83	62	2	0	0	17	127 1/3	108	43	40	37	70
1986—	New York (N.L.)	14	9	.609	3.02	75	0	0	0	22	128	107	48	43	42	65
1987—	New York (N.L.)	7	5	.583	4.16	56	0	0	0	25	88 2/3	95	41	41	28	32
1988—	New York (N.L.)	5	5	.500	2.63	62	0	0	0	16	89	80	31	26	31	46
1989—	New York (N.L.)	1	5	.167	3.31	25	0	0	0	4	35 1/3	34	21	13	16	15
—	Philadelphia (N.L.)■	3	3	.500	1.11	44	0	0	0	19	56 2/3	45	15	7	22	32
1990—	Philadelphia (N.L.)	6	8	.429	3.86	72	0	0	0	22	86 1/3	92	41	37	35	39
1991—	Philadelphia (N.L.)	3	6	.333	3.20	38	0	0	0	3	59	61	28	21	32	28

Year	Team (League)	W	L	Pct.	ERA	G	GS	CG	ShO	Sv.	IP	H	R	ER	BB	SO
	—Los Angeles (N.L.)■	6	3	.667	2.55	33	0	0	0	7	42 1/3	39	12	12	16	22
1992	—Los Angeles (N.L.)	6	10	.375	4.09	65	0	0	0	14	83 2/3	103	46	38	42	50
1993	—Los Angeles (N.L.)	5	3	.625	2.25	54	0	0	0	2	68	76	32	17	30	27
1994	—Los Angeles (N.L.)	0	3	.000	5.23	32	0	0	0	0	41 1/3	50	25	24	22	29
1995	—Texas (A.L.)■	7	4	.636	4.02	64	0	0	0	4	85	86	39	38	34	49
A.L. totals (1 year)		7	4	.636	4.02	64	0	0	0	4	85	86	39	38	34	49
N.L. totals (10 years)		62	65	.488	3.17	618	2	0	0	151	905 2/3	890	383	319	353	455
Major league totals (11 years)		69	69	.500	3.24	682	2	0	0	155	990 2/3	976	422	357	387	504

CHAMPIONSHIP SERIES RECORD

Year	Team (League)	W	L	Pct.	ERA	G	GS	CG	ShO	Sv.	IP	H	R	ER	BB	SO
1986	—New York (N.L.)	0	0	...	0.00	2	0	0	0	0	7	1	0	0	0	3
1988	—New York (N.L.)	0	1	.000	4.50	4	0	0	0	0	6	6	3	3	2	5
Champ. series totals (2 years)		0	1	.000	2.08	6	0	0	0	0	13	7	3	3	2	8

WORLD SERIES RECORD

NOTES: Member of World Series championship team (1986).

Year	Team (League)	W	L	Pct.	ERA	G	GS	CG	ShO	Sv.	IP	H	R	ER	BB	SO
1986	—New York (N.L.)	1	0	1.000	4.91	5	0	0	0	0	7 1/3	10	5	4	6	2

McELROY, CHUCK — P — REDS

PERSONAL: Born October 1, 1967, in Port Arthur, Tex. . . . 6-0/195. . . . Throws left, bats left. . . . Full name: Charles Dwayne McElroy. . . . Name pronounced MACK-il-roy.

HIGH SCHOOL: Lincoln (Port Arthur, Tex.).

TRANSACTIONS/CAREER NOTES: Selected by Philadelphia Phillies organization in eighth round of free-agent draft (June 2, 1986). . . . Traded by Phillies with P Bob Scanlan to Chicago Cubs for P Mitch Williams (April 7, 1991). . . . Traded by Cubs to Cincinnati Reds for P Larry Luebbers, P Mike Anderson and C Darron Cox (December 10, 1993). . . . On disabled list (June 7-23, 1995).

Year	Team (League)	W	L	Pct.	ERA	G	GS	CG	ShO	Sv.	IP	H	R	ER	BB	SO
1986	—Utica (NYP)	4	6	.400	2.95	14	14	5	1	0	94 2/3	85	40	31	28	91
1987	—Spartanburg (SAL)	14	4	.778	3.11	24	21	5	2	0	130 1/3	117	51	45	48	115
	—Clearwater (Fla. St.)	1	0	1.000	0.00	2	2	0	0	0	7 1/3	1	1	0	4	7
1988	—Reading (Eastern)	9	12	.429	4.50	28	26	4	2	0	160	•173	89	*80	70	92
1989	—Reading (Eastern)	3	1	.750	2.68	32	0	0	0	12	47	39	14	14	14	39
	—Scran./W.B. (Int'l)	1	2	.333	2.93	14	0	0	0	3	15 1/3	13	6	5	11	12
	—Philadelphia (N.L.)	0	0	...	1.74	11	0	0	0	0	10 1/3	12	2	2	4	8
1990	—Scran./W.B. (Int'l)	6	8	.429	2.72	57	1	0	0	7	76	62	24	23	34	78
	—Philadelphia (N.L.)	0	1	.000	7.71	16	0	0	0	0	14	24	13	12	10	16
1991	—Chicago (N.L.)■	6	2	.750	1.95	71	0	0	0	3	101 1/3	73	33	22	57	92
1992	—Chicago (N.L.)	4	7	.364	3.55	72	0	0	0	6	83 2/3	73	40	33	51	83
1993	—Chicago (N.L.)	2	2	.500	4.56	49	0	0	0	0	47 1/3	51	30	24	25	31
	—Iowa (Am. Assoc.)	0	1	.000	4.60	9	0	0	0	2	15 2/3	19	10	8	9	13
1994	—Cincinnati (N.L.)■	1	2	.333	2.34	52	0	0	0	5	57 2/3	52	15	15	15	38
1995	—Cincinnati (N.L.)	3	4	.429	6.02	44	0	0	0	0	40 1/3	46	29	27	15	27
Major league totals (7 years)		16	18	.471	3.43	315	0	0	0	14	354 2/3	331	162	135	177	295

McGEE, WILLIE — OF — CARDINALS

PERSONAL: Born November 2, 1958, in San Francisco. . . . 6-1/185. . . . Bats both, throws right. . . . Full name: Willie Dean McGee.

HIGH SCHOOL: Ellis (Richmond, Calif.).

COLLEGE: Diablo Valley College (Calif.).

TRANSACTIONS/CAREER NOTES: Selected by Chicago White Sox organization in seventh round of free-agent draft (June 8, 1976); did not sign. . . . Selected by New York Yankees organization in secondary phase of free-agent draft (January 11, 1977). . . . On disabled list (May 22-June 7 and July 14-August 7, 1980; and April 24-June 4, 1981). . . . Traded by Yankees organization to St. Louis Cardinals organization for P Bob Sykes (October 21, 1981). . . . On Louisville disabled list (April 13-23, 1982). . . . On St. Louis disabled list (March 30-April 29, 1983); included rehabilitation assignment to Arkansas (April 18-29). . . . On disabled list (July 12-27, 1984 and August 3-27, 1986). . . . On disabled list (June 7-July 18, 1989); included rehabilitation assignment to Louisville (July 8-18). . . . On St. Louis disabled list (July 26-August 14, 1989). . . . Traded by Cardinals to Oakland Athletics for OF Felix Jose, 3B Stan Royer and P Daryl Green (August 29, 1990). . . . Granted free agency (November 5, 1990). . . . Signed by San Francisco Giants (December 3, 1990). . . . On San Francisco disabled list (July 12-August 1, 1991); included rehabilitation assignment to Phoenix (July 28-August 1). . . . On disabled list (July 10-30, 1993 and June 8, 1994-remainder of season). . . . Granted free agency (October 14, 1994). . . . Signed by Pawtucket, Boston Red Sox organization (June 6, 1995). . . . Granted free agency (November 3, 1995). . . . Signed by Cardinals (December 15, 1995).

RECORDS: Holds modern N.L. single-season record for highest batting average by switch-hitter (100 or more games)—.353 (1985). . . . Shares major league single-season record for fewest double plays by outfielder who led league in double plays—3 (1991).

HONORS: Won N.L. Gold Glove as outfielder (1983, 1985-86). . . . Named N.L. Player of the Year by The Sporting News (1985). . . . Named outfielder on The Sporting News N.L. All-Star team (1985). . . . Named outfielder on The Sporting News N.L. Silver Slugger team (1985). . . . Named N.L. Most Valuable Player by Baseball Writers' Association of America (1985).

STATISTICAL NOTES: Hit for the cycle (June 23, 1984). . . . Led N.L. in grounding into double plays with 24 in 1987. . . . Tied for N.L. lead in double plays by outfielder with three in 1991. . . . Career major league grand slams: 1.

			BATTING											FIELDING			
Year	Team (League)	Pos.	G	AB	R	H	2B	3B	HR	RBI	Avg.	BB	SO	SB	PO	A	E	Avg.
1977	—Oneonta (NYP)	OF	65	225	31	53	4	3	2	22	.236	13	65	13	103	5	10	.915
1978	—Fort Lauder. (FSL)	OF	124	423	62	106	6	6	0	37	.251	50	78	25	243	12	9	.966
1979	—West Haven (East.)	OF	49	115	21	28	3	1	1	8	.243	13	17	7	88	3	3	.968
	—Fort Lauder. (FSL)	OF	46	176	25	56	8	3	1	18	.318	17	34	16	103	3	2	.981
1980	—Nashville (South.)	OF	78	223	35	63	4	5	1	22	.283	19	39	7	127	6	6	.957
1981	—Nashville (South.)	OF	100	388	77	125	20	5	7	63	.322	24	46	24	203	10	6	.973
1982	—Louisville (A.A.)■	OF	13	55	11	16	2	2	1	3	.291	2	7	5	40	0	1	.976

Year	Team (League)	Pos.	G	AB	R	H	2B	3B	HR	RBI	Avg.	BB	SO	SB	PO	A	E	Avg.
			BATTING												FIELDING			
	—St. Louis (N.L.)	OF	123	422	43	125	12	8	4	56	.296	12	58	24	245	3	11	.958
1983—	St. Louis (N.L.)	OF	147	601	75	172	22	8	5	75	.286	26	98	39	385	7	5	.987
	—Arkansas (Texas)	OF	7	29	5	8	1	1	0	2	.276	4	6	1	7	0	0	1.000
1984—	St. Louis (N.L.)	OF	145	571	82	166	19	11	6	50	.291	29	80	43	374	10	6	.985
1985—	St. Louis (N.L.)	OF	152	612	114	*216	26	*18	10	82	*.353	34	86	56	382	11	9	.978
1986—	St. Louis (N.L.)	OF	124	497	65	127	22	7	7	48	.256	37	82	19	325	9	3	*.991
1987—	St. Louis (N.L.)	OF-SS	153	620	76	177	37	11	11	105	.285	24	90	16	354	10	7	.981
1988—	St. Louis (N.L.)	OF	137	562	73	164	24	6	3	50	.292	32	84	41	348	9	9	.975
1989—	St. Louis (N.L.)	OF	58	199	23	47	10	2	3	17	.236	10	34	8	118	2	3	.976
	—Louisville (A.A.)	OF	8	27	5	11	4	0	0	4	.407	3	4	3	20	1	1	.955
1990—	St. Louis (N.L.)	OF	125	501	76	168	32	5	3	62	*.335	38	86	28	341	13	*16	.957
	—Oakland (A.L.)■	OF-DH	29	113	23	31	3	2	0	15	.274	10	18	3	72	1	1	.986
1991—	San Fran. (N.L.)■	OF	131	497	67	155	30	3	4	43	.312	34	74	17	259	6	6	.978
	—Phoenix (PCL)	OF	4	10	4	5	1	0	0	1	.500	3	1	2	10	0	1	.909
1992—	San Francisco (N.L.)	OF	138	474	56	141	20	2	1	36	.297	29	88	13	231	11	6	.976
1993—	San Francisco (N.L.)	OF	130	475	53	143	28	1	4	46	.301	38	67	10	224	9	5	.979
1994—	San Francisco (N.L.)	OF	45	156	19	44	3	0	5	23	.282	15	24	3	80	2	1	.988
1995—	Pawtucket (Int'l)■	OF	5	21	9	10	0	0	0	2	.476	0	4	2	7	0	1	.875
	—Boston (A.L.)	OF	67	200	32	57	11	3	2	15	.285	9	41	5	101	7	3	.973
American League totals (2 years)			96	313	55	88	14	5	2	30	.281	19	59	8	173	8	4	.978
National League totals (13 years)			1608	6187	822	1845	285	82	66	693	.298	358	951	317	3666	102	87	.977
Major league totals (14 years)			1704	6500	877	1933	299	87	68	723	.297	377	1010	325	3839	110	91	.977

DIVISION SERIES RECORD

Year	Team (League)	Pos.	G	AB	R	H	2B	3B	HR	RBI	Avg.	BB	SO	SB	PO	A	E	Avg.
			BATTING												FIELDING			
1995—	Boston (A.L.)	OF-PH	2	4	0	1	0	0	0	1	.250	0	2	0	0	0	0	...

CHAMPIONSHIP SERIES RECORD

NOTES: Shares single-series record for most triples—2 (1982).... Shares N.L. career records for most triples—3; and most times caught stealing—4.... Shares N.L. single-series record for most times caught stealing—3 (1985).

Year	Team (League)	Pos.	G	AB	R	H	2B	3B	HR	RBI	Avg.	BB	SO	SB	PO	A	E	Avg.
			BATTING												FIELDING			
1982—	St. Louis (N.L.)	OF	3	13	4	4	0	2	1	5	.308	0	5	0	12	0	1	.923
1985—	St. Louis (N.L.)	OF	6	26	6	7	1	0	0	3	.269	3	6	2	18	0	0	1.000
1987—	St. Louis (N.L.)	OF	7	26	2	8	1	1	0	2	.308	0	5	0	16	0	0	1.000
1990—	Oakland (A.L.)	OF-PR-DH	3	9	3	2	1	0	0	0	.222	1	2	2	2	0	0	1.000
Championship series totals (4 years)			19	74	15	21	3	3	1	10	.284	4	18	4	48	0	1	.980

WORLD SERIES RECORD

NOTES: Member of World Series championship team (1982).

Year	Team (League)	Pos.	G	AB	R	H	2B	3B	HR	RBI	Avg.	BB	SO	SB	PO	A	E	Avg.
			BATTING												FIELDING			
1982—	St. Louis (N.L.)	OF	6	25	6	6	0	0	2	5	.240	1	3	2	24	0	0	1.000
1985—	St. Louis (N.L.)	OF	7	27	2	7	2	0	1	2	.259	1	3	1	15	0	0	1.000
1987—	St. Louis (N.L.)	OF	7	27	2	10	2	0	0	4	.370	0	9	0	21	1	1	.957
1990—	Oakland (A.L.)	OF-PH	4	10	1	2	1	0	0	0	.200	0	2	1	5	0	0	1.000
World Series totals (4 years)			24	89	11	25	5	0	3	11	.281	2	17	4	65	1	1	.985

ALL-STAR GAME RECORD

Year	League	Pos.	AB	R	H	2B	3B	HR	RBI	Avg.	BB	SO	SB	PO	A	E	Avg.
			BATTING											FIELDING			
1983—	National	OF	2	0	1	0	0	0	0	.500	0	0	0	2	0	0	1.000
1985—	National	OF	2	0	1	1	0	0	2	.500	0	0	0	1	0	0	1.000
1987—	National	OF	4	0	0	0	0	0	0	.000	0	0	0	2	0	0	1.000
1988—	National	PR-OF	2	0	0	0	0	0	0	.000	0	0	0	1	0	0	1.000
All-Star Game totals (4 years)			10	0	2	1	0	0	2	.200	0	0	0	6	0	0	1.000

McGINNIS, RUSS 3B/C

PERSONAL: Born June 18, 1963, in Coffeyville, Kan.... 6-3/225.... Bats right, throws right.... Full name: Russell Brent McGinnis.
HIGH SCHOOL: Sooner (Bartlesville, Okla.).
COLLEGE: Oklahoma.
TRANSACTIONS/CAREER NOTES: Selected by Milwaukee Brewers organization in 14th round of free-agent draft (June 3, 1985).... Traded by Brewers organization to Oakland Athletics organization for P Bill Mooneyham (June 29, 1987).... Selected by Chicago Cubs organization from A's organization in Rule 5 minor league draft (December 4, 1990).... Granted free agency (October 15, 1991).... Signed by Texas Rangers organization (December 2, 1991).... Granted free agency (October 16, 1992).... Signed by Kansas City Royals organization (December 10, 1992).... On disabled list (July 4-August 13, 1993).... Granted free agency (October 15, 1993).... Re-signed by Omaha, Royals organization (January 1, 1994).... On disabled list (May 12-June 1, 1994).... Granted free agency (October 15, 1994).... Re-signed by Omaha (December 13, 1994).... Released by Royals (May 15, 1995).... Signed by Rochester, Baltimore Orioles organization (June 30, 1995).... On Rochester disabled list (August 15-22, 1995).... Granted free agency (October 16, 1995).
STATISTICAL NOTES: Led Pacific Coast League catchers with 14 errors in 1989.... Led American Association with .414 on-base percentage in 1992.

Year	Team (League)	Pos.	G	AB	R	H	2B	3B	HR	RBI	Avg.	BB	SO	SB	PO	A	E	Avg.
			BATTING												FIELDING			
1985—	Helena (Pioneer)	1B-3B-C	48	150	33	46	7	0	5	38	.307	31	19	2	200	51	10	.962
1986—	Beloit (Midwest)	1B-C-3B	124	413	62	102	24	2	16	59	.247	52	79	5	929	66	17	.983
1987—	Beloit (Midwest)	1B-C-3B	51	189	34	58	10	0	13	35	.307	19	36	1	384	33	7	.983
	—Modesto (Calif.)■	C-3B-1B	47	165	24	42	9	0	8	31	.255	23	33	1	137	21	4	.975

Year	Team (League)	Pos.	G	AB	R	H	2B	3B	HR	RBI	Avg.	BB	SO	SB	PO	A	E	Avg.
			BATTING												FIELDING			
1988—	Huntsville (South.)	C-1B	23	77	9	20	9	0	2	15	.260	7	13	1	82	11	2	.979
	—Tacoma (PCL)	C-1B	63	186	25	47	13	1	2	22	.253	21	38	1	309	30	9	.974
1989—	Tacoma (PCL)	C-1B	110	380	42	105	25	0	7	60	.276	45	78	0	625	59	†15	.979
1990—	Tacoma (PCL)	C-1B	110	359	57	89	19	1	13	77	.248	75	70	2	687	61	8	.989
1991—	Iowa (Am. Assoc.)■	1B-C-3B	111	374	70	105	18	2	15	70	.281	63	68	3	734	64	8	.990
1992—	Okla. City (A.A.)■	3B-C-1B	99	330	63	87	19	1	18	51	.264	79	52	0	320	148	24	.951
	—Texas (A.L.)	C-3B-1B	14	33	2	8	4	0	0	4	.242	3	7	0	45	4	0	1.000
1993—	Omaha (A.A.)■	3B-1B-C	78	275	53	80	20	2	16	54	.291	42	44	1	174	102	7	.975
1994—	Omaha (A.A.)	C-3-1-O	98	344	73	97	21	1	24	70	.282	64	64	1	333	53	8	.980
1995—	Kansas City (A.L.)	1B-3B-OF	3	5	1	0	0	0	0	0	.000	1	1	0	9	0	0	1.000
	—Rochester (Int'l)■	1B-G	20	55	8	10	2	0	3	11	.182	17	19	0	41	2	0	1.000
Major league totals (2 years)			17	38	3	8	4	0	0	4	.211	4	8	0	54	4	0	1.000

McGRIFF, FRED — 1B — BRAVES

PERSONAL: Born October 31, 1963, in Tampa, Fla. . . . 6-3/215. . . . Bats left, throws left. . . . Full name: Frederick Stanley McGriff. . . . Cousin of Terry McGriff, major league catcher with four teams (1987-90 and 1993-94); and uncle of Charles Johnson, catcher, Florida Marlins.

HIGH SCHOOL: Jefferson (Tampa, Fla.).

TRANSACTIONS/CAREER NOTES: Selected by New York Yankees organization in ninth round of free-agent draft (June 8, 1981). . . . Traded by Yankees organization with OF Dave Collins, P Mike Morgan and cash to Toronto Blue Jays for OF/C Tom Dodd and P Dale Murray (December 9, 1982). . . . On disabled list (June 5-August 14, 1985). . . . Traded by Blue Jays with SS Tony Fernandez to San Diego Padres for OF Joe Carter and 2B Roberto Alomar (December 5, 1990). . . . On suspended list (June 23-26, 1992). . . . Traded by Padres to Atlanta Braves for OF Mel Nieves, P Donnie Elliott and OF Vince Moore (July 18, 1993). . . . Granted free agency (November 6, 1995). . . . Re-signed by Braves (December 2, 1995).

RECORDS: Shares major league record for most grand slams in two consecutive games—2 (August 13 and 14, 1991). . . . Shares N.L. single-season record for fewest errors by first baseman who led league in errors—12 (1992).

HONORS: Named first baseman on The Sporting News A.L. All-Star team (1989). . . . Named first baseman on The Sporting News A.L. Silver Slugger team (1989). . . . Named first baseman on The Sporting News N.L. All-Star team (1992-93). . . . Named first baseman on The Sporting News N.L. Silver Slugger team (1992-93).

STATISTICAL NOTES: Led International League first basemen with .992 fielding percentage, 1,219 putouts, 85 assists, 1,314 total chances and 108 double plays in 1986. . . . Tied for International League lead in intentional bases on balls received with eight and in grounding into double plays with 16 in 1986. . . . Led A.L. first basemen with 1,592 total chances and 148 double plays in 1989. . . . Led N.L. with 26 intentional base on balls received in 1991. . . . Led N.L. first basemen with 1077 total chances in 1994. . . . Career major league grand slams: 5.

M

Year	Team (League)	Pos.	G	AB	R	H	2B	3B	HR	RBI	Avg.	BB	SO	SB	PO	A	E	Avg.
			BATTING												FIELDING			
1981—	GC Yankees (GCL)	1B	29	81	6	12	2	0	0	9	.148	11	20	0	176	8	7	.963
1982—	GC Yankees (GCL)	1B	62	217	38	59	11	1	*9	•41	.272	*48	63	6	514	*56	8	.986
1983—	Florence (S. Atl.)■	1B	33	119	26	37	3	1	7	26	.311	20	35	3	250	14	6	.978
	—Kinston (Carolina)	1B	94	350	53	85	14	1	21	57	.243	55	112	3	784	57	10	.988
1984—	Knoxville (South.)	1B	56	189	29	47	13	2	9	25	.249	29	55	0	481	45	10	.981
	—Syracuse (Int'l)	1B	70	238	28	56	10	1	13	28	.235	26	89	0	644	45	3	.996
1985—	Syracuse (Int'l)	1B	51	176	19	40	8	2	5	20	.227	23	53	0	433	37	5	.989
1986—	Syracuse (Int'l)	1B-OF	133	468	69	121	23	4	19	74	.259	83	119	0	†1219	†85	10	†.992
	—Toronto (A.L.)	DH-1B	3	5	1	1	0	0	0	0	.200	0	2	0	3	0	0	1.000
1987—	Toronto (A.L.)	DH-1B	107	295	58	73	16	0	20	43	.247	60	104	3	108	7	2	.983
1988—	Toronto (A.L.)	1B	154	536	100	151	35	4	34	82	.282	79	149	6	1344	93	5	*.997
1989—	Toronto (A.L.)	1B-DH	161	551	98	148	27	3	*36	92	.269	119	131	7	1460	115	*17	.989
1990—	Toronto (A.L.)	1B-DH	153	557	91	167	21	1	35	88	.300	94	108	5	1246	126	6	.996
1991—	San Diego (N.L.)■	1B	153	528	84	147	19	1	31	106	.278	105	135	4	1370	87	14	.990
1992—	San Diego (N.L.)	1B	152	531	79	152	30	4	*35	104	.286	96	108	8	1219	108	•12	.991
1993—	San Diego (N.L.)	1B	83	302	52	83	11	1	18	46	.275	42	55	4	640	47	12	.983
	—Atlanta (N.L.)■	1B	68	255	59	79	18	1	19	55	.310	34	51	1	563	45	5	.992
1994—	Atlanta (N.L.)	1B	113	424	81	135	25	1	34	94	.318	50	76	7	*1004	66	7	.994
1995—	Atlanta (N.L.)	1B##i	144	528	85	148	27	1	27	93	.280	65	99	3	1285	96	5	.996
American League totals (5 years)			578	1944	348	540	99	8	125	305	.278	352	494	21	4161	341	30	.993
National League totals (5 years)			713	2568	440	744	130	9	164	498	.290	392	524	27	6081	449	55	.992
Major league totals (10 years)			1291	4512	788	1284	229	17	289	803	.285	744	1018	48	10242	790	85	.992

DIVISION SERIES RECORD

Year	Team (League)	Pos.	G	AB	R	H	2B	3B	HR	RBI	Avg.	BB	SO	SB	PO	A	E	Avg.
			BATTING												FIELDING			
1995—	Atlanta (N.L.)	1B	4	18	4	6	0	0	2	6	.333	2	3	0	39	2	0	1.000

CHAMPIONSHIP SERIES RECORD

Year	Team (League)	Pos.	G	AB	R	H	2B	3B	HR	RBI	Avg.	BB	SO	SB	PO	A	E	Avg.
			BATTING												FIELDING			
1989—	Toronto (A.L.)	1B	5	21	1	3	0	0	0	3	.143	0	4	0	35	2	1	.974
1993—	Atlanta (N.L.)	1B	6	23	6	10	2	0	1	4	.435	4	7	0	49	4	0	1.000
1995—	Atlanta (N.L.)	1B	4	16	5	7	4	0	0	0	.438	3	0	0	42	4	0	1.000
Championship series totals (3 years)			15	60	12	20	6	0	1	7	.333	7	11	0	126	10	1	.993

WORLD SERIES RECORD

NOTES: Hit home run in first at-bat (October 21, 1995). . . . Member of World Series championship team (1995).

Year	Team (League)	Pos.	G	AB	R	H	2B	3B	HR	RBI	Avg.	BB	SO	SB	PO	A	E	Avg.
			BATTING												FIELDING			
1995—	Atlanta (N.L.)	1B	6	23	5	6	2	0	2	3	.261	3	7	1	68	2	1	.986

ALL-STAR GAME RECORD

NOTES: Named Most Valuable Player (1994).

Year League	Pos.	AB	R	H	2B	3B	HR	RBI	Avg.	BB	SO	SB	PO	A	E	Avg.
		BATTING											FIELDING			
1992— National	1B	3	0	2	0	0	0	1	.667	0	0	0	7	1	0	1.000
1994— National	PH-1B	1	1	1	0	0	1	2	1.000	0	0	0	0	0	0	...
1995— National	1B	3	0	0	0	0	0	0	.000	0	2	0	5	0	0	1.000
All-Star Game totals (3 years)		7	1	3	0	0	1	3	.429	0	2	0	12	1	0	1.000

McGUIRE, RYAN 1B EXPOS

PERSONAL: Born November 23, 1971, in Wilson, N.C. . . . 6-1/195. . . . Bats left, throws left. . . . Full name: Ryan B. McGuire.
HIGH SCHOOL: El Camino Real (Woodland Hills, Calif.).
COLLEGE: UCLA.
TRANSACTIONS/CAREER NOTES: Selected by Boston Red Sox organization in third round of free-agent draft (June 3, 1993). . . . Traded by Red Sox with P Rheal Cormier and P Shayne Bennett to Montreal Expos for SS Wil Cordero and P Bryan Eversgerd (January 10, 1996).
STATISTICAL NOTES: Led Carolina League first basemen with 1,312 total chances in 1994.

Year Team (League)	Pos.	G	AB	R	H	2B	3B	HR	RBI	Avg.	BB	SO	SB	PO	A	E	Avg.
			BATTING											FIELDING			
1993— Fort Lauder. (FSL)	1B	56	213	23	69	12	2	4	38	.324	27	34	2	513	61	5	.991
1994— Lynchburg (Caro.)	1B	*137	489	70	133	29	0	10	73	.272	79	77	10	*1165	*129	18	.986
1995— Trenton (Eastern)	1B	109	414	59	138	29	1	7	59	.333	58	51	11	708	55	10	.987

McGWIRE, MARK 1B ATHLETICS

PERSONAL: Born October 1, 1963, in Pomona, Calif. . . . 6-5/250. . . . Bats right, throws right. . . . Full name: Mark David McGwire. . . . Brother of Dan McGwire, quarterback, Miami Dolphins.
HIGH SCHOOL: Damien (Claremont, Calif.).
COLLEGE: Southern California.
TRANSACTIONS/CAREER NOTES: Selected by Montreal Expos organization in eighth round of free-agent draft (June 8, 1981); did not sign. . . . Selected by Oakland Athletics organization in first round (10th pick overall) of free-agent draft (June 4, 1984). . . . On disabled list (April 11-26, 1989 and August 22-September 11, 1992). . . . Granted free agency (October 26, 1992). . . . Re-signed by A's (December 24, 1992). . . . On disabled list (May 14-September 3, 1993; April 30-June 18 and July 27, 1994-remainder of season). . . . On suspended list (September 4-8, 1993). . . . On disabled list (July 18-August 2 and August 5-26, 1995).
RECORDS: Holds major league rookie-season records for most home runs—49; and extra bases on long hits—183 (1987). . . . Shares major league record for most home runs in two consecutive games—5 (June 27 [3] and 28 [2], 1987 and June 10 [2] and 11 [3], 1995). . . . Shares modern major league record for most runs in two consecutive games—9 (June 27 and 28, 1987). . . . Holds A.L. rookie-season record for highest slugging percentage—.618 (1987).
HONORS: Named College Player of the Year by The Sporting News (1984). . . . Named first baseman on The Sporting News college All-America team (1984). . . . Named A.L. Rookie Player of the Year by The Sporting News (1987). . . . Named A.L. Rookie of the Year by Baseball Writers' Association of America (1987). . . . Won A.L. Gold Glove at first base (1990). . . . Named first baseman on The Sporting News A.L. All-Star team (1992). . . . Named first baseman on The Sporting News A.L. Silver Slugger team (1992).
STATISTICAL NOTES: Led California League third basemen with 239 assists and 354 total chances in 1985. . . . Hit three home runs in one game (June 27, 1987 and June 11, 1995). . . . Led A.L. with .618 slugging percentage in 1987 and .585 in 1992. . . . Led A.L. first basemen with 1,429 total chances in 1990. . . . Career major league grand slams: 6.
MISCELLANEOUS: Member of 1984 U.S. Olympic baseball team.

Year Team (League)	Pos.	G	AB	R	H	2B	3B	HR	RBI	Avg.	BB	SO	SB	PO	A	E	Avg.
			BATTING											FIELDING			
1984— Modesto (Calif.)	1B	16	55	7	11	3	0	1	1	.200	8	21	0	107	6	1	.991
1985— Modesto (Calif.)	3B-1B	138	489	95	134	23	3	•24	•106	.274	96	108	1	105	†240	33	.913
1986— Huntsville (South.)	3B	55	195	40	59	15	0	10	53	.303	46	45	3	34	124	16	.908
— Tacoma (PCL)	3B	78	280	42	89	21	5	13	59	.318	42	67	1	53	126	25	.877
— Oakland (A.L.)	3B	18	53	10	10	1	0	3	9	.189	4	18	0	10	20	6	.833
1987— Oakland (A.L.)	1B-3B-OF	151	557	97	161	28	4	*49	118	.289	71	131	1	1176	101	13	.990
1988— Oakland (A.L.)	1B-OF	155	550	87	143	22	1	32	99	.260	76	117	0	1228	88	9	.993
1989— Oakland (A.L.)	1B-DH	143	490	74	113	17	0	33	95	.231	83	94	1	1170	114	6	.995
1990— Oakland (A.L.)	1B-DH	156	523	87	123	16	0	39	108	.235	*110	116	2	*1329	95	5	.997
1991— Oakland (A.L.)	1B	154	483	62	97	22	0	22	75	.201	93	116	2	1191	##i101	4	.997
1992— Oakland (A.L.)	1B	139	467	87	125	22	0	42	104	.268	90	105	0	1118	71	6	.995
1993— Oakland (A.L.)	1B	27	84	16	28	6	0	9	24	.333	21	19	0	197	14	0	1.000
1994— Oakland (A.L.)	1B-DH	47	135	26	34	3	0	9	25	.252	37	40	0	307	18	4	.988
1995— Oakland (A.L.)	1B-DH	104	317	75	87	13	0	39	90	.274	88	77	1	775	64	*12	.986
Major league totals (10 years)		1094	3659	621	921	150	5	277	747	.252	673	833	7	8501	686	65	.993

CHAMPIONSHIP SERIES RECORD

Year Team (League)	Pos.	G	AB	R	H	2B	3B	HR	RBI	Avg.	BB	SO	SB	PO	A	E	Avg.
			BATTING											FIELDING			
1988— Oakland (A.L.)	1B	4	15	4	5	0	0	1	3	.333	1	5	0	24	2	0	1.000
1989— Oakland (A.L.)	1B	5	18	3	7	1	0	1	3	.389	1	4	0	46	1	1	.979
1990— Oakland (A.L.)	1B	4	13	2	2	0	0	0	2	.154	3	3	0	40	0	0	1.000
1992— Oakland (A.L.)	1B	6	20	1	3	0	0	1	3	.150	5	4	0	46	2	1	.980
Championship series totals (4 years)		19	66	10	17	1	0	3	11	.258	10	16	0	156	5	2	.988

WORLD SERIES RECORD

NOTES: Member of World Series championship team (1989).

Year Team (League)	Pos.	G	AB	R	H	2B	3B	HR	RBI	Avg.	BB	SO	SB	PO	A	E	Avg.
			BATTING											FIELDING			
1988— Oakland (A.L.)	1B	5	17	1	1	0	0	1	1	.059	3	4	0	40	3	0	1.000
1989— Oakland (A.L.)	1B	4	17	0	5	1	0	0	1	.294	1	3	0	28	2	0	1.000
1990— Oakland (A.L.)	1B	4	14	1	3	0	0	0	0	.214	2	4	0	42	1	2	.956
World Series totals (3 years)		13	48	2	9	1	0	1	2	.188	6	11	0	110	6	2	.983

ALL-STAR GAME RECORD

NOTES: Named to A.L. All-Star team; replaced by Rafael Palmeiro due to injury (1991).

Year League	Pos.	AB	R	H	2B	3B	HR	RBI	Avg.	BB	SO	SB	PO	A	E	Avg.
		BATTING											FIELDING			
1987— American	1B	3	0	0	0	0	0	0	.000	0	0	0	7	0	1	.875
1988— American	1B	2	0	1	0	0	0	0	.500	0	1	0	8	0	0	1.000
1989— American	1B	3	0	1	0	0	0	0	.333	0	0	0	5	0	0	1.000
1990— American	1B	2	0	0	0	0	0	0	.000	0	2	0	7	0	0	1.000
1991— American		Selected, did not play—injured.														
1992— American	1B	3	1	1	0	0	0	2	.333	0	0	0	4	0	0	1.000
1995— American		Selected, did not play—injured.														
All-Star Game totals (5 years)		13	1	3	0	0	0	2	.231	0	3	0	31	0	1	.969

McLEMORE, MARK — 2B — RANGERS

PERSONAL: Born October 4, 1964, in San Diego. . . . 5-11/207. . . . Bats both, throws right. . . . Full name: Mark Tremell McLemore.
HIGH SCHOOL: Morse (San Diego).
TRANSACTIONS/CAREER NOTES: Selected by California Angels organization in ninth round of free-agent draft (June 7, 1982). . . . On disabled list (May 15-27, 1985). . . . On California disabled list (May 24-August 2, 1988); included rehabilitation assignments to Palm Springs (July 7-21) and Edmonton (July 22-27). . . . On California disabled list (May 17-August 17, 1990); included rehabilitation assignments to Edmonton (May 24-June 6) and Palm Springs (August 9-13). . . . Traded by Angels to Colorado Springs, Cleveland Indians organization (August 17, 1990), completing deal in which Indians traded C Ron Tingley to Angels for a player to be named later (September 6, 1989). . . . Released by Indians organization (December 13, 1990). . . . Signed by Tucson, Houston Astros organization (March 6, 1991). . . . On Houston disabled list (May 9-June 25, 1991); included rehabilitation assignments to Tucson (May 24-29) and Jackson (June 14-22). . . . Released by Astros (June 25, 1991). . . . Signed by Baltimore Orioles (July 5, 1991). . . . Granted free agency (October 15, 1991). . . . Re-signed by Orioles organization (February 5, 1992). . . . Granted free agency (December 19, 1992). . . . Re-signed by Orioles organization (January 6, 1993). . . . Granted free agency (October 18, 1994). . . . Signed by Texas Rangers (December 13, 1994).
STATISTICAL NOTES: Led California League second basemen with 400 assists and 84 double plays in 1984. . . . Led Pacific Coast League second basemen with 597 total chances and 95 double plays in 1989.

Year Team (League)	Pos.	G	AB	R	H	2B	3B	HR	RBI	Avg.	BB	SO	SB	PO	A	E	Avg.
			BATTING											FIELDING			
1982— Salem (Northwest)	2B-SS	55	165	42	49	6	2	0	25	.297	39	38	14	81	125	11	.949
1983— Peoria (Midwest)	2B-SS	95	329	42	79	7	3	0	18	.240	53	64	15	170	250	24	.946
1984— Redwood (Calif.)	2B-SS	134	482	102	142	8	3	0	45	.295	106	75	59	274	†429	25	.966
1985— Midland (Texas)	2B-SS	117	458	80	124	17	6	2	46	.271	66	59	31	301	339	19	.971
1986— Midland (Texas)	2B	63	237	54	75	9	1	1	29	.316	48	18	38	155	194	13	.964
— Edmonton (PCL)	2B	73	286	41	79	13	1	0	23	.276	39	30	29	173	215	7	.982
— California (A.L.)	2B	5	4	0	0	0	0	0	0	.000	1	2	0	3	10	0	1.000
1987— California (A.L.)	2B-SS-DH	138	433	61	102	13	3	3	41	.236	48	72	25	293	363	17	.975
1988— California (A.L.)	2B-3B-DH	77	233	38	56	11	2	2	16	.240	25	25	13	108	178	6	.979
— Palm Springs (Cal.)	2B	11	44	9	15	3	1	0	6	.341	11	7	7	18	24	1	.977
— Edmonton (PCL)	2B	12	45	7	12	3	0	0	6	.267	4	4	7	35	33	1	.986
1989— Edmonton (PCL)	2B	114	430	60	105	13	2	2	34	.244	49	67	26	*264	323	10	*.983
— California (A.L.)	2B-DH	32	103	12	25	3	1	0	14	.243	7	19	6	55	88	5	.966
1990— California (A.L.)	2B	20	48	4	7	2	0	0	2	.146	4	9	1	14	15	0	1.000
— Edmonton (PCL)	2B-SS	9	39	4	10	2	0	0	3	.256	6	10	0	24	32	4	.933
— Palm Springs (Cal.)	2B	6	22	3	6	0	0	0	2	.273	3	7	0	20	22	0	1.000
— Colo. Springs (PCL)■	2B-3B-SS	14	54	11	15	2	0	1	7	.278	11	8	5	23	40	2	.969
— Cleveland (A.L.)	SS-3B-2B	8	12	2	2	0	0	0	0	.167	0	6	0	23	24	4	.922
1991— Houston (N.L.)■	2B	21	61	6	9	1	0	0	2	.148	6	13	0	25	54	2	.975
— Tucson (PCL)	2B	4	14	2	5	1	0	0	0	.357	2	1	0	8	6	0	1.000
— Jackson (Texas)	2B	7	22	6	5	3	0	1	4	.227	6	3	1	27	24	0	1.000
— Rochester (Int'l)■	2B	57	228	32	64	11	4	1	28	.281	27	29	12	134	166	5	.984
1992— Baltimore (A.L.)	2B-DH	101	228	40	56	7	2	0	27	.246	21	26	11	126	186	7	.978
1993— Baltimore (A.L.)	O-2-3-DH	148	581	81	165	27	5	4	72	.284	64	92	21	335	80	6	.986
1994— Baltimore (A.L.)	2B-OF-DH	104	343	44	88	11	1	3	29	.257	51	50	20	219	269	9	.982
1995— Texas (A.L.)■	OF-2B-DH	129	467	73	122	20	5	5	41	.261	59	71	21	248	184	4	.991
American League totals (9 years)		762	2452	355	623	94	19	17	242	.254	280	372	118	1424	1397	58	.980
National League totals (1 year)		21	61	6	9	1	0	0	2	.148	6	13	0	25	54	2	.975
Major league totals (10 years)		783	2513	361	632	95	19	17	244	.251	286	385	118	1449	1451	60	.980

McMICHAEL, GREG — P — BRAVES

PERSONAL: Born December 1, 1966, in Knoxville, Tenn. . . . 6-3/215. . . . Throws right, bats right. . . . Full name: Gregory Winston McMichael.
HIGH SCHOOL: Webb School of Knoxville (Knoxville, Tenn.).
COLLEGE: Tennessee.
TRANSACTIONS/CAREER NOTES: Selected by Cleveland Indians organization in seventh round of free-agent draft (June 1, 1988). . . . Released by Colorado Springs, Indians organization (April 4, 1991). . . . Signed by Durham, Atlanta Braves organization (April 16, 1991).

Year Team (League)	W	L	Pct.	ERA	G	GS	CG	ShO	Sv.	IP	H	R	ER	BB	SO
1988— Burlington (Appal.)	2	0	1.000	2.57	3	3	1	1	0	21	17	9	6	4	20
— Kinston (Carolina)	4	2	.667	2.68	11	11	2	0	0	77 1/3	57	31	23	18	35
1989— Cant./Akr. (East.)	11	11	.500	3.49	26	•26	8	•5	0	170	164	81	66	64	101
1990— Cant./Akr. (East.)	2	3	.400	3.35	13	4	0	0	0	40 1/3	39	17	15	17	19
— Colo. Springs (PCL)	2	3	.400	5.80	12	12	1	1	0	59	72	45	38	30	34
1991— Durham (Carolina)■	5	6	.455	3.62	36	6	0	0	2	79 2/3	83	34	32	29	82
1992— Greenville (South.)	4	2	.667	1.36	15	4	0	0	1	46 1/3	37	14	7	13	53
— Richmond (Int'l)	6	5	.545	4.38	19	13	0	0	2	90 1/3	89	52	44	34	86
1993— Atlanta (N.L.)	2	3	.400	2.06	74	0	0	0	19	91 2/3	68	22	21	29	89
1994— Atlanta (N.L.)	4	6	.400	3.84	51	0	0	0	21	58 2/3	66	29	25	19	47
1995— Atlanta (N.L.)	7	2	.778	2.79	67	0	0	0	2	80 2/3	64	27	25	32	74
Major league totals (3 years)	13	11	.542	2.77	192	0	0	0	42	231	198	78	71	80	210

DIVISION SERIES RECORD

Year	Team (League)	W	L	Pct.	ERA	G	GS	CG	ShO	Sv.	IP	H	R	ER	BB	SO
1995—	Atlanta (N.L.)	0	0	...	6.75	2	0	0	0	0	1 1/3	1	1	1	2	1

CHAMPIONSHIP SERIES RECORD

Year	Team (League)	W	L	Pct.	ERA	G	GS	CG	ShO	Sv.	IP	H	R	ER	BB	SO
1993—	Atlanta (N.L.)	0	1	.000	6.75	4	0	0	0	0	4	7	3	3	2	1
1995—	Atlanta (N.L.)	1	0	1.000	0.00	3	0	0	0	1	2 2/3	0	0	0	1	2
Champ. series totals (2 years)		1	1	.500	4.05	7	0	0	0	1	6 2/3	7	3	3	3	3

WORLD SERIES RECORD

NOTES: Member of World Series championship team (1995).

Year	Team (League)	W	L	Pct.	ERA	G	GS	CG	ShO	Sv.	IP	H	R	ER	BB	SO
1995—	Atlanta (N.L.)	0	0	...	2.70	3	0	0	0	0	3 1/3	3	2	1	2	2

McMILLON, BILLY — OF — MARLINS

PERSONAL: Born November 17, 1971, in Otero, N.M. . . . 5-11/172. . . . Bats left, throws left. . . . Full name: William E. McMillon.

COLLEGE: Clemson.

TRANSACTIONS/CAREER NOTES: Selected by Florida Marlins organization in eighth round of free-agent draft (June 3, 1993).

STATISTICAL NOTES: Tied for New York-Pennsylvania League lead with four intentional bases on balls received in 1993. . . . Tied for Midwest League lead with nine sacrifice flies in 1994. . . . Led Eastern League with .423 on-base percentage in 1995.

			BATTING											FIELDING			
Year	Team (League)	Pos.	G	AB	R	H	2B	3B	HR	RBI	Avg.	BB	SO	SB	PO	A	E	Avg.
1993—	Elmira (NYP)	OF	57	226	38	69	14	2	6	35	.305	31	43	5	66	1	5	.931
1994—	Kane Co. (Midw.)	OF	•137	496	88	125	25	3	17	*101	.252	*84	99	7	187	9	7	.966
1995—	Portland (Eastern)	OF	*141	518	92	*162	29	3	14	93	.313	*96	90	15	207	14	4	.982

McMURTRY, CRAIG — P

PERSONAL: Born November 5, 1959, in Temple, Tex. . . . 6-5/195. . . . Throws right, bats right. . . . Full name: Joe Craig McMurtry.

HIGH SCHOOL: Troy (Tex.).

JUNIOR COLLEGE: McLennan Community College (Tex.).

TRANSACTIONS/CAREER NOTES: Selected by Atlanta Braves organization in first round (fourth pick overall) of free-agent draft (January 8, 1980). . . . On Atlanta disabled list (July 27-September 1, 1986); included rehabilitation assignment to Greenville (August 14-September 1). . . . Traded by Braves to Toronto Blue Jays for 2B Damaso Garcia and P Luis Leal (February 2, 1987). . . . On Toronto disabled list (March 30-June 18, 1987); included rehabilitation assignment to Knoxville (May 29-June 17). . . . Granted free agency (November 22, 1987). . . . Signed by Texas Rangers (December 8, 1987). . . . On Texas disabled list (April 18-May 5, 1989). . . . On Texas disabled list (May 25-August 20, 1989); included rehabilitation assignments to Sarasota Rangers (August 5-14) and Oklahoma City (August 15-20). . . . Granted free agency (November 13, 1989). . . . Re-signed by Rangers organization (January 5, 1990). . . . Released by Rangers (April 25, 1990). . . . Re-signed by Rangers organization (May 10, 1990). . . . Granted free agency (November 5, 1990). . . . Re-signed by Rangers (January 8, 1991). . . . Released by Oklahoma City (April 4, 1991). . . . Signed by Phoenix, San Francisco Giants organization (April 29, 1991). . . . On disabled list (May 7-18, 1992). . . . Granted free agency (October 15, 1992). . . . Signed by Carolina, Pittsburgh Pirates organization (February 16, 1993). . . . Played in Mexican League (1993). . . . On Buffalo disabled list (June 14-22, 1993). . . . Granted free agency (October 15, 1993). . . . Signed by Tucson, Houston Astros organization (March 2, 1994). . . . On disabled list (May 9-19 and August 26, 1994-remainder of season). . . . On Tucson disabled list (April 19-May 24, 1995). . . . Granted free agency (October 16, 1995).

HONORS: Named International League Pitcher of the Year (1982). . . . Named N.L. Rookie Pitcher of the Year by THE SPORTING NEWS (1983).

Year	Team (League)	W	L	Pct.	ERA	G	GS	CG	ShO	Sv.	IP	H	R	ER	BB	SO
1980—	Savannah (South.)	7	4	.636	3.56	14	13	5	1	0	86	82	40	34	35	37
1981—	Savannah (South.)	*15	11	.577	2.76	28	28	13	2	0	202	168	87	62	95	111
1982—	Richmond (Int'l)	*17	9	.654	3.81	32	##i32	8	1	0	*210	198	98	89	107	96
1983—	Atlanta (N.L.)	15	9	.625	3.08	36	35	6	3	0	224 2/3	204	86	77	88	105
1984—	Atlanta (N.L.)	9	17	.346	4.32	37	30	0	0	0	183 1/3	184	100	88	102	99
1985—	Atlanta (N.L.)	0	3	.000	6.60	17	6	0	0	1	45	56	36	33	27	28
—	Richmond (Int'l)	7	5	.583	3.27	16	16	4	2	0	107 1/3	88	43	39	51	74
1986—	Atlanta (N.L.)	1	6	.143	4.74	37	5	0	0	0	79 2/3	82	46	42	43	50
—	Greenville (South.)	1	1	.500	6.00	3	3	0	0	0	15	13	10	10	9	12
1987—	Knoxville (South.)■	4	2	.667	2.77	12	11	1	0	0	78	64	28	24	20	56
—	Syracuse (Int'l)	5	3	.625	3.52	9	8	1	1	0	53 2/3	46	23	21	15	31
1988—	Okla. City (A.A.)■	2	5	.286	4.35	9	9	2	0	0	49 2/3	55	27	24	21	35
—	Texas (A.L.)	3	3	.500	2.25	32	0	0	0	3	60	37	16	15	24	35
1989—	Texas (A.L.)	0	0	...	7.43	19	0	0	0	0	23	29	21	19	13	14
—	GC Rangers (GCL)	0	1	.000	1.13	4	2	0	0	0	8	3	2	1	2	10
—	Okla. City (A.A.)	0	0	...	3.00	1	0	0	0	0	3	2	1	1	1	1
1990—	Texas (A.L.)	0	3	.000	4.32	23	3	0	0	0	41 2/3	43	25	20	30	14
—	Okla. City (A.A.)	1	1	.500	2.70	6	5	0	0	0	26 2/3	31	15	8	21	19
1991—	Phoenix (PCL)■	10	6	.625	4.38	27	15	1	1	0	113	117	70	55	44	67
1992—	Phoenix (PCL)	5	8	.385	4.23	40	14	1	1	1	129 2/3	140	71	61	59	83
1993—	M.C. Red Devils (Mex.)■	1	2	.333	5.08	17	0	0	0	6	28 1/3	30	17	16	13	25
—	Buffalo (A.A.)■	6	4	.600	3.44	30	13	1	1	1	96 2/3	102	44	37	38	63
1994—	Tucson (Pac. Coast)■	8	4	.667	3.56	29	19	0	0	2	126 1/3	118	55	50	35	109
1995—	Tucson (Pac. Coast)	6	1	.857	1.29	13	13	1	0	0	69 2/3	54	11	10	19	41
—	Houston (N.L.)	0	1	.000	7.84	11	0	0	0	0	10 1/3	15	11	9	9	4
A.L. totals (3 years)		3	6	.333	3.90	74	3	0	0	3	124 2/3	109	62	54	67	63
N.L. totals (5 years)		25	36	.410	4.13	138	76	6	3	1	543	541	279	249	269	286
Major league totals (8 years)		28	42	.400	4.08	212	79	6	3	4	667 2/3	650	341	303	336	349

M

McRAE, BRIAN — OF — CUBS

PERSONAL: Born August 27, 1967, in Bradenton, Fla. . . . 6-0/190. . . . Bats both, throws right. . . . Full name: Brian Wesley McRae. . . . Son of Hal McRae, coach, Cincinnati Reds; outfielder/designated hitter, Reds and Kansas City Royals (1968 and 1970-87); manager, Royals (1991-94); and coach, Royals (1987) and Montreal Expos (1990-91).
HIGH SCHOOL: Blue Springs (Mo.).
TRANSACTIONS/CAREER NOTES: Selected by Kansas City Royals organization in first round (17th pick overall) of free-agent draft (June 3, 1985). . . . Traded by Royals to Chicago Cubs for P Derek Wallace and P Geno Morones (April 5, 1995).
RECORDS: Shares major league single-season record for fewest double plays by outfielder (150 or more games)—0 (1991). . . . Shares major league single-game record for most unassisted double plays by oufielder—1 (August 23, 1992).
STATISTICAL NOTES: Led Northwest League second basemen with 373 total chances in 1986. . . . Tied for Southern League lead in double plays by outfielder with five in 1989. . . . Led N.L. outfielders with 352 total chances in 1995. . . . Career major league grand slams: 2.

			BATTING											FIELDING			
Year Team (League)	Pos.	G	AB	R	H	2B	3B	HR	RBI	Avg.	BB	SO	SB	PO	A	E	Avg.
1985—GC Royals (GCL)	2B-SS	60	217	40	58	6	5	0	23	.267	28	34	27	116	142	18	.935
1986—Eugene (N'west)	2B	72	306	*66	82	10	3	1	29	.268	41	49	28	146	*214	13	*.965
1987—Fort Myers (FSL)	2B	131	481	62	121	14	1	1	31	.252	22	70	33	*284	346	18	.972
1988—Baseball City (FSL)	2B	30	107	18	33	2	0	1	11	.308	9	11	8	70	103	4	.977
—Memphis (South.)	2B	91	288	33	58	13	1	4	15	.201	16	60	13	147	231	18	.955
1989—Memphis (South.)	OF	138	*533	72	121	18	8	5	42	.227	43	65	23	249	11	5	.981
1990—Memphis (South.)	OF	116	470	78	126	24	6	10	64	.268	44	66	21	265	8	7	.975
—Kansas City (A.L.)	OF	46	168	21	48	8	3	2	23	.286	9	29	4	120	1	0	1.000
1991—Kansas City (A.L.)	OF	152	629	86	164	28	9	8	64	.261	24	99	20	405	2	3	.993
1992—Kansas City (A.L.)	OF	149	533	63	119	23	5	4	52	.223	42	88	18	419	8	3	.993
1993—Kansas City (A.L.)	OF	153	627	78	177	28	9	12	69	.282	37	105	23	394	4	7	.983
1994—Kansas City (A.L.)	OF-DH	114	436	71	119	22	6	4	40	.273	54	67	28	252	2	3	.988
1995—Chicago (N.L.)■	OF	137	*580	92	167	38	7	12	48	.288	47	92	27	*345	4	3	.991
American League totals (5 years)		614	2393	319	627	109	32	30	248	.262	166	388	93	1590	17	16	.990
National League totals (1 year)		137	580	92	167	38	7	12	48	.288	47	92	27	345	4	3	.991
Major league totals (6 years)		751	2973	411	794	147	39	42	296	.267	213	480	120	1935	21	19	.990

MEACHAM, RUSTY — P — ROYALS

PERSONAL: Born January 27, 1968, in Stuart, Fla. . . . 6-3/180. . . . Throws right, bats right. . . . Full name: Russell Loren Meacham.
JUNIOR COLLEGE: Indian River Community College (Fla.).
TRANSACTIONS/CAREER NOTES: Selected by Detroit Tigers organization in 33rd round of free-agent draft (June 2, 1987). . . . Claimed on waivers by Kansas City Royals (October 23, 1991). . . . On Kansas City disabled list (May 1-June 4, 1993); included rehabilitation assignment to Omaha (May 18-June 4). . . . On Kansas City disabled list (June 15, 1993-remainder of season).

Year Team (League)	W	L	Pct.	ERA	G	GS	CG	ShO	Sv.	IP	H	R	ER	BB	SO
1988—Fayetteville (S. Atl.)	0	3	.000	6.20	6	5	0	0	0	24 2/3	37	19	17	6	16
—Bristol (Appal.)	•9	1	•.900	*1.43	13	9	2	•2	0	75 1/3	55	14	12	22	85
1989—Fayetteville (S. Atl.)	10	3	.769	2.29	16	15	2	0	0	102	103	33	26	23	74
—Lakeland (Fla. St.)	5	4	.556	1.95	11	9	4	2	0	64 2/3	59	15	14	12	39
1990—London (Eastern)	*15	9	.625	3.13	26	26	•9	•3	0	178	161	70	62	36	123
1991—Toledo (Int'l)	9	7	.563	3.09	26	17	3	1	2	125 1/3	117	53	43	40	70
—Detroit (A.L.)	2	1	.667	5.20	10	4	0	0	0	27 2/3	35	17	16	11	14
1992—Kansas City (A.L.)■	10	4	.714	2.74	64	0	0	0	2	101 2/3	88	39	31	21	64
1993—Kansas City (A.L.)	2	2	.500	5.57	15	0	0	0	0	21	31	15	13	5	13
—Omaha (Am. Assoc.)	0	0	...	4.82	7	0	0	0	0	9 1/3	10	5	5	1	10
1994—Omaha (Am. Assoc.)	1	1	.500	7.00	8	0	0	0	1	9	9	7	7	3	16
—Kansas City (A.L.)	3	3	.500	3.73	36	0	0	0	4	50 2/3	51	23	21	12	36
1995—Kansas City (A.L.)	4	3	.571	4.98	49	0	0	0	2	59 2/3	72	36	33	19	30
Major league totals (5 years)	21	13	.618	3.94	174	4	0	0	8	260 2/3	277	130	114	68	157

MEARES, PAT — SS — TWINS

PERSONAL: Born September 6, 1968, in Salina, Kan. . . . 6-0/188. . . . Bats right, throws right. . . . Full name: Patrick James Meares.
HIGH SCHOOL: Sacred Heart (Salina, Kan.).
COLLEGE: Wichita State.
TRANSACTIONS/CAREER NOTES: Selected by Minnesota Twins organization in 15th round of free-agent draft (June 4, 1990). . . . On disabled list (June 22-July 7, 1994).

			BATTING											FIELDING			
Year Team (League)	Pos.	G	AB	R	H	2B	3B	HR	RBI	Avg.	BB	SO	SB	PO	A	E	Avg.
1990—Kenosha (Midwest)	3B-2B	52	197	26	47	10	2	4	22	.239	25	45	2	35	94	16	.890
1991—Visalia (California)	2B-3B-OF	89	360	53	109	21	4	6	44	.303	24	63	15	155	224	26	.936
1992—Orlando (Southern)	SS	81	300	42	76	19	0	3	23	.253	11	57	5	91	190	35	.889
1993—Portland (PCL)	SS	18	54	6	16	5	0	0	3	.296	3	11	0	28	48	5	.938
—Minnesota (A.L.)	SS	111	346	33	87	14	3	0	33	.251	7	52	4	165	304	19	.961
1994—Minnesota (A.L.)	SS	80	229	29	61	12	1	2	24	.266	14	50	5	133	209	13	.963
1995—Minnesota (A.L.)	SS-OF	116	390	57	105	19	4	12	49	.269	15	68	10	187	317	•18	.966
Major league totals (3 years)		307	965	119	253	45	8	14	106	.262	36	170	19	485	830	50	.963

MECIR, JIM — P — YANKEES

PERSONAL: Born May 16, 1970, in Queens, N.Y. . . . 6-1/195. . . . Throws right, bats both. . . . Full name: James Jason Mecir.
HIGH SCHOOL: Smithtown East (St. James, N.Y.).

COLLEGE: Eckerd (Fla.).

TRANSACTIONS/CAREER NOTES: Selected by Seattle Mariners organization in third round of free-agent draft (June 3, 1991). . . . On disabled list (June 25-August 25, 1992). . . . Traded by Mariners with 1B Tino Martinez and P Jeff Nelson to New York Yankees for P Sterling Hitchcock and 3B Russ Davis (December 7, 1995).

STATISTICAL NOTES: Led California League with 15 hit batsmen in 1993.

Year Team (League)	W	L	Pct.	ERA	G	GS	CG	ShO	Sv.	IP	H	R	ER	BB	SO
1991— San Bern. (Calif.)	3	5	.375	4.22	14	12	0	0	1	70 1/3	72	40	33	37	48
1992— San Bern. (Calif.)	4	5	.444	4.67	14	11	0	0	0	61 2/3	72	40	32	26	53
1993— Riverside (Calif.)	9	11	.450	4.33	26	26	1	0	0	145 1/3	160	89	70	58	85
1994— Jacksonville (Sou.)	6	5	.545	2.69	46	0	0	0	13	80 1/3	73	28	24	35	53
1995— Tacoma (PCL)	1	4	.200	3.10	40	0	0	0	8	69 2/3	63	29	24	28	46
— Seattle (A.L.)	0	0	...	0.00	2	0	0	0	0	4 2/3	5	1	0	2	3
Major league totals (1 year)	0	0	...	0.00	2	0	0	0	0	4 2/3	5	1	0	2	3

MEJIA, MIGUEL — OF — CARDINALS

PERSONAL: Born March 25, 1975, in San Pedro de Macoris Dominican Republic. . . . 6-1/155. . . . Bats right, throws right.

TRANSACTIONS/CAREER NOTES: Signed as non-drafted free agent by Baltimore Orioles organization (January 22, 1992). . . . Selected by Kansas City Royals from Orioles organization in Rule 5 major league draft (December 4, 1995). . . . Traded by Royals to St. Louis Cardinals as part of a three-team deal in which Cardinals sent OF Andre King to Cincinnati Reds for SS Luis Ordaz. Reds then sent P Mike Remlinger to Royals to complete deal (December 4, 1995).

		BATTING												FIELDING			
Year Team (League)	Pos.	G	AB	R	H	2B	3B	HR	RBI	Avg.	BB	SO	SB	PO	A	E	Avg.
1992— Dom. Orioles (DSL)	OF	51	187	42	63	11	0	1	31	.337	30	19	30	93	12	14	.882
1993— Albany (S. Atl.)	OF	23	79	11	13	0	3	0	2	.165	4	22	7	37	1	3	.927
— GC Orioles (GCL)	OF	35	130	21	32	3	3	0	12	.246	13	23	18	80	3	2	.976
1994— Albany (S. Atl.)	OF	22	58	6	10	1	1	0	3	.172	5	20	5	41	4	3	.938
— Bluefield (Appal.)	OF	50	191	34	51	5	5	2	24	.267	17	39	33	86	8	6	.940
1995— Bluefield (Appal.)	OF	51	181	50	54	6	3	3	30	.298	18	30	36	74	5	5	.940
— High Desert (Calif.)	OF	37	119	14	32	6	1	0	12	.269	14	17	16	58	2	3	.952

MEJIA, ROBERTO — 2B — REDS

PERSONAL: Born April 14, 1972, in Hato Mayor, Dominican Republic. . . . 5-11/165. . . . Bats right, throws right. . . . Full name: Roberto Antonio Diaz Mejia.

HIGH SCHOOL: Colegio Adventista (Dominican Republic).

TRANSACTIONS/CAREER NOTES: Signed as non-drafted free agent by Los Angeles Dodgers organization (November 21, 1988). . . . On disabled list (April 29-May 19 and August 18, 1992-remainder of season). . . . Selected by Colorado Rockies in second round (30th pick overall) of expansion draft (November 17, 1992). . . . On Colorado Springs suspended list (June 26-28, 1995). . . . Granted free agency (December 21, 1995). . . . Signed by Cincinnati Reds organization (January 2, 1996).

		BATTING												FIELDING			
Year Team (League)	Pos.	G	AB	R	H	2B	3B	HR	RBI	Avg.	BB	SO	SB	PO	A	E	Avg.
1989— Santo Dom. (DSL)	...	43	136	18	30	5	3	0	20	.221	24	22	7	...	...	...	...
1990— Santo Dom. (DSL)	...	67	246	61	74	19	1	8	74	.301	48	30	9	...	...	...	...
1991— Great Falls (Pio.)	2B	23	84	17	22	6	2	2	14	.262	7	22	3	33	54	3	.967
1992— Vero Beach (FSL)	2B	96	330	42	82	17	1	12	40	.248	37	60	14	148	212	15	.960
1993— Colo. Springs (PCL)■	2B	77	291	51	87	15	2	14	48	.299	18	56	12	166	204	8	.979
— Colorado (N.L.)	2B	65	229	31	53	14	5	5	20	.231	13	63	4	126	184	12	.963
1994— Colorado (N.L.)	2B	38	116	11	28	8	1	4	14	.241	15	33	3	69	94	7	.959
— Colo. Springs (PCL)	2B	73	283	54	80	24	2	6	37	.283	21	49	7	172	213	12	.970
1995— Colo. Springs (PCL)	2B	38	143	18	42	10	2	2	14	.294	7	29	0	80	97	5	.973
— Colorado (N.L.)	2B	23	52	5	8	1	0	1	4	.154	0	17	0	35	30	2	.970
Major league totals (3 years)		126	397	47	89	23	6	10	38	.224	28	113	7	230	308	21	.962

MENDOZA, RAMIRO — P — YANKEES

PERSONAL: Born June 15, 1972, in Los Santos, Panama. . . . 6-2/154. . . . Throws right, bats right.

TRANSACTIONS/CAREER NOTES: Signed as non-drafted free agent by New York Yankees organization (November 13, 1991).

Year Team (League)	W	L	Pct.	ERA	G	GS	CG	ShO	Sv.	IP	H	R	ER	BB	SO
1992— Dominican Yankees (DSL)	10	2	.833	2.13	15	15	5	0	0	109 2/3	93	37	26	28	79
1993— GC Yankees (GCL)	4	5	.444	2.79	15	9	0	0	1	67 2/3	59	26	21	7	61
— Greensboro (S. Atl.)	0	1	.000	2.45	2	0	0	0	0	3 2/3	3	1	1	5	3
1994— Tampa (Fla. St.)	12	6	.667	3.01	22	21	1	0	0	134 1/3	133	54	45	35	110
1995— Norwich (Eastern)	5	6	.455	3.21	19	19	2	1	0	89 2/3	87	39	32	33	68
— Columbus (Int'l)	1	0	1.000	2.57	2	2	0	0	0	14	10	4	4	2	13

MENHART, PAUL — P — MARINERS

PERSONAL: Born March 25, 1969, in St. Louis. . . . 6-2/190. . . . Throws right, bats right. . . . Full name: Paul Gerard Menhart.

HIGH SCHOOL: Robert E. Fitch Senior (Groton, Conn.).

COLLEGE: Western Carolina.

TRANSACTIONS/CAREER NOTES: Selected by Toronto Blue Jays organization in ninth round of free-agent draft (June 4, 1990). . . . On disabled list (August 12-27, 1993 and March 26, 1994-entire season). . . . Traded by Blue Jays with P Edwin Hurtado to Seattle Mariners for P Bill Risley and 2B Miguel Cairo (December 18, 1995).

STATISTICAL NOTES: Pitched 1-0 one-hit, complete-game loss for Toronto against Baltimore (August 2, 1995).

Year	Team (League)	W	L	Pct.	ERA	G	GS	CG	ShO	Sv.	IP	H	R	ER	BB	SO
1990—	St. Cathar. (NYP)	0	5	.000	4.05	8	8	0	0	0	40	34	27	18	19	38
	—Myrtle Beach (SAL)	3	0	1.000	0.59	5	4	1	0	0	30 2/3	18	5	2	5	18
1991—	Dunedin (Fla. St.)	10	6	.625	2.66	20	20	3	0	0	128 1/3	114	42	38	34	114
1992—	Knoxville (South.)	10	11	.476	3.85	28	28	2	1	0	177 2/3	181	85	76	38	104
1993—	Syracuse (Int'l)	9	10	.474	3.64	25	25	4	0	0	151	143	74	61	67	108
1994—								Did not play.								
1995—	Toronto (A.L.)	1	4	.200	4.92	21	9	1	0	0	78 2/3	72	49	43	47	50
	—Syracuse (Int'l)	2	4	.333	6.31	10	10	0	0	0	51 1/3	62	42	36	25	30
Major league totals (1 year)		1	4	.200	4.92	21	9	1	0	0	78 2/3	72	49	43	47	50

MERCED, ORLANDO — OF/1B — PIRATES

PERSONAL: Born November 2, 1966, in San Juan, Puerto Rico. . . . 5-11/183. . . . Bats left, throws right. . . . Full name: Orlando Luis Merced. . . . Name pronounced mer-SED.

HIGH SCHOOL: University Garden (San Juan, Puerto Rico).

TRANSACTIONS/CAREER NOTES: Signed as non-drafted free agent by Pittsburgh Pirates organization (February 22, 1985). . . . On Macon disabled list (April 18-28, 1987). . . . On Watertown disabled list (June 23, 1987-remainder of season).

STATISTICAL NOTES: Led N.L. outfielders with five double plays in 1993. . . . Career major league grand slams: 1.

MISCELLANEOUS: Batted as switch-hitter (1985-92).

							BATTING							FIELDING			
Year	Team (League)	Pos.	G	AB	R	H	2B	3B	HR	RBI	Avg.	BB	SO	SB	PO	A	E	Avg.
1985—	GC Pirates (GCL)	SS-3B-1B	40	136	16	31	6	0	1	13	.228	9	9	3	46	78	28	.816
1986—	Macon (S. Atl.)	OF-3B	65	173	20	34	4	1	2	24	.197	12	38	5	53	15	13	.840
	—Watertown (NYP)	3B-1B-OF	27	89	12	16	0	1	3	9	.180	14	21	6	49	28	10	.885
1987—	Macon (S. Atl.)	OF	4	4	1	0	0	0	0	0	.000	1	3	0	1	1	0	1.000
	—Watertown (NYP)	2B	4	12	4	5	0	1	0	3	.417	1	1	1	11	7	2	.900
1988—	Augusta (S. Atl.)	2B-3B-SS	37	136	19	36	6	3	1	17	.265	7	20	2	35	39	7	.914
	—Salem (Carolina)	3-2-O-S	80	298	47	87	12	7	7	42	.292	27	64	13	77	183	31	.893
1989—	Harrisburg (East.)	1B-OF-3B	95	341	43	82	16	4	6	48	.240	32	66	13	435	32	10	.979
	—Buffalo (A.A.)	1B-OF-3B	35	129	18	44	5	3	1	16	.341	7	26	0	173	15	3	.984
1990—	Buffalo (A.A.)	1B-3B-OF	101	378	52	99	12	6	9	55	.262	46	63	14	689	83	20	.975
	—Pittsburgh (N.L.)	OF-C	25	24	3	5	1	0	0	0	.208	1	9	0	0	0	0	...
1991—	Buffalo (A.A.)	1B	3	12	1	2	0	0	0	0	.167	1	4	1	29	2	0	1.000
	—Pittsburgh (N.L.)	1B-OF	120	411	83	113	17	2	10	50	.275	64	81	8	916	60	12	.988
1992—	Pittsburgh (N.L.)	1B-OF	134	405	50	100	28	5	6	60	.247	52	63	5	906	75	5	.995
1993—	Pittsburgh (N.L.)	OF-1B	137	447	68	140	26	4	8	70	.313	77	64	3	485	31	10	.981
1994—	Pittsburgh (N.L.)	OF-1B	108	386	48	105	21	3	9	51	.272	42	58	4	508	29	5	.991
1995—	Pittsburgh (N.L.)	OF-1B	132	487	75	146	29	4	15	83	.300	52	74	7	374	23	6	.985
Major league totals (6 years)			656	2160	327	609	122	18	48	314	.282	288	349	27	3189	218	38	.989

CHAMPIONSHIP SERIES RECORD

NOTES: Hit home run in first at-bat (October 12, 1991).

							BATTING							FIELDING			
Year	Team (League)	Pos.	G	AB	R	H	2B	3B	HR	RBI	Avg.	BB	SO	SB	PO	A	E	Avg.
1991—	Pittsburgh (N.L.)	1B-PH	3	9	1	2	0	0	1	1	.222	0	1	0	13	0	1	.929
1992—	Pittsburgh (N.L.)	1B-PH	4	10	0	1	1	0	0	2	.100	2	4	0	27	2	1	.967
Championship series totals (2 years)			7	19	1	3	1	0	1	3	.158	2	5	0	40	2	2	.955

MERCEDES, HENRY — C — ROYALS

PERSONAL: Born July 23, 1969, in Santo Domingo, Dominican Republic. . . . 6-1/210. . . . Bats right, throws right. . . . Full name: Henry Felipe Perez Mercedes.

TRANSACTIONS/CAREER NOTES: Signed as non-drafted free agent by Oakland Athletics organization (June 22, 1987). . . . Granted free agency (October 15, 1994). . . . Signed by Omaha, Kansas City Royals organization (November 11, 1994).

STATISTICAL NOTES: Led California League catchers with 21 errors in 1991. . . . Led Pacific Coast League catchers with 12 errors and 10 double plays in 1993.

							BATTING							FIELDING			
Year	Team (League)	Pos.	G	AB	R	H	2B	3B	HR	RBI	Avg.	BB	SO	SB	PO	A	E	Avg.
1987—							Dominican Summer League statistics unavailable.										
1988—	Arizona A's (Ariz.)	C	2	5	1	2	0	0	0	0	.400	0	0	0	13	2	0	1.000
1989—	S. Oregon (N'west)	C-3B	22	61	6	10	0	1	0	1	.164	10	24	0	129	15	3	.980
	—Modesto (Calif.)	C	16	37	6	3	0	0	1	3	.081	7	22	0	81	9	4	.957
	—Madison (Midwest)	C	51	152	11	32	3	0	2	13	.211	22	46	0	304	40	5	.986
1990—	Madison (Midwest)	C-3-2-O	90	282	29	64	13	2	3	37	.227	30	100	6	555	110	9	.987
	—Tacoma (PCL)	C	12	31	3	6	1	0	0	2	.194	3	7	0	46	4	0	1.000
1991—	Modesto (Calif.)	C-3B-P	116	388	55	100	17	3	4	61	.258	68	110	5	551	86	†24	.964
1992—	Tacoma (PCL)	C	85	246	36	57	9	2	0	20	.232	26	60	1	476	62	9	.984
	—Oakland (A.L.)	C	9	5	1	4	0	1	0	1	.800	0	1	0	7	0	1	.875
1993—	Tacoma (PCL)	C-3B-OF	85	256	37	61	13	1	4	32	.238	31	53	1	332	74	†18	.958
	—Oakland (A.L.)	C-DH	20	47	5	10	2	0	0	3	.213	2	15	1	66	10	1	.987
1994—	Tacoma (PCL)	C-3-1-O	66	205	16	39	5	1	1	17	.190	13	60	1	216	33	8	.969
1995—	Omaha (A.A.)■	C-3B	86	275	37	59	12	0	11	37	.215	22	90	2	419	71	8	.984
	—Kansas City (A.L.)	C	23	43	7	11	2	0	0	9	.256	8	13	0	62	8	1	.986
Major league totals (3 years)			52	95	13	25	4	1	0	13	.263	10	29	1	135	18	3	.981

RECORD AS PITCHER

Year	Team (League)	W	L	Pct.	ERA	G	GS	CG	ShO	Sv.	IP	H	R	ER	BB	SO
1991—	Modesto (Calif.)	0	1	.000	81.00	1	0	0	0	0	1	4	9	9	6	2

MERCEDES, JOSE — P — BREWERS

PERSONAL: Born March 5, 1971, in El Seibo, Dominican Republic. . . . 6-1/199. . . . Throws right, bats right. . . . Full name: Jose Miguel Mercedes.

TRANSACTIONS/CAREER NOTES: Signed as non-drafted free agent by Baltimore Orioles organization (August 10, 1989). . . . Selected by Milwaukee Brewers from Orioles organization in Rule 5 major league draft (December 13, 1993). . . . On Milwaukee disabled list (April 2-May 30, 1994); included rehabilitation assignments to El Paso (April 30-May 14) and New Orleans (May 14-28). . . . On disabled list (May 14, 1995-remainder of season).

Year	Team (League)	W	L	Pct.	ERA	G	GS	CG	ShO	Sv.	IP	H	R	ER	BB	SO
1990—		Dominican Summer League statistics unavailable.														
1991—		Dominican Summer League statistics unavailable.														
1992—	GC Orioles (GCL)	2	3	.400	1.78	8	5	2	0	0	35 1/3	31	12	7	13	21
	—Kane Co. (Mid.)	3	2	.600	2.66	8	8	2	•2	0	47 1/3	40	26	14	15	45
1993—	Bowie (Eastern)	6	8	.429	4.78	26	23	3	0	0	147	170	86	78	65	75
1994—	El Paso (Texas)■	2	0	1.000	4.66	3	0	0	0	0	9 2/3	13	6	5	4	8
	—New Orleans (A.A.)	0	0	...	4.91	3	3	0	0	0	18 1/3	19	10	10	8	7
	—Milwaukee (A.L.)	2	0	1.000	2.32	19	0	0	0	0	31	22	9	8	16	11
1995—	Milwaukee (A.L.)	0	1	.000	9.82	5	0	0	0	0	7 1/3	12	9	8	8	6
Major league totals (2 years)		2	1	.667	3.76	24	0	0	0	0	38 1/3	34	18	16	24	17

MERCKER, KENT — P — ORIOLES

PERSONAL: Born February 1, 1968, in Dublin, O. . . . 6-2/195. . . . Throws left, bats left. . . . Full name: Kent Franklin Mercker.

HIGH SCHOOL: Dublin (O.).

TRANSACTIONS/CAREER NOTES: Selected by Atlanta Braves organization in first round (fifth pick overall) of free-agent draft (June 2, 1986). . . . On disabled list (March 30-May 6, 1990 and August 9-24, 1991). . . . Traded by Braves to Baltimore Orioles for P Joe Borowski and P Rachaad Stewart (December 17, 1995).

HONORS: Named Carolina League co-Pitcher of the Year (1988).

STATISTICAL NOTES: Pitched six innings, combining with Mark Wohlers (two innings) and Alejandro Pena (one inning) in 1-0 no-hit victory against San Diego (September 11, 1991). . . . Pitched 6-0 no-hit victory against Los Angeles (April 8, 1994).

Year	Team (League)	W	L	Pct.	ERA	G	GS	CG	ShO	Sv.	IP	H	R	ER	BB	SO
1986—	GC Braves (GCL)	4	3	.571	2.47	9	8	0	0	0	47 1/3	37	21	13	16	42
1987—	Durham (Carolina)	0	1	.000	5.40	3	3	0	0	0	11 2/3	11	8	7	6	14
1988—	Durham (Carolina)	11	4	.733	*2.75	19	19	5	0	0	127 2/3	102	44	39	47	159
	—Greenville (South.)	3	1	.750	3.35	9	9	0	0	0	48 1/3	36	20	18	26	60
1989—	Richmond (Int'l)	9	12	.429	3.20	27	•27	4	0	0	168 2/3	107	66	60	*95	*144
	—Atlanta (N.L.)	0	0	...	12.46	2	1	0	0	0	4 1/3	8	6	6	6	4
1990—	Richmond (Int'l)	5	4	.556	3.55	12	10	0	0	1	58 1/3	60	30	23	27	69
	—Atlanta (N.L.)	4	7	.364	3.17	36	0	0	0	7	48 1/3	43	22	17	24	39
1991—	Atlanta (N.L.)	5	3	.625	2.58	50	4	0	0	6	73 1/3	56	23	21	35	62
1992—	Atlanta (N.L.)	3	2	.600	3.42	53	0	0	0	6	68 1/3	51	27	26	35	49
1993—	Atlanta (N.L.)	3	1	.750	2.86	43	6	0	0	0	66	52	24	21	36	59
1994—	Atlanta (N.L.)	9	4	.692	3.45	20	17	2	1	0	112 1/3	90	46	43	45	111
1995—	Atlanta (N.L.)	7	8	.467	4.15	29	26	0	0	0	143	140	73	66	61	102
Major league totals (7 years)		31	25	.554	3.49	233	54	2	1	19	515 2/3	440	221	200	242	426

DIVISION SERIES RECORD

Year	Team (League)	W	L	Pct.	ERA	G	GS	CG	ShO	Sv.	IP	H	R	ER	BB	SO
1995—	Atlanta (N.L.)	0	0	...	0.00	1	0	0	0	0	1/3	0	0	0	0	0

CHAMPIONSHIP SERIES RECORD

NOTES: Shares single-series record for most games pitched—5 (1993).

Year	Team (League)	W	L	Pct.	ERA	G	GS	CG	ShO	Sv.	IP	H	R	ER	BB	SO
1991—	Atlanta (N.L.)	0	1	.000	13.50	1	0	0	0	0	2/3	0	1	1	2	0
1992—	Atlanta (N.L.)	0	0	...	0.00	2	0	0	0	0	3	1	0	0	1	1
1993—	Atlanta (N.L.)	0	0	...	1.80	5	0	0	0	0	5	3	1	1	2	4
Champ. series totals (3 years)		0	1	.000	2.08	8	0	0	0	0	8 2/3	4	2	2	5	5

WORLD SERIES RECORD

NOTES: Member of World Series championship team (1995).

Year	Team (League)	W	L	Pct.	ERA	G	GS	CG	ShO	Sv.	IP	H	R	ER	BB	SO
1991—	Atlanta (N.L.)	0	0	...	0.00	2	0	0	0	0	1	0	0	0	0	1
1995—	Atlanta (N.L.)	0	0	...	4.50	1	0	0	0	0	2	1	1	1	2	2
World Series totals (2 years)		0	0	...	3.00	3	0	0	0	0	3	1	1	1	2	3

MERULLO, MATT — C

PERSONAL: Born August 4, 1965, in Ridgefield, Conn. . . . 6-2/200. . . . Bats left, throws right. . . . Full name: Matthew Bates Merullo. . . . Grandson of Lennie Merullo Sr., infielder, Chicago Cubs (1941-47); and son of Lennie Merullo Jr., minor league infielder (1961-64).

HIGH SCHOOL: Fairfield (Conn.) College Prep.

COLLEGE: North Carolina.

TRANSACTIONS/CAREER NOTES: Selected by Chicago White Sox organization in seventh round of free-agent draft (June 2, 1986). . . . On Vancouver disabled list (July 9-17 and July 25-September 16, 1992). . . . Traded by White Sox organization to Cleveland Indians organization for OF Ken Ramos (March 30, 1994). . . . Granted free agency (October 15, 1994). . . . Signed by Salt Lake, Minnesota Twins organization (December 16, 1994). . . . Granted free agency (October 6, 1995).

STATISTICAL NOTES: Led Southern League with 21 passed balls in 1988. . . . Led Southern League catchers with 18 errors in 1990. . . . Career major league grand slams: 1.

M

Year	Team (League)	Pos.	G	AB	R	H	2B	3B	HR	RBI	Avg.	BB	SO	SB	PO	A	E	Avg.
				BATTING											FIELDING			
1986—	Peninsula (Caro.)	C	64	208	21	63	12	2	3	35	.303	19	16	1	225	26	6	.977
1987—	Day. Beach (FSL)	C-1B-OF	70	250	26	65	11	6	4	47	.260	20	18	1	227	28	6	.977
—	Birm. (Southern)	C	48	167	13	46	7	0	2	17	.275	6	20	1	278	24	8	.974
1988—	Birm. (Southern)	C-1B	125	449	58	117	26	0	6	60	.261	40	59	3	640	60	14	.980
1989—	Vancouver (PCL)	C	3	9	0	2	1	0	0	2	.222	2	1	0	19	1	1	.952
—	Chicago (A.L.)	C	31	81	5	18	1	0	1	8	.222	6	14	0	100	10	3	.973
—	Birm. (Southern)	C	33	119	19	35	6	0	3	23	.294	16	15	0	149	10	1	.994
1990—	Birm. (Southern)	C-1B	102	378	57	110	26	1	8	50	.291	34	49	2	561	51	†24	.962
1991—	Chicago (A.L.)	C-1B-DH	80	140	8	32	1	0	5	21	.229	9	18	0	159	14	2	.989
—	Birm. (Southern)	C	8	28	5	6	0	0	2	3	.214	2	4	0	25	3	1	.966
1992—	Chicago (A.L.)	C-DH	24	50	3	9	1	1	0	3	.180	1	8	0	64	3	2	.971
—	Vancouver (PCL)	C-1B	14	45	2	8	1	1	1	4	.178	1	2	0	54	4	2	.967
1993—	Nashville (A.A.)	C-1B	103	352	50	117	30	1	12	65	*.332	28	47	0	435	40	8	.983
—	Chicago (A.L.)	DH	8	20	1	1	0	0	0	0	.050	0	1	0	...	...	...	...
1994—	Charlotte (Int'l)■	C	112	417	52	125	20	6	12	75	.300	25	47	2	405	38	10	.978
—	Cleveland (A.L.)	C	4	10	1	1	0	0	0	0	.100	2	1	0	22	0	1	.957
1995—	Minnesota (A.L.)■	C-DH-1B	76	195	19	55	14	1	1	27	.282	14	27	0	215	13	3	.987
Major league totals (6 years)			223	496	37	116	17	2	7	59	.234	32	69	0	560	40	11	.982

MESA, JOSE — P — INDIANS

PERSONAL: Born May 22, 1966, in Azua, Dominican Republic. . . . 6-3/225. . . . Throws right, bats right. . . . Full name: Jose Ramon Mesa.

HIGH SCHOOL: Santa School (Azua, Dominican Republic).

TRANSACTIONS/CAREER NOTES: Signed as non-drafted free agent by Toronto Blue Jays organization (October 31, 1981). . . . On Kinston disabled list (August 27, 1984-remainder of season). . . . Traded by Blue Jays organization to Baltimore Orioles (September 4, 1987), completing deal in which Orioles traded P Mike Flanagan to Blue Jays for P Oswald Peraza and a player to be named later (August 31, 1987). . . . On Rochester disabled list (April 18-May 16 and June 30, 1988-remainder of season; May 27, 1989-remainder of season; and August 21-September 5, 1991). . . . Traded by Orioles to Cleveland Indians for OF Kyle Washington (July 14, 1992). . . . On suspended list (April 5-8, 1993).

HONORS: Named A.L. Fireman of the Year by The Sporting News (1995).

STATISTICAL NOTES: Tied for Carolina League lead with nine hit batsmen in 1985.

MISCELLANEOUS: Appeared in one game as pinch-runner for Baltimore (1991).

Year	Team (League)	W	L	Pct.	ERA	G	GS	CG	ShO	Sv.	IP	H	R	ER	BB	SO
1982—	GC Blue Jays (GCL)	6	4	.600	2.70	13	12	6	*3	1	83 1/3	58	34	25	20	40
1983—	Florence (S. Atl.)	6	12	.333	5.48	28	27	1	0	0	141 1/3	153	*116	86	93	91
1984—	Florence (S. Atl.)	4	3	.571	3.76	7	7	0	0	0	38 1/3	38	24	16	25	35
—	Kinston (Carolina)	5	2	.714	3.91	10	9	0	0	0	50 2/3	51	23	22	28	24
1985—	Kinston (Carolina)	5	10	.333	6.16	30	20	0	0	1	106 2/3	110	89	73	79	71
1986—	Vent. County (Calif.)	10	6	.625	3.86	24	24	2	1	0	142 1/3	141	71	61	58	113
—	Knoxville (South.)	2	2	.500	4.35	9	8	2	1	0	41 1/3	40	32	20	23	30
1987—	Knoxville (South.)	10	•13	.435	5.21	35	*35	4	2	0	*193 1/3	*206	*131	*112	104	115
—	Baltimore (A.L.)■	1	3	.250	6.03	6	5	0	0	0	31 1/3	38	23	21	15	17
1988—	Rochester (Int'l)	0	3	.000	8.62	11	2	0	0	0	15 2/3	21	20	15	14	15
1989—	Rochester (Int'l)	0	2	.000	5.40	7	1	0	0	0	10	10	6	6	6	3
—	Hagerstown (East.)	0	0	...	1.38	3	3	0	0	0	13	9	2	2	4	12
1990—	Hagerstown (East.)	5	5	.500	3.42	15	15	3	1	0	79	77	35	30	30	72
—	Rochester (Int'l)	1	2	.333	2.42	4	4	0	0	0	26	21	11	7	12	23
—	Baltimore (A.L.)	3	2	.600	3.86	7	7	0	0	0	46 2/3	37	20	20	27	24
1991—	Baltimore (A.L.)	6	11	.353	5.97	23	23	2	1	0	123 2/3	151	86	82	62	64
—	Rochester (Int'l)	3	3	.500	3.86	8	8	1	1	0	51 1/3	37	25	22	30	48
1992—	Baltimore (A.L.)	3	8	.273	5.19	13	12	0	0	0	67 2/3	77	41	39	27	22
—	Cleveland (A.L.)■	4	4	.500	4.16	15	15	1	1	0	93	92	45	43	43	40
1993—	Cleveland (A.L.)	10	12	.455	4.92	34	33	3	0	0	208 2/3	232	122	114	62	118
1994—	Cleveland (A.L.)	7	5	.583	3.82	51	0	0	0	2	73	71	33	31	26	63
1995—	Cleveland (A.L.)	3	0	1.000	1.13	62	0	0	0	*46	64	49	9	8	17	58
Major league totals (7 years)		37	45	.451	4.55	211	95	6	2	48	708	747	379	358	279	406

DIVISION SERIES RECORD

Year	Team (League)	W	L	Pct.	ERA	G	GS	CG	ShO	Sv.	IP	H	R	ER	BB	SO
1995—	Cleveland (A.L.)	0	0	...	0.00	2	0	0	0	0	2	0	0	0	2	0

CHAMPIONSHIP SERIES RECORD

Year	Team (League)	W	L	Pct.	ERA	G	GS	CG	ShO	Sv.	IP	H	R	ER	BB	SO
1995—	Cleveland (A.L.)	0	0	...	2.25	4	0	0	0	1	4	3	1	1	1	1

WORLD SERIES RECORD

Year	Team (League)	W	L	Pct.	ERA	G	GS	CG	ShO	Sv.	IP	H	R	ER	BB	SO
1995—	Cleveland (A.L.)	1	0	1.000	4.50	2	0	0	0	1	4	5	2	2	1	4

ALL-STAR GAME RECORD

Year	League	W	L	Pct.	ERA	GS	CG	ShO	Sv.	IP	H	R	ER	BB	SO
1995—	American	0	0	...	0.00	0	0	0	0	1	0	0	0	0	1

MICELI, DAN — P — PIRATES

PERSONAL: Born September 9, 1970, in Newark, N.J. . . . 6-0/216. . . . Throws right, bats right. . . . Full name: Daniel Miceli.

HIGH SCHOOL: Dr. Phillips (Orlando, Fla.).

TRANSACTIONS/CAREER NOTES: Signed as non-drafted free agent by Kansas City Royals organization (March 7, 1990). . . . Traded by Royals with P Jon Lieber to Pittsburgh Pirates for P Stan Belinda (July 31, 1993).

Year	Team (League)	W	L	Pct.	ERA	G	GS	CG	ShO	Sv.	IP	H	R	ER	BB	SO
1990—	GC Royals (GCL)	3	4	.429	3.91	*27	0	0	0	4	53	45	27	23	29	48
1991—	Eugene (N'west)	0	1	.000	2.14	25	0	0	0	10	33 2/3	18	8	8	18	43
1992—	Appleton (Midw.)	1	1	.500	1.93	23	0	0	0	9	23 1/3	12	6	5	4	44
	—Memphis (South.)	3	0	1.000	1.91	32	0	0	0	4	37 2/3	20	10	8	13	46
1993—	Memphis (South.)	6	4	.600	4.60	40	0	0	0	7	58 2/3	54	30	30	39	68
	—Carolina (South.)■	0	2	.000	5.11	13	0	0	0	10	12 1/3	11	8	7	4	19
	—Pittsburgh (N.L.)	0	0	...	5.06	9	0	0	0	0	5 1/3	6	3	3	3	4
1994—	Buffalo (A.A.)	1	1	.500	1.88	19	0	0	0	2	24	15	5	5	6	31
	—Pittsburgh (N.L.)	2	1	.667	5.93	28	0	0	0	2	27 1/3	28	19	18	11	27
1995—	Pittsburgh (N.L.)	4	4	.500	4.66	58	0	0	0	21	58	61	30	30	28	56
Major league totals (3 years)		6	5	.545	5.06	95	0	0	0	23	90 2/3	95	52	51	42	87

MIESKE, MATT — OF — BREWERS

PERSONAL: Born February 13, 1968, in Midland, Mich. . . . 6-0/192. . . . Bats right, throws right. . . . Full name: Matthew Todd Mieske. . . . Name pronounced MEE-skee.
HIGH SCHOOL: Bay City Western (Auburn, Mich.).
COLLEGE: Western Michigan.
TRANSACTIONS/CAREER NOTES: Selected by Oakland Athletics organization in 20th round of free-agent draft (June 5, 1989); did not sign. . . . Selected by San Diego Padres organization in 17th round of free-agent draft (June 4, 1990). . . . Traded by Padres organization with P Ricky Bones and IF Jose Valentin to Milwaukee Brewers organization for 3B Gary Sheffield and P Geoff Kellogg (March 27, 1992). . . . On New Orleans disabled list (May 25-June 10 and June 13-July 29, 1993).
HONORS: Named Northwest League Most Valuable Player (1990). . . . Named California League Most Valuable Player (1991).
STATISTICAL NOTES: Led Northwest League with 155 total bases in 1990. . . . Led Northwest League outfielders with 148 total chances in 1990. . . . Led California League with 261 total bases and .456 on-base percentage in 1991. . . . Career major league grand slams: 2.

			BATTING												FIELDING			
Year	Team (League)	Pos.	G	AB	R	H	2B	3B	HR	RBI	Avg.	BB	SO	SB	PO	A	E	Avg.
1990—	Spokane (N'west)	OF	*76	*291	*59	99	20	0	*12	*63	.340	45	43	26	*134	7	7	.953
1991—	High Desert (Calif.)	OF	•133	492	108	*168	*36	6	15	119	*.341	*94	82	39	258	14	*15	.948
1992—	Denver (A.A.)■	OF	134	*524	80	140	29	11	19	77	.267	39	90	13	252	*23	*13	.955
1993—	New Orleans (A.A.)	OF	60	219	36	57	14	2	8	22	.260	27	46	6	114	4	2	.983
	—Milwaukee (A.L.)	OF	23	58	9	14	0	0	3	7	.241	4	14	0	43	1	3	.936
1994—	Milwaukee (A.L.)	OF-DH	84	259	39	67	13	1	10	38	.259	21	62	3	154	7	4	.976
	—New Orleans (A.A.)	OF	2	8	2	2	0	0	1	3	.250	1	1	1	2	0	0	1.000
1995—	Milwaukee (A.L.)	OF-DH	117	267	42	67	13	1	12	48	.251	27	45	2	177	7	4	.979
Major league totals (3 years)			224	584	90	148	26	2	25	93	.253	52	121	5	374	15	11	.973

MILLER, KEITH — 3B

PERSONAL: Born June 12, 1963, in Midland, Mich. . . . 5-11/185. . . . Bats right, throws right. . . . Full name: Keith Alan Miller.
HIGH SCHOOL: All Saints (Bay City, Mich.).
COLLEGE: Oral Roberts.
TRANSACTIONS/CAREER NOTES: Selected by Cleveland Indians organization in 24th round of free-agent draft (June 5, 1981); did not sign. . . . Selected by New York Yankees organization in second round of free-agent draft (June 4, 1984); pick received as compensation for San Diego Padres signing free-agent P Goose Gossage. Contract was later voided after it was discovered Miller had a pre-existing knee injury. . . . Signed as non-drafted free agent by New York Mets organization (September 6, 1984). . . . On disabled list (April 8-May 20, 1986). . . . On New York disabled list (June 29-September 1, 1987); included rehabilitation assignment to Tidewater (August 21-September 1). . . . On disabled list (April 25-May 17 and August 15-September 1, 1990; and May 27-June 16, 1991). . . . Traded by Mets with OF Kevin McReynolds and IF Gregg Jefferies to Kansas City Royals for P Bret Saberhagen and IF Bill Pecota (December 11, 1991). . . . On disabled list (May 18-June 2 and July 11-August 14, 1992). . . . On Kansas City disabled list (April 6-21, 1993). . . . On Kansas City disabled list (June 5-August 23, 1993); included rehabilitation assignment to Omaha (August 16-23). . . . Granted free agency (December 20, 1993). . . . Re-signed by Royals (December 22, 1993). . . . On Kansas City disabled list (March 25-July 14); included rehabilitation assignment to Omaha (June 21-July 10). . . . Granted free agency (October 24, 1994). . . . Re-signed by Royals organization (December 13, 1994). . . . Released by Royals (May 15, 1995).
STATISTICAL NOTES: Tied for Texas League lead in being hit by pitch with seven in 1986.

			BATTING												FIELDING			
Year	Team (League)	Pos.	G	AB	R	H	2B	3B	HR	RBI	Avg.	BB	SO	SB	PO	A	E	Avg.
1985—	Lynchburg (Caro.)	3B-2B-OF	89	325	51	98	16	5	7	54	.302	39	52	14	103	203	25	.924
	—Jackson (Texas)	2B-SS	46	165	17	37	8	1	3	22	.224	12	38	8	108	132	8	.968
1986—	Jackson (Texas)	2B	94	353	80	116	23	4	5	36	.329	62	56	23	198	272	19	.961
1987—	Tidewater (Int'l)	2B-OF	53	202	29	50	9	1	6	22	.248	14	36	14	112	129	5	.980
	—New York (N.L.)	2B	25	51	14	19	2	2	0	1	.373	2	6	8	21	38	2	.967
1988—	Tidewater (Int'l)	2-S-3-O	42	171	23	48	11	1	1	15	.281	12	19	8	81	111	12	.941
	—New York (N.L.)	2-S-3-O	40	70	9	15	1	1	1	5	.214	6	10	0	34	24	5	.921
1989—	Tidewater (Int'l)	2-O-S-3	48	184	33	49	8	2	1	15	.266	18	24	12	89	109	8	.961
	—New York (N.L.)	2-O-S-3	57	143	15	33	7	0	1	7	.231	5	27	6	90	52	5	.966
1990—	New York (N.L.)	OF-2B-SS	88	233	42	60	8	0	1	12	.258	23	46	16	168	21	4	.979
1991—	New York (N.L.)	2-O-3-S	98	275	41	77	22	1	4	23	.280	23	44	14	165	154	10	.970
1992—	Kansas City (A.L.)■	2B-OF-DH	106	416	57	118	24	4	4	38	.284	31	46	16	230	250	15	.970
1993—	Kansas City (A.L.)	3-DH-O-2	37	108	9	18	3	0	0	3	.167	8	19	3	18	35	6	.898
	—Omaha (A.A.)	3B	6	24	2	7	1	1	0	2	.292	0	2	1	2	8	1	.909
1994—	Omaha (A.A.)	3B-2B-OF	15	49	7	9	2	1	0	3	.184	6	10	2	26	19	3	.938
	—Kansas City (A.L.)	OF-3B	5	15	1	2	0	0	0	0	.133	0	3	0	7	2	0	1.000
1995—	Kansas City (A.L.)	DH-OF	9	15	2	5	0	0	1	3	.333	2	4	0	5	1	0	1.000
	—Omaha (A.A.)	OF	7	20	3	5	2	0	0	2	.250	4	2	1	2	0	0	1.000
American League totals (4 years)			157	554	69	143	27	4	5	44	.258	41	72	19	260	288	21	.963
National League totals (5 years)			308	772	121	204	40	4	7	48	.264	59	133	44	478	289	26	.967
Major league totals (9 years)			465	1326	190	347	67	8	12	92	.262	100	205	63	738	577	47	.965

MILLER, KURT — P — MARLINS

PERSONAL: Born August 24, 1972, in Tucson, Ariz. . . . 6-5/205. . . . Throws right, bats right. . . . Full name: Kurt Everett Miller.
HIGH SCHOOL: Bowie (Tex.), Tulsa (Okla.) Union and West (Bakersfield, Calif.).
TRANSACTIONS/CAREER NOTES: Selected by Pittsburgh Pirates organization in first round (fifth pick overall) of free-agent draft (June 4, 1990). . . . On Augusta disabled list (July 10-August 3, 1991). . . . Traded by Pirates with a player to be named later to Texas Rangers for 3B Steve Buechele (August 30, 1991); Rangers acquired P Hector Fajardo to complete deal (September 6, 1991). . . . Traded by Rangers with P Robb Nen to Florida Marlins for P Cris Carpenter (July 17, 1993).
STATISTICAL NOTES: Tied for Texas League lead with four balks in 1992.

Year	Team (League)	W	L	Pct.	ERA	G	GS	CG	ShO	Sv.	IP	H	R	ER	BB	SO
1990	—Welland (NYP)	3	2	.600	3.29	14	12	0	0	0	65 2/3	59	39	24	37	62
1991	—Augusta (S. Atl.)	6	7	.462	2.50	21	21	2	2	0	115 1/3	89	49	32	57	103
1992	—Charlotte (Fla. St.)■	5	4	.556	2.39	12	12	0	0	0	75 1/3	51	23	20	29	58
	—Tulsa (Texas)	7	5	.583	3.68	16	15	0	0	0	88	82	42	36	35	73
1993	—Tulsa (Texas)	6	8	.429	5.06	18	18	0	0	0	96	102	69	54	45	68
	—Edmonton (PCL)■	3	3	.500	4.50	9	9	0	0	0	48	42	24	24	34	19
1994	—Edmonton (PCL)	7	*13	.350	6.88	23	23	0	0	0	125 2/3	164	105	96	64	58
	—Florida (N.L.)	1	3	.250	8.10	4	4	0	0	0	20	26	18	18	7	11
1995	—Charlotte (Int'l)	8	11	.421	4.62	22	22	0	0	0	126 2/3	143	76	65	55	83
Major league totals (1 year)		1	3	.250	8.10	4	4	0	0	0	20	26	18	18	7	11

MILLER, ORLANDO — SS — ASTROS

PERSONAL: Born January 13, 1969, in Changuinola, Panama. . . . 6-1/180. . . . Bats right, throws right. . . . Full name: Orlando Salmon Miller.
TRANSACTIONS/CAREER NOTES: Signed as non-drafted free agent by New York Yankees organization (September 17, 1987). . . . Traded by Yankees organization to Houston Astros organization for IF Dave Silvestri and a player to be named later (March 13, 1990); Yankees acquired P Daven Bond to complete deal (June 11, 1990). . . . On Jackson disabled list (May 10-June 8, 1991). . . . On disabled list (April 8-24, 1993 and August 26-September 10, 1995).
STATISTICAL NOTES: Led South Atlantic League shortstops with 93 double plays in 1990.

				BATTING										FIELDING			
Year	Team (League)	Pos.	G	AB	R	H	2B	3B	HR	RBI	Avg.	BB	SO	SB	PO	A	E	Avg.
1988	—Fort Lauder. (FSL)	SS	3	11	0	3	0	0	0	1	.273	0	1	0	4	4	0	1.000
	—GC Yankees (GCL)	2B-SS	14	44	5	8	1	0	0	5	.182	3	10	1	19	30	5	.907
1989	—Oneonta (NYP)	2-S-3-0	58	213	29	62	5	2	1	25	.291	6	37	8	96	124	9	.961
1990	—Asheville (S. Atl.)■	SS	121	438	60	137	29	6	4	62	.313	25	52	12	208	348	*47	.922
1991	—Jackson (Texas)	SS	23	70	5	13	6	0	1	5	.186	5	13	0	31	66	12	.890
	—Osceola (Fla. St.)	SS	74	272	27	81	11	2	0	36	.298	13	30	1	106	205	24	.928
1992	—Jackson (Texas)	SS	115	379	51	100	26	5	5	53	.264	16	75	7	132	254	22	.946
	—Tucson (PCL)	SS	10	37	4	9	0	0	2	8	.243	1	2	0	10	26	1	.973
1993	—Tucson (PCL)	SS	122	471	86	143	29	16	16	89	.304	20	95	2	180	389	*33	.945
1994	—Tucson (PCL)	SS-2B	93	338	54	87	16	6	10	55	.257	16	77	3	154	296	29	.939
	—Houston (N.L.)	SS-2B	16	40	3	13	0	1	2	9	.325	2	12	1	12	30	0	1.000
1995	—Houston (N.L.)	SS	92	324	36	85	20	1	5	36	.262	22	71	3	131	270	15	.964
Major league totals (2 years)			108	364	39	98	20	2	7	45	.269	24	83	4	143	300	15	.967

MILLER, TREVER — P — TIGERS

PERSONAL: Born May 29, 1973, in Louisville, Ky. . . . 6-3/175. . . . Throws left, bats right. . . . Full name: Trever Douglas Miller.
HIGH SCHOOL: Trinity (Louisville, Ky.).
TRANSACTIONS/CAREER NOTES: Selected by Detroit Tigers organization in supplemental round ("sandwich pick" between first and second round, 41st pick overall) of free-agent draft (June 3, 1991); pick received as part of compensation for Atlanta Braves signing Type A free agent C Mike Heath.
STATISTICAL NOTES: Tied for Appalachian League lead with seven home runs allowed in 1991.

Year	Team (League)	W	L	Pct.	ERA	G	GS	CG	ShO	Sv.	IP	H	R	ER	BB	SO
1991	—Bristol (Appal.)	2	7	.222	5.67	13	13	0	0	0	54	60	44	34	29	46
1992	—Bristol (Appal.)	3	•8	.273	4.93	12	12	1	0	0	69 1/3	75	45	38	27	64
1993	—Fayetteville (S. Atl.)	8	13	.381	4.19	28	28	2	0	0	161	151	99	75	67	116
1994	—Trenton (Eastern)	7	•16	.304	4.39	26	26	*6	0	0	174 1/3	*198	95	85	51	73
1995	—Jacksonville (Sou.)	8	2	.800	2.72	31	16	3	2	0	122 1/3	122	46	37	34	77

MILLS, ALAN — P — ORIOLES

PERSONAL: Born October 18, 1966, in Lakeland, Fla. . . . 6-1/192. . . . Throws right, bats both. . . . Full name: Alan Bernard Mills.
HIGH SCHOOL: Kathleen (Fla.).
JUNIOR COLLEGE: Polk Community College (Fla.).
TRANSACTIONS/CAREER NOTES: Selected by Boston Red Sox organization in first round (13th pick overall) of free-agent draft (January 14, 1986); did not sign. . . . Selected by California Angels organization in secondary phase of free-agent draft (June 2, 1986). . . . Traded by Angels organization to New York Yankees organization (June 22, 1987), completing deal in which Angels traded P Ron Romanick and a player to be named later to Yankees for C Butch Wynegar (December 19, 1986). . . . Traded by Yankees to Baltimore Orioles for two players to be named later (February 29, 1992); Yankees acquired P Francisco de la Rosa (February 29, 1992) and P Mark Carper (June 8, 1992) to complete deal. . . . On suspended list (June 26-30, 1993). . . . On Rochester disabled list (July 4-September 16, 1995).

Year	Team (League)	W	L	Pct.	ERA	G	GS	CG	ShO	Sv.	IP	H	R	ER	BB	SO
1986	—Salem (Northwest)	6	6	.500	4.63	14	14	1	0	0	83 2/3	77	58	43	60	50
1987	—Prin. William (Caro.)■	2	11	.154	6.09	35	8	0	0	1	85 2/3	102	75	58	64	53
1988	—Prin. William (Caro.)	3	8	.273	4.13	42	5	0	0	4	93 2/3	93	56	43	43	59
1989	—Prin. William (Caro.)	6	1	.857	0.91	26	0	0	0	7	39 2/3	22	5	4	13	44

Year	Team (League)	W	L	Pct.	ERA	G	GS	CG	ShO	Sv.	IP	H	R	ER	BB	SO
	—Fort Lauder. (FSL)	1	4	.200	3.77	22	0	0	0	6	31	40	15	13	9	25
1990—	New York (A.L.)	1	5	.167	4.10	36	0	0	0	0	41 2/3	48	21	19	33	24
	—Columbus (Int'l)	3	3	.500	3.38	17	0	0	0	6	29 1/3	22	11	11	14	30
1991—	Columbus (Int'l)	7	5	.583	4.43	38	15	0	0	8	113 2/3	109	65	56	75	77
	—New York (A.L.)	1	1	.500	4.41	6	2	0	0	0	16 1/3	16	9	8	8	11
1992—	Rochester (Int'l)■	0	1	.000	5.40	3	0	0	0	1	5	6	3	3	2	8
	—Baltimore (A.L.)	10	4	.714	2.61	35	3	0	0	2	103 1/3	78	33	30	54	60
1993—	Baltimore (A.L.)	5	4	.556	3.23	45	0	0	0	4	100 1/3	80	39	36	51	68
1994—	Baltimore (A.L.)	3	3	.500	5.16	47	0	0	0	2	45 1/3	43	26	26	24	44
1995—	Baltimore (A.L.)	3	0	1.000	7.43	21	0	0	0	0	23	30	20	19	18	16
	—Rochester (Int'l)	0	1	.000	0.00	1	1	0	0	0	2 2/3	2	6	0	5	2
	—GC Orioles (GCL)	0	0	...	0.00	1	1	0	0	0	2	3	0	0	2	1
Major league totals (6 years)		23	17	.575	3.76	190	5	0	0	8	330	295	148	138	188	223

MIMBS, MARK — P — RANGERS

PERSONAL: Born February 13, 1969, in Macon, Ga. . . . 6-2/180. . . . Throws left, bats left. . . . Full name: Mark Ivey Mimbs. . . . Twin brother of Mike Mimbs, pitcher, Philadelphia Phillies.

HIGH SCHOOL: Windsor Academy (Macon, Ga.).

COLLEGE: Mercer (Ga.).

TRANSACTIONS/CAREER NOTES: Selected by Los Angeles Dodgers organization in 25th round of free-agent draft (June 4, 1990). . . . On Albuquerque disabled list (April 7-May 5 and May 20, 1994-remainder of season). . . . On disabled list (July 16-August 26, 1995). . . . Selected by Texas Rangers from Dodgers organization in Rule 5 major league draft (December 4, 1995).

Year	Team (League)	W	L	Pct.	ERA	G	GS	CG	ShO	Sv.	IP	H	R	ER	BB	SO
1990—	Great Falls (Pio.)	7	4	.636	3.23	14	•14	0	0	0	78	69	32	28	29	*94
1991—	Bakersfield (Calif.)	12	6	.667	2.22	27	25	0	0	0	170	134	49	42	59	164
1992—	Albuquerque (PCL)	0	4	.000	6.10	12	7	0	0	0	48 2/3	58	34	33	19	32
	—San Antonio (Tex.)	1	5	.167	3.61	13	13	0	0	0	82 1/3	78	43	33	22	55
1993—	Albuquerque (PCL)	0	1	.000	10.13	19	1	0	0	1	18 2/3	20	21	21	16	12
	—San Antonio (Tex.)	3	3	.500	1.60	49	0	0	0	10	67 2/3	49	21	12	18	77
1994—	Albuquerque (PCL)	1	0	1.000	4.05	6	0	0	0	0	6 2/3	8	3	3	0	9
	—Bakersfield (Calif.)	0	0	...	0.00	1	0	0	0	0	1 2/3	3	0	0	0	0
1995—	Albuquerque (PCL)	6	5	.545	2.97	23	16	1	0	0	106	105	40	35	22	96

MIMBS, MICHAEL — P — PHILLIES

PERSONAL: Born February 13, 1969, in Macon, Ga. . . . 6-2/190. . . . Throws left, bats left. . . . Full name: Michael Randall Mimbs. . . . Twin brother of Mark Mimbs, pitcher, Texas Rangers.

HIGH SCHOOL: Windsor Academy (Macon, Ga.).

COLLEGE: Mercer (Ga.).

TRANSACTIONS/CAREER NOTES: Selected by Los Angeles Dodgers organization in 24th round of free-agent draft (June 4, 1990). . . . Released by Albuquerque, Dodgers organization (March 31, 1993). . . . Signed by St. Paul, independent (May 1993). . . . Signed by Harrisburg, Montreal Expos organization (January 24, 1994). . . . Selected by Philadelphia Phillies from Expos organization in Rule 5 major league draft (December 5, 1994).

Year	Team (League)	W	L	Pct.	ERA	G	GS	CG	ShO	Sv.	IP	H	R	ER	BB	SO
1990—	Great Falls (Pio.)	0	0	...	4.05	3	0	0	0	0	6 2/3	4	5	3	5	7
	—Yakima (N'west)	4	3	.571	3.88	12	12	0	0	0	67 1/3	58	36	29	39	72
1991—	Vero Beach (FSL)	•12	4	.750	2.67	24	22	1	1	0	141 2/3	124	52	42	70	132
1992—	San Antonio (Tex.)	10	8	.556	4.23	24	22	2	0	1	129 2/3	132	65	61	73	87
1993—	St. Paul (Northern)■	8	2	.800	3.20	20	16	1	0	0	98 1/3	94	48	35	45	97
1994—	Harrisburg (East.)■	11	4	.733	3.46	32	21	2	1	0	153 2/3	130	69	59	61	145
1995—	Philadelphia (N.L.)■	9	7	.563	4.15	35	19	2	1	1	136 2/3	127	70	63	75	93
Major league totals (1 year)		9	7	.563	4.15	35	19	2	1	1	136 2/3	127	70	63	75	93

MINOR, BLAS — P — METS

PERSONAL: Born March 20, 1966, in Merced, Calif. . . . 6-3/203. . . . Throws right, bats right. . . . Full name: Blas Minor Jr. . . . Name pronounced BLOSS.

HIGH SCHOOL: Atwater (Calif.).

JUNIOR COLLEGE: Merced (Calif.) College.

COLLEGE: Arizona State.

TRANSACTIONS/CAREER NOTES: Selected by Kansas City Royals organization in 11th round of free-agent draft (January 9, 1985); did not sign. . . . Selected by Philadelphia Phillies organization in secondary phase of free-agent draft (June 3, 1985); did not sign. . . . Selected by Phillies organization in secondary phase of free-agent draft (January 14, 1986); did not sign. . . . Selected by Pittsburgh Pirates organization in sixth round of free-agent draft (June 1, 1988). . . . On Buffalo disabled list (June 8-24 and June 28-August 12, 1991). . . . On suspended list (September 3-8, 1993). . . . Claimed on waivers by New York Mets (November 4, 1994). . . . On disabled list (July 24-August 24, 1995).

Year	Team (League)	W	L	Pct.	ERA	G	GS	CG	ShO	Sv.	IP	H	R	ER	BB	SO
1988—	Princeton (Appal.)	0	1	.000	4.41	15	0	0	0	7	16 1/3	18	10	8	5	23
1989—	Salem (Carolina)	3	5	.375	3.63	39	4	0	0	0	86 2/3	91	43	35	31	62
1990—	Harrisburg (East.)	6	4	.600	3.06	38	6	0	0	5	94	81	41	32	29	98
	—Buffalo (A.A.)	0	1	.000	3.38	1	0	0	0	0	2 2/3	2	1	1	2	2
1991—	Buffalo (A.A.)	2	2	.500	5.75	17	3	0	0	0	36	46	27	23	15	25
	—Carolina (South.)	0	0	...	2.84	3	2	0	0	0	12 2/3	9	4	4	7	18
1992—	Buffalo (A.A.)	5	4	.556	2.43	45	7	0	0	18	96 1/3	72	30	26	26	60
	—Pittsburgh (N.L.)	0	0	...	4.50	1	0	0	0	0	2	3	2	1	0	0
1993—	Pittsburgh (N.L.)	8	6	.571	4.10	65	0	0	0	2	94 1/3	94	43	43	26	84
1994—	Pittsburgh (N.L.)	0	1	.000	8.05	17	0	0	0	1	19	27	17	17	9	17
	—Buffalo (A.A.)	1	2	.333	2.98	33	3	0	0	11	51 1/3	47	17	17	12	61
1995—	New York (N.L.)■	4	2	.667	3.66	35	0	0	0	1	46 2/3	44	21	19	13	43
Major league totals (4 years)		12	9	.571	4.44	118	0	0	0	4	162	168	83	80	48	144

MINTZ, STEVE — P — GIANTS

PERSONAL: Born November 28, 1968, in Wilmington, N.C. . . . 5-11/190. . . . Throws right, bats left. . . . Full name: Stephen Wayne Mintz.
HIGH SCHOOL: North Brunswick (N.C.).
COLLEGE: Mount Olive (N.C.).
TRANSACTIONS/CAREER NOTES: Selected by Los Angeles Dodgers organization in 17th round of free-agent draft (June 4, 1990). . . . Released by Albuquerque, Dodgers organization (March 31, 1993). . . . Signed by New Britain, Boston Red Sox organization (April 21, 1993). . . . On disabled list (April 30-May 13, 1993). . . . Granted free agency (October 15, 1993). . . . Signed by Phoenix, San Francisco Giants organization (December 15, 1993).

Year	Team (League)	W	L	Pct.	ERA	G	GS	CG	ShO	Sv.	IP	H	R	ER	BB	SO
1990—	Yakima (N'west)	4	3	.571	3.88	12	12	0	0	0	67 1/3	58	36	29	39	72
1991—	Bakersfield (Calif.)	6	6	.500	4.30	28	11	0	0	3	92	85	56	44	58	101
1992—	Vero Beach (FSL)	3	6	.333	3.13	43	2	0	0	6	77 2/3	66	29	27	30	66
1993—	New Britain (East.)■	2	4	.333	2.08	43	1	0	0	7	69 1/3	52	22	16	30	51
1994—	Shreveport (Texas)■	10	2	*.833	2.20	30	0	0	0	0	65 1/3	45	29	16	22	42
	—Phoenix (PCL)	0	1	.000	5.50	24	0	0	0	3	36	40	24	22	13	27
1995—	Phoenix (PCL)	5	2	.714	2.39	31	0	0	0	7	49	42	16	13	21	36
	—San Francisco (N.L.)	1	2	.333	7.45	14	0	0	0	0	19 1/3	26	16	16	12	7
Major league totals (1 year)		1	2	.333	7.45	14	0	0	0	0	19 1/3	26	16	16	12	7

MIRANDA, ANGEL — P — BREWERS

PERSONAL: Born November 9, 1969, in Arecibo, Puerto Rico. . . . 6-1/195. . . . Throws left, bats left. . . . Full name: Angel Luis Miranda.
HIGH SCHOOL: Maria Cadillo (Arecibo, Puerto Rico).
TRANSACTIONS/CAREER NOTES: Signed as non-drafted free agent by Milwaukee Brewers organization (March 4, 1987). . . . Loaned by Brewers organization to Butte, independent (March 4, 1987). . . . On Milwaukee disabled list (March 27-June 1, 1993); included rehabilitation assignment to New Orleans (May 4-June 1). . . . On Milwaukee disabled list (March 21-June 28, 1994); included rehabilitation assignments to Beloit (June 4-11) and New Orleans (June 11-25). . . . On disabled list (June 27-July 29, 1995).
STATISTICAL NOTES: Led American Association with six balks in 1992.

Year	Team (League)	W	L	Pct.	ERA	G	GS	CG	ShO	Sv.	IP	H	R	ER	BB	SO
1987—	Butte (Pioneer)	1	1	.500	3.74	12	0	0	0	0	21 2/3	15	13	9	10	28
	—Helena (Pioneer)■	0	1	.000	2.49	13	0	0	0	3	21 2/3	12	9	6	16	32
1988—	Stockton (Calif.)■	0	1	.000	7.18	16	0	0	0	2	26 1/3	20	30	21	37	36
	—Helena (Pioneer)	5	2	.714	3.86	14	11	0	0	0	60 2/3	54	32	26	58	75
1989—	Beloit (Midwest)	6	5	.545	0.86	43	0	0	0	16	63	39	13	6	32	88
1990—	Stockton (Calif.)	9	4	.692	2.66	52	9	2	1	24	108 1/3	75	37	32	49	138
1991—	El Paso (Texas)	4	2	.667	2.54	38	0	0	0	11	74 1/3	55	27	21	41	86
	—Denver (Am. Assoc.)	0	1	.000	6.17	11	0	0	0	2	11 2/3	10	9	8	17	14
1992—	Denver (Am. Assoc.)	6	12	.333	4.77	28	27	1	1	0	160 1/3	183	100	85	*77	122
1993—	New Orleans (A.A.)	0	1	.000	3.44	9	2	0	0	0	18 1/3	11	8	7	10	24
	—Milwaukee (A.L.)	4	5	.444	3.30	22	17	2	0	0	120	100	53	44	52	88
1994—	Beloit (Midwest)	0	0	. . .	2.70	2	2	0	0	0	10	11	3	3	1	14
	—New Orleans (A.A.)	0	1	.000	3.46	3	3	0	0	0	13	11	5	5	7	9
	—Milwaukee (A.L.)	2	5	.286	5.28	8	8	1	0	0	46	39	28	27	27	24
1995—	Milwaukee (A.L.)	4	5	.444	5.23	30	10	0	0	1	74	83	47	43	49	45
Major league totals (3 years)		10	15	.400	4.28	60	35	3	0	1	240	222	128	114	128	157

MISURACA, MIKE — P

PERSONAL: Born August 21, 1968, in Long Beach, Calif. . . . 6-0/188. . . . Throws right, bats right. . . . Full name: Michael William Misuraca.
HIGH SCHOOL: Glendora (Calif.).
TRANSACTIONS/CAREER NOTES: Signed as non-drafted free agent by Minnesota Twins organization (July 20, 1988). . . . On temporarily inactive list (May 1-June 1, 1991). . . . Granted free agency (December 21, 1995).
STATISTICAL NOTES: Led Pacific Coast League with eight hit batsmen in 1995.

Year	Team (League)	W	L	Pct.	ERA	G	GS	CG	ShO	Sv.	IP	H	R	ER	BB	SO
1989—	Kenosha (Midwest)	1	5	.167	5.28	9	9	0	0	0	46	47	32	27	15	30
	—Elizabeth. (App.)	•10	3	.769	2.53	13	13	9	*2	0	*103	92	34	29	33	89
1990—	Kenosha (Midwest)	9	9	.500	3.33	26	26	1	0	0	167 1/3	164	81	62	57	116
1991—	Visalia (California)	7	9	.438	4.27	21	19	2	1	0	116	131	65	55	39	82
1992—	Miracle (Florida State)	7	14	.333	3.61	28	*28	3	1	0	157	163	84	63	63	107
1993—	Nashville (South.)	6	6	.500	3.82	25	17	2	1	0	113	103	57	48	40	80
1994—	Nashville (South.)	8	4	.667	3.63	17	17	0	0	0	106 2/3	115	56	43	22	80
	—Salt Lake (PCL)	3	5	.375	5.21	10	10	1	0	0	65 2/3	88	43	38	13	51
1995—	Salt Lake (PCL)	9	6	.600	5.34	31	19	1	0	0	143 1/3	174	93	85	36	67

MITCHELL, LARRY — P — PHILLIES

PERSONAL: Born October 16, 1971, in Flint, Mich. . . . 6-1/219. . . . Throws right, bats right. . . . Full name: Larry Paul Mitchell II.
HIGH SCHOOL: Charlottesville (Va.).
COLLEGE: James Madison.
TRANSACTIONS/CAREER NOTES: Selected by Philadelphia Phillies organization in fifth round of free-agent draft (June 1, 1992).
STATISTICAL NOTES: Led Eastern League with 15 wild pitches in 1994.

Year	Team (League)	W	L	Pct.	ERA	G	GS	CG	ShO	Sv.	IP	H	R	ER	BB	SO
1992—	Martinsville (App.)	1	0	1.000	1.42	3	3	0	0	0	19	17	8	3	6	18
	—Batavia (NYP)	7	2	.778	2.63	10	10	3	1	0	65	63	25	19	11	58
1993—	Spartanburg (SAL)	6	6	.500	4.10	19	19	4	•2	0	116 1/3	113	55	53	54	114
	—Clearwater (Fla. St.)	4	4	.500	3.00	9	9	1	0	0	57	50	23	19	21	45
1994—	Reading (Eastern)	10	13	.435	3.97	30	*30	2	0	0	165 1/3	143	91	73	*103	128
1995—	Reading (Eastern)	6	11	.353	5.54	25	24	1	1	0	128 1/3	136	85	79	72	107

MLICKI, DAVE — P — METS

PERSONAL: Born June 8, 1968, in Cleveland. . . . 6-4/190. . . . Throws right, bats right. . . . Full name: David John Mlicki. . . . Brother of Doug Mlicki, pitcher, Houston Astros organization. . . . Name pronounced muh-LICK-ee.
HIGH SCHOOL: Cheyenne Mountain (Colorado Springs, Colo.).
COLLEGE: Oklahoma State.
TRANSACTIONS/CAREER NOTES: Selected by Seattle Mariners organization in 23rd round of free-agent draft (June 5, 1989); did not sign. . . . Selected by Cleveland Indians organization in 17th round of free-agent draft (June 4, 1990). . . . On Cleveland disabled list (April 4-August 4, 1993); included rehabilitation assignment to Canton/Akron (July 19-August 4). . . . Traded by Indians organization with P Jerry DiPoto, P Paul Byrd and a player to be named later to New York Mets organization for OF Jeromy Burnitz and P Joe Roa (November 18, 1994); Mets acquired 2B Jesus Azuaje to complete deal (December 6, 1994).
STATISTICAL NOTES: Led International League with 26 home runs allowed in 1994.

Year Team (League)	W	L	Pct.	ERA	G	GS	CG	ShO	Sv.	IP	H	R	ER	BB	SO
1990—Burlington (Appal.)	3	1	.750	3.50	8	1	0	0	0	18	16	11	7	6	17
—Watertown (NYP)	3	0	1.000	3.38	7	4	0	0	0	32	33	15	12	11	28
1991—Columbus (S. Atl.)	8	6	.571	4.20	22	19	2	0	0	115 2/3	101	70	54	70	136
1992—Cant./Akr. (East.)	11	9	.550	3.60	27	*27	2	0	0	172 2/3	143	77	69	•80	146
—Cleveland (A.L.)	0	2	.000	4.98	4	4	0	0	0	21 2/3	23	14	12	16	16
1993—Cant./Akr. (East.)	2	1	.667	0.39	6	6	0	0	0	23	15	2	1	8	21
—Cleveland (A.L.)	0	0	...	3.38	3	3	0	0	0	13 1/3	11	6	5	6	7
1994—Charlotte (Int'l)	6	10	.375	4.25	28	28	0	0	0	165 1/3	179	85	78	64	152
1995—New York (N.L.)■	9	7	.563	4.26	29	25	0	0	0	160 2/3	160	82	76	54	123
A.L. totals (2 years)	0	2	.000	4.37	7	7	0	0	0	35	34	20	17	22	23
N.L. totals (1 year)	9	7	.563	4.26	29	25	0	0	0	160 2/3	160	82	76	54	123
Major league totals (3 years)	9	9	.500	4.28	36	32	0	0	0	195 2/3	194	102	93	76	146

MLICKI, DOUG — P — ASTROS

PERSONAL: Born April 12, 1971, in Cleveland. . . . 6-3/175. . . . Throws right, bats right. . . . Full name: Douglas James Mlicki. . . . Brother of Dave Mlicki, pitcher, New York Mets. . . . Name pronounced muh-LICK-ee.
COLLEGE: Ohio University.
TRANSACTIONS/CAREER NOTES: Selected by Houston Astros organization in 12th round of free-agent draft (June 1, 1992).
STATISTICAL NOTES: Led Florida State League with 16 home runs allowed in 1993.

Year Team (League)	W	L	Pct.	ERA	G	GS	CG	ShO	Sv.	IP	H	R	ER	BB	SO
1992—Auburn (NYP)	1	6	.143	2.99	14	13	0	0	0	81 1/3	50	35	27	30	83
1993—Osceola (Florida St.)	11	10	.524	3.91	26	23	0	0	0	158 2/3	158	81	69	65	111
1994—Jackson (Texas)	13	7	.650	3.38	23	23	1	0	0	138 2/3	107	62	52	54	130
1995—Jackson (Texas)	8	3	.727	2.79	16	16	2	0	0	96 2/3	73	41	30	33	72
—Tucson (Pac. Coast)	1	2	.333	5.56	6	6	0	0	0	34	44	27	21	6	22

MOEHLER, BRIAN — P — TIGERS

PERSONAL: Born December 3, 1971, in Rockingham, N.C. . . . 6-3/195. . . . Throws right, bats right. . . . Full name: Brian Merritt Moehler.
COLLEGE: North Carolina-Greensboro.
TRANSACTIONS/CAREER NOTES: Selected by Detroit Tigers organization in sixth round of free-agent draft (June 3, 1993).

Year Team (League)	W	L	Pct.	ERA	G	GS	CG	ShO	Sv.	IP	H	R	ER	BB	SO
1993—Niag. Falls (NYP)	6	5	.545	3.22	12	11	0	0	0	58 2/3	51	33	21	27	38
1994—Lakeland (Fla. St.)	12	12	.500	3.01	26	25	5	2	0	164 2/3	153	66	55	65	92
1995—Jacksonville (Sou.)	8	10	.444	4.82	28	27	0	0	0	162 1/3	176	94	87	52	89

MOHLER, MIKE — P — ATHLETICS

PERSONAL: Born July 26, 1968, in Dayton, O. . . . 6-2/195. . . . Throws left, bats right. . . . Full name: Michael Ross Mohler.
HIGH SCHOOL: East Ascension (Gonzales, La.).
COLLEGE: Nicholls State (La.).
TRANSACTIONS/CAREER NOTES: Selected by Oakland Athletics organization in 42nd round of free-agent draft (June 5, 1989). . . . On Tacoma disabled list (April 7-May 24, 1994).

Year Team (League)	W	L	Pct.	ERA	G	GS	CG	ShO	Sv.	IP	H	R	ER	BB	SO
1990—Madison (Midwest)	1	1	.500	3.41	42	2	0	0	1	63 1/3	56	34	24	32	72
1991—Modesto (Calif.)	9	4	.692	2.86	21	20	1	0	0	122 2/3	106	48	39	45	98
—Huntsville (South.)	4	2	.667	3.57	8	8	0	0	0	53	55	22	21	20	27
1992—Huntsville (South.)	3	8	.273	3.59	44	6	0	0	3	80 1/3	72	41	32	39	56
1993—Oakland (A.L.)	1	6	.143	5.60	42	9	0	0	0	64 1/3	57	45	40	44	42
1994—Modesto (Calif.)	1	1	.500	2.76	7	5	0	0	1	29 1/3	21	9	9	6	29
—Tacoma (PCL)	1	3	.250	3.53	17	11	0	0	0	63 2/3	66	31	25	21	50
—Oakland (A.L.)	0	1	.000	7.71	1	1	0	0	0	2 1/3	2	3	2	2	4
1995—Edmonton (PCL)	2	1	.667	2.60	29	0	0	0	5	45	40	16	13	20	28
—Oakland (A.L.)	1	1	.500	3.04	28	0	0	0	1	23 2/3	16	8	8	18	15
Major league totals (3 years)	2	8	.200	4.98	71	10	0	0	1	90 1/3	75	56	50	64	61

MOLITOR, PAUL — DH/1B — TWINS

PERSONAL: Born August 22, 1956, in St. Paul, Minn. . . . 6-0/190. . . . Bats right, throws right. . . . Full name: Paul Leo Molitor.
HIGH SCHOOL: Cretin (St. Paul).
COLLEGE: Minnesota.

TRANSACTIONS/CAREER NOTES: Selected by St. Louis Cardinals organization in 28th round of free-agent draft (June 5, 1974); did not sign. . . . Selected by Milwaukee Brewers organization in first round (third pick overall) of free-agent draft (June 7, 1977). . . . On disabled list (June 24-July 18, 1980; May 3-August 12, 1981; May 2, 1984-remainder of season; August 13-28, 1985; May 10-30, June 2-17 and June 19-July 8, 1986; and April 30-May 26 and June 27-July 16, 1987). . . . Granted free agency (November 9, 1987). . . . Re-signed by Brewers (January 5, 1988). . . . On disabled list (March 30-April 14, 1989). . . . On Milwaukee disabled list (April 2-27, 1990). . . . On Milwaukee disabled list (June 17-July 30, 1990); included rehabilitation assignment to Beloit (July 28). . . . Granted free agency (October 30, 1992). . . . Signed by Toronto Blue Jays (December 7, 1992). . . . Granted free agency (November 3, 1995). . . . Signed by Minnesota Twins (December 5, 1995).
RECORDS: Shares major league record for most stolen bases in one inning—3 (July 26, 1987, first inning). . . . Holds A.L. single-season record for most stolen bases without being caught stealing—20 (1994).
HONORS: Named shortstop on The Sporting News college All-America team (1977). . . . Named Midwest League Most Valuable Player (1977). . . . Named A.L. Rookie Player of the Year by The Sporting News (1978). . . . Named designated hitter on The Sporting News A.L. All-Star team (1987 and 1993-94). . . . Named designated hitter on The Sporting News A.L. Silver Slugger team (1987-88 and 1993).
STATISTICAL NOTES: Hit three home runs in one game (May 12, 1982). . . . Led A.L. third basemen with 29 errors and 48 double plays in 1982. . . . Hit for the cycle (May 15, 1991). . . . Career major league grand slams: 2.

				BATTING											FIELDING			
Year	**Team (League)**	**Pos.**	**G**	**AB**	**R**	**H**	**2B**	**3B**	**HR**	**RBI**	**Avg.**	**BB**	**SO**	**SB**	**PO**	**A**	**E**	**Avg.**
1977	—Burlington (Midw.)	SS	64	228	52	79	12	0	8	50	.346	47	25	14	83	207	28	.912
1978	—Milwaukee (A.L.)	2-S-DH-3	125	521	73	142	26	4	6	45	.273	19	54	30	253	401	22	.967
1979	—Milwaukee (A.L.)	2B-SS-DH	140	584	88	188	27	16	9	62	.322	48	48	33	309	440	16	.979
1980	—Milwaukee (A.L.)	2-S-DH-3	111	450	81	137	29	2	9	37	.304	48	48	34	260	336	20	.968
1981	—Milwaukee (A.L.)	OF-DH	64	251	45	67	11	0	2	19	.267	25	29	10	119	4	3	.976
1982	—Milwaukee (A.L.)	3B-DH-SS	160	*666	*136	201	26	8	19	71	.302	69	93	41	134	350	†32	.938
1983	—Milwaukee (A.L.)	3B-DH	152	608	95	164	28	6	15	47	.270	59	74	41	105	343	16	.966
1984	—Milwaukee (A.L.)	3B-DH	13	46	3	10	1	0	0	6	.217	2	8	1	7	21	2	.933
1985	—Milwaukee (A.L.)	3B-DH	140	576	93	171	28	3	10	48	.297	54	80	21	126	263	19	.953
1986	—Milwaukee (A.L.)	3B-DH-OF	105	437	62	123	24	6	9	55	.281	40	81	20	86	171	15	.945
1987	—Milwaukee (A.L.)	DH-3B-2B	118	465	*114	164	*41	5	16	75	.353	69	67	45	60	113	5	.972
1988	—Milwaukee (A.L.)	3B-DH-2B	154	609	115	190	34	6	13	60	.312	71	54	41	87	188	17	.942
1989	—Milwaukee (A.L.)	3B-DH-2B	155	615	84	194	35	4	11	56	.315	64	67	27	106	287	18	.956
1990	—Milwaukee (A.L.)	2-1-DH-3	103	418	64	119	27	6	12	45	.285	37	51	18	463	222	10	.986
	—Beloit (Midwest)	DH	1	4	1	2	0	0	1	1	.500	0	0	0	...	...	...	...
1991	—Milwaukee (A.L.)	DH-1B	158	*665	*133	*216	32	•13	17	75	.325	77	62	19	389	32	6	.986
1992	—Milwaukee (A.L.)	DH-1B	158	609	89	195	36	7	12	89	.320	73	66	31	461	26	2	.996
1993	—Toronto (A.L.)■	DH-1B	160	636	121	*211	37	5	22	111	.332	77	71	22	178	14	3	.985
1994	—Toronto (A.L.)	DH-1B	*115	454	86	155	30	4	14	75	.341	55	48	20	47	3	0	1.000
1995	—Toronto (A.L.)	DH	130	525	63	142	31	2	15	60	.270	61	57	12	0	0	0	...
Major league totals (18 years)			2261	9135	1545	2789	503	97	211	1036	.305	948	1058	466	3190	3214	206	.969

DIVISION SERIES RECORD

				BATTING											FIELDING			
Year	**Team (League)**	**Pos.**	**G**	**AB**	**R**	**H**	**2B**	**3B**	**HR**	**RBI**	**Avg.**	**BB**	**SO**	**SB**	**PO**	**A**	**E**	**Avg.**
1981	—Milwaukee (A.L.)	OF	5	20	2	5	0	0	1	1	.250	2	5	0	12	0	0	1.000

CHAMPIONSHIP SERIES RECORD

NOTES: Holds single-series record for most consecutive hits—6 (1993). . . . Shares career record for most consecutive hits—6 (1993).

				BATTING											FIELDING			
Year	**Team (League)**	**Pos.**	**G**	**AB**	**R**	**H**	**2B**	**3B**	**HR**	**RBI**	**Avg.**	**BB**	**SO**	**SB**	**PO**	**A**	**E**	**Avg.**
1982	—Milwaukee (A.L.)	3B	5	19	4	6	1	0	2	5	.316	2	3	1	4	11	2	.882
1993	—Toronto (A.L.)	DH	6	23	7	9	2	1	1	5	.391	3	3	0	...	...	...	...
Championship series totals (2 years)			11	42	11	15	3	1	3	10	.357	5	6	1	4	11	2	.882

WORLD SERIES RECORD

NOTES: Named Most Valuable Player (1993). . . . Holds single-game records for most hits—5; and most singles—5 (October 12, 1982). . . . Shares single-series record for most runs—10 (1993). . . . Shares single-game record (nine innings) for most at-bats—6 (October 12, 1982). . . . Member of World Series championship team (1993).

				BATTING											FIELDING			
Year	**Team (League)**	**Pos.**	**G**	**AB**	**R**	**H**	**2B**	**3B**	**HR**	**RBI**	**Avg.**	**BB**	**SO**	**SB**	**PO**	**A**	**E**	**Avg.**
1982	—Milwaukee (A.L.)	3B	7	31	5	11	0	0	0	3	.355	2	4	1	4	9	0	1.000
1993	—Toronto (A.L.)	DH-3B-1B	6	24	10	12	2	2	2	8	.500	3	0	1	7	3	0	1.000
World Series totals (2 years)			13	55	15	23	2	2	2	11	.418	5	4	2	11	12	0	1.000

ALL-STAR GAME RECORD

			BATTING											FIELDING			
Year	**League**	**Pos.**	**AB**	**R**	**H**	**2B**	**3B**	**HR**	**RBI**	**Avg.**	**BB**	**SO**	**SB**	**PO**	**A**	**E**	**Avg.**
1980	—American		Selected, did not play—injured.														
1985	—American	3B-OF	1	0	0	0	0	0	0	.000	0	0	0	0	0	0	...
1988	—American	2B	3	0	0	0	0	0	0	.000	0	1	0	1	2	0	1.000
1991	—American	3B	0	0	0	0	0	0	0	...	0	0	0	0	0	0	...
1992	—American	PH-1B	2	0	1	0	0	0	0	.500	0	1	0	5	0	1	.833
1993	—American	DH	1	0	0	0	0	0	0	.000	1	0	0	...	...	...	...
1994	—American	PH	1	0	0	0	0	0	0	.000	0	0	0	...	...	...	...
All-Star Game totals (6 years)			8	0	1	0	0	0	0	.125	1	2	0	6	2	1	.889

MONDESI, RAUL — OF — DODGERS

PERSONAL: Born March 12, 1971, in San Cristobal, Dominican Republic. . . . 5-11/212. . . . Bats right, throws right. . . . Name pronounced MON-de-see.
HIGH SCHOOL: Liceo Manuel Maria Valencia (Dominican Republic).
TRANSACTIONS/CAREER NOTES: Signed as non-drafted free agent by Los Angeles Dodgers organization (June 6, 1988). . . . On Bakersfield disabled list (May 8-July 5, 1991). . . . On Albuquerque disabled list (May 8-16, 1992). . . . On San Antonio disabled list (June 2-16, June 24-August 10 and August 24, 1992-remainder of season).

HONORS: Named N.L. Rookie Player of the Year by THE SPORTING NEWS (1994). . . . Named N.L. Rookie of the Year by Baseball Writers' Association of America (1994). . . . Won N.L. Gold Glove as outfielder (1995).
STATISTICAL NOTES: Career major league grand slams: 1.

			BATTING												FIELDING			
Year	Team (League)	Pos.	G	AB	R	H	2B	3B	HR	RBI	Avg.	BB	SO	SB	PO	A	E	Avg.
1990—	Great Falls (Pio.)	OF	44	175	35	53	10	4	8	31	.303	11	30	30	65	4	1	.986
1991—	Bakersfield (Calif.)	OF	28	106	23	30	7	2	3	13	.283	5	21	9	42	5	3	.940
—	San Antonio (Tex.)	OF	53	213	32	58	11	5	5	26	.272	8	47	8	101	6	4	.964
—	Albuquerque (PCL)	OF	2	9	3	3	0	1	0	0	.333	0	1	1	0	0	1	.000
1992—	Albuquerque (PCL)	OF	35	138	23	43	4	7	4	15	.312	9	35	2	89	8	7	.933
—	San Antonio (Tex.)	OF	18	68	8	18	2	2	2	14	.265	1	24	3	31	6	1	.974
1993—	Albuquerque (PCL)	OF	110	425	65	119	22	7	12	65	.280	18	85	13	211	10	10	.957
—	Los Angeles (N.L.)	OF	42	86	13	25	3	1	4	10	.291	4	16	4	55	3	3	.951
1994—	Los Angeles (N.L.)	OF	112	434	63	133	27	8	16	56	.306	16	78	11	206	*16	8	.965
1995—	Los Angeles (N.L.)	OF	139	536	91	153	23	6	26	88	.285	33	96	27	282	*16	6	.980
Major league totals (3 years)			293	1056	167	311	53	15	46	154	.295	53	190	42	543	35	17	.971

DIVISION SERIES RECORD

			BATTING												FIELDING			
Year	Team (League)	Pos.	G	AB	R	H	2B	3B	HR	RBI	Avg.	BB	SO	SB	PO	A	E	Avg.
1995—	Los Angeles (N.L.)	OF	3	9	0	2	0	0	0	1	.222	0	2	0	8	0	0	1.000

ALL-STAR GAME RECORD

			BATTING											FIELDING			
Year	League	Pos.	AB	R	H	2B	3B	HR	RBI	Avg.	BB	SO	SB	PO	A	E	Avg.
1995—	National	OF	1	0	0	0	0	0	0	.000	0	0	0	2	0	0	1.000

MONDS, WONDER — OF — BRAVES

PERSONAL: Born January 11, 1973, in Fort Pierce, Fla. . . . 6-3/190. . . . Bats right, throws right. . . . Full name: Wonderful Terrific Monds.
COLLEGE: Tennessee State.
TRANSACTIONS/CAREER NOTES: Selected by Atlanta Braves organization in 50th round of free-agent draft (June 3, 1993). . . . On Durham disabled list (May 19-July 3, 1995).

			BATTING												FIELDING			
Year	Team (League)	Pos.	G	AB	R	H	2B	3B	HR	RBI	Avg.	BB	SO	SB	PO	A	E	Avg.
1993—	Idaho Falls (Pio.)	OF	60	214	47	64	13	8	4	35	.299	25	43	16	73	8	7	.920
1994—	Macon (S. Atl.)	OF	104	365	70	106	23	12	10	41	.290	22	82	41	180	17	5	.975
—	Durham (Carolina)	OF	18	53	7	11	2	0	2	10	.208	2	11	5	21	1	0	1.000
1995—	GC Braves (GCL)	OF	4	15	1	2	0	0	0	1	.133	1	8	2	8	0	0	1.000
—	Durham (Carolina)	OF	81	297	44	83	17	0	6	33	.279	17	63	28	112	9	2	.984

MONTELEONE, RICH — P

PERSONAL: Born March 22, 1963, in Tampa, Fla. . . . 6-2/214. . . . Throws right, bats right. . . . Full name: Richard Monteleone. . . . Name pronounced MON-ta-lee-YONE.
HIGH SCHOOL: Tampa (Fla.) Catholic.
TRANSACTIONS/CAREER NOTES: Selected by Detroit Tigers organization in first round (20th pick overall) of free-agent draft (June 7, 1982). . . . Traded by Tigers organization to Seattle Mariners for 3B Darnell Coles (December 12, 1985). . . . Released by Mariners organization (May 9, 1988). . . . Signed by Edmonton, California Angels organization (May 13, 1988). . . . Traded by Angels organization with OF Claudell Washington to New York Yankees for OF Luis Polonia (April 28, 1990). . . . Granted free agency (October 15, 1993). . . . Signed by San Francisco Giants organization (November 9, 1993). . . . On disabled list (May 16-June 17, 1994). . . . Released by Giants (November 22, 1994). . . . Signed by Chunichi Dragons of Japan Central League (1995). . . . Released by Dragons (July 1995). . . . Signed by Vancouver, California Angels organization (August 8, 1995). . . . Granted free agency (December 21, 1995).
STATISTICAL NOTES: Led Appalachian League pitchers with eight home runs allowed in 1982.

Year	Team (League)	W	L	Pct.	ERA	G	GS	CG	ShO	Sv.	IP	H	R	ER	BB	SO
1982—	Bristol (Appal.)	4	6	.400	3.89	12	12	2	0	0	71 2/3	66	41	31	23	52
1983—	Lakeland (Fla. St.)	9	8	.529	4.11	24	24	1	0	0	142 1/3	146	80	65	80	124
—	Birmingham (Sou.)	1	1	.500	7.20	3	3	0	0	0	15	25	12	12	6	9
1984—	Birmingham (Sou.)	7	8	.467	4.66	19	19	4	0	0	123 2/3	116	69	64	67	74
—	Evansville (A.A.)	5	3	.625	4.50	11	11	2	0	0	64	64	33	32	36	42
1985—	Nashville (A.A.)	6	12	.333	5.08	27	26	3	0	0	145 1/3	149	89	82	87	97
1986—	Calgary (PCL)■	8	12	.400	5.28	39	21	0	0	0	158 2/3	177	108	93	*89	101
1987—	Seattle (A.L.)	0	0	. . .	6.43	3	0	0	0	0	7	10	5	5	4	2
—	Calgary (PCL)	6	*13	.316	5.51	51	0	0	0	15	65 1/3	59	45	40	63	38
1988—	Calgary (PCL)	0	0	. . .	12.54	10	0	0	0	0	9 1/3	21	19	13	4	5
—	Edmonton (PCL)■	4	7	.364	4.46	20	16	3	1	0	113	120	65	56	23	93
—	California (A.L.)	0	0	. . .	0.00	3	0	0	0	0	4 1/3	4	0	0	1	3
1989—	Edmonton (PCL)	3	6	.333	3.47	13	8	2	0	0	57	50	23	22	16	47
—	California (A.L.)	2	2	.500	3.18	24	0	0	0	0	39 2/3	39	15	14	13	27
1990—	Edmonton (PCL)	1	0	1.000	1.93	5	1	0	0	1	14	7	3	3	4	9
—	Columbus (Int'l)■	4	4	.500	2.24	38	0	0	0	9	64 1/3	51	17	16	23	60
—	New York (A.L.)	0	1	.000	6.14	5	0	0	0	0	7 1/3	8	5	5	2	8
1991—	Columbus (Int'l)	1	3	.250	2.12	32	0	0	0	17	46 2/3	36	15	11	7	52
—	New York (A.L.)	3	1	.750	3.64	26	0	0	0	0	47	42	27	19	19	34
1992—	New York (A.L.)	7	3	.700	3.30	47	0	0	0	0	92 2/3	82	35	34	27	62
1993—	New York (A.L.)	7	4	.636	4.94	42	0	0	0	0	85 2/3	85	52	47	35	50
1994—	San Francisco (N.L.)■	4	3	.571	3.18	39	0	0	0	0	45 1/3	43	18	16	13	16
1995—	Chunichi (Jp. Cn.)■	2	4	.333	6.55	11	0	0	0	0	44	55	32	32	17	19

M

Year	Team (League)	W	L	Pct.	ERA	G	GS	CG	ShO	Sv.	IP	H	R	ER	BB	SO
	—Vancouver (PCL)■	1	0	1.000	3.24	7	1	0	0	1	16 2/3	19	7	6	3	7
	—California (A.L.)	1	0	1.000	2.00	9	0	0	0	0	9	8	2	2	3	5
A.L. totals (8 years)		20	11	.645	3.87	159	0	0	0	0	292 2/3	278	141	126	104	191
N.L. totals (1 year)		4	3	.571	3.18	39	0	0	0	0	45 1/3	43	18	16	13	16
Major league totals (9 years)		24	14	.632	3.78	198	0	0	0	0	338	321	159	142	117	207

MONTGOMERY, JEFF — P — ROYALS

PERSONAL: Born January 7, 1962, in Wellston, O. . . . 5-11/180. . . . Throws right, bats right. . . . Full name: Jeffrey Thomas Montgomery.
HIGH SCHOOL: Wellston (O.).
COLLEGE: Marshall (bachelor of science degree in computer science, 1984).
TRANSACTIONS/CAREER NOTES: Selected by Cincinnati Reds organization in ninth round of free-agent draft (June 6, 1983). . . . Traded by Reds to Kansas City Royals for OF Van Snider (February 15, 1988). . . . Granted free agency (November 8, 1995). . . . Re-signed by Royals (December 15, 1995).
RECORDS: Shares major league record for striking out side on nine pitches (April 29, 1990, eighth inning).
HONORS: Named A.L. Fireman of the Year by The Sporting News (1993).

Year	Team (League)	W	L	Pct.	ERA	G	GS	CG	ShO	Sv.	IP	H	R	ER	BB	SO
1983	—Billings (Pioneer)	6	2	.750	2.42	20	0	0	0	5	44 2/3	31	13	12	13	90
1984	—Tampa (Fla. St.)	5	3	.625	2.44	31	0	0	0	•14	44 1/3	29	15	12	30	56
	—Vermont (Eastern)	2	0	1.000	2.13	22	0	0	0	4	25 1/3	14	7	6	24	20
1985	—Vermont (Eastern)	5	3	.625	2.05	*53	1	0	0	9	101	63	25	23	48	89
1986	—Denver (Am. Assoc.)	11	7	.611	4.39	30	22	2	2	1	151 2/3	162	88	74	57	78
1987	—Nashville (A.A.)	8	5	.615	4.14	24	21	1	0	0	139	132	76	64	51	121
	—Cincinnati (N.L.)	2	2	.500	6.52	14	1	0	0	0	19 1/3	25	15	14	9	13
1988	—Omaha (Am. Assoc.)■	1	2	.333	1.91	20	0	0	0	13	28 1/3	15	6	6	11	36
	—Kansas City (A.L.)	7	2	.778	3.45	45	0	0	0	1	62 2/3	54	25	24	30	47
1989	—Kansas City (A.L.)	7	3	.700	1.37	63	0	0	0	18	92	66	16	14	25	94
1990	—Kansas City (A.L.)	6	5	.545	2.39	73	0	0	0	24	94 1/3	81	36	25	34	94
1991	—Kansas City (A.L.)	4	4	.500	2.90	67	0	0	0	33	90	83	32	29	28	77
1992	—Kansas City (A.L.)	1	6	.143	2.18	65	0	0	0	39	82 2/3	61	23	20	27	69
1993	—Kansas City (A.L.)	7	5	.583	2.27	69	0	0	0	•45	87 1/3	65	22	22	23	66
1994	—Kansas City (A.L.)	2	3	.400	4.03	42	0	0	0	27	44 2/3	48	21	20	15	50
1995	—Kansas City (A.L.)	2	3	.400	3.43	54	0	0	0	31	65 2/3	60	27	25	25	49
A.L. totals (8 years)		36	31	.537	2.60	478	0	0	0	218	619 1/3	518	202	179	207	546
N.L. totals (1 year)		2	2	.500	6.52	14	1	0	0	0	19 1/3	25	15	14	9	13
Major league totals (9 years)		38	33	.535	2.72	492	1	0	0	218	638 2/3	543	217	193	216	559

ALL-STAR GAME RECORD

Year	League	W	L	Pct.	ERA	GS	CG	ShO	Sv.	IP	H	R	ER	BB	SO
1992	—American	0	0	. . .	27.00	0	0	0	0	2/3	2	2	2	0	0
1993	—American	0	0	. . .	0.00	0	0	0	0	1	0	0	0	0	1
All-Star totals (2 years)		0	0	. . .	10.80	0	0	0	0	1 2/3	2	2	2	0	1

MONTGOMERY, STEVE — P — CARDINALS

PERSONAL: Born December 25, 1970, in Westminster, Calif. . . . 6-4/210. . . . Throws right, bats right. . . . Full name: Steven L. Montgomery.
HIGH SCHOOL: Fountain Valley (Calif.).
COLLEGE: Pepperdine.
TRANSACTIONS/CAREER NOTES: Selected by St. Louis Cardinals organization in third round of free-agent draft (June 1, 1992).

Year	Team (League)	W	L	Pct.	ERA	G	GS	CG	ShO	Sv.	IP	H	R	ER	BB	SO
1993	—St. Petersburg (FSL)	2	1	.667	2.66	14	5	0	0	3	40 2/3	33	14	12	9	34
	—Arkansas (Texas)	3	3	.500	3.94	6	6	0	0	0	32	34	17	14	12	19
1994	—Arkansas (Texas)	4	5	.444	3.28	50	9	0	0	2	107	97	43	39	33	73
1995	—Arkansas (Texas)	5	2	.714	3.25	*55	0	0	0	*36	61	52	22	22	22	56

MOORE, MARCUS — P — REDS

PERSONAL: Born November 2, 1970, in Oakland, Calif. . . . 6-5/195. . . . Throws right, bats both. . . . Full name: Marcus Braymont Moore.
HIGH SCHOOL: John F. Kennedy (Richmond, Calif.).
TRANSACTIONS/CAREER NOTES: Selected by California Angels organization in 17th round of free-agent draft (June 1, 1988). . . . Traded by Angels organization to Toronto Blue Jays organization for C Ken Rivers (December 4, 1990); completing deal in which Angels traded OF Devon White, P Willie Fraser and a player to be named later to Blue Jays for OF Junior Felix, IF Luis Sojo and a player to be named later (December 2, 1990). . . . Selected by Colorado Rockies in third round (56th pick overall) of expansion draft (November 17, 1992). . . . Traded by Rockies to Cincinnati Reds for IF Chris Sexton (April 10, 1995).

Year	Team (League)	W	L	Pct.	ERA	G	GS	CG	ShO	Sv.	IP	H	R	ER	BB	SO
1989	—Bend (Northwest)	2	5	.286	4.52	14	14	1	0	0	81 2/3	84	55	41	51	74
1990	—Quad City (Midw.)	*16	5	.762	3.31	27	27	2	1	0	160 1/3	150	83	59	106	160
1991	—Dunedin (Fla. St.)■	6	13	.316	3.70	27	25	2	0	0	160 2/3	139	78	66	*99	115
1992	—Knoxville (South.)	5	10	.333	5.59	36	14	1	0	0	106 1/3	110	82	66	79	85
1993	—Central Valley (Cal.)■	1	0	1.000	0.75	8	0	0	0	2	12	7	3	1	9	15
	—Colo. Springs (PCL)	1	5	.167	4.47	30	0	0	0	4	44 1/3	54	26	22	29	38
	—Colorado (N.L.)	3	1	.750	6.84	27	0	0	0	0	26 1/3	30	25	20	20	13
1994	—Colorado (N.L.)	1	1	.500	6.15	29	0	0	0	0	33 2/3	33	26	23	21	33
	—Colo. Springs (PCL)	3	4	.429	8.00	19	8	0	0	0	54	67	59	48	61	54
1995	—Indianapolis (A.A.)■	1	0	1.000	4.97	7	1	0	0	1	12 2/3	13	8	7	14	6
	—Chattanooga (Sou.)	6	1	.857	4.98	36	0	0	0	2	43 1/3	31	24	24	34	57
Major league totals (2 years)		4	2	.667	6.45	56	0	0	0	0	60	63	51	43	41	46

MOORE, MIKE P

PERSONAL: Born November 26, 1959, in Eakly, Okla. . . . 6-4/205. . . . Throws right, bats right. . . . Full name: Michael Wayne Moore.
HIGH SCHOOL: Eakly (Okla.).
COLLEGE: Oral Roberts.
TRANSACTIONS/CAREER NOTES: Selected by St. Louis Cardinals organization in third round of free-agent draft (June 6, 1978); did not sign. . . . Selected by Seattle Mariners organization in first round (first pick overall) of free-agent draft (June 8, 1981). . . . Granted free agency (November 4, 1988). . . . Signed by Oakland Athletics (November 28, 1988). . . . On disabled list (July 20-August 6, 1991). . . . Granted free agency (October 30, 1992). . . . Signed by Detroit Tigers (December 9, 1992). . . . Released by Tigers (September 5, 1995).
HONORS: Named righthanded pitcher on The Sporting News college All-America team (1981).
STATISTICAL NOTES: Struck out 16 batters in one game (August 19, 1988). . . . Led A.L. with 22 wild pitches in 1992. . . . Pitched 3-0 one-hit, complete-game victory against Kansas City (July 25, 1993). . . . Pitched 9-0 one-hit, complete-game victory against Oakland (August 23, 1993). . . . Led A.L. with 35 home runs allowed in 1993.
MISCELLANEOUS: Made an out in only appearance as pinch-hitter (1987). . . . Appeared in one game as pinch-runner (1991).

Year	Team (League)	W	L	Pct.	ERA	G	GS	CG	ShO	Sv.	IP	H	R	ER	BB	SO
1981—	Lynn (Eastern)	6	5	.545	3.64	13	13	6	2	0	94	83	42	38	34	81
1982—	Seattle (A.L.)	7	14	.333	5.36	28	27	1	1	0	144 1/3	159	91	86	79	73
—	Salt Lake (PCL)	0	0	...	4.50	1	1	0	0	0	8	9	4	4	5	6
1983—	Seattle (A.L.)	6	8	.429	4.71	22	21	3	2	0	128	130	75	67	60	108
—	Salt Lake (PCL)	4	4	.500	3.61	11	11	4	1	0	82 1/3	78	48	33	54	80
1984—	Seattle (A.L.)	7	17	.292	4.97	34	33	6	0	0	212	236	127	117	85	158
1985—	Seattle (A.L.)	17	10	.630	3.46	35	34	14	2	0	247	230	100	95	70	155
1986—	Seattle (A.L.)	11	13	.458	4.30	38	•37	11	1	1	266	*279	141	127	94	146
1987—	Seattle (A.L.)	9	*19	.321	4.71	33	33	12	0	0	231	*268	145	*121	84	115
1988—	Seattle (A.L.)	9	15	.375	3.78	37	32	9	3	1	228 2/3	196	104	96	63	182
1989—	Oakland (A.L.)■	19	11	.633	2.61	35	35	6	3	0	241 2/3	193	82	70	83	172
1990—	Oakland (A.L.)	13	15	.464	4.65	33	33	3	0	0	199 1/3	204	113	103	84	73
1991—	Oakland (A.L.)	17	8	.680	2.96	33	33	3	1	0	210	176	75	69	105	153
1992—	Oakland (A.L.)	17	12	.586	4.12	36	•36	2	0	0	223	229	113	102	103	117
1993—	Detroit (A.L.)■	13	9	.591	5.22	36	•36	4	3	0	213 2/3	227	135	124	89	89
1994—	Detroit (A.L.)	11	10	.524	5.42	25	•25	4	0	0	154 1/3	152	97	93	•89	62
1995—	Detroit (A.L.)	5	•15	.250	7.53	25	25	1	0	0	132 2/3	179	118	111	68	64
Major league totals (14 years)		161	176	.478	4.39	450	440	79	16	2	2831 2/3	2858	1516	1381	1156	1667

CHAMPIONSHIP SERIES RECORD

Year	Team (League)	W	L	Pct.	ERA	G	GS	CG	ShO	Sv.	IP	H	R	ER	BB	SO
1989—	Oakland (A.L.)	1	0	1.000	0.00	1	1	0	0	0	7	3	1	0	2	3
1990—	Oakland (A.L.)	1	0	1.000	1.50	1	1	0	0	0	6	4	1	1	1	5
1992—	Oakland (A.L.)	0	2	.000	7.45	2	2	0	0	0	9 2/3	11	9	8	5	7
Champ. series totals (3 years)		2	2	.500	3.57	4	4	0	0	0	22 2/3	18	11	9	8	15

WORLD SERIES RECORD

NOTES: Shares single-game record for most wild pitches—2 (October 15, 1989). . . . Member of World Series championship team (1989).

Year	Team (League)	W	L	Pct.	ERA	G	GS	CG	ShO	Sv.	IP	H	R	ER	BB	SO
1989—	Oakland (A.L.)	2	0	1.000	2.08	2	2	0	0	0	13	9	3	3	3	10
1990—	Oakland (A.L.)	0	1	.000	6.75	1	1	0	0	0	2 2/3	8	6	2	0	1
World Series totals (2 years)		2	1	.667	2.87	3	3	0	0	0	15 2/3	17	9	5	3	11

ALL-STAR GAME RECORD

Year	League	W	L	Pct.	ERA	GS	CG	ShO	Sv.	IP	H	R	ER	BB	SO
1989—	American	0	0	...	0.00	0	0	0	0	1	0	0	0	0	1

MORANDINI, MICKEY 2B PHILLIES

PERSONAL: Born April 22, 1966, in Kittanning, Pa. . . . 5-11/176. . . . Bats left, throws right. . . . Full name: Michael Robert Morandini. . . . Name pronounced MOR-an-DEEN-ee.
HIGH SCHOOL: Leechburg (Pa.) Area.
COLLEGE: Indiana.
TRANSACTIONS/CAREER NOTES: Selected by Pittsburgh Pirates organization in seventh round of free-agent draft (June 2, 1987); did not sign. . . . Selected by Philadelphia Phillies organization in fifth round of free-agent draft (June 1, 1988).
STATISTICAL NOTES: Led International League second basemen with 271 putouts, 419 assists and 701 total chances in 1990.
MISCELLANEOUS: Member of 1988 U.S. Olympic baseball team. . . . Turned unassisted triple play while playing second base (September 20, 1992, sixth inning); ninth player ever to accomplish feat and first ever by second baseman during regular season.

			BATTING												FIELDING			
Year	Team (League)	Pos.	G	AB	R	H	2B	3B	HR	RBI	Avg.	BB	SO	SB	PO	A	E	Avg.
1989—	Spartanburg (SAL)	SS	63	231	43	78	19	1	1	30	.338	35	45	18	87	198	10	.966
—	Clearwater (FSL)	SS	17	63	14	19	4	1	0	4	.302	7	8	3	20	59	2	.975
—	Reading (Eastern)	SS	48	188	39	66	12	1	5	29	.351	23	32	5	73	137	10	.955
1990—	Scran./W.B. (Int'l)	2B-SS	139	503	76	131	24	*10	1	31	.260	60	90	16	†271	†419	11	.984
—	Philadelphia (N.L.)	2B	25	79	9	19	4	0	1	3	.241	6	19	3	37	61	1	.990
1991—	Scran./W.B. (Int'l)	2B	12	46	7	12	4	0	1	9	.261	5	6	2	19	38	1	.983
—	Philadelphia (N.L.)	2B	98	325	38	81	11	4	1	20	.249	29	45	13	183	254	6	.986
1992—	Philadelphia (N.L.)	2B-SS	127	422	47	112	8	8	3	30	.265	25	64	8	239	336	6	.990
1993—	Philadelphia (N.L.)	2B	120	425	57	105	19	9	3	33	.247	34	73	13	208	288	5	.990
1994—	Philadelphia (N.L.)	2B	87	274	40	80	16	5	2	26	.292	34	33	10	167	216	6	.985
1995—	Philadelphia (N.L.)	2B	127	494	65	140	34	7	6	49	.283	42	80	9	269	336	7	.989
Major league totals (6 years)			584	2019	256	537	92	33	16	161	.266	170	314	56	1103	1491	31	.988

CHAMPIONSHIP SERIES RECORD

				BATTING											FIELDING			
Year	Team (League)	Pos.	G	AB	R	H	2B	3B	HR	RBI	Avg.	BB	SO	SB	PO	A	E	Avg.
1993	—Philadelphia (N.L.)	2B-PH	4	16	1	4	0	1	0	2	.250	0	3	1	8	9	1	.944

WORLD SERIES RECORD

				BATTING											FIELDING			
Year	Team (League)	Pos.	G	AB	R	H	2B	3B	HR	RBI	Avg.	BB	SO	SB	PO	A	E	Avg.
1993	—Philadelphia (N.L.)	PH-2B	3	5	1	1	0	0	0	0	.200	1	2	0	2	0	0	1.000

ALL-STAR GAME RECORD

			BATTING											FIELDING			
Year	League	Pos.	AB	R	H	2B	3B	HR	RBI	Avg.	BB	SO	SB	PO	A	E	Avg.
1995	—National	2B	1	0	0	0	0	0	0	.000	0	1	0	0	1	0	1.000

MORDECAI, MIKE — 2B — BRAVES

PERSONAL: Born December 13, 1967, in Birmingham, Ala. . . . 5-11/175. . . . Bats right, throws right. . . . Full name: Michael Howard Mordecai.

HIGH SCHOOL: Hewitt-Trussville (Ala.).

COLLEGE: South Alabama.

TRANSACTIONS/CAREER NOTES: Selected by Pittsburgh Pirates organization in 33rd round of free-agent draft (June 2, 1986); did not sign. . . . Selected by Atlanta Braves organization in sixth round of free-agent draft (June 5, 1989). . . . On disabled list (April 8-29, 993).

				BATTING											FIELDING			
Year	Team (League)	Pos.	G	AB	R	H	2B	3B	HR	RBI	Avg.	BB	SO	SB	PO	A	E	Avg.
1989	—Burlington (Midw.)	SS-3B	65	241	39	61	11	1	1	22	.253	33	43	12	80	163	21	.920
	—Greenville (South.)	3B-2B	4	8	0	3	0	0	0	1	.375	1	1	0	4	6	0	1.000
1990	—Durham (Carolina)	SS	72	271	42	76	11	7	3	36	.280	42	45	10	111	221	29	.920
1991	—Durham (Carolina)	SS	109	397	52	104	15	2	4	42	.262	40	58	30	164	302	27	.945
1992	—Greenville (South.)	SS	65	222	31	58	13	1	4	31	.261	29	31	9	93	204	11	.964
	—Richmond (Int'l)	SS-2B-3B	36	118	12	29	3	0	1	6	.246	5	19	0	48	101	10	.937
1993	—Richmond (Int'l)	2-S-3-O-C-1	72	205	29	55	8	1	2	14	.268	14	33	10	98	145	9	.964
1994	—Richmond (Int'l)	SS-1B-3B	99	382	67	107	25	1	14	57	.280	35	50	14	117	279	22	.947
	—Atlanta (N.L.)	SS	4	4	1	1	0	0	1	3	.250	1	0	0	1	4	0	1.000
1995	—Atlanta (N.L.)	2-1-3-S-O	69	75	10	21	6	0	3	11	.280	9	16	0	39	31	0	1.000
Major league totals (2 years)			73	79	11	22	6	0	4	14	.278	10	16	0	40	35	0	1.000

DIVISION SERIES RECORD

				BATTING											FIELDING			
Year	Team (League)	Pos.	G	AB	R	H	2B	3B	HR	RBI	Avg.	BB	SO	SB	PO	A	E	Avg.
1995	—Atlanta (N.L.)	PH-SS	2	3	1	2	1	0	0	2	.667	0	0	0	1	0	0	1.000

CHAMPIONSHIP SERIES RECORD

				BATTING											FIELDING			
Year	Team (League)	Pos.	G	AB	R	H	2B	3B	HR	RBI	Avg.	BB	SO	SB	PO	A	E	Avg.
1995	—Atlanta (N.L.)	PH-SS	2	2	0	0	0	0	0	0	.000	0	1	0	0	0	0	...

WORLD SERIES RECORD

NOTES: Member of World Series championship team (1995).

				BATTING											FIELDING			
Year	Team (League)	Pos.	G	AB	R	H	2B	3B	HR	RBI	Avg.	BB	SO	SB	PO	A	E	Avg.
1995	—Atlanta (N.L.)	SS-DH	3	3	0	1	0	0	0	0	.333	0	1	0	0	6	0	1.000

MOREL, RAMON — P — PIRATES

PERSONAL: Born August 15, 1974, in Villa Gonzalez, Dominican Republic. . . . 6-2/193. . . . Throws right, bats right. . . . Full name: Ramon Rafael Morel.

HIGH SCHOOL: Milagro Hernandez (Dominican Republic).

TRANSACTIONS/CAREER NOTES: Signed as non-drafted free agent by Pittsburgh Pirates organization (May 29, 1991).

Year	Team (League)	W	L	Pct.	ERA	G	GS	CG	ShO	Sv.	IP	H	R	ER	BB	SO
1991	—DSL Pirates (DSL)	3	3	.500	3.60	16	1	0	0	0	25	25	20	10	16	14
1992	—DSL Pirates (DSL)	2	0	1.000	1.06	3	3	0	0	0	17	12	2	2	7	9
	—GC Pirates (GCL)	2	2	.500	4.34	14	2	1	1	0	45 2/3	49	26	22	11	29
1993	—Welland (NYP)	7	8	.467	4.21	16	16	0	0	0	77	90	45	36	21	51
1994	—Augusta (S. Atl.)	10	7	.588	2.83	28	27	2	1	0	168 2/3	157	69	53	24	152
1995	—Lynchburg (Caro.)	3	7	.300	3.47	12	12	1	1	0	72 2/3	80	35	28	13	44
	—Carolina (South.)	3	3	.500	3.52	10	10	0	0	0	69	71	31	27	10	34
	—Pittsburgh (N.L.)	0	1	.000	2.84	5	0	0	0	0	6 1/3	6	2	2	2	3
Major league totals (1 year)		0	1	.000	2.84	5	0	0	0	0	6 1/3	6	2	2	2	3

MORGAN, MIKE — P — CARDINALS

PERSONAL: Born October 8, 1959, in Tulare, Calif. . . . 6-2/220. . . . Throws right, bats right. . . . Full name: Michael Thomas Morgan.

HIGH SCHOOL: Valley (Las Vegas).

TRANSACTIONS/CAREER NOTES: Selected by Oakland Athletics organization in first round (fourth pick overall) of free-agent draft (June 6, 1978). . . . On disabled list (May 14-June 27, 1980). . . . Traded by A's organization to New York Yankees for SS Fred Stanley and a player to be named later (November 3, 1980); A's acquired 2B Brian Doyle to complete deal (November 17, 1980). . . . On disabled list (April 9-22, 1981). . . . Traded by Yankees with OF/1B Dave Collins, 1B Fred McGriff and cash to Toronto Blue Jays for P Dale Murray and OF/C Tom Dodd

(December 9, 1982). . . . On Toronto disabled list (July 2-August 23, 1983); included rehabilitation assignment to Syracuse (August 1-18). . . . Selected by Seattle Mariners from Blue Jays organization in Rule 5 major league draft (December 3, 1984). . . . On Seattle disabled list (April 17, 1985-remainder of season); included rehabilitation assignment to Calgary (July 19-22). . . . Traded by Mariners to Baltimore Orioles for P Ken Dixon (December 9, 1987). . . . On Baltimore disabled list (June 9-July 19, 1988); included rehabilitation assignment to Rochester (June 30-July 17). . . . On Baltimore disabled list (August 12, 1988-remainder of season). . . . Traded by Orioles to Los Angeles Dodgers for OF Mike Devereaux (March 12, 1989). . . . Granted free agency (October 28, 1991). . . . Signed by Chicago Cubs (December 3, 1991). . . . On disabled list (June 14-29, 1993; May 9-27, June 2-22 and July 28, 1994-remainder of season). . . . On Chicago disabled list (April 24-May 25, 1995); included rehabilitation assignment to Orlando (May 15-25). . . . Traded by Cubs with 3B/OF Paul Torres and C Francisco Morales to St. Louis Cardinals for 3B Todd Zeile and cash (June 16, 1995). . . . On St. Louis disabled list (July 4-24, 1995). . . . Granted free agency (November 6, 1995). . . . Re-signed by Cardinals (December 7, 1995).

Year	Team (League)	W	L	Pct.	ERA	G	GS	CG	ShO	Sv.	IP	H	R	ER	BB	SO
1978	—Oakland (A.L.)	0	3	.000	7.50	3	3	1	0	0	12	19	12	10	8	0
	—Vancouver (PCL)	5	6	.455	5.58	14	14	5	1	0	92	109	67	57	54	31
1979	—Ogden (Pac. Coast)	5	5	.500	3.48	13	13	6	0	0	101	93	48	39	49	42
	—Oakland (A.L.)	2	10	.167	5.96	13	13	2	0	0	77	102	57	51	50	17
1980	—Ogden (Pac. Coast)	6	9	.400	5.40	20	20	3	0	0	115	135	79	69	77	46
1981	—Nashville (South.)■	8	7	.533	4.42	26	26	7	0	0	169	164	97	83	83	100
1982	—New York (A.L.)	7	11	.389	4.37	30	23	2	0	0	150 1/3	167	77	73	67	71
1983	—Toronto (A.L.)■	0	3	.000	5.16	16	4	0	0	0	45 1/3	48	26	26	21	22
	—Syracuse (Int'l)	0	3	.000	5.59	5	4	0	0	1	19 1/3	20	12	12	13	17
1984	—Syracuse (Int'l)	13	11	.542	4.07	34	28	10	•4	1	*185 2/3	167	•101	84	•100	105
1985	—Seattle (A.L.)■	1	1	.500	12.00	2	2	0	0	0	6	11	8	8	5	2
	—Calgary (PCL)	0	0	...	4.50	1	1	0	0	0	2	3	1	1	0	0
1986	—Seattle (A.L.)	11	•17	.393	4.53	37	33	9	1	1	216 1/3	243	122	109	86	116
1987	—Seattle (A.L.)	12	17	.414	4.65	34	31	8	2	0	207	245	117	107	53	85
1988	—Baltimore (A.L.)■	1	6	.143	5.43	22	10	2	0	1	71 1/3	70	45	43	23	29
	—Rochester (Int'l)	0	2	.000	4.76	3	3	0	0	0	17	19	10	9	6	7
1989	—Los Angeles (N.L.)■	8	11	.421	2.53	40	19	0	0	0	152 2/3	130	51	43	33	72
1990	—Los Angeles (N.L.)	11	15	.423	3.75	33	33	6	•4	0	211	216	100	88	60	106
1991	—Los Angeles (N.L.)	14	10	.583	2.78	34	33	5	1	1	236 1/3	197	85	73	61	140
1992	—Chicago (N.L.)■	16	8	.667	2.55	34	34	6	1	0	240	203	80	68	79	123
1993	—Chicago (N.L.)	10	15	.400	4.03	32	32	1	1	0	207 2/3	206	100	93	74	111
1994	—Chicago (N.L.)	2	10	.167	6.69	15	15	1	0	0	80 2/3	111	65	60	35	57
1995	—Orlando (Southern)	0	2	.000	7.59	2	2	0	0	0	10 2/3	13	9	9	7	5
	—St. Louis (N.L.)■	5	6	.455	3.88	17	17	1	0	0	106 2/3	114	48	46	25	46
A.L. totals (8 years)		34	68	.333	4.89	157	119	24	3	2	785 1/3	905	464	427	313	342
N.L. totals (7 years)		66	75	.468	3.43	205	183	20	7	1	1235	1177	529	471	367	655
Major league totals (15 years)		100	143	.412	4.00	362	302	44	10	3	2020 1/3	2082	993	898	680	997

ALL-STAR GAME RECORD

Year	League	W	L	Pct.	ERA	GS	CG	ShO	Sv.	IP	H	R	ER	BB	SO
1991	—National	0	0	...	0.00	0	0	0	0	1	0	0	0	0	1

MORMAN, ALVIN — P — ASTROS

PERSONAL: Born January 6, 1969, in Rockingham, N.C. . . . 6-3/210. . . . Throws left, bats left.

HIGH SCHOOL: Richmond Senior (Rockingham, N.C.).

COLLEGE: Wingate (N.C.).

TRANSACTIONS/CAREER NOTES: Selected by Houston Astros organization in 39th round of free-agent draft (June 3, 1991). . . . On disabled list (August 26, 1993-remainder of season and May 23-June 14, 1995). . . . On temporarily inactive list (July 25-August 2, 1994).

Year	Team (League)	W	L	Pct.	ERA	G	GS	CG	ShO	Sv.	IP	H	R	ER	BB	SO
1991	—GC Astros (GCL)	1	0	1.000	2.16	11	0	0	0	1	16 2/3	15	7	4	5	24
	—Osceola (Florida St.)	0	0	...	1.50	3	0	0	0	0	6	5	3	1	2	3
1992	—Asheville (S. Atl.)	8	0	1.000	1.55	57	0	0	0	15	75 1/3	60	17	13	26	70
1993	—Jackson (Texas)	8	2	*.800	2.96	19	19	0	0	0	97 1/3	77	35	32	28	101
1994	—Tucson (Pac. Coast)	3	7	.300	5.11	58	0	0	0	5	74	84	51	42	26	49
1995	—Tucson (Pac. Coast)	5	1	.833	3.91	45	0	0	0	3	48 1/3	50	26	21	20	36

MORMAN, RUSS — 1B/OF — MARLINS

PERSONAL: Born April 28, 1962, in Independence, Mo. . . . 6-4/215. . . . Bats right, throws right. . . . Full name: Russell Lee Morman.

HIGH SCHOOL: William Chrisman (Independence, Mo.).

JUNIOR COLLEGE: Iowa Western Community College.

COLLEGE: Wichita State.

TRANSACTIONS/CAREER NOTES: Selected by Kansas City Royals organization in seventh round of free-agent draft (January 13, 1981); did not sign. . . . Selected by Chicago White Sox organization in first round (28th pick overall) of free-agent draft (June 6, 1983); pick received as compensation for Oakland Athletics signing Type B free-agent SS Bill Almon. . . . Released by White Sox (November 20, 1989). . . . Signed by Omaha, Kansas City Royals organization (December 21, 1989). . . . Granted free agency (October 16, 1991). . . . Signed by Cincinnati Reds organization (November 12, 1991). . . . Released by Nashville, Reds organization (March 26, 1992). . . . Re-signed by Nashville (May 22, 1992). . . . Released by Nashville (September 25, 1992). . . . Signed by Pittsburgh Pirates organization (January 12, 1993). . . . On disabled list (June 23-30, 1993). . . . Granted free agency (October 15, 1993). . . . Signed by Edmonton, Florida Marlins organization (February 4, 1994). . . . On Florida disabled list (July 29-August 19, 1995); included rehabilitation assignment to Charlotte (August 14-18). . . . Granted free agency (October 16, 1995). . . . Re-signed by Marlins organization (November 7, 1995).

RECORDS: Shares major league record for most hits in one inning in first major league game—2 (August 3, 1986, fourth inning).

HONORS: Named first baseman on The Sporting News college All-America team (1983).

STATISTICAL NOTES: Led Eastern League with .512 slugging percentage in 1985. . . . Led Eastern League first basemen with .988 fielding percentage and 79 assists in 1985. . . . Led American Association third basemen with 23 double plays in 1986.

Year	Team (League)	Pos.	G	AB	R	H	2B	3B	HR	RBI	Avg.	BB	SO	SB	PO	A	E	Avg.
			BATTING												FIELDING			
1983—	Glens Falls (East.)	1B	71	233	29	57	9	1	3	32	.245	40	65	8	591	43	7	.989
1984—	Appleton (Midw.)	1B-OF	122	424	68	111	17	7	7	80	.262	80	93	29	823	43	10	.989
1985—	Glens Falls (East.)	1B-3B-OF	119	422	64	131	24	5	17	81	.310	65	51	11	905	†81	12	†.988
—	Buffalo (A.A.)	1B	21	64	16	19	3	1	7	14	.297	10	16	2	144	7	2	.987
1986—	Buffalo (A.A.)	3B-OF	106	365	52	97	17	2	13	57	.266	54	58	3	87	201	24	.923
—	Chicago (A.L.)	1B	49	159	18	40	5	0	4	17	.252	16	36	1	342	26	4	.989
1987—	Hawaii (PCL)	1B-OF	89	294	52	79	19	2	9	53	.269	60	56	5	410	28	3	.993
1988—	Vancouver (PCL)	1B-OF	69	257	40	77	8	1	5	45	.300	32	48	4	370	21	3	.992
—	Chicago (A.L.)	1B-OF-DH	40	75	8	18	2	0	0	3	.240	3	17	0	114	5	2	.983
1989—	Vancouver (PCL)	1B-OF	61	216	18	60	14	1	1	23	.278	18	41	1	163	12	3	.983
—	Chicago (A.L.)	1B	37	58	5	13	2	0	0	8	.224	6	16	1	157	13	2	.988
1990—	Omaha (A.A.)■	1-O-3-2	121	436	67	130	14	9	13	81	.298	51	78	21	665	59	5	.993
—	Kansas City (A.L.)	OF-1B-DH	12	37	5	10	4	2	1	3	.270	3	3	0	27	4	0	1.000
1991—	Kansas City (A.L.)	1B-OF-DH	12	23	1	6	0	0	0	1	.261	1	5	0	47	3	0	1.000
—	Omaha (A.A.)	1B-OF-P	88	316	46	83	15	3	7	50	.263	43	53	10	564	41	7	.989
1992—	Nashville (A.A.)■	1B	101	384	53	119	31	2	14	63	.310	36	60	5	773	59	8	.990
1993—	Buffalo (A.A.)■	1B	119	409	79	131	34	2	22	77	.320	48	59	0	814	60	8	.991
1994—	Edmonton (PCL)■	1B-3B-P	114	406	69	142	30	2	19	82	.350	36	62	9	818	80	6	.993
—	Florida (N.L.)	1B	13	33	2	7	0	1	1	2	.212	2	9	0	66	9	1	.987
1995—	Charlotte (Int'l)	1B-OF	44	169	28	53	7	1	6	36	.314	14	22	2	416	23	2	.995
—	Florida (N.L.)	OF-1B	34	72	9	20	2	1	3	7	.278	3	12	0	31	2	1	.971
American League totals (5 years)			150	352	37	87	13	2	5	32	.247	29	77	2	687	51	8	.989
National League totals (2 years)			47	105	11	27	2	2	4	9	.257	5	21	0	97	11	2	.982
Major league totals (7 years)			197	457	48	114	15	4	9	41	.249	34	98	2	784	62	10	.988

RECORD AS PITCHER

Year	Team (League)	W	L	Pct.	ERA	G	GS	CG	ShO	Sv.	IP	H	R	ER	BB	SO
1991—	Omaha (Am. Assoc.)	0	0	...	0.00	1	0	0	0	0	1	0	0	0	0	0
1994—	Edmonton (PCL)	0	0	...	54.00	1	0	0	0	0	1/3	0	2	2	3	0

MORRIS, BOBBY — 2B — CUBS

PERSONAL: Born November 22, 1972, in Hammond, Ind. . . . 6-0/190. . . . Bats left, throws right. . . . Full name: Robert David Morris. . . . Brother of Hal Morris, first baseman, Cincinnati Reds.

HIGH SCHOOL: Munster (Ind.).

COLLEGE: Iowa.

TRANSACTIONS/CAREER NOTES: Selected by Chicago Cubs organization in ninth round of free-agent draft (June 3, 1993). . . . On disabled list (August 10-September 1, 1995).

STATISTICAL NOTES: Led Appalachian League second basemen with 20 errors in 1993. . . . Led Midwest League with .443 on-base percentage in 1994.

Year	Team (League)	Pos.	G	AB	R	H	2B	3B	HR	RBI	Avg.	BB	SO	SB	PO	A	E	Avg.
			BATTING												FIELDING			
1993—	Hunting. (Appal.)	2B-3B	50	170	29	49	8	3	1	24	.288	24	29	6	84	123	†20	.912
1994—	Peoria (Midwest)	2B	101	362	61	128	33	1	7	64	.354	53	63	7	184	226	25	.943
1995—	Daytona (Fla. St.)	2B	95	344	44	106	18	2	2	55	.308	38	46	22	109	133	*24	.910

MORRIS, HAL — 1B — REDS

PERSONAL: Born April 9, 1965, in Fort Rucker, Ala. . . . 6-4/210. . . . Bats left, throws left. . . . Full name: William Harold Morris. . . . Brother of Bobby Morris, second baseman, Chicago Cubs organization.

HIGH SCHOOL: Munster (Ind.).

COLLEGE: Michigan.

TRANSACTIONS/CAREER NOTES: Selected by New York Yankees organization in eighth round of free-agent draft (June 2, 1986). . . . On Albany/Colonie disabled list (August 14, 1986-remainder of season). . . . Traded by Yankees with P Rodney Imes to Cincinnati Reds for P Tim Leary and OF Van Snider (December 12, 1989). . . . On Cincinnati disabled list (April 16-May 17, 1992); included rehabilitation assignment to Nashville (May 14-17). . . . On Cincinnati disabled list (August 5-21, 1992). . . . On Cincinnati disabled list (March 27-June 7, 1993); included rehabilitation assignment to Indianapolis (June 4-7). . . . On suspended list (August 10, 1993). . . . On Cincinnati disabled list (June 18-July 13, 1995); included rehabilitation assignment to Indianapolis (July 7-10). . . . Granted free agency (November 2, 1995). . . . Re-signed by Reds (December 6, 1995).

STATISTICAL NOTES: Career major league grand slams: 1.

Year	Team (League)	Pos.	G	AB	R	H	2B	3B	HR	RBI	Avg.	BB	SO	SB	PO	A	E	Avg.
			BATTING												FIELDING			
1986—	Oneonta (NYP)	1B	36	127	26	48	9	2	3	30	.378	18	15	1	317	26	3	.991
—	Alb./Colon. (East.)	1B	25	79	7	17	5	0	0	4	.215	4	10	0	203	19	2	.991
1987—	Alb./Colon. (East.)	1B-OF	135	*530	65	*173	31	4	5	73	.326	36	43	7	1086	79	17	.986
1988—	Columbus (Int'l)	OF-1B	121	452	41	134	19	4	3	38	.296	36	62	8	543	26	8	.986
—	New York (A.L.)	OF-DH	15	20	1	2	0	0	0	0	.100	0	9	0	7	0	0	1.000
1989—	Columbus (Int'l)	1B-OF	111	417	70	136	24	1	17	66	*.326	28	47	5	636	67	9	.987
—	New York (A.L.)	OF-1B-DH	15	18	2	5	0	0	0	4	.278	1	4	0	12	0	0	1.000
1990—	Cincinnati (N.L.)■	1B-OF	107	309	50	105	22	3	7	36	.340	21	32	9	595	53	4	.994
—	Nashville (A.A.)	OF	16	64	8	22	5	0	1	10	.344	5	10	4	23	1	1	.960
1991—	Cincinnati (N.L.)	1B-OF	136	478	72	152	33	1	14	59	.318	46	61	10	979	100	9	.992
1992—	Cincinnati (N.L.)	1B	115	395	41	107	21	3	6	53	.271	45	53	6	841	86	1	*.999
—	Nashville (A.A.)	1B	2	6	1	1	1	0	0	0	.167	2	1	0	13	3	0	1.000
1993—	Indianapolis (A.A.)	1B	3	13	4	6	0	1	1	5	.462	1	2	0	26	3	0	1.000
—	Cincinnati (N.L.)	1B	101	379	48	120	18	0	7	49	.317	34	51	2	746	75	5	.994
1994—	Cincinnati (N.L.)	1B	112	436	60	146	30	4	10	78	.335	34	62	6	901	80	6	.994
1995—	Cincinnati (N.L.)	1B	101	359	53	100	25	2	11	51	.279	29	58	1	757	72	5	.994

Year	Team (League)	Pos.	G	AB	R	H	2B	3B	HR	RBI	Avg.	BB	SO	SB	PO	A	E	Avg.
			BATTING												FIELDING			
	— Indianapolis (A.A.)......	1B	2	5	2	2	0	0	0	1	.400	1	0	0	13	2	0	1.000
American League totals (2 years)			30	38	3	7	0	0	0	4	.184	1	13	0	19	0	0	1.000
National League totals (6 years)			672	2356	324	730	149	13	55	326	.310	209	317	34	4819	466	30	.994
Major league totals (8 years)			702	2394	327	737	149	13	55	330	.308	210	330	34	4838	466	30	.994

DIVISION SERIES RECORD

Year	Team (League)	Pos.	G	AB	R	H	2B	3B	HR	RBI	Avg.	BB	SO	SB	PO	A	E	Avg.
			BATTING												FIELDING			
1995	— Cincinnati (N.L.).........	1B	3	10	5	5	1	0	0	2	.500	3	1	1	22	2	0	1.000

CHAMPIONSHIP SERIES RECORD

Year	Team (League)	Pos.	G	AB	R	H	2B	3B	HR	RBI	Avg.	BB	SO	SB	PO	A	E	Avg.
			BATTING												FIELDING			
1990	— Cincinnati (N.L.).........	1B-PH	5	12	3	5	1	0	0	1	.417	1	0	0	20	2	0	1.000
1995	— Cincinnati (N.L.).........	1B-PH	4	12	0	2	1	0	0	1	.167	1	1	1	27	3	0	1.000
Championship series totals (2 years)			9	24	3	7	2	0	0	2	.292	2	1	1	47	5	0	1.000

WORLD SERIES RECORD

NOTES: Member of World Series championship team (1990).

Year	Team (League)	Pos.	G	AB	R	H	2B	3B	HR	RBI	Avg.	BB	SO	SB	PO	A	E	Avg.
			BATTING												FIELDING			
1990	— Cincinnati (N.L.).........	1B-DH	4	14	0	1	0	0	0	2	.071	1	1	0	18	1	0	1.000

MOSQUERA, JULIO — C — BLUE JAYS

PERSONAL: Born January 29, 1972, in Panama City, Panama. . . . 6-0/185. . . . Bats right, throws right. . . . Full name: Julio Alberto Mosquera.
TRANSACTIONS/CAREER NOTES: Signed as non-drafted free agent by Toronto Blue Jays organization (May 16, 1991).
STATISTICAL NOTES: Led Pioneer League with 13 passed balls in 1994. . . . Led South Atlantic League catchers with .991 fielding percentage in 1995.

Year	Team (League)	Pos.	G	AB	R	H	2B	3B	HR	RBI	Avg.	BB	SO	SB	PO	A	E	Avg.
			BATTING												FIELDING			
1991	— Dom. Blue Jays (DSL)	C	42	136	20	29	3	0	0	10	.213	8	12	3	...	...	...	...
1992	— Dom. Blue Jays (DSL)	C	67	235	47	85	12	1	3	39	.362	17	20	17	207	94	14	.956
1993	— GC Blue Jays (GCL)....	C-SS	35	108	9	28	3	2	0	15	.259	8	16	3	180	39	8	.965
1994	— Medicine Hat (Pio.)	C	59	229	33	78	17	1	2	44	.341	18	35	3	299	*70	11	.971
1995	— Hagerstown (SAL)......	C-1B	108	406	64	118	22	5	3	46	.291	29	53	5	641	103	7	†.991

MOTA, JOSE — IF/OF — ROYALS

PERSONAL: Born March 16, 1965, in Santo Domingo, Dominican Republic. . . . 5-9/155. . . . Bats both, throws right. . . . Full name: Jose Manuel Mota. . . . Son of Manny Mota, coach, Los Angeles Dodgers and major league outfielder with four teams (1962-80 and 1982); brother of Andy Mota, infielder, Houston Astros (1991); brother of Gary Mota, outfielder, Philadelphia Phillies organization; and brother of Domingo Mota, infielder, Kansas City Royals organization.
HIGH SCHOOL: Calasanz (Santo Domingo, Dominican Republic).
COLLEGE: Cal State Fullerton.
TRANSACTIONS/CAREER NOTES: Selected by Chicago White Sox organization in second round of free-agent draft (June 3, 1985). . . . Traded by White Sox organization to Texas Rangers organization (December 12, 1985), completing deal in which Rangers traded IF Wayne Tolleson and P Dave Schmidt to White Sox for IF Scott Fletcher, P Ed Correa and a player to be named later (November 25, 1985). . . . On Tulsa disabled list (May 14-24, 1986). . . . Contract sold by Rangers organization to Los Angeles Dodgers organization (June 24, 1987). . . . Selected by Oakland Athletics from Dodgers organization in Rule 5 major league draft (December 6, 1988). . . . Traded by Oakland A's to San Diego Padres organization as part of a three-way deal in which A's organization acquired OF Peter Kuld from Cleveland Indians organization (June 3, 1989); Indians organization acquired OF/P Brian Brooks to complete deal (June 11, 1989). . . . Granted free agency (October 15, 1991). . . . Signed by Kansas City Royals organization (November 22, 1991). . . . On Omaha disabled list (April 6-24, 1995). . . . On Kansas City disabled list (June 3-September 5, 1995); included rehabilitation assignments to Omaha (July 24-30 and August 22-September 3). . . . Granted free agency (October 16, 1995). . . . Re-signed by Royals organization (November 24, 1995).
HONORS: Named second baseman on The Sporting News college All-America team (1985).

Year	Team (League)	Pos.	G	AB	R	H	2B	3B	HR	RBI	Avg.	BB	SO	SB	PO	A	E	Avg.
			BATTING												FIELDING			
1985	— Niag. Falls (NYP)........	2B	65	254	35	77	9	2	0	27	.303	28	29	8	154	156	16	.951
	— Buffalo (A.A.)............	2B	6	18	3	5	0	0	0	1	.278	2	0	0	10	12	0	1.000
1986	— Tulsa (Texas)■..........	3B	41	158	26	51	7	3	1	11	.323	22	13	14	53	102	8	.951
	— Okla. City (A.A.)..........	2B	71	255	38	71	9	1	0	20	.278	24	43	7	129	201	*14	.959
1987	— Tulsa (Texas)	2B	21	71	11	15	2	0	0	4	.211	13	12	2	43	51	3	.969
	— San Antonio (Tex.)■..	2B	54	190	23	50	4	3	0	11	.263	21	34	3	95	139	5	.979
1988	— San Antonio (Tex.)	OF-2B-3B	82	214	32	56	11	1	1	18	.262	27	35	10	56	32	3	.967
	— Albuquerque (PCL).....	2B-SS	6	15	4	5	0	0	0	1	.333	3	3	1	2	10	0	1.000
1989	— Huntsville (South.)■..	2B	27	81	15	11	1	0	0	6	.136	30	15	3	57	54	5	.957
	— Wichita (Texas)■	S-O-2-3	41	109	17	35	5	1	1	9	.321	17	21	3	57	64	1	.992
1990	— Las Vegas (PCL)	S-O-3-2	92	247	44	74	4	4	4	21	.300	42	35	2	64	117	8	.958
1991	— Las Vegas (PCL)	2-S-3-O	107	377	56	109	10	2	1	37	.289	54	48	15	173	310	15	.970
	— San Diego (N.L.)	2B	17	36	4	8	0	0	0	2	.222	2	7	0	24	27	2	.962
1992	— Omaha (A.A.)■	2B-SS-OF	131	469	45	108	11	0	3	28	.230	41	56	21	215	348	13	.977
1993	— Omaha (A.A.)............	SS-2B-3B	105	330	46	93	11	2	3	35	.282	34	34	27	127	211	13	.963
1994	— Omaha (A.A.)............	2B-SS	100	358	60	92	13	6	0	32	.257	47	41	25	172	276	15	.968
1995	— Omaha (A.A.)............	SS-2B-OF	27	87	6	28	4	0	0	10	.322	6	9	1	34	52	4	.956
	— Kansas City (A.L.)	2B	2	2	0	0	0	0	0	0	.000	0	0	0	1	3	0	1.000
American League totals (1 year)			2	2	0	0	0	0	0	0	.000	0	0	0	1	3	0	1.000
National League totals (1 year)			17	36	4	8	0	0	0	2	.222	2	7	0	24	27	2	.962
Major league totals (2 years)			19	38	4	8	0	0	0	2	.211	2	7	0	25	30	2	.965

MOTEN, SCOTT — P — CUBS

PERSONAL: Born April 12, 1972, in Sun Valley, Calif. . . . 6-1/195. . . . Throws right, bats right. . . . Full name: Christopher Scott Moten.
HIGH SCHOOL: Bellflower (Calif.).
COLLEGE: Cerritos (Calif.).
TRANSACTIONS/CAREER NOTES: Selected by Minnesota Twins organization in 29th round of free-agent draft (June 3, 1991). . . . Claimed on waivers by Chicago Cubs (November 3, 1995).

Year	Team (League)	W	L	Pct.	ERA	G	GS	CG	ShO	Sv.	IP	H	R	ER	BB	SO
1992—	Elizabeth. (App.)	•8	1	.889	2.40	13	12	1	1	0	78 2/3	60	31	21	32	71
1993—	Fort Wayne (Midw.)	7	11	.389	5.05	30	22	0	0	1	140 2/3	152	99	79	63	141
1994—	Fort Myers (Fla. St.)	8	4	.667	2.16	44	1	0	0	7	96	87	32	23	38	68
	—Nashville (South.)	0	1	.000	3.86	3	0	0	0	0	4 2/3	5	4	2	2	4
1995—	New Britain (East.)	8	5	.615	3.94	40	1	0	0	3	75 1/3	65	40	33	36	43

MOTTOLA, CHAD — OF — REDS

PERSONAL: Born October 15, 1971, in Augusta, Ga. . . . 6-3/220. . . . Bats right, throws right. . . . Full name: Charles Edward Mottola.
HIGH SCHOOL: St. Thomas Aquinas (Fort Lauderdale, Fla.).
COLLEGE: Central Florida.
TRANSACTIONS/CAREER NOTES: Selected by Cincinnati Reds organization in first round (fifth pick overall) of free-agent draft (June 1, 1992). . . . On disabled list (May 11-20, 1994).

				BATTING											FIELDING			
Year	Team (League)	Pos.	G	AB	R	H	2B	3B	HR	RBI	Avg.	BB	SO	SB	PO	A	E	Avg.
1992—	Billings (Pioneer)	OF	57	213	53	61	8	3	12	37	.286	25	43	12	89	9	3	.970
1993—	Winst.-Salem (Car.)	OF	137	493	76	138	25	3	21	91	.280	62	109	13	214	*20	*15	.940
1994—	Chatt. (South.)	OF	118	402	44	97	19	1	7	41	.241	30	68	9	230	17	1	.996
1995—	Chatt. (South.)	OF	51	181	32	53	13	1	10	39	.293	13	32	1	106	6	3	.974
	—Indianapolis (A.A.)	OF	69	239	40	62	11	1	8	37	.259	20	50	8	151	11	4	.976

MOUTON, JAMES — OF — ASTROS

PERSONAL: Born December 29, 1968, in Denver. . . . 5-9/175. . . . Bats right, throws right. . . . Full name: James Raleigh Mouton. . . . Name pronounced MOO-tawn.
HIGH SCHOOL: Luther Burbank Senior (Sacramento, Calif.).
COLLEGE: St. Mary's (Calif.).
TRANSACTIONS/CAREER NOTES: Selected by New York Yankees organization in 42nd round of free-agent draft (June 2, 1987); did not sign. . . . Selected by Minnesota Twins organization in eighth round of free-agent draft (June 4, 1990); did not sign. . . . Selected by Houston Astros organization in seventh round of free-agent draft (June 3, 1991). . . . On Houston disabled list (June 12-30, 1995); included rehabilitation assignment to Tucson (June 27-30).
HONORS: Named Pacific Coast League Most Valuable Player (1993).
STATISTICAL NOTES: Led New York-Pennsylvania League in caught stealing with 18 in 1991. . . . Led New York-Pennsylvania League second basemen with 382 total chances in 1991. . . . Led Florida State League second basemen with 623 total chances in 1992. . . . Led Pacific Coast League with 286 total bases and tied for lead in caught stealing with 18 in 1993. . . . Led Pacific Coast League second basemen with 674 total chances and 75 double plays in 1993. . . . Career major league grand slams: 1.

				BATTING											FIELDING			
Year	Team (League)	Pos.	G	AB	R	H	2B	3B	HR	RBI	Avg.	BB	SO	SB	PO	A	E	Avg.
1991—	Auburn (NYP)	2B	76	288	71	76	15	*10	2	40	.264	55	32	*60	*170	184	*28	.927
1992—	Osceola (Fla. St.)	2B	133	507	*110	143	•30	6	11	62	.282	71	78	*51	*288	294	*41	.934
1993—	Tucson (PCL)	2B	134	*546	*126	*172	*42	12	16	92	.315	72	82	40	*277	*354	*43	.936
1994—	Houston (N.L.)	OF	99	310	43	76	11	0	2	16	.245	27	69	24	163	5	3	.982
	—Tucson (PCL)	OF	4	17	2	7	1	0	1	1	.412	2	3	1	7	1	0	1.000
1995—	Tucson (PCL)	OF	3	11	1	5	0	0	1	1	.455	0	2	0	1	0	1	.500
	—Houston (N.L.)	OF	104	298	42	78	18	2	4	27	.262	25	59	25	136	4	0	1.000
Major league totals (2 years)			203	608	85	154	29	2	6	43	.253	52	128	49	299	9	3	.990

MOUTON, LYLE — OF — WHITE SOX

PERSONAL: Born May 13, 1969, in Lafayette, La. . . . 6-4/240. . . . Bats right, throws right. . . . Full name: Lyle Joseph Mouton. . . . Name pronounced MOO-tawn.
HIGH SCHOOL: St. Thomas More (Lafayette, La.).
COLLEGE: Louisiana State.
TRANSACTIONS/CAREER NOTES: Selected by New York Yankees organization in fifth round of free-agent draft (June 3, 1991). . . . Traded by Yankees to Chicago White Sox (April 22, 1995), completing deal in which White Sox traded P Jack McDowell to Yankees for P Keith Heberling and a player to be named later (December 14, 1994).

				BATTING											FIELDING			
Year	Team (League)	Pos.	G	AB	R	H	2B	3B	HR	RBI	Avg.	BB	SO	SB	PO	A	E	Avg.
1991—	Oneonta (NYP)	OF	70	272	53	84	11	2	7	41	.309	31	38	15	106	5	5	.957
1992—	Prin. William (Car.)	OF	50	189	28	50	14	1	6	34	.265	17	42	4	49	5	4	.931
	—Albany (Eastern)	OF	64	214	25	46	12	2	2	27	.215	24	55	1	102	1	0	1.000
1993—	Albany (Eastern)	OF	135	491	74	125	22	3	16	76	.255	50	125	18	189	9	5	.975
1994—	Alb./Colon. (East.)	OF-3B	74	274	42	84	23	1	12	42	.307	27	62	7	118	4	2	.984
	—Columbus (Int'l)	OF	59	204	26	64	14	5	4	32	.314	14	45	5	99	5	1	.990
1995—	Nashville (A.A.)■	OF	71	267	40	79	17	0	8	41	.296	23	58	10	123	8	3	.978
	—Chicago (A.L.)	OF-DH	58	179	23	54	16	0	5	27	.302	19	46	1	93	5	1	.990
Major league totals (1 year)			58	179	23	54	16	0	5	27	.302	19	46	1	93	5	1	.990

MOYER, JAMIE — P — RED SOX

PERSONAL: Born November 18, 1962, in Sellersville, Pa. . . . 6-0/170. . . . Throws left, bats left. . . . Son-in-law of Digger Phelps, ESPN college basketball analyst, and Notre Dame basketball coach (1971-72 through 1990-91).
HIGH SCHOOL: Souderton (Pa.) Area.
COLLEGE: St. Joseph's (Pa.).
TRANSACTIONS/CAREER NOTES: Selected by Chicago Cubs organization in sixth round of free-agent draft (June 4, 1984). . . . Traded by Cubs with OF Rafael Palmeiro and P Drew Hall to Texas Rangers for P Mitch Williams, P Paul Kilgus, P Steve Wilson, IF Curtis Wilkerson, IF Luis Benitez and OF Pablo Delgado (December 5, 1988). . . . On Texas disabled list (May 31-September 1, 1989); included rehabilitation assignments to Gulf Coast Rangers (August 5-14) and Tulsa (August 15-24). . . . Released by Rangers (November 13, 1990). . . . Signed by Louisville, St. Louis Cardinals organization (January 9, 1991). . . . Released by Cardinals (October 14, 1991). . . . Signed by Cubs organization (January 8, 1992). . . . Released by Iowa, Cubs organization (March 30, 1992). . . . Signed by Toledo, Detroit Tigers organization (May 24, 1992). . . . Granted free agency (December 8, 1992). . . . Signed by Baltimore Orioles organization (December 14, 1992). . . . Granted free agency (November 1, 1995). . . . Signed by Boston Red Sox (December 22, 1995).
STATISTICAL NOTES: Led American Association with 16 home runs allowed in 1991.

Year	Team (League)	W	L	Pct.	ERA	G	GS	CG	ShO	Sv.	IP	H	R	ER	BB	SO
1984	Geneva (NYP)	•9	3	.750	1.89	14	14	5	2	0	*104 2/3	59	27	22	31	*120
1985	Winst.-Salem (Car.)	8	2	.800	2.30	12	12	6	2	0	94	82	36	24	22	94
	—Pittsfield (Eastern)	7	6	.538	3.72	15	15	3	0	0	96 2/3	99	49	40	32	51
1986	Pittsfield (Eastern)	3	1	.750	0.88	6	6	0	0	0	41	27	10	4	16	42
	—Iowa (Am. Assoc.)	3	2	.600	2.55	6	6	2	0	0	42 1/3	25	14	12	11	25
	—Chicago (N.L.)	7	4	.636	5.05	16	16	1	1	0	87 1/3	107	52	49	42	45
1987	Chicago (N.L.)	12	15	.444	5.10	35	33	1	0	0	201	210	127	*114	97	147
1988	Chicago (N.L.)	9	15	.375	3.48	34	30	3	1	0	202	212	84	78	55	121
1989	Texas (A.L.)■	4	9	.308	4.86	15	15	1	0	0	76	84	51	41	33	44
	—GC Rangers (GCL)	1	0	1.000	1.64	3	3	0	0	0	11	8	4	2	1	18
	—Tulsa (Texas)	1	1	.500	5.11	2	2	1	1	0	12 1/3	16	8	7	3	9
1990	Texas (A.L.)	2	6	.250	4.66	33	10	1	0	0	102 1/3	115	59	53	39	58
1991	St. Louis (N.L.)■	0	5	.000	5.74	8	7	0	0	0	31 1/3	38	21	20	16	20
	—Louisville (A.A.)	5	10	.333	3.80	20	20	1	0	0	125 2/3	125	64	53	43	69
1992	Toledo (Int'l)■	10	8	.556	2.86	21	20	5	0	0	138 2/3	128	48	44	37	80
1993	Rochester (Int'l)■	6	0	1.000	1.67	8	8	1	1	0	54	42	13	10	13	41
	—Baltimore (A.L.)	12	9	.571	3.43	25	25	3	1	0	152	154	63	58	38	90
1994	Baltimore (A.L.)	5	7	.417	4.77	23	23	0	0	0	149	158	81	79	38	87
1995	Baltimore (A.L.)	8	6	.571	5.21	27	18	0	0	0	115 2/3	117	70	67	30	65
A.L. totals (5 years)		31	37	.456	4.51	123	91	5	1	0	595	628	324	298	178	344
N.L. totals (4 years)		28	39	.418	4.50	93	86	5	2	0	521 2/3	567	284	261	210	333
Major league totals (9 years)		59	76	.437	4.51	216	177	10	3	0	1116 2/3	1195	608	559	388	677

MUELLER, BILL — 3B/2B — GIANTS

PERSONAL: Born March 17, 1971, in Maryland Heights, Mo. . . . 5-11/175. . . . Bats both, throws right. . . . Full name: William Mueller.
HIGH SCHOOL: DeSmet (Creve Coeur, Mo.).
COLLEGE: Southwest Missouri State.
TRANSACTIONS/CAREER NOTES: Selected by San Francisco Giants organization in 15th round of free-agent draft (June 3, 1993).
STATISTICAL NOTES: Led California League with .435 on-base percentage in 1994.

				BATTING											FIELDING			
Year	Team (League)	Pos.	G	AB	R	H	2B	3B	HR	RBI	Avg.	BB	SO	SB	PO	A	E	Avg.
1993	Everett (N'west)	2B	58	200	31	60	8	2	1	24	.300	42	17	13	86	143	8	.966
1994	San Jose (Calif.)	3B-2B-SS	120	431	79	130	20	•9	5	72	.302	*103	47	4	83	276	29	.925
1995	Shreveport (Texas)	3B-2B	88	330	56	102	16	2	1	39	.309	53	36	6	52	169	5	.978
	—Phoenix (PCL)	3B-2B	41	172	23	51	13	6	2	19	.297	19	31	0	26	85	7	.941

MULHOLLAND, TERRY — P

PERSONAL: Born March 9, 1963, in Uniontown, Pa. . . . 6-3/212. . . . Throws left, bats right. . . . Full name: Terence John Mulholland.
HIGH SCHOOL: Laurel Highlands (Uniontown, Pa.).
COLLEGE: Marietta College (O.).
TRANSACTIONS/CAREER NOTES: Selected by San Francisco Giants organization in first round (24th pick overall) of free-agent draft (June 4, 1984); pick received as compensation for Detroit Tigers signing free-agent IF Darrell Evans. . . . On San Francisco disabled list (August 1, 1988-remainder of season). . . . Traded by Giants with P Dennis Cook and 3B Charlie Hayes to Philadelphia Phillies for P Steve Bedrosian and a player to be named later (June 18, 1989); Giants organization acquired IF Rick Parker to complete deal (August 7, 1989). . . . On Philadelphia disabled list (June 12-28, 1990); included rehabilitation assignment to Scranton/Wilkes-Barre (June 23-24). . . . Traded by Phillies with a player to be named later to New York Yankees for P Bobby Munoz, 2B Kevin Jordan and P Ryan Karp (February 9, 1994); Yankees acquired P Jeff Patterson to complete deal (November 8, 1994). . . . Granted free agency (October 17, 1994). . . . Signed by Giants (April 8, 1995). . . . On San Francisco disabled list (June 6-July 4, 1995); included rehabilitation assignment to Phoenix (June 23-July 4). . . . Granted free agency (November 3, 1995).
STATISTICAL NOTES: Pitched 6-0 no-hit victory for Philadelphia against San Francisco (August 15, 1990).
MISCELLANEOUS: Appeared in one game as pinch-runner (1991). . . . Appeared in one game as pinch-runner with San Francisco (1995).

Year	Team (League)	W	L	Pct.	ERA	G	GS	CG	ShO	Sv.	IP	H	R	ER	BB	SO
1984	Everett (N'west)	1	0	1.000	0.00	3	3	0	0	0	19	10	2	0	4	15
	—Fresno (California)	5	2	.714	2.95	9	9	0	0	0	42 2/3	32	17	14	36	39
1985	Shreveport (Texas)	9	8	.529	2.90	26	26	8	*3	0	176 2/3	166	79	57	87	122
1986	Phoenix (PCL)	8	5	.615	4.46	17	17	3	0	0	111	112	60	55	56	77
	—San Francisco (N.L.)	1	7	.125	4.94	15	10	0	0	0	54 2/3	51	33	30	35	27
1987	Phoenix (PCL)	7	12	.368	5.07	37	*29	3	1	1	172 1/3	200	*124	•97	90	94
1988	Phoenix (PCL)	7	3	.700	3.58	19	14	3	2	0	100 2/3	116	45	40	44	57

M

Year	Team (League)	W	L	Pct.	ERA	G	GS	CG	ShO	Sv.	IP	H	R	ER	BB	SO
	—San Francisco (N.L.)	2	1	.667	3.72	9	6	2	1	0	46	50	20	19	7	18
1989	—San Francisco (N.L.)	0	0	...	4.09	5	1	0	0	0	11	15	5	5	4	6
	—Phoenix (PCL)	4	5	.444	2.99	13	10	3	0	0	78 1/3	67	30	26	26	61
	—Philadelphia (N.L.)■	4	7	.364	5.00	20	17	2	1	0	104 1/3	122	61	58	32	60
1990	—Philadelphia (N.L.)	9	10	.474	3.34	33	26	6	1	0	180 2/3	172	78	67	42	75
	—Scran./W.B. (Int'l)	0	1	.000	3.00	1	1	0	0	0	6	9	4	2	2	2
1991	—Philadelphia (N.L.)	16	13	.552	3.61	34	34	8	3	0	232	231	100	93	49	142
1992	—Philadelphia (N.L.)	13	11	.542	3.81	32	32	*12	2	0	229	227	101	97	46	125
1993	—Philadelphia (N.L.)	12	9	.571	3.25	29	28	7	2	0	191	177	80	69	40	116
1994	—New York (A.L.)■	6	7	.462	6.49	24	19	2	0	0	120 2/3	150	94	87	37	72
1995	—San Francisco (N.L.)■	5	13	.278	5.80	29	24	2	0	0	149	190	112	96	38	65
	—Phoenix (PCL)	0	0	...	2.25	1	1	0	0	0	4	4	3	1	1	4
A.L. totals (1 year)		6	7	.462	6.49	24	19	2	0	0	120 2/3	150	94	87	37	72
N.L. totals (8 years)		62	71	.466	4.01	206	178	39	10	0	1197 2/3	1235	590	534	293	634
Major league totals (9 years)		68	78	.466	4.24	230	197	41	10	0	1318 1/3	1385	684	621	330	706

CHAMPIONSHIP SERIES RECORD

Year	Team (League)	W	L	Pct.	ERA	G	GS	CG	ShO	Sv.	IP	H	R	ER	BB	SO
1993	—Philadelphia (N.L.)	0	1	.000	7.20	1	1	0	0	0	5	9	5	4	1	2

WORLD SERIES RECORD

Year	Team (League)	W	L	Pct.	ERA	G	GS	CG	ShO	Sv.	IP	H	R	ER	BB	SO
1993	—Philadelphia (N.L.)	1	0	1.000	6.75	2	2	0	0	0	10 2/3	14	8	8	3	5

ALL-STAR GAME RECORD

Year	League	W	L	Pct.	ERA	GS	CG	ShO	Sv.	IP	H	R	ER	BB	SO
1993	—National	0	0	...	4.50	1	0	0	0	2	1	1	1	2	0

MULLIGAN, SEAN — C — PADRES

PERSONAL: Born April 25, 1970, in Lynwood, Calif. . . . 6-2/210. . . . Bats right, throws right. . . . Full name: Sean Patrick Mulligan.
HIGH SCHOOL: Rubidoux (Riverside, Calif.).
COLLEGE: Illinois.
TRANSACTIONS/CAREER NOTES: Selected by San Diego Padres organization in fourth round of free-agent draft (June 3, 1991). . . . On suspended list (July 7-14, 1993).

						BATTING									FIELDING			
Year	Team (League)	Pos.	G	AB	R	H	2B	3B	HR	RBI	Avg.	BB	SO	SB	PO	A	E	Avg.
1991	—Char., S.C. (S. Atl.)	C	60	215	24	56	9	3	4	30	.260	17	56	4	327	48	9	.977
1992	—Waterloo (Midw.)	C	79	278	24	70	13	1	5	43	.252	20	62	1	231	18	4	.984
	—High Desert (Calif.)	C	35	118	14	19	4	0	4	14	.161	11	38	0	153	17	6	.966
1993	—Rancho Cuca. (Cal.)	C	79	268	29	75	10	3	6	36	.280	34	33	1	251	23	10	.965
1994	—Rancho Cuca. (Cal.)	C	66	243	45	74	18	1	9	49	.305	24	39	1	300	27	3	.991
	—Wichita (Texas)	C-1B	56	208	29	73	14	0	1	30	.351	11	25	2	315	36	3	.992
1995	—Las Vegas (PCL)	C	101	339	34	93	20	1	7	43	.274	27	61	0	439	33	6	.987

MUNOZ, BOBBY — P — PHILLIES

PERSONAL: Born March 3, 1968, in Rio Piedras, Puerto Rico. . . . 6-7/259. . . . Throws right, bats right. . . . Full name: Roberto Munoz.
HIGH SCHOOL: Hialeah (Fla.) Miami Lakes.
JUNIOR COLLEGE: Palm Beach Junior College (Fla.) and Polk Community College (Fla.).
TRANSACTIONS/CAREER NOTES: Selected by New York Yankees organization in 15th round of free-agent draft (June 1, 1988). . . . Traded by Yankees with 2B Kevin Jordan and P Ryan Karp to Philadelphia Phillies for P Terry Mulholland and a player to be named later (February 9, 1994); Yankees acquired P Jeff Patterson to complete deal (November 8, 1994). . . . On Philadelphia disabled list (April 18-July 22 and August 3, 1995-remainder of season); included rehabilitation assignments to Reading (June 19-July 10) and Scranton/Wilkes-Barre (July 10-17).

Year	Team (League)	W	L	Pct.	ERA	G	GS	CG	ShO	Sv.	IP	H	R	ER	BB	SO
1989	—GC Yankees (GCL)	1	1	.500	3.48	2	2	0	0	0	10 1/3	5	4	4	4	13
	—Fort Lauder. (FSL)	1	2	.333	4.73	3	3	0	0	0	13 1/3	16	8	7	7	2
1990	—Greensboro (S. Atl.)	5	12	.294	3.73	25	24	0	0	0	132 2/3	133	70	55	58	100
1991	—Fort Lauder. (FSL)	5	8	.385	2.33	19	19	4	2	0	108	91	45	28	40	53
	—Columbus (Int'l)	0	1	.000	24.00	1	1	0	0	0	3	8	8	8	3	2
1992	—Alb./Colon. (East.)	7	5	.583	3.28	22	22	0	0	0	112 1/3	96	55	41	70	66
1993	—Columbus (Int'l)	3	1	.750	1.44	22	1	0	0	10	31 1/3	24	6	5	8	16
	—New York (A.L.)	3	3	.500	5.32	38	0	0	0	0	45 2/3	48	27	27	26	33
1994	—Philadelphia (N.L.)■	7	5	.583	2.67	21	14	1	0	1	104 1/3	101	40	31	35	59
	—Scran./W.B. (Int'l)	2	3	.400	2.12	6	5	0	0	0	34	27	9	8	14	24
1995	—Reading (Eastern)	0	4	.000	10.80	4	4	0	0	0	15	28	19	18	3	8
	—Scran./W.B. (Int'l)	1	0	1.000	0.56	2	2	1	1	0	16	8	2	1	3	10
	—Philadelphia (N.L.)	0	2	.000	5.74	3	3	0	0	0	15 2/3	15	13	10	9	6
A.L. totals (1 year)		3	3	.500	5.32	38	0	0	0	0	45 2/3	48	27	27	26	33
N.L. totals (2 years)		7	7	.500	3.08	24	17	1	0	1	120	116	53	41	44	65
Major league totals (3 years)		10	10	.500	3.69	62	17	1	0	1	165 2/3	164	80	68	70	98

MUNOZ, MIKE — P — ROCKIES

PERSONAL: Born July 12, 1965, in Baldwin Park, Calif. . . . 6-2/192. . . . Throws left, bats left. . . . Full name: Michael Anthony Munoz.
HIGH SCHOOL: Bishop Amat (La Puente, Calif.).
COLLEGE: Cal Poly Pomona.

TRANSACTIONS/CAREER NOTES: Selected by Los Angeles Dodgers organization in third round of free-agent draft (June 2, 1986).... Traded by Dodgers organization to Detroit Tigers for P Mike Wilkins (September 30, 1990).... Granted free agency (May 12, 1993).... Signed by Colorado Springs, Colorado Rockies organization (May 14, 1993).

Year	Team (League)	W	L	Pct.	ERA	G	GS	CG	ShO	Sv.	IP	H	R	ER	BB	SO
1986—	Great Falls (Pio.)	4	4	.500	3.21	14	14	2	2	0	81 1/3	85	44	29	38	49
1987—	Bakersfield (Calif.)	8	7	.533	3.74	52	12	2	0	9	118	125	68	49	43	80
1988—	San Antonio (Tex.)	7	2	.778	1.00	56	0	0	0	14	71 2/3	63	18	8	24	71
1989—	Albuquerque (PCL)	6	4	.600	3.08	60	0	0	0	6	79	72	32	27	40	81
	—Los Angeles (N.L.)	0	0	...	16.88	3	0	0	0	0	2 2/3	5	5	5	2	3
1990—	Los Angeles (N.L.)	0	1	.000	3.18	8	0	0	0	0	5 2/3	6	2	2	3	2
	—Albuquerque (PCL)	4	1	.800	4.25	49	0	0	0	6	59 1/3	65	33	28	19	40
1991—	Toledo (Int'l)■	2	3	.400	3.83	38	1	0	0	8	54	44	30	23	35	38
	—Detroit (A.L.)	0	0	...	9.64	6	0	0	0	0	9 1/3	14	10	10	5	3
1992—	Detroit (A.L.)	1	2	.333	3.00	65	0	0	0	2	48	44	16	16	25	23
1993—	Detroit (A.L.)	0	1	.000	6.00	8	0	0	0	0	3	4	2	2	6	1
	—Colo. Springs (PCL)■	1	2	.333	1.67	40	0	0	0	3	37 2/3	46	10	7	9	30
	—Colorado (N.L.)	2	1	.667	4.50	21	0	0	0	0	18	21	12	9	9	16
1994—	Colorado (N.L.)	4	2	.667	3.74	57	0	0	0	1	45 2/3	37	22	19	31	32
1995—	Colorado (N.L.)	2	4	.333	7.42	64	0	0	0	2	43 2/3	54	38	36	27	37
	A.L. totals (3 years)	1	3	.250	4.18	79	0	0	0	2	60 1/3	62	28	28	36	27
	N.L. totals (5 years)	8	8	.500	5.52	153	0	0	0	3	115 2/3	123	79	71	72	90
	Major league totals (7 years)	9	11	.450	5.06	232	0	0	0	5	176	185	107	99	108	117

DIVISION SERIES RECORD

Year	Team (League)	W	L	Pct.	ERA	G	GS	CG	ShO	Sv.	IP	H	R	ER	BB	SO
1995—	Colorado (N.L.)	0	1	.000	13.50	4	0	0	0	0	1 1/3	4	2	2	1	1

MUNOZ, NOE — C — DODGERS

PERSONAL: Born December 3, 1970, in Ecatepec, Mexico.... 6-2/180.... Bats right, throws right.
HIGH SCHOOL: Emiliano Zapata (Mexico).
TRANSACTIONS/CAREER NOTES: Signed as non-drafted free agent by Los Angeles Dodgers organization (September 15, 1993).

			BATTING												FIELDING			
Year	Team (League)	Pos.	G	AB	R	H	2B	3B	HR	RBI	Avg.	BB	SO	SB	PO	A	E	Avg.
1994—	San Antonio (Tex.)	C	51	137	12	31	4	2	2	14	.226	3	21	1	315	24	3	.991
	—Bakersfield (Calif.)	C	8	26	4	7	2	0	0	3	.269	3	5	0	61	7	0	1.000
1995—	Reynoso (Mex.)■	C	36	121	23	38	8	0	1	22	.314	19	17	0	185	25	6	.972
	—Albuquerque (PCL)■	C	23	58	1	13	1	0	0	3	.224	2	8	0	89	16	1	.991
	—Los Angeles (N.L.)	C	2	1	0	0	0	0	0	0	.000	0	0	0	6	0	0	1.000
	Major league totals (1 year)		2	1	0	0	0	0	0	0	.000	0	0	0	6	0	0	1.000

MUNOZ, OSCAR — P — ORIOLES

PERSONAL: Born September 25, 1969, in Hialeah, Fla.... 6-3/210.... Throws right, bats right.... Full name: Juan Oscar Munoz.
HIGH SCHOOL: Christopher Columbus (Miami).
COLLEGE: Miami (Fla.).
TRANSACTIONS/CAREER NOTES: Selected by Cleveland Indians organization in fifth round of free-agent draft (June 4, 1990).... Traded by Indians organization with P Curt Leskanic to Minnesota Twins organization for 1B Paul Sorrento (March 28, 1992).... On disabled list (April 9-16 and June 19-August 21, 1992).... Claimed on waivers by Baltimore Orioles (November 20, 1995).
HONORS: Named Southern League Pitcher of the Year (1993).
STATISTICAL NOTES: Pitched 1-0 no-hit victory for Kinston against Prince William (May 26, 1991).

Year	Team (League)	W	L	Pct.	ERA	G	GS	CG	ShO	Sv.	IP	H	R	ER	BB	SO
1990—	Watertown (NYP)	1	1	.500	1.69	2	2	0	0	0	10 2/3	8	2	2	3	9
	—Kinston (Carolina)	7	0	1.000	2.39	9	9	2	1	0	64	43	18	17	18	55
1991—	Kinston (Carolina)	6	3	.667	1.44	14	14	2	1	0	93 2/3	60	23	15	36	111
	—Cant./Akr. (East.)	3	8	.273	5.72	15	15	2	1	0	85	88	54	54	51	71
1992—	Orlando (Southern)■	3	5	.375	5.05	14	12	1	0	0	67 2/3	73	44	38	32	74
1993—	Nashville (South.)■	11	4	•.733	3.08	20	20	1	0	0	131 2/3	123	56	45	51	139
	—Portland (PCL)	2	2	.500	4.31	5	5	0	0	0	31 1/3	29	18	15	17	29
1994—	Salt Lake (PCL)	9	8	.529	5.88	26	26	1	0	0	139 1/3	180	113	91	68	100
	—Nashville (South.)	3	0	1.000	0.41	3	3	2	1	0	22	16	1	1	5	21
1995—	Salt Lake (PCL)	8	6	.571	4.95	19	19	1	1	0	112 2/3	121	67	62	35	74
	—Minnesota (A.L.)	2	1	.667	5.60	10	3	0	0	0	35 1/3	40	28	22	17	25
	Major league totals (1 year)	2	1	.667	5.60	10	3	0	0	0	35 1/3	40	28	22	17	25

MUNOZ, PEDRO — OF

PERSONAL: Born September 19, 1968, in Ponce, Puerto Rico.... 5-10/208.... Bats right, throws right.... Full name: Pedro Javier Munoz.
HIGH SCHOOL: Dr. Pila (Ponce, Puerto Rico).
TRANSACTIONS/CAREER NOTES: Signed as non-drafted free agent by Toronto Blue Jays organization (May 31, 1985).... On disabled list (July 30-August 28, 1987).... Traded by Blue Jays organization with 2B Nelson Liriano to Minnesota Twins for P John Candelaria (July 27, 1990).... On Minnesota disabled list (July 15-30, 1991 and July 1-26, 1993).... Granted free agency (December 21, 1995).
STATISTICAL NOTES: Tied for South Atlantic League lead with four intentional bases on balls received in 1986.... Career major league grand slams: 1.

			BATTING												FIELDING			
Year	Team (League)	Pos.	G	AB	R	H	2B	3B	HR	RBI	Avg.	BB	SO	SB	PO	A	E	Avg.
1985—	GC Blue Jays (GCL)	OF	40	145	14	38	3	0	2	17	.262	9	20	4	46	2	1	.980

M

Year	Team (League)	Pos.	G	AB	R	H	2B	3B	HR	RBI	Avg.	BB	SO	SB	PO	A	E	Avg.
			BATTING												FIELDING			
1986—	Florence (S. Atl.)	OF	122	445	69	131	16	5	14	82	.294	54	100	9	197	14	9	.959
1987—	Dunedin (Fla. St.)	OF	92	341	55	80	11	5	8	44	.235	34	74	13	4	1	0	1.000
1988—	Dunedin (Fla. St.)	OF	133	481	59	141	21	7	8	73	.293	52	87	15	164	8	*15	.920
1989—	Knoxville (South.)	OF	122	442	54	118	15	4	19	65	.267	20	85	10	55	3	1	.983
1990—	Syracuse (Int'l)	OF	86	317	41	101	22	3	7	56	.319	24	64	16	110	4	6	.950
—	Portland (PCL)■	OF	30	110	19	35	4	0	5	21	.318	15	18	8	51	1	3	.945
—	Minnesota (A.L.)	OF-DH	22	85	13	23	4	1	0	5	.271	2	16	3	34	1	1	.972
1991—	Portland (PCL)	OF	56	212	33	67	19	2	5	28	.316	19	42	9	109	2	2	.982
—	Minnesota (A.L.)	OF-DH	51	138	15	39	7	1	7	26	.283	9	31	3	89	3	1	.989
1992—	Minnesota (A.L.)	OF-DH	127	418	44	113	16	3	12	71	.270	17	90	4	220	8	3	.987
1993—	Minnesota (A.L.)	OF	104	326	34	76	11	1	13	38	.233	25	97	1	172	5	3	.983
1994—	Minnesota (A.L.)	OF-DH	75	244	35	72	15	2	11	36	.295	19	67	0	110	1	4	.965
1995—	Minnesota (A.L.)	DH-OF-1B	104	376	45	113	17	0	18	58	.301	19	86	0	29	4	5	.868
Major league totals (6 years)			483	1587	186	436	70	8	61	234	.275	91	387	11	654	22	17	.975

MURPHY, ROB — P — PADRES

PERSONAL: Born May 26, 1960, in Miami. . . . 6-2/215. . . . Throws left, bats left. . . . Full name: Robert Albert Murphy Jr.

HIGH SCHOOL: Christopher Columbus (Miami).

COLLEGE: Florida.

TRANSACTIONS/CAREER NOTES: Selected by Milwaukee Brewers organization in 29th round of free-agent draft (June 6, 1978); did not sign. . . . Selected by Cincinnati Reds organization in secondary phase of free-agent draft (January 13, 1981). . . . Traded by Reds with 1B Nick Esasky to Boston Red Sox for 1B Todd Benzinger, P Jeff Sellers and a player to be named later (December 13, 1988); Reds acquired P Luis Vasquez to complete deal (January 12, 1989). . . . Traded by Red Sox to Seattle Mariners for P Mike Gardiner (April 1, 1991). . . . Granted free agency (December 20, 1991). . . . Signed by Houston Astros organization (January 27, 1992). . . . On Houston disabled list (May 3-22, 1992). . . . Granted free agency (October 29, 1992). . . . Signed by St. Louis Cardinals (January 7, 1993). . . . Claimed on waivers by New York Yankees (August 3, 1994). . . . Granted free agency (October 28, 1994). . . . Signed by Albuquerque, Los Angeles Dodgers organization (April 12, 1995). . . . Released by Dodgers (May 16, 1995). . . . Signed by Charlotte, Florida Marlins organization (June 12, 1995). . . . Released by Marlins (July 24, 1995). . . . Signed by San Diego Padres organization (January 19, 1996).

Year	Team (League)	W	L	Pct.	ERA	G	GS	CG	ShO	Sv.	IP	H	R	ER	BB	SO
1981—	Tampa (Fla. St.)	6	8	.429	4.54	25	20	2	0	0	105	109	73	53	67	58
1982—	Ced. Rap. (Midw.)	3	7	.300	4.04	31	9	0	0	0	89	92	62	40	61	96
1983—	Ced. Rap. (Midw.)	6	10	.375	3.33	36	18	2	1	2	140 2/3	120	66	52	69	137
1984—	Vermont (Eastern)	2	3	.400	2.71	45	1	0	0	•15	69 2/3	57	23	21	35	69
1985—	Denver (Am. Assoc.)	5	5	.500	4.61	41	0	0	0	5	84	94	55	43	57	66
—	Cincinnati (N.L.)	0	0	...	6.00	2	0	0	0	0	3	2	2	2	2	1
1986—	Denver (Am. Assoc.)	3	4	.429	1.90	27	0	0	0	7	42 2/3	33	12	9	24	36
—	Cincinnati (N.L.)	6	0	1.000	0.72	34	0	0	0	1	50 1/3	26	4	4	21	36
1987—	Cincinnati (N.L.)	8	5	.615	3.04	87	0	0	0	3	100 2/3	91	37	34	32	99
1988—	Cincinnati (N.L.)	0	6	.000	3.08	*76	0	0	0	3	84 2/3	69	31	29	38	74
1989—	Boston (A.L.)■	5	7	.417	2.74	74	0	0	0	9	105	97	38	32	41	107
1990—	Boston (A.L.)	0	6	.000	6.32	68	0	0	0	7	57	85	46	40	32	54
1991—	Seattle (A.L.)■	0	1	.000	3.00	57	0	0	0	4	48	47	17	16	19	34
1992—	Houston (N.L.)■	3	1	.750	4.04	59	0	0	0	0	55 2/3	56	28	25	21	42
1993—	St. Louis (N.L.)■	5	7	.417	4.87	73	0	0	0	1	64 2/3	73	37	35	20	41
1994—	St. Louis (N.L.)	4	3	.571	3.79	50	0	0	0	2	40 1/3	35	18	17	13	25
—	New York (A.L.)■	0	0	...	16.20	3	0	0	0	0	1 2/3	3	3	3	0	0
1995—	Los Angeles (N.L.)■	0	1	.000	12.60	6	0	0	0	0	5	6	7	7	3	2
—	Charlotte (Int'l)■	0	0	...	0.00	3	0	0	0	2	3	2	0	0	0	1
—	Florida (N.L.)	1	1	.500	9.82	8	0	0	0	0	7 1/3	8	9	8	5	5
A.L. totals (4 years)		5	14	.263	3.87	202	0	0	0	20	211 2/3	232	104	91	92	195
N.L. totals (8 years)		27	24	.529	3.52	395	0	0	0	10	411 2/3	366	173	161	155	325
Major league totals (11 years)		32	38	.457	3.64	597	0	0	0	30	623 1/3	598	277	252	247	520

CHAMPIONSHIP SERIES RECORD

Year	Team (League)	W	L	Pct.	ERA	G	GS	CG	ShO	Sv.	IP	H	R	ER	BB	SO
1990—	Boston (A.L.)	0	0	...	13.50	1	0	0	0	0	2/3	2	1	1	1	0

MURRAY, EDDIE — 1B/DH — INDIANS

PERSONAL: Born February 24, 1956, in Los Angeles. . . . 6-2/220. . . . Bats both, throws right. . . . Full name: Eddie Clarence Murray. . . . Brother of Rich Murray, first baseman, San Francisco Giants (1980 and 1983); brother of Leon Murray, minor league first baseman (1970); brother of Charles Murray, minor league outfielder (1962-66 and 1969); and brother of Venice Murray, minor league first baseman (1978).

HIGH SCHOOL: Locke (Los Angeles).

COLLEGE: Cal State Los Angeles.

TRANSACTIONS/CAREER NOTES: Selected by Baltimore Orioles organization in third round of free-agent draft (June 5, 1973). . . . On disabled list (July 10-August 7, 1986). . . . Traded by Orioles to Los Angeles Dodgers for P Brian Holton, P Ken Howell and SS Juan Bell (December 4, 1988). . . . Granted free agency (October 29, 1991). . . . Signed by New York Mets (November 27, 1991). . . . Granted free agency (November 1, 1993). . . . Signed by Cleveland Indians (December 2, 1993). . . . On disabled list (July 3-August 1, 1995). . . . Granted free agency (November 6, 1995). . . . Re-signed by Indians (December 7, 1995).

RECORDS: Holds major league career records for most games with switch-hit home runs—11; most games by first baseman—2,412; and most assists by first baseman—1,864. . . . Shares A.L. single-season record for games with switch-hit home runs—2 (1982, 1987). . . . Holds A.L. career record for most game-winning RBIs—117. . . . Holds A.L. single-season records for most consecutive games with one or more hits by switch-hitter—22 (1984); and most intentional bases on balls by switch-hitter—25 (1984). . . . Holds N.L. single-season record for most double plays by first baseman (150 or more games)—88 (1990). . . . Shares N.L. single-season record for fewest errors by first baseman who led league in errors—12 (1992).

HONORS: Named Appalachian League Player of the Year (1973). . . . Named A.L. Rookie of the Year by Baseball Writers' Association of America (1977). . . . Won A.L. Gold Glove at first base (1982-84). . . . Named first baseman on The Sporting News A.L. All-Star team (1983).

. . . Named first baseman on The Sporting News A.L. Silver Slugger team (1983-84). . . . Named first baseman on The Sporting News N.L. All-Star team (1990). . . . Named first baseman on The Sporting News N.L. Silver Slugger team (1990).

STATISTICAL NOTES: Led Florida State League with 212 total bases in 1974. . . . Led Florida State League first basemen with 113 double plays in 1974. . . . Switch-hit home runs in one game 11 times (August 3, 1977; August 29, 1979, second game, two righthanded and one lefthanded; August 16, 1981; April 24 and August 26, 1982; August 26, 1985, two lefthanded and one righthanded; May 8 and May 9, 1987; April 18 and June 9, 1990; and April 21, 1994). . . . Led A.L. first basemen with 1,615 total chances in 1978, 1,694 in 1984 and 1,526 in 1987. . . . Led A.L. first basemen with 1,504 putouts in 1978. . . . Hit three home runs in one game (August 29, 1979, second game; September 14, 1980, 13 innings; and August 26, 1985). . . . Led A.L. with .410 on-base percentage and 19 game-winning RBIs in 1984. . . . Led A.L. with 25 intentional bases on balls received in 1984 and tied for lead with 18 in 1982. . . . Led A.L. first basemen with 152 double plays in 1984, 146 in 1987 and tied for lead with 154 in 1985. . . . Led N.L. first basemen with .996 fielding percentage, 137 assists and 122 double plays in 1989. . . . Tied for N.L. lead with 21 intentional bases on balls received in 1990. . . . Career major league grand slams: 17.

			BATTING												FIELDING			
Year	Team (League)	Pos.	G	AB	R	H	2B	3B	HR	RBI	Avg.	BB	SO	SB	PO	A	E	Avg.
1973—	Bluefield (Appal.)	1B	50	188	34	54	6	0	11	32	.287	19	46	6	421	14	13	.971
1974—	Miami (Florida St.)	1B	131	460	64	133	*29	7	12	63	.289	58	85	4	*1114	*51	*25	.979
—	Asheville (South.)	1B	2	7	1	2	2	0	0	2	.286	1	1	0	17	0	0	1.000
1975—	Asheville (South.)	1B-3B	124	436	66	115	13	5	17	68	.264	53	79	7	637	58	15	.979
1976—	Charlotte (South.)	1B	88	299	46	89	15	2	12	46	.298	43	41	11	746	45	9	.989
—	Rochester (Int'l)	1B-OF-3B	54	168	35	46	6	2	11	40	.274	34	27	3	291	13	5	.984
1977—	Baltimore (A.L.)	DH-1B	160	611	81	173	29	2	27	88	.283	48	104	0	482	20	4	.992
1978—	Baltimore (A.L.)	1B-3B-DH	161	610	85	174	32	3	27	95	.285	70	97	6	†1507	112	6	.996
1979—	Baltimore (A.L.)	1B-DH	159	606	90	179	30	2	25	99	.295	72	78	10	*1456	107	10	.994
1980—	Baltimore (A.L.)	1B-DH	158	621	100	186	36	2	32	116	.300	54	71	7	1369	77	9	.994
1981—	Baltimore (A.L.)	1B	99	378	57	111	21	2	•22	*78	.294	40	43	2	899	*91	1	*.999
1982—	Baltimore (A.L.)	1B-DH	151	550	87	174	30	1	32	110	.316	70	82	7	1269	97	4	*.997
1983—	Baltimore (A.L.)	1B-DH	156	582	115	178	30	3	33	111	.306	86	90	5	1393	114	10	.993
1984—	Baltimore (A.L.)	1B-DH	•162	588	97	180	26	3	29	110	.306	*107	87	10	*1538	*143	13	.992
1985—	Baltimore (A.L.)	1B-DH	156	583	111	173	37	1	31	124	.297	84	68	5	1338	152	*19	.987
1986—	Baltimore (A.L.)	1B-DH	137	495	61	151	25	1	17	84	.305	78	49	3	1045	88	13	.989
1987—	Baltimore (A.L.)	1B-DH	160	618	89	171	28	3	30	91	.277	73	80	1	1371	145	10	.993
1988—	Baltimore (A.L.)	1B-DH	161	603	75	171	27	2	28	84	.284	75	78	5	867	106	11	.989
1989—	Los Angeles (N.L.)■	1B-3B	160	594	66	147	29	1	20	88	.247	87	85	7	1316	†137	6	†.996
1990—	Los Angeles (N.L.)	1B	155	558	96	184	22	3	26	95	.330	82	64	8	1180	113	10	.992
1991—	Los Angeles (N.L.)	1B-3B	153	576	69	150	23	1	19	96	.260	55	74	10	1327	128	7	.995
1992—	New York (N.L.)■	1B	156	551	64	144	37	2	16	93	.261	66	74	4	1283	96	•12	.991
1993—	New York (N.L.)	1B	154	610	77	174	28	1	27	100	.285	40	61	2	1319	111	18	.988
1994—	Cleveland (A.L.)■	DH-1B	108	433	57	110	21	1	17	76	.254	31	53	8	243	14	3	.988
1995—	Cleveland (A.L.)	DH-1B	113	436	68	141	21	0	21	82	.323	39	65	5	160	22	3	.984
American League totals (14 years)			2041	7714	1173	2272	393	26	371	1348	.295	927	1045	74	14937	1288	116	.993
National League totals (5 years)			778	2889	372	799	139	8	108	472	.277	330	358	31	6425	585	53	.992
Major league totals (19 years)			2819	10603	1545	3071	532	34	479	1820	.290	1257	1403	105	21362	1873	169	.993

DIVISION SERIES RECORD

			BATTING												FIELDING			
Year	Team (League)	Pos.	G	AB	R	H	2B	3B	HR	RBI	Avg.	BB	SO	SB	PO	A	E	Avg.
1995—	Cleveland (A.L.)	DH	3	13	3	5	0	1	1	3	.385	2	1	0	...	...	...	...

CHAMPIONSHIP SERIES RECORD

NOTES: Shares single-game record for most runs—4 (October 7, 1983).

			BATTING												FIELDING			
Year	Team (League)	Pos.	G	AB	R	H	2B	3B	HR	RBI	Avg.	BB	SO	SB	PO	A	E	Avg.
1979—	Baltimore (A.L.)	1B	4	12	3	5	0	0	1	5	.417	5	2	0	44	3	2	.959
1983—	Baltimore (A.L.)	1B	4	15	5	4	0	0	1	3	.267	3	3	1	34	3	1	.974
1995—	Cleveland (A.L.)	DH	6	24	2	6	1	0	1	3	.250	2	3	0	...	...	...	...
Championship series totals (3 years)			14	51	10	15	1	0	3	11	.294	10	8	1	78	6	3	.966

WORLD SERIES RECORD

NOTES: Member of World Series championship team (1983).

			BATTING												FIELDING			
Year	Team (League)	Pos.	G	AB	R	H	2B	3B	HR	RBI	Avg.	BB	SO	SB	PO	A	E	Avg.
1979—	Baltimore (A.L.)	1B	7	26	3	4	1	0	1	2	.154	4	4	1	60	7	0	1.000
1983—	Baltimore (A.L.)	1B	5	20	2	5	0	0	2	3	.250	1	4	0	46	1	1	.979
1995—	Cleveland (A.L.)	1B-DH	6	19	1	2	0	0	1	3	.105	5	4	0	27	0	0	1.000
World Series totals (3 years)			18	65	6	11	1	0	4	8	.169	10	12	1	133	8	1	.993

ALL-STAR GAME RECORD

			BATTING										FIELDING			
Year	League	Pos.	AB	R	H	2B	3B	HR	RBI	Avg.	BB	SO	SB	PO	A	E	Avg.
1978—	American							Did not play.									
1981—	American	PH-1B	2	0	0	0	0	0	0	.000	0	0	0	2	1	0	1.000
1982—	American	PH-1B	1	0	0	0	0	0	0	.000	1	0	0	4	0	0	1.000
1983—	American	1B	2	0	0	0	0	0	0	.000	0	0	0	4	0	0	1.000
1984—	American	1B	2	0	1	1	0	0	0	.500	0	1	0	3	0	0	1.000
1985—	American	1B	3	0	0	0	0	0	0	.000	0	0	0	5	2	0	1.000
1986—	American							Did not play.									
1991—	National	1B	1	0	0	0	0	0	0	.000	0	1	0	3	0	0	1.000
All-Star Game totals (6 years)			11	0	1	1	0	0	0	.091	1	2	0	21	3	0	1.000

MURRAY, GLENN — OF — RED SOX

PERSONAL: Born November 23, 1970, in Manning, S.C. . . . 6-2/225. . . . Bats right, throws right. . . . Full name: Glenn Everett Murray.

HIGH SCHOOL: Manning (S.C.).

TRANSACTIONS/CAREER NOTES: Selected by Montreal Expos organization in second round of free-agent draft (June 5, 1989).... Traded by Expos to Boston Red Sox for a player to be named later (March 23, 1994); Expos acquired OF Derek Vinyard to complete deal (September 15, 1994).... On disabled list (May 15-24, 1995).

STATISTICAL NOTES: Led International League in being hit by pitch with 11 in 1995.

			BATTING												FIELDING			
Year	**Team (League)**	**Pos.**	**G**	**AB**	**R**	**H**	**2B**	**3B**	**HR**	**RBI**	**Avg.**	**BB**	**SO**	**SB**	**PO**	**A**	**E**	**Avg.**
1989—	GC Expos (GCL)	3B-OF	27	87	10	15	6	2	0	7	.172	6	30	8	10	26	8	.818
—	Jamestown (NYP)	3B	3	10	1	3	1	0	0	1	.300	1	1	0	0	1	1	.500
1990—	Jamestown (NYP)	OF	53	165	20	37	8	4	1	14	.224	21	43	12	48	6	5	.915
1991—	Rockford (Midw.)	OF	124	479	73	113	16	*14	5	60	.236	77	136	22	222	5	7	.970
1992—	W.P. Beach (FSL)	OF	119	414	79	96	14	5	13	41	.232	*75	*150	26	229	11	1	.996
1993—	Harrisburg (East.)	OF	127	475	82	120	21	4	26	96	.253	56	111	16	270	6	7	.975
1994—	Pawtucket (Int'l)■	OF	130	465	74	104	17	1	25	64	.224	55	134	9	223	1	*10	.957
1995—	Pawtucket (Int'l)	OF	104	336	66	82	15	0	25	66	.244	34	109	5	227	5	6	.975

MURRAY, MATT — P — RED SOX

PERSONAL: Born September 26, 1970, in Boston.... 6-5/235.... Throws right, bats left.... Full name: Matthew Michael Murray.

HIGH SCHOOL: Loomis Chaffee (Windsor, Conn.).

TRANSACTIONS/CAREER NOTES: Selected by Atlanta Braves organization in second round of free-agent draft (June 1, 1988); pick received as compensation for Philadelphia Phillies signing Type B free-agent P David Palmer.... On disabled list (May 1-July 10 and July 20, 1991-remainder of season).... On Greenville disabled list (April 9-September 16, 1992).... On Atlanta disabled list (April 3-July 11, 1993); included rehabilitation assignment to Macon (June 15-July 11).... Traded by Braves organization to Boston Red Sox organization for OF Marc Lewis and P Mike Jacobs (August 31, 1995), completing deal in which Red Sox acquired P Mike Stanton and a player to be named later for two players to be named later (July 31, 1995).

Year	**Team (League)**	**W**	**L**	**Pct.**	**ERA**	**G**	**GS**	**CG**	**ShO**	**Sv.**	**IP**	**H**	**R**	**ER**	**BB**	**SO**
1988—	Pulaski (Appal.)	2	4	.333	4.17	13	8	0	0	1	54	48	32	25	26	76
1989—	GC Braves (GCL)	1	0	1.000	0.00	2	2	0	0	0	7	3	0	0	0	10
—	Sumter (S. Atl.)	3	5	.375	4.33	12	12	0	0	0	72 2/3	62	37	35	22	69
1990—	Burlington (Midw.)	11	7	.611	3.26	26	26	6	3	0	163	139	72	59	61	134
1991—	Durham (Carolina)	1	0	1.000	1.29	2	2	0	0	0	7	5	1	1	0	7
1992—								Did not play.								
1993—	Macon (S. Atl.)	7	3	.700	1.83	15	15	3	0	0	83 2/3	70	24	17	27	77
1994—	Durham (Carolina)	6	7	.462	3.79	15	15	1	0	0	97 1/3	93	43	41	22	76
—	Greenville (South.)	3	4	.429	5.08	12	12	0	0	0	67 1/3	89	43	38	31	48
1995—	Greenville (South.)	4	0	1.000	1.53	5	5	0	0	0	29 1/3	20	5	5	8	25
—	Richmond (Int'l)	10	3	.769	2.78	19	19	0	0	0	123	108	41	38	34	78
—	Atlanta (N.L.)	0	2	.000	6.75	4	1	0	0	0	10 2/3	10	8	8	5	3
—	Boston (A.L.)■	0	1	.000	18.90	2	1	0	0	0	3 1/3	11	10	7	3	1
A.L. totals (1 year)		0	1	.000	18.90	2	1	0	0	0	3 1/3	11	10	7	3	1
N.L. totals (1 year)		0	2	.000	6.75	4	1	0	0	0	10 2/3	10	8	8	5	3
Major league totals (1 year)		0	3	.000	9.64	6	2	0	0	0	14	21	18	15	8	4

MUSSINA, MIKE — P — ORIOLES

PERSONAL: Born December 8, 1968, in Williamsport, Pa.... 6-2/185.... Throws right, bats right.... Full name: Michael Cole Mussina.... Name pronounced myoo-SEEN-uh.

HIGH SCHOOL: Montoursville (Pa.).

COLLEGE: Stanford (degree in economics, 1990).

TRANSACTIONS/CAREER NOTES: Selected by Baltimore Orioles organization in 11th round of free-agent draft (June 2, 1987); did not sign.... Selected by Orioles organization in first round (20th pick overall) of free-agent draft (June 4, 1990).... On Rochester disabled list (May 5-12, 1991).... On Baltimore disabled list (July 22-August 20, 1993); included rehabilitation assignment to Bowie (August 9-20).

HONORS: Named International League Most Valuable Pitcher (1991).... Named righthanded pitcher on THE SPORTING NEWS A.L. All-Star team (1995).

STATISTICAL NOTES: Pitched 8-0 one-hit, complete-game victory against Texas (July 17, 1992).

Year	**Team (League)**	**W**	**L**	**Pct.**	**ERA**	**G**	**GS**	**CG**	**ShO**	**Sv.**	**IP**	**H**	**R**	**ER**	**BB**	**SO**
1990—	Hagerstown (East.)	3	0	1.000	1.49	7	7	2	1	0	42 1/3	34	10	7	7	40
—	Rochester (Int'l)	0	0	...	1.35	2	2	0	0	0	13 1/3	8	2	2	4	15
1991—	Rochester (Int'l)	10	4	.714	2.87	19	19	3	1	0	122 1/3	108	42	39	31	107
—	Baltimore (A.L.)	4	5	.444	2.87	12	12	2	0	0	87 2/3	77	31	28	21	52
1992—	Baltimore (A.L.)	18	5	*.783	2.54	32	32	8	4	0	241	212	70	68	48	130
1993—	Baltimore (A.L.)	14	6	.700	4.46	25	25	3	2	0	167 2/3	163	84	83	44	117
—	Bowie (Eastern)	1	0	1.000	2.25	2	2	0	0	0	8	5	2	2	1	10
1994—	Baltimore (A.L.)	16	5	.762	3.06	24	24	3	0	0	176 1/3	163	63	60	42	99
1995—	Baltimore (A.L.)	*19	9	.679	3.29	32	32	7	*4	0	221 2/3	187	86	81	50	158
Major league totals (5 years)		71	30	.703	3.22	125	125	23	10	0	894 1/3	802	334	320	205	556

ALL-STAR GAME RECORD

Year	**League**	**W**	**L**	**Pct.**	**ERA**	**GS**	**CG**	**ShO**	**Sv.**	**IP**	**H**	**R**	**ER**	**BB**	**SO**
1992—	American	0	0	...	0.00	0	0	0	0	1	0	0	0	0	0
1993—	American						Did not play.								
1994—	American	0	0	...	0.00	0	0	0	0	1	1	0	0	0	1
All-Star totals (2 years)		0	0	...	0.00	0	0	0	0	2	1	0	0	0	1

MYERS, GREG — C — TWINS

PERSONAL: Born April 14, 1966, in Riverside, Calif.... 6-2/215.... Bats left, throws right.... Full name: Gregory Richard Myers.

HIGH SCHOOL: Riverside (Calif.) Polytechnical.
TRANSACTIONS/CAREER NOTES: Selected by Toronto Blue Jays organization in third round of free-agent draft (June 4, 1984).... On disabled list (June 17, 1988-remainder of season).... On Toronto disabled list (March 26-June 5, 1989); included rehabilitation assignment to Knoxville (May 17-June 5).... On Toronto disabled list (May 5-25, 1990); included rehabilitation assignment to Syracuse (May 21-24).... Traded by Blue Jays with OF Rob Ducey to California Angels for P Mark Eichhorn (July 30, 1992).... On California disabled list (August 27, 1992-remainder of season).... On California disabled list (April 24-June 21, 1994); included rehabilitation assignments to Lake Elsinore (May 20-June 6 and June 13-21).... On disabled list (April 21-May 6, June 1-21 and September 30, 1995-remainder of season).... Granted free agency (November 3, 1995).... Signed by Minnesota Twins (December 8, 1995).
STATISTICAL NOTES: Led California League catchers with 967 total chances in 1986.... Led International League catchers with 698 total chances in 1987.

				BATTING											FIELDING			
Year	Team (League)	Pos.	G	AB	R	H	2B	3B	HR	RBI	Avg.	BB	SO	SB	PO	A	E	Avg.
1984—	Medicine Hat (Pio.)	C	38	133	20	42	9	0	2	20	.316	16	6	0	216	24	4	.984
1985—	Florence (S. Atl.)	C	134	489	52	109	19	2	5	62	.223	39	54	0	551	61	7	*.989
1986—	Ventura (Calif.)	C	124	451	65	133	23	4	20	79	.295	43	46	9	*849	99	19	.980
1987—	Syracuse (Int'l)	C	107	342	35	84	19	1	10	47	.246	22	46	3	*637	50	11	.984
—	Toronto (A.L.)	C	7	9	1	1	0	0	0	0	.111	0	3	0	24	1	0	1.000
1988—	Syracuse (Int'l)	C	34	120	18	34	7	1	7	21	.283	8	24	1	63	9	1	.986
1989—	Knoxville (South.)	C	29	90	11	30	10	0	5	19	.333	3	16	1	130	12	1	.993
—	Toronto (A.L.)	C-DH	17	44	0	5	2	0	0	1	.114	2	9	0	46	6	0	1.000
—	Syracuse (Int'l)	C	24	89	8	24	6	0	1	11	.270	4	9	0	60	7	1	.985
1990—	Toronto (A.L.)	C	87	250	33	59	7	1	5	22	.236	22	33	0	411	30	3	.993
—	Syracuse (Int'l)	C	3	11	0	2	1	0	0	2	.182	1	1	0	14	0	0	1.000
1991—	Toronto (A.L.)	C	107	309	25	81	22	0	8	36	.262	21	45	0	484	37	11	.979
1992—	Toronto (A.L.)	C	22	61	4	14	6	0	0	13	.230	5	5	0	92	13	1	.991
—	California (A.L.)■	C-DH	8	17	0	4	1	0	0	0	.235	0	6	0	33	3	0	1.000
1993—	California (A.L.)	C-DH	108	290	27	74	10	0	7	40	.255	17	47	3	369	44	6	.986
1994—	California (A.L.)	C-DH	45	126	10	31	6	0	2	8	.246	10	27	0	194	28	2	.991
—	Lake Elsinore (Calif.)	C	10	32	4	8	2	0	0	5	.250	2	6	0	31	3	0	1.000
1995—	California (A.L.)	C-DH	85	273	35	71	12	2	9	38	.260	17	49	0	341	21	4	.989
Major league totals (8 years)			486	1379	135	340	66	3	32	158	.247	94	224	3	1994	183	27	.988

CHAMPIONSHIP SERIES RECORD

				BATTING											FIELDING			
Year	Team (League)	Pos.	G	AB	R	H	2B	3B	HR	RBI	Avg.	BB	SO	SB	PO	A	E	Avg.
1991—	Toronto (A.L.)								Did not play.									

MYERS, MIKE — P — TIGERS

PERSONAL: Born June 26, 1969, in Cook County, Ill.... 6-3/195.... Throws left, bats left.... Full name: Michael Stanley Myers.
HIGH SCHOOL: Crystal Lake (Ill.) Central.
COLLEGE: Iowa State.
TRANSACTIONS/CAREER NOTES: Selected by San Francisco Giants organization in fourth round of free-agent draft (June 4, 1990).... On Clinton disabled list (June 3-September 16, 1991; April 9-June 2 and June 21-July 6, 1992).... Selected by Florida Marlins from Giants organization in Rule 5 major league draft (December 7, 1992).... On Edmonton disabled list (April 13-June 7, 1994).... On Florida disabled list (June 7-August 5, 1994); included rehabilitation assignment to Brevard County (June 23-July 11).... Traded by Marlins to Detroit Tigers (August 9, 1995), completing deal in which Marlins acquired P Buddy Groom for a player to be named later (August 7, 1995).
STATISTICAL NOTES: Led Pacific Coast League with 10 hit batsmen in 1993.

Year	Team (League)	W	L	Pct.	ERA	G	GS	CG	ShO	Sv.	IP	H	R	ER	BB	SO
1990—	Everett (N'west)	4	5	.444	3.90	15	14	1	0	0	85 1/3	91	43	37	30	73
1991—	Clinton (Midwest)	5	3	.625	2.62	11	11	1	0	0	65 1/3	61	23	19	18	59
1992—	San Jose (Calif.)	5	1	.833	2.30	8	8	0	0	0	54 2/3	43	20	14	17	40
—	Clinton (Midwest)	1	2	.333	1.19	7	7	0	0	0	37 2/3	28	11	5	8	32
1993—	Edmonton (PCL)■	7	14	.333	5.18	27	27	3	0	0	161 2/3	195	109	93	52	112
1994—	Edmonton (PCL)	1	5	.167	5.55	12	11	0	0	0	60	78	42	37	21	55
—	Brevard Co. (FSL)	0	0	...	0.79	3	2	0	0	0	11 1/3	7	1	1	4	15
1995—	Charlotte (Int'l)	0	5	.000	5.65	37	0	0	0	0	36 2/3	41	25	23	15	24
—	Florida (N.L.)	0	0	...	0.00	2	0	0	0	0	2	1	0	0	3	0
—	Toledo (Int'l)■	0	0	...	4.32	6	0	0	0	0	8 1/3	6	4	4	3	8
—	Detroit (A.L.)	1	0	1.000	9.95	11	0	0	0	0	6 1/3	10	7	7	4	4
A.L. totals (1 year)		1	0	1.000	9.95	11	0	0	0	0	6 1/3	10	7	7	4	4
N.L. totals (1 year)		0	0	...	0.00	2	0	0	0	0	2	1	0	0	3	0
Major league totals (1 year)		1	0	1.000	7.56	13	0	0	0	0	8 1/3	11	7	7	7	4

MYERS, RANDY — P — ORIOLES

PERSONAL: Born September 19, 1962, in Vancouver, Wash.... 6-1/230.... Throws left, bats left.... Full name: Randall Kirk Myers.
HIGH SCHOOL: Evergreen (Vancouver, Wash.).
JUNIOR COLLEGE: Clark Community College (Wash.).
TRANSACTIONS/CAREER NOTES: Selected by Cincinnati Reds organization in third round of free-agent draft (January 12, 1982); did not sign.... Selected by New York Mets organization in secondary phase of free-agent draft (June 7, 1982).... Traded by Mets with P Kip Gross to Cincinnati Reds for P John Franco and OF Don Brown (December 6, 1989).... Traded by Reds to San Diego Padres for OF/2B Bip Roberts and a player to be named later (December 8, 1991); Reds acquired OF Craig Pueschner to complete deal (December 9, 1991).... Granted free agency (October 26, 1992).... Signed by Chicago Cubs (December 9, 1992).... Granted free agency (November 3, 1995).... Signed by Baltimore Orioles (December 14, 1995).
RECORDS: Shares N.L. single-game record for most consecutive strikeouts by relief pitcher—6 (September 8, 1990).... Holds N.L. single-season record for most saves—53 (1993).
HONORS: Named Carolina League Pitcher of the Year (1984).... Named N.L. Fireman of the Year by The Sporting News (1993 and 1995).

STATISTICAL NOTES: Tied for Appalachian League lead with three balks in 1982.

MISCELLANEOUS: Had sacrifice hit in one game as pinch-hitter (1992). . . . Grounded into a double play in one game as pinch-hitter (1993).

Year	Team (League)	W	L	Pct.	ERA	G	GS	CG	ShO	Sv.	IP	H	R	ER	BB	SO
1982—	Kingsport (Appal.)	6	3	.667	4.12	13	•13	1	0	0	74 1/3	68	49	34	69	•86
1983—	Columbia (S. Atl.)	14	10	.583	3.63	28	•28	3	0	0	173 1/3	146	94	70	108	164
1984—	Lynchburg (Caro.)	13	5	.722	*2.06	23	22	•7	1	0	157	123	46	36	61	171
—	Jackson (Texas)	2	1	.667	2.06	5	5	1	0	0	35	29	14	8	16	35
1985—	Jackson (Texas)	4	8	.333	3.96	19	19	2	1	0	120 1/3	99	61	53	69	116
—	Tidewater (Int'l)	1	1	.500	1.84	8	7	0	0	0	44	40	13	9	20	25
—	New York (N.L.)	0	0	...	0.00	1	0	0	0	0	2	0	0	0	1	2
1986—	Tidewater (Int'l)	6	7	.462	2.35	45	0	0	0	12	65	44	19	17	44	79
—	New York (N.L.)	0	0	...	4.22	10	0	0	0	0	10 2/3	11	5	5	9	13
1987—	New York (N.L.)	3	6	.333	3.96	54	0	0	0	6	75	61	36	33	30	92
—	Tidewater (Int'l)	0	0	...	4.91	5	0	0	0	3	7 1/3	6	4	4	4	13
1988—	New York (N.L.)	7	3	.700	1.72	55	0	0	0	26	68	45	15	13	17	69
1989—	New York (N.L.)	7	4	.636	2.35	65	0	0	0	24	84 1/3	62	23	22	40	88
1990—	Cincinnati (N.L.)■	4	6	.400	2.08	66	0	0	0	31	86 2/3	59	24	20	38	98
1991—	Cincinnati (N.L.)	6	13	.316	3.55	58	12	1	0	6	132	116	61	52	80	108
1992—	San Diego (N.L.)■	3	6	.333	4.29	66	0	0	0	38	79 2/3	84	38	38	34	66
1993—	Chicago (N.L.)■	2	4	.333	3.11	73	0	0	0	*53	75 1/3	65	26	26	26	86
1994—	Chicago (N.L.)	1	5	.167	3.79	38	0	0	0	21	40 1/3	40	18	17	16	32
1995—	Chicago (N.L.)	1	2	.333	3.88	57	0	0	0	*38	55 2/3	49	25	24	28	59
Major league totals (11 years)		34	49	.410	3.17	543	12	1	0	243	709 2/3	592	271	250	319	713

CHAMPIONSHIP SERIES RECORD

NOTES: Named N.L. Championship Series co-Most Valuable Player (1990). . . . Shares N.L. single-series record for most saves—3 (1990).

Year	Team (League)	W	L	Pct.	ERA	G	GS	CG	ShO	Sv.	IP	H	R	ER	BB	SO
1988—	New York (N.L.)	2	0	1.000	0.00	3	0	0	0	0	4 2/3	1	0	0	2	0
1990—	Cincinnati (N.L.)	0	0	...	0.00	4	0	0	0	3	5 2/3	2	0	0	3	7
Champ. series totals (2 years)		2	0	1.000	0.00	7	0	0	0	3	10 1/3	3	0	0	5	7

WORLD SERIES RECORD

NOTES: Member of World Series championship team (1990).

Year	Team (League)	W	L	Pct.	ERA	G	GS	CG	ShO	Sv.	IP	H	R	ER	BB	SO
1990—	Cincinnati (N.L.)	0	0	...	0.00	3	0	0	0	1	3	2	0	0	0	3

ALL-STAR GAME RECORD

Year	League	W	L	Pct.	ERA	GS	CG	ShO	Sv.	IP	H	R	ER	BB	SO
1990—	National	0	0	...	0.00	0	0	0	0	1	1	0	0	2	0
1994—	National	0	0	...	0.00	0	0	0	0	1	1	0	0	0	1
1995—	National	0	0	...	0.00	0	0	0	1	1	0	0	0	1	0
All-Star totals (3 years)		0	0	...	0.00	0	0	0	1	3	2	0	0	3	1

MYERS, ROD — P — CUBS

PERSONAL: Born June 26, 1969, in Rockford, Ill. . . . 6-1/200. . . . Throws right, bats right. . . . Full name: Rodney Myers.

HIGH SCHOOL: Rockford (Ill.) East.

COLLEGE: Wisconsin.

TRANSACTIONS/CAREER NOTES: Selected by Kansas City Royals organization in 12th round of free-agent draft (June 4, 1990). . . . On disabled list (May 17-June 3 and June 21-September 15, 1994; and June 30-July 21, 1995). . . . Selected by Chicago Cubs from Royals organization in Rule 5 major league draft (December 4, 1995).

Year	Team (League)	W	L	Pct.	ERA	G	GS	CG	ShO	Sv.	IP	H	R	ER	BB	SO
1990—	Eugene (N'west)	0	2	.000	1.19	6	4	0	0	0	22 2/3	19	9	3	13	17
1991—	Appleton (Midw.)	1	1	.500	2.60	9	4	0	0	0	27 2/3	22	9	8	26	29
1992—	Lethbridge (Pio.)	5	•8	.385	4.01	15	15	*5	0	0	*103 1/3	93	57	46	61	76
1993—	Rockford (Midw.)	7	3	.700	1.79	12	12	5	2	0	85 1/3	65	22	17	18	65
—	Memphis (South.)	3	6	.333	5.62	12	12	1	1	0	65 2/3	73	46	41	32	42
1994—	Wilmington (Caro.)	1	1	.500	4.82	4	0	0	0	1	9 1/3	9	6	5	1	9
—	Memphis (South.)	5	1	.833	1.03	42	0	0	0	9	69 2/3	45	20	8	29	53
1995—	Omaha (Am. Assoc.)	4	5	.444	4.10	38	0	0	0	2	48 1/3	52	26	22	19	38

MYERS, ROD — OF — ROYALS

PERSONAL: Born January 14, 1973, in Conroe, Tex. . . . 6-0/190. . . . Bats left, throws left. . . . Full name: Rodney Demond Myers.

HIGH SCHOOL: Conroe (Tex.).

TRANSACTIONS/CAREER NOTES: Selected by Kansas City Royals organization in 13th round of free-agent draft (June 3, 1991).

				BATTING										FIELDING			
Year	Team (League)	Pos.	G	AB	R	H	2B	3B	HR	RBI	Avg.	BB	SO	SB	PO	A	E	Avg.
1991—	GC Royals (GCL)	OF	44	133	14	37	2	3	1	18	.278	6	27	12	45	2	1	.979
—	Baseball City (FSL)	OF	4	11	1	2	0	0	0	0	.182	0	5	1	4	0	0	1.000
1992—	Appleton (Midw.)	OF	71	218	31	48	10	2	4	30	.220	39	67	25	132	5	10	.932
1993—	Rockford (Midw.)	OF	129	474	69	123	24	5	9	68	.259	58	117	49	208	10	7	.969
1994—	Wilmington (Caro.)	OF	126	457	76	120	20	4	12	65	.263	67	93	31	168	5	7	.961
1995—	Wichita (Texas)	OF-1B	131	499	71	*153	22	6	7	62	.307	34	77	29	262	8	10	.964

NABHOLZ, CHRIS — P — METS

PERSONAL: Born January 5, 1967, in Harrisburg, Pa. . . . 6-5/217. . . . Throws left, bats left. . . . Full name: Christopher William Nabholz. . . . Name pronounced NAB-holts.

HIGH SCHOOL: Pottsville (Pa.).

COLLEGE: Towson State.

TRANSACTIONS/CAREER NOTES: Selected by Cleveland Indians organization in 30th round of free-agent draft (June 3, 1985); did not sign. . . . Selected by Montreal Expos organization in second round of free-agent draft (June 1, 1988). . . . On Montreal disabled list (June 16-August 4, 1991); included rehabilitation assignment to Indianapolis (July 16-August 4). . . . On Montreal disabled list (August 11-September 11, 1993); included rehabilitation assignment to Ottawa (August 31-September 11). . . . Traded by Expos to Indians for P J.J. Thobe and 1B Dave Duplessis (February 14, 1994). . . . On Cleveland disabled list (May 22-July 1, 1994); included rehabilitation assignment to Charlotte (June 12-July 1). . . . Traded by Indians with P Steve Farr to Boston Red Sox for P Jeff Russell (July 1, 1994). . . . Granted free agency (December 23, 1994). . . . Signed by Iowa, Chicago Cubs organization (April 8, 1995). . . . On Chicago disabled list (May 11-June 15, 1995); included rehabilitation assignment to Iowa (June 13-15). . . . Granted free agency (October 13, 1995). . . . Signed by New York Mets (November 20, 1995).

STATISTICAL NOTES: Pitched 2-0 one-hit, complete-game victory for Montreal against New York (September 20, 1990). . . . Pitched eight innings, combining with Bruce Walton (one inning) in 4-0 no-hit victory for Ottawa against Richmond (May 24, 1993).

Year	Team (League)	W	L	Pct.	ERA	G	GS	CG	ShO	Sv.	IP	H	R	ER	BB	SO
1989	Rockford (Midw.)	13	5	.722	2.18	24	23	3	3	0	161 1/3	132	54	39	41	149
1990	Jacksonville (Sou.)	7	2	.778	3.03	11	11	0	0	0	74 1/3	62	28	25	27	77
	Montreal (N.L.)	6	2	.750	2.83	11	11	1	1	0	70	43	23	22	32	53
	Indianapolis (A.A.)	0	6	.000	4.83	10	10	0	0	0	63 1/3	66	38	34	28	44
1991	Montreal (N.L.)	8	7	.533	3.63	24	24	1	0	0	153 2/3	134	66	62	57	99
	Indianapolis (A.A.)	2	2	.500	1.86	4	4	0	0	0	19 1/3	13	5	4	5	16
1992	Montreal (N.L.)	11	12	.478	3.32	32	32	1	1	0	195	176	80	72	74	130
1993	Montreal (N.L.)	9	8	.529	4.09	26	21	1	0	0	116 2/3	100	57	53	63	74
	Ottawa (Int'l)	1	1	.500	4.39	5	5	0	0	0	26 2/3	24	15	13	7	20
1994	Cleveland (A.L.)■	0	1	.000	11.45	6	4	0	0	0	11	23	16	14	9	5
	Charlotte (Int'l)	3	1	.750	2.66	4	4	0	0	0	23 2/3	20	8	7	3	11
	Boston (A.L.)■	3	4	.429	6.64	8	8	0	0	0	42	44	32	31	29	23
1995	Iowa (Am. Assoc.)■	0	2	.000	6.41	6	5	0	0	0	19 2/3	27	17	14	12	16
	Chicago (N.L.)	0	1	.000	5.40	34	0	0	0	0	23 1/3	22	15	14	14	21
A.L. totals (1 year)		3	5	.375	7.64	14	12	0	0	0	53	67	48	45	38	28
N.L. totals (5 years)		34	30	.531	3.59	127	88	4	2	0	558 2/3	475	241	223	240	377
Major league totals (6 years)		37	35	.514	3.94	141	100	4	2	0	611 2/3	542	289	268	278	405

NAEHRING, TIM — 3B — RED SOX

PERSONAL: Born February 1, 1967, in Cincinnati. . . . 6-2/203. . . . Bats right, throws right. . . . Full name: Timothy James Naehring. . . . Name pronounced NAIR-ring.

HIGH SCHOOL: LaSalle (Cincinnati).

COLLEGE: Miami of Ohio.

TRANSACTIONS/CAREER NOTES: Selected by Boston Red Sox organization in eighth round of free-agent draft (June 1, 1988). . . . On Boston disabled list (August 16, 1990-remainder of season and May 18, 1991-remainder of season). . . . On Boston disabled list (July 25-September 3, 1992); included rehabilitation assignment to Pawtucket (August 22-September 3). . . . On Boston disabled list (April 1-July 2, 1993); included rehabilitation assignment to Pawtucket (June 13-July 2). . . . On Boston disabled list (June 7-July 6, 1994); included rehabilitation assignment to Pawtucket (July 2-6).

				BATTING											FIELDING			
Year	Team (League)	Pos.	G	AB	R	H	2B	3B	HR	RBI	Avg.	BB	SO	SB	PO	A	E	Avg.
1988	Elmira (NYP)	SS	19	59	6	18	3	0	1	13	.305	8	11	0	25	51	6	.927
	Winter Haven (FSL)	SS	42	141	17	32	7	0	0	10	.227	19	24	1	77	136	20	.914
1989	Lynchburg (Caro.)	SS	56	209	24	63	7	1	4	37	.301	23	30	2	72	131	12	.944
	Pawtucket (Int'l)	SS-3B	79	273	32	75	16	1	3	31	.275	27	41	2	118	192	21	.937
1990	Pawtucket (Int'l)	SS-3B-2B	82	290	45	78	16	1	15	47	.269	37	56	0	126	240	16	.958
	Boston (A.L.)	SS-3B-2B	24	85	10	23	6	0	2	12	.271	8	15	0	36	66	9	.919
1991	Boston (A.L.)	SS-3B-2B	20	55	1	6	1	0	0	3	.109	6	15	0	17	53	3	.959
1992	Boston (A.L.)	S-2-3-DH-O	72	186	12	43	8	0	3	14	.231	18	31	0	95	170	3	.989
	Pawtucket (Int'l)	2B	11	34	7	10	0	0	2	5	.294	8	6	1	22	39	3	.953
1993	Pawtucket (Int'l)	3B-SS-2B	55	202	38	62	9	1	7	36	.307	35	27	0	79	133	4	.981
	Boston (A.L.)	2-DH-3-S	39	127	14	42	10	0	1	17	.331	10	26	1	45	44	2	.978
1994	Boston (A.L.)	2-3-1-S-DH	80	297	41	82	18	1	7	42	.276	30	56	1	190	183	6	.984
	Pawtucket (Int'l)	2B-3B	4	15	2	2	2	0	0	3	.133	1	2	0	2	5	1	.875
1995	Boston (A.L.)	3B-DH	126	433	61	133	27	2	10	57	.307	77	66	0	85	244	16	.954
Major league totals (6 years)			361	1183	139	329	70	3	23	145	.278	149	209	2	468	760	39	.969

DIVISION SERIES RECORD

				BATTING											FIELDING			
Year	Team (League)	Pos.	G	AB	R	H	2B	3B	HR	RBI	Avg.	BB	SO	SB	PO	A	E	Avg.
1995	Boston (A.L.)	3B	3	13	2	4	0	0	1	1	.308	0	1	0	5	5	0	1.000

NAGY, CHARLES — P — INDIANS

PERSONAL: Born May 5, 1967, in Fairfield, Conn. . . . 6-3/200. . . . Throws right, bats left. . . . Full name: Charles Harrison Nagy. . . . Name pronounced NAG-ee.

HIGH SCHOOL: Roger Ludlowe (Fairfield, Conn.).

COLLEGE: Connecticut.

TRANSACTIONS/CAREER NOTES: Selected by Cleveland Indians organization in first round (17th pick overall) of free-agent draft (June 1, 1988); pick received as part of compensation for San Francisco Giants signing Type A free-agent OF Brett Butler. . . . On Cleveland disabled

list (May 16-October 1, 1993); included rehabilitation assignment to Canton/Akron (June 10-24).
HONORS: Named Carolina League Pitcher of the Year (1989).
STATISTICAL NOTES: Pitched 6-0 one-hit, complete-game victory against Baltimore (August 8, 1992).
MISCELLANEOUS: Member of 1988 U.S. Olympic baseball team.

Year	Team (League)	W	L	Pct.	ERA	G	GS	CG	ShO	Sv.	IP	H	R	ER	BB	SO
1989	—Kinston (Carolina)	8	4	.667	1.51	13	13	6	*4	0	95 1/3	69	22	16	24	99
	—Cant./Akr. (East.)	4	5	.444	3.35	15	14	2	0	0	94	102	44	35	32	65
1990	—Cant./Akr. (East.)	13	8	.619	2.52	23	23	•9	0	0	175	132	62	49	39	99
	—Cleveland (A.L.)	2	4	.333	5.91	9	8	0	0	0	45 2/3	58	31	30	21	26
1991	—Cleveland (A.L.)	10	15	.400	4.13	33	33	6	1	0	211 1/3	228	103	97	66	109
1992	—Cleveland (A.L.)	17	10	.630	2.96	33	33	10	3	0	252	245	91	83	57	169
1993	—Cleveland (A.L.)	2	6	.250	6.29	9	9	1	0	0	48 2/3	66	38	34	13	30
	—Cant./Akr. (East.)	0	0	...	1.13	2	2	0	0	0	8	8	1	1	2	4
1994	—Cleveland (A.L.)	10	8	.556	3.45	23	23	3	0	0	169 1/3	175	76	65	48	108
1995	—Cleveland (A.L.)	16	6	.727	4.55	29	29	2	1	0	178	194	95	90	61	139
Major league totals (6 years)		57	49	.538	3.97	136	135	22	5	0	905	966	434	399	266	581

DIVISION SERIES RECORD

Year	Team (League)	W	L	Pct.	ERA	G	GS	CG	ShO	Sv.	IP	H	R	ER	BB	SO
1995	—Cleveland (A.L.)	1	0	1.000	1.29	1	1	0	0	0	7	4	1	1	5	6

CHAMPIONSHIP SERIES RECORD

NOTES: Shares A.L. single-game record for most consecutive strikeouts—4 (October 13, 1995).

Year	Team (League)	W	L	Pct.	ERA	G	GS	CG	ShO	Sv.	IP	H	R	ER	BB	SO
1995	—Cleveland (A.L.)	0	0	...	1.13	1	1	0	0	0	8	5	2	1	0	6

WORLD SERIES RECORD

Year	Team (League)	W	L	Pct.	ERA	G	GS	CG	ShO	Sv.	IP	H	R	ER	BB	SO
1995	—Cleveland (A.L.)	0	0	...	6.43	1	1	0	0	0	7	8	5	5	1	4

ALL-STAR GAME RECORD

Year	League	W	L	Pct.	ERA	GS	CG	ShO	Sv.	IP	H	R	ER	BB	SO
1992	—American	0	0	...	0.00	0	0	0	0	1	0	0	0	0	1

NARCISSE, TYRONE — P — BREWERS

PERSONAL: Born February 4, 1972, in Port Arthur, Tex. . . . 6-5/205. . . . Throws right, bats right. . . . Full name: Tyrone Davis Narcisse.
HIGH SCHOOL: Lincoln (Port Arthur, Tex.).
TRANSACTIONS/CAREER NOTES: Selected by San Diego Padres organization in ninth round of free-agent draft (June 4, 1990). . . . Released by Padres organization (May 3, 1992). . . . Signed by Houston Astros organization (June 13, 1992). . . . Selected by Milwaukee Brewers from Astros organization in Rule 5 major league draft (December 4, 1995).

Year	Team (League)	W	L	Pct.	ERA	G	GS	CG	ShO	Sv.	IP	H	R	ER	BB	SO
1990	—Arizona Padres (Ariz.)	0	0	...	5.06	7	1	0	0	0	10 2/3	13	11	6	6	6
1991	—Arizona Padres (Ariz.)	2	3	.400	7.47	11	10	0	0	0	37 1/3	43	41	31	37	23
1992	—GC Astros (GCL)■	3	2	.600	4.93	11	6	0	0	0	34 2/3	31	25	19	24	32
1993	—Asheville (S. Atl.)	6	12	.333	4.38	29	•29	2	0	0	160 1/3	173	95	78	66	114
1994	—Osceola (Florida St.)	7	11	.389	4.87	26	26	2	0	0	146	153	91	79	57	86
1995	—Jackson (Texas)	5	*14	.263	3.24	27	27	2	0	0	163 2/3	140	76	59	60	93

NATAL, BOB — C — MARLINS

PERSONAL: Born November 13, 1965, in Long Beach, Calif. . . . 5-11/190. . . . Bats right, throws right. . . . Full name: Robert Marcel Natal.
HIGH SCHOOL: Hilltop (Chula Vista, Calif.).
COLLEGE: UC San Diego.
TRANSACTIONS/CAREER NOTES: Selected by Montreal Expos organization in 13th round of free-agent draft (June 2, 1987). . . . Selected by Florida Marlins in third round (55th pick overall) of expansion draft (November 17, 1992). . . . On Florida disabled list (June 2-23, 1993); included rehabilitation assignment to Edmonton (June 14-23).
STATISTICAL NOTES: Led Florida State League catchers with 765 total chances in 1988.

			BATTING												FIELDING			
Year	Team (League)	Pos.	G	AB	R	H	2B	3B	HR	RBI	Avg.	BB	SO	SB	PO	A	E	Avg.
1987	—Jamestown (NYP)	C	57	180	26	58	8	4	7	32	.322	12	25	6	321	52	6	.984
1988	—W.P. Beach (FSL)	C	113	387	47	93	17	0	6	51	.240	29	50	3	*671	77	17	.978
1989	—Jacksonv. (South.)	C	46	141	12	29	8	1	0	11	.206	9	24	2	324	37	7	.981
	—W.P. Beach (FSL)	C	15	48	5	6	0	0	1	2	.125	9	9	1	68	24	3	.968
1990	—Jacksonv. (South.)	C	62	171	23	42	7	1	7	25	.246	14	42	0	344	46	10	.975
1991	—Indianapolis (A.A.)	C	16	41	2	13	4	0	0	9	.317	6	9	1	62	5	2	.971
	—Harrisburg (East.)	C	100	336	47	86	16	3	13	53	.256	49	90	1	453	45	4	.992
1992	—Indianapolis (A.A.)	C-OF	96	344	50	104	19	3	12	50	.302	28	42	3	468	54	5	.991
	—Montreal (N.L.)	C	5	6	0	0	0	0	0	0	.000	1	1	0	10	0	1	.909
1993	—Edmonton (PCL)■	C	17	66	16	21	6	1	3	16	.318	8	10	0	119	19	2	.986
	—Florida (N.L.)	C	41	117	3	25	4	1	1	6	.214	6	22	1	196	18	0	1.000
1994	—Edmonton (PCL)	C	37	115	12	32	5	2	3	19	.278	9	18	1	184	31	1	.995
	—Florida (N.L.)	C	10	29	2	8	2	0	0	2	.276	5	5	1	50	9	1	.983
1995	—Florida (N.L.)	C	16	43	2	10	2	1	2	6	.233	1	9	0	80	3	1	.988
	—Charlotte (Int'l)	C-3B-1B	53	191	23	60	14	0	3	24	.314	11	23	0	271	49	2	.994
Major league totals (4 years)			72	195	7	43	8	2	3	14	.221	13	37	2	336	30	3	.992

NAULTY, DAN — P — TWINS

PERSONAL: Born January 6, 1970, in Los Angeles. . . . 6-6/211. . . . Throws right, bats right.
COLLEGE: Cal State-Fullerton.
TRANSACTIONS/CAREER NOTES: Selected by Minnesota Twins organization in 14th round of free-agent draft (June 1, 1992).

Year Team (League)	W	L	Pct.	ERA	G	GS	CG	ShO	Sv.	IP	H	R	ER	BB	SO
1992— Kenosha (Midwest)	0	1	.000	5.50	6	2	0	0	0	18	22	12	11	7	14
1993— Fort Myers (Fla. St.)	0	3	.000	5.70	7	6	0	0	0	30	41	22	19	14	20
— Fort Wayne (Midw.)	6	8	.429	3.26	18	18	3	2	0	116	101	45	42	48	96
1994— Fort Myers (Fla. St.)	8	4	.667	2.95	16	15	1	0	0	88 1/3	78	35	29	32	83
— Nashville (South.)	0	7	.000	5.89	9	9	0	0	0	47 1/3	48	32	31	22	29
1995— Salt Lake (PCL)	2	6	.250	5.18	42	8	0	0	4	90 1/3	92	55	52	2	76

NAVARRO, JAIME — P — CUBS

PERSONAL: Born March 27, 1968, in Bayamon, Puerto Rico. . . . 6-4/230. . . . Throws right, bats right. . . . Son of Julio Navarro, pitcher, Los Angeles Angels, Detroit Tigers and Atlanta Braves (1962-66 and 1970).
HIGH SCHOOL: Luis Pales Matos (Bayamon, Puerto Rico).
COLLEGE: Miami-Dade Community College-New World Center.
TRANSACTIONS/CAREER NOTES: Selected by Baltimore Orioles organization in second round of free-agent draft (January 14, 1986); did not sign. . . . Selected by Orioles organization in secondary phase of free-agent draft (June 2, 1986); did not sign. . . . Selected by Milwaukee Brewers organization in third round of free-agent draft (June 2, 1987). . . . Granted free agency (April 7, 1995). . . . Signed by Chicago Cubs (April 9, 1995). . . . Granted free agency (November 1, 1995). . . . Re-signed by Cubs (December 8, 1995).
RECORDS: Shares A.L. single-season record for most sacrifice flies allowed—17 (1993).
STATISTICAL NOTES: Led A.L. with five balks in 1990.

Year Team (League)	W	L	Pct.	ERA	G	GS	CG	ShO	Sv.	IP	H	R	ER	BB	SO
1987— Helena (Pioneer)	4	3	.571	3.57	13	13	3	0	0	85 2/3	87	37	34	18	95
1988— Stockton (Calif.)	15	5	.750	3.09	26	23	8	2	0	174 2/3	148	70	60	74	151
1989— El Paso (Texas)	5	2	.714	2.47	11	11	1	0	0	76 2/3	61	29	21	35	78
— Denver (Am. Assoc.)	1	1	.500	3.60	3	3	1	0	0	20	24	8	8	7	17
— Milwaukee (A.L.)	7	8	.467	3.12	19	17	1	0	0	109 2/3	119	47	38	32	56
1990— Milwaukee (A.L.)	8	7	.533	4.46	32	22	3	0	1	149 1/3	176	83	74	41	75
— Denver (Am. Assoc.)	2	3	.400	4.20	6	6	1	0	0	40 2/3	41	27	19	14	28
1991— Milwaukee (A.L.)	15	12	.556	3.92	34	34	10	2	0	234	237	117	102	73	114
1992— Milwaukee (A.L.)	17	11	.607	3.33	34	34	5	3	0	246	224	98	91	64	100
1993— Milwaukee (A.L.)	11	12	.478	5.33	35	34	5	1	0	214 1/3	254	135	*127	73	114
1994— Milwaukee (A.L.)	4	9	.308	6.62	29	10	0	0	0	89 2/3	115	71	66	35	65
1995— Chicago (N.L.)■	14	6	.700	3.28	29	29	1	1	0	200 1/3	194	79	73	56	128
A.L. totals (6 years)	62	59	.512	4.30	183	151	24	6	1	1043	1125	551	498	318	524
N.L. totals (1 year)	14	6	.700	3.28	29	29	1	1	0	200 1/3	194	79	73	56	128
Major league totals (7 years)	76	65	.539	4.13	212	180	25	7	1	1243 1/3	1319	630	571	374	652

NEAGLE, DENNY — P — PIRATES

PERSONAL: Born September 13, 1968, in Gambrills, Md. . . . 6-2/225. . . . Throws left, bats left. . . . Full name: Dennis Edward Neagle Jr. . . . Name pronounced NAY-ghul.
HIGH SCHOOL: Arundel (Gambrills, Md.).
COLLEGE: Minnesota.
TRANSACTIONS/CAREER NOTES: Selected by Minnesota Twins organization in third round of free-agent draft (June 5, 1989). . . . On Portland disabled list (April 5-23, 1991). . . . On Minnesota disabled list (July 28-August 12, 1991). . . . Traded by Twins with OF Midre Cummings to Pittsburgh Pirates for P John Smiley (March 17, 1992).
STATISTICAL NOTES: Career major league grand slams: 1.
MISCELLANEOUS: Appeared in one game as pinch-runner (1992). . . . Appeared in one game as pinch-runner (1995).

Year Team (League)	W	L	Pct.	ERA	G	GS	CG	ShO	Sv.	IP	H	R	ER	BB	SO
1989— Elizabeth. (App.)	1	2	.333	4.50	6	3	0	0	1	22	20	11	11	8	32
— Kenosha (Midwest)	2	1	.667	1.65	6	6	1	1	0	43 2/3	25	9	8	16	40
1990— Visalia (California)	8	0	1.000	1.43	10	10	0	0	0	63	39	13	10	16	92
— Orlando (Southern)	12	3	.800	2.45	17	17	4	1	0	121 1/3	94	40	33	31	94
1991— Portland (PCL)	9	4	.692	3.27	19	17	1	1	0	104 2/3	101	41	38	32	94
— Minnesota (A.L.)	0	1	.000	4.05	7	3	0	0	0	20	28	9	9	7	14
1992— Pittsburgh (N.L.)■	4	6	.400	4.48	55	6	0	0	2	86 1/3	81	46	43	43	77
1993— Pittsburgh (N.L.)	3	5	.375	5.31	50	7	0	0	1	81 1/3	82	49	48	37	73
— Buffalo (A.A.)	0	0	...	0.00	3	0	0	0	0	3 1/3	3	0	0	2	6
1994— Pittsburgh (N.L.)	9	10	.474	5.12	24	24	2	0	0	137	135	80	78	49	122
1995— Pittsburgh (N.L.)	13	8	.619	3.43	31	•31	5	1	0	•209 2/3	*221	91	80	45	150
A.L. totals (1 year)	0	1	.000	4.05	7	3	0	0	0	20	28	9	9	7	14
N.L. totals (4 years)	29	29	.500	4.36	160	68	7	1	3	514 1/3	519	266	249	174	422
Major league totals (5 years)	29	30	.492	4.35	167	71	7	1	3	534 1/3	547	275	258	181	436

CHAMPIONSHIP SERIES RECORD

Year Team (League)	W	L	Pct.	ERA	G	GS	CG	ShO	Sv.	IP	H	R	ER	BB	SO
1992— Pittsburgh (N.L.)	0	0	...	27.00	2	0	0	0	0	1 2/3	4	5	5	3	0

ALL-STAR GAME RECORD

Year League	W	L	Pct.	ERA	GS	CG	ShO	Sv.	IP	H	R	ER	BB	SO
1995— National	0	0	...	0.00	0	0	0	0	1	1	0	0	0	1

NELSON, JEFF — P — YANKEES

PERSONAL: Born November 17, 1966, in Baltimore. . . . 6-8/235. . . . Throws right, bats right. . . . Full name: Jeffrey Allen Nelson.
HIGH SCHOOL: Catonsville (Md.).
JUNIOR COLLEGE: Catonsville (Md.) Community College.
TRANSACTIONS/CAREER NOTES: Selected by Los Angeles Dodgers organization in 22nd round of free-agent draft (June 4, 1984). . . . On disabled list (April 10-June 4, 1986). . . . Selected by Calgary, Seattle Mariners organization from Dodgers organization in Rule 5 minor league draft (December 9, 1986). . . . On disabled list (July 16, 1989-remainder of season). . . . Traded by Mariners with 1B Tino Martinez and P Jim Mecir to New York Yankees for P Sterling Hitchcock and 3B Russ Davis (December 7, 1995).
MISCELLANEOUS: Appeared in one game as outfielder with no chances with Seattle (1993).

Year	Team (League)	W	L	Pct.	ERA	G	GS	CG	ShO	Sv.	IP	H	R	ER	BB	SO
1984	—Great Falls (Pio.)	0	0	...	54.00	1	0	0	0	0	2/3	3	4	4	3	1
	—GC Dodgers (GCL)	0	0	...	1.35	9	0	0	0	0	13 1/3	6	3	2	6	7
1985	—GC Dodgers (GCL)	0	5	.000	5.51	14	7	0	0	0	47 1/3	72	50	29	32	31
1986	—Great Falls (Pio.)	0	0	...	13.50	3	0	0	0	0	2	5	3	3	3	1
	—Bakersfield (Calif.)	0	7	.000	6.69	24	11	0	0	0	71 1/3	79	83	53	84	37
1987	—Salinas (Calif.)■	3	7	.300	5.74	17	16	1	0	0	80	80	61	51	71	43
1988	—San Bern. (Calif.)	8	9	.471	5.54	27	27	1	1	0	149 1/3	163	115	92	91	94
1989	—Williamsport (East.)	7	5	.583	3.31	15	15	2	0	0	92 1/3	72	41	34	53	61
1990	—Williamsport (East.)	1	4	.200	6.44	10	10	0	0	0	43 1/3	65	35	31	18	14
	—Peninsula (Caro.)	2	2	.500	3.15	18	7	1	1	6	60	47	21	21	25	49
1991	—Jacksonville (Sou.)	4	0	1.000	1.27	21	0	0	0	12	28 1/3	23	5	4	9	34
	—Calgary (PCL)	3	4	.429	3.90	28	0	0	0	21	32 1/3	39	19	14	15	26
1992	—Calgary (PCL)	1	0	1.000	0.00	2	0	0	0	0	3 2/3	0	0	0	1	0
	—Seattle (A.L.)	1	7	.125	3.44	66	0	0	0	6	81	71	34	31	44	46
1993	—Calgary (PCL)	1	0	1.000	1.17	5	0	0	0	1	7 2/3	6	1	1	2	6
	—Seattle (A.L.)	5	3	.625	4.35	71	0	0	0	1	60	57	30	29	34	61
1994	—Seattle (A.L.)	0	0	...	2.76	28	0	0	0	0	42 1/3	35	18	13	20	44
	—Calgary (PCL)	1	4	.200	2.84	18	0	0	0	8	25 1/3	21	9	8	7	30
1995	—Seattle (A.L.)	7	3	.700	2.17	62	0	0	0	2	78 2/3	58	21	19	27	96
Major league totals (4 years)		13	13	.500	3.16	227	0	0	0	9	262	221	103	92	125	247

DIVISION SERIES RECORD

Year	Team (League)	W	L	Pct.	ERA	G	GS	CG	ShO	Sv.	IP	H	R	ER	BB	SO
1995	—Seattle (A.L.)	0	1	.000	3.18	3	0	0	0	0	5 2/3	7	2	2	3	7

CHAMPIONSHIP SERIES RECORD

Year	Team (League)	W	L	Pct.	ERA	G	GS	CG	ShO	Sv.	IP	H	R	ER	BB	SO
1995	—Seattle (A.L.)	0	0	...	0.00	3	0	0	0	0	3	3	0	0	5	3

NEN, ROBB — P — MARLINS

PERSONAL: Born November 28, 1969, in San Pedro, Calif. . . . 6-4/200. . . . Throws right, bats right. . . . Full name: Robert Allen Nen. . . . Son of Dick Nen, first baseman, Los Angeles Dodgers, Washington Senators and Chicago Cubs (1963, 1965-68 and 1970).
HIGH SCHOOL: Los Alamitos (Calif.).
TRANSACTIONS/CAREER NOTES: Selected by Texas Rangers organization in 32nd round of free-agent draft (June 2, 1987). . . . On Charlotte disabled list (beginning of season-April 26 and May 6-May 24, 1990). . . . On disabled list (April 23-June 10, June 28-July 8 and July 11-September 3, 1991; and May 7-September 9, 1992). . . . On Texas disabled list (June 12-July 17, 1993); included rehabilitation assignment to Oklahoma City (June 21-July 17). . . . Traded by Rangers with P Kurt Miller to Florida Marlins for P Cris Carpenter (July 17, 1993).

Year	Team (League)	W	L	Pct.	ERA	G	GS	CG	ShO	Sv.	IP	H	R	ER	BB	SO
1987	—GC Rangers (GCL)	0	0	...	7.71	2	0	0	0	0	2 1/3	4	2	2	3	4
1988	—Gastonia (S. Atl.)	0	5	.000	7.45	14	10	0	0	0	48 1/3	69	57	40	45	36
	—Butte (Pioneer)	4	5	.444	8.75	14	13	0	0	0	48 1/3	65	55	47	45	30
1989	—Gastonia (S. Atl.)	7	4	.636	2.41	24	24	1	1	0	138 1/3	96	47	37	76	146
1990	—Charlotte (Fla. St.)	1	4	.200	3.69	11	11	1	0	0	53 2/3	44	28	22	36	38
	—Tulsa (Texas)	0	5	.000	5.06	7	7	0	0	0	26 2/3	23	20	15	21	21
1991	—Tulsa (Texas)	0	2	.000	5.79	6	6	0	0	0	28	24	21	18	20	23
1992	—Tulsa (Texas)	1	1	.500	2.16	4	4	1	0	0	25	21	7	6	2	20
1993	—Texas (A.L.)	1	1	.500	6.35	9	3	0	0	0	22 2/3	28	17	16	26	12
	—Okla. City (A.A.)	0	2	.000	6.67	6	5	0	0	0	28 1/3	45	22	21	18	12
	—Florida (N.L.)■	1	0	1.000	7.02	15	1	0	0	0	33 1/3	35	28	26	20	27
1994	—Florida (N.L.)	5	5	.500	2.95	44	0	0	0	15	58	46	20	19	17	60
1995	—Florida (N.L.)	0	7	.000	3.29	62	0	0	0	23	65 2/3	62	26	24	23	68
A.L. totals (1 year)		1	1	.500	6.35	9	3	0	0	0	22 2/3	28	17	16	26	12
N.L. totals (3 years)		6	12	.333	3.96	121	1	0	0	38	157	143	74	69	60	155
Major league totals (3 years)		7	13	.350	4.26	130	4	0	0	38	179 2/3	171	91	85	86	167

NEVIN, PHIL — 3B/OF — TIGERS

PERSONAL: Born January 19, 1971, in Fullerton, Calif. . . . 6-2/180. . . . Bats right, throws right. . . . Full name: Phillip Joseph Nevin.
HIGH SCHOOL: El Dorado (Placentia, Calif.).
COLLEGE: Cal State Fullerton.
TRANSACTIONS/CAREER NOTES: Selected by Los Angeles Dodgers organization in third round of free-agent draft (June 5, 1989); did not sign. . . . Selected by Houston Astros organization in first round (first pick overall) of free-agent draft (June 1, 1992). . . . On Tucson disabled list (July 12-30, 1995). . . . Traded by Astros to Detroit Tigers (August 15, 1995), completing deal in which Astros acquired P Mike Henneman for a player to be named later (August 10, 1995).
HONORS: Named Golden Spikes Award winner by USA Baseball (1992). . . . Named third baseman on The Sporting News college All-America team (1992).
STATISTICAL NOTES: Led Pacific Coast League third basemen with .891 fielding percentage in 1993. . . . Led Pacific Coast League in ground-

ing into double plays with 21 in 1994. . . . Led Pacific Coast League third basemen with 31 errors and 32 double plays in 1994.
MISCELLANEOUS: Member of 1992 U.S. Olympic baseball team.

			BATTING											FIELDING			
Year	Team (League)	Pos.	G	AB	R	H	2B	3B	HR	RBI	Avg.	BB	SO	SB	PO	A	E	Avg.
1993—	Tucson (PCL)	3B-OF	123	448	67	128	21	3	10	93	.286	52	99	8	68	187	29	†.898
1994—	Tucson (PCL)	3B-OF	118	445	67	117	20	1	12	79	.263	55	101	3	73	240	†32	.907
1995—	Tucson (PCL)	3B	62	223	31	65	16	0	7	41	.291	27	39	2	39	128	14	.923
—	Houston (N.L.)	3B	18	60	4	7	1	0	0	1	.117	7	13	1	10	32	3	.933
—	Toledo (Int'l)■	OF	7	23	3	7	2	0	1	3	.304	1	5	0	2	0	0	1.000
—	Detroit (A.L.)	OF-DH	29	96	9	21	3	1	2	12	.219	11	27	0	50	2	2	.963
American League totals (1 year)			29	96	9	21	3	1	2	12	.219	11	27	0	50	2	2	.963
National League totals (1 year)			18	60	4	7	1	0	0	1	.117	7	13	1	10	32	3	.933
Major league totals (1 year)			47	156	13	28	4	1	2	13	.179	18	40	1	60	34	5	.949

NEWFIELD, MARC OF PADRES

PERSONAL: Born October 19, 1972, in Sacramento, Calif. . . . 6-4/205. . . . Bats right, throws right. . . . Full name: Marc Alexander Newfield.
HIGH SCHOOL: Marina (Huntington Beach, Calif.).
TRANSACTIONS/CAREER NOTES: Selected by Seattle Mariners organization in first round (sixth pick overall) of free-agent draft (June 4, 1990). . . . On disabled list (June 3, 1992-remainder of season). . . . Traded by Mariners with P Ron Villone to San Diego Padres for P Andy Benes and a player to be named later (July 31, 1995); Mariners acquired P Greg Keagle to complete deal (September 16, 1995).
HONORS: Named Arizona League Most Valuable Player (1990).

			BATTING											FIELDING			
Year	Team (League)	Pos.	G	AB	R	H	2B	3B	HR	RBI	Avg.	BB	SO	SB	PO	A	E	Avg.
1990—	Ariz. Mariners (Ariz.)	1B-OF	51	192	34	60	•13	2	6	38	.313	25	20	4	358	13	5	.987
1991—	San Bern. (Calif.)	OF-1B	125	440	64	132	22	3	11	68	.300	59	90	12	245	10	8	.970
—	Jacksonv. (South.)	OF-1B	6	26	4	6	3	0	0	2	.231	0	8	0	16	0	1	.941
1992—	Jacksonv. (South.)	OF	45	162	15	40	12	0	4	19	.247	12	34	1	17	1	0	1.000
1993—	Jacksonv. (South.)	1B-OF	91	336	48	103	18	0	19	51	.307	33	35	1	435	21	3	.993
—	Seattle (A.L.)	DH-OF	22	66	5	15	3	0	1	7	.227	2	8	0	0	0	0	. . .
1994—	Calgary (PCL)	OF	107	430	89	150	*44	2	19	83	.349	42	58	0	136	1	9	.938
—	Seattle (A.L.)	DH-OF	12	38	3	7	1	0	1	4	.184	2	4	0	2	0	0	1.000
1995—	Tacoma (PCL)	OF	53	198	30	55	11	0	5	30	.278	19	30	1	55	1	2	.966
—	Seattle (A.L.)	OF	24	85	7	16	3	0	3	14	.188	3	16	0	44	0	0	1.000
—	Las Vegas (PCL)■	OF-1B	20	70	10	24	5	1	3	12	.343	3	11	2	54	2	1	.982
—	San Diego (N.L.)	OF	21	55	6	17	5	1	1	7	.309	2	8	0	24	1	0	1.000
American League totals (3 years)			58	189	15	38	7	0	5	25	.201	7	28	0	46	0	0	1.000
National League totals (1 year)			21	55	6	17	5	1	1	7	.309	2	8	0	24	1	0	1.000
Major league totals (3 years)			79	244	21	55	12	1	6	32	.225	9	36	0	70	1	0	1.000

NEWSON, WARREN OF RANGERS

PERSONAL: Born July 3, 1964, in Newnan, Ga. . . . 5-7/202. . . . Bats left, throws left. . . . Full name: Warren Dale Newson.
HIGH SCHOOL: Newnan (Ga.).
COLLEGE: Middle Georgia College.
TRANSACTIONS/CAREER NOTES: Selected by San Diego Padres organization in fourth round of free-agent draft (January 14, 1986). . . . Traded by Padres with IF Joey Cora and IF Kevin Garner to Chicago White Sox organization for P Adam Peterson and P Steve Rosenberg (March 31, 1991). . . . On Nashville disabled list (April 29-May 22, 1993). . . . Traded by White Sox to Seattle Mariners for a player to be named later (July 18, 1995); White Sox acquired P Jeff Darwin to complete deal (October 9, 1995). . . . Released by Mariners (November 16, 1995). . . . Signed by Texas Rangers (December 6, 1995).
STATISTICAL NOTES: Led Texas League with 10 intentional bases on balls received in 1989.

			BATTING											FIELDING			
Year	Team (League)	Pos.	G	AB	R	H	2B	3B	HR	RBI	Avg.	BB	SO	SB	PO	A	E	Avg.
1986—	Spokane (N'west)	OF	54	159	29	37	8	1	2	31	.233	47	37	3	54	3	3	.950
1987—	Char., S.C. (S. Atl.)	OF	58	191	50	66	12	2	7	32	.346	52	35	13	81	4	2	.977
—	Reno (California)	OF	51	165	44	51	7	2	6	28	.309	39	34	2	60	5	8	.890
1988—	Riverside (Calif.)	OF	130	438	99	130	23	•7	*22	91	.297	107	102	36	182	7	11	.945
1989—	Wichita (Texas)	OF	128	427	94	130	20	6	18	70	.304	*103	99	20	191	15	5	.976
1990—	Las Vegas (PCL)	OF	123	404	80	123	20	3	13	58	.304	83	110	13	146	4	10	.938
1991—	Vancouver (PCL)■	OF	33	111	19	41	12	1	2	19	.369	30	26	5	53	1	0	1.000
—	Chicago (A.L.)	OF-DH	71	132	20	39	5	0	4	25	.295	28	34	2	48	3	2	.962
1992—	Chicago (A.L.)	OF-DH	63	136	19	30	3	0	1	11	.221	37	38	3	67	5	0	1.000
—	Vancouver (PCL)	OF	19	59	7	15	0	0	0	9	.254	16	21	3	42	1	1	.977
1993—	Nashville (A.A.)	OF	61	176	40	60	8	2	4	21	.341	38	38	5	74	7	1	.988
—	Chicago (A.L.)	DH-OF	26	40	9	12	0	0	2	6	.300	9	12	0	5	0	0	1.000
1994—	Chicago (A.L.)	OF-DH	63	102	16	26	5	0	2	7	.255	14	23	1	46	1	1	.979
1995—	Chicago (A.L.)	OF-DH	51	85	19	20	0	2	3	9	.235	23	27	1	44	1	1	.978
—	Seattle (A.L.)■	OF	33	72	15	21	2	0	2	6	.292	16	18	1	33	1	1	.971
Major league totals (5 years)			307	567	98	148	15	2	14	64	.261	127	152	8	243	11	5	.981

DIVISION SERIES RECORD

			BATTING											FIELDING			
Year	Team (League)	Pos.	G	AB	R	H	2B	3B	HR	RBI	Avg.	BB	SO	SB	PO	A	E	Avg.
1995—	Seattle (A.L.)	PH	1	1	0	0	0	0	0	0	.000	0	1	0	. . .	. . .	. . .	. . .

CHAMPIONSHIP SERIES RECORD

			BATTING											FIELDING			
Year	Team (League)	Pos.	G	AB	R	H	2B	3B	HR	RBI	Avg.	BB	SO	SB	PO	A	E	Avg.
1993—	Chicago (A.L.)	DH-PH	2	5	1	1	0	0	1	1	.200	0	1	0	. . .	. . .	. . .	. . .

N

NICHOLS, ROD — P — BRAVES

PERSONAL: Born December 29, 1964, in Burlington, Ia. . . . 6-2/190. . . . Throws right, bats right. . . . Full name: Rodney Lea Nichols.
HIGH SCHOOL: Highland (Alberquerque, N.M.).
COLLEGE: New Mexico.
TRANSACTIONS/CAREER NOTES: Selected by Cleveland Indians organization in fifth round of free-agent draft (June 3, 1985). . . . On disabled list (July 12-August 18, 1986). . . . On Cleveland disabled list (March 26-May 12, 1988). . . . On Cleveland disabled list (March 19-June 12, 1989); included rehabilitation assignment to Colorado Springs (May 24-June 12). . . . Granted free agency (December 19, 1992). . . . Signed by Los Angeles Dodgers organization (January 15, 1993). . . . Granted free agency (October 15, 1993). . . . Signed by Omaha, Kansas City Royals organization (January 26, 1994). . . . Granted free agency (October 15, 1994). . . . Signed by Richmond, Atlanta Braves organization (February 1, 1995).

Year	Team (League)	W	L	Pct.	ERA	G	GS	CG	ShO	Sv.	IP	H	R	ER	BB	SO
1985—	Batavia (NYP)	5	5	.500	3.00	13	13	3	0	0	84	74	40	28	33	93
1986—	Waterloo (Midw.)	8	5	.615	4.06	20	20	3	1	0	115 1/3	128	56	52	21	83
1987—	Kinston (Carolina)	4	2	.667	4.02	9	8	1	1	0	56	53	27	25	14	61
	— Williamsport (East.)	4	3	.571	3.69	16	16	1	0	0	100	107	53	41	33	60
1988—	Kinston (Carolina)	3	1	.750	4.50	4	4	0	0	0	24	26	13	12	15	19
	— Colo. Springs (PCL)	2	6	.250	5.68	10	9	2	0	0	58 2/3	69	41	37	17	43
	— Cleveland (A.L.)	1	7	.125	5.06	11	10	3	0	0	69 1/3	73	41	39	23	31
1989—	Colo. Springs (PCL)	8	1	.889	3.58	10	10	2	1	0	65 1/3	57	28	26	30	41
	— Cleveland (A.L.)	4	6	.400	4.40	15	11	0	0	0	71 2/3	81	42	35	24	42
1990—	Cleveland (A.L.)	0	3	.000	7.88	4	2	0	0	0	16	24	14	14	6	3
	— Colo. Springs (PCL)	12	9	.571	5.13	22	22	4	•2	0	133 1/3	160	84	76	48	74
1991—	Cleveland (A.L.)	2	11	.154	3.54	31	16	3	1	1	137 1/3	145	63	54	30	76
1992—	Cleveland (A.L.)	4	3	.571	4.53	30	9	0	0	0	105 1/3	114	58	53	31	56
	— Colo. Springs (PCL)	3	3	.500	5.67	9	9	1	0	0	54	65	39	34	16	35
1993—	Albuquerque (PCL)■	8	5	.615	4.30	21	21	3	1	0	127 2/3	132	68	61	50	79
	— Los Angeles (N.L.)	0	1	.000	5.68	4	0	0	0	0	6 1/3	9	5	4	2	3
1994—	Omaha (Am. Assoc.)■	5	10	.333	5.64	33	22	3	1	1	142	163	102	89	52	92
1995—	Richmond (Int'l)■	1	2	.333	2.53	41	3	0	0	•25	57	54	16	16	6	57
	— Atlanta (N.L.)	0	0	...	5.40	5	0	0	0	0	6 2/3	14	11	4	5	3
	A.L. totals (5 years)	11	30	.268	4.39	91	48	6	1	1	399 2/3	437	218	195	114	208
	N.L. totals (2 years)	0	1	.000	5.54	9	0	0	0	0	13	23	16	8	7	6
	Major league totals (7 years)	11	31	.262	4.43	100	48	6	1	1	412 2/3	460	234	203	121	214

NICHTING, CHRIS — P — RANGERS

PERSONAL: Born May 13, 1966, in Cincinnati. . . . 6-1/205. . . . Throws right, bats right. . . . Full name: Christopher Thomas Nichting. . . . Name pronounced NICK-ting.
HIGH SCHOOL: Elder (Cincinnati).
COLLEGE: Northwestern.
TRANSACTIONS/CAREER NOTES: Selected by Los Angeles Dodgers organization in third round of free-agent draft (June 2, 1987). . . . On San Antonio disabled list (April 10, 1990-entire season). . . . On Yakima disabled list (June 17, 1991-remainder of season). . . . On San Antonio disabled list (August 12, 1992-remainder of season). . . . On Albuquerque disabled list (April 8-July 2, 1993). . . . On Vero Beach disabled list (July 15-26 and July 28, 1993-remainder of season). . . . On San Antonio disabled list (April 7-23, 1994). . . . Granted free agency (October 15, 1994). . . . Signed by Texas Rangers (November 18, 1994). . . . On Oklahoma City suspended list (June 8-10, 1995).

N

Year	Team (League)	W	L	Pct.	ERA	G	GS	CG	ShO	Sv.	IP	H	R	ER	BB	SO
1988—	Vero Beach (FSL)	11	4	.733	2.09	21	19	5	1	1	138	90	40	32	51	*151
1989—	San Antonio (Tex.)	4	*14	.222	5.03	26	26	2	0	0	154	160	96	86	*101	*136
1990—								Did not play.								
1991—								Did not play.								
1992—	Albuquerque (PCL)	1	3	.250	7.93	10	9	0	0	0	42	64	42	37	23	25
	— San Antonio (Tex.)	4	5	.444	2.52	13	13	0	0	0	78 2/3	58	25	22	37	81
1993—	Vero Beach (FSL)	0	1	.000	4.15	4	4	0	0	0	17 1/3	18	9	8	6	18
1994—	San Antonio (Tex.)	3	4	.429	1.64	21	8	0	0	1	65 2/3	47	21	12	34	74
	— Albuquerque (PCL)	2	2	.500	7.40	10	7	0	0	0	41 1/3	61	39	34	28	25
1995—	Okla. City (A.A.)■	5	5	.500	2.13	23	7	3	•2	1	67 2/3	58	19	16	19	72
	— Texas (A.L.)	0	0	...	7.03	13	0	0	0	0	24 1/3	36	19	19	13	6
	Major league totals (1 year)	0	0	...	7.03	13	0	0	0	0	24 1/3	36	19	19	13	6

NIED, DAVID — P — ROCKIES

PERSONAL: Born December 22, 1968, in Dallas. . . . 6-2/185. . . . Throws right, bats right. . . . Full name: David Glen Nied. . . . Name pronounced NEED.
HIGH SCHOOL: Duncanville (Tex.).
TRANSACTIONS/CAREER NOTES: Selected by Atlanta Braves organization in 14th round of free-agent draft (June 2, 1987). . . . Selected by Colorado Rockies in first round (first pick overall) of expansion draft (November 17, 1992). . . . On Colorado disabled list (May 28-September 4, 1993); included rehabilitation assignments to Central Valley (August 19-24) and Colorado Springs (August 24-September 4). . . . On Colorado disabled list (April 18-August 5, 1995); included rehabilitation assignments to Portland (July 11-16), New Haven (July 16-21) and Colorado Springs (July 21-August 5). . . . On Colorado Springs disabled list (August 30, 1995-remainder of season).
STATISTICAL NOTES: Tied for South Atlantic League lead with 15 home runs allowed in 1988.

Year	Team (League)	W	L	Pct.	ERA	G	GS	CG	ShO	Sv.	IP	H	R	ER	BB	SO
1988—	Sumter (S. Atl.)	12	9	.571	3.76	27	27	3	1	0	165 1/3	156	78	69	53	133
1989—	Durham (Carolina)	5	2	.714	6.63	12	12	0	0	0	58 1/3	74	47	43	23	38
	— Burlington (Midw.)	5	6	.455	3.83	13	12	2	1	0	80	78	38	34	23	73
1990—	Durham (Carolina)	1	1	.500	3.83	10	10	0	0	0	42 1/3	38	19	18	14	27
	— Burlington (Midw.)	5	3	.625	2.25	10	9	1	1	0	64	55	21	16	10	66
1991—	Greenville (South.)	7	3	.700	2.41	15	15	1	0	0	89 2/3	79	26	24	20	101

Year	Team (League)	W	L	Pct.	ERA	G	GS	CG	ShO	Sv.	IP	H	R	ER	BB	SO
	— Durham (Carolina)	8	3	.727	1.56	13	12	2	•2	0	80 2/3	46	19	14	23	77
1992	— Richmond (Int'l)	*14	9	.609	2.84	26	26	*7	2	0	168	144	73	53	44	*159
	— Atlanta (N.L.)	3	0	1.000	1.17	6	2	0	0	0	23	10	3	3	5	19
1993	— Colorado (N.L.)■	5	9	.357	5.17	16	16	1	0	0	87	99	53	50	42	46
	— Central Valley (Cal.)	0	1	.000	3.00	1	1	0	0	0	3	3	2	1	3	3
	— Colo. Springs (PCL)	0	2	.000	9.00	3	3	0	0	0	15	24	17	15	6	11
1994	— Colorado (N.L.)	9	7	.563	4.80	22	22	2	1	0	122	137	70	65	47	74
1995	— Portland (Northwest)	0	0	...	0.00	1	1	0	0	0	3	1	0	0	1	5
	— New Haven (East.)	0	0	...	8.10	1	1	0	0	0	3 1/3	4	3	3	0	0
	— Colo. Springs (PCL)	1	1	.500	4.99	7	7	0	0	0	30 2/3	31	18	17	25	21
	— Colorado (N.L.)	0	0	...	20.77	2	0	0	0	0	4 1/3	11	10	10	3	3
Major league totals (4 years)		17	16	.515	4.87	46	40	3	1	0	236 1/3	257	136	128	97	142

WORLD SERIES RECORD

Year	Team (League)	W	L	Pct.	ERA	G	GS	CG	ShO	Sv.	IP	H	R	ER	BB	SO
1992	— Atlanta (N.L.)	Did not play.														

NIEVES, MELVIN — OF — PADRES

PERSONAL: Born December 28, 1971, in San Juan, Puerto Rico. . . . 6-2/210. . . . Bats both, throws right. . . . Full name: Melvin Ramos Nieves. . . . Name pronounced nee-EV-es.

HIGH SCHOOL: Ivis Pales Matos (Santa Rosa, Puerto Rico).

TRANSACTIONS/CAREER NOTES: Signed as non-drafted free agent by Atlanta Braves organization (May 20, 1988). . . . On disabled list (April 11-June 13, 1991). . . . On Richmond disabled list (May 18-26, 1993). . . . Traded by Braves with P Donnie Elliott and OF Vince Moore to San Diego Padres for 1B Fred McGriff (July 18, 1993).

STATISTICAL NOTES: Career major league grand slams: 2.

			BATTING											FIELDING			
Year	Team (League)	Pos.	G	AB	R	H	2B	3B	HR	RBI	Avg.	BB	SO	SB	PO	A	E	Avg.
1988	— GC Braves (GCL)	OF	56	170	16	30	6	0	1	12	.176	20	53	5	100	1	2	.981
1989	— Pulaski (Appal.)	OF	64	231	43	64	16	3	9	46	.277	30	59	6	45	1	6	.885
1990	— Sumter (S. Atl.)	OF	126	459	60	130	24	7	9	59	.283	53	125	10	227	7	11	.955
1991	— Durham (Carolina)	OF	64	201	31	53	11	0	9	25	.264	40	53	3	75	8	5	.943
1992	— Durham (Carolina)	OF	31	106	18	32	9	1	8	32	.302	17	33	4	61	4	2	.970
	— Greenville (South.)	OF	100	350	61	99	23	5	18	76	.283	52	98	6	127	9	5	.965
	— Atlanta (N.L.)	OF	12	19	0	4	1	0	0	1	.211	2	7	0	8	0	3	.727
1993	— Richmond (Int'l)	OF	78	273	38	76	10	3	10	36	.278	25	84	4	124	5	7	.949
	— Las Vegas (PCL)■	OF	43	159	31	49	10	1	7	24	.308	18	42	2	79	4	1	.988
	— San Diego (N.L.)	OF	19	47	4	9	0	0	2	3	.191	3	21	0	27	0	2	.931
1994	— Las Vegas (PCL)	OF-1B	111	406	81	125	17	6	25	92	.308	58	*138	1	170	4	10	.946
	— San Diego (N.L.)	OF	10	19	2	5	1	0	1	4	.263	3	10	0	11	1	0	1.000
1995	— San Diego (N.L.)	OF-1B	98	234	32	48	6	1	14	38	.205	19	88	2	106	5	2	.982
Major league totals (4 years)			139	319	38	66	8	1	17	46	.207	27	126	2	152	6	7	.958

NILSSON, DAVE — C — BREWERS

PERSONAL: Born December 14, 1969, in Brisbane, Queensland, Australia. . . . 6-3/231. . . . Bats left, throws right. . . . Full name: David Wayne Nilsson.

HIGH SCHOOL: Kedron (Brisbane, Australia).

TRANSACTIONS/CAREER NOTES: Signed as non-drafted free agent by Milwaukee Brewers organization (February 9, 1987). . . . On disabled list (April 30-May 26, 1990). . . . On Denver disabled list (August 13, 1991-remainder of season). . . . On Milwaukee disabled list (July 6-24, 1992); included rehabilitation assignment to Denver (July 16-24). . . . On Milwaukee disabled list (March 27-April 14, 1993); included rehabilitation assignment to El Paso (April 5-14). . . . On Milwaukee disabled list (May 18-June 22, 1993); included rehabilitation assignment to New Orleans (May 26-June 13). . . . On Milwaukee disabled list (April 16, 1995); included rehabilitation assignments to Beloit (June 10-14), El Paso (June 14-21) and New Orleans (June 21-24).

STATISTICAL NOTES: Career major league grand slams: 2.

			BATTING											FIELDING			
Year	Team (League)	Pos.	G	AB	R	H	2B	3B	HR	RBI	Avg.	BB	SO	SB	PO	A	E	Avg.
1987	— Helena (Pioneer)	C	55	188	36	74	13	0	1	21	.394	5	7	0	329	28	7	.981
1988	— Beloit (Midwest)	C-1B	95	332	28	74	15	2	4	41	.223	25	49	2	526	64	6	.990
1989	— Stockton (Calif.)	C-2B	125	472	59	115	16	6	5	56	.244	50	76	2	703	66	13	.983
1990	— Stockton (Calif.)	C-1B-3B	107	359	70	104	22	3	7	47	.290	43	36	6	600	86	12	.983
1991	— El Paso (Texas)	C-3B	65	249	52	104	24	3	5	57	.418	27	14	4	348	46	8	.980
	— Denver (A.A.)	C-1B-3B	28	95	10	22	8	0	1	14	.232	17	16	1	146	16	2	.988
1992	— Denver (A.A.)	C-1B-3B	66	240	38	76	16	7	3	39	.317	23	19	10	350	51	6	.985
	— Milwaukee (A.L.)	C-1B-DH	51	164	15	38	8	0	4	25	.232	17	18	2	231	16	2	.992
1993	— El Paso (Texas)	C	5	17	5	8	1	0	1	7	.471	2	4	1	31	9	0	1.000
	— Milwaukee (A.L.)	C-DH-1B	100	296	35	76	10	2	7	40	.257	37	36	3	457	33	9	.982
	— New Orleans (A.A.)	C	17	61	9	21	6	0	1	9	.344	5	6	0	55	7	1	.984
1994	— Milwaukee (A.L.)	C-DH-1B	109	397	51	109	28	3	12	69	.275	34	61	1	315	15	2	.994
1995	— Beloit (Midwest)	DH	3	11	2	6	3	0	1	7	.545	2	0	0	0	0	0	...
	— El Paso (Texas)	OF	5	15	1	7	1	0	1	4	.467	0	1	1	4	0	0	1.000
	— New Orleans (A.A.)	OF	3	9	1	4	0	0	1	4	.444	2	0	0	2	0	0	1.000
	— Milwaukee (A.L.)	O-DH-1-C	81	263	41	73	12	1	12	53	.278	24	41	2	117	7	2	.984
Major league totals (4 years)			341	1120	142	296	58	6	35	187	.264	112	156	8	1120	71	15	.988

N

NITKOWSKI, C.J. — P — TIGERS

PERSONAL: Born March 3, 1973, in Suffren, N.Y. . . . 6-3/190. . . . Throws left, bats left. . . . Full name: Christopher J. Nitkowski.
HIGH SCHOOL: Don Bosco (N.J.).
COLLEGE: St. John's.
TRANSACTIONS/CAREER NOTES: Selected by Cincinnati Reds organization in first round (ninth pick overall) of free-agent draft (June 2, 1994). . . . Traded by Reds with P David Tuttle and a player to be named later to Detroit Tigers for P David Wells (July 31, 1995); Tigers acquired IF Mark Lewis to complete deal (November 16, 1995).

Year Team (League)	W	L	Pct.	ERA	G	GS	CG	ShO	Sv.	IP	H	R	ER	BB	SO
1994— Chattanooga (Sou.)	6	3	.667	3.50	14	14	0	0	0	74 2/3	61	30	29	40	60
1995— Chattanooga (Sou.)	4	2	.667	2.50	8	8	0	0	0	50 1/3	39	20	14	20	52
— Indianapolis (A.A.)	0	2	.000	5.20	6	6	0	0	0	27 2/3	28	16	16	10	21
— Cincinnati (N.L.)	1	3	.250	6.12	9	7	0	0	0	32 1/3	41	25	22	15	18
— Detroit (A.L.)■	1	4	.200	7.09	11	11	0	0	0	39 1/3	53	32	31	20	13
A.L. totals (1 year)	1	4	.200	7.09	11	11	0	0	0	39 1/3	53	32	31	20	13
N.L. totals (1 year)	1	3	.250	6.12	9	7	0	0	0	32 1/3	41	25	22	15	18
Major league totals (1 year)	2	7	.222	6.66	20	18	0	0	0	71 2/3	94	57	53	35	31

NIXON, OTIS — OF — BLUE JAYS

PERSONAL: Born January 9, 1959, in Evergreen, N.C. . . . 6-2/180. . . . Bats both, throws right. . . . Full name: Otis Junior Nixon. . . . Brother of Donell Nixon, outfielder, Seattle Mariners, San Francisco Giants and Baltimore Orioles (1985, 1987-89 and 1990).
HIGH SCHOOL: Columbus (N.C.).
COLLEGE: Louisburg (N.C.) College.
TRANSACTIONS/CAREER NOTES: Selected by Cincinnati Reds organization in 21st round of free-agent draft (June 6, 1978); did not sign. . . . Selected by California Angels organization in secondary phase of free-agent draft (January 9, 1979); did not sign. . . . Selected by New York Yankees organization in secondary phase of free-agent draft (June 5, 1979). . . . Traded by Yankees with P George Frazier and a player to be named later to Cleveland Indians for 3B Toby Harrah and a player to be named later (February 5, 1984); Yankees organization acquired P Rick Browne and Indians organization acquired P Guy Elston to complete deal (February 8, 1984). . . . Granted free agency (October 15, 1987). . . . Signed by Indianapolis, Montreal Expos organization (March 5, 1988). . . . Traded by Expos with 3B Boi Rodriguez to Atlanta Braves for C Jimmy Kremers and a player to be named later (April 1, 1991); Sumter, Expos organization, acquired P Keith Morrison to complete deal (June 3, 1991). . . . On suspended list (August 13-16, 1991). . . . On disqualified list (September 16, 1991-April 24, 1992). . . . Granted free agency (November 11, 1991). . . . Re-signed by Braves (December 12, 1991). . . . Granted free agency (October 25, 1993). . . . Signed by Boston Red Sox (December 7, 1993). . . . Traded by Red Sox with 3B Luis Ortiz to Texas Rangers for DH/OF Jose Canseco (December 9, 1994). . . . Granted free agency (November 3, 1995). . . . Signed by Toronto Blue Jays (December 7, 1995).
RECORDS: Shares modern major league single-game record for most stolen bases—6 (June 16, 1991).
STATISTICAL NOTES: Led Appalachian League third basemen with .945 fielding percentage, 52 putouts, 120 assists, 182 total chances and 12 double plays in 1979. . . . Led International League in caught stealing with 29 in 1983. . . . Led International League outfielders with .992 fielding percentage, 363 putouts and 371 total chances in 1983. . . . Led A.L. in caught stealing with 21 in 1995.

			BATTING											FIELDING			
Year Team (League)	**Pos.**	**G**	**AB**	**R**	**H**	**2B**	**3B**	**HR**	**RBI**	**Avg.**	**BB**	**SO**	**SB**	**PO**	**A**	**E**	**Avg.**
1979— Paintsville (Appal.)	3B-SS	63	203	58	58	10	3	1	25	.286	*57	40	5	†54	†122	11	†.941
1980— Greensboro (S. Atl.)	3B-SS	136	493	*124	137	12	5	3	48	.278	*113	88	*67	164	308	36	.929
1981— Nashville (South.)	SS	127	407	89	102	9	2	0	20	.251	*110	101	71	198	348	*56	.907
1982— Nashville (South.)	SS-2B	72	283	47	80	3	2	0	20	.283	59	56	61	126	211	23	.936
— Columbus (Int'l)	2B-SS	59	207	43	58	4	0	0	14	.280	49	41	46	104	169	14	.951
1983— Columbus (Int'l)	OF-2B	138	*557	*129	*162	11	6	0	41	.291	96	83	*94	†385	24	4	†.990
— New York (A.L.)	OF	13	14	2	2	0	0	0	0	.143	1	5	2	14	1	1	.938
1984— Cleveland (A.L.)■	OF	49	91	16	14	0	0	0	1	.154	8	11	12	81	3	0	1.000
— Maine (Int'l)	OF	72	253	42	70	5	1	0	22	.277	44	45	39	206	7	1	.995
1985— Cleveland (A.L.)	OF-DH	104	162	34	38	4	0	3	9	.235	8	27	20	129	5	4	.971
1986— Cleveland (A.L.)	OF-DH	105	95	33	25	4	1	0	8	.263	13	12	23	90	3	3	.969
1987— Cleveland (A.L.)	OF-DH	19	17	2	1	0	0	0	1	.059	3	4	2	21	0	0	1.000
— Buffalo (A.A.)	OF	59	249	51	71	13	4	2	23	.285	34	30	36	170	3	3	.983
1988— Indianapolis (A.A.)■	OF	67	235	52	67	6	3	0	19	.285	43	28	40	130	1	1	.992
— Montreal (N.L.)	OF	90	271	47	66	8	2	0	15	.244	28	42	46	176	2	1	.994
1989— Montreal (N.L.)	OF	126	258	41	56	7	2	0	21	.217	33	36	37	160	2	2	.988
1990— Montreal (N.L.)	OF-SS	119	231	46	58	6	2	1	20	.251	28	33	50	149	6	1	.994
1991— Atlanta (N.L.)■	OF	124	401	81	119	10	1	0	26	.297	47	40	72	218	6	3	.987
1992— Atlanta (N.L.)	OF	120	456	79	134	14	2	2	22	.294	39	54	41	333	6	3	.991
1993— Atlanta (N.L.)	OF	134	461	77	124	12	3	1	24	.269	61	63	47	308	4	3	.990
1994— Boston (A.L.)■	OF	103	398	60	109	15	1	0	25	.274	55	65	42	254	4	3	.989
1995— Texas (A.L.)■	OF	139	589	87	174	21	2	0	45	.295	58	85	50	357	4	4	.989
American League totals (7 years)		532	1366	234	363	44	4	3	89	.266	146	209	151	946	20	15	.985
National League totals (6 years)		713	2078	371	557	57	12	4	128	.268	236	268	293	1344	26	13	.991
Major league totals (13 years)		1245	3444	605	920	101	16	7	217	.267	382	477	444	2290	46	28	.988

CHAMPIONSHIP SERIES RECORD

NOTES: Shares N.L. single-game record for most hits—4 (October 10, 1992).

			BATTING											FIELDING			
Year Team (League)	**Pos.**	**G**	**AB**	**R**	**H**	**2B**	**3B**	**HR**	**RBI**	**Avg.**	**BB**	**SO**	**SB**	**PO**	**A**	**E**	**Avg.**
1992— Atlanta (N.L.)	OF	7	28	5	8	2	0	0	2	.286	4	4	3	16	0	0	1.000
1993— Atlanta (N.L.)	OF	6	23	3	8	2	0	0	4	.348	5	6	0	13	0	0	1.000
Championship series totals (2 years)		13	51	8	16	4	0	0	6	.314	9	10	3	29	0	0	1.000

WORLD SERIES RECORD

			BATTING											FIELDING			
Year Team (League)	**Pos.**	**G**	**AB**	**R**	**H**	**2B**	**3B**	**HR**	**RBI**	**Avg.**	**BB**	**SO**	**SB**	**PO**	**A**	**E**	**Avg.**
1992— Atlanta (N.L.)	OF	6	27	3	8	1	0	0	1	.296	1	3	5	18	0	0	1.000

NIXON, TROT — OF — RED SOX

PERSONAL: Born April 11, 1974, in Durham, N.C. . . . 6-2/196. . . . Bats left, throws left. . . . Full name: Christopher Trotman Nixon.
HIGH SCHOOL: New Hanover (Wilmington, N.C.).
TRANSACTIONS/CAREER NOTES: Selected by Boston Red Sox organization in first round (seventh pick overall) of free-agent draft (June 3, 1993). . . . On disabled list (July 12, 1994-remainder of season).

			BATTING												FIELDING			
Year	Team (League)	Pos.	G	AB	R	H	2B	3B	HR	RBI	Avg.	BB	SO	SB	PO	A	E	Avg.
1994—	Lynchburg (Caro.)	OF	71	264	33	65	12	0	12	43	.246	44	53	10	143	8	4	.974
1995—	Sarasota (FSL)	OF	73	264	43	80	11	4	5	39	.303	45	46	7	140	4	2	.986
—	Trenton (Eastern)	OF	25	94	9	15	3	1	2	8	.160	7	20	2	66	2	0	1.000

NOKES, MATT — C — BREWERS

PERSONAL: Born October 31, 1963, in San Diego. . . . 6-1/210. . . . Bats left, throws right. . . . Full name: Matthew Dodge Nokes.
HIGH SCHOOL: Patrick Henry (San Diego).
TRANSACTIONS/CAREER NOTES: Selected by San Francisco Giants organization in 20th round of free-agent draft (June 8, 1981). . . . Traded by Giants with P Dave LaPoint and P Eric King to Detroit Tigers for P Juan Berenguer, C Bob Melvin and a player to be named later (October 7, 1985); Giants acquired P Scott Medvin to complete deal (December 11, 1985). . . . On disabled list (June 19-August 3, 1989). . . . Traded by Tigers to New York Yankees for P Lance McCullers and P Clay Parker (June 4, 1990). . . . On disabled list (June 21-July 7, 1993). . . . On New York disabled list (April 26-June 29, 1994); included rehabilitation assignments to Albany (June 13-17) and Columbus (June 17-29). . . . Granted free agency (October 18, 1994). . . . Signed by Baltimore Orioles (December 9, 1994). . . . Released by Orioles (June 19, 1995). . . . Signed by Colorado Springs, Colorado Rockies organization (July 20, 1995). . . . On Colorado disabled list (July 31-September 4, 1995); included rehabilitation assignment to Colorado Springs (August 14-17). . . . Released by Rockies (October 10, 1995). . . . Signed by Milwaukee Brewers organization (December 21, 1995).
HONORS: Named catcher on The Sporting News A.L. All-Star team (1987). . . . Named catcher on The Sporting News A.L. Silver Slugger team (1987).
STATISTICAL NOTES: Led Pioneer League with 19 passed balls in 1981. . . . Led California League catchers with nine double plays in 1983. . . . Led Texas League catchers with six double plays in 1985. . . . Tied for American Association lead in errors by catcher with 13 in 1986. . . . Career major league grand slams: 6.

			BATTING												FIELDING			
Year	Team (League)	Pos.	G	AB	R	H	2B	3B	HR	RBI	Avg.	BB	SO	SB	PO	A	E	Avg.
1981—	Great Falls (Pio.)	C	44	146	14	33	6	2	0	13	.226	11	23	0	288	35	*13	.961
1982—	Clinton (Midwest)	C	82	247	19	53	12	0	3	23	.215	15	44	1	363	41	13	.969
1983—	Fresno (California)	C	125	429	62	138	26	6	14	82	.322	60	92	0	595	62	16	.976
1984—	Shreveport (Texas)	C	97	308	32	89	19	2	11	61	.289	30	34	0	400	31	8	.982
1985—	Shreveport (Texas)	C	105	344	52	101	24	1	14	56	.294	41	47	2	520	40	12	.979
—	San Francisco (N.L.)	C	19	53	3	11	2	0	2	5	.208	1	9	0	84	2	2	.977
1986—	Nashville (A.A.)■	C-1B-OF	125	428	55	122	25	4	10	71	.285	30	41	2	502	50	‡18	.968
—	Detroit (A.L.)	C	7	24	2	8	1	0	1	2	.333	1	1	0	43	2	0	1.000
1987—	Detroit (A.L.)	C-DH-O-3	135	461	69	133	14	2	32	87	.289	35	70	2	600	32	5	.992
1988—	Detroit (A.L.)	C-DH	122	382	53	96	18	0	16	53	.251	34	58	0	574	45	7	.989
1989—	Detroit (A.L.)	C-DH	87	268	15	67	10	0	9	39	.250	17	37	1	235	26	6	.978
1990—	Detroit (A.L.)	DH-C	44	111	12	30	5	1	3	8	.270	4	14	0	55	7	1	.984
—	New York (A.L.)■	C-DH-OF	92	240	21	57	4	0	8	32	.238	20	33	2	182	27	1	.995
1991—	New York (A.L.)	C-DH	135	456	52	122	20	0	24	77	.268	25	49	3	690	48	6	.992
1992—	New York (A.L.)	C	121	384	42	86	9	1	22	59	.224	37	62	0	552	47	4	.993
1993—	New York (A.L.)	C-DH	76	217	25	54	8	0	10	35	.249	16	31	0	245	19	2	.992
1994—	New York (A.L.)	C-DH-1B	28	79	11	23	3	0	7	19	.291	5	16	0	106	6	3	.974
—	Alb./Colon. (East.)	C	3	11	1	4	1	0	0	3	.364	1	1	0	21	2	0	1.000
—	Columbus (Int'l)	C-1B	11	38	8	11	1	0	5	11	.289	2	6	0	55	4	0	1.000
1995—	Baltimore (A.L.)■	C-DH	26	49	4	6	1	0	2	6	.122	4	11	0	83	5	1	.989
—	Colo. Springs (PCL)■	C	12	37	7	8	2	0	4	10	.216	2	4	0	43	3	1	.979
—	Colorado (N.L.)	C	10	11	1	2	1	0	0	0	.182	1	4	0	10	0	1	.909
American League totals (10 years)			873	2671	306	682	93	4	134	417	.255	198	382	8	3365	264	36	.990
National League totals (2 years)			29	64	4	13	3	0	2	5	.203	2	13	0	94	2	3	.970
Major league totals (11 years)			902	2735	310	695	96	4	136	422	.254	200	395	8	3459	266	39	.990

CHAMPIONSHIP SERIES RECORD

			BATTING												FIELDING			
Year	Team (League)	Pos.	G	AB	R	H	2B	3B	HR	RBI	Avg.	BB	SO	SB	PO	A	E	Avg.
1987—	Detroit (A.L.)	C-PH-DH	5	14	2	2	0	0	1	2	.143	1	4	0	11	2	0	1.000

ALL-STAR GAME RECORD

			BATTING											FIELDING			
Year	League	Pos.	AB	R	H	2B	3B	HR	RBI	Avg.	BB	SO	SB	PO	A	E	Avg.
1987—	American	C	2	0	0	0	0	0	0	.000	0	0	0	8	0	0	1.000

NOMO, HIDEO — P — DODGERS

PERSONAL: Born August 31, 1968, in Osaka, Japan. . . . 6-2/210. . . . Throws right, bats right.
TRANSACTIONS/CAREER NOTES: Selected by Kintetsu Buffaloes in first round of 1989 Japanese free-agent draft. . . . Signed as free agent by Los Angeles Dodgers organization (February 8, 1995). . . . On Albuquerque temporarily inactive list (April 3-27, 1995).
HONORS: Named N.L. Rookie Pitcher of the Year by The Sporting News (1995). . . . Named N.L. Rookie of the Year by Baseball Writers' Association of America (1995).
STATISTICAL NOTES: Struck out 16 batters in one game (June 14, 1995). . . . Pitched 3-0 one-hit, complete-game victory against San Francisco (August 5, 1995). . . . Led N.L. with 19 wild pitches and five balks in 1995.
MISCELLANEOUS: Member of 1988 Japanese Olympic baseball team.

Year	Team (League)	W	L	Pct.	ERA	G	GS	CG	ShO	Sv.	IP	H	R	ER	BB	SO
1990—	Kintetsu (Jap. Pac.)	*18	8	.692	*2.91	29	27	21	2	0	235	167	...	76	*109	*287
1991—	Kintetsu (Jap. Pac.)	*17	11	.607	3.05	31	29	22	*4	1	242 1/3	183	...	82	*128	*287
1992—	Kintetsu (Jap. Pac.)	*18	8	.692	2.66	30	29	17	*5	0	216 2/3	150	...	64	*117	*228
1993—	Kintetsu (Jap. Pac.)	*17	12	.586	3.70	32	32	14	2	0	243 1/3	*201	...	100	*148	*276
1994—	Kintetsu (Jap. Pac.)	8	7	.533	3.63	17	17	6	0	0	114	...	...	46	86	126
1995—	Bakersfield (Calif.)■	0	1	.000	3.38	1	1	0	0	0	5 1/3	6	2	2	1	6
—	Los Angeles (N.L.)	13	6	.684	2.54	28	28	4	•3	0	191 1/3	124	63	54	78	*236
Major league totals (1 year)		13	6	.684	2.54	28	28	4	3	0	191 1/3	124	63	54	78	236

DIVISION SERIES RECORD

Year	Team (League)	W	L	Pct.	ERA	G	GS	CG	ShO	Sv.	IP	H	R	ER	BB	SO
1995—	Los Angeles (N.L.)	0	1	.000	9.00	1	1	0	0	0	5	7	5	5	2	6

ALL-STAR GAME RECORD

Year	League	W	L	Pct.	ERA	GS	CG	ShO	Sv.	IP	H	R	ER	BB	SO
1995—	National	0	0	...	0.00	1	0	0	0	2	1	0	0	0	3

NORMAN, LES — OF — ROYALS

PERSONAL: Born February 25, 1969, in Warren, Mich. . . . 6-1/185. . . . Bats right, throws right. . . . Full name: Leslie Eugene Norman.
HIGH SCHOOL: Reed-Custer (Braidwood, Ill.).
COLLEGE: College of St. Francis (Ill.).
TRANSACTIONS/CAREER NOTES: Selected by Boston Red Sox organization in 26th round of free-agent draft (June 4, 1990); did not sign. . . . Selected by Kansas City Royals organization in 25th round of free-agent draft (June 3, 1991).
STATISTICAL NOTES: Led Southern League outfielders with 17 assists in 1993. . . . Led Southern League outfielders with .996 fielding percentage in 1994.

			BATTING												FIELDING			
Year	Team (League)	Pos.	G	AB	R	H	2B	3B	HR	RBI	Avg.	BB	SO	SB	PO	A	E	Avg.
1991—	Eugene (N'west)	OF	30	102	14	25	4	1	2	18	.245	9	18	2	65	5	3	.959
1992—	Appleton (Midw.)	OF-1B-3B	59	218	38	82	17	1	4	47	.376	22	18	8	119	20	3	.979
—	Memphis (South.)	OF	72	271	32	74	14	5	3	20	.273	22	37	4	124	9	4	.971
1993—	Memphis (South.)	OF-1B	133	484	78	141	32	5	17	81	.291	50	88	11	273	†17	10	.967
1994—	Memphis (South.)	OF-1B	106	383	53	101	19	4	13	55	.264	36	44	7	242	14	2	†.992
1995—	Omaha (A.A.)	OF-1B	83	313	46	89	19	3	9	33	.284	18	48	5	180	9	4	.979
—	Kansas City (A.L.)	OF-DH	24	40	6	9	0	1	0	4	.225	6	6	0	22	1	1	.958
Major league totals (1 year)			24	40	6	9	0	1	0	4	.225	6	6	0	22	1	1	.958

NORTON, GREG — 3B — WHITE SOX

PERSONAL: Born July 6, 1972, in San Leandro, Calif. . . . 6-1/190. . . . Bats both, throws right. . . . Full name: Gregory Norton.
HIGH SCHOOL: Bishop O'dowd (Oakland, Calif.).
COLLEGE: Oklahoma.
TRANSACTIONS/CAREER NOTES: Selected by San Francisco Giants organization in seventh round of free-agent draft (June 4, 1990); did not sign. . . . Selected by Chicago White Sox organization in second round of free-agent draft (June 3, 1993).
STATISTICAL NOTES: Led Midwest League third basemen with 387 total chances in 1994.

			BATTING												FIELDING			
Year	Team (League)	Pos.	G	AB	R	H	2B	3B	HR	RBI	Avg.	BB	SO	SB	PO	A	E	Avg.
1993—	GC Whi. Sox (GCL)	3B	3	9	1	2	0	0	0	2	.222	1	1	0	1	7	0	1.000
—	Hickory (S. Atl.)	3B-SS	71	254	36	62	12	2	4	36	.244	41	44	0	57	161	17	.928
1994—	South Bend (Mid.)	3B	127	477	73	137	22	2	6	64	.287	62	71	5	92	*265	30	.922
1995—	Birm. (Southern)	3B	133	469	65	162	23	2	6	60	.345	64	90	19	102	277	25	*.938

NUNEZ, SERGIO — 2B — ROYALS

PERSONAL: Born January 3, 1975, in Santo Domingo, Dominican Republic. . . . 5-11/155. . . . Bats right, throws right. . . . Full name: Sergio Augusto Nunez.
HIGH SCHOOL: Lico Secuonderio Las Americas (Santo Domingo, Dominican Republic).
TRANSACTIONS/CAREER NOTES: Signed as non-drafted free agent by Kansas City Royals organization (November 15, 1991).
STATISTICAL NOTES: Tied for Dominican Summer League lead with seven intentional bases on balls received in 1993. . . . Led Gulf Coast League with 130 total bases, .560 slugging percentage and .474 on-base percentage in 1994. . . . Tied for Gulf Coast League lead in caught stealing with 12 in 1994.

			BATTING												FIELDING			
Year	Team (League)	Pos.	G	AB	R	H	2B	3B	HR	RBI	Avg.	BB	SO	SB	PO	A	E	Avg.
1992—	Dom. Royals (DSL)	2B-SS	62	202	49	61	4	5	0	30	.302	31	21	29	123	169	24	.924
1993—	Dom. Royals (DSL)	IF	70	249	63	85	18	2	2	35	.341	50	17	32	171	214	16	.960
1994—	GC Royals (GCL)	2B	59	232	*64	*92	9	7	5	24	*.397	32	17	*37	123	176	10	.968
1995—	Wilmington (Caro.)	2B	124	460	63	109	10	2	4	25	.237	51	66	33	231	313	26	.954

NUNNALLY, JON — OF — ROYALS

PERSONAL: Born November 9, 1971, in Pelham, N.C. . . . 5-10/190. . . . Bats left, throws right. . . . Full name: Jonathan Keith Nunnally.
JUNIOR COLLEGE: Miami-Dade (South) Community College.
TRANSACTIONS/CAREER NOTES: Selected by Cleveland Indians organization in third round of free-agent draft (June 1, 1992). . . . Selected by Kansas City Royals from Indians organization in Rule 5 major league draft (December 5, 1994).
STATISTICAL NOTES: Hit home run in first major league at-bat (April 29, 1995).

Year Team (League)	Pos.	G	AB	R	H	2B	3B	HR	RBI	Avg.	BB	SO	SB	PO	A	E	Avg.
			BATTING											FIELDING			
1992—Watertown (NYP)	OF	69	246	39	59	10	4	5	43	.240	32	55	12	146	2	8	.949
1993—Columbus (S. Atl.)	2B-OF	125	438	81	110	15	2	15	56	.251	63	108	17	226	202	25	.945
1994—Kinston (Carolina)	OF	132	483	70	129	29	2	22	74	.267	64	125	23	263	*14	9	.969
1995—Kansas City (A.L.)■	OF-DH	119	303	51	74	15	6	14	42	.244	51	86	6	197	5	6	.971
Major league totals (1 year)		119	303	51	74	15	6	14	42	.244	51	86	6	197	5	6	.971

OBANDO, SHERMAN — OF — ORIOLES

PERSONAL: Born January 23, 1970, in Bocas del Toro, Panama. . . . 6-4/215. . . . Bats right, throws right. . . . Full name: Sherman Omar Obando.

TRANSACTIONS/CAREER NOTES: Signed as non-drafted free agent by New York Yankees organization (September 17, 1987). . . . On Prince William disabled list (May 3-July 25, 1991). . . . On disabled list (April 9-May 11, 1992). . . . Selected by Baltimore Orioles from Yankees organization in Rule 5 major league draft (December 7, 1992). . . . On Baltimore disabled list (May 25-June 24, 1993); included rehabilitation assignment to Bowie (June 4-23). . . . On Baltimore disabled list (June 26-July 11, 1993).

STATISTICAL NOTES: Led International League with .603 slugging percentage in 1994.

Year Team (League)	Pos.	G	AB	R	H	2B	3B	HR	RBI	Avg.	BB	SO	SB	PO	A	E	Avg.
			BATTING											FIELDING			
1988—GC Yankees (GCL)	OF	49	172	26	44	10	2	4	27	.256	16	32	8	55	3	3	.951
1989—Oneonta (NYP)	OF	70	276	50	86	*23	3	6	45	.312	16	45	8	50	0	6	.893
1990—Prin. William (Car.)	OF	121	439	67	117	24	6	10	67	.267	42	85	5	156	4	7	.958
1991—GC Yankees (GCL)	DH	4	17	3	5	2	0	0	1	.294	1	2	0	...	...	...	...
—Prin. William (Car.)	OF	42	140	25	37	11	1	7	31	.264	19	28	0	19	1	0	1.000
1992—Alb./Colon. (East.)	1B	109	381	71	107	19	3	17	56	.281	32	67	3	430	32	11	.977
1993—Baltimore (A.L.)■	DH-OF	31	92	8	25	2	0	3	15	.272	4	26	0	13	0	1	.929
—Bowie (Eastern)	OF-1B	19	58	8	14	2	0	3	12	.241	9	11	1	32	0	1	.970
1994—Rochester (Int'l)	OF	109	403	67	133	*36	7	20	69	.330	30	53	1	97	5	3	.971
1995—Baltimore (A.L.)	DH-OF	16	38	0	10	1	0	0	3	.263	2	12	1	12	0	1	.923
—Rochester (Int'l)	OF-1B	85	324	42	96	26	6	9	53	.296	29	57	1	184	15	8	.961
Major league totals (2 years)		47	130	8	35	3	0	3	18	.269	6	38	1	25	0	2	.926

O'BRIEN, CHARLIE — C — BLUE JAYS

PERSONAL: Born May 1, 1961, in Tulsa, Okla. . . . 6-2/205. . . . Bats right, throws right. . . . Full name: Charles Hugh O'Brien. . . . Brother of John O'Brien, minor league first baseman, St. Louis Cardinals organization (1991-93).

HIGH SCHOOL: Bishop Kelley (Tulsa, Okla.).

JUNIOR COLLEGE: McLennan Community College (Tex.).

COLLEGE: Wichita State.

TRANSACTIONS/CAREER NOTES: Selected by Texas Rangers organization in 14th round of free-agent draft (June 6, 1978); did not sign. . . . Selected by Seattle Mariners organization in 21st round of free-agent draft (June 8, 1981); did not sign. . . . Selected by Oakland Athletics organization in fifth round of free-agent draft (June 7, 1982). . . . On disabled list (July 31, 1983-remainder of season). . . . On Albany/Colonie disabled list (April 13-May 15, 1984). . . . Traded by A's organization with IF Steve Kiefer, P Mike Fulmer and P Pete Kendrick to Milwaukee Brewers for P Moose Haas (March 30, 1986). . . . Traded by Brewers with a player to be named later to New York Mets for two players to be named later (August 30, 1990); Brewers acquired P Julio Machado and P Kevin Brown (September 7, 1990) and Mets acquired P Kevin Carmody (September 11, 1990) to complete deal. . . . Granted free agency (October 29, 1993). . . . Signed by Atlanta Braves (November 26, 1993). . . . Granted free agency (October 30, 1995). . . . Signed by Toronto Blue Jays (December 14, 1995).

Year Team (League)	Pos.	G	AB	R	H	2B	3B	HR	RBI	Avg.	BB	SO	SB	PO	A	E	Avg.
			BATTING											FIELDING			
1982—Medford (N'west)	C	17	60	11	17	3	0	3	14	.283	10	10	0	116	18	4	.971
—Modesto (Calif.)	C	41	140	23	42	6	0	3	32	.300	20	19	7	239	44	5	.983
1983—Alb./Colon. (East.)	C-1B	92	285	50	83	12	1	14	56	.291	52	39	3	478	82	11	.981
1984—Modesto (Calif.)	C	9	32	8	9	2	0	1	5	.281	2	4	1	41	8	0	1.000
—Tacoma (PCL)	C-OF	69	195	33	44	11	0	9	22	.226	28	31	0	260	39	0	1.000
1985—Huntsville (South.)	C	33	115	20	24	5	0	7	16	.209	16	20	0	182	29	5	.977
—Oakland (A.L.)	C	16	11	3	3	1	0	0	1	.273	3	3	0	23	0	1	.958
—Modesto (Calif.)	C	9	27	5	8	4	1	1	2	.296	2	5	0	33	8	1	.976
—Tacoma (PCL)	C	18	57	5	9	4	0	0	7	.158	6	17	0	110	9	3	.975
1986—Vancouver (PCL)■	C	6	17	1	2	0	0	0	1	.118	4	4	0	22	3	2	.926
—El Paso (Texas)	C-OF-1B	92	336	72	109	20	3	15	75	.324	50	30	0	437	43	4	.992
1987—Denver (A.A.)	C	80	266	37	75	12	1	8	35	.282	41	33	5	415	53	6	.987
—Milwaukee (A.L.)	C	10	35	2	7	3	1	0	0	.200	4	4	0	78	11	0	1.000
1988—Denver (A.A.)	C	48	153	16	43	5	0	4	25	.281	19	19	1	243	44	3	.990
—Milwaukee (A.L.)	C	40	118	12	26	6	0	2	9	.220	5	16	0	210	20	2	.991
1989—Milwaukee (A.L.)	C	62	188	22	44	10	0	6	35	.234	21	11	0	314	36	5	.986
1990—Milwaukee (A.L.)	C	46	145	11	27	7	2	0	11	.186	11	26	0	217	24	2	.992
—New York (N.L.)■	C	28	68	6	11	3	0	0	9	.162	10	8	0	191	21	3	.986
1991—New York (N.L.)	C	69	168	16	31	6	0	2	14	.185	17	25	0	396	37	4	.991
1992—New York (N.L.)	C	68	156	15	33	12	0	2	13	.212	16	18	0	287	44	7	.979
1993—New York (N.L.)	C	67	188	15	48	11	0	4	23	.255	14	14	1	325	39	5	.986
1994—Atlanta (N.L.)■	C	51	152	24	37	11	0	8	28	.243	15	24	0	308	26	3	.991
1995—Atlanta (N.L.)	C	67	198	18	45	7	0	9	23	.227	29	40	0	446	23	4	.992
American League totals (5 years)		174	497	50	107	27	3	8	56	.215	44	60	0	842	91	10	.989
National League totals (6 years)		350	930	94	205	50	0	25	110	.220	101	129	1	1953	190	26	.988
Major league totals (10 years)		524	1427	144	312	77	3	33	166	.219	145	189	1	2795	281	36	.988

DIVISION SERIES RECORD

Year Team (League)	Pos.	G	AB	R	H	2B	3B	HR	RBI	Avg.	BB	SO	SB	PO	A	E	Avg.
			BATTING											FIELDING			
1995—Atlanta (N.L.)	C	2	5	0	1	0	0	0	0	.200	1	1	0	8	1	0	1.000

CHAMPIONSHIP SERIES RECORD

			BATTING											FIELDING			
Year	Team (League)	Pos.	G	AB	R	H	2B	3B	HR	RBI	Avg.	BB	SO	SB	PO	A	E	Avg.
1995—	Atlanta (N.L.)	C-PH	2	5	1	2	0	0	1	3	.400	0	1	0	3	1	0	1.000

WORLD SERIES RECORD

NOTES: Member of World Series championship team (1995).

			BATTING											FIELDING			
Year	Team (League)	Pos.	G	AB	R	H	2B	3B	HR	RBI	Avg.	BB	SO	SB	PO	A	E	Avg.
1995—	Atlanta (N.L.)	C	2	3	0	0	0	0	0	0	.000	0	0	0	7	2	0	1.000

OCHOA, ALEX — OF — METS

PERSONAL: Born March 29, 1972, in Miami Lakes, Fla. . . . 6-0/185. . . . Bats right, throws right. . . . Full name: Alex Ochoa.
HIGH SCHOOL: Hialeah (Fla.) Miami Lakes.
TRANSACTIONS/CAREER NOTES: Selected by Baltimore Orioles organization in third round of free-agent draft (June 3, 1991). . . . Traded by Orioles with OF Damon Buford to New York Mets for 3B/OF Bobby Bonilla and a player to be named later (July 28, 1995); Orioles acquired P Jimmy Williams to complete deal (August 17, 1995).
STATISTICAL NOTES: Led Carolina League in grounding into double plays with 15 in 1993. . . . Led Eastern League with 12 sacrifice flies in 1994. . . . Tied for Eastern League lead in double plays by outfielder with five in 1994. . . . Led International League outfielders with 249 putouts and 266 total chances in 1995.

			BATTING											FIELDING			
Year	Team (League)	Pos.	G	AB	R	H	2B	3B	HR	RBI	Avg.	BB	SO	SB	PO	A	E	Avg.
1991—	GC Orioles (GCL)	OF	53	179	26	55	8	3	1	30	.307	16	14	11	45	3	2	.960
1992—	Kane Co. (Midw.)	OF	133	499	65	147	22	7	1	59	.295	58	55	31	225	•17	•12	.953
1993—	Frederick (Caro.)	OF	137	532	84	147	29	5	13	90	.276	46	67	34	169	13	11	.943
1994—	Bowie (Eastern)	OF	134	519	77	156	25	2	14	82	.301	49	67	28	237	*22	6	.977
1995—	Rochester (Int'l)	OF	91	336	41	92	18	2	8	46	.274	26	50	17	183	9	5	.975
—	Norfolk (Int'l)■	OF	34	123	17	38	6	2	2	15	.309	14	12	7	§66	1	2	.971
—	New York (N.L.)	OF	11	37	7	11	1	0	0	0	.297	2	10	1	20	1	0	1.000
Major league totals (1 year)			11	37	7	11	1	0	0	0	.297	2	10	1	20	1	0	1.000

OFFERMAN, JOSE — SS — ROYALS

PERSONAL: Born November 8, 1968, in San Pedro de Macoris, Dominican Republic. . . . 6-0/190. . . . Bats both, throws right. . . . Full name: Jose Antonio Dono Offerman.
HIGH SCHOOL: Colegio Biblico Cristiano (Dominican Republic).
TRANSACTIONS/CAREER NOTES: Signed as non-drafted free agent by Los Angeles Dodgers organization (July 24, 1986). . . . Traded by Dodgers to Kansas City Royals for P Billy Brewer (December 17, 1995).
HONORS: Named Minor League Player of the Year by THE SPORTING NEWS (1990). . . . Named Pacific Coast League Player of the Year (1990).
STATISTICAL NOTES: Tied for Pioneer League lead in caught stealing with 10 in 1988. . . . Tied for Pacific Coast League lead in caught stealing with 18 in 1990. . . . Led Pacific Coast League shortstops with 36 errors in 1990. . . . Hit home run in first major league at-bat (August 19, 1990). . . . Led N.L. with 25 sacrifice hits in 1993.

			BATTING											FIELDING			
Year	Team (League)	Pos.	G	AB	R	H	2B	3B	HR	RBI	Avg.	BB	SO	SB	PO	A	E	Avg.
1987—			Dominican Summer League statistics unavailable.															
1988—	Great Falls (Pio.)	SS	60	251	75	83	11	5	2	28	.331	38	42	*57	82	143	18	*.926
1989—	Bakersfield (Calif.)	SS	62	245	53	75	9	4	2	22	.306	35	48	37	94	179	30	.901
—	San Antonio (Tex.)	SS	68	278	47	80	6	3	2	22	.288	40	39	32	106	168	20	.932
1990—	Albuquerque (PCL)	SS-2B	117	454	104	148	16	11	0	56	.326	71	81	*60	174	361	†36	.937
—	Los Angeles (N.L.)	SS	29	58	7	9	0	0	1	7	.155	4	14	1	30	40	4	.946
1991—	Albuquerque (PCL)	SS	79	289	58	86	8	4	0	29	.298	47	58	32	126	241	17	.956
—	Los Angeles (N.L.)	SS	52	113	10	22	2	0	0	3	.195	25	32	3	50	121	10	.945
1992—	Los Angeles (N.L.)	SS	149	534	67	139	20	8	1	30	.260	57	98	23	208	398	*42	.935
1993—	Los Angeles (N.L.)	SS	158	590	77	159	21	6	1	62	.269	71	75	30	250	454	*37	.950
1994—	Los Angeles (N.L.)	SS	72	243	27	51	8	4	1	25	.210	38	38	2	123	195	11	.967
—	Albuquerque (PCL)	SS	56	224	43	74	7	5	1	31	.330	37	48	9	91	196	13	.957
1995—	Los Angeles (N.L.)	SS	119	429	69	123	14	6	4	33	.287	69	67	2	165	312	*35	.932
Major league totals (6 years)			579	1967	257	503	65	24	8	160	.256	264	324	61	826	1520	139	.944

DIVISION SERIES RECORD

			BATTING											FIELDING			
Year	Team (League)	Pos.	G	AB	R	H	2B	3B	HR	RBI	Avg.	BB	SO	SB	PO	A	E	Avg.
1995—	Los Angeles (N.L.)	PR	1	0	0	0	0	0	0	0	...	0	0	0	...	...	...	...

ALL-STAR GAME RECORD

			BATTING										FIELDING			
Year	League	Pos.	AB	R	H	2B	3B	HR	RBI	Avg.	BB	SO	SB	PO	A	E	Avg.
1995—	National	SS	0	0	0	0	0	0	0	...	0	0	0	0	0	0	...

OGDEN, JAMIE — OF — TWINS

PERSONAL: Born January 19, 1972, in South St. Paul, Minn. . . . 6-5/233. . . . Bats left, throws left. . . . Full name: Jamie Ogden.
HIGH SCHOOL: White Bear Lake (Minn.).
TRANSACTIONS/CAREER NOTES: Selected by Minnesota Twins organization in third round of free-agent draft (June 4, 1990); pick recieved as part of compensation for Pittsburgh Pirates signing Type C free-agent 2B Wally Backman.

Year	Team (League)	Pos.	G	AB	R	H	2B	3B	HR	RBI	Avg.	BB	SO	SB	PO	A	E	Avg.
				BATTING											FIELDING			
1990—	GC Twins (GCL)	1B	28	101	11	20	1	2	0	5	.198	7	41	2	199	19	5	.978
1991—	GC Twins (GCL)	1B-OF	37	122	22	39	9	•7	2	25	.320	11	30	8	257	12	6	.978
1992—	Kenosha (Midwest)	OF	108	372	36	91	14	3	3	51	.245	52	108	9	126	7	6	.957
1993—	Fort Myers (FSL)	OF	118	396	37	96	22	4	8	46	.242	34	89	7	217	16	7	.971
1994—	Fort Myers (FSL)	OF	69	251	32	66	12	0	7	22	.263	16	52	12	74	4	2	.975
1995—	New Britain (East.)	OF	117	384	54	109	22	1	13	61	.284	48	90	6	660	44	9	.987

OGEA, CHAD — P — INDIANS

PERSONAL: Born November 9, 1970, in Lake Charles, La. . . . 6-2/200. . . . Throws right, bats left. . . . Full name: Chad Wayne Ogea. . . . Name pronounced OH-jay.
HIGH SCHOOL: St. Louis (Lake Charles, La.).
COLLEGE: Louisiana State.
TRANSACTIONS/CAREER NOTES: Selected by Cleveland Indians organization in third round of free-agent draft (June 3, 1991).
STATISTICAL NOTES: Led International League with 26 home runs allowed in 1993.

Year	Team (League)	W	L	Pct.	ERA	G	GS	CG	ShO	Sv.	IP	H	R	ER	BB	SO
1992—	Kinston (Carolina)	13	3	.813	3.49	21	21	•5	•2	0	139 1/3	135	61	54	29	123
—	Cant./Akr. (East.)	6	1	.857	2.20	7	7	1	1	0	49	38	12	12	12	40
1993—	Charlotte (Int'l)	•13	8	.619	3.82	29	•29	0	0	0	181 1/3	169	91	77	54	135
1994—	Charlotte (Int'l)	9	10	.474	3.85	24	23	6	0	1	163 2/3	146	80	70	34	113
—	Cleveland (A.L.)	0	1	.000	6.06	4	1	0	0	0	16 1/3	21	11	11	10	11
1995—	Buffalo (A.A.)	0	1	.000	4.58	4	4	0	0	0	17 2/3	16	12	9	8	11
—	Cleveland (A.L.)	8	3	.727	3.05	20	14	1	0	0	106 1/3	95	38	36	29	57
Major league totals (2 years)		8	4	.667	3.45	24	15	1	0	0	122 2/3	116	49	47	39	68

CHAMPIONSHIP SERIES RECORD

Year	Team (League)	W	L	Pct.	ERA	G	GS	CG	ShO	Sv.	IP	H	R	ER	BB	SO
1995—	Cleveland (A.L.)	0	0	...	0.00	1	0	0	0	0	2/3	1	0	0	0	2

OJALA, KIRT — P — YANKEES

PERSONAL: Born December 24, 1968, in Kalamazoo, Mich. . . . 6-2/210. . . . Throws left, bats left. . . . Full name: Kirt Stanley Ojala. . . . Name pronounced oh-JAH-la.
HIGH SCHOOL: Portage (Mich.) Central.
COLLEGE: Michigan.
TRANSACTIONS/CAREER NOTES: Selected by New York Yankees organization in fourth round of free-agent draft (June 4, 1990). . . . On disabled list (April 9-23, 1992). . . . Selected by Oakland Athletics from Yankees organization in Rule 5 major league draft (December 7, 1992). . . . Returned to Yankees organization (March 27, 1993).

Year	Team (League)	W	L	Pct.	ERA	G	GS	CG	ShO	Sv.	IP	H	R	ER	BB	SO
1990—	Oneonta (NYP)	7	2	.778	2.16	14	14	1	0	0	79	75	28	19	43	87
1991—	Prin. William (Caro.)	8	7	.533	2.53	25	23	1	0	0	156 2/3	120	52	44	61	112
1992—	Alb./Colon. (East.)	12	8	.600	3.62	24	23	2	1	0	151 2/3	130	71	61	•80	116
1993—	Columbus (Int'l)	8	9	.471	5.50	31	20	0	0	0	126	145	85	77	71	83
—	Alb./Colon. (East.)	1	0	1.000	0.00	1	1	0	0	0	6 1/3	5	0	0	2	6
1994—	Columbus (Int'l)	11	7	.611	3.83	25	23	1	1	0	148	157	78	63	46	81
1995—	Columbus (Int'l)	8	7	.533	3.95	32	20	0	0	1	145 2/3	138	74	64	54	107

O'LEARY, TROY — OF — RED SOX

PERSONAL: Born August 4, 1969, in Compton, Calif. . . . 6-0/196. . . . Bats left, throws left. . . . Full name: Troy Franklin O'Leary.
HIGH SCHOOL: Cypress (Calif.).
TRANSACTIONS/CAREER NOTES: Selected by Milwaukee Brewers organization in 13th round of free-agent draft (June 2, 1987). . . . Claimed on waivers by Boston Red Sox (April 14, 1995).
HONORS: Named Texas League Most Valuable Player (1992).
STATISTICAL NOTES: Led Pioneer League with 144 total bases in 1989. . . . Led Texas League with 227 total bases and .399 on-base percentage in 1992. . . . Led Texas League outfielders with 242 total chances in 1992.

Year	Team (League)	Pos.	G	AB	R	H	2B	3B	HR	RBI	Avg.	BB	SO	SB	PO	A	E	Avg.
				BATTING											FIELDING			
1987—	Helena (Pioneer)	OF	3	5	0	2	0	0	0	1	.400	0	0	0	0	0	0	...
1988—	Helena (Pioneer)	OF	67	203	40	70	11	1	0	27	.345	30	32	10	64	4	3	.958
1989—	Beloit (Midwest)	OF	42	115	7	21	4	0	0	8	.183	15	20	1	55	1	1	.982
—	Helena (Pioneer)	OF	•68	263	54	*89	16	3	11	*56	.338	28	43	9	92	6	3	.970
1990—	Beloit (Midwest)	OF	118	436	73	130	29	1	6	62	.298	41	90	12	184	14	8	.961
—	Stockton (Calif.)	OF	2	6	1	3	1	0	0	0	.500	2	1	0	3	0	1	.750
1991—	Stockton (Calif.)	OF	126	418	63	110	20	4	5	46	.263	73	96	4	163	4	3	.982
1992—	El Paso (Texas)	OF	*135	*506	*92	*169	27	8	5	79	*.334	59	87	28	*220	11	*11	.955
1993—	New Orleans (A.A.)	OF-1B	111	388	65	106	32	1	7	59	.273	43	61	6	189	8	6	.970
—	Milwaukee (A.L.)	OF	19	41	3	12	3	0	0	3	.293	5	9	0	32	1	0	1.000
1994—	New Orleans (A.A.)	OF-1B	63	225	44	74	18	5	8	43	.329	32	37	10	99	10	2	.982
—	Milwaukee (A.L.)	OF-DH	27	66	9	18	1	1	2	7	.273	5	12	1	37	2	0	1.000
1995—	Boston (A.L.)■	OF-DH	112	399	60	123	31	6	10	49	.308	29	64	5	196	6	5	.976
Major league totals (3 years)			158	506	72	153	35	7	12	59	.302	39	85	6	265	9	5	.982

O

OLERUD, JOHN 1B BLUE JAYS

PERSONAL: Born August 5, 1968, in Seattle. . . . 6-5/218. . . . Bats left, throws left. . . . Full name: John Garrett Olerud. . . . Son of John E. Olerud, minor league catcher (1965-70). . . . Name pronounced OH-luh-rude.
HIGH SCHOOL: Interlake (Bellevue, Wash.).
COLLEGE: Washington State.
TRANSACTIONS/CAREER NOTES: Selected by New York Mets organization in 27th round of free-agent draft (June 2, 1986); did not sign. . . . Selected by Toronto Blue Jays organization in third round of free-agent draft (June 5, 1989).
RECORDS: Shares A.L. single-season records for most intentional bases on balls received—33 (1993); and most intentional bases on balls received by lefthanded hitter—33 (1993).
STATISTICAL NOTES: Tied for A.L. lead with 10 sacrifice flies in 1991. . . . Led A.L. with 33 intentional bases on balls received and .473 on-base percentage in 1993. . . . Career major league grand slams: 1.

		BATTING												FIELDING			
Year Team (League)	**Pos.**	**G**	**AB**	**R**	**H**	**2B**	**3B**	**HR**	**RBI**	**Avg.**	**BB**	**SO**	**SB**	**PO**	**A**	**E**	**Avg.**
1989—Toronto (A.L.)	1B-DH	6	8	2	3	0	0	0	0	.375	0	1	0	19	2	0	1.000
1990—Toronto (A.L.)	DH-1B	111	358	43	95	15	1	14	48	.265	57	75	0	133	10	2	.986
1991—Toronto (A.L.)	1B-DH	139	454	64	116	30	1	17	68	.256	68	84	0	1120	78	5	.996
1992—Toronto (A.L.)	1B-DH	138	458	68	130	28	0	16	66	.284	70	61	1	1057	81	7	.994
1993—Toronto (A.L.)	1B-DH	158	551	109	200	*54	2	24	107	*.363	114	65	0	1160	97	10	.992
1994—Toronto (A.L.)	1B-DH	108	384	47	114	29	2	12	67	.297	61	53	1	824	68	6	.993
1995—Toronto (A.L.)	1B	135	492	72	143	32	0	8	54	.291	84	54	0	1099	89	4	.997
Major league totals (7 years)		795	2705	405	801	188	6	91	410	.296	454	393	2	5412	425	34	.994

CHAMPIONSHIP SERIES RECORD

		BATTING												FIELDING			
Year Team (League)	**Pos.**	**G**	**AB**	**R**	**H**	**2B**	**3B**	**HR**	**RBI**	**Avg.**	**BB**	**SO**	**SB**	**PO**	**A**	**E**	**Avg.**
1991—Toronto (A.L.)	1B	5	19	1	3	0	0	0	3	.158	3	1	0	40	3	0	1.000
1992—Toronto (A.L.)	1B	6	23	4	8	2	0	1	4	.348	2	5	0	51	1	0	1.000
1993—Toronto (A.L.)	1B	6	23	5	8	1	0	0	3	.348	4	1	0	48	9	1	.983
Championship series totals (3 years)		17	65	10	19	3	0	1	10	.292	9	7	0	139	13	1	.993

WORLD SERIES RECORD

NOTES: Member of World Series championship teams (1992 and 1993).

		BATTING												FIELDING			
Year Team (League)	**Pos.**	**G**	**AB**	**R**	**H**	**2B**	**3B**	**HR**	**RBI**	**Avg.**	**BB**	**SO**	**SB**	**PO**	**A**	**E**	**Avg.**
1992—Toronto (A.L.)	1B	4	13	2	4	0	0	0	0	.308	0	4	0	25	3	0	1.000
1993—Toronto (A.L.)	1B	5	17	5	4	1	0	1	2	.235	4	1	0	36	0	0	1.000
World Series totals (2 years)		9	30	7	8	1	0	1	2	.267	4	5	0	61	3	0	1.000

ALL-STAR GAME RECORD

		BATTING											FIELDING			
Year League	**Pos.**	**AB**	**R**	**H**	**2B**	**3B**	**HR**	**RBI**	**Avg.**	**BB**	**SO**	**SB**	**PO**	**A**	**E**	**Avg.**
1993—American	1B	2	0	0	0	0	0	0	.000	0	0	0	4	0	0	1.000

OLIVA, JOSE 3B CARDINALS

PERSONAL: Born March 3, 1971, in San Pedro de Macoris, Dominican Republic. . . . 6-3/215. . . . Bats right, throws right. . . . Full name: Jose Galvez Oliva.
TRANSACTIONS/CAREER NOTES: Signed as non-drafted free agent by Texas Rangers organization (November 12, 1987). . . . On Charlotte disabled list (July 16-25, 1991). . . . Traded by Rangers organization to Atlanta Braves organization for P Charlie Leibrandt and P Pat Gomez (December 9, 1992). . . . Traded by Braves to St. Louis Cardinals for OF Anton French (August 25, 1995).
STATISTICAL NOTES: Led Texas League third basemen with 328 total chances and tied for lead with 15 double plays in 1992.

		BATTING												FIELDING			
Year Team (League)	**Pos.**	**G**	**AB**	**R**	**H**	**2B**	**3B**	**HR**	**RBI**	**Avg.**	**BB**	**SO**	**SB**	**PO**	**A**	**E**	**Avg.**
1988—GC Rangers (GCL)	SS	27	70	5	15	3	0	1	11	.214	3	14	0	16	43	6	.908
1989—Butte (Pioneer)	SS-3B	41	114	18	24	2	3	4	13	.211	14	41	4	38	94	15	.898
1990—Gastonia (S. Atl.)	SS-3B-2B	120	387	43	81	25	1	10	52	.209	26	104	9	163	284	44	.910
1991—Charlotte (Fla. St.)	3B-SS	108	383	55	92	17	4	•14	59	.240	44	108	9	79	154	16	.936
—GC Rangers (GCL)	3B	3	11	0	1	1	0	0	1	.091	2	3	0	4	3	0	1.000
1992—Tulsa (Texas)	3B	124	445	57	120	28	6	16	75	.270	40	135	4	*75	*225	28	.915
1993—Richmond (Int'l)■	3B-SS	125	412	63	97	20	6	21	65	.235	35	134	1	44	206	19	.929
1994—Richmond (Int'l)	3B	99	371	52	94	17	0	24	64	.253	25	92	2	40	217	14	.948
—Atlanta (N.L.)	3B	19	59	9	17	5	0	6	11	.288	7	10	0	9	32	3	.932
1995—Atlanta (N.L.)	3B-1B	48	109	7	17	4	0	5	12	.156	7	22	0	14	41	6	.902
—St. Louis (N.L.)■	3B-1B	22	74	8	9	1	0	2	8	.122	5	24	0	27	32	1	.983
Major league totals (2 years)		89	242	24	43	10	0	13	31	.178	19	56	0	50	105	10	.939

OLIVARES, OMAR P TIGERS

PERSONAL: Born July 6, 1967, in Mayaguez, Puerto Rico. . . . 6-1/193. . . . Throws right, bats right. . . . Full name: Omar Palqu Olivares. . . . Son of Ed Olivares, outfielder, St. Louis Cardinals (1960-61).
HIGH SCHOOL: Hostos (Mayaguez, Puerto Rico).
TRANSACTIONS/CAREER NOTES: Signed as non-drafted free agent by San Diego Padres organization (September 15, 1986). . . . Traded by Padres organization to St. Louis Cardinals for OF Alex Cole and P Steve Peters (February 27, 1990). . . . On St. Louis disabled list (May 27-June 13, 1992 and June 4-20, 1993). . . . Granted free agency (April 7, 1995). . . . Signed by Colorado Rockies (April 9, 1995). . . . Claimed on waivers by Philadelphia Phillies (July 11, 1995). . . . Granted free agency (October 16, 1995). . . . Signed by Detroit Tigers (December 20, 1995).

RECORDS: Shares major league single-season record for fewest double plays by pitcher who led league in double plays—4 (1992).
STATISTICAL NOTES: Tied for Texas League lead with 10 hit batsmen in 1989.
MISCELLANEOUS: Appeared in one game as pinch-runner and singled and scored in three games as pinch-hitter (1992). . . . Appeared in one game as pinch-runner and made an out in one game as pinch-hitter (1993). . . . Made an out in one game as pinch-hitter with St. Louis (1994). . . . Appeared in one game as pinch runner with Colorado (1995). . . . Hit two-run home run in only game as pinch-hitter with Philadelphia (1995).

Year	Team (League)	W	L	Pct.	ERA	G	GS	CG	ShO	Sv.	IP	H	R	ER	BB	SO
1987—	Char., S.C. (S. Atl.)	4	14	.222	4.60	31	24	5	0	0	170 1/3	182	107	87	57	86
1988—	Char., S.C. (S. Atl.)	13	6	.684	2.23	24	24	*10	3	0	185 1/3	166	63	46	43	94
—	Riverside (Calif.)	3	0	1.000	1.16	4	3	1	0	0	23 1/3	18	9	3	9	16
1989—	Wichita (Texas)	12	11	.522	3.39	26	26	6	1	0	*185 2/3	175	87	70	61	79
1990—	Louisville (A.A.)■	10	11	.476	2.82	23	23	5	2	0	159 1/3	127	58	50	59	88
—	St. Louis (N.L.)	1	1	.500	2.92	9	6	0	0	0	49 1/3	45	17	16	17	20
1991—	St. Louis (N.L.)	11	7	.611	3.71	28	24	0	0	1	167 1/3	148	72	69	61	91
—	Louisville (A.A.)	1	2	.333	3.47	6	6	0	0	0	36 1/3	39	15	14	16	27
1992—	St. Louis (N.L.)	9	9	.500	3.84	32	30	1	0	0	197	189	84	84	63	124
1993—	St. Louis (N.L.)	5	3	.625	4.17	58	9	0	0	1	118 2/3	134	60	55	54	63
1994—	Louisville (A.A.)	2	1	.667	4.37	9	9	0	0	0	47 1/3	47	24	23	16	38
—	St. Louis (N.L.)	3	4	.429	5.74	14	12	1	0	1	73 2/3	84	53	47	37	26
1995—	Colo. Springs (PCL)■	0	1	.000	5.40	3	2	0	0	0	11 2/3	14	7	7	2	6
—	Colorado (N.L.)	1	3	.250	7.39	11	6	0	0	0	31 2/3	44	28	26	21	15
—	Philadelphia (N.L.)■	0	1	.000	5.40	5	0	0	0	0	10	11	6	6	2	7
—	Scran./W.B. (Int'l)	0	3	.000	4.87	7	7	0	0	0	44 1/3	49	25	24	20	28
Major league totals (6 years)		30	28	.517	4.21	157	87	2	0	3	647 2/3	655	320	303	255	346

OLIVER, DARREN P RANGERS

PERSONAL: Born October 6, 1970, in Kansas City, Mo. . . . 6-2/200. . . . Throws left, bats right. . . . Full name: Darren Christopher Oliver. . . . Son of Bob Oliver, major league first baseman/outfielder with five teams (1965 and 1969-75).
HIGH SCHOOL: Rio Linda (Calif.) Senior.
TRANSACTIONS/CAREER NOTES: Selected by Texas Rangers organization in third round of free-agent draft (June 1, 1988). . . . On Gulf Coast disabled list (April 6-August 9, 1990). . . . On disabled list (May 1, 1991-remainder of season). . . . On Tulsa disabled list (July 1, 1992-remainder of season). . . . On disabled list (June 27, 1995-remainder of season).

Year	Team (League)	W	L	Pct.	ERA	G	GS	CG	ShO	Sv.	IP	H	R	ER	BB	SO
1988—	GC Rangers (GCL)	5	1	.833	2.15	12	9	0	0	0	54 1/3	39	16	13	18	59
1989—	Gastonia (S. Atl.)	8	7	.533	3.16	24	23	2	1	0	122 1/3	86	54	43	82	108
1990—	GC Rangers (GCL)	0	0	...	0.00	3	3	0	0	0	6	1	1	0	1	7
—	Gastonia (S. Atl.)	0	0	...	13.50	1	1	0	0	0	2	1	3	3	4	2
1991—	Charlotte (Fla. St.)	0	1	.000	4.50	2	2	0	0	0	8	6	4	4	3	12
1992—	Charlotte (Fla. St.)	1	0	1.000	0.72	8	2	1	1	2	25	11	2	2	10	33
—	Tulsa (Texas)	0	1	.000	3.14	3	3	0	0	0	14 1/3	15	9	5	4	14
1993—	Tulsa (Texas)	7	5	.583	1.96	46	0	0	0	6	73 1/3	51	18	16	41	77
—	Texas (A.L.)	0	0	...	2.70	2	0	0	0	0	3 1/3	2	1	1	1	4
1994—	Texas (A.L.)	4	0	1.000	3.42	43	0	0	0	2	50	40	24	19	35	50
—	Okla. City (A.A.)	0	0	...	0.00	6	0	0	0	1	7 1/3	1	0	0	3	6
1995—	Texas (A.L.)	4	2	.667	4.22	17	7	0	0	0	49	47	25	23	32	39
Major league totals (3 years)		8	2	.800	3.78	62	7	0	0	2	102 1/3	89	50	43	68	93

OLIVER, JOE C

PERSONAL: Born July 24, 1965, in Memphis, Tenn. . . . 6-3/220. . . . Bats right, throws right. . . . Full name: Joseph Melton Oliver.
HIGH SCHOOL: Boone (Orlando, Fla.).
TRANSACTIONS/CAREER NOTES: Selected by Cincinnati Reds organization in second round of free-agent draft (June 6, 1983); pick received as compensation for New York Yankees signing Type A free-agent P Bob Shirley. . . . On disabled list (April 23-May 6, 1986 and April 12, 1994-remainder of season). . . . Released by Reds (November 3, 1994). . . . Signed by New Orleans, Milwaukee Brewers organization (March 24, 1995). . . . On Milwaukee disabled list (July 14-August 15, 1995); included rehabilitation assignment to New Orleans (August 10-15). . . . Granted free agency (October 31, 1995).
STATISTICAL NOTES: Led Pioneer League catchers with .989 fielding percentage, 425 putouts, 38 assists and 468 total chances in 1983. . . . Led Midwest League catchers with 855 total chances and 30 passed balls in 1984. . . . Led Florida State League catchers with 84 assists and 33 passed balls in 1985. . . . Led American Association catchers with 13 errors in 1989. . . . Tied for N.L. lead with 16 passed balls in 1990. . . . Led N.L. catchers with 925 putouts and 997 total chances in 1992. . . . Career major league grand slams: 3.

			BATTING												FIELDING			
Year	Team (League)	Pos.	G	AB	R	H	2B	3B	HR	RBI	Avg.	BB	SO	SB	PO	A	E	Avg.
1983—	Billings (Pioneer)	C-1B	56	186	21	40	4	0	4	28	.215	15	47	1	†426	†39	5	†.989
1984—	Ced. Rap. (Midw.)	C	102	335	34	73	11	0	3	29	.218	17	83	2	*757	85	13	.985
1985—	Tampa (Fla. St.)	C-1B	112	386	38	104	23	2	7	62	.269	32	75	1	615	†94	16	.978
1986—	Vermont (Eastern)	C	84	282	32	78	18	1	6	41	.277	21	47	2	383	62	14	.969
1987—	Vermont (Eastern)	C-1B	66	236	31	72	13	2	10	60	.305	17	30	0	247	35	10	.966
1988—	Nashville (A.A.)	C	73	220	19	45	7	2	4	24	.205	18	39	0	413	37	7	.985
—	Chatt. (South.)	C	28	105	9	26	6	0	3	12	.248	5	19	0	176	15	0	1.000
1989—	Nashville (A.A.)	C-1B	71	233	22	68	13	0	6	31	.292	13	35	0	388	37	†13	.970
—	Cincinnati (N.L.)	C	49	151	13	41	8	0	3	23	.272	6	28	0	260	21	4	.986
1990—	Cincinnati (N.L.)	C	121	364	34	84	23	0	8	52	.231	37	75	1	686	59	6	*.992
1991—	Cincinnati (N.L.)	C	94	269	21	58	11	0	11	41	.216	18	53	0	496	40	11	.980
1992—	Cincinnati (N.L.)	C-1B	143	485	42	131	25	1	10	57	.270	35	75	2	†926	64	8	.992
1993—	Cincinnati (N.L.)	C-1B-OF	139	482	40	115	28	0	14	75	.239	27	91	0	825	70	7	.992
1994—	Cincinnati (N.L.)	C	6	19	1	4	0	0	1	5	.211	2	3	0	48	2	1	.980
1995—	Milwaukee (A.L.)■	C-DH-1B	97	337	43	92	20	0	12	51	.273	27	66	2	414	40	8	.983
—	New Orleans (A.A.)	C	4	13	0	1	1	0	0	0	.077	0	3	0	14	7	0	1.000
American League totals (1 year)			97	337	43	92	20	0	12	51	.273	27	66	2	414	40	8	.983
National League totals (6 years)			552	1770	151	433	95	1	47	253	.245	125	325	3	3241	256	37	.990
Major league totals (7 years)			649	2107	194	525	115	1	59	304	.249	152	391	5	3655	296	45	.989

CHAMPIONSHIP SERIES RECORD

			BATTING											FIELDING			
Year Team (League)	Pos.	G	AB	R	H	2B	3B	HR	RBI	Avg.	BB	SO	SB	PO	A	E	Avg.
1990— Cincinnati (N.L.)	C	5	14	1	2	0	0	0	0	.143	0	2	0	27	1	0	1.000

WORLD SERIES RECORD

NOTES: Member of World Series championship team (1990).

			BATTING											FIELDING			
Year Team (League)	Pos.	G	AB	R	H	2B	3B	HR	RBI	Avg.	BB	SO	SB	PO	A	E	Avg.
1990— Cincinnati (N.L.)	C	4	18	2	6	3	0	0	2	.333	0	1	0	27	1	3	.903

OLSON, GREGG — P — CARDINALS

PERSONAL: Born October 11, 1966, in Omaha, Neb. . . . 6-4/212. . . . Throws right, bats right. . . . Full name: Gregg William Olson.
HIGH SCHOOL: Northwest (Omaha, Neb.).
COLLEGE: Auburn.
TRANSACTIONS/CAREER NOTES: Selected by Baltimore Orioles organization in first round (fourth pick overall) of free-agent draft (June 1, 1988). . . . On disabled list (August 9-September 20, 1993). . . . Granted free agency (December 20, 1993). . . . Signed by Atlanta Braves (February 8, 1994). . . . On Atlanta disabled list (March 26-May 30, 1994); included rehabilitation assignment to Richmond (May 14-30). . . . Granted free agency (December 23, 1994). . . . Signed by Cleveland Indians organization (March 24, 1995). . . . On Buffalo disabled list (April 6-14, 1995). . . . Contract sold by Buffalo to Kansas City Royals (July 24, 1995). . . . Granted free agency (November 1, 1995). . . . Signed by St. Louis Cardinals organization (January 23, 1996).
RECORDS: Holds A.L. rookie-season record for most saves—27 (1989).
HONORS: Named righthanded pitcher on THE SPORTING NEWS college All-America team (1988). . . . Named A.L. Rookie of the Year by Baseball Writers' Association of America (1989).
STATISTICAL NOTES: Pitched one inning, combining with starter Bob Milacki (six innings), Mike Flanagan (one inning) and Mark Williamson (one inning) in 2-0 no-hit victory against Oakland (July 13, 1991).
MISCELLANEOUS: Struck out in only plate appearance (1993).

Year Team (League)	W	L	Pct.	ERA	G	GS	CG	ShO	Sv.	IP	H	R	ER	BB	SO
1988— Hagerstown (Caro.)	1	0	1.000	2.00	8	0	0	0	4	9	5	2	2	2	9
— Charlotte (South.)	0	1	.000	5.87	8	0	0	0	1	15 1/3	24	13	10	6	22
— Baltimore (A.L.)	1	1	.500	3.27	10	0	0	0	0	11	10	4	4	10	9
1989— Baltimore (A.L.)	5	2	.714	1.69	64	0	0	0	27	85	57	17	16	46	90
1990— Baltimore (A.L.)	6	5	.545	2.42	64	0	0	0	37	74 1/3	57	20	20	31	74
1991— Baltimore (A.L.)	4	6	.400	3.18	72	0	0	0	31	73 2/3	74	28	26	29	72
1992— Baltimore (A.L.)	1	5	.167	2.05	60	0	0	0	36	61 1/3	46	14	14	24	58
1993— Baltimore (A.L.)	0	2	.000	1.60	50	0	0	0	29	45	37	9	8	18	44
1994— Richmond (Int'l)■	0	0	. . .	1.59	8	2	0	0	2	11 1/3	8	3	2	8	13
— Atlanta (N.L.)	0	2	.000	9.20	16	0	0	0	1	14 2/3	19	15	15	13	10
1995— Buffalo (A.A.)■	1	0	1.000	2.49	18	0	0	0	13	21 2/3	16	6	6	9	25
— Cleveland (A.L.)	0	0	. . .	13.50	3	0	0	0	0	2 2/3	5	4	4	2	0
— Omaha (Am. Assoc.)■	0	0	. . .	0.00	1	0	0	0	0	1	0	0	0	1	1
— Kansas City (A.L.)	3	3	.500	3.26	20	0	0	0	3	30 1/3	23	11	11	17	21
A.L. totals (7 years)	20	24	.455	2.42	343	0	0	0	163	383 1/3	309	107	103	177	368
N.L. totals (1 year)	0	2	.000	9.20	16	0	0	0	1	14 2/3	19	15	15	13	10
Major league totals (8 years)	20	26	.435	2.67	359	0	0	0	164	398	328	122	118	190	378

ALL-STAR GAME RECORD

Year League	W	L	Pct.	ERA	GS	CG	ShO	Sv.	IP	H	R	ER	BB	SO
1990— American						Did not play.								

O'NEILL, PAUL — OF — YANKEES

PERSONAL: Born February 25, 1963, in Columbus, O. . . . 6-4/215. . . . Bats left, throws left. . . . Full name: Paul Andrew O'Neill. . . . Son of Charles O'Neill, minor league pitcher (1945-48).
HIGH SCHOOL: Brookhaven (Columbus, O.).
COLLEGE: Otterbein College (O.).
TRANSACTIONS/CAREER NOTES: Selected by Cincinnati Reds organization in fourth round of free-agent draft (June 8, 1981). . . . On disabled list (May 10-July 16, 1986). . . . On Cincinnati disabled list (July 21-September 1, 1989); included rehabilitation assignment to Nashville (August 27-September 1). . . . Traded by Reds with 1B Joe DeBerry to New York Yankees for OF Roberto Kelly (November 3, 1992). . . . On disabled list (May 7-23, 1995).
STATISTICAL NOTES: Led American Association outfielders with 19 assists and eight double plays in 1985. . . . Hit three home runs in one game (August 31, 1995). . . . Career major league grand slams: 2.

			BATTING											FIELDING			
Year Team (League)	Pos.	G	AB	R	H	2B	3B	HR	RBI	Avg.	BB	SO	SB	PO	A	E	Avg.
1981— Billings (Pioneer)	OF	66	241	37	76	7	2	3	29	.315	21	35	6	87	4	5	.948
1982— Ced. Rap. (Midw.)	OF	116	386	50	105	19	2	8	71	.272	21	79	12	137	7	8	.947
1983— Tampa (Fla. St.)	OF-1B	121	413	62	115	23	7	8	51	.278	56	70	20	218	14	10	.959
— Waterbury (East.)	OF	14	43	6	12	0	0	0	6	.279	6	8	2	26	0	0	1.000
1984— Vermont (Eastern)	OF	134	475	70	126	31	5	16	76	.265	52	72	29	246	5	7	.973
1985— Denver (A.A.)	OF-1B	*137	*509	63	*155	*32	3	7	74	.305	28	73	5	248	†20	7	.975
— Cincinnati (N.L.)	OF	5	12	1	4	1	0	0	1	.333	0	2	0	3	1	0	1.000
1986— Cincinnati (N.L.)	PH	3	2	0	0	0	0	0	0	.000	1	1	0	. . .	. . .	. . .	. . .
— Denver (A.A.)	OF	55	193	20	49	9	2	5	27	.254	9	28	1	98	7	4	.963
1987— Cincinnati (N.L.)	OF-1B-P	84	160	24	41	14	1	7	28	.256	18	29	2	90	2	4	.958
— Nashville (A.A.)	OF	11	37	12	11	0	0	3	6	.297	5	5	1	19	1	0	1.000
1988— Cincinnati (N.L.)	OF-1B	145	485	58	122	25	3	16	73	.252	38	65	8	410	13	6	.986
1989— Cincinnati (N.L.)	OF	117	428	49	118	24	2	15	74	.276	46	64	20	223	7	4	.983
— Nashville (A.A.)	OF	4	12	1	4	0	0	0	0	.333	3	1	1	7	1	0	1.000
1990— Cincinnati (N.L.)	OF	145	503	59	136	28	0	16	78	.270	53	103	13	271	12	2	.993

Year	Team (League)	Pos.	G	AB	R	H	2B	3B	HR	RBI	Avg.	BB	SO	SB	PO	A	E	Avg.
			BATTING												FIELDING			
1991—	Cincinnati (N.L.)	OF	152	532	71	136	36	0	28	91	.256	73	107	12	301	13	2	.994
1992—	Cincinnati (N.L.)	OF	148	496	59	122	19	1	14	66	.246	77	85	6	291	12	1	*.997
1993—	New York (A.L.)■	OF-DH	141	498	71	155	34	1	20	75	.311	44	69	2	230	7	2	.992
1994—	New York (A.L.)	OF-DH	103	368	68	132	25	1	21	83	*.359	72	56	5	203	7	1	.995
1995—	New York (A.L.)	OF-DH	127	460	82	138	30	4	22	96	.300	71	76	1	220	3	3	.987
American League totals (3 years)			371	1326	221	425	89	6	63	254	.321	187	201	8	653	17	6	.991
National League totals (8 years)			799	2618	321	679	147	7	96	411	.259	306	456	61	1589	60	19	.989
Major league totals (11 years)			1170	3944	542	1104	236	13	159	665	.280	493	657	69	2242	77	25	.989

DIVISION SERIES RECORD

Year	Team (League)	Pos.	G	AB	R	H	2B	3B	HR	RBI	Avg.	BB	SO	SB	PO	A	E	Avg.
			BATTING												FIELDING			
1995—	New York (A.L.)	OF-PH	5	18	5	6	0	0	3	6	.333	5	5	0	13	0	0	1.000

CHAMPIONSHIP SERIES RECORD

Year	Team (League)	Pos.	G	AB	R	H	2B	3B	HR	RBI	Avg.	BB	SO	SB	PO	A	E	Avg.
			BATTING												FIELDING			
1990—	Cincinnati (N.L.)	OF	5	17	1	8	3	0	1	4	.471	1	1	1	9	2	0	1.000

WORLD SERIES RECORD

NOTES: Member of World Series championship team (1990).

Year	Team (League)	Pos.	G	AB	R	H	2B	3B	HR	RBI	Avg.	BB	SO	SB	PO	A	E	Avg.
			BATTING												FIELDING			
1990—	Cincinnati (N.L.)	OF	4	12	2	1	0	0	0	1	.083	5	2	1	11	0	0	1.000

ALL-STAR GAME RECORD

Year	League	Pos.	AB	R	H	2B	3B	HR	RBI	Avg.	BB	SO	SB	PO	A	E	Avg.
			BATTING											FIELDING			
1991—	National	OF	2	0	0	0	0	0	0	.000	0	1	0	0	0	0	...
1994—	American	PH	1	0	0	0	0	0	0	.000	0	0	0	...	...	...	...
1995—	American	OF	1	0	0	0	0	0	0	.000	0	0	0	0	0	0	...
All-Star Game totals (3 years)			4	0	0	0	0	0	0	.000	0	1	0	0	0	0	...

RECORD AS PITCHER

Year	Team (League)	W	L	Pct.	ERA	G	GS	CG	ShO	Sv.	IP	H	R	ER	BB	SO
1987—	Cincinnati (N.L.)	0	0	...	13.50	1	0	0	0	0	2	2	3	3	4	2

ONTIVEROS, STEVE — P

PERSONAL: Born March 5, 1961, in Tularosa, N.M. . . . 6-0/190. . . . Throws right, bats right. . . . Full name: Steven Ontiveros. . . . Name pronounced AHN-tih-VAIR-oss.

HIGH SCHOOL: St. Joseph (South Bend, Ind.).

COLLEGE: Michigan.

TRANSACTIONS/CAREER NOTES: Selected by Oakland Athletics organization in second round of free-agent draft (June 7, 1982). . . . On West Haven temporarily inactive list (July 27-August 6, 1982). . . . On disabled list (April 16-August 8, 1984). . . . On Tacoma disabled list (April 16-28, 1985). . . . On disabled list (July 24-September 14, 1986). . . . On Oakland disabled list (March 30-April 24, 1987); included rehabilitation assignment to Tacoma (April 21-24). . . . On disabled list (June 12-August 2 and August 3, 1988-remainder of season). . . . Released by A's (December 21, 1988). . . . Signed by Philadelphia Phillies organization (February 16, 1989). . . . On Philadelphia disabled list (April 20-June 6, 1989); included rehabilitation assignment to Scranton/Wilkes-Barre (May 14-22). . . . On Philadelphia disabled list (June 21, 1989-remainder of season); included rehabilitation assignment to Scranton/Wilkes-Barre (June 28). . . . On Philadelphia disabled list (March 30-September 8, 1990); included rehabilitation assignments to Clearwater (August 2-16) and Reading (August 17-19 and August 27-September 2). . . . On disabled list (March 29, 1991-entire season); included rehabilitation assignments to Scranton/Wilkes-Barre (April 28-May 15 and August 22-September 2). . . . Granted free agency (November 11, 1991). . . . Signed by Toledo, Detroit Tigers organization (February 28, 1992). . . . On Toledo disabled list (April 9-16, 1992). . . . Released by Toledo (April 16, 1992). . . . Signed by Portland, Minnesota Twins organization (April 5, 1993). . . . Traded by Twins organization to Seattle Mariners organization for OF Greg Shockey (August 10, 1993). . . . Granted free agency (October 8, 1993). . . . Signed by A's (January 31, 1994). . . . Granted free agency (October 24, 1994). . . . Re-signed by A's (April 11, 1995). . . . On disabled list (July 16-August 24, 1995). . . . Granted free agency (November 1, 1995).

STATISTICAL NOTES: Pitched 3-0 one-hit, complete-game victory against New York (May 27, 1995).

MISCELLANEOUS: Appeared in one game as pinch-runner (1986). . . . Appeared in two games as pinch-runner (1988).

Year	Team (League)	W	L	Pct.	ERA	G	GS	CG	ShO	Sv.	IP	H	R	ER	BB	SO
1982—	Medford (N'west)	1	0	1.000	0.00	4	0	0	0	0	8	3	0	0	4	9
—	West Haven (East.)	2	2	.500	6.33	16	2	0	0	0	27	34	26	19	12	28
1983—	Alb./Colon. (East.)	8	4	.667	3.75	32	13	5	0	5	129 2/3	131	62	54	36	91
1984—	Madison (Midwest)	3	1	.750	2.05	5	5	2	0	0	30 2/3	23	10	7	6	26
—	Tacoma (PCL)	1	1	.500	7.94	2	2	0	0	0	11 1/3	18	11	10	5	6
1985—	Tacoma (PCL)	3	0	1.000	2.94	15	0	0	0	2	33 2/3	26	13	11	21	30
—	Oakland (A.L.)	1	3	.250	1.93	39	0	0	0	8	74 2/3	45	17	16	19	36
1986—	Oakland (A.L.)	2	2	.500	4.71	46	0	0	0	10	72 2/3	72	40	38	25	54
1987—	Tacoma (PCL)	0	0	...	3.00	1	1	0	0	0	3	1	1	1	2	1
—	Oakland (A.L.)	10	8	.556	4.00	35	22	2	1	1	150 2/3	141	78	67	50	97
1988—	Oakland (A.L.)	3	4	.429	4.61	10	10	0	0	0	54 2/3	57	32	28	21	30
1989—	Philadelphia (N.L.)■	2	1	.667	3.82	6	5	0	0	0	30 2/3	34	15	13	15	12
—	Scran./W.B. (Int'l)	0	0	...	0.00	1	1	0	0	0	3 1/3	3	0	0	3	0
1990—	Clearwater (Fla. St.)	0	0	...	2.35	3	3	0	0	0	7 2/3	4	2	2	3	2
—	Reading (Eastern)	0	2	.000	9.00	2	2	0	0	0	6	7	6	6	2	8
—	Philadelphia (N.L.)	0	0	...	2.70	5	0	0	0	0	10	9	3	3	3	6
1991—	Scran./W.B. (Int'l)	2	1	.667	2.90	7	7	0	0	0	31	29	11	10	10	21
1992—								Did not play.								
1993—	Portland (PCL)■	7	6	.538	2.87	20	16	2	0	0	103 1/3	90	40	33	20	73
—	Seattle (A.L.)■	0	2	.000	1.00	14	0	0	0	0	18	18	3	2	6	13

Year	Team (League)	W	L	Pct.	ERA	G	GS	CG	ShO	Sv.	IP	H	R	ER	BB	SO
1994—	Oakland (A.L.)■	6	4	.600	*2.65	27	13	2	0	0	$115\frac{1}{3}$	93	39	34	26	56
1995—	Oakland (A.L.)	9	6	.600	4.37	22	22	2	1	0	$129\frac{2}{3}$	144	75	63	38	77
A.L. totals (7 years)		31	29	.517	3.63	193	67	6	2	19	$615\frac{2}{3}$	570	284	248	185	363
N.L. totals (2 years)		2	1	.667	3.54	11	5	0	0	0	$40\frac{2}{3}$	43	18	16	18	18
Major league totals (9 years)		33	30	.524	3.62	204	72	6	2	19	$656\frac{1}{3}$	613	302	264	203	381

ALL-STAR GAME RECORD

Year	League	W	L	Pct.	ERA	GS	CG	ShO	Sv.	IP	H	R	ER	BB	SO
1995—	American	0	1	.000	13.50	0	0	0	0	$\frac{2}{3}$	1	1	1	0	1

OQUENDO, JOSE — 2B/SS — CARDINALS

PERSONAL: Born July 4, 1963, in Rio Piedras, Puerto Rico. . . . 5-10/171. . . . Bats both, throws right. . . . Full name: Jose Manuel Oquendo. . . . Name pronounced oh-KEN-doh.

HIGH SCHOOL: Villamallo (Rio Piedras, Puerto Rico).

TRANSACTIONS/CAREER NOTES: Signed as non-drafted free agent by New York Mets organization (April 15, 1979). . . . Traded by Mets organization with P Mark Jason Davis to St. Louis Cardinals organization for SS Angel Salazar and P John Young (April 2, 1985). . . . On St. Louis disabled list (April 7-June 2, 1992); included rehabilitation assignments to Arkansas (May 11-13) and Louisville (May 23-June 2). . . . On St. Louis disabled list (June 9-July 13, 1992); included rehabilitation assignment to Louisville (July 7-13). . . . On St. Louis disabled list (July 22-September 1, 1992); included rehabilitation assignment to Louisville (August 20-31). . . . On St. Louis disabled list (August 9, 1993-remainder of season). . . . Granted free agency (November 1, 1995). . . . Re-signed by Cardinals organization (December 7, 1995).

RECORDS: Holds major league single-season records for highest fielding percentage by second baseman (150 or more games)—.996; and fewest errors—3 (1990). . . . Shares major league single-season record for fewest double plays by second baseman (150 or more games)—65 (1990). . . . Holds N.L. single-season record for fewest chances accepted by second baseman (150 games or more)—678 (1990).

STATISTICAL NOTES: Led Northwest League shortstops with 40 errors in 1979. . . . Led Carolina League with 13 sacrifice hits in 1980. . . . Led International League with 14 sacrifice hits in 1982. . . . Led American Association with 15 sacrifice hits in 1985. . . . Led American Association shortstops with 591 total chances in 1985. . . . Led N.L. second basemen with 346 putouts, 500 assists, 851 total chances and 106 double plays in 1989. . . . Led N.L. second basemen with .994 fielding percentage in 1989 and .996 in 1990.

				BATTING										FIELDING			
Year	Team (League)	Pos.	G	AB	R	H	2B	3B	HR	RBI	Avg.	BB	SO	SB	PO	A	E	Avg.
1979—	Grays Har. (N'west)	SS-2B	64	220	24	50	8	0	1	14	.227	33	45	9	90	177	†40	.870
1980—	Lynchburg (Caro.)	SS	109	301	38	51	10	3	0	26	.169	47	59	14	126	358	31	*.940
1981—	Lynchburg (Caro.)	SS	124	393	59	98	8	6	0	38	.249	71	61	38	169	390	23	*.960
1982—	Tidewater (Int'l)	SS	114	337	40	72	8	3	0	22	.214	41	50	24	186	337	25	.954
1983—	Tidewater (Int'l)	SS	13	34	3	4	0	0	0	3	.118	5	6	2	20	23	4	.915
—	New York (N.L.)	SS	120	328	29	70	7	0	1	17	.213	19	60	8	182	326	21	.960
1984—	New York (N.L.)	SS	81	189	23	42	5	0	0	10	.222	15	26	10	95	152	7	.972
—	Tidewater (Int'l)	SS	38	113	8	18	1	0	1	8	.159	5	14	8	54	111	2	.988
1985—	Louisville (A.A.)■	SS	133	384	38	81	8	1	1	30	.211	24	41	13	*227	341	23	.961
1986—	St. Louis (N.L.)	S-2-3-O	76	138	20	41	4	1	0	13	.297	15	20	2	52	94	8	.948
1987—	St. Louis (N.L.)	IF-OF-P	116	248	43	71	9	0	1	24	.286	54	29	4	149	133	4	.986
1988—	St. Louis (N.L.)	I-O-C-P	148	451	36	125	10	1	7	46	.277	52	40	4	268	315	11	.981
1989—	St. Louis (N.L.)	2B-SS-1B	•163	556	59	162	28	7	1	48	.291	79	59	3	†356	†523	6	†.993
1990—	St. Louis (N.L.)	2B-SS	156	469	38	118	17	5	1	37	.252	74	46	1	294	403	4	†.994
1991—	St. Louis (N.L.)	2B-SS-P	127	366	37	88	11	4	1	26	.240	67	48	1	271	368	9	.986
1992—	St. Louis (N.L.)	2B-SS	14	35	3	9	3	1	0	3	.257	5	3	0	18	30	1	.980
—	Arkansas (Texas)	2B	2	7	3	3	0	0	0	1	.429	0	0	0	3	2	0	1.000
—	Louisville (A.A.)	SS-2B	20	64	8	17	2	0	0	6	.266	11	3	0	36	55	5	.948
1993—	St. Louis (N.L.)	SS-2B	46	73	7	15	0	0	0	4	.205	12	8	0	52	82	1	.993
1994—	St. Louis (N.L.)	SS-2B	55	129	13	34	2	2	0	9	.264	21	16	1	53	98	4	.974
1995—	St. Louis (N.L.)	2-S-3-O	88	220	31	46	8	3	2	17	.209	35	21	1	134	210	6	.983
Major league totals (12 years)			1190	3202	339	821	104	24	14	254	.256	448	376	35	1924	2734	82	.983

CHAMPIONSHIP SERIES RECORD

				BATTING										FIELDING			
Year	Team (League)	Pos.	G	AB	R	H	2B	3B	HR	RBI	Avg.	BB	SO	SB	PO	A	E	Avg.
1987—	St. Louis (N.L.)	OF-3B-PH	5	12	3	2	0	0	1	4	.167	3	2	0	7	0	0	1.000

WORLD SERIES RECORD

				BATTING										FIELDING			
Year	Team (League)	Pos.	G	AB	R	H	2B	3B	HR	RBI	Avg.	BB	SO	SB	PO	A	E	Avg.
1987—	St. Louis (N.L.)	3B-OF	7	24	2	6	0	0	0	2	.250	1	4	0	8	10	0	1.000

RECORD AS PITCHER

Year	Team (League)	W	L	Pct.	ERA	G	GS	CG	ShO	Sv.	IP	H	R	ER	BB	SO
1987—	St. Louis (N.L.)	0	0	. . .	27.00	1	0	0	0	0	1	4	3	3	1	0
1988—	St. Louis (N.L.)	0	1	.000	4.50	1	0	0	0	0	4	4	2	2	6	1
1991—	St. Louis (N.L.)	0	0	. . .	27.00	1	0	0	0	0	1	2	3	3	0	1
Major league totals (3 years)		0	1	.000	12.00	3	0	0	0	0	6	10	8	8	7	2

OQUIST, MIKE — P

PERSONAL: Born May 30, 1968, in La Junta, Colo. . . . 6-2/170. . . . Throws right, bats right. . . . Full name: Michael Lee Oquist. . . . Name pronounced OH-kwist.

HIGH SCHOOL: La Junta (Colo.).

COLLEGE: Arkansas.

TRANSACTIONS/CAREER NOTES: Selected by Baltimore Orioles organization in 13th round of free-agent draft (June 5, 1989). . . . Granted free agency (October 16, 1995).

Year	Team (League)	W	L	Pct.	ERA	G	GS	CG	ShO	Sv.	IP	H	R	ER	BB	SO
1989—	Erie (N.Y.-Penn)	7	4	.636	3.59	15	15	1	1	0	97 2/3	86	43	39	25	109
1990—	Frederick (Caro.)	9	8	.529	2.81	25	25	3	1	0	166 1/3	134	64	52	48	*170
1991—	Hagerstown (East.)	10	9	.526	4.06	27	26	1	0	0	166 1/3	168	82	75	62	136
1992—	Rochester (Int'l)	10	12	.455	4.11	26	24	5	0	0	153 1/3	164	80	70	45	111
1993—	Rochester (Int'l)	9	8	.529	3.50	28	21	2	1	0	149 1/3	144	62	58	41	128
	— Baltimore (A.L.)	0	0	...	3.86	5	0	0	0	0	11 2/3	12	5	5	4	8
1994—	Rochester (Int'l)	3	2	.600	3.73	13	8	0	0	3	50 2/3	54	23	21	15	36
	— Baltimore (A.L.)	3	3	.500	6.17	15	9	0	0	0	58 1/3	75	41	40	30	39
1995—	Baltimore (A.L.)	2	1	.667	4.17	27	0	0	0	0	54	51	27	25	41	27
	— Rochester (Int'l)	0	0	...	5.25	7	0	0	0	2	12	17	8	7	5	11
Major league totals (3 years)		5	4	.556	5.08	47	9	0	0	0	124	138	73	70	75	74

ORELLANO, RAFAEL — P — RED SOX

PERSONAL: Born April 28, 1973, in Humacao, Puerto Rico. . . . 6-2/160. . . . Throws left, bats left. . . . Full name: Rafael A. Orellano.
TRANSACTIONS/CAREER NOTES: Signed as non-drafted free agent by Boston Red Sox organization (November 7, 1992). . . . On disabled list (July 26, 1993-remainder of season).

Year	Team (League)	W	L	Pct.	ERA	G	GS	CG	ShO	Sv.	IP	H	R	ER	BB	SO
1993—	Utica (NYP)	1	2	.333	5.79	11	0	0	0	2	18 2/3	22	15	12	7	13
1994—	GC Red Sox (GCL)	1	0	1.000	2.03	4	3	0	0	0	13 1/3	6	3	3	4	10
	— Sarasota (Fla. St.)	11	3	*.786	2.40	16	16	2	1	0	97 1/3	68	28	26	25	103
1995—	Trenton (Eastern)	11	7	.611	3.09	27	27	2	0	0	*186 2/3	146	68	64	72	*160

ORIE, KEVIN — SS — CUBS

PERSONAL: Born September 1, 1972, in West Chester, Pa. . . . 6-4/210. . . . Bats right, throws right. . . . Full name: Kevin Leonard Orie.
HIGH SCHOOL: Upper St. Clair (Pa.).
COLLEGE: Indiana.
TRANSACTIONS/CAREER NOTES: Selected by Chicago Cubs organization in supplemental round ("sandwich pick" between first and second round, 29th pick overall) of free-agent draft (June 3, 1993); pick received as part of compensation for Atlanta Braves signing Type A free-agent P Greg Maddux. . . . On disabled list (May 3, 1994-remainder of season).

				BATTING											FIELDING			
Year	Team (League)	Pos.	G	AB	R	H	2B	3B	HR	RBI	Avg.	BB	SO	SB	PO	A	E	Avg.
1993—	Peoria (Midwest)	SS-OF	65	238	28	64	17	1	7	45	.269	21	51	3	77	149	12	.950
1994—	Daytona (Fla. St.)	DH	6	17	4	7	3	1	1	5	.412	8	4	0	...	...	...	...
1995—	Daytona (Fla. St.)	3B	119	409	54	100	17	4	9	51	.244	42	71	5	80	204	26	.916

OROSCO, JESSE — P — ORIOLES

PERSONAL: Born April 21, 1957, in Santa Barbara, Calif. . . . 6-2/205. . . . Throws left, bats right. . . . Name pronounced oh-ROSS-koh.
HIGH SCHOOL: Santa Barbara (Calif.).
COLLEGE: Santa Barbara (Calif.) City College.
TRANSACTIONS/CAREER NOTES: Selected by St. Louis Cardinals organization in seventh round of free-agent draft (January 11, 1977); did not sign. . . . Selected by Minnesota Twins organization in second round of free-agent draft (January 10, 1978). . . . Traded by Twins organization to New York Mets (February 7, 1979), completing deal in which Twins traded P Greg Field and a player to be named later to Mets for P Jerry Koosman (December 8, 1978). . . . Traded by Mets as part of an eight-player, three-team deal in which Mets sent Orosco to Oakland Athletics (December 11, 1987). A's then traded Orosco, SS Alfredo Griffin and P Jay Howell to Los Angeles Dodgers for P Bob Welch, P Matt Young and P Jack Savage. A's then traded Savage, P Wally Whitehurst and P Kevin Tapani to Mets. . . . Granted free agency (November 4, 1988). . . . Signed by Cleveland Indians (December 3, 1988). . . . Traded by Indians to Milwaukee Brewers for a player to be named later (December 6, 1991); deal settled in cash. . . . Granted free agency (November 5, 1992). . . . Re-signed by Brewers (December 4, 1992). . . . Granted free agency (October 15, 1994). . . . Signed by Baltimore Orioles (April 9, 1995).
MISCELLANEOUS: Appeared in one game as outfielder with one putout (1986). . . . Struck out in only plate appearance (1993).

Year	Team (League)	W	L	Pct.	ERA	G	GS	CG	ShO	Sv.	IP	H	R	ER	BB	SO
1978—	Elizabeth. (App.)	4	4	.500	1.13	20	0	0	0	6	40	29	7	5	20	48
1979—	Tidewater (Int'l)■	4	4	.500	3.89	16	15	1	0	0	81	82	45	35	43	55
	— New York (N.L.)	1	2	.333	4.89	18	2	0	0	0	35	33	20	19	22	22
1980—	Jackson (Texas)	4	4	.500	3.68	37	1	0	0	3	71	52	36	29	62	85
1981—	Tidewater (Int'l)	9	5	.643	3.31	46	10	0	0	8	87	80	39	32	32	81
	— New York (N.L.)	0	1	.000	1.59	8	0	0	0	1	17	13	4	3	6	18
1982—	New York (N.L.)	4	10	.286	2.72	54	2	0	0	4	109 1/3	92	37	33	40	89
1983—	New York (N.L.)	13	7	.650	1.47	62	0	0	0	17	110	76	27	18	38	84
1984—	New York (N.L.)	10	6	.625	2.59	60	0	0	0	31	87	58	29	25	34	85
1985—	New York (N.L.)	8	6	.571	2.73	54	0	0	0	17	79	66	26	24	34	68
1986—	New York (N.L.)	8	6	.571	2.33	58	0	0	0	21	81	64	23	21	35	62
1987—	New York (N.L.)	3	9	.250	4.44	58	0	0	0	16	77	78	41	38	31	78
1988—	Los Angeles (N.L.)■	3	2	.600	2.72	55	0	0	0	9	53	41	18	16	30	43
1989—	Cleveland (A.L.)■	3	4	.429	2.08	69	0	0	0	3	78	54	20	18	26	79
1990—	Cleveland (A.L.)	5	4	.556	3.90	55	0	0	0	2	64 2/3	58	35	28	38	55
1991—	Cleveland (A.L.)	2	0	1.000	3.74	47	0	0	0	0	45 2/3	52	20	19	15	36
1992—	Milwaukee (A.L.)■	3	1	.750	3.23	59	0	0	0	1	39	33	15	14	13	40
1993—	Milwaukee (A.L.)	3	5	.375	3.18	57	0	0	0	8	56 2/3	47	25	20	17	67
1994—	Milwaukee (A.L.)	3	1	.750	5.08	40	0	0	0	0	39	32	26	22	26	36
1995—	Baltimore (A.L.)■	2	4	.333	3.26	*65	0	0	0	3	49 2/3	28	19	18	27	58
A.L. totals (7 years)		21	19	.525	3.36	392	0	0	0	17	372 2/3	304	160	139	162	371
N.L. totals (9 years)		50	49	.505	2.73	427	4	0	0	116	648 1/3	521	225	197	270	549
Major league totals (16 years)		71	68	.511	2.96	819	4	0	0	133	1021	825	385	336	432	920

CHAMPIONSHIP SERIES RECORD

NOTES: Holds single-series record for most games won—3 (1986).

Year	Team (League)	W	L	Pct.	ERA	G	GS	CG	ShO	Sv.	IP	H	R	ER	BB	SO
1986—	New York (N.L.)	3	0	1.000	3.38	4	0	0	0	0	8	5	3	3	2	10
1988—	Los Angeles (N.L.)	0	0	...	7.71	4	0	0	0	0	2 1/3	4	2	2	3	0
Champ. series totals (2 years)		3	0	1.000	4.35	8	0	0	0	0	10 1/3	9	5	5	5	10

WORLD SERIES RECORD

NOTES: Member of World Series championship teams (1986 and 1988).

Year	Team (League)	W	L	Pct.	ERA	G	GS	CG	ShO	Sv.	IP	H	R	ER	BB	SO
1986—	New York (N.L.)	0	0	...	0.00	4	0	0	0	2	5 2/3	2	0	0	0	6
1988—	Los Angeles (N.L.)							Did not play.								
World Series totals (1 year)		0	0	...	0.00	4	0	0	0	2	5 2/3	2	0	0	0	6

ALL-STAR GAME RECORD

Year	League	W	L	Pct.	ERA	GS	CG	ShO	Sv.	IP	H	R	ER	BB	SO
1983—	National	0	0	...	0.00	0	0	0	0	1/3	0	0	0	0	1
1984—	National						Did not play.								
All-Star totals (1 year)		0	0	...	0.00	0	0	0	0	1/3	0	0	0	0	1

ORSULAK, JOE — OF — MARLINS

PERSONAL: Born May 31, 1962, in Glen Ridge, N.J. . . . 6-1/205. . . . Bats left, throws left. . . . Full name: Joseph Michael Orsulak. . . . Name pronounced OR-suh-lack.

HIGH SCHOOL: Parsippany (N.J.).

TRANSACTIONS/CAREER NOTES: Selected by Pittsburgh Pirates organization in sixth round of free-agent draft (June 3, 1980). . . . On temporarily inactive list (July 10-27, 1981). . . . On disabled list (May 25-June 9, 1985). . . . On Pittsburgh disabled list (March 31-May 22, 1987); included rehabilitation assignment to Vancouver (May 4-22). . . . Traded by Pirates to Baltimore Orioles for SS Terry Crowley Jr. and 3B Rico Rossy (November 6, 1987). . . . On disabled list (August 16-September 1, 1992). . . . Granted free agency (October 28, 1992). . . . Signed by New York Mets (December 18, 1992). . . . Granted free agency (November 11, 1995). . . . Signed by Florida Marlins (December 5, 1995).

STATISTICAL NOTES: Tied for South Atlantic League lead in double plays by outfielder with four in 1981. . . . Led Pacific Coast League outfielders with 367 total chances and eight double plays in 1983. . . . Career major league grand slams: 2.

			BATTING											FIELDING			
Year	Team (League)	Pos.	G	AB	R	H	2B	3B	HR	RBI	Avg.	BB	SO	SB	PO	A	E	Avg.
1981—	Greenwood (S. Atl.)	OF	118	460	80	145	18	8	6	70	.315	29	32	18	249	16	4	*.985
1982—	Alexandria (Caro.)	OF-1B	129	463	92	134	18	4	14	65	.289	47	46	28	286	7	10	.967
1983—	Hawaii (PCL)	OF	139	538	87	154	12	•13	10	58	.286	48	41	38	*341	•18	8	.978
—	Pittsburgh (N.L.)	OF	7	11	0	2	0	0	0	1	.182	0	2	0	2	2	0	1.000
1984—	Hawaii (PCL)	OF	98	388	51	110	19	12	3	53	.284	29	38	14	258	6	2	.992
—	Pittsburgh (N.L.)	OF	32	67	12	17	1	2	0	3	.254	1	7	3	41	1	0	1.000
1985—	Pittsburgh (N.L.)	OF	121	397	54	119	14	6	0	21	.300	26	27	24	229	10	6	.976
1986—	Pittsburgh (N.L.)	OF	138	401	60	100	19	6	2	19	.249	28	38	24	193	11	4	.981
1987—	Vancouver (PCL)	OF	39	143	20	33	6	1	1	12	.231	17	21	2	58	2	2	.968
1988—	Baltimore (A.L.)■	OF	125	379	48	109	21	3	8	27	.288	23	30	9	228	6	5	.979
1989—	Baltimore (A.L.)	OF-DH	123	390	59	111	22	5	7	55	.285	41	35	5	250	10	4	.985
1990—	Baltimore (A.L.)	OF-DH	124	413	49	111	14	3	11	57	.269	46	48	6	267	5	3	.989
1991—	Baltimore (A.L.)	OF-DH	143	486	57	135	22	1	5	43	.278	28	45	6	273	*22	1	.997
1992—	Baltimore (A.L.)	OF-DH	117	391	45	113	18	3	4	39	.289	28	34	5	228	9	4	.983
1993—	New York (N.L.)■	OF-1B	134	409	59	116	15	4	8	35	.284	28	25	5	231	10	5	.980
1994—	New York (N.L.)	OF-1B	96	292	39	76	3	0	8	42	.260	16	21	4	148	8	3	.981
1995—	New York (N.L.)	OF-1B	108	290	41	82	19	2	1	37	.283	19	35	1	111	4	4	.966
American League totals (5 years)			632	2059	258	579	97	15	35	221	.281	166	192	31	1246	52	17	.987
National League totals (7 years)			636	1867	265	512	71	20	19	158	.274	118	155	61	955	46	22	.978
Major league totals (12 years)			1268	3926	523	1091	168	35	54	379	.278	284	347	92	2201	98	39	.983

O

ORTIZ, LUIS — 3B — RANGERS

PERSONAL: Born May 25, 1970, in Santo Domingo, Dominican Republic. . . . 6-0/195. . . . Bats right, throws right. . . . Full name: Luis Alberto Ortiz.

HIGH SCHOOL: De La Salle Dominican (Santo Domingo, Dominican Republic).

COLLEGE: Union University (Tenn.).

TRANSACTIONS/CAREER NOTES: Selected by Boston Red Sox organization in eighth round of free-agent draft (June 3, 1991). . . . On Pawtucket disabled list (June 26-July 15, 1993 and July 31, 1994-remainder of season). . . . Traded by Red Sox with OF Otis Nixon to Texas Rangers for DH/OF Jose Canseco (December 9, 1994).

			BATTING											FIELDING			
Year	Team (League)	Pos.	G	AB	R	H	2B	3B	HR	RBI	Avg.	BB	SO	SB	PO	A	E	Avg.
1991—	GC Red Sox (GCL)	3B	42	153	21	51	11	2	4	29	.333	8	9	2	30	67	7	.933
1992—	Lynchburg (Caro.)	3B	94	355	43	103	27	1	10	61	.290	22	55	4	37	97	20	.870
1993—	Pawtucket (Int'l)	3B-OF	102	402	45	118	28	1	18	81	.294	13	74	1	45	114	12	.930
—	Boston (A.L.)	3B-DH	9	12	0	3	0	0	0	1	.250	0	2	0	2	2	0	1.000
1994—	Pawtucket (Int'l)	3B-1B	81	317	47	99	15	3	6	36	.312	29	29	1	69	112	17	.914
—	Boston (A.L.)	DH	7	18	3	3	2	0	0	6	.167	1	5	0	...	...	...	...
1995—	Okla. City (A.A.)■	3B-1B	47	170	19	52	10	5	2	20	.306	8	20	1	35	93	9	.934
—	Texas (A.L.)	3B-DH	41	108	10	25	5	2	1	18	.231	6	18	0	9	43	8	.867
Major league totals (3 years)			57	138	13	31	7	2	1	25	.225	7	25	0	11	45	8	.875

OSBORNE, DONOVAN P CARDINALS

PERSONAL: Born June 21, 1969, in Roseville, Calif. . . . 6-2/195. . . . Throws left, bats left. . . . Full name: Donovan Alan Osborne.
HIGH SCHOOL: Carson (Carson City, Nev.).
COLLEGE: UNLV.
TRANSACTIONS/CAREER NOTES: Selected by Montreal Expos organization in ninth round of free-agent draft (June 2, 1987); did not sign. . . . Selected by St. Louis Cardinals organization in first round (13th pick overall) of free-agent draft (June 4, 1990). . . . On St. Louis disabled list (April 2, 1994-entire season). . . . On St. Louis disabled list (May 15-July 14, 1995); included rehabilitation assignments to Arkansas and Louisville (June 28-July 14).
HONORS: Named lefthanded pitcher on The Sporting News college All-America team (1989).
MISCELLANEOUS: Appeared in three games as pinch-runner (1993).

Year	Team (League)	W	L	Pct.	ERA	G	GS	CG	ShO	Sv.	IP	H	R	ER	BB	SO
1990—	Hamilton (NYP)	0	2	.000	3.60	4	4	0	0	0	20	21	8	8	5	14
—	Savannah (S. Atl.)	2	2	.500	2.61	6	6	1	0	0	41 1/3	40	20	12	7	28
1991—	Arkansas (Texas)	8	12	.400	3.63	26	26	3	0	0	166	178	82	67	43	130
1992—	St. Louis (N.L.)	11	9	.550	3.77	34	29	0	0	0	179	193	91	75	38	104
1993—	St. Louis (N.L.)	10	7	.588	3.76	26	26	1	0	0	155 2/3	153	73	65	47	83
1994—								Did not play.								
1995—	St. Louis (N.L.)	4	6	.400	3.81	19	19	0	0	0	113 1/3	112	58	48	34	82
—	Arkansas (Texas)	0	1	.000	2.45	2	2	0	0	0	11	12	4	3	2	6
—	Louisville (A.A.)	0	1	.000	3.86	1	1	0	0	0	7	8	3	3	0	3
Major league totals (3 years)		25	22	.532	3.78	79	74	1	0	0	448	458	222	188	119	269

OSUNA, ANTONIO P DODGERS

PERSONAL: Born April 12, 1973, in Sinaloa, Mexico. . . . 5-11/160. . . . Throws right, bats right. . . . Full name: Antonio Pedro Osuna.
HIGH SCHOOL: Secondaria Federal (Mexico).
TRANSACTIONS/CAREER NOTES: Signed as non-drafted free agent by Los Angeles Dodgers organization (June 12, 1991). . . . On suspended list (April 8-July 17, 1993). . . . On San Antonio disabled list (April 8-June 6, 1994). . . . On Los Angeles disabled list (May 19-June 16, 1995); included rehabilitation assignment to San Bernardino (June 6-16).

Year	Team (League)	W	L	Pct.	ERA	G	GS	CG	ShO	Sv.	IP	H	R	ER	BB	SO
1991—	GC Dodgers (GCL)	0	0	...	0.82	8	0	0	0	4	11	8	5	1	0	13
—	Yakima (N'west)	0	0	...	3.20	13	0	0	0	5	25 1/3	18	10	9	8	39
1992—	M.C. Tigers (Mex.)	13	7	.650	4.05	28	26	3	1	0	166 2/3	181	80	75	74	129
1993—	Bakersfield (Calif.)	0	2	.000	4.91	14	2	0	0	2	18 1/3	19	10	10	5	20
1994—	San Antonio (Tex.)	1	2	.333	0.98	35	0	0	0	19	46	19	6	5	18	53
—	Albuquerque (PCL)	0	0	...	0.00	6	0	0	0	4	6	5	1	0	1	8
1995—	Los Angeles (N.L.)	2	4	.333	4.43	39	0	0	0	0	44 2/3	39	22	22	20	46
—	San Bern. (Calif.)	0	0	...	1.29	5	0	0	0	0	7	3	1	1	5	11
—	Albuquerque (PCL)	0	1	.000	4.42	19	0	0	0	11	18 1/3	15	9	9	9	19
Major league totals (1 year)		2	4	.333	4.43	39	0	0	0	0	44 2/3	39	22	22	20	46

DIVISION SERIES RECORD

Year	Team (League)	W	L	Pct.	ERA	G	GS	CG	ShO	Sv.	IP	H	R	ER	BB	SO
1995—	Los Angeles (N.L.)	0	1	.000	2.70	3	0	0	0	0	3 1/3	3	1	1	1	3

OTANEZ, WILLIS 3B MARINERS

PERSONAL: Born April 19, 1973, in Cotui, Dominican Republic. . . . 5-11/150. . . . Bats right, throws right. . . . Full name: Willis A. Otanez. . . . Name pronounced oh-TAHN-yez.
HIGH SCHOOL: Liceo Miguel Angel Garcia (Cotui, Dominican Republic).
TRANSACTIONS/CAREER NOTES: Signed as non-drafted free agent by Los Angeles Dodgers organization (February 10, 1990). . . . Traded by Dodgers with 2B Miguel Cairo to Seattle Mariners for 3B Mike Blowers (November 29, 1995).

				BATTING											FIELDING			
Year	Team (League)	Pos.	G	AB	R	H	2B	3B	HR	RBI	Avg.	BB	SO	SB	PO	A	E	Avg.
1990—	Santo Dom. (DSL)	...	70	267	44	84	18	0	1	46	.315	51	24	4	...	...	...	...
1991—	Great Falls (Pio.)	SS-3B	58	222	38	64	9	2	6	39	.288	19	34	3	64	124	22	.895
1992—	Vero Beach (FSL)	SS-3B	117	390	27	86	18	0	3	27	.221	24	60	2	160	305	33	.934
1993—	Bakersfield (Calif.)	3B-SS-2B	95	325	34	85	11	2	10	39	.262	29	63	1	76	211	25	.920
1994—	Vero Beach (FSL)	3B	131	476	77	132	27	1	19	72	.277	53	98	4	*109	302	23	.947
1995—	Vero Beach (FSL)	3B	92	354	39	92	24	0	10	53	.260	28	59	1	59	186	20	.925
—	San Antonio (Tex.)	3B	27	100	8	24	4	1	1	7	.240	6	25	0	18	48	3	.957

O

OTERO, RICKY OF PHILLIES

PERSONAL: Born April 15, 1972, in Vega Baja, Puerto Rico. . . . 5-7/150. . . . Bats both, throws right. . . . Full name: Ricardo Otero.
HIGH SCHOOL: Lino Padron Rivera (Vega Baja, Puerto Rico).
TRANSACTIONS/CAREER NOTES: Selected by Toronto Blue Jays organization in 65th round of free-agent draft (June 5, 1989); did not sign. . . . Selected by New York Mets organization in 45th round of free-agent draft (June 4, 1990). . . . On suspended list (April 17-29 and August 27-29, 1994). . . . Traded by Mets to Philadelphia Phillies for OF Phil Geisler (December 14, 1995).
STATISTICAL NOTES: Led Appalachian League with six sacrifice flies and tied for league lead with five intentional bases on balls received and two double plays by outfielder in 1991. . . . Tied for International League lead in caught stealing with 13 in 1995. . . . Led International League outfielders with five double plays in 1995.

				BATTING											FIELDING			
Year	Team (League)	Pos.	G	AB	R	H	2B	3B	HR	RBI	Avg.	BB	SO	SB	PO	A	E	Avg.
1991—	Kingsport (Appal.)	OF	66	236	47	*81	16	3	7	52	*.343	35	32	12	122	7	2	.985
—	Pittsfield (NYP)	OF	6	24	4	7	0	0	0	2	.292	2	1	4	11	1	1	.923

Year Team (League)	Pos.	BATTING G	AB	R	H	2B	3B	HR	RBI	Avg.	BB	SO	SB	FIELDING PO	A	E	Avg.
1992—Columbia (S. Atl.)	OF	90	353	57	106	24	4	8	60	.300	38	53	39	203	15	10	.956
—St. Lucie (Fla. St.)	OF	40	151	20	48	8	4	0	19	.318	9	11	10	94	6	1	.990
1993—Binghamton (East.)	OF	124	503	63	133	21	10	2	54	.264	38	57	29	238	9	6	.976
1994—Binghamton (East.)	OF	128	531	96	156	31	*9	7	57	.294	50	49	33	264	6	4	.985
1995—New York (N.L.)	OF	35	51	5	7	2	0	0	1	.137	3	10	2	31	1	0	1.000
—Norfolk (Int'l)	OF	72	295	37	79	8	6	1	23	.268	27	33	16	147	12	5	.970
Major league totals (1 year)		35	51	5	7	2	0	0	1	.137	3	10	2	31	1	0	1.000

OWEN, SPIKE SS/2B

PERSONAL: Born April 19, 1961, in Cleburne, Tex. . . . 5-10/170. . . . Bats both, throws right. . . . Full name: Spike Dee Owen. . . . Brother of Dave Owen, shortstop, Chicago Cubs and Kansas City Royals (1983-85 and 1988).
HIGH SCHOOL: Cleburne (Tex.).
COLLEGE: Texas.
TRANSACTIONS/CAREER NOTES: Selected by Seattle Mariners organization in first round (sixth pick overall) of free-agent draft (June 7, 1982). . . . On disabled list (July 15-August 1, 1985). . . . Traded by Mariners with OF Dave Henderson to Boston Red Sox for IF Rey Quinones, a player to be named later and cash (August 19, 1986); as part of deal, Mariners claimed P Mike Brown and P Mike Trujillo on waivers from Red Sox (August 22, 1986). Mariners acquired OF John Christensen to complete deal (September 25, 1986). . . . Traded by Red Sox with P Dan Gakeler to Montreal Expos for P John Dopson and SS Luis Rivera (December 8, 1988). . . . On disabled list (July 17-August 1, 1989 and July 20-August 4, 1992). . . . Granted free agency (October 26, 1992). . . . Signed by New York Yankees (December 4, 1992). . . . Traded by Yankees with cash to California Angels for P Jose Musset (December 9, 1993). . . . On California disabled list (July 6-August 1, 1995); included rehabilitation assignment to Lake Elsinore (July 28-August 1). . . . Granted free agency (November 3, 1995).
RECORDS: Shares modern major league single-game record for most runs—6 (August 21, 1986). . . . Holds N.L. single-season record for most consecutive errorless games by shortstop—63 (April 9-June 22, 1990).
HONORS: Named shortstop on The Sporting News college All-America team (1982).
STATISTICAL NOTES: Led A.L. shortstops with 767 total chances and 133 double plays in 1986.

Year Team (League)	Pos.	BATTING G	AB	R	H	2B	3B	HR	RBI	Avg.	BB	SO	SB	FIELDING PO	A	E	Avg.
1982—Lynn (Eastern)	SS	78	241	32	64	9	2	1	27	.266	44	33	18	106	207	9	.972
1983—Salt Lake (PCL)	SS	72	256	58	68	8	9	1	32	.266	57	23	22	111	212	14	.958
—Seattle (A.L.)	SS	80	306	36	60	11	3	2	21	.196	24	44	10	122	233	11	.970
1984—Seattle (A.L.)	SS	152	530	67	130	18	8	3	43	.245	46	63	16	245	463	17	.977
1985—Seattle (A.L.)	SS	118	352	41	91	10	6	6	37	.259	34	27	11	196	361	14	.975
1986—Seattle (A.L.)	SS	112	402	46	99	22	6	0	35	.246	34	42	1	209	372	17	.972
—Boston (A.L.)■	SS	42	126	21	23	2	1	1	10	.183	17	9	3	70	95	4	.976
1987—Boston (A.L.)	SS	132	437	50	113	17	7	2	48	.259	53	43	11	176	336	13	.975
1988—Boston (A.L.)	SS-DH	89	257	40	64	14	1	5	18	.249	27	27	0	102	192	10	.967
1989—Montreal (N.L.)■	SS	142	437	52	102	17	4	6	41	.233	76	44	3	232	388	13	*.979
1990—Montreal (N.L.)	SS	149	453	55	106	24	5	5	35	.234	70	60	8	216	340	6	*.989
1991—Montreal (N.L.)	SS	139	424	39	108	22	8	3	26	.255	42	61	2	189	376	8	.986
1992—Montreal (N.L.)	SS	122	386	52	104	16	3	7	40	.269	50	30	9	188	300	9	.982
1993—New York (A.L.)■	SS-DH	103	334	41	78	16	2	2	20	.234	29	30	3	116	312	14	.968
1994—California (A.L.)■	3-S-1-DH-2	82	268	30	83	17	2	3	37	.310	49	17	2	64	139	8	.962
1995—California (A.L.)	3B-SS-2B	82	218	17	50	9	3	1	28	.229	18	22	3	65	95	6	.964
—Lake Elsinore (Calif.)	2B-3B	3	10	1	2	1	0	0	0	.200	2	2	0	0	3	0	1.000
American League totals (9 years)		992	3230	389	791	136	39	25	297	.245	331	324	60	1365	2598	114	.972
National League totals (4 years)		552	1700	198	420	79	20	21	142	.247	238	195	22	825	1404	36	.984
Major league totals (13 years)		1544	4930	587	1211	215	59	46	439	.246	569	519	82	2190	4002	150	.976

CHAMPIONSHIP SERIES RECORD

Year Team (League)	Pos.	BATTING G	AB	R	H	2B	3B	HR	RBI	Avg.	BB	SO	SB	FIELDING PO	A	E	Avg.
1986—Boston (A.L.)	SS	7	21	5	9	0	1	0	3	.429	2	2	1	12	21	5	.868
1988—Boston (A.L.)	PH	1	0	0	0	0	0	0	0	...	0	0	0	...	...	...	...
Championship series totals (2 years)		8	21	5	9	0	1	0	3	.429	2	2	1	12	21	5	.868

WORLD SERIES RECORD

Year Team (League)	Pos.	BATTING G	AB	R	H	2B	3B	HR	RBI	Avg.	BB	SO	SB	FIELDING PO	A	E	Avg.
1986—Boston (A.L.)	SS	7	20	2	6	0	0	0	2	.300	5	6	0	10	13	0	1.000

OWENS, ERIC 3B/2B REDS

PERSONAL: Born February 3, 1971, in Danville, Va. . . . 6-1/185. . . . Bats right, throws right. . . . Full name: Eric Blake Owens.
HIGH SCHOOL: Tunstall (Dry Fork, Va.).
COLLEGE: Ferrum (Va.).
TRANSACTIONS/CAREER NOTES: Selected by Cincinnati Reds organization in fourth round of free-agent draft (June 1, 1992). . . . On Indianapolis disabled list (August 20-September 11, 1995).
HONORS: Named American Association Most Valuable Player (1995).
STATISTICAL NOTES: Led Pioneer League shortstops with 28 errors in 1992.

Year Team (League)	Pos.	BATTING G	AB	R	H	2B	3B	HR	RBI	Avg.	BB	SO	SB	FIELDING PO	A	E	Avg.
1992—Billings (Pioneer)	SS-3B	67	239	41	72	10	3	3	26	.301	23	22	15	82	164	†29	.895
1993—Winst.-Salem (Car.)	SS	122	487	74	132	25	4	10	63	.271	53	69	21	*215	347	34	.943
1994—Chatt. (South.)	3B-2B	134	523	73	133	17	3	3	36	.254	54	86	38	151	266	40	.912
1995—Indianapolis (A.A.)	2B	108	427	*86	134	24	•8	12	63	.314	52	61	*33	219	274	*17	.967
—Cincinnati (N.L.)	3B	2	2	0	2	0	0	0	1	1.000	0	0	0	0	0	0	...
Major league totals (1 year)		2	2	0	2	0	0	0	1	1.000	0	0	0	0	0	0	...

OWENS, JAYHAWK — C — ROCKIES

PERSONAL: Born February 10, 1969, in Cincinnati. . . . 6-1/213. . . . Bats right, throws right. . . . Full name: Claude Jayhawk Owens II.
HIGH SCHOOL: Glen Este (Cincinnati).
COLLEGE: Middle Tennessee State.
TRANSACTIONS/CAREER NOTES: Selected by Boston Red Sox organization in 25th round of free-agent draft (June 2, 1987); did not sign. . . . Selected by Minnesota Twins organization in third round of free-agent draft (June 4, 1990). . . . On disabled list (April 12-June 5, 1991 and August 13-September 6, 1992). . . . Selected by Colorado Rockies in first round (23rd pick overall) of expansion draft (November 17, 1992). . . . On Colorado Springs disabled list (August 11-30 and September 5-12, 1994).
STATISTICAL NOTES: Tied for Southern League lead in errors by catcher with 14 in 1992. . . . Tied for Pacific Coast League lead in double plays by catcher with eight in 1995.

			BATTING											FIELDING			
Year Team (League)	Pos.	G	AB	R	H	2B	3B	HR	RBI	Avg.	BB	SO	SB	PO	A	E	Avg.
1990— Kenosha (Midwest)	OF-C	66	216	31	51	9	2	5	30	.236	39	59	15	133	8	5	.966
1991— Visalia (California)	OF	65	233	33	57	17	1	6	33	.245	35	70	14	123	6	1	.992
1992— Orlando (Southern)	C-OF	102	330	50	88	24	0	4	30	.267	36	67	10	656	62	‡14	.981
1993— Colo. Springs (PCL)■	C-OF-1B	55	174	24	54	11	3	6	43	.310	21	56	5	207	18	10	.957
— Colorado (N.L.)	C	33	86	12	18	5	0	3	6	.209	6	30	1	138	19	7	.957
1994— Colo. Springs (PCL)	C-OF	77	257	43	69	11	7	6	44	.268	32	66	3	417	43	6	.987
— Colorado (N.L.)	C	6	12	4	3	0	1	0	1	.250	3	3	0	25	3	0	1.000
1995— Colo. Springs (PCL)	C	70	221	47	65	13	5	12	48	.294	20	61	2	390	46	5	.989
— Colorado (N.L.)	C	18	45	7	11	2	0	4	12	.244	2	15	0	79	6	1	.988
Major league totals (3 years)		57	143	23	32	7	1	7	19	.224	11	48	1	242	28	8	.971

DIVISION SERIES RECORD

			BATTING											FIELDING			
Year Team (League)	Pos.	G	AB	R	H	2B	3B	HR	RBI	Avg.	BB	SO	SB	PO	A	E	Avg.
1995— Colorado (N.L.)	C	1	1	0	0	0	0	0	0	.000	0	1	0	2	1	0	1.000

PACHECO, ALEX — P — EXPOS

PERSONAL: Born July 19, 1973, in Caracas, Venezuela. . . . 6-3/200. . . . Throws right, bats right. . . . Full name: Alexander Melchor Pacheco.
HIGH SCHOOL: Francisco Fajardo (Caracas, Venezuela).
TRANSACTIONS/CAREER NOTES: Signed as non-drafted free agent by Montreal Expos organization (November 13, 1989).

Year Team (League)	W	L	Pct.	ERA	G	GS	CG	ShO	Sv.	IP	H	R	ER	BB	SO
1990— GC Expos (GCL)	1	0	1.000	5.19	6	0	0	0	0	8 2/3	11	7	5	4	5
1991— GC Expos (GCL)	3	0	1.000	5.08	15	4	0	0	1	44 1/3	56	32	25	26	19
1992— Jamestown (NYP)	3	3	.500	5.54	16	5	0	0	0	50 1/3	53	36	31	29	32
1993— Jamestown (NYP)	0	1	.000	3.21	6	1	0	0	0	14	11	7	5	4	15
— Burlington (Midw.)	3	5	.375	4.19	13	7	0	0	1	43	47	31	20	12	24
1994— Burlington (Midw.)	3	8	.273	5.14	37	4	0	0	5	68 1/3	79	51	39	22	69
— WP Beach (FSL)	1	0	1.000	2.25	9	0	0	0	0	12	9	3	3	4	12
1995— Harrisburg (East.)	9	7	.563	4.27	45	0	0	0	4	86 1/3	76	45	41	31	88
— Ottawa (Int'l)	1	0	1.000	6.23	4	0	0	0	0	8 2/3	8	6	6	5	4

PAGLIARULO, MIKE — 3B — RANGERS

PERSONAL: Born March 15, 1960, in Medford, Mass. . . . 6-2/195. . . . Bats left, throws right. . . . Full name: Michael Timothy Pagliarulo. . . . Son of Charles Pagliarulo, minor league infielder (1958). . . . Name pronounced PAL-ya-ROO-lo.
HIGH SCHOOL: Medford (Mass.).
COLLEGE: Miami (Fla.).
TRANSACTIONS/CAREER NOTES: Selected by New York Yankees organization in sixth round of free-agent draft (June 8, 1981). . . . On disabled list (July 25-August 11, 1988). . . . Traded by Yankees with P Don Schulze to San Diego Padres for P Walt Terrell and a player to be named later (July 22, 1989); Yankees acquired P Fred Toliver to complete deal (September 27, 1989). . . . Granted free agency (November 5, 1990). . . . Signed by Minnesota Twins (January 25, 1991). . . . Granted free agency (November 11, 1991). . . . Re-signed by Twins (January 7, 1992). . . . On Minnesota disabled list (March 28-April 14, 1992). . . . On Minnesota disabled list (April 22-July 23, 1992); included rehabilitation assignment to Fort Myers (July 14-23). . . . Granted free agency (October 30, 1992). . . . Re-signed by Twins (April 3, 1993). . . . Traded by Twins to Baltimore Orioles for a player to be named later (August 15, 1993); Twins acquired P Erik Schullstrom to complete deal (August 16, 1993). . . . Granted free agency (November 2, 1993). . . . Signed by Seibu Lions of Japan Pacific League (December 1, 1993). . . . Signed as free agent Oklahoma City, Texas Rangers organization (March 30, 1995). . . . On disabled list (August 16-September 1, 1995). . . . Granted free agency (November 3, 1995). . . . Re-signed by Rangers organization (January 9, 1996).
STATISTICAL NOTES: Led New York-Pennsylvania League with eight intentional bases on balls received in 1981. . . . Led New York-Pennsylvania League third basemen with 214 total chances in 1981. . . . Led Southern League third basemen with 433 total chances in 1983. . . . Career major league grand slams: 5.

			BATTING											FIELDING			
Year Team (League)	Pos.	G	AB	R	H	2B	3B	HR	RBI	Avg.	BB	SO	SB	PO	A	E	Avg.
1981— Oneonta (NYP)	3B	72	245	32	53	9	4	2	28	.216	38	47	13	40	*159	15	.930
1982— Greensboro (S. Atl.)	3B	123	403	79	113	22	0	22	79	.280	83	76	7	73	*278	27	.929
1983— Nashville (South.)	3B	135	450	82	117	19	4	19	80	.260	59	100	8	*98	*315	20	*.954
1984— Columbus (Int'l)	3B-SS	58	146	24	31	5	1	7	25	.212	18	30	0	27	95	13	.904
— New York (A.L.)	3B	67	201	24	48	15	3	7	34	.239	15	46	0	44	106	7	.955
1985— New York (A.L.)	3B	138	380	55	91	16	2	19	62	.239	45	86	0	67	187	13	.951
1986— New York (A.L.)	3B-SS	149	504	71	120	24	3	28	71	.238	54	120	4	104	283	19	.953
1987— New York (A.L.)	3B-1B	150	522	76	122	26	3	32	87	.234	53	111	1	97	297	17	.959
1988— New York (A.L.)	3B	125	444	46	96	20	1	15	67	.216	37	104	1	82	232	19	.943
1989— New York (A.L.)	3B-DH	74	223	19	44	10	0	4	16	.197	19	43	1	25	122	10	.936
— San Diego (N.L.)■	3B	50	148	12	29	7	0	3	14	.196	18	39	2	19	83	7	.936
1990— San Diego (N.L.)	3B	128	398	29	101	23	2	7	38	.254	39	66	1	79	200	13	.955

Year	Team (League)	Pos.	G	AB	R	H	2B	3B	HR	RBI	Avg.	BB	SO	SB	PO	A	E	Avg.
			BATTING												FIELDING			
1991—	Minnesota (A.L.)■	3B-2B	121	365	38	102	20	0	6	36	.279	21	55	1	56	248	11	.965
1992—	Minnesota (A.L.)	3B-DH	42	105	10	21	4	0	0	9	.200	1	17	1	11	64	3	.962
	—Fort Myers (FSL)	3B	6	20	2	4	2	0	0	2	.200	4	2	1	3	14	2	.895
1993—	Minnesota (A.L.)	3B	83	253	31	74	16	4	3	23	.292	18	34	6	42	137	3	.984
	—Baltimore (A.L.)■	3B-1B	33	117	24	38	9	0	6	21	.325	8	15	0	53	49	5	.953
1994—	Seibu (Jp. Pac.)■	3B	80	285	39	75	17	3	7	47	.263	43	69	3	...	...	...	...
1995—	Texas (A.L.)■	3B-1B	86	241	27	56	16	0	4	27	.232	15	49	0	111	121	7	.971
American League totals (10 years)			1068	3355	421	812	176	16	124	453	.242	286	680	15	692	1846	114	.957
National League totals (2 years)			178	546	41	130	30	2	10	52	.238	57	105	3	98	283	20	.950
Major league totals (11 years)			1246	3901	462	942	206	18	134	505	.241	343	785	18	790	2129	134	.956

CHAMPIONSHIP SERIES RECORD

Year	Team (League)	Pos.	G	AB	R	H	2B	3B	HR	RBI	Avg.	BB	SO	SB	PO	A	E	Avg.
			BATTING												FIELDING			
1991—	Minnesota (A.L.)	3B-PH	5	15	4	5	1	0	1	3	.333	0	2	0	4	10	0	1.000

WORLD SERIES RECORD

NOTES: Member of World Series championship team (1991).

Year	Team (League)	Pos.	G	AB	R	H	2B	3B	HR	RBI	Avg.	BB	SO	SB	PO	A	E	Avg.
			BATTING												FIELDING			
1991—	Minnesota (A.L.)	3B-PH	6	11	1	3	0	0	1	2	.273	1	2	0	3	3	0	1.000

PAGNOZZI, TOM — C — CARDINALS

PERSONAL: Born July 30, 1962, in Tucson, Ariz. . . . 6-1/190. . . . Bats right, throws right. . . . Full name: Thomas Alan Pagnozzi. . . . Brother of Tim Pagnozzi, minor league shortstop (1976); and brother of Mike Pagnozzi, minor league pitcher (1975-78). . . . Name pronounced pag-NAHZ-ee.

HIGH SCHOOL: Rincon (Tucson, Ariz.).

JUNIOR COLLEGE: Central Arizona College.

COLLEGE: Arkansas.

TRANSACTIONS/CAREER NOTES: Selected by Milwaukee Brewers organization in 24th round of free-agent draft (January 12, 1982); did not sign. . . . Selected by St. Louis Cardinals organization in eighth round of free-agent draft (June 6, 1983). . . . On St. Louis disabled list (May 8-June 17, 1993); included rehabilitation assignment to Louisville (June 2-17). . . . On St. Louis disabled list (March 29-May 5, 1994); included rehabilitation assignment to Louisville (April 23-May 5). . . . On St. Louis disabled list (July 18-August 26, 1995); included rehabilitation assignment to Louisville (August 17-26).

RECORDS: Shares N.L. single-season records for highest fielding percentage by catcher (100 or more games)—.999 (1992); and fewest errors by catcher (100 or more games)—1 (1992).

HONORS: Won N.L. Gold Glove at catcher (1991-92 and 1994).

STATISTICAL NOTES: Led N.L. catchers with .998 fielding percentage in 1994. . . . Career major league grand slams: 2.

Year	Team (League)	Pos.	G	AB	R	H	2B	3B	HR	RBI	Avg.	BB	SO	SB	PO	A	E	Avg.
			BATTING												FIELDING			
1983—	Erie (NYP)	C	45	168	28	52	9	1	6	22	.310	14	34	3	183	20	3	.985
	—Macon (S. Atl.)	C	18	57	7	14	2	1	0	6	.246	6	13	0	125	18	8	.947
1984—	Springfield (Midw.)	C	114	396	57	112	20	4	10	68	.283	31	75	3	667	*90	12	.984
1985—	Arkansas (Texas)	C-1B	41	139	15	43	7	1	5	29	.309	13	21	0	243	27	1	.996
	—Louisville (A.A.)	C	76	268	29	72	13	2	5	40	.269	21	47	0	266	25	4	.986
1986—	Louisville (A.A.)	C	30	106	12	31	4	0	1	18	.292	6	21	0	160	19	3	.984
1987—	Louisville (A.A.)	C-3B	84	320	53	100	20	2	14	71	.313	30	50	0	427	43	6	.987
	—St. Louis (N.L.)	C-1B	27	48	8	9	1	0	2	9	.188	4	13	1	61	5	0	1.000
1988—	St. Louis (N.L.)	1B-C-3B	81	195	17	55	9	0	0	15	.282	11	32	0	340	30	4	.989
1989—	St. Louis (N.L.)	C-1B-3B	52	80	3	12	2	0	0	3	.150	6	19	0	100	9	2	.982
1990—	St. Louis (N.L.)	C-1B	69	220	20	61	15	0	2	23	.277	14	37	1	345	39	4	.990
1991—	St. Louis (N.L.)	C-1B	140	459	38	121	24	5	2	57	.264	36	63	9	682	81	7	.991
1992—	St. Louis (N.L.)	C	139	485	33	121	26	3	7	44	.249	28	64	2	688	53	1	*.999
1993—	St. Louis (N.L.)	C	92	330	31	85	15	1	7	41	.258	19	30	1	421	44	4	.991
	—Louisville (A.A.)	C	12	43	5	12	3	0	1	1	.279	2	3	0	51	6	2	.966
1994—	Louisville (A.A.)	C	10	25	4	6	3	0	0	3	.240	6	6	0	32	3	0	1.000
	—St. Louis (N.L.)	C-1B	70	243	21	66	12	1	7	40	.272	21	39	0	370	41	1	†.998
1995—	St. Louis (N.L.)	C	62	219	17	47	14	1	2	15	.215	11	31	0	336	38	2	.995
	—Louisville (A.A.)	C	5	16	4	8	2	0	1	3	.500	1	0	0	19	0	0	1.000
Major league totals (9 years)			732	2279	188	577	118	11	29	247	.253	150	328	14	3343	340	25	.993

CHAMPIONSHIP SERIES RECORD

Year	Team (League)	Pos.	G	AB	R	H	2B	3B	HR	RBI	Avg.	BB	SO	SB	PO	A	E	Avg.
			BATTING												FIELDING			
1987—	St. Louis (N.L.)	PH	1	1	0	0	0	0	0	0	.000	0	0	0	...	...	...	...

WORLD SERIES RECORD

Year	Team (League)	Pos.	G	AB	R	H	2B	3B	HR	RBI	Avg.	BB	SO	SB	PO	A	E	Avg.
			BATTING												FIELDING			
1987—	St. Louis (N.L.)	DH-PH	2	4	0	1	0	0	0	0	.250	0	0	0	...	...	...	...

ALL-STAR GAME RECORD

Year	League	Pos.	AB	R	H	2B	3B	HR	RBI	Avg.	BB	SO	SB	PO	A	E	Avg.
			BATTING											FIELDING			
1992—	National	PH	1	0	0	0	0	0	0	.000	0	0	0	...	...	...	...

P

PAIGE, CAREY — P — BLUE JAYS

PERSONAL: Born March 2, 1974, in Abilene, Tex. . . . 6-3/175. . . . Throws right, bats right. . . . Full name: Carey Don Paige.
HIGH SCHOOL: Cooper (Abilene, Tex.).
TRANSACTIONS/CAREER NOTES: Selected by Atlanta Braves organization in third round of free-agent draft (June 1, 1992). . . . On Durham disabled list (April 6-May 15, 1995). . . . Selected by Toronto Blue Jays from Braves organization in Rule 5 major league draft (December 4, 1995).

Year	Team (League)	W	L	Pct.	ERA	G	GS	CG	ShO	Sv.	IP	H	R	ER	BB	SO
1992—	GC Braves (GCL)	0	3	.000	3.83	13	7	0	0	0	40	31	19	17	17	39
1993—	Danville (Appal.)	2	4	.333	4.21	13	13	0	0	0	66 1/3	59	37	31	32	58
1994—	Macon (S. Atl.)	8	6	.571	1.70	19	19	1	0	0	105 2/3	87	32	20	33	119
	—Durham (Carolina)	2	2	.500	4.71	6	6	0	0	0	28 2/3	31	19	15	13	25
1995—	Durham (Carolina)	5	3	.625	3.38	10	10	1	0	0	64	53	24	24	15	37
	—Greenville (South.)	1	4	.200	5.01	7	7	0	0	0	41 1/3	45	30	23	11	26

PAINTER, LANCE — P — ROCKIES

PERSONAL: Born July 21, 1967, in Bedford, England. . . . 6-1/197. . . . Throws left, bats left. . . . Full name: Lance T. Painter.
HIGH SCHOOL: Nicolet (Glendale, Wis.).
COLLEGE: Wisconsin.
TRANSACTIONS/CAREER NOTES: Selected by San Diego Padres organization in 25th round of free-agent draft (June 4, 1990). . . . Selected by Colorado Rockies in second round (34th pick overall) of expansion draft (November 17, 1992). . . . On disabled list (April 17-May 6, 1995).
STATISTICAL NOTES: Led Texas League with 10 hit batsmen in 1992.
MISCELLANEOUS: Received base on balls in only appearance as pinch-hitter with Colorado (1995).

Year	Team (League)	W	L	Pct.	ERA	G	GS	CG	ShO	Sv.	IP	H	R	ER	BB	SO
1990—	Spokane (N'west)	7	3	.700	1.51	23	1	0	0	3	71 2/3	45	18	12	15	104
1991—	Waterloo (Midw.)	14	8	.636	2.30	28	28	7	*4	0	200	162	64	51	57	201
1992—	Wichita (Texas)	10	5	*.667	3.53	27	•27	1	1	0	163 1/3	138	74	64	55	137
1993—	Colo. Springs (PCL)■	9	7	.563	4.30	23	22	•4	1	0	138	165	90	66	44	91
	—Colorado (N.L.)	2	2	.500	6.00	10	6	1	0	0	39	52	26	26	9	16
1994—	Colo. Springs (PCL)	4	3	.571	4.79	13	13	1	0	0	71 1/3	83	42	38	28	59
	—Colorado (N.L.)	4	6	.400	6.11	15	14	0	0	0	73 2/3	91	51	50	26	41
1995—	Colorado (N.L.)	3	0	1.000	4.37	33	1	0	0	1	45 1/3	55	23	22	10	36
	—Colo. Springs (PCL)	0	3	.000	5.96	11	4	0	0	0	25 2/3	32	20	17	11	12
Major league totals (3 years)		9	8	.529	5.58	58	21	1	0	1	158	198	100	98	45	93

DIVISION SERIES RECORD

NOTES: Struck out in only appearance as pinch-hitter (1995).

Year	Team (League)	W	L	Pct.	ERA	G	GS	CG	ShO	Sv.	IP	H	R	ER	BB	SO
1995—	Colorado (N.L.)	0	0	...	5.40	1	1	0	0	0	5	5	3	3	2	4

PALACIOS, VICENTE — P

PERSONAL: Born July 19, 1963, in Mataloma, Mexico. . . . 6-3/175. . . . Throws right, bats right. . . . Full name: Vicente Hernandez Diaz Palacios. . . . Name pronounced puh-LAH-see-os.
HIGH SCHOOL: Secundaria Tecnica (Soleda Vera Cruz, Mexico).
TRANSACTIONS/CAREER NOTES: Signed as free agent by Aguila of Mexican League (April 23, 1982). . . . Contract sold by Aguila to Chicago White Sox organization (July 20, 1984). . . . Loaned by White Sox organization to Mexico City Reds of Mexican League (May 28-September 3, 1985). . . . Loaned by White Sox to Aguila of Mexican League (April 5-September 1, 1986). . . . Released by White Sox organization (November 10, 1986). . . . Signed by Pittsburgh Pirates organization (December 4, 1986). . . . Selected by Milwaukee Brewers from Pirates organization in Rule 5 major league draft (December 8, 1986). . . . Returned to Pirates (April 3, 1987). . . . On disabled list (April 1-June 12 and July 4, 1989-remainder of season). . . . On Pittsburgh disabled list (August 8-September 6, 1991); included rehabilitation assignment to Buffalo (August 28-September 6). . . . On disabled list (June 19, 1992-remainder of season). . . . Released by Pirates (November 18, 1992). . . . Signed by San Diego Padres organization (February 1, 1993). . . . Released by Padres (March 29, 1993). . . . Played in Mexican League (1993). . . . Signed as free agent by Louisville, St. Louis Cardinals organization (December 23, 1993). . . . On disabled list (June 22, 1995-remainder of season). . . . Released by Cardinals (November 15, 1995).
STATISTICAL NOTES: Led Mexican League with three balks in 1983. . . . Tied for Eastern League lead with four balks in 1985. . . . Pitched 10-0 one-hit, complete-game victory against Houston (July 19, 1994).

Year	Team (League)	W	L	Pct.	ERA	G	GS	CG	ShO	Sv.	IP	H	R	ER	BB	SO
1982—								Did not play.								
1983—	Aguila (Mexican)	12	6	.667	2.61	22	22	10	3	0	165 1/3	121	53	48	60	125
1984—	Aguila (Mexican)	7	8	.467	3.52	24	20	7	1	4	128	117	64	50	79	120
	—Glens Falls (East.)■	1	2	.333	2.49	5	5	0	0	0	25 1/3	23	12	7	11	10
1985—	Glens Falls (East.)	1	1	.500	4.76	8	4	0	0	1	39 2/3	44	25	21	29	20
	—Mex. City Reds (Mex.)■	7	2	.778	3.87	13	13	4	1	0	74 1/3	86	44	32	44	49
1986—	Aguila (Mexican)■	5	14	.263	4.41	23	20	11	2	1	138 2/3	157	75	68	78	121
1987—	Vancouver (PCL)■	13	5	.722	*2.58	27	26	7	*5	0	*185	140	63	53	85	*148
	—Pittsburgh (N.L.)	2	1	.667	4.30	6	4	0	0	0	29 1/3	27	14	14	9	13
1988—	Pittsburgh (N.L.)	1	2	.333	6.66	7	3	0	0	0	24 1/3	28	18	18	15	15
	—Buffalo (A.A.)	3	0	1.000	1.99	5	5	1	1	0	31 2/3	26	7	7	5	23
1989—	Buffalo (A.A.)	0	2	.000	7.20	2	2	0	0	0	10	9	8	8	8	8
1990—	Buffalo (A.A.)	13	7	.650	3.43	28	28	5	0	0	183 2/3	173	77	70	53	137
	—Pittsburgh (N.L.)	0	0	...	0.00	7	0	0	0	3	15	4	0	0	2	8
1991—	Pittsburgh (N.L.)	6	3	.667	3.75	36	7	1	1	3	81 2/3	69	34	34	38	64
	—Buffalo (A.A.)	0	0	...	1.42	3	0	0	0	2	6 1/3	7	1	1	2	8
1992—	Pittsburgh (N.L.)	3	2	.600	4.25	20	8	0	0	0	53	56	25	25	27	33
1993—	Yuc.-Aguas. (Mex.)■	4	4	.500	3.94	38	2	0	0	20	59 1/3	47	27	26	40	57
1994—	St. Louis (N.L.)■	3	8	.273	4.44	31	17	1	1	1	117 2/3	104	60	58	43	95
1995—	St. Louis (N.L.)	2	3	.400	5.80	20	5	0	0	0	40 1/3	48	29	26	19	34
Major league totals (7 years)		17	19	.472	4.36	127	44	2	2	7	361 1/3	336	180	175	153	262

PALMEIRO, ORLANDO — OF — ANGELS

PERSONAL: Born January 19, 1969, in Hoboken, N.J. . . . 5-11/155. . . . Bats left, throws right. . . . Cousin of Rafael Palmeiro, first baseman, Baltimore Orioles. . . . Name pronounced pal-MAIR-oh.
HIGH SCHOOL: Southridge (Miami).
JUNIOR COLLEGE: Miami-Dade Community College.
COLLEGE: Miami (Fla.).
TRANSACTIONS/CAREER NOTES: Selected by California Angels organization in 33rd round of free-agent draft (June 3, 1991). . . . On disabled list (September 1-26, 1994).
STATISTICAL NOTES: Tied for Northwest League lead in double plays by outfielder with two in 1991. . . . Led Texas League with 18 sacrifice hits in 1993. . . . Led Texas League outfielders with 328 total chances in 1993. . . . Led Pacific Coast League in caught stealing with 16 in 1994. . . . Led Pacific Coast League with 11 sacrifice hits in 1995.

		BATTING												FIELDING			
Year Team (League)	Pos.	G	AB	R	H	2B	3B	HR	RBI	Avg.	BB	SO	SB	PO	A	E	Avg.
1991—Boise (Northwest)	OF	70	277	56	77	11	2	1	24	.278	33	22	8	130	8	2	*.986
1992—Quad City (Midw.)	OF	127	451	83	143	22	4	0	41	*.317	56	41	31	211	9	6	.973
1993—Midland (Texas)	OF	131	*535	85	163	19	5	0	64	.305	42	35	18	*307	12	9	.973
1994—Vancouver (PCL)	OF	117	458	79	150	28	4	1	47	.328	58	46	21	254	6	1	.996
1995—Vancouver (PCL)	OF	107	398	66	122	21	4	0	47	.307	41	34	16	192	4	1	*.995
—California (A.L.)	OF-DH	15	20	3	7	0	0	0	1	.350	1	1	0	7	0	0	1.000
Major league totals (1 year)		15	20	3	7	0	0	0	1	.350	1	1	0	7	0	0	1.000

PALMEIRO, RAFAEL — 1B — ORIOLES

PERSONAL: Born September 24, 1964, in Havana, Cuba. . . . 6-0/188. . . . Bats left, throws left. . . . Full name: Rafael Corrales Palmeiro. . . . Cousin of Orlando Palmeiro, outfielder, California Angels organization. . . . Name pronounced pal-MAIR-oh.
HIGH SCHOOL: Jackson (Miami).
COLLEGE: Mississippi State (degree in commercial art).
TRANSACTIONS/CAREER NOTES: Selected by New York Mets organization in eighth round of free-agent draft (June 7, 1982); did not sign. . . . Selected by Chicago Cubs organization in first round (22nd pick overall) of free-agent draft (June 3, 1985); pick received as compensation for San Diego Padres signing Type A free-agent P Tim Stoddard. . . . Traded by Cubs with P Jamie Moyer and P Drew Hall to Texas Rangers for P Mitch Williams, P Paul Kilgus, P Steve Wilson, IF Curtis Wilkerson, IF Luis Benitez and OF Pablo Delgado (December 5, 1988). . . . Granted free agency (October 25, 1993). . . . Signed by Baltimore Orioles (December 12, 1993).
HONORS: Named outfielder on The Sporting News college All-America team (1985). . . . Named Eastern League Most Valuable Player (1986).
STATISTICAL NOTES: Led Eastern League with 225 total bases, 13 sacrifice flies and 13 intentional bases on balls received in 1986. . . . Led A.L. first basemen with 1,540 total chances and 133 double plays in 1993. . . . Career major league grand slams: 2.

		BATTING												FIELDING			
Year Team (League)	Pos.	G	AB	R	H	2B	3B	HR	RBI	Avg.	BB	SO	SB	PO	A	E	Avg.
1985—Peoria (Midwest)	OF	73	279	34	83	22	4	5	51	.297	31	34	9	113	7	1	.992
1986—Pittsfield (Eastern)	OF	•140	509	66	*156	29	2	12	*95	.306	54	32	15	248	9	3	*.988
—Chicago (N.L.)	OF	22	73	9	18	4	0	3	12	.247	4	6	1	34	2	4	.900
1987—Iowa (Am. Assoc.)	OF-1B	57	214	36	64	14	3	11	41	.299	22	22	4	150	13	2	.988
—Chicago (N.L.)	OF-1B	84	221	32	61	15	1	14	30	.276	20	26	2	176	9	1	.995
1988—Chicago (N.L.)	OF-1B	152	580	75	178	41	5	8	53	.307	38	34	12	322	11	5	.985
1989—Texas (A.L.)■	1B-DH	156	559	76	154	23	4	8	64	.275	63	48	4	1167	*119	12	.991
1990—Texas (A.L.)	1B-DH	154	598	72	*191	35	6	14	89	.319	40	59	3	1215	91	7	.995
1991—Texas (A.L.)	1B-DH	159	631	115	203	*49	3	26	88	.322	68	72	4	1305	96	*12	.992
1992—Texas (A.L.)	1B-DH	159	608	84	163	27	4	22	85	.268	72	83	2	1251	*143	7	.995
1993—Texas (A.L.)	1B	160	597	*124	176	40	2	37	105	.295	73	85	22	*1388	*147	5	.997
1994—Baltimore (A.L.)■	1B	111	436	82	139	32	0	23	76	.319	54	63	7	959	66	4	.996
1995—Baltimore (A.L.)	1B	143	554	89	172	30	2	39	104	.310	62	65	3	1181	*119	4	.997
American League totals (7 years)		1042	3983	642	1198	236	21	169	611	.301	432	475	45	8466	781	51	.995
National League totals (3 years)		258	874	116	257	60	6	25	95	.294	62	66	15	532	22	10	.982
Major league totals (10 years)		1300	4857	758	1455	296	27	194	706	.300	494	541	60	8998	803	61	.994

ALL-STAR GAME RECORD

		BATTING											FIELDING			
Year League	Pos.	AB	R	H	2B	3B	HR	RBI	Avg.	BB	SO	SB	PO	A	E	Avg.
1988—National	PH-OF	0	0	0	0	0	0	0	...	1	0	0	1	0	0	1.000
1991—American	1B	0	0	0	0	0	0	0	...	1	0	0	2	0	0	1.000
All-Star Game totals (2 years)		0	0	0	0	0	0	0	...	2	0	0	3	0	0	1.000

P

PALMER, DEAN — 3B — RANGERS

PERSONAL: Born December 27, 1968, in Tallahassee, Fla. . . . 6-2/195. . . . Bats right, throws right. . . . Full name: Dean William Palmer.
HIGH SCHOOL: Florida (Tallahassee, Fla.).
TRANSACTIONS/CAREER NOTES: Selected by Texas Rangers organization in third round of free-agent draft (June 2, 1986). . . . On disabled list (July 19, 1988-remainder of season; April 28-May 13, 1994; and June 4-September 22, 1995).
STATISTICAL NOTES: Led Texas League third basemen with 30 errors in 1989. . . . Led A.L. third basemen with 29 errors in 1993. . . . Career major league grand slams: 4.

		BATTING												FIELDING			
Year Team (League)	Pos.	G	AB	R	H	2B	3B	HR	RBI	Avg.	BB	SO	SB	PO	A	E	Avg.
1986—GC Rangers (GCL)	3B	50	163	19	34	7	1	0	12	.209	22	34	6	25	75	13	.885
1987—Gastonia (S. Atl.)	3B	128	484	51	104	16	0	9	54	.215	36	126	5	58	209	*59	.819
1988—Charlotte (Fla. St.)	3B	74	305	38	81	12	1	4	35	.266	15	69	0	49	144	28	.873
1989—Tulsa (Texas)	3B-SS	133	498	82	125	32	5	*25	90	.251	41	*152	15	85	213	†31	.906

				BATTING											FIELDING			
Year	Team (League)	Pos.	G	AB	R	H	2B	3B	HR	RBI	Avg.	BB	SO	SB	PO	A	E	Avg.
	—Texas (A.L.)	3-DH-S-O	16	19	0	2	2	0	0	1	.105	0	12	0	3	4	2	.778
1990—	Tulsa (Texas)	3B	7	24	4	7	0	1	3	9	.292	4	10	0	9	6	3	.833
	—Okla. City (A.A.)	3B-1B	88	316	33	69	17	4	12	39	.218	20	106	1	206	110	21	.938
1991—	Okla. City (A.A.)	3B-OF	60	234	45	70	11	2	*22	59	.299	20	61	4	49	105	11	.933
	—Texas (A.L.)	3B-OF-DH	81	268	38	50	9	2	15	37	.187	32	98	0	69	75	9	.941
1992—	Texas (A.L.)	3B	152	541	74	124	25	0	26	72	.229	62	*154	10	124	254	22	.945
1993—	Texas (A.L.)	3B-SS	148	519	88	127	31	2	33	96	.245	53	154	11	86	258	†29	.922
1994—	Texas (A.L.)	3B	93	342	50	84	14	2	19	59	.246	26	89	3	50	179	*22	.912
1995—	Texas (A.L.)	3B	36	119	30	40	6	0	9	24	.336	21	21	1	19	72	5	.948
Major league totals (6 years)			526	1808	280	427	87	6	102	289	.236	194	528	25	351	842	89	.931

PANIAGUA, JOSE — P — EXPOS

PERSONAL: Born August 20, 1973, in San Jose De Ocoa, Dominican Republic. . . . 6-2/185. . . . Throws right, bats right. . . . Full name: Jose Luis Sanchez Paniagua.

TRANSACTIONS/CAREER NOTES: Signed as non-drafted free agent by Montreal Expos organization (September 17, 1990).

Year	Team (League)	W	L	Pct.	ERA	G	GS	CG	ShO	Sv.	IP	H	R	ER	BB	SO
1992—	DSL Expos (DSL)	3	7	.300	4.15	13	13	3	1	0	73 2/3	69	50	34	46	60
1993—	GC Expos (GCL)	3	0	1.000	0.67	4	4	1	0	0	27	13	2	2	5	25
1994—	WP Beach (FSL)	9	9	.500	3.64	26	26	1	0	0	141	131	82	57	54	110
1995—	Harrisburg (East.)	7	•12	.368	5.34	25	25	2	1	0	126 1/3	140	84	75	62	89

PAQUETTE, CRAIG — 3B — ATHLETICS

PERSONAL: Born March 28, 1969, in Long Beach, Calif. . . . 6-0/190. . . . Bats right, throws right. . . . Full name: Craig Howard Paquette.

HIGH SCHOOL: Ranchos Alamitos (Garden Grove, Calif.).

COLLEGE: Golden West College (Calif.).

TRANSACTIONS/CAREER NOTES: Selected by Minnesota Twins organization in 36th round of free-agent draft (June 2, 1987); did not sign. . . . Selected by Oakland Athletics organization in eighth round of free-agent draft (June 5, 1989). . . . On Modesto disabled list (April 10-May 5, 1991). . . . On Huntsville disabled list (June 1-11, 1991). . . . On Tacoma disabled list (July 18, 1994-remainder of season).

STATISTICAL NOTES: Tied for Northwest League lead with 163 total bases in 1989. . . . Led Northwest League third basemen with .936 fielding percentage and 12 double plays in 1989. . . . Led Southern League third basemen with 349 total chances in 1992. . . . Career major league grand slams: 1.

				BATTING											FIELDING			
Year	Team (League)	Pos.	G	AB	R	H	2B	3B	HR	RBI	Avg.	BB	SO	SB	PO	A	E	Avg.
1989—	S. Oregon (N'west)	3B-SS-2B	71	277	53	93	*22	3	14	56	.336	30	46	9	61	155	15	†.935
1990—	Modesto (Calif.)	3B	130	495	65	118	23	4	15	59	.238	47	123	8	*88	218	26	*.922
1991—	Huntsville (South.)	3B-1B	102	378	50	99	18	1	8	60	.262	28	87	0	51	132	16	.920
1992—	Huntsville (South.)	3B	115	450	59	116	25	4	17	71	.258	29	118	13	69	*248	*32	.908
	—Tacoma (PCL)	3B	17	66	10	18	7	0	2	11	.273	2	16	3	14	33	3	.940
1993—	Tacoma (PCL)	3B-SS-2B	50	183	29	49	8	0	8	29	.268	14	54	3	32	116	15	.908
	—Oakland (A.L.)	3B-DH-OF	105	393	35	86	20	4	12	46	.219	14	108	4	82	165	13	.950
1994—	Tacoma (PCL)	3B	65	245	39	70	12	3	17	48	.286	14	48	3	40	166	14	.936
	—Oakland (A.L.)	3B	14	49	0	7	2	0	0	0	.143	0	14	1	14	22	0	1.000
1995—	Oakland (A.L.)	3-O-S-1	105	283	42	64	13	1	13	49	.226	12	88	5	72	92	8	.953
Major league totals (3 years)			224	725	77	157	35	5	25	95	.217	26	210	10	168	279	21	.955

PARENT, MARK — C — TIGERS

PERSONAL: Born September 16, 1961, in Ashland, Ore. . . . 6-5/240. . . . Bats right, throws right. . . . Full name: Mark Alan Parent.

HIGH SCHOOL: Anderson (Calif.).

TRANSACTIONS/CAREER NOTES: Selected by San Diego Padres organization in fourth round of free-agent draft (June 5, 1979). . . . On suspended list (August 27, 1983-remainder of season). . . . On disabled list (September 4, 1984-remainder of season). . . . Traded by Padres to Texas Rangers for 3B Scott Coolbaugh (December 12, 1990). . . . On Texas disabled list (March 9-September 6, 1991); included rehabilitation assignment to Oklahoma City (August 31-September 5). . . . Granted free agency (October 8, 1991). . . . Signed by Baltimore Orioles organization (February 5, 1992). . . . On Rochester disabled list (April 10-17, 1992). . . . Released by Orioles (December 2, 1993). . . . Signed by Chicago Cubs organization (December 14, 1993). . . . Claimed on waivers by Pittsburgh Pirates (October 11, 1994). . . . Traded by Pirates to Cubs for a player to be named later (August 31, 1995). . . . Granted free agency (October 31, 1995). . . . Signed by Detroit Tigers (December 13, 1995).

STATISTICAL NOTES: Led Northwest League catchers with .979 fielding percentage in 1980. . . . Led Carolina League catchers with 16 double plays in 1981. . . . Led Pacific Coast League catchers with .988 fielding percentage in 1987. . . . Led International League catchers with eight double plays in 1992. . . . Tied for International League lead in double plays by catcher with 11 in 1993.

				BATTING											FIELDING			
Year	Team (League)	Pos.	G	AB	R	H	2B	3B	HR	RBI	Avg.	BB	SO	SB	PO	A	E	Avg.
1979—	Walla Walla (N'west)	C-OF	40	126	8	24	4	0	1	11	.190	8	31	8	229	34	6	.978
1980—	Reno (California)	C	30	99	8	20	3	0	0	12	.202	16	12	0	128	23	2	.987
	—Grays Har. (N'west)	C-1B	66	230	29	55	11	2	7	32	.239	17	30	1	381	38	9	†.979
1981—	Salem (Carolina)	C	123	438	44	103	16	3	6	47	.235	37	90	10	*694	87	*28	.965
1982—	Amarillo (Texas)	C	26	89	12	17	3	1	1	13	.191	11	13	2	100	6	2	.981
	—Salem (Carolina)	C-1B	99	360	39	81	15	2	6	41	.225	32	58	2	475	64	12	.978
1983—	Beaumont (Texas)	C	81	282	38	71	22	1	7	33	.252	33	35	1	464	71	10	*.982
1984—	Beaumont (Texas)	C-1B	111	380	52	109	24	3	7	60	.287	38	39	1	674	68	7	.991
1985—	Las Vegas (PCL)	C-1B	105	361	36	87	23	3	7	45	.241	29	58	1	586	54	6	.991
1986—	Las Vegas (PCL)	C-1B	86	267	29	77	10	4	5	40	.288	23	25	0	344	40	5	.987
	—San Diego (N.L.)	C	8	14	1	2	0	0	0	0	.143	1	3	0	16	0	2	.889

Year	Team (League)	Pos.	G	AB	R	H	2B	3B	HR	RBI	Avg.	BB	SO	SB	PO	A	E	Avg.
			BATTING												FIELDING			
1987—	Las Vegas (PCL)	C-1-3-O	105	387	50	113	23	2	4	43	.292	38	53	2	556	58	8	†.987
—	San Diego (N.L.)	C	12	25	0	2	0	0	0	2	.080	0	9	0	36	3	0	1.000
1988—	San Diego (N.L.)	C	41	118	9	23	3	0	6	15	.195	6	23	0	203	15	3	.986
1989—	San Diego (N.L.)	C-1B	52	141	12	27	4	0	7	21	.191	8	34	1	246	17	0	1.000
1990—	San Diego (N.L.)	C	65	189	13	42	11	0	3	16	.222	16	29	1	324	31	3	.992
1991—	Okla. City (A.A.)■	C	5	8	0	2	0	0	0	1	.250	0	1	0	4	0	0	1.000
—	Texas (A.L.)	C	3	1	0	0	0	0	0	0	.000	0	1	0	5	0	0	1.000
1992—	Rochester (Int'l)■	C	101	356	52	102	24	0	17	69	.287	35	64	4	588	49	4	.994
—	Baltimore (A.L.)	C	17	34	4	8	1	0	2	4	.235	3	7	0	73	7	1	.988
1993—	Rochester (Int'l)	C	92	332	47	82	15	0	14	56	.247	40	71	0	549	63	3	*.995
—	Baltimore (A.L.)	C-DH	22	54	7	14	2	0	4	12	.259	3	14	0	83	5	1	.989
1994—	Chicago (N.L.)■	C	44	99	8	26	4	0	3	16	.263	13	24	0	184	21	5	.976
1995—	Pittsburgh (N.L.)■	C	69	233	25	54	9	0	15	33	.232	23	62	0	365	39	4	.990
—	Chicago (N.L.)■	C	12	32	5	8	2	0	3	5	.250	3	7	0	66	5	0	1.000
American League totals (3 years)			42	89	11	22	3	0	6	16	.247	6	22	0	161	12	2	.989
National League totals (7 years)			303	851	73	184	33	0	37	108	.216	70	191	2	1440	131	17	.989
Major league totals (10 years)			345	940	84	206	36	0	43	124	.219	76	213	2	1601	143	19	.989

PARK, CHAN HO — P — DODGERS

PERSONAL: Born June 30, 1973, in Kong Ju City, Korea. . . . 6-2/195. . . . Throws right, bats right.
HIGH SCHOOL: Kong Ju (Kong Ju City, Korea).
COLLEGE: Han Yang University (Seoul, Korea).
TRANSACTIONS/CAREER NOTES: Signed as non-drafted free agent by Los Angeles Dodgers organization (January 14, 1994). . . . On Albuquerque disabled list (July 16-29, 1995).

Year	Team (League)	W	L	Pct.	ERA	G	GS	CG	ShO	Sv.	IP	H	R	ER	BB	SO
1994—	Los Angeles (N.L.)	0	0	...	11.25	2	0	0	0	0	4	5	5	5	5	6
—	San Antonio (Tex.)	5	7	.417	3.55	20	20	0	0	0	101 1/3	91	52	40	57	100
1995—	Albuquerque (PCL)	6	7	.462	4.91	23	22	0	0	0	110	93	64	60	76	101
—	Los Angeles (N.L.)	0	0	...	4.50	2	1	0	0	0	4	2	2	2	2	7
Major league totals (2 years)		0	0	...	7.88	4	1	0	0	0	8	7	7	7	7	13

PARKER, RICK — OF — DODGERS

PERSONAL: Born March 20, 1963, in Kansas City, Mo. . . . 6-0/185. . . . Bats right, throws right. . . . Full name: Richard Allen Parker.
HIGH SCHOOL: Oak Park (Kansas City, Mo.).
COLLEGE: Southwest Missouri State and Texas.
TRANSACTIONS/CAREER NOTES: Selected by Philadelphia Phillies organization in 16th round of free-agent draft (June 3, 1985). . . . Traded by Phillies organization to Phoenix, San Francisco Giants organization (August 7, 1989), completing deal in which Phillies traded P Steve Bedrosian and a player to be named later to Giants for P Dennis Cook, P Terry Mulholland and 3B Charlie Hayes (June 18, 1989). . . . On San Francisco disabled list (March 25-May 16, 1991); included rehabilitation assignment to Phoenix (April 27-May 16). . . . Released by Giants (December 9, 1991). . . . Signed by Tucson, Houston Astros organization (January 3, 1992). . . . Granted free agency (October 4, 1992). . . . Re-signed by Tucson (December 14, 1992). . . . Granted free agency (October 4, 1993). . . . Signed by New York Mets organization (December 16, 1993). . . . On New York disabled list (May 29-June 24, 1994). . . . Granted free agency (October 16, 1994). . . . Signed by Albuquerque, Los Angeles Dodgers organization (January 24, 1995).

Year	Team (League)	Pos.	G	AB	R	H	2B	3B	HR	RBI	Avg.	BB	SO	SB	PO	A	E	Avg.
			BATTING												FIELDING			
1985—	Bend (Northwest)	SS	55	205	45	51	9	1	2	20	.249	40	42	14	79	143	25	.899
1986—	Spartanburg (SAL)	SS	62	233	39	69	7	3	5	28	.296	36	39	14	87	169	18	.934
—	Clearwater (FSL)	SS	63	218	24	51	10	2	0	15	.234	21	29	8	94	197	21	.933
1987—	Clearwater (FSL)	2B-SS-3B	101	330	56	83	13	3	3	34	.252	31	36	6	130	234	27	.931
1988—	Reading (Eastern)	3-O-1-2-S	116	362	50	93	13	3	3	47	.257	36	50	24	174	114	18	.941
1989—	Reading (Eastern)	3B-OF-SS	103	388	59	92	7	*9	3	32	.237	42	62	17	123	91	22	.907
—	Phoenix (PCL)■	3B-OF-SS	18	68	5	18	2	2	0	11	.265	2	14	1	25	32	1	.983
1990—	Phoenix (PCL)	3B-OF-2B	44	173	38	58	7	4	1	18	.335	17	17	13	57	51	2	.982
—	San Francisco (N.L.)	O-2-S-3	54	107	19	26	5	0	2	14	.243	10	15	6	45	3	2	.960
1991—	Phoenix (PCL)	OF-3B-SS	85	297	41	89	10	9	6	41	.300	26	35	16	132	58	11	.945
—	San Francisco (N.L.)	OF	13	14	0	1	0	0	0	1	.071	1	5	0	5	0	0	1.000
1992—	Tucson (PCL)■	O-3-1-S	105	319	51	103	10	11	4	38	.323	28	36	20	61	9	5	.933
1993—	Tucson (PCL)	OF-3B-1B	29	120	28	37	9	3	2	12	.308	14	20	6	77	3	3	.964
—	Houston (N.L.)	OF-SS-2B	45	45	11	15	3	0	0	4	.333	3	8	1	18	0	0	1.000
1994—	Norfolk (Int'l)■	O-2-S-3	73	228	29	61	9	0	2	16	.268	29	39	9	94	27	4	.968
—	New York (N.L.)	OF	8	16	1	1	0	0	0	0	.063	0	2	0	14	1	0	1.000
1995—	Albuquerque (PCL)■	O-2-3-S	58	175	33	49	7	2	1	14	.280	27	17	1	83	7	2	.978
—	Los Angeles (N.L.)	OF-3B-SS	27	29	3	8	0	0	0	4	.276	2	4	1	20	1	0	1.000
Major league totals (5 years)			147	211	34	51	8	0	2	23	.242	16	34	8	102	5	2	.982

P

PARRA, JOSE — P — TWINS

PERSONAL: Born November 28, 1972, in Jacagua Santiago, Dominican Republic. . . . 5-11/165. . . . Throws right, bats right. . . . Full name: Jose Miguel Parra.
HIGH SCHOOL: Liceo Evangelico Jacagua (Dominican Republic).
TRANSACTIONS/CAREER NOTES: Signed as non-drafted free agent by Los Angeles Dodgers organization (December 7, 1989). . . . On disabled list (May 15-June 17 and August 13, 1993-remainder of season). . . . Traded by Dodgers with 3B/1B Ron Coomer, P Greg Hansell and a player to be named later to Minnesota Twins for P Kevin Tapani and P Mark Guthrie (July 31, 1995); Twins acquired OF Chris Latham to

complete deal (October 30, 1995).

Year Team (League)	W	L	Pct.	ERA	G	GS	CG	ShO	Sv.	IP	H	R	ER	BB	SO
1989— Santo Dom. (DSL)	8	1	.889	1.87	13	11	4	3	2	67 1/3	60	21	14	20	51
1990— GC Dodgers (GCL)	5	3	.625	2.67	10	10	1	0	0	57 1/3	50	22	17	18	50
1991— Great Falls (Pio.)	4	6	.400	6.16	14	14	1	1	0	64 1/3	86	58	44	18	55
1992— Bakersfield (Calif.)	7	8	.467	3.59	24	23	3	0	0	143	151	73	57	47	107
— San Antonio (Tex.)	2	0	1.000	6.14	3	3	0	0	0	14 2/3	22	12	10	7	7
1993— San Antonio (Tex.)	1	8	.111	3.15	17	17	0	0	0	111 1/3	103	46	39	12	87
1994— Albuquerque (PCL)	10	10	.500	4.78	27	27	1	0	0	145	190	92	77	38	90
1995— Albuquerque (PCL)	3	2	.600	5.13	12	10	1	1	1	52 2/3	62	33	30	17	33
— Los Angeles (N.L.)	0	0	...	4.35	8	0	0	0	0	10 1/3	10	8	5	6	7
— Minnesota (A.L.)■	1	5	.167	7.59	12	12	0	0	0	61 2/3	83	59	52	22	29
A.L. totals (1 year)	1	5	.167	7.59	12	12	0	0	0	61 2/3	83	59	52	22	29
N.L. totals (1 year)	0	0	...	4.35	8	0	0	0	0	10 1/3	10	8	5	6	7
Major league totals (1 year)	1	5	.167	7.13	20	12	0	0	0	72	93	67	57	28	36

PARRETT, JEFF — P — CARDINALS

PERSONAL: Born August 26, 1961, in Indianapolis. . . . 6-3/195. . . . Throws right, bats right. . . . Full name: Jeffrey Dale Parrett.
HIGH SCHOOL: Lafayette (Lexington, Ky.).
COLLEGE: Kentucky.
TRANSACTIONS/CAREER NOTES: Selected by Milwaukee Brewers organization in ninth round of free-agent draft (June 6, 1983). . . . Selected by Montreal Expos from Brewers organization in Rule 5 major league draft (December 10, 1985). . . . On disabled list (July 16-August 14, 1988). . . . Traded by Expos with P Floyd Youmans to Philadelphia Phillies for P Kevin Gross (December 6, 1988). . . . On disabled list (April 29-May 22, 1989). . . . Traded by Phillies with two players to be named later to Atlanta Braves for OF Dale Murphy and a player to be named later (August 3, 1990); Scranton/Wilkes-Barre, Phillies organization, acquired P Tommy Greene (August 9, 1990) and Braves acquired OF Jim Vatcher (August 9, 1990) and SS Victor Rosario (September 4, 1990) to complete deal. . . . Released by Braves (December 9, 1991). . . . Signed by Oakland Athletics organization (February 7, 1992). . . . Granted free agency (December 19, 1992). . . . Signed by Colorado Rockies (January 21, 1993). . . . On disabled list (July 29, 1993-remainder of season). . . . Released by Rockies (November 10, 1993). . . . Signed by Omaha, Kansas City Royals organization (May 24, 1994). . . . On Omaha disabled list (May 24-June 29, 1994). . . . Granted free agency (October 15, 1994). . . . Signed by New Jersey, St. Louis Cardinals organization (April 8, 1995). . . . Granted free agency (October 31, 1995). . . . Re-signed by Cardinals (December 7, 1995).

Year Team (League)	W	L	Pct.	ERA	G	GS	CG	ShO	Sv.	IP	H	R	ER	BB	SO
1983— Paintsville (Appal.)	2	0	1.000	2.12	3	3	0	0	0	17	12	6	4	8	21
— Beloit (Midwest)	2	2	.500	4.02	10	8	0	0	0	47	40	26	21	29	34
1984— Beloit (Midwest)	4	3	.571	4.52	29	5	1	1	2	91 2/3	76	50	46	71	95
1985— Stockton (Calif.)	7	4	.636	*2.75	45	2	0	0	11	127 2/3	97	50	39	75	120
1986— Montreal (N.L.)■	0	1	.000	4.87	12	0	0	0	0	20 1/3	19	11	11	13	21
— Indianapolis (A.A.)	2	5	.286	4.96	25	8	0	0	2	69	54	44	38	35	76
1987— Indianapolis (A.A.)	2	1	.667	2.01	20	0	0	0	9	22 1/3	15	5	5	13	17
— Montreal (N.L.)	7	6	.538	4.21	45	0	0	0	6	62	53	33	29	30	56
1988— Montreal (N.L.)	12	4	.750	2.65	61	0	0	0	6	91 2/3	66	29	27	45	62
1989— Philadelphia (N.L.)■	12	6	.667	2.98	72	0	0	0	6	105 2/3	90	43	35	44	98
1990— Philadelphia (N.L.)	4	9	.308	5.18	47	5	0	0	1	81 2/3	92	51	47	36	69
— Atlanta (N.L.)■	1	1	.500	3.00	20	0	0	0	1	27	27	11	9	19	17
1991— Atlanta (N.L.)	1	2	.333	6.33	18	0	0	0	1	21 1/3	31	18	15	12	14
— Richmond (Int'l)	2	7	.222	4.52	19	14	0	0	0	79 2/3	72	45	40	46	88
1992— Oakland (A.L.)■	9	1	.900	3.02	66	0	0	0	0	98 1/3	81	35	33	42	78
1993— Colorado (N.L.)■	3	3	.500	5.38	40	6	0	0	1	73 2/3	78	47	44	45	66
1994— Omaha (Am. Assoc.)	0	3	.000	3.96	12	4	0	0	0	38 2/3	34	21	17	14	35
1995— St. Louis (N.L.)■	4	7	.364	3.64	59	0	0	0	0	76 2/3	71	33	31	28	71
A.L. totals (1 year)	9	1	.900	3.02	66	0	0	0	0	98 1/3	81	35	33	42	78
N.L. totals (8 years)	44	39	.530	3.99	374	11	0	0	22	560	527	276	248	272	474
Major league totals (9 years)	53	40	.570	3.84	440	11	0	0	22	658 1/3	608	311	281	314	552

CHAMPIONSHIP SERIES RECORD

Year Team (League)	W	L	Pct.	ERA	G	GS	CG	ShO	Sv.	IP	H	R	ER	BB	SO
1992— Oakland (A.L.)	0	0	...	11.57	3	0	0	0	0	2 1/3	6	3	3	0	1

PARRIS, STEVE — P — PIRATES

PERSONAL: Born December 17, 1967, in Joliet, Ill. . . . 6-0/190. . . . Throws right, bats right. . . . Full name: Steven Michael Parris.
HIGH SCHOOL: Joliet (Ill.) West.
COLLEGE: College of St. Francis (Ill).
TRANSACTIONS/CAREER NOTES: Selected by Philadelphia Phillies organization in fifth round of free-agent draft (June 5, 1989). . . . Claimed on waivers by Los Angeles Dodgers (April 19, 1993). . . . Claimed on waivers by Seattle Mariners (April 26, 1993). . . . On Jacksonville disabled list (May 12-June 23 and July 17-31, 1993). . . . Released by Mariners (July 31, 1993). . . . Signed by Salem, Pittsburgh Pirates organization (June 24, 1994).

Year Team (League)	W	L	Pct.	ERA	G	GS	CG	ShO	Sv.	IP	H	R	ER	BB	SO
1989— Batavia (NYP)	3	5	.375	3.92	13	10	1	0	0	66 2/3	69	38	29	20	46
1990— Batavia (NYP)	7	1	*.875	2.64	14	14	0	0	0	81 2/3	70	34	24	22	50
1991— Clearwater (Fla. St.)	7	5	.583	3.39	43	6	0	0	1	93	101	43	35	25	59
1992— Reading (Eastern)	5	7	.417	4.64	18	14	0	0	0	85 1/3	94	55	44	21	60
— Scran./W.B. (Int'l)	3	3	.500	4.03	11	6	0	0	1	51 1/3	57	25	23	17	29
1993— Scran./W.B. (Int'l)	0	0	...	12.71	3	0	0	0	0	5 2/3	9	9	8	3	4
— Jacksonville (Sou.)■	0	1	.000	5.93	7	1	0	0	0	13 2/3	15	9	9	6	5
1994— Salem (Carolina)■	3	3	.500	3.63	17	7	0	0	0	57	58	24	23	21	48
1995— Carolina (South.)	9	1	.900	2.51	14	14	2	2	0	89 2/3	61	25	25	16	86
— Pittsburgh (N.L.)	6	6	.500	5.38	15	15	1	1	0	82	89	49	49	33	61
Major league totals (1 year)	6	6	.500	5.38	15	15	1	1	0	82	89	49	49	33	61

P

PARRISH, LANCE — C — PIRATES

PERSONAL: Born June 15, 1956, in McKeesport, Pa. . . . 6-3/224. . . . Bats right, throws right. . . . Full name: Lance Michael Parrish.
HIGH SCHOOL: Walnut (Calif.).
TRANSACTIONS/CAREER NOTES: Selected by Detroit Tigers organization in first round (16th pick overall) of free-agent draft (June 5, 1974). . . . On disabled list (July 31-September 29, 1986). . . . Granted free agency (November 12, 1986) . . . Signed by Philadelphia Phillies (March 13, 1987). . . . On disabled list (July 13-28, 1988). . . . Traded by Phillies to California Angels for P David Holdridge (October 3, 1988). . . . On California disabled list (June 10-25, 1991; May 5-28 and June 8-23, 1992). . . . Released by Angels (June 23, 1992). . . . Signed by Seattle Mariners (June 28, 1992). . . . Granted free agency (November 3, 1992). . . . Signed by Los Angeles Dodgers organization (January 8, 1993). . . . Released by Albuquerque, Dodgers organization (May 7, 1993). . . . Signed by Cleveland Indians (May 7, 1993). . . . Released by Indians (May 30, 1993). . . . Signed by Tigers organization (February 14, 1994). . . . Contract sold by Toledo, Tigers organization to Pittsburgh Pirates (April 30, 1994). . . . Granted free agency (October 25, 1994). . . . Signed by Omaha, Kansas City Royals organization (February 7, 1995). . . . Traded by Royals to Toronto Blue Jays organization for future considerations (April 22, 1995). . . . Granted free agency (November 2, 1995). . . . Signed by Pirates organization (January 4, 1996).
HONORS: Named catcher on The Sporting News A.L. Silver Slugger team (1980, 1982-84, 1986 and 1990). . . . Named catcher on The Sporting News A.L. All-Star team (1982 and 1984). . . . Won A.L. Gold Glove at catcher (1983-85).
STATISTICAL NOTES: Led Florida State League catchers with eight double plays and 31 passed balls in 1975. . . . Led Southern League with 22 passed balls in 1976. . . . Led American Association catchers with 10 double plays and 21 passed balls in 1977. . . . Led A.L. with 21 passed balls in 1979, 19 in 1991 and tied for lead with 17 in 1980. . . . Led A.L. with 13 sacrifice flies in 1983. . . . Led A.L. catchers with 772 total chances in 1983. . . . Led A.L. catchers with 11 double plays in 1984 and 15 in 1990. . . . Led N.L. catchers with 12 passed balls and tied for lead with 11 double plays in 1988. . . . Led A.L. catchers with 88 assists in 1990. . . . Career major league grand slams: 7.

			BATTING											FIELDING			
Year Team (League)	**Pos.**	**G**	**AB**	**R**	**H**	**2B**	**3B**	**HR**	**RBI**	**Avg.**	**BB**	**SO**	**SB**	**PO**	**A**	**E**	**Avg.**
1974—Bristol (Appal.)	3B-OF	68	253	45	54	11	1	11	46	.213	32	*92	2	36	83	22	.844
1975—Lakeland (Fla. St.)	C	100	341	30	75	15	2	5	37	.220	30	85	0	460	50	7	.986
1976—Montgomery (Sou.)	C	107	340	46	75	9	2	14	55	.221	38	95	0	*600	*79	11	*.984
1977—Evansville (A.A.)	C	115	416	74	116	21	2	25	90	.279	56	105	2	*722	*82	11	*.987
—Detroit (A.L.)	C	12	46	10	9	2	0	3	7	.196	5	12	0	76	6	0	1.000
1978—Detroit (A.L.)	C	85	288	37	63	11	3	14	41	.219	11	71	0	353	39	5	.987
1979—Detroit (A.L.)	C	143	493	65	136	26	3	19	65	.276	49	105	6	707	*79	9	.989
1980—Detroit (A.L.)	C-DH-1-0	144	553	79	158	34	6	24	82	.286	31	109	6	607	67	7	.990
1981—Detroit (A.L.)	C-DH	96	348	39	85	18	2	10	46	.244	34	52	2	407	40	3	.993
1982—Detroit (A.L.)	C-OF	133	486	75	138	19	2	32	87	.284	40	99	3	627	76	8	.989
1983—Detroit (A.L.)	C-DH	155	605	80	163	42	3	27	114	.269	44	106	1	695	73	4	.995
1984—Detroit (A.L.)	C-DH	147	578	75	137	16	2	33	98	.237	41	120	2	720	67	7	.991
1985—Detroit (A.L.)	C-DH	140	549	64	150	27	1	28	98	.273	41	90	2	695	53	5	.993
1986—Detroit (A.L.)	C-DH	91	327	53	84	6	1	22	62	.257	38	83	0	483	48	6	.989
1987—Philadelphia (N.L.)■	C	130	466	42	114	21	0	17	67	.245	47	104	0	724	66	9	.989
1988—Philadelphia (N.L.)	C-1B	123	424	44	91	17	2	15	60	.215	47	93	0	640	73	9	.988
1989—California (A.L.)■	C-DH	124	433	48	103	12	1	17	50	.238	42	104	1	638	63	5	.993
1990—California (A.L.)	C-1B-DH	133	470	54	126	14	0	24	70	.268	46	107	2	794	†90	6	.993
1991—California (A.L.)	C-DH-1B	119	402	38	87	12	0	19	51	.216	35	117	0	670	57	2	.997
1992—California (A.L.)	C-DH	24	83	7	19	2	0	4	11	.229	5	22	0	107	8	3	.975
—Seattle (A.L.)■	C-1B-DH	69	192	19	45	11	1	8	21	.234	19	48	1	276	15	3	.990
1993—Albuquerque (PCL)■	C	11	33	4	9	2	0	0	1	.273	5	4	0	67	7	0	1.000
—Cleveland (A.L.)■	C	10	20	2	4	1	0	1	2	.200	4	5	1	47	10	3	.950
1994—Toledo (Int'l)■	C-1B	15	51	6	17	3	0	1	5	.333	5	7	0	60	5	1	.985
—Pittsburgh (N.L.)■	C-1B	40	126	10	34	5	0	3	16	.270	18	28	1	228	15	4	.984
1995—Toronto (A.L.)■	C-DH	70	178	15	36	9	0	4	22	.202	15	52	0	346	41	0	1.000
American League totals (16 years)		1695	6051	760	1543	262	25	289	927	.255	500	1302	27	8248	832	76	.992
National League totals (3 years)		293	1016	96	239	43	2	35	143	.235	112	225	1	1592	154	22	.988
Major league totals (19 years)		1988	7067	856	1782	305	27	324	1070	.252	612	1527	28	9840	986	98	.991

CHAMPIONSHIP SERIES RECORD

			BATTING											FIELDING			
Year Team (League)	**Pos.**	**G**	**AB**	**R**	**H**	**2B**	**3B**	**HR**	**RBI**	**Avg.**	**BB**	**SO**	**SB**	**PO**	**A**	**E**	**Avg.**
1984—Detroit (A.L.)	C	3	12	1	3	1	0	1	3	.250	0	3	0	21	2	0	1.000

WORLD SERIES RECORD

NOTES: Member of World Series championship team (1984).

			BATTING											FIELDING			
Year Team (League)	**Pos.**	**G**	**AB**	**R**	**H**	**2B**	**3B**	**HR**	**RBI**	**Avg.**	**BB**	**SO**	**SB**	**PO**	**A**	**E**	**Avg.**
1984—Detroit (A.L.)	C	5	18	3	5	1	0	1	2	.278	3	2	1	30	3	1	.971

ALL-STAR GAME RECORD

NOTES: Named to A.L. All-Star team for 1985 game; replaced by Rich Gedman due to injury.

		BATTING											FIELDING			
Year League	**Pos.**	**AB**	**R**	**H**	**2B**	**3B**	**HR**	**RBI**	**Avg.**	**BB**	**SO**	**SB**	**PO**	**A**	**E**	**Avg.**
1980—American	C	1	0	0	0	0	0	0	.000	0	1	0	0	0	0	...
1982—American	C	2	0	1	1	0	0	0	.500	0	0	0	2	3	0	1.000
1983—American	C	2	0	0	0	0	0	0	.000	0	1	0	1	0	0	1.000
1984—American	C	2	0	0	0	0	0	0	.000	0	2	0	3	1	1	.800
1985—American		Selected, did not play—injured.														
1986—American	C	3	0	0	0	0	0	0	.000	0	0	0	4	0	0	1.000
1988—National	C	1	0	0	0	0	0	0	.000	0	0	0	0	0	0	...
1990—American	PH-C	1	1	1	0	0	0	0	1.000	0	0	0	3	0	0	1.000
All-Star Game totals (7 years)		12	1	2	1	0	0	0	.167	0	4	0	13	4	1	.944

P

PATTERSON, BOB — P — CUBS

PERSONAL: Born May 16, 1959, in Jacksonville, Fla. . . . 6-2/192. . . . Throws left, bats right. . . . Full name: Robert Chandler Patterson.
HIGH SCHOOL: Wade Hampton (Greenville, S.C.).
COLLEGE: East Carolina (degree in industrial technology).
TRANSACTIONS/CAREER NOTES: Selected by San Diego Padres organization in 21st round of free-agent draft (June 7, 1982). . . . Traded by Padres to Pittsburgh Pirates for OF Marvell Wynne (April 3, 1986). . . . On disabled list (April 28, 1988-remainder of season). . . . Released by Pirates (November 20, 1992). . . . Signed by Texas Rangers organization (December 8, 1992). . . . Granted free agency (October 4, 1993). . . . Signed by California Angels organization (January 18, 1994). . . . Granted free agency (December 23, 1994). . . . Re-signed by Angels organization (April 16, 1995). . . . Granted free agency (November 2, 1995). . . . Signed by Chicago Cubs (January 16, 1996).

Year	Team (League)	W	L	Pct.	ERA	G	GS	CG	ShO	Sv.	IP	H	R	ER	BB	SO
1982—	GC Padres (GCL)	4	3	.571	2.94	8	6	3	0	0	52	60	18	17	7	65
—	Reno (California)	1	0	1.000	3.55	4	4	1	1	0	25 1/3	28	11	10	5	10
1983—	Beaumont (Texas)	8	4	.667	4.01	43	9	2	0	11	116 2/3	107	61	52	36	97
1984—	Las Vegas (PCL)	8	9	.471	3.27	*60	7	1	0	13	143 1/3	129	63	52	37	97
1985—	Las Vegas (PCL)	10	11	.476	3.14	42	20	7	1	6	186 1/3	187	80	65	52	146
—	San Diego (N.L.)	0	0	...	24.75	3	0	0	0	0	4	13	11	11	3	1
1986—	Hawaii (Pac. Coast)■	9	6	.600	3.40	25	21	6	1	1	156	146	68	59	44	*137
—	Pittsburgh (N.L.)	2	3	.400	4.95	11	5	0	0	0	36 1/3	49	20	20	5	20
1987—	Pittsburgh (N.L.)	1	4	.200	6.70	15	7	0	0	0	43	49	34	32	22	27
—	Vancouver (PCL)	5	2	.714	2.12	14	12	5	1	0	89	62	21	21	30	92
1988—	Buffalo (A.A.)	2	0	1.000	2.32	4	4	1	0	0	31	26	12	8	4	20
1989—	Buffalo (A.A.)	12	6	.667	3.35	31	25	4	1	1	177 1/3	177	69	66	35	103
—	Pittsburgh (N.L.)	4	3	.571	4.05	12	3	0	0	1	26 2/3	23	13	12	8	20
1990—	Pittsburgh (N.L.)	8	5	.615	2.95	55	5	0	0	5	94 2/3	88	33	31	21	70
1991—	Pittsburgh (N.L.)	4	3	.571	4.11	54	1	0	0	2	65 2/3	67	32	30	15	57
1992—	Pittsburgh (N.L.)	6	3	.667	2.92	60	0	0	0	9	64 2/3	59	22	21	23	43
1993—	Texas (A.L.)■	2	4	.333	4.78	52	0	0	0	1	52 2/3	59	28	28	11	46
1994—	California (A.L.)■	2	3	.400	4.07	47	0	0	0	1	42	35	21	19	15	30
1995—	California (A.L.)	5	2	.714	3.04	62	0	0	0	0	53 1/3	48	18	18	13	41
A.L. totals (3 years)		9	9	.500	3.95	161	0	0	0	2	148	142	67	65	39	117
N.L. totals (7 years)		25	21	.543	4.22	210	21	0	0	17	335	348	165	157	97	238
Major league totals (10 years)		34	30	.531	4.14	371	21	0	0	19	483	490	232	222	136	355

CHAMPIONSHIP SERIES RECORD

Year	Team (League)	W	L	Pct.	ERA	G	GS	CG	ShO	Sv.	IP	H	R	ER	BB	SO
1990—	Pittsburgh (N.L.)	0	0	...	0.00	2	0	0	0	1	1	1	0	0	2	0
1991—	Pittsburgh (N.L.)	0	0	...	0.00	1	0	0	0	0	2	1	0	0	0	3
1992—	Pittsburgh (N.L.)	0	0	...	5.40	2	0	0	0	0	1 2/3	3	1	1	1	1
Champ. series totals (3 years)		0	0	...	1.93	5	0	0	0	1	4 2/3	5	1	1	3	4

PATTERSON, DANNY — P — RANGERS

PERSONAL: Born February 17, 1971, in San Gabriel, Calif. . . . 6-0/175. . . . Throws right, bats right. . . . Full name: Danny Shane Patterson.
HIGH SCHOOL: San Gabriel (Calif.).
JUNIOR COLLEGE: Cerritos College (Calif.).
TRANSACTIONS/CAREER NOTES: Selected by Texas Rangers organization in 47th round of free-agent draft (June 5, 1989).

Year	Team (League)	W	L	Pct.	ERA	G	GS	CG	ShO	Sv.	IP	H	R	ER	BB	SO
1990—	Butte (Pioneer)	0	3	.000	6.35	13	3	0	0	1	28 1/3	36	23	20	14	18
1991—	GC Rangers (GCL)	5	3	.625	3.24	11	9	0	0	0	50	43	21	18	12	46
1992—	Gastonia (S. Atl.)	4	6	.400	3.59	23	21	3	1	0	105 1/3	106	47	42	33	84
1993—	Charlotte (Fla. St.)	5	6	.455	2.51	47	0	0	0	7	68	55	22	19	28	41
1994—	Tulsa (Texas)	1	4	.200	1.64	30	1	0	0	6	44	35	13	8	17	33
—	Charlotte (Fla. St.)	1	0	1.000	4.61	7	0	0	0	0	13 2/3	13	7	7	5	9
1995—	Tulsa (Texas)	2	2	.500	6.19	26	0	0	0	5	36 1/3	45	27	25	13	24
—	Okla. City (A.A.)	1	0	1.000	1.65	14	0	0	0	2	27 1/3	23	8	5	9	9

PATTERSON, JEFF — P — GIANTS

PERSONAL: Born October 1, 1968, in Anaheim, Calif. . . . 6-2/200. . . . Throws right, bats right. . . . Full name: Jeffrey Simmons Patterson.
HIGH SCHOOL: Loara (Anaheim, Calif.).
JUNIOR COLLEGE: Cypress (Calif.) College.
TRANSACTIONS/CAREER NOTES: Selected by Philadelphia Phillies organization in 58th round of free-agent draft (June 1, 1988). . . . Traded by Phillies to New York Yankees (November 8, 1994), completing deal in which Yankees traded P Pedro Munoz, 2B Kevin Jordan and P Ryan Karp to Phillies for P Terry Mulholland and a player to be named later (February 9, 1994). . . . Granted free agency (October 12, 1995). . . . Signed by San Francisco Giants organization (November 10, 1995).

Year	Team (League)	W	L	Pct.	ERA	G	GS	CG	ShO	Sv.	IP	H	R	ER	BB	SO
1989—	Martinsville (App.)	2	4	.333	3.61	7	7	0	0	0	42 1/3	35	23	17	12	44
—	Batavia (NYP)	2	4	.333	2.87	9	7	1	1	1	53 1/3	44	19	17	11	41
1990—	Clearwater (Fla. St.)	3	6	.333	2.96	11	11	0	0	0	67	63	34	22	22	28
1991—	Spartanburg (SAL)	9	8	.529	4.42	35	10	2	1	9	114	103	60	56	41	114
1992—	Clearwater (Fla. St.)	2	1	.667	1.98	30	0	0	0	14	36 1/3	29	11	8	11	33
—	Reading (Eastern)	3	1	.750	4.60	26	0	0	0	13	31 1/3	30	16	16	14	22
—	Scran./W.B. (Int'l)	2	1	.667	2.63	11	0	0	0	1	13 2/3	10	4	4	8	11
1993—	Scran./W.B. (Int'l)	7	5	.583	2.69	•62	0	0	0	8	93 2/3	79	32	28	42	68
1994—	Scran./W.B. (Int'l)	6	4	.600	4.60	52	2	0	0	5	94	102	50	48	48	64
1995—	New York (A.L.)■	0	0	...	2.70	3	0	0	0	0	3 1/3	3	1	1	3	3
—	Columbus (Int'l)	5	3	.625	3.61	33	0	0	0	0	62 1/3	56	30	25	30	36
Major league totals (1 year)		0	0	...	2.70	3	0	0	0	0	3 1/3	3	1	1	3	3

P

PATTERSON, JOHN — 2B

PERSONAL: Born February 11, 1967, in Key West, Fla. . . . 5-9/168. . . . Bats both, throws right. . . . Full name: John Allen Patterson.
HIGH SCHOOL: Trevor G. Browne (Phoenix).
JUNIOR COLLEGE: Central Arizona College.
COLLEGE: Grand Canyon (Ariz.).
TRANSACTIONS/CAREER NOTES: Selected by San Diego Padres organization in third round of free-agent draft (January 14, 1986); did not sign. . . . Selected by San Francisco Giants organization in 23rd round of free-agent draft (June 1, 1988). . . . On disabled list (April 1, 1989-entire season). . . . On San Francisco disabled list (May 7-23, 1992). . . . On San Francisco disabled list (March 27-September 1, 1993); included rehabilitation assignment to San Jose (August 13-September 1). . . . Granted free agency (October 24, 1995).
STATISTICAL NOTES: Career major league grand slams: 1.

			BATTING												FIELDING			
Year Team (League)	**Pos.**	**G**	**AB**	**R**	**H**	**2B**	**3B**	**HR**	**RBI**	**Avg.**	**BB**	**SO**	**SB**	**PO**	**A**	**E**	**Avg.**
1988—Everett (N'west)	2B-SS	58	232	37	58	10	4	0	26	.250	18	27	21	89	97	9	.954
1989—								Did not play.									
1990—San Jose (Calif.)	2B	131	530	91	160	23	6	4	66	.302	46	74	29	247	322	26	.956
1991—Shreveport (Texas)	2B	117	464	81	137	31	13	4	56	.295	30	63	41	242	299	15	.973
1992—San Francisco (N.L.)	2B-OF	32	103	10	19	1	1	0	4	.184	5	24	5	66	54	4	.968
—Phoenix (PCL)	2B-OF-3B	93	362	52	109	20	6	2	37	.301	33	45	22	185	239	9	.979
1993—San Jose (Calif.)	2B	16	68	8	16	7	0	1	14	.235	7	12	6	2	2	0	1.000
—San Francisco (N.L.)	PH	16	16	1	3	0	0	1	2	.188	0	5	0	...	...	...	...
1994—San Francisco (N.L.)	2B	85	240	36	57	10	1	3	32	.238	16	43	13	121	163	6	.979
1995—San Francisco (N.L.)	2B	95	205	27	42	5	3	1	14	.205	14	41	4	114	112	4	.983
Major league totals (4 years)		228	564	74	121	16	5	5	52	.215	35	113	22	301	329	14	.978

PAVLAS, DAVE — P — YANKEES

PERSONAL: Born August 12, 1962, in Frankfurt, West Germany. . . . 6-7/195. . . . Throws right, bats right. . . . Full name: David Lee Pavlas.
HIGH SCHOOL: Shiner (Tex.).
COLLEGE: Rice.
TRANSACTIONS/CAREER NOTES: Signed as non-drafted free agent by Chicago Cubs organization (December 15, 1984). . . . Traded by Cubs organization to Texas Rangers organization (June 6, 1987), completing deal in which Rangers traded P Mike Mason to Cubs for a player to be named later (May 15, 1987). . . . Contract sold by Rangers organization to Cubs organization (January 3, 1990). . . . Released by Cubs (September 5, 1991). . . . Signed by Greenville, Atlanta Braves organization (February 9, 1992). . . . Released by Greenville (March 31, 1992). . . . Played in Mexican League (1992). . . . Signed by Iowa, Cubs organization (July 26, 1992). . . . Granted free agency (October 15, 1992). . . . Signed by Buffalo, Pittsburgh Pirates organization (June 1, 1993). . . . Loaned by Buffalo to Mexico City Red Devils of Mexican League (June 1, 1993-remainder of season). . . . Granted free agency (October 15, 1993). . . . Signed by New York Yankees organization (February 8, 1995). . . . On Columbus disabled list (April 21-28, 1995). . . . Granted free agency (October 16, 1995). . . . Re-signed by Yankees organization (January 19, 1996).
HONORS: Named Carolina League Pitcher of the Year (1986).
STATISTICAL NOTES: Led American Association with 10 hit batsmen in 1990.

Year Team (League)	**W**	**L**	**Pct.**	**ERA**	**G**	**GS**	**CG**	**ShO**	**Sv.**	**IP**	**H**	**R**	**ER**	**BB**	**SO**
1985—Peoria (Midwest)	8	3	.727	2.62	17	15	3	1	1	110	90	40	32	32	86
1986—Winst.-Salem (Car.)	14	6	.700	3.84	28	26	5	2	0	173 1/3	172	91	74	57	143
1987—Pittsfield (Eastern)	6	1	.857	3.80	7	7	0	0	0	45	49	25	19	17	27
—Tulsa (Texas)■	1	6	.143	7.69	13	12	0	0	0	59 2/3	79	51	51	27	46
1988—Tulsa (Texas)	5	2	.714	1.98	26	5	1	0	2	77 1/3	52	26	17	18	69
—Okla. City (A.A.)	3	1	.750	4.47	13	8	0	0	0	52 1/3	59	29	26	28	40
1989—Okla. City (A.A.)	2	*14	.125	4.70	29	21	4	0	0	143 2/3	175	89	75	67	94
1990—Iowa (Am. Assoc.)■	8	3	.727	3.26	53	3	0	0	8	99 1/3	84	38	36	48	96
—Chicago (N.L.)	2	0	1.000	2.11	13	0	0	0	0	21 1/3	23	7	5	6	12
1991—Iowa (Am. Assoc.)	5	6	.455	3.98	61	0	0	0	7	97 1/3	92	49	43	43	54
—Chicago (N.L.)	0	0	...	18.00	1	0	0	0	0	1	3	2	2	0	0
1992—Jalisco (Mexican)■	1	4	.200	2.61	12	4	1	0	4	41 1/3	35	16	12	10	25
—Iowa (Am. Assoc.)■	3	3	.500	3.38	12	4	0	0	0	37 1/3	43	20	14	8	34
1993—M.C. Red Devils (Mex.)■	5	3	.625	3.49	11	11	1	0	0	56 2/3	59	24	22	19	32
1994—							Did not play.								
1995—Columbus (Int'l)■	3	3	.500	2.61	48	0	0	0	18	58 2/3	43	19	17	20	51
—New York (A.L.)	0	0	...	3.18	4	0	0	0	0	5 2/3	8	2	2	0	3
A.L. totals (1 year)	0	0	...	3.18	4	0	0	0	0	5 2/3	8	2	2	0	3
N.L. totals (2 years)	2	0	1.000	2.82	14	0	0	0	0	22 1/3	26	9	7	6	12
Major league totals (3 years)	2	0	1.000	2.89	18	0	0	0	0	28	34	11	9	6	15

PAVLIK, ROGER — P — RANGERS

PERSONAL: Born October 4, 1967, in Houston. . . . 6-2/220. . . . Throws right, bats right. . . . Full name: Roger Allen Pavlik.
HIGH SCHOOL: Aldine (Houston).
TRANSACTIONS/CAREER NOTES: Selected by Texas Rangers organization in second round of free-agent draft (June 2, 1986). . . . On disabled list (June 21, 1986-remainder of season; June 4-August 6, 1987; and April 29-May 6 and May 23-July 29, 1991). . . . On Texas disabled list (March 25-May 15, 1994); included rehabilitation assignments to Charlotte (April 23-May 10) and Oklahoma City (May 10-15). . . . On Texas disabled list (June 12-July 2, 1994); included rehabilitation assignment to Oklahoma City (June 27-July 2). . . . On Texas disabled list (July 3-24, 1994); included rehabilitation assignment to Oklahoma City (July 7-27).
STATISTICAL NOTES: Pitched 5 1/3 innings, combining with reliever Steve Peters (2 2/3 innings) for eight no-hit innings in a 1-0 loss to Indianapolis (April 17, 1991).

Year Team (League)	**W**	**L**	**Pct.**	**ERA**	**G**	**GS**	**CG**	**ShO**	**Sv.**	**IP**	**H**	**R**	**ER**	**BB**	**SO**
1986—							Did not play.								
1987—Gastonia (S. Atl.)	2	7	.222	4.95	15	14	0	0	0	67 1/3	66	46	37	42	55
1988—Gastonia (S. Atl.)	2	12	.143	4.59	18	16	0	0	0	84 1/3	94	65	43	58	89

Year	Team (League)	W	L	Pct.	ERA	G	GS	CG	ShO	Sv.	IP	H	R	ER	BB	SO
	— Butte (Pioneer)	4	0	1.000	4.59	8	8	1	1	0	49	45	29	25	34	56
1989—	Charlotte (Fla. St.)	3	8	.273	3.41	26	22	1	1	1	118 2/3	92	60	45	72	98
1990—	Charlotte (Fla. St.)	5	3	.625	2.44	11	11	1	0	0	66 1/3	50	21	18	40	76
	— Tulsa (Texas)	6	5	.545	2.33	16	16	2	1	0	100 1/3	66	29	26	71	91
1991—	Okla. City (A.A.)	0	5	.000	5.19	8	7	0	0	0	26	19	21	15	26	43
1992—	Okla. City (A.A.)	7	5	.583	2.98	18	18	0	0	0	117 2/3	90	44	39	51	104
	— Texas (A.L.)	4	4	.500	4.21	13	12	1	0	0	62	66	32	29	34	45
1993—	Okla. City (A.A.)	3	2	.600	1.70	6	6	0	0	0	37	26	12	7	14	32
	— Texas (A.L.)	12	6	.667	3.41	26	26	2	0	0	166 1/3	151	67	63	80	131
1994—	Charlotte (Fla. St.)	2	1	.667	1.08	3	3	0	0	0	16 2/3	13	2	2	2	15
	— Okla. City (A.A.)	2	2	.500	3.10	5	5	0	0	0	29	26	11	10	7	38
	— Texas (A.L.)	2	5	.286	7.69	11	11	0	0	0	50 1/3	61	45	43	30	31
1995—	Texas (A.L.)	10	10	.500	4.37	31	31	2	1	0	191 2/3	174	96	93	90	149
Major league totals (4 years)		28	25	.528	4.36	81	80	5	1	0	470 1/3	452	240	228	234	356

PEGUES, STEVE — OF — MARINERS

PERSONAL: Born May 21, 1968, in Pontotoc, Miss. . . . 6-2/190. . . . Bats right, throws right. . . . Full name: Steven Antone Pegues. . . . Name pronounced peh-GEEZE.

HIGH SCHOOL: Pontotoc (Miss.).

TRANSACTIONS/CAREER NOTES: Selected by Detroit Tigers organization in first round (21st pick overall) of free-agent draft (June 2, 1987). . . . Claimed on waivers by San Diego Padres (March 20, 1992). . . . On disabled list (April 9-May 7, May 25-June 1 and July 18-August 26, 1993). . . . Granted free agency (April 1, 1994). . . . Signed by Cincinnati Reds organization (April 7, 1994). . . . Granted free agency (July 27, 1994). . . . Signed by Pittsburgh Pirates (July 29, 1994). . . . Granted free agency (October 11, 1995). . . . Signed by Seattle Mariners organization (December 14, 1995).

STATISTICAL NOTES: Led Pacific Coast League outfielders with 24 assists in 1992.

				BATTING											FIELDING			
Year	Team (League)	Pos.	G	AB	R	H	2B	3B	HR	RBI	Avg.	BB	SO	SB	PO	A	E	Avg.
1987—	Bristol (Appal.)	OF	59	236	36	67	6	5	2	23	.284	16	42	22	114	4	10	.922
1988—	Fayetteville (SAL)	OF	118	437	50	112	7	5	6	46	.256	21	90	21	240	13	12	.955
1989—	Fayetteville (SAL)	OF	70	269	35	83	11	6	1	38	.309	15	52	16	127	8	2	.985
	— Lakeland (Fla. St.)	OF	55	193	24	49	7	2	0	15	.254	7	19	12	115	3	2	.983
1990—	London (Eastern)	OF	126	483	48	131	22	5	8	63	.271	12	58	17	244	7	•9	.965
1991—	London (Eastern)	OF	56	216	24	65	3	2	6	26	.301	8	24	4	69	4	1	.986
	— Toledo (Int'l)	OF	68	222	21	50	13	3	4	23	.225	3	31	8	84	7	4	.958
1992—	Las Vegas (PCL)■	OF-1B	123	376	51	99	21	4	9	56	.263	7	64	12	203	†24	9	.962
1993—	Las Vegas (PCL)	OF	68	270	52	95	20	5	9	50	.352	7	43	12	103	5	2	.982
1994—	Indianapolis (A.A.)■	OF	63	245	36	71	16	11	6	29	.290	6	44	10	134	2	4	.971
	— Cincinnati (N.L.)	OF	11	10	1	3	0	0	0	0	.300	1	3	0	5	0	1	.833
	— Pittsburgh (N.L.)■	OF	7	26	1	10	2	0	0	2	.385	1	2	1	8	0	0	1.000
1995—	Pittsburgh (N.L.)	OF	82	171	17	42	8	0	6	16	.246	4	36	1	81	2	4	.954
Major league totals (2 years)			100	207	19	55	10	0	6	18	.266	6	41	2	94	2	5	.950

PEMBERTON, RUDY — OF — RANGERS

PERSONAL: Born December 17, 1969, in San Pedro de Macoris, Dominican Republic. . . . 6-1/185. . . . Bats right, throws right. . . . Full name: Rudy Hector Perez Pemberton.

TRANSACTIONS/CAREER NOTES: Signed as non-drafted free agent by Detroit Tigers organization (June 7, 1987). . . . On disabled list (April 7-May 10, 1994). . . . Granted free agency (October 3, 1995). . . . Signed by Texas Rangers organization (December 19, 1995).

STATISTICAL NOTES: Tied for Florida State League lead in being hit by pitch with 13 in 1992.

				BATTING											FIELDING			
Year	Team (League)	Pos.	G	AB	R	H	2B	3B	HR	RBI	Avg.	BB	SO	SB	PO	A	E	Avg.
1987—		Dominican Summer League statistics unavailable.																
1988—	Bristol (Appal.)	OF	6	5	2	0	0	0	0	0	.000	1	3	0	0	0	0	...
1989—	Bristol (Appal.)	OF	56	214	40	58	9	2	6	39	.271	14	43	19	84	4	5	.946
1990—	Fayetteville (SAL)	OF	127	454	59	126	14	5	6	61	.278	42	91	12	192	12	10	.953
1991—	Lakeland (Fla. St.)	OF	111	375	40	86	15	2	3	36	.229	25	52	25	184	9	9	.955
1992—	Lakeland (Fla. St.)	OF	104	343	41	91	16	5	3	43	.265	21	37	25	147	17	3	.982
1993—	London (Eastern)	OF	124	471	70	130	22	4	15	67	.276	24	80	14	215	11	8	.966
1994—	Toledo (Int'l)	OF	99	360	49	109	13	3	12	58	.303	18	62	30	182	5	8	.959
1995—	Detroit (A.L.)	OF-DH	12	30	3	9	3	1	0	3	.300	1	5	0	15	0	0	1.000
	— Toledo (Int'l)	OF	67	224	31	77	15	3	7	23	.344	15	36	8	59	2	3	.953
Major league totals (1 year)			12	30	3	9	3	1	0	3	.300	1	5	0	15	0	0	1.000

P

PENA, ALEJANDRO — P — MARLINS

PERSONAL: Born June 25, 1959, in Cambiaso, Dominican Republic. . . . 6-1/228. . . . Throws right, bats right. . . . Full name: Alejandro Vasquez Pena.

TRANSACTIONS/CAREER NOTES: Signed as non-drafted free agent by Los Angeles Dodgers organization (September 10, 1978). . . . On disabled list (April 8-September 5, 1985). . . . On Los Angeles disabled list (March 23-May 26, 1986); included rehabilitation assignment to Vero Beach (May 2-19). . . . On disabled list (July 27-August 17, 1987). . . . Granted free agency (November 4, 1988). . . . Re-signed by Dodgers (November 7, 1988). . . . On disabled list (July 8-23, 1989). . . . Traded by Dodgers with OF Mike Marshall to New York Mets for OF Juan Samuel (December 20, 1989). . . . Traded by Mets to Atlanta Braves for P Tony Castillo and a player to be named later (August 28, 1991); Mets acquired P Joe Roa to complete deal (August 29, 1991). . . . Granted free agency (November 1, 1991). . . . Re-signed by Braves (February 28, 1992). . . . On disabled list (May 31-June 18 and August 21-September 5, 1992). . . . Granted free agency (November 3, 1992). . . . Signed by Pittsburgh Pirates (December 10, 1992). . . . On disabled list (March 22, 1993-entire season). . . . On Pittsburgh disabled list (March 25-May 1, 1994); included rehabilitation assignment to Buffalo (April 26-29). . . . Released by Pirates (June 30, 1994). . . . Signed by

Pawtucket, Boston Red Sox organization (April 23, 1995). . . . Released by Red Sox (June 13, 1995). . . . Signed by Charlotte, Florida Marlins organization (June 27, 1995). . . . Traded by Marlins to Braves for a player to be named later (August 31, 1995); Marlins acquired P Chris Seelbach to complete deal (September 15, 1995). . . . Granted free agency (November 3, 1995). . . . Signed by Marlins organization (December 12, 1995).

STATISTICAL NOTES: Pitched one inning, combining with starter Kent Mercker (six innings) and Mark Wohlers (two innings) in 1-0 no-hit victory for Atlanta against San Diego (September 11, 1991).

Year	Team (League)	W	L	Pct.	ERA	G	GS	CG	ShO	Sv.	IP	H	R	ER	BB	SO
1979—	Clinton (Midwest)	3	3	.500	4.18	21	5	0	0	0	71	53	39	33	44	57
1980—	Vero Beach (FSL)	10	3	.769	3.21	35	3	0	0	8	73	57	32	26	41	46
1981—	Albuquerque (PCL)	2	5	.286	1.61	38	0	0	0	*22	56	36	12	10	21	40
	—Los Angeles (N.L.)	1	1	.500	2.88	14	0	0	0	2	25	18	8	8	11	14
1982—	Los Angeles (N.L.)	0	2	.000	4.79	29	0	0	0	0	35 2/3	37	24	19	21	20
	—Albuquerque (PCL)	1	1	.500	5.34	16	0	0	0	5	28 2/3	37	18	17	10	27
1983—	Los Angeles (N.L.)	12	9	.571	2.75	34	26	4	3	1	177	152	67	54	51	120
1984—	Los Angeles (N.L.)	12	6	.667	*2.48	28	28	8	•4	0	199 1/3	186	67	55	46	135
1985—	Los Angeles (N.L.)	0	1	.000	8.31	2	1	0	0	0	4 1/3	7	5	4	3	2
1986—	Vero Beach (FSL)	0	2	.000	7.47	4	4	0	0	0	15 2/3	22	15	13	4	11
	—Los Angeles (N.L.)	1	2	.333	4.89	24	10	0	0	1	70	74	40	38	30	46
1987—	Los Angeles (N.L.)	2	7	.222	3.50	37	7	0	0	11	87 1/3	82	41	34	37	76
1988—	Los Angeles (N.L.)	6	7	.462	1.91	60	0	0	0	12	94 1/3	75	29	20	27	83
1989—	Los Angeles (N.L.)	4	3	.571	2.13	53	0	0	0	5	76	62	20	18	18	75
1990—	New York (N.L.)■	3	3	.500	3.20	52	0	0	0	5	76	71	31	27	22	76
1991—	New York (N.L.)	6	1	.857	2.71	44	0	0	0	4	63	63	20	19	19	49
	—Atlanta (N.L.)■	2	0	1.000	1.40	15	0	0	0	11	19 1/3	11	3	3	3	13
1992—	Atlanta (N.L.)	1	6	.143	4.07	41	0	0	0	15	42	40	19	19	13	34
1993—								Did not play.								
1994—	Buffalo (A.A.)■	0	0	. . .	0.00	2	2	0	0	0	2	1	0	0	0	4
	—Pittsburgh (N.L.)	3	2	.600	5.02	22	0	0	0	7	28 2/3	22	16	16	10	27
1995—	Boston (A.L.)■	1	1	.500	7.40	17	0	0	0	0	24 1/3	33	23	20	12	25
	—Charlotte (Int'l)■	0	0	. . .	0.96	9	0	0	0	5	9 1/3	2	1	1	1	7
	—Florida (N.L.)	2	0	1.000	1.50	13	0	0	0	0	18	11	3	3	3	21
	—Atlanta (N.L.)■	0	0	. . .	4.15	14	0	0	0	0	13	11	6	6	4	18
A.L. totals (1 year)		1	1	.500	7.40	17	0	0	0	0	24 1/3	33	23	20	12	25
N.L. totals (14 years)		55	50	.524	3.00	482	72	12	7	74	1029	922	399	343	318	809
Major league totals (14 years)		56	51	.523	3.10	499	72	12	7	74	1053 1/3	955	422	363	330	834

DIVISION SERIES RECORD

Year	Team (League)	W	L	Pct.	ERA	G	GS	CG	ShO	Sv.	IP	H	R	ER	BB	SO
1995—	Atlanta (N.L.)	2	0	1.000	0.00	3	0	0	0	0	3	3	0	0	1	2

CHAMPIONSHIP SERIES RECORD

NOTES: Shares single-series record for most wild pitches—4 (1991). . . . Shares N.L. single-series record for most saves—3 (1991).

Year	Team (League)	W	L	Pct.	ERA	G	GS	CG	ShO	Sv.	IP	H	R	ER	BB	SO
1981—	Los Angeles (N.L.)	0	0	. . .	0.00	2	0	0	0	0	2 1/3	1	0	0	0	0
1983—	Los Angeles (N.L.)	0	0	. . .	6.75	1	0	0	0	0	2 2/3	4	2	2	1	3
1988—	Los Angeles (N.L.)	1	1	.500	4.15	3	0	0	0	1	4 1/3	1	2	2	5	1
1991—	Atlanta (N.L.)	0	0	. . .	0.00	4	0	0	0	3	4 1/3	1	0	0	0	4
1995—	Atlanta (N.L.)	0	0	. . .	0.00	3	0	0	0	0	3	2	0	0	1	4
Champ. series totals (5 years)		1	1	.500	2.16	13	0	0	0	4	16 2/3	9	4	4	7	12

WORLD SERIES RECORD

NOTES: Member of World Series championship teams (1981, 1988 and 1995).

Year	Team (League)	W	L	Pct.	ERA	G	GS	CG	ShO	Sv.	IP	H	R	ER	BB	SO
1981—	Los Angeles (N.L.)							Did not play.								
1988—	Los Angeles (N.L.)	1	0	1.000	0.00	2	0	0	0	0	5	2	0	0	1	7
1991—	Atlanta (N.L.)	0	1	.000	3.38	3	0	0	0	0	5 1/3	6	2	2	3	7
1995—	Atlanta (N.L.)	0	1	.000	9.00	2	0	0	0	0	1	3	1	1	2	0
World Series totals (3 years)		1	2	.333	2.38	7	0	0	0	0	11 1/3	11	3	3	6	14

PENA, GERONIMO 2B

PERSONAL: Born March 29, 1967, in Distrito Nacional, Dominican Republic. . . . 6-1/195. . . . Bats both, throws right.

HIGH SCHOOL: Distrito Nacional (Dominican Republic).

TRANSACTIONS/CAREER NOTES: Signed as non-drafted free agent by St. Louis Cardinals organization (August 9, 1984). . . . On St. Louis disabled list (March 25-June 5, 1989); included rehabilitation assignment to St. Petersburg (May 29-June 5). . . . On St. Louis disabled list (March 28-May 26, 1992); included rehabilitation assignment to Louisville (May 11-18 and May 21-25). . . . On St. Louis disabled list (June 28-August 17, 1992); included rehabilitation assignments to Louisville (July 16-20 and August 4-17). . . . On St. Louis disabled list (July 6-September 3, 1993); included rehabilitation assignments to Louisville (August 23-September 3). . . . On disabled list (August 3, 1994-remainder of season). . . . On St. Louis disabled list (May 4-29, June 16-July 1 and August 3, 1995-remainder of season); included rehabilitation assignment to Louisville (May 22-29). . . . Granted free agency (December 21, 1995).

STATISTICAL NOTES: Led Appalachian League with four intentional bases on balls received in 1986. . . . Led South Atlantic League second basemen with 324 putouts, 342 assists, 29 errors, 695 total chances and 80 double plays in 1987. . . . Led Florida State League second basemen with 723 total chances and 103 double plays in 1988. . . . Led American Association in being hit by pitch with 18 in 1990. . . . Led American Association third basemen with 20 errors in 1990. . . . Switch-hit home runs in one game (April 17, 1994).

MISCELLANEOUS: Batted righthanded only (1986-87).

			BATTING											FIELDING			
Year	Team (League)	Pos.	G	AB	R	H	2B	3B	HR	RBI	Avg.	BB	SO	SB	PO	A	E	Avg.
1985—	S.F. de Mac. (DSL)	. . .	46	120	31	31	5	0	0	15	.258	23	18	13	. . .	. . .	. . .	. . .
1986—	Johns. City (App.)	2B	56	202	*55	60	7	4	3	20	.297	46	33	27	108	144	7	.973
1987—	Savannah (S. Atl.)	2B-SS	134	505	95	136	28	3	9	51	.269	73	98	*80	†325	†343	†29	.958
1988—	St. Peters. (FSL)	2B	130	484	82	125	25	10	4	35	.258	88	103	35	*301	*402	20	*.972

Year	Team (League)	Pos.	G	AB	R	H	2B	3B	HR	RBI	Avg.	BB	SO	SB	PO	A	E	Avg.
			BATTING												FIELDING			
1989—	St. Peters. (FSL)	2B	6	21	2	4	1	0	0	2	.190	3	6	2	9	19	1	.966
—	Arkansas (Texas)	2B	77	267	61	79	16	8	9	44	.296	38	68	14	177	208	14	.965
1990—	Louisville (A.A.)	2B-3B	118	390	65	97	24	6	6	35	.249	69	116	24	153	261	†27	.939
—	St. Louis (N.L.)	2B	18	45	5	11	2	0	0	2	.244	4	14	1	24	30	1	.982
1991—	St. Louis (N.L.)	2B-OF	104	185	38	45	8	3	5	17	.243	18	45	15	101	146	6	.976
1992—	St. Louis (N.L.)	2B	62	203	31	62	12	1	7	31	.305	24	37	13	125	184	5	.984
—	Louisville (A.A.)	2B	28	101	16	25	9	4	3	12	.248	13	27	4	70	68	5	.965
1993—	St. Louis (N.L.)	2B	74	254	34	65	19	2	5	30	.256	25	71	13	140	200	12	.966
—	Louisville (A.A.)	2B	7	23	4	4	1	0	0	0	.174	1	4	1	10	18	0	1.000
1994—	St. Louis (N.L.)	2B-3B	83	213	33	54	13	1	11	34	.254	24	54	9	120	170	3	.990
1995—	St. Louis (N.L.)	2B	32	101	20	27	6	1	1	8	.267	16	30	3	50	73	3	.976
—	Louisville (A.A.)	2B	6	21	5	8	1	0	2	6	.381	3	1	0	9	16	2	.926
Major league totals (6 years)			373	1001	161	264	60	8	29	122	.264	111	251	54	560	803	30	.978

PENA, TONY — C — INDIANS

PERSONAL: Born June 4, 1957, in Monte Cristi, Dominican Republic. . . . 6-0/185. . . . Bats right, throws right. . . . Full name: Antonio Francisco Padilla Pena. . . . Brother of Ramon Pena, pitcher, Detroit Tigers (1989).

HIGH SCHOOL: Liceo Marti (Monte Cristi, Dominican Republic).

TRANSACTIONS/CAREER NOTES: Signed as non-drafted free agent by Pittsburgh Pirates organization (July 22, 1975). . . . Traded by Pirates to St. Louis Cardinals for OF Andy Van Slyke, C Mike LaValliere and P Mike Dunne (April 1, 1987). . . . On St. Louis disabled list (April 11-May 22, 1987); included rehabilitation assignment to Louisville (May 19-22). . . . Granted free agency (November 13, 1989). . . . Signed by Boston Red Sox (November 27, 1989). . . . Granted free agency (October 29, 1993). . . . Signed by Cleveland Indians organization (February 7, 1994). . . . Granted free agency (October 25, 1994). . . . Re-signed by Indians organization (December 13, 1994). . . . Granted free agency (November 2, 1995). . . . Re-signed by Indians (December 6, 1995).

HONORS: Named catcher on The Sporting News N.L. All-Star team (1983). . . . Won N.L. Gold Glove at catcher (1983-85). . . . Won A.L. Gold Glove at catcher (1991).

STATISTICAL NOTES: Led Carolina League catchers with nine double plays and tied for lead with 16 passed balls in 1977. . . . Led Eastern League catchers with 14 double plays in 1979. . . . Led N.L. catchers with 1,075 total chances in 1983, 999 in 1984 and 1,034 in 1985. . . . Led N.L. catchers with 15 double plays in 1984 and 13 in 1989. . . . Led N.L. catchers with 100 assists in 1985. . . . Led N.L. catchers with 18 errors in 1986. . . . Tied for N.L. lead in grounding into double plays with 21 in 1986. . . . Led N.L. catchers with .994 fielding percentage in 1988 and .997 in 1989. . . . Led A.L. catchers with 864 putouts and 943 total chances in 1990. . . . Led A.L. catchers with 929 total chances and 15 double plays in 1991. . . . Led A.L. catchers with 12 double plays in 1992. . . . Career major league grand slams: 3.

Year	Team (League)	Pos.	G	AB	R	H	2B	3B	HR	RBI	Avg.	BB	SO	SB	PO	A	E	Avg.
			BATTING												FIELDING			
1976—	GC Pirates (GCL)	O-1-C-3	33	110	10	23	2	2	1	11	.209	4	17	5	108	14	4	.968
—	Char., S.C. (W. Car.)	C	14	49	4	11	2	0	1	8	.224	4	7	0	64	7	2	.973
1977—	Char., S.C. (W. Car.)	C	29	101	10	24	4	0	3	16	.238	7	21	2	172	19	6	.970
—	Salem (Carolina)	C	84	319	36	88	15	3	7	46	.276	14	60	3	*470	*66	*17	.969
1978—	Shreveport (Texas)	C	104	348	34	80	14	0	8	42	.230	15	96	3	637	54	*25	.965
1979—	Buffalo (Eastern)	C	134	515	89	161	16	4	34	97	.313	39	83	5	*768	*120	*26	.972
1980—	Portland (PCL)	C	124	452	57	148	24	13	9	77	.327	29	75	5	*639	85	•23	.969
—	Pittsburgh (N.L.)	C	8	21	1	9	1	1	0	1	.429	0	4	0	38	2	2	.952
1981—	Pittsburgh (N.L.)	C	66	210	16	63	9	1	2	17	.300	8	23	1	286	41	5	.985
1982—	Pittsburgh (N.L.)	C	138	497	53	147	28	4	11	63	.296	17	57	2	763	89	16	.982
1983—	Pittsburgh (N.L.)	C	151	542	51	163	22	3	15	70	.301	31	73	6	*976	90	9	.992
1984—	Pittsburgh (N.L.)	C	147	546	77	156	27	2	15	78	.286	36	79	12	*895	*95	9	.991
1985—	Pittsburgh (N.L.)	C-1B	147	546	53	136	27	2	10	59	.249	29	67	12	925	†102	12	.988
1986—	Pittsburgh (N.L.)	C-1B	144	510	56	147	26	2	10	52	.288	53	69	9	824	99	†18	.981
1987—	St. Louis (N.L.)■	C-1B-OF	116	384	40	82	13	4	5	44	.214	36	54	6	624	51	8	.988
—	Louisville (A.A.)	C	2	8	0	3	0	0	0	0	.375	0	2	0	7	1	0	1.000
1988—	St. Louis (N.L.)	C-1B	149	505	55	133	23	1	10	51	.263	33	60	6	796	72	6	†.993
1989—	St. Louis (N.L.)	C-OF	141	424	36	110	17	2	4	37	.259	35	33	5	675	70	2	†.997
1990—	Boston (A.L.)■	C-1B	143	491	62	129	19	1	7	56	.263	43	71	8	†866	74	5	.995
1991—	Boston (A.L.)	C	141	464	45	107	23	2	5	48	.231	37	53	8	*864	60	5	.995
1992—	Boston (A.L.)	C	133	410	39	99	21	1	1	38	.241	24	61	3	*786	57	6	.993
1993—	Boston (A.L.)	C-DH	126	304	20	55	11	0	4	19	.181	25	46	1	698	53	4	.995
1994—	Cleveland (A.L.)■	C	40	112	18	33	8	1	2	10	.295	9	11	0	209	17	1	.996
1995—	Cleveland (A.L.)	C	91	263	25	69	15	0	5	28	.262	14	44	1	508	36	7	.987
American League totals (6 years)			674	2044	209	492	97	5	24	199	.241	152	286	21	3931	297	28	.993
National League totals (10 years)			1207	4185	438	1146	193	22	82	472	.274	278	519	59	6802	711	87	.989
Major league totals (16 years)			1881	6229	647	1638	290	27	106	671	.263	430	805	80	10733	1008	115	.990

DIVISION SERIES RECORD

Year	Team (League)	Pos.	G	AB	R	H	2B	3B	HR	RBI	Avg.	BB	SO	SB	PO	A	E	Avg.
			BATTING												FIELDING			
1995—	Cleveland (A.L.)	C	2	2	1	1	0	0	1	1	.500	0	0	0	5	0	0	1.000

CHAMPIONSHIP SERIES RECORD

Year	Team (League)	Pos.	G	AB	R	H	2B	3B	HR	RBI	Avg.	BB	SO	SB	PO	A	E	Avg.
			BATTING												FIELDING			
1987—	St. Louis (N.L.)	C	7	21	5	8	0	1	0	0	.381	3	4	1	55	5	0	1.000
1990—	Boston (A.L.)	C	4	14	0	3	0	0	0	0	.214	0	0	0	22	4	1	.963
1995—	Cleveland (A.L.)	C	4	6	1	2	1	0	0	0	.333	1	0	0	15	1	0	1.000
Championship series totals (3 years)			15	41	6	13	1	1	0	0	.317	4	4	1	92	10	1	.990

WORLD SERIES RECORD

Year	Team (League)	Pos.	G	AB	R	H	2B	3B	HR	RBI	Avg.	BB	SO	SB	PO	A	E	Avg.
			BATTING												FIELDING			
1987—	St. Louis (N.L.)	C-DH	7	22	2	9	1	0	0	4	.409	3	2	1	32	1	1	.971
1995—	Cleveland (A.L.)	C	2	6	0	1	0	0	0	0	.167	0	0	0	7	1	0	1.000
World Series totals (2 years)			9	28	2	10	1	0	0	4	.357	3	2	1	39	2	1	.976

ALL-STAR GAME RECORD

Year	League	Pos.	AB	R	H	2B	3B	HR	RBI	Avg.	BB	SO	SB	PO	A	E	Avg.
			BATTING											FIELDING			
1982—	National	PR-C	1	0	0	0	0	0	0	.000	0	0	1	3	0	0	1.000
1984—	National	C	0	0	0	0	0	0	0	...	0	0	0	2	0	0	1.000
1985—	National	C	0	0	0	0	0	0	0	...	0	1	0	4	1	0	1.000
1986—	National	PR	0	0	0	0	0	0	0	...	0	0	0	...	...	...	...
1989—	National	PH-C	2	0	0	0	0	0	0	.000	0	0	0	2	0	0	1.000
All-Star Game totals (5 years)			3	0	0	0	0	0	0	.000	0	1	1	11	1	0	1.000

PENDLETON, TERRY — 3B — MARLINS

PERSONAL: Born July 16, 1960, in Los Angeles. . . . 5-9/195. . . . Bats both, throws right. . . . Full name: Terry Lee Pendleton.
HIGH SCHOOL: Channel Island (Oxnard, Calif.).
JUNIOR COLLEGE: Oxnard (Calif.) College.
COLLEGE: Fresno State.
TRANSACTIONS/CAREER NOTES: Selected by St. Louis Cardinals organization in seventh round of free-agent draft (June 7, 1982). . . . On disabled list (April 8-May 23 and July 16-September 5, 1983; June 15-30, 1985; May 28-June 24, 1988; and April 24-May 9, 1990). . . . Granted free agency (November 5, 1990). . . . Signed by Atlanta Braves (December 3, 1990). . . . On Atlanta disabled list (June 21-July 25, 1994); included rehabilitation assignment to Greenville (July 23-25). . . . Granted free agency (October 24, 1994). . . . Signed by Florida Marlins (April 7, 1995). . . . On suspended list (June 17-21, 1995).
HONORS: Won N.L. Gold Glove at third base (1987, 1989 and 1992). . . . Named N.L. Comeback Player of the Year by The Sporting News (1991). . . . Named third baseman on The Sporting News N.L. All-Star team (1991). . . . Named N.L. Most Valuable Player by Baseball Writers' Association of America (1991).
STATISTICAL NOTES: Led American Association third basemen with .964 fielding percentage and 88 putouts in 1984. . . . Led N.L. third basemen with 133 putouts and 371 assists in 1986. . . . Led N.L. third basemen with 524 total chances in 1986, 512 in 1987, 520 in 1989, 481 in 1991 and 477 in 1992. . . . Led N.L. third basemen with 36 double plays in 1986 and 31 in 1991. . . . Tied for N.L. lead with 303 total bases in 1991. . . . Career major league grand slams: 3.

Year	Team (League)	Pos.	G	AB	R	H	2B	3B	HR	RBI	Avg.	BB	SO	SB	PO	A	E	Avg.
				BATTING											FIELDING			
1982—	Johns. City (App.)	2B	43	181	38	58	14	•4	4	27	.320	12	28	13	79	105	17	.915
—	St. Peters. (FSL)	2B	20	69	4	18	2	1	1	7	.261	2	18	1	41	51	2	.979
1983—	Arkansas (Texas)	2B	48	185	29	51	10	3	4	20	.276	9	26	7	94	135	7	.970
1984—	Louisville (A.A.)	3B-2B	91	330	52	98	23	5	4	44	.297	24	51	6	†91	157	10	†.961
—	St. Louis (N.L.)	3B	67	262	37	85	16	3	1	33	.324	16	32	20	59	155	13	.943
1985—	St. Louis (N.L.)	3B	149	559	56	134	16	3	5	69	.240	37	75	17	129	361	18	.965
1986—	St. Louis (N.L.)	3B-OF	159	578	56	138	26	5	1	59	.239	34	59	24	†133	†371	20	.962
1987—	St. Louis (N.L.)	3B	159	583	82	167	29	4	12	96	.286	70	74	19	117	*369	26	.949
1988—	St. Louis (N.L.)	3B	110	391	44	99	20	2	6	53	.253	21	51	3	75	239	12	.963
1989—	St. Louis (N.L.)	3B	162	613	83	162	28	5	13	74	.264	44	81	9	113	*392	15	*.971
1990—	St. Louis (N.L.)	3B	121	447	46	103	20	2	6	58	.230	30	58	7	91	248	19	.947
1991—	Atlanta (N.L.)■	3B	153	586	94	*187	34	8	22	86	*.319	43	70	10	108	*349	24	.950
1992—	Atlanta (N.L.)	3B	160	640	98	•199	39	1	21	105	.311	37	67	5	*133	*325	19	.960
1993—	Atlanta (N.L.)	3B	161	633	81	172	33	1	17	84	.272	36	97	5	*128	319	19	.959
1994—	Atlanta (N.L.)	3B	77	309	25	78	18	3	7	30	.252	12	57	2	60	149	11	.950
—	Greenville (South.)	3B	2	6	0	3	1	0	0	2	.500	0	1	0	1	1	1	.667
1995—	Florida (N.L.)■	3B	133	513	70	149	32	1	14	78	.290	38	84	1	•104	250	18	.952
Major league totals (12 years)			1611	6114	772	1673	311	38	125	825	.274	418	805	122	1250	3527	214	.957

CHAMPIONSHIP SERIES RECORD

NOTES: Shares record for most at-bats in one inning—2 (October 13, 1985, second inning). . . . Holds N.L. career record for most games—32; and most at-bats—129. . . . Shares N.L. single-series record for most at-bats—30 (1991 and 1992).

Year	Team (League)	Pos.	G	AB	R	H	2B	3B	HR	RBI	Avg.	BB	SO	SB	PO	A	E	Avg.
				BATTING											FIELDING			
1985—	St. Louis (N.L.)	3B	6	24	2	5	1	0	0	4	.208	1	3	0	6	18	1	.960
1987—	St. Louis (N.L.)	3B	6	19	3	4	0	1	0	1	.211	0	6	0	3	11	0	1.000
1991—	Atlanta (N.L.)	3B	7	30	1	5	1	1	0	1	.167	1	3	0	5	11	0	1.000
1992—	Atlanta (N.L.)	3B	7	30	2	7	2	0	0	3	.233	0	2	0	4	18	0	1.000
1993—	Atlanta (N.L.)	3B	6	26	4	9	1	0	1	5	.346	0	2	0	7	5	0	1.000
Championship series totals (5 years)			32	129	12	30	5	2	1	14	.233	2	16	0	25	63	1	.989

WORLD SERIES RECORD

Year	Team (League)	Pos.	G	AB	R	H	2B	3B	HR	RBI	Avg.	BB	SO	SB	PO	A	E	Avg.
				BATTING											FIELDING			
1985—	St. Louis (N.L.)	3B	7	23	3	6	1	1	0	3	.261	3	2	0	6	14	1	.952
1987—	St. Louis (N.L.)	DH-PH	3	7	2	3	0	0	0	1	.429	1	1	2	...	...	...	...
1991—	Atlanta (N.L.)	3B	7	30	6	11	3	0	2	3	.367	3	1	0	3	20	2	.920
1992—	Atlanta (N.L.)	3B	6	25	2	6	2	0	0	2	.240	1	5	0	4	19	0	1.000
World Series totals (4 years)			23	85	13	26	6	1	2	9	.306	8	9	2	13	53	3	.957

ALL-STAR GAME RECORD

Year	League	Pos.	AB	R	H	2B	3B	HR	RBI	Avg.	BB	SO	SB	PO	A	E	Avg.
			BATTING											FIELDING			
1992—	National	3B	2	0	1	0	0	0	0	.500	0	0	0	0	2	0	1.000

PENN, SHANNON — 2B — TIGERS

PERSONAL: Born September 11, 1969, in Cincinnati. . . . 5-10/163. . . . Bats both, throws right. . . . Full name: Shannon Dion Penn.
HIGH SCHOOL: Withrow (Cincinnati).

P

JUNIOR COLLEGE: Southwestern Michigan, then Lakeland (O.).
TRANSACTIONS/CAREER NOTES: Selected by Texas Rangers organization in 58th round of free-agent draft (June 1, 1988). . . . Released by Gastonia, Rangers organization (July 4, 1991). . . . Signed by Detroit Tigers organization (December 23, 1991). . . . On Toledo disabled list (July 30-August 21, 1995).
STATISTICAL NOTES: Led Pioneer League second basemen with 281 total chances in 1990. . . . Led International League second basemen with .978 fielding percentage in 1994.

			BATTING											FIELDING			
Year Team (League)	**Pos.**	**G**	**AB**	**R**	**H**	**2B**	**3B**	**HR**	**RBI**	**Avg.**	**BB**	**SO**	**SB**	**PO**	**A**	**E**	**Avg.**
1989— GC Rangers (GCL)	2B	47	147	19	32	2	1	0	8	.218	20	27	17	68	71	5	.965
1990— Butte (Pioneer)	2B	60	197	38	64	4	2	0	18	.325	15	35	9	*110	154	*17	.940
1991— Gastonia (S. Atl.)	2B	48	129	22	28	5	0	0	6	.217	11	30	7	70	113	10	.948
1992— Niag. Falls (NYP)■	2B-3B-SS	70	253	47	69	9	2	3	25	.273	28	52	31	107	160	15	.947
1993— London (Eastern)	2B-OF	128	493	78	128	13	6	0	36	.260	54	95	*53	197	311	23	.957
1994— Toledo (Int'l)	2B-SS	114	444	63	126	14	6	2	33	.284	30	96	*45	204	318	12	†.978
1995— Detroit (A.L.)	2B	3	9	0	3	0	0	0	0	.333	1	2	0	10	9	3	.864
— Toledo (Int'l)	2B	63	218	41	54	4	1	1	15	.248	17	40	15	106	173	11	.962
Major league totals (1 year)		3	9	0	3	0	0	0	0	.333	1	2	0	10	9	3	.864

PENNINGTON, BRAD — P — RED SOX

PERSONAL: Born April 14, 1969, in Salem, Ind. . . . 6-5/215. . . . Throws left, bats left. . . . Full name: Brad Lee Pennington.
HIGH SCHOOL: Eastern (Pekin, Ind.).
JUNIOR COLLEGE: Vincennes (Ind.) University.
COLLEGE: Bellarmine College (Ky.).
TRANSACTIONS/CAREER NOTES: Selected by Baltimore Orioles organization in 12th round of free-agent draft (June 5, 1989). . . . Traded by Orioles organization to Cincinnati Reds for OF Danny Clyburn and P Tony Nieto (June 16, 1995). . . . Granted free agency (October 16, 1995). . . . Signed by Boston Red Sox (November 8, 1995).
STATISTICAL NOTES: Tied for Appalachian League lead with 14 wild pitches in 1989.

Year Team (League)	**W**	**L**	**Pct.**	**ERA**	**G**	**GS**	**CG**	**ShO**	**Sv.**	**IP**	**H**	**R**	**ER**	**BB**	**SO**
1989— Bluefield (Appal.)	2	•7	.222	6.58	15	14	0	0	0	64 1/3	50	58	47	*74	81
1990— Wausau (Midwest)	4	9	.308	5.18	32	18	1	0	0	106	81	89	61	*121	142
1991— Frederick (Caro.)	1	4	.200	3.92	36	0	0	0	13	43 2/3	32	23	19	44	58
— Kane Co. (Mid.)	0	2	.000	5.87	23	0	0	0	4	23	16	17	15	25	43
1992— Frederick (Caro.)	1	0	1.000	2.00	8	0	0	0	2	9	5	3	2	4	16
— Hagerstown (East.)	1	2	.333	2.54	19	0	0	0	7	28 1/3	20	9	8	17	33
— Rochester (Int'l)	1	3	.250	2.08	29	0	0	0	5	39	12	10	9	33	56
1993— Rochester (Int'l)	1	2	.333	3.45	17	0	0	0	8	15 2/3	12	11	6	13	19
— Baltimore (A.L.)	3	2	.600	6.55	34	0	0	0	4	33	34	25	24	25	39
1994— Baltimore (A.L.)	0	1	.000	12.00	8	0	0	0	0	6	9	8	8	8	7
— Rochester (Int'l)	6	8	.429	5.32	35	9	0	0	3	86 1/3	68	59	51	74	89
1995— Baltimore (A.L.)	0	1	.000	8.10	8	0	0	0	0	6 2/3	3	7	6	11	10
— Cincinnati (N.L.)■	0	0	...	5.59	6	0	0	0	0	9 2/3	9	8	6	11	7
— Indianapolis (A.A.)	0	0	...	10.29	11	2	0	0	0	14	17	19	16	21	11
A.L. totals (3 years)	3	4	.429	7.49	50	0	0	0	4	45 2/3	46	40	38	44	56
N.L. totals (1 year)	0	0	...	5.59	6	0	0	0	0	9 2/3	9	8	6	11	7
Major league totals (3 years)	3	4	.429	7.16	56	0	0	0	4	55 1/3	55	48	44	55	63

PERCIBAL, BILLY — P — ORIOLES

PERSONAL: Born February 2, 1974, in San Pedro de Macoris, Dominican Republic. . . . 6-1/156. . . . Throws right, bats right. . . . Full name: William Percibal.
TRANSACTIONS/CAREER NOTES: Signed as non-drafted free agent by Baltimore Orioles organization (August 2, 1991).

Year Team (League)	**W**	**L**	**Pct.**	**ERA**	**G**	**GS**	**CG**	**ShO**	**Sv.**	**IP**	**H**	**R**	**ER**	**BB**	**SO**
1992— GC Orioles (GCL)	2	1	.667	8.10	16	0	0	0	0	26 2/3	42	26	24	7	25
1993— Bluefield (Appal.)	6	0	1.000	3.81	13	13	0	0	0	82 2/3	71	48	35	33	81
1994— Albany (S. Atl.)	13	9	.591	3.56	28	•28	3	2	0	169 1/3	160	80	67	90	132
1995— High Desert (Calif.)	7	6	.538	3.23	21	20	2	0	0	128	123	63	46	55	105
— Bowie (Eastern)	1	0	1.000	0.00	2	2	0	0	0	14	7	0	0	7	7

PERCIVAL, TROY — P — ANGELS

PERSONAL: Born August 9, 1969, in Fontana, Calif. . . . 6-3/200. . . . Throws right, bats right. . . . Full name: Troy Eugene Percival. . . . Name pronounced PER-sih-vol.
HIGH SCHOOL: Moreno Valley (Calif.).
COLLEGE: UC Riverside.
TRANSACTIONS/CAREER NOTES: Selected by California Angels organization in sixth round of free-agent draft (June 5, 1990). . . . On Palm Springs disabled list (June 3-July 2, 1992). . . . On disabled list (May 28, 1993-remainder of season).

Year Team (League)	**W**	**L**	**Pct.**	**ERA**	**G**	**GS**	**CG**	**ShO**	**Sv.**	**IP**	**H**	**R**	**ER**	**BB**	**SO**
1991— Boise (Northwest)	2	0	1.000	1.41	28	0	0	0	*12	38 1/3	23	7	6	18	63
1992— Palm Springs (Cal.)	1	1	.500	5.06	11	0	0	0	2	10 2/3	6	7	6	8	16
— Midland (Texas)	3	0	1.000	2.37	20	0	0	0	5	19	18	5	5	11	21
1993— Vancouver (PCL)	0	1	.000	6.27	18	0	0	0	4	18 2/3	24	14	13	13	19
1994— Vancouver (PCL)	2	6	.250	4.13	49	0	0	0	15	61	63	31	28	29	73
1995— California (A.L.)	3	2	.600	1.95	62	0	0	0	3	74	37	19	16	26	94
Major league totals (1 year)	3	2	.600	1.95	62	0	0	0	3	74	37	19	16	26	94

RECORD AS POSITION PLAYER

			BATTING											FIELDING			
Year	Team (League)	Pos.	G	AB	R	H	2B	3B	HR	RBI	Avg.	BB	SO	SB	PO	A	E	Avg.
1990—	Boise (Northwest)	C	29	79	12	16	0	0	0	5	.203	19	25	0	215	25	5	.980

PEREZ, CARLOS — P — EXPOS

PERSONAL: Born January 14, 1971, in Nigua, Dominican Republic. . . . 6-3/195. . . . Throws left, bats left. . . . Full name: Carlos Gross Perez. . . . Brother of Melido Perez, pitcher, New York Yankees; brother of Pascual Perez, major league pitcher with four teams (1980-85 and 1987-92); brother of Vladimir Perez, minor league pitcher (1986-94); brother of Dario Perez, minor league pitcher (1988-94); and brother of Valerio Perez, minor league pitcher (1983-84).

TRANSACTIONS/CAREER NOTES: Signed as non-drafted free agent by Montreal Expos organization (January 7, 1988). . . . On disabled list (April 9-24 and May 18-July 7, 1992). . . . On suspended list (July 7-October 22, 1992).

Year	Team (League)	W	L	Pct.	ERA	G	GS	CG	ShO	Sv.	IP	H	R	ER	BB	SO
1989—	DSL Expos (DSL)	3	3	.500	3.07	16	4	0	0	2	44	25	21	15	32	45
1990—	GC Expos (GCL)	3	1	.750	2.52	13	2	0	0	2	35 2/3	24	14	10	15	38
1991—	Sumter (S. Atl.)	2	2	.500	2.44	16	12	0	0	0	73 2/3	57	29	20	32	69
1992—	Rockford (Midw.)	0	1	.000	5.79	7	1	0	0	1	9 1/3	12	7	6	5	8
1993—	Burlington (Midw.)	1	0	1.000	3.24	12	1	0	0	0	16 2/3	13	6	6	9	21
—	San Bern. (Calif.)	8	7	.533	3.44	20	18	0	0	0	131	120	57	50	44	98
1994—	Harrisburg (East.)	7	2	.778	1.94	12	11	2	2	1	79	55	27	17	18	69
—	Ottawa (Int'l)	7	5	.583	3.33	17	17	3	0	0	119	130	50	44	41	82
1995—	Montreal (N.L.)	10	8	.556	3.69	28	23	2	1	0	141 1/3	142	61	58	28	106
Major league totals (1 year)		10	8	.556	3.69	28	23	2	1	0	141 1/3	142	61	58	28	106

ALL-STAR GAME RECORD

Year	League	W	L	Pct.	ERA	GS	CG	ShO	Sv.	IP	H	R	ER	BB	SO
1995—	National	0	0	...	0.00	0	0	0	0	1/3	1	0	0	1	0

PEREZ, DANNY — OF — BREWERS

PERSONAL: Born February 26, 1971, in El Paso, Tex. . . . 5-10/188. . . . Bats right, throws right. . . . Full name: Daniel Perez.

HIGH SCHOOL: El Paso Hanks (Tex.).

COLLEGE: Oklahoma State.

TRANSACTIONS/CAREER NOTES: Selected by Milwaukee Brewers organization in 21st round of free-agent draft (June 1, 1992). . . . On El Paso suspended list (July 7-12, 1994). . . . On New Orleans disabled list (May 22-July 18, 1995).

			BATTING											FIELDING			
Year	Team (League)	Pos.	G	AB	R	H	2B	3B	HR	RBI	Avg.	BB	SO	SB	PO	A	E	Avg.
1992—	Helena (Pioneer)	OF	33	104	12	22	3	0	1	13	.212	10	17	3	50	5	1	.982
1993—	Beloit (Midwest)	OF	106	377	70	113	17	6	10	59	.300	56	64	23	180	9	2	.990
—	Stockton (Calif.)	OF	10	24	4	7	3	1	0	0	.292	2	5	2	11	0	0	1.000
1994—	Stockton (Calif.)	OF	9	33	7	9	0	0	0	3	.273	7	7	2	12	2	0	1.000
—	El Paso (Texas)	OF	115	440	88	143	19	*17	6	73	.325	45	79	9	197	15	4	.981
1995—	New Orleans (A.A.)	DH	12	34	5	10	1	0	0	0	.294	5	9	0	...	...	...	...
—	El Paso (Texas)	DH	22	76	16	21	1	1	0	7	.276	4	14	1	...	...	...	...

PEREZ, EDDIE — C/1B — BRAVES

PERSONAL: Born May 4, 1968, in Cuidad Ojeda, Venezuela. . . . 6-1/175. . . . Bats right, throws right.

HIGH SCHOOL: Doctor Raul Cuenca (Cuidad Ojeda, Venezuela).

TRANSACTIONS/CAREER NOTES: Signed as non-drafted free agent by Atlanta Braves organization (September 27, 1986).

STATISTICAL NOTES: Led South Atlantic League catchers with 13 double plays in 1989. . . . Tied for International League lead in errors by catcher with 11 in 1994. . . . Led International League catchers with 539 putouts, 69 assists and 615 total chances in 1995. . . . Tied for International League lead with seven double plays in 1995.

NOTES: Member of World Series championship team (1995); did not play.

			BATTING											FIELDING			
Year	Team (League)	Pos.	G	AB	R	H	2B	3B	HR	RBI	Avg.	BB	SO	SB	PO	A	E	Avg.
1987—	GC Braves (GCL)	C	31	89	8	18	1	0	1	5	.202	8	14	0	161	31	4	.980
1988—	Burlington (Midw.)	C-1B	64	186	14	43	8	0	4	19	.231	10	33	1	245	42	11	.963
1989—	Sumter (S. Atl.)	C-1B	114	401	39	93	21	0	5	44	.232	44	68	2	760	96	16	.982
1990—	Sumter (S. Atl.)	C-1B	41	123	11	22	7	1	3	17	.179	14	18	0	315	32	3	.991
—	Durham (Carolina)	C-1B	31	93	9	22	1	0	3	10	.237	1	12	0	197	17	3	.986
1991—	Durham (Carolina)	C-1B	92	277	38	75	10	1	9	41	.271	17	33	0	497	55	8	.986
—	Greenville (South.)	1B	1	4	0	1	0	0	0	0	.250	0	1	0	9	0	0	1.000
1992—	Greenville (South.)	C-1B	91	275	28	63	16	0	6	41	.229	24	41	3	631	64	14	.980
1993—	Greenville (South.)	1B-C	28	84	15	28	6	0	6	17	.333	2	8	1	146	19	3	.982
1994—	Richmond (Int'l)	C-1B	113	388	37	101	16	2	9	49	.260	18	47	1	718	80	‡12	.985
1995—	Richmond (Int'l)	C-1B	92	324	31	86	19	0	5	40	.265	12	58	1	†540	†69	7	.989
—	Atlanta (N.L.)	C-1B	7	13	1	4	1	0	1	4	.308	0	2	0	34	2	0	1.000
Major league totals (1 year)			7	13	1	4	1	0	1	4	.308	0	2	0	34	2	0	1.000

PEREZ, EDUARDO — 3B — ANGELS

PERSONAL: Born September 11, 1969, in Cincinnati. . . . 6-4/215. . . . Bats right, throws right. . . . Full name: Eduardo Antanacio Perez. . . . Son of Tony Perez, director of international relations, Florida Marlins; major league infielder with four teams (1964-86) and manager, Cincinnati Reds (1993); and brother of Victor Perez, minor league outfielder/first baseman (1990).

HIGH SCHOOL: Robinson (Santurce, Puerto Rico).
COLLEGE: Florida State.
TRANSACTIONS/CAREER NOTES: Selected by California Angels organization in first round (17th pick overall) of free-agent draft (June 3, 1991).... On Palm Springs disabled list (May 9-19, 1992).... On Vancouver disabled list (June 26-July 7, 1994).

			BATTING											FIELDING			
Year Team (League)	Pos.	G	AB	R	H	2B	3B	HR	RBI	Avg.	BB	SO	SB	PO	A	E	Avg.
1991— Boise (Northwest)	OF-1B	46	160	35	46	13	0	1	22	.288	19	39	12	87	6	3	.969
1992— Palm Springs (Cal.)	3B-SS-OF	54	204	37	64	8	4	3	35	.314	23	33	14	30	90	16	.882
— Midland (Texas)	3B-OF-1B	62	235	27	54	8	1	3	23	.230	22	49	19	53	97	13	.920
1993— Vancouver (PCL)	3B-1B-OF	96	363	66	111	23	6	12	70	.306	28	83	21	98	174	23	.922
— California (A.L.)	3B-DH	52	180	16	45	6	2	4	30	.250	9	39	5	24	101	5	.962
1994— California (A.L.)	1B	38	129	10	27	7	0	5	16	.209	12	29	3	305	15	1	.997
— Vancouver (PCL)	3B	61	219	37	65	14	3	7	38	.297	34	53	9	35	116	12	.926
— Ariz. Angels (Ariz.)	3B	1	3	0	0	0	0	0	0	.000	1	1	0	0	3	0	1.000
1995— Vancouver (PCL)	3B-1B	69	246	39	80	12	7	6	37	.325	25	34	6	94	90	6	.968
— California (A.L.)	3B-DH	29	71	9	12	4	1	1	7	.169	12	9	0	16	37	7	.883
Major league totals (3 years)		119	380	35	84	17	3	10	53	.221	33	77	8	345	153	13	.975

PEREZ, MELIDO — P — YANKEES

PERSONAL: Born February 15, 1966, in Costa Verde, Dominican Republic.... 6-4/210.... Throws right, bats right.... Brother of Carlos Perez, pitcher, Montreal Expos; brother of Pascual Perez, major league pitcher with four teams (1980-85 and 1987-92); brother of Vladimir Perez, minor league pitcher (1986-94); brother of Dario Perez, minor league pitcher (1988-94); and brother of Valerio Perez, minor league pitcher (1983-84).
HIGH SCHOOL: San Gregorio de Nigua (San Cristobal, Dominican Republic).
TRANSACTIONS/CAREER NOTES: Signed as non-drafted free agent by Kansas City Royals organization (July 22, 1983).... Traded by Royals with P John Davis, P Chuck Mount and P Greg Hibbard to Chicago White Sox for P Floyd Bannister and IF Dave Cochrane (December 10, 1987).... Traded by White Sox with P Robert Wickman and P Domingo Jean to New York Yankees for 2B Steve Sax and cash (January 10, 1992).... On disabled list (April 1-18, 1993).... On New York disabled list (July 1-September 8, 1995); included rehabilitation assignment to Norwich (August 29-September 8).
STATISTICAL NOTES: Tied for Northwest League lead with 13 home runs allowed and two balks in 1985.... Pitched six-inning, 8-0 no-hit victory against New York (July 12, 1990).

Year Team (League)	W	L	Pct.	ERA	G	GS	CG	ShO	Sv.	IP	H	R	ER	BB	SO
1984— Char., S.C. (S. Atl.)	5	7	.417	4.35	16	15	0	0	0	89	99	52	43	19	55
1985— Eugene (N'west)	6	7	.462	5.44	17	•15	2	0	0	101	116	65	*61	35	88
1986— Burlington (Midw.)	10	12	.455	3.70	28	23	*13	1	0	170 1/3	148	83	70	49	153
1987— Fort Myers (Fla. St.)	4	3	.571	2.38	8	8	5	1	0	64 1/3	51	20	17	7	51
— Memphis (South.)	8	5	.615	3.43	20	20	5	2	0	133 2/3	125	60	51	20	126
— Kansas City (A.L.)	1	1	.500	7.84	3	3	0	0	0	10 1/3	18	12	9	5	5
1988— Chicago (A.L.)■	12	10	.545	3.79	32	32	3	1	0	197	186	105	83	72	138
1989— Chicago (A.L.)	11	14	.440	5.01	31	31	2	0	0	183 1/3	187	106	102	90	141
1990— Chicago (A.L.)	13	14	.481	4.61	35	35	3	3	0	197	177	111	101	86	161
1991— Chicago (A.L.)	8	7	.533	3.12	49	8	0	0	1	135 2/3	111	49	47	52	128
1992— New York (A.L.)■	13	16	.448	2.87	33	33	10	1	0	247 2/3	212	94	79	93	218
1993— New York (A.L.)	6	14	.300	5.19	25	25	0	0	0	163	173	103	94	64	148
1994— New York (A.L.)	9	4	.692	4.10	22	22	1	0	0	151 1/3	134	74	69	58	109
1995— New York (A.L.)	5	5	.500	5.58	13	12	1	0	0	69 1/3	70	46	43	31	44
— Norwich (Eastern)	1	0	1.000	0.00	2	2	0	0	0	9	7	0	0	3	9
Major league totals (9 years)	78	85	.479	4.17	243	201	20	5	1	1354 2/3	1268	700	627	551	1092

PEREZ, MIKE — P — CUBS

PERSONAL: Born October 19, 1964, in Yauco, Puerto Rico.... 6-0/200.... Throws right, bats right.... Full name: Michael Irvin Perez.
HIGH SCHOOL: Yauco (Puerto Rico).
JUNIOR COLLEGE: San Jose (Calif.) City College.
COLLEGE: Troy (Ala.) State.
TRANSACTIONS/CAREER NOTES: Selected by St. Louis Cardinals organization in 12th round of free-agent draft (June 2, 1986).... On Louisville disabled list (July 25-August 6, 1991).... On St. Louis disabled list (July 6-August 15, 1993); included rehabilitation assignment to Arkansas (August 7-15).... On St. Louis disabled list (April 25-May 25 and July 16, 1994-remainder of season).... Granted free agency (December 23, 1994).... Signed by Iowa, Chicago Cubs organization (April 11, 1995).

Year Team (League)	W	L	Pct.	ERA	G	GS	CG	ShO	Sv.	IP	H	R	ER	BB	SO
1986— Johns. City (App.)	3	5	.375	2.97	18	8	2	0	3	72 2/3	69	35	24	22	72
1987— Springfield (Midw.)	6	2	.750	0.85	58	0	0	0	*41	84 1/3	47	12	8	21	119
1988— Arkansas (Texas)	1	3	.250	11.30	11	0	0	0	0	14 1/3	18	18	18	13	17
— St. Petersburg (FSL)	2	2	.500	2.08	35	0	0	0	17	43 1/3	24	12	10	16	45
1989— Arkansas (Texas)	4	6	.400	3.64	57	0	0	0	*33	76 2/3	68	34	31	32	74
1990— Louisville (A.A.)	7	7	.500	4.28	•57	0	0	0	*31	67 1/3	64	34	32	33	69
— St. Louis (N.L.)	1	0	1.000	3.95	13	0	0	0	1	13 2/3	12	6	6	3	5
1991— St. Louis (N.L.)	0	2	.000	5.82	14	0	0	0	0	17	19	11	11	7	7
— Louisville (A.A.)	3	5	.375	6.13	37	0	0	0	4	47	54	38	32	25	39
1992— St. Louis (N.L.)	9	3	.750	1.84	77	0	0	0	0	93	70	23	19	32	46
1993— St. Louis (N.L.)	7	2	.778	2.48	65	0	0	0	7	72 2/3	65	24	20	20	58
— Arkansas (Texas)	0	0	...	7.36	4	0	0	0	0	3 2/3	7	3	3	0	4
1994— St. Louis (N.L.)	2	3	.400	8.71	36	0	0	0	12	31	52	32	30	10	20
1995— Chicago (N.L.)■	2	6	.250	3.66	68	0	0	0	2	71 1/3	72	30	29	27	49
Major league totals (6 years)	21	16	.568	3.47	273	0	0	0	22	298 2/3	290	126	115	99	185

PEREZ, ROBERT — OF — BLUE JAYS

PERSONAL: Born June 4, 1969, in Bolivar, Venezuela. . . . 6-3/215. . . . Bats right, throws right. . . . Full name: Robert Alexander Jimenez Perez.

HIGH SCHOOL: Raul Leoni Otero (Bolivar, Venezuela).

TRANSACTIONS/CAREER NOTES: Signed as non-drafted free agent by Toronto Blue Jays organization (May 1, 1989).

STATISTICAL NOTES: Led International League outfielders with 303 total chances in 1993. . . . Tied for International League lead in grounding into double plays with 19 in 1993. . . . Led International League in grounding into double plays with 21 in 1994. . . . Tied for International League lead with eight sacrifice flies in 1994. . . . Led International League with 249 total bases in 1995.

			BATTING												FIELDING			
Year	Team (League)	Pos.	G	AB	R	H	2B	3B	HR	RBI	Avg.	BB	SO	SB	PO	A	E	Avg.
1989—	Santo Dom. (DSL)	OF	52	219	34	*79	*20	3	5	40	.361	21	23	5	...	...	...	...
1990—	St. Cathar. (NYP)	OF	52	207	21	54	10	2	5	25	.261	8	34	7	80	5	1	.988
	—Myrtle Beach (SAL)	OF	21	72	8	21	2	0	1	10	.292	3	9	2	40	1	1	.976
1991—	Dunedin (Fla. St.)	OF	127	480	50	*145	28	6	4	50	*.302	22	72	8	160	10	5	.971
	—Syracuse (Int'l)	OF	4	20	2	4	1	0	0	1	.200	0	2	0	5	0	1	.833
1992—	Knoxville (South.)	OF	*139	•526	59	137	25	5	9	59	.260	13	87	11	241	13	7	.973
1993—	Syracuse (Int'l)	OF	138	524	72	154	26	10	12	64	.294	24	65	13	278	•13	*12	.960
1994—	Syracuse (Int'l)	OF	128	510	63	155	28	3	10	65	.304	27	76	4	231	8	9	.964
	—Toronto (A.L.)	OF	4	8	0	1	0	0	0	0	.125	0	1	0	3	1	0	1.000
1995—	Syracuse (Int'l)	OF	122	502	70	*172	*38	6	9	67	*.343	13	60	7	208	7	8	.964
	—Toronto (A.L.)	OF	17	48	2	9	2	0	1	3	.188	0	5	0	30	0	0	1.000
Major league totals (2 years)			21	56	2	10	2	0	1	3	.179	0	6	0	33	1	0	1.000

PEREZ, TOMAS — SS — BLUE JAYS

PERSONAL: Born December 29, 1973, in Barquisimeto, Venezuela. . . . 5-11/175. . . . Bats both, throws right. . . . Full name: Tomas Orlando Perez.

TRANSACTIONS/CAREER NOTES: Signed as non-drafted free agent by Montreal Expos organization (July 11, 1991). . . . Selected by California Angels from Expos organization in Rule 5 major league draft (December 5, 1994). . . . Contract sold by Angels to Toronto Blue Jays (December 5, 1994).

STATISTICAL NOTES: Led Midwest League shortstops with 217 putouts and 65 double plays in 1994.

			BATTING												FIELDING			
Year	Team (League)	Pos.	G	AB	R	H	2B	3B	HR	RBI	Avg.	BB	SO	SB	PO	A	E	Avg.
1992—	Dom. Expos (DSL)	IF	44	151	35	46	7	0	1	19	.305	27	20	12	112	138	12	.954
1993—	GC Expos (GCL)	SS	52	189	27	46	3	1	2	21	.243	23	25	8	*121	*205	12	*.964
1994—	Burlington (Midw.)	SS-2B	119	465	76	122	22	1	8	47	.262	48	78	8	†221	347	34	.944
1995—	Toronto (A.L.)■	SS-2B-3B	41	98	12	24	3	1	1	8	.245	7	18	0	48	77	5	.962
Major league totals (1 year)			41	98	12	24	3	1	1	8	.245	7	18	0	48	77	5	.962

PEREZ, YORKIS — P — MARLINS

PERSONAL: Born September 30, 1967, in Bajos de Haina, Dominican Republic. . . . 6-0/180. . . . Throws left, bats left. . . . Full name: Yorkis Miguel Perez.

TRANSACTIONS/CAREER NOTES: Signed as non-drafted free agent by Minnesota Twins organization (February 23, 1983). . . . Traded by Twins organization with P Neal Heaton, P Al Cardwood and C Jeff Reed to Montreal Expos for P Jeff Reardon and C Tom Nieto (February 3, 1987). . . . Granted free agency (October 15, 1990). . . . Signed by Atlanta Braves organization (January 1991). . . . Traded by Braves with P Turk Wendell to Chicago Cubs for P Mike Bielecki and C Damon Berryhill (September 29, 1991). . . . Released by Cubs (December 11, 1991). . . . Signed by Yomiuri Giants of Japan Central League (1992). . . . Released by Yomiuri (August 17, 1992). . . . Signed as free agent by Jacksonville, Seattle Mariners organization (August 19, 1992). . . . Released by Mariners organization (January 11, 1993). . . . Signed by Montreal Expos organization (February 15, 1993). . . . Granted free agency (October 15, 1993). . . . Signed by Edmonton, Florida Marlins organization (December 15, 1993). . . . On Florida disabled list (June 10-30, 1994); included rehabilitation assignment to Portland (June 25-30).

Year	Team (League)	W	L	Pct.	ERA	G	GS	CG	ShO	Sv.	IP	H	R	ER	BB	SO
1983—	Elizabeth. (App.)	0	1	.000	20.25	3	1	0	0	0	4	5	9	9	9	6
1984—	Elizabeth. (App.)	0	0	...	0.00	1	0	0	0	0	1 1/3	1	0	0	1	1
1985—	Santiago (DSL)	6	8	.429	3.17	21	16	7	2	1	122	104	58	43	63	69
1986—	Kenosha (Midwest)	4	11	.267	5.15	31	18	3	0	0	131	120	81	75	88	144
1987—	WP Beach (FSL)■	6	2	.750	2.34	15	15	3	0	0	100	78	36	26	46	111
	—Jacksonville (Sou.)	2	7	.222	4.05	12	10	1	1	1	60	61	34	27	30	60
1988—	Jacksonville (Sou.)	8	12	.400	5.82	27	25	2	1	0	130	142	96	84	94	105
1989—	WP Beach (FSL)	7	6	.538	2.76	18	12	0	0	1	94 2/3	62	34	29	54	85
	—Jacksonville (Sou.)	4	3	.571	3.60	20	0	0	0	0	35	25	16	14	34	50
1990—	Jacksonville (Sou.)	2	2	.500	6.00	28	2	0	0	1	42	36	34	28	34	39
	—Indianapolis (A.A.)	1	1	.500	2.31	9	0	0	0	0	11 2/3	8	5	3	6	8
1991—	Richmond (Int'l)■	•12	3	•.800	3.79	36	10	0	0	1	107	99	47	45	53	102
	—Chicago (N.L.)■	1	0	1.000	2.08	3	0	0	0	0	4 1/3	2	1	1	2	3
1992—	Yomiuri (Jp. Cen.)■	0	1	.000	7.11	3	...	...	...	0	6 1/3	8	...	5	3	6
1993—	Harrisburg (East.)■	4	2	.667	3.45	34	0	0	0	3	44 1/3	49	26	17	20	58
	—Ottawa (Int'l)	0	1	.000	3.60	20	0	0	0	5	20	14	12	8	7	17
1994—	Florida (N.L.)■	3	0	1.000	3.54	44	0	0	0	0	40 2/3	33	18	16	14	41
	—Portland (Eastern)	0	0	...	0.00	2	0	0	0	0	2	1	0	0	0	2
1995—	Florida (N.L.)	2	6	.250	5.21	69	0	0	0	1	46 2/3	35	29	27	28	47
Major league totals (3 years)		6	6	.500	4.32	116	0	0	0	1	91 2/3	70	48	44	44	91

PERRY, GERALD 1B

PERSONAL: Born October 30, 1960, in Savannah, Ga. . . . 6-0/201. . . . Bats left, throws right. . . . Full name: Gerald June Perry. . . . Nephew of Dan Driessen, major league first baseman with five teams (1973-87).

HIGH SCHOOL: H.E. McCracken (Buffton, N.C.).

TRANSACTIONS/CAREER NOTES: Selected by Atlanta Braves organization in 11th round of free-agent draft (June 6, 1978). . . . On disabled list (June 19-July 4, 1988; June 6-21 and July 10, 1989-remainder of season). . . . Traded by Braves with P Jim LeMasters to Kansas City Royals for P Charlie Leibrandt and P Rick Luecken (December 15, 1989). . . . Granted free agency (November 5, 1990). . . . Signed by St. Louis Cardinals (December 13, 1990). . . . Granted free agency (October 25, 1993). . . . Re-signed by Cardinals (December 21, 1993). . . . Granted free agency (October 27, 1994). . . . Re-signed by Cardinals (April 7, 1995). . . . Released by Cardinals (August 31, 1995).

STATISTICAL NOTES: Led Gulf Coast League first basemen with 46 double plays in 1978. . . . Led Carolina League first basemen with 109 double plays in 1980. . . . Career major league grand slams: 1.

		BATTING												FIELDING			
Year Team (League)	Pos.	G	AB	R	H	2B	3B	HR	RBI	Avg.	BB	SO	SB	PO	A	E	Avg.
1978— GC Braves (GCL)	1B	*55	191	32	51	*12	3	1	26	.267	23	23	7	*479	*37	6	*.989
1979— Greenw. (W. Car.)	1B	109	400	69	133	17	4	9	71	*.333	56	63	35	881	59	19	.980
1980— Durham (Carolina)	1B	138	497	102	124	19	5	15	92	.249	94	77	37	*1296	93	16	.989
1981— Savannah (South.)	1B	137	476	71	132	18	3	19	84	.277	69	95	22	1221	86	18	.986
1982— Richmond (Int'l)	1B	133	492	94	146	22	4	15	92	.297	91	79	39	1110	94	•17	.986
1983— Richmond (Int'l)	1B	113	423	81	133	21	8	13	71	.314	73	55	26	943	88	11	.989
— Atlanta (N.L.)	1B-OF	27	39	5	14	2	0	1	6	.359	5	4	0	55	0	1	.982
1984— Atlanta (N.L.)	1B-OF	122	347	52	92	12	2	7	47	.265	61	38	15	550	28	12	.980
1985— Atlanta (N.L.)	1B-OF	110	238	22	51	5	0	3	13	.214	23	28	9	541	37	9	.985
1986— Richmond (Int'l)	OF-1B	107	384	69	125	30	5	10	75	.326	58	41	11	394	25	7	.984
— Atlanta (N.L.)	OF-1B	29	70	6	19	2	0	2	11	.271	8	4	0	24	1	2	.926
1987— Atlanta (N.L.)	1B-OF	142	533	77	144	35	2	12	74	.270	48	63	42	1297	72	14	.990
1988— Atlanta (N.L.)	1B	141	547	61	164	29	1	8	74	.300	36	49	29	1282	106	•17	.988
1989— Atlanta (N.L.)	1B	72	266	24	67	11	0	4	21	.252	32	28	10	618	51	9	.987
1990— Kansas City (A.L.)■	DH-1B	133	465	57	118	22	2	8	57	.254	39	56	17	394	40	6	.986
1991— St. Louis (N.L.)■	1B-OF	109	242	29	58	8	4	6	36	.240	22	34	15	413	29	5	.989
1992— St. Louis (N.L.)	1B	87	143	13	34	8	0	1	18	.238	15	23	3	221	11	3	.987
1993— St. Louis (N.L.)	1B-OF	96	98	21	33	5	0	4	16	.337	18	23	1	79	3	2	.976
1994— St. Louis (N.L.)	1B	60	77	12	25	7	0	3	18	.325	15	12	1	96	4	1	.990
1995— St. Louis (N.L.)	1B	65	79	4	13	4	0	0	5	.165	6	12	0	69	3	0	1.000
American League totals (1 year)		133	465	57	118	22	2	8	57	.254	39	56	17	394	40	6	.986
National League totals (12 years)		1060	2679	326	714	128	9	51	339	.267	289	318	125	5245	345	75	.987
Major league totals (13 years)		1193	3144	383	832	150	11	59	396	.265	328	374	142	5639	385	81	.987

PERRY, HERBERT 1B INDIANS

PERSONAL: Born September 15, 1969, in Mayo, Fla. . . . 6-2/215. . . . Bats right, throws right. . . . Full name: Herbert Edward Perry Jr.

HIGH SCHOOL: Lafayette (Mayo, Fla.).

COLLEGE: Florida.

TRANSACTIONS/CAREER NOTES: Selected by Cleveland Indians organization in second round of free-agent draft (June 3, 1991). . . . On disabled list (June 18-July 13, 1991 and July 23, 1993-remainder of season).

STATISTICAL NOTES: Led Eastern League in being hit by pitch with 15 in 1993.

		BATTING												FIELDING			
Year Team (League)	Pos.	G	AB	R	H	2B	3B	HR	RBI	Avg.	BB	SO	SB	PO	A	E	Avg.
1991— Watertown (NYP)	DH	14	52	3	11	2	0	0	5	.212	8	7	0	...	...	...	...
1992— Kinston (Carolina)	1B-OF-3B	121	449	74	125	16	1	19	77	.278	46	89	12	297	39	5	.985
1993— Cant./Akr. (East.)	1B-3B-OF	89	327	52	88	21	1	9	55	.269	37	47	7	378	86	10	.979
1994— Charlotte (Int'l)	1B-3B-OF	102	376	67	123	20	4	13	70	.327	41	55	9	747	55	6	.993
— Cleveland (A.L.)	1B-3B	4	9	1	1	0	0	0	1	.111	3	1	0	25	5	1	.968
1995— Buffalo (A.A.)	1B	49	180	27	57	14	1	2	17	.317	15	18	1	419	44	3	.994
— Cleveland (A.L.)	1B-DH-3B	52	162	23	51	13	1	3	23	.315	13	28	1	391	30	0	1.000
Major league totals (2 years)		56	171	24	52	13	1	3	24	.304	16	29	1	416	35	1	.998

DIVISION SERIES RECORD

		BATTING												FIELDING			
Year Team (League)	Pos.	G	AB	R	H	2B	3B	HR	RBI	Avg.	BB	SO	SB	PO	A	E	Avg.
1995— Cleveland (A.L.)	PH	1	1	0	0	0	0	0	0	.000	0	0	0	...	...	...	...

CHAMPIONSHIP SERIES RECORD

		BATTING												FIELDING			
Year Team (League)	Pos.	G	AB	R	H	2B	3B	HR	RBI	Avg.	BB	SO	SB	PO	A	E	Avg.
1995— Cleveland (A.L.)	1B	3	8	0	0	0	0	0	0	.000	1	3	0	30	0	0	1.000

WORLD SERIES RECORD

		BATTING												FIELDING			
Year Team (League)	Pos.	G	AB	R	H	2B	3B	HR	RBI	Avg.	BB	SO	SB	PO	A	E	Avg.
1995— Cleveland (A.L.)	1B	3	5	0	00	0	0	0	0	.000	0	2	0	13	2	0	1.000

PERSON, ROBERT P METS

PERSONAL: Born October 6, 1969, in Lowell, Mass. . . . 5-11/180. . . . Throws right, bats right. . . . Full name: Robert Alan Person.

HIGH SCHOOL: University City (Mo.).

JUNIOR COLLEGE: Seminole (Okla.) Junior College.

TRANSACTIONS/CAREER NOTES: Selected by Cleveland Indians organization in 25th round of free-agent draft (June 5, 1989). . . . Loaned by Indians organization to Bend, independent (June 12-25, 1991). . . . Traded by Indians organization to Chicago White Sox organization for P Grady Hall (June 27, 1991). . . . On disabled list (April 10-May 13, 1992). . . . Selected by Florida Marlins in second round (47th pick overall) of expansion draft (November 17, 1992). . . . Granted free agency (December 19, 1992). . . . Re-signed by Edmonton, Marlins organization (January 8, 1993). . . . Traded by Marlins organization to New York Mets organization for P Steve Long (March 30, 1994).

Year	Team (League)	W	L	Pct.	ERA	G	GS	CG	ShO	Sv.	IP	H	R	ER	BB	SO
1989	—Burlington (Appal.)	0	1	.000	3.18	10	5	0	0	1	34	23	13	12	17	19
1990	—Watertown (NYP)	1	0	1.000	1.10	5	2	0	0	0	16 1/3	8	2	2	7	19
	—Kinston (Carolina)	1	0	1.000	2.70	4	3	0	0	0	16 2/3	17	6	5	9	7
	—GC Indians (GCL)	0	2	.000	7.36	8	0	0	0	2	7 1/3	10	7	6	4	8
1991	—Kinston (Carolina)	3	5	.375	4.67	11	11	0	0	0	52	56	37	27	42	45
	—Bend (Northwest)■	1	1	.500	3.60	2	2	0	0	0	10	6	6	4	5	6
	—South Bend (Midw.)■	4	3	.571	3.30	13	13	0	0	0	76 1/3	50	35	28	56	66
1992	—Sarasota (Fla. St.)	5	7	.417	3.59	19	18	1	0	0	105 1/3	90	48	42	62	85
1993	—High Desert (Calif.)■	12	10	.545	4.69	28	26	4	0	0	169	184	*115	88	48	107
1994	—Binghamton (East.)■	9	6	.600	3.45	31	23	3	2	0	159	124	68	61	68	130
1995	—Binghamton (East.)	5	4	.556	3.11	26	7	1	0	7	66 2/3	46	27	23	25	65
	—Norfolk (Int'l)	2	1	.667	4.50	5	4	0	0	0	32	30	17	16	13	33
	—New York (N.L.)	1	0	1.000	0.75	3	1	0	0	0	12	5	1	1	2	10
Major league totals (1 year)		1	0	1.000	0.75	3	1	0	0	0	12	5	1	1	2	10

RECORD AS POSITION PLAYER

				BATTING											FIELDING		
Year	Team (League)	Pos.	G	AB	R	H	2B	3B	HR	RBI	Avg.	BB	SO	SB	PO	A	E	Avg.
1990	—GC Indians (GCL)	OF	24	46	6	4	0	0	0	3	.087	10	12	1	10	2	0	1.000

PETAGINE, ROBERTO 1B PADRES

PERSONAL: Born June 7, 1971, in Nueva Esparita, Venezuela. . . . 6-1/170. . . . Bats left, throws left. . . . Full name: Roberto Antonio Petagine. . . . Name pronounced PET-uh-GHEEN.

TRANSACTIONS/CAREER NOTES: Signed as non-drafted free agent by Houston Astros organization (February 13, 1990). . . . On Tucson disabled list (April 30-June 11, 1994). . . . Traded by Astros with 3B Ken Caminiti, OF Steve Finley, SS Andujar Cedeno, P Brian Williams and a player to be named later to San Diego Padres for OF Phil Plantier, OF Derek Bell, P Pedro Martinez, P Doug Brocail, IF Craig Shipley and SS Ricky Gutierrez (December 28, 1994).

HONORS: Named Texas League Player of the Year (1993).

STATISTICAL NOTES: Led Gulf Coast League first basemen with .990 fielding percentage and 46 double plays in 1990. . . . Led Texas League with .442 on-base percentage and 14 intentional bases on balls received in 1993.

				BATTING											FIELDING			
Year	Team (League)	Pos.	G	AB	R	H	2B	3B	HR	RBI	Avg.	BB	SO	SB	PO	A	E	Avg.
1990	—GC Astros (GCL)	1B-OF	55	187	35	54	5	4	2	24	.289	26	23	9	474	36	5	†.990
1991	—Burlington (Midw.)	1B	124	432	72	112	24	1	12	58	.259	71	74	7	940	60	22	.978
1992	—Osceola (Fla. St.)	1B	86	307	52	90	22	4	7	49	.293	47	47	3	701	74	10	.987
	—Jackson (Texas)	1B	21	70	8	21	4	0	4	12	.300	6	15	1	151	15	0	1.000
1993	—Jackson (Texas)	1B	128	437	73	146	*36	2	15	90	*.334	*84	89	6	1033	*110	14	.988
1994	—Houston (N.L.)	1B	8	7	0	0	0	0	0	0	.000	1	3	0	3	0	0	1.000
	—Tucson (PCL)	1B	65	247	53	78	19	0	10	44	.316	35	54	3	597	35	10	.984
1995	—San Diego (N.L.)■	1B-OF	89	124	15	29	8	0	3	17	.234	26	41	0	263	22	1	.997
	—Las Vegas (PCL)	1B	19	56	8	12	2	1	1	5	.214	13	17	1	110	7	3	.975
Major league totals (2 years)			97	131	15	29	8	0	3	17	.221	27	44	0	266	22	1	.997

PETERS, CHRIS P PIRATES

PERSONAL: Born January 28, 1972, in Fort Thomas, Ky. . . . 6-1/162. . . . Throws left, bats left. . . . Full name: Christopher Michael Peters.

HIGH SCHOOL: Peters Township (McMurray, Pa.).

COLLEGE: Indiana.

TRANSACTIONS/CAREER NOTES: Selected by Pittsburgh Pirates organization in 37th round of free-agent draft (June 3, 1993).

Year	Team (League)	W	L	Pct.	ERA	G	GS	CG	ShO	Sv.	IP	H	R	ER	BB	SO
1993	—Welland (NYP)	1	0	1.000	4.55	16	0	0	0	0	27 2/3	33	16	14	20	25
1994	—Augusta (S. Atl.)	4	5	.444	4.30	54	0	0	0	4	60 2/3	51	34	29	33	83
	—Salem (Carolina)	1	0	1.000	13.50	3	0	0	0	0	3 1/3	5	5	5	1	2
1995	—Lynchburg (Caro.)	11	5	.688	2.43	24	24	3	*3	0	144 2/3	126	57	39	35	132
	—Carolina (South.)	2	0	1.000	1.29	2	2	0	0	0	14	9	2	2	2	7

PETERSON, CHARLES OF PIRATES

PERSONAL: Born May 8, 1974, in Laurens, S.C. . . . 6-3/203. . . . Bats right, throws right. . . . Full name: Charles Edward Peterson.

HIGH SCHOOL: Laurens (S.C.).

TRANSACTIONS/CAREER NOTES: Selected by Pittsburgh Pirates organization in first round (22nd pick overall) of free-agent draft (June 3, 1993).

				BATTING											FIELDING			
Year	Team (League)	Pos.	G	AB	R	H	2B	3B	HR	RBI	Avg.	BB	SO	SB	PO	A	E	Avg.
1993	—GC Pirates (GCL)	OF	49	188	28	57	11	3	1	23	.303	22	22	8	75	7	5	.943
1994	—Augusta (S. Atl.)	OF	108	415	55	106	14	6	4	40	.255	35	78	27	172	11	11	.943
1995	—Lynchburg (Caro.)	OF	107	391	61	107	9	4	7	51	.274	43	73	31	192	11	8	.962
	—Carolina (South.)	OF	20	70	13	23	3	1	0	7	.329	9	15	2	40	2	1	.977

PETKOVSEK, MARK — P — CARDINALS

PERSONAL: Born November 18, 1965, in Beaumont, Tex. . . . 6-0/185. . . . Throws right, bats right. . . . Full name: Mark Joseph Petkovsek. . . . Name pronounced PET-kie-zeck.
HIGH SCHOOL: Kelly (Beaumont, Tex.).
COLLEGE: Texas.
TRANSACTIONS/CAREER NOTES: Selected by Texas Rangers organization in supplemental round ("sandwich pick" between first and second round, 29th pick overall) of free-agent draft (June 2, 1987); pick received as compensation for New York Yankees signing Type A free-agent OF Gary Ward. . . . Granted free agency (October 16, 1991). . . . Signed by Pittsburgh Pirates organization (January 22, 1992). . . . Granted free agency (October 15, 1992). . . . Re-signed by Pirates organization (November 9, 1992). . . . On Buffalo disabled list (July 4-23, 1993). . . . Granted free agency (October 12, 1993). . . . Signed by Tucson, Houston Astros organization (March 4, 1994). . . . On disabled list (July 20-August 12, 1994). . . . Granted free agency (October 15, 1994). . . . Signed by St. Louis Cardinals organization (November 18, 1994). . . . On Louisville suspended list (May 12-17, 1995).
STATISTICAL NOTES: Pitched 5-0 no-hit victory against Colorado Springs (May 16, 1994).

Year	Team (League)	W	L	Pct.	ERA	G	GS	CG	ShO	Sv.	IP	H	R	ER	BB	SO
1987	— GC Rangers (GCL)	0	0	...	3.18	3	1	0	0	0	5 2/3	4	2	2	2	7
	— Charlotte (Fla. St.)	3	4	.429	4.02	11	10	0	0	0	56	67	36	25	17	23
1988	— Charlotte (Fla. St.)	10	11	.476	2.97	28	28	7	•5	0	175 2/3	156	71	58	42	95
1989	— Tulsa (Texas)	8	5	.615	3.47	21	21	1	0	0	140	144	63	54	35	66
	— Okla. City (A.A.)	0	4	.000	7.34	6	6	0	0	0	30 2/3	39	27	25	18	8
1990	— Okla. City (A.A.)	7	*14	.333	5.25	28	28	2	1	0	151	*187	*103	88	42	81
1991	— Okla. City (A.A.)	9	8	.529	4.93	25	24	3	1	0	149 2/3	162	89	82	38	67
	— Texas (A.L.)	0	1	.000	14.46	4	1	0	0	0	9 1/3	21	16	15	4	6
1992	— Buffalo (A.A.)■	8	8	.500	3.53	32	22	1	0	1	150 1/3	150	76	59	44	49
1993	— Buffalo (A.A.)	3	4	.429	4.33	14	11	1	0	0	70 2/3	74	38	34	16	27
	— Pittsburgh (N.L.)	3	0	1.000	6.96	26	0	0	0	0	32 1/3	43	25	25	9	14
1994	— Tucson (Pac. Coast)■	10	7	.588	4.62	25	23	1	1	0	138 1/3	176	87	71	40	69
1995	— Louisville (A.A.)■	4	1	.800	2.32	8	8	2	1	0	54 1/3	38	16	14	8	30
	— St. Louis (N.L.)	6	6	.500	4.00	26	21	1	1	0	137 1/3	136	71	61	35	71
A.L. totals (1 year)		0	1	.000	14.46	4	1	0	0	0	9 1/3	21	16	15	4	6
N.L. totals (2 years)		9	6	.600	4.56	52	21	1	1	0	169 2/3	179	96	86	44	85
Major league totals (3 years)		9	7	.563	5.08	56	22	1	1	0	179	200	112	101	48	91

PETTITTE, ANDY — P — YANKEES

PERSONAL: Born June 15, 1972, in Baton Rouge, La. . . . 6-5/235. . . . Throws left, bats left. . . . Full name: Andrew Eugene Pettitte.
HIGH SCHOOL: Deer Park (Tex.).
COLLEGE: San Jacinto College (Tex.).
TRANSACTIONS/CAREER NOTES: Selected by New York Yankees organization in 22nd round of free-agent draft (June 4, 1990); did not sign. . . . Signed as non-drafted free agent by Yankees organization (May 25, 1991). . . . On Albany temporarily inactive list (June 5-10, 1994).

Year	Team (League)	W	L	Pct.	ERA	G	GS	CG	ShO	Sv.	IP	H	R	ER	BB	SO
1991	— GC Yankees (GCL)	4	1	.800	0.98	6	6	0	0	0	36 2/3	16	6	4	8	51
	— Oneonta (NYP)	2	2	.500	2.18	6	6	1	0	0	33	33	18	8	16	32
1992	— Greensboro (S. Atl.)	10	4	.714	2.20	27	27	2	1	0	168	141	53	41	55	130
1993	— Prin. William (Caro.)	11	9	.550	3.04	26	26	2	1	0	159 2/3	146	68	54	47	129
	— Albany (S. Atl.)	1	0	1.000	3.60	1	1	0	0	0	5	5	4	2	2	6
1994	— Alb./Colon. (East.)	7	2	.778	2.71	11	11	0	0	0	73	60	32	22	18	50
	— Columbus (Int'l)	7	2	.778	2.98	16	16	3	0	0	96 2/3	101	40	32	21	61
1995	— Columbus (Int'l)	0	0	...	0.00	2	2	0	0	0	11 2/3	7	0	0	0	8
	— New York (A.L.)	12	9	.571	4.17	31	26	3	0	0	175	183	86	81	63	114
Major league totals (1 year)		12	9	.571	4.17	31	26	3	0	0	175	183	86	81	63	114

DIVISION SERIES RECORD

Year	Team (League)	W	L	Pct.	ERA	G	GS	CG	ShO	Sv.	IP	H	R	ER	BB	SO
1995	— New York (A.L.)	0	0	...	5.14	1	1	0	0	0	7	9	4	4	3	0

PHILLIPS, J.R. — 1B — GIANTS

PERSONAL: Born April 29, 1970, in West Covina, Calif. . . . 6-1/185. . . . Bats left, throws left. . . . Full name: Charles Gene Phillips.
HIGH SCHOOL: Bishop Amat (La Puente, Calif.).
TRANSACTIONS/CAREER NOTES: Selected by California Angels organization in fourth round of free-agent draft (June 1, 1988). . . . Claimed on waivers by San Francisco Giants (December 17, 1992). . . . On Phoenix disabled list (August 14, 1994-remainder of season).
STATISTICAL NOTES: Led Northwest League first basemen with 641 putouts, 42 assists and 691 total chances in 1990. . . . Led California League first basemen with 1,166 putouts, 1,272 total chances and 117 double plays in 1991. . . . Led Texas League first basemen with 1,222 putouts, 100 assists, 17 errors, 1,339 total chances and 106 double plays in 1992. . . . Led Pacific Coast League first basemen with 1,135 putouts, 93 assists, 28 errors and 1,256 total chances in 1993.

			BATTING											FIELDING			
Year	Team (League)	Pos.	G	AB	R	H	2B	3B	HR	RBI	Avg.	BB	SO	SB	PO	A	E	Avg.
1988	— Bend (Northwest)	OF-1B	56	210	24	40	8	0	4	23	.190	21	70	3	197	9	3	.986
1989	— Quad City (Midw.)	1B-OF	125	442	41	85	29	1	8	50	.192	49	146	3	954	46	20	.980
1990	— Palm Springs (Cal.)	1B	46	162	14	32	4	1	1	15	.198	10	58	3	436	26	16	.967
	— Boise (Northwest)	1B-OF	70	237	30	46	6	0	10	34	.194	19	78	1	†642	†42	8	.988
1991	— Palm Springs (Cal.)	1B-P	130	471	64	117	22	2	20	70	.248	57	*144	15	†1166	94	12	.991
1992	— Midland (Texas)	1B-OF	127	497	58	118	32	4	14	77	.237	32	*165	5	†1223	†100	†17	.987
1993	— Phoenix (PCL)■	1B-OF	134	506	80	133	35	2	*27	94	.263	53	127	7	†1138	†93	†29	.977
	— San Francisco (N.L.)	1B	11	16	1	5	1	1	1	4	.313	0	5	0	32	2	1	.971
1994	— Phoenix (PCL)	1B	95	360	69	108	28	5	27	79	.300	45	96	4	782	78	6	.993
	— San Francisco (N.L.)	1B	15	38	1	5	0	0	1	3	.132	1	13	1	79	10	1	.989
1995	— San Francisco (N.L.)	1B-OF	92	231	27	45	9	0	9	28	.195	19	69	1	536	37	4	.993
Major league totals (3 years)			118	285	29	55	10	1	11	35	.193	20	87	2	647	49	6	.991

P

RECORD AS PITCHER

Year	Team (League)	W	L	Pct.	ERA	G	GS	CG	ShO	Sv.	IP	H	R	ER	BB	SO
1991—	Palm Springs (Cal.)...........	0	0	...	4.50	2	0	0	0	0	2	3	1	1	2	3

PHILLIPS, TONY — 3B/OF — WHITE SOX

PERSONAL: Born April 25, 1959, in Atlanta. . . . 5-10/175. . . . Bats both, throws right. . . . Full name: Keith Anthony Phillips.
HIGH SCHOOL: Roswell (Ga.).
COLLEGE: New Mexico Military Institute.
TRANSACTIONS/CAREER NOTES: Selected by Seattle Mariners organization in 16th round of free-agent draft (June 7, 1977); did not sign. . . . Selected by Montreal Expos organization in secondary phase of free-agent draft (January 10, 1978). . . . On West Palm Beach temporarily inactive list (April 11-May 4, 1978). . . . Traded by Expos organization with cash to San Diego Padres for 1B Willie Montanez (August 31, 1980). . . . Traded by Padres organization with P Eric Mustad and IF Kevin Bell to Oakland Athletics organization for P Bob Lacey and P Roy Moretti (March 27, 1981). . . . On Oakland disabled list (March 26-August 22, 1985); included rehabilitation assignments to Tacoma (July 30-August 5 and August 7-20). . . . On disabled list (August 14-October 3, 1986). . . . On Oakland disabled list (July 12-August 28, 1987); included rehabilitation assignment to Tacoma (August 20-28). . . . Released by A's (December 21, 1987). . . . Re-signed by A's (March 9, 1988). . . . On Oakland disabled list (May 18-July 8, 1988); included rehabilitation assignment to Tacoma (June 16-July 4). . . . Granted free agency (November 13, 1989). . . . Signed by Detroit Tigers (December 5, 1989). . . . Traded by Tigers to California Angels for OF Chad Curtis (April 12, 1995). . . . On suspended list (August 8-11, 1995). . . . Granted free agency (October 31, 1995). . . . Signed by Chicago White Sox (January 20, 1996).
RECORDS: Shares major league single-game record (nine innings) for most assists by second baseman—12 (July 6, 1986).
STATISTICAL NOTES: Led Southern League shortstops with 42 errors in 1980. . . . Led Eastern League in being hit by pitch with 10 in 1981. . . . Hit for the cycle (May 16, 1986). . . . Led A.L. third basemen with 19 errors in 1995. . . . Career major league grand slams: 1.

				BATTING										FIELDING			
Year	Team (League)	Pos.	G	AB	R	H	2B	3B	HR	RBI	Avg.	BB	SO	SB	PO	A	E	Avg.
1978—	W.P. Beach (FSL)........	3B-SS-2B	32	54	8	9	0	0	0	3	.167	9	7	2	13	33	5	.902
—	Jamestown (NYP)......	SS-2B-3B	52	152	24	29	5	2	1	17	.191	27	24	3	73	146	16	.932
1979—	W.P. Beach (FSL)........	2B-SS	60	203	30	47	5	1	0	18	.232	36	26	7	120	156	21	.929
—	Memphis (South.)......	SS-2B	52	156	31	44	4	2	3	11	.282	19	13	3	68	134	18	.918
1980—	Memphis (South.)......	SS-2B	136	502	100	125	18	4	5	41	.249	*98	89	50	226	408	†42	.938
1981—	West Haven (East.)■..	SS	131	461	79	114	25	3	9	64	.247	67	69	40	200	391	*33	.947
—	Tacoma (PCL)...........	2B-SS	4	11	1	4	1	0	0	2	.364	0	0	0	8	10	0	1.000
1982—	Tacoma (PCL)...........	SS	86	300	76	89	18	5	4	47	.297	73	63	29	138	236	30	.926
—	Oakland (A.L.)...........	SS	40	81	11	17	2	2	0	8	.210	12	26	2	46	95	7	.953
1983—	Oakland (A.L.)...........	S-2-3-DH	148	412	54	102	12	3	4	35	.248	48	69	16	218	383	30	.952
1984—	Oakland (A.L.)...........	SS-2B-OF	154	451	62	120	24	3	4	37	.266	42	86	10	255	391	28	.958
1985—	Tacoma (PCL)...........	3B-2B	20	69	9	9	1	0	0	5	.130	8	28	3	15	36	4	.927
—	Oakland (A.L.)...........	3B-2B	42	161	23	45	12	2	4	17	.280	13	34	3	54	103	3	.981
1986—	Oakland (A.L.)...........	2-3-O-DH-S	118	441	76	113	14	5	5	52	.256	76	82	15	191	326	13	.975
1987—	Oakland (A.L.)...........	2-3-S-O-DH	111	379	48	91	20	0	10	46	.240	57	76	7	179	299	14	.972
—	Tacoma (PCL)...........	2B-3B	7	26	5	9	2	1	1	6	.346	4	3	1	8	10	0	1.000
1988—	Tacoma (PCL)...........	S-O-2-3	16	59	10	16	0	0	2	8	.271	12	13	0	25	27	2	.963
—	Oakland (A.L.)...........	3-O-2-S-1-DH	79	212	32	43	8	4	2	17	.203	36	50	0	84	80	10	.943
1989—	Oakland (A.L.)...........	2-3-S-O-1	143	451	48	118	15	6	4	47	.262	58	66	3	184	321	15	.971
1990—	Detroit (A.L.)■..........	3-2-S-O-DH	152	573	97	144	23	5	8	55	.251	99	85	19	180	368	23	.960
1991—	Detroit (A.L.).............	O-3-2-DH-S	146	564	87	160	28	4	17	72	.284	79	95	10	269	237	8	.984
1992—	Detroit (A.L.).............	O-2-DH-3-S	159	606	*114	167	32	3	10	64	.276	114	93	12	301	195	11	.978
1993—	Detroit (A.L.).............	O-2-DH-3	151	566	113	177	27	0	7	57	.313	*132	102	16	321	165	13	.974
1994—	Detroit (A.L.).............	OF-2B-DH	114	438	91	123	19	3	19	61	.281	95	105	13	254	42	6	.980
1995—	California (A.L.)■.......	3B-OF-DH	139	525	119	137	21	1	27	61	.261	113	135	13	166	179	†20	.945
Major league totals (14 years)			1696	5860	975	1557	257	41	121	629	.266	974	1104	139	2702	3184	201	.967

CHAMPIONSHIP SERIES RECORD

				BATTING										FIELDING			
Year	Team (League)	Pos.	G	AB	R	H	2B	3B	HR	RBI	Avg.	BB	SO	SB	PO	A	E	Avg.
1988—	Oakland (A.L.)...........	OF-2B	2	7	0	2	1	0	0	0	.286	1	3	0	10	0	0	1.000
1989—	Oakland (A.L.)...........	2B-3B	5	18	1	3	1	0	0	1	.167	2	4	2	4	14	0	1.000
Championship series totals (2 years)			7	25	1	5	2	0	0	1	.200	3	7	2	14	14	0	1.000

WORLD SERIES RECORD

NOTES: Member of World Series championship team (1989).

				BATTING										FIELDING			
Year	Team (League)	Pos.	G	AB	R	H	2B	3B	HR	RBI	Avg.	BB	SO	SB	PO	A	E	Avg.
1988—	Oakland (A.L.)...........	OF-2B	2	4	1	1	0	0	0	0	.250	1	2	2	3	5	0	1.000
1989—	Oakland (A.L.)...........	2B-3B-OF	4	17	2	4	1	0	1	3	.235	0	3	0	8	15	0	1.000
World Series totals (2 years)			6	21	3	5	1	0	1	3	.238	1	5	2	11	20	0	1.000

P

PHOENIX, STEVE — P

PERSONAL: Born January 31, 1968, in Phoenix. . . . 6-2/175. . . . Throws right, bats right. . . . Full name: Steven Robert Phoenix.
HIGH SCHOOL: Valhalla (El Cajon, Calif.).
COLLEGE: Grand Canyon (Ariz.).
TRANSACTIONS/CAREER NOTES: Signed as non-drafted free agent by Oakland Athletics organization (June 19, 1990). . . . On Huntsville disabled list (June 12-August 1, 1993). . . . Granted free agency (October 27, 1995).

Year	Team (League)	W	L	Pct.	ERA	G	GS	CG	ShO	Sv.	IP	H	R	ER	BB	SO
1990—	Arizona A's (Ariz.)..............	3	1	.750	1.45	6	6	0	0	0	31	25	14	5	4	31
—	Modesto (Calif.)................	4	1	.800	4.58	6	6	0	0	0	37 1/3	43	21	19	10	23
1991—	Madison (Midwest)............	3	0	1.000	2.95	7	2	0	0	2	21 1/3	26	8	7	10	19
—	Modesto (Calif.)................	5	2	.714	3.74	27	3	1	1	2	84 1/3	87	44	35	33	65
—	Huntsville (South.)............	0	0	...	6.00	2	/0	0	0	0	3	7	3	2	1	3

Year	Team (League)	W	L	Pct.	ERA	G	GS	CG	ShO	Sv.	IP	H	R	ER	BB	SO
1992—	Huntsville (South.)	11	5	.688	2.79	32	24	0	0	0	174	179	68	54	36	124
1993—	Huntsville (South.)	2	2	.500	1.40	11	0	0	0	1	19⅓	13	5	3	5	15
—	Tacoma (PCL)	0	2	.000	6.97	11	5	0	0	0	31	42	27	24	27	21
1994—	Huntsville (South.)	6	2	.750	1.29	38	0	0	0	20	48⅔	42	9	7	16	40
—	Tacoma (PCL)	0	2	.000	1.23	20	0	0	0	9	22	16	5	3	4	16
—	Oakland (A.L.)	0	0	...	6.23	2	0	0	0	0	4⅓	4	3	3	2	3
1995—	Edmonton (PCL)	4	3	.571	4.50	40	0	0	0	5	64	66	36	32	28	28
—	Oakland (A.L.)	0	0	...	32.40	1	0	0	0	0	1⅔	3	6	6	3	3
Major league totals (2 years)		0	0	...	13.50	3	0	0	0	0	6	7	9	9	5	6

PIAZZA, MIKE — C — DODGERS

PERSONAL: Born September 4, 1968, in Norristown, Pa. . . . 6-3/215. . . . Bats right, throws right. . . . Full name: Michael Joseph Piazza. . . . Name pronounced pee-AH-za.

HIGH SCHOOL: Phoenixville (Pa.) Area.

JUNIOR COLLEGE: Miami-Dade (North) Community College.

TRANSACTIONS/CAREER NOTES: Selected by Los Angeles Dodgers organization in 62nd round of free-agent draft (June 1, 1988). . . . On disabled list (May 11-June 4, 1995).

HONORS: Named N.L. Rookie Player of the Year by The Sporting News (1993). . . . Named catcher on The Sporting News N.L. All-Star team (1993-95). . . . Named catcher on The Sporting News N.L. Silver Slugger team (1993-95). . . . Named N.L. Rookie of the Year by Baseball Writers' Association of America (1993).

STATISTICAL NOTES: Led California League with .540 slugging percentage and in grounding into double plays with 19 in 1991. . . . Led N.L. catchers with 98 assists and tied for lead with 11 errors in 1993. . . . Led N.L. catchers with 866 total chances and 12 passed balls in 1995. . . . Career major league grand slams: 4.

			BATTING												FIELDING			
Year	Team (League)	Pos.	G	AB	R	H	2B	3B	HR	RBI	Avg.	BB	SO	SB	PO	A	E	Avg.
1989—	Salem (Northwest)	C	57	198	22	53	11	0	8	25	.268	13	51	0	230	21	6	.977
1990—	Vero Beach (FSL)	C-1B	88	272	27	68	20	0	6	45	.250	11	68	0	428	38	16	.967
1991—	Bakersfield (Calif.)	C-1B	117	448	71	124	27	2	29	80	.277	47	83	0	723	69	15	.981
1992—	San Antonio (Tex.)	C	31	114	18	43	11	0	7	21	.377	13	18	0	189	22	4	.981
—	Albuquerque (PCL)	C-1B	94	358	54	122	22	5	16	69	.341	37	57	1	550	50	9	.985
—	Los Angeles (N.L.)	C	21	69	5	16	3	0	1	7	.232	4	12	0	94	7	1	.990
1993—	Los Angeles (N.L.)	C-1B	149	547	81	174	24	2	35	112	.318	46	86	3	901	†98	‡11	.989
1994—	Los Angeles (N.L.)	C	107	405	64	129	18	0	24	92	.319	33	65	1	640	38	*10	.985
1995—	Los Angeles (N.L.)	C	112	434	82	150	17	0	32	93	.346	39	80	1	*805	52	9	.990
Major league totals (4 years)			389	1455	232	469	62	2	92	304	.322	122	243	5	2440	195	31	.988

DIVISION SERIES RECORD

			BATTING												FIELDING			
Year	Team (League)	Pos.	G	AB	R	H	2B	3B	HR	RBI	Avg.	BB	SO	SB	PO	A	E	Avg.
1995—	Los Angeles (N.L.)	C	3	14	1	3	1	0	1	1	.214	0	2	0	31	0	0	1.000

ALL-STAR GAME RECORD

			BATTING										FIELDING			
Year	League	Pos.	AB	R	H	2B	3B	HR	RBI	Avg.	BB	SO	SB	PO	A	E	Avg.
1993—	National	C	1	0	0	0	0	0	0	.000	0	1	0	3	0	0	1.000
1994—	National	C	4	0	1	0	0	0	1	.250	0	0	0	6	0	0	1.000
1995—	National	C	3	1	1	0	0	1	1	.333	0	0	0	6	1	0	1.000
All-Star Game totals (3 years)			8	1	2	0	0	1	2	.250	0	1	0	15	1	0	1.000

PICHARDO, HIPOLITO — P — ROYALS

PERSONAL: Born August 22, 1969, in Jicome Esperanza, Dominican Republic. . . . 6-1/185. . . . Throws right, bats right. . . . Full name: Hipolito Antonio Pichardo. . . . Name pronounced ee-POL-uh-toe puh-CHAR-doh.

HIGH SCHOOL: Liceo Enriguillo (Jicome Esperanza, Dominican Republic).

TRANSACTIONS/CAREER NOTES: Signed as non-drafted free agent by Kansas City Royals organization (December 16, 1987). . . . On disabled list (August 14-September 1, 1993 and August 15-September 1, 1995).

STATISTICAL NOTES: Pitched 8-0 one-hit, complete-game victory for Kansas City against Boston (July 21, 1992).

Year	Team (League)	W	L	Pct.	ERA	G	GS	CG	ShO	Sv.	IP	H	R	ER	BB	SO
1988—	GC Royals (GCL)	0	0	...	13.50	1	0	0	0	0	1⅓	3	2	2	1	3
1989—	Appleton (Midw.)	5	4	.556	2.97	12	12	2	0	0	75⅔	58	29	25	18	50
1990—	Baseball City (FSL)	1	6	.143	3.80	11	10	0	0	0	45	47	28	19	25	40
1991—	Memphis (South.)	3	11	.214	4.27	34	11	0	0	0	99	116	56	47	38	75
1992—	Memphis (South.)	0	0	...	0.64	2	2	0	0	0	14	13	2	1	1	10
—	Kansas City (A.L.)	9	6	.600	3.95	31	24	1	1	0	143⅔	148	71	63	49	59
1993—	Kansas City (A.L.)	7	8	.467	4.04	30	25	2	0	0	165	183	85	74	53	70
1994—	Kansas City (A.L.)	5	3	.625	4.92	45	0	0	0	3	67⅔	82	42	37	24	36
1995—	Kansas City (A.L.)	8	4	.667	4.36	44	0	0	0	1	64	66	34	31	30	43
Major league totals (4 years)		29	21	.580	4.19	150	49	3	1	4	440⅓	479	232	205	156	208

PICKETT, RICKY — P — GIANTS

PERSONAL: Born January 19, 1970, in Fort Worth, Texas . . . 6-1/200. . . . Throws left, bats left. . . . Full name: Cecil Lee Pickett.

HIGH SCHOOL: Eastern Hills (Fort Worth, Tex.).

JUNIOR COLLEGE: Northeastern Oklahoma A&M.

TRANSACTIONS/CAREER NOTES: Selected by Cincinnati Reds organization in 28th round of free-agent draft (June 1, 1992). . . . Traded by

Reds organization with OF Deion Sanders, P John Roper, P Scott Service and 1B Dave McCarty to San Francisco Giants organization for P Mark Portugal, P Dave Burba and OF Darren Lewis (July 21, 1995).

Year	Team (League)	W	L	Pct.	ERA	G	GS	CG	ShO	Sv.	IP	H	R	ER	BB	SO
1992—	Billings (Pioneer)	1	2	.333	2.35	20	4	0	0	2	53 2/3	35	21	14	28	41
1993—	Char., W.Va. (S. Atl.)	1	2	.333	6.75	44	1	0	0	0	44	42	40	33	48	65
1994—	Char., W.Va. (S. Atl.)	1	1	.500	1.98	28	0	0	0	13	27 1/3	14	8	6	20	48
	—Winst.-Salem (Car.)	2	1	.667	3.75	21	0	0	0	4	24	16	11	10	23	33
1995—	Chattanooga (Sou.)	4	5	.444	3.28	40	0	0	0	9	46 2/3	22	20	17	44	69
	—Shreveport (Texas)■	2	0	1.000	1.71	14	0	0	0	3	21	9	5	4	9	23

PIERCE, JEFF — P — RED SOX

PERSONAL: Born June 7, 1969, in Poughkeepsie, N.Y. . . . 6-1/187. . . . Throws right, bats right. . . . Full name: Jeffrey Charles Pierce.
HIGH SCHOOL: F.D. Roosevelt (Hyde Park, N.Y.).
JUNIOR COLLEGE: Dutchess Community College (N.Y.).
COLLEGE: North Carolina State.
TRANSACTIONS/CAREER NOTES: Signed as non-drafted free agent by Chicago White Sox organization (June 10, 1991). . . . On Birmingham disabled list (June 20-July 9, 1993). . . . Traded by White Sox with P Johnny Ruffin to Cincinnati Reds for P Tim Belcher (July 31, 1993). . . . Claimed on waivers by Boston Red Sox (March 18, 1994). . . . On Pawtucket disabled list (July 28-September 14, 1995).

Year	Team (League)	W	L	Pct.	ERA	G	GS	CG	ShO	Sv.	IP	H	R	ER	BB	SO
1992—	South Bend (Midw.)	3	5	.375	2.07	52	0	0	0	30	69 2/3	46	22	16	18	88
	—Sarasota (Fla. St.)	0	0	...	0.00	1	0	0	0	0	2/3	0	0	0	0	1
1993—	Birmingham (Sou.)	3	4	.429	2.59	33	0	0	0	18	48 2/3	34	16	14	7	45
	—Chattanooga (Sou.)■	0	0	...	2.61	13	0	0	0	4	20 2/3	17	6	6	9	22
1994—	New Britain (East.)■	1	2	.333	2.29	29	0	0	0	10	39 1/3	31	13	10	12	54
	—Pawtucket (Int'l)	6	1	.857	3.43	32	0	0	0	2	60 1/3	53	27	23	21	57
1995—	Boston (A.L.)	0	3	.000	6.60	12	0	0	0	0	15	16	12	11	14	12
	—Pawtucket (Int'l)	4	2	.667	4.14	23	3	0	0	0	41 1/3	34	21	19	16	43
Major league totals (1 year)		0	3	.000	6.60	12	0	0	0	0	15	16	12	11	14	12

RECORD AS POSITION PLAYER

				BATTING											FIELDING			
Year	Team (League)	Pos.	G	AB	R	H	2B	3B	HR	RBI	Avg.	BB	SO	SB	PO	A	E	Avg.
1991—	Utica (N.Y.-Penn)	OF	50	158	22	38	10	4	0	24	.241	25	26	4	46	0	3	.939

PIRKL, GREG — 1B — MARINERS

PERSONAL: Born August 7, 1970, in Long Beach, Calif. . . . 6-5/240. . . . Bats right, throws right. . . . Full name: Gregory Daniel Pirkl.
HIGH SCHOOL: Los Alamitos (Calif.).
TRANSACTIONS/CAREER NOTES: Selected by Seattle Mariners organization in second round of free-agent draft (June 1, 1988). . . . On disabled list (May 31-June 22 and July 3, 1990-remainder of season). . . . On Calgary disabled list (June 6-15, 1994). . . . On Seattle disabled list (June 22-September 1, 1995); included rehabilitation assignment to Tacoma (July 29-August 27).
STATISTICAL NOTES: Led Northwest League with 22 passed balls in 1988. . . . Led Pacific Coast League with 10 sacrifice flies in 1993. . . . Led Pacific Coast League first basemen with 21 double plays in 1993.

				BATTING											FIELDING			
Year	Team (League)	Pos.	G	AB	R	H	2B	3B	HR	RBI	Avg.	BB	SO	SB	PO	A	E	Avg.
1988—	Belling. (N'west)	C	65	246	22	59	6	0	6	35	.240	12	59	1	227	19	9	.965
1989—	Belling. (N'west)	C	70	265	31	68	6	0	8	36	.257	23	51	4	296	23	9	.973
1990—	San Bern. (Calif.)	C	58	207	37	61	10	0	5	28	.295	13	34	3	325	40	9	.976
1991—	San Bern. (Calif.)	C-1B	63	239	32	75	13	1	14	53	.314	12	43	4	412	33	11	.976
	—Peninsula (Caro.)	C-1B	64	239	20	63	16	0	6	41	.264	9	42	0	322	31	5	.986
1992—	Jacksonv. (South.)	1B-C	59	227	25	66	11	1	10	29	.291	9	45	0	473	35	5	.990
	—Calgary (PCL)	1B	79	286	30	76	21	3	6	32	.266	14	64	4	625	44	7	.990
1993—	Calgary (PCL)	1B-3B	115	445	67	137	24	1	21	94	.308	13	50	3	920	72	14	.986
	—Seattle (A.L.)	1B-DH	7	23	1	4	0	0	1	4	.174	0	4	0	42	5	0	1.000
1994—	Seattle (A.L.)	DH-1B	19	53	7	14	3	0	6	11	.264	1	12	0	56	1	1	.983
	—Calgary (PCL)	1B	87	353	69	112	21	0	22	72	.317	24	58	1	614	45	13	.981
1995—	Seattle (A.L.)	1B-DH	10	17	2	4	0	0	0	0	.235	1	7	0	32	3	0	1.000
	—Tacoma (PCL)	1B	47	174	29	51	8	2	15	44	.293	14	28	1	276	19	5	.983
Major league totals (3 years)			36	93	10	22	3	0	7	15	.237	2	23	0	130	9	1	.993

PISCIOTTA, MARC — P — PIRATES

PERSONAL: Born August 7, 1970, in Edison, N.J. . . . 6-5/227. . . . Throws right, bats right. . . . Full name: Marc George Pisciotta. . . . Brother of Scott Pisciotta, pitcher, Montreal Expos organization. . . . Name pronounced pih-SHO-tuh.
HIGH SCHOOL: George Walton Comprehensive (Marietta, Ga.).
COLLEGE: Georgia Tech.
TRANSACTIONS/CAREER NOTES: Selected by Pittsburgh Pirates organization in 19th round of free-agent draft (June 3, 1991). . . . On disabled list (May 22-June 19, 1992). . . . Selected by Colorado Rockies from Pirates organization in Rule 5 major league draft (December 13, 1993). . . . Returned to Pirates organization (March 28, 1994).

Year	Team (League)	W	L	Pct.	ERA	G	GS	CG	ShO	Sv.	IP	H	R	ER	BB	SO
1991—	Welland (NYP)	1	1	.500	0.26	24	0	0	0	8	34	16	4	1	20	47
1992—	Augusta (S. Atl.)	4	5	.444	4.54	20	12	1	0	1	79 1/3	91	51	40	43	54
1993—	Augusta (S. Atl.)	5	2	.714	2.68	34	0	0	0	12	43 2/3	31	18	13	17	49
	—Salem (Carolina)	0	0	...	2.95	20	0	0	0	12	18 1/3	23	13	6	13	13
1994—	Salem (Carolina)	1	4	.200	1.53	31	0	0	0	19	29 1/3	24	14	5	13	23
	—Carolina (South.)	3	4	.429	5.61	26	0	0	0	5	25 2/3	32	21	16	15	21
1995—	Carolina (South.)	6	4	.600	4.15	56	0	0	0	9	69 1/3	60	37	32	45	57

PITTSLEY, JAMES — P — ROYALS

PERSONAL: Born April 3, 1974, in DuBois, Pa. . . . 6-7/215. . . . Throws right, bats right. . . . Full name: James Michael Pittsley.
HIGH SCHOOL: DuBois (Pa.) High.
TRANSACTIONS/CAREER NOTES: Selected by Kansas City Royals organization in first round (17th pick overall) of free-agent draft (June 1, 1992); pick received as part of compensation for San Diego Padres signing Type A free agent IF Kurt Stillwell. . . . On disabled list (May 29-June 6 and July 29-September 13, 1993). . . . On Kansas City disabled list (August 17, 1995-remainder of season).

Year	Team (League)	W	L	Pct.	ERA	G	GS	CG	ShO	Sv.	IP	H	R	ER	BB	SO
1992—	GC Royals (GCL)	4	1	.800	3.32	9	9	0	0	0	43 1/3	27	16	16	15	47
—	Baseball City (FSL)	0	0	...	0.00	1	1	0	0	0	3	2	0	0	1	4
1993—	Rockford (Midw.)	5	5	.500	4.26	15	15	2	1	0	80 1/3	76	43	38	32	87
1994—	Wilmington (Caro.)	11	5	.688	3.17	27	27	1	1	0	161 2/3	154	73	57	42	*171
1995—	Omaha (Am. Assoc.)	4	1	.800	3.21	8	8	0	0	0	47 2/3	38	20	17	16	39
—	Kansas City (A.L.)	0	0	...	13.50	1	1	0	0	0	3 1/3	7	5	5	1	0
Major league totals (1 year)		0	0	...	13.50	1	1	0	0	0	3 1/3	7	5	5	1	0

PLANTIER, PHIL — OF — TIGERS

PERSONAL: Born January 27, 1969, in Manchester, N.H. . . . 5-11/195. . . . Bats left, throws right. . . . Full name: Phillip Alan Plantier. . . . Name pronounced plan-TEER.
HIGH SCHOOL: Poway (Calif.).
TRANSACTIONS/CAREER NOTES: Selected by Boston Red Sox organization in 11th round of free-agent draft (June 2, 1987). . . . On Pawtucket disabled list (August 28-September 4, 1992). . . . Traded by Red Sox to San Diego Padres for P Jose Melendez (December 9, 1992). . . . On disabled list (April 26-May 11, 1993). . . . Traded by Padres with OF Derek Bell, P Pedro Martinez, P Doug Brocail, IF Craig Shipley and SS Ricky Gutierrez to Houston Astros for 3B Ken Caminiti, OF Steve Finley, SS Andujar Cedeno, 1B Robert Petagine, P Brian Williams and a player to be named later (December 28, 1994). . . . On Houston disabled list (May 17-July 7, 1995); included rehabilitation assignments to Tucson (June 1-5 and July 2-7). . . . Traded by Astros to Padres for P Jeff Tabaka and P Rich Loiselle (July 19, 1995). . . . Released by Padres (November 20, 1995). . . . Signed by Detroit Tigers (December 7, 1995).
HONORS: Named Carolina League Most Valuable Player (1989).
STATISTICAL NOTES: Led Carolina League with 242 total bases, .546 slugging percentage and tied for lead with seven intentional bases on balls received in 1989. . . . Led International League with .549 slugging percentage in 1990. . . . Career major league grand slams: 1.

				BATTING											FIELDING			
Year	Team (League)	Pos.	G	AB	R	H	2B	3B	HR	RBI	Avg.	BB	SO	SB	PO	A	E	Avg.
1987—	Elmira (NYP)	3B	28	80	7	14	2	0	2	9	.175	9	9	0	12	34	12	.793
1988—	Winter Haven (FSL)	OF-3B-2B	111	337	29	81	13	1	4	32	.240	51	62	0	106	72	18	.908
1989—	Lynchburg (Caro.)	OF	131	443	73	133	26	1	*27	*105	.300	74	122	4	140	10	8	.949
1990—	Pawtucket (Int'l)	OF	123	430	83	109	22	3	*33	79	.253	62	*148	1	245	8	*14	.948
—	Boston (A.L.)	DH-OF	14	15	1	2	1	0	0	3	.133	4	6	0	0	0	0	...
1991—	Pawtucket (Int'l)	OF-3B	84	298	69	91	19	4	16	61	.305	65	64	6	173	6	0	1.000
—	Boston (A.L.)	OF-DH	53	148	27	49	7	1	11	35	.331	23	38	1	80	1	2	.976
1992—	Boston (A.L.)	OF-DH	108	349	46	86	19	0	7	30	.246	44	83	2	148	6	4	.975
—	Pawtucket (Int'l)	OF	12	40	7	17	0	0	5	14	.425	6	6	0	23	1	0	1.000
1993—	San Diego (N.L.)■	OF	138	462	67	111	20	1	34	100	.240	61	124	4	272	14	3	.990
1994—	San Diego (N.L.)	OF	96	341	44	75	21	0	18	41	.220	36	91	3	158	5	2	.988
1995—	Houston (N.L.)■	OF	22	68	12	17	2	0	4	15	.250	11	19	0	25	0	1	.962
—	Tucson (PCL)	OF	10	24	6	6	2	0	1	4	.250	5	4	0	9	0	0	1.000
—	San Diego (N.L.)■	OF	54	148	21	38	4	0	5	19	.257	17	29	1	64	5	3	.958
American League totals (3 years)			175	512	74	137	27	1	18	68	.268	71	127	3	228	7	6	.975
National League totals (3 years)			310	1019	144	241	47	1	61	175	.237	125	263	8	519	24	9	.984
Major league totals (6 years)			485	1531	218	378	74	2	79	243	.247	196	390	11	747	31	15	.981

PLESAC, DAN — P — PIRATES

PERSONAL: Born February 4, 1962, in Gary, Ind. . . . 6-5/217. . . . Throws left, bats left. . . . Full name: Daniel Thomas Plesac. . . . Name pronounced PLEE-sack.
HIGH SCHOOL: Crown Point (Ind.).
COLLEGE: North Carolina State.
TRANSACTIONS/CAREER NOTES: Selected by St. Louis Cardinals organization in second round of free-agent draft (June 3, 1980); did not sign. . . . Selected by Milwaukee Brewers organization in first round (26th pick overall) of free-agent draft (June 6, 1983). . . . Granted free agency (October 27, 1992). . . . Signed by Chicago Cubs (December 8, 1992). . . . Granted free agency (October 25, 1994). . . . Signed by Pittsburgh Pirates (November 9, 1994).
STATISTICAL NOTES: Led Appalachian League pitchers with three balks in 1983.

Year	Team (League)	W	L	Pct.	ERA	G	GS	CG	ShO	Sv.	IP	H	R	ER	BB	SO
1983—	Paintsville (Appal.)	*9	1	.900	3.50	14	14	2	0	0	82 1/3	76	44	32	57	*85
1984—	Stockton (Calif.)	6	6	.500	3.32	16	16	2	0	0	108 1/3	106	51	40	50	101
—	El Paso (Texas)	2	2	.500	3.46	7	7	0	0	0	39	43	19	15	16	24
1985—	El Paso (Texas)	12	5	.706	4.97	25	24	2	0	0	150 1/3	171	91	83	68	128
1986—	Milwaukee (A.L.)	10	7	.588	2.97	51	0	0	0	14	91	81	34	30	29	75
1987—	Milwaukee (A.L.)	5	6	.455	2.61	57	0	0	0	23	79 1/3	63	30	23	23	89
1988—	Milwaukee (A.L.)	1	2	.333	2.41	50	0	0	0	30	52 1/3	46	14	14	12	52
1989—	Milwaukee (A.L.)	3	4	.429	2.35	52	0	0	0	33	61 1/3	47	16	16	17	52
1990—	Milwaukee (A.L.)	3	7	.300	4.43	66	0	0	0	24	69	67	36	34	31	65
1991—	Milwaukee (A.L.)	2	7	.222	4.29	45	10	0	0	8	92 1/3	92	49	44	39	61
1992—	Milwaukee (A.L.)	5	4	.556	2.96	44	4	0	0	1	79	64	28	26	35	54
1993—	Chicago (N.L.)■	2	1	.667	4.74	57	0	0	0	0	62 2/3	74	37	33	21	47
1994—	Chicago (N.L.)	2	3	.400	4.61	54	0	0	0	1	54 2/3	61	30	28	13	53
1995—	Pittsburgh (N.L.)■	4	4	.500	3.58	58	0	0	0	3	60 1/3	53	26	24	27	57
A.L. totals (7 years)		29	37	.439	3.21	365	14	0	0	133	524 1/3	460	207	187	186	448
N.L. totals (3 years)		8	8	.500	4.31	169	0	0	0	4	177 2/3	188	93	85	61	157
Major league totals (10 years)		37	45	.451	3.49	534	14	0	0	137	702	648	300	272	247	605

P

ALL-STAR GAME RECORD

Year League	W	L	Pct.	ERA	GS	CG	ShO	Sv.	IP	H	R	ER	BB	SO
1987— American	0	0	...	0.00	0	0	0	0	1	0	0	0	0	1
1988— American	0	0	...	0.00	0	0	0	0	1/3	0	0	0	0	1
1989— American	0	0	...	...	0	0	0	0	0	1	0	0	0	0
All-Star totals (3 years)	0	0	...	0.00	0	0	0	0	1 1/3	1	0	0	0	2

PLUNK, ERIC — P — INDIANS

PERSONAL: Born September 3, 1963, in Wilmington, Calif. . . . 6-6/220. . . . Throws right, bats right. . . . Full name: Eric Vaughn Plunk.
HIGH SCHOOL: Bellflower (Calif.).
COLLEGE: Cal State Dominguez Hills.
TRANSACTIONS/CAREER NOTES: Selected by New York Yankees organization in fourth round of free-agent draft (June 8, 1981). . . . On disabled list (August 11-26, 1983). . . . Traded by Yankees with OF Stan Javier, P Jay Howell, P Jose Rijo and P Tim Birtsas to Oakland Athletics for OF Rickey Henderson, P Bert Bradley and cash (December 5, 1984). . . . On disabled list (July 2-17, 1988). . . . Traded by A's with P Greg Cadaret and OF Luis Polonia to New York Yankees for OF Rickey Henderson (June 21, 1989). . . . Released by Yankees (November 20, 1991). . . . Signed by Syracuse, Toronto Blue Jays organization (December 12, 1991). . . . Released by Syracuse (March 27, 1992). . . . Signed by Canton/Akron, Cleveland Indians organization (April 9, 1992). . . . Granted free agency (October 27, 1992). . . . Re-signed by Indians (November 12, 1992).
STATISTICAL NOTES: Tied for Florida State League lead with seven balks in 1984. . . . Led A.L. with six balks in 1986.

Year Team (League)	W	L	Pct.	ERA	G	GS	CG	ShO	Sv.	IP	H	R	ER	BB	SO
1981— GC Yankees (GCL)	3	4	.429	3.83	11	11	1	0	0	54	56	29	23	20	47
1982— Paintsville (Appal.)	6	3	.667	4.64	12	8	4	0	0	64	63	35	33	30	59
1983— Fort Lauder. (FSL)	8	10	.444	2.74	20	20	5	•4	0	125	115	55	38	63	109
1984— Fort Lauder. (FSL)	12	12	.500	2.86	28	28	7	1	0	176 1/3	153	85	56	*123	*152
1985— Huntsville (South.)■	8	2	.800	3.40	13	13	2	1	0	79 1/3	61	36	30	56	68
— Tacoma (PCL)	0	5	.000	5.77	11	10	0	0	0	53	51	41	34	50	43
1986— Tacoma (PCL)	2	3	.400	4.68	6	6	0	0	0	32 2/3	25	18	17	33	31
— Oakland (A.L.)	4	7	.364	5.31	26	15	0	0	0	120 1/3	91	75	71	102	98
1987— Oakland (A.L.)	4	6	.400	4.74	32	11	0	0	2	95	91	53	50	62	90
— Tacoma (PCL)	1	1	.500	1.56	24	0	0	0	9	34 2/3	21	8	6	17	56
1988— Oakland (A.L.)	7	2	.778	3.00	49	0	0	0	5	78	62	27	26	39	79
1989— Oakland (A.L.)	1	1	.500	2.20	23	0	0	0	1	28 2/3	17	7	7	12	24
— New York (A.L.)■	7	5	.583	3.69	27	7	0	0	0	75 2/3	65	36	31	52	61
1990— New York (A.L.)	6	3	.667	2.72	47	0	0	0	0	72 2/3	58	27	22	43	67
1991— New York (A.L.)	2	5	.286	4.76	43	8	0	0	0	111 2/3	128	69	59	62	103
1992— Cant./Akr. (East.)■	1	2	.333	1.72	9	0	0	0	0	15 2/3	11	4	3	5	19
— Cleveland (A.L.)	9	6	.600	3.64	58	0	0	0	4	71 2/3	61	31	29	38	50
1993— Cleveland (A.L.)	4	5	.444	2.79	70	0	0	0	15	71	61	29	22	30	77
1994— Cleveland (A.L.)	7	2	.778	2.54	41	0	0	0	3	71	61	25	20	37	73
1995— Cleveland (A.L.)	6	2	.750	2.67	56	0	0	0	2	64	48	19	19	27	71
Major league totals (10 years)	57	44	.564	3.73	472	41	0	0	32	859 2/3	743	398	356	504	793

DIVISION SERIES RECORD

Year Team (League)	W	L	Pct.	ERA	G	GS	CG	ShO	Sv.	IP	H	R	ER	BB	SO
1995— Cleveland (A.L.)	0	0	...	0.00	1	0	0	0	0	1 1/3	1	0	0	1	1

CHAMPIONSHIP SERIES RECORD

Year Team (League)	W	L	Pct.	ERA	G	GS	CG	ShO	Sv.	IP	H	R	ER	BB	SO
1988— Oakland (A.L.)	0	0	...	0.00	1	0	0	0	0	1/3	1	0	0	0	1
1995— Cleveland (A.L.)	0	0	...	9.00	3	0	0	0	0	2	1	2	2	3	2
Champ. series totals (2 years)	0	0	...	7.71	4	0	0	0	0	2 1/3	2	2	2	3	3

WORLD SERIES RECORD

Year Team (League)	W	L	Pct.	ERA	G	GS	CG	ShO	Sv.	IP	H	R	ER	BB	SO
1988— Oakland (A.L.)	0	0	...	0.00	2	0	0	0	0	1 2/3	0	0	0	0	3
1995— Cleveland (A.L.)					Did not play.										

POLONIA, LUIS — OF

PERSONAL: Born October 27, 1964, in Santiago City, Dominican Republic. . . . 5-8/160. . . . Bats left, throws left. . . . Full name: Luis Andrew Almonte Polonia. . . . Name pronounced po-LONE-yuh.
HIGH SCHOOL: San Francisco (Santiago City, Dominican Republic).
TRANSACTIONS/CAREER NOTES: Signed as non-drafted free agent by Oakland Athletics organization (January 3, 1984). . . . Traded by A's with P Greg Cadaret and P Eric Plunk to New York Yankees for OF Rickey Henderson (June 21, 1989). . . . Traded by Yankees to California Angels for OF Claudell Washington and P Rich Monteleone (April 28, 1990). . . . On suspended list (September 30-October 3, 1992). . . . Granted free agency (October 27, 1993). . . . Signed by Yankees (December 20, 1993). . . . Traded by Yankees to Atlanta Braves for OF Troy Hughes (August 11, 1995). . . . Granted free agency (November 2, 1995).
STATISTICAL NOTES: Led Midwest League in caught stealing with 24 in 1984. . . . Led Pacific Coast League in caught stealing with 21 in 1986. . . . Led A.L. in caught stealing with 23 in 1991 and 21 in 1992 and tied for lead with 24 in 1993. . . . Career major league grand slams: 1.
MISCELLANEOUS: Batted as switch-hitter (1984-86 and Tacoma, 1987-88).

		BATTING											FIELDING			
Year Team (League)	Pos.	G	AB	R	H	2B	3B	HR	RBI	Avg.	BB	SO	SB	PO	A	E	Avg.
1984— Madison (Midwest)	OF	135	*528	103	*162	21	10	8	64	.307	57	95	55	202	9	10	.955
1985— Huntsville (South.)	OF	130	515	82	149	15	*18	2	36	.289	58	53	39	236	13	12	.954
1986— Tacoma (PCL)	OF	134	*549	98	*165	20	4	3	63	.301	52	65	36	*318	8	10	.970
1987— Tacoma (PCL)	OF	14	56	18	18	1	2	0	8	.321	14	6	4	28	1	1	.967
— Oakland (A.L.)	OF-DH	125	435	78	125	16	10	4	49	.287	32	64	29	235	2	5	.979
1988— Tacoma (PCL)	OF	65	254	58	85	13	5	2	27	.335	29	28	31	129	7	7	.951

Year	Team (League)	Pos.	G	AB	R	H	2B	3B	HR	RBI	Avg.	BB	SO	SB	PO	A	E	Avg.
				BATTING											FIELDING			
	—Oakland (A.L.)	OF-DH	84	288	51	84	11	4	2	27	.292	21	40	24	155	3	2	.988
1989	—Oakland (A.L.)	OF-DH	59	206	31	59	6	4	1	17	.286	9	15	13	126	3	2	.985
	—New York (A.L.)■	OF-DH	66	227	39	71	11	2	2	29	.313	16	29	9	105	6	2	.982
1990	—New York (A.L.)	DH	11	22	2	7	0	0	0	3	.318	0	1	1	...	...	...	...
	—California (A.L.)■	OF-DH	109	381	50	128	7	9	2	32	.336	25	42	20	142	3	3	.980
1991	—California (A.L.)	OF-DH	150	604	92	179	28	8	2	50	.296	52	74	48	246	9	5	.981
1992	—California (A.L.)	OF-DH	149	577	83	165	17	4	0	35	.286	45	64	51	192	8	4	.980
1993	—California (A.L.)	OF-DH	152	576	75	156	17	6	1	32	.271	48	53	55	286	12	5	.983
1994	—New York (A.L.)■	OF-DH	95	350	62	109	21	6	1	36	.311	37	36	20	155	9	4	.976
1995	—New York (A.L.)	OF	67	238	37	62	9	3	2	15	.261	25	29	10	132	5	0	1.000
	—Atlanta (N.L.)■	OF	28	53	6	14	7	0	0	2	.264	3	9	3	9	0	0	1.000
American League totals (9 years)			1067	3904	600	1145	143	56	17	325	.293	310	447	280	1774	60	32	.983
National League totals (1 year)			28	53	6	14	7	0	0	2	.264	3	9	3	9	0	0	1.000
Major league totals (9 years)			1095	3957	606	1159	150	56	17	327	.293	313	456	283	1783	60	32	.983

DIVISION SERIES RECORD

Year	Team (League)	Pos.	G	AB	R	H	2B	3B	HR	RBI	Avg.	BB	SO	SB	PO	A	E	Avg.
				BATTING											FIELDING			
1995	—Atlanta (N.L.)	PH	3	3	0	1	0	0	0	2	.333	0	1	1	...	...	...	...

CHAMPIONSHIP SERIES RECORD

Year	Team (League)	Pos.	G	AB	R	H	2B	3B	HR	RBI	Avg.	BB	SO	SB	PO	A	E	Avg.
				BATTING											FIELDING			
1988	—Oakland (A.L.)	PR-OF-PH	3	5	0	2	0	0	0	0	.400	1	2	0	2	0	0	1.000
1995	—Atlanta (N.L.)	OF-PR-PH	3	2	0	1	0	0	0	1	.500	0	0	0	0	0	0	...
Championship series totals (2 years)			6	7	0	3	0	0	0	1	.429	1	2	0	2	0	0	1.000

WORLD SERIES RECORD

NOTES: Member of World Series championship team (1995).

Year	Team (League)	Pos.	G	AB	R	H	2B	3B	HR	RBI	Avg.	BB	SO	SB	PO	A	E	Avg.
				BATTING											FIELDING			
1988	—Oakland (A.L.)	PH-OF	3	9	1	1	0	0	0	0	.111	0	2	0	2	0	0	1.000
1995	—Atlanta (N.L.)	PH-OF	4	14	3	4	1	0	1	4	.286	1	3	1	3	0	0	1.000
World Series totals (2 years)			7	23	4	5	1	0	1	4	.217	1	5	1	5	0	0	1.000

POOLE, JIM P INDIANS

PERSONAL: Born April 28, 1966, in Rochester, N.Y. . . . 6-2/203. . . . Throws left, bats left. . . . Full name: James Richard Poole.

HIGH SCHOOL: South College (Philadelphia).

COLLEGE: Georgia Tech.

TRANSACTIONS/CAREER NOTES: Selected by Los Angeles Dodgers organization in 34th round of free-agent draft (June 2, 1987); did not sign. . . . Selected by Dodgers organization in ninth round of free-agent draft (June 1, 1988). . . . Traded by Dodgers with cash to Texas Rangers for P Steve Allen and P David Lynch (December 30, 1990). . . . Claimed on waivers by Baltimore Orioles (May 31, 1991). . . . On Baltimore disabled list (April 3-June 23, 1992); included rehabilitation assignments to Hagerstown (May 25-June 12) and Rochester (June 12-23). . . . Granted free agency (December 23, 1994). . . . Signed by Buffalo, Cleveland Indians organization (March 18, 1995).

Year	Team (League)	W	L	Pct.	ERA	G	GS	CG	ShO	Sv.	IP	H	R	ER	BB	SO
1988	—Vero Beach (FSL)	1	1	.500	3.77	10	0	0	0	0	14 1/3	13	7	6	9	12
1989	—Vero Beach (FSL)	11	4	.733	1.61	*60	0	0	0	19	78 1/3	57	16	14	24	93
	—Bakersfield (Calif.)	0	0	...	0.00	1	0	0	0	0	1 2/3	2	1	0	0	1
1990	—San Antonio (Tex.)	6	7	.462	2.40	54	0	0	0	16	63 2/3	55	31	17	27	77
	—Los Angeles (N.L.)	0	0	...	4.22	16	0	0	0	0	10 2/3	7	5	5	8	6
1991	—Okla. City (A.A.)■	0	0	...	0.00	10	0	0	0	3	12 1/3	4	0	0	1	14
	—Texas (A.L.)	0	0	...	4.50	5	0	0	0	1	6	10	4	3	3	4
	—Rochester (Int'l)■	3	2	.600	2.79	27	0	0	0	9	29	29	11	9	9	25
	—Baltimore (A.L.)	3	2	.600	2.00	24	0	0	0	0	36	19	10	8	9	34
1992	—Hagerstown (East.)	0	1	.000	2.77	7	3	0	0	0	13	14	4	4	1	4
	—Rochester (Int'l)	1	6	.143	5.31	32	0	0	0	10	42 1/3	40	26	25	18	30
	—Baltimore (A.L.)	0	0	...	0.00	6	0	0	0	0	3 1/3	3	3	0	1	3
1993	—Baltimore (A.L.)	2	1	.667	2.15	55	0	0	0	2	50 1/3	30	18	12	21	29
1994	—Baltimore (A.L.)	1	0	1.000	6.64	38	0	0	0	0	20 1/3	32	15	15	11	18
1995	—Buffalo (A.A.)■	0	0	...	27.00	1	1	0	0	0	2 2/3	7	8	8	2	0
	—Cleveland (A.L.)	3	3	.500	3.75	42	0	0	0	0	50 1/3	40	22	21	17	41
A.L. totals (5 years)		9	6	.600	3.19	170	0	0	0	3	166 1/3	134	72	59	62	129
N.L. totals (1 year)		0	0	...	4.22	16	0	0	0	0	10 2/3	7	5	5	8	6
Major league totals (6 years)		9	6	.600	3.25	186	0	0	0	3	177	141	77	64	70	135

DIVISION SERIES RECORD

Year	Team (League)	W	L	Pct.	ERA	G	GS	CG	ShO	Sv.	IP	H	R	ER	BB	SO
1995	—Cleveland (A.L.)	0	0	...	5.40	1	0	0	0	0	1 2/3	2	1	1	1	2

CHAMPIONSHIP SERIES RECORD

Year	Team (League)	W	L	Pct.	ERA	G	GS	CG	ShO	Sv.	IP	H	R	ER	BB	SO
1995	—Cleveland (A.L.)	0	0	...	0.00	1	0	0	0	0	1	0	0	0	0	2

WORLD SERIES RECORD

Year	Team (League)	W	L	Pct.	ERA	G	GS	CG	ShO	Sv.	IP	H	R	ER	BB	SO
1995	—Cleveland (A.L.)	0	1	.000	3.86	2	0	0	0	0	2 1/3	1	1	1	0	1

PORTUGAL, MARK — P — REDS

PERSONAL: Born October 30, 1962, in Los Angeles. . . . 6-0/190. . . . Throws right, bats right. . . . Full name: Mark Steven Portugal.
HIGH SCHOOL: Norwalk (Calif.).
TRANSACTIONS/CAREER NOTES: Signed as non-drafted free agent by Minnesota Twins organization (October 23, 1980). . . . On Toledo disabled list (July 22-August 2, 1985). . . . On Minnesota disabled list (August 7-28, 1988). . . . Traded by Twins to Houston Astros for a player to be named later (December 4, 1988); Twins organization acquired P Todd McClure to complete deal (December 7, 1988). . . . On disabled list (July 18-August 13, 1991). . . . On Houston disabled list (June 13-July 4 and July 10-September 23, 1992). . . . Granted free agency (October 25, 1993). . . . Signed by San Francisco Giants (November 21, 1993). . . . On disabled list (June 17-July 3 and August 6, 1994-remainder of season). . . . Traded by Giants with OF Darren Lewis and P Dave Burba to Cincinnati Reds for OF Deion Sanders, P John Roper, P Ricky Pickett, P Scott Service and IF Dave McCarty (July 21, 1995).
HONORS: Named pitcher on The Sporting News N.L. Silver Slugger team (1994).
STATISTICAL NOTES: Led Appalachian League with 12 wild pitches, 11 home runs allowed and tied for lead with five hit batsmen in 1981. . . . Tied for N.L. lead in games started by pitcher with 31 in 1995.
MISCELLANEOUS: Appeared in one game as pinch-runner (1991).

Year	Team (League)	W	L	Pct.	ERA	G	GS	CG	ShO	Sv.	IP	H	R	ER	BB	SO
1981	—Elizabeth. (App.)	7	1	.875	3.71	14	13	2	0	1	85	65	41	35	39	65
1982	—Wis. Rap. (Midw.)	9	8	.529	4.01	36	15	4	1	2	119	110	62	53	62	95
1983	—Visalia (California)	10	5	.667	4.18	24	23	2	0	0	131 1/3	142	77	61	84	132
1984	—Orlando (Southern)	14	7	.667	2.98	27	27	10	3	0	196	171	80	65	113	110
1985	—Toledo (Int'l)	8	5	.615	3.78	19	19	5	1	0	128 2/3	129	60	54	60	89
	—Minnesota (A.L.)	1	3	.250	5.55	6	4	0	0	0	24 1/3	24	16	15	14	12
1986	—Toledo (Int'l)	5	1	.833	2.60	6	6	3	1	0	45	34	15	13	23	30
	—Minnesota (A.L.)	6	10	.375	4.31	27	15	3	0	1	112 2/3	112	56	54	50	67
1987	—Minnesota (A.L.)	1	3	.250	7.77	13	7	0	0	0	44	58	40	38	24	28
	—Portland (PCL)	1	10	.091	6.00	17	16	2	0	0	102	108	75	68	50	69
1988	—Portland (PCL)	2	0	1.000	1.37	3	3	1	1	0	19 2/3	15	3	3	8	9
	—Minnesota (A.L.)	3	3	.500	4.53	26	0	0	0	3	57 2/3	60	30	29	17	31
1989	—Tucson (Pac. Coast)■	7	5	.583	3.78	17	17	5	0	0	116 2/3	107	55	49	32	90
	—Houston (N.L.)	7	1	.875	2.75	20	15	2	1	0	108	91	34	33	37	86
1990	—Houston (N.L.)	11	10	.524	3.62	32	32	1	0	0	196 2/3	187	90	79	67	136
1991	—Houston (N.L.)	10	12	.455	4.49	32	27	1	0	1	168 1/3	163	91	84	59	120
1992	—Houston (N.L.)	6	3	.667	2.66	18	16	1	1	0	101 1/3	76	32	30	41	62
1993	—Houston (N.L.)	18	4	*.818	2.77	33	33	1	1	0	208	194	75	64	77	131
1994	—San Francisco (N.L.)■	10	8	.556	3.93	21	21	1	0	0	137 1/3	135	68	60	45	87
1995	—San Francisco (N.L.)	5	5	.500	4.15	17	17	1	0	0	104	106	56	48	34	63
	—Cincinnati (N.L.)■	6	5	.545	3.82	14	§14	0	0	0	77 2/3	79	35	33	22	33
A.L. totals (4 years)		11	19	.367	5.13	72	26	3	0	4	238 2/3	254	142	136	105	138
N.L. totals (7 years)		73	48	.603	3.52	187	175	8	3	1	1101 1/3	1031	481	431	382	718
Major league totals (11 years)		84	67	.556	3.81	259	201	11	3	5	1340	1285	623	567	487	856

CHAMPIONSHIP SERIES RECORD

Year	Team (League)	W	L	Pct.	ERA	G	GS	CG	ShO	Sv.	IP	H	R	ER	BB	SO
1995	—Cincinnati (N.L.)	0	1	.000	36.00	1	0	0	0	0	1	3	4	4	1	0

POSADA, JORGE — C — YANKEES

PERSONAL: Born August 17, 1971, in Santurce, Puerto Rico. . . . 6-2/205. . . . Bats both, throws right. . . . Full name: Jorge Rafael Posada.
HIGH SCHOOL: Colegio Alejandrino (Puerto Rico).
TRANSACTIONS/CAREER NOTES: Selected by New York Yankees organization in 24th round of free-agent draft (June 4, 1990). . . . On disabled list (July 26-September 4, 1994). . . . On Columbus disabled list (May 3-12, 1995).
STATISTICAL NOTES: Led New York-Pennsylvania League second basemen with 42 double plays in 1991. . . . Led Carolina League with 38 passed balls in 1993. . . . Tied for Carolina League lead in intentional bases on balls received with four in 1993. . . . Tied for International League lead in errors by catcher with 11 in 1994. . . . Tied for International League lead in double plays by catcher with seven in 1995. . . . Led International League with 14 passed balls in 1995.

				BATTING											FIELDING			
Year	Team (League)	Pos.	G	AB	R	H	2B	3B	HR	RBI	Avg.	BB	SO	SB	PO	A	E	Avg.
1991	—Oneonta (NYP)	2B-C	71	217	34	51	5	5	4	33	.235	51	51	6	172	205	21	.947
1992	—Greensboro (S. Atl.)	C-3B	101	339	60	94	22	4	12	58	.277	58	87	11	263	39	11	.965
1993	—Prin. William (Car.)	C-3B	118	410	71	106	27	2	17	61	.259	67	90	17	677	98	15	.981
	—Albany (Eastern)	C	7	25	3	7	0	0	0	0	.280	2	7	0	39	7	2	.958
1994	—Columbus (Int'l)	C-OF	92	313	46	75	13	3	11	48	.240	32	81	5	425	39	‡11	.977
1995	—Columbus (Int'l)	C	108	368	60	94	32	5	8	51	.255	54	101	4	500	58	4	*.993
	—New York (A.L.)	C	1	0	0	0	0	0	0	0	...	0	0	0	1	0	0	1.000
Major league totals (1 year)			1	0	0	0	0	0	0	0	...	0	0	0	1	0	0	1.000

DIVISION SERIES RECORD

				BATTING											FIELDING			
Year	Team (League)	Pos.	G	AB	R	H	2B	3B	HR	RBI	Avg.	BB	SO	SB	PO	A	E	Avg.
1995	—New York (A.L.)	PR	1	0	1	0	0	0	0	0	...	0	0	0	...	...	...	...

POTTS, MICHAEL — P — BRAVES

PERSONAL: Born September 5, 1970, in Langdale, Ala. . . . 5-9/170. . . . Throws left, bats left. . . . Full name: Michael Larry Potts.
HIGH SCHOOL: Lithonia (Ga.).
COLLEGE: Gordon College (Ga.).
TRANSACTIONS/CAREER NOTES: Selected by Cleveland Indians organization in 16th round of free-agent draft (June 5, 1989); did not sign. . . . Selected by Atlanta Braves organization in 18th round of free-agent draft (June 4, 1990). . . . On disabled list (May 24-June 5, 1993).

Year	Team (League)	W	L	Pct.	ERA	G	GS	CG	ShO	Sv.	IP	H	R	ER	BB	SO
1990—	GC Braves (GCL)	5	2	.714	3.46	23	1	0	0	4	39	30	23	15	25	39
1991—	Macon (S. Atl.)	8	5	.615	3.49	34	11	2	2	1	95 1/3	64	45	37	50	75
1992—	Durham (Carolina)	6	8	.429	4.02	30	21	0	0	1	127 2/3	104	75	57	71	123
1993—	Greenville (South.)	7	6	.538	3.88	25	25	1	0	0	141 2/3	131	79	61	86	116
1994—	Richmond (Int'l)	6	3	.667	3.68	52	0	0	0	2	85 2/3	75	41	35	43	66
1995—	Richmond (Int'l)	5	5	.500	3.79	38	1	0	0	1	73 2/3	79	35	31	37	52

POWELL, JAY — P — MARLINS

PERSONAL: Born January 19, 1972, in Meridian, Miss. . . . 6-4/225. . . . Throws right, bats right. . . . Full name: James Willard Powell Jr. . . . Brother-in-law of Bud Brown, defensive back, Miami Dolphins (1984-88).

HIGH SCHOOL: West Lauderdale (Collinsville, Miss.).

COLLEGE: Mississippi State.

TRANSACTIONS/CAREER NOTES: Selected by San Diego Padres organization in 11th round of free-agent draft (June 4, 1990); did not sign. . . . Selected by Baltimore Orioles organization in first round (19th pick overall) of free-agent draft (June 3, 1993). . . . On disabled list (April 7-26, 1994). . . . Traded by Orioles organization to Florida Marlins organization for IF Bret Barberie (December 6, 1994).

Year	Team (League)	W	L	Pct.	ERA	G	GS	CG	ShO	Sv.	IP	H	R	ER	BB	SO
1993—	Albany (S. Atl.)	0	2	.000	4.55	6	6	0	0	0	27 2/3	29	19	14	13	29
1994—	Frederick (Caro.)	7	7	.500	4.96	26	20	0	0	1	123 1/3	132	79	68	54	87
1995—	Portland (Eastern)■	5	4	.556	1.87	50	0	0	0	*24	53	42	12	11	15	53
—	Florida (N.L.)	0	0	...	1.08	9	0	0	0	0	8 1/3	7	2	1	6	4
Major league totals (1 year)		0	0	...	1.08	9	0	0	0	0	8 1/3	7	2	1	6	4

POWELL, ROSS — P

PERSONAL: Born January 24, 1968, in Grand Rapids, Mich. . . . 6-0/180. . . . Throws left, bats left. . . . Full name: Ross John Powell.

HIGH SCHOOL: Cedar Springs (Mich.).

COLLEGE: Michigan.

TRANSACTIONS/CAREER NOTES: Selected by Cincinnati Reds organization in third round of free-agent draft (June 5, 1989). . . . Traded by Reds with P Marty Lister to Houston Astros for C Eddie Taubensee (April 19, 1994). . . . Traded by Astros organization to Pittsburgh Pirates organization for a player to be named later (July 28, 1995). . . . Granted free agency (October 11, 1995).

STATISTICAL NOTES: Led American Association with 27 home runs allowed in 1993.

Year	Team (League)	W	L	Pct.	ERA	G	GS	CG	ShO	Sv.	IP	H	R	ER	BB	SO
1989—	Ced. Rap. (Midw.)	7	4	.636	3.54	13	13	1	1	0	76 1/3	68	37	30	23	58
1990—	Chattanooga (Sou.)	8	•14	.364	1.31	29	27	•6	1	0	185	172	29	27	57	132
—	Nashville (A.A.)	0	0	...	3.38	3	0	0	0	0	2 2/3	1	1	1	0	4
1991—	Nashville (A.A.)	8	8	.500	4.37	24	24	1	0	0	129 2/3	125	74	63	63	82
1992—	Chattanooga (Sou.)	4	1	.800	1.26	14	5	0	0	1	57 1/3	43	9	8	17	56
—	Nashville (A.A.)	4	8	.333	3.38	25	12	0	0	0	93 1/3	89	37	35	42	84
1993—	Indianapolis (A.A.)	10	10	.500	4.11	28	27	4	0	0	179 2/3	159	89	82	71	133
—	Cincinnati (N.L.)	0	3	.000	4.41	9	1	0	0	0	16 1/3	13	8	8	6	17
1994—	Indianapolis (A.A.)	1	1	.500	6.52	4	1	0	0	0	9 2/3	16	10	7	11	11
—	Tucson (Pac. Coast)■	4	2	.667	5.99	16	10	0	0	1	67 2/3	81	47	45	27	45
—	Houston (N.L.)	0	0	...	1.23	12	0	0	0	0	7 1/3	6	1	1	5	5
1995—	Houston (N.L.)	0	0	...	11.00	15	0	0	0	0	9	16	12	11	11	8
—	Tucson (Pac. Coast)	3	3	.500	3.08	13	4	0	0	1	38	37	16	13	15	34
—	Pittsburgh (N.L.)■	0	2	.000	5.23	12	3	0	0	0	20 2/3	20	14	12	10	12
Major league totals (3 years)		0	5	.000	5.40	48	4	0	0	0	53 1/3	55	35	32	32	42

POZO, ARQUIMEDEZ — 2B — MARINERS

PERSONAL: Born August 24, 1973, in Santo Domingo, Dominican Republic. . . . 5-10/160. . . . Bats right, throws right.

TRANSACTIONS/CAREER NOTES: Signed as non-drafted free agent by Seattle Mariners organization (August 26, 1990).

			BATTING												FIELDING			
Year	Team (League)	Pos.	G	AB	R	H	2B	3B	HR	RBI	Avg.	BB	SO	SB	PO	A	E	Avg.
1991—		Dominican Summer League statistics unavailable.																
1992—	San Bern. (Calif.)	2B	54	199	33	52	8	4	3	19	.261	20	41	13	105	157	15	.946
—	Belling. (N'west)	2B	39	149	37	48	12	0	7	21	.322	20	24	9	85	129	10	.955
1993—	Riverside (Calif.)	2B	127	515	98	176	44	6	13	83	.342	56	56	10	249	*367	•24	.963
1994—	Jacksonv. (South.)	2B	119	447	70	129	31	1	14	54	.289	32	43	11	240	349	17	.972
1995—	Tacoma (PCL)	2B-3B	122	450	57	135	19	6	10	62	.300	26	31	3	191	304	17	.967
—	Seattle (A.L.)	2B	1	1	0	0	0	0	0	0	.000	0	0	0	0	1	0	1.000
Major league totals (1 year)			1	1	0	0	0	0	0	0	.000	0	0	0	0	1	0	1.000

PRATT, TODD — C

PERSONAL: Born February 9, 1967, in Bellevue, Neb. . . . 6-3/224. . . . Bats right, throws right. . . . Full name: Todd Alan Pratt.

HIGH SCHOOL: Hilltop (Chula Vista, Calif.).

TRANSACTIONS/CAREER NOTES: Selected by Boston Red Sox organization in sixth round of free-agent draft (June 3, 1985). . . . Selected by Cleveland Indians organization from Red Sox organization in Rule 5 minor league draft (December 7, 1987). . . . Returned to Red Sox organization (March 1988). . . . Granted free agency (October 15, 1991). . . . Signed by Baltimore Orioles organization (November 13, 1991). . . . Selected by Philadelphia Phillies from Orioles organization in Rule 5 major league draft (December 9, 1991). . . . On Philadelphia disabled list (April 28-May 27, 1993); included rehabilitation assignment to Scranton/Wilkes-Barre (May 23-27). . . . Granted free agency (December 23, 1994). . . . Signed by Iowa, Chicago Cubs organization (April 8, 1995). . . . Granted free agency (October 16, 1995).

STATISTICAL NOTES: Led South Atlantic League catchers with 660 putouts and nine double plays and tied for lead with 13 errors in 1986.

. . . Led Eastern League catchers with 11 errors in 1989.

			BATTING											FIELDING			
Year Team (League)	Pos.	G	AB	R	H	2B	3B	HR	RBI	Avg.	BB	SO	SB	PO	A	E	Avg.
1985— Elmira (NYP)	C	39	119	7	16	1	1	0	5	.134	10	27	0	254	29	6	.979
1986— Greensboro (S. Atl.)	C-1B	107	348	63	84	16	0	12	56	.241	75	114	0	†826	55	‡15	.983
1987— Winter Haven (FSL)	C-1B-OF	118	407	57	105	22	0	12	65	.258	70	94	0	672	64	15	.980
1988— New Britain (East.)	C-1B	124	395	41	89	15	2	8	49	.225	41	110	1	540	46	15	.975
1989— New Britain (East.)	C-1B	109	338	30	77	17	1	2	35	.228	44	66	1	435	42	†11	.977
1990— New Britain (East.)	C-1B	70	195	15	45	14	1	2	22	.231	18	56	0	166	15	4	.978
1991— Pawtucket (Int'l)	C-1B	68	219	68	64	16	0	11	41	.292	23	42	0	236	21	4	.985
1992— Reading (Eastern)■	C	41	132	20	44	6	1	6	26	.333	24	28	2	90	6	3	.970
— Scran./W.B. (Int'l)	C-1B	41	125	20	40	9	1	7	28	.320	30	14	1	152	16	4	.977
— Philadelphia (N.L.)	C	16	46	6	13	1	0	2	10	.283	4	12	0	65	4	2	.972
1993— Philadelphia (N.L.)	C	33	87	8	25	6	0	5	13	.287	5	19	0	169	7	2	.989
— Scran./W.B. (Int'l)	C	3	9	1	2	1	0	0	1	.222	3	1	0	11	0	0	1.000
1994— Philadelphia (N.L.)	C	28	102	10	20	6	1	2	9	.196	12	29	0	172	8	0	1.000
1995— Iowa (Am. Assoc.)■	C-1B	23	58	3	19	1	0	0	5	.328	4	17	0	82	8	2	.978
— Chicago (N.L.)	C	25	60	3	8	2	0	0	4	.133	6	21	0	149	9	3	.981
Major league totals (4 years)		102	295	27	66	15	1	9	36	.224	27	81	0	555	28	7	.988

CHAMPIONSHIP SERIES RECORD

			BATTING											FIELDING			
Year Team (League)	Pos.	G	AB	R	H	2B	3B	HR	RBI	Avg.	BB	SO	SB	PO	A	E	Avg.
1993— Philadelphia (N.L.)	C	1	1	0	0	0	0	0	0	.000	0	1	0	1	0	0	1.000

WORLD SERIES RECORD

			BATTING											FIELDING			
Year Team (League)	Pos.	G	AB	R	H	2B	3B	HR	RBI	Avg.	BB	SO	SB	PO	A	E	Avg.
1993— Philadelphia (N.L.)								Did not play.									

PRIDE, CURTIS — OF

PERSONAL: Born December 17, 1968, in Washington, D.C. . . . 6-0/200. . . . Bats left, throws right. . . . Full name: Curtis John Pride.
HIGH SCHOOL: John F. Kennedy (Silver Spring, Md.).
COLLEGE: William & Mary (received degree).
TRANSACTIONS/CAREER NOTES: Selected by New York Mets organization in 10th round of free-agent draft (June 2, 1986). . . . Granted free agency (October 15, 1992). . . . Signed by Ottawa, Montreal Expos organization (December 8, 1992). . . . On Ottawa disabled list (April 7-May 13, July 6-15 and August 7-14, 1994). . . . Granted free agency (October 16, 1995).

			BATTING											FIELDING			
Year Team (League)	Pos.	G	AB	R	H	2B	3B	HR	RBI	Avg.	BB	SO	SB	PO	A	E	Avg.
1986— Kingsport (Appal.)	OF	27	46	5	5	0	0	1	4	.109	6	24	5	17	1	0	1.000
1987— Kingsport (Appal.)	OF	31	104	22	25	4	0	1	9	.240	16	34	14	39	3	5	.894
1988— Kingsport (Appal.)	OF	70	268	*59	76	13	1	8	27	.284	50	48	23	118	6	5	.961
1989— Pittsfield (NYP)	OF	55	212	35	55	7	3	6	23	.259	25	47	9	105	3	4	.964
1990— Columbia (S. Atl.)	OF	53	191	38	51	4	4	6	25	.267	21	45	11	72	4	11	.874
1991— St. Lucie (Fla. St.)	OF	116	392	57	102	21	7	9	37	.260	43	94	24	199	5	4	.981
1992— Binghamton (East.)	OF	118	388	54	88	15	3	10	42	.227	47	110	14	214	3	8	.964
1993— Harrisburg (East.)■	OF	50	180	51	64	6	3	15	39	.356	12	36	21	69	0	2	.972
— Ottawa (Int'l)	OF	69	262	55	79	11	4	6	22	.302	34	61	29	136	3	2	.986
— Montreal (N.L.)	OF	10	9	3	4	1	1	1	5	.444	0	3	1	2	0	0	1.000
1994— W.P. Beach (FSL)	OF	3	8	5	6	1	0	1	3	.750	4	2	2	11	0	0	1.000
— Ottawa (Int'l)	OF	82	300	56	77	16	4	9	32	.257	39	81	22	164	1	3	.982
1995— Ottawa (Int'l)	OF	42	154	25	43	8	3	4	24	.279	12	35	8	69	5	2	.974
— Montreal (N.L.)	OF	48	63	10	11	1	0	0	2	.175	5	16	3	23	0	2	.920
Major league totals (2 years)		58	72	13	15	2	1	1	7	.208	5	19	4	25	0	2	.926

PRIETO, ARIEL — P — ATHLETICS

PERSONAL: Born October 22, 1969, in Havana, Cuba. . . . 6-3/225. . . . Throws right, bats right.
TRANSACTIONS/CAREER NOTES: Selected by Oakland Athletics organization in first round (fifth pick overall) of free-agent draft (June 1, 1995). . . . On disabled list (August 19-September 3, 1995).

Year Team (League)	W	L	Pct.	ERA	G	GS	CG	ShO	Sv.	IP	H	R	ER	BB	SO
1995— Oakland (A.L.)	2	6	.250	4.97	14	9	1	0	0	58	57	35	32	32	37

PRINCE, TOM — C — DODGERS

PERSONAL: Born August 13, 1964, in Kankakee, Ill. . . . 5-11/185. . . . Bats right, throws right. . . . Full name: Thomas Albert Prince.
HIGH SCHOOL: Bradley Bourbonnais (Kankakee, Ill.).
JUNIOR COLLEGE: Kankakee (Ill.) Community College.
TRANSACTIONS/CAREER NOTES: Selected by Atlanta Braves organization in eighth round of free-agent draft (January 11, 1983); did not sign. . . . Selected by Braves organization in secondary phase of free-agent draft (June 6, 1983); did not sign. . . . Selected by Pittsburgh Pirates organization in secondary phase of free-agent draft (January 17, 1984). . . . On Pittsburgh disabled list (August 13-September 1, 1991); included rehabilitation assignment to Buffalo (August 28-September 1). . . . Granted free agency (October 15, 1993). . . . Signed by Albuquerque, Los Angeles Dodgers organization (November 12, 1993). . . . On Albuquerque disabled list (April 30-May 7, 1994). . . . Released by Dodgers (December 5, 1994). . . . Re-signed by Dodgers organization (January 5, 1995). . . . On Los Angeles disabled list (June 4-July 10, 1995); included rehabilitation assignment to Albuquerque (June 26-July 10). . . . Granted free agency (October 15, 1995). . . . Re-signed by Dodgers organization (November 1, 1995).
STATISTICAL NOTES: Led South Atlantic League catchers with 930 total chances, 10 double plays and 27 passed balls in 1985. . . . Led

Carolina League catchers with 954 total chances and 15 passed balls in 1986. . . . Led Eastern League catchers with 721 total chances and nine double plays in 1987. . . . Led American Association catchers with 12 double plays in 1992. . . . Led Pacific Coast League catchers with 677 total chances and nine double plays in 1994.

							BATTING								FIELDING			
Year	Team (League)	Pos.	G	AB	R	H	2B	3B	HR	RBI	Avg.	BB	SO	SB	PO	A	E	Avg.
1984—	Watertown (NYP)	C-3B	23	69	6	14	3	0	2	13	.203	9	13	0	155	26	2	.989
—	GC Pirates (GCL)	C-1B	18	48	4	11	0	0	1	6	.229	8	10	1	75	16	4	.958
1985—	Macon (S. Atl.)	C	124	360	60	75	20	1	10	42	.208	96	92	13	*810	*101	*19	.980
1986—	Prin. William (Car.)	C	121	395	59	100	34	1	10	47	.253	50	74	4	*821	•113	20	.979
1987—	Harrisburg (East.)	C	113	365	41	112	23	2	6	54	.307	51	46	6	*622	*88	•11	.985
—	Pittsburgh (N.L.)	C	4	9	1	2	1	0	1	2	.222	0	2	0	14	3	0	1.000
1988—	Buffalo (A.A.)	C	86	304	35	79	16	0	14	42	.260	23	53	3	456	51	*12	.977
—	Pittsburgh (N.L.)	C	29	74	3	13	2	0	0	6	.176	4	15	0	108	8	2	.983
1989—	Buffalo (A.A.)	C	65	183	21	37	8	1	6	33	.202	22	30	2	312	22	5	.985
—	Pittsburgh (N.L.)	C	21	52	1	7	4	0	0	5	.135	6	12	1	85	11	4	.960
1990—	Pittsburgh (N.L.)	C	4	10	1	1	0	0	0	0	.100	1	2	0	16	1	0	1.000
—	Buffalo (A.A.)	C-1B	94	284	38	64	13	0	7	37	.225	39	46	4	461	62	8	.985
1991—	Pittsburgh (N.L.)	C-1B	26	34	4	9	3	0	1	2	.265	7	3	0	53	9	1	.984
—	Buffalo (A.A.)	C	80	221	29	46	8	3	6	32	.208	37	31	3	379	61	5	.989
1992—	Pittsburgh (N.L.)	C-3B	27	44	1	4	2	0	0	5	.091	6	9	1	76	8	2	.977
—	Buffalo (A.A.)	C-OF	75	244	34	64	17	0	9	35	.262	20	35	3	307	50	8	.978
1993—	Pittsburgh (N.L.)	C	66	179	14	35	14	0	2	24	.196	13	38	1	271	31	5	.984
1994—	Albuquerque (PCL)■	C	103	330	61	94	31	2	20	54	.285	51	67	2	593	*75	9	.987
—	Los Angeles (N.L.)	C	3	6	2	2	0	0	0	1	.333	1	3	0	11	1	0	1.000
1995—	Los Angeles (N.L.)	C	18	40	3	8	2	1	1	4	.200	4	10	0	71	8	1	.988
—	Albuquerque (PCL)	C	61	192	30	61	15	0	7	36	.318	27	41	0	310	34	4	.989
Major league totals (9 years)			198	448	30	81	28	1	5	49	.181	42	94	3	705	80	15	.981

PUCKETT, KIRBY — OF — TWINS

PERSONAL: Born March 14, 1961, in Chicago. . . . 5-9/233. . . . Bats right, throws right.

HIGH SCHOOL: Calumet (Chicago).

JUNIOR COLLEGE: Triton College (Ill.).

COLLEGE: Bradley.

TRANSACTIONS/CAREER NOTES: Selected by Minnesota Twins organization in first round (third pick overall) of free-agent draft (January 12, 1982). . . . Granted free agency (October 28, 1992). . . . Re-signed by Twins (December 4, 1992).

RECORDS: Shares major league single-season record for most at-bats with no sacrifice flies—680 (1986). . . . Shares major league record for most consecutive years leading league in hits—3 (1987-89). . . . Shares major league single-game records for most doubles—4 (May 13, 1989); and most doubles in two consecutive games—6 (May 13 [4] and 14 [2], 1989). . . . Shares modern major league record for most hits in first game in majors (nine innings)—4 (May 8, 1984). . . . Holds A.L. record for most hits in two consecutive nine-inning games—10 (August 29 [4] and 30 [6], 1987). . . . Shares A.L. career record for most seasons with 400 or more putouts by outfielder—5.

HONORS: Named California League Player of the Year (1983). . . . Named outfielder on The Sporting News A.L. All-Star team (1986-89, 1992 and 1994). . . . Named outfielder on The Sporting News A.L. Silver Slugger team (1986-89, 1992 and 1994). . . . Won A.L. Gold Glove as outfielder (1986-89 and 1991-92).

STATISTICAL NOTES: Led Appalachian League with 135 total bases in 1982. . . . Led California League outfielders with five double plays in 1983. . . . Led A.L. outfielders with 492 total chances in 1985, 465 in 1988 and 455 in 1989. . . . Hit for the cycle (August 1, 1986). . . . Collected six hits in one game (August 30, 1987 and May 23, 1991). . . . Led A.L. with 358 total bases in 1988 and 313 in 1992. . . . Led A.L. in grounding into double plays with 27 in 1991. . . . Career major league grand slams: 7.

							BATTING								FIELDING			
Year	Team (League)	Pos.	G	AB	R	H	2B	3B	HR	RBI	Avg.	BB	SO	SB	PO	A	E	Avg.
1982—	Elizabeth. (Appal.)	OF	65	*275	*65	*105	15	3	3	35	*.382	25	27	•43	133	*11	5	.966
1983—	Visalia (California)	OF	138	*548	105	172	29	7	9	97	.314	46	62	48	253	*22	5	.982
1984—	Toledo (Int'l)	OF	21	80	9	21	2	0	1	5	.263	4	14	8	35	1	3	.923
—	Minnesota (A.L.)	OF	128	557	63	165	12	5	0	31	.296	16	69	14	438	*16	3	.993
1985—	Minnesota (A.L.)	OF	161	*691	80	199	29	13	4	74	.288	41	87	21	*465	19	8	.984
1986—	Minnesota (A.L.)	OF	161	680	119	223	37	6	31	96	.328	34	99	20	429	8	6	.986
1987—	Minnesota (A.L.)	OF-DH	157	624	96	•207	32	5	28	99	.332	32	91	12	341	8	5	.986
1988—	Minnesota (A.L.)	OF	158	*657	109	*234	42	5	24	121	.356	23	83	6	*450	12	3	.994
1989—	Minnesota (A.L.)	OF-DH	159	635	75	*215	45	4	9	85	*.339	41	59	11	*438	13	4	.991
1990—	Minnesota (A.L.)	O-DH-2-3-S	146	551	82	164	40	3	12	80	.298	57	73	5	354	9	4	.989
1991—	Minnesota (A.L.)	OF	152	611	92	195	29	6	15	89	.319	31	78	11	373	13	6	.985
1992—	Minnesota (A.L.)	O-DH-3-2-S	160	639	104	*210	38	4	19	110	.329	44	97	17	394	9	3	.993
1993—	Minnesota (A.L.)	OF-DH	156	622	89	184	39	3	22	89	.296	47	93	8	312	13	2	.994
1994—	Minnesota (A.L.)	OF-DH	108	439	79	139	32	3	20	*112	.317	28	47	6	204	*13	3	.986
1995—	Minnesota (A.L.)	O-DH-2-3-S	137	538	83	169	39	0	23	99	.314	56	89	3	195	10	4	.981
Major league totals (12 years)			1783	7244	1071	2304	414	57	207	1085	.318	450	965	134	4393	143	51	.989

CHAMPIONSHIP SERIES RECORD

NOTES: Named A.L. Championship Series Most Valuable Player (1991). . . . Shares A.L. single-game record for most at-bats—6 (October 12, 1987).

							BATTING								FIELDING			
Year	Team (League)	Pos.	G	AB	R	H	2B	3B	HR	RBI	Avg.	BB	SO	SB	PO	A	E	Avg.
1987—	Minnesota (A.L.)	OF	5	24	3	5	1	0	1	3	.208	0	5	1	7	0	0	1.000
1991—	Minnesota (A.L.)	OF	5	21	4	9	1	0	2	6	.429	1	4	0	13	1	0	1.000
Championship series totals (2 years)			10	45	7	14	2	0	3	9	.311	1	9	1	20	1	0	1.000

WORLD SERIES RECORD

NOTES: Shares record for most at-bats in one inning—2 (October 18, 1987, fourth inning). . . . Shares single-game record for most runs—4 (October 24, 1987). . . . Member of World Series championship teams (1987 and 1991).

Year	Team (League)	Pos.	G	AB	R	H	2B	3B	HR	RBI	Avg.	BB	SO	SB	PO	A	E	Avg.
			BATTING												FIELDING			
1987—	Minnesota (A.L.)	OF	7	28	5	10	1	1	0	3	.357	2	1	1	15	1	1	.941
1991—	Minnesota (A.L.)	OF	7	24	4	6	0	1	2	4	.250	5	7	1	16	1	0	1.000
World Series totals (2 years)			14	52	9	16	1	2	2	7	.308	7	8	2	31	2	1	.971

ALL-STAR GAME RECORD

NOTES: Named Most Valuable Player (1993).

Year	League	Pos.	AB	R	H	2B	3B	HR	RBI	Avg.	BB	SO	SB	PO	A	E	Avg.
			BATTING											FIELDING			
1986—	American	OF	3	0	1	0	0	0	0	.333	1	0	1	5	0	0	1.000
1987—	American	PH-OF	4	0	0	0	0	0	0	.000	0	3	0	1	0	0	1.000
1988—	American	OF	1	0	0	0	0	0	0	.000	0	0	0	1	0	0	1.000
1989—	American	OF	3	1	1	0	0	0	0	.333	0	0	0	0	0	0	...
1990—	American	PH-OF	1	0	1	0	0	0	0	1.000	0	0	0	1	0	0	1.000
1991—	American	OF	1	0	0	0	0	0	0	.000	0	0	0	0	0	0	...
1992—	American	OF	3	1	1	0	0	0	0	.333	0	1	0	2	0	0	1.000
1993—	American	OF	3	1	2	1	0	1	2	.667	0	0	0	1	0	0	1.000
1994—	American	OF	3	0	1	0	0	0	1	.333	0	0	0	1	0	0	1.000
1995—	American	OF	2	0	0	0	0	0	0	.000	0	1	0	2	0	0	1.000
All-Star Game totals (10 years)			24	3	7	1	0	1	3	.292	1	5	1	14	0	0	1.000

PUGH, TIM — P — REDS

PERSONAL: Born January 26, 1967, in Lake Tahoe, Calif. . . . 6-6/225. . . . Throws right, bats right. . . . Full name: Timothy Dean Pugh.
HIGH SCHOOL: Bartlesville (Okla.).
COLLEGE: Oklahoma State.
TRANSACTIONS/CAREER NOTES: Selected by Toronto Blue Jays organization in eighth round of free-agent draft (June 1, 1988); did not sign. . . . Selected by Cincinnati Reds organization in sixth round of free-agent draft (June 5, 1989). . . . On Indianapolis disabled list (June 17-July 29, 1994).
STATISTICAL NOTES: Pitched 8-0 one-hit, complete-game victory against San Diego (September 29, 1993).
MISCELLANEOUS: Struck out in only appearance as pinch-hitter with Cincinnati (1995).

Year	Team (League)	W	L	Pct.	ERA	G	GS	CG	ShO	Sv.	IP	H	R	ER	BB	SO
1989—	Billings (Pioneer)	2	6	.250	3.94	13	13	2	0	0	77 2/3	81	44	34	25	72
1990—	Char., W.Va. (S. Atl.)	*15	6	.714	1.93	27	27	*8	2	0	177 1/3	142	58	38	56	153
1991—	Chattanooga (Sou.)	3	1	.750	1.64	5	5	0	0	0	38 1/3	20	7	7	11	24
—	Nashville (A.A.)	7	11	.389	3.81	23	23	3	1	0	148 2/3	130	68	63	56	89
1992—	Nashville (A.A.)	•12	9	.571	3.55	27	27	3	2	0	169 2/3	165	75	67	65	117
—	Cincinnati (N.L.)	4	2	.667	2.58	7	7	0	0	0	45 1/3	47	15	13	13	18
1993—	Cincinnati (N.L.)	10	15	.400	5.26	31	27	3	1	0	164 1/3	200	102	96	59	94
1994—	Cincinnati (N.L.)	3	3	.500	6.04	10	9	1	0	0	47 2/3	60	37	32	26	24
—	Indianapolis (A.A.)	2	3	.400	4.60	9	7	1	1	0	45	50	26	23	15	21
1995—	Indianapolis (A.A.)	2	4	.333	4.68	6	6	1	1	0	42 1/3	42	24	22	14	20
—	Cincinnati (N.L.)	6	5	.545	3.84	28	12	0	0	0	98 1/3	100	46	42	32	38
Major league totals (4 years)		23	25	.479	4.63	76	55	4	1	0	355 2/3	407	200	183	130	174

PULLIAM, HARVEY — OF — ROCKIES

PERSONAL: Born October 20, 1967, in San Francisco. . . . 6-0/218. . . . Bats right, throws right. . . . Full name: Harvey Jerome Pulliam Jr.
HIGH SCHOOL: McAteer (San Francisco).
TRANSACTIONS/CAREER NOTES: Selected by Kansas City Royals organization in third round of free-agent draft (June 2, 1986). . . . Granted free agency (October 15, 1993). . . . Signed by Las Vegas, San Diego Padres organization (March 1, 1994). . . . On disabled list (June 16-28, 1994). . . . Granted free agency (October 15, 1994). . . . Signed by Colorado Springs, Colorado Rockies organization (January 31, 1995).
STATISTICAL NOTES: Led Pacific Coast League with .614 slugging percentage in 1995. . . . Led Pacific Coast League with 10 intentional bases on balls received in 1995. . . . Led Pacific Coast League outfielders with six double plays in 1995.

Year	Team (League)	Pos.	G	AB	R	H	2B	3B	HR	RBI	Avg.	BB	SO	SB	PO	A	E	Avg.
			BATTING												FIELDING			
1986—	GC Royals (GCL)	OF	48	168	14	35	3	0	4	23	.208	8	33	3	62	5	4	.944
1987—	Appleton (Midw.)	OF	110	395	54	109	20	1	9	55	.276	26	79	21	195	8	6	.971
1988—	Baseball City (FSL)	OF	132	457	56	111	19	4	4	42	.243	34	87	21	289	9	6	.980
1989—	Memphis (South.)	OF	116	417	67	121	28	8	10	67	.290	44	65	5	157	8	5	.971
—	Omaha (A.A.)	OF	7	22	3	4	2	0	0	2	.182	3	6	0	12	1	0	1.000
1990—	Omaha (A.A.)	OF	123	436	72	117	18	5	16	72	.268	49	82	9	188	12	4	.980
1991—	Omaha (A.A.)	OF	104	346	35	89	18	2	6	39	.257	31	62	2	162	12	3	.983
—	Kansas City (A.L.)	OF	18	33	4	9	1	0	3	4	.273	3	9	0	21	1	2	.917
1992—	Omaha (A.A.)	OF	100	359	55	97	12	2	16	60	.270	32	53	4	168	7	1	.994
—	Kansas City (A.L.)	DH-OF	4	5	2	1	1	0	0	0	.200	1	3	0	3	0	0	1.000
1993—	Kansas City (A.L.)	OF	27	62	7	16	5	0	1	6	.258	2	14	0	33	0	1	.971
—	Omaha (A.A.)	OF	54	208	28	55	10	0	5	26	.264	17	36	1	102	7	6	.948
1994—	Las Vegas (PCL)■	OF	95	314	48	72	10	0	20	53	.229	21	65	0	144	6	4	.974
1995—	Colo. Springs (PCL)■	OF	115	407	90	133	30	6	*25	•91	.327	49	59	6	186	8	3	.985
—	Colorado (N.L.)	OF	5	5	1	2	1	0	1	3	.400	0	2	0	0	0	0	...
American League totals (3 years)			49	100	13	26	7	0	4	10	.260	6	26	0	57	1	3	.951
National League totals (1 year)			5	5	1	2	1	0	1	3	.400	0	2	0	0	0	0	...
Major league totals (4 years)			54	105	14	28	8	0	5	13	.267	6	28	0	57	1	3	.951

PULSIPHER, BILL — P — METS

PERSONAL: Born October 9, 1973, in Fort Benning, Ga. . . . 6-3/200. . . . Throws left, bats left. . . . Full name: William Thomas Pulsipher.
HIGH SCHOOL: Fairfax (Va.).
TRANSACTIONS/CAREER NOTES: Selected by New York Mets organization in second round of free-agent draft (June 3, 1991).
STATISTICAL NOTES: Tied for Eastern League lead with four balks in 1994.

Year	Team (League)	W	L	Pct.	ERA	G	GS	CG	ShO	Sv.	IP	H	R	ER	BB	SO
1992	Pittsfield (NYP)	6	3	.667	2.84	14	14	0	0	0	95	88	40	30	56	83
1993	Capital City (S. Atl.)	2	3	.400	2.08	6	6	1	0	0	43 1/3	34	17	10	12	29
—	St. Lucie (Fla. St.)	7	3	.700	2.24	13	13	3	1	0	96 1/3	63	27	24	39	102
1994	Binghamton (East.)	14	9	.609	3.22	28	28	5	1	0	*201	179	90	72	89	171
1995	Norfolk (Int'l)	6	4	.600	3.14	13	13	•4	2	0	91 2/3	84	36	32	33	63
—	New York (N.L.)	5	7	.417	3.98	17	17	2	0	0	126 2/3	122	58	56	45	81
Major league totals (1 year)		5	7	.417	3.98	17	17	2	0	0	126 2/3	122	58	56	45	81

PYE, EDDIE — 2B

PERSONAL: Born February 13, 1967, in Columbia, Tenn. . . . 5-10/175. . . . Bats right, throws right. . . . Full name: Robert Edward Pye.
HIGH SCHOOL: Columbia (Tenn.) Central.
COLLEGE: Middle Tennessee State.
TRANSACTIONS/CAREER NOTES: Selected by Los Angeles Dodgers organization in 10th round of free-agent draft (June 1, 1988). . . . On disabled list (April 21-28 and May 7, 1991-remainder of season). . . . On temporarily inactive list (May 2-22, 1992). . . . On Albuquerque disabled list (July 24-August 4, 1994). . . . Granted free agency (October 16, 1995).
STATISTICAL NOTES: Led Texas League second basemen with 23 errors in 1990.

				BATTING											FIELDING			
Year	Team (League)	Pos.	G	AB	R	H	2B	3B	HR	RBI	Avg.	BB	SO	SB	PO	A	E	Avg.
1988	Great Falls (Pio.)	2B-SS	61	237	50	71	8	4	2	30	.300	29	26	19	89	163	12	.955
1989	Bakersfield (Calif.)	2B-SS	129	488	59	126	21	2	8	47	.258	41	87	19	220	371	32	.949
1990	San Antonio (Tex.)	2B-SS	119	455	67	113	18	7	2	44	.248	45	68	19	216	379	†23	.963
1991	Albuquerque (PCL)	2B	12	30	4	13	1	0	1	8	.433	4	4	1	18	18	2	.947
1992	Albuquerque (PCL)	3B-2B	72	222	30	67	11	2	1	25	.302	13	41	6	52	115	13	.928
1993	Albuquerque (PCL)	2B-SS-3B	101	365	53	120	21	7	7	66	.329	32	43	5	182	254	12	.973
1994	Albuquerque (PCL)	2B-SS	100	361	79	121	19	6	2	42	.335	48	43	11	206	287	9	.982
—	Los Angeles (N.L.)	2B-SS	7	10	2	1	0	0	0	0	.100	1	4	0	4	13	0	1.000
1995	Albuquerque (PCL)	2B-SS-3B	84	302	49	89	20	1	3	32	.295	30	36	11	132	196	13	.962
—	Los Angeles (N.L.)	3B	7	8	0	0	0	0	0	0	.000	0	4	0	0	0	0	...
Major league totals (2 years)			14	18	2	1	0	0	0	0	.056	1	8	0	4	13	0	1.000

QUANTRILL, PAUL — P — BLUE JAYS

PERSONAL: Born November 3, 1968, in London, Ont. . . . 6-1/185. . . . Throws right, bats left. . . . Full name: Paul John Quantrill.
HIGH SCHOOL: Okemos (Mich.).
COLLEGE: Wisconsin.
TRANSACTIONS/CAREER NOTES: Selected by Los Angeles Dodgers organization in 26th round of free-agent draft (June 2, 1986); did not sign. . . . Selected by Boston Red Sox organization in sixth round of free-agent draft (June 5, 1989). . . . Traded by Red Sox with OF Billy Hatcher to Philadelphia Phillies for OF Wes Chamberlain and P Mike Sullivan (May 31, 1994). . . . Traded by Phillies to Toronto Blue Jays for 3B Howard Battle and P Ricardo Jordan (December 6, 1995).

Year	Team (League)	W	L	Pct.	ERA	G	GS	CG	ShO	Sv.	IP	H	R	ER	BB	SO
1989	GC Red Sox (GCL)	0	0	...	0.00	2	0	0	0	2	5	2	0	0	0	5
—	Elmira (NYP)	5	4	.556	3.43	20	7	•5	0	2	76	90	37	29	12	57
1990	Winter Haven (FSL)	2	5	.286	4.14	7	7	1	0	0	45 2/3	46	24	21	6	14
—	New Britain (East.)	7	11	.389	3.53	22	22	1	1	0	132 2/3	148	65	52	23	53
1991	New Britain (East.)	2	1	.667	2.06	5	5	1	0	0	35	32	14	8	8	18
—	Pawtucket (Int'l)	10	7	.588	4.45	25	23	•6	2	0	155 2/3	169	81	77	30	75
1992	Pawtucket (Int'l)	6	8	.429	4.46	19	18	4	1	0	119	143	63	59	20	56
—	Boston (A.L.)	2	3	.400	2.19	27	0	0	0	1	49 1/3	55	18	12	15	24
1993	Boston (A.L.)	6	12	.333	3.91	49	14	1	1	1	138	151	73	60	44	66
1994	Boston (A.L.)	1	1	.500	3.52	17	0	0	0	0	23	25	10	9	5	15
—	Philadelphia (N.L.)■	2	2	.500	6.00	18	1	0	0	1	30	39	21	20	10	13
—	Scran./W.B. (Int'l)	3	3	.500	3.47	8	8	1	1	0	57	55	25	22	6	36
1995	Philadelphia (N.L.)	11	12	.478	4.67	33	29	0	0	0	179 1/3	212	102	93	44	103
A.L. totals (3 years)		9	16	.360	3.47	93	14	1	1	2	210 1/3	231	101	81	64	105
N.L. totals (2 years)		13	14	.481	4.86	51	30	0	0	1	209 1/3	251	123	113	54	116
Major league totals (4 years)		22	30	.423	4.16	144	44	1	1	3	419 2/3	482	224	194	118	221

RAABE, BRIAN — 2B/3B — TWINS

PERSONAL: Born November 5, 1967, in New Ulm, Minn. . . . 5-9/170. . . . Bats right, throws right. . . . Full name: Brian Charles Raabe.
HIGH SCHOOL: New Ulm (Minn.).
COLLEGE: Minnesota.
TRANSACTIONS/CAREER NOTES: Selected by Minnesota Twins organization in 41st round of free-agent draft (June 4, 1990).

				BATTING											FIELDING			
Year	Team (League)	Pos.	G	AB	R	H	2B	3B	HR	RBI	Avg.	BB	SO	SB	PO	A	E	Avg.
1990	Visalia (California)	2B	42	138	11	34	3	2	0	17	.246	10	9	5	98	98	2	.990
1991	Visalia (California)	2B-3B-P	85	311	36	80	3	1	1	22	.257	40	14	15	120	198	2	.994

Year	Team (League)	Pos.	G	AB	R	H	2B	3B	HR	RBI	Avg.	BB	SO	SB	PO	A	E	Avg.
				BATTING											FIELDING			
1992—	Miracle (Florida State)	2B	102	361	52	104	16	2	2	32	.288	48	17	7	231	300	5	*.991
—	Orlando (Southern)	2B-P	32	108	12	30	6	0	2	6	.278	2	2	0	47	83	1	.992
1993—	Nashville (South.)	2-3-S-P	134	524	80	150	23	2	6	52	.286	56	28	18	139	308	16	.965
1994—	Salt Lake (PCL)	2B-SS-3B	123	474	78	152	26	3	3	49	.321	50	11	9	185	300	7	.986
1995—	Salt Lake (PCL)	2B-3B-SS	112	440	88	134	32	6	3	60	.305	45	14	15	120	249	6	.984
—	Minnesota (A.L.)	2B-3B	6	14	4	3	0	0	0	1	.214	1	0	0	5	8	0	1.000
Major league totals (1 year)			6	14	4	3	0	0	0	1	.214	1	0	0	5	8	0	1.000

RECORD AS PITCHER

Year	Team (League)	W	L	Pct.	ERA	G	GS	CG	ShO	Sv.	IP	H	R	ER	BB	SO
1991—	Visalia (California)	0	0	...	0.00	1	0	0	0	0	1	0	0	0	0	0
1992—	Orlando (Southern)	0	0	...	0.00	1	0	0	0	0	2/3	1	0	0	0	0
1993—	Nashville (South.)	0	0	...	54.00	1	0	0	0	0	1	8	6	6	0	0

RADINSKY, SCOTT — P — DODGERS

PERSONAL: Born March 3, 1968, in Glendale, Calif. . . . 6-3/204. . . . Throws left, bats left. . . . Full name: Scott David Radinsky.

HIGH SCHOOL: Simi Valley (Calif.).

TRANSACTIONS/CAREER NOTES: Selected by Chicago White Sox organization in third round of free-agent draft (June 2, 1986). . . . On Chicago disabled list (March 2, 1994-entire season). . . . On Chicago disabled list (July 17-August 15, 1995); included rehabilitation assignment to South Bend (August 1-15). . . . Granted free agency (December 21, 1995). . . . Signed by Los Angeles Dodgers organization (January 16, 1996).

Year	Team (League)	W	L	Pct.	ERA	G	GS	CG	ShO	Sv.	IP	H	R	ER	BB	SO
1986—	GC White Sox (GCL)	1	0	1.000	3.38	7	7	0	0	0	26 2/3	24	20	10	17	18
1987—	Peninsula (Caro.)	1	7	.125	5.77	12	8	0	0	0	39	43	30	25	32	37
—	GC White Sox (GCL)	3	3	.500	2.31	11	10	0	0	0	58 1/3	43	23	15	39	41
1988—	GC White Sox (GCL)	0	0	...	5.40	5	0	0	0	0	3 1/3	2	2	2	4	7
1989—	South Bend (Midw.)	7	5	.583	1.75	53	0	0	0	31	61 2/3	39	21	12	19	83
1990—	Chicago (A.L.)	6	1	.857	4.82	62	0	0	0	4	52 1/3	47	29	28	36	46
1991—	Chicago (A.L.)	5	5	.500	2.02	67	0	0	0	8	71 1/3	53	18	16	23	49
1992—	Chicago (A.L.)	3	7	.300	2.73	68	0	0	0	15	59 1/3	54	21	18	34	48
1993—	Chicago (A.L.)	8	2	.800	4.28	73	0	0	0	4	54 2/3	61	33	26	19	44
1994—								Did not play.								
1995—	Chicago (A.L.)	2	1	.667	5.45	46	0	0	0	1	38	46	23	23	17	14
—	South Bend (Midw.)	0	0	...	0.00	6	0	0	0	2	9 2/3	5	0	0	0	11
Major league totals (5 years)		24	16	.600	3.62	316	0	0	0	32	275 2/3	261	124	111	129	201

CHAMPIONSHIP SERIES RECORD

Year	Team (League)	W	L	Pct.	ERA	G	GS	CG	ShO	Sv.	IP	H	R	ER	BB	SO
1993—	Chicago (A.L.)	0	0	...	10.80	4	0	0	0	0	1 2/3	3	4	2	1	1

RADKE, BRAD — P — TWINS

PERSONAL: Born October 27, 1972, in Eau Claire, Wis. . . . 6-2/186. . . . Throws right, bats right. . . . Full name: Brad William Radke.

HIGH SCHOOL: Jesuit (Tampa, Fla.).

TRANSACTIONS/CAREER NOTES: Selected by Minnesota Twins organization in eighth round of free-agent draft (June 3, 1991).

STATISTICAL NOTES: Led A.L. with 32 home runs allowed in 1995.

Year	Team (League)	W	L	Pct.	ERA	G	GS	CG	ShO	Sv.	IP	H	R	ER	BB	SO
1991—	GC Twins (GCL)	3	4	.429	3.08	10	9	1	0	1	49 2/3	41	21	17	14	46
1992—	Kenosha (Midwest)	10	10	.500	2.93	26	25	4	1	0	165 2/3	149	70	54	47	127
1993—	Fort Myers (Fla. St.)	3	5	.375	3.82	14	14	0	0	0	92	85	42	39	21	69
—	Nashville (South.)	2	6	.250	4.62	13	13	1	0	0	76	81	42	39	16	76
1994—	Nashville (South.)	12	9	.571	2.66	29	*28	5	1	0	186 1/3	167	66	55	34	123
1995—	Minnesota (A.L.)	11	14	.440	5.32	29	28	2	1	0	181	195	112	107	47	75
Major league totals (1 year)		11	14	.440	5.32	29	28	2	1	0	181	195	112	107	47	75

RAINES, TIM — OF — YANKEES

PERSONAL: Born September 16, 1959, in Sanford, Fla. . . . 5-8/186. . . . Bats both, throws right. . . . Full name: Timothy Raines. . . . Brother of Ned Raines, minor league outfielder (1978-80).

HIGH SCHOOL: Seminole (Sanford, Fla.).

TRANSACTIONS/CAREER NOTES: Selected by Montreal Expos organization in fifth round of free-agent draft (June 7, 1977). . . . On disabled list (May 23-June 5, 1978). . . . Granted free agency (November 12, 1986). . . . Re-signed by Expos (May 2, 1987). . . . On disabled list (June 24-July 9, 1988 and June 25-July 10, 1990). . . . Traded by Expos with P Jeff Carter and a player to be named later to Chicago White Sox for OF Ivan Calderon and P Barry Jones (December 23, 1990); White Sox acquired P Mario Brito to complete deal (February 15, 1991). . . . On Chicago disabled list (April 10-May 22, 1993); included rehabilitation assignment to Nashville (May 19-22). . . . Granted free agency (November 1, 1993). . . . Re-signed by White Sox (December 22, 1993). . . . Traded by White Sox to New York Yankees for future considerations (December 28, 1995).

RECORDS: Holds major league single-season record for most intentional bases on balls received by switch-hitter—26 (1987). . . . Holds A.L. career record for most consecutive stolen bases without being caught stealing—40 (July 23, 1993 through August 4, 1995). . . . Shares A.L. single-game record for most consecutive times reached base safely—7 (April 20, 1994, 12 innings).

HONORS: Named Minor League Player of the Year by The Sporting News (1980). . . . Named N.L. Rookie Player of the Year by The Sporting News (1981). . . . Named outfielder on The Sporting News N.L. All-Star team (1983 and 1986). . . . Won The Sporting News Gold Shoe Award (1984). . . . Named outfielder on The Sporting News N.L. Silver Slugger team (1986).

STATISTICAL NOTES: Led N.L. outfielders with 21 assists in 1983. . . . Led N.L. with .413 on-base percentage in 1986. . . . Hit for the cycle (August 16, 1987). . . . Switch-hit home runs in one game (July 16, 1988 and August 31, 1993). . . . Hit three home runs in one game (April

R

18, 1994). . . . Career major league grand slams: 5.

			BATTING											FIELDING			
Year Team (League)	Pos.	G	AB	R	H	2B	3B	HR	RBI	Avg.	BB	SO	SB	PO	A	E	Avg.
1977— GC Expos (GCL)	2B-3B-OF	49	161	28	45	6	2	0	21	.280	27	16	29	79	72	13	.921
1978— W.P. Beach (FSL)	2B-SS	100	359	67	103	10	0	0	23	.287	64	44	57	219	273	24	.953
1979— Memphis (South.)	2B	•145	552	*104	160	25	10	5	50	.290	90	51	59	*341	*413	*23	.970
— Montreal (N.L.)	PR	6	0	3	0	0	0	0	0	...	0	0	2	...	...	...	...
1980— Denver (A.A.)	2B	108	429	105	152	23	•11	6	64	*.354	61	42	*77	226	338	16	.972
— Montreal (N.L.)	2B-OF	15	20	5	1	0	0	0	0	.050	6	3	5	15	16	0	1.000
1981— Montreal (N.L.)	OF-2B	88	313	61	95	13	7	5	37	.304	45	31	*71	162	8	4	.977
1982— Montreal (N.L.)	OF-2B	156	647	90	179	32	8	4	43	.277	75	83	*78	293	126	8	.981
1983— Montreal (N.L.)	OF-2B	156	615	*133	183	32	8	11	71	.298	97	70	*90	314	†23	4	.988
1984— Montreal (N.L.)	OF-2B	160	622	106	192	•38	9	8	60	.309	87	69	*75	420	8	6	.986
1985— Montreal (N.L.)	OF	150	575	115	184	30	13	11	41	.320	81	60	70	284	8	2	.993
1986— Montreal (N.L.)	OF	151	580	91	194	35	10	9	62	*.334	78	60	70	270	13	6	.979
1987— Montreal (N.L.)	OF	139	530	*123	175	34	8	18	68	.330	90	52	50	297	9	4	.987
1988— Montreal (N.L.)	OF	109	429	66	116	19	7	12	48	.270	53	44	33	235	5	3	.988
1989— Montreal (N.L.)	OF	145	517	76	148	29	6	9	60	.286	93	48	41	253	7	1	.996
1990— Montreal (N.L.)	OF	130	457	65	131	11	5	9	62	.287	70	43	49	239	3	6	.976
1991— Chicago (A.L.)■	OF-DH	155	609	102	163	20	6	5	50	.268	83	68	51	273	12	3	.990
1992— Chicago (A.L.)	OF-DH	144	551	102	162	22	9	7	54	.294	81	48	45	312	12	2	.994
1993— Chicago (A.L.)	OF	115	415	75	127	16	4	16	54	.306	64	35	21	200	5	0	*1.000
— Nashville (A.A.)	OF	3	11	3	5	1	0	0	2	.455	2	0	2	3	0	0	1.000
1994— Chicago (A.L.)	OF	101	384	80	102	15	5	10	52	.266	61	43	13	204	3	4	.981
1995— Chicago (A.L.)	OF-DH	133	502	81	143	25	4	12	67	.285	70	52	13	193	7	4	.980
American League totals (5 years)		648	2461	440	697	98	28	50	277	.283	359	246	143	1182	39	13	.989
National League totals (12 years)		1405	5305	934	1598	273	81	96	552	.301	775	563	634	2782	226	44	.986
Major league totals (17 years)		2053	7766	1374	2295	371	109	146	829	.296	1134	809	777	3964	265	57	.987

CHAMPIONSHIP SERIES RECORD

NOTES: Holds single-series record for most singles—10 (1993). . . . Shares A.L. single-series record for most hits—12 (1993).

			BATTING											FIELDING			
Year Team (League)	Pos.	G	AB	R	H	2B	3B	HR	RBI	Avg.	BB	SO	SB	PO	A	E	Avg.
1981— Montreal (N.L.)	OF	5	21	1	5	2	0	0	1	.238	0	3	0	9	0	0	1.000
1993— Chicago (A.L.)	OF	6	27	5	12	2	0	0	1	.444	2	2	1	12	2	0	1.000
Championship series totals (2 years)		11	48	6	17	4	0	0	2	.354	2	5	1	21	2	0	1.000

ALL-STAR GAME RECORD

NOTES: Named Most Valuable Player (1987).

		BATTING											FIELDING			
Year League	Pos.	AB	R	H	2B	3B	HR	RBI	Avg.	BB	SO	SB	PO	A	E	Avg.
1981— National	PR-OF	0	0	0	0	0	0	0	...	0	0	0	1	0	0	1.000
1982— National	OF	1	0	0	0	0	0	0	.000	1	1	1	0	0	0	...
1983— National	OF	3	0	0	0	0	0	0	.000	0	1	1	2	0	0	1.000
1984— National	OF	1	0	0	0	0	0	0	.000	0	1	0	4	0	0	1.000
1985— National	PH-OF	0	1	0	0	0	0	0	...	1	0	0	0	0	0	...
1986— National	PH-OF	2	0	0	0	0	0	0	.000	0	1	0	1	0	0	1.000
1987— National	OF	3	0	3	0	1	0	2	1.000	0	0	1	1	0	0	1.000
All-Star Game totals (7 years)		10	1	3	0	1	0	2	.300	2	4	3	9	0	0	1.000

RALSTON, KRIS P ROYALS

PERSONAL: Born August 8, 1971, in Carthage, Mo. . . . 6-2/200. . . . Throws right, bats right. . . . Full name: Kristopher Mance Ralston.
HIGH SCHOOL: Carthage (Mo.).
JUNIOR COLLEGE: Crowder (Mo.).
COLLEGE: Central Missouri State.
TRANSACTIONS/CAREER NOTES: Selected by Kansas City Royals organization in 21st round of free-agent draft (June 3, 1993).

Year Team (League)	W	L	Pct.	ERA	G	GS	CG	ShO	Sv.	IP	H	R	ER	BB	SO
1993— Eugene (N'west)	7	3	.700	2.74	15	15	1	0	0	82	52	29	25	36	75
1994— Wilmington (Caro.)	10	4	.714	2.39	20	18	2	1	0	109 1/3	84	36	29	38	102
1995— Wichita (Texas)	9	4	.692	3.56	18	16	0	0	0	93 2/3	85	40	37	28	84

RAMIREZ, ANGEL OF BLUE JAYS

PERSONAL: Born January 24, 1973, in Azua, Dominican Republic. . . . 6-0/170. . . . Bats right, throws right. . . . Full name: Angel Emilio Ramirez.
TRANSACTIONS/CAREER NOTES: Signed as non-drafted free agent by Toronto Blue Jays organization (May 16, 1991).
STATISTICAL NOTES: Led Pioneer League outfielders with 145 total chances in 1993. . . . Led Florida State League outfielders with 348 total chances in 1995.

			BATTING											FIELDING			
Year Team (League)	Pos.	G	AB	R	H	2B	3B	HR	RBI	Avg.	BB	SO	SB	PO	A	E	Avg.
1991— Dom. Blue Jays (DSL)	OF	49	183	29	52	6	3	8	23	.284	12	24	11	...	...	...	...
1992— Dom. Blue Jays (DSL)	OF	70	283	64	92	14	11	2	59	.325	17	34	10	103	6	4	.965
1993— St. Cathar. (NYP)	OF	6	22	2	6	1	0	0	2	.273	0	7	0	11	0	1	.917
— Medicine Hat (Pio.)	OF	62	227	40	80	8	5	4	30	.352	8	43	15	*131	8	6	.959
1994— Hagerstown (SAL)	OF	117	454	71	127	17	14	9	51	.280	21	103	21	213	10	8	.965
1995— Dunedin (Fla. St.)	OF	131	*541	78	149	19	5	8	52	.275	21	99	17	*320	17	*11	.968

RAMIREZ, HECTOR — P — METS

PERSONAL: Born December 15, 1971, in El Seybo, Dominican Republic. . . . 6-3/218. . . . Throws right, bats right. . . . Full name: Hector Benvenido Ramirez.

HIGH SCHOOL: Liceo Local (El Seybo, Dominican Republic).

TRANSACTIONS/CAREER NOTES: Signed as non-drafted free agent by New York Mets organization (August 22, 1988).

STATISTICAL NOTES: Tied for Florida State League lead with eight balks in 1994.

Year	Team (League)	W	L	Pct.	ERA	G	GS	CG	ShO	Sv.	IP	H	R	ER	BB	SO
1989—	GC Mets (GCL)	0	5	.000	4.50	15	5	0	0	0	42	35	29	21	24	14
1990—	GC Mets (GCL)	3	5	.375	4.26	11	8	1	0	0	50 2/3	54	34	24	21	43
1991—	Kingsport (Appal.)	8	2	.800	2.65	14	13	0	0	0	85	83	39	25	28	64
1992—	Columbia (S. Atl.)	5	4	.556	3.61	17	17	1	0	0	94 2/3	93	50	38	33	53
1993—	GC Mets (GCL)	1	0	1.000	0.00	1	1	0	0	0	7	5	1	0	1	6
—	Capital City (S. Atl.)	4	6	.400	5.34	14	14	0	0	0	64	86	51	38	23	42
1994—	St. Lucie (Fla. St.)	11	12	.478	3.43	27	27	•6	1	0	*194	*202	86	74	50	110
1995—	Binghamton (East.)	4	•12	.250	4.60	20	20	2	0	0	123 1/3	127	69	63	48	63

RAMIREZ, MANNY — OF — INDIANS

PERSONAL: Born May 30, 1972, in Santo Domingo, Dominican Republic. . . . 6-0/190. . . . Bats right, throws right. . . . Full name: Manuel Aristides Ramirez.

HIGH SCHOOL: George Washington (New York).

TRANSACTIONS/CAREER NOTES: Selected by Cleveland Indians organization in first round (13th pick overall) of free-agent draft (June 3, 1991). . . . On disabled list (July 10, 1992-remainder of season).

HONORS: Named Appalachian League Most Valuable Player (1991). . . . Named outfielder on THE SPORTING NEWS A.L. All-Star team (1995). . . . Named outfielder on THE SPORTING NEWS A.L. Silver Slugger team (1995).

STATISTICAL NOTES: Led Appalachian League with 146 total bases and .679 slugging percentage in 1991. . . . Career major league grand slams: 1.

			BATTING												FIELDING			
Year	Team (League)	Pos.	G	AB	R	H	2B	3B	HR	RBI	Avg.	BB	SO	SB	PO	A	E	Avg.
1991—	Burlington (Appal.)	OF	59	215	44	70	11	4	*19	*63	.326	34	41	7	83	2	3	.966
1992—	Kinston (Carolina)	OF	81	291	52	81	18	4	13	63	.278	45	74	1	128	3	6	.956
1993—	Cant./Akr. (East.)	OF	89	344	67	117	32	0	17	79	*.340	45	68	2	142	4	5	.967
—	Charlotte (Int'l)	OF	40	145	38	46	12	0	14	36	.317	27	35	1	70	3	3	.961
—	Cleveland (A.L.)	DH-OF	22	53	5	9	1	0	2	5	.170	2	8	0	3	0	0	1.000
1994—	Cleveland (A.L.)	OF-DH	91	290	51	78	22	0	17	60	.269	42	72	4	150	7	1	.994
1995—	Cleveland (A.L.)	OF-DH	137	484	85	149	26	1	31	107	.308	75	112	6	220	3	5	.978
Major league totals (3 years)			250	827	141	236	49	1	50	172	.285	119	192	10	373	10	6	.985

DIVISION SERIES RECORD

			BATTING												FIELDING			
Year	Team (League)	Pos.	G	AB	R	H	2B	3B	HR	RBI	Avg.	BB	SO	SB	PO	A	E	Avg.
1995—	Cleveland (A.L.)	OF	3	12	1	0	0	0	0	0	.000	1	2	0	3	0	0	1.000

CHAMPIONSHIP SERIES RECORD

			BATTING												FIELDING			
Year	Team (League)	Pos.	G	AB	R	H	2B	3B	HR	RBI	Avg.	BB	SO	SB	PO	A	E	Avg.
1995—	Cleveland (A.L.)	OF	6	21	2	6	0	0	2	2	.286	2	5	0	9	0	0	1.000

WORLD SERIES RECORD

			BATTING												FIELDING			
Year	Team (League)	Pos.	G	AB	R	H	2B	3B	HR	RBI	Avg.	BB	SO	SB	PO	A	E	Avg.
1995—	Cleveland (A.L.)	OF	6	18	2	4	0	0	1	2	.222	4	5	1	8	0	0	1.000

ALL-STAR GAME RECORD

			BATTING											FIELDING			
Year	League	Pos.	AB	R	H	2B	3B	HR	RBI	Avg.	BB	SO	SB	PO	A	E	Avg.
1995—	American	PH-OF	0	0	0	0	0	0	0	...	2	0	0	2	0	0	1.000

RANDA, JOE — 3B — ROYALS

PERSONAL: Born December 18, 1969, in Milwaukee. . . . 5-11/190. . . . Bats right, throws right. . . . Full name: Joseph Gregory Randa.

HIGH SCHOOL: Kettle Moraine Public (Wales, Wis.).

JUNIOR COLLEGE: Indian River Community College (Fla.).

COLLEGE: Tennessee.

TRANSACTIONS/CAREER NOTES: Selected by California Angels organization in 30th round of free-agent draft (June 5, 1989); did not sign. . . . Selected by Kansas City Royals organization in 11th round of free-agent draft (June 3, 1991).

HONORS: Named Northwest League Most Valuable Player (1991).

STATISTICAL NOTES: Led Northwest League with 150 total bases and .438 on-base percentage in 1991. . . . Led Northwest League third basemen with 182 total chances and 12 double plays in 1991. . . . Led Southern League with 10 sacrifice flies in 1993. . . . Led American Association third basemen with 433 total chances and 28 double plays in 1994.

			BATTING												FIELDING			
Year	Team (League)	Pos.	G	AB	R	H	2B	3B	HR	RBI	Avg.	BB	SO	SB	PO	A	E	Avg.
1991—	Eugene (N'west)	3B	72	275	53	*93	20	2	11	59	.338	46	29	6	*57	*111	14	*.923
1992—	Appleton (Midw.)	3B	72	266	55	80	13	0	5	43	.301	34	37	6	53	137	12	.941
—	Baseball City (FSL)	3B-SS	51	189	22	52	7	0	1	12	.275	12	21	4	43	105	6	.961
1993—	Memphis (South.)	3B	131	505	74	149	31	5	11	72	.295	39	64	8	*97	309	25	.942
1994—	Omaha (A.A.)	3B	127	455	65	125	27	2	10	51	.275	30	49	5	*85	*324	*24	.945

							BATTING								FIELDING		
Year	Team (League)	Pos.	G	AB	R	H	2B	3B	HR	RBI	Avg.	BB	SO	SB	PO	A	E	Avg.
1995—	Omaha (A.A.)	3B	64	233	33	64	10	2	8	33	.275	22	33	2	42	96	6	.958
—	Kansas City (A.L.)	3B-2B-DH	34	70	6	12	2	0	1	5	.171	6	17	0	15	44	3	.952
Major league totals (1 year)			34	70	6	12	2	0	1	5	.171	6	17	0	15	44	3	.952

RAPP, PAT — P — MARLINS

PERSONAL: Born July 13, 1967, in Jennings, La. . . . 6-3/215. . . . Throws right, bats right. . . . Full name: Patrick Leland Rapp.
HIGH SCHOOL: Sulphur (La.).
JUNIOR COLLEGE: Hinds Community College (Miss.).
COLLEGE: Southern Mississippi.
TRANSACTIONS/CAREER NOTES: Selected by San Francisco Giants organization in 15th round of free-agent draft (June 5, 1989). . . . Selected by Florida Marlins in first round (10th pick overall) of expansion draft (November 17, 1992).
STATISTICAL NOTES: Pitched 17-0 one-hit, complete-game victory against Colorado (September 17, 1995).
MISCELLANEOUS: Appeared in one game as pinch-runner (1994).

Year	Team (League)	W	L	Pct.	ERA	G	GS	CG	ShO	Sv.	IP	H	R	ER	BB	SO
1989—	Pocatello (Pioneer)	4	6	.400	5.30	16	12	1	0	0	73	90	54	43	29	40
1990—	Clinton (Midwest)	14	10	.583	2.64	27	26	4	0	0	167 1/3	132	60	49	79	132
1991—	San Jose (Calif.)	7	5	.583	2.50	16	15	1	0	0	90	88	41	25	37	73
—	Shreveport (Texas)	6	2	.750	2.69	10	10	1	1	0	60 1/3	52	23	18	22	46
1992—	Phoenix (PCL)	7	8	.467	3.05	39	12	2	1	3	121	115	54	41	40	79
—	San Francisco (N.L.)	0	2	.000	7.20	3	2	0	0	0	10	8	8	8	6	3
1993—	Edmonton (PCL)■	8	3	.727	3.43	17	17	•4	1	0	107 2/3	89	45	41	34	93
—	Florida (N.L.)	4	6	.400	4.02	16	16	1	0	0	94	101	49	42	39	57
1994—	Florida (N.L.)	7	8	.467	3.85	24	23	2	1	0	133 1/3	132	67	57	69	75
1995—	Charlotte (Int'l)	0	1	.000	6.00	1	1	0	0	0	6	6	4	4	1	5
—	Florida (N.L.)	14	7	.667	3.44	28	28	3	2	0	167 1/3	158	72	64	76	102
Major league totals (4 years)		25	23	.521	3.80	71	69	6	3	0	404 2/3	399	196	171	190	237

RASMUSSEN, DENNIS — P

PERSONAL: Born April 18, 1959, in Los Angeles. . . . 6-7/235. . . . Throws left, bats left. . . . Full name: Dennis Lee Rasmussen. . . . Grandson of Bill Brubaker, infielder, Pittsburgh Pirates and Boston Braves (1932-40 and 1943).
HIGH SCHOOL: Bear Creek (Lakewood, Colo.).
COLLEGE: Creighton.
TRANSACTIONS/CAREER NOTES: Selected by Pittsburgh Pirates organization in 18th round of free-agent draft (June 7, 1977); did not sign. . . . Selected by California Angels organization in first round (17th pick overall) of free-agent draft (June 3, 1980); pick received as compensation for Houston Astros signing free-agent P Nolan Ryan. . . . Traded by Angels organization to New York Yankees (November 24, 1982), completing deal in which Yankees traded P Tommy John to Angels for a player to be named later (August 31, 1982). . . . Traded by Yankees organization with 2B Edwin Rodriguez to San Diego Padres (September 12, 1983), completing deal in which Padres traded P John Montefusco to Yankees for two players to be named later (August 26, 1983). . . . Traded by Padres with a player to be named later to Yankees organization for 3B Graig Nettles (March 30, 1984); Yankees organization acquired P Darin Cloninger to complete deal (April 26, 1984). . . . Traded by Yankees to Cincinnati Reds for P Bill Gullickson (August 26, 1987). . . . Traded by Reds to Padres for P Candy Sierra (June 8, 1988). . . . Granted free agency (November 5, 1990). . . . Re-signed by Padres (January 9, 1991). . . . On San Diego disabled list (March 31-May 25, 1991); included rehabilitation assignment to Las Vegas (April 23-May 22). . . . Granted free agency (October 28, 1991). . . . Signed by Rochester, Baltimore Orioles organization (January 31, 1992). . . . Released by Rochester (June 2, 1992). . . . Signed by Iowa, Chicago Cubs organization (June 5, 1992). . . . On Chicago disabled list (July 2-21, 1992). . . . Released by Cubs (July 24, 1992). . . . Signed by Omaha, Kansas City Royals organization (July 27, 1992). . . . On Kansas City disabled list (March 26-April 27, 1993); included rehabilitation assignment to Omaha (April 15-27). . . . On Kansas City disabled list (May 13-June 20, 1993); included rehabilitation assignment to Omaha (May 22-June 20). . . . Granted free agency (October 29, 1993). . . . Signed by Phoenix, San Francisco Giants organization (January 31, 1994). . . . Released by Phoenix (May 2, 1994). . . . Signed by Omaha, Royals organization (May 27, 1994). . . . Granted free agency (October 15, 1994). . . . Re-signed by Omaha (November 15, 1994). . . . Released by Royals (July 7, 1995).
STATISTICAL NOTES: Led Eastern League with 18 wild pitches in 1981. . . . Led N.L. with 28 home runs allowed in 1990. . . . Pitched 2-0 one-hit, complete-game victory for Kansas City against California (September 29, 1992).
MISCELLANEOUS: Doubled with three RBIs in only appearance as pinch-hitter (1990). . . . Struck out in only appearance as pinch-hitter with San Diego (1991).

Year	Team (League)	W	L	Pct.	ERA	G	GS	CG	ShO	Sv.	IP	H	R	ER	BB	SO
1980—	Salinas (Calif.)	4	6	.400	5.45	11	11	4	1	0	76	69	51	46	52	63
1981—	Holyoke (Eastern)	8	12	.400	3.98	24	24	6	1	0	156	134	95	69	99	125
1982—	Spokane (PCL)	11	8	.579	5.03	27	27	4	2	0	171 2/3	166	110	96	*113	162
1983—	Columbus (Int'l)■	•13	10	.565	4.57	28	•28	8	1	0	181	161	106	92	108	*187
—	San Diego (N.L.)■	0	0	. . .	1.98	4	1	0	0	0	13 2/3	10	5	3	8	13
1984—	Columbus (Int'l)■	4	1	.800	3.09	6	6	3	1	0	43 2/3	24	15	15	27	30
—	New York (A.L.)	9	6	.600	4.57	24	24	1	0	0	147 2/3	127	79	75	60	110
1985—	New York (A.L.)	3	5	.375	3.98	22	16	2	0	0	101 2/3	97	56	45	42	63
—	Columbus (Int'l)	0	3	.000	3.80	7	7	1	0	0	45	41	24	19	25	43
1986—	New York (A.L.)	18	6	.750	3.88	31	31	3	1	0	202	160	91	87	74	131
1987—	New York (A.L.)	9	7	.563	4.75	26	25	2	0	0	146	145	78	77	55	89
—	Columbus (Int'l)	1	0	1.000	1.29	1	1	0	0	0	7	5	1	1	0	4
—	Cincinnati (N.L.)■	4	1	.800	3.97	7	7	0	0	0	45 1/3	39	22	20	12	39
1988—	Cincinnati (N.L.)	2	6	.250	5.75	11	11	1	1	0	56 1/3	68	36	36	22	27
—	San Diego (N.L.)■	14	4	.778	2.55	20	20	6	0	0	148 1/3	131	48	42	36	85
1989—	San Diego (N.L.)	10	10	.500	4.26	33	33	1	0	0	183 2/3	190	100	87	72	87
1990—	San Diego (N.L.)	11	15	.423	4.51	32	32	3	1	0	187 2/3	217	110	94	62	86
1991—	Las Vegas (PCL)	1	3	.250	5.47	5	5	1	0	0	26 1/3	23	18	16	15	12
—	San Diego (N.L.)	6	13	.316	3.74	24	24	1	1	0	146 2/3	155	74	61	49	75
1992—	Rochester (Int'l)■	0	7	.000	5.67	9	9	1	0	0	46	49	33	29	22	33
—	Iowa (Am. Assoc.)■	1	1	.500	4.76	2	2	0	0	0	11 1/3	15	7	6	3	6

Year	Team (League)	W	L	Pct.	ERA	G	GS	CG	ShO	Sv.	IP	H	R	ER	BB	SO
	—Chicago (N.L.)	0	0	...	10.80	3	1	0	0	0	5	7	6	6	2	0
	—Omaha (Am. Assoc.)■	3	3	.500	1.42	11	6	3	2	0	50 2/3	37	14	8	17	44
	—Kansas City (A.L.)	4	1	.800	1.43	5	5	1	1	0	37 2/3	25	7	6	6	12
1993	—Omaha (Am. Assoc.)	7	8	.467	5.03	17	17	3	1	0	105 2/3	124	68	59	27	59
	—Kansas City (A.L.)	1	2	.333	7.45	9	4	0	0	0	29	40	25	24	14	12
1994	—Phoenix (PCL)■	1	2	.333	4.20	5	5	1	0	0	30	39	17	14	7	12
	—Omaha (Am. Assoc.)■	10	7	.588	3.24	20	18	*9	2	0	139	135	59	50	36	84
1995	—Omaha (Am. Assoc.)	6	3	.667	2.89	10	10	3	1	0	65 1/3	63	22	21	17	51
	—Kansas City (A.L.)	0	1	.000	9.00	5	1	0	0	0	10	13	10	10	8	6
A.L. totals (7 years)		44	28	.611	4.33	122	106	9	2	0	674	607	346	324	259	423
N.L. totals (7 years)		47	49	.490	3.99	134	129	12	3	0	786 2/3	817	401	349	263	412
Major league totals (12 years)		91	77	.542	4.15	256	235	21	5	0	1460 2/3	1424	747	673	522	835

RATLIFF, JON — P — TIGERS

PERSONAL: Born December 22, 1971, in Syracuse, N.Y. . . . 6-5/200. . . . Throws right, bats right. . . . Full name: Jon Charles Ratliff.
HIGH SCHOOL: Liverpool (N.Y.).
COLLEGE: Lemoyne (N.Y.).
TRANSACTIONS/CAREER NOTES: Selected by San Diego Padres organization in 22nd round of free-agent draft (June 4, 1990); did not sign. . . . Selected by Chicago Cubs organization in first round (24th pick overall) of free-agent draft (June 3, 1993); pick received as part of compensation for Atlanta Braves signing Type A free-agent P Greg Maddux. . . . Selected by Detroit Tigers from Cubs organization in Rule 5 major league draft (December 4, 1995).

Year	Team (League)	W	L	Pct.	ERA	G	GS	CG	ShO	Sv.	IP	H	R	ER	BB	SO
1993	—Geneva (NYP)	1	1	.500	3.21	3	3	0	0	0	14	12	8	5	8	7
	—Daytona (Fla. St.)	2	4	.333	3.95	8	8	0	0	0	41	50	29	18	23	15
1994	—Daytona (Fla. St.)	3	2	.600	3.50	8	8	1	0	0	54	64	23	21	5	17
	—Iowa (Am. Assoc.)	1	3	.250	5.40	5	4	0	0	0	28 1/3	39	19	17	7	10
	—Orlando (Southern)	1	9	.100	5.63	12	12	1	0	0	62 1/3	78	44	39	26	19
1995	—Orlando (Southern)	10	5	.667	3.47	26	25	1	1	0	140	143	67	54	42	94

READY, RANDY — IF/OF

PERSONAL: Born January 8, 1960, in San Mateo, Calif. . . . 5-11/184. . . . Bats right, throws right. . . . Full name: Randy Max Ready.
HIGH SCHOOL: John F. Kennedy (Fremont, Calif.).
COLLEGE: Cal State Hayward and Mesa College (Colo.).
TRANSACTIONS/CAREER NOTES: Selected by Milwaukee Brewers organization in fifth round of free-agent draft (June 3, 1980). . . . On Vancouver disabled list (August 21, 1984-remainder of season). . . . On Milwaukee disabled list (April 30-June 19, 1985); included rehabilitation assignment to Vancouver (June 1-19). . . . Traded by Brewers to San Diego Padres for a player to be named later (June 12, 1986); Brewers organization acquired IF Tim Pyznarski to complete deal (October 29, 1986). . . . On San Diego disabled list (June 19-July 7, 1986). . . . On Las Vegas disabled list (July 22, 1986-remainder of season). . . . Traded by Padres with OF John Kruk to Philadelphia Phillies for OF Chris James (June 2, 1989). . . . On disabled list (June 7-July 11, 1991). . . . Granted free agency (October 28, 1991). . . . Signed by Oakland Athletics (January 14, 1992). . . . On disabled list (April 5-21 and June 17-July 8, 1992). . . . Granted free agency (October 27, 1992). . . . Signed by Omaha, Kansas City Royals organization (March 2, 1993). . . . Released by Omaha (April 8, 1993). . . . Signed by Rochester, Baltimore Orioles organization (May 7, 1993). . . . Released by Rochester (August 9, 1993). . . . Signed by Montreal Expos (August 10, 1993). . . . Granted free agency (November 3, 1993). . . . Re-signed by Expos organization (December 14, 1993). . . . Released by Ottawa, Expos organization (March 30, 1994). . . . Re-signed by Ottawa (March 31, 1994). . . . On Ottawa disabled list (April 13-22 and May 2-25, 1994). . . . Released by Ottawa (June 24, 1994). . . . Signed by Philadelphia Phillies (June 24, 1994). . . . Granted free agency (October 1994). . . . Re-signed by Scranton, Phillies organization (April 8, 1995). . . . Released by Phillies (July 17, 1995).
RECORDS: Shares A.L. single-game record for most innings played by third baseman—25 (May 8, finished May 9, 1984; fielded 24 1/3 innings).
STATISTICAL NOTES: Led Midwest League third basemen with 22 double plays in 1981. . . . Led Texas League with 281 total bases in 1982. . . . Led Texas League third basemen with 456 total chances and 27 double plays in 1982. . . . Career major league grand slams: 1.

				BATTING												FIELDING			
Year	Team (League)	Pos.	G	AB	R	H	2B	3B	HR	RBI	Avg.	BB	SO	SB	PO	A	E	Avg.
1980	—Butte (Pioneer)	SS-2B-3B	61	226	*65	85	*23	4	8	50	*.376	57	32	2	86	174	22	.922
1981	—Burlington (Midw.)	3B	110	367	74	113	17	0	17	56	.308	85	54	7	72	216	21	*.932
1982	—El Paso (Texas)	3B	132	475	*122	*178	33	5	20	99	*.375	92	48	13	*115	*312	•29	.936
1983	—Vancouver (PCL)	3B	116	407	82	134	28	1	13	59	.329	*99	59	24	136	231	24	.939
	—Milwaukee (A.L.)	DH-3B	12	37	8	15	3	2	1	6	.405	6	3	0	5	8	0	1.000
1984	—Milwaukee (A.L.)	3B	37	123	13	23	6	1	3	13	.187	14	18	0	29	76	6	.946
	—Vancouver (PCL)	2B-3B	43	151	48	49	7	4	3	18	.325	43	21	10	74	125	6	.971
1985	—Milwaukee (A.L.)	O-3-2-DH	48	181	29	48	9	5	1	21	.265	14	23	0	93	14	1	.991
	—Vancouver (PCL)	OF-3B-2B	52	190	33	62	12	3	4	29	.326	30	14	14	60	35	7	.931
1986	—Milwaukee (A.L.)	O-2-3-DH	23	79	8	15	4	0	1	4	.190	9	9	2	35	21	3	.949
	—San Diego (N.L.)■	3B	1	3	0	0	0	0	0	0	.000	0	1	0	0	2	1	.667
	—Las Vegas (PCL)	3B-OF	10	38	5	14	4	0	1	8	.368	6	2	1	12	10	0	1.000
1987	—San Diego (N.L.)	3B-2B-OF	124	350	69	108	26	6	12	54	.309	67	44	7	124	220	15	.958
1988	—San Diego (N.L.)	3B-2B-OF	114	331	43	88	16	2	7	39	.266	39	38	6	112	153	11	.960
1989	—San Diego (N.L.)	3B-2B-OF	28	67	4	17	2	1	0	5	.254	11	6	0	16	36	2	.963
	—Philadelphia (N.L.)■	OF-3B-2B	72	187	33	50	11	1	8	21	.267	31	31	4	64	36	7	.935
1990	—Philadelphia (N.L.)	OF-2B	101	217	26	53	9	1	1	26	.244	29	35	3	78	86	2	.988
1991	—Philadelphia (N.L.)	2B	76	205	32	51	10	1	1	20	.249	47	25	2	127	145	3	.989
1992	—Oakland (A.L.)■	O-DH-3-2-1	61	125	17	25	2	0	3	17	.200	25	23	1	53	19	5	.935
1993	—Rochester (Int'l)■	3-O-1-2	84	305	48	88	17	3	9	46	.289	50	37	4	156	70	6	.974
	—Montreal (N.L.)■	2B-1B-3B	40	134	22	34	8	1	1	10	.254	23	8	2	135	92	8	.966
1994	—Ottawa (Int'l)	2B-1B-SS	39	127	16	26	3	2	2	16	.205	22	14	1	44	77	3	.976
	—Philadelphia (N.L.)■	2B-3B	17	42	5	16	1	0	1	3	.381	8	6	0	18	27	0	1.000
1995	—Philadelphia (N.L.)	1B-2B	23	29	3	4	0	0	0	0	.138	3	6	0	29	2	1	.969
American League totals (5 years)			181	545	75	126	24	8	9	61	.231	68	76	3	215	138	15	.959
National League totals (9 years)			596	1565	237	421	83	13	31	178	.269	258	200	24	703	799	50	.968
Major league totals (13 years)			777	2110	312	547	107	21	40	239	.259	326	276	27	918	937	65	.966

CHAMPIONSHIP SERIES RECORD

Year	Team (League)	Pos.	G	AB	R	H	2B	3B	HR	RBI	Avg.	BB	SO	SB	PO	A	E	Avg.
			BATTING												FIELDING			
1992—	Oakland (A.L.)	PH	1	1	0	0	0	0	0	0	.000	0	1	0	...	...	...	...

REBOULET, JEFF — IF — TWINS

PERSONAL: Born April 30, 1964, in Dayton, O. . . . 6-0/171. . . . Bats right, throws right. . . . Full name: Jeffrey Allen Reboulet. . . . Name pronounced REB-uh-lay.
HIGH SCHOOL: Alter (Kettering, O.).
COLLEGE: Louisiana State.
TRANSACTIONS/CAREER NOTES: Selected by Houston Astros organization in 26th round of free-agent draft (June 3, 1985); did not sign. . . Selected by Minnesota Twins organization in 10th round of free-agent draft (June 2, 1986).
STATISTICAL NOTES: Led Southern League shortstops with 602 total chances in 1988. . . . Led Pacific Coast League with 17 sacrifice hits in 1991. . . . Led Pacific Coast League shortstops with 649 total chances and 99 double plays in 1991.

Year	Team (League)	Pos.	G	AB	R	H	2B	3B	HR	RBI	Avg.	BB	SO	SB	PO	A	E	Avg.
			BATTING												FIELDING			
1986—	Visalia (California)	SS	72	254	54	73	13	1	0	29	.287	54	33	14	118	188	20	.939
1987—	Orlando (Southern)	SS-2B-3B	129	422	52	108	15	1	1	35	.256	58	56	9	220	370	26	.958
1988—	Orlando (Southern)	SS	125	439	57	112	24	2	4	41	.255	53	55	18	*225	347	30	.950
—	Portland (PCL)	2B-SS	4	12	0	1	0	0	0	1	.083	3	2	0	8	13	1	.955
1989—	Portland (PCL)	S-2-3-O	26	65	9	16	1	0	0	3	.246	12	11	2	38	62	7	.935
—	Orlando (Southern)	SS-2B-OF	81	291	43	63	5	1	0	26	.216	49	33	11	129	228	22	.942
1990—	Orlando (Southern)	2-3-S-O-1	97	287	43	66	12	2	2	28	.230	57	37	10	131	230	12	.968
1991—	Portland (PCL)	SS	134	391	50	97	27	3	3	46	.248	57	52	5	*202	415	*32	.951
1992—	Portland (PCL)	SS	48	161	21	46	11	1	2	21	.286	35	18	3	72	141	7	.968
—	Minnesota (A.L.)	S-3-2-O-DH	73	137	15	26	7	1	1	16	.190	23	26	3	71	163	5	.979
1993—	Minnesota (A.L.)	S-3-2-O-DH	109	240	33	62	8	0	1	15	.258	35	37	5	122	215	6	.983
1994—	Minnesota (A.L.)	S-2-1-3-O-DH	74	189	28	49	11	1	3	23	.259	18	23	0	150	131	7	.976
1995—	Minnesota (A.L.)	S-3-1-2-C	87	216	39	63	11	0	4	23	.292	27	34	1	164	160	4	.988
Major league totals (4 years)			343	782	115	200	37	2	9	77	.256	103	120	9	507	669	22	.982

REED, JEFF — C — ROCKIES

PERSONAL: Born November 12, 1962, in Joliet, Ill. . . . 6-2/190. . . . Bats left, throws right. . . . Full name: Jeffrey Scott Reed. . . . Brother of Curtis Reed, minor league outfielder (1977-84).
HIGH SCHOOL: West (Joliet, Ill.).
TRANSACTIONS/CAREER NOTES: Selected by Minnesota Twins organization in first round (12th pick overall) of free-agent draft (June 3, 1980). . . . Traded by Twins organization with P Neal Heaton, P Al Cardwood and P Yorkis Perez to Montreal Expos for P Jeff Reardon and C Tom Nieto (February 3, 1987). . . . On Montreal disabled list (April 20-May 25, 1987); included rehabilitation assignment to Indianapolis (May 19-25). . . . Traded by Expos with OF Herm Winningham and P Randy St. Claire to Cincinnati Reds for OF Tracy Jones and P Pat Pacillo (July 13, 1988). . . . On disabled list (July 1-19, 1991). . . . On Cincinnati disabled list (April 26-September 1, 1992); included rehabilitation assignment to Nashville (August 17-September 1). . . . Granted free agency (October 27, 1992). . . . Signed by San Francisco Giants organization (January 15, 1993). . . . On San Francisco disabled list (June 30-August 3, 1993); included rehabilitation assignment to San Jose (July 21-22 and July 30-August 3). . . . Granted free agency (November 3, 1995). . . . Signed by Colorado Rockies (December 18, 1995).
RECORDS: Holds modern N.L. record for most errors by catcher in one inning—3 (July 28, 1987, seventh inning).
STATISTICAL NOTES: Led California League catchers with 758 total chances and tied for lead with nine double plays in 1982. . . . Led Southern League catchers with 714 total chances and 12 double plays in 1983. . . . Led International League catchers with 720 total chances in 1985. . . . Career major league grand slams: 1.

Year	Team (League)	Pos.	G	AB	R	H	2B	3B	HR	RBI	Avg.	BB	SO	SB	PO	A	E	Avg.
			BATTING												FIELDING			
1980—	Elizabeth. (Appal.)	C	65	225	39	64	15	1	1	20	.284	51	23	2	269	*41	9	.972
1981—	Wis. Rap. (Midw.)	C	106	312	63	73	12	1	4	34	.234	86	36	4	547	*93	7	.989
—	Orlando (Southern)	C	3	4	0	1	0	0	0	0	.250	1	0	0	4	1	0	1.000
1982—	Visalia (California)	C	125	395	69	130	19	2	5	54	.329	78	32	1	*642	•106	10	.987
1983—	Orlando (Southern)	C	118	379	52	100	16	5	6	45	.264	76	40	2	*618	*88	8	*.989
—	Toledo (Int'l)	C	14	41	5	7	1	1	0	3	.171	5	9	0	77	6	1	.988
1984—	Minnesota (A.L.)	C	18	21	3	3	3	0	0	1	.143	2	6	0	41	2	1	.977
—	Toledo (Int'l)	C	94	301	30	80	16	3	3	35	.266	37	35	1	546	43	5	*.992
1985—	Toledo (Int'l)	C	122	404	53	100	15	3	5	36	.248	59	49	1	*627	*81	12	.983
—	Minnesota (A.L.)	C	7	10	2	2	0	0	0	0	.200	0	3	0	9	3	0	1.000
1986—	Minnesota (A.L.)	C	68	165	13	39	6	1	2	9	.236	16	19	1	332	19	2	.994
—	Toledo (Int'l)	C	25	71	10	22	5	3	1	14	.310	17	9	0	108	22	2	.985
1987—	Montreal (N.L.)■	C	75	207	15	44	11	0	1	21	.213	12	20	0	357	36	12	.970
—	Indianapolis (A.A.)	C	5	17	0	3	0	0	0	0	.176	1	2	0	27	2	0	1.000
1988—	Montreal (N.L.)	C	43	123	10	27	3	2	0	9	.220	13	22	1	197	20	1	.995
—	Indianapolis (A.A.)	C	8	22	1	7	3	0	0	1	.318	2	2	0	30	11	0	1.000
—	Cincinnati (N.L.)■	C	49	142	10	33	6	0	1	7	.232	15	19	0	271	18	2	.993
1989—	Cincinnati (N.L.)	C	102	287	16	64	11	0	3	23	.223	34	46	0	504	50	7	.988
1990—	Cincinnati (N.L.)	C	72	175	12	44	8	1	3	16	.251	24	26	0	358	26	5	.987
1991—	Cincinnati (N.L.)	C	91	270	20	72	15	2	3	31	.267	23	38	0	527	29	5	.991
1992—	Nashville (A.A.)	C	14	25	1	6	1	0	1	2	.240	2	7	0	47	4	0	1.000
—	Cincinnati (N.L.)	C	15	25	2	4	0	0	0	2	.160	1	4	0	29	2	0	1.000
1993—	San Fran. (N.L.)■	C	66	119	10	31	3	0	6	12	.261	16	22	0	180	14	0	1.000
—	San Jose (Calif.)	C	4	10	2	5	1	0	0	2	.500	1	0	0	19	2	0	1.000
1994—	San Francisco (N.L.)	C	50	103	11	18	3	0	1	7	.175	11	21	0	138	9	1	.993
1995—	San Francisco (N.L.)	C	66	113	12	30	2	0	0	9	.265	20	17	0	175	21	1	.995
American League totals (3 years)			93	196	18	44	9	1	2	10	.224	18	28	1	382	24	3	.993
National League totals (9 years)			629	1564	118	367	62	5	18	137	.235	169	235	1	2736	225	34	.989
Major league totals (12 years)			722	1760	136	411	71	6	20	147	.234	187	263	2	3118	249	37	.989

R

CHAMPIONSHIP SERIES RECORD

Year	Team (League)	Pos.	G	AB	R	H	2B	3B	HR	RBI	Avg.	BB	SO	SB	PO	A	E	Avg.
				BATTING											FIELDING			
1990—	Cincinnati (N.L.)	C	4	7	0	0	0	0	0	0	.000	2	0	0	24	1	0	1.000

WORLD SERIES RECORD

NOTES: Member of World Series championship team (1990).

Year	Team (League)	Pos.	G	AB	R	H	2B	3B	HR	RBI	Avg.	BB	SO	SB	PO	A	E	Avg.
				BATTING											FIELDING			
1990—	Cincinnati (N.L.)								Did not play.									

REED, JODY — 2B — PADRES

PERSONAL: Born July 26, 1962, in Tampa, Fla. . . . 5-9/165. . . . Bats right, throws right. . . . Full name: Jody Eric Reed.
HIGH SCHOOL: Brandon (Fla.).
JUNIR COLLEGE: Manatee Junior College (Fla.).
COLLEGE: Florida State (degree in criminology, 1985).
TRANSACTIONS/CAREER NOTES: Selected by Texas Rangers organization in third round of free-agent draft (January 12, 1982); did not sign. . . . Selected by San Francisco Giants organization in secondary phase of free-agent draft (June 7, 1982); did not sign. . . . Selected by Rangers organization in secondary phase of free-agent draft (June 6, 1983); did not sign. . . . Selected by Boston Red Sox organization in eighth round of free-agent draft (June 4, 1984). . . . Selected by Colorado Rockies in first round (13th pick overall) of expansion draft (November 17, 1992). . . . Traded by Rockies to Los Angeles Dodgers for P Rudy Seanez (November 17, 1992). . . . On disabled list (June 16-July 15, 1993). . . . Granted free agency (October 25, 1993). . . . Signed by Milwaukee Brewers organization (February 3, 1994). . . . Granted free agency (October 18, 1994). . . . Signed by San Diego Padres (April 19, 1995). . . . Granted free agency (November 11, 1995). . . . Re-signed by Padres (December 19, 1995).
RECORDS: Shares major league record for most doubles in one inning—2 (September 8, 1991, third inning). . . . Shares modern major league record for most long hits in one inning—2 (September 8, 1991, third inning).
STATISTICAL NOTES: Led Florida State League shortstops with 101 double plays in 1985. . . . Led International League shortstops with 683 total chances and 86 double plays in 1987. . . . Led A.L. second basemen with 587 total chances and 72 double plays in 1994.

Year	Team (League)	Pos.	G	AB	R	H	2B	3B	HR	RBI	Avg.	BB	SO	SB	PO	A	E	Avg.
				BATTING											FIELDING			
1984—	Winter Haven (FSL)	SS	77	273	46	74	14	1	0	20	.271	52	19	9	128	271	26	.939
1985—	Winter Haven (FSL)	SS	134	489	*95	157	25	1	0	45	*.321	*94	26	16	*256	*478	37	*.952
1986—	New Britain (East.)	SS	60	218	33	50	12	1	0	11	.229	52	9	10	114	190	14	.956
—	Pawtucket (Int'l)	SS	69	227	27	64	11	0	1	30	.282	31	18	8	115	222	12	.966
1987—	Pawtucket (Int'l)	SS	136	510	77	151	22	2	7	51	.296	69	23	9	*236	*427	20	.971
—	Boston (A.L.)	SS-2B-3B	9	30	4	9	1	1	0	8	.300	4	0	1	11	26	0	1.000
1988—	Boston (A.L.)	S-2-3-DH	109	338	60	99	23	1	1	28	.293	45	21	1	147	282	11	.975
1989—	Boston (A.L.)	S-2-3-O-DH	146	524	76	151	42	2	3	40	.288	73	44	4	255	423	19	.973
1990—	Boston (A.L.)	2B-SS-DH	155	598	70	173	•45	0	5	51	.289	75	65	4	278	478	16	.979
1991—	Boston (A.L.)	2B	153	618	87	175	42	2	5	60	.283	60	53	6	312	444	14	.982
1992—	Boston (A.L.)	2B-DH	143	550	64	136	27	1	3	40	.247	62	44	7	304	472	14	.982
1993—	Los Angeles (N.L.)■	2B	132	445	48	123	21	2	2	31	.276	38	40	1	280	413	5	*.993
1994—	Milwaukee (A.L.)■	2B	108	399	48	108	22	0	2	37	.271	57	34	5	*231	*353	3	*.995
1995—	San Diego (N.L.)■	2B-SS	131	445	58	114	18	1	4	40	.256	59	38	6	304	366	4	.994
American League totals (7 years)			823	3057	409	851	202	7	19	264	.278	376	261	28	1538	2478	77	.981
National League totals (2 years)			263	890	106	237	39	3	6	71	.266	97	78	7	584	779	9	.993
Major league totals (9 years)			1086	3947	515	1088	241	10	25	335	.276	473	339	35	2122	3257	86	.984

CHAMPIONSHIP SERIES RECORD

Year	Team (League)	Pos.	G	AB	R	H	2B	3B	HR	RBI	Avg.	BB	SO	SB	PO	A	E	Avg.
				BATTING											FIELDING			
1988—	Boston (A.L.)	SS	4	11	0	3	1	0	0	0	.273	2	1	0	3	10	0	1.000
1990—	Boston (A.L.)	2B-SS	4	15	0	2	0	0	0	1	.133	0	2	0	11	11	0	1.000
Championship series totals (2 years)			8	26	0	5	1	0	0	1	.192	2	3	0	14	21	0	1.000

REED, RICK — P — METS

PERSONAL: Born August 16, 1964, in Huntington, W.Va. . . . 6-0/200. . . . Throws right, bats right. . . . Full name: Richard Allen Reed.
HIGH SCHOOL: Huntington (W.Va.).
COLLEGE: Marshall.
TRANSACTIONS/CAREER NOTES: Selected by Pittsburgh Pirates organization in 26th round of free-agent draft (June 2, 1986). . . . On Buffalo disabled list (May 2-13, 1991). . . . Granted free agency (April 3, 1992). . . . Signed by Omaha, Kansas City Royals organization (April 4, 1992). . . . Granted free agency (August 5, 1993). . . . Signed by Oklahoma City, Texas Rangers organization (August 11, 1993). . . . Claimed on waivers by Cincinnati Reds (May 13, 1994). . . . On Indianapolis disabled list (May 29-June 9, 1995). . . . Granted free agency (October 16, 1995). . . . Signed by New York Mets organization (November 7, 1995).
HONORS: Named American Association Most Valuable Pitcher (1991).

Year	Team (League)	W	L	Pct.	ERA	G	GS	CG	ShO	Sv.	IP	H	R	ER	BB	SO
1986—	GC Pirates (GCL)	0	2	.000	3.75	8	3	0	0	0	24	20	12	10	6	15
—	Macon (S. Atl.)	0	0	. . .	2.84	1	1	0	0	0	6 1/3	5	3	2	2	1
1987—	Macon (S. Atl.)	8	4	.667	2.50	46	0	0	0	7	93 2/3	80	38	26	29	92
1988—	Salem (Carolina)	6	2	.750	2.74	15	8	4	1	0	72 1/3	56	28	22	17	73
—	Harrisburg (East.)	1	0	1.000	1.13	2	2	0	0	0	16	11	2	2	2	17
—	Buffalo (A.A.)	5	2	.714	1.64	10	9	3	2	0	77	62	15	14	12	50
—	Pittsburgh (N.L.)	1	0	1.000	3.00	2	2	0	0	0	12	10	4	4	2	6
1989—	Buffalo (A.A.)	9	8	.529	3.72	20	20	3	0	0	125 2/3	130	58	52	28	75
—	Pittsburgh (N.L.)	1	4	.200	5.60	15	7	0	0	0	54 2/3	62	35	34	11	34
1990—	Buffalo (A.A.)	7	4	.636	3.46	15	15	2	2	0	91	82	37	35	21	63
—	Pittsburgh (N.L.)	2	3	.400	4.36	13	8	1	1	1	53 2/3	62	32	26	12	27
1991—	Buffalo (A.A.)	*14	4	*.778	*2.15	25	25	•5	2	0	167 2/3	151	45	40	26	102

Year	Team (League)	W	L	Pct.	ERA	G	GS	CG	ShO	Sv.	IP	H	R	ER	BB	SO
	—Pittsburgh (N.L.)	0	0	...	10.38	1	1	0	0	0	4 1/3	8	6	5	1	2
1992	—Omaha (Am. Assoc.)■	5	4	.556	4.35	11	10	3	0	1	62	67	33	30	12	35
	—Kansas City (A.L.)	3	7	.300	3.68	19	18	1	1	0	100 1/3	105	47	41	20	49
1993	—Omaha (Am. Assoc.)	11	4	.733	3.09	19	19	3	*2	0	128 1/3	116	48	44	14	58
	—Kansas City (A.L.)	0	0	...	9.82	1	0	0	0	0	3 2/3	6	4	4	1	3
	—Okla. City (A.A.)■	1	3	.250	4.19	5	5	1	0	0	34 1/3	43	20	16	2	21
	—Texas (A.L.)	1	0	1.000	2.25	2	0	0	0	0	4	6	1	1	1	2
1994	—Okla. City (A.A.)	1	1	.500	3.86	2	2	0	0	0	11 2/3	10	5	5	0	8
	—Texas (A.L.)	1	1	.500	5.94	4	3	0	0	0	16 2/3	17	13	11	7	12
	—Indianapolis (A.A.)■	9	5	.643	4.68	21	21	3	1	0	140 1/3	162	80	73	19	79
1995	—Indianapolis (A.A.)	11	4	.733	3.33	22	21	3	1	0	135	127	60	50	26	92
	—Cincinnati (N.L.)	0	0	...	5.82	4	3	0	0	0	17	18	12	11	3	10
A.L. totals (3 years)		5	8	.385	4.11	26	21	1	1	0	124 2/3	134	65	57	29	66
N.L. totals (5 years)		4	7	.364	5.08	35	21	1	1	1	141 2/3	160	89	80	29	79
Major league totals (8 years)		9	15	.375	4.63	61	42	2	2	1	266 1/3	294	154	137	58	145

REED, STEVE — P — ROCKIES

PERSONAL: Born March 11, 1966, in Los Angeles. . . . 6-2/212. . . . Throws right, bats right. . . . Full name: Steven Vincent Reed.
HIGH SCHOOL: Chatsworth (Calif.).
COLLEGE: Lewis-Clark State College (Idaho).
TRANSACTIONS/CAREER NOTES: Signed as non-drafted free agent by San Francisco Giants organization (June 24, 1988). . . . On disabled list (July 17-August 13, 1990). . . . Selected by Colorado Rockies in third round (60th pick overall) of expansion draft (November 17, 1992).

Year	Team (League)	W	L	Pct.	ERA	G	GS	CG	ShO	Sv.	IP	H	R	ER	BB	SO
1988	—Pocatello (Pioneer)	4	1	.800	2.54	31	0	0	0	*13	46	42	20	13	8	49
1989	—Clinton (Midwest)	5	3	.625	1.05	60	0	0	0	26	94 2/3	54	16	11	38	104
	—San Jose (Calif.)	0	0	...	0.00	2	0	0	0	0	2	0	0	0	1	3
1990	—Shreveport (Texas)	3	1	.750	1.64	45	1	0	0	8	60 1/3	53	20	11	20	59
1991	—Shreveport (Texas)	2	0	1.000	0.83	15	0	0	0	7	21 2/3	17	2	2	3	26
	—Phoenix (PCL)	2	3	.400	4.31	41	0	0	0	6	56 1/3	62	33	27	12	46
1992	—Shreveport (Texas)	1	0	1.000	0.62	27	0	0	0	23	29	18	3	2	0	33
	—Phoenix (PCL)	0	1	.000	3.48	29	0	0	0	20	31	27	13	12	10	30
	—San Francisco (N.L.)	1	0	1.000	2.30	18	0	0	0	0	15 2/3	13	5	4	3	11
1993	—Colorado (N.L.)■	9	5	.643	4.48	64	0	0	0	3	84 1/3	80	47	42	30	51
	—Colo. Springs (PCL)	0	0	...	0.00	11	0	0	0	7	12 1/3	8	1	0	3	10
1994	—Colorado (N.L.)	3	2	.600	3.94	*61	0	0	0	3	64	79	33	28	26	51
1995	—Colorado (N.L.)	5	2	.714	2.14	71	0	0	0	3	84	61	24	20	21	79
Major league totals (4 years)		18	9	.667	3.41	214	0	0	0	9	248	233	109	94	80	192

DIVISION SERIES RECORD

Year	Team (League)	W	L	Pct.	ERA	G	GS	CG	ShO	Sv.	IP	H	R	ER	BB	SO
1995	—Colorado (N.L.)	0	0	...	0.00	3	0	0	0	0	2 2/3	2	0	0	1	3

REESE, POKEY — SS — REDS

PERSONAL: Born June 10, 1973, in Columbia, S.C. . . . 5-11/180. . . . Bats right, throws right. . . . Full name: Calvin Reese.
HIGH SCHOOL: Lower Richland (Hopkins, S.C.).
TRANSACTIONS/CAREER NOTES: Selected by Cincinnati Reds organization in first round (20th pick overall) of free-agent draft (June 3, 1991). . . . On disabled list (June 23-July 22, 1995).

				BATTING										FIELDING			
Year	Team (League)	Pos.	G	AB	R	H	2B	3B	HR	RBI	Avg.	BB	SO	SB	PO	A	E	Avg.
1991	—Princeton (Appal.)	SS	62	231	30	55	8	3	3	27	.238	23	44	10	93	146	*31	.885
1992	—Char., W.Va. (SAL)	SS	106	380	50	102	19	3	6	53	.268	24	75	19	181	287	34	.932
1993	—Chatt. (South.)	SS	102	345	35	73	17	4	3	37	.212	23	77	8	181	300	25	.951
1994	—Chatt. (South.)	SS	134	484	77	130	23	4	12	49	.269	43	75	21	*221	362	38	.939
1995	—Indianapolis (A.A.)	SS	89	343	51	82	21	1	10	46	.239	36	81	8	131	258	27	.935

REKAR, BRYAN — P — ROCKIES

PERSONAL: Born June 3, 1972, in Oak Lawn, Ill. . . . 6-3/210. . . . Throws right, bats right.
HIGH SCHOOL: Providence Catholic (New Lenox, Ill.).
COLLEGE: Bradley.
TRANSACTIONS/CAREER NOTES: Selected by Colorado Rockies organization in second round of free-agent draft (June 3, 1993).

Year	Team (League)	W	L	Pct.	ERA	G	GS	CG	ShO	Sv.	IP	H	R	ER	BB	SO
1993	—Bend (Northwest)	3	5	.375	4.08	13	13	1	0	0	75	81	36	34	18	59
1994	—Central Valley (Cal.)	6	6	.500	3.48	22	19	0	0	0	111 1/3	120	52	43	31	91
1995	—New Haven (East.)	6	3	.667	2.13	12	12	1	1	0	80 1/3	65	28	19	16	80
	—Colo. Springs (PCL)	4	2	.667	1.49	7	7	2	1	0	48 1/3	29	10	8	13	39
	—Colorado (N.L.)	4	6	.400	4.98	15	14	1	0	0	85	95	51	47	24	60
Major league totals (1 year)		4	6	.400	4.98	15	14	1	0	0	85	95	51	47	24	60

RELAFORD, DESI — SS — MARINERS

PERSONAL: Born September 16, 1973, in Valdosta, Ga. . . . 5-8/155. . . . Bats both, throws right. . . . Full name: Desmond Lamont Relaford.
HIGH SCHOOL: Sandalwood (Jacksonville, Fla.).

TRANSACTIONS/CAREER NOTES: Selected by Seattle Mariners organization in fourth round of free-agent draft (June 3, 1991).
STATISTICAL NOTES: Led California League shortstops with 601 total chances in 1992. . . . Led Southern League shortstops with 35 errors in 1993.

					BATTING									FIELDING			
Year	Team (League)	Pos.	G	AB	R	H	2B	3B	HR	RBI	Avg.	BB	SO	SB	PO	A	E	Avg.
1991—	Ariz. Mariners (Ariz.)	SS-2B	46	163	36	44	7	3	0	18	.270	22	24	17	58	126	24	.885
1992—	Peninsula (Caro.)	SS	130	445	53	96	18	1	3	34	.216	39	88	27	167	*382	*52	.913
1993—	Jacksonv. (South.)	SS-2B-3B	133	472	49	115	16	4	8	47	.244	50	103	16	157	386	†38	.935
1994—	Jacksonv. (South.)	SS	37	143	24	29	7	3	3	11	.203	22	28	10	71	119	4	.979
	—Riverside (Calif.)	SS	99	374	95	116	27	5	5	59	.310	78	78	27	125	296	36	.921
1995—	Port City (Southern)	SS-2B	90	352	51	101	11	2	7	27	.287	41	58	25	134	276	31	.930
	—Tacoma (PCL)	2B-SS	30	113	20	27	5	1	2	7	.239	13	24	6	52	93	6	.960

REMLINGER, MIKE — P — ROYALS

PERSONAL: Born March 26, 1966, in Middletown, N.Y. . . . 6-0/195. . . . Throws left, bats left. . . . Full name: Michael John Remlinger. . . . Name pronounced REM-lynn-jer.
HIGH SCHOOL: Carver (Plymouth, Mass.).
COLLEGE: Dartmouth.
TRANSACTIONS/CAREER NOTES: Selected by San Francisco Giants organization in first round (16th pick overall) of free-agent draft (June 2, 1987). . . . On disabled list (April 30, 1988-remainder of season). . . . Traded by Giants with OF Kevin Mitchell to Seattle Mariners for P Bill Swift, P Mike Jackson and P Dave Burba (December 11, 1991). . . . On Jacksonville disabled list (July 30, 1992-remainder of season). . . . Granted free agency (October 15, 1993). . . . Signed by New York Mets organization (November 22, 1993). . . . Traded by Mets to Cincinnati Reds for OF Cobi Cradle (May 11, 1995). . . . Granted free agency (October 6, 1995). . . . Traded by Reds to Kansas City Royals as part of a three-team deal in which Reds sent SS Luis Ordaz to St. Louis Cardinals for OF Andre King. Royals then sent OF Miguel Mejia to Cardinals to complete deal (December 4, 1995).
RECORDS: Shares major league record for pitching shutout in first major league game (June 15, 1991).

Year	Team (League)	W	L	Pct.	ERA	G	GS	CG	ShO	Sv.	IP	H	R	ER	BB	SO
1987—	Everett (N'west)	0	0	. . .	3.60	2	1	0	0	0	5	1	2	2	5	11
	—Clinton (Midwest)	2	1	.667	3.30	6	5	0	0	0	30	21	12	11	14	43
	—Shreveport (Texas)	4	2	.667	2.36	6	6	0	0	0	34 1/3	14	11	9	22	51
1988—	Shreveport (Texas)	1	0	1.000	0.69	3	3	0	0	0	13	7	4	1	4	18
1989—	Shreveport (Texas)	4	6	.400	2.98	16	16	0	0	0	90 2/3	68	43	30	73	92
	—Phoenix (PCL)	1	6	.143	9.21	11	10	0	0	0	43	51	47	44	52	28
1990—	Shreveport (Texas)	9	11	.450	3.90	25	25	2	1	0	147 2/3	149	82	64	72	75
1991—	Phoenix (PCL)	5	5	.500	6.38	19	19	1	1	0	108 2/3	134	86	77	59	68
	—San Francisco (N.L.)	2	1	.667	4.37	8	6	1	1	0	35	36	17	17	20	19
1992—	Calgary (PCL)■	1	7	.125	6.65	21	11	0	0	0	70 1/3	97	65	52	48	24
	—Jacksonville (Sou.)	1	1	.500	3.46	5	5	0	0	0	26	25	15	10	11	21
1993—	Calgary (PCL)	4	3	.571	5.53	19	18	0	0	0	84 2/3	100	57	52	52	51
	—Jacksonville (Sou.)	1	3	.250	6.58	7	7	0	0	0	39 2/3	40	30	29	19	23
1994—	Norfolk (Int'l)■	2	4	.333	3.14	12	9	0	0	0	63	57	29	22	25	45
	—New York (N.L.)	1	5	.167	4.61	10	9	0	0	0	54 2/3	55	30	28	35	33
1995—	New York (N.L.)	0	1	.000	6.35	5	0	0	0	0	5 2/3	7	5	4	2	6
	—Cincinnati (N.L.)■	0	0	. . .	9.00	2	0	0	0	0	1	2	1	1	3	1
	—Indianapolis (A.A.)	5	3	.625	4.05	41	1	0	0	0	46 2/3	40	24	21	32	58
Major league totals (3 years)		3	7	.300	4.67	25	15	1	1	0	96 1/3	100	53	50	60	59

RENTERIA, EDGAR — SS — MARLINS

PERSONAL: Born August 7, 1975, in Barranquilla, Colombia. . . . 6-1/172. . . . Bats right, throws right. . . . Full name: Edgar E. Renteria.
HIGH SCHOOL: Instituto Los Alpes (Barranquilla, Colombia).
TRANSACTIONS/CAREER NOTES: Signed as non-drafted free agent by Florida Marlins organization (February 14, 1992).

					BATTING									FIELDING			
Year	Team (League)	Pos.	G	AB	R	H	2B	3B	HR	RBI	Avg.	BB	SO	SB	PO	A	E	Avg.
1992—	GC Marlins (GCL)	SS	43	163	25	47	8	1	0	9	.288	8	29	10	56	152	*24	.897
1993—	Kane Co. (Midw.)	SS	116	384	40	78	8	0	1	35	.203	35	94	7	•173	306	34	.934
1994—	Brevard County (FSL)	SS	128	439	46	111	15	1	0	36	.253	35	56	6	167	372	23	.959
1995—	Portland (Eastern)	SS	135	508	70	147	15	7	7	68	.289	32	85	30	179	379	33	.944

REYES, AL — P — BREWERS

PERSONAL: Born April 10, 1971, in San Cristobal, Dominican Republic. . . . 6-1/193. . . . Throws right, bats right. . . . Full name: Rafael Alberto Reyes.
TRANSACTIONS/CAREER NOTES: Signed as non-drafted free agent by Montreal Expos organization (February 17, 1988). . . . On disabled list (May 23, 1991-remainder of season). . . . Selected by Milwaukee Brewers from Expos organization in Rule 5 major league draft (December 5, 1994). . . . On disabled list (July 19, 1995-remainder of season).

Year	Team (League)	W	L	Pct.	ERA	G	GS	CG	ShO	Sv.	IP	H	R	ER	BB	SO
1989—	DSL Expos (DSL)	3	4	.429	2.79	12	10	1	0	0	71	68	36	22	33	49
1990—	WP Beach (FSL)	5	4	.556	4.74	16	10	0	0	1	57	58	32	30	32	47
1991—	Rockford (Midw.)	0	1	.000	5.56	3	3	0	0	0	11 1/3	14	8	7	2	10
1992—	Albany (S. Atl.)	0	2	.000	3.95	27	0	0	0	4	27 1/3	24	14	12	13	29
1993—	Burlington (Midw.)	7	6	.538	2.68	53	0	0	0	11	74	52	33	22	26	80
1994—	Harrisburg (East.)	2	2	.500	3.25	60	0	0	0	*35	69 1/3	68	26	25	13	60
1995—	Milwaukee (A.L.)■	1	1	.500	2.43	27	0	0	0	1	33 1/3	19	9	9	18	29
Major league totals (1 year)		1	1	.500	2.43	27	0	0	0	1	33 1/3	19	9	9	18	29

REYES, CARLOS — P — ATHLETICS

PERSONAL: Born April 4, 1969, in Miami. . . . 6-1/190. . . . Throws right, bats both. . . . Full name: Carlos Alberto Reyes Jr.
HIGH SCHOOL: Tampa (Fla.) Catholic.
JUNIOR COLLEGE: Brevard Community College (Fla.).
COLLEGE: Florida Southern.
TRANSACTIONS/CAREER NOTES: Signed as non-drafted free agent by Atlanta Braves organization (June 21, 1991). . . . Selected by Oakland Athletics from Braves organization in Rule 5 major league draft (December 13, 1993). . . . On Oakland disabled list (July 18-August 4, 1994); included rehabilitation assignment to Modesto (July 25-30).

Year	Team (League)	W	L	Pct.	ERA	G	GS	CG	ShO	Sv.	IP	H	R	ER	BB	SO
1991—	GC Braves (GCL)	3	2	.600	1.77	20	0	0	0	5	45 2/3	44	15	9	9	37
1992—	Macon (S. Atl.)	2	3	.400	2.10	23	0	0	0	2	60	57	16	14	11	57
—	Durham (Carolina)	2	1	.667	2.43	21	0	0	0	5	40 2/3	31	11	11	10	33
1993—	Greenville (South.)	8	1	.889	2.06	33	2	0	0	2	70	64	22	16	24	57
—	Richmond (Int'l)	1	0	1.000	3.77	18	1	0	0	1	28 2/3	30	12	12	11	30
1994—	Oakland (A.L.)■	0	3	.000	4.15	27	9	0	0	1	78	71	38	36	44	57
—	Modesto (Calif.)	0	0	. . .	0.00	3	3	0	0	0	5	2	0	0	0	3
1995—	Oakland (A.L.)	4	6	.400	5.09	40	1	0	0	0	69	71	43	39	28	48
Major league totals (2 years)		4	9	.308	4.59	67	10	0	0	1	147	142	81	75	72	105

REYNOLDS, SHANE — P — ASTROS

PERSONAL: Born March 26, 1968, in Bastrop, La. . . . 6-3/210. . . . Throws right, bats right. . . . Full name: Richard Shane Reynolds.
HIGH SCHOOL: Ouachita Christian (Monroe, La.).
JUNIOR COLLEGE: Faulkner State Junior College (Ala.).
COLLEGE: Texas.
TRANSACTIONS/CAREER NOTES: Selected by Houston Astros organization in third round of free-agent draft (June 5, 1989).
MISCELLANEOUS: Appeared in one game as pinch-runner (1995).

Year	Team (League)	W	L	Pct.	ERA	G	GS	CG	ShO	Sv.	IP	H	R	ER	BB	SO
1989—	Auburn (NYP)	3	2	.600	2.31	6	6	1	0	0	35	36	16	9	14	23
—	Asheville (S. Atl.)	5	3	.625	3.68	8	8	2	1	0	51 1/3	53	25	21	21	33
1990—	Chatt. (South.)	9	10	.474	4.81	29	27	2	1	0	155 1/3	•181	104	83	70	92
1991—	Jackson (Texas)	8	9	.471	4.47	27	•27	2	0	0	151	165	93	75	62	116
1992—	Tucson (Pac. Coast)	9	8	.529	3.68	25	22	2	0	1	142	156	73	58	34	106
—	Houston (N.L.)	1	3	.250	7.11	8	5	0	0	0	25 1/3	42	22	20	6	10
1993—	Tucson (Pac. Coast)	10	6	.625	3.62	25	20	2	0	1	139 1/3	147	74	56	21	106
—	Houston (N.L.)	0	0	. . .	0.82	5	1	0	0	0	11	11	4	1	6	10
1994—	Houston (N.L.)	8	5	.615	3.05	33	14	1	1	0	124	128	46	42	21	110
1995—	Houston (N.L.)	10	11	.476	3.47	30	30	3	2	0	189 1/3	196	87	73	37	175
Major league totals (4 years)		19	19	.500	3.50	76	50	4	3	0	349 2/3	377	159	136	70	305

REYNOSO, ARMANDO — P — ROCKIES

PERSONAL: Born May 1, 1966, in San Luis Potosi, Mexico. . . . 6-0/204. . . . Throws right, bats right. . . . Full name: Martia Armando Gutierrez Reynoso. . . . Name pronounced ray-NO-so.
HIGH SCHOOL: Escuela Secandaria Mita del Estado (Jalisco, Mexico).
TRANSACTIONS/CAREER NOTES: Signed as free agent by Saltillo of Mexican League. . . . Contract sold by Saltillo to Atlanta Braves organization (August 15, 1990). . . . Selected by Colorado Rockies in third round (58th pick overall) of expansion draft (November 17, 1992). . . . On disabled list (May 21, 1994-remainder of season). . . . On Colorado disabled list (April 17-June 18, 1995); included rehabilitation assignments to Colorado Springs (May 9-20 and June 8-14).
STATISTICAL NOTES: Led International League with six balks in 1991 and five in 1992. . . . Tied for International League lead with 10 hit batsmen in 1991.
MISCELLANEOUS: Appeared in one game as pinch-runner with Colorado (1993).

Year	Team (League)	W	L	Pct.	ERA	G	GS	CG	ShO	Sv.	IP	H	R	ER	BB	SO
1988—	Saltillo (Mexican)	11	11	.500	4.30	32	29	10	2	2	180	176	98	86	85	92
1989—	Saltillo (Mexican)	13	9	.591	3.48	27	25	7	2	0	160 1/3	155	78	62	64	107
1990—	Saltillo (Mexican)	*20	3	.870	2.60	27	•27	12	5	0	200 2/3	174	61	58	73	*170
—	Richmond (Int'l)■	3	1	.750	2.25	4	3	0	0	0	24	26	7	6	7	15
1991—	Richmond (Int'l)	10	6	.625	*2.61	22	19	3	•3	0	131	117	44	38	39	97
—	Atlanta (N.L.)	2	1	.667	6.17	6	5	0	0	0	23 1/3	26	18	16	10	10
1992—	Richmond (Int'l)	12	9	.571	2.66	28	27	4	1	0	169 1/3	156	65	50	52	108
—	Atlanta (N.L.)	1	0	1.000	4.70	3	1	0	0	1	7 2/3	11	4	4	2	2
1993—	Colo. Springs (PCL)■	2	1	.667	3.22	4	4	0	0	0	22 1/3	19	10	8	8	22
—	Colorado (N.L.)	12	11	.522	4.00	30	30	4	0	0	189	206	101	84	63	117
1994—	Colorado (N.L.)	3	4	.429	4.82	9	9	1	0	0	52 1/3	54	30	28	22	25
1995—	Colo. Springs (PCL)	2	1	.667	1.57	5	5	0	0	0	23	14	4	4	6	17
—	Colorado (N.L.)	7	7	.500	5.32	20	18	0	0	0	93	116	61	55	36	40
Major league totals (5 years)		25	23	.521	4.61	68	63	5	0	1	365 1/3	413	214	187	133	194

DIVISION SERIES RECORD

Year	Team (League)	W	L	Pct.	ERA	G	GS	CG	ShO	Sv.	IP	H	R	ER	BB	SO
1995—	Colorado (N.L.)	0	0	. . .	0.00	1	0	0	0	0	1	2	0	0	0	0

RHODES, ARTHUR — P — ORIOLES

PERSONAL: Born October 24, 1969, in Waco, Tex. . . . 6-2/206. . . . Throws left, bats left. . . . Full name: Arthur Lee Rhodes Jr. . . . Brother of Ricky Rhodes, minor league pitcher, New York Yankees organization (1988-92).

HIGH SCHOOL: LaVega (Waco, Tex.).

TRANSACTIONS/CAREER NOTES: Selected by Baltimore Orioles organization in second round of free-agent draft (June 1, 1988).... On Hagerstown disabled list (May 13-June 5, 1991).... On Baltimore disabled list (May 16-August 2, 1993); included rehabilitation assignment to Rochester (July 4-August 2).... On Baltimore disabled list (May 2-20, 1994); included rehabilitation assignment to Frederick (May 16-20).... On Baltimore disabled list (August 25, 1995-remainder of season).

HONORS: Named Eastern League Pitcher of the Year (1991).

Year	Team (League)	W	L	Pct.	ERA	G	GS	CG	ShO	Sv.	IP	H	R	ER	BB	SO
1988—	Bluefield (Appal.)	3	4	.429	3.31	11	7	0	0	0	35 1/3	29	17	13	15	44
1989—	Erie (NYP)	2	0	1.000	1.16	5	5	1	0	0	31	13	7	4	10	45
	—Frederick (Caro.)	2	2	.500	5.18	7	6	0	0	0	24 1/3	19	16	14	19	28
1990—	Frederick (Caro.)	4	6	.400	2.12	13	13	3	0	0	80 2/3	62	25	19	21	103
	—Hagerstown (East.)	3	4	.429	3.73	12	12	0	0	0	72 1/3	62	32	30	39	60
1991—	Hagerstown (East.)	7	4	.636	2.70	19	19	2	2	0	106 2/3	73	37	32	47	115
	—Baltimore (A.L.)	0	3	.000	8.00	8	8	0	0	0	36	47	35	32	23	23
1992—	Rochester (Int'l)	6	6	.500	3.72	17	17	1	0	0	101 2/3	84	48	42	46	115
	—Baltimore (A.L.)	7	5	.583	3.63	15	15	2	1	0	94 1/3	87	39	38	38	77
1993—	Baltimore (A.L.)	5	6	.455	6.51	17	17	0	0	0	85 2/3	91	62	62	49	49
	—Rochester (Int'l)	1	1	.500	4.05	6	6	0	0	0	26 2/3	26	12	12	15	33
1994—	Baltimore (A.L.)	3	5	.375	5.81	10	10	3	2	0	52 2/3	51	34	34	30	47
	—Frederick (Caro.)	0	0	...	0.00	1	1	0	0	0	5	3	0	0	0	7
	—Rochester (Int'l)	7	5	.583	2.79	15	15	3	0	0	90 1/3	70	41	28	34	86
1995—	Rochester (Int'l)	2	1	.667	2.70	4	4	1	0	0	30	27	12	9	8	33
	—Baltimore (A.L.)	2	5	.286	6.21	19	9	0	0	0	75 1/3	68	53	52	48	77
Major league totals (5 years)		17	24	.415	5.70	69	59	5	3	0	344	344	223	218	188	273

RHODES, TUFFY — OF

PERSONAL: Born August 21, 1968, in Cincinnati.... 6-0/195.... Bats left, throws left.... Full name: Karl Derrick Rhodes.

HIGH SCHOOL: Western Hills (Cincinnati).

TRANSACTIONS/CAREER NOTES: Selected by Houston Astros organization in third round of free-agent draft (June 2, 1986).... On Tucson disabled list (May 28-July 1, 1992).... Granted free agency (April 23, 1993).... Signed by Omaha, Kansas City Royals organization (April 27, 1993).... Traded by Royals to Chicago Cubs as part of a three-way deal in which Cubs sent P Paul Assenmacher to New York Yankees and Yankees sent P John Habyan to Royals (July 30, 1993).... Claimed on waivers by Boston Red Sox (May 26, 1995).... Granted free agency (October 16, 1995).

STATISTICAL NOTES: Tied for Southern League lead in double plays by outfielder with five in 1989.... Led American Association with 295 total bases, 112 runs, 43 doubles and .602 slugging percentage in 1993.... Hit three home runs in one game (April 4, 1994).

				BATTING										FIELDING			
Year	Team (League)	Pos.	G	AB	R	H	2B	3B	HR	RBI	Avg.	BB	SO	SB	PO	A	E	Avg.
1986—	GC Astros (GCL)	OF	*62	222	36	65	10	3	0	22	.293	32	33	14	113	6	0	*1.000
1987—	Asheville (S. Atl.)	OF	129	413	62	104	16	4	3	50	.252	77	82	43	163	14	9	.952
1988—	Osceola (Fla. St.)	OF-2B	132	452	69	128	4	2	1	34	.283	81	53	64	232	14	2	.992
1989—	Columbus (South.)	OF	•143	520	81	134	25	5	4	63	.258	93	105	18	262	15	11	.962
1990—	Tucson (PCL)	OF	107	385	68	106	24	11	3	59	.275	47	75	24	214	*20	8	.967
	—Houston (N.L.)	OF	39	86	12	21	6	1	1	3	.244	13	12	4	61	2	3	.955
1991—	Houston (N.L.)	OF	44	136	7	29	3	1	1	12	.213	14	26	2	87	4	4	.958
	—Tucson (PCL)	OF	84	308	45	80	17	1	1	46	.260	38	47	5	140	11	9	.944
1992—	Tucson (PCL)	OF	94	332	62	96	16	10	2	54	.289	55	63	8	210	13	6	.974
	—Houston (N.L.)	OF	5	4	0	0	0	0	0	0	.000	0	2	0	0	0	0	...
1993—	Houston (N.L.)	OF	5	2	0	0	0	0	0	0	.000	0	0	0	2	0	0	1.000
	—Omaha (A.A.)■	OF	88	365	81	116	31	2	23	64	.318	38	60	10	135	13	6	.961
	—Iowa (A.A.)■	OF	35	125	§31	40	§12	1	7	25	.320	20	22	6	57	4	2	.968
	—Chicago (N.L.)	OF	15	52	12	15	2	1	3	7	.288	11	9	2	31	1	1	.970
1994—	Chicago (N.L.)	OF	95	269	39	63	17	0	8	19	.234	33	64	6	142	4	5	.967
1995—	Chicago (N.L.)	OF	13	16	2	2	0	0	0	2	.125	0	4	0	8	0	1	.889
	—Boston (A.L.)■	OF	10	25	2	2	1	0	0	1	.080	3	4	0	18	0	1	.947
	—Pawtucket (Int'l)	OF	69	246	40	70	13	3	10	43	.285	34	46	8	172	6	6	.967
American League totals (1 year)			10	25	2	2	1	0	0	1	.080	3	4	0	18	0	1	.947
National League totals (6 years)			216	565	72	130	28	3	13	43	.230	71	117	14	331	11	14	.961
Major league totals (6 years)			226	590	74	132	29	3	13	44	.224	74	121	14	349	11	15	.960

RICCI, CHUCK — P — RED SOX

PERSONAL: Born November 20, 1968, in Abington, Pa.... 6-2/180.... Throws right, bats right.... Full name: Charles Mark Ricci.... Name pronounced RICH-ee.

HIGH SCHOOL: Shawnee (Medford, N.J.).

TRANSACTIONS/CAREER NOTES: Selected by Baltimore Orioles organization in fourth round of free-agent draft (June 2, 1987).... On Hagerstown disabled list (July 15-September 14, 1992).... Granted free agency (October 15, 1993).... Signed by Philadelphia Phillies organization (April 7, 1994).... Granted free agency (October 16, 1995).... Signed by Boston Red Sox organization (December 26, 1995).

STATISTICAL NOTES: Led Appalachian League with 11 home runs allowed in 1987.

Year	Team (League)	W	L	Pct.	ERA	G	GS	CG	ShO	Sv.	IP	H	R	ER	BB	SO
1987—	Bluefield (Appal.)	5	5	.500	6.50	13	12	0	0	0	62 1/3	74	52	45	38	40
1988—	Bluefield (Appal.)	4	6	.400	6.66	14	14	1	0	0	73	92	61	54	48	73
1989—	Waterloo (Midw.)	10	12	.455	2.98	29	25	•9	0	0	181 1/3	160	89	60	59	89
1990—	Frederick (Caro.)	7	12	.368	4.41	26	18	2	1	0	122 1/3	126	79	60	47	94
1991—	Frederick (Caro.)	12	14	.462	3.11	30	*29	2	0	0	173 2/3	148	91	60	84	144
1992—	Frederick (Caro.)	0	0	...	0.00	1	0	0	0	0	2 1/3	2	1	0	1	2
	—Hagerstown (East.)	1	4	.200	5.77	20	6	0	0	0	57 2/3	58	40	37	47	58
1993—	Bowie (Eastern)	7	4	.636	3.20	34	1	0	0	5	81 2/3	72	35	29	20	83
	—Rochester (Int'l)	0	0	...	5.63	4	0	0	0	0	8	11	5	5	3	6

R

Year	Team (League)	W	L	Pct.	ERA	G	GS	CG	ShO	Sv.	IP	H	R	ER	BB	SO
1994—	Reading (Eastern)■	1	0	1.000	0.00	14	0	0	0	0	19	10	1	0	4	23
—	Scran./W.B. (Int'l)	4	3	.571	4.04	44	1	0	0	6	64 2/3	60	30	29	22	72
1995—	Scran./W.B. (Int'l)	4	3	.571	2.49	*68	0	0	0	•25	65	48	22	18	24	66
—	Philadelphia (N.L.)	1	0	1.000	1.80	7	0	0	0	0	10	9	2	2	3	9
Major league totals (1 year)		1	0	1.000	1.80	7	0	0	0	0	10	9	2	2	3	9

RIGHETTI, DAVE P

PERSONAL: Born November 28, 1958, in San Jose, Calif. . . . 6-4/219. . . . Throws left, bats left. . . . Full name: David Allen Righetti. . . . Son of Leo Righetti, minor league infielder (1944-49 and 1951-57); and brother of Steven Righetti, minor league third baseman (1977-79). . . . Name pronounced rih-GET-tee.

HIGH SCHOOL: Pioneer (San Jose, Calif.).

COLLEGE: San Jose (Calif.) City College.

TRANSACTIONS/CAREER NOTES: Selected by Texas Rangers organization in first round (ninth pick overall) of free-agent draft (January 11, 1977). . . . On disabled list (July 31-September 2, 1978). . . . Traded by Rangers organization with P Mike Griffin, P Paul Mirabella, OF Juan Beniquez and OF Greg Jemison to New York Yankees for P Sparky Lyle, P Larry McCall, P Dave Rajsich, C Mike Heath, SS Domingo Ramos and cash (November 10, 1978). . . . On West Haven disabled list (May 21-June 28, 1979). . . . On Columbus disabled list (June 28-July 20 and August 2-23, 1979). . . . On disabled list (June 17-July 2, 1984). . . . Granted free agency (November 9, 1987). . . . Re-signed by Yankees (December 23, 1987). . . . Granted free agency (November 5, 1990). . . . Signed by San Francisco Giants (December 4, 1990). . . . Released by Giants (November 9, 1993). . . . Signed by Oakland Athletics (December 23, 1993). . . . Released by A's (April 27, 1994). . . . Signed by Toronto Blue Jays organization (May 13, 1994). . . . Released by Blue Jays (October 11, 1994). . . . Signed by Nashville, Chicago White Sox organization (April 12, 1995). . . . Granted free agency (November 9, 1995).

HONORS: Named A.L. Rookie Pitcher of the Year by The Sporting News (1981). . . . Named A.L. Rookie of the Year by Baseball Writers' Association of America (1981). . . . Named A.L. Fireman of the Year by The Sporting News (1986). . . . Named A.L. co-Fireman of the Year by The Sporting News (1987).

STATISTICAL NOTES: Pitched 4-0 no-hit victory against Boston (July 4, 1983).

MISCELLANEOUS: Singled in only appearance as pinch-hitter (1992).

Year	Team (League)	W	L	Pct.	ERA	G	GS	CG	ShO	Sv.	IP	H	R	ER	BB	SO
1977—	Asheville (W. Caro.)	11	3	*.786	3.14	17	16	3	0	0	109	98	47	38	53	101
1978—	Tulsa (Texas)	5	5	.500	3.16	13	13	6	0	0	91	66	40	32	49	127
1979—	West Haven (East.)■	4	3	.571	1.96	11	11	3	0	0	69	45	23	15	45	78
—	Columbus (Int'l)	3	2	.600	2.93	8	6	3	2	0	40	22	13	13	19	44
—	New York (A.L.)	0	1	.000	3.71	3	3	0	0	0	17	10	7	7	10	13
1980—	Columbus (Int'l)	6	10	.375	4.63	24	23	4	1	0	142	124	79	73	*101	139
1981—	Columbus (Int'l)	5	0	1.000	1.00	7	7	2	2	0	45	30	8	5	26	50
—	New York (A.L.)	8	4	.667	2.06	15	15	2	0	0	105	75	25	24	38	89
1982—	New York (A.L.)	11	10	.524	3.79	33	27	4	0	1	183	155	88	77	*108	163
—	Columbus (Int'l)	1	0	1.000	2.81	4	4	1	0	0	25 2/3	22	11	8	12	33
1983—	New York (A.L.)	14	8	.636	3.44	31	31	7	2	0	217	194	96	83	67	169
1984—	New York (A.L.)	5	6	.455	2.34	64	0	0	0	31	96 1/3	79	29	25	37	90
1985—	New York (A.L.)	12	7	.632	2.78	74	0	0	0	29	107	96	36	33	45	92
1986—	New York (A.L.)	8	8	.500	2.45	74	0	0	0	*46	106 2/3	88	31	29	35	83
1987—	New York (A.L.)	8	6	.571	3.51	60	0	0	0	31	95	95	45	37	44	77
1988—	New York (A.L.)	5	4	.556	3.52	60	0	0	0	25	87	86	35	34	37	70
1989—	New York (A.L.)	2	6	.250	3.00	55	0	0	0	25	69	73	32	23	26	51
1990—	New York (A.L.)	1	1	.500	3.57	53	0	0	0	36	53	48	24	21	26	43
1991—	San Francisco (N.L.)■	2	7	.222	3.39	61	0	0	0	24	71 2/3	64	29	27	28	51
1992—	San Francisco (N.L.)	2	7	.222	5.06	54	4	0	0	3	78 1/3	79	47	44	36	47
1993—	San Francisco (N.L.)	1	1	.500	5.70	51	0	0	0	1	47 1/3	58	31	30	17	31
1994—	Oakland (A.L.)■	0	0	...	16.71	7	0	0	0	0	7	13	13	13	9	4
—	Knoxville (South.)■	1	1	.500	2.21	7	4	0	0	0	20 1/3	20	12	5	4	18
—	Toronto (A.L.)	0	1	.000	6.75	13	0	0	0	0	13 1/3	9	10	10	10	10
1995—	Nashville (A.A.)■	4	5	.444	3.23	16	15	1	1	0	83 2/3	81	40	30	20	44
—	Chicago (A.L.)	3	2	.600	4.20	10	9	0	0	0	49 1/3	65	24	23	18	29
A.L. totals (13 years)		77	64	.546	3.28	552	85	13	2	224	1205 2/3	1086	495	439	510	983
N.L. totals (3 years)		5	15	.250	4.61	166	4	0	0	28	197 1/3	201	107	101	81	129
Major league totals (16 years)		82	79	.509	3.46	718	89	13	2	252	1403	1287	602	540	591	1112

DIVISION SERIES RECORD

Year	Team (League)	W	L	Pct.	ERA	G	GS	CG	ShO	Sv.	IP	H	R	ER	BB	SO
1981—	New York (A.L.)	2	0	1.000	1.00	2	1	0	0	0	9	8	1	1	3	10

CHAMPIONSHIP SERIES RECORD

Year	Team (League)	W	L	Pct.	ERA	G	GS	CG	ShO	Sv.	IP	H	R	ER	BB	SO
1981—	New York (A.L.)	1	0	1.000	0.00	1	1	0	0	0	6	4	0	0	2	4

WORLD SERIES RECORD

Year	Team (League)	W	L	Pct.	ERA	G	GS	CG	ShO	Sv.	IP	H	R	ER	BB	SO
1981—	New York (A.L.)	0	0	...	13.50	1	1	0	0	0	2	5	3	3	2	1

ALL-STAR GAME RECORD

Year	League	W	L	Pct.	ERA	GS	CG	ShO	Sv.	IP	H	R	ER	BB	SO
1986—	American	0	0	...	0.00	0	0	0	0	2/3	2	0	0	0	0
1987—	American	0	0	...	0.00	0	0	0	0	1/3	1	0	0	0	0
All-Star totals (2 years)		0	0	...	0.00	0	0	0	0	1	3	0	0	0	0

RIGHTNOWAR, RON P

PERSONAL: Born September 5, 1964, in Toledo, O. . . . 6-3/190. . . . Throws right, bats right. . . . Full name: Ronald Gene Rightnowar.

HIGH SCHOOL: Whitmer (Toledo, O.).

COLLEGE: Eastern Michigan.

TRANSACTIONS/CAREER NOTES: Signed as non-drafted free agent by Detroit Tigers organization (September 30, 1986). . . . On Toledo disabled list (April 10-18 and June 10-21, 1991; April 8-May 5 and July 22-August 10, 1993). . . . Traded by Tigers organization to Milwaukee Brewers organization for a player to be named later (August 28, 1993); Tigers acquired OF/IF Damon Riesgo to complete deal (December 14, 1993). . . . Granted free agency (October 16, 1995).

Year	Team (League)	W	L	Pct.	ERA	G	GS	CG	ShO	Sv.	IP	H	R	ER	BB	SO
1987	—Fayetteville (S. Atl.)	7	7	.500	4.96	39	10	2	0	6	101 2/3	115	70	56	37	65
1988	—Lakeland (Fla. St.)	2	0	1.000	1.46	17	2	0	0	0	49 1/3	41	19	8	11	32
1989	—London (Eastern)	2	8	.200	5.00	36	7	2	0	5	108	132	63	60	34	46
1990	—London (Eastern)	2	2	.500	3.25	23	0	0	0	4	44 1/3	40	20	16	9	33
	—Toledo (Int'l)	4	5	.444	4.74	28	0	0	0	6	38	46	24	20	10	28
	—Niag. Falls (NYP)	1	0	1.000	0.00	1	1	1	0	0	7	4	0	0	1	9
1991	—London (Eastern)	2	1	.667	3.91	15	0	0	0	3	25 1/3	27	13	11	8	18
	—Toledo (Int'l)	1	1	.500	3.94	23	0	0	0	3	29 2/3	30	15	13	15	5
1992	—Toledo (Int'l)	3	2	.600	6.16	34	0	0	0	3	57	68	43	39	18	33
1993	—Toledo (Int'l)	2	2	.500	3.55	22	6	0	0	1	58 1/3	57	32	23	19	32
	—New Orleans (A.A.)■	0	0	...	10.38	4	0	0	0	0	8 2/3	19	10	10	2	8
1994	—New Orleans (A.A.)	8	2	.800	2.25	51	2	0	0	11	88	62	25	22	21	79
1995	—New Orleans (A.A.)	1	1	.500	2.67	25	0	0	0	10	30 1/3	37	16	9	9	22
	—Milwaukee (A.L.)	2	1	.667	5.40	34	0	0	0	1	36 2/3	35	23	22	18	22
Major league totals (1 year)		2	1	.667	5.40	34	0	0	0	1	36 2/3	35	23	22	18	22

RIJO, JOSE — P — REDS

PERSONAL: Born May 13, 1965, in San Cristobal, Dominican Republic. . . . 6-3/215. . . . Throws right, bats right. . . . Full name: Jose Antonio Abreau Rijo. . . . Name pronounced REE-ho.

TRANSACTIONS/CAREER NOTES: Signed as non-drafted free agent by New York Yankees organization (August 1, 1980). . . . Traded by Yankees organization with OF Stan Javier, P Jay Howell, P Eric Plunk and P Tim Birtsas to Oakland Athletics for OF Rickey Henderson, P Bert Bradley and cash (December 5, 1984). . . . Traded by A's organization with P Tim Birtsas to Cincinnati Reds for OF Dave Parker (December 8, 1987). . . . On disabled list (August 18-September 8, 1988 and July 17-September 1, 1989). . . . On Cincinnati disabled list (June 29-July 21, 1990); included rehabilitation assignment to Nashville (July 16-20). . . . On disabled list (June 21-July 25, 1991; April 18-May 3, 1992; June 2-17, 1995; and July 19, 1995-remainder of season).

HONORS: Named Florida State League Most Valuable Player (1983). . . . Named righthanded pitcher on The Sporting News N.L. All-Star team (1991).

STATISTICAL NOTES: Led Pacific Coast League with 11 balks in 1985. . . . Struck out 16 batters in one game (April 19, 1986). . . . Tied for N.L. lead with five balks in 1990. . . . Pitched 6-0 one-hit, complete-game victory against Colorado (September 25, 1993).

MISCELLANEOUS: Struck out in only appearance as pinch-hitter (1991).

Year	Team (League)	W	L	Pct.	ERA	G	GS	CG	ShO	Sv.	IP	H	R	ER	BB	SO
1981	—GC Yankees (GCL)	3	3	.500	4.50	11	1	0	0	1	22	37	16	11	7	22
1982	—Paintsville (Appal.)	8	4	.667	2.50	13	12	6	•3	0	79 1/3	76	33	22	22	66
1983	—Fort Lauder. (FSL)	*15	5	.750	*1.68	21	21	*15	•4	0	160 1/3	129	38	30	43	152
	—Nashville (South.)	3	2	.600	2.68	5	5	3	0	0	40 1/3	31	12	12	22	32
1984	—New York (A.L.)	2	8	.200	4.76	24	5	0	0	2	62 1/3	74	40	33	33	47
	—Columbus (Int'l)	3	3	.500	4.41	11	11	0	0	0	65 1/3	67	35	32	40	47
1985	—Tacoma (PCL)■	7	10	.412	2.90	24	24	3	1	0	149	116	64	48	*108	*179
	—Oakland (A.L.)	6	4	.600	3.53	12	9	0	0	0	63 2/3	57	26	25	28	65
1986	—Oakland (A.L.)	9	11	.450	4.65	39	26	4	0	1	193 2/3	172	116	100	108	176
1987	—Oakland (A.L.)	2	7	.222	5.90	21	14	1	0	0	82 1/3	106	67	54	41	67
	—Tacoma (PCL)	2	4	.333	3.95	9	8	0	0	0	54 2/3	44	27	24	28	67
1988	—Cincinnati (N.L.)■	13	8	.619	2.39	49	19	0	0	0	162	120	47	43	63	160
1989	—Cincinnati (N.L.)	7	6	.538	2.84	19	19	1	1	0	111	101	39	35	48	86
1990	—Cincinnati (N.L.)	14	8	.636	2.70	29	29	7	1	0	197	151	65	59	78	152
	—Nashville (A.A.)	0	0	...	8.31	1	1	0	0	0	4 1/3	5	4	4	2	2
1991	—Cincinnati (N.L.)	15	6	•.714	2.51	30	30	3	1	0	204 1/3	165	69	57	55	172
1992	—Cincinnati (N.L.)	15	10	.600	2.56	33	33	2	0	0	211	185	67	60	44	171
1993	—Cincinnati (N.L.)	14	9	.609	2.48	36	•36	2	1	0	257 1/3	218	76	71	62	*227
1994	—Cincinnati (N.L.)	9	6	.600	3.08	26	*26	2	0	0	172 1/3	177	73	59	52	171
1995	—Cincinnati (N.L.)	5	4	.556	4.17	14	14	0	0	0	69	76	33	32	22	62
A.L. totals (4 years)		19	30	.388	4.75	96	54	5	0	3	402	409	249	212	210	355
N.L. totals (8 years)		92	57	.617	2.71	236	206	17	4	0	1384	1193	469	416	424	1201
Major league totals (12 years)		111	87	.561	3.16	332	260	22	4	3	1786	1602	718	628	634	1556

CHAMPIONSHIP SERIES RECORD

Year	Team (League)	W	L	Pct.	ERA	G	GS	CG	ShO	Sv.	IP	H	R	ER	BB	SO
1990	—Cincinnati (N.L.)	1	0	1.000	4.38	2	2	0	0	0	12 1/3	10	6	6	7	15

WORLD SERIES RECORD

NOTES: Named Most Valuable Player (1990). . . . Member of World Series championship team (1990).

Year	Team (League)	W	L	Pct.	ERA	G	GS	CG	ShO	Sv.	IP	H	R	ER	BB	SO
1990	—Cincinnati (N.L.)	2	0	1.000	0.59	2	2	0	0	0	15 1/3	9	1	1	5	14

ALL-STAR GAME RECORD

Year	League	W	L	Pct.	ERA	GS	CG	ShO	Sv.	IP	H	R	ER	BB	SO
1994	—National	Selected, did not play—injured.													

RILEY, MARQUIS — OF — ANGELS

PERSONAL: Born December 27, 1970, in Ashdown, Ark. . . . 5-11/170. . . . Bats right, throws right. . . . Full name: Marquis Jevel Riley.

HIGH SCHOOL: Ashdown (Ark.).

COLLEGE: Central Arkansas.

TRANSACTIONS/CAREER NOTES: Selected by California Angels organization in second round of free-agent draft (June 1, 1992); pick received as part of compensation for Chicago White Sox signing Type C free agent P Kirk McCaskill. . . . On Midland disabled list (May 10-27, 1994).
STATISTICAL NOTES: Led California League outfielders with 314 total chances in 1993. . . . Led California League in caught stealing with 25 in 1993. . . . Led Pacific Coast League outfielders with 330 total chances in 1995.

			BATTING											FIELDING			
Year	Team (League)	Pos.	G	AB	R	H	2B	3B	HR	RBI	Avg.	BB	SO	SB	PO	A	E	Avg.
1992	—Boise (Northwest)	OF	52	201	47	48	12	1	0	12	.239	37	29	7	95	1	2	*.980
1993	—Palm Springs (Cal.)	OF	130	508	93	134	10	2	1	42	.264	90	117	69	*297	12	5	*.984
1994	—Midland (Texas)	OF	93	374	68	107	12	4	1	29	.286	35	57	32	190	7	8	.961
	—Vancouver (PCL)	OF	4	14	3	3	0	0	0	1	.214	3	3	1	9	0	1	.900
1995	—Vancouver (PCL)	OF	120	477	70	125	6	6	0	43	.262	49	69	29	*326	2	2	.994

RIPKEN, BILLY 2B/SS ORIOLES

PERSONAL: Born December 16, 1964, in Havre de Grace, Md. . . . 6-1/187. . . . Bats right, throws right. . . . Full name: William Oliver Ripken. . . . Son of Cal Ripken Sr., minor league catcher (1957-62 and 1964), manager, Baltimore Orioles (1987-88), and coach, Orioles (1976-86 and 1989-92); and brother of Cal Ripken Jr., shortstop, Orioles.
HIGH SCHOOL: Aberdeen (Md.).
TRANSACTIONS/CAREER NOTES: Selected by Baltimore Orioles organization in 11th round of free-agent draft (June 7, 1982). . . . On disabled list (April 20-May 3, 1984; June 23-July 6, 1985; March 27-April 14 and August 23-September 7, 1989; and August 5-20, 1990). . . . On Baltimore disabled list (July 15-August 15, 1991); included rehabilitation assignments to Frederick (August 12-13) and Hagerstown (August 13-15). . . . Released by Orioles (December 11, 1992). . . . Signed by Texas Rangers organization (February 1, 1993). . . . On Texas disabled list (May 13-28 and June 21-September 1, 1993). . . . Granted free agency (October 4, 1993). . . . Re-signed by Rangers organization (December 18, 1993). . . . On disabled list (May 10-25 and July 16, 1994-remainder of season). . . . Granted free agency (October 14, 1994). . . . Signed by Buffalo, Cleveland Indians organization (March 25, 1995). . . . Granted free agency (November 2, 1995). . . . Signed by Orioles organization (December 23, 1995).
STATISTICAL NOTES: Led Southern League second basemen with 723 total chances and 79 double plays in 1986. . . . Tied for Southern League lead in grounding into double plays with 21 in 1986. . . . Tied for A.L. lead with 17 sacrifice hits in 1990. . . . Tied for American Association lead with eight sacrifice flies in 1995. . . . Led American Association shortstops with .978 fielding percentage, 389 assists and 80 double plays in 1995.

			BATTING											FIELDING			
Year	Team (League)	Pos.	G	AB	R	H	2B	3B	HR	RBI	Avg.	BB	SO	SB	PO	A	E	Avg.
1982	—Bluefield (Appal.)	SS-3B-2B	27	45	8	11	1	0	0	4	.244	8	6	0	15	17	3	.914
1983	—Bluefield (Appal.)	SS-3B	48	152	24	33	6	0	0	13	.217	12	13	7	82	145	23	.908
1984	—Hagerstown (Car.)	SS-2B	115	409	48	94	15	3	2	40	.230	36	64	3	187	358	28	.951
1985	—Charlotte (South.)	SS	18	51	2	7	1	0	0	3	.137	6	4	0	18	52	4	.946
	—Day. Beach (FSL)	SS-3B-2B	67	222	23	51	11	0	0	18	.230	22	24	7	90	198	8	.973
1986	—Charlotte (South.)	2B	141	530	58	142	20	3	5	62	.268	24	47	9	*305	*395	*23	.968
1987	—Rochester (Int'l)	2B-SS	74	238	32	68	15	0	0	11	.286	21	24	7	154	200	9	.975
	—Baltimore (A.L.)	2B	58	234	27	72	9	0	2	20	.308	21	23	4	133	162	3	.990
1988	—Baltimore (A.L.)	2B-3B-DH	150	512	52	106	18	1	2	34	.207	33	63	8	310	440	12	.984
1989	—Baltimore (A.L.)	2B	115	318	31	76	11	2	2	26	.239	22	53	1	255	335	9	.985
1990	—Baltimore (A.L.)	2B	129	406	48	118	28	1	3	38	.291	28	43	5	250	366	8	.987
1991	—Baltimore (A.L.)	2B	104	287	24	62	11	1	0	14	.216	15	31	0	201	284	7	.986
	—Frederick (Caro.)	DH	1	4	2	1	0	0	0	1	.250	0	1	0	...	...	...	...
	—Hagerstown (East.)	2B	1	5	1	3	0	0	0	0	.600	0	0	1	2	1	0	1.000
1992	—Baltimore (A.L.)	2B-DH	111	330	35	76	15	0	4	36	.230	18	26	2	217	317	4	*.993
1993	—Texas (A.L.)■	2B-SS-3B	50	132	12	25	4	0	0	11	.189	11	19	0	80	123	2	.990
1994	—Texas (A.L.)	3-2-S-1	32	81	9	25	5	0	0	6	.309	3	11	2	29	50	2	.975
1995	—Buffalo (A.A.)■	SS-2B	130	448	51	131	34	1	4	56	.292	28	38	6	163	†401	12	†.979
	—Cleveland (A.L.)	2B-3B	8	17	4	7	0	0	2	3	.412	0	3	0	7	6	0	1.000
Major league totals (9 years)			757	2317	242	567	101	5	15	188	.245	151	272	22	1482	2083	47	.987

RIPKEN, CAL SS ORIOLES

PERSONAL: Born August 24, 1960, in Havre de Grace, Md. . . . 6-4/220. . . . Bats right, throws right. . . . Full name: Calvin Edwin Ripken Jr. . . . Son of Cal Ripken Sr., minor league catcher (1957-62 and 1964), manager, Baltimore Orioles (1987-88), and coach, Orioles (1976-86 and 1989-92); and brother of Bill Ripken, second baseman/shorstop, Orioles organization.
HIGH SCHOOL: Aberdeen (Md.).
TRANSACTIONS/CAREER NOTES: Selected by Baltimore Orioles organization in second round of free-agent draft (June 6, 1978).
RECORDS: Holds major league career records for most consecutive games played—2,153 (May 30, 1982 to present); most home runs by shortstop—319; most years leading league in games by shortstop—11; most consecutive games by shortstop—2,126; and most years leading league in double plays by shortstop—8. . . . Shares major league career record for most years played all club's games—13. . . . Holds major league single-season records for most at-bats without a triple—646 (1989); highest fielding percentage by shortstop—.996 (1990); fewest errors by shortstop (150 or more games)—3 (1990); most consecutive errorless games by shortstop—95 (April 14 through July 27, 1990); and most consecutive chances accepted by shortstop without an error—431 (April 14-July 28, 1990, first game). . . . Holds A.L. career record for most years leading league in putouts by shortstop—6. . . . Holds A.L. single-season record for most assists by shortstop—583 (1984). . . . Shares A.L. career record for most years leading league in assists by shortstop—7.
HONORS: Named A.L. Rookie Player of the Year by The Sporting News (1982). . . . Named A.L. Rookie of the Year by Baseball Writers' Association of America (1982). . . . Named Major League Player of the Year by The Sporting News (1983 and 1991). . . . Named A.L. Player of the Year by The Sporting News (1983 and 1991). . . . Named shortstop on The Sporting News A.L. All-Star team (1983-85, 1989, 1991 and 1993-95). . . . Named shortstop on The Sporting News A.L. Silver Slugger team (1983-86, 1989, 1991 and 1993-94). . . . Named A.L. Most Valuable Player by Baseball Writers' Association of America (1983 and 1991). . . . Won A.L. Gold Glove at shortstop (1991-92). . . . Named Sportsman of the Year by The Sporting News (1995).
STATISTICAL NOTES: Tied for Appalachian League lead in double plays by shortstop with 31 in 1978. . . . Led Southern League third basemen with .933 fielding percentage, 119 putouts, 268 assists, 415 total chances and 34 double plays in 1980. . . . Tied for Southern League lead with nine sacrifice flies in 1980. . . . Led A.L. shortstops with 831 total chances in 1983, 906 in 1984, 815 in 1989, 806 in 1991 and 738 in 1993. . . . Led A.L. shortstops with 113 double plays in 1983, 122 in 1984, 123 in 1985, 119 in 1989, 114 in 1991, 119 in 1992, 72 in 1994 and 100 in 1995. . . . Hit for the cycle (May 6, 1984). . . . Tied for A.L. lead with 15 game-winning RBIs in 1986. . . . Tied for A.L. lead

R

with 10 sacrifice flies in 1988. . . . Led A.L. with 368 total bases in 1991. . . . Career major league grand slams: 4.

Year Team (League)	Pos.	G	AB	R	H	2B	3B	HR	RBI	Avg.	BB	SO	SB	PO	A	E	Avg.
			BATTING											FIELDING			
1978— Bluefield (Appal.)........	SS	63	239	27	63	7	1	0	24	.264	24	46	1	*92	204	*33	.900
1979— Miami (Florida St.).....	3B-SS-2B	105	393	51	119	*28	1	5	54	.303	31	64	4	149	260	30	.932
— Charlotte (South.).......	3B	17	61	6	11	0	1	3	8	.180	3	13	1	13	26	3	.929
1980— Charlotte (South.).......	3B-SS	•144	522	91	144	28	5	25	78	.276	77	81	4	†151	†341	35	†.934
1981— Rochester (Int'l).........	3B-SS	114	437	74	126	31	4	23	75	.288	66	85	0	128	320	21	.955
— Baltimore (A.L.)..........	SS-3B	23	39	1	5	0	0	0	0	.128	1	8	0	13	30	3	.935
1982— Baltimore (A.L.)..........	SS-3B	160	598	90	158	32	5	28	93	.264	46	95	3	221	440	19	.972
1983— Baltimore (A.L.)..........	SS	•162	*663	*121	*211	*47	2	27	102	.318	58	97	0	272	*534	25	.970
1984— Baltimore (A.L.)..........	SS	•162	641	103	195	37	7	27	86	.304	71	89	2	*297	*583	26	.971
1985— Baltimore (A.L.)..........	SS	161	642	116	181	32	5	26	110	.282	67	68	2	*286	474	26	.967
1986— Baltimore (A.L.)..........	SS	162	627	98	177	35	1	25	81	.282	70	60	4	240	*482	13	.982
1987— Baltimore (A.L.)..........	SS	*162	624	97	157	28	3	27	98	.252	81	77	3	240	*480	20	.973
1988— Baltimore (A.L.)..........	SS	161	575	87	152	25	1	23	81	.264	102	69	2	*284	480	21	.973
1989— Baltimore (A.L.)..........	SS	•162	646	80	166	30	0	21	93	.257	57	72	3	*276	*531	8	.990
1990— Baltimore (A.L.)..........	SS	161	600	78	150	28	4	21	84	.250	82	66	3	242	435	3	*.996
1991— Baltimore (A.L.)..........	SS	•162	650	99	210	46	5	34	114	.323	53	46	6	*267	*528	11	*.986
1992— Baltimore (A.L.)..........	SS	*162	637	73	160	29	1	14	72	.251	64	50	4	*287	445	12	.984
1993— Baltimore (A.L.)..........	SS	*162	*641	87	165	26	3	24	90	.257	65	58	1	226	*495	17	.977
1994— Baltimore (A.L.)..........	SS	112	444	71	140	19	3	13	75	.315	32	41	1	132	321	7	*.985
1995— Baltimore (A.L.)..........	SS	144	550	71	144	33	2	17	88	.262	52	59	0	206	409	7	*.989
Major league totals (15 years)		2218	8577	1272	2371	447	42	327	1267	.276	901	955	34	3489	6667	218	.979

CHAMPIONSHIP SERIES RECORD

Year Team (League)	Pos.	G	AB	R	H	2B	3B	HR	RBI	Avg.	BB	SO	SB	PO	A	E	Avg.
			BATTING											FIELDING			
1983— Baltimore (A.L.)..........	SS	4	15	5	6	2	0	0	1	.400	2	3	0	7	11	0	1.000

WORLD SERIES RECORD

NOTES: Member of World Series championship team (1983).

Year Team (League)	Pos.	G	AB	R	H	2B	3B	HR	RBI	Avg.	BB	SO	SB	PO	A	E	Avg.
			BATTING											FIELDING			
1983— Baltimore (A.L.)..........	SS	5	18	2	3	0	0	0	1	.167	3	4	0	6	14	0	1.000

ALL-STAR GAME RECORD

NOTES: Named Most Valuable Player (1991). . . . Shares single-game record for most at-bats in nine-inning game—5 (July 12, 1994).

Year League	Pos.	AB	R	H	2B	3B	HR	RBI	Avg.	BB	SO	SB	PO	A	E	Avg.
		BATTING											FIELDING			
1983— American....................	SS	0	0	0	0	0	0	0	. . .	1	0	0	1	0	0	1.000
1984— American....................	SS	3	0	0	0	0	0	0	.000	0	0	0	0	0	0	. . .
1985— American....................	SS	3	0	1	0	0	0	0	.333	0	0	0	2	1	0	1.000
1986— American....................	SS	4	0	0	0	0	0	0	.000	0	0	0	0	1	0	1.000
1987— American....................	SS	2	0	1	0	0	0	0	.500	0	0	0	0	5	0	1.000
1988— American....................	SS	3	0	0	0	0	0	0	.000	1	0	0	1	4	0	1.000
1989— American....................	SS	3	0	1	1	0	0	0	.333	0	0	0	0	0	0	. . .
1990— American....................	SS	2	0	0	0	0	0	0	.000	0	0	0	1	1	0	1.000
1991— American....................	SS	3	1	2	0	0	1	3	.667	0	0	0	2	1	0	1.000
1992— American....................	SS	3	0	1	0	0	0	1	.333	0	0	0	1	1	0	1.000
1993— American....................	SS	3	0	0	0	0	0	0	.000	0	1	0	1	2	0	1.000
1994— American....................	SS	5	0	1	1	0	0	0	.200	0	2	0	1	2	0	1.000
1995— American....................	SS	3	0	2	0	0	0	0	.667	0	0	0	2	1	0	1.000
All-Star Game totals (13 years)		37	1	9	2	0	1	4	.243	2	3	0	12	19	0	1.000

RISLEY, BILL — P — BLUE JAYS

PERSONAL: Born May 29, 1967, in Chicago. . . . 6-2/215. . . . Throws right, bats right. . . . Full name: William Charles Risley. . . . Name pronounced RIZZ-lee.

HIGH SCHOOL: Marist (Chicago).

TRANSACTIONS/CAREER NOTES: Selected by Cincinnati Reds organization in 14th round of free-agent draft (June 2, 1987). . . . Traded by Reds with P John Wetteland to Montreal Expos for OF Dave Martinez, P Scott Ruskin and SS Willie Greene (December 11, 1991). . . . On Indianapolis disabled list (April 9-20 and May 16-June 3, 1992). . . . On Ottawa disabled list (April 8-23 and June 30-July 10, 1993). . . . Claimed on waivers by Seattle Mariners (March 17, 1994). . . . On Seattle disabled list (May 29-June 13, 1995); included rehabilitation assignment to Tacoma (June 12-13). . . . Traded by Mariners with 2B Miguel Cairo to Toronto Blue Jays for P Edwin Hurtado and P Paul Menhart (December 18, 1995).

STATISTICAL NOTES: Tied for Southern League lead with five balks in 1991.

Year Team (League)	W	L	Pct.	ERA	G	GS	CG	ShO	Sv.	IP	H	R	ER	BB	SO
1987— GC Reds (GCL)..................	1	4	.200	1.89	11	11	0	0	0	52 1/3	38	24	11	26	50
1988— Greensboro (S. Atl.)...........	8	4	.667	4.11	23	23	3	3	0	120 1/3	82	60	55	84	135
1989— Ced. Rap. (Midw.)..............	9	10	.474	3.90	27	27	2	0	0	140 2/3	87	72	61	81	128
1990— Ced. Rap. (Midw.)..............	8	9	.471	2.81	22	22	•7	1	0	137 2/3	99	51	43	68	123
1991— Chattanooga (Sou.)............	5	7	.417	3.16	19	19	3	0	0	108 1/3	81	48	38	60	77
— Nashville (A.A.)..................	3	5	.375	4.91	8	8	1	0	0	44	45	27	24	26	32
1992— Indianapolis (A.A.)■	5	8	.385	6.40	25	15	0	0	0	95 2/3	105	69	68	47	64
— Montreal (N.L.)..................	1	0	1.000	1.80	1	1	0	0	0	5	4	1	1	1	2
1993— Ottawa (Int'l)......................	2	4	.333	2.69	41	0	0	0	1	63 2/3	51	26	19	34	74
— Montreal (N.L.)..................	0	0	. . .	6.00	2	0	0	0	0	3	2	3	2	2	2
1994— Calgary (PCL)■..................	0	0	. . .	3.00	6	1	0	0	1	12	13	5	4	4	15
— Seattle (A.L.).....................	9	6	.600	3.44	37	0	0	0	0	52 1/3	31	20	20	19	61
1995— Tacoma (PCL).....................	0	0	. . .	0.00	1	0	0	0	0	1	0	0	0	1	2
— Seattle (A.L.).....................	2	1	.667	3.13	45	0	0	0	1	60 1/3	55	21	21	18	65
A.L. totals (2 years)..................	11	7	.611	3.28	82	0	0	0	1	112 2/3	86	41	41	37	126
N.L. totals (2 years)..................	1	0	1.000	3.38	3	1	0	0	0	8	6	4	3	3	4
Major league totals (4 years)......	12	7	.632	3.28	85	1	0	0	1	120 2/3	92	45	44	40	130

DIVISION SERIES RECORD

Year	Team (League)	W	L	Pct.	ERA	G	GS	CG	ShO	Sv.	IP	H	R	ER	BB	SO
1995—	Seattle (A.L.)	0	0	...	6.00	4	0	0	0	1	3	2	2	2	0	1

CHAMPIONSHIP SERIES RECORD

Year	Team (League)	W	L	Pct.	ERA	G	GS	CG	ShO	Sv.	IP	H	R	ER	BB	SO
1995—	Seattle (A.L.)	0	0	...	0.00	3	0	0	0	0	2 2/3	2	0	0	1	2

RITCHIE, TODD — P — TWINS

PERSONAL: Born November 7, 1971, in Portsmouth, Va. . . . 6-3/190. . . . Throws right, bats right. . . . Full name: Todd Everett Ritchie.

HIGH SCHOOL: Duncanville (Tex.).

TRANSACTIONS/CAREER NOTES: Selected by Minnesota Twins organization in first round (12th pick overall) of free-agent draft (June 4, 1990). . . . On disabled list (August 19, 1991-remainder of season; June 24-July 9, 1993; and April 28, 1994-remainder of season).

Year	Team (League)	W	L	Pct.	ERA	G	GS	CG	ShO	Sv.	IP	H	R	ER	BB	SO
1990—	Elizabeth. (App.)	5	2	.714	1.94	11	11	1	0	0	65	45	22	14	24	49
1991—	Kenosha (Midwest)	7	6	.538	3.55	21	21	0	0	0	116 2/3	113	53	46	50	101
1992—	Visalia (California)	11	9	.550	5.06	28	•28	3	1	0	172 2/3	193	113	97	65	129
1993—	Nashville (South.)	3	2	.600	3.66	12	10	0	0	0	46 2/3	46	21	19	15	41
1994—	Nashville (South.)	0	2	.000	4.24	4	4	0	0	0	17	24	10	8	7	9
1995—	New Britain (East.)	4	9	.308	5.73	24	21	0	0	0	113	135	78	72	54	60

RITZ, KEVIN — P — ROCKIES

PERSONAL: Born June 8, 1965, in Eatonstown, N.J. . . . 6-4/222. . . . Throws right, bats right. . . . Full name: Kevin D. Ritz.

HIGH SCHOOL: Davis County (Ia.).

JUNIOR COLLEGE: Indian Hills Community College (Ia.).

COLLEGE: William Penn (Ia.).

TRANSACTIONS/CAREER NOTES: Selected by San Francisco Giants organization in fourth round of free-agent draft (January 9, 1985); did not sign. . . . Selected by Detroit Tigers organization in secondary phase of free-agent draft (June 3, 1985). . . . On Detroit disabled list (August 4, 1992-remainder of season). . . . Selected by Colorado Rockies in second round (46th pick overall) of expansion draft (November 17, 1992). . . . On disabled list (April 4, 1993-entire season). . . . Released by Rockies (October 12, 1993). . . . Re-signed by Rockies organization (December 1, 1993).

Year	Team (League)	W	L	Pct.	ERA	G	GS	CG	ShO	Sv.	IP	H	R	ER	BB	SO
1986—	Gastonia (S. Atl.)	1	2	.333	4.21	7	7	0	0	0	36 1/3	29	19	17	21	34
—	Lakeland (Fla. St.)	3	9	.250	5.57	18	15	0	0	1	85 2/3	114	60	53	45	39
1987—	Glens Falls (East.)	8	8	.500	4.89	25	25	1	0	0	152 2/3	171	95	83	71	78
1988—	Glens Falls (East.)	8	10	.444	3.82	26	26	4	2	0	136 2/3	115	68	58	70	75
1989—	Toledo (Int'l)	7	8	.467	3.16	16	16	1	0	0	102 2/3	95	48	36	60	74
—	Detroit (A.L.)	4	6	.400	4.38	12	12	1	0	0	74	75	41	36	44	56
1990—	Toledo (Int'l)	3	6	.333	5.22	20	18	0	0	0	89 2/3	93	68	52	59	57
—	Detroit (A.L.)	0	4	.000	11.05	4	4	0	0	0	7 1/3	14	12	9	14	3
1991—	Toledo (Int'l)	8	7	.533	3.28	20	19	3	0	0	126 1/3	116	50	46	60	105
—	Detroit (A.L.)	0	3	.000	11.74	11	5	0	0	0	15 1/3	17	22	20	22	9
1992—	Detroit (A.L.)	2	5	.286	5.60	23	11	0	0	0	80 1/3	88	52	50	44	57
1993—		Did not play.														
1994—	Colo. Springs (PCL)■	5	0	1.000	1.29	9	3	1	1	0	35	26	6	5	6	27
—	Colorado (N.L.)	5	6	.455	5.62	15	15	0	0	0	73 2/3	88	49	46	35	53
1995—	Colorado (N.L.)	11	11	.500	4.21	31	28	0	0	2	173 1/3	171	91	81	65	120
	A.L. totals (4 years)	6	18	.250	5.85	50	32	1	0	0	177	194	127	115	124	125
	N.L. totals (2 years)	16	17	.485	4.63	46	43	0	0	2	247	259	140	127	100	173
	Major league totals (6 years)	22	35	.386	5.14	96	75	1	0	2	424	453	267	242	224	298

DIVISION SERIES RECORD

Year	Team (League)	W	L	Pct.	ERA	G	GS	CG	ShO	Sv.	IP	H	R	ER	BB	SO
1995—	Colorado (N.L.)	0	0	...	7.71	2	1	0	0	0	7	12	7	6	3	5

RIVERA, MARIANO — P — YANKEES

PERSONAL: Born November 29, 1969, in Panama City, Panama. . . . 6-4/168. . . . Throws right, bats right.

TRANSACTIONS/CAREER NOTES: Signed as non-drafted free agent by New York Yankees organization (February 17, 1990). . . . On disabled list (April 10-May 19, July 11-28 and August 12-September 8, 1992). . . . On Albany/Colonie disabled list (April 9-June 28, 1993). . . . On Greensboro disabled list (September 6, 1993-remainder of season). . . . On Tampa disabled list (April 23-May 9, 1994). . . . On Columbus disabled list (August 4-14, 1994).

STATISTICAL NOTES: Pitched seven-inning, 3-0 no-hit victory against Gulf Coast Pirates (August 31, 1990). . . . Pitched five-inning 3-0 no-hit victory for Columbus against Rochester (June 26, 1995).

Year	Team (League)	W	L	Pct.	ERA	G	GS	CG	ShO	Sv.	IP	H	R	ER	BB	SO
1990—	GC Yankees (GCL)	5	1	.833	*0.17	22	1	1	1	1	52	17	3	1	7	58
1991—	Greensboro (S. Atl.)	4	9	.308	2.75	29	15	1	0	0	114 2/3	103	48	35	36	123
1992—	Fort Lauder. (FSL)	5	3	.625	2.28	10	10	3	1	0	59 1/3	40	17	15	5	42
1993—	Greensboro (S. Atl.)	1	0	1.000	2.06	10	10	0	0	0	39 1/3	31	12	9	15	32
—	GC Yankees (GCL)	0	1	.000	2.25	2	2	0	0	0	4	2	1	1	1	6
1994—	Tampa (Fla. St.)	3	0	1.000	2.21	7	7	0	0	0	36 2/3	34	12	9	12	27
—	Alb./Colon. (East.)	3	0	1.000	2.27	9	9	0	0	0	63 1/3	58	20	16	8	39
—	Columbus (Int'l)	4	2	.667	5.81	6	6	1	0	0	31	34	22	20	10	23
1995—	Columbus (Int'l)	2	2	.500	2.10	7	7	1	1	0	30	25	10	7	3	30
—	New York (A.L.)	5	3	.625	5.51	19	10	0	0	0	67	71	43	41	30	51
	Major league totals (1 year)	5	3	.625	5.51	19	10	0	0	0	67	71	43	41	30	51

DIVISION SERIES RECORD

Year	Team (League)	W	L	Pct.	ERA	G	GS	CG	ShO	Sv.	IP	H	R	ER	BB	SO
1995—	New York (A.L.)	1	0	1.000	0.00	3	0	0	0	0	5 1/3	3	0	0	1	8

RIVERA, ROBERTO P CUBS

PERSONAL: Born January 1, 1969, in Bayamon, Puerto Rico. . . . 6-0/200. . . . Throws left, bats left. . . . Full name: Roberto Diaz Rivera.
HIGH SCHOOL: Dr. Augustin Stahl (Bayamon, Puerto Rico).
TRANSACTIONS/CAREER NOTES: Signed as non-drafted free agent by Cleveland Indians organization (January 24, 1988). . . . On disabled list (May 22-June 23, 1992). . . . Released by Indians organization (October 18, 1993). . . . Signed by Chicago Cubs organization (December 10, 1993).

Year	Team (League)	W	L	Pct.	ERA	G	GS	CG	ShO	Sv.	IP	H	R	ER	BB	SO
1988	GC Indians (GCL)	6	5	.545	3.25	14	12	1	1	0	69 1/3	64	32	25	21	38
1989	Burlington (Appal.)	3	4	.429	3.51	18	2	1	0	2	51 1/3	44	24	20	16	42
1990	Watertown (NYP)	4	4	.500	3.60	14	13	2	1	0	85	85	43	34	10	63
1991	Columbus (S. Atl.)	7	1	.875	1.65	30	1	0	0	3	49	48	15	9	12	36
	—Kinston (Carolina)	1	0	1.000	4.35	10	0	0	0	0	10 1/3	10	6	5	2	9
1992	Kinston (Carolina)	3	5	.375	3.25	24	8	4	1	1	88 2/3	83	35	32	11	56
1993	Cant./Akr. (East.)	0	1	.000	5.02	8	0	0	0	0	14 1/3	22	8	8	3	6
	—Kinston (Carolina)	2	3	.400	6.17	19	1	0	0	0	35	44	26	24	4	32
1994	Peoria (Midwest)■	3	1	.750	2.33	14	0	0	0	0	19 1/3	27	6	5	3	13
	—Orlando (Southern)	3	2	.600	2.76	34	0	0	0	4	45 2/3	45	14	14	11	31
1995	Orlando (Southern)	6	2	.750	2.38	49	0	0	0	6	68	50	18	18	11	34
	—Chicago (N.L.)	0	0	...	5.40	7	0	0	0	0	5	8	3	3	2	2
Major league totals (1 year)		0	0	...	5.40	7	0	0	0	0	5	8	3	3	2	2

RIVERA, RUBEN OF YANKEES

PERSONAL: Born November 14, 1973, in Chorrera, Panama. . . . 6-3/200. . . . Bats right, throws right. . . . Full name: Ruben Moreno Rivera.
TRANSACTIONS/CAREER NOTES: Signed as non-drafted free agent by New York Yankees organization (November 21, 1990).
HONORS: Named New York-Pennsylvania League Most Valuable Player (1993). . . . Named South Atlantic League Most Valuable Player (1994).
STATISTICAL NOTES: Led New York-Pennsylvania League outfielders with three double plays in 1993. . . . Led South Atlantic League with .573 slugging percentage in 1994.

			BATTING												FIELDING			
Year	Team (League)	Pos.	G	AB	R	H	2B	3B	HR	RBI	Avg.	BB	SO	SB	PO	A	E	Avg.
1991	Santo Dom. (DSL)	...	51	170	27	34	3	2	2	16	.200	23	37	14				...
1992	GC Yankees (GCL)	OF	53	194	37	53	10	3	1	20	.273	42	49	21	67	10	4	.951
1993	Oneonta (NYP)	OF	55	199	45	55	7	6	13	47	.276	32	66	12	111	9	3	.976
1994	Greensboro (S. Atl.)	OF	105	400	83	115	24	3	•28	81	.288	47	125	36	217	14	5	.979
	—Tampa (Fla. St.)	OF	34	134	18	35	4	3	5	20	.261	8	38	12	76	6	2	.976
1995	Norwich (Eastern)	OF	71	256	49	75	16	8	9	39	.293	37	77	16	176	7	3	.984
	—Columbus (Int'l)	OF	48	174	37	47	8	2	15	35	.270	26	62	8	113	6	3	.975
	—New York (A.L.)	OF	5	1	0	0	0	0	0	0	.000	0	1	0	2	0	0	1.000
Major league totals (1 year)			5	1	0	0	0	0	0	0	.000	0	1	0	2	0	0	1.000

ROA, JOE P INDIANS

PERSONAL: Born October 11, 1971, in Southfield, Mich. . . . 6-1/195. . . . Throws right, bats right. . . . Full name: Joe Rodger Roa. . . . Name pronounced ROE-ah.
HIGH SCHOOL: Hazel Park (Mich.).
TRANSACTIONS/CAREER NOTES: Selected by Atlanta Braves organization in 18th round of free-agent draft (June 5, 1989). . . . Traded by Braves to New York Mets organization (August 29, 1991), completing deal in which Mets traded P Alejandro Pena to Braves for P Tony Castillo and a player to be named (August 28, 1991). . . . On Norfolk suspended list (July 31-August 2, 1994). . . . Traded by Mets organization with OF Jeromy Burnitz to Cleveland Indians organization for P Dave Mlicki, P Paul Byrd, P Jerry DiPoto and a player to be named (November 18, 1994); Mets acquired 2B Jesus Azuaje to complete deal (December 6, 1994).

Year	Team (League)	W	L	Pct.	ERA	G	GS	CG	ShO	Sv.	IP	H	R	ER	BB	SO
1989	GC Braves (GCL)	2	2	.500	2.89	13	4	0	0	0	37 1/3	40	18	12	10	21
1990	Pulaski (Appal.)	4	2	.667	2.97	14	11	3	1	0	75 2/3	55	29	25	26	49
1991	Macon (S. Atl.)	13	3	.813	2.17	30	18	4	2	1	141	106	46	34	33	96
1992	St. Lucie (Fla. St.)■	9	7	.563	3.63	26	24	2	1	0	156 1/3	176	80	63	15	61
1993	Binghamton (East.)	12	7	.632	3.87	32	23	2	1	0	167 1/3	190	80	72	24	73
1994	Binghamton (East.)	2	1	.667	1.80	3	3	0	0	0	20	18	6	4	1	11
	—Norfolk (Int'l)	8	8	.500	3.49	25	25	5	0	0	167 2/3	184	82	65	34	74
1995	Buffalo (A.A.)■	*17	3	.850	3.50	25	24	3	0	0	164 2/3	168	71	64	28	93
	—Cleveland (A.L.)	0	1	.000	6.00	1	1	0	0	0	6	9	4	4	2	0
Major league totals (1 year)		0	1	.000	6.00	1	1	0	0	0	6	9	4	4	2	0

ROBERSON, KEVIN OF METS

PERSONAL: Born January 29, 1968, in Decatur, Ill. . . . 6-4/210. . . . Bats both, throws right. . . . Full name: Kevin Lynn Roberson. . . . Name pronounced RO-ber-son.
HIGH SCHOOL: Eisenhower (Decatur, Ill).
JUNIOR COLLEGE: Parkland College (Ill.).
TRANSACTIONS/CAREER NOTES: Selected by Chicago Cubs organization in 16th round of free-agent draft (June 1, 1988). . . . On disabled list (June 6-September 14, 1992). . . . On Chicago disabled list (July 5, 1994-remainder of season). . . . Claimed on waivers by Seattle Mariners (July 7, 1995). . . . Granted free agency (October 16, 1995). . . . Signed by Norfolk, New York Mets organization (November 12, 1995).
STATISTICAL NOTES: Led South Atlantic League outfielders with seven double plays in 1989.

Year	Team (League)	Pos.	BATTING G	AB	R	H	2B	3B	HR	RBI	Avg.	BB	SO	SB	FIELDING PO	A	E	Avg.
1988—	Wytheville (Appal.)	OF	63	225	39	47	12	2	3	29	.209	40	86	3	93	4	6	.942
1989—	Char., W.Va. (SAL)	OF	126	429	49	109	19	1	13	57	.254	70	•149	3	210	18	7	.970
1990—	Winst.-Salem (Car.)	OF	85	313	49	84	23	3	5	45	.268	25	70	7	136	4	6	.959
—	Charlotte (South.)	OF	31	119	14	29	6	2	5	16	.244	8	25	2	63	1	0	1.000
1991—	Charlotte (South.)	OF	136	507	77	130	24	2	19	67	.256	39	*129	17	259	7	4	.985
1992—	Iowa (Am. Assoc.)	OF	51	197	25	60	15	4	6	34	.305	5	46	0	87	1	4	.957
1993—	Iowa (Am. Assoc.)	OF	67	263	48	80	20	1	16	50	.304	19	66	3	110	4	4	.966
—	Chicago (N.L.)	OF	62	180	23	34	4	1	9	27	.189	12	48	0	77	2	3	.963
1994—	Iowa (Am. Assoc.)	OF	19	67	9	21	8	0	3	17	.313	4	19	0	33	0	0	1.000
—	Chicago (N.L.)	OF	44	55	8	12	4	0	4	9	.218	2	14	0	7	1	2	.800
1995—	Chicago (N.L.)	OF	32	38	5	7	1	0	4	6	.184	6	14	0	8	0	0	1.000
—	Tacoma (PCL)■	OF	42	157	17	37	6	1	6	17	.236	19	51	1	51	2	1	.981
Major league totals (3 years)			138	273	36	53	9	1	17	42	.194	20	76	0	92	3	5	.950

ROBERSON, SID — P — BREWERS

PERSONAL: Born September 7, 1971, in Jacksonville, Fla. . . . 5-9/170. . . . Throws left, bats left. . . . Full name: Sidney Dean Roberson.
HIGH SCHOOL: Orange Park (Fla.).
COLLEGE: North Florida.
TRANSACTIONS/CAREER NOTES: Selected by Milwaukee Brewers organization in 29th round of free-agent draft (June 1, 1992).
HONORS: Named California League Pitcher of the Year (1993). . . . Named Texas League Pitcher of the Year (1994).
STATISTICAL NOTES: Led Texas League with 17 hit batsmen in 1994.

Year	Team (League)	W	L	Pct.	ERA	G	GS	CG	ShO	Sv.	IP	H	R	ER	BB	SO
1992—	Helena (Pioneer)	4	4	.500	3.46	9	8	1	0	0	65	68	32	25	18	65
1993—	Stockton (Calif.)	12	8	.600	*2.60	24	23	•6	1	0	166	157	68	48	34	87
1994—	El Paso (Texas)	*15	8	.652	2.83	25	25	*8	0	0	*181 1/3	190	70	57	48	119
1995—	New Orleans (A.A.)	0	2	.000	7.62	4	3	0	0	0	13	20	11	11	10	8
—	Milwaukee (A.L.)	6	4	.600	5.76	26	13	0	0	0	84 1/3	102	55	54	37	40
Major league totals (1 year)		6	4	.600	5.76	26	13	0	0	0	84 1/3	102	55	54	37	40

ROBERTS, BIP — 2B/OF — ROYALS

PERSONAL: Born October 27, 1963, in Berkeley, Calif. . . . 5-7/165. . . . Bats both, throws right. . . . Full name: Leon Joseph Roberts III.
HIGH SCHOOL: Skyline (Oakland, Calif.).
JUNIOR COLLEGE: Chabot (Calif.).
COLLEGE: UNLV.
TRANSACTIONS/CAREER NOTES: Selected by Pittsburgh Pirates organization in fifth round of free-agent draft (June 8, 1981); did not sign. . . . Selected by Pirates organization in secondary phase of free-agent draft (June 7, 1982). . . . On suspended list (June 30-July 3, 1985). . . . Selected by San Diego Padres from Pirates organization in Rule 5 major league draft (December 10, 1985). . . . On disabled list (May 21-June 5, 1986 and August 17-September 9, 1991). . . . Traded by Padres with a player to be named later to Cincinnati Reds for P Randy Myers (December 8, 1991); Reds acquired OF Craig Pueschner to complete deal (December 9, 1991). . . . On disabled list (July 2-17 and August 4, 1993-remainder of season). . . . Granted free agency (October 26, 1993). . . . Signed by Padres (January 10, 1994). . . . Granted free agency (October 20, 1994). . . . Re-signed by Padres (December 23, 1994). . . . On San Diego disabled list (June 28-July 13 and July 14-August 22, 1995); included rehabilitation assignments to Rancho Cucamonga (August 18-19) and Las Vegas (August 19-22). . . . Traded by Padres with P Bryan Wolff to Kansas City Royals for 1B Wally Joyner and P Aaron Dorlarque (December 21, 1995).
RECORDS: Shares N.L. single-season record for most consecutive hits—10 (September 19, 20, 22 [second game] and 23, 1992; one base on balls).
STATISTICAL NOTES: Led South Atlantic League second basemen with .962 fielding percentage and tied for lead with 76 double plays in 1983. . . . Led Carolina League second basemen with 654 total chances and 91 double plays in 1984. . . . Career major league grand slams: 1.

Year	Team (League)	Pos.	BATTING G	AB	R	H	2B	3B	HR	RBI	Avg.	BB	SO	SB	FIELDING PO	A	E	Avg.
1982—	GC Pirates (GCL)	2B	6	23	4	7	1	0	0	1	.304	2	4	4	14	15	0	1.000
—	Greenwood (S. Atl.)	2B	33	107	15	23	3	1	0	6	.215	15	18	10	52	82	7	.950
1983—	Greenwood (S. Atl.)	2B-SS	122	438	78	140	20	5	6	63	.320	69	43	27	273	311	24	†.961
1984—	Prin. William (Car.)	2B	134	498	81	*150	25	5	8	77	.301	44	63	50	*282	352	20	*.969
1985—	Nashua (Eastern)	2B	105	401	64	109	19	5	1	23	.272	29	43	•40	217	249	•29	.941
1986—	San Diego (N.L.)■	2B	101	241	34	61	5	2	1	12	.253	14	29	14	166	172	10	.971
1987—	Las Vegas (PCL)	2B-OF-3B	98	359	66	110	18	10	1	38	.306	37	39	27	147	150	8	.974
1988—	Las Vegas (PCL)	3B-OF-2B	100	343	73	121	21	8	7	51	.353	32	45	29	103	130	17	.932
—	San Diego (N.L.)	2B-3B	5	9	1	3	0	0	0	0	.333	1	2	0	2	3	1	.833
1989—	San Diego (N.L.)	O-3-S-2	117	329	81	99	15	8	3	25	.301	49	45	21	134	113	9	.965
1990—	San Diego (N.L.)	O-3-S-2	149	556	104	172	36	3	9	44	.309	55	65	46	227	160	13	.968
1991—	San Diego (N.L.)	2B-OF	117	424	66	119	13	3	3	32	.281	37	71	26	239	185	10	.977
1992—	Cincinnati (N.L.)■	OF-2B-3B	147	532	92	172	34	6	4	45	.323	62	54	44	209	152	7	.981
1993—	Cincinnati (N.L.)	2-0-3-S	83	292	46	70	13	0	1	18	.240	38	46	26	152	176	6	.982
1994—	San Diego (N.L.)■	2B-OF	105	403	52	129	15	5	2	31	.320	39	57	21	178	221	9	.978
1995—	San Diego (N.L.)	OF-2B-SS	73	296	40	90	14	0	2	25	.304	17	36	20	135	88	4	.982
—	Rancho Cuca. (Cal.)	DH	1	3	1	0	0	0	0	0	.000	1	1	1	0	0	0	...
—	Las Vegas (PCL)	SS-2B	3	12	1	4	0	0	0	2	.333	0	3	1	2	15	1	.944
Major league totals (9 years)			897	3082	516	915	145	27	25	232	.297	312	405	218	1442	1270	69	.975

ALL-STAR GAME RECORD

Year	League	Pos.	BATTING AB	R	H	2B	3B	HR	RBI	Avg.	BB	SO	SB	FIELDING PO	A	E	Avg.
1992—	National	OF	2	1	2	0	0	0	2	1.000	0	0	0	0	0	0	...

ROBERTS, BRETT — P — TWINS

PERSONAL: Born March 24, 1970, in Portsmouth, O. . . . 6-7/230. . . . Throws right, bats right.
HIGH SCHOOL: South Webster (O.).
COLLEGE: Morehead State.
TRANSACTIONS/CAREER NOTES: Selected by Cincinnati Reds organization in 33rd round of free-agent draft (June 1, 1988); did not sign. . . . Selected by Minnesota Twins organization in fourth round of free-agent draft (June 3, 1991). . . . On temporarily inactive list (June 19-July 6 and July 15-August 1, 1995).
MISCELLANEOUS: Selected by Sacramento Kings in second round (54th pick overall) of 1992 NBA draft.

Year	Team (League)	W	L	Pct.	ERA	G	GS	CG	ShO	Sv.	IP	H	R	ER	BB	SO
1991	—Elizabeth. (App.)	3	0	1.000	2.25	6	6	1	0	0	28	21	8	7	10	27
1992	—Kenosha (Midwest)	1	1	.500	5.56	7	6	6	0	0	22 2/3	23	18	14	15	23
1993	—Fort Myers (Fla. St.)	9	*16	.360	4.35	28	•28	3	0	0	173 2/3	184	93	*84	86	106
1994	—Fort Myers (Fla. St.)	6	7	.462	4.32	21	21	1	0	0	116 2/3	123	71	56	47	75
	—Nashville (South.)	2	1	.667	6.75	5	5	0	0	0	20	30	18	15	12	11
1995	—New Britain (East.)	11	9	.550	3.41	28	28	•5	1	0	174	162	72	66	50	135

ROBERTS, LONELL — OF — BLUE JAYS

PERSONAL: Born June 7, 1971, in Bloomington, Calif. . . . 6-0/180. . . . Bats both, throws right. . . . Full name: Lonell Dashawn Roberts.
HIGH SCHOOL: Bloomington (Calif.).
TRANSACTIONS/CAREER NOTES: Selected by Toronto Blue Jays organization in eighth round of free-agent draft (June 5, 1989).

				BATTING											FIELDING			
Year	Team (League)	Pos.	G	AB	R	H	2B	3B	HR	RBI	Avg.	BB	SO	SB	PO	A	E	Avg.
1989	—Medicine Hat (Pio.)	OF	29	78	2	11	1	0	0	6	.141	7	27	3	42	0	2	.955
1990	—Medicine Hat (Pio.)	OF	38	118	14	25	2	0	0	8	.212	6	29	8	35	4	1	.975
1991	—Myrtle Beach (SAL)	OF	110	388	39	86	7	2	2	27	.222	27	84	35	153	9	8	.953
1992	—St. Cathar. (NYP)	OF	62	244	37	50	3	1	0	11	.205	19	75	33	94	7	2	.981
	—Knoxville (South.)	OF	5	14	1	0	0	0	0	0	.000	1	4	1	15	1	0	1.000
1993	—Hagerstown (SAL)	OF	131	501	78	120	21	4	3	46	.240	53	103	54	254	10	12	.957
1994	—Dunedin (Fla. St.)	OF	118	490	74	132	18	3	3	31	.269	32	104	*61	221	13	4	.983
1995	—Knoxville (South.)	OF	116	454	66	107	12	3	1	29	.236	27	97	57	159	3	9	.947

ROBERTSON, RICH — P — TWINS

PERSONAL: Born September 15, 1968, in Nacogdoches, Tex. . . . 6-4/175. . . . Throws left, bats left. . . . Full name: Richard Wayne Robertson.
HIGH SCHOOL: Waller (Tex.).
JUNIOR COLLEGE: San Jacinto College (Tex.).
COLLEGE: Texas A&M.
TRANSACTIONS/CAREER NOTES: Selected by San Diego Padres organization in 32nd round of free-agent draft (June 5, 1989); did not sign. . . . Selected by Pittsburgh Pirates organization in ninth round of free-agent draft (June 4, 1990). . . . On Buffalo disabled list (June 10-19, 1993). . . . Claimed on waivers by Minnesota Twins (November 4, 1994).

Year	Team (League)	W	L	Pct.	ERA	G	GS	CG	ShO	Sv.	IP	H	R	ER	BB	SO
1990	—Welland (NYP)	3	4	.429	3.08	16	13	0	0	0	64 1/3	51	34	22	55	80
1991	—Augusta (S. Atl.)	4	7	.364	4.99	13	12	1	0	0	74	73	52	41	51	62
	—Salem (Carolina)	2	4	.333	4.93	12	11	0	0	0	45 2/3	34	32	25	42	32
1992	—Salem (Carolina)	3	0	1.000	3.41	6	6	0	0	0	37	29	18	14	10	27
	—Carolina (South.)	6	7	.462	3.03	20	20	1	1	0	124 2/3	127	51	42	41	107
1993	—Buffalo (A.A.)	9	8	.529	4.28	23	23	2	0	0	132 1/3	141	67	63	52	71
	—Pittsburgh (N.L.)	0	1	.000	6.00	9	0	0	0	0	9	15	6	6	4	5
1994	—Buffalo (A.A.)	5	10	.333	3.11	18	17	0	0	0	118 2/3	112	47	41	36	71
	—Pittsburgh (N.L.)	0	0	...	6.89	8	0	0	0	0	15 2/3	20	12	12	10	8
1995	—Salt Lake (PCL)■	5	0	1.000	2.44	7	7	1	0	0	44 1/3	31	13	12	12	40
	—Minnesota (A.L.)	2	0	1.000	3.83	25	4	1	0	0	51 2/3	48	28	22	31	38
A.L. totals (1 year)		2	0	1.000	3.83	25	4	1	0	0	51 2/3	48	28	22	31	38
N.L. totals (2 years)		0	1	.000	6.57	17	0	0	0	0	24 2/3	35	18	18	14	13
Major league totals (3 years)		2	1	.667	4.72	42	4	1	0	0	76 1/3	83	46	40	45	51

ROBINSON, KEN — P — BLUE JAYS

PERSONAL: Born November 3, 1969, in Barberton, O. . . . 5-9/170. . . . Throws right, bats right. . . . Full name: Kenneth Neal Robinson.
COLLEGE: Florida State.
TRANSACTIONS/CAREER NOTES: Selected by Toronto Blue Jays organization in 10th round of free-agent draft (June 3, 1991).

Year	Team (League)	W	L	Pct.	ERA	G	GS	CG	ShO	Sv.	IP	H	R	ER	BB	SO
1991	—Medicine Hat (Pio.)	0	1	.000	3.86	6	2	0	0	0	11 2/3	12	8	5	5	18
1992	—Myrtle Beach (SAL)	1	0	1.000	2.82	20	0	0	0	1	38 1/3	25	12	12	30	45
1993	—Hagerstown (S. Atl.)	4	7	.364	4.65	40	0	0	0	7	71 2/3	74	43	37	31	65
1994	—Hagerstown (S. Atl.)	4	1	.800	3.20	10	0	0	0	1	19 2/3	15	8	7	4	27
	—Dunedin (Fla. St.)	1	1	.500	1.80	5	0	0	0	0	10	6	2	2	4	16
	—Syracuse (Int'l)	4	2	.667	3.74	30	3	0	0	0	55 1/3	46	27	23	25	48
1995	—Syracuse (Int'l)	5	3	.625	3.22	38	0	0	0	2	50 1/3	37	18	18	12	61
	—Toronto (A.L.)	1	2	.333	3.69	21	0	0	0	0	39	25	21	16	22	31
Major league totals (1 year)		1	2	.333	3.69	21	0	0	0	0	39	25	21	16	22	31

R

RODRIGUEZ, ALEX — SS — MARINERS

PERSONAL: Born July 27, 1975, in New York. . . . 6-3/195. . . . Bats right, throws right. . . . Full name: Alexander Emmanuel Rodriguez.
HIGH SCHOOL: Westminister Christian (Miami).
TRANSACTIONS/CAREER NOTES: Selected by Seattle Mariners organization in first round (first pick overall) of free-agent draft (June 3, 1993).

			BATTING											FIELDING			
Year Team (League)	**Pos.**	**G**	**AB**	**R**	**H**	**2B**	**3B**	**HR**	**RBI**	**Avg.**	**BB**	**SO**	**SB**	**PO**	**A**	**E**	**Avg.**
1993—								Did not play.									
1994—Appleton (Midw.)	SS	65	248	49	79	17	6	14	55	.319	24	44	16	86	185	19	.934
—Jacksonv. (South.)	SS	17	59	7	17	4	1	1	8	.288	10	13	2	17	63	3	.964
—Seattle (A.L.)	SS	17	54	4	11	0	0	0	2	.204	3	20	3	20	45	6	.915
—Calgary (PCL)	SS	32	119	22	37	7	4	6	21	.311	8	25	2	45	104	3	.980
1995—Tacoma (PCL)	SS	54	214	37	77	12	3	15	45	.360	18	44	2	90	157	10	.961
—Seattle (A.L.)	SS-DH	48	142	15	33	6	2	5	19	.232	6	42	4	56	106	8	.953
Major league totals (2 years)		65	196	19	44	6	2	5	21	.224	9	62	7	76	151	14	.942

DIVISION SERIES RECORD

			BATTING											FIELDING			
Year Team (League)	**Pos.**	**G**	**AB**	**R**	**H**	**2B**	**3B**	**HR**	**RBI**	**Avg.**	**BB**	**SO**	**SB**	**PO**	**A**	**E**	**Avg.**
1995—Seattle (A.L.)	SS-PR	1	1	1	0	0	0	0	0	.000	0	0	0	0	0	0	...

CHAMPIONSHIP SERIES RECORD

			BATTING											FIELDING			
Year Team (League)	**Pos.**	**G**	**AB**	**R**	**H**	**2B**	**3B**	**HR**	**RBI**	**Avg.**	**BB**	**SO**	**SB**	**PO**	**A**	**E**	**Avg.**
1995—Seattle (A.L.)	PH	1	1	0	0	0	0	0	0	.000	0	1	0	...	...	...	...

RODRIGUEZ, CARLOS — SS — RED SOX

PERSONAL: Born November 1, 1967, in Mexico City, Mexico. . . . 5-9/160. . . . Bats both, throws right. . . . Full name: Carlos Marquez Rodriguez.
TRANSACTIONS/CAREER NOTES: Contract sold by Mexico City Tigers of Mexican League to New York Yankees organization (March 20, 1987). . . . Granted free agency (October 15, 1993). . . . Signed by Boston Red Sox organization (December 8, 1993). . . . Released by Red Sox (December 5, 1994). . . . Re-signed by Pawtucket, Red Sox organization (January 9, 1995). . . . On Pawtucket disabled list (April 6-July 5, 1995).
STATISTICAL NOTES: Led Gulf Coast League shortstops with .950 fielding percentage, 78 putouts, 167 assists and 258 total chances in 1987. . . . Led Florida State League with 21 sacrifice hits in 1989.

			BATTING											FIELDING			
Year Team (League)	**Pos.**	**G**	**AB**	**R**	**H**	**2B**	**3B**	**HR**	**RBI**	**Avg.**	**BB**	**SO**	**SB**	**PO**	**A**	**E**	**Avg.**
1987—GC Yankees (GCL)	SS-2B	50	115	15	18	0	0	0	11	.157	23	8	2	†79	†168	13	†.950
1988—Fort Lauder. (FSL)	SS-2B	124	461	39	110	15	1	0	36	.239	23	30	3	241	363	18	.971
1989—Fort Lauder. (FSL)	SS	102	353	48	85	15	1	0	26	.241	49	25	9	180	279	14	*.970
—Alb./Colon. (East.)	SS	36	107	15	27	4	2	0	8	.252	13	4	1	46	107	5	.968
1990—Alb./Colon. (East.)	SS	18	75	10	21	4	0	0	7	.280	2	2	1	23	58	3	.964
—Columbus (Int'l)	SS	71	220	31	60	12	0	0	16	.273	30	8	3	90	232	6	.982
1991—Columbus (Int'l)	SS	73	212	32	54	9	3	0	21	.255	42	13	1	138	236	11	.971
—New York (A.L.)	SS-2B	15	37	1	7	0	0	0	2	.189	1	2	0	11	34	2	.957
1992—Alb./Colon. (East.)	SS-2B-P	112	381	37	100	18	2	2	38	.262	29	26	3	194	339	13	.976
—Columbus (Int'l)	2B	1	4	0	0	0	0	0	0	.000	0	1	0	2	5	0	1.000
1993—Columbus (Int'l)	S-2-1-3-P	57	154	25	39	9	1	1	11	.253	20	10	2	78	114	1	.995
—Alb./Colon. (East.)	SS	38	152	16	56	14	1	0	30	.368	12	9	2	48	97	9	.942
1994—Pawtucket (Int'l)■	SS	47	165	24	46	5	1	3	25	.279	17	14	4	83	136	4	.982
—Boston (A.L.)	SS-2B-3B	57	174	15	50	14	1	1	13	.287	11	13	1	85	132	6	.973
1995—Pawtucket (Int'l)	SS	40	133	19	39	7	0	0	13	.293	20	8	1	51	99	6	.962
—GC Red Sox (GCL)	2B-SS	13	42	12	9	3	0	0	0	.214	9	3	0	20	24	2	.957
—Boston (A.L.)	2B-SS-3B	13	30	5	10	2	0	0	5	.333	2	2	0	16	27	1	.977
Major league totals (3 years)		85	241	21	67	16	1	1	20	.278	14	17	1	112	193	9	.971

RECORD AS PITCHER

Year Team (League)	**W**	**L**	**Pct.**	**ERA**	**G**	**GS**	**CG**	**ShO**	**Sv.**	**IP**	**H**	**R**	**ER**	**BB**	**SO**
1992—Alb./Colon. (East.)	0	0	...	0.00	1	0	0	0	0	1	1	0	0	0	0
1993—Columbus (Int'l)	0	0	...	0.00	1	0	0	0	0	1	2	0	0	0	0

RODRIGUEZ, FELIX — P — DODGERS

PERSONAL: Born December 5, 1972, in Montecristi, Dominican Republic. . . . 6-1/180. . . . Throws right, bats right. . . . Full name: Felix Antonio Rodriguez.
HIGH SCHOOL: Liceo Bijiador (Montecristy, Dominican Republic).
TRANSACTIONS/CAREER NOTES: Signed as non-drafted free agent by Los Angeles Dodgers organization (October 17, 1989). . . . On disabled list (August 11, 1992-remainder of season). . . . On Albuquerque disabled list (July 5-18, 1995).
STATISTICAL NOTES: Pitched 11-0 no-hit victory against Sarasota (August 28, 1993).

Year Team (League)	**W**	**L**	**Pct.**	**ERA**	**G**	**GS**	**CG**	**ShO**	**Sv.**	**IP**	**H**	**R**	**ER**	**BB**	**SO**
1993—Vero Beach (FSL)	8	8	.500	3.75	32	20	2	1	0	132	109	71	55	71	80
1994—San Antonio (Tex.)	6	8	.429	4.03	26	26	0	0	0	136 1/3	106	70	61	*88	126
1995—Albuquerque (PCL)	3	2	.600	4.24	14	11	0	0	0	51	52	29	24	26	46
—Los Angeles (N.L.)	1	1	.500	2.53	11	0	0	0	0	10 2/3	11	3	3	5	5
Major league totals (1 year)	1	1	.500	2.53	11	0	0	0	0	10 2/3	11	3	3	5	5

RECORD AS POSITION PLAYER

Year Team (League)	Pos.	G	AB	R	H	2B	3B	HR	RBI	Avg.	BB	SO	SB	PO	A	E	Avg.
		BATTING												FIELDING			
1990—Santo Domingo (DSL)	...	63	241	23	55	10	0	2	33	.228	15	52	4	...	...	...	...
1991—G.C. Dodgers (GCL) ...	C	45	139	15	37	8	1	2	21	.266	6	32	1	161	18	5	.973
1992—Great Falls (Pio.)	C-OF	32	110	20	32	8	0	2	20	.291	1	16	2	221	33	2	.992

RODRIGUEZ, FRANK — P — TWINS

PERSONAL: Born December 11, 1972, in Brooklyn, N.Y. . . . 6-0/195. . . . Throws right, bats right. . . . Full name: Francisco Rodriguez.
HIGH SCHOOL: Eastern District (Brooklyn, N.Y.).
COLLEGE: Howard College (Big Spring, Tex.).
TRANSACTIONS/CAREER NOTES: Selected by Boston Red Sox in second round of free-agent draft (June 4, 1990); pick received as compensation for Atlanta Braves signing of Type B free agent 1B Nick Esasky. . . . Traded by Red Sox with a player to be named later to Minnesota Twins for P Rick Aguilera (July 6, 1995); Twins acquired OF J.J. Johnson to complete deal (October 11, 1995).

Year Team (League)	W	L	Pct.	ERA	G	GS	CG	ShO	Sv.	IP	H	R	ER	BB	SO
1992—Lynchburg (Caro.)	12	7	.632	3.09	25	25	1	0	0	148 2/3	125	56	51	65	129
1993—New Britain (East.)	7	11	.389	3.74	28	26	•4	1	0	170 2/3	147	79	71	78	151
1994—Pawtucket (Int'l)	8	13	.381	3.92	28	28	*8	1	0	*186	182	95	81	60	*160
1995—Boston (A.L.)	0	2	.000	10.57	9	2	0	0	0	15 1/3	21	19	18	10	14
—Pawtucket (Int'l)	1	1	.500	4.00	13	2	0	0	2	27	19	12	12	8	18
—Minnesota (A.L.)■	5	6	.455	5.38	16	16	0	0	0	90 1/3	93	64	54	47	45
Major league totals (1 year)	5	8	.385	6.13	25	18	0	0	0	105 2/3	114	83	72	57	59

RECORD AS POSITION PLAYER

Year Team (League)	Pos.	G	AB	R	H	2B	3B	HR	RBI	Avg.	BB	SO	SB	PO	A	E	Avg.
		BATTING												FIELDING			
1991—GC Red Sox (GCL)	SS	3	14	3	7	0	1	0	3	.500	0	1	0	9	10	1	.950
—Elmira (NYP)	SS	67	255	36	69	5	3	6	31	.271	13	38	3	95	209	24	.927

RODRIGUEZ, HENRY — OF/1B — EXPOS

PERSONAL: Born November 8, 1967, in Santo Domingo, Dominican Republic. . . . 6-1/205. . . . Bats left, throws left. . . . Full name: Henry Anderson Lorenzo Rodriguez.
HIGH SCHOOL: Liceo Republica de Paraguay.
TRANSACTIONS/CAREER NOTES: Signed as non-drafted free agent by Los Angeles Dodgers organization (July 14, 1985). . . . Traded by Dodgers with IF Jeff Treadway to Montreal Expos for OF Roberto Kelly and P Joey Eischen (May 23, 1995). . . . On Montreal disabled list (June 2-September 1, 1995); included rehabilitation assignment to Ottawa (August 7-16).
HONORS: Named Texas League Most Valuable Player (1990).
STATISTICAL NOTES: Tied for Gulf Coast League lead with seven intentional bases on balls received in 1987. . . . Led Texas League with 14 sacrifice flies in 1990. . . . Tied for Pacific Coast League lead with 10 sacrifice flies in 1992.

Year Team (League)	Pos.	G	AB	R	H	2B	3B	HR	RBI	Avg.	BB	SO	SB	PO	A	E	Avg.
		BATTING												FIELDING			
1987—GC Dodgers (GCL)	1B-SS	49	148	23	49	7	3	0	15	*.331	16	15	3	309	23	6	.982
1988—Santo Dom. (DSL)	...	19	21	9	8	2	0	0	10	.381	10	6	4	...	...	...	...
—Salem (Northwest)	1B	72	291	47	84	14	4	2	39	.289	21	42	14	585	*38	7	.989
1989—Vero Beach (FSL)	1B-OF	126	433	53	123	*33	1	10	73	.284	48	58	7	1072	66	12	.990
—Bakersfield (Calif.)	1B	3	9	2	2	0	0	1	2	.222	0	3	0	8	0	0	1.000
1990—San Antonio (Tex.)	OF	129	495	82	144	22	9	*28	*109	.291	61	66	5	223	5	10	.958
1991—Albuquerque (PCL)	OF-1B	121	446	61	121	22	5	10	67	.271	25	62	4	234	12	5	.980
1992—Albuquerque (PCL)	1B-OF	94	365	59	111	21	5	14	72	.304	31	57	1	484	41	10	.981
—Los Angeles (N.L.)	OF-1B	53	146	11	32	7	0	3	14	.219	8	30	0	68	8	3	.962
1993—Albuquerque (PCL)	1B-OF	46	179	26	53	13	5	4	30	.296	14	37	1	277	18	5	.983
—Los Angeles (N.L.)	OF-1B	76	176	20	39	10	0	8	23	.222	11	39	1	127	9	1	.993
1994—Los Angeles (N.L.)	OF-1B	104	306	33	82	14	2	8	49	.268	17	58	0	198	9	2	.990
1995—Los Angeles (N.L.)	OF-1B	21	80	6	21	4	1	1	10	.263	5	17	0	37	0	0	1.000
—Montreal (N.L.)■	1B-OF	24	58	7	12	0	0	1	5	.207	6	11	0	88	7	1	.990
—Ottawa (Int'l)	DH	4	15	0	3	1	0	0	2	.200	1	4	0	0	0	0	...
Major league totals (4 years)		278	766	77	186	35	3	21	101	.243	47	155	1	518	33	7	.987

RODRIGUEZ, IVAN — C — RANGERS

PERSONAL: Born November 30, 1971, in Vega Baja, Puerto Rico. . . . 5-9/205. . . . Bats right, throws right.
HIGH SCHOOL: Lina Padron Rivera (Vega Baja, Puerto Rico).
TRANSACTIONS/CAREER NOTES: Signed as non-drafted free agent by Texas Rangers organization (July 27, 1988). . . . On disabled list (June 6-27, 1992).
HONORS: Won A.L. Gold Glove at catcher (1992-95). . . . Named catcher on The Sporting News A.L. All-Star team (1994-95). . . . Named catcher on The Sporting News A.L. Silver Slugger team (1994-95).
STATISTICAL NOTES: Led South Atlantic League catchers with 34 double plays in 1989. . . . Led Florida State League catchers with 842 total chances in 1990.

Year Team (League)	Pos.	G	AB	R	H	2B	3B	HR	RBI	Avg.	BB	SO	SB	PO	A	E	Avg.
		BATTING												FIELDING			
1989—Gastonia (S. Atl.)	C	112	386	38	92	22	1	7	42	.238	21	58	2	691	*96	11	.986
1990—Charlotte (Fla. St.)	C	109	408	48	117	17	7	2	55	.287	12	50	1	*727	101	14	.983
1991—Tulsa (Texas)	C	50	175	16	48	7	2	3	28	.274	6	27	1	210	33	3	.988
—Texas (A.L.)	C	88	280	24	74	16	0	3	27	.264	5	42	0	517	62	10	.983
1992—Texas (A.L.)	C-DH	123	420	39	109	16	1	8	37	.260	24	73	0	763	85	*15	.983
1993—Texas (A.L.)	C-DH	137	473	56	129	28	4	10	66	.273	29	70	8	801	76	8	.991
1994—Texas (A.L.)	C	99	363	56	108	19	1	16	57	.298	31	42	6	600	44	5	.992
1995—Texas (A.L.)	C-DH	130	492	56	149	32	2	12	67	.303	16	48	0	707	*67	8	.990
Major league totals (5 years)		577	2028	231	569	111	8	49	254	.281	105	275	14	3388	334	46	.988

ALL-STAR GAME RECORD

NOTES: Shares single-game record for most at-bats in nine-inning game—5 (July 12, 1994).

		BATTING											FIELDING			
Year League	Pos.	AB	R	H	2B	3B	HR	RBI	Avg.	BB	SO	SB	PO	A	E	Avg.
1992— American	C	2	0	0	0	0	0	0	.000	0	1	0	4	0	0	1.000
1993— American	C	2	1	1	1	0	0	0	.500	0	0	0	3	0	0	1.000
1994— American	C	5	1	2	0	0	0	0	.400	0	1	0	5	0	0	1.000
1995— American	C	3	0	0	0	0	0	0	.000	0	1	0	6	1	0	1.000
All-Star Game totals (4 years)		12	2	3	1	0	0	0	.250	0	3	0	18	1	0	1.000

RODRIGUEZ, RICH — P — REDS

PERSONAL: Born March 1, 1963, in Downey, Calif. . . . 6-0/200. . . . Throws left, bats left. . . . Full name: Richard Anthony Rodriguez.
HIGH SCHOOL: Mountain View (El Monte, Calif.).
COLLEGE: Tennessee.
TRANSACTIONS/CAREER NOTES: Selected by Kansas City Royals organization in 17th round of free-agent draft (June 8, 1981); did not sign. . . . Selected by New York Mets organization in ninth round of free-agent draft (June 4, 1984). . . . Traded by Mets organization to Wichita, San Diego Padres organization, for 1B Brad Pounders and 1B Bill Stevenson (January 13, 1989). . . . Traded by Padres with 3B Gary Sheffield to Florida Marlins for P Trevor Hoffman, P Jose Martinez and P Andres Berumen (June 24, 1993). . . . Released by Marlins (March 29, 1994). . . . Signed by St. Louis Cardinals (April 1, 1994). . . . On disabled list (April 27, 1995-remainder of season). . . . Released by Cardinals (November 20, 1995). . . . Signed by Cincinnati Reds organization (January 2, 1996).
MISCELLANEOUS: Appeared in one game as pinch-runner (1991). . . . Had sacrifice hit in only appearance as pinch-hitter (1992).

Year Team (League)	W	L	Pct.	ERA	G	GS	CG	ShO	Sv.	IP	H	R	ER	BB	SO
1984— Little Falls (NYP)	2	1	.667	2.80	25	1	0	0	0	35 1/3	28	21	11	36	27
1985— Columbia (S. Atl.)	6	3	.667	4.03	49	3	0	0	6	80 1/3	89	41	36	36	71
1986— Lynchburg (Caro.)	2	1	.667	3.57	36	0	0	0	3	45 1/3	37	20	18	19	38
— Jackson (Texas)	3	4	.429	9.00	13	5	1	0	0	33	51	35	33	15	15
1987— Lynchburg (Caro.)	3	1	.750	2.78	*69	0	0	0	5	68	69	23	21	26	59
1988— Jackson (Texas)	2	7	.222	2.87	47	1	0	0	6	78 1/3	66	35	25	42	68
1989— Wichita (Texas)■	8	3	.727	3.63	54	0	0	0	8	74 1/3	74	30	30	37	40
1990— Las Vegas (PCL)	3	4	.429	3.51	27	2	0	0	8	59	50	24	23	22	46
— San Diego (N.L.)	1	1	.500	2.83	32	0	0	0	1	47 2/3	52	17	15	16	22
1991— San Diego (N.L.)	3	1	.750	3.26	64	1	0	0	0	80	66	31	29	44	40
1992— San Diego (N.L.)	6	3	.667	2.37	61	1	0	0	0	91	77	28	24	29	64
1993— San Diego (N.L.)	2	3	.400	3.30	34	0	0	0	2	30	34	15	11	9	22
— Florida (N.L.)■	0	1	.000	4.11	36	0	0	0	1	46	39	23	21	24	21
1994— St. Louis (N.L.)■	3	5	.375	4.03	56	0	0	0	0	60 1/3	62	30	27	26	43
1995— St. Louis (N.L.)	0	0	...	0.00	1	0	0	0	0	1 2/3	0	0	0	0	0
Major league totals (6 years)	15	14	.517	3.20	284	2	0	0	4	356 2/3	330	144	127	148	212

RODRIGUEZ, STEVE — 2B — TIGERS

PERSONAL: Born November 29, 1970, in Las Vegas. . . . 5-8/170. . . . Bats right, throws right. . . . Full name: Steven James Rodriguez.
HIGH SCHOOL: Valley (Las Vegas).
COLLEGE: Pepperdine.
TRANSACTIONS/CAREER NOTES: Selected by Boston Red Sox organization in fifth round of free-agent draft (June 1, 1992). . . . On Pawtucket disabled list (June 27-July 17, 1994). . . . Claimed on waivers by Detroit Tigers (September 8, 1995).
STATISTICAL NOTES: Led Carolina League second basemen with 236 putouts, 348 assists and 606 total chances in 1993.

			BATTING												FIELDING			
Year Team (League)	Pos.	G	AB	R	H	2B	3B	HR	RBI	Avg.	BB	SO	SB	PO	A	E	Avg.
1992— Winter Haven (FSL)	2B	26	87	13	15	0	0	1	5	.172	9	17	4	44	78	7	.946
1993— Lynchburg (Caro.)	2B-SS	120	493	78	135	26	3	3	42	.274	31	69	20	†236	†350	22	.964
1994— New Britain (East.)	2B-SS	38	159	25	45	5	2	0	14	.283	9	14	8	74	117	1	.995
— Pawtucket (Int'l)	2B	62	233	28	70	11	0	1	21	.300	14	30	11	102	156	2	.992
1995— Pawtucket (Int'l)	2B	82	324	39	78	16	3	1	24	.241	25	34	12	167	191	9	.975
— Boston (A.L.)	SS-DH-2B	6	8	1	1	0	0	0	0	.125	1	1	1	1	4	1	.833
— Detroit (A.L.)■	2B-SS	12	31	4	6	1	0	0	0	.194	5	9	1	21	34	1	.982
Major league totals (1 year)		18	39	5	7	1	0	0	0	.179	6	10	2	22	38	2	.968

ROGERS, BRYAN — P — METS

PERSONAL: Born October 30, 1967, in Hollister, Calif. . . . 5-11/170. . . . Throws right, bats right. . . . Full name: Bryan Alan Rogers.
HIGH SCHOOL: Hollister (Calif.).
JUNIOR COLLEGE: Gavilan (Calif.).
COLLEGE: Sonoma State (Calif.).
TRANSACTIONS/CAREER NOTES: Selected by New York Mets organization in 39th round of free-agent draft (June 1, 1988). . . . On Binghamton disabled list (June 27-July 4, 1992). . . . On Binghamton suspended list (August 17-19, 1994).

Year Team (League)	W	L	Pct.	ERA	G	GS	CG	ShO	Sv.	IP	H	R	ER	BB	SO
1988— Kingsport (Appal.)	2	3	.400	6.32	15	2	0	0	0	31 1/3	30	33	22	14	35
1989— Columbia (S. Atl.)	3	2	.600	3.12	14	4	0	0	3	43 1/3	36	16	15	14	36
1990— St. Lucie (Fla. St.)	9	8	.529	3.09	29	19	5	0	4	148 2/3	127	66	51	26	96
1991— Williamsport (East.)	6	8	.429	4.72	41	0	0	0	15	61	73	33	32	18	33
1992— Binghamton (East.)	3	2	.600	4.33	22	0	0	0	1	35 1/3	37	21	17	7	20
— St. Lucie (Fla. St.)	2	4	.333	2.93	17	0	0	0	2	30 2/3	24	12	10	7	17
1993— Binghamton (East.)	5	4	.556	2.34	*62	0	0	0	8	84 2/3	80	29	22	25	42
1994— Norfolk (Int'l)	2	2	.500	5.40	20	0	0	0	0	30	35	19	18	10	8
— Binghamton (East.)	5	1	.833	1.65	41	0	0	0	11	60	49	17	11	14	46
1995— Norfolk (Int.)	8	3	.727	2.21	56	0	0	0	10	77 1/3	58	22	19	22	50

R

ROGERS, JIMMY — P — BLUE JAYS

PERSONAL: Born January 3, 1967, in Tulsa, Okla. . . . 6-2/205. . . . Throws right, bats right. . . . Full name: James Randall Rogers.
HIGH SCHOOL: Daniel Webster (Tulsa, Okla.).
JUNIOR COLLEGE: Seminole (Okla.) Junior College.
TRANSACTIONS/CAREER NOTES: Selected by Toronto Blue Jays organization in 16th round of free-agent draft (June 2, 1986). . . . On disabled list (April 9-September 8, 1992; April 8-May 15 and June 15-22, 1993).
HONORS: Named South Atlantic League Most Outstanding Pitcher (1988).

Year	Team (League)	W	L	Pct.	ERA	G	GS	CG	ShO	Sv.	IP	H	R	ER	BB	SO
1987—	St. Cathar. (NYP)	2	4	.333	3.36	13	12	0	0	0	56 1/3	46	33	21	24	60
1988—	Myrtle Beach (SAL)	*18	4	*.818	3.35	33	•32	2	0	0	188 1/3	145	84	70	95	*198
1989—	Knoxville (South.)	12	10	.545	4.56	32	*30	1	0	0	158	136	89	80	132	120
1990—	Knoxville (South.)	9	12	.429	4.47	32	30	2	1	0	173 1/3	179	98	86	104	113
1991—	Knoxville (South.)	7	11	.389	3.31	28	27	4	•3	0	168 1/3	140	70	62	90	122
1992—								Did not play.								
1993—	Knoxville (South.)	7	7	.500	4.04	19	19	0	0	0	100 1/3	107	54	45	33	80
1994—	Syracuse (Int'l)	5	4	.556	4.60	31	10	0	0	0	94	82	51	48	49	69
1995—	Syracuse (Int'l)	3	4	.429	3.05	38	0	0	0	1	73 2/3	65	26	25	31	82
—	Toronto (A.L.)	2	4	.333	5.70	19	0	0	0	0	23 2/3	21	15	15	18	13
Major league totals (1 year)		2	4	.333	5.70	19	0	0	0	0	23 2/3	21	15	15	18	13

ROGERS, KENNY — P — YANKEES

PERSONAL: Born November 10, 1964, in Savannah, Ga. . . . 6-1/205. . . . Throws left, bats left. . . . Full name: Kenneth Scott Rogers.
HIGH SCHOOL: Plant City (Fla.).
TRANSACTIONS/CAREER NOTES: Selected by Texas Rangers organization in 39th round of free-agent draft (June 7, 1982). . . . On Tulsa disabled list (April 12-30, 1986). . . . Granted free agency (October 31, 1995). . . . Signed by New York Yankees (December 30, 1995).
STATISTICAL NOTES: Tied for A.L. lead with five balks in 1993. . . . Pitched 4-0 perfect game against California (July 28, 1994).

Year	Team (League)	W	L	Pct.	ERA	G	GS	CG	ShO	Sv.	IP	H	R	ER	BB	SO
1982—	GC Rangers (GCL)	0	0	...	0.00	2	0	0	0	0	3	0	0	0	0	4
1983—	GC Rangers (GCL)	4	1	.800	2.36	15	6	0	0	1	53 1/3	40	21	14	20	36
1984—	Burlington (Midw.)	4	7	.364	3.98	39	4	1	0	3	92 2/3	87	52	41	33	93
1985—	Day. Beach (FSL)	0	1	.000	7.20	6	0	0	0	0	10	12	9	8	11	9
—	Burlington (Midw.)	2	5	.286	2.84	33	4	2	1	4	95	67	34	30	62	96
1986—	Tulsa (Texas)	0	3	.000	9.91	10	4	0	0	0	26 1/3	39	30	29	18	23
—	Salem (Carolina)	2	7	.222	6.27	12	12	0	0	0	66	75	54	46	26	46
1987—	Charlotte (Fla. St.)	0	3	.000	4.76	5	3	0	0	0	17	17	13	9	8	14
—	Tulsa (Texas)	1	5	.167	5.35	28	6	0	0	2	69	80	51	41	35	59
1988—	Tulsa (Texas)	4	6	.400	4.00	13	13	2	0	0	83 1/3	73	43	37	34	76
—	Charlotte (Fla. St.)	2	0	1.000	1.27	8	6	0	0	1	35 1/3	22	8	5	11	26
1989—	Texas (A.L.)	3	4	.429	2.93	73	0	0	0	2	73 2/3	60	28	24	42	63
1990—	Texas (A.L.)	10	6	.625	3.13	69	3	0	0	15	97 2/3	93	40	34	42	74
1991—	Texas (A.L.)	10	10	.500	5.42	63	9	0	0	5	109 2/3	121	80	66	61	73
1992—	Texas (A.L.)	3	6	.333	3.09	*81	0	0	0	6	78 2/3	80	32	27	26	70
1993—	Texas (A.L.)	16	10	.615	4.10	35	33	5	0	0	208 1/3	210	108	95	71	140
1994—	Texas (A.L.)	11	8	.579	4.46	24	24	6	2	0	167 1/3	169	93	83	52	120
1995—	Texas (A.L.)	17	7	.708	3.38	31	31	3	1	0	208	192	87	78	76	140
Major league totals (7 years)		70	51	.579	3.88	376	100	14	3	28	943 1/3	925	468	407	370	680

ALL-STAR GAME RECORD

Year	League	W	L	Pct.	ERA	GS	CG	ShO	Sv.	IP	H	R	ER	BB	SO
1995—	American	0	0	...	9.00	0	0	0	0	1	1	1	1	0	2

ROGERS, KEVIN — P — PIRATES

PERSONAL: Born August 20, 1968, in Cleveland, Miss. . . . 6-1/198. . . . Throws left, bats left. . . . Full name: Charles Kevin Rogers.
HIGH SCHOOL: Cleveland (Miss.).
JUNIOR COLLEGE: Mississippi Delta Junior College.
TRANSACTIONS/CAREER NOTES: Selected by San Francisco Giants organization in ninth round of free-agent draft (June 1, 1988). . . . On disabled list (May 2, 1994-remainder of season). . . . On San Francisco disabled list (April 22, 1995-entire season); included rehabilitation assignments to San Jose (April 29-May 4 and May 14-17) and Phoenix (June 8-12). . . . Claimed on waivers by Pittsburgh Pirates (October 26, 1995).

Year	Team (League)	W	L	Pct.	ERA	G	GS	CG	ShO	Sv.	IP	H	R	ER	BB	SO
1988—	Pocatello (Pioneer)	2	8	.200	6.20	13	13	1	0	0	69 2/3	73	51	48	35	71
1989—	Clinton (Midwest)	13	8	.619	2.55	29	•28	4	0	0	169 1/3	128	74	48	78	168
1990—	San Jose (Calif.)	14	5	.737	3.61	28	26	1	1	0	172	143	86	69	68	*186
1991—	Shreveport (Texas)	4	6	.400	3.36	22	22	2	0	0	118	124	63	44	54	108
1992—	Shreveport (Texas)	8	5	.615	2.58	16	16	2	2	0	101	87	34	29	29	110
—	Phoenix (PCL)	3	3	.500	4.00	11	11	1	1	0	69 2/3	63	34	31	22	62
—	San Francisco (N.L.)	0	2	.000	4.24	6	6	0	0	0	34	37	17	16	13	26
1993—	San Francisco (N.L.)	2	2	.500	2.68	64	0	0	0	0	80 2/3	71	28	24	28	62
1994—	San Francisco (N.L.)	0	0	...	3.48	9	0	0	0	0	10 1/3	10	4	4	6	7
1995—	San Jose (Calif.)	0	2	.000	1.80	4	4	0	0	0	10	10	2	2	1	5
—	Phoenix (PCL)	0	0	...	4.15	3	1	0	0	0	4 1/3	9	2	2	2	1
Major league totals (3 years)		2	4	.333	3.17	79	6	0	0	0	125	118	49	44	47	95

ROJAS, MEL — P — EXPOS

PERSONAL: Born December 10, 1966, in Haina, Dominican Republic. . . . 5-11/195. . . . Throws right, bats right. . . . Full name: Melquiades Rojas. . . . Nephew of Felipe Alou, manager, Montreal Expos, and major league outfielder/first baseman with six teams (1958-74); nephew of Matty Alou, major league outfielder with six teams (1960-74); nephew of Jesus Alou, major league outfielder with four teams (1963-75 and 1978-79); brother of Francisco Rojas, minor league outfielder (1978-79); and cousin of Moises Alou, outfielder, Expos. . . . Name pronounced RO-hoss.

HIGH SCHOOL: Liceo Manresa (Santo Domingo, Dominican Republic).

TRANSACTIONS/CAREER NOTES: Signed as non-drafted free agent by Montreal Expos organization (November 7, 1985). . . . On Rockford disabled list (May 7-June 14, 1988). . . . On West Palm Beach disabled list (August 8, 1988-remainder of season). . . . On Indianapolis disabled list (June 26-July 5, 1991). . . . On disabled list (July 4-19, 1993).

Year	Team (League)	W	L	Pct.	ERA	G	GS	CG	ShO	Sv.	IP	H	R	ER	BB	SO
1986—	GC Expos (GCL)	4	5	.444	4.88	13	12	1	0	0	55 1/3	63	39	30	37	34
1987—	Burlington (Midw.)	8	9	.471	3.80	25	25	4	1	0	158 2/3	146	84	67	67	100
1988—	Rockford (Midw.)	6	4	.600	2.45	12	12	0	0	0	73 1/3	52	30	20	29	72
—	WP Beach (FSL)	1	0	1.000	3.60	2	2	0	0	0	5	4	2	2	1	4
1989—	Jacksonville (Sou.)	10	7	.588	2.49	34	12	1	1	5	112	62	39	31	57	104
1990—	Indianapolis (A.A.)	2	4	.333	3.13	17	17	0	0	0	97 2/3	84	42	34	47	64
—	Montreal (N.L.)	3	1	.750	3.60	23	0	0	0	1	40	34	17	16	24	26
1991—	Montreal (N.L.)	3	3	.500	3.75	37	0	0	0	6	48	42	21	20	13	37
—	Indianapolis (A.A.)	4	2	.667	4.10	14	10	0	0	1	52 2/3	50	29	24	14	55
1992—	Indianapolis (A.A.)	2	1	.667	5.40	4	0	0	0	0	8 1/3	10	5	5	3	7
—	Montreal (N.L.)	7	1	.875	1.43	68	0	0	0	10	100 2/3	71	17	16	34	70
1993—	Montreal (N.L.)	5	8	.385	2.95	66	0	0	0	10	88 1/3	80	39	29	30	48
1994—	Montreal (N.L.)	3	2	.600	3.32	58	0	0	0	16	84	71	35	31	21	84
1995—	Montreal (N.L.)	1	4	.200	4.12	59	0	0	0	30	67 2/3	69	32	31	29	61
Major league totals (6 years)		22	19	.537	3.00	311	0	0	0	73	428 2/3	367	161	143	151	326

RONAN, MARC — C — YANKEES

PERSONAL: Born September 19, 1969, in Ozark, Ala. . . . 6-2/190. . . . Bats left, throws right. . . . Full name: Edward Marcus Ronan.

HIGH SCHOOL: H.B. Plant (Tampa, Fla.).

COLLEGE: Florida State.

TRANSACTIONS/CAREER NOTES: Selected by St. Louis Cardinals organization in third round of free-agent draft (June 4, 1990). . . . On suspended list (May 13-15, 1995). . . . Traded by Cardinals organization to Milwaukee Brewers organization for a player to be named later (October 19, 1995). . . . Selected by New York Yankees from Brewers organization in Rule 5 major league draft (December 4, 1995).

STATISTICAL NOTES: Led Midwest League catchers with 919 total chances in 1992.

				BATTING										FIELDING			
Year	Team (League)	Pos.	G	AB	R	H	2B	3B	HR	RBI	Avg.	BB	SO	SB	PO	A	E	Avg.
1990—	Hamilton (NYP)	C-1B	56	167	14	38	6	0	1	15	.228	15	37	1	357	43	9	.978
1991—	Savannah (S. Atl.)	C	108	343	39	81	10	1	0	45	.236	38	54	11	678	87	9	.988
1992—	Springfield (Midw.)	C	110	376	45	81	19	2	6	48	.215	23	58	4	*818	90	11	.988
1993—	St. Peters. (FSL)	C-OF	25	87	13	27	5	0	0	6	.310	6	10	0	155	30	2	.989
—	Arkansas (Texas)	C	96	281	33	60	16	1	7	34	.214	26	47	1	564	65	4	*.994
—	St. Louis (N.L.)	C	6	12	0	1	0	0	0	0	.083	0	5	0	29	0	0	1.000
1994—	Louisville (A.A.)	C	84	269	32	64	11	2	2	21	.238	12	43	3	525	38	5	.991
1995—	Louisville (A.A.)	C	78	225	15	48	8	0	0	8	.213	14	42	4	417	35	3	*.993
Major league totals (1 year)			6	12	0	1	0	0	0	0	.083	0	5	0	29	0	0	1.000

ROPER, JOHN — P — REDS

PERSONAL: Born November 21, 1971, in Southern Pines, N.C. . . . 6-0/175. . . . Throws right, bats right. . . . Full name: John Christopher Roper.

HIGH SCHOOL: Hoke County (Raeford, N.C.).

TRANSACTIONS/CAREER NOTES: Selected by Cincinnati Reds organization in 12th round of free-agent draft (June 4, 1990). . . . On disabled list (July 6-August 21, 1992). . . . On Indianapolis disabled list (May 27-June 6, 1993). . . . On Cincinnati disabled list (June 19-July 19, 1993). . . . On Cincinnati disabled list (May 1-June 12, 1995); including rehabilitation assignments to Chattanooga (May 19-30) and Indianapolis (May 30-June 10). . . . On Indianapolis disabled list (July 16-21, 1995). . . . Traded by Reds with OF Deion Sanders, P Ricky Pickett, P Scott Service and IF Dave McCarty to San Francisco Giants for OF Darren Lewis, P Mark Portugal and P Dave Burba (July 21, 1995). . . . On Phoenix disabled list (July 23-September 2, 1995). . . . Claimed on waivers by Reds (October 26, 1995).

STATISTICAL NOTES: Pitched 1-0 no-hit victory against Birmingham (August 28, 1992, first game).

Year	Team (League)	W	L	Pct.	ERA	G	GS	CG	ShO	Sv.	IP	H	R	ER	BB	SO
1990—	GC Reds (GCL)	7	2	.778	0.97	13	•13	0	0	0	74	41	10	8	31	76
1991—	Char., W.Va. (S. Atl.)	14	9	.609	2.27	27	•27	5	•3	0	186 2/3	135	59	47	67	*189
1992—	Chattanooga (Sou.)	10	9	.526	4.10	20	20	1	1	0	120 2/3	115	57	55	37	99
1993—	Indianapolis (A.A.)	3	5	.375	4.45	12	12	0	0	0	54 2/3	56	33	27	30	42
—	Cincinnati (N.L.)	2	5	.286	5.63	16	15	0	0	0	80	92	51	50	36	54
1994—	Indianapolis (A.A.)	7	0	1.000	2.17	8	8	1	0	0	58	48	17	14	10	33
—	Cincinnati (N.L.)	6	2	.750	4.50	16	15	0	0	0	92	90	49	46	30	51
1995—	Cincinnati (N.L.)	0	0	...	10.29	2	2	0	0	0	7	13	9	8	4	6
—	Chattanooga (Sou.)	0	0	...	1.00	3	3	0	0	0	9	5	1	1	1	6
—	Indianapolis (A.A.)	2	5	.286	4.97	8	8	0	0	0	41 2/3	47	26	23	16	23
—	Phoenix (PCL)■	0	1	.000	9.00	1	1	0	0	0	3	5	3	3	0	2
—	San Francisco (N.L.)	0	0	...	27.00	1	0	0	0	0	1	2	3	3	2	0
Major league totals (3 years)		8	7	.533	5.35	35	32	0	0	0	180	197	112	107	72	111

ROSSELLI, JOE P GIANTS

PERSONAL: Born May 28, 1972, in Burbank, Calif. . . . 6-1/170. . . . Throws left, bats right. . . . Full name: Joseph D. Rosselli.
HIGH SCHOOL: Mission Hills (Calif.)-Alemany.
TRANSACTIONS/CAREER NOTES: Selected by San Francisco Giants organization in supplemental round ("sandwich pick" between second and third round) of free-agent draft (June 4, 1990); pick received as compensation for Cleveland Indians signing Type C free-agent OF Candy Maldonado. . . . On disabled list (August 1-20, 1992 and April 29, 1993-remainder of season). . . . On Phoenix disabled list (August 1-8, 1994). . . . On San Francisco disabled list (May 14-July 2, 1995); included rehabilitation assignment to Phoenix (June 16-July 2).
HONORS: Named California League Pitcher of the Year (1992).

Year	Team (League)	W	L	Pct.	ERA	G	GS	CG	ShO	Sv.	IP	H	R	ER	BB	SO
1990—	Everett (N'west)	4	4	.500	4.71	15	15	0	0	0	78 1/3	87	47	41	29	90
1991—	Clinton (Midwest)	8	7	.533	3.10	22	22	2	0	0	153 2/3	144	70	53	49	127
1992—	San Jose (Calif.)	11	4	.733	*2.41	22	22	4	0	0	149 2/3	145	50	40	46	111
1993—	Shreveport (Texas)	0	1	.000	3.13	4	4	0	0	0	23	22	9	8	7	19
1994—	Shreveport (Texas)	7	2	.778	1.89	14	14	2	•2	0	90 2/3	67	24	19	17	54
	—Phoenix (PCL)	1	8	.111	4.94	13	13	0	0	0	74 2/3	96	46	41	15	35
1995—	San Francisco (N.L.)	2	1	.667	8.70	9	5	0	0	0	30	39	29	29	20	7
	—Phoenix (PCL)	4	3	.571	4.99	13	13	1	0	0	79 1/3	94	47	44	12	34
Major league totals (1 year)		2	1	.667	8.70	9	5	0	0	0	30	39	29	29	20	7

ROWLAND, RICH C BLUE JAYS

PERSONAL: Born February 25, 1967, in Cloverdale, Calif. . . . 6-1/215. . . . Bats right, throws right. . . . Full name: Richard Garnet Rowland.
HIGH SCHOOL: Cloverdale (Calif.).
JUNIOR COLLEGE: Mendocino Community College (Calif.).
TRANSACTIONS/CAREER NOTES: Selected by Detroit Tigers organization in 17th round of free-agent draft (June 1, 1988). . . . On Toledo disabled list (May 3-27, 1991). . . . Traded by Tigers to Boston Red Sox for C John Flaherty (April 1, 1994). . . . Granted free agency (October 16, 1995). . . . Signed by Toronto Blue Jays organization (December 6, 1995).
STATISTICAL NOTES: Tied for International League lead in grounding into double plays with 20 in 1992. . . . Led International League catchers with 68 assists in 1992.

				BATTING											FIELDING			
Year	Team (League)	Pos.	G	AB	R	H	2B	3B	HR	RBI	Avg.	BB	SO	SB	PO	A	E	Avg.
1988—	Bristol (Appal.)	C	56	186	29	51	10	1	4	41	.274	27	39	1	253	31	7	.976
1989—	Fayetteville (SAL)	C	108	375	43	102	17	1	9	59	.272	54	98	4	527	66	11	.982
1990—	London (Eastern)	C	47	161	22	46	10	0	8	30	.286	20	33	1	231	24	3	.988
	—Toledo (Int'l)	C	62	192	28	50	12	0	7	22	.260	15	33	2	305	39	*13	.964
	—Detroit (A.L.)	C-DH	7	19	3	3	1	0	0	0	.158	2	4	0	29	0	1	.967
1991—	Toledo (Int'l)	C	109	383	56	104	26	0	13	68	.272	60	77	4	614	78	4	*.994
	—Detroit (A.L.)	C-DH	4	4	0	1	0	0	0	1	.250	1	2	0	2	1	0	1.000
1992—	Toledo (Int'l)	C-1B	136	473	75	111	19	1	25	82	.235	56	112	9	628	†68	6	.991
	—Detroit (A.L.)	C-DH-3-1	6	14	2	3	0	0	0	0	.214	3	3	0	12	1	0	1.000
1993—	Toledo (Int'l)	C	96	325	58	87	24	2	21	59	.268	51	72	1	569	64	8	.988
	—Detroit (A.L.)	C-DH	21	46	2	10	3	0	0	4	.217	5	16	0	75	7	1	.988
1994—	Boston (A.L.)■	C-DH-1B	46	118	14	27	3	0	9	20	.229	11	35	0	196	12	6	.972
1995—	Boston (A.L.)	C-DH	14	29	1	5	1	0	0	1	.172	0	11	0	39	3	1	.977
	—Pawtucket (Int'l)	C-1B-3B	34	124	20	32	7	0	8	24	.258	7	24	0	205	10	3	.986
Major league totals (6 years)			98	230	22	49	8	0	9	26	.213	22	71	0	353	24	9	.977

RUEBEL, MATT P PIRATES

PERSONAL: Born October 16, 1969, in Cincinnati. . . . 6-2/180. . . . Throws left, bats left. . . . Full name: Matthew Alexander Ruebel.
COLLEGE: Oklahoma.
TRANSACTIONS/CAREER NOTES: Selected by Pittsburgh Pirates organization in third round of free-agent draft (June 3, 1991).

Year	Team (League)	W	L	Pct.	ERA	G	GS	CG	ShO	Sv.	IP	H	R	ER	BB	SO
1991—	Welland (NYP)	1	1	.500	1.95	6	6	0	0	0	27 2/3	16	9	6	11	27
	—Augusta (S. Atl.)	3	4	.429	3.83	8	8	2	1	0	47	43	26	20	25	35
1992—	Augusta (S. Atl.)	5	2	.714	2.78	12	10	1	0	0	64 2/3	53	26	20	19	65
	—Salem (Carolina)	1	6	.143	4.71	13	13	1	0	0	78 1/3	77	49	41	43	46
1993—	Salem (Carolina)	1	4	.200	5.94	19	1	0	0	0	33 1/3	34	31	22	32	29
	—Augusta (S. Atl.)	5	5	.500	2.42	23	7	1	1	0	63 1/3	51	28	17	34	50
1994—	Salem (Carolina)	6	6	.500	3.44	21	13	0	0	0	86 1/3	87	49	33	27	72
	—Carolina (South.)	1	1	.500	6.61	6	3	0	0	0	16 1/3	28	15	12	3	14
1995—	Carolina (South.)	13	5	.722	2.76	27	27	4	*3	0	169 1/3	150	68	52	45	136

RUETER, KIRK P EXPOS

PERSONAL: Born December 1, 1970, in Centralia, Ill. . . . 6-3/195. . . . Throws left, bats left. . . . Full name: Kirk Wesley Rueter. . . . Name pronounced REE-ter.
HIGH SCHOOL: Nashville (Ill.) Community.
COLLEGE: Murray State.
TRANSACTIONS/CAREER NOTES: Selected by Montreal Expos organization in 19th round of free-agent draft (June 3, 1991).
HONORS: Named N.L. Rookie Pitcher of the Year by The Sporting News (1993).
STATISTICAL NOTES: Pitched 1-0 one-hit, complete-game victory for Montreal against San Francisco (August 27, 1995).

Year	Team (League)	W	L	Pct.	ERA	G	GS	CG	ShO	Sv.	IP	H	R	ER	BB	SO
1991—	GC Expos (GCL)	1	1	.500	0.95	5	4	0	0	0	19	16	5	2	4	19
	—Sumter (S. Atl.)	3	1	.750	1.33	8	5	0	0	0	40 2/3	32	8	6	10	27

Year	Team (League)	W	L	Pct.	ERA	G	GS	CG	ShO	Sv.	IP	H	R	ER	BB	SO
1992—	Rockford (Midw.)	11	9	.550	2.58	26	26	6	•2	0	174 1/3	150	68	50	36	153
1993—	Harrisburg (East.)	5	0	1.000	1.36	9	8	1	1	0	59 2/3	47	10	9	7	36
	—Ottawa (Int'l)	4	2	.667	2.70	7	7	1	0	0	43 1/3	46	20	13	3	27
	—Montreal (N.L.)	8	0	1.000	2.73	14	14	1	0	0	85 2/3	85	33	26	18	31
1994—	Montreal (N.L.)	7	3	.700	5.17	20	20	0	0	0	92 1/3	106	60	53	23	50
	—Ottawa (Int'l)	0	0	...	4.50	1	1	0	0	0	2	1	1	1	0	1
1995—	Montreal (N.L.)	5	3	.625	3.23	9	9	1	1	0	47 1/3	38	17	17	9	28
	—Ottawa (Int'l)	9	7	.563	3.06	20	20	3	1	0	120 2/3	120	50	41	25	67
Major league totals (3 years)		20	6	.769	3.83	43	43	2	1	0	225 1/3	229	110	96	50	109

RUFFCORN, SCOTT — P — WHITE SOX

PERSONAL: Born December 29, 1969, in New Braunfels, Tex. . . . 6-4/210. . . . Throws right, bats right. . . . Full name: Scott Patrick Ruffcorn.
HIGH SCHOOL: S.F. Austin (Austin, Tex.).
COLLEGE: Baylor.
TRANSACTIONS/CAREER NOTES: Selected by Atlanta Braves organization in 39th round of free-agent draft (June 1, 1988); did not sign. . . . Selected by Chicago White Sox organization in first round (25th pick overall) of free-agent draft (June 3, 1991). . . . On Nashville disabled list (May 28-August 17, 1995).

Year	Team (League)	W	L	Pct.	ERA	G	GS	CG	ShO	Sv.	IP	H	R	ER	BB	SO
1991—	GC White Sox (GCL)	0	0	...	3.18	4	2	0	0	0	11 1/3	8	7	4	5	15
	—South Bend (Midw.)	1	3	.250	3.92	9	9	0	0	0	43 2/3	35	26	19	25	45
1992—	Sarasota (Fla. St.)	14	5	.737	2.19	25	24	2	0	0	160 1/3	122	53	39	39	140
1993—	Birmingham (Sou.)	9	4	.692	2.73	20	20	3	*3	0	135	108	47	41	52	*141
	—Chicago (A.L.)	0	2	.000	8.10	3	2	0	0	0	10	9	11	9	10	2
	—Nashville (A.A.)	2	2	.500	2.80	7	6	1	0	0	45	30	16	14	8	44
1994—	Chicago (A.L.)	0	2	.000	12.79	2	2	0	0	0	6 1/3	15	11	9	5	3
	—Nashville (A.A.)	*15	3	•.833	2.72	24	24	3	•3	0	165 2/3	139	57	50	40	144
1995—	Nashville (A.A.)	0	0	...	108.00	2	2	0	0	0	1/3	3	4	4	3	0
	—Birmingham (Sou.)	0	2	.000	5.63	3	3	0	0	0	16	17	11	10	10	13
	—GC White Sox (GCL)	0	0	...	0.90	3	3	0	0	0	10	7	4	1	5	7
	—Chicago (A.L.)	0	0	...	7.88	4	0	0	0	0	8	10	7	7	13	5
Major league totals (3 years)		0	4	.000	9.25	9	4	0	0	0	24 1/3	34	29	25	28	10

RUFFIN, BRUCE — P — ROCKIES

PERSONAL: Born October 4, 1963, in Lubbock, Tex. . . . 6-2/215. . . . Throws left, bats both. . . . Full name: Bruce Wayne Ruffin.
HIGH SCHOOL: J.M. Hanks (El Paso, Tex.).
COLLEGE: Texas.
TRANSACTIONS/CAREER NOTES: Selected by Philadelphia Phillies organization in 31st round of free-agent draft (June 7, 1982); did not sign. . . . Selected by Phillies organization in second round of free-agent draft (June 3, 1985); pick received as compensation for Pittsburgh Pirates signing free-agent OF Sixto Lezcano. . . . Traded by Phillies to Milwaukee Brewers for SS/3B Dale Sveum (December 11, 1991). . . . Granted free agency (November 5, 1992). . . . Signed by Colorado Rockies (December 7, 1992). . . . On Colorado disabled list (May 29-June 17 and June 26-August 22, 1995); included rehabilitation assignment to New Haven (August 16-20).
MISCELLANEOUS: Struck out in only appearance as pinch-hitter (1990).

Year	Team (League)	W	L	Pct.	ERA	G	GS	CG	ShO	Sv.	IP	H	R	ER	BB	SO
1985—	Clearwater (Fla. St.)	5	5	.500	2.88	14	14	3	1	0	97	87	33	31	34	74
1986—	Reading (Eastern)	8	4	.667	3.29	16	13	4	2	0	90 1/3	89	41	33	26	68
	—Philadelphia (N.L.)	9	4	.692	2.46	21	21	6	0	0	146 1/3	138	53	40	44	70
1987—	Philadelphia (N.L.)	11	14	.440	4.35	35	35	3	1	0	204 2/3	236	118	99	73	93
1988—	Philadelphia (N.L.)	6	10	.375	4.43	55	15	3	0	3	144 1/3	151	86	71	80	82
1989—	Philadelphia (N.L.)	6	10	.375	4.44	24	23	1	0	0	125 2/3	152	69	62	62	70
	—Scran./W.B. (Int'l)	5	1	.833	4.68	9	9	0	0	0	50	44	28	26	39	44
1990—	Philadelphia (N.L.)	6	13	.316	5.38	32	25	2	1	0	149	178	99	89	62	79
1991—	Scran./W.B. (Int'l)	4	5	.444	4.66	13	13	1	0	0	75 1/3	82	43	39	41	50
	—Philadelphia (N.L.)	4	7	.364	3.78	31	15	1	1	0	119	125	52	50	38	85
1992—	Milwaukee (A.L.)■	1	6	.143	6.67	25	6	1	0	0	58	66	43	43	41	45
	—Denver (Am. Assoc.)	3	0	1.000	0.94	4	4	1	0	0	28 2/3	28	12	3	8	17
1993—	Colorado (N.L.)■	6	5	.545	3.87	59	12	0	0	2	139 2/3	145	71	60	69	126
1994—	Colorado (N.L.)	4	5	.444	4.04	56	0	0	0	16	55 2/3	55	28	25	30	65
1995—	Colorado (N.L.)	0	1	.000	2.12	37	0	0	0	11	34	26	8	8	19	23
	—New Haven (East.)	0	0	...	0.00	2	2	0	0	0	2	1	0	0	0	2
A.L. totals (1 year)		1	6	.143	6.67	25	6	1	0	0	58	66	43	43	41	45
N.L. totals (9 years)		52	69	.430	4.06	350	146	16	3	32	1118 1/3	1206	584	504	477	693
Major league totals (10 years)		53	75	.414	4.19	375	152	17	3	32	1176 1/3	1272	627	547	518	738

DIVISION SERIES RECORD

Year	Team (League)	W	L	Pct.	ERA	G	GS	CG	ShO	Sv.	IP	H	R	ER	BB	SO
1995—	Colorado (N.L.)	0	0	...	2.70	4	0	0	0	0	3 1/3	3	1	1	2	2

RUFFIN, JOHNNY — P — REDS

PERSONAL: Born July 29, 1971, in Butler, Ala. . . . 6-3/170. . . . Throws right, bats right. . . . Full name: Johnny Renando Ruffin.
HIGH SCHOOL: Choctaw County (Butler, Ala.).
TRANSACTIONS/CAREER NOTES: Selected by Chicago White Sox organization in fourth round of free-agent draft (June 1, 1988). . . . Traded by White Sox with P Jeff Pierce to Cincinnati Reds for P Tim Belcher (July 31, 1993). . . . On Cincinnati disabled list (September 1, 1995-remainder of season).
STATISTICAL NOTES: Pitched 6-1 no-hit victory against Charlotte (June 14, 1991, second game).

Year	Team (League)	W	L	Pct.	ERA	G	GS	CG	ShO	Sv.	IP	H	R	ER	BB	SO
1988—	GC White Sox (GCL)	4	2	.667	2.30	13	11	1	0	0	58 2/3	43	27	15	22	31
1989—	Utica (NYP)	4	8	.333	3.36	15	15	0	0	0	88 1/3	67	43	33	46	92
1990—	South Bend (Midw.)	7	6	.538	4.17	24	24	0	0	0	123	117	86	57	82	92
1991—	Sarasota (Fla. St.)	11	4	.733	3.23	26	26	6	2	0	158 2/3	126	68	57	62	117
1992—	Birmingham (Sou.)	0	7	.000	6.04	10	10	0	0	0	47 2/3	51	48	32	34	44
	—Sarasota (Fla. St.)	3	7	.300	5.89	23	8	0	0	0	62 2/3	56	46	41	41	61
1993—	Birmingham (Sou.)	0	4	.000	2.82	11	0	0	0	2	22 1/3	16	9	7	9	23
	—Nashville (A.A.)	3	4	.429	3.30	29	0	0	0	1	60	48	24	22	16	69
	—Indianapolis (A.A.)■	1	1	.500	1.35	3	0	0	0	1	6 2/3	3	1	1	2	6
	—Cincinnati (N.L.)	2	1	.667	3.58	21	0	0	0	2	37 2/3	36	16	15	11	30
1994—	Cincinnati (N.L.)	7	2	.778	3.09	51	0	0	0	1	70	57	26	24	27	44
1995—	Cincinnati (N.L.)	0	0	...	1.35	10	0	0	0	0	13 1/3	4	3	2	11	11
	—Indianapolis (A.A.)	3	1	.750	2.90	36	1	0	0	0	49 2/3	27	19	16	37	58
Major league totals (3 years)		9	3	.750	3.05	82	0	0	0	3	121	97	45	41	49	85

RUMER, TIM — P — RANGERS

PERSONAL: Born August 8, 1969, in Philadelphia. . . . 6-3/205. . . . Throws left, bats left. . . . Full name: Timothy Day Rumer.
HIGH SCHOOL: Princeton (N.J.).
COLLEGE: Duke.
TRANSACTIONS/CAREER NOTES: Selected by New York Yankees organization in eighth round of free-agent draft (June 4, 1990). . . . On disabled list (April 9, 1993-entire season). . . . Selected by Texas Rangers from Yankees organization in Rule 5 major league draft (December 4, 1995).
STATISTICAL NOTES: Led International League with 16 hit batsmen in 1995.

Year	Team (League)	W	L	Pct.	ERA	G	GS	CG	ShO	Sv.	IP	H	R	ER	BB	SO
1990—	GC Yankees (GCL)	6	3	.667	1.70	12	12	2	0	0	74	34	23	14	21	88
1991—	Fort Lauder. (FSL)	10	7	.588	2.89	24	23	3	2	0	149 1/3	125	59	48	49	112
1992—	Prin. William (Caro.)	10	7	.588	3.59	23	23	1	0	0	128	122	61	51	34	105
1993—								Did not play.								
1994—	Alb./Colon. (East.)	8	10	.444	3.11	25	25	2	1	0	150 2/3	127	61	52	75	130
1995—	Columbus (Int'l)	10	8	.556	5.22	28	25	0	0	0	141 1/3	156	98	82	*76	110

RUSSELL, JEFF — P

PERSONAL: Born September 2, 1961, in Cincinnati. . . . 6-3/205. . . . Throws right, bats right. . . . Full name: Jeffrey Lee Russell.
HIGH SCHOOL: Wyoming (Cincinnati).
JUNIOR COLLEGE: Gulf Coast Community College (Fla.).
TRANSACTIONS/CAREER NOTES: Selected by Cincinnati Reds organization in fifth round of free-agent draft (June 5, 1979). . . . On disabled list (May 5-June 10 and July 28, 1982-remainder of season). . . . On Denver disabled list (May 22-June 10, 1985). . . . Traded by Reds to Texas Rangers organization (July 23, 1985), completing deal in which Rangers traded 3B Buddy Bell to Reds for OF Duane Walker and a player to be named later (July 19, 1985). . . . On Texas disabled list (March 25-May 15, 1987); included rehabilitation assignments to Charlotte (April 26-May 4) and Oklahoma City (May 5-15). . . . On Texas disabled list (May 29-September 10, 1990); included rehabilitation assignment to Charlotte (July 30-August 3). . . . Traded by Rangers with OF Ruben Sierra, P Bobby Witt and cash to Oakland Athletics for OF Jose Canseco (August 31, 1992). . . . Granted free agency (October 26, 1992). . . . Signed by Boston Red Sox (March 1, 1993). . . . On disabled list (August 29-September 28, 1993). . . . Traded by Red Sox to Cleveland Indians for P Chris Nabholz and P Steve Farr (July 1, 1994). . . . Granted free agency (October 26, 1994). . . . Signed by Rangers (April 11, 1995). . . . On disabled list (June 27-July 13 and August 2-17, 1995). . . . Granted free agency (November 11, 1995).
HONORS: Named A.L. Fireman of the Year by THE SPORTING NEWS (1989).
MISCELLANEOUS: Made an out in only appearance as pinch-hitter (1988).

Year	Team (League)	W	L	Pct.	ERA	G	GS	CG	ShO	Sv.	IP	H	R	ER	BB	SO
1980—	Eugene (N'west)	6	5	.545	3.00	13	13	3	0	0	90	80	47	30	50	75
1981—	Tampa (Fla. St.)	10	4	.714	2.01	22	21	5	2	0	143	109	51	32	48	92
1982—	Waterbury (East.)	6	4	.600	2.37	14	12	2	1	0	79 2/3	67	27	21	23	88
1983—	Indianapolis (A.A.)	5	5	.500	3.55	18	17	5	0	1	119	106	51	47	44	98
	—Cincinnati (N.L.)	4	5	.444	3.03	10	10	2	0	0	68 1/3	58	30	23	22	40
1984—	Cincinnati (N.L.)	6	*18	.250	4.26	33	30	4	2	0	181 2/3	186	97	86	65	101
1985—	Denver (Am. Assoc.)	6	4	.600	4.22	16	16	1	1	0	102 1/3	94	51	48	46	81
	—Okla. City (A.A.)■	1	0	1.000	2.77	2	2	2	00	0	13	11	4	4	5	13
	—Texas (A.L.)	3	6	.333	7.55	13	13	0	0	0	62	85	55	52	27	44
1986—	Okla. City (A.A.)	4	1	.800	3.95	11	11	1	0	0	70 2/3	63	32	31	38	34
	—Texas (A.L.)	5	2	.714	3.40	37	0	0	0	2	82	74	40	31	31	54
1987—	Charlotte (Fla. St.)	0	0	...	2.45	2	2	0	0	0	11	8	3	3	5	3
	—Okla. City (A.A.)	0	0	...	1.42	4	0	0	0	0	6 1/3	5	1	1	1	5
	—Texas (A.L.)	5	4	.556	4.44	52	2	0	0	3	97 1/3	109	56	48	52	56
1988—	Texas (A.L.)	10	9	.526	3.82	34	24	5	1	0	188 2/3	183	86	80	66	88
1989—	Texas (A.L.)	6	4	.600	1.98	71	0	0	0	*38	72 2/3	45	21	16	24	77
1990—	Texas (A.L.)	1	5	.167	4.26	27	0	0	0	10	25 1/3	23	15	12	16	16
	—Charlotte (Fla. St.)	0	1	.000	...	1	0	0	0	0	0	1	1	1	0	0
1991—	Texas (A.L.)	6	4	.600	3.29	68	0	0	0	30	79 1/3	71	36	29	26	52
1992—	Texas (A.L.)	2	3	.400	1.91	51	0	0	0	28	56 2/3	51	14	12	22	43
	—Oakland (A.L.)■	2	0	1.000	0.00	8	0	0	0	2	9 2/3	4	0	0	3	5
1993—	Boston (A.L.)■	1	4	.200	2.70	51	0	0	0	33	46 2/3	39	16	14	14	45
1994—	Boston (A.L.)	0	5	.000	5.14	29	0	0	0	12	28	30	17	16	13	18
	—Cleveland (A.L.)■	1	1	.500	4.97	13	0	0	0	5	12 2/3	13	8	7	3	10
1995—	Texas (A.L.)■	1	0	1.000	3.03	37	0	0	0	20	32 2/3	36	12	11	9	21
A.L. totals (11 years)		43	47	.478	3.72	491	39	5	1	183	793 2/3	763	376	328	306	529
N.L. totals (2 years)		10	23	.303	3.92	43	40	6	2	0	250	244	127	109	87	141
Major league totals (13 years)		53	70	.431	3.77	534	79	11	3	183	1043 2/3	1007	503	437	393	670

CHAMPIONSHIP SERIES RECORD

Year	Team (League)	W	L	Pct.	ERA	G	GS	CG	ShO	Sv.	IP	H	R	ER	BB	SO
1992—	Oakland (A.L.)	1	0	1.000	9.00	3	0	0	0	0	2	2	2	2	4	0

ALL-STAR GAME RECORD

Year	League	W	L	Pct.	ERA	GS	CG	ShO	Sv.	IP	H	R	ER	BB	SO
1988—	American	0	0	...	0.00	0	0	0	0	1	1	0	0	1	0
1989—	American	0	0	...	9.00	0	0	0	0	1	1	1	1	1	0
All-Star totals (2 years)		0	0	...	4.50	0	0	0	0	2	2	1	1	2	0

RYAN, KEN — P — RED SOX

PERSONAL: Born October 24, 1968, in Pawtucket, R.I. . . . 6-3/230. . . . Throws right, bats right. . . . Full name: Kenneth Frederick Ryan Jr.
HIGH SCHOOL: Seekonk (Mass.).
TRANSACTIONS/CAREER NOTES: Signed as non-drafted free agent by Boston Red Sox organization (June 16, 1986).

Year	Team (League)	W	L	Pct.	ERA	G	GS	CG	ShO	Sv.	IP	H	R	ER	BB	SO
1986—	Elmira (NYP)	2	2	.500	5.82	13	1	0	0	0	21 2/3	20	14	14	21	22
1987—	Greensboro (S. Atl.)	3	12	.200	5.49	28	19	2	0	0	121 1/3	139	88	74	63	75
1988—	Lynchburg (Caro.)	2	7	.222	6.18	19	14	0	0	0	71 1/3	79	51	49	45	49
1989—	Winter Haven (FSL)	8	8	.500	3.15	24	22	3	0	0	137	114	58	48	81	78
1990—	Lynchburg (Caro.)	6	•14	.300	5.13	28	•28	3	1	0	161 1/3	182	104	92	82	109
1991—	Winter Haven (FSL)	1	3	.250	2.05	21	1	0	0	1	52 2/3	40	15	12	19	53
—	New Britain (East.)	1	2	.333	1.73	14	0	0	0	1	26	23	7	5	12	26
—	Pawtucket (Int'l)	1	0	1.000	4.91	9	0	0	0	1	18 1/3	15	11	10	11	14
1992—	New Britain (East.)	1	4	.200	1.95	44	0	0	0	22	50 2/3	44	17	11	24	51
—	Pawtucket (Int'l)	2	0	1.000	2.08	9	0	0	0	7	8 2/3	6	2	2	4	6
—	Boston (A.L.)	0	0	...	6.43	7	0	0	0	1	7	4	5	5	5	5
1993—	Boston (A.L.)	7	2	.778	3.60	47	0	0	0	1	50	43	23	20	29	49
—	Pawtucket (Int'l)	0	2	.000	2.49	18	0	0	0	8	25 1/3	18	9	7	17	22
1994—	Sarasota (Fla. St.)	0	0	...	3.68	8	0	0	0	1	7 1/3	6	3	3	2	11
—	Boston (A.L.)	2	3	.400	2.44	42	0	0	0	13	48	46	14	13	17	32
1995—	Boston (A.L.)	0	4	.000	4.96	28	0	0	0	7	32 2/3	34	20	18	24	34
—	Trenton (Eastern)	0	2	.000	5.82	11	0	0	0	2	17	23	13	11	5	16
—	Pawtucket (Int'l)	0	1	.000	6.30	9	0	0	0	0	10	12	7	7	4	6
Major league totals (4 years)		9	9	.500	3.66	124	0	0	0	22	137 2/3	127	62	56	75	120

RYAN, MATT — P — PIRATES

PERSONAL: Born March 30, 1972, in Chattanooga, Tenn. . . . 6-5/185. . . . Throws right, bats right. . . . Full name: William Mathew Ryan.
HIGH SCHOOL: Kirby (Memphis, Tenn.).
COLLEGE: Mississippi.
TRANSACTIONS/CAREER NOTES: Selected by Pittsburgh Pirates organization in 25th round of free-agent draft (June 3, 1993). . . . On Calgary disabled list (July 18-August 11, 1995).

Year	Team (League)	W	L	Pct.	ERA	G	GS	CG	ShO	Sv.	IP	H	R	ER	BB	SO
1993—	GC Pirates (GCL)	1	1	.500	2.33	9	0	0	0	2	19 1/3	17	8	5	9	20
—	Welland (NYP)	0	1	.000	2.08	16	0	0	0	5	17 1/3	11	10	4	12	25
1994—	Augusta (S. Atl.)	2	1	.667	1.14	33	0	0	0	13	39 1/3	29	12	5	7	49
—	Salem (Carolina)	2	2	.500	1.91	25	0	0	0	7	28 1/3	27	12	6	8	13
1995—	Carolina (South.)	2	1	.667	1.57	44	0	0	0	26	46	33	10	8	19	23
—	Calgary (PCL)	0	0	...	1.93	5	0	0	0	1	4 2/3	5	1	1	1	2

SABERHAGEN, BRET — P — ROCKIES

PERSONAL: Born April 11, 1964, in Chicago Heights, Ill. . . . 6-1/200. . . . Throws right, bats right. . . . Full name: Bret William Saberhagen. . . . Name pronounced SAY-ber-HAY-gun.
HIGH SCHOOL: Cleveland (Reseda, Calif.).
TRANSACTIONS/CAREER NOTES: Selected by Kansas City Royals organization in 19th round of free-agent draft (June 7, 1982). . . . On disabled list (August 10-September 1, 1986; July 16-September 10, 1990; and June 15-July 13, 1991). . . . Traded by Royals with IF Bill Pecota to New York Mets for OF Kevin McReynolds, IF Gregg Jefferies and 2B Keith Miller (December 11, 1991). . . . On disabled list (May 16-July 18 and August 2-September 7, 1992 and August 3, 1993-remainder of season). . . . On suspended list (April 3-8, 1994). . . . Traded by Mets with a player to be named later to Colorado Rockies for P Juan Acevedo and P Arnold Gooch (July 31, 1995); Rockies acquired P David Swanson to complete deal (August 4, 1995).
HONORS: Named A.L. Pitcher of the Year by The Sporting News (1985 and 1989). . . . Named righthanded pitcher on The Sporting News A.L. All-Star team (1985 and 1989). . . . Named A.L. Cy Young Award winner by Baseball Writers' Association of America (1985 and 1989). . . . Named A.L. Comeback Player of the Year by The Sporting News (1987). . . . Won A.L. Gold Glove at pitcher (1989).
STATISTICAL NOTES: Pitched 7-0 no-hit victory against Chicago (August 26, 1991).
MISCELLANEOUS: Appeared in one game as pinch-runner (1984). . . . Appeared in three games as pinch-runner (1989).

Year	Team (League)	W	L	Pct.	ERA	G	GS	CG	ShO	Sv.	IP	H	R	ER	BB	SO
1983—	Fort Myers (Fla. St.)	10	5	.667	2.30	16	16	3	1	0	109 2/3	98	34	28	19	82
—	Jacksonville (Sou.)	6	2	.750	2.91	11	11	2	1	0	77 1/3	66	31	25	29	48
1984—	Kansas City (A.L.)	10	11	.476	3.48	38	18	2	1	1	157 2/3	138	71	61	36	73
1985—	Kansas City (A.L.)	20	6	.769	2.87	32	32	10	1	0	235 1/3	211	79	75	38	158
1986—	Kansas City (A.L.)	7	12	.368	4.15	30	25	4	2	0	156	165	77	72	29	112
1987—	Kansas City (A.L.)	18	10	.643	3.36	33	33	15	4	0	257	246	99	96	53	163
1988—	Kansas City (A.L.)	14	16	.467	3.80	35	35	9	0	0	260 2/3	*271	122	110	59	171
1989—	Kansas City (A.L.)	*23	6	.793	*2.16	36	35	*12	4	0	*262 1/3	209	74	63	43	193
1990—	Kansas City (A.L.)	5	9	.357	3.27	20	20	5	0	0	135	146	52	49	28	87
1991—	Kansas City (A.L.)	13	8	.619	3.07	28	28	7	2	0	196 1/3	165	76	67	45	136

Year Team (League)	W	L	Pct.	ERA	G	GS	CG	ShO	Sv.	IP	H	R	ER	BB	SO
1992—New York (N.L.)■	3	5	.375	3.50	17	15	1	1	0	97 2/3	84	39	38	27	81
1993—New York (N.L.)	7	7	.500	3.29	19	19	4	1	0	139 1/3	131	55	51	17	93
1994—New York (N.L.)	14	4	.778	2.74	24	24	4	0	0	177 1/3	169	58	54	13	143
1995—New York (N.L.)	5	5	.500	3.35	16	16	3	0	0	110	105	45	41	20	71
—Colorado (N.L.)■	2	1	.667	6.28	9	9	0	0	0	43	60	33	30	13	29
A.L. totals (8 years)	110	78	.585	3.21	252	226	64	14	1	1660 1/3	1551	650	593	331	1093
N.L. totals (4 years)	31	22	.585	3.39	85	83	12	2	0	567 1/3	549	230	214	90	417
Major league totals (12 years)	141	100	.585	3.26	337	309	76	16	1	2227 2/3	2100	880	807	421	1510

DIVISION SERIES RECORD

Year Team (League)	W	L	Pct.	ERA	G	GS	CG	ShO	Sv.	IP	H	R	ER	BB	SO
1995—Colorado (N.L.)	0	1	.000	11.25	1	1	0	0	0	4	7	6	5	1	3

CHAMPIONSHIP SERIES RECORD

Year Team (League)	W	L	Pct.	ERA	G	GS	CG	ShO	Sv.	IP	H	R	ER	BB	SO
1984—Kansas City (A.L.)	0	0	...	2.25	1	1	0	0	0	8	6	3	2	1	5
1985—Kansas City (A.L.)	0	0	...	6.14	2	2	0	0	0	7 1/3	12	5	5	2	6
Champ. series totals (2 years)	0	0	...	4.11	3	3	0	0	0	15 1/3	18	8	7	3	11

WORLD SERIES RECORD

NOTES: Named Most Valuable Player (1985).... Member of World Series championship team (1985).

Year Team (League)	W	L	Pct.	ERA	G	GS	CG	ShO	Sv.	IP	H	R	ER	BB	SO
1985—Kansas City (A.L.)	2	0	1.000	0.50	2	2	2	1	0	18	11	1	1	1	10

ALL-STAR GAME RECORD

Year League	W	L	Pct.	ERA	GS	CG	ShO	Sv.	IP	H	R	ER	BB	SO
1987—American	0	0	...	0.00	1	0	0	0	3	1	0	0	0	0
1990—American	1	0	1.000	0.00	0	0	0	0	2	0	0	0	0	1
1994—National	Did not play.													
All-Star totals (2 years)	1	0	1.000	0.00	1	0	0	0	5	1	0	0	0	1

SABO, CHRIS — 3B — REDS

PERSONAL: Born January 19, 1962, in Detroit.... 6-0/185.... Bats right, throws right.... Full name: Christopher Andrew Sabo.... Name pronounced SAY-bo.

HIGH SCHOOL: Detroit Catholic Central.

COLLEGE: Michigan.

TRANSACTIONS/CAREER NOTES: Selected by Montreal Expos organization in 30th round of free-agent draft (June 3, 1980); did not sign. ... Selected by Cincinnati Reds organization in second round of free-agent draft (June 6, 1983).... On Cincinnati disabled list (June 27-September 1, 1989); included rehabilitation assignment to Nashville (August 7-11).... On Cincinnati disabled list (April 8-23, 1992); included rehabilitation assignment to Nashville (April 17-21).... On disabled list (May 31-June 15, 1993).... Granted free agency (October 25, 1993).... Signed by Baltimore Orioles (January 14, 1994).... On disabled list (May 7-22, 1994).... Granted free agency (October 12, 1994).... Signed by Chicago White Sox (April 11, 1995).... Released by White Sox (June 5, 1995).... Signed by Louisville, St. Louis Cardinals organization (June 8, 1995).... On St. Louis disabled list (June 26-September 11, 1995); included rehabilitation assignment to St. Petersburg (August 13-September 1).... Released by Cardinals (September 11, 1995).... Signed by Reds organization (December 7, 1995).

RECORDS: Shares major league single-game record (nine innings) for most assists by third baseman—11 (April 7, 1988).

HONORS: Named third baseman on The Sporting News college All-America team (1983).... Named N.L. Rookie of the Year by Baseball Writers' Association of America (1988).

STATISTICAL NOTES: Led Eastern League third basemen with .943 fielding percentage in 1984.... Led Eastern League third basemen with 236 assists in 1985.... Led N.L. third basemen with .966 fielding percentage and 31 double plays in 1988.... Career major league grand slams: 3.

			BATTING											FIELDING			
Year Team (League)	Pos.	G	AB	R	H	2B	3B	HR	RBI	Avg.	BB	SO	SB	PO	A	E	Avg.
1983—Ced. Rap. (Midw.)	3B	77	274	43	75	11	6	12	37	.274	26	39	15	43	130	9	.951
1984—Vermont (Eastern)	3B-2B	125	441	44	94	19	1	5	38	.213	44	62	10	80	210	21	†.932
1985—Vermont (Eastern)	3B-SS	124	428	66	119	19	0	11	46	.278	50	39	7	97	†236	18	.949
1986—Denver (A.A.)	3B	129	432	83	118	26	2	10	60	.273	48	53	9	83	202	9	*.969
1987—Nashville (A.A.)	3B	91	315	56	92	19	3	7	51	.292	37	25	23	43	137	12	.938
1988—Cincinnati (N.L.)	3B-SS	137	538	74	146	40	2	11	44	.271	29	52	46	75	318	14	†.966
1989—Cincinnati (N.L.)	3B	82	304	40	79	21	1	6	29	.260	25	33	14	36	145	11	.943
—Nashville (A.A.)	3B	7	30	0	5	2	0	0	3	.167	0	0	0	7	5	1	.923
1990—Cincinnati (N.L.)	3B	148	567	95	153	38	2	25	71	.270	61	58	25	70	273	12	*.966
1991—Cincinnati (N.L.)	3B	153	582	91	175	35	3	26	88	.301	44	79	19	86	255	12	.966
1992—Cincinnati (N.L.)	3B	96	344	42	84	19	3	12	43	.244	30	54	4	60	159	9	.961
—Nashville (A.A.)	DH	3	11	3	4	0	0	1	1	.364	1	1	0	...	...	...	...
1993—Cincinnati (N.L.)	3B	148	552	86	143	33	2	21	82	.259	43	105	6	79	242	11	.967
1994—Baltimore (A.L.)■	3B-OF-DH	68	258	41	66	15	3	11	42	.256	20	38	1	52	50	4	.962
1995—Chicago (A.L.)■	DH-1B-3B	20	71	10	18	5	0	1	8	.254	3	12	2	10	1	1	.917
—Louisville (A.A.)■	1B	9	28	5	11	0	0	1	4	.393	1	4	0	32	4	0	1.000
—St. Louis (N.L.)	1B-3B	5	13	0	2	1	0	0	3	.154	1	2	1	11	3	1	.933
—St. Peters. (FSL)	1B-3B-OF	14	39	10	9	0	0	2	7	.231	10	6	1	58	9	1	.985
American League totals (2 years)		88	329	51	84	20	3	12	50	.255	23	50	3	62	51	5	.958
National League totals (7 years)		769	2900	428	782	187	13	101	360	.270	233	383	115	417	1395	70	.963
Major league totals (8 years)		857	3229	479	866	207	16	113	410	.268	256	433	118	479	1446	75	.963

CHAMPIONSHIP SERIES RECORD

			BATTING											FIELDING			
Year Team (League)	Pos.	G	AB	R	H	2B	3B	HR	RBI	Avg.	BB	SO	SB	PO	A	E	Avg.
1990—Cincinnati (N.L.)	3B	6	22	1	5	0	0	1	3	.227	1	4	0	7	7	0	1.000

WORLD SERIES RECORD

NOTES: Shares record for most home runs in two consecutive innings—2 (October 19, 1990, second and third innings). . . . Member of World Series championship team (1990).

		BATTING												FIELDING			
Year Team (League)	Pos.	G	AB	R	H	2B	3B	HR	RBI	Avg.	BB	SO	SB	PO	A	E	Avg.
1990— Cincinnati (N.L.)	3B	4	16	2	9	1	0	2	5	.563	2	2	0	3	14	0	1.000

ALL-STAR GAME RECORD

		BATTING											FIELDING			
Year League	Pos.	AB	R	H	2B	3B	HR	RBI	Avg.	BB	SO	SB	PO	A	E	Avg.
1988— National	PR	0	0	0	0	0	0	0	. . .	0	0	1	. . .	. . .	. . .	. . .
1990— National	3B	2	0	0	0	0	0	0	.000	0	0	0	0	2	0	1.000
1991— National	3B	2	0	0	0	0	0	0	.000	0	0	0	1	0	0	1.000
All-Star Game totals (3 years)		4	0	0	0	0	0	0	.000	0	0	1	1	2	0	1.000

SACKINSKY, BRIAN — P — ORIOLES

PERSONAL: Born June 22, 1971, in Pittsburgh. . . . 6-4/220. . . . Throws right, bats right. . . . Full name: Brian Walter Sackinsky.
HIGH SCHOOL: South Park (Library, Pa.).
COLLEGE: Stanford.
TRANSACTIONS/CAREER NOTES: Selected by Baltimore Orioles organization in 39th round of free-agent draft (June 5, 1989); did not sign. . . . Selected by Orioles organization in second round of free-agent draft (June 1, 1992). . . . On disabled list (May 15-June 6 and July 17, 1995-remainder of season).
STATISTICAL NOTES: Led Eastern League with 24 home runs allowed in 1994.

Year Team (League)	W	L	Pct.	ERA	G	GS	CG	ShO	Sv.	IP	H	R	ER	BB	SO
1992— Frederick (Caro.)	0	3	.000	13.06	5	3	0	0	0	10 1/3	20	15	15	6	10
— Bluefield (Appal.)	2	2	.500	3.58	5	5	0	0	0	27 2/3	30	15	11	9	33
1993— Albany (S. Atl.)	3	4	.429	3.20	9	8	0	0	0	50 2/3	50	29	18	16	41
— Frederick (Caro.)	6	8	.429	3.20	18	18	1	0	0	121	117	55	43	37	112
1994— Bowie (Eastern)	11	7	.611	3.36	28	26	4	0	0	177	165	73	66	39	145
1995— Rochester (Int'l)	3	3	.500	4.60	14	11	0	0	0	62 2/3	70	33	32	10	42

SAENZ, OLMEDO — 3B — WHITE SOX

PERSONAL: Born October 8, 1970, in Herrera, Panama. . . . 6-0/185. . . . Bats right, throws right. . . . Full name: Olmedo Sanchez Saenz. . . Name pronounced SIGNS.
TRANSACTIONS/CAREER NOTES: Signed as non-drafted free agent by Chicago White Sox organization (May 11, 1990).
STATISTICAL NOTES: Led American Association third basemen with 395 total chances in 1995.

		BATTING												FIELDING			
Year Team (League)	Pos.	G	AB	R	H	2B	3B	HR	RBI	Avg.	BB	SO	SB	PO	A	E	Avg.
1991— South Bend (Mid.)	3B	56	192	23	47	10	1	2	22	.245	21	48	5	29	68	12	.890
— Sarasota (Fla. St.)	3B	5	19	1	2	0	1	0	2	.105	2	0	0	5	11	3	.842
1992— South Bend (Mid.)	3B-1B	132	493	66	121	26	4	7	59	.245	36	52	16	113	294	48	.895
1993— South Bend (Mid.)	3B	13	50	3	18	4	1	0	7	.360	7	7	1	11	31	4	.913
— Sarasota (Fla. St.)	3B	33	121	13	31	9	4	0	27	.256	9	18	3	15	55	5	.933
— Birm. (Southern)	3B	49	173	30	60	17	2	6	29	.347	20	21	2	38	87	14	.899
1994— Nashville (A.A.)	3B	107	383	48	100	27	2	12	59	.261	30	57	3	76	167	22	.917
— Chicago (A.L.)	3B	5	14	2	2	0	1	0	0	.143	0	5	0	3	5	0	1.000
1995— Nashville (A.A.)	3B	111	415	60	126	26	1	13	74	.304	45	60	0	*82	*289	*24	*.939
Major league totals (1 year)		5	14	2	2	0	1	0	0	.143	0	5	0	3	5	0	1.000

SAGER, A.J. — P

PERSONAL: Born March 3, 1965, in Columbus, O. . . . 6-4/220. . . . Throws right, bats right. . . . Full name: Anthony Joseph Sager.
HIGH SCHOOL: Watkins Memorial (Kirkersville, O.).
COLLEGE: Toledo (received degree).
TRANSACTIONS/CAREER NOTES: Selected by San Diego Padres organization in 10th round of free-agent draft (June 1, 1988). . . . Granted free agency (October 15, 1994). . . . Signed by Colorado Springs, Colorado Rockies organization (December 7, 1994). . . . Granted free agency (October 16, 1995).

Year Team (League)	W	L	Pct.	ERA	G	GS	CG	ShO	Sv.	IP	H	R	ER	BB	SO
1988— Spokane (N'west)	8	3	.727	5.11	15	15	2	0	0	98 2/3	*123	*67	*56	27	74
1989— Char., S.C. (S. Atl.)	•14	9	.609	3.38	26	25	6	2	0	167 2/3	166	77	63	40	105
1990— Wichita (Texas)	11	•12	.478	5.48	26	26	2	1	0	154 1/3	*200	*105	*94	29	79
1991— Las Vegas (PCL)	7	5	.583	4.71	18	18	3	2	0	109	127	63	57	20	61
— Wichita (Texas)	4	3	.571	4.13	10	10	1	0	0	65 1/3	69	35	30	16	31
1992— Las Vegas (PCL)	1	7	.125	7.95	30	3	0	0	1	60	89	57	53	17	40
1993— Wichita (Texas)	5	3	.625	3.19	11	11	2	1	0	73 1/3	69	30	26	16	49
— Las Vegas (PCL)	6	5	.545	3.70	21	11	2	1	1	90	91	49	37	18	58
1994— San Diego (N.L.)	1	4	.200	5.98	22	3	0	0	0	46 2/3	62	34	31	16	26
— Las Vegas (PCL)	1	4	.200	4.43	23	2	0	0	5	40 2/3	57	24	20	8	23
1995— Colo. Springs (PCL)■	8	5	.615	3.50	23	22	1	1	0	133 2/3	153	61	52	23	80
— Colorado (N.L.)	0	0	. . .	7.36	10	0	0	0	0	14 2/3	19	16	12	7	10
Major league totals (2 years)	1	4	.200	6.31	32	3	0	0	0	61 1/3	81	50	43	23	36

S

SALKELD, ROGER — P — REDS

PERSONAL: Born March 6, 1971, in Burbank, Calif. . . . 6-5/215. . . . Throws right, bats right. . . . Full name: Roger W. Salkeld. . . . Grandson of Bill Salkeld, catcher with Pittsburgh Pirates, Boston Braves and Chicago White Sox (1945-50).
HIGH SCHOOL: Saugus (Calif.).
TRANSACTIONS/CAREER NOTES: Selected by Seattle Mariners organization in first round (third pick overall) of free-agent draft (June 5, 1989). . . . On disabled list (April 6-21, 1990). . . . On Calgary disabled list (April 9, 1992-entire season and April 8-June 22, 1993). . . . Traded by Mariners organization to Cincinnati Reds organization for P Tim Belcher (May 15, 1995).

Year	Team (League)	W	L	Pct.	ERA	G	GS	CG	ShO	Sv.	IP	H	R	ER	BB	SO
1989—	Bellingham (N'west)	2	2	.500	1.29	8	6	0	0	0	42	27	17	6	10	55
1990—	San Bern. (Calif.)	11	5	.688	3.40	25	25	2	0	0	153 1/3	140	77	58	83	167
1991—	Jacksonville (Sou.)	8	8	.500	3.05	23	23	5	0	0	153 2/3	131	56	52	55	159
—	Calgary (PCL)	2	1	.667	5.12	4	4	0	0	0	19 1/3	18	16	11	13	21
1992—								Did not play.								
1993—	Jacksonville (Sou.)	4	3	.571	3.27	14	14	0	0	0	77	71	39	28	29	56
—	Seattle (A.L.)	0	0	...	2.51	3	2	0	0	0	14 1/3	13	4	4	4	13
1994—	Calgary (PCL)	3	7	.300	6.15	13	13	0	0	0	67 1/3	74	54	46	39	54
—	Seattle (A.L.)	2	5	.286	7.17	13	13	0	0	0	59	76	47	47	45	46
1995—	Tacoma (PCL)	1	0	1.000	1.80	4	3	0	0	1	15	8	4	3	7	11
—	Indianapolis (A.A.)■	12	2	*.857	4.22	20	20	1	0	0	119 1/3	96	60	56	57	86
Major league totals (2 years)		2	5	.286	6.26	16	15	0	0	0	73 1/3	89	51	51	49	59

SALMON, TIM — OF — ANGELS

PERSONAL: Born August 24, 1968, in Long Beach, Calif. . . . 6-3/220. . . . Bats right, throws right. . . . Full name: Timothy James Salmon. . . . Name pronounced SA-mon.
HIGH SCHOOL: Greenway (Phoenix).
COLLEGE: Grand Canyon (Ariz.).
TRANSACTIONS/CAREER NOTES: Selected by Atlanta Braves organization in 18th round of free-agent draft (June 2, 1986); did not sign. . . . Selected by California Angels organization in third round of free-agent draft (June 5, 1989). . . . On disabled list (May 12-23 and May 27-August 7, 1990; and July 18-August 3, 1994).
RECORDS: Shares A.L. record for most hits in three consecutive games—13 (May 10 [4], 11 [4]and 13 [5], 1994).
HONORS: Named Minor League Player of the Year by The Sporting News (1992). . . . Named Pacific Coast League Most Valuable Player (1992). . . . Named A.L. Rookie Player of the Year by The Sporting News (1993). . . . Named A.L. Rookie of the Year by Baseball Writers' Association of America (1993). . . . Named outfielder on The Sporting News A.L. All-Star team (1995). . . . Named outfielder on The Sporting News Silver Slugger team (1995).
STATISTICAL NOTES: Led Pacific Coast League with 275 total bases, .672 slugging percentage and .469 on-base percentage in 1992. . . . Led A.L. outfielders with four double plays in 1994. . . . Career major league grand slams: 2.

				BATTING										FIELDING			
Year	Team (League)	Pos.	G	AB	R	H	2B	3B	HR	RBI	Avg.	BB	SO	SB	PO	A	E	Avg.
1989—	Bend (Northwest)	OF	55	196	37	48	6	5	6	31	.245	33	60	2	84	7	4	.958
1990—	Palm Springs (Cal.)	OF	36	118	19	34	6	0	2	21	.288	21	44	11	63	3	1	.985
—	Midland (Texas)	OF	27	97	17	26	3	1	3	16	.268	18	38	1	51	6	3	.950
1991—	Midland (Texas)	OF	131	465	100	114	26	4	23	94	.245	*89	*166	12	265	16	10	.966
1992—	Edmonton (PCL)	OF	118	409	•101	142	38	4	*29	*105	.347	91	103	9	231	14	3	.988
—	California (A.L.)	OF	23	79	8	14	1	0	2	6	.177	11	23	1	40	1	2	.953
1993—	California (A.L.)	OF-DH	142	515	93	146	35	1	31	95	.283	82	135	5	335	12	7	.980
1994—	California (A.L.)	OF	100	373	67	107	18	2	23	70	.287	54	102	1	219	9	8	.966
1995—	California (A.L.)	OF-DH	143	537	111	177	34	3	34	105	.330	91	111	5	320	7	4	.988
Major league totals (4 years)			408	1504	279	444	88	6	90	276	.295	238	371	12	914	29	21	.978

SAMUEL, JUAN — 1B/OF — BLUE JAYS

PERSONAL: Born December 9, 1960, in San Pedro de Macoris, Dominican Republic. . . . 5-11/170. . . . Bats right, throws right. . . . Full name: Juan Milton Samuel. . . . Name pronounced sam-WELL.
HIGH SCHOOL: Licey Puerto Rico.
TRANSACTIONS/CAREER NOTES: Signed as non-drafted free agent by Philadelphia Phillies organization (April 29, 1980). . . . On Philadelphia disabled list (April 13-May 2, 1986 and April 1-19, 1989). . . . Traded by Phillies to New York Mets for OF Lenny Dykstra, P Roger McDowell and a player to be named later (June 18, 1989); Phillies organization acquired P Tom Edens to complete deal (July 27, 1989). . . . Traded by Mets to Los Angeles Dodgers for P Alejandro Pena and OF Mike Marshall (December 20, 1989). . . . Granted free agency (November 5, 1990). . . . Re-signed by Dodgers (December 16, 1990). . . . Granted free agency (October 28, 1991). . . . Re-signed by Dodgers (February 27, 1992). . . . On Los Angeles disabled list (April 28-June 11, 1992). . . . Released by Dodgers (July 30, 1992). . . . Signed by Kansas City Royals (August 6, 1992). . . . Granted free agency (October 21, 1992). . . . Signed by Cincinnati Reds organization (December 11, 1992). . . . Granted free agency (October 25, 1993). . . . Signed by Detroit Tigers organization (February 14, 1994). . . . Granted free agency (October 25, 1994). . . . Re-signed by Tigers organization (April 17, 1995). . . . Traded by Tigers to Royals for a player to be named later (September 8, 1995); Tigers acquired OF Phil Hiatt to complete deal (September 14, 1995). . . . Granted free agency (November 2, 1995). . . . Signed by Toronto Blue Jays organization (January 16, 1996).
RECORDS: Holds major league single-season records for most at-bats by righthander—701 (1984); and fewest sacrifice hits with most at-bats—0 (1984). . . . Shares major league record for most consecutive seasons leading league in strikeouts—4 (1984-1987). . . . Shares major league single-game record (nine innings) for most assists by second baseman—12 (April 20, 1985). . . . Holds N.L. single-season record for most at-bats—701 (1984).
HONORS: Named Carolina League Most Valuable Player (1982). . . . Named N.L. Rookie Player of the Year by The Sporting News (1984). . . . Named second baseman on The Sporting News N.L. All-Star team (1987). . . . Named second baseman on The Sporting News N.L. Silver Slugger team (1987).
STATISTICAL NOTES: Led Northwest League in caught stealing with 10 in 1980. . . . Led South Atlantic League second basemen with 739 total chances and 82 double plays in 1981. . . . Led Carolina League second basemen with 721 total chances and 82 double plays in 1982. . . . Led Carolina League with 283 total bases and tied for lead in being hit by pitch with 15 in 1982. . . . Led N.L. second basemen with 826

total chances in 1987. . . . Led N.L. second basemen with 343 putouts and 92 double plays in 1988. . . . Career major league grand slams: 2.

				BATTING											FIELDING			
Year	Team (League)	Pos.	G	AB	R	H	2B	3B	HR	RBI	Avg.	BB	SO	SB	PO	A	E	Avg.
1980—	Cent. Ore. (N'west)	2B	69	*298	66	84	11	2	17	44	.282	17	*87	25	162	188	*30	.921
1981—	Spartanburg (SAL)	2B	135	512	88	127	22	8	11	74	.248	36	132	53	*280	*409	*50	.932
1982—	Peninsula (Caro.)	2B	135	494	*111	158	29	6	28	94	.320	31	124	64	*244	*442	*35	.951
1983—	Reading (Eastern)	2B	47	184	36	43	10	0	11	39	.234	8	50	19	121	127	14	.947
	—Portland (PCL)	2B	65	261	59	86	14	8	15	52	.330	22	46	33	110	168	15	.949
	—Philadelphia (N.L.)	2B	18	65	14	18	1	2	2	5	.277	4	16	3	44	54	9	.916
1984—	Philadelphia (N.L.)	2B	160	*701	105	191	36	•19	15	69	.272	28	*168	72	388	438	*33	.962
1985—	Philadelphia (N.L.)	2B	161	*663	101	175	31	13	19	74	.264	33	•141	53	*389	463	15	.983
1986—	Philadelphia (N.L.)	2B	145	591	90	157	36	12	16	78	.266	26	*142	42	290	440	*25	.967
1987—	Philadelphia (N.L.)	2B	160	*655	113	178	37	*15	28	100	.272	60	*162	35	*374	434	*18	.978
1988—	Philadelphia (N.L.)	2B-OF-3B	157	629	68	153	32	9	12	67	.243	39	151	33	†351	387	16	.979
1989—	Philadelphia (N.L.)	OF	51	199	32	49	3	1	8	20	.246	18	45	11	133	2	1	.993
	—New York (N.L.)■	OF	86	333	37	76	13	1	3	28	.228	24	75	31	206	4	3	.986
1990—	Los Angeles (N.L.)■	2B-OF	143	492	62	119	24	3	13	52	.242	51	126	38	273	262	16	.971
1991—	Los Angeles (N.L.)	2B	153	594	74	161	22	6	12	58	.271	49	133	23	300	442	17	.978
1992—	Los Angeles (N.L.)	2B-OF	47	122	7	32	3	1	0	15	.262	7	22	2	76	77	5	.968
	—Kansas City (A.L.)■	OF-2B	29	102	15	29	5	3	0	8	.284	7	27	6	45	29	6	.925
1993—	Cincinnati (N.L.)■	2-1-3-O	103	261	31	60	10	4	4	26	.230	23	53	9	151	172	10	.970
1994—	Detroit (A.L.)■	O-DH-2-1	59	136	32	42	9	5	5	21	.309	10	26	5	82	28	1	.991
1995—	Detroit (A.L.)	1-DH-O-2	76	171	28	48	10	1	10	34	.281	24	38	5	289	35	9	.973
	—Kansas City (A.L.)■	DH-OF-1B	15	34	3	6	0	0	2	5	.176	5	11	1	11	0	0	1.000
American League totals (3 years)			179	443	78	125	24	9	17	68	.282	46	102	17	427	92	16	.970
National League totals (11 years)			1384	5305	734	1369	248	86	132	592	.258	362	1234	352	2975	3175	168	.973
Major league totals (13 years)			1563	5748	812	1494	272	95	149	660	.260	408	1336	369	3402	3267	184	.973

CHAMPIONSHIP SERIES RECORD

				BATTING											FIELDING			
Year	Team (League)	Pos.	G	AB	R	H	2B	3B	HR	RBI	Avg.	BB	SO	SB	PO	A	E	Avg.
1983—	Philadelphia (N.L.)	PR	1	0	0	0	0	0	0	0	...	0	0	0	...	...	...	...

WORLD SERIES RECORD

				BATTING											FIELDING			
Year	Team (League)	Pos.	G	AB	R	H	2B	3B	HR	RBI	Avg.	BB	SO	SB	PO	A	E	Avg.
1983—	Philadelphia (N.L.)	PR-PH	3	1	0	0	0	0	0	0	.000	0	0	0	...	...	...	...

ALL-STAR GAME RECORD

NOTES: Holds single-game record for most putouts by second baseman—7 (July 14, 1987). . . . Shares single-game record for most chances accepted by second baseman—9 (July 14, 1987).

			BATTING										FIELDING			
Year	League	Pos.	AB	R	H	2B	3B	HR	RBI	Avg.	BB	SO	SB	PO	A	E	Avg.
1984—	National							Did not play.									
1987—	National	2B	4	0	0	0	0	0	0	.000	0	1	0	7	2	0	1.000
1991—	National	2B	1	0	1	0	0	0	0	1.000	0	0	0	2	1	0	1.000
All-Star Game totals (2 years)			5	0	1	0	0	0	0	.200	0	1	0	9	3	0	1.000

SANCHEZ, REY — SS — CUBS

PERSONAL: Born October 5, 1967, in Rio Piedras, Puerto Rico. . . . 5-9/175. . . . Bats right, throws right. . . . Full name: Rey Francisco Guadalupe Sanchez.

HIGH SCHOOL: Live Oak (Morgan Hill, Calif.).

TRANSACTIONS/CAREER NOTES: Selected by Texas Rangers organization in 13th round of free-agent draft (June 2, 1986). . . . Traded by Rangers organization to Chicago Cubs organization for IF Bryan House (January 3, 1990). . . . On disabled list (April 6, 1990-entire season). . . . On Chicago disabled list (May 6-21, 1992); included rehabilitation assignment to Iowa (May 13-21). . . . On disabled list (July 24-August 9, 1995).

STATISTICAL NOTES: Led Gulf Coast League shortstops with .932 fielding percentage in 1986. . . . Led American Association shortstops with 104 double plays in 1989. . . . Led American Association shortstops with 596 total chances and 81 double plays in 1992.

				BATTING											FIELDING			
Year	Team (League)	Pos.	G	AB	R	H	2B	3B	HR	RBI	Avg.	BB	SO	SB	PO	A	E	Avg.
1986—	GC Rangers (GCL)	SS-2B	52	169	27	49	3	1	0	23	.290	41	18	10	69	158	15	†.938
1987—	Gastonia (S. Atl.)	SS	50	160	19	35	1	2	1	10	.219	22	17	6	88	162	18	.933
	—Butte (Pioneer)	SS	49	189	36	69	10	6	0	25	.365	21	12	22	84	162	12	.953
1988—	Charlotte (Fla. St.)	SS	128	418	60	128	6	5	0	38	.306	35	24	29	226	*415	35	.948
1989—	Okla. City (A.A.)	SS	134	464	38	104	10	4	1	39	.224	21	50	4	*237	*418	29	*.958
1990—									Did not play.									
1991—	Iowa (Am. Assoc.)■	SS	126	417	60	121	16	5	2	46	.290	37	27	13	204	*375	17	*.971
	—Chicago (N.L.)	SS-2B	13	23	1	6	0	0	0	2	.261	4	3	0	11	25	0	1.000
1992—	Chicago (N.L.)	SS-2B	74	255	24	64	14	3	1	19	.251	10	17	2	148	202	9	.975
	—Iowa (Am. Assoc.)	SS-2B	20	76	12	26	3	0	0	3	.342	4	1	6	31	77	5	.956
1993—	Chicago (N.L.)	SS	105	344	35	97	11	2	0	28	.282	15	22	1	158	316	15	.969
1994—	Chicago (N.L.)	2B-SS-3B	96	291	26	83	13	1	0	24	.285	20	29	2	152	278	9	.979
1995—	Chicago (N.L.)	2B-SS	114	428	57	119	22	2	3	27	.278	14	48	6	195	351	7	.987
Major league totals (5 years)			402	1341	143	369	60	8	4	100	.275	63	119	11	664	1172	40	.979

SANDBERG, RYNE — 2B — CUBS

PERSONAL: Born September 18, 1959, in Spokane, Wash. . . . 6-2/190. . . . Bats right, throws right. . . . Full name: Ryne Dee Sandberg.

HIGH SCHOOL: North Central (Spokane, Wash.).

S

TRANSACTIONS/CAREER NOTES: Selected by Philadelphia Phillies organization in 20th round of free-agent draft (June 6, 1978). . . . Traded by Phillies with SS Larry Bowa to Chicago Cubs for SS Ivan DeJesus (January 27, 1982). . . . On disabled list (June 14-July 11, 1987). . . . On Chicago disabled list (March 27-April 30, 1993); included rehabilitation assignments to Daytona (April 25-27) and Orlando (April 27-29). . . . On voluntarily retired list (June 13, 1994-October 31, 1995).

RECORDS: Holds major league career records for highest fielding percentage by second baseman—.990; and most consecutive errorless games by second baseman—123 (June 21, 1989 through May 17, 1990). . . . Holds major league single-season record for most consecutive errorless games by second baseman—90 (June 21 through October 1, 1989). . . . Shares major league career record for most years with 500 or more assists by second baseman—6. . . . Shares major league single-game record for most assists by second baseman—12 (June 12, 1983).

HONORS: Won N.L. Gold Glove at second base (1983-91). . . . Named Major League Player of the Year by The Sporting News (1984). . . . Named N.L. Player of the Year by The Sporting News (1984). . . . Named second baseman on The Sporting News N.L. All-Star team (1984 and 1988-92). . . . Named second baseman on The Sporting News N.L. Silver Slugger team (1984-85 and 1988-92). . . . Named N.L. Most Valuable Player by Baseball Writers' Association of America (1984).

STATISTICAL NOTES: Led Pioneer League shortstops with 39 double plays in 1978. . . . Led Western Carolinas League shortstops with 80 double plays in 1979. . . . Led Eastern League shortstops with .964 fielding percentage, 386 assists and 81 double plays in 1980. . . . Led N.L. second basemen with .986 fielding percentage, 571 assists and 126 double plays in 1983. . . . Led N.L. second basemen with 914 total chances in 1983, 870 in 1984, 824 in 1988 and 830 in 1992. . . . Led N.L. with 344 total bases in 1990. . . . Career major league grand slams: 3.

		BATTING												FIELDING			
Year Team (League)	Pos.	G	AB	R	H	2B	3B	HR	RBI	Avg.	BB	SO	SB	PO	A	E	Avg.
1978—Helena (Pioneer)	SS	56	190	34	59	6	6	1	23	.311	26	42	15	92	*200	24	.924
1979—Spartan. (W. Caro.)	SS	•138	*539	83	133	21	7	4	47	.247	64	95	21	134	*467	35	*.945
1980—Reading (Eastern)	SS-3B	129	490	95	152	21	12	11	79	.310	73	72	32	156	†388	20	†.965
1981—Okla. City (A.A.)	SS-2B	133	519	78	152	17	5	9	62	.293	48	94	32	229	396	21	.967
—Philadelphia (N.L.)	SS-2B	13	6	2	1	0	0	0	0	.167	0	1	0	7	7	0	1.000
1982—Chicago (N.L.)■	3B-2B	156	635	103	172	33	5	7	54	.271	36	90	32	136	373	12	.977
1983—Chicago (N.L.)	2B-SS	158	633	94	165	25	4	8	48	.261	51	79	37	330	†572	13	†.986
1984—Chicago (N.L.)	2B	156	636	*114	200	36	•19	19	84	.314	52	101	32	314	*550	6	*.993
1985—Chicago (N.L.)	2B-SS	153	609	113	186	31	6	26	83	.305	57	97	54	353	501	12	.986
1986—Chicago (N.L.)	2B	154	627	68	178	28	5	14	76	.284	46	79	34	309	*492	5	*.994
1987—Chicago (N.L.)	2B	132	523	81	154	25	2	16	59	.294	59	79	21	294	375	10	.985
1988—Chicago (N.L.)	2B	155	618	77	163	23	8	19	69	.264	54	91	25	291	*522	11	.987
1989—Chicago (N.L.)	2B	157	606	•104	176	25	5	30	76	.290	59	85	15	294	466	6	.992
1990—Chicago (N.L.)	2B	155	615	*116	188	30	3	*40	100	.306	50	84	25	278	*469	8	.989
1991—Chicago (N.L.)	2B	158	585	104	170	32	2	26	100	.291	87	89	22	267	*515	4	*.995
1992—Chicago (N.L.)	2B	158	612	100	186	32	8	26	87	.304	68	73	17	283	*539	8	.990
1993—Daytona (Fla. St.)	2B	2	5	2	1	0	0	1	2	.200	1	0	0	3	4	0	1.000
—Orlando (Southern)	2B	4	9	0	2	0	0	0	1	.222	3	1	0	3	8	0	1.000
—Chicago (N.L.)	2B	117	456	67	141	20	0	9	45	.309	37	62	9	209	347	7	.988
1994—Chicago (N.L.)	2B	57	223	36	53	9	5	5	24	.238	23	40	2	96	202	4	.987
1995—								Did not play.									
Major league totals (14 years)		1879	7384	1179	2133	349	72	245	905	.289	679	1050	325	3461	5930	106	.989

CHAMPIONSHIP SERIES RECORD

		BATTING												FIELDING			
Year Team (League)	Pos.	G	AB	R	H	2B	3B	HR	RBI	Avg.	BB	SO	SB	PO	A	E	Avg.
1984—Chicago (N.L.)	2B	5	19	3	7	2	0	0	2	.368	3	2	3	13	18	1	.969
1989—Chicago (N.L.)	2B	5	20	6	8	3	1	1	4	.400	3	4	0	7	11	0	1.000
Championship series totals (2 years)		10	39	9	15	5	1	1	6	.385	6	6	3	20	29	1	.980

ALL-STAR GAME RECORD

		BATTING											FIELDING			
Year League	Pos.	AB	R	H	2B	3B	HR	RBI	Avg.	BB	SO	SB	PO	A	E	Avg.
1984—National	2B	4	0	1	0	0	0	0	.250	0	0	1	0	0	0	...
1985—National	2B	1	1	0	0	0	0	0	.000	1	0	0	0	3	0	1.000
1986—National	2B	3	0	0	0	0	0	0	.000	0	0	0	0	2	1	.667
1987—National	2B	2	0	0	0	0	0	0	.000	0	0	0	0	2	0	1.000
1988—National	2B	4	0	1	0	0	0	0	.250	0	2	0	2	2	0	1.000
1989—National	2B	3	0	0	0	0	0	0	.000	0	2	0	2	4	0	1.000
1990—National	2B	3	0	0	0	0	0	0	.000	0	0	0	1	2	0	1.000
1991—National	2B	3	0	1	1	0	0	0	.333	0	0	0	2	1	0	1.000
1992—National	2B	2	0	0	0	0	0	0	.000	0	1	0	2	3	0	1.000
1993—National	2B	1	0	0	0	0	0	0	.000	1	0	0	0	2	0	1.000
All-Star Game totals (10 years)		26	1	3	1	0	0	0	.115	2	5	1	9	21	1	.968

SANDERS, DEION OF

PERSONAL: Born August 9, 1967, in Fort Myers, Fla. . . . 6-1/195. . . . Bats left, throws left. . . . Full name: Deion Luwynn Sanders.

HIGH SCHOOL: North Fort Myers (Fla.).

COLLEGE: Florida State.

TRANSACTIONS/CAREER NOTES: Selected by Kansas City Royals organization in sixth round of free-agent draft (June 3, 1985); did not sign. . . . Selected by New York Yankees organization in 30th round of free-agent draft (June 1, 1988). . . . On disqualified list (August 1-September 24, 1990). . . . Released by Yankees organization (September 24, 1990). . . . Signed by Atlanta Braves (January 29, 1991). . . . Placed on Richmond temporarily inactive list (August 1, 1991). . . . On disqualified list (April 29-May 21, 1993). . . . On disabled list (August 22-September 6, 1993). . . . Traded by Braves to Cincinnati Reds for OF Roberto Kelly and P Roger Etheridge (May 29, 1994). . . . On Cincinnati disabled list (June 1-July 16, 1995); included rehabilitation assignment to Chattanooga (July 12-14). . . . Traded by Reds with P John Roper, P Ricky Pickett, P Scott Service and IF Dave McCarty to San Francisco Giants for OF Darren Lewis, P Mark Portugal and P Dave Burba (July 21, 1995). . . . Granted free agency (December 21, 1995).

STATISTICAL NOTES: Led N.L. in caught stealing with 16 in 1994.

MISCELLANEOUS: Only person in history to play in both the World Series (1992) and Super Bowl (1994 and 1995 seasons).

Year	Team (League)	Pos.	G	AB	R	H	2B	3B	HR	RBI	Avg.	BB	SO	SB	PO	A	E	Avg.
			BATTING												FIELDING			
1988—	GC Yankees (GCL)......	OF	17	75	7	21	4	2	0	6	.280	2	10	11	33	1	2	.944
—	Fort Lauder. (FSL)......	OF	6	21	5	9	2	0	0	2	.429	1	3	2	22	2	0	1.000
—	Columbus (Int'l).........	OF	5	20	3	3	1	0	0	0	.150	1	4	1	13	0	0	1.000
1989—	Alb./Colon. (East.)......	OF	33	119	28	34	2	2	1	6	.286	11	20	17	79	3	0	1.000
—	New York (A.L.).........	OF	14	47	7	11	2	0	2	7	.234	3	8	1	30	1	1	.969
—	Columbus (Int'l).........	OF	70	259	38	72	12	7	5	30	.278	22	46	16	165	0	4	.976
1990—	New York (A.L.).........	OF-DH	57	133	24	21	2	2	3	9	.158	13	27	8	69	2	2	.973
—	Columbus (Int'l).........	OF	22	84	21	27	7	1	2	10	.321	17	15	9	49	1	0	1.000
1991—	Atlanta (N.L.)■..........	OF	54	110	16	21	1	2	4	13	.191	12	23	11	57	3	3	.952
—	Richmond (Int'l).........	OF	29	130	20	34	6	3	5	16	.262	10	28	12	73	1	1	.987
1992—	Atlanta (N.L.)............	OF	97	303	54	92	6	*14	8	28	.304	18	52	26	174	4	3	.983
1993—	Atlanta (N.L.)............	OF	95	272	42	75	18	6	6	28	.276	16	42	19	137	1	2	.986
1994—	Atlanta (N.L.)............	OF	46	191	32	55	10	0	4	21	.288	16	28	19	99	0	2	.980
—	Cincinnati (N.L.)■......	OF	46	184	26	51	7	4	0	7	.277	16	35	19	110	2	0	1.000
1995—	Cincinnati (N.L.).........	OF	33	129	19	31	2	3	1	10	.240	9	18	16	88	2	3	.968
—	Chatt. (South.)...........	OF	2	7	1	4	0	0	1	2	.571	0	1	1	3	1	0	1.000
—	San Franc. (N.L.)■.....	OF	52	214	29	61	9	5	5	18	.285	18	42	8	127	0	2	.984
American League totals (2 years)			71	180	31	32	4	2	5	16	.178	16	35	9	99	3	3	.971
National League totals (5 years)			423	1403	218	386	53	34	28	125	.275	105	240	118	792	12	15	.982
Major league totals (7 years)			494	1583	249	418	57	36	33	141	.264	121	275	127	891	15	18	.981

CHAMPIONSHIP SERIES RECORD

Year	Team (League)	Pos.	G	AB	R	H	2B	3B	HR	RBI	Avg.	BB	SO	SB	PO	A	E	Avg.
			BATTING												FIELDING			
1992—	Atlanta (N.L.)............	OF-PH	4	5	0	0	0	0	0	0	.000	0	3	0	1	0	0	1.000
1993—	Atlanta (N.L.)............	PH-OF-PR	5	3	0	0	0	0	0	0	.000	0	1	0	0	0	0	...
Championship series totals (2 years)			9	8	0	0	0	0	0	0	.000	0	4	0	1	0	0	1.000

WORLD SERIES RECORD

Year	Team (League)	Pos.	G	AB	R	H	2B	3B	HR	RBI	Avg.	BB	SO	SB	PO	A	E	Avg.
			BATTING												FIELDING			
1992—	Atlanta (N.L.)............	OF	4	15	4	8	2	0	0	1	.533	2	1	5	5	1	0	1.000

RECORD AS FOOTBALL PLAYER

TRANSACTIONS/CAREER NOTES: Selected by Atlanta Falcons in first round (fifth pick overall) of 1989 NFL draft. . . . Signed by Falcons (September 7, 1989). . . . On reserve/did not report list (July 27-August 13, 1990). . . . Granted roster exemption for one game (September 1992). . . . On reserve/did not report list (July 23-October 14, 1993). . . . Designated by Falcons as transition player (February 15, 1994). . . . Free agency status changed by Falcons from transitional to unconditional (April 28, 1994). . . . Signed by San Francisco 49ers (September 15, 1994). . . . Granted unconditional free agency (February 17, 1995). . . . Signed by Dallas Cowboys (September 9, 1995).

HONORS: Named defensive back on The Sporting News college All-America team (1986-1988). . . . Jim Thorpe Award winner (1988). . . . Named cornerback on The Sporting News NFL All-Pro team (1991, 1992, 1994 and 1995). . . . Played in Pro Bowl (1991-1994 seasons). . . . Named kick returner on The Sporting News NFL All-Pro team (1992).

PRO STATISTICS: 1989—Caught one pass for minus eight yards and recovered one fumble. 1990—Recovered two fumbles. 1991—Caught one pass for 17 yards and recovered one fumble. 1992—Rushed once for minus four yards, caught three passes for 45 yards (15.0-yard avg.) and a touchdown and recovered two fumbles. 1993—Caught six passes for 106 yards (17.7-yard avg.) and a touchdown. 1995—Caught two passes for 25 yards and rushed twice for nine yards.

MISCELLANEOUS: Plays cornerback.

Year	Team	G	No.	Yds.	Avg.	TD	No.	No.	Yds.	Avg.	TD	No.	Yds.	Avg.	TD	TD	Pts.	Fum.
			INTERCEPTIONS				SACKS	PUNT RETURNS				KICKOFF RETURNS				TOTAL		
1989—	Atlanta NFL................	15	5	52	10.4	0	0.0	28	307	11.0	*1	35	725	20.7	0	1	6	2
1990—	Atlanta NFL................	16	3	153	51.0	2	0.0	29	250	8.6	*1	39	851	21.8	0	3	18	4
1991—	Atlanta NFL................	15	6	119	19.8	1	1.0	21	170	8.1	0	26	576	22.2	*1	2	12	1
1992—	Atlanta NFL................	13	3	105	35.0	0	0.0	13	41	3.2	0	40	*1067	26.7	*2	3	18	3
1993—	Atlanta NFL................	11	7	91	13.0	0	0.0	2	21	10.5	0	7	169	24.1	0	1	6	0
1994—	San Francisco NFL	14	6	303	50.5	3	0.0	0	0	0.0	0	0	0	0.0	0	3	18	0
1995—	Dallas NFL.................	9	2	34	17.0	0	0.0	1	54	54.0	0	1	15	15.0	0	0	0	0
Pro totals (7 years)............		93	32	857	26.8	6	1.0	94	843	9.0	2	148	3403	23.0	3	13	78	10

SANDERS, REGGIE OF REDS

PERSONAL: Born December 1, 1967, in Florence, S.C. . . . 6-1/185. . . . Bats right, throws right. . . . Full name: Reginald Laverne Sanders.

HIGH SCHOOL: Wilson (Florence, S.C.).

COLLEGE: Spartanburg (S.C.) Methodist.

TRANSACTIONS/CAREER NOTES: Selected by Cincinnati Reds organization in seventh round of free-agent draft (June 2, 1987). . . . On disabled list (July 11-September 15, 1988 and July 15-September 5, 1989). . . . On Chattanooga disabled list (June 30-July 26, 1991). . . . On Cincinnati disabled list (August 24-September 20, 1991; and May 13-29 and July 17-August 2, 1992). . . . On suspended list (June 3-9, 1994).

HONORS: Named Midwest League Most Valuable Player (1990). . . . Named outfielder on The Sporting News N.L. All-Star team (1995).

STATISTICAL NOTES: Hit three home runs in one game (August 15, 1995).

Year	Team (League)	Pos.	G	AB	R	H	2B	3B	HR	RBI	Avg.	BB	SO	SB	PO	A	E	Avg.
			BATTING												FIELDING			
1988—	Billings (Pioneer)........	SS	17	64	11	15	1	1	0	3	.234	6	4	10	18	33	3	.944
1989—	Greensboro (S. Atl.)...	SS	81	315	53	91	18	5	9	53	.289	29	63	21	125	169	42	.875
1990—	Ced. Rap. (Midw.)......	OF	127	466	89	133	21	4	17	63	.285	59	97	40	241	10	10	.962
1991—	Chatt. (South.)...........	OF	86	302	50	95	15	•8	8	49	.315	41	67	15	158	2	3	.982
—	Cincinnati (N.L.).........	OF	9	40	6	8	0	0	1	3	.200	0	9	1	22	0	0	1.000
1992—	Cincinnati (N.L.).........	OF	116	385	62	104	26	6	12	36	.270	48	98	16	262	11	6	.978
1993—	Cincinnati (N.L.).........	OF	138	496	90	136	16	4	20	83	.274	51	118	27	312	3	8	.975
1994—	Cincinnati (N.L.).........	OF	107	400	66	105	20	8	17	62	.263	41	*114	21	218	12	6	.975
1995—	Cincinnati (N.L.).........	OF	133	484	91	148	36	6	28	99	.306	69	122	36	268	12	5	.982
Major league totals (5 years)			503	1805	315	501	98	24	78	283	.278	209	461	101	1082	38	25	.978

DIVISION SERIES RECORD

				BATTING										FIELDING			
Year	Team (League)	Pos.	G	AB	R	H	2B	3B	HR	RBI	Avg.	BB	SO	SB	PO	A	E	Avg.
1995—	Cincinnati (N.L.)	OF	3	13	3	2	1	0	1	2	.154	1	9	2	7	0	1	.875

CHAMPIONSHIP SERIES RECORD

				BATTING										FIELDING			
Year	Team (League)	Pos.	G	AB	R	H	2B	3B	HR	RBI	Avg.	BB	SO	SB	PO	A	E	Avg.
1995—	Cincinnati (N.L.)	OF	4	16	0	2	0	0	0	0	.125	2	10	0	7	0	1	.875

ALL-STAR GAME RECORD

			BATTING										FIELDING			
Year	League	Pos.	AB	R	H	2B	3B	HR	RBI	Avg.	BB	SO	SB	PO	A	E	Avg.
1995—	National	OF	1	0	0	0	0	0	0	.000	0	1	0	0	0	0	...

SANDERS, SCOTT — P — PADRES

PERSONAL: Born March 25, 1969, in Hannibal, Mo. . . . 6-4/220. . . . Throws right, bats right. . . . Full name: Scott Gerald Sanders.
HIGH SCHOOL: Thibodaux (La.).
COLLEGE: Nicholls State (La.).
TRANSACTIONS/CAREER NOTES: Selected by San Diego Padres organization in supplemental round ("sandwich pick" between first and second round, 32nd pick overall) of free-agent draft (June 4, 1990); pick received as part of compensation for Kansas City Royals signing Type A free-agent P Mark Davis. . . . On disabled list (May 1-17, 1994). . . . On San Diego disabled list (July 18, 1995-remainder of season); included rehabilitation assignment to Las Vegas (August 28-September 1).
STATISTICAL NOTES: Tied for N.L. lead with 10 wild pitches in 1994.

Year	Team (League)	W	L	Pct.	ERA	G	GS	CG	ShO	Sv.	IP	H	R	ER	BB	SO
1990—	Waterloo (Midw.)	2	2	.500	4.86	7	7	0	0	0	37	43	21	20	21	29
—	Spokane (N'west)	2	1	.667	0.95	3	3	0	0	0	19	12	3	2	5	21
1991—	Waterloo (Midw.)	3	0	1.000	0.68	4	4	0	0	0	26 1/3	17	2	2	6	18
—	High Desert (Calif.)	9	6	.600	3.66	21	21	4	2	0	132 2/3	114	72	54	72	93
1992—	Wichita (Texas)	7	5	.583	3.49	14	14	0	0	0	87 2/3	85	35	34	37	95
—	Las Vegas (PCL)	3	6	.333	5.50	14	12	1	1	0	72	97	49	44	31	51
1993—	Las Vegas (PCL)	5	10	.333	4.96	24	24	•4	0	0	152 1/3	170	101	84	62	*161
—	San Diego (N.L.)	3	3	.500	4.13	9	9	0	0	0	52 1/3	54	32	24	23	37
1994—	San Diego (N.L.)■	4	8	.333	4.78	23	20	0	0	1	111	103	63	59	48	109
1995—	San Diego (N.L.)	5	5	.500	4.30	17	15	1	0	0	90	79	46	43	31	88
—	Las Vegas (PCL)	0	0	...	0.00	1	1	0	0	0	3	3	0	0	1	2
Major league totals (3 years)		12	16	.429	4.48	49	44	1	0	1	253 1/3	236	141	126	102	234

SANDERSON, SCOTT — P — ANGELS

PERSONAL: Born July 22, 1956, in Dearborn, Mich. . . . 6-5/192. . . . Throws right, bats right. . . . Full name: Scott Douglas Sanderson.
HIGH SCHOOL: Glenbrook North (Northbrook, Ill.).
COLLEGE: Vanderbilt.
TRANSACTIONS/CAREER NOTES: Selected by Kansas City Royals organization in 11th round of free-agent draft (June 5, 1974); did not sign. . . . Selected by Montreal Expos organization in third round of free-agent draft (June 7, 1977). . . . On disabled list (July 5-September 1, 1983). . . . Traded by Expos with IF Al Newman to San Diego Padres for P Gary Lucas (December 7, 1983); traded by Padres to Chicago Cubs for 1B Carmelo Martinez, P Craig Lefferts and 3B Fritz Connally (December 7, 1983). . . . On Chicago disabled list (June 1-July 5, 1984); included rehabilitation assignment to Lodi (June 29-July 5). . . . On disabled list (August 14, 1985-remainder of season; March 29-April 24 and June 22-July 7, 1987). . . . On Chicago disabled list (April 5-August 23, 1988); included rehabilitation assignments to Peoria (June 25-29) and Iowa (June 30-July 11). . . . Granted free agency (November 4, 1988). . . . Re-signed by Cubs (December 7, 1988). . . . Granted free agency (November 13, 1989). . . . Signed by Oakland Athletics (December 13, 1989). . . . Granted free agency (November 5, 1990). . . . Re-signed by A's (December 19, 1990). . . . Contract sold by A's to New York Yankees (December 31, 1990). . . . Granted free agency (October 28, 1992). . . . Signed by California Angels (February 11, 1993). . . . Claimed on waivers by San Francisco Giants (August 3, 1993). . . . Granted free agency (November 1, 1993). . . . Signed by Chicago White Sox organization (March 1, 1994). . . . Granted free agency (October 27, 1994). . . . Signed by Vancouver, Angels organization (April 18, 1995). . . . On disabled list (June 1, 1995-remainder of season). . . . Granted free agency (November 8, 1995). . . . Re-signed by Angels organization (December 7, 1995).
RECORDS: Shares major league record for most home runs allowed in one inning—4 (May 2, 1992, fifth inning). . . . Shares N.L. record for most consecutive home runs allowed in one inning—3 (July 11, 1982, second inning).
STATISTICAL NOTES: Pitched 4-0 one-hit, complete-game victory against San Francisco (May 8, 1979). . . . Pitched 2-0 one-hit, complete-game victory against California (July 11, 1991).

Year	Team (League)	W	L	Pct.	ERA	G	GS	CG	ShO	Sv.	IP	H	R	ER	BB	SO
1977—	WP Beach (FSL)	5	2	.714	2.68	10	10	2	1	0	57	58	22	17	23	37
1978—	Memphis (South.)	5	3	.625	4.03	9	9	1	0	0	58	55	32	26	19	44
—	Denver (Am. Assoc.)	4	2	.667	6.06	9	9	1	0	0	49	47	35	33	30	36
—	Montreal (N.L.)	4	2	.667	2.51	10	9	1	1	0	61	52	20	17	21	50
1979—	Montreal (N.L.)	9	8	.529	3.43	34	24	5	3	1	168	148	69	64	54	138
1980—	Montreal (N.L.)	16	11	.593	3.11	33	33	7	3	0	211	206	76	73	56	125
1981—	Montreal (N.L.)	9	7	.563	2.96	22	22	4	1	0	137	122	50	45	31	77
1982—	Montreal (N.L.)	12	12	.500	3.46	32	32	7	0	0	224	212	98	86	58	158
1983—	Montreal (N.L.)	6	7	.462	4.65	18	16	0	0	1	81 1/3	98	50	42	20	55
1984—	Chicago (N.L.)■	8	5	.615	3.14	24	24	3	0	0	140 2/3	140	54	49	24	76
—	Lodi (California)	0	1	.000	3.60	1	1	0	0	0	5	7	2	2	0	2
1985—	Chicago (N.L.)	5	6	.455	3.12	19	19	2	0	0	121	100	49	42	27	80
1986—	Chicago (N.L.)	9	11	.450	4.19	37	28	1	1	1	169 2/3	165	85	79	37	124
1987—	Chicago (N.L.)	8	9	.471	4.29	32	22	0	0	2	144 2/3	156	72	69	50	106
1988—	Peoria (Midwest)	0	0	...	0.00	1	1	0	0	0	5	4	1	0	0	3
—	Iowa (Am. Assoc.)	1	0	1.000	4.73	3	3	0	0	0	13 1/3	13	7	7	2	4
—	Chicago (N.L.)	1	2	.333	5.28	11	0	0	0	0	15 1/3	13	9	9	3	6

Year Team (League)	W	L	Pct.	ERA	G	GS	CG	ShO	Sv.	IP	H	R	ER	BB	SO
1989— Chicago (N.L.)	11	9	.550	3.94	37	23	2	0	0	146 1/3	155	69	64	31	86
1990— Oakland (A.L.)■	17	11	.607	3.88	34	34	2	1	0	206 1/3	205	99	89	66	128
1991— New York (A.L.)■	16	10	.615	3.81	34	34	2	2	0	208	200	95	88	29	130
1992— New York (A.L.)	12	11	.522	4.93	33	33	2	1	0	193 1/3	220	116	106	64	104
1993— California (A.L.)■	7	11	.389	4.46	21	21	4	1	0	135 1/3	153	77	67	27	66
— San Francisco (N.L.)■	4	2	.667	3.51	11	8	0	0	0	48 2/3	48	20	19	7	36
1994— Chicago (A.L.)■	8	4	.667	5.09	18	14	1	0	0	92	110	57	52	12	36
1995— California (A.L.)■	1	3	.250	4.12	7	7	0	0	0	39 1/3	48	23	18	4	23
A.L. totals (6 years)	61	50	.550	4.32	147	143	11	5	0	874 1/3	936	467	420	202	487
N.L. totals (13 years)	102	91	.529	3.55	320	260	32	9	5	1668 2/3	1615	721	658	419	1117
Major league totals (18 years)	163	141	.536	3.82	467	403	43	14	5	2543	2551	1188	1078	621	1604

DIVISION SERIES RECORD

Year Team (League)	W	L	Pct.	ERA	G	GS	CG	ShO	Sv.	IP	H	R	ER	BB	SO
1981— Montreal (N.L.)	0	0	...	6.75	1	1	0	0	0	2 2/3	4	4	2	2	2

CHAMPIONSHIP SERIES RECORD

Year Team (League)	W	L	Pct.	ERA	G	GS	CG	ShO	Sv.	IP	H	R	ER	BB	SO
1981— Montreal (N.L.)							Did not play.								
1984— Chicago (N.L.)	0	0	...	5.79	1	1	0	0	0	4 2/3	6	3	3	1	2
1989— Chicago (N.L.)	0	0	...	0.00	1	0	0	0	0	2	2	0	0	0	1
1990— Oakland (A.L.)							Did not play.								
Champ. series totals (2 years)	0	0	...	4.05	2	1	0	0	0	6 2/3	8	3	3	1	3

WORLD SERIES RECORD

Year Team (League)	W	L	Pct.	ERA	G	GS	CG	ShO	Sv.	IP	H	R	ER	BB	SO
1990— Oakland (A.L.)	0	0	...	10.80	2	0	0	0	0	1 2/3	4	2	2	1	0

ALL-STAR GAME RECORD

Year League	W	L	Pct.	ERA	GS	CG	ShO	Sv.	IP	H	R	ER	BB	SO
1991— American						Did not play.								

SANFORD, MO — P — RANGERS

PERSONAL: Born December 24, 1966, in Americus, Ga. . . . 6-6/225. . . . Throws right, bats right. . . . Full name: Meredith Leroy Sanford Jr.
HIGH SCHOOL: Starkville (Miss.).
COLLEGE: Alabama.
TRANSACTIONS/CAREER NOTES: Selected by New York Yankees organization in third round of free-agent draft (June 4, 1984); did not sign. . . . Selected by Cincinnati Reds organization in 32nd round of free-agent draft (June 1, 1988). . . . Selected by Colorado Rockies in third round (62nd pick overall) of expansion draft (November 17, 1992). . . . Granted free agency (December 20, 1993). . . . Signed by Minnesota Twins organization (January 5, 1994). . . . On Salt Lake disabled list (July 17, 1995-remainder of season). . . . Granted free agency (October 3, 1995). . . . Signed by Texas Rangers organization (December 6, 1995).
STATISTICAL NOTES: Pitched 7-0 no-hit victory against Myrtle Beach (June 2, 1989).

Year Team (League)	W	L	Pct.	ERA	G	GS	CG	ShO	Sv.	IP	H	R	ER	BB	SO
1988— GC Reds (GCL)	3	4	.429	3.23	14	11	0	0	1	53	34	24	19	25	64
1989— Greensboro (S. Atl.)	12	6	.667	2.81	25	25	3	1	0	153 2/3	112	52	48	64	160
1990— Ced. Rap. (Midw.)	13	4	.765	2.74	25	25	2	1	0	157 2/3	112	50	48	55	180
1991— Chattanooga (Sou.)	7	4	.636	2.74	16	16	1	1	0	95 1/3	69	37	29	55	124
— Nashville (A.A.)	3	0	1.000	1.60	5	5	2	2	0	33 2/3	19	7	6	22	38
— Cincinnati (N.L.)	1	2	.333	3.86	5	5	0	0	0	28	19	14	12	15	31
1992— Nashville (A.A.)	8	8	.500	5.68	25	25	0	0	0	122	128	81	77	65	129
— Chattanooga (Sou.)	4	0	1.000	1.35	4	4	1	1	0	26 2/3	13	5	4	6	28
1993— Colo. Springs (PCL)■	3	6	.333	5.23	20	17	0	0	0	105	103	64	61	57	104
— Colorado (N.L.)	1	2	.333	5.30	11	6	0	0	0	35 2/3	37	25	21	27	36
1994— Salt Lake (PCL)■	7	5	.583	4.87	37	11	0	0	4	125 2/3	121	74	68	52	141
1995— Minnesota (A.L.)	0	0	...	5.30	11	0	0	0	0	18 2/3	16	11	11	16	17
— Salt Lake (PCL)	0	1	.000	6.35	4	0	0	0	0	5 2/3	6	4	4	4	8
A.L. totals (1 year)	0	0	...	5.30	11	0	0	0	0	18 2/3	16	11	11	16	17
N.L. totals (2 years)	2	4	.333	4.66	16	11	0	0	0	63 2/3	56	39	33	42	67
Major league totals (3 years)	2	4	.333	4.81	27	11	0	0	0	82 1/3	72	50	44	58	84

SANTANA, JULIO — P — RANGERS

PERSONAL: Born January 20, 1974, in San Pedro de Macoris, Dominican Republic. . . . 6-0/175. . . . Throws right, bats right. . . . Full name: Julio Franklin Santana. . . . Nephew of Rico Carty, major league outfielder with seven teams (1963-79).
TRANSACTIONS/CAREER NOTES: Signed as non-drafted free agent by Texas Rangers organization (February 18, 1990).

Year Team (League)	W	L	Pct.	ERA	G	GS	CG	ShO	Sv.	IP	H	R	ER	BB	SO
1992— San Pedro (DSL)	0	1	.000	3.24	4	1	0	0	0	8 1/3	8	5	3	7	5
1993— GC Rangers (GCL)	4	1	.800	1.38	*26	0	0	0	7	39	31	9	6	7	50
1994— Char., W.Va. (S. Atl.)	6	7	.462	2.46	16	16	0	0	0	91 1/3	65	38	25	44	103
— Tulsa (Texas)	7	2	.778	2.90	11	11	2	0	0	71 1/3	50	26	23	41	45
1995— Okla. City (A.A.)	0	2	.000	39.00	2	2	0	0	0	3	9	14	13	7	6
— Charlotte (Fla. St.)	0	3	.000	3.73	5	5	1	0	0	31 1/3	32	16	13	16	27
— Tulsa (Texas)	6	4	.600	3.23	15	15	3	0	0	103	91	40	37	52	71

RECORD AS POSITION PLAYER

			BATTING											FIELDING			
Year Team (League)	Pos.	G	AB	R	H	2B	3B	HR	RBI	Avg.	BB	SO	SB	PO	A	E	Avg.
1990— San Pedro (DSL)	...	11	34	4	7	0	0	1	3	.206	5	7	0	...	...	...	...
1991— San Pedro (DSL)	...	55	161	27	42	7	0	2	12	.261	27	37	5	...	...	...	...
1992— San Pedro (DSL)	OF-IF	17	48	7	11	2	0	2	2	.229	11	8	0	50	2	4	.929

SANTANGELLO, F.P. — 3B/OF — EXPOS

PERSONAL: Born October 24, 1967, in Livonia, Mich. . . . 5-10/170. . . . Bats both, throws right. . . . Full name: Frank Payl Santangello.
COLLEGE: Miami (Fla.).
TRANSACTIONS/CAREER NOTES: Selected by Montreal Expos organization in 20th round of free-agent draft (June 5, 1989). . . . On disabled list (April 21-May 2, 1994).
STATISTICAL NOTES: Led Eastern League with 13 sacrifice hits in 1991.

			BATTING											FIELDING			
Year Team (League)	Pos.	G	AB	R	H	2B	3B	HR	RBI	Avg.	BB	SO	SB	PO	A	E	Avg.
1989—Jamestown (NYP)	2B	2	6	0	3	1	0	0	0	.500	1	0	1	5	5	2	.833
—W.P. Beach (FSL)	SS-2B-OF	57	173	18	37	4	0	0	14	.214	23	12	3	32	67	8	.925
1990—W.P. Beach (FSL)	S-O-2-3	116	394	63	109	19	2	0	38	.277	51	49	22	151	202	22	.941
1991—Harrisburg (East.)	2-O-S-3	132	462	78	113	12	7	5	42	.245	74	45	21	234	253	16	.968
1992—Indianapolis (A.A.)	O-2-S-3	137	462	83	123	25	0	5	34	.266	62	58	12	291	119	4	.990
1993—Ottawa (Int'l)	O-S-3-2	131	453	86	124	21	2	4	45	.274	59	52	18	246	186	14	.969
1994—Ottawa (Int'l)	O-2-S-3	119	413	62	104	28	1	5	41	.252	59	64	7	235	140	12	.969
1995—Ottawa (Int'l)	3-2-O-S-C	95	267	37	68	15	3	2	25	.255	32	22	7	89	185	10	.965
—Montreal (N.L.)	OF-2B	35	98	11	29	5	1	1	9	.296	12	9	1	47	0	1	.979
Major league totals (1 year)		35	98	11	29	5	1	1	9	.296	12	9	1	47	0	1	.979

SANTIAGO, BENITO — C

PERSONAL: Born March 9, 1965, in Ponce, Puerto Rico. . . . 6-1/185. . . . Bats right, throws right. . . . Full name: Benito Rivera Santiago. . . . Name pronounced SAHN-tee-AH-go.
HIGH SCHOOL: John F. Kennedy (Ponce, Puerto Rico).
TRANSACTIONS/CAREER NOTES: Signed as non-drafted free agent by San Diego Padres organization (September 1, 1982). . . . On disabled list (June 21-July 2, 1985). . . . On San Diego disabled list (June 15-August 10, 1990); included rehabilitation assignment to Las Vegas (August 2-9). . . . On San Diego disabled list (May 31-July 11, 1992); included rehabilitation assignment to Las Vegas (July 7-11). . . . Granted free agency (October 26, 1992). . . . Signed by Florida Marlins (December 16, 1992). . . . On suspended list (May 5-9, 1994). . . . Granted free agency (October 20, 1994). . . . Signed by Cincinnati Reds (April 17, 1995). . . . On disabled list (May 8-July 4, 1995). . . . Granted free agency (October 31, 1995).
RECORDS: Holds major league rookie-season record for most consecutive games batted safely—34 (August 25-October 2, 1987). . . . Shares major league single-season record for fewest passed balls (100 or more games)—0 (1992).
HONORS: Named N.L. Rookie Player of the Year by The Sporting News (1987). . . . Named catcher on The Sporting News N.L. All-Star team (1987, 1989 and 1991). . . . Named catcher on The Sporting News N.L. Silver Slugger team (1987-88 and 1990-91). . . . Named N.L. Rookie of the Year by Baseball Writers' Association of America (1987). . . . Won N.L. Gold Glove at catcher (1988-90).
STATISTICAL NOTES: Led Florida State League catchers with 26 passed balls and 12 double plays in 1983. . . . Led Texas League catchers with 78 assists and 16 passed balls in 1985. . . . Led Pacific Coast League catchers with 655 total chances in 1986. . . . Led N.L. with 22 passed balls in 1987, 14 in 1989 and 23 in 1993. . . . Led N.L. in grounding into double plays with 21 in 1991. . . . Tied for N.L. lead in double plays by catcher with 11 in 1988 and 14 in 1991. . . . Led N.L. catchers with 100 assists and 14 errors in 1991. . . . Led N.L. catchers with .996 fielding percentage in 1995. . . . Career major league grand slams: 3.

			BATTING											FIELDING			
Year Team (League)	Pos.	G	AB	R	H	2B	3B	HR	RBI	Avg.	BB	SO	SB	PO	A	E	Avg.
1983—Miami (Florida St.)	C	122	429	34	106	25	3	5	56	.247	11	79	3	471	*69	*21	.963
1984—Reno (California)	C	114	416	64	116	20	6	16	83	.279	36	75	5	692	96	25	.969
1985—Beaumont (Texas)	C-1B-3B	101	372	55	111	16	6	5	52	.298	16	59	12	525	†78	15	.976
1986—Las Vegas (PCL)	C	117	437	55	125	26	3	17	71	.286	17	81	19	*563	71	*21	.968
—San Diego (N.L.)	C	17	62	10	18	2	0	3	6	.290	2	12	0	80	7	5	.946
1987—San Diego (N.L.)	C	146	546	64	164	33	2	18	79	.300	16	112	21	817	80	*22	.976
1988—San Diego (N.L.)	C	139	492	49	122	22	2	10	46	.248	24	82	15	725	*75	*12	.985
1989—San Diego (N.L.)	C	129	462	50	109	16	3	16	62	.236	26	89	11	685	81	*20	.975
1990—San Diego (N.L.)	C	100	344	42	93	8	5	11	53	.270	27	55	5	538	51	12	.980
—Las Vegas (PCL)	C	6	20	5	6	2	0	1	8	.300	3	1	0	25	5	0	1.000
1991—San Diego (N.L.)	C-OF	152	580	60	155	22	3	17	87	.267	23	114	8	830	†100	†14	.985
1992—San Diego (N.L.)	C	106	386	37	97	21	0	10	42	.251	21	52	2	584	53	*12	.982
—Las Vegas (PCL)	C	4	13	3	4	0	0	1	2	.308	1	1	0	13	2	0	1.000
1993—Florida (N.L.)■	C-OF	139	469	49	108	19	6	13	50	.230	37	88	10	740	64	11	.987
1994—Florida (N.L.)	C	101	337	35	92	14	2	11	41	.273	25	57	1	511	*66	5	.991
1995—Cincinnati (N.L.)■	C-1B	81	266	40	76	20	0	11	44	.286	24	48	2	480	35	2	†.996
Major league totals (10 years)		1110	3944	436	1034	177	23	120	510	.262	225	709	75	5990	612	115	.983

DIVISION SERIES RECORD

			BATTING											FIELDING			
Year Team (League)	Pos.	G	AB	R	H	2B	3B	HR	RBI	Avg.	BB	SO	SB	PO	A	E	Avg.
1995—Cincinnati (N.L.)	C	3	9	2	3	0	0	1	3	.333	3	3	0	20	0	0	1.000

CHAMPIONSHIP SERIES RECORD

			BATTING											FIELDING			
Year Team (League)	Pos.	G	AB	R	H	2B	3B	HR	RBI	Avg.	BB	SO	SB	PO	A	E	Avg.
1995—Cincinnati (N.L.)	C	4	13	0	3	0	0	0	0	.231	2	3	0	23	1	0	1.000

ALL-STAR GAME RECORD

		BATTING											FIELDING			
Year League	Pos.	AB	R	H	2B	3B	HR	RBI	Avg.	BB	SO	SB	PO	A	E	Avg.
1989—National	C	1	0	0	0	0	0	0	.000	0	1	0	0	0	1	.000
1990—National		Selected, did not play—injured.														
1991—National	C	3	0	0	0	0	0	0	.000	0	1	0	4	0	0	1.000
1992—National	C	1	0	0	0	0	0	0	.000	0	1	0	3	0	0	1.000
All-Star Game totals (3 years)		5	0	0	0	0	0	0	.000	0	3	0	7	0	1	.875

SANTOS, HENRY — P — BREWERS

PERSONAL: Born January 17, 1973, in Santiago, Dominican Republic. . . . 6-1/175. . . . Throws left, bats left. . . . Full name: Henry A. Santos.
TRANSACTIONS/CAREER NOTES: Signed as non-drafted free agent by Detroit Tigers organization (September 7, 1989). . . . Traded by Tigers to Milwaukee Brewers for OF Duane Singleton (January 23, 1996).

Year	Team (League)	W	L	Pct.	ERA	G	GS	CG	ShO	Sv.	IP	H	R	ER	BB	SO
1990—	Dominican Tigers (DSL)	1	9	.100	6.67	18	13	2	0	0	79 2/3	88	83	59	65	79
1991—	Dominican Tigers (DSL)	1	9	.100	3.86	17	14	2	0	0	84	68	60	36	71	100
1992—	Bristol (Appal.)	0	1	.000	6.60	12	0	0	0	0	15	17	18	11	12	16
1993—	Niag. Falls (NYP)	2	1	.667	2.34	7	7	0	0	0	42 1/3	29	15	11	17	50
—	Fayetteville (S. Atl.)	3	2	.600	4.70	8	8	0	0	0	44	43	25	23	30	29
1994—	Fayetteville (S. Atl.)	4	8	.333	3.92	15	15	0	0	0	82 2/3	76	44	36	42	57
—	Lakeland (Fla. St.)	1	6	.143	7.69	11	11	0	0	0	52 2/3	88	52	45	34	35
1995—	Lakeland (Fla. St.)	5	6	.455	4.24	35	10	0	0	0	97 2/3	111	59	46	40	80
—	Toledo (Int'l)	0	1	.000	6.75	1	0	0	0	0	2 2/3	3	2	2	2	4

SASSER, MACKEY — C/OF

PERSONAL: Born August 3, 1962, in Fort Gaines, Ga. . . . 6-1/210. . . . Bats left, throws right. . . . Full name: Mack Daniel Sasser Jr.
HIGH SCHOOL: Godby (Tallahassee, Fla.).
JUNIOR COLLEGE: George C. Wallace Community College (Ala.).
COLLEGE: Troy (Ala.) State.
TRANSACTIONS/CAREER NOTES: Selected by San Francisco Giants organization in fifth round of free-agent draft (January 17, 1984). . . . Traded by Giants organization with cash to Pittsburgh Pirates organization for P Don Robinson (July 31, 1987). . . . Traded by Pirates with P Tim Drummond to New York Mets for 1B Randy Milligan and P Scott Henion (March 26, 1988). . . . Granted free agency (December 19, 1992). . . . Signed by Seattle Mariners (December 23, 1992). . . . On disabled list (March 26-April 21, 1993). . . . On suspended list (July 27-30, 1993). . . . On Seattle disabled list (April 10-May 2, 1994); included rehabilitation assignment to Calgary (April 23-May 2). . . . Released by Mariners (May 6, 1994). . . . Signed by Wichita, San Diego Padres organization (May 20, 1994). . . . Released by Wichita (June 26, 1994). . . . Signed by Tabasco of Mexican League (July 1994) . . . Signed as free agent by Buffalo, Pirates organization (December 12, 1994). . . . Released by Pirates (May 16, 1995).
STATISTICAL NOTES: Led California League with 245 total bases in 1985. . . . Led California League with 19 passed balls in 1985. . . . Led Texas League with 13 intentional bases on balls received in 1986. . . . Led Pacific Coast League catchers with 584 putouts, 16 errors and 663 total chances in 1987. . . . Led N.L. catchers with 14 errors in 1990. . . . Career major league grand slams: 1.

			BATTING												FIELDING			
Year	Team (League)	Pos.	G	AB	R	H	2B	3B	HR	RBI	Avg.	BB	SO	SB	PO	A	E	Avg.
1984—	Clinton (Midwest)	1-3-O-C	118	428	57	125	20	5	6	65	.292	30	46	15	526	95	17	.973
—	Fresno (California)	OF-3B-1B	16	62	8	17	1	1	0	6	.274	3	6	1	24	15	4	.907
1985—	Fresno (California)	O-C-1-3	133	497	79	168	27	4	14	102	.338	36	35	3	402	42	14	.969
1986—	Shreveport (Texas)	C-1B-OF	120	441	52	129	29	5	5	72	.293	44	36	4	577	66	10	.985
1987—	Phoe.-Vanc. (PCL)	C-3B-1B	115	400	53	127	24	1	3	56	.318	32	19	3	†588	72	†18	.973
—	San Francisco (N.L.)	C	2	4	0	0	0	0	0	0	.000	0	0	0	7	0	0	1.000
—	Pittsburgh (N.L.)■	C	12	23	2	5	0	0	0	2	.217	0	2	0	22	0	0	1.000
1988—	New York (N.L.)■	C-3B-OF	60	123	9	35	10	1	1	17	.285	6	9	0	235	17	6	.977
1989—	New York (N.L.)	C-3B	72	182	17	53	14	2	1	22	.291	7	15	0	335	19	3	.992
1990—	New York (N.L.)	C-1B	100	270	31	83	14	0	6	41	.307	15	19	0	501	43	†14	.975
1991—	New York (N.L.)	C-OF-1B	96	228	18	62	14	2	5	35	.272	9	19	0	271	21	3	.990
1992—	New York (N.L.)	C-1B-OF	92	141	7	34	6	0	2	18	.241	3	10	0	131	5	1	.993
1993—	Seattle (A.L.)■	O-DH-C-1	83	188	18	41	10	2	1	21	.218	15	30	1	60	4	3	.955
1994—	Seattle (A.L.)	C-OF	3	4	0	0	0	0	0	0	.000	0	0	0	0	0	0	...
—	Calgary (PCL)	C-OF	8	29	2	8	2	0	1	1	.276	0	3	0	19	1	0	1.000
—	Wichita (Texas)■	1B-OF-C	28	104	13	29	5	0	4	13	.279	6	7	2	199	17	1	.995
—	Tabasco (Mexican)■	1B-OF	29	108	12	32	4	2	1	9	.296	6	3	1	166	18	1	.995
1995—	Pittsburgh (N.L.)■	C	14	26	1	4	1	0	0	0	.154	0	0	0	35	3	0	1.000
American League totals (2 years)			86	192	18	41	10	2	1	21	.214	15	30	1	60	4	3	.955
National League totals (7 years)			448	997	85	276	59	5	15	135	.277	40	74	0	1537	108	27	.984
Major league totals (9 years)			534	1189	103	317	69	7	16	156	.267	55	104	1	1597	112	30	.983

CHAMPIONSHIP SERIES RECORD

			BATTING												FIELDING			
Year	Team (League)	Pos.	G	AB	R	H	2B	3B	HR	RBI	Avg.	BB	SO	SB	PO	A	E	Avg.
1988—	New York (N.L.)	PH-C	4	5	0	1	0	0	0	0	.200	0	1	0	2	0	0	1.000

SCANLAN, BOB — P

PERSONAL: Born August 9, 1966, in Los Angeles. . . . 6-8/215. . . . Throws right, bats right. . . . Full name: Robert Guy Scanlan Jr.
HIGH SCHOOL: Harvard (North Hollywood, Calif.).
TRANSACTIONS/CAREER NOTES: Selected by Philadelphia Phillies organization in 25th round of free-agent draft (June 4, 1984). . . . Traded by Phillies with P Chuck McElroy to Chicago Cubs organization for P Mitch Williams (April 7, 1991). . . . On suspended list (September 30-October 4, 1992 and September 17-20, 1993). . . . Traded by Cubs to Milwaukee Brewers for P Rafael Novoa and OF Mike Carter (December 19, 1993). . . . On Milwaukee disabled list (June 12-August 21, 1995); included rehabilitation assignment to New Orleans (August 4-21). . . . Released by Brewers (December 18, 1995).
STATISTICAL NOTES: Led International League with 17 wild pitches in 1988.

Year	Team (League)	W	L	Pct.	ERA	G	GS	CG	ShO	Sv.	IP	H	R	ER	BB	SO
1984—	GC Phillies (GCL)	0	2	.000	6.48	13	6	0	0	0	33 1/3	43	31	24	30	17
1985—	Spartanburg (SAL)	8	12	.400	4.14	26	25	4	0	0	152 1/3	160	95	70	53	108
1986—	Clearwater (Fla. St.)	8	12	.400	4.15	24	22	5	0	0	125 2/3	146	73	58	45	51
1987—	Reading (Eastern)	*15	5	.750	5.10	27	26	3	1	0	164	187	98	93	55	91
1988—	Maine (Int'l)	5	*18	.217	5.59	28	27	4	1	0	161	181	*110	*100	50	79
1989—	Reading (Eastern)	6	10	.375	5.78	31	17	4	1	0	118 1/3	124	88	•76	58	63

Year	Team (League)	W	L	Pct.	ERA	G	GS	CG	ShO	Sv.	IP	H	R	ER	BB	SO
1990—	Scran./W.B. (Int'l)	8	1	.889	4.85	23	23	1	0	0	130	128	79	70	59	74
1991—	Iowa (Am. Assoc.)■	2	0	1.000	2.95	4	3	0	0	0	18 1/3	14	8	6	10	15
	—Chicago (N.L.)	7	8	.467	3.89	40	13	0	0	1	111	114	60	48	40	44
1992—	Chicago (N.L.)	3	6	.333	2.89	69	0	0	0	14	87 1/3	76	32	28	30	42
1993—	Chicago (N.L.)	4	5	.444	4.54	70	0	0	0	0	75 1/3	79	41	38	28	44
1994—	Milwaukee (A.L.)■	2	6	.250	4.11	30	12	0	0	2	103	117	53	47	28	65
1995—	Milwaukee (A.L.)	4	7	.364	6.59	17	14	0	0	0	83 1/3	101	66	61	44	29
	—New Orleans (A.A.)	0	1	.000	5.40	3	3	0	0	0	11 2/3	17	7	7	3	5
A.L. totals (2 years)		6	13	.316	5.22	47	26	0	0	2	186 1/3	218	119	108	72	94
N.L. totals (3 years)		14	19	.424	3.75	179	13	0	0	15	273 2/3	269	133	114	98	130
Major league totals (5 years)		20	32	.385	4.34	226	39	0	0	17	460	487	252	222	170	224

SCARSONE, STEVE — IF — GIANTS

PERSONAL: Born April 11, 1966, in Anaheim, Calif. . . . 6-2/195. . . . Bats right, throws right. . . . Full name: Steven Wayne Scarsone. . . . Name pronounced scar-SONE-ee.

HIGH SCHOOL: Canyon (Anaheim, Calif.).

COLLEGE: Santa Ana (Calif.) College.

TRANSACTIONS/CAREER NOTES: Selected by Philadelphia Phillies organization in second round of free-agent draft (January 14, 1986). . . . Traded by Phillies to Baltimore Orioles for SS Juan Bell (August 11, 1992). . . . Traded by Orioles to San Francisco Giants for OF Mark Leonard (March 20, 1993). . . . On San Francisco disabled list (March 31-June 1, 1993). . . . On Phoenix disabled list (June 22-29, 1993).

STATISTICAL NOTES: Led Northwest League second basemen with 147 putouts, 29 errors and 45 double plays in 1986. . . . Led International League second basemen with 20 errors in 1991. . . . Led International League second basemen with 304 assists, 26 errors and 77 double plays in 1992.

				BATTING										FIELDING			
Year	Team (League)	Pos.	G	AB	R	H	2B	3B	HR	RBI	Avg.	BB	SO	SB	PO	A	E	Avg.
1986—	Bend (Northwest)	2B-SS	65	219	42	48	10	•4	4	21	.219	30	51	11	†149	188	†30	.918
1987—	Char., W.Va. (SAL)	SS-2B-3B	95	259	35	56	11	1	1	17	.216	31	64	8	127	212	25	.931
1988—	Clearwater (FSL)	SS-3B-2B	125	456	51	120	21	4	8	46	.263	18	93	14	179	326	33	.939
1989—	Reading (Eastern)	2B-SS	75	240	30	43	5	0	4	22	.179	15	67	2	171	200	11	.971
1990—	Clearwater (FSL)	2B	59	211	20	58	9	5	3	23	.275	19	57	3	116	147	13	.953
	—Reading (Eastern)	2B-SS	74	245	26	65	12	1	3	23	.265	14	63	0	141	206	8	.977
1991—	Reading (Eastern)	2B	15	49	6	15	0	0	3	3	.306	4	15	2	43	54	3	.970
	—Scran./W.B. (Int'l)	2B-SS	111	405	52	111	20	6	6	38	.274	19	81	10	222	343	†21	.964
1992—	Scran./W.B. (Int'l)	2B	89	325	43	89	23	4	11	48	.274	24	74	10	174	†253	†19	.957
	—Philadelphia (N.L.)	2B	7	13	1	2	0	0	0	0	.154	1	6	0	3	3	0	1.000
	—Rochester (Int'l)■	2B-3B	23	82	13	21	3	0	1	12	.256	6	12	3	36	†57	†7	.930
	—Baltimore (A.L.)	2B-3B-SS	11	17	2	3	0	0	0	0	.176	1	6	0	6	8	2	.875
1993—	Phoenix (PCL)■	2-3-S-1	19	70	13	18	1	2	3	9	.257	8	21	2	36	48	3	.966
	—San Francisco (N.L.)	2B-3B-1B	44	103	16	26	9	0	2	15	.252	4	32	0	53	44	1	.990
1994—	San Francisco (N.L.)	2-3-1-S	52	103	21	28	8	0	2	13	.272	10	20	0	66	80	2	.986
1995—	San Francisco (N.L.)	3B-2B-1B	80	233	33	62	10	3	11	29	.266	18	82	3	135	113	11	.958
American League totals (1 year)			11	17	2	3	0	0	0	0	.176	1	6	0	6	8	2	.875
National League totals (4 years)			183	452	71	118	27	3	15	57	.261	33	140	3	257	240	14	.973
Major league totals (4 years)			194	469	73	121	27	3	15	57	.258	34	146	3	263	248	16	.970

SCHALL, GENE — 1B/OF — PHILLIES

PERSONAL: Born June 5, 1970, in Abington, Pa. . . . 6-3/206. . . . Bats right, throws right. . . . Full name: Eugene David Schall.

HIGH SCHOOL: LaSalle (Philadelphia).

COLLEGE: Villanova.

TRANSACTIONS/CAREER NOTES: Selected by Philadelphia Phillies organization in fourth round of free-agent draft (June 3, 1991). . . . On disabled list (August 5, 1991-remainder of season).

STATISTICAL NOTES: Led International League first basemen with with 1,041 putouts, 75 assists, 14 errors, 1,130 total chances and 103 double plays in 1994.

				BATTING										FIELDING			
Year	Team (League)	Pos.	G	AB	R	H	2B	3B	HR	RBI	Avg.	BB	SO	SB	PO	A	E	Avg.
1991—	Batavia (NYP)	1B	13	44	5	15	1	0	2	8	.341	3	16	0	28	5	0	1.000
1992—	Spartanburg (SAL)	OF	77	276	44	74	13	1	8	41	.268	29	52	3	89	9	2	.980
	—Clearwater (FSL)	OF	40	133	16	33	4	2	4	19	.248	14	29	1	56	1	2	.966
1993—	Reading (Eastern)	1B-OF	82	285	51	93	12	4	15	60	.326	24	56	2	298	25	1	.997
	—Scran./W.B. (Int'l)	1B	40	139	16	33	6	1	4	16	.237	19	38	4	287	28	3	.991
1994—	Scran./W.B. (Int'l)	1B-OF	127	463	54	132	35	4	16	89	.285	50	86	9	†1045	†76	†14	.988
1995—	Scran./W.B. (Int'l)	OF-1B-3B	92	320	52	100	25	4	12	63	.313	49	54	3	431	25	4	.991
	—Philadelphia (N.L.)	1B-OF	24	65	2	15	2	0	0	5	.231	6	16	0	115	10	2	.984
Major league totals (1 year)			24	65	2	15	2	0	0	5	.231	6	16	0	115	10	2	.984

SCHEID, RICH — P

PERSONAL: Born February 3, 1965, in Staten Island, N.Y. . . . 6-3/200. . . . Throws left, bats left. . . . Full name: Richard Paul Scheid. . . . Name pronounced SHYD.

HIGH SCHOOL: Tottenville (Staten Island, N.Y.).

COLLEGE: Seton Hall.

TRANSACTIONS/CAREER NOTES: Selected by New York Yankees organization in second round of free-agent draft (June 2, 1986). . . . Traded by Yankees organization with P Bob Tewksbury and P Dean Wilkins to Chicago Cubs organization for P Steve Trout (July 13, 1987). . . . Traded by Cubs to Chicago White Sox organization for P Chuck Mount (December 22, 1989). . . . Traded by White Sox to Houston Astros for a player to be named later (July 4, 1992); White Sox acquired IF Eric Yelding to complete deal (July 10, 1992). . . . Released by Astros (January 21, 1993). . . . Signed by Edmonton, Florida Marlins organization (February 10, 1993). . . . Granted free agency (October 12, 1995).

Year Team (League)	W	L	Pct.	ERA	G	GS	CG	ShO	Sv.	IP	H	R	ER	BB	SO
1986— Oneonta (N.Y.-Penn)	9	3	.750	2.23	15	15	3	1	0	93	62	30	23	32	100
1987— Fort Lauder. (FSL)	7	0	1.000	2.95	9	8	1	0	0	55	43	25	18	29	49
— Alb./Colon. (East.)	2	3	.400	5.44	9	9	1	1	0	48	44	33	29	33	33
— Pittsfield (Eastern)■	2	0	1.000	7.39	11	6	0	0	0	28	44	27	23	19	13
1988— Pittsfield (Eastern)	6	6	.500	3.73	24	20	1	0	1	118 1/3	119	58	49	62	75
1989— Iowa (Am. Assoc.)	0	0	...	4.91	7	0	0	0	0	7 1/3	8	6	4	10	7
— Charlotte (South.)	4	1	.800	4.08	17	6	1	0	0	46 1/3	43	30	21	27	37
1990— Birmingham (Sou.)■	2	1	.667	2.22	25	1	0	0	4	44 2/3	37	17	11	21	37
— Vancouver (PCL)	2	2	.500	3.20	20	2	0	0	0	39 1/3	37	19	14	24	38
1991— Vancouver (PCL)	6	7	.462	6.08	47	0	0	0	3	66 2/3	65	46	45	33	57
1992— Vancouver (PCL)	1	2	.333	2.80	29	0	0	0	0	35 1/3	29	13	11	28	24
— Tucson (Pac. Coast)■	2	3	.400	2.53	12	8	0	0	1	57	49	23	16	23	34
— Houston (N.L.)	0	1	.000	6.00	7	1	0	0	0	12	14	8	8	6	8
1993— Edmonton (PCL)■	5	7	.417	5.07	38	12	0	0	0	110	130	68	62	38	84
1994— Edmonton (PCL)	9	4	.692	4.05	17	17	2	•2	0	102 1/3	110	50	46	41	86
— Florida (N.L.)	1	3	.250	3.34	8	5	0	0	0	32 1/3	35	18	12	8	17
1995— Florida (N.L.)	0	0	...	6.10	6	0	0	0	0	10 1/3	14	7	7	7	10
— Charlotte (Int'l)	1	4	.200	5.93	19	8	0	0	0	54 2/3	74	40	36	15	37
Major league totals (3 years)	1	4	.200	4.45	21	6	0	0	0	54 2/3	63	33	27	21	35

SCHILLING, CURT — P — PHILLIES

PERSONAL: Born November 14, 1966, in Anchorage, Alaska. . . . 6-4/226. . . . Throws right, bats right. . . . Full name: Curtis Montague Schilling.

HIGH SCHOOL: Shadow Mountain (Phoenix).

COLLEGE: Yavapai College (Ariz.).

TRANSACTIONS/CAREER NOTES: Selected by Boston Red Sox organization in second round of free-agent draft (January 14, 1986). . . . Traded by Red Sox organization with OF Brady Anderson to Baltimore Orioles for P Mike Boddicker (July 29, 1988). . . . Traded by Orioles with P Pete Harnisch and OF Steve Finley to Houston Astros for 1B Glenn Davis (January 10, 1991). . . . Traded by Astros to Philadelphia Phillies for P Jason Grimsley (April 2, 1992). . . . On Philadelphia disabled list (May 17-July 25, 1994); included rehabilitation assignments to Scranton/Wilkes-Barre (July 10-15) and Reading (July 15-20). . . . On disabled list (July 19, 1995-remainder of season).

STATISTICAL NOTES: Tied for International League lead with six balks in 1989. . . . Pitched 2-1 one-hit, complete-game victory against New York (September 9, 1992).

Year Team (League)	W	L	Pct.	ERA	G	GS	CG	ShO	Sv.	IP	H	R	ER	BB	SO
1986— Elmira (NYP)	7	3	.700	2.59	16	15	2	1	0	93 2/3	92	34	27	30	75
1987— Greensboro (S. Atl.)	8	*15	.348	3.82	29	28	7	3	0	184	179	96	78	65	*189
1988— New Britain (East.)	8	5	.615	2.97	21	17	4	1	0	106	91	44	35	40	62
— Charlotte (South.)■	5	2	.714	3.18	7	7	2	1	0	45 1/3	36	19	16	23	32
— Baltimore (A.L.)	0	3	.000	9.82	4	4	0	0	0	14 2/3	22	19	16	10	4
1989— Rochester (Int'l)	•13	11	.542	3.21	27	•27	•9	•3	0	*185 1/3	176	76	66	59	109
— Baltimore (A.L.)	0	1	.000	6.23	5	1	0	0	0	8 2/3	10	6	6	3	6
1990— Rochester (Int'l)	4	4	.500	3.92	15	14	1	0	0	87 1/3	95	46	38	25	83
— Baltimore (A.L.)	1	2	.333	2.54	35	0	0	0	3	46	38	13	13	19	32
1991— Houston (N.L.)■	3	5	.375	3.81	56	0	0	0	8	75 2/3	79	35	32	39	71
— Tucson (Pac. Coast)	0	1	.000	3.42	13	0	0	0	3	23 2/3	16	9	9	12	21
1992— Philadelphia (N.L.)■	14	11	.560	2.35	42	26	10	4	2	226 1/3	165	67	59	59	147
1993— Philadelphia (N.L.)	16	7	.696	4.02	34	34	7	2	0	235 1/3	234	114	105	57	186
1994— Philadelphia (N.L.)	2	8	.200	4.48	13	13	1	0	0	82 1/3	87	42	41	28	58
— Scran./W.B. (Int'l)	0	0	...	1.80	2	2	0	0	0	10	6	2	2	5	6
— Reading (Eastern)	0	0	...	0.00	1	1	0	0	0	4	6	0	0	1	4
1995— Philadelphia (N.L.)	7	5	.583	3.57	17	17	1	0	0	116	96	52	46	26	114
A.L. totals (3 years)	1	6	.143	4.54	44	5	0	0	3	69 1/3	70	38	35	32	42
N.L. totals (5 years)	42	36	.538	3.46	162	90	19	6	10	735 2/3	661	310	283	209	576
Major league totals (8 years)	43	42	.506	3.56	206	95	19	6	13	805	731	348	318	241	618

CHAMPIONSHIP SERIES RECORD

NOTES: Named N.L. Championship Series Most Valuable Player (1993). . . . Holds single-game records for most consecutive strikeouts; and most consecutive strikeouts from start of the game—5 (October 6, 1993).

Year Team (League)	W	L	Pct.	ERA	G	GS	CG	ShO	Sv.	IP	H	R	ER	BB	SO
1993— Philadelphia (N.L.)	0	0	...	1.69	2	2	0	0	0	16	11	4	3	5	19

WORLD SERIES RECORD

Year Team (League)	W	L	Pct.	ERA	G	GS	CG	ShO	Sv.	IP	H	R	ER	BB	SO
1993— Philadelphia (N.L.)	1	1	.500	3.52	2	2	1	1	0	15 1/3	13	7	6	5	9

SCHMIDT, CURT — P — EXPOS

PERSONAL: Born March 16, 1970, in Miles City, Mont. . . . 6-5/200. . . . Throws right, bats right. . . . Full name: Curtis A. Schmidt.

HIGH SCHOOL: Custer County (Miles City, Mont.).

COLLEGE: Kansas.

TRANSACTIONS/CAREER NOTES: Selected by Montreal Expos organization in 41st round of free-agent draft (June 1, 1992).

Year Team (League)	W	L	Pct.	ERA	G	GS	CG	ShO	Sv.	IP	H	R	ER	BB	SO
1992— Jamestown (NYP)	3	4	.429	2.70	29	1	1	1	2	63 1/3	42	21	19	29	61
— WP Beach (FSL)	0	0	...	0.00	3	0	0	0	0	5	3	0	0	1	3
1993— GC Expos (GCL)	1	0	1.000	0.00	1	1	0	0	0	5	1	0	0	1	7
— WP Beach (FSL)	4	6	.400	3.17	44	2	0	0	5	65 1/3	63	32	23	25	51
1994— Harrisburg (East.)	6	2	.750	1.88	53	0	0	0	5	71 2/3	51	19	15	29	75
1995— Montreal (N.L.)	0	0	...	6.97	11	0	0	0	0	10 1/3	15	8	8	9	7
— Ottawa (Int'l)	5	0	1.000	2.22	43	0	0	0	15	52 2/3	40	14	13	18	38
Major league totals (1 year)	0	0	...	6.97	11	0	0	0	0	10 1/3	15	8	8	9	7

SCHMIDT, JASON — P — BRAVES

PERSONAL: Born January 29, 1973, in Kelso, Wash. . . . 6-5/185. . . . Throws right, bats right. . . . Full name: Jason David Schmidt.
HIGH SCHOOL: Kelso (Wash.).
TRANSACTIONS/CAREER NOTES: Selected by Atlanta Braves organization in eighth round of free-agent draft (June 3, 1991).
MISCELLANEOUS: Received base on balls in only appearance as pinch-hitter with Atlanta (1995).

Year	Team (League)	W	L	Pct.	ERA	G	GS	CG	ShO	Sv.	IP	H	R	ER	BB	SO
1991	—GC Braves (GCL)	3	4	.429	2.38	11	11	0	0	0	45 1/3	32	21	12	23	44
1992	—Pulaski (Appal.)	3	4	.429	4.01	11	11	0	0	0	58 1/3	38	36	26	31	56
	—Macon (S. Atl.)	0	3	.000	4.01	7	7	0	0	0	24 2/3	31	18	11	19	33
1993	—Durham (Carolina)	7	11	.389	4.94	22	22	0	0	0	116 2/3	128	69	64	47	110
1994	—Greenville (South.)	8	7	.533	3.65	24	24	1	0	0	140 2/3	135	64	57	54	131
1995	—Atlanta (N.L.)	2	2	.500	5.76	9	2	0	0	0	25	27	17	16	18	19
	—Richmond (Int'l)	8	6	.571	*2.25	19	19	0	0	0	116	97	40	29	48	95
Major league totals (1 year)		2	2	.500	5.76	9	2	0	0	0	25	27	17	16	18	19

SCHMIDT, JEFF — P — ANGELS

PERSONAL: Born February 21, 1971, in Northfield, Minn. . . . 6-5/190. . . . Throws right, bats right. . . . Full name: Jeffrey Thomas Schmidt.
HIGH SCHOOL: La Crosse (Wis.) Central.
COLLEGE: Minnesota.
TRANSACTIONS/CAREER NOTES: Selected by California Angels organization in supplemental round ("sandwich pick" between first and second round, 39th pick overall) of free-agent draft (June 1, 1992); pick received as part of compensation for Kansas City Royals signing Type A free agent 1B Wally Joyner.
STATISTICAL NOTES: Led Texas League with 18 wild pitches in 1995.

Year	Team (League)	W	L	Pct.	ERA	G	GS	CG	ShO	Sv.	IP	H	R	ER	BB	SO
1992	—Boise (Northwest)	1	6	.143	4.47	11	11	00	0	0	52 1/3	55	41	26	18	41
1993	—Ced. Rap. (Midw.)	3	•14	.176	4.90	26	25	3	0	0	152 1/3	166	*105	83	58	107
1994	—Lake Elsinore (California)	1	5	.167	4.11	39	11	0	0	12	92	94	54	42	28	70
1995	—Midland (Texas)	4	12	.250	5.83	20	20	0	0	0	100 1/3	127	75	65	48	46

SCHMIDT, TOM — 3B — TIGERS

PERSONAL: Born February 12, 1973, in Towson, Md. . . . 6-3/200. . . . Bats right, throws right. . . . Full name: Thomas William Schmidt.
HIGH SCHOOL: Loyola (Towson, Md.).
COLLEGE: Brevard (Fla.).
TRANSACTIONS/CAREER NOTES: Selected by Colorado Rockies organization in 24th round of free-agent draft (June 1, 1992). . . . Claimed on waivers by Detroit Tigers (November 20, 1995).

				BATTING											FIELDING			
Year	Team (League)	Pos.	G	AB	R	H	2B	3B	HR	RBI	Avg.	BB	SO	SB	PO	A	E	Avg.
1992	—Bend (Northwest)	3B	68	249	39	64	13	1	7	27	.257	24	78	17	40	111	17	.899
1993	—Central Vall. (Cal.)	3B	126	478	61	117	15	1	19	62	.245	40	107	5	73	217	*34	.895
1994	—Central Vall. (Cal.)	3B	99	334	36	81	8	1	9	50	.243	52	100	3	60	188	20	.925
1995	—New Haven (East.)	3B	115	423	55	92	25	3	6	49	.217	24	99	2	*79	181	*30	.897

SCHOFIELD, DICK — SS — ANGELS

PERSONAL: Born November 21, 1962, in Springfield, Ill. . . . 5-10/179. . . . Bats right, throws right. . . . Full name: Richard Craig Schofield. . . . Son of John Richard (Dick) Schofield, major league infielder with seven teams (1953-71).
HIGH SCHOOL: Sacred Heart-Griffin (Springfield, Ill.).
TRANSACTIONS/CAREER NOTES: Selected by California Angels organization in first round (third pick overall) of free-agent draft (June 8, 1981). . . . On disabled list (July 1-24, 1984; July 13-August 11, 1987; April 12-May 6 and August 11-September 21, 1989). . . . On California disabled list (March 31-June 6, 1990); included rehabilitation assignment to Edmonton (May 31-June 5). . . . Granted free agency (November 1, 1991). . . . Re-signed by Angels (January 17, 1992). . . . Traded by Angels to New York Mets for P Julio Valera and a player to be named later (April 12, 1992); Angels acquired P Julian Vasquez to complete deal (October 6, 1992). . . . Granted free agency (October 28, 1992). . . . Signed by Toronto Blue Jays organization (January 15, 1993). . . . On Toronto disabled list (May 13-September 1, 1993); included rehabilitation assignment to Dunedin (August 14-September 1). . . . Granted free agency (October 25, 1994). . . . Signed by Albuquerque, Los Angeles Dodgers organization (April 15, 1995). . . . Released by Dodgers (May 16, 1995). . . . Signed by Vancouver, Angels organization (August 4, 1995). . . . On Vancouver disabled list (August 5-16, 1995). . . . Granted free agency (November 9, 1995). . . . Re-signed by Angels organization (December 6, 1995).
STATISTICAL NOTES: Led Pioneer League shortstops with 102 putouts in 1981. . . . Led A.L. shortstops with .984 fielding percentage in 1987. . . . Led A.L. shortstops with 125 double plays in 1988. . . . Career major league grand slams: 5.

				BATTING											FIELDING			
Year	Team (League)	Pos.	G	AB	R	H	2B	3B	HR	RBI	Avg.	BB	SO	SB	PO	A	E	Avg.
1981	—Idaho Falls (Pio.)	SS-2B	66	226	59	63	10	1	6	31	.279	*68	60	13	†102	201	22	.932
1982	—Danville (Midwest)	SS	92	308	80	111	21	*10	12	53	*.360	70	66	17	129	249	23	.943
	—Redwood (Calif.)	SS	33	102	15	25	3	3	1	8	.245	17	20	6	35	103	3	.979
	—Spokane (PCL)	SS-3B	7	30	4	9	4	1	1	12	.300	3	6	0	7	20	0	1.000
1983	—Edmonton (PCL)	SS-3B	139	521	91	148	30	7	16	94	.284	72	105	9	220	402	30	.954
	—California (A.L.)	SS	21	54	4	11	2	0	3	4	.204	6	8	0	24	67	7	.929
1984	—California (A.L.)	SS	140	400	39	77	10	3	4	21	.193	33	79	5	218	420	12	*.982
1985	—California (A.L.)	SS	147	438	50	96	19	3	8	41	.219	35	70	11	261	397	25	.963
1986	—California (A.L.)	SS	139	458	67	114	17	6	13	57	.249	48	55	23	246	389	18	.972
1987	—California (A.L.)	SS-2B-DH	134	479	52	120	17	3	9	46	.251	37	63	19	205	351	9	†.984
1988	—California (A.L.)	SS	155	527	61	126	11	6	6	34	.239	40	57	20	278	492	13	*.983
1989	—California (A.L.)	SS	91	302	42	69	11	2	4	26	.228	28	47	9	118	276	7	.983

Year	Team (League)	Pos.	G	AB	R	H	2B	3B	HR	RBI	Avg.	BB	SO	SB	PO	A	E	Avg.
			BATTING												FIELDING			
1990—	Edmonton (PCL)	SS	5	18	4	7	1	0	1	4	.389	3	4	0	6	14	1	.952
—	California (A.L.)	SS	99	310	41	79	8	1	1	18	.255	52	61	3	170	318	17	.966
1991—	California (A.L.)	SS	134	427	44	96	9	3	0	31	.225	50	69	8	186	398	15	.975
1992—	California (A.L.)	SS	1	3	0	1	0	0	0	0	.333	1	0	0	3	1	0	1.000
—	New York (N.L.)■	SS	142	420	52	86	18	2	4	36	.205	60	82	11	205	391	7	*.988
1993—	Toronto (A.L.)■	SS	36	110	11	21	1	2	0	5	.191	16	25	3	61	106	4	.977
—	Dunedin (Fla. St.)	SS	11	30	4	6	2	0	0	4	.200	3	7	0	14	13	1	.964
1994—	Toronto (A.L.)	SS	95	325	38	83	14	1	4	32	.255	34	62	7	150	235	11	.972
1995—	Los Angeles (N.L.)■	SS-3B	9	10	0	1	0	0	0	0	.100	1	3	0	3	9	0	1.000
—	Vancouver (PCL)■	SS	16	53	5	10	4	0	0	9	.189	3	3	0	24	44	5	.932
—	California (A.L.)	SS	12	20	1	5	0	0	0	2	.250	4	2	0	8	23	0	1.000
American League totals (13 years)			1204	3853	450	898	119	30	52	317	.233	384	598	108	1928	3473	138	.975
National League totals (2 years)			151	430	52	87	18	2	4	36	.202	61	85	11	208	400	7	.989
Major league totals (13 years)			1355	4283	502	985	137	32	56	353	.230	445	683	119	2136	3873	145	.976

CHAMPIONSHIP SERIES RECORD

Year	Team (League)	Pos.	G	AB	R	H	2B	3B	HR	RBI	Avg.	BB	SO	SB	PO	A	E	Avg.
			BATTING												FIELDING			
1986—	California (A.L.)	SS	7	30	4	9	1	0	1	2	.300	1	5	1	13	23	2	.947
1993—	Toronto (A.L.)		Did not play.															
Championship series totals (1 year)			7	30	4	9	1	0	1	2	.300	1	5	1	13	23	2	.947

WORLD SERIES RECORD

NOTES: Member of World Series championship team (1993).

Year	Team (League)	Pos.	G	AB	R	H	2B	3B	HR	RBI	Avg.	BB	SO	SB	PO	A	E	Avg.
			BATTING												FIELDING			
1993—	Toronto (A.L.)		Did not play.															

SCHOUREK, PETE — P — REDS

PERSONAL: Born May 10, 1969, in Austin, Tex. . . . 6-5/205. . . . Throws left, bats left. . . . Full name: Peter Alan Schourek. . . . Name pronounced SHUR-ek.

HIGH SCHOOL: George C. Marshall (Falls Church, Va.).

TRANSACTIONS/CAREER NOTES: Selected by New York Mets organization in second round of free-agent draft (June 2, 1987). . . . On disabled list (June 17, 1988-remainder of season). . . . Claimed on waivers by Cincinnati Reds (April 7, 1994).

HONORS: Named lefthanded pitcher on The Sporting News N.L. All-Star team (1995).

STATISTICAL NOTES: Pitched 9-0 one-hit, complete-game victory against Montreal (September 10, 1991).

MISCELLANEOUS: Appeared in one game as pinch-runner with New York (1992).

Year	Team (League)	W	L	Pct.	ERA	G	GS	CG	ShO	Sv.	IP	H	R	ER	BB	SO
1987—	Kingsport (Appal.)	4	5	.444	3.68	12	12	2	0	0	78 1/3	70	37	32	34	57
1988—		Did not play.														
1989—	Columbia (S. Atl.)	5	9	.357	2.85	27	19	5	1	1	136	120	66	43	66	131
—	St. Lucie (Fla. St.)	0	0	...	2.25	2	1	0	0	0	4	3	1	1	2	4
1990—	St. Lucie (Fla. St.)	4	1	.800	0.97	5	5	2	2	0	37	29	4	4	8	28
—	Tidewater (Int'l)	1	0	1.000	2.57	2	2	1	1	0	14	9	4	4	5	14
—	Jackson (Texas)	11	4	.733	3.04	19	19	1	0	0	124 1/3	109	53	42	39	94
1991—	Tidewater (Int'l)	1	1	.500	2.52	4	4	0	0	0	25	18	7	7	10	17
—	New York (N.L.)	5	4	.556	4.27	35	8	1	1	2	86 1/3	82	49	41	43	67
1992—	Tidewater (Int'l)	2	5	.286	2.73	8	8	2	1	0	52 2/3	46	20	16	23	42
—	New York (N.L.)	6	8	.429	3.64	22	21	0	0	0	136	137	60	55	44	60
1993—	New York (N.L.)	5	12	.294	5.96	41	18	0	0	0	128 1/3	168	90	85	45	72
1994—	Cincinnati (N.L.)■	7	2	.778	4.09	22	10	0	0	0	81 1/3	90	39	37	29	69
1995—	Cincinnati (N.L.)	18	7	.720	3.22	29	29	2	0	0	190 1/3	158	72	68	45	160
Major league totals (5 years)		41	33	.554	4.14	149	86	3	1	2	622 1/3	635	310	286	206	428

DIVISION SERIES RECORD

Year	Team (League)	W	L	Pct.	ERA	G	GS	CG	ShO	Sv.	IP	H	R	ER	BB	SO
1995—	Cincinnati (N.L.)	1	0	1.000	2.57	1	1	0	0	0	7	5	2	2	3	5

CHAMPIONSHIP SERIES RECORD

Year	Team (League)	W	L	Pct.	ERA	G	GS	CG	ShO	Sv.	IP	H	R	ER	BB	SO
1995—	Cincinnati (N.L.)	0	1	.000	1.26	2	2	0	0	0	14 1/3	14	2	2	3	13

SCHRENK, STEVE — P — WHITE SOX

PERSONAL: Born November 20, 1968, in Great Lakes, Ill. . . . 6-3/185. . . . Throws right, bats right. . . . Full name: Steven Wayne Schrenk.

HIGH SCHOOL: North Marion (Aurora, Ore.).

TRANSACTIONS/CAREER NOTES: Selected by Chicago White Sox organization in fourth round of free-agent draft (June 2, 1987). . . . On disabled list (April 11-September 3, 1991). . . . On Nashville disabled list (April 21, 1995-remainder of season).

Year	Team (League)	W	L	Pct.	ERA	G	GS	CG	ShO	Sv.	IP	H	R	ER	BB	SO
1987—	GC White Sox (GCL)	1	2	.333	0.95	8	6	1	1	0	28 1/3	23	10	3	12	19
1988—	South Bend (Midw.)	3	7	.300	5.00	21	18	1	0	0	90	95	63	50	37	58
1989—	South Bend (Midw.)	5	2	.714	4.33	16	16	1	1	0	79	71	44	38	44	49
1990—	South Bend (Midw.)	7	6	.538	2.95	20	14	2	1	0	103 2/3	79	44	34	25	92
1991—	GC White Sox (GCL)	1	3	.250	2.92	11	7	0	0	0	37	30	20	12	6	39
1992—	Sarasota (Fla. St.)	15	2	.882	2.05	25	22	4	2	1	154	130	48	35	40	113
—	Birmingham (Sou.)	1	1	.500	3.65	2	2	0	0	0	12 1/3	13	5	5	11	9
1993—	Birmingham (Sou.)	5	1	.833	1.17	8	8	2	1	0	61 2/3	31	11	8	7	51

Year	Team (League)	W	L	Pct.	ERA	G	GS	CG	ShO	Sv.	IP	H	R	ER	BB	SO
	—Nashville (A.A.)	6	8	.429	3.90	21	20	0	0	0	$122\frac{1}{3}$	117	61	53	47	78
1994	—Nashville (A.A.)	14	6	.700	3.48	29	28	2	1	0	$178\frac{2}{3}$	175	82	69	69	134
1995	—GC White Sox (GCL)	0	1	.000	0.00	2	2	0	0	0	7	5	2	0	0	6

SCHULLSTROM, ERIK P

PERSONAL: Born March 25, 1969, in San Diego. . . . 6-5/220. . . . Throws right, bats right. . . . Full name: Erik Paul Schullstrom.
HIGH SCHOOL: Alameda (Calif.).
COLLEGE: Fresno State.
TRANSACTIONS/CAREER NOTES: Selected by Toronto Blue Jays organization in 24th round of free-agent draft (June 2, 1987); did not sign. . . . Selected by Baltimore Orioles organization in second round of free-agent draft (June 4, 1990). . . . On Frederick disabled list (April 11-May 8 and May 14-31, 1991). . . . Traded by Orioles organization with a player to be named later to San Diego Padres organization for P Craig Lefferts (August 31, 1992); Padres acquired IF Ricky Gutierrez to complete deal (September 4, 1992). . . . Claimed on waivers by Orioles (April 1, 1993). . . . Traded by Orioles to Minnesota Twins (August 16, 1993), completing deal in which Twins traded 3B Mike Pagliarulo to Orioles for a player to be named later (August 15, 1993). . . . Granted free agency (November 20, 1995).
STATISTICAL NOTES: Pitched 2-0 no-hit victory for Frederick against Kinston (July 3, 1991).

Year	Team (League)	W	L	Pct.	ERA	G	GS	CG	ShO	Sv.	IP	H	R	ER	BB	SO
1990	—Wausau (Midwest)	0	2	.000	4.66	5	5	0	0	0	$19\frac{1}{3}$	20	12	10	7	21
	—Frederick (Caro.)	2	0	1.000	3.46	2	2	0	0	0	13	9	5	5	6	8
1991	—Frederick (Caro.)	5	6	.455	3.05	19	17	1	1	0	$85\frac{2}{3}$	70	32	29	45	73
	—Hagerstown (East.)	1	0	1.000	2.77	2	2	0	0	0	13	11	5	4	3	9
1992	—Hagerstown (East.)	5	9	.357	3.61	23	22	2	0	0	127	120	66	51	63	128
	—Las Vegas (PCL)■	1	0	1.000	0.00	1	1	0	0	0	5	3	0	0	3	4
1993	—Bowie (Eastern)■	5	10	.333	4.27	24	14	2	0	1	$109\frac{2}{3}$	119	63	52	45	97
	—Nashville (South.)■	1	0	1.000	4.85	4	3	0	0	0	13	16	7	7	6	11
1994	—Nashville (South.)	1	2	.333	2.63	26	0	0	0	8	41	36	14	12	6	43
	—Salt Lake (PCL)	0	1	.000	3.97	8	0	0	0	2	$11\frac{1}{3}$	12	5	5	3	8
	—Minnesota (A.L.)	0	0	...	2.77	9	0	0	0	1	13	13	7	4	5	13
1995	—Salt Lake (PCL)	2	0	1.000	4.66	10	0	0	0	2	$9\frac{2}{3}$	12	5	5	4	8
	—Minnesota (A.L.)	0	0	...	6.89	37	0	0	0	0	47	66	36	36	22	21
Major league totals (2 years)		0	0	...	6.00	46	0	0	0	1	60	79	43	40	27	34

SCHUTZ, CARL P BRAVES

PERSONAL: Born August 22, 1971, in Hammond, La. . . . 5-11/200. . . . Throws left, bats left. . . . Full name: Carl James Schutz.
COLLEGE: Southeastern Louisiana.
TRANSACTIONS/CAREER NOTES: Selected by Atlanta Braves organization in third round (June 3, 1993).

Year	Team (League)	W	L	Pct.	ERA	G	GS	CG	ShO	Sv.	IP	H	R	ER	BB	SO
1993	—Danville (Appal.)	1	0	1.000	0.61	13	0	0	0	4	$14\frac{2}{3}$	6	1	1	6	25
	—Greenville (S. Atl.)	2	1	.667	5.06	22	0	0	0	3	$21\frac{1}{3}$	17	17	12	22	19
1994	—Durham (Carolina)	3	3	.500	4.89	53	0	0	0	20	$53\frac{1}{3}$	35	30	29	46	81
1995	—Greenville (South.)	3	7	.300	4.94	51	0	0	0	26	$58\frac{1}{3}$	53	36	32	36	56

SCOTT, TIM P EXPOS

PERSONAL: Born November 16, 1966, in Hanford, Calif. . . . 6-2/205. . . . Throws right, bats right. . . . Full name: Timothy Dale Scott.
HIGH SCHOOL: Hanford (Calif.).
TRANSACTIONS/CAREER NOTES: Selected by Los Angeles Dodgers organization in second round of free-agent draft (June 4, 1984). . . . On disabled list (July 23, 1985-remainder of season and April 11-May 15, 1986). . . . Granted free agency (October 15, 1990). . . . Signed by San Diego Padres organization (November 1, 1990). . . . Traded by Padres to Montreal Expos for IF/OF Archi Cianfrocco (June 23, 1993). . . . On disabled list (June 6-21, 1994).

Year	Team (League)	W	L	Pct.	ERA	G	GS	CG	ShO	Sv.	IP	H	R	ER	BB	SO
1984	—Great Falls (Pio.)	5	4	.556	4.38	13	13	3	•2	0	78	90	58	38	44	38
1985	—Bakersfield (Calif.)	3	4	.429	5.80	12	10	2	0	0	$63\frac{2}{3}$	84	46	41	28	31
1986	—Vero Beach (FSL)	5	4	.556	3.40	20	13	3	1	0	$95\frac{1}{3}$	113	44	36	24	37
1987	—Bakersfield (Calif.)	2	3	.400	4.45	7	5	1	0	0	$32\frac{1}{3}$	33	19	16	10	29
	—San Antonio (Tex.)	0	1	.000	16.88	2	2	0	0	0	$5\frac{1}{3}$	14	10	10	2	6
1988	—Bakersfield (Calif.)	4	7	.364	3.64	36	2	0	0	7	$64\frac{1}{3}$	52	34	26	26	59
1989	—San Antonio (Tex.)	4	2	.667	3.71	48	0	0	0	4	68	71	30	28	36	64
1990	—San Antonio (Tex.)	3	3	.500	2.85	30	0	0	0	7	$47\frac{1}{3}$	35	17	15	14	52
	—Albuquerque (PCL)	2	1	.667	4.20	17	0	0	0	3	15	14	9	7	14	15
1991	—Las Vegas (PCL)■	8	8	.500	5.19	41	11	0	0	0	111	133	78	64	39	74
	—San Diego (N.L.)	0	0	...	9.00	2	0	0	0	0	1	2	2	1	0	1
1992	—Las Vegas (PCL)	1	2	.333	2.25	24	0	0	0	15	28	20	8	7	3	28
	—San Diego (N.L.)	4	1	.800	5.26	34	0	0	0	0	$37\frac{2}{3}$	39	24	22	21	30
1993	—San Diego (N.L.)	2	0	1.000	2.39	24	0	0	0	0	$37\frac{2}{3}$	38	13	10	15	30
	—Montreal (N.L.)■	5	2	.714	3.71	32	0	0	0	1	34	31	15	14	19	35
1994	—Montreal (N.L.)	5	2	.714	2.70	40	0	0	0	1	$53\frac{1}{3}$	51	17	16	18	37
1995	—Montreal (N.L.)	2	0	1.000	3.98	62	0	0	0	2	$63\frac{1}{3}$	52	30	28	23	57
Major league totals (5 years)		18	5	.783	3.61	194	0	0	0	4	227	213	101	91	96	190

SEANEZ, RUDY P DODGERS

PERSONAL: Born October 20, 1968, in Brawley, Calif. . . . 5-10/185. . . . Throws right, bats right. . . . Full name: Rudy Caballero Seanez. . . . Name pronounced see-AHN-yez.
HIGH SCHOOL: Brawley (Calif.) Union.

TRANSACTIONS/CAREER NOTES: Selected by Cleveland Indians organization in fourth round of free-agent draft (June 10, 1986).... On disabled list (May 4-July 11 and August 9-29, 1987).... On Cleveland disabled list (April 1-16, 1991).... On Cleveland disabled list (July 30-September 2, 1991); included rehabilitation assignment to Colorado Springs (August 14-September 2).... Traded by Indians to Los Angeles Dodgers for P Dennis Cook and P Mike Christopher (December 10, 1991).... On disabled list (March 29, 1992-entire season).... Traded by Dodgers to Colorado Rockies for 2B Jody Reed (November 17, 1992).... On Colorado disabled list (April 4-July 16, 1993); included rehabilitation assignments to Central Valley (June 16-July 4) and Colorado Springs (July 4-15).... Granted free agency (July 16, 1993).... Signed by Las Vegas, San Diego Padres organization (July 22, 1993).... Released by Padres (November 18, 1993).... Signed by Dodgers organization (January 12, 1994).... On Los Angeles disabled list (May 28-June 16, 1995); included rehabilitation assignment to San Bernardino (June 9-16).

STATISTICAL NOTES: Pitched 4-0 no-hit victory against Pulaski (August 2, 1986).

Year Team (League)	W	L	Pct.	ERA	G	GS	CG	ShO	Sv.	IP	H	R	ER	BB	SO
1986—Burlington (Appal.)	5	2	.714	3.20	13	12	1	1	0	76	59	37	27	32	56
1987—Waterloo (Midw.)	0	4	.000	6.75	10	10	0	0	0	34 2/3	35	29	26	23	23
1988—Waterloo (Midw.)	6	6	.500	4.69	22	22	1	1	0	113 1/3	98	69	59	68	93
1989—Kinston (Carolina)	8	10	.444	4.14	25	25	1	0	0	113	94	66	52	*111	149
—Colo. Springs (PCL)	0	0	...	0.00	1	0	0	0	0	1	1	0	0	0	0
—Cleveland (A.L.)	0	0	...	3.60	5	0	0	0	0	5	1	2	2	4	7
1990—Cant./Akr. (East.)	1	0	1.000	2.16	15	0	0	0	5	16 2/3	9	4	4	12	27
—Cleveland (A.L.)	2	1	.667	5.60	24	0	0	0	0	27 1/3	22	17	17	25	24
—Colo. Springs (PCL)	1	4	.200	6.75	12	0	0	0	1	12	15	10	9	10	7
1991—Colo. Springs (PCL)	0	0	...	7.27	16	0	0	0	0	17 1/3	17	14	14	22	19
—Cant./Akr. (East.)	4	2	.667	2.58	25	0	0	0	7	38 1/3	17	12	11	30	73
—Cleveland (A.L.)	0	0	...	16.20	5	0	0	0	0	5	10	12	9	7	7
1992—■	Did not play.														
1993—Central Valley (Cal.)■	0	2	.000	9.72	5	1	0	0	0	8 1/3	9	9	9	11	7
—Colo. Springs (PCL)	0	0	...	9.00	3	0	0	0	0	3	3	3	3	1	5
—Las Vegas (PCL)■	0	1	.000	6.41	14	0	0	0	0	19 2/3	24	15	14	11	14
—San Diego (N.L.)	0	0	...	13.50	3	0	0	0	0	3 1/3	8	6	5	2	1
1994—Albuquerque (PCL)■	2	1	.667	5.32	20	0	0	0	9	22	28	14	13	13	26
—Los Angeles (N.L.)	1	1	.500	2.66	17	0	0	0	0	23 2/3	24	7	7	9	18
1995—Los Angeles (N.L.)	1	3	.250	6.75	37	0	0	0	3	34 2/3	39	27	26	18	29
—San Bern. (Calif.)■	2	0	1.000	0.00	4	0	0	0	1	6	2	0	0	3	5
A.L. totals (3 years)	2	1	.667	6.75	34	0	0	0	0	37 1/3	33	31	28	36	38
N.L. totals (3 years)	2	4	.333	5.55	57	0	0	0	3	61 2/3	71	40	38	29	48
Major league totals (6 years)	4	5	.444	6.00	91	0	0	0	3	99	104	71	66	65	86

SEEFRIED, TATE — 1B — YANKEES

PERSONAL: Born April 22, 1972, in Seattle.... 6-4/205.... Bats left, throws right.... Full name: Tate Carsten Seefried.... Name pronounced SEE-freed.

HIGH SCHOOL: El Segundo (Calif.).

TRANSACTIONS/CAREER NOTES: Selected by New York Yankees organization in third round of free-agent draft (June 4, 1990).

STATISTICAL NOTES: Tied for New York-Pennsylvania League lead with seven sacrifice flies in 1991.... Led New York-Pennsylvania League first basemen with 725 total chances and 56 double plays in 1991.... Led South Atlantic League first basemen with 1,388 total chances in 1992.... Tied for Carolina League lead with four intentional bases on balls received in 1993.... Led Carolina League first basemen with 1,234 total chances in 1993.

			BATTING											FIELDING			
Year Team (League)	Pos.	G	AB	R	H	2B	3B	HR	RBI	Avg.	BB	SO	SB	PO	A	E	Avg.
1990—GC Yankees (GCL)	1B	52	178	15	28	3	0	0	20	.157	22	53	2	418	30	6	.987
1991—Oneonta (NYP)	1B	73	264	40	65	19	0	7	51	.246	32	65	12	*667	46	*12	.983
1992—Greensboro (S. Atl.)	1B	*141	532	73	129	23	5	20	90	.242	51	166	8	*1257	*118	13	*.991
1993—Prin. William (Car.)	1B	125	464	63	123	25	4	21	89	.265	50	*150	8	*1127	91	16	.987
1994—Alb./Colon. (East.)	1B	118	444	63	100	14	2	27	83	.225	48	*149	1	945	88	7	*.993
1995—Norwich (Eastern)	1B	77	274	34	62	18	1	5	33	.226	31	86	0	497	39	6	.989
—Columbus (Int'l)	1B	29	110	7	18	6	0	1	12	.164	1	34	0	271	25	2	.993

SEELBACH, CHRIS — P — MARLINS

PERSONAL: Born December 18, 1972, in Lufkin, Tex.... 6-4/180.... Throws right, bats right.... Full name: Christopher Don Seelbach.

HIGH SCHOOL: Lufkin (Tex.).

TRANSACTIONS/CAREER NOTES: Selected by Atlanta Braves organization in fourth round of free-agent draft (June 3, 1991).... Traded by Braves to Florida Marlins (September 15, 1995), completing deal in which Braves acquired P Alejandro Pena for a player to be named later (August 31, 1995).

Year Team (League)	W	L	Pct.	ERA	G	GS	CG	ShO	Sv.	IP	H	R	ER	BB	SO
1991—GC Braves (GCL)	0	1	.000	4.20	4	4	0	0	0	15	13	7	7	6	19
1992—Macon (S. Atl.)	9	11	.450	3.20	27	27	1	0	0	157 1/3	134	65	56	68	144
1993—Durham (Carolina)	9	9	.500	4.93	25	25	0	0	0	131 1/3	133	85	72	74	112
1994—Greenville (South.)	4	6	.400	2.33	15	15	2	0	0	92 2/3	64	26	24	38	79
—Richmond (Int'l)	3	5	.375	4.84	12	11	0	0	0	61 1/3	68	37	33	36	35
1995—Richmond (Int'l)	4	6	.400	4.66	14	14	1	0	0	73 1/3	64	39	38	39	65
—Greenville (South.)	6	0	1.000	1.64	9	9	1	1	0	60 1/3	38	15	11	30	65

SEFCIK, KEVIN — 3B/2B — PHILLIES

PERSONAL: Born February 10, 1971, in Oak Lawn, Ill.... 5-10/175.... Bats right, throws right.... Full name: Kevin John Sefcik.

HIGH SCHOOL: Victor Andrews (Tinley Park, Ill.).

COLLEGE: St. Xavier (Ill.).

S

TRANSACTIONS/CAREER NOTES: Selected by Philadelphia Phillies organization in 33rd round of free-agent draft (June 3, 1993).
STATISTICAL NOTES: Led New York-Pennsylvania League second basemen with 212 assists and 359 total chances in 1993.

			BATTING											FIELDING			
Year Team (League)	Pos.	G	AB	R	H	2B	3B	HR	RBI	Avg.	BB	SO	SB	PO	A	E	Avg.
1993—Batavia (NYP)	2B-3B	74	281	49	84	24	4	2	28	.299	27	22	20	136	†216	16	.957
1994—Clearwater (FSL)	3B-2B	130	516	83	147	29	8	2	46	.285	49	43	30	91	293	21	.948
1995—Scran./W.B. (Int'l)	2B	7	26	5	9	6	1	0	6	.346	3	1	0	13	16	0	1.000
—Reading (Eastern)	SS-3B	128	508	68	138	18	4	4	46	.272	38	48	14	166	349	18	.966
—Philadelphia (N.L.)	3B	5	4	1	0	0	0	0	0	.000	0	2	0	0	1	0	1.000
Major league totals (1 year)		5	4	1	0	0	0	0	0	.000	0	2	0	0	1	0	1.000

SEGUI, DAVID 1B EXPOS

PERSONAL: Born July 19, 1966, in Kansas City, Kan. . . . 6-1/202. . . . Bats both, throws left. . . . Full name: David Vincent Segui. . . . Son of Diego Segui, major league pitcher with five teams (1962-75 and 1977); and brother of Dan Segui, minor league infielder (1987-90). . . . Name pronounced seh-GHEE.
HIGH SCHOOL: Bishop Ward (Kansas City, Kan.).
JUNIOR COLLEGE: Kansas City Kansas Community College.
COLLEGE: Louisiana Tech.
TRANSACTIONS/CAREER NOTES: Selected by Baltimore Orioles organization in 18th round of free-agent draft (June 2, 1987). . . . On Rochester disabled list (April 19-26, 1991). . . . On suspended list (August 16-19, 1993). . . . Traded by Orioles to New York Mets for SS Kevin Baez and P Tom Wegmann (March 27, 1994). . . . On disabled list (June 20-July 5, 1994). . . . Traded by Mets to Montreal Expos for P Reid Cornelius (June 8, 1995).
STATISTICAL NOTES: Led N.L. first basemen with .996 fielding percentage in 1994. . . . Career major league grand slams: 1.

			BATTING											FIELDING			
Year Team (League)	Pos.	G	AB	R	H	2B	3B	HR	RBI	Avg.	BB	SO	SB	PO	A	E	Avg.
1988—Hagerstown (Car.)	1B-OF	60	190	35	51	12	4	3	31	.268	22	23	0	342	25	9	.976
1989—Frederick (Caro.)	1B	83	284	43	90	19	0	10	50	.317	41	32	2	707	47	4	.995
—Hagerstown (East.)	1B	44	173	22	56	14	1	1	27	.324	16	16	0	381	30	1	.998
1990—Rochester (Int'l)	1B-OF	86	307	55	103	28	0	2	51	.336	45	28	5	704	62	3	.996
—Baltimore (A.L.)	1B-DH	40	123	14	30	7	0	2	15	.244	11	15	0	283	26	3	.990
1991—Rochester (Int'l)	1B-OF	28	96	9	26	2	0	1	10	.271	15	6	1	165	15	0	1.000
—Baltimore (A.L.)	OF-1B-DH	86	212	15	59	7	0	2	22	.278	12	19	1	264	23	3	.990
1992—Baltimore (A.L.)	1B-OF	115	189	21	44	9	0	1	17	.233	20	23	1	406	35	1	.998
1993—Baltimore (A.L.)	1B-DH	146	450	54	123	27	0	10	60	.273	58	53	2	1152	98	5	.996
1994—New York (N.L.)■	1B-OF	92	336	46	81	17	1	10	43	.241	33	43	0	695	52	5	†.993
1995—New York (N.L.)	OF-1B	33	73	9	24	3	1	2	11	.329	12	9	1	56	5	0	1.000
—Montreal (N.L.)■	1B-OF	97	383	59	117	22	3	10	57	.305	28	38	1	840	70	3	.997
American League totals (4 years)		387	974	104	256	50	0	15	114	.263	101	110	4	2105	182	12	.995
National League totals (2 years)		222	792	114	222	42	5	22	111	.280	73	90	2	1591	127	8	.995
Major league totals (6 years)		609	1766	218	478	92	5	37	225	.271	174	200	6	3696	309	20	.995

SEITZER, KEVIN 3B/1B BREWERS

PERSONAL: Born March 26, 1962, in Springfield, Ill. . . . 5-11/193. . . . Bats right, throws right. . . . Full name: Kevin Lee Seitzer. . . . Name pronounced SITE-ser.
HIGH SCHOOL: Lincoln (Ill.).
COLLEGE: Eastern Illinois (bachelor of science degree in industrial electronics).
TRANSACTIONS/CAREER NOTES: Selected by Kansas City Royals organization in 11th round of free-agent draft (June 6, 1983). . . . On disabled list (April 27-May 31, 1991). . . . Released by Royals (March 26, 1992). . . . Signed by Milwaukee Brewers (April 5, 1992). . . . Granted free agency (October 27, 1992). . . . Signed by Oakland Athletics (February 1, 1993). . . . Released by A's (July 26, 1993). . . . Signed by Brewers (July 29, 1993). . . . Granted free agency (October 29, 1993). . . . Re-signed by Brewers (February 11, 1994). . . . On Milwaukee disabled list (May 10-June 14, 1994); included rehabilitation assignment to Beloit (June 11-14). . . . Granted free agency (November 1, 1995). . . . Re-signed by Brewers (December 7, 1995).
HONORS: Named South Atlantic League Most Valuable Player (1984).
STATISTICAL NOTES: Led Pioneer League third basemen with 122 assists and 172 total chances in 1983. . . . Led South Atlantic League third basemen with 409 total chances in 1984. . . . Tied for American Association lead in being hit by pitch with nine in 1986. . . . Collected six hits in one game (August 2, 1987). . . . Tied for A.L. lead in errors by third baseman with 22 in 1987. . . . Led A.L. third basemen with 26 errors in 1988. . . . Led A.L. third basemen with .969 fielding percentage in 1992. . . . Career major league grand slams: 3.

			BATTING											FIELDING			
Year Team (League)	Pos.	G	AB	R	H	2B	3B	HR	RBI	Avg.	BB	SO	SB	PO	A	E	Avg.
1983—Butte (Pioneer)	3B-SS	68	238	60	82	14	1	2	45	.345	46	36	11	52	†124	21	.893
1984—Char., S.C. (S. Atl.)	3B	•141	489	*96	*145	26	5	8	79	.297	*118	70	23	80	*279	*50	.878
1985—Fort Myers (FSL)	1B-3B	90	290	61	91	10	5	3	46	.314	85	30	28	569	88	9	.986
—Memphis (South.)	3B-1B-OF	52	187	26	65	6	2	1	20	.348	25	21	9	79	51	10	.929
1986—Memphis (South.)	1B	4	11	4	3	0	0	0	1	.273	7	1	2	28	3	1	.969
—Omaha (A.A.)	OF-1B-3B	129	432	86	138	20	11	13	74	.319	89	57	20	338	39	9	.977
—Kansas City (A.L.)	1B-OF-3B	28	96	16	31	4	1	2	11	.323	19	14	0	224	19	3	.988
1987—Kansas City (A.L.)	3-1-O-DH	161	641	105	•207	33	8	15	83	.323	80	85	12	290	315	‡24	.962
1988—Kansas City (A.L.)	3B-OF-DH	149	559	90	170	32	5	5	60	.304	72	64	10	93	297	†26	.938
1989—Kansas City (A.L.)	3-S-O-1	160	597	78	168	17	2	4	48	.281	102	76	17	118	277	20	.952
1990—Kansas City (A.L.)	3B-2B	158	622	91	171	31	5	6	38	.275	67	66	7	118	281	19	.955
1991—Kansas City (A.L.)	3B-DH	85	234	28	62	11	3	1	25	.265	29	21	4	45	127	11	.940
1992—Milwaukee (A.L.)■	3B-2B-1B	148	540	74	146	35	1	5	71	.270	57	44	13	102	277	12	†.969
1993—Oakland (A.L.)■	3-1-DH-O-2-P	73	255	24	65	10	2	4	27	.255	27	33	4	205	89	7	.977
—Milwaukee (A.L.)■	3-1-DH-O-2-S	47	162	21	47	6	0	7	30	.290	17	15	3	70	61	5	.963
1994—Milwaukee (A.L.)	3B-1B-DH	80	309	44	97	24	2	5	49	.314	30	38	2	329	104	11	.975
—Beloit (Midwest)	3B	3	12	3	4	3	0	0	3	.333	0	0	2	1	6	0	1.000
1995—Milwaukee (A.L.)	3B-1B-DH	132	492	56	153	33	3	5	69	.311	64	57	2	340	181	10	.981
Major league totals (10 years)		1221	4507	627	1317	236	32	59	511	.292	564	513	74	1934	2028	148	.964

S

ALL-STAR GAME RECORD

Year	League	Pos.	AB	R	H	2B	3B	HR	RBI	Avg.	BB	SO	SB	PO	A	E	Avg.
			BATTING											FIELDING			
1987—	American	3B	2	0	0	0	0	0	0	.000	1	0	0	0	0	0	...
1995—	American	PH-3B	2	0	0	0	0	0	0	.000	0	0	0	0	0	0	...
All-Star Game totals (2 years)			4	0	0	0	0	0	0	.000	1	0	0	0	0	0	...

RECORD AS PITCHER

Year	Team (League)	W	L	Pct.	ERA	G	GS	CG	ShO	Sv.	IP	H	R	ER	BB	SO
1993—	Oakland (A.L.)	0	0	...	0.00	1	0	0	0	0	1/3	0	0	0	0	1

SELE, AARON — P — RED SOX

PERSONAL: Born June 25, 1970, in Golden Valley, Minn. . . . 6-5/218. . . . Throws right, bats right. . . . Full name: Aaron Helmer Sele. . . . Name pronounced SEE-lee.

HIGH SCHOOL: North Kitsap (Poulsbo, Wash.).

COLLEGE: Washington State.

TRANSACTIONS/CAREER NOTES: Selected by Minnesota Twins organization in 37th round of free-agent draft (June 1, 1988); did not sign. . . . Selected by Boston Red Sox organization in first round (23rd pick overall) of free-agent draft (June 3, 1991). . . . On Boston disabled list (May 24, 1995-remainder of season); included rehabilitation assignments to Trenton (June 19-22), Sarasota (July 10-21 and August 7-16) and Pawtucket (August 16-23).

HONORS: Named A.L. Rookie Pitcher of the Year by The Sporting News (1993). . . . Named International League Most Valuable Pitcher (1993).

STATISTICAL NOTES: Led Carolina League with 14 hit batsmen in 1992. . . . Tied for A.L. lead with nine hit batsmen in 1994.

Year	Team (League)	W	L	Pct.	ERA	G	GS	CG	ShO	Sv.	IP	H	R	ER	BB	SO
1991—	Winter Haven (FSL)	3	6	.333	4.96	13	11	4	0	1	69	65	42	38	32	51
1992—	Lynchburg (Caro.)	13	5	.722	2.91	20	19	2	1	0	127	104	51	41	46	112
—	New Britain (East.)	2	1	.667	6.27	7	6	1	0	0	33	43	29	23	15	29
1993—	Pawtucket (Int'l)	8	2	.800	2.19	14	14	2	1	0	94 1/3	74	30	23	23	87
—	Boston (A.L.)	7	2	.778	2.74	18	18	0	0	0	111 2/3	100	42	34	48	93
1994—	Boston (A.L.)	8	7	.533	3.83	22	22	2	0	0	143 1/3	140	68	61	60	105
1995—	Boston (A.L.)	3	1	.750	3.06	6	6	0	0	0	32 1/3	32	14	11	14	21
—	Trenton (Eastern)	0	1	.000	3.38	2	2	0	0	0	8	8	3	3	2	9
—	Sarasota (Fla. St.)	0	0	...	0.00	2	2	0	0	0	7	6	0	0	1	8
—	Pawtucket (Int'l)	0	0	...	9.00	2	2	0	0	0	5	9	5	5	2	1
Major league totals (3 years)		18	10	.643	3.32	46	46	2	0	0	287 1/3	272	124	106	122	219

SERAFINI, DAN — P — TWINS

PERSONAL: Born January 25, 1974, in San Francisco. . . . 6-1/180. . . . Throws left, bats both.

HIGH SCHOOL: Serra (San Mateo, Calif.).

TRANSACTIONS/CAREER NOTES: Selected by Minnesota Twins organization in first round (26th pick overall) of free-agent draft (June 1, 1992).

Year	Team (League)	W	L	Pct.	ERA	G	GS	CG	ShO	Sv.	IP	H	R	ER	BB	SO
1992—	GC Twins (GCL)	1	0	1.000	3.64	8	6	0	0	0	29 2/3	27	16	12	15	33
1993—	Fort Wayne (Midw.)	10	8	.556	3.65	27	27	1	1	0	140 2/3	117	72	57	83	147
1994—	Fort Myers (Fla. St.)	9	9	.500	4.61	23	23	2	1	0	136 2/3	149	84	70	57	130
1995—	New Britain (East.)	12	9	.571	3.38	27	27	1	1	0	162 2/3	155	74	61	72	123
—	Salt Lake (PCL)	0	0	...	6.75	1	0	0	0	1	4	4	3	3	1	4

SERVAIS, SCOTT — C — CUBS

PERSONAL: Born June 4, 1967, in LaCrosse, Wis. . . . 6-2/205. . . . Bats right, throws right. . . . Full name: Scott Daniel Servais. . . . Name pronounced SER-viss.

HIGH SCHOOL: Westby (Wis.).

COLLEGE: Creighton.

TRANSACTIONS/CAREER NOTES: Selected by New York Mets organization in second round of free-agent draft (June 3, 1985); did not sign. . . . Selected by Houston Astros organization in third round of free-agent draft (June 1, 1988). . . . On Tucson disabled list (June 29-July 1, 1991). . . . On Houston disabled list (August 4-September 7, 1991). . . . Traded by Astros with OF Luis Gonzalez to Chicago Cubs for C Rick Wilkins (June 28, 1995). . . . On Chicago disabled list (July 10-August 3, 1995).

STATISTICAL NOTES: Tied for Pacific Coast League lead in double plays by catcher with nine in 1990. . . . Led N.L. catchers with 12 errors in 1995.

MISCELLANEOUS: Member of 1988 U.S. Olympic baseball team.

Year	Team (League)	Pos.	G	AB	R	H	2B	3B	HR	RBI	Avg.	BB	SO	SB	PO	A	E	Avg.
				BATTING											FIELDING			
1989—	Osceola (Fla. St.)	C-1B	46	153	16	41	9	0	2	23	.268	16	35	0	168	24	4	.980
—	Columbus (South.)	C	63	199	20	47	5	0	1	22	.236	19	42	0	330	45	3	.992
1990—	Tucson (PCL)	C	89	303	37	66	11	3	5	37	.218	18	61	0	453	63	9	.983
1991—	Tucson (PCL)	C	60	219	34	71	12	0	2	27	.324	13	19	0	350	33	6	.985
—	Houston (N.L.)	C	16	37	0	6	3	0	0	6	.162	4	8	0	77	4	1	.988
1992—	Houston (N.L.)	C	77	205	12	49	9	0	0	15	.239	11	25	0	386	27	2	.995
1993—	Houston (N.L.)	C	85	258	24	63	11	0	11	32	.244	22	45	0	493	40	2	.996
1994—	Houston (N.L.)	C	78	251	27	49	15	1	9	41	.195	10	44	0	481	29	2	.996
1995—	Houston (N.L.)	C	28	89	7	20	10	0	1	12	.225	9	15	0	198	17	5	.977
—	Chicago (N.L.)■	C	52	175	31	50	12	0	12	35	.286	23	37	2	328	33	§7	.981
Major league totals (5 years)			336	1015	101	237	60	1	33	141	.233	79	174	2	1963	150	19	.991

SERVICE, SCOTT — P — GIANTS

PERSONAL: Born February 26, 1967, in Cincinnati. . . . 6-6/226. . . . Throws right, bats right. . . . Full name: David Scott Service.
HIGH SCHOOL: Aiken (Cincinnati).
TRANSACTIONS/CAREER NOTES: Signed as non-drafted free agent by Philadelphia Phillies organization (August 24, 1985). . . . Granted free agency (October 11, 1990). . . . Signed by Montreal Expos organization (November 15, 1990). . . . Released by Expos organization (July 19, 1991). . . . Played with Chunichi Dragons of Japan Central League (August 1991). . . . Signed by Expos organization (January 10, 1992). . . . Granted free agency (June 8, 1992). . . . Signed by Nashville, Cincinnati Reds organization (June 9, 1992). . . . On Indianapolis disabled list (May 15-22, 1993). . . . Claimed on waivers by Colorado Rockies (June 28, 1993). . . . Claimed on waivers by Reds (July 7, 1993). . . . On Indianapolis disabled list (April 17-24, 1994). . . . Released by Reds (November 17, 1994). . . . Re-signed by Indianapolis, Reds organization (February 24, 1995). . . . Traded by Reds organization with OF Deion Sanders, P John Roper, P Ricky Pickett and IF Dave McCarty to San Francisco Giants for OF Darren Lewis, P Mark Portugal and P Dave Burba (July 21, 1995).
STATISTICAL NOTES: Led American Association with .800 winning percentage in 1992.
MISCELLANEOUS: Made an out in only appearance as pinch-hitter with Cincinnati (1993).

Year Team (League)	W	L	Pct.	ERA	G	GS	CG	ShO	Sv.	IP	H	R	ER	BB	SO
1986—Spartanburg (SAL)	1	6	.143	5.83	14	9	1	0	0	58 2/3	68	44	38	34	49
—Utica (NYP)	5	4	.556	2.67	10	10	2	0	0	70 2/3	65	30	21	18	43
—Clearwater (Fla. St.)	1	2	.333	3.20	4	4	1	1	0	25 1/3	20	10	9	15	19
1987—Reading (Eastern)	0	3	.000	7.78	5	4	0	0	0	19 2/3	22	19	17	16	12
—Clearwater (Fla. St.)	13	4	.765	2.48	21	21	5	2	0	137 2/3	127	46	38	32	73
1988—Reading (Eastern)	3	4	.429	2.86	10	9	1	1	0	56 2/3	52	25	18	22	39
—Maine (Int'l)	8	8	.500	3.67	19	18	1	0	0	110 1/3	109	51	45	31	87
—Philadelphia (N.L.)	0	0	...	1.69	5	0	0	0	0	5 1/3	7	1	1	1	6
1989—Scran./W.B. (Int'l)	3	1	.750	2.16	23	0	0	0	6	33 1/3	27	8	8	23	23
—Reading (Eastern)	6	6	.500	3.26	23	10	1	1	1	85 2/3	71	36	31	23	82
1990—Scran./W.B. (Int'l)	5	4	.556	4.76	45	9	0	0	2	96 1/3	96	56	51	44	94
1991—Indianapolis (A.A.)■	6	7	.462	2.97	18	17	3	1	0	121 1/3	83	42	40	39	91
—Chunichi (Jp. Cn.)■	0	0	...	9.00	1	...	...	...	0	1	...	...	1	0	0
1992—Indianapolis (A.A.)■	2	0	1.000	0.74	13	0	0	0	2	24 1/3	12	3	2	9	25
—Montreal (N.L.)	0	0	...	14.14	5	0	0	0	0	7	15	11	11	5	11
—Nashville (A.A.)■	6	2	§.750	2.29	39	2	0	0	4	70 2/3	54	22	18	35	87
1993—Indianapolis (A.A.)	4	2	.667	4.45	21	1	0	0	2	30 1/3	25	16	15	17	28
—Colorado (N.L.)■	0	0	...	9.64	3	0	0	0	0	4 2/3	8	5	5	1	3
—Cincinnati (N.L.)■	2	2	.500	3.70	26	0	0	0	2	41 1/3	36	19	17	15	40
1994—Indianapolis (A.A.)	5	5	.500	2.31	40	0	0	0	13	58 1/3	35	16	15	27	67
—Cincinnati (N.L.)	1	2	.333	7.36	6	0	0	0	0	7 1/3	8	9	6	3	5
1995—Indianapolis (A.A.)	4	1	.800	2.18	36	0	0	0	18	41 1/3	33	13	10	15	48
—San Francisco (N.L.)■	3	1	.750	3.19	28	0	0	0	0	31	18	11	11	20	30
Major league totals (5 years)	6	5	.545	4.75	73	0	0	0	2	96 2/3	92	56	51	45	95

SEXTON, JEFF — P — INDIANS

PERSONAL: Born October 4, 1971, in Westminster, Calif. . . . 6-2/190. . . . Throws right, bats right. . . . Full name: Jeffrey Scott Sexton.
TRANSACTIONS/CAREER NOTES: Signed as non-drafted free agent by Cleveland Indians organization (June 22, 1993).

Year Team (League)	W	L	Pct.	ERA	G	GS	CG	ShO	Sv.	IP	H	R	ER	BB	SO
1993—Watertown (NYP)	1	1	.500	2.67	17	1	1	•1	2	33 2/3	35	15	10	10	30
1994—Watertown (NYP)	1	0	1.000	0.39	10	0	0	0	3	23	19	3	1	7	16
—Columbus (S. Atl.)	1	0	1.000	3.60	14	2	0	0	1	30	17	13	12	9	35
1995—Columbus (S. Atl.)	6	2	.750	2.19	14	13	2	2	0	82 1/3	66	27	20	16	71
—Kinston (Carolina)	5	1	.833	2.53	8	8	2	1	0	57	52	17	16	7	41

SHARPERSON, MIKE — 2B/3B — PADRES

PERSONAL: Born October 4, 1961, in Orangeburg, S.C. . . . 6-3/208. . . . Bats right, throws right. . . . Full name: Michael Tyrone Sharperson.
HIGH SCHOOL: Wilkinson (Orangeburg, S.C.).
JUNIOR COLLEGE: DeKalb Community College South (Ga.).
TRANSACTIONS/CAREER NOTES: Selected by Pittsburgh Pirates organization in 41st round of free-agent draft (June 5, 1979); did not sign. . . . Selected by Montreal Expos organization in secondary phase of free-agent draft (January 8, 1980); did not sign. . . . Selected by Detroit Tigers organization in fourth round of free-agent draft (January 13, 1981); did not sign. . . . Selected by Toronto Blue Jays organization in secondary phase of free-agent draft (June 8, 1981). . . . On disabled list (August 14, 1983-remainder of season). . . . Traded by Blue Jays organization to Los Angeles Dodgers for P Juan Guzman (September 22, 1987). . . . On disabled list (May 8-30, 1991). . . . Granted free agency (October 8, 1993). . . . Re-signed by Dodgers organization (February 23, 1994). . . . Released by Dodgers organization (April 2, 1994). . . . Signed by Pawtucket, Boston Red Sox organization (May 26, 1994). . . . Released by Pawtucket (July 17, 1994). . . . Signed by Iowa, Chicago Cubs organization (July 27, 1994). . . . Granted free agency (October 15, 1994). . . . Signed by Richmond, Atlanta Braves organization (January 20, 1995). . . . On Richmond suspended list (April 6-9, 1995). . . . Granted free agency (October 3, 1995). . . . Signed by San Diego Padres organization (November 29, 1995).
STATISTICAL NOTES: Led Southern League second basemen with 775 total chances and 103 double plays in 1984. . . . Led International League second basemen with 286 putouts and 666 total chances in 1985. . . . Tied for International League lead in double plays by third baseman with 16 in 1987.

			BATTING											FIELDING			
Year Team (League)	Pos.	G	AB	R	H	2B	3B	HR	RBI	Avg.	BB	SO	SB	PO	A	E	Avg.
1982—Florence (S. Atl.)	SS-3B	111	326	51	83	16	1	3	33	.255	59	59	28	136	261	33	.923
1983—Kinston (Carolina)	S-3-2-C	90	361	55	96	8	1	5	41	.266	39	65	20	148	286	19	.958
1984—Knoxville (South.)	2B	140	542	86	165	25	7	4	48	.304	48	66	20	*331	*423	21	.973
1985—Syracuse (Int'l)	2B-SS	134	*536	*86	*155	19	*7	1	59	.289	71	75	14	†291	372	17	.975
1986—Syracuse (Int'l)	2B-3B	133	519	*86	*150	18	*9	4	45	.289	69	67	17	258	376	18	.972
1987—Toronto (A.L.)	2B	32	96	4	20	4	1	0	9	.208	7	15	2	64	69	4	.971
—Syracuse (Int'l)	3B-2B	88	338	67	101	21	5	5	26	.299	40	41	13	81	152	8	.967

				BATTING											FIELDING			
Year	Team (League)	Pos.	G	AB	R	H	2B	3B	HR	RBI	Avg.	BB	SO	SB	PO	A	E	Avg.
	—Los Angeles (N.L.)■	3B-2B	10	33	7	9	2	0	0	1	.273	4	5	0	4	28	1	.970
1988	—Albuquerque (PCL)	2B-3B-SS	56	210	55	67	10	2	0	30	.319	31	25	19	88	173	12	.956
	—Los Angeles (N.L.)	2B-3B-SS	46	59	8	16	1	0	0	4	.271	1	12	0	19	31	2	.962
1989	—Albuquerque (PCL)	2B-3B-SS	98	359	81	111	15	7	3	48	.309	66	46	17	114	250	14	.963
	—Los Angeles (N.L.)	2-1-3-S	27	28	2	7	3	0	0	5	.250	4	7	0	11	8	0	1.000
1990	—Los Angeles (N.L.)	3-S-2-1	129	357	42	106	14	2	3	36	.297	45	39	15	152	193	15	.958
1991	—Los Angeles (N.L.)	3-S-1-2	105	216	24	60	11	2	2	20	.278	25	24	1	89	107	4	.980
1992	—Los Angeles (N.L.)	2B-3B-SS	128	317	48	95	21	0	3	36	.300	47	33	2	120	220	13	.963
1993	—Los Angeles (N.L.)	2-3-S-O-1	73	90	13	23	4	0	2	10	.256	5	17	2	29	38	5	.931
1994	—Pawtucket (Int'l)■	3B-2B	37	131	16	39	10	0	0	13	.298	21	17	5	31	77	6	.947
	—Iowa (Am. Assoc.)■	3-1-2-S	31	90	16	25	3	2	5	16	.278	9	14	3	67	29	2	.980
1995	—Richmond (Int'l)■	3B-1B-2B	87	298	42	95	16	1	3	47	.319	35	34	7	78	138	5	.977
	—Atlanta (N.L.)	3B	7	7	1	1	1	0	0	2	.143	0	2	0	0	0	0	...
American League totals (1 year)			32	96	4	20	4	1	0	9	.208	7	15	2	64	69	4	.971
National League totals (8 years)			525	1107	145	317	57	4	10	114	.286	131	139	20	424	625	40	.963
Major league totals (8 years)			557	1203	149	337	61	5	10	123	.280	138	154	22	488	694	44	.964

CHAMPIONSHIP SERIES RECORD

				BATTING											FIELDING			
Year	Team (League)	Pos.	G	AB	R	H	2B	3B	HR	RBI	Avg.	BB	SO	SB	PO	A	E	Avg.
1988	—Los Angeles (N.L.)	PH-SS-3B	2	1	0	0	0	0	0	1	.000	1	0	0	1	0	0	1.000

ALL-STAR GAME RECORD

			BATTING										FIELDING			
Year	League	Pos.	AB	R	H	2B	3B	HR	RBI	Avg.	BB	SO	SB	PO	A	E	Avg.
1992	—National	3B	1	0	0	0	0	0	0	.000	0	1	0	1	0	0	1.000

SHAW, JEFF — P — REDS

PERSONAL: Born July 7, 1966, in Washington Court House, O. . . . 6-2/200. . . . Throws right, bats right. . . . Full name: Jeffrey Lee Shaw.
HIGH SCHOOL: Washington Senior (Washington Court House, O.).
JUNIOR COLLEGE: Cuyahoga Community College-Western Campus (O.).
COLLEGE: Rio Grande (O.) College.
TRANSACTIONS/CAREER NOTES: Selected by Cleveland Indians organization in first round (first pick overall) of free-agent draft (January 14, 1986). . . . Granted free agency (October 16, 1992). . . . Signed by Omaha, Kansas City Royals organization (November 9, 1992). . . . Traded by Royals organization with C Tim Spehr to Montreal Expos organization for P Mark Gardner and P Doug Piatt (December 9, 1992). . . . Granted free agency (February 17, 1995). . . . Re-signed by Ottawa (April 9, 1995). . . . Traded by Expos to Chicago White Sox for P Jose DeLeon (August 28, 1995). . . . Granted free agency (December 21, 1995). . . . Signed by Cincinnati Reds organization (January 2, 1996).
STATISTICAL NOTES: Led Eastern League with 14 hit batsmen in 1989. . . . Tied for Pacific Coast League lead with 10 hit batsmen in 1992.

Year	Team (League)	W	L	Pct.	ERA	G	GS	CG	ShO	Sv.	IP	H	R	ER	BB	SO
1986	—Batavia (NYP)	8	4	.667	2.44	14	12	3	1	0	88 2/3	79	32	24	35	71
1987	—Waterloo (Midw.)	11	11	.500	3.52	28	*28	6	*4	0	184 1/3	192	89	72	56	117
1988	—Williamsport (East.)	5	*19	.208	3.63	27	•27	6	1	0	163 2/3	•173	*94	66	75	61
1989	—Cant./Akr. (East.)	7	10	.412	3.62	30	22	6	3	0	154 1/3	134	84	62	67	95
1990	—Colo. Springs (PCL)	10	3	.769	4.29	17	16	4	0	0	98 2/3	98	54	47	52	55
	—Cleveland (A.L.)	3	4	.429	6.66	12	9	0	0	0	48 2/3	73	38	36	20	25
1991	—Colo. Springs (PCL)	6	3	.667	4.64	12	12	1	0	0	75 2/3	77	47	39	25	55
	—Cleveland (A.L.)	0	5	.000	3.36	29	1	0	0	1	72 1/3	72	34	27	27	31
1992	—Colo. Springs (PCL)	10	5	.667	4.76	25	24	1	0	0	155	174	88	82	45	84
	—Cleveland (A.L.)	0	1	.000	8.22	2	1	0	0	0	7 2/3	7	7	7	4	3
1993	—Ottawa (Int'l)■	0	0	...	0.00	2	1	0	0	0	4	5	0	0	2	1
	—Montreal (N.L.)	2	7	.222	4.14	55	8	0	0	0	95 2/3	91	47	44	32	50
1994	—Montreal (N.L.)	5	2	.714	3.88	46	0	0	0	1	67 1/3	67	32	29	15	47
1995	—Montreal (N.L.)	1	6	.143	4.62	50	0	0	0	3	62 1/3	58	35	32	26	45
	—Chicago (A.L.)■	0	0	...	6.52	9	0	0	0	0	9 2/3	12	7	7	1	6
A.L. totals (4 years)		3	10	.231	5.01	52	11	0	0	1	138 1/3	164	86	77	52	65
N.L. totals (3 years)		8	15	.348	4.19	151	8	0	0	4	225 1/3	216	114	105	73	142
Major league totals (6 years)		11	25	.306	4.50	203	19	0	0	5	363 2/3	380	200	182	125	207

SHEAFFER, DANNY — C — CARDINALS

PERSONAL: Born August 2, 1961, in Jacksonville, Fla. . . . 6-0/190. . . . Bats right, throws right. . . . Full name: Danny Todd Sheaffer.
HIGH SCHOOL: Red Land (Lewisberry, Pa.).
JUNIOR COLLEGE: Harrisburg (Pa.) Junior College.
COLLEGE: Clemson.
TRANSACTIONS/CAREER NOTES: Selected by Boston Red Sox organization in first round (20th pick overall) of free-agent draft (January 13, 1981). . . . On disabled list (May 3-14, 1982). . . . Granted free agency (October 15, 1988). . . . Signed by Colorado Springs, Cleveland Indians organization (November 15, 1988). . . . Granted free agency (October 15, 1989). . . . Signed by Buffalo, Pittsburgh Pirates organization (November 25, 1989). . . . Granted free agency (October 15, 1990). . . . Signed by Minnesota Twins organization (December 20, 1990). . . . Granted free agency (October 15, 1992). . . . Signed by Colorado Rockies organization (October 29, 1992). . . . Granted free agency (October 15, 1994). . . . Signed by Louisville, St. Louis Cardinals organization (December 19, 1994).
STATISTICAL NOTES: Led Florida State League with 14 errors in 1982. . . . Led Pacific Coast League catchers with .994 fielding percentage in 1992. . . . Career major league grand slams: 1.

				BATTING											FIELDING			
Year	Team (League)	Pos.	G	AB	R	H	2B	3B	HR	RBI	Avg.	BB	SO	SB	PO	A	E	Avg.
1981	—Elmira (NYP)	C	62	198	39	57	9	0	8	29	.288	23	38	2	220	35	5	.981
	—Bristol (Eastern)	C-2B	8	12	0	0	0	0	0	1	.000	0	3	0	16	3	0	1.000
1982	—Winter Haven (FSL)	C-3B	82	260	20	65	4	0	5	25	.250	18	37	2	316	51	†16	.958

Year	Team (League)	Pos.	BATTING G	AB	R	H	2B	3B	HR	RBI	Avg.	BB	SO	SB	FIELDING PO	A	E	Avg.
1983—	Winst.-Salem (Car.)....	C-1B-OF	112	380	48	105	14	2	15	63	.276	36	50	1	427	44	6	.987
1984—	New Britain (East.).....	C-OF	93	303	33	73	10	0	1	27	.241	29	31	2	438	47	6	.988
1985—	Pawtucket (Int'l).........	C	77	243	24	63	9	0	8	33	.259	17	35	0	289	18	6	.981
1986—	Pawtucket (Int'l).........	C-OF	79	265	34	90	16	1	2	30	.340	10	24	9	380	39	5	.988
1987—	Boston (A.L.).............	C	25	66	5	8	1	0	1	5	.121	0	14	0	121	5	3	.977
	—Pawtucket (Int'l).........	C-1B-OF	69	242	32	62	13	2	2	25	.256	6	29	6	346	32	5	.987
1988—	Pawtucket (Int'l).........	C-1-3-O	98	299	30	82	17	1	1	28	.274	18	32	20	509	58	6	.990
1989—	Colo. Springs (PCL)■	OF-3B	107	401	62	113	26	2	3	47	.282	24	39	6	136	11	10	.936
	—Cleveland (A.L.)..........	DH-3B-OF	7	16	1	1	0	0	0	0	.063	2	2	0	4	0	0	1.000
1990—	Buffalo (A.A.)■..........	C-OF-1B	55	144	23	35	7	0	2	19	.243	11	14	4	163	10	5	.972
1991—	Portland (PCL)■........	C-1-O-2	93	330	46	100	14	2	1	43	.303	26	35	2	448	39	11	.978
1992—	Portland (PCL)...........	C-OF-3B	116	442	54	122	23	4	5	56	.276	21	36	3	605	66	4	†.994
1993—	Colorado (N.L.)■.......	C-1-O-3	82	216	26	60	9	1	4	32	.278	8	15	2	337	32	2	.995
1994—	Colorado (N.L.)..........	C-1B-OF	44	110	11	24	4	0	1	12	.218	10	11	0	182	16	1	.995
1995—	St. Louis (N.L.)■........	C-1B-3B	76	208	24	48	10	1	5	30	.231	23	38	0	391	43	3	.993
American League totals (2 years)			32	82	6	9	1	0	1	5	.110	2	16	0	125	5	3	.977
National League totals (3 years)			202	534	61	132	23	2	10	74	.247	41	64	2	910	91	6	.994
Major league totals (5 years)			234	616	67	141	24	2	11	79	.229	43	80	2	1035	96	9	.992

SHEETS, ANDY — SS — MARINERS

PERSONAL: Born November 19, 1971, in Baton Rouge, La. . . . 6-2/180. . . . Bats right, throws right.

HIGH SCHOOL: St. Amant (La.).

COLLEGE: Tulane, then Louisiana State.

TRANSACTIONS/CAREER NOTES: Selected by Seattle Mariners organization in fourth round of free-agent draft (June 1, 1992).

Year	Team (League)	Pos.	BATTING G	AB	R	H	2B	3B	HR	RBI	Avg.	BB	SO	SB	FIELDING PO	A	E	Avg.
1993—	Riverside (Calif.).........	SS	52	176	23	34	9	1	1	12	.193	17	51	2	80	159	17	.934
	—Appleton (Midw.).......	SS-2B-OF	69	259	32	68	10	4	1	25	.263	20	59	7	98	194	11	.964
1994—	Riverside (Calif.).........	SS	31	100	17	27	5	1	2	10	.270	16	22	6	39	95	14	.905
	—Jacksonv. (South.).....	SS	70	232	26	51	12	0	0	17	.220	20	54	3	105	205	17	.948
	—Calgary (PCL)............	SS	26	93	22	32	8	1	2	16	.344	11	20	1	32	80	2	.982
1995—	Tacoma (PCL).............	SS	132	437	57	128	29	9	2	47	.293	32	83	8	157	382	27	.952

SHEFFIELD, GARY — OF — MARLINS

PERSONAL: Born November 18, 1968, in Tampa, Fla. . . . 5-11/190. . . . Bats right, throws right. . . . Full name: Gary Antonian Sheffield. . . . Nephew of Dwight Gooden, pitcher, New York Yankees organization.

HIGH SCHOOL: Hillsborough (Tampa, Fla.).

TRANSACTIONS/CAREER NOTES: Selected by Milwaukee Brewers organization in first round (sixth pick overall) of free-agent draft (June 2, 1986). . . . On Milwaukee disabled list (July 14-September 9, 1989). . . . On suspended list (August 31-September 3, 1990). . . . On disabled list (June 15-July 3 and July 25, 1991-remainder of season). . . . Traded by Brewers with P Geoff Kellogg to San Diego Padres for P Ricky Bones, IF Jose Valentin and OF Matt Mieske (March 27, 1992). . . . Traded by Padres with P Rich Rodriguez to Florida Marlins for P Trevor Hoffman, P Jose Martinez and P Andres Berumen (June 24, 1993). . . . On Florida suspended list (July 9-12, 1993). . . . On Florida disabled list (May 10-25 and May 28-June 12, 1994); included rehabilitation assignment to Portland (June 10-12). . . . On disabled list (June 11-September 1, 1995).

HONORS: Named Minor League co-Player of the Year by The Sporting News (1988). . . . Named Major League Player of the Year by The Sporting News (1992). . . . Named N.L. Comeback Player of the Year by The Sporting News (1992). . . . Named third baseman on The Sporting News N.L. All-Star team (1992). . . . Named third baseman on The Sporting News N.L. Silver Slugger team (1992).

STATISTICAL NOTES: Led Pioneer League shortstops with 34 double plays in 1986. . . . Led California League shortstops with 77 double plays in 1987. . . . Led N.L. with 323 total bases in 1992. . . . Career major league grand slams: 3.

Year	Team (League)	Pos.	BATTING G	AB	R	H	2B	3B	HR	RBI	Avg.	BB	SO	SB	FIELDING PO	A	E	Avg.
1986—	Helena (Pioneer)........	SS	57	222	53	81	12	2	15	*71	.365	20	14	14	97	149	24	.911
1987—	Stockton (Calif.).........	SS	129	469	84	130	23	3	17	*103	.277	81	49	25	235	345	39	.937
1988—	El Paso (Texas)...........	SS-3B-OF	77	296	70	93	19	3	19	65	.314	35	41	5	130	206	23	.936
	—Denver (A.A.).............	3B-SS	57	212	42	73	9	5	9	54	.344	21	22	8	54	97	8	.950
	—Milwaukee (A.L.)........	SS	24	80	12	19	1	0	4	12	.238	7	7	3	39	48	3	.967
1989—	Milwaukee (A.L.)........	SS-3B-DH	95	368	34	91	18	0	5	32	.247	27	33	10	100	238	16	.955
	—Denver (A.A.).............	SS	7	29	3	4	1	1	0	0	.138	2	0	0	2	6	0	1.000
1990—	Milwaukee (A.L.)........	3B	125	487	67	143	30	1	10	67	.294	44	41	25	98	254	25	.934
1991—	Milwaukee (A.L.)........	3B-DH	50	175	25	34	12	2	2	22	.194	19	15	5	29	65	8	.922
1992—	San Diego (N.L.)■.....	3B	146	557	87	184	34	3	33	100	*.330	48	40	5	99	299	16	.961
1993—	San Diego (N.L.)........	3B	68	258	34	76	12	2	10	36	.295	18	30	5	41	102	15	.905
	—Florida (N.L.)■..........	3B	72	236	33	69	8	3	10	37	.292	29	34	12	38	123	19	.894
1994—	Florida (N.L.).............	OF	87	322	61	89	16	1	27	78	.276	51	50	12	154	7	5	.970
	—Portland (Eastern)......	OF	2	7	1	2	1	0	0	0	.286	1	3	0	3	0	0	1.000
1995—	Florida (N.L.).............	OF	63	213	46	69	8	0	16	46	.324	55	45	19	109	5	7	.942
American League totals (4 years)			294	1110	138	287	61	3	21	133	.259	97	96	43	266	605	52	.944
National League totals (4 years)			436	1586	261	487	78	9	96	297	.307	201	199	53	441	536	62	.940
Major league totals (8 years)			730	2696	399	774	139	12	117	430	.287	298	295	96	707	1141	114	.942

ALL-STAR GAME RECORD

Year	League	Pos.	BATTING AB	R	H	2B	3B	HR	RBI	Avg.	BB	SO	SB	FIELDING PO	A	E	Avg.
1992—	National.....................	3B	2	0	0	0	0	0	0	.000	0	0	0	0	0	0	...
1993—	National.....................	3B	3	1	2	0	0	1	2	.667	0	0	0	0	2	0	1.000
All-Star Game totals (2 years)			5	1	2	0	0	1	2	.400	0	0	0	0	2	0	1.000

SHEPHERD, KEITH — P — ORIOLES

PERSONAL: Born January 21, 1968, in Wabash, Ind. . . . 6-2/235. . . . Throws right, bats right. . . . Full name: Keith Wayne Shepherd.
HIGH SCHOOL: Wabash (Ind.).
TRANSACTIONS/CAREER NOTES: Selected by Pittsburgh Pirates organization in 11th round of free-agent draft (June 2, 1986). . . . Selected by Omaha, Kansas City Royals organization, from Salem, Pirates organization, in Rule 5 minor league draft (December 6, 1988). . . . Released by Royals organization (July 24, 1989). . . . Signed by Cleveland Indians organization (July 24, 1989). . . . Loaned by Indians organization to Reno, independent (April 4, 1990). . . . On Reno suspended list (May 2-June 11, 1990). . . . Returned to Indians organization (June 11, 1990). . . . Released by Indians organization (October 22, 1990). . . . Signed by Chicago White Sox organization (March 12, 1991). . . . Traded by White Sox to Philadelphia Phillies for IF Dale Sveum (August 10, 1992). . . . Selected by Colorado Rockies in second round (50th pick overall) of expansion draft (November 17, 1992). . . . On Colorado suspended list (June 21-29, 1993). . . . Traded by Rockies organization to Boston Red Sox organization for P Brian Conroy (June 3, 1994). . . . On Sarasota disabled list (July 13-25, 1994). . . . On Boston disabled list (May 1-June 5, 1995). . . . Released by Red Sox (June 5, 1995). . . . Signed by Charlotte, Florida Marlins organization (June 15, 1995). . . . On Charlotte disabled list (July 8-26, 1995). . . . Released by Charlotte (July 26, 1995). . . . Signed by Baltimore Orioles organization (December 27, 1995).

Year Team (League)	W	L	Pct.	ERA	G	GS	CG	ShO	Sv.	IP	H	R	ER	BB	SO
1986— GC Pirates (GCL)	0	4	.000	6.06	8	2	0	0	0	16 1/3	16	17	11	15	12
1987— Watertown (NYP)	5	2	.714	4.20	17	13	1	1	0	70 2/3	66	40	33	42	57
1988— Augusta (S. Atl.)	7	3	.700	4.02	16	16	1	1	0	85	71	45	38	50	49
— Salem (Carolina)	2	3	.400	5.83	8	5	0	0	0	29 1/3	26	24	19	29	15
1989— Baseball City (FSL)■	1	7	.125	4.94	11	10	0	0	0	47 1/3	45	33	26	32	20
— Kinston (Carolina)■	1	2	.333	2.86	8	2	0	0	0	28 1/3	25	11	9	15	23
1990— Reno (California)■	1	4	.200	5.40	25	5	0	0	0	25	22	25	15	18	16
— Watertown (NYP)■	3	3	.500	2.48	24	0	0	0	3	54 1/3	41	22	15	29	55
1991— South Bend (Midw.)■	1	2	.333	0.51	31	0	0	0	10	35 1/3	17	4	2	19	38
— Sarasota (Fla. St.)	1	1	.500	2.72	18	0	0	0	2	39 2/3	33	16	12	20	24
1992— Birmingham (Sou.)	3	3	.500	2.14	40	0	0	0	7	71 1/3	50	19	17	20	64
— Reading (Eastern)■	0	1	.000	2.78	4	3	0	0	0	22 2/3	17	7	7	4	9
— Philadelphia (N.L.)	1	1	.500	3.27	12	0	0	0	2	22	19	10	8	6	10
1993— Colo. Springs (PCL)■	3	6	.333	6.78	37	1	0	0	8	67 2/3	90	61	51	44	57
— Colorado (N.L.)	1	3	.250	6.98	14	1	0	0	1	19 1/3	26	16	15	4	7
1994— Colo. Springs (PCL)	0	1	.000	9.10	18	0	0	0	1	29 2/3	40	33	30	22	21
— Pawtucket (Int'l)■	0	3	.000	9.15	6	4	0	0	0	20 2/3	37	22	21	9	8
— Sarasota (Fla. St.)	0	0	...	3.00	20	0	0	0	7	21	12	7	7	12	21
1995— Boston (A.L.)	0	0	...	36.00	2	0	0	0	0	1	4	4	4	2	0
— Charlotte (Int'l)■	1	1	.500	21.21	4	0	0	0	0	4 2/3	11	11	11	3	2
A.L. totals (1 year)	0	0	...	36.00	2	0	0	0	0	1	4	4	4	2	0
N.L. totals (2 years)	2	4	.333	5.01	26	1	0	0	3	41 1/3	45	26	23	10	17
Major league totals (3 years)	2	4	.333	5.74	28	1	0	0	3	42 1/3	49	30	27	12	17

SHIPLEY, CRAIG — SS/3B — PADRES

PERSONAL: Born January 7, 1963, in Sydney, Australia. . . . 6-1/190. . . . Bats right, throws right. . . . Full name: Craig Barry Shipley.
HIGH SCHOOL: Epping (Sydney, Australia).
COLLEGE: Alabama.
TRANSACTIONS/CAREER NOTES: Signed as non-drafted free agent by Los Angeles Dodgers organization (May 28, 1984). . . . On Albuquerque disabled list (May 5-June 6, 1986). . . . Traded by Dodgers to New York Mets organization for C John Gibbons (April 1, 1988). . . . On disabled list (beginning of season-August 20, 1990). . . . Selected by San Diego Padres organization from Mets organization in Rule 5 minor league draft (December 2, 1990). . . . On Las Vegas disabled list (April 11-May 2, 1991). . . . On disabled list (May 6-23, 1993 and April 25-May 20, 1994). . . . Traded by Padres with OF Phil Plantier, OF Derek Bell, P Pedro Martinez, P Doug Brocail and SS Ricky Gutierrez to Houston Astros for 3B Ken Caminiti, OF Steve Finley, SS Andujar Cedeno, 1B Robert Petagine, P Brian Williams and a player to be named later (December 28, 1994). . . . Granted free agency (December 21, 1995). . . . Signed by Padres (January 5, 1996).
STATISTICAL NOTES: Career major league grand slams: 1.

		BATTING												FIELDING			
Year Team (League)	Pos.	G	AB	R	H	2B	3B	HR	RBI	Avg.	BB	SO	SB	PO	A	E	Avg.
1984— Vero Beach (FSL)	SS	85	293	56	82	11	2	0	28	.280	52	44	18	137	216	17	.954
1985— Albuquerque (PCL)	SS	124	414	50	100	9	2	0	30	.242	22	43	24	202	367	21	.964
1986— Albuquerque (PCL)	SS	61	203	33	59	8	2	0	16	.291	11	23	6	99	173	18	.938
— Los Angeles (N.L.)	SS-2B-3B	12	27	3	3	1	0	0	4	.111	2	5	0	16	18	3	.919
1987— Albuquerque (PCL)	SS	49	139	17	31	6	1	1	15	.223	13	19	6	70	101	9	.950
— San Antonio (Tex.)	3B	33	127	14	30	5	3	2	9	.236	5	17	2	19	56	3	.962
— Los Angeles (N.L.)	SS-3B	26	35	3	9	1	0	0	2	.257	0	6	0	15	28	3	.935
1988— Jackson (Texas)■	SS	89	335	41	88	14	3	6	41	.263	24	40	6	141	266	16	.962
— Tidewater (Int'l)	2B-SS-3B	40	151	12	41	5	0	1	13	.272	4	15	0	54	110	2	.988
1989— Tidewater (Int'l)	SS-3B-2B	44	131	6	27	1	0	2	9	.206	7	22	0	48	110	6	.963
— New York (N.L.)	SS-3B	4	7	3	1	0	0	0	0	.143	0	1	0	0	4	0	1.000
1990— Tidewater (Int'l)	PH-PR	4	3	1	0	0	0	0	0	.000	0	1	0	...	...	...	...
1991— Las Vegas (PCL)■	SS-2B	65	230	27	69	9	5	5	34	.300	10	32	2	83	177	6	.977
— San Diego (N.L.)	SS-2B	37	91	6	25	3	0	1	6	.275	2	14	0	39	70	7	.940
1992— San Diego (N.L.)	SS-2B-3B	52	105	7	26	6	0	0	7	.248	2	21	1	52	74	1	.992
1993— San Diego (N.L.)	S-3-2-O	105	230	25	54	9	0	4	22	.235	10	31	12	84	121	7	.967
1994— San Diego (N.L.)	3-S-2-O-1	81	240	32	80	14	4	4	30	.333	9	28	6	65	108	9	.951
1995— Houston (N.L.)■	3-S-2-1	92	232	23	61	8	1	3	24	.263	8	28	6	43	116	3	.981
Major league totals (8 years)		409	967	102	259	42	5	12	95	.268	33	134	25	314	539	33	.963

SHUEY, PAUL — P — INDIANS

PERSONAL: Born September 16, 1970, in Lima, O. . . . 6-3/215. . . . Throws right, bats right. . . . Full name: Paul Kenneth Shuey.
HIGH SCHOOL: Millbrook (Raleigh, N.C.).
COLLEGE: North Carolina.

TRANSACTIONS/CAREER NOTES: Selected by Cleveland Indians organization in first round (second pick overall) of free-agent draft (June 1, 1992). . . . On Cleveland disabled list (June 27-July 21, 1994); included rehabilitation assignment to Charlotte (July 5-21). . . . On Cleveland disabled list (May 4-22, 1995). . . . On Buffalo disabled list (June 2-July 10, 1995).
RECORDS: Shares major league record for most strikeouts in one inning—4 (May 14, 1994, ninth inning).

Year	Team (League)	W	L	Pct.	ERA	G	GS	CG	ShO	Sv.	IP	H	R	ER	BB	SO
1992—	Columbus (S. Atl.)	5	5	.500	3.35	14	14	0	0	0	78	62	35	29	47	73
1993—	Cant./Akr. (East.)	4	8	.333	7.30	27	7	0	0	0	61 2/3	76	50	50	36	41
—	Kinston (Carolina)	1	0	1.000	4.84	15	0	0	0	0	22 1/3	29	12	12	8	27
1994—	Kinston (Carolina)	1	0	1.000	3.75	13	0	0	0	8	12	10	5	5	3	16
—	Cleveland (A.L.)	0	1	.000	8.49	14	0	0	0	5	11 2/3	14	11	11	12	16
—	Charlotte (Int'l)	2	1	.667	1.93	20	0	0	0	10	23 1/3	15	9	5	10	25
1995—	Cleveland (A.L.)	0	2	.000	4.26	7	0	0	0	0	6 1/3	5	4	3	5	5
—	Buffalo (A.A.)	1	2	.333	2.63	25	0	0	0	11	27 1/3	21	9	8	7	27
Major league totals (2 years)		0	3	.000	7.00	21	0	0	0	5	18	19	15	14	17	21

SHUMPERT, TERRY — 2B

PERSONAL: Born August 16, 1966, in Paducah, Ky. . . . 5-11/185. . . . Bats right, throws right. . . . Full name: Terrance Darnell Shumpert.
HIGH SCHOOL: Paducah (Ky.) Tilghman.
COLLEGE: Kentucky.
TRANSACTIONS/CAREER NOTES: Selected by Kansas City Royals organization in second round of free-agent draft (June 2, 1987). . . . On disabled list (July 19-August 13, 1989). . . . On Kansas City disabled list (June 3-September 10, 1990); included rehabilitation assignment to Omaha (August 7-25). . . . On Kansas City disabled list (August 7-September 7, 1992). . . . Traded by Royals to Boston Red Sox for a player to be named later (December 13, 1994). . . . Granted free agency (October 6, 1995).
STATISTICAL NOTES: Led American Association with 21 sacrifice hits in 1993. . . . Career major league grand slams: 1.

			BATTING												FIELDING			
Year	Team (League)	Pos.	G	AB	R	H	2B	3B	HR	RBI	Avg.	BB	SO	SB	PO	A	E	Avg.
1987—	Eugene (N'west)	2B	48	186	38	54	16	1	4	22	.290	27	41	16	81	107	11	.945
1988—	Appleton (Midw.)	2B-OF	114	422	64	102	*37	2	7	38	.242	56	90	36	235	266	20	.962
1989—	Omaha (A.A.)	2B	113	355	54	88	29	2	4	22	.248	25	63	23	218	295	*22	.959
1990—	Omaha (A.A.)	2B	39	153	24	39	6	4	2	12	.255	14	28	18	72	95	7	.960
—	Kansas City (A.L.)	2B-DH	32	91	7	25	6	1	0	8	.275	2	17	3	56	74	3	.977
1991—	Kansas City (A.L.)	2B	144	369	45	80	16	4	5	34	.217	30	75	17	249	368	16	.975
1992—	Kansas City (A.L.)	2B-DH-SS	36	94	6	14	5	1	1	11	.149	3	17	2	50	77	4	.969
—	Omaha (A.A.)	2B-SS	56	210	23	42	12	0	1	14	.200	13	33	3	113	154	9	.967
1993—	Omaha (A.A.)	2B	111	413	70	124	29	1	14	59	.300	41	62	*36	190	303	14	.972
—	Kansas City (A.L.)	2B	8	10	0	1	0	0	0	0	.100	2	2	1	11	11	0	1.000
1994—	Kansas City (A.L.)	2-3-DH-S	64	183	28	44	6	2	8	24	.240	13	39	18	70	129	8	.961
1995—	Boston (A.L.)■	2-3-S-DH	21	47	6	11	3	0	0	3	.234	4	13	3	21	35	2	.966
—	Pawtucket (Int'l)	3B-2B-OF	37	133	17	36	7	0	2	11	.271	14	27	10	29	69	11	.899
Major league totals (6 years)			305	794	92	175	36	8	14	80	.220	54	163	44	457	694	33	.972

SIDDALL, JOE — C — MARLINS

PERSONAL: Born October 25, 1967, in Windsor, Ont. . . . 6-1/195. . . . Bats left, throws right. . . . Full name: Joseph Todd Siddall.
HIGH SCHOOL: Assumption College (Windsor, Ont.).
COLLEGE: Central Michigan.
TRANSACTIONS/CAREER NOTES: Signed as non-drafted free agent by Montreal Expos organization (August 5, 1987). . . . Granted free agency (October 16, 1995). . . . Signed by Florida Marlins organization (November 30, 1995).
STATISTICAL NOTES: Led New York-Pennsylvania League catchers with seven double plays in 1988. . . . Led Midwest League with 19 passed balls in 1989.

			BATTING												FIELDING			
Year	Team (League)	Pos.	G	AB	R	H	2B	3B	HR	RBI	Avg.	BB	SO	SB	PO	A	E	Avg.
1988—	Jamestown (NYP)	C	53	178	18	38	5	3	1	16	.213	14	29	5	298	50	4	.989
1989—	Rockford (Midw.)	C	98	313	36	74	15	2	4	38	.236	26	56	8	656	91	12	.984
1990—	W.P. Beach (FSL)	C	106	349	29	78	12	1	0	32	.223	20	55	6	644	*105	7	*.991
1991—	Harrisburg (East.)	C	76	235	28	54	6	1	1	23	.230	23	53	8	401	36	7	.984
1992—	Harrisburg (East.)	C	95	288	26	68	12	0	2	27	.236	29	55	4	199	28	1	.996
1993—	Ottawa (Int'l)	C-O-1-3	48	136	14	29	6	0	1	16	.213	19	33	2	221	33	5	.981
—	Montreal (N.L.)	C-OF-1B	19	20	0	2	1	0	0	1	.100	1	5	0	33	5	0	1.000
1994—	Ottawa (Int'l)	C	38	110	9	19	2	1	3	13	.173	10	21	1	194	26	0	1.000
1995—	Ottawa (Int'l)	C-3B	83	248	26	53	14	2	1	23	.214	23	42	3	348	57	5	.988
—	Montreal (N.L.)	C	7	10	4	3	0	0	0	1	.300	3	3	0	14	1	2	.882
Major league totals (2 years)			26	30	4	5	1	0	0	2	.167	4	8	0	47	6	2	.964

SIERRA, RUBEN — OF — YANKEES

PERSONAL: Born October 6, 1965, in Rio Piedras, Puerto Rico. . . . 6-1/200. . . . Bats both, throws right. . . . Full name: Ruben Angel Garcia Sierra.
HIGH SCHOOL: Dr. Secario Rosario (Rio Piedras, Puerto Rico).
TRANSACTIONS/CAREER NOTES: Signed as non-drafted free agent by Texas Rangers organization (November 21, 1982). . . . Traded by Rangers with P Jeff Russell, P Bobby Witt and cash to Oakland Athletics for OF Jose Canseco (August 31, 1992). . . . Granted free agency (October 26, 1992). . . . Re-signed by A's (December 21, 1992). . . . On Oakland disabled list (July 7-22, 1995). . . . Traded by A's with P Jason Beverlin to New York Yankees for OF/DH Danny Tartabull (July 28, 1995).
HONORS: Named A.L. Player of the Year by The Sporting News (1989). . . . Named outfielder on The Sporting News A.L. All-Star team (1989). . . . Named outfielder on The Sporting News A.L. Silver Slugger team (1989).

STATISTICAL NOTES: Switch-hit home runs in one game (September 13, 1986; August 27, 1988; June 8, 1989; and June 7, 1994). . . . Led A.L. with 12 sacrifice flies in 1987. . . . Led A.L. outfielders with six double plays in 1987. . . . Led A.L. with 344 total bases and .543 slugging percentage in 1989. . . . Career major league grand slams: 3.
MISCELLANEOUS: Batted righthanded only (1983).

S

		BATTING												FIELDING			
Year Team (League)	Pos.	G	AB	R	H	2B	3B	HR	RBI	Avg.	BB	SO	SB	PO	A	E	Avg.
1983—GC Rangers (GCL)	OF	48	182	26	44	7	3	1	26	.242	16	38	3	67	6	4	.948
1984—Burlington (Midw.)	OF	•138	482	55	127	33	5	6	75	.263	49	97	13	239	18	*20	.928
1985—Tulsa (Texas)	OF	*137	*545	63	138	34	*8	13	74	.253	35	111	22	234	12	*15	.943
1986—Okla. City (A.A.)	OF	46	189	31	56	11	2	9	41	.296	15	27	8	114	4	2	.983
—Texas (A.L.)	OF-DH	113	382	50	101	13	10	16	55	.264	22	65	7	200	7	6	.972
1987—Texas (A.L.)	OF	158	*643	97	169	35	4	30	109	.263	39	114	16	272	•17	11	.963
1988—Texas (A.L.)	OF-DH	156	615	77	156	32	2	23	91	.254	44	91	18	310	11	7	.979
1989—Texas (A.L.)	OF	•162	634	101	194	35	*14	29	*119	.306	43	82	8	313	13	9	.973
1990—Texas (A.L.)	OF-DH	159	608	70	170	37	2	16	96	.280	49	86	9	283	7	10	.967
1991—Texas (A.L.)	OF	161	661	110	203	44	5	25	116	.307	56	91	16	305	15	7	.979
1992—Texas (A.L.)	OF-DH	124	500	66	139	30	6	14	70	.278	31	59	12	224	6	7	.970
—Oakland (A.L.)■	OF-DH	27	101	17	28	4	1	3	17	.277	14	9	2	59	0	0	1.000
1993—Oakland (A.L.)	OF-DH	158	630	77	147	23	5	22	101	.233	52	97	25	291	9	7	.977
1994—Oakland (A.L.)	OF-DH	110	426	71	114	21	1	23	92	.268	23	64	8	155	8	*9	.948
1995—Oakland (A.L.)	OF-DH	70	264	40	70	17	0	12	42	.265	24	42	4	89	1	4	.957
—New York (A.L.)■	DH-OF	56	215	33	56	15	0	7	44	.260	22	34	1	18	1	1	.950
Major league totals (10 years)		1454	5679	809	1547	306	50	220	952	.272	419	834	126	2519	95	78	.971

DIVISION SERIES RECORD

		BATTING												FIELDING			
Year Team (League)	Pos.	G	AB	R	H	2B	3B	HR	RBI	Avg.	BB	SO	SB	PO	A	E	Avg.
1995—New York (A.L.)	DH	5	23	2	4	2	0	2	5	.174	2	7	0	...	...	...	...

CHAMPIONSHIP SERIES RECORD

		BATTING												FIELDING			
Year Team (League)	Pos.	G	AB	R	H	2B	3B	HR	RBI	Avg.	BB	SO	SB	PO	A	E	Avg.
1992—Oakland (A.L.)	OF	6	24	4	8	2	1	1	7	.333	2	1	1	12	0	0	1.000

ALL-STAR GAME RECORD

		BATTING											FIELDING			
Year League	Pos.	AB	R	H	2B	3B	HR	RBI	Avg.	BB	SO	SB	PO	A	E	Avg.
1989—American	OF	3	1	2	0	0	0	1	.667	0	0	0	1	0	0	1.000
1991—American	OF	2	0	0	0	0	0	0	.000	0	2	0	0	0	0	...
1992—American	OF	2	2	1	0	0	1	2	.500	0	0	0	1	0	0	1.000
1994—American	OF	2	0	1	0	0	0	0	.500	0	0	0	1	0	0	1.000
All-Star Game totals (4 years)		9	3	4	0	0	1	3	.444	0	2	0	3	0	0	1.000

SIEVERT, MARK — P — BLUE JAYS

PERSONAL: Born February 16, 1973, in Janesville, Wis. . . . 6-4/195. . . . Throws right, bats left. . . . Full name: Mark Andrew Sievert.
HIGH SCHOOL: Northwestern Prep (Watertown, Wis.).
TRANSACTIONS/CAREER NOTES: Signed as non-drafted free agent by Toronto Blue Jays organization (August 24, 1991). . . . On disabled list (June 18, 1992-remainder of season).
STATISTICAL NOTES: Pitched 2-0 no-hit victory against Utica (August 5, 1994, second game).

Year Team (League)	W	L	Pct.	ERA	G	GS	CG	ShO	Sv.	IP	H	R	ER	BB	SO
1992—							Did not pitch.								
1993—Medicine Hat (Pio.)	6	3	.667	5.00	15	15	0	0	0	63	63	40	35	30	52
1994—St. Cathar. (NYP)	7	4	.636	3.09	14	14	1	1	1	81 2/3	59	30	28	28	82
1995—Hagerstown (S. Atl.)	12	6	.667	2.91	27	27	3	0	0	160 2/3	126	59	52	46	140

SILVA, JOSE — P — BLUE JAYS

PERSONAL: Born December 19, 1973, in Tijuana, Mexico. . . . 6-5/210. . . . Throws right, bats right. . . . Full name: Jose Leonel Silva.
HIGH SCHOOL: Hilltop (Chula Vista, Calif.).
TRANSACTIONS/CAREER NOTES: Selected by Toronto Blue Jays organization in sixth round of free-agent draft (June 3, 1991). . . . On disabled list (April 6-August 17, 1995).

Year Team (League)	W	L	Pct.	ERA	G	GS	CG	ShO	Sv.	IP	H	R	ER	BB	SO
1992—GC Blue Jays (GCL)	6	4	.600	2.28	12	•12	0	0	0	59 1/3	42	23	15	18	78
1993—Hagerstown (S. Atl.)	12	5	.706	2.52	24	24	0	0	0	142 2/3	103	50	40	62	161
1994—Dunedin (Fla. St.)	0	2	.000	3.77	8	7	0	0	0	43	41	32	18	24	41
—Knoxville (South.)	4	8	.333	4.14	16	16	1	1	0	91 1/3	89	47	42	31	71
1995—Knoxville (South.)	0	0	...	9.00	3	0	0	0	0	2	3	2	2	6	2

SILVESTRI, DAVE — SS — EXPOS

PERSONAL: Born September 29, 1967, in St. Louis. . . . 6-0/196. . . . Bats right, throws right. . . . Full name: David Joseph Silvestri.
HIGH SCHOOL: Parkway Central (St. Louis).
COLLEGE: Missouri.
TRANSACTIONS/CAREER NOTES: Selected by Houston Astros in second round of free-agent draft (June 1, 1988); pick received as compensation for New York Yankees signing Type B free-agent OF Jose Cruz. . . . Traded by Astros organization with a player to be named later to Yankees organization for IF Orlando Miller (March 13, 1990); Yankees acquired P Daven Bond to complete deal (June 11, 1990). . . . On New York disabled list (May 13-30, 1995). . . . Traded by Yankees to Montreal Expos for OF Tyrone Horne (July 16, 1995).

STATISTICAL NOTES: Led Florida State League shortstops with 221 putouts, 473 assists, 726 total chances and 93 double plays in 1989. . . . Led Carolina League shortstops with 622 total chances and 96 double plays in 1990. . . . Led Eastern League shortstops with 84 double plays in 1991.
MISCELLANEOUS: Member of 1988 U.S. Olympic baseball team.

					BATTING										FIELDING			
Year Team (League)	**Pos.**	**G**	**AB**	**R**	**H**	**2B**	**3B**	**HR**	**RBI**	**Avg.**	**BB**	**SO**	**SB**	**PO**	**A**	**E**	**Avg.**
1989—Osceola (Fla. St.)	SS-1B	129	437	67	111	20	1	2	50	.254	68	72	28	†238	†475	32	.957
1990—Prin. William (Car.)■	SS	131	465	74	120	30	7	5	56	.258	77	90	37	218	*382	22	*.965
—Alb./Colon. (East.)	SS	2	7	0	2	0	0	0	2	.286	0	1	0	3	5	1	.889
1991—Alb./Colon. (East.)	SS	*140	512	*97	134	31	8	19	83	.262	83	126	20	218	*362	•32	.948
1992—Columbus (Int'l)	SS	118	420	83	117	25	5	13	73	.279	58	110	19	*195	265	11	*.977
—New York (A.L.)	SS	7	13	3	4	0	2	0	1	.308	0	3	0	4	12	2	.889
1993—Columbus (Int'l)	SS-3B-OF	120	428	76	115	26	4	20	65	.269	68	127	6	183	299	16	.968
—New York (A.L.)	SS-3B	7	21	4	6	1	0	1	4	.286	5	3	0	9	20	3	.906
1994—Columbus (Int'l)	2-S-3-O-1	114	394	72	99	19	2	25	83	.251	*83	129	18	174	235	19	.956
—New York (A.L.)	2B-3B-SS	12	18	3	2	0	1	1	2	.111	4	9	0	14	16	1	.968
1995—New York (A.L.)	2-DH-1-S	17	21	4	2	0	0	1	4	.095	4	9	0	28	13	0	1.000
—Montreal (N.L.)■	S-3-1-2-O	39	72	12	19	6	0	2	7	.264	9	27	2	34	36	1	.986
American League totals (4 years)		43	73	14	14	1	3	3	11	.192	13	24	0	55	61	6	.951
National League totals (1 year)		39	72	12	19	6	0	2	7	.264	9	27	2	34	36	1	.986
Major league totals (4 years)		82	145	26	33	7	3	5	18	.228	22	51	2	89	97	7	.964

SIMAS, BILL — P — WHITE SOX

PERSONAL: Born November 28, 1971, in Hanford, Calif. . . . 6-3/220. . . . Throws right, bats left. . . . Full name: William Anthony Simas Jr.
HIGH SCHOOL: St. Joseph (Calif.).
COLLEGE: Fresno (Calif.) City College.
TRANSACTIONS/CAREER NOTES: Selected by California Angels organization in sixth round of free-agent draft (June 1, 1992). . . . Traded by Angels with P Andrew Lorraine, P John Snyder and OF McKay Christensen to Chicago White Sox for P Jim Abbott and P Tim Fortugno (July 27, 1995).

Year Team (League)	**W**	**L**	**Pct.**	**ERA**	**G**	**GS**	**CG**	**ShO**	**Sv.**	**IP**	**H**	**R**	**ER**	**BB**	**SO**
1992—Boise (Northwest)	6	5	.545	3.95	14	12	0	0	1	70 2/3	82	44	31	29	39
1993—Ced. Rap. (Midw.)	5	8	.385	4.95	35	6	0	0	6	80	93	60	44	36	62
1994—Lake Elsinore (California)	5	2	.714	2.11	37	0	0	0	13	47	44	17	11	10	34
—Midland (Texas)	2	0	1.000	0.59	13	0	0	0	6	15 1/3	5	1	1	2	12
1995—Vancouver (PCL)	6	3	.667	3.55	30	0	0	0	6	38	44	19	15	14	44
—Nashville (A.A.)■	1	1	.500	3.86	7	0	0	0	0	11 2/3	12	5	5	3	12
—Chicago (A.L.)	1	1	.500	2.57	14	0	0	0	0	14	15	5	4	10	16
Major league totals (1 year)	1	1	.500	2.57	14	0	0	0	0	14	15	5	4	10	16

SIMMS, MIKE — OF — ASTROS

PERSONAL: Born January 12, 1967, in Orange, Calif. . . . 6-4/185. . . . Bats right, throws right. . . . Full name: Michael Howard Simms.
HIGH SCHOOL: Esperanza (Calif.).
TRANSACTIONS/CAREER NOTES: Selected by Houston Astros organization in sixth round of free-agent draft (June 3, 1985). . . . On disabled list (May 11-28, 1989). . . . On Tucson disabled list (July 31-August 16, 1992). . . . Granted free agency (March 30, 1993). . . . Signed by San Diego Padres organization (April 7, 1993). . . . Granted free agency (October 15, 1993). . . . Signed by Pittsburgh Pirates (December 15, 1993). . . . Released by Buffalo, Pirates organization (April 28, 1994). . . . Signed by Tucson (May 2, 1994). . . . Granted free agency (October 15, 1994).
STATISTICAL NOTES: Led South Atlantic League with 264 total bases in 1987. . . . Led South Atlantic League first basemen with 1,089 putouts, 19 errors and 1,158 total chances in 1987. . . . Led Pacific Coast League first basemen with 19 errors in 1990.

					BATTING										FIELDING			
Year Team (League)	**Pos.**	**G**	**AB**	**R**	**H**	**2B**	**3B**	**HR**	**RBI**	**Avg.**	**BB**	**SO**	**SB**	**PO**	**A**	**E**	**Avg.**
1985—GC Astros (GCL)	1B	21	70	10	19	2	1	3	18	.271	6	26	0	186	7	5	.975
1986—GC Astros (GCL)	1B	54	181	33	47	14	1	4	37	.260	22	48	2	433	28	7	.985
1987—Asheville (S. Atl.)	1B-3B	133	469	93	128	19	0	*39	100	.273	73	*167	7	†1089	52	†19	.984
1988—Osceola (Fla. St.)	1B	123	428	63	104	19	1	16	73	.243	76	130	9	1143	41	22	.982
1989—Columbus (South.)	1B	109	378	64	97	21	3	20	81	.257	66	110	12	938	44	10	.990
1990—Tucson (PCL)	1B-3B-OF	124	421	75	115	34	5	13	72	.273	74	*135	3	1013	75	†19	.983
—Houston (N.L.)	1B	12	13	3	4	1	0	1	2	.308	0	4	0	20	1	0	1.000
1991—Tucson (PCL)	OF-1B	85	297	53	73	20	2	15	59	.246	36	94	2	325	25	8	.978
—Houston (N.L.)	OF	49	123	18	25	5	0	3	16	.203	18	38	1	44	4	6	.889
1992—Tucson (PCL)	OF-1B	116	404	73	114	22	6	11	75	.282	61	107	7	476	29	11	.979
—Houston (N.L.)	OF-1B	15	24	1	6	1	0	1	3	.250	2	9	0	10	2	0	1.000
1993—Las Vegas (PCL)■	1-O-3-P	129	414	74	111	25	2	24	80	.268	67	114	1	774	46	13	.984
1994—Buffalo (A.A.)■	OF	18	55	10	13	5	0	4	8	.236	4	13	0	26	0	0	1.000
—Tucson (PCL)■	1B-OF-3B	100	373	76	107	34	6	20	85	.287	51	79	9	555	32	9	.985
—Houston (N.L.)	OF	6	12	1	1	1	0	0	0	.083	0	5	1	6	0	1	.857
1995—Houston (N.L.)	1B-OF	50	121	14	31	4	0	9	24	.256	13	28	1	221	17	1	.996
—Tucson (PCL)	1B-OF	85	319	56	94	26	8	13	66	.295	35	65	10	424	30	8	.983
Major league totals (5 years)		132	293	37	67	12	0	14	45	.229	33	84	3	301	24	8	.976

RECORD AS PITCHER

Year Team (League)	**W**	**L**	**Pct.**	**ERA**	**G**	**GS**	**CG**	**ShO**	**Sv.**	**IP**	**H**	**R**	**ER**	**BB**	**SO**
1993—Las Vegas (PCL)	0	0	. . .	0.00	1	0	0	0	0	2/3	1	0	0	0	0

SINGLETON, CHRIS — OF — GIANTS

PERSONAL: Born August 15, 1972, in Martinez, Calif. . . . 6-2/195. . . . Bats left, throws left. . . . Full name: Christopher V. Singleton.
HIGH SCHOOL: Pinole (Calif.) Valley.

COLLEGE: Nevada.
TRANSACTIONS/CAREER NOTES: Selected by San Francisco Giants organization in second round of free-agent draft (June 3, 1993).

			BATTING												FIELDING			
Year	Team (League)	Pos.	G	AB	R	H	2B	3B	HR	RBI	Avg.	BB	SO	SB	PO	A	E	Avg.
1993—	Everett (N'west)	OF	58	219	39	58	14	4	3	18	.265	18	46	14	106	6	3	.974
1994—	San Jose (Calif.)	OF	113	425	51	106	17	5	2	49	.249	27	62	19	248	10	13	.952
1995—	San Jose (Calif.)	OF	94	405	55	112	13	5	2	31	.277	17	49	33	142	6	7	.955

S

SINGLETON, DUANE — OF — TIGERS

PERSONAL: Born August 6, 1972, in Staten Island, N.Y. . . . 6-1/177. . . . Bats left, throws right. . . . Full name: Duane Earl Singleton.
HIGH SCHOOL: McKee Vocational & Technical (Staten Island, N.Y.).
TRANSACTIONS/CAREER NOTES: Selected by Milwaukee Brewers organization in fifth round of free-agent draft (June 4, 1990). . . . Loaned by Brewers organization to Salinas, independent (June 7-July 3, 1992). . . . On El Paso disabled list (June 20-27, 1994). . . . On New Orleans suspended list (July 6-8, 1995). . . . Traded by Brewers to Detroit Tigers for P Henry Santos (January 28, 1996).
STATISTICAL NOTES: Led Arizona League outfielders with two double plays in 1990. . . . Led California League outfielders with 20 assists in 1992. . . . Led California League outfielders with five double plays in 1992. . . . Tied for American Association lead in caught stealing with 15 in 1995.

			BATTING												FIELDING			
Year	Team (League)	Pos.	G	AB	R	H	2B	3B	HR	RBI	Avg.	BB	SO	SB	PO	A	E	Avg.
1990—	Ariz. Brewers (Ariz.)	OF	45	126	30	30	6	1	1	12	.238	*43	37	7	67	6	3	.961
1991—	Beloit (Midwest)	OF	101	388	57	112	13	7	3	44	.289	40	57	42	155	*25	6	.968
1992—	Salinas (Calif.)■	OF	19	72	6	22	5	2	1	8	.306	6	11	4	31	3	0	1.000
—	Stockton (Calif.)■	OF	97	389	73	112	15	10	5	51	.288	39	66	34	196	§17	9	.959
1993—	El Paso (Texas)	OF	125	456	52	105	21	6	2	61	.230	34	90	23	288	*20	8	.975
1994—	El Paso (Texas)	OF	39	139	25	40	11	3	2	24	.288	19	33	10	65	5	3	.959
—	Stockton (Calif.)	OF	38	134	31	39	6	0	4	13	.291	18	23	15	87	5	2	.979
—	New Orleans (A.A.)	OF	41	133	26	37	4	5	0	14	.278	18	26	6	114	2	2	.983
—	Milwaukee (A.L.)	OF	2	0	0	0	0	0	0	0	...	0	0	0	2	0	0	1.000
1995—	New Orleans (A.A.)	OF-1B-3B	106	355	48	95	10	4	4	29	.268	39	63	31	168	13	4	.978
—	Milwaukee (A.L.)	OF	13	31	0	2	0	0	0	0	.065	1	10	1	22	1	0	1.000
Major league totals (2 years)			15	31	0	2	0	0	0	0	.065	1	10	1	24	1	0	1.000

SIROTKA, MIKE — P — WHITE SOX

PERSONAL: Born May 13, 1971, in Chicago. . . . 6-1/200. . . . Throws left, bats left. . . . Full name: Michael R. Sirotka.
HIGH SCHOOL: Westfield (Houston).
COLLEGE: Louisiana State.
TRANSACTIONS/CAREER NOTES: Selected by Chicago White Sox organization in 15th round of free-agent draft (June 3, 1993). . . . On Hickory disabled list (July 1-28, 1993). . . . On South Bend temporarily inactive list (August 27-October 4, 1993).

Year	Team (League)	W	L	Pct.	ERA	G	GS	CG	ShO	Sv.	IP	H	R	ER	BB	SO
1993—	GC White Sox (GCL)	0	0	...	0.00	3	0	0	0	0	5	4	1	0	2	8
—	South Bend (Midw.)	0	1	.000	6.10	7	1	0	0	0	10 1/3	12	8	7	6	12
1994—	South Bend (Midw.)	12	9	.571	3.07	27	27	8	2	0	196 2/3	183	99	67	56	173
1995—	Birmingham (Sou.)	7	6	.538	3.20	16	16	1	0	0	101 1/3	95	42	36	22	79
—	Chicago (A.L.)	1	2	.333	4.19	6	6	0	0	0	34 1/3	39	16	16	17	19
—	Nashville (A.A.)	1	5	.167	2.83	8	8	0	0	0	54	51	21	17	13	34
Major league totals (1 year)		1	2	.333	4.19	6	6	0	0	0	34 1/3	39	16	16	17	19

SLAUGHT, DON — C — REDS

PERSONAL: Born September 11, 1958, in Long Beach, Calif. . . . 6-1/185. . . . Bats right, throws right. . . . Full name: Donald Martin Slaught.
HIGH SCHOOL: Rolling Hills (Palos Verdes, Calif.).
JUNIOR COLLEGE: El Camino College (Calif.).
COLLEGE: UCLA (bachelor of science degree in economics, 1983).
TRANSACTIONS/CAREER NOTES: Selected by Milwaukee Brewers organization in 19th round of free-agent draft (June 5, 1979); did not sign. . . . Selected by Kansas City Royals organization in seventh round of free-agent draft (June 3, 1980). . . . On Omaha disabled list (August 16-September 29, 1981 and April 21-May 15, 1982). . . . On disabled list (May 16-June 1, 1983). . . . Traded by Royals to Texas Rangers as part of a six-player, four-team deal in which Royals acquired C Jim Sundberg from Brewers, Mets organization acquired P Frank Wills from Royals, Brewers acquired P Danny Darwin and a player to be named later from Rangers and P Tim Leary from Mets (January 18, 1985); Brewers organization acquired C Bill Hance from Rangers to complete deal (January 30, 1985). . . . On disabled list (August 9-26, 1985). . . . On Texas disabled list (May 18-July 4, 1986); included rehabilitation assignment to Oklahoma City (July 1-4). . . . Traded by Rangers to New York Yankees for a player to be named later (November 2, 1987); Rangers acquired P Brad Arnsberg to complete deal (November 10, 1987). . . . On disabled list (May 15-June 20, 1988). . . . Traded by Yankees to Pittsburgh Pirates for P Jeff D. Robinson and P Willie Smith (December 4, 1989). . . . On disabled list (June 30-July 16, 1990). . . . Granted free agency (November 5, 1990). . . . Re-signed by Pirates (December 19, 1990). . . . On disabled list (July 22-August 13, 1991). . . . On Pittsburgh disabled list (March 28-April 23, 1992); included rehabilitation assignment to Buffalo (April 17-20). . . . On Pittsburgh disabled list (May 2-June 19 and July 21-August 31, 1995); included rehabilitation assignments to Gulf Coast Pirates (May 31-June 8) and Carolina (June 15-18). . . . Granted free agency (November 1, 1995). . . . Signed by Cincinnati Reds organization (January 2, 1996).
STATISTICAL NOTES: Career major league grand slams: 1.

			BATTING												FIELDING			
Year	Team (League)	Pos.	G	AB	R	H	2B	3B	HR	RBI	Avg.	BB	SO	SB	PO	A	E	Avg.
1980—	Fort Myers (FSL)	C	50	176	13	46	9	0	2	16	.261	16	11	3	175	34	4	.981
1981—	Jacksonv. (South.)	C-1B	96	379	45	127	21	2	6	44	.335	32	44	13	482	61	9	.984
—	Omaha (A.A.)	C	22	71	10	21	4	0	2	8	.296	4	7	3	91	7	3	.970
1982—	Omaha (A.A.)	C	53	206	29	55	10	1	4	16	.267	7	20	6	216	25	5	.980

Year	Team (League)	Pos.	G	AB	R	H	2B	3B	HR	RBI	Avg.	BB	SO	SB	PO	A	E	Avg.
			BATTING												FIELDING			
	—Kansas City (A.L.)	C	43	115	14	32	6	0	3	8	.278	9	12	0	156	7	1	.994
1983	—Kansas City (A.L.)	C-DH	83	276	21	86	13	4	0	28	.312	11	27	3	299	18	12	.964
1984	—Kansas City (A.L.)	C-DH	124	409	48	108	27	4	4	42	.264	20	55	0	547	44	11	.982
1985	—Texas (A.L.)■	C	102	343	34	96	17	4	8	35	.280	20	41	5	550	33	6	.990
1986	—Texas (A.L.)	C-DH	95	314	39	83	17	1	13	46	.264	16	59	3	533	40	4	.993
	—Okla. City (A.A.)	C	3	12	2	4	1	0	0	1	.333	0	3	0	6	1	0	1.000
1987	—Texas (A.L.)	C-DH	95	237	25	53	15	2	8	16	.224	24	51	0	429	39	7	.985
1988	—New York (A.L.)■	C-DH	97	322	33	91	25	1	9	43	.283	24	54	1	496	24	•11	.979
1989	—New York (A.L.)	C-DH	117	350	34	88	21	3	5	38	.251	30	57	1	493	44	5	.991
1990	—Pittsburgh (N.L.)■	C	84	230	27	69	18	3	4	29	.300	27	27	0	345	36	8	.979
1991	—Pittsburgh (N.L.)	C-3B	77	220	19	65	17	1	1	29	.295	21	32	1	338	31	5	.987
1992	—Buffalo (A.A.)	C	2	6	1	2	0	0	0	1	.333	0	0	0	15	3	0	1.000
	—Pittsburgh (N.L.)	C	87	255	26	88	17	3	4	37	.345	17	23	2	365	35	5	.988
1993	—Pittsburgh (N.L.)	C	116	377	34	113	19	2	10	55	.300	29	56	2	539	51	4	.993
1994	—Pittsburgh (N.L.)	C	76	240	21	69	7	0	2	21	.288	34	31	0	425	36	3	.994
1995	—Pittsburgh (N.L.)	C	35	112	13	34	6	0	0	13	.304	9	8	0	220	9	1	.996
	—Carolina (South.)	C	3	12	1	3	1	0	0	1	.250	0	3	0	24	1	0	1.000
American League totals (8 years)			756	2366	248	637	141	19	50	256	.269	154	356	13	3503	249	57	.985
National League totals (6 years)			475	1434	140	438	84	9	21	184	.305	137	177	5	2232	198	26	.989
Major league totals (14 years)			1231	3800	388	1075	225	28	71	440	.283	291	533	18	5735	447	83	.987

CHAMPIONSHIP SERIES RECORD

Year	Team (League)	Pos.	G	AB	R	H	2B	3B	HR	RBI	Avg.	BB	SO	SB	PO	A	E	Avg.
			BATTING												FIELDING			
1984	—Kansas City (A.L.)	C	3	11	0	4	0	0	0	0	.364	0	0	0	17	0	3	.850
1990	—Pittsburgh (N.L.)	C	4	11	0	1	1	0	0	1	.091	2	3	0	22	1	1	.958
1991	—Pittsburgh (N.L.)	C-PH	6	17	0	4	0	0	0	1	.235	1	4	0	30	5	0	1.000
1992	—Pittsburgh (N.L.)	C-PH	5	12	5	4	1	0	1	5	.333	6	3	0	17	1	0	1.000
Championship series totals (4 years)			18	51	5	13	2	0	1	7	.255	9	10	0	86	7	4	.959

SLOCUMB, HEATHCLIFF — P — PHILLIES

PERSONAL: Born June 7, 1966, in Jamaica, N.Y. . . . 6-3/220. . . . Throws right, bats right.
HIGH SCHOOL: John Bowne (Flushing, N.Y.).
TRANSACTIONS/CAREER NOTES: Signed as non-drafted free agent by New York Mets organization (July 10, 1984). . . . Selected by Chicago Cubs organization from Mets organization in Rule 5 minor league draft (December 9, 1986). . . . Traded by Cubs to Cleveland Indians for SS Jose Hernandez (June 1, 1993). . . . Traded by Indians to Philadelphia Phillies for OF Ruben Amaro (November 2, 1993).
STATISTICAL NOTES: Led Carolina League with 19 wild pitches in 1988.

Year	Team (League)	W	L	Pct.	ERA	G	GS	CG	ShO	Sv.	IP	H	R	ER	BB	SO
1984	—Kingsport (Appal.)	0	0	...	0.00	1	0	0	0	0	1/3	0	1	0	1	0
	—Little Falls (NYP)	0	0	...	11.00	4	1	0	0	0	9	8	11	11	16	10
1985	—Kingsport (Appal.)	3	2	.600	3.78	11	9	1	0	0	52 1/3	47	32	22	31	29
1986	—Little Falls (NYP)	3	1	.750	1.65	25	0	0	0	1	43 2/3	24	17	8	36	41
1987	—Winst.-Salem (Car.)■	1	2	.333	6.26	9	4	0	0	0	27 1/3	26	25	19	26	27
	—Peoria (Midwest)	10	4	.714	2.60	16	16	3	1	0	103 2/3	97	44	30	42	81
1988	—Winst.-Salem (Car.)	6	6	.500	4.96	25	19	2	1	1	119 2/3	122	75	66	90	78
1989	—Peoria (Midwest)	5	3	.625	1.78	49	0	0	0	22	55 2/3	31	16	11	33	52
1990	—Charlotte (South.)	3	1	.750	2.15	43	0	0	0	12	50 1/3	50	20	12	32	37
	—Iowa (Am. Assoc.)	3	2	.600	2.00	20	0	0	0	1	27	16	10	6	18	21
1991	—Chicago (N.L.)	2	1	.667	3.45	52	0	0	0	1	62 2/3	53	29	24	30	34
	—Iowa (Am. Assoc.)	1	0	1.000	4.05	12	0	0	0	1	13 1/3	10	8	6	6	9
1992	—Chicago (N.L.)	0	3	.000	6.50	30	0	0	0	1	36	52	27	26	21	27
	—Iowa (Am. Assoc.)	1	3	.250	2.59	36	1	0	0	7	41 2/3	36	13	12	16	47
1993	—Iowa (Am. Assoc.)	1	0	1.000	1.50	10	0	0	0	7	12	7	2	2	8	10
	—Chicago (N.L.)	1	0	1.000	3.38	10	0	0	0	0	10 2/3	7	5	4	4	4
	—Cleveland (A.L.)■	3	1	.750	4.28	20	0	0	0	0	27 1/3	28	14	13	16	18
	—Charlotte (Int'l)	3	2	.600	3.56	23	0	0	0	1	30 1/3	25	14	12	11	25
1994	—Philadelphia (N.L.)■	5	1	.833	2.86	52	0	0	0	0	72 1/3	75	32	23	28	58
1995	—Philadelphia (N.L.)	5	6	.455	2.89	61	0	0	0	32	65 1/3	64	26	21	35	63
A.L. totals (1 year)		3	1	.750	4.28	20	0	0	0	0	27 1/3	28	14	13	16	18
N.L. totals (5 years)		13	11	.542	3.57	205	0	0	0	34	247	251	119	98	118	186
Major league totals (5 years)		16	12	.571	3.64	225	0	0	0	34	274 1/3	279	133	111	134	204

ALL-STAR GAME RECORD

Year	League	W	L	Pct.	ERA	GS	CG	ShO	Sv.	IP	H	R	ER	BB	SO
1995	—National	1	0	1.000	0.00	0	0	0	0	1	1	0	0	0	2

SLUSARSKI, JOE — P

PERSONAL: Born December 19, 1966, in Indianapolis. . . . 6-4/195. . . . Throws right, bats right. . . . Full name: Joseph Andrew Slusarski.
HIGH SCHOOL: Griffin (Springfield, Ill.).
JUNIOR COLLEGE: Lincoln Land Community College (Ill.).
COLLEGE: New Orleans.
TRANSACTIONS/CAREER NOTES: Selected by Seattle Mariners organization in sixth round of free-agent draft (June 2, 1987); did not sign. . . . Selected by Oakland Athletics organization in second round of free-agent draft (June 1, 1988). . . . On Huntsville disabled list (May 18-25, 1990). . . . On Tacoma disabled list (August 2-11, 1992 and July 22-August 11, 1993). . . . Released by Tacoma (May 11, 1994). . . . Signed by Reading, Philadelphia Phillies organization (June 3, 1994). . . . Granted free agency (October 15, 1994). . . . Signed by Cleveland Indians organization (January 20, 1995). . . . Released by Indians organization (April 24, 1995). . . . Signed by New Orleans, Milwaukee

Brewers organization (May 19, 1995). . . . Granted free agency (October 16, 1995).
STATISTICAL NOTES: Led California League with 15 home runs allowed in 1989.
MISCELLANEOUS: Member of 1988 U.S. Olympic baseball team.

Year	Team (League)	W	L	Pct.	ERA	G	GS	CG	ShO	Sv.	IP	H	R	ER	BB	SO
1989—	Modesto (Calif.)	•13	10	.565	3.18	27	27	4	1	0	184	155	78	65	50	160
1990—	Huntsville (South.)	6	8	.429	4.47	17	17	2	0	0	108 2/3	114	65	54	35	75
—	Tacoma (PCL)	4	2	.667	3.40	9	9	0	0	0	55 2/3	54	24	21	22	37
1991—	Oakland (A.L.)	5	7	.417	5.27	20	19	1	0	0	109 1/3	121	69	64	52	60
—	Tacoma (PCL)	4	2	.667	2.72	7	7	0	0	0	46 1/3	42	20	14	10	25
1992—	Oakland (A.L.)	5	5	.500	5.45	15	14	0	0	0	76	85	52	46	27	38
—	Tacoma (PCL)	2	4	.333	3.77	11	10	0	0	0	57 1/3	67	30	24	18	26
1993—	Tacoma (PCL)	7	5	.583	4.76	24	21	1	1	0	113 1/3	133	67	60	40	61
—	Oakland (A.L.)	0	0	...	5.19	2	1	0	0	0	8 2/3	9	5	5	11	1
1994—	Tacoma (PCL)	2	3	.400	6.03	7	7	0	0	0	37 1/3	45	28	25	11	24
—	Reading (Eastern)■	1	2	.333	4.63	5	4	0	0	0	23 1/3	25	15	12	5	17
—	Scran./W.B. (Int'l)	2	3	.400	7.82	10	4	0	0	0	38	50	36	33	10	29
1995—	Buffalo (A.A.)■	1	1	.500	6.32	4	2	0	0	0	15 2/3	18	12	11	4	9
—	New Orleans (A.A.)■	1	1	.500	1.12	33	0	0	0	11	48 1/3	37	10	6	11	30
—	Milwaukee (A.L.)	1	1	.500	5.40	12	0	0	0	0	15	21	11	9	6	6
Major league totals (4 years)		11	13	.458	5.34	49	34	1	0	0	209	236	137	124	96	105

SMALL, AARON — P — MARINERS

PERSONAL: Born November 23, 1971, in Oxnard, Calif. . . . 6-5/208. . . . Throws right, bats right. . . . Full name: Aaron James Small.
HIGH SCHOOL: South Hills (Covina, Calif.).
TRANSACTIONS/CAREER NOTES: Selected by Toronto Blue Jays organization in 22nd round of free-agent draft (June 5, 1989). . . . Traded by Blue Jays to Florida Marlins for a player to be named later (April 26, 1995); Blue Jays acquired P Ernie Delgado to complete deal (September 19, 1995). . . . On Charlotte disabled list (May 3-June 14, 1995). . . . Claimed on waivers by Seattle Mariners (January 23, 1996).

Year	Team (League)	W	L	Pct.	ERA	G	GS	CG	ShO	Sv.	IP	H	R	ER	BB	SO
1989—	Medicine Hat (Pio.)	1	7	.125	5.86	15	14	0	0	0	70 2/3	80	55	46	31	40
1990—	Myrtle Beach (SAL)	9	9	.500	2.80	27	27	1	0	0	147 2/3	150	72	46	56	96
1991—	Dunedin (Fla. St.)	8	7	.533	2.73	24	23	1	0	0	148 1/3	129	51	45	42	92
1992—	Knoxville (South.)	5	12	.294	5.27	27	24	2	1	0	135	152	94	79	61	79
1993—	Knoxville (South.)	4	4	.500	3.39	48	9	0	0	16	93	99	44	35	40	44
1994—	Knoxville (South.)	5	5	.500	2.99	29	11	1	1	5	96 1/3	92	37	32	38	75
—	Syracuse (Int'l)	3	2	.600	2.22	13	0	0	0	0	24 1/3	19	8	6	9	15
—	Toronto (A.L.)	0	0	...	9.00	1	0	0	0	0	2	5	2	2	2	0
1995—	Syracuse (Int'l)	0	0	...	5.40	1	0	0	0	0	1 2/3	3	1	1	1	2
—	Charlotte (Int'l)■	2	1	.667	2.88	33	0	0	0	10	40 2/3	36	15	13	10	31
—	Florida (N.L.)	1	0	1.000	1.42	7	0	0	0	0	6 1/3	7	2	1	6	5
A.L. totals (1 year)		0	0	...	9.00	1	0	0	0	0	2	5	2	2	2	0
N.L. totals (1 year)		1	0	1.000	1.42	7	0	0	0	0	6 1/3	7	2	1	6	5
Major league totals (2 years)		1	0	1.000	3.24	8	0	0	0	0	8 1/3	12	4	3	8	5

SMALL, MARK — P — ASTROS

PERSONAL: Born November 12, 1967, in Portland, Ore. . . . 6-3/205. . . . Throws right, bats right. . . . Full name: Mark Allen Small.
HIGH SCHOOL: West Seattle (Seattle, Wash.).
COLLEGE: Washington State.
TRANSACTIONS/CAREER NOTES: Selected by Kansas City Royals organization in 59th round of free-agent draft (June 2, 1987); did not sign. . . . Selected by Houston Astros organization in 17th round of free-agent draft (June 5, 1989). . . . On disabled list (July 3-23, 1992 and April 19-26, 1995).

Year	Team (League)	W	L	Pct.	ERA	G	GS	CG	ShO	Sv.	IP	H	R	ER	BB	SO
1989—	Auburn (NYP)	0	1	.000	5.03	10	3	0	0	2	19 2/3	17	13	11	11	23
1990—	Asheville (S. Atl.)	3	4	.429	4.15	34	0	0	0	6	52	54	36	24	37	34
1991—	Osceola (Florida St.)	3	0	1.000	1.61	26	0	0	0	2	44 2/3	30	10	8	19	44
1992—	Osceola (Florida St.)	5	9	.357	3.86	22	20	1	0	0	105	97	56	45	38	69
1993—	Jackson (Texas)	7	2	.778	3.19	51	0	0	0	0	84 2/3	71	34	30	41	64
1994—	Jackson (Texas)	3	1	.750	3.86	16	0	0	0	3	21	22	16	9	10	14
—	Tucson (Pac. Coast)	8	5	.615	5.27	41	0	0	0	4	70	86	48	41	34	30
1995—	Tucson (Pac. Coast)	3	3	.500	4.09	51	0	0	0	19	66	74	32	30	19	51

SMILEY, JOHN — P — REDS

PERSONAL: Born March 17, 1965, in Phoenixville, Pa. . . . 6-4/210. . . . Throws left, bats left. . . . Full name: John Patrick Smiley.
HIGH SCHOOL: Perkiomen Valley (Graterford, Pa.).
TRANSACTIONS/CAREER NOTES: Selected by Pittsburgh Pirates organization in 12th round of free-agent draft (June 6, 1983). . . . On disabled list (April 27-May 27, 1984 and May 19-July 1, 1990). . . . Traded by Pirates to Minnesota Twins for P Denny Neagle and OF Midre Cummings (March 17, 1992). . . . Granted free agency (October 26, 1992). . . . Signed by Cincinnati Reds (December 1, 1992). . . . On disabled list (July 3, 1993-remainder of season and August 22-September 6, 1995).
STATISTICAL NOTES: Tied for Gulf Coast League lead with five home runs allowed in 1983. . . . Pitched 2-1 one-hit, complete-game victory against Montreal (June 3, 1988). . . . Pitched 4-0 one-hit, complete-game victory against New York (April 17, 1991).

Year	Team (League)	W	L	Pct.	ERA	G	GS	CG	ShO	Sv.	IP	H	R	ER	BB	SO
1983—	GC Pirates (GCL)	3	4	.429	5.92	12	12	0	0	0	65 1/3	69	45	*43	27	42
1984—	Macon (S. Atl.)	5	11	.313	3.95	21	19	2	0	1	130	119	73	57	41	73
1985—	Prin. William (Caro.)	2	2	.500	5.14	10	10	0	0	0	56	64	36	32	27	45
—	Macon (S. Atl.)	3	8	.273	4.67	16	16	1	1	0	88 2/3	84	55	46	37	70
1986—	Prin. William (Caro.)	2	4	.333	3.10	48	2	0	0	14	90	64	35	31	40	93

Year	Team (League)	W	L	Pct.	ERA	G	GS	CG	ShO	Sv.	IP	H	R	ER	BB	SO
	—Pittsburgh (N.L.)	1	0	1.000	3.86	12	0	0	0	0	11 2/3	4	6	5	4	9
1987	—Pittsburgh (N.L.)	5	5	.500	5.76	63	0	0	0	4	75	69	49	48	50	58
1988	—Pittsburgh (N.L.)	13	11	.542	3.25	34	32	5	1	0	205	185	81	74	46	129
1989	—Pittsburgh (N.L.)	12	8	.600	2.81	28	28	8	1	0	205 1/3	174	78	64	49	123
1990	—Pittsburgh (N.L.)	9	10	.474	4.64	26	25	2	0	0	149 1/3	161	83	77	36	86
1991	—Pittsburgh (N.L.)	•20	8	•.714	3.08	33	32	2	1	0	207 2/3	194	78	71	44	129
1992	—Minnesota (A.L.)■	16	9	.640	3.21	34	34	5	2	0	241	205	93	86	65	163
1993	—Cincinnati (N.L.)■	3	9	.250	5.62	18	18	2	0	0	105 2/3	117	69	66	31	60
1994	—Cincinnati (N.L.)	11	10	.524	3.86	24	24	1	1	0	158 2/3	169	80	68	37	112
1995	—Cincinnati (N.L.)	12	5	.706	3.46	28	27	1	0	0	176 2/3	173	72	68	39	124
A.L. totals (1 year)		16	9	.640	3.21	34	34	5	2	0	241	205	93	86	65	163
N.L. totals (9 years)		86	66	.566	3.76	266	186	21	4	4	1295	1246	596	541	336	830
Major league totals (10 years)		102	75	.576	3.67	300	220	26	6	4	1536	1451	689	627	401	993

DIVISION SERIES RECORD

Year	Team (League)	W	L	Pct.	ERA	G	GS	CG	ShO	Sv.	IP	H	R	ER	BB	SO
1995	—Cincinnati (N.L.)	0	0	...	3.00	1	1	0	0	0	6	9	2	2	0	1

CHAMPIONSHIP SERIES RECORD

Year	Team (League)	W	L	Pct.	ERA	G	GS	CG	ShO	Sv.	IP	H	R	ER	BB	SO
1990	—Pittsburgh (N.L.)	0	0	...	0.00	1	0	0	0	0	2	2	0	0	0	0
1991	—Pittsburgh (N.L.)	0	2	.000	23.63	2	2	0	0	0	2 2/3	8	8	7	1	3
1995	—Cincinnati (N.L.)	0	0	...	3.60	1	1	0	0	0	5	5	2	2	0	1
Champ. series totals (3 years)		0	2	.000	8.38	4	3	0	0	0	9 2/3	15	10	9	1	4

ALL-STAR GAME RECORD

Year	League	W	L	Pct.	ERA	GS	CG	ShO	Sv.	IP	H	R	ER	BB	SO
1991	—National	0	0	...	...	0	0	0	0	0	1	1	1	0	0
1995	—National	0	0	...	9.00	0	0	0	0	2	2	2	2	0	0
All-Star totals (2 years)		0	0	...	13.50	0	0	0	0	2	3	3	3	0	0

SMITH, BOBBY 3B BRAVES

PERSONAL: Born May 10, 1974, in Oakland, Calif. . . . 6-3/190. . . . Bats right, throws right. . . . Full name: Robert Eugene Smith.
HIGH SCHOOL: Fremont (Oakland, Calif.).
TRANSACTIONS/CAREER NOTES: Selected by Atlanta Braves organization in 11th round of free-agent draft (June 1, 1992).
STATISTICAL NOTES: Tied for Carolina League lead in grounding into double plays with 19 in 1994. . . . Led Carolina League third basemen with 388 total chances and 27 double plays in 1994.

				BATTING											FIELDING			
Year	Team (League)	Pos.	G	AB	R	H	2B	3B	HR	RBI	Avg.	BB	SO	SB	PO	A	E	Avg.
1992	—GC Braves (GCL)	3B	57	217	31	51	9	1	3	28	.235	17	55	5	37	115	15	.910
1993	—Macon (S. Atl.)	3B	108	384	53	94	16	7	4	38	.245	23	81	12	65	167	30	.885
1994	—Durham (Carolina)	3B	127	478	49	127	27	2	12	71	.266	41	112	18	104	253	31	*.920
1995	—Greenville (South.)	3B	127	444	75	116	27	3	14	58	.261	40	109	12	*120	265	26	.937

SMITH, CAM P TIGERS

PERSONAL: Born September 20, 1973, in Brooklyn, N.Y. . . . 6-3/195. . . . Throws right, bats right. . . . Full name: Cameron Smith.
COLLEGE: Ithaca (N.Y.) College.
TRANSACTIONS/CAREER NOTES: Selected by Detroit Tigers organization in third round of free-agent draft (June 3, 1993).
STATISTICAL NOTES: Led South Atlantic League with 21 wild pitches and 18 hit batsmen in 1995.

Year	Team (League)	W	L	Pct.	ERA	G	GS	CG	ShO	Sv.	IP	H	R	ER	BB	SO
1993	—Bristol (Appal.)	3	1	.750	3.58	9	7	1	0	0	37 2/3	25	22	15	22	33
	—Niag. Falls (NYP)	0	0	...	18.00	2	2	0	0	0	5	12	11	10	6	0
1994	—Fayetteville (S. Atl.)	5	13	.278	6.06	26	26	1	0	0	133 2/3	133	100	90	86	128
1995	—Fayetteville (S. Atl.)	13	8	.619	3.81	29	*29	2	2	0	149	110	75	63	87	166

SMITH, DANNY P RANGERS

PERSONAL: Born April 20, 1969, in St. Paul, Minn. . . . 6-5/195. . . . Throws left, bats left. . . . Full name: Daniel Scott Smith.
HIGH SCHOOL: Apple Valley (Minn.).
COLLEGE: Creighton.
TRANSACTIONS/CAREER NOTES: Selected by Minnesota Twins organization in 22nd round of free-agent draft (June 2, 1987); did not sign. . . . Selected by Texas Rangers organization in first round (16th pick overall) of free-agent draft (June 4, 1990). . . . On Tulsa disabled list (August 5-20, 1992). . . . On Texas disabled list (March 27-May 18, 1993); included rehabilitation assignment to Charlotte (May 17-18). . . . On Oklahoma City disabled list (June 23-September 1, 1993). . . . On Texas disabled list (September 1, 1993-remainder of season). . . . On Texas disabled list (March 26-June 2, 1994); included rehabilitation assignment to Charlotte (May 28-June 2). . . . On disabled list (April 16, 1995-entire season).
HONORS: Named Texas League Pitcher of the Year (1992).

Year	Team (League)	W	L	Pct.	ERA	G	GS	CG	ShO	Sv.	IP	H	R	ER	BB	SO
1990	—Butte (Pioneer)	2	0	1.000	3.65	5	5	0	0	0	24 2/3	23	10	10	6	27
	—Tulsa (Texas)	3	2	.600	3.76	7	7	0	0	0	38 1/3	27	16	16	16	32
1991	—Okla. City (A.A.)	4	*17	.190	5.52	28	27	3	0	0	151 2/3	*195	*114	*93	75	85
1992	—Tulsa (Texas)	11	7	.611	*2.52	24	23	4	*3	0	146 1/3	110	48	41	34	122
	—Texas (A.L.)	0	3	.000	5.02	4	2	0	0	0	14 1/3	18	8	8	8	5
1993	—Charlotte (Fla. St.)	1	0	1.000	0.00	1	1	0	0	0	7	3	0	0	0	5
	—Okla. City (A.A.)	1	2	.333	4.70	3	3	0	0	0	15 1/3	16	11	8	5	12

Year	Team (League)	W	L	Pct.	ERA	G	GS	CG	ShO	Sv.	IP	H	R	ER	BB	SO
1994—	Charlotte (Fla. St.)	0	0	...	0.00	2	0	0	0	0	3 2/3	2	0	0	2	3
—	Okla. City (A.A.)	2	1	.667	2.84	10	2	0	0	2	25 1/3	27	9	8	9	15
—	Texas (A.L.)	1	2	.333	4.30	13	0	0	0	0	14 2/3	18	11	7	12	9
1995—		Did not play.														
Major league totals (2 years)		1	5	.167	4.66	17	2	0	0	0	29	36	19	15	20	14

SMITH, DWIGHT — OF — BRAVES

PERSONAL: Born November 8, 1963, in Tallahassee, Fla. . . . 5-11/195. . . . Bats left, throws right. . . . Full name: John Dwight Smith.

HIGH SCHOOL: Wade Hampton (Varnville, S.C.).

COLLEGE: Spartanburg (S.C.) Methodist.

TRANSACTIONS/CAREER NOTES: Selected by Toronto Blue Jays organization in third round of free-agent draft (January 17, 1984); did not sign. . . . Selected by Chicago Cubs organization in secondary phase of free-agent draft (June 4, 1984). . . . On Chicago disabled list (July 8-August 5, 1993); included rehabilitation assignment to Daytona (July 30-August 4). . . . Granted free agency (December 20, 1993). . . . Signed by California Angels (February 1, 1994). . . . Traded by Angels to Baltimore Orioles for a player to be named later (June 14, 1994); Angels acquired OF Bo Ortiz to complete deal (July 14, 1994). . . . Granted free agency (December 23, 1994). . . . Signed by Atlanta Braves (April 12, 1995). . . . Granted free agency (October 31, 1995). . . . Re-signed by Braves (January 8, 1996).

STATISTICAL NOTES: Tied for Appalachian League lead in double plays by outfielder with three in 1984. . . . Led Midwest League outfielders with 296 total chances in 1986. . . . Led Eastern League with 270 total bases and tied for lead in caught stealing with 18 in 1987. . . . Career major league grand slams: 2.

			BATTING												FIELDING			
Year	Team (League)	Pos.	G	AB	R	H	2B	3B	HR	RBI	Avg.	BB	SO	SB	PO	A	E	Avg.
1984—	Pikeville (Appal.)	OF	61	195	42	46	6	2	1	17	.236	52	47	*39	77	8	•9	.904
1985—	Geneva (NYP)	OF	73	232	44	67	11	2	4	32	.289	31	33	30	81	4	7	.924
1986—	Peoria (Midwest)	OF	124	471	92	146	22	*11	11	57	.310	59	92	53	*272	11	13	.956
1987—	Pittsfield (Eastern)	OF	130	498	*111	168	28	10	18	72	.337	67	79	*60	214	8	•14	.941
1988—	Iowa (Am. Assoc.)	OF	129	505	76	148	26	3	9	48	.293	54	90	25	216	11	*15	.938
1989—	Iowa (Am. Assoc.)	OF	21	83	11	27	7	3	2	7	.325	7	11	6	39	2	4	.911
—	Chicago (N.L.)	OF	109	343	52	111	19	6	9	52	.324	31	51	9	188	7	5	.975
1990—	Chicago (N.L.)	OF	117	290	34	76	15	0	6	27	.262	28	46	11	139	4	2	.986
1991—	Chicago (N.L.)	OF	90	167	16	38	7	2	3	21	.228	11	32	2	73	3	3	.962
1992—	Chicago (N.L.)	OF	109	217	28	60	10	3	3	24	.276	13	40	9	93	2	2	.979
—	Iowa (Am. Assoc.)	OF	3	8	1	2	1	0	0	1	.250	2	2	0	2	0	0	1.000
1993—	Chicago (N.L.)	OF	111	310	51	93	17	5	11	35	.300	25	51	8	163	5	8	.955
—	Daytona (Fla. St.)	OF	5	16	3	5	4	0	0	2	.313	3	4	0	3	0	0	1.000
1994—	California (A.L.)■	OF-DH	45	122	19	32	5	1	5	18	.262	7	20	2	50	2	5	.912
—	Baltimore (A.L.)■	OF-DH	28	74	12	23	2	1	3	12	.311	5	17	0	31	0	2	.939
1995—	Atlanta (N.L.)■	OF	103	131	16	33	8	2	3	21	.252	13	35	0	24	0	2	.923
American League totals (1 year)			73	196	31	55	7	2	8	30	.281	12	37	2	81	2	7	.922
National League totals (6 years)			639	1458	197	411	76	18	35	180	.282	121	255	39	680	21	22	.970
Major league totals (7 years)			712	1654	228	466	83	20	43	210	.282	133	292	41	761	23	29	.964

DIVISION SERIES RECORD

			BATTING												FIELDING			
Year	Team (League)	Pos.	G	AB	R	H	2B	3B	HR	RBI	Avg.	BB	SO	SB	PO	A	E	Avg.
1995—	Atlanta (N.L.)	PH	4	3	0	2	1	0	0	1	.667	0	0	0	...	...	...	...

CHAMPIONSHIP SERIES RECORD

NOTES: Shares record for most at-bats in one inning—2 (October 5, 1989, first inning).

			BATTING												FIELDING			
Year	Team (League)	Pos.	G	AB	R	H	2B	3B	HR	RBI	Avg.	BB	SO	SB	PO	A	E	Avg.
1989—	Chicago (N.L.)	OF	4	15	2	3	1	0	0	0	.200	2	2	1	10	0	0	1.000
1995—	Atlanta (N.L.)	PH	1	2	0	0	0	0	0	0	.000	0	0	0	...	...	...	...
Championship series totals (2 years)			5	17	2	3	1	0	0	0	.176	2	2	1	10	0	0	1.000

WORLD SERIES RECORD

NOTES: Member of World Series championship team (1995).

			BATTING												FIELDING			
Year	Team (League)	Pos.	G	AB	R	H	2B	3B	HR	RBI	Avg.	BB	SO	SB	PO	A	E	Avg.
1995—	Atlanta (N.L.)	PH	3	2	0	1	0	0	0	0	.500	1	0	0	...	...	...	...

SMITH, LEE — P — ANGELS

PERSONAL: Born December 4, 1957, in Jamestown, La. . . . 6-6/269. . . . Throws right, bats right. . . . Full name: Lee Arthur Smith.

HIGH SCHOOL: Castor (La.).

COLLEGE: Northwestern (La.) State.

TRANSACTIONS/CAREER NOTES: Selected by Chicago Cubs organization in second round of free-agent draft (June 4, 1975). . . . On disabled list (April 21-May 6, 1986). . . . Traded by Cubs to Boston Red Sox for P Al Nipper and P Calvin Schiraldi (December 8, 1987). . . . Traded by Red Sox to St. Louis Cardinals for OF Tom Brunansky (May 4, 1990). . . . Traded by Cardinals to New York Yankees for P Richard Batchelor (August 31, 1993). . . . Granted free agency (October 25, 1993). . . . Signed by Baltimore Orioles (January 29, 1994). . . . Granted free agency (October 24, 1994). . . . Signed by California Angels (December 14, 1994).

RECORDS: Holds major league career records for most saves—471; and most consecutive errorless games by pitcher—546 (July 5, 1982 through September 22, 1992). . . . Holds N.L. career record for most saves—340.

HONORS: Named N.L. co-Fireman of the Year by The Sporting News (1983 and 1992). . . . Named N.L Fireman of the Year by The Sporting News (1991). . . . Named A.L. Fireman of the Year by The Sporting News (1994).

STATISTICAL NOTES: Tied for American Association lead with 16 wild pitches in 1980.

Year	Team (League)	W	L	Pct.	ERA	G	GS	CG	ShO	Sv.	IP	H	R	ER	BB	SO
1975—	GC Cubs (GCL)	3	5	.375	2.32	10	10	2	1	0	62	35	23	16	*49	35
1976—	Pomp. Beach (FSL)	4	8	.333	5.35	26	18	2	1	0	101	120	76	60	74	52

S

Year	Team (League)	W	L	Pct.	ERA	G	GS	CG	ShO	Sv.	IP	H	R	ER	BB	SO
1977—	Pomp. Beach (FSL)	10	4	.714	4.29	26	18	4	0	0	130	131	67	62	85	82
1978—	Midland (Texas)	8	10	.444	5.98	30	25	3	0	0	155	161	122	103	*128	71
1979—	Midland (Texas)	9	5	.643	4.93	35	9	0	0	1	104	122	65	57	85	46
1980—	Wichita (Am. Assoc.)	4	7	.364	3.70	50	2	0	0	15	90	70	49	37	56	63
—	Chicago (N.L.)	2	0	1.000	2.86	18	0	0	0	0	22	21	9	7	14	17
1981—	Chicago (N.L.)	3	6	.333	3.49	40	1	0	0	1	67	57	31	26	31	50
1982—	Chicago (N.L.)	2	5	.286	2.69	72	5	0	0	17	117	105	38	35	37	99
1983—	Chicago (N.L.)	4	10	.286	1.65	66	0	0	0	*29	103 1/3	70	23	19	41	91
1984—	Chicago (N.L.)	9	7	.563	3.65	69	0	0	0	33	101	98	42	41	35	86
1985—	Chicago (N.L.)	7	4	.636	3.04	65	0	0	0	33	97 2/3	87	35	33	32	112
1986—	Chicago (N.L.)	9	9	.500	3.09	66	0	0	0	31	90 1/3	69	32	31	42	93
1987—	Chicago (N.L.)	4	10	.286	3.12	62	0	0	0	36	83 2/3	84	30	29	32	96
1988—	Boston (A.L.)■	4	5	.444	2.80	64	0	0	0	29	83 2/3	72	34	26	37	96
1989—	Boston (A.L.)	6	1	.857	3.57	64	0	0	0	25	70 2/3	53	30	28	33	96
1990—	Boston (A.L.)	2	1	.667	1.88	11	0	0	0	4	14 1/3	13	4	3	9	17
—	St. Louis (N.L.)■	3	4	.429	2.10	53	0	0	0	27	68 2/3	58	20	16	20	70
1991—	St. Louis (N.L.)	6	3	.667	2.34	67	0	0	0	*47	73	70	19	19	13	67
1992—	St. Louis (N.L.)	4	9	.308	3.12	70	0	0	0	*43	75	62	28	26	26	60
1993—	St. Louis (N.L.)	2	4	.333	4.50	55	0	0	0	43	50	49	25	25	9	49
—	New York (A.L.)■	0	0	...	0.00	8	0	0	0	3	8	4	0	0	5	11
1994—	Baltimore (A.L.)■	1	4	.200	3.29	41	0	0	0	*33	38 1/3	34	16	14	11	42
1995—	California (A.L.)■	0	5	.000	3.47	52	0	0	0	37	49 1/3	42	19	19	25	43
A.L. totals (6 years)		13	16	.448	3.06	240	0	0	0	131	264 1/3	218	103	90	120	305
N.L. totals (12 years)		55	71	.437	2.91	703	6	0	0	340	948 2/3	830	332	307	332	890
Major league totals (16 years)		68	87	.439	2.95	943	6	0	0	471	1213	1048	435	397	452	1195

CHAMPIONSHIP SERIES RECORD

Year	Team (League)	W	L	Pct.	ERA	G	GS	CG	ShO	Sv.	IP	H	R	ER	BB	SO
1984—	Chicago (N.L.)	0	1	.000	9.00	2	0	0	0	1	2	3	2	2	0	3
1988—	Boston (A.L.)	0	1	.000	8.10	2	0	0	0	0	3 1/3	6	3	3	1	4
Champ. series totals (2 years)		0	2	.000	8.44	4	0	0	0	1	5 1/3	9	5	5	1	7

ALL-STAR GAME RECORD

Year	League	W	L	Pct.	ERA	GS	CG	ShO	Sv.	IP	H	R	ER	BB	SO
1983—	National	0	0	...	9.00	0	0	0	0	1	2	2	1	0	1
1987—	National	1	0	1.000	0.00	0	0	0	0	3	2	0	0	0	4
1991—	National						Did not play.								
1992—	National						Did not play.								
1993—	National						Did not play.								
1994—	American	0	0	...	18.00	0	0	0	0	1	1	2	2	1	0
1995—	American						Did not play.								
All-Star totals (3 years)		1	0	1.000	5.40	0	0	0	0	5	5	4	3	1	5

SMITH, MARK — OF — ORIOLES

PERSONAL: Born May 7, 1970, in Pasadena, Calif. . . . 6-4/195. . . . Bats right, throws right. . . . Full name: Mark Edward Smith.
HIGH SCHOOL: Arcadia (Calif.).
COLLEGE: Southern California.
TRANSACTIONS/CAREER NOTES: Selected by Baltimore Orioles organization in first round (ninth pick overall) of free-agent draft (June 3, 1991).

			BATTING												FIELDING			
Year	Team (League)	Pos.	G	AB	R	H	2B	3B	HR	RBI	Avg.	BB	SO	SB	PO	A	E	Avg.
1991—	Frederick (Caro.)	OF	38	148	20	37	5	1	4	29	.250	9	24	1	49	1	1	.980
1992—	Hagerstown (East.)	OF	128	472	51	136	*32	6	4	62	.288	45	55	15	226	9	4	.983
1993—	Rochester (Int'l)	OF	129	485	69	136	27	1	12	68	.280	37	90	4	261	9	7	.975
1994—	Rochester (Int'l)	OF	114	437	69	108	27	1	19	66	.247	35	88	4	207	9	5	.977
—	Baltimore (A.L.)	OF	3	7	0	1	0	0	0	2	.143	0	2	0	8	0	0	1.000
1995—	Rochester (Int'l)	OF	96	364	55	101	25	3	12	66	.277	24	69	7	167	4	7	.961
—	Baltimore (A.L.)	OF-DH	37	104	11	24	5	0	3	15	.231	12	22	3	60	2	0	1.000
Major league totals (2 years)			40	111	11	25	5	0	3	17	.225	12	24	3	68	2	0	1.000

SMITH, OZZIE — SS — CARDINALS

PERSONAL: Born December 26, 1954, in Mobile, Ala. . . . 5-10/180. . . . Bats both, throws right. . . . Full name: Osborne Earl Smith.
HIGH SCHOOL: Locke (Los Angeles).
COLLEGE: Cal Poly San Luis Obispo (received degree).
TRANSACTIONS/CAREER NOTES: Selected by Detroit Tigers organization in seventh round of free-agent draft (June 8, 1976); did not sign. . . . Selected by San Diego Padres organization in fourth round of free-agent draft (June 7, 1977). . . . Traded by Padres to St. Louis Cardinals for SS Garry Templeton (February 11, 1982). . . . On disabled list (July 14-August 19, 1984; March 31-April 15, 1989; and June 16-July 1, 1992). . . . Granted free agency (November 2, 1992). . . . Re-signed by Cardinals (December 6, 1992). . . . On suspended list (June 14-16, 1994). . . . On disabled list (May 18-August 18, 1995).
RECORDS: Holds major league records for most assists by shortop—8,213; most double plays by shortstop—1,554; most years with 500 or more assists by shortstop—8; and most years leading league in assists and chances accepted by shortstop—8. . . . Holds major league single-season records for most assists by shortstop—621 (1980); fewest chances accepted by shortstop who led league in chances accepted—692 (1989); and fewest double plays by shortstop who led league in double plays—79 (1991). . . . Shares major league record for most double plays by shortstop in extra-inning game—6 (August 25, 1979, 19 innings). . . . Holds N.L. career records for most games by shortstop—2,459. . . . Holds N.L. single-season record for fewest errors by shortstop (150 or more games)—8 (1991). . . . Holds N.L. record for most years leading league in fielding percentage by shortstop (100 or more games)—7. . . . Shares N.L. records for most consecutive years leading league in assists by shortstop—4 (1979-82); highest fielding percentage by shortstop (150 or more games)—.987 (1987 and 1991);

and most years leading league in double plays by shortstop—5. . . . Shares modern N.L. record for most consecutive years leading league in fielding percentage by shortstop (100 or more games)—4 (1984-87).

HONORS: Won N.L. Gold Glove at shortstop (1980-92). . . . Named shortstop on The Sporting News N.L. All-Star team (1982, 1984-87). . . . Named shortstop on The Sporting News N.L. Silver Slugger team (1987).

STATISTICAL NOTES: Led Northwest League shortstops with 40 double plays in 1977. . . . Led N.L. with 28 sacrifice hits in 1978 and 23 in 1980. . . . Led N.L. shortstops with 933 total chances in 1980, 658 in 1981, 844 in 1983, 827 in 1985, 771 in 1987, 775 in 1988 and 709 in 1989. . . . Led N.L. shortstops with 113 double plays in 1980, 111 in 1987, 79 in 1991 and tied for lead with 94 in 1984 and 96 in 1986.

			BATTING											FIELDING			
Year Team (League)	Pos.	G	AB	R	H	2B	3B	HR	RBI	Avg.	BB	SO	SB	PO	A	E	Avg.
1977—Walla Walla (N'west) ..	SS	•68	*287	*69	87	10	2	1	35	.303	40	12	*30	130	*254	23	*.943
1978—San Diego (N.L.)	SS	159	590	69	152	17	6	1	46	.258	47	43	40	264	548	25	.970
1979—San Diego (N.L.)	SS	156	587	77	124	18	6	0	27	.211	37	37	28	256	*555	20	.976
1980—San Diego (N.L.)	SS	158	609	67	140	18	5	0	35	.230	71	49	57	*288	*621	24	.974
1981—San Diego (N.L.)	SS	•110	*450	53	100	11	2	0	21	.222	41	37	22	220	*422	16	*.976
1982—St. Louis (N.L.)■	SS	140	488	58	121	24	1	2	43	.248	68	32	25	279	*535	13	*.984
1983—St. Louis (N.L.)...........	SS	159	552	69	134	30	6	3	50	.243	64	36	34	*304	519	21	.975
1984—St. Louis (N.L.)...........	SS	124	412	53	106	20	5	1	44	.257	56	17	35	233	437	12	*.982
1985—St. Louis (N.L.)...........	SS	158	537	70	148	22	3	6	54	.276	65	27	31	264	*549	14	*.983
1986—St. Louis (N.L.)...........	SS	153	514	67	144	19	4	0	54	.280	79	27	31	229	453	15	*.978
1987—St. Louis (N.L.)...........	SS	158	600	104	182	40	4	0	75	.303	89	36	43	245	*516	10	*.987
1988—St. Louis (N.L.)...........	SS	153	575	80	155	27	1	3	51	.270	74	43	57	234	*519	22	.972
1989—St. Louis (N.L.)...........	SS	155	593	82	162	30	8	2	50	.273	55	37	29	209	*483	17	.976
1990—St. Louis (N.L.)...........	SS	143	512	61	130	21	1	1	50	.254	61	33	32	212	378	12	.980
1991—St. Louis (N.L.)...........	SS	150	550	96	157	30	3	3	50	.285	83	36	35	244	387	8	*.987
1992—St. Louis (N.L.)...........	SS	132	518	73	153	20	2	0	31	.295	59	34	43	232	420	10	.985
1993—St. Louis (N.L.)...........	SS	141	545	75	157	22	6	1	53	.288	43	18	21	251	451	19	.974
1994—St. Louis (N.L.)...........	SS	98	381	51	100	18	3	3	30	.262	38	26	6	135	291	8	*.982
1995—St. Louis (N.L.)...........	SS	44	156	16	31	5	1	0	11	.199	17	12	4	60	129	7	.964
Major league totals (18 years)		2491	9169	1221	2396	392	67	26	775	.261	1047	580	573	4159	8213	273	.978

CHAMPIONSHIP SERIES RECORD

NOTES: Named N.L. Championship Series Most Valuable Player (1985).

			BATTING											FIELDING			
Year Team (League)	Pos.	G	AB	R	H	2B	3B	HR	RBI	Avg.	BB	SO	SB	PO	A	E	Avg.
1982—St. Louis (N.L.)...........	SS	3	9	0	5	0	0	0	3	.556	3	0	1	4	11	0	1.000
1985—St. Louis (N.L.)...........	SS	6	23	4	10	1	1	1	3	.435	3	1	1	6	16	0	1.000
1987—St. Louis (N.L.)...........	SS	7	25	2	5	0	1	0	1	.200	3	4	0	10	19	1	.967
Championship series totals (3 years)		16	57	6	20	1	2	1	7	.351	9	5	2	20	46	1	.985

WORLD SERIES RECORD

NOTES: Member of World Series championship team (1982).

			BATTING											FIELDING			
Year Team (League)	Pos.	G	AB	R	H	2B	3B	HR	RBI	Avg.	BB	SO	SB	PO	A	E	Avg.
1982—St. Louis (N.L.)...........	SS	7	24	3	5	0	0	0	1	.208	3	0	1	22	17	0	1.000
1985—St. Louis (N.L.)...........	SS	7	23	1	2	0	0	0	0	.087	4	0	1	10	16	1	.963
1987—St. Louis (N.L.)...........	SS	7	28	3	6	0	0	0	2	.214	2	3	2	7	19	0	1.000
World Series totals (3 years)		21	75	7	13	0	0	0	3	.173	9	3	4	39	52	1	.989

ALL-STAR GAME RECORD

		BATTING											FIELDING			
Year League	Pos.	AB	R	H	2B	3B	HR	RBI	Avg.	BB	SO	SB	PO	A	E	Avg.
1981—National......................	SS	0	0	0	0	0	0	0	...	2	0	0	1	0	0	1.000
1982—National......................	PR-SS	0	0	0	0	0	0	0	...	0	0	0	0	1	0	1.000
1983—National......................	SS	2	1	1	0	0	0	0	.500	0	0	0	0	0	0	...
1984—National......................	SS	3	0	0	0	0	0	0	.000	0	0	1	3	0	0	1.000
1985—National......................	SS	4	0	0	0	0	0	0	.000	0	0	0	1	3	0	1.000
1986—National......................	SS	1	0	0	0	0	0	0	.000	0	0	0	3	2	0	1.000
1987—National......................	SS	2	0	0	0	0	0	0	.000	0	0	0	3	2	1	.833
1988—National......................	SS	2	0	0	0	0	0	0	.000	0	1	0	1	4	0	1.000
1989—National......................	SS	4	0	1	0	0	0	0	.250	0	0	0	1	3	0	1.000
1990—National......................	SS	1	0	0	0	0	0	0	.000	0	0	0	1	1	0	1.000
1991—National......................	SS	1	0	0	0	0	0	0	.000	1	0	0	0	1	0	1.000
1992—National......................	SS	3	0	1	1	0	0	0	.333	0	1	0	1	1	0	1.000
1994—National......................	SS	3	0	1	0	0	0	0	.333	0	0	0	1	2	0	1.000
1995—National......................		Selected, did not play—injured.														
All-Star Game totals (13 years)		26	1	4	1	0	0	0	.154	3	2	1	16	20	1	.973

SMITH, PETE P

PERSONAL: Born February 27, 1966, in Weymouth, Mass. . . . 6-2/200. . . . Throws right, bats right. . . . Full name: Peter John Smith.

HIGH SCHOOL: Burlington (Mass.).

TRANSACTIONS/CAREER NOTES: Selected by Philadelphia Phillies organization in first round (21st pick overall) of free-agent draft (June 4, 1984). . . . Traded by Phillies organization with C Ozzie Virgil to Atlanta Braves for P Steve Bedrosian and OF Milt Thompson (December 10, 1985). . . . On Atlanta disabled list (June 25-September 3, 1990); included rehabilitation assignment to Greenville (August 26-September 2). . . . On Atlanta disabled list (April 4-May 23, 1991); included rehabilitation assignments to Macon (April 12-24) and Richmond (April 24-May 9 and May 13-14). . . . On disabled list (July 25-September 1, 1993). . . . Traded by Braves to New York Mets for OF Dave Gallagher (November 24, 1993). . . . On disabled list (July 18-August 7, 1994). . . . Granted free agency (October 25, 1994). . . . Signed by Cincinnati Reds (December 1, 1994). . . . Released by Reds (June 27, 1995). . . . Signed by Charlotte, Florida Marlins organization (July 1, 1995). . . . Granted free agency (October 16, 1995).

STATISTICAL NOTES: Led N.L. with seven balks in 1989. . . . Pitched seven-inning, 1-0 no-hit victory for Richmond against Rochester (May 3, 1992). . . . Led N.L. with 25 home runs allowed in 1994.

MISCELLANEOUS: Appeared in one game as pinch-runner (1989).

Year	Team (League)	W	L	Pct.	ERA	G	GS	CG	ShO	Sv.	IP	H	R	ER	BB	SO
1984—	GC Phillies (GCL)	1	2	.333	1.46	8	8	0	0	0	37	28	11	6	16	35
1985—	Clearwater (Fla. St.)	12	10	.545	3.29	26	25	4	1	0	153	135	68	56	80	86
1986—	Greenville (South.)■	1	8	.111	5.85	24	19	0	0	0	104 2/3	117	88	68	78	64
1987—	Greenville (South.)	9	9	.500	3.35	29	25	5	1	1	177 1/3	162	76	66	67	119
	—Atlanta (N.L.)	1	2	.333	4.83	6	6	0	0	0	31 2/3	39	21	17	14	11
1988—	Atlanta (N.L.)	7	15	.318	3.69	32	32	5	3	0	195 1/3	183	89	80	88	124
1989—	Atlanta (N.L.)	5	14	.263	4.75	28	27	1	0	0	142	144	83	75	57	115
1990—	Atlanta (N.L.)	5	6	.455	4.79	13	13	3	0	0	77	77	45	41	24	56
	—Greenville (South.)	0	0	...	0.00	2	2	0	0	0	3 1/3	1	0	0	0	2
1991—	Macon (S. Atl.)	0	0	...	8.38	3	3	0	0	0	9 2/3	15	11	9	2	14
	—Richmond (Int'l)	3	3	.500	7.24	10	10	1	0	0	51	66	44	41	24	41
	—Atlanta (N.L.)	1	3	.250	5.06	14	10	0	0	0	48	48	33	27	22	29
1992—	Richmond (Int'l)	7	4	.636	2.14	15	15	4	1	0	109 1/3	75	27	26	24	93
	—Atlanta (N.L.)	7	0	1.000	2.05	12	11	2	1	0	79	63	19	18	28	43
1993—	Atlanta (N.L.)	4	8	.333	4.37	20	14	0	0	0	90 2/3	92	45	44	36	53
1994—	New York (N.L.)■	4	10	.286	5.55	21	21	1	0	0	131 1/3	145	83	81	42	62
1995—	Cincinnati (N.L.)■	1	2	.333	6.66	11	2	0	0	0	24 1/3	30	19	18	7	14
	—Charlotte (Int'l)■	2	1	.667	3.86	10	8	0	0	0	49	51	21	21	17	20
Major league totals (9 years)		35	60	.368	4.40	157	136	12	4	0	819 1/3	821	437	401	318	507

CHAMPIONSHIP SERIES RECORD

Year	Team (League)	W	L	Pct.	ERA	G	GS	CG	ShO	Sv.	IP	H	R	ER	BB	SO
1992—	Atlanta (N.L.)	0	0	...	2.45	2	0	0	0	0	3 2/3	2	1	1	3	3

WORLD SERIES RECORD

Year	Team (League)	W	L	Pct.	ERA	G	GS	CG	ShO	Sv.	IP	H	R	ER	BB	SO
1992—	Atlanta (N.L.)	0	0	...	0.00	1	0	0	0	0	3	3	0	0	0	0

SMITH, ZANE — P

PERSONAL: Born December 28, 1960, in Madison, Wis. . . . 6-1/207. . . . Throws left, bats left. . . . Full name: Zane William Smith.
HIGH SCHOOL: North Platte (Neb.).
COLLEGE: Indiana State.
TRANSACTIONS/CAREER NOTES: Selected by Atlanta Braves organization in third round of free-agent draft (June 7, 1982). . . . On disabled list (August 5-September 1, 1985 and August 25, 1988-remainder of season). . . . Traded by Braves to Montreal Expos for P Sergio Valdez, P Nate Minchey and OF Kevin Dean (July 2, 1989). . . . Traded by Expos to Pittsburgh Pirates for P Scott Ruskin, SS Willie Greene and a player to be named later (August 8, 1990); Expos acquired OF Moises Alou to complete deal (August 16, 1990). . . . Granted free agency (November 5, 1990). . . . Re-signed by Pirates (December 6, 1990). . . . On disabled list (July 15-August 8 and August 15-September 22, 1992). . . . On Pittsburgh disabled list (March 26-June 16, 1993); included rehabilitation assignment to Carolina (May 11-29). . . . On Pittsburgh disabled list (September 8, 1993-remainder of season). . . . Granted free agency (October 25, 1994). . . . Signed by Boston Red Sox (April 18, 1995). . . . On Boston disabled list (April 25-May 14 and August 7-26, 1995); included rehabilitation assignment to Pawtucket (August 17-22). . . . Granted free agency (November 1, 1995).
HONORS: Named lefthanded pitcher on The Sporting News N.L. All-Star team (1987).
STATISTICAL NOTES: Led N.L. batters with 14 sacrifice hits in 1987. . . . Pitched 1-0 one-hit, complete-game victory for Pittsburgh against New York (Septmber 5, 1990). . . . Pitched 6-0 one-hit, complete-game victory against St. Louis (May 29, 1991).
MISCELLANEOUS: Appeared in four games as pinch-runner (1988). . . . Appeared in three games as pinch-runner and made an out in only appearance as pinch-hitter with Atlanta (1989). . . . Doubled with an RBI and scored in only appearance as pinch-hitter with Montreal (1989). . . . Doubled with an RBI in only appearance as pinch-hitter with Montreal (1990). . . . Struck out in only appearance as pinch-hitter (1991). . . . Struck out twice and received a base on balls in three games as pinch-hitter (1992). . . . Struck out in only appearance as pinch-hitter (1994).

Year	Team (League)	W	L	Pct.	ERA	G	GS	CG	ShO	Sv.	IP	H	R	ER	BB	SO
1982—	Anderson (S. Atl.)	5	3	.625	6.86	12	10	1	1	1	63	65	53	48	34	32
1983—	Durham (Carolina)	9	•15	.375	4.90	27	27	7	0	0	170 2/3	183	109	93	83	126
1984—	Greenville (South.)	7	0	1.000	1.65	9	9	3	1	0	60	47	13	11	23	35
	—Richmond (Int'l)	7	4	.636	4.15	19	19	3	0	0	123 2/3	113	62	57	65	68
	—Atlanta (N.L.)	1	0	1.000	2.25	3	3	0	0	0	20	16	7	5	13	16
1985—	Atlanta (N.L.)	9	10	.474	3.80	42	18	2	2	0	147	135	70	62	80	85
1986—	Atlanta (N.L.)	8	16	.333	4.05	38	32	3	1	1	204 2/3	209	109	92	105	139
1987—	Atlanta (N.L.)	15	10	.600	4.09	36	•36	9	3	0	242	245	*130	110	91	130
1988—	Atlanta (N.L.)	5	10	.333	4.30	23	22	3	0	0	140 1/3	159	72	67	44	59
1989—	Atlanta (N.L.)	1	12	.077	4.45	17	17	0	0	0	99	102	65	49	33	58
	—Montreal (N.L.)■	0	1	.000	1.50	31	0	0	0	2	48	39	11	8	19	35
1990—	Montreal (N.L.)	6	7	.462	3.23	22	21	1	0	0	139 1/3	141	57	50	41	80
	—Pittsburgh (N.L.)■	6	2	.750	1.30	11	10	3	2	0	76	55	20	11	9	50
1991—	Pittsburgh (N.L.)	16	10	.615	3.20	35	35	6	3	0	228	234	95	81	29	120
1992—	Pittsburgh (N.L.)	8	8	.500	3.06	23	22	4	3	0	141	138	56	48	19	56
1993—	Carolina (South.)	1	2	.333	3.05	4	4	0	0	0	20 2/3	20	10	7	5	13
	—Pittsburgh (N.L.)	3	7	.300	4.55	14	14	1	0	0	83	97	43	42	22	32
1994—	Pittsburgh (N.L.)	10	8	.556	3.27	25	24	2	1	0	157	162	67	57	34	57
1995—	Boston (A.L.)■	8	8	.500	5.61	24	21	0	0	0	110 2/3	144	78	69	23	47
	—Pawtucket (Int'l)	0	0	...	0.00	1	1	0	0	0	7	5	0	0	0	5
A.L. totals (1 year)		8	8	.500	5.61	24	21	0	0	0	110 2/3	144	78	69	23	47
N.L. totals (11 years)		88	101	.466	3.56	320	254	34	15	3	1725 1/3	1732	802	682	539	917
Major league totals (12 years)		96	109	.468	3.68	344	275	34	15	3	1836	1876	880	751	562	964

DIVISION SERIES RECORD

Year	Team (League)	W	L	Pct.	ERA	G	GS	CG	ShO	Sv.	IP	H	R	ER	BB	SO
1995—	Boston (A.L.)	0	1	.000	6.75	1	0	0	0	0	1 1/3	1	1	1	0	0

CHAMPIONSHIP SERIES RECORD

Year	Team (League)	W	L	Pct.	ERA	G	GS	CG	ShO	Sv.	IP	H	R	ER	BB	SO
1990—	Pittsburgh (N.L.)	0	2	.000	6.00	2	1	0	0	0	9	14	6	6	1	8
1991—	Pittsburgh (N.L.)	1	1	.500	0.61	2	2	0	0	0	14 2/3	15	1	1	3	10
Champ. series totals (2 years)		1	3	.250	2.66	4	3	0	0	0	23 2/3	29	7	7	4	18

SMOLTZ, JOHN — P — BRAVES

PERSONAL: Born May 15, 1967, in Warren, Mich. . . . 6-3/185. . . . Throws right, bats right. . . . Full name: John Andrew Smoltz.
HIGH SCHOOL: Waverly (Lansing, Mich.).
TRANSACTIONS/CAREER NOTES: Selected by Detroit Tigers organization in 22nd round of free-agent draft (June 3, 1985). . . . Traded by Tigers organization to Atlanta Braves for P Doyle Alexander (August 12, 1987). . . . On suspended list (June 20-29, 1994).
RECORDS: Shares major league record for most home runs allowed in one inning—4 (June 19, 1994, first inning).
STATISTICAL NOTES: Tied for Florida State League lead with six balks in 1986. . . . Led N.L. with 14 wild pitches in 1990, 20 in 1991 and 17 in 1992. . . . Struck out 15 batters in one game (May 24, 1992).
MISCELLANEOUS: Appeared in three games as pinch-runner and struck out in only appearance in pinch-hitter (1989). . . . Appeared in four games as pinch-runner (1990). . . . Appeared in two games as pinch-runner (1991). . . . Struck out in only appearance as pinch-hitter (1992).

Year Team (League)	W	L	Pct.	ERA	G	GS	CG	ShO	Sv.	IP	H	R	ER	BB	SO
1986— Lakeland (Fla. St.)	7	8	.467	3.56	17	14	2	1	0	96	86	44	38	31	47
1987— Glens Falls (East.)	4	10	.286	5.68	21	21	0	0	0	130	131	89	82	81	86
— Richmond (Int'l)■	0	1	.000	6.19	3	3	0	0	0	16	17	11	11	11	5
1988— Richmond (Int'l)	10	5	.667	2.79	20	20	3	0	0	135 1/3	118	49	42	37	115
— Atlanta (N.L.)	2	7	.222	5.48	12	12	0	0	0	64	74	40	39	33	37
1989— Atlanta (N.L.)	12	11	.522	2.94	29	29	5	0	0	208	160	79	68	72	168
1990— Atlanta (N.L.)	14	11	.560	3.85	34	34	6	2	0	231 1/3	206	109	99	*90	170
1991— Atlanta (N.L.)	14	13	.519	3.80	36	36	5	0	0	229 2/3	206	101	97	77	148
1992— Atlanta (N.L.)	15	12	.556	2.85	35	•35	9	3	0	246 2/3	206	90	78	80	*215
1993— Atlanta (N.L.)	15	11	.577	3.62	35	35	3	1	0	243 2/3	208	104	98	100	208
1994— Atlanta (N.L.)	6	10	.375	4.14	21	21	1	0	0	134 2/3	120	69	62	48	113
1995— Atlanta (N.L.)	12	7	.632	3.18	29	29	2	1	0	192 2/3	166	76	68	72	193
Major league totals (8 years)	90	82	.523	3.53	231	231	31	7	0	1550 2/3	1346	668	609	572	1252

DIVISION SERIES RECORD

Year Team (League)	W	L	Pct.	ERA	G	GS	CG	ShO	Sv.	IP	H	R	ER	BB	SO
1995— Atlanta (N.L.)	0	0	...	7.94	1	1	0	0	0	5 2/3	5	5	5	1	6

CHAMPIONSHIP SERIES RECORD

NOTES: Named N.L. Championship Series Most Valuable Player (1992). . . . Shares major league career record for most strikeouts—46. . . . Shares N.L. career record for most games won—4. . . . Shares N.L. single-series record for most bases on balls allowed—10 (1992).

Year Team (League)	W	L	Pct.	ERA	G	GS	CG	ShO	Sv.	IP	H	R	ER	BB	SO
1991— Atlanta (N.L.)	2	0	1.000	1.76	2	2	1	1	0	15 1/3	14	3	3	3	15
1992— Atlanta (N.L.)	2	0	1.000	2.66	3	3	0	0	0	20 1/3	14	7	6	10	19
1993— Atlanta (N.L.)	0	1	.000	0.00	1	1	0	0	0	6 1/3	8	2	0	5	10
1995— Atlanta (N.L.)	0	0	...	2.57	1	1	0	0	0	7	7	2	2	2	2
Champ. series totals (4 years)	4	1	.800	2.02	7	7	1	1	0	49	43	14	11	20	46

WORLD SERIES RECORD

NOTES: Appeared in one game as pinch-runner (1992). . . . Member of World Series championship team (1995).

Year Team (League)	W	L	Pct.	ERA	G	GS	CG	ShO	Sv.	IP	H	R	ER	BB	SO
1991— Atlanta (N.L.)	0	0	...	1.26	2	2	0	0	0	14 1/3	13	2	2	1	11
1992— Atlanta (N.L.)	1	0	1.000	2.70	2	2	0	0	0	13 1/3	13	5	4	7	12
1995— Atlanta (N.L.)	0	0	...	15.43	1	1	0	0	0	2 1/3	6	4	4	2	4
World Series totals (3 years)	1	0	1.000	3.00	5	5	0	0	0	30	32	11	10	10	27

ALL-STAR GAME RECORD

NOTES: Shares single-game record for most wild pitches—2 (July 13, 1993). . . . Shares record for most wild pitches in one inning—2 (July 13, 1993, sixth inning).

Year League	W	L	Pct.	ERA	GS	CG	ShO	Sv.	IP	H	R	ER	BB	SO
1989— National	0	1	.000	9.00	0	0	0	0	1	2	1	1	0	0
1992— National	0	0	...	0.00	0	0	0	0	1/3	1	0	0	0	0
1993— National	0	0	...	0.00	0	0	0	0	1/3	0	0	0	1	0
All-Star totals (3 years)	0	1	.000	5.40	0	0	0	0	1 2/3	3	1	1	1	0

SNOPEK, CHRIS — 3B/SS — WHITE SOX

PERSONAL: Born September 20, 1970, in Cynthiana, Ky. . . . 6-1/185. . . . Bats right, throws right. . . . Full name: Christopher Charles Snopek.
HIGH SCHOOL: Harrison County (Cynthiana, Ky.).
COLLEGE: Mississippi.
TRANSACTIONS/CAREER NOTES: Selected by Texas Rangers organization in 11th round of free-agent draft (June 5, 1989); did not sign. . . . Selected by Chicago White Sox organization in sixth round of free-agent draft (June 1, 1992).
STATISTICAL NOTES: Led New York-Pennsylvania League third baseman with 18 double plays in 1992. . . . Led Southern League third basemen with 29 double plays in 1994.

			BATTING											FIELDING			
Year Team (League)	Pos.	G	AB	R	H	2B	3B	HR	RBI	Avg.	BB	SO	SB	PO	A	E	Avg.
1992— Utica (NYP)	3B-SS	73	245	49	69	15	1	2	29	.282	*52	44	14	48	151	11	.948
1993— South Bend (Mid.)	3B	22	72	20	28	8	1	5	18	.389	15	13	1	19	51	3	.959
— Sarasota (Fla. St.)	3B-SS	107	371	61	91	21	4	10	50	.245	65	67	3	94	240	24	.933
1994— Birm. (Southern)	3B-SS	106	365	58	96	25	3	6	54	.263	58	49	9	89	312	25	.941
1995— Nashville (A.A.)	SS-3B	113	393	56	127	23	4	12	55	.323	50	72	2	133	358	32	.939
— Chicago (A.L.)	3B-SS	22	68	12	22	4	0	1	7	.324	9	12	1	25	31	2	.966
Major league totals (1 year)		22	68	12	22	4	0	1	7	.324	9	12	1	25	31	2	.966

SNOW, J.T. — 1B — ANGELS

PERSONAL: Born February 26, 1968, in Long Beach, Calif. . . . 6-2/202. . . . Bats both, throws left. . . . Full name: Jack Thomas Snow Jr. . . . Son of Jack Snow, wide receiver, Los Angeles Rams (1965-75).

HIGH SCHOOL: Los Alamitos (Calif.).
COLLEGE: Arizona.
TRANSACTIONS/CAREER NOTES: Selected by New York Yankees organization in fifth round of free-agent draft (June 5, 1989). . . . Traded by Yankees with P Jerry Nielsen and P Russ Springer to California Angels for P Jim Abbott (December 6, 1992).
HONORS: Named International League Most Valuable Player (1992). . . . Won A.L. Gold Glove at first base (1995).
STATISTICAL NOTES: Led New York-Pennsylvania League first basemen with 649 total chances in 1989. . . . Led Carolina League in grounding into double plays with 20 in 1990. . . . Led Carolina League first basemen with 1,298 total chances and 120 double plays in 1990. . . . Tied for Eastern League lead with 10 sacrifice flies in 1991. . . . Led Eastern League first basemen with 1,200 total chances in 1991. . . . Led International League with 11 intentional bases on balls received in 1992. . . . Led International League first basemen with .995 fielding percentage, 1,097 putouts, 93 assists, 1,196 total chances and 107 double plays in 1992. . . . Career major league grand slams: 2.

			BATTING											FIELDING			
Year Team (League)	Pos.	G	AB	R	H	2B	3B	HR	RBI	Avg.	BB	SO	SB	PO	A	E	Avg.
1989—Oneonta (NYP)	1B	73	274	41	80	18	2	8	51	.292	29	35	4	*590	53	6	*.991
1990—Prin. William (Car.)	1B	*138	520	57	133	25	1	8	72	.256	46	65	2	*1208	*78	12	.991
1991—Alb./Colon. (East.)	1B	132	477	78	133	33	3	13	76	.279	67	78	5	*1102	90	8	*.993
1992—Columbus (Int'l)	1B-OF	135	492	81	154	26	4	15	78	•.313	70	65	3	†1103	†93	8	†.993
—New York (A.L.)	1B-DH	7	14	1	2	1	0	0	2	.143	5	5	0	43	2	0	1.000
1993—California (A.L.)■	1B	129	419	60	101	18	2	16	57	.241	55	88	3	1010	81	6	.995
—Vancouver (PCL)	1B	23	94	19	32	9	1	5	24	.340	10	13	0	200	13	2	.991
1994—Vancouver (PCL)	1B	53	189	35	56	13	2	8	43	.296	22	32	1	413	42	1	.998
—California (A.L.)	1B	61	223	22	49	4	0	8	30	.220	19	48	0	489	37	2	.996
1995—California (A.L.)	1B	143	544	80	157	22	1	24	102	.289	52	91	2	1161	57	4	.997
Major league totals (4 years)		340	1200	163	309	45	3	48	191	.258	131	232	5	2703	177	12	.996

SODOWSKY, CLINT P TIGERS

PERSONAL: Born July 13, 1972, in Ponca City, Okla. . . . 6-3/180. . . . Throws right, bats left. . . . Full name: Clint Rea Sodowsky.
JUNIOR COLLEGE: Connors State (Okla.).
TRANSACTIONS/CAREER NOTES: Selected by Detroit Tigers organization in ninth round of free-agent draft (June 3, 1991). . . . On disabled list (August 29-September 13, 1994). . . . On Jacksonville suspended list (May 15-16, 1995).

Year Team (League)	W	L	Pct.	ERA	G	GS	CG	ShO	Sv.	IP	H	R	ER	BB	SO
1991—Bristol (Appal.)	0	5	.000	3.76	14	8	0	0	0	55	49	34	23	34	44
1992—Bristol (Appal.)	2	2	.500	3.54	15	6	0	0	0	56	46	35	22	29	48
1993—Fayetteville (S. Atl.)	14	10	.583	5.09	27	27	1	0	0	155 2/3	177	101	88	51	80
1994—Lakeland (Fla. St.)	6	3	.667	3.83	19	18	1	1	0	110 1/3	111	58	47	34	73
1995—Jacksonville (Sou.)	5	5	.500	2.55	19	19	5	•3	0	123 2/3	102	46	35	50	77
—Toledo (Int'l)	5	1	.833	2.85	9	9	1	0	0	60	47	21	19	30	32
—Detroit (A.L.)	2	2	.500	5.01	6	6	0	0	0	23 1/3	24	15	13	18	14
Major league totals (1 year)	2	2	.500	5.01	6	6	0	0	0	23 1/3	24	15	13	18	14

SOJO, LUIS SS/2B MARINERS

PERSONAL: Born January 3, 1966, in Barquisimeto, Venezuela. . . . 5-11/175. . . . Bats right, throws right. . . . Name pronounced SO-ho.
TRANSACTIONS/CAREER NOTES: Signed as non-drafted free agent by Toronto Blue Jays organization (January 3, 1986). . . . Traded by Blue Jays with OF Junior Felix and a player to be named later to California Angels for OF Devon White, P Willie Fraser and a player to be named later (December 2, 1990); Blue Jays acquired P Marcus Moore and Angels acquired C Ken Rivers to complete deal (December 4, 1990). . . . Traded by Angels to Blue Jays for 3B Kelly Gruber and cash (December 8, 1992). . . . On Toronto disabled list (May 10-30, 1993). . . . Granted free agency (October 15, 1993). . . . Signed by Seattle Mariners organization (January 10, 1994). . . . On Seattle disabled list (June 7-23, 1995); included rehabilitation assignment to Tacoma (June 19-23).
STATISTICAL NOTES: Led International League shortstops with .957 fielding percentage in 1989. . . . Led International League with nine sacrifice flies in 1990. . . . Led A.L. with 19 sacrifice hits in 1991. . . . Career major league grand slams: 1.

			BATTING											FIELDING			
Year Team (League)	Pos.	G	AB	R	H	2B	3B	HR	RBI	Avg.	BB	SO	SB	PO	A	E	Avg.
1986—						Dominican Summer League statistics unavailable.											
1987—Myrtle Beach (SAL)	S-2-3-O	72	223	23	47	5	4	2	15	.211	17	18	5	104	123	14	.942
1988—Myrtle Beach (SAL)	SS	135	*536	83	*155	22	5	5	56	.289	35	35	14	191	407	28	.955
1989—Syracuse (Int'l)	SS-2B	121	482	54	133	20	5	3	54	.276	21	42	9	170	348	23	†.957
1990—Syracuse (Int'l)	2B-SS	75	297	39	88	12	3	6	25	.296	14	23	10	138	212	10	.972
—Toronto (A.L.)	2-S-O-3-DH	33	80	14	18	3	0	1	9	.225	5	5	1	34	31	5	.929
1991—California (A.L.)■	2-S-3-O-DH	113	364	38	94	14	1	3	20	.258	14	26	4	233	335	11	.981
1992—Edmonton (PCL)	3B-2B-SS	37	145	22	43	9	1	1	24	.297	9	17	4	32	106	4	.972
—California (A.L.)	2B-3B-SS	106	368	37	100	12	3	7	43	.272	14	24	7	196	293	9	.982
1993—Toronto (A.L.)■	SS-2B-3B	19	47	5	8	2	0	0	6	.170	4	2	0	24	35	2	.967
—Syracuse (Int'l)	2-O-3-S-1	43	142	17	31	7	2	1	12	.218	8	12	2	46	60	4	.964
1994—Calgary (PCL)■	SS-2B	24	102	19	33	9	3	1	18	.324	10	7	5	36	81	2	.983
—Seattle (A.L.)	2-S-DH-3	63	213	32	59	9	2	6	22	.277	8	25	2	97	186	7	.976
1995—Seattle (A.L.)	SS-2B-OF	102	339	50	98	18	2	7	39	.289	23	19	4	141	221	9	.976
—Tacoma (PCL)	2B-SS	4	17	1	3	0	0	1	1	.176	0	2	0	4	9	0	1.000
Major league totals (6 years)		436	1411	176	377	58	8	24	139	.267	68	101	18	725	1101	43	.977

DIVISION SERIES RECORD

			BATTING											FIELDING			
Year Team (League)	Pos.	G	AB	R	H	2B	3B	HR	RBI	Avg.	BB	SO	SB	PO	A	E	Avg.
1995—Seattle (A.L.)	SS	5	20	0	5	0	0	0	3	.250	0	3	0	9	15	1	.960

CHAMPIONSHIP SERIES RECORD

			BATTING											FIELDING			
Year Team (League)	Pos.	G	AB	R	H	2B	3B	HR	RBI	Avg.	BB	SO	SB	PO	A	E	Avg.
1995—Seattle (A.L.)	SS	6	20	0	5	2	0	0	1	.250	0	2	0	9	18	1	.964

SORRENTO, PAUL — 1B — MARINERS

PERSONAL: Born November 17, 1965, in Somerville, Mass. . . . 6-2/220. . . . Bats left, throws right. . . . Full name: Paul Anthony Sorrento.
HIGH SCHOOL: St. John's Preparatory (Danvers, Mass.).
COLLEGE: Florida State.
TRANSACTIONS/CAREER NOTES: Selected by California Angels organization in fourth round of free-agent draft (June 2, 1986). . . . Traded by Angels organization with P Mike Cook and P Rob Wassenaar to Minnesota Twins for P Bert Blyleven and P Kevin Trudeau (November 3, 1988). . . . Traded by Twins to Cleveland Indians for P Oscar Munoz and P Curt Leskanic (March 28, 1992). . . . Granted free agency (December 21, 1995). . . . Signed by Seattle Mariners (January 3, 1996).
STATISTICAL NOTES: Led Southern League first basemen with 103 double plays in 1989. . . . Led Pacific Coast League first basemen with 14 errors in 1991. . . . Career major league grand slams: 3.

		BATTING												FIELDING			
Year Team (League)	**Pos.**	**G**	**AB**	**R**	**H**	**2B**	**3B**	**HR**	**RBI**	**Avg.**	**BB**	**SO**	**SB**	**PO**	**A**	**E**	**Avg.**
1986—Quad Cities (Mid.)	OF	53	177	33	63	11	2	6	34	.356	24	40	0	83	7	1	.989
—Palm Springs (Cal.)	OF	16	62	5	15	3	0	1	7	.242	4	15	0	16	1	1	.944
1987—Palm Springs (Cal.)	OF	114	370	66	83	14	2	8	45	.224	78	95	1	123	10	4	.971
1988—Palm Springs (Cal.)	1B-OF	133	465	91	133	30	6	14	99	.286	110	101	3	719	55	18	.977
1989—Orlando (Southern)■	1B	140	509	81	130	*35	2	27	*112	.255	84	119	1	1070	41	*24	.979
—Minnesota (A.L.)	1B-DH	14	21	2	5	0	0	0	1	.238	5	4	0	13	0	0	1.000
1990—Portland (PCL)	1B-OF	102	354	59	107	27	1	19	72	.302	64	95	3	695	52	13	.983
—Minnesota (A.L.)	DH-1B	41	121	11	25	4	1	5	13	.207	12	31	1	118	7	1	.992
1991—Portland (PCL)	1B-OF	113	409	59	126	30	2	13	79	.308	62	65	1	933	58	†14	.986
—Minnesota (A.L.)	1B-DH	26	47	6	12	2	0	4	13	.255	4	11	0	70	7	0	1.000
1992—Cleveland (A.L.)■	1B-DH	140	458	52	123	24	1	18	60	.269	51	89	0	996	78	8	.993
1993—Cleveland (A.L.)	1B-OF-DH	148	463	75	119	26	1	18	65	.257	58	121	3	1015	86	6	.995
1994—Cleveland (A.L.)	1B-DH	95	322	43	90	14	0	14	62	.280	34	68	0	798	59	4	.995
1995—Cleveland (A.L.)	1B-DH	104	323	50	76	14	0	25	79	.235	51	71	1	816	58	7	.992
Major league totals (7 years)		568	1755	239	450	84	3	84	293	.256	215	395	5	3826	295	26	.994

DIVISION SERIES RECORD

		BATTING												FIELDING			
Year Team (League)	**Pos.**	**G**	**AB**	**R**	**H**	**2B**	**3B**	**HR**	**RBI**	**Avg.**	**BB**	**SO**	**SB**	**PO**	**A**	**E**	**Avg.**
1995—Cleveland (A.L.)	1B	3	10	2	3	0	0	0	1	.300	2	3	0	27	5	2	.941

CHAMPIONSHIP SERIES RECORD

		BATTING												FIELDING			
Year Team (League)	**Pos.**	**G**	**AB**	**R**	**H**	**2B**	**3B**	**HR**	**RBI**	**Avg.**	**BB**	**SO**	**SB**	**PO**	**A**	**E**	**Avg.**
1991—Minnesota (A.L.)	PH	1	1	0	0	0	0	0	0	.000	0	1	0	...	...	...	...
1995—Cleveland (A.L.)	1B	4	13	2	2	1	0	0	0	.154	2	3	0	34	1	2	.946
Championship series totals (2 years)		5	14	2	2	1	0	0	0	.143	2	4	0	34	1	2	.946

WORLD SERIES RECORD

NOTES: Member of World Series championship team (1991).

		BATTING												FIELDING			
Year Team (League)	**Pos.**	**G**	**AB**	**R**	**H**	**2B**	**3B**	**HR**	**RBI**	**Avg.**	**BB**	**SO**	**SB**	**PO**	**A**	**E**	**Avg.**
1991—Minnesota (A.L.)	PH-1B	3	2	0	0	0	0	0	0	.000	1	2	0	1	1	0	1.000
1995—Cleveland (A.L.)	1B-PH	6	11	0	2	1	0	0	0	.182	0	4	0	19	2	1	.955
World Series totals (2 years)		9	13	0	2	1	0	0	0	.154	1	6	0	20	3	1	.958

SOSA, SAMMY — OF — CUBS

PERSONAL: Born November 12, 1968, in San Pedro de Macoris, Dominican Republic. . . . 6-0/190. . . . Bats right, throws right. . . . Full name: Samuel Sosa.
TRANSACTIONS/CAREER NOTES: Signed as non-drafted free agent by Texas Rangers organization (July 30, 1985). . . . Traded by Rangers with SS Scott Fletcher and P Wilson Alvarez to Chicago White Sox for OF Harold Baines and IF Fred Manrique (July 29, 1989). . . . Traded by White Sox with P Ken Patterson to Chicago Cubs for OF George Bell (March 30, 1992). . . . On Chicago disabled list (June 13-July 27, 1992); included rehabilitation assignment to Iowa (July 21-27). . . . On Chicago disabled list (August 7-September 16, 1992).
HONORS: Named outfielder on The Sporting News N.L. All-Star team (1995). . . . Named outfielder on The Sporting News N.L. Silver Slugger team (1995).
STATISTICAL NOTES: Led Gulf Coast League with 96 total bases in 1986. . . . Tied for South Atlantic League lead in double plays by outfielder with four in 1987. . . . Collected six hits in one game (July 2, 1993). . . . Tied for N.L. lead in double plays by outfielder with four in 1995.

		BATTING												FIELDING			
Year Team (League)	**Pos.**	**G**	**AB**	**R**	**H**	**2B**	**3B**	**HR**	**RBI**	**Avg.**	**BB**	**SO**	**SB**	**PO**	**A**	**E**	**Avg.**
1986—GC Rangers (GCL)	OF	61	229	38	63	*19	1	4	28	.275	22	51	11	92	9	•6	.944
1987—Gastonia (S. Atl.)	OF	129	519	73	145	27	4	11	59	.279	21	123	22	183	12	17	.920
1988—Charlotte (Fla. St.)	OF	131	507	70	116	13	*12	9	51	.229	35	106	42	227	11	7	.971
1989—Texas (A.L.)	OF-DH	25	84	8	20	3	0	1	3	.238	0	20	0	33	1	2	.944
—Chicago (A.L.)■	OF	33	99	19	27	5	0	3	10	.273	11	27	7	61	1	2	.969
—Okla. City (A.A.)	OF	10	39	2	4	2	0	0	3	.103	2	8	4	22	0	2	.917
—Vancouver (PCL)	OF	13	49	7	18	3	0	1	5	.367	0	20	0	43	1	0	1.000
1990—Chicago (A.L.)	OF	153	532	72	124	26	10	15	70	.233	33	150	32	315	14	*13	.962
1991—Chicago (A.L.)	OF-DH	116	316	39	64	10	1	10	33	.203	14	98	13	214	6	6	.973
—Vancouver (PCL)	OF	32	116	19	31	7	2	3	19	.267	17	32	9	95	2	3	.970
1992—Chicago (N.L.)■	OF	67	262	41	68	7	2	8	25	.260	19	63	15	145	4	6	.961
—Iowa (Am. Assoc.)	OF	5	19	3	6	2	0	0	1	.316	1	2	5	14	0	0	1.000
1993—Chicago (N.L.)	OF	159	598	92	156	25	5	33	93	.261	38	135	36	344	17	9	.976
1994—Chicago (N.L.)	OF	105	426	59	128	17	6	25	70	.300	25	92	22	248	5	7	.973
1995—Chicago (N.L.)	OF	•144	564	89	151	17	3	36	119	.268	58	134	34	320	13	*13	.962
American League totals (3 years)		327	1031	138	235	44	11	29	116	.228	58	295	52	623	22	23	.966
National League totals (4 years)		475	1850	281	503	66	16	102	307	.272	140	424	107	1057	39	35	.969
Major league totals (7 years)		802	2881	419	738	110	27	131	423	.256	198	719	159	1680	61	58	.968

ALL-STAR GAME RECORD

Year	League	Pos.	AB	R	H	2B	3B	HR	RBI	Avg.	BB	SO	SB	PO	A	E	Avg.
			BATTING											FIELDING			
1995—	National	OF	1	0	0	0	0	0	0	.000	0	0	0	2	0	0	1.000

SPARKS, STEVE — P — BREWERS

PERSONAL: Born July 2, 1965, in Tulsa, Okla. . . . 6-0/187. . . . Throws right, bats right. . . . Full name: Steven William Sparks.
HIGH SCHOOL: Holland Hall (Tulsa, Okla.).
COLLEGE: Sam Houston State.
TRANSACTIONS/CAREER NOTES: Selected by Milwaukee Brewers organization in fifth round of free-agent draft (June 2, 1987).

Year	Team (League)	W	L	Pct.	ERA	G	GS	CG	ShO	Sv.	IP	H	R	ER	BB	SO
1987—	Helena (Pioneer)	6	3	.667	4.68	10	9	2	0	0	57 2/3	68	44	30	20	47
1988—	Beloit (Midwest)	9	13	.409	3.79	25	24	5	1	0	164	162	80	69	51	96
1989—	Stockton (Calif.)	•13	5	.722	2.41	23	22	3	2	0	164	125	55	44	53	126
1990—	Stockton (Calif.)	10	7	.588	3.69	19	19	5	1	0	129 1/3	136	63	53	31	77
—	El Paso (Texas)	1	2	.333	6.53	7	6	1	0	0	30 1/3	43	24	22	15	17
1991—	Stockton (Calif.)	9	10	.474	3.06	24	24	•8	2	0	179 2/3	160	70	61	98	139
—	El Paso (Texas)	1	2	.333	9.53	4	4	0	0	0	17	30	22	18	9	10
1992—	El Paso (Texas)	9	8	.529	5.37	28	22	3	0	1	140 2/3	159	99	84	50	79
1993—	New Orleans (A.A.)	9	13	.409	3.84	29	•28	*7	1	0	*180 1/3	174	89	77	*80	104
1994—	New Orleans (A.A.)	10	12	.455	4.46	28	27	5	1	0	*183 2/3	183	101	91	68	105
1995—	Milwaukee (A.L.)	9	11	.450	4.63	33	27	3	0	0	202	210	111	104	86	96
Major league totals (1 year)		9	11	.450	4.63	33	27	3	0	0	202	210	111	104	86	96

SPEHR, TIM — C — EXPOS

PERSONAL: Born July 2, 1966, in Excelsior Springs, Mo. . . . 6-2/200. . . . Bats right, throws right. . . . Full name: Timothy Joseph Spehr. . . . Name pronounced SPEAR.
HIGH SCHOOL: Richfield (Waco, Tex.).
COLLEGE: Arizona State.
TRANSACTIONS/CAREER NOTES: Selected by Kansas City Royals organization in fifth round of free-agent draft (June 1, 1988). . . . On disabled list (June 25-July 27, 1988). . . . On Baseball City disabled list (April 7-May 21, 1989). . . . Traded by Royals organization with P Jeff Shaw to Montreal Expos organization for P Mark Gardner and P Doug Piatt (December 9, 1992). . . . On disabled list (July 31, 1995-remainder of season).
STATISTICAL NOTES: Led American Association catchers with 730 total chances and 14 double plays in 1990. . . . Tied for American Association lead in being hit by pitch with 11 in 1992. . . . Career major league grand slams: 1.

Year	Team (League)	Pos.	G	AB	R	H	2B	3B	HR	RBI	Avg.	BB	SO	SB	PO	A	E	Avg.
				BATTING											FIELDING			
1988—	Appleton (Midw.)	C	31	110	15	29	3	0	5	22	.264	10	28	3	146	14	7	.958
1989—	Baseball City (FSL)	C	18	64	8	16	5	0	1	7	.250	5	17	1	63	7	1	.986
—	Memphis (South.)	C	61	216	22	42	9	0	8	23	.194	16	59	1	274	36	5	.984
1990—	Omaha (A.A.)	C	102	307	42	69	10	2	6	34	.225	41	88	5	*658	67	5	*.993
1991—	Omaha (A.A.)	C	72	215	27	59	14	2	6	26	.274	25	48	3	402	53	8	.983
—	Kansas City (A.L.)	C	37	74	7	14	5	0	3	14	.189	9	18	1	190	19	3	.986
1992—	Omaha (A.A.)	C	109	336	48	85	22	0	15	42	.253	61	89	4	577	65	7	.989
1993—	Montreal (N.L.)■	C	53	87	14	20	6	0	2	10	.230	6	20	2	166	22	9	.954
—	Ottawa (Int'l)	C	46	141	15	28	6	1	4	13	.199	14	35	2	248	24	6	.978
1994—	Montreal (N.L.)	C-OF	52	36	8	9	3	1	0	5	.250	4	11	2	104	6	0	1.000
1995—	Montreal (N.L.)	C	41	35	4	9	5	0	1	3	.257	6	7	0	92	12	1	.990
American League totals (1 year)			37	74	7	14	5	0	3	14	.189	9	18	1	190	19	3	.986
National League totals (3 years)			146	158	26	38	14	1	3	18	.241	16	38	4	362	40	10	.976
Major league totals (4 years)			183	232	33	52	19	1	6	32	.224	25	56	5	552	59	13	.979

SPIERS, BILL — 2B — ASTROS

PERSONAL: Born June 5, 1966, in Orangeburg, S.C. . . . 6-2/190. . . . Bats left, throws right. . . . Full name: William James Spiers III. . . . Name pronounced SPY-ers.
HIGH SCHOOL: Wade Hampton Academy (Orangeburg, S.C.).
COLLEGE: Clemson.
TRANSACTIONS/CAREER NOTES: Selected by Milwaukee Brewers organization in first round (13th pick overall) of free-agent draft (June 2, 1987). . . . On Milwaukee disabled list (April 6-May 15, 1990); included rehabilitation assignment to Denver (April 27-May 14). . . . On Milwaukee disabled list (April 5-September 2, 1992); included rehabilitation assignments to Beloit (May 6-15 and August 20-September 2). . . . Granted free agency (December 20, 1993). . . . Re-signed by Brewers (December 21, 1993). . . . Claimed on waivers by New York Mets (October 25, 1994). . . . On New York disabled list (May 15-June 5 and June 26-July 16, 1995); included rehabilitation assignment to Norfolk (May 22-June 5). . . . Granted free agency (November 3, 1995). . . . Signed by Houston Astros organization (January 10, 1996).
HONORS: Named shortstop on The Sporting News college All-America team (1987).
STATISTICAL NOTES: Career major league grand slams: 2.

Year	Team (League)	Pos.	G	AB	R	H	2B	3B	HR	RBI	Avg.	BB	SO	SB	PO	A	E	Avg.
				BATTING											FIELDING			
1987—	Helena (Pioneer)	SS	6	22	4	9	1	0	0	3	.409	3	3	2	8	6	6	.700
—	Beloit (Midwest)	SS	64	258	43	77	10	1	3	26	.298	15	38	11	111	160	20	.931
1988—	Stockton (Calif.)	SS	84	353	68	95	17	3	5	52	.269	42	41	27	140	240	19	.952
—	El Paso (Texas)	SS	47	168	22	47	5	2	3	21	.280	15	20	4	73	141	13	.943
1989—	Milwaukee (A.L.)	S-3-2-DH-1	114	345	44	88	9	3	4	33	.255	21	63	10	164	295	21	.956
—	Denver (A.A.)	SS	14	47	9	17	2	1	2	8	.362	5	6	1	32	33	2	.970

Year	Team (League)	Pos.	G	AB	R	H	2B	3B	HR	RBI	Avg.	BB	SO	SB	PO	A	E	Avg.
			BATTING												FIELDING			
1990—	Denver (A.A.)	SS	11	38	6	12	0	0	1	7	.316	10	8	1	22	23	2	.957
—	Milwaukee (A.L.)	SS	112	363	44	88	15	3	2	36	.242	16	46	11	159	326	12	.976
1991—	Milwaukee (A.L.)	SS-DH-OF	133	414	71	117	13	6	8	54	.283	34	55	14	201	345	17	.970
1992—	Beloit (Midwest)	SS	16	55	9	13	3	0	0	7	.236	7	7	4	12	28	3	.930
—	Milwaukee (A.L.)	S-2-DH-3	12	16	2	5	2	0	0	2	.313	1	4	1	6	6	0	1.000
1993—	Milwaukee (A.L.)	2-0-S-DH	113	340	43	81	8	4	2	36	.238	29	51	9	213	231	13	.972
1994—	Milwaukee (A.L.)	3-S-DH-0-1	73	214	27	54	10	1	0	17	.252	19	42	7	70	129	8	.961
1995—	New York (N.L.)■	3B-2B	63	72	5	15	2	1	0	11	.208	12	15	0	13	30	7	.860
—	Norfolk (Int'l)	2B-3B	12	41	4	9	2	0	0	4	.220	8	6	0	23	29	4	.929
American League totals (6 years)			557	1692	231	433	57	17	16	178	.256	120	261	52	813	1332	71	.968
National League totals (1 year)			63	72	5	15	2	1	0	11	.208	12	15	0	13	30	7	.860
Major league totals (7 years)			620	1764	236	448	59	18	16	189	.254	132	276	52	826	1362	78	.966

SPIEZIO, SCOTT — 3B — ATHLETICS

PERSONAL: Born September 21, 1972, in Joliet, Ill. . . . 6-2/195. . . . Bats both, throws right. . . . Full name: Scott Edward Spiezio. . . . Son of Ed Spiezio, third baseman, St. Louis Cardinals, San Diego Padres and Chicago White Sox (1964-72).
HIGH SCHOOL: Morris (Ill.).
COLLEGE: Illinois.
TRANSACTIONS/CAREER NOTES: Selected by Oakland Athletics organization in sixth round of free-agent draft (June 3, 1993).
STATISTICAL NOTES: Led California League third basemen with .948 fielding percentage in 1994. . . . Led Southern League with 14 sacrifice flies in 1995. . . . Led Southern League third basemen with 424 total chances, 291 assists, 29 errors and 34 double plays in 1995.

Year	Team (League)	Pos.	G	AB	R	H	2B	3B	HR	RBI	Avg.	BB	SO	SB	PO	A	E	Avg.
			BATTING												FIELDING			
1993—	S. Oregon (N'west)	3B-1B	31	125	32	41	10	2	3	19	.328	16	18	0	76	40	9	.928
—	Modesto (Calif.)	3B-1B	32	110	12	28	9	1	1	13	.255	23	19	1	42	51	5	.949
1994—	Modesto (Calif.)	3B-1B-SS	127	453	84	127	32	5	14	68	.280	88	72	5	66	281	18	†.951
1995—	Huntsville (South.)	3B-1B-2B	141	528	78	149	33	8	13	86	.282	67	78	10	122	†295	†29	.935

SPOLJARIC, PAUL — P — BLUE JAYS

PERSONAL: Born September 24, 1970, in Kelowna, B.C. . . . 6-3/212. . . . Throws left, bats right. . . . Full name: Paul Nikola Spoljaric. . . . Name pronounced spole-JAIR-ick.
HIGH SCHOOL: Springvalley Secondary (Kelowna, B.C.).
COLLEGE: Douglas College (B.C.).
TRANSACTIONS/CAREER NOTES: Signed as non-drafted free agent by Toronto Blue Jays organization (August 26, 1989).
HONORS: Named South Atlantic League Most Outstanding Pitcher (1992).

Year	Team (League)	W	L	Pct.	ERA	G	GS	CG	ShO	Sv.	IP	H	R	ER	BB	SO
1990—	Medicine Hat (Pio.)	3	7	.300	4.34	15	13	0	0	1	66 1/3	57	43	32	35	62
1991—	St. Cathar. (NYP)	0	2	.000	4.82	4	4	0	0	0	18 2/3	21	14	10	9	21
1992—	Myrtle Beach (SAL)	10	8	.556	2.82	26	26	1	0	0	162 2/3	111	68	51	58	161
1993—	Dunedin (Fla. St.)	3	0	1.000	1.38	4	4	0	0	0	26	16	5	4	12	29
—	Knoxville (South.)	4	1	.800	2.28	7	7	0	0	0	43 1/3	30	12	11	22	51
—	Syracuse (Int'l)	8	7	.533	5.29	18	18	1	1	0	95 1/3	97	63	56	52	88
1994—	Toronto (A.L.)	0	1	.000	38.57	2	1	0	0	0	2 1/3	5	10	10	9	2
—	Syracuse (Int'l)	1	5	.167	5.70	8	8	0	0	0	47 1/3	47	37	30	28	38
—	Knoxville (South.)	6	5	.545	3.62	17	16	0	0	0	102	88	50	41	48	79
1995—	Syracuse (Int'l)	2	10	.167	4.93	43	9	0	0	10	87 2/3	69	51	48	54	108
Major league totals (1 year)		0	1	.000	38.57	2	1	0	0	0	2 1/3	5	10	10	9	2

SPRAGUE, ED — 3B — BLUE JAYS

PERSONAL: Born July 25, 1967, in Castro Valley, Calif. . . . 6-2/205. . . . Bats right, throws right. . . . Full name: Edward Nelson Sprague. . . . Son of Ed Sprague, major league pitcher with four teams (1968-69 and 1971-76); and husband of Kristen Babb, Olympic gold-medal synchronized swimmer (1992). . . . Name pronounced SPRAYGH.
HIGH SCHOOL: St. Mary's (Stockton, Calif.).
COLLEGE: Stanford.
TRANSACTIONS/CAREER NOTES: Selected by Boston Red Sox organization in 26th round of free-agent draft (June 3, 1985); did not sign. . . . Selected by Toronto Blue Jays organization in first round (25th pick overall) of free-agent draft (June 1, 1988). . . . On suspended list (August 8-10, 1993).
STATISTICAL NOTES: Led International League third basemen with 31 errors and 364 total chances and tied for lead with 240 assists in 1990. . . . Led A.L. in grounding into double plays with 23 in 1993. . . . Led A.L. third basemen with 98 putouts in 1994 and 133 in 1995. . . . Led A.L. in being hit by pitch with 15 in 1995. . . . Career major league grand slams: 2.
MISCELLANEOUS: Member of 1988 U.S. Olympic baseball team.

Year	Team (League)	Pos.	G	AB	R	H	2B	3B	HR	RBI	Avg.	BB	SO	SB	PO	A	E	Avg.
			BATTING												FIELDING			
1989—	Dunedin (Fla. St.)	3B	52	192	21	42	9	2	7	23	.219	16	40	1	33	86	14	.895
—	Syracuse (Int'l)	3B	86	288	23	60	14	1	5	33	.208	18	73	0	51	149	*25	.889
1990—	Syracuse (Int'l)	3B-1B-C	142	*519	60	124	23	5	20	75	.239	31	100	4	171	‡246	†35	.923
1991—	Syracuse (Int'l)	C-3B	23	88	24	32	8	0	5	25	.364	10	21	2	111	17	6	.955
—	Toronto (A.L.)	3-1-C-DH	61	160	17	44	7	0	4	20	.275	19	43	0	167	72	14	.945
1992—	Syracuse (Int'l)	C-1B-3B	100	369	49	102	18	2	16	50	.276	44	73	0	438	44	12	.976
—	Toronto (A.L.)	C-1-DH-3	22	47	6	11	2	0	1	7	.234	3	7	0	82	5	1	.989
1993—	Toronto (A.L.)	3B	150	546	50	142	31	1	12	73	.260	32	85	1	*127	232	17	.955
1994—	Toronto (A.L.)	3B-1B	109	405	38	97	19	1	11	44	.240	23	95	1	†117	147	14	.950
1995—	Toronto (A.L.)	3B-1B-DH	144	521	77	127	27	2	18	74	.244	58	96	0	†167	234	17	.959
Major league totals (5 years)			486	1679	188	421	86	4	46	218	.251	135	326	2	660	690	63	.955

CHAMPIONSHIP SERIES RECORD

Year	Team (League)	Pos.	G	AB	R	H	2B	3B	HR	RBI	Avg.	BB	SO	SB	PO	A	E	Avg.
			BATTING												FIELDING			
1991—	Toronto (A.L.)								Did not play.									
1992—	Toronto (A.L.)	PH	2	2	0	1	0	0	0	0	.500	0	1	0	...	...	...	...
1993—	Toronto (A.L.)	3B	6	21	0	6	0	1	0	4	.286	2	4	0	5	9	0	1.000
Championship series totals (2 years)			8	23	0	7	0	1	0	4	.304	2	5	0	5	9	0	1.000

WORLD SERIES RECORD

NOTES: Hit home run in first at-bat (October 18, 1992). . . . Member of World Series championship team (1992 and 1993).

Year	Team (League)	Pos.	G	AB	R	H	2B	3B	HR	RBI	Avg.	BB	SO	SB	PO	A	E	Avg.
			BATTING												FIELDING			
1992—	Toronto (A.L.)	PH-1B	3	2	1	1	0	0	1	2	.500	1	0	0	0	0	0	...
1993—	Toronto (A.L.)	3B-PH-1B	5	15	0	1	0	0	0	2	.067	1	6	0	4	9	2	.867
World Series totals (2 years)			8	17	1	2	0	0	1	4	.118	2	6	0	4	9	2	.867

SPRINGER, DENNIS — P — ANGELS

PERSONAL: Born February 12, 1965, in Fresno, Calif. . . . 5-10/190. . . . Throws right, bats right. . . . Full name: Dennis LeRoy Springer.
HIGH SCHOOL: Washington (Fresno, Calif.).
COLLEGE: Fresno State.
TRANSACTIONS/CAREER NOTES: Selected by Los Angeles Dodgers organization in 21st round of free-agent draft (June 2, 1987). . . . On San Antonio disabled list (April 19-27, 1992). . . . On disabled list (August 24-September 6, 1993). . . . Granted free agency (October 15, 1993). . . . Signed by Philadelphia Phillies organization (May 19, 1994). . . . Granted free agency (December 21, 1995). . . . Signed by California Angels organization (January 5, 1996).

Year	Team (League)	W	L	Pct.	ERA	G	GS	CG	ShO	Sv.	IP	H	R	ER	BB	SO
1987—	Great Falls (Pio.)	4	3	.571	2.88	23	5	1	0	6	65 2/3	70	38	21	16	54
1988—	Bakersfield (Calif.)	13	7	.650	3.27	32	20	6	•4	2	154	135	75	56	62	108
1989—	San Antonio (Tex.)	6	8	.429	3.15	19	19	4	1	0	140	128	58	49	46	89
—	Albuquerque (PCL)	4	1	.800	4.83	8	7	0	0	0	41	58	28	22	14	18
1990—	San Antonio (Tex.)	8	6	.571	3.31	24	24	3	0	0	*163 1/3	147	76	60	73	77
1991—	San Antonio (Tex.)	10	10	.500	4.43	30	24	2	0	0	164 2/3	153	96	81	91	*138
1992—	San Antonio (Tex.)	6	7	.462	4.35	18	18	4	0	0	122	114	61	59	49	73
—	Albuquerque (PCL)	2	7	.222	5.66	11	11	1	0	0	62	70	45	39	22	36
1993—	Albuquerque (PCL)	3	8	.273	5.99	35	18	0	0	0	130 2/3	173	104	87	39	69
1994—	Reading (Eastern)■	5	8	.385	3.40	24	19	2	0	2	135	125	74	51	44	118
1995—	Scran./W.B. (Int'l)	10	11	.476	4.68	30	23	4	0	0	171	163	*101	89	47	115
—	Philadelphia (N.L.)	0	3	.000	4.84	4	4	0	0	0	22 1/3	21	15	12	9	15
Major league totals (1 year)		0	3	.000	4.84	4	4	0	0	0	22 1/3	21	15	12	9	15

SPRINGER, RUSS — P — PHILLIES

PERSONAL: Born November 7, 1968, in Alexandria, La. . . . 6-4/205. . . . Throws right, bats right. . . . Full name: Russell Paul Springer.
HIGH SCHOOL: Grant (Dry Prong, La.).
COLLEGE: Louisiana State.
TRANSACTIONS/CAREER NOTES: Selected by New York Yankees organization in seventh round of free-agent draft (June 5, 1989). . . . Traded by Yankees with 1B J.T. Snow and P Jerry Nielsen to California Angels for P Jim Abbott (December 6, 1992). . . . On California disabled list (August 2, 1993-remainder of season). . . . Traded by Angels to Philadelphia Phillies (August 15, 1995), completing deal in which Angles acquired OF Dave Gallagher from Phillies for 2B Kevin Flora and a player to be named later (August 9, 1995).

Year	Team (League)	W	L	Pct.	ERA	G	GS	CG	ShO	Sv.	IP	H	R	ER	BB	SO
1989—	GC Yankees (GCL)	3	0	1.000	1.50	6	6	0	0	0	24	14	8	4	10	34
1990—	GC Yankees (GCL)	0	2	.000	1.20	4	4	0	0	0	15	10	6	2	4	17
—	Greensboro (S. Atl.)	2	3	.400	3.67	10	10	0	0	0	56 1/3	51	33	23	31	51
1991—	Fort Lauder. (FSL)	5	9	.357	3.49	25	25	2	0	0	152 1/3	118	68	59	62	139
—	Alb./Colon. (East.)	1	0	1.000	1.80	2	2	0	0	0	15	9	4	3	6	16
1992—	Columbus (Int'l)	8	5	.615	2.69	20	20	1	0	0	123 2/3	89	46	37	54	95
—	New York (A.L.)	0	0	...	6.19	14	0	0	0	0	16	18	11	11	10	12
1993—	Vancouver (PCL)■	5	4	.556	4.27	11	9	1	0	0	59	58	37	28	33	40
—	California (A.L.)	1	6	.143	7.20	14	9	1	0	0	60	73	48	48	32	31
1994—	Vancouver (PCL)	7	4	.636	3.04	12	12	•4	0	0	83	77	35	28	19	58
—	California (A.L.)	2	2	.500	5.52	18	5	0	0	2	45 2/3	53	28	28	14	28
1995—	Vancouver (PCL)	2	0	1.000	3.44	6	6	0	0	0	34	24	16	13	23	23
—	California (A.L.)	1	2	.333	6.10	19	6	0	0	1	51 2/3	60	37	35	25	38
—	Philadelphia (N.L.)■	0	0	...	3.71	14	0	0	0	0	26 2/3	22	11	11	10	32
A.L. totals (4 years)		4	10	.286	6.33	65	20	1	0	3	173 1/3	204	124	122	81	109
N.L. totals (1 year)		0	0	...	3.71	14	0	0	0	0	26 2/3	22	11	11	10	32
Major league totals (4 years)		4	10	.286	5.99	79	20	1	0	3	200	226	135	133	91	141

STAHOVIAK, SCOTT — 3B — TWINS

PERSONAL: Born March 6, 1970, in Waukegan, Ill. . . . 6-5/222. . . . Bats left, throws right. . . . Full name: Scott Edmund Stahoviak. . . . Name pronounced stuh-HO-vee-ak.
HIGH SCHOOL: Carmel (Mundelein, Ill.).
COLLEGE: Creighton.
TRANSACTIONS/CAREER NOTES: Selected by Minnesota Twins organization in 27th round of free-agent draft (June 1, 1988); did not sign. . . . Selected by Twins organization in supplemental round ("sandwich pick" between first and second round, 27th pick overall) of free-agent draft (June 3, 1991); pick received as compensation for California Angels signing Type A free-agent 3B Gary Gaetti. . . . On Nashville disabled list (May 12-June 24, 1993).

			BATTING												FIELDING			
Year	Team (League)	Pos.	G	AB	R	H	2B	3B	HR	RBI	Avg.	BB	SO	SB	PO	A	E	Avg.
1991—	Visalia (California)	3B	43	158	29	44	9	1	1	25	.278	22	28	9	31	89	12	.909
1992—	Visalia (California)	3B	110	409	62	126	26	3	5	68	.308	82	66	17	92	181	*40	.872
1993—	Nashville (South.)	3-1-S-O	93	331	40	90	25	1	12	56	.272	56	95	10	89	150	24	.909
—	Minnesota (A.L.)	3B	20	57	1	11	4	0	0	1	.193	3	22	0	9	38	4	.922
1994—	Salt Lake (PCL)	3B-1B	123	437	96	139	41	6	13	94	.318	70	90	6	303	204	31	.942
1995—	Salt Lake (PCL)	3B-1B	9	33	6	10	1	0	0	5	.303	6	3	2	36	16	0	1.000
—	Minnesota (A.L.)	1B-3B-DH	94	263	28	70	19	0	3	23	.266	30	61	5	503	91	5	.992
Major league totals (2 years)			114	320	29	81	23	0	3	24	.253	33	83	5	512	129	9	.986

STAIRS, MATT — OF — ATHLETICS

PERSONAL: Born February 27, 1969, in Fredericton, New Brunswick, Canada. . . . 5-9/175. . . . Bats left, throws right. . . . Full name: Matthew Wade Stairs.

HIGH SCHOOL: Fredericton (New Brunswick).

TRANSACTIONS/CAREER NOTES: Signed as non-drafted free agent by Montreal Expos organization (January 17, 1989). . . . On disabled list (May 16-23, 1991). . . . On Ottawa disabled list (May 7-18, 1993). . . . Released by Expos (June 8, 1993). . . . Signed by Chunichi Dragons of Japan Central League (June 1993). . . . Signed as free agent by Expos organization (December 15, 1993). . . . Traded by Expos with P Pete Young to Boston Red Sox for a player to be named later and cash (February 18, 1994). . . . Granted free agency (October 14, 1995). . . . Signed by Oakland Athletics organization (December 1, 1995).

HONORS: Named Eastern League Most Valuable Player (1991).

STATISTICAL NOTES: Led Eastern League with .509 slugging percentage, 257 total bases and tied for lead with eight intentional bases on balls received in 1991.

MISCELLANEOUS: Member of 1988 Canadian Olympic baseball team.

			BATTING												FIELDING			
Year	Team (League)	Pos.	G	AB	R	H	2B	3B	HR	RBI	Avg.	BB	SO	SB	PO	A	E	Avg.
1989—	W.P. Beach (FSL)	3B-SS-2B	36	111	12	21	3	1	1	9	.189	9	18	0	21	66	4	.956
—	Jamestown (NYP)	2B-3B	14	43	8	11	1	0	1	5	.256	3	5	1	15	35	6	.893
—	Rockford (Midw.)	3B	44	141	20	40	9	2	2	14	.284	15	29	5	30	62	7	.929
1990—	W.P. Beach (FSL)	3B-2B	55	183	30	62	9	3	3	30	.339	41	19	15	40	112	17	.899
—	Jacksonv. (South.)	3-0-2-S	79	280	26	71	17	0	3	34	.254	22	43	5	76	107	22	.893
1991—	Harrisburg (East.)	2B-3B-OF	129	505	87	*168	30	•10	13	78	*.333	66	47	23	193	314	22	.958
1992—	Indianapolis (A.A.)	OF	110	401	57	107	23	4	11	56	.267	49	61	11	188	11	3	.985
—	Montreal (N.L.)	OF	13	30	2	5	2	0	0	5	.167	7	7	0	14	0	1	.933
1993—	Ottawa (Int'l)	OF	34	125	18	35	4	2	3	20	.280	11	15	4	49	4	0	1.000
—	Montreal (N.L.)	OF	6	8	1	3	1	0	0	2	.375	0	1	0	1	0	0	1.000
—	Chunichi (Jp. Cn.)■	...	60	132	10	33	6	0	6	23	.250	7	34	1	...	...	...	...
1994—	New Britain (East.)■	OF-1B	93	317	44	98	25	2	9	61	.309	53	38	10	106	12	3	.975
1995—	Pawtucket (Int'l)	OF	75	271	40	77	17	0	13	56	.284	29	41	3	79	13	0	1.000
—	Boston (A.L.)	OF-DH	39	88	8	23	7	1	1	17	.261	4	14	0	19	2	2	.913
American League totals (1 year)			39	88	8	23	7	1	1	17	.261	4	14	0	19	2	2	.913
National League totals (2 years)			19	38	3	8	3	0	0	7	.211	7	8	0	15	0	1	.938
Major league totals (3 years)			58	126	11	31	10	1	1	24	.246	11	22	0	34	2	3	.923

DIVISION SERIES RECORD

			BATTING												FIELDING			
Year	Team (League)	Pos.	G	AB	R	H	2B	3B	HR	RBI	Avg.	BB	SO	SB	PO	A	E	Avg.
1995—	Boston (A.L.)	PH	1	1	0	0	0	0	0	0	.000	0	1	0	...	...	...	...

STANKIEWICZ, ANDY — IF — EXPOS

PERSONAL: Born August 10, 1964, in Inglewood, Calif. . . . 5-9/165. . . . Bats right, throws right. . . . Full name: Andrew Neal Stankiewicz.

HIGH SCHOOL: St. Paul (Sante Fe Springs, Calif.).

COLLEGE: Pepperdine.

TRANSACTIONS/CAREER NOTES: Selected by Kansas City Royals organization in 26th round of free-agent draft (June 7, 1982); did not sign. . . . Selected by Detroit Tigers organization in 18th round of free-agent draft (June 3, 1985); did not sign. . . . Selected by New York Yankees organization in 12th round of free-agent draft (June 2, 1986). . . . On disabled list (May 16-31, 1992). . . . On Columbus disabled list (August 18-26, 1993). . . . Traded by Yankees with P Domingo Jean to Houston Astros for P Xavier Hernandez (November 27, 1993). . . . On Houston disabled list (July 6-August 7, 1994); included rehabilitation assignment to Jackson (August 1-7). . . . On Houston disabled list (May 29-June 26, 1995); included rehabilitation assignment to Tuscon (June 18-26). . . . Granted free agency (October 16, 1995). . . . Signed by Montreal Expos organization (December 20, 1995).

STATISTICAL NOTES: Led Eastern League with 11 sacrifice flies in 1989. . . . Led Eastern League second basemen with 615 total chances and 85 double plays in 1989.

			BATTING												FIELDING			
Year	Team (League)	Pos.	G	AB	R	H	2B	3B	HR	RBI	Avg.	BB	SO	SB	PO	A	E	Avg.
1986—	Oneonta (NYP)	2B-SS	59	216	51	64	8	3	0	17	.296	38	41	14	107	152	12	.956
1987—	Fort Lauder. (FSL)	2B	119	456	80	140	18	7	2	47	.307	62	84	26	233	347	16	.973
1988—	Alb./Colon. (East.)	2B	109	414	63	111	20	2	1	33	.268	39	53	15	230	325	*16	.972
—	Columbus (Int'l)	2B	29	114	4	25	0	0	0	4	.219	6	25	2	56	97	3	.981
1989—	Alb./Colon. (East.)	2B	133	498	*74	133	26	2	4	49	.267	57	59	*41	*242	*369	4	*.993
1990—	Columbus (Int'l)	2B-SS-3B	135	446	68	102	14	4	1	48	.229	71	63	25	237	399	10	.985
1991—	Columbus (Int'l)	2-S-3-P	125	372	47	101	12	4	1	41	.272	29	45	29	220	324	15	.973
1992—	New York (A.L.)	SS-2B-DH	116	400	52	107	22	2	2	25	.268	38	42	9	185	346	12	.978
1993—	Columbus (Int'l)	2B-3B-SS	90	331	45	80	12	5	0	32	.242	29	46	12	138	265	6	.985
—	New York (A.L.)	2-3-DH-S	16	9	5	0	0	0	0	0	.000	1	1	0	7	15	0	1.000
1994—	Houston (N.L.)■	SS-2B-3B	37	54	10	14	3	0	1	5	.259	12	12	1	12	45	0	1.000
—	Jackson (Texas)	2B-SS	5	12	1	5	0	0	0	3	.417	0	0	0	8	7	1	.938
1995—	Houston (N.L.)	SS-2B-3B	43	52	6	6	1	0	0	7	.115	12	19	4	20	59	1	.988
—	Tucson (PCL)	SS-2B-3B	25	87	16	24	4	0	1	15	.276	14	8	3	36	81	3	.975
American League totals (2 years)			132	409	57	107	22	2	2	25	.262	39	43	9	192	361	12	.979
National League totals (2 years)			80	106	16	20	4	0	1	12	.189	24	31	5	32	104	1	.993
Major league totals (4 years)			212	515	73	127	26	2	3	37	.247	63	74	14	224	465	13	.981

RECORD AS PITCHER

Year	Team (League)	W	L	Pct.	ERA	G	GS	CG	ShO	Sv.	IP	H	R	ER	BB	SO
1991—	Columbus (Int'l)	0	0	...	0.00	1	0	0	0	0	1/3	1	0	0	1	0

S

STANLEY, MIKE — C — RED SOX

PERSONAL: Born June 25, 1963, in Fort Lauderdale, Fla. . . . 6-0/190. . . . Bats right, throws right. . . . Full name: Robert Michael Stanley.
HIGH SCHOOL: St. Thomas Aquinas (Fort Lauderdale, Fla.).
COLLEGE: Florida.
TRANSACTIONS/CAREER NOTES: Selected by Texas Rangers organization in 16th round of free-agent draft (June 3, 1985). . . . On disabled list (July 24-August 14, 1988 and August 18-September 2, 1989). . . . Granted free agency (November 15, 1990). . . . Re-signed by Rangers organization (February 4, 1991). . . . Granted free agency (October 14, 1991). . . . Signed by Columbus, New York Yankees organization (January 21, 1992). . . . On disabled list (May 14-29, 1994). . . . Granted free agency (November 1, 1995). . . . Signed by Boston Red Sox (December 14, 1995).
HONORS: Named catcher on The Sporting News A.L. All-Star team (1993). . . . Named catcher on The Sporting News A.L. Silver Slugger team (1993).
STATISTICAL NOTES: Hit three home runs in one game (August 10, 1995, first game). . . . Career major league grand slams: 8.

			BATTING												FIELDING			
Year	Team (League)	Pos.	G	AB	R	H	2B	3B	HR	RBI	Avg.	BB	SO	SB	PO	A	E	Avg.
1985—	Salem (Carolina)	1B-C	4	9	2	5	0	0	0	3	.556	1	1	0	19	1	1	.952
—	Burlington (Midw.)	C-1B-OF	13	42	8	13	2	0	1	6	.310	6	5	0	45	2	0	1.000
—	Tulsa (Texas)	C-1-O-2	46	165	24	51	10	0	3	17	.309	24	18	6	289	18	6	.981
1986—	Tulsa (Texas)	C-1B-3B	67	235	41	69	16	2	6	35	.294	34	26	5	379	45	2	.995
—	Texas (A.L.)	3-C-DH-O	15	30	4	10	3	0	1	1	.333	3	7	1	14	8	1	.957
—	Okla. City (A.A.)	C-3B-1B	56	202	37	74	13	3	5	49	.366	44	42	1	206	55	9	.967
1987—	Okla. City (A.A.)	C-1B	46	182	43	61	8	3	13	54	.335	29	36	2	277	32	2	.994
—	Texas (A.L.)	C-1-DH-O	78	216	34	59	8	1	6	37	.273	31	48	3	389	26	7	.983
1988—	Texas (A.L.)	C-DH-1-3	94	249	21	57	8	0	3	27	.229	37	62	0	342	17	4	.989
1989—	Texas (A.L.)	C-DH-1-3	67	122	9	30	3	1	1	11	.246	12	29	1	117	8	3	.977
1990—	Texas (A.L.)	C-DH-3-1	103	189	21	47	8	1	2	19	.249	30	25	1	261	25	4	.986
1991—	Texas (A.L.)	C-1-3-DH-O	95	181	25	45	13	1	3	25	.249	34	44	0	288	20	6	.981
1992—	New York (A.L.)■	C-DH-1B	68	173	24	43	7	0	8	27	.249	33	45	0	287	30	6	.981
1993—	New York (A.L.)	C-DH	130	423	70	129	17	1	26	84	.305	57	85	1	652	46	3	*.996
1994—	New York (A.L.)	C-1B-DH	82	290	54	87	20	0	17	57	.300	39	56	0	442	35	5	.990
1995—	New York (A.L.)	C-DH	118	399	63	107	29	1	18	83	.268	57	106	1	651	35	5	.993
Major league totals (10 years)			850	2272	325	614	116	6	85	371	.270	333	507	8	3443	250	44	.988

DIVISION SERIES RECORD

			BATTING												FIELDING			
Year	Team (League)	Pos.	G	AB	R	H	2B	3B	HR	RBI	Avg.	BB	SO	SB	PO	A	E	Avg.
1995—	New York (A.L.)	C	4	16	2	5	0	0	1	3	.313	2	1	0	30	0	1	.968

ALL-STAR GAME RECORD

			BATTING											FIELDING			
Year	League	Pos.	AB	R	H	2B	3B	HR	RBI	Avg.	BB	SO	SB	PO	A	E	Avg.
1995—	American	C	1	0	0	0	0	0	0	.000	0	0	0	3	0	0	1.000

STANTON, MIKE — P — RED SOX

PERSONAL: Born June 2, 1967, in Houston. . . . 6-1/190. . . . Throws left, bats left. . . . Full name: William Michael Stanton.
HIGH SCHOOL: Midland (Tex.).
JUNIOR COLLEGE: Alvin (Tex.) Community College.
TRANSACTIONS/CAREER NOTES: Selected by Atlanta Braves organization in 13th round of free-agent draft (June 2, 1987). . . . On Atlanta disabled list (April 27, 1990-remainder of season); included rehabilitation assignments to Greenville (May 31-June 5 and August 21-29). . . . Granted free agency (December 23, 1994). . . . Re-signed by Braves (April 12, 1995). . . . Traded by Braves with a player to be named later to Boston Red Sox for two players to be named later (July 31, 1995); Red Sox acquired P Matt Murray and Braves acquired OF Marc Lewis and P Mike Jacobs to complete deal (August 31, 1995).

Year	Team (League)	W	L	Pct.	ERA	G	GS	CG	ShO	Sv.	IP	H	R	ER	BB	SO
1987—	Pulaski (Appal.)	4	8	.333	3.24	15	13	3	2	0	83 1/3	64	37	30	42	82
1988—	Burlington (Midw.)	11	5	.688	3.62	30	23	1	1	0	154	154	86	62	69	160
—	Durham (Carolina)	1	0	1.000	1.46	2	2	1	1	0	12 1/3	14	3	2	5	14
1989—	Greenville (South.)	4	1	.800	1.58	47	0	0	0	19	51 1/3	32	10	9	31	58
—	Richmond (Int'l)	2	0	1.000	0.00	13	0	0	0	8	20	6	0	0	13	20
—	Atlanta (N.L.)	0	1	.000	1.50	20	0	0	0	7	24	17	4	4	8	27
1990—	Atlanta (N.L.)	0	3	.000	18.00	7	0	0	0	2	7	16	16	14	4	7
—	Greenville (South.)	0	1	.000	1.59	4	4	0	0	0	5 2/3	7	1	1	3	4
1991—	Atlanta (N.L.)	5	5	.500	2.88	74	0	0	0	7	78	62	27	25	21	54
1992—	Atlanta (N.L.)	5	4	.556	4.10	65	0	0	0	8	63 2/3	59	32	29	20	44
1993—	Atlanta (N.L.)	4	6	.400	4.67	63	0	0	0	27	52	51	35	27	29	43
1994—	Atlanta (N.L.)	3	1	.750	3.55	49	0	0	0	3	45 2/3	41	18	18	26	35
1995—	Atlanta (N.L.)	1	1	.500	5.59	26	0	0	0	1	19 1/3	31	14	12	6	13
—	Boston (A.L.)■	1	0	1.000	3.00	22	0	0	0	0	21	17	9	7	8	10
A.L. totals (1 year)		1	0	1.000	3.00	22	0	0	0	0	21	17	9	7	8	10
N.L. totals (7 years)		18	21	.462	4.01	304	0	0	0	55	289 2/3	277	146	129	114	223
Major league totals (7 years)		19	21	.475	3.94	326	0	0	0	55	310 2/3	294	155	136	122	233

DIVISION SERIES RECORD

Year	Team (League)	W	L	Pct.	ERA	G	GS	CG	ShO	Sv.	IP	H	R	ER	BB	SO
1995—	Boston (A.L.)	0	0	...	0.00	1	0	0	0	0	2 1/3	1	0	0	0	4

CHAMPIONSHIP SERIES RECORD

NOTES: Shares single-series record for most games pitched—5 (1992).

Year Team (League)	W	L	Pct.	ERA	G	GS	CG	ShO	Sv.	IP	H	R	ER	BB	SO
1991—Atlanta (N.L.)	0	0	...	2.45	3	0	0	0	0	3 2/3	4	1	1	3	3
1992—Atlanta (N.L.)	0	0	...	0.00	5	0	0	0	0	4 1/3	2	1	0	2	5
1993—Atlanta (N.L.)	0	0	...	0.00	1	0	0	0	0	1	1	0	0	1	0
Champ. series totals (3 years)	0	0	...	1.00	9	0	0	0	0	9	7	2	1	6	8

WORLD SERIES RECORD

Year Team (League)	W	L	Pct.	ERA	G	GS	CG	ShO	Sv.	IP	H	R	ER	BB	SO
1991—Atlanta (N.L.)	1	0	1.000	0.00	5	0	0	0	0	7 1/3	5	0	0	2	7
1992—Atlanta (N.L.)	0	0	...	0.00	4	0	0	0	1	5	3	0	0	2	1
World Series totals (2 years)	1	0	1.000	0.00	9	0	0	0	1	12 1/3	8	0	0	4	8

STEINBACH, TERRY C ATHLETICS

PERSONAL: Born March 2, 1962, in New Ulm, Minn. . . . 6-1/195. . . . Bats right, throws right. . . . Full name: Terry Lee Steinbach. . . . Brother of Tom Steinbach, minor league outfielder (1983).

HIGH SCHOOL: New Ulm (Minn.).

COLLEGE: Minnesota.

TRANSACTIONS/CAREER NOTES: Selected by Cleveland Indians organization in 16th round of free-agent draft (June 3, 1980); did not sign. . . . Selected by Oakland Athletics organization in ninth round of free-agent draft (June 6, 1983). . . . On disabled list (May 6-June 1, 1988; July 3-28, 1990; and April 10-25, 1992). . . . Granted free agency (October 26, 1992). . . . Re-signed by A's (December 14, 1992). . . . On disabled list (August 16, 1993-remainder of season and August 13-29, 1995).

HONORS: Named Southern League Most Valuable Player (1986).

STATISTICAL NOTES: Led Northwest League third basemen with 122 assists and tied for lead with 17 errors in 1983. . . . Led Midwest League third basemen with 31 double plays in 1984. . . . Led Southern League with 22 passed balls in 1986. . . . Hit home run in first major league at-bat (September 12, 1986). . . . Led A.L. catchers with 15 errors in 1991. . . . Led A.L. catchers with .998 fielding percentage in 1994. . . . Career major league grand slams: 6.

		BATTING												FIELDING			
Year Team (League)	Pos.	G	AB	R	H	2B	3B	HR	RBI	Avg.	BB	SO	SB	PO	A	E	Avg.
1983—Medford (N'west)	3B-OF-1B	62	219	42	69	16	0	6	38	.315	28	22	8	105	†124	‡21	.916
1984—Madison (Midwest)	3B-1B-P	135	474	57	140	24	6	11	79	.295	49	59	5	107	257	27	.931
1985—Huntsville (South.)	C-3-1-O-P	128	456	64	124	31	3	9	72	.272	45	36	4	187	43	6	.975
1986—Huntsville (South.)	C-1B-3B	138	505	113	164	33	2	24	*132	.325	94	74	10	620	73	14	.980
—Oakland (A.L.)	C	6	15	3	5	0	0	2	4	.333	1	0	0	21	4	1	.962
1987—Oakland (A.L.)	C-3-DH-1	122	391	66	111	16	3	16	56	.284	32	66	1	642	44	10	.986
1988—Oakland (A.L.)	C-3-1-DH-O	104	351	42	93	19	1	9	51	.265	33	47	3	536	58	9	.985
1989—Oakland (A.L.)	C-O-1-DH-3	130	454	37	124	13	1	7	42	.273	30	66	1	612	47	11	.984
1990—Oakland (A.L.)	C-DH-1B	114	379	32	95	15	2	9	57	.251	19	66	0	401	31	5	.989
1991—Oakland (A.L.)	C-1B-DH	129	456	50	125	31	1	6	67	.274	22	70	2	639	53	†15	.979
1992—Oakland (A.L.)	C-1B-DH	128	438	48	122	20	1	12	53	.279	45	58	2	598	72	10	.985
1993—Oakland (A.L.)	C-1B-DH	104	389	47	111	19	1	10	43	.285	25	65	3	524	47	7	.988
1994—Oakland (A.L.)	C-DH-1B	103	369	51	105	21	2	11	57	.285	26	62	2	597	59	1	†.998
1995—Oakland (A.L.)	C-1B	114	406	43	113	26	1	15	65	.278	25	74	1	686	57	6	.992
Major league totals (10 years)		1054	3648	419	1004	180	13	97	495	.275	258	574	15	5256	472	75	.987

CHAMPIONSHIP SERIES RECORD

		BATTING												FIELDING			
Year Team (League)	Pos.	G	AB	R	H	2B	3B	HR	RBI	Avg.	BB	SO	SB	PO	A	E	Avg.
1988—Oakland (A.L.)	C	2	4	0	1	0	0	0	0	.250	2	0	0	12	0	0	1.000
1989—Oakland (A.L.)	C-DH	4	15	0	3	0	0	0	1	.200	1	5	0	17	0	0	1.000
1990—Oakland (A.L.)	C	3	11	2	5	0	0	0	1	.455	1	2	0	11	0	0	1.000
1992—Oakland (A.L.)	C	6	24	1	7	0	0	1	5	.292	2	7	0	30	7	0	1.000
Championship series totals (4 years)		15	54	3	16	0	0	1	7	.296	6	14	0	70	7	0	1.000

WORLD SERIES RECORD

NOTES: Member of World Series championship team (1989).

		BATTING												FIELDING			
Year Team (League)	Pos.	G	AB	R	H	2B	3B	HR	RBI	Avg.	BB	SO	SB	PO	A	E	Avg.
1988—Oakland (A.L.)	C-DH	3	11	0	4	1	0	0	0	.364	0	2	0	11	3	0	1.000
1989—Oakland (A.L.)	C	4	16	3	4	0	1	1	7	.250	2	1	0	27	2	0	1.000
1990—Oakland (A.L.)	C	3	8	0	1	0	0	0	0	.125	0	1	0	8	1	0	1.000
World Series totals (3 years)		10	35	3	9	1	1	1	7	.257	2	4	0	46	6	0	1.000

ALL-STAR GAME RECORD

NOTES: Named Most Valuable Player (1988). . . . Hit home run in first at-bat (July 12, 1988).

		BATTING											FIELDING			
Year League	Pos.	AB	R	H	2B	3B	HR	RBI	Avg.	BB	SO	SB	PO	A	E	Avg.
1988—American	C	1	1	1	0	0	1	2	1.000	0	0	0	3	1	1	.800
1989—American	C	3	0	1	0	0	0	0	.333	0	0	0	6	1	0	1.000
1993—American	C	2	0	1	1	0	0	1	.500	0	1	0	6	0	0	1.000
All-Star Game totals (3 years)		6	1	3	1	0	1	3	.500	0	1	0	15	2	1	.944

RECORD AS PITCHER

Year Team (League)	W	L	Pct.	ERA	G	GS	CG	ShO	Sv.	IP	H	R	ER	BB	SO
1984—Madison (Midwest)	0	0	...	9.00	2	0	0	0	0	3	2	4	3	4	0
1985—Huntsville (South.)	0	0	...	0.00	1	0	0	0	0	1	0	0	0	0	0

STEPHENSON, GARRETT — P — ORIOLES

PERSONAL: Born January 2, 1972, in Takoma Park, Md. . . . 6-4/195. . . . Throws right, bats right. . . . Full name: Garrett Charles Stephenson.
HIGH SCHOOL: Linganore (Frederick, Md.), then Boonsboro (Md.).
JUNIOR COLLEGE: Ricks (Idaho).
COLLEGE: Idaho State.
TRANSACTIONS/CAREER NOTES: Selected by Baltimore Orioles organization in 18th round of free-agent draft (June 1, 1992).
STATISTICAL NOTES: Led Eastern League with 23 home runs allowed and 18 hit batsmen in 1995.

Year	Team (League)	W	L	Pct.	ERA	G	GS	CG	ShO	Sv.	IP	H	R	ER	BB	SO
1992—	Bluefield (Appal.)	3	1	.750	4.73	12	3	0	0	0	32 1/3	35	22	17	7	30
1993—	Albany (S. Atl.)	16	7	.696	2.84	30	24	3	•2	1	171 1/3	142	65	54	44	147
1994—	Frederick (Caro.)	7	5	.583	4.02	18	17	1	0	0	107 1/3	91	62	48	36	133
	—Bowie (Eastern)	3	2	.600	5.15	7	7	1	1	0	36 2/3	47	22	21	11	32
1995—	Bowie (Eastern)	7	10	.412	3.64	29	*29	1	0	0	175 1/3	154	87	71	47	139

STEVENS, DAVE — P — TWINS

PERSONAL: Born March 4, 1970, in Fullerton, Calif. . . . 6-3/205. . . . Throws right, bats right. . . . Full name: David James Stevens.
HIGH SCHOOL: La Habra (Calif.).
COLLEGE: Fullerton (Calif.) College.
TRANSACTIONS/CAREER NOTES: Selected by Chicago Cubs organization in 20th round of free-agent draft (June 5, 1989). . . . On disabled list (June 17-July 4, 1991). . . . On Iowa disabled list (April 8-May 20, 1993). . . . Traded by Cubs with C Matt Walbeck to Minnesota Twins for P Willie Banks (November 24, 1993).

Year	Team (League)	W	L	Pct.	ERA	G	GS	CG	ShO	Sv.	IP	H	R	ER	BB	SO
1990—	Hunting. (Appal.)	2	4	.333	4.61	13	11	0	0	0	56 2/3	48	44	29	47	55
1991—	Geneva (NYP)	2	3	.400	2.85	9	9	1	0	0	47 1/3	49	20	15	14	44
1992—	Charlotte (South.)	9	13	.409	3.91	26	26	2	0	0	149 2/3	147	79	65	53	89
1993—	Iowa (Am. Assoc.)	4	0	1.000	4.19	24	0	0	0	4	34 1/3	24	16	16	14	29
	—Orlando (Southern)	6	1	.857	4.22	11	11	1	1	0	70 1/3	69	36	33	35	49
1994—	Salt Lake (PCL)■	6	2	.750	1.67	23	0	0	0	3	43	41	13	8	16	30
	—Minnesota (A.L.)	5	2	.714	6.80	24	0	0	0	0	45	55	35	34	23	24
1995—	Minnesota (A.L.)	5	4	.556	5.07	56	0	0	0	10	65 2/3	74	40	37	32	47
	Major league totals (2 years)	10	6	.625	5.77	80	0	0	0	10	110 2/3	129	75	71	55	71

STEVERSON, TODD — OF — TIGERS

PERSONAL: Born November 15, 1971, in Los Angeles. . . . 6-2/194. . . . Bats right, throws right. . . . Full name: Todd Anthony Steverson. . . . Cousin of Ron LeFlore, outfielder with Detroit Tigers, Montreal Expos and Chicago White Sox (1974-82).
HIGH SCHOOL: Culver City (Calif.).
COLLEGE: Arizona State.
TRANSACTIONS/CAREER NOTES: Selected by St. Louis Cardinals organization in sixth round of free-agent draft (June 5, 1989); did not sign. . . . Selected by Toronto Blue Jays organization in first round (25th pick overall) of free-agent draft (June 1, 1992). . . . Selected by Detroit Tigers from Blue Jays organization in Rule 5 major league draft (December 5, 1994). . . . On Detroit disabled list (June 16-September 1, 1995); included rehabilitation assignments to Toledo (July 7-16 and August 22-31).
STATISTICAL NOTES: Tied for New York-Pennsylvania League lead in double plays by outfielder with two in 1992.

			BATTING												FIELDING			
Year	Team (League)	Pos.	G	AB	R	H	2B	3B	HR	RBI	Avg.	BB	SO	SB	PO	A	E	Avg.
1992—	St. Cathar. (NYP)	OF	65	225	26	47	9	9	6	24	.209	20	83	23	94	7	4	.962
1993—	Dunedin (Fla. St.)	OF-2B	106	413	68	112	32	4	11	54	.271	44	118	15	149	5	1	.994
1994—	Knoxville (South.)	OF	124	415	59	109	24	5	9	38	.263	71	112	20	186	9	8	.961
1995—	Detroit (A.L.)■	OF-DH	30	42	11	11	0	0	2	6	.262	6	10	2	22	1	0	1.000
	—Toledo (Int'l)	OF	9	28	6	3	0	0	1	1	.107	5	13	0	8	1	2	.818
	Major league totals (1 year)		30	42	11	11	0	0	2	6	.262	6	10	2	22	1	0	1.000

STEWART, DAVE — P

PERSONAL: Born February 19, 1957, in Oakland, Calif. . . . 6-2/200. . . . Throws right, bats right. . . . Full name: David Keith Stewart.
HIGH SCHOOL: St. Elizabeth (Oakland, Calif.).
JUNIOR COLLEGE: Merritt College (Calif.).
COLLEGE: Cal State Hayward.
TRANSACTIONS/CAREER NOTES: Selected by Los Angeles Dodgers organization in 16th round of free-agent draft (June 4, 1975). . . . Traded by Dodgers with a player to be named later to Texas Rangers for P Rick Honeycutt (August 19, 1983); Rangers acquired P Ricky Wright to complete deal (September 16, 1983). . . . Traded by Rangers to Philadelphia Phillies for P Rick Surhoff (September 13, 1985). . . . Released by Phillies (May 9, 1986). . . . Signed by Tacoma, Oakland Athletics organization (May 23, 1986). . . . On disabled list (May 9-26, 1991 and June 30-July 24, 1992). . . . Granted free agency (October 29, 1992). . . . Signed by Toronto Blue Jays (December 8, 1992). . . . On disabled list (April 3-May 13, 1993). . . . Granted free agency (October 20, 1994). . . . Signed by A's (April 8, 1995). . . . Announced retirement (July 23, 1995).
RECORDS: Shares A.L. single-season record for fewest complete games by pitcher who led league in complete games—11 (1990).
HONORS: Named righthanded pitcher on THE SPORTING NEWS A.L. All-Star team (1988).
STATISTICAL NOTES: Tied for Midwest League lead with three balks in 1977. . . . Pitched 2-0 one-hit, complete-game victory against Seattle (August 4, 1988). . . . Led A.L. with 16 balks in 1988. . . . Pitched 5-0 no-hit victory against Toronto (June 29, 1990).

Year	Team (League)	W	L	Pct.	ERA	G	GS	CG	ShO	Sv.	IP	H	R	ER	BB	SO
1975—	Bellingham (N'west)	0	5	.000	5.51	22	5	1	0	2	49	59	46	30	49	37
1976—	Danville (Midwest)	0	2	.000	16.20	4	3	0	0	0	10	17	20	18	16	10
	—Bellingham (N'west)	1	1	.500	5.04	24	2	0	0	1	50	47	35	28	58	53
1977—	Clinton (Midwest)	*17	4	*.810	2.15	24	24	•15	•3	0	176	152	52	42	72	144

Year	Team (League)	W	L	Pct.	ERA	G	GS	CG	ShO	Sv.	IP	H	R	ER	BB	SO
	—Albuquerque (PCL)	1	0	1.000	4.50	1	1	0	0	0	6	4	3	3	6	3
1978—	San Antonio (Tex.)	14	12	.538	3.68	28	•28	5	2	0	*193	181	99	79	97	130
	—Los Angeles (N.L.)	0	0	...	0.00	1	0	0	0	0	2	1	0	0	0	1
1979—	Albuquerque (PCL)	11	12	.478	5.24	28	26	5	1	1	170	198	112	99	81	105
1980—	Albuquerque (PCL)	•15	10	.600	3.70	31	*29	11	0	1	*202	189	94	83	89	125
1981—	Los Angeles (N.L.)	4	3	.571	2.51	32	0	0	0	6	43	40	13	12	14	29
1982—	Los Angeles (N.L.)	9	8	.529	3.81	45	14	0	0	1	146 1/3	137	72	62	49	80
1983—	Los Angeles (N.L.)	5	2	.714	2.96	46	1	0	0	8	76	67	28	25	33	54
	—Texas (A.L.)■	5	2	.714	2.14	8	8	2	0	0	59	50	15	14	17	24
1984—	Texas (A.L.)	7	14	.333	4.73	32	27	3	0	0	192 1/3	193	106	101	87	119
1985—	Texas (A.L.)	0	6	.000	5.42	42	5	0	0	4	81 1/3	86	53	49	37	64
	—Philadelphia (N.L.)■	0	0	...	6.23	4	0	0	0	0	4 1/3	5	4	3	4	2
1986—	Philadelphia (N.L.)	0	0	...	6.57	8	0	0	0	0	12 1/3	15	9	9	4	9
	—Tacoma (PCL)■	0	0	...	0.00	1	0	0	0	0	3	4	1	0	1	3
	—Oakland (A.L.)	9	5	.643	3.74	29	17	4	1	0	149 1/3	137	67	62	65	102
1987—	Oakland (A.L.)	•20	13	.606	3.68	37	37	8	1	0	261 1/3	224	121	107	105	205
1988—	Oakland (A.L.)	21	12	.636	3.23	37	*37	•14	2	0	*275 2/3	240	111	99	110	192
1989—	Oakland (A.L.)	21	9	.700	3.32	36	•36	8	0	0	257 2/3	*260	105	95	69	155
1990—	Oakland (A.L.)	22	11	.667	2.56	36	•36	•11	•4	0	*267	226	84	76	83	166
1991—	Oakland (A.L.)	11	11	.500	5.18	35	•35	2	1	0	226	245	*135	*130	105	144
1992—	Oakland (A.L.)	12	10	.545	3.66	31	31	2	0	0	199 1/3	175	96	81	79	130
1993—	Toronto (A.L.)■	12	8	.600	4.44	26	26	0	0	0	162	146	86	80	72	96
1994—	Toronto (A.L.)	7	8	.467	5.87	22	22	1	0	0	133 1/3	151	89	87	62	111
1995—	Oakland (A.L.)■	3	7	.300	6.89	16	16	0	0	0	81	101	65	62	39	58
A.L. totals (13 years)		150	116	.564	4.00	387	333	55	9	4	2345 1/3	2234	1133	1043	930	1566
N.L. totals (6 years)		18	13	.581	3.52	136	15	0	0	15	284	265	126	111	104	175
Major league totals (16 years)		168	129	.566	3.95	523	348	55	9	19	2629 1/3	2499	1259	1154	1034	1741

DIVISION SERIES RECORD

Year	Team (League)	W	L	Pct.	ERA	G	GS	CG	ShO	Sv.	IP	H	R	ER	BB	SO
1981—	Los Angeles (N.L.)	0	2	.000	40.50	2	0	0	0	0	2/3	4	3	3	0	1

CHAMPIONSHIP SERIES RECORD

NOTES: Named A.L. Championship Series Most Valuable Player (1990 and 1993). . . . Holds career records for most games won—8; most games won by undefeated pitcher—8; most innings pitched—75 1/3; and most bases on balls issued—25. . . . Shares A.L. single-series record for most games won—2 (1989-90 and 1993).

Year	Team (League)	W	L	Pct.	ERA	G	GS	CG	ShO	Sv.	IP	H	R	ER	BB	SO
1988—	Oakland (A.L.)	1	0	1.000	1.35	2	2	0	0	0	13 1/3	9	2	2	6	11
1989—	Oakland (A.L.)	2	0	1.000	2.81	2	2	0	0	0	16	13	5	5	3	9
1990—	Oakland (A.L.)	2	0	1.000	1.13	2	2	0	0	0	16	8	2	2	2	4
1992—	Oakland (A.L.)	1	0	1.000	2.70	2	2	1	0	0	16 2/3	14	5	5	6	7
1993—	Toronto (A.L.)	2	0	1.000	2.03	2	2	0	0	0	13 1/3	8	3	3	8	8
Champ. series totals (5 years)		8	0	1.000	2.03	10	10	1	0	0	75 1/3	52	17	17	25	39

WORLD SERIES RECORD

NOTES: Named Most Valuable Player (1989). . . . Member of World Series championship teams (1981, 1989 and 1993).

Year	Team (League)	W	L	Pct.	ERA	G	GS	CG	ShO	Sv.	IP	H	R	ER	BB	SO
1981—	Los Angeles (N.L.)	0	0	...	0.00	2	0	0	0	0	1 2/3	1	0	0	2	1
1988—	Oakland (A.L.)	0	1	.000	3.14	2	2	0	0	0	14 1/3	12	7	5	5	5
1989—	Oakland (A.L.)	2	0	1.000	1.69	2	2	1	1	0	16	10	3	3	2	14
1990—	Oakland (A.L.)	0	2	.000	2.77	2	2	1	0	0	13	10	6	4	6	5
1993—	Toronto (A.L.)	0	1	.000	6.75	2	2	0	0	0	12	10	9	9	8	8
World Series totals (5 years)		2	4	.333	3.32	10	8	2	1	0	57	43	25	21	23	33

ALL-STAR GAME RECORD

Year	League	W	L	Pct.	ERA	GS	CG	ShO	Sv.	IP	H	R	ER	BB	SO
1989—	American	0	0	...	18.00	1	0	0	0	1	3	2	2	2	0

STEWART, SHANNON — OF — BLUE JAYS

PERSONAL: Born February 25, 1974, in Cincinnati. . . . 6-1/195. . . . Bats right, throws right. . . . Full name: Shannon Harold Stewart.
HIGH SCHOOL: Southridge (Miami).
TRANSACTIONS/CAREER NOTES: Selected by Toronto Blue Jays organization in first round (19th pick overall) of free-agent draft (June 1, 1992); pick received as part of compensation for Los Angeles Dodgers signing Type A free-agent P Tom Candiotti. . . . On disabled list (June 13-September 13, 1994).

			BATTING											FIELDING			
Year	Team (League)	Pos.	G	AB	R	H	2B	3B	HR	RBI	Avg.	BB	SO	SB	PO	A	E	Avg.
1992—	GC Blue Jays (GCL)	OF	50	172	44	40	1	0	1	11	.233	24	27	*32	81	1	1	.988
1993—	St. Cathar. (NYP)	OF	75	*301	•53	84	15	2	3	29	.279	33	43	25	81	0	0	1.000
1994—	Hagerstown (SAL)	OF	56	225	39	73	10	5	4	25	.324	23	39	15	92	4	1	.990
1995—	Knoxville (South.)	OF	138	498	89	143	24	6	5	55	.287	*89	61	42	283	6	6	.980
	—Toronto (A.L.)	OF	12	38	2	8	0	0	0	1	.211	5	5	2	20	1	1	.955
Major league totals (1 year)			12	38	2	8	0	0	0	1	.211	5	5	2	20	1	1	.955

STINNETT, KELLY — C — BREWERS

PERSONAL: Born February 14, 1970, in Lawton, Okla. . . . 5-11/195. . . . Bats right, throws right. . . . Full name: Kelly Lee Stinnett. . . . Name pronounced stih-NET.
HIGH SCHOOL: Lawton (Okla.).
JUNIOR COLLEGE: Seminole (Okla.) Junior College.
TRANSACTIONS/CAREER NOTES: Selected by Cleveland Indians organization in 11th round of free-agent draft (June 5, 1989). . . . Selected

by New York Mets from Indians organization in Rule 5 major league draft (December 13, 1993). . . . Traded by Mets to Milwaukee Brewers for P Cory Lidle (January 17, 1996).
STATISTICAL NOTES: Led New York-Pennsylvania League catchers with 18 errors in 1990. . . . Led South Atlantic League catchers with 27 errors in 1991.

			BATTING											FIELDING			
Year	**Team (League)**	**Pos.**	**G**	**AB**	**R**	**H**	**2B**	**3B**	**HR**	**RBI**	**Avg.**	**BB**	**SO**	**SB**	**PO**	**A**	**E**	**Avg.**
1990—	Watertown (NYP)	C-1B	60	192	29	46	10	2	2	21	.240	40	43	3	348	48	†18	.957
1991—	Columbus (S. Atl.)	C-1B	102	384	49	101	15	1	14	74	.263	26	70	4	685	100	†28	.966
1992—	Cant./Akr. (East.)	C	91	296	37	84	10	0	6	32	.284	16	43	7	560	57	*13	.979
1993—	Charlotte (Int'l)	C	98	288	42	79	10	3	6	33	.274	17	52	0	495	48	8	.985
1994—	New York (N.L.)■	C	47	150	20	38	6	2	2	14	.253	11	28	2	211	20	5	.979
1995—	New York (N.L.)	C	77	196	23	43	8	1	4	18	.219	29	65	2	380	22	7	.983
Major league totals (2 years)			124	346	43	81	14	3	6	32	.234	40	93	4	591	42	12	.981

STOCKER, KEVIN — SS — PHILLIES

PERSONAL: Born February 13, 1970, in Spokane, Wash. . . . 6-1/175. . . . Bats both, throws right. . . . Full name: Kevin Douglas Stocker.
HIGH SCHOOL: Central Valley (Veradale, Wash.).
COLLEGE: Washington.
TRANSACTIONS/CAREER NOTES: Selected by Philadelphia Phillies organization in second round of free-agent draft (June 3, 1991). . . . On Philadelphia disabled list (April 28-June 1, 1994); included rehabilitation assignment to Scranton (May 28-June 1).

			BATTING											FIELDING			
Year	**Team (League)**	**Pos.**	**G**	**AB**	**R**	**H**	**2B**	**3B**	**HR**	**RBI**	**Avg.**	**BB**	**SO**	**SB**	**PO**	**A**	**E**	**Avg.**
1991—	Spartanburg (SAL)	SS	70	250	26	55	11	1	0	20	.220	31	37	15	83	176	18	.935
1992—	Clearwater (FSL)	SS	63	244	43	69	13	4	1	33	.283	27	31	15	102	220	16	.953
—	Reading (Eastern)	SS	62	240	31	60	9	2	1	13	.250	22	30	17	100	172	14	.951
1993—	Scran./W.B. (Int'l)	SS	83	313	54	73	14	1	3	17	.233	29	56	17	122	248	15	.961
—	Philadelphia (N.L.)	SS	70	259	46	84	12	3	2	31	.324	30	43	5	118	202	14	.958
1994—	Philadelphia (N.L.)	SS	82	271	38	74	11	2	2	28	.273	44	41	2	118	253	16	.959
—	Scran./W.B. (Int'l)	SS	4	13	1	4	1	0	0	2	.308	1	0	0	5	11	0	1.000
1995—	Philadelphia (N.L.)	SS	125	412	42	90	14	3	1	32	.218	43	75	6	147	383	17	.969
Major league totals (3 years)			277	942	126	248	37	8	5	91	.263	117	159	13	383	838	47	.963

CHAMPIONSHIP SERIES RECORD

			BATTING											FIELDING			
Year	**Team (League)**	**Pos.**	**G**	**AB**	**R**	**H**	**2B**	**3B**	**HR**	**RBI**	**Avg.**	**BB**	**SO**	**SB**	**PO**	**A**	**E**	**Avg.**
1993—	Philadelphia (N.L.)	SS	6	22	0	4	1	0	0	1	.182	2	5	0	10	13	1	.958

WORLD SERIES RECORD

			BATTING											FIELDING			
Year	**Team (League)**	**Pos.**	**G**	**AB**	**R**	**H**	**2B**	**3B**	**HR**	**RBI**	**Avg.**	**BB**	**SO**	**SB**	**PO**	**A**	**E**	**Avg.**
1993—	Philadelphia (N.L.)	SS	6	19	1	4	1	0	0	1	.211	5	5	0	8	13	0	1.000

STOTTLEMYRE, TODD — P — CARDINALS

PERSONAL: Born May 20, 1965, in Yakima, Wash. . . . 6-3/200. . . . Throws right, bats left. . . . Full name: Todd Vernon Stottlemyre. . . . Son of Mel Stottlemyre Sr., pitching coach, Houston Astros; pitcher, New York Yankees (1964-74) and pitching coach, New York Mets (1984-93); and brother of Mel Stottlemyre Jr., pitcher, Kansas City Royals (1990).
HIGH SCHOOL: A.C. Davis (Yakima, Wash.).
COLLEGE: Yakima (Wash.) Valley College.
TRANSACTIONS/CAREER NOTES: Selected by New York Yankees organization in fifth round of free-agent draft (June 6, 1983); did not sign. . . . Selected by St. Louis Cardinals organization in secondary phase of free-agent draft (January 9, 1985); did not sign. . . . Selected by Toronto Blue Jays organization in secondary phase of free-agent draft (June 3, 1985). . . . On disabled list (June 20-July 13, 1992). . . . On suspended list (September 23-28, 1992). . . . On disabled list (May 23-June 13, 1993). . . . Granted free agency (October 18, 1994). . . . Signed by Oakland Athletics (April 11, 1995). . . . Traded by A's to St. Louis Cardinals for OF Allen Battle, P Bret Wagner, P Jay Witasick and P Carl Dale (January 9, 1996).
STATISTICAL NOTES: Pitched 9-0 one-hit, complete-game victory against Chicago (August 26, 1992). . . . Struck out 15 batters in one game (June 16, 1995).

Year	**Team (League)**	**W**	**L**	**Pct.**	**ERA**	**G**	**GS**	**CG**	**ShO**	**Sv.**	**IP**	**H**	**R**	**ER**	**BB**	**SO**
1986—	Vent. County (Calif.)	9	4	.692	2.43	17	17	2	0	0	103 2/3	76	39	28	36	104
—	Knoxville (South.)	8	7	.533	4.18	18	18	1	0	0	99	93	56	46	49	81
1987—	Syracuse (Int'l)	11	•13	.458	4.44	34	*34	1	0	0	186 2/3	189	•103	*92	*87	143
1988—	Toronto (A.L.)	4	8	.333	5.69	28	16	0	0	0	98	109	70	62	46	67
—	Syracuse (Int'l)	5	0	1.000	2.05	7	7	1	0	0	48 1/3	36	12	11	8	51
1989—	Toronto (A.L.)	7	7	.500	3.88	27	18	0	0	0	127 2/3	137	56	55	44	63
—	Syracuse (Int'l)	3	2	.600	3.23	10	9	2	0	0	55 2/3	46	23	20	15	45
1990—	Toronto (A.L.)	13	17	.433	4.34	33	33	4	0	0	203	214	101	98	69	115
1991—	Toronto (A.L.)	15	8	.652	3.78	34	34	1	0	0	219	194	97	92	75	116
1992—	Toronto (A.L.)	12	11	.522	4.50	28	27	6	2	0	174	175	99	87	63	98
1993—	Toronto (A.L.)	11	12	.478	4.84	30	28	1	1	0	176 2/3	204	107	95	69	98
1994—	Toronto (A.L.)	7	7	.500	4.22	26	19	3	1	1	140 2/3	149	67	66	48	105
1995—	Oakland (A.L.)■	14	7	.667	4.55	31	31	2	0	0	209 2/3	228	117	106	80	205
Major league totals (8 years)		83	77	.519	4.41	237	206	17	4	1	1348 2/3	1410	714	661	494	867

CHAMPIONSHIP SERIES RECORD

Year	**Team (League)**	**W**	**L**	**Pct.**	**ERA**	**G**	**GS**	**CG**	**ShO**	**Sv.**	**IP**	**H**	**R**	**ER**	**BB**	**SO**
1989—	Toronto (A.L.)	0	1	.000	7.20	1	1	0	0	0	5	7	4	4	2	3
1991—	Toronto (A.L.)	0	1	.000	9.82	1	1	0	0	0	3 2/3	7	4	4	1	3
1992—	Toronto (A.L.)	0	0	...	2.45	1	0	0	0	0	3 2/3	3	1	1	0	1
1993—	Toronto (A.L.)	0	1	.000	7.50	1	1	0	0	0	6	6	5	5	4	4
Champ. series totals (4 years)		0	3	.000	6.87	4	3	0	0	0	18 1/3	23	14	14	7	11

WORLD SERIES RECORD

NOTES: Shares records for most bases on balls allowed in one inning—4 (October 20, 1993, first inning); and most consecutive bases on balls allowed in one inning—3 (October 20, 1993, first inning). . . . Member of World Series championship teams (1992 and 1993).

Year	Team (League)	W	L	Pct.	ERA	G	GS	CG	ShO	Sv.	IP	H	R	ER	BB	SO
1992—	Toronto (A.L.)	0	0	...	0.00	4	0	0	0	0	3 2/3	4	0	0	0	4
1993—	Toronto (A.L.)	0	0	...	27.00	1	1	0	0	0	2	3	6	6	4	1
World Series totals (2 years)		0	0	...	9.53	5	1	0	0	0	5 2/3	7	6	6	4	5

S

STOVALL, DAROND — OF — EXPOS

PERSONAL: Born January 3, 1973, in St. Louis. . . . 6-1/185. . . . Bats both, throws left. . . . Full name: Darond T. Stovall.
HIGH SCHOOL: Althoff Catholic (Belleville, Ill.).
TRANSACTIONS/CAREER NOTES: Selected by St. Louis Cardinals organization in fifth round of free-agent draft (June 3, 1991). . . . Traded by Cardinals organization with P Bryan Eversgerd and P Kirk Bullinger to Montreal Expos organization for P Ken Hill (April 5, 1995).
STATISTICAL NOTES: Led Florida State League outfielders with 339 total chances in 1994.

				BATTING										FIELDING			
Year	Team (League)	Pos.	G	AB	R	H	2B	3B	HR	RBI	Avg.	BB	SO	SB	PO	A	E	Avg.
1991—	Johns. City (App.)	OF	48	134	16	19	2	2	0	5	.142	23	63	9	69	2	5	.934
1992—	Savannah (S. Atl.)	OF	135	450	51	92	13	7	7	40	.204	63	138	20	250	8	12	.956
1993—	Springfield (Midw.)	OF	*135	460	73	118	19	4	20	81	.257	53	143	18	247	6	11	.958
1994—	St. Peters. (FSL)	OF	134	507	68	113	20	6	15	69	.223	62	*154	24	*328	7	4	.988
1995—	W.P. Beach (FSL)■	OF	121	461	52	107	22	2	4	51	.232	44	117	18	283	13	3	.990

STRANGE, DOUG — 2B — MARINERS

PERSONAL: Born April 13, 1964, in Greenville, S.C. . . . 6-1/185. . . . Bats both, throws right. . . . Full name: Joseph Douglas Strange.
HIGH SCHOOL: Wade Hampton (Greenville, S.C.).
COLLEGE: North Carolina State.
TRANSACTIONS/CAREER NOTES: Selected by Detroit Tigers organization in seventh round of free-agent draft (June 3, 1985). . . . Traded by Tigers to Houston Astros organization for IF/OF Lou Frazier (March 30, 1990). . . . Released by Astros organization (May 25, 1990). . . . Signed by Chicago Cubs organization (June 11, 1990). . . . Granted free agency (December 19, 1992). . . . Signed by Texas Rangers organization (January 11, 1993). . . . On disabled list (July 2-17, 1994). . . . Granted free agency (December 23, 1994). . . . Signed by Tacoma, Seattle Mariners organization (April 5, 1995).
STATISTICAL NOTES: Led Florida State League third basemen with 116 putouts and tied for lead with 20 double plays in 1986. . . . Led American Association third basemen with 16 double plays in 1990. . . . Led American Association with 10 intentional bases on balls received in 1991.
MISCELLANEOUS: Batted righthanded only (Glens Falls, 1987).

				BATTING										FIELDING			
Year	Team (League)	Pos.	G	AB	R	H	2B	3B	HR	RBI	Avg.	BB	SO	SB	PO	A	E	Avg.
1985—	Bristol (Appal.)	OF-2B-3B	65	226	43	69	16	1	6	45	.305	22	30	6	84	59	11	.929
1986—	Lakeland (Fla. St.)	3B-1B	126	466	59	119	29	4	2	63	.255	65	59	18	†202	215	37	.919
1987—	Glens Falls (East.)	3-2-0-S	115	431	63	130	31	1	13	70	.302	31	53	5	110	214	20	.942
—	Toledo (Int'l)	3B	16	45	7	11	2	0	1	5	.244	4	7	3	14	28	3	.933
1988—	Toledo (Int'l)	3B-SS-1B	82	278	23	56	8	2	6	19	.201	8	38	9	52	126	13	.932
—	Glens Falls (East.)	3B	57	218	32	61	11	1	1	36	.280	16	28	11	45	112	12	.929
1989—	Toledo (Int'l)	3B-SS	83	304	38	75	15	2	8	42	.247	34	49	8	108	197	17	.947
—	Detroit (A.L.)	3B-2B-SS	64	196	16	42	4	1	1	14	.214	17	36	3	53	118	19	.900
1990—	Tucson (PCL)■	3B-SS	37	98	7	22	3	0	0	7	.224	8	23	0	9	47	9	.862
—	Iowa (Am. Assoc.)■	3B-2B-SS	82	269	31	82	17	1	5	35	.305	28	42	6	58	149	16	.928
1991—	Iowa (Am. Assoc.)	3-2-1-S-0	131	509	76	149	35	5	8	56	.293	49	75	10	263	273	21	.962
—	Chicago (N.L.)	3B	3	9	0	4	1	0	0	1	.444	0	1	1	1	3	1	.800
1992—	Iowa (Am. Assoc.)	2B-3B	55	212	32	65	16	1	4	26	.307	9	32	3	84	126	16	.929
—	Chicago (N.L.)	3B-2B	52	94	7	15	1	0	1	5	.160	10	15	1	24	51	6	.926
1993—	Texas (A.L.)■	2B-3B-SS	145	484	58	124	29	0	7	60	.256	43	69	6	276	374	13	.980
1994—	Texas (A.L.)	2B-3B-OF	73	226	26	48	12	1	5	26	.212	15	38	1	88	175	11	.960
1995—	Seattle (A.L.)■	3-2-0-DH	74	155	19	42	9	2	2	21	.271	10	25	0	39	69	5	.956
American League totals (4 years)			356	1061	119	256	54	4	15	121	.241	85	168	10	456	736	48	.961
National League totals (2 years)			55	103	7	19	2	0	1	6	.184	10	16	2	25	54	7	.919
Major league totals (6 years)			411	1164	126	275	56	4	16	127	.236	95	184	12	481	790	55	.959

DIVISION SERIES RECORD

				BATTING										FIELDING			
Year	Team (League)	Pos.	G	AB	R	H	2B	3B	HR	RBI	Avg.	BB	SO	SB	PO	A	E	Avg.
1995—	Seattle (A.L.)	3B-PH	2	4	0	0	0	0	0	1	.000	1	1	0	0	0	0	...

CHAMPIONSHIP SERIES RECORD

				BATTING										FIELDING			
Year	Team (League)	Pos.	G	AB	R	H	2B	3B	HR	RBI	Avg.	BB	SO	SB	PO	A	E	Avg.
1995—	Seattle (A.L.)	PH-3B	4	4	0	0	0	0	0	0	.000	0	2	0	2	3	0	1.000

STRAWBERRY, DARRYL — OF

PERSONAL: Born March 12, 1962, in Los Angeles. . . . 6-6/215. . . . Bats left, throws left. . . . Full name: Darryl Eugene Strawberry. . . . Brother of Michael Strawberry, minor league outfielder (1980-81).
HIGH SCHOOL: Crenshaw (Los Angeles).
TRANSACTIONS/CAREER NOTES: Selected by New York Mets organization in first round (first pick overall) of free-agent draft (June 3, 1980). . . . On disabled list (May 12-June 28, 1985). . . . Granted free agency (November 5, 1990). . . . Signed by Los Angeles Dodgers (November

8, 1990). . . . On disabled list (June 18-July 3, 1991; May 14-July 6 and July 21-September 1, 1992). . . . On Los Angeles disabled list (May 13-June 5, 1993); included rehabilitation assignment to Albuquerque (May 28-June 5). . . . On Los Angeles disabled list (June 17, 1993-remainder of season and April 4-May 26, 1994). . . . Released by Dodgers (May 26, 1994). . . . Signed by San Francisco Giants organization (June 19, 1994). . . . On suspended list (February 6-June 19, 1995). . . . Released by Giants (February 8, 1995). . . . Signed by New York Yankees organization (June 19, 1995). . . . On Columbus disabled list (June 22-July 4, 1995). . . . Granted free agency (November 30, 1995).

HONORS: Named Texas League Most Valuable Player (1982). . . . Named N.L. Rookie Player of the Year by The Sporting News (1983). . . . Named N.L. Rookie of the Year by Baseball Writers' Association of America (1983). . . . Named outfielder on The Sporting News N.L. All-Star team (1988 and 1990). . . . Named outfielder on The Sporting News N.L. Silver Slugger team (1988 and 1990).

STATISTICAL NOTES: Led Texas League in slugging percentage with .602 and in caught stealing with 22 in 1982. . . . Hit three home runs in one game (August 5, 1985). . . . Led N.L. with .545 slugging percentage in 1988. . . . Led Gulf Coast League with five intentional bases on balls received in 1995. . . . Career major league grand slams: 6.

		BATTING												FIELDING			
Year Team (League)	Pos.	G	AB	R	H	2B	3B	HR	RBI	Avg.	BB	SO	SB	PO	A	E	Avg.
1980—Kingsport (Appal.)	OF	44	157	27	42	5	2	5	20	.268	20	39	5	55	4	3	.952
1981—Lynchburg (Caro.)	OF	123	420	84	107	22	6	13	78	.255	82	105	31	173	8	13	.933
1982—Jackson (Texas)	OF	129	435	93	123	19	9	*34	97	.283	*100	145	45	211	8	9	.961
1983—Tidewater (Int'l)	OF	16	57	12	19	4	1	3	13	.333	14	18	7	22	0	4	.846
—New York (N.L.)	OF	122	420	63	108	15	7	26	74	.257	47	128	19	232	8	4	.984
1984—New York (N.L.)	OF	147	522	75	131	27	4	26	97	.251	75	131	27	276	11	6	.980
1985—New York (N.L.)	OF	111	393	78	109	15	4	29	79	.277	73	96	26	211	5	2	.991
1986—New York (N.L.)	OF	136	475	76	123	27	5	27	93	.259	72	141	28	226	10	6	.975
1987—New York (N.L.)	OF	154	532	108	151	32	5	39	104	.284	97	122	36	272	6	8	.972
1988—New York (N.L.)	OF	153	543	101	146	27	3	*39	101	.269	85	127	29	297	4	9	.971
1989—New York (N.L.)	OF	134	476	69	107	26	1	29	77	.225	61	105	11	272	4	8	.972
1990—New York (N.L.)	OF	152	542	92	150	18	1	37	108	.277	70	110	15	268	10	3	.989
1991—Los Angeles (N.L.)■	OF	139	505	86	134	22	4	28	99	.265	75	125	10	209	11	5	.978
1992—Los Angeles (N.L.)	OF	43	156	20	37	8	0	5	25	.237	19	34	3	67	2	1	.986
1993—Los Angeles (N.L.)	OF	32	100	12	14	2	0	5	12	.140	16	19	1	37	1	4	.905
—Albuquerque (PCL)	OF	5	19	3	6	2	0	1	2	.316	2	5	1	7	0	0	1.000
1994—Phoenix (PCL)■	OF	3	10	3	3	0	0	2	3	.300	0	4	0	4	0	0	1.000
—San Francisco (N.L.)	OF	29	92	13	22	3	1	4	17	.239	19	22	0	61	1	2	.969
1995—GC Yankees (GCL)■	OF	7	20	3	5	2	0	0	4	.250	9	5	2	3	1	0	1.000
—Tampa (Fla. St.)	DH	2	9	1	2	1	0	1	2	.222	1	2	0	...	...	...	...
—Columbus (Int'l)	OF	22	83	20	25	3	1	7	29	.301	15	17	1	9	0	0	1.000
—New York (A.L.)	DH-OF	32	87	15	24	4	1	3	13	.276	10	22	0	18	2	2	.909
American League totals (1 year)		32	87	15	24	4	1	3	13	.276	10	22	0	18	2	2	.909
National League totals (12 years)		1352	4756	793	1232	222	35	294	886	.259	709	1160	205	2428	73	58	.977
Major league totals (13 years)		1384	4843	808	1256	226	36	297	899	.259	719	1182	205	2446	75	60	.977

DIVISION SERIES RECORD

		BATTING												FIELDING			
Year Team (League)	Pos.	G	AB	R	H	2B	3B	HR	RBI	Avg.	BB	SO	SB	PO	A	E	Avg.
1995—New York (A.L.)	PH	2	2	0	0	0	0	0	0	.000	0	1	0	...	...	...	...

CHAMPIONSHIP SERIES RECORD

NOTES: Shares single-series record for most strikeouts—12 (1986). . . . Shares N.L. single-series record for most at-bats—30 (1988).

		BATTING												FIELDING			
Year Team (League)	Pos.	G	AB	R	H	2B	3B	HR	RBI	Avg.	BB	SO	SB	PO	A	E	Avg.
1986—New York (N.L.)	OF	6	22	4	5	1	0	2	5	.227	3	12	1	9	0	0	1.000
1988—New York (N.L.)	OF	7	30	5	9	2	0	1	6	.300	2	5	0	11	0	0	1.000
Championship series totals (2 years)		13	52	9	14	3	0	3	11	.269	5	17	1	20	0	0	1.000

WORLD SERIES RECORD

NOTES: Member of World Series championship team (1986).

		BATTING												FIELDING			
Year Team (League)	Pos.	G	AB	R	H	2B	3B	HR	RBI	Avg.	BB	SO	SB	PO	A	E	Avg.
1986—New York (N.L.)	OF	7	24	4	5	1	0	1	1	.208	4	6	3	19	0	0	1.000

ALL-STAR GAME RECORD

		BATTING											FIELDING			
Year League	Pos.	AB	R	H	2B	3B	HR	RBI	Avg.	BB	SO	SB	PO	A	E	Avg.
1984—National	OF	2	0	1	0	0	0	0	.500	0	1	0	0	0	0	...
1985—National	OF	1	2	1	0	0	0	0	1.000	1	0	1	3	0	0	1.000
1986—National	OF	2	0	1	0	0	0	0	.500	0	1	0	1	0	0	1.000
1987—National	OF	2	0	0	0	0	0	0	.000	0	0	0	0	0	0	...
1988—National	OF	4	0	1	0	0	0	0	.250	0	1	0	4	0	0	1.000
1989—National		Selected, did not play—injured.														
1990—National	OF	1	0	0	0	0	0	0	.000	0	1	0	3	1	1	.800
1991—National		Selected, did not play—injured.														
All-Star Game totals (6 years)		12	2	4	0	0	0	0	.333	1	4	1	11	1	1	.923

STUBBS, FRANKLIN 1B/OF

PERSONAL: Born October 21, 1960, in Laurinburg, N.C. . . . 6-2/209. . . . Bats left, throws left. . . . Full name: Franklin Lee Stubbs.

HIGH SCHOOL: Richmond (Hamlet, N.C.).

COLLEGE: Virginia Tech.

TRANSACTIONS/CAREER NOTES: Selected by Los Angeles Dodgers organization in first round (19th pick overall) of free-agent draft (June 7, 1982). . . . On disabled list (July 5, 1982-remainder of season; August 3-24, 1987; and August 20, 1989-remainder of season). . . . Traded by Dodgers to Houston Astros for P Terry Wells (April 1, 1990). . . . Granted free agency (November 5, 1990). . . . Signed by Milwaukee Brewers (December 5, 1990). . . . Granted free agency (January 20, 1993). . . . Signed by Montreal Expos organization (February 22, 1993). . . . Released by Expos (March 29, 1993). . . . Signed by Boston Red Sox organization (May 11, 1993). . . . Granted free agency (October 15,

1993). . . . Played in Mexico (1994). . . . Signed by Toledo, Detroit Tigers organization (December 20, 1994). . . . On disabled list (July 17-August 12, 1995). . . . Granted free agency (November 2, 1995).
RECORDS: Shares major league single-game record for fewest putouts by first baseman—0 (July 25, 1990).
HONORS: Named first baseman on THE SPORTING NEWS college All-America team (1982).
STATISTICAL NOTES: Led N.L. first basemen with .994 fielding percentage in 1987. . . . Career major league grand slams: 3.

			BATTING											FIELDING			
Year Team (League)	**Pos.**	**G**	**AB**	**R**	**H**	**2B**	**3B**	**HR**	**RBI**	**Avg.**	**BB**	**SO**	**SB**	**PO**	**A**	**E**	**Avg.**
1982— Vero Beach (FSL)	1B	16	54	6	11	1	1	3	5	.204	6	13	2	134	3	3	.979
1983— San Antonio (Tex.)	1B-OF	47	173	35	54	8	3	12	52	.312	29	32	5	425	23	5	.989
— Albuquerque (PCL)	OF-1B	76	267	49	74	16	3	16	58	.277	41	53	3	106	3	6	.948
1984— Los Angeles (N.L.)	1B-OF	87	217	22	42	2	3	8	17	.194	24	63	2	417	37	4	.991
— Albuquerque (PCL)	OF-1B	29	108	26	35	5	5	6	24	.324	12	23	3	36	4	2	.952
1985— Albuquerque (PCL)	1B-OF	132	421	86	118	23	5	32	93	.280	83	105	23	945	87	14	.987
— Los Angeles (N.L.)	1B	10	9	0	2	0	0	0	2	.222	0	3	0	11	0	0	1.000
1986— Los Angeles (N.L.)	OF-1B	132	420	55	95	11	1	23	58	.226	37	107	7	244	14	7	.974
1987— Los Angeles (N.L.)	1B-OF	129	386	48	90	16	3	16	52	.233	31	85	8	830	79	5	†.995
1988— Los Angeles (N.L.)	1B-OF	115	242	30	54	13	0	8	34	.223	23	61	11	530	57	13	.978
1989— Los Angeles (N.L.)	OF-1B	69	103	11	30	6	0	4	15	.291	16	27	3	70	5	3	.962
1990— Houston (N.L.)■	1B-OF	146	448	59	117	23	2	23	71	.261	48	114	19	609	43	6	.991
1991— Milwaukee (A.L.)■	1B-OF-DH	103	362	48	77	16	2	11	38	.213	35	71	13	828	82	9	.990
1992— Milwaukee (A.L.)	1B-DH-OF	92	288	37	66	11	1	9	42	.229	27	68	11	525	63	8	.987
1993— Pawtucket (Int'l)■	1B	94	334	47	79	18	1	15	58	.237	51	82	3	389	28	7	.983
1994— Yucatan (Mexican)■	2B-1B-OF	40	134	21	33	8	0	3	13	.246	24	25	6	351	11	4	.989
1995— Detroit (A.L.)■	1B-OF-DH	62	116	13	29	11	0	2	19	.250	19	27	0	155	5	5	.970
American League totals (3 years)		257	766	98	172	38	3	22	99	.225	81	166	24	1508	150	22	.987
National League totals (7 years)		688	1825	225	430	71	9	82	249	.236	179	460	50	2711	235	38	.987
Major league totals (10 years)		945	2591	323	602	109	12	104	348	.232	260	626	74	4219	385	60	.987

CHAMPIONSHIP SERIES RECORD

			BATTING											FIELDING			
Year Team (League)	**Pos.**	**G**	**AB**	**R**	**H**	**2B**	**3B**	**HR**	**RBI**	**Avg.**	**BB**	**SO**	**SB**	**PO**	**A**	**E**	**Avg.**
1988— Los Angeles (N.L.)	1B-PH	4	8	0	2	0	0	0	0	.250	0	4	0	16	2	0	1.000

WORLD SERIES RECORD

NOTES: Member of World Series championship team (1988).

			BATTING											FIELDING			
Year Team (League)	**Pos.**	**G**	**AB**	**R**	**H**	**2B**	**3B**	**HR**	**RBI**	**Avg.**	**BB**	**SO**	**SB**	**PO**	**A**	**E**	**Avg.**
1988— Los Angeles (N.L.)	1B	5	17	3	5	2	0	0	2	.294	1	3	0	34	0	0	1.000

STULL, EVERETT — P — EXPOS

PERSONAL: Born August 24, 1971, in Fort Riley, Kan. . . . 6-3/200. . . . Throws right, bats right. . . . Full name: Everett James Stull.
HIGH SCHOOL: Redan (Stone Mountain, Ga.).
COLLEGE: Tennessee State.
TRANSACTIONS/CAREER NOTES: Selected by Montreal Expos organization in third round of free-agent draft (June 1, 1992).
STATISTICAL NOTES: Led New York-Pennsylvania League with 18 wild pitches in 1992.

Year Team (League)	**W**	**L**	**Pct.**	**ERA**	**G**	**GS**	**CG**	**ShO**	**Sv.**	**IP**	**H**	**R**	**ER**	**BB**	**SO**
1992— Jamestown (NYP)	3	5	.375	5.40	14	14	0	0	0	63 1/3	52	49	38	*61	64
1993— Burlington (Midw.)	4	9	.308	3.83	15	15	0	0	0	82 1/3	68	44	35	59	85
1994— WP Beach (FSL)	10	10	.500	3.31	27	26	3	1	0	147	116	60	54	78	165
1995— Harrisburg (East.)	3	•12	.200	5.54	24	24	0	0	0	126 2/3	114	88	78	79	132

STURTZE, TANYON — P — CUBS

PERSONAL: Born October 12, 1970, in Worcester, Mass. . . . 6-5/205. . . . Throws right, bats right. . . . Full name: Tanyon James Sturtze. . . Name pronounced STURTS.
HIGH SCHOOL: St. Peter-Marian (Worcester, Mass.).
JUNIOR COLLEGE: Quinsigamond Community College (Mass.).
TRANSACTIONS/CAREER NOTES: Selected by Oakland Athletics organization in 23rd round of free-agent draft (June 4, 1990). . . . On Huntsville disabled list (April 7-16, 1994). . . . Selected by Chicago Cubs from A's organization in Rule 5 major league draft (December 5, 1994).
STATISTICAL NOTES: Pitched 5-0 no-hit victory against Chattanooga (June 13, 1993).

Year Team (League)	**W**	**L**	**Pct.**	**ERA**	**G**	**GS**	**CG**	**ShO**	**Sv.**	**IP**	**H**	**R**	**ER**	**BB**	**SO**
1990— Arizona A's (Ariz.)	2	5	.286	5.44	12	10	0	0	0	48	55	41	29	27	30
1991— Madison (Midwest)	10	5	.667	3.09	27	27	0	0	0	163	136	77	56	58	88
1992— Modesto (Calif.)	7	11	.389	3.75	25	25	1	0	0	151	143	72	63	78	126
1993— Huntsville (South.)	5	12	.294	4.78	28	•28	1	1	0	165 2/3	169	102	*88	85	112
1994— Huntsville (South.)	6	3	.667	3.22	17	17	1	0	0	103 1/3	100	40	37	39	63
— Tacoma (PCL)	4	5	.444	4.04	11	9	0	0	0	64 2/3	73	36	29	34	28
1995— Chicago (N.L.)■	0	0	...	9.00	2	0	0	0	0	2	2	2	2	1	0
— Iowa (Am. Assoc.)	4	7	.364	6.80	23	17	1	1	0	86	108	66	65	42	48
Major league totals (1 year)	0	0	...	9.00	2	0	0	0	0	2	2	2	2	1	0

STYNES, CHRIS — 2B — ROYALS

PERSONAL: Born January 19, 1973, in Queens, N.Y. . . . 5-9/175. . . . Bats right, throws right. . . . Full name: Christopher Desmond Stynes.
HIGH SCHOOL: Boca Raton (Fla.).
TRANSACTIONS/CAREER NOTES: Selected by Toronto Blue Jays in third round of free-agent draft (June 3, 1991). . . . Traded by Blue Jays with P David Sinnes and IF Tony Medrano to Kansas City Royals for P David Cone (April 6, 1995).

STATISTICAL NOTES: Tied for Florida State League lead in double plays by third basemen with 22 in 1993. . . . Led Southern League with 237 total bases in 1994.

				BATTING											FIELDING			
Year	Team (League)	Pos.	G	AB	R	H	2B	3B	HR	RBI	Avg.	BB	SO	SB	PO	A	E	Avg.
1991—	GC Blue Jays (GCL)	3B	57	219	29	67	15	1	4	39	.306	9	39	10	42	*138	8	*.957
1992—	Myrtle Beach (SAL)	3B	127	489	67	139	36	0	7	46	.284	16	43	28	86	208	26	.919
1993—	Dunedin (Fla. St.)	3B	123	496	72	151	28	5	7	48	.304	25	40	19	83	234	21	*.938
1994—	Knoxville (South.)	2B	136	*545	79	*173	32	4	8	79	.317	23	36	28	247	•366	20	.968
1995—	Omaha (A.A.)■	2B-3B	83	306	51	84	12	5	9	42	.275	27	24	4	144	204	13	.964
—	Kansas City (A.L.)	2B-DH	22	35	7	6	1	0	0	2	.171	4	3	0	21	35	1	.982
Major league totals (1 year)			22	35	7	6	1	0	0	2	.171	4	3	0	21	35	1	.982

SULLIVAN, SCOTT — P — REDS

PERSONAL: Born March 13, 1971, in Tuscaloosa, Ala. . . . 6-4/210. . . . Throws right, bats right. . . . Full name: William Scott Sullivan.
HIGH SCHOOL: Pickens Academy (Carrollton, Ala.).
COLLEGE: Auburn.
TRANSACTIONS/CAREER NOTES: Selected by Cincinnati Reds organization in second round of free-agent draft (June 3, 1993). . . . On Indianapolis disabled list (August 21, 1995-remainder of season).

Year	Team (League)	W	L	Pct.	ERA	G	GS	CG	ShO	Sv.	IP	H	R	ER	BB	SO
1993—	Billings (Pioneer)	5	0	1.000	1.67	18	7	2	2	3	54	33	13	10	25	79
1994—	Chattanooga (Sou.)	11	7	.611	3.41	34	13	2	0	7	121 1/3	101	60	46	40	111
1995—	Indianapolis (A.A.)	4	3	.571	3.53	44	0	0	0	1	58 2/3	51	31	23	24	54
—	Cincinnati (N.L.)	0	0	...	4.91	3	0	0	0	0	3 2/3	4	2	2	2	2
Major league totals (1 year)		0	0	...	4.91	3	0	0	0	0	3 2/3	4	2	2	2	2

SUPPAN, JEFF — P — RED SOX

PERSONAL: Born January 2, 1975, in Oklahoma City. . . . 6-2/203. . . . Throws right, bats right. . . . Full name: Jeffrey Scot Suppan.
HIGH SCHOOL: Crespi (Encino, Calif.).
TRANSACTIONS/CAREER NOTES: Selected by Boston Red Sox organization in second round of free-agent draft (June 3, 1993). . . . On Trenton disabled list (April 9-29, 1995).

Year	Team (League)	W	L	Pct.	ERA	G	GS	CG	ShO	Sv.	IP	H	R	ER	BB	SO
1993—	GC Red Sox (GCL)	4	3	.571	2.18	10	9	2	1	0	57 2/3	52	20	14	16	64
1994—	Sarasota (Fla. St.)	•13	7	.650	3.26	27	27	4	2	0	174	153	74	63	50	*173
1995—	Trenton (Eastern)	6	2	.750	2.36	15	15	1	1	0	99	86	35	26	26	88
—	Boston (A.L.)	1	2	.333	5.96	8	3	0	0	0	22 2/3	29	15	15	5	19
—	Pawtucket (Int'l)	2	3	.400	5.32	7	7	0	0	0	45 2/3	50	29	27	9	32
Major league totals (1 year)		1	2	.333	5.96	8	3	0	0	0	22 2/3	29	15	15	5	19

SURHOFF, B.J. — 3B/OF — ORIOLES

PERSONAL: Born August 4, 1964, in Bronx, N.Y. . . . 6-1/200. . . . Bats left, throws right. . . . Full name: William James Surhoff. . . . Son of Dick Surhoff, forward, New York Knicks and Milwaukee Hawks of National Basketball Association (1952-53 and 1953-54); and brother of Rich Surhoff, pitcher, Philadelphia Phillies and Texas Rangers (1985).
HIGH SCHOOL: Rye (N.Y.).
COLLEGE: North Carolina.
TRANSACTIONS/CAREER NOTES: Selected by New York Yankees organization in fifth round of free-agent draft (June 7, 1982); did not sign. . . . Selected by Milwaukee Brewers organization in first round (first pick overall) of free-agent draft (June 3, 1985). . . . On suspended list (August 23-25, 1990). . . . On Milwaukee disabled list (March 25-April 16, April 20-May 23 and July 7, 1994-remainder of season); included rehabilitation assignments to El Paso (April 12-16) and New Orleans (May 17-23). . . . Granted free agency (October 20, 1994). . . . Re-signed by New Orleans, Brewers organization (April 7, 1995). . . . Granted free agency (November 6, 1995). . . . Signed by Baltimore Orioles (December 20, 1995).
HONORS: Named College Player of the Year by The Sporting News (1985). . . . Named catcher on The Sporting News college All-America team (1985).
STATISTICAL NOTES: Tied for Pacific Coast League lead in double plays by catcher with 10 in 1986. . . . Led A.L. catchers with 68 assists in 1991. . . . Career major league grand slams: 2.
MISCELLANEOUS: Member of 1984 U.S. Olympic baseball team.

				BATTING											FIELDING			
Year	Team (League)	Pos.	G	AB	R	H	2B	3B	HR	RBI	Avg.	BB	SO	SB	PO	A	E	Avg.
1985—	Beloit (Midwest)	C	76	289	39	96	13	4	7	58	.332	22	35	10	475	44	3	.994
1986—	Vancouver (PCL)	C	116	458	71	141	19	3	5	59	.308	29	30	21	539	70	7	*.989
1987—	Milwaukee (A.L.)	C-3-DH-1	115	395	50	118	22	3	7	68	.299	36	30	11	648	56	11	.985
1988—	Milwaukee (A.L.)	C-3-1-S-O	139	493	47	121	21	0	5	38	.245	31	49	21	550	94	8	.988
1989—	Milwaukee (A.L.)	C-DH-3B	126	436	42	108	17	4	5	55	.248	25	29	14	530	58	10	.983
1990—	Milwaukee (A.L.)	C-3B	135	474	55	131	21	4	6	59	.276	41	37	18	619	62	12	.983
1991—	Milwaukee (A.L.)	C-DH-3-O-2	143	505	57	146	19	4	5	68	.289	26	33	5	665	†71	4	.995
1992—	Milwaukee (A.L.)	C-1-DH-O-3	139	480	63	121	19	1	4	62	.252	46	41	14	699	74	6	.992
1993—	Milwaukee (A.L.)	3-O-1-C-DH	148	552	66	151	38	3	7	79	.274	36	47	12	175	220	18	.956
1994—	El Paso (Texas)	OF	3	12	2	3	1	0	0	0	.250	0	2	0	3	0	0	1.000
—	Milwaukee (A.L.)	3-C-1-O-DH	40	134	20	35	11	2	5	22	.261	16	14	0	121	29	4	.974
—	New Orleans (A.A.)	3-O-C-1	5	19	3	6	2	0	0	1	.316	1	2	0	21	3	0	1.000
1995—	Milwaukee (A.L.)	O-1-C-DH	117	415	72	133	26	3	13	73	.320	37	43	7	530	44	5	.991
Major league totals (9 years)			1102	3884	472	1064	194	24	57	524	.274	294	323	102	4537	708	78	.985

S

SUZUKI, MAKOTO — P — MARINERS

PERSONAL: Born May 31, 1975, in Kobe, Japan. . . . 6-3/195. . . . Throws right, bats right.
HIGH SCHOOL: Takigawa Daini (Kobe, Japan).
TRANSACTIONS/CAREER NOTES: Played with Salinas, independent (August 30, 1992). . . . Signed as non-drafted free agent by Seattle Mariners organization (September 5, 1993). . . . On disabled list (April 19-June 15 and July 10, 1994-remainder of season).

Year	Team (League)	W	L	Pct.	ERA	G	GS	CG	ShO	Sv.	IP	H	R	ER	BB	SO
1992—	Salinas (Calif.)	0	0	. . .	0.00	1	0	0	0	0	1	0	0	0	0	1
1993—	San Bern. (Calif.)	4	4	.500	3.68	48	1	0	0	12	$80^2/_3$	59	37	33	56	87
1994—	Jacksonville (Sou.)	1	0	1.000	2.84	8	0	0	0	1	$12^2/_3$	15	4	4	6	10
1995—	Riverside (Calif.)	0	1	.000	4.70	6	0	0	0	0	$7^2/_3$	10	4	4	6	6
	—Ariz. Mariners (Ariz.)	1	0	1.000	6.75	4	3	0	0	0	4	5	4	3	0	3

SWARTZBAUGH, DAVE — P — CUBS

PERSONAL: Born February 11, 1968, in Middletown, O. . . . 6-2/210. . . . Throws right, bats right. . . . Full name: David Theodore Swartzbaugh.
HIGH SCHOOL: Middletown (O.).
COLLEGE: Miami of Ohio.
TRANSACTIONS/CAREER NOTES: Selected by Chicago Cubs organization in ninth round of free-agent draft (June 5, 1989). . . . On Iowa disabled list (April 6-13, 1995).

Year	Team (League)	W	L	Pct.	ERA	G	GS	CG	ShO	Sv.	IP	H	R	ER	BB	SO
1989—	Geneva (NYP)	2	3	.400	4.92	18	10	0	0	0	75	81	59	41	35	77
1990—	Peoria (Midwest)	8	11	.421	3.82	29	•29	5	2	0	$169^2/_3$	147	88	72	89	128
1991—	Peoria (Midwest)	0	5	.000	1.83	5	5	1	0	0	$34^1/_3$	21	16	7	15	31
	—Winst.-Salem (Car.)	10	4	.714	1.83	15	15	2	1	0	$93^2/_3$	71	22	19	42	73
	—Charlotte (South.)	0	1	.000	10.13	1	1	0	0	0	$5^1/_3$	6	7	6	3	5
1992—	Charlotte (South.)	7	10	.412	3.65	27	27	5	2	0	165	134	78	67	62	111
1993—	Iowa (Am. Assoc.)	4	6	.400	5.30	26	9	0	0	1	$86^2/_3$	90	57	51	44	69
	—Orlando (Southern)	1	3	.250	4.23	10	9	1	0	0	66	52	33	31	18	59
1994—	Orlando (Southern)	2	4	.333	3.30	42	1	0	0	2	79	70	36	29	19	70
	—Iowa (Am. Assoc.)	1	0	1.000	8.38	10	0	0	0	0	$19^1/_3$	24	18	18	15	14
1995—	Iowa (Am. Assoc.)	3	0	1.000	1.53	30	0	0	0	0	47	33	10	8	18	38
	—Orlando (Southern)	4	0	1.000	2.48	16	0	0	0	0	29	18	10	8	7	37
	—Chicago (N.L.)	0	0	. . .	0.00	7	0	0	0	0	$7^1/_3$	5	2	0	3	5
Major league totals (1 year)		0	0	. . .	0.00	7	0	0	0	0	$7^1/_3$	5	2	0	3	5

SWEENEY, MARK — OF — CARDINALS

PERSONAL: Born October 26, 1969, in Framingham, Mass. . . . 6-1/195. . . . Bats left, throws left. . . . Full name: Mark Patrick Sweeney.
HIGH SCHOOL: Holliston (Mass.).
COLLEGE: Maine.
TRANSACTIONS/CAREER NOTES: Selected by Los Angeles Dodgers organization in 39th round of free-agent draft (June 4, 1990); did not sign. . . . Selected by California Angels organization in ninth round of free-agent draft (June 3, 1991). . . . Traded by Angels organization with a player to be named later to St. Louis Cardinals for P John Habyan (July 8, 1995).

			BATTING											FIELDING			
Year	Team (League)	Pos.	G	AB	R	H	2B	3B	HR	RBI	Avg.	BB	SO	SB	PO	A	E	Avg.
1991—	Boise (Northwest)	OF	70	234	45	66	10	3	4	34	.282	*51	42	9	81	2	4	.954
1992—	Quad City (Midw.)	OF	120	424	65	115	20	5	14	76	.271	47	85	15	205	5	4	.981
1993—	Palm Springs (Cal.)	OF-1B	66	245	41	87	18	3	3	47	.355	42	29	9	145	2	7	.955
	—Midland (Texas)	OF	51	188	41	67	13	2	9	32	.356	27	22	1	85	3	1	.989
1994—	Vancouver (PCL)	1B-OF	103	344	59	98	12	3	8	49	.285	59	50	3	330	12	2	.994
	—Midland (Texas)	OF-1B	14	50	13	15	3	0	3	18	.300	10	10	1	66	5	2	.973
1995—	Vancouver (PCL)	OF-1B	69	226	48	78	14	2	7	59	.345	43	33	3	102	2	2	.981
	—Louisville (A.A.)■	1B	22	76	15	28	8	0	2	22	.368	14	8	2	176	19	2	.990
	—St. Louis (N.L.)	1B-OF	37	77	5	21	2	0	2	13	.273	10	15	1	153	11	2	.988
Major league totals (1 year)			37	77	5	21	2	0	2	13	.273	10	15	1	153	11	2	.988

SWEENEY, MIKE — C — ROYALS

PERSONAL: Born July 22, 1973, in Orange, Calif. . . . 6-1/195. . . . Bats right, throws right. . . . Full name: Michael John Sweeney.
HIGH SCHOOL: Ontario (Calif.).
TRANSACTIONS/CAREER NOTES: Selected by Kansas City Royals organization in 10th round of free-agent draft (June 3, 1991). . . . On disabled list (May 24-July 5, 1994).
STATISTICAL NOTES: Led Carolina League with .548 slugging percentage in 1995.

			BATTING											FIELDING			
Year	Team (League)	Pos.	G	AB	R	H	2B	3B	HR	RBI	Avg.	BB	SO	SB	PO	A	E	Avg.
1991—	GC Royals (GCL)	C-1B	38	102	8	22	3	0	1	11	.216	11	9	1	124	16	4	.972
1992—	Eugene (N'west)	C	59	199	17	44	12	1	4	28	.221	13	54	3	367	42	14	.967
1993—	Eugene (N'west)	C	53	175	32	42	10	2	6	29	.240	30	41	1	364	46	7	.983
1994—	Rockford (Midw.)	C	86	276	47	83	20	3	10	52	.301	55	43	0	453	54	6	.988
1995—	Wilmington (Caro.)	C-3B	99	332	61	103	23	1	18	53	*.310	60	39	6	575	45	7	.989
	—Kansas City (A.L.)	C	4	4	1	1	0	0	0	0	.250	0	0	0	7	0	1	.875
Major league totals (1 year)			4	4	1	1	0	0	0	0	.250	0	0	0	7	0	1	.875

SWIFT, BILL P ROCKIES

PERSONAL: Born October 27, 1961, in South Portland, Me. . . . 6-0/197. . . . Throws right, bats right. . . . Full name: William Charles Swift.
HIGH SCHOOL: South Portland (Portland, Me.).
COLLEGE: Maine.
TRANSACTIONS/CAREER NOTES: Selected by Minnesota Twins organization in second round of free-agent draft (June 6, 1983); did not sign. . . . Selected by Seattle Mariners organization in first round (second pick overall) of free-agent draft (June 4, 1984). . . . On disabled list (May 6-21, 1985 and April 22, 1987-remainder of season). . . . On Seattle disabled list (March 28-April 27, 1989); included rehabilitation assignment to San Bernardino (April 18-27). . . . On disabled list (April 11-26, 1991). . . . Traded by Mariners with P Mike Jackson and P Dave Burba to San Francisco Giants for OF Kevin Mitchell and P Mike Remlinger (December 11, 1991). . . . On disabled list (May 23-June 21 and August 25-September 9, 1992; May 18-June 6 and June 24-July 21, 1994). . . . Granted free agency (October 15, 1994). . . . Signed by Colorado Rockies (April 8, 1995). . . . On disabled list (May 28-June 16 and July 26-September 1, 1995).
MISCELLANEOUS: Member of 1984 U.S. Olympic baseball team. . . . Appeared in five games as pinch-runner (1992). . . . Appeared in one game as pinch-runner (1994).

Year	Team (League)	W	L	Pct.	ERA	G	GS	CG	ShO	Sv.	IP	H	R	ER	BB	SO
1985	—Chattanooga (Sou.)	2	1	.667	3.69	7	7	0	0	0	39	34	16	16	21	21
	—Seattle (A.L.)	6	10	.375	4.77	23	21	0	0	0	120 2/3	131	71	64	48	55
1986	—Seattle (A.L.)	2	9	.182	5.46	29	17	1	0	0	115 1/3	148	85	70	55	55
	—Calgary (PCL)	4	4	.500	3.95	10	8	3	1	1	57	57	33	25	22	29
1987	—Calgary (PCL)	0	0	...	8.84	5	5	0	0	0	18 1/3	32	22	18	13	5
1988	—Seattle (A.L.)	8	12	.400	4.59	38	24	6	1	0	174 2/3	199	99	89	65	47
1989	—San Bern. (Calif.)	1	0	1.000	0.00	2	2	0	0	0	10	8	0	0	2	4
	—Seattle (A.L.)	7	3	.700	4.43	37	16	0	0	1	130	140	72	64	38	45
1990	—Seattle (A.L.)	6	4	.600	2.39	55	8	0	0	6	128	135	46	34	21	42
1991	—Seattle (A.L.)	1	2	.333	1.99	71	0	0	0	17	90 1/3	74	22	20	26	48
1992	—San Francisco (N.L.)■	10	4	.714	*2.08	30	22	3	2	1	164 2/3	144	41	38	43	77
1993	—San Francisco (N.L.)	21	8	.724	2.82	34	34	1	1	0	232 2/3	195	82	73	55	157
1994	—San Francisco (N.L.)	8	7	.533	3.38	17	17	0	0	0	109 1/3	109	49	41	31	62
1995	—Colorado (N.L.)■	9	3	.750	4.94	19	19	0	0	0	105 2/3	122	62	58	43	68
A.L. totals (6 years)		30	40	.429	4.04	253	86	7	1	24	759	827	395	341	253	292
N.L. totals (4 years)		48	22	.686	3.09	100	92	4	3	1	612 1/3	570	234	210	172	364
Major league totals (10 years)		78	62	.557	3.62	353	178	11	4	25	1371 1/3	1397	629	551	425	656

DIVISION SERIES RECORD

Year	Team (League)	W	L	Pct.	ERA	G	GS	CG	ShO	Sv.	IP	H	R	ER	BB	SO
1995	—Colorado (N.L.)	0	0	...	6.00	1	1	0	0	0	6	7	4	4	2	3

SWINDELL, GREG P ASTROS

PERSONAL: Born January 2, 1965, in Fort Worth, Tex. . . . 6-3/225. . . . Throws left, bats right. . . . Full name: Forest Gregory Swindell. . . . Name pronounced swin-DELL.
HIGH SCHOOL: Sharpstown (Tex.).
COLLEGE: Texas.
TRANSACTIONS/CAREER NOTES: Selected by Cleveland Indians organization in first round (second pick overall) of free-agent draft (June 2, 1986). . . . On disabled list (June 30, 1987-remainder of season and July 26-August 30, 1989). . . . Traded by Indians to Cincinnati Reds for P Jack Armstrong, P Scott Scudder and P Joe Turek (November 15, 1991). . . . On disabled list (August 23-September 7, 1992). . . . Granted free agency (October 26, 1992). . . . Signed by Houston Astros (December 4, 1992). . . . On disabled list (July 6-26, 1993).
HONORS: Named lefthanded pitcher on The Sporting News college All-America team (1985-86).
STATISTICAL NOTES: Struck out 15 batters in one game (May 10, 1987).
MISCELLANEOUS: Struck out in only appearance as pinch-hitter (1995).

Year	Team (League)	W	L	Pct.	ERA	G	GS	CG	ShO	Sv.	IP	H	R	ER	BB	SO
1986	—Waterloo (Midw.)	2	1	.667	1.00	3	3	0	0	0	18	12	2	2	3	25
	—Cleveland (A.L.)	5	2	.714	4.23	9	9	1	0	0	61 2/3	57	35	29	15	46
1987	—Cleveland (A.L.)	3	8	.273	5.10	16	15	4	1	0	102 1/3	112	62	58	37	97
1988	—Cleveland (A.L.)	18	14	.563	3.20	33	33	12	4	0	242	234	97	86	45	180
1989	—Cleveland (A.L.)	13	6	.684	3.37	28	28	5	2	0	184 1/3	170	71	69	51	129
1990	—Cleveland (A.L.)	12	9	.571	4.40	34	34	3	0	0	214 2/3	245	110	105	47	135
1991	—Cleveland (A.L.)	9	16	.360	3.48	33	33	7	0	0	238	241	112	92	31	169
1992	—Cincinnati (N.L.)■	12	8	.600	2.70	31	30	5	3	0	213 2/3	210	72	64	41	138
1993	—Houston (N.L.)■	12	13	.480	4.16	31	30	1	1	0	190 1/3	215	98	88	40	124
1994	—Houston (N.L.)	8	9	.471	4.37	24	24	1	0	0	148 1/3	175	80	72	26	74
1995	—Houston (N.L.)	10	9	.526	4.47	33	26	1	1	0	153	180	86	76	39	96
A.L. totals (6 years)		60	55	.522	3.79	153	152	32	7	0	1043	1059	487	439	226	756
N.L. totals (4 years)		42	39	.519	3.83	119	110	8	5	0	705 1/3	780	336	300	146	432
Major league totals (10 years)		102	94	.520	3.80	272	262	40	12	0	1748 1/3	1839	823	739	372	1188

ALL-STAR GAME RECORD

Year	League	W	L	Pct.	ERA	GS	CG	ShO	Sv.	IP	H	R	ER	BB	SO
1989	—American	0	0	...	0.00	0	0	0	0	1 2/3	2	0	0	0	3

TABAKA, JEFF P ASTROS

PERSONAL: Born January 17, 1964, in Barberton, O. . . . 6-2/195. . . . Throws left, bats right. . . . Full name: Jeffrey Jon Tabaka. . . . Name pronounced tuh-BAW-kuh.
HIGH SCHOOL: Copley (O.) Senior.
COLLEGE: Kent.
TRANSACTIONS/CAREER NOTES: Selected by Montreal Expos organization in free-agent draft (June 2, 1986). . . . On West Palm Beach disabled list (May 2-June 23, 1988). . . . Selected by Philadelphia Phillies from Expos organization in Rule 5 major league draft (December 5,

1988); Expos waived right to reclaim him as part of deal in which Expos traded P Floyd Youmans and P Jeff Parrett to Phillies for P Kevin Gross (December 6, 1988). . . . Released by Reading, Phillies organization (July 26, 1991). . . . Signed by Milwaukee Brewers organization (August 8, 1991). . . . On disabled list (June 18-July 4, 1992). . . . Granted free agency (October 15, 1992). . . . Re-signed by Brewers (October 30, 1992). . . . Selected by Florida Marlins in third round (71st pick overall) of expansion draft (November 17, 1992). . . . Granted free agency (March 21, 1993). . . . Signed by New Orleans, Brewers organization (March 26, 1993). . . . Granted free agency (October 15, 1993). . . . Re-signed by Brewers organization (January 6, 1994). . . . Released by New Orleans (April 2, 1994). . . . Signed by Pittsburgh Pirates organization (April 3, 1994). . . . Claimed on waivers by San Diego Padres (May 12, 1994). . . . Traded by Padres with P Rich Loiselle to Houston Astros for OF Phil Plantier (July 19, 1995).

MISCELLANEOUS: Made two outs in one game as designated hitter with New Orleans (1993).

Year Team (League)	W	L	Pct.	ERA	G	GS	CG	ShO	Sv.	IP	H	R	ER	BB	SO
1986—Jamestown (NYP)	2	4	.333	4.30	13	9	0	0	0	52 1/3	51	31	25	34	57
1987—WP Beach (FSL)	8	6	.571	4.17	28	15	0	0	5	95	90	46	44	58	71
1988—WP Beach (FSL)	7	5	.583	1.71	16	16	2	2	0	95	71	38	18	34	52
—Jacksonville (Sou.)	1	0	1.000	6.55	2	2	0	0	0	11	14	8	8	5	7
1989—Reading (Eastern)■	8	7	.533	4.65	21	17	6	1	0	100 2/3	109	59	52	54	80
—Scran./W.B. (Int'l)	0	4	.000	6.32	6	6	0	0	0	31 1/3	32	26	22	23	15
1990—Clearwater (Fla. St.)	5	2	.714	3.03	8	5	0	0	0	35 2/3	39	17	12	18	23
1991—Reading (Eastern)	4	8	.333	5.07	21	20	1	1	0	108 1/3	117	65	61	78	68
—Stockton (Calif.)■	0	2	.000	5.19	4	4	0	0	0	17 1/3	19	11	10	16	19
1992—El Paso (Texas)■	9	5	.643	2.52	50	0	0	0	10	82	67	23	23	38	75
1993—New Orleans (A.A.)	6	6	.500	3.24	53	0	0	0	1	58 1/3	50	26	21	30	63
1994—Buffalo (A.A.)■	1	0	1.000	3.38	9	0	0	0	1	5 1/3	3	2	2	4	4
—Pittsburgh (N.L.)	0	0	...	18.00	5	0	0	0	0	4	4	8	8	8	2
—San Diego (N.L.)■	3	1	.750	3.89	34	0	0	0	1	37	28	21	16	19	30
1995—Las Vegas (PCL)	0	1	.000	1.99	19	0	0	0	6	22 2/3	16	6	5	14	27
—San Diego (N.L.)	0	0	...	7.11	10	0	0	0	0	6 1/3	10	5	5	5	6
—Houston (N.L.)■	1	0	1.000	2.22	24	0	0	0	0	24 1/3	17	6	6	12	19
Major league totals (2 years)	4	1	.800	4.40	73	0	0	0	1	71 2/3	59	40	35	44	57

T

TAPANI, KEVIN P

PERSONAL: Born February 18, 1964, in Des Moines, Ia. . . . 6-0/188. . . . Throws right, bats right. . . . Full name: Kevin Ray Tapani. . . . Name pronounced TAP-uh-nee.

HIGH SCHOOL: Escanaba (Mich.).

COLLEGE: Central Michigan (degree in finance, 1987).

TRANSACTIONS/CAREER NOTES: Selected by Chicago Cubs organization in ninth round of free-agent draft (June 3, 1985); did not sign. . . . Selected by Oakland Athletics organization in second round of free-agent draft (June 2, 1986). . . . Traded by A's as part of an eight-player, three-team deal in which New York Mets traded P Jesse Orosco to A's (December 11, 1987). A's traded Orosco, SS Alfredo Griffin and P Jay Howell to Los Angeles Dodgers for P Bob Welch, P Matt Young and P Jack Savage. A's then traded Savage, P Wally Whitehurst and Tapani to Mets. . . . Traded by Mets with P Tim Drummond to Portland, Minnesota Twins organization (August 1, 1989), as partial completion of deal in which Twins traded P Frank Viola to Mets for P Rick Aguilera, P David West and three players to be named later (July 31, 1989); Twins acquired P Jack Savage to complete deal (October 16, 1989). . . . On disabled list (August 17-September 10, 1990). . . . Traded by Twins with P Mark Guthrie to Los Angeles Dodgers for 1B/3B Ron Coomer, P Greg Hansell, P Jose Parra and a player to be named later (July 31, 1995); Twins acquired OF Chris Latham to complete deal (October 30, 1995). . . . Granted free agency (December 21, 1995).

Year Team (League)	W	L	Pct.	ERA	G	GS	CG	ShO	Sv.	IP	H	R	ER	BB	SO
1986—Medford (N'west)	1	0	1.000	0.00	2	2	0	0	0	8 1/3	6	3	0	3	9
—Modesto (Calif.)	6	1	.857	2.48	11	11	1	0	0	69	74	26	19	22	44
—Huntsville (South.)	1	0	1.000	6.00	1	1	0	0	0	6	8	4	4	1	2
—Tacoma (PCL)	0	1	.000	15.43	1	1	0	0	0	2 1/3	5	6	4	1	1
1987—Modesto (Calif.)	10	7	.588	3.76	24	24	6	1	0	148 1/3	122	74	62	60	121
1988—St. Lucie (Fla. St.)■	1	0	1.000	1.42	3	3	0	0	0	19	17	5	3	4	11
—Jackson (Texas)	5	1	.833	2.74	24	5	0	0	3	62 1/3	46	23	19	19	35
1989—Tidewater (Int'l)	7	5	.583	3.47	17	17	2	1	0	109	113	49	42	25	63
—New York (N.L.)	0	0	...	3.68	3	0	0	0	0	7 1/3	5	3	3	4	2
—Portland (PCL)■	4	2	.667	2.20	6	6	1	0	0	41	38	15	10	12	30
—Minnesota (A.L.)	2	2	.500	3.86	5	5	0	0	0	32 2/3	34	15	14	8	21
1990—Minnesota (A.L.)	12	8	.600	4.07	28	28	1	1	0	159 1/3	164	75	72	29	101
1991—Minnesota (A.L.)	16	9	.640	2.99	34	34	4	1	0	244	225	84	81	40	135
1992—Minnesota (A.L.)	16	11	.593	3.97	34	34	4	1	0	220	226	103	97	48	138
1993—Minnesota (A.L.)	12	15	.444	4.43	36	35	3	1	0	225 2/3	243	123	111	57	150
1994—Minnesota (A.L.)	11	7	.611	4.62	24	24	4	1	0	156	181	86	80	39	91
1995—Minnesota (A.L.)	6	11	.353	4.92	20	20	3	1	0	133 2/3	155	79	73	34	88
—Los Angeles (N.L.)■	4	2	.667	5.05	13	11	0	0	0	57	72	37	32	14	43
A.L. totals (7 years)	75	63	.543	4.06	181	180	19	6	0	1171 1/3	1228	565	528	255	724
N.L. totals (2 years)	4	2	.667	4.90	16	11	0	0	0	64 1/3	77	40	35	18	45
Major league totals (7 years)	79	65	.549	4.10	197	191	19	6	0	1235 2/3	1305	605	563	273	769

DIVISION SERIES RECORD

Year Team (League)	W	L	Pct.	ERA	G	GS	CG	ShO	Sv.	IP	H	R	ER	BB	SO
1995—Los Angeles (N.L.)	0	0	...	81.00	2	0	0	0	0	1/3	0	3	3	4	1

CHAMPIONSHIP SERIES RECORD

Year Team (League)	W	L	Pct.	ERA	G	GS	CG	ShO	Sv.	IP	H	R	ER	BB	SO
1991—Minnesota (A.L.)	0	1	.000	7.84	2	2	0	0	0	10 1/3	16	9	9	3	9

WORLD SERIES RECORD

NOTES: Member of World Series championship team (1991).

Year Team (League)	W	L	Pct.	ERA	G	GS	CG	ShO	Sv.	IP	H	R	ER	BB	SO
1991—Minnesota (A.L.)	1	1	.500	4.50	2	2	0	0	0	12	13	6	6	2	7

TARASCO, TONY — OF — EXPOS

PERSONAL: Born December 9, 1970, in New York. . . . 6-1/205. . . . Bats left, throws right. . . . Full name: Anthony Giacinto Tarasco.
HIGH SCHOOL: Santa Monica (Calif.).
TRANSACTIONS/CAREER NOTES: Selected by Atlanta Braves organization in 15th round of free-agent draft (June 1, 1988). . . . On disabled list (August 4-September 12, 1991). . . . Traded by Braves with OF Roberto Kelly and P Esteban Yan to Montreal Expos for OF Marquis Grissom (April 6, 1995).

		BATTING												FIELDING			
Year Team (League)	Pos.	G	AB	R	H	2B	3B	HR	RBI	Avg.	BB	SO	SB	PO	A	E	Avg.
1988—Idaho Falls (Pio.)	OF	7	10	1	0	0	0	0	1	.000	5	2	1	2	0	1	.667
—GC Braves (GCL)	OF	21	64	10	15	6	1	0	4	.234	7	7	3	25	1	1	.963
1989—Pulaski (Appal.)	OF	49	156	22	53	8	2	2	22	.340	21	20	7	45	4	3	.942
1990—Sumter (S. Atl.)	OF	107	355	42	94	13	3	3	37	.265	37	57	9	173	14	9	.954
1991—Durham (Carolina)	OF	78	248	31	62	8	2	12	38	.250	21	64	11	119	6	3	.977
1992—Greenville (South.)	OF-2B	133	489	73	140	22	2	15	54	.286	27	84	33	209	17	5	.978
1993—Richmond (Int'l)	OF	93	370	73	122	15	7	15	53	.330	36	54	19	143	8	2	.987
—Atlanta (N.L.)	OF	24	35	6	8	2	0	0	2	.229	0	5	0	11	0	0	1.000
1994—Atlanta (N.L.)	OF	87	132	16	36	6	0	5	19	.273	9	17	5	42	1	0	1.000
1995—Montreal (N.L.)■	OF	126	438	64	109	18	4	14	40	.249	51	78	24	230	7	5	.979
Major league totals (3 years)		237	605	86	153	26	4	19	61	.253	60	100	29	283	8	5	.983

CHAMPIONSHIP SERIES RECORD

		BATTING												FIELDING			
Year Team (League)	Pos.	G	AB	R	H	2B	3B	HR	RBI	Avg.	BB	SO	SB	PO	A	E	Avg.
1993—Atlanta (N.L.)	OF-PR	2	1	0	0	0	0	0	0	.000	0	1	0	0	0	0	...

TARTABULL, DANNY — DH/OF — WHITE SOX

PERSONAL: Born October 30, 1962, in Miami. . . . 6-1/204. . . . Bats right, throws right. . . . Full name: Danilo Mora Tartabull. . . . Son of Jose Tartabull, outfielder, Kansas City A's, Boston Red Sox and Oakland A's (1962-70); and brother of Jose Tartabull Jr., minor league outfielder (1986-88).
HIGH SCHOOL: Carol City (Miami).
TRANSACTIONS/CAREER NOTES: Selected by Cincinnati Reds organization in third round of free-agent draft (June 3, 1980). . . . Selected by Seattle Mariners organization in player compensation pool draft (January 20, 1983); pick received as compensation for Chicago White Sox signing free-agent P Floyd Bannister (December 13, 1982). . . . On disabled list (May 15-30, 1986). . . . Traded by Mariners with P Rick Luecken to Kansas City Royals for P Scott Bankhead, P Steve Shields and OF Mike Kingery (December 10, 1986). . . . On disabled list (June 15-30, 1989; April 11-May 18 and July 14-31, 1990). . . . Granted free agency (October 28, 1991). . . . Signed by New York Yankees (January 6, 1992). . . . On disabled list (April 21-May 8 and July 27-August 14, 1992; and May 25-June 15, 1993). . . . Traded by Yankees to Oakland Athletics for OF Ruben Sierra and P Jason Beverlin (July 28, 1995). . . . On Oakland disabled list (August 3-September 1, 1995). . . Traded by A's to Chicago White Sox for P Andrew Lorraine and OF Charles Poe (January 22, 1996).
HONORS: Named Florida State League Most Valuable Player (1981). . . . Named Pacific Coast League Player of the Year (1985).
STATISTICAL NOTES: Led Florida State League third basemen with 29 errors in 1981. . . . Led Pacific Coast League shortstops with 68 double plays in 1984. . . . Led Pacific Coast League with .615 slugging percentage and 291 total bases in 1985. . . . Led Pacific Coast League shortstops with 35 errors in 1985. . . . Led A.L. with 21 game-winning RBIs in 1987. . . . Hit three home runs in one game (July 6, 1991). . . . Led A.L. with .593 slugging percentage in 1991. . . . Career major league grand slams: 10.

		BATTING												FIELDING			
Year Team (League)	Pos.	G	AB	R	H	2B	3B	HR	RBI	Avg.	BB	SO	SB	PO	A	E	Avg.
1980—Billings (Pioneer)	3B-OF-2B	59	157	33	47	10	0	2	27	.299	37	24	7	34	54	14	.863
1981—Tampa (Fla. St.)	3B-2B	127	422	86	131	*28	10	14	81	*.310	90	77	11	150	248	†39	.911
1982—Waterbury (East.)	2B	126	409	64	93	17	3	17	63	.227	89	120	12	237	306	*32	.944
1983—Chatt. (South.)■	2B	128	481	95	145	32	7	13	66	.301	47	63	25	252	405	23	.966
1984—Salt Lake (PCL)	SS	116	418	69	127	22	9	13	73	.304	57	69	11	181	333	24	.955
—Seattle (A.L.)	SS-2B	10	20	3	6	1	0	2	7	.300	2	3	0	8	21	2	.935
1985—Calgary (PCL)	SS-3B	125	473	102	142	14	3	*43	*109	.300	67	123	17	181	399	†36	.942
—Seattle (A.L.)	SS-3B	19	61	8	20	7	1	1	7	.328	8	14	1	28	43	4	.947
1986—Seattle (A.L.)	O-2-DH-3	137	511	76	138	25	6	25	96	.270	61	157	4	233	111	18	.950
1987—Kansas City (A.L.)■	OF-DH	158	582	95	180	27	3	34	101	.309	79	136	9	228	11	6	.976
1988—Kansas City (A.L.)	OF-DH	146	507	80	139	38	3	26	102	.274	76	119	8	227	8	9	.963
1989—Kansas City (A.L.)	OF-DH	133	441	54	118	22	0	18	62	.268	69	123	4	108	3	2	.982
1990—Kansas City (A.L.)	OF-DH	88	313	41	84	19	0	15	60	.268	36	93	1	81	1	3	.965
1991—Kansas City (A.L.)	OF-DH	132	484	78	153	35	3	31	100	.316	65	121	6	190	4	7	.965
1992—New York (A.L.)■	OF-DH	123	421	72	112	19	0	25	85	.266	103	115	2	143	3	3	.980
1993—New York (A.L.)	DH-OF	138	513	87	128	33	2	31	102	.250	92	156	0	88	3	2	.978
1994—New York (A.L.)	DH-OF	104	399	68	102	24	1	19	67	.256	66	111	1	43	1	0	1.000
1995—New York (A.L.)	DH-OF	59	192	25	43	12	0	6	28	.224	33	54	0	27	1	0	1.000
—Oakland (A.L.)■	DH-OF	24	88	9	23	4	0	2	7	.261	10	28	0	1	0	0	1.000
Major league totals (12 years)		1271	4532	696	1246	266	19	235	824	.275	700	1230	36	1405	210	56	.966

ALL-STAR GAME RECORD

		BATTING											FIELDING			
Year League	Pos.	AB	R	H	2B	3B	HR	RBI	Avg.	BB	SO	SB	PO	A	E	Avg.
1991—American	DH	2	0	0	0	0	0	0	.000	0	1	0	...	...	...	...

TATUM, JIM — C — RED SOX

PERSONAL: Born October 9, 1967, in San Diego. . . . 6-2/200. . . . Bats right, throws right. . . . Full name: James Ray Tatum Jr.
HIGH SCHOOL: Santana (Santee, Calif.).
TRANSACTIONS/CAREER NOTES: Selected by San Diego Padres organization in third round of free-agent draft (June 3, 1985). . . . Released by Padres organization (June 8, 1988). . . . Signed as free agent by Cleveland Indians organization (September 14, 1989). . . . Released by

Indians organization (May 24, 1990). . . . Signed by Milwaukee Brewers organization (June 21, 1990). . . . Selected by Colorado Rockies in second round (44th pick overall) of expansion draft (November 17, 1992). . . . Granted free agency (December 20, 1993). . . . Re-signed by Rockies organization (December 23, 1993). . . . Granted free agency (October 15, 1994). . . . Re-signed by Rockies (November 2, 1994). . . . Granted free agency (October 16, 1995). . . . Signed by Boston Red Sox (November 1, 1995).

HONORS: Named American Association Most Valuable Player (1992).

STATISTICAL NOTES: Led Northwest League third basemen with 149 assists, 27 errors, 214 total chances and 11 double plays in 1985. . . . Led South Atlantic League third basemen with 35 errors and 29 double plays in 1986. . . . Led South Atlantic League third basemen with 257 assists and tied for lead with 368 total chances in 1987. . . . Led Texas League in sacrifice flies with 20, in being hit by pitch with 15 and in grounding into double plays with 21 in 1991. . . . Led American Association with 261 total bases and 11 sacrifice flies in 1992. . . . Led Pacific Coast League with 10 sacrifice flies in 1994. . . . Career major league grand slams: 1.

			BATTING											FIELDING			
Year	**Team (League)**	**Pos.**	**G**	**AB**	**R**	**H**	**2B**	**3B**	**HR**	**RBI**	**Avg.**	**BB**	**SO**	**SB**	**PO**	**A**	**E**	**Avg.**
1985—	Spokane (N'west).......	3B-SS	74	281	21	64	9	1	1	32	.228	20	60	0	51	†168	†30	.880
1986—	Char., S.C. (S. Atl.).....	3B-2B-SS	120	431	55	112	19	2	10	62	.260	41	83	2	81	232	†41	.884
1987—	Char., S.C. (S. Atl.).....	3B-SS-2B	128	468	52	131	22	2	9	72	.280	46	65	8	87	†259	24	.935
1988—	Wichita (Texas)	3B	118	402	38	105	26	1	8	54	.261	30	73	2	*97	195	27	.915
1989—	....							Did not play.										
1990—	Cant./Akr. (East.)■.....	3B-1B	30	106	6	19	6	0	2	11	.179	6	19	1	57	51	12	.900
	—Stockton (Calif.)■.....	3B-1B	70	260	41	68	16	0	12	59	.262	13	49	4	160	108	7	.975
1991—	El Paso (Texas)..........	S-3-C-1-P	130	493	99	158	27	8	18	128	.320	63	79	5	190	263	31	.936
1992—	Denver (A.A.)..............	3B-OF	130	492	74	*162	*36	3	19	101	*.329	40	87	8	90	272	25	.935
	—Milwaukee (A.L.)	3B	5	8	0	1	0	0	0	0	.125	1	2	0	6	2	0	1.000
1993—	Colorado (N.L.)■	1B-3B-OF	92	98	7	20	5	0	1	12	.204	5	27	0	45	5	2	.962
	—Colo. Springs (PCL) ...	3B-1B	13	45	5	10	2	0	2	7	.222	2	9	0	8	21	3	.906
1994—	Colo. Springs (PCL) ...	C-3-O-1	121	439	76	154	43	1	21	97	.351	44	84	2	372	106	16	.968
1995—	Colo. Springs (PCL) ...	3B-C	27	93	17	30	7	0	6	18	.323	6	21	0	15	39	4	.931
	—Colorado (N.L.)	OF-C	34	34	4	8	1	1	0	4	.235	1	7	0	4	0	0	1.000
American League totals (1 year)			5	8	0	1	0	0	0	0	.125	1	2	0	6	2	0	1.000
National League totals (2 years)			126	132	11	28	6	1	1	16	.212	6	34	0	49	5	2	.964
Major league totals (3 years)			131	140	11	29	6	1	1	16	.207	7	36	0	55	7	2	.969

RECORD AS PITCHER

Year	**Team (League)**	**W**	**L**	**Pct.**	**ERA**	**G**	**GS**	**CG**	**ShO**	**Sv.**	**IP**	**H**	**R**	**ER**	**BB**	**SO**
1991—	El Paso (Texas)......................	0	0	. . .	0.00	1	0	0	0	0	1	1	0	0	0	0

TAUBENSEE, EDDIE C REDS

PERSONAL: Born October 31, 1968, in Beeville, Tex. . . . 6-4/205. . . . Bats left, throws right. . . . Full name: Edward Kenneth Taubensee. . . . Name pronounced TAW-ben-see.

HIGH SCHOOL: Lake Howell (Casselberry, Fla.).

TRANSACTIONS/CAREER NOTES: Selected by Cincinnati Reds organization in sixth round of free-agent draft (June 2, 1986). . . . Selected by Oakland Athletics from Reds organization in Rule 5 major league draft (December 3, 1990). . . . Claimed on waivers by Cleveland Indians (April 4, 1991). . . . Traded by Indians with P Willie Blair to Houston Astros for OF Kenny Lofton and IF Dave Rohde (December 10, 1991). . . . Traded by Astros to Reds for P Ross Powell and P Marty Lister (April 19, 1994).

STATISTICAL NOTES: Led Pioneer League with 19 passed balls in 1987. . . . Tied for South Atlantic League lead in double plays by catcher with seven in 1988.

			BATTING											FIELDING			
Year	**Team (League)**	**Pos.**	**G**	**AB**	**R**	**H**	**2B**	**3B**	**HR**	**RBI**	**Avg.**	**BB**	**SO**	**SB**	**PO**	**A**	**E**	**Avg.**
1986—	GC Reds (GCL)..........	C-1B	35	107	8	21	3	0	1	11	.196	11	33	0	208	27	8	.967
1987—	Billings (Pioneer)........	C	55	162	24	43	7	0	5	28	.265	25	47	2	344	29	6	.984
1988—	Greensboro (S. Atl.) ...	C	103	330	36	85	16	1	10	41	.258	44	93	8	640	70	15	.979
	—Chatt. (South.)............	C	5	12	2	2	0	0	1	1	.167	3	4	0	17	5	1	.957
1989—	Ced. Rap. (Midw.)	C	59	196	25	39	5	0	8	22	.199	25	55	4	400	9	1	.998
	—Chatt. (South.)............	C	45	127	11	24	2	0	3	13	.189	11	28	0	213	31	6	.976
1990—	Ced. Rap. (Midw.)	C	122	417	57	108	21	1	16	62	.259	51	98	11	795	94	16	.982
1991—	Cleveland (A.L.)■.......	C	26	66	5	16	2	1	0	8	.242	5	16	0	89	6	2	.979
	—Colo. Springs (PCL) ...	C	91	287	53	89	23	3	13	39	.310	31	61	0	412	47	12	.975
1992—	Houston (N.L.)■	C	104	297	23	66	15	0	5	28	.222	31	78	2	557	66	5	.992
	—Tucson (PCL)	C	20	74	13	25	8	1	1	10	.338	8	17	0	127	10	4	.972
1993—	Houston (N.L.)	C	94	288	26	72	11	1	9	42	.250	21	44	1	551	41	5	.992
1994—	Houston (N.L.)	C	5	10	0	1	0	0	0	0	.100	0	3	0	19	2	0	1.000
	—Cincinnati (N.L.)■	C	61	177	29	52	8	2	8	21	.294	15	28	2	362	17	4	.990
1995—	Cincinnati (N.L.)	C-1B	80	218	32	62	14	2	9	44	.284	22	52	2	338	22	6	.984
American League totals (1 year)			26	66	5	16	2	1	0	8	.242	5	16	0	89	6	2	.979
National League totals (4 years)			344	990	110	253	48	5	31	135	.256	89	205	7	1827	148	20	.990
Major league totals (5 years)			370	1056	115	269	50	6	31	143	.255	94	221	7	1916	154	22	.989

CHAMPIONSHIP SERIES RECORD

			BATTING											FIELDING			
Year	**Team (League)**	**Pos.**	**G**	**AB**	**R**	**H**	**2B**	**3B**	**HR**	**RBI**	**Avg.**	**BB**	**SO**	**SB**	**PO**	**A**	**E**	**Avg.**
1995—	Cincinnati (N.L.)	PH-C	2	2	0	1	0	0	0	0	.500	0	0	0	0	0	0	. . .

TAVAREZ, JESUS OF MARLINS

PERSONAL: Born March 26, 1971, in Santo Domingo, Dominican Republic. . . . 6-0/170. . . . Bats both, throws right. . . . Full name: Jesus Rafael Tavarez. . . . Name pronounced tuh-VARE-ez.

TRANSACTIONS/CAREER NOTES: Signed as non-drafted free agent by Seattle Mariners organization (June 8, 1989). . . . On disabled list (April 20-May 20, 1992). . . . Selected by Florida Marlins in first round (26th pick overall) of expansion draft (November 17, 1992). . . . On disabled list (May 18-June 4, 1993). . . . On Florida disabled list (June 11-27, 1995).

STATISTICAL NOTES: Tied for Carolina League lead in double plays by outfielder with four in 1990.
MISCELLANEOUS: Batted righthanded only (1990-92).

		BATTING												FIELDING			
Year Team (League)	Pos.	G	AB	R	H	2B	3B	HR	RBI	Avg.	BB	SO	SB	PO	A	E	Avg.
1989—					Dominican Summer League statistics unavailable.												
1990— Peninsula (Caro.)	OF	108	379	39	90	10	1	0	32	.237	20	79	40	228	•12	9	.964
1991— San Bern. (Calif.)........	OF	124	466	80	132	11	3	5	41	.283	39	78	69	231	9	9	.964
1992— Jacksonv. (South.)	OF	105	392	38	101	9	2	3	25	.258	23	54	29	208	7	5	.977
1993— High Desert (Calif.)■ .	OF	109	444	104	130	21	8	7	71	.293	57	66	47	194	10	9	.958
1994— Portland (Eastern)......	OF	89	353	60	101	11	8	2	32	.286	35	63	20	171	3	6	.967
— Florida (N.L.).............	OF	17	39	4	7	0	0	0	4	.179	1	5	1	28	1	0	1.000
1995— Charlotte (Int'l)...........	OF	39	140	15	42	6	2	1	8	.300	9	19	7	92	2	2	.979
— Florida (N.L.).............	OF	63	190	31	55	6	2	2	13	.289	16	27	7	118	1	0	1.000
Major league totals (2 years)		80	229	35	62	6	2	2	17	.271	17	32	8	146	2	0	1.000

TAVAREZ, JULIAN — P — INDIANS

PERSONAL: Born May 22, 1973, in Santiago, Dominican Republic. . . . 6-2/165. . . . Throws right, bats right.
HIGH SCHOOL: Santiago (Dominican Republic) Public School.
TRANSACTIONS/CAREER NOTES: Signed as non-drafted free agent by Cleveland Indians organization (March 16, 1990).
HONORS: Named A.L. Rookie Pitcher of the Year by The Sporting News (1995).
STATISTICAL NOTES: Led Appalachian League with 10 hit batsmen in 1993.

Year Team (League)	W	L	Pct.	ERA	G	GS	CG	ShO	Sv.	IP	H	R	ER	BB	SO
1990— DSL Indians (DSL)............	5	5	.500	3.29	14	12	3	0	0	82	85	53	30	48	33
1991— DSL Indians (DSL)............	8	2	.800	2.67	19	18	1	0	0	121 1/3	95	41	36	28	75
1992— Burlington (Appal.)............	6	3	.667	2.68	14	*14	2	•2	0	87 1/3	86	41	26	12	69
1993— Kinston (Carolina)............	11	5	.688	2.42	18	18	2	0	0	119	102	48	32	28	107
— Cant./Akr. (East.)...............	2	1	.667	0.95	3	2	1	1	0	19	14	2	2	1	11
— Cleveland (A.L.)...................	2	2	.500	6.57	8	7	0	0	0	37	53	29	27	13	19
1994— Charlotte (Int'l)..................	•15	6	.714	3.48	26	26	2	2	0	176	167	79	68	43	102
— Cleveland (A.L.)...................	0	1	.000	21.60	1	1	0	0	0	1 2/3	6	8	4	1	0
1995— Cleveland (A.L.)..................	10	2	.833	2.44	57	0	0	0	0	85	76	36	23	21	68
Major league totals (3 years)......	12	5	.706	3.93	66	8	0	0	0	123 2/3	135	73	54	35	87

DIVISION SERIES RECORD

Year Team (League)	W	L	Pct.	ERA	G	GS	CG	ShO	Sv.	IP	H	R	ER	BB	SO
1995— Cleveland (A.L.)..................	0	0	...	6.75	3	0	0	0	0	2 2/3	5	2	2	0	3

CHAMPIONSHIP SERIES RECORD

Year Team (League)	W	L	Pct.	ERA	G	GS	CG	ShO	Sv.	IP	H	R	ER	BB	SO
1995— Cleveland (A.L.)..................	0	1	.000	2.70	4	0	0	0	0	3 1/3	3	1	1	1	2

WORLD SERIES RECORD

Year Team (League)	W	L	Pct.	ERA	G	GS	CG	ShO	Sv.	IP	H	R	ER	BB	SO
1995— Cleveland (A.L.)..................	0	0	...	0.00	5	0	0	0	0	4 1/3	3	0	0	2	1

TAYLOR, BRIEN — P — YANKEES

PERSONAL: Born December 26, 1971, in Beaufort, N.C. . . . 6-3/220. . . . Throws left, bats left. . . . Full name: Brien M. Taylor.
HIGH SCHOOL: East Cateret (Beaufort, N.C.).
TRANSACTIONS/CAREER NOTES: Selected by New York Yankees organization in first round (first pick overall) of free-agent draft (June 3, 1991). . . . On Columbus disabled list (April 7, 1994-entire season; April 6-June 22 and June 30-August 9, 1995).
STATISTICAL NOTES: Led Florida State League with 10 balks in 1992.

Year Team (League)	W	L	Pct.	ERA	G	GS	CG	ShO	Sv.	IP	H	R	ER	BB	SO
1992— Fort Lauder. (FSL).............	6	8	.429	2.57	27	27	0	0	0	161 1/3	121	60	46	66	*187
1993— Albany (Eastern)................	13	7	.650	3.48	27	27	1	0	0	163	127	83	63	*102	150
1994—							Did not play.								
1995— GC Yankees (GCL)..............	2	5	.286	6.08	11	11	0	0	0	40	29	37	27	*54	38

TAYLOR, SCOTT M. — P

PERSONAL: Born October 3, 1966, in Topeka, Kan. . . . 6-3/200. . . . Throws right, bats right. . . . Full name: Scott Michael Taylor.
HIGH SCHOOL: Arkansas City (Kan.).
COLLEGE: Kansas.
TRANSACTIONS/CAREER NOTES: Selected by Seattle Mariners organization in 15th round of free-agent draft (June 1, 1988). . . . Traded by Mariners organization to Atlanta Braves organization for OF Dennis Hood (December 10, 1990). . . . Released by Greenville, Braves organization (June 18, 1992). . . . Signed by El Paso, Milwaukee Brewers organization (June 25, 1992). . . . Traded by Brewers organization to Texas Rangers for OF David Hulse (April 14, 1995). . . . Granted free agency (October 16, 1995).
STATISTICAL NOTES: Pitched 6-0 no-hit victory against Buffalo (August 12, 1994).

Year Team (League)	W	L	Pct.	ERA	G	GS	CG	ShO	Sv.	IP	H	R	ER	BB	SO
1989— Wausau (Midwest)............	9	7	.563	3.22	16	16	6	2	0	106 1/3	92	49	38	37	65
— Williamsport (East.)...........	1	4	.200	5.75	10	7	1	0	0	40 2/3	49	26	26	20	22
1990— San Bern. (Calif.)...............	8	8	.500	5.41	34	21	1	0	1	126 1/3	148	100	76	69	86
1991— Durham (Carolina)■	10	3	.769	2.18	24	16	2	0	3	111 1/3	94	32	27	33	78
— Greenville (South.).............	3	4	.429	4.19	8	7	1	1	0	43	49	25	20	16	26
1992— Greenville (South.)............	1	1	.500	6.69	22	4	0	0	1	39	44	31	29	18	20
— El Paso (Texas)■.............	4	2	.667	3.48	11	9	0	0	0	54 1/3	45	21	21	19	37
1993— El Paso (Texas)...................	6	6	.500	3.80	17	16	1	0	0	104 1/3	105	53	44	31	76

Year	Team (League)	W	L	Pct.	ERA	G	GS	CG	ShO	Sv.	IP	H	R	ER	BB	SO
	—New Orleans (A.A.)	5	1	.833	2.31	12	8	1	0	0	62 1/3	48	17	16	21	47
1994—	New Orleans (A.A.)	14	9	.609	4.29	28	27	4	1	0	165 2/3	177	88	79	59	106
1995—	New Orleans (A.A.)	1	0	1.000	2.38	2	2	0	0	0	11 1/3	10	3	3	3	9
	—Okla. City (A.A.)■	7	8	.467	3.66	22	19	1	1	0	118	122	59	48	38	65
	—Texas (A.L.)	1	2	.333	9.39	3	3	0	0	0	15 1/3	25	16	16	5	10
Major league totals (1 year)		1	2	.333	9.39	3	3	0	0	0	15 1/3	25	16	16	5	10

TELEMACO, AMAURY — P — CUBS

PERSONAL: Born January 19, 1974, in Higuey, Dominican Republic. . . . 6-3/210. . . . Throws right, bats right. . . . Full name: Amaury Regalado Telemaco. . . . Name pronounced AH-mer-ee tel-ah-MAH-ko.

TRANSACTIONS/CAREER NOTES: Signed as non-drafted free agent by Chicago Cubs organization (May 23, 1991). . . . On temporarily inactive list (August 17, 1993-remainder of season). . . . On Orlando disabled list (August 23-September 8, 1994).

Year	Team (League)	W	L	Pct.	ERA	G	GS	CG	ShO	Sv.	IP	H	R	ER	BB	SO
1991—	Puerta Plata (DSL)	3	3	.500	3.55	15	13	0	0	0	66	81	43	26	32	43
1992—	Hunting. (Appal.)	3	5	.375	4.01	12	12	2	0	0	76 1/3	71	45	34	17	*93
	—Peoria (Midwest)	0	1	.000	7.94	2	1	0	0	0	5 2/3	9	5	5	5	5
1993—	Peoria (Midwest)	8	11	.421	3.45	23	23	3	0	0	143 2/3	129	69	55	54	133
1994—	Daytona (Fla. St.)	7	3	.700	3.40	11	11	2	0	0	76 2/3	62	35	29	23	59
	—Orlando (Southern)	3	5	.375	3.45	12	12	2	0	0	62 2/3	56	29	24	20	49
1995—	Orlando (Southern)	8	8	.500	3.29	22	22	3	1	0	147 2/3	112	60	54	42	151

TELGHEDER, DAVID — P — ATHLETICS

PERSONAL: Born November 11, 1966, in Middletown, N.Y. . . . 6-3/212. . . . Throws right, bats right. . . . Full name: David William Telgheder. . . . Name pronounced tell-GATOR.

HIGH SCHOOL: Minisink Valley (Slate Hill, N.Y.).

COLLEGE: Massachusetts (received degree, 1989).

TRANSACTIONS/CAREER NOTES: Selected by New York Mets organization in 31st round of free-agent draft (June 5, 1989). . . . On Norfolk disabled list (September 1-8, 1994). . . . Granted free agency (October 16, 1995). . . . Signed by Oakland Athletics organization (November 21, 1995).

STATISTICAL NOTES: Pitched 1-0 no-hit victory against Pawtucket (May 15, 1992).

Year	Team (League)	W	L	Pct.	ERA	G	GS	CG	ShO	Sv.	IP	H	R	ER	BB	SO
1989—	Pittsfield (NYP)	5	3	.625	2.45	13	7	4	1	2	58 2/3	43	18	16	9	65
1990—	Columbia (S. Atl.)	9	3	.750	1.54	14	13	5	1	0	99 1/3	79	22	17	10	81
	—St. Lucie (Fla. St.)	9	4	.692	3.00	14	14	3	0	0	96	84	38	32	14	77
1991—	Williamsport (East.)	•13	11	.542	3.60	28	26	1	0	0	167 2/3	185	81	67	33	90
1992—	Tidewater (Int'l)	6	*14	.300	4.21	28	27	3	2	0	169	173	87	79	36	118
1993—	Norfolk (Int'l)	7	3	.700	2.95	13	12	0	0	1	76 1/3	81	29	25	19	52
	—New York (N.L.)	6	2	.750	4.76	24	7	0	0	0	75 2/3	82	40	40	21	35
1994—	New York (N.L.)	0	1	.000	7.20	6	0	0	0	0	10	11	8	8	8	4
	—Norfolk (Int'l)	8	10	.444	3.40	23	23	3	2	0	158 2/3	156	65	60	26	83
1995—	Norfolk (Int'l)	5	4	.556	2.24	29	11	0	0	3	92 1/3	77	34	23	8	75
	—New York (N.L.)	1	2	.333	5.61	7	4	0	0	0	25 2/3	34	18	16	7	16
Major league totals (3 years)		7	5	.583	5.17	37	11	0	0	0	111 1/3	127	66	64	36	55

TETTLETON, MICKEY — OF/DH/C — RANGERS

PERSONAL: Born September 16, 1960, in Oklahoma City. . . . 6-2/212. . . . Bats both, throws right. . . . Full name: Mickey Lee Tettleton.

HIGH SCHOOL: Southeast (Oklahoma City).

COLLEGE: Oklahoma State.

TRANSACTIONS/CAREER NOTES: Selected by Oakland Athletics organization in fifth round of free-agent draft (June 8, 1981). . . . On disabled list (July 16-August 13, 1982). . . . On Oakland disabled list (August 4-25, 1985); included rehabilitation assignment to Modesto (August 21-25). . . . On Oakland disabled list (May 9-June 16, 1986); included rehabilitation assignment to Modesto (May 23-June 13). . . . On Oakland disabled list (July 22-August 6, 1987); included rehabilitation assignment to Modesto (August 2-6). . . . Released by A's (March 28, 1988). . . . Signed by Rochester, Baltimore Orioles organization (April 5, 1988). . . . On disabled list (August 5-September 2, 1989). . . . Granted free agency (November 5, 1990). . . . Re-signed by Orioles (December 19, 1990). . . . Traded by Orioles to Detroit Tigers for P Jeff M. Robinson (January 11, 1991). . . . Granted free agency (October 18, 1994). . . . Signed by Texas Rangers (April 13, 1995). . . . Granted free agency (November 3, 1995). . . . Re-signed by Rangers (December 9, 1995).

RECORDS: Holds major league single-season record for most strikeouts by switch-hitter—160 (1990).

HONORS: Named catcher on The Sporting News A.L. All-Star team (1989 and 1991-92). . . . Named catcher on The Sporting News A.L. Silver Slugger team (1989 and 1991-92).

STATISTICAL NOTES: Tied for Eastern League lead with eight intentional bases on balls received in 1984. . . . Led Eastern League catchers with .993 fielding percentage in 1984. . . . Switch-hit home runs in one game three times (June 13, 1988; May 7, 1993, 12 innings; and April 28, 1995). . . . Led A.L. catchers with .996 fielding percentage in 1992. . . . Career major league grand slams: 6.

				BATTING											FIELDING			
Year	Team (League)	Pos.	G	AB	R	H	2B	3B	HR	RBI	Avg.	BB	SO	SB	PO	A	E	Avg.
1981—	Modesto (Calif.)	C-OF-1B	48	138	28	34	3	0	5	19	.246	46	33	2	235	31	14	.950
1982—	Modesto (Calif.)	C-OF	88	253	44	63	18	0	8	37	.249	63	46	4	424	36	8	.983
1983—	Modesto (Calif.)	C-OF	124	378	55	92	18	2	7	62	.243	82	71	1	582	46	11	.983
1984—	Alb./Colon. (East.)	C-O-1-3-S	86	281	32	65	18	0	5	47	.231	52	52	2	368	42	3	†.993
	—Oakland (A.L.)	C	33	76	10	20	2	1	1	5	.263	11	21	0	112	10	1	.992
1985—	Oakland (A.L.)	C-DH	78	211	23	53	12	0	3	15	.251	28	59	2	344	24	4	.989
	—Modesto (Calif.)	C	4	14	1	3	3	0	0	2	.214	0	4	0	20	1	0	1.000
1986—	Oakland (A.L.)	C	90	211	26	43	9	0	10	35	.204	39	51	7	463	32	8	.984
	—Modesto (Calif.)	C	15	42	14	10	1	0	2	8	.238	19	9	2	40	3	2	.956

Year	League	Pos.		AB	R	H	2B	3B	HR	RBI	Avg.	BB	SO	SB	PO	A	E	Avg.
			BATTING												FIELDING			
1987—	Oakland (A.L.)	C-1B-DH	82	211	19	41	3	0	8	26	.194	30	65	1	435	29	6	.987
—	Modesto (Calif.)	C	3	11	4	4	1	0	2	2	.364	1	4	0	5	0	0	1.000
1988—	Rochester (Int'l)■	C-OF	19	41	9	10	3	1	1	4	.244	9	15	0	71	7	3	.963
—	Baltimore (A.L.)	C	86	283	31	74	11	1	11	37	.261	28	70	0	361	31	3	.992
1989—	Baltimore (A.L.)	C-DH	117	411	72	106	21	2	26	65	.258	73	117	3	297	42	2	.994
1990—	Baltimore (A.L.)	C-DH-1-O	135	444	68	99	21	2	15	51	.223	106	160	2	458	39	5	.990
1991—	Detroit (A.L.)■	C-DH-O-1	154	501	85	132	17	2	31	89	.263	101	131	3	562	55	6	.990
1992—	Detroit (A.L.)	C-DH-1-O	157	525	82	125	25	0	32	83	.238	•122	137	0	481	47	2	≠.996
1993—	Detroit (A.L.)	1-C-O-DH	152	522	79	128	25	4	32	110	.245	109	139	3	724	47	6	.992
1994—	Detroit (A.L.)	C-1-DH-O	107	339	57	84	18	2	17	51	.248	97	98	0	368	31	5	.988
1995—	Texas (A.L.)■	O-DH-1-C	134	429	76	102	19	1	32	78	.238	107	110	0	185	10	3	.985
Major league totals (12 years)			1325	4163	628	1007	183	15	218	645	.242	851	1158	21	4790	397	51	.990

ALL-STAR GAME RECORD

Year	League	Pos.	AB	R	H	2B	3B	HR	RBI	Avg.	BB	SO	SB	PO	A	E	Avg.
			BATTING											FIELDING			
1989—	American	C	1	0	0	0	0	0	0	.000	0	0	0	2	0	0	1.000
1994—	American	PH	0	0	0	0	0	0	0	...	1	0	0	...	...	...	...
All-Star Game totals (2 years)			1	0	0	0	0	0	0	.000	1	0	0	2	0	0	1.000

TEWKSBURY, BOB — P — PADRES

PERSONAL: Born November 30, 1960, in Concord, N.H. . . . 6-4/205. . . . Throws right, bats right. . . . Full name: Robert Alan Tewksbury.
HIGH SCHOOL: Merrimack (Penacook, N.H.).
COLLEGE: Rutgers and St. Leo College (Fla.).
TRANSACTIONS/CAREER NOTES: Selected by New York Yankees organization in 19th round of free-agent draft (June 8, 1981). . . . On Fort Lauderdale disabled list (April 8-June 7, 1983). . . . On disabled list (April 9-27, 1984). . . . On Albany/Colonie disabled list (June 10-25, 1985). . . . Traded by Yankees with P Rich Scheid and P Dean Wilkins to Chicago Cubs for P Steve Trout (July 13, 1987). . . . On Chicago disabled list (August 13, 1987-remainder of season and May 22-June 12, 1988). . . . Granted free agency (October 15, 1988). . . . Signed by St. Louis Cardinals (December 16, 1988). . . . Granted free agency (October 17, 1994). . . . Signed by Texas Rangers (April 10, 1995). . . . On Texas disabled list (July 23-August 26, 1995); included rehabilitation assignment to Charlotte (August 22-26). . . . Granted free agency (November 3, 1995). . . . Signed by San Diego Padres (December 18, 1995).
STATISTICAL NOTES: Pitched 5-0 one-hit, complete-game victory for St. Louis against Houston (August 17, 1990).
MISCELLANEOUS: Struck out in only appearance as pinch-hitter with Texas (1995).

Year	Team (League)	W	L	Pct.	ERA	G	GS	CG	ShO	Sv.	IP	H	R	ER	BB	SO
1981—	Oneonta (NYP)	7	3	.700	3.60	14	14	6	1	0	85	85	43	34	37	62
1982—	Fort Lauder. (FSL)	*15	4	.789	*1.88	24	23	•13	*5	1	182 1/3	146	46	38	47	92
1983—	Fort Lauder. (FSL)	2	0	1.000	0.00	2	2	1	0	0	16	6	1	0	1	5
—	Nashville (South.)	5	1	.833	2.82	7	7	3	0	0	51	49	20	16	10	15
1984—	Nashville (South.)	11	9	.550	2.83	26	26	6	0	0	172	185	69	54	42	78
1985—	Alb./Colon. (East.)	6	5	.545	3.54	17	17	4	2	0	106 2/3	101	48	42	19	63
—	Columbus (Int'l)	3	0	1.000	1.02	6	6	1	1	0	44	27	5	5	5	21
1986—	New York (A.L.)	9	5	.643	3.31	23	20	2	0	0	130 1/3	144	58	48	31	49
—	Columbus (Int'l)	1	0	1.000	2.70	2	2	0	0	0	10	6	3	3	2	4
1987—	New York (A.L.)	1	4	.200	6.75	8	6	0	0	0	33 1/3	47	26	25	7	12
—	Columbus (Int'l)	6	1	.857	2.53	11	11	3	0	0	74 2/3	68	23	21	11	32
—	Chicago (N.L.)■	0	4	.000	6.50	7	3	0	0	0	18	32	15	13	13	10
1988—	Iowa (Am. Assoc.)	4	2	.667	3.76	10	10	2	2	0	67	73	28	28	10	43
—	Chicago (N.L.)	0	0	...	8.10	1	1	0	0	0	3 1/3	6	5	3	2	1
1989—	Louisville (A.A.)■	•13	5	.722	2.43	28	28	2	1	0	*189	170	63	51	34	72
—	St. Louis (N.L.)	1	0	1.000	3.30	7	4	1	1	0	30	25	12	11	10	17
1990—	St. Louis (N.L.)	10	9	.526	3.47	28	20	3	2	1	145 1/3	151	67	56	15	50
—	Louisville (A.A.)	3	2	.600	2.43	6	6	0	0	0	40 2/3	41	15	11	3	22
1991—	St. Louis (N.L.)	11	12	.478	3.25	30	30	3	0	0	191	206	86	69	38	75
1992—	St. Louis (N.L.)	16	5	*.762	2.16	33	32	5	0	0	233	217	63	56	20	91
1993—	St. Louis (N.L.)	17	10	.630	3.83	32	32	2	0	0	213 2/3	*258	99	91	20	97
1994—	St. Louis (N.L.)	12	10	.545	5.32	24	24	4	1	0	155 2/3	*190	97	92	22	79
1995—	Texas (A.L.)■	8	7	.533	4.58	21	21	4	1	0	129 2/3	169	75	66	20	53
—	Charlotte (Fla. St.)	1	0	1.000	0.00	1	1	0	0	0	6	3	0	0	0	4
A.L. totals (3 years)		18	16	.529	4.26	52	47	6	1	0	293 1/3	360	159	139	58	114
N.L. totals (8 years)		67	50	.573	3.55	162	146	18	4	1	990	1085	444	391	140	420
Major league totals (10 years)		85	66	.563	3.72	214	193	24	5	1	1283 1/3	1445	603	530	198	534

ALL-STAR GAME RECORD

Year	League	W	L	Pct.	ERA	GS	CG	ShO	Sv.	IP	H	R	ER	BB	SO
1992—	National	0	0	...	21.60	0	0	0	0	1 2/3	4	4	4	1	0

THOBE, J.J. — P — RED SOX

PERSONAL: Born November 19, 1970, in Covington, Ky. . . . 6-6/200. . . . Throws right, bats right. . . . Full name: John Joseph Thobe. . . . Brother of Tom Thobe, pitcher, Atlanta Braves.
JUNIOR COLLEGE: Rancho Santiago (Calif.).
TRANSACTIONS/CAREER NOTES: Selected by Cleveland Indians organization in seventh round of free-agent draft (June 1, 1992). . . . On Kinston disabled list (August 31-September 12, 1993). . . . On Harrisburg disabled list (June 14-July 16, 1994). . . . Traded by Indians organization with 1B Dave Duplessis to Montreal Expos organization for P Chris Nabholz (February 14, 1994). . . . On Kinston disabled list (August 31-September 12, 1995). . . . Claimed on waivers by Boston Red Sox (October 12, 1995).

Year	Team (League)	W	L	Pct.	ERA	G	GS	CG	ShO	Sv.	IP	H	R	ER	BB	SO
1993—	Columbus (S. Atl.)	11	2	.846	*1.91	19	19	2	0	0	132	105	36	28	25	106
—	Kinston (Carolina)	1	2	.333	3.13	4	4	0	0	0	23	26	11	8	9	11
1994—	WP Beach (FSL)■	1	1	.500	3.75	2	2	0	0	0	12	14	5	5	2	4
—	Harrisburg (East.)	7	8	.467	4.33	21	21	1	0	0	120 2/3	129	73	58	24	57
1995—	Ottawa (Int'l)	5	8	.385	3.27	55	0	0	0	5	88	79	37	32	16	36
—	Montreal (N.L.)	0	0	...	9.00	4	0	0	0	0	4	6	4	4	3	0
Major league totals (1 year)		0	0	...	9.00	4	0	0	0	0	4	6	4	4	3	0

THOBE, TOM — P — BRAVES

PERSONAL: Born September 3, 1969, in Covington, Ky. . . . 6-6/195. . . . Throws left, bats left. . . . Full name: Thomas Neal Thobe. . . . Brother of J.J. Thobe, pitcher, Boston Red Sox.
HIGH SCHOOL: Edison (Huntington Beach, Calif.).
JUNIOR COLLEGE: Golden West (Huntington Beach, Calif.).
TRANSACTIONS/CAREER NOTES: Selected by Chicago Cubs organization in 38th round of free-agent draft (June 2, 1987). . . . Released by Cubs organization (1988). . . . Signed by Atlanta Braves organization (June 6, 1988).

Year Team (League)	W	L	Pct.	ERA	G	GS	CG	ShO	Sv.	IP	H	R	ER	BB	SO
1988—Wytheville (Appal.)	3	3	.500	8.95	18	5	0	0	0	57 1/3	90	66	57	30	31
1989—						Out of organized baseball.									
1990—						Out of organized baseball.									
1991—						Out of organized baseball.									
1992—						Out of organized baseball.									
1993—Macon (S. Atl.)■	7	5	.583	2.69	43	0	0	0	5	70 1/3	70	25	21	16	55
1994—Greenville (South.)	7	6	.538	2.54	51	0	0	0	9	63 2/3	56	21	18	26	52
1995—Richmond (Int'l)	7	0	1.000	1.84	48	2	1	1	5	88	65	27	18	26	57
—Atlanta (N.L.)	0	0	...	10.80	3	0	0	0	0	3 1/3	7	4	4	0	2
Major league totals (1 year)	0	0	...	10.80	3	0	0	0	0	3 1/3	7	4	4	0	2

THOMAS, FRANK — 1B — WHITE SOX

PERSONAL: Born May 27, 1968, in Columbus, Ga. . . . 6-5/257. . . . Bats right, throws right. . . . Full name: Frank Edward Thomas.
HIGH SCHOOL: Columbus (Ga.).
COLLEGE: Auburn.
TRANSACTIONS/CAREER NOTES: Selected by Chicago White Sox organization in first round (seventh pick overall) of free-agent draft (June 5, 1989).
RECORDS: Shares A.L. single-season record for most intentional bases on balls received by righthanded batter—29 (1995).
HONORS: Named first baseman on The Sporting News college All-America team (1989). . . . Named designated hitter on The Sporting News A.L. All-Star team (1991). . . . Named designated hitter on The Sporting News A.L. Silver Slugger team (1991). . . . Named Major League Player of the Year by The Sporting News (1993). . . . Named first baseman on The Sporting News A.L. All-Star team (1993-94). . . . Named first baseman on The Sporting News A.L. Silver Slugger team (1993-94). . . . Named A.L. Most Valuable Player by Baseball Writers' Association of America (1993-94).
STATISTICAL NOTES: Led Southern League with .581 slugging percentage and .487 on-base percentage in 1990. . . . Led A.L. with .453 on-base percentage in 1991, .439 in 1992 and .487 in 1994. . . . Led A.L. first basemen with 1,533 total chances in 1992. . . . Led A.L. with .729 slugging percentage in 1994. . . . Led A.L. with 12 sacrifice flies in 1995. . . . Led A.L. with 29 intentional bases on balls received in 1995. . . . Career major league grand slams: 3.

		BATTING												FIELDING			
Year Team (League)	Pos.	G	AB	R	H	2B	3B	HR	RBI	Avg.	BB	SO	SB	PO	A	E	Avg.
1989—GC Whi. Sox (GCL)	1B	17	52	8	19	5	0	1	11	.365	10	24	4	130	8	2	.986
—Sarasota (Fla. St.)	1B	55	188	27	52	9	1	4	30	.277	31	33	0	420	31	7	.985
1990—Birm. (Southern)	1B	109	353	85	114	27	5	18	71	.323	*112	74	7	954	77	14	.987
—Chicago (A.L.)	1B-DH	60	191	39	63	11	3	7	31	.330	44	54	0	428	26	5	.989
1991—Chicago (A.L.)	DH-1B	158	559	104	178	31	2	32	109	.318	*138	112	1	459	27	2	.996
1992—Chicago (A.L.)	1B-DH	160	573	108	185	•46	2	24	115	.323	•122	88	6	*1428	92	13	.992
1993—Chicago (A.L.)	1B-DH	153	549	106	174	36	0	41	128	.317	112	54	4	1222	83	15	.989
1994—Chicago (A.L.)	1B-DH	113	399	*106	141	34	1	38	101	.353	*109	61	2	735	45	7	.991
1995—Chicago (A.L.)	1B-DH	•145	493	102	152	27	0	40	111	.308	*136	74	3	738	34	7	.991
Major league totals (6 years)		789	2764	565	893	185	8	182	595	.323	661	443	16	5010	307	49	.991

CHAMPIONSHIP SERIES RECORD

NOTES: Holds single-series record for most bases on balls received—10 (1993). . . . Shares single-game record for most bases on balls received—4 (October 5, 1993).

		BATTING												FIELDING			
Year Team (League)	Pos.	G	AB	R	H	2B	3B	HR	RBI	Avg.	BB	SO	SB	PO	A	E	Avg.
1993—Chicago (A.L.)	1B-DH	6	17	2	6	0	0	1	3	.353	10	5	0	24	3	0	1.000

ALL-STAR GAME RECORD

		BATTING											FIELDING			
Year League	Pos.	AB	R	H	2B	3B	HR	RBI	Avg.	BB	SO	SB	PO	A	E	Avg.
1993—American	PH-DH	1	0	1	0	0	0	0	1.000	0	0	0	...	...	...	...
1994—American	1B	2	1	2	0	0	0	1	1.000	1	0	0	6	0	0	1.000
1995—American	1B	2	1	1	0	0	1	2	.500	0	0	0	5	1	0	1.000
All-Star Game totals (3 years)		5	2	4	0	0	1	3	.800	1	0	0	11	1	0	1.000

THOMAS, LARRY — P — WHITE SOX

PERSONAL: Born October 25, 1969, in Miami. . . . 6-1/195. . . . Throws left, bats right. . . . Full name: Larry Wayne Thomas Jr.
HIGH SCHOOL: Winthrop (Mass.).
COLLEGE: Maine.
TRANSACTIONS/CAREER NOTES: Selected by Chicago White Sox organization in second round of free-agent draft (June 3, 1991). . . . On disabled list (July 3-14, 1994).

Year Team (League)	W	L	Pct.	ERA	G	GS	CG	ShO	Sv.	IP	H	R	ER	BB	SO
1991—Utica (NYP)	1	3	.250	1.47	11	10	0	0	0	73 1/3	55	22	12	25	61
—Birmingham (Sou.)	0	0	...	3.00	2	0	0	0	0	6	6	3	2	4	2
1992—Sarasota (Fla. St.)	5	0	1.000	1.62	8	8	0	0	0	55 2/3	44	14	10	7	50
—Birmingham (Sou.)	8	6	.571	*1.94	17	17	3	0	0	120 2/3	102	32	26	30	72

Year	Team (League)	W	L	Pct.	ERA	G	GS	CG	ShO	Sv.	IP	H	R	ER	BB	SO
1993—	Nashville (A.A.)	4	6	.400	5.99	18	18	1	0	0	100 2/3	114	73	67	32	67
—	Sarasota (Fla. St.)	4	2	.667	2.48	8	8	3	2	0	61 2/3	52	19	17	15	27
—	Birmingham (Sou.)	0	1	.000	5.14	1	1	0	0	0	7	9	5	4	1	5
1994—	Birmingham (Sou.)	5	10	.333	4.63	24	24	1	0	0	144	159	96	74	53	77
1995—	Birmingham (Sou.)	4	1	.800	1.34	35	0	0	0	2	40 1/3	24	9	6	15	47
—	Chicago (A.L.)	0	0	...	1.32	17	0	0	0	0	13 2/3	8	2	2	6	12
Major league totals (1 year)		0	0	...	1.32	17	0	0	0	0	13 2/3	8	2	2	6	12

THOMAS, MIKE — P

PERSONAL: Born September 2, 1969, in Sacramento, Calif. . . . 6-2/200. . . . Throws left, bats left. . . . Full name: Michael Steven Thomas.
HIGH SCHOOL: Cabot (Ark.).
JUNIOR COLLEGE: Labette Community Junior College (Kan.).
TRANSACTIONS/CAREER NOTES: Selected by New York Mets organization in 23rd round of free-agent draft (June 5, 1989). . . . Traded by Mets with P Ron Darling to Montreal Expos organization for P Tim Burke (July 15, 1991). . . . Selected by Cleveland Indians from Expos organization in Rule 5 major league draft (December 9, 1991). . . . Returned to Expos (April 2, 1992). . . . Granted free agency (October 15, 1993). . . . Signed by Milwaukee Brewers organization (November 30, 1993). . . . On Milwaukee disabled list (July 13-30, 1995); included rehabilitation assignment to New Orleans (July 21-30). . . . On New Orleans disabled list (August 7-21, 1995). . . . Released by Brewers organization (August 21, 1995).

Year	Team (League)	W	L	Pct.	ERA	G	GS	CG	ShO	Sv.	IP	H	R	ER	BB	SO
1989—	GC Mets (GCL)	2	0	1.000	1.44	8	3	0	0	0	31 1/3	23	5	5	14	34
—	Kingsport (Appal.)	1	2	.333	6.52	6	3	0	0	0	19 1/3	13	16	14	17	17
1990—	Pittsfield (NYP)	3	3	.500	2.67	28	3	0	0	3	64	51	23	19	29	80
1991—	Columbia (S. Atl.)	4	2	.667	2.41	30	0	0	0	15	41	28	15	11	30	59
—	Sumter (S. Atl.)■	4	1	.800	3.95	19	0	0	0	5	27 1/3	25	13	12	18	30
1992—	Rockford (Midw.)	5	9	.357	3.58	28	17	1	0	2	113	98	52	45	51	108
1993—	WP Beach (FSL)	1	3	.250	3.29	25	0	0	0	9	27 1/3	19	13	10	23	28
—	Harrisburg (East.)	2	2	.500	4.73	25	0	0	0	6	32 1/3	34	18	17	19	40
1994—	El Paso (Texas)■	2	3	.400	3.39	50	0	0	0	20	66 1/3	57	36	25	42	59
1995—	Milwaukee (A.L.)	0	0	...	0.00	1	0	0	0	0	1 1/3	2	0	0	1	0
—	New Orleans (A.A.)	0	1	.000	4.05	35	0	0	0	1	33 1/3	37	18	15	18	28
Major league totals (1 year)		0	0	...	0.00	1	0	0	0	0	1 1/3	2	0	0	1	0

THOME, JIM — 3B — INDIANS

PERSONAL: Born August 27, 1970, in Peoria, Ill. . . . 6-4/220. . . . Bats left, throws right. . . . Full name: James Howard Thome. . . . Name pronounced TOE-me.
HIGH SCHOOL: Limestone (Bartonville, Ill.).
COLLEGE: Illinois Central.
TRANSACTIONS/CAREER NOTES: Selected by Cleveland Indians organization in 13th round of free-agent draft (June 5, 1989). . . . On Cleveland disabled list (March 28-May 18, 1992); included rehabilitation assignment to Canton/Akron (May 9-18). . . . On Cleveland disabled list (May 20-June 15, 1992); included rehabilitation assignment to Canton/Akron (June 1-15).
HONORS: Named International League Most Valuable Player (1993). . . . Named third baseman on The Sporting News A.L. All-Star team (1995).
STATISTICAL NOTES: Led International League with .441 on-base percentage in 1993. . . . Hit three home runs in one game (July 22, 1994).

				BATTING											FIELDING			
Year	Team (League)	Pos.	G	AB	R	H	2B	3B	HR	RBI	Avg.	BB	SO	SB	PO	A	E	Avg.
1989—	GC Indians (GCL)	SS-3B	55	186	22	44	5	3	0	22	.237	21	33	6	65	144	21	.909
1990—	Burlington (Appal.)	3B	34	118	31	44	7	1	12	34	.373	27	18	6	28	79	11	.907
—	Kinston (Carolina)	3B	33	117	19	36	4	1	4	16	.308	24	26	4	10	66	8	.905
1991—	Cant./Akr. (East.)	3B	84	294	47	99	20	2	5	45	.337	44	58	8	41	167	17	.924
—	Colo. Springs (PCL)	3B	41	151	20	43	7	3	2	28	.285	12	29	0	28	84	6	.949
—	Cleveland (A.L.)	3B	27	98	7	25	4	2	1	9	.255	5	16	1	12	60	8	.900
1992—	Colo. Springs (PCL)	3B	12	48	11	15	4	1	2	14	.313	6	16	0	9	20	8	.784
—	Cleveland (A.L.)	3B	40	117	8	24	3	1	2	12	.205	10	34	2	21	61	11	.882
—	Cant./Akr. (East.)	3B	30	107	16	36	9	2	1	14	.336	24	30	0	11	35	4	.920
1993—	Charlotte (Int'l)	3B	115	410	85	136	21	4	25	*102	*.332	76	94	1	67	226	15	.951
—	Cleveland (A.L.)	3B	47	154	28	41	11	0	7	22	.266	29	36	2	29	86	6	.950
1994—	Cleveland (A.L.)	3B	98	321	58	86	20	1	20	52	.268	46	84	3	62	173	15	.940
1995—	Cleveland (A.L.)	3B-DH	137	452	92	142	29	3	25	73	.314	97	113	4	75	214	16	.948
Major league totals (5 years)			349	1142	193	318	67	7	55	168	.278	187	283	12	199	594	56	.934

DIVISION SERIES RECORD

				BATTING											FIELDING			
Year	Team (League)	Pos.	G	AB	R	H	2B	3B	HR	RBI	Avg.	BB	SO	SB	PO	A	E	Avg.
1995—	Cleveland (A.L.)	3B	3	13	1	2	0	0	1	3	.154	1	6	0	6	6	0	1.000

CHAMPIONSHIP SERIES RECORD

				BATTING											FIELDING			
Year	Team (League)	Pos.	G	AB	R	H	2B	3B	HR	RBI	Avg.	BB	SO	SB	PO	A	E	Avg.
1995—	Cleveland (A.L.)	3B	5	15	2	4	0	0	2	5	.267	2	3	0	1	5	1	.857

WORLD SERIES RECORD

				BATTING											FIELDING			
Year	Team (League)	Pos.	G	AB	R	H	2B	3B	HR	RBI	Avg.	BB	SO	SB	PO	A	E	Avg.
1995—	Cleveland (A.L.)	3B-PH	6	19	1	4	1	0	1	2	.211	2	5	0	3	5	1	.889

THOMPSON, JUSTIN — P — TIGERS

PERSONAL: Born March 8, 1973, in San Antonio, Tex. . . . 6-3/175. . . . Throws left, bats left. . . . Full name: Justin Willard Thompson.
HIGH SCHOOL: Klein Oak (Spring, Tex.).
TRANSACTIONS/CAREER NOTES: Selected by Detroit Tigers organization in supplemental round ("sandwich pick" between first and second round, 32nd pick overall) of free-agent draft (June 3, 1991); pick received as part of compensation for Minnesota Twins signing Type A free agent P Jack Morris. . . . On Trenton disabled list (April 8, 1994-entire season).

Year	Team (League)	W	L	Pct.	ERA	G	GS	CG	ShO	Sv.	IP	H	R	ER	BB	SO
1991—	Bristol (Appal.)	2	5	.286	3.60	10	10	0	0	0	50	45	29	20	24	60
1992—	Fayetteville (S. Atl.)	4	4	.500	2.18	20	19	0	0	0	95	79	32	23	40	88
1993—	Lakeland (Fla. St.)	4	4	.500	3.56	11	11	0	0	0	55 2/3	65	25	22	16	46
—	London (Eastern)	3	6	.333	4.09	14	14	1	0	0	83 2/3	96	51	38	37	72
1994—								Did not play.								
1995—	Lakeland (Fla. St.)	2	1	.667	4.88	6	6	0	0	0	24	30	13	13	8	20
—	Jacksonville (Sou.)	6	7	.462	3.73	18	18	3	0	0	123	110	55	51	38	98

THOMPSON, MARK — P — ROCKIES

PERSONAL: Born April 7, 1971, in Russellville, Ky. . . . 6-2/205. . . . Throws right, bats right. . . . Full name: Mark Radford Thompson.
HIGH SCHOOL: Logan County (Russellville, Ky.).
COLLEGE: Kentucky.
TRANSACTIONS/CAREER NOTES: Selected by Colorado Rockies organization in second round of free-agent draft (June 1, 1992). . . . On Colorado Springs disabled list (June 30-September 7, 1993; August 9-18 and August 27-September 5, 1994).

Year	Team (League)	W	L	Pct.	ERA	G	GS	CG	ShO	Sv.	IP	H	R	ER	BB	SO
1992—	Bend (Northwest)	8	4	.667	1.95	16	•16	*4	0	0	*106 1/3	81	32	23	31	*102
1993—	Central Valley (Cal.)	3	2	.600	2.20	11	11	0	0	0	69 2/3	46	19	17	18	72
—	Colo. Springs (PCL)	3	0	1.000	2.70	4	4	2	0	0	33 1/3	31	13	10	11	22
1994—	Colo. Springs (PCL)	8	9	.471	4.49	23	23	•4	1	0	140 1/3	169	83	70	57	82
—	Colorado (N.L.)	1	1	.500	9.00	2	2	0	0	0	9	16	9	9	8	5
1995—	Colorado (N.L.)	2	3	.400	6.53	21	5	0	0	0	51	73	42	37	22	30
—	Colo. Springs (PCL)	5	3	.625	6.10	11	10	0	0	0	62	73	43	42	25	38
Major league totals (2 years)		3	4	.429	6.90	23	7	0	0	0	60	89	51	46	30	35

DIVISION SERIES RECORD

Year	Team (League)	W	L	Pct.	ERA	G	GS	CG	ShO	Sv.	IP	H	R	ER	BB	SO
1995—	Colorado (N.L.)	0	0	...	0.00	1	0	0	0	1	1	0	0	0	0	0

THOMPSON, MILT — OF — DODGERS

PERSONAL: Born January 5, 1959, in Washington, D.C. . . . 5-11/203. . . . Bats left, throws right. . . . Full name: Milton Bernard Thompson.
HIGH SCHOOL: Col. Zadok Magruder (Rockville, Md.).
COLLEGE: Howard.
TRANSACTIONS/CAREER NOTES: Selected by Atlanta Braves organization in second round of free-agent draft (January 9, 1979). . . . Traded by Braves with P Steve Bedrosian to Philadelphia Phillies for C Ozzie Virgil and P Pete Smith (December 10, 1985). . . . Traded by Phillies to St. Louis Cardinals for C Steve Lake and OF Curt Ford (December 16, 1988). . . . Granted free agency (October 27, 1992). . . . Signed by Phillies (December 9, 1992). . . . Traded by Phillies to Houston Astros for P Tom Edens (July 31, 1994). . . . Granted free agency (October 26, 1994). . . . Re-signed by Astros (December 20, 1994). . . . Granted free agency (November 1, 1995). . . . Signed by Los Angeles Dodgers organization (January 12, 1996).
STATISTICAL NOTES: Led Southern League outfielders with 336 total chances in 1982. . . . Led Southern League in caught stealing with 19 in 1982. . . . Led International League outfielders with 341 total chances in 1984.

			BATTING												FIELDING			
Year	Team (League)	Pos.	G	AB	R	H	2B	3B	HR	RBI	Avg.	BB	SO	SB	PO	A	E	Avg.
1979—	Greenw. (W. Car.)	OF	53	145	31	27	4	1	2	16	.186	32	39	16	85	8	3	.969
—	Kingsport (Appal.)	OF	26	94	22	31	8	4	1	11	.330	16	17	13	58	4	1	.984
1980—	Durham (Carolina)	OF	68	255	49	74	12	3	2	36	.290	42	62	38	159	8	5	.971
—	Savannah (South.)	OF	71	278	35	83	7	3	1	15	.299	19	67	22	133	11	6	.960
1981—	Savannah (South.)	OF	140	493	92	135	18	2	4	31	.274	87	105	46	226	17	8	.968
1982—	Savannah (South.)	OF	•144	526	83	132	20	7	6	45	.251	87	145	*68	*312	10	14	.958
—	Richmond (Int'l)	OF	3	6	2	1	0	0	0	0	.167	1	3	1	4	0	0	1.000
1983—	Richmond (Int'l)	OF	12	32	12	8	1	0	0	3	.250	10	5	6	30	0	1	.968
—	Savannah (South.)	OF-1B	115	386	84	117	21	4	5	36	.303	83	76	46	295	15	7	.978
1984—	Richmond (Int'l)	OF	134	503	•91	145	11	3	4	40	.288	83	86	47	*317	13	11	.968
—	Atlanta (N.L.)	OF	25	99	16	30	1	0	2	4	.303	11	11	14	37	6	2	.956
1985—	Richmond (Int'l)	OF	82	312	52	98	10	1	2	22	.314	32	30	34	209	3	4	.981
—	Atlanta (N.L.)	OF	73	182	17	55	7	2	0	6	.302	7	36	9	78	2	3	.964
1986—	Philadelphia (N.L.)■	OF	96	299	38	75	7	1	6	23	.251	26	62	19	212	1	2	.991
—	Portland (PCL)	OF	41	161	26	56	10	2	1	16	.348	15	20	21	101	1	1	.990
1987—	Philadelphia (N.L.)	OF	150	527	86	159	26	9	7	43	.302	42	87	46	354	4	4	.989
1988—	Philadelphia (N.L.)	OF	122	378	53	109	16	2	2	33	.288	39	59	17	278	5	5	.983
1989—	St. Louis (N.L.)■	OF	155	545	60	158	28	8	4	68	.290	39	91	27	348	5	8	.978
1990—	St. Louis (N.L.)	OF	135	418	42	91	14	7	6	30	.218	39	60	25	232	4	7	.971
1991—	St. Louis (N.L.)	OF	115	326	55	100	16	5	6	34	.307	32	53	16	207	8	2	.991
1992—	St. Louis (N.L.)	OF	109	208	31	61	9	1	4	17	.293	16	39	18	74	1	2	.974
1993—	Philadelphia (N.L.)■	OF	129	340	42	89	14	2	4	44	.262	40	57	9	162	6	1	.994
1994—	Philadelphia (N.L.)	OF	87	220	29	60	7	0	3	30	.273	23	28	7	119	1	0	*1.000
—	Houston (N.L.)■	OF	9	21	5	6	0	0	1	3	.286	1	2	2	7	1	0	1.000
1995—	Houston (N.L.)	OF	92	132	14	29	9	0	2	19	.220	14	37	4	45	2	1	.979
Major league totals (12 years)			1297	3695	488	1022	154	37	47	354	.277	329	622	213	2153	46	37	.983

CHAMPIONSHIP SERIES RECORD

			BATTING											FIELDING			
Year Team (League)	Pos.	G	AB	R	H	2B	3B	HR	RBI	Avg.	BB	SO	SB	PO	A	E	Avg.
1993—Philadelphia (N.L.)......	OF-PH-PR	6	13	2	3	1	0	0	0	.231	1	2	0	8	0	1	.889

WORLD SERIES RECORD

			BATTING											FIELDING			
Year Team (League)	Pos.	G	AB	R	H	2B	3B	HR	RBI	Avg.	BB	SO	SB	PO	A	E	Avg.
1993—Philadelphia (N.L.)......	OF-PR	5	16	3	5	1	1	1	6	.313	1	2	0	10	0	1	.909

THOMPSON, ROBBY 2B GIANTS

PERSONAL: Born May 10, 1962, in West Palm Beach, Fla. . . . 5-11/173. . . . Bats right, throws right. . . . Full name: Robert Randall Thompson.
HIGH SCHOOL: Forest Hill (West Palm Beach, Fla.).
JUNIOR COLLEGE: Palm Beach Junior College (Fla.).
COLLEGE: Florida.
TRANSACTIONS/CAREER NOTES: Selected by Oakland Athletics organization in second round of free-agent draft (January 12, 1982); did not sign. . . . Selected by Seattle Mariners organization in secondary phase of free-agent draft (June 7, 1982); did not sign. . . . Selected by San Francisco Giants organization in secondary phase of free-agent draft (June 6, 1983). . . . On disabled list (April 28-May 13, 1987; April 29-May 22, 1992; and July 5-22, 1993). . . . Granted free agency (October 26, 1993). . . . Re-signed by Giants (November 13, 1993). . . . On San Francisco disabled list (May 9-June 26, 1994); included rehabilitation assignment to Phoenix (June 21-25). . . . On San Francisco disabled list (July 5, 1994-remainder of season and May 26-June 10, 1995).
RECORDS: Holds major league single-game record for most times caught stealing—4 (June 27, 1986, 12 innings).
HONORS: Named N.L. Rookie Player of the Year by The Sporting News (1986). . . . Named second baseman on The Sporting News N.L. All-Star team (1993). . . . Won N.L. Gold Glove at second base (1993). . . . Named second baseman on The Sporting News N.L. Silver Slugger team (1993).
STATISTICAL NOTES: Led Texas League second basemen with .982 fielding percentage, 291 putouts, 664 total chances and 91 double plays in 1985. . . . Led N.L. with 18 sacrifice hits in 1986. . . . Tied for N.L. lead in being hit by pitch with 13 in 1989. . . . Tied for N.L. lead in double plays by second baseman with 94 in 1990. . . . Hit for the cycle (April 22, 1991). . . . Led N.L. second basemen with 98 double plays in 1991 and 101 in 1992. . . . Career major league grand slams: 2.

			BATTING											FIELDING			
Year Team (League)	Pos.	G	AB	R	H	2B	3B	HR	RBI	Avg.	BB	SO	SB	PO	A	E	Avg.
1983—Fresno (California)......	2B	64	220	33	57	8	1	4	23	.259	18	62	4	118	185	11	.965
1984—Fresno (California)......	2B-SS-3B	102	325	53	81	11	0	8	43	.249	47	85	21	182	280	24	.951
1985—Shreveport (Texas).....	2B-SS	121	449	85	117	20	7	9	40	.261	65	101	28	†292	366	12	†.982
1986—San Francisco (N.L.) ..	2B-SS	149	549	73	149	27	3	7	47	.271	42	112	12	255	451	17	.976
1987—San Francisco (N.L.) ..	2B	132	420	62	110	26	5	10	44	.262	40	91	16	246	341	17	.972
1988—San Francisco (N.L.) ..	2B	138	477	66	126	24	6	7	48	.264	40	111	14	255	365	14	.978
1989—San Francisco (N.L.) ..	2B	148	547	91	132	26	*11	13	50	.241	51	133	12	307	425	8	.989
1990—San Francisco (N.L.) ..	2B	144	498	67	122	22	3	15	56	.245	34	96	14	287	441	8	.989
1991—San Francisco (N.L.) ..	2B	144	492	74	129	24	5	19	48	.262	63	95	14	320	402	11	.985
1992—San Francisco (N.L.) ..	2B	128	443	54	115	25	1	14	49	.260	43	75	5	296	382	15	.978
1993—San Francisco (N.L.) ..	2B	128	494	85	154	30	2	19	65	.312	45	97	10	273	384	8	.988
1994—San Francisco (N.L.) ..	2B	35	129	13	27	8	2	2	7	.209	15	32	3	67	121	2	.989
—Phoenix (PCL)...........	2B	4	11	2	4	2	0	0	1	.364	2	4	1	7	9	1	.941
1995—San Francisco (N.L.) ..	2B	95	336	51	75	15	0	8	23	.223	42	76	1	181	238	3	.993
Major league totals (10 years)		1241	4385	636	1139	227	38	114	437	.260	415	918	101	2487	3550	103	.983

CHAMPIONSHIP SERIES RECORD

			BATTING											FIELDING			
Year Team (League)	Pos.	G	AB	R	H	2B	3B	HR	RBI	Avg.	BB	SO	SB	PO	A	E	Avg.
1987—San Francisco (N.L.) ..	2B-PH	7	20	4	2	0	1	1	2	.100	5	7	2	11	19	1	.968
1989—San Francisco (N.L.) ..	2B	5	18	5	5	0	0	2	3	.278	3	2	0	10	13	0	1.000
Championship series totals (2 years)		12	38	9	7	0	1	3	5	.184	8	9	2	21	32	1	.981

WORLD SERIES RECORD

			BATTING											FIELDING			
Year Team (League)	Pos.	G	AB	R	H	2B	3B	HR	RBI	Avg.	BB	SO	SB	PO	A	E	Avg.
1989—San Francisco (N.L.) ..	2B-PH	4	11	0	1	0	0	0	2	.091	0	4	0	4	10	0	1.000

ALL-STAR GAME RECORD

NOTES: Named to N.L. All-Star team for 1988 game; replaced by Bob Walk due to injury. . . . Named to N.L. All-Star team for 1993 game; replaced by Gregg Jefferies due to injury.

		BATTING											FIELDING			
Year League	Pos.	AB	R	H	2B	3B	HR	RBI	Avg.	BB	SO	SB	PO	A	E	Avg.
1988— National.....................	Selected, did not play—injured.															
1993— National.....................	Selected, did not play—injured.															

THOMPSON, RYAN OF METS

PERSONAL: Born November 4, 1967, in Chestertown, Md. . . . 6-3/215. . . . Bats right, throws right. . . . Full name: Ryan Orlando Thompson.
HIGH SCHOOL: Kent County (Rock Hall, Md.).
TRANSACTIONS/CAREER NOTES: Selected by Toronto Blue Jays organization in 13th round of free-agent draft (June 2, 1987). . . . On disabled list (May 29-June 7, 1991). . . . On Syracuse disabled list (May 4-11 and July 20-27, 1992). . . . Traded by Blue Jays to New York Mets (September 1, 1992), completing deal in which Mets traded P David Cone to Blue Jays for IF Jeff Kent and a player to be named later (August 27, 1992). . . . On New York disabled list (April 18-May 30 and July 18-August 18, 1995); included rehabilitation assignments to Norfolk (May 13-30) and Binghamton (August 16-18).
STATISTICAL NOTES: Career major league grand slams: 1.

Year	Team (League)	Pos.	G	AB	R	H	2B	3B	HR	RBI	Avg.	BB	SO	SB	PO	A	E	Avg.
				BATTING											FIELDING			
1987—	Medicine Hat (Pio.)	OF	40	110	13	27	3	1	1	9	.245	6	34	1	56	2	4	.935
1988—	St. Cathar. (NYP)	OF	23	57	13	10	4	0	0	2	.175	24	21	2	29	1	4	.882
—	Dunedin (Fla. St.)	OF	17	29	2	4	0	0	1	2	.138	2	12	0	11	0	0	1.000
1989—	St. Cathar. (NYP)	OF	74	278	39	76	14	1	6	36	.273	16	60	9	111	•11	5	.961
1990—	Dunedin (Fla. St.)	OF	117	438	56	101	15	5	6	37	.231	20	100	18	237	7	7	.972
1991—	Knoxville (South.)	OF	114	403	48	97	14	3	8	40	.241	26	88	17	222	5	4	.983
1992—	Syracuse (Int'l)	OF	112	429	74	121	20	7	14	46	.282	43	114	10	270	8	4	.986
—	New York (N.L.)■	OF	30	108	15	24	7	1	3	10	.222	8	24	2	77	2	1	.988
1993—	New York (N.L.)	OF	80	288	34	72	19	2	11	26	.250	19	81	2	228	4	3	.987
—	Norfolk (Int'l)	OF	60	224	39	58	11	2	12	34	.259	24	81	6	138	4	4	.973
1994—	New York (N.L.)	OF	98	334	29	75	14	1	18	59	.225	28	94	1	274	5	3	.989
1995—	Norfolk (Int'l)	OF	15	53	7	18	3	0	2	11	.340	4	15	4	15	2	0	1.000
—	New York (N.L.)	OF	75	267	39	67	13	0	7	31	.251	19	77	3	193	4	3	.985
—	Binghamton (East.)	OF	2	8	2	4	0	0	1	4	.500	1	2	0	2	0	0	1.000
Major league totals (4 years)			283	997	117	238	53	4	39	126	.239	74	276	8	772	15	10	.987

T

THOMSON, JOHN P ROCKIES

PERSONAL: Born October 1, 1973, in Vicksburg, Miss. . . . 6-3/175. . . . Throws right, bats right.
JUNIOR COLLEGE: Blinn (Tex.).
TRANSACTIONS/CAREER NOTES: Selected by Colorado Rockies organization in seventh round of free-agent draft (June 3, 1993).
STATISTICAL NOTES: Tied for Arizona League lead with 14 wild pitches in 1993.

Year	Team (League)	W	L	Pct.	ERA	G	GS	CG	ShO	Sv.	IP	H	R	ER	BB	SO
1993—	Ariz. Rockies (Ariz.)	3	5	.375	4.62	11	11	0	0	0	50 2/3	43	40	26	31	36
1994—	Asheville (S. Atl.)	6	6	.500	2.85	19	15	1	1	0	88 1/3	70	34	28	33	79
—	Central Valley (Cal.)	3	1	.750	3.28	9	8	0	0	0	49 1/3	43	20	18	18	41
1995—	New Haven (Eastern)	7	8	.467	4.18	26	24	0	0	0	131 1/3	132	69	61	56	82

THURMAN, GARY OF METS

PERSONAL: Born November 12, 1964, in Indianapolis. . . . 5-10/180. . . . Bats right, throws right. . . . Full name: Gary Montez Thurman Jr.
HIGH SCHOOL: Indianapolis North Central.
TRANSACTIONS/CAREER NOTES: Selected by Kansas City Royals organization in first round (21st pick overall) of free-agent draft (June 6, 1983). . . . On Kansas City disabled list (March 26-April 13, 1989). . . . On Kansas City disabled list (May 10-July 26, 1989); included rehabilitation assignment to Omaha (June 15-July 26). . . . On disabled list (August 6-September 9, 1991). . . . Claimed on waivers by Detroit Tigers (March 26, 1993). . . . Granted free agency (December 20, 1993). . . . Signed by Chicago White Sox organization (February 10, 1994). . . . Granted free agency (October 15, 1994). . . . Signed by Tacoma, Seattle Mariners organization (December 12, 1994). . . . Granted free agency (October 16, 1995). . . . Signed by New York Mets organization (December 20, 1995).
STATISTICAL NOTES: Led Gulf Coast League outfielders with 143 total chances in 1983. . . . Tied for South Atlantic League lead in caught stealing with 17 in 1984. . . . Led South Atlantic League outfielders with 329 total chances in 1984. . . . Led Florida State League outfielders with 396 total chances in 1985. . . . Tied for American Association lead in double plays by outfielder with six in 1987.

Year	Team (League)	Pos.	G	AB	R	H	2B	3B	HR	RBI	Avg.	BB	SO	SB	PO	A	E	Avg.
				BATTING											FIELDING			
1983—	GC Royals (GCL)	OF	59	203	32	52	8	2	0	19	.256	34	*58	31	*127	*13	3	.979
1984—	Char., S.C. (S. Atl.)	OF	129	478	71	109	6	8	6	51	.228	81	127	44	*311	5	13	.960
1985—	Fort Myers (FSL)	OF	134	453	68	137	9	9	0	45	.302	68	93	*70	*368	18	10	.975
1986—	Memphis (South.)	OF	131	525	88	164	24	12	7	62	.312	56	81	53	277	5	11	.962
—	Omaha (A.A.)	OF	3	2	1	1	0	0	0	0	.500	2	0	2	2	0	0	1.000
1987—	Omaha (A.A.)	OF	115	450	88	132	14	9	8	39	.293	48	84	*58	283	11	•8	.974
—	Kansas City (A.L.)	OF	27	81	12	24	2	0	0	5	.296	8	20	7	61	5	2	.971
1988—	Omaha (A.A.)	OF	106	422	77	106	12	6	3	40	.251	38	80	35	195	16	6	.972
—	Kansas City (A.L.)	OF-DH	35	66	6	11	1	0	0	2	.167	4	20	5	36	1	2	.949
1989—	Kansas City (A.L.)	OF-DH	72	87	24	17	2	1	0	5	.195	15	26	16	54	2	3	.949
—	Omaha (A.A.)	OF	17	64	5	14	3	2	0	3	.219	7	18	5	34	1	2	.946
1990—	Kansas City (A.L.)	OF	23	60	5	14	3	0	0	3	.233	2	12	1	32	0	0	1.000
—	Omaha (A.A.)	OF	98	381	65	126	14	8	0	26	.331	31	68	39	163	6	6	.966
1991—	Kansas City (A.L.)	OF	80	184	24	51	9	0	2	13	.277	11	42	15	129	2	4	.970
1992—	Kansas City (A.L.)	OF-DH	88	200	25	49	6	3	0	20	.245	9	34	9	138	5	2	.986
1993—	Detroit (A.L.)■	OF-DH	75	89	22	19	2	2	0	13	.213	11	30	7	54	3	3	.950
1994—	Nashville (A.A.)■	OF	130	470	76	124	17	•12	5	60	.264	35	85	20	264	11	4	.986
1995—	Tacoma (PCL)■	OF	93	363	65	109	10	12	5	46	.300	20	62	22	180	13	7	.965
—	Seattle (A.L.)	OF	13	25	3	8	2	0	0	3	.320	1	3	5	15	0	0	1.000
Major league totals (8 years)			413	792	121	193	27	6	2	64	.244	61	187	65	519	18	16	.971

TIMLIN, MIKE P BLUE JAYS

PERSONAL: Born March 10, 1966, in Midland, Tex. . . . 6-4/210. . . . Throws right, bats right. . . . Full name: Michael August Timlin.
HIGH SCHOOL: Midland (Tex.).
COLLEGE: Southwestern University (Tex.).
TRANSACTIONS/CAREER NOTES: Selected by Toronto Blue Jays organization in fifth round of free-agent draft (June 2, 1987). . . . On disabled list (April 4-May 2, 1989 and August 2-17, 1991). . . . On Toronto disabled list (March 27-June 12, 1992); included rehabilitation assignments to Dunedin (April 11-15 and May 24-June 5) and Syracuse (June 5-12). . . . On disabled list (May 25-June 9, 1994). . . . On Toronto disabled list (June 22-August 18, 1995); included rehabilitation assignment to Syracuse (July 31-August 18).
STATISTICAL NOTES: Led South Atlantic League with 19 hit batsmen in 1988.

Year	Team (League)	W	L	Pct.	ERA	G	GS	CG	ShO	Sv.	IP	H	R	ER	BB	SO
1987—	Medicine Hat (Pio.)	4	8	.333	5.14	13	12	2	0	0	75 1/3	79	50	43	26	66
1988—	Myrtle Beach (SAL)	10	6	.625	2.86	35	22	0	0	0	151	119	68	48	77	106
1989—	Dunedin (Fla. St.)	5	8	.385	3.25	33	7	1	0	7	88 2/3	90	44	32	36	64
1990—	Dunedin (Fla. St.)	7	2	.778	1.43	42	0	0	0	22	50 1/3	36	11	8	16	46
—	Knoxville (South.)	1	2	.333	1.73	17	0	0	0	8	26	20	6	5	7	21
1991—	Toronto (A.L.)	11	6	.647	3.16	63	3	0	0	3	108 1/3	94	43	38	50	85
1992—	Dunedin (Fla. St.)	0	0	...	0.90	6	1	0	0	1	10	9	2	1	2	7
—	Syracuse (Int'l)	0	1	.000	8.74	7	1	0	0	3	11 1/3	15	11	11	5	7
—	Toronto (A.L.)	0	2	.000	4.12	26	0	0	0	1	43 2/3	45	23	20	20	35
1993—	Toronto (A.L.)	4	2	.667	4.69	54	0	0	0	1	55 2/3	63	32	29	27	49
—	Dunedin (Fla. St.)	0	0	...	1.00	4	0	0	0	1	9	4	1	1	0	8
1994—	Toronto (A.L.)	0	1	.000	5.18	34	0	0	0	2	40	41	25	23	20	38
1995—	Toronto (A.L.)	4	3	.571	2.14	31	0	0	0	5	42	38	13	10	17	36
—	Syracuse (Int'l)	1	1	.500	1.04	8	0	0	0	0	17 1/3	13	6	2	4	13
Major league totals (5 years)		19	14	.576	3.73	208	3	0	0	12	289 2/3	281	136	120	134	243

CHAMPIONSHIP SERIES RECORD

Year	Team (League)	W	L	Pct.	ERA	G	GS	CG	ShO	Sv.	IP	H	R	ER	BB	SO
1991—	Toronto (A.L.)	0	1	.000	3.18	4	0	0	0	0	5 2/3	5	4	2	2	5
1992—	Toronto (A.L.)	0	0	...	6.75	2	0	0	0	0	1 1/3	4	1	1	0	1
1993—	Toronto (A.L.)	0	0	...	3.86	1	0	0	0	0	2 1/3	3	1	1	0	2
Champ. series totals (3 years)		0	1	.000	3.86	7	0	0	0	0	9 1/3	12	6	4	2	8

WORLD SERIES RECORD

NOTES: Member of World Series championship teams (1992 and 1993).

Year	Team (League)	W	L	Pct.	ERA	G	GS	CG	ShO	Sv.	IP	H	R	ER	BB	SO
1992—	Toronto (A.L.)	0	0	...	0.00	2	0	0	0	1	1 1/3	0	0	0	0	0
1993—	Toronto (A.L.)	0	0	...	0.00	2	0	0	0	0	2 1/3	2	0	0	0	4
World Series totals (2 years)		0	0	...	0.00	4	0	0	0	1	3 2/3	2	0	0	0	4

TIMMONS, OZZIE — OF — CUBS

PERSONAL: Born September 18, 1970, in Tampa, Fla. . . . 6-2/220. . . . Bats right, throws right. . . . Full name: Osborne Llewellyn Timmons.
HIGH SCHOOL: Brandon (Fla.).
COLLEGE: University of Tampa (Fla.).
TRANSACTIONS/CAREER NOTES: Selected by Chicago White Sox organization in 44th round of free-agent draft (June 1, 1988); did not sign. . . . Selected by Chicago Cubs organization in fifth round of free-agent draft (June 3, 1991). . . . On disabled list (August 9, 1993-remainder of season).

			BATTING											FIELDING			
Year	Team (League)	Pos.	G	AB	R	H	2B	3B	HR	RBI	Avg.	BB	SO	SB	PO	A	E	Avg.
1991—	Geneva (NYP)	OF	73	294	35	65	10	1	•12	47	.221	18	39	4	118	3	4	.968
1992—	Winst.-Salem (Car.)	OF	86	305	64	86	18	0	18	56	.282	58	46	11	90	7	1	.990
—	Charlotte (South.)	OF	36	122	13	26	7	0	3	13	.213	12	26	2	41	3	1	.978
1993—	Orlando (Southern)	OF	107	359	65	102	22	2	18	58	.284	62	80	5	169	14	6	.968
1994—	Iowa (Am. Assoc.)	OF	126	440	63	116	30	2	22	66	.264	36	93	0	228	14	6	.976
1995—	Chicago (N.L.)	OF	77	171	30	45	10	1	8	28	.263	13	32	3	63	1	2	.970
Major league totals (1 year)			77	171	30	45	10	1	8	28	.263	13	32	3	63	1	2	.970

TINGLEY, RON — C — ANGELS

PERSONAL: Born May 27, 1959, in Presque Isle, Me. . . . 6-2/194. . . . Bats right, throws right. . . . Full name: Ronald Irvin Tingley.
HIGH SCHOOL: Ramona (Riverside, Calif.).
TRANSACTIONS/CAREER NOTES: Selected by San Diego Padres organization in 10th round of free-agent draft (June 7, 1977). . . . On disabled list (April 10-29, 1980). . . . Traded by Padres organization to Seattle Mariners organization for SS Bill Wrona (April 1, 1984). . . . On disabled list (April 7-August 10, 1984). . . . Granted free agency (October 15, 1984). . . . Signed by Calgary, Mariners organization (January 15, 1985). . . . Granted free agency (October 15, 1985). . . . Signed by Richmond, Atlanta Braves organization (November 19, 1985). . . . Released by Braves organization (June 19, 1986). . . . Signed by Maine, Cleveland Indians organization (June 23, 1986). . . . Traded by Indians organization to California Angels for a player to be named later (September 6, 1989); Colorado Springs, Indians organization, acquired IF Mark McLemore to complete deal (August 17, 1990). . . . On California disabled list (August 4-September 1, 1990). . . . Granted free agency (October 15, 1990). . . . Re-signed by Angels organization (December 6, 1990). . . . Granted free agency (October 7, 1993). . . . Signed by Edmonton, Florida Marlins organization (November 3, 1993). . . . Granted free agency (June 30, 1994). . . . Signed by Nashville, Chicago White Sox organization (July 2, 1994). . . . On Chicago disabled list (July 24, 1994-remainder of season). . . . Released by White Sox (November 10, 1994). . . . Signed by Toledo, Detroit Tigers organization (December 17, 1994). . . . Released by Tigers (October 12, 1995). . . . Signed by Angels organization (December 14, 1995).
STATISTICAL NOTES: Tied for N.L. lead with 10 passed balls in 1994. . . . Career major league grand slams: 1.

			BATTING											FIELDING			
Year	Team (League)	Pos.	G	AB	R	H	2B	3B	HR	RBI	Avg.	BB	SO	SB	PO	A	E	Avg.
1977—	Walla Walla (N'west)	OF	21	33	8	5	0	0	1	3	.152	2	9	0	5	2	0	1.000
1978—	Walla Walla (N'west)	OF-C	43	140	22	29	2	0	2	21	.207	21	38	2	149	16	8	.954
1979—	Santa Clara (Calif.)	C-OF-P	52	143	11	29	4	1	0	17	.203	18	37	0	258	42	8	.974
—	Amarillo (Texas)	C-OF	30	90	16	23	4	1	1	6	.256	14	17	2	133	17	4	.974
1980—	Reno (California)	C-OF	65	204	37	61	3	3	3	35	.299	33	35	46	333	46	10	.974
1981—	Amarillo (Texas)	C-1B-OF	116	379	72	109	9	*10	13	60	.288	52	98	8	607	47	11	.983
1982—	Hawaii (PCL)	C	115	362	45	95	13	8	6	42	.262	56	103	11	540	77	12	.981
—	San Diego (N.L.)	C	8	20	0	2	0	0	0	0	.100	0	7	0	40	4	2	.957
1983—	Las Vegas (PCL)	C	92	294	44	83	15	6	10	48	.282	39	85	9	449	55	12	.977
1984—	Salt Lake (PCL)■	C	3	2	1	1	0	0	1	1	.500	0	1	0	3	0	0	1.000
1985—	Calgary (PCL)	C-OF	83	277	36	70	11	3	11	47	.253	30	74	3	399	51	10	.978

Year Team (League)	Pos.	G	AB	R	H	2B	3B	HR	RBI	Avg.	BB	SO	SB	PO	A	E	Avg.
		BATTING												FIELDING			
1986— Richmond (Int'l)■	C	9	23	1	4	0	0	0	1	.174	0	9	1	40	3	0	1.000
— Maine (Int'l)■	C	49	151	12	31	2	1	3	12	.205	12	27	1	240	20	6	.977
1987— Buffalo (A.A.)	C-1B-3B	57	167	27	45	8	5	5	30	.269	25	42	1	306	37	6	.983
1988— Colo. Springs (PCL)	C	44	130	11	37	5	1	3	20	.285	12	23	1	234	22	0	1.000
— Cleveland (A.L.)	C	9	24	1	4	0	0	1	2	.167	2	8	0	48	6	0	1.000
1989— Colo. Springs (PCL)	C-1B	66	207	28	54	8	2	6	39	.261	19	49	2	349	45	12	.970
— California (A.L.)■	C	4	3	0	1	0	0	0	0	.333	1	0	0	7	1	1	.889
1990— Edmonton (PCL)	C	54	172	27	46	9	2	5	23	.267	21	39	1	284	35	8	.976
— California (A.L.)	C	5	3	0	0	0	0	0	0	.000	1	1	0	12	0	0	1.000
1991— Edmonton (PCL)	C	17	55	11	16	5	0	3	15	.291	8	14	1	65	9	3	.961
— California (A.L.)	C	45	115	11	23	7	0	1	13	.200	8	34	1	222	32	3	.988
1992— California (A.L.)	C	71	127	15	25	2	1	3	8	.197	13	35	0	270	35	4	.987
1993— California (A.L.)	C	58	90	7	18	7	0	0	12	.200	9	22	1	200	20	1	.995
1994— Florida (N.L.)■	C	19	52	4	9	3	1	1	2	.173	5	18	0	91	10	1	.990
— Nashville (A.A.)■	C	6	16	1	2	1	0	0	1	.125	1	7	0	34	3	0	1.000
— Chicago (A.L.)	C	5	5	0	0	0	0	0	0	.000	0	2	0	16	0	0	1.000
1995— Detroit (A.L.)■	C-1B	54	124	14	28	8	1	4	18	.226	15	38	0	199	19	2	.991
American League totals (8 years)		251	491	48	99	24	2	9	53	.202	49	140	2	974	113	11	.990
National League totals (2 years)		27	72	4	11	3	1	1	2	.153	5	25	0	131	14	3	.980
Major league totals (9 years)		278	563	52	110	27	3	10	55	.195	54	165	2	1105	127	14	.989

RECORD AS PITCHER

Year Team (League)	W	L	Pct.	ERA	G	GS	CG	ShO	Sv.	IP	H	R	ER	BB	SO
1979— Santa Clara (Calif.)	0	0	...	9.00	1	0	0	0	0	1	4	5	1	2	2

TINSLEY, LEE — OF — RED SOX

PERSONAL: Born March 4, 1969, in Shelbyville, Ky. . . . 5-10/196. . . . Bats both, throws right. . . . Full name: Lee Owen Tinsley.

HIGH SCHOOL: Shelby County (Ky.).

TRANSACTIONS/CAREER NOTES: Selected by Oakland Athletics organization in first round (11th pick overall) of free-agent draft (June 2, 1987). . . . Traded by A's with P Apolinar Garcia to Cleveland Indians for 3B Brook Jacoby (July 26, 1991). . . . Claimed on waivers by Seattle Mariners (September 21, 1992). . . . Traded by Mariners to Boston Red Sox for a player to be named later (March 22, 1994); Mariners acquired P Jim Smith to complete deal (September 15, 1994). . . . On Boston disabled list (May 19-June 8 and August 23-September 8, 1995); included rehabilitation assignment to Trenton (June 4-8).

STATISTICAL NOTES: Tied for Northwest League lead in caught stealing with 10 in 1988. . . . Led Midwest League outfielders with 320 total chances in 1990.

Year Team (League)	Pos.	G	AB	R	H	2B	3B	HR	RBI	Avg.	BB	SO	SB	PO	A	E	Avg.
			BATTING											FIELDING			
1987— Medford (N'west)	OF	45	132	22	23	3	2	0	13	.174	35	57	9	77	2	4	.952
1988— S. Oregon (N'west)	OF	72	256	56	64	8	2	3	28	.250	*66	*106	*42	127	6	6	.957
1989— Madison (Midwest)	OF	123	397	51	72	10	2	6	31	.181	67	*177	19	274	7	8	.972
1990— Madison (Midwest)	OF	132	482	88	121	14	12	12	59	.251	78	*175	44	*302	7	11	.966
1991— Huntsville (South.)	OF	92	303	47	68	7	6	2	24	.224	52	97	36	175	3	7	.962
— Cant./Akr. (East.)■	OF	38	139	26	41	7	2	3	8	.295	18	37	18	56	1	2	.966
1992— Colo. Springs (PCL)	OF	27	81	19	19	2	1	0	4	.235	16	19	3	42	1	1	.977
— Cant./Akr. (East.)	OF	96	349	65	100	9	8	5	38	.287	42	82	18	226	5	5	.979
1993— Seattle (A.L.)■	OF-DH	11	19	2	3	1	0	1	2	.158	2	9	0	9	0	1	.900
— Calgary (PCL)	OF	111	450	95	136	25	*18	10	63	.302	50	98	34	241	4	3	.988
1994— Boston (A.L.)■	OF-DH	78	144	27	32	4	0	2	14	.222	19	36	13	113	1	1	.991
1995— Boston (A.L.)	OF	100	341	61	97	17	1	7	41	.284	39	74	18	228	4	5	.979
— Trenton (Eastern)	OF	4	18	3	7	1	0	0	3	.389	1	5	1	4	0	0	1.000
Major league totals (3 years)		189	504	90	132	22	1	10	57	.262	60	119	31	350	5	7	.981

DIVISION SERIES RECORD

Year Team (League)	Pos.	G	AB	R	H	2B	3B	HR	RBI	Avg.	BB	SO	SB	PO	A	E	Avg.
			BATTING											FIELDING			
1995— Boston (A.L.)	OF	1	5	0	0	0	0	0	0	.000	1	2	0	1	0	0	1.000

TOMBERLIN, ANDY — OF

PERSONAL: Born November 7, 1966, in Monroe, N.C. . . . 5-11/160. . . . Bats left, throws left. . . . Full name: Andy Lee Tomberlin.

HIGH SCHOOL: Piedmont (Monroe, N.C.).

TRANSACTIONS/CAREER NOTES: Signed as non-drafted free agent by Atlanta Braves organization (August 16, 1985). . . . On disabled list (April 10-May 28, 1991). . . . Granted free agency (October 15, 1992). . . . Signed by Buffalo, Pittsburgh Pirates organization (November 24, 1992). . . . On Buffalo disabled list (May 22-June 5 and June 30-July 27, 1993). . . . Granted free agency (October 13, 1993). . . . Signed by Pawtucket, Boston Red Sox organization (February 4, 1994). . . . On Boston disabled list (June 9-July 26, 1994). . . . Granted free agency (October 6, 1994). . . . Signed by Oakland Athletics organization (December 11, 1994). . . . On Edmonton disabled list (August 2-September 12, 1995). . . . Granted free agency (October 16, 1995).

STATISTICAL NOTES: Tied for Carolina League lead with seven intentional base on balls received in 1989.

Year Team (League)	Pos.	G	AB	R	H	2B	3B	HR	RBI	Avg.	BB	SO	SB	PO	A	E	Avg.
			BATTING											FIELDING			
1986— Sumter (S. Atl.)	P	13	1	0	0	0	0	0	0	.000	1	1	0	2	2	2	.667
— Pulaski (Appal.)	P	3	4	2	1	0	0	0	0	.250	2	1	0	0	5	0	1.000
1987— Pulaski (Appal.)	P	14	7	1	2	0	0	0	1	.286	0	0	0	1	9	1	.909
1988— Burlington (Midw.)	OF	43	134	24	46	7	3	3	18	.343	22	33	7	62	6	3	.958
— Durham (Carolina)	OF-P	83	256	43	77	16	3	6	35	.301	49	42	16	152	2	3	.981
1989— Durham (Carolina)	OF-1B-P	119	363	63	102	13	2	16	61	.281	54	82	35	442	16	1	.998

Year	Team (League)	Pos.	G	AB	R	H	2B	3B	HR	RBI	Avg.	BB	SO	SB	PO	A	E	Avg.
				BATTING											FIELDING			
1990—	Greenville (South.)	OF-P	60	196	31	61	9	1	4	25	.311	20	35	9	95	4	3	.971
—	Richmond (Int'l)	OF-1B	80	283	36	86	19	3	4	31	.304	39	43	11	180	9	4	.979
1991—	Richmond (Int'l)	OF	93	329	47	77	13	2	2	24	.234	41	85	10	192	1	1	.995
1992—	Richmond (Int'l)	OF	118	406	69	110	16	5	9	47	.271	41	102	12	184	9	3	.985
1993—	Buffalo (A.A.)■	OF-P	68	221	41	63	11	6	12	45	.285	18	48	3	104	7	5	.957
—	Pittsburgh (N.L.)	OF	27	42	4	12	0	1	1	5	.286	2	14	0	9	1	0	1.000
1994—	Pawtucket (Int'l)■	OF	54	189	38	63	12	2	13	39	.333	22	60	11	90	4	2	.979
—	Boston (A.L.)	OF-DH-P	18	36	1	7	0	1	1	1	.194	6	12	1	12	2	0	1.000
1995—	Edmonton (PCL)■	OF	14	52	9	13	3	0	2	7	.250	5	15	0	25	1	2	.929
—	Oakland (A.L.)	OF-DH	46	85	15	18	0	0	4	10	.212	5	22	4	45	1	1	.979
American League totals (2 years)			64	121	16	25	0	1	5	11	.207	11	34	5	57	3	1	.984
National League totals (1 year)			27	42	4	12	0	1	1	5	.286	2	14	0	9	1	0	1.000
Major league totals (3 years)			91	163	20	37	0	2	6	16	.227	13	48	5	66	4	1	.986

RECORD AS PITCHER

Year	Team (League)	W	L	Pct.	ERA	G	GS	CG	ShO	Sv.	IP	H	R	ER	BB	SO
1986—	Sumter (S. Atl.)	1	0	1.000	4.62	13	0	0	0	0	25 1/3	18	17	13	27	22
—	Pulaski (Appal.)	2	0	1.000	2.12	3	3	0	0	0	17	13	4	4	9	15
1987—	Pulaski (Appal.)	4	2	.667	4.43	12	6	0	0	0	44 2/3	35	23	22	29	51
1988—	Durham (Carolina)	0	0	...	0.00	1	0	0	0	0	1	0	0	0	0	0
1989—	Durham (Carolina)	0	0	...	18.00	1	0	0	0	0	1	2	2	2	2	2
1990—	Greenville (South.)	0	0	...	0.00	1	0	0	0	0	1	1	0	0	1	1
1993—	Buffalo (A.A.)■	0	0	...	0.00	2	0	0	0	0	2	0	0	0	3	1
1994—	Boston (A.L.)	0	0	...	0.00	1	0	0	0	0	2	1	0	0	1	1
Major league totals (1 year)		0	0	...	0.00	1	0	0	0	0	2	1	0	0	1	1

TORRES, DILSON — P — ROYALS

PERSONAL: Born May 31, 1970, in Sur Edo Aragua, Venezuela. . . . 6-3/200. . . . Throws right, bats right. . . . Full name: Dilson Dario Torres.

TRANSACTIONS/CAREER NOTES: Signed as non-drafted free agent by Toronto Blue Jays organization (December 10, 1990). . . . Selected by Omaha, Kansas City Royals organization, from Knoxville, Blue Jays organization, in Rule 5 minor league draft (December 13, 1993).

Year	Team (League)	W	L	Pct.	ERA	G	GS	CG	ShO	Sv.	IP	H	R	ER	BB	SO
1991—	Santo Dom. (DSL)	3	3	.500	0.96	18	3	0	0	7	47	29	13	5	32	41
1992—	Santo Dom. (DSL)	2	0	1.000	1.62	25	0	0	0	14	39	26	9	7	14	43
1993—	St. Cathar. (NYP)	1	4	.200	3.13	17	0	0	0	3	23	21	13	8	6	23
1994—	Wilmington (Caro.)■	7	2	.778	1.37	15	9	0	0	2	59 1/3	47	15	9	15	49
—	Memphis (South.)	6	0	1.000	1.83	10	9	0	0	0	59	47	15	12	10	47
1995—	Kansas City (A.L.)	1	2	.333	6.09	24	2	0	0	0	44 1/3	56	30	30	17	28
—	Omaha (Am. Assoc.)	3	1	.750	2.63	5	5	1	1	0	27 1/3	28	11	8	7	12
Major league totals (1 year)		1	2	.333	6.09	24	2	0	0	0	44 1/3	56	30	30	17	28

TORRES, SALOMON — P — MARINERS

PERSONAL: Born March 11, 1972, in San Pedro de Macoris, Dominican Republic. . . . 5-11/165. . . . Throws right, bats right. . . . Full name: Salomon Ramirez Torres.

HIGH SCHOOL: Centro Academico Rogus (San Pedro de Macoris, Dominican Republic).

TRANSACTIONS/CAREER NOTES: Signed as non-drafted free agent by San Francisco Giants organization (September 15, 1989). . . . Traded by Giants to Seattle Mariners for P Shawn Estes and IF Wilson Delgado (May 21, 1995).

HONORS: Named Midwest League Most Valuable Player (1991).

Year	Team (League)	W	L	Pct.	ERA	G	GS	CG	ShO	Sv.	IP	H	R	ER	BB	SO
1990—	San Pedro (DSL)	11	1	.917	0.50	13	13	6	0	0	90	44	15	5	30	101
1991—	Clinton (Midwest)	•16	5	.762	*1.41	28	28	*8	3	0	*210 1/3	148	48	33	47	*214
1992—	Shreveport (Texas)	6	10	.375	4.21	25	25	4	2	0	162 1/3	167	93	76	34	151
1993—	Shreveport (Texas)	7	4	.636	2.70	12	12	2	1	0	83 1/3	67	27	25	12	67
—	Phoenix (PCL)	7	4	.636	3.50	14	14	•4	1	0	105 1/3	105	43	41	27	99
—	San Francisco (N.L.)	3	5	.375	4.03	8	8	0	0	0	44 2/3	37	21	20	27	23
1994—	San Francisco (N.L.)	2	8	.200	5.44	16	14	1	0	0	84 1/3	95	55	51	34	42
—	Phoenix (PCL)	5	6	.455	4.22	13	13	0	0	0	79	85	49	37	31	64
1995—	San Francisco (N.L.)	0	1	.000	9.00	4	1	0	0	0	8	13	8	8	7	2
—	Phoenix (PCL)	0	0	...	0.00	1	0	0	0	0	2	2	0	0	0	5
—	Tacoma (PCL)■	1	1	.500	3.21	5	4	0	0	0	28	20	10	10	13	19
—	Seattle (A.L.)	3	8	.273	6.00	16	13	1	0	0	72	87	53	48	42	45
A.L. totals (1 year)		3	8	.273	6.00	16	13	1	0	0	72	87	53	48	42	45
N.L. totals (3 years)		5	14	.263	5.19	28	23	1	0	0	137	145	84	79	68	67
Major league totals (3 years)		8	22	.267	5.47	44	36	2	0	0	209	232	137	127	110	112

TRACHSEL, STEVE — P — CUBS

PERSONAL: Born October 31, 1970, in Oxnard, Calif. . . . 6-4/205. . . . Throws right, bats right. . . . Full name: Stephen Christopher Trachsel. . . . Name pronounced TRACK-sul.

HIGH SCHOOL: Troy (Fullerton, Calif.).

JUNIOR COLLEGE: Fullerton (Calif.) College.

COLLEGE: Long Beach State.

TRANSACTIONS/CAREER NOTES: Selected by Chicago Cubs organization in eighth round of free-agent draft (June 3, 1991). . . . On Chicago disabled list (July 20-August 4, 1994).

HONORS: Named N.L. Rookie Pitcher of the Year by The Sporting News (1994).

STATISTICAL NOTES: Pitched 4-2 no-hit victory for Winston-Salem against Peninsula (July 12, 1991, second game).

Year	Team (League)	W	L	Pct.	ERA	G	GS	CG	ShO	Sv.	IP	H	R	ER	BB	SO
1991—	Geneva (NYP)	1	0	1.000	1.26	2	2	0	0	0	14 1/3	10	2	2	6	7
—	Winst.-Salem (Car.)	4	4	.500	3.67	12	12	1	0	0	73 2/3	70	38	30	19	69
1992—	Charlotte (South.)	•13	8	.619	3.06	29	•29	5	2	0	*191	180	76	65	35	135
1993—	Iowa (Am. Assoc.)	13	6	.684	3.96	27	26	1	1	0	170 2/3	170	78	75	45	135
—	Chicago (N.L.)	0	2	.000	4.58	3	3	0	0	0	19 2/3	16	10	10	3	14
1994—	Chicago (N.L.)	9	7	.563	3.21	22	22	1	0	0	146	133	57	52	54	108
—	Iowa (Am. Assoc.)	0	2	.000	10.00	2	2	0	0	0	9	11	10	10	7	8
1995—	Chicago (N.L.)	7	13	.350	5.15	30	29	2	0	0	160 2/3	174	104	92	76	117
Major league totals (3 years)		16	22	.421	4.25	55	54	3	0	0	326 1/3	323	171	154	133	239

TRAMMELL, ALAN — SS — TIGERS

PERSONAL: Born February 21, 1958, in Garden Grove, Calif. . . . 6-0/185. . . . Bats right, throws right. . . . Full name: Alan Stuart Trammell. . . . Name pronounced TRAM-ull.

HIGH SCHOOL: Kearney (San Diego).

TRANSACTIONS/CAREER NOTES: Selected by Detroit Tigers organization in second round of free-agent draft (June 8, 1976). . . . On disabled list (July 9-31, 1984; June 29-July 17, 1988; June 4-23, 1989; July 18-August 13, 1991; and May 16, 1992-remainder of season). . . . Granted free agency (November 6, 1992). . . . Re-signed by Tigers (December 2, 1992). . . . On disabled list (April 2-17, 1993). . . . Granted free agency (October 28, 1993). . . . Re-signed by Tigers (November 3, 1993). . . . Granted free agency (October 25, 1994). . . . Re-signed by Tigers (April 8, 1995). . . . On disabled list (April 21-May 6, 1995). . . . Granted free agency (December 21, 1995). . . . Re-signed by Tigers (January 24, 1996).

HONORS: Named Southern League Most Valuable Player (1977). . . . Won A.L. Gold Glove at shortstop (1980-81 and 1983-84). . . . Named A.L. Comeback Player of the Year by The Sporting News (1983). . . . Named shortstop on The Sporting News A.L. All-Star team (1987-88 and 1990). . . . Named shortstop on The Sporting News A.L. Silver Slugger team (1987-88 and 1990).

STATISTICAL NOTES: Led A.L. with 16 sacrifice hits in 1981 and 15 in 1983. . . . Led A.L. shortstops with 102 double plays in 1990. . . . Career major league grand slams: 5.

			BATTING												FIELDING			
Year	Team (League)	Pos.	G	AB	R	H	2B	3B	HR	RBI	Avg.	BB	SO	SB	PO	A	E	Avg.
1976—	Bristol (Appal.)	SS	41	140	27	38	2	2	0	7	.271	26	20	8	59	131	12	.941
—	Montgomery (Sou.)	SS	21	56	4	10	0	0	0	2	.179	7	12	3	40	64	2	.981
1977—	Montgomery (Sou.)	SS	134	454	78	132	9	*19	3	50	.291	56	92	4	188	397	27	.956
—	Detroit (A.L.)	SS	19	43	6	8	0	0	0	0	.186	4	12	0	15	34	2	.961
1978—	Detroit (A.L.)	SS	139	448	49	120	14	6	2	34	.268	45	56	3	239	421	14	.979
1979—	Detroit (A.L.)	SS	142	460	68	127	11	4	6	50	.276	43	55	17	245	388	26	.961
1980—	Detroit (A.L.)	SS	146	560	107	168	21	5	9	65	.300	69	63	12	225	412	13	.980
1981—	Detroit (A.L.)	SS	105	392	52	101	15	3	2	31	.258	49	31	10	181	347	9	.983
1982—	Detroit (A.L.)	SS	157	489	66	126	34	3	9	57	.258	52	47	19	259	459	16	.978
1983—	Detroit (A.L.)	SS	142	505	83	161	31	2	14	66	.319	57	64	30	236	367	13	.979
1984—	Detroit (A.L.)	SS-DH	139	555	85	174	34	5	14	69	.314	60	63	19	180	314	10	.980
1985—	Detroit (A.L.)	SS	149	605	79	156	21	7	13	57	.258	50	71	14	225	400	15	.977
1986—	Detroit (A.L.)	SS-DH	151	574	107	159	33	7	21	75	.277	59	57	25	238	445	22	.969
1987—	Detroit (A.L.)	SS	151	597	109	205	34	3	28	105	.343	60	47	21	222	421	19	.971
1988—	Detroit (A.L.)	SS	128	466	73	145	24	1	15	69	.311	46	46	7	195	355	11	.980
1989—	Detroit (A.L.)	SS-DH	121	449	54	109	20	3	5	43	.243	45	45	10	188	396	9	.985
1990—	Detroit (A.L.)	SS-DH	146	559	71	170	37	1	14	89	.304	68	55	12	232	409	14	.979
1991—	Detroit (A.L.)	SS-DH	101	375	57	93	20	0	9	55	.248	37	39	11	131	296	9	.979
1992—	Detroit (A.L.)	SS-DH	29	102	11	28	7	1	1	11	.275	15	4	2	46	80	3	.977
1993—	Detroit (A.L.)	S-3-O-DH	112	401	72	132	25	3	12	60	.329	38	38	12	113	238	9	.975
1994—	Detroit (A.L.)	SS-DH	76	292	38	78	17	1	8	28	.267	16	35	3	117	181	10	.968
1995—	Detroit (A.L.)	SS-DH	74	223	28	60	12	0	2	23	.269	27	19	3	86	158	5	.980
Major league totals (19 years)			2227	8095	1215	2320	410	55	184	987	.287	840	847	230	3373	6121	229	.976

CHAMPIONSHIP SERIES RECORD

			BATTING												FIELDING			
Year	Team (League)	Pos.	G	AB	R	H	2B	3B	HR	RBI	Avg.	BB	SO	SB	PO	A	E	Avg.
1984—	Detroit (A.L.)	SS	3	11	2	4	0	1	1	3	.364	3	1	0	1	8	0	1.000
1987—	Detroit (A.L.)	SS	5	20	3	4	1	0	0	2	.200	1	2	0	6	9	1	.938
Championship series totals (2 years)			8	31	5	8	1	1	1	5	.258	4	3	0	7	17	1	.960

WORLD SERIES RECORD

NOTES: Named Most Valuable Player (1984). . . . Shares single-game record for batting in all club's runs—4 (October 13, 1984). . . . Member of World Series championship team (1984).

			BATTING												FIELDING			
Year	Team (League)	Pos.	G	AB	R	H	2B	3B	HR	RBI	Avg.	BB	SO	SB	PO	A	E	Avg.
1984—	Detroit (A.L.)	SS	5	20	5	9	1	0	2	6	.450	2	2	1	8	9	1	.944

ALL-STAR GAME RECORD

NOTES: Named to A.L. All-Star team for 1984 game; replaced by Alfredo Griffin due to injury. . . . Named to A.L. All-Star team for 1988 game; replaced by Cal Ripken Jr. due to injury.

			BATTING											FIELDING			
Year	League	Pos.	AB	R	H	2B	3B	HR	RBI	Avg.	BB	SO	SB	PO	A	E	Avg.
1980—	American	SS	0	0	0	0	0	0	0	...	0	0	0	0	0	0	...
1984—	American		Selected, did not play—injured.														
1985—	American	SS	1	0	0	0	0	0	0	.000	0	0	0	0	0	0	...
1987—	American	PH	1	0	0	0	0	0	0	.000	0	0	0	...	...	...	...
1988—	American		Selected, did not play—injured.														
1990—	American	PH	1	0	0	0	0	0	0	.000	0	0	0	...	...	...	...
All-Star Game totals (4 years)			3	0	0	0	0	0	0	.000	0	0	0	0	0	0	...

TREADWAY, JEFF 3B/2B

PERSONAL: Born January 22, 1963, in Columbus, Ga. . . . 5-11/175. . . . Bats left, throws right. . . . Full name: Hugh Jeffery Treadway.
HIGH SCHOOL: Griffin (Ga.).
JUNIOR COLLEGE: Middle Georgia College.
COLLEGE: Georgia.
TRANSACTIONS/CAREER NOTES: Selected by Montreal Expos organization in 18th round of free-agent draft (January 13, 1981); did not sign. . . . Signed as non-drafted free agent by Cincinnati Reds organization (January 29, 1984). . . . On disabled list (August 28-September 24, 1988). . . . Contract sold by Reds to Atlanta Braves (March 25, 1989). . . . On Atlanta disabled list (March 10-June 26, 1992); included rehabilitation assignment to Greenville (June 22-26). . . . Released by Braves (November 20, 1992). . . . Signed by Cleveland Indians organization (December 17, 1992). . . . Granted free agency (October 27, 1993). . . . Signed by Los Angeles Dodgers organization (December 14, 1993). . . . On disabled list (May 28-June 20, 1994). . . . Traded by Dodgers with OF Henry Rodriguez to Montreal Expos for OF Roberto Kelly and P Joey Eischen (May 23, 1995). . . . On Montreal disabled list (June 6-24, 1995). . . . Announced retirement (September 15, 1995).
STATISTICAL NOTES: Hit three home runs in one game (May 26, 1990).

			BATTING											FIELDING			
Year	**Team (League)**	**Pos.**	**G**	**AB**	**R**	**H**	**2B**	**3B**	**HR**	**RBI**	**Avg.**	**BB**	**SO**	**SB**	**PO**	**A**	**E**	**Avg.**
1984	Tampa (Fla. St.)	3B-2B	119	372	44	115	16	0	0	44	.309	54	40	13	128	184	25	.926
1985	Vermont (Eastern)	2B	129	431	63	130	17	1	2	49	.302	71	40	6	271	332	15	.976
1986	Vermont (Eastern)	2B	33	122	18	41	8	1	1	16	.336	23	12	3	68	102	5	.971
	—Denver (A.A.)	2B-3B	72	204	20	67	11	4	3	23	.328	19	12	3	75	153	6	.974
1987	Nashville (A.A.)	2B	123	409	66	129	28	5	7	59	.315	52	41	2	236	362	12	*.980
	—Cincinnati (N.L.)	2B	23	84	9	28	4	0	2	4	.333	2	6	1	44	48	4	.958
1988	Cincinnati (N.L.)	2B-3B	103	301	30	76	19	4	2	23	.252	27	30	2	189	253	8	.982
1989	Atlanta (N.L.)■	2B-3B	134	473	58	131	18	3	8	40	.277	30	38	3	273	341	12	.981
1990	Atlanta (N.L.)	2B	128	474	56	134	20	2	11	59	.283	25	42	3	241	360	15	.976
1991	Atlanta (N.L.)	2B	106	306	41	98	17	2	3	32	.320	23	19	2	155	206	15	.960
1992	Greenville (South.)	2B	4	11	1	5	2	0	0	1	.455	2	1	0	8	10	0	1.000
	—Atlanta (N.L.)	2B-3B	61	126	5	28	6	1	0	5	.222	9	16	1	53	85	1	.993
1993	Cleveland (A.L.)■	3B-2B-DH	97	221	25	67	14	1	2	27	.303	14	21	1	46	111	10	.940
1994	Los Angeles (N.L.)■	2B-3B	52	67	14	20	3	0	0	5	.299	5	8	1	21	37	3	.951
1995	Los Angeles (N.L.)	3B-2B	17	17	2	2	0	1	0	3	.118	0	2	0	1	1	0	1.000
	—Montreal (N.L.)■	2B-3B	41	50	4	12	2	0	0	10	.240	5	2	0	11	16	0	1.000
American League totals (1 year)			97	221	25	67	14	1	2	27	.303	14	21	1	46	111	10	.940
National League totals (8 years)			665	1898	219	529	89	13	26	181	.279	126	163	13	988	1347	58	.976
Major league totals (9 years)			762	2119	244	596	103	14	28	208	.281	140	184	14	1034	1458	68	.973

CHAMPIONSHIP SERIES RECORD

			BATTING											FIELDING			
Year	**Team (League)**	**Pos.**	**G**	**AB**	**R**	**H**	**2B**	**3B**	**HR**	**RBI**	**Avg.**	**BB**	**SO**	**SB**	**PO**	**A**	**E**	**Avg.**
1991	Atlanta (N.L.)	2B	1	3	0	1	0	0	0	0	.333	0	0	0	2	2	0	1.000
1992	Atlanta (N.L.)	PH-2B	3	3	1	2	0	0	0	0	.667	0	1	0	0	1	0	1.000
Championship series totals (2 years)			4	6	1	3	0	0	0	0	.500	0	1	0	2	3	0	1.000

WORLD SERIES RECORD

			BATTING											FIELDING			
Year	**Team (League)**	**Pos.**	**G**	**AB**	**R**	**H**	**2B**	**3B**	**HR**	**RBI**	**Avg.**	**BB**	**SO**	**SB**	**PO**	**A**	**E**	**Avg.**
1991	Atlanta (N.L.)	PH-2B	3	4	1	1	0	0	0	0	.250	1	2	0	1	3	1	.800
1992	Atlanta (N.L.)	PH	1	1	0	0	0	0	0	0	.000	0	0	0	...	...	...	...
World Series totals (2 years)			4	5	1	1	0	0	0	0	.200	1	2	0	1	3	1	.800

TREMIE, CHRIS C WHITE SOX

PERSONAL: Born October 17, 1969, in Houston. . . . 6-0/200. . . . Bats right, throws right. . . . Full name: Christopher James Tremie.
HIGH SCHOOL: South Houston (Houston).
COLLEGE: Houston.
TRANSACTIONS/CAREER NOTES: Selected by Houston Astros organization in 41st round of free-agent draft (June 1, 1988); did not sign. . . . Selected by Chicago White Sox organization in 39th round of free-agent draft (June 1, 1992). . . . On disabled list (July 22, 1992-remainder of season).
STATISTICAL NOTES: Led Southern League catchers with 13 double plays in 1994.

			BATTING											FIELDING			
Year	**Team (League)**	**Pos.**	**G**	**AB**	**R**	**H**	**2B**	**3B**	**HR**	**RBI**	**Avg.**	**BB**	**SO**	**SB**	**PO**	**A**	**E**	**Avg.**
1992	Utica (NYP)	C	6	16	1	1	0	0	0	0	.063	0	5	0	37	5	1	.977
1993	Hickory (S. Atl.)	C	49	155	7	29	6	1	1	17	.187	9	26	0	343	44	4	.990
	—GC Whi. Sox (GCL)	C	2	4	0	0	0	0	0	0	.000	0	0	0	11	0	0	1.000
	—Sarasota (Fla. St.)	C	14	37	2	6	1	0	0	5	.162	2	4	0	71	13	0	1.000
1994	Birm. (Southern)	C	92	302	32	68	13	0	2	29	.225	17	44	4	561	70	6	.991
1995	Nashville (A.A.)	C	67	190	13	38	4	0	2	16	.200	13	37	0	394	30	1	.998
	—Chicago (A.L.)	C-DH	10	24	0	4	0	0	0	0	.167	1	2	0	39	2	1	.976
Major league totals (1 year)			10	24	0	4	0	0	0	0	.167	1	2	0	39	2	1	.976

TRINIDAD, HECTOR P TWINS

PERSONAL: Born September 8, 1973, in Los Angeles. . . . 6-2/190. . . . Throws right, bats right.
HIGH SCHOOL: Pioneer (Whittier, Calif.).
TRANSACTIONS/CAREER NOTES: Selected by Chicago Cubs organization in sixth round of free-agent draft (June 3, 1991). . . . Sent by Cubs organization to Minnesota Twins organization (October 21, 1994); deal arranged as compensation to Twins for Cubs signing Andy MacPhail as chief operating officer and president (September 9, 1994).

Year	Team (League)	W	L	Pct.	ERA	G	GS	CG	ShO	Sv.	IP	H	R	ER	BB	SO
1991—	Hunting. (Appal.)	6	3	.667	2.87	12	10	2	0	0	69	64	28	22	11	61
1992—	Geneva (NYP)	8	6	.571	2.40	15	•15	2	0	0	93 2/3	78	33	25	13	70
1993—	Peoria (Midwest)	7	6	.538	2.47	22	22	4	0	0	153	142	56	42	29	118
—	Orlando (Southern)	1	3	.250	6.57	4	4	1	0	0	24 2/3	34	19	18	7	13
1994—	Daytona (Fla. St.)	11	9	.550	3.23	28	27	4	1	0	175 2/3	171	72	63	40	142
1995—	New Britain (East.)■	4	11	.267	4.61	23	22	0	0	0	121	137	67	62	22	92

TROMBLEY, MIKE — P — TWINS

PERSONAL: Born April 14, 1967, in Springfield, Mass. . . . 6-2/208. . . . Throws right, bats right. . . . Full name: Michael Scott Trombley.
HIGH SCHOOL: Minnechaug Regional (Wilbraham, Mass.).
COLLEGE: Duke.
TRANSACTIONS/CAREER NOTES: Selected by Minnesota Twins organization in 14th round of free-agent draft (June 5, 1989).
STATISTICAL NOTES: Pitched 3-0 no-hit victory against Knoxville (August 8, 1991). . . . Led Pacific Coast League with 18 home runs allowed in 1992.

Year	Team (League)	W	L	Pct.	ERA	G	GS	CG	ShO	Sv.	IP	H	R	ER	BB	SO
1989—	Kenosha (Midwest)	5	1	.833	3.12	12	3	0	0	2	49	45	23	17	13	41
—	Visalia (California)	2	2	.500	2.14	6	6	2	1	0	42	31	12	10	11	36
1990—	Visalia (California)	14	6	.700	3.43	27	25	3	1	0	176	163	79	67	50	164
1991—	Orlando (Southern)	12	7	.632	2.54	27	27	7	2	0	*191	153	65	54	57	*175
1992—	Portland (PCL)	10	8	.556	3.65	25	25	2	0	0	165	149	70	67	58	*138
—	Minnesota (A.L.)	3	2	.600	3.30	10	7	0	0	0	46 1/3	43	20	17	17	38
1993—	Minnesota (A.L.)	6	6	.500	4.88	44	10	0	0	2	114 1/3	131	72	62	41	85
1994—	Minnesota (A.L.)	2	0	1.000	6.33	24	0	0	0	0	48 1/3	56	36	34	18	32
—	Salt Lake (PCL)	4	4	.500	5.04	11	10	0	0	0	60 2/3	75	37	34	20	63
1995—	Salt Lake (PCL)	5	3	.625	3.62	12	12	0	0	0	69 2/3	71	32	28	26	59
—	Minnesota (A.L.)	4	8	.333	5.62	20	18	0	0	0	97 2/3	107	68	61	42	68
Major league totals (4 years)		15	16	.484	5.11	98	35	0	0	2	306 2/3	337	196	174	118	223

TUCKER, MICHAEL — OF — ROYALS

PERSONAL: Born June 25, 1971, in South Boston, Va. . . . 6-2/185. . . . Bats left, throws right. . . . Full name: Michael Anthony Tucker.
HIGH SCHOOL: Bluestone (Skipwith, Va.).
COLLEGE: Longwood (Va.).
TRANSACTIONS/CAREER NOTES: Selected by Kansas City Royals organization in first round (10th pick overall) of free-agent draft (June 1, 1992).

				BATTING											FIELDING			
Year	Team (League)	Pos.	G	AB	R	H	2B	3B	HR	RBI	Avg.	BB	SO	SB	PO	A	E	Avg.
1993—	Wilmington (Caro.)	2B	61	239	42	73	14	2	6	44	.305	34	49	12	120	157	10	.965
—	Memphis (South.)	2B	72	244	38	68	7	4	9	35	.279	42	51	12	153	176	13	.962
1994—	Omaha (A.A.)	OF	132	485	75	134	16	7	21	77	.276	69	111	11	196	11	•7	.967
1995—	Kansas City (A.L.)	OF-DH	62	177	23	46	10	0	4	17	.260	18	51	2	67	3	1	.986
—	Omaha (A.A.)	OF	71	275	37	84	18	4	4	28	.305	24	39	11	133	11	2	.986
Major league totals (1 year)			62	177	23	46	10	0	4	17	.260	18	51	2	67	3	1	.986

TUCKER, SCOOTER — C — ROYALS

PERSONAL: Born November 18, 1966, in Greenville, Miss. . . . 6-2/205. . . . Bats right, throws right. . . . Full name: Eddie Jack Tucker.
HIGH SCHOOL: Washington (Greenville, Miss.).
COLLEGE: Delta State (Miss.).
TRANSACTIONS/CAREER NOTES: Selected by San Francisco Giants organization in fifth round of free-agent draft (June 1, 1988). . . . Claimed on waivers by Houston Astros (September 25, 1991). . . . On disabled list (July 3-10, 1994). . . . Traded by Astros to Cleveland Indians for P Matt Williams (May 15, 1995). . . . Claimed on waivers by Atlanta Braves (June 29, 1995). . . . Granted free agency (October 16, 1995). . . . Signed by Kansas City Royals organization (December 7, 1995).
STATISTICAL NOTES: Led Texas League catchers with .995 fielding percentage, 673 putouts, 70 assists and 747 total chances in 1991. . . . Led Pacific Coast League catchers with .993 fielding percentage in 1994.

				BATTING											FIELDING			
Year	Team (League)	Pos.	G	AB	R	H	2B	3B	HR	RBI	Avg.	BB	SO	SB	PO	A	E	Avg.
1988—	Everett (N'west)	C	45	153	24	40	5	0	3	23	.261	30	34	0	237	23	1	.996
1989—	Clinton (Midwest)	C-OF	126	426	44	105	20	2	3	43	.246	58	80	6	649	60	10	.986
1990—	San Jose (Calif.)	C-OF	123	439	59	123	28	2	5	71	.280	71	69	9	599	88	11	.984
1991—	Shreveport (Texas)	C-3B	110	352	49	100	29	1	4	49	.284	48	57	3	†673	†71	4	†.995
1992—	Tucson (PCL)■	C	83	288	36	87	15	1	1	29	.302	28	35	5	517	56	5	.991
—	Houston (N.L.)	C	20	50	5	6	1	0	0	3	.120	3	13	1	75	6	2	.976
1993—	Tucson (PCL)	C-1B-3B	98	318	54	87	20	2	1	37	.274	47	37	1	621	69	5	.993
—	Houston (N.L.)	C	9	26	1	5	1	0	0	3	.192	2	3	0	56	3	0	1.000
1994—	Tucson (PCL)	C-1B	113	408	64	131	38	1	14	80	.321	48	56	3	625	64	7	†.990
1995—	Houston (N.L.)	C	5	7	1	2	0	0	1	1	.286	0	0	0	7	1	0	1.000
—	Cleveland (A.L.)■	C	17	20	2	0	0	0	0	0	.000	5	4	0	53	3	1	.982
—	Richmond (Int'l)■	C	22	66	5	11	3	1	0	6	.167	8	16	0	107	16	2	.984
American League totals (1 year)			17	20	2	0	0	0	0	0	.000	5	4	0	53	3	1	.982
National League totals (3 years)			34	83	7	13	2	0	1	7	.157	5	16	1	138	10	2	.987
Major league totals (3 years)			51	103	9	13	2	0	1	7	.126	10	20	1	191	13	3	.986

TURNER, CHRIS — C — ANGELS

PERSONAL: Born March 23, 1969, in Bowling Green, Ky. . . . 6-1/190. . . . Bats right, throws right. . . . Full name: Christopher Wan Turner.
HIGH SCHOOL: Warren Central (Bowling Green, Ky.).
COLLEGE: Western Kentucky (degree in psychology, 1991).
TRANSACTIONS/CAREER NOTES: Selected by California Angels organization in seventh round of free-agent draft (June 3, 1991).
STATISTICAL NOTES: Led Northwest League catchers with .997 fielding percentage in 1991. . . . Led Pacific Coast League with 17 passed balls in 1993.

			BATTING												FIELDING			
Year	Team (League)	Pos.	G	AB	R	H	2B	3B	HR	RBI	Avg.	BB	SO	SB	PO	A	E	Avg.
1991	—Boise (Northwest)	C-OF	52	163	26	37	5	0	2	29	.227	32	32	10	360	39	2	†.995
1992	—Quad City (Midw.)	C-1B	109	330	66	83	18	1	9	53	.252	85	65	8	727	98	9	.989
1993	—Vancouver (PCL)	C-1B	90	283	50	78	12	1	4	57	.276	49	44	6	524	56	6	.990
	—California (A.L.)	C	25	75	9	21	5	0	1	13	.280	9	16	1	116	14	1	.992
1994	—California (A.L.)	C	58	149	23	36	7	1	1	12	.242	10	29	3	268	29	1	.997
	—Vancouver (PCL)	C	3	10	1	2	1	0	0	1	.200	0	2	0	10	1	1	.917
1995	—Vancouver (PCL)	C-3-1-0	80	282	44	75	20	2	3	48	.266	34	54	3	345	49	6	.985
	—California (A.L.)	C	5	10	0	1	0	0	0	1	.100	0	3	0	17	2	0	1.000
Major league totals (3 years)			88	234	32	58	12	1	2	26	.248	19	48	4	401	45	2	.996

TYLER, BRAD — 2B — ORIOLES

PERSONAL: Born March 3, 1969, in Aurora, Ind. . . . 6-2/175. . . . Bats left, throws right. . . . Full name: Brad William Tyler.
HIGH SCHOOL: South Dearborn (Aurora, Ind.).
COLLEGE: Evansville.
TRANSACTIONS/CAREER NOTES: Selected by Baltimore Orioles organization in sixth round of free-agent draft (June 4, 1990).

			BATTING												FIELDING			
Year	Team (League)	Pos.	G	AB	R	H	2B	3B	HR	RBI	Avg.	BB	SO	SB	PO	A	E	Avg.
1990	—Wausau (Midwest)	S-2-0-3	57	190	31	44	4	3	2	24	.232	44	45	11	77	122	6	.971
1991	—Kane Co. (Midw.)	2B	60	199	35	54	10	3	3	29	.271	44	25	5	121	142	16	.943
	—Frederick (Caro.)	2B-3B-OF	56	187	26	48	6	0	4	26	.257	33	33	3	94	140	14	.944
1992	—Frederick (Caro.)	2B	54	185	34	47	11	2	3	22	.254	43	34	9	109	152	15	.946
	—Hagerstown (East.)	2B	83	256	41	57	9	1	2	21	.223	34	45	23	118	203	16	.953
1993	—Bowie (Eastern)	2-0-3-1	129	437	85	103	24	*17	10	44	.236	84	89	24	240	311	21	.963
1994	—Rochester (Int'l)	2-3-1-0	101	314	38	82	15	8	7	43	.261	38	69	7	114	179	16	.948
1995	—Rochester (Int'l)	2B-OF	114	361	60	93	17	3	17	52	.258	*71	63	10	197	253	14	.970

UNROE, TIM — 3B/1B — BREWERS

PERSONAL: Born October 7, 1970, in Round Lake Beach, Ill. . . . 6-3/200. . . . Bats right, throws right. . . . Full name: Timothy Brian Unroe.
COLLEGE: Lewis (Ill.).
TRANSACTIONS/CAREER NOTES: Selected by Milwaukee Brewers organization in 28th round of free-agent draft (June 1, 1992).
HONORS: Named Texas League Player of the Year (1994).
STATISTICAL NOTES: Led Pioneer League third basemen with 62 putouts, 155 assists, 16 double plays and 236 total chances in 1992. . . . Led California League third basemen with .936 fielding percentage, 78 putouts, 244 assists and 344 total chances in 1993. . . . Led Texas League with 242 total bases and nine sacrifice flies in 1994.

			BATTING												FIELDING			
Year	Team (League)	Pos.	G	AB	R	H	2B	3B	HR	RBI	Avg.	BB	SO	SB	PO	A	E	Avg.
1992	—Helena (Pioneer)	3B-1B	74	266	61	74	13	2	*16	58	.278	47	91	3	†70	†155	20	.918
1993	—Stockton (Calif.)	3B-OF	108	382	57	96	21	6	12	63	.251	36	96	9	†81	†244	23	†.934
1994	—El Paso (Texas)	3B-1B-OF	126	474	*97	*147	36	7	15	*103	.310	42	107	14	383	203	19	.969
1995	—New Orleans (A.A.)	3B-1B-OF	102	371	43	97	21	2	6	45	.261	18	94	4	373	160	12	.978
	—Milwaukee (A.L.)	1B	2	4	0	1	0	0	0	0	.250	0	0	0	11	0	0	1.000
Major league totals (1 year)			2	4	0	1	0	0	0	0	.250	0	0	0	11	0	0	1.000

URBANI, TOM — P — CARDINALS

PERSONAL: Born January 21, 1968, in Santa Cruz, Calif. . . . 6-1/190. . . . Throws left, bats left. . . . Full name: Thomas James Urbani.
HIGH SCHOOL: Harbor (Santa Cruz, Calif.).
JUNIOR COLLEGE: Cabrillo College (Calif.).
COLLEGE: Long Beach State.
TRANSACTIONS/CAREER NOTES: Selected by Kansas City Royals organization in 33rd round of free-agent draft (June 2, 1986); did not sign. . . . Selected by Texas Rangers organization in 34th round of free-agent draft (June 1, 1988); did not sign. . . . Selected by Minnesota Twins organization in 29th round of free-agent draft (June 5, 1989); did not sign. . . . Selected by St. Louis Cardinals organization in 13th round of free-agent draft (June 4, 1990). . . . On St. Louis disabled list (May 22-June 13, 1995).

Year	Team (League)	W	L	Pct.	ERA	G	GS	CG	ShO	Sv.	IP	H	R	ER	BB	SO
1990	—Johns. City (App.)	4	3	.571	3.35	9	9	0	0	0	48 1/3	43	35	18	15	40
	—Hamilton (NYP)	0	4	.000	6.15	5	5	0	0	0	26 1/3	33	26	18	15	17
1991	—Springfield (Midw.)	3	2	.600	2.08	8	8	0	0	0	47 2/3	45	20	11	6	42
	—St. Petersburg (FSL)	8	7	.533	2.35	19	19	2	1	0	118 2/3	109	39	31	25	64
1992	—Arkansas (Texas)	4	6	.400	1.93	10	10	2	1	0	65 1/3	49	23	14	15	41
	—Louisville (A.A.)	4	5	.444	4.67	16	16	0	0	0	88 2/3	91	50	46	37	46
1993	—Louisville (A.A.)	9	5	.643	2.47	18	13	0	0	1	94 2/3	86	29	26	23	65
	—St. Louis (N.L.)	1	3	.250	4.65	18	9	0	0	0	62	73	44	32	26	33
1994	—St. Louis (N.L.)	3	7	.300	5.15	20	10	0	0	0	80 1/3	98	48	46	21	43
	—Louisville (A.A.)	4	2	.667	5.77	7	7	0	0	0	43 2/3	51	31	28	11	42
1995	—Louisville (A.A.)	1	1	.500	2.93	2	2	0	0	0	15 1/3	16	6	5	5	11
	—St. Louis (N.L.)	3	5	.375	3.70	24	13	0	0	0	82 2/3	99	40	34	21	52
Major league totals (3 years)		7	15	.318	4.48	62	32	0	0	0	225	270	132	112	68	128

URBINA, UGUETH — P — EXPOS

PERSONAL: Born February 15, 1974, in Caracas, Venezuela. . . . 6-2/185. . . . Throws right, bats right. . . . Full name: Ugueth Urtain Urbina. . . . Name pronounced OOO-get.
HIGH SCHOOL: Liceo Peres Bonalde (Miranda, Venezuala).
TRANSACTIONS/CAREER NOTES: Signed as non-drafted free agent by Montreal Expos organization (July 2, 1990). . . . On disabled list (April 8-17, 1994). . . . On temporarily inactive list (May 9-June 6, 1994). . . . On Ottawa disabled list (August 10-September 14, 1995).

Year	Team (League)	W	L	Pct.	ERA	G	GS	CG	ShO	Sv.	IP	H	R	ER	BB	SO
1991—	GC Expos (GCL)	3	3	.500	2.29	10	10	3	•1	0	63	58	24	16	10	51
1992—	Albany (S. Atl.)	7	•13	.350	3.22	24	24	5	2	0	142 1/3	111	68	51	54	100
1993—	Burlington (Midw.)	2	3	.400	4.50	10	8	0	0	0	46	41	31	23	22	30
	— Harrisburg (East.)	4	5	.444	3.99	11	11	3	1	0	70	66	32	31	32	45
1994—	Harrisburg (East.)	9	3	.750	3.28	21	21	0	0	0	120 2/3	95	49	44	43	86
1995—	WP Beach (FSL)	1	0	1.000	0.00	2	2	0	0	0	9	4	0	0	1	11
	— Ottawa (Int'l)	6	2	.750	3.04	13	11	2	1	0	68	46	26	23	26	55
	— Montreal (N.L.)	2	2	.500	6.17	7	4	0	0	0	23 1/3	26	17	16	14	15
Major league totals (1 year)		2	2	.500	6.17	7	4	0	0	0	23 1/3	26	17	16	14	15

URSO, SAL — P — MARINERS

PERSONAL: Born January 19, 1972, in Tampa, Fla. . . . 5-11/190. . . . Throws left, bats right. . . . Full name: Salvatore Jude Urso.
HIGH SCHOOL: Plant (Tampa, Fla.).
TRANSACTIONS/CAREER NOTES: Selected by Seattle Mariners organization in 36th round of free-agent draft (June 4, 1990). . . . On disabled list (April 8-May 17, 1993).

Year	Team (League)	W	L	Pct.	ERA	G	GS	CG	ShO	Sv.	IP	H	R	ER	BB	SO
1990—	Ariz. Mariners (Ariz.)	3	2	.600	3.02	20	0	0	0	1	50 2/3	36	25	17	23	63
1991—	Peninsula (Caro.)	0	3	.000	3.06	46	0	0	0	8	61 2/3	74	36	21	30	44
1992—	San Bern. (Calif.)	0	1	.000	5.08	37	0	0	0	1	51 1/3	66	34	29	32	40
1993—	Appleton (Midw.)	4	4	.500	3.35	36	1	0	0	2	53 2/3	57	24	20	24	50
1994—	Riverside (Calif.)	1	2	.333	5.97	30	1	0	0	0	34 2/3	44	27	23	14	26
1995—	Port City (Southern)	2	0	1.000	2.17	51	0	0	0	1	45 2/3	41	13	11	21	44

VALDES, ISMAEL — P — DODGERS

PERSONAL: Born August 21, 1973, in Victoria, Mexico. . . . 6-3/207. . . . Throws right, bats right.
HIGH SCHOOL: CBTIS #119 (Victoria, Mexico).
TRANSACTIONS/CAREER NOTES: Signed as non-drafted free agent by Los Angeles Dodgers (June 14, 1991). . . . Loaned by Dodgers organization to Mexico City Tigers of Mexican League (April 21-June 26, 1992 and March 17-August 19, 1993).

Year	Team (League)	W	L	Pct.	ERA	G	GS	CG	ShO	Sv.	IP	H	R	ER	BB	SO
1991—	GC Dodgers (GCL)	2	2	.500	2.32	10	10	0	0	0	50 1/3	44	15	13	13	44
1992—	La Vega (DSL)	3	0	1.000	1.42	6	0	0	0	0	38	27	9	6	17	34
	— M.C. Tigers (Mex.)■	0	0	. . .	19.64	5	0	0	0	0	3 2/3	15	9	8	1	2
1993—	San Antonio (Tex.)■	1	0	1.000	1.38	3	2	0	0	0	13	12	2	2	0	11
	— M.C. Tigers (Mex.)■	16	7	.696	3.94	26	25	11	1	0	173 2/3	192	87	76	55	113
1994—	San Antonio (Tex.)■	2	3	.400	3.38	8	8	0	0	0	53 1/3	54	22	20	9	55
	— Albuquerque (PCL)	4	1	.800	3.40	8	8	0	0	0	45	44	21	17	13	39
	— Los Angeles (N.L.)	3	1	.750	3.18	21	1	0	0	0	28 1/3	21	10	10	10	28
1995—	Los Angeles (N.L.)	13	11	.542	3.05	33	27	6	2	1	197 2/3	168	76	67	51	150
Major league totals (2 years)		16	12	.571	3.07	54	28	6	2	1	226	189	86	77	61	178

DIVISION SERIES RECORD

Year	Team (League)	W	L	Pct.	ERA	G	GS	CG	ShO	Sv.	IP	H	R	ER	BB	SO
1995—	Los Angeles (N.L.)	0	0	. . .	0.00	1	1	0	0	0	7	3	2	0	1	6

VALDES, MARC — P — MARLINS

PERSONAL: Born December 20, 1971, in Dayton, O. . . . 6-0/187. . . . Throws right, bats right. . . . Full name: Marc Christopher Valdes.
HIGH SCHOOL: Jesuit (Tampa, Fla.).
COLLEGE: Florida.
TRANSACTIONS/CAREER NOTES: Selected by Cincinnati Reds organization in 20th round of free-agent draft (June 4, 1990); did not sign. . . . Selected by Florida Marlins organization in first round (27th pick overall) of free-agent draft (June 3, 1993).

Year	Team (League)	W	L	Pct.	ERA	G	GS	CG	ShO	Sv.	IP	H	R	ER	BB	SO
1993—	Elmira (NYP)	0	2	.000	5.59	3	3	0	0	0	9 2/3	8	9	6	7	15
1994—	Kane Co. (Mid.)	7	4	.636	2.95	11	11	2	0	0	76 1/3	62	30	25	21	68
	— Portland (Eastern)	8	4	.667	2.55	15	15	0	0	0	99	77	31	28	39	70
1995—	Charlotte (Int'l)	9	•13	.409	4.86	27	27	3	2	0	170 1/3	189	98	•92	59	104
	— Florida (N.L.)	0	0	. . .	14.14	3	3	0	0	0	7	17	13	11	9	2
Major league totals (1 year)		0	0	. . .	14.14	3	3	0	0	0	7	17	13	11	9	2

VALDES, PEDRO — OF/1B — CUBS

PERSONAL: Born June 29, 1973, in Fajardo, Puerto Rico. . . . 6-1/180. . . . Bats left, throws left. . . . Full name: Pedro Jose Manzo Valdes.
HIGH SCHOOL: Carlos Escobar (Loiza, Puerto Rico).
TRANSACTIONS/CAREER NOTES: Selected by Chicago Cubs organization in 12th round of free-agent draft (June 4, 1990).
STATISTICAL NOTES: Led Southern League outfielders with six double plays in 1995.

				BATTING											FIELDING			
Year	Team (League)	Pos.	G	AB	R	H	2B	3B	HR	RBI	Avg.	BB	SO	SB	PO	A	E	Avg.
1991—	Hunting. (Appal.)	OF	49	152	17	44	11	1	0	16	.289	17	30	5	66	4	6	.921
1992—	Peoria (Midwest)	OF	33	112	8	26	7	0	0	20	.232	7	32	0	32	1	1	.971

Year	Team (League)	Pos.	G	AB	R	H	2B	3B	HR	RBI	Avg.	BB	SO	SB	PO	A	E	Avg.
				BATTING											FIELDING			
	—Geneva (NYP)	OF-1B	66	254	27	69	10	0	5	24	.272	3	33	4	210	18	9	.962
1993	—Peoria (Midwest)	OF-1B	65	234	33	74	11	1	7	36	.316	10	40	2	51	2	1	.981
	—Daytona (Fla. St.)	OF-1B	60	230	27	66	16	1	8	49	.287	9	30	3	176	7	3	.984
1994	—Orlando (Southern)	OF	116	365	39	103	14	4	1	37	.282	20	45	2	177	12	7	.964
1995	—Orlando (Southern)	OF	114	426	57	128	28	3	7	68	.300	37	77	3	172	11	4	.979

VALDEZ, CARLOS P GIANTS

PERSONAL: Born December 26, 1971, in Nizao Bani, Dominican Republic. . . . 5-11/175. . . . Throws right, bats right. . . . Full name: Carlos Luis Valdez.

TRANSACTIONS/CAREER NOTES: Signed as non-drafted free agent by San Francisco Giants organization (April 6, 1990). . . . On Arizona suspended list (July 29-30, 1991). . . . On Dominican Giants suspended list (August 18-September 8, 1992).

Year	Team (League)	W	L	Pct.	ERA	G	GS	CG	ShO	Sv.	IP	H	R	ER	BB	SO
1990	—Dominican Giants (DSL)	5	4	.556	3.48	13	12	2	0	1	75	77	46	29	31	47
1991	—Arizona Giants (Ariz.)	2	3	.400	5.68	13	10	0	0	0	63 1/3	73	48	40	32	48
1992	—Dominican Giants (DSL)	1	1	.500	2.45	5	4	1	0	1	29 1/3	30	14	8	8	35
	—Arizona Giants (Ar.)	3	1	.750	0.00	6	0	0	0	0	14 2/3	7	2	0	5	14
	—Everett (N'west)	0	1	.000	1.42	3	0	0	0	0	6 1/3	4	2	1	7	6
1993	—Clinton (Midwest)	4	7	.364	3.99	35	2	0	0	3	90 1/3	74	47	40	44	85
1994	—San Jose (Calif.)	8	6	.571	4.51	36	17	0	0	0	123 2/3	109	70	62	61	116
1995	—Shreveport (Texas)	3	2	.600	1.27	22	3	0	0	5	64	40	11	9	14	51
	—Phoenix (PCL)	1	0	1.000	2.76	18	0	0	0	2	29 1/3	29	10	9	13	30
	—San Francisco (N.L.)	0	1	.000	6.14	11	0	0	0	0	14 2/3	19	10	10	8	7
Major league totals (1 year)		0	1	.000	6.14	11	0	0	0	0	14 2/3	19	10	10	8	7

VALDEZ, SERGIO P GIANTS

PERSONAL: Born September 7, 1965, in Elias Pina, Dominican Republic. . . . 6-1/190. . . . Throws right, bats right. . . . Full name: Sergio Sanchez Valdez.

TRANSACTIONS/CAREER NOTES: Signed as non-drafted free agent by Montreal Expos organization (June 18, 1983). . . . On West Palm Beach disabled list (May 17-June 3, 1984). . . . Traded by Expos organization with P Nate Minchey and OF Kevin Dean to Atlanta Braves for P Zane Smith (July 2, 1989). . . . Claimed on waivers by Cleveland Indians (April 30, 1990). . . . Released by Indians (March 25, 1991). . . . Re-signed by Indians organization (April 3, 1991). . . . Granted free agency (October 16, 1991). . . . Signed by Montreal Expos organization (December 10, 1991). . . . On Ottawa disabled list (April 24-May 16, 1993). . . . Granted free agency (October 15, 1993). . . . Signed by Boston Red Sox organization (February 10, 1994). . . . Granted free agency (October 15, 1994). . . . Signed by Phoenix, San Francisco Giants organization (January 2, 1995).

Year	Team (League)	W	L	Pct.	ERA	G	GS	CG	ShO	Sv.	IP	H	R	ER	BB	SO
1983	—Calgary (Pioneer)	6	3	.667	5.57	13	13	1	0	0	72 2/3	88	55	45	31	41
1984	—WP Beach (FSL)	0	0	. . .	8.74	5	0	0	0	0	11 1/3	15	11	11	8	6
	—Jamestown (NYP)	2	7	.222	4.03	13	12	5	1	0	76	78	47	34	33	46
1985	—Utica (NYP)	6	5	.545	3.07	15	•15	5	0	0	105 2/3	98	53	36	36	86
1986	—WP Beach (FSL)	*16	6	.727	2.47	24	24	6	•4	0	145 2/3	119	48	40	46	108
	—Montreal (N.L.)	0	4	.000	6.84	5	5	0	0	0	25	39	20	19	11	20
1987	—Indianapolis (A.A.)	10	7	.588	5.12	27	27	2	•2	0	158 1/3	191	108	90	64	*128
1988	—Indianapolis (A.A.)	5	4	.556	3.43	14	14	0	0	0	84	80	38	32	28	61
1989	—Indianapolis (A.A.)	6	3	.667	3.28	19	12	0	0	1	90 2/3	78	38	33	26	81
	—Atlanta (N.L.)■	1	2	.333	6.06	19	1	0	0	0	32 2/3	31	24	22	17	26
1990	—Atlanta (N.L.)	0	0	. . .	6.75	6	0	0	0	0	5 1/3	6	4	4	3	3
	—Cleveland (A.L.)■	6	6	.500	4.75	24	13	0	0	0	102 1/3	109	62	54	35	63
	—Colo. Springs (PCL)	4	3	.571	5.19	7	7	2	1	0	43 1/3	55	29	25	13	33
1991	—Colo. Springs (PCL)	4	•12	.250	4.11	26	15	4	0	0	131 1/3	139	67	60	27	71
	—Cleveland (A.L.)	1	0	1.000	5.51	6	0	0	0	0	16 1/3	15	11	10	5	11
1992	—Indianapolis (A.A.)■	4	2	.667	3.75	13	8	0	0	0	62 1/3	59	29	26	13	41
	—Montreal (N.L.)	0	2	.000	2.41	27	0	0	0	0	37 1/3	25	12	10	12	32
1993	—Ottawa (Int'l)	5	3	.625	3.12	30	4	0	0	1	83 2/3	77	31	29	22	53
	—Montreal (N.L.)	0	0	. . .	9.00	4	0	0	0	0	3	4	4	3	1	2
1994	—Sarasota (Fla. St.)■	1	2	.333	4.31	5	5	0	0	0	31 1/3	45	17	15	3	25
	—Pawtucket (Int'l)	8	6	.571	3.26	26	9	1	0	0	99 1/3	94	42	36	29	67
	—Boston (A.L.)	0	1	.000	8.16	12	1	0	0	0	14 1/3	25	14	13	8	4
1995	—Phoenix (PCL)■	6	7	.462	4.45	18	18	2	0	0	109 1/3	117	58	54	25	64
	—San Francisco (N.L.)	4	5	.444	4.75	13	11	1	0	0	66 1/3	78	43	35	17	29
A.L. totals (3 years)		7	7	.500	5.21	42	14	0	0	0	133	149	87	77	48	78
N.L. totals (6 years)		5	13	.278	4.93	74	17	1	0	0	169 2/3	183	107	93	61	112
Major league totals (8 years)		12	20	.375	5.06	116	31	1	0	0	302 2/3	332	194	170	109	190

VALENTIN, JOHN SS RED SOX

PERSONAL: Born February 18, 1967, in Mineola, N.Y. . . . 6-0/185. . . . Bats right, throws right. . . . Full name: John William Valentin. . . . Name pronounced VAL-en-tin.

HIGH SCHOOL: St. Anthony (Jersey City, N.J.).

COLLEGE: Seton Hall.

TRANSACTIONS/CAREER NOTES: Selected by Boston Red Sox organization in fifth round of free-agent draft (June 1, 1988). . . . On Boston disabled list (April 1-20, 1993); included rehabilitation assignment to Pawtucket (April 16-20). . . . On Boston disabled list (May 4-June 6, 1994); included rehabilitation assignment to Pawtucket (May 31-June 6).

HONORS: Named shortstop on The Sporting News A.L. Silver Slugger team (1995).

STATISTICAL NOTES: Led New York-Pennsylvania League shortstops with .949 fielding percentage in 1988. . . . Hit three home runs in one game (June 2, 1995). . . . Led A.L. shortstops with 659 total chances in 1995. . . . Career major league grand slams: 2.

MISCELLANEOUS: Turned unassisted triple play while playing shortstop (July 8, 1994, sixth inning); 10th player ever to accomplish feat.

			BATTING											FIELDING			
Year	**Team (League)**	**Pos.**	**G**	**AB**	**R**	**H**	**2B**	**3B**	**HR**	**RBI**	**Avg.**	**BB**	**SO**	**SB**	**PO**	**A**	**E**	**Avg.**
1988—	Elmira (N.Y.-Penn)	SS-3B	60	207	18	45	5	1	2	16	.217	36	35	5	96	175	14	†.951
1989—	Winter Haven (FSL)	SS-3B	55	215	27	58	13	1	3	18	.270	13	29	4	99	177	12	.958
—	Lynchburg (Caro.)	SS	75	264	47	65	7	2	8	34	.246	41	40	5	105	220	16	.953
1990—	New Britain (East.)	SS	94	312	20	68	18	1	2	31	.218	25	46	1	139	266	21	.951
1991—	New Britain (East.)	SS	23	81	8	16	3	0	0	5	.198	9	14	1	50	65	3	.975
—	Pawtucket (Int'l)	SS	100	329	52	87	22	4	9	49	.264	60	42	0	184	300	25	.951
1992—	Pawtucket (Int'l)	SS	97	331	47	86	18	1	9	29	.260	48	50	1	148	*358	20	.962
—	Boston (A.L.)	SS	58	185	21	51	13	0	5	25	.276	20	17	1	79	182	10	.963
1993—	Pawtucket (Int'l)	SS	2	9	3	3	0	0	1	1	.333	0	1	0	8	9	0	1.000
—	Boston (A.L.)	SS	144	468	50	130	40	3	11	66	.278	49	77	3	238	432	20	.971
1994—	Boston (A.L.)	SS-DH	84	301	53	95	26	2	9	49	.316	42	38	3	134	242	8	.979
—	Pawtucket (Int'l)	SS	5	18	2	6	0	0	1	2	.333	3	4	0	7	16	3	.885
1995—	Boston (A.L.)	SS	135	520	108	155	37	2	27	102	.298	81	67	20	227	*414	•18	.973
Major league totals (4 years)			421	1474	232	431	116	7	52	242	.292	192	199	27	678	1270	56	.972

DIVISION SERIES RECORD

			BATTING											FIELDING			
Year	**Team (League)**	**Pos.**	**G**	**AB**	**R**	**H**	**2B**	**3B**	**HR**	**RBI**	**Avg.**	**BB**	**SO**	**SB**	**PO**	**A**	**E**	**Avg.**
1995—	Boston (A.L.)	SS	3	12	1	3	1	0	1	2	.250	3	1	0	5	5	1	.909

VALENTIN, JOSE — SS — BREWERS

PERSONAL: Born October 12, 1969, in Manati, Puerto Rico. . . . 5-10/166. . . . Bats left, throws right. . . . Full name: Jose Antonio Valentin. . . . Brother of Jose J. Valentin, infielder, Minnesota Twins organization. . . . Name pronounced VAL-un-TEEN.

TRANSACTIONS/CAREER NOTES: Signed as non-drafted free agent by San Diego Padres organization (October 12, 1986). . . . On disabled list (April 16-May 1 and May 18-July 11, 1990). . . . Traded by Padres with P Ricky Bones and OF Matt Mieske to Milwaukee Brewers for 3B Gary Sheffield and P Geoff Kellogg (March 27, 1992).

STATISTICAL NOTES: Led Texas League shortstops with 658 total chances in 1991. . . . Led American Association shortstops with 639 total chances and 70 double plays in 1992. . . . Led American Association shortstops with 211 putouts and 80 double plays in 1993. . . . Led A.L. shortstops with 20 errors in 1994. . . . Career major league grand slams: 2.

			BATTING											FIELDING			
Year	**Team (League)**	**Pos.**	**G**	**AB**	**R**	**H**	**2B**	**3B**	**HR**	**RBI**	**Avg.**	**BB**	**SO**	**SB**	**PO**	**A**	**E**	**Avg.**
1987—	Spokane (N'west)	SS	70	244	52	61	8	2	2	24	.250	35	38	8	101	175	26	.914
1988—	Char., S.C. (S. Atl.)	SS	133	444	56	103	20	1	6	44	.232	45	83	11	204	412	60	.911
1989—	Riverside (Calif.)	SS	114	381	40	74	10	5	10	41	.194	37	93	8	*227	333	*46	.924
—	Wichita (Texas)	SS-3B	18	49	8	12	1	0	2	5	.245	5	12	1	26	45	8	.899
1990—	Wichita (Texas)	SS	11	36	4	10	2	0	0	2	.278	5	7	2	14	33	2	.959
1991—	Wichita (Texas)	SS	129	447	73	112	22	5	17	68	.251	55	115	8	176	*442	40	.939
1992—	Denver (A.A.)■	SS	*139	492	78	118	19	11	3	45	.240	53	99	9	*187	*414	*38	.941
—	Milwaukee (A.L.)	SS-2B	4	3	1	0	0	0	0	1	.000	0	0	0	1	1	1	.667
1993—	New Orleans (A.A.)	SS-1B	122	389	56	96	22	5	9	53	.247	47	87	9	†212	351	29	.951
—	Milwaukee (A.L.)	SS	19	53	10	13	1	2	1	7	.245	7	16	1	20	51	6	.922
1994—	Milwaukee (A.L.)	S-2-DH-3	97	285	47	68	19	0	11	46	.239	38	75	12	151	336	†20	.961
1995—	Milwaukee (A.L.)	SS-DH-3B	112	338	62	74	23	3	11	49	.219	37	83	16	164	335	15	.971
Major league totals (4 years)			232	679	120	155	43	5	23	103	.228	82	174	29	336	723	42	.962

VALENZUELA, FERNANDO — P — PADRES

PERSONAL: Born November 1, 1960, in Navojoa, Sonora, Mexico. . . . 5-11/202. . . . Throws left, bats left. . . . Full name: Fernando Anguamea Valenzuela. . . . Name pronounced VAL-en-ZWAY-luh.

TRANSACTIONS/CAREER NOTES: Contract sold by Puebla of Mexican League to Los Angeles Dodgers organization (July 6, 1979). . . . On disabled list (July 31-September 26, 1988). . . . Granted free agency (November 13, 1989). . . . Re-signed by Dodgers (December 15, 1989). . . . Granted free agency (November 5, 1990). . . . Re-signed by Dodgers (December 19, 1990). . . . Released by Dodgers (March 28, 1991). . . . Signed by California Angels organization (May 20, 1991). . . . On California disabled list (June 13-July 5, 1991). . . . Released by Angels (July 5, 1991). . . . Re-signed by Angels organization (July 10, 1991). . . . Released by Angels organization (September 10, 1991). . . . Signed by Toledo, Detroit Tigers organization (March 20, 1992). . . . Loaned by Toledo to Jalisco of Mexican League (March 20-June 3, 1992). . . . Contract acquired by Jalisco from Tigers organization (June 3, 1992). . . . Signed as free agent by Baltimore Orioles organization (February 27, 1993). . . . Granted free agency (October 29, 1993). . . . Signed by Jalisco (1994). . . . Signed as free agent by Philadelphia Phillies (June 24, 1994). . . . Granted free agency (October 1994). . . . Signed by Las Vegas, San Diego Padres organization (April 5, 1995). . . . Granted free agency (November 11, 1995). . . . Re-signed by Padres (December 7, 1995).

RECORDS: Shares modern major league rookie-season record for most shutout games won or tied—8 (1981). . . . Shares N.L. single-season record for fewest assists by pitcher who led league in assists—47 (1986).

HONORS: Named Major League Player of the Year by The Sporting News (1981). . . . Named N.L. Pitcher of the Year by The Sporting News (1981). . . . Named N.L. Rookie Pitcher of the Year by The Sporting News (1981). . . . Named lefthanded pitcher on The Sporting News N.L. All-Star team (1981 and 1986). . . . Named pitcher on The Sporting News N.L. Silver Slugger team (1981 and 1983). . . . Named N.L. Cy Young Award winner by Baseball Writers' Association of America (1981). . . . Named N.L. Rookie of the Year by Baseball Writers' Association of America (1981). . . . Won N.L. Gold Glove at pitcher (1986).

STATISTICAL NOTES: Led Mexican Center League with 13 wild pitches in 1978. . . . Struck out 15 batters in one game (May 23, 1984). . . . Led N.L. with 14 wild pitches in 1987. . . . Pitched 6-0 no-hit victory against St. Louis (June 29, 1990).

MISCELLANEOUS: Appeared in one game as outfielder with no chances (1982). . . . Struck out twice in two appearances as pinch-hitter (1989). . . . Doubled and singled in two appearances as pinch-hitter (1990). . . . Appeared in one game as first baseman with two putouts (1989).

Year	**Team (League)**	**W**	**L**	**Pct.**	**ERA**	**G**	**GS**	**CG**	**ShO**	**Sv.**	**IP**	**H**	**R**	**ER**	**BB**	**SO**
1978—	Guana. (Mex. Cen.)	5	6	.455	2.23	16	13	6	0	1	93	88	46	23	46	*91
1979—	Yucatan (Mexican)	10	12	.455	2.49	26	26	12	2	0	181	157	68	50	70	141

Year	Team (League)	W	L	Pct.	ERA	G	GS	CG	ShO	Sv.	IP	H	R	ER	BB	SO
	—Lodi (California)■	1	2	.333	1.13	3	3	0	0	0	24	21	10	3	3	18
1980	—San Antonio (Tex.)	13	9	.591	3.10	27	25	11	4	0	174	156	70	60	70	*162
	—Los Angeles (N.L.)	2	0	1.000	0.00	10	0	0	0	1	18	8	2	0	5	16
1981	—Los Angeles (N.L.)	13	7	.650	2.48	25	•25	*11	*8	0	*192	140	55	53	61	*180
1982	—Los Angeles (N.L.)	19	13	.594	2.87	37	37	18	4	0	285	247	105	91	83	199
1983	—Los Angeles (N.L.)	15	10	.600	3.75	35	35	9	4	0	257	245	*122	107	99	189
1984	—Los Angeles (N.L.)	12	17	.414	3.03	34	34	12	2	0	261	218	109	88	*106	240
1985	—Los Angeles (N.L.)	17	10	.630	2.45	35	35	14	5	0	272 1/3	211	92	74	101	208
1986	—Los Angeles (N.L.)	*21	11	.656	3.14	34	34	*20	3	0	269 1/3	226	104	94	85	242
1987	—Los Angeles (N.L.)	14	14	.500	3.98	34	34	•12	1	0	251	*254	120	111	*124	190
1988	—Los Angeles (N.L.)	5	8	.385	4.24	23	22	3	0	1	142 1/3	142	71	67	76	64
1989	—Los Angeles (N.L.)	10	13	.435	3.43	31	31	3	0	0	196 2/3	185	89	75	98	116
1990	—Los Angeles (N.L.)	13	13	.500	4.59	33	33	5	2	0	204	223	112	*104	77	115
1991	—Palm Springs (Cal.)■	0	0	...	0.00	1	1	0	0	0	4	4	1	0	3	2
	—Midland (Texas)	3	1	.750	1.96	4	4	1	1	0	23	18	5	5	6	17
	—California (A.L.)	0	2	.000	12.15	2	2	0	0	0	6 2/3	14	10	9	3	5
	—Edmonton (PCL)	3	3	.500	7.12	7	7	0	0	0	36 2/3	48	34	29	17	36
1992	—Jalisco (Mexican)■	10	9	.526	3.86	22	22	•13	0	0	156 1/3	154	81	67	51	98
1993	—Baltimore (A.L.)■	8	10	.444	4.94	32	31	5	2	0	178 2/3	179	104	98	79	78
	—Rochester (Int'l)	0	1	.000	10.80	1	1	0	0	0	3 1/3	6	4	4	3	1
	—Bowie (Eastern)	0	0	...	1.50	1	1	0	0	0	6	4	1	1	0	4
1994	—Jalisco (Mexican)■	10	3	.769	2.67	17	17	8	0	0	118	133	56	35	39	73
	—Philadelphia (N.L.)■	1	2	.333	3.00	8	7	0	0	0	45	42	16	15	7	19
1995	—San Diego (N.L.)■	8	3	.727	4.98	29	15	0	0	0	90 1/3	101	53	50	34	57
A.L. totals (2 years)		8	12	.400	5.20	34	33	5	2	0	185 1/3	193	114	107	82	83
N.L. totals (13 years)		150	121	.554	3.37	368	342	107	29	2	2484	2242	1050	929	956	1835
Major league totals (15 years)		158	133	.543	3.49	402	375	112	31	2	2669 1/3	2435	1164	1036	1038	1918

DIVISION SERIES RECORD

Year	Team (League)	W	L	Pct.	ERA	G	GS	CG	ShO	Sv.	IP	H	R	ER	BB	SO
1981	—Los Angeles (N.L.)	1	0	1.000	1.06	2	2	1	0	0	17	10	2	2	3	10

CHAMPIONSHIP SERIES RECORD

NOTES: Holds N.L. single-game record for most bases on balls allowed—8 (October 14, 1985).... Shares N.L. single-series record for most bases on balls allowed—10 (1985).

Year	Team (League)	W	L	Pct.	ERA	G	GS	CG	ShO	Sv.	IP	H	R	ER	BB	SO
1981	—Los Angeles (N.L.)	1	1	.500	2.45	2	2	0	0	0	14 2/3	10	4	4	5	10
1983	—Los Angeles (N.L.)	1	0	1.000	1.13	1	1	0	0	0	8	7	1	1	4	5
1985	—Los Angeles (N.L.)	1	0	1.000	1.88	2	2	0	0	0	14 1/3	11	3	3	10	13
Champ. series totals (3 years)		3	1	.750	1.95	5	5	0	0	0	37	28	8	8	19	28

WORLD SERIES RECORD

NOTES: Member of World Series championship team (1981).

Year	Team (League)	W	L	Pct.	ERA	G	GS	CG	ShO	Sv.	IP	H	R	ER	BB	SO
1981	—Los Angeles (N.L.)	1	0	1.000	4.00	1	1	1	0	0	9	9	4	4	7	6

ALL-STAR GAME RECORD

NOTES: Shares single-game record for most consecutive strikeouts—5 (July 15, 1986).

Year	League	W	L	Pct.	ERA	GS	CG	ShO	Sv.	IP	H	R	ER	BB	SO
1981	—National	0	0	...	0.00	1	0	0	0	1	2	0	0	0	0
1982	—National	0	0	...	0.00	0	0	0	0	2/3	0	0	0	2	0
1983	—National						Did not play.								
1984	—National	0	0	...	0.00	0	0	0	0	2	2	0	0	0	3
1985	—National	0	0	...	0.00	0	0	0	0	1	0	0	0	1	1
1986	—National	0	0	...	0.00	0	0	0	0	3	1	0	0	0	5
All-Star totals (5 years)		0	0	...	0.00	1	0	0	0	7 2/3	5	0	0	3	9

VALLE, DAVE — C — RANGERS

PERSONAL: Born October 30, 1960, in Bayside, N.Y. . . . 6-2/220. . . . Bats right, throws right. . . . Brother of John Valle, minor league outfielder (1972-84). . . . Name pronounced VALLEY.

HIGH SCHOOL: Holy Cross (Flushing, N.Y.).

TRANSACTIONS/CAREER NOTES: Selected by Seattle Mariners organization in second round of free-agent draft (June 6, 1978). . . . On disabled list (July 26-August 25, 1979; June 24-July 3, 1981; April 13-June 20 and June 27-July 7, 1983). . . . On Salt Lake City disabled list (May 4-17 and June 9-25, 1984). . . . On Seattle disabled list (April 26-July 19, 1985); included rehabilitation assignment to Calgary (June 26-July 12). . . . On disabled list (April 17-May 7, 1987 and July 23-September 2, 1988). . . . On Seattle disabled list (May 30-July 6, 1989); included rehabilitation assignment to Calgary (July 4-6). . . . On disabled list (May 18-June 17, 1990). . . . On suspended list (July 21-24, 1991). . . . On disabled list (May 9-26, 1992). . . . Granted free agency (October 26, 1993). . . . Signed by Boston Red Sox (December 30, 1993). . . . Traded by Red Sox to Milwaukee Brewers for OF Tom Brunansky (June 16, 1994). . . . On Milwaukee disabled list (July 7-22, 1994). . . . Granted free agency (October 21, 1994). . . . Signed by Texas Rangers (December 6, 1994).

STATISTICAL NOTES: Led Northwest League catchers with six double plays and tied for lead with 23 passed balls in 1978. . . . Led California League catchers with 102 assists in 1980. . . . Led A.L. catchers with .997 fielding percentage in 1990. . . . Led A.L. in being hit by pitch with 17 in 1993. . . . Tied for A.L. lead in double plays by catcher with 13 in 1993. . . . Career major league grand slams: 1.

			BATTING											FIELDING			
Year	Team (League)	Pos.	G	AB	R	H	2B	3B	HR	RBI	Avg.	BB	SO	SB	PO	A	E	Avg.
1978	—Belling. (N'west)	C	57	167	12	34	2	0	2	21	.204	16	34	3	*338	65	10	.976
1979	—Alexandria (Caro.)	C	58	169	17	36	5	0	6	25	.213	23	24	1	290	44	11	.968
1980	—San Jose (Calif.)	C-P	119	430	81	126	14	0	12	70	.293	50	54	6	570	†102	17	.975
1981	—Lynn (Eastern)	C	93	318	38	82	16	0	11	54	.258	36	48	3	445	56	6	.988
1982	—Salt Lake (PCL)	C-1B	75	234	28	49	11	1	4	28	.209	26	26	0	347	49	11	.973
1983	—Chatt. (South.)	C-1B	53	176	20	42	11	0	3	22	.239	24	28	0	239	24	4	.985

Year	Team (League)	Pos.	G	AB	R	H	2B	3B	HR	RBI	Avg.	BB	SO	SB	PO	A	E	Avg.
			BATTING												FIELDING			
1984—	Salt Lake (PCL)	C	86	284	54	79	13	1	12	54	.278	45	36	0	433	34	6	.987
	—Seattle (A.L.)	C	13	27	4	8	1	0	1	4	.296	1	5	0	56	5	0	1.000
1985—	Seattle (A.L.)	C	31	70	2	11	1	0	0	4	.157	1	17	0	117	7	3	.976
	—Calgary (PCL)	C	42	131	17	45	8	0	6	26	.344	20	19	0	202	11	1	.995
1986—	Calgary (PCL)	C	105	353	71	110	21	2	21	72	.312	41	43	5	404	61	6	.987
	—Seattle (A.L.)	C-1B	22	53	10	18	3	0	5	15	.340	7	7	0	90	3	2	.979
1987—	Seattle (A.L.)	C-DH-1-O	95	324	40	83	16	3	12	53	.256	15	46	2	422	34	5	.989
1988—	Seattle (A.L.)	C-DH-1B	93	290	29	67	15	2	10	50	.231	18	38	0	490	47	6	.989
1989—	Seattle (A.L.)	C	94	316	32	75	10	3	7	34	.237	29	32	0	496	52	4	.993
	—Calgary (PCL)	C	2	6	0	0	0	0	0	0	.000	0	0	0	6	0	0	1.000
1990—	Seattle (A.L.)	C-1B	107	308	37	66	15	0	7	33	.214	45	48	1	633	44	2	†.997
1991—	Seattle (A.L.)	C	132	324	38	63	8	1	8	32	.194	34	49	0	676	52	6	.992
1992—	Seattle (A.L.)	C	124	367	39	88	16	1	9	30	.240	27	58	0	606	62	7	.990
1993—	Seattle (A.L.)	C	135	423	48	109	19	0	13	63	.258	48	56	1	*881	71	5	.995
1994—	Boston (A.L.)■	C-1B	30	76	6	12	2	1	1	5	.158	9	18	0	156	5	3	.982
	—Milwaukee (A.L.)■	C-DH	16	36	8	14	6	0	1	5	.389	9	4	0	47	2	0	1.000
1995—	Texas (A.L.)■	C-1B	36	75	7	18	3	0	0	5	.240	6	18	1	157	13	1	.994
Major league totals (12 years)			928	2689	300	632	115	11	74	333	.235	249	396	5	4827	397	44	.992

RECORD AS PITCHER

Year	Team (League)	W	L	Pct.	ERA	G	GS	CG	ShO	Sv.	IP	H	R	ER	BB	SO
1980—	San Jose (Calif.)	0	0	...	0.00	1	0	0	0	0	1	1	0	0	2	2

V

VANDER WAL, JOHN 1B/OF ROCKIES

PERSONAL: Born April 29, 1966, in Grand Rapids, Mich. . . . 6-2/198. . . . Bats left, throws left. . . . Full name: John Henry Vander Wal.
HIGH SCHOOL: Hudsonville (Mich.).
COLLEGE: Western Michigan.
TRANSACTIONS/CAREER NOTES: Selected by Houston Astros organization in eighth round of free-agent draft (June 4, 1984); did not sign. . . . Selected by Montreal Expos organization in third round of free-agent draft (June 2, 1987). . . . Contract sold by Expos with OF Ronnie Hall to Colorado Rockies (March 31, 1994).
RECORDS: Holds major league single-season record for most hits by pinch-hitter—28 (1995).

Year	Team (League)	Pos.	G	AB	R	H	2B	3B	HR	RBI	Avg.	BB	SO	SB	PO	A	E	Avg.
			BATTING												FIELDING			
1987—	Jamestown (NYP)	OF	18	69	24	33	12	3	3	15	.478	3	14	3	20	0	0	1.000
	—W.P. Beach (FSL)	OF	50	189	29	54	11	2	2	22	.286	30	25	8	103	1	3	.972
1988—	W.P. Beach (FSL)	OF	62	231	50	64	15	2	10	33	.277	32	40	11	109	3	1	.991
	—Jacksonv. (South.)	OF	58	208	22	54	14	0	3	14	.260	17	49	3	99	0	0	1.000
1989—	Jacksonv. (South.)	OF	71	217	30	55	9	2	6	24	.253	22	51	2	72	3	1	.987
1990—	Indianapolis (A.A.)	OF	51	135	16	40	6	0	2	14	.296	13	28	0	48	4	2	.963
	—Jacksonv. (South.)	OF	77	277	45	84	25	3	8	40	.303	39	46	6	106	4	1	.991
1991—	Indianapolis (A.A.)	OF	133	478	84	140	36	8	15	71	.293	79	118	8	197	7	1	*.995
	—Montreal (N.L.)	OF	21	61	4	13	4	1	1	8	.213	1	18	0	29	0	0	1.000
1992—	Montreal (N.L.)	OF-1B	105	213	21	51	8	2	4	20	.239	24	36	3	122	6	2	.985
1993—	Montreal (N.L.)	1B-OF	106	215	34	50	7	4	5	30	.233	27	30	6	271	14	4	.986
1994—	Colorado (N.L.)■	1B-OF	91	110	12	27	3	1	5	15	.245	16	31	2	106	3	0	1.000
1995—	Colorado (N.L.)	1B-OF	105	101	15	35	8	1	5	21	.347	16	23	1	51	4	2	.965
Major league totals (5 years)			428	700	86	176	30	9	20	94	.251	84	138	12	579	27	8	.987

DIVISION SERIES RECORD

Year	Team (League)	Pos.	G	AB	R	H	2B	3B	HR	RBI	Avg.	BB	SO	SB	PO	A	E	Avg.
			BATTING												FIELDING			
1995—	Colorado (N.L.)	PH	4	4	0	0	0	0	0	0	.000	0	2	0	...	...	...	...

VANEGMOND, TIM P

PERSONAL: Born May 31, 1969, in Shreveport, La. . . . 6-2/180. . . . Throws right, bats right. . . . Full name: Timothy Layne Vanegmond. . . . Name pronounced VAN-eg-mond.
HIGH SCHOOL: East Coweta (Senoia, Ga.).
JUNIOR COLLEGE: Southern Union State Junior College (Ala.).
COLLEGE: Jacksonville (Ala.) State.
TRANSACTIONS/CAREER NOTES: Selected by Boston Red Sox organization in 17th round of free-agent draft (June 3, 1991). . . . On Boston disabled list (April 25-May 10, 1995). . . . On Pawtucket disabled list (June 29-July 28 and August 30, 1995-remainder of season). . . . Granted free agency (December 21, 1995).
STATISTICAL NOTES: Led Carolina League with 18 wild pitches in 1992. . . . Pitched 2-0 no-hit victory against Prince William (June 1, 1992). . . . Led Eastern League with 14 hit batsmen in 1993.

Year	Team (League)	W	L	Pct.	ERA	G	GS	CG	ShO	Sv.	IP	H	R	ER	BB	SO
1991—	GC Red Sox (GCL)	2	0	1.000	0.60	3	2	0	0	1	15	6	1	1	1	20
	—Winter Haven (FSL)	4	5	.444	3.03	13	10	4	2	2	68 1/3	69	32	23	23	47
1992—	Lynchburg (Caro.)	12	4	.750	3.42	28	27	2	1	0	173 2/3	161	73	66	52	140
1993—	New Britain (East.)	6	12	.333	3.97	29	*29	1	1	0	*190 1/3	182	*99	84	44	*163
1994—	Pawtucket (Int'l)	9	5	.643	3.77	20	20	1	0	0	119 1/3	110	58	50	42	87
	—Boston (A.L.)	2	3	.400	6.34	7	7	1	0	0	38 1/3	38	27	27	21	22
1995—	Pawtucket (Int'l)	5	3	.625	3.92	12	12	0	0	0	66 2/3	66	32	29	21	47
	—Boston (A.L.)	0	1	.000	9.45	4	1	0	0	0	6 2/3	9	7	7	6	5
Major league totals (2 years)		2	4	.333	6.80	11	8	1	0	0	45	47	34	34	27	27

VanLANDINGHAM, WILLIAM — P — GIANTS

PERSONAL: Born July 16, 1970, in Columbia, Tenn. . . . 6-2/210. . . . Throws right, bats right. . . . Full name: William Joseph VanLandingham.
HIGH SCHOOL: Battle Ground Academy (Franklin, Tenn.).
COLLEGE: Kentucky.
TRANSACTIONS/CAREER NOTES: Selected by San Francisco Giants organization in fifth round of free-agent draft (June 3, 1991). . . . On San Jose disabled list (May 30-July 14, 1992). . . . On San Francisco disabled list (April 24-June 6, 1995); included rehabilitation assignment to San Jose (May 30-June 6).
STATISTICAL NOTES: Led Northwest League with 25 wild pitches in 1991.

Year Team (League)	W	L	Pct.	ERA	G	GS	CG	ShO	Sv.	IP	H	R	ER	BB	SO
1991—Everett (N'west)	•8	4	.667	4.09	15	15	0	0	0	77	58	43	35	*79	86
1992—San Jose (Calif.)	1	3	.250	5.57	6	6	0	0	0	21	22	18	13	13	18
—Clinton (Midwest)	0	4	.000	5.67	10	10	0	0	0	54	49	40	34	29	59
1993—San Jose (Calif.)	•14	8	.636	5.12	27	•27	1	0	0	163 1/3	167	103	*93	87	*171
—Phoenix (PCL)	0	1	.000	6.43	1	1	0	0	0	7	8	6	5	0	2
1994—Shreveport (Texas)	4	3	.571	2.81	8	8	1	0	0	51 1/3	41	21	16	11	45
—San Francisco (N.L.)	8	2	.800	3.54	16	14	0	0	0	84	70	37	33	43	56
—Phoenix (PCL)	1	1	.500	2.48	5	5	0	0	0	29	21	15	8	14	29
1995—San Jose (Calif.)	1	0	1.000	0.00	1	1	0	0	0	6 2/3	4	0	0	2	5
—San Francisco (N.L.)	6	3	.667	3.67	18	18	1	0	0	122 2/3	124	58	50	40	95
Major league totals (2 years)	14	5	.737	3.61	34	32	1	0	0	206 2/3	194	95	83	83	151

VAN POPPEL, TODD — P — ATHLETICS

PERSONAL: Born December 9, 1971, in Hinsdale, Ill. . . . 6-5/210. . . . Throws right, bats right. . . . Full name: Todd Matthew Van Poppel.
HIGH SCHOOL: St. Martin (Arlington, Tex.).
TRANSACTIONS/CAREER NOTES: Selected by Oakland Athletics organization in first round (14th pick overall) of free-agent draft (June 4, 1990); pick received as part of compensation for Milwaukee Brewers signing Type A free-agent DH Dave Parker. . . . On disabled list (May 28-September 11, 1992).

Year Team (League)	W	L	Pct.	ERA	G	GS	CG	ShO	Sv.	IP	H	R	ER	BB	SO
1990—S. Oregon (N'west)	1	1	.500	1.13	5	5	0	0	0	24	10	5	3	9	32
—Madison (Midwest)	2	1	.667	3.95	3	3	0	0	0	13 2/3	8	11	6	10	17
1991—Huntsville (South.)	6	*13	.316	3.47	24	24	1	1	0	132 1/3	118	69	51	90	115
—Oakland (A.L.)	0	0	...	9.64	1	1	0	0	0	4 2/3	7	5	5	2	6
1992—Tacoma (PCL)	4	2	.667	3.97	9	9	0	0	0	45 1/3	44	22	20	35	29
1993—Tacoma (PCL)	4	8	.333	5.83	16	16	0	0	0	78 2/3	67	53	51	54	71
—Oakland (A.L.)	6	6	.500	5.04	16	16	0	0	0	84	76	50	47	62	47
1994—Oakland (A.L.)	7	10	.412	6.09	23	23	0	0	0	116 2/3	108	80	79	•89	83
1995—Oakland (A.L.)	4	8	.333	4.88	36	14	1	0	0	138 1/3	125	77	75	56	122
Major league totals (4 years)	17	24	.415	5.39	76	54	1	0	0	343 2/3	316	212	206	209	258

VanRYN, BEN — P — ANGELS

PERSONAL: Born August 9, 1971, in Fort Wayne, Ind. . . . 6-5/185. . . . Throws left, bats left. . . . Full name: Benjamin Ashley VanRyn. . . . Name pronounced van-RIN.
HIGH SCHOOL: East Noble (Kendallville, Ind.).
TRANSACTIONS/CAREER NOTES: Selected by Montreal Expos organization in supplemental round ("sandwich pick" between first and second round, 37th pick overall) of free-agent draft (June 4, 1990); pick received as part of compensation for New York Yankees signing Type A free-agent P Pascual Perez. . . . On Sumter disabled list (July 25-August 1, 1991). . . . Traded by Expos organization to Los Angeles Dodgers organization for OF Marc Griffin (December 10, 1991). . . . Traded by Dodgers to Cincinnati Reds for P William Brunson (December 16, 1994). . . . Claimed on waivers by California Angels (May 9, 1995).
HONORS: Named Texas League Pitcher of the Year (1993).

Year Team (League)	W	L	Pct.	ERA	G	GS	CG	ShO	Sv.	IP	H	R	ER	BB	SO
1990—GC Expos (GCL)	5	3	.625	1.74	10	9	0	0	0	51 2/3	44	13	10	15	56
1991—Sumter (S. Atl.)	2	13	.133	6.50	20	20	0	0	0	109 1/3	122	96	79	61	77
—Jamestown (NYP)	3	3	.500	5.01	6	6	1	0	0	32 1/3	37	19	18	12	23
1992—Vero Beach (FSL)■	10	7	.588	3.20	26	25	1	1	0	137 2/3	125	58	49	54	108
1993—San Antonio (Tex.)	*14	4	.778	*2.21	21	21	1	0	0	134 1/3	118	43	33	37	144
—Albuquerque (PCL)	1	4	.200	10.73	6	6	0	0	0	24 1/3	35	30	29	17	9
1994—Albuquerque (PCL)	4	1	.800	6.39	12	9	0	0	0	50 2/3	75	42	36	24	44
—San Antonio (Tex.)	8	3	.727	2.99	17	17	0	0	0	102 1/3	93	42	34	35	72
1995—Chattanooga (Sou.)■	0	1	.000	9.24	5	3	0	0	0	12 2/3	22	18	13	6	6
—Vancouver (PCL)■	2	0	1.000	3.07	11	5	0	0	0	29 1/3	29	10	10	9	20
—Midland (Texas)	1	1	.500	2.78	19	0	0	0	1	32 1/3	33	10	10	12	24

VAN SLYKE, ANDY — OF

PERSONAL: Born December 21, 1960, in Utica, N.Y. . . . 6-2/198. . . . Bats left, throws right. . . . Full name: Andrew James Van Slyke.
HIGH SCHOOL: New Hartford (N.Y.).
TRANSACTIONS/CAREER NOTES: Selected by St. Louis Cardinals organization in first round (sixth pick overall) of free-agent draft (June 5, 1979). . . . On disabled list (June 8, 1979-entire season and April 10-May 14, 1981). . . . Traded by Cardinals with C Mike LaValliere and P Mike Dunne to Pittsburgh Pirates for C Tony Pena (April 1, 1987). . . . On disabled list (April 17-May 12, 1989). . . . On Pittsburgh disabled list (June 15-August 27, 1993); included rehabilitation assignment to Carolina (August 16-19, 1993). . . . Granted free agency (October 21, 1994). . . . Signed by Baltimore Orioles (April 21, 1995). . . . On Baltimore disabled list (May 11-26 and May 31-June 16 1995); included rehabilitation assignments to Bowie (June 11-14) and Frederick (June 14-16). . . . Traded by Orioles to Philadelphia Phillies for P Gene Harris (June 18, 1995). . . . On Philadelphia disabled list (June 21-July 17, 1995). . . . Granted free agency (November 3, 1995).

RECORDS: Shares major league single-game record for most unassisted double plays by outfielder—1 (July 7, 1992).
HONORS: Named N.L. Player of the Year by THE SPORTING NEWS (1988). . . . Named outfielder on THE SPORTING NEWS N.L. All-Star team (1988 and 1992). . . . Won N.L. Gold Glove as outfielder (1988-92). . . . Named outfielder on THE SPORTING NEWS N.L. Silver Slugger team (1988 and 1992).
STATISTICAL NOTES: Tied for N.L. lead in double plays by outfielder with four in 1985, six in 1987 and five in 1989. . . . Led N.L. with 13 sacrifice flies in 1988. . . . Led N.L. outfielders with 422 total chances in 1988. . . . Career major league grand slams: 1.

		BATTING												FIELDING			
Year Team (League)	Pos.	G	AB	R	H	2B	3B	HR	RBI	Avg.	BB	SO	SB	PO	A	E	Avg.
1979—								Did not play.									
1980—Gastonia (S. Atl.)........	OF	126	426	62	115	15	4	8	59	.270	70	68	19	177	16	•16	.923
1981—St. Peters. (FSL).........	OF	94	282	42	62	11	3	1	25	.220	47	55	10	168	10	5	.973
1982—Arkansas (Texas)........	OF	123	416	83	116	13	*11	16	70	.279	61	85	37	266	17	7	.976
1983—Louisville (A.A.)..........	3B-1B-OF	54	220	52	81	21	4	6	41	.368	31	30	13	201	78	16	.946
—St. Louis (N.L.)...........	OF-3B-1B	101	309	51	81	15	5	8	38	.262	46	64	21	203	59	6	.978
1984—St. Louis (N.L.)...........	OF-3B-1B	137	361	45	88	16	4	7	50	.244	63	71	28	357	82	8	.982
1985—St. Louis (N.L.)...........	OF-1B	146	424	61	110	25	6	13	55	.259	47	54	34	237	13	1	.996
1986—St. Louis (N.L.)...........	OF-1B	137	418	48	113	23	7	13	61	.270	47	85	21	415	34	8	.982
1987—Pittsburgh (N.L.)■.....	OF-1B	157	564	93	165	36	11	21	82	.293	56	122	34	338	10	4	.989
1988—Pittsburgh (N.L.)........	OF	154	587	101	169	23	*15	25	100	.288	57	126	30	*406	12	4	.991
1989—Pittsburgh (N.L.)........	OF-1B	130	476	64	113	18	9	9	53	.237	47	100	16	344	9	4	.989
1990—Pittsburgh (N.L.)........	OF	136	493	67	140	26	6	17	77	.284	66	89	14	326	6	8	.976
1991—Pittsburgh (N.L.)........	OF	138	491	87	130	24	7	17	83	.265	71	85	10	273	8	1	.996
1992—Pittsburgh (N.L.)........	OF	154	614	103	•199	*45	12	14	89	.324	58	99	12	421	11	5	.989
1993—Pittsburgh (N.L.)........	OF	83	323	42	100	13	4	8	50	.310	24	40	11	205	2	1	.995
—Carolina (South.)........	OF	2	4	0	0	0	0	0	1	.000	1	3	0	0	0	0	...
1994—Pittsburgh (N.L.)........	OF	105	374	41	92	18	3	6	30	.246	52	72	7	239	9	2	.992
1995—Baltimore (A.L.)■.......	OF	17	63	6	10	1	0	3	8	.159	5	15	0	42	2	1	.978
—Bowie (Eastern)..........	OF	2	6	2	3	0	0	0	2	.500	3	0	0	4	0	0	1.000
—Frederick (Caro.).........	OF	1	2	1	0	0	0	0	0	.000	2	1	1	3	0	0	1.000
—Philadelphia (N.L.)■ ..	OF	63	214	26	52	10	2	3	16	.243	28	41	7	117	5	2	.984
American League totals (1 year)		17	63	6	10	1	0	3	8	.159	5	15	0	42	2	1	.978
National League totals (13 years)		1641	5648	829	1552	292	91	161	784	.275	662	1048	245	3881	260	54	.987
Major league totals (13 years)		1658	5711	835	1562	293	91	164	792	.274	667	1063	245	3923	262	55	.987

CHAMPIONSHIP SERIES RECORD

		BATTING												FIELDING			
Year Team (League)	Pos.	G	AB	R	H	2B	3B	HR	RBI	Avg.	BB	SO	SB	PO	A	E	Avg.
1985—St. Louis (N.L.)...........	OF-PR	5	11	1	1	0	0	0	1	.091	2	1	0	6	0	0	1.000
1990—Pittsburgh (N.L.)........	OF	6	24	3	5	1	1	0	3	.208	1	7	1	13	1	0	1.000
1991—Pittsburgh (N.L.)........	OF	7	25	3	4	2	0	1	2	.160	5	5	1	18	1	0	1.000
1992—Pittsburgh (N.L.)........	OF	7	29	1	8	3	1	0	4	.276	1	5	0	20	0	0	1.000
Championship series totals (4 years)		25	89	8	18	6	2	1	10	.202	9	18	2	57	2	0	1.000

WORLD SERIES RECORD

		BATTING												FIELDING			
Year Team (League)	Pos.	G	AB	R	H	2B	3B	HR	RBI	Avg.	BB	SO	SB	PO	A	E	Avg.
1985—St. Louis (N.L.)...........	OF-PH-PR	6	11	0	1	0	0	0	0	.091	0	5	0	8	0	0	1.000

ALL-STAR GAME RECORD

		BATTING											FIELDING			
Year League	Pos.	AB	R	H	2B	3B	HR	RBI	Avg.	BB	SO	SB	PO	A	E	Avg.
1988—National.....................	OF	2	0	0	0	0	0	0	.000	0	0	0	2	0	0	1.000
1992—National.....................	OF	2	0	0	0	0	0	0	.000	0	0	0	0	0	0	...
1993—National.....................							Selected, did not play—injured.									
All-Star Game totals (2 years)		4	0	0	0	0	0	0	.000	0	0	0	2	0	0	1.000

VARSHO, GARY OF

PERSONAL: Born June 20, 1961, in Marshfield, Wis. . . . 5-11/190. . . . Bats left, throws right. . . . Full name: Gary Andrew Varsho.
HIGH SCHOOL: Marshfield (Wis.).
COLLEGE: Wisconsin-Oshkosh.
TRANSACTIONS/CAREER NOTES: Selected by Chicago Cubs organization in fifth round of free-agent draft (June 7, 1982). . . . On disabled list (August 13, 1986-remainder of season). . . . Traded by Cubs to Pittsburgh Pirates for OF Steve Carter (March 29, 1991). . . . Claimed on waivers by Cincinnati Reds (November 25, 1992). . . . Granted free agency (October 7, 1993). . . . Signed by Pirates organization (January 5, 1994). . . . Released by Buffalo, Pirates organization (March 28, 1994). . . . Re-signed by Buffalo (March 29, 1994). . . . On temporarily inactive list (April 14-19, 1994). . . . Granted free agency (October 14, 1994). . . . Signed by Scranton/Wilkes-Barre, Philadelphia Phillies organization (April 20, 1995). . . . On disabled list (July 16-August 8, 1995). . . . Granted free agency (October 4, 1995).
STATISTICAL NOTES: Led California League second basemen with 71 double plays in 1983. . . . Led Texas League second basemen with 650 total chances in 1984. . . . Led American Association in caught stealing with 17 in 1987.

		BATTING												FIELDING			
Year Team (League)	Pos.	G	AB	R	H	2B	3B	HR	RBI	Avg.	BB	SO	SB	PO	A	E	Avg.
1982—Quad Cities (Mid.)......	2B	76	271	52	68	9	4	3	40	.251	49	50	30	190	180	14	.964
1983—Salinas (Calif.)...........	2B	131	490	69	129	16	*13	3	57	.263	49	108	46	284	339	•33	.950
1984—Midland (Texas)..........	2B	128	429	65	112	15	6	8	50	.261	49	86	27	*286	335	*29	.955
1985—Pittsfield (Eastern)......	1B-OF	115	418	62	101	14	6	3	37	.242	40	53	•40	670	51	6	.992
1986—Pittsfield (Eastern)......	OF-1B-2B	107	399	75	106	18	5	13	44	.266	38	52	*45	213	14	6	.974
1987—Iowa (Am. Assoc.)......	OF	132	504	87	152	23	9	9	48	.302	41	65	37	227	18	6	.976
1988—Iowa (Am. Assoc.)......	OF	66	234	46	65	16	5	4	26	.278	18	38	8	120	6	2	.984
—Chicago (N.L.)...........	OF	46	73	6	20	3	0	0	5	.274	1	6	5	29	0	3	.906
1989—Chicago (N.L.)...........	OF	61	87	10	16	4	2	0	6	.184	4	13	3	25	1	2	.929

Year	Team (League)	Pos.	G	AB	R	H	2B	3B	HR	RBI	Avg.	BB	SO	SB	PO	A	E	Avg.
			BATTING												FIELDING			
	—Iowa (Am. Assoc.)	OF	31	112	13	26	3	1	2	13	.232	9	21	6	67	4	3	.959
1990	—Iowa (Am. Assoc.)	OF-1B-3B	63	229	35	69	9	0	7	33	.301	25	35	18	202	15	7	.969
	—Chicago (N.L.)	OF	46	48	10	12	4	0	0	1	.250	1	6	2	2	0	0	1.000
1991	—Pittsburgh (N.L.)■	OF-1B	99	187	23	51	11	2	4	23	.273	19	34	9	95	2	1	.990
1992	—Pittsburgh (N.L.)	OF	103	162	22	36	6	3	4	22	.222	10	32	5	62	1	1	.984
1993	—Cincinnati (N.L.)■	OF	77	95	8	22	6	0	2	11	.232	9	19	1	27	1	0	1.000
	—Indianapolis (A.A.)	OF-1B	32	121	19	35	8	1	3	18	.289	15	13	1	69	0	4	.945
1994	—Buffalo (A.A.)■	OF	18	57	7	19	1	2	2	8	.333	1	5	1	22	0	0	1.000
	—Pittsburgh (N.L.)	OF-1B	67	82	15	21	6	3	0	5	.256	4	19	0	25	0	2	.926
1995	—Philadelphia (N.L.)■	OF	72	103	7	26	1	1	0	11	.252	7	17	2	31	0	2	.939
Major league totals (8 years)			571	837	101	204	41	11	10	84	.244	55	146	27	296	5	11	.965

CHAMPIONSHIP SERIES RECORD

Year	Team (League)	Pos.	G	AB	R	H	2B	3B	HR	RBI	Avg.	BB	SO	SB	PO	A	E	Avg.
			BATTING												FIELDING			
1991	—Pittsburgh (N.L.)	PH	2	2	0	1	0	0	0	0	.500	0	1	0	...	...	...	...
1992	—Pittsburgh (N.L.)	PH-OF	2	2	0	1	0	0	0	0	.500	0	0	0	0	0	0	...
Championship series totals (2 years)			4	4	0	2	0	0	0	0	.500	0	1	0	0	0	0	...

VAUGHN, GREG — OF — BREWERS

V

PERSONAL: Born July 3, 1965, in Sacramento, Calif. . . . 6-0/202. . . . Bats right, throws right. . . . Full name: Gregory Lamont Vaughn.

HIGH SCHOOL: John F. Kennedy (Sacramento, Calif.).

JUNIOR COLLEGE: Sacramento (Calif.) City College.

COLLEGE: Miami (Fla.).

TRANSACTIONS/CAREER NOTES: Selected by St. Louis Cardinals organization in fifth round of free-agent draft (January 17, 1984); did not sign. . . . Selected by Milwaukee Brewers organization in secondary phase of free-agent draft (June 4, 1984); did not sign. . . . Selected by Pittsburgh Pirates organization in secondary phase of free-agent draft (January 9, 1985); did not sign. . . . Selected by California Angels organization in secondary phase of free-agent draft (June 3, 1985); did not sign. . . . Selected by Brewers organization in secondary phase of free-agent draft (June 2, 1986). . . . On disabled list (May 26-June 10, 1990). . . . On Milwaukee disabled list (April 8-27, 1994); included rehabilitation assignment to Beloit (April 25-27).

HONORS: Named Midwest League co-Most Valuable Player (1987). . . . Named American Association Most Valuable Player (1989).

STATISTICAL NOTES: Led Midwest League with 292 total bases in 1987. . . . Led Texas League with 279 total bases in 1988. . . . Led American Association with .548 slugging percentage in 1989. . . . Career major league grand slams: 1.

Year	Team (League)	Pos.	G	AB	R	H	2B	3B	HR	RBI	Avg.	BB	SO	SB	PO	A	E	Avg.
			BATTING												FIELDING			
1986	—Helena (Pioneer)	OF	66	258	64	75	13	2	16	54	.291	30	69	23	99	5	3	.972
1987	—Beloit (Midwest)	OF	139	492	*120	150	31	6	*33	105	.305	102	115	36	247	11	10	.963
1988	—El Paso (Texas)	OF	131	505	*104	152	*39	2	*28	*105	.301	63	120	22	216	12	7	.970
1989	—Denver (A.A.)	OF	110	387	74	107	17	5	*26	*92	.276	62	94	20	140	4	3	.980
	—Milwaukee (A.L.)	OF-DH	38	113	18	30	3	0	5	23	.265	13	23	4	32	1	2	.943
1990	—Milwaukee (A.L.)	OF-DH	120	382	51	84	26	2	17	61	.220	33	91	7	195	8	7	.967
1991	—Milwaukee (A.L.)	OF-DH	145	542	81	132	24	5	27	98	.244	62	125	2	315	5	2	.994
1992	—Milwaukee (A.L.)	OF-DH	141	501	77	114	18	2	23	78	.228	60	123	15	288	6	3	.990
1993	—Milwaukee (A.L.)	OF-DH	154	569	97	152	28	2	30	97	.267	89	118	10	214	1	3	.986
1994	—Milwaukee (A.L.)	OF-DH	95	370	59	94	24	1	19	55	.254	51	93	9	162	5	3	.982
	—Beloit (Midwest)	DH	2	6	1	1	0	0	0	0	.167	4	1	0	...	...	...	...
1995	—Milwaukee (A.L.)	DH	108	392	67	88	19	1	17	59	.224	55	89	10	...	...	...	...
Major league totals (7 years)			801	2869	450	694	142	13	138	471	.242	363	662	57	1206	26	20	.984

ALL-STAR GAME RECORD

Year	League	Pos.	AB	R	H	2B	3B	HR	RBI	Avg.	BB	SO	SB	PO	A	E	Avg.
			BATTING											FIELDING			
1993	—American	OF	1	1	1	0	0	0	0	1.000	0	0	0	0	0	0	...

VAUGHN, MO — 1B — RED SOX

PERSONAL: Born December 15, 1967, in Norwalk, Conn. . . . 6-1/240. . . . Bats left, throws right. . . . Full name: Maurice Samuel Vaughn.

HIGH SCHOOL: Trinity Pawling Prep (Pawling, N.Y.).

COLLEGE: Seton Hall.

TRANSACTIONS/CAREER NOTES: Selected by Boston Red Sox organization in first round (23rd pick overall) of free-agent draft (June 9, 1989).

HONORS: Named first baseman on The Sporting News A.L. All-Star team (1995). . . . Named first baseman on The Sporting News A.L. Silver Slugger team (1995). . . . Named A.L. Most Valuable Player by Baseball Writers' Association of America (1995).

STATISTICAL NOTES: Led A.L. with 20 intentional bases on balls received in 1994. . . . Led A.L. first basemen with 103 double plays in 1994. . . . Led A.L. first basemen with 1,368 total chances and 128 double plays in 1995. . . . Career major league grand slams: 5.

Year	Team (League)	Pos.	G	AB	R	H	2B	3B	HR	RBI	Avg.	BB	SO	SB	PO	A	E	Avg.
			BATTING												FIELDING			
1989	—New Britain (East.)	1B	73	245	28	68	15	0	8	38	.278	25	47	1	541	45	•10	.983
1990	—Pawtucket (Int'l)	1B	108	386	62	114	26	1	22	72	.295	44	87	3	828	60	11	.988
1991	—Pawtucket (Int'l)	1B	69	234	35	64	10	0	14	50	.274	60	44	2	432	24	3	.993
	—Boston (A.L.)	1B-DH	74	219	21	57	12	0	4	32	.260	26	43	2	378	26	6	.985
1992	—Boston (A.L.)	1B-DH	113	355	42	83	16	2	13	57	.234	47	67	3	741	57	*15	.982
	—Pawtucket (Int'l)	1B	39	149	15	42	6	0	6	28	.282	18	35	1	368	15	8	.980
1993	—Boston (A.L.)	1B-DH	152	539	86	160	34	1	29	101	.297	79	130	4	1110	70	*16	.987
1994	—Boston (A.L.)	1B-DH	111	394	65	122	25	1	26	82	.310	57	112	4	880	57	10	.989
1995	—Boston (A.L.)	1B-DH	140	550	98	165	28	3	39	•126	.300	68	*150	11	*1262	95	11	.992
Major league totals (5 years)			590	2057	312	587	115	7	111	398	.285	277	502	24	4371	305	58	.988

DIVISION SERIES RECORD

Year	Team (League)	Pos.	G	AB	R	H	2B	3B	HR	RBI	Avg.	BB	SO	SB	PO	A	E	Avg.
				BATTING											FIELDING			
1995—	Boston (A.L.)	1B	3	14	0	0	0	0	0	0	.000	1	7	0	27	2	0	1.000

ALL-STAR GAME RECORD

Year	League	Pos.	AB	R	H	2B	3B	HR	RBI	Avg.	BB	SO	SB	PO	A	E	Avg.
			BATTING											FIELDING			
1995—	American	1B	2	0	0	0	0	0	0	.000	0	2	0	4	0	0	1.000

VELANDIA, JORGE — SS — PADRES

PERSONAL: Born January 12, 1975, in Miranda, Venezuela. . . . 5-9/160. . . . Bats right, throws right. . . . Full name: Jorge Macias Velandia.

TRANSACTIONS/CAREER NOTES: Signed as non-drafted free agent by Detroit Tigers organization (January 15, 1992). . . . Traded by Tigers organization with 3B Scott Livingstone to San Diego Padres organization for P Gene Harris (May 11, 1994).

Year	Team (League)	Pos.	G	AB	R	H	2B	3B	HR	RBI	Avg.	BB	SO	SB	PO	A	E	Avg.
				BATTING											FIELDING			
1992—	Bristol (Appal.)	SS-2B	45	119	20	24	6	1	0	9	.202	15	16	3	54	88	12	.922
1993—	Niag. Falls (NYP)	SS	72	212	30	41	11	0	1	22	.193	19	48	22	82	186	24	.918
—	Fayetteville (SAL)	SS-2B-3B	37	106	15	17	4	0	0	11	.160	13	21	5	47	94	9	.940
1994—	Lakeland (Fla. St.)	SS-2B-3B	22	60	8	14	4	0	0	3	.233	6	14	0	40	56	4	.960
—	Springfield (Midw.)■	SS-2B	98	290	42	71	14	0	4	36	.245	21	46	5	118	303	26	.942
1995—	Memphis (South.)	SS	63	186	23	38	10	2	4	17	.204	14	37	0	88	152	12	.952
—	Las Vegas (PCL)	SS	66	206	25	54	12	3	0	25	.262	13	37	0	97	190	*31	.903

V

VELARDE, RANDY — SS/3B — ANGELS

PERSONAL: Born November 24, 1962, in Midland, Tex. . . . 6-0/192. . . . Bats right, throws right. . . . Full name: Randy Lee Velarde. . . . Name pronounced vel-ARE-dee.

HIGH SCHOOL: Robert E. Lee (Midland, Tex.).

COLLEGE: Lubbock (Tex.) Christian College.

TRANSACTIONS/CAREER NOTES: Selected by Chicago White Sox organization in 19th round of free-agent draft (June 3, 1985). . . . Traded by White Sox organization with P Pete Filson to New York Yankees for P Scott Nielsen and IF Mike Soper (January 5, 1987). . . . On New York disabled list (August 9-29, 1989). . . . On New York disabled list (June 6-July 30, 1993); included rehabilitation assignment to Albany/Colonie (July 24-30). . . . Granted free agency (December 23, 1994). . . . Re-signed by Oneonta, Yankees organization (April 12, 1995). . . . Granted free agency (November 2, 1995). . . . Signed by California Angels (November 21, 1995).

STATISTICAL NOTES: Led Midwest League shortstops with 52 errors in 1986.

Year	Team (League)	Pos.	G	AB	R	H	2B	3B	HR	RBI	Avg.	BB	SO	SB	PO	A	E	Avg.
				BATTING											FIELDING			
1985—	Niag. Falls (NYP)	O-S-2-3	67	218	28	48	7	3	1	16	.220	35	72	8	124	117	15	.941
1986—	Appleton (Midw.)	SS-3B-OF	124	417	55	105	31	4	11	50	.252	58	96	13	205	300	†54	.903
—	Buffalo (A.A.)	SS	9	20	2	4	1	0	0	2	.200	2	4	1	9	28	3	.925
1987—	Alb./Colon. (East.)■	SS-OF	71	263	40	83	20	2	7	32	.316	25	47	8	128	254	17	.957
—	Columbus (Int'l)	SS	49	185	21	59	10	6	5	33	.319	15	36	8	100	164	16	.943
—	New York (A.L.)	SS	8	22	1	4	0	0	0	1	.182	0	6	0	8	20	2	.933
1988—	Columbus (Int'l)	SS-2B-3B	78	293	39	79	23	4	5	37	.270	25	71	7	123	271	25	.940
—	New York (A.L.)	2B-SS-3B	48	115	18	20	6	0	5	12	.174	8	24	1	72	98	8	.955
1989—	Columbus (Int'l)	SS-3B	103	387	59	103	26	3	11	53	.266	38	105	3	150	295	22	.953
—	New York (A.L.)	3B-SS	33	100	12	34	4	2	2	11	.340	7	14	0	26	61	4	.956
1990—	New York (A.L.)	3-S-O-2-DH	95	229	21	48	6	2	5	19	.210	20	53	0	70	159	12	.950
1991—	New York (A.L.)	3B-SS-OF	80	184	19	45	11	1	1	15	.245	18	43	3	64	148	15	.934
1992—	New York (A.L.)	S-3-O-2	121	412	57	112	24	1	7	46	.272	38	78	7	179	257	15	.967
1993—	New York (A.L.)	O-S-3-DH	85	226	28	68	13	2	7	24	.301	18	39	2	102	92	9	.956
—	Alb./Colon. (East.)	SS-OF	5	17	2	4	0	0	1	2	.235	2	2	0	6	12	2	.900
1994—	New York (A.L.)	S-3-O-2	77	280	47	78	16	1	9	34	.279	22	61	4	92	188	19	.936
1995—	New York (A.L.)	2-S-O-3	111	367	60	102	19	1	7	46	.278	55	64	5	168	258	10	.977
Major league totals (9 years)			658	1935	263	511	99	10	43	208	.264	186	382	22	781	1281	94	.956

DIVISION SERIES RECORD

Year	Team (League)	Pos.	G	AB	R	H	2B	3B	HR	RBI	Avg.	BB	SO	SB	PO	A	E	Avg.
				BATTING											FIELDING			
1995—	New York (A.L.)	2B-3B-OF	5	17	3	3	0	0	0	1	.176	6	4	0	15	11	1	.963

VENTURA, ROBIN — 3B — WHITE SOX

PERSONAL: Born July 14, 1967, in Santa Maria, Calif. . . . 6-1/198. . . . Bats left, throws right. . . . Full name: Robin Mark Ventura.

HIGH SCHOOL: Righetti (Santa Maria, Calif.).

COLLEGE: Oklahoma State.

TRANSACTIONS/CAREER NOTES: Selected by Chicago White Sox organization in first round (10th pick overall) of free-agent draft (June 1, 1988). . . . On suspended list (August 23-25, 1993).

RECORDS: Shares major league single-game record for most grand slams—2 (September 4, 1995).

HONORS: Named College Player of the Year by The Sporting News (1987-88). . . . Named third baseman on The Sporting News college All-America team (1987-88). . . . Named Golden Spikes Award winner by USA Baseball (1988). . . . Won A.L. Gold Glove at third base (1991-93).

STATISTICAL NOTES: Led Southern League with 12 intentional bases on balls received in 1989. . . . Led Southern League third basemen with .930 fielding percentage and tied for lead with 21 double plays in 1989. . . . Led A.L. third basemen with 134 putouts and 18 errors in 1991. . . . Led A.L. third basemen with 141 putouts, 372 assists, 536 total chances and tied for lead with 29 double plays in 1992. . . . Led A.L. third basemen with 404 total chances in 1993. . . . Led A.L. third basemen with 22 double plays in 1994. . . . Career major league grand slams: 7.

MISCELLANEOUS: Member of 1988 U.S. Olympic baseball team.

			BATTING											FIELDING			
Year Team (League)	**Pos.**	**G**	**AB**	**R**	**H**	**2B**	**3B**	**HR**	**RBI**	**Avg.**	**BB**	**SO**	**SB**	**PO**	**A**	**E**	**Avg.**
1989— Birm. (Southern)	3B-1B-2B	129	454	75	126	25	2	3	67	.278	93	51	9	108	249	27	†.930
— Chicago (A.L.)	3B	16	45	5	8	3	0	0	7	.178	8	6	0	17	33	2	.962
1990— Chicago (A.L.)	3B-1B	150	493	48	123	17	1	5	54	.249	55	53	1	116	268	25	.939
1991— Chicago (A.L.)	3B-1B	157	606	92	172	25	1	23	100	.284	80	67	2	†225	291	†18	.966
1992— Chicago (A.L.)	3B-1B	157	592	85	167	38	1	16	93	.282	93	71	2	†141	†375	23	.957
1993— Chicago (A.L.)	3B-1B	157	554	85	145	27	1	22	94	.262	105	82	1	119	278	14	.966
1994— Chicago (A.L.)	3B-1B-SS	109	401	57	113	15	1	18	78	.282	61	69	3	89	180	20	.931
1995— Chicago (A.L.)	3B-1B-DH	135	492	79	145	22	0	26	93	.295	75	98	4	201	216	19	.956
Major league totals (7 years)		881	3183	451	873	147	5	110	519	.274	477	446	13	908	1641	121	.955

CHAMPIONSHIP SERIES RECORD

			BATTING											FIELDING			
Year Team (League)	**Pos.**	**G**	**AB**	**R**	**H**	**2B**	**3B**	**HR**	**RBI**	**Avg.**	**BB**	**SO**	**SB**	**PO**	**A**	**E**	**Avg.**
1993— Chicago (A.L.)	3B-1B	6	20	2	4	0	0	1	5	.200	6	6	0	9	6	1	.938

ALL-STAR GAME RECORD

		BATTING											FIELDING			
Year League	**Pos.**	**AB**	**R**	**H**	**2B**	**3B**	**HR**	**RBI**	**Avg.**	**BB**	**SO**	**SB**	**PO**	**A**	**E**	**Avg.**
1992— American	3B	2	1	2	1	0	0	1	1.000	0	0	0	1	1	0	1.000

VERAS, QUILVIO — 2B — MARLINS

PERSONAL: Born April 3, 1971, in Santo Domingo, Dominican Republic. . . . 5-9/166. . . . Bats both, throws right. . . . Full name: Quilvio Alberto Perez Veras.

HIGH SCHOOL: Victor E. Liz (Santo Domingo, Dominican Republic).

TRANSACTIONS/CAREER NOTES: Signed as non-drafted free agent by New York Mets organization (November 22, 1989). . . . On suspended list (July 31-August 2, 1994). . . . On disabled list (August 7-15, 1994). . . . Traded by Mets to Florida Marlins for OF Carl Everett (November 29, 1994).

STATISTICAL NOTES: Tied for Appalachian League lead in double plays by second baseman with 30 in 1991. . . . Led Appalachian League second basemen with 282 total chances in 1991. . . . Led South Atlantic League in on-base percentage with .441 and in caught stealing with 35 in 1992. . . . Led Eastern League in on-base percentage with .430 and in caught stealing with 19 in 1993. . . . Led Eastern League second basemen with 669 total chances in 1993. . . . Led International League in caught stealing with 18 in 1994. . . . Led International League second basemen with 589 total chances and 84 double plays in 1994. . . . Led N.L. in caught stealing with 21 in 1995. . . . Career major league grand slams: 1.

			BATTING											FIELDING			
Year Team (League)	**Pos.**	**G**	**AB**	**R**	**H**	**2B**	**3B**	**HR**	**RBI**	**Avg.**	**BB**	**SO**	**SB**	**PO**	**A**	**E**	**Avg.**
1990— GC Mets (GCL)	2B	30	98	26	29	3	3	1	5	.296	19	16	16	45	76	3	.976
— Kingsport (Appal.)	2B	24	94	21	36	6	0	1	14	.383	13	14	9	55	79	8	.944
1991— Kingsport (Appal.)	2B	64	226	*54	76	11	4	1	16	.336	36	28	38	*113	*161	8	.972
— Pittsfield (NYP)	2B-SS	5	15	3	4	0	1	0	2	.267	5	1	2	16	16	1	.970
1992— Columbia (S. Atl.)	2B	117	414	97	132	24	10	2	40	*.319	84	52	*66	208	313	20	.963
1993— Binghamton (East.)	2B	128	444	87	136	19	7	2	51	.306	*91	62	52	*274	*372	23	.966
1994— Norfolk (Int'l)	2B	123	457	71	114	22	4	0	43	.249	59	56	40	*267	*308	*14	.976
1995— Florida (N.L.)■	2B-OF	124	440	86	115	20	7	5	32	.261	80	68	*56	299	315	9	.986
Major league totals (1 year)		124	440	86	115	20	7	5	32	.261	80	68	56	299	315	9	.986

VERES, DAVE — P — EXPOS

PERSONAL: Born October 19, 1966, in Montgomery, Ala. . . . 6-2/195. . . . Throws right, bats right. . . . Full name: David Scott Veres. . . . Name pronounced VER-es.

HIGH SCHOOL: Gresham (Ore.).

JUNIOR COLLEGE: Mount Hood Community College (Ore.).

TRANSACTIONS/CAREER NOTES: Selected by Oakland Athletics organization in fourth round of free-agent draft (January 14, 1986). . . . Traded by A's organization to Los Angeles Dodgers organization for P Kevin Campbell (January 15, 1991). . . . Loaned by Dodgers organization to Mexico City Tigers of Mexican League (April 3-May 15, 1992). . . . Released by Albuquerque, Dodgers organization (May 15, 1992). . . . Signed by Houston Astros organization (May 28, 1992). . . . Traded by Astros with C Raul Chavez to Montreal Expos for 3B Sean Berry (December 20, 1995).

STATISTICAL NOTES: Tied for California League lead with 29 wild pitches in 1987. . . . Led Southern League with 16 wild pitches in 1989.

Year Team (League)	**W**	**L**	**Pct.**	**ERA**	**G**	**GS**	**CG**	**ShO**	**Sv.**	**IP**	**H**	**R**	**ER**	**BB**	**SO**
1986— Medford (N'west)	5	2	.714	3.26	15	•15	0	0	0	77 1/3	58	38	28	57	60
1987— Modesto (Calif.)	8	9	.471	4.79	26	26	2	0	0	148 1/3	124	90	79	108	124
1988— Modesto (Calif.)	4	11	.267	3.31	19	19	3	0	0	125	100	61	46	78	91
— Huntsville (South.)	3	4	.429	4.15	8	8	0	0	0	39	50	20	18	15	17
1989— Huntsville (South.)	8	11	.421	4.86	29	28	2	1	0	159 1/3	160	93	86	83	105
1990— Tacoma (PCL)	11	8	.579	4.69	32	23	2	0	1	151 2/3	136	90	79	88	88
1991— Albuquerque (PCL)■	7	6	.538	4.47	57	3	0	0	5	100 2/3	89	52	50	52	81
1992— M.C. Tigers (Mex.)■	1	5	.167	8.10	14	1	0	0	1	23 1/3	29	21	21	12	12
— Tucson (Pac. Coast)■	2	3	.400	5.30	29	1	0	0	0	52 2/3	60	36	31	17	46
1993— Tucson (Pac. Coast)	6	10	.375	4.90	43	15	1	0	5	130 1/3	156	88	71	32	122
1994— Tucson (Pac. Coast)	1	1	.500	1.88	16	0	0	0	1	24	17	8	5	10	19
— Houston (N.L.)	3	3	.500	2.41	32	0	0	0	1	41	39	13	11	7	28
1995— Houston (N.L.)	5	1	.833	2.26	72	0	0	0	1	103 1/3	89	29	26	30	94
Major league totals (2 years)	8	4	.667	2.31	104	0	0	0	2	144 1/3	128	42	37	37	122

VERES, RANDY — P — MARLINS

PERSONAL: Born November 25, 1965, in San Francisco. . . . 6-3/210. . . . Throws right, bats right. . . . Full name: Randolph Ruhland Veres. . . . Name pronounced VER-es.
HIGH SCHOOL: Cordova (Rancho Cordova, Calif.).
COLLEGE: Sacramento (Calif.) City College.
TRANSACTIONS/CAREER NOTES: Selected by New York Mets organization in 32nd round of free-agent draft (June 4, 1984); did not sign. . . . Selected by Milwaukee Brewers organization in secondary phase of free-agent draft (January 9, 1985). . . . On disabled list (August 17, 1986-remainder of season). . . . Signed as free agent by Richmond, Atlanta Braves organization (May 3, 1991). . . . Released by Richmond (June 12, 1991). . . . Signed by Phoenix, San Francisco Giants organization (June 19, 1991). . . . Granted free agency (September 15, 1991). . . . Re-signed by Giants organization (October 11, 1991). . . . On disabled list (May 16-September 8, 1992). . . . Granted free agency (October 15, 1992). . . . Signed by Canton/Akron, Cleveland Indians organization (June 15, 1993). . . . On disabled list (July 9-16, 1993). . . . Granted free agency (October 15, 1993). . . . Signed by Chicago Cubs (December 3, 1993). . . . Released by Cubs (November 15, 1994). . . . Signed by Charlotte, Florida Marlins organization (March 12, 1995). . . . On Charlotte disabled list (April 6-25, 1995). . . . On Florida disabled list (September 4, 1995-remainder of season).

Year	Team (League)	W	L	Pct.	ERA	G	GS	CG	ShO	Sv.	IP	H	R	ER	BB	SO
1985—	Helena (Pioneer)	7	4	.636	3.84	13	13	3	2	0	77 1/3	66	43	33	36	67
1986—	Beloit (Midwest)	4	12	.250	3.89	23	22	3	1	0	113 1/3	132	78	49	52	87
1987—	Beloit (Midwest)	10	6	.625	3.12	21	21	6	0	0	127	132	63	44	52	98
1988—	Stockton (Calif.)	8	4	.667	3.35	20	14	1	1	0	110	94	54	41	77	96
	— El Paso (Texas)	3	2	.600	3.66	6	6	0	0	0	39 1/3	35	18	16	12	31
1989—	El Paso (Texas)	2	3	.400	4.78	8	8	0	0	0	43 1/3	43	29	23	25	41
	— Denver (Am. Assoc.)	6	7	.462	3.95	17	17	2	1	0	107	108	57	47	38	80
	— Milwaukee (A.L.)	0	1	.000	4.32	3	1	0	0	0	8 1/3	9	5	4	4	8
1990—	Denver (Am. Assoc.)	1	6	.143	5.19	16	7	0	0	2	50 1/3	60	36	29	27	36
	— Milwaukee (A.L.)	0	3	.000	3.67	26	0	0	0	1	41 2/3	38	17	17	16	16
1991—	Richmond (Int'l)■	0	2	.000	5.04	9	3	0	0	0	25	32	14	14	10	12
	— Phoenix (PCL)■	3	0	1.000	3.56	19	1	0	0	1	43	42	26	17	14	41
1992—	Phoenix (PCL)	0	2	.000	8.10	12	0	0	0	1	13 1/3	14	12	12	13	13
1993—	Cant./Akr. (East.)■	1	5	.167	4.89	13	12	0	0	0	57	59	33	31	19	49
1994—	Iowa (Am. Assoc.)■	5	6	.455	2.93	33	3	0	0	5	55 1/3	43	25	18	11	42
	— Chicago (N.L.)	1	1	.500	5.59	10	0	0	0	0	9 2/3	12	6	6	2	5
1995—	Charlotte (Int'l)■	1	0	1.000	2.70	6	0	0	0	1	6 2/3	3	2	2	5	5
	— Florida (N.L.)	4	4	.500	3.88	47	0	0	0	1	48 2/3	46	25	21	22	31
A.L. totals (2 years)		0	4	.000	3.78	29	1	0	0	1	50	47	22	21	20	24
N.L. totals (2 years)		5	5	.500	4.17	57	0	0	0	1	58 1/3	58	31	27	24	36
Major league totals (4 years)		5	9	.357	3.99	86	1	0	0	2	108 1/3	105	53	48	44	60

VIANO, JAKE — P — ROCKIES

PERSONAL: Born September 4, 1973, in Los Altos, Calif. . . . 5-10/177. . . . Throws right, bats right. . . . Full name: Jacob Viano.
JUNIOR COLLEGE: Long Beach (Calif.) City College.
TRANSACTIONS/CAREER NOTES: Selected by Colorado Rockies organization in 11th round of free-agent draft (June 3, 1993).

Year	Team (League)	W	L	Pct.	ERA	G	GS	CG	ShO	Sv.	IP	H	R	ER	BB	SO
1993—	Ariz. Rockies (Ar.)	2	2	.500	3.27	22	1	0	0	1	33	24	15	12	6	32
1994—	Asheville (S. Atl.)	4	1	.800	1.35	41	0	0	0	23	53 1/3	36	11	8	24	58
	— New Haven (Eastern)	0	3	.000	2.38	8	0	0	0	0	11 1/3	7	7	3	8	14
1995—	New Haven (Eastern)	3	6	.333	3.38	57	0	0	0	19	72	51	31	27	38	85

VILLONE, RON — P — PADRES

PERSONAL: Born January 16, 1970, in Englewood, N.J. . . . 6-3/235. . . . Throws left, bats left. . . . Full name: Ronald Thomas Villone Jr.
COLLEGE: Massachusetts.
TRANSACTIONS/CAREER NOTES: Selected by Seattle Mariners in first round (14th pick overall) of free-agent draft (June 1, 1992). . . . On disabled list (April 19-26, 1994). . . . Traded by Mariners with OF Marc Newfield to San Diego Padres for P Andy Benes and a player to be named later (July 31, 1995); Mariners acquired P Greg Keagle to complete deal (September 16, 1995).
MISCELLANEOUS: Member of 1992 U.S. Olympic baseball team.

Year	Team (League)	W	L	Pct.	ERA	G	GS	CG	ShO	Sv.	IP	H	R	ER	BB	SO
1993—	Riverside (Calif.)	7	4	.636	4.21	16	16	0	0	0	83 1/3	74	47	39	62	82
	— Jacksonville (Sou.)	3	4	.429	4.38	11	11	0	0	0	63 2/3	49	34	31	41	66
1994—	Jacksonville (Sou.)	6	7	.462	3.86	41	5	0	0	8	79 1/3	56	37	34	68	94
1995—	Seattle (A.L.)	0	2	.000	7.91	19	0	0	0	0	19 1/3	20	19	17	23	26
	— Tacoma (PCL)	1	0	1.000	0.61	22	0	0	0	13	29 2/3	9	6	2	19	43
	— San Diego (N.L.)■	2	1	.667	4.21	19	0	0	0	1	25 2/3	24	12	12	11	37
A.L. totals (1 year)		0	2	.000	7.91	19	0	0	0	0	19 1/3	20	19	17	23	26
N.L. totals (1 year)		2	1	.667	4.21	19	0	0	0	1	25 2/3	24	12	12	11	37
Major league totals (1 year)		2	3	.400	5.80	38	0	0	0	1	45	44	31	29	34	63

VINA, FERNANDO — 2B — BREWERS

PERSONAL: Born April 16, 1969, in Sacramento, Calif. . . . 5-9/170. . . . Bats left, throws right. . . . Name pronounced VEEN-ya.
HIGH SCHOOL: Valley (Sacramento, Calif.).
JUNIOR COLLEGE: Cosumnes River College (Calif.) and Sacramento (Calif.) City College.
COLLEGE: Arizona State.
TRANSACTIONS/CAREER NOTES: Selected by New York Yankees organization in 51st round of free-agent draft (June 1, 1988); did not sign. . . . Selected by New York Mets organization in ninth round of free-agent draft (June 4, 1990). . . . Selected by Seattle Mariners from Mets

organization in Rule 5 major league draft (December 7, 1992). . . . Returned to Mets organization (June 15, 1993). . . . On New York disabled list (May 22-June 6, 1994). . . . On Norfolk disabled list (August 30-September 6, 1994). . . . Traded by Mets to Milwaukee Brewers (December 22, 1994), completing deal in which Brewers traded P Doug Henry for two players to be named later (November 30, 1994); Brewers acquired C Javier Gonzalez as partial completion of deal (December 6, 1994).

STATISTICAL NOTES: Tied for South Atlantic League lead in caught stealing with 22 in 1991. . . . Led South Atlantic League second basemen with 600 total chances and 61 double plays in 1991. . . . Led Florida State League second basemen with 85 double plays in 1992. . . . Led N.L. in being hit by pitch with 12 in 1994.

			BATTING											FIELDING			
Year Team (League)	Pos.	G	AB	R	H	2B	3B	HR	RBI	Avg.	BB	SO	SB	PO	A	E	Avg.
1991—Columbia (S. Atl.)	2B	129	498	77	135	23	6	6	50	.271	46	27	42	194	*385	21	*.965
1992—St. Lucie (Fla. St.)	2B	111	421	61	124	15	5	1	42	.295	32	26	36	219	*360	17	.971
—Tidewater (Int'l)	2B	11	30	3	6	0	0	0	2	.200	0	2	0	16	28	1	.978
1993—Seattle (A.L.)■	2B-SS-DH	24	45	5	10	2	0	0	2	.222	4	3	6	28	40	0	1.000
—Norfolk (Int'l)■	SS-2B-OF	73	287	24	66	6	4	4	27	.230	7	17	16	146	232	14	.964
1994—New York (N.L.)	2-3-S-O	79	124	20	31	6	0	0	6	.250	12	11	3	46	59	4	.963
—Norfolk (Int'l)	SS-2B	6	17	2	3	0	0	0	1	.176	1	1	1	9	11	1	.952
1995—Milwaukee (A.L.)■	2B-SS-3B	113	288	46	74	7	7	3	29	.257	22	28	6	194	245	8	.982
American League totals (2 years)		137	333	51	84	9	7	3	31	.252	26	31	12	222	285	8	.984
National League totals (1 year)		79	124	20	31	6	0	0	6	.250	12	11	3	46	59	4	.963
Major league totals (3 years)		216	457	71	115	15	7	3	37	.252	38	42	15	268	344	12	.981

VINAS, JULIO — C — WHITE SOX

PERSONAL: Born February 14, 1973, in Miami. . . . 6-1/205. . . . Bats right, throws right. . . . Full name: Julio C. Vinas.

HIGH SCHOOL: American (Hialeah, Fla.).

TRANSACTIONS/CAREER NOTES: Selected by Chicago White Sox organization in 33rd round of free-agent draft (June 3, 1991).

			BATTING											FIELDING			
Year Team (League)	Pos.	G	AB	R	H	2B	3B	HR	RBI	Avg.	BB	SO	SB	PO	A	E	Avg.
1991—GC Whi. Sox (GCL)	1B-C-OF	50	187	21	42	9	0	3	29	.225	19	40	2	381	31	13	.969
1992—Utica (NYP)	C-1B	47	151	22	37	6	4	0	24	.245	11	29	1	320	37	9	.975
—South Bend (Mid.)	C-1B	33	94	7	16	3	0	0	10	.170	9	17	1	220	20	5	.980
1993—South Bend (Mid.)	C	55	188	24	60	15	1	9	37	.319	12	29	1	333	30	12	.968
—Sarasota (Fla. St.)	C	18	65	5	16	2	1	1	7	.246	5	13	0	93	14	2	.982
1994—South Bend (Mid.)	C	121	466	68	118	31	1	9	75	.253	43	75	0	697	90	8	.990
1995—Birm. (Southern)	C-1B	102	372	47	100	16	2	6	61	.269	37	80	3	425	53	10	.980

VIOLA, FRANK — P

PERSONAL: Born April 19, 1960, in East Meadow, N.Y. . . . 6-4/210. . . . Throws left, bats left. . . . Full name: Frank John Viola Jr. . . . Name pronounced vy-OH-luh.

HIGH SCHOOL: East Meadow (New York).

COLLEGE: St. John's.

TRANSACTIONS/CAREER NOTES: Selected by Kansas City Royals organization in 16th round of free-agent draft (June 6, 1978); did not sign. . . . Selected by Minnesota Twins organization in second round of free-agent draft (June 8, 1981). . . . Traded by Twins to New York Mets for P Rick Aguilera, P David West and three players to be named later (July 31, 1989); Portland, Twins organization, acquired P Kevin Tapani and P Tim Drummond (August 1, 1989), and Twins acquired P Jack Savage to complete deal (October 16, 1989). . . . Granted free agency (October 28, 1991). . . . Signed by Boston Red Sox (January 2, 1992). . . . On disabled list (May 4, 1994-remainder of season). . . . Granted free agency (October 20, 1994). . . . Signed by Toronto Blue Jays organization (April 24, 1995). . . . On Dunedin disabled list (June 15-July 10, 1995). . . . Released by Blue Jays organization (July 25, 1995). . . . Signed by Indianapolis, Cincinnati Reds organization (July 25, 1995). . . . On Cincinnati disabled list (September 22, 1995-remainder of season). . . . Granted free agency (November 1, 1995).

RECORDS: Holds major league single-season record for fewest innings pitched for league leader—249 2/3 (1990).

HONORS: Named A.L. Pitcher of the Year by The Sporting News (1988). . . . Named lefthanded pitcher on The Sporting News A.L. All-Star team (1988). . . . Named A.L. Cy Young Award winner by Baseball Writers' Association of America (1988). . . . Named lefthanded pitcher on The Sporting News N.L. All-Star team (1990).

STATISTICAL NOTES: Pitched 1-0 one-hit, complete-game victory against Toronto (September 30, 1992).

Year Team (League)	W	L	Pct.	ERA	G	GS	CG	ShO	Sv.	IP	H	R	ER	BB	SO
1981—Orlando (Southern)	5	4	.556	3.43	17	15	2	0	0	97	112	47	37	33	50
1982—Toledo (Int'l)	2	3	.400	3.88	8	8	2	0	0	58	61	27	25	18	34
—Minnesota (A.L.)	4	10	.286	5.21	22	22	3	1	0	126	152	77	73	38	84
1983—Minnesota (A.L.)	7	15	.318	5.49	35	34	4	0	0	210	242	*141	*128	92	127
1984—Minnesota (A.L.)	18	12	.600	3.21	35	35	10	4	0	257 2/3	225	101	92	73	149
1985—Minnesota (A.L.)	18	14	.563	4.09	36	36	9	0	0	250 2/3	262	*136	114	68	135
1986—Minnesota (A.L.)	16	13	.552	4.51	37	•37	7	1	0	245 2/3	257	136	123	83	191
1987—Minnesota (A.L.)	17	10	.630	2.90	36	36	7	1	0	251 2/3	230	91	81	66	197
1988—Minnesota (A.L.)	*24	7	*.774	2.64	35	35	7	2	0	255 1/3	236	80	75	54	193
1989—Minnesota (A.L.)	8	12	.400	3.79	24	24	7	1	0	175 2/3	171	80	74	47	138
—New York (N.L.)■	5	5	.500	3.38	12	12	2	1	0	85 1/3	75	35	32	27	73
1990—New York (N.L.)	20	12	.625	2.67	35	•35	7	3	0	*249 2/3	227	83	74	60	182
1991—New York (N.L.)	13	15	.464	3.97	35	35	3	0	0	231 1/3	*259	112	102	54	132
1992—Boston (A.L.)■	13	12	.520	3.44	35	35	6	1	0	238	214	99	91	89	121
1993—Boston (A.L.)	11	8	.579	3.14	29	29	2	1	0	183 2/3	180	76	64	72	91
1994—Boston (A.L.)	1	1	.500	4.65	6	6	0	0	0	31	34	17	16	17	9
1995—Dunedin (Fla. St.)■	0	1	.000	3.97	3	3	0	0	0	11 1/3	12	9	5	3	8
—Indianapolis (A.A.)■	3	3	.500	4.09	6	6	0	0	0	33	33	17	15	6	25
—Cincinnati (N.L.)	0	1	.000	6.28	3	3	0	0	0	14 1/3	20	11	10	3	4
A.L. totals (11 years)	137	114	.546	3.77	330	329	62	12	0	2225 1/3	2203	1034	931	699	1435
N.L. totals (4 years)	38	33	.535	3.38	85	85	12	4	0	580 2/3	581	241	218	144	391
Major league totals (14 years)	175	147	.543	3.69	415	414	74	16	0	2806	2784	1275	1149	843	1826

CHAMPIONSHIP SERIES RECORD

Year	Team (League)	W	L	Pct.	ERA	G	GS	CG	ShO	Sv.	IP	H	R	ER	BB	SO
1987—	Minnesota (A.L.)	1	0	1.000	5.25	2	2	0	0	0	12	14	8	7	5	9

WORLD SERIES RECORD

NOTES: Named Most Valuable Player (1987). . . . Member of World Series championship team (1987).

Year	Team (League)	W	L	Pct.	ERA	G	GS	CG	ShO	Sv.	IP	H	R	ER	BB	SO
1987—	Minnesota (A.L.)	2	1	.667	3.72	3	3	0	0	0	19¹/₃	17	8	8	3	16

ALL-STAR GAME RECORD

Year	League	W	L	Pct.	ERA	GS	CG	ShO	Sv.	IP	H	R	ER	BB	SO
1988—	American	1	0	1.000	0.00	1	0	0	0	2	0	0	0	0	1
1990—	National	0	0	...	0.00	0	0	0	0	1	1	0	0	0	0
1991—	National	0	0	...	0.00	0	0	0	0	1	0	0	0	1	0
All-Star totals (3 years)		1	0	1.000	0.00	1	0	0	0	4	1	0	0	1	1

VITIELLO, JOE — 1B — ROYALS

PERSONAL: Born April 11, 1970, in Cambridge, Mass. . . . 6-3/230. . . . Bats right, throws right. . . . Full name: Joseph David Vitiello. . . . Name pronounced VIT-ee-ELL-oh.

HIGH SCHOOL: Stoneham (Mass.).

COLLEGE: Alabama.

TRANSACTIONS/CAREER NOTES: Selected by New York Yankees organization in 31st round of free-agent draft (June 1, 1988); did not sign. . . . Selected by Kansas City Royals organization in first round (seventh pick overall) of free-agent draft (June 3, 1991). . . . On disabled list (April 12-23, 1992; June 2-11, 1993; and May 23-June 16, 1994).

STATISTICAL NOTES: Led American Association with .440 on-base percentage in 1994.

				BATTING										FIELDING			
Year	Team (League)	Pos.	G	AB	R	H	2B	3B	HR	RBI	Avg.	BB	SO	SB	PO	A	E	Avg.
1991—	Eugene (N'west)	OF-1B	19	64	16	21	2	0	6	21	.328	11	18	1	49	4	1	.981
—	Memphis (South.)	OF-1B	36	128	15	28	4	1	0	18	.219	23	36	0	77	4	1	.988
1992—	Baseball City (FSL)	1B	115	400	52	113	16	1	8	65	.283	46	101	0	879	44	13	.986
1993—	Memphis (South.)	1B	117	413	62	119	25	2	15	66	.288	57	95	2	830	53	•17	.981
1994—	Omaha (A.A.)	1B	98	352	46	121	28	3	10	61	*.344	56	63	3	605	46	8	.988
1995—	Kansas City (A.L.)	DH-1B	53	130	13	33	4	0	7	21	.254	8	25	0	51	3	1	.982
—	Omaha (A.A.)	1B-OF	59	229	33	64	14	2	12	42	.279	12	50	0	225	21	4	.984
Major league totals (1 year)			53	130	13	33	4	0	7	21	.254	8	25	0	51	3	1	.982

VIZCAINO, JOSE — SS — METS

PERSONAL: Born March 26, 1968, in San Cristobal, Dominican Republic. . . . 6-1/180. . . . Bats both, throws right. . . . Full name: Jose Luis Pimental Vizcaino. . . . Name pronounced VIS-ky-EE-no.

HIGH SCHOOL: Americo Tolentino (Palenque de San Cristobal, Dominican Republic).

TRANSACTIONS/CAREER NOTES: Signed as non-drafted free agent by Los Angeles Dodgers organization (February 18, 1986). . . . Traded by Dodgers to Chicago Cubs for IF Greg Smith (December 14, 1990). . . . On disabled list (April 20-May 6 and August 26-September 16, 1992). . . . Traded by Cubs to New York Mets for P Anthony Young and P Ottis Smith (March 30, 1994).

STATISTICAL NOTES: Led Gulf Coast League shortstops with 23 double plays in 1987. . . . Led Pacific Coast League shortstops with 611 total chances and 82 double plays in 1989. . . . Tied for N.L. lead in fielding percentage by shortstop with .984 and assists by shortstop with 411 in 1995.

				BATTING										FIELDING			
Year	Team (League)	Pos.	G	AB	R	H	2B	3B	HR	RBI	Avg.	BB	SO	SB	PO	A	E	Avg.
1987—	GC Dodgers (GCL)	SS-1B	49	150	26	38	5	1	0	12	.253	22	24	8	73	107	13	.933
1988—	Bakersfield (Calif.)	SS	122	433	77	126	11	4	0	38	.291	50	54	13	185	340	30	.946
1989—	Albuquerque (PCL)	SS	129	434	60	123	10	4	1	44	.283	33	41	16	*191	*390	*30	.951
—	Los Angeles (N.L.)	SS	7	10	2	2	0	0	0	0	.200	0	1	0	6	9	2	.882
1990—	Albuquerque (PCL)	2B-SS	81	276	46	77	10	2	2	38	.279	30	33	13	141	229	14	.964
—	Los Angeles (N.L.)	SS-2B	37	51	3	14	1	1	0	2	.275	4	8	1	23	27	2	.962
1991—	Chicago (N.L.)■	3B-SS-2B	93	145	7	38	5	0	0	10	.262	5	18	2	49	118	7	.960
1992—	Chicago (N.L.)	SS-3B-2B	86	285	25	64	10	4	1	17	.225	14	35	3	93	195	9	.970
1993—	Chicago (N.L.)	SS-3B-2B	151	551	74	158	19	4	4	54	.287	46	71	12	217	410	17	.974
1994—	New York (N.L.)■	SS	103	410	47	105	13	3	3	33	.256	33	62	1	136	291	13	.970
1995—	New York (N.L.)	SS-2B	135	509	66	146	21	5	3	56	.287	35	76	8	189	‡411	10	‡.984
Major league totals (7 years)			612	1961	224	527	69	17	11	172	.269	137	271	27	713	1461	60	.973

VIZQUEL, OMAR — SS — INDIANS

PERSONAL: Born April 24, 1967, in Caracas, Venezuela. . . . 5-9/165. . . . Bats both, throws right. . . . Full name: Omar Enrique Vizquel. . . . Name pronounced vis-KEL.

HIGH SCHOOL: Francisco Espejo (Caracas, Venezuela).

TRANSACTIONS/CAREER NOTES: Signed as non-drafted free agent by Seattle Mariners organization (April 1, 1984). . . . On Seattle disabled list (April 7-May 13, 1990); included rehabilitation assignments to Calgary (May 3-7) and San Bernardino (May 8-12). . . . On Seattle disabled list (April 13-May 11, 1992); included rehabilitation assignment to Calgary (May 5-11). . . . Traded by Mariners to Cleveland Indians for SS Felix Fermin, 1B Reggie Jefferson and cash (December 20, 1993). . . . On Cleveland disabled list (April 23-June 13, 1994); included rehabilitation assignment to Charlotte (June 6-13).

HONORS: Won A.L. Gold Glove at shortstop (1993-95).

STATISTICAL NOTES: Led Midwest League shortstops with .969 fielding percentage in 1986. . . . Tied for A.L. lead in double plays by shortstop with 108 in 1993. . . . Career major league grand slams: 1.

MISCELLANEOUS: Batted righthanded only (1984-88).

V

Year	Team (League)	Pos.	G	AB	R	H	2B	3B	HR	RBI	Avg.	BB	SO	SB	PO	A	E	Avg.
			BATTING												FIELDING			
1984—	Butte (Pioneer)	SS-2B	15	45	7	14	2	0	0	4	.311	3	8	2	13	29	5	.894
1985—	Belling. (N'west)	SS-2B	50	187	24	42	9	0	5	17	.225	12	27	4	85	175	19	.932
1986—	Wausau (Midwest)	SS-2B	105	352	60	75	13	2	4	28	.213	64	56	19	153	328	16	†.968
1987—	Salinas (Calif.)	SS-2B	114	407	61	107	12	8	0	38	.263	57	55	25	81	295	25	.938
1988—	Vermont (Eastern)	SS	103	374	54	95	18	2	2	35	.254	42	44	30	173	268	19	*.959
—	Calgary (PCL)	SS	33	107	10	24	2	3	1	12	.224	5	14	2	43	92	6	.957
1989—	Calgary (PCL)	SS	7	28	3	6	2	0	0	3	.214	3	4	0	15	14	0	1.000
—	Seattle (A.L.)	SS	143	387	45	85	7	3	1	20	.220	28	40	1	208	388	18	.971
1990—	Calgary (PCL)	SS	48	150	18	35	6	2	0	8	.233	13	10	4	70	142	6	.972
—	San Bern. (Calif.)	SS	6	28	5	7	0	0	0	3	.250	3	1	1	11	21	3	.914
—	Seattle (A.L.)	SS	81	255	19	63	3	2	2	18	.247	18	22	4	103	239	7	.980
1991—	Seattle (A.L.)	SS-2B	142	426	42	98	16	4	1	41	.230	45	37	7	224	422	13	.980
1992—	Seattle (A.L.)	SS	136	483	49	142	20	4	0	21	.294	32	38	15	223	403	7	*.989
—	Calgary (PCL)	SS	6	22	0	6	1	0	0	2	.273	1	3	0	14	21	1	.972
1993—	Seattle (A.L.)	SS-DH	158	560	68	143	14	2	2	31	.255	50	71	12	245	475	15	.980
1994—	Cleveland (A.L.)■	SS	69	286	39	78	10	1	1	33	.273	23	23	13	113	204	6	.981
—	Charlotte (Int'l)	SS	7	26	3	7	1	0	0	1	.269	2	1	1	11	18	1	.967
1995—	Cleveland (A.L.)	SS	136	542	87	144	28	0	6	56	.266	59	59	29	210	405	9	.986
Major league totals (7 years)			865	2939	349	753	98	16	13	220	.256	255	290	81	1326	2536	75	.981

DIVISION SERIES RECORD

Year	Team (League)	Pos.	G	AB	R	H	2B	3B	HR	RBI	Avg.	BB	SO	SB	PO	A	E	Avg.
			BATTING												FIELDING			
1995—	Cleveland (A.L.)	SS	3	12	2	2	1	0	0	4	.167	2	2	1	4	11	0	1.000

CHAMPIONSHIP SERIES RECORD

Year	Team (League)	Pos.	G	AB	R	H	2B	3B	HR	RBI	Avg.	BB	SO	SB	PO	A	E	Avg.
			BATTING												FIELDING			
1995—	Cleveland (A.L.)	SS	6	23	2	2	1	0	0	2	.087	5	2	3	9	21	0	1.000

WORLD SERIES RECORD

Year	Team (League)	Pos.	G	AB	R	H	2B	3B	HR	RBI	Avg.	BB	SO	SB	PO	A	E	Avg.
			BATTING												FIELDING			
1995—	Cleveland (A.L.)	SS	6	23	3	4	0	1	0	1	.174	3	5	1	12	22	0	1.000

VOIGT, JACK — OF

PERSONAL: Born May 17, 1966, in Sarasota, Fla. . . . 6-1/175. . . . Bats right, throws right. . . . Full name: John David Voigt.

HIGH SCHOOL: Venice (Fla.).

COLLEGE: Louisiana State.

TRANSACTIONS/CAREER NOTES: Selected by Baltimore Orioles organization in ninth round of free-agent draft (June 2, 1987). . . . Traded by Orioles to Texas Rangers for P John Dettmer (May 16, 1995). . . . Traded by Rangers organization to Boston Red Sox organization for P Chris Howard (August 31, 1995). . . . Granted free agency (October 16, 1995).

STATISTICAL NOTES: Led New York-Pennsylvania League third basemen with .941 fielding percentage and 16 double plays in 1987. . . . Led Carolina League third basemen with .990 fielding percentage in 1989. . . . Led Eastern League with 11 sacrifice flies in 1990.

Year	Team (League)	Pos.	G	AB	R	H	2B	3B	HR	RBI	Avg.	BB	SO	SB	PO	A	E	Avg.
			BATTING												FIELDING			
1987—	Newark (NY-Penn)	3B-1B	63	219	41	70	10	1	11	52	*.320	33	45	1	63	141	11	†.949
—	Hagerstown (Car.)	1B	2	9	0	1	0	0	0	1	.111	1	4	0	9	0	2	.818
1988—	Hagerstown (Car.)	OF-1B	115	367	62	83	18	2	12	42	.226	66	92	5	213	11	6	.974
1989—	Frederick (Caro.)	OF-1B	127	406	61	107	26	5	10	77	.264	62	106	17	189	16	2	†.990
1990—	Hagerstown (East.)	OF	126	418	55	107	26	2	12	70	.256	59	97	5	249	12	6	.978
1991—	Hagerstown (East.)	OF	29	90	15	22	3	0	0	6	.244	15	19	6	8	0	0	1.000
—	Rochester (Int'l)	OF-1B-3B	83	267	46	72	12	4	6	35	.270	40	53	9	198	32	3	.987
1992—	Rochester (Int'l)	OF-1B-3B	129	443	74	126	23	4	16	64	.284	58	102	9	330	36	10	.973
—	Baltimore (A.L.)	PR	1	0	0	0	0	0	0	0	...	0	0	0	...	...	...	...
1993—	Rochester (Int'l)	OF-3B-1B	18	61	16	22	6	1	3	11	.361	9	14	0	38	5	1	.977
—	Baltimore (A.L.)	O-DH-1-3	64	152	32	45	11	1	6	23	.296	25	33	1	101	6	1	.991
1994—	Baltimore (A.L.)	OF-1B-DH	59	141	15	34	5	0	3	20	.241	18	25	0	114	5	2	.983
—	Bowie (Eastern)	1B-3B-OF	41	154	26	48	9	1	6	35	.312	26	26	5	222	36	1	.996
1995—	Baltimore (A.L.)	DH-1B	3	1	1	1	0	0	0	0	1.000	0	0	0	1	1	0	1.000
—	Texas (A.L.)■	OF-1B-DH	33	62	8	10	3	0	2	8	.161	10	14	0	55	2	1	.983
—	Tulsa (Texas)	OF-1B	4	16	1	3	0	0	1	3	.188	2	5	1	8	1	0	1.000
Major league totals (4 years)			160	356	56	90	19	1	11	51	.253	53	72	1	271	14	4	.986

VOLLMER, SCOTT — C — WHITE SOX

PERSONAL: Born February 9, 1971, in Anaheim, Calif. . . . 6-1/185. . . . Bats right, throws right. . . . Full name: Scott S. Vollmer.

COLLEGE: Pepperdine.

TRANSACTIONS/CAREER NOTES: Selected by Chicago White Sox organization in 17th round of free-agent draft (June 3, 1993).

Year	Team (League)	Pos.	G	AB	R	H	2B	3B	HR	RBI	Avg.	BB	SO	SB	PO	A	E	Avg.
			BATTING												FIELDING			
1993—	GC Whi. Sox (GCL)	C-2B	43	132	19	36	9	0	0	11	.273	17	11	3	228	27	6	.977
1994—	Hickory (S. Atl.)	C	110	420	52	115	24	4	7	81	.274	39	63	0	732	64	*15	.982
1995—	Birm. (Southern)	C	81	258	35	61	5	0	6	39	.236	42	39	0	554	70	5	*.992

VOSBERG, ED — P — RANGERS

PERSONAL: Born September 28, 1961, in Tucson, Ariz. . . . 6-1/190. . . . Throws left, bats left. . . . Full name: Edward John Vosberg.
HIGH SCHOOL: Salpointe (Tucson, Ariz.).
COLLEGE: Arizona.
TRANSACTIONS/CAREER NOTES: Selected by St. Louis Cardinals organization in third round of free-agent draft (June 5, 1979); did not sign. . . . Selected by Toronto Blue Jays organization in 11th round of free-agent draft (June 7, 1982); did not sign. . . . Selected by San Diego Padres organization in third round of free-agent draft (June 6, 1983). . . . Traded by Padres organization to Houston Astros organization for C Dan Walters (December 13, 1988). . . . Traded by Astros organization to Los Angeles Dodgers organization (August 1, 1989), completing deal in which Dodgers organization traded OF Javier Ortiz to Astros organization for a player to be named later (July 22, 1989). . . . Granted free agency (October 15, 1989). . . . Signed by Phoenix, San Francisco Giants organization (March 13, 1990). . . . Granted free agency (October 15, 1990). . . . Signed by California Angels organization (December 4, 1990). . . . Released by Angels organization (May 11, 1991). . . . Signed by Calgary, Seattle Mariners organization (May 20, 1991). . . . Released by Mariners organization (July 10, 1991). . . . Pitched in Italy (1992). . . . Signed by Iowa, Chicago Cubs organization (March 17, 1993). . . . Granted free agency (October 15, 1993). . . . Signed by Oakland Athletics organization (December 3, 1993). . . . Granted free agency (October 15, 1994). . . . Re-signed by A's organization (November 11, 1994). . . . Selected by Los Angeles Dodgers from A's organization in Rule 5 major league draft (December 5, 1994). . . . Granted free agency (April 24, 1995). . . . Signed by Texas Rangers organization (April 26, 1995).
STATISTICAL NOTES: Led Pacific Coast League with 11 balks in 1987.

Year	Team (League)	W	L	Pct.	ERA	G	GS	CG	ShO	Sv.	IP	H	R	ER	BB	SO
1983—	Reno (California)	6	6	.500	3.87	15	15	3	0	0	97 2/3	111	61	42	39	70
—	Beaumont (Texas)	1	0	1.000	0.00	1	1	1	1	0	7	2	0	0	2	1
1984—	Beaumont (Texas)	13	•11	.542	3.43	27	•27	5	2	0	183 2/3	196	87	70	74	100
1985—	Beaumont (Texas)	9	11	.450	3.91	27	•27	2	1	0	175	178	92	76	69	124
1986—	Las Vegas (PCL)	7	8	.467	4.72	25	24	2	1	0	129 2/3	136	80	68	64	93
—	San Diego (N.L.)	0	1	.000	6.59	5	3	0	0	0	13 2/3	17	11	10	9	8
1987—	Las Vegas (PCL)	9	8	.529	3.92	34	24	3	0	0	167 2/3	154	88	73	97	98
1988—	Las Vegas (PCL)	11	7	.611	4.15	45	11	1	0	2	128	137	67	59	56	75
1989—	Tucson (Pac. Coast)■	4	7	.364	6.78	23	14	0	0	1	87 2/3	122	70	66	49	68
—	Albuquerque (PCL)■	2	1	.667	2.70	12	0	0	0	0	20	17	8	6	5	18
1990—	Phoenix (PCL)■	1	3	.250	2.65	24	0	0	0	3	34	36	14	10	16	28
—	San Francisco (N.L.)	1	1	.500	5.55	18	0	0	0	0	24 1/3	21	16	15	12	12
1991—	Edmonton (PCL)■	0	1	.000	6.28	12	0	0	0	0	14 1/3	19	10	10	5	14
—	Calgary (PCL)■	0	2	.000	7.23	16	0	0	0	2	23 2/3	38	26	19	12	15
1992—						Italian League statistics unavailable.										
1993—	Iowa (Am. Assoc.)■	5	1	.833	3.57	52	0	0	0	3	63	67	32	25	22	64
1994—	Tacoma (PCL)■	4	2	.667	3.35	26	1	0	0	3	53 2/3	39	21	20	19	54
—	Oakland (A.L.)	0	2	.000	3.95	16	0	0	0	0	13 2/3	16	7	6	5	12
1995—	Okla. City (A.A.)■	1	0	1.000	0.00	1	0	0	0	0	1 2/3	1	0	0	1	2
—	Texas (A.L.)	5	5	.500	3.00	44	0	0	0	4	36	32	15	12	16	36
A.L. totals (2 years)		5	7	.417	3.26	60	0	0	0	4	49 2/3	48	22	18	21	48
N.L. totals (2 years)		1	2	.333	5.92	23	3	0	0	0	38	38	27	25	21	20
Major league totals (4 years)		6	9	.400	4.41	83	3	0	0	4	87 2/3	86	49	43	42	68

WADE, TERRELL — P — BRAVES

PERSONAL: Born January 25, 1973, in Rembert, S.C. . . . 6-3/205. . . . Throws left, bats left. . . . Full name: Hawatha Terrell Wade.
HIGH SCHOOL: Hillcrest (S.C.).
TRANSACTIONS/CAREER NOTES: Signed as non-drafted free agent by Atlanta Braves organization (June 17, 1991). . . . On Greenville disabled list (April 7-August 9, 1994).

Year	Team (League)	W	L	Pct.	ERA	G	GS	CG	ShO	Sv.	IP	H	R	ER	BB	SO
1991—	GC Braves (GCL)	2	0	1.000	6.26	10	2	0	0	0	23	29	17	16	15	22
1992—	Idaho Falls (Pio.)	1	4	.200	6.44	13	11	0	0	0	50 1/3	59	46	36	42	54
1993—	Macon (S. Atl.)	8	2	.800	1.73	14	14	0	0	0	83 1/3	57	16	16	36	121
—	Durham (Carolina)	2	1	.667	3.27	5	5	0	0	0	33	26	13	12	18	47
—	Greenville (South.)	2	1	.667	3.21	8	8	1	1	0	42	32	16	15	29	40
1994—	Greenville (South.)	9	3	.750	3.83	21	21	0	0	0	105 2/3	87	49	45	58	105
—	Richmond (Int'l)	2	2	.500	2.63	4	4	0	0	0	24	23	9	7	15	26
1995—	Richmond (Int'l)	10	9	.526	4.56	24	23	1	0	0	142	137	76	72	63	124
—	Atlanta (N.L.)	0	1	.000	4.50	3	0	0	0	0	4	3	2	2	4	3
Major league totals (1 year)		0	1	.000	4.50	3	0	0	0	0	4	3	2	2	4	3

WAGNER, BILLY — P — ASTROS

PERSONAL: Born June 25, 1971, in Tannersville, Va. . . . 5-11/180. . . . Throws left, bats left. . . . Full name: William Edward Wagner.
HIGH SCHOOL: Tazewell (Va.).
COLLEGE: Ferrum (Va.).
TRANSACTIONS/CAREER NOTES: Selected by Houston Astros organization in first round (12th pick overall) of free-agent draft (June 3, 1993).

Year	Team (League)	W	L	Pct.	ERA	G	GS	CG	ShO	Sv.	IP	H	R	ER	BB	SO
1993—	Auburn (NYP)	1	3	.250	4.08	7	7	0	0	0	28 2/3	25	19	13	25	31
1994—	Quad City (Midw.)	8	9	.471	3.29	26	26	2	0	0	153	99	71	56	*91	*204
1995—	Jackson (Texas)	2	2	.500	2.57	12	12	0	0	0	70	49	25	20	36	77
—	Tucson (Pac. Coast)	5	3	.625	3.18	13	13	0	0	0	76 1/3	70	28	27	32	80
—	Houston (N.L.)	0	0	...	0.00	1	0	0	0	0	1/3	0	0	0	0	0
Major league totals (1 year)		0	0	...	0.00	1	0	0	0	0	1/3	0	0	0	0	0

WAGNER, PAUL — P — PIRATES

PERSONAL: Born November 14, 1967, in Milwaukee. . . . 6-1/209. . . . Throws right, bats right. . . . Full name: Paul Alan Wagner.
HIGH SCHOOL: Washington (Germantown, Wis.).
COLLEGE: Illinois State.
TRANSACTIONS/CAREER NOTES: Selected by Pittsburgh Pirates organization in 12th round of free-agent draft (June 5, 1989). . . . On disabled list (August 3-19, 1993 and July 3-21, 1995).
STATISTICAL NOTES: Pitched 4-0 one-hit, complete-game victory against Colorado (August 29, 1995).
MISCELLANEOUS: Made an out in only appearance as pinch-hitter (1995).

Year	Team (League)	W	L	Pct.	ERA	G	GS	CG	ShO	Sv.	IP	H	R	ER	BB	SO
1989—	Welland (NYP)	4	5	.444	4.47	13	10	0	0	0	50 1/3	54	34	25	15	30
1990—	Augusta (S. Atl.)	7	7	.500	2.75	35	1	0	0	4	72	71	30	22	30	71
—	Salem (Carolina)	0	1	.000	5.00	11	4	0	0	2	36	39	22	20	17	28
1991—	Salem (Carolina)	11	6	.647	3.12	25	25	5	•2	0	158 2/3	124	70	55	60	113
1992—	Carolina (South.)	6	6	.500	3.03	19	19	2	1	0	121 2/3	104	52	41	47	101
—	Pittsburgh (N.L.)	2	0	1.000	0.69	6	1	0	0	0	13	9	1	1	5	5
—	Buffalo (A.A.)	3	3	.500	5.49	8	8	0	0	0	39 1/3	51	27	24	14	19
1993—	Pittsburgh (N.L.)	8	8	.500	4.27	44	17	1	1	2	141 1/3	143	72	67	42	114
1994—	Pittsburgh (N.L.)	7	8	.467	4.59	29	17	1	0	0	119 2/3	136	69	61	50	86
1995—	Pittsburgh (N.L.)	5	*16	.238	4.80	33	25	3	1	1	165	174	96	88	72	120
Major league totals (4 years)		22	32	.407	4.45	112	60	5	2	3	439	462	238	217	169	325

WAKEFIELD, TIM — P — RED SOX

PERSONAL: Born August 2, 1966, in Melbourne, Fla. . . . 6-2/205. . . . Throws right, bats right. . . . Full name: Timothy Stephen Wakefield.
HIGH SCHOOL: Eau Gallie (Melbourne, Fla.).
COLLEGE: Florida Tech.
TRANSACTIONS/CAREER NOTES: Selected by Pittsburgh Pirates organization in eighth round of free-agent draft (June 1, 1988). . . . Released by Pirates (April 20, 1995). . . . Signed by Boston Red Sox organization (April 26, 1995).
HONORS: Named N.L. Rookie Pitcher of the Year by The Sporting News (1992). . . . Named A.L. Comeback Player of the Year by The Sporting News (1995).
STATISTICAL NOTES: Led Carolina League with 24 home runs allowed in 1990. . . . Led American Association with 27 home runs allowed and 23 hit batsmen in 1994.
MISCELLANEOUS: Appeared in one game as pinch-runner with Pittsburgh (1992).

Year	Team (League)	W	L	Pct.	ERA	G	GS	CG	ShO	Sv.	IP	H	R	ER	BB	SO
1989—	Welland (NYP)	1	1	.500	3.40	18	1	0	0	2	39 2/3	30	17	15	21	42
1990—	Salem (Carolina)	10	•14	.417	4.73	28	•28	2	0	0	*190 1/3	*187	109	*100	*85	127
1991—	Carolina (South.)	15	8	.652	2.90	26	25	•8	1	0	183	155	68	59	51	120
—	Buffalo (A.A.)	0	1	.000	11.57	1	1	0	0	0	4 2/3	8	6	6	1	4
1992—	Buffalo (A.A.)	10	3	.769	3.06	20	20	*6	1	0	135 1/3	122	52	46	51	71
—	Pittsburgh (N.L.)	8	1	.889	2.15	13	13	4	1	0	92	76	26	22	35	51
1993—	Pittsburgh (N.L.)	6	11	.353	5.61	24	20	3	2	0	128 1/3	145	83	80	75	59
—	Carolina (South.)	3	5	.375	6.99	9	9	1	0	0	56 2/3	68	48	44	22	36
1994—	Buffalo (A.A.)	5	*15	.250	5.84	30	•29	4	1	0	175 2/3	*197	*127	*114	*98	83
1995—	Pawtucket (Int'l)■	2	1	.667	2.52	4	4	0	0	0	25	23	10	7	9	14
—	Boston (A.L.)	16	8	.667	2.95	27	27	6	1	0	195 1/3	163	76	64	68	119
A.L. totals (1 year)		16	8	.667	2.95	27	27	6	1	0	195 1/3	163	76	64	68	119
N.L. totals (2 years)		14	12	.538	4.17	37	33	7	3	0	220 1/3	221	109	102	110	110
Major league totals (3 years)		30	20	.600	3.59	64	60	13	4	0	415 2/3	384	185	166	178	229

DIVISION SERIES RECORD

Year	Team (League)	W	L	Pct.	ERA	G	GS	CG	ShO	Sv.	IP	H	R	ER	BB	SO
1995—	Boston (A.L.)	0	1	.000	11.81	1	1	0	0	0	5 1/3	5	7	7	5	4

CHAMPIONSHIP SERIES RECORD

NOTES: Shares single-series record for most complete games—2 (1992). . . . Shares N.L. career record for most complete games—2.

Year	Team (League)	W	L	Pct.	ERA	G	GS	CG	ShO	Sv.	IP	H	R	ER	BB	SO
1992—	Pittsburgh (N.L.)	2	0	1.000	3.00	2	2	2	0	0	18	14	6	6	5	7

RECORD AS POSITION PLAYER

			BATTING											FIELDING			
Year	Team (League)	Pos.	G	AB	R	H	2B	3B	HR	RBI	Avg.	BB	SO	SB	PO	A	E	Avg.
1988—	Watertown (NYP)	1B	54	159	24	30	6	2	3	20	.189	25	57	3	377	25	8	.980
1989—	Augusta (S. Atl.)	3B-1B	11	34	5	8	2	1	0	5	.235	1	14	1	27	6	3	.917
—	Welland (NYP)	3-2-1	36	63	7	13	4	0	1	3	.206	3	21	1	26	31	8	.877

WALBECK, MATT — C — TWINS

PERSONAL: Born October 2, 1969, in Sacramento, Calif. . . . 5-11/188. . . . Bats both, throws right. . . . Full name: Matthew Lovick Walbeck.
HIGH SCHOOL: Sacramento (Calif.).
TRANSACTIONS/CAREER NOTES: Selected by Chicago Cubs organization in eighth round of free-agent draft (June 2, 1987). . . . On Winston-Salem disabled list (April 12-July 11, 1990). . . . On Charleston, W.Va. disabled list (September 5, 1992-remainder of season). . . . Traded by Cubs with P Dave Stevens to Minnesota Twins for P Willie Banks (November 24, 1993).
STATISTICAL NOTES: Tied for Carolina League lead with 10 sacrifice flies in 1991. . . . Led American Association catchers with 561 total chances and tied for lead with nine double plays in 1993. . . . Career major league grand slams: 1.
MISCELLANEOUS: Batted righthanded only (1987-89).

			BATTING											FIELDING			
Year	Team (League)	Pos.	G	AB	R	H	2B	3B	HR	RBI	Avg.	BB	SO	SB	PO	A	E	Avg.
1987—	Wytheville (Appal.)	C	51	169	24	53	9	3	1	28	.314	22	39	0	293	22	1	*.997

Year Team (League)	Pos.	G	AB	R	H	2B	3B	HR	RBI	Avg.	BB	SO	SB	PO	A	E	Avg.
		BATTING												FIELDING			
1988— Char., W.Va. (SAL)	C	104	312	28	68	9	0	2	24	.218	30	44	7	549	68	14	.978
1989— Peoria (Midwest)	C	94	341	38	86	19	0	4	47	.252	20	47	5	605	72	11	.984
1990— Peoria (Midwest)	C	25	66	2	15	1	0	0	5	.227	5	7	1	137	16	2	.987
1991— Winst.-Salem (Car.)	C	91	260	25	70	11	0	3	41	.269	20	23	3	473	64	12	.978
1992— Charlotte (South.)	C-1B	105	385	48	116	22	1	7	42	.301	33	56	0	552	80	10	.984
1993— Chicago (N.L.)	C	11	30	2	6	2	0	1	6	.200	1	6	0	49	2	0	1.000
— Iowa (Am. Assoc.)	C	87	331	31	93	18	2	6	43	.281	18	47	1	496	*64	1	*.998
1994— Minnesota (A.L.)■	C-DH	97	338	31	69	12	0	5	35	.204	17	37	1	496	45	4	.993
1995— Minnesota (A.L.)	C	115	393	40	101	18	1	1	44	.257	25	71	3	604	35	6	.991
American League totals (2 years)		212	731	71	170	30	1	6	79	.233	42	108	4	1100	80	10	.992
National League totals (1 year)		11	30	2	6	2	0	1	6	.200	1	6	0	49	2	0	1.000
Major league totals (3 years)		223	761	73	176	32	1	7	85	.231	43	114	4	1149	82	10	.992

WALKER, LARRY — OF — ROCKIES

PERSONAL: Born December 1, 1966, in Maple Ridge, B.C. . . . 6-3/225. . . . Bats left, throws right. . . . Full name: Larry Kenneth Robert Walker.

HIGH SCHOOL: Maple Ridge (B.C.) Senior Secondary School.

TRANSACTIONS/CAREER NOTES: Signed as non-drafted free agent by Montreal Expos organization (November 14, 1984). . . . On disabled list (April 4, 1988-entire season; June 28-July 13, 1991; and May 26-June 10, 1993). . . . On suspended list (June 24-28, 1994). . . . Granted free agency (October 24, 1994). . . . Signed by Colorado Rockies (April 8, 1995).

HONORS: Named outfielder on The Sporting News N.L. All-Star team (1992). . . . Won N.L. Gold Glove as outfielder (1992-93). . . . Named outfielder on The Sporting News N.L. Silver Slugger team (1992).

STATISTICAL NOTES: Career major league grand slams: 1.

Year Team (League)	Pos.	G	AB	R	H	2B	3B	HR	RBI	Avg.	BB	SO	SB	PO	A	E	Avg.
		BATTING												FIELDING			
1985— Utica (NYP)	1B-3B	62	215	24	48	8	2	2	26	.223	18	57	12	354	62	8	.981
1986— Burlington (Midw.)	OF-3B	95	332	67	96	12	6	29	74	.289	46	112	16	106	51	10	.940
— W.P. Beach (FSL)	OF	38	113	20	32	7	5	4	16	.283	26	32	2	44	5	0	1.000
1987— Jacksonv. (South.)	OF	128	474	91	136	25	7	26	83	.287	67	120	24	263	9	9	.968
1988—		Did not play.															
1989— Indianapolis (A.A.)	OF	114	385	68	104	18	2	12	59	.270	50	87	36	241	*18	*11	.959
— Montreal (N.L.)	OF	20	47	4	8	0	0	0	4	.170	5	13	1	19	2	0	1.000
1990— Montreal (N.L.)	OF	133	419	59	101	18	3	19	51	.241	49	112	21	249	12	4	.985
1991— Montreal (N.L.)	OF-1B	137	487	59	141	30	2	16	64	.290	42	102	14	536	36	6	.990
1992— Montreal (N.L.)	OF	143	528	85	159	31	4	23	93	.301	41	97	18	269	16	2	.993
1993— Montreal (N.L.)	OF-1B	138	490	85	130	24	5	22	86	.265	80	76	29	316	16	6	.982
1994— Montreal (N.L.)	OF-1B	103	395	76	127	44	2	19	86	.322	47	74	15	423	29	9	.980
1995— Colorado (N.L.)■	OF	131	494	96	151	31	5	36	101	.306	49	72	16	225	13	3	.988
Major league totals (7 years)		805	2860	464	817	178	21	135	485	.286	313	546	114	2037	124	30	.986

DIVISION SERIES RECORD

Year Team (League)	Pos.	G	AB	R	H	2B	3B	HR	RBI	Avg.	BB	SO	SB	PO	A	E	Avg.
		BATTING												FIELDING			
1995— Colorado (N.L.)	OF	4	14	3	3	0	0	1	3	.214	3	4	1	3	0	0	1.000

ALL-STAR GAME RECORD

Year League	Pos.	AB	R	H	2B	3B	HR	RBI	Avg.	BB	SO	SB	PO	A	E	Avg.
		BATTING											FIELDING			
1992— National	PH	1	0	1	0	0	0	0	1.000	0	0	0	...	...	...	...

WALKER, MIKE — P — PHILLIES

PERSONAL: Born October 4, 1966, in Chicago. . . . 6-1/205. . . . Throws right, bats right. . . . Full name: Michael Charles Walker.

HIGH SCHOOL: Hernando (Brooksville, Fla.).

JUNIOR COLLEGE: Seminole Community College (Fla.).

TRANSACTIONS/CAREER NOTES: Selected by Montreal Expos organization in 14th round of free-agent draft (June 4, 1984); did not sign. . . . Selected by Expos organization in secondary phase of free-agent draft (January 9, 1985); did not sign. . . . Selected by Cleveland Indians organization in second round of free-agent draft (January 14, 1986). . . . Released by Indians (November 27, 1991). . . . Signed by Detroit Tigers organization (December 19, 1991). . . . Granted free agency (October 15, 1992). . . . Signed by Canton/Akron, Indians organization (February 8, 1993). . . . Released by Canton/Akron (March 30, 1993). . . . Signed by Orlando, Chicago Cubs organization (June 22, 1993). . . . Granted free agency (October 15, 1993). . . . Re-signed by Iowa, Cubs organization (January 7, 1994). . . . Granted free agency (October 7, 1994). . . . Re-signed by Iowa (November 3, 1994). . . . Granted free agency (October 9, 1995). . . . Signed by Philadelphia Phillies organization (January 19, 1996).

STATISTICAL NOTES: Led Eastern League with 17 wild pitches in 1988. . . . Led Pacific Coast League with 21 home runs allowed and 14 hit batsmen in 1989.

Year Team (League)	W	L	Pct.	ERA	G	GS	CG	ShO	Sv.	IP	H	R	ER	BB	SO
1986— Burlington (Appal.)	4	6	.400	5.89	14	13	1	0	0	70 1/3	75	*65	•46	45	42
1987— Waterloo (Midw.)	11	7	.611	3.59	23	23	*8	1	0	145 1/3	133	74	58	68	144
— Kinston (Carolina)	3	0	1.000	2.61	3	3	0	0	0	20 2/3	17	7	6	14	19
1988— Williamsport (East.)	*15	7	.682	3.72	28	•27	3	0	0	*164 1/3	162	82	68	74	*144
— Cleveland (A.L.)	0	1	.000	7.27	3	1	0	0	0	8 2/3	8	7	7	10	7
1989— Colo. Springs (PCL)	6	*15	.286	5.79	28	•28	4	0	0	168	193	*124	*108	*93	97
1990— Colo. Springs (PCL)	2	7	.222	5.58	18	12	0	0	1	79	96	62	49	36	50
— Cant./Akr. (East.)	1	0	1.000	0.00	1	1	0	0	0	7	4	0	0	4	3
— Cleveland (A.L.)	2	6	.250	4.88	18	11	0	0	0	75 2/3	82	49	41	42	34
1991— Cant./Akr. (East.)	9	4	.692	2.79	45	1	0	0	11	77 1/3	68	36	24	45	42
— Cleveland (A.L.)	0	1	.000	2.08	5	0	0	0	0	4 1/3	6	1	1	2	2

Year	Team (League)	W	L	Pct.	ERA	G	GS	CG	ShO	Sv.	IP	H	R	ER	BB	SO
1992—	Toledo (Int'l)■	2	8	.200	5.83	42	1	0	0	4	78 2/3	102	62	51	44	44
1993—	Orlando (Southern)■	2	3	.400	7.31	16	2	0	0	1	28 1/3	42	26	23	9	21
—	Iowa (Am. Assoc.)	1	1	.500	2.70	12	0	0	0	0	23 1/3	22	8	7	9	11
1994—	Iowa (Am. Assoc.)	6	2	.750	2.99	56	0	0	0	8	87 1/3	80	33	29	34	56
1995—	Chicago (N.L.)	1	3	.250	3.22	42	0	0	0	1	44 2/3	45	22	16	24	20
—	Iowa (Am. Assoc.)	1	1	.500	4.10	16	1	0	0	0	26 1/3	22	13	12	19	13
A.L. totals (3 years)		2	8	.200	4.97	26	12	0	0	0	88 2/3	96	57	49	54	43
N.L. totals (1 year)		1	3	.250	3.22	42	0	0	0	1	44 2/3	45	22	16	24	20
Major league totals (4 years)		3	11	.214	4.39	68	12	0	0	1	133 1/3	141	79	65	78	63

WALKER, PETE — P — METS

PERSONAL: Born April 8, 1969, in Beverly, Mass. . . . 6-2/195. . . . Throws right, bats right. . . . Full name: Peter Brian Walker.
HIGH SCHOOL: East Lyme (Conn.).
COLLEGE: Connecticut.
TRANSACTIONS/CAREER NOTES: Selected by New York Mets organization in seventh round of free-agent draft (June 4, 1990). . . . On disabled list (June 6-18, 1992 and April 25-May 9, 1993). . . . On Norfolk disabled list (April 7-May 16, 1994). . . . On Norfolk suspended list (August 5-6, 1994).

Year	Team (League)	W	L	Pct.	ERA	G	GS	CG	ShO	Sv.	IP	H	R	ER	BB	SO
1990—	Pittsfield (NYP)	5	7	.417	4.16	16	13	1	0	0	80	74	43	37	46	73
1991—	St. Lucie (Fla. St.)	10	12	.455	3.21	26	25	1	0	0	151 1/3	145	77	54	52	95
1992—	Binghamton (East.)	7	12	.368	4.12	24	23	4	0	0	139 2/3	159	77	64	46	72
1993—	Binghamton (East.)	4	9	.308	3.44	45	10	0	0	19	99 1/3	89	45	38	46	89
1994—	St. Lucie (Fla. St.)	0	0	...	2.25	3	0	0	0	0	4	3	2	1	1	5
—	Norfolk (Int'l)	2	4	.333	3.97	37	0	0	0	3	47 2/3	48	22	21	24	42
1995—	Norfolk (Int'l)	5	2	.714	3.91	34	1	0	0	8	48 1/3	51	24	21	16	39
—	New York (N.L.)	1	0	1.000	4.58	13	0	0	0	0	17 2/3	24	9	9	5	5
Major league totals (1 year)		1	0	1.000	4.58	13	0	0	0	0	17 2/3	24	9	9	5	5

WALKER, WADE — P — CUBS

PERSONAL: Born September 18, 1971, in Baton Rouge, La. . . . 6-1/190. . . . Throws right, bats right. . . . Full name: Wade Michael Walker.
HIGH SCHOOL: St. Amant (La.).
COLLEGE: Northwestern (La.) State.
TRANSACTIONS/CAREER NOTES: Selected by Chicago Cubs organization in 16th round of free-agent draft (June 3, 1993).
STATISTICAL NOTES: Tied for New York-Pennsylvania League lead with nine sacrifice flies allowed in 1993.

Year	Team (League)	W	L	Pct.	ERA	G	GS	CG	ShO	Sv.	IP	H	R	ER	BB	SO
1993—	Geneva (NYP)	5	2	.714	3.12	13	13	1	0	0	83 2/3	76	38	29	36	47
1994—	Peoria (Midwest)	14	12	.538	3.99	28	•28	4	1	0	178 1/3	192	*108	79	72	117
1995—	Daytona (Fla. St.)	8	6	.571	2.53	25	24	2	1	0	135	113	50	38	36	117

WALL, DONNE — P — ASTROS

PERSONAL: Born July 11, 1967, in Potosi, Mo. . . . 6-1/180. . . . Throws right, bats right. . . . Full name: Donnell Lee Wall.
HIGH SCHOOL: Festus (Mo.).
JUNIOR COLLEGE: Jefferson (Mo.), then Meramec (Mo.).
COLLEGE: Southwestern Louisiana.
TRANSACTIONS/CAREER NOTES: Selected by Houston Astros organization in 18th round of free-agent draft (June 5, 1989). . . . On disabled list (May 27-June 16, 1994).
HONORS: Named Pacific Coast League Most Valuable Player (1995).
STATISTICAL NOTES: Led South Atlantic League with 18 home runs allowed in 1990.

Year	Team (League)	W	L	Pct.	ERA	G	GS	CG	ShO	Sv.	IP	H	R	ER	BB	SO
1989—	Auburn (N.Y.-Penn)	7	0	*1.000	1.79	12	8	3	1	1	65 1/3	45	17	13	12	69
1990—	Asheville (S. Atl.)	6	8	.429	5.18	28	22	1	0	1	132	149	87	76	47	111
1991—	Burlington (Midw.)	7	5	.583	2.03	16	16	3	1	0	106 2/3	73	30	24	21	102
—	Osceola (Florida St.)	6	3	.667	2.09	12	12	4	2	0	77 1/3	55	22	18	11	62
1992—	Osceola (Florida St.)	3	1	.750	2.63	7	7	0	0	0	41	37	13	12	8	30
—	Jackson (Texas)	9	6	.600	3.54	18	18	2	0	0	114 1/3	114	51	45	26	99
1993—	Tucson (Pac. Coast)	6	4	.600	3.83	25	22	0	0	0	131 2/3	147	73	56	25	89
1994—	Tucson (Pac. Coast)	11	8	.579	4.43	26	24	2	2	0	148 1/3	171	87	73	35	84
1995—	Tucson (Pac. Coast)	*17	6	.739	*3.30	28	•28	0	0	0	*177 1/3	190	72	65	32	*119
—	Houston (N.L.)	3	1	.750	5.55	6	5	0	0	0	24 1/3	33	19	15	5	16
Major league totals (1 year)		3	1	.750	5.55	6	5	0	0	0	24 1/3	33	19	15	5	16

WALLACE, B.J. — P — PHILLIES

PERSONAL: Born May 18, 1971, in Mobile, Ala. . . . 6-3/195. . . . Throws left, bats right. . . . Full name: Billy Lyle Wallace Jr.
HIGH SCHOOL: Monroe Academy (Monroeville, Ala.).
COLLEGE: Mississippi State.
TRANSACTIONS/CAREER NOTES: Selected by Montreal Expos organization in first round (third pick overall) of free-agent draft (June 1, 1992). . . . On disabled list (April 13-May 1 and June 4-September 26, 1994; and April 17, 1995-entire season). . . . Selected by Philadelphia Phillies from Expos organization in Rule 5 major league draft (December 4, 1995).
STATISTICAL NOTES: Led Florida State League with 11 hit batsmen in 1993.
MISCELLANEOUS: Member of 1992 U.S. Olympic baseball team.

Year	Team (League)	W	L	Pct.	ERA	G	GS	CG	ShO	Sv.	IP	H	R	ER	BB	SO
1993—	WP Beach (FSL)	11	8	.579	3.28	25	24	0	0	0	137 1/3	112	61	50	65	126
1994—	Harrisburg (East.)	1	3	.250	4.81	8	8	1	1	0	43	34	27	23	27	30
1995—		Did not play.														

WALLACE, DEREK — P — METS

PERSONAL: Born September 1, 1971, in Van Nuys, Calif. . . . 6-3/185. . . . Throws right, bats right. . . . Full name: Derek Robert Wallace.
HIGH SCHOOL: Chatsworth (Calif.).
COLLEGE: Pepperdine.
TRANSACTIONS/CAREER NOTES: Selected by Pittsburgh Pirates organization in 36th round of free-agent draft (June 5, 1989); did not sign. . . . Selected by Chicago Cubs organization in first round (11th pick overall) of free-agent draft (June 1, 1992). . . . Traded by Cubs with P Geno Morones to Kansas City Royals for OF Brian McRae (April 5, 1995). . . . Traded by Royals organization with a player to be named later to New York Mets organization for P Jason Jacome and P Allen McDill (July 21, 1995); Mets acquired P John Carter to complete deal (November 16, 1995).
STATISTICAL NOTES: Led Florida State League with 11 balks in 1993.

Year	Team (League)	W	L	Pct.	ERA	G	GS	CG	ShO	Sv.	IP	H	R	ER	BB	SO
1992—	Peoria (Midwest)	0	1	.000	4.91	2	0	0	0	0	3 2/3	3	2	2	1	2
1993—	Daytona (Fla. St.)	5	6	.455	4.20	14	12	0	0	1	79 1/3	85	50	37	23	34
—	Iowa (Am. Assoc.)	0	0	. . .	11.25	1	1	0	0	0	4	8	5	5	1	2
—	Orlando (Southern)	5	7	.417	5.03	15	15	2	0	0	96 2/3	105	59	54	28	69
1994—	Orlando (Southern)	2	9	.182	5.74	33	12	1	0	8	89 1/3	95	61	57	31	49
—	Iowa (Am. Assoc.)	0	1	.000	4.15	5	0	0	0	1	4 1/3	4	4	2	4	3
1995—	Wichita (Texas)■	4	3	.571	4.40	26	0	0	0	6	43	51	23	21	13	24
—	Binghamton (East.)■	0	1	.000	5.28	15	0	0	0	2	15 1/3	11	9	9	9	8

WALLACE, KENT — P — YANKEES

PERSONAL: Born August 22, 1970, in Paducah, Ky. . . . 6-3/195. . . . Throws right, bats left. . . . Full name: Kent Edwin Wallace.
HIGH SCHOOL: Reidland (Paducah, Ky.).
COLLEGE: Southern Illinois, then Murray State.
TRANSACTIONS/CAREER NOTES: Selected by New York Yankees organization in 14th round of free-agent draft (June 1, 1992). . . . On disabled list (May 27-June 14 and July 2, 1993-remainder of season).

Year	Team (League)	W	L	Pct.	ERA	G	GS	CG	ShO	Sv.	IP	H	R	ER	BB	SO
1992—	Oneonta (NYP)	8	4	.667	2.55	14	14	1	1	0	81 1/3	76	32	23	11	55
1993—	Greensboro (S. Atl.)	4	2	.667	3.00	13	10	2	1	2	66	63	31	22	12	49
1994—	Tampa (Fla. St.)	6	3	.667	2.09	39	0	0	0	7	77 2/3	60	23	18	22	61
1995—	Norwich (Eastern)	7	6	.538	3.52	18	16	0	0	0	94 2/3	93	41	37	24	72
—	Columbus (Int'l)	4	1	.800	3.02	9	9	0	0	0	50 2/3	44	19	17	11	31

W

WALLACH, TIM — 3B — ANGELS

PERSONAL: Born September 14, 1957, in Huntington Park, Calif. . . . 6-3/202. . . . Bats right, throws right. . . . Full name: Timothy Charles Wallach.
HIGH SCHOOL: University (Irvine, Calif.).
JUNIOR COLLEGE: Saddleback Community College (Calif.).
COLLEGE: Cal State Fullerton.
TRANSACTIONS/CAREER NOTES: Selected by California Angels organization in eighth round of free-agent draft (June 6, 1978); did not sign. . . . Selected by Montreal Expos organization in first round (10th pick overall) of free-agent draft (June 5, 1979). . . . Traded by Expos to Los Angeles Dodgers for SS Tim Barker (December 24, 1992). . . . On disabled list (July 18-August 9, 1993). . . . Granted free agency (October 15, 1994). . . . Re-signed by Dodgers (December 13, 1994). . . . On Los Angeles disabled list (April 22-May 20 and August 27-September 11, 1995); included rehabilitation assignments to Albuquerque (May 4-6) and San Bernardino (May 16-20). . . . Granted free agency (November 6, 1995). . . . Signed by Angels organization (December 5, 1995).
HONORS: Named Golden Spikes Award winner by USA Baseball (1979). . . . Named College Player of the Year by The Sporting News (1979). . . . Named first baseman on The Sporting News college All-America team (1979). . . . Named third baseman on The Sporting News N.L. All-Star team (1985 and 1987). . . . Won N.L. Gold Glove at third base (1985, 1988 and 1990). . . . Named third baseman on The Sporting News N.L. Silver Slugger team (1985 and 1987). . . . Named N.L. Comeback Player of the Year by The Sporting News (1994).
STATISTICAL NOTES: Hit home run in first major league at-bat (September 6, 1980). . . . Led American Association with 295 total bases and tied for lead with nine sacrifice flies in 1980. . . . Led N.L. third basemen with 132 putouts in 1982, 162 in 1984, 128 in 1987 and 123 in 1988. . . . Led N.L. third basemen with 332 assists in 1984. . . . Led N.L. third basemen with 515 total chances in 1984 and 549 in 1985. . . . Led N.L. third basemen with 29 double plays in 1984, 34 in 1985 and tied for lead with 31 in 1988. . . . Led N.L. in being hit by pitch with 10 in 1986. . . . Tied for N.L. lead with 16 game-winning RBIs in 1987. . . . Hit three home runs in one game (May 4, 1987). . . . Led N.L. in grounding into double plays with 21 in 1989. . . . Led N.L. third basemen with .976 fielding percentage in 1995. . . . Career major league grand slams: 5.

				BATTING											FIELDING			
Year	Team (League)	Pos.	G	AB	R	H	2B	3B	HR	RBI	Avg.	BB	SO	SB	PO	A	E	Avg.
1979—	Memphis (South.)	1B-3B	75	257	50	84	16	4	18	51	.327	37	53	0	290	35	4	.988
1980—	Denver (A.A.)	3B-OF-1B	134	512	103	144	29	7	36	124	.281	51	92	1	222	147	21	.946
—	Montreal (N.L.)	OF-1B	5	11	1	2	0	0	1	2	.182	1	5	0	12	0	0	1.000
1981—	Montreal (N.L.)	OF-1B-3B	71	212	19	50	9	1	4	13	.236	15	37	0	207	31	1	.996
1982—	Montreal (N.L.)	3B-OF-1B	158	596	89	160	31	3	28	97	.268	36	81	6	†132	287	23	.948
1983—	Montreal (N.L.)	3B	156	581	54	156	33	3	19	70	.269	55	97	0	*151	262	19	.956
1984—	Montreal (N.L.)	3B-SS	160	582	55	143	25	4	18	72	.246	50	101	3	†162	†332	21	.959
1985—	Montreal (N.L.)	3B	155	569	70	148	36	3	22	81	.260	38	79	9	*148	*383	18	.967
1986—	Montreal (N.L.)	3B	134	480	50	112	22	1	18	71	.233	44	72	8	94	270	16	.958
1987—	Montreal (N.L.)	3B-P	153	593	89	177	*42	4	26	123	.298	37	98	9	†128	292	21	.952
1988—	Montreal (N.L.)	3B-2B	159	592	52	152	32	5	12	69	.257	38	88	2	†124	329	18	.962

Year	Team (League)	Pos.	G	AB	R	H	2B	3B	HR	RBI	Avg.	BB	SO	SB	PO	A	E	Avg.
			BATTING												FIELDING			
1989—	Montreal (N.L.)	3B-P	154	573	76	159	•42	0	13	77	.277	58	81	3	113	302	18	.958
1990—	Montreal (N.L.)	3B	161	626	69	185	37	5	21	98	.296	42	80	6	128	309	21	.954
1991—	Montreal (N.L.)	3B	151	577	60	130	22	1	13	73	.225	50	100	2	107	310	14	*.968
1992—	Montreal (N.L.)	3B-1B	150	537	53	120	29	1	9	59	.223	50	90	2	689	244	15	.984
1993—	Los Angeles (N.L.)■	3B-1B	133	477	42	106	19	1	12	62	.222	32	70	0	121	229	15	.959
1994—	Los Angeles (N.L.)	3B	113	414	68	116	21	1	23	78	.280	46	80	0	*81	176	11	.959
1995—	Albuquerque (PCL)	3B	1	3	1	1	0	0	0	1	.333	0	2	0	0	1	0	1.000
—	San Bern. (Calif.)	3B	4	15	2	7	3	0	0	4	.467	0	3	0	2	8	1	.909
—	Los Angeles (N.L.)	3B-1B	97	327	24	87	22	2	9	38	.266	27	69	0	61	156	5	†.977
Major league totals (16 years)			2110	7747	871	2003	422	35	248	1083	.259	619	1228	50	2458	3912	236	.964

DIVISION SERIES RECORD

Year	Team (League)	Pos.	G	AB	R	H	2B	3B	HR	RBI	Avg.	BB	SO	SB	PO	A	E	Avg.
			BATTING												FIELDING			
1981—	Montreal (N.L.)	OF	4	4	1	1	1	0	0	0	.250	4	0	0	4	0	0	1.000
1995—	Los Angeles (N.L.)	3B	3	12	0	1	0	0	0	0	.083	1	3	0	1	2	0	1.000
Division series totals (2 years)			7	16	1	2	1	0	0	0	.125	5	3	0	5	2	0	1.000

CHAMPIONSHIP SERIES RECORD

Year	Team (League)	Pos.	G	AB	R	H	2B	3B	HR	RBI	Avg.	BB	SO	SB	PO	A	E	Avg.
			BATTING												FIELDING			
1981—	Montreal (N.L.)	PH	1	1	0	0	0	0	0	0	.000	0	0	0	...	...	...	...

ALL-STAR GAME RECORD

Year	League	Pos.	AB	R	H	2B	3B	HR	RBI	Avg.	BB	SO	SB	PO	A	E	Avg.
			BATTING											FIELDING			
1984—	National	3B	1	0	0	0	0	0	0	.000	0	0	0	0	0	0	...
1985—	National	3B	2	1	1	1	0	0	0	.500	1	1	0	1	1	0	1.000
1987—	National	3B	3	0	0	0	0	0	0	.000	0	0	0	0	2	0	1.000
1989—	National	3B	1	0	0	0	0	0	0	.000	0	0	0	0	0	0	...
1990—	National	3B	2	0	0	0	0	0	0	.000	0	0	0	0	0	0	...
All-Star Game totals (5 years)			9	1	1	1	0	0	0	.111	1	1	0	1	3	0	1.000

RECORD AS PITCHER

Year	Team (League)	W	L	Pct.	ERA	G	GS	CG	ShO	Sv.	IP	H	R	ER	BB	SO
1987—	Montreal (N.L.)	0	0	...	0.00	1	0	0	0	0	1	1	0	0	0	0
1989—	Montreal (N.L.)	0	0	...	9.00	1	0	0	0	0	1	2	1	1	0	0
Major league totals (2 years)		0	0	...	4.50	2	0	0	0	0	2	3	1	1	0	0

WALTON, JEROME — OF — BRAVES

PERSONAL: Born July 8, 1965, in Newnan, Ga. . . . 6-1/185. . . . Bats right, throws right. . . . Full name: Jerome O'Terrell Walton.

HIGH SCHOOL: Enterprise (Ala.).

JUNIOR COLLEGE: Enterprise (Ala.) State Junior College.

TRANSACTIONS/CAREER NOTES: Selected by Chicago Cubs organization in second round of free-agent draft (January 14, 1986). . . . On Chicago disabled list (May 11-June 11, 1989); included rehabilitation assignment to Iowa (June 6-11). . . . On Chicago disabled list (June 18-August 2, 1990); included rehabilitation assignment to Iowa (July 29-August 1). . . . On Chicago disabled list (March 28-April 24, 1992); included rehabilitation assignment to Iowa (April 17-24). . . . On Iowa disabled list (July 1-September 14, 1992). . . . Granted free agency (December 19, 1992). . . . Signed by California Angels organization (January 29, 1993). . . . On Vancouver disabled list (July 19-August 20, 1993). . . . Released by Angels organization (August 20, 1993). . . . Signed by Cincinnati Reds organization (November 4, 1993). . . . On disabled list (July 1-23 and July 27, 1994-remainder of season). . . . Granted free agency (December 21, 1995). . . . Signed by Atlanta Braves (January 3, 1996).

HONORS: Named N.L. Rookie Player of the Year by The Sporting News (1989). . . . Named N.L. Rookie of the Year by Baseball Writers' Association of America (1989).

STATISTICAL NOTES: Led Appalachian League outfielders with 128 putouts and 131 total chances and tied for lead with two double plays in 1986. . . . Led Midwest League in caught stealing with 25 in 1987.

Year	Team (League)	Pos.	G	AB	R	H	2B	3B	HR	RBI	Avg.	BB	SO	SB	PO	A	E	Avg.
			BATTING												FIELDING			
1986—	Wytheville (Appal.)	OF-3B	62	229	48	66	7	4	5	34	.288	28	40	21	†130	7	3	.979
1987—	Peoria (Midwest)	OF	128	472	102	158	24	11	6	38	.335	91	91	49	255	9	7	.974
1988—	Pittsfield (Eastern)	OF	120	414	64	137	26	2	3	49	*.331	41	69	42	270	11	2	*.993
1989—	Chicago (N.L.)	OF	116	475	64	139	23	3	5	46	.293	27	77	24	289	2	3	.990
—	Iowa (Am. Assoc.)	OF	4	18	4	6	1	0	1	3	.333	1	5	2	8	0	0	1.000
1990—	Chicago (N.L.)	OF	101	392	63	103	16	2	2	21	.263	50	70	14	247	3	6	.977
—	Iowa (Am. Assoc.)	OF	4	16	3	3	0	0	1	1	.188	2	4	0	6	1	0	1.000
1991—	Chicago (N.L.)	OF	123	270	42	59	13	1	5	17	.219	19	55	7	170	2	3	.983
1992—	Iowa (Am. Assoc.)	OF	7	27	8	8	2	1	0	3	.296	4	6	1	10	0	0	1.000
—	Chicago (N.L.)	OF	30	55	7	7	0	1	0	1	.127	9	13	1	34	0	2	.944
1993—	California (A.L.)■	DH-OF	5	2	2	0	0	0	0	0	.000	1	2	1	2	0	0	1.000
—	Vancouver (PCL)	OF	54	176	34	55	11	1	2	20	.313	16	24	5	82	3	0	1.000
1994—	Cincinnati (N.L.)■	OF-1B	46	68	10	21	4	0	1	9	.309	4	12	1	57	1	1	.983
1995—	Cincinnati (N.L.)	OF-1B	102	162	32	47	12	1	8	22	.290	17	25	10	110	2	2	.982
American League totals (1 year)			5	2	2	0	0	0	0	0	.000	1	2	1	2	0	0	1.000
National League totals (6 years)			518	1422	218	376	68	8	21	116	.264	126	252	57	907	10	17	.982
Major league totals (7 years)			523	1424	220	376	68	8	21	116	.264	127	254	58	909	10	17	.982

DIVISION SERIES RECORD

Year	Team (League)	Pos.	G	AB	R	H	2B	3B	HR	RBI	Avg.	BB	SO	SB	PO	A	E	Avg.
			BATTING												FIELDING			
1995—	Cincinnati (N.L.)	OF-PH	3	3	0	0	0	0	0	0	.000	1	1	0	3	0	0	1.000

CHAMPIONSHIP SERIES RECORD

NOTES: Shares records for most at-bats—2; hits—2; and singles—2, in one inning (October 5, 1989, first inning).

		BATTING											FIELDING		
Year Team (League)	Pos.	G	AB	R	H	2B	3B	HR	RBI	Avg.	BB	SO	SB	PO	A	E	Avg.
1989—Chicago (N.L.)	OF	5	22	4	8	0	0	0	2	.364	2	2	0	11	0	0	1.000
1995—Cincinnati (N.L.)	OF	2	7	0	0	0	0	0	0	.000	0	2	0	6	0	0	1.000
Championship series totals (2 years)		7	29	4	8	0	0	0	2	.276	2	4	0	17	0	0	1.000

WARD, BRYAN — P — MARLINS

PERSONAL: Born January 28, 1972, in Bristol, Pa. . . . 6-2/210. . . . Throws left, bats left.
COLLEGE: South Carolina-Aiken.
TRANSACTIONS/CAREER NOTES: Selected by Florida Marlins organization in 20th round of free-agent draft (June 3, 1993).

Year Team (League)	W	L	Pct.	ERA	G	GS	CG	ShO	Sv.	IP	H	R	ER	BB	SO
1993—Elmira (NYP)	2	5	.286	4.99	14	11	0	0	0	61 1/3	82	41	34	26	63
1994—Kane Co. (Mid.)	3	4	.429	3.40	47	0	0	0	11	55 2/3	46	27	21	21	62
1995—Brevard County (FSL)	5	1	.833	2.88	11	11	0	0	0	72	68	27	23	17	65
—Portland (Eastern)	7	3	.700	4.50	20	11	1	1	2	72	70	42	36	31	71

WARD, DUANE — P

PERSONAL: Born May 28, 1964, in Parkview, N.M. . . . 6-4/225. . . . Throws right, bats right. . . . Full name: Roy Duane Ward.
HIGH SCHOOL: Farmington (N.M.).
TRANSACTIONS/CAREER NOTES: Selected by Atlanta Braves organization in first round (ninth pick overall) of free-agent draft (June 7, 1982). . . . On disabled list (May 7-29 and July 14-August 7, 1984). . . . Traded by Braves organization to Toronto Blue Jays for P Doyle Alexander (July 6, 1986). . . . On Toronto disabled list (March 25, 1994-entire season); included rehabilitation assignment to Dunedin (June 30-July 7). . . . On Toronto disabled list (May 12-June 2, 1995); included rehabilitation assignment to Syracuse (May 16-30). . . . On Toronto disabled list (June 23, 1995-entire season); included rehabilitation assignment to Dunedin (July 10-14). . . . Granted free agency (November 2, 1995).

Year Team (League)	W	L	Pct.	ERA	G	GS	CG	ShO	Sv.	IP	H	R	ER	BB	SO
1982—GC Braves (GCL)	2	3	.400	4.53	8	8	1	0	0	45 2/3	45	25	23	24	31
—Anderson (S. Atl.)	1	2	.333	5.32	5	4	0	0	0	23 2/3	24	16	14	15	18
1983—Durham (Carolina)	11	13	.458	4.29	28	28	6	2	0	178 1/3	165	103	85	75	115
1984—Greenville (South.)	4	9	.308	4.99	21	20	4	0	0	104 2/3	108	71	58	57	54
1985—Greenville (South.)	11	10	.524	4.20	28	24	3	0	0	150	141	83	70	*105	100
—Richmond (Int'l)	0	1	.000	11.81	5	1	0	0	0	5 1/3	8	9	7	8	3
1986—Atlanta (N.L.)	0	1	.000	7.31	10	0	0	0	0	16	22	13	13	8	8
—Richmond (Int'l)	1	1	.500	3.38	6	6	0	0	0	34 2/3	34	13	13	23	17
—Syracuse (Int'l)■	6	4	.600	4.23	14	14	3	0	0	83	91	43	39	29	50
—Toronto (A.L.)	0	1	.000	13.50	2	1	0	0	0	2	3	4	3	4	1
1987—Toronto (A.L.)	1	0	1.000	6.94	12	1	0	0	0	11 2/3	14	9	9	12	10
—Syracuse (Int'l)	2	2	.500	3.89	46	3	0	0	14	76 1/3	59	35	33	42	67
1988—Toronto (A.L.)	9	3	.750	3.30	64	0	0	0	15	111 2/3	101	46	41	60	91
1989—Toronto (A.L.)	4	10	.286	3.77	66	0	0	0	15	114 2/3	94	55	48	58	122
1990—Toronto (A.L.)	2	8	.200	3.45	73	0	0	0	11	127 2/3	101	51	49	42	112
1991—Toronto (A.L.)	7	6	.538	2.77	*81	0	0	0	23	107 1/3	80	36	33	33	132
1992—Toronto (A.L.)	7	4	.636	1.95	79	0	0	0	12	101 1/3	76	27	22	39	103
1993—Toronto (A.L.)	2	3	.400	2.13	71	0	0	0	•45	71 2/3	49	17	17	25	97
1994—Dunedin (Fla. St.)	1	0	1.000	4.50	3	1	0	0	0	4	4	2	2	0	4
1995—Toronto (A.L.)	0	1	.000	27.00	4	0	0	0	0	2 2/3	11	10	8	5	3
—Syracuse (Int'l)	1	1	.500	15.00	6	0	0	0	0	6	14	10	10	2	4
—Dunedin (Fla. St.)	0	1	.000	6.23	3	2	0	0	0	4 1/3	4	3	3	1	4
A.L. totals (9 years)	32	36	.471	3.18	452	2	0	0	121	650 2/3	529	255	230	278	671
N.L. totals (1 year)	0	1	.000	7.31	10	0	0	0	0	16	22	13	13	8	8
Major league totals (9 years)	32	37	.464	3.28	462	2	0	0	121	666 2/3	551	268	243	286	679

CHAMPIONSHIP SERIES RECORD

Year Team (League)	W	L	Pct.	ERA	G	GS	CG	ShO	Sv.	IP	H	R	ER	BB	SO
1989—Toronto (A.L.)	0	0	...	7.36	2	0	0	0	0	3 2/3	6	3	3	3	5
1991—Toronto (A.L.)	0	1	.000	6.23	2	0	0	0	1	4 1/3	4	3	3	1	6
1992—Toronto (A.L.)	1	0	1.000	6.75	3	0	0	0	0	4	5	3	3	1	2
1993—Toronto (A.L.)	0	0	...	5.79	4	0	0	0	2	4 2/3	4	3	3	3	8
Champ. series totals (4 years)	1	1	.500	6.48	11	0	0	0	3	16 2/3	19	12	12	8	21

WORLD SERIES RECORD

NOTES: Shares single-series record for most games won as relief pitcher—2 (1992). . . . Member of World Series championship teams (1992 and 1993).

Year Team (League)	W	L	Pct.	ERA	G	GS	CG	ShO	Sv.	IP	H	R	ER	BB	SO
1992—Toronto (A.L.)	2	0	1.000	0.00	4	0	0	0	0	3 1/3	1	0	0	1	6
1993—Toronto (A.L.)	1	0	1.000	1.93	4	0	0	0	2	4 2/3	3	2	1	0	7
World Series totals (2 years)	3	0	1.000	1.13	8	0	0	0	2	8	4	2	1	1	13

ALL-STAR GAME RECORD

Year League	W	L	Pct.	ERA	GS	CG	ShO	Sv.	IP	H	R	ER	BB	SO
1993—American	0	0	...	0.00	0	0	0	0	1	0	0	0	0	2

WARD, TURNER — OF — BREWERS

PERSONAL: Born April 11, 1965, in Orlando, Fla. . . . 6-2/198. . . . Bats both, throws right. . . . Full name: Turner Max Ward.
HIGH SCHOOL: Satsuma (Ala.).
COLLEGE: South Alabama.

TRANSACTIONS/CAREER NOTES: Selected by New York Yankees organization in 18th round of free-agent draft (June 2, 1986). . . . Traded by Yankees organization with C Joel Skinner to Cleveland Indians organization for OF Mel Hall (March 19, 1989). . . . On Gulf Coast Indians disabled list (April 7-July 24, 1989). . . . Traded by Indians with P Tom Candiotti to Toronto Blue Jays for P Denis Boucher, OF Glenallen Hill, OF Mark Whiten and a player to be named later (June 27, 1991); Indians acquired cash to complete deal (October 15, 1991). . . . On Toronto disabled list (August 2-September 1, 1993); included rehabilitation assignment to Knoxville (August 21-September 1). . . . Claimed on waivers by Milwaukee Brewers (November 24, 1993). . . . On Milwaukee disabled list (June 7-22, July 2-19 and July 24, 1995-remainder of season); included rehabilitation assignments to Beloit (July 17-19) and New Orleans (August 10-17 and August 31-September 5).
STATISTICAL NOTES: Led Pacific Coast League outfielders with 292 putouts and 308 total chances in 1990.

			BATTING											FIELDING			
Year Team (League)	**Pos.**	**G**	**AB**	**R**	**H**	**2B**	**3B**	**HR**	**RBI**	**Avg.**	**BB**	**SO**	**SB**	**PO**	**A**	**E**	**Avg.**
1986—Oneonta (NYP)	OF-1B-3B	63	221	42	62	4	1	1	19	.281	31	39	6	97	6	5	.954
1987—Fort Lauder. (FSL)	OF-3B	130	493	83	145	15	2	7	55	.294	64	83	25	332	11	8	.977
1988—Columbus (Int'l)	OF	134	490	55	123	24	1	7	50	.251	48	100	28	223	5	1	*.996
1989—GC Indians (GCL)■	DH	4	15	2	3	0	0	0	1	.200	2	2	1	...	...	...	...
—Cant./Akr. (East.)	OF	30	93	19	28	5	1	0	3	.301	15	16	1	2	0	0	1.000
1990—Colo. Springs (PCL)	OF-2B	133	495	89	148	24	9	6	65	.299	72	70	22	†292	7	9	.971
—Cleveland (A.L.)	OF-DH	14	46	10	16	2	1	1	10	.348	3	8	3	20	2	1	.957
1991—Cleveland (A.L.)	OF	40	100	11	23	7	0	0	5	.230	10	16	0	65	1	0	1.000
—Colo. Springs (PCL)	OF	14	51	5	10	1	1	1	3	.196	6	9	2	30	0	1	.968
—Toronto (A.L.)■	OF	8	13	1	4	0	0	0	2	.308	1	2	0	5	0	0	1.000
—Syracuse (Int'l)	OF	59	218	40	72	11	3	7	32	.330	47	22	9	136	5	0	1.000
1992—Toronto (A.L.)	OF	18	29	7	10	3	0	1	3	.345	4	4	0	18	1	0	1.000
—Syracuse (Int'l)	OF	81	280	41	67	10	2	10	29	.239	44	43	7	143	3	5	.967
1993—Toronto (A.L.)	OF-1B	72	167	20	32	4	2	4	28	.192	23	26	3	97	2	1	.990
—Knoxville (South.)	OF	7	23	6	6	2	0	0	2	.261	7	3	3	20	0	0	1.000
1994—Milwaukee (A.L.)■	OF-3B	102	367	55	85	15	2	9	45	.232	52	68	6	260	9	4	.985
1995—Milwaukee (A.L.)	OF-DH	44	129	19	34	3	1	4	16	.264	14	21	6	81	5	1	.989
—Beloit (Midwest)	OF	2	5	0	0	0	0	0	0	.000	3	1	0	1	0	0	1.000
—New Orleans (A.A.)	OF	11	33	3	8	1	1	1	3	.242	4	10	0	9	0	1	.900
Major league totals (6 years)		298	851	123	204	34	6	19	109	.240	107	145	18	546	20	7	.988

WARE, JEFF — P — BLUE JAYS

PERSONAL: Born November 11, 1970, in Norfolk, Va. . . . 6-3/195. . . . Throws right, bats right. . . . Full name: Jeffrey Allan Ware.
HIGH SCHOOL: First Colonial (Virginia Beach, Va.).
TRANSACTIONS/CAREER NOTES: Selected by Toronto Blue Jays organization in supplemental round ("sandwich pick" between first and second round, 35th pick overall) of free-agent draft (June 3, 1991); pick received as part of compensation for Chicago White Sox signing Type A free-agent OF/DH George Bell. . . . On Dunedin disabled list (April 8-1993 entire season). . . . On disabled list (April 7-July 9, 1994).

Year Team (League)	**W**	**L**	**Pct.**	**ERA**	**G**	**GS**	**CG**	**ShO**	**Sv.**	**IP**	**H**	**R**	**ER**	**BB**	**SO**
1992—Dunedin (Fla. St.)	5	3	.625	2.63	12	12	1	1	0	75 1/3	64	26	22	30	49
1993—							Did not play.								
1994—Knoxville (South.)	0	7	.000	6.87	10	10	0	0	0	38	50	32	29	16	31
1995—Syracuse (Int'l)	7	0	1.000	3.00	16	16	0	0	0	75	62	29	25	46	76
—Toronto (A.L.)	2	1	.667	5.47	5	5	0	0	0	26 1/3	28	18	16	21	18
Major league totals (1 year)	2	1	.667	5.47	5	5	0	0	0	26 1/3	28	18	16	21	18

WASDIN, JOHN — P — ATHLETICS

PERSONAL: Born August 5, 1972, in Fort Belvoir, Va. . . . 6-2/190. . . . Throws right, bats right. . . . Full name: John Truman Wasdin.
HIGH SCHOOL: Amos P. Godby (Tallahassee, Fla.).
COLLEGE: Florida State.
TRANSACTIONS/CAREER NOTES: Selected by New York Yankees organization in 41st round of free-agent draft (June 4, 1990); did not sign. . . . Selected by Oakland Athletics organization in first round (25th pick overall) of free-agent draft (June 3, 1993).
STATISTICAL NOTES: Led Pacific Coast League with 26 home runs allowed in 1995.

Year Team (League)	**W**	**L**	**Pct.**	**ERA**	**G**	**GS**	**CG**	**ShO**	**Sv.**	**IP**	**H**	**R**	**ER**	**BB**	**SO**
1993—Arizona A's (Ariz.)	0	0	...	3.00	1	1	0	0	0	3	3	1	1	0	1
—Madison (Midwest)	2	3	.400	1.86	9	9	0	0	0	48 1/3	32	11	10	9	40
—Modesto (Calif.)	0	3	.000	3.86	3	3	0	0	0	16 1/3	17	9	7	4	11
1994—Modesto (Calif.)	3	1	.750	1.69	6	4	0	0	0	26 2/3	17	6	5	5	30
—Huntsville (South.)	12	3	.800	3.43	21	21	0	0	0	141 2/3	126	61	54	29	108
1995—Edmonton (PCL)	12	8	.600	5.52	29	•28	2	1	0	174 1/3	193	117	107	38	111
—Oakland (A.L.)	1	1	.500	4.67	5	2	0	0	0	17 1/3	14	9	9	3	6
Major league totals (1 year)	1	1	.500	4.67	5	2	0	0	0	17 1/3	14	9	9	3	6

WASZGIS, B.J. — C — ORIOLES

PERSONAL: Born August 24, 1970, in Omaha, Neb. . . . 6-2/210. . . . Bats right, throws right. . . . Full name: Robert Michael Waszgis Jr. . . . Name pronounced WAZ-gis.
HIGH SCHOOL: South (Omaha, Neb.).
JUNIOR COLLEGE: Fort Scott (Kan.).
COLLEGE: McNeese State.
TRANSACTIONS/CAREER NOTES: Selected by Philadelphia Phillies organization in 21st round of free agent draft (June 4, 1990); did not sign. . . . Selected by Baltimore Orioles organization in 10th round of free-agent draft (June 3, 1991).
STATISTICAL NOTES: Led Carolina League catchers with 78 assists and 21 passed balls in 1994. . . . Led Eastern League catchers with 782 putouts, 16 errors, 23 passed balls and 887 total chances in 1995.

			BATTING											FIELDING			
Year Team (League)	**Pos.**	**G**	**AB**	**R**	**H**	**2B**	**3B**	**HR**	**RBI**	**Avg.**	**BB**	**SO**	**SB**	**PO**	**A**	**E**	**Avg.**
1991—Bluefield (Appal.)	C	12	35	8	8	1	0	3	8	.229	5	11	3	71	11	1	.988
1992—Kane Co. (Midw.)	C-1B	111	340	39	73	18	1	11	47	.215	54	94	3	517	71	14	.977

Year	Team (League)	Pos.	G	AB	R	H	2B	3B	HR	RBI	Avg.	BB	SO	SB	PO	A	E	Avg.
			BATTING												FIELDING			
1993—	Albany (S. Atl.)	C	86	300	45	92	25	3	8	52	.307	27	55	4	369	49	8	.981
	— Frederick (Caro.)	C	31	109	12	27	4	0	3	9	.248	9	30	1	159	23	2	.989
1994—	Frederick (Caro.)	C-1B	122	426	76	120	16	3	21	*100	.282	65	94	6	688	†84	16	.980
1995—	Bowie (Eastern)	C-1B	130	438	53	111	22	0	10	50	.253	70	91	2	†783	89	†16	.982

WATKINS, PAT — OF — REDS

PERSONAL: Born September 2, 1972, in Raleigh, N.C. . . . 6-2/185. . . . Bats right, throws right. . . . Full name: William Patrick Watkins.
HIGH SCHOOL: Garner (N.C.).
COLLEGE: East Carolina.
TRANSACTIONS/CAREER NOTES: Selected by Cincinnati Reds organization in supplemental round ("sandwich pick" between first and second round, 32nd pick overall) of free-agent draft (June 3, 1993); pick recieved as part of compensation for Houston Astros signing Type A free-agent P Greg Swindell.
STATISTICAL NOTES: Led Carolina League with 267 total bases in 1994. . . . Tied for Carolina League lead in double plays by outfielder with four in 1994.

Year	Team (League)	Pos.	G	AB	R	H	2B	3B	HR	RBI	Avg.	BB	SO	SB	PO	A	E	Avg.
			BATTING												FIELDING			
1993—	Billings (Pioneer)	OF	66	235	46	63	10	3	6	30	.268	22	44	15	123	5	2	.985
1994—	Winst.-Salem (Car.)	OF	132	*524	*107	*152	24	5	27	83	.290	62	84	31	262	13	7	.975
1995—	Winst.-Salem (Car.)	OF	27	107	14	22	3	1	4	13	.206	10	24	1	51	5	1	.982
	— Chatt. (South.)	OF	105	358	57	104	26	2	12	57	.291	33	53	5	185	8	8	.960

WATKINS, SCOTT — P — TWINS

PERSONAL: Born May 15, 1970, in Tulsa, Okla. . . . 6-3/180. . . . Throws left, bats left. . . . Full name: Scott Allen Watkins.
COLLEGE: Oklahoma State.
TRANSACTIONS/CAREER NOTES: Selected by Minnesota Twins organization in 23rd round of free-agent draft (June 1, 1992).

Year	Team (League)	W	L	Pct.	ERA	G	GS	CG	ShO	Sv.	IP	H	R	ER	BB	SO
1992—	Kenosha (Midwest)	2	5	.286	3.69	27	0	0	0	1	46 1/3	43	21	19	14	58
1993—	Fort Wayne (Midw.)	2	0	1.000	3.26	15	0	0	0	1	30 1/3	26	13	11	9	31
	— Fort Myers (Fla. St.)	2	2	.500	2.93	20	0	0	0	3	27 2/3	27	14	9	12	41
	— Nashville (South.)	0	1	.000	5.94	13	0	0	0	0	16 2/3	19	15	11	7	17
1994—	Nashville (South.)	1	0	1.000	4.61	11	0	0	0	3	13 2/3	13	9	7	4	11
	— Salt Lake (PCL)	2	6	.250	6.75	46	0	0	0	3	57 1/3	73	46	43	28	47
1995—	Salt Lake (PCL)	4	2	.667	2.80	45	0	0	0	*20	54 2/3	45	18	17	13	57
	— Minnesota (A.L.)	0	0	...	5.40	27	0	0	0	0	21 2/3	22	14	13	11	11
Major league totals (1 year)		0	0	...	5.40	27	0	0	0	0	21 2/3	22	14	13	11	11

WATSON, ALLEN — P — GIANTS

PERSONAL: Born November 18, 1970, in Jamaica, N.Y. . . . 6-3/190. . . . Throws left, bats left. . . . Full name: Allen Kenneth Watson.
HIGH SCHOOL: Christ the King (Queens, N.Y.).
COLLEGE: New York State Institute of Technology.
TRANSACTIONS/CAREER NOTES: Selected by St. Louis Cardinals organization in first round (21st pick overall) of free-agent draft (June 3, 1991); pick received as part of compensation for Toronto Blue Jays signing Type A free-agent P Ken Dayley. . . . On Savannah disabled list (August 19, 1991-remainder of season). . . . On suspended list (June 25-July 3, 1994). . . . On St. Louis disabled list (June 7-July 8, 1995); included rehabilitation assignments to Arkansas (June 21-26) and Louisville (June 26-July 8). . . . Traded by Cardinals with P Rich DeLucia and P Doug Creek to San Francisco Giants for SS Royce Clayton and a player to be named later (December 14, 1995); Cardinals acquired 2B Chris Wimmer to complete deal (January 16, 1996).

Year	Team (League)	W	L	Pct.	ERA	G	GS	CG	ShO	Sv.	IP	H	R	ER	BB	SO
1991—	Hamilton (NYP)	1	1	.500	2.52	8	8	0	0	0	39 1/3	22	15	11	17	46
	— Savannah (S. Atl.)	1	1	.500	3.95	3	3	0	0	0	13 2/3	16	7	6	8	12
1992—	St. Petersburg (FSL)	5	4	.556	1.91	14	14	2	0	0	89 2/3	81	31	19	18	80
	— Arkansas (Texas)	8	5	.615	2.15	14	14	3	1	0	96 1/3	77	24	23	23	93
	— Louisville (A.A.)	1	0	1.000	1.46	2	2	0	0	0	12 1/3	8	4	2	5	9
1993—	Louisville (A.A.)	5	4	.556	2.91	17	17	2	0	0	120 2/3	101	46	39	31	86
	— St. Louis (N.L.)	6	7	.462	4.60	16	15	0	0	0	86	90	53	44	28	49
1994—	St. Louis (N.L.)	6	5	.545	5.52	22	22	0	0	0	115 2/3	130	73	71	53	74
1995—	St. Louis (N.L.)	7	9	.438	4.96	21	19	0	0	0	114 1/3	126	68	63	41	49
	— Louisville (A.A.)	2	2	.500	2.63	4	4	1	1	0	24	20	10	7	6	19
	— Arkansas (Texas)	1	0	1.000	0.00	1	1	0	0	0	5	4	1	0	0	7
Major league totals (3 years)		19	21	.475	5.07	59	56	0	0	0	316	346	194	178	122	172

WATTS, BRANDON — P — DODGERS

PERSONAL: Born September 13, 1972, in Ruston, La. . . . 6-3/195. . . . Throws left, bats left.
HIGH SCHOOL: Ruston (La.).
TRANSACTIONS/CAREER NOTES: Selected by Los Angeles Dodgers organization in seventh round of free-agent draft (June 3, 1991). . . . On Yakima suspended list (July 10, 1993-remainder of season). . . . On Yakima disabled list (June 16, 1994-remainder of season). . . . On disabled list (April 14-June 14, 1995).

Year	Team (League)	W	L	Pct.	ERA	G	GS	CG	ShO	Sv.	IP	H	R	ER	BB	SO
1991—	GC Dodgers (GCL)	1	3	.250	4.64	12	5	0	0	1	33	28	20	17	25	30
1992—	GC Dodgers (GCL)	2	1	.667	3.00	4	4	1	1	0	24	15	9	8	8	19
	— Great Falls (Pio.)	1	1	.500	5.09	13	0	0	0	1	17 2/3	12	11	10	14	15
1993—	Vero Beach (FSL)	0	1	.000	4.08	8	0	0	0	0	17 2/3	14	11	8	16	12
	— Yakima (N'west)	0	2	.000	8.00	2	2	0	0	0	9	8	8	8	7	12
1994—								Did not play.								
1995—	Vero Beach (FSL)	5	3	.625	4.04	13	8	0	0	0	49	46	29	22	22	42

WEATHERS, DAVE — P — MARLINS

PERSONAL: Born September 25, 1969, in Lawrenceburg, Tenn. . . . 6-3/220. . . . Throws right, bats right. . . . Full name: John David Weathers.
HIGH SCHOOL: Loretto (Tenn.).
JUNIOR COLLEGE: Motlow State Community College (Tenn.).
TRANSACTIONS/CAREER NOTES: Selected by Toronto Blue Jays organization in third round of free-agent draft (June 1, 1988). . . . On Syracuse disabled list (May 11-July 31, 1992). . . . Selected by Florida Marlins in second round (29th pick overall) of expansion draft (November 17, 1992). . . . On Florida disabled list (June 26-July 13, 1995); included rehabilitation assignment to Brevard County (July 4-10).
MISCELLANEOUS: Appeared in two games as pinch-runner (1994).

Year	Team (League)	W	L	Pct.	ERA	G	GS	CG	ShO	Sv.	IP	H	R	ER	BB	SO
1988	St. Cathar. (NYP)	4	4	.500	3.02	15	12	0	0	0	62 2/3	58	30	21	26	36
1989	Myrtle Beach (SAL)	11	•13	.458	3.86	31	*31	2	0	0	172 2/3	163	99	74	86	111
1990	Dunedin (Fla. St.)	10	7	.588	3.70	27	•27	2	0	0	158	158	82	65	59	96
1991	Knoxville (South.)	10	7	.588	2.45	24	22	5	2	0	139 1/3	121	51	38	49	114
	—Toronto (A.L.)	1	0	1.000	4.91	15	0	0	0	0	14 2/3	15	9	8	17	13
1992	Syracuse (Int'l)	1	4	.200	4.66	12	10	0	0	0	48 1/3	48	29	25	21	30
	—Toronto (A.L.)	0	0	. . .	8.10	2	0	0	0	0	3 1/3	5	3	3	2	3
1993	Edmonton (PCL)■	11	4	•.733	3.83	22	22	3	1	0	141	150	77	60	47	117
	—Florida (N.L.)	2	3	.400	5.12	14	6	0	0	0	45 2/3	57	26	26	13	34
1994	Florida (N.L.)	8	12	.400	5.27	24	24	0	0	0	135	166	87	79	59	72
1995	Florida (N.L.)	4	5	.444	5.98	28	15	0	0	0	90 1/3	104	68	60	52	60
	—Brevard Co. (FSL)	0	0	. . .	0.00	1	1	0	0	0	4	4	0	0	1	3
A.L. totals (2 years)		1	0	1.000	5.50	17	0	0	0	0	18	20	12	11	19	16
N.L. totals (3 years)		14	20	.412	5.48	66	45	0	0	0	271	327	181	165	124	166
Major league totals (5 years)		15	20	.429	5.48	83	45	0	0	0	289	347	193	176	143	182

WEAVER, ERIC — P — DODGERS

PERSONAL: Born August 4, 1973, in Springfield, Ill. . . . 6-5/230. . . . Throws right, bats right. . . . Full name: James Eric Weaver.
HIGH SCHOOL: Illiopolis (Ill.).
TRANSACTIONS/CAREER NOTES: Signed as non-drafted free agent by Los Angeles Dodgers organization (July 22, 1991). . . . On disabled list (May 1-August 31, 1994).
STATISTICAL NOTES: Pitched 2-1 no-hit victory against Fort Lauderdale (July 17, 1992, first game).

Year	Team (League)	W	L	Pct.	ERA	G	GS	CG	ShO	Sv.	IP	H	R	ER	BB	SO
1992	Vero Beach (FSL)	4	11	.267	4.12	19	18	1	0	0	89 2/3	73	52	41	57	73
1993	Bakersfield (Calif.)	6	11	.353	4.28	28	•27	0	0	0	157 2/3	135	89	75	*118	110
1994	Vero Beach (FSL)	1	3	.250	6.75	7	7	0	0	0	24	28	20	18	9	22
1995	San Antonio (Tex.)	8	11	.421	4.07	27	26	1	0	0	141 2/3	147	83	64	72	105

WEBER, NEIL — P — EXPOS

PERSONAL: Born December 6, 1972, in Newport Beach, Calif. . . . 6-5/215. . . . Throws left, bats left. . . . Full name: Neil Aaron Weber.
HIGH SCHOOL: Corona Del Mar (Newport Beach, Calif.).
JUNIOR COLLEGE: Cuesta College (Calif.).
TRANSACTIONS/CAREER NOTES: Selected by Montreal Expos organization in eighth round of free-agent draft (June 3, 1993).

Year	Team (League)	W	L	Pct.	ERA	G	GS	CG	ShO	Sv.	IP	H	R	ER	BB	SO
1993	Jamestown (NYP)	6	5	.545	2.77	16	•16	2	•1	0	94 1/3	84	46	29	36	80
1994	WP Beach (FSL)	9	7	.563	3.20	25	24	1	0	0	135	113	58	48	62	134
1995	Harrisburg (East.)	6	11	.353	5.01	28	28	0	0	0	152 2/3	157	98	*85	*90	119

WEBSTER, LENNY — C — PHILLIES

PERSONAL: Born February 10, 1965, in New Orleans. . . . 5-9/202. . . . Bats right, throws right. . . . Full name: Leonard Irell Webster.
HIGH SCHOOL: Lutcher (La.).
COLLEGE: Grambling State.
TRANSACTIONS/CAREER NOTES: Selected by Minnesota Twins organization in 16th round of free-agent draft (June 7, 1982); did not sign. . . . Selected by Twins organization in 21st round of free-agent draft (June 3, 1985). . . . Traded by Twins to Montreal Expos organization for a player to be named later (March 14, 1994). . . . Granted free agency (December 23, 1994). . . . Signed by Scranton, Philadelphia Phillies organization (April 7, 1995).
HONORS: Named Midwest League Most Valuable Player (1988).

			BATTING											FIELDING			
Year	Team (League)	Pos.	G	AB	R	H	2B	3B	HR	RBI	Avg.	BB	SO	SB	PO	A	E	Avg.
1986	Kenosha (Midwest)	C	22	65	2	10	2	0	0	8	.154	10	12	0	87	9	0	1.000
	—Elizabeth. (Appal.)	C	48	152	29	35	4	0	3	14	.230	22	21	1	88	11	3	.971
1987	Kenosha (Midwest)	C	52	140	17	35	7	0	3	17	.250	17	20	2	228	29	5	.981
1988	Kenosha (Midwest)	C	129	465	82	134	23	2	11	87	.288	71	47	3	606	96	14	.980
1989	Visalia (California)	C	63	231	36	62	7	0	5	39	.268	27	27	2	352	57	4	.990
	—Orlando (Southern)	C	59	191	29	45	7	0	2	17	.236	44	20	2	293	46	4	.988
	—Minnesota (A.L.)	C	14	20	3	6	2	0	0	1	.300	3	2	0	32	0	0	1.000
1990	Orlando (Southern)	C	126	455	69	119	31	0	8	71	.262	68	57	0	629	70	9	.987
	—Minnesota (A.L.)	C	2	6	1	2	1	0	0	0	.333	1	1	0	9	0	0	1.000
1991	Portland (PCL)	C	87	325	43	82	18	0	7	34	.252	24	32	1	477	65	6	*.989
	—Minnesota (A.L.)	C	18	34	7	10	1	0	3	8	.294	6	10	0	61	10	1	.986
1992	Minnesota (A.L.)	C-DH	53	118	10	33	10	1	1	13	.280	9	11	0	190	11	1	.995
1993	Minnesota (A.L.)	C-DH	49	106	14	21	2	0	1	8	.198	11	8	1	177	13	0	1.000
1994	Montreal (N.L.)■	C	57	143	13	39	10	0	5	23	.273	16	24	0	237	19	1	.996

Year	Team (League)	Pos.	G	AB	R	H	2B	3B	HR	RBI	Avg.	BB	SO	SB	PO	A	E	Avg.
				BATTING											FIELDING			
1995—	Philadelphia (N.L.)■ ..	C	49	150	18	40	9	0	4	14	.267	16	27	0	274	18	3	.990
American League totals (5 years)			136	284	35	72	16	1	5	30	.254	30	32	1	469	34	2	.996
National League totals (2 years)			106	293	31	79	19	0	9	37	.270	32	51	0	511	37	4	.993
Major league totals (7 years)			242	577	66	151	35	1	14	67	.262	62	83	1	980	71	6	.994

WEBSTER, MITCH OF

PERSONAL: Born May 16, 1959, in Larned, Kan. . . . 6-1/191. . . . Bats both, throws left. . . . Full name: Mitchell Dean Webster.

HIGH SCHOOL: Larned (Kan.).

TRANSACTIONS/CAREER NOTES: Selected by Los Angeles Dodgers organization in 23rd round of free-agent draft (June 7, 1977). . . . Selected by Syracuse, Toronto Blue Jays organization from Dodgers organization in Rule 5 minor league draft (December 4, 1979). . . . Traded by Blue Jays organization to Montreal Expos for a player to be named later (June 22, 1985); Blue Jays organization acquired P Cliff Young to complete deal (September 10, 1985). . . . Traded by Expos to Chicago Cubs for OF Dave Martinez (July 14, 1988). . . . On disabled list (May 14-29, 1989). . . . Traded by Cubs to Cleveland Indians for OF Dave Clark (November 20, 1989). . . . Traded by Indians to Pittsburgh Pirates for P Mike York (May 16, 1991). . . . Traded by Pirates to Dodgers for OF Jose Gonzales (July 3, 1991). . . . Granted free agency (October 30, 1991). . . . Re-signed by Dodgers (December 6, 1991). . . . Granted free agency (October 27, 1992). . . . Re-signed by Dodgers (December 4, 1992). . . . Granted free agency (October 24, 1994). . . . Re-signed by Albuquerque, Dodgers organization (April 7, 1995). . . . On disabled list (August 15-September 5, 1995). . . . Granted free agency (October 14, 1995).

RECORDS: Shares major league single-season record for fewest double plays by outfielder (150 or more games)—0 (1987).

STATISTICAL NOTES: Led International League outfielders with 385 total chances and five double plays in 1982. . . . Career major league grand slams: 3.

Year	Team (League)	Pos.	G	AB	R	H	2B	3B	HR	RBI	Avg.	BB	SO	SB	PO	A	E	Avg.
				BATTING											FIELDING			
1977—	Lethbridge (Pio.)	OF	55	168	45	59	4	0	0	31	.351	36	21	13	81	3	8	.913
1978—	Clinton (Midwest).......	OF	45	157	18	38	3	1	0	9	.242	19	26	8	92	6	7	.933
—	Lethbridge (Pio.)	OF	55	182	58	58	5	1	0	18	.319	45	22	18	77	3	0	*1.000
1979—	Clinton (Midwest).......	OF	123	473	95	*154	17	7	2	40	*.326	58	54	10	*272	10	10	.966
1980—	Syracuse (Int'l)■........	OF	49	161	23	35	4	2	1	12	.217	8	18	4	112	3	5	.958
—	Kinston (Carolina)	OF	65	258	43	76	7	3	0	28	.295	21	21	16	129	8	5	.965
1981—	Knoxville (South.).......	OF	140	554	89	163	26	6	1	42	.294	45	56	52	317	7	10	.970
1982—	Syracuse (Int'l)...........	OF	137	513	95	144	21	7	13	68	.281	67	55	12	*367	16	2	*.995
1983—	Syracuse (Int'l)...........	OF-1B	135	462	77	120	26	8	9	45	.260	68	60	21	266	16	10	.966
—	Toronto (A.L.).............	OF-DH	11	11	2	2	0	0	0	0	.182	1	1	0	5	0	0	1.000
1984—	Toronto (A.L.).............	OF-DH-1B	26	22	9	5	2	1	0	4	.227	1	7	0	16	0	2	.889
—	Syracuse (Int'l)...........	OF	95	360	60	108	22	5	3	25	.300	51	36	16	239	7	7	.972
1985—	Toronto (A.L.).............	OF-DH	4	1	0	0	0	0	0	0	.000	0	0	0	0	0	0	...
—	Syracuse (Int'l)...........	OF	47	189	32	52	5	3	3	23	.275	20	24	5	83	10	1	.989
—	Montreal (N.L.)■........	OF	74	212	32	58	8	2	11	30	.274	20	33	15	133	3	1	.993
1986—	Montreal (N.L.)...........	OF	151	576	89	167	31	*13	8	49	.290	57	78	36	325	12	8	.977
1987—	Montreal (N.L.)...........	OF	156	588	101	165	30	8	15	63	.281	70	95	33	266	8	5	.982
1988—	Montreal (N.L.)...........	OF	81	259	33	66	5	2	2	13	.255	36	37	12	153	2	1	.994
—	Chicago (N.L.)■.........	OF	70	264	36	70	11	6	4	26	.265	19	50	10	169	1	5	.971
1989—	Chicago (N.L.)............	OF	98	272	40	70	12	4	3	19	.257	30	55	14	161	3	6	.965
1990—	Cleveland (A.L.)■.......	OF-1B-DH	128	437	58	110	20	6	12	55	.252	20	61	22	345	3	5	.986
1991—	Cleveland (A.L.)..........	OF	13	32	2	4	0	0	0	0	.125	3	9	2	24	0	0	1.000
—	Pittsburgh (N.L.)■.....	OF	36	97	9	17	3	4	1	0	.175	9	31	0	50	2	2	.963
—	Los Angeles (N.L.)■ ..	OF-1B	58	74	12	21	5	1	1	10	.284	9	21	0	37	0	0	1.000
1992—	Los Angeles (N.L.)	OF	135	262	33	70	12	5	6	35	.267	27	49	11	130	0	3	.977
1993—	Los Angeles (N.L.)	OF	88	172	26	42	6	2	2	14	.244	11	24	4	75	1	4	.950
1994—	Los Angeles (N.L.)	OF	82	84	16	23	4	0	4	12	.274	8	13	1	29	0	0	1.000
1995—	Los Angeles (N.L.)	OF	54	56	6	10	1	1	1	3	.179	4	14	0	12	0	0	1.000
American League totals (5 years)			182	503	71	121	22	7	12	59	.241	25	78	24	390	3	7	.983
National League totals (10 years)			1083	2916	433	779	128	48	58	274	.267	300	500	136	1540	32	35	.978
Major league totals (13 years)			1265	3419	504	900	150	55	70	333	.263	325	578	160	1930	35	42	.979

DIVISION SERIES RECORD

Year	Team (League)	Pos.	G	AB	R	H	2B	3B	HR	RBI	Avg.	BB	SO	SB	PO	A	E	Avg.
				BATTING											FIELDING			
1995—	Los Angeles (N.L.)	PH	2	2	0	0	0	0	0	0	.000	0	0	0	...	...	...	...

CHAMPIONSHIP SERIES RECORD

Year	Team (League)	Pos.	G	AB	R	H	2B	3B	HR	RBI	Avg.	BB	SO	SB	PO	A	E	Avg.
				BATTING											FIELDING			
1989—	Chicago (N.L.)...........	OF-PH	3	3	0	1	0	0	0	0	.333	0	0	0	0	0	0	...

WEGER, WES SS/2B BREWERS

PERSONAL: Born October 3, 1970, in Madison, Fla. . . . 6-0/176. . . . Bats right, throws right. . . . Full name: Wesley Wayne Weger.

HIGH SCHOOL: Lake Mary (Fla.).

COLLEGE: Stetson (Fla.).

TRANSACTIONS/CAREER NOTES: Selected by Milwaukee Brewers organization in ninth round of free-agent draft (June 1, 1992). . . . On El Paso disabled list (April 7, 1994-entire season).

STATISTICAL NOTES: Led Texas League shortstops with 592 total chances in 1993.

Year	Team (League)	Pos.	G	AB	R	H	2B	3B	HR	RBI	Avg.	BB	SO	SB	PO	A	E	Avg.
				BATTING											FIELDING			
1992—	Helena (Pioneer)	SS-2B	36	133	36	57	9	1	5	31	.429	22	9	7	46	134	8	.957
—	Stockton (Calif.)	SS	32	120	26	31	7	2	1	18	.258	20	17	3	55	96	8	.950

Year	Team (League)	Pos.	G	AB	R	H	2B	3B	HR	RBI	Avg.	BB	SO	SB	PO	A	E	Avg.
						BATTING									FIELDING			
1993—	El Paso (Texas)	SS	123	471	69	137	24	5	5	53	.291	31	44	9	*205	*349	*38	.936
1994—									Did not play.									
1995—	El Paso (Texas)	SS-3B	45	160	22	41	9	2	0	19	.256	10	14	1	62	103	12	.932
	—New Orleans (A.A.)	2B-3B-SS	64	234	28	67	16	0	2	24	.286	10	31	0	124	162	9	.969

WEGMAN, BILL P

PERSONAL: Born December 19, 1962, in Cincinnati. . . . 6-5/235. . . . Throws right, bats right. . . . Full name: William Edward Wegman.

HIGH SCHOOL: Oak Hill (Cincinnati).

TRANSACTIONS/CAREER NOTES: Selected by Milwaukee Brewers organization in fifth round of free-agent draft (June 8, 1981). . . . On Vancouver disabled list (June 18-August 11, 1984). . . . On disabled list (August 7-22, 1987; May 21-June 7, 1988; and June 1, 1989-remainder of season). . . . On Milwaukee disabled list (June 3, 1990-remainder of season); included rehabilitation assignment to Beloit (June 27). . . . On Milwaukee disabled list (April 5-May 3, 1991); included rehabilitation assignments to Beloit (April 13-30) and Denver (April 30-May 3). . . . On disabled list (July 7-September 14, 1993 and May 4-30, 1994). . . . Granted free agency (November 3, 1995).

STATISTICAL NOTES: Led California League with five balks in 1983. . . . Led Pacific Coast League with 21 home runs allowed in 1985.

MISCELLANEOUS: Appeared in two games as pinch-runner (1986). . . . Appeared in one game as pinch-runner (1988).

Year	Team (League)	W	L	Pct.	ERA	G	GS	CG	ShO	Sv.	IP	H	R	ER	BB	SO
1981—	Butte (Pioneer)	6	5	.545	4.17	14	13	4	0	0	82	94	51	38	44	47
1982—	Beloit (Midwest)	12	6	.667	2.81	25	25	10	1	0	179 2/3	176	77	56	38	129
1983—	Stockton (Calif.)	*16	5	.762	*1.30	24	23	•15	•4	0	186 2/3	149	33	27	45	135
1984—	El Paso (Texas)	4	5	.444	2.67	10	10	4	0	0	64	62	25	19	15	42
	—Vancouver (PCL)	0	3	.000	1.95	6	3	0	0	1	27 2/3	30	11	6	8	16
1985—	Vancouver (PCL)	10	11	.476	4.02	28	28	8	2	0	188	187	93	84	52	113
	—Milwaukee (A.L.)	2	0	1.000	3.57	3	3	0	0	0	17 2/3	17	8	7	3	6
1986—	Milwaukee (A.L.)	5	12	.294	5.13	35	32	2	0	0	198 1/3	217	120	113	43	82
1987—	Milwaukee (A.L.)	12	11	.522	4.24	34	33	7	0	0	225	229	113	106	53	102
1988—	Milwaukee (A.L.)	13	13	.500	4.12	32	31	4	1	0	199	207	104	91	50	84
1989—	Milwaukee (A.L.)	2	6	.250	6.71	11	8	0	0	0	51	69	44	38	21	27
1990—	Denver (Am. Assoc.)	1	0	1.000	3.29	3	3	0	0	0	13 2/3	10	5	5	7	14
	—Milwaukee (A.L.)	2	2	.500	4.85	8	5	1	1	0	29 2/3	37	21	16	6	20
	—Beloit (Midwest)	0	0	...	0.00	1	1	0	0	0	2	1	0	0	1	2
1991—	Beloit (Midwest)	0	2	.000	1.64	3	3	0	0	0	11	11	5	2	1	12
	—Denver (Am. Assoc.)	0	0	...	2.57	1	1	0	0	0	7	6	2	2	1	1
	—Milwaukee (A.L.)	15	7	.682	2.84	28	28	7	2	0	193 1/3	176	76	61	40	89
1992—	Milwaukee (A.L.)	13	14	.481	3.20	35	35	7	0	0	261 2/3	251	104	93	55	127
1993—	Milwaukee (A.L.)	4	14	.222	4.48	20	18	5	0	0	120 2/3	135	70	60	34	50
1994—	Milwaukee (A.L.)	8	4	.667	4.51	19	19	0	0	0	115 2/3	140	64	58	26	59
1995—	Milwaukee (A.L.)	5	7	.417	5.35	37	4	0	0	2	70 2/3	89	45	42	21	50
Major league totals (11 years)		81	90	.474	4.16	262	216	33	4	2	1482 2/3	1567	769	685	352	696

WEHNER, JOHN 3B/OF PIRATES

PERSONAL: Born June 29, 1967, in Pittsburgh. . . . 6-3/206. . . . Bats right, throws right. . . . Full name: John Paul Wehner. . . . Name pronounced WAY-ner.

HIGH SCHOOL: Carrick (Pittsburgh).

COLLEGE: Indiana.

TRANSACTIONS/CAREER NOTES: Selected by Pittsburgh Pirates organization in seventh round of free-agent draft (June 1, 1988). . . . On Pittsburgh disabled list (August 29-October 7, 1991 and July 20, 1994-remainder of season).

STATISTICAL NOTES: Led New York-Pennsylvania League third basemen with 219 total chances and 14 double plays in 1988. . . . Led Carolina League third basemen with 403 total chances and tied for lead with 24 double plays in 1989. . . . Led Eastern League third basemen with 476 total chances and 40 double plays in 1990.

Year	Team (League)	Pos.	G	AB	R	H	2B	3B	HR	RBI	Avg.	BB	SO	SB	PO	A	E	Avg.
						BATTING									FIELDING			
1988—	Watertown (NYP)	3B	70	265	41	73	6	0	3	31	.275	21	39	18	*65	137	17	.922
1989—	Salem (Carolina)	3B	*137	*515	69	*155	32	6	14	73	.301	42	81	21	*89	*278	36	.911
1990—	Harrisburg (East.)	3B	•138	*511	71	147	27	1	4	62	.288	40	51	24	*109	*317	*50	.895
1991—	Carolina (South.)	3B-1B	61	234	30	62	5	1	3	21	.265	24	32	17	182	134	10	.969
	—Buffalo (A.A.)	3B	31	112	18	34	9	2	1	15	.304	14	12	6	30	69	8	.925
	—Pittsburgh (N.L.)	3B	37	106	15	36	7	0	0	7	.340	7	17	3	23	65	6	.936
1992—	Buffalo (A.A.)	2B-1B-3B	60	223	37	60	13	2	7	27	.269	29	30	10	226	122	7	.980
	—Pittsburgh (N.L.)	3B-1B-2B	55	123	11	22	6	0	0	4	.179	12	22	3	96	64	4	.976
1993—	Pittsburgh (N.L.)	OF-3B-2B	29	35	3	5	0	0	0	0	.143	6	10	0	17	8	0	1.000
	—Buffalo (A.A.)	3B-2B-OF	89	330	61	83	22	2	7	34	.252	40	53	17	133	256	17	.958
1994—	Buffalo (A.A.)	OF-3B-2B	88	330	52	100	19	3	7	44	.303	32	36	21	131	113	11	.957
	—Pittsburgh (N.L.)	3B	2	4	1	1	1	0	0	3	.250	0	1	0	0	2	0	1.000
1995—	Calgary (PCL)	3B-2B-OF	40	158	30	52	12	2	4	24	.329	12	16	8	36	98	12	.918
	—Pittsburgh (N.L.)	0-3-C-S	52	107	13	33	0	3	0	5	.308	10	17	3	35	29	0	1.000
Major league totals (5 years)			175	375	43	97	14	3	0	19	.259	35	67	9	171	168	10	.971

CHAMPIONSHIP SERIES RECORD

Year	Team (League)	Pos.	G	AB	R	H	2B	3B	HR	RBI	Avg.	BB	SO	SB	PO	A	E	Avg.
						BATTING									FIELDING			
1992—	Pittsburgh (N.L.)	PH	2	2	0	0	0	0	0	0	.000	0	2	0	...	...	...	...

WEISS, WALT SS ROCKIES

PERSONAL: Born November 28, 1963, in Tuxedo, N.Y. . . . 6-0/178. . . . Bats both, throws right. . . . Full name: Walter William Weiss Jr.

HIGH SCHOOL: Suffern (N.Y.).

COLLEGE: North Carolina.

TRANSACTIONS/CAREER NOTES: Selected by Baltimore Orioles organization in 10th round of free-agent draft (June 7, 1982); did not sign. . . . Selected by Oakland Athletics organization in first round (11th pick overall) of free-agent draft (June 3, 1985). . . . On Oakland disabled list (May 18-July 31, 1989); included rehabilitation assignments to Tacoma (July 18-25) and Modesto (July 26-31). . . . On disabled list (August 23-September 7, 1990; April 15-30 and June 7, 1991-remainder of season). . . . On Oakland disabled list (March 30-June 3, 1992); included rehabilitation assignment to Tacoma (May 26-June 3). . . . Traded by A's to Florida Marlins for C Eric Helfand and a player to be named later (November 17, 1992); A's acquired P Scott Baker from Marlins to complete deal (November 20, 1992). . . . Granted free agency (October 25, 1993). . . . Signed by Colorado Rockies (January 7, 1994). . . . Granted free agency (November 3, 1995). . . . Re-signed by Rockies (December 6, 1995).

HONORS: Named A.L. Rookie Player of the Year by The Sporting News (1988). . . . Named A.L. Rookie of the Year by Baseball Writers' Association of America (1988).

STATISTICAL NOTES: Led N.L. shortstops with 99 double plays in 1995. . . . Career major league grand slams: 1.

			BATTING												FIELDING			
Year	Team (League)	Pos.	G	AB	R	H	2B	3B	HR	RBI	Avg.	BB	SO	SB	PO	A	E	Avg.
1985	—Pocatello (Pioneer)	SS	40	158	19	49	9	3	0	21	.310	12	18	6	51	126	11	.941
	—Modesto (Calif.)	SS	30	122	17	24	4	1	0	7	.197	12	20	3	36	97	7	.950
1986	—Madison (Midwest)	SS	84	322	50	97	15	5	2	54	.301	33	66	12	143	251	20	.952
	—Huntsville (South.)	SS	46	160	19	40	2	1	0	13	.250	11	39	5	72	142	11	.951
1987	—Huntsville (South.)	SS	91	337	43	96	16	2	1	32	.285	47	67	23	152	259	17	.960
	—Oakland (A.L.)	SS-DH	16	26	3	12	4	0	0	1	.462	2	2	1	8	30	1	.974
	—Tacoma (PCL)	SS	46	179	35	47	4	3	0	17	.263	28	31	8	76	140	11	.952
1988	—Oakland (A.L.)	SS	147	452	44	113	17	3	3	39	.250	35	56	4	254	431	15	.979
1989	—Oakland (A.L.)	SS	84	236	30	55	11	0	3	21	.233	21	39	6	106	195	15	.953
	—Tacoma (PCL)	SS	2	9	1	1	1	0	0	1	.111	0	0	0	0	3	1	.750
	—Modesto (Calif.)	SS	5	8	1	3	0	0	0	1	.375	4	1	0	6	9	0	1.000
1990	—Oakland (A.L.)	SS	138	445	50	118	17	1	2	35	.265	46	53	9	194	373	12	.979
1991	—Oakland (A.L.)	SS	40	133	15	30	6	1	0	13	.226	12	14	6	64	99	5	.970
1992	—Tacoma (PCL)	SS	4	13	2	3	1	0	0	3	.231	2	1	0	8	14	1	.957
	—Oakland (A.L.)	SS	103	316	36	67	5	2	0	21	.212	43	39	6	144	270	19	.956
1993	—Florida (N.L.)■	SS	158	500	50	133	14	2	1	39	.266	79	73	7	229	406	15	.977
1994	—Colorado (N.L.)■	SS	110	423	58	106	11	4	1	32	.251	56	58	12	157	318	13	.973
1995	—Colorado (N.L.)	SS	137	427	65	111	17	3	1	25	.260	98	57	15	201	406	16	.974
American League totals (6 years)			528	1608	178	395	60	7	8	130	.246	159	203	32	770	1398	67	.970
National League totals (3 years)			405	1350	173	350	42	9	3	96	.259	233	188	34	587	1130	44	.975
Major league totals (9 years)			933	2958	351	745	102	16	11	226	.252	392	391	66	1357	2528	111	.972

DIVISION SERIES RECORD

			BATTING												FIELDING			
Year	Team (League)	Pos.	G	AB	R	H	2B	3B	HR	RBI	Avg.	BB	SO	SB	PO	A	E	Avg.
1995	—Colorado (N.L.)	SS	4	12	1	2	0	0	0	0	.167	3	3	1	6	12	0	1.000

CHAMPIONSHIP SERIES RECORD

			BATTING												FIELDING			
Year	Team (League)	Pos.	G	AB	R	H	2B	3B	HR	RBI	Avg.	BB	SO	SB	PO	A	E	Avg.
1988	—Oakland (A.L.)	SS	4	15	2	5	2	0	0	2	.333	0	4	0	7	10	0	1.000
1989	—Oakland (A.L.)	SS-PR	4	9	2	1	1	0	0	0	.111	1	1	1	5	9	0	1.000
1990	—Oakland (A.L.)	SS	2	7	2	0	0	0	0	0	.000	2	2	0	2	7	1	.900
1992	—Oakland (A.L.)	SS	3	6	1	1	0	0	0	0	.167	2	1	2	5	6	0	1.000
Championship series totals (4 years)			13	37	7	7	3	0	0	2	.189	5	8	3	19	32	1	.981

WORLD SERIES RECORD

NOTES: Member of World Series championship team (1989).

			BATTING												FIELDING			
Year	Team (League)	Pos.	G	AB	R	H	2B	3B	HR	RBI	Avg.	BB	SO	SB	PO	A	E	Avg.
1988	—Oakland (A.L.)	SS	5	16	1	1	0	0	0	0	.063	0	1	0	5	11	1	.941
1989	—Oakland (A.L.)	SS	4	15	3	2	0	0	1	1	.133	2	2	0	7	8	0	1.000
World Series totals (2 years)			9	31	4	3	0	0	1	1	.097	2	3	0	12	19	1	.969

WELLS, BOB — P — MARINERS

PERSONAL: Born November 1, 1966, in Yakima, Wash. . . . 6-0/180. . . . Throws right, bats right. . . . Full name: Robert Lee Wells.

HIGH SCHOOL: Eisenhower (Yakima, Wash.).

JUNIOR COLLEGE: Spokane Falls Community College (Wash.).

TRANSACTIONS/CAREER NOTES: Signed as non-drafted free agent by Philadelphia Phillies organization (August 18, 1988). . . . On Reading disabled list (July 21, 1991-remainder of season). . . . On Scranton/Wilkes-Barre disabled list (April 9-28, 1992). . . . On Reading disabled list (June 9, 1992-remainder of season and April 8-June 13, 1993). . . . Claimed on waivers by Seattle Mariners (June 30, 1994).

Year	Team (League)	W	L	Pct.	ERA	G	GS	CG	ShO	Sv.	IP	H	R	ER	BB	SO
1989	—Martinsville (App.)	0	0	...	4.50	4	0	0	0	0	6	8	5	3	2	3
1990	—Spartanburg (SAL)	5	8	.385	2.87	20	19	2	0	0	113	94	47	36	40	73
	—Clearwater (Fla. St.)	0	2	.000	4.91	6	1	0	0	1	14 2/3	17	9	8	6	11
1991	—Clearwater (Fla. St.)	7	2	.778	3.11	24	9	1	0	0	75 1/3	63	27	26	19	66
	—Reading (Eastern)	1	0	1.000	3.60	1	1	0	0	0	5	4	2	2	1	3
1992	—Clearwater (Fla. St.)	1	0	1.000	3.86	9	0	0	0	5	9 1/3	10	4	4	3	9
	—Reading (Eastern)	0	1	.000	1.17	3	3	0	0	0	15 1/3	12	2	2	5	11
1993	—Clearwater (Fla. St.)	1	0	1.000	0.98	12	1	0	0	2	27 2/3	23	5	3	6	24
	—Scran./W.B. (Int'l)	1	1	.500	2.79	11	0	0	0	0	19 1/3	19	7	6	5	8
1994	—Reading (Eastern)	1	3	.250	2.79	14	0	0	0	4	19 1/3	18	6	6	3	19
	—Philadelphia (N.L.)	1	0	1.000	1.80	6	0	0	0	0	5	4	1	1	3	3
	—Scran./W.B. (Int'l)	0	2	.000	2.45	11	0	0	0	0	14 2/3	18	6	4	6	13
	—Calgary (PCL)■	3	2	.600	6.54	6	6	0	0	0	31 2/3	43	27	23	9	17
	—Seattle (A.L.)	1	0	1.000	2.25	1	0	0	0	0	4	4	1	1	1	3
1995	—Seattle (A.L.)	4	3	.571	5.75	30	4	0	0	0	76 2/3	88	51	49	39	38
A.L. totals (2 years)		5	3	.625	5.58	31	4	0	0	0	80 2/3	92	52	50	40	41
N.L. totals (1 year)		1	0	1.000	1.80	6	0	0	0	0	5	4	1	1	3	3
Major league totals (2 years)		6	3	.667	5.36	37	4	0	0	0	85 2/3	96	53	51	43	44

DIVISION SERIES RECORD

Year	Team (League)	W	L	Pct.	ERA	G	GS	CG	ShO	Sv.	IP	H	R	ER	BB	SO
1995—	Seattle (A.L.)	0	0	...	9.00	1	0	0	0	0	1	2	1	1	1	0

CHAMPIONSHIP SERIES RECORD

Year	Team (League)	W	L	Pct.	ERA	G	GS	CG	ShO	Sv.	IP	H	R	ER	BB	SO
1995—	Seattle (A.L.)	0	0	...	3.00	1	0	0	0	0	3	2	1	1	2	2

WELLS, DAVID — P — ORIOLES

PERSONAL: Born May 20, 1963, in Torrance, Calif. . . . 6-4/225. . . . Throws left, bats left. . . . Full name: David Lee Wells.
HIGH SCHOOL: Point Loma (San Diego).
TRANSACTIONS/CAREER NOTES: Selected by Toronto Blue Jays organization in second round of free-agent draft (June 7, 1982). . . . On Knoxville disabled list (June 28, 1984-remainder of season). . . . On disabled list (April 10, 1985-entire season). . . . On Knoxville disabled list (July 7-August 20, 1986). . . . Released by Blue Jays (March 30, 1993). . . . Signed by Detroit Tigers (April 3, 1993). . . . On disabled list (August 1-20, 1993). . . . Granted free agency (October 28, 1993). . . . Re-signed by Tigers (December 13, 1993). . . . On Detroit disabled list (April 19-June 6, 1994); included rehabilitation assignment to Lakeland (May 27-June 6). . . . Traded by Tigers to Cincinnati Reds for P C.J. Nitkowski, P David Tuttle and a player to be named later (July 31, 1995); Tigers acquired IF Mark Lewis to complete deal (November 16, 1995). . . . Traded by Reds to Baltimore Orioles for OF Curtis Goodwin and OF Trovin Valdez (December 26, 1995).

Year	Team (League)	W	L	Pct.	ERA	G	GS	CG	ShO	Sv.	IP	H	R	ER	BB	SO
1982—	Medicine Hat (Pio.)	4	3	.571	5.18	12	12	1	0	0	64 1/3	71	42	37	32	53
1983—	Kinston (Carolina)	6	5	.545	3.73	25	25	5	0	0	157	141	81	65	71	115
1984—	Kinston (Carolina)	1	6	.143	4.71	7	7	0	0	0	42	51	29	22	19	44
—	Knoxville (South.)	3	2	.600	2.59	8	8	3	1	0	59	58	22	17	17	34
1985—		Did not play.														
1986—	Florence (S. Atl.)	0	0	...	3.55	4	1	0	0	0	12 2/3	7	6	5	9	14
—	Ventura (Calif.)	2	1	.667	1.89	5	2	0	0	0	19	13	5	4	4	26
—	Knoxville (South.)	1	3	.250	4.05	10	7	1	0	0	40	42	24	18	18	32
—	Syracuse (Int'l)	0	1	.000	9.82	3	0	0	0	0	3 2/3	6	4	4	1	2
1987—	Syracuse (Int'l)	4	6	.400	3.87	43	12	0	0	6	109 1/3	102	49	47	32	106
—	Toronto (A.L.)	4	3	.571	3.99	18	2	0	0	1	29 1/3	37	14	13	12	32
1988—	Toronto (A.L.)	3	5	.375	4.62	41	0	0	0	4	64 1/3	65	36	33	31	56
—	Syracuse (Int'l)	0	0	...	0.00	6	0	0	0	3	5 2/3	7	1	0	2	8
1989—	Toronto (A.L.)	7	4	.636	2.40	54	0	0	0	2	86 1/3	66	25	23	28	78
1990—	Toronto (A.L.)	11	6	.647	3.14	43	25	0	0	3	189	165	72	66	45	115
1991—	Toronto (A.L.)	15	10	.600	3.72	40	28	2	0	1	198 1/3	188	88	82	49	106
1992—	Toronto (A.L.)	7	9	.438	5.40	41	14	0	0	2	120	138	84	72	36	62
1993—	Detroit (A.L.)■	11	9	.550	4.19	32	30	0	0	0	187	183	93	87	42	139
1994—	Lakeland (Fla. St.)	0	0	...	0.00	2	2	0	0	0	6	5	1	0	0	3
—	Detroit (A.L.)	5	7	.417	3.96	16	16	5	1	0	111 1/3	113	54	49	24	71
1995—	Detroit (A.L.)	10	3	.769	3.04	18	18	3	0	0	130 1/3	120	54	44	37	83
—	Cincinnati (N.L.)■	6	5	.545	3.59	11	11	3	0	0	72 2/3	74	34	29	16	50
A.L. totals (9 years)		73	56	.566	3.78	303	133	10	1	13	1116	1075	520	469	304	742
N.L. totals (1 year)		6	5	.545	3.59	11	11	3	0	0	72 2/3	74	34	29	16	50
Major league totals (9 years)		79	61	.564	3.77	314	144	13	1	13	1188 2/3	1149	554	498	320	792

DIVISION SERIES RECORD

Year	Team (League)	W	L	Pct.	ERA	G	GS	CG	ShO	Sv.	IP	H	R	ER	BB	SO
1995—	Cincinnati (N.L.)	1	0	1.000	0.00	1	1	0	0	0	6 1/3	6	1	0	1	8

CHAMPIONSHIP SERIES RECORD

Year	Team (League)	W	L	Pct.	ERA	G	GS	CG	ShO	Sv.	IP	H	R	ER	BB	SO
1989—	Toronto (A.L.)	0	0	...	0.00	1	0	0	0	0	1	0	1	0	2	1
1991—	Toronto (A.L.)	0	0	...	2.35	4	0	0	0	0	7 2/3	6	2	2	2	9
1992—	Toronto (A.L.)	Did not play.														
1995—	Cincinnati (N.L.)	0	1	.000	4.50	1	1	0	0	0	6	8	3	3	2	3
Champ. series totals (3 years)		0	1	.000	3.07	6	1	0	0	0	14 2/3	14	6	5	6	13

WORLD SERIES RECORD

NOTES: Member of World Series championship team (1992).

Year	Team (League)	W	L	Pct.	ERA	G	GS	CG	ShO	Sv.	IP	H	R	ER	BB	SO
1992—	Toronto (A.L.)	0	0	...	0.00	4	0	0	0	0	4 1/3	1	0	0	2	3

ALL-STAR GAME RECORD

Year	League	W	L	Pct.	ERA	GS	CG	ShO	Sv.	IP	H	R	ER	BB	SO
1995—	American	0	0	...	0.00	0	0	0	0	1/3	0	0	0	0	1

WENDELL, TURK — P — CUBS

PERSONAL: Born May 19, 1967, in Pittsfield, Mass. . . . 6-2/195. . . . Throws right, bats left. . . . Full name: Steven John Wendell.
HIGH SCHOOL: Wahconah Regional (Dalton, Mass.).
COLLEGE: Quinnipiac College (Conn.).
TRANSACTIONS/CAREER NOTES: Selected by Atlanta Braves organization in fifth round of free-agent draft (June 1, 1988). . . . Traded by Braves with P Yorkis Perez to Chicago Cubs for P Mike Bielecki and C Damon Berryhill (September 29, 1991). . . . On disabled list (May 4, 1992-remainder of season). . . . On Chicago disabled list (April 16-May 27, 1995); included rehabilitation assignments to Daytona (May 5-15) and Orlando (May 15-27).

Year	Team (League)	W	L	Pct.	ERA	G	GS	CG	ShO	Sv.	IP	H	R	ER	BB	SO
1988—	Pulaski (Appal.)	3	•8	.273	3.83	14	14	*6	1	0	*101	85	50	43	30	87
1989—	Burlington (Midw.)	9	11	.450	2.21	22	22	•9	*5	0	159	127	63	39	41	153
—	Greenville (South.)	0	0	...	9.82	1	1	0	0	0	3 2/3	7	5	4	1	3
—	Durham (Carolina)	2	0	1.000	1.13	3	3	1	0	0	24	13	4	3	6	27
1990—	Durham (Carolina)	1	3	.250	1.86	6	5	1	0	0	38 2/3	24	10	8	15	26
—	Greenville (South.)	4	9	.308	5.74	36	13	1	1	2	91	105	70	58	48	85

Year	Team (League)	W	L	Pct.	ERA	G	GS	CG	ShO	Sv.	IP	H	R	ER	BB	SO
1991—	Greenville (South.)	11	3	*.786	2.56	25	20	1	1	0	147 2/3	130	47	42	51	122
	— Richmond (Int'l)	0	2	.000	3.43	3	3	1	0	0	21	20	9	8	16	18
1992—	Iowa (Am. Assoc.)■	2	0	1.000	1.44	4	4	0	0	0	25	17	7	4	15	12
1993—	Iowa (Am. Assoc.)	10	8	.556	4.60	25	25	3	0	0	148 2/3	148	88	76	47	110
	— Chicago (N.L.)	1	2	.333	4.37	7	4	0	0	0	22 2/3	24	13	11	8	15
1994—	Iowa (Am. Assoc.)	11	6	.647	2.95	23	23	6	•3	0	168	141	58	55	28	118
	— Chicago (N.L.)	0	1	.000	11.93	6	2	0	0	0	14 1/3	22	20	19	10	9
1995—	Daytona (Fla. St.)	0	0	...	1.17	4	2	0	0	0	7 2/3	5	2	1	1	8
	— Orlando (Southern)	1	0	1.000	3.86	5	0	0	0	1	7	6	3	3	4	7
	— Chicago (N.L.)	3	1	.750	4.92	43	0	0	0	0	60 1/3	71	35	33	24	50
Major league totals (3 years)		4	4	.500	5.83	56	6	0	0	0	97 1/3	117	68	63	42	74

WENGERT, DON — P — ATHLETICS

PERSONAL: Born November 6, 1969, in Sioux City, Ia. . . . 6-2/205. . . . Throws right, bats right. . . . Full name: Donald Paul Wengert. . . . Brother of Bill Wengert, pitcher, Boston Red Sox organization.

HIGH SCHOOL: Heelan Catholic (Sioux City, Ia.).

COLLEGE: Iowa State.

TRANSACTIONS/CAREER NOTES: Selected by Cincinnati Reds organization in 60th round of free-agent draft (June 1, 1988); did not sign. . . . Selected by Oakland Athletics organization in fourth round of free-agent draft (June 1, 1992). . . . On Oakland disabled list (July 30-August 18, 1995); included rehabilitation assignment to Edmonton (August 7-18).

Year	Team (League)	W	L	Pct.	ERA	G	GS	CG	ShO	Sv.	IP	H	R	ER	BB	SO
1992—	S. Oregon (N'west)	2	0	1.000	1.46	6	5	1	0	0	37	32	6	6	7	29
	— Madison (Midwest)	3	4	.429	3.38	7	7	0	0	0	40	42	20	15	17	29
1993—	Madison (Midwest)	6	5	.545	3.32	13	13	2	0	0	78 2/3	79	30	29	18	46
	— Modesto (Calif.)	3	6	.333	4.73	12	12	0	0	0	70 1/3	75	42	37	29	43
1994—	Modesto (Calif.)	4	1	.800	2.95	10	7	0	0	2	42 2/3	40	15	14	11	52
	— Huntsville (South.)	6	4	.600	3.26	17	17	1	0	0	99 1/3	86	43	36	33	92
1995—	Oakland (A.L.)	1	1	.500	3.34	19	0	0	0	0	29 2/3	30	14	11	12	16
	— Edmonton (PCL)	1	1	.500	7.38	16	6	0	0	1	39	55	32	32	16	20
Major league totals (1 year)		1	1	.500	3.34	19	0	0	0	0	29 2/3	30	14	11	12	16

WEST, DAVID — P — PHILLIES

PERSONAL: Born September 1, 1964, in Memphis, Tenn. . . . 6-6/247. . . . Throws left, bats left. . . . Full name: David Lee West.

HIGH SCHOOL: Craigmont (Memphis, Tenn.).

TRANSACTIONS/CAREER NOTES: Selected by New York Mets organization in fourth round of free-agent draft (June 6, 1983). . . . Traded by Mets with P Rick Aguilera and three players to be named later to Minnesota Twins for P Frank Viola (July 31, 1989); Portland, Twins organization, acquired P Kevin Tapani and P Tim Drummond (August 1, 1989), and Twins acquired P Jack Savage to complete deal (October 16, 1989). . . . On disabled list (September 7, 1990-remainder of season). . . . On Minnesota disabled list (April 7-July 2, 1991); included rehabilitation assignments to Orlando (May 12-15) and Portland (June 14-July 2). . . . Traded by Twins to Philadelphia Phillies for P Mike Hartley (December 5, 1992). . . . On Philadelphia disabled list (May 14-June 16 and July 7, 1995-remainder of season); included rehabilitation assignments to Scranton/Wilkes-Barre (June 5-9) and Reading (June 9-16).

STATISTICAL NOTES: Led New York-Pennsylvania League with 16 wild pitches in 1984. . . . Pitched 3-0 no-hit victory against Spartanburg (August 14, 1985). . . . Pitched six innings, combining with Larry Casian (two innings) and Greg Johnson (one inning) in 5-0 no-hit victory for Portland against Vancouver (June 7, 1992).

Year	Team (League)	W	L	Pct.	ERA	G	GS	CG	ShO	Sv.	IP	H	R	ER	BB	SO
1983—	GC Mets (GCL)	2	4	.333	2.85	12	10	0	0	0	53 2/3	41	28	17	52	56
1984—	Columbia (S. Atl.)	3	5	.375	6.23	12	12	0	0	0	60 2/3	41	47	42	68	60
	— Little Falls (NYP)	6	4	.600	3.34	13	11	0	0	0	62	43	35	23	62	79
1985—	Columbia (S. Atl.)	10	9	.526	4.56	26	25	5	2	0	150	105	97	76	*111	194
1986—	Lynchburg (Caro.)	1	6	.143	5.16	13	13	1	0	0	75	76	50	43	53	70
	— Columbia (S. Atl.)	10	3	.769	2.91	13	13	3	1	0	92 2/3	74	41	30	56	101
1987—	Jackson (Texas)	10	7	.588	2.81	25	25	4	•2	0	166 2/3	152	67	52	*81	*186
1988—	Tidewater (Int'l)	12	4	*.750	*1.80	23	23	7	1	0	160 1/3	106	42	32	*97	143
	— New York (N.L.)	1	0	1.000	3.00	2	1	0	0	0	6	6	2	2	3	3
1989—	Tidewater (Int'l)	7	4	.636	2.37	12	12	5	1	0	87 1/3	60	31	23	29	69
	— New York (N.L.)	0	2	.000	7.40	11	2	0	0	0	24 1/3	25	20	20	14	19
	— Minnesota (A.L.)■	3	2	.600	6.41	10	5	0	0	0	39 1/3	48	29	28	19	31
1990—	Minnesota (A.L.)	7	9	.438	5.10	29	27	2	0	0	146 1/3	142	88	83	78	92
1991—	Minnesota (A.L.)	4	4	.500	4.54	15	12	0	0	0	71 1/3	66	37	36	28	52
	— Orlando (Southern)	0	0	...	0.00	1	1	0	0	0	1/3	0	0	0	0	0
	— Portland (PCL)	1	1	.500	6.32	4	4	0	0	0	15 2/3	12	11	11	12	15
1992—	Portland (PCL)	7	6	.538	4.43	19	18	1	0	0	101 2/3	88	51	50	65	87
	— Minnesota (A.L.)	1	3	.250	6.99	9	3	0	0	0	28 1/3	32	24	22	20	19
1993—	Philadelphia (N.L.)■	6	4	.600	2.92	76	0	0	0	3	86 1/3	60	37	28	51	87
1994—	Philadelphia (N.L.)	4	10	.286	3.55	31	14	0	0	0	99	74	44	39	61	83
1995—	Philadelphia (N.L.)	3	2	.600	3.79	8	8	0	0	0	38	34	17	16	19	25
	— Scran./W.B. (Int'l)	1	0	1.000	0.00	1	1	1	1	0	7	2	0	0	0	6
	— Reading (Eastern)	0	0	...	1.50	1	1	0	0	0	6	2	1	1	3	8
A.L. totals (4 years)		15	18	.455	5.33	63	47	2	0	0	285 1/3	288	178	169	145	194
N.L. totals (5 years)		14	18	.438	3.73	128	25	0	0	3	253 2/3	199	120	105	148	217
Major league totals (8 years)		29	36	.446	4.58	191	72	2	0	3	539	487	298	274	293	411

CHAMPIONSHIP SERIES RECORD

Year	Team (League)	W	L	Pct.	ERA	G	GS	CG	ShO	Sv.	IP	H	R	ER	BB	SO
1991—	Minnesota (A.L.)	1	0	1.000	0.00	2	0	0	0	0	5 2/3	1	0	0	4	4
1993—	Philadelphia (N.L.)	0	0	...	13.50	3	0	0	0	0	2 2/3	5	5	4	2	5
Champ. series totals (2 years)		1	0	1.000	4.32	5	0	0	0	0	8 1/3	6	5	4	6	9

WORLD SERIES RECORD

NOTES: Member of World Series championship team (1991).

Year Team (League)	W	L	Pct.	ERA	G	GS	CG	ShO	Sv.	IP	H	R	ER	BB	SO
1991—Minnesota (A.L.)	0	0	...	...	2	0	0	0	0	0	2	4	4	4	0
1993—Philadelphia (N.L.)	0	0	...	27.00	3	0	0	0	0	1	5	3	3	1	0
World Series totals (2 years)	0	0	...	63.00	5	0	0	0	0	1	7	7	7	5	0

WETTELAND, JOHN — P — YANKEES

PERSONAL: Born August 21, 1966, in San Mateo, Calif. . . . 6-2/215. . . . Throws right, bats right. . . . Full name: John Karl Wetteland.
HIGH SCHOOL: Cardinal Newman (Santa Rosa, Calif.).
COLLEGE: College of San Mateo (Calif.).
TRANSACTIONS/CAREER NOTES: Selected by New York Mets organization in 12th round of free-agent draft (June 4, 1984); did not sign. . . . Selected by Los Angeles Dodgers organization in secondary phase of free-agent draft (January 9, 1985). . . . Selected by Detroit Tigers from Dodgers organization in Rule 5 major league draft (December 7, 1987). . . . Returned to Dodgers organization (March 29, 1988). . . . On Albuquerque disabled list (May 1-8 and June 3-29, 1991). . . . Traded by Dodgers with P Tim Belcher to Cincinnati Reds for OF Eric Davis and P Kip Gross (November 25, 1991). . . . Traded by Reds with P Bill Risley to Montreal Expos for OF Dave Martinez, P Scott Ruskin and SS Willie Greene (December 11, 1991). . . . On Montreal disabled list (March 23-April 23, 1993); included rehabilitation assignment to West Palm Beach (April 18-23). . . . On disabled list (April 18-May 4, 1994). . . . Traded by Expos to New York Yankees for OF Fernando Seguignol, a player to be named later and cash (April 5, 1995).
STATISTICAL NOTES: Tied for Florida State League lead with 11 home runs allowed and 17 wild pitches in 1987. . . . Led Texas League with 22 wild pitches in 1988.

Year Team (League)	W	L	Pct.	ERA	G	GS	CG	ShO	Sv.	IP	H	R	ER	BB	SO
1985—Great Falls (Pio.)	1	1	.500	3.92	11	2	0	0	0	20 2/3	17	10	9	15	23
1986—Bakersfield (Calif.)	0	7	.000	5.78	15	12	4	0	0	67	71	50	43	46	38
—Great Falls (Pio.)	4	3	.571	5.45	12	12	1	0	0	69 1/3	70	51	42	40	59
1987—Vero Beach (FSL)	12	7	.632	3.13	27	27	7	2	0	175 2/3	150	81	61	92	144
1988—San Antonio (Tex.)	10	8	.556	3.88	25	25	3	1	0	162 1/3	141	74	70	•77	140
1989—Albuquerque (PCL)	5	3	.625	3.65	10	10	1	0	0	69	61	28	28	20	73
—Los Angeles (N.L.)	5	8	.385	3.77	31	12	0	0	1	102 2/3	81	46	43	34	96
1990—Los Angeles (N.L.)	2	4	.333	4.81	22	5	0	0	0	43	44	28	23	17	36
—Albuquerque (PCL)	2	2	.500	5.59	8	5	1	0	0	29	27	19	18	13	26
1991—Albuquerque (PCL)	4	3	.571	2.79	41	4	0	0	20	61 1/3	48	22	19	26	55
—Los Angeles (N.L.)	1	0	1.000	0.00	6	0	0	0	0	9	5	2	0	3	9
1992—Montreal (N.L.)■	4	4	.500	2.92	67	0	0	0	37	83 1/3	64	27	27	36	99
1993—WP Beach (FSL)	0	0	...	0.00	2	2	0	0	0	3	0	0	0	0	6
—Montreal (N.L.)	9	3	.750	1.37	70	0	0	0	43	85 1/3	58	17	13	28	113
1994—Montreal (N.L.)	4	6	.400	2.83	52	0	0	0	25	63 2/3	46	22	20	21	68
1995—New York (A.L.)■	1	5	.167	2.93	60	0	0	0	31	61 1/3	40	22	20	14	66
A.L. totals (1 year)	1	5	.167	2.93	60	0	0	0	31	61 1/3	40	22	20	14	66
N.L. totals (6 years)	25	25	.500	2.93	248	17	0	0	106	387	298	142	126	139	421
Major league totals (7 years)	26	30	.464	2.93	308	17	0	0	137	448 1/3	338	164	146	153	487

DIVISION SERIES RECORD

Year Team (League)	W	L	Pct.	ERA	G	GS	CG	ShO	Sv.	IP	H	R	ER	BB	SO
1995—New York (A.L.)	0	1	.000	14.54	3	0	0	0	0	4 1/3	8	7	7	2	5

WHISENANT, MATT — P — MARLINS

PERSONAL: Born June 8, 1971, in Los Angeles. . . . 6-3/215. . . . Throws left, bats both. . . . Full name: Matthew Michael Whisenant.
HIGH SCHOOL: La Canada (Calif.).
JUNIOR COLLEGE: Glendale (Ariz.) Community College.
TRANSACTIONS/CAREER NOTES: Selected by Philadelphia Phillies organization in 18th round of free-agent draft (June 5, 1989). . . . Traded by Phillies organization with P Joel Adamson to Florida Marlins organization for P Danny Jackson (November 17, 1992). . . . On disabled list (July 13, 1993-remainder of season).

Year Team (League)	W	L	Pct.	ERA	G	GS	CG	ShO	Sv.	IP	H	R	ER	BB	SO
1990—Princeton (Appal.)	0	0	...	11.40	9	2	0	0	0	15	16	27	19	20	25
1991—Batavia (NYP)	2	1	.667	2.45	11	10	0	0	0	47 2/3	31	19	13	42	55
1992—Spartanburg (SAL)	11	7	.611	3.23	27	27	2	0	0	150 2/3	117	69	54	85	151
1993—Kane Co. (Mid.)■	2	6	.250	4.69	15	15	0	0	0	71	68	45	37	56	74
1994—Brevard Co. (FSL)	6	9	.400	3.38	28	26	5	1	0	160	125	71	60	82	103
1995—Portland (East.)	10	6	.625	3.50	23	22	2	0	0	128 2/3	106	57	50	65	107

WHITAKER, LOU — 2B

PERSONAL: Born May 12, 1957, in Brooklyn, N.Y. . . . 5-11/180. . . . Bats left, throws right. . . . Full name: Louis Rodman Whitaker.
HIGH SCHOOL: Martinsville (Va.).
TRANSACTIONS/CAREER NOTES: Selected by Detroit Tigers organization in fifth round of free-agent draft (June 4, 1975). . . . On disabled list (May 3-14, 1977 and June 13-28, 1979). . . . Granted free agency (November 2, 1992). . . . Re-signed by Tigers (December 7, 1992). . . . On disabled list (April 21-May 12, 1995). . . . Granted free agency (November 7, 1995).
HONORS: Named Florida State League Most Valuable Player (1976). . . . Named A.L. Rookie of the Year by Baseball Writers' Association of America (1978). . . . Named second baseman on The Sporting News A.L. All-Star team (1983-84). . . . Named second baseman on The Sporting News A.L. Silver Slugger team (1983-85 and 1987). . . . Won A.L. Gold Glove at second base (1983-85).
STATISTICAL NOTES: Led Florida State League second basemen with 30 double plays in 1976. . . . Led A.L. second basemen with 811 total chances and 120 double plays in 1982. . . . Career major league grand slams: 4.

			BATTING											FIELDING			
Year Team (League)	Pos.	G	AB	R	H	2B	3B	HR	RBI	Avg.	BB	SO	SB	PO	A	E	Avg.
1975—Bristol (Appal.)	3B-SS	42	114	17	27	6	1	1	17	.237	25	13	1	38	82	16	.882
1976—Lakeland (Fla. St.)	3B	124	343	*70	129	12	5	1	62	.376	55	51	48	*99	*267	*30	*.924
1977—Montgomery (Sou.)	2B	107	396	*81	111	13	4	3	48	.280	58	52	38	208	285	15	.970

Year	Team (League)	Pos.	G	AB	R	H	2B	3B	HR	RBI	Avg.	BB	SO	SB	PO	A	E	Avg.
			BATTING												FIELDING			
	— Detroit (A.L.)	2B	11	32	5	8	1	0	0	2	.250	4	6	2	17	18	0	1.000
1978	— Detroit (A.L.)	2B-DH	139	484	71	138	12	7	3	58	.285	61	65	7	301	458	17	.978
1979	— Detroit (A.L.)	2B	127	423	75	121	14	8	3	42	.286	78	66	20	280	369	9	.986
1980	— Detroit (A.L.)	2B	145	477	68	111	19	1	1	45	.233	73	79	8	340	428	12	.985
1981	— Detroit (A.L.)	2B	•109	335	48	88	14	4	5	36	.263	40	42	5	227	*354	9	.985
1982	— Detroit (A.L.)	2B-DH	152	560	76	160	22	8	15	65	.286	48	58	11	331	*470	10	*.988
1983	— Detroit (A.L.)	2B	161	643	94	206	40	6	12	72	.320	67	70	17	299	447	13	.983
1984	— Detroit (A.L.)	2B	143	558	90	161	25	1	13	56	.289	62	63	6	290	405	15	.979
1985	— Detroit (A.L.)	2B	152	609	102	170	29	8	21	73	.279	80	56	6	314	414	11	.985
1986	— Detroit (A.L.)	2B	144	584	95	157	26	6	20	73	.269	63	70	13	276	421	11	.984
1987	— Detroit (A.L.)	2B	149	604	110	160	38	6	16	59	.265	71	108	13	275	416	17	.976
1988	— Detroit (A.L.)	2B	115	403	54	111	18	2	12	55	.275	66	61	2	218	284	8	.984
1989	— Detroit (A.L.)	2B-DH	148	509	77	128	21	1	28	85	.251	89	59	6	*327	393	11	.985
1990	— Detroit (A.L.)	2B-DH	132	472	75	112	22	2	18	60	.237	74	71	8	286	372	6	.991
1991	— Detroit (A.L.)	2B-DH	138	470	94	131	26	2	23	78	.279	90	45	4	255	361	4	*.994
1992	— Detroit (A.L.)	2B-DH	130	453	77	126	26	0	19	71	.278	81	46	6	256	312	9	.984
1993	— Detroit (A.L.)	2B	119	383	72	111	32	1	9	67	.290	78	46	3	236	322	11	.981
1994	— Detroit (A.L.)	2B-DH	92	322	67	97	21	2	12	43	.301	41	47	2	136	246	12	.970
1995	— Detroit (A.L.)	2B-DH	84	249	36	73	14	0	14	44	.293	31	41	4	107	163	4	.985
Major league totals (19 years)			2390	8570	1386	2369	420	65	244	1084	.276	1197	1099	143	4771	6653	189	.984

CHAMPIONSHIP SERIES RECORD

Year	Team (League)	Pos.	G	AB	R	H	2B	3B	HR	RBI	Avg.	BB	SO	SB	PO	A	E	Avg.
			BATTING												FIELDING			
1984	— Detroit (A.L.)	2B	3	14	3	2	0	0	0	0	.143	0	3	0	5	6	0	1.000
1987	— Detroit (A.L.)	2B	5	17	4	3	0	0	1	1	.176	7	3	1	11	14	0	1.000
Championship series totals (2 years)			8	31	7	5	0	0	1	1	.161	7	6	1	16	20	0	1.000

WORLD SERIES RECORD

NOTES: Member of World Series championship team (1984).

Year	Team (League)	Pos.	G	AB	R	H	2B	3B	HR	RBI	Avg.	BB	SO	SB	PO	A	E	Avg.
			BATTING												FIELDING			
1984	— Detroit (A.L.)	2B	5	18	6	5	2	0	0	0	.278	4	4	0	15	18	0	1.000

ALL-STAR GAME RECORD

NOTES: Named to A.L. All-Star team for 1987 game; replaced by Harold Reynolds due to injury.

Year	League	Pos.	AB	R	H	2B	3B	HR	RBI	Avg.	BB	SO	SB	PO	A	E	Avg.
			BATTING											FIELDING			
1983	— American	PH-2B	1	1	1	0	1	0	2	1.000	0	0	0	1	0	0	1.000
1984	— American	2B	3	0	2	1	0	0	0	.667	0	0	0	0	5	0	1.000
1985	— American	2B	2	0	0	0	0	0	0	.000	0	0	0	1	1	0	1.000
1986	— American	2B	2	1	1	0	0	1	2	.500	0	1	0	0	3	0	1.000
1987	— American		Selected, did not play—injured.														
All-Star Game totals (4 years)			8	2	4	1	1	1	4	.500	0	1	0	2	9	0	1.000

WHITE, DERRICK 1B

PERSONAL: Born October 12, 1969, in San Rafael, Calif. . . . 6-1/220. . . . Bats right, throws right. . . . Full name: Derrick Ramon White.
HIGH SCHOOL: Terra Linda (San Rafael, Calif.).
JUNIOR COLLEGE: Santa Rosa (Calif.) Junior College.
COLLEGE: Oklahoma.
TRANSACTIONS/CAREER NOTES: Selected by Minnesota Twins organization in 23rd round of free-agent draft (June 5, 1989); did not sign. . . . Selected by Philadelphia Phillies organization in ninth round of free-agent draft (June 4, 1990); did not sign. . . . Selected by Montreal Expos organization in sixth round of free-agent draft (June 3, 1991). . . . On Ottawa disabled list (April 8-May 4, 1993). . . . Released by Ottawa (June 14, 1994). . . . Signed by Portland, Florida Marlins organization (June 23, 1994). . . . Granted free agency (October 15, 1994). . . . Signed by Toledo, Detroit Tigers organization (November 16, 1994). . . . Released by Tigers (October 12, 1995).
STATISTICAL NOTES: Led Eastern League first basemen with 1,294 total chances and 110 double plays in 1992.

Year	Team (League)	Pos.	G	AB	R	H	2B	3B	HR	RBI	Avg.	BB	SO	SB	PO	A	E	Avg.
			BATTING												FIELDING			
1991	— Jamestown (NYP)	OF-1B	72	271	46	89	10	4	6	50	.328	40	46	8	402	18	8	.981
1992	— Harrisburg (East.)	1B	134	495	63	137	19	2	13	81	.277	40	73	17	*1178	*106	10	*.992
1993	— W.P. Beach (FSL)	1B	6	25	1	5	0	0	0	1	.200	1	2	2	38	4	0	1.000
	— Ottawa (Int'l)	1B	67	249	32	70	15	1	4	29	.281	20	52	10	632	49	8	.988
	— Montreal (N.L.)	1B	17	49	6	11	3	0	2	4	.224	2	12	2	129	8	1	.993
	— Harrisburg (East.)	1B	21	79	14	18	1	0	2	12	.228	5	17	2	171	11	2	.989
1994	— Ottawa (Int'l)	1B-OF	47	99	13	21	4	0	0	9	.212	8	25	4	179	11	2	.990
	— Portland (Eastern)■	OF-1B	74	264	39	71	13	2	4	34	.269	28	52	14	137	12	3	.980
1995	— Toledo (Int'l)■	OF-1B	87	309	50	82	15	3	14	49	.265	29	65	6	327	20	9	.975
	— Detroit (A.L.)	1B-OF-DH	39	48	3	9	2	0	0	2	.188	0	7	1	55	5	2	.968
American League totals (1 year)			39	48	3	9	2	0	0	2	.188	0	7	1	55	5	2	.968
National League totals (1 year)			17	49	6	11	3	0	2	4	.224	2	12	2	129	8	1	.993
Major league totals (2 years)			56	97	9	20	5	0	2	6	.206	2	19	3	184	13	3	.985

WHITE, DEVON OF MARLINS

PERSONAL: Born December 29, 1962, in Kingston, Jamaica. . . . 6-2/190. . . . Bats both, throws right. . . . Full name: Devon Markes White. . . . Name pronounced de-VON.
HIGH SCHOOL: Park West (New York).

W

TRANSACTIONS/CAREER NOTES: Selected by California Angels organization in sixth round of free-agent draft (June 8, 1981). . . . On suspended list (June 11-12 and July 19, 1982-remainder of season). . . . On Edmonton disabled list (May 12-22, 1986). . . . On disabled list (May 7-June 10, 1988). . . . Traded by Angels organization with P Willie Fraser and a player to be named later to Toronto Blue Jays for OF Junior Felix, IF Luis Sojo and a player to be named later (December 2, 1990); Blue Jays acquired P Marcus Moore and Angels acquired C Ken Rivers to complete deal (December 4, 1990). . . . Granted free agency (November 1, 1995). . . . Signed by Florida Marlins (November 21, 1995).
RECORDS: Shares major league record for most stolen bases in one inning—3 (September 9, 1989, sixth inning).
HONORS: Won A.L. Gold Glove as outfielder (1988-89 and 1991-95).
STATISTICAL NOTES: Led Midwest League outfielders with 286 total chances in 1983. . . . Led California League outfielders with 351 total chances in 1984. . . . Led Pacific Coast League outfielders with 339 total chances in 1986. . . . Switch-hit home runs in one game three times (June 23, 1987; June 29, 1990; and June 1, 1992). . . . Led A.L. outfielders with 449 total chances in 1987, 448 in 1991 and 458 in 1992. . . . Career major league grand slams: 3.

				BATTING											FIELDING			
Year	**Team (League)**	**Pos.**	**G**	**AB**	**R**	**H**	**2B**	**3B**	**HR**	**RBI**	**Avg.**	**BB**	**SO**	**SB**	**PO**	**A**	**E**	**Avg.**
1981—	Idaho Falls (Pio.)	OF-3B-1B	30	106	10	19	2	0	0	10	.179	12	34	4	33	10	3	.935
1982—	Danville (Midwest)	OF	57	186	21	40	6	1	1	11	.215	11	41	11	89	3	8	.920
1983—	Peoria (Midwest)	OF	117	430	69	109	17	6	13	66	.253	36	124	32	267	8	11	.962
—	Nashua (Eastern)	OF	17	70	11	18	7	2	0	2	.257	7	22	5	37	0	3	.925
1984—	Redwood (Calif.)	OF	138	520	101	147	25	5	7	55	.283	56	118	36	*322	16	13	.963
1985—	Midland (Texas)	OF	70	260	52	77	10	4	4	35	.296	35	46	38	176	10	4	.979
—	Edmonton (PCL)	OF	66	277	53	70	16	5	4	39	.253	24	77	21	205	6	2	.991
—	California (A.L.)	OF	21	7	7	1	0	0	0	0	.143	1	3	3	10	1	0	1.000
1986—	Edmonton (PCL)	OF	112	461	84	134	25	10	14	60	.291	31	90	*42	317	•16	6	.982
—	California (A.L.)	OF	29	51	8	12	1	1	1	3	.235	6	8	6	49	0	2	.961
1987—	California (A.L.)	OF	159	639	103	168	33	5	24	87	.263	39	135	32	*424	16	9	.980
1988—	California (A.L.)	OF	122	455	76	118	22	2	11	51	.259	23	84	17	364	7	9	.976
1989—	California (A.L.)	OF-DH	156	636	86	156	18	13	12	56	.245	31	129	44	430	10	5	.989
1990—	California (A.L.)	OF	125	443	57	96	17	3	11	44	.217	44	116	21	302	11	9	.972
—	Edmonton (PCL)	OF	14	55	9	20	4	4	0	6	.364	7	12	4	31	1	3	.914
1991—	Toronto (A.L.)■	OF	156	642	110	181	40	10	17	60	.282	55	135	33	*439	8	1	*.998
1992—	Toronto (A.L.)	OF-DH	153	641	98	159	26	7	17	60	.248	47	133	37	*443	8	7	.985
1993—	Toronto (A.L.)	OF	146	598	116	163	42	6	15	52	.273	57	127	34	399	6	3	.993
1994—	Toronto (A.L.)	OF	100	403	67	109	24	6	13	49	.270	21	80	11	268	3	6	.978
1995—	Toronto (A.L.)	OF	101	427	61	121	23	5	10	53	.283	29	97	11	261	7	3	.989
Major league totals (11 years)			1268	4942	789	1284	246	58	131	515	.260	353	1047	249	3389	77	54	.985

CHAMPIONSHIP SERIES RECORD

NOTES: Holds career record for highest batting average (50 or more at-bats)—.392. . . . Holds single-series record for most times caught stealing—4 (1992). . . . Shares A.L. single-series record for most hits—12 (1993). . . . Shares A.L. single-game record for most at-bats—6 (October 11, 1992, 11 innings).

				BATTING											FIELDING			
Year	**Team (League)**	**Pos.**	**G**	**AB**	**R**	**H**	**2B**	**3B**	**HR**	**RBI**	**Avg.**	**BB**	**SO**	**SB**	**PO**	**A**	**E**	**Avg.**
1986—	California (A.L.)	OF-PR	4	2	2	1	0	0	0	0	.500	0	1	0	3	0	0	1.000
1991—	Toronto (A.L.)	OF	5	22	5	8	1	0	0	0	.364	2	3	3	16	0	0	1.000
1992—	Toronto (A.L.)	OF	6	23	2	8	2	0	0	2	.348	5	6	0	16	0	1	.941
1993—	Toronto (A.L.)	OF	6	27	3	12	1	1	1	2	.444	1	5	0	15	0	0	1.000
Championship series totals (4 years)			21	74	12	29	4	1	1	4	.392	8	15	3	50	0	1	.980

WORLD SERIES RECORD

NOTES: Member of World Series championship teams (1992 and 1993).

				BATTING											FIELDING			
Year	**Team (League)**	**Pos.**	**G**	**AB**	**R**	**H**	**2B**	**3B**	**HR**	**RBI**	**Avg.**	**BB**	**SO**	**SB**	**PO**	**A**	**E**	**Avg.**
1992—	Toronto (A.L.)	OF	6	26	2	6	1	0	0	2	.231	0	6	1	22	0	0	1.000
1993—	Toronto (A.L.)	OF	6	24	8	7	3	2	1	7	.292	4	7	1	16	0	0	1.000
World Series totals (2 years)			12	50	10	13	4	2	1	9	.260	4	13	2	38	0	0	1.000

ALL-STAR GAME RECORD

				BATTING									FIELDING			
Year	**League**	**Pos.**	**AB**	**R**	**H**	**2B**	**3B**	**HR**	**RBI**	**Avg.**	**BB**	**SO**	**SB**	**PO**	**A**	**E**	**Avg.**
1989—	American	OF	1	0	0	0	0	0	0	.000	0	0	0	0	0	0	. . .
1993—	American	OF	2	1	1	1	0	0	1	.500	0	0	1	1	0	0	1.000
All-Star Game totals (2 years)			3	1	1	1	0	0	1	.333	0	0	1	1	0	0	1.000

WHITE, GABE — P — REDS

PERSONAL: Born November 20, 1971, in Sebring, Fla. . . . 6-2/200. . . . Throws left, bats left. . . . Full name: Gabriel Allen White.
HIGH SCHOOL: Sebring (Fla.).
TRANSACTIONS/CAREER NOTES: Selected by Montreal Expos organization in supplemental round ("sandwich pick" between first and second round, 28th pick overall) of free-agent draft (June 4, 1990); pick received as part of compensation for California Angels signing Type A free-agent P Mark Langston. . . . On Harrisburg disabled list (July 2-27, 1993). . . . On Ottawa disabled list (April 7-May 6, 1994). . . . Traded by Expos to Cincinnati Reds for 2B Jhonny Carvajal (December 15, 1995).
RECORDS: Shares N.L. record for most consecutive home runs allowed in one inning—3 (July 7, 1995, second inning).

Year	**Team (League)**	**W**	**L**	**Pct.**	**ERA**	**G**	**GS**	**CG**	**ShO**	**Sv.**	**IP**	**H**	**R**	**ER**	**BB**	**SO**
1990—	GC Expos (GCL)	4	2	.667	3.14	11	11	1	0	0	57 1/3	50	21	20	12	41
1991—	Sumter (S. Atl.)	6	9	.400	3.26	24	24	5	0	0	149	127	73	54	53	140
1992—	Rockford (Midw.)	14	8	.636	2.84	27	27	7	0	0	187	148	73	59	61	*176
1993—	Harrisburg (East.)	7	2	.778	2.16	16	16	2	1	0	100	80	30	24	28	80
—	Ottawa (Int'l)	2	1	.667	3.12	6	6	1	1	0	40 1/3	38	15	14	6	28
1994—	WP Beach (FSL)	1	0	1.000	1.50	1	1	0	0	0	6	2	2	1	1	4
—	Ottawa (Int'l)	8	3	.727	5.05	14	14	0	0	0	73	77	49	41	28	63
—	Montreal (N.L.)	1	1	.500	6.08	7	5	0	0	1	23 2/3	24	16	16	11	17
1995—	Ottawa (Int'l)	2	3	.400	3.90	12	12	0	0	0	62 1/3	58	31	27	17	37
—	Montreal (N.L.)	1	2	.333	7.01	19	1	0	0	0	25 2/3	26	21	20	9	25
Major league totals (2 years)		2	3	.400	6.57	26	6	0	0	1	49 1/3	50	37	36	20	42

WHITE, RICK P

PERSONAL: Born December 23, 1968, in Springfield, O. . . . 6-4/215. . . . Throws right, bats right. . . . Full name: Richard Allen White.
HIGH SCHOOL: Kenton Ridge (Springfield, O.).
JUNIOR COLLEGE: Paducah (Ky.) Community College.
TRANSACTIONS/CAREER NOTES: Selected by Pittsburgh Pirates organization in 15th round of free-agent draft (June 4, 1990). . . . On Carolina disabled list (May 15-July 6, 1993). . . . On Buffalo disabled list (August 28-September 4, 1993). . . . On Pittsburgh disabled list (April 14-May 17, 1995); included rehabilitation assignment to Gulf Coast Pirates (April 26-May 17). . . . Granted free agency (December 21, 1995).

Year	Team (League)	W	L	Pct.	ERA	G	GS	CG	ShO	Sv.	IP	H	R	ER	BB	SO
1990	— GC Pirates (GCL)	3	1	.750	0.76	7	6	0	0	0	35 2/3	26	11	3	4	27
	— Welland (NYP)	1	4	.200	3.26	9	5	1	0	0	38 2/3	39	19	14	14	43
1991	— Augusta (S. Atl.)	4	4	.500	3.00	34	0	0	0	6	63	68	26	21	18	52
	— Salem (Carolina)	2	3	.400	4.66	13	5	1	0	1	46 1/3	41	27	24	9	36
1992	— Salem (Carolina)	7	9	.438	3.80	18	18	•5	0	0	120 2/3	116	58	51	24	70
	— Carolina (South.)	1	7	.125	4.21	10	10	1	0	0	57 2/3	59	32	27	18	45
1993	— Carolina (South.)	4	3	.571	3.50	12	12	1	0	0	69 1/3	59	29	27	12	52
	— Buffalo (A.A.)	0	3	.000	3.54	7	3	0	0	0	28	25	13	11	8	16
1994	— Pittsburgh (N.L.)	4	5	.444	3.82	43	5	0	0	6	75 1/3	79	35	32	17	38
1995	— Pittsburgh (N.L.)	2	3	.400	4.75	15	9	0	0	0	55	66	33	29	18	29
	— Calgary (PCL)	6	4	.600	4.20	14	11	1	0	0	79 1/3	97	40	37	10	56
Major league totals (2 years)		6	8	.429	4.21	58	14	0	0	6	130 1/3	145	68	61	35	67

WHITE, RONDELL OF EXPOS

PERSONAL: Born February 23, 1972, in Milledgeville, Ga. . . . 6-1/205. . . . Bats right, throws right. . . . Full name: Rondell Bernard White.
HIGH SCHOOL: Jones County (Gray, Ga.).
TRANSACTIONS/CAREER NOTES: Selected by Montreal Expos organization in first round (24th pick overall) of free-agent draft (June 4, 1990); pick received as part of compensation for California Angels signing Type A free-agent P Mark Langston.
STATISTICAL NOTES: Led Gulf Coast League with 96 total bases in 1990. . . . Hit for the cycle (June 11, 1995, 13 innings). . . . Collected six hits in one game (June 11, 1995). . . . Career major league grand slams: 1.

			BATTING											FIELDING			
Year	Team (League)	Pos.	G	AB	R	H	2B	3B	HR	RBI	Avg.	BB	SO	SB	PO	A	E	Avg.
1990	— GC Expos (GCL)	OF	57	221	33	66	7	4	5	34	.299	17	33	10	71	1	2	.973
1991	— Sumter (S. Atl.)	OF	123	465	80	122	23	6	13	68	.262	57	109	50	215	6	3	*.987
1992	— W.P. Beach (FSL)	OF	111	450	80	142	10	*12	4	41	.316	46	78	42	187	2	3	.984
	— Harrisburg (East.)	OF	21	89	22	27	7	1	2	7	.303	6	14	6	29	1	2	.938
1993	— Harrisburg (East.)	OF	90	372	72	122	16	10	12	52	.328	22	72	21	179	4	1	.995
	— Ottawa (Int'l)	OF	37	150	28	57	8	2	7	32	.380	12	20	10	79	0	1	.988
	— Montreal (N.L.)	OF	23	73	9	19	3	1	2	15	.260	7	16	1	33	0	0	1.000
1994	— Montreal (N.L.)	OF	40	97	16	27	10	1	2	13	.278	9	18	1	34	1	2	.946
	— Ottawa (Int'l)	OF	42	169	23	46	7	0	7	18	.272	15	17	9	91	4	2	.979
1995	— Montreal (N.L.)	OF	130	474	87	140	33	4	13	57	.295	41	87	25	270	5	4	.986
Major league totals (3 years)			193	644	112	186	46	6	17	85	.289	57	121	27	337	6	6	.983

WHITEN, MARK OF PHILLIES

PERSONAL: Born November 25, 1966, in Pensacola, Fla. . . . 6-3/235. . . . Bats both, throws right. . . . Full name: Mark Anthony Whiten. . . . Name pronounced WHITT-en.
HIGH SCHOOL: Pensacola (Fla.).
JUNIOR COLLEGE: Pensacola (Fla.) Junior College.
TRANSACTIONS/CAREER NOTES: Selected by Toronto Blue Jays organization in fifth round of free-agent draft (January 14, 1986). . . . On Toronto suspended list (May 23-25, 1991). . . . Traded by Blue Jays with P Denis Boucher, OF Glenallen Hill and a player to be named later to Cleveland Indians for P Tom Candiotti and OF Turner Ward (June 27, 1991); Indians acquired cash to complete deal (October 15, 1991). . . . Traded by Indians to St. Louis Cardinals for P Mark Clark and SS Juan Andujar (March 31, 1993). . . . On St. Louis disabled list (April 18-May 5, 1994); included rehabilitation assignment to Louisville (May 2-5). . . . Traded by Cardinals with P Rheal Cormier to Boston Red Sox for 3B Scott Cooper, P Cory Bailey and a player to be named later (April 8, 1995). . . . On Boston disabled list (May 22-June 9, 1995); included rehabilitation assignment to Pawtucket (June 2-9). . . . Traded by Red Sox to Philadelphia Phillies for 1B Dave Hollins (July 24, 1995).
RECORDS: Shares major league single-game records for most home runs—4 (September 7, 1993, second game); and most runs batted in—12 (September 7, 1993, second game). . . . Shares major league record for most runs batted in during doubleheader—13 (September 7, 1993). . . . Shares N.L. record for most runs batted in during two consecutive games—13 (September 7, 1993, first and second games).
STATISTICAL NOTES: Tied for Pioneer League lead in being hit by pitch with six in 1986. . . . Led South Atlantic League outfielders with 322 total chances and tied for lead with four double plays in 1987. . . . Led South Atlantic League in being hit by pitch with 16 and tied for lead in intentional bases on balls received with 10 in 1987. . . . Led Southern League in being hit by pitch with 11 in 1989. . . . Hit four home runs in one game (September 7, 1993, second game). . . . Switch-hit home runs in one game (September 14, 1993). . . . Career major league grand slams: 2.
MISCELLANEOUS: Batted righthanded only (1988-89).

			BATTING											FIELDING			
Year	Team (League)	Pos.	G	AB	R	H	2B	3B	HR	RBI	Avg.	BB	SO	SB	PO	A	E	Avg.
1986	— Medicine Hat (Pio.)	OF	•70	270	53	81	16	3	10	44	.300	29	56	22	111	9	*10	.923
1987	— Myrtle Beach (SAL)	OF	*139	494	90	125	22	5	15	64	.253	76	149	49	*292	*18	12	.963
1988	— Dunedin (Fla. St.)	OF	99	385	61	97	8	5	7	37	.252	41	69	17	200	*21	9	.961
	— Knoxville (South.)	OF	28	108	20	28	3	1	2	9	.259	12	20	6	62	3	4	.942
1989	— Knoxville (South.)	OF	129	423	75	109	13	6	12	47	.258	60	114	11	223	17	8	.968
1990	— Syracuse (Int'l)	OF	104	390	65	113	19	4	14	48	.290	37	72	14	158	14	6	.966
	— Toronto (A.L.)	OF-DH	33	88	12	24	1	1	2	7	.273	7	14	2	60	3	0	1.000
1991	— Toronto (A.L.)	OF	46	149	12	33	4	3	2	19	.221	11	35	0	90	2	0	1.000

W

Year	Team (League)	Pos.	G	AB	R	H	2B	3B	HR	RBI	Avg.	BB	SO	SB	PO	A	E	Avg.
			BATTING												FIELDING			
	—Cleveland (A.L.)■	OF-DH	70	258	34	66	14	4	7	26	.256	19	50	4	166	11	7	.962
1992—	Cleveland (A.L.)	OF-DH	148	508	73	129	19	4	9	43	.254	72	102	16	321	14	7	.980
1993—	St. Louis (N.L.)■	OF	152	562	81	142	13	4	25	99	.253	58	110	15	329	9	10	.971
1994—	St. Louis (N.L.)	OF	92	334	57	98	18	2	14	53	.293	37	75	10	234	9	9	.964
	—Louisville (A.A.)	OF	3	10	2	3	1	0	1	3	.300	1	1	0	3	0	0	1.000
1995—	Boston (A.L.)■	OF-DH	32	108	13	20	3	0	1	10	.185	8	23	1	52	4	0	1.000
	—Pawtucket (Int'l)	OF	28	102	19	29	3	1	4	13	.284	19	30	4	43	4	3	.940
	—Philadelphia (N.L.)■	OF	60	212	38	57	10	1	11	37	.269	31	63	7	105	4	4	.965
American League totals (4 years)			329	1111	144	272	41	12	21	105	.245	117	224	23	689	34	14	.981
National League totals (3 years)			304	1108	176	297	41	7	50	189	.268	126	248	32	668	22	23	.968
Major league totals (6 years)			633	2219	320	569	82	19	71	294	.256	243	472	55	1357	56	37	.974

WHITESIDE, MATT — P — RANGERS

PERSONAL: Born August 8, 1967, in Charleston, Mo. . . . 6-0/205. . . . Throws right, bats right. . . . Full name: Matthew Christopher Whiteside.
HIGH SCHOOL: Charleston (Mo.).
COLLEGE: Arkansas State (degree in physical education).
TRANSACTIONS/CAREER NOTES: Selected by Texas Rangers organization in 25th round of free-agent draft (June 4, 1990). . . . On disabled list (May 9-25, 1995).

Year	Team (League)	W	L	Pct.	ERA	G	GS	CG	ShO	Sv.	IP	H	R	ER	BB	SO
1990—	Butte (Pioneer)	4	4	.500	3.45	18	5	0	0	2	57 1/3	57	33	22	25	45
1991—	Gastonia (S. Atl.)	3	1	.750	2.15	48	0	0	0	29	62 2/3	44	19	15	21	71
1992—	Tulsa (Texas)	0	1	.000	2.41	33	0	0	0	21	33 2/3	31	9	9	3	30
	—Okla. City (A.A.)	1	0	1.000	0.79	12	0	0	0	8	11 1/3	7	1	1	3	13
	—Texas (A.L.)	1	1	.500	1.93	20	0	0	0	4	28	26	8	6	11	13
1993—	Texas (A.L.)	2	1	.667	4.32	60	0	0	0	1	73	78	37	35	23	39
	—Okla. City (A.A.)	2	1	.667	5.56	8	0	0	0	1	11 1/3	17	7	7	8	10
1994—	Texas (A.L.)	2	2	.500	5.02	47	0	0	0	1	61	68	40	34	28	37
1995—	Texas (A.L.)	5	4	.556	4.08	40	0	0	0	3	53	48	24	24	19	46
Major league totals (4 years)		10	8	.556	4.14	167	0	0	0	9	215	220	109	99	81	135

WHITESIDE, SEAN — P — TIGERS

PERSONAL: Born April 19, 1971, in Lakeland, Fla. . . . 6-4/190. . . . Throws left, bats left. . . . Full name: David Sean Whiteside.
COLLEGE: UNC Charlotte.
TRANSACTIONS/CAREER NOTES: Selected by Detroit Tigers organization in 11th round of free-agent draft (June 1, 1992). . . . On disabled list (July 4-August 2, 1993).

Year	Team (League)	W	L	Pct.	ERA	G	GS	CG	ShO	Sv.	IP	H	R	ER	BB	SO
1992—	Niag. Falls (NYP)	8	4	.667	2.45	15	11	0	0	0	69 2/3	54	26	19	24	72
1993—	Fayetteville (S. Atl.)	3	5	.375	4.65	24	16	0	0	0	100 2/3	113	68	52	41	85
1994—	Lakeland (Fla. St.)	0	2	.000	1.15	13	0	0	0	2	31 1/3	21	6	4	12	39
	—Trenton (Eastern)	2	2	.500	2.45	25	0	0	0	5	36 2/3	26	13	10	15	31
1995—	Detroit (A.L.)	0	0	...	14.73	2	0	0	0	0	3 2/3	7	6	6	4	2
	—Jacksonville (Sou.)	2	0	1.000	3.78	27	1	0	0	0	33 1/3	34	17	14	20	17
Major league totals (1 year)		0	0	...	14.73	2	0	0	0	0	3 2/3	7	6	6	4	2

WHITMORE, DARRELL — OF — MARLINS

PERSONAL: Born November 18, 1968, in Front Royal, Va. . . . 6-1/210. . . . Bats left, throws right. . . . Full name: Darrell Lamont Whitmore.
HIGH SCHOOL: Warren County (Front Royal, Va.).
COLLEGE: West Virginia.
TRANSACTIONS/CAREER NOTES: Selected by Toronto Blue Jays organization in 10th round of free-agent draft (June 2, 1987); did not sign. . . . Selected by Blue Jays organization in 58th round of free-agent draft (June 1, 1988); did not sign. . . . Selected by Cleveland Indians organization in second round of free-agent draft (June 4, 1990); pick received as compensation for Seattle Mariners signing Type B free-agent 1B Pete O'Brien. . . . On temporarily inactive list (July 2, 1991-remainder of season). . . . Selected by Florida Marlins in first round (16th pick overall) of expansion draft (November 17, 1992). . . . On Edmonton suspended list (August 14-24, 1994). . . . On disabled list (June 4, 1995-remainder of season).

Year	Team (League)	Pos.	G	AB	R	H	2B	3B	HR	RBI	Avg.	BB	SO	SB	PO	A	E	Avg.
			BATTING												FIELDING			
1990—	Burlington (Appal.)	OF	30	112	18	27	3	2	0	13	.241	9	30	9	28	1	4	.879
1991—	Watertown (NYP)	OF	6	19	2	7	2	1	0	9	.368	3	2	0	0	0	0	...
1992—	Kinston (Carolina)	OF	121	443	71	124	22	2	10	52	.280	56	92	17	184	6	8	.960
1993—	Edmonton (PCL)■	OF	73	273	52	97	24	2	9	62	.355	22	53	11	171	7	4	.978
	—Florida (N.L.)	OF	76	250	24	51	8	2	4	19	.204	10	72	4	140	3	3	.979
1994—	Edmonton (PCL)	OF	115	421	72	119	24	5	20	61	.283	41	76	14	203	7	8	.963
	—Florida (N.L.)	OF	9	22	1	5	1	0	0	0	.227	3	5	0	14	0	0	1.000
1995—	Florida (N.L.)	OF	27	58	6	11	2	0	1	2	.190	5	15	0	24	0	1	.960
Major league totals (3 years)			112	330	31	67	11	2	5	21	.203	18	92	4	178	3	4	.978

WHITTEN, CASEY — P — INDIANS

PERSONAL: Born May 23, 1972, in Evansville, Ind. . . . 6-0/175. . . . Throws left, bats left. . . . Full name: Charles Kenneth Whitten.
HIGH SCHOOL: Gibson Southern (Fort Branch, Ind.).
COLLEGE: Indiana State.

TRANSACTIONS/CAREER NOTES: Selected by Cleveland Indians organization in second round of free-agent draft (June 3, 1993).... On disabled list (August 14, 1995-remainder of season).

Year	Team (League)	W	L	Pct.	ERA	G	GS	CG	ShO	Sv.	IP	H	R	ER	BB	SO
1993—	Watertown (NYP)	6	3	.667	2.42	14	14	0	0	0	81 2/3	75	28	22	18	81
1994—	Kinston (Carolina)	9	10	.474	4.28	27	27	0	0	0	153 1/3	127	78	73	64	148
1995—	Cant./Akr. (East.)	9	8	.529	3.31	20	20	2	1	0	114 1/3	100	49	42	38	91

WICKANDER, KEVIN — P — BREWERS

PERSONAL: Born January 4, 1965, in Fort Dodge, Ia.... 6-3/205.... Throws left, bats left.... Full name: Kevin Dean Wickander.... Name pronounced WICK-and-er.

HIGH SCHOOL: Cortez (Phoenix).

COLLEGE: Grand Canyon (Ariz.).

TRANSACTIONS/CAREER NOTES: Selected by Cleveland Indians organization in second round of free-agent draft (June 2, 1986).... On disabled list (May 31, 1990-remainder of season).... On Colorado Springs temporarily inactive list (May 25-June 29, 1991).... Traded by Indians to Cincinnati Reds for a player to be named later (May 7, 1993); Indians acquired P Todd Ruyak to complete deal (June 4, 1993).... On Cincinnati disabled list (June 2-21, 1993); included rehabilitation assignment to Indianapolis (June 16-21).... On Cincinnati disabled list (July 2-19, 1993).... Granted free agency (October 15, 1993).... Signed by Toledo, Detroit Tigers organization (January 23, 1995).... On Detroit disabled list (July 14-August 4, 1995).... Traded by Tigers to Milwaukee Brewers for a player to be named later (August 29, 1995); Tigers acquired OF Derek Hacopian to complete deal (September 2, 1995).

Year	Team (League)	W	L	Pct.	ERA	G	GS	CG	ShO	Sv.	IP	H	R	ER	BB	SO
1986—	Batavia (NYP)	3	4	.429	2.72	11	9	0	0	0	46 1/3	30	19	14	27	63
1987—	Kinston (Carolina)	9	6	.600	3.42	25	25	2	1	0	147 1/3	128	69	56	75	118
1988—	Williamsport (East.)	1	0	1.000	0.63	24	0	0	0	16	28 2/3	14	3	2	9	33
	—Colo. Springs (PCL)	0	2	.000	7.16	19	0	0	0	0	32 2/3	44	30	26	27	22
1989—	Colo. Springs (PCL)	1	3	.250	2.95	45	0	0	0	11	42 2/3	40	14	14	27	41
	—Cleveland (A.L.)	0	0	...	3.38	2	0	0	0	0	2 2/3	6	1	1	2	0
1990—	Cleveland (A.L.)	0	1	.000	3.65	10	0	0	0	0	12 1/3	14	6	5	4	10
1991—	Cant./Akr. (East.)	1	2	.333	3.96	20	0	0	0	0	25	24	14	11	13	21
	—Colo. Springs (PCL)	1	0	1.000	2.45	11	0	0	0	2	11	8	3	3	5	9
1992—	Colo. Springs (PCL)	0	0	...	1.64	8	0	0	0	2	11	4	2	2	6	18
	—Cleveland (A.L.)	2	0	1.000	3.07	44	0	0	0	1	41	39	14	14	28	38
1993—	Cleveland (A.L.)	0	0	...	4.15	11	0	0	0	0	8 2/3	15	7	4	3	3
	—Cincinnati (N.L.)■	1	0	1.000	6.75	33	0	0	0	0	25 1/3	32	20	19	19	20
	—Indianapolis (A.A.)	0	0	...	0.00	1	1	0	0	0	3	2	0	0	1	2
1994—		Did not play.														
1995—	Toledo (Int'l)■	2	1	.667	2.13	16	0	0	0	1	12 2/3	11	3	3	5	8
	—Detroit (A.L.)	0	0	...	2.60	21	0	0	0	1	17 1/3	18	6	5	9	9
	—Milwaukee (A.L.)■	0	0	...	0.00	8	0	0	0	0	6	1	0	0	3	2
A.L. totals (5 years)		2	1	.667	2.97	96	0	0	0	2	88	93	34	29	49	62
N.L. totals (1 year)		1	0	1.000	6.75	33	0	0	0	0	25 1/3	32	20	19	19	20
Major league totals (5 years)		3	1	.750	3.81	129	0	0	0	2	113 1/3	125	54	48	68	82

WICKMAN, BOB — P — YANKEES

PERSONAL: Born February 6, 1969, in Green Bay, Wis.... 6-1/212.... Throws right, bats right.... Full name: Robert Joe Wickman.

HIGH SCHOOL: Oconto Falls (Wis.).

COLLEGE: Wisconsin-Whitewater.

TRANSACTIONS/CAREER NOTES: Selected by Chicago White Sox organization in second round of free-agent draft (June 4, 1990).... Traded by White Sox organization with P Melido Perez and P Domingo Jean to New York Yankees organization for 2B Steve Sax and cash (January 10, 1992).

Year	Team (League)	W	L	Pct.	ERA	G	GS	CG	ShO	Sv.	IP	H	R	ER	BB	SO
1990—	GC White Sox (GCL)	2	0	1.000	2.45	2	2	0	0	0	11	7	4	3	1	15
	—Sarasota (Fla. St.)	0	1	.000	1.98	2	2	0	0	0	13 2/3	17	7	3	4	8
	—South Bend (Midw.)	7	2	.778	1.38	9	9	3	0	0	65 1/3	50	16	10	16	50
1991—	Sarasota (Fla. St.)	5	1	.833	2.05	7	7	1	1	0	44	43	16	10	11	32
	—Birmingham (Sou.)	6	10	.375	3.56	20	20	4	1	0	131 1/3	127	68	52	50	81
1992—	Columbus (Int'l)■	12	5	.706	2.92	23	23	2	1	0	157	131	61	51	55	108
	—New York (A.L.)	6	1	.857	4.11	8	8	0	0	0	50 1/3	51	25	23	20	21
1993—	New York (A.L.)	14	4	.778	4.63	41	19	1	1	4	140	156	82	72	69	70
1994—	New York (A.L.)	5	4	.556	3.09	*53	0	0	0	6	70	54	26	24	27	56
1995—	New York (A.L.)	2	4	.333	4.05	63	1	0	0	1	80	77	38	36	33	51
Major league totals (4 years)		27	13	.675	4.10	165	28	1	1	11	340 1/3	338	171	155	149	198

DIVISION SERIES RECORD

Year	Team (League)	W	L	Pct.	ERA	G	GS	CG	ShO	Sv.	IP	H	R	ER	BB	SO
1995—	New York (A.L.)	0	0	...	0.00	3	0	0	0	0	3	5	0	0	0	3

WIDGER, CHRIS — C — MARINERS

PERSONAL: Born May 21, 1971, in Wilmington, Del.... 6-3/195.... Bats right, throws right.... Full name: Christopher Jon Widger.... Nephew of Mike Widger, linebacker, Montreal Alouettes and Ottawa Rough Riders of Canadian Football League (1970-78).

HIGH SCHOOL: Pennsville (N.J.).

COLLEGE: George Mason.

TRANSACTIONS/CAREER NOTES: Selected by Seattle Mariners organization in third round of free-agent draft (June 1, 1992).... On disabled list (June 6-16, 1993).

				BATTING										FIELDING			
Year	Team (League)	Pos.	G	AB	R	H	2B	3B	HR	RBI	Avg.	BB	SO	SB	PO	A	E	Avg.
1992—	Belling. (N'west)	C	51	166	28	43	7	2	5	30	.259	22	36	8	266	39	4	*.987
1993—	Riverside (Calif.)	C-OF	97	360	44	95	28	2	9	58	.264	19	64	5	472	63	14	.974

W

Year	Team (League)	Pos.	G	AB	R	H	2B	3B	HR	RBI	Avg.	BB	SO	SB	PO	A	E	Avg.
				BATTING											FIELDING			
1994—	Jacksonv. (South.)	C-OF-1B	116	388	58	101	15	3	16	59	.260	39	69	8	564	73	13	.980
1995—	Tacoma (PCL)	C-OF	50	174	29	48	11	1	9	21	.276	9	29	0	189	22	4	.981
—	Seattle (A.L.)	C-OF-DH	23	45	2	9	0	0	1	2	.200	3	11	0	64	1	0	1.000
Major league totals (1 year)			23	45	2	9	0	0	1	2	.200	3	11	0	64	1	0	1.000

DIVISION SERIES RECORD

Year	Team (League)	Pos.	G	AB	R	H	2B	3B	HR	RBI	Avg.	BB	SO	SB	PO	A	E	Avg.
				BATTING											FIELDING			
1995—	Seattle (A.L.)	C	2	3	0	0	0	0	0	0	.000	0	3	0	14	0	0	1.000

CHAMPIONSHIP SERIES RECORD

Year	Team (League)	Pos.	G	AB	R	H	2B	3B	HR	RBI	Avg.	BB	SO	SB	PO	A	E	Avg.
				BATTING											FIELDING			
1995—	Seattle (A.L.)	C	3	1	0	0	0	0	0	0	.000	0	1	0	7	0	0	1.000

WILKINS, RICK — C — ASTROS

PERSONAL: Born June 4, 1967, in Jacksonville, Fla. . . . 6-2/215. . . . Bats left, throws right. . . . Full name: Richard David Wilkins.

HIGH SCHOOL: The Bolles School (Jacksonville, Fla.).

JUNIOR COLLEGE: Florida Community College-Jacksonville.

COLLEGE: Furman.

TRANSACTIONS/CAREER NOTES: Selected by Chicago Cubs organization in 23rd round of free-agent draft (June 2, 1986). . . . On Chicago disabled list (June 2-28, 1995). . . . Traded by Cubs to Houston Astros for OF Luis Gonzalez and C Scott Servais (June 28, 1995). . . . On Houston disabled list (July 2-September 5, 1995); included rehabilitation assignments to Jackson (August 28-September 1) and Tucson (September 1-5).

STATISTICAL NOTES: Led Appalachian League with eight intentional bases on balls received in 1987. . . . Led Appalachian League catchers with .989 fielding percentage, 483 putouts and 540 total chances and tied for lead with six double plays in 1987. . . . Led Midwest League catchers with 984 total chances in 1988. . . . Led Carolina League catchers with 860 total chances and tied for lead with eight double plays in 1989. . . . Led Southern League catchers with 857 total chances, 11 double plays and 15 passed balls in 1990. . . . Career major league grand slams: 1.

Year	Team (League)	Pos.	G	AB	R	H	2B	3B	HR	RBI	Avg.	BB	SO	SB	PO	A	E	Avg.
				BATTING											FIELDING			
1987—	Geneva (NYP)	C-1B	75	243	35	61	8	2	8	43	.251	58	40	7	†503	51	7	†.988
1988—	Peoria (Midwest)	C	137	490	54	119	30	1	8	63	.243	67	110	4	*864	*101	*19	.981
1989—	Winst.-Salem (Car.)	C	132	445	61	111	24	1	12	54	.249	50	87	6	*764	*78	*18	.979
1990—	Charlotte (South.)	C	127	449	48	102	18	1	17	71	.227	43	95	4	*740	*103	14	.984
1991—	Iowa (Am. Assoc.)	C-OF	38	107	12	29	3	1	5	14	.271	11	17	1	204	24	3	.987
—	Chicago (N.L.)	C	86	203	21	45	9	0	6	22	.222	19	56	3	373	42	3	.993
1992—	Chicago (N.L.)	C	83	244	20	66	9	1	8	22	.270	28	53	0	408	47	3	.993
—	Iowa (Am. Assoc.)	C	47	155	20	43	11	2	5	28	.277	19	42	0	177	18	2	.990
1993—	Chicago (N.L.)	C	136	446	78	135	23	1	30	73	.303	50	99	2	717	89	3	.996
1994—	Chicago (N.L.)	C-1B	100	313	44	71	25	2	7	39	.227	40	86	4	550	51	4	.993
1995—	Chicago (N.L.)	C-1B	50	162	24	31	2	0	6	14	.191	36	51	0	294	31	4	.988
—	Houston (N.L.)■	C	15	40	6	10	1	0	1	5	.250	10	10	0	87	4	0	1.000
—	Jackson (Texas)	C	4	11	0	0	0	0	0	0	.000	3	2	0	23	1	0	1.000
—	Tucson (PCL)	C	4	12	0	4	0	0	0	4	.333	2	0	0	27	4	0	1.000
Major league totals (5 years)			470	1408	193	358	69	4	58	175	.254	183	355	9	2429	264	17	.994

WILLIAMS, BERNIE — OF — YANKEES

PERSONAL: Born September 13, 1968, in San Juan, Puerto Rico. . . . 6-2/205. . . . Bats both, throws right. . . . Full name: Bernabe Figueroa Williams.

TRANSACTIONS/CAREER NOTES: Signed as non-drafted free agent by New York Yankees organization (September 13, 1985). . . . On disabled list (July 15, 1988-remainder of season and May 13-June 7, 1993).

RECORDS: Shares major league single-game record (nine innings) for most strikeouts—5 (August 21, 1991). . . . Shares major league record for most doubles in one inning—2 (June 22, 1994, seventh inning). . . . Shares modern major league record for most long hits in one inning—2 (June 22, 1994, seventh inning).

STATISTICAL NOTES: Led Gulf Coast League outfielders with 123 total chances in 1986. . . . Tied for Gulf Coast League lead in caught stealing with 12 in 1986. . . . Led Eastern League in caught stealing with 18 in 1990. . . . Led Eastern League outfielders with 307 total chances and tied for lead with four double plays in 1990. . . . Switch-hit home runs in one game (June 6, 1994). . . . Led A.L. outfielders with 441 total chances in 1995. . . . Career major league grand slams: 2.

MISCELLANEOUS: Batted righthanded only (1986-88).

Year	Team (League)	Pos.	G	AB	R	H	2B	3B	HR	RBI	Avg.	BB	SO	SB	PO	A	E	Avg.
				BATTING											FIELDING			
1986—	GC Yankees (GCL)	OF	61	230	*45	62	5	3	2	25	.270	39	40	33	*117	3	3	.976
1987—	Fort Lauder. (FSL)	OF	25	71	11	11	3	0	0	4	.155	18	22	9	49	1	0	1.000
—	Oneonta (NYP)	OF	25	93	13	32	4	0	0	15	.344	10	14	9	40	0	2	.952
1988—	Prin. William (Car.)	OF	92	337	72	113	16	7	7	45	*.335	65	65	29	186	8	5	.975
1989—	Columbus (Int'l)	OF	50	162	21	35	8	1	2	16	.216	25	38	11	112	2	1	.991
—	Alb./Colon. (East.)	OF	91	314	63	79	11	8	11	42	.252	60	72	26	180	5	5	.974
1990—	Alb./Colon. (East.)	OF	134	466	*91	131	28	5	8	54	.281	*98	97	*39	*288	15	4	.987
1991—	Columbus (Int'l)	OF	78	306	52	90	14	6	8	37	.294	38	43	9	164	2	1	.994
—	New York (A.L.)	OF	85	320	43	76	19	4	3	34	.238	48	57	10	230	3	5	.979
1992—	New York (A.L.)	OF	62	261	39	73	14	2	5	26	.280	29	36	7	187	5	1	.995
—	Columbus (Int'l)	OF	95	363	68	111	23	•9	8	50	.306	52	61	20	205	2	2	.990
1993—	New York (A.L.)	OF	139	567	67	152	31	4	12	68	.268	53	106	9	366	5	4	.989
1994—	New York (A.L.)	OF	108	408	80	118	29	1	12	57	.289	61	54	16	277	7	3	.990
1995—	New York (A.L.)	OF	144	563	93	173	29	9	18	82	.307	75	98	8	*432	1	•8	.982
Major league totals (5 years)			538	2119	322	592	122	20	50	267	.279	266	351	50	1492	21	21	.986

DIVISION SERIES RECORD

Year	Team (League)	Pos.	G	AB	R	H	2B	3B	HR	RBI	Avg.	BB	SO	SB	PO	A	E	Avg.
			BATTING												FIELDING			
1995—	New York (A.L.)	OF	5	21	8	9	2	0	2	5	.429	7	3	1	13	0	0	1.000

WILLIAMS, BRIAN — P — TIGERS

PERSONAL: Born February 15, 1969, in Lancaster, S.C. . . . 6-2/225. . . . Throws right, bats right. . . . Full name: Brian O'Neal Williams.
HIGH SCHOOL: Lewisville (Fort Lawn, S.C.).
COLLEGE: South Carolina.
TRANSACTIONS/CAREER NOTES: Selected by Pittsburgh Pirates organization in third round of free-agent draft (June 2, 1987); did not sign. . . . Selected by Houston Astros organization in supplemental round ("sandwich pick" between first and second round, 31st pick overall) of free-agent draft (June 4, 1990); pick received as part of compensation for San Francisco Giants signing Type A free-agent OF Kevin Bass. . . . On Tucson disabled list (May 25-June 1, 1992). . . . On Houston disabled list (August 5-20, 1993); included rehabilitation assignment to Tucson (August 15-20). . . . On Houston disabled list (August 1-September 19, 1994). . . . Traded by Astros with 3B Ken Caminiti, OF Steve Finley, SS Andujar Cedeno, 1B Robert Petagine and a player to be named later to San Diego Padres for OF Phil Plantier, OF Derek Bell, P Pedro Martinez, P Doug Brocail, IF Craig Shipley and SS Ricky Gutierrez (December 28, 1994). . . . Granted free agency (December 21, 1995). . . . Signed by Detroit Tigers (January 10, 1996).
MISCELLANEOUS: Appeared in four games as pinch-runner with Houston (1992).

Year	Team (League)	W	L	Pct.	ERA	G	GS	CG	ShO	Sv.	IP	H	R	ER	BB	SO
1990—	Auburn (NYP)	0	0	. . .	4.05	3	3	0	0	0	6 2/3	6	5	3	6	7
1991—	Osceola (Florida St.)	6	4	.600	2.91	15	15	0	0	0	89 2/3	72	41	29	40	67
	— Jackson (Texas)	2	1	.667	4.20	3	3	0	0	0	15	17	8	7	7	15
	— Tucson (Pac. Coast)	0	1	.000	4.93	7	7	0	0	0	38 1/3	39	25	21	22	29
	— Houston (N.L.)	0	1	.000	3.75	2	2	0	0	0	12	11	5	5	4	4
1992—	Tucson (Pac. Coast)	6	1	.857	4.50	12	12	0	0	0	70	78	37	35	26	58
	— Houston (N.L.)	7	6	.538	3.92	16	16	0	0	0	96 1/3	92	44	42	42	54
1993—	Houston (N.L.)	4	4	.500	4.83	42	5	0	0	3	82	76	48	44	38	56
	— Tucson (Pac. Coast)	1	0	1.000	0.00	2	0	0	0	0	3	1	0	0	0	3
1994—	Houston (N.L.)	6	5	.545	5.74	20	13	0	0	0	78 1/3	112	64	50	41	49
	— Tucson (Pac. Coast)	2	0	1.000	2.21	3	3	0	0	0	20 1/3	22	6	5	9	17
1995—	San Diego (N.L.)■	3	10	.231	6.00	44	6	0	0	0	72	79	54	48	38	75
Major league totals (5 years)		20	26	.435	4.99	124	42	0	0	3	340 2/3	370	215	189	163	238

W

WILLIAMS, EDDIE — 1B — TIGERS

PERSONAL: Born November 1, 1964, in Shreveport, La. . . . 6-0/210. . . . Bats right, throws right. . . . Full name: Edward Laquan Williams.
HIGH SCHOOL: Hoover (San Diego).
TRANSACTIONS/CAREER NOTES: Selected by New York Mets organization in first round (fourth pick overall) of free-agent draft (June 6, 1983). . . . Traded by Mets organization with P Matt Bullinger and P Jay Tibbs to Cincinnati Reds for P Bruce Berenyi (June 15, 1984). . . . Selected by Cleveland Indians from Reds organization in Rule 5 major league draft (December 10, 1985). . . . Traded by Indians to Chicago White Sox for P Joel Davis and P Ed Wojna (January 23, 1989). . . . Granted free agency (October 15, 1989). . . . Signed by Las Vegas, San Diego Padres organization (December 21, 1989). . . . Contract sold by Padres to Fukuoka Daiei Hawks of Japan Pacific League (December 2, 1990). . . . Released by Fukuoka (September 1991). . . . Signed by Greenville, Atlanta Braves organization (February 16, 1992). . . . Released by Richmond, Braves organization (May 14, 1992). . . . Signed by Denver, Milwaukee Brewers organization (November 30, 1992). . . . Released by New Orleans, Brewers organization (April 19, 1993). . . . Signed by Las Vegas, Padres organization (December 17, 1993). . . . Granted free agency (December 21, 1995). . . . Signed by Detroit Tigers (January 2, 1996).
HONORS: Named Midwest League Most Valuable Player (1985).
STATISTICAL NOTES: Led Midwest League in being hit by pitch with 15 in 1985. . . . Led American Association third basemen with 352 total chances, 24 double plays, 237 assists, and 27 errors in 1987. . . . Led American Association in being hit by pitch with 15 in 1987. . . . Led Pacific Coast League in being hit by pitch with 12 in 1988. . . . Career major league grand slams: 2.

Year	Team (League)	Pos.	G	AB	R	H	2B	3B	HR	RBI	Avg.	BB	SO	SB	PO	A	E	Avg.
			BATTING												FIELDING			
1983—	Little Falls (NYP)	3B	50	190	30	50	6	2	6	28	.263	19	41	3	50	53	13	.888
1984—	Columbia (S. Atl.)	3B	43	152	17	28	4	2	3	24	.184	15	31	1	24	76	16	.862
	— Tampa (Fla. St.)■	3B	50	138	20	35	8	0	2	16	.254	25	23	0	25	43	11	.861
1985—	Ced. Rap. (Midw.)	3B	119	406	71	106	13	3	20	83	.261	62	101	5	83	204	33	.897
1986—	Cleveland (A.L.)■	OF	5	7	2	1	0	0	0	1	.143	0	3	0	0	0	0	. . .
	— Waterbury (East.)	3B	62	214	24	51	10	0	7	30	.238	28	41	3	39	100	15	.903
1987—	Buffalo (A.A.)	3B-SS	131	488	90	142	29	2	22	85	.291	55	117	6	88	†237	†27	.923
	— Cleveland (A.L.)	3B	22	64	9	11	4	0	1	4	.172	9	19	0	17	37	1	.982
1988—	Colo. Springs (PCL)	3B-SS-1B	101	365	53	110	24	3	12	58	.301	18	51	0	93	177	29	.903
	— Cleveland (A.L.)	3B	10	21	3	4	0	0	0	1	.190	0	3	0	3	18	0	1.000
1989—	Chicago (A.L.)■	3B	66	201	25	55	8	0	3	10	.274	18	31	1	37	123	16	.909
	— Vancouver (PCL)	3B-1B	35	114	12	28	8	0	1	13	.246	15	18	1	8	10	4	.818
1990—	Las Vegas (PCL)■	3B-1B	93	348	59	110	29	2	17	75	.316	42	47	0	106	121	17	.930
	— San Diego (N.L.)	3B	14	42	5	12	3	0	3	4	.286	5	6	0	5	21	3	.897
1991—	Fukuoka (Jp. Pac.)■	3B	49	163	20	41	. . .	. . .	5	16	.252	21	32	2	. . .	. . .	. . .	. . .
1992—	Richmond (Int'l)■	3B	24	74	8	15	3	0	1	5	.203	3	9	0	7	26	5	.868
1993—	New Orleans (A.A.)■	3B-1B	8	27	2	7	0	1	1	4	.259	7	4	0	14	13	1	.964
1994—	Las Vegas (PCL)■	1B-3B	59	219	48	77	12	1	20	54	.352	24	34	0	276	49	4	.988
	— San Diego (N.L.)	1B-3B	49	175	32	58	11	1	11	42	.331	15	26	0	383	29	5	.988
1995—	San Diego (N.L.)	1B	97	296	35	77	11	1	12	47	.260	23	47	0	571	49	7	.989
American League totals (4 years)			103	293	39	71	12	0	4	16	.242	27	56	1	57	178	17	.933
National League totals (3 years)			160	513	72	147	25	2	26	93	.287	43	79	0	959	99	15	.986
Major league totals (7 years)			263	806	111	218	37	2	30	109	.270	70	135	1	1016	277	32	.976

WILLIAMS, GEORGE C ATHLETICS

PERSONAL: Born April 22, 1969, in La Crosse, Wis. . . . 5-10/190. . . . Bats both, throws right. . . . Full name: George Erik Williams.
HIGH SCHOOL: La Crosse (Wis.) Central.
COLLEGE: Texas-Pan American.
TRANSACTIONS/CAREER NOTES: Selected by Oakland Athletics organization in 24th round of free-agent draft (June 3, 1991). . . . On disabled list (April 7-June 23, 1994).
STATISTICAL NOTES: Tied for Midwest League lead with six intentional bases on balls received in 1992. . . . Career major league grand slams: 1.

			BATTING												FIELDING			
Year	Team (League)	Pos.	G	AB	R	H	2B	3B	HR	RBI	Avg.	BB	SO	SB	PO	A	E	Avg.
1991—	S. Oregon (N'west).....	C-3B	55	174	24	41	10	0	2	24	.236	38	36	9	126	44	6	.966
1992—	Madison (Midwest)....	C-OF	115	349	56	106	18	2	5	42	.304	76	53	9	455	57	18	.966
1993—	Huntsville (South.).....	C-OF-3B	124	434	80	128	26	2	14	77	.295	67	66	6	430	63	11	.978
1994—	West. Mich. (Mid.).....	C	63	221	40	67	20	1	8	48	.303	44	47	6	21	3	0	1.000
1995—	Edmonton (PCL)........	C-OF	81	290	53	90	20	0	13	55	.310	50	52	0	310	44	7	.981
	—Oakland (A.L.)..........	C-DH	29	79	13	23	5	1	3	14	.291	11	21	0	58	7	3	.956
Major league totals (1 year)			29	79	13	23	5	1	3	14	.291	11	21	0	58	7	3	.956

WILLIAMS, GERALD OF YANKEES

PERSONAL: Born August 10, 1966, in New Orleans. . . . 6-2/190. . . . Bats right, throws right. . . . Full name: Gerald Floyd Williams.
COLLEGE: Grambling State.
TRANSACTIONS/CAREER NOTES: Selected by New York Yankees organization in 14th round of free-agent draft (June 2, 1987).
STATISTICAL NOTES: Led Carolina League outfielders with 307 total chances in 1989. . . . Led International League outfielders with 354 total chances in 1992. . . . Tied for International League lead in double plays by outfielder with five in 1992. . . . Career major league grand slams: 1.

			BATTING												FIELDING			
Year	Team (League)	Pos.	G	AB	R	H	2B	3B	HR	RBI	Avg.	BB	SO	SB	PO	A	E	Avg.
1987—	Oneonta (NYP)...........	OF	29	115	26	42	6	2	2	29	.365	16	18	6	68	3	3	.959
1988—	Prin. William (Car.).....	OF	54	159	20	29	3	0	2	18	.182	15	47	6	71	2	3	.961
	—Fort Lauder. (FSL)......	OF	63	212	21	40	7	2	2	17	.189	16	56	4	163	2	6	.965
1989—	Prin. William (Car.).....	OF	134	454	63	104	19	6	13	69	.229	51	120	15	*292	7	8	.974
1990—	Fort Lauder. (FSL).......	OF	50	204	25	59	4	5	7	43	.289	16	52	19	115	1	3	.975
	—Alb./Colon. (East.)......	OF	96	324	54	81	17	2	13	58	.250	35	74	18	210	6	7	.969
1991—	Alb./Colon. (East.)......	OF	45	175	28	50	15	0	5	32	.286	18	26	18	109	4	3	.974
	—Columbus (Int'l).........	OF	61	198	20	51	8	3	2	27	.258	16	39	9	124	1	3	.977
1992—	Columbus (Int'l).........	OF	*142	547	92	*156	31	6	16	86	.285	38	98	36	*332	*14	8	.977
	—New York (A.L.)..........	OF	15	27	7	8	2	0	3	6	.296	0	3	2	20	1	2	.913
1993—	Columbus (Int'l).........	OF	87	336	53	95	19	6	8	38	.283	20	66	29	191	6	3	.985
	—New York (A.L.)..........	OF-DH	42	67	11	10	2	3	0	6	.149	1	14	2	41	2	2	.956
1994—	New York (A.L.)..........	OF-DH	57	86	19	25	8	0	4	13	.291	4	17	1	43	2	2	.957
1995—	New York (A.L.)..........	OF-DH	100	182	33	45	18	2	6	28	.247	22	34	4	138	6	1	.993
Major league totals (4 years)			214	362	70	88	30	5	13	53	.243	27	68	9	242	11	7	.973

DIVISION SERIES RECORD

			BATTING												FIELDING			
Year	Team (League)	Pos.	G	AB	R	H	2B	3B	HR	RBI	Avg.	BB	SO	SB	PO	A	E	Avg.
1995—	New York (A.L.)..........	OF-PR	5	5	1	0	0	0	0	0	.000	2	3	0	7	1	0	1.000

WILLIAMS, KEITH OF GIANTS

PERSONAL: Born April 21, 1972, in Bedford, Pa. . . . 6-0/190. . . . Bats right, throws right. . . . Full name: David Keith Williams.
HIGH SCHOOL: Bedford (Pa.).
COLLEGE: Clemson.
TRANSACTIONS/CAREER NOTES: Selected by San Francisco Giants organization in seventh round of free-agent draft (June 3, 1993).
STATISTICAL NOTES: Led Northwest League with 154 total bases in 1993.

			BATTING												FIELDING			
Year	Team (League)	Pos.	G	AB	R	H	2B	3B	HR	RBI	Avg.	BB	SO	SB	PO	A	E	Avg.
1993—	Everett (N'west)..........	OF	75	288	57	*87	21	5	12	49	.302	48	73	21	106	3	3	.973
1994—	San Jose (Calif.).........	OF	128	504	91	151	30	8	21	97	.300	60	102	4	197	6	3	*.985
1995—	Shreveport (Texas).....	OF	75	275	39	84	20	1	9	55	.305	23	39	5	109	4	4	.966
	—Phoenix (PCL)............	OF	24	83	7	25	4	1	2	14	.301	5	11	0	38	1	0	1.000

WILLIAMS, MATT 3B GIANTS

PERSONAL: Born November 28, 1965, in Bishop, Calif. . . . 6-2/216. . . . Bats right, throws right. . . . Full name: Matthew Derrick Williams. . . . Grandson of Bartholomew (Bart) Griffith, outfielder/first baseman, Brooklyn Dodgers and Washington Senators (1922-24).
HIGH SCHOOL: Carson (Nev.).
COLLEGE: UNLV.
TRANSACTIONS/CAREER NOTES: Selected by New York Mets organization in 27th round of free-agent draft (June 6, 1983); did not sign. . . . Selected by San Francisco Giants organization in first round (third pick overall) of free-agent draft (June 2, 1986). . . . On disabled list (June 28-July 14, 1993). . . . On San Francisco disabled list (June 4-August 19, 1995); included rehabilitation assignments to San Jose (July 24-25 and August 13-19).
HONORS: Named shortstop on The Sporting News college All-America team (1986). . . . Named third baseman on The Sporting News N.L. All-Star team (1990 and 1993-94). . . . Named third baseman on The Sporting News N.L. Silver Slugger team (1990 and 1993-94). . . . Won N.L. Gold Glove at third base (1991 and 1993-94).

STATISTICAL NOTES: Led N.L. third basemen with 33 double plays in 1990 and 1992 and 34 in 1993. . . . Tied for N.L. lead in total chances by third baseman with 465 in 1990. . . . Led N.L. third basemen with 131 putouts in 1991. . . . Led N.L. third basemen with 326 total chances in 1994. . . . Career major league grand slams: 5.

			BATTING												FIELDING			
Year	Team (League)	Pos.	G	AB	R	H	2B	3B	HR	RBI	Avg.	BB	SO	SB	PO	A	E	Avg.
1986—	Everett (N'west)	SS	4	17	3	4	0	1	1	10	.235	1	4	0	5	10	2	.882
—	Clinton (Midwest)	SS	68	250	32	60	14	3	7	29	.240	23	62	3	89	150	10	.960
1987—	Phoenix (PCL)	3B-2B-SS	56	211	36	61	15	2	6	37	.289	19	53	6	53	136	14	.931
—	San Francisco (N.L.)	SS-3B	84	245	28	46	9	2	8	21	.188	16	68	4	110	234	9	.975
1988—	Phoenix (PCL)	3-S-2-O	82	306	45	83	19	1	12	51	.271	13	56	6	56	173	13	.946
—	San Francisco (N.L.)	3B-SS	52	156	17	32	6	1	8	19	.205	8	41	0	48	108	7	.957
1989—	San Francisco (N.L.)	3B-SS	84	292	31	59	18	1	18	50	.202	14	72	1	90	168	10	.963
—	Phoenix (PCL)	3B-SS-OF	76	284	61	91	20	2	26	61	.320	32	51	9	57	197	11	.958
1990—	San Francisco (N.L.)	3B	159	617	87	171	27	2	33	*122	.277	33	138	7	*140	306	19	.959
1991—	San Francisco (N.L.)	3B-SS	157	589	72	158	24	5	34	98	.268	33	128	5	†134	295	16	.964
1992—	San Francisco (N.L.)	3B	146	529	58	120	13	5	20	66	.227	39	109	7	105	289	*23	.945
1993—	San Francisco (N.L.)	3B	145	579	105	170	33	4	38	110	.294	27	80	1	117	266	12	.970
1994—	San Francisco (N.L.)	3B	112	445	74	119	16	3	*43	96	.267	33	87	1	79	*235	12	.963
1995—	San Francisco (N.L.)	3B	76	283	53	95	17	1	23	65	.336	30	58	2	49	178	10	.958
—	San Jose (Calif.)	3B	4	11	2	2	0	0	1	2	.182	0	3	0	0	4	0	1.000
Major league totals (9 years)			1015	3735	525	970	163	24	225	647	.260	233	781	28	872	2079	118	.962

CHAMPIONSHIP SERIES RECORD

NOTES: Holds N.L. single-series record for most runs batted in—9 (1989).

			BATTING												FIELDING			
Year	Team (League)	Pos.	G	AB	R	H	2B	3B	HR	RBI	Avg.	BB	SO	SB	PO	A	E	Avg.
1987—	San Francisco (N.L.)								Did not play.									
1989—	San Francisco (N.L.)	3B-SS	5	20	2	6	1	0	2	9	.300	0	2	0	5	12	0	1.000
Championship series totals (1 year)			5	20	2	6	1	0	2	9	.300	0	2	0	5	12	0	1.000

WORLD SERIES RECORD

			BATTING												FIELDING			
Year	Team (League)	Pos.	G	AB	R	H	2B	3B	HR	RBI	Avg.	BB	SO	SB	PO	A	E	Avg.
1989—	San Francisco (N.L.)	SS-3B	4	16	1	2	0	0	1	1	.125	0	6	0	4	12	0	1.000

ALL-STAR GAME RECORD

			BATTING											FIELDING			
Year	League	Pos.	AB	R	H	2B	3B	HR	RBI	Avg.	BB	SO	SB	PO	A	E	Avg.
1990—	National	PH	1	0	0	0	0	0	0	.000	0	1	0	...	...	...	...
1994—	National	3B	3	0	0	0	0	0	0	.000	0	2	0	0	1	1	.500
1995—	National						Selected, did not play—injured.										
All-Star Game totals (2 years)			4	0	0	0	0	0	0	.000	0	3	0	0	1	1	.500

WILLIAMS, MIKE — P — PHILLIES

PERSONAL: Born July 29, 1968, in Radford, Va. . . . 6-2/195. . . . Throws right, bats right. . . . Full name: Michael Darren Williams.
HIGH SCHOOL: Giles (Pearisburg, Va.).
COLLEGE: Virginia Tech.
TRANSACTIONS/CAREER NOTES: Selected by Philadelphia Phillies organization in 14th round of free-agent draft (June 4, 1990).

Year	Team (League)	W	L	Pct.	ERA	G	GS	CG	ShO	Sv.	IP	H	R	ER	BB	SO
1990—	Batavia (NYP)	2	3	.400	2.30	27	0	0	0	11	47	39	17	12	13	42
1991—	Clearwater (Fla. St.)	7	3	.700	1.74	14	14	2	1	0	93 1/3	65	23	18	14	76
—	Reading (Eastern)	7	5	.583	3.69	16	15	2	1	0	102 1/3	93	44	42	36	51
1992—	Reading (Eastern)	1	2	.333	5.17	3	3	0	0	0	15 2/3	17	10	9	7	12
—	Scran./W.B. (Int'l)	9	1	*.900	2.43	16	16	3	1	0	92 2/3	84	26	25	30	59
—	Philadelphia (N.L.)	1	1	.500	5.34	5	5	1	0	0	28 2/3	29	20	17	7	5
1993—	Scran./W.B. (Int'l)	9	2	*.818	2.87	14	13	1	1	0	97 1/3	93	34	31	16	53
—	Philadelphia (N.L.)	1	3	.250	5.29	17	4	0	0	0	51	50	32	30	22	33
1994—	Philadelphia (N.L.)	2	4	.333	5.01	12	8	0	0	0	50 1/3	61	31	28	20	29
—	Scran./W.B. (Int'l)	2	7	.222	5.79	14	14	1	0	0	84	91	55	54	36	53
1995—	Philadelphia (N.L.)	3	3	.500	3.29	33	8	0	0	0	87 2/3	78	37	32	29	57
—	Scran./W.B. (Int'l)	0	1	.000	4.66	3	3	1	0	0	9 2/3	8	5	5	2	8
Major league totals (4 years)		7	11	.389	4.42	67	25	1	0	0	217 2/3	218	120	107	78	124

WILLIAMS, MITCH — P

PERSONAL: Born November 17, 1964, in Santa Ana, Calif. . . . 6-4/205. . . . Throws left, bats left. . . . Full name: Mitchell Steven Williams. . . . Brother of Bruce Williams, minor league pitcher (1981-85).
HIGH SCHOOL: West Linn (Ore.).
TRANSACTIONS/CAREER NOTES: Selected by San Diego Padres organization in eighth round of free-agent draft (June 7, 1982). . . . Selected by Texas Rangers from Padres organization in Rule 5 major league draft (December 3, 1984). . . . Returned to Padres organization (April 6, 1985). . . . Traded by Padres organization to Rangers for 3B Randy Asadoor (April 6, 1985). . . . On suspended list (May 2-4, 1988). . . . Traded by Rangers with P Paul Kilgus, P Steve Wilson, IF Curtis Wilkerson, IF Luis Benitez and OF Pablo Delgado to Chicago Cubs for OF Rafael Palmeiro, P Jamie Moyer and P Drew Hall (December 5, 1988). . . . On disabled list (June 12-July 12, 1990). . . . Traded by Cubs to Philadelphia Phillies for P Chuck McElroy and P Bob Scanlan (April 7, 1991). . . . Granted free agency (October 31, 1991). . . . Re-signed by Phillies (December 18, 1991). . . . Traded by Phillies to Houston Astros for P Doug Jones and P Jeff Juden (December 2, 1993). . . . Released by Astros (May 31, 1994). . . . Signed by California Angels (November 30, 1994). . . . Released by Angels (June 19, 1995).
RECORDS: Holds major league rookie-season record for most games pitched—80 (1986).
STATISTICAL NOTES: Led Northwest League pitchers with 14 wild pitches and tied for lead with two balks in 1983.

Year	Team (League)	W	L	Pct.	ERA	G	GS	CG	ShO	Sv.	IP	H	R	ER	BB	SO
1982—	Wal. Walla (N'west)	3	4	.429	4.78	12	12	0	0	0	58 1/3	37	37	31	*72	66
1983—	Reno (California)	1	7	.125	7.14	11	11	0	0	0	58	58	56	46	60	44
—	Spokane (N'west)	7	6	.538	4.48	14	•14	3	1	0	92 1/3	84	51	•46	55	87
1984—	Reno (California)	9	8	.529	4.99	26	26	3	1	0	164	163	113	91	127	165
1985—	Salem (Carolina)■	6	9	.400	5.45	22	21	1	0	0	99	57	64	60	*117	138
—	Tulsa (Texas)	2	2	.500	4.64	6	6	0	0	0	33	17	24	17	48	37
1986—	Texas (A.L.)	8	6	.571	3.58	*80	0	0	0	8	98	69	39	39	79	90
1987—	Texas (A.L.)	8	6	.571	3.23	85	1	0	0	6	108 2/3	63	47	39	94	129
1988—	Texas (A.L.)	2	7	.222	4.63	67	0	0	0	18	68	48	38	35	47	61
1989—	Chicago (N.L.)■	4	4	.500	2.64	*76	0	0	0	36	81 2/3	71	27	24	52	67
1990—	Chicago (N.L.)	1	8	.111	3.93	59	2	0	0	16	66 1/3	60	38	29	50	55
1991—	Philadelphia (N.L.)■	12	5	.706	2.34	69	0	0	0	30	88 1/3	56	24	23	62	84
1992—	Philadelphia (N.L.)	5	8	.385	3.78	66	0	0	0	29	81	69	39	34	64	74
1993—	Philadelphia (N.L.)	3	7	.300	3.34	65	0	0	0	43	62	56	30	23	44	60
1994—	Houston (N.L.)■	1	4	.200	7.65	25	0	0	0	6	20	21	17	17	24	21
1995—	California (A.L.)■	1	2	.333	6.75	20	0	0	0	0	10 2/3	13	10	8	21	9
A.L. totals (4 years)		19	21	.475	3.82	252	1	0	0	32	285 1/3	193	134	121	241	289
N.L. totals (6 years)		26	36	.419	3.38	360	2	0	0	160	399 1/3	333	175	150	296	361
Major league totals (10 years)		45	57	.441	3.56	612	3	0	0	192	684 2/3	526	309	271	537	650

CHAMPIONSHIP SERIES RECORD

Year	Team (League)	W	L	Pct.	ERA	G	GS	CG	ShO	Sv.	IP	H	R	ER	BB	SO
1989—	Chicago (N.L.)	0	0	...	0.00	2	0	0	0	0	1	1	0	0	0	2
1993—	Philadelphia (N.L.)	2	0	1.000	1.69	4	0	0	0	2	5 1/3	6	2	1	2	5
Champ. series totals (2 years)		2	0	1.000	1.42	6	0	0	0	2	6 1/3	7	2	1	2	7

WORLD SERIES RECORD

Year	Team (League)	W	L	Pct.	ERA	G	GS	CG	ShO	Sv.	IP	H	R	ER	BB	SO
1993—	Philadelphia (N.L.)	0	2	.000	20.25	3	0	0	0	1	2 2/3	5	6	6	4	1

ALL-STAR GAME RECORD

Year	League	W	L	Pct.	ERA	GS	CG	ShO	Sv.	IP	H	R	ER	BB	SO
1989—	National	0	0	...	0.00	0	0	0	0	1	0	0	0	1	1

WILLIAMS, REGGIE — OF

PERSONAL: Born May 5, 1966, in Laurens, S.C. . . . 6-1/185. . . . Bats both, throws right. . . . Full name: Reginald Bernard Williams.
HIGH SCHOOL: Laurens (S.C.) District 55.
COLLEGE: South Carolina-Aiken.
TRANSACTIONS/CAREER NOTES: Selected by San Francisco Giants organization in 25th round of free-agent draft (June 1, 1988). . . . Released by Giants organization (June 20, 1989). . . . Signed by Boise, independent (July 20, 1989). . . . Signed as free agent by California Angels organization (February 15, 1990). . . . On Quad City disabled list (April 12-May 22, 1991). . . . Traded by Angels to Los Angeles Dodgers for P Mike James (October 26, 1993). . . . Released by Dodgers (October 13, 1994). . . . Re-signed by Dodgers (April 11, 1995). . . . Granted free agency (October 16, 1995).
STATISTICAL NOTES: Led Northwest League with 10 caught stealing in 1988. . . . Led Pacific Coast League outfielders with 324 total chances in 1992 and 303 in 1993. . . . Tied for Pacific Coast League lead in double plays by outfielder with four in 1993.

			BATTING												FIELDING			
Year	Team (League)	Pos.	G	AB	R	H	2B	3B	HR	RBI	Avg.	BB	SO	SB	PO	A	E	Avg.
1988—	Everett (N'west)	OF	60	223	52	56	8	1	3	29	.251	47	43	36	131	4	4	.971
1989—	Clinton (Midwest)	OF	68	236	38	46	9	2	3	18	.195	29	66	14	146	7	3	.981
—	Boise (Northwest)■	OF	42	153	33	41	5	1	3	14	.268	24	29	18	64	3	2	.971
1990—	Quad City (Midw.)■	OF	58	189	50	46	11	2	3	12	.243	39	60	24	110	6	1	.991
1991—	Midland (Texas)	OF	83	319	77	99	12	3	1	30	.310	62	67	21	187	9	7	.966
—	Palm Springs (Cal.)	OF	14	44	10	13	1	0	1	2	.295	21	15	6	33	1	1	.971
1992—	Edmonton (PCL)	OF	139	519	96	141	26	9	3	64	.272	88	110	44	*313	8	3	.991
—	California (A.L.)	OF-DH	14	26	5	6	1	1	0	2	.231	1	10	0	26	0	0	1.000
1993—	Vancouver (PCL)	OF	130	481	92	132	17	6	2	53	.274	*88	99	*50	*293	6	4	.987
1994—	Albuquerque (PCL)■	OF	104	288	55	90	15	8	4	42	.313	33	62	21	137	6	4	.973
1995—	Los Angeles (N.L.)	OF	15	11	2	1	0	0	0	1	.091	2	3	0	6	0	0	1.000
—	Albuquerque (PCL)	OF	66	234	44	73	15	5	6	29	.312	30	46	6	141	10	0	1.000
American League totals (1 year)			14	26	5	6	1	1	0	2	.231	1	10	0	26	0	0	1.000
National League totals (1 year)			15	11	2	1	0	0	0	1	.091	2	3	0	6	0	0	1.000
Major league totals (2 years)			29	37	7	7	1	1	0	3	.189	3	13	0	32	0	0	1.000

WILLIAMS, SHAD — P — ANGELS

PERSONAL: Born March 10, 1971, in Fresno, Calif. . . . 6-0/185. . . . Throws right, bats right. . . . Full name: Shad Clayton Williams.
HIGH SCHOOL: San Joaquin Memorial (Fresno, Calif.).
COLLEGE: Fresno (Calif.) City College.
TRANSACTIONS/CAREER NOTES: Selected by California Angels organization in 17th round of free-agent draft (June 3, 1991). . . . On Midland disabled list (April 19-May 24, 1994).
STATISTICAL NOTES: Pitched 7-0 no-hit victory for Midland against Arkansas (May 28, 1994, second game).

Year	Team (League)	W	L	Pct.	ERA	G	GS	CG	ShO	Sv.	IP	H	R	ER	BB	SO
1992—	Quad City (Midw.)	13	11	.542	3.26	27	26	7	0	0	179 1/3	161	81	65	55	152
1993—	Midland (Texas)	7	10	.412	4.71	27	•27	2	0	0	175 2/3	192	100	92	65	91
1994—	Midland (Texas)	3	0	1.000	1.11	5	5	1	1	0	32 1/3	13	4	4	4	29
—	Vancouver (PCL)	4	6	.400	4.60	16	16	1	1	0	86	100	61	44	30	42
1995—	Vancouver (PCL)	9	7	.563	3.37	25	25	3	1	0	149 2/3	142	65	56	48	114

WILLIAMS, TODD — P — ATHLETICS

PERSONAL: Born February 13, 1971, in Syracuse, N.Y. . . . 6-3/185. . . . Throws right, bats right. . . . Full name: Todd Michael Williams.
HIGH SCHOOL: East Syracuse (N.Y.) Minoa.
JUNIOR COLLEGE: Onondaga Community College (N.Y.).
TRANSACTIONS/CAREER NOTES: Selected by Los Angeles Dodgers organization in 54th round of free-agent draft (June 4, 1990). . . . On disabled list (April 7-16, 1994). . . . Traded by Dodgers to Oakland Athletics for P Matt McDonald (September 8, 1995).

Year	Team (League)	W	L	Pct.	ERA	G	GS	CG	ShO	Sv.	IP	H	R	ER	BB	SO
1991—	Great Falls (Pio.)	5	2	.714	2.72	28	0	0	0	8	53	50	26	16	24	59
1992—	Bakersfield (Calif.)	0	0	. . .	2.30	13	0	0	0	9	15 2/3	11	4	4	7	11
	— San Antonio (Tex.)	7	4	.636	3.27	39	0	0	0	13	44	47	17	16	23	35
1993—	Albuquerque (PCL)	5	5	.500	4.99	*65	0	0	0	*21	70 1/3	87	44	39	31	56
1994—	Albuquerque (PCL)	4	2	.667	3.11	59	0	0	0	13	72 1/3	78	29	25	17	30
1995—	Los Angeles (N.L.)	2	2	.500	5.12	16	0	0	0	0	19 1/3	19	11	11	7	8
	— Albuquerque (PCL)	4	1	.800	3.38	25	0	0	0	0	45 1/3	59	21	17	15	23
Major league totals (1 year)		2	2	.500	5.12	16	0	0	0	0	19 1/3	19	11	11	7	8

WILLIAMS, WOODY — P — BLUE JAYS

PERSONAL: Born August 19, 1966, in Houston. . . . 6-0/190. . . . Throws right, bats right. . . . Full name: Gregory Scott Williams.
HIGH SCHOOL: Cy-Fair (Houston).
COLLEGE: Houston.
TRANSACTIONS/CAREER NOTES: Selected by Toronto Blue Jays organization in 28th round of free-agent draft (June 1, 1988). . . . On disabled list (April 9-May 17, 1992). . . . On Toronto disabled list (July 17, 1995-remainder of season); included rehabilitation assignment to Syracuse (August 15-25).

Year	Team (League)	W	L	Pct.	ERA	G	GS	CG	ShO	Sv.	IP	H	R	ER	BB	SO
1988—	St. Cathar. (NYP)	8	2	.800	1.54	12	12	2	0	0	76	48	22	13	21	58
	— Knoxville (South.)	2	2	.500	3.81	6	4	0	0	0	28 1/3	27	13	12	12	25
1989—	Dunedin (Fla. St.)	3	5	.375	2.32	20	9	0	0	3	81 1/3	63	26	21	27	60
	— Knoxville (South.)	3	5	.375	3.55	14	12	2	•2	1	71	61	32	28	33	51
1990—	Knoxville (South.)	7	9	.438	3.14	42	12	0	0	5	126	111	55	44	39	74
	— Syracuse (Int'l)	0	1	.000	10.00	3	0	0	0	0	9	15	10	10	4	8
1991—	Knoxville (South.)	3	2	.600	3.59	18	1	0	0	3	42 2/3	42	18	17	14	37
	— Syracuse (Int'l)	3	4	.429	4.12	31	0	0	0	6	54 2/3	52	27	25	27	37
1992—	Syracuse (Int'l)	6	8	.429	3.13	25	16	1	0	1	120 2/3	115	46	42	41	81
1993—	Syracuse (Int'l)	1	1	.500	2.20	12	0	0	0	3	16 1/3	15	5	4	5	16
	— Toronto (A.L.)	3	1	.750	4.38	30	0	0	0	0	37	40	18	18	22	24
	— Dunedin (Fla. St.)	0	0	. . .	0.00	2	0	0	0	0	4	0	0	0	2	2
1994—	Toronto (A.L.)	1	3	.250	3.64	38	0	0	0	0	59 1/3	44	24	24	33	56
	— Syracuse (Int'l)	0	0	. . .	0.00	1	0	0	0	1	1 2/3	0	0	0	0	1
1995—	Toronto (A.L.)	1	2	.333	3.69	23	3	0	0	0	53 2/3	44	23	22	28	41
	— Syracuse (Int'l)	0	0	. . .	3.52	5	1	0	0	1	7 2/3	5	3	3	5	13
Major league totals (3 years)		5	6	.455	3.84	91	3	0	0	0	150	128	65	64	83	121

WILLIS, CARL — P

PERSONAL: Born December 28, 1960, in Danville, Va. . . . 6-4/213. . . . Throws right, bats left. . . . Full name: Carl Blake Willis.
HIGH SCHOOL: Piedmont Academy (Providence, N.C.).
COLLEGE: UNC Wilmington.
TRANSACTIONS/CAREER NOTES: Selected by San Francisco Giants organization in 31st round of free-agent draft (June 7, 1982); did not sign. . . . Selected by Detroit Tigers organization in 23rd round of free-agent draft (June 6, 1983). . . . Traded by Tigers to Cincinnati Reds (September 1, 1984), completing deal in which Reds traded P Bill Scherrer to Tigers for cash and a player to be named later (August 27, 1984). . . . Selected by California Angels from Reds organization in Rule 5 major league draft (December 10, 1985). . . . Returned to Reds organization (April 6, 1986). . . . Traded by Reds organization to Chicago White Sox for OF Darrell Pruitt (January 19, 1988). . . . Selected by Edmonton, Angels organization, from White Sox organization in Rule 5 minor league draft (December 6, 1988). . . . Granted free agency (October 22, 1989). . . . Signed by Colorado Springs, Cleveland Indians organization (December 20, 1989). . . . Granted free agency (October 15, 1990). . . . Signed by Portland, Minnesota Twins organization (December 12, 1990). . . . On Minnesota disabled list (March 30-May 14, 1993); included rehabilitation assignment to Portland (May 6-14). . . . Granted free agency (October 12, 1994). . . . Re-signed by Salt Lake, Twins organization (April 6, 1995). . . . Released by Twins (May 4, 1995). . . . Signed by Vancouver, Angels organization (June 27, 1995). . . . Granted free agency (October 16, 1995).

Year	Team (League)	W	L	Pct.	ERA	G	GS	CG	ShO	Sv.	IP	H	R	ER	BB	SO
1983—	Bristol (Appal.)	0	1	.000	3.38	2	0	0	0	0	2 2/3	0	1	1	4	3
	— Lakeland (Fla. St.)	3	0	1.000	0.00	4	0	0	0	0	9 2/3	6	0	0	5	7
	— Birmingham (Sou.)	3	1	.750	3.98	14	0	0	0	2	20 1/3	16	9	9	7	13
1984—	Evansville (A.A.)	5	3	.625	3.73	40	1	0	0	16	60 1/3	59	26	25	20	27
	— Detroit (A.L.)	0	2	.000	7.31	10	2	0	0	0	16	25	13	13	5	4
	— Cincinnati (N.L.)■	0	1	.000	3.72	7	0	0	0	1	9 2/3	8	4	4	2	3
1985—	Cincinnati (N.L.)	1	0	1.000	9.22	11	0	0	0	1	13 2/3	21	18	14	5	6
	— Denver (Am. Assoc.)	4	4	.500	4.15	37	1	0	0	8	78	82	39	36	30	27
1986—	Denver (Am. Assoc.)	1	3	.250	4.68	20	1	0	0	8	32 2/3	29	22	17	16	16
	— Cincinnati (N.L.)	1	3	.250	4.47	29	0	0	0	0	52 1/3	54	29	26	32	24
1987—	Nashville (A.A.)	6	4	.600	3.33	53	0	0	0	5	83 2/3	97	39	31	30	54
1988—	Vancouver (PCL)■	4	4	.500	4.22	40	1	0	0	4	64	77	36	30	16	44
	— Chicago (A.L.)	0	0	. . .	8.25	6	0	0	0	0	12	17	12	11	7	6
1989—	Edmonton (PCL)■	5	7	.417	3.69	36	10	0	0	5	112 1/3	137	54	46	36	47
1990—	Colo. Springs (PCL)■	5	3	.625	6.39	41	6	0	0	2	98 2/3	136	80	70	32	42
1991—	Portland (PCL)■	1	1	.500	1.64	3	1	0	0	0	11	5	4	2	0	0
	— Minnesota (A.L.)	8	3	.727	2.63	40	0	0	0	2	89	76	31	26	19	53
1992—	Minnesota (A.L.)	7	3	.700	2.72	59	0	0	0	1	79 1/3	73	25	24	11	45

Year	Team (League)	W	L	Pct.	ERA	G	GS	CG	ShO	Sv.	IP	H	R	ER	BB	SO
1993—	Portland (PCL)	0	0	...	2.25	2	0	0	0	0	4	6	2	1	1	2
—	Minnesota (A.L.)	3	0	1.000	3.10	53	0	0	0	5	58	56	23	20	17	44
1994—	Minnesota (A.L.)	2	4	.333	5.92	49	0	0	0	3	59 1/3	89	48	39	12	37
1995—	Minnesota (A.L.)	0	0	...	94.50	3	0	0	0	0	2/3	5	7	7	5	0
—	Vancouver (PCL)■	2	2	.500	4.11	20	0	0	0	1	35	40	17	16	11	17
A.L. totals (7 years)		20	12	.625	4.01	220	2	0	0	11	314 1/3	341	159	140	76	189
N.L. totals (3 years)		2	4	.333	5.23	47	0	0	0	2	75 2/3	83	51	44	39	33
Major league totals (9 years)		22	16	.579	4.25	267	2	0	0	13	390	424	210	184	115	222

CHAMPIONSHIP SERIES RECORD

Year	Team (League)	W	L	Pct.	ERA	G	GS	CG	ShO	Sv.	IP	H	R	ER	BB	SO
1991—	Minnesota (A.L.)	0	0	...	0.00	3	0	0	0	0	5 1/3	2	0	0	0	3

WORLD SERIES RECORD

NOTES: Member of World Series championship team (1991).

Year	Team (League)	W	L	Pct.	ERA	G	GS	CG	ShO	Sv.	IP	H	R	ER	BB	SO
1991—	Minnesota (A.L.)	0	0	...	5.14	4	0	0	0	0	7	6	4	4	2	2

WILSON, DAN — C — MARINERS

PERSONAL: Born March 25, 1969, in Arlington Heights, Ill. . . . 6-3/202. . . . Bats right, throws right. . . . Full name: Daniel Allen Wilson.
HIGH SCHOOL: Barrington (Ill.).
COLLEGE: Minnesota.
TRANSACTIONS/CAREER NOTES: Selected by New York Mets organization in 26th round of free-agent draft (June 2, 1987); did not sign. . . . Selected by Cincinnati Reds organization in first round (seventh pick overall) of free-agent draft (June 4, 1990). . . . Traded by Reds with P Bobby Ayala to Seattle Mariners for P Erik Hanson and 2B Bret Boone (November 2, 1993).
STATISTICAL NOTES: Led American Association catchers with 810 total chances in 1992. . . . Led A.L. catchers with 952 total chances in 1995.

			BATTING												FIELDING			
Year	Team (League)	Pos.	G	AB	R	H	2B	3B	HR	RBI	Avg.	BB	SO	SB	PO	A	E	Avg.
1990—	Char., W.Va. (SAL)	C	32	113	16	28	9	1	2	17	.248	13	17	0	190	24	1	.995
1991—	Char., W.Va. (SAL)	C	52	197	25	62	11	1	3	29	.315	25	21	1	355	41	3	.992
—	Chatt. (South.)	C	81	292	32	75	19	2	2	38	.257	21	39	2	486	49	4	.993
1992—	Nashville (A.A.)	C	106	366	27	92	16	1	4	34	.251	31	58	1	*733	*69	*8	.990
—	Cincinnati (N.L.)	C	12	25	2	9	1	0	0	3	.360	3	8	0	42	4	0	1.000
1993—	Cincinnati (N.L.)	C	36	76	6	17	3	0	0	8	.224	9	16	0	146	9	1	.994
—	Indianapolis (A.A.)	C	51	191	18	50	11	1	1	17	.262	19	31	1	314	24	2	.994
1994—	Seattle (A.L.)■	C	91	282	24	61	14	2	3	27	.216	10	57	1	602	45	*9	.986
1995—	Seattle (A.L.)	C	119	399	40	111	22	3	9	51	.278	33	63	2	*895	52	5	.995
American League totals (2 years)			210	681	64	172	36	5	12	78	.253	43	120	3	1497	97	14	.991
National League totals (2 years)			48	101	8	26	4	0	0	11	.257	12	24	0	188	13	1	.995
Major league totals (4 years)			258	782	72	198	40	5	12	89	.253	55	144	3	1685	110	15	.992

DIVISION SERIES RECORD

			BATTING												FIELDING			
Year	Team (League)	Pos.	G	AB	R	H	2B	3B	HR	RBI	Avg.	BB	SO	SB	PO	A	E	Avg.
1995—	Seattle (A.L.)	C	5	17	0	2	0	0	0	1	.118	2	6	0	34	1	0	1.000

CHAMPIONSHIP SERIES RECORD

			BATTING												FIELDING			
Year	Team (League)	Pos.	G	AB	R	H	2B	3B	HR	RBI	Avg.	BB	SO	SB	PO	A	E	Avg.
1995—	Seattle (A.L.)	C	6	16	0	0	0	0	0	0	.000	0	4	0	35	3	1	.974

WILSON, ENRIQUE — SS — INDIANS

PERSONAL: Born July 27, 1975, in Santo Domingo, Dominican Republic. . . . 5-11/160. . . . Bats both, throws right. . . . Full name: Enrique Martes Wilson.
HIGH SCHOOL: Liceo Ramon Amelio Jiminez (Santo Domingo, Dominican Republic).
TRANSACTIONS/CAREER NOTES: Signed as non-drafted free agent by Minnesota Twins organization (April 15, 1992). . . . Traded by Twins organization to Cleveland Indians organization (February 21, 1994), completing deal in which Twins acquired P Shawn Bryant for a player to be named later (February 21, 1994).
STATISTICAL NOTES: Led South Atlantic League shortstops with 625 total chances and 66 double plays in 1994. . . . Led Carolina League with 10 sacrifice flies in 1995.

			BATTING												FIELDING			
Year	Team (League)	Pos.	G	AB	R	H	2B	3B	HR	RBI	Avg.	BB	SO	SB	PO	A	E	Avg.
1992—	GC Twins (GCL)	SS	13	44	12	15	1	0	0	8	.341	4	4	3	9	26	4	.897
1993—	Elizabeth. (Appal.)	SS-3B	58	197	42	57	8	4	13	50	.289	14	18	5	50	139	19	.909
1994—	Columbus (S. Atl.)■	SS	133	512	82	143	28	12	10	72	.279	44	34	21	*185	*407	33	.947
1995—	Kinston (Carolina)	SS-2B	117	464	55	124	24	•7	6	52	.267	25	38	18	181	375	21	.964

WILSON, GARY — P — PIRATES

PERSONAL: Born January 1, 1970, in Arcata, Calif. . . . 6-3/190. . . . Throws right, bats right. . . . Full name: Gary Morris Wilson.
HIGH SCHOOL: Arcata (Calif.).
COLLEGE: Cal State Sacramento.
TRANSACTIONS/CAREER NOTES: Selected by Pittsburgh Pirates organization in 18th round of free-agent draft (June 1, 1992). . . . On Calgary disabled list (June 25-July 5 and July 6-August 15, 1995).

Year	Team (League)	W	L	Pct.	ERA	G	GS	CG	ShO	Sv.	IP	H	R	ER	BB	SO
1992—	Welland (NYP)	3	2	.600	1.06	13	4	0	0	0	42 1/3	27	9	5	13	40
—	Augusta (S. Atl.)	2	3	.400	3.67	7	7	0	0	0	41 2/3	43	22	17	7	27
1993—	Augusta (S. Atl.)	3	7	.300	5.47	20	6	0	0	0	51	66	35	31	11	42

Year	Team (League)	W	L	Pct.	ERA	G	GS	CG	ShO	Sv.	IP	H	R	ER	BB	SO
	—Salem (Carolina)	5	5	.500	5.74	15	15	0	0	0	78 1/3	102	58	50	25	54
1994	—Salem (Carolina)	3	1	.750	2.31	6	6	1	1	0	35	41	12	9	4	26
	—Carolina (South.)	8	5	.615	2.56	22	22	*7	2	0	161 2/3	144	55	46	37	97
1995	—Pittsburgh (N.L.)	0	1	.000	5.02	10	0	0	0	0	14 1/3	13	8	8	5	8
	—Calgary (PCL)	1	2	.333	5.51	6	4	0	0	0	16 1/3	19	16	10	9	12
	—Carolina (South.)	0	0	...	0.00	1	1	0	0	0	4 2/3	0	0	0	3	5
Major league totals (1 year)		0	1	.000	5.02	10	0	0	0	0	14 1/3	13	8	8	5	8

WILSON, NIGEL — OF — REDS

PERSONAL: Born January 12, 1970, in Oshawa, Ont. . . . 6-1/185. . . . Bats left, throws left. . . . Full name: Nigel Edward Wilson.
HIGH SCHOOL: Ajax (Ont.).
TRANSACTIONS/CAREER NOTES: Signed as non-drafted free agent by Toronto Blue Jays organization (July 30, 1987). . . . Selected by Florida Marlins in first round (second pick overall) of expansion draft (November 17, 1992). . . . On Edmonton disabled list (June 18-July 24, 1993 and May 7-June 7, 1994). . . . Claimed on waivers by Cincinnati Reds (April 22, 1995). . . . Released by Reds (April 23, 1995). . . . Re-signed by Indianapolis, Reds organization (April 25, 1995).
STATISTICAL NOTES: Led Florida State League with 217 total bases and .477 slugging percentage in 1991. . . . Led Southern League with 269 total bases in 1992. . . . Tied for Pacific Coast League lead in being hit by pitch with 10 in 1993.

				BATTING											FIELDING			
Year	Team (League)	Pos.	G	AB	R	H	2B	3B	HR	RBI	Avg.	BB	SO	SB	PO	A	E	Avg.
1988	—St. Cathar. (NYP)	OF	40	103	12	21	1	2	2	11	.204	12	32	8	50	3	5	.914
1989	—St. Cathar. (NYP)	OF	42	161	17	35	5	2	4	18	.217	11	50	8	37	2	3	.929
1990	—Myrtle Beach (SAL)	OF	110	440	77	120	23	9	16	62	.273	30	71	22	127	7	10	.931
1991	—Dunedin (Fla. St.)	OF	119	455	64	137	18	*13	12	55	.301	29	99	27	196	7	8	.962
1992	—Knoxville (South.)	OF	137	521	85	143	•34	7	26	69	.274	33	137	13	192	6	9	.957
1993	—Edmonton (PCL)■	OF	96	370	66	108	26	7	17	68	.292	25	108	8	121	13	2	.985
	—Florida (N.L.)	OF	7	16	0	0	0	0	0	0	.000	0	11	0	4	0	0	1.000
1994	—Edmonton (PCL)	OF	87	314	50	97	24	1	12	62	.309	22	79	2	121	10	4	.970
1995	—Indianapolis (A.A.)■	OF	82	304	53	95	27	3	17	51	.313	13	95	5	111	4	5	.958
	—Cincinnati (N.L.)	OF	5	7	0	0	0	0	0	0	.000	0	4	0	2	0	0	1.000
Major league totals (2 years)			12	23	0	0	0	0	0	0	.000	0	15	0	6	0	0	1.000

WILSON, PAUL — P — METS

PERSONAL: Born March 28, 1973, in Orlando, Fla. . . . 6-5/235. . . . Throws right, bats right. . . . Full name: Paul Anthony Wilson.
HIGH SCHOOL: William R. Boone (Orlando, Fla.).
COLLEGE: Florida State.
TRANSACTIONS/CAREER NOTES: Selected by New York Mets organization in first round (first pick overall) of free-agent draft (June 2, 1994).
STATISTICAL NOTES: Named Eastern League Pitcher of the Year (1995).

Year	Team (League)	W	L	Pct.	ERA	G	GS	CG	ShO	Sv.	IP	H	R	ER	BB	SO
1994	—GC Mets (GCL)	0	2	.000	3.00	3	3	0	0	0	12	8	4	4	4	13
	—St. Lucie (Fla. St.)	0	5	.000	5.06	8	8	0	0	0	37 1/3	32	23	21	17	37
1995	—Binghamton (East.)	6	3	.667	*2.17	16	16	4	1	0	120 1/3	89	34	29	24	127
	—Norfolk (Int.)	5	3	.600	2.85	10	10	*4	1	0	66 1/3	59	25	21	20	67

WILSON, TREVOR — P — REDS

PERSONAL: Born June 7, 1966, in Torrance, Calif. . . . 6-0/204. . . . Throws left, bats left. . . . Full name: Trevor Kirk Wilson.
HIGH SCHOOL: Oregon City (Ore.).
COLLEGE: Oregon State.
TRANSACTIONS/CAREER NOTES: Selected by San Francisco Giants organization in eighth round of free-agent draft (June 3, 1985). . . . On San Francisco disabled list (August 22-September 6, 1990 and March 27-April 18, 1992). . . . On suspended list (June 26-29, 1992). . . . On San Francisco disabled list (May 21-June 5, 1993). . . . On San Francisco disabled list (July 3-August 10, 1993); included rehabilitation assignment to San Jose (August 3-10). . . . On San Francisco disabled list (August 24-September 15, 1993). . . . On disabled list (March 23, 1994-entire season). . . . Granted free agency (December 23, 1994). . . . Re-signed by Giants (April 7, 1995). . . . On San Francisco disabled list (June 20-July 17 and August 13, 1995-remainder of season); included rehabilitation assignments to San Jose (July 8-17 and August 31-September 8). . . . Granted free agency (November 1, 1995). . . . Signed by Cincinnati Reds (January 12, 1996).
RECORDS: Shares major league record for striking out side on nine pitches (June 7, 1992, ninth inning).
STATISTICAL NOTES: Tied for Northwest League lead with two balks in 1985. . . . Pitched 6-0 one-hit, complete-game victory for San Francisco against San Diego (June 13, 1990). . . . Tied for N.L. lead with seven balks in 1992.
MISCELLANEOUS: Appeared in one game as pinch-runner with San Francisco (1989). . . . Appeared in one game as pinch-runner (1992). . . . Appeared in one game as pinch-runner and struck out in only appearance as pinch-hitter with San Francisco (1995).

Year	Team (League)	W	L	Pct.	ERA	G	GS	CG	ShO	Sv.	IP	H	R	ER	BB	SO
1985	—Everett (N'west)	2	4	.333	4.23	17	7	0	0	3	55 1/3	67	36	26	26	50
1986	—Clinton (Midwest)	6	11	.353	4.27	34	21	0	0	2	130 2/3	126	70	62	64	84
1987	—Clinton (Midwest)	10	6	.625	2.01	26	26	3	2	0	161 1/3	130	60	36	77	146
1988	—Shreveport (Texas)	5	4	.556	1.86	12	11	0	0	0	72 2/3	55	19	15	23	53
	—Phoenix (PCL)	2	3	.400	5.05	11	9	0	0	0	51 2/3	49	35	29	33	49
	—San Francisco (N.L.)	0	2	.000	4.09	4	4	0	0	0	22	25	14	10	8	15
1989	—Phoenix (PCL)	7	7	.500	3.12	23	20	2	0	0	115 1/3	109	49	40	76	77
	—San Francisco (N.L.)	2	3	.400	4.35	14	4	0	0	0	39 1/3	28	20	19	24	22
1990	—Phoenix (PCL)	5	5	.500	3.82	11	10	2	1	0	66	63	31	28	44	45
	—San Francisco (N.L.)	8	7	.533	4.00	27	17	3	2	0	110 1/3	87	52	49	49	66
1991	—San Francisco (N.L.)	13	11	.542	3.56	44	29	2	1	0	202	173	87	80	77	139
1992	—San Francisco (N.L.)	8	14	.364	4.21	26	26	1	1	0	154	152	82	72	64	88
1993	—San Francisco (N.L.)	7	5	.583	3.60	22	18	1	0	0	110	110	45	44	40	57
	—San Jose (Calif.)	1	0	1.000	0.00	2	2	0	0	0	10	4	0	0	3	8
1995	—San Francisco (N.L.)							Did not play.								
1995	—San Francisco (N.L.)	3	4	.429	3.92	17	17	0	0	0	82 2/3	82	42	36	38	38
	—San Jose (Calif.)	0	1	.000	1.35	2	2	0	0	0	6 2/3	5	4	1	3	5
Major league totals (7 years)		41	46	.471	3.87	154	115	7	4	0	720 1/3	657	342	310	300	425

WINFIELD, DAVE DH/OF

PERSONAL: Born October 3, 1951, in St. Paul, Minn. . . . 6-6/245. . . . Bats right, throws right. . . . Full name: David Mark Winfield.
HIGH SCHOOL: St. Paul (Minn.) Central.
COLLEGE: Minnesota (received degree).
TRANSACTIONS/CAREER NOTES: Selected by Baltimore Orioles organization in 40th round of free-agent draft (June 5, 1969); did not sign. . . . Selected by San Diego Padres organization in first round (fourth pick overall) of free-agent draft (June 5, 1973). . . . Granted free agency (October 22, 1980). . . . Signed by New York Yankees (December 15, 1980). . . . On disabled list (May 20-June 4, 1982; April 16-May 1, 1984; and March 19, 1989-entire season). . . . Traded by Yankees to California Angels for P Mike Witt (May 11, 1990). . . . Granted free agency (October 30, 1991). . . . Signed by Toronto Blue Jays (December 19, 1991). . . . Granted free agency (November 2, 1992). . . . Signed by Minnesota Twins (December 17, 1992). . . . On disabled list (July 7-23, 1994). . . . Traded by Twins to Cleveland Indians for a player to be named later (August 31, 1994). . . . Granted free agency (October 17, 1994). . . . Signed by Indians (April 5, 1995). . . . On disabled list (June 11-July 17 and August 12-September 1, 1995). . . . Granted free agency (November 6, 1995).
HONORS: Named outfielder on The Sporting News college All-America team (1973). . . . Named outfielder on The Sporting News N.L. All-Star team (1979). . . . Won N.L. Gold Glove as outfielder (1979-80). . . . Named outfielder on The Sporting News A.L. Silver Slugger team (1981-85). . . . Named outfielder on The Sporting News A.L. All-Star team (1982-84). . . . Won A.L. Gold Glove as outfielder (1982-85 and 1987). . . . Named A.L. Comeback Player of the Year by The Sporting News (1990). . . . Named designated hitter on The Sporting News A.L. All-Star team (1992). . . . Named designated hitter on The Sporting News A.L. Silver Slugger team (1992).
STATISTICAL NOTES: Led N.L. with 333 total bases and 24 intentional bases on balls received in 1979. . . . Hit three home runs in one game (April 13, 1991). . . . Hit for the cycle (June 24, 1991). . . . Career major league grand slams: 11.
MISCELLANEOUS: Selected by Atlanta Hawks in fifth round (79th pick overall) of 1973 NBA draft. . . . Selected by Utah Stars in sixth round (58th pick overall) of 1973 ABA draft. . . . Selected by Minnesota Vikings in 17th round (429th pick overall) of 1973 NFL draft.

			BATTING												FIELDING			
Year	Team (League)	Pos.	G	AB	R	H	2B	3B	HR	RBI	Avg.	BB	SO	SB	PO	A	E	Avg.
1973—	San Diego (N.L.)	OF-1B	56	141	9	39	4	1	3	12	.277	12	19	0	65	1	3	.957
1974—	San Diego (N.L.)	OF	145	498	57	132	18	4	20	75	.265	40	96	9	276	11	•12	.960
1975—	San Diego (N.L.)	OF	143	509	74	136	20	2	15	76	.267	69	82	23	302	9	9	.972
1976—	San Diego (N.L.)	OF	137	492	81	139	26	4	13	69	.283	65	78	26	304	*15	6	.982
1977—	San Diego (N.L.)	OF	157	615	104	169	29	7	25	92	.275	58	75	16	368	15	11	.972
1978—	San Diego (N.L.)	OF-1B	158	587	88	181	30	5	24	97	.308	55	81	21	328	8	7	.980
1979—	San Diego (N.L.)	OF	159	597	97	184	27	10	34	*118	.308	85	71	15	344	14	5	.986
1980—	San Diego (N.L.)	OF	162	558	89	154	25	6	20	87	.276	79	83	23	273	20	4	.987
1981—	New York (A.L.)■	OF-DH	105	388	52	114	25	1	13	68	.294	43	41	11	196	1	3	.985
1982—	New York (A.L.)	OF-DH	140	539	84	151	24	8	37	106	.280	45	64	5	279	*17	8	.974
1983—	New York (A.L.)	OF	152	598	99	169	26	8	32	116	.283	58	77	15	313	5	7	.978
1984—	New York (A.L.)	OF	141	567	106	193	34	4	19	100	.340	53	71	6	306	3	2	.994
1985—	New York (A.L.)	OF-DH	155	633	105	174	34	6	26	114	.275	52	96	19	316	13	3	.991
1986—	New York (A.L.)	OF-DH-3B	154	565	90	148	31	5	24	104	.262	77	106	6	292	9	5	.984
1987—	New York (A.L.)	OF-DH	156	575	83	158	22	1	27	97	.275	76	96	5	253	6	3	.989
1988—	New York (A.L.)	OF-DH	149	559	96	180	37	2	25	107	.322	69	88	9	276	3	3	.989
1989—									Did not play.									
1990—	New York (A.L.)	OF-DH	20	61	7	13	3	0	2	6	.213	4	13	0	12	0	0	1.000
—	California (A.L.)■	OF-DH	112	414	63	114	18	2	19	72	.275	48	68	0	165	7	2	.989
1991—	California (A.L.)	OF-DH	150	568	75	149	27	4	28	86	.262	56	109	7	198	7	2	.990
1992—	Toronto (A.L.)■	DH-OF	156	583	92	169	33	3	26	108	.290	82	89	2	52	1	0	1.000
1993—	Minnesota (A.L.)■	DH-OF-1B	143	547	72	148	27	2	21	76	.271	45	106	2	91	3	0	1.000
1994—	Minnesota (A.L.)	DH-OF	77	294	35	74	15	3	10	43	.252	31	51	2	3	0	0	1.000
1995—	Cleveland (A.L.)■	DH	46	115	11	22	5	0	2	4	.191	14	26	1	0	0	0	...
American League totals (14 years)			1856	7006	1070	1976	361	49	311	1207	.282	753	1101	90	2752	75	38	.987
National League totals (8 years)			1117	3997	599	1134	179	39	154	626	.284	463	585	133	2260	93	57	.976
Major league totals (22 years)			2973	11003	1669	3110	540	88	465	1833	.283	1216	1686	223	5012	168	95	.982

DIVISION SERIES RECORD

			BATTING												FIELDING			
Year	Team (League)	Pos.	G	AB	R	H	2B	3B	HR	RBI	Avg.	BB	SO	SB	PO	A	E	Avg.
1981—	New York (A.L.)	OF	5	20	2	7	3	0	0	0	.350	1	5	0	10	1	0	1.000

CHAMPIONSHIP SERIES RECORD

NOTES: Shares A.L. single-game record for most at-bats—6 (October 11, 1992, 11 innings).

			BATTING												FIELDING			
Year	Team (League)	Pos.	G	AB	R	H	2B	3B	HR	RBI	Avg.	BB	SO	SB	PO	A	E	Avg.
1981—	New York (A.L.)	OF	3	13	2	2	1	0	0	2	.154	2	2	1	6	0	0	1.000
1992—	Toronto (A.L.)	DH	6	24	7	6	1	0	2	3	.250	4	2	0	...	...	...	...
Championship series totals (2 years)			9	37	9	8	2	0	2	5	.216	6	4	1	6	0	0	1.000

WORLD SERIES RECORD

NOTES: Member of World Series championship team (1992).

			BATTING												FIELDING			
Year	Team (League)	Pos.	G	AB	R	H	2B	3B	HR	RBI	Avg.	BB	SO	SB	PO	A	E	Avg.
1981—	New York (A.L.)	OF	6	22	0	1	0	0	0	1	.045	5	4	1	13	1	0	1.000
1992—	Toronto (A.L.)	OF-DH	6	22	0	5	1	0	0	3	.227	2	3	0	7	0	0	1.000
World Series totals (2 years)			12	44	0	6	1	0	0	4	.136	7	7	1	20	1	0	1.000

ALL-STAR GAME RECORD

NOTES: Holds career record for most doubles—7. . . . Shares record for most consecutive games with one or more hits—7. . . . Shares single-game record for most at-bats in nine-inning game—5 (July 17, 1979).

			BATTING											FIELDING			
Year	League	Pos.	AB	R	H	2B	3B	HR	RBI	Avg.	BB	SO	SB	PO	A	E	Avg.
1977—	National	OF	2	0	2	1	0	0	2	1.000	0	0	0	1	0	0	1.000
1978—	National	OF	2	1	1	0	0	0	0	.500	0	0	0	1	0	0	1.000
1979—	National	OF	5	1	1	1	0	0	1	.200	0	1	0	3	0	0	1.000
1980—	National	OF	2	0	0	0	0	0	1	.000	0	0	0	2	0	0	1.000
1981—	American	OF	4	0	0	0	0	0	0	.000	1	0	0	0	1	0	1.000
1982—	American	OF	2	0	1	0	0	0	0	.500	0	0	0	0	0	0	...

Year	League	Pos.	AB	R	H	2B	3B	HR	RBI	Avg.	BB	SO	SB	PO	A	E	Avg.
			BATTING											FIELDING			
1983—	American	OF	3	2	3	1	0	0	1	1.000	0	0	0	3	0	0	1.000
1984—	American	OF	4	0	1	1	0	0	0	.250	0	0	0	2	1	0	1.000
1985—	American	OF	3	0	1	0	0	0	0	.333	0	0	1	0	0	0	...
1986—	American	OF	1	1	1	1	0	0	0	1.000	0	0	0	0	0	0	...
1987—	American	OF	5	0	1	1	0	0	0	.200	1	0	0	2	0	0	1.000
1988—	American	OF	3	1	1	1	0	0	0	.333	0	0	0	1	0	0	1.000
All-Star Game totals (12 years)			36	6	13	7	0	0	5	.361	2	1	1	15	2	0	1.000

WITASICK, JAY — P — ATHLETICS

PERSONAL: Born August 28, 1972, in Baltimore. . . . 6-4/205. . . . Throws right, bats right. . . . Full name: Gerald A. Witasick.
HIGH SCHOOL: C Milton Wright (Bel Air, Md.).
JUNIOR COLLEGE: Brevard (Fla.).
COLLEGE: Maryland-Baltimore County.
TRANSACTIONS/CAREER NOTES: Selected by St. Louis Cardinals organization in second round of free-agent draft (June 3, 1993). . . . On disabled list (July 17, 1995-remainder of season). . . . Traded by Cardinals with OF Allen Battle, P Bret Wagner and P Carl Dale to Oakland Athletics for P Todd Stottlemyre (January 9, 1996).

Year	Team (League)	W	L	Pct.	ERA	G	GS	CG	ShO	Sv.	IP	H	R	ER	BB	SO
1993—	Johns. City (App.)	4	3	.571	4.12	12	12	0	0	0	67 2/3	65	42	31	19	74
—	Savannah (S. Atl.)	1	0	1.000	4.50	1	1	0	0	0	6	7	3	3	2	8
1994—	Madison (Midwest)	10	4	.714	2.32	18	18	2	0	0	112 1/3	74	36	29	42	141
1995—	St. Petersburg (FSL)	7	7	.500	2.74	18	18	1	1	0	105	80	39	32	36	109
—	Arkansas (Texas)	2	4	.333	6.88	7	7	0	0	0	34	46	29	26	16	26

WITT, BOBBY — P — RANGERS

PERSONAL: Born May 11, 1964, in Arlington, Va. . . . 6-2/205. . . . Throws right, bats right. . . . Full name: Robert Andrew Witt.
HIGH SCHOOL: Canton (Mass.).
COLLEGE: Oklahoma.
TRANSACTIONS/CAREER NOTES: Selected by Cincinnati Reds organization in seventh round of free-agent draft (June 7, 1982); did not sign. . . . Selected by Texas Rangers organization in first round (third pick overall) of free-agent draft (June 3, 1985). . . . On Texas disabled list (May 21-June 20, 1987); included rehabilitation assignments to Oklahoma City (June 7-12) and Tulsa (June 13). . . . On Texas disabled list (May 27-July 31, 1991); included rehabilitation assignment to Oklahoma City (July 22-29). . . . Traded by Rangers with OF Ruben Sierra, P Jeff Russell and cash to Oakland Athletics for OF Jose Canseco (August 31, 1992). . . . Granted free agency (October 26, 1994). . . . Signed by Florida Marlins (April 9, 1995). . . . Traded by Marlins to Rangers for two players to be named later (August 8, 1995); Marlins acquired P Wilson Heredia (August 11, 1995) and OF Scott Podsednik (October 2, 1995) to complete deal. . . . Granted free agency (November 3, 1995). . . . Re-signed by Rangers (December 23, 1995).
RECORDS: Shares major league record for most strikeouts in one inning—4 (August 2, 1987, second inning).
HONORS: Named righthanded pitcher on The Sporting News college All-America team (1985).
STATISTICAL NOTES: Led A.L. with 22 wild pitches in 1986 and tied for lead with 16 in 1988. . . . Pitched 4-0 one-hit, complete-game victory against Kansas City (June 23, 1994).
MISCELLANEOUS: Member of 1984 U.S. Olympic baseball team. . . . Struck out in only appearance as pinch-hitter with Texas (1987). . . . Appeared in two games as pinch-runner (1990). . . . Appeared in one game as pinch-runner (1994). . . . Appeared in two games as pinch-runner with Florida (1995).

Year	Team (League)	W	L	Pct.	ERA	G	GS	CG	ShO	Sv.	IP	H	R	ER	BB	SO
1985—	Tulsa (Texas)	0	6	.000	6.43	11	8	0	0	0	35	26	26	25	44	39
1986—	Texas (A.L.)	11	9	.550	5.48	31	31	0	0	0	157 2/3	130	104	96	*143	174
1987—	Texas (A.L.)	8	10	.444	4.91	26	25	1	0	0	143	114	82	78	*140	160
—	Okla. City (A.A.)	1	0	1.000	9.00	1	1	0	0	0	5	5	5	5	3	2
—	Tulsa (Texas)	0	1	.000	5.40	1	1	0	0	0	5	5	9	3	6	2
1988—	Texas (A.L.)	8	10	.444	3.92	22	22	13	2	0	174 1/3	134	83	76	101	148
—	Okla. City (A.A.)	4	6	.400	4.34	11	11	3	0	0	76 2/3	69	42	37	47	70
1989—	Texas (A.L.)	12	13	.480	5.14	31	31	5	1	0	194 1/3	182	123	•111	*114	166
1990—	Texas (A.L.)	17	10	.630	3.36	33	32	7	1	0	222	197	98	83	110	221
1991—	Texas (A.L.)	3	7	.300	6.09	17	16	1	1	0	88 2/3	84	66	60	74	82
—	Okla. City (A.A.)	1	1	.500	1.13	2	2	0	0	0	8	3	1	1	8	12
1992—	Texas (A.L.)	9	13	.409	4.46	25	25	0	0	0	161 1/3	152	87	80	95	100
—	Oakland (A.L.)■	1	1	.500	3.41	6	6	0	0	0	31 2/3	31	12	12	19	25
1993—	Oakland (A.L.)	14	13	.519	4.21	35	33	5	1	0	220	226	112	103	91	131
1994—	Oakland (A.L.)	8	10	.444	5.04	24	24	5	3	0	135 2/3	151	88	76	70	111
1995—	Florida (N.L.)■	2	7	.222	3.90	19	19	1	0	0	110 2/3	104	52	48	47	95
—	Texas (A.L.)■	3	4	.429	4.55	10	10	1	0	0	61 1/3	81	35	31	21	46
A.L. totals (10 years)		94	100	.485	4.56	260	255	38	9	0	1590	1482	890	806	978	1364
N.L. totals (1 year)		2	7	.222	3.90	19	19	1	0	0	110 2/3	104	52	48	47	95
Major league totals (10 years)		96	107	.473	4.52	279	274	39	9	0	1700 2/3	1586	942	854	1025	1459

CHAMPIONSHIP SERIES RECORD

Year	Team (League)	W	L	Pct.	ERA	G	GS	CG	ShO	Sv.	IP	H	R	ER	BB	SO
1992—	Oakland (A.L.)	0	0	...	18.00	1	0	0	0	0	1	2	2	2	1	1

WITTE, TREY — P — EXPOS

PERSONAL: Born January 15, 1970, in Houston. . . . 6-1/190. . . . Throws right, bats right. . . . Full name: Laurence Joseph Witte.
HIGH SCHOOL: Jersey Village (Houston).
COLLEGE: Texas A&M.
TRANSACTIONS/CAREER NOTES: Selected by Seattle Mariners organization in ninth round of free agent draft (June 3, 1991). . . . Selected by Montreal Expos from Mariners organization in Rule 5 major league draft (December 4, 1995).

Year	Team (League)	W	L	Pct.	ERA	G	GS	CG	ShO	Sv.	IP	H	R	ER	BB	SO
1991—	Bellingham (N'west)	2	2	.500	2.20	27	0	0	0	8	45	27	12	11	31	44
1992—	San Bern. (Calif.)	1	1	.500	6.63	21	0	0	0	1	36 2/3	58	36	27	11	27
1993—	Appleton (Midw.)	3	9	.250	4.26	28	14	1	0	0	101 1/3	111	57	48	22	62
1994—	Riverside (Calif.)	4	3	.571	4.31	25	0	0	0	0	54 1/3	57	29	26	15	45
1995—	Port City (Southern)	3	2	.600	1.73	48	0	0	0	11	62 1/3	48	17	12	14	39

WOHLERS, MARK — P — BRAVES

PERSONAL: Born January 23, 1970, in Holyoke, Mass. . . . 6-4/207. . . . Throws right, bats right. . . . Full name: Mark Edward Wohlers.
HIGH SCHOOL: Holyoke (Mass.).
TRANSACTIONS/CAREER NOTES: Selected by Atlanta Braves organization in eighth round of free-agent draft (June 1, 1988).
RECORDS: Shares major league record for most strikeouts in one inning—4 (June 7, 1995, ninth inning).
HONORS: Named Southern League Outstanding Pitcher (1991).
STATISTICAL NOTES: Pitched two innings, combining with starter Kent Mercker (six innings) and Alejandro Pena (one inning) in 1-0 no-hit victory for Atlanta against San Diego (September 11, 1991).

Year	Team (League)	W	L	Pct.	ERA	G	GS	CG	ShO	Sv.	IP	H	R	ER	BB	SO
1988—	Pulaski (Appal.)	5	3	.625	3.32	13	9	1	0	0	59 2/3	47	37	22	50	49
1989—	Sumter (S. Atl.)	2	7	.222	6.49	14	14	0	0	0	68	74	55	49	59	51
—	Pulaski (Appal.)	1	1	.500	5.48	14	8	0	0	0	46	48	36	28	28	50
1990—	Greenville (South.)	0	1	.000	4.02	14	0	0	0	6	15 2/3	14	7	7	14	20
—	Sumter (S. Atl.)	5	4	.556	1.88	37	2	0	0	5	52 2/3	27	13	11	20	85
1991—	Greenville (South.)	0	0	...	0.57	28	0	0	0	21	31 1/3	9	4	2	13	44
—	Richmond (Int'l)	1	0	1.000	1.03	23	0	0	0	11	26 1/3	23	4	3	12	22
—	Atlanta (N.L.)	3	1	.750	3.20	17	0	0	0	2	19 2/3	17	7	7	13	13
1992—	Richmond (Int'l)	0	2	.000	3.93	27	2	0	0	9	34 1/3	32	16	15	17	33
—	Atlanta (N.L.)	1	2	.333	2.55	32	0	0	0	4	35 1/3	28	11	10	14	17
1993—	Richmond (Int'l)	1	3	.250	1.84	25	0	0	0	4	29 1/3	21	7	6	11	39
—	Atlanta (N.L.)	6	2	.750	4.50	46	0	0	0	0	48	37	25	24	22	45
1994—	Atlanta (N.L.)	7	2	.778	4.59	51	0	0	0	1	51	51	35	26	33	58
1995—	Atlanta (N.L.)	7	3	.700	2.09	65	0	0	0	25	64 2/3	51	16	15	24	90
Major league totals (5 years)		24	10	.706	3.38	211	0	0	0	32	218 2/3	184	94	82	106	223

DIVISION SERIES RECORD

Year	Team (League)	W	L	Pct.	ERA	G	GS	CG	ShO	Sv.	IP	H	R	ER	BB	SO
1995—	Atlanta (N.L.)	0	1	.000	6.75	3	0	0	0	2	2 2/3	6	2	2	2	4

CHAMPIONSHIP SERIES RECORD

Year	Team (League)	W	L	Pct.	ERA	G	GS	CG	ShO	Sv.	IP	H	R	ER	BB	SO
1991—	Atlanta (N.L.)	0	0	...	0.00	3	0	0	0	0	1 2/3	3	0	0	1	1
1992—	Atlanta (N.L.)	0	0	...	0.00	3	0	0	0	0	3	2	0	0	1	2
1993—	Atlanta (N.L.)	0	1	.000	3.38	4	0	0	0	0	5 1/3	2	2	2	3	10
1995—	Atlanta (N.L.)	1	0	1.000	1.80	4	0	0	0	0	5	2	1	1	0	8
Champ. series totals (4 years)		1	1	.500	1.80	14	0	0	0	0	15	9	3	3	5	21

WORLD SERIES RECORD

NOTES: Member of World Series championship team (1995).

Year	Team (League)	W	L	Pct.	ERA	G	GS	CG	ShO	Sv.	IP	H	R	ER	BB	SO
1991—	Atlanta (N.L.)	0	0	...	0.00	3	0	0	0	0	1 2/3	2	0	0	2	1
1992—	Atlanta (N.L.)	0	0	...	0.00	2	0	0	0	0	2/3	0	0	0	1	0
1995—	Atlanta (N.L.)	0	0	...	1.80	4	0	0	0	0	5	4	1	1	3	3
World Series totals (3 years)		0	0	...	1.23	9	0	0	0	0	7 1/3	6	1	1	6	4

WOJCIECHOWSKI, STEVE — P — ATHLETICS

PERSONAL: Born July 29, 1970, in Blue Island, Ill. . . . 6-2/185. . . . Throws left, bats left. . . . Full name: Steven Joseph Wojciechowski. . . . Name pronounced wo-jo-KOW-ski.
HIGH SCHOOL: Thornton Fractional North (Calumet City, Ill.).
COLLEGE: St. Xavier (Ill.).
TRANSACTIONS/CAREER NOTES: Selected by Oakland Athletics organization in fourth round of free-agent draft (June 3, 1991). . . . On disabled list (June 16-August 6, 1992).

Year	Team (League)	W	L	Pct.	ERA	G	GS	CG	ShO	Sv.	IP	H	R	ER	BB	SO
1991—	S. Oregon (N'west)	2	5	.286	3.76	16	11	0	0	0	67	74	45	28	29	50
1992—	Modesto (Calif.)	6	3	.667	3.53	14	14	0	0	0	66 1/3	60	32	26	27	53
1993—	Modesto (Calif.)	8	2	.800	2.55	14	14	1	1	0	84 2/3	64	29	24	36	52
—	Huntsville (South.)	4	6	.400	5.32	13	13	1	1	0	67 2/3	91	50	40	30	52
1994—	Huntsville (South.)	10	5	.667	3.10	27	26	1	0	0	177	148	72	61	62	114
1995—	Edmonton (PCL)	6	3	.667	3.69	14	12	2	1	0	78	75	37	32	21	39
—	Oakland (A.L.)	2	3	.400	5.18	14	7	0	0	0	48 2/3	51	28	28	28	13
Major league totals (1 year)		2	3	.400	5.18	14	7	0	0	0	48 2/3	51	28	28	28	13

WOLCOTT, BOB — P — MARINERS

PERSONAL: Born September 8, 1973, in Huntington Beach, Calif. . . . 6-0/190. . . . Throws right, bats right. . . . Full name: Robert William Wolcott.
HIGH SCHOOL: North (Medford, Ore.).
TRANSACTIONS/CAREER NOTES: Selected by Seattle Mariners organization in second round of free-agent draft (June 1, 1992).

Year	Team (League)	W	L	Pct.	ERA	G	GS	CG	ShO	Sv.	IP	H	R	ER	BB	SO
1992—	Bellingham (N'west)	0	1	.000	6.85	9	7	0	0	0	22 1/3	25	18	17	19	17
1993—	Bellingham (N'west)	8	4	.667	2.64	15	15	1	0	0	95 1/3	70	31	28	26	79
1994—	Riverside (Calif.)	14	8	.636	2.84	26	26	•5	1	0	*180 2/3	173	75	57	50	142

Year	Team (League)	W	L	Pct.	ERA	G	GS	CG	ShO	Sv.	IP	H	R	ER	BB	SO
	—Calgary (PCL)	0	1	.000	3.00	1	1	0	0	0	6	6	2	2	3	5
1995	—Port City (Southern)	7	3	.700	2.20	12	12	2	1	0	86	60	26	21	13	53
	—Tacoma (PCL)	6	3	.667	4.08	13	13	2	1	0	79 1/3	94	49	36	16	43
	—Seattle (A.L.)	3	2	.600	4.42	7	6	0	0	0	36 2/3	43	18	18	14	19
Major league totals (1 year)		3	2	.600	4.42	7	6	0	0	0	36 2/3	43	18	18	14	19

CHAMPIONSHIP SERIES RECORD

Year	Team (League)	W	L	Pct.	ERA	G	GS	CG	ShO	Sv.	IP	H	R	ER	BB	SO
1995	—Seattle (A.L.)	1	0	1.000	2.57	1	1	0	0	0	7	8	2	2	5	2

WOMACK, TONY — SS — PIRATES

PERSONAL: Born September 25, 1969, in Danville, Va. . . . 5-9/155. . . . Bats left, throws right. . . . Full name: Anthony Darrell Womack.
HIGH SCHOOL: Gretna (Va.).
COLLEGE: Guilford (N.C.).
TRANSACTIONS/CAREER NOTES: Selected by Pittsburgh Pirates organization in seventh round of free-agent draft (June 3, 1991). . . . On disabled list (April 17-26 and August 28, 1992-remainder of season).
STATISTICAL NOTES: Tied for American Association lead with 12 sacrifice hits in 1994.

				BATTING										FIELDING			
Year	Team (League)	Pos.	G	AB	R	H	2B	3B	HR	RBI	Avg.	BB	SO	SB	PO	A	E	Avg.
1991	—Welland (NYP)	SS-2B	45	166	30	46	3	0	1	8	.277	17	39	26	78	109	16	.921
1992	—Augusta (S. Atl.)	SS-2B	102	380	62	93	8	3	0	18	.245	41	59	50	186	291	40	.923
1993	—Salem (Carolina)	SS	72	304	41	91	11	3	2	18	.299	13	34	28	130	223	28	.927
	—Carolina (South.)	SS	60	247	41	75	7	2	0	23	.304	17	34	21	102	169	11	.961
	—Pittsburgh (N.L.)	SS	15	24	5	2	0	0	0	0	.083	3	3	2	11	22	1	.971
1994	—Buffalo (A.A.)	SS-2B	106	421	40	93	9	2	0	18	.221	19	76	41	211	283	22	.957
	—Pittsburgh (N.L.)	2B-SS	5	12	4	4	0	0	0	1	.333	2	3	0	3	6	2	.818
1995	—Calgary (PCL)	2B-SS	30	107	12	30	3	1	0	6	.280	12	11	7	37	94	5	.963
	—Carolina (South.)	SS-2B	82	332	52	85	9	4	1	19	.256	19	36	27	126	241	18	.953
Major league totals (2 years)			20	36	9	6	0	0	0	1	.167	5	6	2	14	28	3	.933

WOODALL, BRAD — P — BRAVES

PERSONAL: Born June 25, 1969, in Atlanta. . . . 6-0/175. . . . Throws left, bats both. . . . Full name: David Bradley Woodall.
HIGH SCHOOL: Spring Valley (Columbia, S.C.).
COLLEGE: North Carolina.
TRANSACTIONS/CAREER NOTES: Signed as non-drafted free agent by Atlanta Braves (June 10, 1991). . . . On Greenville disabled list (April 8-May 3, 1993). . . . On Richmond disabled list (July 8-August 18, 1995).
HONORS: Named International League Pitcher of the Year (1994).

Year	Team (League)	W	L	Pct.	ERA	G	GS	CG	ShO	Sv.	IP	H	R	ER	BB	SO
1991	—Idaho Falls (Pio.)	4	1	.800	1.37	28	0	0	0	11	39 1/3	29	9	6	19	57
	—Durham (Carolina)	0	0	...	2.45	4	0	0	0	0	7 1/3	4	3	2	4	14
1992	—Durham (Carolina)	1	2	.333	2.13	24	0	0	0	4	42 1/3	30	11	10	11	51
	—Greenville (South.)	3	4	.429	3.20	21	1	0	0	1	39 1/3	26	15	14	17	45
1993	—Durham (Carolina)	3	1	.750	3.00	6	5	1	1	0	30	21	10	10	6	27
	—Idaho Falls (Pio.)	2	4	.333	3.38	8	7	1	0	0	53 1/3	43	24	20	24	38
	—Richmond (Int'l)	5	3	.625	4.21	10	9	0	0	0	57 2/3	59	32	27	16	45
1994	—Richmond (Int'l)	•15	6	.714	*2.38	27	27	4	*3	0	185 2/3	159	62	49	49	137
	—Atlanta (N.L.)	0	1	.000	4.50	1	1	0	0	0	6	5	3	3	2	2
1995	—Atlanta (N.L.)	1	1	.500	6.10	9	0	0	0	0	10 1/3	13	10	7	8	5
	—Richmond (Int'l)	4	4	.500	5.10	13	11	0	0	0	65 1/3	70	39	37	17	44
Major league totals (2 years)		1	2	.333	5.51	10	1	0	0	0	16 1/3	18	13	10	10	7

WOODS, BRIAN — P — WHITE SOX

PERSONAL: Born June 7, 1971, in Belleville, N.J. . . . 6-6/212. . . . Throws right, bats right.
COLLEGE: Farleigh Dickinson.
TRANSACTIONS/CAREER NOTES: Selected by Chicago White Sox organization in 20th round of free-agent draft (June 3, 1993).
STATISTICAL NOTES: Pitched seven innings, combining with Arthur Vazquez (two innngs), in 8-0 no-hit victory against Salem (April 8, 1995).

Year	Team (League)	W	L	Pct.	ERA	G	GS	CG	ShO	Sv.	IP	H	R	ER	BB	SO
1993	—GC White Sox (GCL)	0	0	...	2.25	2	2	0	0	0	8	4	3	2	6	6
	—Hickory (S. Atl.)	2	5	.286	2.51	10	10	0	0	0	61	49	20	17	31	53
	—South Bend (Midw.)	0	1	.000	3.86	2	1	0	0	0	7	7	5	3	3	4
1994	—South Bend (Midw.)	4	12	.250	3.90	20	18	2	0	0	115 1/3	108	65	50	49	107
1995	—Prin. William (Caro.)	9	*15	.375	5.17	27	27	3	0	0	139 1/3	155	89	80	53	102

WORRELL, TIM — P — PADRES

PERSONAL: Born July 5, 1967, in Pasadena, Calif. . . . 6-4/220. . . . Throws right, bats right. . . . Full name: Timothy Howard Worrell. . . . Brother of Todd Worrell, pitcher, Los Angeles Dodgers. . . . Name pronounced wor-RELL.
HIGH SCHOOL: Maranatha (Sierra Madre, Calif.).
COLLEGE: Biola College (Calif.).
TRANSACTIONS/CAREER NOTES: Selected by San Diego Padres organization in 20th round of free-agent draft (June 5, 1989). . . . On disabled list (April 19, 1994-remainder of season). . . . On San Diego disabled list (April 24-September 1, 1995); included rehabilitation assignments to Rancho Cucamonga (May 3-17 and August 1-10) and Las Vegas (May 17-June 1 and August 10-30).
STATISTICAL NOTES: Pitched 2-0 no-hit victory for Las Vegas against Phoenix (September 5, 1992).

W

Year	Team (League)	W	L	Pct.	ERA	G	GS	CG	ShO	Sv.	IP	H	R	ER	BB	SO
1989—								Did not play.								
1990—	Char., S.C. (S. Atl.)	5	8	.385	4.64	20	19	3	0	0	110 2/3	120	65	57	28	68
1991—	Waterloo (Midw.)	8	4	.667	3.34	14	14	3	2	0	86 1/3	70	36	32	33	83
	—High Desert (Calif.)	5	2	.714	4.24	11	11	2	0	0	63 2/3	65	32	30	33	70
1992—	Wichita (Texas)	8	6	.571	2.86	19	19	1	1	0	125 2/3	115	46	40	32	109
	—Las Vegas (PCL)	4	2	.667	4.26	10	10	1	1	0	63 1/3	61	32	30	19	32
1993—	Las Vegas (PCL)	5	6	.455	5.48	15	14	2	0	0	87	102	61	53	26	89
	—San Diego (N.L.)	2	7	.222	4.92	21	16	0	0	0	100 2/3	104	63	55	43	52
1994—	San Diego (N.L.)	0	1	.000	3.68	3	3	0	0	0	14 2/3	9	7	6	5	14
1995—	Rancho Cuca. (Cal.)	0	2	.000	5.16	9	3	0	0	1	22 2/3	25	17	13	6	17
	—Las Vegas (PCL)	0	2	.000	6.00	10	3	0	0	0	24	27	21	16	17	18
	—San Diego (N.L.)	1	0	1.000	4.73	9	0	0	0	0	13 1/3	16	7	7	6	13
Major league totals (3 years)		3	8	.273	4.76	33	19	0	0	0	128 2/3	129	77	68	54	79

WORRELL, TODD — P — DODGERS

PERSONAL: Born September 28, 1959, in Arcadia, Calif. . . . 6-5/222. . . . Throws right, bats right. . . . Full name: Todd Roland Worrell. . . . Brother of Tim Worrell, pitcher, San Diego Padres organization. . . . Name pronounced wor-RELL.

HIGH SCHOOL: Maranatha (Sierra Madre, Calif.).

COLLEGE: Biola College, Calif. (degree in Christian education).

TRANSACTIONS/CAREER NOTES: Selected by St. Louis Cardinals organization in first round (21st pick overall) of free-agent draft (June 7, 1982). . . . On St. Louis disabled list (May 14-June 7, 1989); included rehabilitation assignment to Louisville (June 6-7). . . . On St. Louis disabled list (March 31, 1990-entire season). . . . On St. Louis disabled list (April 4, 1991-entire season); included rehabilitation assignment to Louisville (May 4-10). . . . Granted free agency (October 26, 1992). . . . Signed by Los Angeles Dodgers (December 9, 1992). . . . On Los Angeles disabled list (April 8-May 27, 1993); included rehabilitation assignment to Bakersfield (May 23-27). . . . On Los Angeles disabled list (June 11-July 15, 1993); included rehabilitation assignment to Albuquerque (June 30-July 15). . . . On disabled list (May 5-23, 1994).

RECORDS: Holds major league rookie-season record for most saves—36 (1986).

HONORS: Named righthanded pitcher on The Sporting News college All-America team (1982). . . . Named N.L. Rookie Pitcher of the Year by The Sporting News (1986). . . . Named N.L. Fireman of the Year by The Sporting News (1986). . . . Named N.L. Rookie of the Year by Baseball Writers' Association of America (1986).

MISCELLANEOUS: Appeared in two games as outfielder with no chances (1986). . . . Appeared in one game as outfielder with no chances (1987 and St. Louis 1989).

Year	Team (League)	W	L	Pct.	ERA	G	GS	CG	ShO	Sv.	IP	H	R	ER	BB	SO
1982—	Erie (NYP)	4	1	.800	3.31	9	8	0	0	0	51 2/3	52	23	19	15	57
1983—	Louisville (A.A.)	4	2	.667	4.74	15	14	1	0	0	79 2/3	76	49	42	42	46
	—Arkansas (Texas)	5	2	.714	3.07	10	10	4	0	0	70 1/3	57	33	24	37	74
1984—	Arkansas (Texas)	3	10	.231	4.49	18	18	5	0	0	100 1/3	109	72	50	67	88
	—St. Petersburg (FSL)	3	2	.600	2.09	8	7	2	0	0	47 1/3	41	22	11	24	33
1985—	Louisville (A.A.)	8	6	.571	3.60	34	17	2	1	11	127 2/3	114	59	51	47	*126
	—St. Louis (N.L.)	3	0	1.000	2.91	17	0	0	0	5	21 2/3	17	7	7	7	17
1986—	St. Louis (N.L.)	9	10	.474	2.08	74	0	0	0	*36	103 2/3	86	29	24	41	73
1987—	St. Louis (N.L.)	8	6	.571	2.66	75	0	0	0	33	94 2/3	86	29	28	34	92
1988—	St. Louis (N.L.)	5	9	.357	3.00	68	0	0	0	32	90	69	32	30	34	78
1989—	St. Louis (N.L.)	3	5	.375	2.96	47	0	0	0	20	51 2/3	42	21	17	26	41
	—Louisville (A.A.)	0	0	...	0.00	1	1	0	0	0	1	0	0	0	0	1
1990—								Did not play.								
1991—	Louisville (A.A.)	0	0	...	18.00	3	3	0	0	0	3	4	6	6	3	4
1992—	St. Louis (N.L.)	5	3	.625	2.11	67	0	0	0	3	64	45	15	15	25	64
1993—	Los Angeles (N.L.)■	1	1	.500	6.05	35	0	0	0	5	38 2/3	46	28	26	11	31
	—Bakersfield (Calif.)	0	0	...	0.00	2	2	0	0	0	2	1	0	0	0	5
	—Albuquerque (PCL)	1	0	1.000	1.04	7	2	0	0	0	8 2/3	7	2	1	2	13
1994—	Los Angeles (N.L.)	6	5	.545	4.29	38	0	0	0	11	42	37	21	20	12	44
1995—	Los Angeles (N.L.)	4	1	.800	2.02	59	0	0	0	32	62 1/3	50	15	14	19	61
Major league totals (9 years)		44	40	.524	2.86	480	0	0	0	177	568 2/3	478	197	181	209	501

CHAMPIONSHIP SERIES RECORD

NOTES: Appeared in one game as outfielder (1987).

Year	Team (League)	W	L	Pct.	ERA	G	GS	CG	ShO	Sv.	IP	H	R	ER	BB	SO
1985—	St. Louis (N.L.)	1	0	1.000	1.42	4	0	0	0	0	6 1/3	4	1	1	2	3
1987—	St. Louis (N.L.)	0	0	...	2.08	3	0	0	0	1	4 1/3	4	1	1	1	6
Champ. series totals (2 years)		1	0	1.000	1.69	7	0	0	0	1	10 2/3	8	2	2	3	9

WORLD SERIES RECORD

NOTES: Shares single-game record for most consecutive strikeouts—6 (October 24, 1985).

Year	Team (League)	W	L	Pct.	ERA	G	GS	CG	ShO	Sv.	IP	H	R	ER	BB	SO
1985—	St. Louis (N.L.)	0	1	.000	3.86	3	0	0	0	1	4 2/3	4	2	2	2	6
1987—	St. Louis (N.L.)	0	0	...	1.29	4	0	0	0	2	7	6	1	1	4	3
World Series totals (2 years)		0	1	.000	2.31	7	0	0	0	3	11 2/3	10	3	3	6	9

ALL-STAR GAME RECORD

Year	League	W	L	Pct.	ERA	GS	CG	ShO	Sv.	IP	H	R	ER	BB	SO
1988—	National	0	0	...	0.00	0	0	0	0	1	0	0	0	0	0
1995—	National						Did not play.								
All-Star totals (1 years)		0	0	...	0.00	0	0	0	0	1	0	0	0	0	0

WORTHINGTON, CRAIG — 3B — RANGERS

PERSONAL: Born April 17, 1965, in Los Angeles. . . . 6-0/200. . . . Bats right, throws right. . . . Full name: Craig Richard Worthington.

HIGH SCHOOL: Cantwell (Pico Rivera, Calif.).

COLLEGE: Cerritos College (Calif.).

TRANSACTIONS/CAREER NOTES: Selected by New York Mets organization in sixth round of free-agent draft (January 17, 1984); did not sign. . . . Selected by Houston Astros organization in secondary phase of free-agent draft (June 4, 1984); did not sign. . . . Selected by Chicago Cubs organization in secondary phase of free-agent draft (January 9, 1985); did not sign. . . . Selected by Baltimore Orioles organization in secondary phase of free-agent draft (June 3, 1985). . . . On Baltimore disabled list (May 21-June 29, 1991); included rehabilitation assignment to Rochester (June 11-29). . . . On Rochester disabled list (July 4-September 5, 1991). . . . Traded by Orioles with P Tom Martin to San Diego Padres for P Jim Lewis and OF Steve Martin (February 17, 1992). . . . Released by Padres (March 30, 1992). . . . Signed by Colorado Springs, Cleveland Indians organization (April 18, 1992). . . . Released by Indians (September 23, 1992). . . . Signed by Cubs organization (February 8, 1993). . . . Granted free agency (October 15, 1993). . . . Re-signed by Iowa, Cubs organization (March 9, 1994). . . . Granted free agency (October 15, 1994). . . . Signed by Indianapolis, Cincinnati Reds organization (November 5, 1994). . . . Selected by Philadelphia Phillies from Reds organization in Rule 5 major league draft (December 5, 1994). . . . Returned to Reds organization (April 19, 1995). . . . Traded by Reds organization to Texas Rangers for 1B Stephen Larkin (August 16, 1995).

HONORS: Named International League Player of the Year (1988). . . . Named A.L. Rookie Player of the Year by The Sporting News (1989).

STATISTICAL NOTES: Led International League third basemen with 310 total chances and tied for lead with 16 double plays in 1987. . . . Led International League third basemen with 91 putouts and 319 total chances in 1988. . . . Led American Association third basemen with .940 fielding percentage, 71 putouts, 240 assists and 331 total chances in 1993. . . . Led American Association third basemen with .973 fielding percentage in 1994.

		BATTING												FIELDING			
Year Team (League)	**Pos.**	**G**	**AB**	**R**	**H**	**2B**	**3B**	**HR**	**RBI**	**Avg.**	**BB**	**SO**	**SB**	**PO**	**A**	**E**	**Avg.**
1985— Bluefield (Appal.)	3B	39	129	33	44	9	1	7	20	.341	10	19	3	32	68	12	.893
1986— Hagerstown (Car.)	3B	132	480	85	144	35	1	15	*105	.300	82	58	7	92	249	32	.914
1987— Rochester (Int'l)	3B	109	383	46	99	14	1	7	50	.258	32	62	0	*79	*211	*20	*.935
1988— Rochester (Int'l)	3B-SS	121	430	53	105	25	1	16	73	.244	39	93	3	†91	209	19	.940
— Baltimore (A.L.)	3B	26	81	5	15	2	0	2	4	.185	9	24	1	20	53	3	.961
1989— Baltimore (A.L.)	3B	145	497	57	123	23	0	15	70	.247	61	114	1	113	277	20	.951
1990— Baltimore (A.L.)	3B-DH	133	425	46	96	17	0	8	44	.226	63	96	1	90	218	18	.945
1991— Baltimore (A.L.)	3B	31	102	11	23	3	0	4	12	.225	12	14	0	26	51	2	.975
— Rochester (Int'l)	3B	19	57	10	17	4	0	2	9	.298	6	8	0	10	13	1	.958
1992— Colo. Springs (PCL)■	3B	90	319	47	94	25	0	6	57	.295	33	67	0	47	169	17	.927
— Cleveland (A.L.)	3B	9	24	0	4	0	0	0	2	.167	2	4	0	6	18	4	.857
1993— Iowa (Am. Assoc.)■	3B-1B	132	469	63	128	23	0	13	66	.273	59	91	1	†77	†241	20	†.941
1994— Iowa (Am. Assoc.)	3B-1B-P	122	365	58	105	18	0	17	69	.288	55	74	4	109	205	10	†.969
1995— Indianapolis (A.A.)	3B-1B	81	277	48	88	19	0	9	41	.318	31	51	1	245	140	9	.977
— Cincinnati (N.L.)	1B-3B	10	18	1	5	1	0	1	2	.278	2	1	0	26	4	0	1.000
— Texas (A.L.)■	3B	26	68	4	15	4	0	2	6	.221	7	8	0	13	36	1	.980
American League totals (6 years)		370	1197	123	276	49	0	31	138	.231	154	260	3	268	653	48	.950
National League totals (1 year)		10	18	1	5	1	0	1	2	.278	2	1	0	26	4	0	1.000
Major league totals (6 years)		380	1215	124	281	50	0	32	140	.231	156	261	3	294	657	48	.952

RECORD AS PITCHER

Year Team (League)	W	L	Pct.	ERA	G	GS	CG	ShO	Sv.	IP	H	R	ER	BB	SO
1994— Iowa (Am. Assoc.)	0	0	. . .	13.50	1	0	0	0	0	2/3	2	2	1	0	0

YAN, ESTEBAN — P — EXPOS

PERSONAL: Born June 22, 1974, in Campha Deleseybo, Dominican Republic. . . . 6-4/230. . . . Throws right, bats right.

TRANSACTIONS/CAREER NOTES: Signed as non-drafted free agent by Atlanta Braves organization (November 21, 1990). . . . Traded by Braves with OF Roberto Kelly and OF Tony Tarasco to Montreal Expos for OF Marquis Grissom (April 6, 1995).

STATISTICAL NOTES: Led South Atlantic League with six balks in 1994.

Year Team (League)	W	L	Pct.	ERA	G	GS	CG	ShO	Sv.	IP	H	R	ER	BB	SO
1991— San Pedro (DSL)	4	1	.800	3.63	18	11	0	0	0	72	61	36	29	26	34
1992— San Pedro (DSL)	12	3	.800	1.32	16	16	7	4	0	115 2/3	85	37	17	23	86
1993— Danville (Appal.)	4	7	.364	3.03	14	14	0	0	0	71 1/3	73	46	24	24	50
1994— Macon (S. Atl.)	11	12	.478	3.27	28	•28	4	•3	0	170 2/3	155	85	62	34	121
1995— W.P. Beach (FSL)■	6	8	.429	3.07	24	21	1	0	1	137 2/3	139	63	47	33	89

YOUNG, ANTHONY — P — ASTROS

PERSONAL: Born January 19, 1966, in Houston. . . . 6-2/220. . . . Throws right, bats right. . . . Full name: Anthony Wayne Young.

HIGH SCHOOL: Furr (Houston).

COLLEGE: Houston.

TRANSACTIONS/CAREER NOTES: Selected by Montreal Expos organization in 10th round of free-agent draft (June 4, 1984); did not sign. . . . Selected by New York Mets organization in 38th round of free-agent draft (June 2, 1987). . . . On disabled list (July 19, 1989-remainder of season and June 11-18, 1990). . . . Traded by Mets with P Ottis Smith to Chicago Cubs for IF Jose Vizcaino (March 30, 1994). . . . On disabled list (July 10-26 and July 27, 1994-remainder of season). . . . On Chicago disabled list (April 24-June 13, 1995); included rehabilitation assignment to Daytona (May 15-June 13). . . . On Chicago disabled list (June 23-July 21, 1995); included rehabilitation assignment to Iowa (July 14-21). . . . Granted free agency (December 21, 1995). . . . Signed by Houston Astros organization (January 5, 1996).

RECORDS: Holds major league record for most consecutive games lost—27 (May 6, 1992 through July 24, 1993). . . . Holds modern N.L. rookie-season record for most consecutive games lost—14 (1992). . . . Holds N.L. record for most consecutive games lost at start of season—13 (April 9-July 24, 1993). . . . Shares N.L. record for most consecutive home runs allowed in one inning—3 (April 15, 1994, first inning).

HONORS: Named Texas League Pitcher of the Year (1990).

Year Team (League)	W	L	Pct.	ERA	G	GS	CG	ShO	Sv.	IP	H	R	ER	BB	SO
1987— Little Falls (NYP)	3	4	.429	4.53	14	9	0	0	0	53 2/3	58	37	27	25	48
1988— Little Falls (NYP)	3	5	.375	2.20	15	10	4	0	0	73 2/3	51	33	18	34	75
1989— Columbia (S. Atl.)	9	6	.600	3.49	21	17	8	1	0	129	115	60	50	55	127
1990— Jackson (Texas)	*15	3	.833	*1.65	23	23	3	1	0	158	116	38	29	52	95
1991— Tidewater (Int'l)	7	9	.438	3.73	25	25	3	1	0	164	172	74	68	67	93
— New York (N.L.)	2	5	.286	3.10	10	8	0	0	0	49 1/3	48	20	17	12	20
1992— New York (N.L.)	2	14	.125	4.17	52	13	1	0	15	121	134	66	56	31	64
1993— New York (N.L.)	1	16	.059	3.77	39	10	1	0	3	100 1/3	103	62	42	42	62
— Norfolk (Int'l)	1	1	.500	1.13	3	3	0	0	0	16	14	2	2	5	8
1994— Chicago (N.L.)■	4	6	.400	3.92	20	19	0	0	0	114 2/3	103	57	50	46	65
1995— Daytona (Fla. St.)	0	0	. . .	5.63	6	1	0	0	0	8	5	5	5	4	3
— Orlando (Southern)	0	0	. . .	0.00	2	2	0	0	0	5	6	1	0	3	5
— Chicago (N.L.)	3	4	.429	3.70	32	1	0	0	2	41 1/3	47	20	17	14	15
— Iowa (Am. Assoc.)	0	1	.000	11.25	3	1	0	0	0	4	9	5	5	4	6
Major league totals (5 years)	12	45	.211	3.84	153	51	2	0	20	426 2/3	435	225	182	145	226

YOUNG, DMITRI — 1B/OF — CARDINALS

PERSONAL: Born October 11, 1973, in Vicksburg, Miss. . . . 6-2/210. . . . Bats both, throws right. . . . Full name: Dmitri Dell Young.
HIGH SCHOOL: Rio Mesa (Oxnard, Calif.).
TRANSACTIONS/CAREER NOTES: Selected by St. Louis Cardinals organization in first round (fourth pick overall) of free-agent draft (June 3, 1991). . . . On disabled list (June 2-9, 1994). . . . On Arkansas suspended list (August 1-11 and August 17-27, 1995).
STATISTICAL NOTES: Led Texas League with 14 intentional bases on balls received in 1994. . . . Led Texas League first basemen with 15 errors in 1994.

			BATTING												FIELDING			
Year	Team (League)	Pos.	G	AB	R	H	2B	3B	HR	RBI	Avg.	BB	SO	SB	PO	A	E	Avg.
1991	Johns. City (App.)	3B	37	129	22	33	10	0	2	22	.256	21	28	2	19	49	5	.932
1992	Springfield (Midw.)	3B	135	493	74	153	*36	6	14	72	.310	51	94	14	66	239	42	.879
1993	St. Peters. (FSL)	3B-1B	69	270	31	85	13	3	5	43	.315	24	28	3	260	90	10	.972
	—Arkansas (Texas)	1B-3B	45	166	13	41	11	2	3	21	.247	9	29	4	348	29	7	.982
1994	Arkansas (Texas)	OF-1B	125	453	53	123	33	2	8	54	.272	36	60	0	485	44	†16	.971
1995	Arkansas (Texas)	OF	97	367	54	107	18	6	10	62	.292	30	46	2	116	5	9	.931
	—Louisville (A.A.)	OF	2	7	3	2	0	0	0	0	.286	1	1	0	3	0	1	.750

YOUNG, ERIC — 2B — ROCKIES

PERSONAL: Born May 18, 1967, in New Brunswick, N.J. . . . 5-9/170. . . . Bats right, throws right. . . . Full name: Eric Orlando Young.
HIGH SCHOOL: New Brunswick (N.J.).
COLLEGE: Rutgers.
TRANSACTIONS/CAREER NOTES: Selected by Los Angeles Dodgers organization in 43rd round of free-agent draft (June 5, 1989). . . . Selected by Colorado Rockies in first round (11th pick overall) of expansion draft (November 17, 1992).
STATISTICAL NOTES: Led Florida State League second basemen with 24 errors in 1990. . . . Led Texas League in caught stealing with 26 in 1991. . . . Led Texas League second basemen with .974 fielding percentage in 1991. . . . Tied for N.L. lead in errors by second baseman with 11 in 1995.

			BATTING												FIELDING			
Year	Team (League)	Pos.	G	AB	R	H	2B	3B	HR	RBI	Avg.	BB	SO	SB	PO	A	E	Avg.
1989	GC Dodgers (GCL)	2B	56	197	53	65	11	5	2	22	.330	33	16	*41	104	128	*15	.939
1990	Vero Beach (FSL)	2B-OF	127	460	*101	132	23	7	2	50	.287	69	35	*76	156	218	†25	.937
1991	San Antonio (Tex.)	2B-OF	127	461	82	129	17	4	3	35	.280	67	36	*70	206	282	13	†.974
	—Albuquerque (PCL)	2B	1	5	0	2	0	0	0	0	.400	0	0	0	1	2	0	1.000
1992	Albuquerque (PCL)	2B	94	350	61	118	16	5	3	49	.337	33	18	28	210	287	•20	.961
	—Los Angeles (N.L.)	2B	49	132	9	34	1	0	1	11	.258	8	9	6	85	114	9	.957
1993	Colorado (N.L.)■	2B-OF	144	490	82	132	16	8	3	42	.269	63	41	42	254	230	18	.964
1994	Colorado (N.L.)	OF-2B	90	228	37	62	13	1	7	30	.272	38	17	18	97	4	2	.981
1995	Colorado (N.L.)	2B-OF	120	366	68	116	21	•9	6	36	.317	49	29	35	180	230	11	†.974
Major league totals (4 years)			403	1216	196	344	51	18	17	119	.283	158	96	101	616	578	40	.968

DIVISION SERIES RECORD

			BATTING												FIELDING			
Year	Team (League)	Pos.	G	AB	R	H	2B	3B	HR	RBI	Avg.	BB	SO	SB	PO	A	E	Avg.
1995	Colorado (N.L.)	2B	4	16	3	7	1	0	1	2	.438	2	2	1	8	13	3	.875

YOUNG, ERNIE — OF — ATHLETICS

PERSONAL: Born July 8, 1969, in Chicago. . . . 6-1/190. . . . Bats right, throws right. . . . Full name: Ernest Wesley Young.
HIGH SCHOOL: Mendel Catholic (Chicago).
COLLEGE: Lewis (Ill.).
TRANSACTIONS/CAREER NOTES: Selected by Oakland Athletics organization in 10th round of free-agent draft (June 4, 1990). . . . On disabled list (July 11, 1992-remainder of season).
STATISTICAL NOTES: Led California League with .635 slugging percentage in 1993.

			BATTING												FIELDING			
Year	Team (League)	Pos.	G	AB	R	H	2B	3B	HR	RBI	Avg.	BB	SO	SB	PO	A	E	Avg.
1990	S. Oregon (N'west)	OF	50	168	34	47	6	2	6	23	.280	29	53	4	62	5	2	.971
1991	Madison (Midwest)	OF	114	362	75	92	19	2	15	71	.254	58	115	20	204	9	7	.968
1992	Modesto (Calif.)	OF	74	253	55	63	12	4	11	33	.249	47	74	11	126	11	6	.958
1993	Modesto (Calif.)	OF	85	301	83	92	18	6	23	71	.306	72	92	23	178	8	3	.984
	—Huntsville (South.)	OF	45	120	26	25	5	0	5	15	.208	24	36	8	97	8	4	.963
1994	Huntsville (South.)	OF	72	257	45	89	19	4	14	55	.346	37	45	5	98	13	2	.982
	—Oakland (A.L.)	OF-DH	11	30	2	2	1	0	0	3	.067	1	8	0	22	1	1	.958
	—Tacoma (PCL)	OF	29	102	19	29	4	0	6	16	.284	13	27	0	53	2	2	.965
1995	Edmonton (PCL)	OF	95	347	70	96	21	4	15	72	.277	49	73	2	194	7	6	.971
	—Oakland (A.L.)	OF	26	50	9	10	3	0	2	5	.200	8	12	0	35	0	2	.946
Major league totals (2 years)			37	80	11	12	4	0	2	8	.150	9	20	0	57	1	3	.951

YOUNG, KEVIN — 1B — PIRATES

PERSONAL: Born June 16, 1969, in Alpena, Mich. . . . 6-2/231. . . . Bats right, throws right. . . . Full name: Kevin Stacey Young.
HIGH SCHOOL: Washington (Kansas City, Kan.).
JUNIOR COLLEGE: Kansas City Kansas Community College.
COLLEGE: Southern Mississippi.
TRANSACTIONS/CAREER NOTES: Selected by Pittsburgh Pirates organization in seventh round of free-agent draft (June 4, 1990). . . . On Pittsburgh disabled list (July 24-August 8, 1995).

STATISTICAL NOTES: Tied for Southern League lead in errors by third baseman with 26 in 1991. . . . Tied for American Association lead in being hit by pitch with 11 in 1992. . . . Led American Association third basemen with 300 assists, 32 errors, 436 total chances and 41 double plays in 1992. . . . Led N.L. first basemen with .998 fielding percentage in 1993.

			BATTING												FIELDING			
Year	Team (League)	Pos.	G	AB	R	H	2B	3B	HR	RBI	Avg.	BB	SO	SB	PO	A	E	Avg.
1990—	Welland (NYP)	SS	72	238	46	58	16	2	5	30	.244	31	36	10	*79	118	26	.883
1991—	Salem (Carolina)	3B	56	201	38	63	12	4	6	28	.313	20	34	3	54	93	12	.925
—	Carolina (South.)	3B-1B	75	263	36	90	19	6	3	33	.342	15	38	9	157	116	‡28	.907
—	Buffalo (A.A.)	3B-1B	4	9	1	2	1	0	0	2	.222	0	0	1	6	6	2	.857
1992—	Buffalo (A.A.)	3B-1B	137	490	*91	154	29	6	8	65	.314	67	67	18	129	†313	†32	.932
—	Pittsburgh (N.L.)	3B-1B	10	7	2	4	0	0	0	4	.571	2	0	1	3	1	1	.800
1993—	Pittsburgh (N.L.)	1B-3B	141	449	38	106	24	3	6	47	.236	36	82	2	1122	112	3	†.998
1994—	Pittsburgh (N.L.)	1B-3B-OF	59	122	15	25	7	2	1	11	.205	8	34	0	179	45	3	.987
—	Buffalo (A.A.)	3B-1B	60	228	26	63	14	5	5	27	.276	15	45	6	59	162	4	.982
1995—	Calgary (PCL)	3B-1B	45	163	24	58	23	1	8	34	.356	15	21	6	144	85	12	.950
—	Pittsburgh (N.L.)	3B-1B	56	181	13	42	9	0	6	22	.232	8	53	1	58	110	12	.933
Major league totals (4 years)			266	759	68	177	40	5	13	84	.233	54	169	4	1362	268	19	.988

ZAUN, GREG — C — ORIOLES

PERSONAL: Born April 14, 1971, in Glendale, Calif. . . . 5-10/170. . . . Bats both, throws right. . . . Full name: Gregory Owen Zaun. . . . Nephew of Rick Dempsey, major league catcher with six teams (1969-92).

HIGH SCHOOL: St. Francis (La Canada, Calif.).

TRANSACTIONS/CAREER NOTES: Selected by Baltimore Orioles organization in 17th round of free-agent draft (June 5, 1989). . . . On Bowie disabled list (June 17-July 15, 1993).

STATISTICAL NOTES: Led Appalachian League catchers with 460 putouts and 501 total chances in 1990. . . . Led Midwest League catchers with 796 total chances in 1991. . . . Led Carolina League catchers with 746 putouts, 91 assists, 18 errors, 855 total chances and 10 double plays in 1992. . . . Led International League catchers with 841 total chances and 11 double plays in 1994.

			BATTING												FIELDING			
Year	Team (League)	Pos.	G	AB	R	H	2B	3B	HR	RBI	Avg.	BB	SO	SB	PO	A	E	Avg.
1990—	Wausau (Midwest)	C	37	100	3	13	0	1	1	7	.130	7	17	0	270	26	3	.990
—	Bluefield (Appal.)	C-3-S-P	61	184	29	55	5	2	2	21	.299	23	15	5	†462	34	10	.980
1991—	Kane Co. (Midw.)	C	113	409	67	112	17	5	4	51	.274	50	41	4	*697	83	16	.980
1992—	Frederick (Caro.)	C-2B	108	383	54	96	18	6	6	52	.251	42	45	3	†746	†91	†18	.979
1993—	Bowie (Eastern)	C-2-3-P	79	258	25	79	10	0	3	38	.306	27	26	4	423	51	10	.979
—	Rochester (Int'l)	C	21	78	10	20	4	2	1	11	.256	6	11	0	141	18	4	.975
1994—	Rochester (Int'l)	C	123	388	61	92	16	4	7	43	.237	56	72	4	*750	82	9	*.989
1995—	Rochester (Int'l)	C	42	140	26	41	13	1	6	18	.293	14	21	0	243	18	3	.989
—	Baltimore (A.L.)	C	40	104	18	27	5	0	3	14	.260	16	14	1	216	13	3	.987
Major league totals (1 year)			40	104	18	27	5	0	3	14	.260	16	14	1	216	13	3	.987

RECORD AS PITCHER

Year	Team (League)	W	L	Pct.	ERA	G	GS	CG	ShO	Sv.	IP	H	R	ER	BB	SO
1990—	Bluefield (Appal.)	0	0	...	0.00	1	0	0	0	0	1	1	0	0	1	1
1993—	Bowie (Eastern)	0	0	...	0.00	1	0	0	0	0	2 1/3	1	0	0	0	0

ZEILE, TODD — 3B — PHILLIES

PERSONAL: Born September 9, 1965, in Van Nuys, Calif. . . . 6-1/200. . . . Bats right, throws right. . . . Full name: Todd Edward Zeile. . . . Husband of Julianne McNamara, Olympic gold-medal gymnast (1984). . . . Name pronounced ZEEL.

HIGH SCHOOL: Hart (Newhall, Calif.).

COLLEGE: UCLA.

TRANSACTIONS/CAREER NOTES: Selected by Kansas City Royals organization in 30th round of free-agent draft (June 6, 1983); did not sign. . . . Selected by St. Louis Cardinals organization in supplemental round ("sandwich pick" between second and third round 55th pick overall) of free-agent draft (June 2, 1986); pick received as compensation for New York Yankees signing Type C free-agent IF Ivan DeJesus. . . . On St. Louis disabled list (April 23-May 9, 1995); included rehabilitation assignment to Louisville (May 6-9). . . . Traded by Cardinals with cash to Chicago Cubs for P Mike Morgan, 3B/OF Paul Torres and C Francisco Morales (June 16, 1995). . . . Granted free agency (December 21, 1995). . . . Signed by Philadelphia Phillies (December 22, 1995).

RECORDS: Holds N.L. single-season record for fewest putouts by third baseman (150 or more games)—83 (1993).

HONORS: Named Midwest League co-Most Valuable Player (1987).

STATISTICAL NOTES: Led New York-Pennsylvania League with six sacrifice flies in 1986. . . . Tied for New York-Pennsylvania League lead in double plays by catcher with seven in 1986. . . . Led Texas League catchers with 687 putouts and 761 total chances in 1988. . . . Led American Association catchers with .992 fielding percentage and 17 passed balls in 1989. . . . Career major league grand slams: 3.

			BATTING												FIELDING			
Year	Team (League)	Pos.	G	AB	R	H	2B	3B	HR	RBI	Avg.	BB	SO	SB	PO	A	E	Avg.
1986—	Erie (NYP)	C	70	248	40	64	14	1	14	*63	.258	37	52	5	407	*66	8	.983
1987—	Springfield (Midw.)	C-3B	130	487	94	142	24	4	25	*106	.292	70	85	1	867	79	14	.985
1988—	Arkansas (Texas)	C-OF-1B	129	430	95	117	33	2	19	75	.272	83	64	6	†697	66	10	.987
1989—	Louisville (A.A.)	C-3B-1B	118	453	71	131	26	3	19	85	.289	45	78	0	583	71	6	†.991
—	St. Louis (N.L.)	C	28	82	7	21	3	1	1	8	.256	9	14	0	125	10	4	.971
1990—	St. Louis (N.L.)	C-3-1-O	144	495	62	121	25	3	15	57	.244	67	77	2	648	106	15	.980
1991—	St. Louis (N.L.)	3B	155	565	76	158	36	3	11	81	.280	62	94	17	124	290	*25	.943
1992—	St. Louis (N.L.)	3B	126	439	51	113	18	4	7	48	.257	68	70	7	81	235	13	.960
—	Louisville (A.A.)	3B	21	74	11	23	4	1	5	13	.311	9	13	0	15	41	5	.918
1993—	St. Louis (N.L.)	3B	157	571	82	158	36	1	17	103	.277	70	76	5	83	310	33	.923
1994—	St. Louis (N.L.)	3B	113	415	62	111	25	1	19	75	.267	52	56	1	66	224	12	.960
1995—	Louisville (A.A.)	1B	2	8	0	1	0	0	0	0	.125	0	2	0	11	1	1	.923
—	St. Louis (N.L.)	1B	34	127	16	37	6	0	5	22	.291	18	23	1	310	30	7	.980
—	Chicago (N.L.)■	3B-OF-1B	79	299	34	68	16	0	9	30	.227	16	53	0	52	134	12	.939
Major league totals (7 years)			836	2993	390	787	165	13	84	424	.263	362	463	33	1489	1339	121	.959

Y Z

ZOSKY, EDDIE SS

PERSONAL: Born February 10, 1968, in Whittier, Calif. . . . 6-0/180. . . . Bats right, throws right. . . . Full name: Edward James Zosky. . . . Name pronounced ZAH-skee.

HIGH SCHOOL: St. Paul's (Sante Fe Springs, Calif.).

COLLEGE: Fresno State.

TRANSACTIONS/CAREER NOTES: Selected by New York Mets organization in fifth round of free-agent draft (June 2, 1986); did not sign. . . . Selected by Toronto Blue Jays organization in first round (19th pick overall) of free-agent draft (June 5, 1989). . . . On Toronto disabled list (March 26-August 11, 1993); included rehabilitation assignments to Hagerstown (July 26-August 2) and Syracuse (August 2-11). . . . On disabled list (June 29-August 10, 1994). . . . Traded by Blue Jays to Florida Marlins for a player to be named later (November 18, 1994); Blue Jays acquired P Scott Pace to complete deal (December 14, 1994). . . . Granted free agency (October 16, 1995).

HONORS: Named shortstop on The Sporting News college All-America team (1989).

STATISTICAL NOTES: Led Southern League shortstops with 80 double plays in 1990. . . . Led International League shortstops with 616 total chances and 88 double plays in 1991.

			BATTING											FIELDING			
Year	Team (League)	Pos.	G	AB	R	H	2B	3B	HR	RBI	Avg.	BB	SO	SB	PO	A	E	Avg.
1989—	Knoxville (South.)	SS	56	208	21	46	5	3	2	14	.221	10	32	1	94	135	8	.966
1990—	Knoxville (South.)	SS	115	450	53	122	20	7	3	45	.271	26	72	3	*196	295	31	*.941
1991—	Syracuse (Int'l)	SS	119	511	69	135	18	4	6	39	.264	35	82	9	*221	*371	24	*.961
	—Toronto (A.L.)	SS	18	27	2	4	1	1	0	2	.148	0	8	0	12	26	0	1.000
1992—	Syracuse (Int'l)	SS	96	342	31	79	11	6	4	38	.231	19	53	3	123	249	27	.932
	—Toronto (A.L.)	SS	8	7	1	2	0	1	0	1	.286	0	2	0	2	10	1	.923
1993—	Hagerstown (SAL)	SS	5	20	2	2	0	0	0	1	.100	2	1	0	10	15	0	1.000
	—Syracuse (Int'l)	SS	28	93	9	20	5	0	0	8	.215	1	20	0	48	71	5	.960
1994—	Syracuse (Int'l)	2B-SS-3B	85	284	41	75	15	3	7	37	.264	9	46	3	120	212	15	.957
1995—	Florida (N.L.)■	SS-2B	6	5	0	1	0	0	0	0	.200	0	0	0	1	2	1	.750
	—Charlotte (Int'l)	SS-2B-3B	92	312	27	77	15	2	3	42	.247	7	48	2	161	279	15	.967
American League totals (2 years)			26	34	3	6	1	2	0	3	.176	0	10	0	14	36	1	.980
National League totals (1 year)			6	5	0	1	0	0	0	0	.200	0	0	0	1	2	1	.750
Major league totals (3 years)			32	39	3	7	1	2	0	3	.179	0	10	0	15	38	2	.964

MAJOR LEAGUE MANAGERS

ALOU, FELIPE — EXPOS

PERSONAL: Born May 12, 1935, in Haina, Dominican Republic. . . . 6-1/195. . . . Batted right, threw right. . . . Full name: Felipe Rojas Alou. . . . Father of Moises Alou, outfielder, Montreal Expos; brother of Jesus Alou, major league outfielder with four teams (1965-75 and 1978-79); brother of Matty Alou, major league outfielder with six teams (1960-74); and uncle of Mel Rojas, pitcher, Expos.
COLLEGE: University of Santo Domingo (Dominican Republic).
TRANSACTIONS/CAREER NOTES: Signed as free agent by New York Giants organization (November 14, 1955). . . . Giants franchise moved from New York to San Francisco (1958). . . . Traded by Giants with P Billy Hoeft, C Ed Bailey and a player to be named later to Milwaukee Braves for P Bob Hendley, P Bob Shaw and C Del Crandall (December 3, 1963); Braves acquired IF Ernie Bowman to complete deal (January 8, 1964). . . . On disabled list (June 24-July 25, 1964). . . . Braves franchise moved from Milwaukee to Atlanta (1966). . . . Traded by Braves to Oakland Athletics for P Jim Nash (December 3, 1969). . . . Traded by A's to New York Yankees for P Rob Gardner and P Ron Klimkowski (April 9, 1971). . . . Contract sold by Yankees to Montreal Expos (September 5, 1973). . . . Contract sold by Expos to Milwaukee Brewers (December 7, 1973). . . . Released by Brewers (April 29, 1974).
HONORS: Named first baseman on The Sporting News N.L. All-Star team (1966).
STATISTICAL NOTES: Led N.L. with 355 total bases in 1966. . . . Career major league grand slams: 2.

			BATTING												FIELDING			
Year	Team (League)	Pos.	G	AB	R	H	2B	3B	HR	RBI	Avg.	BB	SO	SB	PO	A	E	Avg.
1956	—Lake Charl. (Evan.).....	OF	5	9	1	2	0	0	0	1	.222	...	...	0	6	1	0	1.000
	—Cocoa (Florida St.).....	OF-3B	119	445	111	169	15	6	21	99	*.380	68	40	*48	199	60	23	.918
1957	—Minneapolis (A.A.).....	OF	24	57	7	12	2	0	0	3	.211	5	8	1	32	1	1	.971
	—Springfield (East.)......	OF-3B	106	359	45	110	14	3	12	71	.306	27	29	18	215	26	9	.964
1958	—Phoenix (PCL)...........	OF	55	216	61	69	16	2	13	42	.319	17	24	10	150	3	3	.981
	—San Francisco (N.L.) ..	OF	75	182	21	46	9	2	4	16	.253	19	34	4	126	2	2	.985
1959	—San Francisco (N.L.) ..	OF	95	247	38	68	13	2	10	33	.275	17	38	5	111	2	3	.974
1960	—San Francisco (N.L.) ..	OF	106	322	48	85	17	3	8	44	.264	16	42	10	156	5	7	.958
1961	—San Francisco (N.L.) ..	OF	132	415	59	120	19	0	18	52	.289	26	41	11	196	10	2	.990
1962	—San Francisco (N.L.) ..	OF	154	561	96	177	30	3	25	98	.316	33	66	10	262	7	8	.971
1963	—San Francisco (N.L.) ..	OF	157	565	75	159	31	9	20	82	.281	27	87	11	279	9	4	.986
1964	—Milwaukee (N.L.)■.....	OF-1B	121	415	60	105	26	3	9	51	.253	30	41	5	329	12	5	.986
1965	—Milwaukee (N.L.)........	O-1-3-S	143	555	80	165	29	2	23	78	.297	31	63	8	626	43	6	.991
1966	—Atlanta (N.L.).............	1-O-3-S	154	*666	*122	*218	32	6	31	74	.327	24	51	5	935	64	13	.987
1967	—Atlanta (N.L.).............	1B-OF	140	574	76	157	26	3	15	43	.274	32	50	6	864	34	9	.990
1968	—Atlanta (N.L.).............	OF	160	*662	72	•210	37	5	11	57	.317	48	56	12	379	8	8	.980
1969	—Atlanta (N.L.).............	OF	123	476	54	134	13	1	5	32	.282	23	23	4	260	4	3	.989
1970	—Oakland (A.L.)■..........	OF-1B	154	575	70	156	25	3	8	55	.271	32	31	10	290	11	7	.977
1971	—Oakland (A.L.)...........	OF	2	8	0	2	1	0	0	0	.250	0	1	0	7	0	0	1.000
	—New York (A.L.)■.......	OF-1B	131	461	52	133	20	6	8	69	.289	32	24	5	506	23	4	.992
1972	—New York (A.L.)..........	1B-OF	120	324	33	90	18	1	6	37	.278	22	27	1	669	54	7	.990
1973	—New York (A.L.)..........	1B-OF	93	280	25	66	12	0	4	27	.236	9	25	0	512	31	7	.987
	—Montreal (N.L.)■........	OF-1B	19	48	4	10	1	0	1	4	.208	2	4	0	30	3	0	1.000
1974	—Milwaukee (A.L.)■	OF	3	3	0	0	0	0	0	0	.000	0	2	0	0	0	1	.000
American League totals (5 years)			503	1651	180	447	76	10	26	188	.271	95	110	16	1984	119	26	.988
National League totals (13 years)			1579	5688	805	1654	283	39	180	664	.291	328	596	91	4553	203	70	.985
Major league totals (17 years)			2082	7339	985	2101	359	49	206	852	.286	423	706	107	6537	322	96	.986

CHAMPIONSHIP SERIES RECORD

			BATTING												FIELDING			
Year	Team (League)	Pos.	G	AB	R	H	2B	3B	HR	RBI	Avg.	BB	SO	SB	PO	A	E	Avg.
1969	—Atlanta (N.L.).............	PH	1	1	0	0	0	0	0	0	.000	0	0	0	...	...	...	...

WORLD SERIES RECORD

			BATTING												FIELDING			
Year	Team (League)	Pos.	G	AB	R	H	2B	3B	HR	RBI	Avg.	BB	SO	SB	PO	A	E	Avg.
1962	—San Francisco (N.L.) ..	OF	7	26	2	7	1	1	0	1	.269	1	4	0	8	0	1	.889

ALL-STAR GAME RECORD

			BATTING											FIELDING			
Year	League	Pos.	AB	R	H	2B	3B	HR	RBI	Avg.	BB	SO	SB	PO	A	E	Avg.
1962	—National.....................	OF	0	0	0	0	0	0	1	...	0	0	0	0	0	0	...
1966	—National.....................							Did not play.									
1968	—National.....................	OF	0	0	0	0	0	0	0	...	0	0	0	0	0	0	...
All-Star Game totals (2 years)			0	0	0	0	0	0	1	...	0	0	0	0	0	0	...

RECORD AS MANAGER

BACKGROUND: Spring training instructor, Montreal Expos (1976). . . . Coach, Expos (1979-80, 1984 and October 8, 1991-May 22, 1992).
HONORS: Named Florida State League Manager of the Year (1990). . . . Named N.L. Manager of the Year by The Sporting News (1994). . . . Named N.L. Manager of the Year by Baseball Writers' Association of America (1994).

		REGULAR SEASON				POSTSEASON							
						Playoff		Champ. Series		World Series		All-Star Game	
Year	Team (League)	W	L	Pct.	Pos.	W	L	W	L	W	L	W	L
1977	—West Palm Beach (Florida State)	77	55	.583	1st (S)	1	2	—	—	—	—	—	—
1978	—Memphis (Southern)...............................	71	73	.493	2nd (W)	—	—	—	—	—	—	—	—
1981	—Denver (American Association)	76	60	.559	2nd (W)	4	0	—	—	—	—	—	—
1982	—Wichita (American Association)...............	70	67	.511	2nd (W)	—	—	—	—	—	—	—	—
1983	—Wichita (American Association)...............	65	71	.478	3rd (W)	—	—	—	—	—	—	—	—
1985	—Indianapolis (American Association)	61	81	.430	4th (E)	—	—	—	—	—	—	—	—

Year	Team (League)	W	L	Pct.	Pos.	Playoff W	Playoff L	Champ. Series W	Champ. Series L	World Series W	World Series L	All-Star Game W	All-Star Game L
		REGULAR SEASON				POSTSEASON							
1986	West Palm Beach (Florida State)	80	55	.593	1st (S)	3	3	—	—	—	—	—	—
1987	West Palm Beach (Florida State)	75	63	.543	2nd (S)	—	—	—	—	—	—	—	—
1988	West Palm Beach (Florida State)	41	27	.603	2nd (E)	—	—	—	—	—	—	—	—
	—(Second half)	30	36	.455	3rd (E)	2	2	—	—	—	—	—	—
1989	West Palm Beach (Florida State)	39	31	.557	T2nd (E)	—	—	—	—	—	—	—	—
	—(Second half)	35	33	.515	2nd (E)	—	—	—	—	—	—	—	—
1990	West Palm Beach (Florida State)	49	19	.721	1st (E)	—	—	—	—	—	—	—	—
	—(Second half)	43	21	.672	1st (E)	3	3	—	—	—	—	—	—
1991	West Palm Beach (Florida State)	33	31	.516	4th (E)	—	—	—	—	—	—	—	—
	—(Second half)	39	28	.582	2nd (E)	6	1	—	—	—	—	—	—
1992	Montreal (N.L.)	70	55	.560	2nd (E)	—	—	—	—	—	—	—	—
1993	Montreal (N.L.)	94	68	.580	2nd (E)	—	—	—	—	—	—	—	—
1994	Montreal (N.L.)	74	40	.649		—	—	—	—	—	—	—	—
1995	Montreal (N.L.)	66	78	.458	5th (E)	—	—	—	—	—	—	1	0
Major league totals (4 years)		304	241	.558		—	—	—	—	—	—	1	0

NOTES:

1977—Lost to St. Petersburg in semifinals.
1978—Memphis tied one game.
1981—Defeated Omaha for league championship.
1986—Defeated Winter Haven, two games to none, in semifinals; lost to St. Petersburg, three games to one, in league championship.
1988—Defeated Vero Beach, two games to none, in first round; lost to Osceola, two games to none, in semifinals.
1990—Defeated Lakeland, two games to one, in semifinals; lost to Vero Beach, two games to one, in league championship.
1991—Defeated Vero Beach, two games to one, in first round; defeated Lakeland, two games to none, in semifinals; defeated Clearwater, two games to none, in league championship.
1992—Replaced Montreal manager Tom Runnells with club in fourth place and record of 17-20 (May 22).
1994—Montreal was in first place in N.L. East at time of season-ending strike (August 12).

BAKER, DUSTY — GIANTS

PERSONAL: Born June 15, 1949, in Riverside, Calif. . . . 6-2/200. . . . Batted right, threw right. . . . Full name: Johnnie B. Baker Jr.
HIGH SCHOOL: Del Campo (Fair Oaks, Calif.).
COLLEGE: American River College (Calif.).
TRANSACTIONS/CAREER NOTES: Selected by Atlanta Braves organization in 26th round of free-agent draft (June 6, 1967). . . . On West Palm Beach restricted list (April 5-June 13, 1968). . . . On Atlanta military list (January 24-April 3, 1969 and June 17-July 3, 1972). . . . Traded by Braves with 1B/3B Ed Goodson to Los Angeles Dodgers for OF Jimmy Wynn, 2B Lee Lacy, 1B/OF Tom Paciorek and IF Jerry Royster (November 17, 1975). . . . Released on waivers by Dodgers (February 10, 1984); San Francisco Giants claim rejected (February 16, 1984). . . . Granted free agency (February 21, 1984). . . . Signed by Giants (April 1, 1984). . . . On restricted list (April 2-11, 1984). . . . Traded by Giants to Oakland Athletics for P Ed Puikunas and C Dan Winters (March 24, 1985). . . . Granted free agency (November 10, 1986).
RECORDS: Shares major league records for most plate appearances, most at-bats and most times faced pitcher as batsman in one inning—3 (September 20, 1972, second inning); and most stolen bases in one inning—3 (June 27, 1984, third inning). . . . Holds N.L. single-season record for fewest chances accepted by outfielder (150 or more games)—235 (1977).
HONORS: Named outfielder on THE SPORTING NEWS N.L. All-Star team (1980). . . . Named outfielder on THE SPORTING NEWS N.L. Silver Slugger team (1980-81). . . . Won N.L. Gold Glove as outfielder (1981).
STATISTICAL NOTES: Led N.L. outfielders with 407 total chances in 1973. . . . Career major league grand slams: 4.

Year	Team (League)	Pos.	G	AB	R	H	2B	3B	HR	RBI	Avg.	BB	SO	SB	PO	A	E	Avg.
				BATTING											FIELDING			
1967	Austin (Texas)	OF	9	39	6	9	1	0	0	1	.231	2	7	0	17	0	1	.944
1968	W.P. Beach (FSL)	OF	6	21	2	4	0	0	0	2	.190	1	4	0	6	2	0	1.000
	—Greenw. (W. Car.)	OF	52	199	45	68	11	3	6	39	.342	23	39	6	82	1	3	.965
	—Atlanta (N.L.)	OF	6	5	0	2	0	0	0	0	.400	0	1	0	0	0	0	...
1969	Shreveport (Texas)	OF	73	265	40	68	5	1	9	31	.257	36	41	2	135	10	3	.980
	—Richmond (Int'l)	OF-3B	25	89	7	22	4	0	0	8	.247	11	22	3	40	9	4	.925
	—Atlanta (N.L.)	OF	3	7	0	0	0	0	0	0	.000	0	3	0	2	0	0	1.000
1970	Richmond (Int'l)	OF	118	461	97	150	29	3	11	51	.325	53	45	10	236	10	7	.972
	—Atlanta (N.L.)	OF	13	24	3	7	0	0	0	4	.292	2	4	0	11	1	3	.800
1971	Richmond (Int'l)	OF-3B	80	341	62	106	23	2	11	41	.311	25	37	10	136	13	4	.974
	—Atlanta (N.L.)	OF	29	62	2	14	2	0	0	4	.226	1	14	0	29	1	0	1.000
1972	Atlanta (N.L.)	OF	127	446	62	143	27	2	17	76	.321	45	68	4	344	8	4	.989
1973	Atlanta (N.L.)	OF	159	604	101	174	29	4	21	99	.288	67	72	24	*390	10	7	.983
1974	Atlanta (N.L.)	OF	149	574	80	147	35	0	20	69	.256	71	87	18	359	10	7	.981
1975	Atlanta (N.L.)	OF	142	494	63	129	18	2	19	72	.261	67	57	12	287	10	3	.990
1976	Los Angeles (N.L.)■	OF	112	384	36	93	13	0	4	39	.242	31	54	2	254	3	1	.996
1977	Los Angeles (N.L.)	OF	153	533	86	155	26	1	30	86	.291	58	89	2	227	8	3	.987
1978	Los Angeles (N.L.)	OF	149	522	62	137	24	1	11	66	.262	47	66	12	250	13	4	.985
1979	Los Angeles (N.L.)	OF	151	554	86	152	29	1	23	88	.274	56	70	11	289	14	3	.990
1980	Los Angeles (N.L.)	OF	153	579	80	170	26	4	29	97	.294	43	66	12	308	5	3	.991
1981	Los Angeles (N.L.)	OF	103	400	48	128	17	3	9	49	.320	29	43	10	181	8	2	.990
1982	Los Angeles (N.L.)	OF	147	570	80	171	19	1	23	88	.300	56	62	17	226	7	6	.975
1983	Los Angeles (N.L.)	OF	149	531	71	138	25	1	15	73	.260	72	59	7	249	4	5	.981
1984	San Fran. (N.L.)■	OF	100	243	31	71	7	2	3	32	.292	40	27	4	112	1	3	.974
1985	Oakland (A.L.)■	1B-OF-DH	111	343	48	92	15	1	14	52	.268	50	47	2	465	29	5	.990
1986	Oakland (A.L.)	OF-DH-1B	83	242	25	58	8	0	4	19	.240	27	37	0	90	4	0	1.000
American League totals (2 years)			194	585	73	150	23	1	18	71	.256	77	84	2	555	33	5	.992
National League totals (17 years)			1845	6532	891	1831	297	22	224	942	.280	685	842	135	3518	103	54	.985
Major league totals (19 years)			2039	7117	964	1981	320	23	242	1013	.278	762	926	137	4073	136	59	.986

DIVISION SERIES RECORD

Year	Team (League)	Pos.	G	AB	R	H	2B	3B	HR	RBI	Avg.	BB	SO	SB	PO	A	E	Avg.
				BATTING											FIELDING			
1981—	Los Angeles (N.L.)	OF	5	18	2	3	1	0	0	1	.167	2	0	0	12	0	0	1.000

CHAMPIONSHIP SERIES RECORD

NOTES: Named N.L. Championship Series Most Valuable Player (1977). . . . Shares single-game record for most grand slams—1 (October 5, 1977). . . . Shares record for most runs batted in in one inning—4 (October 5, 1977, fourth inning). . . . Shares N.L. single-game record for most hits—4 (October 7, 1978).

Year	Team (League)	Pos.	G	AB	R	H	2B	3B	HR	RBI	Avg.	BB	SO	SB	PO	A	E	Avg.
				BATTING											FIELDING			
1977—	Los Angeles (N.L.)	OF	4	14	4	5	1	0	2	8	.357	2	3	0	3	0	0	1.000
1978—	Los Angeles (N.L.)	OF	4	15	1	7	2	0	0	1	.467	3	0	0	5	0	0	1.000
1981—	Los Angeles (N.L.)	OF	5	19	3	6	1	0	0	3	.316	1	0	0	10	0	1	.909
1983—	Los Angeles (N.L.)	OF	4	14	4	5	1	0	1	1	.357	2	0	0	9	0	0	1.000
Championship series totals (4 years)			17	62	12	23	5	0	3	13	.371	8	3	0	27	0	1	.964

WORLD SERIES RECORD

NOTES: Member of World Series championship team (1981).

Year	Team (League)	Pos.	G	AB	R	H	2B	3B	HR	RBI	Avg.	BB	SO	SB	PO	A	E	Avg.
				BATTING											FIELDING			
1977—	Los Angeles (N.L.)	OF	6	24	4	7	0	0	1	5	.292	0	2	0	11	0	1	.917
1978—	Los Angeles (N.L.)	OF	6	21	2	5	0	0	1	1	.238	1	3	0	12	0	0	1.000
1981—	Los Angeles (N.L.)	OF	6	24	3	4	0	0	0	1	.167	1	6	0	13	0	0	1.000
World Series totals (3 years)			18	69	9	16	0	0	2	7	.232	2	11	0	36	0	1	.973

ALL-STAR GAME RECORD

Year	League	Pos.	AB	R	H	2B	3B	HR	RBI	Avg.	BB	SO	SB	PO	A	E	Avg.
			BATTING											FIELDING			
1981—	National	OF	2	0	1	0	0	0	0	.500	0	0	0	2	0	0	1.000
1982—	National	OF	2	0	0	0	0	0	0	.000	0	0	0	0	0	0	...
All-Star Game totals (2 years)			4	0	1	0	0	0	0	.250	0	0	0	2	0	0	1.000

RECORD AS MANAGER

BACKGROUND: Coach, San Francisco Giants (1988-92). . . . Manager, Scottsdale Scorpions, Giants organization, Arizona Fall League (1992, record: 20-22, second place/Northern Division).

HONORS: Named N.L. Manager of the Year by the Baseball Writers' Association of America (1993). . . . Coach, N.L. All-Star team (1994).

Year	Team (League)	W	L	Pct.	Pos.	Playoff W	Playoff L	Champ. Series W	Champ. Series L	World Series W	World Series L	All-Star Game W	All-Star Game L
		REGULAR SEASON				POSTSEASON							
1993—	San Francisco (N.L.)	103	59	.636	2nd (W)	—	—	—	—	—	—	—	—
1994—	San Francisco (N.L.)	55	60	.478		—	—	—	—	—	—	—	—
1995—	San Francisco (N.L.)	67	77	.465	4th (W)	—	—	—	—	—	—	—	—
Major league totals (3 years)		225	196	.534		—	—	—	—	—	—	—	—

NOTES:

1994—San Francisco was in second place in N.L. West at time of season-ending strike (August 12).

BAYLOR, DON — ROCKIES

PERSONAL: Born June 28, 1949, in Austin, Tex. . . . 6-1/220. . . . Batted right, threw right. . . . Full name: Donald Edward Baylor. . . . Cousin of Pat Ballage, safety, Indianapolis Colts (1986-87).

HIGH SCHOOL: Stephen F. Austin (Austin, Tex.).

TRANSACTIONS/CAREER NOTES: Selected by Baltimore Orioles organization in second round of free-agent draft (June 6, 1967). . . . Traded by Orioles with P Mike Torrez and P Paul Mitchell to Oakland Athletics for OF Reggie Jackson, P Ken Holtzman and P Bill Van Bommel (April 2, 1976). . . . Granted free agency (November 1, 1976). . . . Signed by California Angels (November 16, 1976). . . . On disabled list (May 11-June 26, 1980). . . . Granted free agency (November 10, 1982). . . . Signed by New York Yankees (December 1, 1982). . . . Traded by Yankees to Boston Red Sox for DH Mike Easler (March 28, 1986). . . . Traded by Red Sox to Minnesota Twins for a player to be named later (August 31, 1987); Red Sox acquired P Enrique Rios to complete deal (December 18, 1987). . . . Released by Twins (December 21, 1987). . . . Signed by A's (February 9, 1988). . . . Granted free agency (November 4, 1988).

RECORDS: Holds major league career record for most times hit by pitch—267. . . . Shares major league records for most consecutive home runs in two consecutive games—4 (July 1 [1] and 2 [3], 1975, bases on balls included); and most long hits in opening game of season—4 (2 doubles, 1 triple, 1 home run, April 6, 1973). . . . Shares major league record for most times caught stealing in one inning—2 (June 15, 1974, ninth inning). . . . Shares modern major league single-game record for most at-bats—7 (August 25, 1979). . . . Holds A.L. single-season record for most times hit by pitch—35 (1986).

HONORS: Named Appalachian League Player of the Year (1967). . . . Named Minor League Player of the Year by The Sporting News (1970). . . . Named A.L. Player of the Year by The Sporting News (1979). . . . Named A.L. Most Valuable Player by Baseball Writers' Association of America (1979). . . . Named designated hitter on The Sporting News A.L. All-Star team (1979 and 1985-86). . . . Named designated hitter on The Sporting News A.L. Silver Slugger team (1983, 1985-86).

STATISTICAL NOTES: Led Appalachian League with 135 total bases and tied for lead in caught stealing with 6 in 1967. . . . Led Texas League in being hit by pitch with 13 in 1969. . . . Led International League with 296 total bases in 1970. . . . Led International League in being hit by pitch with 19 in 1970 and 16 in 1971. . . . Led A.L. in being hit by pitch with 13 in 1973, 20 in 1976, 18 in 1978, 23 in 1984, 24 in 1985, 35 in 1986, 28 in 1987 and tied for lead with 13 in 1975. . . . Hit three home runs in one game (July 2, 1975). . . . Led A.L. with 12 sacrifice flies in 1978. . . . Led A.L. with 21 game-winning RBIs in 1982. . . . Career major league grand slams: 12.

Year	Team (League)	Pos.	G	AB	R	H	2B	3B	HR	RBI	Avg.	BB	SO	SB	PO	A	E	Avg.
				BATTING											FIELDING			
1967—	Bluefield (Appal.)	OF	•67	246	50	*85	10	*8	8	47	*.346	35	52	*26	106	5	5	.957
1968—	Stockton (Calif.)	OF	68	244	52	90	6	3	7	40	.369	35	65	14	135	3	7	.952
—	Elmira (Eastern)	OF	6	24	4	8	1	1	1	3	.333	3	4	1	10	1	0	1.000
—	Rochester (Int'l)	OF	15	46	4	10	2	0	0	4	.217	3	17	1	29	1	4	.882

Year	Team (League)	Pos.	G	AB	R	H	2B	3B	HR	RBI	Avg.	BB	SO	SB	PO	A	E	Avg.
				BATTING											FIELDING			
1969—	Miami (Florida St.)	OF	17	56	13	21	5	4	3	24	.375	7	8	3	30	2	3	.914
—	Dall./Fort W. (Tex.)	OF	109	406	71	122	17	•10	11	57	.300	48	77	19	241	7	*13	.950
1970—	Rochester (Int'l)	OF	•140	508	*127	166	*34	*15	22	107	.327	76	99	26	286	5	7	.977
—	Baltimore (A.L.)	OF	8	17	4	4	0	0	0	4	.235	2	3	1	15	0	0	1.000
1971—	Rochester (Int'l)	OF	136	492	104	154	•31	10	20	95	.313	79	73	25	210	4	9	.960
—	Baltimore (A.L.)	OF	1	2	0	0	0	0	0	1	.000	2	1	0	4	0	0	1.000
1972—	Baltimore (A.L.)	OF-1B	102	320	33	81	13	3	11	38	.253	29	50	24	206	4	5	.977
1973—	Baltimore (A.L.)	OF-1B-DH	118	405	64	116	20	4	11	51	.286	35	48	32	228	10	6	.975
1974—	Baltimore (A.L.)	OF-1B	137	489	66	133	22	1	10	59	.272	43	56	29	260	2	5	.981
1975—	Baltimore (A.L.)	OF-DH-1B	145	524	79	148	21	6	25	76	.282	53	64	32	286	8	5	.983
1976—	Oakland (A.L.)■	OF-1B-DH	157	595	85	147	25	1	15	68	.247	58	72	52	781	45	12	.986
1977—	California (A.L.)■	OF-DH-1B	154	561	87	141	27	0	25	75	.251	62	76	26	280	16	7	.977
1978—	California (A.L.)	DH-OF-1B	158	591	103	151	26	0	34	99	.255	56	71	22	194	9	6	.971
1979—	California (A.L.)	OF-DH-1B	•162	628	*120	186	33	3	36	*139	.296	71	51	22	203	3	5	.976
1980—	California (A.L.)	OF-DH	90	340	39	85	12	2	5	51	.250	24	32	6	119	4	4	.969
1981—	California (A.L.)	DH-1B-OF	103	377	52	90	18	1	17	66	.239	42	51	3	38	3	0	1.000
1982—	California (A.L.)	DH	157	608	80	160	24	1	24	93	.263	57	69	10	...	...	...	...
1983—	New York (A.L.)■	DH-OF-1B	144	534	82	162	33	3	21	85	.303	40	53	17	23	2	1	.962
1984—	New York (A.L.)	DH-OF	134	493	84	129	29	1	27	89	.262	38	68	1	8	0	1	.889
1985—	New York (A.L.)	DH	142	477	70	110	24	1	23	91	.231	52	90	0	...	...	...	...
1986—	Boston (A.L.)■	DH-1B-OF	160	585	93	139	23	1	31	94	.238	62	111	3	71	4	1	.987
1987—	Boston (A.L.)	DH	108	339	64	81	8	0	16	57	.239	40	47	5	...	...	...	...
—	Minnesota (A.L.)■	DH	20	49	3	14	1	0	0	6	.286	5	12	0	...	...	...	...
1988—	Oakland (A.L.)■	DH	92	264	28	58	7	0	7	34	.220	34	44	0	...	...	...	...
Major league totals (19 years)			2292	8198	1236	2135	366	28	338	1276	.260	805	1069	285	2716	110	58	.980

CHAMPIONSHIP SERIES RECORD

NOTES: Holds career record for most clubs played with—5. . . . Holds single-series record for most runs batted in—10 (1982). . . . Shares single-game records for most times reached base safely—5 (October 8, 1986); and most grand slams—1 (October 9, 1982). . . . Shares record for most runs batted in in one inning—4 (October 9, 1982, eighth inning). . . . Holds A.L. record for most consecutive games with one or more hits—12 (1982 [last three games], 1986-87). . . . Shares A.L. single-game record for most runs batted in—5 (October 5, 1982).

Year	Team (League)	Pos.	G	AB	R	H	2B	3B	HR	RBI	Avg.	BB	SO	SB	PO	A	E	Avg.
				BATTING											FIELDING			
1973—	Baltimore (A.L.)	OF-PH	4	11	3	3	0	0	0	1	.273	3	5	0	7	0	0	1.000
1974—	Baltimore (A.L.)	OF-DH	4	15	0	4	0	0	0	0	.267	0	2	0	9	0	0	1.000
1979—	California (A.L.)	DH-OF	4	16	2	3	0	0	1	2	.188	1	2	0	4	0	0	1.000
1982—	California (A.L.)	DH	5	17	2	5	1	1	1	10	.294	2	0	0	...	...	...	...
1986—	Boston (A.L.)	DH	7	26	6	9	3	0	1	2	.346	4	5	0	...	...	...	...
1987—	Minnesota (A.L.)	PH-DH	2	5	0	2	0	0	0	1	.400	0	0	0	...	...	...	...
1988—	Oakland (A.L.)	DH	2	6	0	0	0	0	0	1	.000	1	2	0	...	...	...	...
Championship series totals (7 years)			28	96	13	26	4	1	3	17	.271	11	16	0	20	0	0	1.000

WORLD SERIES RECORD

NOTES: Shares record for most at-bats in one inning—2 (October 17, 1987, fourth inning). . . . Member of World Series championship team (1987).

Year	Team (League)	Pos.	G	AB	R	H	2B	3B	HR	RBI	Avg.	BB	SO	SB	PO	A	E	Avg.
				BATTING											FIELDING			
1986—	Boston (A.L.)	DH-PH	4	11	1	2	1	0	0	1	.182	1	3	0	...	...	...	...
1987—	Minnesota (A.L.)	DH-PH	5	13	3	5	0	0	1	3	.385	1	1	0	...	...	...	...
1988—	Oakland (A.L.)	PH	1	1	0	0	0	0	0	0	.000	0	1	0	...	...	...	...
World Series totals (3 years)			10	25	4	7	1	0	1	4	.280	2	5	0	...	...	...	...

ALL-STAR GAME RECORD

Year	League	Pos.	AB	R	H	2B	3B	HR	RBI	Avg.	BB	SO	SB	PO	A	E	Avg.
			BATTING											FIELDING			
1979—	American	OF	4	2	2	1	0	0	1	.500	0	0	0	1	0	0	1.000

RECORD AS MANAGER

BACKGROUND: Special assistant to general manager, Milwaukee Brewers (September 5-December 4, 1989). . . . Coach, Brewers (December 4, 1989-91). . . . Coach, St. Louis Cardinals (1992).

HONORS: Coach, N.L. All-Star team (1994). . . . Named N.L. Manager of the Year by The Sporting News (1995). . . . Named N.L. Manager of the Year by Baseball Writers' Association of America (1995).

Year	Team (League)	W	L	Pct.	Pos.	Playoff W	Playoff L	Champ. Series W	Champ. Series L	World Series W	World Series L	All-Star Game W	All-Star Game L
		REGULAR SEASON				POSTSEASON							
1993—	Colorado (N.L.)	67	95	.414	6th (W)	—	—	—	—	—	—	—	—
1994—	Colorado (N.L.)	53	64	.453		—	—	—	—	—	—	—	—
1995—	Colorado (N.L.)	77	67	.535	2nd (W)	1	3	—	—	—	—	—	—
Major league totals (3 years)		197	226	.466		1	3	—	—	—	—	—	—

NOTES:

1994—Colorado was in third place in N.L. West at time of season-ending strike (August 12).

1995—Lost to Atlanta in N.L. divisional playoff.

BELL, BUDDY — TIGERS

PERSONAL: Born August 27, 1951, in Pittsburgh. . . . 6-3/200. . . . Batted right, threw right. . . . Full name: David Gus Bell. . . . Father of David Bell, second baseman, St. Louis Cardinals; father of Mike Bell, third baseman, Texas Rangers organization; and son of Gus Bell, major league outfielder with four teams (1950-64).

HIGH SCHOOL: Moeller (Cincinnati).
COLLEGE: Xavier, then Miami of Ohio.
TRANSACTIONS/CAREER NOTES: Selected by Cleveland Indians organization in 16th round of free-agent draft (June 5, 1969). . . . On disabled list (May 27-June 17 and August 8-September 1, 1974). . . . Traded by Indians to Texas Rangers for 3B Toby Harrah (December 8, 1978). . . . On disabled list (June 9-24, 1980). . . . Traded by Rangers to Cincinnati Reds for OF Duane Walker and a player to be named later (July 19, 1985); Rangers organization acquired P Jeff Russell to complete deal (July 23, 1985). . . . On Cincinnati disabled list (March 26-April 10 and April 14-May 11, 1988). . . . Traded by Reds to Houston Astros for a player to be named later (June 19, 1988); Reds organization acquired P Carl Grovom to complete deal (October 20, 1988). . . . On Houston disabled list (August 4-19, 1988). . . . Released by Astros (December 21, 1988). . . . Signed by Rangers (January 9, 1989). . . . On disabled list (April 8-28, 1989). . . . Announced retirement (June 24, 1989).
HONORS: Won A.L. Gold Glove at third base (1979-84). . . . Named third baseman on THE SPORTING NEWS A.L. All-Star team (1981 and 1984). . . . Named third baseman on THE SPORTING NEWS A.L. Silver Slugger team (1984).
STATISTICAL NOTES: Led Gulf Coast League second basemen with 26 double plays in 1969. . . . Led A.L. third basemen with 144 putouts and 44 double plays in 1973. . . . Led A.L. third basemen with 495 total chances in 1978, 361 in 1981, 540 in 1982 and 523 in 1983. . . . Tied for A.L. lead in double plays by third basemen with 30 in 1978. . . . Led A.L. third basemen with 364 assists in 1979 and 281 in 1981. . . . Led A.L. third basemen with .981 fielding percentage in 1980 and .976 in 1982. . . . Led A.L. with 10 sacrifice flies in 1981. . . . Career major league grand slams: 8.

			BATTING											FIELDING			
Year Team (League)	Pos.	G	AB	R	H	2B	3B	HR	RBI	Avg.	BB	SO	SB	PO	A	E	Avg.
1969—Sarasota (Gulf Coast).	2B	51	170	18	39	4	•3	3	24	.229	17	15	3	119	108	7	*.970
1970—W. Caro.	3B-2B-SS	121	442	81	117	19	3	12	75	.265	44	43	9	116	189	27	.919
1971—Wichita (A.A.)	3-2-S-O	129	470	65	136	23	1	11	59	.289	42	51	7	*139	203	16	.955
1972—Cleveland (A.L.)	OF-3B	132	466	49	119	21	1	9	36	.255	34	29	5	284	23	3	.990
1973—Cleveland (A.L.)	3B-OF	156	631	86	169	23	7	14	59	.268	49	47	7	†146	363	22	.959
1974—Cleveland (A.L.)	3B	116	423	51	111	15	1	7	46	.262	35	29	1	112	274	15	.963
1975—Cleveland (A.L.)	3B	153	553	66	150	20	4	10	59	.271	51	72	6	*146	330	25	.950
1976—Cleveland (A.L.)	3B-1B	159	604	75	170	26	2	7	60	.281	44	49	3	109	331	20	.957
1977—Cleveland (A.L.)	3B-OF	129	479	64	140	23	4	11	64	.292	45	63	1	134	253	16	.960
1978—Cleveland (A.L.)	3B	142	556	71	157	27	8	6	62	.282	39	43	1	125	*355	15	.970
1979—Texas (A.L.)■	3B-SS	•162	*670	89	200	42	3	18	101	.299	30	45	5	147	†429	17	.971
1980—Texas (A.L.)	3B-SS	129	490	76	161	24	4	17	83	.329	40	39	3	125	282	8	†.981
1981—Texas (A.L.)	3B-SS	97	360	44	106	16	1	10	64	.294	42	30	3	67	†284	14	.962
1982—Texas (A.L.)	3B-SS	148	537	62	159	27	2	13	67	.296	70	50	5	*131	397	13	†.976
1983—Texas (A.L.)	3B	156	618	75	171	35	3	14	66	.277	50	48	3	123	*383	17	.967
1984—Texas (A.L.)	3B	148	553	88	174	36	5	11	83	.315	63	54	2	129	323	•20	.958
1985—Texas (A.L.)	3B	84	313	33	74	13	3	4	32	.236	33	21	3	70	192	16	.942
—Cincinnati (N.L.)■	3B	67	247	28	54	15	2	6	36	.219	34	27	0	54	105	9	.946
1986—Cincinnati (N.L.)	3B-2B	155	568	89	158	29	3	20	75	.278	73	49	2	105	291	10	.975
1987—Cincinnati (N.L.)	3B	143	522	74	148	19	2	17	70	.284	71	39	4	93	241	7	*.979
1988—Cincinnati (N.L.)	3B-1B	21	54	3	10	0	0	0	3	.185	7	3	0	14	26	2	.952
—Houston (N.L.)■	3B-1B	74	269	24	68	10	1	7	37	.253	19	29	1	74	114	13	.935
1989—Texas (A.L.)■	3B-1B	34	82	4	15	4	0	0	3	.183	7	10	0	10	13	0	1.000
American League totals (15 years)		1945	7335	933	2076	352	48	151	885	.283	632	629	48	1858	4232	221	.965
National League totals (4 years)		460	1660	218	438	73	8	50	221	.264	204	147	7	340	777	41	.965
Major league totals (18 years)		2405	8995	1151	2514	425	56	201	1106	.279	836	776	55	2198	5009	262	.965

ALL-STAR GAME RECORD

		BATTING											FIELDING			
Year League	Pos.	AB	R	H	2B	3B	HR	RBI	Avg.	BB	SO	SB	PO	A	E	Avg.
1973—American	PH	1	0	1	0	1	0	0	1.000	0	0	0	0	0	0	...
1980—American	3B	2	0	0	0	0	0	0	.000	0	1	0	0	2	0	1.000
1981—American	3B	1	0	0	0	0	0	1	.000	0	0	0	1	2	0	1.000
1982—American	PH-3B	3	0	0	0	0	0	0	.000	0	2	0	0	1	1	.500
1984—American	3B	1	0	0	0	0	0	0	.000	0	0	0	0	1	0	1.000
All-Star Game totals (5 years)		8	0	1	0	1	0	1	.125	0	3	0	1	6	1	.875

RECORD AS MANAGER

BACKGROUND: Minor league hitting instructor, Cleveland Indians organization (1990). . . . Director of minor league instruction, Chicago White Sox organization (1991-93). . . . Coach, Indians (1994-95).

BEVINGTON, TERRY — WHITE SOX

PERSONAL: Born July 7, 1956, in Akron, O. . . . 6-2/190. . . . Batted right, threw right. . . . Full name: Terry Paul Bevington.
HIGH SCHOOL: Santa Monica (Calif.).
TRANSACTIONS/CAREER NOTES: Selected by New York Yankees organization in fourth round of free-agent draft (June 5, 1974). . . . On Fort Lauderdale disabled list (April 20-June 30, 1976). . . . Released by Yankees organization (July 5, 1977). . . . Signed by Milwaukee Brewers organization (February 7, 1978).

			BATTING											FIELDING			
Year Team (League)	Pos.	G	AB	R	H	2B	3B	HR	RBI	Avg.	BB	SO	SB	PO	A	E	Avg.
1974—Johns. City (App.)	OF-C-1B	63	222	33	44	10	0	2	30	.198	34	36	2	220	21	9	.964
1975—Oneonta (NYP)	C	60	193	24	51	11	1	2	23	.264	25	19	3	389	46	8	.982
1976—Oneonta (NYP)	DH	2	3	0	0	0	0	0	0	.000	0	1	0	0	0	0	...
1977—Fort Lauder. (FSL)	C	23	60	7	13	1	0	1	8	.217	5	7	0	61	14	1	.987
1978—Burlington (Midw.)■	C	63	179	22	43	14	0	4	23	.240	22	31	8	226	17	8	.968
1979—Holyoke (Eastern)	C	83	214	26	54	12	0	4	21	.252	31	31	8	333	42	11	.972
1980—Vancouver (PCL)	C	33	86	13	29	5	0	1	8	.337	14	7	6	110	13	4	.969
—Burlington (Midw.)	C	39	117	14	31	7	0	2	11	.265	13	9	11	199	20	9	.961

RECORD AS MANAGER

BACKGROUND: Player/coach, Burlington (June 12, 1980-remainder of season). . . . Coach, Chicago White Sox (1989-June 1, 1995).

Year	Team (League)	REGULAR SEASON W	L	Pct.	Pos.	POSTSEASON Playoff W	L	Champ. Series W	L	World Series W	L	All-Star Game W	L
1981—	Burlington (Midwest)	21	45	.318	T3rd (S)	—	—	—	—	—	—	—	—
	— (Second half)	33	36	.478	3rd (S)	—	—	—	—	—	—	—	—
1982—	Beloit (Midwest)	71	68	.511	2nd (C)	—	—	—	—	—	—	—	—
1983—	Stockton (California)	44	24	.647	1st (N)	—	—	—	—	—	—	—	—
	— (Second half)	35	35	.500	3rd (N)	1	2	—	—	—	—	—	—
1984—	El Paso (Texas)	37	30	.552	2nd (W)	—	—	—	—	—	—	—	—
	— (Second half)	35	33	.515	2nd (W)	—	—	—	—	—	—	—	—
1985—	El Paso (Texas)	39	29	.574	1st (W)	—	—	—	—	—	—	—	—
	— (Second half)	47	21	.691	1st (W)	0	4	—	—	—	—	—	—
1986—	Vancouver (Pacific Coast)	42	24	.636	1st (N)	—	—	—	—	—	—	—	—
	— (Second half)	43	29	.597	1st (N)	—	—	—	—	—	—	—	—
1987—	Denver (American Association)	79	61	.564	1st	7	3	—	—	—	—	—	—
1988—	Vancouver (Pacific Coast)	42	29	.592	1st (N)	—	—	—	—	—	—	—	—
	— (Second half)	43	28	.606	1st (N)	4	3	—	—	—	—	—	—
1995—	Chicago (A.L.)	57	56	.504	3rd (C)	—	—	—	—	—	—	—	—
Major league totals (1 year)		57	56	.504		—	—	—	—	—	—	—	—

NOTES:

1983—Lost to Redwood in playoffs.
1985—Lost to Jackson in league championship.
1986—Defeated Tacoma, three games to none, in playoffs; lost to Las Vegas, three games to two, in league championship.
1987—Defeated Oklahoma City, three games to two, in playoffs; lost to Indianapolis, four games to one, in league championship.
1988—Defeated Portland, three games to one, in playoffs; lost to Las Vegas, three games to one, in league championship.
1995—Replaced Chicago manager Gene Lamont with club in fourth place and record of 11-20 (June 2). On suspended list (August 1-5).

BOCHY, BRUCE — PADRES

PERSONAL: Born April 16, 1955, in Landes de Boussac, France. . . . 6-4/225. . . . Batted right, threw right. . . . Full name: Bruce Douglas Bochy. . . . Brother of Joe Bochy, catcher, Minnesota Twins organization (1969-72). . . . Name pronounced BO-chee.

HIGH SCHOOL: Melbourne (Fla.).

COLLEGE: Florida State.

TRANSACTIONS/CAREER NOTES: Selected by Chicago White Sox organization in eighth round of free-agent draft (January 9, 1975); did not sign. . . . Selected by Houston Astros organization in secondary phase of free-agent draft (June 4, 1975). . . . Traded by Astros to New York Mets organization for two players to be named later (February 11, 1981); Astros acquired IF Randy Rodgers and C Stan Hough to complete deal (April 3, 1981). . . . Released by Mets (January 21, 1983). . . . Signed by Las Vegas, San Diego Padres organization (February 23, 1983). . . . On disabled list (April 13-May 6, 1987). . . . Granted free agency (November 9, 1987). . . . Signed as player/coach by Las Vegas (1988).

STATISTICAL NOTES: Tied for Florida State League lead with 12 passed balls in 1977.

Year	Team (League)	Pos.	G	BATTING AB	R	H	2B	3B	HR	RBI	Avg.	BB	SO	SB	FIELDING PO	A	E	Avg.
1975—	Covington (Appal.)	C	37	145	31	49	9	0	4	34	.338	11	18	0	231	36	4	.985
1976—	Columbus (South.)	C	69	230	9	53	6	0	0	16	.230	14	30	0	266	45	6	.981
	— Dubuque (Midw.)	C-1B	30	103	9	25	4	0	1	8	.243	12	11	1	165	25	5	.974
1977—	Cocoa (Florida St.)	C	128	430	40	109	18	2	3	35	.253	35	50	0	*492	67	12	.979
1978—	Columbus (South.)	C	79	261	25	70	10	2	7	34	.268	13	30	0	419	49	7	.985
	— Houston (N.L.)	C	54	154	8	41	8	0	3	15	.266	11	35	0	268	35	8	.974
1979—	Houston (N.L.)	C	56	129	11	28	4	0	1	6	.217	17	25	0	198	29	7	.970
1980—	Houston (N.L.)	C-1B	22	22	0	4	1	0	0	0	.182	0	0	0	19	1	0	1.000
1981—	Tidewater (Int'l)■	C	85	269	23	61	11	2	8	38	.227	22	47	0	253	35	3	.990
1982—	Tidewater (Int'l)	C	81	251	32	57	11	0	15	52	.227	19	47	2	427	57	5	.990
	— New York (N.L.)	C-1B	17	49	4	15	4	0	2	8	.306	4	6	0	92	8	4	.962
1983—	Las Vegas (PCL)■	C	42	145	28	44	8	1	11	33	.303	15	25	3	157	21	3	.983
	— San Diego (N.L.)	C	23	42	2	9	1	1	0	3	.214	0	9	0	51	5	0	1.000
1984—	Las Vegas (PCL)	C	34	121	18	32	7	0	7	22	.264	17	13	0	189	17	2	.990
	— San Diego (N.L.)	C	37	92	10	21	5	1	4	15	.228	3	21	0	147	12	2	.988
1985—	San Diego (N.L.)	C	48	112	16	30	2	0	6	13	.268	6	30	0	148	11	2	.988
1986—	San Diego (N.L.)	C	63	127	16	32	9	0	8	22	.252	14	23	1	202	22	2	.991
1987—	San Diego (N.L.)	C	38	75	8	12	3	0	2	11	.160	11	21	0	95	7	4	.962
1988—	Las Vegas (PCL)	C	53	147	17	34	5	0	5	13	.231	17	28	0	207	19	3	.987
Major league totals (9 years)			358	802	75	192	37	2	26	93	.239	66	170	1	1220	130	29	.979

CHAMPIONSHIP SERIES RECORD

Year	Team (League)	Pos.	G	BATTING AB	R	H	2B	3B	HR	RBI	Avg.	BB	SO	SB	FIELDING PO	A	E	Avg.
1980—	Houston (N.L.)	C	1	1	0	0	0	0	0	0	.000	0	0	0	5	1	0	1.000

WORLD SERIES RECORD

Year	Team (League)	Pos.	G	BATTING AB	R	H	2B	3B	HR	RBI	Avg.	BB	SO	SB	FIELDING PO	A	E	Avg.
1984—	San Diego (N.L.)	PH	1	1	0	1	0	0	0	0	1.000	0	0	0	...	...	...	...

RECORD AS MANAGER

BACKGROUND: Player/coach, Las Vegas, San Diego Padres organization (1988). . . . Coach, Padres (1993-94).

Year	Team (League)	W	L	Pct.	Pos.	Playoff W	Playoff L	Champ. Series W	Champ. Series L	World Series W	World Series L	All-Star Game W	All-Star Game L
		REGULAR SEASON				POSTSEASON							
1989—	Spokane (Northwest)	41	34	.547	1st (N)	2	1	—	—	—	—	—	—
1990—	Riverside (California)	35	36	.493	4th (S)	—	—	—	—	—	—	—	—
	—(Second half)	29	42	.408	5th (S)	—	—	—	—	—	—	—	—
1991—	High Desert (California)	31	37	.456	3rd (S)	—	—	—	—	—	—	—	—
	—(Second half)	42	26	.618	1st (S)	6	2	—	—	—	—	—	—
1992—	Wichita (Texas)	39	29	.574	1st (W)	6	1	—	—	—	—	—	—
	—(Second half)	31	37	.456	4th (W)	—	—	—	—	—	—	—	—
1995—	San Diego (N.L.)	70	74	.486	3rd (W)	—	—	—	—	—	—	—	—
Major league totals (1 year)		70	74	.486		—	—	—	—	—	—	—	—

NOTES:

1989—Defeated Southern Oregon in league championship.

1991—Defeated Bakersfield, three games to none, in semifinals; defeated Stockton, three games to two, in league championship.

1992—Defeated El Paso, two games to one, in semifinals; defeated Shreveport, four games to none, in league championship.

BOONE, BOB — ROYALS

PERSONAL: Born November 19, 1947, in San Diego. . . . 6-2/207. . . . Batted right, threw right. . . . Full name: Robert Raymond Boone. . . . Son of Ray Boone, major league infielder with six teams (1948-60); brother of Rodney Boone, minor league catcher/outfielder (1972-75); father of Bret Boone, second baseman, Cincinnati Reds; and father of Aaron Boone, third baseman, Cincinnati Reds organization.

HIGH SCHOOL: Crawford (San Diego).

COLLEGE: Stanford (bachelor of arts degree in psychology, 1969).

TRANSACTIONS/CAREER NOTES: Selected by Philadelphia Phillies organization in 20th round of free-agent draft (June 5, 1969). . . . On military list (May 26, 1970-remainder of season). . . . On disabled list (April 10-June 4, 1971). . . . Contrcat sold by Phillies to California Angels (December 6, 1981). . . . Granted free agency (November 12, 1986). . . . Re-signed by Angels (May 1, 1987). . . . Granted free agency (October 24, 1988). . . . Signed by Kansas City Royals (November 30, 1988). . . . On disabled list (May 17-July 20, 1990). . . . Granted free agency (November 5, 1990). . . . Signed by Tacoma, Oakland Athletics organization (May 31, 1993). . . . Released by Tacoma (June 1, 1993).

RECORDS: Holds major league career record for most years by catcher (100 or more games)—15.

HONORS: Named catcher on The Sporting News N.L. All-Star team (1976). . . . Won N.L. Gold Glove at catcher (1978-79). . . . Won A.L. Gold Glove at catcher (1982,86-89).

STATISTICAL NOTES: Tied for Carolina League lead in double plays by third baseman with 18 in 1969. . . . Led Northwestern League catchers with 18 passed balls and 13 double plays in 1972. . . . Led N.L. catchers with 924 total chances in 1974. . . . Led N.L. catchers with .991 fielding percentage in 1978. . . . Led A.L. catchers with 745 total chances in 1982 and 823 in 1989. . . . Led A.L. catchers with 12 double plays in 1983, 15 in 1985 and 16 in 1986. . . . Career major league grand slams: 2.

Year	Team (League)	Pos.	G	AB	R	H	2B	3B	HR	RBI	Avg.	BB	SO	SB	PO	A	E	Avg.
			BATTING												FIELDING			
1969—	Ral./Durham (Car.)	3B	80	300	45	90	13	1	5	46	.300	19	24	0	71	160	20	.920
1970—	Reading (Eastern)	3B	20	80	12	23	2	0	2	10	.288	7	9	0	28	38	7	.904
1971—	Reading (Eastern)	3B-C-SS	92	328	41	87	14	3	4	37	.265	28	28	1	206	138	17	.953
1972—	Eugene (N'west)	C	138	513	77	158	32	4	17	67	.308	45	35	2	*699	*77	*24	.970
	—Philadelphia (N.L.)	C	16	51	4	14	1	0	1	4	.275	5	7	1	66	7	5	.936
1973—	Philadelphia (N.L.)	C	145	521	42	136	20	2	10	61	.261	41	36	3	868	*89	10	.990
1974—	Philadelphia (N.L.)	C	146	488	41	118	24	3	3	52	.242	35	29	3	*825	77	*22	.976
1975—	Philadelphia (N.L.)	C-3B	97	289	28	71	14	2	2	20	.246	32	14	1	459	48	5	.990
1976—	Philadelphia (N.L.)	C-1B	121	361	40	98	18	2	4	54	.271	45	44	2	587	39	6	.991
1977—	Philadelphia (N.L.)	C-3B	132	440	55	125	26	4	11	66	.284	42	54	5	654	83	8	.989
1978—	Philadelphia (N.L.)	C-1B-OF	132	435	48	123	18	4	12	62	.283	46	37	2	650	55	8	†.989
1979—	Philadelphia (N.L.)	C-3B	119	398	38	114	21	3	9	58	.286	49	33	1	527	66	8	.987
1980—	Philadelphia (N.L.)	C	141	480	34	110	23	1	9	55	.229	48	41	3	741	88	*18	.979
1981—	Philadelphia (N.L.)	C	76	227	19	48	7	0	4	24	.211	22	16	2	365	32	6	.985
1982—	California (A.L.)■	C	143	472	42	121	17	0	7	58	.256	39	34	0	*650	*87	8	.989
1983—	California (A.L.)	C	142	468	46	120	18	0	9	52	.256	24	42	4	606	*83	*14	.980
1984—	California (A.L.)	C	139	450	33	91	16	1	3	32	.202	25	45	3	660	*71	12	.984
1985—	California (A.L.)	C	150	460	37	114	17	0	5	55	.248	37	35	1	670	71	10	.987
1986—	California (A.L.)	C	144	442	48	98	12	2	7	49	.222	43	30	1	812	*84	11	.988
1987—	Palm Springs (Cal.)	C	3	9	0	1	1	0	0	0	.111	1	0	0	17	4	1	.955
	—California (A.L.)	C-DH	128	389	42	94	18	0	3	33	.242	35	36	0	684	56	*13	.983
1988—	California (A.L.)	C	122	352	38	104	17	0	5	39	.295	29	26	2	506	*66	8	.986
1989—	Kansas City (A.L.)■	C	131	405	33	111	13	2	1	43	.274	49	37	3	*752	64	7	.991
1990—	Kansas City (A.L.)	C	40	117	11	28	3	0	0	9	.239	17	12	1	243	19	4	.985
American League totals (9 years)			1139	3555	330	881	131	5	40	370	.248	298	297	15	5583	601	87	.986
National League totals (10 years)			1125	3690	349	957	172	21	65	456	.259	365	311	23	5742	584	96	.985
Major league totals (19 years)			2264	7245	679	1838	303	26	105	826	.254	663	608	38	11325	1185	183	.986

DIVISION SERIES RECORD

Year	Team (League)	Pos.	G	AB	R	H	2B	3B	HR	RBI	Avg.	BB	SO	SB	PO	A	E	Avg.
			BATTING												FIELDING			
1981—	Philadelphia (N.L.)	C	3	5	0	0	0	0	0	0	.000	0	0	0	10	2	0	1.000

CHAMPIONSHIP SERIES RECORD

NOTES: Holds career record for most sacrifice hits—5. . . . Shares single-series records for most consecutive hits—5; most singles—9 (1986); and most sacrifice hits—2 (1982). . . . Shares A.L. career record for most consecutive hits—5.

Year	Team (League)	Pos.	G	AB	R	H	2B	3B	HR	RBI	Avg.	BB	SO	SB	PO	A	E	Avg.
			BATTING												FIELDING			
1976—	Philadelphia (N.L.)	C	3	7	0	2	0	0	0	1	.286	1	0	0	8	2	0	1.000
1977—	Philadelphia (N.L.)	C	4	10	1	4	0	0	0	0	.400	0	0	0	18	2	0	1.000
1978—	Philadelphia (N.L.)	C	3	11	0	2	0	0	0	0	.182	0	1	0	16	2	1	.947

Year	Team (League)	Pos.	G	AB	R	H	2B	3B	HR	RBI	Avg.	BB	SO	SB	PO	A	E	Avg.
			BATTING												FIELDING			
1980—	Philadelphia (N.L.)	C	5	18	1	4	0	0	0	2	.222	1	2	0	22	3	0	1.000
1982—	California (A.L.)	C	5	16	3	4	0	0	1	4	.250	0	2	0	30	3	0	1.000
1986—	California (A.L.)	C	7	22	4	10	0	0	1	2	.455	1	3	0	33	3	0	1.000
Championship series totals (6 years)			27	84	9	26	0	0	2	9	.310	3	8	0	127	15	1	.993

WORLD SERIES RECORD

NOTES: Member of World Series championship team (1980).

Year	Team (League)	Pos.	G	AB	R	H	2B	3B	HR	RBI	Avg.	BB	SO	SB	PO	A	E	Avg.
			BATTING												FIELDING			
1980—	Philadelphia (N.L.)	C	6	17	3	7	2	0	0	4	.412	4	0	0	49	3	0	1.000

ALL-STAR GAME RECORD

Year	League	Pos.	AB	R	H	2B	3B	HR	RBI	Avg.	BB	SO	SB	PO	A	E	Avg.
			BATTING											FIELDING			
1976—	National	C	2	0	0	0	0	0	0	.000	0	0	0	5	0	0	1.000
1978—	National	C	1	1	1	0	0	0	2	1.000	0	0	0	3	1	0	1.000
1979—	National	C	2	1	1	0	0	0	0	.500	0	0	0	0	0	0	...
1983—	American	C	0	0	0	0	0	0	0	...	0	0	0	1	0	0	1.000
All-Star Game totals (4 years)			5	2	2	0	0	0	2	.400	0	0	0	9	1	0	1.000

RECORD AS MANAGER

BACKGROUND: Coach, Cincinnati Reds (1994).

Year	Team (League)	W	L	Pct.	Pos.	Playoff W	Playoff L	Champ. Series W	Champ. Series L	World Series W	World Series L	All-Star Game W	All-Star Game L
		REGULAR SEASON				POSTSEASON							
1992—	Tacoma (Pacific Coast)	26	45	.366	5th (N)	—	—	—	—	—	—	—	—
	—(Second half)	30	42	.417	5th (N)	—	—	—	—	—	—	—	—
1993—	Tacoma (Pacific Coast)	30	42	.417	5th (N)	—	—	—	—	—	—	—	—
	—(Second half)	37	35	.514	3rd (N)	—	—	—	—	—	—	—	—
1995—	Kansas City (A.L.)	70	74	.486	2nd (C)	—	—	—	—	—	—	—	—
Major league totals (1 year)		70	74	.486		—	—	—	—	—	—	—	—

COLLINS, TERRY — ASTROS

PERSONAL: Born May 27, 1949, in Midland, Mich. . . . 5-8/160. . . . Batted left, threw right. . . . Full name: Terry Lee Collins.
HIGH SCHOOL: Midland (Mich.).
COLLEGE: Eastern Michigan (bachelor of science degree).
TRANSACTIONS/CAREER NOTES: Selected by Pittsburgh Pirates organization in 19th round of free-agent draft (June 8, 1971). . . . Released by Pirates organization (January 7, 1974). . . . Signed by Los Angeles Dodgers organization (January 14, 1974). . . . On disabled list (July 2-August 6, 1976). . . . Served as player/coach for Waterbury (1975) and Albuquerque (1977). . . . Released by Dodgers organization (February 28, 1978). . . . Signed by Dodgers organization as coach (March 13, 1978). . . . Released by Dodgers organization (May 14, 1978). . . . Signed by Dodgers organization as player (May 14, 1978). . . . On disabled list (June 26-July 6, 1978). . . . Signed as player/coach for Albuquerque for 1979. . . . On temporarily inactive list (entire 1979 season). . . . Released by Dodgers organization (December 7, 1979). . . . Signed by Dodgers organization as coach (January 30, 1980). . . . Signed by Dodgers organization as player/coach (May 18, 1980). . . . On disabled list (May 29-July 1 and July 12-August 17, 1980). . . . Released by Dodgers organization (September 18, 1980). . . . Signed by Dodgers organization as player/manager (August 17, 1984). . . . Released as player by Dodgers organization (September 28, 1984).
STATISTICAL NOTES: Led New York-Pennsylvania League shortstops with 310 total chances and 37 double plays in 1971.

Year	Team (League)	Pos.	G	AB	R	H	2B	3B	HR	RBI	Avg.	BB	SO	SB	PO	A	E	Avg.
			BATTING												FIELDING			
1971—	Niag. Falls (NYP)	SS	70	265	51	81	12	3	1	26	.306	36	35	12	*112	*179	19	*.939
1972—	Salem (Carolina)	2B	126	459	77	116	17	7	1	41	.253	70	75	8	*254	333	*25	.959
1973—	Sherbrooke (East.)	2-O-3-P-S	114	324	52	76	9	0	0	20	.235	59	54	7	177	206	12	.970
1974—	Waterbury (East.)■	2B-SS	86	230	28	46	3	2	1	23	.200	46	42	2	144	243	11	.972
1975—	Waterbury (East.)	SS	4	9	2	1	0	0	0	1	.111	3	2	0	3	9	2	.857
	—Albuquerque (PCL)	2B-SS-3B	64	153	24	48	5	4	0	10	.314	18	19	2	87	53	11	.927
1976—	Albuquerque (PCL)	3B-OF-SS	67	174	23	42	4	5	2	24	.241	19	21	6	46	64	3	.973
1977—	Albuquerque (PCL)	2-3-S-P	54	158	27	39	6	3	0	15	.247	32	21	2	64	113	9	.952
1978—	Albuquerque (PCL)	2-3-S-P-O-1	72	217	29	60	9	4	1	22	.276	21	20	4	115	162	12	.958
1979—									Did not play.									
1980—	Albuquerque (PCL)	DH	11	14	1	2	0	0	0	1	.143	3	4	1	...	...	...	...
1981—									Did not play.									
1982—									Did not play.									
1983—									Did not play.									
1984—	Albuquerque (PCL)	SS-2B	3	6	1	1	0	0	0	0	.167	0	0	0	5	3	0	1.000

RECORD AS PITCHER

Year	Team (League)	W	L	Pct.	ERA	G	GS	CG	ShO	Sv.	IP	H	R	ER	BB	SO
1973—	Sherbrooke (East.)	0	0	...	2.25	3	0	0	0	2	4	3	1	1	3	0
1977—	Albuquerque (PCL)	0	0	...	0.00	1	0	0	0	0	2	2	0	0	0	1
1978—	Albuquerque (PCL)	0	0	...	0.00	2	0	0	0	1	3	1	0	0	1	1

RECORD AS MANAGER

BACKGROUND: Player/coach, Waterbury, Dodgers organization (1975). . . . Player/coach, Albuquerque, Dodgers organization (1977-80). . . . Coach, Pittsburgh Pirates (November 26, 1991-November 17, 1993).

HONORS: Named Minor League Manager of the Year by The Sporting News (1987). . . . Named Pacific Coast League Manager of the Year (1988). . . . Coach, N.L. All-Star team (1995).

	REGULAR SEASON				POSTSEASON							
					Playoff		Champ. Series		World Series		All-Star Game	
Year Team (League)	W	L	Pct.	Pos.	W	L	W	L	W	L	W	L
1981—Lodi (California)	30	40	.429	7th	—	—	—	—	—	—	—	—
—(Second half)	43	27	.614	T2nd	5	2	—	—	—	—	—	—
1982—Vero Beach (Florida State)	38	31	.551	2nd (S)	—	—	—	—	—	—	—	—
—(Second half)	42	22	.656	1st (S)	1	2	—	—	—	—	—	—
1983—San Antonio (Texas)	33	34	.493	3rd (W)	—	—	—	—	—	—	—	—
—(Second half)	3	4	.429		—	—	—	—	—	—	—	—
—Albuquerque, second half (Pacific Coast)	42	26	.618	1st (S)	3	5	—	—	—	—	—	—
1984—Albuquerque (Pacific Coast)	36	36	.500	5th (S)	—	—	—	—	—	—	—	—
—(Second half)	26	45	.366	5th (S)	—	—	—	—	—	—	—	—
1985—Albuquerque (Pacific Coast)	36	35	.507	4th (S)	—	—	—	—	—	—	—	—
—(Second half)	31	41	.431	4th (S)	—	—	—	—	—	—	—	—
1986—Albuquerque (Pacific Coast)	28	43	.394	5th (S)	—	—	—	—	—	—	—	—
—(Second half)	26	45	.366	5th (S)	—	—	—	—	—	—	—	—
1987—Albuquerque (Pacific Coast)	43	27	.614	1st (S)	—	—	—	—	—	—	—	—
—(Second half)	34	38	.472	4th (S)	6	1	—	—	—	—	—	—
1988—Albuquerque (Pacific Coast)	38	33	.535	2nd (S)	—	—	—	—	—	—	—	—
—(Second half)	48	23	.676	1st (S)	0	3	—	—	—	—	—	—
1989—Buffalo (American Association)	80	62	.563	2nd (E)	—	—	—	—	—	—	—	—
1990—Buffalo (American Association)	85	62	.578	2nd (E)	—	—	—	—	—	—	—	—
1991—Buffalo (American Association)	81	62	.566	1st (E)	2	3	—	—	—	—	—	—
1994—Houston (N.L.)	66	49	.574		—	—	—	—	—	—	—	—
1995—Houston (N.L.)	76	68	.528	2nd (C)	—	—	—	—	—	—	—	—
Major league totals (2 years)	142	117	.548		—	—	—	—	—	—	—	—

NOTES:

1981—Defeated Reno, two games to one, in semifinals; defeated Visalia, three games to two, in league championship.

1982—Lost to Fort Lauderdale in playoffs.

1983—Replaced Albuquerque manager Del Crandall (June 29). Defeated Las Vegas, three games to two, in playoffs; lost to Portland, three games to none, in league championship.

1987—Defeated Las Vegas, three games to none, in playoffs; defeated Calgary, three games to one, in league championship.

1988—Lost to Las Vegas in playoffs.

1991—Lost to Denver in league championship.

1994—Houston was in second place in N.L. Central at time of season-ending strike (August 12).

COX, BOBBY — BRAVES

PERSONAL: Born May 21, 1941, in Tulsa, Okla. . . . 6-0/185. . . . Batted right, threw right. . . . Full name: Robert Joe Cox.

HIGH SCHOOL: Selma (Calif.).

TRANSACTIONS/CAREER NOTES: Signed by Los Angeles Dodgers organization (1959). . . . Selected by Chicago Cubs organization from Dodgers organization in Rule 5 minor league draft (November 30, 1964). . . . Acquired by Atlanta Braves organization (1966). . . . On Austin disabled list (May 8-18 and May 30-June 9, 1966). . . . On disabled list (May 1-June 12, 1967). . . . Traded by Braves to New York Yankees for C Bob Tillman and P Dale Roberts (December 7, 1967); Roberts later was transferred to Richmond. . . . On disabled list (May 28-June 18, 1970). . . . Released by Yankees organization (September 22, 1970). . . . Signed by Fort Lauderdale, Yankees organization (July 17, 1971). . . . Released as player by Fort Lauderdale (August 28, 1971).

STATISTICAL NOTES: Led Alabama-Florida League shortstops with 71 double plays in 1961. . . . Led Pacific Coast League third basemen with .954 fielding percentage in 1965.

		BATTING												FIELDING			
Year Team (League)	Pos.	G	AB	R	H	2B	3B	HR	RBI	Avg.	BB	SO	SB	PO	A	E	Avg.
1960—Reno (California)	2B	125	440	99	112	20	5	13	75	.255	95	129	28	282	*385	*39	.945
1961—Salem (Northwest)	2B	14	44	3	9	2	0	0	2	.205	0	14	0	25	25	2	.962
—Pan. City (Ala.-Fla.)	2B	92	335	66	102	27	4	17	73	.304	48	72	17	220	247	8	*.983
1962—Salem (Northwest)	3B-2B	*141	514	83	143	26	7	16	82	.278	63	119	7	174	296	28	.944
1963—Albuquerque (Tex.)	3B	17	53	5	15	2	0	2	5	.283	3	12	1	8	27	1	.972
—Great Falls (Pio.)	3B	109	407	103	137	*31	4	19	85	.337	73	84	7	82	211	21	*.933
1964—Albuquerque (Tex.)	2B	138	523	98	152	29	13	16	91	.291	52	84	8	*322	*415	*28	.963
1965—Salt Lake (PCL)■	3B-2B	136	473	58	125	32	1	12	55	.264	35	96	1	133	337	22	†.955
1966—Tacoma (PCL)	3B-2B	10	34	2	4	1	0	0	4	.118	6	9	0	23	15	0	1.000
—Austin (Texas)■	2B-3B	92	339	35	77	11	1	7	30	.227	25	55	7	140	216	12	.967
1967—Richmond (Int'l)	3B-1B	99	350	52	104	17	4	14	51	.297	34	73	3	84	136	8	.965
1968—New York (A.L.)■	3B	135	437	33	100	15	1	7	41	.229	41	85	3	98	279	17	.957
1969—New York (A.L.)	3B-2B	85	191	17	41	7	1	2	17	.215	34	41	0	50	147	11	.947
1970—Syracuse (Int'l)	3B-SS-2B	90	251	34	55	15	0	9	30	.219	49	40	0	86	163	13	.950
1971—Fort Lauder. (FSL)	2B-P	4	9	1	1	0	0	0	0	.111	1	0	0	4	5	0	1.000
Major league totals (2 years)		220	628	50	141	22	2	9	58	.225	75	126	3	148	426	28	.953

RECORD AS PITCHER

Year Team (League)	W	L	Pct.	ERA	G	GS	CG	ShO	Sv.	IP	H	R	ER	BB	SO
1971—Fort Lauder. (FSL)	0	1	.000	5.40	3	0	0	0	0	10	15	9	6	5	4

RECORD AS MANAGER

BACKGROUND: Minor league instructor, New York Yankees (October 28, 1970-March 24, 1971). . . . Player/manager, Fort Lauderdale, Yankees organization (1971). . . . Coach, Yankees (1977).

HONORS: Coach, A.L. All-Star team (1985). . . . Named Major League Manager of the Year by The Sporting News (1985). . . . Named A.L. Manager of the Year by the Baseball Writers' Association of America (1985). . . . Named N.L. Manager of the Year by The Sporting News (1991 and 1993). . . . Named N.L. Manager of the Year by the Baseball Writers' Association of America (1991).

Year	Team (League)	REGULAR SEASON W	L	Pct.	Pos.	POSTSEASON Playoff W	L	Champ. Series W	L	World Series W	L	All-Star Game W	L
1971	—Fort Lauderdale (Florida State)	71	70	.504	4th (E)	—	—	—	—	—	—	—	—
1972	—West Haven (Eastern)	84	56	.600	1st (A)	3	0	—	—	—	—	—	—
1973	—Syracuse (International)	76	70	.521	3rd (A)	—	—	—	—	—	—	—	—
1974	—Syracuse (International)	74	70	.514	2nd (N)	—	—	—	—	—	—	—	—
1975	—Syracuse (International)	72	64	.529	3rd	—	—	—	—	—	—	—	—
1976	—Syracuse (International)	82	57	.590	2nd	6	1	—	—	—	—	—	—
1978	—Atlanta (N.L.)	69	93	.426	6th (W)	—	—	—	—	—	—	—	—
1979	—Atlanta (N.L.)	66	94	.413	6th (W)	—	—	—	—	—	—	—	—
1980	—Atlanta (N.L.)	81	80	.503	4th (W)	—	—	—	—	—	—	—	—
1981	—Atlanta (N.L.)	25	29	.463	4th (W)	—	—	—	—	—	—	—	—
	—(Second half)	25	27	.481	5th (W)	—	—	—	—	—	—	—	—
1982	—Toronto (A.L.)	78	84	.481	T6th (E)	—	—	—	—	—	—	—	—
1983	—Toronto (A.L.)	89	73	.549	4th (E)	—	—	—	—	—	—	—	—
1984	—Toronto (A.L.)	89	73	.549	2nd (E)	—	—	—	—	—	—	—	—
1985	—Toronto (A.L.)	99	62	.615	1st (E)	—	—	3	4	—	—	—	—
1990	—Atlanta (N.L.)	40	57	.412	6th (W)	—	—	—	—	—	—	—	—
1991	—Atlanta (N.L.)	94	68	.580	1st (W)	—	—	4	3	3	4	—	—
1992	—Atlanta (N.L.)	98	64	.605	1st (W)	—	—	4	3	2	4	0	1
1993	—Atlanta (N.L.)	104	58	.642	1st (W)	—	—	2	4	—	—	0	1
1994	—Atlanta (N.L.)	68	46	.596		—	—	—	—	—	—	—	—
1995	—Atlanta (N.L.)	90	54	.625	1st (E)	3	1	4	0	4	2	—	—
American League totals (4 years)		355	292	.549		—	—	3	4	—	—	—	—
National League totals (10 years)		760	670	.531		3	1	14	10	9	10	0	2
Major league totals (14 years)		1115	962	.537		3	1	17	14	9	10	0	2

NOTES:

1972—Defeated Three Rivers in playoff.

1976—Defeated Memphis, three games to none, in playoffs; defeated Richmond, three games to one, in league championship.

1985—Lost to Kansas City in A.L. Championship Series.

1990—Replaced Atlanta manager Russ Nixon with club in sixth place and record of 25-40 (June 22).

1991—Defeated Pittsburgh in N.L. Championship Series; lost to Minnesota in World Series.

1992—Defeated Pittsburgh in N.L. Championship Series; lost to Toronto in World Series.

1993—Lost to Philadelphia in N.L. Championship Series.

1994—Atlanta was in second place in N.L. East at time of season-ending strike (August 12).

1995—Defeated Colorado in N.L. divisional playoff; defeated Cincinnati in N.L. Championship Series; defeated Cleveland in World Series.

FREGOSI, JIM — PHILLIES

PERSONAL: Born April 4, 1942, in San Francisco. . . . 6-2/197. . . . Batted right, threw right. . . . Full name: James Louis Fregosi. . . . Father of Jim Fregosi Jr., minor league shortstop (1985-87).

HIGH SCHOOL: Serra (San Mateo, Calif.).

COLLEGE: Menlo College (Calif.).

TRANSACTIONS/CAREER NOTES: Signed by Boston Red Sox organization (September 6, 1959). . . . Selected by Los Angeles Angels in A.L. expansion draft (December 14, 1960). . . . On disabled list (July 12-August 5, 1961). . . . Traded by Angels to New York Mets for P Nolan Ryan, P Don Rose, OF Leroy Stanton and C Francisco Estrada (December 10, 1971). . . . Traded by Mets to Texas Rangers for a player to be named later (July 11, 1973); deal settled in cash. . . . On disabled list (April 22-May 12, 1977). . . . Traded by Rangers to Pittsburgh Pirates for 1B/C Ed Kirkpatrick (June 15, 1977). . . . Released by Pirates in order to accept managerial position with California Angels (June 1, 1978).

RECORDS: Shares major league single-game record for most double plays started by shortstop (nine-inning game)—5 (May 1, 1966, first game).

HONORS: Named shortstop on The Sporting News A.L. All-Star team (1964 and 1967). . . . Won A.L. Gold Glove at shortstop (1967).

STATISTICAL NOTES: Tied for American Association lead in double plays by shortstop with 100 in 1961. . . . Led American League with 15 sacrifice hits in 1965. . . . Led American League shortstops with 125 double plays in 1966 and tied for lead with 92 in 1968. . . . Led American League shortstops with 531 assists and tied for lead with 35 errors in 1966. . . . Career major league grand slams: 1.

Year	Team (League)	Pos.	G	BATTING AB	R	H	2B	3B	HR	RBI	Avg.	BB	SO	SB	FIELDING PO	A	E	Avg.
1960	—Alpine (Soph.)	IF-OF	112	404	96	108	17	7	6	58	.267	74	99	4	198	261	39	.922
1961	—Dall./Fort W. (A.A.)	SS	150	516	54	131	18	4	6	50	.254	50	70	6	247	*495	*53	.933
	—Los Angeles (A.L.)	SS	11	27	7	6	0	0	0	3	.222	1	4	0	12	22	2	.944
1962	—Dall./Fort W. (A.A.)	SS-OF	64	219	25	62	9	3	1	14	.283	32	37	1	94	164	22	.921
	—Los Angeles (A.L.)	SS	58	175	15	51	3	4	3	23	.291	18	27	2	96	150	15	.943
1963	—Los Angeles (A.L.)	SS	154	592	83	170	29	12	9	50	.287	36	104	2	271	446	27	.964
1964	—Los Angeles (A.L.)	SS	147	505	86	140	22	9	18	72	.277	72	87	8	225	421	23	.966
1965	—California (A.L.)	SS	161	602	66	167	19	7	15	64	.277	54	107	13	*312	481	26	.968
1966	—California (A.L.)	SS-1B	162	611	78	154	32	7	13	67	.252	67	89	17	299	†531	†35	.960
1967	—California (A.L.)	SS	151	590	75	171	23	6	9	56	.290	49	77	9	258	435	25	.965
1968	—California (A.L.)	SS	159	614	77	150	21	*13	9	49	.244	60	101	9	273	454	29	.962
1969	—California (A.L.)	SS	161	580	78	151	22	6	12	47	.260	93	86	9	255	465	21	.972
1970	—California (A.L.)	SS-1B	158	601	95	167	33	5	22	82	.278	69	92	0	313	475	20	.975
1971	—California (A.L.)	SS-1B-OF	107	347	31	81	15	1	5	33	.233	39	61	2	241	251	22	.957
1972	—New York (N.L.)■	3B-SS-1B	101	340	31	79	15	4	5	32	.232	38	71	0	91	162	15	.944
1973	—New York (N.L.)	S-3-1-O	45	124	7	29	4	1	0	11	.234	20	25	1	47	70	9	.929
	—Texas (A.L.)■	3B-1B-SS	45	157	25	42	6	2	6	16	.268	12	31	0	98	53	5	.968
1974	—Texas (A.L.)	1B-3B	78	230	31	60	5	0	12	34	.261	22	41	0	331	73	5	.988
1975	—Texas (A.L.)	1B-DH-3B	77	191	25	50	5	0	7	33	.262	20	39	0	356	35	6	.985
1976	—Texas (A.L.)	1B-DH-3B	58	133	17	31	7	0	2	12	.233	23	33	2	183	18	2	.990
1977	—Texas (A.L.)	1B-DH	13	28	4	7	1	0	1	5	.250	3	4	0	31	4	0	1.000
	—Pittsburgh (N.L.)■	1B-3B	36	56	10	16	1	1	3	16	.286	13	10	2	99	5	2	.981
1978	—Pittsburgh (N.L.)	3B-1B-2B	20	20	3	4	1	0	0	1	.200	6	8	0	14	4	2	.900
American League totals (16 years)			1700	5983	793	1598	243	72	143	646	.267	638	983	73	3554	4314	263	.968
National League totals (4 years)			202	540	51	128	21	6	8	60	.237	77	114	3	251	241	28	.946
Major league totals (18 years)			1902	6523	844	1726	264	78	151	706	.265	715	1097	76	3805	4555	291	.966

ALL-STAR GAME RECORD

Year League	Pos.	AB	R	H	2B	3B	HR	RBI	Avg.	BB	SO	SB	PO	A	E	Avg.
		BATTING											FIELDING			
1964— American	SS	4	1	1	0	0	0	1	.250	0	1	0	4	1	0	1.000
1966— American	SS	2	0	0	0	0	0	0	.000	0	1	0	0	1	0	1.000
1967— American	SS	4	0	1	0	0	0	0	.250	0	2	0	2	3	0	1.000
1968— American	SS	3	0	1	1	0	0	0	.333	0	1	0	1	6	0	1.000
1969— American	SS	1	0	0	0	0	0	0	.000	0	0	0	0	0	0	...
1970— American	PH	1	0	0	0	0	0	0	.000	0	0	0	...	...	...	...
All-Star Game totals (6 years)		15	1	3	1	0	0	1	.200	0	5	0	7	11	0	1.000

RECORD AS MANAGER

BACKGROUND: Special assignment scout and coach, Philadelphia Phillies (1989-90).... Minor league pitching instructor and special assignment scout, Phillies (beginning of 1991 season-April 23, 1991).

HONORS: Named American Association Manager of the Year (1983).... Named American Association co-Manager of the Year (1985).... Named Minor League Manager of the Year by The Sporting News (1985).... Coach, A.L. All-Star team (1987).... Coach, N.L. All-Star team (1993).

Year Team (League)	W	L	Pct.	Pos.	Playoff W	Playoff L	Champ. Series W	Champ. Series L	World Series W	World Series L	All-Star Game W	All-Star Game L
	REGULAR SEASON				POSTSEASON							
1978— California (A.L.)	62	54	.534	T2nd (W)	—	—	—	—	—	—	—	—
1979— California (A.L.)	88	74	.543	1st (W)	—	—	1	3	—	—	—	—
1980— California (A.L.)	65	95	.406	6th (W)	—	—	—	—	—	—	—	—
1981— California (A.L.)	22	25	.468		—	—	—	—	—	—	—	—
1983— Louisville (American Association)	78	57	.578	1st (E)	3	6	—	—	—	—	—	—
1984— Louisville (American Association)	79	76	.510	4th	8	3	—	—	—	—	—	—
1985— Louisville (American Association)	74	68	.521	1st (E)	4	1	—	—	—	—	—	—
1986— Louisville (American Association)	32	34	.485	3rd (E)	—	—	—	—	—	—	—	—
— Chicago (A.L.)	45	51	.469	5th (W)	—	—	—	—	—	—	—	—
1987— Chicago (A.L.)	77	85	.475	5th (W)	—	—	—	—	—	—	—	—
1988— Chicago (A.L.)	71	90	.441	5th (W)	—	—	—	—	—	—	—	—
1991— Philadelphia (N.L.)	74	75	.497	3rd (E)	—	—	—	—	—	—	—	—
1992— Philadelphia (N.L.)	70	92	.432	6th (E)	—	—	—	—	—	—	—	—
1993— Philadelphia (N.L.)	97	65	.599	1st (E)	—	—	4	2	2	4	—	—
1994— Philadelphia (N.L.)	54	61	.470		—	—	—	—	—	—	1	0
1995— Philadelphia (N.L.)	69	75	.479	T2nd (E)	—	—	—	—	—	—	—	—
American League totals (7 years)	430	474	.476		—	—	1	3	—	—	—	—
National League totals (5 years)	364	368	.497		—	—	4	2	2	4	1	0
Major league totals (12 years)	794	842	.485		—	—	5	5	2	4	1	0

NOTES:

1978—Replaced California manager Dave Garcia with club in third place and record of 25-21 (June 1).

1979—Lost to Baltimore in A.L. Championship Series.

1981—Replaced as California manager by Gene Mauch with club in fourth place (May 28).

1983—Defeated Oklahoma City, three games to two, in playoff; lost to Denver, four games to none, in championship playoff.

1984—Defeated Indianapolis, four games to two, in playoff; defeated Denver, four games to one, in championship playoff.

1985—Defeated Oklahoma City, four games to one, in championship playoff.

1986—Replaced manager Tony La Russa (26-38) and interim manager Doug Rader (1-1) with club in fifth place and record of 27-39 (June 22).

1991—Replaced Philadelphia manager Nick Leyva with club in sixth place and record of 4-9 (April 23).

1993—Defeated Atlanta in N.L. Championship Series; lost to Toronto in World Series.

1994—Philadelphia was in fourth place in N.L. East at time of season-ending strike (August 12).

GARNER, PHIL — BREWERS

PERSONAL: Born April 30, 1949, in Jefferson City, Tenn.... 5-10/177.... Batted right, threw right.... Full name: Philip Mason Garner.

HIGH SCHOOL: Beardon (Knoxville, Tenn.).

COLLEGE: Tennessee (degree in general business, 1973).

TRANSACTIONS/CAREER NOTES: Selected by Montreal Expos organization in eighth round of free-agent draft (June 4, 1970); did not sign. ... Selected by Oakland Athletics organization in secondary phase of free-agent draft (January 13, 1971).... Traded by A's with IF Tommy Helms and P Chris Batton to Pittsburgh Pirates for P Doc Medich, P Dave Giusti, P Rick Langford, P Doug Bair, OF Mitchell Page and OF Tony Armas (March 15, 1977).... On Pittsburgh disabled list (April 2-23, 1981).... Traded by Pirates to Houston Astros for 2B Johnny Ray and two players to be named later (August 31, 1981); Pirates organization acquired OF Kevin Houston and P Randy Niemann to complete deal (September 9, 1981).... Granted free agency (November 12, 1986).... Re-signed by Astros (January 6, 1987).... Traded by Astros to Los Angeles Dodgers for a player to be named later (June 19, 1987); Astros organization acquired P Jeff Edwards to complete deal (June 26, 1987).... Granted free agency (November 9, 1987).... Signed by San Francisco Giants (January 28, 1988).... On San Francisco disabled list (April 13-September 2, 1988); included rehabilitation assignment to Phoenix (August 5-24).... Granted free agency (November 3, 1988).

RECORDS: Shares major league record for most grand slams in two consecutive games—2 (September 14 and 15, 1978).... Shares N.L. single-month record for most grand slams—2 (September 1978).

STATISTICAL NOTES: Led Pacific Coast League third basemen with 104 putouts, 261 assists, 35 errors, 400 total chances and 23 double plays in 1973.... Led A.L. second basemen with 26 errors in 1975.... Led A.L. second basemen with 865 total chances in 1976.... Led N.L. second basemen with 499 assists, 21 errors, 869 total chances and 116 double plays in 1980.... Career major league grand slams: 3.

Year Team (League)	Pos.	G	AB	R	H	2B	3B	HR	RBI	Avg.	BB	SO	SB	PO	A	E	Avg.
			BATTING											FIELDING			
1971— Burlington (Midw.)	3B	116	439	73	122	22	4	11	70	.278	49	73	8	*122	203	29	.918
1972— Birm. (Southern)	3B	71	264	45	74	10	6	12	40	.280	27	43	3	74	116	13	.936
— Iowa (Am. Assoc.)	3B	70	247	33	60	18	4	9	22	.243	30	73	7	50	140	10	.950
1973— Tucson (PCL)	3B-2B	138	516	87	149	23	12	14	73	.289	72	90	3	†107	†270	†35	.915
— Oakland (A.L.)	3B	9	5	0	0	0	0	0	0	.000	0	3	0	2	3	0	1.000
1974— Tucson (PCL)	3B-SS	96	388	78	128	29	10	11	51	.330	53	58	8	92	182	15	.948
— Oakland (A.L.)	3B-SS-2B	30	28	4	5	1	0	0	1	.179	1	5	1	11	24	1	.972

Year	Team (League)	Pos.	G	AB	R	H	2B	3B	HR	RBI	Avg.	BB	SO	SB	PO	A	E	Avg.
				BATTING											FIELDING			
1975—	Oakland (A.L.)	2B-SS	•160	488	46	120	21	5	6	54	.246	30	65	4	355	427	†26	.968
1976—	Oakland (A.L.)	2B	159	555	54	145	29	12	8	74	.261	36	71	35	378	*465	22	.975
1977—	Pittsburgh (N.L.)■	3B-2B-SS	153	585	99	152	35	10	17	77	.260	55	65	32	223	351	17	.971
1978—	Pittsburgh (N.L.)	3B-2B-SS	154	528	66	138	25	9	10	66	.261	66	71	27	258	389	28	.959
1979—	Pittsburgh (N.L.)	3B-2B-SS	150	549	76	161	32	8	11	59	.293	55	74	17	234	396	22	.966
1980—	Pittsburgh (N.L.)	2B-SS	151	548	62	142	27	6	5	58	.259	46	53	32	349	†500	†21	.976
1981—	Pittsburgh (N.L.)	2B	56	181	22	46	6	2	1	20	.254	21	21	4	121	148	9	.968
—	Houston (N.L.)■	2B	31	113	13	27	3	1	0	6	.239	15	11	6	62	102	3	.982
1982—	Houston (N.L.)	2B-3B	155	588	65	161	33	8	13	83	.274	40	92	24	285	464	17	.978
1983—	Houston (N.L.)	3B	154	567	76	135	24	2	14	79	.238	63	84	18	100	311	24	.945
1984—	Houston (N.L.)	3B-2B	128	374	60	104	17	6	4	45	.278	43	63	3	136	251	12	.970
1985—	Houston (N.L.)	3B-2B	135	463	65	124	23	10	6	51	.268	34	72	4	101	229	21	.940
1986—	Houston (N.L.)	3B-2B	107	313	43	83	14	3	9	41	.265	30	45	12	66	152	23	.905
1987—	Houston (N.L.)	SS-2B	43	112	15	25	5	0	3	15	.223	8	20	1	28	55	2	.976
—	Los Angeles (N.L.)■	3B-2B-SS	70	126	14	24	4	0	2	8	.190	20	24	5	37	89	11	.920
1988—	San Fran. (N.L.)■	3B	15	13	0	2	0	0	0	1	.154	1	3	0	0	0	0	...
—	Phoenix (PCL)	2B-3B	17	45	5	12	2	1	1	5	.267	4	4	0	12	22	0	1.000
American League totals (4 years)			358	1076	104	270	51	17	14	129	.251	67	144	40	746	919	49	.971
National League totals (12 years)			1502	5060	676	1324	248	65	95	609	.262	497	698	185	2000	3437	210	.963
Major league totals (16 years)			1860	6136	780	1594	299	82	109	738	.260	564	842	225	2746	4356	259	.965

DIVISION SERIES RECORD

Year	Team (League)	Pos.	G	AB	R	H	2B	3B	HR	RBI	Avg.	BB	SO	SB	PO	A	E	Avg.
				BATTING											FIELDING			
1981—	Houston (N.L.)	2B	5	18	1	2	0	0	0	0	.111	3	3	0	6	8	1	.933

CHAMPIONSHIP SERIES RECORD

Year	Team (League)	Pos.	G	AB	R	H	2B	3B	HR	RBI	Avg.	BB	SO	SB	PO	A	E	Avg.
				BATTING											FIELDING			
1975—	Oakland (A.L.)	2B	3	5	0	0	0	0	0	0	.000	0	1	0	7	4	1	.917
1979—	Pittsburgh (N.L.)	2B-SS	3	12	4	5	0	1	1	1	.417	1	0	0	8	9	0	1.000
1986—	Houston (N.L.)	3B	3	9	1	2	1	0	0	2	.222	1	2	0	1	9	0	1.000
Championship series totals (3 years)			9	26	5	7	1	1	1	3	.269	2	3	0	16	22	1	.974

WORLD SERIES RECORD

NOTES: Shares single-series record for collecting one or more hits in each game (1979). . . . Member of World Series championship team (1979).

Year	Team (League)	Pos.	G	AB	R	H	2B	3B	HR	RBI	Avg.	BB	SO	SB	PO	A	E	Avg.
				BATTING											FIELDING			
1979—	Pittsburgh (N.L.)	2B	7	24	4	12	4	0	0	5	.500	3	1	0	21	23	2	.957

ALL-STAR GAME RECORD

Year	League	Pos.	AB	R	H	2B	3B	HR	RBI	Avg.	BB	SO	SB	PO	A	E	Avg.
			BATTING											FIELDING			
1976—	American	2B	1	0	0	0	0	0	0	.000	0	1	0	1	1	0	1.000
1980—	National	2B	2	1	1	0	0	0	0	.500	1	1	1	1	3	0	1.000
1981—	National	2B	0	0	0	0	0	0	0	...	0	0	0	0	0	0	...
All-Star Game totals (3 years)			3	1	1	0	0	0	0	.333	1	2	1	2	4	0	1.000

RECORD AS MANAGER

BACKGROUND: Coach, Houston Astros (1989-91).
HONORS: Coach, A.L. All-Star team (1995).

Year	Team (League)	W	L	Pct.	Pos.	Playoff W	Playoff L	Champ. Series W	Champ. Series L	World Series W	World Series L	All-Star Game W	All-Star Game L
		REGULAR SEASON				POSTSEASON							
1992—	Milwaukee (A.L.)	92	70	.568	2nd (E)	—	—	—	—	—	—	—	—
1993—	Milwaukee (A.L.)	69	93	.426	7th (E)	—	—	—	—	—	—	—	—
1994—	Milwaukee (A.L.)	53	62	.461		—	—	—	—	—	—	—	—
1995—	Milwaukee (A.L.)	65	79	.451	4th (C)	—	—	—	—	—	—	—	—
Major league totals (4 years)		279	304	.479		—	—	—	—	—	—	—	—

NOTES:
1993—On suspended list (September 24-27).
1994—Milwaukee was in fifth place in A.L. Central at time of season-ending strike (August 12).
1995—On suspended list (July 27-31).

GASTON, CITO — BLUE JAYS

PERSONAL: Born March 17, 1944, in San Antonio. . . . 6-4/210. . . . Batted right, threw right. . . . Full name: Clarence Edwin Gaston.
HIGH SCHOOL: Holy Cross (Corpus Christi, Tex.).
TRANSACTIONS/CAREER NOTES: Signed by Milwaukee Braves organization (March 22, 1964). . . . On Binghamton disabled list (May 26-July 6, 1964). . . . On disabled list (August 2-29, 1965). . . . Braves franchise moved from Milwaukee to Atlanta (1966). . . . Selected by San Diego Padres in expansion draft (October 14, 1968). . . . On disabled list (May 17-June 2, 1972). . . . Traded by Padres to Braves for P Danny Frisella (November 7, 1974). . . . Contract sold by Braves to Pittsburgh Pirates (September 22, 1978). . . . Granted free agency (November 2, 1978). . . . Signed by Santo Domingo of Inter-American League (April 10, 1979). . . . On suspended list (June 21-30, 1979). . . . Granted free agency when Inter-American League folded (June 30, 1979). . . . Signed by Leon of Mexican League (July 22, 1979).
STATISTICAL NOTES: Led New York-Pennsylvania League with 255 total bases in 1966. . . . Career major league grand slams: 1.

Year	Team (League)	Pos.	G	AB	R	H	2B	3B	HR	RBI	Avg.	BB	SO	SB	PO	A	E	Avg.
			BATTING												FIELDING			
1964—	Binghamton (NYP)	OF	11	21	1	5	2	0	1	4	.238	1	9	0	8	0	1	.889
—	Greenville (W. Car.)	OF	49	165	15	38	6	3	0	16	.230	8	47	1	62	5	5	.931
1965—	W.P. Beach (FSL)	OF	70	202	14	38	5	3	0	9	.188	33	50	0	111	4	5	.958
1966—	Batavia (NYP)	OF	114	433	84	143	18	5	*28	*104	.330	59	84	8	214	12	13	.946
—	Austin (Texas)	OF	4	10	2	3	1	1	0	4	.300	2	2	0	10	0	0	1.000
1967—	Austin (Texas)	OF	136	505	72	154	24	6	10	70	.305	45	104	6	274	8	12	.959
—	Atlanta (N.L.)	OF	9	25	1	3	0	1	0	1	.120	0	5	1	7	1	2	.800
1968—	Richmond (Int'l)	OF	21	71	9	17	4	0	2	8	.239	8	21	0	43	0	0	1.000
—	Shreveport (Texas)	OF	96	340	49	95	15	4	6	57	.279	28	55	12	203	3	9	.958
1969—	San Diego (N.L.)■	OF	129	391	20	90	11	7	2	28	.230	24	117	4	243	12	11	.959
1970—	San Diego (N.L.)	OF	146	584	92	186	26	9	29	93	.318	41	142	4	310	7	8	.975
1971—	San Diego (N.L.)	OF	141	518	57	118	13	9	17	61	.228	24	121	1	271	8	5	.982
1972—	San Diego (N.L.)	OF	111	379	30	102	14	0	7	44	.269	22	76	0	158	10	4	.977
1973—	San Diego (N.L.)	OF	133	476	51	119	18	4	16	57	.250	20	88	0	198	16	•12	.947
1974—	San Diego (N.L.)	OF	106	267	19	57	11	0	6	33	.213	16	51	0	119	7	1	.992
1975—	Atlanta (N.L.)■	OF-1B	64	141	17	34	4	0	6	15	.241	17	33	1	80	2	3	.965
1976—	Atlanta (N.L.)	OF-1B	69	134	15	39	4	0	4	25	.291	13	21	1	58	2	1	.984
1977—	Atlanta (N.L.)	OF-1B	56	85	6	23	4	0	3	21	.271	5	19	1	44	4	1	.980
1978—	Atlanta (N.L.)	OF-1B	60	118	5	27	1	0	1	9	.229	3	20	0	66	2	3	.958
—	Pittsburgh (N.L.)■	OF	2	2	1	1	0	0	0	0	.500	0	0	0	0	0	0	...
1979—	San Dom. (In.-Am.)■	...	40	148	22	48	5	0	1	14	.324	...	...	1	...	...	...	...
—	Leon (Mexican)■	OF	24	83	5	28	2	0	1	8	.337	10	16	0	24	0	0	1.000
1980—	Leon (Mexican)	1B	48	185	16	44	5	0	4	27	.238	11	26	0	126	3	3	.977
Major league totals (11 years)			1026	3120	314	799	106	30	91	387	.256	185	693	13	1554	71	51	.970

ALL-STAR GAME RECORD

Year	League	Pos.	AB	R	H	2B	3B	HR	RBI	Avg.	BB	SO	SB	PO	A	E	Avg.
			BATTING											FIELDING			
1970—	National	OF	2	0	0	0	0	0	0	.000	1	0	0	2	0	0	1.000

RECORD AS MANAGER

BACKGROUND: Minor league instructor, Atlanta Braves organization (1981). . . . Coach, Toronto Blue Jays (1982-May 15, 1989).
HONORS: Coach, A.L. All-Star team (1991).

Year	Team (League)	W	L	Pct.	Pos.	Playoff W	Playoff L	Champ. Series W	Champ. Series L	World Series W	World Series L	All-Star Game W	All-Star Game L
		REGULAR SEASON				POSTSEASON							
1989—	Toronto (A.L.)	77	49	.611	1st (E)	—	—	1	4	—	—	—	—
1990—	Toronto (A.L.)	86	76	.531	2nd (E)	—	—	—	—	—	—	—	—
1991—	Toronto (A.L.)	91	71	.562	1st (E)	—	—	1	4	—	—	—	—
1992—	Toronto (A.L.)	96	66	.593	1st (E)	—	—	4	2	4	2	—	—
1993—	Toronto (A.L.)	95	67	.586	1st (E)	—	—	4	2	4	2	1	0
1994—	Toronto (A.L.)	55	60	.478		—	—	—	—	—	—	0	1
1995—	Toronto (A.L.)	56	88	.389	5th (E)	—	—	—	—	—	—	—	—
Major league totals (7 years)		556	477	.538		—	—	10	12	8	4	1	1

NOTES:

1989—Replaced Toronto manager Jimy Williams with club in seventh place and record of 12-24 (May 15); lost to Oakland in A.L. Championship Series.

1991—Record includes time taken off because of back injury (August 21-September 27); Blue Jays were 19-14 under temporary manager Gene Tenace during that time; lost to Minnesota in A.L. Championship Series.

1992—Defeated Oakland in A.L. Championship Series; defeated Atlanta in World Series.

1993—Defeated Chicago in A.L. Championship Series; defeated Philadelphia in World Series.

1994—On suspended list (May 27-30); club went 2-1 under bench coach Gene Tenace. Toronto was in third place in A.L. East at time of season-ending strike (August 12).

GREEN, DALLAS — METS

PERSONAL: Born August 4, 1934, in Newport, Del. . . . 6-5/210. . . . Threw right, batted left. . . . Full name: George Dallas Green Jr. . . . Father of John Green, minor league pitcher (1985-90).
HIGH SCHOOL: Conrad (Wilmington, Del.).
COLLEGE: Delaware (bachelor of science degree, 1981).
TRANSACTIONS/CAREER NOTES: Signed as free agent by Philadelphia Phillies organization (June 9, 1955). . . . On disabled list (May 25-June 12, 1959). . . . Contract sold by Phillies organization to Washington Senators (April 11, 1965). . . . Returned to Phillies organization (May 11, 1965). . . . Contract sold by Phillies organization to New York Mets organization (July 22, 1966). . . . Returned to Phillies organization (August 10, 1966). . . . Served as player/coach for Reading (1967). . . . Released by Phillies (September 22, 1967).

Year	Team (League)	W	L	Pct.	ERA	G	GS	CG	ShO	Sv.	IP	H	R	ER	BB	SO
1955—	Reidsville (Caro.)	1	1	.500	10.06	7	2	1	0	...	17	25	22	19	16	8
—	Matt. (Miss.-O.V.)	4	3	.571	3.44	11	8	5	3	...	55	43	29	21	42	85
1956—	Salt Lake City (Pio.)	17	12	.586	3.58	33	31	17	1	...	239	182	126	95	*187	*226
1957—	Miami (Int'l)	0	1	.000	10.50	2	2	0	0	...	6	6	8	7	4	5
—	H.P.-Thomas. (Car.)	12	9	.571	4.02	25	20	8	2	...	159	143	84	71	92	147
1958—	Miami (Int'l)	7	10	.412	3.74	31	22	5	0	...	159	135	73	66	70	103
1959—	Buffalo (Int'l)	9	5	.643	2.94	17	15	6	2	...	101	94	39	33	28	72
1960—	Buffalo (Int'l)	3	4	.429	3.36	11	11	4	0	...	75	72	35	28	26	44
—	Philadelphia (N.L.)	3	6	.333	4.05	23	10	5	1	...	109	100	54	49	44	51
1961—	Philadelphia (N.L.)	2	4	.333	4.85	42	10	1	1	...	128	160	77	69	47	51
1962—	Philadelphia (N.L.)	6	6	.500	3.84	37	10	2	0	...	129	145	58	55	43	58
1963—	Philadelphia (N.L.)	7	5	.583	3.23	40	14	4	0	...	120	134	53	43	38	68
1964—	Arkansas (PCL)	4	1	.800	2.63	7	6	2	0	...	48	46	15	14	9	34
—	Philadelphia (N.L.)	2	1	.667	5.79	25	0	0	0	...	42	63	31	27	14	21

Year	Team (League)	W	L	Pct.	ERA	G	GS	CG	ShO	Sv.	IP	H	R	ER	BB	SO
1965—	Washington (A.L.)■	0	0	. . .	3.21	6	2	0	0	. . .	14	14	6	5	3	6
—	Arkansas (PCL)■	12	7	.632	3.66	23	23	12	1	. . .	172	180	81	70	36	119
1966—	San Diego (PCL)	14	9	.609	3.82	26	26	11	3	. . .	184	200	91	78	28	90
—	New York (N.L.)■	0	0	. . .	5.40	4	0	0	0	. . .	5	6	3	3	2	1
1967—	Reading (Eastern)■	6	2	.750	1.77	8	8	7	3	. . .	66	59	20	13	12	42
—	Philadelphia (N.L.)	0	0	. . .	9.00	8	0	0	0	. . .	15	25	16	15	6	12
A.L. totals (1 year)		0	0	. . .	3.21	6	2	0	0	0	14	14	6	5	3	6
N.L. totals (7 years)		20	22	.476	4.29	179	44	12	2	0	548	633	292	261	194	262
Major league totals (8 years)		20	22	.476	4.26	185	46	12	2	0	562	647	298	266	197	268

RECORD AS MANAGER

BACKGROUND: Player/coach, Reading, Philadelphia Phillies organization (1967). . . . Assistant farm director, Phillies (November 19, 1969-June 2, 1972). . . . Director of minor leagues, Phillies (June 2, 1972-August 31, 1979). . . . General manager, Chicago Cubs (1982-87). . . . Scout, New York Mets (1991-May 19, 1993).

HONORS: Named Appalachian League Manager of the Year (1969). . . . Named Major League Executive of the Year by The Sporting News (1984).

		REGULAR SEASON				POSTSEASON							
						Playoff		Champ. Series		World Series		All-Star Game	
Year	Team (League)	W	L	Pct.	Pos.	W	L	W	L	W	L	W	L
1968—	Huron (Northern)	26	43	.377	5th	—	—	—	—	—	—	—	—
1969—	Pulaski (Appalachian)	38	28	.576	1st (N)	—	—	—	—	—	—	—	—
1979—	Philadelphia (N.L.)	19	11	.633	4th (E)	—	—	—	—	—	—	—	—
1980—	Philadelphia (N.L.)	91	71	.562	1st (E)	—	—	3	2	4	2	—	—
1981—	Philadelphia (N.L.)	34	21	.618	1st (E)	—	—	—	—	—	—	1	0
—	(Second half)	25	27	.481	3rd (E)	2	3	—	—	—	—	—	—
1989—	New York (A.L.)	56	65	.463		—	—	—	—	—	—	—	—
1993—	New York (N.L.)	46	78	.371	7th (E)	—	—	—	—	—	—	—	—
1994—	New York (N.L.)	55	58	.487		—	—	—	—	—	—	—	—
1995—	New York (N.L.)	69	75	.479	T2nd (E)	—	—	—	—	—	—	—	—
National League totals (6 years)		339	341	.499		2	3	3	2	4	2	1	0
American League totals (1 year)		56	65	.463		—	—	—	—	—	—	—	—
Major league totals (7 years)		395	406	.493		2	3	3	2	4	2	1	0

NOTES:

1979—Replaced Philadelphia manager Danny Ozark with club in fifth place and record of 65-67 (August 31).
1980—Defeated Houston in N.L. Championship Series; defeated Kansas City in World Series.
1981—Lost to Montreal in divisional playoffs.
1989—Replaced by Bucky Dent as New York manager with club in sixth place (August 18).
1993—Replaced New York manager Jeff Torborg with club in seventh place and record of 13-25 (May 19).
1994—New York was in third place in N.L. East at time of season-ending strike (August 12).

HARGROVE, MIKE — INDIANS

PERSONAL: Born October 26, 1949, in Perryton, Tex. . . . 6-0/195. . . . Batted left, threw left. . . . Full name: Dudley Michael Hargrove.

HIGH SCHOOL: Perryton (Tex.).

COLLEGE: Northwestern State, Okla. (degree in physical education and social sciences).

TRANSACTIONS/CAREER NOTES: Selected by Texas Rangers organization in 25th round of free-agent draft (June 6, 1972). . . . Traded by Rangers with 3B Kurt Bevacqua and C Bill Fahey to San Diego Padres for OF Oscar Gamble, C Dave Roberts and cash (October 25, 1978). . . . Traded by Padres to Cleveland Indians for OF Paul Dade (June 14, 1979). . . . Granted free agency (November 12, 1985).

HONORS: Named Western Carolinas League Player of the Year (1973). . . . Named A.L. Rookie Player of the Year by The Sporting News (1974). . . . Named A.L. Rookie of the Year by Baseball Writers' Association of America (1974).

STATISTICAL NOTES: Led New York-Pennsylvania League first basemen with 58 double plays in 1972. . . . Led Western Carolinas League with 247 total bases in 1973. . . . Led Western Carolinas League first basemen with 118 double plays in 1973. . . . Led A.L. first basemen with 1,489 total chances in 1980. . . . Led A.L. with .432 on-base percentage in 1981. . . . Career major league grand slams: 1.

			BATTING											FIELDING			
Year	Team (League)	Pos.	G	AB	R	H	2B	3B	HR	RBI	Avg.	BB	SO	SB	PO	A	E	Avg.
1972—	Geneva (NYP)	1B	•70	243	38	65	8	0	4	37	.267	52	44	3	*537	•40	10	*.983
1973—	Gastonia (W. Car.)	1B	•130	456	88	*160	*35	8	12	82	*.351	68	47	10	*1121	•77	14	*.988
1974—	Texas (A.L.)	1B-DH-OF	131	415	57	134	18	6	4	66	.323	49	42	0	638	72	9	.987
1975—	Texas (A.L.)	OF-1B-DH	145	519	82	157	22	2	11	62	.303	79	66	4	513	45	13	.977
1976—	Texas (A.L.)	1B	151	541	80	155	30	1	7	58	.287	*97	64	2	1222	110	*21	.984
1977—	Texas (A.L.)	1B	153	525	98	160	28	4	18	69	.305	103	59	2	1393	100	11	.993
1978—	Texas (A.L.)	1B-DH	146	494	63	124	24	1	7	40	.251	*107	47	2	1221	*116	*17	.987
1979—	San Diego (N.L.)■	1B	52	125	15	24	5	0	0	8	.192	25	15	0	323	17	5	.986
—	Cleveland (A.L.)■	OF-1B-DH	100	338	60	110	21	4	10	56	.325	63	40	2	356	16	2	.995
1980—	Cleveland (A.L.)	1B	160	589	86	179	22	2	11	85	.304	111	36	4	*1391	88	10	.993
1981—	Cleveland (A.L.)	1B-DH	94	322	43	102	21	0	2	49	.317	60	16	5	766	76	•9	.989
1982—	Cleveland (A.L.)	1B-DH	160	591	67	160	26	1	4	65	.271	101	58	2	1293	*123	5	.996
1983—	Cleveland (A.L.)	1B-DH	134	469	57	134	21	4	3	57	.286	78	40	0	1098	115	7	.994
1984—	Cleveland (A.L.)	1B	133	352	44	94	14	2	2	44	.267	53	38	0	790	83	8	.991
1985—	Cleveland (A.L.)	1B-DH-OF	107	284	31	81	14	1	1	27	.285	39	29	1	599	66	6	.991
American League totals (12 years)			1614	5439	768	1590	261	28	80	678	.292	940	535	24	11280	1010	118	.990
National League totals (1 year)			52	125	15	24	5	0	0	8	.192	25	15	0	323	17	5	.986
Major league totals (12 years)			1666	5564	783	1614	266	28	80	686	.290	965	550	24	11603	1027	123	.990

ALL-STAR GAME RECORD

			BATTING										FIELDING			
Year	League	Pos.	AB	R	H	2B	3B	HR	RBI	Avg.	BB	SO	SB	PO	A	E	Avg.
1975—	American	PH	1	0	0	0	0	0	0	.000	0	0	0	. . .	. . .	. . .	. . .

RECORD AS MANAGER

BACKGROUND: Minor league coach, Cleveland Indians organization (1986). . . . Coach, Indians (1990-July 6, 1991).

HONORS: Named Carolina League Manager of the Year (1987). . . . Named Pacific Coast League Manager of the Year (1989). . . . Coach, A.L. All-Star team (1994). . . . Named A.L. Manager of the Year by THE SPORTING NEWS (1995).

	REGULAR SEASON				POSTSEASON							
					Playoff		Champ. Series		World Series		All-Star Game	
Year Team (League)	W	L	Pct.	Pos.	W	L	W	L	W	L	W	L
1987— Kinston (Carolina)	33	37	.471	T3rd (S)	—	—	—	—	—	—	—	—
— (Second half)	42	28	.600	1st (S)	3	3	—	—	—	—	—	—
1988— Williamsport (Eastern)	66	73	.475	6th	—	—	—	—	—	—	—	—
1989— Colorado Springs (Pacific Coast)	44	26	.629	1st (S)	—	—	—	—	—	—	—	—
— (Second half)	34	38	.472	3rd (S)	2	3	—	—	—	—	—	—
1991— Cleveland (A.L.)	32	53	.376	7th (E)	—	—	—	—	—	—	—	—
1992— Cleveland (A.L.)	76	86	.469	T4th (E)	—	—	—	—	—	—	—	—
1993— Cleveland (A.L.)	76	86	.469	6th (E)	—	—	—	—	—	—	—	—
1994— Cleveland (A.L.)	66	47	.584		—	—	—	—	—	—	—	—
1995— Cleveland (A.L.)	100	44	.694	1st (C)	3	0	4	2	2	4	—	—
Major league totals (5 years)	350	316	.526		3	0	4	2	2	4	—	—

NOTES:

1987—Defeated Winston-Salem, two games to none, in playoffs; lost to Salem, three games to one, in league championship.

1989—Lost to Albuquerque in playoffs.

1991—Replaced Cleveland manager John McNamara with club in seventh place and record of 25-52 (July 6).

1994—Cleveland was in second place in A.L. Central at time of season-ending strike (August 12).

1995—Defeated Boston in A.L. divisional playoff; defeated Seattle in A.L. Championship Series; lost to Atlanta in World Series.

HOWE, ART — ATHLETICS

PERSONAL: Born December 15, 1946, in Pittsburgh. . . . 6-1/185. . . . Batted right, threw right. . . . Full name: Arthur Henry Howe Jr.

HIGH SCHOOL: Shaler (Glenshaw, Pa.).

COLLEGE: Wyoming (bachelor of science degree in business administration, 1969).

TRANSACTIONS/CAREER NOTES: Signed as free agent by Pittsburgh Pirates organization (June, 1971). . . . On disabled list (August 17-September 2, 1972 and April 13-May 6, 1973). . . . Traded by Pirates to Houston Astros (January 6, 1976), completing deal in which Astros traded 2B Tommy Helms to Pirates for a player to be named later (December 12, 1975). . . . On disabled list (May 12-June 19, 1982 and March 27, 1983-entire season). . . . Granted free agency (November 7, 1983). . . . Signed by St. Louis Cardinals (March 21, 1984). . . . Released by Cardinals (April 22, 1985).

STATISTICAL NOTES: Tied for Carolina League lead in putouts by third baseman with 95 in 1971. . . . Led International League third basemen with 22 errors and 24 double plays in 1972. . . . Career major league grand slams: 1.

			BATTING											FIELDING			
Year Team (League)	Pos.	G	AB	R	H	2B	3B	HR	RBI	Avg.	BB	SO	SB	PO	A	E	Avg.
1971— Salem (Carolina)	3B-SS	114	382	77	133	27	7	12	79	*.348	82	74	11	‡110	221	21	.940
1972— Char., W.Va. (Int'l)	3B-2B-SS	109	365	68	99	21	3	14	53	.271	63	69	8	105	248	†24	.936
1973— Char., W.Va. (Int'l)	3B-2B-SS	119	372	50	85	20	1	8	44	.228	54	70	6	141	229	21	.946
1974— Char., W.Va. (Int'l)	3B	60	207	26	70	17	4	8	36	.338	31	27	4	35	90	9	.933
— Pittsburgh (N.L.)	3B-SS	29	74	10	18	4	1	1	5	.243	9	13	0	11	49	4	.938
1975— Char., W.Va. (Int'l)	3B-2B	11	42	4	15	1	3	0	3	.357	2	4	0	15	23	1	.974
— Pittsburgh (N.L.)	3B-SS	63	146	13	25	9	0	1	10	.171	15	15	1	19	89	7	.939
1976— Memphis (Int'l)■	3B-1B	74	259	50	92	21	3	12	59	.355	34	31	1	93	120	14	.938
— Houston (N.L.)	3B-2B	21	29	0	4	1	0	0	0	.138	6	6	0	17	16	1	.971
1977— Houston (N.L.)	2B-3B-SS	125	413	44	109	23	7	8	58	.264	41	60	0	213	333	8	.986
1978— Houston (N.L.)	2B-3B-1B	119	420	46	123	33	3	7	55	.293	34	41	2	240	302	13	.977
1979— Houston (N.L.)	2B-3B-1B	118	355	32	88	15	2	6	33	.248	36	37	3	188	261	7	.985
1980— Houston (N.L.)	1-3-2-S	110	321	34	91	12	5	10	46	.283	34	29	1	598	86	10	.986
1981— Houston (N.L.)	3B-1B	103	361	43	107	22	4	3	36	.296	41	23	1	67	206	9	.968
1982— Houston (N.L.)	3B-1B	110	365	29	87	15	1	5	38	.238	41	45	2	344	174	7	.987
1983—								Did not play.									
1984— St. Louis (N.L.)■	3-1-2-S	89	139	17	30	5	0	2	12	.216	18	18	0	71	80	3	.981
1985— St. Louis (N.L.)	1B-3B	4	3	0	0	0	0	0	0	.000	0	0	0	5	1	0	1.000
Major league totals (11 years)		891	2626	268	682	139	23	43	293	.260	275	287	10	1773	1597	69	.980

DIVISION SERIES RECORD

			BATTING											FIELDING			
Year Team (League)	Pos.	G	AB	R	H	2B	3B	HR	RBI	Avg.	BB	SO	SB	PO	A	E	Avg.
1981— Houston (N.L.)	3B	5	17	1	4	0	0	1	1	.235	2	1	0	6	9	0	1.000

CHAMPIONSHIP SERIES RECORD

			BATTING											FIELDING			
Year Team (League)	Pos.	G	AB	R	H	2B	3B	HR	RBI	Avg.	BB	SO	SB	PO	A	E	Avg.
1974— Pittsburgh (N.L.)	PH	1	1	0	0	0	0	0	0	.000	0	0	0	...	...	...	...
1980— Houston (N.L.)	1B-PH	5	15	0	3	1	1	0	2	.200	2	2	0	29	3	0	1.000
Championship series totals (2 years)		6	16	0	3	1	1	0	2	.188	2	2	0	29	3	0	1.000

RECORD AS MANAGER

BACKGROUND: Coach, Texas Rangers (May 21, 1985-88). . . . Scout, Los Angeles Dodgers organization (1994). . . . Coach, Colorado Rockies (1995).

HONORS: Coach, N.L. All-Star team (1991).

	REGULAR SEASON				POSTSEASON							
					Playoff		Champ. Series		World Series		All-Star Game	
Year Team (League)	W	L	Pct.	Pos.	W	L	W	L	W	L	W	L
1989— Houston (N.L.)	86	76	.531	3rd (W)	—	—	—	—	—	—	—	—
1990— Houston (N.L.)	75	87	.463	T4th (W)	—	—	—	—	—	—	—	—
1991— Houston (N.L.)	65	97	.401	6th (W)	—	—	—	—	—	—	—	—

Year	Team (League)	W	L	Pct.	Pos.	Playoff W	Playoff L	Champ. Series W	Champ. Series L	World Series W	World Series L	All-Star Game W	All-Star Game L
		REGULAR SEASON				POSTSEASON							
1992	—Houston (N.L.)	81	81	.500	4th (W)	—	—	—	—	—	—	—	—
1993	—Houston (N.L.)	85	77	.525	3rd (W)	—	—	—	—	—	—	—	—
Major league totals (5 years)		392	418	.484		—	—	—	—	—	—	—	—

JOHNSON, DAVEY — ORIOLES

PERSONAL: Born January 30, 1943, in Orlando, Fla. . . . 6-1/182. . . . Batted right, threw right. . . . Full name: David Allen Johnson.

HIGH SCHOOL: Alamo Heights (San Antonio).

COLLEGE: Texas A&M, Trinity University, Tex. (degree in mathematics) and Johns Hopkins.

TRANSACTIONS/CAREER NOTES: Signed as free agent by Baltimore Orioles organization (June 2, 1962). . . . On Rochester disabled list (August 7-September 1, 1965). . . . Traded by Orioles with P Pat Dobson, P Roric Harrison and C Johnny Oates to Atlanta Braves for C Earl Williams and IF Taylor Duncan (November 30, 1972). . . . Released by Braves (April 11, 1975). . . . Signed by Yomiuri Giants of Japan Central League (1975). . . . Released by Yomiuri (January 21, 1977). . . . Signed by Philadelphia Phillies (February 3, 1977). . . . On disabled list (June 15-July 1, 1977). . . . Traded by Phillies to Chicago Cubs for P Larry Anderson (August 6, 1978). . . . Released by Cubs (October 17, 1978). . . . Served as player/manager with Miami of Inter-American League (1979). . . . Granted free agency when league folded (June 30, 1979).

RECORDS: Shares major league single-season records for most home runs by second baseman—42 (1973, also had one home run as pinch-hitter); fewest triples (150 or more games)—0 (1973); and most grand slams by pinch-hitter—2 (1978).

HONORS: Won A.L. Gold Glove at second base (1969-71). . . . Named second baseman on The Sporting News A.L. All-Star team (1970). . . . Named N.L. Comeback Player of the Year by The Sporting News (1973). . . . Named second baseman on The Sporting News N.L. All-Star team (1973).

STATISTICAL NOTES: Led California League shortstops with 63 double plays in 1962. . . . Led A.L. second basemen with 19 errors in 1966. . . . Tied for A.L. lead in putouts by second baseman with 379 in 1970. . . . Tied for A.L. lead with eight sacrifice flies in 1967. . . . Led A.L. second basemen with 103 double plays in 1971. . . . Led N.L. second basemen with 877 total chances and tied for lead with 106 double plays in 1973. . . . Career major league grand slams: 5.

Year	Team (League)	Pos.	G	AB	R	H	2B	3B	HR	RBI	Avg.	BB	SO	SB	PO	A	E	Avg.
				BATTING											FIELDING			
1962	—Stockton (Calif.)	SS	97	343	58	106	18	•12	10	63	.309	43	61	8	135	307	40	*.917
1963	—Elmira (Eastern)	SS-2B	63	233	47	76	11	6	13	42	.326	29	42	12	115	155	12	.957
	—Rochester (Int'l)	2B-OF	63	211	31	52	9	3	6	22	.246	25	39	4	141	138	11	.962
1964	—Rochester (Int'l)	2B-SS	•155	590	87	156	29	14	19	73	.264	71	95	7	326	445	39	.952
1965	—Baltimore (A.L.)	3B-2B-SS	20	47	5	8	3	0	0	1	.170	5	6	3	11	37	3	.941
	—Rochester (Int'l)	SS	52	193	29	58	9	3	4	22	.301	16	34	4	96	161	10	.963
1966	—Baltimore (A.L.)	2B-SS	131	501	47	129	20	3	7	56	.257	31	64	3	294	357	≠20	.970
1967	—Baltimore (A.L.)	2B-3B	148	510	62	126	30	3	10	64	.247	59	82	4	344	351	14	.980
1968	—Baltimore (A.L.)	2B-SS	145	504	50	122	24	4	9	56	.242	44	80	7	294	370	15	.978
1969	—Baltimore (A.L.)	2B-SS	142	511	52	143	34	1	7	57	.280	57	52	3	358	370	12	.984
1970	—Baltimore (A.L.)	2B-SS	149	530	68	149	27	1	10	53	.281	66	68	2	‡382	391	8	.990
1971	—Baltimore (A.L.)	2B	142	510	67	144	26	1	18	72	.282	51	55	3	361	367	12	.984
1972	—Baltimore (A.L.)	2B	118	376	31	83	22	3	5	32	.221	52	68	1	286	307	6	*.990
1973	—Atlanta (N.L.)■	2B	157	559	84	151	25	0	43	99	.270	81	93	5	383	464	*30	.966
1974	—Atlanta (N.L.)	1B-2B	136	454	56	114	18	0	15	62	.251	75	59	1	789	231	11	.989
1975	—Atlanta (N.L.)	PH	1	1	0	1	1	0	0	1	1.000	0	0	0	...	...	...	...
	—Yomiuri (Jp. Cen.)■	3B-SS	91	289	29	57	7	0	13	38	.197	32	71	1	85	157	11	.957
1976	—Yomiuri (Jp. Cen.)	2B-3B-1B	108	371	48	102	16	2	26	74	.275	55	62	1	226	28	11	.958
1977	—Philadelphia (N.L.)■	1B-2B-3B	78	156	23	50	9	1	8	36	.321	23	20	1	299	31	0	1.000
1978	—Philadelphia (N.L.)	2B-3B-1B	44	89	14	17	2	0	2	14	.191	10	19	0	56	41	6	.942
	—Chicago (N.L.)■	3B	12	49	5	15	1	1	2	6	.306	5	9	0	4	22	5	.839
1979	—Miami (In.-Am.)■	1B	10	25	7	6	2	0	1	2	.240	...	...	0	...	...	...	...
American League totals (8 years)			995	3489	382	904	186	16	66	391	.259	365	475	26	2330	2550	90	.982
National League totals (5 years)			428	1308	182	348	56	2	70	218	.266	194	200	7	1531	789	52	.978
Major league totals (13 years)			1423	4797	564	1252	242	18	136	609	.261	559	675	33	3861	3339	142	.981

CHAMPIONSHIP SERIES RECORD

Year	Team (League)	Pos.	G	AB	R	H	2B	3B	HR	RBI	Avg.	BB	SO	SB	PO	A	E	Avg.
				BATTING											FIELDING			
1969	—Baltimore (A.L.)	2B	3	13	2	3	0	0	0	0	.231	2	1	0	5	11	0	1.000
1970	—Baltimore (A.L.)	2B	3	11	4	4	0	0	2	4	.364	1	1	0	11	4	0	1.000
1971	—Baltimore (A.L.)	2B	3	10	2	3	2	0	0	0	.300	3	1	0	5	6	1	.917
1977	—Philadelphia (N.L.)	1B	1	4	0	1	0	0	0	2	.250	0	1	0	8	0	0	1.000
Championship series totals (4 years)			10	38	8	11	2	0	2	6	.289	6	4	0	29	21	1	.980

WORLD SERIES RECORD

Year	Team (League)	Pos.	G	AB	R	H	2B	3B	HR	RBI	Avg.	BB	SO	SB	PO	A	E	Avg.
				BATTING											FIELDING			
1966	—Baltimore (A.L.)	2B	4	14	1	4	1	0	0	1	.286	0	1	0	12	12	0	1.000
1969	—Baltimore (A.L.)	2B	5	16	1	1	0	0	0	0	.063	2	1	0	8	15	0	1.000
1970	—Baltimore (A.L.)	2B	5	16	2	5	2	0	0	2	.313	5	2	0	15	9	0	1.000
1971	—Baltimore (A.L.)	2B	7	27	1	4	0	0	0	3	.148	0	1	0	18	12	0	1.000
World Series totals (4 years)			21	73	5	14	3	0	0	6	.192	7	5	0	53	48	0	1.000

ALL-STAR GAME RECORD

Year	League	Pos.	AB	R	H	2B	3B	HR	RBI	Avg.	BB	SO	SB	PO	A	E	Avg.
			BATTING											FIELDING			
1968	—American	2B	1	0	0	0	0	0	0	.000	0	1	0	1	1	0	1.000
1969	—American	Selected, did not play—injured.															
1970	—American	2B	5	0	1	0	0	0	0	.200	0	1	0	5	1	0	1.000
1973	—National	2B	1	0	0	0	0	0	0	.000	0	0	0	1	1	0	1.000
All-Star Game totals (3 years)			7	0	1	0	0	0	0	.143	0	2	0	7	3	0	1.000

RECORD AS MANAGER

BACKGROUND: Instructor, New York Mets organization (1982). . . . Consultant, Cincinnati Reds (December 31, 1992-May 24, 1993).
HONORS: Coach, N.L. All-Star team (1986).

	REGULAR SEASON				POSTSEASON							
					Playoff		Champ. Series		World Series		All-Star Game	
Year Team (League)	W	L	Pct.	Pos.	W	L	W	L	W	L	W	L
1979— Miami (Inter-American)	43	17	.717	1st	—	—	—	—	—	—	—	—
— (Second half)	8	4	.667	1st	—	—	—	—	—	—	—	—
1981— Jackson (Texas)	39	27	.591	1st (E)	—	—	—	—	—	—	—	—
— (Second half)	29	39	.426	3rd (E)	5	1	—	—	—	—	—	—
1983— Tidewater (International)	71	68	.511	4th	6	3	—	—	—	—	—	—
1984— New York (N.L.)	90	72	.556	2nd (E)	—	—	—	—	—	—	—	—
1985— New York (N.L.)	98	64	.605	2nd (E)	—	—	—	—	—	—	—	—
1986— New York (N.L.)	108	54	.667	1st (E)	—	—	4	2	4	3	—	—
1987— New York (N.L.)	92	70	.568	2nd (E)	—	—	—	—	—	—	1	0
1988— New York (N.L.)	100	60	.625	1st (E)	—	—	3	4	—	—	—	—
1989— New York (N.L.)	87	75	.537	2nd (E)	—	—	—	—	—	—	—	—
1990— New York (N.L.)	20	22	.476		—	—	—	—	—	—	—	—
1993— Cincinnati (N.L.)	53	65	.449	5th (W)	—	—	—	—	—	—	—	—
1994— Cincinnati (N.L.)	66	48	.579		—	—	—	—	—	—	—	—
1995— Cincinnati (N.L.)	85	59	.590	1st (C)	3	0	0	4	—	—	—	—
Major league totals (10 years)	799	589	.576		3	0	7	10	4	3	1	0

NOTES:
1979—Inter-American League folded June 30. Miami finished first in both halves of season and was declared league champion.
1981—Defeated Tulsa, two games to one, in playoffs; defeated San Antonio, three games to none, in league championship.
1983—Defeated Columbus, three games to two, in playoffs; defeated Richmond, three games to one, in league championship.
1986—Defeated Houston in N.L. Championship Series; defeated Boston in World Series.
1988—Lost to Los Angeles in N.L. Championship Series.
1990—Replaced as New York manager by Bud Harrelson, with club in fourth place (May 29).
1993—Replaced Cincinnati manager Tony Perez, with club in fifth place and record of 20-24 (May 24).
1994—Cincinnati was in first place in N.L. Central at time of season-ending strike (August 12).
1995—Defeated Los Angeles in N.L. divisional playoff; lost to Atlanta in N.L. Championship Series.

KELLY, TOM — TWINS

PERSONAL: Born August 15, 1950, in Graceville, Minn. . . . 5-11/185. . . . Batted left, threw left. . . . Full name: Jay Thomas Kelly.
HIGH SCHOOL: St. Mary's (South Amboy, N.J.).
COLLEGE: Monmouth College (N.J.).
TRANSACTIONS/CAREER NOTES: Selected by Seattle Pilots organization in eighth round of free-agent draft (June 7, 1968). . . . Seattle franchise moved to Milwaukee and renamed Brewers (1970). . . . On temporarily inactive list (April 16-20, April 25-30 and August 21, 1970-remainder of season). . . . On military list (August 27, 1970-February 3, 1971). . . . Released by Jacksonville (April 6, 1971). . . . Signed by Charlotte, Minnesota Twins organization (April 28, 1971). . . . Loaned by Twins organization to Rochester, Baltimore Orioles organization (April 5-September 22, 1976). . . . On temporarily inactive list (April 15-19, 1977). . . . On disabled list (July 25-August 4, 1977). . . . Released by Toledo (December 18, 1978). . . . Signed by Visalia, Twins organization (January 2, 1979). . . . Released by Visalia (December 2, 1980).
STATISTICAL NOTES: Led Pacific Coast League outfielders with six double plays in 1972.

		BATTING												FIELDING			
Year Team (League)	Pos.	G	AB	R	H	2B	3B	HR	RBI	Avg.	BB	SO	SB	PO	A	E	Avg.
1968— Newark (NYP)	OF	65	218	50	69	11	4	2	10	.317	43	31	*16	*144	*9	3	.981
1969— Clinton (Midwest)	OF	100	269	47	60	10	2	6	35	.223	82	31	10	158	15	4	.977
1970— Jacksonv. (South.)	OF-1B	93	266	33	64	10	1	8	38	.241	41	37	2	204	19	4	.982
1971— Charlotte (South.)■	1B-OF	100	303	50	89	17	0	6	41	.294	59	52	2	508	38	9	.984
1972— Tacoma (PCL)	OF-1B	132	407	76	114	19	2	10	52	.280	70	95	4	282	19	10	.968
1973— Tacoma (PCL)	OF-1B	114	337	67	87	10	2	17	49	.258	89	64	4	200	20	6	.973
1974— Tacoma (PCL)	OF-1B	115	357	68	110	16	0	18	69	.308	78	41	4	514	41	3	.995
1975— Tacoma (PCL)	OF-1B	62	202	38	51	5	0	9	29	.252	47	36	6	185	12	6	.970
— Minnesota (A.L.)	1B-DH-OF	49	127	11	23	5	0	1	11	.181	15	22	0	360	28	6	.985
1976— Rochester (Int'l)■	OF-1B	127	405	71	117	19	3	18	70	.289	85	71	2	323	28	4	.989
1977— Tacoma (PCL)■	1B-OF-P	113	363	80	99	12	1	12	64	.273	78	61	11	251	15	6	.978
1978— Toledo (Int'l)	1B-OF	119	325	47	74	13	0	10	49	.228	*91	61	2	556	46	5	.992
1979— Visalia (California)	1B-P	2	0	0	0	0	0	0	0	...	1	0	0	3	4	0	1.000
Major league totals (1 year)		49	127	11	23	5	0	1	11	.181	15	22	0	360	28	6	.985

RECORD AS PITCHER

Year Team (League)	W	L	Pct.	ERA	G	GS	CG	ShO	Sv.	IP	H	R	ER	BB	SO
1977— Tacoma (PCL)	0	0	...	6.00	1	0	0	0	0	3	2	2	2	3	0
1979— Visalia (California)	1	0	1.000	2.25	1	1	0	0	0	8	5	3	2	7	2
1980— Visalia (California)	0	0	...	0.69	2	1	0	0	0	13	12	1	1	6	2

RECORD AS MANAGER

BACKGROUND: Player/manager, Tacoma, Minnesota Twins organization (June 1977-remainder of season). . . . Player/coach, Toledo, Twins organization (1978). . . . Coach, Twins (1983-September 11, 1986).
HONORS: Named California League Manager of the Year (1979). . . . Named California League co-Manager of the Year (1980). . . . Named Southern League Manager of the Year (1981). . . . Coach, A.L. All-Star team (1991). . . . Named A.L. Manager of the Year by The Sporting News (1991). . . . Named A.L. Manager of the Year by the Baseball Writers' Association of America (1991).

	REGULAR SEASON				POSTSEASON							
					Playoff		Champ. Series		World Series		All-Star Game	
Year Team (League)	W	L	Pct.	Pos.	W	L	W	L	W	L	W	L
1977— Tacoma (Pacific Coast)	28	26	.519	3rd (W)	—	—	—	—	—	—	—	—
1979— Visalia (California)	44	26	.629	1st (S)	1	2	—	—	—	—	—	—
— (Second half)	42	28	.600	2nd (S)	—	—	—	—	—	—	—	—

Year	Team (League)	REGULAR SEASON W	L	Pct.	Pos.	POSTSEASON Playoff W	L	Champ. Series W	L	World Series W	L	All-Star Game W	L
1980—	Visalia (California)	27	43	.386	4th (S)	—	—	—	—	—	—	—	—
	—(Second half)	44	26	.629	1st (S)	2	3	—	—	—	—	—	—
1981—	Orlando (Southern)	42	27	.609	1st (E)	6	2	—	—	—	—	—	—
	—(Second half)	37	36	.507	3rd (E)	—	—	—	—	—	—	—	—
1982—	Orlando (Southern)	31	38	.449	5th (E)	—	—	—	—	—	—	—	—
	—(Second half)	43	32	.573	2nd (E)	—	—	—	—	—	—	—	—
1986—	Minnesota (A.L.)	12	11	.522	6th (W)	—	—	—	—	—	—	—	—
1987—	Minnesota (A.L.)	85	77	.525	1st (W)	—	—	4	1	4	3	—	—
1988—	Minnesota (A.L.)	91	71	.562	2nd (W)	—	—	—	—	—	—	1	0
1989—	Minnesota (A.L.)	80	82	.494	5th (W)	—	—	—	—	—	—	—	—
1990—	Minnesota (A.L.)	74	88	.457	7th (W)	—	—	—	—	—	—	—	—
1991—	Minnesota (A.L.)	95	67	.586	1st (W)	—	—	4	1	4	3	—	—
1992—	Minnesota (A.L.)	90	72	.556	2nd (W)	—	—	—	—	—	—	1	0
1993—	Minnesota (A.L.)	71	91	.438	T5th (W)	—	—	—	—	—	—	—	—
1994—	Minnesota (A.L.)	53	60	.469		—	—	—	—	—	—	—	—
1995—	Minnesota (A.L.)	56	88	.389	5th (C)	—	—	—	—	—	—	—	—
Major league totals (10 years)		707	707	.500		—	—	8	2	8	6	2	0

NOTES:

1977—Replaced Tacoma manager Del Wilber with record of 40-49 and became player/manager (June).
1979—Lost to San Jose in semifinals.
1980—Defeated Fresno, two games to one, in semifinals; lost to Stockton, three games to none, in league championship.
1981—Defeated Savannah, three games to one, in semifinals; defeated Nashville, three games to one, in league championship.
1986—Replaced Minnesota manager Ray Miller with club in seventh place and record of 59-80 (September 12).
1987—Defeated Detroit in A.L. Championship Series; defeated St. Louis in World Series.
1991—Defeated Toronto in A.L. Championship Series; defeated Atlanta in World Series.
1994—Minnesota was in fourth place in A.L. Central at time of season-ending strike (August 12).

KENNEDY, KEVIN — RED SOX

PERSONAL: Born September 26, 1954, in Los Angeles. . . . 6-3/220. . . . Batted right, threw right. . . . Full name: Kevin Curtis Kennedy.
HIGH SCHOOL: Taft (Woodland Hills, Calif.).
COLLEGE: San Diego State, then Cal State Northridge (degree in accounting).
TRANSACTIONS/CAREER NOTES: Selected by Baltimore Orioles organization in eighth round of free-agent draft (June 8, 1976). . . . On Rochester disabled list (June 10-July 6, 1981). . . . Released by Orioles organization (July 6, 1981). . . . Signed by St. Louis Cardinals organization (July 12, 1981). . . . Released by Cardinals organization (April 25, 1982). . . . Signed by Los Angeles Dodgers organization (April 29, 1982). . . . Granted free agency (October 22, 1982). . . . Served as coach of Lodi, Dodgers organization (February 9-May 16, 1983). . . . Signed as player by Albuquerque, Dodgers organization (May 16, 1983). . . . Released by Albuquerque (June 2, 1983). . . . Re-signed as coach of Lodi (June 2, 1983).
STATISTICAL NOTES: Led International League catchers with 10 double plays in 1979.

Year	Team (League)	Pos.	BATTING G	AB	R	H	2B	3B	HR	RBI	Avg.	BB	SO	SB	FIELDING PO	A	E	Avg.
1976—	Bluefield (Appal.)	C	21	81	9	22	4	0	1	10	.272	10	9	1	160	25	3	.984
	—Charlotte (South.)	C	40	123	21	27	4	0	0	5	.220	18	19	2	210	24	2	.992
1977—	Charlotte (South.)	C	36	115	12	29	7	0	0	14	.252	11	18	0	194	22	7	.969
	—Rochester (Int'l)	C	14	43	2	12	2	0	0	3	.279	0	4	0	67	3	1	.986
1978—	Rochester (Int'l)	C	123	410	46	104	17	2	4	58	.254	41	67	3	548	53	8	.987
1979—	Rochester (Int'l)	C	109	360	28	71	8	4	3	32	.197	26	40	0	586	56	7	.989
1980—	Rochester (Int'l)	C	77	232	21	61	8	0	1	28	.263	21	33	0	318	37	4	.989
1981—	Rochester (Int'l)	C	24	71	5	13	2	0	0	5	.183	4	12	0	91	11	4	.962
	—Springfield (A.A.)■	C	9	23	2	3	1	0	0	0	.130	3	3	0	37	2	0	1.000
1982—	Louisville (A.A.)	C	4	9	0	1	0	0	0	1	.111	2	2	0	18	1	1	.950
	—Albuquerque (PCL)■	C-P	51	137	17	39	5	0	3	20	.285	10	22	3	217	22	7	.972
1983—	Albuquerque (PCL)	C-P	2	3	1	0	0	0	0	2	.000	1	0	0	9	0	0	1.000

RECORD AS PITCHER

Year	Team (League)	W	L	Pct.	ERA	G	GS	CG	ShO	Sv.	IP	H	R	ER	BB	SO
1982—	Albuquerque (PCL)	0	0	. . .	9.00	1	0	0	0	0	1	2	1	1	0	0
1983—	Albuquerque (PCL)	0	0	. . .	0.00	1	0	0	0	0	1 1/3	1	0	0	0	0

RECORD AS MANAGER

BACKGROUND: Coach, Lodi, Los Angeles Dodgers organization (February 9-May 16 and June 2, 1983-remainder of season). . . . Director, minor league field operations, Montreal Expos (October 31, 1991-May 22, 1992). . . . Coach, Expos (May 22, 1992-remainder of season).
HONORS: Named Pioneer League Manager of the Year (1985). . . . Named Pacific Coast League Manager of the Year (1990).

Year	Team (League)	REGULAR SEASON W	L	Pct.	Pos.	POSTSEASON Playoff W	L	Champ. Series W	L	World Series W	L	All-Star Game W	L
1984—	Great Falls (Pioneer)	37	31	.544	2nd (N)	—	—	—	—	—	—	—	—
1985—	Great Falls (Pioneer)	54	16	.771	1st (N)	2	3	—	—	—	—	—	—
1986—	Great Falls (Pioneer)	40	30	.571	2nd	1	3	—	—	—	—	—	—
1987—	Bakersfield (California)	41	31	.569	2nd (S)	0	1	—	—	—	—	—	—
	—(Second half)	37	34	.521	2nd (S)	—	—	—	—	—	—	—	—
1988—	San Antonio (Texas)	42	26	.618	1st (W)	—	—	—	—	—	—	—	—
	—(Second half)	31	34	.477	3rd (W)	0	2	—	—	—	—	—	—
1989—	Albuquerque (Pacific Coast)	36	35	.507	3rd (S)	—	—	—	—	—	—	—	—
	—(Second half)	44	27	.620	1st (S)	4	5	—	—	—	—	—	—
1990—	Albuquerque (Pacific Coast)	46	25	.648	1st (S)	—	—	—	—	—	—	—	—

Year	Team (League)	REGULAR SEASON W	L	Pct.	Pos.	POSTSEASON Playoff W	L	Champ. Series W	L	World Series W	L	All-Star Game W	L
	—(Second half)	45	26	.634	1st (S)	6	2	—	—	—	—	—	—
1991	—Albuquerque (Pacific Coast)	38	30	.559	3rd (S)	—	—	—	—	—	—	—	—
	—(Second half)	42	28	.600	2nd (S)	—	—	—	—	—	—	—	—
1993	—Texas (A.L.)	86	76	.531	2nd (W)	—	—	—	—	—	—	—	—
1994	—Texas (A.L.)	52	62	.456		—	—	—	—	—	—	—	—
1995	—Boston (A.L.)	86	58	.597	1st (E)	0	3	—	—	—	—	—	—
Major league totals (3 years)		224	196	.533		0	3	—	—	—	—	—	—

NOTES:

1985—Lost to Salt Lake City in league championship.
1986—Lost to Salt Lake City in league championship.
1987—Lost to El Paso in one-game playoff for first-half title.
1988—Lost to El Paso in playoffs.
1989—Defeated Colorado Springs, three games to two, in playoffs; lost to Vancouver, three games to one, in league championship.
1990—Defeated Colorado Springs, three games to two, in playoffs; defeated Edmonton, three games to none, in league championship.
1994—Texas was in first place in A.L. West at time of season-ending strike (August 12).
1995—Lost to Cleveland in A.L. divisional playoff.

KNIGHT, RAY — REDS

PERSONAL: Born December 28, 1952, in Albany, Ga. . . . 6-2/190. . . . Batted right, threw right. . . . Full name: Charles Ray Knight. . . . Husband of Nancy Lopez, professional golfer.

HIGH SCHOOL: Dougherty (Albany, Ga.).

TRANSACTIONS/CAREER NOTES: Selected by Cincinnati Reds organization in 10th round of free-agent draft (June 4, 1970). . . . On disabled list (June 21-July 2, 1976 and April 17-May 8, 1978). . . . Traded by Reds to Houston Astros for 1B/OF Cesar Cedeno (December 18, 1981). . . . Traded by Astros to New York Mets for three players to be named later (August 28, 1984); Astros acquired OF Gerald Young, IF Manny Lee (August 31, 1984) and P Mitch Cook (September 10, 1984) to complete deal. . . . On disabled list (March 30-April 20, 1985). . . . Granted free agency (November 12, 1986). . . . Signed by Baltimore Orioles (February 12, 1987). . . . Traded by Orioles to Detroit Tigers for P Mark Thurmond (February 27, 1988). . . . Released by Tigers (November 16, 1988).

RECORDS: Shares major league records for most home runs in one inning—2; and most total bases in one inning—8 (May 13, 1980, fifth inning).

HONORS: Named N.L. Comeback Player of the Year by THE SPORTING NEWS (1986).

STATISTICAL NOTES: Tied for American Association lead in double plays by third basemen with 24 in 1974. . . . Led American Association third basemen with 102 putouts in 1976. . . . Tied for N.L. lead in grounding into double plays with 24 in 1980. . . . Led N.L. in grounding into double plays with 18 in 1981. . . . Career major league grand slams: 4.

Year	Team (League)	Pos.	BATTING G	AB	R	H	2B	3B	HR	RBI	Avg.	BB	SO	SB	FIELDING PO	A	E	Avg.
1971	—Sioux Falls (North.)	OF-IF-P	64	239	34	68	5	2	6	31	.285	26	27	6	69	79	17	.897
1972	—Three Rivers (East.)	OF-IF-P	97	302	25	64	8	1	2	35	.212	21	41	2	102	142	20	.924
1973	—Three Rivers (East.)	0-3-1-2	57	193	41	54	14	2	2	22	.280	28	33	1	76	57	7	.950
	—Indianapolis (A.A.)	3-0-1-P	78	253	20	55	10	4	1	16	.217	24	40	3	72	126	11	.947
1974	—Indianapolis (A.A.)	3B	107	352	36	80	13	4	5	37	.227	17	51	2	94	177	11	*.961
	—Cincinnati (N.L.)	3B	14	11	1	2	1	0	0	2	.182	1	2	0	2	8	0	1.000
1975	—Indianapolis (A.A.)	3B	123	434	58	118	16	5	4	48	.272	40	51	3	*116	227	17	.953
1976	—Indianapolis (A.A.)	3B-1B	110	396	47	106	24	3	10	41	.268	36	50	2	†136	181	13	.961
1977	—Cincinnati (N.L.)	3-2-O-S	80	92	8	24	5	1	1	13	.261	9	16	1	45	45	4	.957
1978	—Cincinnati (N.L.)	3-2-O-S-1	83	65	7	13	3	0	1	4	.200	3	13	0	13	41	7	.885
1979	—Cincinnati (N.L.)	3B	150	551	64	175	37	4	10	79	.318	38	57	4	120	262	15	.962
1980	—Cincinnati (N.L.)	3B	162	618	71	163	39	7	14	78	.264	36	62	1	120	291	13	.969
1981	—Cincinnati (N.L.)	3B	106	386	43	100	23	1	6	34	.259	33	51	2	69	176	11	.957
1982	—Houston (N.L.)■	1B-3B	158	609	72	179	36	6	6	70	.294	48	58	2	1002	186	17	.986
1983	—Houston (N.L.)	1B	145	507	43	154	36	4	9	70	.304	42	62	0	1285	73	9	.993
1984	—Houston (N.L.)	3B-1B	88	278	15	62	10	0	2	29	.223	14	30	0	236	95	7	.979
	—New York (N.L.)■	3B-1B	27	93	13	26	4	0	1	6	.280	7	13	0	20	37	2	.966
1985	—New York (N.L.)	3B-2B-1B	90	271	22	59	12	0	6	36	.218	13	32	1	56	113	7	.960
1986	—New York (N.L.)	3B-1B	137	486	51	145	24	2	11	76	.298	40	63	2	94	204	16	.949
1987	—Baltimore (A.L.)■	3B-1B	150	563	46	144	24	0	14	65	.256	39	90	0	169	284	19	.960
1988	—Detroit (A.L.)■	1B-3B-OF	105	299	34	65	12	2	3	33	.217	20	30	1	438	42	4	.992
American League totals (2 years)			255	862	80	209	36	2	17	98	.242	59	120	1	607	326	23	.976
National League totals (11 years)			1240	3967	410	1102	230	25	67	497	.278	284	459	13	3062	1531	108	.977
Major league totals (13 years)			1495	4829	490	1311	266	27	84	595	.271	343	579	14	3669	1857	131	.977

CHAMPIONSHIP SERIES RECORD

Year	Team (League)	Pos.	BATTING G	AB	R	H	2B	3B	HR	RBI	Avg.	BB	SO	SB	FIELDING PO	A	E	Avg.
1979	—Cincinnati (N.L.)	3B	3	14	0	4	1	0	0	0	.286	0	2	1	0	5	0	1.000
1986	—New York (N.L.)	3B	6	24	1	4	0	0	0	2	.167	1	5	0	5	19	1	.960
Championship series totals (2 years)			9	38	1	8	1	0	0	2	.211	1	7	1	5	24	1	.967

WORLD SERIES RECORD

NOTES: Named Most Valuable Player (1986). . . . Member of World Series championship team (1986).

Year	Team (League)	Pos.	BATTING G	AB	R	H	2B	3B	HR	RBI	Avg.	BB	SO	SB	FIELDING PO	A	E	Avg.
1986	—New York (N.L.)	3B	6	23	4	9	1	0	1	5	.391	2	2	0	5	6	1	.917

ALL-STAR GAME RECORD

Year	League	Pos.	BATTING AB	R	H	2B	3B	HR	RBI	Avg.	BB	SO	SB	FIELDING PO	A	E	Avg.
1980	—National	3B	1	1	1	0	0	0	0	1.000	1	0	1	0	1	0	1.000
1982	—National	3B	3	0	0	0	0	0	0	.000	0	1	0	1	4	0	1.000
All-Star Game totals (2 years)			4	1	1	0	0	0	0	.250	1	1	1	1	5	0	1.000

RECORD AS PITCHER

Year	Team (League)	W	L	Pct.	ERA	G	GS	CG	ShO	Sv.	IP	H	R	ER	BB	SO
1971	—Sioux Falls (North.)	1	1	.500	11.25	3	0	0	0	0	4	5	6	5	5	4
1972	—Three Rivers (East.)	0	0	. . .	2.25	2	0	0	0	0	4	3	1	1	4	2
1973	—Indianapolis (A.A.)	0	0	. . .	4.50	1	0	0	0	0	2	2	1	1	4	0

RECORD AS MANAGER

BACKGROUND: Coach, Cincinnati Reds (1993-94). . . . Assistant manager, Reds (1995).

LA RUSSA, TONY — CARDINALS

PERSONAL: Born October 4, 1944, in Tampa, Fla. . . . 6-0/185. . . . Batted right, threw right. . . . Full name: Anthony La Russa Jr.
HIGH SCHOOL: Jefferson (Tampa, Fla.).
COLLEGE: University of Tampa (Fla.), South Florida (degree in industrial management) and Florida State (law degree, 1980).
TRANSACTIONS/CAREER NOTES: Signed by Kansas City Athletics organization (June 6, 1962). . . . On disabled list (May 9-September 8, 1964; June 3-July 15, 1965; and April 12-May 6 and July 3-September 5, 1967). . . . A's franchise moved from Kansas City to Oakland (October 1967). . . . Contract sold by A's to Atlanta Braves (August 14, 1971). . . . Traded by Braves to Chicago Cubs for P Tom Phoebus (October 20, 1972). . . . Contract sold by Cubs to Pittsburgh Pirates organization (March 23, 1974). . . . Released by Pirates organization (April 4, 1975). . . . Signed by Chicago White Sox organization (April 7, 1975). . . . On disabled list (August 8-18, 1976). . . . Contract sold by White Sox to St. Louis Cardinals organization (December 13, 1976). . . . Released by Cardinals organization (September 29, 1977).
STATISTICAL NOTES: Led International League in being hit by pitch with 11 in 1972.

			BATTING											FIELDING			
Year	Team (League)	Pos.	G	AB	R	H	2B	3B	HR	RBI	Avg.	BB	SO	SB	PO	A	E	Avg.
1962	—Day. Beach (FSL)	SS	64	225	37	58	7	0	1	32	.258	42	47	11	135	173	38	.890
	—Binghamton (East.)	SS-2B	12	43	3	8	0	0	0	4	.186	5	9	2	20	27	8	.855
1963	—Kansas City (A.L.)	SS-2B	34	44	4	11	1	1	0	1	.250	7	12	0	29	25	2	.964
1964	—Lewiston (N'west)	2B-SS	90	329	50	77	22	1	1	25	.234	53	56	10	188	218	18	.958
1965	—Birm. (Southern)	2B	75	259	24	50	11	2	1	18	.193	26	37	5	202	161	21	.945
1966	—Modesto (Calif.)	2B	81	316	67	92	20	1	7	54	.291	44	37	18	201	212	20	.954
	—Mobile (Southern)	2B	51	170	20	50	9	4	4	26	.294	23	24	4	117	133	10	.962
1967	—Birm. (Southern)	2B	41	139	12	32	6	1	5	22	.230	10	11	3	88	120	5	.977
1968	—Oakland (A.L.)	PH	5	3	0	1	0	0	0	0	.333	0	0	0	. . .	. . .	. . .	. . .
	—Vancouver (PCL)	2B	122	455	55	109	16	8	5	29	.240	52	58	4	249	321	14	*.976
1969	—Iowa (Am. Assoc.)	2B	67	235	37	72	11	1	4	27	.306	0	1	5	177	222	15	.964
	—Oakland (A.L.)	PH	8	8	0	0	0	0	0	0	.000	42	30	0	. . .	. . .	. . .	. . .
1970	—Iowa (Am. Assoc.)	2B	22	88	13	22	5	0	2	5	.250	9	14	0	52	59	3	.974
	—Oakland (A.L.)	2B	52	106	6	21	4	1	0	6	.198	15	19	0	67	89	5	.969
1971	—Iowa (Am. Assoc.)	2-3-S-O	28	107	21	31	5	1	2	11	.290	10	11	0	70	85	2	.987
	—Oakland (A.L.)	2B-SS-3B	23	8	3	0	0	0	0	0	.000	0	4	0	8	7	2	.882
	—Atlanta (N.L.)■	2B	9	7	1	2	0	0	0	0	.286	1	1	0	8	6	1	.933
1972	—Richmond (Int'l)	2B	122	389	68	120	13	2	10	42	.308	72	41	0	305	289	20	.967
1973	—Wichita (A.A.)■	2B-1B-3B	106	392	82	123	16	0	5	75	.314	60	46	10	423	213	26	.961
	—Chicago (N.L.)	PR	1	0	1	0	0	0	0	0	. . .	0	0	0	. . .	. . .	. . .	. . .
1974	—Char., W.Va. (Int'l)■	2B	139	457	50	119	17	1	8	35	.260	51	50	4	262	*378	17	.974
1975	—Denver (A.A.)■	3-O-S-2	118	354	87	99	23	2	7	46	.280	70	46	13	95	91	10	.949
1976	—Iowa (Am. Assoc.)	3-2-S-1-O-P	107	332	53	86	11	0	4	34	.259	40	43	10	132	160	22	.930
1977	—New Orleans (A.A.)■	2B-3B	50	128	17	24	2	2	3	6	.188	20	21	0	66	87	7	.956
American League totals (5 years)			122	169	13	33	5	2	0	7	.195	64	65	0	104	121	9	.962
National League totals (2 years)			10	7	2	2	0	0	0	0	.286	1	1	0	8	6	1	.933
Major league totals (6 years)			132	176	15	35	5	2	0	7	.199	65	66	0	112	127	10	.960

RECORD AS PITCHER

Year	Team (League)	W	L	Pct.	ERA	G	GS	CG	ShO	Sv.	IP	H	R	ER	BB	SO
1976	—Iowa (Am. Assoc.)	0	0	. . .	3.00	3	0	0	0	0	3	3	1	1	0	0

RECORD AS MANAGER

BACKGROUND: Coach, St. Louis Cardinals organization (June 20-September 29, 1977). . . . Coach, Chicago White Sox (July 3, 1978-remainder of season).
RECORDS: Shares major league single-season record for most clubs managed—2 (1986).
HONORS: Named Major League Manager of the Year by The Sporting News (1983). . . . Named A.L. Manager of the Year by the Baseball Writers' Association of America (1983, 1988 and 1992). . . . Coach, A.L. All-Star team (1984 and 1987). . . . Named A.L. Manager of the Year by The Sporting News (1988 and 1992).

		REGULAR SEASON				POSTSEASON							
						Playoff		Champ. Series		World Series		All-Star Game	
Year	Team (League)	W	L	Pct.	Pos.	W	L	W	L	W	L	W	L
1978	—Knoxville (Southern)	49	21	.700	1st (W)	—	—	—	—	—	—	—	—
	—(Second half)	4	4	.500		—	—	—	—	—	—	—	—
1979	—Iowa (American Association)	54	52	.509		—	—	—	—	—	—	—	—
	—Chicago (A.L.)	27	27	.500	5th (W)	—	—	—	—	—	—	—	—
1980	—Chicago (A.L.)	70	90	.438	5th (W)	—	—	—	—	—	—	—	—
1981	—Chicago (A.L.)	31	22	.585	3rd (W)	—	—	—	—	—	—	—	—
	—(Second half)	23	30	.434	6th (W)	—	—	—	—	—	—	—	—
1982	—Chicago (A.L.)	87	75	.537	3rd (W)	—	—	—	—	—	—	—	—
1983	—Chicago (A.L.)	99	63	.611	1st (W)	—	—	1	3	—	—	—	—
1984	—Chicago (A.L.)	74	88	.457	T5th (W)	—	—	—	—	—	—	—	—
1985	—Chicago (A.L.)	85	77	.525	3rd (W)	—	—	—	—	—	—	—	—
1986	—Chicago (A.L.)	26	38	.406		—	—	—	—	—	—	—	—
	—Oakland (A.L.)	45	34	.570	T3rd (W)	—	—	—	—	—	—	—	—
1987	—Oakland (A.L.)	81	81	.500	3rd (W)	—	—	—	—	—	—	—	—
1988	—Oakland (A.L.)	104	58	.642	1st (W)	—	—	4	0	1	4	—	—

Year	Team (League)	REGULAR SEASON W	L	Pct.	Pos.	POSTSEASON Playoff W	L	Champ. Series W	L	World Series W	L	All-Star Game W	L
1989—	Oakland (A.L.)	99	63	.611	1st (W)	—	—	4	1	4	0	1	0
1990—	Oakland (A.L.)	103	59	.636	1st (W)	—	—	4	0	0	4	1	0
1991—	Oakland (A.L.)	84	78	.519	4th (W)	—	—	—	—	—	—	1	0
1992—	Oakland (A.L.)	96	66	.593	1st (W)	—	—	2	4	—	—	—	—
1993—	Oakland (A.L.)	68	94	.420	7th (W)	—	—	—	—	—	—	—	—
1994—	Oakland (A.L.)	51	63	.447		—	—	—	—	—	—	—	—
1995—	Oakland (A.L.)	67	77	.465	4th (W)	—	—	—	—	—	—	—	
Major league totals (17 years)		1320	1183	.527		—	—	15	8	5	8	3	0

NOTES:

1978—Became Chicago White Sox coach and replaced as Knoxville manager by Joe Jones, with club in third place (July 3).

1979—Replaced as Iowa manager by Joe Sparks, with club in second place (August 3); replaced Chicago manager Don Kessinger with club in fifth place and record of 46-60 (August 3).

1983—Lost to Baltimore in A.L. Championship Series.

1986—Replaced as White Sox manager by interim manager Doug Rader, with club in sixth place (June 20); replaced Oakland manager Jackie Moore (record of 29-44) and interim manager Jeff Newman (record of 2-8) with club in seventh place and record of 31-52 (July 7).

1988—Defeated Boston in A.L. Championship Series; lost to Los Angeles in World Series.

1989—Defeated Toronto in A.L. Championship Series; defeated San Francisco in World Series.

1990—Defeated Boston in A.L. Championship Series; lost to Cincinnati in World Series.

1992—Lost to Toronto in A.L. Championship Series.

1993—On suspended list (October 1-remainder of season).

1994—Oakland was in second place in A.L. West at time of season-ending strike (August 12).

LACHEMANN, MARCEL — ANGELS

PERSONAL: Born June 13, 1941, in Los Angeles. . . . 6-1/185. . . . Threw right, batted right. . . . Full name: Marcel Ernest Lachemann. . . . Brother of Rene Lachemann, manager, Florida Marlins; and brother of Bill Lachemann, minor league catcher (1955-63). . . . Name pronounced LATCH-man.

HIGH SCHOOL: Dorsey (Los Angeles).

COLLEGE: Southern California (degree in business administration).

TRANSACTIONS/CAREER NOTES: Signed by Kansas City Athletics organization (February 7, 1963). . . . On military list (February 4-June 29, 1964). . . . A's franchise moved from Kansas City to Oakland (October 1967). . . . On temporarily inactive list (August 3-9, 1968 and August 12-17, 1968). . . . Released by A's organization (January 22, 1973). . . . Signed by Montreal Expos organization (February 11, 1973). . . . On disabled list (June 25-July 9, 1973).

Year	Team (League)	W	L	Pct.	ERA	G	GS	CG	ShO	Sv.	IP	H	R	ER	BB	SO
1963—	Day. Beach (FSL)	4	8	.333	4.15	36	9	1	0	8	115	100	68	53	78	99
1964—	Lewiston (N'west)	3	4	.429	2.81	26	1	0	0	7	48	42	17	15	18	33
1965—	Birmingham (Sou.)	4	11	.267	3.32	58	1	0	0	11	95	96	43	35	38	65
1966—	Vancouver (PCL)	1	3	.250	4.18	53	0	0	0	9	97	89	56	45	53	62
1967—	Birmingham (Sou.)	2	2	.500	4.57	35	0	0	0	5	63	62	41	32	29	39
1968—	Birmingham (Sou.)	2	2	.500	0.80	22	0	0	0	6	45	31	8	4	8	33
—	Vancouver (PCL)	1	0	1.000	2.73	14	0	0	0	1	33	40	15	10	7	17
1969—	Iowa (Am. Assoc.)	2	5	.286	2.47	20	0	0	0	5	51	54	16	14	8	36
—	Oakland (A.L.)	4	1	.800	3.95	28	0	0	0	2	43 1/3	43	24	19	19	16
1970—	Iowa (Am. Assoc.)	3	2	.600	2.45	11	0	0	0	4	22	25	8	6	7	17
—	Oakland (A.L.)	3	3	.500	2.78	41	0	0	0	3	58 1/3	58	20	18	18	39
1971—	Iowa (Am. Assoc.)	5	2	.714	3.04	43	1	0	0	11	74	73	36	25	29	37
—	Oakland (A.L.)	0	0	...	54.00	1	0	0	0	0	1/3	2	2	2	1	0
1972—	Iowa (Am. Assoc.)	6	7	.462	4.88	42	0	0	0	5	72	81	47	39	20	49
1973—	Quebec City (East.)■	2	3	.400	4.28	25	1	0	0	2	40	61	26	19	14	20
1974—	WP Beach (FSL)	7	4	.636	7.71	5	0	0	0	0	7	8	6	6	1	5
Major league totals (3 years)		7	4	.636	3.44	70	0	0	0	5	102	103	46	39	38	55

RECORD AS MANAGER

BACKGROUND: Pitching coach, Montreal Expos organization (1973-75). . . . Assistant baseball coach, University of Southern California (1977-81). . . . Minor league pitching instructor, California Angels organization (1982-83). . . . Pitching coach, Angels (1984-92). . . . Pitching coach, Florida Marlins (1993-May 17, 1994).

Year	Team (League)	REGULAR SEASON W	L	Pct.	Pos.	POSTSEASON Playoff W	L	Champ. Series W	L	World Series W	L	All-Star Game W	L
1994—	California (A.L.)	31	44	.413		—	—	—	—	—	—	—	—
1995—	California (A.L.)	78	67	.542	2nd (W)	—	—	—	—	—	—	—	—
Major league totals (2 years)		109	111	.495		—	—	—	—	—	—	—	—

NOTES:

1994—Replaced California manager Buck Rodgers with club in third place, record of 16-24 (May 17). California was in fourth place in A.L. West at time of season-ending baseball strike (August 12).

LACHEMANN, RENE — MARLINS

PERSONAL: Born May 4, 1945, in Los Angeles. . . . 6-0/200. . . . Batted right, threw right. . . . Full name: Rene George Lachemann. . . . Brother of Marcel Lachemann, manager, California Angels; and brother of Bill Lachemann, minor league catcher (1955-63). . . . Name pronounced LATCH-man.

HIGH SCHOOL: Dorsey (Los Angeles).

COLLEGE: Southern California.

TRANSACTIONS/CAREER NOTES: Signed as free agent by Kansas City Athletics organization (September 18, 1963). . . . On Mobile disabled list (July 19-29, 1966). . . . A's franchise moved from Kansas City to Oakland (October 1967). . . . Released by A's organization (October 26, 1972).

STATISTICAL NOTES: Led Midwest League catchers with 14 double plays in 1964. . . . Led Pacific Coast League catchers with 889 total chances and 13 double plays in 1967.

Year	Team (League)	Pos.	G	AB	R	H	2B	3B	HR	RBI	Avg.	BB	SO	SB	PO	A	E	Avg.
			BATTING												FIELDING			
1964—	Burlington (Midw.)	C	99	335	52	94	14	1	*24	82	.281	33	74	0	743	55	10	.988
—	Birm. (Southern)	C	3	6	1	4	1	0	0	1	.667	0	0	0	7	1	0	1.000
1965—	Kansas City (A.L.)	C	92	216	20	49	7	1	9	29	.227	12	57	0	361	27	8	.980
1966—	Mobile (Southern)	C	119	434	48	111	17	1	15	65	.256	32	104	0	819	48	13	.985
—	Kansas City (A.L.)	C	7	5	0	1	1	0	0	0	.200	0	1	0	10	1	0	1.000
1967—	Vancouver (PCL)	C	123	410	26	91	16	0	6	53	.222	31	100	0	*811	68	10	.989
1968—	Oakland (A.L.)	C	19	60	3	9	1	0	0	4	.150	1	11	0	82	5	3	.967
—	Vancouver (PCL)	C-1B	63	193	14	48	7	0	4	14	.249	18	48	0	351	22	7	.982
1969—	Iowa (Am. Assoc.)	1B-C	107	415	47	106	18	1	20	66	.255	35	91	1	782	62	10	.988
1970—	Iowa (Am. Assoc.)	1-3-2-C	61	171	25	44	10	0	5	20	.257	22	36	0	365	29	7	.983
1971—	Iowa (Am. Assoc.)	1-3-C-2	92	314	42	76	16	1	17	48	.242	23	76	1	542	65	10	.984
1972—	Iowa (Am. Assoc.)	1-C-O-3	95	236	25	51	6	0	11	37	.216	44	61	1	347	18	6	.984
Major league totals (3 years)			118	281	23	59	9	1	9	33	.210	13	69	0	453	33	11	.978

RECORD AS MANAGER

BACKGROUND: Coach, Boston Red Sox (October 29, 1984-86). . . . Coach, Oakland Athletics (November 18, 1986-92).

HONORS: Named Southern League Manager of the Year (1976).

Year	Team (League)	W	L	Pct.	Pos.	Playoff W	Playoff L	Champ. Series W	Champ. Series L	World Series W	World Series L	All-Star Game W	All-Star Game L
		REGULAR SEASON				POSTSEASON							
1973—	Burlington (Midwest)	24	23	.511	5th (S)	—	—	—	—	—	—	—	—
—	(Second half)	30	32	.484	3rd (S)	—	—	—	—	—	—	—	—
1974—	Burlington (Midwest)	29	28	.509	2nd (S)	—	—	—	—	—	—	—	—
—	(Second half)	32	31	.508	2nd (S)	—	—	—	—	—	—	—	—
1975—	Modesto (California)	33	37	.471	6th	—	—	—	—	—	—	—	—
—	(Second half)	35	35	.500	5th	—	—	—	—	—	—	—	—
1976—	Chattanooga (Southern)	34	30	.532	1st (W)	—	—	—	—	—	—	—	—
—	(Second half)	36	38	.486	2nd (W)	0	1	—	—	—	—	—	—
1977—	San Jose (Pacific Coast)	64	80	.444	4th	—	—	—	—	—	—	—	—
1978—	San Jose (Pacific Coast)	53	87	.379	5th	—	—	—	—	—	—	—	—
1979—	Spokane (Pacific Coast)	39	32	.549	2nd (N)	—	—	—	—	—	—	—	—
—	(Second half)	29	47	.382	5th (N)	—	—	—	—	—	—	—	—
1980—	Spokane (Pacific Coast)	24	41	.369	5th (N)	—	—	—	—	—	—	—	—
—	(Second half)	36	39	.480	2nd (N)	—	—	—	—	—	—	—	—
1981—	Spokane (Pacific Coast)	11	9	.550		—	—	—	—	—	—	—	—
—	Seattle (A.L.)	15	18	.455	6th (W)	—	—	—	—	—	—	—	—
—	Seattle (second half)	23	29	.442	5th (W)	—	—	—	—	—	—	—	—
1982—	Seattle (A.L.)	76	86	.469	4th (W)	—	—	—	—	—	—	—	—
1983—	Seattle (A.L.)	26	47	.356		—	—	—	—	—	—	—	—
1984—	Milwaukee (A.L.)	67	94	.416	7th (E)	—	—	—	—	—	—	—	—
1993—	Florida (N.L.)	64	98	.395	6th (E)	—	—	—	—	—	—	—	—
1994—	Florida (N.L.)	51	64	.443		—	—	—	—	—	—	—	—
1995—	Florida (N.L.)	67	76	.469	4th (E)	—	—	—	—	—	—	—	—
A.L. totals (4 years)		207	274	.430		—	—	—	—	—	—	—	—
N.L. totals (3 years)		182	238	.433		—	—	—	—	—	—	—	—
Major league totals (7 years)		389	512	.432		—	—	—	—	—	—	—	—>

NOTES:

1976—Lost to Montgomery in one-game playoff in West Division Championship.

1981—Left Spokane (second place) to replace Seattle manager Maury Wills, with club in seventh place and record of 6-18 (May 6).

1983—Replaced as Seattle manager by Del Crandall, with club in seventh place (June 25).

1994—Florida was in fifth place in N.L. East at time of season-ending strike (August 12).

LASORDA, TOM — DODGERS

PERSONAL: Born September 22, 1927, in Norristown, Pa. . . . 5-9/195. . . . Threw left, batted left. . . . Full name: Thomas Charles Lasorda. . . . Name pronounced luh-SORR-duh.

HIGH SCHOOL: Norristown (Pa.).

TRANSACTIONS/CAREER NOTES: On National Defense list (May 14, 1946-February 2, 1948). . . . On disabled list (July 9-19, 1948). . . . Selected by Nashua, Brooklyn Dodgers organization, from Philadelphia Phillies organization in Rule 5 minor league draft (November 24, 1948). . . . Contract sold by Brooklyn Dodgers organization to Kansas City Athletics (March 2, 1956). . . . Traded by A's to New York Yankees for P Wally Burnette and cash (July 11, 1956). . . . Contract sold by Yankees organization to Dodgers organization (May 26, 1957). . . . Released by Dodgers organization (July 9, 1960).

RECORDS: Shares N.L. record for most wild pitches in one inning—3 (May 5, 1955, first inning).

HONORS: Named International League Pitcher of the Year (1958).

STATISTICAL NOTES: Led Canadian-American League with 20 wild pitches in 1948. . . . Led International League with 14 wild pitches in 1953.

Year	Team (League)	W	L	Pct.	ERA	G	GS	CG	ShO	Sv.	IP	H	R	ER	BB	SO
1945—	Concord (N.C. St.)	3	12	.200	4.09	27	13	6	0	...	121	115	84	55	100	91
1946—							In military service.									
1947—							In military service.									
1948—	Schen. (Can.-Am.)	9	12	.429	4.64	32	18	11	0	...	192	180	122	99	153	195
1949—	Greenville (S. Atl.)■	7	7	.500	2.93	45	15	6	0	...	178	141	81	58	138	151
1950—	Montreal (Int'l)	9	4	.692	3.70	31	17	7	0	...	146	136	73	60	82	85
1951—	Montreal (Int'l)	12	8	.600	3.49	31	21	11	1	...	165	145	75	64	87	80

Year	Team (League)	W	L	Pct.	ERA	G	GS	CG	ShO	Sv.	IP	H	R	ER	BB	SO
1952—	Montreal (Int'l)	14	5	.737	3.66	33	27	12	5	...	182	156	90	74	93	77
1953—	Montreal (Int'l)	17	8	.680	2.81	36	29	12	3	...	208	171	77	65	94	122
1954—	Montreal (Int'l)	14	5	.737	3.51	23	21	13	1	...	154	142	66	60	79	75
—	Brooklyn (N.L.)	0	0	...	5.00	4	0	0	0	...	9	8	5	5	5	5
1955—	Brooklyn (N.L.)	0	0	...	13.50	4	1	0	0	...	4	5	6	6	6	4
—	Montreal (Int'l)	9	8	.529	3.27	22	21	11	3	...	143	125	58	52	62	92
1956—	Kansas City (A.L.)■	0	4	.000	6.20	18	5	0	0	...	45	40	38	31	45	28
—	Denver (Am. Assoc.)■	3	4	.429	4.99	16	13	2	0	...	83	94	54	46	34	54
1957—	Denver (Am. Assoc.)	0	2	.000	12.18	6	4	0	0	...	17	29	25	23	6	8
—	Los Angeles (PCL)■	7	10	.412	3.89	29	20	5	1	...	132	134	73	57	59	72
1958—	Montreal (Int'l)	*18	6	.750	2.50	34	31	*16	•5	...	*230	191	77	64	76	126
1959—	Montreal (Int'l)	12	8	.600	3.83	29	28	10	2	...	188	192	93	80	•77	64
1960—	Montreal (Int'l)	2	5	.286	8.20	12	10	1	0	...	45	79	48	41	24	17
A.L. totals (1 year)		0	4	.000	6.20	18	5	0	0	0	45	40	38	31	45	28
N.L. totals (2 years)		0	0	...	7.62	8	1	0	0	0	13	13	11	11	11	9
Major league totals (3 years)		0	4	.000	6.52	26	6	0	0	0	58	53	49	42	56	37

RECORD AS MANAGER

BACKGROUND: Scout, Los Angeles Dodgers (1961-65). . . . Manager, Dodgers farm team in Arizona Instructional League (1969). . . . Coach, Dodgers (1973-76).

HONORS: Named Pioneer League Manager of the Year (1967). . . . Named Pacific Coast League co-Manager of the Year (1970). . . . Named Minor League Manager of the Year by THE SPORTING NEWS (1970). . . . Coach, N.L. All-Star team (1977, 1983-84, 1986 and 1993). . . . Named N.L. Manager of the Year by the Baseball Writers' Association of America (1983 and 1988). . . . Named N.L. co-Manager of the Year by THE SPORTING NEWS (1988).

		REGULAR SEASON				POSTSEASON							
						Playoff		Champ. Series		World Series		All-Star Game	
Year	Team (League)	W	L	Pct.	Pos.	W	L	W	L	W	L	W	L
1965—	Pocatello (Pioneer)	33	33	.500	T2nd	—	—	—	—	—	—	—	—
1966—	Ogden (Pioneer)	39	27	.591	1st	—	—	—	—	—	—	—	—
1967—	Ogden (Pioneer)	41	25	.621	1st	—	—	—	—	—	—	—	—
1968—	Ogden (Pioneer)39	25	.609	1st	—	—	—	—	—	—	—	—	—
1969—	Spokane (Pacific Coast)	71	73	.493	2nd (N)	—	—	—	—	—	—	—	—
1970—	Spokane (Pacific Coast)	94	52	.630	1st (N)	4	0	—	—	—	—	—	—
1971—	Spokane (Pacific Coast)	69	76	.476	3rd (N)	—	—	—	—	—	—	—	—
1972—	Albuquerque (Pacific Coast)	92	56	.622	1st (E)	3	1	—	—	—	—	—	—
1976—	Los Angeles (N.L.)	2	2	.500	2nd (W)	—	—	—	—	—	—	—	—
1977—	Los Angeles (N.L.)	98	64	.605	1st (W)	—	—	3	1	2	4	—	—
1978—	Los Angeles (N.L.)	95	67	.586	1st (W)	—	—	3	1	2	4	1	0
1979—	Los Angeles (N.L.)	79	83	.488	3rd (W)	—	—	—	—	—	—	1	0
1980—	Los Angeles (N.L.)	92	71	.564	2nd (W)	—	—	—	—	—	—	—	—
1981—	Los Angeles (N.L.)	36	21	.632	1st (W)	—	—	—	—	—	—	—	—
—	(Second half)	27	26	.509	4th (W)	3	2	3	2	4	2	—	—
1982—	Los Angeles (N.L.)	88	74	.543	2nd (W)	—	—	—	—	—	—	1	0
1983—	Los Angeles (N.L.)	91	71	.562	1st (W)	—	—	1	3	—	—	—	—
1984—	Los Angeles (N.L.)	79	83	.488	4th (W)	—	—	—	—	—	—	—	—
1985—	Los Angeles (N.L.)	95	67	.586	1st (W)	—	—	2	4	—	—	—	—
1986—	Los Angeles (N.L.)	73	89	.451	5th (W)	—	—	—	—	—	—	—	—
1987—	Los Angeles (N.L.)	73	89	.451	4th (W)	—	—	—	—	—	—	—	—
1988—	Los Angeles (N.L.)	94	67	.584	1st (W)	—	—	4	3	4	1	—	—
1989—	Los Angeles (N.L.)	77	83	.481	4th (W)	—	—	—	—	—	—	0	1
1990—	Los Angeles (N.L.)	86	76	.531	2nd (W)	—	—	—	—	—	—	—	—
1991—	Los Angeles (N.L.)	93	69	.574	2nd (W)	—	—	—	—	—	—	—	—
1992—	Los Angeles (N.L.)	63	99	.389	6th (W)	—	—	—	—	—	—	—	—
1993—	Los Angeles (N.L.)	81	81	.500	4th (W)	—	—	—	—	—	—	—	—
1994—	Los Angeles (N.L.)	58	56	.509		—	—	—	—	—	—	—	—
1995—	Los Angeles (N.L.)	78	66	.542	1st (W)	0	3	—	—	—	—	—	—
Major league totals (20 years)		1558	1404	.526		3	5	16	14	12	11	3	1

NOTES:

1970—Defeated Hawaii in championship playoff.
1972—Defeated Eugene in championship playoff.
1976—Replaced retiring Los Angeles manager Walter Alston with club in second place and record of 90-68 (September 29).
1977—Defeated Philadelphia in N.L. Championship Series; lost to New York Yankees in World Series.
1978—Defeated Philadelphia in N.L. Championship Series; lost to New York Yankees in World Series.
1981—Defeated Houston in N.L. divisional playoffs; defeated Montreal in N.L. Championship Series; defeated New York Yankees in World Series.
1983—Lost to Philadelphia in N.L. Championship Series.
1985—Lost to St. Louis in N.L. Championship Series.
1988—Defeated New York Mets in N.L. Championship Series; defeated Oakland in World Series.
1994—Los Angeles was in first place in N.L. West at time of season-ending strike.
1995—Lost to Cincinnati in N.L. divisional playoff.

LEYLAND, JIM — PIRATES

PERSONAL: Born December 15, 1944, in Toledo, O. . . . 5-11/170. . . . Batted right, threw right. . . . Full name: James Richard Leyland. . . . Name pronounced LEE-lund.

HIGH SCHOOL: Perrysburg (O.).

TRANSACTIONS/CAREER NOTES: Signed as free agent by Detroit Tigers organization (September 21, 1963). . . . On disabled list (June 15-27, 1964). . . . Released by Rocky Mount, Tigers organization (March 27, 1971).

				BATTING										FIELDING			
Year Team (League)	Pos.	G	AB	R	H	2B	3B	HR	RBI	Avg.	BB	SO	SB	PO	A	E	Avg.
1964—Lakeland (Fla. St.)	C	52	129	8	25	0	1	0	8	.194	18	33	1	268	17	6	.979
—Cocoa Tigers (CRL)	C	24	52	2	12	1	1	0	4	.231	13	7	1	122	15	3	.979
1965—Jamestown (NYP)	C-3B-P	82	211	18	50	7	2	1	21	.237	37	44	2	318	36	6	.983
1966—Rocky Mount (Car.)	C	67	173	24	42	6	0	0	16	.243	32	35	0	369	23	1	.997
1967—Montgomery (Sou.)	C	62	171	11	40	3	0	1	16	.234	16	27	0	350	25	6	.984
1968—Montgomery (Sou.)	C-3B-SS	81	264	19	51	3	0	1	20	.193	14	54	2	511	43	7	.988
1969—Montgomery (Sou.)	C	16	39	1	8	0	0	0	1	.205	4	7	0	64	6	3	.959
—Lakeland (Fla. St.)	C-P	60	179	20	43	8	0	1	16	.240	31	17	0	321	28	4	.989
1970—Montgomery (Sou.)	C	2	3	0	0	0	0	0	0	.000	0	0	0	6	0	1	.857

RECORD AS PITCHER

Year Team (League)	W	L	Pct.	ERA	G	GS	CG	ShO	Sv.	IP	H	R	ER	BB	SO
1965—Jamestown (NYP)	0	0	...	0.00	1	0	0	0	...	2	2	0	0	0	1
1969—Lakeland (Fla. St.)	0	0	...	9.00	1	0	0	0	0	2	4	2	2	0	1

RECORD AS MANAGER

BACKGROUND: Coach, Detroit Tigers organization (1970-June 5, 1971); served as player/coach (1970). . . . Coach, Chicago White Sox (1982-85).

HONORS: Named Florida State League Manager of the Year (1977-78). . . . Named American Association Manager of the Year (1979). . . . Named N.L. co-Manager of the Year by THE SPORTING NEWS (1988). . . . Coach, N.L. All-Star team (1990-91 and 1994). . . . Named N.L. Manager of the Year by THE SPORTING NEWS (1990 and 1992). . . . Named N.L. Manager of the Year by the Baseball Writers' Association of America (1990 and 1992).

	REGULAR SEASON				POSTSEASON							
					Playoff		Champ. Series		World Series		All-Star Game	
Year Team (League)	W	L	Pct.	Pos.	W	L	W	L	W	L	W	L
1971—Bristol (Appalachian)	31	35	.470	3rd (S)	—	—	—	—	—	—	—	—
1972—Clinton (Midwest)	22	41	.349	5th (N)	—	—	—	—	—	—	—	—
—(Second half)	27	36	.429	4th (N)	—	—	—	—	—	—	—	—
1973—Clinton (Midwest)	36	26	.581	2nd (N)	—	—	—	—	—	—	—	—
—(Second half)	37	25	.597	1st (N)	0	2	—	—	—	—	—	—
1974—Montgomery (Southern)	61	76	.445	3rd (W)	—	—	—	—	—	—	—	—
1975—Clinton (Midwest)	29	31	.483	4th (S)	—	—	—	—	—	—	—	—
—(Second half)	38	30	.559	2nd (S)	—	—	—	—	—	—	—	—
1976—Lakeland (Florida State)	74	64	.536	2nd (N)	4	0	—	—	—	—	—	—
1977—Lakeland (Florida State)	85	53	.616	1st (N)	5	1	—	—	—	—	—	—
1978—Lakeland (Florida State)	31	38	.449	4th (N)	—	—	—	—	—	—	—	—
—(Second half)	47	22	.681	1st (N)	2	2	—	—	—	—	—	—
1979—Evansville (American Association)	78	58	.574	1st (E)	4	2	—	—	—	—	—	—
1980—Evansville (American Association)	61	74	.452	2nd (E)	—	—	—	—	—	—	—	—
1981—Evansville (American Association)	73	63	.537	1st (E)	1	3	—	—	—	—	—	—
1986—Pittsburgh (N.L.)	64	98	.395	6th (E)	—	—	—	—	—	—	—	—
1987—Pittsburgh (N.L.)	80	82	.494	T4th (E)	—	—	—	—	—	—	—	—
1988—Pittsburgh (N.L.)	85	75	.525	2nd (E)	—	—	—	—	—	—	—	—
1989—Pittsburgh (N.L.)	74	88	.457	5th (E)	—	—	—	—	—	—	—	—
1990—Pittsburgh (N.L.)	95	67	.586	1st (E)	—	—	2	4	—	—	—	—
1991—Pittsburgh (N.L.)	98	64	.605	1st (E)	—	—	3	4	—	—	—	—
1992—Pittsburgh (N.L.)	96	66	.593	1st (E)	—	—	3	4	—	—	—	—
1993—Pittsburgh (N.L.)	75	87	.463	5th (E)	—	—	—	—	—	—	—	—
1994—Pittsburgh (N.L.)	53	61	.465		—	—	—	—	—	—	—	—
1995—Pittsburgh (N.L.)	58	86	.403	5th (C)	—	—	—	—	—	—	—	—
Major league totals (10 years)	778	774	.501		—	—	8	12	—	—	—	—

NOTES:

1973—Lost to Wisconsin Rapids in playoff.

1976—Defeated Miami, two games to none, in semifinals; defeated Tampa, two games to none, in league championship.

1977—Defeated Miami, two games to none, in semifinals; defeated St. Petersburg, three games to one, in league championship.

1978—Defeated St. Petersburg, one game to none, in Northern Division championship; lost to Miami, two games to one, in league championship.

1979—Defeated Oklahoma City in league championship.

1981—Lost to Denver in semifinals.

1985—Served as acting manager of Chicago White Sox (record of 1-1), with club in fourth place, while manager Tony La Russa served a suspension (August 10 and 11).

1990—Lost to Cincinnati in N.L. Championship Series.

1991—Lost to Atlanta in N.L. Championship Series.

1992—Lost to Atlanta in N.L. Championship Series.

1993—On suspended list (August 27-September 1).

1994—Pittsburgh was tied for third place in N.L. Central at time of season-ending baseball strike (August 12).

OATES, JOHNNY — RANGERS

PERSONAL: Born January 21, 1946, in Sylva, N.C. . . . 5-11/185. . . . Batted left, threw right. . . . Full name: Johnny Lane Oates.

HIGH SCHOOL: Prince George (Va.).

COLLEGE: Virginia Tech (received bachelor of science degree in health and physical education).

TRANSACTIONS/CAREER NOTES: Selected by Chicago White Sox organization in second round of free-agent draft (June 1966); did not sign. . . . Selected by Baltimore Orioles organization in secondary phase of free-agent draft (January 28, 1967). . . . On military list (April 21-August 22, 1970). . . . Traded by Orioles with P Pat Dobson, P Roric Harrison and 2B Dave Johnson to Atlanta Braves for C Earl Williams and IF Taylor Duncan (November 30, 1972). . . . On disabled list (July 17-September 2, 1973). . . . Traded by Braves with 1B Dick Allen to Philadelphia Phillies for C Jim Essian, OF Barry Bonnell and cash (May 7, 1975). . . . On disabled list (April 14-June 1, 1976). . . . Traded by Phillies with P Quency Hill to Los Angeles Dodgers for IF Ted Sizemore (December 20, 1976). . . . Released by Dodgers (March 27, 1980). . . . Signed by New York Yankees (April 4, 1980). . . . Granted free agency (November 13, 1980). . . . Re-signed by Yankees organization (January 23, 1981). . . . On Columbus disabled list (August 3-25, 1981). . . . Released by Yankees organization (October 27, 1981).

STATISTICAL NOTES: Led International League catchers with 727 total chances in 1971. . . . Led N.L. with 15 passed balls in 1974. . . . Tied for N.L. lead in double plays by catcher with 10 in 1975.

			BATTING												FIELDING			
Year	Team (League)	Pos.	G	AB	R	H	2B	3B	HR	RBI	Avg.	BB	SO	SB	PO	A	E	Avg.
1967—	Bluefield (Appal.)	C	5	12	5	5	1	0	1	4	.417	2	0	0	23	5	0	1.000
—	Miami (Florida St.)	C-OF	48	156	22	45	5	2	3	19	.288	24	13	2	271	37	8	.975
1968—	Miami (Florida St.)	C-OF	70	194	24	51	9	3	0	23	.263	33	14	2	384	42	3	.993
1969—	Dall./Fort W. (Tex.)	C	66	191	24	55	12	2	1	18	.288	20	9	0	253	42	4	.987
1970—	Rochester (Int'l)	C	9	16	1	6	1	0	0	4	.375	4	2	0	24	2	0	1.000
—	Baltimore (A.L.)	C	5	18	2	5	0	1	0	2	.278	2	0	0	30	1	2	.939
1971—	Rochester (Int'l)	C	114	346	49	96	16	3	7	44	.277	49	31	10	*648	*73	6	.992
1972—	Baltimore (A.L.)	C	85	253	20	66	12	1	4	21	.261	28	31	5	391	31	2	*.995
1973—	Atlanta (N.L.)■	C	93	322	27	80	6	0	4	27	.248	22	31	1	409	57	9	.981
1974—	Atlanta (N.L.)	C	100	291	22	65	10	0	1	21	.223	23	24	2	434	55	4	.992
1975—	Atlanta (N.L.)	C	8	18	0	4	1	0	0	0	.222	1	4	0	21	1	0	1.000
—	Philadelphia (N.L.)■	C	90	269	28	77	14	0	1	25	.286	33	29	1	429	44	5	.990
1976—	Philadelphia (N.L.)	C	37	99	10	25	2	0	0	8	.253	8	12	0	155	15	1	.994
1977—	Los Angeles (N.L.)■	C	60	156	18	42	4	0	3	11	.269	11	11	1	258	37	4	.987
1978—	Los Angeles (N.L.)	C	40	75	5	23	1	0	0	6	.307	5	3	0	77	10	4	.956
1979—	Los Angeles (N.L.)	C	26	46	4	6	2	0	0	2	.130	4	1	0	64	13	2	.975
1980—	New York (A.L.)■	C	39	64	6	12	3	0	1	3	.188	2	3	1	99	10	1	.991
1981—	New York (A.L.)	C	10	26	4	5	1	0	0	0	.192	2	0	0	49	3	2	.963
American League totals (4 years)			139	361	32	88	16	2	5	26	.244	34	34	6	569	45	7	.989
National League totals (7 years)			454	1276	114	322	40	0	9	100	.252	107	115	5	1847	232	29	.986
Major league totals (11 years)			593	1637	146	410	56	2	14	126	.250	141	149	11	2416	277	36	.987

CHAMPIONSHIP SERIES RECORD

			BATTING												FIELDING			
Year	Team (League)	Pos.	G	AB	R	H	2B	3B	HR	RBI	Avg.	BB	SO	SB	PO	A	E	Avg.
1976—	Philadelphia (N.L.)	C	1	1	0	0	0	0	0	0	.000	0	0	0	1	0	0	1.000

WORLD SERIES RECORD

			BATTING												FIELDING			
Year	Team (League)	Pos.	G	AB	R	H	2B	3B	HR	RBI	Avg.	BB	SO	SB	PO	A	E	Avg.
1977—	Los Angeles (N.L.)	C	1	1	0	0	0	0	0	0	.000	0	0	0	1	0	0	1.000
1978—	Los Angeles (N.L.)	C	1	1	0	1	0	0	0	0	1.000	1	0	0	3	1	0	1.000
World Series totals (2 years)			2	2	0	1	0	0	0	0	.500	1	0	0	4	1	0	1.000

RECORD AS MANAGER

BACKGROUND: Player/coach, Columbus, New York Yankees organization (July 30, 1981-remainder of season). . . . Coach, Chicago Cubs (1984-87). . . . Coach, Baltimore Orioles (1989-May 23, 1991).

HONORS: Named International League Manager of the Year (1988). . . . Coach, A.L. All-Star team (1993 and 1995). . . . Named A.L. Manager of the Year by THE SPORTING NEWS (1993).

		REGULAR SEASON				POSTSEASON							
						Playoff		Champ. Series		World Series		All-Star Game	
Year	Team (League)	W	L	Pct.	Pos.	W	L	W	L	W	L	W	L
1982—	Nashville (Southern)	32	38	.457	4th (W)	—	—	—	—	—	—	—	—
—	(Second half)	45	29	.608	1st (W)	6	2	—	—	—	—	—	—
1983—	Columbus (International)	83	57	.593	1st	2	3	—	—	—	—	—	—
1988—	Rochester (International)	77	64	.546	1st (W)	5	5	—	—	—	—	—	—
1991—	Baltimore (A.L.)	54	71	.432	6th (E)	—	—	—	—	—	—	—	—
1992—	Baltimore (A.L.)	89	73	.549	3rd (E)	—	—	—	—	—	—	—	—
1993—	Baltimore (A.L.)	85	77	.525	T3rd (E)	—	—	—	—	—	—	—	—
1994—	Baltimore (A.L.)	63	49	.563		—	—	—	—	—	—	—	—
1995—	Texas (A.L.)	74	70	.514	3rd (W)	—	—	—	—	—	—	—	—
Major league totals (5 years)		365	340	.518		—	—	—	—	—	—	—	—

NOTES:

1982—Defeated Knoxville, three games to one, in playoffs; defeated Jacksonville, three games to one, in league championship.

1983—Lost to Tidewater in playoffs.

1988—Defeated Tidewater, three games to one, in league championship; lost to Indianapolis (American Association), four games to two, in AAA-Alliance championship.

1991—Replaced Baltimore manager Frank Robinson with club in seventh place and record of 13-24 (May 23).

1994—Baltimore was in second place in A.L. East at time of season ending strike (August 12).

PINIELLA, LOU — MARINERS

PERSONAL: Born August 28, 1943, in Tampa, Fla. . . . 6-2/199. . . . Batted right, threw right. . . . Full name: Louis Victor Piniella. . . . Cousin of Dave Magadan, first baseman/third baseman, Chicago Cubs. . . . Name pronounced pin-ELL-uh.

HIGH SCHOOL: Jesuit (Tampa, Fla.).

COLLEGE: Tampa.

TRANSACTIONS/CAREER NOTES: Signed as free agent by Cleveland Indians organization (June 9, 1962). . . . Selected by Washington Senators organization from Jacksonville, Indians organization, in Rule 5 major league draft (November 26, 1962). . . . On military list (March 9-July 20, 1964). . . . Traded by Senators organization to Baltimore Orioles organization (August 4, 1964), completing deal in which Orioles traded P Lester (Buster) Narum to Senators for cash and a player to be named later (March 31, 1964). . . . On suspended list (June 27-29, 1965). . . . Traded by Orioles organization to Indians organization for C Camilo Carreon (March 10, 1966). . . . On temporarily inactive list (May 19-22, 1967). . . . On disabled list (May 22-June 6, 1968). . . . On temporarily inactive list (June 6-25, 1968). . . . Selected by Seattle Pilots in expansion draft (October 15, 1968). . . . Traded by Pilots to Kansas City Royals for OF Steve Whitaker and P John Gelnar (April 1, 1969). . . . On military list (August 7-22, 1969). . . . On disabled list (May 5-June 8, 1971). . . . Traded by Royals with P Ken Wright to New York Yankees for P Lindy McDaniel (December 7, 1973). . . . On disabled list (June 17-July 6, 1975; August 23-September 7, 1981; and March 30-April 22, 1983). . . . Announced retirement (June 17, 1984).

RECORDS: Shares major league record for most assists by outfielder in one inning—2 (May 27, 1974, third inning).
HONORS: Named A.L. Rookie of the Year by Baseball Writers' Association of America (1969).
STATISTICAL NOTES: Led A.L. in grounding into double plays with 25 in 1972. . . . Career major league grand slams: 1.

			BATTING											FIELDING			
Year Team (League)	**Pos.**	**G**	**AB**	**R**	**H**	**2B**	**3B**	**HR**	**RBI**	**Avg.**	**BB**	**SO**	**SB**	**PO**	**A**	**E**	**Avg.**
1962—Selma (Ala.-Fla.)	OF	70	278	40	75	10	5	8	44	.270	10	57	4	94	6	9	.917
1963—Peninsula (Caro.)■	OF	143	548	71	170	29	4	16	77	.310	34	70	8	271	*23	8	.974
1964—Aberdeen (North.)	OF	20	74	8	20	8	3	0	12	.270	6	9	1	37	1	1	.974
—Baltimore (A.L.)■	PH	4	1	0	0	0	0	0	0	.000	0	0	0	...	...	...	...
1965—Elmira (Eastern)	OF	126	490	64	122	29	6	11	64	.249	22	57	5	176	5	7	.963
1966—Portland (PCL)■	OF	133	457	47	132	22	3	7	52	.289	20	52	6	177	11	11	.945
1967—Portland (PCL)	OF	113	396	46	122	20	1	8	56	.308	23	47	2	199	7	6	.972
1968—Portland (PCL)	OF	88	331	49	105	15	3	13	62	.317	19	31	0	167	6	7	.961
—Cleveland (A.L.)	OF	6	5	1	0	0	0	0	1	.000	0	0	1	1	0	0	1.000
1969—Kansas City (A.L.)■	OF	135	493	43	139	21	6	11	68	.282	33	56	2	278	13	7	.977
1970—Kansas City (A.L.)	OF-1B	144	542	54	163	24	5	11	88	.301	35	42	3	250	6	4	.985
1971—Kansas City (A.L.)	OF	126	448	43	125	21	5	3	51	.279	21	43	5	201	6	3	.986
1972—Kansas City (A.L.)	OF	151	574	65	179	*33	4	11	72	.312	34	59	7	275	8	7	.976
1973—Kansas City (A.L.)	OF-DH	144	513	53	128	28	1	9	69	.250	30	65	5	196	9	3	.986
1974—New York (A.L.)■	OF-DH-1B	140	518	71	158	26	0	9	70	.305	32	58	1	270	16	3	.990
1975—New York (A.L.)	OF-DH	74	199	7	39	4	1	0	22	.196	16	22	0	65	5	1	.986
1976—New York (A.L.)	OF-DH	100	327	36	92	16	6	3	38	.281	18	34	0	199	10	4	.981
1977—New York (A.L.)	OF-DH-1B	103	339	47	112	19	3	12	45	.330	20	31	2	86	3	2	.978
1978—New York (A.L.)	OF-DH	130	472	67	148	34	5	6	69	.314	34	36	3	213	4	7	.969
1979—New York (A.L.)	OF-DH	130	461	49	137	22	2	11	69	.297	17	31	3	204	13	4	.982
1980—New York (A.L.)	OF-DH	116	321	39	92	18	0	2	27	.287	29	20	0	157	8	5	.971
1981—New York (A.L.)	OF-DH	60	159	16	44	9	0	5	18	.277	13	9	0	69	2	1	.986
1982—New York (A.L.)	DH-OF	102	261	33	80	17	1	6	37	.307	18	18	0	68	2	0	1.000
1983—New York (A.L.)	OF-DH	53	148	19	43	9	1	2	16	.291	11	12	1	67	4	3	.959
1984—New York (A.L.)	OF-DH	29	86	8	26	4	1	1	6	.302	7	5	0	40	3	0	1.000
Major league totals (18 years)		1747	5867	651	1705	305	41	102	766	.291	368	541	33	2639	112	54	.981

DIVISION SERIES RECORD

			BATTING											FIELDING			
Year Team (League)	**Pos.**	**G**	**AB**	**R**	**H**	**2B**	**3B**	**HR**	**RBI**	**Avg.**	**BB**	**SO**	**SB**	**PO**	**A**	**E**	**Avg.**
1981—New York (A.L.)	DH-PH	4	10	1	2	1	0	1	3	.200	0	0	0	...	...	...	...

CHAMPIONSHIP SERIES RECORD

			BATTING											FIELDING			
Year Team (League)	**Pos.**	**G**	**AB**	**R**	**H**	**2B**	**3B**	**HR**	**RBI**	**Avg.**	**BB**	**SO**	**SB**	**PO**	**A**	**E**	**Avg.**
1976—New York (A.L.)	DH-PH	4	11	1	3	1	0	0	0	.273	0	1	0	...	...	...	...
1977—New York (A.L.)	OF-DH	5	21	1	7	3	0	0	2	.333	0	1	0	9	1	0	1.000
1978—New York (A.L.)	OF	4	17	2	4	0	0	0	0	.235	0	3	0	13	0	0	1.000
1980—New York (A.L.)	OF	2	5	1	1	0	0	1	1	.200	2	1	0	5	0	0	1.000
1981—New York (A.L.)	PH-DH-OF	3	5	2	3	0	0	1	3	.600	0	0	0	0	0	0	...
Championship series totals (5 years)		18	59	7	18	4	0	2	6	.305	2	6	0	27	1	0	1.000

WORLD SERIES RECORD

NOTES: Shares single-series record for collecting one or more hits in each game (1978). . . . Member of World Series championship teams (1977 and 1978).

			BATTING											FIELDING			
Year Team (League)	**Pos.**	**G**	**AB**	**R**	**H**	**2B**	**3B**	**HR**	**RBI**	**Avg.**	**BB**	**SO**	**SB**	**PO**	**A**	**E**	**Avg.**
1976—New York (A.L.)	DH-OF-PH	4	9	1	3	1	0	0	0	.333	0	0	0	1	0	0	1.000
1977—New York (A.L.)	OF	6	22	1	6	0	0	0	3	.273	0	3	0	16	1	1	.944
1978—New York (A.L.)	OF	6	25	3	7	0	0	0	4	.280	0	0	1	14	1	0	1.000
1981—New York (A.L.)	OF-PH	6	16	2	7	1	0	0	3	.438	0	1	1	7	0	0	1.000
World Series totals (4 years)		22	72	7	23	2	0	0	10	.319	0	4	2	38	2	1	.976

ALL-STAR GAME RECORD

		BATTING											FIELDING			
Year League	**Pos.**	**AB**	**R**	**H**	**2B**	**3B**	**HR**	**RBI**	**Avg.**	**BB**	**SO**	**SB**	**PO**	**A**	**E**	**Avg.**
1972—American	PH	1	0	0	0	0	0	0	.000	0	0	0	...	...	...	...

RECORD AS MANAGER

BACKGROUND: Coach, New York Yankees (June 25, 1984-85). . . . Vice-president/general manager, Yankees (beginning of 1988 season-June 22, 1988). . . . Special adviser, Yankees (1989).
HONORS: Named A.L. Manager of the Year by Baseball Writers' Association of America (1995).

	REGULAR SEASON				POSTSEASON							
					Playoff		Champ. Series		World Series		All-Star Game	
Year Team (League)	**W**	**L**	**Pct.**	**Pos.**	**W**	**L**	**W**	**L**	**W**	**L**	**W**	**L**
1986—New York (A.L.)	90	72	.556	2nd (E)	—	—	—	—	—	—	—	—
1987—New York (A.L.)	89	73	.549	4th (E)	—	—	—	—	—	—	—	—
1988—New York (A.L.)	45	48	.484	5th (E)	—	—	—	—	—	—	—	—
1990—Cincinnati (N.L.)	91	71	.562	1st (W)	—	—	4	2	4	0	—	—
1991—Cincinnati (N.L.)	74	88	.457	5th (W)	—	—	—	—	—	—	0	1
1992—Cincinnati (N.L.)	90	72	.556	2nd (W)	—	—	—	—	—	—	—	—
1993—Seattle (A.L.)	82	80	.506	4th (W)	—	—	—	—	—	—	—	—
1994—Seattle (A.L.)	49	63	.438		—	—	—	—	—	—	—	—
1995—Seattle (A.L.)	79	66	.545	1st (W)	3	2	2	4	—	—	—	—
American League totals (6 years)	434	402	.519		3	2	2	4	—	—	—	—
National League totals (3 years)	255	231	.525		—	—	4	2	4	0	0	1
Major league totals (9 years)	689	633	.521		3	2	6	6	4	0	0	1

NOTES:
1988—Replaced New York manager Billy Martin with club in second place and record of 40-28 (June 23).
1990—Defeated Pittsburgh in N.L. Championship Series; defeated Oakland in World Series.
1994—Seattle was in third place in A.L. West at time of season-ending strike (August 12).
1995—Defeated New York in A.L. divisional playoff; lost to Cleveland in A.L. Championship Series.

RIGGLEMAN, JIM — CUBS

PERSONAL: Born December 9, 1952, in Fort Dix, N.J. . . . 5-11/175. . . . Batted right, threw right. . . . Full name: James David Riggleman.
HIGH SCHOOL: Richard Montgomery (Rockville, Md.).
COLLEGE: Frostburg (Md.) State (degree in physical education).
TRANSACTIONS/CAREER NOTES: Selected by Los Angeles Dodgers organization in fourth round of free-agent draft (June 5, 1974). . . . Traded by Dodgers organization to St. Louis Cardinals organization for C Sergio Robles (July 19, 1976). . . . On Springfield disabled list (April 14-July 3, 1978). . . . Released by Arkansas to become coach (May 25, 1981).
STATISTICAL NOTES: Led Eastern League third basemen with 30 double plays in 1975.

			BATTING											FIELDING			
Year Team (League)	Pos.	G	AB	R	H	2B	3B	HR	RBI	Avg.	BB	SO	SB	PO	A	E	Avg.
1974— Waterbury (East.)	2B-3B	80	252	29	67	13	1	8	41	.266	25	56	1	159	175	20	.944
1975— Waterbury (East.)	3B	129	439	61	113	14	7	11	57	.257	54	86	14	109	267	53	.876
1976— Waterbury (East.)	OF-3B	84	287	38	75	14	2	6	39	.261	31	47	4	99	29	18	.877
— Arkansas (Texas)■	3B-OF-1B	47	154	29	46	9	1	5	25	.299	19	13	1	38	73	10	.917
1977— Arkansas (Texas)	3B	27	93	10	26	7	2	0	11	.280	16	9	6	25	48	5	.936
— New Orleans (A.A.)	3B-OF-SS	103	346	52	83	16	0	17	52	.240	34	65	10	88	149	24	.908
1978— Arkansas (Texas)	3B-OF	59	174	34	51	8	1	4	34	.293	43	39	2	29	60	14	.864
1979— Arkansas (Texas)	3B-OF-1B	46	110	17	30	9	0	1	23	.273	13	23	5	34	22	4	.933
— Springfield (A.A.)	3B-OF-1B	35	93	9	22	4	0	2	9	.237	5	26	3	47	4	6	.895
1980— Arkansas (Texas)	3B-OF	127	431	84	127	29	7	21	90	.295	60	67	28	123	243	26	.934
1981— Arkansas (Texas)	OF-3B	37	133	17	32	7	1	1	15	.241	16	29	3	56	22	5	.940

RECORD AS MANAGER

BACKGROUND: Coach, Arkansas, St. Louis Cardinals organization, (May 25, 1981-remainder of season). . . . Coach, Louisville, Cardinals organization (April 13-May 31, 1982). . . . Director of player development, Cardinals (June 21, 1988-remainder of season). . . . Coach, Cardinals (1989-90).
HONORS: Coach, N.L. All-Star team (1995).

	REGULAR SEASON				POSTSEASON							
					Playoff		Champ. Series		World Series		All-Star Game	
Year Team (League)	W	L	Pct.	Pos.	W	L	W	L	W	L	W	L
1982— St. Petersburg (Florida State)	8	4	.667	2nd	—	—	—	—	—	—	—	—
— (Second half)	35	30	.538	2nd	—	—	—	—	—	—	—	—
1983— St. Petersburg (Florida State)	33	35	.485	T3rd	—	—	—	—	—	—	—	—
— (Second half)	37	29	.561	2nd	—	—	—	—	—	—	—	—
1984— St. Petersburg (Florida State)	39	38	.506	3rd	—	—	—	—	—	—	—	—
— (Second half)	32	35	.478	3rd	—	—	—	—	—	—	—	—
1985— Arkansas (Texas)	33	30	.524	1st (E)	—	—	—	—	—	—	—	—
— (Second half)	31	40	.437	4th (E)	0	2	—	—	—	—	—	—
1986— Arkansas (Texas)	35	28	.556	3rd (E)	—	—	—	—	—	—	—	—
— (Second half)	32	39	.451	3rd (E)	—	—	—	—	—	—	—	—
1987— Arkansas (Texas)	36	29	.554	2nd (E)	—	—	—	—	—	—	—	—
— (Second half)	36	34	.514	3rd (E)	—	—	—	—	—	—	—	—
1988— Arkansas (Texas)	30	37	.448	3rd (E)	—	—	—	—	—	—	—	—
— (Second half)	2	1	.667		—	—	—	—	—	—	—	—
1991— Las Vegas (Pacific Coast)	36	34	.514	4th (S)	—	—	—	—	—	—	—	—
— (Second half)	29	41	.414	5th (S)	—	—	—	—	—	—	—	—
1992— Las Vegas (Pacific Coast)	41	31	.569	1st (S)	—	—	—	—	—	—	—	—
— (Second half)	33	39	.458	3rd (S)	2	3	—	—	—	—	—	—
— San Diego (N.L.)	4	8	.333	3rd (W)	—	—	—	—	—	—	—	—
1993— San Diego (N.L.)	61	101	.377	7th (W)	—	—	—	—	—	—	—	—
1994— San Diego (N.L.)	47	70	.402		—	—	—	—	—	—	—	—
1995— Chicago (N.L.)	73	71	.507	3rd (C)	—	—	—	—	—	—	—	—
Major league totals (4 years)	185	250	.425		—	—	—	—	—	—	—	—

NOTES:
1982—Replaced St. Petersburg manager Nick Leyva with club in fourth place and record of 26-30 (June 4).
1985—Lost to Jackson in semifinals.
1988—Replaced as Arkansas manager by Darold Knowles (June 21).
1992—Lost to Colorado Springs in semifinals. Replaced San Diego manager Greg Riddoch with club in third place and record of 78-72 (September 23).
1994—San Diego was in fourth place in N.L. West at time of season-ending baseball strike (August 12).

TORRE, JOE — YANKEES

PERSONAL: Born July 18, 1940, in Brooklyn, N.Y. . . . 6-1/210. . . . Batted right, threw right. . . . Full name: Joseph Paul Torre. . . . Brother of Frank Torre, first baseman, Milwaukee Braves and Philadelphia Phillies (1956-60, 1962-63). . . . Name pronounced TORE-ee.
HIGH SCHOOL: St. Francis Prep (Brooklyn, N.Y.).
TRANSACTIONS/CAREER NOTES: Signed by Jacksonville, Milwaukee Braves organization (August 24, 1959). . . . On military list (September 30, 1962-March 26, 1963). . . . Braves franchise moved from Milwaukee to Atlanta (1966). . . . On disabled list (April 18-May 9, 1968). . . . Traded by Braves to St. Louis Cardinals for 1B Orlando Cepeda (March 17, 1969). . . . Traded by Cardinals to New York Mets for P Tommy Moore and P Ray Sadecki (October 13, 1974). . . . Released as player by Mets (June 18, 1977).
RECORDS: Shares major league single-game record for most times grounded into double play—4 (July 21, 1975).
HONORS: Named catcher on The Sporting News N.L. All-Star team (1964-66). . . . Won N.L. Gold Glove at catcher (1965). . . . Named Major

League Player of the Year by The Sporting News (1971). . . . Named N.L. Player of the Year by The Sporting News (1971). . . . Named third baseman on The Sporting News N.L. All-Star team (1971). . . . Named N.L. Most Valuable Player by Baseball Writers' Association of America (1971).

STATISTICAL NOTES: Led N.L. catchers with .995 fielding percentage in 1964 and .996 in 1968. . . . Led N.L. in grounding into double plays with 26 in 1964, 22 in 1965, 22 in 1967 and 21 in 1968. . . . Led N.L. catchers with 12 double plays in 1967. . . . Led N.L. with 352 total bases in 1971. . . . Hit for the cycle (June 27, 1973). . . . Led N.L. first basemen with 102 assists and 144 double plays in 1974. . . . Career major league grand slams: 3.

			BATTING												FIELDING			
Year	Team (League)	Pos.	G	AB	R	H	2B	3B	HR	RBI	Avg.	BB	SO	SB	PO	A	E	Avg.
1960—	Eau Claire (North.)	C	117	369	63	127	23	3	16	74	*.344	70	45	7	636	64	9	.987
—	Milwaukee (N.L.)	PH	2	2	0	1	0	0	0	0	.500	0	1	0	...	...	...	...
1961—	Louisville (A.A.)	C	27	111	18	38	8	2	3	24	.342	6	9	0	185	14	2	.990
—	Milwaukee (N.L.)	C	113	406	40	113	21	4	10	42	.278	28	60	3	494	50	10	.982
1962—	Milwaukee (N.L.)	C	80	220	23	62	8	1	5	26	.282	24	24	1	325	39	5	.986
1963—	Milwaukee (N.L.)	C-1B-OF	142	501	57	147	19	4	14	71	.293	42	79	1	919	76	6	.994
1964—	Milwaukee (N.L.)	C-1B	154	601	87	193	36	5	20	109	.321	36	67	4	1081	94	7	†.994
1965—	Milwaukee (N.L.)	C-1B	148	523	68	152	21	1	27	80	.291	61	79	0	1022	73	8	.993
1966—	Atlanta (N.L.)	C-1B	148	546	83	172	20	3	36	101	.315	60	61	0	874	87	12	.988
1967—	Atlanta (N.L.)	C-1B	135	477	67	132	18	1	20	68	.277	75	49	2	785	81	8	.991
1968—	Atlanta (N.L.)	C-1B	115	424	45	115	11	2	10	55	.271	34	72	1	733	48	2	†.997
1969—	St. Louis (N.L.)■	1B-C	159	602	72	174	29	6	18	101	.289	66	85	0	1360	91	7	.995
1970—	St. Louis (N.L.)	C-3B-1B	•161	624	89	203	27	9	21	100	.325	70	91	2	651	162	13	.984
1971—	St. Louis (N.L.)	3B	161	634	97	*230	34	8	24	*137	*.363	63	70	4	*136	271	•21	.951
1972—	St. Louis (N.L.)	3B-1B	149	544	71	157	26	6	11	81	.289	54	74	3	336	198	15	.973
1973—	St. Louis (N.L.)	1B-3B	141	519	67	149	17	2	13	69	.287	65	78	2	881	128	12	.988
1974—	St. Louis (N.L.)	1B-3B	147	529	59	149	28	1	11	70	.282	69	68	1	1173	†121	14	.989
1975—	New York (N.L.)■	3B-1B	114	361	33	89	16	3	6	35	.247	35	55	0	172	157	15	.956
1976—	New York (N.L.)	1B-3B	114	310	36	95	10	3	5	31	.306	21	35	1	593	52	7	.989
1977—	New York (N.L.)	1B-3B	26	51	2	9	3	0	1	9	.176	2	10	0	83	3	1	.989
Major league totals (18 years)			2209	7874	996	2342	344	59	252	1185	.297	805	1058	25	11618	1731	163	.988

ALL-STAR GAME RECORD

			BATTING											FIELDING			
Year	League	Pos.	AB	R	H	2B	3B	HR	RBI	Avg.	BB	SO	SB	PO	A	E	Avg.
1963—	National							Did not play.									
1964—	National	C	2	0	0	0	0	0	0	.000	0	0	0	5	0	0	1.000
1965—	National	C	4	1	1	0	0	1	2	.250	0	0	0	5	1	0	1.000
1966—	National	C	3	0	0	0	0	0	0	.000	0	1	0	5	0	0	1.000
1967—	National	C	2	0	0	0	0	0	0	.000	0	0	0	4	1	0	1.000
1970—	National	PH	1	0	0	0	0	0	0	.000	0	0	0	...	...	...	...
1971—	National	3B	3	0	0	0	0	0	0	.000	0	1	0	1	0	0	1.000
1972—	National	3B	3	0	0	0	0	0	0	.000	0	1	0	1	2	0	1.000
1973—	National	1B-3B	3	0	0	0	0	0	0	.000	0	0	0	5	0	0	1.000
All-Star Game totals (8 years)			21	1	1	0	0	1	2	.048	0	3	0	26	4	0	1.000

RECORD AS MANAGER

BACKGROUND: Player/manager, New York Mets (May 31-June 18, 1977).

HONORS: Coach, N.L. All-Star team (1983 and 1992).

		REGULAR SEASON				POSTSEASON							
						Playoff		Champ. Series		World Series		All-Star Game	
Year	Team (League)	W	L	Pct.	Pos.	W	L	W	L	W	L	W	L
1977—	New York (N.L.)	49	68	.419	6th (E)	—	—	—	—	—	—	—	—
1978—	New York (N.L.)	66	96	.407	6th (E)	—	—	—	—	—	—	—	—
1979—	New York (N.L.)	63	99	.389	6th (E)	—	—	—	—	—	—	—	—
1980—	New York (N.L.)	67	95	.414	5th (E)	—	—	—	—	—	—	—	—
1981—	New York (N.L.)	17	34	.333	5th (E)	—	—	—	—	—	—	—	—
—	(Second half)	24	28	.462	4th (E)	—	—	—	—	—	—	—	—
1982—	Atlanta (N.L.)	89	73	.549	1st (W)	—	—	0	3	—	—	—	—
1983—	Atlanta (N.L.)	88	74	.543	2nd (W)	—	—	—	—	—	—	—	—
1984—	Atlanta (N.L.)	80	82	.494	T2nd (W)	—	—	—	—	—	—	—	—
1990—	St. Louis (N.L.)	24	34	.414	6th (E)	—	—	—	—	—	—	—	—
1991—	St. Louis (N.L.)	84	78	.519	2nd (E)	—	—	—	—	—	—	—	—
1992—	St. Louis (N.L.)	83	79	.512	3rd (E)	—	—	—	—	—	—	—	—
1993—	St. Louis (N.L.)	87	75	.537	3rd (E)	—	—	—	—	—	—	—	—
1994—	St. Louis (N.L.)	53	61	.465		—	—	—	—	—	—	—	—
1995—	St. Louis (N.L.)	20	27	.426	4th (C)	—	—	—	—	—	—	—	—
Major league totals (14 years)		894	1003	.471		—	—	0	3	—	—	—	—

NOTES:

1977—Replaced New York manager Joe Frazier with club in sixth place and record of 15-30 (May 31); served as player/manager (May 31-June 18, when released as player).

1982—Lost to St. Louis in N.L. Championship Series.

1990—Replaced St. Louis manager Whitey Herzog (33-47) and interim manager Red Schoendienst (13-11) with club in sixth place and record of 46-58 (August 1). 1994—St. Louis was tied for third place in N.L. Central at time of season-ending strike (August 12).

1995—Replaced as Cardinals manager by interim manager Mike Jorgensen, with club in fourth place (June 16).

1995 A.L. STATISTICAL LEADERS

BATTING

BATTING AVERAGE
.356 Edgar Martinez, Sea.
.333 Chuck Knoblauch, Min.
.330 Tim Salmon, Cal.
.324 Wade Boggs, N.Y.
.323 Eddie Murray, Cle.
.320 B.J. Surhoff, Mil.
.318 Chili Davis, Cal.
.317 Albert Belle, Cle.
.314 Carlos Baerga, Cle.
.314 Jim Thome, Cle.

RUNS
121 Albert Belle, Cle.
121 Edgar Martinez, Sea.
120 Jim Edmonds, Cal.
119 Tony Phillips, Cal.
111 Tim Salmon, Cal.
108 Brady Anderson, Bal.
108 John Valentin, Bos.
107 Chuck Knoblauch, Min.
102 Frank Thomas, Chi.
98 2 Players tied

HITS
186 Lance Johnson, Chi.
182 Edgar Martinez, Sea.
179 Chuck Knoblauch, Min.
177 Tim Salmon, Cal.
175 Carlos Baerga, Cle.
174 Otis Nixon, Tex.
173 Albert Belle, Cle.
173 Bernie Williams, N.Y.
172 Rafael Palmeiro, Bal.
169 Kirby Puckett, Min.

DOUBLES
52 Albert Belle, Cle.
52 Edgar Martinez, Sea.
39 Kirby Puckett, Min.
37 John Valentin, Bos.
35 Tino Martinez, Sea.
34 Tim Salmon, Cal.
34 Chuck Knoblauch, Min.
33 Brady Anderson, Bal.
33 Cal Ripken, Bal.
33 Kevin Seitzer, Mil.

TRIPLES
13 Kenny Lofton, Cle.
12 Lance Johnson, Chi.
10 Brady Anderson, Bal.
9 Bernie Williams, N.Y.
8 Chuck Knoblauch, Min.
7 Roberto Alomar, Tor.
7 Fernando Vina, Mil.

HOME RUNS
50 Albert Belle, Cle.
40 Jay Buhner, Sea.
40 Frank Thomas, Chi.
39 Mark McGwire, Oak.
39 Rafael Palmeiro, Bal.
39 Mo Vaughn, Bos.
35 Gary Gaetti, K.C.
34 Tim Salmon, Cal.
33 Jim Edmonds, Cal.
32 Mickey Tettleton, Tex.

RUNS BATTED IN
126 Albert Belle, Cle.
126 Mo Vaughn, Bos.
121 Jay Buhner, Sea.
113 Edgar Martinez, Sea.
111 Tino Martinez, Sea.
111 Frank Thomas, Chi.
107 Jim Edmonds, Cal.
107 Manny Ramirez, Cle.
105 Tim Salmon, Cal.
104 Rafael Palmeiro, Bal.

TOTAL BASES
377 Albert Belle, Cle.
323 Rafael Palmeiro, Bal.
321 Edgar Martinez, Sea.
319 Tim Salmon, Cal.
316 Mo Vaughn, Bos.
299 Jim Edmonds, Cal.
299 Frank Thomas, Chi.
286 Tino Martinez, Sea.
277 Kirby Puckett, Min.
277 John Valentin, Bos.

ON-BASE PERCENTAGE
.479 Edgar Martinez, Sea.
.454 Frank Thomas, Chi.
.438 Jim Thome, Cle.
.429 Tim Salmon, Cal.
.429 Chili Davis, Cal.
.424 Chuck Knoblauch, Min.
.415 Tim Naehring, Bos.
.412 Wade Boggs, N.Y.
.407 Rickey Henderson, Oak.
.403 Harold Baines, Bal.

SLUGGING PERCENTAGE
.690 Albert Belle, Cle.
.628 Edgar Martinez, Sea.
.606 Frank Thomas, Chi.
.594 Tim Salmon, Cal.
.583 Rafael Palmeiro, Bal.
.575 Mo Vaughn, Bos.
.566 Jay Buhner, Sea.
.558 Manny Ramirez, Cle.
.558 Jim Thome, Cle.
.556 Jose Canseco, Bos.

EXTRA-BASE HITS
103 Albert Belle, Cle.
81 Edgar Martinez, Sea.
71 Rafael Palmeiro, Bal.
71 Tim Salmon, Cal.
70 Mo Vaughn, Bos.
69 Tino Martinez, Sea.
67 Jim Edmonds, Cal.
67 Frank Thomas, Chi.
66 John Valentin, Bos.
63 Jay Buhner, Sea.

STOLEN BASES
54 Kenny Lofton, Cle.
50 Tom Goodwin, K.C.
50 Otis Nixon, Tex.
46 Chuck Knoblauch, Min.
42 Vince Coleman, K.C.-Sea.
40 Lance Johnson, Chi.
36 Stan Javier, Oak.
32 Rickey Henderson, Oak.
30 Roberto Alomar, Tor.
29 Omar Vizquel, Cle.

MULTIHIT GAMES
56 Chuck Knoblauch, Min.
55 Tim Salmon, Cal.
54 Lance Johnson, Chi.
54 Edgar Martinez, Sea.
52 Carlos Baerga, Cle.
51 Rafael Palmeiro, Bal.
51 Kirby Puckett, Min.
50 Albert Belle, Cle.
50 Otis Nixon, Tex.
49 Two players tied

PITCHING

EARNED-RUN AVERAGE
2.48 Randy Johnson, Sea.
2.95 Tim Wakefield, Bos.
3.08 Dennis Martinez, Cle.
3.29 Mike Mussina, Bal.
3.38 Kenny Rogers, Tex.
3.57 David Cone, Tor.-N.Y.
3.60 Kevin Brown, Bal.
3.64 Al Leiter, Tor.
3.70 Jim Abbott, Chi.-Cal.
3.75 Mark Gubicza, K.C.

GAMES
65 Jesse Orosco, Bal.
64 Roger McDowell, Tex.
63 Bob Wickman, N.Y.
63 Bobby Ayala, Sea.
63 Stan Belinda, Bos.
62 Jeff Nelson, Sea.
62 Jose Mesa, Cle.
62 Bob Patterson, Cal.
62 Troy Percival, Cal.
60 Three pitchers tied

INNINGS PITCHED
229.1 David Cone, Tor.-N.Y.
221.2 Mike Mussina, Bal.
217.2 Jack McDowell, N.Y.
214.1 Randy Johnson, Sea.
213.1 Mark Gubicza, K.C.
209.2 Todd Stottlemyre, Oak.
208.0 Kenny Rogers, Tex.
203.2 Alex Fernandez, Chi.
203.0 Chuck Finley, Cal.
202.0 Steve Sparks, Mil.

WINS
19 Mike Mussina, Bal.
18 Randy Johnson, Sea.
18 David Cone, Tor.-N.Y.
17 Kenny Rogers, Tex.
16 Tim Wakefield, Bos.
16 Charles Nagy, Cle.
16 Orel Hershiser, Cle.
15 Five pitchers tied

COMPLETE GAMES
8 Jack McDowell, N.Y.
7 Scott Erickson, Min.-Bal.
7 Mike Mussina, Bal.
6 David Cone, Tor.-N.Y.
6 Randy Johnson, Sea.
6 Tim Wakefield, Bos.
5 Alex Fernandez, Chi.
4 Five pitchers tied

STRIKEOUTS PER 9 INN.
12.3 Randy Johnson, Sea.
8.8 Todd Stottlemyre, Oak.
8.6 Chuck Finley, Cal.
8.3 Kevin Appier, K.C.
7.5 Al Leiter, Tor.
7.5 David Cone, Tor.-N.Y.
7.0 Charles Nagy, Cle.
7.0 Alex Fernandez, Chi.
7.0 Roger Pavlik, Tex.
6.7 Erik Hanson, Bos.

SAVES
46 Jose Mesa, Cle.
37 Lee Smith, Cal.
32 Roberto Hernandez, Chi.
32 Rick Aguilera, Min.-Bos.
31 John Wetteland, N.Y.
31 Jeff Montgomery, K.C.
29 Dennis Eckersley, Oak.
22 Mike Fetters, Mil.
22 Doug Jones, Bal.
20 Jeff Russell, Tex.

SHUTOUTS
4 Mike Mussina, Bal.
3 Randy Johnson, Sea.
2 Scott Erickson, Bal.
2 Alex Fernandez, Chi.
2 Jack McDowell, N.Y.
2 David Cone, Tor.
2 Dennis Martinez, Cle.
2 Mark Gubicza, K.C.

STRIKEOUTS
294 Randy Johnson, Sea.
205 Todd Stottlemyre, Oak.
195 Chuck Finley, Cal.
191 David Cone, Tor.-N.Y.
185 Kevin Appier, K.C.
159 Alex Fernandez, Chi.
158 Mike Mussina, Bal.
157 Jack McDowell, N.Y.
153 Al Leiter, Tor.
149 Roger Pavlik, Tex.

OPP. BATTING AVG. AGAINST
.201 Randy Johnson, Sea.
.221 Kevin Appier, K.C.
.226 Mike Mussina, Bal.
.227 Tim Wakefield, Bos.
.228 David Cone, Tor.-N.Y.
.238 Al Leiter, Tor.
.241 Kevin Brown, Bal.
.243 Kenny Rogers, Tex.
.243 Roger Pavlik, Tex.
.244 Orel Hershiser, Cle.

1995 N.L. STATISTICAL LEADERS

BATTING

BATTING AVERAGE
.368 Tony Gwynn, S.D.
.346 Mike Piazza, L.A.
.340 Dante Bichette, Col.
.334 Derek Bell, Hou.
.326 Mark Grace, Chi.
.319 Barry Larkin, Cin.
.309 Vinny Castilla, Col.
.309 David Segui, N.Y.-Mon.
.306 Gregg Jefferies, Phi.
.306 Reggie Sanders, Cin.

RUNS
123 Craig Biggio, Hou.
109 Barry Bonds, S.F.
104 Steve Finley, S.D.
102 Dante Bichette, Col.
98 Barry Larkin, Cin.
97 Mark Grace, Chi.
96 Larry Walker, Col.
92 Brian McRae, Chi.
91 Raul Mondesi, L.A.
91 Reggie Sanders, Cin.

HITS
197 Dante Bichette, Col.
197 Tony Gwynn, S.D.
180 Mark Grace, Chi.
167 Craig Biggio, Hou.
167 Steve Finley, S.D.
167 Brian McRae, Chi.
164 Eric Karros, L.A.
163 Vinny Castilla, Col.
159 Ken Caminiti, S.D.
158 Barry Larkin, Cin.

DOUBLES
51 Mark Grace, Chi.
38 Dante Bichette, Col.
38 Brian McRae, Chi.
36 Reggie Sanders, Cin.
35 Wil Cordero, Mon.
35 Ray Lankford, St. L.
34 Bret Boone, Cin.
34 Vinny Castilla, Col.
34 Mickey Morandini, Phi.

TRIPLES
9 Brett Butler, N.Y.-L.A.
9 Eric Young, Col.
8 Steve Finley, S.D.
8 Luis Gonzalez, Hou.-Chi.
8 Deion Sanders, Cin.-S.F.

HOME RUNS
40 Dante Bichette, Col.
36 Sammy Sosa, Chi.
36 Larry Walker, Col.
33 Barry Bonds, S.F.
32 Vinny Castilla, Col.
32 Eric Karros, L.A.
32 Mike Piazza, L.A.
31 Andres Galarraga, Col.
29 Ron Gant, Cin.
28 Reggie Sanders, Cin.

RUNS BATTED IN
128 Dante Bichette, Col.
119 Sammy Sosa, Chi.
106 Andres Galarraga, Col.
105 Eric Karros, L.A.
105 Jeff Conine, Fla.
104 Barry Bonds, S.F.
101 Larry Walker, Col.
99 Reggie Sanders, Cin.
94 Ken Caminiti, S.D.

TOTAL BASES
359 Dante Bichette, Col.
300 Larry Walker, Col.
297 Vinny Castilla, Col.
295 Eric Karros, L.A.
292 Barry Bonds, S.F.
285 Mark Grace, Chi.
283 Andres Galarraga, Col.
282 Sammy Sosa, Chi.
280 Reggie Sanders, Cin.
270 Ken Caminiti, S.D.

ON-BASE PERCENTAGE
.431 Barry Bonds, Giants
.406 Craig Biggio, Hou.
.404 Tony Gwynn, S.D.
.403 Walt Weiss, Col.
.400 Mike Piazza, L.A.
.399 Jeff Bagwell, Hou.
.397 Reggie Sanders, Cin.
.395 Mark Grace, Chi.
.394 Barry Larkin, Cin.
.389 Jose Offerman, L.A.

SLUGGING PERCENTAGE
.620 Dante Bichette, Col.
.607 Larry Walker, Col.
.606 Mike Piazza, L.A.
.579 Reggie Sanders, Cin.
.577 Barry Bonds, S.F.
.564 Vinny Castilla, Col.
.554 Ron Gant, Cin.
.535 Eric Karros, L.A.
.520 Jeff Conine, Fla.
.516 Mark Grace, Chi.

EXTRA-BASE HITS
80 Dante Bichette, Col.
72 Larry Walker, Col.
70 Reggie Sanders, Cin.
70 Mark Grace, Chi.
70 Barry Bonds, S.F.
68 Vinny Castilla, Col.
64 Eric Karros, L.A.
63 Andres Galarraga, Col.
62 Ray Lankford, St. L.
59 Ken Caminiti, S.D.

STOLEN BASES
56 Quilvio Veras, Fla.
51 Barry Larkin, Cin.
39 Delino DeShields, L.A.
36 Steve Finley, S.D.
36 Reggie Sanders, Cin.
35 Eric Young, Col.
34 Sammy Sosa, Chi.
33 Craig Biggio, Hou.
32 Brett Butler, N.Y.-L.A.
32 Darren Lewis, S.F.-Cin.

MULTIHIT GAMES
65 Tony Gwynn, S.D.
58 Dante Bichette, Col.
53 Craig Biggio, Hou.
53 Mark Grace, Chi.
52 Brian McRae, Chi.
50 Vinny Castilla, Col.
49 Mike Piazza, L.A.
48 Larry Walker, Col.
48 Barry Larkin, Cin.
46 Terry Pendleton, Fla.

PITCHING

EARNED RUN AVERAGE
1.63 Greg Maddux, Atl.
2.54 Hideo Nomo, L.A.
2.94 Andy Ashby, S.D.
3.05 Ismael Valdes, L.A.
3.08 Tom Glavine, Atl.
3.08 Joey Hamilton, S.D.
3.18 John Smoltz, Atl.
3.21 Frank Castillo, Chi.
3.22 Pete Schourek, Cin.
3.28 Jaime Navarro, Chi.

GAMES
76 Curtis Leskanic, Col.
72 Dave Veres, Hou.
71 Steve Reed, Col.
69 Yorkis Perez, Fla.
68 Todd Jones, Hou.
68 Darren Holmes, Col.
68 Mike Perez, Chi.
67 Greg McMichael, Atl.
65 Mark Wohlers, Atl.

INNINGS PITCHED
209.2 Greg Maddux, Atl.
209.2 Denny Neagle, Pit.
206.1 Ramon Martinez, L.A.
204.1 Joey Hamilton, S.D.
200.1 Jaime Navarro, Chi.
198.2 Tom Glavine, Atl.
197.2 Ismael Valdes, L.A.
195.2 Bobby Jones, N.Y.
195.2 Mark Leiter, S.F.
194.2 Pedro Martinez, Mon.

WINS
19 Greg Maddux, Atl.
18 Pete Schourek, Cin.
17 Ramon Martinez, L.A.
16 Tom Glavine, Atl.
14 John Burkett, Fla.
14 Pedro Martinez, Mon.
14 Jaime Navarro, Chi.
14 Pat Rapp, Fla.

COMPLETE GAMES
10 Greg Maddux, Atl.
7 Mark Leiter, S.F.
6 Ismael Valdes, L.A.
5 Denny Neagle, Pit.
4 John Burkett, Fla.
4 Tyler Green, Phi.
4 Ramon Martinez, L.A.
4 Hideo Nomo, L.A.

STRIKEOUTS PER 9 INN.
11.1 Hideo Nomo, L.A.
9.0 John Smoltz, Atl.
8.3 Shane Reynolds, Hou.
8.0 Pedro Martinez, Mon.
7.8 Kevin Foster, Chi.
7.8 Jeff Fassero, Mon.
7.8 Greg Maddux, Atl.
7.6 Pete Schourek, Cin.
7.3 Steve Avery, Atl.
7.0 Chris Hammond, Fla.

SAVES
38 Randy Myers, Chi.
36 Tom Henke, St. L.
33 Rod Beck, S.F.
32 Heathcliff Slocumb, Phi.
32 Todd Worrell, L.A.
31 Trevor Hoffman, S.D.
30 Mel Rojas, Mon.
29 John Franco, N.Y.
28 Jeff Brantley, Cin.
25 Mark Wohlers, Atl.

SHUTOUTS
3 Greg Maddux, Atl.
3 Hideo Nomo, L.A.
2 10 pitchers tied

STRIKEOUTS
236 Hideo Nomo, L.A.
193 John Smoltz, Atl.
181 Greg Maddux, Atl.
175 Shane Reynolds, Hou.
174 Pedro Martinez, Mon.
164 Jeff Fassero, Mon.
160 Pete Schourek, Cin.
150 Andy Ashby, S.D.
150 Denny Neagle, Pit.
150 Ismael Valdes, L.A.

OPP. BATTING AVG. AGAINST
.182 Hideo Nomo, L.A.
.197 Greg Maddux, Atl.
.227 Pedro Martinez, Mon.
.228 Ismael Valdes, L.A.
.228 Pete Schourek, Cin.
.231 Ramon Martinez, L.A.
.232 John Smoltz, Atl.
.240 Kevin Foster, Chi.
.246 Tom Glavine, Atl.
.246 Joey Hamilton, S.D.